2012
Writer's
MARKET®
DELUXE EDITION

Includes a 1-year online subscription to

Where & How to Sell What You Write

THE ULTIMATE MARKET RESEARCH TOOL FOR WRITERS

To register your *2012 Writer's Market Deluxe Edition* and **start your 1-year online subscription**, scratch off the block below to reveal your activation code*, then go to WritersMarket.com. Click on "Sign Up Now" and enter your contact information and activation code. It's that easy!

UPDATED MARKET LISTINGS FOR YOUR INTEREST AREA
EASY-TO-USE SEARCHABLE DATABASE • RECORD-KEEPING TOOLS
PROFESSIONAL TIPS & ADVICE • INDUSTRY NEWS

*valid through 12/31/12

WritersMarket.com
Where & How to Sell What You Write

Activate your WritersMarket.com subscription to get instant access to:

- **UPDATED LISTINGS IN YOUR WRITING GENRE:** Find additional listings that didn't make it into the book, updated contact information and more. WritersMarket.com provides the most comprehensive database of verified markets available anywhere.

- **EASY-TO-USE SEARCHABLE DATABASE:** Looking for a specific magazine or book publisher? Just type in its name. Or widen your prospects with the Advanced Search. You can also search for listings that have been recently updated!

- **PERSONALIZED TOOLS:** Store your best-bet markets, and use our popular record-keeping tools to track your submissions. Plus, get new and updated market listings, query reminders, and more—every time you log in!

- **PROFESSIONAL TIPS & ADVICE:** From pay rate charts and sample query letters to Q&A's with literary agents and how-to articles, we have the resources freelance writers need.

- **INDUSTRY UPDATES:** Debbie Ridpath Ohi's Market Watch column keeps you up-to-date on the latest publishing industry news, so you'll always be in-the-know.

YOU'LL GET ALL OF THIS WITH YOUR SUBSCRIPTION TO

WritersMarket.com
Where & How to Sell What You Write

12WMI0M

12TH ANNUAL EDITION

2012
Writer's
MARKET
DELUXE EDITION

Robert Lee Brewer, Editor

WRITER'S DIGEST
BOOKS
WritersDigest.com
Cincinnati, Ohio

2012 Writer's Market. Copyright © 2011 F + W Media, Inc. Published by Writer's Digest Books, an imprint of F+W Media, Inc., 4700 East Galbraith Road, Cincinnati, Ohio 45236. Printed and bound in the United States of America. All rights reserved. No part of this book may be reproduced in any form or by any electronic or mechanical means including information storage and retrieval systems without permission in writing from the publisher, except by a reviewer, who may quote brief passages in a review.

Publisher & Editorial Director, Writing Community: Phil Sexton
Managing Editor, Writer's Digest Market Books: Adria Haley

Writer's Market website: www.writersmarket.com
Writer's Digest website: www.writersdigest.com

Distributed in Canada by Fraser Direct
100 Armstrong Avenue
Georgetown, Ontario, Canada L7G 5S4
Tel: (905) 877-4411

Distributed in the U.K. and Europe by F&W Media International
Brunel House, Newton Abbot, Devon, TQ12 4PU, England
Tel: (+44) 1626-323200, Fax: (+44) 1626-323319
E-mail: postmaster@davidandcharles.co.uk

Distributed in Australia by Capricorn Link
P.O. Box 704, Windsor, NSW 2756 Australia
Tel: (02) 4577-3555

Library of Congress Catalog Number 31-20772
ISSN: 0084-2729
ISBN-13: 978-1-59963-226-1
ISBN-13: 978-1-59963-227-8 (*Writer's Market Deluxe Edition*)
ISBN-10: 1-59963-226-8
ISBN-10: 1-59963-227-6 (*Writer's Market Deluxe Edition*)

Attention Booksellers: This is an annual directory of F + W Media, Inc. Return deadline for this edition is December 31, 2012.

Edited by: Robert Lee Brewer
Cover designed by: Jessica Boonstra
Interior designed by: Claudean Wheeler
Production coordinated by: Greg Nock
Cover illustration by: Emily Keafer

CONTENTS

RESOURCES

MARKETS

FROM THE EDITOR

There are few industries that have changed as dramatically as the publishing industry in the 21st century. For one thing, many publishing companies have re-branded themselves as media companies. For another thing, e-books are starting to sell more than printed books from major online retailers. While the changes can seem dizzying at times, I'm sure of one thing: There will always be a need for engaging and talented freelance writers.

The tricky part for these freelancers will be figuring out where the opportunities are and how to take advantage of them. This edition of *Writer's Market* provides a guide of what's happening in the industry now and how to take advantage of these new opportunities.

If freelancers want to make a career out of writing, they need to manage their writing careers like businesses. Recognizing this need, the *2012 Writer's Market* includes articles like "Making the Most of the Money You Earn" and "Recordkeeping and Pricing."

Beyond finding and managing their work, 21st century writers have to step up their game in promoting their writing as well. After all, small businesses have to build their brands if they wish to compete in the marketplace, so freelancers are held to this same standard. That's why the *2012 Writer's Market* includes articles on book trailers, social media, and more.

As always, this book is loaded with opportunities to get published and paid for your writing, whether you're searching for book publishers, magazines, contests, literary agents, or scriptwriting opportunities.

Until next we meet, keep writing and marketing what you write.

Robert Lee Brewer
Senior Content Editor
Writer's Market and WritersMarket.com
http://blog.writersdigest.com/poeticasides
http://twitter.com/robertleebrewer

HOW TO USE *WRITER'S MARKET*

Writer's Market is here to help you decide where and how to submit your writing to appropriate markets. Each listing contains information about the editorial focus of the market, how it prefers material to be submitted, payment information, and other helpful tips.

WHAT'S INSIDE?

Since 1921, *Writer's Market* has been giving you the information you need to knowledgeably approach a market. We've continued to develop improvements to help you access that information more efficiently.

NAVIGATIONAL TOOLS. We've designed the pages of *Writer's Market* with you, the writer, in mind. Within the pages you will find **readable market listings** and **accessible charts and graphs**. One such chart can be found in the ever-popular "How Much Should I Charge?" article. We've taken all of the updated information in this feature and put it into an easy-to-read and navigate chart, making it convenient for you to find the rates that accompany the freelance jobs you're seeking.

Since 1921, *Writer's Market* has been giving you the information you need to knowledgeably approach a market. We've designed it with you, the writer, in mind.

ICONS. There are a variety of icons that appear before each listing. A complete Key to Icons & Abbreviations appears on the back inside cover. Icons let you know whether a listing is new to the book (⊕), a book publisher accepts only agented writers ([A]), comparative pay rates for a magazine ($-$$$$), and more.

ACQUISITION NAMES, ROYALTY RATES AND ADVANCES. In the Book Publishers section, we identify acquisition editors with the boldface word **Contact** to help you get your manuscript to the right person. Royalty rates and advances are also highlighted in boldface, as is other important information on the percentage of first-time writers and unagented writers the company publishes, the number of books published, and the number of manuscripts received each year.

EDITORS, PAY RATES, AND PERCENTAGE OF MATERIAL WRITTEN BY FREELANCE WRITERS. In the Consumer Magazines and Trade Journals sections, we identify to whom you should send your query or article with the boldface word **Contact**. The amount (percentage) of material accepted from freelance writers, and the pay rates for features, columns and departments, and fillers are also highlighted in boldface to help you quickly identify the information you need to know when considering whether to submit your work.

QUERY FORMATS. We asked editors how they prefer to receive queries and have indicated in the listings whether they prefer them by mail, e-mail, fax or phone. Be sure to check an editor's individual preference before sending your query.

ARTICLES. Most of the articles are new to this edition. Writers who want to improve their submission techniques should read the articles in the **Finding Work** section. The **Managing Work** section is geared more toward post-acceptance topics, such as contract negotiation and organization. With self-promotion a

KEY TO ICONS & ABBREVIATIONS

⊕	market new to this edition
[A]	market accepts agented submissions only
⊘	market does not accept unsolicited submissions
🏆	award-winning market
🍁	Canadian market
🌐	market located outside of the U.S. and Canada
↖	online opportunity
$	market pays 0-9¢/word or $0-$150/article
$$	market pays 10-49¢/word or $151-$750/article
$$$	market pays 50-99¢/word or $751-$1,500/article
$$$$	market pays $1/word or over $1,500/article
💬	comment from the editor of *Writer's Market*
🔑	tips to break into a specific market
ms, mss	manuscript(s)
b&w	black & white (photo)
SASE	self-addressed, stamped envelope
SAE	self-addressed envelope
IRC	International Reply Coupon, for use when mailing to countries other than your own

big key in freelance success, there is a section of articles dedicated to this topic too: **Promoting Work**.

IMPORTANT LISTING INFORMATION

1) Listings are based on editorial questionnaires and interviews. They are not advertisements; publishers do not pay for their listings. The markets are not endorsed by *Writer's Market* editors. F + W Media, Inc., Writer's Digest Books, and its employees go to great effort to ascertain the validity of information in this book. However, transactions between users of the information and individuals and/or companies are strictly between those parties.

2) All listings have been verified before publication of this book. If a listing has not changed from last year, then the editor said the market's needs have not changed and the previous listing continues to accurately reflect its policies.

3) *Writer's Market* reserves the right to exclude any listing.

4) When looking for a specific market, check the index. A market may not be listed for one of these reasons:
   - It doesn't solicit freelance material.
   - It doesn't pay for material.
   - It has gone out of business.
   - It has failed to verify or update its listing for this edition.
   - It hasn't answered *Writer's Market* inquiries satisfactorily. (To the best of our ability, and with our readers' help, we try to screen fradulent listings.)

IF WRITER'S MARKET IS NEW TO YOU . . .

A quick look at the **Contents** pages will familiarize you with the arrangement of *Writer's Market*. The three largest sections of the book are the market listings of Book Publishers; Consumer Magazines; and Trade Journals. You will also find other sections of market listings for Literary Agents; Newspapers; Screenwriting Markets; Playwriting Markets; Greeting Card Companies; and Contests & Awards.

Narrowing your search

After you've identified the market categories that interest you, you can begin researching specific markets within each section.

Consumer Magazines and Trade Journals are categorized by subject within their respective sections to make it easier for you to identify markets for your work. If you want to publish an article dealing with parenting, you could look under the Child Care & Parental Guidance category of Consumer Magazines to find an appropriate market. You would want to keep in mind, however, that magazines in other categories might also be interested in your article. (For example, women's magazines publish such material.)

Contests & Awards are categorized by genre of writing. If you want to find journalism contests, you would search the Journalism category; if you have an unpublished novel, check the Fiction category.

Interpreting the markets

Once you've identified companies or publications that cover the subjects in which you're interested, you can begin evaluating specific listings to pinpoint the markets most receptive to your work and most beneficial to you.

In evaluating individual listings, check the location of the company, the types of material it is interested in seeing, submission requirements, and rights and payment policies. Depending on your personal concerns, any of these items could be a deciding factor as you determine which markets you plan to approach. Many listings also include a reporting time.

Check the Glossary for unfamiliar words. Specific symbols and abbreviations are explained in the Key to Icons & Abbreviations appearing on the back inside cover. The most important abbreviation is SASE—self-addressed, stamped envelope.

A careful reading of the listings will reveal that many editors are very specific about their needs. Your chances of success increase if you follow directions to the letter. Often companies do not accept unsolicited manuscripts and return them unread. If a company does not accept unsolicited manuscripts, it is indicated in the listing with a (⊘) icon. (Note: You may still be able to query a market that does not accept unsolicited manuscripts.)

Whenever possible, obtain submission guidelines before submitting material. You can usually obtain guidelines by sending a SASE to the address in the listing. Magazines often post their guidelines on their websites, and many book publishers do so as well. Most of the listings indicate how writer's guidelines are made available. You should also familiarize yourself with the company's publications. Many of the listings contain instructions on how to obtain sample copies, catalogs or market lists. The more research you do upfront, the better your chances of acceptance, publication and payment.

Don't forget your webinar!

To access the webinar that is included with your book, go to writersmarket.com/2012wm and learn how to build your author platform.

Guide to listing features

Below is an example of the market listings you'll find in each section of *Writer's Market*. Note the callouts that identify various format features of the listing.

EASY-TO-USE REFERENCE ICONS

DIRECT E-MAIL ADDRESSES

SPECIFIC CONTACT NAMES

DETAILED SUBMISSION GUIDELINES

SPECIFIC PAY RATES

$ THE GEORGIA REVIEW

The University of Georgia, Athens GA 30602-9009. (706)542-3481. Fax: (706)542-0047. E-mail: garev@uga.edu. Website: www.uga.edu/garev. **Contact:** Stephen Corey, editor. **99% freelance written**. Quarterly journal. Our readers are educated, inquisitive people who read a lot of work in the areas we feature, so they expect only the best in our pages. All work submitted should show evidence that the writer is at least as well-educated and well-read as our readers. Essays should be authoritative but accessible to a range of readers. Estab. 1947. Circ. 3,500. Byline given. Pays on publication. No kill fee. Publishes ms an average of 6 month's after acceptance. Accepts queries by mail. Responds in 2 weeks to queries. Responds in 2-3 months to mss. Sample copy for $10. Guidelines available online.

- No simultaneous or electronic submissions.

NONFICTION Needs essays. For the most part we are not interested in scholarly articles that are narrow in focus and/or overly burdened with footnotes. The ideal essay for *The Georgia Review* is a provocative, thesis-oriented work that can engage both the intelligent general reader and the specialist. **Buys 12-20 mss/year.** Send complete ms. **Pays $40/published page.**

PHOTOS Send photos. Reviews 5x7 prints or larger. Offers no additional payment for photos accepted with ms.

FICTION "We seek original, excellent writing not bound by type. Ordinarily we do not publish novel excerpts or works translated into English, and we strongly discourage authors from submitting these." **Buys 12-20 mss/year.** Send complete ms. **Pays $40/published page.**

POETRY "We seek original, excellent poetry. We do not accept submissions via fax or e-mail. If a submission is known to be included in a book already accepted by a publisher, please notify us of this fact (and of the anticipated date of book publication) in a cover letter." Reads year-round, but submissions postmarked May 15-August 15 will be returned unread. Guidelines available for SASE or on website. Responds in 2-3 months. Always sends prepublication galleys. Acquires first North American serial rights. Reviews books of poetry. "Our poetry reviews range from 500-word 'Book Briefs' on single volumes to 5,000-word essay reviews on multiple volumes." Buys 60-75 poems/year. Submit maximum 5 poems. **Pays $3/line.**

TIPS "Unsolicited manuscripts will not be considered from May 15-August 15 (annually); all such submissions received during that period will be returned unread. Check website for submission guidelines."

BEFORE YOUR FIRST SALE

Everything in life has to start somewhere and that somewhere is always at the beginning. Stephen King, J.K. Rowling, John Grisham, Nora Roberts—they all had to start at the beginning. It would be great to say becoming a writer is as easy as waving a magic wand over your manuscript and "Poof!" you're published, but that's not how it happens. While there's no one true "key" to becoming successful, a long, well-paid writing career *can* happen when you combine four elements:

- Good writing
- Knowledge of writing markets
- Professionalism
- Persistence

Good writing is useless if you don't know which markets will buy your work or how to pitch and sell your writing. If you aren't professional and persistent in your contact with editors, your writing is just that—your writing. But if you are a writer who embraces the above four elements, you have a good chance at becoming a paid, published writer who will reap the benefits of a long and successful career.

As you become more involved with writing, you may read articles or talk to editors and authors with conflicting opinions about the right way to submit your work. The truth is, there are many different routes a writer can follow to get published, but no matter which route you choose, the end is always the same—becoming a published writer.

The following information on submissions has worked for many writers, but it is by no means the be-all-end-all of proper submission guidelines. It's very easy to get wrapped up in the specifics of submitting (Should I put my last name on every page of my manuscript?) and ignore the more important issues (Will this idea on ice fishing in Alaska be appropriate for a regional magazine in Seattle?). Don't allow yourself to become so blinded by submission procedures that you forget common sense. If you use your common sense and develop professional, courteous relations with editors, you will eventually find your own submission style.

DEVELOP YOUR IDEAS, THEN TARGET THE MARKETS

Writers often think of an interesting story, complete the manuscript, and then begin the search for a suitable publisher or magazine. While this approach is common for fiction, poetry and screenwriting, it reduces your chances of success in many nonfiction writing areas. Instead, try choosing categories that interest you and study those sections in *Writer's Market*. Select several listings you consider good prospects for your type of writing. Sometimes the individual listings will even help you generate ideas.

Next, make a list of the potential markets for each idea. Make the initial contact with markets using the method stated in the market listings. If you exhaust your list of possibilities, don't give up. Instead, reevaluate the idea or try another angle. Continue developing ideas and approaching markets. Identify and rank potential markets for an idea and continue the process.

As you submit to the various publications listed in *Writer's Market*, it's important to remember that every magazine is published with a particular audience and slant in mind. Probably the number one complaint we receive from editors is the submissions they receive are completely wrong for their magazines or book line. The first mark of professionalism is to know your market well. Gaining that knowledge starts with *Writer's Market*, but you should also do your own detective work. Search out back issues of the magazines you wish to write for, pick up recent issues at your local newsstand, or visit magazines' websites—anything that will help you figure out what subjects specific magazines publish. This research is also helpful in learning what topics have been covered ad nauseum—the topics you should stay away from or approach in a fresh way. Magazines' websites are invaluable as most post the current issue of the magazine, as well as back issues, and most offer writer's guidelines.

The same advice is true for submitting to book publishers. Research publisher websites for their submission guidelines, recently published titles and their backlist. You can use this information to target your book proposal in a way that fits with a publisher's other titles while not directly competing for sales.

Prepare for rejection and the sometimes lengthy wait. When a submission is returned, check your file folder of potential markets for that idea. Cross off the market that rejected the idea. If the editor has given you suggestions or reasons why the manuscript was not accepted, you might want to incorporate these suggestions when revising your manuscript.

After revising your manuscript mail it to the next market on your list.

Take rejection with a grain of salt

Rejection is a way of life in the publishing world. It's inevitable in a business that deals with such an overwhelming number of applicants for such a limited number of positions. Anyone who has published has lived through many rejections, and writers with thin skin are at a distinct disadvantage. A rejection letter is not a personal attack. It simply indicates your submission is not appropriate for that market. Writers who let rejection dissuade them from pursuing their dream or who react to an editor's "No" with indignation or fury do themselves a disservice. Writers who let rejection stop them do not get published. Resign yourself to facing rejection now. You will live through it, and you'll eventually overcome it.

QUERY AND COVER LETTERS

A query letter is a brief, one-page letter used as a tool to hook an editor and get him interested in your idea. When you send a query letter to a magazine, you are trying to get an editor to buy your idea or article. When you query a book publisher, you are attempting to get an editor interested enough in your idea to request your book proposal or your entire manuscript. (Note: Some book editors prefer to receive book proposals on first contact. Check individual listings for which method editors prefer.)

Here are some basic guidelines to help you create a query that's polished and well-organized. For more tips see "Query Letter Clinic" article.

- **LIMIT IT TO ONE PAGE, SINGLE-SPACED**, and address the editor by name (Mr. or Ms. and the surname). *Note*: Do not assume that a person is a Mr. or Ms. unless it is obvious from the name listed. For example, if you are contacting a D.J. Smith, do not assume that D.J. should be preceded by Mr. or Ms. Instead, address the letter to D.J. Smith.
- **GRAB THE EDITOR'S ATTENTION WITH A STRONG OPENING.** Some magazine queries, for example, begin with a paragraph meant to approximate the lead of the intended article.
- **INDICATE HOW YOU INTEND TO DEVELOP THE ARTICLE OR BOOK.** Give the editor some idea of the work's structure and content.
- **LET THE EDITOR KNOW IF YOU HAVE PHOTOS** or illustrations available to accompany your magazine article.
- **MENTION ANY EXPERTISE OR TRAINING THAT QUALIFIES YOU** to write the article or book. If you've been published before, mention it; if not, don't.
- **END WITH A DIRECT REQUEST TO WRITE THE ARTICLE.** Or, if you're pitching a book, ask for the go-ahead to send in a full proposal or the entire manuscript. Give the editor an idea of the expected length and delivery date of your manuscript.

A common question that arises is: If I don't hear from an editor in the reported response time, how do I know when I can safely send the query to another market? Many writers find it helpful to indicate in their queries that if they don't receive a response from the editor (slightly after the listed reporting time), they will assume the editor is not interested. It's best to take this approach, particularly if your topic is timely.

A brief, single-spaced cover letter is helpful when sending a manuscript as it helps personalize the submission. However, if you have previously queried the editor, use the cover letter to politely and briefly remind the editor of that query—when it was sent, what it contained, etc. "Here is the piece on low-fat cooking that I queried you about on December 12. I look forward to hearing from you at your earliest convenience." Do not use the cover letter as a sales pitch.

If you are submitting to a market that accepts unsolicited manuscripts, a cover letter is useful because it personalizes your submission. You can, and should, include information about the manuscript, yourself, your publishing history, and your qualifications.

In addition to tips on writing queries, "The Query Letter Clinic" article offers eight example query letters, some that work and some that don't, as well as comments on why the letters were either successful or failed to garner an assignment or contract.

Querying for fiction

Fiction is sometimes queried, but more often editors prefer receiving material. Many fiction editors won't decide on a submission until they have seen the complete manuscript. When submitting a fiction book idea, most editors prefer to see at least a synopsis and sample chapters (usually the first three). For fiction published in magazines, most editors want to see the complete short story manuscript. If an editor does request a query for fiction, it should include a description of the main theme and story line, including the conflict and resolution. Take a look at individual listings to see what editors prefer to receive.

QUERY LETTER RESOURCES

The following list of books provide you with more detailed information on writing query letters, cover letters, and book proposals. All titles are published by Writer's Digest Books.

- *Formatting & Submitting Your Manuscript*, 3rd Edition, by Chuck Sambuchino
- *How to Write Attention-Grabbing Query & Cover Letters*, by John Wood
- *How to Write a Book Proposal*, 4th Edition, by Michael Larsen
- *Writer's Market Companion*, 2nd Edition, by Joe Feiertag and Mary Cupito

---

THE SYNOPSIS

Most fiction books are sold by a complete manuscript, but most editors and agents don't have the time to read a complete manuscript of every wannabe writer. As a result, publishing decision makers use the synopsis and sample chapters to help the screening process of fiction. The synopsis, on its most basic level, communicates what the book is about.

The length and depth of a synopsis can change from agent to agent or publisher to publisher. Some will want a synopsis that is 1-2 single-spaced pages; others will want a synopsis that can run up to 25 double-spaced pages. Checking your listings in *Writer's Market*, as well as double-checking with the listing's website, will help guide you in this respect.

The content should cover all the essential points of the novel from beginning to end and in the correct order. The essential points include main characters, main plot points, and, yes, the ending. Of course, your essential points will vary from the editor who wants a 1-page synopsis to the editor who wants a 25-page synopsis.

NONFICTION BOOK PROPOSALS

Most nonfiction books are sold by a book proposal—a package of materials that details what your book is about, who its intended audience is, and how you intend to write the book. It includes some combination of a cover or query letter, an overview, an outline, author's information sheet, and sample chapters. Editors also want to see information about the audience for your book and about titles that compete with your proposed book.

Submitting a nonfiction book proposal

A proposal package should include the following items:

- **A COVER OR QUERY LETTER.** This letter should be a short introduction to the material you include in the proposal.
- **AN OVERVIEW.** This is a brief summary of your book. It should detail your book's subject and give an idea of how that subject will be developed.
- **AN OUTLINE.** The outline covers your book chapter by chapter and should include all major points covered in each chapter. Some outlines are done in traditional outline form, but most are written in paragraph form.
- **AN AUTHOR'S INFORMATION SHEET.** This information should acquaint the editor with your writing background and convince him of your qualifications regarding the subject of your book.
- **SAMPLE CHAPTERS.** Many editors like to see sample chapters, especially for a first book. Sample chapters show the editor how you write and develop ideas from your outline.
- **MARKETING INFORMATION.** Facts about how and to whom your book can be successfully marketed are now expected to accompany every book proposal. If you can provide information about the audience for your book and suggest ways the book publisher can reach those people, you will increase your chances of acceptance.

- **COMPETITIVE TITLE ANALYSIS.** Check the *Subject Guide to Books in Print* for other titles on your topic. Write a one- or two-sentence synopsis of each. Point out how your book differs and improves upon existing topics.

For more information on nonfiction book proposals, read Michael Larsen's *How to Write a Book Proposal* (Writer's Digest Books).

A WORD ABOUT AGENTS

An agent represents a writer's work to publishers, negotiates contracts, follows up to see that contracts are fulfilled, and generally handles a writer's business affairs, leaving the writer free to write. Effective agents are valued for their contacts in the publishing industry, their knowledge about who to approach with certain ideas, their ability to guide an author's career, and their business sense.

While most book publishers listed in *Writer's Market* publish books by unagented writers, some of the larger houses are reluctant to consider submissions that have not reached them through a literary agent. Companies with such a policy are noted by an (**A**) icon at the beginning of the listing, as well as in the submission information within the listing.

Writer's Market includes a list of literary agents who are all members of the Association of Authors' Representatives and who are also actively seeking new and established writers.

MANUSCRIPT FORMAT

You can increase your chances of publication by following a few standard guidelines regarding the physical format of your manuscript. It should be your goal to make your manuscript readable. Follow these suggestions as you would any other suggestions: Use what works for you and discard what doesn't.

In general, when submitting a manuscript, you should use white, 8½×11, 20 lb. paper, and you should also choose a legible, professional looking font (i.e., Times New Roman)—no all-italic or artsy fonts. Your entire manuscript should be double-spaced with a 1½-inch margin on all sides of the page. Once you are ready to print your manuscript, you should print either on a laser printer or an ink-jet printer.

MANUSCRIPT FORMATTING SAMPLE

(1) Your Name   50,000 Words **(3)**
Your Street Address
City State ZIP Code
Day and Evening Phone Numbers
E-mail Address

Website (if applicable)
(2)

TITLE

by

(4) Your Name

(5) You can increase your chances of publication by following a few standard guidelines regarding the physical format of your article or manuscript. It should be your goal to make your manuscript readable. Use these suggestions as you would any other suggestions: Use what works for you and discard what doesn't.

In general, when submitting a manuscript, you should use white, 8½×11, 20-lb. bond paper, and you should also choose a legible, professional-looking font (i.e., Times New Roman)—no all-italic or artsy fonts. Your entire manuscript should be double-spaced with a 1½-inch margin on all sides of the page. Once you are ready to print your article or manuscript, you should print either on a laser printer or an ink-jet printer.

Remember, articles should be written after you send a one-page query letter to an editor, and the editor then asks you to write the article. If, however, you are sending an article "on spec" to an editor, you should send both a query letter and the complete article.

Fiction and poetry is a little different from nonfiction articles, in that it is rarely queried. More often than not, poetry and fiction editors want to review the complete manuscript before making a final decision.

(1) Type your real name (even if you use a pseudonym) and contact information **(2)** Double-space twice **(3)** Estimated word count **(4)** Type your title in capital letters, double-space and type "by," double-space again, and type your name (or pseudonym if you're using one) **(5)** Double-space twice, then indent first paragraph and start text of your manuscript **(6)** On subsequent pages, type your name, a dash, and the page number in the upper left or right corner

ESTIMATING WORD COUNT

Many computers will provide you with a word count of your manuscript. Your editor will count again after editing the manuscript. Although your computer is counting characters, an editor or production editor is more concerned about the amount of space the text will occupy on a page. Several small headlines or subheads, for instance, will be counted the same by your computer as any other word of text. However, headlines and subheads usually employ a different font size than the body text, so an editor may count them differently to be sure enough space has been estimated for larger type.

For short manuscripts, it's often quickest to count each word on a representative page and multiply by the number of pages. You can get a very rough count by multiplying the number of pages in your manuscript by 250 (the average number of words on a double-spaced typewritten page).

PHOTOGRAPHS AND SLIDES

In some cases, the availability of photographs and slides can be the deciding factor as to whether an editor will accept your submission. This is especially true when querying a publication that relies heavily on photographs, illustrations or artwork to enhance the article (i.e., craft magazines, hobby magazines, etc.). In some instances, the publication may offer additional payment for photographs or illustrations.

Check the individual listings to find out which magazines review photographs and what their submission guidelines are. Most publications prefer you do not send photographs with your submission. However, if photographs or illustrations are available, you should indicate that in your query. As with manuscripts, never send the originals of your photographs or illustrations. Instead, send prints or duplicates of slides and transparencies. Also, most magazines and book publishers use digital images.

SEND PHOTOCOPIES

If there is one hard-and-fast rule in publishing, it's this: *Never* send the original (or only) copy of your manuscript. Most editors cringe when they find out a writer has sent the only copy of their manuscript. You should always send photocopies of your manuscript.

Some writers choose to send a self-addressed, stamped postcard with a photocopied submission. In their cover letter they suggest if the editor is not interested in their manuscript, it may be tossed out and a reply sent on the postcard. This method is particularly helpful when sending your submissions to international markets.

MAILING SUBMISSIONS

No matter what size manuscript you're mailing, always include a self-addressed, stamped envelope (SASE) with sufficient return postage. The website for the U.S. Postal Service (www.

usps.com) and the website for the Canadian Post (www.canadapost.ca) both have postage calculators if you are unsure how much postage to affix.

A book manuscript should be mailed in a sturdy, well-wrapped box. Enclose a self-addressed mailing label and paper clip your return postage to the label. However, be aware that some book publishers do not return unsolicited manuscripts, so make sure you know the practice of the publisher before sending any unsolicited material.

Types of mail service

There are many different mailing service options available to you whether you are sending a query letter or a complete manuscript. You can work with the U.S. Postal Service, United Parcel Service, Federal Express, or any number of private mailing companies. The following are the five most common types of mailing services offered by the U.S. Postal Service.

- **FIRST CLASS** is a fairly expensive way to mail a manuscript, but many writers prefer it. First-Class mail generally receives better handling and is delivered more quickly than Standard mail.
- **PRIORITY MAIL** reaches its destination within two or three days.
- **STANDARD MAIL** rates are available for packages, but be sure to pack your materials carefully because they will be handled roughly. To make sure your package will be returned to you if it is undeliverable, print "Return Postage Guaranteed" under your address.
- **CERTIFIED MAIL** must be signed for when it reaches its destination.
- **REGISTERED MAIL** is a high-security method of mailing where the contents are insured. The package is signed in and out of every office it passes through, and a receipt is returned to the sender when the package reaches its destination.

MAILING MANUSCRIPTS

- Fold manuscripts under five pages into thirds, and send in a #10 SASE.
- Mail manuscripts five pages or more unfolded in a 9 X 12 or 10 X 13 SASE.
- For return envelope, fold the envelope in half, address it to yourself, and add a stamp, or, if going to Canada or another international destination, International Reply Coupons (available at most post office branches).
- Don't send by Certified Mail—this is a sign of an amateur.

QUERY LETTER CLINIC

Many great writers ask year after year, "Why is it so hard to get published?" In many cases, these writers have spent years—and possibly thousands of dollars on books and courses—developing their craft. They submit to the appropriate markets, yet rejection is always the end result. The culprit? A weak query letter.

The query letter is often the most important piece of the publishing puzzle. In many cases, it determines whether an editor or agent will even read your manuscript. A good query letter makes a good first impression; a bad query letter earns a swift rejection.

THE ELEMENTS OF A QUERY LETTER

A query letter should sell editors or agents on your idea or convince them to request your finished manuscript. The most effective query letters get into the specifics from the very first line. It's important to remember that the query is a call to action, not a listing of features and benefits.

In addition to selling your idea or manuscript, a query letter can include information on the availability of photographs or artwork. You can include a working title and projected word count. Depending on the piece, you might also mention whether a sidebar might be appropriate and the type of research you plan to conduct. If appropriate, include a tentative deadline and indicate whether the query is being simultaneously submitted.

Biographical information should be included as well, but don't overdo it unless your background actually helps sell the article or proves that you're the only person who could write your proposed piece.

THINGS TO AVOID IN A QUERY LETTER

The query letter is not a place to discuss pay rates. This step comes after an editor has agreed to take on your article or book. Besides making an unprofessional impression on an editor, it can also work to your disadvantage in negotiating your fee. If you ask for too much, an editor may not even contact you to see if a lower rate might work. If you ask for too little, you may start an editorial relationship where you are making far less than the normal rate.

You should also avoid rookie mistakes, such as mentioning that your work is copyrighted or including the copyright symbol on your work. While you want to make it clear that you've researched the market, avoid using flattery as a technique for selling your work. It often has the opposite effect of what you intend. In addition, don't hint that you can rewrite the piece, as this only leads the editor to think there will be a lot of work involved in shaping up your writing.

Also, never admit several other editors or agents have rejected the query. Always treat your new audience as if they are the first place on your list of submission possibilities.

HOW TO FORMAT YOUR QUERY LETTER

It's OK to break writing rules in a short story or article, but you should follow the rules when it comes to crafting an effective query. Here are guidelines for query writing.
- Use a normal font and typeface, such as Times New Roman and 10- or 12-point type.
- Include your name, address, phone number, e-mail address and website, if possible.
- Use a one-inch margin on paper queries.
- Address a specific editor or agent. (Note: The listings in *Writer's Market* provide a contact name for most submissions. It's wise to double-check contact names online or by calling.)
- Limit query letter to one single-spaced page.
- Include self-addressed, stamped envelope or postcard for response with post submissions. Use block paragraph format (no indentations). Thank the editor for considering your query.

WHEN AND HOW TO FOLLOW UP

Accidents do happen. Queries may not reach your intended reader. Staff changes or interoffice mail snafus may end up with your query letter thrown away. Or the editor may have set your query off to the side for further consideration and forgotten it. Whatever the case may be, there are some basic guidelines you should use for your follow-up communication.

Most importantly, wait until the reported response time, as indicated in *Writer's Market* or their submission guidelines, has elapsed before contacting an editor or agent. Then, you should send a short and polite e-mail describing the original query sent, the date it was sent, and asking if they received it or made a decision regarding its fate.

The importance of remaining polite and businesslike when following up cannot be stressed enough. Making a bad impression on an editor can often have a ripple effect—as that editor may share his or her bad experience with other editors at the magazine or publishing company.

HOW THE CLINIC WORKS

As mentioned earlier, the query letter is the most important weapon for getting an assignment or a request for your full manuscript. Published writers know how to craft a well-written, hard-hitting query. What follows are eight queries: four are strong; four are not. Detailed comments show what worked and what did not. As you'll see, there is no cut-and-dried "good" query format; every strong query works on its own merit.

GOOD NONFICTION MAGAZINE QUERY

Jimmy Boaz, editor
American Organic Farmer's Digest
8336 Old Dirt Road
Macon GA 00000

Dear Mr. Boaz,

There are 87 varieties of organic crops grown in the United States, but there's only one farm producing 12 of these—Morganic Corporation. **2**

Located in the heart of Arkansas, this company spent the past decade providing great organic crops at a competitive price helping them grow into the ninth leading organic farming operation in the country. Along the way, they developed the most unique organic offering in North America.

As a seasoned writer with access to Richard Banks, the founder and president of Morganic, I propose writing a profile piece on Banks for your Organic Shakers department. After years of reading this riveting column, I believe the time has come to cover Morganic's rise in the organic farming industry. **3**

This piece would run in the normal 800-1,200 word range with photographs available of Banks and Morganic's operation.

I've been published in *Arkansas Farmer's Deluxe, Organic Farming Today* and in several newspapers. **4**

Thank you for your consideration of this article. I hope to hear from you soon.

Sincerely,

Jackie Service
34 Good St.
Little Rock AR 00000
jackie.service9867@email.com

1 My name is only available on our magazine's website and on the masthead. This writer has done her research. **2** Here's a story that hasn't been pitched before. I didn't know Morganic was so unique in the market. I want to know more. **3** The writer has access to her interview subject, and she displays knowledge of the magazine by pointing out the correct section in which her piece would run. **4** While I probably would've assigned this article based off the idea alone, her past credits do help solidify my decision.

BAD NONFICTION MAGAZINE QUERY

Dear Gentlemen, **1**

I'd like to write the next great article you'll ever publish. My writing credits include expose pieces I've done for local and community newspapers and for my college English classes. I've been writing for years and years. **2**

Your magazine may not be a big one like *Rolling Stone or Sports Illustrated*, but I'm willing to write an interview for you anyway. I know you need material, and I need money. (Don't worry. I won't charge you too much.) **3**

Just give me some people to interview, and I'll do the best job you've ever read. It will be amazing, and I can re-write the piece for you if you don't agree. I'm willing to re-write 20 times if needed. **4**

You better hurry up and assign me an article though, because I've sent out letters to lots of other magazines, and I'm sure to be filled up to capacity very soon. **5**

Later gents,

Carl Bighead
76 Bad Query Lane
Big City NY 00000

1 This is sexist, and it doesn't address any contact specifically. **2** An over-the-top claim by a writer who does not impress me with his publishing background. **3** Insults the magazine and then reassures me he won't charge too much? **4** While I do assign material from time to time, I prefer writers pitch me their own ideas after studying the magazine. **5** I'm sure people aren't going to be knocking down his door anytime soon.

GOOD FICTION MAGAZINE QUERY

Marcus West
88 Piano Drive
Lexington KY 00000

August 8, 2011 **1**

Jeanette Curic, editor
Wonder Stories
45 Noodle Street
Portland OR 00000

Dear Ms. Curic,

Please consider the following 1,200-word story, "Turning to the Melon," a quirky coming-of-age story with a little magical realism thrown in the mix. **2**

After reading *Wonder Stories* for years, I think I've finally written something that would fit with your audience. My previous short story credits include *Stunned Fiction Quarterly* and *Faulty Mindbomb*. **3**

Thank you in advance for considering "Turning to Melon."

Sincerely,

Marcus West
(123) 456-7890
marcusw87452@email.com

Encl: Manuscript and SASE **4**

1 Follows the format we established in our guidelines. Being able to follow directions is more important than many writers realize. **2** Story is in our word count, and the description sounds like the type of story we would consider publishing. **3** It's flattering to know he reads our magazine. While it won't guarantee publication, it does make me a little more hopeful that the story I'm reading will be a good fit. Also, good to know he's been published before. **4** I can figure it out, but it's nice to know what other materials were included in the envelope. This letter is not flashy, but it gives me the basics and puts me in the right frame of mind to read the actual story.

BAD FICTION MAGAZINE QUERY

To: curic@wonderstories808.com ❶
Subject: A Towering Epic Fantasy

Hello there. ❷

I've written a great fantasy epic novel short story of about 25,000 words that may be included in your magazine if you so desire. ❸

More than 20 years, I've spent chained to my desk in a basement writing out the greatest story of our modern time. And it can be yours if you so desire to have it. ❹

Just say the word, and I'll ship it over to you. We can talk money and movie rights after your acceptance. I have big plans for this story, and you can be part of that success. ❺

Yours forever (if you so desire), ❻

Harold
(or Harry for friends)

❶ We do not consider e-mail queries or submissions. ❷ This is a little too informal. ❸ First off, what did he write? An epic novel or short story? Second, 25,000 words is way over our 1,500-word max. ❹ I'm lost for words. ❺ Money and movie rights? We pay moderate rates and definitely don't get involved in movies. ❻ I'm sure the writer was just trying to be nice, but this is a little bizarre and kind of creepy. I do not so desire more contact with "Harry."

GOOD NONFICTION BOOK QUERY

To: corey@bigbookspublishing.com
Subject: Query: Become a Better Parent in 30 Days **1**

Dear Mr. Corey,

2 As a parent of six and a high school teacher for more than 20 years, I know first hand that being a parent is difficult work. Even harder is being a good parent. My proposed title **3** *Taking Care of Yourself and Your Kids: A 30-day Program to Become a Better Parent While Still Living Your Life* would show how to handle real-life situations and still be a good parent.

This book has been years in the making, as it follows the outline I've used successfully in my summer seminars I give on the topic to thousands of parents every year. It really works, because past participants contact me constantly to let me know what a difference my classes have made in their lives. **4**

In addition to marketing and selling *Taking Care of Yourself and Your Kids* at my summer seminars, I would also be able to sell it through my website and promote it through my weekly e-newsletter with over 25,000 subscribers. Of course, it would also make a very nice trade title that I think would sell well in bookstores and possibly retail outlets, such as Wal-Mart and Target. **5**

Please contact me for a copy of my full book proposal today. **6**

Thank you for your consideration.

Marilyn Parent
8647 Query St.
Norman OK 00000
mparent8647@email.com
www.marilynsbetterparents.com

1 Effective subject line. Lets me know exactly what to expect when I open the e-mail. **2** Good lead. Six kids and teaches high school. I already trust her as an expert. **3** Nice title that would fit well with others we currently offer. **4** Her platform as a speaker definitely gets my attention. **5** 25,000 e-mail subscribers? She must have a very good voice to gather that many readers. **6** I was interested after the first paragraph, but every paragraph after made it impossible to not request her proposal.

BAD NONFICTION BOOK QUERY

To: info@bigbookspublishing.com
Subject: a question for you ❶

I really liked this book by Mega Book Publishers called *Build Better Trains in Your Own Backyard*. It was a great book that covered all the basics of model train building. My father and I would read from it together and assemble all the pieces, and it was magical like Christmas all through the year. Why wouldn't you want to publish such a book? ❷

Well, here it is. I've already copyrighted the material for 2006 and can help you promote it if you want to send me on a worldwide book tour. As you can see from my attached digital photo, I'm not the prettiest person, but I am passionate. ❸

There are at least 1,000 model train builders in the United States alone, and there might be even more than that. I haven't done enough research yet, because I don't know if this is an idea that appeals to you. If you give me maybe $500, I could do that research in a day and get back to you on it. ❹

Anyway, this idea is a good one that brings back lots of memories for me.

Jacob ❺

❶ The subject line is so vague I almost deleted this e-mail as spam without even opening it. ❷ The reason we don't publish such a book is easy—we don't do hobby titles. ❸ I'm not going to open an attachment from an unknown sender via e-mail. Also, copyrighting your work years before pitching is the sign of an amateur. ❹ 1,000 possible buyers is a small market, and I'm not going to pay a writer to do research on a proposal. ❺ Not even a last name? Or contact information? At least I won't feel guilty for not responding.

GOOD FICTION BOOK QUERY

Jeremy Mansfield, editor
Novels R Us Publishing
8787 Big Time Street
New York NY 00000

Dear Mr. Mansfield,

My 62,000-word novel, *The Cat Walk,* is a psychologically complex thriller in the same mold as James Patterson's Alex Cross novels, but with a touch of the supernatural a la Stephenie Meyer. **1**

Rebecca Frank is at the top of the modeling world, posing for magazines in exotic locales all over the world and living life to its fullest. Despite all her success, she feels something is missing in her life. Then she runs into Marcus Hunt, a wealthy bachelor with cold blue eyes and an ambiguous past.

Within 24 hours of meeting Marcus, Rebecca's understanding of the world turns upside down, and she finds herself fighting for her life and the love of a man who may not have the ability to return her the favor.

Filled with demons, serial killers, trolls, maniacal clowns and more, *The Cat Walk* follows Rebecca through a gauntlet of trouble and turmoil, leading up to a final climactic realization that may lead to her own unraveling. **2**

The Cat Walk should fit in well with your other titles, such as *Bone Dead* and *Carry Me Home*, though it is a unique story. Your website mentioned supernatural suspense as a current interest, so I hope this is a good match. **3**

My short fiction has appeared in many mystery magazines, including a prize-winning story in *The Mysterious Oregon Quarterly.* This novel is the first in a series that I'm working on (already half-way through the second). **4**

As stated in your guidelines, I've included the first 30 pages. Thank you for considering *The Cat Walk*.

Sincerely,

Merry Plentiful
54 Willow Road
East Lansing MI 00000
merry865423@email.com

1 Novel is correct length and has the suspense and supernatural elements we're seeking. **2** The quick summary sounds like something we would write on the back cover of our paperbacks. That's a good thing, because it identifies the triggers that draw a response out of our readers. **3** She mentions similar titles we've done and that she's done research on our website. She's not afraid to put in a little extra effort. **4** At the moment, I'm not terribly concerned that this book could become a series, but it is something good to file away in the back of my mind for future use.

BAD FICTION BOOK QUERY

Jeremy Mansfield
Novels R Us Publishing
8787 Big Time Street
New York NY 00000

Dear Editor,

My novel has an amazing twist ending that could make it a worldwide phenomenon overnight while you are sleeping. It has spectacular special effects that will probably lead to a multi-million dollar movie deal that will also spawn action figures, lunch boxes, and several other crazy subsidiary rights. I mean, we're talking big-time money here. **1**

I'm not going to share the twist until I have a signed contract that authorizes me to a big bank account, because I don't want to have my idea stolen and used to promote whatever new initiative "The Man" has in mind for media nowadays. Let it be known that you will be rewarded handsomely for taking a chance on me. **2**

Did you know that George Lucas once took a chance on an actor named Harrison Ford by casting him as Han Solo in Star Wars? Look at how that panned out. Ford went on to become a big actor in the Indiana Jones series, *The Fugitive, Blade Runner*, and more. It's obvious that you taking a risk on me could play out in the same dramatic way. **3**

I realize that you've got to make money, and guess what? I want to make money too. So we're on the same page, you and I. We both want to make money, and we'll stop at nothing to do so.

If you want me to start work on this amazing novel with an incredible twist ending, just send a one-page contract agreeing to pay me a lot of money if we hit it big. No other obligations will apply. If it's a bust, I won't sue you for millions. **4**

Sincerely,

Kenzel Pain
92 Bad Writer Road
Austin TX 00000

1 While I love to hear enthusiasm from a writer about his or her work, this kind of unchecked excitement is worrisome for an editor. **2** I need to know the twist to make a decision on whether to accept the manuscript. Plus, I'm troubled by the paranoia and emphasis on making a lot of money. **3** I'm confused. Does he think he's Harrison Ford? **4** So that's the twist: He hasn't even written the novel yet. There's no way I'm going to offer a contract for a novel that hasn't been written by someone with no experience or idea of how the publishing industry works.

PERFECT PITCH:

Pitches That Never Fail

....

by Marc Acito

"A first-time novelist sets the record at a writers conference for the most pitches, leading to a multiple-book deal, awards, translations, excellent reviews and a movie option. An inspiring true success story, a literary version of Seabiscuit, *except the horse is a writer."*

As pitches go, this one's devoid of conflict, but that's the point. This scenario actually happened to me. Hence my qualification for writing this article.

My writing students get nervous when I ask them to pitch their works-in-progress on the first day of class, particularly if they're just starting. "I wouldn't know how to describe it," they say. "I don't know what it's about."

A pitch is simply another story that you're telling. A very, very short one.

And therein lies the problem. To some degree, we can't know what our novel/memoir/screenplay/play/nonfiction book is entirely about until we've gotten it down. But I contend that thinking about the pitch ahead of time helps focus a writer's goals for a piece. It's not just a commercial concern, it's an artistic one.

Writers are storytellers and a pitch is simply another story that you're telling. A very, very short one. Rather than view pitching as if you were a salesman in a bad suit hawking used cars, imagine that you're a pitcher for the Yankees and that the agent or editor is the catcher: They're on your team, so they really want to catch the ball.

Or, put another way, you're a different kind of pitcher, this one full of cool, refreshing water that will fill their empty glass.

But first you've got to get their attention.

THE HOOK

"I need something to grab me right away that tells me exactly why I should want to read this submission (of all the submissions on my desk)," says Christina Pride, senior editor at Hyperion.

A hook is exactly what it sounds like—a way to grab a reader like a mackerel and reel them in. It's not a plot summary, but more like the ad campaign you'd see on a movie poster. Veteran Hollywood screenwriter Cynthia Whitcomb, who teaches the pitching workshop at the Willamette Writers Conference in Portland, Oregon, recommends that writers of all genres start with a hooky tagline like this one from *Raiders of the Lost Ark*:

> *"If adventure had a name, it'd be Indiana Jones."*

That's not just first-rate marketing, it's excellent storytelling.

Here are some of my other favorite taglines for movies based on books, so you can see how easily the concept works for novels:

- "Help is coming from above." (*Charlotte's Web*)
- "From the moment they met it was murder." (*Double Indemnity*)
- "The last man on earth is not alone." (*I am Legend*)
- "Love means never having to say you're sorry." (*Love Story*)

The last one actually isn't true; love means always saying you're sorry, even when you're not, but the thought is provocative and provocation is exactly what you want to do.

When I pitched my first novel, *How I Paid for College,* I always started the same way. First, I looked the catcher right in the eye (this is very important—how else are they going to catch the ball?). Then I said,

> *"Embezzlement. Blackmail. Fraud…High School."*

I began my query letters the same way.

"I always begin my proposals with a question," says Jennifer Basye Sander, co-author of *The Complete Idiots Guide to Getting Published.* "I want to get an editor nodding their head in agreement right away."

No, you're not asking something like, "Are you ready to rock 'n roll?" but instead an open-ended conversation starter like, "Can you be forgiven for sending an innocent man to jail?" (Ian McEwan's *Atonement*) or "What does it take to climb Mount Everest?" (Jon Krakauer's *Into Thin Air*). Particularly useful are "what if?" questions like "What if an amnesiac didn't know he was the world's most wanted assassin?" (Robert Ludlum's *The Bourne Identity*) or "What if Franklin Delano Roosevelt had been defeated by Charles Lindbergh in 1940?" (*The Plot Against America*, Philip Roth).

Acito employs humor in his novels, but there's nothing funny about the effectiveness of his pitches.

The same also holds true for nonfiction. If you sat down in front of an agent and asked, "What if you could trim your belly fat and use it to fuel your car?" trust me, they'd listen. Questions like that make the catcher want to know more. Which is exactly what you do by creating…

THE LOG LINE

No, it's not a country western dance done in a timber mill. And without realizing it, you're already a connoisseur of the genre, having read thousands of log lines in *TV Guide* or imdb. com or the *New York Times* Bestseller List. A log line is a one-sentence summary that states the central conflict of your story. For example:

> *"A teen runaway kills the first person she encounters, then is pursued by the dead woman's sister as she teams up with three strangers to kill again."*

Recognize it? That's *The Wizard of Oz*.
Here's another:

> *"The son of a carpenter leaves on an adventure of self-discovery, rejects sin, dies and rises again transformed."*

Obviously, that's *Pinocchio*.
Okay, seriously, here's the one I did for *How I Paid for College*:

> *"A talented but irresponsible teenager schemes to steal his college tuition money when his wealthy father refuses to pay for him to study acting at Juilliard."*

It's not genius, but it captured the story succinctly by identifying the protagonist, the antagonist, and the conflict between them. In other words, the essential element for any compelling story.

AND HERE'S THE PITCH...

Pitches are often referred to as "elevator pitches" because they should last the length of your average elevator ride—anywhere from 30 seconds to two minutes. Or, for a query letter, one page single-spaced. That's about 350 words, including "Dear Mr. William Morris" and "Your humble servant, Desperate Writer."

Essentially, the pitch is identical to a book jacket blurb: it elaborates on the set-up, offers a few further complications on the central conflict, then gives an indication of how it wraps up. When it comes to the ending, "don't be coy," says Erin Harris, a literary agent at the Irene Skolnick Agency in Manhattan. "Spoil the secrets, and let me know what really happens." Agents and editors want a clear idea of what kind of ride they're getting on before investing hours in your manuscript. Make it easy for them to do their jobs selling it.

> Agents and editors want a clear idea of what kind of ride they're getting on before investing hours in your manuscript.

Nowhere was this clearer to me than when I read the jacket copy of my first novel and saw that it was virtually identical to my query letter.

Indeed, your best practice for learning how to pitch is to read jacket descriptions (leaving out the part about the author being a "bold, original new voice"—that's for others to say).

Or think of it as a very short story, following the structure attributed to writer Alice Adams: Action, Backstory, Development, Climax, End.

It's as easy as ABDCE.

"The best queries convey the feeling that the author understands what the scope, structure, voice, and audience of the book really are," says Rakesh Satyal, senior editor at HarperCollins to authors such as Paul Coelho, Armistead Maupin and Clive Barker. "To misunderstand or miscommunicate any of these things can be truly detrimental."

That's the reason we often resort to the Hollywoody jargon of it's "This meets that," as in "It's *No Country for Old Men* meets *Little Women*." Or it's...

- ...*Die Hard* on a bus (*Speed*)
- ...*Die Hard* in a plane (*Con Air*)
- ...*Die Hard* in a phone booth (*Phone Booth*)
- ...*Die Hard* in a skyscraper (no, wait, that's *Die Hard*).

HOW I PAID FOR COLLEGE

A Tale of Sex, Theft, Friendship and Musical Theater

A novel by Marc Acito

Embezzlement…Blackmail…Fraud…High School.

How I Paid for College is a 97,000-word comic novel about a talented but irresponsible teenager who schemes to steal his college tuition money when his wealthy father refuses to pay for acting school. The story is just true enough to embarrass my family.

It's 1983 in Wallingford, New Jersey, a sleepy bedroom community outside of Manhattan. Seventeen-year-old Edward Zanni, a feckless Ferris Bueller type, is Peter Panning his way through a carefree summer of magic and mischief, sending underwear up flagpoles and re-arranging lawn animals in compromising positions. The fun comes to a screeching halt, however, when Edward's father remarries and refuses to pay for Edward to study acting at Juilliard.

In a word, Edward's screwed. He's ineligible for scholarships because his father earns too much. He's unable to contact his mother because she's off somewhere in Peru trying to commune with the Incan spirits. And, in a sure sign he's destined for a life in the arts, Edward's incapable of holding down a job. ("One little flesh wound is all it takes to get fired as a dog groomer, even if you artfully arrange its hair so the scar doesn't show.")

So Edward turns to his loyal (but immoral) misfit friends to help him steal the tuition money from his father. Disguising themselves as nuns and priests (because who's going to question the motives of a bunch of nuns and priests?) they merrily scheme their way through embezzlement, money laundering, identity theft, forgery and blackmail.

But along the way Edward also learns the value of friendship, hard work and how you're not really a man until you can beat up your father. (Metaphorically, that is.)

How I Paid for College is a farcical coming-of-age story that combines the first-person-smart-ass tone of David Sedaris with the byzantine plot twists of Armistead Maupin. I've written it with the HBO-watching, NPR-listening, Vanity Fair-reading audience in mind.

As a syndicated humor columnist, I'm familiar with this audience. For the past three years, my bi-weekly column, "The Gospel According to Marc," has appeared in 18 alternative newspapers in major markets, including Los Angeles, Chicago and Washington, DC. During that time I've amassed a personal mailing list of over 1,000 faithful readers.

How I Paid for College is a story for anyone who's ever had a dream…and a scheme.

www.MarcAcito.com
(503) 246-2208
Marc@MarcAcito.com
5423 SW Cameron Road, Portland, OR 97221

"I appreciate when agents and authors offer good comp titles," confirms Hyperion's Christina Pride. "It's good shorthand to help me begin to position the book in my mind right from the outset in terms of sensibility and potential audience."

Agent Erin Harris agrees. "For example," she says, "the premise of one book meets the milieu of another book." As in *Pride and Prejudice and Zombies*, an idea I will forever regret not thinking of myself.

When citing comp titles, be certain to invoke the most commercially successful and well-known works to which you can honestly liken yourself. No agent wants to earn 15 percent of *Obscure Literary Title* meets *Total Downer by Author Who Committed Suicide*.

So I steered clear of my lesser-known influences and focused on the big names, saying, "*How I Paid for College* is a farcical coming-of-age story that combines the first-person-smart-ass tone of David Sedaris with the byzantine plot twists of Armistead Maupin."

That line also made it onto the jacket copy.

My book hasn't changed, but I continue to update the pitch as I develop the movie. What started as "*Ferris Bueller* meets *High School Musical*," turned into "A mash-up of *Ocean's 11* and *Glee*." By the time the movie actually gets made it'll be "*iTunes Implant Musical Experience* meets *Scheming Sentient Robots*."

"A word of caution," Harris adds. "Please do not liken your protagonist to Holden Caulfield or your prose style to that of Proust. Truly, it's best to steer clear of the inimitable."

Speaking of the inimitable, while the titles of *Catcher in the Rye* and *Remembrance of Things Past* are poetically evocative, they wouldn't distinguish themselves from the pack in the Too-Much-Information Age. Nowadays, your project is competing for attention with a video of a toddler trapped behind a couch. (I'm serious, Google it, it's got all the makings of great drama: a sympathetic protagonist, conflict, complications, laughter, tears and an uplifting ending. All in two minutes and 27 seconds.)

So while it's not a dictum of the publishing industry (though, given the nosedive the industry has taken, what do *they* know?), I think 21st century writers would do well to title their works in ways that accommodate the searchable keyword culture of the Internet.

In other words, *To Kill a Mockingbird* was fine for 1960, but if you tried promoting it today, you'd end up at the PETA website.

Like the logline, the catchiest titles actually describe what the book is about. Consider:

- *Eat, Pray, Love*
- *Diary of a Wimpy Kid*
- *Sh*t My Dad Says*
- *A Portrait of the Artist as a Young Man*

In those cases, the title is the synopsis. Similarly, some titles, while less clear, include an inherent mystery or question:

- *Sophie's Choice*

- *The Hunger Games*
- *And Then There Were None*
- *The Hitchhiker's Guide to the Galaxy*

Lastly, even if the reader can't know automatically what the title means, it helps if it's simple and memorable, like:

- *Twilight*
- *Valley of the Dolls*
- *The Thorn Birds*
- *Captain Underpants*

One way to tell if you've got an effective title is to submit it to the "Have you read…?" test. If it feels natural coming at the end of that sentence, you're on the right track.

Granted, straightforward titles are easier if you're writing nonfiction like *Trim Your Belly Fat and Use it to Fuel Your Car*. As is the final part of the pitch.

BUILDING A PLATFORM

Along with branding, platform is one of the most overused buzz words of the last decade. "If you are writing nonfiction," Erin Harris says, "it's important to describe your platform and to be a qualified expert on the subject about which you're writing"

In other words, if you're going to write *Teach Your Cat to Tap Dance* you better deliver a tap-dancing cat, along with research about the market for such a book.

For first-time novelists this can prove challenging. But Harris says that every credit truly helps: "If you have pieces published in literary magazines, if you have won awards, or if you have an MFA, my interest is piqued."

That last advice should also pique the interest of every fledgling writer out there. In my case, what actually got me an agent wasn't just the pitch, it was the fact that I met best-selling novelist Chuck Palahniuk at a workshop and he'd read a column of mine in a small alternative newspaper. Ultimately, it's not about who you know, it's about who knows you. So publish wherever you can. You never know who's reading.

Write on.

MARC ACITO is the award-winning author of the comic novels *How I Paid for College* and *Attack of the Theater People*. *How I Paid for College* won the Ken Kesey Award for Fiction, was a Top Teen Pick by the American Library Association and is translated into five languages the author cannot read. A regular contributor to NPR's *All Things Considered*, he teaches story structure online and at NYU. www.MarcAcito.com

PHOTO: Marc Acito

FEATURE ARTICLE WRITING:

The Query in 3 Parts

by Chuck Sambuchino

If you want to write freelance articles for editors, the query letter is your best and most effective tool. It's essentially a one-page business plan for your idea—explaining what the idea is, why it will be a good fit for their publication, and why you're a qualified writer for the assignment.

You see, editors for magazines, newspapers and websites have one thing in common: They're all incredibly busy. They have very little time for anything, so they need to consider article ideas quickly, and that's where your query comes in. It's your pitch, and you have one short page to get their attention and convince them to pay you money in exchange for an assignment. Although there is no "perfect" or "surefire" way to structure a query, I have adopted and slowly tried to refine a three-part approach that seems to work well. Read on, and dig deeper into what comprises a successful, eye-catching query letter.

THE FIRST SECTION: THE HOOK

Nothing works better in a query letter than hooking an editor right away with your idea. By the end of the first sentence, they should be intrigued and want to know more. The first paragraph is designed to pique interest and give them a taste of what your article will be about. It's also the best chance you have in a query to show the flavor of your writing—your voice, for lack of a better term. If the article is going to be light and funny, your intro should reflect that. If it's going to be heavy and serious, make sure your query is, too. Keep in mind that if you are contacting a person you know or through a referral, that is always a great way to start—explaining your connection.

If you don't have a connection or referral, here are a few ways to get an editor's attention immediately with your query:

Start with an eye-catching fact

> Alaska not only has the country's highest ratio of low birth weight babies, the percentage is actually going up yearly.

> Last year's dreaded recession brought countless white wedding plans to a screeching halt. According to David Bridal's recent national survey, 75% of American brides-to-be are searching high and low for a way to still have the wedding of their dreams—without spending a fortune.

With an approach like this, you're aiming to immediately tell the editor that what you have to say is news—and it's important.

Use an interesting tidbit

> There are 87 varieties of organic crops grown in the United States, but there's only one farm producing 12 of these—Morganic Corporation.

> If I asked you which sports hobby was the most popular for retirees in South Florida, you may say bowling or shuffleboard. Perhaps some would even throw out softball or darts—but all those guesses would be wrong. The truth is: The mini-golf movement has hit South Florida big time, and it's taking over everywhere.

When you have a story that isn't hard news (perhaps a feature or profile), an interesting fact works well. Think of it like this: You learned about something and were interested enough to research more and pitch an article. Try to get us interested in the subject just like you were.

Start in media res—in the middle of a story

> It was 2:14 a.m. when a drunk driver smashed into the bedroom of Mike Edson's condo and took the life of his wife.

> I'm right in the middle of my weeklong quest to find the best cheeseburger in DC when a monstrosity known only as "The Goliath" is dropped in front of me on a plate. It's less of a burger than it is a defining moment in your life. I notice my hands are shaking as I reach to pick it up—all three pounds of it.

When your piece focuses on a front-to-back narrative (that can involve you or others), you can always just show an interesting moment right in the middle. This gets us editors asking questions such as "How did he get to this moment?" "Does he finish the burger?" "What was his final decision as to the best burger in the city?" In other words, I want to know more.

THE SECOND SECTION: THE SPECS

If you've done your job, the editor is still reading your query. You've caught their attention with the first sentence then expounded on your idea by putting more meat on the bones. The second part of the query letter is where you take a step back and start to talk about the specs of the article itself. A safe way is to start this paragraph with "I propose an article on …"

With a paragraph or two, your goal is to explain more about the size and scope of the piece, what the article will look like on the page, and, finally, prove to the editor that you read their publication and are familiar with the type of content readers like to see.

Mind the Details

Here are things you want to address/include:

- Estimated length (word count).
- Targeted section of the magazine. Where will this article appear in the publication?
- What kind of story is it? Feature? Profile? Column?
- The slant, if it needs explaining. For example, let's say you hear about a local woman who's planting a rose in town for every soldier that dies fighting the war on terror. You could pitch an article about her to a gardening magazine, a military/patriotic magazine, and a local interest magazine. But each one will need a different focus— a different slant.
- Do you have access to people you will interview? If you are proposing to profile famous screenwriter Charlie Kaufman for *Creative Screenwriting*, you will need to say that you have access to him somehow. Do you want to sit down with Kevin Garnett? How can you secure an interview?
- Do you have access to images or will you provide art/pictures? If you're writing for *Popular Woodworking* or *Ohio Game and Fish*, will you be taking your own photos to provide with the piece? You increase your chances of success if you do so.
- Any sources lined up—or at least the names of whom you would interview. If you are writing a piece on low birth weight, to continue that example, you should quickly list the names of people you will consult and interview for the piece. With luck, you've already spoken with one and have a quote you can include in the query.

THE THIRD SECTION: THE BIO

If an editor is still reading your query by the end, she must love the idea and feel it has promise for their publication. What a writer must do now is convince her as to why they're the ideal person to compose this piece. In other words, she's looking for credentials—a bio.

Elements of a Bio

- Do you have any qualifications of relevance? For example, if you're writing for *Men's Fitness,* do you hold any degrees or certifications in the health field?
- Have you written about this subject before?
- What publications have you written for, if any?

If you have enclosed or attached clips (previously published samples of your writing), say so. You can attach PDF scans of a piece, or simply paste a link to an online article. Ideally, you want to show them clips that have some comparison to what you want to write about. For instance, if you want to do a profile of gymnast who is considered the most promising eight-year-old in the world in her field, then do you have any sample profiles for the editor to see? Mentioning that you write about cars for the local paper shows that you're a professional, but doesn't yet convince her that you can tackle a profile on an eight-year-old.

And if You Have No Credits?

Keep in mind that if you have no clips to include, don't embellish or exaggerate. Just skip the clips part. Thank the editor for considering the submission and wrap up with "Sincerely, (Name)."

The higher you aim for an assignment, the more editors will demand credentials and credits. If you query the local parenting magazine that's usually found for free in supermarkets, you don't need a slew of impressive articles in your pocket. You probably just need a good idea and professional-looking query. But if you want to write for a mid-size magazine like *The Pastel Journal* or *Girlfriends Magazine*, you will likely need some bylines to your name.

QUERY FAQ

Do queries have a specific font or format? Your best bet is to use a normal font and typeface, such as Times New Roman or Arial. Use 10- or 12-point font.

Should I discuss payment in a query? No. If you've done your research, you should have a general idea of what a magazine pays. The payment discussion will come up organically as the conversation goes along. Bringing up payment too quickly may show that you're hard to work with.

Who do I address the letter to? Every publication has a submissions editor—meaning, an individual who is in charge of reviewing queries and accepting good ideas. With a tiny website or magazine, there is likely a staff of one, and the top editor is reviewing everything. For larger publications, such as our magazines here at our publishing house—*Writer's Digest* or *Watercolor Artist*—the top editor is not the contact person for submissions. Seek out a copy of the publication's submission guidelines to get the name of the submissions editor. If in doubt, contact the publication by e-mail or phone and simply ask who to address the letter to and the best e-mail address to use.

Should I mention the work is copyrighted? No. The editors already know this, and mentioning what the editors already know comes off amateurish.

Do editors want to know if it's a simultaneous submission? You don't *have* to mention it, but yes, editors appreciate knowing.

What if the query has been rejected in the past? Don't mention it when contacting editors. Letting them know this just makes the idea sound worse. They get to thinking, "If four other people have rejected it, the idea must not be worth it…"

What if the material's been published before? Let editors know. If what you're pitching is a reprinted article or an excerpt from a book you wrote, that's A-OK—just let them know upfront.

Should writers submit via e-mail vs. snail mail? Once again, check the submission guidelines to see how publications like to get queries. Over the past decade, there has been a gradual yet large shift toward e-queries—and that's a good thing. E-mail queries are quicker and less expensive. If you have the option to submit either way, it makes no real difference.

Can I follow up if I don't hear back? Sure, but check guidelines first. If a magazine says they respond to ideas within six weeks, I'd wait eight before following up. In your follow-up, be polite and humble, simply mentioning that you had not heard back and are afraid the first e-mail got lost in cyberspace, which is why you're resubmitting the original query below (just cut and paste it again).

How do you end a query? A safe bet is always to thank the editor for their time and sign off. If you're querying an agent, ask if you can send some pages of your work (or the full proposal for nonfiction).

BOOK QUERIES

Book queries are slightly different than article queries whether you're submitting to a literary agent or directly to a publisher. Again, there is no surefire format, but they are still one page long and you can still employ a three-part structure—but the three parts will be:

PART 1: THE BASICS. Provide the title, word count and genre/category. Also, why are you contacting this agent/editor? Explain why you picked this agent/editor out of all your options. Explain why they're a great match for your book. Try to establish a connection. If you are contacting by referral, or because you met them at a writers' conference, say so upfront.

PART 2: THE PITCH. This is where you explain what your project is about in 3-10 sentences. If you're writing a novel or memoir, go to the nearest Barnes & Noble and start looking at the backs of DVD boxes and the inside covers of novels. This will get you in the mindset of writing a concise and compelling pitch paragraph. You will see how a pitch is composed and how they're designed to pique your interest but not reveal the ending.

PART 3: THE BIO. Again, list who you are and what credits you have. If you are writing nonfiction, this section—explaining your platform and marketing ability—will be the most important aspect of the letter.

GOOD ARTICLE QUERY

John Q. Writer 7
123 Author Lane Writerville, USA
johnqwriter@email.com
(323) 555-0000

Jan. 30, 2009

Jane Smith, managing editor
New Mexico Magazine
4200 Magazine Blvd. Santa Fe, NM 87501

Ms. Smith: 1

According to the Bible, it took two days for God to create all living creatures. 9 The way New Mexican Regina Gordon sees it, the 48-Hour Film Project involves the same amount of time—with only a slightly less complicated task.

"Every second counts, when you have 48 hours to make a film." That's the motto of the 48-Hour Film Project (www.48hourfilm.com), a nationwide event that challenges local filmmakers to form teams and create four-minute movies—from script to set design to finished product—in 48 hours or less. Albuquerque is no stranger to the fray, and will again participate in the competition in 2009.

Also returning in 2009 is the city's area producer: Gordon. More than 20 area teams competed in 2008—with all of these guerilla filmmakers reporting to one woman—Gordon—who must substitute passion, adrenaline, and insane amounts of coffee for sleep she certainly won't get. So what drives her and other participants to exhaust themselves like they do? I propose an 2 800-word short profile on Gordon and, with it, New Mexico's involvement in the project for *New Mexico Magazine.* (I've already touched based with Gordon.) I believe that a Gordon feature would be a great fit for the "Introducing" section 8 of your magazine. To give readers a feel for what a kinetic, exciting, shoot-from-the-hip experience this is, I would interview Langston to hear anecdotes from last year and discover what lies in store for this year—as a sense of community for the project continues to build in the area.

3 In 2003, I covered Philadelphia's involvement in the project for *Artspike* magazine. Thank you for considering this piece. My résumé and clips are enclosed.

4 Respectfully,
5

John Q. Writer

Encl.: Clips and résumé 6

1 Always address the correct editor 2 Estimated word count 3 Highlight qualifications quickly and effectively 4 Be polite 5 Signature. If you're mailing the letter, leave enough room here to sign your cursive signature. 6 Detail your enclosures 7 One of many letterhead styles you can use 8 Targeting a specific section of the magazine shows you're familiar with the publication 9 A lead designed to hook and pique interest

BAD ARTICLE QUERY

Richard D. Bonehead
123 Mistake Lane Rejectionville, USA [1]

March 24, 2009

Editors
Atlanta Journal-Constitution
[2]

Dear Sir/Ma'am: [3]

I have an idea for a newspaper article. I have a feeling that it would be a controversial and explosive story that would sell a whole bunch of copies—its [4] that good. What I want to do is give you some of my early thoughts, and if you're interested, we can talk some specifics over the phone (though bear with me; my cell phone gets bad reception).

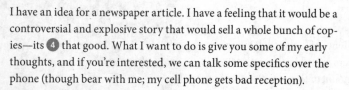

This is what I'm thinking. I write an article on how the social networking juggernaut MySpace [5] is affecting the dating scene in the ATL. Cool, huh? I know that I could have pitched this) to *Atlanta Magazine* or even *People*, but I figured I would give you a shot. For the article, I would need some ideas for sources, and probably some upfront money to buy a laptop. At this point, I'm thinking the article will run about 5,000 words. [6]

My writing influences are Stephen King, James Patterson and Joe Eszterhas. I've blogged on MySpace plenty of times before and I also regularly comment on website forums and message boards, so I think I have the necessary experience to tackle such an article. [7]

I'm offering a seven-day window on this query because I think that's fair. After all, this is a sizzling topic. Please get back to me right quick.

Peace,

Richard D. Bonehead

[1] No e-mail or phone number included [2] Address is missing [3] Not targeting a specific editor shows lack of basic research [4] This simple grammatical error could have been caught with some proofreading [5] Idea is not fleshed out and no indication of how to hook readers [6] Proposed length is way too long for virtually any publication [7] While you want to list credentials, something worse would be to list meaningless accomplishments

GOOD QUERY TO AGENT

(2) Dorien Orion
123 Author Lane
Writerville, USA
(323) 555-0000
johnqwriter@email.com

Mollie Glick

Foundry Literary + Media
33 West 17th St. PH
New York, NY 10011

Dear Ms. Glick: (3)

I am a psychiatrist, published author, and expert for the national media seeking representation for my memoir (1) titled, *Queen of the Road: The True Tale of 47 States, 22,000 Miles, 200 Shoes, 2 Cats, 1 Poodle, a Husband, and a Bus with a Will of Its Own.* Because you are interested in unique voices, I thought we might be a good match.

When Tim first announced he wanted to "chuck it all" and travel around the country in a converted bus for a year, (4) I gave this profound and potentially life-altering notion all the thoughtful consideration it deserved. "Why can't you be like a normal husband with a midlife crisis and have an affair or buy a Corvette?" I asked, adding, "I will never, ever, EVER live on a bus."

What do you get when you cram married shrinks — one in a midlife crisis, the other his materialistic, wise-cracking wife — two cats who hate each other and a Standard Poodle who loves licking them all, into a bus for a year? *Queen of the Road* is a memoir of my dysfunctional, multi-species family's travels to and travails in the 49 continental states.

(5) As a psychiatrist, award-winning author (*I Know You Really Love Me*, Macmillan/Dell) and frequent media expert on psychiatric topics, (including "Larry King," "GMA," "48 Hours," *The New York Times* and *People Magazine*), my life has centered on introspection, analysis and storytelling. Yet, I count among my greatest accomplishments that last year, our bus was featured as the centerfold of *Bus Conversions Magazine*, thus fulfilling my life-long ambition of becoming a Miss September.

If you are interested in sample pages, I would be happy to send them to you via e-mail or snail mail.

Best wishes,

Doreen Orion

Note how this is a nonfiction book, but memoirs are treated as novels because they read like novels. *(Comments provided by Mollie Glick of Foundry Literary + Media.)*

(1) Note how books are "titled," not "entitled." (2) Including full contact information (3) Always address your query to a specific agent. (4) It doesn't take long for Doreen to provide the hook, or "elevator pitch," and quickly explain what her memoir is about. (5) Lastly, Doreen sums up her platform nicely. Her writing credits are impressive, and she's obviously got the connections in place to spread the word about this book once it comes out.

BAD QUERY TO AGENT

Big Time Literary Agency
200 W. Broadway
New York, NY 10125

Dear Agent: **2**

I have just completed my first novel and would like to sell it to a publisher. I have never had a book published but I know this novel will be a bestseller. I'm looking for an agent to help me. I would really appreciate it if you could read over the enclosed chapters and give me some advice on whether you think this a good novel **6** and if it needs any extra work to make it a bestseller.

The Subject of Susan is about 60,000 words long and is geared toward an **4** adult audience. It is all about a headstrong woman named Susan and her trials and tribulations throughout the 1950s and beyond as she makes her way in the legal world after graduating from law school as the only woman in her graduating class. **1**

This is my first novel **3** and while I am not familiar with the legal world, since I'm not a lawyer, I find the subject fascinating and think readers will too. I've written a lot of short stories dealing with women's lives but they were much more romanticized than the story of Susan. Susan is someone you would know in real life. I have spent the last 20 years of my life raising my children **7** and think I have what it takes to become a successful writer.

I own the **5** copyright on this book and would like to discuss possible advances and royalties with you sometime soon.

Thank you very much,

John Q. Writer

1 There is nothing here to indicate how this book will distinguish itself from the thousands of other similar books that have been published. How will this book be different? **2** Always address your query to a specific agent. **3** Never mention that you're a first-time writer or that you have never been published—it singles you out as an amateur. **4** This is vague and tells the agent very little about the book. There is no "hook" to capture the agent's attention. **5** Don't mention copyright information or payment expectations. This is a query to assess an agent's interest in your novel. **6** Don't ask an agent for advice or criticism—that's not the agent's job nor the purpose of the query letter. **7** Don't draw attention to your lack of experience as a writer, and don't mention anything about yourself that is not pertinent to the novel. Keep all your information focused on the book itself.

CHUCK SAMBUCHINO is a freelancer as well as the editor of *Guide to Literary Agents* (www.guidetoliteraryagents.com/blog). He also helmed the third edition of *Formatting & Submitting Your Manuscript* (Writer's Digest Books) and is the author of *How to Survive a Garden Gnome Attack* (Ten Speed Press). More than 600 of his articles have appeared in print.

PHOTO: Al Parrish

THE UNCERTAINLY BRAVE NEW WORLD:

Recent Changes in Publishing

....

by Robert Lee Brewer

When I first started working at F + W Media (a little over 11 years ago), it was called F&W Publishing, and *Writer's Market* had a Compact Disc complement, not a website called WritersMarket.com. Books and magazines were printed for the most part, and social networking was something done in person, not on a computer or "smart" phone.

Of course, things have changed dramatically in just over a decade. Some changes have been driven by technology. Other changes have been driven by the economy. Regardless of why things have changed, it's important for freelancers to understand the new world of publishing and how to make it work for them.

The following snapshots will show writers how the industry has changed and how it is continuing to change. However, I want to make one point perfectly clear: The publishing industry is still dominated by the traditional print models. Whether that will hold true forever is anyone's guess, but for now, traditional print is still where most of the money is. That said, let's look at how the industry is changing.

BOOK PUBLISHING

Until very recently, the main changes in book publishing seemed limited only to where books sold (a progression to online sales) and how well books sold (a slight downward trend as books fight to stay relevant against online competition). However, advancements in e-reader products have started to shift the market in potentially dramatic ways.

For instance, Amazon now sells more e-books than paperback or hardcover books. That's a dramatic shift. At the same time, Amazon's top selling product is its own Kindle e-reading device. This is important because Amazon is the top retailer on the Internet.

With Borders recently filing for bankruptcy and in-store sales at many brick and mortar bookstores trending downward, it's becoming more and more apparent that book sales are moving online. Plus, the definition of the word "book" is morphing into a publication that could be print and/or electronic in nature.

Authors may not be signing hardcover books in the future; they may be signing special edition thumb drives—or providing electronic signatures on e-readers as if signing for a credit card purchase at Wal-Mart or Target.

THREE TOP E-READERS

The e-reader market has been picking up momentum at unbelievable speeds, and it's affecting how publishers and writers approach publication. Here are the three top e-readers:

- **KINDLE.** This is the official e-reader of Amazon. It uses an e-ink screen, which means that it doesn't reflect light and is easier on the eyes. Using e-ink screens also means the screen only displays in black & white.

- **IPAD.** The e-reader developed by Apple has been courting more magazine business than that of book publishing for a few reasons. One, the iPad has a backlit LCD screen, which is a little harder on the eyes for prolonged reading sessions. Two, the iPad displays in color, which suits the needs of magazine publishers. Finally, the iPad is more interactive.

- **NOOK.** Brick-and-mortar booksellers Barnes & Noble developed the Nook to compete with both the Kindle and the iPad, though initially it seems more aligned to the needs of book publishers. Available in both color and e-ink versions, the Nook has the advantage of being available for purchase online and in-store.

MAGAZINES

The magazine industry has been a little more adventurous than book publishing in terms of trying out new models—from using websites to providing digital downloads. In many cases, the experiments have been interesting but not sustainable. The latest trend is to create magazine apps for Apple's iPad.

By the time this book is printed, the kinks in the magazine app market may be straightened out, but at the moment there are a few problems with this latest experiment. Magazine publishers and Apple have been wrestling over how much customer information the publishers can access as well as how much money Apple can claim on sales. Plus, there are even problems with offering subscriptions (as opposed to single issues of magazines).

As with the book publishing specific e-reading devices, competitors are sure to take the initial success of magazine apps and make the market more competitive, which will probably be a good thing for both publishers and freelance writers. Still, this only covers distribution. The future magazine app products will likely do things that print products can't.

Freelance writers may have to write an article but also record a video presentation. Or writers may need to write an interview, but then share video of the interview taking place. Or pitch a game that can be developed to run along with a piece on how to do (blank). The new app environment will require a greater level of creativity and interactivity.

SELF-PUBLISHING

At the beginning of the 21st century, self-publishing was still considered a major no-no for serious writers who wanted to make money writing. Part of the argument had to do with production value; part of the argument had to do with distribution; and another part had to do with predatory tactics used by self-publishing companies. Writers should always be on guard for predators, but the other two problems can now be overcome.

With the rise of social networks, writers now have more access to reputable editors and designers than at any point in the past. As a result, writers can now create wonderfully edited and designed products that readers want. Plus, writers can get programming help to create electronic versions of their books.

The changes to the publishing industry mentioned earlier in this article about book publishers and magazines have not completely leveled the playing field with self-published authors. However, those changes have made it easier for self-published writers to compete. It just takes a lot of hard work and a little creativity.

E-BOOK PRICING: ARE YOU CHASING READERS OR MONEY?

Of course, writers who publish books probably would like both more money and readers. However, some recent developments in self-publishing have me wondering about what the best pricing strategy might be for e-Books.

At the time of this article, Amazon offered 70% royalties to authors for books sold at $2.99 or more. Titles sold below this threshold only earned 35% royalties. Many authors have been experimenting at the lower price point and finding that their sales jump exponentially.

This leads me to wonder if it's better to de-value the price of a book to convert more sales or to keep the price point higher to have a more engaged readership. After all, it would take six sales at 99 cents to equal one sale at $2.99 (from the author's perspective).

From a purely economic perspective, a writer just needs to test each price point and see which one brings in more money. From a purely numbers perspective, a writer might just want the number of readers to be greater and assume that more sales units equals more readers.

This is where things get interesting or confusing—depending upon your interest in math, statistics and behavioral studies. More sales at a lower price point could actually produce fewer engaged readers, because 99-cent e-books could be considered an impulse buy (like a 99-cent phone app).

Many writers and publishers may consider reader engagement an unimportant criterion. Many readers already "gift" books and make impulse buys at higher price points anyway. For many, it really does come down to what makes the most money.

While not everyone will achieve the same level of success that Amanda Hocking and J.A. Konrath have with their self-publishing efforts, freelance writers now have the opportunity to leverage their hard work and creativity in ways that were not available a decade ago. If you're interested in self-publishing, I recommend checking out the self-publishing checklist following this article.

ROBERT LEE BREWER is Senior Content Editor for the Writer's Digest Writing Community. In 2010, he was named Poet Laureate of the Blogosphere by BloggingPoet.com. He frequently speaks on writing and publishing topics at writers conferences. A version of the e-book pricing sidebar was excerpted from his personal blog, My Name Is Not Bob (http://robertleebrewer.blogspot.com).

PHOTO: Al Parrish

SELF-PUBLISHING CHECKLIST

Below is a checklist of essential hurdles to clear when self-publishing your book. This list makes the assumption that you've already completed and polished your manuscript. For more information on self-publishing, check out *The Complete Guide to Self-Publishing*, by Tom and Marilyn Ross (Writer's Digest).

☐ **CREATE PRODUCTION SCHEDULE.** Put a deadline for every step of the process of self-publishing your book. A good rule of thumb is to double your estimates on how long each step will take. It's better to have too much time and hit your dates than constantly have to extend deadlines.

☐ **FIND EDITOR.** Don't skimp on your project and do all the editing yourself. Even editors need editors. Try to find an editor you trust, whether through a recommendation or a search online. Ask for references if the editor is new to you.

☐ **FIND DESIGNER.** Same goes here. Find a good designer to at least handle the cover. If you can have a designer lay out the interior pages too, that's even better.

☐ **DEFINE THE TARGET AUDIENCE.** In nonfiction this is an important step, because knowing the needs of the audience can help with the editing process. Even if you're writing fiction or poetry, it's a good idea to figure out who your audience is, because this will help you with the next few steps.

☐ **FIGURE OUT A PRINT AND DISTRIBUTION PLAN.** This plan should first figure out what the end product will be: printed book, e-book, app, or a combination of options. Then, the plan will define how the products will be created and distributed to readers.

❑ **SET PUBLICATION DATE.** The publication date should be set on your production schedule above. Respect this deadline more than all the others, because the marketing and distribution plans will most likely hinge on this deadline being met.

❑ **PLOT OUT YOUR MARKETING PLAN.** The smartest plan is to have a soft launch date of a week or two (just in case). Then, hard launch into your marketing campaign, which could be as simple as a book release party and social networking mentions, or as involved as a guest blog tour and paid advertising. With self-publishing, it's usually more prudent to spend energy and ideas than money on marketing—at least in the beginning.

❑ **HAVE AN EXCELLENT TITLE.** For nonfiction, titles are easy. Describe what your book is covering in a way that is interesting to your target audience. For fiction and poetry, titles can be a little trickier, but attempt to make your title easy to remember and refer.

❑ **GET ENDORSEMENT.** Time for this should be factored into the production schedule. Contact some authors or experts in a field related to your title and send them a copy of your manuscript to review. Ask them to consider endorsing your book, and if they do, put that endorsement on the cover. Loop in your designer to make this look good.

❑ **REGISTER COPYRIGHT.** Protect your work. Go to http://copyright.gov for more information on how to register your book.

❑ **SECURE ISBN.** An ISBN code helps booksellers track and sell your book. To learn more about securing an ISBN, go to www.isbn.org.

❑ **CREATE TABLE OF CONTENTS AND INDEX (FOR NONFICTION).** The table of contents (TOC) helps organize a nonfiction title and give structure for both the author and the reader. An index serves a similar function for readers, making it easier for them to find the information they want to find. While an index is usually not necessary for fiction or poetry, most poetry collections do use a table of contents to make it easy to locate individual poems.

❑ **INCLUDE AUTHOR BIO.** Readers want to know about the authors of the books they read. Make this information easy to find in the back of the book.

❑ **INCLUDE CONTACT INFORMATION.** In the front of the book, preferably on the copyright and ISBN page, include all contact information, including mailing address and website. E-mail address is optional, but the more options you give the better chance you'll be contacted.

❏ **EXECUTE MARKETING PLAN.** Planning is important, but execution is critical to achieving success. If you're guest posting, finish posts on time and participate in comments section of your blog post. If you're making bookstore appearances, confirm dates and show up a little early—plus invite friends and family to attend.

❏ **KEEP DETAILED ACCOUNTING RECORDS.** For tax purposes, you'll need to keep records of how much money you invest in your project, as well as how much you receive back. Keep accurate and comprehensive records from day one, and you'll be a much happier self-published author.

FINDING WORK ON THE INTERNET:

A Wealth of Writing Opportunities

....

by Rob Spiegel

Welcome to the new world of freelancing. Even if you're pitching to print magazines, there's a good chance the freelance opportunities will involve the publication's web news, e-mail newsletters, podcasts or blogs. Freelancers today are doing most of their writing work on the Internet, for the Internet. The opportunities are widespread, from consumer magazines and trade journals to websites and organizations that need to keep their web content fresh. Even broadcast sites need freelance writers.

There is a wide range of things you can do on the Internet to find new paying markets for your writing. Whether you're targeting print publications or websites, your search and pitches will take place online. The online job boards in the publishing industry list employment opportunities as well as freelance projects. Freelancers' sites list oddball jobs. I once saw the job of writing love snippets for the inside of the wrappers of Dove chocolates posted online.

Seeking out writing work can become an adventure in sleuthing, an activity that warms the heart and boils the blood of every eager freelancer.

You can go to online lists of magazines such as *Writer's Digest* and isolate those that fit your subject expertise. You can also rub elbows with potential writing clients at social networking sites or you can bid on writing jobs at auction sites such as Guru.com and Elance. Finding markets online is fun these days. It's low pressure and there is a surprisingly wide range of opportunity. Seeking out writing work can become an adventure in sleuthing, an activity that warms the heart and boils the blood of every eager freelancer.

PLUG AWAY EVERY DAY

Success in almost any endeavor requires consistent effort and an aggressive learning curve. The best way to find writing work online is to devote a portion of each day to the effort. Most writers have learned that the discipline of daily writing is the best way to develop craft. Successful marketing requires the same consistent effort. I've been most successful at getting new work when I approach it as a daily job. Two hours each day should be plenty. More is even better.

Initially, your time will include listing the different tasks involved in the search. One task could be searching on a particular subject that interests you such as food or soccer and making a list of markets. That effort can be followed by drafting queries for those publications. If you devote at least two hours each day to your search, chances are you'll get somewhere.

THE CLASSIC QUERY IS NOW AN E-MAIL

Most creative people hate sales. Yet the query is essentially a sales letter. If you don't put your heart into it, it's sure to fail. Most writers also hate to boast. Writers don't mind receiving praise, but most writers I know think it's gauche to brag about skills and accomplishments. Yet an effective query does just that. It lays out a great idea that's perfect for the editor, then unequivocally asserts this is the writer—the only writer—who can execute the grand concept. With practice, writers can overcome their false modesty and learn to dash off assignment-getting queries. Queries get easier once you start getting rewarded for the effort.

The advantage of cold calling is you're not up against the same level of competition as a job applicant or a query writer.

If you think writing queries is difficult, try cold calling. For many trade publications and websites run by organizations, the query won't do. Instead, you approach these markets with a direct pitch to help them with their writing. In many ways this takes more creativity and a greater sales ability than a query. After all, magazine editors are expecting queries and they—believe it or not—are happy to receive them. But a cold call can often be experienced as intrusion. The trick is to make the approach seem helpful rather than aggressive, while at the same time, touting skills and accomplishments. Not an easy task. The advantage of cold calling is you're not up against the same level of competition as a job applicant or a query writer.

GENERAL JOB BOARDS AND WRITING JOB BOARDS

There are two job sites devoted to the publishing industry: JournalismJobs.com and MediaBistro.com. JouranlismJobs.com focuses primarily on newspapers and magazines, while MediaBistro.com caters to the book and magazine industries, while also including public relations. Both sites also list jobs for web-only publishers. Many employers advertise on both sites.

While some of the job postings are for freelance positions or projects, the bulk of the listings are for walk-into-the-building employment. One thing to remember when scrolling through the sites is that a job posting is an advertised need. Sometimes you can pitch your writing services as a way to fill that need without hiring an employee. These sites are heavily perused by hungry writers. The trick is to respond to postings the day they show up. After 24 hours, the company has enough resumes to last a year.

SOCIAL NETWORKING SITES

While Facebook may seem like an off-working-hours playland, it is slowly becoming more and more a promotion tool for entrepreneurs. There are ways to communicate on Facebook to attract and keep writing clients. You can create a page specifically designed to be your Internet face as a professional writer. LinkedIn is more specifically designed for business networking. The networking sites are not great for finding new clients immediately, but they can be an excellent tool for staying in touch with clients to make sure you are high-on-the-mind for future projects. I've used LinkedIn to stay in touch with editors who have left a job. When one of those editors gets a new job, you'll know about it. An editor at a new job is always in need of freelancers.

AUCTION AND KNOWLEDGE SITES

Auction sites are filled with jobs just waiting for a writer. Both Guru.com and Elance post writing jobs that freelancers can bid on. The house takes a cut of the price negotiated between the writer and the client. Not all clients are great, but you can often weed out the difficult clients by making reasonable bids and letting the low bidders take the cheap clients. The work-for-hire projects on the auction sites range from writing an article to ghostwriting a book—and everything in between. Some of the projects can turn into regular clients.

Another advantage is the global nature of the sites. I've landed projects in the UK, The Netherlands and Asia. One advantage of these sites is you can sign up to receive notifications for the type of projects that interest you. So instead of scanning the site each day to look for appropriate work, you receive e-mails that describe the posted project.

Most knowledge sites—from About.com to eHow to HowStuffWorks—use freelance writers to run their expert sites. These are significant endeavors. About.com is owned by *The New York Times* and HowStuffWorks is owned by *Discovery* magazine. The guides to these sites are typically freelancers who write articles and blogs about individual subjects, from alternative rock to autism. The sites are a blend of short 300-to-500-word articles, lists of resources and a running blog.

The guides are typically journalists who have covered the subject for a few years or they are practitioners with strong writing skills. The guides usually write two or three new articles each week and blog about three or four times each week. To get the job, guides have to build content in a competitive test. The winning guide is typically paid a monthly fee that increases based on site traffic.

PROFESSIONAL BLOGS

The blog is the new personal column, but with far less structure. Professional blogs written by journalists are a distant cousin of the personal blog. For one, the personal view of the writer is usually restricted to in-the-know info on the subject rather than personal feelings or thoughts. Even though the professional blog retains a professional feel, it still tends to have little formal structure.

The blog is the new personal column, but with far less structure.

A typical professional blog takes on a single subject in 100 to 300 words. Often an entry consists of little more than a heads-up about a recent article of note on the subject, or perhaps a heads-up about a coming conference. Professional blogs can range from politics to food to design engineering. It is becoming very common for websites to use freelancers as bloggers.

ONLINE EDITING

There is a growing need for online editing. As websites proliferate, new opportunities arise for editors who can plow through amateurish copy and turn it into coherent prose that will attract viewers and keep them coming back. Often, these positions are held by freelancers who comb through copy before it's posted—or after it's posted. The advantage of these jobs is they tend to be very stable. The disadvantage for writers is they don't satisfy the urge to write, since they're correcting the work of other writers rather than creating original copy. You typically have to learn the site's individual style and work with a content management system. But the learning curve for style and systems is usually a short month or two.

JOB OR FREELANCE

In the process of seeking freelancing, you will inevitably run into job opportunities. In our increasingly virtual world, online publishers have become comfortable with the notion of hiring a writer who works remotely. The first time I was offered a writing job in the late 1990s—from an editor I was pitching for freelance work—I was shocked. As we moved further into the next decade, opportunities for online writing and editing jobs became more common. In the past two years, I have seriously considered a number of online jobs. The advantage is they come with benefits. The disadvantage is that in most cases they don't pay as well as regular freelancing, even if you take benefits into consideration.

You will be faced with choosing between short-term work and long-term work. At first you'll probably take any work, but in time you will face some choices. On first glance, short-term work looks more attractive. Short-term work comes in the form of projects—a bank's annual report, a long white paper, a book. In most cases short-term work pays more per hour invested. But the advantage of long-term work—an article every month for a magazine, an ongoing blog—is the consistent flow of cash. When you're freelancing, smooth money is more valuable than lumpy money. The difference is also in time. With short-term projects, you're always back to zero-paid marketing when it's over. With long-term work, year after year you're cranking out work and getting regular pay.

CONTENT MANAGEMENT SYSTEMS

While some freelance clients will be happy to receive Word documents containing your articles, others will ask you to work with a content management system. These systems format your copy in preparation for posting. If you're writing a blog, you will probably have to work within the publisher's blogging software. Content systems can be awkward until you learn the hidden tricks, such as posting illustrations and photos. Web publishing software doesn't tend to be intuitive or user friendly. Even more challenging is the notion that your blog will likely go live before an editor has a chance to revise and proof for typos. Often I find out about a typo when a reader catches my mistake and posts it as a comment. The saving grace with content management software is that editors know their systems are cumbersome, so they don't mind stupid questions—and you'll have plenty.

WEBSITES TO SEARCH FOR WORK

Here are the websites mentioned in this article as potential places to find work online:
- About.com http://about.com
- eHow http://ehow.com
- Elance http://elance.com
- Facebook http://facebook.com
- Guru http://guru.com
- HowStuffWorks http://howstuffworks.com

- Journalism Jobs http://journalismjobs.com
- LinkedIn http://linkedin.com
- Media Bistro http://mediabistro.com
- Writer's Digest http://writersdigest.com

EXPERIMENT

The list of writing opportunities on the Internet is long and varied. A winning strategy for finding writing assignments is to play with a number of tactics to discover which ones work. I find it fairly easy to nab article assignments on technical subjects at trade magazines. A friend of mine finds it easy to get work writing blogs on food and soccer. Try different veins until you hit gold. Some Internet-based writing opportunities will be difficult to land, others may come relatively easy. At first it will be hard to tell what will come easy and what will seem nearly impossible. Once you hit that pay dirt, though, there's a good chance you can mine it for years to come.

PHOTO: Letta Gorder

ROB SPIEGEL has been writing for online publications for two decades. He is a former senior editor for *Ecommerce Business* and *Electronic News*. He is a contributing editor (freelancer) for *Automation World, Design News* and *EDN*. He is the launch publisher of *Chile Pepper* magazine, which he sold to return to writing. He is also the author of five books about home-based and Internet businesses.

WRITING FOR ONLINE CONTENT PROVIDERS

by Patricia Woodside

Online content providers, sometimes called "content factories" or "content mills," are all over the Internet. If you've seen search engine results from eHow, Helium or similar sites, you've bumped into an online content provider.

Although some writers have nothing good to say about these sites, content providers offer a legitimate writing opportunity for new and experienced freelancers who do their homework and utilize these sites to meet personal objectives. They may not be the right market for all, but they are worth consideration.

WHAT ARE CONTENT PROVIDERS?

Content providers, such as Demand Studios and Examiner.com, offer writers the opportunity to publish short articles online for pay. Published articles contain general information, instruction or advice, and often are tied to advertisements for related products and services. Some sites specialize in a niche area, such as personal finance, while others publish a wide range of articles based on recent trending topics and popular Internet searches.

Writers for content providers range from new graduates to seasoned journalists to stay-at-home moms.

Writers for content providers range from new graduates to seasoned journalists to stay-at-home moms. The application process usually consists of an online application along with a bio, resume and writing sample. Some sites accept all applicants. Others, like wiseGEEK, require you to work with their editorial staff to publish several articles before acceptance.

Once accepted, you will select topics from a queue of available titles or create your own titles of interest to readers and advertisers. You'll then submit your articles for copyediting, if required. Upon acceptance, your article is published and you receive payment.

LIST OF CONTENT FARMS

Want to investigate examples of content farms? Here is a list of some prominent sites:

- All Experts (allexperts.com)
- Answers (answers.com)
- Ask (ask.com)
- Associated Content (associatedcontent.com)
- BizRate (bizrate.com)
- Buzzle (buzzle.com)
- Bytes (bytes.com)
- ChaCha (chacha.com)
- Demand Media (demandmedia.com)
- eFreedom (efreedom.com)
- eHow (ehow.com)
- Essortment (essortment.com)
- Examiner (examiner.com)
- Expert Village (expertvillage.com)
- Experts Exchange (experts-exchange.com)
- eZine Articles (ezinearticles.com)
- Find Articles (findarticles.com)
- FixYa (fixya.com)
- Gather (gather.com)
- Helium (helium.com)
- Hub Pages (hubpages.com)
- InfoBarrel (infobarrel.com)
- LiveStrong (livestrong.com)
- Mahalo (mahalo.com)
- Question Hub (questionhub.com)
- Squidoo (squidoo.com)
- Suite101 (suite101.com)
- Twenga (twenga.com)
- wiseGEEK (wisegeek.com)
- Yahoo! Answers (answers.yahoo.com)
- Xomba (xomba.com)

RICHES OR RIP-OFF?

Earnings potential is at the heart of why some freelancers frown upon content providers. Upfront payments can be as low as $1 per article, although the average is between $10 and $15. Some providers do not offer upfront payments but rather pay based on "clicks" or a percentage of advertising and sales revenue. Still others, like Gather.com, pay in points that may be traded in for retail gift certificates or cash.

My first online content provider was Examiner.com. I wrote about anything to do with writing in my local area as well as general writing topics. I thought my job was to write. In truth, my job was to market my writing. Payment depended on readership. After nine months of juggling three articles per week for Examiner.com with my other writing tasks, I stopped. I never received a check.

THE CRITICISMS

Low or no payment is the primary but not the only complaint lodged against content providers. Writers lack creative freedom. Research can be faulty and superficial. There is little or low quality editorial support. Writers get trapped into making a quick buck. The writing credits are worthless. These may be valid concerns, but there is another side to the content provider coin.

THE UPSIDE OF ONLINE CONTENT PROVIDERS

Income is only one reason writers elect to publish with content providers. For the new writer, these sites offer a way to break into freelance writing and build confidence before tackling the traditional query process.

New and seasoned writers can pen a few hundred words and receive their first paycheck in as little as one week. Some sites pay monthly. Demand Studios, for example, pays twice weekly via PayPal.

Content providers offer schedule and workload flexibility. Some sites require a minimum number of articles per week or month, but many do not.

Freelancers can establish a byline. You can become an expert specializing in a subject area. You learn to write tight and to hit a deadline. You learn to work with editors. You can expand your writing network through site blogs, forums and social media. Some sites even offer perks like discount buying plans and healthcare coverage.

Although the money is frequently characterized as pennies, it doesn't have to be. A prolific writer or one who develops a niche, masters search engine optimization and drives increasing traffic to his articles can earn hundreds or even thousands of dollars per month.

My second foray into writing for a content provider was markedly different. I opted to write for Demand Studios, which publishes to popular sites such as eHow, LiveStrong and

Answerbag.com. Demand Studios offers style templates, requires source citations and provides copyediting. The number of articles I wrote in a given period depended on my availability and need for extra income. Over the course of 10 months, I earned an average of $10 per title for 66 titles. One, a revenue sharing article, continues to earn residuals. Not a fortune, to be sure, but this site fit my needs for cash flow and writing credits. I rarely took more than 90 minutes to research and write an article. My focus has shifted now to more traditional markets, but I continue to write for them today.

MAKING THE MOST OF ONLINE CONTENT PROVIDERS

Writing for an online content provider can be frustrating and generate little income or it can yield steady money and be a stepping stone to bigger markets. How do you make the most of this opportunity?

- **DEFINE YOUR OBJECTIVES.** What is your purpose in writing for this market and what are your expectations?
- **RESEARCH CONTENT PROVIDERS THAT INTEREST YOU.** Read their posted articles. Use your network to gain insight from the experiences of other writers. Know the minimum writing requirements, the type of editorial support provided, the payment model and pay frequency, whether you will retain copyrights and whether there may be opportunities for higher pay or networking.
- **MONITOR THE TIME YOU SPEND SELECTING, RESEARCHING AND WRITING ARTICLES.** Look for subjects you have familiarity with to minimize your time spent.
- **SEEK WAYS TO MAXIMIZE YOUR EARNINGS.** Use social media to drive traffic to articles depending on pay-per-click or ad revenues. Write about trending topics or timeless subjects.
- **CAPITALIZE ON REPRINT OPPORTUNITIES.** Even if you don't retain your copyright, make the most of your research by taking a different slant for another market, even for rejected pieces.

Online content providers probably won't go away, even with search engines like Google threatening to lower their articles in search results. Content providers are a legitimate market. If they meet your writing needs, write away!

PATRICIA WOODSIDE is a contributing writer for eHow.com and has served as a judge for various writing contests. She's had fiction and nonfiction accepted for publication with regional and national magazines, including *True Romance* and *D-Mars Health & Wellness Journal*. Woodside blogs at the Readin 'N' Writin blog (http://readinnwritin.blogspot.com).

PUBLISHERS & THEIR IMPRINTS

The publishing world is in constant transition. With all the buying, selling, reorganizing, consolidating, and dissolving, it's hard to keep publishers and their imprints straight. To help make sense of these changes, here's a breakdown of major publishers (and their divisions)—who owns whom and which imprints are under each company umbrella. Keep in mind that this information changes frequently. The website of each publisher is provided to help you keep an eye on this ever-evolving business.

HACHETTE BOOK GROUP USA

www.hachettebookgroupusa.com

CENTER STREET
FAITHWORDS
GRAND CENTRAL PUBLISHING
  Business Plus
  5-Spot
  Forever
  Springboard Press
  Twelve
  Vision
  Wellness Central

HACHETTE BOOK GROUP DIGITAL MEDIA
  Hachette Audio

LITTLE, BROWN AND COMPANY
  Back Bay Books
    Bulfinch
  Reagan Arthur Books

LITTLE, BROWN BOOKS FOR YOUNG READERS
  LB Kids
  Poppy

ORBIT

YEN PRESS

HARLEQUIN ENTERPRISES

www.eharlequin.com

HARLEQUIN
  Harlequin American Romance
  Harlequin Bianca

Harlequin Blaze

Harlequin Deseo

Harlequin Historical

Harlequin Intrigue

Harlequin Tiffany

Harlequin Teen

Harlequin Medical Romance

Harlequin NASCAR

Harlequin Presents

Harlequin Romance

Harlequin Superromance

Harlequin eBooks

Harlequin Special Releases

Harlequin Nonfiction

Harlequin Historical Undone

HQN BOOKS

HQN eBooks

LUNA

Luna eBooks

MIRA

Mira eBooks

KIMANI PRESS

Kimani Press Arabesque

Kimani Press Kimani Romance

Kimani Press Kimani TRU

Kimani Press New Spirit

Kimani Press Sepia

Kimani Press Special Releases

Kimani Press eBooks

RED DRESS INK

Red Dress eBooks

SILHOUETTE

Silhouette Desire

Silhouette Nocturne

Silhouette Nocturne Bites

Silhouette Romantic Suspense

Silhouette Special Edition

Silhouette eBooks

SPICE

SPICE Books

SPICE Briefs

STEEPLE HILL

Steeple Hill Café©

Steeple Hill Love Inspired

Steeple Hill Love Inspired Historical

Steeple Hill Love Inspired Suspense

Steeple Hill Women's Fiction

Steeple Hill eBooks

WORLDWIDE LIBRARY

Rogue Angel

Worldwide Mystery

Worldwilde Library eBooks

HARLEQUIN CANADA

HARLEQUIN U.K.

Mills & Boon

HARPERCOLLINS

www.harpercollins.com

HARPERMORROW

Amistad

Avon

Avon A

Avon Inspire

Avon Red

Collins Design

Ecco

Eos

Harper

Harper Business

HarperLuxe

Harper Paperbacks

Harper Perennial

HarperAudio

HarperBibles

HarperCollins e-Books

HarperOne

ItBooks

Rayo

William Morrow

HARPERCOLLINS CHILDREN'S BOOKS

Amistad

Balzer + Bray

Greenwillow Books

HarperCollins

Children's Audio

Harper Festival

HarperTeen

Rayo

Katherine Tegen Books

TOKYOPOP

HarperCollins e-Books

HARPERCOLLINS U.K.

Fourth Estate

HarperPress

HarperPerennial

The Friday Project

HarperThorsons/Element

HarperNonFiction

HarperTrue

HarperSport

HarperFiction

Voyager

Blue Door

Angry Robot

Avon U.K.

HarperCollins Childrens Books

Collins

Collins Geo

Collins Education

Collins Language

HARPERCOLLINS CANADA

HarperCollinsPublishers

Collins Canada

HarperPerennial Canada

HarperTrophyCanada

Phyllis Bruce Books

HARPERCOLLINS AUSTRALIA

HarperCollins

Angus & Robertson

HarperSports

Fourth Estate

Harper Perennial

Collins

Voyager

HARPERCOLLINS INDIA

HARPERCOLLINS NEW ZEALAND

HarperCollins

HarperSports

Flamingo

Voyager

Perennial

ZONDERVAN

Zonderkids

Editorial Vida

Youth Specialties

MACMILLAN US (HOLTZBRINCK)

http://us.macmillan.com

MACMILLAN

Farrar, Straus & Giroux

Faber and Faber, Inc

Farrar, Straus

Hill & Wang

HENRY HOLT & CO.

Henry Holt Books for Young Readers

Holt Paperbacks

Metropolitan

Times

MACMILLAN CHILDREN'S

Feiwel & Friends

Farrar, Straus and Giroux Books
for Young Readers

Kingfisher

Holt Books for Young Readers

Priddy Books

Roaring Brook Press

First Second

Square Fish

PICADOR

PALGRAVE MACMILLAN

TOR/FORGE BOOKS

Tor

Forge

Orb

Tor/Seven Seas

ST. MARTIN'S PRESS

Minotaur Press

Thomas Dunne Books

**BEDFORD, FREEMAN & WORTH
PUBLISHING GROUP**

BEDFORD/ST. MARTIN'S

HAYDEN-MCNEIL

W.H. FREEMAN

WORTH PUBLISHERS

MACMILLAN KIDS

YOUNG LISTENERS

MACMILLAN AUDIO

PENGUIN GROUP (USA), INC.

www.penguingroup.com

PENGUIN ADULT DIVISION

Ace

Alpha

Amy Einhorn Books/Putnam

Avery

Berkley

Current

Dutton

G.P. Putnam's Sons

Gotham

HPBooks

Hudson Street Press

Jeremy P. Tarcher

Jove

NAL

Pamela Dorman Books

Penguin

Penguin Press

Perigree

Plume

Portfolio

Prentice Hall Press

RIVERHEAD

Sentinel

Tarcher

Viking Press

Price Stern Sloan

YOUNG READERS DIVISION

Dial Books for Young Readers

Dutton Children's Books

Firebird

Frederick Warne

Grosset & Dunlap

Philomel

PUFFIN BOOKS
- Razorbill
- Speak
- Viking Books for Young Readers

RANDOM HOUSE, INC. (BERTELSMANN)

www.randomhouse.com

CROWN TRADE GROUP
- Amphoto Books
- Backstage Books
- Billboard Books
- Broadway Business
- Crown
- Crown Business
- Crown Forum
- Clarkson Potter
- Doubleday Religion
- Harmony
- Monacelli Press
- Potter Craft
- Potter Style
- Three Rivers Press
- Ten Speed Press
- Tricycle Press
- Shaye Areheart Books
- Waterbrook Multnomah
- Watson-Guptill

KNOPF DOUBLEDAY PUBLISHING GROUP
- Alfred A. Knopf
- Anchor Books
- Doubleday
- Everyman's Library
- Nan A. Talese
- Pantheon Books
- Schocken Books
- Vintage/Anchor

RANDOM HOUSE PUBLISHING GROUP
- Ballantine Books
- Bantam
- Dell
- Del Rey
- Del Rey/Lucas Books
- The Dial Press
- The Modern Library
- One World
- Presidio Press
- Random House Trade Group
- Random House Trade Paperbacks
- Spectra
- Spiegel and Grau
- Villard Books

RANDOM HOUSE AUDIO PUBLISHING GROUP
- Listening Library
- Random House Audio

RANDOM HOUSE CHILDREN'S BOOKS
- Kids@Random
- Golden Books
- Bantam Books
- David Fickling Books
- Delacorte Press Books for Young Readers
- Delacorte Press Trade Paperbacks
- Disney Books for Young Readers
- Doubleday Books for Young Readers
- Dragonfly
- Laurel-Leaf
- Picturebacks
- Robin Corey Books
- Schwartz and Wade Books
- Wendy Lamb Books
- Yearling

RANDOM HOUSE INFORMATION GROUP
- Fodor's Travel
- Living Language

Prima Games
Princeton Review
RH Puzzles & Games
RH Reference Publishing
Sylvan Learning

RANDOM HOUSE INTERNATIONAL
Arete
McClelland & Stewart Ltd.
Plaza & Janes
RH Australia
RH of Canada Limited
RH Mondadori
RH South America
RH United Kingdom
Transworld UK
Verlagsgruppe RH

SIMON & SCHUSTER

www.simonandschuster.com

SIMON & SCHUSTER ADULT PUBLISHING
Atria Books/Beyond Words
Beach Lane Books
Folger Shakespeare Library

Free Press
Gallery Books
Howard Books
Pocket Books
Scribner
Simon & Schuster
Strebor
The Touchstone & Fireside Group
Pimsleur
Simon & Schuster Audioworks

SIMON & SCHUSTER CHILDREN'S PUBLISHING
Aladdin Paperbacks
Atheneum Books for Young Readers
Libros Para Niños
Little Simon®
Margaret K. McElderry Books
Simon & Schuster Books for Young Readers
Simon Pulse
Simon Spotlight®

SIMON & SCHUSTER INTERNATIONAL
Simon & Schuster Australia
Simon & Schuster Canada
Simon & Schuster UK

THE WRITING ENTREPRENEUR

....

by J.M. Lacey

//

If you are writing full time, or even part time, and you claim the business on your taxes, you are an entrepreneur. Running a business comes with unique challenges and perks. If you are a sole proprietorship, or LLC, and you have no staff, you are marketing your own business, managing contracts and filing your own taxes. So how do you enjoy writing while simultaneously running a business? How can social networking ease your burden? Do your business cards scream amateur? How can you get a client to sign a contract—on your terms? And what really is considered tax deductible for a writer?

THE HAPPY WRITER

Before you even begin your writing business, there are some things to consider to help you build your career.

Kelly James-Enger, author of *Six Figure Freelancing–The Writer's Guide to Making More Money* and freelancer for the last 14 years, says that finding a niche, something you're good at, will help stem the tide of financial insecurity. "Specializing helps set you apart from everyone else and it's easier to get assignments."

To maintain a happy, balanced writing life, she also offers some tips for writers:

- **CHOOSE A MARKET YOU'D LIKE TO WRITE FOR MORE THAN ONCE,** then focus on building relationships.
- **HAVE A DAILY PRODUCTION GOAL,** such as how many queries you plan to send.
- **THINK LONG TERM.** Make sure what you do is leading you in the direction you want to reach.
- **CONSIDER WHAT THE MARKET WILL BEAR,** not just what you want to do. "Don't have all your money come from one source," she adds. "Diversify what you can do."

- **BE CAREFUL ABOUT WORKING NON-STOP.** Have a set time to turn off the e-mail and computer. Avoid working weekends and nights.

GETTING CLIENTS

Things that seem small to you—business cards, websites, stationery—can make a big impression. Prospects will never know how well you write if they can't get past a non-professional set-up.

Get simple, classy, clean and sophisticated cards professionally printed. Include your phone number, mailing, web and e-mail addresses, if you want paying clients to contact you. Your stationery should be the same.

Your website is going to be your most important marketing tool. Make sure your site is personalized, professional and provides the information your prospect will need, such as articles, client list, and portfolio.

....

Your website is going to be your most important marketing tool.

....

There are many books and articles that will tell you to save money and go ahead and design your own site. I disagree 100 percent. Unless you have had training in marketing, design, SEO and html construction, your site will look homemade. Plus, you are too intimate with your own business to have an objective outlook.

Websites aren't as expensive as they used to be, but you will have to dish out a few to several hundred dollars, depending on your needs. To run a business, you have to spend money, and if you pour your investment into anything, it should be your website. Write your own content and save money, but hand the rest over to the professionals. To keep more dollars in your wallet, offer to do a trade with your designer—materials for them and a website for you.

"But I'm a writer," you say, "what does design matter?" If your site looks thrown together, prospects will think your writing is treated the same. And frankly, if your site is difficult to navigate—too much scrolling, tiny fonts, unorganized, dark background—they'll give up looking. No one has that much time or patience.

You also need a professional e-mail address, so get rid of your Yahoo, Gmail and Hotmail, and use your real name. JMLacey@jmlacey.com sounds a lot better than trixie_partygirl@hotmail.com. Save that for your personal accounts.

Next, find work by writing letters, making cold calls, sending e-mails and getting out there. Target businesses (or magazines) for whom you'd like to write. My first major client came via a cold call to another prospect. After I met with the initial contact, she referred me to someone else. I contacted that business immediately, and within three days, I had snagged that client and am still with them over two years later working on multiple projects.

Can social networking help? Yes, if you use it wisely. Join groups like LinkedIn, Facebook and Twitter, but make sure anytime you type a comment or message, it's with the purpose of building your business. You can direct people to your site and blog, but don't ask for their business. Try to type messages and/or guide them to helpful articles and information. Remember the WIIFM—What's In It For Me? It's about *them,* not you. Eventually, your readers will gain confidence in your expert abilities. Be cautious that your networking habits do not become time suckers. Try to have a set time each day, and a set amount of time, to check in with all your networks and forums.

CONTRACTS

Once you have a client, how do you get paid on your terms?

As you establish your business and writing credentials, try to have a solid, though not inflexible idea, of how much you will be paid. Understand what to charge for your level of expertise and geographical area. Most clients, especially corporate clients, prefer project fees instead of hourly rates. So have a base in your head, if you can, of how long something will take you, and come up with a reasonable fee.

Figure out how much you're willing to go down if the client tries to negotiate. Be confident in your figure, but be agreeable with the client. Before I type the contract, I usually state the estimate then ask: "Will that work within your budget?" You want to avoid going too low just to get that project, but don't quote so high you quote yourself out of a job. It takes trial and error, but after a while, you'll learn and gain confidence.

Make sure your contract covers everything unexpected because once you quote a price you can't retract and ask for more. For example, my contracts outline the project and everything that goes with it—three edits, one additional meeting (even via phone), conception, content and design. If the project goes over what was agreed upon—additional edits, meetings, pages, etc.—I charge the additional fee stated in the contract. I also charge extra for commercial photos and anything that might crop up as I go along. But I have to have it covered or I lose money. And don't forget to include the deadline.

Most important, be certain the contract states what you will be paid and when. For my new clients, especially for large projects, I always ask for one-third to one-half down payment. If I'm hiring outside contractors, such as a web designer, I will ask for my contractor's fee in full, if I can, just in case the project flops. All my clients know they will receive an invoice when they've approved the final draft, and my invoice states "payment due upon receipt."

Some commercial clients have their own contracts written by lawyers who really should use writers. If you don't understand something, ask. Contracts are for negotiating. Include your requirements, like the additional charges for extra work. You want to be comfortable signing that contract.

Do not do the work or research until you have it in writing. People will try to get you to "look" at their stuff so you can get a handle on what they want. That's fine, but either wait until you have the contract, or tell them you charge for your research. The reason? You want people to respect you as a professional from the start. Otherwise, they will expect more for nothing.

....

Do not do the work or research until you have it in writing.

....

Target clients that will pay you what you are worth. Again, use your discretion, but be firm. If they start out by saying, "I don't have much money," run, because they don't and you have a business to operate. If they tell you, "We can market you," then unless they are a marketing agency, they can't do anything to help you that you can't do. To run your business effectively, establish yourself as a professional by not catering to the low-paying, time-sucking gigs that will get you nowhere except homeless.

TAX DEDUCTIONS

If you claim your writing on your taxes, then it isn't a hobby. This means that almost everything you do and buy for your business is tax deductible.

So what can you deduct? Pretty much anything office-related (computer, pens), books, magazine subscriptions and conferences are among your deductions. And anything you need that will help you in your research, such as travel expenses. In my case, CDs and concert tickets are included in my write-offs as a classical music writer.

Building your writing business takes time. It can take several months to a few years, but it will happen. The more effort you put into it, the sooner it will thrive. But above all, your professional habits will only increase your chances of being successful.

NEGOTIATING TIPS FOR WRITERS FROM AN EDITOR

While being an editor pays the bills around here, I always see a writer when I look in the mirror. And just to show you how much I care about my fellow writers, I'm going to make my life as an editor potentially more difficult by sharing my negotiating tips for writers.

Different editors surely approach negotiation in their own unique ways, but these are my tips for handling editors like myself.

- **ALWAYS TRY TO NEGOTIATE.** I loathe negotiating. Judging by the lack of negotiation from most of my freelancers, I've concluded that most of them loathe negotiating too. But I think it's important for writers to at least try to negotiate from the beginning, because I take those writers a little more seriously, especially if they...

- **DELIVER THE GOODS ON EACH ASSIGNMENT.** Write an amazing article with great sources and examples, and I'm more likely to offer you a better contract the next time around. If I don't, I may be trying to maintain the status quo, but you should try to nudge me again. And I emphasize nudging.

- **DON'T MAKE YOUR DEMANDS A "MY-WAY-OR-THE-HIGHWAY" SITUATION.** That is, don't make it that kind of situation unless you're willing to take the highway. There have been situations, especially when I'm working with a new freelancer, in which I'm not able or willing to go over my initial offer. There have been very good pitches that I let walk, because I couldn't (or wouldn't) go higher. Believe me, I always wish I could offer more, but I have to fill my pages with great content (not squander it all on a handful of articles). That said...

- **PITCH ME WITH AN IDEA THAT IS UNIQUE AND TRULY HELPFUL FOR MY AUDIENCE.** If you pitch me on an interview or list of query tips, I'm less likely to get excited than if you pitch me on an article that tells writers how to make a living off Twitter in 30 days (and actually have the track record to back up that claim). For instance, Lynn Wasnak, who puts together our "How Much Should I Charge?" piece, is far and away my top paid freelancer, because she has to survey professionals in several different fields of writing. It's a unique piece that is truly helpful for my audience. As such, she has greater negotiating power. Still...

- **CHOOSE YOUR BATTLES.** I advise negotiating each time you get a new assignment. Maybe I'll give a little, maybe I won't. But please pick your battles about what you want to negotiate. Don't fight over every single clause in your contract. That gets annoying on my end, and I'm just too busy to enjoy being annoyed. Related to that...

- **DON'T BE A PEST.** I'm more willing to negotiate with writers who complete their assignments on time and don't contact me every couple days with a revision of an already turned in piece or who try to re-negotiate the fee on an article after I've already assigned the piece. I like it when writers ask questions and want to make sure they understand an assignment, but I don't like to have to constantly haggle over things after we've come to an agreement. That's a good way to not receive any more assignments in the future.

- **THINK OF CREATIVE WAYS TO NEGOTIATE.** Offer to write a sidebar for an extra fee—or a series of blog posts. If the editor is unable to offer more money, ask for more complimentary copies. Or some other related comp that the editor may be able to send your way. Editors like to make writers happy (especially if they do a great job), so help them help you get more out of your relationship.

—Robert Lee Brewer

J.M. LACEY (http://jmlacey.com) is an independent writer, marketing and public relations professional. She has over 14 years worth of experience in journalism, marketing, public relations, and sales, working for both the corporate and nonprofit sectors. She maintains a classical music blog (http://seasonkt.com) and works with small to large businesses creating websites, advertisements, biographies and other marketing and publicity needs. She is also a public speaker and teaches workshops on writing for businesses and on marketing at writing and corporate conferences.

CONTRACT NEGOTIATION

by Jane Choate

You've done it. You've sold your book or story. Hooray! You've accomplished something that most people only dream of. Now comes the fun part—signing the contract. Before you place your John—or Jane—Hancock on the dotted line, however, take a look at the language of the contract.

It's important to remember that whoever drafts the contract drafts it for his advantage. Since contracts are drafted by the publisher, the terms are designed to be most favorable for the publisher, not the author. Almost everything is negotiable; however, some of the terms and conditions (Ts and Cs) are not. Specifically, no publisher is likely to change the clauses that indemnify them if the author is successfully sued for plagiarism.

> Before disputing any clause, it's important to read the entire contract, try to understand each clause (which may require an attorney) and draft a list of clauses you would like changed.

Before disputing any clause, it's important to read the entire contract, try to understand each clause (which may require an attorney) and draft a list of clauses you would like changed. I suggest dividing them into three categories:

- **DEAL BREAKERS**–If this clause isn't changed, you won't sign the contract.
- **IMPORTANT**–Changing this clause is important, but if you can't get it modified, you'll still sign the contract, provided that you get other important clauses changed to your benefit.

- **NICE TO HAVE**–You'd be happy if this clause were modified, but it really isn't important. (Note: It's good to have a few clauses in this category, since it gives you negotiating room. When negotiating, you will *not* tell the publisher which category each point is, so you can "give" on some of these and hold firm on the important ones.)

When actually negotiating the contract, I recommend face-to-face meetings, if possible. If not, use a phone call. E-mail is the least preferred method, since it provides less opportunity for explanations and can result in misunderstandings. In any case, you should have a written list of each of the points you're disputing as well as the wording you would like to see in the contract.

Key points to understand and possibly negotiate:

- **COPYRIGHT**–Depending on what you've written and whether or not you plan to try to sell it again (in its entirety or in part) to another publisher, if the publisher insists on holding the copyright, this could be a deal breaker. On the other hand, if the work is so specialized that you know there are no other markets, you might agree to let the publisher copyright in his name. Ideally, however, the copyright should be in your name.
- **DELIVERY DATE**–When are you required to deliver a completed manuscript? This is one of the more easily negotiated clauses. My advice is to be certain that you can meet the date, because you are technically in breach of contract if you miss it. Breach is NOT a good thing.
- **PAYMENT**–How much will you be paid? When? This is often a difficult clause to negotiate, but it never hurts to try.
- **ACCOUNTING**–If your work will result in royalties, it's important to understand what the accounting period is and how soon after it ends you'll receive royalty statements.

MORE ON ACCOUNTING

Beware of clauses that say that no payment or accounting is due unless it exceeds a specific amount. While the publisher may reasonably want to avoid issuing small checks, you should always receive a statement.

Joint accounting is a concept that stumps many authors. The term means nothing on your first book. It means a great deal, though, if you publish a second book with the same publisher. With joint accounting, all monies from both the first and the second books go into the same pot.

If you haven't earned out the advance on your first book (this is common for a new author on her first book), but the second book does very well, the publisher will "ding" your account for the negative royalty balance on the first one. Obviously it is to your advantage to have this clause eliminated. Ask that each book stand on its own.

- **REVERSION OF RIGHTS**–It is advantageous to the publisher to retain those rights for as long as possible. It is equally advantageous for you, the author, to regain the rights as soon as possible. Why? If you are in possession of the rights, you can re-sell your work to different venues. Regarding short works, I have sold reprint rights to other periodicals after the work is first published. With books, I have had success in selling large print rights once I've regained rights to the book.

- **AUDITING**–If you expect to receive royalties, the contract should include a clause allowing you to audit the publisher's books. This could be your only way of proving that you've been paid the correct amount. Absence of this clause is a red flag.

- **AUTHOR'S COPIES**–I've found this to be one of the more easily negotiated clauses. If the publisher isn't willing or able to increase the advance, they will often agree to give you additional author copies.

....

The goal is to give you as much flexibility as possible and keep you from being locked into one publisher.

....

- **FIRST OPTION**–In typical book contracts, you're asked to give the publisher the right of first refusal on your next book. The language in some contracts seeks to prevent the author from signing another contract with another publisher until the current book is published (publication can be months, perhaps years) after you've completed the manuscript. The key is to make this clause as restrictive as possible. For example, if you've written a book set during the Civil War, you might want this clause to require you to send the publisher your next book set during that period. If you write books in a series, another way to restrict the clause is to agree to give the publisher right of refusal on your next book featuring characters from the contracted book. The goal is to give you as much flexibility as possible and keep you from being locked into one publisher.

- **SALES TERRITORY**–Publishers will want to publish your book in every language through the entire world. If you are agented, your agent will try to keep foreign rights on your behalf and try to sell them directly to foreign publishers. When publishers license translation rights, they split the proceeds received from foreign publishers with the author. If you aren't represented by an agent, ask if there is any flexibility regarding the split. Contracts frequently call for a 50/50 split between publisher and author. You can always ask for a better cut: "What about 75/25 or 60/40?" (With the higher amount going to you, the author.)

- **SPLITS AND SERIALS**–There are two questions with regard to serial rights: First, determine who controls the rights? If you have an agent, he may try to keep control of the serialization rights. Second, ask about the split. It is not uncommon for the author to receive 90 percent of the money from a first serial rights sale. Again, you need to ask. You've lost nothing if you ask and are refused.

Be smart. Be savvy. Remember, you are not just a writer; you are a businessperson.

JANE CHOATE has been writing since man first chiseled his name into a rock. Her credits include 31 books, including *Star Crossed* and *Eden's Garden*, and over 300 articles and short stories for such publications as *Chicken Soup for the Soul*, *The Writer*, *Children's Book Insider*, and others. She is currently working on a romantic suspense.

CONTRACTS 101

....

by Cindy Ferraino

//

After you do a victory dance about getting the book deal you always dreamed about or your article hitting the top of the content list of a popular magazine, the celebration quickly comes to a halt when you realize you are not at the finish line yet. Your heart begins to beat faster because you know the next possible hurdle is just around the corner—the contract. For many, the idea of reviewing a contract is like being back in first grade. You know you have to listen to the teacher when you could be playing outside. You know you have to read this contract but why because there are terms in there that look like an excerpt from a foreign language syllabus.

Before I changed my status to self-employed writer, I was working as a grants and contracts administrator at a large medical university in Philadelphia. I helped shepherd the MD and PhD researchers through the channels of grants and contracts administration. While the researchers provided the technical and scientific pieces that could potentially be the next cure for diabetes, heart disease or cancer, I was there to make sure they did their magic within the confines of a budget and imposed contractual regulations. The budget process was easy but when it came to contract regulations—oh well, that was a different story. I became familiar with the terms such as indemnifications, property and intellectual rights and conditions of payments. In addition to the budget process, I was an integral part of reviewing and negotiating a grant or contract that had the best interests for every party involved.

After my son was born, I left the university and my contracts background went on a brief hiatus. Once my son went off to school, I began freelance writing. After a few writing gigs sprinkled with a few too many rejection slips, I landed an assignment for *Dog Fancy* magazine. I was thrilled and eagerly anticipated the arrival of a contract in my inbox. As

I opened the document, the hiatus had lifted. I read through the contract and was able to send it back within a few hours.

For many new freelancers or writers who have been around the block, contract administration is not something that they can list as a perk on their resume. Instead of searching through the Yellow Pages for a contract lawyer or trying to call in a special favor to a writer friend, there are some easy ways for a newbie writer or even a seasoned writer to review a contract before putting a smiley face next to the dotted line.

TAKE A DEEP BREATH, THEN READ ON

Remember breaking those seals on test booklets and the voice in the background telling you "Please read the directions slowly." As you tried to drown out the voice because your stomach was in knots, little did you know that those imparting words of wisdom would come in handy as you perspired profusely over the legal jargon that unfolded before your eyes. The same words go for contracts.

Many writers, including myself, are anxious to get an assignment under way but the contract carrot continues to loom over our creative minds. "I'm surprised by writers who just skim a contract and then sign it without understanding what it means, "says Kelly James-Enger. James-Enger is the author of books including *Six Figure Freelancing: The Writer's Guide to Making More* (Random House, 2005) and blog Dollarsanddeadlines. blogspot.com. "Most of the language in magazine contracts isn't that complicated, but it can be confusing when you're new to the business."

When I receive a contract from a new publisher or editor, I make a second copy. My children call it "my sloppy copy." I take out a highlighter and begin to mark up the key points of the contract: beginning and end date, conditions of payment, how my relationship is defined by the publisher and what the outline of the article should look like.

The beginning and end date of a contract is crucial. After I recently negotiated a contract, the editor changed the due date of the article in an e-mail. I made sure the contract was changed to reflect the new due date. The conditions of the payments are important

PAYMENT TYPES

There are any number of different arrangements for publishers to pay writers. However, here are three of the most common and what they mean.

- Pays on acceptance. This means that a publisher pays (or cuts a check) for the writer upon acceptance of the manuscript. This is usually the best deal a writer can hope to receive.
- Pays on publication. In these cases, a publisher pays (or cuts a check) for the writer by the publication date of the manuscript. For magazines, this could mean several months after the manuscript was accepted and approved. For books, this could mean more than a year.
- Pays after publication. Sometimes contracts will specify exactly how long after publication. Be wary of contracts that leave it open-ended.

because it will describe when the writer will be paid and by what method. Most publishers have turned to incremental payment schedules or payments to be made online like Pay-Pal. How the publisher considers your contractor status is important. If you're a freelance contract writer, the contract should reflect that as well as identify you as an independent contractor for IRS tax purposes. Finally, the contract will highlight an outline of what your article or proposal should look like.

After I recently negotiated a contract, the editor changed the due date of the article in an e-mail. I made sure the contract was changed to reflect the new due date.

As you slowly digest the terms you are about to agree to for your assignment or book project, you gain a better understanding of what an editor or publisher expects from you and when.

CUTTING TO THE LEGAL CHASE

Once you have had a chance to review a contract, you may be scratching your head and saying, "Okay, now what does this all mean to me as a writer?" James-Enger describes three key areas where writers should keep sharp on when it comes to contracts—Indemnification, Pay and Exclusivity provisions.

INDEMNIFICATION is a publisher's way of saying if something goes wrong, we are not responsible. If a claim is brought against another writer's work, a publisher does not want to be responsible for the legal aftermath but you could be the one receiving a notice in the mail. James-Enger warns writers to be on the lookout for indemnification clauses. "In the U.S., anyone can sue anyone over just about anything," she says. "I'm okay with agreeing to indemnification clauses that specify breaches of contract because I know I'm not going to plagiarize, libel or misquote anyone. But I can't promise that the publication will never be sued by anyone whether or not I actually breached the contract."

CONTRACT TIPS /////////////////////////////////

Even seasoned freelancers can find themselves intimidated by contracts. Here are a few things to consider with your contract:

- **KEEP COPY ON RECORD.** If the contract is sent via e-mail, keep a digital copy, but also print up a hard copy and keep it in an easy-to-find file folder.

- **CHECK FOR RIGHTS.** It's almost never a good idea to sell all rights. But you should also pay attention to whether you're selling any subsidiary or reprint rights. The more rights you release the more payment you should expect (and demand).
- **WHEN PAYMENT.** Make sure you understand when you are to be paid and have it specified in your contract. You may think that payment will come when the article is accepted or published, but different publishers have different policies. Get it in writing.
- **HOW MUCH PAYMENT.** The contract should specify exactly how much you are going to be paid. If there is no payment listed on the contract, the publisher could use your work for free.
- **TURN IN CONTRACT BEFORE ASSIGNMENT.** Don't start working until the contract is signed, and everything is official. As a freelancer, time is as important as money. Don't waste any of your time and effort on any project that is not yet contracted.

PAY is where you want the publisher "to show you the money." Writers need to be aware of how publishers will discuss the terms of payment in the contract. James-Enger advises to have "payment on acceptance." This means you will be paid when the editor agrees to accept your manuscript or article. If there is "no payment on acceptance," some publishers will pay when the article is published. "Push for payment whenever you can," she says.

EXCLUSIVITY PROVISIONS are where a particular publisher will not allow the writer to publish an article or manuscript that is "about the same or similar subject" during the time the publisher runs the piece. Because of the nature of the writing business, James-Enger feels writers need to negotiate this part of the contract. "I specialize in health, fitness and nutrition, and I'm always writing about a similar subject," she says.

WHEN TO HEAD TO THE BARGAINING TABLE

Recently, I became an independent contractor for the American Composites Manufacturing Association (ACMA). When I reviewed the terms of the contract, I was concerned how my independent contractor status was identified. Although I am not an ACMA employee, I wanted to know if I could include my ACMA publications on my resume. Before I signed the contract, I questioned this issue with my editor. My editor told me I may use this opportunity to put on my resume. I signed the contract and finished my assignment.

Writers should be able to talk to an editor or a publisher if there is a question about a term or clause in a contract. "Don't be afraid to talk to the editor about the changes you'd like to make to a contract," James-Enger says. "You don't know what you'll get or if an editor is willing to negotiate it, until you ask."

When writers have to approach an editor for changes to a contract, James-Enger advises writers to act professionally when it comes to the negotiations. "I start out with saying—I am really excited to be working with you on this story and I appreciate the assignment, but I have a couple of issues with the contract that I'd like to talk to you about," she says. "Sure I want a better contract but I also want to maintain a good working relationship with my editor. A scorched-earth policy doesn't benefit any freelancer in the long run."

....

In today's economy, writers are a little more reluctant to ask for a higher rate for an article.

....

Negotiating payment terms is a tricky subject for some writers. Writers want to get the most bang for their buck but they don't want to lose a great writing assignment. Do your research first before you decide to ask an editor for more money to complete the assignment. Double check the publisher's website or look to see if the pay scale is equivalent to other publishers in the particular industry. Some publishers have a set publishing fee whereas others may have a little more wiggle room depending on the type of the assignment given. In today's economy, writers are a little more reluctant to ask for a higher rate for an article. If the publisher seems to be open to discussion about the pay scale, just make sure you approach the situation in a professional manner so as to not turn the publisher away from giving you another assignment.

WHO WILL OWN YOUR WRITING?

Besides payment terms, another area that writers may find themselves on the other end of the negotiation table is with ownership rights. We all want to take credit for the work that we have poured our heart and soul into. Unfortunately, the business of publishing has different ways of saying how a writer can classify their work. Ownership rights vary but the biggest one that writers have a hard time trying to build up a good case against is "all rights." "All rights" is exactly what it means: *hope you are not in love with what you have just written because you will not be able to use it again.*

RIGHTS AND WHAT THEY MEAN

A creative work can be used in many different ways. As the author of the work, you hold all rights to the work in question. When you agree to have your work published, you are granting a publisher the right to use your work in any number of ways. Whether that right is to publish the manuscript for the first time in a publication, or to publish it as many times and in as many ways as a publisher wishes, is up to you—it all depends on the agreed-upon terms. As a general rule, the more rights you license away, the less control you have over your work and the money you're paid. You should strive to keep as many rights to your work as you can.

Writers and editors sometimes define rights in a number of different ways. Below you will find a classification of terms as they relate to rights.

- **FIRST SERIAL RIGHTS.** Rights that the writer offers a newspaper or magazine to publish the manuscript for the first time in any periodical. All other rights remain with the writer. Sometimes the qualifier "North American" is added to these rights to specify a geographical limitation to the license. When content is excerpted from a book scheduled to be published, and it appears in a magazine or newspaper prior to book publication, this is also called first serial rights.

- **ONE-TIME RIGHTS.** Nonexclusive rights (rights that can be licensed to more than one market) purchased by a periodical to publish the work once (also known as simultaneous rights). That is, there is nothing to stop the author from selling the work to other publications at the same time.

- **SECOND SERIAL (REPRINT) RIGHTS.** Nonexclusive rights given to a newspaper or magazine to publish a manuscript after it has already appeared in another newspaper or magazine.

- **ALL RIGHTS.** This is exactly what it sounds like. "All rights" means an author is selling every right he has to a work. If you license all rights to your work, you forfeit the right to ever use the work again. If you think you may want to use the article again, you should avoid submitting to such markets or refuse payment and withdraw your material.

- **ELECTRONIC RIGHTS.** Rights that cover a broad range of electronic media, including websites, CD/DVDs, video games, smart phone apps, and more. The contract should specify if—and which—electronic rights are included. The presumption is unspecified rights remain with the writer.

- **SUBSIDIARY RIGHTS.** Rights, other than book publication rights, that should be covered in a book contract. These may include various serial rights; movie, TV, audio, and other electronic rights; translation rights, etc. The book contract should specify who controls the rights (author or publisher) and what percentage of sales from the licensing of these rights goes to the author.

- **DRAMATIC, TV, AND MOTION PICTURE RIGHTS.** Rights for use of material on the stage, on TV, or in the movies. Often a one-year option to buy such rights is offered (generally for 10 percent of the total price). The party interested in the rights then tries to sell the idea to other people—actors, directors, studios, or TV networks. Some properties are optioned numerous times, but most fail to become full productions. In those cases, the writer can sell the rights again and again.

Sometimes editors don't take the time to specify the rights they are buying. If you sense that an editor is interested in getting stories, but doesn't seem to know what his and the writer's responsibilities are, be wary. In such a case, you'll want to explain what rights you're offering (preferably one-time or first serial rights only) and that you expect additional payment for subsequent use of your work.

The Copyright Law that went into effect January 1, 1978, states writers are primarily selling one-time rights to their work unless they—and the publisher—agree otherwise in writing. Book rights are covered fully by contract between the writer and the book publisher.

In recent months, I have written for two publications that I had given "all rights" to the company. My rationale is that I knew I would never need to use those articles again but I did make sure I was able to include those articles for my byline to show that I have publishing experience.

If you feel that you want to reuse or recycle an article that you had written a few years ago, you might want to consider negotiating an "all rights" clause or maybe going to another publisher. "We don't take all rights so there is no reason for authors to request we change the rights clause," says Angela Hoy, author and owner of WritersWeekly.com and Booklocker. com. "Our contracts were rated 'Outstanding' by Mark Levine (author of *The Fine Print of Self-Publishing*) and has also been called the clearest and fairest in the industry."

James-Enger is also an advocate of negotiating contracts that include an "all rights" clause. "I hate 'all rights' contracts, and try to avoid signing them as they preclude me from ever reselling the piece as a reprint to other markets," she says. "I explain that to editors, and I have been able to get editors to agree to let me retain nonexclusive reprint rights even when they buy all rights—which still lets me market the piece as a reprint." James-Enger also advises that "if the publisher demands all rights, then negotiate if the payment is sub-standard."

So if you are just receiving a contract in the mail for the first time or you are working with a new publisher, you should not be afraid of the legal lingo that blankets the message "we want to work with you." Contracts are meant to protect both the interests of the publishers and writers. Publishers want the commitment from writers that he or she will provide their best work and writers want to be recognized for their best work. But between those contracts lines, the legal lingo can cause writers to feel they need a law degree to review the contract. No, just sit back and relax and enjoy the prose that will take your writing to the next level.

CINDY FERRAINO has been blessed with a variety of assignments, including newspaper articles, magazine articles, ghost-written articles, stories for books, and most recently authoring a book on accounting and bookkeeping terminology, *The Complete Dictionary of Accounting & Bookkeeping Terms Explained Simply* (Atlantic Publishing Group).

MAKING THE MOST OF THE MONEY YOU EARN

....

by Sage Cohen

Writers who manage money well can establish a prosperous writing life that meets their short-term needs and long-term goals. This article will introduce the key financial systems, strategies, attitudes and practices that will help you cultivate a writing life that makes the most of your resources and sustains you over time.

DIVIDING BUSINESS AND PERSONAL EXPENSES

If you are reporting your writing business to the IRS, it is important that you keep the money that flows from this source entirely separate from your personal finances. Here's what you'll need to accomplish this:

- **BUSINESS CHECKING ACCOUNT:** Only two types of money go into this account: money you have been paid for your writing and/or "capital investments" you make by depositing your own money to invest in the business. And only two types of payments are made from this account: business-related expenses (such as: subscriptions, marketing and advertisement, professional development, fax or phone service, postage, computer software and supplies), and "capital draws" which you make to pay yourself.

- **BUSINESS SAVINGS ACCOUNT OR MONEY MARKET ACCOUNT:** This account is the holding pen where your quarterly tax payments will accumulate and earn interest. Money put aside for your retirement account(s) can also be held here.

- **BUSINESS CREDIT CARD:** It's a good idea to have a credit card for your business as a means of emergency preparedness. Pay off the card responsibly every month and this will help you establish a good business credit record, which can be useful down the line should you need a loan for any reason.

When establishing your business banking and credit, shop around for the best deals, such as highest interest rates, lowest (or no) monthly service fees, and free checking. Mint.com is a good source for researching your options.

EXPENSE TRACKING AND RECONCILING

Once your bank accounts are set up, it's time to start tracking and categorizing what you earn and spend. This will ensure that you can accurately report your income and itemize your deductions when tax time rolls around every quarter. Whether you intend to prepare your taxes yourself or have an accountant help you, immaculate financial records will be the key to speed and success in filing your taxes.

For the most effective and consistent expense tracking, I highly recommend that you use a computer program such as QuickBooks. While it may seem simpler to do accounting by hand, I assure you that it isn't. Even a luddite such as I, who can't comprehend the most basic principles of accounting, can use QuickBooks with great aplomb to plug in the proper categories for income and expenses, easily reconcile bank statements, and with a few clicks prepare all of the requisite reports that make it easy to prepare taxes.

PAYING BILLS ONLINE

While it's certainly not imperative, you might want to check out your bank's online bill pay option if you're not using this already. Once you've set up the payee list, you can make payments in a few seconds every month or set up auto payments for expenses that are recurring. Having a digital history of bills paid can also come in handy with your accounting.

MANAGING TAXES

Self-employed people need to pay quarterly taxes. A quick, online search will reveal a variety of tax calculators and other online tools that can help you estimate what your payments should be. Programs such as TurboTax are popular and useful tools for automating and guiding you step-by-step through tax preparation. An accountant can also be helpful in understanding your unique tax picture, identifying and saving the right amount for taxes each quarter, and even determining SEP IRA contribution amounts (described later in this article). The more complex your finances (or antediluvian your accounting skills), the more likely that you'll benefit from this kind of personalized expertise.

Once you have forecasted your taxes either with the help of a specialized, tax-planning program or an accountant, you can establish a plan toward saving the right amount for quarterly payments. For example, once I figured out what my tax bracket was and the approximate percentage of income that needed to be set aside as taxes, I would immediately transfer a percentage of every deposit to my savings account, where it would sit and grow a little interest until quarterly tax time came around. When I could afford to do so, I would also set aside the appropriate percentage of SEP IRA contribution from each deposit so that I'd be ready at end-of-year to deposit as much as I possibly could for retirement.

THE PRINCIPLE TO COMMIT TO IS THIS: Get that tax-earmarked cash out of your hot little hands (i.e., checking account) as soon as you can, and create whatever deterrents you need to leave the money in savings so you'll have it when you need it.

INTELLIGENT INVESTING FOR YOUR CAREER

Your writing business will require not only the investment of your time but also the investment of money. When deciding what to spend and how, consider your values and your budget in these three, key areas:

EDUCATION	MARKETING AND PROMOTION	KEEPING THE WHEELS TURNING
Subscriptions to publications in your field	URL registration and hosting for blogs and websites	Technology and application purchase, servicing and back-up
Memberships to organizations in your field	Contact database subscription (such as Constant Contact) for communicating with your audiences	Office supplies and furniture
Books: on topics you want to learn, or in genres you are cultivating	Business cards and stationery	Insurances for you and/or your business
Conferences and seminars	Print promotions (such as direct mail), giveaways and schwag	Travel, gas, parking
Classes and workshops	Online or print ad placement costs	Phone, fax and e-mail

This is not an absolute formula for spending, by any means—just a snapshot of the types of expenses you may be considering and negotiating over time. My general rule would be: start small and modest with the one or two most urgent and/or inexpensive items in each list, and grow slowly over time as your income grows.

The good news is that these legitimate business expenses may all be deducted from your income—making your net income and tax burden less. Please keep in mind that the IRS allows losses as long as you make a profit for at least three of the first five years you are in business. Otherwise, the IRS will consider your writing a non-deductible hobby.

PREPARATION AND PROTECTION FOR THE FUTURE

As a self-employed writer, in many ways your future is in your hands. Following are some of the health and financial investments that I'd recommend you consider as you build and nurture The Enterprise of You. Please understand that these are a layperson's suggestions. I am by no means an accountant, tax advisor or financial planning guru. I am simply a person who has educated herself on these topics for the sake of her own writing business, made the choices I am recommending and benefited from them. I'd like you to benefit from them, too.

SEP IRAS

Individual Retirement Accounts (IRAs) are investment accounts designed to help individuals save for retirement. But I do recommend that you educate yourself about the Simplified Employee Pension Individual Retirement Account (SEP IRA) and consider opening one if you don't have one already.

A SEP IRA is a special type of IRA that is particularly beneficial to self-employed people. Whereas a Roth IRA has a contribution cap of $5,000 or $6,000, depending on your age, the contribution limit for self-employed people in 2011 is approximately 20% of adjusted earned income, with a maximum contribution of $49,000. Contributions for a SEP IRA are generally 100% tax deductible and investments grow tax deferred. Let's say your adjusted earned income this year is $50,000. This means you'd be able to contribute $10,000 to your retirement account. I encourage you to do some research online or ask your accountant if a SEP IRA makes sense for you.

CREATING A 9-MONTH SAVINGS BUFFER

When you're living month-to-month, you are extremely vulnerable to fluctuation in the economy, client budget changes, life emergencies and every other wrench that could turn a good working groove into a frightening financial rut. The best way to prepare for the unexpected is to start (or continue) developing a savings buffer. The experts these days are suggesting that we accumulate nine months of living expenses to help us navigate transition in a way that we feel empowered rather than scared and desperate to take the next thing that comes along.

When I paid off one of my credit cards in full, I added that monthly payment to the monthly savings transfer.

I started creating my savings buffer by opening the highest-interest money market account I could find and setting up a modest, monthly automatic transfer from my checking account. Then, when I paid off my car after five years of monthly payments, I added my car payment amount to the monthly transfer. (I'd been paying that amount for five years, so I was pretty sure I could continue to pay it to myself.) When I paid off one of my credit cards in full, I added that monthly payment to the monthly savings transfer. Within a year, I had a hefty sum going to savings every month before I had time to think about it, all based on expenses I was accustomed to paying, with money that had never been anticipated in the monthly cash flow.

What can you do today—and tomorrow—to put your money to work for your life, and start being as creative with your savings as you are with language?

DISABILITY INSURANCE

If writing is your livelihood, what happens if you become unable to write? I have writing friends who have become incapacitated and unable to work due to injuries to their brains, backs, hands and eyes. Disability insurance is one way to protect against such emergencies and ensure that you have an income in the unlikely event that you're not physically able to earn one yourself.

Depending on your health, age and budget, monthly disability insurance payments may or may not be within your means or priorities. But you won't know until you learn more about your coverage options. I encourage you to investigate this possibility with several highly rated insurance companies to get the lay of the land for your unique, personal profile and then make an informed decision.

HEALTH INSURANCE

Self-employed writers face tough decisions about health insurance. If you are lucky, there is someone in your family with great health coverage that is also available to you. Without the benefit of group health insurance, chances are that self-insuring costs are high and coverage is low. Just as in disability insurance, age and health status are significant variables in costs and availability of coverage. (Once again, I am no expert on this topic; only a novice who has had to figure things out for myself along the way, sharing the little I know with you.)

Ideally, of course, you'll have reasonably-priced health insurance that helps make preventive care and health maintenance more accessible and protects you in case of a major medical emergency. The following are a few possibilities to check out that could reduce costs and improve access to health coverage:

- Join a group that aggregates its members for group coverage, such as a Chamber of Commerce or AARP. Ask an insurance agent in your area if there are any other group coverage options available to you.

- Consider a high-deductible health plan paired with a Health Savings Account (HSA). Because the deductible is so high, these plans are generally thought to be most useful for a major medical emergency. But an HSA paired with such a plan allows you to put aside a chunk of pre-tax change every year that can be spent on medical expenses or remain in the account where it can be invested and grow. 2011 HSA investment limits, for example, are: $3,050 for individual coverage and $6,150 for family coverage.

Establishing effective financial systems for your writing business will take some time and energy at the front end. I suggest that you pace yourself by taking an achievable step or two each week until you have a baseline of financial management that works for you. Then, you can start moving toward some of your bigger, longer-term goals. Once it's established, your solid financial foundation will pay you in dividends of greater efficiency, insight and peace of mind for the rest of your writing career.

SAGE COHEN is the author of *The Productive Writer: Tips and Tools for Writing More, Stressing Less and Creating Success* and *Writing the Life Poetic: An Invitation to Read and Write Poetry*, both from Writer's Digest Books. She holds an MFA from New York University and a BA from Brown University. Since 1997, Sage has been a freelance marketing communications writer serving clients including: Intuit, Sterling Commerce, Dell, WebMD and Blue Shield. She teaches online classes ranging from poetry to productivity to business writing at pathofpossibility.com.

PHOTO © Nyla Alisia

RECORD KEEPING AND PRICING

....

by Daniel Dern

Being a writer includes many tasks besides the actual act of writing. There's research, marketing, computer maintenance, and, unless you are doing writing strictly as a hobby, financial recordkeeping—keeping track of the money you spend and receive related to your writing activities.

For example, I've been doing freelance writing since 1973, ranging from part-time to full-time... and, along with the writing, research, marketing and sales, et cetera, done my own recordkeeping.

This recordkeeping doesn't have to be complicated or expensive. It's gotten simple bordering on automatic, depending on how you do it.

You'll need to spend a few hours learning what to do and why, and setting up to do it. Jeff Hecht, a full-time science and technology writer who has also sold some science fiction, points out, "You need to understand something about accounting and taxes, even if you use an accountant, because you have to know what's deductible and what isn't, what records to keep, and what information you will have to provide."

After that, it's a few minutes every day or so.

Here's some of my current thoughts and advice on recordkeeping.

[Note: From a tax perspective, this article assumes you are a) a U.S. taxpayer, and b) doing your business activities as an unincorporated individual, which means you file your business income/expense tax information using a Form 1040 Schedule C. If you're already incorporated, or not a U.S. taxpayer, you should know what's in this article already, and some things won't apply to you... but keep reading, you may still learn something useful.)

WHY KEEP FINANCIAL RECORDS OF YOUR BUSINESS

There are several important reasons to keep financial records.

One, so you know how much money you have to pay taxes on (which in turn impacts Reason Number Two).

For example, if you have $65,439 of business income for a calendar year, and $16,222 in business-related expenses, then you have taxable business income of $65,439 - $16,222 = $49,217... the amount you have to report on your Form 1040 under BUSINESS INCOME OR LOSS (which currently is Form 1040 Line 12).

Another way to look at this is: If you don't keep good records of your expenses (which are harder than logging your revenues, as a rule), you'll pay more taxes than you have to, since those business expenses are reducing your total income, which is what you're paying taxes on. Your business expenses become pre-tax rather than post-tax spending... and between Federal income tax, the roughly 16 percent SE (Social Security and Medicare) tax, and any state or city income taxes, that can be between 20 and 50 percent, so good record-keeping can legitimately lower your tax obligation by as much as several thousand dollars a year in taxes. (Depending, of course, on how much you earned, and what your business expenses were—which only good recordkeeping will tell you.)

Convinced yet?

Two, recordkeeping lets you know how well/poorly you're doing in terms of writing as a business activity, income and expensewise. Are you earning less or more than you are spending? Are you earning more—after expenses—than you would working at some other job?

Three, recordkeeping may help you analyze your writing from a business perspective and see what, if anything, might merit being changed. For example, are there seasonal peaks or slumps in work loads? Do some clients (customers) take too long to pay? Are some clients not paying? Do your phone bills seem too high? Can you get some of your supplies at better prices, by changing how you order or switching suppliers? Are you spending more on some events or activities than the resulting business justifies? Accurate records tell you what your gut may only suspect (or might not even suspect).

Rick Telberg, president and chief executive of Bay Street Group, which provides custom research, marketing, strategic consulting, and other services to the professional tax, accounting, and finance sector, stresses the importance of good, organized record-keeping. "Just because you're a writer doesn't mean you are not in business."

WHAT ARE FINANCIAL RECORDS?

Briefly, my definition: "records," a.k.a. "books" or "bookkeeping," means the list of business-related income and business-related expenses.

Business-related INCOME—in accountant-speak, "Accounts Receivable"—as a writer includes money you earn selling articles, stories, books, podcasts—and possibly from writing services, like copyediting, proposal writing, rewriting—and from writing-related activities, e.g., speaking, doing readings, and teaching.

Business-related EXPENDITURES—"Accounts Payable"—refers to money spent to enable you to write. For example, a computer and printer, monthly broadband Internet service, an annual subscription to *Writer's Digest*, professional memberships like SCBWI, office supplies, and professional activities. (More on this below.)

Broadly, "business records" means a list of your relevant monetary transactions. Each item includes the date (month, day, year) and amount.

Income records also include:

- Source—the name of who paid you, e.g., JOE'S FISH MARKET, Susanna Creamcheese, Nicholas' Pizza, Corner Computing.
- Nature of work, e.g. "Royalties, Jan-Mar 2012, Ice Fishing On Mars," "Article, 100 Uses For Old Socks," "Fiction, "Refunds For That Bridge In Brooklyn."

And, if you have invoices (not everyone will), the invoice ID.

FIGURE 1 shows examples of business income records.

> ### A BRIEF RECOMMENDATION FOR INVOICE IDS
>
> Include the year, an absolute tracking number, the client ID, and per-client tracking number—and have this data be part of the file name! So, for example, I have invoice "numbers" like:
>
> Dern-2011-035/SmartBear-01
>
> which would be in a file named:
>
> Dern-2011-SmartBear-01-TestingMobileDevices

FIGURE 1: SAMPLE RECORDS OF BUSINESS INCOME

DATE	INVOICE#	CLIENT#	CLIENT	AMOUNT	PROJECT
Jan 04, 2011	2010-047	NSD-03	NSDuckToll mag	$350.00	Article, "Think Fast! Videoing Your Toller," 800 words
Jan 05, 2011	2010-050	SmartBear-03	SmartBear	$575.00	Article, "Testing Mobile Devices," 2,300 words
Jan 17, 2011	2011-002	CGL-01	Cambridge Globe	$75.00	Article, "Tollers Tolling In The Snow," 400 words
Jan 23, 2011	n/a		DogHouse Press	$382.50	Royalties, 2010 Q2, "Toller Tales: The Restless Urge To Fetch (3rd ed)
Feb 27, 2011	2011-004	FruitBat-01	FruitBatCo	$1,200.00	Case history, "Tablet computers Save $ For Fruit Bat Owners"

Business expense records include, in addition to the date and amount:

- Company, organization, etc. for vendor, supplier, store, etc., their name, e.g., Staples, U.S. Post Office, Fedex, Kinko's, Amazon, AT&T Wireless, Verizon, SouthWest Air, Holiday Inn. For smaller transactions, possibly a general description, like "local newsstand," "yard sale," "airport food," "books from Ernest."
- Nature of item. E.g., broadband, cell phone service, toner for laser printer, stamps, *Maximum PC* magazine (2-year renewal), library fines, batteries, iTunes card, plane fare to SCBWI Winter Conference, etc.

and, depending on how you make payments and how you keep your records:

- Transaction Info, e.g. check #, credit card name, "cash," PayPal
- Notes—details or other miscellaneous information, e.g. "Meet with editor to discuss schedule," "research on hummingbirds, for story," etc.

FIGURE 2 shows examples of business expense records.

FIGURE 2: SAMPLE RECORDS OF BUSINESS EXPENSES

DATE	CATEGORY	WHO	AMOUNT	METHOD	WHAT/NOTES
Jan 12, 2011	DUES&SUBS	Writers Digest	$19.96	Check 437	Renewal, 1 year (8 issues)
Jan 15, 2011	UTILITIES	KiboComm	$89.37	Check 442	Broadband & office tel.
Jan 16, 2011	DUES&SUBS	NSDuckTollClub	$25.00	Check 445	Dues, 1 year
Jan 18, 2011	OFF SUPL	Staples	$23.42	Amex	Paper, binders, misc

It's important—arguably essential—to keep records in a way that lets you find and check specific items, and also lets you get categorized totals. The first reason is to let you check and verify items; the second reason is for having properly sorted totals in preparation for doing your taxes.

"Good recordkeeping means that when it's time to do your taxes, you've got everything in the right place, and, ideally, already sorted and totaled."

"Good recordkeeping means that when it's time to do your taxes, you've got everything in the right place, and, ideally, already sorted and totaled," says Rick Telberg—versus, say, having thrown everything into the proverbial shoebox throughout the year. "It's amazing what 15 minutes a week will yield you in reduced time and aggravation at tax time. Even if you use an accountant to do your taxes, you'll save money by needing less of their time."

WHAT QUALIFIES AS A BUSINESS EXPENSE?

What's a business expense? Your opinion may vary from that of your peers, customers, or friends—for example, you might think that an $800 Barca-Lounger chair for your living room, or a $600 treadmill for your basement, contribute to your "business thinking time" and therefore qualify as business expenses. However, your opinion isn't what matters.

For purposes of doing your taxes, the U.S. Internal Revenue Service (IRS) determines and defines very clearly what constitutes a qualifying expense, and, in some cases, what percentage of a given expense you can claim.

For the official answers, see Instructions for Schedule C: Profit or Loss From A Business.

I also strongly recommend the IRS' Publication 334, Tax Guide for Small Business (For Individuals Who Use Schedule C or C-EZ). Pub 334 tells you exactly what the government wants to know, and what its rules are. Both are available free, as a download, or in hardcopy on request from the IRS, and your local library probably has a copy.

HOW TO CHARGE: SIZE OR TIME

Many writing projects are priced roughly based on word count, but have a fixed price. For example, a 1,500-word article on "Testing Mobile Devices" for one client might be $500, while an 1,800-word one on "Comparing Drupal to Joomla," for a different client, $1,200.

Other projects, like working on a brochure, or doing research, might be a hourly rate, against "Not to Exceed" amounts.

It's essential to establish bounds and limits on project pricing and effort. Your client wants to have a clear cap on the price. You need to have a clear cap on effort for that price, e.g., "Additional drafts, $75/hour," or "If you want an additional 350-word sidebar, that's another $250."

The IRS also has a publication specifically about recordkeeping: Publication 552 (01/2011), Recordkeeping for Individuals.

I urge you to get a copy of each, and read it, slowly and carefully, two or three times. You don't have to do this every year, but it's definitely worth doing at least once. After that, you can just read the "What's New" section.

You may also want to buy or borrow a book or two that explains these. But the IRS is, by definition, the official source regarding what they want. Other books are bound to be correct, and may be clearer, or provide more examples, but the IRS instructions and Publication 334 are your primary sources.

I also suggest you cultivate a business relationship with an accountant or two. Even if you end up doing all your own recordkeeping, bookkeeping and tax prep, it's helpful to have a knowledgeable industry expert on tap for the occasional question or advice. (Be prepared to pay for their time, of course!)

So, what qualifies? Professional memberships and publications are legitimate business expenses, for example. For writers, subscriptions to daily newspapers, e.g., the *New York Times, Washington Post*, and *Boston Globe* are. Ditto a desk, and a chair—even a good ergonomic Herman-Miller Aeron chair (which I haven't yet sprung for) qualifies. Some things may fall into gray areas. Again, read the instructions in the IRS instructions! And feel free to ask fellow writers...but don't accept their opinions blindly.

HOW MUCH TO CHARGE: SETTING (OR AGREEING ON) PRICES

Here's some quick guidelines to setting prices—taken largely from my article "How to Set Prices for Your Services: A Step-by-Step Guide to Calculating What You Must—or CAN—Charge" (http://www.dern.com/hw2price.shtml).

The advice here assumes you are writing for a living. Even if you aren't, it's still worth thinking through your prices—and you shouldn't be undercutting prices of people who are doing this for a living.

First, you need to know how much you would have to charge, to make a living—earn your target salary. This information is the basis for actually setting or agreeing on prices. (Or for deciding you need to look for a new occupation.)

The short answer here (see my "How to set price" article for the long answer) is: Double your current (or target) annual salary, and multiply by between 1.5 and 2, to determine how much you need to earn to replace your salary and benefits, and cover business expenses. Then divide by 1,400—the number of billable/salable hours you have in a year—to get your target hourly rate.

For example: If you were earning $50,000/year, 50,000 times 2 divided by 1,400 equals around $70/hour. If times 1.5, around $55/hour.

Once you know what you have to charge, you can also consider other strategies to base your prices on, which take into account factors like circumstance, bargaining strength, etc.:

- Going Rates. What do your fellow professionals charge; what are prospects paying?
- Paying for Priority. If someone needs immediate, drop-everything service, that often is worth 25-50% more. (Don't be greedy, though.)

Remember that it's legitimate to have sets of prices, such as for large corporations versus start-ups and small businesses; discounts for companies referring or sub-contracting to you; and fixed prices for standard types of projects.

And note: Companies that work regularly with writers (like magazines, and PR agencies) should have set rates and simply tell you what they pay. (But feel free to try and negotiate.)

To help keep track of business expenses (which makes it easier to do the recordkeeping):

- When you buy things, where possible, do business transactions separate from non-business ones. E.g., if you're buying business supplies and school supplies at Staples, CostCo, or wherever, separate the piles, and get them rung up separately.
- Consider a separate checking account and a separate credit card for your business, versus the ones you use for personal expenses. (The separate credit card is particularly good, as interest you pay here is a business expense.)

CATEGORIZING EXPENSES—WHAT INFORMATION DOES THE GOVERNMENT WANT FROM YOU?

Since records for your tax forms are a major goal of business recordkeeping, it makes sense to do your recordkeeping in a way that matches what the government wants.

That means tagging or otherwise categorizing items using the list in Schedule C Part II: EXPENSES, which currently includes (i.e., this is a partial list):

- Advertising
- Car and truck expenses—parking, tolls, and per-mile
- Depreciation and section 179 expense deductions
- Insurance (other than health)—e.g., Business Owner's Policy
- Interest: (Mortgage, other)
- Legal and professional services—accountant, etc.
- Office expense—paper, toner, USB sticks, etc.
- Supplies (not included in Part III)
- Utilities—business phone line, broadband Internet
- Other Expenses—stuff that doesn't readily fall into the other categories

Some of these categories are specific, some are broad. There is no specific category, for example, for "computers"—and it's not necessarily clear where "Web domain registration fees" would go. However, since all numbers end up going into one total—and you're entering totals, not each line item—there's room for judgement calls, or putting those categories into "Other Expenses."

In my recordkeeping, I've typically had more categories than Schedule C has—although over the years, I've combined and simplified some categories—and then combined category totals as needed in my year-end process. For example, my categories include "BOOKS,

MAGAZINES AND MULTIMEDIA" and "DUES AND SUBSCRIPTIONS," both of which get put on my Schedule C under "Other Expenses."

HOW DO YOU KEEP RECORDS?

You need to keep records in a way that's consistent, and clear—and easy for you to do. IRS Publication 552 (01/2011), Recordkeeping for Individuals can help you with this.

These records should be "journaled," that is, written, or entered into a computer file, in a day-by-date order. You might not enter items right when they happen, but it's a bad idea to get more than a few days behind.

Ideally, do this in a way that makes totaling them up easy—like having separate columns for each of the categories that your tax forms want, per above.

You don't need a computer or special software to do this.

You can do this with pen and paper (which I did, for years). For example, with a notebook using accounting paper—or plain old paper. This may be easier if you have a separate column or page for each category.

I began using pen/pencil, accounting paper (a mix of two, three, four and five-column) in a three-ring binder, along with a simple calculator and several folders for filing receipts for the year.

....

There's nothing fancy sophisticated about my spreadsheet. It's just a bunch of columns.

....

A computer will help, though, if used properly.

For example, in the past few years, I've (finally!) started using a spreadsheet, done with Microsoft Excel, and five or 10 three-tab manilla folders for filing receipts.

There's nothing fancy sophisticated about my spreadsheet. It's just a bunch of columns— DATE, VENDOR/SUPPLIER, ITEM(S), CHECK#/ETC, NOTES, and a column for each category, e.g., BOOKS, DUES & SUBSCRIPTIONS, INSURANCE, OFFICE EXPENSES, etc. I have a summing (add items up) row, at the top, for each column; each time I enter a new item, the TOTAL cell automatically updates itself.

(I'll post a generic copy of the spreadsheet to my dern.com website—look for "STUFF I SAID I'D POST"—which you're welcome to use.)

Total cost—less than buying that accounting paper and another three-ring binder, since I already have the computer and a copy of Microsoft Office. Plus the dozen-ish manilla file folders.

You don't have to use a spreadsheet. (I'm doing single-entry bookkeeping, and brief forays into other software were more frustrating than helpful...but I am looking into some new ones that handle expense entry.)

Telberg states, "There's no shortage of software you can run on your computer, or Internet-based services you can use via your Web browser, to keep your records, such as QuickBooks, Quicken Home & Business, FreshBooks, ShowBox, Outright, and Wave Accounting." Some of these, Telberg notes, are just doing bookkeeping, some also offer business tasks like invoicing and analysis.

What's important is that you use the tools, enter items on a regular basis, and make sure you're got a regular backup of your data!

There are a growing number of mobile phone apps, such as ProOnGo Expense (which I haven't tried yet) that can help you record transactions when you are away from your office, by taking pictures of expense receipts and doing a lot of the data entry for you.

What's important is that you use the tools, enter items on a regular basis, and make sure you've got a regular backup of your data! If the file is on your computer, make sure you've got an online backup; if the file is online, make sure you've got a backup locally, or elsewhere online.

SAVING AND FILING RECEIPTS AND RELATED PAPERWORK

For petty expenses, say, under $25, the IRS (and whatever other organizations you might have to show your records to) will take your word for it. In general, get a receipt—and save and file it—whenever possible.

I file and save my receipts—including revenue receipts—using three-tab manilla folders that correspond to my expense categories, one set of folders per year. Like my recordkeeping categories, I've reduced the number of file folder categories over the years. (I don't, for no particular reason, simply have a folder for each recordkeeping category. Go figure.)

To make it easy to find a receipt after I've filed it, when I've entered an item into my business records, I circle and check off the amount on the receipt, and, if it isn't already clear, what the actual item is. If it's a bill that I've paid, I include the date paid and check number, to make it easier to verify without having to dig through my checkbook. Then I file it, trying to put the newest one in the front of the folder.

If you've done a good job of entering this information into your records, you'll almost never actually look at these receipts again. But when you do need to find one, you'll be grateful you're organized.

In terms of keeping receipts, consider getting a scanner—digital copies are now acceptable. (Again, make sure you've got backups!) See IRS Publication 552 for more details about paper versus digital receipts.

And enter the amounts and file the receipts when you get home. Don't wait until the end of the month—or year—to sort, file and enter!

Again, the key is to get, save, enter and file receipts regularly.

SUMMARY: KEEPING PROPER RECORDS REGULARLY IS EASIER AND BETTER THAN NOT

Like I said above, the most important use for this information is to provide the numbers you need for tax purposes, namely, filling out U.S. Form 1040 Schedule C. If you've done your recordkeeping right, you've got all your information in and up-to-date, and the totals are there. If, like me, you've got a few more categories than the Schedule C uses, you'll spend a few minutes adding those totals up.

Otherwise, you're in for days of avoidable stress come April.

And you'll be able to see how well (or poorly) you've done, in terms of writing as a business, and have the information to help decide how you can do better, what expenses to try and cut, or where to spend more.

All for a pad of paper, or little to no additional software, and a few minutes a day.

DANIEL P. DERN has been a freelance writer since 1973 and is based in Newton Center, MA, whose written everything from technology and business journalism and PR, to science fiction, and his Dern Grim Bedtime Tales. His website is www.dern.com, and his blogs include Trying Technology (http://www.TryingTechnology.com) and Dern's PR Tips (http://www.DernsPRTips.com). Contact Daniel at dern@pair.com.

SUBMISSION TRACKER

Recordkeeping is an important tool for the successful freelance writer. It's important to keep accurate records for tax season, but it's equally important to keep accurate submission records. Failure to do so could lead to some embarrassing double submissions or result in missed opportunities to follow up. Plus, an organized writer always impresses editors and agents.

On the next page is a sample submission tracker spreadsheet. You can make copies of the one in this book to help you keep records, or you can create a similar spreadsheet on your computer using a spreadsheet program. WritersMarket.com also provides submission tracking tools as part of the My Markets feature of the site.

This submission tracker has nine columns:

- **MANUSCRIPT TITLE.** This is the title of your manuscript.
- **MARKET.** This is the name of the magazine, book publisher, contest, or other entity to which you've submitted your manuscript.
- **CONTACT NAME.** This is the name of the editor, agent, or other contact who's received your work.
- **DATE SENT.** The date you submitted your manuscript.
- **DATE RETURNED.** The date your manuscript was rejected.
- **DATE ACCEPTED.** The date your manuscript was accepted.
- **DATE PUBLISHED.** The date your manuscript was published.
- **PAYMENT RECEIVED.** Detail any payment received.
- **COMMENTS.** This column is for any other notes about your experience with the market.

SUBMISSION TRACKER

MANUSCRIPT TITLE	MARKET	CONTACT NAME	DATE SENT	DATE RETURNED	DATE ACCEPTED	DATE PUBLISHED	PAYMENT RECEIVED	COMMENTS

PROTECT YOUR DATA:

5 Steps to Do Right Now

by Tony Palermo

Freelance writer and author Katrina Onstad was finishing a particularly difficult assignment for *Chatelaine* magazine when all of a sudden, her monitor turned black. With each passing second, her spirit dropped as she realized that not only had her computer crashed—it had completely died.

"It was very traumatic," said Onstad. "I'd been struggling with the column for days."

She attempted everything to recover her data, including paying close to $300 to a data recovery professional. The most they were able to salvage were some pictures. The column, along with most of her writing, was gone.

To cap it all off, Onstad had to go back to her editor and explain why the column was going to be late. "It was a seriously embarrassing 'cat-ate-my-gym-suit' moment," she said.

Onstad also lost a major draft of her first novel when someone broke into her apartment and stole her laptop. Despite this, she admits that she still doesn't back up her data on a regular basis.

She's not alone. Out of the writers I surveyed, many didn't back up their data at all. In fact, 90 percent of the writers I polled had an incomplete or nonexistent backup and recovery strategy in place.

How about you? If you fall into that 90 percent, fear not, my friend. I've outlined five things that you can do right now to protect your data (and your gym suit.)

1. REALIZE THAT DATA BACKUPS ARE IMPORTANT

Yes, backing up your data really is that important. Your data can be lost a variety of ways. Viruses and other malware? Absolutely. Hardware and software crashes? You bet. Fire, sabotage and theft? Definitely.

WHERE TO GO FOR MORE INFORMATION

Did you know that most Apple Mac and Microsoft Windows based operating systems have built-in tools to help you backup your data? To learn more, check your system's help files and/or manuals. For more up-to-date information, visit HYPERLINK "http://www.apple.com" www.apple.com if your computer is a Mac, or HYPERLINK "http://www.microsoft.com" www.microsoft.com if it is a Windows-based PC.

There are some excellent resources on the Internet that have produced reports comparing the various backup options that are out there. One such website is www.toptenreviews.com. On the top left of the website's main page is a search box. Type "backup" in the search box and then press the search button (it has a picture of a magnifying glass on it). Within the first few search results will be the following three reports:

- Data Backup Software Review 2011
- Online Data Backup Review 2011
- Mac Backup Software Review 2011

Take the time to go through the reports to learn about the different products that are available. It can be a lot to absorb, so if you have questions don't be shy about talking to a technology professional or visiting one of your technology retail outlets.

Even the most successful writers sometimes need help with their computers. Kelly James-Enger is a former attorney turned freelance writer who has published over 700 articles in over 50 national magazines. She has authored, coauthored and ghostwritten 12 books, and also acts as a mentor to other writers. When I asked her how often she backs up her data, she told me that she didn't even know the answer to that question.

No worries for her though because in her own words, she's "married to an awesome IT guy" who also acts as her personal tech support boy. He has her backups fully automated and her data well protected.

My personal favourite is user error; you know, where the problem sits somewhere between the front of the computer and back of the chair?

And, what is data anyways? As a writer, you no doubt think about your articles and books. But what about your accounting files, contact lists, e-mails, music, pictures, research documents and Web favorites? How about your programs and operating system (think MacOS or Microsoft Windows)?

Can you afford to lose any of that data?

Sure, writing is an art but to be financially successful, you have to also think of yourself as a business. After all, you earn your money by writing, or at least hope to, right? So, if one day you lost everything, what impact would that have on your project? How about your livelihood as a writer—your business?

6 WAYS TO PROTECT YOUR WRITING

Below are six strategies for protecting your writing. While these are all good strategies separately, writers should use a combination. It really is better to be safe than sorry.

- **Save as you work.** Don't write for huge chunks of time without hitting the save button. It's hard to get back into "THE ZONE" when you're forced to recreate a scene (or set of scenes).
- **Save files on an online site.** For instance, some writers prefer using Google docs for their writing and Flickr for their images. These sites are good, because your computer could crash, but your files won't be affected.
- **Use external hard drive.** This is a good way to save important files, but if you do this, keep the external hard drive in a separate location than your actual hard drive. After all, the external hard drive won't help out much when a fire, tornado or flood damages your home if it gets destroyed along with the regular hard drive.
- **Find an online backup service.** There are many companies that offer online backup services for reasonable rates. For instance, Carbonite (carbonite.com) offers unlimited data storage for $54.95 per year; Mozy (mozy.com) has rates as low as $5.99 per month.
- **Keep copy offsite.** Step 3 mentions taking this step, but it's advice worth repeating and bolding. A copy only helps in unexpected disasters if it's separated from the original.
- **Print copies.** This is old school, but you could always have a paper copy of writing just in case all the data storage in the world is wiped out by an electromagnetic pulse or intense solar flare. Of course, if that happens, the last thing you might be worried about is whether you have a copy of your unpublished manuscript.

2. EVALUATE YOUR BACKUP OPTIONS

Online, differential, incremental, image, restore—phew—it sounds like a lot of gobbily-gook, doesn't it? With all of the options and technical terminology out there, it can be quite confusing to figure out what you really need.

In general, you have three different backup options: backup your files manually, use an online backup service, or install a backup software program.

The first option, backing up your data manually, is a quick and dirty way of backing up your files. You basically copy your files over to a data key, CD-ROM, DVD or external hard drive. I know of one writer who e-mails copies of her documents to her Hotmail account.

There are a few downsides to a manual backup though. For starters, it relies on you making the time (and remembering) to backup your data. Another problem is knowing exactly what to backup. You might know where you keep your documents and music, but do you know where your contacts and e-mails are stored? How about your accounting files?

For a few dollars a month, another option is to use an online backup service. Unlike a manual backup, with an online service you can schedule when the backup will occur. As scheduled, your files will automatically backup across the Internet and be stored offsite on one of the company's storage systems. One definite advantage is that because they're scheduled, online backups don't rely on you to do them. Another advantage is that the backup files are stored offsite. If your house burns down, a copy of your data is safely stored somewhere else.

One of the downsides to online backups is that they rely on a relatively fast Internet connection. And, even if you do happen to have a fast Internet connection, depending on how much data you have to backup, it can still take a long time to backup or recover your files.

Your other option is to install a backup program on your computer. For the average home user, the price of one of these programs can cost up to $100. The clear advantage to an installed program is that it gives you the option to backup your whole computer, not just your data files. Why is this an advantage, you ask? Well, consider if your computer hard drive fails. Once it's replaced, how long would it take you to reinstall all of your programs and configure your system to just the way you like it? If you had the option to restore your computer to the way it looked at the time of your last backup, it sure could save you a lot of time and heartache.

3. DO SOMETHING—NOW!

Yes, choosing your best backup option will require some thought and research, but you can commit to doing something now. Take the time to manually backup some of your important data. At the very least, e-mail yourself a copy of your most important documents to a Hotmail or Yahoo account. It's not perfect, but some protection is better than none.

4. TEST YOUR BACKUP

This is an important one that is often forgotten. Regardless of what backup method you choose, make sure that you try to recover your files from time-to-time. Be proactive. Discover and eliminate problems beforehand, not at crunch time when you really need your files.

5. STORE A COPY OFFSITE

I touched on it earlier, but again, regardless of whether you backup your files on a DVD, external hard drive or data key, make sure that you store a copy of your backup files somewhere offsite (trade backups with a friend, perhaps). If your place floods or goes up in flames, you'll have some comfort in knowing that a copy of your most important files is safe somewhere else.

COPYRIGHT: THE OTHER FORM OF PROTECTION

Copyright law exists to protect creators of original works. It is also designed to encourage the production of creative works by ensuring that artists and writers hold the rights by which they can profit from their hard work.

The moment you finish a piece of writing—or in fact, the second you begin to pen the manuscript—the law recognizes only you can decide how the work is used. Copyright protects your writing, recognizes you (its sole creator) as its owner, and grants you all the rights and benefits that accompany ownership. With very few exceptions, anything you write today will enjoy copyright protection for your lifetime, plus 70 years. Copyright protects "original works of authorship" that are fixed in a tangible form of expression. Copyright law cannot protect titles, ideas, and facts.

Some writers are under the mistaken impression that a registered copyright with the U.S. Copyright Office (www.copyright.gov) is necessary to protect their work, and that their work is not protected until they "receive" their copyright paperwork from the government. That is not true. You don't have to register your work with the U.S. Copyright Office for it to be protected. Registration of your work does, however, offer some additional protection (specifically, the possibility of recovering punitive damages in an infringement suit) as well as legal proof of the date of copyright.

Most magazines are registered with the U.S. Copyright Office as single collective entities themselves; that is, the works that make up the magazine are not copyrighted individually in the names of the authors. You'll need to register your article yourself if you wish to have the additional protection of copyright (your name, the year of first publication, and the copyright symbol) appended to any published version of your work. You may use the copyright symbol regardless of whether your work has been registered with the U.S. Copyright Office.

One thing you need to pay particular attention to is work-for-hire assignments. If you sign a work-for-hire agreement, you are agreeing that your writing will be done as a work for hire, and you will not control the copyright of the completed work—the person or organization who hired you will be the copyright owner. These arrangements and transfers of exclusive rights must appear in writing to be legal. In fact, it's a good idea to get every publishing agreement you negotiate in writing before the sale.

TONY PALERMO is a freelance writer and journalist who writes regularly for various trade publications, such as Blue Line and The Canadian Journal of Green Building and Design, as well as for several Metroland newspapers. Prior to writing, he spent 15 years in the information technology field where he worked as an independent consultant helping small-to-medium-size business implement cost-effective technology solutions.

TIME MANAGEMENT AND ORGANIZATION FOR WRITERS

....

by Carol Silvis

Do you *wish* you could find time to write, or do you *want* to find time? Unlimited possibilities make it impossible to do everything you *wish*. Spend your time on what you *want* to accomplish.

The last three years I taught full time and authored a textbook, two business books, and newsletter articles. How did I manage with family, work, and community commitments? I *wanted* to write more than I *wished* to do other things. I tracked my time, made writing a priority, eliminated meaningless activities, and created a workable plan. You can do the same.

KNOW WHERE YOUR TIME GOES

Time management is vital to the writer, whose life is often a juggling act. Track where your time goes for several days. You might be surprised to discover how the hours are whittled away by useless activities. Let go of the perpetual overload that eats up the minutes and instead focus on writing.

Nancy Martin, author of nearly 50 popular fiction novels including the Blackbird Sisters mystery series, puts it this way: "Nobody can make time for my writing but me. That's perhaps the first truth a writer needs to acknowledge. Don't keep hoping someone else will create a lovely block of writing time for you. Turn off the TV, limit your Facebook minutes, and go cold turkey on computer games—that's my best advice."

PLAN

What do you want to accomplish? Without a clear direction, procrastination can take hold. Set writing goals and schedule writing time into your day or week. It may not be easy, but it can be done by the serious writer. Consider Timmons Esaias, an instructor in the Writing Popular Fiction MFA Program at Seton Hill University.

With a full-time job, home responsibilities, and an erratic schedule, he says, "I've rarely been able to manage a regular, daily writing schedule. Basically, I'm an afternoon writer for the first draft. I edit best in the mornings." Timmons adapts by carrying projects with him and writing in coffee shops and libraries as well as during his commute. His commitment to writing has resulted in works that have appeared in 15 languages.

Even full-time writers like Martin plan their days. "I try to arrange my writing schedule in a way that sets me up for success. Depending on where I am in the progression of a novel, I try to get to work six to nine hours a day."

MAKE WRITING A PRIORITY

We constantly decide how to spend our time. Serious writers choose to make writing a priority by saying no to other activities. For people hoping to squeeze writing into an already crowded day, suspense novelist and book reviewer Hallie Ephron advises: "Try to write first...commit to writing at least one page every morning before checking e-mail or getting on the Internet."

Ephron follows her own advice as she deals with the responsibilities of giving workshops, guest blogging, traveling to events, maintaining her website, writing articles, and doing interviews. She says, "The competing demands of this kind of career-related but not specific novel-related work are the hardest to keep in bounds...The only way to deal with it is to make myself write first."

When you make writing a priority, push yourself beyond your comfort zone, and stay on track, you will see progress.

....

If you won't respect your own writing time, why should anyone else?

....

Friends and relatives often perceive writers are not working and monopolize their time. Esaias believes writers should turn off all communication devices, including cell phones and e-mail to avoid interruptions. "If you won't respect your own writing time, why should anyone else?" he asks.

What can you do if you have blocked out time to write, but the muse refuses to come? Tackle other writing-related activities. Research, plot, outline, organize your files, stuff envelopes, or search the *Writers' Market* for appropriate publishers and agents for your writing.

Martin studies the work of other authors. "I try to read with a purpose—often making notes of how another writer cranks up tension or plants red herrings or whatever's plaguing me at the time. Or I go word shopping (cull 10 unique or interesting words) to prime my writing pump." She also makes lists of ways to solve story problems.

USE BITS OF TIME

Can't find a large block of time to write? Use minutes. Esaias says, "Most pieces, fiction or nonfiction, tend to have natural sections, and I usually tell myself to work on one section at a time." He suggests learning to force yourself to write about whatever comes into your head and write as fast as you can in bursts. "Don't even stop for spelling."

Break projects down to fit into your schedule (a page, a chapter, or an outline) or start with an easy part (a character snapshot, a plot point, or a scene).

Ephron, writes, "…from 7:30 until maybe 10:30. Then …works in the afternoon, maybe 2-5." She strives for at least 500 new words a day. "Some days it's easier than others," she admits. With 11 published books to her credit, the schedule seems to work.

GET ORGANIZED

Organization is a vital component of time management. When asked if she had tricks to organizing her writing projects that saves time in the long run, Martin said she sets personal deadlines, creates outlines, and has a ruthless critique partner.

Ephron organizes her projects by setting up a main folder for the work in progress and several subfolders for planning, sources, and archive. "Archive is where I put any out-of-date versions of the novel. There's nothing more frustrating than starting to work on your book and realizing that you're working on the wrong file."

Store notes for individual projects in labeled folders and writing related receipts in a large envelope for tax time. Put a container by the door for outgoing items, such as library books and manuscripts to be mailed. Track submissions and responses on a spreadsheet and back-up computer files.

For a time-starved writer, wasting time is not an option. The clock is always ticking.

CAROL SILVIS is the author of *Job Hunting After 50, 101 Ways to Make Yourself Indispensable at Work,* and several college textbooks. She is the president of Pennwriters, Inc., a 440-member writing group. She has also had a dozen creative nonfiction stories and inspirational pieces published in national magazines. For more than two decades, Silvis has trained adults in how to get a job, keep and enjoy it, and get ahead. Learn more about Silvis at www.carolsilvis.com.

PHOTO: Used with permission of author

WRITING CALENDAR

The best way for writers to achieve success is by setting goals. Goals are usually met by writers who give themselves or are given deadlines. Something about having an actual date to hit helps create a sense of urgency in most writers (and editors for that matter). This writing calendar is a great place to keep your important deadlines.

Also, this writing calendar is a good tool for recording upcoming writing events you'd like to attend or contests you'd like to enter. Or use this calendar to block out time for yourself—to just write.

Of course, you can use this calendar to record other special events, especially if you have a habit of remembering to write but of forgetting birthdays or anniversaries. After all, this calendar is now yours. Do with it what you will.

AUGUST 2011

SUN	MON	TUE	WED	THURS	FRI	SAT
	1	2	3	4	5	6
7	8	9	10	11	12	13
14	15	16	17	18	19	20
21	22	23	24	25	26	27
28	29	30	31			

Start a blog and make at least one post per week.

_____

_____

_____

_____

_____

SEPTEMBER 2011

SUN	MON	TUE	WED	THU	FRI	SAT
				1	2	3
4	5	6	7	8	9	10
11	12	13	14	15	16	17
18	19	20	21	22	23	24
25	26	27	28	29	30	

Try sending out one targeted query per day during September.

OCTOBER 2011

SUN	MON	TUE	WED	THU	FRI	SAT
						1
2	3	4	5	6	7	8
9	10	11	12	13	14	15
16	17	18	19	20	21	22
23	24	25	26	27	28	29
30	31					

Are you on Twitter? Try leaving a meaningful tweet daily.

_____

_____

_____

_____

_____

NOVEMBER 2011

SUN	MON	TUE	WED	THU	FRI	SAT
		1	2	3	4	5
6	7	8	9	10	11	12
13	14	15	16	17	18	19
20	21	22	23	24	25	26
27	28	29	30			

Write a novel during November as part of NaNoWriMo!

DECEMBER 2011

SUN	MON	TUE	WED	THU	FRI	SAT
				1	2	3
4	5	6	7	8	9	10
11	12	13	14	15	16	17
18	19	20	21	22	23	24
25	26	27	28	29	30	31

Evaluate your 2011 accomplishments and make 2012 goals.

JANUARY 2012

SUN	MON	TUE	WED	THU	FRI	SAT
1	2	3	4	5	6	7
8	9	10	11	12	13	14
15	16	17	18	19	20	21
22	23	24	25	26	27	28
29	30	31				

Make 2012 your best year freelancing yet!

FEBRUARY 2012

SUN	MON	TUE	WED	THU	FRI	SAT
			1	2	3	4
5	6	7	8	9	10	11
12	13	14	15	16	17	18
19	20	21	22	23	24	25
26	27	28	29			

Use the extra day in February to submit your writing.

_____

_____

_____

_____

_____

MARCH 2012

SUN	MON	TUE	WED	THU	FRI	SAT
				1	2	3
4	5	6	7	8	9	10
11	12	13	14	15	16	17
18	19	20	21	22	23	24
25	26	27	28	29	30	31

Don't wait until April to file your 2011 taxes.

APRIL 2012

SUN	MON	TUE	WED	THU	FRI	SAT
1	2	3	4	5	6	7
8	9	10	11	12	13	14
15	16	17	18	19	20	21
22	23	24	25	26	27	28
29	30					

Write a poem a day for National Poetry Month.

MAY 2012

SUN	MON	TUE	WED	THU	FRI	SAT
		1	2	3	4	5
6	7	8	9	10	11	12
13	14	15	16	17	18	19
20	21	22	23	24	25	26
27	28	29	30	31		

Plan to attend a writing conference this summer.

JUNE 2012

SUN	MON	TUE	WED	THU	FRI	SAT
					1	2
3	4	5	6	7	8	9
10	11	12	13	14	15	16
17	18	19	20	21	22	23
24	25	26	27	28	29	30

Develop one story or article idea each week.

_____

_____

_____

_____

_____

JULY 2012

SUN	MON	TUE	WED	THU	FRI	SAT
1	2	3	4	5	6	7
8	9	10	11	12	13	14
15	16	17	18	19	20	21
22	23	24	25	26	27	28
29	30	31				

Don't forget to keep accurate records for next tax season.

AUGUST 2012

SUN	MON	TUE	WED	THU	FRI	SAT
			1	2	3	4
5	6	7	8	9	10	11
12	13	14	15	16	17	18
19	20	21	22	23	24	25
26	27	28	29	30	31	

Most successful writers read as much as (or more than) they write.

SEPTEMBER 2012

SUN	MON	TUE	WED	THU	FRI	SAT
						1
2	3	4	5	6	7	8
9	10	11	12	13	14	15
16	17	18	19	20	21	22
23	24	25	26	27	28	29
30						

Try an unfamiliar writing style to help you grow as a writer.

OCTOBER 2012

SUN	MON	TUE	WED	THU	FRI	SAT
	1	2	3	4	5	6
7	8	9	10	11	12	13
14	15	16	17	18	19	20
21	22	23	24	25	26	27
28	29	30	31			

Remember to hit the save button when you're writing.

NOVEMBER 2012

SUN	MON	TUE	WED	THU	FRI	SAT
				1	2	3
4	5	6	7	8	9	10
11	12	13	14	15	16	17
18	19	20	21	22	23	24
25	26	27	28	29	30	

Write a novel during November for NaNoWriMo!

DECEMBER 2012

SUN	MON	TUE	WED	THU	FRI	SAT
						1
2	3	4	5	6	7	8
9	10	11	12	13	14	15
16	17	18	19	20	21	22
23	24	25	26	27	28	29
30	31					

If you don't have it yet, find a copy of *2013 Writer's Market*.

LAUNCHING YOUR FREELANCE BUSINESS

by I.J. Schecter

Starting something from scratch takes guts, faith and a healthy dose of stubborn optimism. Some would argue that deciding to launch a freelance writing practice requires a touch of masochism, too. But let's look at this rationally. First, you aren't starting from scratch; you're starting with talent, knowledge, skill, connections, and, probably, the moral support of a good number of people. Second, starting a writing business is no more or less difficult than starting any other type of business, whether a bakery, real estate brokerage or piano-tuning service. Third, you're peddling an extremely valuable product. Most businesses figure out pretty fast that if they don't know how to communicate, they're going to have a hard time winning customers. And in today's world of short attention spans and stimulus overload, the ability to communicate succinctly and powerfully is more valuable than ever.

PRE-WORK

Before putting your name out there, there are a few things you need to take care of. At the top of the list is getting business cards and letterhead printed. When you do start to tell people about your practice, the last thing you want is to be stuck without a card to hand over. And after you do offer it, hopefully prompting a discussion about your potential client's needs, you'll want to send a follow-up letter immediately—but on your own stationery, not some generic one. From the moment you decide to freelance professionally, you must think of yourself as a brand. Most writers feel hesitant about marketing themselves in any specific way because they don't want to cut off other opportunities. But when you're starting out, establishing a firm brand perception—that is, a clear statement about what you do and why it's valuable—is more important than appearing able do it all. Demonstrate expertise in a few specific areas, and others will inevitably find their way into your lap.

SELLING YOURSELF

Almost all writers share an aversion to self-selling—but it's mostly a function of unfair conditioning. That is, they assume they hate marketing themselves before they even try because other writers have convinced them one can't be a good writer and a good salesman at the same time.

The truth is plenty of good writers are natural salesmen, too, but they feel the superficial selling part undermines the authentic writing part. Take a moment to think about it and you'll realize all business-people have to market themselves just like writers do. A restaurateur needs to do more than just open his doors to generate traffic. An investment broker must go beyond merely getting a license if he hopes to succeed. A psychologist wanting to build a practice ought to take a few steps in addition to simply hanging a shingle. And a writer needs to do more than just write. "This job is about sales as much as it is about writing," says Toronto-based freelancer Ian Harvey. "One of the simple rules guiding my practice is this: Hustle, hustle, hustle."

So how does a writer generate buzz? There are several ways: letters, flyers, brochures, newsletters, blogs, samples, cold calls, and so on. When I launched my practice, the first thing I did (after getting business cards and letterhead printed, of course) was to send out hundreds of introductory letters—to those I knew, to those I didn't know, to people, to businesses . . . to just about everyone whose address I could get. I discriminated little in this initial blitz, though naturally with each letter I dropped into the mailbox I became even more nervous that all the money, time and effort I was expending might lead nowhere.

Then I received a phone call. One of my letters had gone to a high school acquaintance working at a company that manufactured and distributed musical compilations on CD. She had received my letter just as her boss was looking for a writer to help write snappy liner notes. Years later, this company remains one of my biggest corporate clients.

Another of my letters went to an old colleague. He had become the head of an executive degree program at a local university and was preparing to design the program brochure, for which a writer was sorely needed. I won the assignment, which led to another three.

The lesson? You truly never know where work is going to come from. More important, you can't count on finding yourself in the right place at the right time; you have to create the possibility of being there.

GROWING PAINS

There are two parts to selling yourself. First is developing the nerve to do it. Second is developing the right type of skin: rhino. "Rejections are part of the game," says Harvey, "but this is the only game in which rejection doesn't mean no. It means not now, or not for me, or not for me right now. It doesn't mean no forever." While it's fair to spend a little time—very little—getting annoyed or frustrated at rejection, it's best to take that annoyed or frustrated energy and pour it into something productive. Few businesses explode overnight; the ones that end up successful demand lots of grunt work up front, reach a minimum threshold after a few years, and then begin to grow in earnest.

WHERE IS YOUR STAPLER?

Many writers and other artists claim that their extreme lack of organization is simply an occupational hazard. Others practically boast about it, claiming it as a distinct imprint of creativity. Whether or not creative types are naturally disinclined toward self-organization, the sooner you decide to get organized and stay organized, the more successful you and your practice will become. Why? Two reasons, one physical, the other mental.

Physically speaking, when your work environment is organized, you spend more time writing and less time trying to locate the calculator or paper clips or this file or that folder. Simple odds dictate that using your time more productively will lead to more work.

The mental aspect is just as important. We all know how aggravating it is having to scramble to find that copy of the current contract for that magazine when we've forgotten what the word count was, or trying desperately to remember where we put the CD with the backup copy of that article after the electrical storm has wiped out our operating system with the deadline looming.

It stands to reason that the less energy you need to put into non-writing activities, the more energy you can direct toward your actual work, improving its overall quality and thereby making you a more desirable commodity. Sure, a little anxiety can be healthy for writing, but it should be anxiety borne of the drive to produce stellar work, not anxiety based on wondering where the stamps got to for the umpteenth time.

Organizing yourself is probably a lot easier than you imagine, and you might even be surprised at how good a little structure makes you feel.

Start small: Buy a box of multicolored file folders, some labels, some CDs or a memory stick, and several upright magazine files. Label one of the magazine files **Contracts**, then place in it different file folders labeled with the subject area for a given contract. For me, these folders include, among others, Bridal, Fitness, Golf, Men's, Gardening, and, of course, Writing and Publishing.

Label another of the magazine files **Current Assignments** and a third **Story Ideas**, and populate them as you did the first. Use consistent colors for specific topics—in other words, gardening always gets a yellow file folder whether it's in the **Story Ideas** or the **Contracts** file. This will make for easy cross-referencing.

And that's just a start. Odds are this small bit of organization will spur you, and soon you'll be creating files for every aspect of your work—character sketches, source notes, dialogue snippets, conferences and retreats, news items.

"Organization is everything," says freelancer Heather Cook, author of *Rookie Reiner: Surviving and Thriving in the Show Pen* (Trafalgar Square Books). "From maintaining accurate records for tax purposes to structuring a weekly plan to include marketing and administrative tasks, it allows me to stay focused and efficient—and that makes my overall work better."

It's imperative you commit to the up-front part. "Most businesses fail because the proprietors underestimate the amount of work required to get the business off the ground and overestimate the revenue in the first year or two," says Paul Lima, a professional writer for over 25 years and author of *The Six-Figure Freelancer*. Adds Vancouver-based freelancer Teresa Murphy, author of more than 1,000 magazine articles, "You need the ability to work 15 hours a day and love it, day in and day out. That means holidays, summer weekends and all-nighters when clients have rush projects. I've worked Boxing Day, New Year's Eve, Easter Sunday until midnight."

Of course, if you've decided to take the plunge in the first place, no doubt you've got this much passion and then some, because, like these professionals, you've realized that, despite the challenges of the writing life, nothing in the world makes you feel happier or more fulfilled.

GAINING, AND SUSTAINING, MOMENTUM

Investing the time and energy at the outset will lead to a point of critical mass—that first small group of people interested in your work, the first pebble in your pond. This could include a magazine editor, the president of a company or a friend needing some editing help. To help that first small ripple expand outward, you need to embed two vital behavioral principles.

1. OVERDELIVERY. Whether you're writing an article for your local newspaper, a marketing brochure for a multinational conglomerate or an essay for your best friend's medical school application, do the very best job you can. Your writing is judged every time you put pen to paper or fingers to keys. Force yourself to knock the ball out of the park at every opportunity and you'll develop the kind of reputation that leads to positive word of mouth, constant repeat business and sparkling testimonials.

2. PROFESSIONALISM. From editors to executives, just about everyone is stretched thin these days—and that's why being known as someone easy to work with can distinguish you from other writers who also deliver solid work. Acting like a professional means a number of things. Dressing a certain way. Acting a certain way. Hitting deadlines. Returning calls and e-mails promptly.

In this business just like any other, people, and circumstances, will irk you—but in almost every case it behooves you to take the high road.

It also means not ever being petty, spiteful or antagonistic. Following the publication of my first short story collection, I lucked into a chance to set up a small table at a prominent outdoor literary festival. Beside me was the editor of an esteemed literary journal—along with her large dog, in a cage a few feet behind us. The dog began barking his head off just as people starting checking out the book tables, and he didn't stop for an hour, scaring off just about anyone who wandered anywhere near me and my book. The woman did nothing. I didn't just want to offer her a few choice words; I wanted to write her a scathing letter several pages long. Friends and family urged me to resist, and, though it was hard, I did. A few years later, when I sent this editor a story for consideration in her journal, she accepted it (though she had no recollection of me from the festival), creating a writing credit that remains one of my most important. The moral? In this business just like any other, people, and circumstances, will irk you—but in almost every case it behooves you to take the high road. Reacting emotionally can only harm you; staying cool can only benefit you.

THE NUMBERS GAME

Writing is dynamic and fluid; it can be endlessly revised, massaged, tweaked, twisted and reversed back over itself. For this reason, it's essential that you get every one of your assignments in writing (no pun intended; OK, slightly intended). Commercial assignments will usually come with a contract; corporate assignments almost never will. To address this, prepare two versions of your own standard agreement. For commercial gigs, this document should include a brief description of the assignment, word count, pay rate, and deadline, along with all the other legal bits you can find by looking up any typical freelance contract. For corporate assignments, it should include a more detailed description of the project (including each piece of work if there are multiple parts), the agreed timeline, the fee (either an overall flat rate or an hourly rate), and, crucially, a definition of completion. For example, in my standard corporate agreement, I have a clause indicating that, for the agreed-upon fee, I will deliver the described work by the noted deadline and then allow two rounds of requested revisions or suggestions from the client, after which I will start charging extra. This creates clear mutual expectations between the client and me and helps avoid awkward conversations toward the end of the project when the senior partner tries to add an arbitrary comma for the third time.

For corporate work, you'll also have to develop the skill of estimating. It's one thing to name an hourly rate when a potential client first asks; it's another to try to come up with a total number of hours based on his incredibly vague description of the assignment. But come up with one you must—only to be met with, in some cases, a response gently questioning why the work ought to take so long. Here we have a quandary: By and large, people vastly underestimate how long good writing actually takes. I've found the best way to deal with this is to be truthful. I tell my clients up front that writing and communications work tends to take quite a bit longer than non-writers imagine, and that, in fact, most projects end up taking 20 percent more hours than I initially estimate because the client themselves didn't realize going in how much would be involved. As long as I deliver good work, this ceases to be an issue.

> It's one thing to name an hourly rate when a potential client first asks; it's another to try to come up with a total number of hours based on his incredibly vague description of the assignment.

How much or how little should you charge for your work? It depends—based on your experience, where you live, and a host of other factors. Make sure, before you enter any negotiation, that you've decided upon the lowest figure you're willing to accept. Or, as freelancer Colette van Haaren puts it, "You need three things in this business: a good nose to sniff out stories, a thick skin for when rejection hits, and a backbone for when you have to negotiate."

SURE I'M WORKING HARD. IN MY HEAD

Only about half my time is spent actually working on assignments. The other half is spent crafting queries, doing research, maintaining correspondence, or, to be honest, just brainstorming. My favorite part of being a writer is that I can work anywhere, since so much of the work is done between my ears. Often someone will ask me a question, and, when I don't answer, my wife will murmur to him or her, "Oh, he's just working." And she's right.

I also believe, however, that the luxury of being able to do mental work represents an important responsibility. During spells when my plate isn't full with deadlines, I don't rest on my laurels. Instead, I record ideas, I query like crazy, I read other writers, I think about new marketing angles. In short, given the nature of my profession, I have no excuse for down time. "If you don't care about your business, no one else will," says freelancer Sharon Aschaiek. "Use slow times to indirectly generate more work—develop new pitches, follow up with previous editors and clients, explore new marketing avenues. Even use the time to take care of accounting and administrative issues. Just don't let yourself get complacent."

ANSWERING THE QUESTION

Friends familiar with your long-time desire to write may good-naturedly tease you about the risk of giving up your thankless but stable 9-to-5 grind to tackle something so daunting. Former colleagues may wonder aloud about your decision. Busybody aunts will gossip about how no one makes money writing and what a nice doctor or lawyer you would have made.

Change their perception by embracing and celebrating your decision rather than timidly defending it. When people ask, "So what are you doing now?" answer with pride and conviction. Don't say, "I thought I'd give freelancing a go and see how it works out," or "I'm going to try being a freelance writer, though I'm not really sure what that means."

Have your "elevator speech"—a business term for the 30-second spiel that describes what you do—always at the ready. When people ask me what I do, I respond, "I'm a freelance writer and communications consultant." If they want to know more, I tell them my practice is divided evenly between commercial writing, like magazine features, and corporate writing, which entails everything from marketing brochures to ghostwriting business books. Suddenly they're intrigued. They see writing as a real, viable, honest-to-goodness business—not because I've dropped figures but because I've spoken about it in a clear, confident manner.

Let's stop apologizing for being writers. I love being one, and I bet you do, too. Tell anyone who asks.

THE BOTTOM LINE

Is freelancing hard work? Sure—damned hard. But it's no harder than any other profession. Like every job, it requires a combination of skill, thoroughness and dependability. The difference is you don't have anyone defining the parameters of the job for you or providing incentives to succeed. The discipline and drive have to come solely from you. Or, in the words of full-time freelancer and book author Lisa Bendall, "All the talent in the world won't help if you aren't willing to put in the time at your desk and actually work. You've got to crack your own whip."

Now get cracking!

I.J. SCHECTER (www.ijschecter.com) is an award-winning writer, interviewer and essayist based in Toronto. His bestselling collection, *Slices: Observations from the Wrong Side of the Fairway* (John Wiley & Sons), is available in bookstores and online. Schecter is also the author of *102 Ways to Earn Money Writing 1,500 Words or Less* (Writer's Digest Books). Schecter provides corporate, creative and technical writing services to a diverse range of clients spanning the globe.

HOW MUCH SHOULD I CHARGE?

....

by Lynn Wasnak

If you're a beginning freelance writer, or don't know many other freelancers, you may wonder how anyone manages to earn enough to eat and pay the rent by writing or performing a mix of writing-related tasks. Yet, smart full-time freelance writers and editors annually gross $35,000 and up—sometimes into the $150,000-200,000 range. These top-earning freelancers rarely have names known to the general public. (Celebrity writers earn fees far beyond the rates cited in this survey.) But, year after year, they sustain themselves and their families on a freelance income, while maintaining control of their hours and their lives.

Such freelancers take writing and editing seriously—it's their business.

Periodically, they sit down and think about the earning potential of their work, and how they can make freelancing more profitable and fun. They know their numbers: what it costs to run their business; what hourly rate they require; how long a job will take. Unless there's a real bonus (a special clip, or a chance to try something new) these writers turn down work that doesn't meet the mark and replace it with a better-paying project.

If you don't know your numbers, take a few minutes to figure them out. Begin by choosing your target annual income—whether it's $25,000 or $100,000. Add in fixed expenses: social security, taxes, and office supplies. Don't forget health insurance and something for your retirement. Once you've determined your annual gross target, divide it by 1,000 billable hours—about 21 hours per week—to determine your target hourly rate.

Remember—this rate is flexible. You can continue doing low-paying work you love as long as you make up for the loss with more lucrative jobs. But you must monitor your rate of earning if you want to reach your goal. If you slip, remind yourself you're in charge. As a freelancer, you can raise prices, chase better-paying jobs, work extra hours, or adjust your spending."

"Sounds great," you may say. "But how do I come up with 1,000 billable hours each year? I'm lucky to find a writing-related job every month or two, and these pay a pittance."

That's where business attitude comes in: network, track your time, join professional organizations, and study the markets. Learn how to query, then query like mad. Take chances by reaching for the next level. Learn to negotiate for a fee you can live on—your plumber does! Then get it in writing.

You'll be surprised how far you can go, and how much you can earn, if you believe in your skills and act on your belief. The rates that follow are a guide to steer you in the right direction.

This report is based on input from sales finalized in 2009 and 2010 only. The data is generated from voluntary surveys completed by members of numerous professional writers' and editors' organizations and specialty groups. We thank these responding groups, listed below, and their members for generously sharing information. If you would like to contribute your input, e-mail lwasnak@fuse.net for a survey.

PARTICIPATING ORGANIZATIONS

Here are the organizations surveyed to compile the "How Much Should I Charge?" pay rate chart. You can also find Professional Organizations in the Resources.

- American Independent Writers (AIW), (202)775-5150. Website: www.amerindy writers.org.
- American Literary Translators Association (ALTA), (972)883-2093. Website: www. utdallas.edu/alta/.
- American Medical Writers Association (AMWA), (301)294-5303. Website: www. amwa.org.
- American Society of Journalists & Authors (ASJA), (212)997-0947. Website: www. asja.org.
- American Society of Media Photographers (ASMP), (215)451-2767. Website: www. asmp.org.
- American Society of Picture Professionals (ASPP), (703)299-0219. Website: www. aspp.com.
- American Translators Association (ATA), (703)683-6100. Website: www.atanet.org.
- Angela Hoy's Writers Weekly. Website: www.writersweekly.com.
- Association of Independents in Radio (AIR), (617)825-4400. Website: www.air media.org.
- Association of Personal Historians (APH). Website: www.personalhistorians.org.
- Educational Freelancers Association (EFA), (212)929-5400. Website: www.the-efa.org.

- Freelance Success (FLX), (877) 731-5411. Website: www.freelancesucess.com.
- International Association of Business Communicators (IABC), (415)544-4700. Website: www.iabc.com.
- Investigative Reporters & Editors (IRE), (573)882-2042. Website: www.ire.org.
- Media Communicators Association International (MCA-I), (888)899-6224. Website: www.mca-i.org.
- National Cartoonists Society (NCS), (407)647-8839. Website: www.reuben.org/main.asp.
- National Writers Union (NWU), (212)254-0279. Website: www.nwu.org.
- National Association of Science Writers (NASW), (510)647-9500. Website: www.nasw.org.
- Society of Professional Journalists (SPJ), (317)927-8000. Website: www.spj.org.
- Society for Technical Communication (STC), (703)522-4114. Website: www.stc.org.
- Women in Film (WIF). Website: www.wif.org.
- Writer's Guild of America East (WGAE), (212)767-7800. Website: www.wgaeast.org.
- Writer's Guild of America West (WGA), (323)951-4000. Website: www.wga.org.

LYNN WASNAK (www.lynnwasnak.com) was directed to the market for her first paid piece of deathless prose ("Fossils in Your Driveway" published by *Journeys* in 1968 for $4) by *Writer's Market*. In the 40 years since, she's made her living as a freelancer and has never looked back.

ADVERTISING & PUBLIC RELATIONS

	PER HOUR			PER PROJECT			OTHER		
	HIGH	LOW	AVG	HIGH	LOW	AVG	HIGH	LOW	AVG
Advertising copywriting	$150	$35	$83	$9,000	$150	$2752	$3/word	25¢/word	$1.56/word
Advertising editing	$125	$20	$64	n/a	n/a	n/a	$1/word	25¢/word	65¢/word
Advertorials	$180	$50	$92	$1,875	$200	$479	$3/word	75¢/word	$1.57/word
Business public relations	$180	$30	$84	n/a	n/a	n/a	$500/day	$200/day	$356/day
Campaign development or product launch	$150	$35	$95	$8,750	$1,500	$4,540	n/a	n/a	n/a
Catalog copywriting	$150	$25	$71	n/a	n/a	n/a	$350/item	$25/item	$116/item
Corporate spokesperson role	$180	$70	$107	n/a	n/a	n/a	$1,200/day	$500/day	$740/day
Direct-mail copywriting	$150	$35	$84	$8,248	$500	$2,839	$4/word $400/page	$1/word $200/page	$2.17/word $314/page
Event promotions/publicity	$125	$30	$75	n/a	n/a	n/a	n/a	n/a	$500/day
Press kits	$180	$30	$82	n/a	n/a	n/a	$850/60sec	$120/60sec	$456/60sec
Press/news release	$180	$30	$78	$1,500	$125	$700	$2/word $750/page	40¢/word $150/page	$1.17/word $348/page
Radio commercials	$99	$30	$72	n/a	n/a	n/a	$850/60sec	$120/60sec	$456/60sec

	PER HOUR			PER PROJECT			OTHER		
	HIGH	LOW	AVG	HIGH	LOW	AVG	HIGH	LOW	AVG
Speech writing/editing for individuals or corporations	$167	$35	$90	$10,000	$2,700	$5,036	$350/minute	$100/minute	$204/minute
BOOK PUBLISHING									
Abstracting and abridging	$125	$30	$74	n/a	n/a	n/a	$2/word	$1/word	$1.48/word
Anthology editing	$80	$23	$51	$7,900	$1,200	$4,588	n/a	n/a	n/a
Book chapter	$100	$35	$60	$2,500	$1,200	$1,758	20¢/word	8¢/word	14¢/word
Book production for clients	$100	$40	$67	n/a	n/a	n/a	$17.50/page	$5/page	$10/page
Book proposal consultation	$125	$25	$66	$1,500	$250	$788	n/a	n/a	n/a
Book publicity for clients	n/a	n/a	n/a	$10,000	$500	$2,000	n/a	n/a	n/a
Book query critique	$100	$50	$72	$500	$75	$202	n/a	n/a	n/a
Children's book writing	$75	$35	$50	n/a	n/a	n/a	$5/word $5,000/adv	$1/word $450/adv	$2.75/word $2,286/adv
Content editing (scholarly/textbook)	$125	$20	$51	$15,000	$500	$4,477	$20/page	$3/page	$6.89/page
Content editing (trade)	$125	$19	$54	$20,000	$1,000	$6,538	$20/page	$3.75/page	$8/page
Copyediting (trade)	$100	$16	$46	$5,500	$2,000	$3,667	$6/page	$1/page	$4.22/page

	PER HOUR			PER PROJECT			OTHER		
	HIGH	LOW	AVG	HIGH	LOW	AVG	HIGH	LOW	AVG
Encyclopedia articles	n/a	n/a	n/a	n/a	n/a	n/a	50¢/word $3,000/item	15¢/word $50/item	35¢/word $933/item
Fiction book writing (own)	n/a	n/a	n/a	n/a	n/a	n/a	$40,000/adv	$525/adv	$14,193/adv
Ghostwriting, as told to	$125	$35	$67	$47,000	$5,500	$22,892	$100/page	$50/page	$87/page
Ghostwriting, no credit	$125	$30	$73	n/a	n/a	n/a	$3/word $500/page	50¢/word $50/page	$1.79/word $206/page
Guidebook writing/editing	n/a	n/a	n/a	n/a	n/a	n/a	$14,000/adv	$10,000/adv	$12,000/adv
Indexing	$60	$22	$35	n/a	n/a	n/a	$12/page	$2/page	$4.72/page
Manuscript evaluation and critique	$100	$23	$66	$2,000	$150	$663			n/a
Manuscript typing	n/a	n/a	$20	n/a	n/a	n/a	$3/page	95¢/page	$1.67/page
Movie novelizations	n/a	n/a	$80	$15,000	$5,000	$9,159	n/a	n/a	n/a
Nonfiction book writing (collaborative)	$125	$40	$80	n/a	n/a	n/a	$110/page $75,000/adv	$50/page $1,300/adv	$80/page $22,684/adv
Nonfiction book writing (own)	$125	$40	$72	n/a	n/a	n/a	$110/page $50,000/adv	$50/page $1,300/adv	$80/page $14,057/adv
Novel synopsis (general)	$60	$30	$45	$450	$150	$292	$100/page	$10/page	$37/page

	PER HOUR			PER PROJECT			OTHER		
	HIGH	LOW	AVG	HIGH	LOW	AVG	HIGH	LOW	AVG
Personal history writing/editing (for clients)	$125	$30	$60	$40,000	$750	$15,038	n/a	n/a	n/a
Proofreading	$75	$15	$31	n/a	n/a	n/a	$5/page	$2/page	$3.26/page
Research for writers or book publishers	$150	$15	$52	n/a	n/a	n/a	$600/day	$450/day	$525/day
Rewriting/structural editing	$120	$25	$67	$50,000	$2,500	$13,929	15¢/word	6¢/word	11¢/word
Translation—literary	n/a	n/a	n/a	$10,000	$7,000	$8,500	20¢/target word	6¢/target word	11¢/target word
Translation—nonfiction/technical	n/a	n/a	n/a	n/a	n/a	n/a	35¢/target word	8¢/target word	16¢/target word
BUSINESS									
Annual reports	$180	$45	$92	$15,000	$500	$5,708	$600	$100	$349
Brochures, booklets, flyers	$150	$30	$81	$15,000	$300	$4,215	$2.50/word $800/page	35¢/word $50/page	$1.21/word $341/page
Business editing (general)	$150	$25	$70	n/a	n/a	n/a	n/a	n/a	n/a
Business letters	$150	$30	$74	n/a	n/a	n/a	$2/word	$1/word	$1.47/word
Business plan	$150	$30	$82	$15,000	$200	$4,100	n/a	n/a	n/a

	PER HOUR			PER PROJECT			OTHER		
	HIGH	LOW	AVG	HIGH	LOW	AVG	HIGH	LOW	AVG
Business writing seminars	$200	$60	$107	$8,600	$550	$2,919	n/a	n/a	n/a
Consultation on communications	$180	$40	$95	n/a	n/a	n/a	$1,200/day	$500/day	$823/day
Copyediting for business	$125	$25	$60	n/a	n/a	n/a	$4/page	$2/page	$3/page
Corporate histories	$180	$35	$86	160,000	$5,000	$54,500	$2/word	$1/word	$1.50/word
Corporate periodicals, editing	$125	$35	$69	n/a	n/a	n/a	$2.50/word	75¢/word	$1.42/word
Corporate periodicals, writing	$135	$35	$78	n/a	n/a	$1,875	$3/word	$1/word	$1.71/word
Corporate profiles	$180	$35	$88	n/a	n/a	$3,000	$2/word	$1/word	$1.50/word
Ghostwriting for business execs	$150	$25	$84	$3,000	$500	$1,393	$2.50/word	50¢/word	$2/word
Ghostwriting for businesses	$250	$35	$109	$3,000	$500	$1,756	n/a	n/a	n/a
Newsletters, desktop publishing/production	$135	$35	$71	$6,600	$1,000	$3,480	$750/page	$150/page	$429/page
Newsletters, editing	$125	$25	$67	n/a	n/a	$3,600	$230/page	$150/page	$185/page
Newsletters, writing	$125	$25	$77	$6,600	$800	$3,567	$5/word $1,250/page	$1/word $150/page	$2.30/word $514/page

	PER HOUR			PER PROJECT			OTHER		
	HIGH	LOW	AVG	HIGH	LOW	AVG	HIGH	LOW	AVG
Translation services for business use	$75	$35	$52	n/a	n/a	n/a	$35/ target word $1.40/ target line	6¢/ target word $1/ target line	$2.30/ target word $1.20/ target line
Resume writing	$100	$60	$72	$500	$150	$287	n/a	n/a	n/a
COMPUTER, INTERNET & TECHNICAL									
Blogging—paid	n/a	n/a	$100	$2,000	$500	$1,240	$500/post	$6/post	$49/post
E-mail copywriting	$125	$35	$85	n/a	n/a	$300	$2/word	30¢/word	91¢/word
Educational webinars	$500	$0	$195	n/a	n/a	n/a	n/a	n/a	n/a
Hardware/Software help screen writing	$95	$60	$81	$6,000	$1,000	$4,000	n/a	n/a	n/a
Hardware/Software manual writing	$165	$30	$80	$23,500	$5,000	$11,500	n/a	n/a	n/a
Internet research	$95	$25	$55	n/a	n/a	n/a	n/a	n/a	n/a
Keyword descriptions	n/a	n/a	n/a	n/a	n/a	n/a	$200/page	$135/page	$165/page
Online videos for clients	$95	$60	$76	n/a	n/a	n/a	n/a	n/a	n/a

	PER HOUR			PER PROJECT			OTHER		
	HIGH	LOW	AVG	HIGH	LOW	AVG	HIGH	LOW	AVG
Social media postings for clients	$95	$30	$62	n/a	n/a	$500	n/a	n/a	$10/word
Technical editing	$150	$25	$65	n/a	n/a	n/a	n/a	n/a	n/a
Technical writing	$160	$30	$80	n/a	n/a	n/a	n/a	n/a	n/a
Web editing	$100	$25	$57	n/a	n/a	n/a	$10/page	$3/page	$5.67/page
Webpage design	$150	$35	$80	$4,000	$200	$1,278	n/a	n/a	n/a
Website or blog promotion	n/a	n/a	n/a	$650	$195	$335	n/a	n/a	n/a
Website reviews	n/a	n/a	n/a	$900	$50	$300	n/a	n/a	n/a
Website search engine optimization	$89	$60	$76	$50,000	$8,000	$12,000	n/a	n/a	n/a
White papers	$135	$25	$82	$10,000	$2,500	$4,927	n/a	n/a	n/a
EDITORIAL/DESIGN PACKAGES									
Desktop publishing	$150	$25	$67	n/a	n/a	n/a	$750/page	$30/page	$202/page
Photo brochures	$125	$65	$87	$15,000	$400	$3,869	$65/picture	$35/picture	$48/picture
Photography	$100	$50	$71	$10,500	$50	$2,100	$2,500/day	$500/day	$1,340/day

	PER HOUR			PER PROJECT			OTHER		
	HIGH	LOW	AVG	HIGH	LOW	AVG	HIGH	LOW	AVG
Photo research	$75	$25	$49	n/a	n/a	n/a	n/a	n/a	n/a
Picture editing	$100	$40	$64	n/a	n/a	n/a	$65/picture	$35/picture	$53/picture
EDUCATIONAL & LITERARY SERVICES									
Author appearances at national events	n/a	n/a	n/a	n/a	n/a	n/a	$500/hour $30,000/event	$100/hour $500/event	$285/hour $5,000/event
Author appearances at regional events	n/a	n/a	n/a	n/a	n/a	n/a	$1,500/event	$50/event	$615/event
Author appearances at local groups	$63	$40	$47	n/a	n/a	n/a	$400/event	$75/event	$219/event
Authors presenting in schools	$125	$25	$78	n/a	n/a	n/a	$350/class	$50/class	$183/class
Educational grant and proposal writing	$100	$35	$67	n/a	n/a	n/a	n/a	n/a	n/a
Manuscript evaluation for theses/dissertations	$100	$15	$53	$1,550	$200	$783	n/a	n/a	n/a
Poetry manuscript critique	$100	$25	$62	n/a	n/a	n/a	n/a	n/a	n/a
Private writing instruction	$60	$50	$57	n/a	n/a	n/a	n/a	n/a	n/a

	PER HOUR			PER PROJECT			OTHER		
	HIGH	LOW	AVG	HIGH	LOW	AVG	HIGH	LOW	AVG
Readings by poets, fiction writers	n/a	n/a	n/a	n/a	n/a	n/a	$3,000/event	$50/event	$225/event
Short story manuscript critique	$150	$30	$75	$175	$50	$112	n/a	n/a	n/a
Teaching adult writing classes	$125	$35	$82	n/a	n/a	n/a	$800/class $5,000/course	$150/class $500/course	$450/class $2,667/course
Writer's workshop panel or class	$220	$30	$92	n/a	n/a	n/a	$5,000/day	$60/day	$1,186/day
Writing for scholarly journals	$100	$40	$63	$450	$100	$285	n/a	n/a	n/a
FILM, VIDEO, TV, RADIO, STAGE									
Book/novel summaries for film producers	n/a	n/a	n/a	n/a	n/a	n/a	$34/page	$15/page	$23/page $120/book
Business film/video scriptwriting	$150	$50	$97	n/a	n/a	$600	$1,000/run min	$50/run min	$334/run min $500/day
Comedy writing for entertainers	n/a	n/a	n/a	n/a	n/a	n/a	$150/joke $500/group	$5/joke $100/group	$50/joke $283/group
Copyediting audiovisuals	$90	$22	$53	n/a	n/a	n/a	n/a	n/a	n/a
Educational or training film/video scriptwriting	$125	$35	$81	n/a	n/a	n/a	$500/run min	$100/run min	$245/run min

	PER HOUR			PER PROJECT			OTHER		
	HIGH	LOW	AVG	HIGH	LOW	AVG	HIGH	LOW	AVG
Feature film options	First 18 months, 10% WGA minimum; 10% minimum each 18-month period thereafter.								
TV options	First 180 days, 5% WGA minimum; 10% minimum each 180-day period thereafter.								
Industrial product film/video scriptwriting	$150	$30	$99	n/a	n/a	n/a	$500/run min	$100/run min	$300/run min
Playwriting for the stage	5-10% box office/Broadway, 6-7% box office/off-Broadway, 10% box office/regional theatre.								
Radio editorials	$70	$50	$60	n/a	n/a	n/a	$200/run min $400/day	$45/run min $250/day	$124/run min $325/day
Radio interviews	n/a	n/a	n/a	$1,500	$150	$683	n/a		
Screenwriting (original screenplay-including treatment)	n/a	n/a	n/a	$117,602	$62,642				$90,122
Script synopsis for agent or film	$2,344/30 min, $4,441/60 min, $6,564/90 min								
Script synopsis for business	$75	$45	$62	n/a	n/a	n/a	n/a		
TV commercials	$99	$60	$81	n/a	n/a	n/a	$2,500/30 sec	$150/30 sec	$1,204/30 sec
TV news story/feature	$1,455/5 min, $2,903/10 min, $4,105/15 min								
TV scripts (non-theatrical)	Prime Time: $33,681/60 min, $47,388/90 min Not Prime Time: $12,857/30 min, $23,370/60 min, $35,122/90 min								

	PER HOUR			PER PROJECT			OTHER		
	HIGH	LOW	AVG	HIGH	LOW	AVG	HIGH	LOW	AVG
TV scripts (teleplay/MOW)	$68,150/120 min								
MAGAZINES & TRADE JOURNALS									
Article manuscript critique	$125	$25	$64	n/a	n/a	n/a	n/a	n/a	n/a
Arts query critique	$100	$50	$75	n/a	n/a	n/a	n/a	n/a	n/a
Arts reviewing	$95	$60	$79	$325	$100	$194	$1.20/word	8¢/word	58¢/word
Book reviews	n/a	n/a	n/a	$900	$25	$338	$1.50/word	15¢/word	68¢/word
City magazine calendar	n/a	n/a	n/a	$250	$50	$140	$1/word	30¢/word	70¢/word
Comic book/strip writing	$200 original story, $500 existing story, $35 short script.								
Consultation on magazine editorial	$150	$30	$81	n/a	n/a	n/a	n/a	n/a	$100/page
Consumer magazine column	n/a	n/a	n/a	$2,500	$75	$898	$2.50/word	37¢/word	$1.13/word
Consumer front-of-book	n/a	n/a	n/a	$850	$350	$600	n/a	n/a	n/a
Content editing	$125	$25	$57	$6,500	$2,000	$3,819	15¢/word	6¢/word	11¢/word
Contributing editor	n/a	n/a	n/a	n/a	n/a	n/a	$156,000/contract	$20,000/contract	$51,000/contract

	PER HOUR			PER PROJECT			OTHER		
	HIGH	LOW	AVG	HIGH	LOW	AVG	HIGH	LOW	AVG
Copyediting magazines	$100	$18	$50	n/a	n/a	n/a	$10/page	$2.90/page	$5.68/page
Fact checking	$125	$15	$46	n/a	n/a	n/a	n/a	n/a	n/a
Gag writing for cartoonists	$35/gag; 25% sale on spec.								
Ghostwriting articles (general)	$200	$30	$102	$3,500	$1,100	$2,229	$10/word	60¢/word	$2.25/word
Magazine research	$100	$15	$47	n/a	n/a	n/a	$500/item	$100/item	$200/item
Proofreading	$75	$15	$35	n/a	n/a	n/a	n/a	n/a	n/a
Reprint fees	n/a	n/a	n/a	$1,500	$20	$461	$1.50/word	10¢/word	73¢/word
Rewriting	$125	$20	$68	n/a	n/a	n/a	n/a	n/a	$50/page
Trade journal feature article	$122	$40	$80	$4,950	$150	$1,412	$3/word	20¢/word	$1.16/word
Transcribing interviews	$180	$90	$50	n/a	n/a	n/a	$3/min	$1/min	$2/min
MEDICAL/SCIENCE									
Medical/scientific conference coverage	$125	$50	$85	n/a	n/a	n/a	$800/day	$300/day	$600/day
Medical/scientific editing	$125	$21	$73	n/a	n/a	n/a	$12.50/page $600/day	$3/page $500/day	$4.40/page $550/day

	PER HOUR			PER PROJECT			OTHER		
	HIGH	LOW	AVG	HIGH	LOW	AVG	HIGH	LOW	AVG
Medical/scientific writing	$250	$30	$95	$5,000	$1,000	$3,354	$2/word	25¢/word	$1.12/word
Medical/scientific multimedia presentations	$100	$50	$75	n/a	n/a	n/a	$100/slide	$50/slide	$77/slide
Medical/scientific proofreading	$125	$18	$64	n/a	n/a	$500	$3/page	$2.50/page	$2.75/page
Pharmaceutical writing	$125	$90	$105	n/a	n/a	n/a	n/a	n/a	n/a
NEWSPAPERS									
Arts reviewing	$69	$30	$53	$200	$15	$101	60¢/word	6¢/word	36¢/word
Book reviews	$69	$45	$58	$350	$15	$140	60¢/word	25¢/word	44¢/word
Column, local	n/a	n/a	n/a	$600	$25	$206	$1/word	38¢/word	65¢/word
Column, self-syndicated	n/a	n/a	n/a	n/a	n/a	n/a	$35/insertion	$4/insertion	$16/insertion
Copyediting	$35	$15	$27	n/a	n/a	n/a	n/a	n/a	n/a
Editing/manuscript evaluation	$75	$25	$35	n/a	n/a	n/a	n/a	n/a	n/a
Feature writing	$79	$40	$63	$1,040	$85	$478	$1.60/word	10¢/word	59¢/word
Investigative reporting	n/a	n/a	n/a	n/a	n/a	n/a	$10,000/grant	$250/grant	$2,250/grant

	PER HOUR			PER PROJECT			OTHER		
	HIGH	LOW	AVG	HIGH	LOW	AVG	HIGH	LOW	AVG
Obituary copy	n/a	n/a	n/a	$225	$35	$124	n/a	n/a	n/a
Proofreading	$45	$15	$23	n/a	n/a	n/a	n/a	n/a	n/a
Stringing	n/a	n/a	n/a	$2,400	$40	$525	n/a	n/a	n/a
NONPROFIT									
Grant writing for nonprofits	$150	$19	$70	$3,000	$500	$1,852	n/a	n/a	n/a
Nonprofit annual reports	$100	$30	$64	n/a	n/a	n/a	n/a	n/a	n/a
Nonprofit writing	$150	$20	$77	$17,600	$200	$4,706	n/a	n/a	n/a
Nonprofit editing	$125	$25	$54	n/a	n/a	n/a	n/a	n/a	n/a
Nonprofit fundraising literature	$110	$35	$74	$3,500	$300	$1,597	$1,000/day	$500/day	$767/day
Nonprofit presentations	$100	$50	$73	n/a	n/a	n/a	n/a	n/a	n/a
Nonprofit public relations	$100	$20	$60	n/a	n/a	n/a	n/a	n/a	n/a
POLITICS/GOVERNMENT									
Government agency writing/editing	$100	$20	$57	n/a	n/a	n/a	$1.25/word	25¢/word	75¢/word

	PER HOUR			PER PROJECT			OTHER		
	HIGH	LOW	AVG	HIGH	LOW	AVG	HIGH	LOW	AVG
Government grant writing/ editing	$150	$19	$68	n/a	n/a	n/a	n/a	n/a	n/a
Government-sponsored research	$100	$35	$66	n/a	n/a	n/a	n/a	n/a	$600/day
Public relations for political campaigns	$150	$40	$86	n/a	n/a	n/a	n/a	n/a	n/a
Speechwriting for government officials	$200	$30	$96	$4,500	$1,000	$2,750	$200/run min	$110/run min	$155/run min
Speechwriting for political campaigns	$150	$60	$101	n/a	n/a	n/a	$200/run min	$100/run min	$162/run min

BUILD A PLATFORM:

Or You'll Miss the Train

....

by Jeff Yeager

"Jeff, you're a wonderful writer!"

Coming from the seasoned New York literary agent, I just wanted those words to hang there, in suspended celebration, while we enjoyed a leisurely lunch at the trendy Manhattan eatery she'd chosen for our meeting. Even though I'm not a dessert fan, I started thinking that maybe I'd stick around after all for some crème brûlée and an espresso or two.

"But the fact is," she continued, "there are lots of wonderful writers—and even lots of truly great writers—who never get a book published." Darn it, so much for basking in the moment. I hadn't even started my salad. Check please!

"The thing that interests me about you, and frankly the reason I agreed to meet with you today, is your platform. I know you're just starting out, but I think publishers will be impressed with the exposure you're already getting and what that means for your platform going forward." I thoughtfully crunched on a crouton from my salad, hoping to suggest that I was contemplating the wisdom of the agent's words. But I'm too honest to be a good bluffer.

"That's fantastic!" I said, enthusiastically spraying the woman I hoped would be my future agent in a shower of soggy crouton crumbs.

"Look," I continued, trying to divert my gaze from what appeared to be an entire crushed baguette clinging to the front of the poor agent's Ann Taylor dress suit. "I really hope you'll agree to represent me, and I want you to know that I always believe in being honest. So I have to confess: I have absolutely no idea what a *platform* is … although I'm delighted that you think I have such a good one."

WHAT THE HECK IS A PLATFORM?

With that awkward self-confessional a few short years ago, I began my journey—and more importantly my education—into the über competitive, promotion-driven world of book publishing.

Simply put, a platform is a writer's capacity to help promote and market his own work to potential readers. It's a writer's ability to attract a fan base of his own, outside of the promotional efforts of his publisher. It's a writer's ability to get his message out to the world.

Ideally, a platform has more than just one plank. For example, it's more than just a strong website or a weekly column in your local newspaper, although either of those planks would be a terrific start. It's a combination of assets, skills, expertise, activities, and professional connections that both strengthen each other and enhance the writer's chances for commercial success.

....

Ideally, a platform has more than just one plank.

....

In my case I was lucky enough to inadvertently receive some national television exposure early in my writing career (see 2008 *Writer's Market* Freelance Success Stories), which I then opportunistically parlayed into more press exposure and a growing network of media contacts. By the time I went looking for a literary agent to represent me in a book deal, I'd only had a few articles published and most of those were online. And while the media visibility I'd received prior to that point was not inconsequential, it wasn't nearly enough to carry a book.

But it was a start, and it proved to an agent—and then to a publisher—that I had the wherewithal to build a viable platform; that I was a horse worth betting on. That was two book deals ago, and my platform has since grown to include professional speaking and television reporting gigs, as well as blogging on a number of high traffic websites and authoring articles for a range of national publications.

At first blush my story might seem plucky to the point of being irrelevant to the careers of most writers. After all, how many newbie writers make their media debut on NBC's *Today* show, as I did? But what I've come to appreciate about platform building is this: Even with luck, you need persistence and promotional savvy, and—even without luck—persistence and promotional savvy is probably all you need.

It's also true what they say about making your own luck. Or, as quote-meister H. Jackson Brown, Jr. puts it, "Opportunity dances with those already on the dance floor." The key to building a successful promotional platform is to make sure you're always out there on the dance floor, shakin' what you got.

PRIORITIES AND GETTING STARTED

Given the laundry list of possible tactics for developing a platform (see sidebar), you need to set priorities in order to use your time and resources effectively, while at the same time remaining flexible enough to quickly act on unanticipated opportunities as they come your way. After all, you never know who's going to ask you to dance once you're out there on the floor.

Logically, the first step is to identify the target audience(s) for your writing. The more focused you can be in defining your audience, the more effective you'll be in reaching out to them. For example, if you're writing a book about dieting, you're obviously looking to reach people who would like to lose weight. But can you be even more specific? Maybe your niche is really middle-aged women hoping to lose weight, or parents who want to help their kids lose weight. Or say you write young adult fiction. Does it appeal more to boys or girls, teens or preteens, urban kids or rural kids, or particular YA book discussion groups, etc.?

Now that you know who your audience is, you need to figure out where and how you can best reach them. This is when the brainstorming really starts. What websites or online discussion boards do they frequent? What magazines and other print publications do they read? Are there certain TV or radio shows that appeal to them? Are there any special events they attend, or clubs or associations they join? In short, what are their favorite dance floors?

Identifying publications, media, and other forums through which you can reach your target audience is a never ending process, because they're constantly changing and you're always looking to expand your platform. When you've tapped into one forum, for example a website that caters to middle-aged women hoping to lose weight, always ask the people you meet there what other websites they visit, magazines they read, books they've enjoyed, and so on. I call this a *progressive focus group*, relying on everyone I meet in my target audience to educate me further about themselves and where I can find more folks just like them.

10 WAYS TO BUILD YOUR PLATFORM

1. Create your own website, keep it current with a blog and other updated content, and make it interactive with forums, contests, surveys, newsletters, a guestbook, etc.

2. Write articles, stories, op-eds, and even letters to the editor for magazines, newsletters, and other print publications read your target audience.

3. Contact other high-traffic websites frequented by your target audience, offer to guest blog or contribute content to them (even for free), link your site to theirs, and participate in their networking forums.

4. Position yourself as *the* go-to source for information regarding your area of expertise by joining related professional organizations, earning certifications, and registering

with online and print directories like LinkedIn.com and *Who's Who*, as well as social networking sites like Facebook and MySpace.

5. Send periodic press releases about yourself, your activities, or some timely aspect of your work/field to targeted print and broadcast media, and offer to sit for an interview—you might be surprised by the response.

6. Hold a publicity event—or dare I say a publicity stunt or gimmick? Challenge your church group to see how much weight they can lose by following the instructions in the diet book you're writing, or hype the mystery novel you're writing by hiding clues around town to the location of the buried treasure—the real treasure might be the media exposure you generate.

7. Give talks, teach classes, offer workshops about your specialty at libraries, schools, churches, and online—but make sure the press knows all about it.

8. Get involved as a volunteer or board member with nonprofit organizations related to your field of interest/expertise; it looks good on your resume and they can be valuable marketing partners for your work.

9. Partner with or co-author a book with a well established, widely recognized expert or celebrity, or try publishing your book through an established franchise like the *Dummies* or *Chicken Soup* serials, where your personal platform is less of a factor.

10. Post your own book trailers and other video content on YouTube, create your own podcasts, or publish your own ezine—even amateurish efforts can catch fire.

IT'S ALL ABOUT CONTENT

Once you've identified your target audience and started building a list of dance floors where they hang out, it's time to introduce yourself, to get to know them, and to make sure they get to know *you*. For most writers, this means providing content; content that helps to establish your reputation, builds name recognition (AKA "brand recognition"), and ideally creates for you a positive notoriety or even celebrity status among members of your target audience.

If you're a nonfiction writer, you typically provide content from the perspective of being an expert in the field (again, a weight loss expert, for example). If you write fiction, the content you provide is hopefully deemed desirable because of your creative and literary prowess. Who wouldn't want to read the words posted on some obscure website by a future J.K. Rowling?

Content, of course, can take many different forms. It's an article or story you get paid handsomely to write for a national magazine, as well as something you write without compensation for an association newsletter read by your target audience. It's the content of your own website and the guest blogs you write for another high-traffic website frequented by your target audience, and it's also every word you type in a chat room where your audience hangs out, even if it's just passing the time of day. It's the talk you give at the local library about what you do for a living. It's the interview you give on radio or national TV.

....

Remember, the most valuable words many authors have ever written are the words they most wish they could take back.

....

The content you provide is the basic building block of your platform, so make sure you have plenty of it and that it reflects the quality and style you want to be associated with. Remember, the most valuable words many authors have ever written are the words they most wish they could take back.

A VIRTUAL PLATFORM?

There's no denying that the Internet has had a profound impact on the enterprises of writing and publishing, and also on the ability of an author to develop a platform. Pre-Internet, writers had to rely on traditional print and broadcast media, as well as public appearances and other in-person networking, to gain visibility and establish credibility.

But is it possible to build a promotional platform entirely through online activities—a *virtual platform*, if you will? If you have your own winning website, soft-market yourself through online chat rooms, maybe blog or contribute content to other sites, will that do the trick?

Timothy Ferriss, author of the bestselling book *The 4 Hour Workweek*, attributes much of his success to viral marketing, particularly his efforts to befriend fellow bloggers who then hyped his book. But viral or old school, it all comes back to content. Ferriss said in an interview with Leo Babauta on writetodone.com, "Marketing can get you an initial wave of customers, but you need a good product to go viral … Focus on making yourself a credible expert vs. pushing a book."

Clearly a strong presence on the Internet can not only be a major plank in an author's platform, but it's also a logical place for many writers to begin building their platforms.

"The barriers (e.g. cost, skill, etc.) for gaining exposure through the Internet are very low," says Kristine Puopolo, Senior Editor with Doubleday Broadway Publishing. "The good news is that almost anyone can publish a blog or create his own website. The bad news is that almost *everyone does* publish a blog and create his own website," she says. Getting noticed on the information superhighway has become increasingly difficult as traffic congestion has increased. "The Internet is a terrific place to create buzz about a book or an author," Puopolo says. "But success is getting that buzz picked up by other media, like TV and print."

So if you were hoping to build your platform solely by sitting at a computer keyboard, Google "try again." Even Ferriss says that his relationships with fellow bloggers were not forged so much over the Internet or even by phone, but by speaking at events they attended and—talk about old school—joining them for some beers afterwards.

5 TOP-O-MIND TIPS

Keep these things in mind as you build your platform, or you'll kick yourself later:

BUILD RELATIONSHIPS, NOT JUST A ROLADEX FILE. Do you still see yourself in the writing business five years from now? Nurture the relationships you develop with press contacts, readers, and the other folks you encounter in the publishing industry, rather than just milking them for a one-off interview, etc. Keep in touch, do them favors, and treat them as friends so that they'll be glad to help you out again in the future.

NO PUBLICITY IS BAD PUBLICITY... or at least that's the way the saying goes. And it's true in a great many cases, particularly when you're just starting out and you're relatively unknown. But also remember that it can be hard to shake an unfavorable reputation once the publicity Gods have saddled you with one, so think twice before jumping at publicity for publicity's sake.

MAILING LISTS ARE GOLDEN. Capturing the names and contact information for everyone you meet—from readers and potential readers to press contacts and booksellers—is key to building your platform. Distribute sign-up lists at your events, collect business cards religiously, and start building a computerized database of your contacts from day one.

REMEMBER THE "SOFT" IN "SOFT-MARKETING." Particularly when it comes to promoting yourself online, in social networking forums, chat rooms, etc., tread lightly. First get to know the community and contribute content that's not self-promotional before you ever start talking about yourself and your writing. I've never encountered an online forum that doesn't have an eager Spam Master (or ten) to bounce you out if you come on too strong with self-promotion.

RECOGNIZE YOUR STRENGTHS AND WEAKNESSES. It's a truly rare and talented writer who has the skills, resources, and time to develop a robust platform without outside help. Consider hiring a publicist, getting professional "media training," taking a public speaking class, or securing other professional assistance to compliment your strengths and weaknesses.

COMMON MYTHS ABOUT PLATFORMS

THAT'S NOT MY JOB, MAN. Talk to anyone in the publishing business, and the answer is always the same: Gone are the days when authors were just expected to write books and publishers were expected to market them, if those golden days ever existed in the first place. Luke Dempsey knows how it works from both sides of the desk. He's the editor-in-chief of Hudson Street Press, a division of Penguin USA, and he's also author of *A Supremely Bad Idea*, published by Bloomsbury in 2008. "These days book promotion is, at best, a partnership between an author and a publisher. If an author has a strong platform, it's also more likely that the publisher will get excited about the project and put their backs into it as well."

ONLY NONFICTION AUTHORS NEED A PLATFORM. It's true that the publishing industry has historically expected most nonfiction authors to have a strong promotional platform of their own. After all, nonfiction writers are usually considered experts regarding their subject matter, and their expertise should be both in demand and validated by appearing in the media, serving as a source, and writing articles and other content related to their field. But as the book industry has become more competitive, fiction writers are now commonly expected to come to the table with a promotional platform as well.

"It used to be that fiction sold pretty much just as a result of good reviews," Puopolo says. "But with so many books on the market today and the increased competition for media attention, a fiction author with a compelling personal story, winning personality, or a degree of celebrity definitely has a leg up." Puopolo says that fiction writers can develop their platforms using some of the same techniques as nonfiction writers (e.g. blogs, personal appearances, etc.), and also with things like "virtually hosting" book discussion groups online or by phone, joining local and national literary organizations, and participating in other genre specific forums. Fiction or nonfiction, Puopolo says effective platforms grow out of the "authenticity" of the author. "Follow who and what you are. Don't try to be something that you aren't."

OKAY, I'VE BUILT MY PLATFORM. NOW I CAN GET BACK TO WRITING. As you probably appreciate by now, your platform is not a static set of achievements, but an evolving portfolio of capacities which will hopefully grow and expand along with your writing career. Everything you write, every media appearance you make, every book talk you give, opens a new avenue for extending and strengthening your platform. You need to start building your platform as soon as you start writing—not when you go shopping for a book deal—and the process continues as long as you continue writing. When it comes to your platform as a writer, it's true what they say: "If you're not growing, you're dying."

CREATING EFFECTIVE PRESS RELEASES

by Lisa Abeyta

I often hear from other writers who take one of my workshops or online classes that they do not know how to market their own work. Writing the entire novel was an easier task than approaching stores, newspapers, or online venues about carrying their book. But whether a writer landed a coveted spot with a major publisher, chose to go with a small local press or ventured into the world of print on demand and vanity presses, it often falls on the shoulders of the author to market their own book. A few fortunate authors will gain access to a publicist through their publisher, but many will be completely on their own.

Writing a press release does not have to be a daunting task. In fact, for anyone who has already written a query letter, you are well on your way to mastering a press release. The goal is the same: catch the reader's attention right away, build interest in your project, and motivate the reader to act on your request.

BASIC PRESS RELEASE FORMAT

Beyond the basics of not using all caps (nobody wants to be shouted at, even if you excited) and checking your grammar, start your press release with the following headline: For Immediate Release. The next line should be in bold and should contain the headline of your press release. Follow this with a very brief paragraph summarizing the content below and then with the body of the press release. Finish with a short About the Author paragraph and end with your contact information, including your address, phone number, email and website.

QUALITY CONTENT IS A MUST

One of the best ways to get your press release past the intern who screens the incessant influx of information is to write your release as a completed article. If your text is compelling, interesting, and complete, you have a much better shot of finding that same text in the Sunday Arts section of the paper. Editors are busy people, and the gift if print-ready text is hard to pass up.

Years ago, when I was working as an artist's representative, I sent press packages to media outlets ahead of each performance in a new city. Editors would often print the press release verbatim, although some would call the artist and conduct an interview. But the press release did its job either way by gaining invaluable publicity before a performance.

Study articles about authors and books. Learn the voice and tone of those articles. Mimic it in your own writing, and you'll be far more likely to generate interest in your project.

WHERE TO SEND YOUR RELEASE

A press release can be a stand alone product or as part of a press package. A package should contain a headshot of yourself and art from your book, both printed and on cd in low and high resolution where possible. The more options you provide, the more likely art will accompany any story published from your press release. It should also include a press copy of the book when possible. You can also attach a sheet with upcoming appearances, other titles, and any other pertinent information.

Press releases can be emailed directly to the appropriate editors or reviewers or uploaded to a variety of online PR distribution sites. And while these sites are great for getting the word out on the web, it is still recommended that you take the time to directly contact the editors who will possibly run your story in print or online. And remember to follow up your press releases with a personal phone call. Nothing will set you apart from the pile of press releases like a friendly follow-up call.

There has been a proliferation of online distribution sites focusing on public relations. Someof these include www/PRWeb.com, www.PRLeap.com, and www.24-7pressrelease.com, and www.epressreleases.com. While many of these sites offer free basic online distribution, there are additional fee-based products for you to consider.

MORE THAN A MEANS TO AN END

Another common misconception, particularly among new authors, is that platform building is simply a step—perhaps even a necessary evil—in getting your book published.

But here's a bright point to end on: From a business perspective, a robust platform *is* an author's business. In manufacturing terms, it's the sum total of *product lines* that a writer has with which to earn a living. And the payout is that in many cases the non-writing product lines that make up an author's platform may grow to be even more lucrative than writing.

Stacey Glick, a literary agent with the prestigious firm Dystel and Goderich in New York, says it best. "The thing you need to understand is that most authors can no longer afford to be one dimensional; that is, just authors," she told me. "An author's appeal to a publisher is largely his platform, and his platform in turn benefits from the books he writes. Round and round you go."

And I always value Stacey Glick's advice. After all, she's not only my agent, but she didn't even send me the dry cleaning bill for her Ann Taylor dress suit.

JEFF YEAGER is the author of *The Ultimate Cheapskate's Road Map to True Riches: A Practical (and Fun) Guide to Enjoying Life More by Spending Less* and *The Cheapskate Next Door: The Surprising Secrets of Americans Living Happily Below Their Means* (both by Broadway). Yeager has appeared as a guest on CNN, ABC News, CNBC, FOX News, PBS, and dozens of local TV stations around the country. www.ultimatecheapskate.com

ON THE ROAD... AGAIN?:

10 Do's & Don'ts for Your Book Tour

....

by Susan Wingate

Willie Nelson's fabulous hit fills many hearts with affability and jubilation as the tune plunks out a paced lilt and the lyrics tell a tale of anticipation for getting back out on the open road.

For the author, however, the book tour means upending our daily schedule in order to sit in a bookstore somewhere in the wild lands of Idaho (because the publicist thought it a good idea) and to wait for someone, anyone to come over simply to chat with you.

One might understand how Nelson would love being on tour. A large part of the musician's life is enjoyed performing in front of audiences. But, for the writer, our enjoyment most often lies with the life we spend close to a friend, our keyboard, as we bang out sentences into our next story, whether that story is fiction or nonfiction.

As a midlist author, I write this article after having recently finished a five-month stint on a traveling book tour for my novel, *Easy as Pie at Bobby's Diner*. The good and not-so-good hang clearly in focus about the tour and I thought other authors who might be considering a book tour might benefit from my experiences.

Thus, I've written ten do's and don'ts to help the adventurous author in you before embarking on what could prove a make-it or break-it venture. With number ten being, possibly, the most important point of all... but, don't jump down to read it now. It will do you no good if you simply skip the previous nine points.

1) **DO** make sure your publicist, publisher and bookstore know when you'll be arriving and whether you have, or not, any books.

2) **DON'T** forget to pack extra books in case the books your publisher means to send, don't arrive. In fact, they just may well forget, entirely, to place *that* order.

3) **DO** make sure that the bookings the publicist has marked "confirmed" on your *confirmed event list* really are confirmed.

4) **DON'T** forget to pack your favorite non-steroidal anti-inflammatory (please check the contents) for the pain that will continue to build behind your left eye and that will end up coursing into your temple, down your neck and that will ultimately settle in your shoulders.

5) **DO** book your flight, hotel, and car when you confirm with your publicist about all dates, times and locations of each city's schedule. (I know. At this point the *confirmed event list* seems rather sketchy, doesn't it? But, you'll plod on, as I did, just to talk to all of those two or three people who will show up at each event.)

6) **DON'T** stand there screaming at the top of your lungs with the *confirmed event list* gripped tightly in your hand, the one you printed out just before leaving your hotel this morning, when the bookstore—the very bookstore you're standing in right now—says they never confirmed any event with any publicist, certainly not yours, and therefore they will NOT be holding an event today.

7) **DO** begin building an itemized list of reasons for your lawyer as to why you want to sue your publisher.

8) **DON'T** speak to anyone at the publisher's office. You will either begin stuttering unintelligibly, or, you'll end up saying things like, "Why, when I get my hands on you, you, you dastardly, flabber-gaster, I'll, I'll..." and *then* you'll begin to stutter unintelligibly.

9) **DO** pack lots of Kleenex or your choice of favorite facial tissue for all of the nights you'll spend weeping uncontrollably and somewhat insanely as you ask yourself, "Why? Why? What was I thinking when I agreed to go on this book tour?!"

10) **DO NOT *EVER*** take a vial of something that looks like Anacin but really is just pretending to be Anacin, and, as it turns out, the contents of this vial are truly some sort of dinosaur tranquilizer your husband had been prescribed for his total knee replacement and, even at this point, do NOT take two. Ever. In the car while you're en route to your next appearance. You'll be out for at least an entire day plus, you could end up spending that day unconscious in some Wendy's parking lot and not comfortably in bed at home...remember home? That place you decided to leave because someone (the publisher) told you a book tour was a good idea?

Naiveté can be a beautiful thing however it is completely ill-advised if you're considering a book tour. And, after reading this, if you still wish to set off on a book tour, be advised to read such books as Lissa Warren's *The Savvy Author's Guide to Book Publicity* or any of the many wonderful how-to guides out there on book promotion and publicity.

Of course, a traveling road show is only one of the two ways to create a buzz for your book. With the advent of the internet, the prospects not only open up but they become much more practical for authors with limited budgets or just a burning desire not to leave your warm happy home. We now have a thing called, virtual book tours.

In my career, I have used both book tour methods—live and virtual. After enduring my latest tour, I have resolved to use the virtual method as much as humanly possible.

> I've used two fabulous Internet book publicists ... The fees for both companies have proven money well-spent and far out-weigh the costs incurred from a live book tour.

I've used two fabulous Internet book publicists, Dorothy Thompson (PumpUpYourBooks. com) and Nikki Leigh (Promo 101 Promotional Services). The fees for both companies have proven money well-spent and far outweigh the costs incurred from a live book tour.

Again, remember, I'm a midlist author. I'm sure James Patterson has tomes of entirely different stories about his book touring experiences. What, with hordes of fans clambering to get at him, forcing their millions of his freshly purchased books into his face for a mere smile, a mere scribble of his autograph. I can only imagine what life on Mr. Patterson's tour might look like, might feel like.

You can be sure, he never accidentally ingested an dinosaur tranquilizer. I'm sure his staff, nurses and all would prevent him from doing that. But, who knows?

SUSAN WINGATE is the author of *Bobby's Diner* (False Bay Books) and *Easy as Pie at Bobby's Diner* (Blue Star Books). Wingate also wrote *A Falling of Law* as JJ Abrams. She writes a monthly column about writing for her local newspaper and is co-host of the talk show Dialogue: Between the Lines. www.susanwingate.com

PHOTO: DiCristina Photography

BOOK TRAILERS:

Reach Your Audience

....

by Darcy Pattison

In 2012, the concept of using video to promote a book will be 10 years old. The term "book trailer" was trademarked in 2002 by Sheila Clover-English for COS Productions. Since then, the form has evolved and become a common element in the mix of marketing and promotion materials. But that doesn't mean book trailers are without controversy.

CONS: IT GOES AGAINST THE GRAIN

One of the biggest objections to book trailers is that it steals the role of imagination from reader by instilling the sound of the character's voice, and a detailed and memorable visual image of the characters. Another objection is that written word should have written-word-promotions. It seems like an oxymoron to promote a novel with a video. While these are valid objections, more and more, authors and publishers are accepting that book trailers are just one more way to reach their audience.

PROS: REACH YOUR AUDIENCE

YOUR AUDIENCE WATCHES VIDEO. Readers are also, by-and-large, consumers of video. Here are the stats: (http://www.reelseo.com/optimize-market-videos-youtube-presentation/).

For example, in April, 2010 in the US, there were more than 30 billion videos watched, approximately 13 billion of those on YouTube.com. About 80 percent of embedded and linked videos on blogs come from YouTube.com.

VIDEOS ARE EFFECTIVE IN GETTING READERS INTERESTED IN A BOOK. Alan Gratz, author of several teen novels (*Samurai Shortstop, Something Rotten, Something Wicked, The Brooklyn Nine,* and *Fantasy Baseball*), said, "I asked a room full of librarians at the 2010 North Carolina School Library Media Association conference if book trailers matter, and was stunned to have the entire room yell, 'Yes! WE love book trailers!'"

Naomi Bates, librarian at Northwest High School Library in Justin, TX, recently surveyed 100 librarians about their usage of book trailers in their school libraries. (http://prezi.com/4knxruygzvuv/book-trailer-survey/) The results were astounding: 99% of librarians thought book trailers were very effective or somewhat effective in presenting a book to students.

It's clear that children and teens are affected by book trailers. Are adults? The answer is a qualified yes. Certainly adults are watching video, just look at the success of YouTube.com. But how many are watching book trailers?

The #1 Hardcover Fiction NY Times Best Seller for the week of January 30, 2011 was *The Inner Circle*, by Brad Meltzer. He was well represented on YouTube.com: a search on returned about 17 videos about Meltzer and his various books. For *The Inner Circle*, there was an official book trailer, video from an author signing, reactions from readers, the author at a book festival and more. The videos were viewed between 650 and 5089 times. It's a small number of views per video, but he does have a video presence; it's a part of his marketing mix.

VIDOES ARE EASY TO DISTRIBUTE. With the advent of YouTube.com and other video sharing sites (GodTube.com, SchoolTube.com, Vimeo, DailyMotion, etc.) it's easy to upload a video and provide links to it. It's true that most viewers will come in the first three weeks of posting (http://www.businessinsider.com/chart-of-the-day-the-lifecycle-of-a-youtube-video-2010-5), but there's also a long tail of viewers, so the trailers promote your book for a long time. In addition, librarians are setting up videos on a loop on digital picture frames or monitors. It creates an increased demand for books promoted with such video displays; often these books have a waiting list for check-out.

DON'T YOU NEED LOTS OF MONEY TO MAKE A BOOK TRAILER?

No. In some ways, the term "book trailer" is unfortunate because it make the inevitable comparison to movie trailers. What's different is that book trailers can fit into one of three aesthetics: movie trailers, PowerPoints or the YouTube Aesthetic. Each aesthetic comes with a different price tag.

1. **MOVIE TRAILER AESTHETIC.** Book trailers that imitate movie trailers have been the Holy Grail. These slick productions are usually created by the publisher and a few authors with big budgets. They are indeed lovely to look at, and if done well, the script pulls in readers. For this aesthetic, big budgets tend to get better results.

   AESTHETICS: *Slick, professional production on all fronts.*

2. **SLIDESHOW AESTHETICS.** On the opposite end of the budget scale is the slideshow book trailer. These are usually author-created and feature a combination of static text and static images. These are likely to created by authors for many years, be-

cause they don't require a big layout of funds. Another reason for their popularity is that this aesthetic is acceptable in schools and in business.

AESTHETICS: *Create the right mood with music, text and images.*

3. **YOUTUBE AESTHETICS.** For book trailers–like any other video–that are mainly used online, there's a more informal aesthetic, one designed for the smaller screens. You-Tube.com thrives on humor, immediacy, and authenticity. Creativity matters more here than pristine audio or video–or budgets. Short videos that allow for easy sharing, remixing, and as the basis for a spoof or parody are perfect for this irreverent media aesthetic.

AESTHETICS: *Creativity and authenticity.*

BOOK TRAILERS TELL STORIES: AND YOU KNOW HOW TO DO THAT!

Regardless of the aesthetic you go for, when you create a book trailer, use your storytelling skills in one of these type stories.

(Playlist: The videos mentioned below are collected on a playlist:http://www.youtube.com/user/BookTrailerManual#grid/user/110AAA374E3E5759.

Or use the video id number to search for each video on YouTube.com.)

1. **STORIES ABOUT THE AUTHOR.** Tell a small, personal story about yourself. Tell something contrary, counterintuitive, or challenge an assumption. Tell about a time you failed, a time you succeeded, explain why you love a certain book or movie. "Such a Pretty Fat" (ID#: K8jnXfVPGfA): Jen Lancaster tells the story of trying to lose weight with humor and honesty.

2. **VALUE IN ACTION STORY.** Tell a story about honesty in action, caring in action, environmentalism in action, youth advocacy in action, etc. Think about what values your book shows about you, then express it in your trailer. "Susane Colasanti talks about SOMETHING LIKE FATE" (ID#: 4AlNtlBzueY): Colasanti talks about her belief in fate and how that value plays out through her story.

3. **GLITZ AND GLAM STORY.** For this type story, link to a celebrity or something popular; or, appeal to something romantic. "Palmer talks about Little Miss Red" (ID#: E9Nr99FsrcI): In homage to the genre of retold fairy tales, Robin Palmer rides in a horse drawn carriage through Central Park as she talks about her book. It's a bit of glam to make the trailer memorable.

4. **WHO AM I? STORY.** People like to hear about your aspirations and beliefs, why you wrote this book, who are you as a writer (honest, thoughtful, insightful, diplomatic, etc.). Try telling a story about a time when you or your work made a difference; or tell a story about someone who taught you how to write, a mentor story. "Hidden Wives Claire Avery Book Trailer" (ID#: wXDvS4cFDXI): This book is about

discovering the sub-culture of polygamy. Avery, along with her sister, discuss their escape from a extreme religious community and emphasis how they triumphed over adversity.

5. **WHY AM I HERE? STORIES.** The idea here is to give the inside story before its widely known, relate a story about the current/upcoming season or event, tell a David v. Goliath (against all odds, I'm here), or tell about a twist in the road to this place in your life. "If I Stay by Gayle Forman" (ID#: 3S3dsvIhAgk): Music is a huge part of author Gayle Forman's book, *If I Stay*. She talks about how the music scene of Eugene, OR, helped shape her poignant novel on the power of love, loss and family.

6. **TEACHING STORY—GIVE ADVICE.** Some stories are meant to teach, explain or deepen understanding about something. Pragmatic, hands-on information always plays well. "Rosalind Wiseman author video for *Boys, Girls and Other Hazardous Materials*" (ID#: QEPaqYyxfzE): In this book—and book trailer—Wiseman gives advice about relationships, wrapped up in a great story of how her students gave her advice.

7. **VISION STORY—HOPE, BELONGING, HAPPINESS, OPTIMISM.** Sometimes the story is about hope, or a vision of a better future. These inspirational stories are often the most popular told. "Peter Hitchens Author Interview—The Rage Against God" (ID#: io1sNfw9-TA): Hitchens explains his journalistic roots, but also is an optimistic explanation of how his life was changed by faith.

8. **I KNOW WHAT YOU ARE THINKING STORY.** These stories try to overcome unspoken objection. "Book Trailer for *Rankin Inlet: A Novel*" (ID#: 8rh-5BP9UF4): Why would a white woman write about the Inuit? In a pro-active stance, Mara Feeney heads off the objection of how a writer can authentically write about a different culture.

As book trailers turn ten years old, they are finding more acceptance in our digital culture. They are here to stay. It's time to study them and learn how to create a compelling one to promote your next book.

Writer and writing teacher **DARCY PATTISON** is the author of *The Book Trailer Manual* (www.booktrailermanual.com) and has been watching and critiquing book related video for several years. As a writing teacher, Darcy is in demand nationwide to teach her Novel Revision Retreat which is based on the workbook, *Novel Metamorphosis: Uncommon Ways to Revise* (Mims House). Learn more about Darcy and her writing at www.darcypattison.com.

THE ART OF PROMOTING:

Advice From the Trenches

....

by Kerrie Flanagan

Author book promotion is not what it used to be. Both traditional and newer online strategies are needed to create an effective marketing plan because publishers now expect authors to carry the majority of the PR responsibilities. Marketing can feel overwhelming for an author but the good news is there are those who have found success in navigating this vast territory.

PLAN AN EVENT

To ensure a good turnout at a book signing or book launch, put in a little extra time to make it an event people will remember. Acclaimed YA author Laura Resau has perfected this idea over the years with the release of each of her books.

"Be creative and think outside the box," says Resau. "Include all ages if possible. Create a fun, lively, warm atmosphere. Make it a party that YOU would attend."

For the launch party of her fourth book, *The Indigo Notebook*, set in Ecuador, her Ecuadorian friend danced and explained the folklore behind the dance. With her latest book, *The Ruby Notebook*, set in France, she hired an accordionist who played while the young kids danced and the crowd enjoyed French pastries. She sets aside time to read excerpts and autograph books.

To promote the event, she uses listservs, her blog, Facebook, an e-newsletter, plus she enlists the help of her friends and writing group members to spread the word. She also sends postcard invitations with the book cover image on front.

"I think people are more likely to come to the release if they have the postcard hanging on their fridge staring at them every day for weeks before the event," she says.

An event can also happen online. For three years in a row, Christina Katz, author of *Get Known Before the Book Deal* and *Writer Mama*, hosted The Writer Mama Back-to-School Giveaway where she gave away a book on her blog every day for 30 days.

"One thing authors need to understand about marketing books today is that if you are not having an ongoing conversation with your fans, you are really missing out on a wealth of opportunities."

"I connected fellow authors with readers and in the process got to know my readers a lot better," said Katz. "One thing authors need to understand about marketing books today is that if you are not having an ongoing conversation with your fans, you are really missing out on the wealth of opportunities."

SPEAK UP

LeAnn Thieman, co-author of 11 Chicken Soup for the Soul books including the *New York Times* best-seller, *Chicken Soup for the Nurses Soul*, finds radio is an effective promotional outlet.

When I am going to be in an area for a speaking event or even just visiting, I call the local stations to see if they are interested in interviewing me on my topic, one I creatively relate to what's happening in the world today.

"There are over 10,000 radio stations in the United States, many with hosts looking for people to interview every day," said Thieman. "When I am going to be in an area for a speaking event or even just visiting, I call the local stations to see if they are interested in interviewing me on my topic, one I creatively relate to what's happening in the world today."

She advises authors to send a copy of their book and a synopsis to the station before the interview. Provide them with questions they can ask and have three to four talking points of your own ready. Weave your own sound bites and messages into the interview, but never overtly promote your book.

Greg Campbell, the best-selling nonfiction author of *Blood Diamonds: Tracing The Deadly Path Of The World's Most Precious Stones*, found promoting himself as an expert speaker to universities, nonprofits and trade shows to be an effective way to promote his books.

"When Scott Selby and I published *Flawless: Inside the Largest Diamond Heist in History*," Campbell said, "we searched for major trade shows on security and offered to speak to attendees about the real-life security failures described in the book. We ended up as keynote speakers at the International Security Conference in Las Vegas, with about 500 people in the audience."

With the help of their publisher, Selby and Campbell arranged to have the local Barnes & Noble set up a table to sell books at the event.

GET SOCIAL

Most authors would agree that staying connected with readers via social media is crucial in any successful publicity plan.

Campbell recently had social media thrust upon him by a pair of fans disappointed in his anemic online presence. They set up a Facebook author fan page as well as an author page on Goodreads.com for him. It pushed him to embrace social media.

"The fact that it took my readers to force me into this realm proved that there were readers out there hungry for information and new content," he said. "Even if it's just 140-character tweets. My education into this realm is continuing, but I plan to begin tweeting and blogging about the content of my newest book several months before it hits the shelves. In this way, I hope to have primed the pump and created online buzz for it long before it's available."

....

The more accessible you are the more readers get a chance to listen to what you have to share.

....

Jane Porter, author of six novels, including her latest, *She's Gone Country*, makes a point to stay connected with her readers.

"Sites like Facebook and Twitter have proved invaluable in providing a different platform to meet with my readers and spread the word," said Porter. "The more accessible you are the more readers get a chance to listen to what you have to share."

Romance author Ashley March finds blog tours highly successful. "I researched blogs and online romance community sites which had good followings and scheduled around 20 days where I visited each website with either an interview or guest blog. I always included a giveaway as a way to create more enthusiasm."

She attributes the buzz and success of her debut novel, *Seducing the Duchess*, with this blog tour.

PARTNER WITH YOUR PUBLISHER

Although publishers do expect authors to take on the role of publicist, it doesn't mean they are not willing to help at all. With her debut novel March took the lead and found her publisher eager to support her efforts.

They sent her book to every major romance reviewer online, provided her with her books to use as giveaways and when she couldn't reach someone at a blog she really wanted to visit, the publisher coordinated that specific blog visit for her. Because of the publisher's support, her March Madness blog party was a success.

"Throughout my debut experience," says March, "I truly felt like we were partners, and that's a great feeling to have."

Katz sums it up best. "Consistent and constant self-promotion are key to publishing success, regardless of whether you self-publish or traditionally publish...It's not any one self-promotion technique an author uses, it's using all of them."

KERRIE FLANAGAN is a freelance writer and the director of Northern Colorado Writers, an organization that supports and encourages writers of all levels and genres. Over the past decade she has published more than 125 articles in national and regional publications, enjoyed two years as contributing editor for Journey magazine, worked in PR for the Fort Collins CVB and for various authors and started The Writing Bug blog. www.KerrieFlanagan.com

PHOTO: Desiree Suchy

BLOGGING BASICS:

Get the Most Out of Your Blog

....

by Robert Lee Brewer

In these days of publishing and media change, writers have to build platforms and learn how to connect to audiences if they want to improve their chances of publication and over-all success. There are many methods of audience connection available to writers, but one of the most important is through blogging.

Since I've spent several years successfully blogging—both personally and profession-ally—I figure I've got a few nuggets of wisdom to pass on to writers who are curious about blogging or who already are.

Here's my quick list of tips:

1. **START BLOGGING TODAY.** If you don't have a blog, use Blogger, WordPress, or some other blogging software to start your blog today. It's free, and you can start off with your very personal "Here I am, world" post.

2. **START SMALL.** Blogs are essentially very simple, but they can get very complicated (for people who like complications). However, I advise bloggers start small and evolve over time.

3. **USE YOUR NAME IN YOUR URL.** This will make it easier for search engines to find you when your audience eventually starts seeking you out by name. For instance, my url is http://robertleebrewer.blogspot.com. If you try Googling "Robert Lee Brewer," you'll notice that My Name Is Not Bob is one of the top 5 search results (behind my other blog: Poetic Asides).

4. **UNLESS YOU HAVE A REASON, USE YOUR NAME AS THE TITLE OF YOUR BLOG.** Again, this helps with search engine results. My Poetic Asides blog includes my name in the title, and it ranks higher than My Name Is Not Bob. However, I felt the play on my name was worth the trade off.

5. **FIGURE OUT YOUR BLOGGING GOALS.** You should return to this step every couple months, because it's natural for your blogging goals to evolve over time. Initially, your blogging goals may be to make a post a week about what you have written, submitted, etc. Over time, you may incorporate guests posts, contests, tips, etc.

6. **BE YOURSELF.** I'm a big supporter of the idea that your image should match your identity. It gets too confusing trying to maintain a million personas. Know who you are and be that on your blog, whether that means you're sincere, funny, sarcastic, etc.

7. **POST AT LEAST ONCE A WEEK.** This is for starters. Eventually, you may find it better to post once a day or multiple times per day. But remember: Start small and evolve over time.

8. **POST RELEVANT CONTENT.** This means that you post things that your readers might actually care to know.

9. **USEFUL AND HELPFUL POSTS WILL ATTRACT MORE VISITORS.** Talking about yourself is all fine and great. I do it myself. But if you share truly helpful advice, your readers will share it with others, and visitors will find you on search engines.

10. **TITLE YOUR POSTS IN A WAY THAT GETS YOU FOUND IN SEARCH ENGINES.** The more specific you can get the better. For instance, the title "Blogging Tips" will most likely get lost in search results. However, the title "Blogging Tips for Writers" specifies which audience I'm targeting and increases the chances of being found on the first page of search results.

11. **LINK TO POSTS IN OTHER MEDIA.** If you have an e-mail newsletter, link to your blog posts in your newsletter. If you have social media accounts, link to your blog posts there. If you have a helpful post, link to it in relevant forums and on message boards.

....

Don't spend a week writing each post. Try to keep it to an hour or two tops and then post.

....

12. **WRITE WELL, BUT BE CONCISE.** At the end of the day, you're writing blog posts, not literary manifestos. Don't spend a week writing each post. Try to keep it to an hour or two tops and then post. Make sure your spelling and grammar are good, but don't stress yourself out too much.

13. **FIND LIKE-MINDED BLOGGERS.** Comment on their blogs regularly and link to them from yours. Eventually, they may do the same. Keep in mind that blogging is a form of social media, so the more you communicate with your peers the more you'll get out of the process.

14. **RESPOND TO COMMENTS ON YOUR BLOG.** Even if it's just a simple "Thanks," respond to your readers if they comment on your blog. After all, you want your readers to be engaged with your blog, and you want them to know that you care they took time to comment.

15. **EXPERIMENT.** Start small, but don't get complacent. Every so often, try something new. For instance, the biggest draw to my Poetic Asides blog are the poetry prompts and challenges I issue to poets. Initially, that was an experiment—one that worked very well. I've tried other experiments that haven't panned out, and that's fine. It's all part of a process.

SEO TIPS FOR WRITERS

Most writers may already know what SEO is. If not, SEO stands for *search engine optimization*. Basically, a site or blog that practices good SEO habits should improve its rankings in search engines, such as Google and Bing. Most huge corporations have realized the importance of SEO and spend enormous sums of time, energy and money on perfecting their SEO practices. However, writers can improve their SEO without going to those same extremes.

In this section, I will use the terms of *site pages* and *blog posts* interchangeably. In both cases, you should be practicing the same SEO strategies (when it makes sense).

Here are my top tips on ways to improve your SEO starting today:

1. **USE APPROPRIATE KEYWORDS.** Make sure that your page displays your main keyword(s) in the page title, content, URL, title tags, page header, image names and tags (if you're including images). All of this is easy to do, but if you feel overwhelmed, just remember to use your keyword(s) in your page title and content (especially in the first and last 50 words of your page).

2. **USE KEYWORDS NATURALLY.** Don't kill your content and make yourself look like a spammer to search engines by overloading your page with your keyword(s). You don't get SEO points for quantity but for quality. Plus, one of the main ways to improve your page rankings is when you...

3. **DELIVER QUALITY CONTENT.** The best way to improve your SEO is by providing content that readers want to share with others by linking to your pages. Some of the top results in search engines can be years old, because the content is so good that people keep coming back. So, incorporate your keywords in a smart way, but make sure it works organically with your content.

4. **UPDATE CONTENT REGULARLY.** If your site looks dead to visitors, then it'll appear that way to search engines too. So update your content regularly. This should be very easy for writers who have blogs. For writers who have sites, incorporate your blog into your site. This will make it easier for visitors to your blog to discover more about you on your site (through your site navigation tools).

5. **LINK BACK TO YOUR OWN CONTENT.** If I have a post on Blogging Tips for Writers, for instance, I'll link back to it if I have a Platform Building post, because the two complement each other. This also helps clicks on my blog, which helps SEO. The one caveat is that you don't go crazy with your linking and that you make sure your links are relevant. Otherwise, you'll kill your traffic, which is not good for your page rankings.

6. **LINK TO OTHERS YOU CONSIDER HELPFUL.** Back in 2000, I remember being ordered by my boss at the time (who didn't last too much longer afterward) to ignore any competitive or complementary websites—no matter how helpful their content—because they were our competitors. You can try basing your online strategy on these principles, but I'm nearly 100 percent confident you'll fail. It's helpful for other sites and your own to link to other great resources. I shine a light on others to help them out (if I find their content truly helpful) in the hopes that they'll do the same if ever they find my content truly helpful for their audience.

7. **GET SPECIFIC WITH YOUR HEADLINES.** If you interview someone on your blog, don't title your post with an interesting quotation. While that strategy may help get readers in the print world, it doesn't help with SEO at all. Instead, title your post as "Interview With (insert name here)." If you have a way to identify the person further, include that in the title too. For instance, when I interview poets on my Poetic Asides blog, I'll title those posts like this: Interview With Poet Erika Meitner. Erika's name is a keyword, but so are the terms *poet* and *interview*.

> If you interview someone on your blog, don't title your post with an interesting quotation. While that strategy may help get readers in the print world, it doesn't help with SEO at all.

8. **USE IMAGES.** Many expert sources state that the use of images can improve SEO, because it shows search engines that the person creating the page is spending a little extra time and effort on the page than a common spammer. However, I'd caution anyone using images to make sure those images are somehow complementary to the content. Don't just throw up a lot of images that have no relevance to anything. At the same time...

9. **OPTIMIZE IMAGES THROUGH STRATEGIC LABELING.** Writers can do this by making sure the image file is labeled using your keyword(s) for the post. Using the Erika Meitner example above (which does include images), I would label the file "Erika Meitner headshot.jpg"—or whatever the image file type happens to be. Writers can

also improve image SEO through the use of captions and ALT tagging. Of course, at the same time, writers should always ask themselves if it's worth going through all that trouble for each image or not. Each writer has to answer that question for him (or her) self.

10. **USE YOUR SOCIAL MEDIA PLATFORM TO SPREAD THE WORD.** Whenever you do something new on your site or blog, you should share that information on your other social media sites, such as Twitter, Facebook, LinkedIn, online forums, etc. This lets your social media connections know that something new is on your site/blog. If it's relevant and/or valuable, they'll let others know. And that's a great way to build your SEO.

Programmers and marketers could get even more involved in the dynamics of SEO optimization, but I think these tips will help most writers out immediately and effectively while still allowing plenty of time and energy for the actual work of writing.

BLOG DESIGN TIPS FOR WRITERS

Design is an important element to any blog's success. But how can you improve your blog's design if you're not a designer? I'm just an editor with an English Lit degree and no formal training in design. However, I've worked in media for more than a decade now and can share some very fundamental and easy tricks to improve the design of your blog.

Here are my seven blog design tips for writers:

1. **USE LISTS.** Whether they're numbered or bullet points, use lists when possible. Lists break up the text and make it easy for readers to follow what you're blogging.

2. **BOLD MAIN POINTS IN LISTS.** Again, this helps break up the text while also highlighting the important points of your post.

3. **USE HEADINGS.** If your posts are longer than 300 words and you don't use lists, then please break up the text by using basic headings.

4. **USE A READABLE FONT.** Avoid using fonts that are too large or too small. Avoid using cursive or weird fonts. Times New Roman or Arial works, but if you want to get "creative," use something similar to those.

5. **LEFT ALIGN.** English-speaking readers are trained to read left to right. If you want to make your blog easier to read, avoid centering or right aligning your text (unless you're purposefully calling out the text).

6. **USE SMALL PARAGRAPHS.** A good rule of thumb is to try and avoid paragraphs that drone on longer than five sentences. I usually try to keep paragraphs to around three sentences myself.

7. **ADD RELEVANT IMAGES.** Personally, I shy away from using too many images. My reason is that I only like to use them if they're relevant. However, images are very

powerful on blogs, so please use them—just make sure they're relevant to your blog post.

If you're already doing everything on my list, keep it up! If you're not, then you might want to re-think your design strategy on your blog. Simply adding a header here and a list there can easily improve the design of a blog post.

GUEST POSTING TIPS FOR WRITERS

Recently, I've broken into guest posting as both a guest poster and as a host of guest posts (over at my Poetic Asides blog). So far, I'm pretty pleased with both sides of the guest posting process. As a writer, it gives me access to an engaged audience I may not usually reach. As a blogger, it provides me with fresh and valuable content I don't have to create. Guest blogging is a rare win-win scenario.

That said, writers could benefit from a few tips on the process of guest posting:

1. **PITCH GUEST POSTS LIKE ONE WOULD PITCH ARTICLES TO A MAGAZINE.** Include what your hook is for the post, what you plan to cover, and a little about who you are. Remember: Your post should somehow benefit the audience of the blog you'd like to guest post.

2. **OFFER PROMOTIONAL COPY OF BOOK (OR OTHER GIVEAWAYS) AS PART OF YOUR GUEST POST.** Having a random giveaway for people who comment on a blog post can help spur conversation and interest in your guest post, which is a great way to get the most mileage out of your guest appearance.

3. **CATER POSTS TO AUDIENCE.** As the editor of *Writer's Market* and *Poet's Market*, I have great range in the topics I can cover. However, if I'm writing a guest post for a fiction blog, I'll write about things of interest to a novelist—not a poet.

4. **MAKE PERSONAL, BUT PROVIDE NUGGET.** Guest posts are a great opportunity for you to really show your stuff to a new audience. You could write a very helpful and impersonal post, but that won't connect with readers the same way as if you write a very helpful and personal post that makes them want to learn more about you (and your blog, your book, your Twitter account, etc.). Speaking of which...

5. **SHARE LINKS TO YOUR WEBSITE, BLOG, SOCIAL NETWORKS, ETC.** After all, you need to make it easy for readers who enjoyed your guest post to learn more about you and your projects. Start the conversation in your guest post and keep it going on your own sites, profiles, etc. And related to that...

6. **PROMOTE YOUR GUEST POST THROUGH YOUR NORMAL CHANNELS ONCE THE POST GOES LIVE.** Your normal audience will want to know where you've been and what you've been doing. Plus, guest posts lend a little extra "street cred" to your projects. But don't stop there...

7. **CHECK FOR COMMENTS ON YOUR GUEST POST AND RESPOND IN A TIMELY MANNER.** Sometimes the comments are the most interesting part of a guest post (no offense). This is where readers can ask more in-depth or related questions, and it's also where you can show your expertise on the subject by being as helpful as possible. And guiding all seven of these tips is this one:

8. **PUT SOME EFFORT INTO YOUR GUEST POST.** Part of the benefit to guest posting is the opportunity to connect with a new audience. Make sure you bring your A-game, because you need to make a good impression if you want this exposure to actually help grow your audience. Don't stress yourself out, but put a little thought into what you submit.

ONE ADDITIONAL TIP: Have fun with it. Passion is what really drives the popularity of blogs. Share your passion and enthusiasm, and readers are sure to be impressed.

TWITTER CHEAT SHEET FOR WRITERS

....

by Robert Lee Brewer

With the publishing (and/or media) industry changing at the speed of light, so are the roles of writers (or content providers), editors (or content managers), agents (or content strategists), etc. One big change for writers (even in fiction, poetry, and other fields) is that they are expected to take an active role in building their own platforms via online and real world networking and exposure. One great tool for this online is Twitter.

It's easy (and free) enough to create a Twitter account, but how can writers take advantage of this social networking tool? What can they logically expect to gain from using it? What is a hashtag anyway? Well, hopefully, this cheat sheet will help.

First, let's look at some basic terminology:

- **TWEET** = Any message sent out to everyone on Twitter. Unless you direct message (DM) someone, everything on Twitter is a Tweet and viewable by anyone.
- **RT** = Retweet. Twitter created a RT-ing tool that makes for easy retweets, but the standard convention is to put an RT and cite the source before reposting something funny or useful that someone else has shared. For example, if I tweeted "Nouns are verbs waiting to happen," you could RT me this way: RT @robertleebrewer Nouns are verbs waiting to happen.
- **DM** = Direct message. These are private and only between people who DM each other.
- **# = HASHTAG.** These are used in front a word (or set of letters) to allow people to easily communicate on a specific topic. For instance, I tweet poetry with other poets on Twitter by using the hashtag #poettalk. Poets can click on the "poettalk" after the hashtag (no space) or they can search on the term "poettalk" in Twitter (right-hand toolbar).

- **#FF** = Follow Friday. This is a nice way to show support for other tweeters on Twitter. On Friday.

Second, here are 10 things you can do to optimize your use of Twitter:

1. **USE YOUR REAL NAME IF POSSIBLE.** Make it easy for people you know or meet to find you on Twitter.

2. **ADD A PROFILE PICTURE.** Preferably this will be a picture of you. People connect better with other people, not cartoons, book covers, logos, etc.

3. **LINK TO A WEBSITE.** Hopefully, you have a blog or website you can link to in your profile. If you don't have a website or blog, make one. Now. And then, link to it from your Twitter profile.

4. **WRITE YOUR BIO.** Make this memorable in some way. You don't have to be funny or cute, but more power to you if you can do this and still make it relevant to who you are.

5. **TWEET REGULARLY.** It doesn't matter if you have only 2 followers (and one is your mom); you still need to tweet daily (or nearly daily) for Twitter to be effective. And remember: If you don't have anything original to add, you can always RT something funny or useful from someone else.

6. **TWEET RELEVANT INFORMATION.** Don't be the person who tweets like this: "I am making a salad;" "I am eating a salad;" "That salad was good;" "I wonder what I'm going to eat next;" etc. These tweets are not interesting or relevant. However, if your salad eating experience rocked your world in a unique way, feel free to share: "Just ate the best salad ever. Now, I'm ready to write a novel."

7. **LINK AND DON'T LINK.** It's good to link to other places and share things you're doing or that you've found elsewhere. At the same time, if all you do is link, people may think you're just trying to sell them stuff all the time.

8. **HAVE A PERSONALITY.** Be yourself. You don't have to be overly cute, funny, smart, etc. Just be yourself and remember that Twitter is all about connecting people. So be a person.

9. **FOLLOW THOSE WORTH FOLLOWING.** Just because you're being followed you don't have to return the follow. For instance, if some local restaurant starts following me, I'm not going to follow them back, because they aren't relevant to me or to my audience.

10. **COMMUNICATE WITH OTHERS.** I once heard someone refer to Twitter as one big cocktail party, and it's true. Twitter is all about communication. If people talk to you or RT you, make sure you talk back and/or thank them. (*Here's a secret: People like to feel involved and acknowledged. I like it; you like it; and so does everyone else.*)

And, of course, if you're not already, please follow me on Twitter @robetleebrewer (http://twitter.com/robertleebrewer)

HERE ARE SOME EXTRA RESOURCES:

- **TwitterGrader.com** (http://twittergrader.com) This site allows you to enter your profile at any given time and find out how you're doing (according to them) in using Twitter effectively. Of course, the grade you receive is bound to not be perfect, but it is a good measuring stick.
- **What the Hashtag?** (http://wthashtag.com) This site allows you to search for hashtags, run reports on them, get transcripts between specific time periods, and more.
- **Hootsuite** (http://hootsuite.com) This is one of many tools that give the ability to Tweet and track your account without even going to Twitter. Many (maybe even most) people use these. There are others, such as TweetDeck, Seesmic, etc. Find one that you like and let it make your social networking life easier to manage.
- **bit.ly** (http://bit.ly) This is one of many URL shortening services out there, which is very helpful when tweeting URL links, since they can easily eat into your 140-character limit on Twitter. This particular one makes it easy for you to track clicks, though I'm sure that's fairly standard.

FACEBOOK VS. LINKEDIN:

Tips for Using Two Social Networking Sites

....

by Robert Lee Brewer

Many writers ask why start a LinkedIn account if they already have a Facebook, or conversely, why start a Facebook if they already have a LinkedIn? That's a fair question, but the answer is simple: Both these sites cater to different audiences, and both of these audiences are important to writers.

LinkedIn is the more professional site of the two. Many professionals use it to make meaningful connections with other like-minded professionals. HR departments use the site to find potential job candidates, and potential job candidates use their LinkedIn profiles as their resumes.

Facebook is a lot less professional, but smart writers treat this site as an important piece to their marketing puzzle. In fact, it's natural for writers to have more fun with their Facebook profiles, but they should still remember that editors, agents, writers, and other professionals may be interested in linking up on Facebook.

FACEBOOK TIPS FOR WRITERS

As of the writing of this article, Facebook is the most popular website on the Internet. Chances are good that you already have a profile on this social networking site. (If you don't have a Facebook profile, then you should create one now, since they're free.) However, you may or may not be optimizing your Facebook use.

Here are some tips for writers who are either new to Facebook or who aren't sure if they're using it the correct way:

1. **COMPLETE YOUR PROFILE.** You don't have to include EVERYTHING, but I'd suggest at least covering these bases: Current City, Birthday (you don't have to include the year), Bio, Education and Work, Contact Information.

2. **MAKE EVERYTHING PUBLIC.** As a writer, you should be using sites like Facebook and Twitter to connect with other writers, editors, agents, and your audience. So make it easy for them to find you and learn more about you by making everything available to the public. That said...

3. **THINK ABOUT YOUR AUDIENCE, FRIENDS, FAMILY, BOSS, FORMER TEACHERS, ETC., IN EVERYTHING YOU DO ON FACEBOOK.** Like it or not, you have to understand that if you are completely public on Facebook (and you should be if you want to connect with your audience) that you need to think about what you do on Facebook before you do it. Because Facebook isn't like Vegas: What happens on Facebook could easily go viral. But don't get paranoid; just use common sense.

> Even though it's virtual, you want your profile to be as human as possible so that you can connect with others.

4. **INCLUDE A PROFILE PICTURE OF YOURSELF.** Don't use a picture of a cute animal, house pet, your children, an animated character, a famous celebrity, a model, etc. Just a nice pic of yourself. Even though it's virtual, you want your profile to be as human as possible so that you can connect with others.

5. **UPDATE YOUR STATUS REGULARLY.** You shouldn't update your status every hour, but once a day is a good pace. This just lets others on Facebook know that you are actively using the site.

6. **COMMUNICATE WITH FRIENDS ON FACEBOOK.** Don't stalk your friends; communicate with them. If you like a friend's status update, comment on it—or at the very least, click the Like button (to acknowledge that you liked their update). Speaking of friends...

7. **BE SELECTIVE ABOUT FRIENDS YOU ADD.** Don't blindly accept every friend request, because some may be bogus, and others may be from serial frienders (people who are trying to hit their friend limits). You want quality friends who share your interests or who you know from the "real world."

8. **BE SELECTIVE ABOUT ADDING APPS.** I'm not a huge fan of apps, because they are a distraction and time killer on Facebook. But there are some that could be useful.

However, don't waste a month of your life playing Farmville or Mafia Wars; you'd be better off completing a crossword or sudoku puzzle.

9. **JOIN RELEVANT GROUPS.** For writers, there are an abundance of groups you could join, from professional organizations to those based around magazines, publishers and literary events. These are great places to connect with other writers. On that same note...

10. **FOLLOW RELEVANT FAN PAGES.** There are many who once had groups that migrated over to using fan pages, so there are fan pages for writing organizations, magazines, publishers, literary events, and more. (I even have a fan page on Facebook; just search for Robert Lee Brewer.)

BONUS TIP: If you have a blog, you can feed your Facebook profile automatically by using the Notes function. All you have to do is go to Notes, click the "Edit import settings" link, and enter your blog url in the correct field. (Note: I had to enter my full url, including the forward slash at the end, before the Notes function accepted my url.)

OTHER SOCIAL NETWORKING SITES

This book contains articles on Twitter, Facebook, and LinkedIn, but there are many other powerful social networking sites on the Internet. Here's a list of some of them:

- **Bebo** (http://bebo.com)
- **Classmates** (http://classmates.com)
- **Digg** (http://digg.com)
- **Flickr** (http://flickr.com)
- **Friendster** (http://friendster.com)
- **Habbo** (http://habbo.com)
- **Hi5** (http://hi5.com)
- **MeetUp** (http://meetup.com)
- **MySpace** (http://myspace.com)
- **Ning** (http://ning.com)
- **Orkut** (http://orkut.com)
- **StumbleUpon** (http://stumbleupon.com)
- **Tagged** (http://tagged.com)
- **Yelp** (http://yelp.com)
- **YouTube** (http://youtube.com)
- **Zorpia** (http://zorpia.com)

LINKEDIN TIPS FOR WRITERS

If Twitter and Facebook are the social networks where writers can just "hang out," then LinkedIn is the one where writers can "network" and make meaningful connections. Some writers may even be able to make connections with editors (like myself) and agents.

Many writers may not use LinkedIn anywhere near as much as they use Facebook or Twitter, but I believe in making yourself easy to find. Having a completed and optimized LinkedIn profile could lead to connections with editors, event coordinators, and other writers.

Here are a few tips I've picked up over time on how to use LinkedIn:

1. **USE YOUR OWN HEAD SHOT FOR YOUR AVATAR.** I recommend this on all social networks, because people want to make "real" connections on these sites. It's hard to take a picture of a family pet or cartoon character seriously.

2. **COMPLETE YOUR PROFILE.** There are many steps to completing your profile, including completing your resume and getting a few recommendations from connections, which leads to the next tip...

3. **GIVE THOUGHTFUL RECOMMENDATIONS TO RECEIVE THEM.** Give if you wish to receive. The recommendations you write will make you feel and look better, but the recommendations you receive in return will truly rock your solar system. Of course, to make and receive recommendations, you'll need to...

4. **SEARCH FOR CONNECTIONS YOU ALREADY HAVE.** These could be "real world" connections and/or connections from other social networks. The ones who are (or have been) most valuable to you are the best to make at first. Then...

5. **MAKE MEANINGFUL CONNECTIONS WITH OTHERS.** Search for other writers, editors, agents, or whoever you think might benefit your writing career. But don't ever spam. Look for meaningful connections and include a note about why you're contacting them through LinkedIn. Remember: Social networking is about *who* you know, not *how many*.

6. **ACCEPT INVITATIONS.** While I think it's a good rule of thumb to be selective about who you invite to connect with you, I also don't see any harm in accepting invitations with abandon—unless they are obviously not a good fit. My reasoning here is that you never know why someone is contacting you. Of course, you can always kill the connection later if it's not working.

7. **MAKE YOUR PROFILE EASY TO FIND.** If possible, work your name into your LinkedIn url. For instance, you can view my LinkedIn profile at http://www.linkedin.

com/in/robertleebrewer. Also, connect to your profile in blog posts and on other social networks.

8. **TAILOR YOUR PROFILE TO THE VISITOR.** It's easy to make me-centric profiles on social networks, because they're asking questions about you. However, remember that these descriptions are more beneficial to you if you're filling them out for the prospective connections you can make on social networking sites. Make it easy for them to figure out who you are, what you do, and how you might improve their lives. As such...

9. **UPDATE YOUR PROFILE REGULARLY WITH USEFUL CONTENT.** You can feed blog posts into your profile easily, and that will keep your profile active. You can also update your status by feeding in tweets or Facebook updates, but I refrain from doing that myself. My reasoning is that my updates are slightly different for each place. However, I can make meaningful tweets and LinkedIn status updates simultaneously by simply adding an #in hashtag to the tweet in question.

10. **JOIN (AND PARTICIPATE) IN GROUPS.** Heck, start your own group if you feel so inclined. Of course, participating in groups will require an extra level of engagement with the site, so this last tip is more an extra credit assignment for those who want to unlock the full potential of LinkedIn.

JANE FRIEDMAN:

Social Media Master Shares Secrets to Success

by Robert Lee Brewer

There are two Jane Friedmans in the publishing business. One is the CEO and Co-Founder of Open Road Integrated Media and the former President and CEO of HarperCollins; the other is a social media guru who owns about everything there is that's labeled JaneFriedman online, including www.janefriedman.com, twitter.com/janefriedman, facebook.com/janefriedman, and well, you get the idea. This other Jane Friedman—who also used to be my boss—is the subject of this interview.

Friedman is the former Publisher and Editorial Director of the Writer's Digest Writing Community and is currently a full-time professor of e-media at the University of Cincinnati—teaching writing and storytelling skills, media ethics, and a range of media-focused classes to traditional students majoring in e-media.

Friedman adds, "I'm still active with Writer's Digest as a contributing editor and blogger, and I teach online classes several times a year on new media topics, such as e-publishing, online marketing, and social media. That keeps me pretty busy! But I am working on a new book for writers forthcoming in 2012 from Writer's Digest."

She also speaks frequently—appearing at more than 200 writing events since 2001, including at events such as BookExpo America, AWP, Digital Book World, and South By Southwest. In 2011, she also served as a panelist to review 2011 grants in literature for the National Endowment for the Arts.

Friedman took a little time out of her hectic schedule to answer the following questions.

In April 2011, you released an e-book, *The Future of Publishing: Enigma Variations*, which analyzes the future of publishing and makes readers laugh at the same time. I assume your April 1 release date was intentionally silly, but that you put quite a bit of effort into making this digital book. Just from a logistics and resources point of view, what went into creating your e-book?

Fortunately, I already had all the skills and tools I needed to create an e-book since I've worked in publishing for nearly 15 years. So it was really about setting aside the time to write, edit, design, and produce the book.

Here are the stages I went through:

- Inspiration and planning stage. I came up with the structure and started outlining what I would write. This was my favorite part, and was accomplished over a week or two, during mini-brainstorm moments.
- Draft stage. In one sitting, I wrote the entire work longhand in about 4–5 hours. That's not typical for me, but it's how things worked out.
- Revision stage. When I typed out my longhand manuscript, I also revised and added content as I went. This took another 4–5 hours.
- Editing stage. I sent my manuscript to two trusted friends (who are also editors, fortunately!), and that feedback process took several days.
- Production stage. While my friends edited the manuscript, I set up the design templates and created the front and back matter in Adobe InDesign. I also created the images at this stage. InDesign is a design and layout program that I've used for many years, so there was no learning curve. Still, this stage took me as much time as writing and revising the book.
- Final production stage. After I had all the edits back, I incorporated them into the final manuscript, dumped the copy into my design template, and took care of all layout and design issues. Then I proofread a hard copy with a friend in one evening, made final corrections in the file, and outputted a PDF that I made available for sale online within minutes. The actual creation of the e-book file was the easiest and quickest part.

As a long-time media professional, did you place any expectations or goals on your title, or is it more of an experiment?

It was a big experiment. I was curious how my online platform would translate into people who would pay to read my writing. Most of my audience is accustomed to getting my advice for free on my blog, in my newsletter, and through various interviews I do online.

I also wanted the experience of seeing how well and what kind of online marketing efforts work, and what channels seemed to be most important for getting the word out. It's interesting to put your online marketing machine (or network) in motion toward a particular goal, and this was the first opportunity I had to measure its strength and reach.

The Future of Publishing offers 14 variations of what the future of publishing holds, and I don't want you to give away too much, but do you have a favorite prediction for the publishing business?

I'm very curious to see if author collectives may develop and gain power, kind of like the United Artists model from the golden age of Hollywood. I don't see any reason why the heavy hitters within popular genres couldn't organize themselves and release their work just as effectively as any traditional publisher.

....

I don't see any reason why the heavy hitters within popular genres couldn't organize themselves and release their work just as effectively as any traditional publisher.

....

I'm also fascinated by the machinations of Amazon, Apple, and Google. Between the three of them, they could become masters of *all* media, and it's been clear for a couple years now that Amazon is not just a retailer, but also a publisher.

As of this interview, you have 70,000 followers on Twitter (@JaneFriedman). I'm sure many writers familiar with Twitter are wondering what your secret is. Have you employed a certain strategy in your use of Twitter?

I'd boil down my strategy to these 3 things:

- Focus and consistency. I am ruthlessly focused on sharing links and tips that are relevant to writing and publishing. I'm not using Twitter casually or as a conversation channel, but as an information channel. Not everyone agrees with that, but people know when they follow me that they'll get high-value links relevant to them.
- Low volume. Some people advise tweeting at least 10-20 times a day, and repeating the same tweets since a tweet's lifespan is so brief (less than 5 minutes). However, I think you're more likely to lose followers by oversharing and duplicating tweets. There's too much noise in this world, and I don't want to be adding any more than I have to. So I rarely repeat myself on Twitter, and there may be some days when I don't tweet at all, or just send out one or two messages. I think people are grateful that I know how to shut up when I don't have something compelling to share.
- Tweet curation. My rise on Twitter is also connected to my weekly blog series, "Best Tweets for Writers." It allows me to share great information from Twitter

for the benefit of everyone, and also honor others who tweet great stuff. I've been running the Best Tweets feature for a couple years now, and it's made me more visible on Twitter than I'd otherwise be.

After more than a decade with F+W Media (which publishes Writer's Market), you decided to leave the publishing and media industry to teach about it at the University of Cincinnati. In what ways has your life changed—if at all—from being a publisher and community leader to being a professor and student leader?

What's funny is that I'm working harder than ever, but I also lead a far more relaxed and enjoyable life, one that's free from the tyranny of hundreds of daily e-mails and countless meetings. I have significantly more freedom to do exactly the kind of work I want to do, and focus on what *I* find meaningful, rather than being told what I must value or prioritize. I've never been so liberated!

I've also had to work on my teaching skills, and learn how to engage students who don't have the same level of intrinsic motivation as those writers I instruct as part of Writer's Digest. So I'm coming up with new curriculum, new exercises, and new ways to teach old topics. Fortunately, this benefits my other professional work too, because I always have a new perspective or insight to discuss on my blog and newsletter.

You've spoken at more than 200 writing events since 2001. Do you have a favorite presentation tip for authors who may be new to speaking at such events?

You can never have a bad presentation if you have good handouts. People LOVE handouts. They have concrete value, people remember your advice better when they can refer to them, and they're also an excellent marketing tool since writers usually save and share handouts.

....

You can never have a bad presentation if you have good handouts. People LOVE handouts.

....

Your personal website is very impressive, incorporating your blogging, tweets, an e-mail newsletter sign up and more. First question, what do you see as the purpose or function of your website for you?

It's the place online that's totally mine. I own it, I decide what happens there, and it collects everything I do in one central place. It has the most comprehensive information about who I am and what I do. No matter where else I am active online (social media, community sites, e-mail, etc.), I always point back to my website so people can find out more and stay in touch by whatever means they prefer.

All serious writers need this kind of hub so they can start learning more about their readers and formalizing a connection with them. Facebook, Twitter, and other sites help you find readers and connect, but those connections can disappear at any moment, or gradually over time. Having your own site gives you more control and insight into your connections, how people are finding you, and why people find you. (You can find out all these things by studying your site analytics.)

Second question, did you launch your current site through your own devices, hire a professional, or through some other means?

I did everything myself. I bought my own domain (JaneFriedman.com) and hosting through GoDaddy. I installed Wordpress on my site, then bought a premium Wordpress theme that looks great without any customization.

I've used Wordpress for many years, so it wasn't difficult to get started with it. I prefer Wordpress because it's free (open source), continually improved and updated, and has amazing support and features because of the huge community that's developed around it. I also love Wordpress because it's a content management system (as opposed to site design software), so it's easy to add loads of content and media without having to know any coding. Just about anyone with a computer and Internet access can do what I did in one (long) evening after watching a few simple online tutorials.

I have thought about hiring a web design professional to kick my site design up a notch—to add some personal style—but I'm more concerned with function and substance right now.

I receive your 3 Happy Things newsletter. Do you feel e-mail can be an important tool for connecting writers and readers?

Being able to directly reach your readers (or most avid fans) is a powerful capability that every author should have. While social media is usually touted as a primary way to build audience, when it comes to online marketing, e-mail is still the most successful and profitable means of interacting with your readership. It's also a tool that you own and isn't subject to the whims of an organization or corporation.

....

Unfortunately, e-mail marketing is probably the No. 1-overlooked means of reader engagement when authors evaluate their overall platform. But it's easy to get started.

....

Unfortunately, e-mail marketing is probably the No. 1 overlooked means of reader engagement when authors evaluate their overall platform. But it's easy to get started. Just sign up with a service like MailChimp, ConstantContact, or AWeber, then publicize the newsletter sign-up link or form. (I like MailChimp because the interface is friendly and intuitive for non-techie people, and it's free to use until you exceed 2,000 names.)

Sending valuable content via e-mail is a way to keep readers updated on what's happening, offer valuable or specialized content (because these will be your most engaged fans), and also gather direct feedback on questions or projects.

It is NOT a way to more easily spam people or overburden them with marketing messages! Treat the medium with respect and care, and you'll see your readership grow.

Personally, I think anyone involved in the publishing and media industry, whether a writer or not, should regularly check in with your There Are No Rules blog. Could you explain what you try to accomplish with this blog for writers who may not be familiar?

In my blog, I emphasize how writers are the ones who are ultimately responsible for the shape and path of their careers. Writers cannot rely on agents, editors, or publishers to be the ones to lead them to success. Writers who do are ultimately disappointed and may end up feeling victimized.

....

Writers cannot rely on agents, editors, or publishers to be the ones to lead them to success. Writers who do are ultimately disappointed and may end up feeling victimized.

....

Because of my fascination with new tools and technologies, I often discuss and feature new media that's giving writers more power and opportunities than ever to get published and find readers. When I say "there are no rules," what I'm saying is: There is no single right way to write better, get published, or have a successful career. You get to decide what that looks like based on your strengths, the qualities of your work, and what attracts readers to you.

Furthermore, given how publishing is rapidly changing from day to day, you can't assume that what worked yesterday will also work today. So I like to offer case studies and Q&As with authors on what innovative efforts are paying off.

I know you have experience with at least a few of the e-reading devices. Do you have a preferred e-reader?

I've been a longtime customer of Amazon, so I invested in a Kindle. I also use an iPad from time to time, but I don't like it as an e-reading device because I find it awkward and heavy for long periods of reading. Also, since my reading is usually black-and-white heavy text, I prefer the non-backlit experience of the Kindle.

The best part about Kindle by far is the frictionless experience of buying books. I buy far more e-books than I ever did physical books because (1) I don't have to worry about storing them or moving them (2) they're cheaper (3) I can get access right away—instant gratification!

If you could only pass on one piece of advice to writers who are seeking to "make a career" out of writing, what would it be?

Think beyond the printed page; think beyond the book. There are so many wonderful, unique ways to deliver a story or spread a message, but we often limit ourselves to thinking of the way it's always been done. It's more possible (and more fun) than ever to make an impact outside of the traditional publishing options. So, think more deeply about who your audience is and how you are most likely to reach them. Think about blog posts, e-newsletters, podcasts, videos, and Twitter accounts. Think about online community sites. Think about personalized experiences. Not every piece of material or content really deserves or needs to appear in print or in a traditionally edited publication. That's not what grants authority any longer. Instead, it's about how you can beautifully match your content or story to the right medium so that it perfectly serves the needs of your audience.

CHUCK SAMBUCHINO:

Educating People on Literary Agents and Garden Gnomes

by Robert Lee Brewer

If you've been to a writing conference (any writing conference) in the past five years, there's a chance you've come into contact with Chuck Sambuchino. As the editor of *Guide to Literary Agents* and *Children's Writer's & Illustrator's Market*, Sambuchino is constantly traveling from one writing event to the next. However, he doesn't let his busy work schedule detract from his real love: writing.

In September 2010, Ten Speed Press released Sambuchino's humor book, *How to Survive a Garden Gnome Attack*. The book quickly became a humor bestseller and has been featured by *Reader's Digest, USA Today, The New York Times* and AOL News. During the week of this interview, it was announced that Sony Pictures Animation picked up an option on the book.

Sambuchino's first title *Formatting & Submitting Your Manuscript,* Third Edition (Writer's Digest Books) covers the nitty gritty details of preparing submissions. Beyond his book writing and editing, Sambuchino is a produced playwright, magazine freelancer, husband, cover band guitarist, chocolate chip cookie fiend, and owner of a flabby-yet-lovable dog named Graham. He also blogs on literary agents through his Guide to Literary Agents blog (guidetoliteraryagents.com/blog) and can be found on Twitter through his handle @ ChuckSambuchino.

What are you currently up to?

I am teaching at a lot of conferences in support of both my work-related books (such as the *2011 Guide to Literary Agents*) and my personal books (such as *How to Survive a Garden Gnome Attack*). At the same time, I have drafted several nonfiction book proposals for new humor books that my agent and I are trying to sell. As she shops them around to publishers, I am keeping myself sane by writing some spec comedy screenplays. I hope to get them to my script manager soon. I have no idea how he will react to them. He could very well burn them.

Besides all that, I still have the 9-to-5 job at Writer's Digest Books keeping me very busy. I am the new editor of the *Children's Writer's & Illustrator's Market*, which is exciting and challenging. I blog. I tweet. I run webinars. Life goes on.

Your Humor/Gnome Defense book, *How to Survive a Garden Gnome Attack*, was released by Ten Speed Press in 2010. That statement provokes a lot of questions, but the first one that I wonder is how did you even develop the idea?

I was thinking about the movie *The Full Monty* (1997). There is a funny scene in it with a garden gnome, and I started to think about how tacky and awful gnomes are. Then I thought: Certainly if gnomes creep me out, they must creep out others. That was the genesis of the idea. I pitched it to my agent, fully expecting her to drop me as a client. Instead, she paused and said "Gnomes? ... I can sell that."

I know you have an agent. Did you hook your agent with the gnome defense pitch, or did you make your connection some other way?

My agent and I connected over another nonfiction book—a very straightforward one celebrating historic theaters around the country that are still in operation today. We got an offer on the book in 2009 but didn't accept it. When that project fell through, my agent asked me what else I had up my sleeve. I passed along a few ideas, the last of which was *Gnome Attack*.

***How to Survive a Garden Gnome Attack* is heavy on the images. Did you have to worry about this side of the process at all? Did you have any input?**

That's a great question. From the beginning, I knew the book would have some kind of art element. When I turned in my sample chapters (as part of my nonfiction book proposal), I paid a local man to draw some funny gnome illustrations to include in the text. I think this was a good move. It helped editors understand that the book would be a mix of text and art.

After Ten Speed Press bought the book, they handled all the art. They opted for color photos and hired a local photographer to shoot them. I was outside the entire process, but kept up to speed and gave the photographer my blessing to go out and shoot some gnomes. Take that last sentence for what you will.

Your book was on the humor bestseller lists in 2010. Can you describe what that process was like?

The first week the book was out, it sold 2,000 copies. And when I saw that number, I just breathed a big sigh of relief. The truth is: Before I keel over, if I'm lucky, I would like

How to Survive a Garden Gnome Attack may or may not save your life someday, but it will make you laugh out loud in parts.

to write a lot of books. And doing that means that I must continue to turn out books that sell at least moderately well. So when the book made the Humor Top 10 alongside names like Chelsea Handler and Jon Stewart, I wasn't so much excited as I was relieved. I mean, if the book just fell on its face, who knows what kinds of roadblocks that would bring about for future projects.

Also, I know you had a book launch party for the book. How did that go? Do you have any tips for other writers on putting a launch party together?

My advice is to do what I did and have not one, but *two* parties. The first party I had was just for close friends and relatives. It was a celebration at a bar with free food and beer. That was a celebration, and it was never intended to make enough money to cover expenses.

....

My advice is to do what I did and have not one, but two parties. The first party I had was just for close friends and relatives. ... The second event I held was at a local bookstore.

....

The second event I held was at a local bookstore. That was more of a formal "release event," with a signing, a reading, a formal Q&A, some storytelling, promotion, a big sign in the store—the works. Both types of events offer their advantages. I suggest both. When you contact a bookstore and want to reserve a date, make sure you have all your information ready. They get lots of requests, so they immediately want to know things such as: publisher, first print run, release date, etc.

Recently, news broke that Robert Zemeckis has attached himself to a Sony Pictures Animation option of *How to Survive a Garden Gnome Attack*. That's got to be a mind-blowing moment. However, I know you and your agent were actively shopping the book. Could you explain what that whole process has been like from your perspective?

From my perspective as a writer, this has all pretty much gone around me, but yes, it is exciting news nonetheless. When *Gnome Attack* came out, my book agent told me she had secured a book-to-film rep in Los Angeles who would try to sell the film rights. (This is standard procedure for almost all books.) I spoke with my new book-to-film rep and we hit it off. At that point, he took the reins. As per standard protocol, he began to send copies of the book to Hollywood producers in the hopes of generating interest in a film adaptation. Some producers thought the idea sounded intriguing; others did not. Life went on.

Then a few months later, we got lucky, plain and simple. We had our hook out there in the ocean of producers when a huge fish came swimming up. Robert Zemeckis was apparently interested in doing a movie about gnomes, as luck would have it, and he got wind of my book. My book-to-film rep got in touch with him and passed aiong the book. A month later. Zemeckis and his production company, ImageMovers, formally attached themselves to the project. The plan was now to use this "packaging" of the book idea and Zemeckis to get a studio to buy the film rights. Before we even had time to shop it everywhere and whet people's appetites, Sony Pictures Animation was alerted to this situation somehow. They called and basically said, "If this book's film rights are for sale and Robert Zemeckis is really attached, then we want it."

That was it. Selling the film rights to a book can be a long and arduous process. We struck gold when Zemeckis came onboard. At that point, the Sony deal happened quickly because of his (monumental) involvement. I mean—the dude won an Oscar!

Keep in mind that all this went around me. I have two great agents who handled this. I was just sitting on the couch making passive-aggressive remarks at my dog.

Your day job is as the editor of *Guide to Literary Agents and Children's Writer's & Illustrator's Market*. What's the most important thing writers should consider before approaching literary agents?

They need to ask themselves: "Is the work ready?" As writers, we keep working on the same project for months (even years) and it just gets to that point where we can't stand looking at it anymore, and want to test the waters. My message to writers everywhere is: Breathe. Put the project on hold for a week or two months, then come back to it. You will have new eyes and will be able to fix problems you never saw before. Never submit a project to an agent if you are aware of any major problems. Typical major problems would be: 1) a novel starts too slow; 2) a novel is too long; 3) a nonfiction author has not yet built up a significant platform that would generate agent interest. If you think your book has a problem, then it does. Fix all major problems before you submit it.

As part of your editor duties, you travel and speak at a lot of writing events. First question, why should writers get out to these events?

How much time do you have? I am a huge proponent of conferences.

Agents and editors are at conferences, so that means you have the chance to mingle with people who can help you get published. There are a variety of courses and sessions to attend—some more on the craft of writing, some more on the business side. Almost all sessions allow for Q&A, so you can get your questions answered. Plus, we all need writer friends who will help us shape our own work before we submit it. Conferences are the places where you make new writing friends for life. If you are thinking of attending a conference, seriously—*go*. Keep in mind you can always combine a vacation with an event. If you have relatives in another city—Seattle or Boston or Dallas or wherever—combine a vacation with a conference (and write off the whole thing!).

Second question, what is your most important presentation tip for writers who might be invited to speak at one?

Give people takeaway tips. People need the nuts and bolts of how to do something. Break the information down and, if possible, provide examples. Be energetic. Crack some jokes. Toss in mentions of your own books and stories, but do it minimally. You won't sell your own book by repeating its title over and over again. You will sell your book through giving a helpful speech and showing you are in command of your subject. If you're an author and are asked to speak, just remember: Make the speech much more than just *your* story.

....

You won't sell our own book by repeating its title over and over again. You will sell your book through giving a helpful speech and showing you are in command of your subject.

....

As an editor who travels a lot, how do manage to write so much? Do you have a routine time of day or week? Some other trick?

I watch very little TV. This keeps me out of the loop at lunch when the conversation turns to "24" or "How I Met Your Mother," but you would be amazed how much time you free up when you simply stop watching TV. Besides that, I just simply *love to write*. Besides hanging out with my wife and dog, there is nothing I would rather be doing than writing.

You maintain the very popular Guide to Literary Agents blog. What's the most important key to blogging success for writers?

I could talk a lot about this, but I'll just cut to the chase and say that the reader must get something out of the posts. People whose blogs are full of posts about themselves and their own books usually go nowhere—because the blog is not really for others; it's for the writers themselves. The more you give, the more you get.

Any tips for writers approaching the humor market?

A lot of the success of your book is simply on the concept and the jokes. If you come up with something that touches a nerve, then it just spreads by word-of-mouth, and there isn't a whole lot of effect you can have on sales one way or the other. My editor once told me my book's biggest two assets would be: 1) the title, and 2) the cover. I believe she was right.

Besides that, try to develop any kind of platform that can supplement sales; and do get an agent, because an agent can help you get published by a bigger house—with publicists who can aid you.

Maybe most importantly for the purposes of protecting our way of life, what is the best way writers can protect themselves against a gnome uprising?

I spill all details in the book, but let me throw out a few here:

- Buy a big ^&*! dog.
- Install motion-activated lights outside.
- Keep a bike handy for when gnomes slash your car tires.
- Do not follow a routine where gnomes can predict your comings and goings.
- Never trust a gnomeowner.
- Remove any pet doors.
- Caulk all house air vents.
- Dig a moat around your house.
- Create quicksand traps for gnomes and bait them with gumdrops and/or a saucer of fine ale.
- For God's sake, remove any lawn gnomes that are on your property!

NICK FLYNN:

Exploring the Unknown Parts of the Self

....

by Robert Lee Brewer

While Nick Flynn had established himself as an award-winning poet previously, he really struck gold in the publishing industry when Norton released his memoir *Another Bullshit Night in Suck City* in 2004. That memoir went on to win the PEN/Martha Albrand Award, was shortlisted for France's Prix Femina, and has been translated into 13 languages. At the time of this interview, Flynn was on set for the filming of the movie which is due for release in 2012.

In 2010, Norton released Flynn's most recent memoir, *The Ticking Is the Bomb*, which is a fragmented story that weaves together his impending fatherhood with his growing outrage and obsession with torture. During the course of the memoir, Flynn meets with some of the Iraqi men depicted in the infamous Abu Ghraib photographs and eventually welcomes his daughter into the world. As with any good memoir, he expertly shares his own process of self-discovery through the world ticking around him.

As a person who makes his living off writing about himself, one might think that Flynn is concerned with how the world interprets his particular literary footprint. However, when I asked him how he hopes people might think of his writing, he answered, "That's probably not for me to say."

What are you currently up to?

For the past seven weeks I've been on the set of the filming of *Another Bullshit Night in Suck City.*

In the beginning of 2010, Norton released your memoir *The Ticking Is the Bomb*, which takes place around the same time as you welcomed your daughter into the world. First, has your daughter changed the way you interpret the world?

Having a daughter, becoming a father, has changed nearly everything. Before it happened, this idea of change sounded like a bad thing, but it turned out that all that changed needed changing anyway. Though her birth did not change, as I mention in the book, my views on torture, as some people claimed it would. I still think it's a very bad idea.

Second, has she altered your writing process at all?

My writing is a bit more focused, perhaps more distilled, these days, simply because—after years of wandering aimlessly in the wilderness, essentially alone—I am now responsible for another human being.

In the book, you write about meeting ex-detainees at Abu Ghraib. One line that I love about the experience after it's over is, "What surprises me is that I forgot that each would be fully human, fully complex." I sometimes feel like that is the appeal of memoirs—that they connect readers with fully human, fully complex people. What do you feel is the most important thing writers can do with their memoirs to make them connect with readers?

Maybe we need to push into the unknown, the unsaid, the unexplored parts of ourselves—

....

The main pitfall is believing your story is somehow special. No matter what you've gone through, there have been many, many others who have gone through the same thing, or are still going through it, or will go through it soon.

....

The Ticking Is the Bomb is your second memoir, so you have a little experience in the genre. What do you consider the greatest challenge in writing a memoir?

It would seem to be the most self-centered of all art forms, but because of that, in order for it to succeed, it has to be as egoless as possible. The main pitfall is believing your story is somehow special. No matter what you've gone through, there have been many, many others who have gone through the same thing, or are still going through it, or will go through it soon. We are merely the ones with words, and this is both a gift and a responsibility.

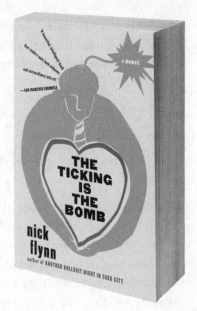

The Ticking Is the Bomb is Flynn's second memoir. His first, *Another Bullshit Night in Suck City*, has been translated into 13 languages and made into a film.

Many writers take many paths to publishing their first book. While I know you write in other genres, I'm wondering how you got your first memoir, *Another Bullshit Night in Suck City*, published. Could you share the story behind that memoir?

> I worked on that book for either seven or nine years, depending on how you count it. Either way, in retrospect, it doesn't seem that long, really—that was the time it took. After I'd been working on it for four (or six) years, I had written about 1,000 pages, maybe 2,000, and I thought 40 were good enough to show someone. I showed them to an agent (Bill Clegg), and he showed them to an editor (Jill Bialosky), and Norton bought it.

That memoir is being turned into a movie that is currently set to release in 2012 with such stars as Robert De Niro, Julianne Moore, and Paul Dano. First question, could you describe the experience of having your memoir turned into a movie?

> This took another seven years, working with a Paul Weitz, who wrote the screenplay and is directing the movie. And I'm glad it took that long, because, again, that was the time it needed.

Second question, have you had any involvement with the script or the filming?

> Paul has shown me every draft, and I've given him notes, and I've been on the set every day for the past seven weeks, sitting beside him.

You're an award-winning poet. Your most recent collection, *The Captain Asks for a Show of Hands*, was released by Graywolf Press in February 2011. Do you feel like your poetry tries to accomplish something that your other forms of writing don't?

I think every art form does something the other forms cannot—poetry is distilled, lyric, mercurial, shimmering, able to inhabit many perspectives from line to line. It moves as fast as film, yet it is at its center meditative.

....

Usually there are several projects going on at one, and I move between them, focusing on one for a few months, then letting it sit for a few months while I work on something else.

....

You've also written a play (*Alice Invents a Little Game* and *Alice Always Wins*) and an instructional book (written with Shirley McPhillips) on how to instruct poetry. How do you decide which projects to write at any given time?

Usually there are several projects going at once, and I move between them, focusing on one for a few months, then letting it sit for a few months while I work on something else. Beyond that, I have very little choice in what I write.

Do you have any sort of writing routine?

Ideally I write for four hours a day. At least, that has been the routine since my daughter has been born, during which time two books have somehow come out.

If you could pass along just one piece of advice to other writers, regardless of genre, what would it be?

Push beyond whatever thresholds you find in your writing.

SANDRA BEASLEY:

Balancing the Fine Line of Truth and a Good Story

....

by Robert Lee Brewer

One of the qualities I love about Sandra Beasley's writing is that it's intelligent without making the reader feel dumb. Beasley is an academic with a sense of humor and an engaging voice, which is probably the main reason she's one of the faster rising new voices in literature.

In fact, I first discovered Beasley through her poetry. She's a very accomplished poet—having released *Theories of Falling* (New Issues) and *I Was the Jukebox* (Norton). Both collections share a fondness for language and inventive storytelling that feels genuine.

In July of 2011, Norton released Beasley's first memoir, *Don't Kill the Birthday Girl*. This memoir is about Beasley real-life experiences as a woman with severe food allergies. These allergies are severe enough that Beasley has had more than her fair share of fatal close calls.

However, Beasley doesn't let her allergies keep her from hitting the road, which is what she's been doing most recently. "For the last two years," says Beasley, "I have toured extensively in support of my books—a pursuit that, ironically, makes it very hard to develop the next book-length project. E-mails, blogging, and freelance pieces take up too many hours of the day. But travel has its own rewards, and I have welcomed the opportunity to glimpse the literary communities anchored by colleges, bookstores, and reading series across the country.

"In particular, my heart has been claimed by Square Books in Oxford, Mississippi, which I first visited as the Ole Miss Summer Poet in Residence in 2010. I've been spending time down there ever since, and I hope to use those experiences as a backdrop for the poems that make up my third collection. I'm also doing a lot of personal grounding—deepening friendships, learning to cook, slowing down and looking at the world around me. It's as Eudora Welty says: 'It's living that makes me want to write, not reading…'"

While in Mississippi, Beasley took a few hours to answer the following questions.

Your most recent book, Don't Kill the Birthday Girl, is a memoir about living your life with food allergies that could possibly end your life. How did you go about getting the book accepted for publication?

I was fortunate to meet my agent, Glen Hartley of Writers' Representatives, through the Maureen Egen Exchange Award offered by *Poets & Writers*. The award is given by genre and by state of residence, so I was the 2008 winner for poetry on behalf of Washington, DC. That meant I was given the opportunity to travel to New York City and meet with a "wish list" of those in the publishing industry. During our meeting, and knowing of prose work I'd been doing for the *Washington Post Magazine*, Glen encouraged me to use my firsthand experience with food allergies to work up a plan for a nonfiction book.

The arc of submitting to Writers' Reps, signing with them, meeting with a few different editors in New York, and ultimately selling the book to Crown, all took place in three or maybe four weeks.

When an agent tells you he's interested in an idea, it's a no-brainer: you give that idea a try. Hammering out a proposal, sample chapter, and outline was an arduous process that took several months and lots of fumbling around online, looking for useful models. But the process of actually selling the book was mercifully fast. The arc of submitting to Writers' Reps, signing with them, meeting with a few different editors in New York, and ultimately selling the book to Crown, all took place in three or maybe four weeks. By six months later I'd quit my job as an editor. It's amazing how quickly one's career path can swerve in a new direction.

In the 2012 Poet's Market, you actually wrote a piece for me on making things up in poetry. Did you find it difficult to really bare everything—the good and the bad—in your memoir?

Who says I bared everything in the memoir? All good writing requires discretion. It's true that I reveal quite a bit about myself, from the ways in which allergies have twisted my self-image to the embarrassing physical dimensions of a reaction. I'm not shy, and I

Beasley is a double threat, writing poetry and nonfiction.

prize the blunt honesty that goes hand-in-hand with humor. That said, I had no interest in exposing my family and loved ones to that same level of scrutiny, so in that way it is not a traditional memoir. This book did not need to be about trotting all the skeletons out of the closet and making them dance. I had too many other interesting threads to follow into the realms of science, pop culture, and food history.

Have your food allergies ever interrupted or affected your writing life?

Food allergies affect every aspect of my life. I wish I could claim Benadryl-induced genius, but the reality is a lot more banal. When traveling for my writing, whether doing research or giving readings, I struggle with the loss of control over my diet. I have to choose between falling into a rut of safe but unappetizing, unhealthy options—a diet of French fries and limp house salads—or working with unfamiliar hosts and restaurants to create a "Sandra-friendly" meal on the fly. Sometimes the latter results in a thrilling taste of regional cuisine. Sometimes the latter results in a trip to the emergency room.

I first discovered your writing through poetry and your most recent collection, I Was the Jukebox, won the 2009 Barnard Women Poets Prize. How do you juggle working on poetry with handling prose? Or is it just whatever comes, comes?

Most writers working in two genres have an instinctive feel for pairing their inspiration with their mode. I began writing prose because some topics that interested me required too much personal or academic back story to examine in poem form. I approach poetry as a space for surreal and philosophical leaps; my prose tends to be researched, conversational, and anchored by firsthand narrative.

What I'm reading primes my productivity to get to work in one or the other genre. When I wake up in the morning and browse the New York Times over breakfast, it puts me in the mindset for prose. If I'm reading poetry (and lots of it, as I tend to do at art colonies), I write more poetry.

You maintain a blog called Chicks Dig Poetry. Do you have any sort of strategy to your blogging?

Strategies are a slippery and sometimes corrosive force in blogging. To me, a blog with a strategy is primarily serving a publicity purpose—or functioning as a trial run for a book project—and no matter how rich the content, I often lose interest because there is no element of surprise. I'm drawn to blogs that serve as a quirky hub of interests, opinions, and confessions belonging to a singular voice (particularly if that voice belongs to an artist I admire). As for "Chicks Dig Poetry," whether I'm offering a report from a recent literary conference, or an ode to DC life, or the video of a favorite TED Talk, or a midnight complaint about a bad allergic reaction, I hope it's that organic range and authenticity that draws people to my blog.

When I'm planning a trip, I look to see if there are neighboring spots within a four-hour drive that might be interested in a visit, and then I use the local literary calendars to figure out whom to query. My needs are modest: a couch to crash on, a fellow writer to visit with, a chance to sell a few books.

It seems like you're always reading somewhere. First question, how do you find all these events to attend?

The truth is that it's a constant hustle—sending lots of emails, being quick and flexible in my replies, saying "yes" whenever possible, and giving a hell of a good reading if I get the opportunity. I host and attend numerous events in Washington, DC, which means I'm developing a network of knowing those who host and give readings in other towns. When I'm planning a trip, I look to see if there are neighboring spots within a four-hour drive that might be interested in a visit, and then I use the local literary calendars to figure out whom to query. My needs are modest: a couch to crash on, a fellow writer to visit with, a chance to sell a few books. I just have to keep the faith in a cumulative payoff, even after a low turnout or fiscally unjustifiable night (and I've had a few).

Second question, do you have any reading or presentation tips you can share with other less experienced writers?

My comments will be specific to poets, since most of what I've given to date is poetry readings. Some readers plow through poem after poem without pause during their sets, either as a matter of nervousness or as a matter of principle, as if to say "My poem should live or die as a standalone text, without surrounding explanation." That's unfair to your audience. As readers, we have the luxury of letting our eye travel up and down the page, revisiting earlier sections and appreciating visual form. As listeners, we only get the one auditory exposure. Why not prepare us? So I suggest writers offer a small anecdote—no more than a minute in length—about the inspiration or technique of each poem before reading it. Mystery is a valuable thing, but not at the expense of losing the room.

Think about which words or breaks can be emphasized in a way that clarifies meaning during the reading. Take a deep breath. Take another one. Slow down. Practice reading at home, so that you're comfortable enough with the text that you can look up to make occasional eye contact with the crowd. Project. Err on the side of reading one poem too few, not one poem too many. And for goodness sakes, please choose and mark your poems in advance. That gratuitous shuffling-of-papers shtick makes everyone antsy.

Have you found that travel helps or hinders your writing? Or just send it in new directions?

In the long term, I have faith that these new landscapes will add depth and variety to my writing. As a nonfiction writer, every day I stumble across stories—snippets of cultural history—that sow the seeds of freelance articles or perhaps even my next book. As a poet, the flora and fauna and vernacular of each place add texture to my work. The trick is to cut myself some slack in the short term, while on the road. Travel is a brutalizing force on the ritualized schedule and unfettered time that I crave as a writer.

You are now a full-time writer. What does this mean for you, and how has it changed your life?

Like so many writers, I fell in love with writing thinking that it equated to quiet afternoons in solitude. But one can reach a stage where being a writer necessitates a heavy amount of social ambassadorship. It's not solely about what's on the page; being a "full-time writer" includes giving readings, attending conferences, mentoring emerging writers, developing a set of philosophies on craft, and engaging in the critical conversation about publishing. Not to mention saving every last receipt and stub for the Schedule C. I'm thrilled to be up to the job, but let's be clear—it is a job, and requires as much diligence and as many to-do lists as anything else that has the power to keep a roof over one's head. It's a gift, it's a calling, it's a way of life, but it's also a job.

This may be a fleeting thing, this life. In two years I could be back in an office, especially if I get the opportunity for hands-on leadership with an arts organization or nonprofit, or as an editor at a magazine. Part of me thrives on that detail work, and there would be undeniable perks—guaranteed health insurance, a retirement plan, access to an industrial-strength copy machine. I miss those things. But for now, I'm where I need to be.

If you could share only one piece of advice with writers, regardless of genre, what would it be?

Don't be afraid of first drafts that are dark, convoluted, or painful. That's probably what your soul most needs to write. Time and good edits can distill and untangle, but time and good edits—even the best edits—cannot compensate for what you do not give yourself permission to write in the first place. Write it! Write it now. Write it all.

JESSICA McCANN:

All Different Kinds of Freelancing

·····························

by Robert Lee Brewer

Bell Bridge Books recently released Jessica McCann's debut novel, *All Different Kinds of Free*. However, McCann didn't quit her day job, which is fine, because she's a professional freelance writer. It's not always easy, but then again, freelancing usually never is.

Of her current schedule, McCann says, "I continue to work as a professional freelance writer and am working on my second novel, another historical. At the same time, I am figuring out how to layer in the additional work required as a debut novelist. A lot of time and effort goes into promoting a published book and nurturing new relationships. A fellow debut author, Laura Munson, recently marveled on Twitter that it's not until after you give birth to your 'book baby' that the real push begins. It made me laugh, because I'm finding it's really true."

In addition to the fiction writing, McCann's reporting and creative nonfiction has appeared in a variety of magazines, including *Business Week, The Writer, Phoenix, Raising Arizona Kids* and *ASU Research* to name a few. Many corporations, universities and nonprofit organizations also tap her to write and edit dynamic communications materials.

McCann recently took a few moments out of her freelancing frenzy to answer the following questions.

Your debut novel, All Different Kinds of Free, was recently released by Bell Bridge Books. How did you sell your novel?

I set about the task of traditional publishing pretty much the old-fashioned way. That began with researching the market, my genre, recent releases, who was publishing what, who was selling what. With a list of about 40 agents who seemed to be a good fit for my book, I sent out query letters and sample chapters 10 to 12 agents at a time. I was fortunate to receive several requests for full reads and several lovely rejections (only a few snarky ones). Then came the call from the Sandra Dijkstra Literary Agency. I had representation, and I was ecstatic. Then the whole process began anew, except that it was my agent who was doing all the research and pitching, while I waited with fingers crossed. When we received an offer from Bell Bridge Books in October 2010, everything suddenly moved very quickly. They loved the book and wanted to fast-track it to release in April 2011, the 150th year anniversary of the Civil War.

The novel already won multiple awards before publication by Bell Bridge Books. What has that experience been like?

That early recognition was so important to my motivation and self-esteem as I chipped away at the manuscript. As a work-in-progress, the novel received semi-finalist nods from the Dana Awards and the William Faulkner-William Wisdom Creative Writing competition. Then it was named a finalist in the Freedom in Fiction prize, and I was given one year to complete the manuscript for grand prize consideration. Each of those nods encouraged me and pushed me to keep writing, revising and sharing my work. Writing a novel, particularly your first novel, is so daunting. It really doesn't take much to derail you. By the time I had completed the novel, winning the Freedom in Fiction prize was truly the icing on the cake. Just knowing that someone, somewhere had already read my novel and liked it made it a little easier to steel myself against the inevitable rejection that comes from agents and editors in the quest to publish.

The novel is inspired by a true story and is historical fiction. Could you explain how (or if) you went about researching your novel?

I really enjoy the research phase of writing. That's often what fuels my creativity, whether I'm writing fiction or nonfiction. Conducting interviews, digging through article archives and books at the library, searching online for little-known facts and resources, watching documentaries—it's a process that helps ideas form in my head, helps me arrange the pieces of my story to create the picture I want my readers to see. *All Different Kinds of Free* was inspired actual events, and so quite a bit of research was needed to write it.

What has been the most surprising part of the book publishing process?

Probably the most surprising part has been how many different aspects there are to it and how hard it is to keep pace with changes in the industry. From big New York publishers, small presses and self-publishing, to hardcover books, trade paperbacks and multiple ebooks, just as much research goes into how to publish a book as it does in writing one. Do you need an agent? How do sales and promotions pan out? Must you have a

McCann may have first made her mark writing freelance nonfiction, but her award-winning novel proves she has fiction chops as well.

so-called platform before you publish? And the list goes on. So it came as a bit of a surprise how much *more* I still have to learn, even though I already had been a published nonfiction writer. Sometimes I think I'll always feel like a novice in this business.

What sort of promotion (if any) have you done for the novel so far?

Because of my professional background in marketing and communications, I actually put together a fairly detailed promotion plan. It addressed pre-release buzz, launch publicity and post-release promotions. I reached out to local media and my social networks. My agent sent advance copies to the major reviewers. And my publisher reached out to independent bookstores, book bloggers and libraries. So promotion has been, and continues to be, a real team effort.

You write communications materials for universities, nonprofit organizations, and other businesses. How did you break into this writing?

I've worked at least part-time as a freelance writer since I was 17 years old. A few years out of high school I landed a full-time job in communications, then as editor of a regional business magazine and finally editor for a custom-book publisher. To make extra money and build up my portfolio, I continued to freelance on the side, mostly by querying magazine editors with story ideas. In 1998, I quit my editing job to freelance full time, which is when I really diversified my writing services to include more communications and marketing work. I've built my business and broken into new markets and industries mostly through one-on-one networking and referrals from past employers and existing clients.

You write freelance nonfiction as well. How do you juggle and prioritize your different writing projects?

My nonfiction writing took top priority for a many years, mostly for economic reasons. When I take on a new nonfiction writing project, I know exactly what is expected and I know I will get paid for it. Fiction is more of a craps shoot. I really only started dabbling with fiction as a way to breathe new life into my nonfiction work, to flex my creative muscles and work my brain in a different way. Once I realized how much I love writing fiction, I found myself scheming for ways to work more of it into my day-to-day writing life. And I keep scheming, especially now that I know I can actually earn some money for my fiction. So the juggling continues and the priorities are in a constant state of flux.

Does the act of nonfiction writing influence your fiction or vice versa?

Very much so. Good fiction writing isn't a whole heck of a lot different than good nonfiction writing. Being efficient with the language, using vivid imagery, telling a compelling story—these are universal to good writing, regardless of the genre. Fiction writing encouraged me to get more creative with my nonfiction; and nonfiction writing encouraged me to be more authentic with my fiction. It's symbiotic.

You have a nice website and more writers are building their followings online. Could you share your online strategy?

Thank you! My website has been another work in progress for me over the past decade or so. It started off as a fairly static site, more of an online portfolio and resume for prospective freelance clients to review. As social media has come of age, my site has also evolved. I've made a conscious decision not to blog (mostly because I don't have the time to consistently post relevant and valuable content). Yet, I've found other ways to keep my site fresh with a live Twitter feed (I guess you could call me a micro-blogger) and with pages like "Books I Love" and "Stuff for Writers" that I update and build upon every month or so.

If you could share only one piece of advice with other writers, what would it be?

Make sure you are writing what you love. Don't allow yourself to become too tempted by hot new literary trends or even big-money corporate-writing contracts. Making the time to write, keeping the motivation alive, weathering the rejection—those are the hardest parts of living a writer's life. Why add to that burden by writing only what others tell you to write? Make sure you are writing something you love.

PROFESSIONAL ORGANIZATIONS

///

AGENTS' ORGANIZATIONS

ASSOCIATION OF AUTHORS' AGENTS (AAA), David Higham Associates Ltd, 5-8 Lower John Street, Golden Square, London W1F 9HA . (020) 7434 5900. E-mail: anthonygoff@david-higham.co.uk. Website: www.agentsassoc.co.uk.

ASSOCIATION OF AUTHORS' REPRESENTATIVES (AAR). E-mail: info@aar-online.org. Website: www.aar-online.org.

ASSOCIATION OF TALENT AGENTS (ATA), 9255 Sunset Blvd., Suite 930, Los Angeles CA 90069. (310)274-0628. Fax: (310)274-5063. E-mail: shellie@agentassociation.com. Website: www. agentassociation.com.

WRITERS' ORGANIZATIONS

ACADEMY OF AMERICAN POETS 584 Broadway, Suite 604, New York NY 10012-5243. (212)274-0343. Fax: (212)274-9427. E-mail: academy@poets.org. Website: www.poets.org.

AMERICAN CRIME WRITERS LEAGUE (ACWL), 17367 Hilltop Ridge Dr., Eureka MO 63205. Website: www.acwl.org.

AMERICAN INDEPENDENT WRITERS (AIW), 1001 Connecticut Ave. NW, Suite 701, Washington DC 20036. (202)775-5150. Fax: (202)775-5810. E-mail: info@aiwriters.org. Website: www.americanindependentwriters.org.

AMERICAN MEDICAL WRITERS ASSOCIATION (AMWA), 30 West Gude Drive, Suite 525, Rockville MD 20850-4347. (301)294-5303. Fax: (301)294-9006. E-mail: amwa@amwa.org. Website: www.amwa.org.

AMERICAN SCREENWRITERS ASSOCIATION (ASA), 269 S. Beverly Dr., Suite 2600, Beverly Hills CA 90212-3807. (866)265-9091. E-mail: asa@goasa.com. Website: www.asascreenwriters.com.

AMERICAN TRANSLATORS ASSOCIATION (ATA), 225 Reinekers Lane, Suite 590, Alexandria VA 22314. (703)683-6100. Fax: (703)683-6122. E-mail: ata@atanet.org. Website: www.atanet.org.

EDUCATION WRITERS ASSOCIATION (EWA), 2122 P St., NW Suite 201, Washington DC 20037. (202)452-9830. Fax: (202)452-9837. E-mail: ewa@ewa.org. Website: www.ewa.org.

GARDEN WRITERS ASSOCIATION (GWA), 10210 Leatherleaf Ct., Manassas VA 20111. (703)257-1032. Fax: (703)257-0213. E-mail: info@gardenwriters.org. Website: www.gardenwriters.org.

HORROR WRITERS ASSOCIATION (HWA), 244 5th Ave., Suite 2767, New York NY 10001. E-mail: hwa@horror.org. Website: www.horror.org.

THE INTERNATIONAL WOMEN'S WRITING GUILD (IWWG),P.O. Box 810, Gracie Station, New York NY 10028-0082. (212)737-7536. Fax: (212)737-9469. E-mail: dirhahn@aol.org. Website: www.iwwg.com.

MYSTERY WRITERS OF AMERICA (MWA), 1140 Broadway, Suite 1507, New York NY 10001. (212)888-8171. Fax: (212)888-8107. E-mail: mwa@mysterywriters.org. Website: www.mysterywriters.org.

NATIONAL ASSOCIATION OF SCIENCE WRITERS (NASW), P.O. Box 7905, Berkeley, CA 94707. (510)647-9500. E-mail: LFriedmann@nasw.org. website: www.nasw.org.

NATIONAL ASSOCIATION OF WOMEN WRITERS (NAWW), 24165 IH-10 W., Suite 217-637, San Antonio TX 78257. Phone/Fax: (866)821-5829. Website: www.naww.org.

ORGANIZATION OF BLACK SCREENWRITERS (OBS). Golden State Mutual Life Insurance Bldg., 1999 West Adams Blvd., Rm. Mezzanine Los Angeles, CA 90018. Website: www.obswriter.com.

OUTDOOR WRITERS ASSOCIATION OF AMERICA (OWAA), 121 Hickory St., Suite 1, Missoula MT 59801. (406)728-7434. Fax: (406)728-7445. E-mail: krhoades@owaa.org. Website: www.owaa.org.

POETRY SOCIETY OF AMERICA (PSA), 15 Gramercy Park, New York NY 10003. (212)254-9628. website: www.poetrysociety.org. Poets & Writers, 90 Broad St., Suite 2100, New York NY 10004. (212)226-3586. Fax: (212)226-3963. Website: www.pw.org.

ROMANCE WRITERS OF AMERICA (RWA), 114615 Benfer Road, Houston TX 77069. (832)717-5200. Fax: (832)717-5201. E-mail: info@rwanational.org. Website: www.rwanational.org.

SCIENCE FICTION AND FANTASY WRITERS OF AMERICA (SFWA), P.O. Box 877, Chestertown MD 21620. E-mail: execdir@sfwa.org. Website: www.sfwa.org.

SOCIETY OF AMERICAN BUSINESS EDITORS & WRITERS (SABEW), University of Missouri, School of Journalism, 30 Neff Annex, Columbia MO 65211. (602) 496-7862. E-mail: sabew@sabew.org. Website: www.sabew.org.

SOCIETY OF AMERICAN TRAVEL WRITERS (SATW), 7044 S. 13 St., Oak Creek WI 53154. (414)908-4949. Fax: (414)768-8001. E-mail: satw@satw.org. Website: www.satw.org.

SOCIETY OF CHILDREN'S BOOK WRITERS & ILLUSTRATORS (SCBWI), 8271 Beverly Blvd., Los Angeles CA 90048. (323)782-1010. Fax: (323)782-1892. E-mail: scbwi@scbwi.org. Website: www.scbwi.org.

WESTERN WRITERS OF AMERICA (WWA). E-mail: spiritfire@kc.rr.com. Website: www.westernwriters.org.

INDUSTRY ORGANIZATIONS

AMERICAN BOOKSELLERS ASSOCIATION (ABA), 200 White Plains Rd., Suite 600, Tarrytown NY 10591. (914)591-2665. Fax: (914)591-2720. E-mail: info@bookweb.org. Website: www.bookweb.org.

AMERICAN SOCIETY OF JOURNALISTS & AUTHORS (ASJA), 1501 Broadway, Suite 302, New York NY 10036. (212)997-0947. Fax: (212)937-2315. E-mail: director@asja.org. Website: www.asja.org.

ASSOCIATION FOR WOMEN IN COMMUNICATIONS (AWC), 3337 Duke St., Alexandria VA 22314. (703)370-7436. Fax: (703)342-4311. E-mail: info@womcom.org. Website: www.womcom.org.

ASSOCIATION OF AMERICAN PUBLISHERS (AAP), 71 5th Ave., 2nd Floor, New York NY 10003. (212)255-0200. Fax: (212)255-7007. Or, 50 F St. NW, Suite 400, Washington DC 20001. (202)347-3375. Fax: (202)347-3690. Website: www.publishers.org.

THE ASSOCIATION OF WRITERS & WRITING PROGRAMS (AWP), Mail Stop 1E3, George Mason University, Fairfax VA 22030. (703)993-4301. Fax: (703)993-4302. E-mail: services@awp-writer.org. website: www.awpwriter.org.

THE AUTHORS GUILD, INC., 31 E. 32nd St., 7th Floor, New York NY 10016. (212)563-5904. Fax: (212)564-5363. E-mail: staff@authorsguild.org. website: www.authorsguild.org.

CANADIAN AUTHORS ASSOCIATION (CAA), P.O. Box 581, Stn. Main Orilla ON L3V 6K5 Canada. (705)653-0323. Fax: (705)653-0593. E-mail: admin@canauthors.org. Website: www.canauthors.org.

CHRISTIAN BOOKSELLERS ASSOCIATION (CBA), P.O. Box 62000, Colorado Springs CO 80962-2000. (800)252-1950. Fax: (719)272-3510. E-mail: info@cbaonline.org. website: www.cba-online.org.

THE DRAMATISTS GUILD OF AMERICA, 1501 Broadway, Suite 701, New York NY 10036. (212)398-9366. Fax: (212)944-0420. Website: www.dramatistsguild.com.

NATIONAL LEAGUE OF AMERICAN PEN WOMEN (NLAPW), 1300 17th St. NW, Washington DC 20036-1973. (202)785-1997. Fax: (202)452-8868. E-mail: nlapw1@verizon.net. Website: www.americanpenwomen.org.

NATIONAL WRITERS ASSOCIATION (NWA), 10940 S. Parker Rd., #508, Parker CO 80134. (303)841-0246. Fax: (303)841-2607. E-mail: natlwritersassn@hotmail.com. Website: www.nationalwriters.com

NATIONAL WRITERS UNION (NWU), 256 West 38th Street, Suite 703, New York, NY 10018. (212)254-0279. Fax: (212)254-0673. E-mail: nwu@nwu.org. Website: www.nwu.org.

PEN AMERICAN CENTER, 588 Broadway, Suite 303, New York NY 10012-3225. (212)334-1660. Fax: (212)334-2181. E-mail: pen@pen.org. Website: www.pen.org.

THE PLAYWRIGHTS GUILD OF CANADA (PGC), 215 Spadina Ave., Suite #210, Toronto ON M5T 2C7 Canada. (416)703-0201. Fax: (416)703-0059. E-mail: info@playwrightsguild.ca. Website: www.playwrightsguild.com.

VOLUNTEER LAWYERS FOR THE ARTS (VLA), One E. 53rd St., 6th Floor, New York NY 10022. (212)319-2787. Fax: (212)752-6575. Website: www.vlany.org.

WOMEN IN FILM (WIF), 6100 Wilshire Blvd., Suite 710, Los Angeles CA 90048. (323)935-2211. Fax: (323)935-2212. E-mail: info@wif.org. Website: www.wif.org.

WOMEN'S NATIONAL BOOK ASSOCIATION (WNBA), P.O. Box 237, FDR Station, New York NY 10150. (212)208-4629. Fax: (212)208-4629. E-mail: publicity@bookbuzz.com. Website: www.wnba-books.org.

WRITERS GUILD OF ALBERTA (WGA), 11759 Groat Rd., Edmonton AB T5M 3K6 Canada. (780)422-8174. Fax: (780)422-2663. E-mail: mail@writersguild.ab.ca. Website: writersguild.ab.ca.

WRITERS GUILD OF AMERICA-EAST (WGA), 555 W. 57th St., Suite 1230, New York NY 10019. (212)767-7800. Fax: (212)582-1909. e-mail: info@wgaeast.org. Website: www.wgaeast.org.

WRITERS GUILD OF AMERICA-WEST (WGA), 7000 W. Third St., Los Angeles CA 90048. (323)951-4000. Fax: (323)782-4800. Website: www.wga.org.

WRITERS UNION OF CANADA (TWUC), 90 Richmond St. E., Suite 200, Toronto ON M5C 1P1 Canada. (416)703-8982. Fax: (416)504-9090. E-mail: info@writersunion.ca. Website: www.writersunion.ca.

GLOSSARY

#10 ENVELOPE. A standard, business-size envelope.

ADVANCE. A sum of money a publisher pays a writer prior to the publication of a book. It is usually paid in installments, such as one-half on signing the contract; one-half on delivery of a complete and satisfactory manuscript.

AGENT. A liaison between a writer and editor or publisher. An agent shops a manuscript around, receiving a commission when the manuscript is accepted. Agents usually take a 10-15% fee from the advance and royalties.

ARC. Advance reader copy.

ASSIGNMENT. Editor asks a writer to produce a specific article for an agreed-upon fee.

AUCTION. Publishers sometimes bid for the acquisition of a book manuscript that has excellent sales prospects. The bids are for the amount of the author's advance, advertising and promotional expenses, royalty percentage, etc. Auctions are conducted by agents.

AVANT-GARDE. Writing that is innovative in form, style, or subject.

BACKLIST. A publisher's list of its books that were not published during the current season, but that are still in print.

BIMONTHLY. Every two months.

BIO. A sentence or brief paragraph about the writer; can include education and work experience.

BIWEEKLY. Every two weeks.

BLOG. Short for weblog. Used by writers to build platform by posting regular commentary, observations, poems, tips, etc.

BLURB. The copy on paperback book covers or hard cover book dust jackets, either promoting the book and the author or featuring testimonials from book reviewers or well-known people in the book's field. Also called flap copy or jacket copy.

BOILERPLATE. A standardized contract.

BOUND GALLEYS. A prepublication edition of a book, usually prepared from photocopies of the final galley proofs; also known as ``bound proofs.'' Designed for promotional purposes, bound galleys serve as the first set of review copies to be mailed out.

BYLINE. Name of the author appearing with the published piece.

CATEGORY FICTION. A term used to include all types of fiction.

CHAPBOOK. A small bookletΔusually paperbackΔof poetry, ballads or tales.

CIRCULATION. The number of subscribers to a magazine.

CLIPS. Samples, usually from newspapers or magazines, of a writer's published work.

COFFEE-TABLE BOOK. An heavily illustrated oversize book.

COMMERCIAL NOVELS. Novels designed to appeal to a broad audience. These are often broken down into categories such as western, mystery and romance. See also genre.

CONTRIBUTOR'S COPIES. Copies of the issues of magazines sent to the author in which the author's work appears.

CO-PUBLISHING. Arrangement where author and publisher share publications costs and profits of a book. Also known as cooperative publishing.

COPYEDITING. Editing a manuscript for grammar, punctuation, printing style and factual accuracy.

COPYRIGHT. A means to protect an author's work. See ``Minding the Details'' for more information.

COVER LETTER. A brief letter that accompanies the manuscript being sent to and agent or editor.

CREATIVE NONFICTION. Nonfictional writing that uses an innovative approach to the subject and creative language.

CRITIQUING SERVICE. Am editing service in which writers pay a fee for comments on the salability or other qualities of their manuscript. Fees vary, as do the quality of the critiques.

CV. Curriculum vita. A brief listing of qualifications and career accomplishments.

ELECTRONIC RIGHTS. Secondary or subsidiary rights dealing with electronic/multimedia formats (i.e., the Internet, CD-ROMs, electronic magazines).

ELECTRONIC SUBMISSION. A submission made by modem or on computer disk.

EROTICA. Fiction or art that is sexually oriented.

EVALUATION FEES. Fees an agent may charge to evaluate material. The extent and quality of this evaluation varies, but comments usually concern the salability of the manuscript.

FAIR USE. A provision of the copyright law that says short passages from copyrighted material may be used without infringing on the owner's rights.

FEATURE. An article giving the reader information of human interest rather than news.

FILLER. A short item used by an editor to "fill" out a newspaper column or magazine page. It could be a joke, an anecdote, etc.

FILM RIGHTS. Rights sold or optioned by the agent/author to a person in the film industry, enabling the book to be made into a movie.

FOREIGN RIGHTS. Translation or reprint rights to be sold abroad.

FRONTLIST. A publisher's list of books that are new to the current season.

GALLEYS. The first typeset version of a manuscript that has not yet been divided into pages.

GENRE. Refers either to a general classification of writing, such as the novel or the poem, or to the categories within those classifications, such as the problem novel or the sonnet.

GHOSTWRITER. A writer who puts into literary form an article, speech, story or book based on another person's ideas or knowledge.

GRAPHIC NOVEL. A story in graphic form, long comic strip, or heavily illustrated story; of 40 pages or more.

HI-LO. A type of fiction that offers a high level of interest for readers at a low reading level.

HIGH CONCEPT. A story idea easily expressed in a quick, one-line description.

HONORARIUM. Token payment--small amount of money, or a byline and copies of the publication.

HOOK. Aspect of the work that sets it apart from others and draws in the reader/viewer.

HOW-TO. Books and magazine articles offering a combination of information and advice in describing how something can be accomplished.

IMPRINT. Name applied to a publisher's specific line of books.

JOINT CONTRACT. A legal agreement between a publisher and two or more authors, establishing provisions for the division of royalties the book generates.

KILL FEE. Fee for a complete article that was assigned and then cancelled.

LEAD TIME. The time between the acquisition of a manuscript by an editor and its actual publication.

LITERARY FICTION. The general category of serious, non-formulaic, intelligent fiction.

MAINSTREAM FICTION. Fiction that transcends popular novel categories such as mystery, romance and science fiction.

MARKETING FEE. Fee charged by some agents to cover marketing expenses. It may be used to cover postage, telephone calls, faxes, photocopying or any other expense incurred in marketing a manuscript.

MASS MARKET. Non-specialized books of wide appeal directed toward a large audience.

MEMOIR. A narrative recounting a writer's (or fictional narrator's) personal or family history; specifics may be altered, though essentially considered nonfiction.

MIDDLE GRADE OR MID-GRADE. The general classification of books written for readers approximately ages 9-11. Also called middle readers.

MIDLIST. Those titles on a publisher's list that are not expected to be big sellers, but are expected to have limited/modest sales.

MODEL RELEASE. A paper signed by the subject of a photograph giving the photographer permission to use the photograph.

MULTIPLE CONTRACT. Book contract with an agreement for a future book(s).

MULTIPLE SUBMISSIONS. Sending more than one book or article idea to a publisher at the same time.

NARRATIVE NONFICTION. A narrative presentation of actual events.

NET ROYALTY. A royalty payment based on the amount of money a book publisher receives on the sale of a book after booksellers' discounts, special sales discounts and returns.

NOVELLA. A short novel, or a long short story; approximately 7,000 to 15,000 words.

ON SPEC. An editor expresses an interest in a proposed article idea and agrees to consider the finished piece for publication "on speculation." The editor is under no obligation to buy the finished manuscript.

ONE-TIME RIGHTS. Rights allowing a manuscript to be published one time. The work can be sold again by the writer without violating the contract.

OPTION CLAUSE. A contract clause giving a publisher the right to publish an author's next book.

PAYMENT ON ACCEPTANCE. The editor sends you a check for your article, story or poem as soon as he decides to publish it.

PAYMENT ON PUBLICATION. The editor doesn't send you a check for your material until it is published.

PEN NAME. The use of a name other than your legal name on articles, stories or books. Also called a pseudonym.

PHOTO FEATURE. Feature in which the emphasis is on the photographs rather than on accompanying written material.

PICTURE BOOK. A type of book aimed at preschoolers to 8-year-olds that tells a story using a combination of text and artwork, or artwork only.

PLATFORM. A writer's speaking experience, interview skills, website and other abilities which help form a following of potential buyers for that author's book.

POD. Print on demand.

PROOFREADING. Close reading and correction of a manuscript's typographical errors.

PROPOSAL. A summary of a proposed book submitted to a publisher, particularly used for nonfiction manuscripts. A proposal often contains an individualized cover letter, one-page overview of the book, marketing information, competitive books, author information, chapter-by-chapter outline, and two to three sample chapters.

QUERY. A letter that sells an idea to an editor or agent. Usually a query is brief (no more than one page) and uses attention-getting prose.

REMAINDERS. Copies of a book that are slow to sell and can be purchased from the publisher at a reduced price.

REPORTING TIME. The time it takes for an editor to report to the author on his/her query or manuscript.

REPRINT RIGHTS. The rights to republish a book after its initial printing.

ROYALTIES, STANDARD HARDCOVER BOOK. 10 percent of the retail price on the first 5,000 copies sold; 121/2 percent on the next 5,000; 15 percent thereafter.

ROYALTIES, STANDARD MASS PAPERBACK BOOK. 4-8 percent of the retail price on the first 150,000 copies sold.

ROYALTIES, STANDARD TRADE PAPERBACK BOOK. No less than 6 percent of list price on the first 20,000 copies; 71/2 percent thereafter.

SASE. Self-addressed, stamped envelope; should be included with all correspondence.

SELF-PUBLISHING. In this arrangement the author pays for manufacturing, production and marketing of his book and keeps all income derived from the book sales.

SEMIMONTHLY. Twice per month.

SEMIWEEKLY. Twice per week.

SERIAL. Published periodically, such as a newspaper or magazine.

SERIAL FICTION. Fiction published in a magazine in installments, often broken off at a suspenseful spot.

SERIAL RIGHTS. The right for a newspaper or magazine to publish sections of a manuscript.

SHORT-SHORT. A complete short story of 1,500 words.

SIDEBAR. A feature presented as a companion to a straight news report (or main magazine article) giving sidelights on human-interest aspects or sometimes elucidating just one aspect of the story.

SIMULTANEOUS SUBMISSIONS. Sending the same article, story or poem to several publishers at the same time. Some publishers refuse to consider such submissions.

SLANT. The approach or style of a story or article that will appeal to readers of a specific magazine.

SLICE-OF-LIFE VIGNETTE. A short fiction piece intended to realistically depict an interesting moment of everyday living.

SLUSH PILE. The stack of unsolicited or misdirected manuscripts received by an editor or book publisher.

SOCIAL NETWORKS. Websites that connect users: sometimes generally, other times around specific interests. Four popular ones at the moment are MySpace, Facebook, Twitter and LinkedIn.

SUBAGENT. An agent handling certain subsidiary rights, usually working in conjuction with the agent who handled the book rights. The percentage paid the book agent is increased to pay the subagent.

SUBSIDIARY RIGHTS. All right other than book publishing rights included in a book publishing contract, such as paperback rights, book club rights and movie rights. Part of an agent's job is to negotiate those rights and advise you on which to sell and which to keep. For more information, read "Minding the Details."

SUBSIDY PUBLISHER. A book publisher who charges the author for the cost to typeset and print his book, the jacket, etc., as opposed to a royalty publisher who pays the author.

SYNOPSIS. A brief summary of a story, novel or play. As part of a book proposal, it is a comprehensive summary condensed in a page or page and a half, single-spaced.

TABLOID. Newspaper format publication on about half the size of the regular newspaper page.

TEARSHEET. Page from a magazine or newspaper containing your printed story, article, poem or ad.

TOC. Table of Contents.

TRADE BOOK. Either a hardcover or softcover book; subject matter frequently concerns a special interest for a general audience; sold mainly in bookstores.

TRADE PAPERBACK. A soft-bound volume, usually around 5X8, published and designed for the general public; available mainly in bookstores.

TRANSLATION RIGHTS. Sold to a foreign agent or foreign publisher.

UNSOLICITED MANUSCRIPT. A story, article, poem or book that an editor did not specifically ask to see.

YA. Young adult books.

LITERARY AGENTS

The literary agencies listed in this section are members of the Association of Authors' Representatives (AAR), which means they do not charge for reading, critiquing or editing. Some agents in this section may charge clients for office expenses. Make sure you have a clear understanding of what these expenses are before signing any agency agreement.

FOR MORE...

The *2012 Guide to Literary Agents* (Writer's Digest Books) offers more than 600 literary agents, as well as information on writers conferences. It also offers a wealth of information on the author/agent relationship and other related topics. Below are explanations of the agent listing subheads.

MEMBER AGENTS Agencies comprised of more than one agent list member agents and to help you determine the most appropriate person for your query letter.

REPRESENTS Here agencies specify what nonfiction and fiction subjects they consider.

HOW TO CONTACT In this section agents specify the type of material they want to receive, how they want to receive it, and how long you should wait for their response.

TERMS Provided here are details of an agent's commission, whether a contract is offered, and any additional office expenses. Standard commissions range from 10-15 percent for domestic sales, and 15-20 percent for foreign or dramatic sales.

❶ 2M COMMUNICATIONS, LTD.

33 W. 17 St., PH, New York NY 10011. (212)741-1509. Fax: (212)691-4460. E-mail: morel@2mcommunications. com. Website: www.2mcommunications.com. **Contact:** Madeleine Morel. Member of AAR. Represents 100 clients. 20% of clients are new/unpublished writers. Currently handles: nonfiction books 100%.

○ Prior to becoming an agent, Ms. Morel worked at a publishing company.

REPRESENTS Nonfiction books. **Considers these nonfiction areas:** autobiography, biography, child guidance, cooking, cultural interests, diet/nutrition, ethnic, foods, health, history, medicine, music, parenting, self-help, women's issues, women's studies, cookbooks.

⚷ This agency specializes in exclusively and non-exclusively representing professional ghostwriters and collaborators. This agency's writers have penned multiple bestsellers. They work closely with other leading literary agents and editors whose high-profile authors require confidential associations.

HOW TO CONTACT Query with SASE. Submit outline, 3 sample chapters. Accepts simultaneous submissions. Responds in 1 week to queries. Responds in 1 month to mss. Obtains most new clients through recommendations from others, solicitations.

TERMS Agent receives 15% commission on domestic sales. Agent receives 20% commission on foreign sales. Offers written contract, binding for 2 years. Charges clients for postage, photocopying, long-distance calls, faxes.

❶ DOMINICK ABEL LITERARY AGENCY, INC.

146 W. 82nd St., #1A, New York NY 10024. (212)877-0710. Fax: (212)595-3133. E-mail: dominick@dalainc. com. Member AAR. Represents 100 clients. Currently handles: adult fiction and nonfiction.

HOW TO CONTACT Query via e-mail.

TERMS Agent receives 15% commission on domestic sales. Agent receives 20% commission on foreign sales.

❶ ADAMS LITERARY

7845 Colony Rd., C4 #215, Charlotte NC 28226. E-mail: info@adamsliterary.com. E-mail: submissions@ adamsliterary.com. Website: www.adamsliterary.com. **Contact:** Tracey Adams, Josh Adams, Quinlan Lee. Member of AAR. Other memberships include SCBWI and WNBA. Currently handles: juvenile books.

MEMBER AGENTS Tracey Adams, Josh Adams, Quinlan Lee.

HOW TO CONTACT "All submissions and queries must be made through the online form on our website. We will not review—and will promptly recycle—any unsolicited submissions or queries we receive by post. Before submitting your work for consideration, please carefully review our complete guidelines. While we have an established client list, we do seek new talent—and we accept submissions from both published and aspiring authors and artists."

❶ ALIVE COMMUNICATIONS, INC.

7680 Goddard St., Suite 200, Colorado Springs CO 80920. (719)260-7080. Fax: (719)260-8223. E-mail: submissions@alivecom.com. Website: www.alivecom. com. **Contact:** Rick Christian. Member of AAR. Other memberships include Authors Guild. Represents 100+ clients. 5% of clients are new/unpublished writers. Currently handles: nonfiction books 50%, novels 40%, juvenile books 10%.

MEMBER AGENTS Rick Christian, president (blockbusters, bestsellers); Lee Hough (popular/commercial nonfiction and fiction, thoughtful spirituality, children's); Andrea Heinecke (thoughtful/inspirational nonfiction, women's fiction/nonfiction, popular/commercial nonfiction & fiction); Joel Kneedler popular/commercial nonfiction and fiction, thoughtful spirituality, children's).

REPRESENTS Nonfiction books, novels, short story collections, novellas. **Considers these nonfiction areas:** autobiography, biography, business, child guidance, economics, how-to, inspirational, parenting, personal improvement, religious, self-help, women's issues, women's studies. **Considers these fiction areas:** adventure, contemporary issues, crime, family saga, historical, humor, inspirational, literary, mainstream, mystery, police, religious, satire, suspense, thriller.

⚷ This agency specializes in fiction, Christian living, how-to and commercial nonfiction. Actively seeking inspirational, literary and mainstream fiction, and work from authors with established track records and platforms. Does not want to receive poetry, scripts or dark themes.

HOW TO CONTACT Query via e-mail. "Be advised that this agency works primarily with well-established, bestselling, and career authors. Always looking for a breakout, blockbuster author with genuine talent." New clients come through recommendations from others.

TERMS Agent receives 15% commission on domestic sales. Offers written contract; 2-month notice must be given to terminate contract.

❶ BETSY AMSTER LITERARY ENTERPRISES

6312 Sw Capitol Hwy #503, Portland OR 97239. Website: www.amsterlit.com. **Contact:** Betsy Amster. Estab. 1992. Member of AAR. Represents more than 65 clients. 35% of clients are new/unpublished writers. Currently handles: nonfiction books 65%, novels 35%.

> ⭕ Prior to opening her agency, Ms. Amster was an editor at Pantheon and Vintage for 10 years, and served as editorial director for the Globe Pequot Press for 2 years.

REPRESENTS Nonfiction books, novels. **Considers these nonfiction areas:** art & design, biography, business, child guidance, cooking/nutrition, current affairs, ethnic, gardening, health/medicine, history, memoirs, money, parenting, popular culture, psychology, science/technology, self-help, sociology, travelogues, social issues, women's issues. **Considers these fiction areas:** ethnic, literary, women's, high quality.

➤ "Actively seeking strong narrative nonfiction, particularly by journalists; outstanding literary fiction (the next Richard Ford or Jhumpa Lahiri); witty, intelligent commerical women's fiction (the next Elinor Lipman or Jennifer Weiner); mysteries that open new worlds to us; and high-profile self-help and psychology, preferably research based." Does not want to receive poetry, children's books, romances, Western, science fiction, action/adventure, screenplays, fantasy, techno thrillers, spy capers, apocalyptic scenarios, or political or religious arguments.

HOW TO CONTACT For adult titles: b.amster.assistant@gmail.com. See submission requirements online at website. The requirements have changed and only e-mail submissions are accepted. Accepts simultaneous submissions. Responds in 1 month to queries. Responds in 2 months to mss. Obtains most new clients through recommendations from others, solicitations, conferences.

TERMS Agent receives 15% commission on domestic sales. Agent receives 20% commission on foreign sales. Offers written contract, binding for 1 year; 3-month notice must be given to terminate contract. Charges for photocopying, postage, long distance phone calls, messengers, galleys/books used in submissions to foreign and film agents and to magazines for first serial rights.

❶ ANDERSON LITERARY MANAGEMENT, LLC

12 W. 19th St., New York NY 10011. (212)645-6045. Fax: (212)741-1936. E-mail: info@andersonliterary.com; kathleen@andersonliterary.com; christine@andersonliterary.com; tess@andersonliterary.com. Website: www.andersonliterary.com/. **Contact:** Kathleen Anderson. Estab. 2006. Member of AAR. Represents 100+ clients. 20% of clients are new/unpublished writers. Currently handles: nonfiction books 50%, novels 50%.

MEMBER AGENTS Kathleen Anderson, Christine Mervart, Tess Taylor.

REPRESENTS Nonfiction books, novels, short story collections, juvenile. **Considers these nonfiction areas:** anthropology, archeology, architecture, art, autobiography, biography, cultural interests, current affairs, dance, design, education, environment, ethnic, gay, government, history, law, lesbian, memoirs, music, nature, politics, psychology, women's issues, women's studies. **Considers these fiction areas:** action, adventure, ethnic, family saga, feminist, frontier, gay, historical, lesbian, literary, mystery, suspense, thriller, westerns, women's, young adult.

➤ "Specializes in adult and young adult literary and commercial fiction, narrative nonfiction, American and European history, literary journalism, nature and travel writing, memoir, and biography." We do not represent science fiction, cookbooks, gardening, craft books or children's picture books. While we love literature in translation, we cannot accept samples of work written in languages other than English.

HOW TO CONTACT Query with SASE. Submit synopsis, first 3 sample chapters, proposal (for nonfiction). Snail mail queries only. Accepts simultaneous submissions. Responds in 6 weeks to queries. Obtains most new clients through recommendations from others, solicitations, conferences.

TERMS Agent receives 15% commission on domestic sales. Offers written contract.

ⓐ ARCADIA

31 Lake Place N., Danbury CT 06810. E-mail: arcadialit@sbcglobal.net. **Contact:** Victoria Gould Pryor. Member of AAR.

REPRESENTS Nonfiction books, literary and commercial fiction. **Considers these nonfiction areas:** biography, business, current affairs, health, history, psychology, science, true crime, women's, investigative journalism; culture; classical music; life transforming self-help.

⚹━ "I'm a very hands-on agent, which is necessary in this competitive marketplace. I work with authors on revisions until whatever we present to publishers is as strong as possible. I represent talented, dedicated, intelligent and ambitious writers who are looking for a longterm relationship based on professional success and mutual respect." Does not want to receive science fiction/fantasy, horror, humor or children's/YA. "We are only able to read fiction submissions from previously published authors."

HOW TO CONTACT No unsolicited submissions. Query with SASE. This agency accepts e-queries (no attachments).

ⓐ THE BALKIN AGENCY, INC.

P.O. Box 222, Amherst MA 01004. (413)322-8697; (978)656-8389. Fax: (413)322-8697. E-mail: rick62838@crocker.com; christinawardlit@mac.com. Website: http://wardbalkin.com. **Contact:** Rick Balkin, president. Christina Ward: P.O. Box 7144, Lowell, MA 01852. Member of AAR. Represents 50 clients. 10% of clients are new/unpublished writers. Currently handles: nonfiction books 85%, 5% reference books .

◯ Prior to opening his agency, Mr. Balkin served as executive editor with Bobbs-Merrill Company.

MEMBER AGENTS Christina Ward (literary fiction: contemporary, historical, mysteries, thrillers. Literary memoirs; creative nonfiction; narrative history; art and culture; biography; psychology; natural history and animal-related narratives; "green" subject areas (alternative lifestyle, shelter, sustainability, local living, permaculture, food systems); nutrition (but probably not cookbooks or diet books); health and medicine; gardening; social thought and commentary).

REPRESENTS Nonfiction books. **Considers these nonfiction areas:** animals, anthropology, current affairs, health, history, how to, nature, popular culture, science, sociology, translation, biography, et alia.

⚹━ This agency specializes in adult nonfiction. Does not want to receive fiction, poetry, screenplays, children's books or computer books.

HOW TO CONTACT Query with SASE. Submit proposal package, outline. Responds in 1 week to queries. Responds in 2 weeks to mss. Obtains most new clients through recommendations from others.

TERMS Agent receives 15% commission on domestic sales. Agent receives 20% commission on foreign sales. Offers written contract, binding for 1 year. This agency charges clients for photocopying and express or foreign mail.

⬤ BARBARA BRAUN ASSOCIATES, INC.

151 West 19th St., 4th floor, New York NY 10011. Fax: (212)604-9041. E-mail: bbasubmissions@gmail.com. Website: www.barbarabraunagency.com. **Contact:** Barbara Braun. Member of AAR.

MEMBER AGENTS Barbara Braun; John F. Baker.

REPRESENTS Nonfiction books, novels. **Considers these nonfiction areas:** We represent both literary and commercial and serious nonfiction, including psychology, biography, history, women's issues, social and political issues, cultural criticism, as well as art, architecture, film, photography, fashion and design. **Considers these fiction areas:** literary and commercial.

⚹━ "Our fiction is strong on women's stories, historical and multicultural stories, as well as mysteries and thrillers. We're interested in narrative nonfiction and books by journalists. We do not represent poetry, science fiction, fantasy, horror, or screenplays. Look online for more details."

HOW TO CONTACT E-mail submissions only marked "query" in subject line. We no longer accept submissions by regular mail. Your query should include: a brief summary of your book, word count, genre, any relevant publishing experience, and the first 5 pages of your manuscript pasted into the body of the e-mail. (NO attachments – we will not open these.)

TERMS Agent receives 15% commission on domestic sales; 20% commission on foreign sales.

⬤ BARBARA HOGENSON AGENCY

165 West End Ave., Suite 19-C, New York NY 10023. (212)874-8084. Fax: (212)362-3011. E-mail: bhogen-

son@aol.com. **Contact:** Barbara Hogenson, Lori Styler, Contract Manager. Member of AAR.

HOW TO CONTACT Query with SASE. Obtains most new clients through recommendations from other clients only.

◐ BARER LITERARY, LLC

270 Lafayette St., Suite 1504, New York NY 10012. (212)691-3513. E-mail: submissions@barerliterary. com. Website: www.barerliterary.com. **Contact:** Julie Barer. Estab. 2004. Member of AAR.

◑ Before becoming an agent, Julie worked at Shakespeare & Co. Booksellers in New York City. She is a graduate of Vassar College.

MEMBER AGENTS Julie Barer.

REPRESENTS Nonfiction books, novels, short story collections. Julie Barer is especially interested in working with emerging writers and developing long-term relationships with new clients. **Considers these nonfiction areas:** biography, ethnic, history, memoirs, popular culture, women's. **Considers these fiction areas:** contemporary issues, ethnic, historical, literary, mainstream.

⌘ This agency no longer accepts young adult submissions.

HOW TO CONTACT Query with SASE; no attachments if query by e-mail. We do not respond to queries via phone or fax.

TERMS Agent receives 15% commission on domestic sales. Agent receives 20% commission on foreign sales. Offers written contract. Charges for photocopying and books ordered.

BLEECKER STREET ASSOCIATES, INC.

217 Thompson St.,, #519, New York NY 10012. (212)677-4492. Fax: (212)388-0001. E-mail: bleeckerst@hotmail.com. **Contact:** Agnes Birnbaum. Member of AAR, RWA, MWA. Represents 60 clients. 20% of clients are new/unpublished writers. Currently handles: nonfiction books 75%, novels 25%.

◑ Prior to becoming an agent, Ms. Birnbaum was a senior editor at Simon & Schuster, Dutton/Signet, and other publishing houses.

REPRESENTS Nonfiction books, novels. **Considers these nonfiction areas:** New Age, animals, biography, business, child, computers, cooking, current affairs, ethnic, government, health, history, how to, memoirs, military, money, nature, popular culture, psychology, religion, science, self help, sociology, sports, true crime, women's. **Considers these fic-**

tion areas: ethnic, historical, literary, mystery, romance, thriller, women's.

⌘ "We're very hands-on and accessible. We try to be truly creative in our submission approaches. We've had especially good luck with first-time authors." Does not want to receive science fiction, westerns, poetry, children's books, academic/scholarly/professional books, plays, scripts, or short stories.

HOW TO CONTACT Query with SASE. No e-mail, phone, or fax queries. Accepts simultaneous submissions. Responds in 2 weeks to queries. Responds in 1 month to mss. "Obtains most new clients through recommendations from others, solicitations, conferences, plus, I will approach someone with a letter if his/her work impresses me."

TERMS Agent receives 15% commission on domestic sales; 25% commission on foreign sales. Offers written contract; 1-month notice to terminate contract. Charges for postage, long distance, fax, messengers, photocopies (not to exceed $200).

◐ BOOKENDS, LLC

136 Long Hill Rd., Gillette NJ 07933. Website: www. bookends-inc.com; bookendslitagency.blogspot.com. **Contact:** Jessica Faust, Kim Lionetti, Jessica Alvarez. Member of AAR, RWA, MWA. Represents 50+ clients. 10% of clients are new/unpublished writers. Currently handles: nonfiction books 50%, novels 50%.

MEMBER AGENTS Jessica Faust (fiction: romance, erotica, women's fiction, mysteries and suspense; nonfiction: business, finance, career, parenting, psychology, women's issues, self-help, health, sex); Kim Lionetti (Kim is only currently considering romance, women's fiction, and young adult queries. If your book is in any of these 3 categories, please be sure to specify "Romance," "Women's Fiction," or "Young Adult" in your e-mail subject line. Any queries that do not follow these guidelines will not be considered); Jessica Alvarez.

REPRESENTS Nonfiction books, novels. **Considers these nonfiction areas:** business, child, ethnic, gay, health, how-to, money, psychology, religion, self-help, sex, true crime, women's. **Considers these fiction areas:** detective, cozies, mainstream, mystery, romance, thriller, women's.

⌘ "BookEnds is currently accepting queries from published and unpublished writers in the areas of romance (and all its sub-genres), erotica, mystery, suspense, women's fiction, and literary fiction. We also do a great deal of nonfiction in the areas of self-help, business, finance, health, pop science, psychology, relationships, parenting, pop culture, true crime, and general nonfiction." BookEnds does not want to receive children's books, screenplays, science fiction, poetry, or technical/military thrillers.

HOW TO CONTACT Review website for guidelines, as they change. BookEnds is no longer accepting unsolicited proposal packages or snail mail queries. Send query in the body of e-mail to only one agent.

BOOKS & SUCH LITERARY AGENCY

52 Mission Circle, Suite 122, PMB 170, Santa Rosa CA 95409. E-mail: representation@booksandsuch.biz. Website: www.booksandsuch.biz. **Contact:** Janet Kobobel Grant, Etta Wilson, Rachel Kent, Mary Keeley. Member of AAR. Member of CBA (associate), American Christian Fiction Writers. Represents 150 clients. 5% of clients are new/unpublished writers. Currently handles: nonfiction books 50%, novels 50%.

Prior to becoming an agent, Ms. Grant was an editor for Zondervan and managing editor for *Focus on the Family*; Ms. Lawton was an author, sculptor and designer of porcelein dolls. Ms. Zurakowski concentrates on material for 20-something or 30-something readers. Ms. Keeley accepts both nonfiction and adult fiction. She previously was an acquisition editor for tyndale publishers

REPRESENTS Nonfiction books, novels. **Considers these nonfiction areas:** humor, religion, self help, women's. **Considers these fiction areas:** contemporary, family, historical, mainstream, religious, romance.

This agency specializes in general and inspirational fiction, romance, and in the Christian booksellers market. Actively seeking well-crafted material that presents Judeo-Christian values, if only subtly.

HOW TO CONTACT Query via e-mail only, no attachments. Accepts simultaneous submissions. Responds in 1 month to queries. "If you don't hear from us asking to see more of your writing within 30 days after you have sent your e-mail, please know that we have read and considered your submission but determined that it would not be a good fit for us." Obtains most new clients through recommendations from others, conferences.

TERMS Agent receives 15% commission on domestic sales. Agent receives 20% commission on foreign sales. Offers written contract; 2-month notice must be given to terminate contract. No additional charges.

GEORGES BORCHARDT, INC.

136 E. 57th St., New York NY 10022. Website: www. gbagency.com. Member of AAR.

MEMBER AGENTS Anne Borchardt; Georges Borchardt; Valerie Borchardt.

This agency specializes in literary fiction and outstanding nonfiction.

HOW TO CONTACT *No unsolicited mss.* Obtains new clients through recommendations from others.

TERMS Agent receives 15% commission on domestic sales. Agent receives 20% commission on foreign sales. Offers written contract.

BRANDT & HOCHMAN LITERARY AGENTS, INC.

1501 Broadway, Suite 2310, New York NY 10036. (212)840-5760. Fax: (212)840-5776. **Contact:** Gail Hochman. Member of AAR. Represents 200 clients.

MEMBER AGENTS Carl Brandt; Gail Hochman; Marianne Merola; Charles Schlessiger; Bill Contardi; Joanne Brownstein.

REPRESENTS Nonfiction books, novels, short story collections, juvenile, journalism. **Considers these nonfiction areas:** autobiography, biography, cultural interests, current affairs, ethnic, government, history, law, politics, women's issues, women's studies. **Considers these fiction areas:** contemporary issues, ethnic, historical, literary, mystery, romance, suspense, thriller, young adult.

HOW TO CONTACT Submit through e-mail or if by post, send one-page query letter with SASE. Accepts simultaneous submissions. Responds in 1 month to queries. Obtains most new clients through recommendations from others.

TERMS Agent receives 15% commission on domestic sales. Agent receives 20% commission on foreign sales. Charges clients for ms duplication or other special expenses agreed to in advance.

BRET ADAMS LTD. AGENCY

448 W. 44th St., New York NY 10036. (212)765-5630. E-mail: literary@bretadamsltd.net. Website: bretadamsltd.net. **Contact:** Colin Hunt, Mark Orsini. Member of AAR. Currently handles: movie scripts, TV scripts, stage plays.

MEMBER AGENTS Bruce Ostler, Mark Orsini.

REPRESENTS Movie scripts, TV scripts, TV movie of the week, theatrical stage play.

☛ Handles theatre/film and TV projects. No books. Cannot accept unsolicited material.

HOW TO CONTACT Professional recommendation.

ⓞ BRICK HOUSE LITERARY AGENTS

80 Fifth Ave., Suite 1101, New York NY 10011. Website: www.brickhouselit.com. **Contact:** Sally Wofford-Girand. Member of AAR.

MEMBER AGENTS Sally Wofford-Girand; Jenni Ferrari-Adler; Melissa Sarver, assistant.

REPRESENTS Nonfiction books, narrative nonfiction. **Considers these nonfiction areas:** cultural interests, ethnic, history, memoirs, nature, science, women's issues, women's studies, biography; food writing; lifestyle; science; natural history. **Considers these fiction areas:** literary, general & juvenile fiction.

☛ Sally's particular areas of interest are: history, memoir, women's issues, cultural studies, and fiction that is both literary and hard to put down (novels like *The Road* or *Blindness)*. Jenni Ferrari-Adler specializes in representing novels, food narrative and cookbooks, and narrative nonfiction. Actively seeking history, memoir, women's issues, cultural studies, literary fiction and quality commercial fiction.

HOW TO CONTACT "E-mail query letter (in body of e-mail, not as attachment) and first page to either Sally or Jenni. We will ask to see more if interested and are sorry that we cannot respond to all queries."

CURTIS BROWN, LTD.

10 Astor Place, New York NY 10003-6935. (212)473-5400. E-mail: gknowlton@cbltd.com. Website: www.curtisbrown.com. **Contact:** Ginger Knowlton. Alternate address: Peter Ginsberg, president at CBSF, 1750 Montgomery St., San Francisco CA 94111. (415)954-8566. Member of AAR. Signatory of WGA.

MEMBER AGENTS Ginger Clark; Katherine Fausset; Holly Frederick, VP; Emilie Jacobson; Elizabeth Hardin; Ginger Knowlton, Exec. VP; Timothy Knowlton, CEO; Laura Blake Peterson; Mitchell Waters. San Francisco Office: Peter Ginsberg (President).

REPRESENTS Nonfiction books, novels, short story collections, juvenile. **Considers these nonfiction areas:** agriculture horticulture, americana, crafts, interior, juvenile, New Age, young, animals, anthropol-

ogy, art, biography, business, child, computers, cooking, current affairs, education, ethnic, gardening, gay, government, health, history, how-to, humor, language, memoirs, military, money, multicultural, music, nature, philosophy, photography, popular culture, psychology, recreation, regional, religion, science, self-help, sex, sociology, software, spirituality, sports, film, translation, travel, true crime, women's, creative nonfiction. **Considers these fiction areas:** contemporary, glitz, New Age, psychic, adventure, comic, confession, detective, erotica, ethnic, experimental, family, fantasy, feminist, gay, gothic, hi lo, historical, horror, humor, juvenile, literary, mainstream, military, multicultural, multimedia, mystery, occult, picture books, plays, poetry, regional, religious, romance, science, short, spiritual, sports, thriller, translation, western, young, womens.

HOW TO CONTACT Prefers to read materials exclusively. *No unsolicited mss.* Responds in 3 weeks to queries. Responds in 5 weeks to mss. Obtains most new clients through recommendations from others, solicitations, conferences.

TERMS Offers written contract. Charges for some postage (overseas, etc.).

⬤ BROWNE & MILLER LITERARY ASSOCIATES

410 S. Michigan Ave., Suite 460, Chicago IL 60605-1465. (312)922-3063. E-mail: mail@browneandmiller.com. Website: www.browneandmiller.com. **Contact:** Danielle Egan-Miller. Estab. 1971. Member of AAR. Other memberships include RWA, MWA, Author's Guild. Represents 150 clients. 2% of clients are new/unpublished writers. Currently handles: nonfiction books 25%, novels 75%.

REPRESENTS Nonfiction books, most genres of commercial adult fiction and nonfiction, as well as select young adult projects. **Considers these nonfiction areas:** agriculture, animals, anthropology, archeology, autobiography, biography, business, child guidance, cooking, crafts, cultural interests, current affairs, economics, environment, ethnic, finance, foods, health, hobbies, horticulture, how-to, humor, inspirational, investigative, medicine, memoirs, money, nature, nutrition, parenting, personal improvement, popular culture, psychology, religious, satire, science, self-help, sociology, sports, technology, true crime, women's issues, women's studies. **Considers these fiction areas:** contemporary issues, crime, detective, erotica, ethnic, family saga, glitz, historical, inspirational, literary, mainstream, mystery, police, religious, romance, sports, suspense, thriller, paranormal.

⊶ "We are partial to talented newcomers and experienced authors who are seeking hands-on career management, highly personal representation, and who are interested in being full partners in their books' successes. We are editorially focused and work closely with our authors through the whole publishing process, from proposal to after publication. We are most interested in commercial women's fiction, especially elegantly crafted, sweeping historicals; edgy, fresh teen/chick/mom/lady lit; and CBA women's fiction by established authors. We are also very keen on literary historical mysteries and literary YA novels. Topical, timely nonfiction projects in a variety of subject areas are also of interest, especially prescriptive how-to, self-help, sports, humor, and pop culture." Does not represent poetry, short stories, plays, original screenplays, articles, children's picture books, software, horror or sci-fi novels.

HOW TO CONTACT Only accepts e-mail queries. Inquiring authors may initially submit one chapter and a synopsis. *No unsolicited mss.* Prefers to read material exclusively. Put submission in the subject line. Send no attachments. Also has online submission form. Responds in 2-4 months to queries. Obtains most new clients through referrals, queries by professional/marketable authors.

TERMS Agent receives 15% commission on domestic sales. Agent receives 20% commission on foreign sales. Offers written contract, binding for 2 years. Charges clients for photocopying, overseas postage.

⊘ BROWN LITERARY AGENCY

410 Seventh St. NW, Naples FL 34120. E-mail: broagent@aol.com. Website: www.brownliteraryagency.com. **Contact:** Roberta Brown. Member of AAR. Other memberships include RWA, Author's Guild. Represents 45 clients. 5% of clients are new/unpublished writers.

REPRESENTS Novels. **Considers these fiction areas:** erotica, romance, women's, single title and category.

⊶ "This agency is selectively reading material at this time."

HOW TO CONTACT Query via e-mail only. Send synopsis and two chapters in Word attachment. Response time varies.

TERMS Agent receives 15% commission on domestic sales. Agent receives 20% commission on foreign sales. Offers written contract; 30-day notice must be given to terminate contract.

⊕ ● KIMBERLEY CAMERON & ASSOCIATES

1550 Tiburon Blvd., #704, Tiburon CA 94920. Fax: (415)789-9177. E-mail: info@kimberleycameron.com. Website: www.kimberleycameron.com. **Contact:** Kimberley Cameron. Member of AAR. 30% of clients are new/unpublished writers. Currently handles: nonfiction books 50%; fiction 50%.

💬 Kimberley Cameron & Associates (formerly The Reece Halsey Agency) has had an illustrious client list of established writers, including the estate of Aldous Huxley, and has represented Upton Sinclair, William Faulkner, and Henry Miller.

MEMBER AGENTS Kimberley Cameron, Amy Burkhardt.

REPRESENTS Nonfiction, fiction. **Considers these nonfiction areas:** biography, current affairs, foods, humor, language, memoirs, popular culture, science, true crime, women's issues, women's studies, lifestyle. **Considers these fiction areas:** adventure, contemporary issues, ethnic, family saga, historical, horror, mainstream, mystery, interlinked short story collections, thriller, women's, and sophisticated/crossover young adult.

⊶ "We are looking for a unique and heartfelt voice that conveys a universal truth."

HOW TO CONTACT Query via e-mail. See our website for submission guidelines. Obtains new clients through recommendations from others, solicitations.

TERMS Agent receives 15% on domestic sales; 10% on film sales. Offers written contract, binding for 1 year.

◑ CAROL MANN AGENCY

55 Fifth Ave., New York NY 10003. (212)206-5635. Fax: (212)675-4809. Website: www.carolmannagency.com/. **Contact:** Eliza Dreier. Member of AAR. Represents roughly 200 clients. 15% of clients are new/unpublished writers. Currently handles: nonfiction books 90%, novels 10%.

MEMBER AGENTS Carol Mann (health/medical, religion, spirituality, self-help, parenting, narrative nonfiction, current affairs); Laura Yorke; Gareth Esersky; Myrsini Stephanides (Nonfiction areas of interest: pop culture and music, humor, narrative nonfiction and memoir, cookbooks; fiction areas of interest: offbeat literary fiction, graphic works, and edgy YA fiction). Joanne Wyckoff (Nonfiction aresas of interest: memoir, narrative nonfiction, personal narrative, psychology, women's issues, education, health and wellness, parenting, serious self-help, natural history); fiction.

REPRESENTS Nonfiction books, novels. **Considers these nonfiction areas:** anthropology, archeology, architecture, art, autobiography, biography, business, child guidance, cultural interests, current affairs, design, ethnic, government, health, history, law, medicine, money, music, parenting, popular culture, politics, psychology, self-help, sociology, sports, women's issues, women's studies. **Considers these fiction areas:** commercial, literary.

8—¶ This agency specializes in current affairs, self-help, popular culture, psychology, parenting, and history. Does not want to receive genre fiction (romance, mystery, etc.).

HOW TO CONTACT Please see website for submission guidelines. Responds in 4 weeks to queries.

TERMS Agent receives 15% commission on domestic sales. Agent receives 20% commission on foreign sales. Offers written contract.

CASTIGLIA LITERARY AGENCY

1155 Camino Del Mar, Suite 510, Del Mar CA 92014. (858)755-8761. Fax: (858)755-7063. E-mail: deborah@castigliaagency.com; win@castiglioagency.com. Website: home.earthlink.net/~mwgconference/id22.html. Member of AAR. Other memberships include PEN. Represents 65 clients. Currently handles: nonfiction books 55%, novels 45%.

MEMBER AGENTS Julie Castiglia; Winifred Golden (science fiction, ethnic, commercial and thriller novels, plus narrative nonfiction and some health books—prefers referrals); Sally Van Haitsma (actively looking for good proposals by way of query letters, and her wish list covers literary and women's fiction, current affairs, architecture, pop culture, and science fiction); Deborah Ritchken (narrative nonfiction, food/cook books, design, France, literary fiction, no genre fiction).

REPRESENTS Nonfiction books, novels. **Considers these nonfiction areas:** animals, anthropology, archeology, autobiography, biography, business, child guidance, cooking, cultural interests, current affairs, economics, environment, ethnic, finance, foods, health, history, inspirational, language, literature, medicine, money, nature, nutrition, psychology, religious, science, technology, women's issues, women's studies. **Considers these fiction areas:** contemporary issues, ethnic, literary, mainstream, mystery, suspense, women's.

8—¶ Does not want to receive horror, screenplays, poetry or academic nonfiction.

HOW TO CONTACT No unsolicited submissions. Query with SASE. No e-mail submissions accepted. Obtains most new clients through recommendations from others, solicitations, conferences.

TERMS Agent receives 15% commission on domestic sales. Agent receives 25% commission on foreign sales. Offers written contract; 6-week notice must be given to terminate contract.

CINE/LIT REPRESENTATION

P.O. Box 802918, Santa Clarita CA 91380-2918. (661)513-0268. Fax: (661)513-0915. **Contact:** Mary Alice Kier. Member of AAR.

MEMBER AGENTS Mary Alice Kier; Anna Cottle.

REPRESENTS Nonfiction books, novels.

8—¶ "Looking for nonfiction books: mainstream, thrillers, mysteries, supernatural, horror, narrative nonfiction, environmental, adventure, biography, travel and pop culture." Does not want to receive Westerns, sci-fi or romance.

HOW TO CONTACT Send query letter with SASE.

DARHANSOFF & VERRILL LITERARY AGENTS

236 W. 26th St., Suite 802, New York NY 10001. (917)305-1300. Fax: (917)305-1400. E-mail: chuck@dvagency.com. Website: www.dvagency.com. Member of AAR. Represents 120 clients. 10% of clients are new/unpublished writers. Currently handles: nonfiction books 25%, novels 60%, story collections 15%.

MEMBER AGENTS Liz Darhansoff; Chuck Verrill, Michele Mortimer.

REPRESENTS Novels, juvenile books, narrative nonfiction, literary fiction, mystery & suspense, young adult.

HOW TO CONTACT Queries welcome via website or with SASE. Obtains most new clients through recommendations from others.

● DAVID BLACK LITERARY AGENCY

335 Adams St., # 2710, Brooklyn NY 11201-3724. (718)852-5500. **Contact:** David Black, owner. Member of AAR. Represents 150 clients. Currently handles: nonfiction books 90%, novels 10%.

MEMBER AGENTS David Black; Susan Raihofer (general nonfiction, literary fiction); Gary Morris (commercial fiction, psychology); Joy E. Tutela (general nonfiction, literary fiction); Leigh Ann Eliseo; Linda Loewenthal (general nonfiction, health, science, psychology, narrative).

REPRESENTS nonfiction books, novels. **Considers these nonfiction areas:** autobiography, biography, business, economics, finance, government, health, history, inspirational, law, medicine, military, money, multicultural, psychology, religious, sports, war, women's issues, women's studies. **Considers these fiction areas:** literary, mainstream, commercial.

8→ This agency specializes in business, sports, politics, and novels.

HOW TO CONTACT Query with SASE. For nonfiction works, send a formal proposal that includes an overview, author bio, chapter outline, a marketing/publicity section, a competition section, and at least one sample chapter. Please also include writing samples, such as newspaper or magazine clips if relevant. (See questions in Guidelines online.) When submitting fiction, please include a synopsis, author bio, and the first 3 chapters of the book (25-50 pages). Accepts simultaneous submissions. Responds in 2 months to queries.

TERMS Agent receives 15% commission on domestic sales. Charges clients for photocopying and books purchased for sale of foreign rights.

◐ DEFIORE & CO.

47 E. 19th St., 3rd Floor, New York NY 10003. (212)925-7744. Fax: (212)925-9803. E-mail: info@defioreandco.com; submissions@defioreandco.com. Website: www.defioreandco.com. **Contact:** Lauren Gilchrist. Member of AAR. Represents 75 clients. 50% of clients are new/unpublished writers. Currently handles: nonfiction books 70%, novels 30%.

○ Prior to becoming an agent, Mr. DeFiore was publisher of Villard Books (1997-1998), editor-in-chief of Hyperion (1992-1997), and editorial director of Delacorte Press (1988-1992).

MEMBER AGENTS Brian DeFiore (popular nonfiction, business, pop culture, parenting, commercial fiction); Laurie Abkemeier (memoir, parenting, business, how-to/self-help, popular science); Kate Garrick (literary fiction, memoir, popular nonfiction); Debra Goldstein (health and diet, wellness); Laura Nolan (cookbooks, memoir, nonfiction); Matthew Elblonk (young adult, popular culture, narrative nonfiction); Karen Gerwin (popular culture, memoir); Caryn Karmatz-Rudy (popular fiction, self-help, narrative nonfiction).

REPRESENTS Nonfiction books, novels. **Considers these nonfiction areas:** autobiography, biography, business, child guidance, cooking, economics, foods, how-to, inspirational, money, multicultural, parenting, popular culture, psychology, religious, self-help, sports, young adult, middle grade. **Considers these fiction areas:** ethnic, literary, mainstream, mystery, suspense, thriller.

8→ "Please be advised that we are not considering children's picture books, poetry, adult science fiction and fantasy, romance, or dramatic projects at this time."

HOW TO CONTACT Query with SASE or e-mail to submissions@defioreandco.com. Please include the word "Query" in the subject line. All attachments will be deleted; please insert all text in the body of the e-mail. For more information about our agents, their individual interests, and their query guidelines, please visit our "About Us" page. Accepts simultaneous submissions. Responds in 3 weeks to queries. Responds in 2 months to mss. Obtains most new clients through recommendations from others.

TERMS Agent receives 15% commission on domestic sales. Agent receives 20% commission on foreign sales. Offers written contract; 10-day notice must be given to terminate contract. Charges clients for photocopying and overnight delivery (deducted only after a sale is made).

DH LITERARY, INC.

P.O. Box 805, Nyack NY 10960-0990. **Contact:** David Hendin. Member of AAR. Represents 10 clients. Currently handles: nonfiction books 80%, novels 10%, scholarly books 10%.

○ Prior to opening his agency, Mr. Hendin served as president and publisher for Pharos Books/World Almanac, as well as senior VP and COO at sister company United Feature Syndicate.

8→ *Not accepting new clients. Please do not send queries or submissions.*

TERMS Agent receives 15% commission on domestic sales. Agent receives 20% commission on foreign sales. Offers written contract, binding for 1 year. Charges for out-of-pocket expenses for overseas postage specifically related to the sale.

● DON CONGDON ASSOCIATES INC.

156 Fifth Ave., Suite 625, New York NY 10010-7002. (212)645-1229. Fax: (212)727-2688. E-mail: dca@doncongdon.com. **Contact:** Don Congdon, Michael Congdon, Susan Ramer, Cristina Concepcion, Maura Kye-Casella, Katie Kotchman, Katie Grimm. Member of AAR. Represents 100 clients. Currently handles: nonfiction books 60%, other 40% fiction.

REPRESENTS Nonfiction books, fiction. **Considers these nonfiction areas:** anthropology, archeology, autobiography, biography, child guidance, cooking, current affairs, dance, environment, film, foods, government, health, history, humor, language, law, literature, medicine, memoirs, military, music, nature, nutrition, parenting, popular culture, politics, psychology, satire, science, technology, theater, travel, true crime, war, women's issues, women's studies, creative nonfiction. **Considers these fiction areas:** action, adventure, contemporary issues, crime, detective, literary, mainstream, mystery, police, short story collections, suspense, thriller, women's.

8→ Especially interested in narrative nonfiction and literary fiction.

HOW TO CONTACT Query with SASE or via e-mail (no attachments). Responds in 3 weeks to queries. Responds in 1 month to mss. Obtains most new clients through recommendations from other authors.

TERMS Agent receives 15% commission on domestic sales. Agent receives 19% commission on foreign sales. Charges client for extra shipping costs, photocopying, copyright fees, book purchases.

● JANIS A. DONNAUD & ASSOCIATES, INC.

525 Broadway, Second Floor, New York NY 10012. (212)431-2664. Fax: (212)431-2667. E-mail: jdonnaud@aol.com; donnaudassociate@aol.com. **Contact:** Janis A. Donnaud. Member of AAR. Signatory of WGA. Represents 40 clients. 5% of clients are new/unpublished writers. Currently handles: nonfiction books 100%.

◯ Prior to opening her agency, Ms. Donnaud was vice president and associate publisher of Random House Adult Trade Group.

REPRESENTS Nonfiction books. **Considers these nonfiction areas:** autobiography, African-American, biography, business, celebrity, child guidance, cooking, current affairs, diet/nutrition, foods, health, humor, medicine, parenting, psychology, satire, women's issues, women's studies, lifestyle.

8→ This agency specializes in health, medical, cooking, humor, pop psychology, narrative nonfiction, biography, parenting, and current affairs. We give a lot of service and attention to clients. Does not want to receive "fiction, poetry, mysteries, juvenile books, romances, science fiction, young adult, religious or fantasy."

HOW TO CONTACT Query with SASE. Submit description of book, 2-3 pages of sample material. Prefers to read materials exclusively. No phone calls. Responds in 1 month to queries. Responds in 1 month to mss. Obtains most new clients through recommendations from others.

TERMS Agent receives 15% commission on domestic sales; 20% on foreign and film sales. Offers written contract; 1-month notice must be given to terminate contract. Charges clients for messengers, photocopying and purchase of books.

⊕ DREISBACH LITERARY MANAGEMENT

PO Box 5379, El Dorado Hills CA 95762. (916)804-5016. E-mail: verna@dreisbachliterary.com. Website: www.dreisbachliterary.com. **Contact:** Verna Dreisbach. Estab. 2007.

REPRESENTS **Considers these nonfiction areas:** animals, biography, business, health, multicultural, parenting, religious, spirituality, travel, true crime, women's issues. **Considers these fiction areas:** literary, mystery, thriller.

8→ "The agency has a particular interest in books with a political, economic or social context. Open to most types of nonfiction. Fiction interests include literary, commercial and YA. Verna's first career as a law enforcement officer gives her a genuine interest and expertise in the genres of mystery, thriller and true crime." Does not want to receive sci-fi, fantasy, horror, poetry, screenplay, Christian or children's books

HOW TO CONTACT E-mail queries only please. No attachments in the query. They will not be opened. No unsolicited manuscripts.

◉ THE LISA EKUS GROUP, LLC

57 North St., Hatfield MA 01038. (413)247-9325. Fax: (413)247-9873. E-mail: LisaEkus@lisaekus.com. Website: www.lisaekus.com. **Contact:** Lisa Ekus-Saffer. Member of AAR.

REPRESENTS Nonfiction books. **Considers these nonfiction areas:** cooking, diet/nutrition, foods, occasionally health/well-being and women's issues.

HOW TO CONTACT Submit a one-page query via e-mail or submit your complete hard copy proposal with title page, proposal contents, concept, bio, marketing, TOC, etc. Include SASE for the return of materials.

◑ THE ELAINE P. ENGLISH LITERARY AGENCY

4710 41st St. NW, Suite D, Washington DC 20016. (202)362-5190. Fax: (202)362-5192. E-mail: queries@elaineenglish.com; elaine@elaineenglish.com; naomi@elaineenglish.com. Website: www.elaineenglish.com/literary.php. **Contact:** Elaine English; Naomi Hackenberg. Member of AAR. Represents 20 clients. 25% of clients are new/unpublished writers. Currently handles: novels 100%.

○ Ms. English has been working in publishing for more than 20 years. She is also an attorney specializing in media and publishing law.

MEMBER AGENTS Elaine English (novels); Naomi Hackenberg (young adult fiction).

REPRESENTS Novels. **Considers these fiction areas:** historical, multicultural, mystery, suspense, thriller, women's, romance (single title, historical, contemporary, romantic, suspense, chick lit, erotic), general women's fiction. The agency is slowly but steadily acquiring in all mentioned areas.

○→ Actively seeking women's fiction, including single-title romances, and young adult fiction. Does not want to receive any science fiction, time travel, or picture books.

HOW TO CONTACT Generally prefers e-queries sent to queries@elaineenglish.com or YA sent to naomi@elaineenglish.com. If requested, submit synopsis, first 3 chapters, SASE. Please check website for further details. Responds in 4-8 weeks to queries; 3 months to requested submissions. Obtains most new clients through recommendations from others, conferences, submissions.

TERMS Agent receives 15% commission on domestic sales. Agent receives 20% commission on foreign sales. Offers written contract; 30-day notice must be given to terminate contract. Charges only for shipping expenses; generally taken from proceeds.

◑ FAYE BENDER LITERARY AGENCY

19 Cheever Place, Brooklyn NY 11231. E-mail: info@fbliterary.com. Website: www.fbliterary.com. **Contact:** Faye Bender. Estab. 2004. Member of AAR.

MEMBER AGENTS Faye Bender.

REPRESENTS Nonfiction books, novels, juvenile. **Considers these nonfiction areas:** biography, memoirs, popular culture, women's issues, women's studies, young adult, narrative; health; popular science. **Considers these fiction areas:** commercial, literary, women's, young adult (middle-grade).

○→ "I choose books based on the narrative voice and strength of writing. I work with previously published and first-time authors." Faye does not represent picture books, genre fiction for adults (western, romance, horror, science fiction, fantasy), business books, spirituality or screenplays.

HOW TO CONTACT Query with SASE and 10 sample pages via mail or e-mail (no attachments). Guidelines online. "Please do not send queries or submissions via registered or certified mail, or by FedEx or UPS requiring signature. We will not return unsolicited submissions weighing more than 16 ounces, even if an SASE is attached. We do not respond to queries via phone or fax."

◑ DIANA FINCH LITERARY AGENCY

116 W. 23rd St., Suite 500, New York NY 10011. E-mail: diana.finch@verizon.net. Website: dianafinchliteraryagency.blogspot.com/. **Contact:** Diana Finch. Member of AAR. Represents 40 clients. 20% of clients are new/unpublished writers. Currently handles: nonfiction books 85%, novels 15%, juvenile books 5%, multimedia 5%.

○ Seeking to represent books that change lives. Prior to opening her agency in 2003, Ms. Finch worked at Ellen Levine Literary Agency for 18 years.

REPRESENTS nonfiction books, novels, scholarly. **Considers these nonfiction areas:** autobiography, biography, business, child guidance, computers, cultural interests, current affairs, dance, economics, environment, ethnic, film, government, health, history, how-to, humor, investigative, juvenile nonfiction, law, medicine, memoirs, military, money, music, parenting, photography, popular culture, politics, psychology, satire, science, self-help, sports, technology, theater, translation, true crime, war, women's issues, women's studies, computers, electronic. **Considers these fiction areas:** action, adventure, crime, detective, ethnic, historical, literary, mainstream, police, thriller, young adult.

⊶ Actively seeking narrative nonfiction, popular science, memoir and health topics. "Does not want romance, mysteries, or children's picture books."

HOW TO CONTACT Query with SASE or via e-mail (no attachments). Accepts simultaneous submissions. Obtains most new clients through recommendations from others.

TERMS Agent receives 15% commission on domestic sales. Agent receives 20% commission on foreign sales. Offers written contract. "I charge for photocopying, overseas postage, galleys, and books purchased, and try to recoup these costs from earnings received for a client, rather than charging outright."

● FRANCES COLLIN, LITERARY AGENT

P.O. Box 33, Wayne PA 19087-0033. E-mail: queries@francescollin.com. Website: www.francescollin.com. **Contact:** Sarah Yake, associate agent. Member of AAR. Represents 90 clients. 1% of clients are new/unpublished writers. Currently handles: nonfiction books 50%, fiction 50%.

REPRESENTS Nonfiction books, fiction, young adult.

⊶ Does not want to receive cookbooks, craft books, poetry, screenplays, or books for young children.

HOW TO CONTACT Query via e-mail describing project (text in the body of the e-mail only, no attachments) to queries@francescollin.com. "Please note that all queries are reviewed by both agents." No phone or fax queries. You may mail queries with a SASE. Accepts simultaneous submissions.

TERMS Agent receives 15% on domestic sales; 20% on foreign sales. Offers written contract.

● BARRY GOLDBLATT LITERARY, LLC

320 Seventh Ave., #266, Brooklyn NY 11215. Fax: (718)360-5453. Website: www.bgliterary.com. **Contact:** Barry Goldblatt. Member of AAR. SCBWI.

MEMBER AGENTS Barry Goldblatt, Joe Monti, Beth Fleisher (kids work and graphic novels; she is particularly interested in finding new voices in mid-dle grade and young adult fantasy, science fiction, mystery, historicals and action adventure).

REPRESENTS Juvenile books. **Considers these fiction areas:** picture books, young adult, middle grade, all genres.

⊶ This agency specializes in children's books of all kinds from picture books to young adult novels, across all over genres.

HOW TO CONTACT E-mail queries query@bgliterary.com, and include the first five pages and a synopsis of the novel pasted into the text of the e-mail. No attachments or links.

◉ GOODMAN ASSOCIATES

500 West End Ave., New York NY 10024-4317. (212)873-4806. Member of AAR.

⊶ Accepting new clients by recommendation only.

● SANFORD J. GREENBURGER ASSOCIATES, INC.

55 Fifth Ave., New York NY 10003. (212)206-5600. Fax: (212)463-8718. E-mail: queryHL@sjga.com. Website: www.greenburger.com. Member of AAR. Represents 500 clients.

MEMBER AGENTS Heide Lange; Faith Hamlin; Dan Mandel; Matthew Bialer; Courtney Miller-Callihan, Michael Harriot, Brenda Bowen (authors and illustrators of children's books for all ages as well as graphic novelists); Lisa Gallagher.

REPRESENTS Nonfiction books and novels. **Considers these nonfiction areas:** Americana, animals, anthropology, archeology, architecture, art, biography, business, computers, cooking, crafts, current affairs, decorating, diet/nutrition, design, education, environment, ethnic, film, foods, gardening, gay/lesbian, government, health, history, horticulture, how-to, humor, interior design, investigative, juvenile nonfiction, language, law, literature, medicine, memoirs, metaphysics, military, money, multicultural, music, New Age, philosophy, photography, popular culture, psychology, recreation, regional, romance, science, sex, sociology, software, sports, theater, translation, travel, true crime, women's issues, women's studies, young adult, software. **Considers these fiction areas:** action, adventure, crime, detective, ethnic, family saga, feminist, gay, glitz, historical, humor, lesbian, literary, mainstream, mystery, police, psychic, regional, satire, sports, supernatural, suspense, thriller.

HOW TO CONTACT Submit query, first 3 chapters, synopsis, brief bio, SASE. Accepts simultaneous submissions. Responds in 2 months to queries and mss. Responds to mss. Obtains most new clients through recommendations from others.

TERMS Agent receives 15% commission on domestic sales. Agent receives 20% commission on foreign sales. Charges for photocopying and books for foreign and subsidiary rights submissions.

✛ 🌑 GREYHAUS LITERARY

3021 20th St., PL SW, Puyallup WA 98373. E-mail: scott@greyhausagency.com. Website: www.greyhausagency.com. **Contact:** Scott Eagan, member RWA. Estab. 2003.

REPRESENTS Fiction, novels. **Considers these fiction areas:** romance, women's.

8—🖈 "We specialize in romance, women's fiction and YA romance." Actively seeking contemporary romance, and stories that are 75,000-100,000 words in length. Does not want sci-fi, fantasy, inspirational, literary, futuristic, erotica, writers targeting e-pubs, young adult.

HOW TO CONTACT Send a query, the first 3 pages and a synopsis of no more than 3 pages. There is also a submission form on this agency's website.

🌑 JOHN HAWKINS & ASSOCIATES, INC.

71 W. 23rd St., Suite 1600, New York NY 10010. (212)807-7040. Fax: (212)807-9555. E-mail: jha@jhalit.com. Website: www.jhalit.com. **Contact:** Moses Cardona (moses@jhalit.com). Member of AAR. Represents over 100 clients. 5-10% of clients are new/unpublished writers. Currently handles: nonfiction books 40%, novels 40%, juvenile books 20%.

MEMBER AGENTS Moses Cardona; Anne Hawkins (ahawkins@jhalit.com); Warren Frazier (frazier@jhalit.com); William Reiss (reiss@jhalit.com).

REPRESENTS Nonfiction books, novels, young adult. **Considers these nonfiction areas:** agriculture, Americana, anthropology, archeology, architecture, art, autobiography, biography, business, cultural interests, current affairs, design, economics, education, ethnic, film, gardening, gay/lesbian, government, health, history, horticulture, how-to, investigative, language, law, medicine, memoirs, money, multicultural, music, philosophy, popular culture, politics, psychology, recreation, science, self-help, sex, sociology, software, theater, travel, true crime, young adult, music, creative nonfiction. **Considers these fiction areas:** action, adventure, crime, detective, ethnic, experimental, family saga, feminist,

frontier, gay, glitz, hi-lo, historical, inspirational, lesbian, literary, mainstream, military, multicultural, multimedia, mystery, police, psychic, religious, short story collections, sports, supernatural, suspense, thriller, translation, war, westerns, women's, young adult.

HOW TO CONTACT Submit query, proposal package, outline, SASE. Accepts simultaneous submissions. Responds in 1 month to queries. Obtains most new clients through recommendations from others.

TERMS Agent receives 15% commission on domestic sales. Agent receives 20% commission on foreign sales. Charges clients for photocopying.

🌑 JANE CHELIUS LITERARY AGENCY

548 Second St., Brooklyn NY 11215. (718)499-0236. Fax: (718)832-7335. E-mail: queries@janechelius.com. Website: www.janechelius.com. Member of AAR.

REPRESENTS Nonfiction books, novels. **Considers these nonfiction areas:** biography, humor, medicine, parenting, popular culture, satire, women's issues, women's studies, natural history; narrative. **Considers these fiction areas:** literary, mystery, suspense.

8—🖈 Does not want to receive fantasy, science fiction, children's books, stage plays, screenplays, or poetry.

HOW TO CONTACT Please see website for submission procedures. Does not consider e-mail queries with attachments. No unsolicited sample chapters or mss. Responds in 3-4-weeks usually.

🌑 JEAN V. NAGGAR LITERARY AGENCY, INC.

216 E. 75th St., Suite 1E, New York NY 10021. (212)794-1082. E-mail: jweltz@jvnla.com; jvnla@jvnla.com. E-mail: jweltz@jvnla.com; jregel@jvnla.com; atasman@jvnla.com; atasman@jvnla.com. Website: www.jvnla.com. **Contact:** Jean Naggar. Member of AAR. Other memberships include PEN, Women's Media Group, Women's Forum. Represents 80 clients. 20% of clients are new/unpublished writers. Currently handles: nonfiction books 35%, novels 45%, juvenile books 15%, scholarly books 5%.

🌑Ms. Naggar has served as president of AAR.

MEMBER AGENTS Jennifer Weltz (subrights, children's, adults); Jessica Regel (young adult, adult, subrights); Jean Naggar taking no new clients. See website for client list; Alice Tasman (adult, children's); Elizabeth Evans (Adult nonfiction, some fiction and YA).

REPRESENTS Nonfiction books, novels. **Considers these nonfiction areas:** biography, child guidance, current affairs, government, health, history, juvenile nonfiction, law, medicine, memoirs, New Age, parenting, politics, psychology, self-help, sociology, travel, women's issues, women's studies. **Considers these fiction areas:** action, adventure, crime, detective, ethnic, family saga, feminist, historical, literary, mainstream, mystery, police, psychic, supernatural, suspense, thriller.

8—⚷ This agency specializes in mainstream fiction and nonfiction and literary fiction with commercial potential.

HOW TO CONTACT Query via e-mail. Prefers to read materials exclusively. No fax queries. Responds in 1 day to queries. Responds in 2 months to mss. Obtains most new clients through recommendations from others.

TERMS Agent receives 15% commission on domestic sales. Agent receives 20% commission on foreign sales. Offers written contract. Charges for overseas mailing, messenger services, book purchases, long-distance telephone, photocopying—all deductible from royalties received.

● WENDY LIPKIND AGENCY

120 E. 81st St., New York NY 10028. (212)628-9653. Fax: (212)585-1306. E-mail: lipkindag@aol.com. **Contact:** Wendy Lipkind. Member of AAR. Represents 40 clients. Currently handles: nonfiction books 100%.

REPRESENTS Nonfiction books. **Considers these nonfiction areas:** autobiography, biography, current affairs, health, history, medicine, science, technology, women's issues, women's studies, social history; narrative nonfiction.

8—⚷ This agency specializes in adult nonfiction.

HOW TO CONTACT Prefers to read materials exclusively. Accepts e-mail queries only (no attachments). Obtains most new clients through recommendations from others.

TERMS Agent receives 15% commission on domestic sales. Agent receives 20% commission on foreign sales. Sometimes offers written contract. Charges clients for foreign postage, messenger service, photocopying, transatlantic calls, faxes.

⊕ ◑ LIVING WORD LITERARY AGENCY

PO Box 40974, Eugene OR 97414. E-mail: livingwordliterary@gmail.com. Website: livingwordliterary.wordpress.com. **Contact:** Kimberly Shumate/Agent. Estab. 2008. Member Evangelical Christian Publishers Association

◔ Kimberly began her employment with Harvest House Publishers as the assistant to the National Sales Manager as well as the International Sales Director.

REPRESENTS Considers these nonfiction areas: health, parenting, self-help, relationships. **Considers these fiction areas:** inspirational, adult fiction, Christian living.

8—⚷ Does not want to receive cookbooks, children's books, science fiction or fantasy, memoirs, screenplays or poetry.

HOW TO CONTACT Submit a query with short synopsis and first chapter via Word document. Agency only responds if interested.

◑ LORETTA BARRETT BOOKS, INC.

220 E. 23rd St., 11th Floor, New York NY 10010. (212)242-3420. E-mail: query@lorettabarrettbooks.com. Website: www.lorettabarrettbooks.com. **Contact:** Loretta A. Barrett, Nick Mullendore, Grabriel Davis. Estab. 1990. Member of AAR. Currently handles: nonfiction books 50%, novels 50%.

◔ Prior to opening her agency, Ms. Barrett was vice president and executive editor at Doubleday and editor-in-chief of Anchor Books.

MEMBER AGENTS Loretta A. Barrett; Nick Mullendore.

REPRESENTS Nonfiction books, novels. **Considers these nonfiction areas:** biography, child guidance, current affairs, ethnic, government, health/nutrition, history, memoirs, money, multicultural, nature, popular culture, psychology, religion, science, self help, sociology, spirituality, sports, women's, young adult, creative nonfiction. **Considers these fiction areas:** contemporary, psychic, adventure, detective, ethnic, family, historical, literary, mainstream, mystery, thriller, young adult.

8—⚷ "The clients we represent include both fiction and nonfiction authors for the general adult trade market. The works they produce encompass a wide range of contemporary topics and themes including commercial thrillers, mysteries, romantic suspense, popular science, memoirs, narrative fiction and current affairs." No children's, juvenile, cookbooks, gardening, science fiction, fantasy novels, historical romance.

HOW TO CONTACT See guidelines online. Use e-mail (no attachments) or if by post, query with SASE.

For hardcopy queries, please send a 1-2 page query letter and a synopsis or chapter outline for your project. In your letter, please include your contact information, any relevant background information on yourself or your project, and a paragraph of description of your project. If you are submitting electronically, then all of this material may be included in the body of your e-mail. Accepts simultaneous submissions. Responds in 3-6 weeks to queries.

TERMS Agent receives 15% commission on domestic sales. Agent receives 20% commission on foreign sales. Offers written contract. Charges clients for shipping and photocopying.

MARIA CARVAINIS AGENCY, INC.

1270 Avenue of the Americas, Suite 2320, New York NY 10019. (212)245-6365. Fax: (212)245-7196. E-mail: mca@mariacarvainisagency.com. **Contact:** Maria Carvainis, Chelsea Gilmore. Member of AAR. Signatory of WGA. Other memberships include Authors Guild, Women's Media Group, ABA, MWA, RWA. Represents 75 clients. 10% of clients are new/unpublished writers. Currently handles: nonfiction books 35%, novels 65%.

○ Prior to opening her agency, Ms. Carvainis spent more than 10 years in the publishing industry as a senior editor with Macmillan Publishing, Basic Books, Avon Books, and Crown Publishers. Ms. Carvainis has served as a member of the AAR Board of Directors and AAR Treasurer, as well as serving as chair of the AAR Contracts Committee. She presently serves on the AAR Royalty Committee. Ms. Gilmore started her publishing career at Oxford University Press, in the Higher Education Group. She then worked at Avalon Books as associate editor. She is most interested in women's fiction, literary fiction, young adult, pop culture, and mystery/suspense.

MEMBER AGENTS Maria Carvainis, president/literary agent; Chelsea Gilmore, literary agent.

REPRESENTS Nonfiction books, novels. **Considers these nonfiction areas:** autobiography, biography, business, economics, history, memoirs, science, technology, women's issues, women's studies. **Considers these fiction areas:** contemporary issues, historical, literary, mainstream, mystery, suspense, thriller, women's, young adult, middle grade.

○—☞ Does not want to receive science fiction or children's picture books.

HOW TO CONTACT Query with SASE. No e-mail accepted. Responds in up to 3 months to mss and to queries in 1 month. Obtains most new clients through recommendations from others, conferences, query letters.

TERMS Agent receives 15% commission on domestic sales. Agent receives 20% commission on foreign sales. Offers written contract. Charges clients for foreign postage and bulk copying.

● THE EVAN MARSHALL AGENCY

6 Tristam Place, Pine Brook NJ 07058-9445. (973)882-1122. Fax: (973)882-3099. E-mail: evanmarshall@optonline.net. **Contact:** Evan Marshall. Member of AAR. Other memberships include MWA, Sisters in Crime. Currently handles: novels 100%.

REPRESENTS Novels. **Considers these fiction areas:** action, adventure, erotica, ethnic, frontier, historical, horror, humor, inspirational, literary, mainstream, mystery, religious, satire, science fiction, suspense, westerns, romance (contemporary, gothic, historical, regency).

HOW TO CONTACT Do not query. Currently accepting clients only by referal from editors and our own clients. Responds in 1 week to queries. Responds in 3 months to mss. Obtains most new clients through recommendations from others.

TERMS Agent receives 15% commission on domestic sales. Agent receives 20% commission on foreign sales. Offers written contract.

● MIRIAM ALTSHULER LITERARY AGENCY

53 Old Post Road N., Red Hook NY 12571. (845)758-9408. Website: www.miriamaltshulerliteraryagency.com. **Contact:** Miriam Altshuler. Estab. 1994. Member of AAR. Represents 40 clients. Currently handles: nonfiction books 45%, novels 45%, story collections 5%, juvenile books 5%.

○ Ms. Altshuler has been an agent since 1982.

REPRESENTS nonfiction books, novels, short story collections, juvenile. **Considers these nonfiction areas:** biography, ethnic, history, language, memoirs, multicultural, music, nature, popular culture, psychology, sociology, film, women's. **Considers these fiction areas:** literary, mainstream, multicultural, some selective children's books.

✂ Literary commercial fiction and nonfiction. Does not want self-help, mystery, how-to, romance, horror, spiritual, fantasy, poetry, screenplays, science fiction or techno-thriller, western.

HOW TO CONTACT Send query; do not send e-mail. If we want to see your ms we will respond via e-mail (if you do not have an e-mail address, please send an SASE. We will only respond if interested in materials. Submit contact info with e-mail address. Prefers to read materials exclusively. Accepts simultaneous submissions. Responds in 3 weeks to mss. Obtains most new clients through recommendations from others.

TERMS Agent receives 15% commission on domestic sales. Agent receives 20% commission on foreign sales. Charges clients for overseas mailing, photocopies, overnight mail when requested by author.

SUSAN ANN PROTTER, LITERARY AGENT

320 Central Park West, Suite 12E, New York NY 10025. **Contact:** Susan Protter. Member of AAR. Other memberships include Authors Guild.

○ Prior to opening her agency, Ms. Protter was associate director of subsidiary rights at Harper & Row Publishers.

HOW TO CONTACT *"We are currently not accepting new unsolicited submissions."*

◑ RICHARD HENSHAW GROUP

22 West 23rd Street, 5th Floor, New York NY 10010. E-mail: submissions@henshaw.com. Website: http://www.richh.addr.com. **Contact:** Rich Henshaw. Member of AAR. Other memberships include SinC, MWA, HWA, SFWA, RWA. 20% of clients are new/unpublished writers. Currently handles: nonfiction books 35%, novels 65%.

○ Prior to opening his agency, Mr. Henshaw served as an agent with Richard Curtis Associates, Inc.

REPRESENTS Nonfiction books, novels. **Considers these nonfiction areas:** animals, autobiography, biography, business, child guidance, cooking, current affairs, dance, economics, environment, foods, gay/lesbian, health, humor, investigative, money, music, New Age, parenting, popular culture, politics, psychology, science, self-help, sociology, sports, technology, true crime, women's issues, women's studies, electronic. **Considers these fiction areas:** action,

adventure, crime, detective, ethnic, family saga, historical, humor, literary, mainstream, mystery, police, psychic, romance, satire, science fiction, sports, supernatural, suspense, thriller.

✂ This agency specializes in thrillers, mysteries, science fiction, fantasy and horror.

HOW TO CONTACT Query with SASE. Accepts multiple submissions. Responds in 3 weeks to queries. Responds in 6 weeks to mss. Obtains most new clients through recommendations from others, solicitations, conferences.

TERMS Agent receives 15% commission on domestic sales. Agent receives 20% commission on foreign sales. No written contract. Charges clients for photocopying and book orders.

◑ RLR ASSOCIATES, LTD.

Literary Department, 7 W. 51st St., New York NY 10019. (212)541-8641. Fax: (212)262-7084. E-mail: sgould@rlrassociates.net. Website: www.rlrassociates.net. **Contact:** Scott Gould. Member of AAR. Represents 50 clients. 25% of clients are new/unpublished writers. Currently handles: nonfiction books 70%, novels 25%, story collections 5%.

REPRESENTS Nonfiction books, novels, short story collections, scholarly. **Considers these nonfiction areas:** animals, anthropology, archeology, art, autobiography, biography, business, child guidance, cooking, cultural interests, current affairs, decorating, diet/nutrition, economics, education, environment, ethnic, foods, gay/lesbian, government, health, history, humor, inspirational, interior design, language, law, memoirs, money, multicultural, music, parenting, photography, popular culture, politics, psychology, religious, science, self-help, sociology, sports, technology, translation, travel, true crime, women's issues, women's studies. **Considers these fiction areas:** action, adventure, cartoon, comic books, crime, detective, ethnic, experimental, family saga, feminist, gay, historical, horror, humor, lesbian, literary, mainstream, multicultural, mystery, police, satire, sports, suspense.

✂ "We provide a lot of editorial assistance to our clients and have connections." Actively seeking fiction, current affairs, history, art, popular culture, health and business. Does not want to receive screenplays.

HOW TO CONTACT Query by either e-mail or mail. Accepts simultaneous submissions. Responds in 4-8 weeks to queries. Obtains most new clients through recommendations from others.

TERMS Agent receives 15% commission on domestic sales. Agent receives 20% commission on foreign sales. Offers written contract.

B.J. ROBBINS LITERARY AGENCY

5130 Bellaire Ave., North Hollywood CA 91607-2908. E-mail: Robbinsliterary@gmail.com. E-mail: amy.bjrobbinsliterary@gmail.com. **Contact:** (Ms.) B.J. Robbins, or Amy Maldonado. Member of AAR. Represents 40 clients. 50% of clients are new/unpublished writers. Currently handles: nonfiction books 50%, novels 50%.

REPRESENTS Nonfiction books, novels. **Considers these nonfiction areas:** autobiography, biography, cultural interests, current affairs, dance, ethnic, film, health, humor, investigative, medicine, memoirs, music, popular culture, psychology, self-help, sociology, sports, theater, travel, true crime, women's issues, women's studies. **Considers these fiction areas:** crime, detective, ethnic, literary, mainstream, mystery, police, sports, suspense, thriller.

HOW TO CONTACT Query with SASE. Submit outline/proposal, 3 sample chapters, SASE. Accepts e-mail queries (no attachments). Accepts simultaneous submissions. Responds in 2-6 weeks to queries. Responds in 6-8 weeks to mss. Obtains most new clients through conferences, referrals.

TERMS Agent receives 15% commission on domestic sales. Agent receives 20% commission on foreign sales. Offers written contract; 3-month notice must be given to terminate contract. This agency charges clients for postage and photocopying (only after sale of ms).

ROBIN STRAUS AGENCY, INC.

229 E. 79th St., Suite 5A, New York NY 10075. (212)472-3282. Fax: (212)472-3833. E-mail: info@robinstrausagency.com. Website: www.robinstrausagency.com/. **Contact:** Ms. Robin Straus. Estab. 1983. Member of AAR.

Prior to becoming an agent, Robin Straus served as a subsidary rights manager at Random House and Doubleday and worked in editorial at Little, Brown.

REPRESENTS Represents high quality adult fiction and nonfiction including literary and commercial fiction, narrative nonfiction, women's fiction, memoirs, history, biographies, books on psychology, popular culture and current affairs, science, parenting, and cookbooks.

Does *not* represent juvenile, young adult, science fiction/fantasy, horror, romance, westerns, poetry or screenplays.

HOW TO CONTACT If you prefer to submit your queries electronically, please note that we do not download manuscripts. All materials must be included in the body of the e-mail. We do not respond to any submissions that do not include a SASE. No metered postage.

TERMS Agent receives 15% commission on domestic sales. Agent receives 20% commission on foreign sales. Offers written contract. Charges for photocopying, express mail services, messenger and foreign postage, galleys and books for submissions, etc. as incurred.

SALLY HILL MCMILLAN & ASSOCIATES, INC.

429 E. Kingston Ave., Charlotte NC 28203. (704)334-0897. **Contact:** Sally Hill McMillan. Member of AAR.

"We are not seeking new clients at this time. Agency specializes in Southern fiction, women's fiction, mystery and practical nonfiction."

HOW TO CONTACT *No unsolicited submissions.*

SANDRA DIJKSTRA LITERARY AGENCY

1155 Camino del Mar, PMB 515, Del Mar CA 92014. (858)755-3115. Fax: (858)794-2822. E-mail: elise@dijkstraagency.com. Website: www.dijkstraagency.com. Member of AAR. Other memberships include Authors Guild, PEN West, Poets and Editors, MWA. Represents 100+ clients. 30% of clients are new/unpublished writers. Currently handles: nonfiction books 50%, novels 45%, juvenile books 5%.

MEMBER AGENTS Sandra Dijkstra; Elise Capron; Jill Marr; Taylor Martindale.

REPRESENTS Nonfiction books, novels. **Considers these nonfiction areas:** Americana, animals, anthropology, archeology, art, business, child guidance, cooking, cultural interests, diet/nutrition, economics, environment, ethnic, foods, gay/lesbian, government, health, history, inspirational, language, law, literature, medicine, memoirs, military, money, parenting, politics, psychology, regional, science, self-help, sociology, technology, travel, war, women's issues, women's studies, Asian studies, juvenile nonfiction, accounting, transportation. **Considers these fiction areas:** erotica, ethnic, fantasy, juvenile, literary, mainstream, mystery, picture books, science fiction, suspense, thriller, graphic novels.

8—π Does not want to receive Western, screenplays, short story collections or poetry.

HOW TO CONTACT "Please see guidelines on our website and please note that we now only accept e-mail submissions. Due to the large number of unsolicited submissions we receive, we are now ONLY able to respond those submissions in which we are interested. Unsolicited submissions in which we are not interested will receive no response." Accepts simultaneous submissions. Responds in about 6 weeks to queries. Obtains most new clients through recommendations from others, solicitations, conferences.

TERMS Agent receives 15% commission on domestic sales. Agent receives 20% commission on foreign sales. Offers written contract. Charges clients for expenses for foreign postage and copying costs if a client requests a hard copy submission to publishers.

● SARAH LAZIN BOOKS

126 Fifth Ave., Suite 300, New York NY 10011. (212)989-5757. Fax: (212)989-1393. E-mail: manuela@lazinbooks.com; slazin@lazinbooks.com. **Contact:** Sarah Lazin. Member of AAR. Represents 75+ clients. Currently handles: nonfiction books 80%, novels 20%.

MEMBER AGENTS Sarah Lazin; Manuela Jessel.

REPRESENTS Nonfiction books, novels. **Considers these nonfiction areas:** narrative nonfiction, history, politics, contemporary affairs, popular culture, music, biography and memoir.

8—π Works with companies who package their books; handles some photography.

HOW TO CONTACT Query with SASE. No e-mail queries. Only accepts queries on referral.

TERMS Agent receives 15% commission on domestic sales. Agent receives 20% commission on foreign sales.

⊘ HAROLD SCHMIDT LITERARY AGENCY

415 W. 23rd St., #6F, New York NY 10011. **Contact:** Harold Schmidt, Acquisitions. Estab. 1984. Member of AAR. Represents 3 clients.

REPRESENTS Nonfiction, fiction. **Considers these fiction areas:** contemporary issues, gay, literary,, original quality fiction with unique narrative voices, high quality psychological suspense and thrillers, likes offbeat/quirky.

8—π Actively seeking novels.

HOW TO CONTACT Query with SASE; do not send material without being asked. No telephone or e-mail queries. Query by mail with SASE or your e-mail address. We will respond if interested. Do not send material unless asked as it cannot be read or returned. No telephone or e-mail queries.

● SHEREE BYKOFSKY ASSOCIATES, INC.

PO Box 706, Brigantine NJ 08203. E-mail: shereebee@aol.com. E-mail: submitbee@aol.com. Website: www.shereebee.com. **Contact:** Sheree Bykofsky. Member of AAR. Other memberships include ASJA, WNBA. Currently handles: nonfiction books 80%, novels 20%.

◌ Prior to opening her agency, Ms. Bykofsky served as executive editor of The Stonesong Press and managing editor of Chiron Press. She is also the author or co-author of more than 20 books, including *The Complete Idiot's Guide to Getting Published.* Ms. Bykofsky teaches publishing at NYU and SEAK, Inc.

MEMBER AGENTS Janet Rosen, associate.

REPRESENTS Nonfiction books, novels. **Considers these nonfiction areas:** Americana, animals, architecture, art, autobiography, biography, business, child guidance, cooking, crafts, creative nonfiction, cultural interests, current affairs, dance, design, economics, education, environment, ethnic, film, finance, foods, gardening, gay, government, health, history, hobbies, humor, language, law, lesbian, memoirs, metaphysics, military, money, multicultural, music, nature, New Age, nutrition, parenting, philosophy, photography, popular culture, politics, psychology, recreation, regional, religious, science, sex, sociology, spirituality, sports, translation, travel, true crime, war, anthropology; creative nonfiction. **Considers these fiction areas:** contemporary issues, literary, mainstream, mystery, suspense.

8—π This agency specializes in popular reference nonfiction, commercial fiction with a literary quality, and mysteries. "I have wide-ranging interests, but it really depends on quality of writing, originality, and how a particular project appeals to me (or not). I take on fiction when I completely love it-it doesn't matter what area or genre." Does not want to receive poetry, material for children, screenplays, westerns, horror, science fiction, or fantasy.

HOW TO CONTACT We only accept e-queries now and will only respond to those in which we are interested. E-mail short queries to submitbee@aol.com. Please, no attachments, snail mail, or phone calls. One-page query, one-page synopsis, and first page of manuscript in the body of the e-mail. Nonfiction: One-page query in the body of the e-mail. We cannot open attached Word files or any other types of attached files. These will be deleted. Accepts simultaneous submissions. Responds in 1 month to requested mss. Obtains most new clients through recommendations from others.

TERMS Agent receives 15% commission on domestic sales. Agent receives 20% commission on foreign sales. Offers written contract, binding for 1 year. Charges for postage, photocopying, fax.

WENDY SHERMAN ASSOCIATES, INC.

27 W. 24th St., New York NY 10010. (212)279-9027. E-mail: wendy@wsherman.com. E-mail: submissions@wsherman.com. Website: www.wsherman.com. **Contact:** Wendy Sherman. Member of AAR. Represents 50 clients. 30% of clients are new/unpublished writers.

Prior to opening the agency, Ms. Sherman served as vice president, executive director, associate publisher, subsidiary rights director, and sales and marketing director for major publishers.

MEMBER AGENTS Wendy Sherman (board member of AAR), Kim Perel.

REPRESENTS **Considers these nonfiction areas:** memoirs, psychology, narrative; practical. **Considers these fiction areas:** mainstream, Mainstream fiction that hits the sweet spot between literary and commercial.

"We specialize in developing new writers, as well as working with more established writers. My experience as a publisher has proven to be a great asset to my clients."

HOW TO CONTACT Query via e-mail Accepts simultaneous submissions. Responds in 1 month to queries. Obtains most new clients through recommendations from others.

TERMS Agent receives 15% commission on domestic sales; 20% commission on foreign and film sales. Offers written contract.

STEELE-PERKINS LITERARY AGENCY

26 Island Ln., Canandaigua NY 14424. (585)396-9290. Fax: (585)396-3579. E-mail: pattiesp@aol.com. **Contact:** Pattie Steele-Perkins. Member of AAR. Other memberships include RWA. Currently handles: novels 100%.

REPRESENTS Novels. **Considers these fiction areas:** romance, women's, All genres: category romance, romantic suspense, historical, contemporary, multi-cultural, and inspirational.

HOW TO CONTACT Submit synopsis and one chapter via e-mail (no attachments) or snail mail. Snail mail submissions require SASE. Accepts simultaneous submissions. Responds in 6 weeks to queries. Obtains most new clients through recommendations from others, queries/solicitations.

TERMS Agent receives 15% commission on domestic sales. Offers written contract, binding for 1 year; 1-month notice must be given to terminate contract.

STERLING LORD LITERISTIC, INC.

65 Bleecker St., 12th Floor, New York NY 10012. (212)780-6050. Fax: (212)780-6095. E-mail: info@sll.com. Website: www.sll.com. Member of AAR. Signatory of WGA. Represents 600 clients. Currently handles: nonfiction books 50%, novels 50%.

MEMBER AGENTS Sterling Lord; Peter Matson; Philippa Brophy (represents journalists, nonfiction writers and novelists, and is most interested in current events, memoir, science, politics, biography, and women's issues); Chris Calhoun; Claudia Cross (a broad range of fiction and nonfiction, from literary fiction to commercial women's fiction and romance novels, to cookbooks, lifestyle titles, memoirs, serious nonfiction on religious and spiritual topics, and books for the CBA marketplace); Robert Guinsler (literary and commercial fiction, journalism, narrative nonfiction with an emphasis on pop culture, science and current events, memoirs and biographies); Laurie Liss (commercial and literary fiction and nonfiction whose perspectives are well developed and unique); Judy Heiblum (fiction and nonfiction writers, looking for distinctive voices that challenge the reader, emotionally or intellectually. She works with journalists, academics, memoirists, and essayists, and is particularly interested in books that explore the intersections of science, culture, history and philosophy. In addition, she is always looking for writers of literary fiction with fresh, uncompromising voices); Neeti Madan (memoir, journalism, history, pop culture, health, lifestyle, women's issues, multicultural books and virtually any intelligent writing on intriguing topics. Neeti is looking for smart, well-written commercial novels, as well as compelling and provocative literary works); George Nicholson (writers and illustrators for children); Jim Rutman; Ira Silverberg; Douglas Stewart (literary fiction, narrative nonfiction, and young adult fiction).

HOW TO CONTACT Query with SASE by snail mail. Include synopsis of the work, a brief proposal or the first three chapters of the manuscript, and brief bio or resume. Does not respond to unsolicited e-mail queries. Responds in 1 month to mss.

TERMS Agent receives 15% commission on domestic sales; 20% commission on foreign sales. Offers written contract. Charges clients for photocopying.

◐ STUART KRICHEVSKY LITERARY AGENCY, INC.

381 Park Ave. S., Suite 428, New York NY 10016. (212)725-5288. Fax: (212)725-5275. E-mail: query@skagency.com. Website: www.skagency.com. Member of AAR.

MEMBER AGENTS Stuart Krichevsky; Shana Cohen (science fiction, fantasy); Jennifer Puglisi (assistant).

REPRESENTS Nonfiction books, novels.

HOW TO CONTACT Submit query, synopsis, 1 sample page via e-mail (no attachments). Snail mail queries also acceptable. Obtains most new clients through recommendations from others, solicitations.

◑ TESSLER LITERARY AGENCY, LLC

27 W. 20th St., Suite 1003, New York NY 10011. (212)242-0466. Fax: (212)242-2366. E-mail: michelle@tessleragency.com. Website: www.tessleragency.com. **Contact:** Michelle Tessler. Member of AAR.

◯ Prior to forming her own agency, Ms. Tessler worked at Carlisle & Co. (now a part of Inkwell Management). She has also worked at the William Morris Agency and the Elaine Markson Literary Agency.

REPRESENTS Nonfiction books, novels.

⌐☞ "The Tessler Agency is a full-service boutique agency that represents writers of literary fiction and high quality nonfiction in the following categories: popular science, reportage, memoir, history, biography, psychology, business and travel."

HOW TO CONTACT Submit query through website only.

● THE AXELROD AGENCY

55 Main St., P.O. Box 357, Chatham NY 12037. (518)392-2100. E-mail: steve@axelrodagency.com. Website: www.axelrodagency.com. **Contact:** Steven Axelrod. Member of AAR. Represents 15-20 clients. 1% of clients are new/unpublished writers. Currently handles: novels 95%.

◯ Prior to becoming an agent, Mr. Axelrod was a book club editor.

REPRESENTS Novels. **Considers these fiction areas:** mystery, romance, women's.

HOW TO CONTACT Query with SASE. Accepts simultaneous submissions. Responds in 3 weeks to queries. Responds in 6 weeks to mss. Obtains most new clients through recommendations from others.

TERMS Agent receives 15% commission on domestic sales. Agent receives 20% commission on foreign sales. No written contract.

THE CHOATE AGENCY, LLC

1320 Bolton Rd., Pelham NY 10803. E-mail: mickey@thechoateagency.com. Website: www.thechoateagency.com. **Contact:** Mickey Choate. Estab. 2004. Member of AAR.

REPRESENTS Nonfiction books, novels. **Considers these nonfiction areas:** history; memoirs by journalists, military or political figures, biography; cookery/food; journalism; military science; narrative; politics; general science; natural science, wine/spirits. **Considers these fiction areas:** historical, mystery, thriller, select literary fiction, strong commercial fiction.

⌐☞ The agency does not handle genre fiction, chic-lit, cozies, romance, self-help, confessional memoirs, spirituality, pop psychology, religion, how-to, New Age titles, children's books, poetry, self-published works or screenplays.

HOW TO CONTACT Query with brief synopsis and bio. This agency prefers e-queries, but accepts snail mail queries with SASE.

● THE HELEN BRANN AGENCY, INC.

94 Curtis Road, Bridgewater CT 06752. Fax: (860)355-2572. Member of AAR.

HOW TO CONTACT Query with SASE.

⊕◑ THE RIGHTS FACTORY

PO Box 499, Station C, Toronto ON M6J 3P6 Canada. (416)966-5367. Website: www.therightsfactory.com.

MEMBER AGENTS Sam Hiyate, Alisha Sevigny, Ali McDonald.

⌐☞ "The Rights Factory is an agency that deals in intellectual property rights to entertainment products, including books, comics & graphic novels, film, television, and video games. We license rights in every territory by representing three types of clients."

HOW TO CONTACT There is a submission form on this agency's website.

THE ROSENBERG GROUP

23 Lincoln Ave., Marblehead MA 01945. (781)990-1341. Fax: (781)990-1344. Website: www.rosenberggroup.com. **Contact:** Barbara Collins Rosenberg. Estab. 1998. Member of AAR. Other memberships include recognized agent of the RWA. Represents 25 clients. 15% of clients are new/unpublished writers. Currently handles: nonfiction books 30%, novels 30%, scholarly books 10%, other 30% college textbooks.

⬤ Prior to becoming an agent, Ms. Rosenberg was a senior editor for Harcourt.

REPRESENTS Nonfiction books, novels, textbooks, college textbooks only. **Considers these nonfiction areas:** current affairs, foods, popular culture, psychology, sports, women's issues, women's studies, women's health, wine/beverages. **Considers these fiction areas:** romance, women's.

⊶ Ms. Rosenberg is well-versed in the romance market (both category and single title). She is a frequent speaker at romance conferences. Actively seeking romance category or single title in contemporary romantic suspense, and the historical subgenres. Does not want to receive inspirational, time travel, futuristic or paranormal.

HOW TO CONTACT Query with SASE. No e-mail or fax queries; will not respond. See guidelines online at website. Responds in 2 weeks to queries. Responds in 4-6 weeks to mss. Obtains most new clients through recommendations from others, solicitations, conferences.

TERMS Agent receives 15% commission on domestic sales. Agent receives 15% commission on foreign sales. Offers written contract; 1-month notice must be given to terminate contract. Charges maximum of $350/year for postage and photocopying.

THE STRINGER LITERARY AGENCY, LLC

E-mail: stringerlit@comcast.net. Website: www.stringerlit.com. **Contact:** Marlene Stringer.

REPRESENTS Considers these nonfiction areas: history, military, music, parenting, science, sports, middle grade. **Considers these fiction areas:** fantasy,

historical, mystery, romance, science fiction, thriller, women's, young adult.

⊶ This agency specializes in fiction. Does not want to receive picture books, plays, short stories or poetry.

HOW TO CONTACT Electronic submissions only. Accepts simultaneous submissions.

SCOTT TREIMEL NY

434 Lafayette St., New York NY 10003. (212)505-8353. E-mail: general@scotttreimelny.com. Website: ScottTreimelNY.blogspot.com; www.ScottTreimelNY.com. **Contact:** John M. Cusick. Member of AAR. Other memberships include Authors Guild, SCBWI. 10% of clients are new/unpublished writers. Currently handles: 100% juvenile/teen books.

⬤ Prior to becoming an agent, Mr. Treimel was an assistant to Marilyn E. Marlow at Curtis Brown, a rights agent for Scholastic, a book packager and rights agent for United Feature Syndicate, a freelance editor, a rights consultant for HarperCollins Children's Books, and the founding director of Warner Bros. Worldwide Publishing.

REPRESENTS Nonfiction books, novels, juvenile, children's, picture books, young adult.

⊶ This agency specializes in tightly focused segments of the trade and institutional markets. Career clients.

HOW TO CONTACT Submissions accepted only via website.

TERMS Agent receives 15% commission on domestic sales. Agent receives 20% commission on foreign sales. Offers verbal or written contract. Charges clients for photocopying, express postage, messengers, and books needed to sell foreign, film and other rights.

TRIDENT MEDIA GROUP

41 Madison Ave., 36th Floor, New York NY 10010. (212)262-4810. E-mail: ellen.assistant@tridentmediagroup.com. Website: www.tridentmediagroup.com. **Contact:** Ellen Levine. Member of AAR.

MEMBER AGENTS Kimberly Whalen, whalen.assistant@tridentmediagroup (commercial fiction and nonfiction, women's fiction, suspense, paranormal and pop culture); Eileen Cope, ecope@tridentmediagroup.com (narrative nonfiction, history, biography, pop culture, health, literary fiction and short story collections); Scott Miller, smiller@tridentmediagroup.com (thrillers, crime, mystery, young adult, children's, narrative nonfiction, current events, military, memoir, literary fiction, graphic novels, pop culture); Alex Glass aglass@tridentmediagroup (thrillers, literary fiction, crime, middle grade, pop culture, young adult, humor and narrative nonfiction); Melissa Flashman, mflashman@tridentmediagroup.com (narrative nonfiction, serious nonfiction, pop culture, lifstyle); Alyssa Henkin, ahenkin@tridentmediagroup.com (juvenile, children's, YA); Stephanie Maclean (romance, women's fiction and young adult); Don Fehr (literary and commercial novelists, narrative nonfiction, memoirs, biography, travel, as well as science/medical/health related titles); Alanna Ramirez (literary fiction, narrative nonfiction, memoir, pop culture, food and wine, and lifestyle books); John Silbersack (commercial and literary fiction, science fiction and fantasy, narrative nonfiction, young adult, and thrillers).

REPRESENTS Nonfiction books, novels, short story collections, juvenile. **Considers these nonfiction areas:** autobiography, biography, current affairs, government, humor, law, memoirs, military, multicultural, popular culture, politics, true crime, war, women's issues, women's studies, young adult. **Considers these fiction areas:** crime, detective, humor, juvenile, literary, military, multicultural, mystery, police, short story collections, suspense, thriller, women's, young adult.

8—⚭ Actively seeking new or established authors in a variety of fiction and nonfiction genres.

HOW TO CONTACT Query with SASE or via e-mail. Check website for more details.

◑ VERITAS LITERARY AGENCY

601 Van Ness Ave., Opera Plaza, Suite E, San Francisco CA 94102. (415)647-6964. Fax: (415)647-6965. E-mail: submissions@veritasliterary.com. Website: www.veritasliterary.com. **Contact:** Katherine Boyle. Member of AAR. Other memberships include Author's Guild.

REPRESENTS Nonfiction books, novels. **Considers these nonfiction areas:** current affairs, memoirs, popular culture, politics, true crime, women's issues, young adult, narrative nonfiction, art and music biography, natural history, health and wellness, psychology, serious religion (no New Age) and popular science. **Considers these fiction areas:** commercial, fantasy, literary, mystery, science fiction, young adult.

8—⚭ Does not want to receive romance, poetry, or children's books.

HOW TO CONTACT This agency accepts short queries or proposals via e-mail only. "If you are sending a proposal or a manuscript after a positive response to a query, please write 'REQUESTED MATERIAL' on the subject line and include the initial query letter."

⊘ RALPH M. VICINANZA LTD.

303 W. 18th St., New York NY 10011. (212)924-7090. Fax: (212)691-9644. Member of AAR.

MEMBER AGENTS Ralph M. Vicinanza; Chris Lotts; Christopher Schelling.

HOW TO CONTACT This agency takes on new clients by professional recommendation only.

TERMS Agent receives 15% commission on domestic sales. Agent receives 20% commission on foreign sales.

● VICKY BIJUR LITERARY AGENCY

333 West End Ave., Apt. 5B, New York NY 10023. E-mail: assistant@vickybijuragency.com. Estab. 1988. Member of AAR.

◯ Vicky Bijur worked at Oxford University Press and with the Charlotte Sheedy Literary Agency. Books she represents have appeared on the New York Times Bestseller List, in the New York Times Notable Books of the Year, Los Angeles Times Best Fiction of the Year, Washington Post Book World Rave Reviews of the Year.

REPRESENTS Nonfiction books, novels. **Considers these nonfiction areas:** cooking, government, health, history, psychology, psychiatry, science, self help, sociology, biography; child care/development; environmental studies; journalism; social sciences.

8—⚭ Does not want science fiction, fantasy, horror, romance, poetry, children's .

HOW TO CONTACT Accepts e-mail queries. Fiction: query and first chapter (if e-mailed, please paste chapter into body of e-mail as I don't open attachments from unfamiliar senders). Nonfiction: query and proposal. No phone or fax queries.

◑ WALES LITERARY AGENCY, INC.

P.O. Box 9426, Seattle WA 98109-0426. (206)284-7114. E-mail: waleslit@waleslit.com. Website: www.waleslit.com. **Contact:** Elizabeth Wales, Neal Swain. Member of AAR. Other memberships include Book Publishers' Northwest, Pacific Northwest Booksellers Association, PEN. Represents 60 clients. 10% of clients are new/unpublished writers. Currently handles: nonfiction books 60%, novels 40%.

Prior to becoming an agent, Ms. Wales worked at Oxford University Press and Viking Penguin.

MEMBER AGENTS Elizabeth Wales; Neal Swain.

This agency specializes in quality fiction and nonfiction. Does not handle screenplays, children's literature, genre fiction, or most category nonfiction.

HOW TO CONTACT Accepts queries sent with cover letter and SASE, and e-mail queries with no attachments. No phone or fax queries. Accepts simultaneous submissions. Responds in 2 weeks to queries, 2 months to mss.

TERMS Agent receives 15% commission on domestic sales; 20% commission on foreign sales.

⊕ ◑ WEED LITERARY

27 West 20th St., New York NY 10011. E-mail: info@weedliterary.com. Website: www.weedliterary.com. **Contact:** Elisabeth Weed. Estab. 2007.

Prior to forming her own agency, Ms. Weed was an agent at Curtis Brown and Trident Media Group.

REPRESENTS Nonfiction, fiction, novels. **Considers these fiction areas:** literary, women's.

This agency specializes in upmarket women's fiction. Does not want to receive picture books, mysteries, thrillers, romance or military.

HOW TO CONTACT Send a query letter.

● THE WENDY WEIL AGENCY, INC.

232 Madison Ave., Suite 1300, New York NY 10016. (212)685-0030. Fax: (212)685-0765. E-mail: wweil@wendyweil.com. Website: www.wendyweil.com. Estab. 1987. Member of AAR. Currently handles: nonfiction books 20%, novels 80%.

MEMBER AGENTS Wendy Weil (commercial fiction, women's fiction, family saga, historical fiction, short stories); Emily Forland; Emma Patterson.

REPRESENTS Nonfiction books, novels.

"The Wendy Weil Agency, Inc. represents fiction and nonfiction for the trade market. We work with literary and commercial fiction, mystery/thriller, memoir, narrative nonfiction, journalism, history, current affairs, books on health, science, popular culture, lifestyle, social activism, and art history. It is a full-service literary agency that handles around 100 authors, among them Pulitzer Prize winners, National Book Award winners, New York Times bestsellers." Does not want to receive screenplays or textbooks.

HOW TO CONTACT "Accepts queries by regular mail and e-mail, however, we cannot guarantee a response to electronic queries. Query letters should be no more than 2 pages, which should include a bit about yourself and an overview of your project. If you'd like, you're welcome to include a separate synopsis along with your query. For queries via regular mail, please be sure to include a SASE for our reply. Snail mail queries are preferred." 4-6 weeks. Obtains most new clients through recommendations from others, solicitations.

◐ TED WEINSTEIN LITERARY MANAGEMENT

307 Seventh Ave., Suite 2407, Dept. GLA, New York NY 10001. E-mail: tw@twliterary.com. E-mail: submissions@twliterary.com. Website: www.twliterary.com. **Contact:** Ted Weinstein. Member of AAR. Represents 75 clients. 50% of clients are new/unpublished writers. Currently handles: nonfiction books 100%.

REPRESENTS Considers these nonfiction areas: biography, business, current affairs, economics, government, health, history, investigative, law, medicine, popular culture, politics, science, self-help, technology, travel, true crime, lifestyle, narrative journalism, popular science.

HOW TO CONTACT Please visit website for detailed guidelines before submitting. E-mail queries **only**. Other Responds in 3 weeks to queries.

TERMS Agent receives 15% commission on domestic sales; 20% on foreign and film sales. Offers written contract, binding for 1 year. Charges clients for photocopying and express shipping.

● WM CLARK ASSOCIATES

186 Fifth Ave., Second Floor, New York NY 10010. (212)675-2784. Fax: (347)-649-9262. E-mail: general@wmclark.com. Website: www.wmclark.com. Estab. 1997. Member of AAR. 50% of clients are new/unpublished writers. Currently handles: nonfiction books 50%, novels 50%.

Prior to opening WCA, Mr. Clark was an agent at the William Morris Agency.

REPRESENTS Nonfiction books, novels. **Considers these nonfiction areas:** architecture, art, autobiography, biography, cultural interests, current affairs, dance, design, ethnic, film, history, inspirational, memoirs, music, politics, popular culture, religious, science, sociology, technology, theater, translation, travel memoir, Eastern Philosophy. **Considers these fiction areas:** contemporary issues, ethnic, historical, literary, mainstream, Southern fiction.

☞ William Clark represents a wide range of titles across all formats to the publishing, motion picture, television, and new media fields on behalf of authors of first fiction and award-winning, bestselling narrative nonfiction, international authors in translation, chefs, musicians, and artists.

HOW TO CONTACT Accepts queries via online form only at www.wmclark.com/queryguidelines.html. We respond to all queries submitted via this form. Responds in 1-2 months to queries.

TERMS Agent receives 15% on domestic sales; 20% on foreign sales. Offers written contract.

AUDREY R. WOLF LITERARY AGENCY

2510 Virginia Ave. NW, #702N, Washington DC 20037. **Contact:** Audrey Wolf. Member of AAR.

HOW TO CONTACT Query with SASE.

⊘ WOLGEMUTH & ASSOCIATES, INC

8600 Crestgate Circle, Orlando FL 32819. (407)909-9445. Fax: (407)909-9446. E-mail: ewolgemuth@wolgemuthandassociates.com. **Contact:** Erik Wolgemuth. Member of AAR. Represents 60 clients. 10% of clients are new/unpublished writers. Currently handles: nonfiction books 90%, novella 2%, juvenile books 5%, multimedia 3%.

💬 "We have been in the publishing business since 1976, having been a marketing executive at a number of houses, a publisher, an author, and a founder and owner of a publishing company."

MEMBER AGENTS Robert D. Wolgemuth; Andrew D. Wolgemuth; Erik S. Wolgemuth.

REPRESENTS Material used by Christian families.

☞ "We are not considering any new material at this time."

TERMS Agent receives 15% commission on domestic sales. Offers written contract, binding for 2-3 years; 30-day notice must be given to terminate contract.

WRITERS HOUSE

21 W. 26th St., New York NY 10010. (212)685-2400. Fax: (212)685-1781. E-mail: mmejias@writershouse.com; smalk@writershouse.com. Website: www.writershouse.com. **Contact:** Michael Mejias. Estab. 1973. Member of AAR. Represents 440 clients. 50% of clients are new/unpublished writers. Currently handles: nonfiction books 25%, novels 40%, juvenile books 35%.

MEMBER AGENTS Albert Zuckerman (major novels, thrillers, women's fiction, important nonfiction).

REPRESENTS Nonfiction books, novels, juvenile. **Considers these nonfiction areas:** animals, art, autobiography, biography, business, child guidance, cooking, decorating, diet/nutrition, economics, film, foods, health, history, humor, interior design, juvenile nonfiction, medicine, military, money, music, parenting, psychology, satire, science, self-help, technology, theater, true crime, women's issues, women's studies. **Considers these fiction areas:** adventure, cartoon, contemporary issues, crime, detective, erotica, ethnic, family saga, fantasy, feminist, frontier, gay, hi-lo, historical, horror, humor, juvenile, literary, mainstream, military, multicultural, mystery, New Age, occult, picture books, police, psychic, regional, romance, spiritual, sports, thriller, translation, war, westerns, women's, young adult, cartoon.

HOW TO CONTACT Query with SASE. Please send us a query letter of no more than 2 pages, which includes your credentials, an explanation of what makes your book unique and special, and a synopsis. (If submitting to Steven Malk: Writers House, 7660 Fay Ave., #338H, La Jolla, CA 92037) Responds in 6-8 weeks to queries. Obtains most new clients through recommendations from authors and editors.

TERMS Agent receives 15% commission on domestic sales. Agent receives 20% commission on foreign sales. Offers written contract, binding for 1 year. Agency charges fees for copying mss/proposals and overseas airmail of books.

BOOK PUBLISHERS

The markets in this year's Book Publishers section offer opportunities in nearly every area of publishing. Large, commercial houses are here as are their smaller counterparts.

When you have compiled a list of publishers interested in books in your subject area, read the detailed listings. Pare down your list by cross-referencing two or three subject areas and eliminating the listings only marginally suited to your book. When you have a good list, send for those publishers' catalogs and manuscript guidelines, or check publishers' websites, which often contain catalog listings, manuscript preparation guidelines, current contact names, and other information helpful to prospective authors. You want to use this information to make sure your book idea is in line with a publisher's list but is not a duplicate of something already published.

You should also visit bookstores and libraries to see if the publisher's books are well represented. When you find a couple of books the house has published that are similar to yours, write or call the company to find out who edited those books. This extra bit of research could be the key to getting your proposal to precisely the right editor.

Publishers prefer different methods of submission on first contact. Most like to see a one-page query. Others will accept a brief proposal package. Some publishers will accept submissions from agents only. Each listing in the Book Publishers section includes specific submission methods, if provided by the publisher.

When you write your one-page query, give an overview of your book, mention the intended audience, the competition for your book (check local bookstore shelves), and what sets your book apart from the competition. You should also include any previous publishing experience or special training relevant to the subject of your book. For more on queries, read "Query Letter Clinic."

Personalize your query by addressing the editor individually and mentioning what you know about the company from its catalog or books. Never send a form letter as a query. Envelopes addressed to "Editor" or "Editorial Department" end up in the dreaded slush pile. Try your best to send your query to the appropriate editor. Editors move around all the time, so it's in your best interest to look online or call the publishing house to make sure the editor you are addressing your query to is still employed by that publisher.

Author-subsidy publishers' not included

Writer's Market is a reference tool to help you sell your writing, and we encourage you to work with publishers that pay a royalty. Subsidy publishing involves paying money to a publishing house to publish a book. The source of the money could be a government, foundation or university grant, or it could be the author of the book. If one of the publishers listed in this book offers you an author-subsidy arrangement (sometimes called "cooperative publishing," "co-publishing," or "joint venture"); or asks you to pay for part or all of the cost of any aspect of publishing (editing services, manuscript critiques, printing, advertising, etc.); or asks you to guarantee the purchase of any number of the books yourself, we would like you to inform us of that company's practices immediately.

INFORMATION AT A GLANCE

There are a number of icons at the beginning of each listing to quickly convey certain information. Different sections of *Writer's Market* include different symbols; check the back inside cover for an explanation of all the symbols used throughout the book.

Publishers, their imprints, and how they are related

In this era of big publishing—and big mergers—the world of publishing has grown even more intertwined. Publishers & Their Imprints lists the imprints and divisions of the largest conglomerate publishers.

Keep in mind that most of the major publishers listed in this family tree do not accept unagented submissions or unsolicited manuscripts. You will find some of these publishers and their imprints listed within the Book Publishers section, though many contain only basic contact information. If you are interested in pursuing any of these publishers, we advise you to see each publisher's website for more information.

🐢 AARDVARK PRESS

P.O. Box 201, Onrus River 7201, South Africa. (27)(28)315-2611. Fax: (27)(28)514-0793. E-mail: publish@aardvark-press.co.za. Website: www.aardvarkpress.co.za.

○ "Our publishing list is closed until further notice."

NONFICTION Subjects include animals, business, economics, cooking, foods, nutrition, nature, environment, sports, travel, leisure, health/recreation, young families. "We look at most nonfiction projects - and if we can't offer to publish (for a myriad reasons including full lists, subject/genre outside our core focus, etc.), we try to provide advice on where an author might improve a proposal, or submit his or her work." Query via e-mail.

ABC-CLIO

Acquisitions Department, P.O. Box 1911, Santa Barbara CA 93116-1911. (805)968-1911. E-mail: ccasey@abc-clio.com. Website: www.abc-clio.com; www.greenwood.com. **Contact:** Cathleen Casey. Estab. 1955. **Publishes 600 titles/year. 20% of books from first-time authors. 90% from unagented writers. Pays variable royalty on net price.** Accepts simultaneous submissions. Catalog and guidelines available online. Online request form.

IMPRINTS ABC-CLIO (serves the history profession, history teachers, and students and scholars of history with a complete line of award-winning databases, books, and eBooks, along with social studies reference and curriculum resources for middle and high school libraries and classrooms); Greenwood Press (high-quality, authoritative reference books and general interest topics across the secondary and higher education curriculum); Praeger (widely regarded to scholarly and professional books in the social sciences and humanities, with emphasis in modern history, military studies, psychology, business, current events and social issues, international affairs, politics, visual and performing arts, and literature); Praeger Security International (insightful and timely material on international security, including defense and foreign policy, strategy, regional security, military history, and terrorism); Libraries Unlimited (professional materials for librarians, media specialists, and teachers).

⚲ ABC-CLIO is an award-winning publisher of reference titles, academic and general interest books, electronic resources, and books for librar-

ians and other professionals. Today, ABC-CLIO publishes under 5 well-respected imprints.

NONFICTION Subjects include business, child guidance, education, government, history, humanities, language, music, psychology, religion, social sciences, sociology, sports, women's issues. No memoirs, drama Query with proposal package, including scope, organization, length of project, whether a complete ms is available or when it will be, CV or résumé and SASE.

TIPS "Looking for reference materials and materials for educated general readers. Many of our authors are college professors who have distinguished credentials and who have published research widely in their fields."

HARRY N. ABRAMS, INC.

Subsidiary of La Martiniere Group, 115 West 18th St., 6th Floor, New York NY 10011. (212)206-7715. Fax: (212)519-1210. E-mail: abrams@abramsbooks.com. Website: www.abramsbooks.com. **Contact:** Managing editor. Estab. 1951. Publishes hardcover and a few paperback originals. **Publishes 250 titles/year.** Responds in 6 months (if interested) to queries.

IMPRINTS Stewart, Tabori & Chang; Abrams Books for Young Readers; Abrams Gifts & Stationary.

○ Does not accept unsolicited materials.

⚲ "We publish *only* high-quality illustrated art books, i.e., art, art history, museum exhibition catalogs, written by specialists and scholars in the field."

NONFICTION Subjects include art, architecture, nature, environment, recreation, outdoor. Requires illustrated material for art and art history, museums. Submit queries, proposals, and mss via mail with SASE. No e-mail submissions. Reviews artwork/photos.

TIPS "We are one of the few publishers who publish almost exclusively illustrated books. We consider ourselves the leading publishers of art books and high-quality artwork in the U.S. Once the author has signed a contract to write a book for our firm the author must finish the manuscript to agreed-upon high standards within the schedule agreed upon in the contract."

Ⓐ ACTION PUBLISHING

P.O. Box 391, Glendale CA 91209. (323)478-1667. Fax: (323)478-1767. Website: www.actionpublishing.com. Estab. 1996.

TIPS "We use a small number of photos. Promo is kept on file for reference if potential interest. If you are sending a book proposal, send query letter first with web link to sample photos if available."

ADAMS MEDIA

Division of F+W Media, Inc., 57 Littlefield St., Avon MA 02322. (508)427-7100. Fax: (800)872-5628. E-mail: paula. munier@fwmedia.com. E-mail: submissions@adams-media.com. Website: www.adamsmedia.com. **Contact:** Paula Munier. Estab. 1980. Publishes hardcover originals, trade paperback originals and reprints. **Publishes more than 250 titles/year. 5,000 queries received/year. 1,500 mss received/year. 40% of books from first-time authors. 40% from unagented writers. Pays standard royalty or makes outright purchase. Pays variable advance.** Publishes book 12-18 months after acceptance of ms. Accepts simultaneous submissions. Responds in 3 months to queries. Guidelines available online.

8—➤ "Adams Media publishes commercial nonfiction, including self-help, inspiration, women's issues, pop psychology, relationships, business, careers, pets, parenting, New Age, gift books, cookbooks, how-to, reference, and humor. Does not return unsolicited materials. Does not accept electronic submissions."

AERONAUTICAL PUBLISHERS

1 Oakglade Circle, Hummelstown PA 17036-9525. (717)566-0468. Fax: (717)566-6423. E-mail: info@possibilitypress.com. Website: www.aeronautical-publishers.com. **Contact:** Mike Markowski, publisher. Estab. 1981. Publishes trade paperback originals. **Pays variable royalty.** Responds in 2 months to queries. Guidelines available online.

IMPRINTS American Aeronautical Archives, Aviation Publishers, Aeronautical Publishers.

8—➤ "Our mission is to help people learn more about aviation and model aviation through the written word."

NONFICTION Subjects include history, aviation, hobbies, recreation, radio control, free flight, indoor models, micro radio control, home-built aircraft, ultralights, and hang gliders. Prefers submission by mail. Include SASE. See guidelines online. Reviews artwork/photos. Do not send originals.

TIPS "Our focus is on books of short to medium length that will serve the emerging needs of the hobby. We also want to help youth get started, while enhancing everyone's enjoyment of the hobby. We are looking for authors who are passionate about the hobby, and will champion their book and the messages of

their books, supported by efforts at promoting and selling their books."

⊕ AFFLUENT PUBLISHING CORPORATION

Affluent Publishing, 1040 Ave.s of the Americas, 24th Floor, New York NY 10018. Website: www.affluent-publishing.com. **Contact:** JB Hamilton, editor (mainstream/contemporary). I. Smushkin, editor (suspense, mystery) Estab. 2008. **Publishes 3 titles/year. 50% of books from first-time authors. 50% from unagented writers. Pays 10-15% royalty on retail price.** Publishes book 24 months after acceptance of ms. Accepts simultaneous submissions. Responds in 2-4 months on queries. Guidelines available online at website.

◯ Does not accept e-mail submissions.

FICTION Subjects include adventure, ethnic, literary, mainstream, mystery, romance, suspense, young adult. Query with SASE.

TIPS "Please follow the submission guidelines posted on our website."

AHSAHTA PRESS

MFA Program in Creative Writing, Boise State University, 1910 University Dr., MS 1525, Boise ID 83725-1525. (208)426-4210. E-mail: ahsahta@boisestate.edu. E-mail: jholmes@boisestate.edu. Website: ahsahta-press.boisestate.edu. **Contact:** Janet Holmes, director. Estab. 1974. Publishes trade paperback originals. **Publishes 7 titles/year. 800 mss received/year. 15% of books from first-time authors. 100% from unagented writers. Pays 8% royalty on retail price.** Publishes book 6-36 months after acceptance of ms. Accepts simultaneous submissions. Responds in 3 months to manuscripts. Book catalog available online.

◯ "Our usual reading period is March 1-May 1, but because of a backlog of accepted manuscripts, *Ahsahta* cannot read unsolicited work until further notice. Please check our site periodically for announcements if you are interested. Ahsahta Press publishes chapbooks only occasionally and by invitation only. During the Sawtooth Poetry Prize Competition (January 1 through March 1) we are not able to consider manuscripts unless they are contest entries. However, we try to respond to submissions within 3 months. The press will continue to read manuscripts for the $1500 Sawtooth Poetry Prize Competition each year between January 1 and March 1. Please see the competition guidelines for more information."

POETRY "We are booked years in advance and are not currently reading manuscripts, with the exception of the Sawtooth Poetry Prize competition, from which we publish 2-3 mss. per year." Submit complete ms.

TIPS "Ahsahta's motto is that poetry is art, so our readers tend to come to us for the unexpected—poetry that makes them think, reflect, and even do something they haven't done before."

ALBERT WHITMAN & COMPANY

250 S. Northwest Highway, Suite 320, Park Ridge IL 60068. (800)255-7675. Fax: (847)581-0039. E-mail: mail@awhitmanco.com. Website: www.albertwhitman.com. **Contact:** Submissions Editor. Wendy McClure, senior editor Estab. 1919. Publishes in original hardcover, paperback, boardbooks. **Publishes 40 titles/year. 10% of books from first-time authors. 50% from unagented writers. On retail price: Pays 10% royalty for novels; 5% for picture books. Pays advance.** Publishes book an average 18 months after acceptance of ms. Accepts simultaneous submissions. Responds within 3 months to queries; 4 months to proposals and mss. "Send a self-addressed, stamped 9×12 envelope with your request, and address your letter to "Catalog Request" at our main address. Please include three first-class stamps (U.S. postage) with your SASE. Unless you specify otherwise, we will send our most recent catalog.". Guidelines available on website.

○ "We have a new policy for unsolicited submissions. After November 1st, 2010, we will respond only to submissions of interest. We read every submission within 4 months of receipt, but we can no longer respond to every one. If you do not receive a response from us after 4 months, we have declined to publish your submission. After November 1st, 2010, please do not enclose an SASE. We will not be returning materials received after that date. Please be sure to include current contact information (mail address, e-mail, and phone number) on cover letter and first page of manuscript."

○━ "Albert Whitman & Company publishes books for the trade, library, and school library market. We have an open submissions policy: we read unsolicited work, which means that it is not necessary for writers to submit through a literary agent. We are interested in reviewing the following types of projects: Picture book manuscripts for ages 2-8; Novels and chap-

ter books for ages 8-12; Young adult novels; Nonfiction for ages 3-12 and YA; Art samples showing pictures of children." Best known for the classic series The Boxcar Children® Mysteries, its highly-praised picture books, novels, and nonfiction titles for ages 2-12, delighting children and reaching out to children of all backgrounds and experiences. "Albert Whitman publishes good books for children on a variety of topics: holidays (i.e., Halloween), special needs (such as diabetes), and problems like divorce. The majority of our titles are picture books with less than 1,500 words. De-emphasizing bedtime stories."

NONFICTION Subjects include Americana, animals, character education, disabilities, family issues, holidays, multicultural, sports, Most of our titles are geared for children in preschool through sixth grade. We are well known for the Boxcar Children® Mysteries and for our Concept Books—those which deal with children's problems and special needs. We also publish picture books, nonfiction, biography, and novels. Reviews artwork/photos. Send photocopies.

FICTION Subjects include juvenile, picture books, sports. "You may send the manuscript in its entirety OR a query letter with synopsis and sample chapters. At this time, we are not seeking manuscripts or writers for the Boxcar Children® Mysteries series."

TIPS "In both picture books and nonfiction, we are seeking stories showing life in other cultures and the variety of multicultural life in the U.S. We also want fiction and nonfiction about mentally or physically challenged children—some recent topics have been autism, stuttering, and diabetes. Look up some of our books first to be sure your submission is appropriate for Albert Whitman & Co.", "We publish trade books that are especially interesting to schools and libraries. We recommend you study our website before submitting your work."

ALEXANDER HAMILTON INSTITUTE

70 Hilltop Rd., Ramsey NJ 07446-1119. (201)825-3377; (800)879-2441. Fax: (201)825-8696. E-mail: editorial@legalworkplace.com. Website: www.legalworkplace.com. **Contact:** Brian L.P. Zevnik, editor-in-chief; Gloria Ju, editor. Estab. 1909. Publishes 3-ring binder and paperback originals. **Publishes 5-10 titles/year. 50 queries received/year. 10 mss received/year. 25% of books from first-time authors. 95% from unagented writers. Pays 5-8% royalty on retail price. Makes**

outright purchase of $3,500-7,000. **Pays $3,500-7,000 advance.** Publishes book 10 months after acceptance of ms. Accepts simultaneous submissions. Responds in 1 month to queries. Responds in 2 months to manuscripts.

8—¬ "Alexander Hamilton Institute publishes management books for upper-level managers and executives. Currently emphasizing legal issues for HR/personnel."

NONFICTION These books combine court case research and practical application of defensible programs. The main audience is US personnel executives and high-level management.

TIPS "We sell exclusively by direct mail or through electronic means to managers and executives. A writer must know his/her field and be able to communicate legal and practical systems and programs."

ALLEN A. KNOLL, PUBLISHERS

200 W. Victoria St., Santa Barbara CA 93101. (805)564-3377. E-mail: bookinfo@knollpublishers.com. Website: www.knollpublishers.com. **Contact:** Submissions. Estab. 1990. Format publishes in hardcover originals.

○ Small independent publisher, publishes a few titles a year. Specializes in "books for intelligent people who read for fun." Books: offset printing; sewn binding. Titles distributed through Ingram, Baker & Taylor.

ALLWORTH PRESS

An imprint of Skyhorse Publishing, 307 West 36th Str., 11th floor, New York NY 10010-4402. (212)777-8395. Fax: (212)777-8261. E-mail: pub@allworth.com. E-mail: bporter@allworth.com. Website: www.allworth.com. **Contact:** Bob Porter, associate publisher. Tad Crawford, publisher Estab. 1989. Publishes hardcover and trade paperback originals. **Publishes 12-18 titles/year. Pays advance.** Responds in 1 month to queries. Responds in 2 months to proposals. Book catalog and ms guidelines free.

8—¬ "Allworth Press publishes business and self-help information for artists, designers, photographers, authors and film and performing artists, as well as books about business, money and the law for the general public. The press also publishes the best of classic and contemporary writing in art and graphic design. Currently emphasizing photography, graphic & industrial design, performing arts, fine arts and crafts, et al."

NONFICTION Subjects include art, architecture, business, economics, film, cinema, stage, music, dance, photography, film, television, graphic design, performing arts, writing, as well as business and legal guides for the public. "We are currently accepting query letters for practical, legal, and technique books targeted to professionals in the arts, including designers, graphic and fine artists, craftspeople, photographers, and those involved in film and the performing arts." Query.

TIPS We are helping creative people in the arts by giving them practical advice about business and success.

ALONDRA PRESS, LLC

4119 Wildacres Dr., Houston TX 77072. E-mail: lark@alondrapress.com. Website: www.alondrapress.com. **Contact:** Pennelope Leight, fiction editor; Solomon Tager, nonfiction editor. Estab. 2007. Publishes trade paperback originals and reprints. **Publishes 4 titles/year. 75% of books from first-time authors. 75% from unagented writers.** Publishes book 8 months after acceptance of ms. Accepts simultaneous submissions. Responds in 1 month to queries and proposals. Responds in 3 month to manuscripts. Guidelines available online.

NONFICTION Subjects include anthropology, archaeology, history, philosophy, psychology, translation. Submit complete ms.

FICTION Subjects include literary, all fiction genres. "Just send us a few pages in an e-mail attachment, or the entire manuscript. We will look at it quickly and tell you if it interests us."

TIPS "Be sure to read our guidelines before sending a submission. We will not respond to authors who do not observe our simple guidelines. Send your submissions in an e-mail attachment only."

ALPINE PUBLICATIONS

38262 Linman Road, Crawford CO 81415. (970)921-5005. Fax: (970)921-5081. E-mail: alpinepubl@aol.com. Website: alpinepub.com. **Contact:** Ms. B.J. McKinney, publisher. Estab. 1975. Publishes hardcover and trade paperback originals and reprints. **Publishes 6-10 titles/year. 40% of books from first-time authors. 95% from unagented writers. Pays 8-15% royalty on wholesale price. Pays advance.** Publishes book 18 months after acceptance of ms. Accepts simultaneous submissions. Responds in 1-3 weeks to queries. Responds in 1 month to proposals and manuscripts. Book catalog available free. Guidelines available online.

IMPRINTS Blue Ribbon Books.

NONFICTION Subjects include animals. Alpine specializes in books that promote the enjoyment of and responsibility for companion animals with emphasis on dogs and horses. No biographies. Reviews artwork/photos. Send photocopies.

TIPS "Our audience is pet owners, breeders, exhibitors, veterinarians, animal trainers, animal care specialists, and judges. Our books are in-depth and most are heavily illustrated. Look up some of our titles before you submit. See what is unique about our books. Write your proposal to suit our guidelines."

AMACOM BOOKS

American Management Association, 1601 Broadway, New York NY 10019-7406. (212)586-8100. Fax: (212)903-8168. E-mail: cparisi@amanet.org; ekadin@amanet.org; rnirkind@amanet.org. Website: www.amacombooks.org; www.amanet.org. **Contact:** Ellen Kadin, executive editor (marketing, career, personal development); Robert Nirkind, senior editor (sales, customer service, project management, finance); Christina Parisi, executive editor (human resources, leadership, training, management). Estab. 1923. Publishes hardcover and trade paperback originals, professional books.

- AMACOM is the publishing arm of the American Management Association, the world's largest training organization for managers and their organizations—advancing the skills of individuals to Dr. business success. AMACOM's books are intended to enhance readers' personal and professional growth, and to help readers meet the challenges of the future by conveying emerging trends and cutting-edge thinking.

NONFICTION Subjects include all business topics. Publishes books for consumer and professional markets, including general business, management, strategic planning, human resources, manufacturing, project management, training, finance, sales, marketing, customer service, career, technology applications, history, real estate, parenting, communications and biography. Submit proposals including brief book description and rationale, TOC, author bio and platform, intended audience, competing books and sample chapters. Proposals returned with SASE only.

AMBASSADOR BOOKS, INC.

Paulist Press, 997 MacArthur Blvd., Mahwah NJ 07430. (201)825-7300; (800)218-1903. Fax: (800)836-3161. E-mail: info@paulistpress.com;ggoggins@paulistpress.com;jconlan@paulistpress.com. Website: www.ambassadorbooks.com. **Contact:** Acquisitions Editor. Publishes hardcover and trade paperback originals. **Publishes 12 titles/year. 500 queries received/year. 100 mss received/year. 50% of books from first-time authors. 90% from unagented writers. Pays 8% royalty on net sales.** Publishes book 18 months after acceptance of ms. Responds in up to 4 months to queries. Book catalog on-line for download, or write for paper catalog.

- Preference is given to non-simultaneous submissions (responds in 1-2 months). Accepts simultaneous submissions.
- We are a Christian publishing company seeking spirituality-focused books for children and adults."

NONFICTION Subjects include creative nonfiction, regional, religion, spirituality, sports, spiritual seeking, spirituality of sports, Catholic themes, intellectual exploration of religious topics, spiritual self-help. Adult books must have spiritual theme. Query with a sample chapter and SASE or complete ms. Children's books published as Ambassador Children's Books, and must have spiritual or self-help topic and 32-page format for ages 3-7, and under 100 pages for juvenile biography and religious topics for ages 8-13. Books with a spiritual theme. Query with proposal and SASE or submit complete ms. Reviews artwork/photos. Send photocopies.

FICTION Not accepted except in adult or juvenile fables. Query with SASE. Submit complete ms.

AMBER COMMUNICATIONS GROUP, INC.

1334 E. Chandler Blvd., Suite 5-D67, Phoenix AZ 85048. Website: www.amberbooks.com. **Contact:** Tony Rose, publisher. Estab. 1998. Publishes trade paperback and mass market paperback originals. Book catalog free or online.

IMPRINTS Amber Books (self-help); Busta Books (celebrity bio); Amber/Wiley (personal finance, beauty); Colossus Books (biographies, famous music personalities); Ambrosia Books (nonfiction, fiction, novels, docudramas).

- Amber Communications Group, Inc. is the nation's largest African-American publisher of self-help books and music biographies.

NONFICTION Subjects include beauty, fashion, history, celebrity memoirs, biographies, multicultural, personal finance, relationship advice. Submit proposal or outline with author biography. Please do not e-mail or mail mss unless requested by publisher. Reviews artwork/photos. Send photocopies, not originals.

FICTION Wants African-American topics and interest. Submit proposal or outline.

TIPS The goal of Amber Communications Group is to expand our catalog comprised of self-help books, and celebrity bio books; and expand our fiction department in print and on software, which pertain to, about, and for the African-American population.

AMERICAN BAR ASSOCIATION PUBLISHING

321 N. Clark St., Chicago IL 60654. (312)988-5000. Fax: (312)988-6030. Website: www.ababooks.org. **Contact:** Kathleen A. Welton, director of book publishing. Estab. 1878. Publishes hardcover and trade paperback originals. **Publishes 100 titles/year. 50 queries received/year. 20% of books from first-time authors. 95% from unagented writers.** Publishes book 6 months after acceptance of ms. Accepts simultaneous submissions. Responds in 1 month to queries. Responds in 1 month to proposals. Responds in 3 months to manuscripts. Book catalog and ms guidelines online.

8→ We are interested in books that help lawyers practice law more effectively, whether it's how to handle clients, structure a real estate deal, or take an antitrust case to court."

NONFICTION Subjects include business, economics, computers, electronics, money, finance, software, legal practice. "Our market is not, generally, the public. Books need to be targeted to lawyers who are seeking solutions to their practice problems. We rarely publish scholarly treatises." All areas of legal practice. Query with SASE.

TIPS "ABA books are written for busy, practicing lawyers. The most successful books have a practical, reader-friendly voice. If you can build in features like checklists, exhibits, sample contracts, flow charts, and tables of cases, please do so. The Association also publishes over 60 major national periodicals in a variety of legal areas. Contact Tim Brandhorst, Deputy Director of book publishing, at the above address for guidelines."

AMERICAN CARRIAGE HOUSE PUBLISHING

P.O. Box 1330, Nevada City CA 95959. (530)432-8860. Fax: (530)432-7379. E-mail: editor@americancar-riagehousepublishing.com. Website: www.ameri-cancarriagehousepublishing.com. **Contact:** Lynn Taylor, editor (parenting, reference, child, women). Estab. 2004. Format publishes in trade paperback and electronic originals. **Publishes 10 titles/year. 40 10% of books from first-time authors. 100% from unagented writers. Pays outright purchase of $300-3,000.** Publishes book 12 months after acceptance of ms. Accepts simultaneous submissions. Responds in 6 months on queries, proposals, and mss. Catalog free on request.

NONFICTION Subjects include child guidance, education, parenting, womens issues, womens studies, young adult. Query with SASE. Reviews artwork/photos. Send photocopies.

FICTION Subjects include religious, spiritual, young adult. Query with SASE.

AMERICAN CATHOLIC PRESS

16565 S. State St., South Holland IL 60473. (312)331-5845. Fax: (708)331-5484. E-mail: acp@acpress.org. Website: www.acpress.org. **Contact:** Rev. Michael Gilligan, PhD, editorial director. Estab. 1967. Publishes hardcover originals and hardcover and paperback reprints. **Publishes 4 titles/year. Makes outright purchase of $25-100.** Guidelines available online.

NONFICTION Subjects include education, music, dance, religion, spirituality. "We publish books on the Roman Catholic liturgy—for the most part, books on religious music and educational books and pamphlets. We also publish religious songs for church use, including Psalms, as well as choral and instrumental arrangements. We are interested in new music, meant for use in church services. Books, or even pamphlets, on the Roman Catholic Mass are especially welcome. We have no interest in secular topics and are not interested in religious poetry of any kind."

TIPS "Most of our sales are by direct mail, although we do work through retail outlets."

AMERICAN CORRECTIONAL ASSOCIATION

206 N. Washington St., Suite 200, Alexandria VA 22314. (703)224-0194. Fax: (703)224-0179. E-mail: aliceh@aca.org;susanc@aca.org;rgibson@aca.org. Website: www.aca.org. **Contact:** Alice Heiserman, manager of publications and research. Estab. 1870. Publishes trade paperback originals. **Publishes 18 titles/year. 90% of books from first-time authors. 100% from unagented writers.** Publishes book 1

year after acceptance of ms. Responds in 4 months to queries. Book catalog available free. Guidelines available online.

☞ American Correctional Association provides practical information on jails, prisons, boot camps, probation, parole, community corrections, juvenile facilities and rehabilitation programs, substance abuse programs, and other areas of corrections."

NONFICTION "We are looking for practical, how-to texts or training materials written for the corrections profession. We are especially interested in books on management, development of first-line supervisors, and security-threat group/management in prisons." No autobiographies or -life accounts by current or former inmates or correctional officers, theses, or dissertations. No fiction or poetry. Query with SASE. Reviews artwork/photos.

TIPS "Authors are professionals in the field of corrections. Our audience is made up of corrections professionals and criminal justice students. No books by inmates or former inmates. This publisher advises out-of-town freelance editors, indexers, and proofreaders to refrain from requesting work from them."

AMERICAN COUNSELING ASSOCIATION

5999 Stevenson Ave., Alexandria VA 22304. (703)823-9800. Fax: (703)823-4786. E-mail: cbaker@counseling.org. Website: www.counseling.org. **Contact:** Carolyn C. Baker, director of publications. Estab. 1952. Publishes paperback originals. **Publishes 10-12 titles/year. 1% of books from first-time authors. 90% from unagented writers.** Accepts simultaneous submissions. Responds in 1 month to queries. Guidelines available free.

☞ The American Counseling Association is dedicated to promoting public confidence and trust in the counseling profession. We publish scholarly texts for graduate level students and mental health professionals. We do not publish books for the general public."

NONFICTION Subjects include education, gay, lesbian, health, multicultural, psychology, religion, sociology, spirituality, women's issues. ACA does not publish self-help books or autobiographies. Query with SASE. Submit proposal package, outline, 2 sample chapters, vitae.

TIPS "Target your market. Your books will not be appropriate for everyone across all disciplines."

AMERICAN FEDERATION OF ASTROLOGERS

6535 S. Rural Rd., Tempe AZ 85283. (480)838-1751. Fax: (480)838-8293. E-mail: info@astrologers.com. Website: www.astrologers.com. Estab. 1938. Publishes trade paperback originals and reprints. **Publishes 10-15 titles/year. 10 queries received/year. 20 mss received/year. 50% of books from first-time authors. 100% from unagented writers. Pays 10% royalty.** Publishes book 10 months after acceptance of ms. Accepts simultaneous submissions. Responds in 6 months to manuscripts. Book catalog available free. Guidelines available free.

☞ American Federation of Astrologers publishes astrology books, calendars, charts, and related aids.

NONFICTION "Our market for beginner books, Sun-sign guides and similar material is limited and we thus publish very few of these. The ideal word count for a book-length manuscript published by AFA is about 40,000 words, although we will consider manuscripts from 20,000 to 60,000 words." Submit complete ms.

TIPS "AFA welcomes articles for *Today's Astrologer*, our monthly journal for members, on any astrological subject. Most articles are 1,500-3,000 words, but we do accept shorter and longer articles. Follow the guidelines online for book manuscripts. You also can e-mail your article to info@astrologers.com, but any charts or illustrations must be submitted as attachments and not embedded in the body of the e-mail or in an attached document."

⊘ AMERICAN PRESS

60 State St., Suite 700, Boston MA 02109. (617)247-0022. E-mail: americanpress@flash.net. Website: www.americanpresspublishers.com. **Contact:** Jana Kirk, editor. Estab. 1911. Publishes college textbooks. **Publishes 25 titles/year. 350 queries received/year. 100 mss received/year. 50% of books from first-time authors. 90% from unagented writers. Pays 5-15% royalty on wholesale price.** Publishes book 9 months after acceptance of ms. Responds in 3 months to queries.

◐ "Mss proposals are welcome in all subjects & disciplines."

NONFICTION Subjects include agriculture, anthropology, archeology, art, architecture, business, economics, education, government, politics, health, medicine, history, horticulture, music, dance, psychology, science, sociology, sports. "We prefer that our authors actually teach courses for which the manuscripts are designed." Query, or submit outline with tentative TOC. *No complete mss.*

AMERICAN QUILTER'S SOCIETY

Schroeder Publishing, P.O. Box 3290, Paducah KY 42002-3290. (270)898-7903. Fax: (270)898-1173. E-mail: editor@aqsquilt.com. Website: www.american-quilter.com. **Contact:** Andi Reynolds, executive book editor (primarily how-to and patterns, but other quilting books sometimes published, including quilt-related fiction). Estab. 1984. Publishes trade paperback titles per year. **Publishes 20-24 titles/year. 100 queries received/year. Multiple submissions okay. 60% of books from first-time authors. Pays 5% royalty on retail price.** Publishes book 12-18 months from manuscript delivery to publication. after acceptance of ms. Accepts simultaneous submissions. Responds in 1 week to 2 months to proposals. Proposal guidelines online.

⚷➻ American Quilter's Society publishes how-to and pattern books for quilters (beginners through intermediate skill level). We are not the publisher for non-quilters writing about quilts."

NONFICTION No queries; proposals only. 1 or 2 completed quilt projects must accompany proposal.

AMERICAN WATER WORKS ASSOCIATION

6666 W. Quincy Ave., Denver CO 80235. (303)347-6278. Fax: (303)794-7310. E-mail: mkozyra@awwa.org. Website: www.awwa.org/communications/books. **Contact:** Scott Millard, Manager, Business & Product Development. Estab. 1881. Publishes hardcover and trade paperback originals. Responds in 4 months to queries. Book catalog and ms guidelines free.

⚷➻ AWWA strives to advance and promote the safety and knowledge of drinking water and related issues to all audiences—from kindergarten through post-doctorate."

NONFICTION Subjects include nature, environment, science, software, drinking water- and wastewater-related topics, operations, treatment, sustainability. Query with SASE. Submit outline, bio, 3 sample chapters. Reviews artwork/photos. Send photocopies.

TIPS "See website to download submission instructions."

AMERICA WEST PUBLISHERS

P.O. Box 2208, Carson City NV 89702-2208. (775)885-0700. Fax: (877)726-2632. E-mail: global@nohoax.

com. Website: www.nohoax.com. **Contact:** George Green, president. Estab. 1985. Publishes hardcover and trade paperback originals and reprints. **Publishes 20 titles/year. 90% of books from first-time authors. 90% from unagented writers. Pays 10% royalty on wholesale price. Pays $300 average advance.** Publishes book 6 months from acceptance to publishing time. after acceptance of ms. Accepts simultaneous submissions. Responds in 1 month to queries. Book catalog and ms guidelines free.

IMPRINTS Bridger House Publishers, Inc.

⚷➻ America West seeks the other side of the picture, political cover-ups, and new health alternatives."

NONFICTION Subjects include business, economics, government, politics, including cover-up, health, medicine, holistic self-help, New Age, UFO-metaphysical. Submit outline, sample chapters. Reviews artwork/photos.

TIPS "We currently have materials in all bookstores that have areas of UFOs; also political and economic nonfiction."

AMHERST MEDIA, INC.

175 Rano St., Suite 200, Buffalo NY 14207. (716)874-4450. Fax: (716)874-4508. E-mail: submissions@amherstmedia.com. Website: www.AmherstMedia.com. **Contact:** Craig Alesse, publisher. Estab. 1974. Publishes trade paperback originals and reprints. **Publishes 30 titles/year. 60% of books from first-time authors. 90% from unagented writers. Pays 6-8% royalty. Pays advance.** Publishes book 1 year. after acceptance of ms. Accepts simultaneous submissions. Responds in 2 months to queries. Book catalog free and online (catalog@amherstmedia.com). Guidelines free and available online.

⚷➻ Amherst Media publishes how-to photography books.

NONFICTION Subjects include photography. Looking for well-written and illustrated photo books. Query with outline, 2 sample chapters, and SASE. Reviews artwork/photos.

TIPS "Our audience is made up of beginning to advanced photographers. If I were a writer trying to market a book today, I would fill the need of a specific audience and self-edit in a tight manner."

⊘ AMIGADGET PUBLISHING CO.

P.O. Box 1696, Lexington SC 29071. E-mail: amigadget@fotoartista.com. Website: www.fotoartista.com/

amigadget. **Contact:** Jay Gross, editor-in-chief. Publishes trade paperback originals. **Publishes 1 titles/year.**

NONFICTION Query via e-mail only. *All unsolicited mss returned unopened.*

TIPS "We are not currently seeking new paper publishing projects, and and we do not publish fiction."

◐, ANAPHORA LITERARY PRESS

104 Banff Dr., Apt. 101, Edinboro PA 16412. (814)273-0004. E-mail: pennsylvaniajournal@gmail.com. E-mail: pennsylvaniajournal@gmail.com. Website: www.anaphoraliterary.wordpress.com. **Contact:** Anna Faktorovich, editor-in-chief (general interest). Estab. 2007. Format publishes in trade paperback originals and reprints; mass market paperback originals and reprints. **Publishes 3 titles/year. 200 queries/year; 100 mss/year 50% of books from first-time authors. 100% from unagented writers. Pays 10-30% royalty on retail price. "We currently publish journals, which are authored by several people. If we publish a novel or a critical book by a single author, we will share our profits with the author."** Publishes book 2 months after acceptance of ms. Accepts simultaneous submissions. Responds in 1 month on queries, proposals, and mss. Catalog and guidelines available online at website.

- ✂— In the Winter of 2010, Anaphora began accepting book-length single-author submissions. We are actively seeking single and multiple-author books in fiction (poetry, novels, and short story collections) and nonfiction (academic, legal, business, journals, edited and un-edited dissertations, biographies, and memoirs). E-mail submissions to pennsylvaniajournal@gmail.com. Profits are split 50/50% with single-author writers. There are no costs to have a book produced by Anaphora. We do not offer any free contributor copies."

NONFICTION Subjects include communications, contemporary culture, creative nonfiction, education, entertainment, games, government, hobbies, humanities, language, literary criticism, literature, memoirs, multicultural, New Age, philosophy, politics, recreation, regional, travel, women's issues, academic, legal, business, journals, edited and un-edited dissertations. "We are actively seeking quality writing that is original, innovative, enlightening, intellectual and otherwise a pleasure to read. Our primary focus in nonfiction is literary criticism; but, there are many other areas

of interest. Send a query letter if you are considering submitting anything in the other fields listed above." Query with SASE. Submit proposal package, including: outline, 1 sample chapter. Submit completed ms. Does not review artwork.

FICTION Subjects include adventure, comic books, confession, contemporary, experimental, fantasy, feminist, gothic, historical, humor, literary, mainstream, military, mystery, occult, picture books, plays, poetry, poetry in translation, regional, short story collections, suspense, war. "We are actively seeking submissions at this time. The genre is not as important as the quality of work. You should have a completed full-length ms ready to be e-mailed or mailed upon request." Looking for single and multiple-author books in fiction (poetry, novels, and short story collections). Query with SASE. Submit proposal package, including synopsis, 1 sample chapter, and completed ms.

POETRY Looking for single and multiple-author books in poetry. Query. Submit 10 sample poems. Submit complete ms.

TIPS "Our audience is academics, college students and graduates, as well as anybody who loves literature. Regardless of profits, we love publishing great books and we enjoy reading submissions. So, if you are reading this book because you love writing and hope to publish as soon as possible, send a query letter or a submission to us. But, remember—proofread your work (most of our editors are English instructors)."

◐ ANDREWS MCMEEL UNIVERSAL

1130 Walnut St., Kansas City MO 64106-2109. (816)932-6700. Website: www.amuniversal.com. **Contact:** Christine Schillig, vice president/editorial director. Estab. 1973. Publishes hardcover and paperback originals. **Publishes 200 titles/year. Pays royalty on retail price or net receipts. Pays advance.**

- ✂— Andrews McMeel publishes general trade books, humor books, miniature gift books, calendars, and stationery products.

NONFICTION Subjects include contemporary culture, general trade, relationships. Also produces gift books. Agented submissions only.

ANGOOR PRESS LLC

2734 Bruchez Pkwy., Unit 103, Denver CO 80234. E-mail: submissions@angoorpress.com. E-mail: submissions@angoorpress.com. Website: www.angoorpress.com. **Contact:** Carolina Maine, Founder, Editor. Estab. 2010. **Publishes 10 titles/year. 50-100% of** books from first-time authors. **100% from unagent-ed writers. Pays 5%-20% on wholesale price in royalties.** Publishes book 6-12 months after acceptance of ms. Responds 3 months to proposals and manuscripts. No catalog available. Manuscript guidelines are free by request.

IMPRINTS Hardcover, Trade paperback, and Electronic originals.

NONFICTION Subjects include contemporary culture, religion. "Essays submitted must be in line with Catholic teaching. Must include author bio." Submit proposal package, and essays in via PDF e-mail attachment. No

FICTION Subjects include adventure, confession, contemporary, ethnic, literary, mainstream, poetry, religious, spiritual. Submit proposal package, including market search, author bio and book marketing plan.

POETRY Submit 2-5 number of sample poems and complete manuscript.

TIPS "Christians."

ANHINGA PRESS

P.O. Box 3665, Tallahassee FL 32315. (850)422-1408. Fax: (850)442-6323. E-mail: info@anhinga.org. Website: www.anhinga.org. **Contact:** Rick Campbell, editor. Publishes hardcover and trade paperback originals. **Publishes 5 titles/year. Pays 10% royalty on retail price. Offers Anhinga Prize of $2,000.** Accepts simultaneous submissions. Responds in 3 months to queries, proposals, and manuscripts. Book catalog and contest for #10 SASE or online. Guidelines available online.

↳ Publishes only full-length collections of poetry (60-80 pages). No individual poems or chapbooks."

POETRY Query with SASE and 10-page sample (not full ms) by mail. No e-mail queries.

APA BOOKS

American Psychological Association, 750 First St., NE, Washington DC 20002-4242. (800)374-2721 or (202)336- 5500. Website: www.apa.org/books. Publishes hardcover and trade paperback originals. Book catalog available online. Guidelines available online.

IMPRINTS Magination Press (children's books).

NONFICTION Subjects include education, gay, lesbian, multicultural, psychology, science, social sciences, sociology, women's issues, women's studies. Submit cv and prospectus with TOC, intended audience, selling points, and outside competition.

TIPS "Our press features scholarly books on empirically supported topics for professionals and students in all areas of psychology."

APPALACHIAN MOUNTAIN CLUB BOOKS

5 Joy St., Boston MA 02108. (617)523-0636. Fax: (617)523-0722. E-mail: amcpublications@outdoors.org. Website: www.outdoors.org. **Contact:** Editor-in-Chief. Estab. 1876. Publishes hardcover and trade paperback originals. Accepts simultaneous submissions. Guidelines available online.

↳ AMC Books are written and published by the experts in the Northeast outdoors. Our mission is to publish authoritative, accurate, and easy-to-use books and maps based on AMC's expertise in outdoor recreation, education, and conservation. We are committed to producing books and maps that appeal to novices and day visitors as well as outdoor enthusiasts in our core activity areas of hiking and paddling. By advancing the interest of the public in outdoor recreation and helping our readers to access backcountry trails and waterways, and by using our books to educate the public about safety, conservation, and stewardship, we support AMC's mission of promoting the protection, enjoyment, and wise use of the Northeast outdoors. We work with the best professional writers possible and draw upon the experience of our programs staff and chapter leaders from Maine to Washington, D.C."

NONFICTION Subjects include nature, environment, recreation, regional, Northeast outdoor recreation, literary nonfiction, guidebooks, Maps that are based on our direct work with land managers and our on-the-ground collection of data on trails, natural features, and points of interest. AMC Books also publishes narrative titles related to outdoor recreation, mountaineering, and adventure, often with a historical perspective. "Appalachian Mountain Club publishes hiking guides, paddling guides, nature, conservation, and mountain-subject guides for America's Northeast. We connect recreation to conservation and education." Query with proposal and the first 3 chapters of your ms to the publications department at AMCpublications@outdoors.org. You can also send them via US Postal Service to AMC Books Editor, Appalachian Mountain Club, 5 Joy St., Boston, MA 02108 with SASE. Reviews artwork/photos. Send on a disk or via weblink.

TIPS "Our audience is outdoor recreationists, conservation-minded hikers and canoeists, family outdoor lovers, armchair enthusiasts. Visit our website for proposal submission guidelines and more information."

ⓐ ARCADE PUBLISHING

307 West 57th St., 11th Floor, New York NY 10018. (212)643-6816. Fax: (212)643-6819. Website: www.arcadepub.com. **Contact:** Jeannette Seaver, publisher/executive editor; Cal Barksdale, executive editor; Casey Ebro, editor; Tessa Aye, assistant editor. Estab. 1988. Publishes hardcover originals, trade paperback reprints. **Publishes 35 titles/year. 5% of books from first-time authors. Pays royalty on retail price. 10 author's copies Pays advance.** Publishes book within 18 months after acceptance of ms. Responds in 2 months to queries. Book catalog and ms guidelines for #10 SASE.

> ☛ Arcade prides itself on publishing top-notch literary nonfiction and fiction, with a significant proportion of foreign writers."

NONFICTION Subjects include history, memoirs, nature, environment, travel, popular science, current events. Agented submissions only. Reviews artwork/photos. Send photocopies.

FICTION Subjects include literary, mainstream, contemporary, short story collections, translation. No romance, historical, science fiction. Agented submissions only.

ARCADIA PUBLISHING

420 Wando Park Blvd., Mt. Pleasant SC 29464. (843)853-2070. Fax: (843)853-0044. E-mail: Please contact the editorial office of your region on our website. Website: www.arcadiapublishing.com. **Contact:** Editorial Director. Estab. 1993. Publishes trade paperback originals. **Publishes 600 titles/year. Pays 8% royalty on retail price.** Publishes book 9 months after acceptance of ms. Accepts simultaneous submissions. Book catalog available online. Guidelines available free.

> ◗ The following submissions e-mail addresses are divided by region: publishingnortheast@arcadiapublishing.com; publishingsouth@arcadiapublishing.com; publishingwest@arcadiapublishing.com; publishingmidwest@arcadiapublishing.com.

> ☛ Arcadia publishes photographic vintage regional histories. We have more than 3,000 Images

of America series in print. We have expanded our California program."

NONFICTION Subjects include history, local, regional. "Arcadia accepts submissions year-round. Our editors seek proposals on local history topics and are able to provide authors with detailed information about our publishing program as well as book proposal submission guidelines. Due to the great demand for titles on local and regional history, we are currently searching for authors to work with us on new photographic history projects. Please contact one of our regional publishing teams if you are interested in submitting a proposal." Specific proposal form to be completed.

TIPS "Writers should know that we only publish history titles. The majority of our books are on a city or region, and contain vintage images with limited text."

⊕ ARCHAIA

1680 Vine St., Suite 912, Los Angeles CA 90028. E-mail: editorial@archaia.com. E-mail: submissions@archaia.com. Website: www.archaia.com. **Contact:** Submissions Editor.

> ◗ Archaia Entertainment, LLC is a multi-award-winning graphic novel publisher with more than 50 renowned publishing brands, including such domestic and international hits as *Artesia, Mouse Guard, The Killer, Gunnerkrigg Court, Awakening, Titanium Rain, Days Missing, Tumor, Syndrome, Okko, The Secret History*, and a line of Jim Henson graphic novels including *Fraggle Rock* and *The Dark Crystal*. Archaia has built an unparalleled reputation for producing meaningful content that perpetually transforms minds, building one of the industry's most visually stunning and eclectic slates of graphic novels. Archaia is the reigning 2010 Graphic Novel Publisher of the Year according to *Ain't it Cool News, Graphic Policy*, and *Comic Related*. Archaia has also successfully emerged as a prolific storyteller in all facets of the entertainment industry, extending its popular brands into film, television, gaming, and branded digital media. Archaia publishes creator-owned comic books and graphic novels in the adventure, fantasy, horror, pulp noir, and science fiction genres that contain idiosyncratic and atypical writing and art. Archaia does not generally hire freelancers

or arrange for freelance work, so submissions should only be for completed book and series proposals. Query with outline/synopsis and pdf of completed pages. Archaia prefers e-mail submissions with pdf attachments. Included info on estimated page count, intended formats, and other technical details. Submissions guidelines on website."

A-R EDITIONS, INC.

8551 Research Way, Suite 180, Middleton WI 53562. (608)203-2565. Fax: (608)831-8200. E-mail: pamela.whitcomb@areditions.com; james.zychowicz@areditions.com. Website: www.areditions.com. **Contact:** Pamela Whitcomb, managing editor (Recent Researches Series); James L. Zychowicz, managing editor (Computer Music and Digital Audio Series, and MLA's Index and Bibliography, Technical Reports, and Basic Manual Series). Estab. 1962. **Publishes 30 titles/year. 40 queries received/year. 30 mss received/year. 75% of books from first-time authors. 100% from unagented writers. Pays royalty or honoraria.** Responds in 1 month to queries. Responds in 3 months to proposals. Responds in 6 months to manuscripts. Book catalog available online. Guidelines available online.

○ "A-R Editions publishes modern critical editions of music based on current musicological research. Each edition is devoted to works by a single composer or to a single genre of composition. The contents are chosen for their potential interest to scholars and performers, then prepared for publication according to the standards that govern the making of all reliable, historical editions."

NONFICTION Subjects include computers, electronics, music, dance, software, historical music editions. Computer Music and Digital Audio Series titles deal with issues tied to digital and electronic media, and include both textbooks and handbooks in this area. Query with SASE. Submit outline. "All material submitted in support of a proposal becomes the property of A-R Editions. Please send photocopies of all important documents (retain your originals). We suggest that you send your proposal either with delivery confirmation or by a service that offers package tracking to avoid misdirected packages."

ARIEL STARR PRODUCTIONS, LTD.

P.O. Box 17, Demarest NJ 07627. E-mail: arielstarrprod@aol.com. E-mail: arielstarrprod@aol.com. **Contact:** Attn: Acquisitions Editor. Estab. 1993. Trade and mass market paperback originals; electronic originals. **Publishes 5 titles/year. Receives 40 queries/year, 4 mss/year. 80% of books from first-time authors. 80% from unagented writers. Pays 5-15% royalty on wholesale price.** Publishes book 12 months after acceptance of ms. Accepts simultaneous submissions. Responds in 2 months on queries and proposals, 6 months on mss. Catalog not available. Guidelines available by e-mail.

○ "Just make sure you submit the query with outline first unless we ask for something else."

NONFICTION Subjects include environment, nature, New Age, religion, spirituality. "We are open to other areas but we ask the person to submit a query letter, one-page outline, and a SASE first; nothing more unless we ask for it." Query with SASE. Reviews artwork/photos; send photocopies.

FICTION Subjects include adventure, fantasy, poetry, religious, science fiction, spiritual. Query with SASE and one-page proposal.

POETRY Query; submit 2 sample poems.

TIPS "We want books that stimulate the brain and inspire the mind. Be honest and decent in your queries."

ARTE PUBLICO PRESS

University of Houston, 452 Cullen Performance Hall, Houston TX 77204-2004. Fax: (713)743-3080. E-mail: submapp@mail.uh.edu. E-mail: submapp@mail.uh.edu. Website: www.artepublicopress.com. **Contact:** Nicolas Kanellos, editor. Estab. 1979. Publishes hardcover originals, trade paperback originals and reprints. **Publishes 25-30 titles/year. 1,000 queries received/yeare. 2,000 mss received/year. 50% of books from first-time authors. 80% from unagented writers. Pays 10% royalty on wholesale price. Provides 20 author's copies; 40% discount on subsequent copies. Pays $1,000-3,000 advance.** Publishes book 2 years. after acceptance of ms. Accepts simultaneous submissions. Responds in 1 month to queries & to proposals. Responds in 4 months to manuscripts. Book catalog available free. Guidelines available online.

IMPRINTS Piñata Books.

○ Arte Publico Press is the oldest and largest publisher of Hispanic literature for children and adults in the United States. "We are a showcase for **Hispanic** literary creativity, arts and culture. Our endeavor is to provide a national forum for U.S.-Hispanic literature."

NONFICTION Subjects include ethnic, language, literature, regional, translation, women's issues, women's studies. Hispanic civil rights issues for new series: The Hispanic Civil Rights Series. Query with SASE. Submit outline, 2 sample chapters.

FICTION Subjects include contemporary, ethnic, literary, mainstream. "Written by U.S.-Hispanics. Query with SASE. Submit outline/proposal, clips, 2 sample chapters. Submit complete ms.

POETRY Submit 10 sample poems.

TIPS "Include cover letter in which you 'sell' your book—why should we publish the book, who will want to read it, why does it matter, etc." "Use our ms submission online form. Format files accepted are: word, plain/text, rich/text files. Other formats will not be accepted. Manuscript files cannot be larger than 5MB. Once editors review your ms, you will receive an e-mail with the decision. Revision process could take up to four (4) months."

ASABI PUBLISHING

Three West Enterprises, (813)579-3506. E-mail: submissions@asabipublishing.com. E-mail: submissions@asabipublishing.com. Website: www.asabipublishing.com. **Contact:** Tressa Sanders, publisher. Estab. 2004. Publishes hardcover, mass market and trade paperback originals. **Publishes 24 titles/year. Accepts submissions electronically only. 90% of books from first-time authors. 90% from unagented writers. Pays 10% royalty on wholesale or list price. Pays up to $500 advance.** Publishes book 6 months after acceptance of ms. Accepts simultaneous submissions. Responds in 1 month to queries and proposals, 2-6 months to mss. Book catalog available online. Guidelines available online and by e-mail.

IMPRINTS Solomon Publishing Group-Sweden

NONFICTION Subjects include agriculture, creative nonfiction, environment, ethnic, gay, health, history, horticulture, lesbian, medicine, nature, psychology, science, sex, social sciences, young adult, skilled trades. Submit 4 sample chapters or completed ms. Submissions must be fully edited by a professional prior to submission. "We do not publish poetry or titles containing religious or spiritual content of any kind." Reviews artwork/photos. Writers should send photocopies.

FICTION Subjects include adventure, confession, erotica, ethnic, experimental, fantasy, gay, horror, juvenile, lesbian, mystery, romance, science fiction, short story collections, suspense, young adult. Submit 4 sample chapters or completed ms.

ASCE PRESS

American Society of Civil Engineers, 1801 Alexander Bell Dr., Reston VA 20191-4382. (703)295-6275. Fax: (703)295-6278. E-mail: bkulamer@asce.org. Website: www.asce.org/pubs. Estab. 1989. **Publishes 10-15 titles/year. 20% of books from first-time authors. 100% from unagented writers.** Request ASCE Press book proposal submission guidelines;. guidelines available online.

8— ASCE Press publishes technical volumes that are useful to practicing civil engineers and civil engineering students, as well as allied professionals. We publish books by individual authors and editors to advance the civil engineering profession. Currently emphasizing geotechnical, structural engineering, sustainable engineering and engineering history. De-emphasizing highly specialized areas with narrow scope."

NONFICTION "We are looking for topics that are useful and instructive to the engineering practitioner." Query with proposal, sample chapters, CV, TOC, and target audience.

TIPS "As a traditional publisher of scientific and technical materials, ASCE Press applies rigorous standards to the expertise, scholarship, readability and attractiveness of its books."

⊕ ASHLAND POETRY PRESS

401 College Ave., Ashland OH 44805. (419)289-5957. Fax: (419)289-5255. E-mail: app@ashland.edu. Website: www.ashland.edu/aupoetry. **Contact:** Sarah M. Wells, Managing Editor. Estab. 1969. Publishes trade paperback originals. **Publishes 2-3 titles/year. 360 mss received/year. 50% of books from first-time authors. 100% from unagented writers. Makes outright purchase of $500-1,000.** Publishes book 10 months after acceptance of ms. Accepts simultaneous submissions. Responds in 1 month to queries. Responds in 6 months to manuscripts. Book catalog available online. Guidelines available online.

POETRY "We accept unsolicited manuscripts through the Snyder Prize competition each spring-the deadline is April 30. Judges are mindful of dedication to craftsmanship and thematic integrity."

TIPS "We rarely publish a title submitted off the transom outside of our Snyder Prize competition."

ASM PRESS

Book division for the American Society for Microbiology, 1752 N. St., NW, Washington DC 20036-2904. (202)737-3600. Fax: (202)942-9342. E-mail: lwilliams@asmusa.org. E-mail: lwilliams@asmusa.org. Website: www.asmpress.org. **Contact:** Lindsay Williams (proposal submissions-books); Gregory Payne, senior editor (all microbiology and related sciences); Eleanor Riemer, consulting editor (food microbiology). Estab. 1899. Publishes hardcover, trade paperback and electronic originals. **Publishes 30 titles/year. 40% of books from first-time authors. 95% from unagented writers. Pays 5-15% royalty on wholesale price. Pays $1,000-10,000 advance.** Publishes book 6-9 months after acceptance of ms. Accepts simultaneous submissions. Responds in 1 month to queries. Responds in 1-2 months to proposals. Responds in 1-4 months to manuscripts. Book catalog available online. Guidelines available online.

NONFICTION Subjects include agriculture, animals, education, health, medicine, history, horticulture, nature, environment, science, microbiology and related sciences. "Must have bona fide academic credentials in which they are writing." Query with SASE or by e-mail. Submit proposal package, outline, prospectus. Proposals for journal articles must be submitted to the journals department at: journals@asmusa.com Reviews artwork/photos. Send photocopies.

TIPS "Credentials are most important."

ASTRAGAL PRESS

Finney Company, 8075 215th St. West, Lakeville MN 55044. (866)543-3045. Fax: (952)669-1968. E-mail: feedback@finneyco.com. Website: www.finneyco.com/books.htm. Estab. 1983. Publishes trade paperback originals and reprints. Accepts simultaneous submissions. Book catalog and ms guidelines free.

Quality books for adults and children that foster an appreciation of Florida's natural communities and fascinating history. "Our primary audience includes those interested in antique tool collecting, metalworking, carriage building, early sciences and early trades, and railroading."

NONFICTION Books on early tools, trades & technology, and railroads. Query with SASE. Submit sample chapters, TOC, book overview, illustration descriptions. Submit complete ms.

TIPS "We sell to niche markets. We are happy to work with knowledgeable amateur authors in developing titles."

ATRIAD PRESS, LLC

13820 Methuen Green, Dallas TX 75240. (972)671-0002. Fax: (214)367-4343. E-mail: ginnie@atriadpress.com. E-mail: editor@atriadpress.com. Website: www.atriadpress.com; www.hauntedencounters.com. **Contact:** Mitchel Whitington, senior editor. Estab. 2002. trade paperback originals. **Writers selected for this collection of personal ghost tales will receive a copy of the book in which their story appears. Authors can purchase additional copies of the books at discounted prices, and re-sell them at book signings, speaking engagements, etc. for additional revenue. A photo and brief bio of the author will be included at the end of the story.** Accepts simultaneous submissions. Book catalog available online. Guidelines available online. If you have any questions regarding the Writer's Guidelines, please contact us by e-mail at editor@atriadpress.com.

We are seeking books on supernatural happenings focused on the State of Texas. The first two titles in this series are: *Tales of Texas Ghosts: Living in a Haunted House* and *Tales of Texas Ghosts: Spirits in the Workplace*. A submission should be based on a , supernatural encounter that you have personally experienced in the State of Texas. Length requirements are somewhat flexible, but stories should be 1000-2000 words. Longer stories will be considered."

NONFICTION "Atriad Press publishes nonfiction Texas genre books only." No poetry, children's books or fiction, please. No family memoirs, either, unless your family was famous, or better yet, infamous. No extreme violence, explicit sexual content, strong language, or any other elements that makes them inappropriate for a teenaged audience. Does not want UFO or angels. Query first. We prefer e-mail rather than postal mail.

TIPS "Manuscripts should be written on an adult level, but please keep in mind that we market to school libraries. Approximate length should be 65,000 words. The market for ghost stories ranges from young to old.

Please check your manuscript carefully for errors in spelling and structure."

ⓐ AVALON BOOKS

Thomas Bouregy & Sons, Inc., 160 Madison Ave., 5th Floor, New York NY 10016. (212)598-0222. Fax: (212)979-1862. E-mail: editorial@avalonbooks.com; avalon@avalonbooks.com; lbrown@avalonbooks.com. E-mail: editorial@avalonbooks.com. Website: www.avalonbooks.com. **Contact:** Lia Brown, editor. Estab. 1950. Format publishes in hardcover originals. **Publishes 60 titles/year. Pays 10% royalty. Pays $1,000 advance** Publishes book 12-18 months after acceptance of ms. Responds in 2-3 months to queries. Guidelines available online.

FICTION "We publish wholesome contemporary romances, mysteries, historical romances and westerns. Our books are read by adults as well as teenagers, and the main characters are all adults. All mysteries are contemporary. We publish contemporary romances, historical romances, mysteries and westerns. Submit first 3 sample chapters, a 2-3 page synopsis and SASE. The manuscripts should be between 50,000-70,000 words. However, if the ms is exceptional, we will accept somewhat longer books. Time period and setting are the author's preference. The historical romances will maintain the high level of reading expected by our readers. The books shall be wholesome fiction, without graphic sex, violence or strong language. " Published *Death in the French Quarter,* by Kent Conwell (mystery); *Judgment at Gold Butte*, by Terrell L. Bowers (western); *Adieu, My Love*, by Lynn Turner (historical romance); *Everything But a Groom*, by Holly Jacobs (romantic comedy). No graphic sex, violence or strong language "We do accept unagented material. We no longer accept e-mail queries. When submitting, include a query letter, a 2-3 page (and no longer) synopsis of the entire ms, and the first three chapters. All submissions must be typed and double spaced. If we think that your novel might be suitable for our list, we will contact you and request that you submit the entire manuscript. **Please note that any unsolicited full manuscripts will not be returned.** There is no need to send your partial to any specific editor at Avalon. The editors read all the genres that are listed above. Address your letter to: **The Editors.** This also goes for e-mail submissions."

TIPS "Avalon Books are geared and marketed for librarians to purchase and distribute."

BACKBEAT BOOKS

Hal Leonard Publishing Group, 33 Plymouth St., Suite 302, Montclair NJ 07042. (800)637-2852. E-mail: medison@halleonard.com. E-mail: medison@halleonard.com. Website: www.backbeatbooks.com. **Contact:** Mike Edison, senior editor (rock, jazz, pop culture). Kristina Radke, publicity Hardcover and trade paperback originals; trade paperback reprints. **Publishes 24 titles/year.**

NONFICTION Subjects include music (rock & roll), pop culture. Query by e-mail.

⊕ BAILIWICK PRESS

309 East Mulberry St., Fort Collins CO 80524. (970) 672-4878. Fax: (970) 672-4731. E-mail: info@bailiwickpress.com. Website: www.bailiwickpress.com.

◯ *"We're a micro-press that produces books and other products that inspire and tell great stories. Our motto is "books with something to say."* We are now considering submissions, agented and unagented, for children's and young adult fiction. We're looking for smart, funny, and layered writing that kids will clamor for. Illustrated fiction is desired but not required. (Illustrators are also invited to send samples.) Make us laugh out loud, ooh and aah, and cry, "Eureka!" Please read the Aldo Zelnick series to determine if we might be on the same page, then fill out our submission form. Please do not send submissions via snail mail. You must complete the online submission form to be considered. If, after completing and submitting the form, you also need to send us an e-mail attachment (such as sample illustrations or excerpts of graphics), you may e-mail them to info@bailiwickpress.com."

⊘ BAKER ACADEMIC

Division of Baker Publishing Group, 6030 E. Fulton Rd., Ada MI 49301. (616)676-9185. Fax: (616)676-2315. Website: www.bakeracademic.com. Estab. 1939. Publishes hardcover and trade paperback originals. **Publishes 50 titles/year. 10% of books from first-time authors. 85% from unagented writers. Pays advance.** Publishes book 1 year after acceptance of ms. Book catalog for 9 ½x12 ½ SAE with 3 first-class stamps. Guidelines for #10 SASE.

◯ "Baker Academic publishes religious academic and professional books for students and church leaders. Does not accept unsolicited queries.", "We will consider unsolicited work only through one of the following Ave. s. Materials sent to our editorial staff through a professional literary agent will be considered. In addition, our staff attends various writers' conferences at which prospective authors can develop relationships with those in the publishing industry. You may also submit your work to the following manuscript submission service, which serve sas a liaison between publishers and prospective authors: Christian Manuscript Submissions, an online service of the Evangelical Christian Publishers' Association: Website: www.christianmanuscriptsubmissions.com; E-mail: info@christianmanuscriptsubmissions.com .

NONFICTION Subjects include anthropology, archeology, education, psychology, religion, women's issues, women's studies, Biblical studies, Christian doctrine, books for pastors and church leaders, contemporary issues.

ⓐ BANCROFT PRESS

P.O. Box 65360, Baltimore MD 21209-9945. (410)358-0658. Fax: (410)764-1967. E-mail: bruceb@bancroftpress.com; HDemchick@bancroftpress.com (if bancrof account is down). Website: www.bancroftpress.com. **Contact:** Bruce Bortz, editor/publisher (health, investments, politics, history, humor, literary novels, mystery/thrillers, chick lit, young adult). Publishes hardcover and trade paperback originals. **Publishes 4-6 titles/year. Pays 6-8% royalty. Pays various royalties on retail price. Pays $750 advance.** Publishes book up to 3 years after acceptance of ms. Accepts simultaneous submissions. Responds in 6-12 months to queries, proposals and manuscripts. Guidelines available online.

○ *The Re-Appearance of Sam Webber*, by Jonathon Scott Fugua is an ALEX Award winner; *Uncovering Sadie's Secrets*, by Libby Sternberg, is an Edgar Award finalist. *The Re-Appearance of Sam Webber*, by Jonathon Scott Fugua is an ALEX Award winner; *Uncovering Sadie's Secrets*, by Libby Sternberg, is an Edgar Award finalist.

⌘ Bancroft Press is a general trade publisher. We publish young adult fiction and adult fiction, as well as occasional nonfiction. Our only mandate is 'books that enlighten.'"

NONFICTION Subjects include business, economics, government, politics, health, medicine, money, finance, regional, sports, women's issues, women's studies, popular culture. "We advise writers to visit the website." All quality books on any subject of interest to the publisher. Submit proposal package, outline, 2 sample chapters, competition/market survey.

FICTION Subjects include ethnic, general, feminist, gay, lesbian, historical, humor, literary, mainstream, contemporary, military, war, mystery, amateur sleuth, cozy, police procedural, private eye/hardboiled, regional, science fiction, hard science fiction/technological, soft/sociological, translation, frontier sage, traditional, young adult, historical, problem novels, series, thrillers.

TIPS "We advise writers to visit our website and to be familiar with our previous work. Patience is the number one attribute contributors must have. It takes us a very long time to get through submitted material, because we are such a small company. Also, we only publish 4-6 books per year, so it may take a long time for your optioned book to be published. We like to be able to market our books to be used in schools and in libraries. We prefer fiction that bucks trends and moves in a new direction. We are especially interested in mysteries and humor (especially humorous mysteries)."

ⓐⓞ BANTAM BOOKS

Imprint of Random House Children's Books/Random House, Inc., 1745 Broadway, New York NY 10019. (212)782-9000. Website: www.randomhouse.com/kids; www.randomhouse.com/teens.

○ Not seeking mss at this time.

BARRICADE BOOKS, INC.

185 Bridge Plaza N., Suite 309, Fort Lee NJ 07024. (201)944-7600. Fax: (201)917-4951. Website: www.barricadebooks.com. **Contact:** Carole Stuart, publisher. Estab. 1991. Publishes hardcover and trade paperback originals, trade paperback reprints. **Publishes 12 titles/year. 200 queries received/year. 100 mss received/year. 80% of books from first-time authors. 50% from unagented writers. Pays 10-12% royalty on retail price for hardcover. Pays advance.** Publishes book 18 months after acceptance of ms. Responds in 1 month to queries.

⌘ Barricade Books publishes nonfiction, mostly of the controversial type, and books we can promote with authors who can talk about their topics on radio and television and to the press."

NONFICTION Subjects include business, economics, ethnic, gay, lesbian, government, politics, health, medicine, history, nature, environment, psychology, sociology, crime. We look for quality nonfiction manuscripts—preferably with a controversial lean. Query with SASE. Submit outline, 1-2 sample chapters. Material will not be returned or responded to without SASE. We do not accept proposals on disk or via e-mail. Reviews artwork/photos. Send photocopies.

TIPS "Do your homework. Visit bookshops to find publishers who are doing the kinds of books you want to write. Always submit to a person—not just 'Editor.' Always enclose a SASE or you may not get a response."

BASIC HEALTH PUBLICATIONS, INC.

28812 Top of the World Dr., Laguna Beach CA 92651. (949)715-7327. Fax: (949)715-7328. Website: www.basichealthpub.com. **Contact:** Norman Goldfind, publisher. Estab. 2001. Publishes hardcover trade paperback and mass market paperback originals and reprints. Accepts simultaneous submissions. Book catalog available online. Guidelines for #10 SASE.

NONFICTION Subjects include health, medicine. "We are very highly focused on health, alternative medicine, nutrition, and fitness. Must be well researched and documented with appropriate references. Writing should be aimed at lay audience but also be able to cross over to professional market." Submit proposal package, outline, 2-3 sample chapters, introduction.

TIPS "Our audience is over 30, well educated, middle to upper income. We prefer writers with professional credentials (M.D.s, Ph.D.s, N.D.s, etc.), or writers with backgrounds in health and medicine."

BAYLOR UNIVERSITY PRESS

One Bear Place 97363, Waco TX 76798. (254)710-3164; 3522. Fax: (254)710-3440. E-mail: carey_newman@baylor.edu. Website: www.baylorpress.com. **Contact:** Dr. Carey C. Newman, Director. Publishes hardcover and trade paperback originals. **Publishes 30 titles/year. Pays 10% royalty on wholesale price.** Publishes book 1 year after acceptance of ms. Accepts simultaneous submissions. Responds in 2 months to proposals. Guidelines available online.

8—π We publish contemporary and historical scholarly works about culture, religion, politics, science, and the arts."

NONFICTION Submit outline, 1-3 sample chapters.

BEARMANOR MEDIA

P.O. Box 1129, Duncan OK 73534. (580)252-3547. Fax: (814)690-1559. E-mail: Books@Benohmart.com. Website: www.Bearmanormedia.com. **Contact:** Ben Ohmart, publisher. Estab. 2000. Publishes trade paperback originals and reprints. **Publishes 70 titles/year. 90% of books from first-time authors. 90% from unagented writers. Negotiable per project. Pays upon acceptance.** Accepts simultaneous submissions. Responds only if interested. Book catalog vailable online, or free with a 9×12 SASE submission.

NONFICTION Subjects include old-time radio, voice actors, old movies, classic television. Query with SASE. E-mail queries preferred. Submit proposal package, outline, list of credits on the subject.

TIPS "My readers love the past. Radio, old movies, old television. My own tastes include voice actors and scripts, especially of radio and television no longer available. I prefer books on subjects that haven't previously been covered as full books. It doesn't matter to me if you're a first-time author or have a track record. Just know your subject!"

BEAR STAR PRESS

185 Hollow Oak Dr., Cohasset CA 95973. (530)891-0360. Website: www.bearstarpress.com. **Contact:** Beth Spencer, publisher/editor. Estab. 1996. Publishes trade paperback originals. **Publishes 1-3 titles/year. Pays $1,000, and 25 copies to winner of annual Dorothy Brunsman contest.** Publishes book 9 months after acceptance of ms. Accepts simultaneous submissions. Responds in 2 weeks to queries. Guidelines available online.

8—π Bear Star is committed to publishing the best poetry it can attract. Each year it sponsors the Dorothy Brunsman contest, open to poets from Western and Pacific states. From time to time we add to our list other poets from our target area whose work we admire."

FICTION "Founded in 1996, Bear Star is committed to publishing the best writing it can attract from the Mountain and Pacific time zones, as well as Alaska and Hawaii. The west abounds in first-rate writers, and we are proud to be part of the poetry renaissance occurring here now. Each year we award the Dorothy Brunsman Poetry Prize ($1,000 and publication) to a writer from the region." Use our Online form. Manuscripts should be between 50 and 65 pages in length. All work must be original and accompanied by a $20 reading fee. Previously published poems can be included in your manuscript if you retain the copyright (this is standard).

POETRY Wants well-crafted poems. No restrictions as to form, subject matter, style, or purpose. "Poets should enter our annual book competition. Other books are occasionally solicited by publisher, sometimes from among contestants who didn't win." Query and submit complete ms. Online form.

TIPS "Send your best work, consider its arrangement. A 'wow' poem early keeps me reading."

BEDFORD/ST. MARTIN'S

Division of Macmillan Publishers, Boston Office, 75 Arlington St., Boston MA 02116. (617)399-4000. E-mail: contactus@bedfordstmartins.com. Website: www.bedfordstmartins.com. Estab. 1981. **Publishes 200 titles/year.** Book catalog available online.

Publishes college textbooks. Subjects include English composition, literature, history, communications, philosophy, music. Photos used for text illustrations, promotional materials, book covers. Examples of recently published titles: Bartholomae/Petrosky, *Ways of Reading*, Ninth Edition (text illustration, book cover); McCornack, *Reflect and Relate*, Second Edition (text illustration, book cover).

FREDERIC C. BEIL, PUBLISHER, INC.

609 Whitaker St., Savannah GA 31401. (912)233-2446. Fax: (912)233-6456. E-mail: books@beil.com. Website: www.beil.com. **Contact:** Mary Ann Bowman, editor. Estab. 1982. Publishes hardcover originals and reprints. **Publishes 13 titles/year. 3,500 queries received/year. 13 mss received/year. 80% of books from first-time authors. 100% from unagented writers. Pays 7 ½% royalty on retail price.** Publishes book 20 months after acceptance of ms. Accepts simultaneous submissions. Responds in 1 week to queries. Book catalog available free.

IMPRINTS The Sandstone Press; Hypermedia, Inc.

Frederic C. Beil publishes in the fields of history, literature, and biography.

NONFICTION Subjects include art, architecture, history, language, literature, book arts. Query with SASE. Reviews artwork/photos. Send photocopies.

FICTION Subjects include historical, literary, regional, short story collections, translation, biography. Query with SASE.

TIPS Our objectives are (1) to offer to the reading public carefully selected texts of lasting value; (2) to adhere to high standards in the choice of materials and in bookmaking craftsmanship; (3) to produce books that exemplify good taste in format and design; and (4) to maintain the lowest cost consistent with quality.

BELLEVUE LITERARY PRESS

New York University School of Medicine, Dept. of Medicine, NYU School of Medicine, 550 First Ave., OBV 612, New York NY 10016. (212) 263-7802. E-mail: BLPsubmissions@gmail.com. Website: http://blpress.org. **Contact:** Erika Goldman, editorial director. Estab. 2005.

Publishes literary and authoritative fiction and nonfiction at the nexus of the arts and the sciences, with a special focus on medicine. As our authors explore cultural and historical representations of the human body, illness, and health, they address the impact of scientific and medical practice on the individual and society."

NONFICTION "If you have a completed manuscript, a sample of a manuscript or a proposal that fits our mission as a press feel free to submit it to us by postal mail. Please keep in mind that at this time we are unable to return manuscripts. We will also accept short proposals by e-mail. You may submit them to either Erika Goldman or her assistant Leslie Hodgkins at: leslie.hodgkins@med.nyu.edu."

TIPS "We are a project of New York University's School of Medicine and while our standards reflect NYU's excellence in scholarship, humanistic medicine, and science, our authors need not be affiliated with NYU. We are not a university press and do not receive any funding from NYU. Our publishing operations are financed exclusively by foundation grants, private donors, and book sales revenue."

BENBELLA BOOKS

10300 N. Central Expy., Suite 400, Dallas TX 75231. Website: www.benbellabooks.com. **Contact:** Glenn Yeffeth, publisher. Estab. 2001. Hardcover and trade paperback originals. **Publishes 20-25 titles/year. Pays 6-15% royalty on retail price.** Publishes book 10 months after acceptance of ms. Accepts simultaneous submissions. Guidelines available online.

NONFICTION Subjects include pop contemporary culture, cooking, foods, nutrition, health, medicine, literary criticism, money, finance, science. Submit proposal package, including: outline, 2 sample chapters (via e-mail).

☼ BENDALL BOOKS

P.O. BOX 115, Mill Bay BC V0R2P0, CA. (250)743-2946. Fax: (250)743-2910. E-mail: admin@bendallbooks.com. Website: www.bendallbooks.com. **Contact:** Mary Moore, publisher. Publishes trade paperback originals. **Publishes 1 titles/year. 30 queries received/year. 5 mss received/year. 50% of books from first-time authors. 100% from unagented writers. Pays 5-15% royalty on wholesale price.** Publishes book 1 year after acceptance of ms. Book catalog available free. Guidelines available online.

NONFICTION Subjects include education.

BENTLEY PUBLISHERS

1734 Massachusetts Ave., Cambridge MA 02138. (617)547-4170. Fax: (617)876-9235. E-mail: michael.bentley@bentleypublishers.com. Website: www.bentleypublishers.com. **Contact:** Michael Bentley, president. Estab. 1950. Publishes hardcover and trade paperback originals and reprints. Book catalog and ms guidelines online and with 9×12 SASE with 4 first-class stamps.

NONFICTION Subjects include Automotive subjects only. Query with SASE. Submit sample chapters, bio, synopsis, target market. Rreviews artwork/photos.

TIPS "Our audience is composed of serious, intelligent automobile, sports car, and racing enthusiasts, automotive technicians and high-performance tuners."

BERRETT-KOEHLER PUBLISHERS, INC.

235 Montgomery St., Suite 650, San Francisco CA 94104. (415)288-0260. Fax: (415)362-2512. E-mail: bkpub@bkpub.com. Website: www.bkconnection.com. **Contact:** Jeevan Sivasubramaniam, sr. man. editor. Publishes hardcover & trade paperback originals, mass market paperback originals, hardcover & trade paperback reprints. **Publishes 40 titles/year. 1,300 queries received/year. 800 mss received/year. 20-30% of books from first-time authors. 70% from unagented writers. Pays 10-20% royalty.** Publishes book 10 months after acceptance of ms. Accepts simultaneous submissions. Responds in 1 month to queries, proposals & manuscripts. Book catalog available online. Guidelines available online.

&— Berrett-Koehler Publishers' mission is to publish books that support the movement toward a world that works for all. Our titles promote positive change at personal, organizational and societal levels." Please see proposal guidelines online.

NONFICTION Subjects include business, economics, community, government, politics, New Age, spirituality. Submit proposal package, outline, bio, 1-2 sample chapters. Hard-copy proposals only. Do not e-mail, fax, or phone please. Reviews artwork/photos. Send photocopies or originals with SASE.

TIPS "Our audience is business leaders. Use common sense, do your research."

BETTERWAY HOME BOOKS

Imprint of F+W Media, Inc., 4700 E. Galbraith Rd., Cincinnati OH 45236. (513)531-2690, ext. 11467. E-mail: jacqueline.musser@fwmedia.com. Website: www.fwmedia.com. **Contact:** Jacqueline Musser, acquisitions editor. Publishes trade paperback and hardcover originals. **Publishes 6-8 titles/year. 6 queries received/year 60% of books from first-time authors. 95% from unagented writers. Pays 8-10% royalty on wholesale price. Pays $2,500-3,000 advance.** Publishes book 18 months after acceptance of ms. Accepts simultaneous submissions. Responds in 3 month to queries and proposals.

NONFICTION Subjects include house and home, basic home repair and home improvement, home organization, homemaking. Query with SASE. Submit proposal package, outline, 1 sample chapter. Reviews artwork/photos. Send photocopies and PDFs (if submitting electronically).

TIPS "Looking for authors who are back to nature and a simple living approach."

✿ BIOGRAPHICAL PUBLISHING COMPANY

95 Sycamore Dr., Prospect CT 06712-1493. (203)758-3661. Fax: (253)793-2618. E-mail: biopub@aol.com. Website: www.biopub.co.cc. **Contact:** John R. Guevin, editor. Estab. 1991. Hardcover originals & reprints; trade paperback originals & reprints. **Publishes 6 titles/year. Receives 300 queries/year; 25 mss/year. 50% of books from first-time authors. 90% from unagented writers. Pays 90-95% royalty on wholesale price.** Publishes book 4 months. after acceptance of ms. Responds in 1 month on queries, proposals, & mss. Catalog & guidelines free on request.

NONFICTION Subjects include animals, career guidance, child guidance, community, cooking, counseling, education, environment, ethnic, finance, foods, games, gardening, government, health, history, hobbies, house and home, humanities, language, literature, medicine, memoirs, military, money, muticultural, nature, nutrition, politics, psychology, public affairs, recreation, regional, science, social sciences, spirituality. Query with SASE; submit completed ms. Reviews artwork/photos. Send photocopies.

FICTION Subjects include adventure, contemporary, ethnic, historical, humor, juvenile, literary, mainstream, military, multicultural, mystery, picture books, poetry, regional, religious, romance, science fiction, short story collections, spiritual, sports, suspense, war, western, young adult. Query with SASE; submit completed ms.

POETRY Query; submit complete ms.

BIRCH BOOK PRESS

P.O. Box 81, Delhi NY 13753. Fax: (607)746-7453. E-mail: birchbrook@copper.net. Website: www.birchbrookpress.info. **Contact:** Tom Tolnay, editor/publisher; Barbara dela Cuesta, assoc. editor. Estab. 1982. Occasionally publishes trade paperback originals. **Publishes 4 titles/year. 200+ queries received/year; 200+ mss received/year 95% from unagented writers. Pays modest royalty on acceptance.** Publishes book Acceptance to publication is 10-18 months. after acceptance of ms. Accepts simultaneous submissions. Responds in 3 to 6 months to mss. Book catalog available online.

IMPRINTS Birch Brook Press; Birch Brook Impressions. "Letterpress editions are printed in our own shop."

"No manuscripts, inquiries only."

Birch Brook Press "is a letterpress book printer/typesetter/designer that uses monies from these activities to publish several titles of its own each year with cultural and literary interest." Specializes in literary work, flyfishing, baseball, outdoors, theme anthologies, occasional translations of classics, and books about books. Has published *Woodstoves & Ravens* by Robert Farmer, *Shadwell Hills*, by Rebecca Lilly, *Seasons of Defiance* by Lance Lee, *And This is What Happens Next*, by Marcus Rome, *Jack's Beans* by Tom Smith, and *Tony's World*, by Barry Wallenstein. Publishes 4 paperbacks and/or hardbacks/year. Specializes "mostly in anthologies with specific themes." Books are "handset letterpress editions printed in our own shop." **Offers occasional co-op contract.**

NONFICTION Subjects include film, music (rare), nonfiction of cultural interest, including stage, opera, including outdoors.

POETRY Query first with a few sample poems or chapters, or send entire ms. No e-mail submissions; submissions by postal mail only. "Must include SASE with submissions." Occasionally comments on rejected poems. Guidelines available for SASE. Pays from $5-25 for publication in anthology. Royalty on co-op contracts. Order sample books by visiting our online catalog at: www.birchbookpress.info.

TIPS "Write well on subjects of interest to BBP, such as outdoors, flyfishing, baseball, music, literary stories and occasional novellas, books about books."

BKMK PRESS

University of Missouri-Kansas City, 5101 Rockhill Rd., Kansas City MO 64110-2499. (816)235-2558. Fax: (816)235-2611. E-mail: bkmk@umkc.edu. Website: www.umkc.edu/bkmk. **Contact:** Ben Furnish, managing editor. Estab. 1971. Publishes trade paperback originals. **Publishes 4/year titles/year.** Accepts simultaneous submissions. Responds in 4-6 months to queries. Guidelines available online.

BkMk Press publishes fine literature. Reading period January-June."

NONFICTION Creative nonfiction essays. Submit 25-50 pp. sample and SASE.

FICTION Subjects include literary, short story collections. Query with SASE.

POETRY Submit 10 sample poems and SASE.

TIPS "We skew toward readers of literature, particularly contemporary writing. Because of our limited number of titles published per year, we discourage apprentice writers or 'scattershot' submissions."

BLACK DOME PRESS CORP.

1011 Route 296, Hensonville NY 12439. (518)734-6357. Fax: (518)734-5802. E-mail: blackdomep@aol.com. Website: www.blackdomepress.com. Estab. 1990. Publishes cloth and trade paperback originals and reprints. Accepts simultaneous submissions. Book catalog and guidelines available online.

Do not send the entire work. Mail a cover letter, table of contents, introduction, sample chapter (or two), and your C.V. or brief biography to the Editor. Please do not send computer disks or submit your proposal via e-mail. If your book will include illustrations, please send us copies of sample illustrations. Do not send originals.

NONFICTION Subjects include history, nature, environment, photography, regional, New York state, Native Americans, grand hotels, genealogy, colonial life, French & Indian War (NYS), American Revolution (NYS), quilting, architecture, railroads, hiking and kayaking guidebooks. New York state regional material only. Submit proposal package, outline, bio.

TIPS "Our audience is comprised of New York state residents, tourists, and visitors."

✚ BLACK OCEAN

P.O. Box 52030, Boston MA 02205. (617)304-9011. Fax: (617)849-5678. E-mail: carrie@blackocean.org. Website: www.blackocean.org. **Contact:** Carrie Olivia Adams, poetry editor. Estab. 2006. **Publishes 3 titles/year.** Responds in 6 months to mss.

POETRY Wants poetry that is well-considered, risks itself, and by its beauty and/or bravery disturbs a tiny corner of the universe. Manuscripts are selected through open submission. Books are 60+ pages. Book/chapbook mss may include previously published poems. We have an open submission period in May of each year; specific guidelines are updated and posted on our website in the months preceding.

BLACK ROSE WRITING

P.O. Box 1540, Castroville TX 78009. E-mail: creator@blackrosewriting.com. Website: www.blackrosewriting.com. **Contact:** Reagan Rothe. Accepts simultaneous submissions. Responds in 1-2 months to mss. Please see submission guidelines online before contacting.

✂ Black Rose Writing is an independent publishing house that believes in developing a personal relationship with our authors." "We publish only one genre..our genre. Publishes nonfiction books, novels, short story collections, novellas, juvenile. Actively seeking fiction, novels and short story collections. We are seeking growth in an array of different genres and searching for new publicity venues for our authors everyday. Black Rose Writing doesn't promise our authors the world, leading them to become overwhelmed by the competitive and difficult venture. We are honest with our authors, and we give them the insight to generate solid leads without wasting their time. Black Rose Writing is able to promote, showcase, and produce

your dedicated stories through the company itself and with our publishing/printing connections. We want to make your writing successes possible and eliminate the fear of a toilsome and lengthy experience."

NONFICTION Subjects include science, sports, young adult. Query with SASE. Submit synopsis, author bio.

FICTION Subjects include adventure, fantasy, historical, horror, humor, juvenile, mainstream, mystery, picture books, plays, romance, short story collections, sports, western, young adult, detective.

TIPS "Please query first with synopsis and author information. Allow 3-4 weeks for response. Always check spelling and do not forward your initial contact e-mails."

BLACK VELVET SEDUCTIONS PUBLISHING

1350-C W. Southport, Box 249, Indianapolis IN 46217. (888)556-2750. E-mail: lauriesanders@blackvelvetseductions.com. Website: www.blackvelvetseductions.com. **Contact:** Laurie Sanders, acquisitions editor. Estab. 2005. Publishes trade paperback and electronic originals and reprints. **Publishes about 20 titles/year. 500 queries received/year. 1,000 mss received/year. 90% of books from first-time authors. 100% from unagented writers. Pays 10% royalty for paperbacks; 50% royalty for electronic books.** Publishes book 6-12 months after acceptance of ms. Accepts simultaneous submissions. Responds in 6 months to queries. Responds in 8 months to proposals. Responds in 8-12 months to mss. Catalog free or online. Guidelines online (guidelines@blackvelvetseductions.com).

IMPRINTS Forbidden Experiences (erotic romance of all types); Tender Destinations (sweet romance of all types); Sensuous Journeys (sensuous romance of all types); Amorous Adventures (romantic suspense); Erotic relationship stories (erotic short stories, usually including spanking, with a romantic relationship at their core).

✂ We publish two types of material: 1) romance novels and short stories and 2) romantic stories involving spanking between consenting adults. We look for well-crafted stories with a high degree of emotional impact. No first person point of view. All material must be in third person point of view." Publishes trade paperback and electronic originals. "We have a high interest in republishing backlist titles in electronic and trade paperback formats once rights have reverted to the author." Accepts only complete manuscripts. Query with SASE. Submit complete ms.

FICTION Subjects include erotic romance, historical romance, multicultural romance, romance, short story collections romantic stories, romantic suspense, western romance. All stories must have a strong romance element. "There are very few sexual taboos in our erotic line. We tend to give our authors the widest latitude. If it is safe, sane, and consensual we will allow our authors latitude to show us the eroticism. However, we will not consider manuscripts with any of the following: bestiality (sex with animals), necrophilia (sex with dead people), pedophillia (sex with children)." Only accepts electronic submissions.

TIPS "We publish romance and erotic romance. We look for books written in very deep point of view."

BLOOMBERG PRESS

Imprint of Bloomberg L.P., 731 Lexington Ave., New York NY 10022. Website: www.bloomberg.com/books. Estab. 1995. Publishes hardcover and trade paperback originals. **Publishes 18-22 titles/year. 200 queries received/year. 20 mss received/year. 45% from unagented writers. Pays negotiable, competitive royalty. Pays negotiable advance. for trade books** Publishes book 9 months after acceptance of ms. Accepts simultaneous submissions. With SASE, responds in 1 month to queries. Book catalog for 10×13 envelope and 5 First-Class stamps.

IMPRINTS Bloomberg Professional Library.

- "Bloomberg Press has published books for financial professionals as well as books of general interest on investing, economics, current affairs and policy affecting investors. The books are written by leading practitioners and authorities, including BLOOMBERG NEWS® reporters and columnists, and are published in more than 20 different languages."
- Bloomberg Press publishes professional books for practitioners in the financial markets. We publish commercially successful, very high-quality books that stand out clearly from the competition by their brevity, ease of use, sophistication, and abundance of practical tips and strategies; books readers need, will use, and appreciate.

NONFICTION Subjects include business, economics, money, finance, professional books on finance, investment and financial services, and books for financial advisors. We are looking for authorities and for experienced service journalists. Do not send us unfocused books containing general information already covered by books in the marketplace. We do not publish business, management, leadership, or career books. Submit outline, sample chapters, SAE with sufficient postage. Submit complete ms.

TIPS *Bloomberg Professional Library:* Audience is upscale, financial professionals—traders, dealers, brokers, planners and advisors, financial managers, money managers, company executives, sophisticated investors. Authors are experienced financial journalists and/or financial professionals nationally prominent in their specialty for some time who have proven an ability to write a successful book. Research Bloomberg and look at our books in a library or bookstore, and peruse our website.

BLUE MOON BOOKS, INC.

327 Elk Ave., P.O. Box 908, Crested Butte CO 81224. (970)349-0504. E-mail: bluemoonbookscb@yahoo. com. Website: http://bluemoonbookscb.com. Estab. 1987. Publishes trade paperback and mass market paperback originals. Book catalog available free.

- Blue Moon Books is strictly an erotic press; largely fetish-oriented material, B&D, S&M, etc.
- Blue Moon Books is strictly an erotic press; largely fetish-oriented material, B&D, S&M, etc.

FICTION Subjects include erotica. *No unsolicited mss.*

BLUE POPPY PRESS

Imprint of Blue Poppy Enterprises, Inc., 1990 57th Court Unit A, Boulder CO 80301-2733. (303)447-8372. Fax: (303)245-8362. E-mail: info@bluepoppy.com. Website: www.bluepoppy.com. **Contact:** Bob Flaws, editor-in-chief. Estab. 1981. Publishes hardcover and trade paperback originals. **Publishes 3-4 titles/year. 50 queries received/year. 5-10 mss received/year. 30-40% of books from first-time authors. 100% from unagented writers. Pays 8-12% royalty.** Publishes book 1 year after acceptance of ms. Responds in 1 month to queries. Book catalog available free. Guidelines available online.

- "Blue Poppy Press is dedicated to expanding and improving the English language literature on acupuncture and Asian medicine for both professional practitioners and lay readers."

NONFICTION Subjects include ethnic, health, medicine. We only publish books on acupuncture and Oriental medicine by authors who can read Chinese and have a minimum of 5 years clinical experience. We also require all our authors to use Wiseman's *Glossary of Chinese Medical Terminology* as their standard for technical terms. Query with SASE. Submit outline, 1 sample chapter.

TIPS "Audience is practicing acupuncturists interested in alternatives in healthcare, preventive medicine, Chinese philosophy, and medicine."

BNA BOOKS

Imprint of The Bureau of National Affairs, Inc., 1801 S. Bell St., Arlington VA 22202. (703)341-5777. Fax: (703)341-1610. E-mail: books@bna.com. Website: www. bnabooks.com. **Contact:** Jim Fattibene, acquisitions manager. Estab. 1929. Publishes hardcover and softcover originals. Accepts simultaneous submissions. Book catalog available online. Guidelines available online.

⬭ BNA Books publishes professional reference books written by lawyers, for lawyers.

NONFICTION No fiction, biographies, bibliographies, cookbooks, religion books, humor, or trade books. Submit detailed TOC or outline, cv, intended market, estimated word length.

TIPS "Our audience is made up of practicing lawyers and law librarians. We look for authoritative and comprehensive treatises that can be supplemented or revised every year or 2 on legal subjects of interest to those audiences."

💲⬤☯🚫⬤🔣🚫 BOA EDITIONS, LTD.

250 North Goodman St., Suite 306, Rochester NY 14607. (585)546-3410. Fax: (585)546-3913. E-mail: conners@boaeditions.org; hall@boaeditions.org. Website: www.boaeditions.org. **Contact:** Peter Conners, editor. Melissa Hall, Development Director/Office Manager Estab. 1976. Publishes hardcover and trade paperback originals. **Publishes 11-13 titles/year. 1,000 queries received/year. 700 mss received/year. 15% of books from first-time authors. 90% from unagented writers. Negotiates royalties. Pays variable advance.** Publishes book 18 months after acceptance of ms. Accepts simultaneous submissions. Responds in 1 week to queries. Responds in 5 months to manuscripts. Book catalog available online. Guidelines available online.

⛏ BOA Editions publishes distinguished collections of poetry, fiction and poetry in transla-

tion. Our goal is to publish the finest American contemporary poetry, fiction and poetry in translation."

FICTION Subjects include literary, poetry, poetry in translation, short story collections. "We now publish literary fiction through our American Reader Series. While aesthetic quality is subjective, our fiction will be by authors more concerned with the artfulness of their writing than the twists and turns of plot. Our strongest current interest is in short story collections (and short-short story collections), although we will consider novels. We strongly advise you to read our first published fiction collections." "We are temporarily closed to novel/collection submissions."

POETRY "Readers who, like Whitman, expect of the poet to 'indicate more than the beauty and dignity which always attach to dumb real objects . . They expect him to indicate the path between reality and their souls,' are the audience of BOA's books."

⊕ BOBO STRATEGY

2506 N. Clark, #301, Chicago IL 60614. E-mail: info@ bobostrategy.com. E-mail: submissions@bobostrategy. com. Website: www.bobostrategy.com. **Contact:** Chris Cunliffe, editor-in-chief. Estab. 2008. Trade paperback originals. **Publishes 1-5 titles/year. Pays 0-10% royalty on retail price; outright purchase up to $2,500.** Publishes book Acceptance to publication time is 6 months. after acceptance of ms. Accepts simultaneous submissions. Responds in 1 month on queries & proposals; responds in 2 months on mss. Catalog online at website. Guidelines available by e-mail.

⛏ We seek writing that brings clarity and simplicity to the complex. If your idea is good, we may be willing to take a chance on you."

NONFICTION Subjects include architecture, art, chess, creative nonfiction, government, humanities, memoirs, politics, regional, travel, world affairs. Query with SASE; submit proposal package, including: outline, 1 sample chapter. E-mail preferred. Reviews artwork; send photocopies. E-mail preferred.

FICTION Subjects include poetry, regional, short story collections. Query; submit proposal package, including: synopsis, 1 sample chapter. E-mail preferred.

⊕ BOLD STROKES BOOKS, INC.

P.O. Box 249, Valley Falls NY 12185. (518)753-6642. Fax: (518)753-6648. E-mail: publisher@boldstrokesbooks.com. E-mail: submissions@boldstrokesbooks. com. Website: www.boldstrokesbooks.com. **Contact:**

Len Barot, acq. director (general/genre gay/lesbian fiction). Trade paperback originals and reprints; electronic originals and reprints. **Publishes 60+ titles/year. 300 queries/year; 300 mss/year. 10-20% of books from first-time authors. 95% from unagented writers. Pays 7-10% royalty on retail price.** Publishes book 12-16 months after acceptance of ms. 1 month/queries; 2 months/proposals; 4 months/mss. Catalog free on request - PDF. Guidelines online at website.

IMPRINTS BSB Fiction (publishes 48/year), Matinee Books Romances (8/year), Victory Editions Lesbian Fiction (6/year), Liberty Editions Gay Fiction (8/year), Soliloquy Young Adul (12/yr), Heat Stroke Erotica (12/yr)

NONFICTION Subjects include gay, lesbian, memoirs, young adult. Submit completed ms with bio, cover letter, and synopsis electronically only. Does not review artwork.

FICTION Subjects include adventure, erotica, fantasy, gay, gothic, historical, horror, lesbian, literary, mainstream, mystery, romance, science fiction, suspense, western, young adult. "Submissions should have a gay, lesbian, transgendered, or bisexual focus and should be positive and life-affirming." Submit completed ms with bio, cover letter, and synopsis—electronically only.

TIPS "We are particularly interested in authors who are interested in craft enhancement, technical development, and exploring and expanding traditional genre definitions and boundaries and are looking for a long-term publishing relationship ."

⊘ BRANDEN PUBLISHING CO., INC.

P.O. Box 812094, Wellesley MA 02482. (781)235-3634. Fax: (781)235-3634. E-mail: branden@brandenbooks.com. Website: www.brandenbooks.com. **Contact:** Adolph Caso, editor. Estab. 1909. Publishes hardcover and trade paperback originals, reprints, and software. **Publishes 15 titles/year. 80% of books from first-time authors. 90% from unagented writers.** Publishes book 10 months after acceptance of ms. Responds in 1 month to queries.

IMPRINTS International Pocket Library and Popular Technology; Four Seas and Brashear; Branden Books.

⁍ Branden publishes books by or about women, children, military, Italian-American, or African-American themes."

NONFICTION Subjects include Americana, art, architecture, computers, electronics, contemporary culture, education, ethnic, government, politics, health,

medicine, history, military, war, music, dance, photography, sociology, software, classics. "Especially looking for about 10 manuscripts on national and international subjects, including biographies of well-known individuals. Currently specializing in Americana, Italian-American, African-American." No religion or philosophy. *No unsolicited mss* Paragraph query only with SASE. No telephone, e-mail, or fax inquiries. Reviews artwork/photos.

FICTION Subjects include ethnic, histories, integration, historical, literary, military, war, religious, historical-reconstructive, short story collections, translation. Looking for contemporary, fast pace, modern society. No science, mystery, experimental, horor, or pornography. *No unsolicited mss* Query with SASE. Paragraph query only with author bio.

BRENNER INFORMATION GROUP

Imprint of Brenner Microcomputing, Inc., P.O. Box 721000, San Diego CA 92172. (858)538-0093. Fax: (Call first). E-mail: brenner@brennerbooks.com. Website: www.brennerbooks.com. **Contact:** Deedee Ade, acquisitions manager (pricing & ranges). Estab. 1982. Publishes trade paperback and electronic originals specializing in pricing and performance time standards. **Publishes 4 titles/year. 4 ms and 6 queries received/year. 1% of books from first-time authors. 1% from unagented writers. Pays 5-15% royalty on wholesale price. Pays $0-1,000 advance.** Publishes book 1 year after acceptance of ms. Accepts simultaneous submissions. Responds in 1 month to queries, proposals, and manuscripts.

BREWERS PUBLICATIONS

Imprint of Brewers Association, 736 Pearl St., Boulder CO 80302. (303)447-0816. Fax: (303)447-2825. E-mail: kristi@brewersassociation.org; webmaster@brewersassociation.org. Website: beertown.org. **Contact:** Kristi Switzer, publisher. Estab. 1986. Publishes hardcover and trade paperback originals. **Publishes 2 titles/year. 50% of books from first-time authors. 100% from unagented writers. Pays small advance.** Publishes book 9 months after acceptance of ms. Accepts simultaneous submissions. Responds in 3 months to relevant queries. Only those submissions relevant to our needs will receive a response to queries. Guidelines available online.

⁍ Brewers Publications is the largest publisher of books on beer-related subjects."

NONFICTION "We only publish nonfiction books of interest to amateur and professional brewers. Our authors have many years of brewing experience and in-depth practical knowledge of their subject. We are not interested in fiction, drinking games or beer/bar reviews. If your book is not about how to make beer, then do not waste your time or ours by sending it. Those determined to fit our needs will subscribe to and read *Zymurgy* and *The New Brewer*." Query first with proposal and sample chapter.

☉ BRIGHTER BOOKS PUBLISHING HOUSE

Brighter Brains, Inc., 5765 Turner Rd., Unit 1, Suite #409, Nanaimo B.C. V9T 6M4, Canada. (250)933-6463. E-mail: info@brighterbooks.com. E-mail: submissions@brighterbooks.com. Website: www.brighterbooks.com. **Contact:** Angela Souza, senior/chief editor and Art Acquisitions (picture books, middle readers, young adult, educational material). Dean Jurgensen, senior editor (sciences, technology, information). Estab. 2009. Hardcover and electronic originals; hardcover and trade paperback reprints; trade paperback originals and reprints. **Publishes 10-15 titles/year. 50% of books from first-time authors. 50% from unagented writers. Pays royalty on wholesale price. Advances are negotiable.** Publishes book 12 months after acceptance of ms. Accepts simultaneous submissions. Responds in 2 months on queries and proposals; 3-4 months on manuscripts. Catalog available online at website. Guidelines online at website and by e-mail at info@brighterbooks.com.

IMPRINTS Juvenile: Picture books; young readers; middle reader; young adults.

NONFICTION , animals, art/architecture, child guidance/parenting, computers/electronics, crafts, education, entertainment/games, hobbies, money/finance for kids, nature/environment, science. "We focus on high-quality reading for children and also unique methods of teaching things to both adults and children." Query with SASE. Submit proposal package, including: outline, 3 sample chapters, and introduction. Submit completed ms for picture books and younger readers. Reviews artwork/photos. "We prefer digital samples, but photocopies are fine as well."

FICTION Subjects include adventure, fantasy, humor, juvenile, multicultural, multimedia, mystery, picture books, science fiction, young adult. "We are looking for a return to the quality of writing found in classical works of literature. We want to publish truly great fiction, no matter the target audience or age level. We

believe that by exposing children and young adults to excellent literature on a day-to-day basis, we can change their lives, making them better thinkers, more creative and well-adjusted. Books change people, and we want to do our part to make it a positive change." Query with SASE. Submit proposal package, including synopsis, 3 sampe chapters. Submit coompleted ms for picture books and young readers.

TIPS "Our fiction readers are smart boys and girls of all ages who are looking for characters they can relate to, and love to read. Our El-Hi readers are looking for a different way of learning school subjects. They may have learning difficulties with traditional methods. Our adult readers are well educated, and looking for well-written books about their subject of interest. 55% of work must be Canadian or Resident. However, we are still looking for talent worldwide."

BRIGHT MOUNTAIN BOOKS, INC.

206 Riva Ridge Dr., Fairview NC 28730. (828)628-1768. Fax: (828)628-1755. E-mail: booksbmb@charter.net. Website: www.brightmountainbooks.com. **Contact:** Cynthia F. Bright, Senior Editor. Martha Fullington, editor Estab. 1983. Publishes trade paperback originals and reprints. **Publishes 3 titles/year. 50% of books from first-time authors. 100% from unagented writers. Pays royalty.** Responds in 1 month to queries. Responds in 5 months to manuscripts.

IMPRINTS Historical Images, Ridgetop Books.

☞ Currently, Bright Mountain Books has nearly forty titles in print, all written by local authors or having subject matter relevant to the region of the Southern Appalachian Mountains.

NONFICTION Subjects include history, regional. "Our current emphasis is on regional titles set in the Southern Appalachians and Carolinas, which can include nonfiction by local writers." Query with SASE.

☉ BROKEN JAW PRESS

Box 596, STN A, Fredericton NB E3B 5A6, Canada. (506)454-5127. E-mail: editors@brokenjaw.com. Website: www.brokenjaw.com. **Contact:** Editorial Board. "Publishes almost exclusively Canadian-authored literary trade paperback originals and reprints". **Publishes 3-6 titles/year. 20% of books from first-time authors. 100% from unagented writers. Pays 10% royalty on retail price. Pays $0-500 advance.** Publishes book 18 months after acceptance of ms. Responds in 1 year to manuscripts. Book catalog for 6×9 SAE with 2 first-class Canadian stamps in Canada or download PDF from website. Guidelines available online.

IMPRINTS Book Rat; Broken Jaw Press; SpareTime Editions; Dead Sea Physh Products; Maritimes Arts Projects Productions.

⚷ We publish poetry, fiction, drama and literary nonfiction, including translations and multi-lingual books."

NONFICTION Subjects include history, literature, literary criticism, regional, women's issues, women's studies, contemporary culture.

FICTION Subjects include Literary novel and short story collections, poetry.

TIPS "Unsolicited queries and manuscripts are not welcome at this time."

BROOKS BOOKS

3720 N. Woodridge Dr., Decatur IL 62526. E-mail: brooksbooks@sbcglobal.net. Website: www.brooks-bookshaiku.com. **Contact:** Randy Brooks, editor (haiku poetry, tanka poetry). Publishes hardcover, trade paperback, & electronic originals. **Publishes 2-3 titles/year. 100 queries received/year. 25 mss received/year. 10% of books from first-time authors. 100% from un-agented writers. Outright purchase based on whole-sale value of 10% of a press run.** Publishes book 6-12 months after acceptance of ms. Responds in 2 months to queries. Responds in 3 months to proposals and manuscripts. Book catalog free on request or online at website. Guidelines free on request, for #10 SASE.

IMPRINTS Brooks Books

⚷ Brooks Books, formerly High/Coo Press, pub-lishes English-language haiku books, chap-books, magazines, and bibliographies."

POETRY "We celebrate English language haiku by promoting & publishing in a variety of media. Our goal is to share our joy of the art of reading & writing haiku through our little chapbook-size magazine, *Mayfly*. Also, we celebrate the art of haiga, lifetime contributions of haiku writers, the integration of visu-al arts (photography or painting) and contemporary English language haiku by leading poets. Query.

TIPS "The best haiku capture human perception— moments of being alive conveyed through sensory images. They do not explain nor describe nor pro-vide philosophical or political commentary. Haiku are gifts of the here and now, deliberately incomplete so that the reader can enter into the haiku moment to open the gift and experience the feelings and insights

of that moment for his or her self. Our readership in-cludes the haiku community, readers of contemporary poetry, teachers and students of Japanese literature and contemporary Japanese poetics."

⊘ CALAMARI PRESS

Via Titta Scarpetta #28, Rome 00153, Italy. E-mail: derek@calamaripress.net. Website: www.calamari-press.com. Publishes paperback originals. **Publishes 1-2/year titles/year. Pays in author's copies.** Pub-lishes book Manuscript published 2-6 months after acceptance. after acceptance of ms. Responds to mss in 2 weeks. Writer's guidelines on website.

⚷ Calamari Press publishes books of literary text and art. Publishes 1-2 books/year. Manu-scripts are selected by invitation. Occasionally has open submission period— check website. Helps to be published in *SleepingFish* first." See separate listing in magazines/journals. Order books through the website, Powell's, or SPD.

FICTION Query with outline/synopsis and 3 sample chapters. Accepts queries by e-mail only. Include brief bio. Send SASE or IRC for return of ms.

CAMINO BOOKS, INC.

P.O. Box 59026, Philadelphia PA 19102. (215)413-1917. Fax: (215)413-3255. Website: www.caminobooks.com. **Contact:** E. Jutkowitz, publisher. Estab. 1987. Pub-lishes hardcover and trade paperback originals. **Pub-lishes 8 titles/year. 20% of books from first-time authors. Pays $2,000 average advance.** Publishes book 12 months after acceptance of ms. Responds in 2 weeks to queries. Guidelines available online.

⚷ Camino Books, Inc., publishes nonfiction of re-gional interest to the Mid-Atlantic states."

NONFICTION Subjects include agriculture, Ameri-cana, art, architecture, child guidance, cooking, foods, nutrition, ethnic, gardening, government, politics, history, regional, travel. Query with SASE. Submit outline, sample chapters.

TIPS "The books must be of interest to readers in the Middle Atlantic states, or they should have a clearly defined niche, such as cookbooks."

↻ CANADIAN LIBRARY ASSOCIATION

(613)232-9625. Fax: (613)563-9895. E-mail: publish-ing@cla.ca. Website: www.cla.ca.

⚷ The **Canadian Library Association** is an award-winning not-for-profit organization, serving as the national voice of the Canadian library and information community and delivering a range of value-added services to professional librarians, library technicians, trustees and the organizations that employ them. To help keep you up-to-date, CLA distributes a bi-weekly e-newsletter chock full of timely news, people highlights, career spotlights, Shop Class specials, conference and award updates. CLA gladly welcomes submissions. Please e-mail a short news item (4-5 lines maximum) to Judy Green at jgreen@cla.ca by noon, Wednesday on a CLA Digest week. Please see schedule online for submission deadlines. *Feliciter* is the only national magazine dedicated to serving the Canadian library and information services community. Each issue of *Feliciter* contains opinion pieces, columns, and feature articles on professional concerns and developments, along with news of the Canadian Library Association. *Feliciter* is published six times a year by the Canadian Library Association. Annual subscriptions are $95.00. See themes online. If you would like to suggest a theme (and/or volunteer to be a guest editor), please contact Judy Green at CLA (jgreen@cla.ca). If you are interested in contributing to a theme issue, please contact the guest editor for that issue. We are also interested in receiving articles on any topic as we try to have space in each issue for articles that are not related to the theme. If you would like to submit an article for consideration, please send it to publishing@cla.ca."

TIPS Call for Proposals for CLA 2011 Conference in Halifax at **The World Trade & Convention Centre**: May 25 - 28, 2011. The call for presentation proposals is closed. Poster submissions are still being accepted. Contact Wendy Walton for more information, wwalton@cla.ca. The preliminary program will be available in early February. Proposed Sessions: To view current submissions please click on the link http://cla.pwwebhost.com/titles.php.

CAROLINA WREN PRESS

120 Morris St., Durham NC 27701. (919)560-2738. E-mail: carolinawrenpress@earthlink.net. Website: www.carolinawrenpress.org. **Contact:** Andrea Selch, president. Estab. 1976. Publishes book 1 year after acceptance of ms. Responds in 3 months to queries. Responds in 6 months to manuscripts. Guidelines available online.

"We are no longer accepting general submissions of poetry and fiction. We welcome submissions to our two contests, which run in alternate years. Reads unsolicited mss of fiction and nonfiction from September 1 to December 1 and poetry and children's lit from February 1 to June 1, but prefers writers to wait and enter their contests—poetry contest in Fall 2012 and 2014; Doris Bawkin Award for Writing by a Woman - prose fiction (a collection of short stories or a novel) or memoir. Submissions are accepted in odd-numbered autumns, with a final deadline of December 1st, 2011, 2013, 2015, etc. There is a $20 reading fee for this contest. Full guidelines should be followed - check the website in late summer to see the current guidelines. See below for poetry contest."

We publish poetry, fiction, nonfiction, biography, autobiography, literary nonfiction work by, and/or about people of color, women, gay/lesbian issues, health and mental health topics in children's literature."

NONFICTION Subjects include biography, autobiography, literary nonfiction work by, and/or about people of color, women, gay/lesbian issues, health and mental health topics in children's literature.

FICTION Subjects include ethnic, experimental, poetry, feminist, gay, lesbian, literary, short story collections. "We are especially interested in children's literature on the subjects of health, illness, mental illness, healing, etc." Query by mail only with SASE

POETRY Query first to see if submissions are open. If so, send 10 pages of sample poems and cover letter with brief bio and publication credits. Include SASE for reply only. Responds to queries in 3 months; to mss in 6 months. Payment varies.

TIPS Manuscripts are read year-round, but reply time is long unless submitting for a contest.

CARTWHEEL BOOKS

Imprint of Scholastic Trade Division, 557 Broadway, New York NY 10012. (212)343-6100. Website: www.scholastic.com. Estab. 1991. Publishes novelty books, easy readers, board books, hardcover and trade paperback originals. Accepts simultaneous submissions. Book catalog for 9×12 SASE. Guidelines available free.

Cartwheel Books publishes innovative books for children, up to age 8. We are looking for 'novelties' that are books first, play objects second. Even without its gimmick, a Cartwheel Book should stand alone as a valid piece of children's literature.

NONFICTION Subjects include animals, history, music, dance, nature, environment, recreation, science, sports. Cartwheel Books publishes for the very young, therefore nonfiction should be written in a manner that is accessible to preschoolers through 2nd grade. Often writers choose topics that are too narrow or 'special' and do not appeal to the mass market. Also, the text and vocabulary are frequently too difficult for our young audience. Accepts mss from agents, previously published authors only. Reviews artwork/photos. Send Please do not send original artwork.

FICTION Subjects include humor, juvenile, mystery, picture books. Again, the subject should have mass market appeal for very young children. Humor can be helpful, but not necessary. Mistakes writers make are a reading level that is too difficult, a topic of no interest or too narrow, or manuscripts that are too long. Accepts mss from agents, previ

TIPS Audience is young children, ages 0-8. Know what types of books the publisher does. Some manuscripts that don't work for one house may be perfect for another. Check out bookstores or catalogs to see where your writing would 'fit' best.

CATHOLIC UNIVERSITY OF AMERICA PRESS

620 Michigan Ave. NE, 240 Leahy Hall, Washington DC 20064. (202)319-5052. Fax: (202)319-4985. E-mail: cua-press@cua.edu. Website: cuapress.cua.edu. **Contact:** James C. Kruggel, acquisitions editor (philosophy, theology); Dr. David J. McGonagle, director (all other fields). Estab. 1939. **Publishes 30-35 titles/year. 50% of books from first-time authors. 100% from unagented writers. Pays variable royalty on net receipts.** Publishes book 18 months after acceptance of ms. Responds in 5 days to queries. Book catalog on request. Guidelines available online.

⌖— The Catholic University of America Press publishes in the fields of history (ecclesiastical and secular), literature and languages, philosophy, political theory, social studies, and theology. "We have interdisciplinary emphasis on patristics, and medieval studies. We publish works of original scholarship intended for academic libraries, scholars and other professionals and works that offer a synthesis of knowledge of

the subject of interest to a general audience or suitable for use in college and university classrooms."

NONFICTION Subjects include government, politics, history, language, literature, philosophy, religion, Church-state relations. No unrevised doctoral dissertations. Length: 40,000-120,000 words. Query with outline, sample chapter, cv, and list of previous publications.

TIPS Scholarly monographs and works suitable for adoption as supplementary reading material in courses have the best chance.

CAVE HOLLOW PRESS

P.O. Drawer J, Warrensburg MO 64093. E-mail: gbcrump@cavehollowpress.com. Website: www.cavehollowpress.com. **Contact:** G.B. Crump, editor. Estab. 2001. Publishes trade paperback originals. **Publishes 1 titles/year. 70 queries received/year. 6 mss received/year. 80% of books from first-time authors. 100% from unagented writers. Pays 7-12% royalty on wholesale price. Pays negotiable amount in advance.** Publishes book 1 year after acceptance of ms. Accepts simultaneous submissions. Responds in 1-2 months to queries and proposals. Responds in 3-6 months to manuscripts. Book catalog for #10 SASE. Guidelines available free.

FICTION Subjects include: mainstream, contemporary. "Our website is updated frequently to reflect the current type of fiction Cave Hollow Press is seeking." Query with SASE.

TIPS "Our audience varies based on the type of book we are publishing. We specialize in Missouri and Midwest regional fiction. We are interested in talented writers from Missouri and the surrounding Midwest. Check our submission guidelines on the website for what type of fiction we are interested in currently."

CAXTON PRESS

312 Main St., Caldwell ID 83605-3299. (208)459-7421. Fax: (208)459-7450. E-mail: sgipson@caxtonpress.com. Website: caxtonpress.com. **Contact:** Wayne Cornell, editor (Western Americana, regional nonfiction). Estab. 1907. Publishes hardcover and trade paperback originals. **Publishes 6-10 titles/year. 50% of books from first-time authors. 60% from unagented writers. Pays royalty. Pays advance.** Publishes book 18 months after acceptance of ms. Accepts simultaneous submissions. Responds in 3 months to queries.

Book catalog for 9×12 envelope and first-class stamps. Guidelines available online.

☛ Western Americana nonfiction remains our focus. We define Western Americana as almost any topic that deals with the people or culture of the west, past and present. Currently emphasizing regional issues—primarily Pacific Northwest. De-emphasizing coffee table or photograph-intensive books."

NONFICTION Subjects include Americana, history, regional. "We need good Western Americana, especially the Northwest, emphasis on serious, narrative nonfiction." Query. Reviews artwork/photos.

TIPS "Books to us never can or will be primarily articles of merchandise to be produced as cheaply as possible and to be sold like slabs of bacon or packages of cereal over the counter. If there is anything that is really worthwhile in this mad jumble we call the 21st century, it should be books."

⊕ CENTER FOR THANATOLOGY RESEARCH & EDUCATION, INC.

391 Atlantic Ave., Brooklyn NY 11217. (718)858-3026. E-mail: thanatology@pipeline.com. Website: www.thanatology.org. **Contact:** Director. Estab. 1980. **Publishes 7 titles/year. 10 queries received/year. 3 mss received/year. 15% of books from first-time authors. 100% from unagented writers. Pays 10% royalty on wholesale price.** Publishes book 9 months after acceptance of ms. Responds in 1 month to queries. Responds in 1 month to proposals. Book catalog and ms guidelines free.

NONFICTION Subjects include education, health, medicine, humanities, psychology, religion, social sciences, sociology, women's issues, women's studies, anthropology. All proposals we feel are applicable are sent to a board of professional readers for comment. Query with SASE. Reviews artwork/photos. Send photocopies.

POETRY We are open to appropriate submissions. Query.

TIPS We serve 2 different audiences: One is physicians/social workers/nurses dealing with dying patients and bereaved families. The second relates to all aspects of cemetery lore: recording, preservation, description, art of.

CENTERSTREAM PUBLISHING

P.O. Box 17878, Anaheim Hills CA 92817. (714)779-9390. Fax: (714)779-9390. E-mail: Centerstrm@aol.com. Website: www.centerstream-usa.com. **Contact:**

Ron Middlebrook, Cindy Middlebrook, owners. Estab. 1980. Publishes music hardcover and mass market paperback originals, trade paperback and mass market paperback reprints. **Publishes 12 titles/year. 15 queries received/year. 15 mss received/year. 80% of books from first-time authors. 100% from unagented writers. Pays 10-15% royalty on wholesale price. Pays $300-3,000 advance.** Publishes book 8 months after acceptance of ms. Accepts simultaneous submissions. Responds in 3 months to queries. Book catalog and ms guidelines for #10 SASE.

☛ Centerstream publishes music history and instructional books, all instruments plus DVDs.

NONFICTION Query with SASE.

CHALICE PRESS

1221 Locust St., Suite 670, St. Louis MO 63103. (314)231-8500. Fax: (314)231-8524. E-mail: submissions@chalicepress.com. Website: www.chalicepress.com. **Contact:** Cyrus N. White, president and publisher. Publishes hardcover and trade paperback originals. **Publishes 35 titles/year. 300 queries received/year. 250 mss received/year. 10% of books from first-time authors. 100% from unagented writers.** Publishes book 1 year after acceptance of ms. Accepts simultaneous submissions. Responds in 1 month to queries. Responds in 2 months to proposals. Responds in 3 months to manuscripts. Book catalog available online. Guidelines available online.

NONFICTION Subjects include religion, Christian spirituality. Submit proposal package, outline, 1-2 sample chapters.

TIPS "We publish for professors, church ministers, and lay Christian readers."

⊕ CHANNEL LAKE, INC.

P.O. Box 1771, New York NY 10156-1771. (800)592-1566. Fax: (866)794-5507. E-mail: info@channellake.com. E-mail: submissions@channellake.com. Website: www.touristtown.com; www.channellake.com. **Contact:** Dirk Vanderwilt, publisher (travel guide books). Estab. 2005. Trade paperback originals. **Publishes 8-10 titles/year. 75% of books from first-time authors. 75% from unagented writers. Pays 6-10% royal on retail price.** Publishes book 3 months after acceptance of ms. Accepts simultaneous submissions. Responds in 1 month on queries, proposals, and manuscripts. Catalog available online at www.touristtown.com. Guidelines free on request.

IMPRINTS Tourist Town Guides, Dirk Vanderwilt,

Publisher

NONFICTION Subjects include travel guide books. "We strongly suggest that you query us before sending a completed manuscript. Our editorial team has very strict content and formatting requirements. Contact us for details." Query. Does not review artwork/photos.

TIPS "Our books are 'local interest' and 'travel books' that are marketed and sold near or in the destination city. Our audience is primarily tourists and vacationers to the destination city. Query first for ms guidelines. The query should include the destination city (U.S. only) that you are interested in writing about."

CHARLESBRIDGE PUBLISHING

85 Main St., Watertown MA 02472. (617)926-0329. Fax: (617)926-5720. E-mail: tradeart@charlesbridge.com. Website: www.charlesbridge.com. **Contact:** Submissions Editors. Estab. 1980. Publishes hardcover and trade paperback nonfiction and fiction, children's books for the trade and library markets. **Publishes 30 titles/year. 10-20% of books from first-time authors. 80% from unagented writers. Pays royalty. Pays advance.** Publishes book 2-4 years after acceptance of ms. Responds in 3 months. If you have not heard back from us after 3 months, you may assume we do not have a place for your project and submit it elsewhere. Guidelines available online.

IMPRINTS Charlesbridge, Imagine Publishing

○ "We're always interested in innovative approaches to a difficult genre, the nonfiction picture book."

&— Charlesbridge publishes high-quality books for children, with a goal of creating lifelong readers and lifelong learners. Our books encourage reading and discovery in the classroom, library, and home. We believe that books for children should offer accurate information, promote a positive worldview, and embrace a child's innate sense of wonder and fun. To this end, we continually strive to seek new voices, new visions, and new directions in children's literature."

NONFICTION Subjects include animals, creative nonfiction, history, multicultural, nature, environment, science, social science. Strong interest in nature, environment, social studies, and other topics for trade and library markets. *Exclusive submissions only.* "Charlesbridge accepts unsolicited manuscripts submitted exclusively to us for a period of three months.

'Exclusive Submission' should be written on all envelopes and cover letters." Please submit only one or two chapters at a time. For nonfiction books longer than 30 manuscript pages, send a detailed proposal, a chapter outline, and one to three chapters of text. Manuscripts should be typed and double-spaced. Please do not submit material by e-mail, by fax, or on a computer disk. Illustrations are not necessary. Please make a copy of your manuscript, as we cannot be responsible for submissions lost in the mail. Include your name and address on the first page of your manuscript and in your cover letter. Be sure to list any previously published work or relevant writing experience.

FICTION Strong stories with enduring themes. Charlesbridge publishes both picture books and transitional bridge books (books ranging from early readers to middle-grade chapter books). Our fiction titles include lively, plot-Dr.n stories with strong, engaging characters. No alphabet books, board books, coloring books, activity books, or books with audiotapes or CD-ROMs. *Exclusive submissions only.* "Charlesbridge accepts unsolicited manuscripts submitted exclusively to us for a period of three months. 'Exclusive Submission' should be written on all envelopes and cover letters." Please submit only one or two manuscript(s) at a time. For picture books and shorter bridge books, please send a complete manuscript. For fiction books longer than 30 manuscript pages, please send a detailed plot synopsis, a chapter outline, and three chapters of text. Manuscripts should be typed and double-spaced. Please do not submit material by e-mail, by fax, or on a computer disk. Illustrations are not necessary. Please make a copy of your manuscript, as we cannot be responsible for submissions lost in the mail. Include your name and address on the first page of your manuscript and in your cover letter. Be sure to list any previously published work or relevant writing experience.

TIPS "To become acquainted with our publishing program, we encourage you to review our books and visit our website (www.charlesbridge.com), where you will find our catalog. To request a printed catalog, please send a 9"×12" SASE with $2.50 in postage."

CHARLES RIVER MEDIA

Course Technology PTR, Cengage Learning, Inc., 20 Channel Center St., Boston MA **02210**. E-mail: **info@ gameprogramminggems.com**. E-mail: emi.smith@ cengage.com. Website: www.gameprogramminggems.com. **Contact:** Emi Smith, sr. acq. editor. **Publishes**

60 titles/year. 1,000 queries received/year. 250 mss received/year. 20% of books from first-time authors. 90% from unagented writers. Pays 5-20% royalty on wholesale price. Pays $3,000-20,000 advance. Publishes book 4 months after acceptance of ms. Accepts simultaneous submissions. Responds in 2 weeks to queries. Book catalog for #10 SASE. Guidelines available online.

NONFICTION Subjects include computers, electronics. Query with SASE. Submit proposal package, outline, resume, 2 sample chapters. Reviews artwork/photos. Send photocopies and GIF, TIFF, or PDF files.

TIPS "We are very receptive to detailed proposals by first-time or nonagented authors. Consult our website for proposal outlines. Manuscripts must be completed within 6 months of contract signing."

CHELSEA GREEN PUBLISHING CO.

P.O. Box 428, White River Junction VT 05001-0428. (802)295-6300. Fax: (802)295-6444. E-mail: submissions@chelseagreen.com; jpraded@chelseagreen.com. Website: www.chelseagreen.com. **Contact:** Joni Praded, editorial director. Estab. 1984. Publishes hardcover and trade paperback originals and reprints. **Publishes 18-25 titles/year. 600-800 queries received/year. 200-300 mss received/year. 30% of books from first-time authors. 80% from unagented writers. Pays royalty on publisher's net. Pays $2,500-10,000 advance.** Publishes book 18 months after acceptance of ms. Responds in 2 weeks to queries. Responds in 1 month to proposals. Responds in 1 month to manuscripts. Book catalog free or online. Guidelines available online.

8—☛ Chelsea Green's Science writers series publishes books on cutting-edge topics that advance science and the role it can play in preserving or creating sustainable civilizations and ecosystems."

NONFICTION Subjects include agriculture, alternative lifestyles, ethical & sustainable business, environment, foods, organic gardening, health, green building, progressive politics, science, social justice, simple living, renewable energy; and other sustainability topics. We only rarely publish cookbooks. We prefer electronic queries and proposals via e-mail (as a single attachment). If sending via snail mail, submissions will only be returned with SASE. Please review our guidelines carefully before submitting. Reviews artwork/photos.

FICTION We do not publish fiction or children's books.

TIPS "Our readers and our authors are passionate about finding sustainable and viable solutions to contemporary challenges in the fields of energy, food production, economics, and building. It would be helpful for prospective authors to have a look at several of our current books, as well as our website."

CHICAGO REVIEW PRESS

814 N. Franklin, Chicago IL 60610-3109. (312)337-0747. Fax: (312)337-5110. E-mail: frontdesk@chicagoreviewpress.com. Website: www.chicagoreviewpress.com. **Contact:** Cynthia Sherry, publisher (general nonfiction, children's nonfiction); Yuval Taylor, senior editor (general nonfiction, especially performing arts-related); Jerome Pohlen, senior editor (popular science, children's nonfiction); Susan Bradanini Betz, senior editor (African-American, Latino-American, progressive politics). Estab. 1973. Publishes hardcover and trade paperback originals, and trade paperback reprints. **Publishes 40-50 titles/year. 400 queries received/year. 800 mss received/year. 50% of books from first-time authors. 50% from unagented writers. Pays 7-12 ½% royalty. Pays $3,000-10,000 average advance.** Publishes book 18 months after acceptance of ms. Accepts simultaneous submissions. Responds in 3 months to queries. ms guidelines for #10 SASE or online at website.

IMPRINTS Lawrence Hill Books (contact Susan Bradanini Betz); A Cappella Books (contact Yuval Taylor) ; Zephyr Press (contact Jerome Pohlen).

8—☛ Chicago Review Press publishes intelligent nonfiction on timely subjects for educated readers with special interests. Does not accept fiction submissions.

NONFICTION Subjects include architecture, art, child guidance, creative nonfiction, education, environment, gardening, health, history, hobbies, memoirs, muticultural, music, nature, recreation, regional, science. Query with outline, TOC, and 1-2 sample chapters.

TIPS "Along with a table of contents and 1-2 sample chapters, also send a cover letter and a list of credentials with your proposal. Also, provide the following information in your cover letter: audience, market, and competition—who is the book written for and what sets it apart from what's already out there."

CHILDREN'S BRAINS ARE YUMMY (CBAY) BOOKS

P.O. Box 92411, Austin TX 78709. (512)789-1004. Fax: (512)473-7710. E-mail: submissions@cbaybooks.com.

Website: www.cbaybooks.com. **Contact:** Madeline Smoot, Publisher. Estab. 2008. **Publishes 8 titles/year. 30% of books from first-time authors. 0% from un-agented writers.**

FICTION Subjects include adventure, mystery, science fiction, suspense, folktales. "CBAY Books currently focuses on quality fantasy and science fiction books for the middle grade and teen markets. Although we are exploring the possibility of publishing fantasy and science fiction books in the future, we are not seeking submissions for them at this time. We do welcome books that mix genres – a fantasy mystery for example – but since our press currently has a narrow focus, all submissions need to have fantasy or science fiction elements to fit in with our list."

TIPS "CBAY Books only accepts unsolicited submissions from authors at specific times for specific genres. Please check the website to see if we are accepting books at this time. Manuscripts received when submissions are closed are not read."

CHILDREN'S PRESS/FRANKLIN WATTS

Imprint of Scholastic, Inc., 90 Old Sherman Turnpike, Danbury CT 06816. Website: scholastic.com/librarypublishing; http://www.scholastic.com/internationalschools/childrenspress.htm. Estab. 1946. Publishes nonfiction hardcover originals. Book catalog for #10 SASE.

"Children's Press publishes 90% nonfiction for the school and library market, and 10% early reader fiction and nonfiction. Our books support textbooks and closely relate to the elementary and middle-school curriculum. Franklin Watts publishes nonfiction for middle and high school curriculum."

NONFICTION Subjects include animals, anthropology, archeology, art, architecture, ethnic, health, medicine, history, hobbies, multicultural, music, dance, nature, environment, science, sports, general children's nonfiction. We publish nonfiction books that supplement the school curriculum. No fiction, poetry, folktales, cookbooks or novelty books. Query with SASE.

TIPS Most of this publisher's books are developed in-house; less than 5% come from unsolicited submissions. However, they publish several series for which they always need new books. Study catalogs to discover possible needs.

CHILD'S PLAY (INTERNATIONAL) LTD.

Children's Play International, Ashworth Rd. Bridgemead, Swindon, Wiltshire SN5 7YD, United Kingdom. E-mail: allday@childs-play.com; neil@childs-play.com; office@childs-play.com. Website: www.childs-play.com. **Contact:** Sue Baker, Neil Burden, manuscript acquisitions. Annie Kubler, art director Estab. 1972.

Specializes in nonfiction, fiction, educational material, multicultural material. Produces 30 picture books/year; 10 young readers/year; 2 middle readers/year. 20% of books by first-time authors. "A child's early years are more important than any other. This is when children learn most about the world around them and the language they need to survive and grow. Child's Play aims to create exactly the right material for this all-important time."

TIPS "Look at our website to see the kind of work we do before sending. Do not send cartoons. We do not publish novels. We do publish lots of books with pictures of babies/toddlers.", "Look at our website to see the kind of work we do before sending. Do not send cartoons. We do not publish novels. We do publish lots of books with pictures of babies/toddlers."

CHILD WELFARE LEAGUE OF AMERICA

E-mail: books@cwla.org. Website: www.cwla.org/pubs. **Contact:** Acquisitions Editor. Publishes hardcover and trade paperback originals. Accepts simultaneous submissions. Book catalog and ms guidelines online.

IMPRINTS CWLA Press (child welfare professional publications); Child & Family Press (children's books and parenting books for the general public).

CWLA is a privately supported, nonprofit, membership-based organization committed to preserving, protecting, and promoting the well-being of all children and their families.

NONFICTION Subjects include child guidance, sociology. Submit complete ms and proposal with outline, TOC, sample chapter, intended audience, and SASE.

TIPS We are looking for positive, kid-friendly books for ages 3-9. We are looking for books that have a positive message—a feel-good book.

CHIVALRY BOOKSHELF

3305 Mayfair Ln., Highland Village TX 75077. (978)418-4774. Fax: (978)418-4774. E-mail: brian@chivalrybookshelf.com. E-mail: csr@chivalrybookshelf.com. Website: www.chivalrybookshelf.com.

Contact: Brian R. Price, publisher (history, art, philosophy, political science, military, martial arts, fencing). Estab. 1996. Publishes hardcover and trade paperback originals and reprints. **Publishes 12 titles/ year. 75 queries received/year. 25 mss received/year. 50% of books from first-time authors. 90% from unagented writers. Pays 5-12% royalty.** Publishes book 6 months after acceptance of ms. Responds in 1 month to queries. Responds in 1 month to proposals. Responds in 2 months to manuscripts. Book catalog available free. Guidelines available online.

NONFICTION Subjects include art, architecture, creative nonfiction, education, government, politics, history, military, war, recreation, sports, martial arts/ fencing especially, translation. "Chivalry Bookshelf began focusing on new works and important reprints relating to arms and armour, medieval knighthood, and related topics. Since then, we have become the largest publisher of books relating to 'Western' or 'historical' martial arts, including translations, interpretations, and fascimile reproductions done in partnership with major museums such as the J. Paul Getty Museum and the British Royal Armouries." Query with SASE if mailing, e-mail or fax. Submit proposal package, outline, 1 sample chapter, sample illustrations. Submit complete ms. Reviews artwork/photos.

TIPS "The bulk of our books are intended for serious amateur scholars and students of history and martial arts. The authors we select tend to have a strong voice, are well read in their chosen field, and submit relatively clean manuscripts."

CHOSEN BOOKS

a division of Baker Publishing Group, 3985 Bradwater St., Fairfax VA 22031-3702. (703)764-8250. Fax: (703)764-3995. E-mail: jcampbell@chosenbooks.com. Website: www.chosenbooks.com. **Contact:** Jane Campbell, editorial director. Estab. 1971. Publishes hardcover and trade paperback originals. **Publishes 20 titles/year. 10% of books from first-time authors. 99% from un-agented writers. Pays small advance.** Publishes book 12-18 months after acceptance of ms. Accepts simultaneous submissions. Responds in 3 months to queries. Guidelines sent electronically on request.

We publish well-crafted books that recognize the gifts and ministry of the Holy Spirit, and help the reader live a more empowered and effective life for Jesus Christ."

NONFICTION "We publish books reflecting the current acts of the Holy Spirit in the world, books with a charismatic Christian orientation, or thematic first-person narrative: query briefly by e-mail first." No New Age, poetry, fiction, autobiographies, biographies, compilations, Bible studies, booklets, academic, or children's books. Submit synopsis, chapter outline, 2 chapters, resume and SASE or e-mail address. No computer disks. E-mail attachments okay.

TIPS "We look for solid, practical advice for the growing and maturing Christian from authors with professional or personal experience platforms. No chronicling of life events, please. Narratives have to be theme-Dr.n. State the topic or theme of your book clearly in your query."

CHRISTIAN BOOKS TODAY LTD

136 Main St., Buckshaw Village Chorley, Lancashire PR7 7BZ, UK. E-mail: submissions@christianbookstoday.com. Website: www.christianbookstoday.com. **Contact:** Jason Richardson, MD (nonfiction); Lynda McIntosh, Editor (fiction). Estab. 2009. Format publishes in trade paperback originals/reprints and electronic originals/reprints. **Publishes 39 titles/year. 100% of books from first-time authors. 100% from unagented writers. Pays 10% royalty on retail price.** Publishes book 6 months after acceptance of ms. Accepts simultaneous submissions. Responds 1 month on queries and 2 months on proposals/manuscripts. Catalog and guidelines available online at www.christianbookstoday.com.

NONFICTION Subjects include spirituality, Christian/Catholic. "The big issues- homosexuality, the Latin Mass, Mega Churches falling numbers, interfaith relationships, atheism—will get our attention." Query with SASE. Submit outline, 3 sample chapters and electronic submissions in RTF only please. No

FICTION Subjects include adventure, poetry, religious, spiritual, Catholic/Christian. "We're looking for writers who write about life as a Catholic, warts and all! Tackle the big issues but in a tasteful way. Life doesn't always conform to doctrine! Moralizing will not appeal to a broader audience. Catholic writers, not Catholic writing. In your cover letter PLEASE tell us to whom your work will appeal and why." Query with SASE. Submit proposal package, including synopsis, 3 sample chapters and by e-mail in RTF document format.

TIPS "We appeal to an audience of practicing Christians, Catholics in particular. We are not interested in Hallmark-ish work but writing by Catholics, rather Catholic writing. If you want to take a risk in subject, you are particularly encouraged to submit. Catholic or general Christian life is real life to us."

CHRISTIAN ED. PUBLISHERS

P.O. Box 26639, San Diego CA 92196. E-mail: crogers@cehouse.com. Website: www.christianedwarehouse.com. **Contact:** Janet Ackelson, assistant editor. Acquisitions: Janet Ackelson, assistant editor; Carol Rogers, managing editor; Nicole Tom, production coordinator. **Work purchased outright from authors for 3¢/word. Pays illustrators $18-20/page.** Responds in 1 month. Book catalog available for 9×12 SAE and 4 first-class stamps. Ms and art guidelines available for SASE or via e-mail.

○ Publishes 110 Bible curriculum titles/year.

⌐ Christian Ed. Publishers is an independent, nondenominational, evangelical company founded over 50 years ago to produce Christ-centered curriculum materials based on the Word of God for thousands of churches of different denominations throughout the world. Our mission is to introduce children, teens, and adults to a personal faith in Jesus Christ, and to help them grow in their faith and service to the Lord. We publish materials that teach moral and spiritual values while training individuals for a lifetime of Christian service. Currently emphasizing Bible curriculum for preschool-preteen ages, including program and student books and take-home papers—all handled by our assigned freelance writers only. Do not send unsolicited manuscripts. Ask for a writer's application."

FICTION "We publish fiction for Bible club take-home papers. All fiction is on assignment only."

TIPS "Read our guidelines carefully before sending us a manuscript or illustrations. Do not send unsolicited manuscripts. All writing and illustrating is done on assignment only and must be age-appropriate (preschool-6th grade). Ask for a writer's application. Do not send manuscripts."

CHRONICLE BOOKS

680 Second St., San Francisco CA 94107. (415)537-4200. Fax: (415)537-4460. Website: www.chroniclebooks.com. **Contact:** Adult Trade Division. Estab. 1966. Publishes hardcover and trade paperback originals. **Publishes 175 titles/year.** Publishes book 18

months after acceptance of ms. Accepts simultaneous submissions. Responds in 3 months to queries. Book catalog for 11X14 envelope and 5 First-Class stamps. Guidelines available online.

IMPRINTS Chronicle Books for Children; GiftWorks (ancillary products, such as stationery, gift books).

⌐ Inspired by the enduring magic and importance of books, our objective is to create and distribute exceptional publishing that is instantly recognizable for its spirit, creativity and value. This objective informs our business relationships and endeavors, be they with customers, authors, suppliers or colleagues."

NONFICTION Subjects include art, architecture, cooking, foods, nutrition, gardening, nature, environment, photography, recreation, regional, design, pop culture, interior design. Query or submit outline/synopsis with artwork and sample chapters

FICTION Submit complete ms.

CHRONICLE BOOKS FOR CHILDREN

680 Second St., San Francisco CA 94107. (415)537-4200. Fax: (415)537-4460. E-mail: frontdesk@chroniclebooks.com. Website: www.chroniclekids.com. **Contact:** Children's Division. Publishes hardcover and trade paperback originals. **Publishes 50-60 titles/year. 30,000 queries received/year. 6% of books from first-time authors. 25% from unagented writers. Pays 8% royalty. Pays variable advance.** Publishes book 18-24 months after acceptance of ms. Accepts simultaneous submissions. Responds in 2-4 weeks to queries. Responds in 6 months to manuscripts. Book catalog for 9×12 envelope and 3 First-Class stamps. Guidelines available online.

⌐ Chronicle Books for Children publishes an eclectic mixture of traditional and innovative children's books. Our aim is to publish books that inspire young readers to learn and grow creatively while helping them discover the joy of reading. We're looking for quirky, bold artwork and subject matter. Currently emphasizing picture books. De-emphasizing young adult."

NONFICTION Subjects include animals, art, architecture, multicultural, nature, environment, science. Query with synopsis. Reviews artwork/photos.

FICTION Subjects include mainstream, contemporary, multicultural, young adult, picture books. We do not accept proposals by fax, via e-mail, or on disk.

When submitting artwork, either as a part of a project or as samples for review, do not send original art.

TIPS "We are interested in projects that have a unique bent to them—be it in subject matter, writing style, or illustrative technique. As a small list, we are looking for books that will lend our list a distinctive flavor. Primarily we are interested in fiction and nonfiction picture books for children ages up to eight years, and nonfiction books for children ages up to twelve years. We publish board, pop-up, and other novelty formats as well as picture books. We are also interested in early chapter books, middle grade fiction, and young adult projects."

CHURCH GROWTH INSTITUTE

P.O. Box 7, Elkton MD 21922-0007. (434)525-0022. Fax: (434)525-0608. E-mail: cgimail@churchgrowth.org. Website: www.churchgrowth.org. **Contact:** Cindy Spear, administrator/resource development director. Estab. 1978. Publishes electronic books (pdf), 3-ring-bound manuals, mixed media resource packets. **Publishes 3 titles/year. Pays 6% royalty on retail price.** Publishes book 1 year after acceptance of ms. Accepts simultaneous submissions. Responds in 3 months to queries. Book catalog for 9×12 envelope and 4 first-class stamps. ms guidelines given after query and outline is received.

⌛ Our mission is to provide practical resources to help pastors, churches, and individuals reach their potential for Christ; to promote spiritual and numerical growth in churches, thereby leading Christians to maturity and lost people to Christ; and to equip pastors so they can equip their church members to do the work of the ministry."

NONFICTION Subjects include education, religion, church-growth related, ministry, how-to manuals, spiritual growth, relationship-building, evangelism. "Accepted manuscripts will be adapted to our resource packet, manual, or inventory format. All material must be practical and easy for the average Christian to understand. Material should originate from a conservative Christian view and cover topics that will help churches grow, through leadership training, self-evaluation, and new or unique ministries, or enhancing existing ministries. Self-discovery inventories regarding spiritual growth, relationship improvement, etc., are hot items." Query, or submit outline and brief explanation of what the packet will accomplish in the local church and whether it is leadership or lay oriented. Queries accepted by mail or e-mail. No phone queries. Reviews artwork/photos. Send photos or images on CD (in TIFF, EPS, or PDF format).

TIPS "We are not accepting textbooks, and are publishing few new printed materials this year-most are online or downloads. Concentrate on how-to manuals and ministry evaluation and diagnostic tools and spiritual or relationship-oriented 'inventories' for individual Christians."

CLARION BOOKS

Houghton Mifflin Co., 215 Park Ave. S., New York NY 10003. Website: www.houghtonmifflinbooks.com; www.hmco.com. **Contact:** Dinah Stevenson, vice president and publisher; Jennifer B. Greene, senior editor (contemporary fiction, picture books for all ages, nonfiction); Jennifer Wingertzahn, editor (fiction, picture books); Lynne Polvino, editor (fiction, nonfiction, picture books). Estab. 1965. Publishes hardcover originals for children. *Identify multiple submissions.* **Publishes 50 titles/year. Pays 5-10% royalty on retail price. Pays minimum of $4,000 advance.** Publishes book 2 years after acceptance of ms. Responds in 2 months to queries. Guidelines for #10 SASE or online.

🔒 "We are no longer responding to your unsolicited submission unless we are interested in publishing it. Please do not include a SASE. Submissions will be recycled, and you will not hear from us regarding the status of your submission unless we are interested. We regret that we cannot respond personally to each submission, but we do consider each and every submission we receive."

⌛ Clarion Books publishes picture books, nonfiction, and fiction for infants through grade 12. Avoid telling your stories in verse unless you are a professional poet."

NONFICTION Subjects include Americana, history, language, literature, nature, environment, photography, holiday. No unsolicited mss. Query with SASE. Submit proposal package, sample chapters, SASE. Reviews artwork/photos. Send photocopies.

FICTION Subjects include adventure, historical, humor, suspense, strong character studies, contemporary. "Clarion is highly selective in the areas of historical fiction, fantasy, and science fiction. A novel must be superlatively written in order to find a place on the list. Mss that arrive without an SASE of adequate size will *not* be responded to or returned. Accepts fiction translations." Submit complete ms. No queries, please. Send to only *one* Clarion editor.

TIPS "Looks for freshness, enthusiasm—in short, life."

CLARITY PRESS, INC.

3277 Roswell Rd. NE, #469, Atlanta GA 30305. (877)613-1495. Fax: (404)231-3899 and (877)613-7868. E-mail: claritypress@usa.net. Website: www.clarity-press.com. **Contact:** Diana G. Collier, editorial director (contemporary social justice issues). Estab. 1984. Publishes hardcover and trade paperback originals. **Publishes 4 titles/year.** Accepts simultaneous submissions. Responds to queries if interested.

NONFICTION Subjects include ethnic, world affairs, human rights/socioeconomic and minority issues. Publishes books on contemporary global issues in US, Middle East and Africa. Query by e-mail only with synopsis, TOC, résumé, publishing history.

TIPS "Check our titles on the website."

CLEIS PRESS

Cleis Press & Viva Editions, 2246 Sixth St., Berkeley CA 94710. (510)845-8000 or (800)780-2279. Fax: (510)845-8001. E-mail: cleis@cleispress.com. E-mail: bknight@cleispress.com. Website: www.cleispress.com and www.vivaeditions.com. **Contact:** Brenda Knight, associate publisher. Kara Wuest, publishing coordinator; Frédérique Delacoste, art director Estab. 1980. Publishes books that inform, enlighten, and entertain. Areas of interest include gift, inspiration, health, family and childcare, self-help, women's issues, reference, cooking. "We do our best to bring readers quality books that celebrate life, inspire the mind, revive the spirit, and enhance lives all around. Our authors are practical visionaries; people who offer deep wisdom in a hopeful and helpful manner.". **Publishes 45 titles/year. 2,000 10% of books from first-time authors. 90% from unagented writers. Pays royalty on retail price.** Publishes book 2 years after acceptance of ms. Responds in 1 month to queries.

IMPRINTS Viva Edition.

➤ Cleis Press publishes provocative, intelligent books in the areas of sexuality, gay and lesbian studies, erotica, fiction, gender studies, and human rights.

NONFICTION Subjects include gay, lesbian, women's issues, women's studies, sexual politics. "Cleis Press is interested in books on topics of sexuality,

human rights and women's and gay and lesbian literature. Please consult our website first to be certain that your book fits our list." Query or submit outline and sample chapters

FICTION Subjects include feminist, gay, lesbian, literary. "We are looking for high quality fiction and nonfiction." "Submit complete ms. *Writer's Market* recommends sending a query with SASE first."

TIPS "Be familiar with publishers' catalogs; be absolutely aware of your audience; research potential markets; present fresh new ways of looking at your topic; avoid 'PR' language and include publishing history in query letter."

CLOVER PARK PRESS

P.O. Box 5067-WS, Santa Monica CA 90409-5067. E-mail: submissions@cloverparkpress.com. Website: www.cloverparkpress.com. **Contact:** Martha Grant, acquisitions editor. Estab. 1991. Publishes hardcover and trade paperback originals. **Publishes 1-3 titles/year. 800 queries received/year. 500 mss received/year. 90% of books from first-time authors. 80% from unagented writers. Pays royalty. Makes outright purchase. Pays modest advance.** Publishes book less than 12 months after acceptance of ms. Accepts simultaneous submissions. Responds in 1-4 months to queries, proposals, and to manuscripts. Book catalog available online. Guidelines for #10 SASE. Current list and guidelines available on website.

NONFICTION Subjects include California (history, natural history, travel, culture or the arts), creative nonfiction, multicultural, nature, environment, regional, science, travel, women's issues, women's studies, world affairs. Please do not send memoir, or personal stories about struggles with alcoholism, addiction, spousal or child abuse, or illness. Query with SASE. Proposal package should contain outline, bio, 30-50 pages (including the first chapter), SASE. Begin your query by e-mail with WS-Query. E-mail queries preferred. Do not telephone.

TIPS "Our audience is primarily women, high school, and college students, readers with curiosity about the world. Initial contact by e-mail or query letter. We welcome good writing. Have patience, we will respond."

COLLEGE PRESS PUBLISHING CO.

P.O.Box 1132, 2111 N. Main St., Suite C, Joplin MO 64801. (800)289-3300. Fax: (417)623-1929. Website: www.collegepress.com. **Contact:** Acquisitions Editor. Estab. 1959. Publishes hardcover and trade paperback originals and reprints. Accepts simultaneous submissions. Responds in 3 months to proposals. Responds in 2 months to mss. Book catalog for 9×12 envelope and 5 first-class stamps. Guidelines available online. **IMPRINTS** HeartSpring Publishing (nonacademic Christian, inspirational, devotional and Christian fiction).

☛ College Press is a traditional Christian publishing house. Seeks proposals for Bible studies, topical studies (biblically based), apologetic studies, historical biographies of Christians, Sunday/Bible School curriculum (adult electives).

NONFICTION Seeks Bible studies, topical studies, apologetic studies, historical biographies of Christians, and Sunday/Bible school curriculum. No poetry, games/puzzles, books on prophecy from a premillennial or dispensational viewpoint, or any book without a Christian message. Query with SASE. Always send a proposal or query letter first and requested manuscripts to: Acquisitions Editor.

TIPS "Our core market is Christian Churches/Churches of Christ and conservative evangelical Christians. Have your material critically reviewed prior to sending it. Make sure that it is non-Calvinistic and that it leans more amillennial (if it is apocalyptic writing)."

⊘ COMMON COURAGE PRESS

One Red Barn Rd., Box 702, Monroe ME 04951. (207)525-0900. Fax: (207)525-3068. Website: www.commoncouragepress.com. Estab. 1991. Publishes hardcover and trade paperback originals and trade paperback reprints. Book catalog available online. Guidelines available online.

○ "We are not accepting unsolicited submissions at this time.", "Nonfiction leftist, activist, political, history, feminist, media issues are our niche."

NONFICTION Subjects include anthropology, archeology, creative nonfiction, ethnic, gay, lesbian, government, politics, health, medicine, history, military, war, multicultural, nature, environment, science. Unsolicited mss returned unopened. Reviews artwork/photos.

TIPS Audience consists of left-wing activists, college audiences.

CONCORDIA PUBLISHING HOUSE

3558 S. Jefferson Ave., St. Louis MO 63118. E-mail: publicity@cph.org;rosemary.parkinson@cph.org. Website: www.cph.org. **Contact:** Peggy Kuethe, senior

editor (children's product, adult devotional, women's resources); Dawn Weinstock, managing production editor (adult nonfiction on Christian spirituality and culture, academic works of interest in Lutheran markets). Estab. 1869. Publishes hardcover and trade paperback originals. Guidelines available online.

☛ Concordia publishes Protestant, inspirational, theological, family, and juvenile material. All mss must conform to the doctrinal tenets of The Lutheran Church—Missouri Synod. No longer publishes fiction."

NONFICTION Subjects include child guidance, religion, science, child guidance in Christian context, inspirational.

TIPS "Do not send finished artwork with the manuscript. If sketches will help in the presentation of the manuscript, they may be sent. If stories are taken from the Bible, they should follow the Biblical account closely. Liberties should not be taken in fantasizing Biblical stories."

CONSORTIUM PUBLISHING

640 Weaver Hill Rd., West Greenwich RI 02817-2261. (401)397-9838. Fax: (401)392-1926. E-mail: ConsortiumPub@msn.com. Website: consortiumpublishing. tripod.com/consortiumpub/index.html. **Contact:** John M. Carlevale, chief of publications. Estab. 1990. Publishes trade paperback originals and reprints. **Publishes 12 titles/year. 150 queries received/year. 50 mss received/year. 50% of books from first-time authors. 95% from unagented writers. Pays 10-15% royalty.** Publishes book 3 months after acceptance of ms. Responds in 2 months to queries. Book catalog online and ms guidelines for #10 SASE.

☛ Consortium publishes books for all levels of the education market."

NONFICTION Subjects include business, economics, child guidance, education, government, politics, health, medicine, history, music, dance, nature, environment, psychology, science, sociology, women's issues, women's studies. Query, or submit proposal package, including TOC, outline, 1 sample chapter, and SASE. Reviews artwork/photos. Send photocopies.

TIPS "Audience is college and high school students and instructors, elementary school teachers and other trainers."

CONSUMER PRESS

13326 SW 28 St., Suite 102, Ft. Lauderdale FL 33330. (954)370-9153. E-mail: info@consumerpress.com.

Contact: Joseph Pappas, editorial director. Estab. 1989. Publishes trade paperback originals. **Publishes 2-5 titles/year. Pays royalty on wholesale price or on retail price, as per agreement.** Book catalog available free.

IMPRINTS Women's Publications.

○ "Consumer Press is a full-spectrum publishing company specializing in literary works by noted personalities. Known for innovation and excellence in copy development, book design, publicity, and distribution, we provide an array of related services for the seasoned or first-time author. Our staff collaborates closely with clients from planning to promotion, with a focus on perennial exposure and global recognition of each title."

NONFICTION Subjects include child guidance, health, medicine, money, finance, women's issues, women's studies, homeowner guides, building/remodeling, food/nutrition. Query with SASE, call, e-mail, or use online submission form.

⊘ COPPER CANYON PRESS

P.O. Box 271, Bldg. 313, Port Townsend WA 98368. (360)385-4925. Fax: (360)385-4985. E-mail: poetry@coppercanyonpress.org. Website: www.coppercanyonpress.org. **Contact:** Editor. Estab. 1972. Publishes trade paperback originals and occasional cloth-bound editions. **Publishes 18 titles/year. 2,000 queries received/year. 1,500 mss received/year. 0% of books from first-time authors. 95% from unagented writers. Pays royalty.** Publishes book 2 years after acceptance of ms. Responds in 4 months to queries. Book catalog & guidelines available online.

IMPRINTS Ausable Press, Chase Twichell.

8—★ Copper Canyon Press is dedicated to publishing poetry in a wide range of styles and from a full range of the world's cultures."

POETRY *No unsolicited mss.*

TIPS "CCP publishes poetry exclusively and is the largest poetry publisher in the U.S. We will not review queries if guidelines are not followed. We will read queries from poets who have published a book. Please read our query guidelines."

CORWIN PRESS, INC.

2455 Teller Rd., Thousand Oaks CA 91320. (800)818-7243. Fax: (805)499-2692. E-mail: cathy.hernandez@corwinpress.com. Website: www.corwinpress.com. **Contact:** Cathy Hernandez, acquisitions editor (con-

tent, curriculum). Hudson Perigo, Executive Editor (classroom management, new teacher induction, general teaching methods); phone: (323)378-6324; E-mail: hudson.perigo@corwin.com; Jessica Allan, Senior Acquisitions Editor (science, special education, gifted education, early childhood education, and counseling), Telephone: (908)277-1447; E-mail: jessica.allan@corwin.com. Estab. 1990. Publishes hardcover and paperback originals. **Publishes 240 titles/year.** Publishes book 7 months after acceptance of ms. Responds in 1-2 months to queries. Guidelines available online.

○ "Corwin Press, Inc., publishes leading-edge, user-friendly publications for education professionals."

NONFICTION Subjects include education. Seeking fresh insights, conclusions, and recommendations for action. Prefers theory or research-based books that provide real-world examples and practical, hands-on strategies to help busy educators be successful. Professional-level publications for administrators, teachers, school specialists, policymakers, researchers and others involved with Pre K-12 education. No textbooks that simply summarize existing knowledge or mass-market books. Query with SASE.

COUNCIL ON SOCIAL WORK EDUCATION

1701 Duke St., Suite 200, Alexandria VA 22314-4703. (703)683-8080. Fax: (703)683-8099. E-mail: info@cswe.org. Website: www.cswe.org. **Contact:** Elizabeth Simon, publications manager. Estab. 1952. Publishes trade paperback originals. **Publishes 4 titles/year. 12 queries received/year. 8 mss received/year. 25% of books from first-time authors. 100% from unagented writers. Pays sliding royalty scale, starting at 10%** Publishes book 1 year after acceptance of ms. Responds in 2 months to queries. Responds in 3 months to proposals and manuscripts. Book catalog and ms guidelines free via website or with SASE.

8—★ Council on Social Work Education produces books and resources for social work educators, students and practitioners."

NONFICTION Subjects include education, sociology, social work. Books for social work and other educators. Query via e-mail only with proposal package, including CV, outline, expected audience, and 2 sample chapters.

TIPS "Audience is Social work educators and students and others in the helping professions. Check areas of publication interest on website."

THE COUNTRYMAN PRESS

P.O. Box 748, Woodstock VT 05091-0748. (802)457-4826. Fax: (802)457-1678. E-mail: countrymanpress@wwnorton.com;khummel@wwnorton.com. Website: www.countrypress.com. Estab. 1973. Publishes hardcover originals, trade paperback originals and reprints. **Publishes 60 titles/year. 1,000 queries received/year. 30% of books from first-time authors. 70% from unagented writers. Pays 5-15% royalty on retail price. Pays $1,000-5,000 advance.** Publishes book 18 months after acceptance of ms. Accepts simultaneous submissions. Responds in 2 months to proposals. Book catalog available free. Guidelines available online.

IMPRINTS Backcountry Guides, Berkshire House.

8— Countryman Press publishes books that encourage physical fitness and appreciation for and understanding of the natural world, self-sufficiency, and adventure."

NONFICTION Subjects include cooking, foods, nutrition, gardening, history, nature, environment, recreation, regional, travel, country living. "We publish several series of regional recreation guidebooks—hiking, bicycling, walking, fly-fishing, canoeing, kayaking—and are looking to expand them. We're also looking for books of national interest on travel, gardening, rural living, nature, and fly-fishing." Submit proposal package, outline, bio, 3 sample chapters, market information, SASE. Reviews artwork/photos. Send photocopies.

COUNTRYSPORT PRESS

Down East Enterprises, P.O. Box 679, Camden ME 04843. (207)594-9544. Fax: (207)594-0147. E-mail: msteere@countrysportpress.com. Website: www.countrysportpress.com. **Contact:** Michael Steere, managing editor. Estab. 1988. Publishes hardcover originals and reprints. **Publishes 4 titles/year. 20% of books from first-time authors. 90% from unagented writers. Pays royalty on wholesale or retail price. Pays variable advance.** Publishes book 1 year after acceptance of ms. Accepts simultaneous submissions. Responds in 1 month to queries. Responds in 3 months to proposals. Responds in 3 months to manuscripts. Book catalog free via website or with SASE.

○ E-mail queries only. Submissions of mss or proposals via e-mail will not be considered.

8— Our audience is upscale sportsmen with interests in wingshooting, fly fishing, fine guns and other outdoor activities.

NONFICTION Subjects include sports, wingshooting. We are looking for high-quality writing that is often reflective, anecdotal, and that offers a complete picture of an outdoor experience. Query with SASE. Submit outline, 3 sample chapters.

COVENANT COMMUNICATIONS, INC.

920 E. State Rd., American Fork UT 84003. (801)756-9966. Fax: (801)756-1049. E-mail: info@covenant-lds.com. E-mail: submissions@covenant-lds.com. Website: www.covenant-lds.com. **Contact:** Kathryn Jenkins, managing editor. Estab. 1958. **Publishes 80-100 titles/year. 350 queries, 1,200 mss 60% of books from first-time authors. 99% from unagented writers. Pays 6 ½-15% royalty on retail price.** Publishes book 6 months to a year after acceptance of ms. Accepts simultaneous submissions. Responds in 1 month on queries & proposals; 4 months on manuscripts. Guidelines available online.

8— Currently emphasizing inspirational, doctrinal, historical, biography. Our fiction is also expanding, and we are looking for new approaches to LDS literature and storytelling."

NONFICTION Subjects include history, religion, spirituality. "We target an exclusive audience of members of The Church of Jesus Christ of Latter-day Saints. All mss must be written for that audience." Submit complete ms. Reviews artwork. Send photocopies.

FICTION Subjects include adventure, historical, mystery, regional, religious, romance, spiritual, suspense. "We publish exclusively to the 'Mormon' (The Church of Jesus Christ of Latter-Day Saints) market. Fiction must feature characters who are members of that church, grappling with issues relevant to that religion." Submit complete ms.

TIPS "Our audience is exclusively LDS (Latter-Day Saints, 'Mormon')." We do not accept manuscripts that do not have a strong LDS theme or feature strong LDS characters.

COWLEY PUBLICATIONS

Rowman & Littlefield, 4501 Forbes Blvd., Suite 200, Lanham MD 20706. Website: www.rowmanlittlefield.com/imprints/cowley.shtml. **Contact:** Sarah Stanton, acquisitions editor. Estab. 1979. Publishes cloth and paperback originals. **Publishes 5-10 titles/year. 500 queries received/year. 300 mss received/year. 50% of books from first-time authors. 90% from unagented writers. Pays 8-15% royalty on net. Pays $0-3,000 advance.** Publishes book 12-18 months after acceptance of ms. Accepts simultaneous submissions. Responds in

3 months to queries; 3 months to proposals. Book catalog available online. Guidelines available online.

○ Purchased by Rowman & Littlefield Publishing Group.

NONFICTION Subjects include religion, spirituality. "We publish books and resources for those seeking spiritual and theological formation. We are committed to developing a new generation of writers and teachers who will encourage people to think and pray in new ways about spirituality, reconciliation, and the future. We are interested in the many ways that faith and spirituality intersect with the world, in arts, social concerns, ethics, and so on." Query with SASE. Submit proposal package, outline, 1 sample chapter, other materials as specified online.

CQ PRESS

2300 N St., NW, Suite 800, Washington DC 20037. (202)729-1800. E-mail: ckiino@cqpress.com; pmcgeehon@cqpress.com; dghart@cqpress.com; apedolsky@cqpress.com. Website: www.cqpress.com. **Contact:** Doug Goldenberg-Hart, Shana Wagger (library/reference); Clarisse Kiino (college); Priscilla McGeehon, Executive Editor, (History); Doug Goldenberg-Hart, Acquisitions Editor; Andrea Pedolsky, Chief, Editorial Acquisitions. Estab. 1945. Publishes hardcover and online paperback titles. Accepts simultaneous submissions. Book catalog available free.

IMPRINTS College, Library/Reference, Staff Directories; CQ Electronic Library/CQ Researcher.

○ CQ Press seeks to educate the public by publishing authoritative works on American and international politics, policy, and people.

NONFICTION Subjects include government, politics, history. "We are interested in American government, public administration, comparative government, and international relations." Submit proposal package, outline, bio.

TIPS Our books present important information on American government and politics, and related issues, with careful attention to accuracy, thoroughness, and readability.

CRAFTSMAN BOOK CO.

6058 Corte Del Cedro, Carlsbad CA 92011. (760)438-7828 or (800)829-8123. Fax: (760)438-0398. Website: www.craftsman-book.com. **Contact:** Laurence D. Jacobs, editorial manager. Estab. 1957. Publishes paperback originals. **Publishes 12 titles/year. 85% of books from first-time authors. 98% from unagented writ-**

ers. **Pays 7 ½-12 ½% royalty on wholesale price or retail price.** Publishes book Acceptance to publication is 2 years. after acceptance of ms. Accepts simultaneous submissions. Responds in 2 months to queries. Book catalog and ms guidelines free.

⌖ Publishes how-to manuals for professional builders. Currently emphasizing construction software.

NONFICTION All titles are related to construction for professional builders. Query with SASE. Reviews artwork/photos.

TIPS "The book submission should be loaded with step-by-step instructions, illustrations, charts, reference data, forms, samples, cost estimates, rules of thumb, and examples that solve actual problems in the builder's office and in the field. It must cover the subject completely, become the owner's primary reference on the subject, have a high utility-to-cost ratio, and help the owner make a better living in his chosen field."

CREATIVE HOMEOWNER

24 Park Way, Upper Saddle River NJ 07458. (201)934-7100, ext. 375. Fax: (201)934-8971 or (201)934-7541. E-mail: info@creativehomeowner.com; rweisman@creativehomeowner.com; mdolan@creativehomeowner.com. Website: www.creativehomeowner.com. **Contact:** Rich Weisman, president; Mary Dolan, photo researcher. Estab. 1978. Publishes trade paperback originals. Book catalog available free.

⌖ Creative Homeowner is a leading and trusted source for the best information, inspiration, and instruction related to the house and home. Over the past 25 years, Creative Homeowner has grown significantly to include titles covering all aspects of decorating and design; home repair and improvement; house plans; and gardening and landscaping. Creative Homeowner's books and online information are known by consumers for their complete and easy-to-follow instructions, up-to-date information, and extensive use of color photography. Among its best-selling titles are *Decorating with Architectural Trimwork, Wiring, and Landscaping with Stone.*

NONFICTION Subjects include gardening, Home remodeling/building. Query, or submit proposal package, including competitive books (short analysis), outline, and SASE Reviews artwork/photos.

CRESCENT MOON PUBLISHING

P.O. Box 393, Maidstone Kent ME14 5XU, UK. (44)(162)272-9593. E-mail: cresmopub@yahoo.co.uk. Website: www.crescentmoon.org.uk. **Contact:** Jeremy Robinson, director (arts, media, cinema, literature); Cassidy Hushes (visual arts). Estab. 1988. Publishes hardcover and trade paperback originals. **Publishes 25 titles/year. 300 queries received/year. 400 mss received/year. 1% of books from first-time authors. 1% from unagented writers. Pays royalty. Pays negotiable advance.** Publishes book 18 months after acceptance of ms. Accepts simultaneous submissions. Responds in 2 months to queries; 4 months to proposals and mss. Book catalog and ms guidelines free.

IMPRINTS *Joe's Press, Pagan America Magazine, Passion Magazine.*

Our mission is to publish the best in contemporary work, in poetry, fiction, and critical studies, and selections from the great writers. Currently emphasizing nonfiction (media, film, music, painting). De-emphasizing children's books."

NONFICTION Subjects include Americana, art, architecture, gardening, government, politics, language, literature, music, dance, philosophy, religion, travel, women's issues, women's studies, cinema, the media, cultural studies. Query with SASE. Submit outline, 2 sample chapters, bio. Reviews artwork/photos. Send photocopies.

FICTION Subjects include erotica, experimental, feminist, gay, lesbian, literary, short story collections, translation. "We do not publish much fiction at present but will consider high quality new work." Query with SASE. Submit outline, clips, 2 sample chapters, bio.

POETRY "We prefer a small selection of the poet's very best work at first. We prefer free verse or non-rhyming poetry. Do not send too much material." Query and submit 6 sample poems.

TIPS "Our audience is interested in new contemporary writing."

CRICKET BOOKS

Imprint of Carus Publishing, 70 E. Lake St., Suite 300, Chicago IL 60601. (603)924-7209. Fax: (603)924-7380. Website: www.cricketmag.com. **Contact:** Submissions Editor. Estab. 1999. Publishes hardcover originals. **Publishes 5 titles/year. Open to first-time authors.** Publishes book 18 months after acceptance of ms.

Currently not accepting queries or ms. Check website for submissions details and updates.

Cricket Books publishes picture books, chapter books, and middle-grade novels.

FICTION Subjects include juvenile, adventure, easy-to-read, fantasy/science fiction, historical, horror, mystery/suspense, problem novels, sports, westerns.

TIPS "Take a look at the recent titles to see what sort of materials we're interested in, especially for nonfiction. Please note that we aren't doing the sort of strictly educational nonfiction that other publishers specialize in."

CROSS-CULTURAL COMMUNICATIONS

Cross-Cultural Literary Editions, Ltd.; Express Editions; Ostrich Editions, 239 Wynsum Ave., Merrick NY 11566-4725. (516)869-5635. Fax: (516)379-1901. E-mail: cccpoetry@aol.com. Website: www.cross-culturalcommunications.com. **Contact:** Stanley H. Barkan, publisher/editor-in-chief (bilingual poetry); Bebe Barkan, Mia Barkan Clarke, art editors (complementary art to poetry editions). Estab. 1971. Publishes hardcover and trade paperback originals. **Publishes 10 titles/year. 200 queries received/year. 50 mss received/year. 25% of books from first-time authors. 100% from unagented writers.** Publishes book 12 months after acceptance of ms. Responds in 1 month to proposals. Responds in 2 months to manuscripts. Book catalog (sample flyers) for #10 SASE.

IMPRINTS Expressive Editions (contact Mia Barkan Clarke).

NONFICTION Subjects include language, literature, memoirs, multicultural. Query first; we basically do not want the focus on nonfiction. Query with SASE. Reviews artwork/photos. Send photocopies.

FICTION Subjects include historical, multicultural, poetry, poetry in translation, translation, Bilingual poetry. Do not query until late 2011 (overcommitted, celebrating 40th anniversary). For bilingual poetry submit 3-6 short poems in original language with English translation, a brief (3-5 lines) bio of the author and translator(s). Query with SASE.

POETRY Query.

TIPS "Best chance: poetry from a translation."

CROSSQUARTER PUBLISHING GROUP

P.O. Box 23749, Santa Fe NM 87502. E-mail: info@crossquarter.com. Website: www.crossquarter.com. **Contact:** Anthony Ravenscroft, Acquisitions. Publishes trade paperback originals and reprints. **Publishes 5-10 titles/year. 1,200 queries received/year. 90% of books from first-time authors. Pays 8-10% royalty on wholesale or retail price.** Publishes book 1-2 years after acceptance of ms. Accepts simultaneous submissions. Responds in 3 months to queries. Book catalog for $1.75. Guidelines available online.

○ Query letters are required. *No unsolicited mss.*

⚷ We emphasize personal sovereignty, self responsibility and growth with pagan or pagan-friendly emphasis for young adults and adults."

NONFICTION Subjects include health, medicine, nature, environment, New Age, philosophy, psychology, religion, pagan only, spirituality, autobiography. Query with SASE. Reviews artwork/photos. Send photocopies.

FICTION Subjects include science fiction, visionary fiction. Query with SASE.

TIPS "Our audience is earth-conscious people looking to grow into balance of body, mind, heart and spirit."

Ⓐ CROWN BUSINESS

Random House, Inc., 1745 Broadway, New York NY 10019. (212)572-2275. Fax: (212)572-6192. E-mail: crownbiz@randomhouse.com. Website: crownpublishing.com. Estab. 1995. Publishes hardcover and trade paperback originals. Accepts simultaneous submissions. Book catalog available online.

○ *Agented submissions only.*

NONFICTION Subjects include business, economics, money, finance, management. Query with proposal package including outline, 1-2 sample chapters, market analysis and information on author platform.

Ⓐ Ⓞ CROWN PUBLISHING GROUP

Imprint of Random House, Inc., 1745 Broadway, New York NY 10019. (212)782-9000. E-mail: CrownBiz@randomhouse.com. Website: www.randomhouse.com/crown. Estab. 1933. Publishes popular fiction and nonfiction hardcover originals.

IMPRINTS Bell Tower; Broadway Business; Clarkson Potter; Crown Business; Crown Forum; Harmony Books; Shaye Arehart Books; Three Rivers Press.

○ *Agented submissions only.* See website for more details.

CYCLOTOUR GUIDE BOOKS

P.O. Box 10585, Rochester NY 10585-0585. (585)244-6157. Fax: (585)244-6157. E-mail: cyclotour@cyclotour.com. Website: www.cyclotour.com. Estab. 1994.

Trade paperback originals. **Publishes 2 titles/year. Receives 25 queries/year and 2 mss/year. 50% of books from first-time authors. 100% from unagented writers.** Publishes book 24 months after acceptance of ms. Accepts simultaneous submissions. Responds in 1 month to queries, proposals, and mss. Book catalog and ms guidelines online.

NONFICTION Subjects include sports (bicycle only), travel (bicycle tourism). No narrative accounts of their bicycle tour without distance indicators. Query with SASE. Reviews artwork/photos as part of ms package. Send photocopies.

TIPS Bicyclists. Folks with a dream of bicycle touring. "Check your grammar and spelling. Write logically."

DANIEL & DANIEL PUBLISHERS, INC.

P.O. Box 2790, McKinleyville CA 95519. (707)839-3495. Fax: (707)839-3242. E-mail: dandd@daniel-publishing.com. Website: www.danielpublishing.com. **Contact:** John Daniel, publisher. Estab. 1980. Publishes hardcover originals and trade paperback originals. **Publishes 12 (or fewer) titles/year. 50% first-time authors% of books from first-time authors. 90% unagented authors% from unagented writers. Pays 10%-60% royalty on wholesale price, depending on which imprint Pays $0-500 advance for John Daniel & Co. Pays $1,000 advance for Perseverance Press. No advance for Fifthian Press.** Publishes book 12 months from acceptance to publication. after acceptance of ms. Accepts simultaneous submissions. Responds in 1 month to queries and proposals; 2 months to mss. Book catalog and guidelines available online.

IMPRINTS John Daniel & Company; Fithian Press (belle lettres: fiction, poetry, memoir, essay); Perseverance Press (literary mysteries).

○ Accepts simultaneous submissions for John Daniel & Co. and Fithian Press; but acquisitions for Perseverance Press are by invitation only.

⚷ Publishes fiction and nonfiction; but very little poetry.

NONFICTION Subjects include: creative nonfiction, memoirs. "We seldom publish books over 70,000 words. Other than that, we're looking for books that are important and well-written." Query with SASE. Submit proposal package, outline, 5 pages.

FICTION Subjects include: literary, short story collections. Query with SASE. Submit proposal package, clips, 5 pages.

POETRY "We publish very little poetry, I'm sorry to say." Query and submit complete ms.

TIPS "Audience includes literate, intelligent general readers. We are very small and very cautious, and we publish fewer books each year, so any submission to us is a long shot. But we welcome your submissions, by mail or e-mail only, please. We don't want submissions by phone, fax or disk."

DANTE UNIVERSITY OF AMERICA PRESS, INC.

P.O. Box 812158, Wellesley MA 02482. Fax: (781)790-1056. E-mail: danteu@danteuniversity.org. Website: www.danteuniversity.org/dpress.html. **Contact:** Josephine Tanner, president. Estab. 1975. Publishes hardcover and trade paperback originals and reprints plus Kindle and Nook editions. **Publishes 5 titles/year. 50% of books from first-time authors. 50% from unagented writers. Pays royalty. Pays negotiable advance.** Publishes book 10 months after acceptance of ms. Responds in 2 months to queries.

8—✒ The Dante University Press exists to bring quality, educational books pertaining to our Italian heritage as well as the historical and political studies of America. Profits from the sale of these publications benefit the Foundation, bringing Dante University closer to a reality."

NONFICTION Subjects include history, Italian-American, humanities, translation, from Italian and Latin, general scholarly nonfiction, Renaissance thought and letter, Italian language and linguistics, Italian-American culture, bilingual education. Query with SASE. Reviews artwork/photos.

FICTION Translations from Italian and Latin. Query with SASE.

POETRY There is a chance that we would use Renaissance poetry translations.

JONATHAN DAVID PUBLISHERS, INC.

68-22 Eliot Ave., Middle Village NY 11379-1194. (718)456-8611. Fax: (718)894-2818. E-mail: submission@jdbooks.com. Website: www.jdbooks.com. **Contact:** David Kolatch, editorial director. Estab. 1948. Publishes hardcover and trade paperback originals and reprints. **Publishes 20-25 titles/year. 50% of books from first-time authors. 90% from unagented writers. Pays royalty, or makes outright purchase.** Publishes book 18 months after acceptance of ms. Responds in 1 month to queries. Responds in 1 month to proposals.

Responds in 2 months to manuscripts. Book catalog available online. Guidelines available online.

8—✒ Jonathan David publishes popular Judaica.

NONFICTION Subjects include cooking, foods, nutrition, creative nonfiction, ethnic, multicultural, religion, sports. Query with SASE. Submit proposal package, outline, résumé, 3 sample chapters. Reviews artwork/photos. Send photocopies.

DAWBERT PRESS, INC.

Submissions Department, P.O. Box 67, Duxbury MA 02331. (781)934-7202. E-mail: editor@dawbert.com. Website: www.dawbert.com. **Contact:** Allison Elliott, editor. Publishes mass market paperback originals. **Publishes 3 titles/year. Pays 5-10% royalty on retail price.** Publishes book months after acceptance of ms. Accepts simultaneous submissions. Guidelines available online.

NONFICTION Subjects include travel, recreation. We publish only travel and recreation books. Submit outline. Reviews artwork/photos. Send photocopies.

DAW BOOKS, INC.

Distributed by Penguin Group (USA), 375 Hudson St., New York NY 10014-3658. (212)366-2096. Fax: (212)366-2090. Website: www.dawbooks.com. **Contact:** Peter Stampfel, submissions editor. Estab. 1971. Publishes hardcover and paperback originals and reprints. **Publishes 50-60 titles/year. Pays in royalties with an advance negotiable on a book-by-book basis.** Responds in 3 months to manuscripts. Guidelines available online.

○ Simultaneous submissions not accepted, unless prior arrangements are made by agent.

8—✒ DAW Books publishes science fiction and fantasy.

NONFICTION We do not want any nonfiction.

FICTION "Currently seeking modern urban fantasy and paranormals. We like character-Dr.n books with appealing protagonists, engaging plots, and well-constructed worlds. We accept both agented and unagented manuscripts.". Submit entire ms, cover letter, SASE.

DAWN PUBLICATIONS

12402 Bitney Springs Rd., Nevada City CA 95959. (530)274-7775. Fax: (530)274-7778. Website: www.dawnpub.com. **Contact:** Glenn Hovemann, editor. Estab. 1979. Publishes hardcover and trade paperback originals. **Publishes 6 titles/year. 2,500 que-**

ries or mss received/year. **15% of books from first-time authors. 90% from unagented writers. Pays advance.** Publishes book 1 to 2 years after acceptance of ms. Accepts simultaneous submissions. Responds in 2 months to queries. Book catalog available online. Guidelines available online.

○ Dawn accepts mss submissions by e-mail; follow instructions posted on website. Submissions by mail still OK.

☞ Dawn Publications is dedicated to inspiring in children a sense of appreciation for all life on earth. Dawn looks for nature awareness and appreciation titles that promote a relationship with the natural world and specific habitats, usually through inspiring treatment and nonfiction."

NONFICTION Subjects include animals, nature, environment.

TIPS "Publishes mostly creative nonfiction with lightness and inspiration." Looking for "picture books expressing nature awareness with inspirational quality leading to enhanced self-awareness. Does not publish anthropomorphic works; no animal dialogue."

DBS PRODUCTIONS

P.O. Box 1894, Charlottesville VA 22903. (800)745-1581. Fax: (434)293-5502. E-mail: info@dbs-sar.com. Website: www.dbs-sar.com. **Contact:** Bob Adams, publisher. Estab. 1989. Publishes hardcover and trade paperback originals. **Publishes 4 titles/year. 10 queries received/year. 10% of books from first-time authors. 100% from unagented writers. Pays 5-20% royalty on retail price.** Publishes book 1 year after acceptance of ms. Responds in 2 weeks to queries. Book catalog available on request or on website. Guidelines for #10 SASE.

○ "dBS Productions produces search and rescue and outdoor first-aid related materials and courses. It offers a selection of publications, videotapes, management kits and tools, and instructional modules."

NONFICTION Subjects include health, medicine. Submit proposal package, outline, 2 sample chapters. Reviews artwork/photos. Send photocopies.

ⒶⲞ DELACORTE PRESS BOOKS FOR YOUNG READERS

Imprint of Random House Children's Books/Random House, Inc., 1745 Broadway, New York NY 10019. (212)782-9000. Website: www.randomhouse.com/kids; www.randomhouse.com/teens.

○ Although not currently accepting unsolicited mss, mss are being sought for 2 contests: Delacorte Dell Yearling Contest for a First Middle-Grade Novel and Delacorte Press Contest for a First Young Adult Novel. Submission guidelines can be found online at www.randomhouse.com/kids/writingcontests.

Ⓐ DEL REY BOOKS

Imprint of Random House Publishing Group, 1745 Broadway, 18th Floor, New York NY 10019. (212)782-9000. E-mail: delrey@randomhouse.com. Website: www.randomhouse.com. Estab. 1977. Publishes hardcover, trade paperback, and mass market originals and mass market paperback reprints. **Pays royalty on retail price. Pays competitive advance.**

☞ Del Rey publishes top level fantasy, alternate history, and science fiction.

FICTION Subjects include fantasy, should have the practice of magic as an essential element of the plot, science fiction, well-plotted novels with good characterizations, exotic locales and detailed alien creatures, alternate history. Agented submissions only.

TIPS "Del Rey is a reader's house. Pay particular attention to plotting, strong characters, and dramatic, satisfactory conclusions. It must be/feel believable. That's what the readers like. In terms of mass market, we basically created the field of fantasy bestsellers. Not that it didn't exist before, but we put the mass into mass market."

DEMONTREVILLE PRESS, INC.

P.O. Box 835, Lake Elmo MN 55042-0835. E-mail: publisher@demontrevillepress.com. Website: www.demontrevillepress.com. **Contact:** Kevin Clemens, publisher (automotive fiction and nonfiction). Estab. 2006. Publishes trade paperback originals and reprints. **Publishes 4 titles/year. 150 queries received/year. 100 mss received/year. 90% of books from first-time authors. 90% from unagented writers. Pays 20% royalty on sale price.** Publishes book 18 months after acceptance of ms. Accepts simultaneous submissions. Responds in 3 months to queries. Responds in 4 months to proposals. Responds in 6 months to manuscripts. Book catalog available online. Guidelines available online.

NONFICTION Subjects include current events, automotive, environment, motorcycle. "We want novel length automotive or motorcycle historicals and/or adventures. Environmental energy and infrastructure books wanted." Submit proposal package online, outline, 3 sample chapters, bio. Reviews artwork/photos. Do not send photos until requested.

FICTION Subjects include current events, environment, adventure, mystery, sports, young adult, automotive, motorcycle. "We want novel length automotive or motorcycle historicals and/or adventures." Submit proposal package, 3 sample chapters, clips, bio.

TIPS "Environmental, energy and transportation nonfiction works are now being accepted. Automotive and motorcycle enthusiasts, adventurers, environmentalists and history buffs make up our audience."

ⓐ DIAL BOOKS FOR YOUNG READERS

Imprint of Penguin Group USA, 345 Hudson St., New York NY 10014. (212)366-2000. Website: www.penguin.com/youngreaders. **Contact:** Submissions Editor. Estab. 1961. Publishes hardcover originals. **Publishes 50 titles/year. 5,000 queries received/year. 20% of books from first-time authors. Pays royalty. Pays varies advance.** Responds in 4-6 months to queries. Book catalog for 9 X12 envelope and 4 First-Class stamps.

> ☛ Dial Books for Young Readers publishes quality picture books for ages 18 months-6 years; lively, believable novels for middle readers and young adults; and occasional nonfiction for middle readers and young adults."

NONFICTION Accepts unsolicited queries.

FICTION Subjects include adventure, fantasy, juvenile, picture books, young adult. Especially looking for lively and well-written novels for middle grade and young adult children involving a convincing plot and believable characters. The subject matter or theme should not already be overworked in previously published books. The approach must not be demeaning to any minority group, nor should the roles of female characters (or others) be stereotyped, though we don't think books should be didactic, or in any way message-y. No topics inappropriate for the juvenile, young adult, and middle grade audiences. No plays. Accepts unsolicited queries & up to 10 pages for longer works and unsolicited mss for picture books.

TIPS "Our readers are anywhere from preschool age to teenage. Picture books must have strong plots, lots of action, unusual premises, or universal themes treated with freshness and originality. Humor works well in these books. A very well-thought-out and intelligently presented book has the best chance of being taken on. Genre isn't as much of a factor as presentation."

DIVERSION PRESS

P.O. Box 270, Campbell Hall, New York NY 10916. E-mail: diversionpress@yahoo.com. Website: www.diversionpress.com. **Contact:** Attn: Acquisition Editor. Estab. 2008. Publishes hardcover, trade and mass market paperback originals. **Publishes 5-10 titles/year. 75% of books from first-time authors. 100% from unagented writers. Pays 10% royalty on wholesale price.** Publishes book 12-29 months after acceptance of ms. Responds in 2 weeks to queries. Responds in 1 month to proposals. Guidelines available online.

NONFICTION Subjects include Americana, animals, community, contemporary culture, education, ethnic, government, politics, health, medicine, history, hobbies, humanities, language, literature, literary criticism, memoirs, military, war, multicultural, philosophy, psychology, recreation, regional, science, social sciences, sociology, travel, women's issues, women's studies, world affairs. "The editors have doctoral degrees and are interested in a broad range of academic works. We are also interested in how-to, slice of life, and other nonfiction areas." Does not review works that are sexually explicit, religious, or put children in a bad light. Send query/proposal first. Mss accepted by request only. Reviews artwork/photos. Send photocopies.

FICTION Subjects include adventure, fantasy, gothic, historical, horror, humor, literary, mainstream, contemporary, mystery, poetry, science fiction, short story collections, suspense, young adult. "We will happily consider any children's or young adult books if they are illustrated. If your story has potential to become a series, please address that in your proposal. Fiction short stories and poetry will be considered for our anthology series. See website for details on how to submit your ms."

POETRY "Poetry will be considered for anthology series and for our poetry award." Submit 5 sample poems.

TIPS "Read our website and blog prior to submitting. We like short, concise queries. Tell us why your book is different, not like other books. Give us a realistic idea of what you will do to market your book—that you will actually do. We will ask for more information if we are interested."

⊕ DIVERTIR

P.O. Box 232, North Salem NH 03073. E-mail: info@divertirpublishing.com. E-mail: query@divertirpublishing.com. Website: http://divertirpublishing.com/. **Contact:** Dr. Kenneth Tupper, Publisher (nonfiction). Estab. 2009. Format publishes in trade paperback and electronic originals. **Publishes 6-12 titles/year. 100% of books from first-time authors. 100% from unagented writers. Pays 10-15% royalty on wholesale price (for novels and nonfiction); outright purchase: $10-50 (for short stories) with additional bonus payments to authors when certain sales milestones are met.** Publishes book 6-9 months after acceptance of ms. Responds in 1-2 months on queries; 3-4 months on proposals and mss. Catalog available online at http://divertirpublishing.com/bookstore.aspx. Guidelines online at website: http://divertirpublishing.com/authorinfo.aspx.

NONFICTION Subjects include astrology, community, contemporary culture, cooking, crafts, creative nonfiction, government, history, hobbies, New Age, photography, politics, psychic, psychology, religion, spirituality, world affairs. "We are particularly interested in the following: political/social commentary, current events, history, humor and satire, crafts and hobbies, inspirational, self-help, religious and spiritual, and metaphysics." Reviews artwork/photos as part of the ms package. Submit electronically.

FICTION Subjects include adventure, contemporary, fantasy, gothic, historical, horror, humor, literary, mainstream, mystery, occult, poetry, religious, romance, science fiction, short story collections, spiritual, translation, young adult. "We are particularly interested in the following: science fiction, fantasy, historical, alternate history, contemporary mythology, mystery and suspense, paranormal, and urban fantasy. Electronically submit proposal package, including synopsis and query letter with author's bio.

POETRY Query.

TIPS "We are currently accepting submissions in the following areas: Fictional Satire (submissions deadline 3/15), Noir (submissions deadline 5/15), Poetry (submissions dealine 3/15). Please see our Author Info page (online) for more information."

Ⓐ ⊘ DK PUBLISHING, INC.

Pearson Plc, 375 Hudson St., New York NY 10014. (646) 674-4000. Website: www.dk.com. **Pays royalty or flat fee.**

○ "DK Publishing is world renowned for its distinctive, highly visual books that inform, inspire, and entertain readers of all ages. Publisher of the recent New York Times bestsellers *Real Sex for Real Women* by Dr. Laura Berman, *Do Not Open*, and *Star Wars: The Clone Wars: The Visual Guide* among others, DK also publishes the award-winning Eyewitness series for children and Eyewitness Travel Guides. BradyGames and Rough Guides are also available from DK, a division of Penguin Group (USA)."

⌐─┬ Publishes picture books for middle-grade and older readers. Also, illustrated reference books for adults and children.

FICTION Agented submissions only.

DORAL PUBLISHING, INC.

3 Burroughs, Irvine CA 92618. (800)633-5385. E-mail: doralpub@mindspring.com. Website: www.doralpub.com. **Contact:** Alvin Grossman, publisher; Joe Liddy, marketing manager (purebred dogs). Estab. 1986. Publishes hardcover and trade paperback originals. **Publishes 10 titles/year. 30 queries received/year. 15 mss received/year. 85% from unagented writers. Pays 10% royalty on wholesale price.** Publishes book 6 months after acceptance of ms. Responds in 2 months to queries. Book catalog available free. Guidelines for #10 SASE.

○ "Doral Publishing publishes only books about dogs and dog-related topics, mostly geared for pure-bred dog owners and showing. Currently emphasizing breed books."

NONFICTION Subjects include animals, health, medicine. "We are looking for new ideas. No flowery prose. Manuscripts should be literate, intelligent, but easy to read. Subjects must be dog-related." Query with SASE. Submit outline, 2 sample chapters. Reviews artwork/photos. Send photocopies.

FICTION Subjects include juvenile. Subjects must center around dogs. Either the main character should be a dog or a dog should play an integral role. Query with SASE.

TIPS "We are currently expanding and are looking for new topics and fresh ideas while staying to our niche. While we will steadfastly maintain that market—we are always looking for excellent breed books—we also want to explore more 'mainstream' topics."

Ⓐ⊘ DOUBLEDAY BOOKS
FOR YOUNG READERS

Imprint of Random House Children's Books/Random House, Inc., 1745 Broadway, New York NY 10019. (212)782-9000. Website: www.randomhouse.com/kids.

○ Trade picture book list, from preschool to age 8. Not accepting any unsolicited book mss at this time.

Ⓐ DOUBLEDAY RELIGIOUS PUBLISHING

The Crown Publishing Group, a Division of Random House, Inc., 1745 Broadway, New York NY 10019. (212)782-9000. Website: www.randomhouse.com; http://crownpublishing.com. Estab. 1897. Publishes hardcover and trade paperback originals and reprints. Accepts simultaneous submissions.

IMPRINTS Image Books; Galilee; New Jerusalem Bible; Three Leaves Press.

○ "Random House, Inc. does not accept unsolicited submissions, proposals, manuscripts, or submission queries via e-mail at this time. If you would like to have your work or manuscript considered for publication by a major book publisher, we recommend that you work with an established literary agent. Each agency has manuscript submission guidelines."

NONFICTION Agented submissions only.

DOVER PUBLICATIONS, INC.

31 E. 2nd St., Mineola NY 11501. (516)294-7000. Fax: (516)873-1401. E-mail: hr@doverpublications.com. Website: www.doverpublications.com. **Contact:** John Grafton (math/science reprints). Estab. 1941. Publishes trade paperback originals and reprints. **Publishes 660 titles/year. Makes outright purchase.** Accepts simultaneous submissions. Book catalog available online.

○ Covers subjects from A - W, including Poetry - Fine Art - Recipes - Games - Puzzles - Famous Quotations - Clip Art - Great Literature - Craft Projects - Photography - Coloring Pages.

NONFICTION Subjects include agriculture, Americana, animals, anthropology, archeology, art, architecture, cooking, foods, nutrition, health, medicine, history, hobbies, language, literature, music, dance, nature, environment, philosophy, photography, religion, science, sports, translation, travel. Publishes mostly reprints. Accepts original paper doll collections, game books, coloring books (juvenile). Query with SASE. Reviews artwork/photos.

DOWN EAST BOOKS

Imprint of Down East Enterprise, Inc., P.O. Box 679, Camden ME 04843-0679. (207)594-9544, 800-766-1670. Fax: (207)594-7215. E-mail: jviehman@downeast.com; editorial@downeast.com. E-mail: submissions@downeast.com. Website: www.downeast.com. **Contact:** Paul Doiron, editor-in-chief. John Viehman, publisher Estab. 1967. Publishes hardcover and trade paperback originals, trade paperback reprints. **Publishes 24-30 titles/year. 50% of books from first-time authors. 90% from unagented writers. Pays $500 average advance.** Publishes book 1 year after acceptance of ms. Accepts simultaneous submissions. Responds in 3 months to queries. Send SASE for ms guidelines. Send 9×12 SASE for guidelines, plus recent catalog.

⟞ Down East Books publishes books that capture and illuminate the unique beauty and character of New England's history, culture, and wild places.

NONFICTION Subjects include Americana, history, nature, environment, recreation, regional, sports. Books about the New England region, Maine in particular. All of our regional books must have a Maine or New England emphasis. Query with SASE. Do not send CD, DVD, or disk. Reviews artwork/photos.

FICTION Subjects include juvenile, mainstream, contemporary, regional. We publish 2-4 juvenile titles/year (fiction and nonfiction), and 0-1 adult fiction titles/year. Query with SASE.

DOWN THE SHORE PUBLISHING

Box 100, West Creek NJ 08092. Fax: (609)597-0422. E-mail: dtsbooks@comcast.net. Website: www.down-the-shore.com. Publishes hardcover and trade paperback originals and reprints. **Publishes 4-10 titles/year. Pays royalty on wholesale or retail price, or makes outright purchase.** Accepts simultaneous submissions. Responds in 3 months to queries. Book catalog for 8×10 SAE with 2 first-class stamps or on website. Guidelines available online.

⟞ Bear in mind that our market is regional-New Jersey, the Jersey Shore, the mid-Atlantic, and seashore and coastal subjects."

NONFICTION Subjects include Americana, art, architecture, history, nature, environment, regional. Query with SASE. Submit proposal package, 1-2 sample chapters, synopsis. Reviews artwork/photos. Send photocopies.

FICTION Subjects include regional. Query with SASE. Submit proposal package, clips, 1-2 sample chapters.
POETRY "We do not publish poetry, unless it is to be included as part of an anthology."
TIPS "Carefully consider whether your proposal is a good fit for our established market."

Ⓐ⊘ DRAGONFLY

Imprint of Random House Children's Books/Random House, Inc., 1745 Broadway, New York NY 10019. (212)782-9000. Website: www.randomhouse.com.

> Quality reprint paperback imprint for paperback books. *Does not accept mss.*

DUFOUR EDITIONS

P.O. Box 7, 124 Byers Road, Chester Springs PA 19425. (610)458-5005 or (800)869-5677. Fax: (610)458-7103. E-mail: orders@dufoureditions.com. Website: www.dufoureditions.com. Estab. 1948. Publishes hardcover originals, trade paperback originals and reprints. **Publishes 3-4 titles/year. 200 queries received/year. 15 mss received/year. 20-30% of books from first-time authors. 80% from unagented writers. Pays $100-500 advance.** Publishes book 18 months after acceptance of ms. Accepts simultaneous submissions. Responds in 3 months to queries. Responds in 3 months to proposals. Responds in 6 months to manuscripts. Book catalog available free.

> We publish literary fiction by good writers which is well received and achieves modest sales. De-emphsazing poetry and nonfiction.

NONFICTION Subjects include history, translation. Query with SASE. Reviews artwork/photos. Send photocopies.
FICTION Subjects include literary, short story collections, translation. We like books that are slightly offbeat, different and well-written. Query with SASE.
POETRY Query.
TIPS Audience is sophisticated, literate readers especially interested in foreign literature and translations, and a strong Irish-Celtic focus, as well as work from U.S. writers. Check to see if the publisher is really a good match for your subject matter.

DUQUESNE UNIVERSITY PRESS

600 Forbes Ave., Pittsburgh PA 15282. (412)396-6610. Fax: (412)396-5984. E-mail: wadsworth@duc.edu. Website: www.dupress.duq.edu. **Contact:** Susan Wadsworth-Booth, director. Estab. 1927. Publishes hardcover and trade paperback originals. **Publishes 8-12 titles/year. 400 queries received/year. 65 mss received/year. 30% of books from first-time authors. 95% from unagented writers. Pays royalty on net price. Pays (some) advance.** Publishes book 1 year after acceptance of ms. Responds in 1 month to proposals. Responds in 3 months to manuscripts. Book catalog and ms guidelines for #10 SASE. Guidelines available online.

> Duquesne publishes scholarly monographs in the fields of literary studies (medieval & Renaissance), continental philosophy, ethics, religious studies and existential psychology. Interdisciplinary works are also of interest. Duquesne University Press does NOT publish fiction, poetry, children's books, technical or "hard" science works, or unrevised theses or dissertations."

NONFICTION Subjects include language, literature, philosophy, continental, psychology, existential, religion. "We look for quality of scholarship." For scholarly books, query or submit outline, 1 sample chapter, and SASE.

Ⓐ⊘ DUTTON ADULT TRADE

Imprint of Penguin Group (USA), Inc., 375 Hudson St., New York NY 10014. (212)366-2000. Website: us.penguingroup.com. Estab. 1852. Publishes hardcover originals. **Pays royalty. Pays negotiable advance.** Accepts simultaneous submissions. Book catalog for #10 SASE.

> *Does not accept unsolicited ms. Agented submissions only.* "Query letters **only** (must include SASE) A query letter should be typed and, ideally, fit on one page. Please include a brief synopsis of your manuscript and your publishing credits, if any."

> *Dutton* publishes hardcover, original, mainstream, and contemporary fiction and nonfiction in the areas of memoir, self-help, politics, psychology, and science for a general readership.", "Dutton currently publishes 45 hardcovers a year, roughly half fiction and half nonfiction. It is currently home to many #1 *New York Times* bestselling authors, most notably **Harlan Coben**, author of *Hold Tight*, **Ken Follett**, author of *Pillars of the Earth* and *World Without End*, **Eckhart Tolle**, author of *A New Earth*, and **Al Franken**, author of *The Truth*. Dutton also publishes the *New York Times* bestselling authors **Eric Jerome Dickey**, author of *Pleasure*

and *Waking with Enemies*, **Raymond Khoury**, author of *The Last Templar* and *The Sanctuary*, **John Lescroart**, author of *Betrayal* and *The Suspect*, **John Hodgman**, author of *The Areas of My Expertise* and *More Information Than You Require*, **John Jakes**, author of *Charleston* and *The Gods of Newport*, **Jenny McCarthy**, author of *Baby Laughs* and *Louder than Words*, and **Daniel Levitin**, author of *This is Your Brain on Music* and *The World in Six Songs*."

NONFICTION Agented submissions only. *No unsolicited mss.*

FICTION Subjects include adventure, historical, literary, mainstream, contemporary, mystery, short story collections, suspense. Agented submissions only. *No unsolicited mss.*

TIPS Write the complete manuscript and submit it to an agent or agents. They will know exactly which editor will be interested in a project.

DUTTON CHILDREN'S BOOKS

Imprint of Penguin Group (USA), Inc., 375 Hudson St., New York NY 10014. E-mail: duttonpublicity@us.penguingroup.com. Website: www.penguin.com. **Contact:** Acquisitions Editor. Estab. 1852. Publishes hardcover originals as well as novelty formats. **Publishes 100 titles/year. 15% of books from first-time authors. Pays royalty on retail price. Pays advance.**

○ "Cultivating the creative talents of authors and illustrators and publishing books with purpose and heart continue to be the mission and joy at Dutton."

○━ Dutton Children's Books publishes high-quality fiction and nonfiction for readers ranging from preschoolers to young adults on a variety of subjects. Currently emphasizing middle-grade and young adult novels that offer a fresh perspective. De-emphasizing photographic nonfiction and picture books that teach a lesson. Approximately 80 new hardcover titles are published every year, fiction and nonfiction for babies through young adults.

NONFICTION Subjects include animals, history, US, nature, environment, science. Query with SASE.

FICTION Dutton Children's Books has a diverse, general interest list that includes picture books; easy-to-read books; and fiction for all ages, from first chapter books to young adult readers. Query with SASE.

EAGLE'S VIEW PUBLISHING

168 West 12th St., Ogden UT 84310. (801)393-3991. Fax: (801)393-4647. E-mail: sales@eaglefeathertrading.com. Website: www.eaglesviewpub.com. **Contact:** Denise Knight, editor-in-chief. Estab. 1982. Publishes trade paperback originals. **Publishes 2-4 titles/year. 40 queries received/year. 20 mss received/year. 90% of books from first-time authors. 100% from unagented writers. Pays 8-10% royalty on net selling price.** Publishes book 12 months or more after acceptance of ms. Accepts simultaneous submissions. Responds in 1 year to proposals. Book catalog and ms guidelines for $4.00.

○━ Eagle's View primarily publishes how-to craft books with a subject related to historical or contemporary Native American/Mountain Man/frontier crafts/bead crafts. Currently emphasizing bead-related craft books. De-emphasizing history except for historical Indian crafts."

NONFICTION Subjects include anthropology, archaeology, Native American crafts, ethnic, Native American, history, American frontier historical patterns and books, hobbies, crafts, especially beadwork. Submit outline, 1-2 sample chapters. Reviews artwork/photos. Send photocopies and sample illustrations.

TIPS "We will not be publishing any new beaded earrings books for the foreseeable future. We are interested in other craft projects using seed beads, especially books that feature a variety of items, not just different designs for 1 item."

EAKIN PRESS

P.O. Box 21235, Waco TX 76702. (254)235-6161. Fax: (254)235-6230. Website: www.eakinpress.com. **Contact:** Kris Gholson, assoc. pub. Estab. 1978. Publishes hardcover and paperback originals and reprints. Accepts simultaneous submissions. Responds in up to 1 year to queries. Book catalog for $1.25. Guidelines available online.

○ No electronic submissions.

○━ Our top priority is to cover the history and culture of the Southwest, especially Texas and Oklahoma. We also have successfully published titles related to ethnic studies. We publish very little fiction, other than for children."

NONFICTION Subjects include Americana, Western, business, economics, cooking, foods, nutrition, ethnic, history, military, war, regional, sports, African American studies. Juvenile nonfiction: includes biographies of historic personalities, prefer with Texas or regional interest, or nature studies; and easy-read illustrated books for grades 1-3. Submit sample chapters, bio, synopsis, publishing credits, SASE.

FICTION Subjects include historical, juvenile. Juvenile fiction for grades K-12, preferably relating to Texas and the Southwest or contemporary. No adult fiction. Query or submit outline/synopsis

EASTLAND PRESS

P.O. Box 99749, Seattle WA 98139. (206)217-0204. Fax: (206)217-0205. E-mail: info@eastlandpress.com. Website: www.eastlandpress.com. **Contact:** John O'Connor, Managing Editor. Estab. 1981. Publishes hardcover and trade paperback originals. **Publishes 4-6 titles/year. 25 queries received/year. 30% of books from first-time authors. 90% from unagented writers. Pays 12-15% royalty on receipts.** Publishes book 12 to 24 months after acceptance of ms. Accepts simultaneous submissions. Responds in 1 month to queries.

⁂ Eastland Press is interested in textbooks for practitioners of alternative medical therapies, primarily Chinese and physical therapies, and related bodywork."

NONFICTION Subjects include health, medicine. "We prefer that a manuscript be completed or close to completion before we will consider publication. Proposals are rarely considered, unless submitted by a published author or teaching institution." Submit outline and 2-3 sample chapters. Reviews artwork/photos. Send photocopies.

⟳ EDGE SCIENCE FICTION AND FANTASY PUBLISHING/TESSERACT BOOKS

Hades Publications, Box 1714, Calgary AB T2P 2L7, Canada. (403)254-0160. Fax: (403)254-0456. E-mail: publisher@hadespublications.com. Website: www.edgewebsite.com. **Contact:** Editorial Manager. Estab. 1996.

TIPS "Send us your best, polished, completed manuscript. Use proper manuscript format. Take the time before you submit to get a critique from people who can offer you useful advice. When in doubt, visit our website for helpful resources, FAQs and other tips."

EDUCATOR'S INTERNATIONAL PRESS, INC.

18 Colleen Rd., Troy NY 12180. (518)271-9886. Fax: (518)266-9422. E-mail: bill@edint.com. Website: www.edint.com. **Contact:** William Clockel, publisher. Estab. 1996. Publishes hardcover and trade paperback

originals and reprints. Accepts simultaneous submissions. Book catalog and ms guidelines free.

⁂ Educator's International publishes books in all aspects of education, broadly conceived, from pre-kindergarten to postgraduate. We specialize in texts, professional books, videos and other materials for students, faculty, practitioners and researchers. We also publish a full list of books in the areas of women's studies, and social and behavioral sciences."

NONFICTION Subjects include education, language, literature, philosophy, psychology, software, women's studies. Submit TOC, outline, 2-3 chapters, resumè with SASE. Reviews artwork/photos.

TIPS Audience is professors, students, researchers, individuals, libraries.

EDUPRESS, INC.

P.O. Box 8610, Madison WI 53708-8610. (800)694-5827. E-mail: edupress@highsmith.com. Website: www.edupressinc.com. Estab. 1979. Publishes trade paperback originals. Book catalog and ms guidelines free.

⁂ Edupress, Inc., publishes supplemental curriculum resources for PK-6th grade. Currently emphasizing reading and math materials, as well as science and social studies.

NONFICTION Subjects include education, resources for pre-school through middle school.

TIPS "Audience is classroom teachers and homeschool parents."

EERDMANS BOOKS FOR YOUNG READERS

2140 Oak Industrial Dr. NE, Grand Rapids MI 49505. E-mail: youngreaders@eerdmans.com; gbrown@eerdmans.com. Website: www.eerdmans.com/youngreaders. **Contact:** Shannon White, Acquisitions Editor.

○ "We accept unsolicited submissions. We respond within 4 months only to submissions we are interested in publishing."

⁂ We are seeking books that encourage independent thinking, problem-solving, creativity, acceptance, kindness. Books that encourage moral values without being didactic or preachy."Board books, picture books, middle reader fiction, young adult fiction, nonfiction, illustrated storybooks. 6,000 mss received/year. Pays 5-7% royalty on retail price. Publishes middle reader and YA books in 1 year; publishes picture books in 2-3 years. "We do not accept or reply to queries or submissions via e-mail or fax to queries. Responds in 3-4 months for exclusive submissions sent to Eerdmans Books for Young Readers, clearly marked no answer to manuscripts". Do not call or e-mail to inquire about the status of your manuscript. "Right now we are not acquiring books that revolve around a holiday. (No Christmas, Thanksgiving, Easter, Halloween, Fourth of July, Hanukkah books.)" Reviews artwork/photos. Send color photocopies rather than original art. "We do not publish retold or original fairy tales, nor do we publish books about witches or ghosts or vampires." Send exclusive ms submissions (marked so on outside of envelope) to acquisitions editor. *A River of Words*, by Jen Bryant, illustrated by Melissa Sweet (2009) Caldecott Honor Book); *Garmann's Summer*, by Stian Hole (2009 Batchelder Honor Book); *Ethan, Suspended*, by Pamela Ehrenberg (novel); *Attack of the Turtle*, by Drew Carlson (novel)." A submission stands out when it's obvious that someone put time into it—the publisher's name and address is spelled correctly, the package is neat, and all of our submission requirements have been followed precisely. We look for short, concise cover letters that explain why the ms fits with our list, and/or how the ms fills an important need in the world of children's literature. Send EXCLUSIVE ms submissions to acquisitions editor. We regret that due to the volume of material we receive, we cannot comment on ms we are unable to accept."

FICTION Send exclusive ms submissions (marked so on outside of envelope) to acquisitions editor.

TIPS "Find out who Eerdmans is before submitting a manuscript. Look at our website, request a catalog, and check out our books." "Find out who Eerdmans is before submitting a manuscript. Look at our website, request a catalog, and check out our books."

WILLIAM B. EERDMANS PUBLISHING CO.

2140 Oak Industrial Dr. NE, Grand Rapids MI 49505. (616)459-4591. Fax: (616)459-6540. E-mail: info@eerdmans.com. Website: www.eerdmans.com. **Contact:** Jon Pott, editor-in-chief. Estab. 1911. Publishes hardcover and paperback originals and reprints. Accepts simultaneous submissions. Responds in 4 weeks to queries, possibly longer for mss. Please include e-mail and/or SASE. Book catalog and ms guidelines free.

IMPRINTS Eerdmans Books for Young Readers.

○ Will not respond to or accept mss, proposals, or queries sent by e-mail or fax.

The majority of our adult publications are religious and most of these are academic or semi-academic in character (as opposed to inspirational or celebrity books), though we also publish general trade books on the Christian life. Our nonreligious titles, most of them in regional history or on social issues, aim, similarly, at an educated audience."

NONFICTION Subjects include history, religious, language, literature, philosophy, of religion, psychology, regional, history, religion, sociology, translation, Biblical studies. "We prefer that writers take the time to notice if we have published anything at all in the same category as their manuscript before sending it to us." Query with TOC, 2-3 sample chapters, and SASE for return of ms. Reviews artwork/photos.

FICTION Subjects include religious, children's, general, fantasy. Query with SASE.

⊕ ELIXIRIST

P.O. Box 17132, Sugar Land TX 77496. E-mail: support@elixirist.com. E-mail: submissions@elixirist.com. Website: www.elixirist.com. **Contact:** Juanita Samborski, Acquisitions Editor (romance, comedy, chicklit, urban fantasy); Sean Samborski, Publisher (speculative, comedy, horror, literary). Estab. 2010. Format publishes in trade paperback, mass market paperback, and electronic originals. **Publishes 12/year titles/year. 50% of books from first-time authors. 100% from unagented writers. Pays 6-12% royalty on retail price.** Publishes book 6-12 months after acceptance of ms. Accepts simultaneous submissions. Responds in 12 months on queries, proposals, and mss. Catalog and guidelines available for SASE.

A small, commercial publisher dealing primarily in the print market in multiple genre formats.

NONFICTION Subjects include Americana, community, creative nonfiction, dance, hobbies, humanities, literary criticism, memoirs, music, philosophy, public affairs, sex, social sciences, sociology, sports, travel, womens issues, womens studies, world affairs, young adult. Query with SASE; submit proposal package, including outline and 3 sample chapters. Reviews artwork/photos as part of the ms package.

FICTION Subjects include adventure, comic books, contemporary, experimental, fantasy, gothic, historical, horror, humor, juvenile, literary, mainstream, mystery, occult, religious, romance, science fiction, sports, suspense, western, young adult, speculative subgenres. Query with SASE; submit synopsis and 3 sample chapters.

TIPS "We publish novels in genres ranging from young adult to literary, multi-genres appealing to both male and female readers."

ELLORA'S CAVE PUBLISHING, INC.

1056 Home Ave., Akron OH 44310. E-mail: service@ ellorascave.com. E-mail: submissions@ellorascave. com. Website: www.ellorascave.com. **Contact:** Raelene Gorlinsky, managing editor; Kelli collins, editor-in-chief. Estab. 2000. Publishes electronic originals and reprints; print books. **Pays 37.5% royalty on gross (cover price).** Accepts simultaneous submissions. Responds in 2 months to queries and to proposals. Responds in 2-6 months to manuscripts. Guidelines available online.

FICTION , Erotic Romance of every subgenre, including gay/lesbian, menage and more, and BDSM. All must be under genre romance. All must have erotic content or author must be willing to add sex during editing. Submit query letter, full synopsis, first three chapters, and last chapter.

TIPS "Our audience is romance readers who want explicit sexual detail. They come to us because we offer not erotica, but Romantica™—sex with romance, plot, emotion. In addition to erotic romance with happy-ever-after endings, we also publish pure erotica, detailing sexual adventure, experimentation, and coming of age."

⊕ ELOHI GADUGI / THE HABIT OF RAINY NIGHTS PRESS

2727 NE 13th Ave., #2, Portland OR 97212-3221. E-mail: editors@elohigadugi.org. E-mail: editors@elohigadugi.org. Website: http://rainynightspress.org. **Contact:** Patricia McLean, Nonfiction Editor (Narrative Nonfiction). Duane Poncy, Fiction Editor (General Fiction, Native American); Ger Kileen, Poetry Editor Estab. 2003. Format publishes in electronic originals. **Publishes 2-3 projected titles/year. 4-5 queries. 90% of books from first-time authors. 100% from unagented writers. Pays 8-12% royalty on retail price (50-60% of wholesale for ebooks)** Publishes

book 9 months after acceptance of ms. Accepts simultaneous submissions. Responds in 1-2 months on queries; 2-3 months on mss. Catalog and guidelines available online at website.

IMPRINTS The Habit of Rainy Nights Press (Patricia McLean or Duane Poncy, Editors); Elohi Gadugi Books / Elohi Gadugi Digital (Duane Poncy, Editor).

NONFICTION Subjects include creative nonfiction, environment, ethnic, memoirs, multicultural, nature. "At this time we are only interested in Native American culture and narrative nonfiction which addresses contemporary environmental, social, political, or indigenous issues from a progressive viewpoint." Submit completed ms via e-mail only. Reviews artwork/photos; writers should send jpeg digital images.

FICTION Subjects include contemporary, ethnic, fantasy, historical, literary, mainstream, multicultural, mystery, poetry, poetry in translation, science fiction, suspense, translation, young adult. "We publish emerging writers whose fiction explores the important concerns of the contemporary world with depth and compassion. Have a strong narrative voice and character-Dr.n story. We don't particularly care for the current trend of books about 'me.' We are not adverse to magical realism, poetic language, and books that take a chance." Submit completed ms via e-mail only.

POETRY "All poetry should have a strong narrative quality. Have something to say!" No academic or experimental poetry. Submit 5-6 sample poems; submit complete ms.

TIPS "Respect your work. Make sure it is ready for publication. Polish, polish, polish. We cannot consider books that need a lot of basic cleaning up. Have something to say—we are not interested in using up vital resources to publish fluff."

EMIS, INC.

P.O. Box 270666, Fort Collins CO 80527-0077. (214)349-0077; (800)225-0694. Fax: (970)672-8606. Website: www.emispub.com. **Contact:** Lynda Blake, president. Publishes trade paperback originals. **Publishes 2 titles/year. Pays 12% royalty on retail price.** Responds in 3 months to queries. Book catalog available free. Guidelines available free.

○ "Medical text designed for physicians; fit in the lab coat pocket as a quick reference. Currently emphasizing women's health."

NONFICTION Subjects include health, medicine, psychology, women's health/medicine. Submit 3 sample chapters with SASE.

TIPS Audience is medical professionals and medical product manufacturers and distributors.

⊘⊘ ENCOUNTER BOOKS

900 Broadway, Suite 400, New York NY 10003-1239. (212)871-6310. Fax: (212)871-6311. E-mail: read@encounterbooks.com. Website: www.encounterbooks.com. **Contact:** Acquisitions. Hardcover originals and trade paperback reprints. Accepts simultaneous submissions. Book catalog free or online. Guidelines available online.

> ○ *Accepts agented material only. No unsolicited mss/queries.* Reading period is March 1-November 1.
>
> ⊶ Encounter Books publishes serious nonfiction—books that can alter our society, challenge our morality, stimulate our imaginations—in the areas of history, politics, religion, biography, education, public policy, current affairs, and social sciences.

NONFICTION Subjects include child guidance, education, ethnic, government, politics, health, medicine, history, language, literature, memoirs, military, war, multicultural, philosophy, psychology, religion, science, sociology, women's issues, women's studies, gender studies. Submit proposal package, including outline and 1 sample chapter, SASE. Do not send via e-mail.

ENGLISH TEA ROSE PRESS

The Wild Rose Press, P.O. Box 708, Adams Basin NY 14410-0708. (585)752-8770. E-mail: queryus@thewildrosepress.com. Website: www.thewildrosepress.com. **Contact:** Nicole D'Arienzo, editor. Estab. 2006. Format publishes in paperback originals, reprints, and e-books in a POD format. *Does not accept unsolicited mss.* **Pays royalty of 7% minimum; 35% maximum.** Publishes book 1 year after acceptance of ms. Responds to queries in 4 weeks; to mss in 12 weeks. Writer's guidelines available on website.

> ○ "English Tea Rose stories encompass historical romances set before 1900 which are not set on American soil. Send us your medieval knights, Vikings, Scottish highlanders, marauding pirates, and ladies and gentlemen of the Ton. English Tea Rose romances should have strong conflict and be emotionally Dr.n; and, whether the story is medieval, Regency,

set during the renaissance, or any other pre-1900 time, they must stay to their period in historical accuracy and flavor. English Tea Roses can range from sweet to spicy, but should not contain overly explicit language." Published 5 debut authors last year. Publishes approximately 10 fiction titles/year. Member: EPIC, Romance Writers of America. Distributes/promotes titles through major distribution chains, including Ingrams, Baker & Taylor, Sony, Amazon.com, Kindle, as well as smaller and online distributors. *Does not accept unsolicited mss.* Agented fiction less than 1%. Always comments on rejected mss. Sends prepublication galleys to author.

FICTION , Wants contemporary, futuristic/time travel, gothic, historical, regency, romantic suspense, erotic, and paranormal romances. Plans several anthologies "in several lines of the company in the next year, including Cactus Rose, Yellow Rose, American Rose, Black Rose, and Scarlet Rose.". Send query letter with outline and a list of publishing credits. Include estimated word count, brief bio, and list of publishing credits.

TIPS "Polish your manuscript, make it as error free as possible, and follow our submission guidelines."

ENSLOW PUBLISHERS, INC.

40 Industrial Rd., Box 398, Berkeley Heights NJ 07922. (973)771-9400. E-mail: customerservice@enslow.com. Website: www.enslow.com. **Contact:** Brian D. Enslow, editor. Estab. 1977. Publishes hardcover originals. 10% require freelance illustration. **Publishes 250 titles/year. Pays royalty on net price with advance or flat fee. Pays advance.** Publishes book 1 year after acceptance of ms. Responds in 1 month to queries. Guidelines for #10 SASE.

IMPRINTS MyReportLinks.com Books, Enslow Elementary.

> ○ "Enslow publishes hardcover nonfiction series books for young adults and school-age children."

NONFICTION Subjects include health, medicine, history, recreation, sports, science, sociology. "Interested in new ideas for series of books for young people." No fiction, fictionalized history, or dialogue.

TIPS "We love to receive resumes from experienced writers with good research skills who can think like young people."

EPICENTER PRESS, INC.

P.O. Box 82368, Kenmore WA 98028. Fax: (425)481-8253. E-mail: info@epicenterpress.com. Website: www.epicenterpress.com. **Contact:** Lael Morgan, 420 Ferry Rd., Saco, ME 04072. Estab. 1987. Publishes hardcover and trade paperback originals. **Publishes 4-8 titles/year. 200 queries received/year. 100 mss received/year. 75% of books from first-time authors. 90% from unagented writers.** Publishes book 12-24 months after acceptance of ms. Responds in 3 months to queries. Book catalog and ms guidelines on website.

○ "Our affiliated company, Aftershocks Media, provides a range of services to self-publisher industry distributors."

⚷ We are a regional press founded in Alaska whose interests include but are not limited to the arts, history, environment, and diverse cultures and lifestyles of the North Pacific and high latitudes."

NONFICTION Subjects include animals, ethnic, history, nature, environment, recreation, regional, women's issues. "Our focus is Alaska and the Pacific Northwest. We do not encourage nonfiction titles from outside this region." Submit outline and 3 sample chapters. Reviews artwork/photos. Send photocopies.

TIPS *Bering Sea Blues*, by Joe Upton; *Surviving the Island of Grace*, by Leslie Leyland Fields.

⊘ ERIE CANAL PRODUCTIONS

4 Farmdale St., Clinton NY 13323. E-mail: eriecanal@juno.com. Website: www.eriecanalproductions.com. **Contact:** Scott Fiesthumel, president. Estab. 2001. Publishes trade paperback originals. **Publishes 1-2 titles/year. 50% of books from first-time authors. 100% from unagented writers. Pays negotiable royalty on net profits.** Responds in 1 month to queries. Book catalog available free.

NONFICTION Subjects include Americana, history, sports. Query with SASE. *All unsolicited mss returned unopened.*

TIPS "We publish nonfiction books that look at historical places, events, and people along the traditional route of the Erie Canal through New York State."

ETC PUBLICATIONS

1456 Rodeo Rd., Palm Springs CA 92262. (760)316-9695; (866)514-9969. Fax: (760)316-9681. Website: www.etcpublications.com. **Contact:** Dr. Richard W. Hostrop, publisher (education and social sciences); Lee Ona S. Hostrop, editorial director (history and works suitable below the college level). Estab. 1972. Publishes hardcover and paperback originals. **Publishes 6-12 titles/year. 75% of books from first-time authors. 90% from unagented writers. Offers 5-15% royalty, based on wholesale and retail price.** Publishes book 9 months after acceptance of ms.

○ "ETC is primarily concerned with publishing nonfiction works that are interesting and useful to the reader. Books for schools - students, teachers, staff, and administrators - are preferred. Other nonfiction types, as evidenced by the website, are welcomed for review as well."

⚷ ETC publishes works that further learning as opposed to entertainment.

NONFICTION Subjects include education, translation, in above areas. Submit complete ms with SASE. Reviews artwork/photos.

TIPS Special consideration is given to those authors who are capable and willing to submit their completed work in camera-ready, typeset form. We are particularly interested in works suitable for both the Christian school market and homeschoolers; e.g., state history texts below the high school level with a Christian-oriented slant.

EXECUTIVE EXCELLENCE PUBLISHING

1806 North 1120 West, Provo UT 84604. (801)375-4060. Fax: (801)377-5960. E-mail: editorial@eep.com. Website: www.eep.com. **Contact:** Ken Shelton, editor in chief. Estab. 1984. Publishes hardcover and trade paperback originals and trade paperback reprints. **Publishes 4 titles/year. 300 queries received/year. 150 mss received/year. 35% of books from first-time authors. 95% from unagented writers. Pays 15% on cash received and 50% of subsidary right proceeds.** Publishes book 6-9 months after acceptance of ms. Accepts simultaneous submissions. Responds in 1 month to queries, proposals and manuscripts. Book catalog free or on website.

⚷ Executive Excellence publishes business and self-help titles. We help you-the busy person, executive or entrepreneur-to find a wiser, better way to live your life and lead your organization. Currently emphasizing business innovations for general management and leadership (from the personal perspective). De-emphasizing technical or scholarly textbooks on operational processes and financial management or workbooks."

NONFICTION Subjects include business, economics, leadership/management. Submit proposal package, including outline, 1-2 sample chapters and author bio, company information.

TIPS "Executive Excellence Publishing is an established publishing house with a strong niche in the marketplace. Our magazines, *Leadership Excellence*, *Sales and Service Excellence* and *Personal Excellence*, are distributed monthly in countries across the world. Our authors are on the cutting edge in their fields of leadership, self-help and business and organizational development. We are always looking for strong new talent with something to say, and a burning desire to say it. We expect authors to invest in their work. We do not offer all-expense paid ego trips."

⊕ F+W CRIME

1213 N. Sherman Ave. #306, Madison WI 53704. E-mail: info@tyrusbooks.com. Website: tyrusbooks.com. **Contact:** Benjamin LeRoy, publisher and community leader.

○ With acquisitin of Tyrus Books, F+W Media, Inc. will enter the fiction market in partnership with Benjamin LeRoy.

FICTION F+W Crime will release as many 200 e-book-only titles with select print releases. Currently not open to submissions.

F+W MEDIA, INC. (BOOK DIVISION)

4700 E. Galbraith Rd., Cincinnati OH 45236. (513)531-2690. Website: www.fwmedia.com. **Contact:** President: Sara Domville, President: David Blansfield; Publisher and Editorial Director, Karen Cooper (Adams Media), Publisher and Editorial Director, Dianne Wheeler (Antiques & Collectibles), Publisher and Editorial Director, Jeff Pozorski (Automotives), Publisher and Editorial Director, Jamie Markle (Art), Publisher and Editorial Director, Stephen Bateman (David & Charles), Publisher and Editorial Director, Gary Lynch (Design), Publisher and Editorial Director, Jim Schlender (Firearms & Knives), Publisher and Editorial Director, Patty Craft (Horticulture), Publisher and Editorial Director, Scott Tappa (Numismatics), Publisher and Editorial Director, Brad Rucks (Outdoors), Publisher and Editorial Director, Dean Listle (Sports, Construction Trade), Publisher and Editorial Director, Steve Shanesy (Woodworking), Publisher and Editorial Director, Phil Sexton (Writer's Digest, HOW Books). Estab. 1913. Publishes trade pa-

perback originals and reprints. **Publishes 400+ titles/year.** Guidelines available online.

IMPRINTS Adams Media (general interest series); David & Charles (crafts, equestrian, railroads, soft crafts); HOW Books (graphic design, illustrated, humor, pop culture); IMPACT Books (fantasy art, manga, creative comics and popular culture); Krause Books (antiques and collectibles, automotive, coins and paper money, comics, crafts, games, firearms, militaria, outdoors and hunting, records and CDs, sports, toys); Memory Makers (scrapbooking); North Light Books (crafts, decorative painting, fine art); Popular Woodworking Books (shop skills, woodworking); Warman's (antiques and collectibles, field guides); Writer's Digest Books (writing and reference).

○ Please see individual listings for specific submission information about the company's imprints.

⊶ In October 2008, F+W Media moved from a divisionally structured company to a Community structure, wherein the Publisher and Editorial Director for each community has full responsibility for the books, magazines, online, events, and educational products associated with their community. F+W Media produces more than 400 new books per year, maintains a backlist of more than 2,500 titles, publishes 39 magazines, owns and operates dozens of informational and subscription-based Web sites, and operates a growing number of successful consumer shows annually."

● FABER & FABER LTD

3 Queen Square, London WC1N 3AU. 020 7465 0045. Fax: 020 7465 0034. Website: www.faber.co.uk. **Contact:** Lee Brackstone, Hannah Griffiths, Angus Cargill, (fiction); Walter Donohue, (film); Dinah Wood, (plays); Julian Loose, Neil Belton, (nonfiction); Paul Keegan, (poetry); Belinda Matthews, (music); Suzy Jenvy, Julia Wells, (children's). Estab. 1925. Publishes hardcover and paperback originals and reprints. **Publishes 200 titles/year. Pays royalty. Pays varying advances with each project. advance.** Accepts simultaneous submissions. Responds in 12 weeks to manuscripts. Book catalog available online.

○ Faber & Faber will consider unsolicited proposals for poetry only.

⊶ Faber & Faber have rejuvenated their nonfiction, music and children's titles in recent years and the film and drama lists remain market leaders.

NONFICTION Subjects include art, architecture, contemporary culture, cooking, foods, nutrition, creative nonfiction, government, politics, history, humanities, literary criticism, memoirs, military, war, multicultural, music, dance, psychology, recreation, science, sports, travel, world affairs, Children's. *No unsolicited nonfiction submissions*

FICTION Subjects include adventure, ethnic, experimental, fantasy, historical, humor, literary, mystery, plays, poetry, short story collections, spiritual, sports, suspense, young adult, Drama, Plays, Screenplays, Children's Fiction, Arts & Literature. No unsolicited fiction submissions

POETRY Address poetry to 'Poetry Submissions Department' and include an SAE for return. For more information, ring 020 7465 0045. Submit 6 sample poems.

TIPS Explore the website and downloadable book catalogues thoroughly to get a feel for the lists in all categories and genres.

FACTS ON FILE, INC.

Infobase Publishing, 132 W. 31st St., 17th Floor, New York NY 10001. (800)322-8755. Fax: (800)678-3633. E-mail: llikoff@factsonfile.com; custserv@factsonfile.com. Website: www.factsonfile.com. **Contact:** Laurie Likoff, Editorial Director (science, fashion, natural history); Frank Darmstadt (science & technology, nature, reference); Owen Lancer, senior editor (American history, women's studies); James Chambers, trade editor (health, pop culture, crime, sports); Jeff Soloway, acquisitions editor (language/literature). Estab. 1941. Publishes hardcover originals and reprints. **Publishes 135-150 titles/year. 25% from unagented writers. Pays 10% royalty on retail price. Pays $5,000-10,000 advance.** Accepts simultaneous submissions. Responds in 2 months to queries. Book catalog available free. Guidelines available online.

IMPRINTS Checkmark Books.

- Facts on File produces high-quality reference materials on a broad range of subjects for the school library market and the general nonfiction trade.

NONFICTION Subjects include contemporary culture, education, health, medicine, history, language, literature, multicultural, recreation, religion, sports, careers, entertainment, natural history, popular culture. "We publish serious, informational books for a targeted audience. All our books must have strong library interest, but we also distribute books effectively to the trade. Our library books fit the junior and senior high school curriculum." No computer books, technical books, cookbooks, biographies (except YA), pop psychology, humor, fiction or poetry. Query or submit outline and sample chapter with SASE. No submissions returned without SASE.

TIPS "Our audience is school and public libraries for our more reference-oriented books and libraries, schools and bookstores for our less reference-oriented informational titles."

FAIRLEIGH DICKINSON UNIVERSITY PRESS

285 Madison Ave., M-GH2-01, Madison NJ 07940. (973)443-8564. Fax: (973)443-8364. E-mail: fdupress@fdu.edu. Website: www.fdupress.org. **Contact:** Harry Keyishian, director. Estab. 1967. Publishes hardcover originals and occasional paperbacks. **Publishes 30-40 titles/year. 33% of books from first-time authors. 95% from unagented writers.** Publishes book approximately 1 year after acceptance of ms. Responds in 2 weeks to queries.

- "Contract is arranged through Associated University Presses of Cranbury, New Jersey. We are a selection committee only. Non-author subsidy publishes 2% of books."

- Fairleigh Dickinson publishes scholarly books for the academic market, in the humanities and social sciences.

NONFICTION Subjects include agriculture, art, architecture, business, economics, contemporary culture, ethnic, film, cinema, stage, gay, lesbian, government, politics, history, local, literary criticism, multicultural, music, dance, philosophy, psychology, regional, religion, sociology, translation, women's issues, women's studies, world affairs, Civil War, film, Jewish studies, scholarly editions. "The Press discourages submissions of unrevised dissertations. We do look for scholarly editions of literary works in all fields, in English, or translation. We welcome inquiries about essay collections if the majority of the material is previously unpublished; that the essays have a unifying and consistent theme, and that the editors provide a substantial scholarly introduction." No nonscholarly books. We do not publish textbooks, or original fiction, poetry or plays. Query with outline, detailed abstract, and sample chapters (if possible). Reviews artwork/photos. Send only copies of illustrations during the evaluation process.

TIPS "Press books are reviewed regularly in leading academic circles. Each year between 150,000-200,000 brochures are mailed to announce new works. Research must be up-to-date. Poor reviews result when bibliographies and notes don't reflect current research. We follow Chicago Manual of Style (15th edition) in scholarly citation. We welcome proposals for essay collections, including unpublished conference papers if they relate to a strong central theme and have scholarly merit. For further details, consult our online catalog."

Ⓐ⊘ FARRAR, STRAUS & GIROUX/BOOKS FOR YOUNG READERS

Books for Young Readers, 175 Fifth Ave., New York NY 10010. (646)307-5151. Website: www.fsgkidsbooks.com. **Contact:** Children's Editorial Department. Estab. 1946. Publishes hardcover originals and trade paperback reprints. **Publishes 75 titles/year. 6,000 queries and mss received/year. 5% of books from first-time authors. 50% from unagented writers. Pays 2-6% royalty on retail price for paperbacks, 3-10% for hardcovers. Pays $3,000-25,000 advance.** Publishes book 18 months after acceptance of ms. Accepts simultaneous submissions. Responds in 2 months to queries. Responds in 3 months to manuscripts. For catalog fax request or e-mail to: childrens.publicity@fsgbooks.com. Guidelines available online.

IMPRINTS Frances Foster Books.

➤ We publish original and well-written material for all ages."

FICTION Subjects include juvenile, picture books, young adult, nonfiction. Do not query picture books; just send manuscript. Do not fax or e-mail queries or manuscripts. Query with SASE. Hard copy submissions only.

TIPS Audience is full age range, preschool to young adult. Specializes in literary fiction.

FATHER'S PRESS

2424 SE 6th St., Lee's Summit MO 64063. (816)600-6288. E-mail: mike@fatherspress.com. Website: www.fatherspress.com. **Contact:** Mike Smitley, owner (fiction, nonfiction). Estab. 2006. Publishes hardcover, trade paperback, and mass market paperback originals and reprints. **Publishes 6-10 titles/year. Pays 10-15% royalty on wholesale price.** Publishes book 6 months after acceptance of ms. Responds in 1 month to queries and proposals. Responds in 3 months to manuscripts. Guidelines available online.

NONFICTION Subjects include animals, cooking, foods, nutrition, creative nonfiction, history, military, war, nature, regional, religion, travel, women's issues, world affairs. Query with SASE. Unsolicited mss returned unopened. Call or e-mail first. Reviews artwork/photos. Send photocopies.

FICTION Subjects include adventure, historical, juvenile, literary, mainstream, contemporary, military, war, mystery, regional, religious, suspense, western, young adult. Query with SASE. Unsolicited mss returned unopened. Call or e-mail first.

FENCE BOOKS

Science Library 320, Univ. of Albany, 1400 Washington Ave., Albany NY 12222. (518)591-8162. E-mail: fence.fencebooks@gmail.com. E-mail: robfence@gmail.com. Website: www.fenceportal.org. **Contact:** Rob Arnold, Submissions Manager. Hardcover originals. Guidelines available online.

➤ Fence is closed to submissions right now. We'll have another reading period in the Spring. Fence Books offers 2 book contests (in addition to the National Poetry Series) with 2 sets of guidelines and entry forms on our website."

FICTION Subjects include poetry.

POETRY Enter National Poetry Series Contest. See Open Competition Guidelines online. Also the annual Fence Books Motherwell Prize 2011 ($5,000) for a first or second book of poetry by a woman. Submit 48-60 pages during the month of November; and Fence Modern Poets Series 2011, for a poet writing in English at any stage in his or her career. $25 entry fee. Submissions may be sent through regular USPS mail, UPS, Fedex-type couriers, or certified mail.

TIPS "At present Fence Books is a self-selecting publisher; mss come to our attention through our contests and through editors' investigations. We hope to become open to submissions of poetry and fiction mss in the near future."

FERGUSON PUBLISHING CO.

Infobase Publishing, 132 W. 31st St., 17th Floor, New York NY 10001. (800)322-8755. E-mail: editorial@factsonfile.com. Website: www.infobasepublishing.com. **Contact:** Editorial Director. Estab. 1940. Publishes hardcover and trade paperback originals. **Publishes 50 titles/year. Pays by project.** Responds in 6 months to queries. Guidelines available online.

◑ "Please provide an overview of the subject you wish to write on, the intended audience, a brief description of the contents, and a sample chapter or headword list. It is not advisable to send a complete manuscript at this point. Include a list of the relevant competition and an indication of how your book will improve upon the competition or fill a specific niche in the market. Include a brief curriculum vitae or your writing accomplishments and relevant experience. Send or e-mail your proposal to: Editorial Director."

⌘━┳ We are primarily a career education publisher that publishes for schools and libraries. We need writers who have expertise in a particular career or career field (for possible full-length books on a specific career or field)."

NONFICTION "We publish work specifically for the elementary/junior high/high school/college library reference market. Works are generally encyclopedic in nature. Our current focus is career encyclopedias and young adult career sets and series. We consider manuscripts that cross over into the trade market." No mass market, poetry, scholarly, or juvenile books, please. Query or submit an outline and 1 sample chapter.

TIPS "We like writers who know the market—former or current librarians or teachers or guidance counselors."

FILTER PRESS, LLC

P.O. Box 95, Palmer Lake CO 80133-0095. (719)481-2420; (888)570-2663. Fax: (719)481-2420. E-mail: info@filterpressbooks.com. Website: www.filterpressbooks.com. **Contact:** Doris Baker, president. Estab. 1957. Publishes trade paperback originals and reprints. **Publishes 4-6 titles/year. Pays 10-12% royalty on wholesale price.** Publishes book 12-18 months after acceptance of ms.

◖ "Filter Press specializes in nonfiction of the West.","Please submit in hardcopy (not a computer disk) to our address."

NONFICTION Subjects include Americana, anthropology, archeology, ethnic, history, regional, crafts and crafts people of the Southwest. Query with outline and SASE. Reviews artwork/photos.

FINNEY COMPANY, INC.

8075 215th St. W., Lakeville MN 55044. (952)469-6699. Fax: (952)469-1968. E-mail: feedback@finneyco.com. Website: www.finneyco.com. **Contact:** Alan E. Krysan, president. Publishes trade paperback orig-

inals. **Publishes 2 titles/year. Pays 10% royalty on wholesale price. Pays advance.** Publishes book 1 year after acceptance of ms. Responds in 10-12 weeks to queries.

NONFICTION Subjects include business, economics, education, career exploration/development. Finney publishes career development educational materials. Query with SASE. Reviews artwork/photos.

FIRE ENGINEERING BOOKS & VIDEOS

Imprint of PennWell Corp., 1421 S. Sheridan Rd., Tulsa OK 74112. (918)831-9410. Fax: (918)831-9555. E-mail: FireBookEditor@pennwell.com; sales@pennwell.com. Website: www.pennwellbooks.com. **Contact:** Maria Patterson. Publishes hardcover and softcover originals. Responds in 1 month to proposals. Book catalog available free.

⌘━┳ Fire Engineering publishes textbooks relevant to firefighting and training. Currently emphasizing strategy and tactics, reserve training, preparedness for terrorist threats, natural disasters, first response to fires and emergencies."

NONFICTION Submit proposal via e-mail.

TIPS No human-interest stories; technical training only.

FLASHLIGHT PRESS

527 Empire Blvd., Brooklyn NY 11225. (718)288-8300. Fax: (718)972-6307. E-mail: editor@flashlightpress.com. Website: www.flashlightpress.com. **Contact:** Shari Dash Greenspan, editor. Estab. 2004. Publishes hardcover and trade paperback originals. **1,200 queries received/year. 120 mss received/year. Pays 8-10% royalty on wholesale price.** Publishes book 36 months after acceptance of ms. Accepts simultaneous submissions. Responds in 1 month to queries. Responds in 3 months to manuscripts. Book catalog available online. Guidelines available online.

FICTION "Only publishes fiction (2 picture books/year), so we're extremely selective. Looking for gems."

TIPS "Our audience is 4-8 years old. Follow our online submissions guide."

FLORICANTO PRESS

Inter American Development, 650 Castro St., Suite 120-331, Mountain View CA 94041-2055. (415)552-1879. Fax: (702)995-1410. E-mail: info@floricantopress.com. Website: www.floricantopress.com. **Contact:** Roberto Cabello-Argandoña. Estab. 1982. Publishes hardcover and trade paperback originals and reprints. Book catalog for #10 SASE. Guidelines available online.

8—⚬ Floricanto Press is dedicated to promoting Latino thought and culture."

NONFICTION Subjects include anthropology, archeology, cooking, foods, nutrition, ethnic, Hispanic, health, medicine, history, language, literature, psychology, women's issues, women's studies. "We are looking primarily for nonfiction popular (but serious) titles that appeal to the general public on Hispanic subjects." Submit ms with word count, author bio, SASE.

TIPS "Audience is general public interested in Hispanic culture. We need authors that are willing to promote their work heavily."

FLORIDA ACADEMIC PRESS

P.O. Box 540, Gainesville FL 32602. (352)332-5104. Fax: (352)331-6003. E-mail: fapress@gmail.com. E-mail: submissions by hard copy only. Website: www.floridaacademicpress.com. Max Vargas, CEO (fiction/nonfiction/scholarly) Estab. 1997. Hardcover and trade paperback originals. **Publishes 4-8 titles/year. 2,000 queries received/year. 1,200 mss received/year. 90% of books from first-time authors. 100% from unagented writers. 5-8% royalty on retail price and higher on sales of 2,500+ copies a year.** Publishes book 3 months after acceptance of ms. Responds in 2 months on mss if rejected; 3-4 months if sent for external review. Catalog available online.

NONFICTION Subjects include government/politics, philosophy, psychology, social sciences, world affairs. We only assess complete mss that do not require extensive copy-editing. SASE returns. Submit completed ms only and c.v. Query letters or works in progress of little interest—submit only final ms. Reviews artwork/photos. Send photocopies.

FICTION Subjects include historical, literary. No poetry, poetry in translation, religious or short story collections. Submit completed ms.

TIPS "Match our needs—do not send blindly. Books we accept for publication must be submitted in camera-ready format. The Press covers all publication/promotional expenditures."

FLYING PEN PRESS LLC

20000 Mitchell Place, Suite 25, Denver CO 80249. (303)375-0499. Fax: (303)375-0499. E-mail: GeneralInquiries@FlyingPenPress.com; Publisher@FlyingPenPress.com. E-mail: Submissions@FlyingPenPress.

com. Website: www.flyingpenpress.com. **Contact:** David A. Rozansky, publisher. Estab. 2007. Trade paperback and electronic originals. **Publishes 5/2010 titles/year. 120 queries/year; 360 mss/year. 55% of books from first-time authors. 88% from unagented writers. Pays 35-46% royalty; share of gross profits (net receipts less printing costs). No advances.** Publishes book 6 months after acceptance of ms. Accepts simultaneous submissions. Responds in less than 1 month on queries/proposals; 6 months on mss. Catalog free on request; available online at website http://www.flyingpenpress.com/catalog. Guidelines free on request and available online.

NONFICTION Subjects include alternative lifestyles, Americana, animals, anthropology, archaeology, business, career guidance, child guidance, communications, community, computers, contemporary culture, counseling, creative nonfiction, economics, electronics, entertainment, environment, ethnic, finance, games, government, health, history, hobbies, humanities, labor, language, literature, medicine, memoirs, military, money, muticultural, nature, parenting, philosophy, politics, public affairs, recreation, regional (CO, S.W. U.S., Nat'l Parks, Rocky Mountains), science, social sciences, sociology, software, translation, transportation, travel, war, world affairs, aviation, aerospace, game books, travel guides, puzzle books. Submit book proposals and completed ms by e-mail only. No unsolicited mss. Reviews artwork/photos. Send JPG, TIF, or PDF files.

FICTION Subjects include adventure, comic books, contemporary, ethnic, experimental, fantasy, gothic, historical, horror, humor, literary, mainstream, military, multicultural, mystery, regional, romance, science fiction, short story collections, sports, suspense, translation, western. "We have changed our focus to be platform centric. We seek ideas for series, and we invite trademark holders and blogging personalities to submit ideas for a line of books." Submit completed ms by e-mail only.

TIPS "Create a series concept that will attract readers, which we can then assign to writers for several books in the line. Trademarked characters, movie and TV tie-ins, and popular blogs are suitable platforms."

⊙ FODOR'S TRAVEL PUBLICATIONS, INC.

Imprint of Random House, Inc., 1745 Broadway, New York NY 10019. E-mail: editors@fodors.com. Website: www.fodors.com. **Contact:** Editorial Director. Estab.

1936. Publishes trade paperback originals. **Most titles are collective works, with contributions as works for hire. Most contributions are updates of previously published volumes.** Accepts simultaneous submissions. Responds in 2 months to queries. Book catalog available free.

○ "If you're interested in working for Fodor's as a travel writer, send your resume and writing clips, together with a cover letter explaining your qualifications and areas of expertise, to editors@fodors.com. You may also mail materials to: Fodor's Travel Publications, Researcher Writer Positions, 1745 Broadway, 15th floor, New York, NY 10019. Remember that most Fodor's writers live in the areas they cover. Note that we do not accept unsolicited manuscripts."

⚓ Fodor's publishes travel books on many regions and countries.

NONFICTION Subjects include travel. We are interested in unique approaches to favorite destinations. Writers seldom review our catalog or our list and often query about books on topics that we're already covering. Beyond that, it's important to review competition and to say what the proposed book will add. Do not send originals without first querying as to our interest in the project. We're not interested in travel literature or in proposals for general travel guidebooks. Agented submissions only. Submit proposal and résumé via mail.

TIPS In preparing your query or proposal, remember that it's the only argument Fodor's will hear about why your book will be a good one, and why you think it will sell; and it's also best evidence of your ability to create the book you propose. Craft your proposal well and carefully so that it puts your best foot forward.

FOREIGN POLICY ASSOCIATION

470 Park Ave. S., New York NY 10016. (212)481-8100. Fax: (212)481-9275. E-mail: info@fpa.org; rnolan@fpa.org. Website: www.fpa.org. Publishes 2 periodicals, an annual eight episode PBS Television series with DVD and an occasional hardcover and trade paperback original. Accepts simultaneous submissions. Book catalog available free.

IMPRINTS Headline Series (quarterly); Great Decisions (annual).

⚓ The Foreign Policy Association, a nonpartisan, not-for-profit educational organization founded in 1918, is a catalyst for developing awareness, understanding of and informed opinion on US foreign policy and global issues. Through its balanced, nonpartisan publications, FPA seeks to encourage individuals in schools, communities and the workplace to participate in the foreign policy process.

NONFICTION Subjects include government, politics, history, foreign policy.

TIPS "Audience is students and people with an interest, but not necessarily any expertise, in foreign policy and international relations."

FORTRESS PRESS

P.O. Box 1209, Minneapolis MN 55440-1209. (612)330-3300. Website: www.fortresspress.com. Publishes hardcover and trade paperback originals. **Pays royalty on retail price.** Accepts simultaneous submissions. Book catalog free (call 1-800-328-4648). Guidelines available online.

⚓ Fortress Press publishes academic books in Biblical studies, theology, Christian ethics, church history, and professional books in pastoral care and counseling."

NONFICTION Subjects include religion, women's issues, women's studies, church history, African-American studies. Query with annotated TOC, brief cv, sample pages, SASE. Please study guidelines before submitting.

FORT ROSS INC. INTERNATIONAL RIGHTS

26 Arthur Place, Yonkers NY 10701. (914)375-6448. E-mail: fortross@optonline.net. Website: www.fortrossinc.com. **Contact:** Dr. Kartsev, executive director. Estab. 1992. Format publishes in hardcover and paperback originals. **Publishes Ernest Hemingway,** *Moveable Feast*, **Restored Edition (in Russian) titles/ year.** Publishes book 12 months after acceptance of ms. Accepts simultaneous submissions. Responds in 1 month to queries and proposals; 3 months to mss.

⚓ Generally, we publish Russia-related books in English or Russian. Sometimes we publish various fiction and nonfiction books in collaboration with the east European publishers in translation. We are looking mainly for well-established authors." Publishes paperback originals. Receives 100 queries received/year;100 mss received/year. Pays 6-8% royalty on wholesale price or makes outright purchase of $500-1,500; negotiable advance.

FORWARD MOVEMENT

412 Sycamore St., Cincinnati OH 45202-4195. (513)721-6659; (800)543-1813. Fax: (513)721-0729. E-mail: rschmidt@forwarddaybyday.com. Website: www. forwardmovement.org. **Contact:** Rev. Dr. Richard H. Schmidt, editor & director. Estab. 1934. **Publishes 30 titles/year.** Responds in 1 month. Book catalog and ms guidelines free. Guidelines available online.

○ "Forward Movement is an official agency of the Episcopal Church. In addition to Forward Day by Day, our daily devotional guide, we publish other books and tracts related to the life and concerns of the Christian church, especially within the Anglican Communion. These typically include material introducing the Episcopal Church, meditations and spiritual readings, prayers, liturgical resources, biblical reflections, and material on stewardship, church history, issues before the church, and Christian healing."

⛏ Forward Movement was established 'to help reinvigorate the life of the church.' Many titles focus on the life of prayer, where our relationship with God is centered, death, marriage, baptism, recovery, joy, the Episcopal Church and more. Currently emphasizing prayer/spirituality."

NONFICTION Subjects include religion. "We are an agency of the Episcopal Church.", "There is a special need for tracts of under 8 pages. (A page usually runs about 200 words.) On rare occasions, we publish a full-length book." Query with SASE or by e-mail with complete ms attached.

FICTION Subjects include juvenile.

TIPS "Audience is primarily Episcopalians and other Christians."

WALTER FOSTER PUBLISHING, INC.

3 Wrigley, Suite A, Irvine CA 92618. (800)426-0099. Fax: (949)380-7575. E-mail: info@walterfoster.com. Website: www.walterfoster.com. Estab. 1922. Publishes trade paperback originals.

⛏ Walter Foster publishes instructional how-to/ craft instruction as well as licensed products."

FOX CHAPEL PUBLISHING

1970 Broad St., East Petersburg PA 17520. (800)457-9112. Fax: (717)560-4702. E-mail: CustomerService@ FoxChapelPublishing.com. Website: www.foxchapel-publishing.com. **Contact:** Peg Couch, acquisitions editor. Publishes hardcover and trade paperback originals and trade paperback reprints. **Publishes 25-40 titles/ year. 50% of books from first-time authors. 100% from unagented writers. Pays royalty or makes outright purchase. Pays variable advance.** Publishes book 6-18 months after acceptance of ms. Accepts simultaneous submissions. Responds in 2 months to queries.

⛏ Fox Chapel publishes woodworking, woodcarving, and design titles for professionals and hobbyists.

NONFICTION Submission guidelines on website Reviews artwork/photos. Send photocopies.

TIPS "We're looking for knowledgeable artists, craftspeople and woodworkers, all experts in their fields, to write books of lasting value."

FREDERICK FELL PUBLISHERS, INC.

2131 Hollywood Blvd., Suite 305, Hollywood FL 33020. (954)925-5242. Fax: (954)925-5244. E-mail: fellpub@ aol.com. Website: www.fellpub.com. **Contact:** Barbara Newman, senior editor. Publishes hardcover and trade paperback originals. **Publishes 40 titles/year. 4,000 queries received/year. 1,000 mss received/year. 95% of books from first-time authors. 95% from unagented writers. Pays negotiable royalty on retail price. Pays up to $10,000 advance.** Publishes book 1 year after acceptance of ms. Accepts simultaneous submissions. Responds in 1 month to queries. Responds in 3 months to proposals. Guidelines available online.

⛏ Fell has launched 25 titles in the *Know-It-All* series. We will be publishing over 125 titles in all genres. Prove to us that your title is the best in this exciting nonfiction format."

NONFICTION Subjects include business, economics, child guidance, education, ethnic, film, cinema, stage, health, medicine, hobbies, money, finance, spirituality. "We are reviewing in all categories. Advise us of the top 3 competitive titles for your work and the reasons why the public would benefit by having your book published." Submit proposal package, including outline, 3 sample chapters, author bio, publicity ideas, market analysis. Reviews artwork/photos. Send photocopies.

TIPS "We are most interested in well-written, timely nonfiction with strong sales potential. We will not consider topics that appeal to a small, select audience. Learn markets and be prepared to help with sales and promotion. Show us how your book is unique or better than the competition."

⬤ FREE PRESS

Simon & Schuster, 1230 Ave. of the Americas, New York NY 10020. (212)698-7000. Fax: (212)632-4989. Website: www.simonsays.com. **Contact:** Bruce Nichols, vice president/senior editor (history/serious nonfiction). Estab. 1947. **Publishes 85 titles/year. 15% of books from first-time authors. 10% from unagented writers. Pays variable royalty. Pays advance.** Publishes book 1 year after acceptance of ms. Responds in 2 months to queries.

  ○ "Simon & Schuster does not accept unsolicited manuscripts. We suggest that prospective authors submit their manuscripts through a professional literary agent."

⊶🖙 The Free Press publishes nonfiction.

NONFICTION *Does not accept unagented submissions.*

FREE SPIRIT PUBLISHING, INC.

217 Fifth Ave. N., Suite 200, Minneapolis MN 55401-1299. (612)338-2068. Fax: (612)337-5050. E-mail: acquisitions@freespirit.com. Website: www.freespirit.com. **Contact:** Acquisitions Editor. Estab. 1983. Publishes trade paperback originals and reprints. **Publishes 12-18 titles/year. 5% of books from first-time authors. 75% from unagented writers. Pays advance.** Book catalog and ms guidelines online.

  ○ Free Spirit does not accept fiction, poetry or storybook submissions.

⊶🖙 We believe passionately in empowering kids to learn to think for themselves and make their own good choices."

NONFICTION Subjects include child guidance, education, pre-K-12, study and social sciences skills, special needs, differentiation but not textbooks or basic skills books like reading, counting, etc., health, medicine, mental/emotional health for/about children, psychology for/about children, sociology for/about children. "Many of our authors are educators, mental health professionals, and youth workers involved in helping kids and teens." No fiction or picture storybooks, poetry, single biographies or autobiographies, books with mythical or animal characters, or books with religious or New Age content. "We are not looking for academic or religious materials, or books that analyze problems with the nation's school systems." Query with cover letter stating qualifications, intent, and intended audience and market analysis (how your book stands out from the field), along with outline, 2 sample chapters, rèsumè, SASE. Do not send original copies of work.

TIPS "Our books are issue-oriented, jargon-free, and solution-focused. Our audience is children, teens, teachers, parents and youth counselors. We are especially concerned with kids' social and emotional well-being and look for books with ready-to-use strategies for coping with today's issues at home or in school—written in every-day language. We are not looking for academic or religious materials, or books that analyze problems with the nation's school systems. Instead, we want books that offer practical, positive advice so kids can help themselves and parents and teachers can help kids succeed."

FRONT ST.

Boyds Mills Press, 815 Church St., Honesdale PA 18431. Website: www.frontSt.books.com. **Contact:** Acquisitions Editor. Estab. 1994. Publishes hardcover originals and trade paperback reprints. **Publishes 10-15 titles/year. 2,000 queries received/year. 5,000 mss received/year. 30% of books from first-time authors. 60% from unagented writers. Pays royalty on retail price. Pays advance.** Publishes book 1 year after acceptance of ms. Accepts simultaneous submissions. Responds in 3 months. Book catalog available online. Guidelines available online.

⊶🖙 We are an independent publisher of books for children and young adults."

FICTION Subjects include adventure, historical, humor, juvenile, literary, picture books, young adult, adventure, fantasy/science fiction fiction, historical, mystery/suspense, problem novels, sports. Query with SASE. Submit complete ms, if under 100 pages, with SASE. keeps illustration samples on file. Reviews artwork/photos w/ms. Send photocopies. "High-quality fiction for children and young adults." Publishes hardcover originals and trade paperback reprints. Books: coated paper; offset printing; case binding; 4-color illustrations. Averages 15 fiction titles/year. Distributes titles through independent sales reps, wholesalers, and via order line directly from Front St.. Promotes titles through sales and professional conferences, sales reps, reviews, catalogs, web site, and direct marketing.

POETRY Submit 25 sample poems.

TIPS "Read through our recently published titles and review our website. Check to see what's on the market and in our catalog before submitting your story. Feel free to query us if you're not sure."

⊕ FUNNELBRAIN LLC

28310 Roadside Dr., Suite 229, Agoura Hills CA 91301. E-mail: writers@funnelbrain.com. Website: www.funnelbrain.com. **Contact:** Jack Dennison, executive chairman. Joe DeTuno, CEO Estab. 2008. Electronic originals and reprints. **Publishes 100-1,000 titles/year. Pays 50% royalty on retail price.** Accepts simultaneous submissions. Responds in 1 month on queries, proposals, and mss. We typically respond within 5 business days. Catalog available online. Guidelines available online and by e-mail.

NONFICTION "We are looking for writers with expertise and enthusiasm in all academic subject areas, as well as non-academic subjects. We target an audience of middle school, high school, and college students, as well as lifelong learners. Writers will do well to focus on a particular niche where the writer has expertise. All queries should be via e-mail."

FICTION Fiction categories and requirements are the same as for nonfiction.

POETRY "We have no plans to publish poetry, but flashcards and quizzes about poetry are welcome."

TIPS "Writers submitting queries or proposals should describe their areas of expertise or interest and qualifications. If possible, writers should identify the particular niche audience they expect their flashcards to serve. While broad topics are welcome, more specific and narrowly focused topics will tend to perform better and face less competition."

⊕ FUTURECYCLE PRESS

313 Pan Will Rd., Mineral Bluff GA 30559. (706)622-4454. E-mail: submissions@futurecycle.org. Website: www.futurecycle.org. **Contact:** Robert S. King, director & editor-in-chief. Estab. 2007.

GAMBIT PUBLISHING

1725 W. Glenlake Ave., #1W, Chicago IL 60660. E-mail: gailglaser@gambitpublishingonline.com. E-mail: editor@gambitpublishingonline.com. Website: www.gambitpublishingonline.com. **Contact:** Gail Glaser, Editor (film, biography, popular culture). Format publishes in hardcover originals and reprints; trade paperback originals and reprints; mass market paperback originals and reprints; electronic originals and reprints. **Publishes 4 titles/year. 75% of books from first-time authors. 100% from unagented writers. Pays 10-60% royalty on retail price. No advance.** Publishes book 3 months after acceptance

of ms. Accepts simultaneous submissions. Responds in 1 month on queries, proposals, and manuscripts. Catalog available online and for #10 SASE. Guidelines free by e-mail at website.

NONFICTION Subjects include architecture, art, contemporary culture, cooking, creative nonfiction, dance, entertainment, environment, games, history, hobbies, house and home, humanities, language, literary criticism, marine subjects, memoirs, military, money, multicultural, music, nature, photography, recreation, regional, sex, social sciences, travel, womens issues, womens studies, film, criticism. Reviews artwork only if necessary to the book. Send photocopies.

FICTION Subjects include adventure, comic books, contemporary, feminist, historical, humor, juvenile, literary, mainstream, military, multicultural, mystery, picture books, plays, poetry, regional, short story collections, suspense, war, western. "We're primarily interestsed in movies, tv, pop culture, but will look over many other subjects." Query with SASE. Submit proposal package, including synopsis, 2 sample chapters. Submit completed mss.

POETRY "We are open to most poetry." Query. Submit 3 sample poems. Submit complete ms.

GASLIGHT PUBLICATIONS

P.O. Box 1344, Studio City CA 91614. Website: http://playerspress.home.att.net/gaslight_catalogue.htm. Estab. 1960.

TIPS "Please send only Sherlock Holmes material. Other stuff just wastes time and money."

GAUTHIER PUBLICATIONS, INC.

Frog Legs Ink, P.O. Box 806241, Saint Clair Shores MI 48080. Fax: (586)279-1515. E-mail: info@gauthierpublications.com. E-mail: submissions@gauthierpublications.com. Website: www.eatabook.com. **Contact:** Elizabeth Gauthier, Creative Director (Children's/Fiction). Hardcover originals and trade paperback originals. **Publishes 10 titles/year. 50% of books from first-time authors. 50% from unagented writers. Pays 5-10% royalty on retail price.** Guidelines available for #10 SASE, or online at website http://gauthierpublications.com, or by e-mail at: submissions@gauthierpublications.com.

IMPRINTS Frog Legs Ink, Hungry Goat Press, Dragon-Fish Comics.

◐ Frog Legs Ink (imprint) is always looking for new writers and illustrators. We are currently looking for Horror/Thriller short stories for an upcoming collection.

NONFICTION Subjects include creative nonfiction, photography, self help. Query with SASE.

FICTION Subjects include adventure, confession, ethnic, experimental, fantasy, feminist, gothic, historical, horror, humor, juvenile, literary, mainstream, contemporary, military, war, multicultural, multimedia, mystery, plays, poetry, poetry in translation, regional, religious, romance. "We are particularly interested in mystery, thriller, graphic novels, horror and Young Adult areas for the upcoming year. We do, however, consider most subjects if they are intriguing and well written." Query with SASE. "Please do not send full ms unless we ask for it If we are interested we will request a few sample chapters and outline. Since we do take the time to read and consider each piece response can take up to 8 weeks. Mailed submissions without SASE included are destroyed if we are not interested."

POETRY "We are particularly interested in mystery, thriller, graphic novels, horror and Young Adult areas for the upcoming year. We do, however, consider most subjects if they are intriguing and well written." Query with SASE.

⊘ GAY SUNSHINE PRESS AND LEYLAND PUBLICATIONS

P.O. Box 410690, San Francisco CA 94141-0690. Website: www.leylandpublications.com. **Contact:** Winston Leyland, editor. Estab. 1975. Publishes hardcover originals, trade paperback originals and reprints. **Publishes 2-3 titles/year. Pays royalty, or makes outright purchase.** Responds in 6 weeks to queries. Responds in 2 months to manuscripts. Book catalog for $1.

○ "Gay History, Sex, Politics, and Culture are the focus of the quality books published by San Francisco's Gay Sunshine. Under the direction of Winston Leyland, Gay Sunshine Press has published gay male books as part of the burgeoning Gay Cultural Renaissance, defined as 'a rediscovery of the Gay Cultural heritage and its expression through art, music, literature, film and in many other ways.' To date these Gay Sunshine books include work by such famous writers as Gore Vidal, Christopher Isherwood, Tennessee Williams, Jean Genet, Allen Ginsberg, as well as much work by younger American writers, and gay literature in translation from other cultures (Japan, China, Latin America, Russia)."

Gay history, sex, politics, and culture are the focus of the quality books published by Gay Sunshine Press. Leyland Publications publishes books on popular aspects of gay sexuality and culture.

NONFICTION "We're interested in innovative literary nonfiction which deals with gay lifestyles." No long personal accounts, academic or overly formal titles. Query with SASE. *All unsolicited mss returned unopened.*

FICTION Subjects include erotica, experimental, historical, literary, mystery, science fiction, translation, All gay male material only. Interested in innovative well-written novels on gay themes; also short story collections. "We have a high literary standard for fiction. We desire fiction on gay themes of high literary quality and prefer writers who have already had work published in books or literary magazines. We also publish erotica—short stories and novels." Query with SASE. *All unsolicited mss returned.*

GEM GUIDES BOOK CO.

1275 W. 9th St., Upland CA 91786. (626)855-1611. Fax: (626)855-1610. E-mail: gembooks@aol.com. Website: www.gemguidesbooks.com. **Contact:** Greg Warner, editor. Estab. 1965. **Publishes 6-8 titles/year. 60% of books from first-time authors. 100% from unagented writers. Pays 6-10% royalty on retail price.** Publishes book 1 year after acceptance of ms. Accepts simultaneous submissions. Responds in 5 months to queries.

IMPRINTS Gembooks.

Gem Guides prefers nonfiction books for the hobbyist in rocks and minerals; lapidary and jewelry-making; crystals and crystal healing; travel and recreation guide books for the West and Southwest; and other regional local interest. Currently emphasizing how-to, field guides, West/Southwest regional interest. De-emphasizing stories, history, poetry."

NONFICTION Subjects include history, Western, hobbies, rockhounding, prospecting, lapidary, jewelry craft, nature, recreation, regional, Western US, science, earth, travel. Query with outline/synopsis and sample chapters with SASE. Reviews artwork/photos.

TIPS "We have a general audience of people interested in recreational activities. Publishers plan and have specific book lines in which they specialize. Learn about the publisher and submit materials compatible with that publisher's product line."

⊕ GENEALOGICAL PUBLISHING CO., INC.

3600 Clipper Mill Rd., Baltimore MD 21211. (410)837-8271. Fax: (410)752-8492. E-mail: info@genealogical.com. E-mail: jgaronzi@genealogical.com. Website: www.genealogical.com. **Contact:** Joe Garonzik, mktg. dir. (history & genealogy). Estab. 1959. Hardcover and trade paperback originals and reprints. **Publishes 100 titles/year. 100 queries/year; 20 mss/year. 10% of books from first-time authors. 99% from unagented writers. 10-15% royalty on wholesale price.** Publishes book 6 months after acceptance of ms. Accepts simultaneous submissions. Responds in 1 month on queries, proposals, and mss. Catalog free on request.
NONFICTION Subjects include Americana, ethnic, history, hobbies. Submit outline, 1 sample chapter. Reviews artwork/photos as part of the mss package.
TIPS "Our audience is genealogy hobbyists."

GENESIS PRESS, INC.

P.O. Box 101, Columbus MS 39701. (888)463-4461. Fax: (662)329-9399. E-mail: customerservice@genesis-press.com. Website: www.genesis-press.com. Estab. 1993. Publishes hardcover and trade paperback originals and reprints. Responds in 2 months to queries. Responds in 4 months to manuscripts. Guidelines available online.
IMPRINTS Indigo (romance); Black Coral (fiction); Indigo Love Spectrum (interracial romance); Indigo After Dark (erotica); Obsidian (thriller/myster); Indigo Glitz (love stories for young adults); Indigo Vibe (for stylish audience under 35 years old); Mount Blue (Christian); Inca Books (teens); Sage (self-help/inspirational).
← Genesis Press is the largest privately owned African-American book publisher in the country. Genesis has steadily increased its reach, and now brings its readers everything from suspense and science fiction to Christian-oriented romance and nonfiction.
NONFICTION Submit outline, 3 sample chapters, SASE. If you would like your ms returned, you must follow all the rules on our website. Please use Priority or First Class mail-no Media Mail, Fed Ex, and no metered mail. We cannot return partials or manuscripts outside the US . No International Reply Coupons, please.

FICTION Subjects include adventure, erotica, ethnic, multicultural, mystery, romance, science fiction, women's. Submit clips, 3 sample chapters, SASE.
TIPS Be professional. Always include a cover letter and SASE. Follow the submission guidelines posted on our website or send SASE for a copy.

⊘ GIFTED EDUCATION PRESS

10201 Yuma Court, Manassas VA 20109. (703)369-5017. E-mail: mfisher345@comcast.net. Website: www.giftedpress.com. **Contact:** Maurice Fisher, publisher. Estab. 1981. Publishes trade paperback originals. **Publishes 5 titles/year. 20 queries received/year. 10 mss received/year. 90% of books from first-time authors. 100% from unagented writers. Pays 10% royalty on retail price.** Publishes book 4 months after acceptance of ms. Accepts simultaneous submissions. Responds in 1 month to queries, proposals and manuscripts. Book catalog available online. Guidelines available online.
← Searching for rigorous texts on teaching science, math and humanities to gifted students."
NONFICTION Subjects include child guidance, computers, electronics, education, history, humanities, philosophy, science, teaching, math, biology, Shakespeare, chemistry, physics, creativity. Query with SASE. *All unsolicited mss returned unopened.* Reviews artwork/photos.
TIPS "Audience includes teachers, parents, gift program supervisors, professors. "Be knowledgeable about your subject. Write clearly and don't use educational jargon."

GIVAL PRESS

Gival Press, LLC, P.O. Box 3812, Arlington VA 22203. (703)351-0079. E-mail: givalpress@yahoo.com. Website: www.givalpress.com. **Contact:** Robert L. Giron, editor-in-chief (Area of interest: literary). Estab. 1998. Publishes trade paperback, electronic originals, and reprints. **Publishes 5-6 titles/year. over 200 queries received/year. 60 mss received/year. 50% of books from first-time authors. 70% from unagented writers. Royalties (% varies).** Publishes book 12 months after acceptance of ms. Accepts simultaneous submissions. Responds in 1 month to queries, 3 months to proposals & mss. Book catalog available online, free on request/for #10 SASE. Guidelines available online, by e-mail, free on request/for #10 SASE.
NONFICTION Subjects include gay, lesbian, memoirs, multicultural, translation, womens issues, wom-

ens studies, scholarly. Submit between October-December only. Always query first via e-mail; provide plan/ms content, bio, and supportive material. Reviews artwork/photos; query first.

FICTION Subjects include gay, lesbian, literary, multicultural, poetry, translation. Always query first via e-mail; provide description, author's bio, and supportive material.

POETRY Query via e-mail; provide description, bio, etc.; submit 5-6 sample poems via e-mail.

TIPS "Our audience is those who read literary works with depth to the work. Visit our website-there is much to be read/learned from the numerous pages."

⊕ GLB PUBLISHERS

1028 Howard St., #503, San Francisco CA 94103. (415)621-8307. E-mail: glbpubs@glbpubs.com. Website: www.glbpubs.com. Estab. 1990. Hardcover, trade paperback, and electronic originals; trade paperback and electronic reprints. **Publishes 4-5 titles/year. Receives 50 queries/year; 40 mss/year 20% of books from first-time authors. 90% from unagented writers. Pays 10-25% royalty on retail price** Publishes book 2-3 months after acceptance of ms. Responds in 2 weeks on queries and proposals; 1 month on mss. Catalog and guidelines free on request and online at website.

NONFICTION Subjects include alternative lifestyles, child guidance, contemporary culture, creative nonfiction, entertainment, ethnic, gay, government, health, history, humanities, lesbian, medicine, memoirs, multicultural, New Age, photography, politics, social sciences, travel, women's issues. Must apply to and be appropriate for gays, lesbians, bisexuals, transgenders. Submit completed ms. Reviews artwork/photos. Send originals or scanned files.

FICTION Subjects include adventure, erotica, fantasy, feminist, gay, gothic, historical, humor, literary, multicultural, mystery, plays, poetry, romance, science fiction, short story collections, suspense, western, young adult. "Must be gay, lesbian, bisexual, or transgender subjects." Submit completed ms.

POETRY Submit completed ms.

TIPS "Our audience consists of 'adults of all ages.'"

GLENBRIDGE PUBLISHING, LTD.

19923 E. Long Ave., Centennial CO 80016. (800)986-4135; (720)870-8381. Fax: (720)230-1209. Website: www.glenbridgepublishing.com. **Contact:** Editor. Estab. 1986. Publishes hardcover originals and reprints,

trade paperback originals. **Publishes 6-8 titles/year. Pays 10% royalty.** Publishes book 1 year after acceptance of ms. Accepts simultaneous submissions. Responds in 2 months to queries. Book catalog available online. Guidelines for #10 SASE.

⟁ Glenbridge has an eclectic approach to publishing. We look for titles that have long-term capabilities."

NONFICTION Subjects include Americana, animals, business, economics, education, environment, family, finance, parenting, writing, film, theatre, communication, cooking, foods, nutrition, health, medicine, history, philosophy, politics & government, psychology, sociology. Publishers for over 23 years, offering books from every genre, with the aim of uplifting, educating, and entertaining. Send e-mail on their website. Query with outline/synopsis, sample chapters.

Ⓐ ⊘ DAVID R. GODINE, PUBLISHER, INC.

9 Hamilton Place, Boston MA 02108. (617)451-9600. Fax: (617)350-0250. E-mail: info@godine.com. Website: www.godine.com. Estab. 1970. Publishes hardcover and trade paperback originals and reprints. **Publishes 35 titles/year. Pays royalty on retail price.** Publishes book 3 years after acceptance of ms. Book catalog for 5X8 envelope and 3 First-Class stamps.

⟁ Our particular strengths are books about the history and design of the written word, literary essays, and the best of world fiction in translation. We also have an unusually strong list of children's books, all of them printed in their entirety with no cuts, deletions, or side-stepping to keep the political watchdogs happy."

NONFICTION Subjects include Americana, art, architecture, gardening, literary criticism, nature, environment, photography, book arts, typography. *No unsolicited mss*

FICTION Subjects include historical, literary, translation, literature, novels. *No unsolicited mss*

TIPS "Please visit our website for more information about our books and detailed submission policy. No phone calls, please."

GOLDEN WEST BOOKS

P.O. Box 80250, San Marino CA 91118. (626)458-8148. Fax: (626)458-8148. E-mail: trainbook@earthlink.net. Website: www.goldenwestbooks.com. **Contact:** Donald Duke, publisher. Publishes hardcover originals. **Publishes 3-4 titles/year. 8-10 queries received/**

year. 5 mss received/year. 75% of books from first-time authors. 100% from unagented writers. Pays 8-10% royalty on wholesale price. Pays no advance. Publishes book 3 months after acceptance of ms. Responds in 3 months to queries. Book catalog and ms guidelines free.

- ⭕ "We are always interested in new material. Please use the form online to contact us; we will follow up with you as soon as possible."
- 💥 Golden West Books specializes in railroad history."

NONFICTION Subjects include Americana, history. Query with SASE. Reviews artwork/photos.

GOLLEHON PRESS, INC.

6157 28th St. SE, Grand Rapids MI 49546. (616)949-3515. Fax: (616)949-8674. E-mail: editorial@gollehonbooks.com. Website: www.gollehonbooks.com. **Contact:** Lori Adams, editor. Publishes hardcover, trade paperback, and mass market paperback originals. **Publishes 6-8 titles/year. 100 queries received/year. 30 mss received/year. 85% of books from first-time authors. 90% from unagented writers. Pays 7% royalty on retail price. Pays $500-1,000 advance.** Publishes book usually 6 months after acceptance of ms. Accepts simultaneous submissions. Responds in 1 month (if interested) to proposals. Responds in 2 months to manuscripts. Book catalog and ms guidelines online.

- 💥 Currently emphasizing theology (life of Christ), political, current events, pets (dogs only, rescue/heroic), self-help, and gardening. *No unsolicited mss*; brief proposals only with first 5 pages of Chapter 1. Writer must have strong credentials to author work."

NONFICTION Submit brief proposal package only with bio and first 5 pages of Chapter 1. "We do not return materials unless we specifically request the full manuscript." Reviews artwork/photos. Send Writer must be sure he/she owns all rights to photos, artwork, illustrations, etc., submitted for consideration (all submissions must be free of any third-party claims). Never send original photos or art.

TIPS "Mail brief book proposal, bio, and a few sample pages only. We will request a full manuscript if interested. We cannot respond to all queries. Full manuscript will be returned if we requested it, and if writer provides SASE. We do not return proposals. Simultaneous submissions are encouraged."

⊕ GOODMAN BECK PUBLISHING

P.O. Box 253, Attn: Senior Editor, Norwood NJ 07648-2428. (201)403-3097. E-mail: info@goodmanbeck.com. Website: www.goodmanbeck.com. **Contact:** Senior Editor. Estab. 2007. Format publishes in trade paperback originals and reprints; mass market paperback originals and reprints. **Publishes 5-6 titles/year. 65% of books from first-time authors. 90% from unagented writers. Pays 10% royalty on retail price** Publishes book 6-9 months from acceptance to publishing time. after acceptance of ms. Accepts simultaneous submissions. Responds in 1 month on queries and proposals; 2 months on mss. Catalog or guidelines are not available.

- ⭕ "Our audience is adults trying to cope with this 'upside down world.' With our self-help books, we are trying to improve the world one book at a time."
- 💥 Our primary interest at this time is mental health, personal growth, aging well, positive psychology, accessible spirituality, and self-help."

NONFICTION Subjects include creative nonfiction, health, medicine, philosophy, psychology, spirituality. No religious or political works, textbooks, or how-to books at this time. Query with SASE. Reviews artwork/photos. Send photocopies.

FICTION Subjects include contemporary, mainstream, mystery, poetry, short story collections, suspense. "Fiction books should be able to generate a passionate response from our adult readers." No science fiction, romance novels. Query with SASE.

POETRY "We are interested in zen-inspired haiku and non-embellished, non-rhyming, egoless poems. Read Mary Oliver." Query, submit 3 sample poems.

TIPS "Your book should be enlightening and marketable. Be prepared to have a comprehensive marketing plan. You will be very involved."

THE GRADUATE GROUP

P.O. Box 370351, West Hartford CT 06137-0351. (860)233-2330. Fax: (860)233-2330. E-mail: graduategroup@hotmail.com. Website: www.graduategroup.com. **Contact:** Mara Whitman, partner; Robert Whitman, vice president. Estab. 1964. Publishes trade paperback originals. **Publishes 50 titles/year. 100 queries received/year. 70 mss received/year. 60% of books from first-time authors. 85% from unagented writers. Pays 20% - royalty on retail price.** Publishes book 3 months after acceptance of ms. Accepts simultaneous submissions. Responds in 1 month to queries. Book catalog available free. Guidelines available online.

8—➤ The Graduate Group helps college and graduate students better prepare themselves for rewarding careers and helps people advance in the workplace. Currently emphasizing test preparation, career advancement, and materials for prisoners, law enforcement, books on unique careers.

NONFICTION Subjects include business, economics, education, government, politics, health, medicine, money, finance, law enforcement. Submit complete ms and SASE with sufficient postage.

TIPS "We are open to all submissions."

GRAND CANYON ASSOCIATION

1824 S. Thompson St., Suite 205, Flagstaff AZ 86001. (928)863-3878. Fax: (928)779-7279. E-mail: tberger@grandcanyon.org. Website: www.grandcanyon.org. **Contact:** Todd R. Berger, Director of Publishing. (Grand Canyon-related geology, natural history, outdoor activities, human history, photography, ecology, etc., posters, postcards and other non-book products). Estab. 1932. Publishes hardcover originals and reprints, and trade paperback originals and reprints. **200 queries received/year. Pays royalty on wholesale price. Makes outright purchase.** Accepts simultaneous submissions. Responds in 2 months to queries, proposals and manuscripts. Book catalog available online. Ms guidelines available by e-mail.

NONFICTION Subjects include Grand Canyon-related animals; anthropology; archaeology; architecture; children's books (fiction & nonfiction); general nonfiction; history; nature; environment; photography; recreation; regional; science; sports; travel; geology. The mission of the Grand Canyon Association (GCA) is to help preserve and protect Grand Canyon National Park by cultivating support through education and understanding of the park. Grand Canyon Association (GCA) is a nonprofit organization established to support education, research, and other programs for the benefit of Grand Canyon National Park and its visitors. GCA operates bookstores throughout the park, publishes books and other materials related to the Grand Canyon region, supports wildlife surveys and other research, funds acquisitions for the park's research library, and produces a wide variety of free publications and exhibits for park visitors. Since 1932, GCA has provided Grand Canyon National Park with over $23 million in financial support.

Query with SASE. Submit proposal package, outline, 3-4 sample chapters, list of publication credits, and samples of previous work. Submit complete ms. Reviews artwork/photos. Send transparencies, color or b&w prints, or digital samples of images.

TIPS "Do not send any proposals that are not directly related to the Grand Canyon or do not have educational value about the Grand Canyon."

GRANITE PUBLISHING, LLC

P.O. Box 1429, Columbus NC 28722. (828)894-8444. Fax: (828)894-8454. E-mail: brian@granitepublishing.us; eileen@souledout.org. Website: www.granitepublishing.us/index.html. **Contact:** Brian Crissey. Publishes trade paperback originals and reprints. **Publishes 4 titles/year. 50 queries received/year. 150 mss received/year. 70% of books from first-time authors. 90% from unagented writers. Pays 7 ½-10% royalty.** Publishes book 16 months after acceptance of ms. Accepts simultaneous submissions. Responds in 6 months to manuscripts.

IMPRINTS Wild Flower Press; Swan-Raven & Co.; Agents of Change.

○ Granite Publishing accepts only a few very fine manuscripts in our niches each year, and those that are accepted must follow our rigid guidelines online at: http://www.granitepublishing.us/root/SubmissionGuidelines.html. Our Little Granite Books imprint publishes only our own writings for children

8—➤ Granite Publishing strives to preserve the Earth by publishing books that develop new wisdom about our emerging planetary citizenship, bringing information from the outerworlds to our world. Currently emphasizing indigenous ideas, planetary healing."

NONFICTION Subjects include New Age, planetary paradigm shift. Submit proposal. Reviews artwork/photos. Send photocopies.

GRAYWOLF PRESS

250 Third Ave. North, Suite 600, Minneapolis MN 55401. E-mail: wolves@graywolfpress.org. Website: www.graywolfpress.org. **Contact:** Katie Dublinski, editorial manager (nonfiction, fiction). Estab. 1974. Publishes trade cloth and paperback originals. **Publishes 23 titles/year. 3,000 queries received/year. 20% of books from first-time authors. 50% from unagented writers. Pays royalty on retail price. Pays $1,000-25,000 advance.** Publishes book 18 months after ac-

ceptance of ms. Responds in 3 months to queries. Book catalog available free. Guidelines available online.

⊶ Graywolf Press is an independent, nonprofit publisher dedicated to the creation and promotion of thoughtful and imaginative contemporary literature essential to a vital and diverse culture."

NONFICTION Subjects include contemporary culture, language, literature, culture. Query with SASE.
FICTION Subjects include short story collections, literary novels. "Familiarize yourself with our list first." No genre books (romance, western, science fiction, suspense) Query with SASE. Please do not fax or e-mail.
POETRY "We are interested in linguistically challenging work." Query with SASE.

GREAT NORTHWEST PUBLISHING & DIST. CO., INC.

P.O. Box 212383, Anchorage AK 99521-2383. (907)373-0122. Fax: (907)376-0122. E-mail: aob-billing@alaskaoutdoorbooks.com. Website: www.alaskaoutdoorbooks.com. **Contact:** Marvin Clark. Estab. 1979. Publishes hardcover originals, trade paperback originals, hardcover reprints and trade paperback reprints. **Publishes 2 titles/year. 75 queries received/year. 20 mss received/year. 80% of books from first-time authors. 100% from unagented writers. Pays 10% royalty on wholesale price.** Publishes book 18 months after acceptance of ms. Accepts simultaneous submissions. Responds in 2 weeks to queries. Book catalog available online. Guidelines available free.

⊶ Great Northwest Publishing now is able to offer hunters and outdoorsmen its 'Alaska Outdoor Books' library. Each volume is a carefully selected work, written by an authentic Alaska Big game hunting and outdoor authority."

NONFICTION , hunting and Alaska. "We are interested only in works from authors with personal knowledge or experience in the matters written about." Query with SASE. Submit complete ms. Reviews artwork/photos. Send photocopies.
TIPS Audience includes upscale outdoorsmen and others interested in the Alaska outdoors.

GREAT POTENTIAL PRESS

7025 E. 1st Ave. Suite 5, Scottsdale AZ 85251. (602)954-4200. Fax: (602)954-0185. E-mail: info@giftedbooks.com. Website: www.giftedbooks.com. **Contact:** Janet Gore, editor, or James T. Webb, Ph.D., president. Estab. 1986. Publishes trade paperback originals. **Publishes**
6-10 titles/year. 75 queries received/year. 20-30 mss received/year. 50% of books from first-time authors. 100% from unagented writers. Pays 10% royalty on retail price.** Publishes book 6-12 months after acceptance of ms. Accepts simultaneous submissions. Responds in 2 months to queries. Responds in 3 months to proposals. Responds in 4 months to manuscripts. Book catalog free or on website. Guidelines available online.

⊶ Specializes in nonfiction books that address academic, social and emotional issues of gifted and talented children and adults."

NONFICTION Subjects include child guidance, education, multicultural, psychology, translation, travel, women's issues, gifted/talented children and adults, misdiagnosis of gifted, parenting gifted, teaching gifted, meeting the social and emotional needs of gifted and talented, and strategies for working with gifted children and adults. Submit proposal package, including preface or introduction, TOC, chapter outline, 2-3 sample chapters and an explanation of how work differs from similar published books.
TIPS "Manuscripts should be clear, cogent, and well-written and should pertain to gifted, talented, and creative persons and/or issues."

GREAT QUOTATIONS PUBLISHING

8102 Lemont Rd., #300, Woodridge IL 60517. (630)390-3580. **Contact:** Ringo Suek, acquisitions editor (humor, relationships, Christian); Jan Stob, acquisitions editor (children's). Estab. 1991. **Publishes 30 titles/year. 1,500 queries received/year. 1,200 mss received/year. 50% of books from first-time authors. 80% from unagented writers.** Publishes book 6 months after acceptance of ms. Accepts simultaneous submissions. Responds in 6 months with SASE to queries. Call them if no response. Book catalog for $2. Guidelines for #10 SASE.

⊶ Great Quotations seeks original material for the following general categories: humor, inspiration, motivation, success, romance, tributes to mom/dad/grandma/grandpa, etc. Currently emphasizing humor, relationships. De-emphasizing poetry, self-help. We publish new books twice a year, in July and in January."

NONFICTION Subjects include business, economics, child guidance, nature, environment, religion, sports, women's issues, women's studies. "We look for subjects with identifiable markets, appealing to the general public. We publish humorous books or others requiring multicolor illustration on the inside. We don't publish highly controversial subject matter." Submit outline, 2 sample chapters. Reviews artwork/photos. Send photocopies and transparencies.

TIPS "Our books are physically small and generally a very quick read with short sentences. They are available at gift shops and book shops throughout the country. We are aware that most of our books are bought on impulse and given as gifts. We need strong, clever, descriptive titles; beautiful cover art; and brief, positive, upbeat text. Be prepared to submit final ms on computer disk, according to our specifications. (It is not necessary to try to format the typesetting of your ms to look like a finished book.)"

GREAT SOURCE EDUCATION GROUP

Houghton Mifflin Harcourt, Editorial Department, 181 Ballardvale St., Wilmington MA 01887. Website: www.greatsource.com. Guidelines available online.

➤ Great Source's main publishing efforts are instructional and focus on the school market. For all materials, the reading level must be appropriate to the skill level of the students and the nature of the materials.

NONFICTION Reading, writing, language arts, math, and science. Material must be appealing to students, proven classroom effective, be consistent with current research.

GREENE BARK PRESS

P.O. Box 1108, Bridgeport CT 06601. (610)434-2802. Fax: (610)434-2803. E-mail: service@greenebarkpress.com. Website: www.greenebarkpress.com. **Contact:** Thomas J. Greene, publisher; Tara Maroney, associate publisher. Estab. 1991. Publishes hardcover originals. **Publishes 1-5 titles/year. 100 queries received/year. 6,000 mss received/year. 60% of books from first-time authors. 100% from unagented writers. Pays 10-15% royalty on wholesale price.** Publishes book 1 year after acceptance of ms. Accepts simultaneous submissions. Responds in 2 months to queries. Responds in 6 months to manuscripts. Guidelines for SASE.

➤ Greene Bark Press only publishes books for children and young adults, mainly picture and read-to books. All of our titles appeal to the imagination and encourage children to read and explore the world through books. We only publish chil-

dren's fiction-all subjects-but in reading picture book format appealing to ages 3-9 or all ages."

FICTION Subjects include juvenile. Submit complete ms. No queries or ms by e-mail.

TIPS "Audience is children who read to themselves and others. Mothers, fathers, grandparents, godparents who read to their respective children, grandchildren. Include SASE, be prepared to wait, do not inquire by telephone."

GREENWILLOW BOOKS

HarperCollins Publishers, 1350 Ave. of the Americas, New York NY 10019. (212)207-7000. Website: www.harperchildrens.com. Estab. 1974. Publishes hardcover originals and reprints.

➤ Greenwillow Books publishes quality picture books and fiction for young readers of all ages, and nonfiction primarily for children under seven years of age. "We hope that at the heart of each book there is honesty, emotion and depth—conveyed by an author or an artist who has something that is worth saying to children and who says it in a way that is worth reading."

FICTION Subjects include fantasy, humor, literary, mystery, picture books. Juvenile.

TIPS Currently not accepting unsolicited mail, mss or queries.

GREENWOOD PRESS

ABC-CLIO, 130 Cremona Dr., Santa Barbara CA 93117. (805)968-1911. E-mail: CustomerService@abc-clio.com. Website: www.abc-clio.com. **Contact:** Vince Burns, vice president of editorial. Publishes hardcover originals. **Publishes 200 titles/year. 1,000 queries received/year. 25% of books from first-time authors. Pays variable royalty on net price. Pays rare advance.** Publishes book 1 year after acceptance of ms. Accepts simultaneous submissions. Responds in 6 months to queries. Book catalog and ms guidelines online.

➤ Greenwood Press publishes reference materials for high school, public and academic libraries in the humanities and the social and hard sciences.

NONFICTION Subjects include humanities, literary criticism, social sciences, humanities and the social and hard sciences. Query with proposal package, including scope, organization, length of project, whether complete ms is available or when it will be, cv or resume and SASE. *No unsolicited mss.*

GREENWOOD PUBLISHING GROUP

Reed-Elsevier (USA) Inc., 88 Post Rd. W, Box 5007, Westport CT 06881-5007. (203)226-3571. Fax: (203)222-6009; 203-222-1502. E-mail: achiffolo@abc-clio.com. Website: www.greenwood.com. **Contact:** See website for list of contact editors by subject area. **Pays variable royalty on net price.** Accepts simultaneous submissions. Book catalog available online. Guidelines available online.

IMPRINTS Praeger (general nonfiction in the social sciences, business, and humanities for public library patrons); Greenwood Press (reference titles for middle, high school, public, and academic libraries); Praeger Security International (nonfiction dealing with security studies broadly defined).

➤ The Greenwood Publishing Group consists of 3 distinguished imprints with one unifying purpose: to provide the best possible reference and general interest resources in the humanities and the social and hard sciences."

NONFICTION Subjects include business, economics, child guidance, education, government, politics, history, humanities, language, literature, music, dance, psychology, religion, social sciences, sociology, sports, women's issues, women's studies. Query with proposal package, including scope, organization, length of project, whether a complete ms is available or when it will be, CV or resume and SASE.

TIPS "No interest in fiction, drama, poetry—looking for reference materials and materials for educated general readers. Many of our authors are college professors who have distinguished credential and who have published research widely in their fields. Greenwood Publishing maintains an excellent website, providing complete catalog, ms guidelines and editorial contacts."

GROSSET & DUNLAP PUBLISHERS

Penguin Putnam Inc., 345 Hudson St., New York NY 10014. Website: www.penguingroup.com. Estab. 1898. Publishes hardcover (few) and mass market paperback originals. **Publishes 100-125 titles/year. Pays royalty. Pays advance.**

○ *Not currently accepting submissions.*

➤ Grosset & Dunlap publishes children's books that show children that reading is fun, with books that speak to their interests, and that are affordable so that children can build a home library of their own. Focus on licensed properties, series and readers.

NONFICTION Subjects include nature, environment, science. Agented submissions only.

FICTION Subjects include juvenile. All book formats except for picture books. Submit a summary and the first chapter or two for longer works Agented submissions only.

TIPS Nonfiction that is particularly topical or of wide interest in the mass market; new concepts for novelty format for preschoolers; and very well-written easy readers on topics that appeal to primary graders have the best chance of selling to our firm.

GROUNDWOOD BOOKS

110 Spadina Ave.Suite 801, Toronto ON M5V 2K4, Canada. E-mail: nfroman@groundwoodbooks.com. Website: www.groundwoodbooks.com.

➤ Groundwood Books. Publishes 10 picture books/year; 3 young readers/year; 5 middle readers/year; 5 young adult titles/year, approximately 2 nonfiction titles/year. 10% of books by first-time authors.

TIPS "Try to familiarize yourself with our list before submitting to judge whether or not your work is appropriate for Groundwood. Visit our website for guidelines (http://www.groundwoodbooks.com/gw_guidelines.cgm)."

GROUP PUBLISHING, INC.

1515 Cascade Ave., Loveland CO 80539. Website: www.group.com. **Contact:** Kerri Loesche, contract & copyright administrator. Estab. 1974. Publishes trade paperback originals. **Publishes 65 titles/year. 500 queries received/year. 500 mss received/year. 40% of books from first-time authors. 95% from unagented writers. Pays up to 10% royalty on wholesale price or makes outright purchase or work for hire. Pays up to $1,000 advance.** Publishes book 18 months after acceptance of ms. Accepts simultaneous submissions. Responds in 1 month to queries. Responds in 6 months to proposals andmanuscripts. Book catalog for 9×12 envelope and 2 First-Class stamps. Guidelines available online at www.group-publishing.com/submissions.asp.

➤ Our mission is to equip churches to help children, youth, and adults grow in their relationship with Jesus."

NONFICTION Subjects include education, religion. "We're an interdenominational publisher of resource materials for people who work with adults, youth or children in a Christian church setting. We also publish materials for use directly by youth or children (such as devotional books, workbooks or Bibles stories). Everything we do is based on concepts of active and interactive learning as described in *Why Nobody Learns Much of Anything at Church: And How to Fix It*, by Thom and Joani Schultz. We need new, practical, hands-on, innovative, out-of-the-box ideas—things that no one's doing.. yet." Query with SASE. Submit proposal package, outline, 3 sample chapters, cover letter, introduction to book, and sample activities if appropriate.

TIPS "Our audience consists of pastors, Christian education directors, youth leaders, and Sunday school teachers."

➕🅐 GROVE/ATLANTIC, INC.

841 Broadway, 4th Floor, New York NY 10003. (212)614-7850. Fax: (212)614-7886. E-mail: info@ groveatlantic.com. Website: www.groveatlantic.com. **Contact:** Morgan Entrekin, publisher (fiction, history, spsorts, current affairs); Elisabeth Schmitz, exec. editor (literary fiction, memoirs). Publishes hardcover and trade paperback originals, and reprints. **Publishes 100 titles/year. 1,000+ queries received/year. 1,000+ mss received/year. 10% of books from first-time authors. 0% from unagented writers. Pays 7 ½-12 ½% royalty. Makes outright purchase of $5-500,000.** Publishes book 9 months after acceptance of ms. Accepts simultaneous submissions. Responds in 1 month to queries. Responds in 2 months to proposals. Responds in 4 months to manuscripts. Book catalog available online.

IMPRINTS Black Cat, Atlantic Monthly Press, Grove Press.

NONFICTION Subjects include art, architecture, business, economics, creative nonfiction, education, government, politics, language, literature, memoirs, military, war, philosophy, psychology, science, social sciences, sports, translation. Agented submissions only.

FICTION Subjects include erotica, horror, literary, science fiction, short story collections, suspense, western. Agented submissions only.

GRYPHON HOUSE, INC.

10770 Columbia Pike, Suite 201, Silver Spring MD 20901. (800)638-0928. Fax: (301)595-0051. E-mail: kathy@ghbooks.com. Website: www.gryphonhouse.

com. **Contact:** Kathy Charner, editor-in-chief. Estab. 1981. Publishes trade paperback originals. **Publishes 12-15 titles/year. Pays royalty on wholesale price.** Responds in 3-6 months to queries. Guidelines available online.

➤ Gryphon House publishes books that teachers and parents of young children (birth-age 8) consider essential to their daily lives."

NONFICTION Subjects include child guidance, education, early childhood. Currently emphasizing social-emotional intelligence and classroom management; de-emphasizing literacy after-school activities. "We prefer to receive a letter of inquiry and/or a proposal, rather than the entire manuscript. Please include: The proposed title The purpose of the book, Table of contents, Introductory material, 20-40 sample pages of the actual book. In addition, please describe the book, including the intended audience, why teachers will want to buy it, how it is different from other similar books already published, and what qualifications you possess that make you the appropriate person to write the book. If you have a writing sample that demonstrates that you write clear, compelling prose, please include it with your letter."

GRYPHON PUBLICATIONS

P.O. Box 209, Brooklyn NY 11228-0209. Website: www.gryphonbooks.com. **Contact:** Gary Lovisi, owner/publisher. Publishes trade paperback originals and reprints. **Publishes 10 titles/year. 500 queries received/year. 1,000 mss received/year. 20% of books from first-time authors. 90% from unagented writers. Makes outright purchase by contract, price varies. Pays no advance.** Publishes book 1-2 years after acceptance of ms. Responds in 1 month to queries. Book catalog and ms guidelines for #10 SASE.

IMPRINTS Paperback Parade Magazine; Hardboiled Magazine; Gryphon Books; Gryphon Doubles.

➤ I publish very genre-oriented work (science fiction, crime, pulps) and nonfiction on these topics, authors and artists. It's best to query with an idea first."

NONFICTION Subjects include hobbies, language, literature, book collecting. "We need well-written, well-researched articles, but query first on topic and length. Writers should not submit material that is not fully developed/researched." Query with SASE. Reviews artwork/photos. Send photocopies; slides, transparencies may be necessary later.

FICTION "We want cutting-edge fiction, under 3,000 words with impact."

TIPS "We are very particular about novels and book-length work. A first-timer has a better chance with a short story or article. On anything over 4,000 words do not send manuscript, send only query letter with SASE. Always query **first** with an SASE."

GULF PUBLISHING COMPANY

2 Greenway Plaza, Suite 1020, Houston TX 77046. (713)529-4301. Fax: (713)520-4433. E-mail: svb@gulfpub.com. Website: www.gulfpub.com. **Contact:** Katie Hammon. Estab. 1916. Hardcover originals and reprints; electronic originals and reprints. **Publishes 12-15 titles/year. 3-5 queries and mss received in a year. 30% of books from first-time authors. 80% from unagented writers. Royalties on retail price. Pays $1,000-$1,500 advance.** Publishes book 8-9 months after acceptance of ms. Accepts simultaneous submissions. 2 months on queries; 1 month on proposals and mss. Catalog free on request. Guidelines available by e-mail.

⚷➤ Gulf Publishing Company is the leading publisher to the oil and gas industry. Our specialized publications reach over 100,000 people involved in energy industries worldwide. Our magazines and catalogs help readers keep current with information important to their field and allow advertisers to reach their customers in all segments of petroleum operations. More than half of Gulf Publishing Company's editorial staff have engineering degrees. The others are thoroughly trained and experienced business journalists and editors."

NONFICTION , Engineering. "We don't publish a lot in the year, therefore we are able to focus more on marketing and sales—we are hoping to grow in the future." Submit outline, 1-2 sample chapters, completed ms. Reviews artwork. Send high res. file formats with high dpi in b&w.

TIPS "Our audience would be engineers, engineering students, academia, professors, well managers, construction engineers. We recommend getting contributors to help with the writing process—this provides a more comprehensive overview for technical and scientific books. Work harder on artwork. It's expensive and time-consuming for a publisher to redraw a lot of the figures."

🅰 GUN DIGEST BOOKS

F+W Media, 700 East State St., Iola WI 54990. (888)457-2873. E-mail: kevin.michalowski@fwmedia.com. Website: www.gundigest.com; www.krause.com. **Contact:** Kevin Michalowski, senior editor (all aspects of firearms history, scholarship, nonpolitical literature). Estab. 1944. Hardcover, trade paperback, mass market paperback, and electronic originals (all). **Publishes 25 titles/year. 75 submissions received/year. 30% of books from first-time authors. 80% from unagented writers. 10 min. to 20% max. (rare) royalty on wholesale price. $2,800-$5,000** Publishes book 7 months after acceptance of ms. Accepts simultaneous submissions. Responds immediately on queries, 2 months on proposals and manuscripts. Catalog online at website: www.krause.com. Guidelines available by e-mail at: corrina.peterson@fwmedia.com.

NONFICTION , Firearms, hunting-related titles only. "Must have mainstream appeal and not be too narrowly focused." Submit proposal package, including outline, 2 sample chapters, and author bio; submit completed manuscript. Review artwork/photos (required); high-res digital only (.jpg.tif)

TIPS "Our audience is shooters, collectors, hunters, outdoors enthusiasts. We prefer not to work through agents."

HACHAI PUBLISHING

527 Empire Boulevard, Brooklyn NY 11225. (718)633-0100. Fax: (718)633-0103. Website: www.hachai.com. **Contact:** Devorah Leah Rosenfeld, editor. Estab. 1988. Publishes hardcover originals. **Publishes 4 titles/year. Makes outright purchase of $600 and up.** Accepts simultaneous submissions. Responds in 2 months to manuscripts. Book catalog available free. Guidelines available online.

⚷➤ Hachai is dedicated to producing high quality Jewish children's literature, ages 2-10. Story should promote universal values such as sharing, kindness, etc.

NONFICTION Subjects include ethnic, religion. Submit complete ms, SASE. Reviews artwork/photos. Send photocopies.

TIPS We are looking for books that convey the traditional Jewish experience in modern times or long ago; traditional Jewish observance such as Sabbath and holidays and mitzvos such as mezuzah, blessings etc.; positive character traits (middos) such as honesty, charity, respect, sharing, etc. We are also interested in historical fiction for young readers (7-10) written with a traditional Jewish perspective and highlighting the relevance of Torah in making important choices. Please, no animal stories, romance, violence, preachy sermonizing.

⊕, HADLEY RILLE BOOKS

P.O. Box 25466, Overland Park KS 66225. E-mail: subs@hadleyrillebooks.com. Website: www.hadleyrillebooks.com. **Contact:** Eric T. Reynolds, editor/publisher.

One story from *Golden Age SF: Tales of a Bygone Future* (2006) selected for David Hartwell and Kathryn Cramer's *Year's Best SF* #12, another selected for Rich Horton's *Space Opera 2007*. Two stories reprinted in Gardner Dozois' *The Year's Best Science Fiction #2* and ten stories received honorable mentions. One story from *Golden Age SF: Tales of a Bygone Future* (2006) selected for David Hartwell and Kathryn Cramer's *Year's Best SF* #12, another selected for Rich Horton's *Space Opera 2007*. Two stories reprinted in Gardner Dozois' *The Year's Best Science Fiction #2* and ten stories received honorable mentions.

FICTION We currently don't have any anthologies open for submissions, but we will in the future. Please check back periodically. We only accept e-mail queries and submissions and for 2010 only during the months of January, February, June, July, November, December.

TIPS "We aim to produce books that are aligned with current interest in the genres. Anthology markets are somewhat rare in SF these days, we feel there aren't enough good anthologies being published each year and part of our goal is to present the best that we can. We like stories that fit well within the guidelines of the particular anthology for which we are soliciting manuscripts. Aside from that, we want stories with strong characters (not necessarily characters with strong personalities, flawed characters are welcome). We want a sense of wonder and awe. We want to feel the world around the character and so scene description is important (however, this doesn't always require a lot of text, just set the scene well so we don't wonder where the character is). We strongly recommend workshopping the story or having it critiqued in some way by readers familiar with the genre. We prefer clicheés be kept to a bare minimum in the prose and avoid re-working old story lines."

HALF HALT PRESS, INC.

P.O. Box 67, Boonsboro MD 21713. (301)733-7119. Fax: (301)733-7408. E-mail: mail@halfhaltpress.com. Website: www.halfhaltpress.com. **Contact:** Elizabeth Rowland, publisher. Estab. 1986. Publishes 90% hardcover and trade paperback originals and 10% reprints. **Publishes 10 titles/year. 25% of books from first-time authors. 50% from unagented writers. Pays 10-12 ½% royalty on retail price.** Publishes book 1 year after acceptance of ms.

We publish high-quality nonfiction on equestrian topics—books that help riders and trainers do something better."

NONFICTION Subjects include animals, horses, sports. "We need serious instructional works by authorities in the field on horse-related topics, broadly defined." Query with SASE. Reviews artwork/photos.

TIPS "Writers have the best chance selling us well-written, unique works that teach serious horse people how to do something better. Offer a straightforward presentation, letting the work speak for itself, without hype or hard sell. Allow the publisher to contact the writer, without frequent calling to check status. As the publisher/author relationship becomes close and is based on working well together, early impressions may be important, even to the point of being a consideration in acceptance for publication."

HAMPTON ROADS PUBLISHING CO., INC.

665 Third St., Suite 400, San Francisco CA 94107. E-mail: submissions@hrpub.com. E-mail: submissions@redwheelweiser.com. Website: www.hrpub.com. **Contact:** Ms. Pat Bryce, Acquisitions Editor. Estab. 1989. Publishes hardcover and trade paperback originals. Publishes and distributes hardcover and paperback originals on subjects including metaphysics, health, complementary medicine, visionary fiction, and other related topics. **Publishes 35-40 titles/year. 1,000 queries received/year. 1,500 mss received/year. 50% of books from first-time authors. 70% from unagented writers. Pays royalty. Pays $1,000-50,000 advance.** Publishes book 1 year after acceptance of ms. Accepts simultaneous submissions. Responds in 2-4 months to queries. Responds in 1 month to proposals. Responds in 6-12 months to manuscripts. Guidelines available online.

"Please know that we only publish a handful of books every year, and that we pass on many well written, important works, simply because we cannot publish them all. We review each and every proposal very carefully. However, due to the volume of inquiries, we cannot respond to them all individually. Please give us 30 days to review your proposal. If you do not hear back from us within that time, this means we have decided to pursue other book ideas that we feel fit better within our plan."

☞ Our reason for being is to impact, uplift, and contribute to positive change in the world. We publish books that will enrich and empower the evolving consciousness of mankind. Though we are not necessarily limited in scope, we are most interested in manuscripts on the following subjects: Body/Mind/Spirit, Health and Healing, Self-Help. Please be advised that at the moment we are not accepting: Fiction or Novelized material that does not pertain to body/mind/spirit, Channeled writing." "

NONFICTION Subjects include New Age, spirituality. Query with SASE. Submit synopsis, SASE. No longer accepting electronic submissions. Reviews artwork/photos. Send photocopies.

FICTION Subjects include literary, spiritual, Visionary fiction, past-life fiction based on actual memories. Fiction should have 1 or more of the following themes: spiritual, inspirational, metaphysical, i.e., past-life recall, out-of-body experiences, near-death experience, paranormal. Query with SASE. Submit outline, 2 sample chapters, clips. Submit complete ms.

HANCOCK HOUSE PUBLISHERS

Hancock Wildlife Foundation, 1431 Harrison Ave., Blaine WA 98230-5005. (604)538-1114. Fax: (604)538-2262. E-mail: karen@hancockwildlife.org. Website: www.hancockwildlife.org. **Contact:** David Hancock. Estab. 1971. Publishes hardcover and trade paperback originals and reprints. **Publishes 12-20 titles/year. 50% of books from first-time authors. 90% from unagented writers. Pays 10% royalty.** Publishes book up to 1 year after acceptance of ms. Accepts simultaneous submissions. Book catalog available free. Guidelines available online.

☞ Hancock House Publishers is the largest North American publisher of wildlife and Native Indian titles. We also cover Pacific Northwest, fishing, history, Canadiana, biographies. We are seeking agriculture, natural history, animal husbandry, conservation, and popular science titles with a regional (Pacific Northwest), na-

tional, or international focus. Currently emphasizing nonfiction wildlife, cryptozoology, guide books, native history, biography, fishing."

NONFICTION Subjects include agriculture, animals, ethnic, history, horticulture, nature, environment, regional. Centered around Pacific Northwest, local history, nature guide books, international ornithology, and Native Americans. Submit proposal package, outline, 3 sample chapters, selling points, SASE. Reviews artwork/photos. Send photocopies.

HANSER PUBLICATIONS

6915 Valley Ave., Cincinnati OH 45244. (513)527-8800; (800)950-8977. Fax: (513)527-8801. E-mail: info@hanserpublications.com. Website: www.hanserpublications.com. **Contact:** Development Editor. Estab. 1993. Publishes hardcover and paperback originals, and digital educational and training programs. **Publishes 10-15 titles/year. 100 queries received/year. 10-20 mss received/year. 50% of books from first-time authors. 100% from unagented writers.** Publishes book 10 months after acceptance of ms. Accepts simultaneous submissions. Responds in 2 weeks to queries. Responds in 1 month to proposals and manuscripts. Book catalog available free. Guidelines available online.

◯ "Hanser Publications is currently seeking technical experts with strong writing skills to author training and reference books and related products focused on various aspects of the manufacturing industry. Our goal is to provide manufacturing professionals with insightful, easy-to-reference information, and to educate and prepare students for technical careers through accessible, concise training manuals. Do your publishing ideas match this goal? If so, we'd like to hear from you. Submit your detailed product proposals, resume of credentials, and a brief writing sample to: Development Editor, Prospective Authors."

☞ Hanser Publications publishes books and electronic media for the manufacturing (both metalworking and plastics) industries. Publications range from basic training materials to advanced reference books."

NONFICTION "We publish how-to texts, references, technical books, and computer-based learning materials for the manufacturing industries. Titles include award-winning management books, encyclopedic references, and leading references." Submit outline, sample chapters, resume, preface, and comparison to competing or similar titles.

TIPS "E-mail submissions speed up response time."

ⒶⓄ HARCOURT, INC., TRADE DIVISION

Imprint of Houghton Mifflin Harcourt Book Group, 215 Park Ave. S., New York NY 10003. Website: www.harcourtbooks.com. Publishes hardcover and trade paperback originals and trade paperback reprints. **Publishes 120 titles/year. 5% of books from first-time authors. 5% from unagented writers. Pays 6-15% royalty on retail price. Pays $2,000 minimum advance.** Accepts simultaneous submissions. Book catalog for 9×12 envelope and first-class stamps. Guidelines available online.

NONFICTION *No unsolicited mss.* Agented submissions only.

FICTION Agented submissions only.

Ⓐ HARPERBUSINESS

Imprint of HarperCollins General Books Group, 10 E. 53rd St., New York NY 10022. (212)207-7000. Website: www.harpercollins.com. Estab. 1991. Publishes hardcover, trade paperback originals and reprints. **Pays royalty on retail price. Pays advance.** Accepts simultaneous submissions.

⬭ "The gold standard of business book publishing for 50 years, Harper Business brings you innovative, authoritative, and creative works from world-class thinkers. Building upon this rich legacy of paradigm-shifting books, Harper Business authors continue to help readers see the future and to lead and live successfully."

⛏ HarperBusiness publishes the inside story on ideas that will shape business practices with cutting-edge information and visionary concepts.

NONFICTION Subjects include business, economics, Marketing subjects. We don't publish how-to, textbooks or things for academic market; no reference (tax or mortgage guides), our reference department does that. Proposals need to be top notch. We tend not to publish people who have no business standing. Must have business credentials. Agented submissions only.

ⒶⓄ HARPERCOLLINS CHILDREN'S BOOKS GROUP

Imprint of HarperCollins Children's Books Group, 10 East 53rd St., New York NY 10022. (212)207-7000. Website: www.harperchildrens.com. **Contact:** Jennifer Deason. Publishes hardcover and paperback originals.

IMPRINTS Amistad; Julie Andrews Collection; Avon; Balzer and Bray; Greenwillow Books; HarperAudio; HarperCollins Children's Books; HarperFestival; HarperTempest; Rayo; Katherine Tegen Books.

⛏ *No unsolicited mss and/or unagented mss or queries.* The volume of these submissions is so large that we cannot give them the attention they deserve. Such submissions will not be reviewed or returned."

NONFICTION *No unsolicited mss or queries.* Agented submissions only.

FICTION Subjects include picture books, young adult, chapter books, middle grade, early readers. Agented submissions only. *No unsolicited mss or queries.*

HARVARD BUSINESS REVIEW PRESS

Imprint of Harvard Business School Publishing Corp., 60 Harvard Way, Boston MA 02163. (617)783-7400. Fax: (617)783-7489. E-mail: cschinke@harvardbusiness.org. Website: www.hbr.org. **Contact:** Courtney Schinke, Editorial Coordinator. Estab. 1984. Publishes hardcover originals and several paperback series. **Publishes 40-50 titles/year. Pays escalating royalty on retail price. Advances vary depending on author and market for the book.** Accepts simultaneous submissions. Responds in 1 month to proposals and manuscripts. Book catalog available online. Guidelines available online.

⛏ The Harvard Business Review Press publishes books for senior and general managers and business scholars. Harvard Business Review Press is the source of the most influential ideas and conversations that shape business worldwide.

NONFICTION Submit proposal package, outline, sample chapters.

TIPS "We do not publish books on real estate, personal finance or business parables."

THE HARVARD COMMON PRESS

535 Albany St., 5th Floor, Boston MA 02118-2500. (617)423-5803. Fax: (617)695-9794. E-mail: info@harvardpress.com. E-mail: editorial@harvardcommonpress.com. Website: www.harvardcommonpress.com. **Contact:** Valerie Cimino, executive editor. Estab. 1976. Publishes hardcover and trade paperback originals and reprints. **Publishes 16 titles/year. 20% of books from first-time authors. 40% from unagented writers. Pays royalty. Pays average $2,500-10,000 advance.** Pub-

lishes book 1 year after acceptance of ms. Accepts simultaneous submissions. Responds in 2 months to queries. Book catalog for 9×12 envelope and 3 first-class stamps. Guidelines for #10 SASE or online.

IMPRINTS Gambit Books.

8—➤ We want strong, practical books that help people gain control over a particular area of their lives. Currently emphasizing cooking, child care/parenting, health. De-emphasizing general instructional books, travel."

NONFICTION Subjects include child guidance, cooking, foods, nutrition, health, medicine. A large percentage of our list is made up of books about cooking, child care, and parenting; in these areas we are looking for authors who are knowledgeable, if not experts, and who can offer a different approach to the subject. We are open to good nonfiction proposals that show evidence of strong organization and writing, and clearly demonstrate a need in the marketplace. First-time authors are welcome. Submit outline. Potential authors may also submit a query letter or e-mail of no more than 300 words, rather than a full proposal; if interested, we will ask to see a proposal. Queries and questions may be sent via e-mail. We will not consider e-mail attachments containing proposals. No phone calls, please.

TIPS "We are demanding about the quality of proposals; in addition to strong writing skills and thorough knowledge of the subject matter, we require a detailed analysis of the competition."

🅐⊘ HARVEST HOUSE PUBLISHERS

990 Owen Loop N., Eugene OR 97402. (541)343-0123. Fax: (541)302-0731. Website: www.harvesthousepublishers.com. Estab. 1974. Publishes hardcover, trade paperback, and mass market paperback originals and reprints. **Publishes 160 titles/year. 1,500 queries received/year. 1,000 mss received/year. 1% of books from first-time authors. Pays royalty.**

NONFICTION Subjects include anthropology, archeology, business, economics, child guidance, health, medicine, money, finance, religion, women's issues, women's studies, Bible studies. *No unsolicited mss.*

FICTION *No unsolicited mss, proposals, or artwork.* Agented submissions only.

TIPS "For first time/nonpublished authors we suggest building their literary résumé by submitting to magazines, or perhaps accruing book contributions."

HASTINGS HOUSE/DAYTRIPS PUBLISHERS

LINI LLC, P.O. Box 908, Winter Park FL 32790-0908. (407)339-3600; (800)206-7822. Fax: (407)339-5900. E-mail: hastingshousebooks.com. Website: www.hastingshousebooks.com. **Contact:** Earl Steinbicker, senior travel editor (edits Daytrips Series). Publishes trade paperback originals and reprints. **Publishes 20 titles/year. 600 queries received/year. 900 mss received/year. 10% of books from first-time authors. 40% from unagented writers.** Publishes book 6-10 months after acceptance of ms. Responds in 2 months to queries.

○ "We are primarily focused on expanding our Daytrips Travel Series (facts/guide) nationally and internationally. Currently de-emphasizing all other subjects."

NONFICTION Subjects include travel. Submit outline. Query.

HATALA GEROPRODUCTS

P.O. Box 42, Greentop MO 63546. E-mail: editor@geroproducts.com. Website: www.geroproducts.com. **Contact:** Mark Hatala, Ph.D., president (psychology, travel, relationships). Estab. 2002. Publishes hardcover and trade paperback originals. **Publishes 3-4 titles/year. 120 queries received/year. 50 mss received/year. 30% of books from first-time authors. 80% from unagented writers. Pays 5-7½% royalty on retail price. Pays $250-500 advance.** Publishes book 18 months after acceptance of ms. Accepts simultaneous submissions. Responds in 1 month to queries. Responds in 2 months to proposals and manuscripts. Guidelines available online.

NONFICTION Subjects include health, medicine, psychology, sex, travel, seniors, advice. Books should be of interest to older (60+) adults. Romance, relationships, advice, travel, how-to books are most appropriate. All books are larger print; so manuscripts should be around 50,000 words. Query with SASE. Submit proposal package, outline, 3 sample chapters, SASE.

TIPS "Audience is men and women (but particularly women) over age 60. Books need to be pertinent to the lives of older Americans. No memoirs or poetry."

HAWK PUBLISHING GROUP

7107 S. Yale Ave., #345, Tulsa OK 74136. (918)492-3677. Fax: (918)492-2120. Website: www.hawkpublishing.com. Estab. 1999. Publishes hardcover and trade paperback originals. **Publishes 6-8 titles/year. 25% of** books from first-time authors. **50% from unagented writers. Pays royalty.** Publishes book 1-2 years after acceptance of ms. Accepts simultaneous submissions. Guidelines available online.

IMPRINTS Art Works, Earth Works, Paper Works

○ "Hawk Publishing is a royalty paying small press publisher of nonfiction instructional pamphlets, guides, cards, books and fine art photographic posters by some of today's most critically acclaimed artists, craftsmen, experts and hobbyists. We'll have three main imprints to start.", "We will print various lengths from pamphlet or booklet form to actual books. We may also offer some manuscripts in ebook formats, where appropriate. Currently, manuscripts with a large number of graphics do not readily lend themselves to ebook formats, so we will make decisions on ebook offerings on a case by case basis."

⚷ Please visit our website and read the submission guidelines before sending anything to us. The best way to learn what might interest us is to visit the website, read the information there, look at the books, and perhaps even read a few of them."

NONFICTION "Looking for subjects of broad appeal and interest."

FICTION Looking for good books of all kinds. Not interested in juvenile, poetry, or short story collections. Does not want childrens or young adult books. "Submissions will not be returned, so send only copies. No SASE. No submissions by e-mail or by 'cerified mail' or any other service that requires a signature." Replies only if interested. If you have not heard from us within 3 months after the receipt of your submission, you may safely assume that we were not able to find a place for it in our list."

TIPS "Prepare a professional submission and follow the guidelines. The simple things really do count; use 12 pt. pitch with 1-inch margins and only send what is requested."

Ⓐ HAY HOUSE, INC.

P.O. Box 5100, Carlsbad CA 92018-5100. (760)431-7695. Fax: (760)431-6948. E-mail: editorial@hayhouse.com. Website: www.hayhouse.com. **Contact:** East-coast acquisitions: Patty Gift (pgift@hayhouse.com), West-coast acquisitions: Alex Freemon (afreemon@hayhouse.com). Estab. 1985. Publishes hardcover and trade paperback originals. **Publishes 50 titles/year. Pays standard royalty.** Accepts simultaneous submissions. Guidelines available online.

IMPRINTS Hay House Lifestyles; New Beginnings Press; SmileyBooks.

⚷ We publish books, audios, and videos that help heal the planet."

NONFICTION Subjects include cooking, foods, nutrition, education, health, medicine, money, finance, nature, environment, New Age, philosophy, psychology, sociology, women's issues, women's studies, mind/body/spirit. "Hay House is interested in a variety of subjects as long as they have a positive self-help slant to them. No poetry, children's books, or negative concepts that are not conducive to helping/healing ourselves or our planet." Accepts e-mail submissions from agents

TIPS "Our audience is concerned with our planet, the healing properties of love, and general self-help principles. If I were a writer trying to market a book today, I would research the market thoroughly to make sure there weren't already too many books on the subject I was interested in writing about. Then I would make sure I had a unique slant on my idea. Simultaneous submissions from agents must include SASE's."

HEALTH COMMUNICATIONS, INC.

3201 SW 15th St., Deerfield Beach FL 33442. (954)360-0909, ext. 232. Fax: (954)360-0034. E-mail: christianb@hcibooks.com. Website: www.hciworldwide.com. **Contact:** Christian Blonshine. Estab. 1976. Publishes hardcover and trade paperback nonfiction only. **Publishes 60 titles/year.** Responds in 3-6 months to queries and proposals. Guidelines available online.

⚷ We are the Life Issues Publisher. Health Communications, Inc., strives to help people grow and improve their lives, from physical and emotional health to finances and interpersonal relationships."

NONFICTION Subjects include child guidance, health, parenting, psychology, women's issues, women's studies, young adult, Self-help.

HEALTH PROFESSIONS PRESS

P.O. Box 10624, Baltimore MD 21285-0624. (410)337-9585. Fax: (410)337-8539. E-mail: mmagnus@healthpropress.com. Website: www.healthpropress.com. **Contact:** Mary Magnus, director of publications (aging, long-term care, health administration). Publishes hardcover and trade paperback originals. **Publishes 6-8 titles/year. 70 queries received/year. 12 mss re-**

ceived/year. **50% of books from first-time authors. 100% from unagented writers. Pays 8-18% royalty on wholesale price.** Publishes book 10 months after acceptance of ms. Accepts simultaneous submissions. Responds in 1 month to queries. Responds in 3 months to proposals. Responds in 4 months to manuscripts. Book catalog free or online. Guidelines available online.

⚷☛ We are a specialty publisher. Our primary audiences are professionals, students, and educated consumers interested in topics related to aging and eldercare."

NONFICTION Subjects include health, medicine, psychology. Query with SASE. Submit proposal package, outline, resume, 1-2 sample chapters, cover letter.

WILLIAM S. HEIN & CO., INC.

1285 Main St., Buffalo NY 14209-1987. (716)882-2600. Fax: (716)883-8100. E-mail: mail@wshein.com. Website: www.wshein.com. **Contact:** Sheila Jarrett, publications manager. Estab. 1961. **Publishes 30 titles/year. 80 queries received/year. 40 mss received/year. 30% of books from first-time authors. 100% from unagented writers. Pays 10-20% royalty on net price.** Publishes book 9 months after acceptance of ms. Accepts simultaneous submissions. Responds in 3 months to queries. Book catalog available online. Guidelines: send e-mail for info and mss proposal form.

⚷☛ William S. Hein & Co. publishes reference books for law librarians, legal researchers, and those interested in legal writing. Currently emphasizing legal research, legal writing, and legal education."

NONFICTION Subjects include education, government, politics, women's issues, world affairs, legislative histories.

❧ HEINEMANN EDUCATIONAL PUBLISHERS

P.O. Box 781940, Sandton 2146, South Africa. (27)(11)322-8600. Fax: 086 687 7822. E-mail: customerliaison@heinemann.co.za. Website: www.heinemann.co.za.

⚷☛ Interested in textbooks for primary schools, literature and textbooks for secondary schools, and technical publishing for colleges/universities.

NONFICTION Subjects include animals, art, architecture, business, economics, education, ethnic,

health, medicine, history, humanities, language, literature, music, dance, psychology, regional, religion, science, social sciences, sports, math, engineering, management, nursing, marketing.

HENDRICK-LONG PUBLISHING CO., INC.

10635 Tower Oaks, Suite D, Houston TX 77070. 832-912-READ. Fax: (832)912-7353. E-mail: hendricklong@att.net. Website: hendricklongpublishing.com. **Contact:** Vilma Long. Estab. 1969. Publishes hardcover and trade paperback originals and hardcover reprints. **Publishes 4 titles/year. 90% from unagented writers. Pays royalty on selling price. Pays advance.** Publishes book 18 months after acceptance of ms. Responds in 3 months to queries. Book catalog for 8½×11 or 9×12 SASE with 4 first-class stamps. Guidelines available online.

⚷☛ Hendrick-Long publishes historical fiction and nonfiction about Texas and the Southwest for children and young adults."

NONFICTION Subjects include history, regional. Subject must be Texas related; other subjects cannot be considered. We are particularly interested in material from educators that can be used in the classroom as workbooks, math, science, history with a Texas theme or twist. Query, or submit outline and 2 sample chapters. Reviews artwork/photos. Send photocopies.

FICTION Subjects include juvenile, young adult. Query with SASE. Submit outline, clips, 2 sample chapters.

HENDRICKSON PUBLISHERS, INC.

140 Summit St., P.O. Box 3473, Peabody MA 01961-3473. Fax: (978)573-8276. E-mail: editorial@hendrickson.com; orders@hendrickson.com. Website: www.hendrickson.com. **Contact:** Shirley Decker-Lucke, editorial director. Estab. 1983. Publishes trade reprints, bibles, and scholarly material in the areas of New Testament; Hebrew Bible; religion and culture; patristics; Judaism; and practical, historical, and Biblical theology. **Publishes 35 titles/year. 800 queries received/year. 10% of books from first-time authors. 90% from unagented writers.** Publishes book an average of 1 year after acceptance of ms. Responds in 3-4 months to queries. Book catalog and ms guidelines for #10 SASE.

⚷☛ Hendrickson is an academic publisher of books that give insight into Bible understanding (academically) and encourage spiritual growth (popular trade). Currently emphasizing Biblical helps and reference, ministerial helps, and Biblical studies."

NONFICTION Subjects include religion. "No longer accepting unsolicited manuscripts or book proposals. Cannot return material sent or respond to all queries." Submit outline, sample chapters, and CV.

HERITAGE BOOKS, INC.

100 Railroad Ave., #104, Westminster MD 21157. (866)282-2689. E-mail: Info@HeritageBooks.com. E-mail: Submissions@HeritageBooks.com. Website: www.heritagebooks.com. **Contact:** Editorial Director. Estab. 1978. Publishes hardcover and paperback originals and reprints. **Publishes 200 titles/year. 25% of books from first-time authors. 100% from unagented writers. Pays 10% royalty on list price** Accepts simultaneous submissions. Responds in 3 months to queries. Book catalog and ms guidelines free.

- Our goal is to celebrate life by exploring all aspects of American life: settlement, development, wars, and other significant events, including family histories, memoirs, etc. Currently emphasizing early American life, early wars and conflicts, ethnic studies."

NONFICTION Subjects include Americana, ethnic, origins and research guides, history, memoirs, military, war, regional, history. Query with SASE. Submit outline via e-mail. Reviews artwork/photos.

TIPS "The quality of the book is of prime importance; next is its relevance to our fields of interest."

HERITAGE HOUSE PUBLISHING CO., LTD.

#340-1105 Pandora Ave., Victoria BC V8V 3P9, Canada. 250-360-0829. E-mail: editorial@heritagehouse.ca. Website: www.heritagehouse.ca. **Contact:** Vivian Sinclair, Managing Editor. Publishes mostly trade paperback and some hardcovers. **Publishes 25-30 titles/year. 200 queries received/year. 100 mss received/year. 50% of books from first-time authors. 90% from unagented writers. Pays 12-15% royalty on net proceeds. Advances are rarely paid.** Publishes book Usually 1-2 years after acceptance of ms. Accepts simultaneous submissions. Responds in 6 months to queries. Catalogue and guidelines available online.

- Heritage House publishes books that celebrate the historical and cultural heritage of Canada, particularly Western Canada and, to an extent, the Pacific Northwest. We also publish some titles of national interest and a series of books aimed at young and casual readers,

called *Amazing Stories*. We accept simultaneous submissions, but indicate on your query that it is a simultaneous submission."

NONFICTION Subjects include contemporary culture, history, regional, sociology, adventure. Writers should include a sample of their writing, an overview sample of photos or illustrations to support the text, and a brief letter describing who they are writing for. Query with SASE. Include synopsis, outline, 2-3 sample chapters with indication of illustrative material available, and marketing strategy.

TIPS "Our books appeal to residents of and visitors to the northwest quadrant of the continent. We're looking for good stories and good storytellers. We focus on work by Canadian authors."

HEYDAY BOOKS

Acquisitions Editor, Box 9145, Berkeley CA 94709-9145. Fax: (510)549-1889. E-mail: heyday@heydaybooks.com. Website: www.heydaybooks.com. **Contact:** Gayle Wattawa, acquisitions editor. Estab. 1974. Publishes hardcover originals, trade paperback originals and reprints. **Publishes 12-15 titles/year. 50% of books from first-time authors. 90% from unagented writers. Pays 8% royalty on net price.** Publishes book 10 months after acceptance of ms. Responds in 2 months to queries and manuscripts. Book catalog for 7×9 SAE with 3 first-class stamps.

- "Heyday is a small publisher with a focus on California and the West. We publish books on cultural and natural history, especially native history, and California art and literature. Take a look at our catalog for a better idea of the kinds of books we publish."

- Heyday Books publishes nonfiction books and literary anthologies with a strong California focus. We publish books about Native Americans, natural history, history, literature, and recreation, with a strong California focus."

NONFICTION Subjects include Americana, ethnic, history, nature, environment, recreation, regional, travel. Books about California only. Query with outline and synopsis. "Query or proposal by traditional post. Include a cover letter introducing yourself and your qualifications, a brief description of your project, a table of contents and list of illustrations, notes on the market you are trying to reach and why your book will appeal to them, a sample chapter, and a SASE if you would like us to return these materials to you." Reviews artwork/photos.

HIBBARD PUBLISHERS

P.O. Box 73182, Lynnwood Ridge 0040, South Africa. (27)(12)804-3990. Fax: (27)(12)804-1240. E-mail: publisher@hibbard.co.za;tersia@hibbard.co.za. Website: www.hibbard.co.za.

IMPRINTS Bard (literature/academic); Thandi Art Press (African language literature); Galactic (math workbooks/poster series); Manx (fiction); Manx Juvenile (children's); GSAT (arts & culture); Five Star Study Guides.

Our mission is to take the products of our authors' dreams and efforts, and to transform and shape these into the best possible product for end users, i.e. readers, teachers, learners and their parents."

TIPS "When the pressure is on, we make use of the services of some of the best free-lancers in various fields."

HIGHLAND PRESS PUBLISHING

P.O. Box 2292, High Springs FL 32655. (386) 454-3927. Fax: (386) 454-3927. E-mail: The.Highland.Press@gmail.com. E-mail: Submissions.hp@gmail.com. Website: www.highlandpress.org. **Contact:** Leanne Burroughs, CEO (fiction); she will forward all mss to appropriate editor. Estab. 2005. Paperback originals. **Publishes 30/year titles/year. 90% from unagented writers. Pays royalties 7.5-8%** Publishes book within 18 months after acceptance of ms. Accepts simultaneous submissions. Responds in 8 weeks to queries; responds in 3-12 months to mss. Catalog and guidelines available online at website.

FICTION Send query letter. Query with outline/synopsis and sample chapters. Accepts queries by snail mail, e-mail. Include estimated word count, target market.

TIPS Special interests: Children's ms must come with illustrator. "We will always be looking for good historical manuscripts. In addition, we are actively seeking inspirational romances and Regency period romances." Numerous romance anthologies are planned. Topics and word count are posted on the Website. Writers should query with their proposal. After the submission deadline has passed, editors select the stories., "I don't publish based on industry trends. We buy what we like and what we believe readers are looking for. However, often this proves to be the genres and time-periods larger publishers are not currently interested in. Be professional at all times. Present your manuscript in the best possible light. Be sure you have run spell check and that the manuscript has been vetted by at least one critique partner, preferably more. Many times we receive manuscripts that have wonderful stories involved, but would take far too much time to edit to make it marketable."

HIGH TIDE PRESS

2081 Calistoga Dr., Suite 2N, New Lenox IL 60451. (815)717-3780. Website: www.hightidepress.com. **Contact:** Monica Regan, senior editor. Estab. 1995. Publishes hardcover and trade paperback originals. **Publishes 2-3 titles/year. 20 queries received/year. 3 mss received/year. 50% of books from first-time authors. 100% from unagented writers. Pays royalty. Percentages vary.** Publishes book Publishes book up to 12 months after acceptance. after acceptance of ms. Accepts simultaneous submissions. Responds in 0-6 months to queries and proposals. Book catalog available online. Guidelines available online at website http://www.hightidepress.com/main/submissions.php.

High Tide Press is a leading provider of resources for disability and nonprofit professionals - publications and training materials on intellectual/developmental disabilities, behavioral health, and nonprofit management."

NONFICTION Subjects include business, economics, education, health, medicine, how-to, human services, nonprofit management, psychology, reference, All of these topics as they relate to developmental, learning and intellectual disabilities, behavioral health, and human services management. "We do not publish personal stories. We produce materials for direct support staff, managers and professionals in the fields of disabilities and human services, as well as educators." Query via e-mail.

TIPS "Our readers are leaders and managers, mostly in the field of human services, and especially those who serve persons with intellectual disabilities or behavioral health needs."

HIPPOPOTAMUS PRESS

22 Whitewell Rd., Frome Somerset BA11 4EL, UK. (44)(173)466-6653. E-mail: rjhippopress@aol.com. **Contact:** R. John, editor; M. Pargitter (poetry); Anna Martin (translation). Estab. 1974. Publishes hardcover and trade paperback originals. **Publishes 6-12 titles/year. 90% of books from first-time authors. 90% from unagented writers. Pays 7 ½-10% royalty on retail price. Pays ad-**

vance. Publishes book 10 months after acceptance of ms. Accepts simultaneous submissions. Responds in 1 month to queries. Book catalog available free.

8→ Hippopotamus Press publishes first, full collections of verse by those well represented in the mainstream poetry magazines of the English-speaking world."

NONFICTION Subjects include language, literature, translation. Query with SASE. Submit complete ms.

POETRY "Read one of our authors—Poets often make the mistake of submitting poetry without knowing the type of verse we publish." Query and submit complete ms.

TIPS "We publish books for a literate audience. We have a strong link to the Modernist tradition. Read what we publish."

HISTORY PUBLISHING COMPANY, INC.

P.O. Box 700, Palisades NY 10964. Fax: (845)231-6167. E-mail: djb@historypublishingco.com. Website: www. historypublishingco.com. **Contact:** Don Bracken, Editorial Director. Estab. 2001. Publishes hardcover and trade paperback originals and electronic books. **Publishes 20 titles/year. 50% of books from first-time authors. 75% from unagented writers. Pays 7-10% royalty on wholesale list price. Does not pay advances to unpublished authors.** Publishes book 1 year after acceptance of ms. Responds in 2 months to full manuscripts. Guidelines on website.

NONFICTION Subjects include Nonfiction: Americana, business, economics, contemporary culture, creative nonfiction, government, politics, history, military, war, social sciences, sociology, world affairs. Query with SASE. Submit proposal package, outline, 3 sample chapters. Submit complete ms. Reviews artwork/photos. Send photocopies.

TIPS "We focus on an audience interested in the events that shaped the world we live in and the events of today that continue to shape that world. Focus on interesting and serious events that will appeal to the contemporary reader who likes easy-to-read history that flows from one page to the next."

HIS WORK CHRISTIAN PUBLISHING

P.O. Box 563, Ward Cove AK 99928. (206)274-8474. Fax: (614)388-0664 eFax. E-mail: hiswork@hiswork-pub.com. Website: www.hisworkpub.com. **Contact:** Angela J. Perez, acquisitions editor. Estab. 2005. Publishes trade paperback and electronic originals and reprints; also, hardcover originals. **Publishes 3-5 titles/**

year. 100% from unagented writers. Pays 10-20% royalty on wholesale price. Publishes book 12-24 months after acceptance of ms. Accepts simultaneous submissions. Responds in 1-3 months to queries. Responds in 1-2 months to requested manuscripts. Book catalog available online. "Guidelines available online and updated regularly. Please check these before submitting to see what we are looking for.".

NONFICTION Subjects include child guidance, cooking, foods, nutrition, creative nonfiction, gardening, health, medicine, history, hobbies, language, literature, memoirs, money, finance, music, dance, photography, recreation, religion, sports. "We only accept Christian material or material that does not go against Christian standards. This is a very strict policy that we enforce. Please keep this in mind before deciding to submit your work to us." Submit query/proposal package, 3 sample chapters, clips. Reviews artwork/photos. Send photocopies.

FICTION Subjects include humor, juvenile, mystery, picture books, poetry, religious, short story collections, sports, suspense, young adult. Submit query/proposal package, 3 sample chapters, clips.

POETRY "We only plan to publish 1-2 titles per year in poetry. Send us only your best work." Submit 15 sample poems.

TIPS "Audience is children and adults who are looking for the entertainment and relaxation you can only get from jumping into a good book. Submit only your best work to us. Submit only in the genres we are interested in publishing. Do not submit work that is not suitable for a Christian audience."

➕Ⓐ HOPEWELL PUBLICATIONS

P.O. Box 11, Titusville NJ 08560. Website: www.hope-pubs.com. **Contact:** E. Martin, publisher. Estab. 2002. Format publishes in hardcover, trade paperback, & electronic originals; trade paperback & electronic reprints. **Publishes 20-30 titles/year. Receives 2,000 queries/year; 500 mss/year. 25% of books from first-time authors. 75% from unagented writers. Pays royalty on retail price.** Publishes book 6-12 months after acceptance of ms. Accepts simultaneous submissions. Responds in 3 months on queries; 6 months on proposals; 9 months on mss. Catalog online at website. Guidelines online at website (e-mail query guidelines).

IMPRINTS Egress Books, Legacy Classics.

○ "Hopewell Publications specializes in classic reprints—books with proven sales records that have gone out of print—and the occasional new title of interest. Our catalog spans from one to sixty years of publication history. We print fiction and nonfiction, and we accept agented and unagented materials. Books are only accepted after a formal e-mail query. Please follow our online query guidelines. While it may take months for us to respond, your query will be read, and if we are interested, we will contact you."

NONFICTION , All nonfiction subjects acceptable. Query online using our online guidelines.

FICTION Subjects include adventure, contemporary, experimental, fantasy, gay, historical, humor, juvenile, literary, mainstream, mystery, plays, short story collections, spiritual, suspense, young adult, All fiction subjects acceptable. Query online using our online guidelines.

HOW BOOKS

Imprint of F+W Media, Inc., 4700 E. Galbraith Rd., Cincinnati OH 45236. (513)531-2690. E-mail: megan.patrick@fwmedia.com. Website: www.howdesign.com. **Contact:** Megan Patrick, acquisitions editor. Estab. 1985. Publishes hardcover and trade paperback originals. **Publishes 15 titles/year. 50 queries received/year. 5 mss received/year. 50% of books from first-time authors. 50% from unagented writers. Pays 10% royalty on wholesale price. Pays $2,000-6,000 advance.** Publishes book 18-24 months after acceptance of ms. Accepts simultaneous submissions. Responds in 1 month to queries and proposals. Responds in 3 months to manuscripts. Book catalog available online. Guidelines available online.

NONFICTION Needs graphic design, creativity, pop culture. "We look for material that reflects the cutting edge of trends, graphic design, and culture. Nearly all HOW Books are intensely visual, and authors must be able to create or supply art/illustration for their books." Query with SASE. Submit proposal package, outline, 1 sample chapter, sample art or sample design. Reviews artwork/photos. Send photocopies and PDF's (if submitting electronically).

TIPS "Audience comprised of graphic designers. Your art, design, or concept."

HQN BOOKS

Imprint of Harlequin, 233 Broadway, Suite 1001, New York NY 10279. Website: e.harlequin.com; www.hqn.com. **Contact:** Tracy Farrell, executive editor. Publishes hardcover, trade paperback, and mass market paperback originals. **Pays royalty. Pays advance.**

○ "HQN publishes romance in all subgenres - historical, contemporary, romantic suspense, paranormal - as long as the story's central focus is romance. Prospective authors can familiarize themselves with the wide range of books we publish by reading work by some of our current authors. These include Susan Andersen, Beth Ciotta, Nicola Cornick, Victoria Dahl, Susan Grant, Kristan Higgins, Susan Mallery, Kasey Michaels, Linda Lael Miller, Diana Palmer, Carly Phillips, Rosemary Rogers, Meryl Sawyer, Gena Showalter, Christina Skye, and Bertrice Small. The imprint is looking for a wide range of authors from known romance stars to first-time authors. At the moment, we are accepting only agented submissions - unagented authors may send a query letter to determine if their project suits our needs. Please send your projects to our New York Editorial Office."

FICTION Subjects include romance, contemporary and historical. Accepts unagented material. Length: 90,000 words.

HUNTER HOUSE PUBLISHERS

P.O. Box 2914, 1515 ½ Park St., Alameda CA 94501-0914. (510)865-5282. E-mail: ordering@hunterhouse.com. E-mail: acquisitions@hunterhouse.com. Website: www.hunterhouse.com. **Contact:** Jeanne Brondino, acquisitions editor; Kiran S. Rana, publisher. Estab. 1978. Publishes trade paperback originals and reprints. **Publishes 10-12 titles/year. 300 queries received/year. 100 mss received/year. 50% of books from first-time authors. 90% from unagented writers. Pays 10-20% royalty on net receipts Pays $500-3,000 advance.** Publishes book 18 months after acceptance of ms. Accepts simultaneous submissions. Responds in 2 months to queries. Responds in 3 months to proposals. Book catalog available online at website. Guidelines available online and by e-mail request.

○━ Hunter House publishes health books (especially women's health), self-help health, sexuality and couple relationships, violence prevention and intervention. De-emphasizing reference, self-help psychology.

NONFICTION Subjects include child guidance, community, health, medicine, nutrition, parenting, psychology, sex, women's issues, self-help, women's health, fitness, relationships, sexuality, personal growth, and violence prevention. Health books (especially women's health) should focus on self-help, health. Family books: Our current focus is sexuality and couple relationships, and alternative lifestyles to high stress. Community topics include violence prevention/violence intervention. We also publish specialized curriculam for counselors and educators in the areas of violence prevention and trauma in children. We do not publish fiction, autobiography, or general children's books, so those types of works get returned right away. Query with proposal package, including synopsis, TOC, and chapter outline, two sample chapters, target audience information, competition, and what distinguishes the book. We look for computer printouts of good quality or e-mail. Please inform us if a manuscript is available on computer disk (IBM format is preferable). Reviews artwork/photos. Send photocopies. Proposals generally not returned, requested mss returned with SASE. Reviews artwork/photos as part of ms package.

TIPS "Audience is concerned people who are looking to educate themselves and their community about real-life issues that affect them. Please send as much information as possible about who your audience is, how your book addresses their needs, and how you reach that audience in your ongoing work." , "Include a marketing plan. Explain how you will help us market your book. Have a Facebook account, Twitter, or a blog. List any professional organization to which you are a member."

IBEX PUBLISHERS

P.O. Box 30087, Bethesda MD 20824. (301)718-8188. Fax: (301)907-8707. E-mail: info@ibexpub.com. Website: www.ibexpublishers.com. Estab. 1979. Publishes hardcover and trade paperback originals and reprints. **Publishes 10-12 titles/year. Payment varies.** Accepts simultaneous submissions. Book catalog available free.

IMPRINTS Iranbooks Press.

➤ IBEX publishes books about Iran and the Middle East and about Persian culture and literature."

NONFICTION Subjects include cooking, foods, nutrition, language, literature. Query with SASE, or submit proposal package, including outline and 2 sample chapters.

POETRY "Translations of Persian poets will be considered."

✚💬 IBIS EDITIONS

P.O. Box 8074, German Colony Jerusalem 91080, Israel. E-mail: iibis@netvision.net.il. Website: www.ibiseditions.com. **Contact:** Peter Cole, editor (poetry). Adina Hoffman, editor (essays and criticism). Estab. 1998.

➤ Publishes Levant-related books of poetry and belletristic prose. The press publishes translations from Hebrew, Arabic, Greek, French, and the other languages of the region. New writing is published, though special attention is paid to overlooked works from the recent and distant past. Ibis aims to make a modest contribution to the literature of this part of the world by drawing together a group of writers and translators whom both politics and market-forces would otherwise keep far apart, or out of print altogether. Ibis is motivated by the belief that literary work, especially when translated into a common language, can serve as an important vehicle for the promotion of understanding between individuals and peoples, and for the discovery of common ground."

ICONOGRAFIX, INC.

1830A Hanley Rd., P.O. Box 446, Hudson WI 54016. (715)381-9755. Fax: (715)381-9756. E-mail: dcfrautschi@iconografixinc.com. Website: www.enthusiastbooks.com. **Contact:** Dylan Frautschi, editorial director. Estab. 1992. Publishes trade paperback originals. **Publishes 24 titles/year. 100 queries received/year. 20 mss received/year. 50% of books from first-time authors. 100% from unagented writers. Pays 8-12% royalty on wholesale price. Pays $1,000-3,000 advance.** Publishes book 1 year after acceptance of ms. Accepts simultaneous submissions. Responds in 1 month to queries. Responds in 3 months to proposals and manuscripts. Book catalog and ms guidelines free.

➤ Iconografix publishes special, historical-interest photographic books for transportation equipment enthusiasts. Currently emphasizing emergency vehicles, buses, trucks, railroads, automobiles, auto racing, construction equipment, snowmobiles."

NONFICTION Subjects include Americana, photos from archives of historic places, objects, people, history, hobbies, military, war, transportation (older photos of specific vehicles). Interested in photo archives. Query with SASE, or submit proposal package, including outline. Reviews artwork/photos. Send photocopies.

IDYLL ARBOR, INC.

39129 264th Ave. SE, Enumclaw WA 98022. (360)825-7797. Fax: (360)825-5670. E-mail: editors@idyllarbor. com. Website: www.idyllarbor.com. **Contact:** Tom Blaschko. Estab. 1984. Publishes hardcover and trade paperback originals, and trade paperback reprints. **Publishes 6 titles/year. 50% of books from first-time authors. 100% from unagented writers. Pays 8-15% royalty on wholesale price or retail price.** Publishes book 1 year after acceptance of ms. Accepts simultaneous submissions. Responds in 1 month to queries. Responds in 2 months to proposals. Responds in 6 months to manuscripts. Book catalog and ms guidelines free.

IMPRINTS Issues Press; Pine Winds Press.

☛ Idyll Arbor publishes practical information on the current state and art of healthcare practice. Currently emphasizing therapies (recreational, aquatic, occupational, music, horticultural), and activity directors in long-term care facilities. Issues Press looks at problems in society from video games to returning veterans and their problems reintegrating into the civilian world. Pine Winds Press publishes books about strange phenomena such as Bigfoot."

NONFICTION Subjects include health, medicine, for therapists, activity directors, psychology, recreational therapy, horticulture (used in long-term care activities or health care therapy). "Idyll Arbor is currently developing a line of books under the imprint Issues Press, which treats emotional issues in a clear-headed manner. The latest books are *Barrier-Free Theatre, Diet Myths BUSTED, and Visits from the Forest People.* Another series of *Personal Health* books explains a condition or a closely related set of medical or psychological conditions. The target audience is the person or the family of the person with the condition. We want to publish a book that explains a condition at the level of de-

tail expected of the average primary care physician so that our readers can address the situation intelligently with specialists. We look for manuscripts from authors with recent clinical experience. Good grounding in theory is required, but practical experience is more important." Query preferred with outline and 1 sample chapter. Reviews artwork/photos. Send photocopies.

TIPS "The books must be useful for the health practitioner who meets face to face with patients or the books must be useful for teaching undergraduate and graduate level classes. We are especially looking for therapists with a solid clinical background to write on their area of expertise."

ILIUM PRESS

2407 S. Sonora Dr., Spokane WA 99037-9011, United States. (509)928-7950. E-mail: contact@iliumpress. com. E-mail: submissions@iliumpress.com. Website: www.iliumpress.com. **Contact:** John Lemon, Owner/editor (literature, epic poetry, how-to). Estab. 2010. Format publishes in trade paperback originals and reprints, electronic originals and reprints. **Publishes 5-10 titles/year. Pays 20%-50% royalties on wholesale price.** Publishes book 6 months after acceptance of ms. Responds in 1 month on queries/proposals and 3 months on manuscripts. Guidelines available on website www.iliumpress.com.

NONFICTION Subjects include contemporary culture, memoirs, music. "Mostly interested in alternative music bio and small business how-to that appeals to urban hipster crowd-DIY music, art, creative work and its promotion." Query with SASE (preferred). Submit proposal package, including outline, 3 sample chapters and SASE.

FICTION Subjects include adventure, erotica, literary, mystery, poetry, poetry in translation, science fiction, noir, gritty mystery; focus on epic narrative poetry; dystopiad sci-fi. "See website for guidelines and preferred styles." Query with SASE. Submit proposal package, including synopsis, 3 sample chapters and SASE.

POETRY "I am primarily interested in epic, narrative book-length poems. See website for details." Query. Submit 3 sample chapters.

TIPS "Read submission guidelines on my website."

IMAGE COMICS

Submissions, c/o Image Comics, 2134 Allston Way, 2nd Floor, Berkeley CA 94704. E-mail: submissions@

imagecomics.com. Website: www.imagecomics.com.
Contact: Eric Stephenson, publisher. Estab. 1992.

☞ Publishes comic books, graphic novels. See this
company's website for detailed guidelines.

IMMEDIUM

P.O. Box 31846, San Francisco CA 94131. (415)452-
8546. Fax: (360)937-6272. E-mail: submissions@im-
medium.com. Website: www.immedium.com. **Contact:** Amy Ma, acquisitions editor. Estab. 2005. Publishes hardcover and trade paperback originals. **Publishes 4 titles/year. 50 queries received/year. 25 mss
received/year. 50% of books from first-time authors.
90% from unagented writers. Pays 5% royalty on
wholesale price. Pays on publication.** Publishes book
24 months after acceptance of ms. Accepts simultaneous submissions. Responds in 1 month to queries.
Responds in 2 months to proposals. Responds in 3
months to mss. Catalog available online. Guidelines
available online.

☞ *Immedium* focuses on publishing eye-catching
children's picture books, Asian American topics, and contemporary arts, popular culture,
and multicultural issues."

NONFICTION Subjects include art, architecture,
multicultural. Query with SASE. Submit proposal
package, outline, 2 sample chapters. Submit complete
ms. Reviews artwork/photos. Send photocopies.

FICTION Subjects include comic books, picture
books. Submit complete ms.

TIPS "Our audience is children and parents. Please
visit our site."

IMPACT BOOKS

Imprint of F+W Media, Inc., 4700 E. Galbraith Rd.,
Cincinnati OH 45236. (513)531-2690. Fax: (513)531-
2686. E-mail: pam.wissman@fwmedia.com. Website:
www.northlightshop.com; www.impact-books.com.
Contact: Pamela Wissman, Editorial Director (art instruction for fantasy, comics, manga, anime, popular culture, graffiti, science fiction, cartooning, body
art). Estab. 2004. Publishes trade paperback originals
and reprints. **Publishes 8-9 titles/year. 50 queries re-
ceived/year. 10-12 mss received/year. 80% of books
from first-time authors. 100% from unagented
writers.** Publishes book 11 months after acceptance
of ms. Accepts simultaneous submissions. Responds
in 4 months to queries. Responds in 4 months to proposals. Responds in 2 months to manuscripts. Book
catalog available free. Guidelines available online.

☞ IMPACT Books publishes titles that emphasize illustrated how-to-draw-manga, graffiti,
fantasy and comics art instruction. Currently
emphasizing fantasy art, traditional American
comics styles, including humor; and Japanese-
style (manga and anime) and graffiti. This market is for experienced artists who are willing
to work with an IMPACT editor to produce
a step-by-step how-to book about the artist's
creative process. See also separate listing for
F+W Media in this section.

NONFICTION Subjects include art, art instruction,
contemporary culture, creative nonfiction, hobbies.
Submit proposal package, outline, 1 sample chapter,
at least 1 example of sample art. Reviews artwork/
photos. Send digital art, hard copies, or anything that
represents the art well, preferably in the form the author plans to submit art if contracted.

TIPS "Audience comprised primarily of 12- to 18-
year-old beginners along the lines of comic buyers,
in general—mostly teenagers—but also appealing to
a broader audience of young adults 19-30 who need
basic techniques. Art must appeal to teenagers and be
submitted in a form that will reproduce well. Authors
need to know how to teach beginners step-by-step. A
sample step-by-step demonstration is important."

INFORMATION TODAY, INC.

143 Old Marlton Pike, Medford NJ 08055. (609)654-
6266. Fax: (609)654-4309. E-mail: jbryans@infoto-
day.com. Website: www.infotoday.com. **Contact:**
John B. Bryans, editor-in-chief/publisher. Publishes
hardcover and trade paperback originals. **Publishes
15-20 titles/year. 200 queries received/year. 30 mss
received/year. 30% of books from first-time authors.
90% from unagented writers. Pays 10-15% royalty
on wholesale price. Pays $500-2,500 advance.** Pub-
lishes book 9 months after acceptance of ms. Accepts
simultaneous submissions. Responds in 1 month
to queries. Responds in 2 months to proposals. Responds in 3 months to manuscripts. Book catalog free
or on website. Proposal guidelines free or via e-mail
as attachment.

IMPRINTS ITI (academic, scholarly, library science);
CyberAge Books (high-end consumer and business
technology books-emphasis on Internet topics
including online research).

☞ We look for highly-focused coverage of cutting-edge technology topics. Written by es-

tablished experts and targeted to a tech-savvy readership. Virtually all our titles focus on how information is accessed, used, shared, and transformed into knowledge that can benefit people, business, and society. Currently emphasizing Internet/online technologies, including their social significance: biography, how-to, technical, reference, scholarly. De-emphasizing fiction."

NONFICTION Subjects include business, economics, computers, electronics, education, science, Internet and cyberculture. Query with SASE. Reviews artwork/photos. Send photocopies.

TIPS "Our readers include scholars, academics, indexers, librarians, information professionals (ITI imprint), as well as high-end consumer and business users of Internet/WWW/online technologies, and people interested in the marriage of technology with issues of social significance (i.e., cyberculture)."

INGALLS PUBLISHING GROUP, INC

P.O. Box 2500, Banner Elk NC 28604. E-mail: editor@ingallspublishinggroup.com; sales@ingallspublishinggroup.com. Website: www.ingallspublishinggroup.com. **Contact:** Rebecca Owen. Estab. 2001. Publishes hardcover originals, paperback originals and paperback reprints. **Pays 10% royalty.** Publishes book Publishes ms 6 months-2 years after acceptance. after acceptance of ms. Accepts simultaneous submissions. Responds in 6 weeks to queries or mss. Guidelines available online.

⊶ We are a small regional house focusing on popular fiction and memoir. At present, we are most interested in regional fiction, historical fiction and mystery fiction." Exploring digital technologies for printing and e-books. Member IBPA, MWA, SIBA. Accepts unsolicited mss. Query first. Will specifically request if interested in reading synopsis and 3 sample chapters. Accepts queries by e-mail. Include estimated word count, brief bio, list of publishing credits. Agented fiction 10%. Accepts electronic submissions. No submissions on disk. Often comments on rejected mss.

FICTION Subjects include historical, mystery, regional. Query first. Will specifically request if interested in reading synopsis and 3 sample chapters. Accepts queries by e-mail. Include estimated word count, brief bio, list of publishing credits. No submissions on disk.

INNOVATIVEKIDS®

Submissions, 50 Washington St., Norwalk CT 06854. E-mail: info@innovativekids.com. Website: www.innovativekids.com. Estab. 1999. Trade and mass market paperback originals. **Publishes 50 titles/year. Pays outright purchase** Publishes book 12 months after acceptance of ms. Accepts simultaneous submissions. Respond in 3 months on manuscripts. Catalog or

NONFICTION Subjects include animals, crafts, education, entertainment, games. Submit manuscript via mail. Reviews artwork/photos; other original art.

TIPS "Our audience is children from birth to age 12."

☉ INSOMNIAC PRESS

520 Princess Ave., London ON N6B 2B8, Canada. (416)504-6270. E-mail: mike@insomniacpress.com. Website: www.insomniacpress.com. **Contact:** Mike O'Connor, publisher. Gillian Urbankiewicz, assistant ed. Estab. 1992. Publishes trade paperback originals and reprints, mass market paperback originals, and electronic originals and reprints. **Publishes 20 titles/year. 250 queries received/year. 1,000 mss received/year. 50% of books from first-time authors. 80% from unagented writers. Pays 10-15% royalty on retail price. Pays $500-1,000 advance.** Publishes book 6 months after acceptance of ms. Accepts simultaneous submissions. Guidelines available online.

NONFICTION Subjects include business, creative nonfiction, gay, lesbian, government, politics, health, medicine, language, literature, money, finance, multicultural, religion, crime. Very interested in areas such as crime and well-written and well-researched nonfiction on topics of wide interest. Query via e-mail, submit proposal package including outline, 2 sample chapters, or submit complete ms. Reviews artwork/photos. Send photocopies.

FICTION Subjects include comic books, ethnic, experimental, gay, lesbian, humor, literary, mainstream, multicultural, mystery, poetry, suspense. "We publish a mix of commercial (mysteries) and literary fiction." Query via e-mail, submit proposal.

POETRY "Our poetry publishing is limited to 2-4 books per year and we are often booked up a year or two in advance." Submit complete ms.

TIPS "We envision a mixed readership that appreciates up-and-coming literary fiction and poetry as well as solidly researched and provocative nonfiction. Peruse our website and familiarize yourself with what we've published in the past."

INTERNATIONAL PRESS

P.O. Box 43502, Somerville MA 02143. (617)623-3855. Fax: (617)623-3101. E-mail: ipb-mgmt@intlpress.com. Website: www.intlpress.com. **Contact:** Brian Bianchini, general manager (research math and physics). Estab. 1992. Publishes hardcover originals and reprints. **Publishes 12 titles/year. 200 queries received/year. 500 mss received/year. 10% of books from first-time authors. 100% from unagented writers. Pays 3-10% royalty.** Publishes book 6 months after acceptance of ms. Responds in 5 months to queries and proposals. Responds in 1 year to manuscripts. Book catalog available free. Guidelines available online.

○ With close ties to the Chinese math community and the community of Chinese American mathematicians, International Press is developing a strong partnership with publishers and distributors of academic books throughout China.

☞ International Press of Boston, Inc. is an academic publishing company that welcomes book publication inquiries from prospective authors on all topics in Mathematics and Physics. International Press also publishes high-level mathematics and mathematical physics book titles and textbooks.

NONFICTION Subjects include science. All our books will be in research mathematics. Authors need to provide ready to print latex files. Submit complete ms. Reviews artwork/photos. Send EPS files.

TIPS "Audience is PhD mathematicians, researchers and students."

INTERNATIONAL WEALTH SUCCESS

P.O. Box 186, Merrick NY 11570-0186. (516)766-5850. Fax: (516)766-5919. Website: www.iwsmoney.com. **Contact:** Tyler G. Hicks, editor. Estab. 1967. **Publishes 10 titles/year. 100% of books from first-time authors. 100% from unagented writers. Pays 10% royalty on wholesale or retail price. Offers usual advance of $1,000, but this varies depending on author's reputation and nature of book. Buys all rights.** Publishes book 4 months after acceptance of ms. Responds in 1 month to queries. Book catalog and ms guidelines for 9×12 SAE with 3 first-class stamps.

○ "Our mission is to publish books, newsletters, and self-study courses aimed at helping be-

ginners and experienced business people start, and succeed in, their own small business in the fields of real estate, import-export, mail order, licensing, venture capital, financial brokerage, etc. The large number of layoffs and downsizings have made our publications of greater importance to people seeking financial independence in their own business, free of layoff threats and snarling bosses."

NONFICTION Subjects include business, economics, financing, business success, venture capital, etc. Techniques, methods, sources for building wealth. Highly personal, how-to-do-it with plenty of case histories. Books are aimed at wealth builders and are highly sympathetic to their problems. These publications present a wide range of business opportunities while providing practical, hands-on, step-by-step instructions aimed at helping readers achieve their personal goals in as short a time as possible while adhering to ethical and professional business standards. Length: 60,000-70,000 words. Query. Reviews artwork/photos.

TIPS "With the mass layoffs in large and medium-size companies there is an increasing interest in owning your own business. So we focus on more how-to, hands-on material on owning—and becoming successful in—one's own business of any kind. Our market is the BWB—Beginning Wealth Builder. This person has so little money that financial planning is something they never think of. Instead, they want to know what kind of a business they can get into to make some money without a large investment. Write for this market and you have millions of potential readers. Remember—there are a lot more people without money than with money."

⊘◗ INTERVARSITY PRESS

P.O. Box 1400, Downers Grove IL 60515-1426. E-mail: e-mail@ivpress.com. Website: www.ivpress.com/submissions. **Contact:** David Zimmerman, associate editor (Likewise); Cindy Bunch, Sr. editor (IVP Connect, Formatio); Mike Gibson, associate editor (academic, reference); Gary Deddo, sr. ed. (IVP Academic) or Dan Reid, sr. ed. (reference, academic); Al Hsu, assoc. ed. (IVP Books). Estab. 1947. Publishes hardcover originals, trade paperback and mass market paperback originals. **Publishes 110-130 titles/year. 450 queries received/year. 900 mss received/year. 13% of books from first-time authors. 86% from unagented writers. Pays 14-16% royalty on retail price.**

Outright purchase is $75-1,500. Pays negotiable advance. Publishes book 18 months after acceptance of ms. Accepts simultaneous submissions. Responds in 3 months to proposals "from pastors, professors, or previously published authors. We are unable to respond to other proposals or queries.". Book catalog for 9 ×12 SAE and 5 first-class stamps, or online at website. Guidelines available online.

IMPRINTS IVP Academic; IVP Connect; IVP Books.

○ "We think of ourselves as the leading publisher of thoughtful Christian books, and we envision our audience to be similarly thoughtful about their Christian lives—people who really want to think through what it means to be a Christ-follower and to live biblically, and then take some concrete steps toward living more in that direction."

8—¬ InterVarsity Press publishes a full line of books from an evangelical Christian perspective targeted to an open-minded audience. We serve those in the university, the church, and the world, by publishing books from an evangelical Christian perspective."

NONFICTION Subjects include business, child guidance, contemporary culture, economics, ethinic, government, history, memoirs, multicultural, philosophy, psychology, religion, science, social sciences, sociology, spirituality, women's issues, women's studies. "InterVarsity Press publishes a full line of books from an evangelical Christian perspective targeted to an open-minded audience. We serve those in the university, the church, and the world, by publishing books from an evangelical Christian perspective." Very few business/economics, child guidance/parenting, memoirs. Query with SASE. Does not review artwork.

TIPS "The best way to submit to us is to go to a conference where one of our editors are. Networking is key. We're seeking writers who have good ideas and a presence/platform where they've been testing their ideas out (a church, university, on a prominent blog). We need authors who will bring resources to the table for helping to publicize and sell their books (speaking at seminars and conferences, writing for national magazines or newspapers, etc.)."

🜨 IRISH ACADEMIC PRESS

2 Brookside, Dundrum Road, Dundrum Dublin 14, Ireland. (353)(1)2989937. Fax: (353)(1)2982783. E-mail: info@iap.ie. E-mail: lisa.hyde@iap.ie. Website: www.iap.ie. **Contact:** Lisa Hyde, editor. Estab. 1974. **Publishes 15 titles/year. Pays royalty.** Accepts simultaneous submissions. Guidelines available free.

IMPRINTS Vallentine-Mitchell Publishers.

○ Request submission guidelines before submitting.

NONFICTION Subjects include art, architecture, government, politics, history, literary criticism, military, war, womens issues, womens studies, genealogy, Irish history. Does not want fiction or poetry. Query with SASE. Submit proposal package, outline, resume, publishing history, bio, target audience, competing books, SASE.

IRON GATE PUBLISHING

P.O. Box 999, Niwot CO 80544-0999. (303)530-2551. Fax: (303)530-5273. E-mail: editor@irongate.com. Website: www.irongate.com. **Contact:** Dina C. Carson, publisher (how-to, genealogy, local history). Publishes hardcover and trade paperback originals. **Publishes 6-10 titles/year. 100 queries received/year. 20 mss received/year. 30% of books from first-time authors. 10% from unagented writers. Pays royalty on a case-by-case basis.** Publishes book 1 year after acceptance of ms. Accepts simultaneous submissions. Responds in 2 months to proposals. Book catalog and writer's guidelines free or online.

IMPRINTS Reunion Solutions Press; KinderMed Press.

8—¬ Our readers are people who are looking for solid, how-to advice on planning reunions or self-publishing a genealogy."

NONFICTION , hobbies, genealogy, local history, reunions, party planning. Query with SASE, or submit proposal package, including outline, 2 sample chapters, and marketing summary. Reviews artwork/photos. Send photocopies.

TIPS "Please look at the other books we publish and tell us in your query letter why your book would fit into our line of books."

JAIN PUBLISHING CO.

P.O. Box 3523, Fremont CA 94539. (510)659-8272. Fax: (510)659-0501. E-mail: mail@jainpub.com. Website: www.jainpub.com. **Contact:** M. Jain, editor-in-chief. Estab. 1989. Publishes hardcover and paperback originals and reprints. **Publishes 12-15 titles/year. 300 queries received/year. 100% from unagented writers. Pays 5-15% royalty on net sales.** Publishes book 12-24 months after acceptance of ms. Responds in 3 months to manuscripts. Book catalog and ms guidelines online.

8—☞ Jain Publishing Co. publishes college textbooks and supplements, as well as professional and scholarly references, e-books and e-courses. It also publishes in the areas of humanities and societies pertaining specifically to ask, commonly categorized as "Asian Studies".

NONFICTION Subjects include humanities, social sciences, Asian studies, medical, business, scientific/technical. Submit proposal package, publishing history. Reviews artwork/photos. Send photocopies.

✪ J. GORDON SHILLINGFORD PUBLISHING INC.

P.O. Box 86, RPO Corydon Ave., Winnipeg MB R3M 3S3, Canada. Phone/Fax: (204)779-6967. E-mail: jgshill@allstream.net. Website: www.jgshillingford.com. **Contact:** Clarise Foster, poetry editor; Glenda MacFarlane, drama editor, Gordon Shillingford, nonfiction editor. Estab. 1993. Publishes trade paperback originals. **Publishes 14 titles/year. 100 queries received/year. 50 mss received/year. 15% of books from first-time authors. 60% from unagented writers. Pays 10% royalty on retail price.** Accepts simultaneous submissions. Responds in 3-6 months to queries. Book catalog available online. Guidelines available online.

8—☞ Publishes nonfiction, drama, and poetry. Does not publish fiction, self-help or children's material. Only publishes Canadian citizens.

NONFICTION Subjects include government, politics, social history. Query with CV, 2-page sample, SASE.

JIST PUBLISHING

7321 Shadeland Station, Suite 200, Indianapolis IN 46256-3923, United States. (317)613-4200. Fax: (317)845-1052. E-mail: spines@jist.com. Website: www.jist.com. **Contact:** Susan Pines, associate publisher (career and education reference and library titles, assessments, videos, e-products); Lori Cates Hand, product line manager, trade and workbooks (Career, job search, and education trade and workbook titles). Estab. 1981. Hardcover and trade paperback originals. **Publishes 60 titles/year. Receives 40 submissions/year 25% of books from first-time authors. 75% from unagented writers. Pays 8-10% royalty on net receipts. Pays advance: 12 months.** Accepts simultaneous submissions. Responds in 6

months to queries, proposals, and mss. Book catalog available online. Guidelines available online.

8—☞ Our purpose is to provide quality job search, career development, occupational, and life skills information, products, and services that help people manage and improve their lives and careers-and the lives of others. Publishes practical, self-directed tools and training materials that are used in employment and training, education, and business settings. Whether reference books, trade books, assessment tools, workbooks, or videos, JIST products foster self-directed job-search attitudes and behaviors."

NONFICTION Subjects include: business, economics, education. Specializes in job search, career development, occupational information, character education, and domestic abuse topics. "We want text/workbook formats that would be useful in a school or other institutional setting. We also publish trade titles for all reading levels. Will consider books for professional staff and educators, appropriate software and videos." Submit proposal package, including outline, 1 sample chapter, and author resume, competitive analysis, marketing ideas. Does not review artwork/photos.

TIPS "Our audiences are students, job seekers, and career changers of all ages and occupations who want to find good jobs quickly and improve their futures. We sell materials through the trade as well as to institutional markets like schools, colleges, and one-stop career centers."

JOURNEYFORTH

Imprint of BJU Press, 1700 Wade Hampton Blvd., Greenville SC 29614. (864)242-5100, ext. 4350. Fax: (864)298-0268. E-mail: jb@bju.edu. Website: www.journeyforth.com. **Contact:** Nancy Lohr. Estab. 1974. Publishes paperback originals. **Publishes 25 titles/year. 10% of books from first-time authors. 8% from unagented writers. Pays royalty.** Publishes book 12-18 months after acceptance of ms. Does accept simultaneous submissions. Responds in 1 month to queries. Responds in 3 months to manuscripts. Book catalog available free. Guidelines available online at www.bjupress.com/books/freelance.php.

8—☞ Small independent publisher of trustworthy novels and biographies for readers pre-school through high school from a conservative Christian perspective, Christian living books, and Bible studies for adults."

NONFICTION Subjects include animals, contemporary culture, creative nonfiction, environment, history, music, nature, religion, spirituality, sports, young adult. Nonfiction Christian living, Bible studies, church and ministry, church history. We produce books for the adult Christian market that are from a conservative Christian worldview.

FICTION Subjects include adventure, historical, animal, easy-to-read, series, mystery, sports, children's/juvenile, suspense, young adult, western. Our fiction is all based on a moral and Christian worldview. Does not want short stories. Submit 5 sample chapters, synopsis, SASE.

TIPS "Study the publisher's guidelines. No picture books and no submissions by e-mail."

🅐 KANE/MILLER BOOK PUBLISHERS

Kane/Miller: A Division of EDC Publishing, 4901 Morena Blvd., Suite 213, San Diego CA 92117. (858)456-0540. Fax: (858)456-9641. E-mail: info@kanemiller.com. E-mail: submissions@kanemiller.com. Website: www.kanemiller.com. **Contact:** Kira Lynn, Editorial Department. Estab. 1985. Responds in 90 days.

> 💬 "We like to think that a child reading a Kane Miller book will see parallels between his own life and what might be the unfamiliar setting and characters of the story. And that by seeing how a character who is somehow or in some way dissimilar - an outsider - finds a way to fit comfortably into a culture or community or situation while maintaining a healthy sense of self and self-dignity, she might be empowered to do the same."

> ⚷ Kane/Miller Book Publishers is a division of EDC Publishing, specializing in award-winning children's books from around the world. Our books bring the children of the world closer to each other, sharing stories and ideas, while exploring cultural differences and similarities. Although we continue to look for books from other countries, we are now actively seeking works that convey cultures and communities within the US. We are looking for picture book fiction and nonfiction on those subjects which may be defined as particularly American: sports such as baseball, historical events, American biographies, American folk tales, etc. We are committed to expanding our early

and middle-grade fiction list. We're interested in great stories with engaging characters in all genres (mystery, fantasy, adventure, historical, etc.) and, as with picture books, especially those with particularly American subjects. All submissions sent via **USPS** should be sent to: Editorial Department. Please do not send anything requiring a signature. Work submitted for consideration may also be sent via e-mail. Please send either the complete picture book ms, the published book (with a summary and outline in English, if that is not the language of origin) or a synopsis of the work and two sample chapters. DO NOT SEND ORIGINALS. Illustrators may send color copies, tear sheets, or other non-returnable illustration samples. If you have a website with additional samples of your work, please include the web address. Please do not send original artwork, or samples on CD. A SASE must be included if you send your submission via USPS; otherwise you will not receive a reply. If we wish to follow up, we will notify you."

NONFICTION Subjects include Americana, history, sports, young adult.

FICTION Subjects include adventure, fantasy, historical, juvenile, mystery, picture books.

⊕ KAR-BEN PUBLISHING

Lerner Publishing Group, 241 First Ave. N., Minneapolis MN 55401. (612)332-3344 x229. Fax: 612-332-7615. E-mail: Editorial@Karben.com. Website: www.Karben.com. Estab. 1974. Publishes hardcover, trade paperback and electronic originals. **Publishes 12-15 titles/year. 800 mss received/year. 70% of books from first-time authors. 70% from unagented writers. Pays 3-5% royalty on NET price. Pays $500-2,500 advance.** Publishes book Most manuscripts published within 24 months. after acceptance of ms. Accepts simultaneous submissions. Responds to all inquiries. Book catalog available online; free upon request. Guidelines available online.

NONFICTION Subjects include Jewish content children's books only. "In addition to traditional Jewish-themed stories about Jewish holidays, history, folktales and other subjects, we especially seek stories that reflect the rich diversity of the contemporary Jewish community." No textbooks, games, or educational materials. Submit completed ms. Reviews artwork separately. Send website info where illustration samples are available for review.

FICTION Subjects include juvenile; Jewish content only. "We seek picture book mss of about 1,000 words on Jewish-themed topics for children." Submit full ms. Picture books only. Recent titles include: *Benno and the Night of Broken Glass, Sammy Spider's First Shavuot, Yuvi's Candy Tree, Zishe the Strongman*.

TIPS "Authors: Do a literature search to make sure similar title doesn't already exist. Illustrators: Look at our online catalog for a sense of what we like—bright colors and lively composition."

KINDRED PRODUCTIONS

1310 Taylor Ave., Winnipeg MB R3M 3Z6, Canada. (204)669-6575. Fax: (204)654-1865. E-mail: kindred@mbconf.ca. Website: www.kindredproductions.com. **Contact:** Renita Kornelsen, Acquisitions. Publishes trade paperback originals and reprints. **Publishes 3 titles/year. 1% of books from first-time authors. 100% from unagented writers.** Publishes book 18 months after acceptance of ms. Accepts simultaneous submissions. Responds in 3 months to queries. Responds in 5 months to manuscripts. Guidelines available by e-mail request.

Kindred Productions publishes, promotes, and markets print and nonprint resources that will shape our Christian faith and discipleship from a Mennonite Brethren perspective. Currently emphasizing Mennonite Brethren Resources. De-emphasizing personal experience, biographical. No children's books or fiction."

NONFICTION Subjects include religion, historical, i. "Our books cater primarily to our Mennonite Brethren denomination readers." Query with SASE. Submit outline, 2-3 sample chapters.

TIPS "Most of our books are sold to churches, religious bookstores, and schools. We are concentrating on books with a Mennonite Brethren perspective. We do not accept children's manuscripts."

KITSUNE BOOKS

P.O. Box 1154, Crawfordville FL 32326-1154. E-mail: contact@kitsunebooks.com. Website: www.kitsunebooks.com. **Contact:** Lynn Holschuh, Assistant Editor. Estab. 2006. Publishes trade paperback originals and reprints. **Publishes 4-5 titles/year. 600+ queries received/year. 70 mss received/year. 30% of books from first-time authors. 50% from unagented writers. Pays**

10% royalty on retail price. Pays $300-600 advance. Publishes book 12-18 months after acceptance of ms. Accepts simultaneous submissions. Responds in 2-4 weeks to queries. Responds in 1-3 months to proposals. Responds in 6-9 months to manuscripts. Book catalog and guidelines available online.

NONFICTION Subjects include memoirs, New Age, spirituality, literary commentary, yoga/fitness. Write for the general reader, but demonstrate a thorough, authoritative knowledge of your subject. No cookbooks, how-to, specific religion books Query via e-mail only. If you insist on sending a postal letter, you must include SASE. No hardcopy submissions unless requested. Reviews artwork/photos.

FICTION Subjects include literary, mainstream, contemporary, dark fantasy, short story collections, poetry, speculative, noir, magical realism. "We are looking for carefully written fiction that's slightly off the beaten path-interesting novels that don't fit easily into any one category. Graceful command of the language is a plus; technical command of grammar/language mechanics a must. Our latest short story collection is in the Raymond Carver tradition. Looking for authors with a unique voice and style." No children's picture books, crime thrillers, mystery, romance, war, westerns, juvenile fiction. Query via e-mail. No hardcopy submissions, no previously published material.

POETRY "You must be able to submit a complete collection, not just a random sampling of unrelated poems. The collection should have a clear theme or structure." Query and submit 3 sample poems.

TIPS "Our readership is eclectic, with a taste for the unusual, the artistic and the unexpected. Kitsune Books caters to lovers of literature, poetry, and well-designed and researched nonfiction. We prefer to deal with mss electronically rather than receiving printouts (saves trees). Please read our category guidelines carefully. Although we do accept some genre fiction, please look carefully at what we don't accept before you submit. Interesting novels that don't fit easily into any one category are considered. No self-published material."

ALFRED A. KNOPF

1745 Broadway, 21st Floor, New York NY 10019. Website: knopf.knopfdoubleday.com. **Contact:** Senior editor. Estab. 1915.

KOENISHA PUBLICATIONS

3196 53rd St., Hamilton MI 49419-9626. Phone/Fax: (269)751-4100. E-mail: koenisha@macatawa.org. Website: www.koenisha.com. **Contact:** Sharolett Koenig, publisher; Earl Leon, acquisition editor. Publishes trade paperback originals. **Publishes 10-12 titles/year. 500 queries received/year. 500 mss received/year. 95% of books from first-time authors. 100% from unagented writers.** Publishes book 1 year after acceptance of ms. Guidelines available online.

NONFICTION *Not accepting submissions from new authors at this time.*

FICTION Subjects include humor, mainstream, contemporary, mystery, romance, suspense, young adult. "We do not accept manuscripts that contain unnecessary foul language, explicit sex or gratuitous violence." Query with SASE. Submit proposal package, clips, 3 sample chapters.

POETRY Submit 3 sample poems.

TIPS "We're not interested in books written to suit a particular line or house or because it's trendy. Instead write a book from your heart—the inspiration or idea that kept you going through the writing process."

KRAUSE PUBLICATIONS

A Division of F+W Media, Inc., 700 E. State St., Iola WI 54990. (715)445-2214. Fax: (715)445-4087. Website: www.krausebooks.com. **Contact:** Paul Kennedy (antiques and collectibles, music, sports, militaria); Corrina Peterson (firearms); Brian Lovett (outdoors); Candy Wiza (Simple Living); Debbie Bradley (Numismatics). Publishes hardcover and trade paperback originals. **Publishes 80 titles/year. 200 queries received/year. 40 mss received/year. 50% of books from first-time authors. 95% from unagented writers. Pays advance. Photo budget.** Publishes book 18 months after acceptance of ms. Responds in 3 months to proposals. Responds in 2 months to manuscripts. Book catalog for free or on website. Guidelines available free upon request.

�➔ We are the world's largest hobby and collectibles publisher."

NONFICTION Submit proposal package, including outline, table of contents, a sample chapter, and letter explaining your project's unique contributions. Reviews artwork/photos. Accepts only digital photography. Send sample photos.

TIPS Audience consists of serious hobbyists. "Your work should provide a unique contribution to the special interest."

LADYBUGPRESS

New Voices / LadybugPress, 16964 Columbia River Dr., Sonora CA 95370-9111. (209)694-8340. E-mail: georgia@ladybugbooks.com. Website: www.ladybugbooks.com. **Contact:** Georgia Jones, editor-in-chief (new authors). Irma Hudson, editor (nonfiction) Estab. 1996. Trade paperback and electronic originals. **Publishes 4-6 trade titles/year. 50 queries/year; 30 mss/year. 90% of books from first-time authors. 100% from unagented writers. Pays 40-45% royalty on wholesale price.** Publishes book 2 months after acceptance of ms. Accepts simultaneous submissions. Responds in 1 month on queries/proposals, 2 months/mss. Catalog and guidelines available online or by CD.

IMPRINTS LadybugPress, NewVoices, Ladybug Productions, Partners in Publishing, Voices, NewVoices Poetry.

◯ Recently won a national book award for audio book and would love to see more high quality audio proposals. Owns print facility and likes seeing creative and color print proposals.

NONFICTION Subjects include alternative lifestyles, contemporary culture, creative nonfiction, dance, music, social sciences, women's issues, world affairs. Our primary interest is in women's issues and peace. Query with SASE; We prefer e-mail submissions. Reviews artwork/photos; send electronic files.

FICTION Subjects include contemporary, feminist, historical, literary, mainstream, poetry. "Our tastes are eclectic." Submit proposal package, including synopsis; prefers electronic submissions, georgia@ladbugbooks.com.

POETRY "We like new poets but can only do poetry in our subsidized program, Partners in Publishing." Query.

TIPS "We have a lot of information on our website, and have several related sites that give an overview of who we are and what we like to see. Take advantage of this and it will help you make good decisions about submissions."

▲◎ LAUREL-LEAF

Imprint of Random House Children's Books/Random House, Inc., 1745 Broadway, New York NY 10019. (212)782-9000. Website: www.randomhouse.com/teens.

○ Quality reprint paperback imprint for young adult paperback books. *Does not accept unsolicited mss.*

LECTIO PUBLISHERS

P.O. Box 11435, Randhart 1457, South Africa. Phone/Fax: (27)(11)907-3053. E-mail: lectio@iafrica.com. Website: www.lectio.co.za.

⊶ Publishes educational and health materials (comics, books, wall charts, teaching aids) used by government departments.

NONFICTION Subjects include health, medicine, science, social sciences, math, life skills, sexuality, arts/culture, technology.

LEGACY PRESS

P.O. Box 261129, San Diego CA 92196. (858)277-1167. E-mail: editor@rainbowpublishers.com. Website: www.rainbowpublishers.com; www.legacypresskids. com. **Contact:** Editorial Department. Estab. 1979.

TIPS "Our Rainbow imprint publishes reproducible books for teachers of children in Christian ministries, including crafts, activities, games and puzzles. Our Legacy imprint publishes titles for children such as devotionals, fiction and Christian living. Please write for guidelines and study the market before submitting material."

HAL LEONARD BOOKS

Hal Leonard Publishing Group, 33 Plymouth St., Suite 302, Montclair NJ 07042. (973)337-5034. Fax: (973)337-5227. **Contact:** John Cerullo, Publisher. Kristina Radka **Publishes 30 titles/year.**

NONFICTION Subjects include music. Query with SASE.

LETHE PRESS

118 Heritage Ave., Maple Shade NJ 08052. (609)410-7391. E-mail: editor@lethepressbooks.com. Website: www.lethepressbooks.com. **Contact:** Steve Berman, publisher. Estab. 2001.

ARTHUR A. LEVINE BOOKS

Scholastic, Inc., 557 Broadway, New York NY 10012. Website: www.arthuralevinebooks.com. Estab. 1996. Publishes hardback and soft cover prints and reprints.

LIFE CYCLE BOOKS

P.O. Box 1008, Niagara Falls NY 14304. (416)690-5860. Fax: (416)690-8532. Website: www.lifecyclebooks. com. **Contact:** Paul Broughton, general manager. Estab. 1973. Publishes trade paperback originals and re-

prints, and mass market reprints. **Publishes 6 titles/year. 100+ queries received/year. 50% of books from first-time authors. 100% from unagented writers. Pays 8-10% royalty on wholesale price. Pays $250-1,000 advance.** Publishes book 1 year after acceptance of ms. Responds in 1 month to queries. Responds in 1 month to proposals. Responds in 1 month to manuscripts. Book catalog available online.

NONFICTION Subjects include health, medicine, religion, social sciences, womens issues, womens studies. We specialize in human life issues. Query with SASE. Submit complete ms. Reviews artwork/photos.

LIGHTHOUSE POINT PRESS

100 First Ave., Suite 525, Pittsburgh PA 15222-1517. (412)323-9320. Fax: (412)323-9334. E-mail: ryearick@yearick-millea.com. **Contact:** Ralph W. Yearick, publisher (business/career/general nonfiction). Estab. 1993. Publishes hardcover and trade paperback originals. **Pays 5-10% royalty on retail price.** Responds in 6 months to queries. Queries by e-mail: info@yearick-millea.com.

⊶ Lighthouse Point Press specializes in business/career nonfiction titles, and books that help readers improve their quality of life. We do not re-publish self-published books."

NONFICTION Subjects include business, economics. "We are open to all types of submissions related to general nonfiction, but most interested in business/career manuscripts." Submit proposal package, outline, 1-2 sample chapters and bio. Complete manuscripts preferred.

TIPS "When submitting a manuscript or proposal, please tell us what you see as the target market/audience for the book. Also, be very specific about what you are willing to do to promote the book."

LILLENAS PUBLISHING CO.

Imprint of Lillenas Drama Resources, P.O. Box 419527, Kansas City MO 64109. (816)931-1900. Fax: (816)412-8390. E-mail: drama@lillenas.com. Website: www. lillenasdrama.com. **Contact:** Drama editor (Christian drama). Publishes mass market paperback and electronic originals. **Publishes 50+ titles/year. Pays royalty on net price. Makes outright purchase.** Responds in 4-6 months. See guidelines online.

⊶ We purchase only original, previously unpublished materials. Also, we require that all scripts be performed at least once before it is submitted for consideration. We do not accept scripts that are sent via fax or e-mail. Direct all manuscripts to the Drama Resources Editor."

NONFICTION Subjects include religion, life issues. No musicals. Query with SASE. Submit complete ms.

FICTION "Looking for sketch and monologue collections for all ages – adults, children and youth. For these collections, we request 12 - 15 scripts to be submitted at one time. Unique treatments of spiritual themes, relevant issues and biblical messages are of interest. Contemporary full-length and one-act plays that have conflict, characterization, and a spiritual context that is neither a sermon nor an apologetic for youth and adults. We also need wholesome so-called secular full-length scripts for dinner theatres and schools." No musicals.

TIPS "We never receive too many manuscripts."

LINDEN PUBLISHING, INC.

2006 S. Mary, Fresno CA 93721. (559)233-6633. Fax: (559)233-6933. E-mail: richard@lindenpub.com. Website: www.lindenpub.com. **Contact:** Richard Sorsky, president; Kent Sorsky, vice president. Estab. 1976. Publishes trade paperback originals; hardcover and trade paperback reprints. **Publishes 10-12 titles/year. 30+ queries received/year. 5-15 mss received/year. 40% of books from first-time authors. 50% from unagented writers. Pays 7½ -12% royalty on wholesale price. Pays $500-6,000 advance.** Publishes book 18 months after acceptance of ms. Responds in 1 month to queries and proposals. Book catalog available online. Guidelines available via e-mail.

NONFICTION Subjects include history, regional, hobbies, woodworking, Regional California history. Submit proposal package, outline, 3 sample chapters, bio. Reviews artwork/photos. Send electronic files, if available.

LISTEN & LIVE AUDIO

P.O. Box 817, Roseland NJ 07068. E-mail: alisa@listenandlive.com. Website: www.listenandlive.com. **Contact:** Alisa Weberman, publisher. **Publishes 30+ titles/year.** Catalog available online.

Independent audiobook publisher. "We also license audiobooks for the download market. We specialize in the following genres: Fiction, Mystery, Nonfiction, Self-help, Business, Children's, and Teen."

LITTLE, BROWN AND CO.

Hachette Book Group USA, 1271 Ave. of the Americas, New York NY 10020. (212)522-8700. Fax: (212)522-

2067. Website: www.hachettebookgroupusa.com. Estab. 1837. Publishes hardcover originals and paperback originals and reprints.

"Unsolicited manuscripts, submissions and queries will not be answered. If you are interested in having a manuscript considered for publication, we recommend that you first enlist the services of an established literary agent."

One of the country's oldest and most distinguished publishing houses, Little, Brown is committed to publishing fiction of the highest quality and nonfiction of lasting significance, by many of America's finest writers."

LLEWELLYN PUBLICATIONS

Imprint of Llewellyn Worldwide, Ltd., 2143 Wooddale Dr., Woodbury MN 55125. (651)291-1970. Fax: (651)291-1908. E-mail: Publicity@llewellyn.com. Website: www.llewellyn.com. **Contact:** Acquisitions Editor. Estab. 1901. Publishes trade and mass market paperback originals. **Publishes 100+ titles/year. 30% of books from first-time authors. 50% from unagented writers. Pays 10% royalty on wholesale or retail price.** Accepts simultaneous submissions. Responds in 3 months to queries. Book catalog for 9×12 SAE with 4 first-class stamps.

Llewellyn publishes New Age fiction and nonfiction exploring new worlds of mind and spirit. Currently emphasizing astrology, alternative health and healing, tarot. De-emphasizing fiction, channeling."

NONFICTION Subjects include cooking, foods, nutrition, health, medicine, nature, environment, New Age, psychology, women's issues, women's studies. Submit outline, sample chapters. Reviews artwork/photos.

LOUISIANA STATE UNIVERSITY PRESS

3990 W. Lakeshore Dr., Baton Rouge LA 70808. (225)578-6294. Fax: (225)578-6461. E-mail: mkc@lsu.edu. Website: www.lsu.edu/lsupress. **Contact:** MK Callaway, Director. Exec. Editor: John Easterly (poetry, fiction, literary studies); Sr. Ed.: Rand Dotson (U.S. History & Southern Studies). Estab. 1935. Publishes hardcover and paperback originals, and reprints. Publishes 8 poetry titles per year and 2 works of original fiction as part of the Yellow Shoe Fiction series. **Publishes 80-90 titles/year. 33% of books from first-time authors. 95% from unagented writers. Pays royalty.** Publishes book 1 year after acceptance of ms. Responds in 1 month to queries. Book catalog and ms guidelines free and online.

8—★ Publishes in the fall and spring.

NONFICTION Subjects include Americana, animals, anthropology, archeology, art, architecture, ethnic, government, politics, history, language, literature, literary criticism, memoirs, military, war, Civil & WWII, music, dance, Southern, Jazz, nature, environment, philosophy, Political, photography, regional, sociology, women's issues, women's studies, world affairs, geography and environmental studies. "We publish general interest books about Louisiana and the South, Atlantic and European and World History. Prizes are regularly awarded to LSU Press authors for the excellence of their general body of work. All books must undergo a rigorous approval process." Query with SASE. Submit proposal package, outline, sample chapters, cover letter, resume. *No unsolicited submissions by e-mail attachment.*

FICTION Query with SASE. Submit proposal package, sample chapters, resume, clips, and cover letter.

POETRY A highly respected publisher of collections by poets such as Claudia Emerson, David Kirby, Brendan Galvin, Fred Chappell, Marilyn Nelson, and Henry Taylor. Publisher of the Southern Messenger Poets series edited by Dave Smith." "No unsolicited poetry mss. for the foreseeable future. We have filled our slots until 2014."

LOVING HEALING PRESS INC.

5145 Pontiac Trail, Ann Arbor MI 48105-9627. (888)761-6268. Fax: (734)663-6861. E-mail: info@lovinghealing.com. Website: www.lovinghealing.com. **Contact:** Victor R. Volkman, senior editor (psychology, self-help, personal growth, trauma recovery). Estab. 2003. Hardcover originals and reprints; Trade paperback originals and reprints. **Publishes 20 titles/year. Receives 200 queries/year; 100 mss/year 50% of books from first-time authors. 80% from unagented writers. Pays 6-12% royalty on retail price.** Publishes book 10 months after acceptance of ms. Accepts simultaneous submissions. Responds in 1 month on queries and proposals, 2 months on mss. Catalog available online at website. Guidelines online at website http://lovinghealing.com/aboutus.

NONFICTION Subjects include child guidance, health, memoirs, psychology, social work. We are primarily interested in self-help books which are person-centered and non-judgmental. Submit proposal package, including: outline, 3 sample chapters; submit completed ms. Reviews artwork/photos as part of the ms package; send JPEG files.

FICTION Subjects include multicultural, social change. Submit completed ms.

⊕ LRP PUBLICATIONS, INC.

P.O. Box 980, Horsham PA 19044. (215)784-0860. Fax: (215)784-9639. E-mail: dshadovitz@lrp.com. Website: www.lrp.com. **Contact:** See website for contacts by product group. Estab. 1977. Publishes hardcover and trade paperback originals. **Pays royalty.** Book catalog available free. Guidelines available free.

○ "LRP publishes two industry-leading magazines, *Human Resource Executive*® and *Risk & Insurance*®, as well as hundreds of newsletters, books, videos and case reporters in the fields of: human resources, federal employment, workers' compensation, public employment law, disability, bankruptcy, education administration and law."

NONFICTION Subjects include business, economics, education. Submit proposal package, outline.

⊘ LUCENT BOOKS

Attn: Publisher - Lucent Books, 27500 Drake Rd., Farmington Hills MI 48331. E-mail: kristine.burns@cengage.com. Website: www.gale.com/lucent. **Contact:** Kristine Burns. Estab. 1988.

8—★ Lucent Books is a nontrade publisher of nonfiction for the middle school audience providing students with resource material for academic studies and for independent learning.

NONFICTION Potential writers should familiarize themselves with the material. All are works for hire, by assignment only. *No unsolicited mss.* E-mail query with cover letter, résumé and list of publications to kristine.burns@cengage.com.

THE LYONS PRESS

Imprint of The Globe Pequot Press, Inc., Box 480, 246 Goose Lane, Guilford CT 06437. (203)458-4500. Fax: (203)458-4668. E-mail: info@globepequot.com. Website: www.lyonspress.com. **Contact:** Janice Goldklang, exec. editor (general nonfiction, memoir, bio, cooking, history, current events), Keith Wallman, senior editor (military history, martial arts, narrative nonfiction, sports, current affairs); Mary Norris, senior editor (narrative nonfiction, adventure, women's issues, cooking, bio, memoir, self-help, animals, cooking); Holly Rubino, editor (narrative nonfiction, home). Estab. 1984 (Lyons & Burford), 1997 (The Lyons Press). Publishes hardcover and trade paperback originals and reprints. **Pays $3,000-25,000 advance.** Accepts simultaneous submissions. Responds in 4 months to queries, proposals and to manuscripts. Book catalog available online. Guidelines available online.

- ○ The Lyons Press has teamed up to develop books with The Explorers Club, Orvis, L.L. Bean, *Field & Stream*, Outward Bound, Buckmasters, and *Golf Magazine*.
- ⌐ The Lyons Press publishes practical and literary books, chiefly centered on outdoor subjects— natural history, all sports, gardening, horses, fishing, hunting, survival, self-reliant living, plus cooking, memoir, bio, nonfiction.

NONFICTION Subjects include agriculture, Americana, animals, art & reference, cooking, foods & wine, nutrition, history, military, war, nature, environment, recreation, sports, adventure, fitness, the sea, woodworking. Visit our website and note the featured categories. Query with SASE. Submit proposal package, outline, 3 sample chapters. marketing description. Reviews artwork/photos. Send photocopies and nonoriginal prints.

MAGNUS PRESS

P.O. Box 2666, Carlsbad CA 92018. (760)806-3743. Fax: (760)806-3689. E-mail: magnuspres@aol.com. Website: www.magnuspress.com. **Contact:** Warren Angel, editorial director. Estab. 1997. Publishes trade paperback originals and reprints. **Publishes 1-3 titles/year. 120 queries received/year. 75 mss received/ year. 44% of books from first-time authors. 89% from unagented writers. Pays 6-15% royalty on retail price.** Publishes book 12 months after acceptance of ms. Accepts simultaneous submissions. Responds in 1 month to queries, proposals and manuscripts. Book catalog and ms guidelines for #10 SASE.

IMPRINTS Canticle Books.

NONFICTION Subjects include religion, from a Christian perspective. "Writers must be well-grounded in Biblical knowledge and must be able to communicate effectively with the lay person." Submit proposal package, outline, sample chapters, bio.

TIPS "Magnus Press's audience is mainly Christian lay persons, but also includes anyone interested in spirituality and/or Biblical studies and the church. Study our listings and catalog; learn to write effectively for an average reader; read any one of our published books."

MAIN ST. RAG PUBLISHING COMPANY

P.O. Box 690100, Charlotte NC 28227-7001. (704)573-2516. E-mail: editor@mainSt.rag.com. Website: www.mainSt.rag.com. **Contact:** M. Scott Douglas, publisher, editor. Estab. 1996. Responds in 3-6 weeks to queries.

IMPRINTS Pure Heart Press (We will publish anything the author or editor is willing to finance.)

- ⌐ There are 4 ways to get a book of poetry published:1) self-publish using our imprint;2) Enter one of our contests;3) Be invited;4) Be recommended."

NONFICTION Subjects include art, architecture, (we prefer eclectic art, architecture.), creative nonfiction, photography, interview, reviews, essays. "Pissing off politicians, corporations, zealots, and/or lawyers is acceptable and encouraged." Nothing derogatory on the basis of race, gender, sexual orientation, or religious persuasion. Query with SASE. Reviews artwork/photos.

FICTION Subjects include literary, poetry, cartoons, short fiction. "See Current themes online. Address to Short Fiction Anthology for consideration for our anthology." "We are not open to unsolicited submissions of full-length mss. of short fiction." Query with SASE. Submit 2 short stories.

POETRY "We are interested in any style, subject, with emphasis on edgier materials, and we enjoy humor. We prefer work alive with the poet's own experiences. We don't want much formal poetry, but will consider it if formal poems maintain the integrity of the form without becoming stiff, uninteresting, or losing their vitality. Poems of 40 lines or less are more acceptable. Submit 6 pages per submission, 1 typed page per 8.5 X 11 page." "We are not interested in the graphic details of your love life. We are least likely to accept garden poetry, poetry about poems or Greek & Roman mythology." Query.

TIPS "You can request a free electronic newsletter which is a reference for writers, readers and publishers by providing limited information and directing them to links and e-mails. Current features include: Call for Submissions; Contests; and New Releases. (No e-mail submissions unless overseas, reviews, images, subscribers to *The MainSt. Rag*.) In all cases, query prior to submitting for instructions."

MANAGEMENT ADVISORY PUBLICATIONS

P.O. Box 81151, Wellesley Hills MA 02481-0001. (781)235-2895. Fax: (781)235-5446. E-mail: info@masp.com. Website: www.masp.com. **Contact:** Jay

Kuong, editor (corporate governance, compliance, security, audit, IT, business continuity). Estab. 1972. Mass market paperback originals. **Publishes 2-10 titles/year. 25 queries/year; 10 mss/year. 5% of books from first-time authors. Pays 5-10% royalty on wholesale price.** Publishes book 3-6 months after acceptance of ms. Responds in 4 months on queries. Catalog not available.

NONFICTION Subjects include business, computers, economics, electronics. Submit proposal package.

TIPS "Our audience is primarily business and IT professionals and University and Company libraries."

⊕ MANDALA PUBLISHING

10 Paul Dr., San Rafael CA 94903. (415)526-1370. E-mail: **info@mandalapublishing.com**. Website: www.mandalapublishing.com. **Contact:** Lisa Fitzpatrick, associate publisher (Hindu philosophy, music, and art). Estab. 1989. Publishes hardcover, trade paperback, and electronic originals. **Publishes 12 titles/year. 200 queries received/year. 100 mss received/year. 40% of books from first-time authors. 100% from unagented writers. Pays 3-15% royalty on retail price.** Publishes book 8 months after acceptance of ms. Accepts simultaneous submissions. Responds in 6 months to queries. Responds in 6 months to proposals. Responds in 6 months to manuscripts. Book catalog available online.

NONFICTION Subjects include alternative, cooking, foods, nutrition, education, health, medicine, philosophy, photography, religion, spirituality. We specialize in preserving and promoting the Vedic tradition by producing high quality, fully illustrated coffee table books, gift items, stationery, posters, etc., for modern general audiences. Query with SASE. Reviews artwork/photos. Send photocopies and thumbnails.

FICTION Subjects include juvenile, religious, spiritual. Query with SASE.

MARINE TECHNIQUES PUBLISHING

126 Western Ave., Suite 266, Augusta ME 04330-7249. (207)622-7984. Fax: (207)621-0821. E-mail: info@marinetechpublishing.com. Website: www.marinetechpublishing.com. **Contact:** James L. Pelletier, president/owner(commercial maritime); Maritime Associates Globally (commercial maritime). Estab. 1983. Trade paperback originals and reprints. **Publishes 2-5 titles/year. 100+ queries received/year. 40+ mss received/year. 50% of books from first-time authors. 75% from unagented writers. Pays 25-55% royalty on wholesale or retail price. Makes outright pur-**
chase. Publishes book 6-12 months after acceptance of ms. Accepts simultaneous submissions. Responds in 2 months to queries, proposals, and manuscripts. Book catalog available online, by e-mail, and for #10 SASE for $5. Guidelines available by e-mail, and for #10 SASE for $5.

☛ Publishes only books related to the commercial marine/maritime industry."

NONFICTION Subjects include maritime education, marine subjects, counseling, career guidance, maritime labor, marine engineering, global water transportation, marine subjects, water transportation. "We are concerned with 'maritime related works' and not recreational boating, but rather commercial maritime industries, such as deep-sea water transportation, offshore oil & gas, inland towing, coastal tug boat, 'water transportation industries.'" Submit proposal package, including all sample chapters; submit completed ms. Reviews artwork/photos as part of the ms package; send photocopies.

FICTION Subjects include adventure, military, war, maritime. Must be commercial maritime/marine related. Submit proposal package, including all sample chapters. Submit complete ms.

TIPS "Audience consists of commercial marine/maritime firms, persons employed in all aspects of the marine/maritime commercial water-transportation-related industries and recreational fresh and salt water fields, persons interested in seeking employment in the commercial marine industry; firms seeking to sell their products and services to vessel owners, operators, and managers; shipyards, vessel repair yards, recreational and yacht boat building and national and international ports and terminals involved with the commercial marine industry globally worldwide, etc."

⊘ MARLOR PRESS, INC.

4304 Brigadoon Dr., St. Paul MN 55126. (651)484-4600. E-mail: marlin.marlor@minn.net. **Contact:** Marlin Bree, publisher. Estab. 1981. Publishes trade paperback originals. **Publishes 2 titles/year. 100 queries received/year. 25 mss received/year. 100% of books from first-time authors. Pays 8-10% royalty on wholesale price.** Publishes book 1 year after acceptance of ms. Responds in 3-6 weeks to queries.

☛ Currently emphasizing general interest nonfiction children's books and nonfiction boating books."

NONFICTION Subjects include travel, boating. Primarily how-to stuff. *No unsolicited mss.* No anecdotal reminiscences or biographical materials. No fiction or poetry. Query first; submit outline with sample chapters only when requested. Do not send full ms. Reviews artwork/photos.

MARTIN SISTERS PUBLISHING, LLC

P.O. Box 1749, Barbourville KY 40906-1499. E-mail: publisher@martinsisterspublishing.com. Website: http://www.martinsisterspublishing.com. **Contact:** Denise Melton, Publisher/Editor (Fiction/nonfiction); Melissa Newman, Publisher/Editor (Fiction/nonfiction). Estab. 2011. Firm/imprint publishes trade and mass market paperback originals; electronic originals. **Publishes 12 titles/year. 75% of books from first-time authors. 100% from unagented writers. Pays 7.5% royalty/max on retail price. No advance offered.** Publishes book Time between acceptance of ms and publication is 6 months. after acceptance of ms. Accepts simultaneous submissions. Responds in 1 month on queries, 2 months on proposals, 3-6 months on mss. Catalog and guidelines available online.

IMPRINTS Ivy House Books - Literary/Mainstream Fiction; Rainshower Books - Christian Fiction and nonfiction; Skyvine Books - Science Fiction/Fantasy/Paranormal; Romance; Martin Sisters Books - nonfiction/Short Story Collections/Coffee Table Books/Cookbooks; Barefoot Books - Young Adult. Query Ms. Newman or Ms. Melton for all imprints listed at submissions@martinsisterspublishing.com.

NONFICTION Subjects include Americana, child guidance, contemporary culture, cooking, creative nonfiction, education, gardening, history, house and home, humanities, labor, language, law, literature, memoirs, money, nutrition, parenting, psychology, regional, sociology, spirituality, womens issues, womens studies, western. Send query letter only to submissions@martinsisterspublishing.com Does not review artwork.

FICTION Subjects include adventure, confession, fantasy, historical, humor, juvenile, literary, mainstream, military, mystery, poetry in translation, regional, religious, romance, science fiction, short story collections, spiritual, sports, suspense, war, western, young adult.

MAUPIN HOUSE PUBLISHING, INC.

2416 NW 71st Place, Gainesville FL 32653. (800)524-0634. Fax: (352)373-5546. E-mail: info@maupin-house.com. Website: www.maupinhouse.com. **Contact:** Julie Graddy, publisher (areas of interest: education, professional development). Publishes trade paperback originals and reprints. **Publishes 6-8 titles/year. 60% of books from first-time authors. 100% from unagented writers. Pays 10% royalty on retail price.** Publishes book 6-18 months after acceptance of ms. Accepts simultaneous submissions. Responds in less than 1 month to queries, proposals, and mss. Catalog and guidelines free on request and available online at website and by e-mail at: publisher@maupinhouse.com.

Maupin House publishes professional resource books for language arts teachers K-12."

NONFICTION Subjects include education, language arts, literacy and the arts, reading comprehension, writing workshop. "Study the website to understand our publishing preferences. Successful authors are all teachers or former teachers." Query with SASE or via e-mail. Submit proposal package, including outline, 1-2 sample chapters, and TOC/marketing ideas. Reviews artwork/photos as part of the mss package. Writers should send photocopies, digital

TIPS "Our audience is K-12 educators, teachers. Be familiar with our publishing areas and tell us why your book idea is better/different than what is out there. How do you plan to promote it? Successful authors help promote books via speaking engagements, conferences, etc."

MAVERICK MUSICALS AND PLAYS

89 Bergann Rd., Maleny QLD 4552, Australia. Phone/Fax: (61)(7)5494-4007. E-mail: helen@mavmuse.com. Website: www.mavmuse.com. **Contact:** The Editor. Estab. 1978. Guidelines available online.

FICTION Subjects include plays and musicals. "Looking for two-act musicals and one- and two-act plays. See website for more details."

MAY DAVENPORT, PUBLISHERS

26313 Purissima Rd., Los Altos Hills CA 94022. (650)947-1275. Fax: (650)947-1373. E-mail: mdbooks@earthlink.net. Website: www.maydavenportpublishers.com. **Contact:** May Davenport, editor/publisher. Estab. 1976. Publishes hardcover and paperback originals. **Publishes 4 titles/year. 95% of books from first-time authors. 100% from unagented writers. Pays 15% royalty on retail price (if book sells). Pays no advance.** Publishes book 12 months after acceptance of ms. Responds in 1 month to queries. Book catalog and ms guidelines for #10 SASE.

🔑 May Davenport publishes literature for teenagers (before they graduate from high school) as supplementary literary material in English courses nationwide. Looking particularly for authors able to write for the teen Internet generation who don't like to read in-depth. Currently emphasizing more upper-level subjects for teens."

NONFICTION Subjects include Americana, language, literature, humorous memoirs for children/young adults. "For children ages 6-8: stories to read with pictures to color in 500 words. For preteens and young adults: Exhibit your writing skills and entertain them with your literary tools." Query with SASE.

FICTION Subjects include humor, literary. "We want to focus on novels junior and senior high school teachers can read aloud, share with their reluctant readers in their classrooms." Query with SASE.

TIPS "Just write your fictional novel humorously. If you can't write that way, create youthful characters so teachers, as well as 15-18-year-old high school readers, will laugh at your descriptive passages and contemporary dialogue. Avoid 1-sentence paragraphs. The audience we want to reach is today's high-tech teens who are talented with digital cameras hooked up to computers. Show them what you can do 'in print' for them and their equipment."

MCFARLAND & CO., INC., PUBLISHERS

Box 611, Jefferson NC 28640. (336)246-4460. Fax: (336)246-5018. E-mail: info@mcfarlandpub.com. Website: www.mcfarlandpub.com. **Contact:** Steve Wilson, editorial director (automotive, general); David Alff, editor (general); Gary Mitchem, acquisitions editor (general, baseball). Estab. 1979. Publishes hardcover and quality paperback originals; a nontrade publisher. **Publishes 350 titles/year. 50% of books from first-time authors. 95% from unagented writers.** Publishes book 10 months after acceptance of ms. Responds in 1 month to queries. Guidelines available online.

🔑 McFarland publishes serious nonfiction in a variety of fields, including general reference, performing arts, popular culture, sports (particularly baseball); women's studies, librarianship, literature, Civil War, history and international studies. Currently emphasizing medieval history, automotive history. De-emphasizing memoirs."

NONFICTION Subjects include art, architecture, automotive, health, medicine, history, military, war/war, popular contemporary culture, music, dance, recreation, sociology, world affairs, sports (very strong), African-American studies (very strong). Reference books are particularly wanted—fresh material (i.e., not in head-to-head competition with an established title). We prefer manuscripts of 250 or more double-spaced pages or at least 75,000 words. No fiction, New Age, exposes, poetry, children's books, devotional/inspirational works, Bible studies, or personal essays. Query with SASE. Submit outline, sample chapters. Reviews artwork/photos.

TIPS "We want well-organized knowledge of an area in which there is not information coverage at present, plus reliability so we don't feel we have to check absolutely everything. Our market is worldwide and libraries are an important part. McFarland also publishes six journals: the *Journal of Information Ethics*, *North Korean Review*, *Base Ball: A Journal of the Early GameBlack Ball: A Negro Leagues Journal*, *Clues: A Journal of Detection*, and *Minerva Journal of Women and War*."

⊕ MC PRESS

P.O. Box 4886, Ketchum ID 83340. Fax: (208)639-1231. E-mail: duptmor@mcpressonline.com. Website: www.mcpressonline.com. **Contact:** David Uptmor, publisher. Estab. 2001. Publishes trade paperback originals. **Publishes 40 titles/year. 100 queries received/year. 50 mss received/year. 5% of books from first-time authors. 5% from unagented writers. Pays 10-16% royalty on wholesale price.** Publishes book 5 months after acceptance of ms. Accepts simultaneous submissions. Responds in 1 month to queries, proposals and manuscripts. Book catalog and ms guidelines free.

IMPRINTS MC Press, IBM Press.

NONFICTION Subjects include computers, electronics. "We specialize in computer titles targeted at IBM technologies." Submit proposal package, outline, 2 sample chapters, abstract. Reviews artwork/photos. Send photocopies.

⊕ ME & MI PUBLISHING

English-Spanish Foundation, 400 South Knoll, Suite B, Wheaton IL 60187. Fax: (630)588-9804. Website: www.memima.com. **Contact:** Mark Wesley, acquisition editor (pre-K-1). Estab. 2001. Publishes hardcover originals. **Publishes 10 titles/year. 30 queries received/year. 30 mss received/year. 30% of books from first-time authors. 70% from unagented writers. Pays 5% royalty on wholesale price. Makes outright purchase of 1,000-3,000.** Publishes book 1 year after acceptance of ms. Accepts simultaneous submissions. Responds in 1 month to queries. Responds in 3 months to proposals. Responds in 4 months to manuscripts. Book catalog available online. Guidelines available via e-mail.

NONFICTION Subjects include ethnic, language, literature, multicultural. Submit complete ms. Reviews artwork/photos. Send photocopies.

TIPS "Our audience is pre-K to 2nd grade. Our books are bilingual (Spanish and English)."

MEADOWBROOK PRESS

5451 Smetana Dr., Minnetonka MN 55343. Fax: (952)930-1940. E-mail: info@meadowbrookpress.com. Website: www.meadowbrookpress.com. **Contact:** Art Director. Estab. 1974. Publishes trade paperback originals and reprints. **1,500 queries received/year. 10% of books from first-time authors. Pays 7 ½% royalty. Pays small advance.** Publishes book 18 months-2 years after acceptance of ms. Accepts simultaneous submissions. Responds only if interested to queries. Book catalog for #10 SASE. Guidelines available online.

"We are not currently accepting unsolicited manuscripts or queries for the following genres: adult fiction, adult poetry, humor, and children's fiction. Also note that we do not currently publish picture books for children, travel titles, scholarly, or literary works. For children's poetry guidelines, please go to our website."

NONFICTION Subjects include child guidance, cooking, foods, nutrition, pregnancy. "We prefer a query first; then we will request an outline and/or sample material. Send for guidelines." No children's fiction, academic, or biography. Query or submit outline with sample chapters.

POETRY Children's poetry books.

TIPS "Always send for guidelines before submitting material. Always submit nonreturnable copies; we do not respond to queries or submissions unless interested."

MELLEN POETRY PRESS

P.O. Box 450, Lewiston NY 14092-0450. (716)754-2266. Fax: (716)754-4056. E-mail: jrupnow@mellen-press.com. Website: www.mellenpress.com. **Contact:** Dr. John Rupnow, acquisitions. Estab. 1973.

We are a non-subsidy academic publisher of books in the humanities and social sciences. Our sole criterion for publication is that a manuscript makes a contribution to scholarship. We publish monographs, critical editions, collections, translations, revisionist studies, constructive essays, bibliographies, dictionaries, grammars and dissertations. We publish in English, French, German, Spanish, Italian, Portuguese, Welsh and Russian. Our books are well reviewed and acquired by research libraries worldwide. The *Press* also publishes over 100 continuing series, several academic journals, and the research generated by several scholarly institutes."

MEMORY MAKERS BOOKS

Imprint of F+W Media, Inc., 4700 E. Galbraith Rd., Cincinnati OH 45236. Website: www.memorymakersmagazine.com. **Contact:** Christine Doyle, editorial director. Estab. 1998. Publishes trade paperback originals. **Publishes 3 titles/year. 70% of books from first-time authors. 95% from unagented writers. Pays royalty. Pays advance.** Publishes book 12-15 months after acceptance of ms. Accepts simultaneous submissions. Responds in 2 months to queries.

Memory Makers Books exclusively publishes titles for the consumer scrapbooking industry in the form of fresh and innovative scrapbooking books. Authors who submit proposal packages must be outstanding scrapbook artists, as well as apt photographers and writers. Authors must possess a well-rounded knowledge of the industry in order to present their special book idea in a concise and complete proposal package to ensure proper evaluation."

NONFICTION Subjects include crafts/scrapbooking. "Submit a proposal package that includes 40-word synopsis of the book; detailed outline (front and back matter, chapters, sidebars) for a 128-page book; no less than 10 pieces of sample art (jpgs) that illustrate the subject/techniques to be covered in the book; a brief biography and published clips."

TIPS "Our readers are savvy scrapbook and paper artists—from beginning to advanced—who are on the lookout for cutting-edge scrapbooking techniques with photo illustration that they can re-create in their own albums with their own photos and journaling. Study our books to see how we present material, then pitch us something fresh, innovative and unlike anything other consumer scrapbooking publishers are producing."

MENC: THE NATIONAL ASSOCIATION FOR MUSIC EDUCATION

MENC, 1806 Robert Fulton Dr., Reston VA 20191-4348. Fax: (703)860-1531. E-mail: ellaw@menc.org. Website: www.menc.org. **Contact:** Ella Wilcox, editor. Sue Rarus, Dir. of Informaton Resources and Publications Estab. 1907. **Pays royalty on retail price.**

⊶ JOURNALS: See www.menc.org for our guidelines for contributors. Our mission is to advance music education by encouraging the study and making of music by all. *Music Educators Journal* and *Teaching Music* are two of our journal publications. *Music Educators Journal (MEJ)* encourages music education professionals who are MENC members to submit mss about all phases of music education in schools and communities, practical instructional techniques, teaching philosophy, and current issues in music teaching and learning. (See separate listing for Teaching Music.) BOOKS: Publishes hardcover and trade paperback originals. Publishes 10 titles/year. 75 queries received/year. 50 mss received/year. 40% of books from first-time authors. 100% from unagented writers. Pays royalty on retail price. Publishes book 1-2 years after acceptance of ms. Responds in 2 months to queries. Responds in 4 months to proposals. Book catalog available online. Guidelines available online.

NONFICTION Subjects include child guidance, education, multicultural, music, dance, music education. Mss evaluated by professional music educators. Submit proposal package, outline, 1-3 sample chapters, bio, CV, marketing strategy. For journal articles, submit electronically to http://mc.manuscriptcentral.com/mej. Authors will be required to set up an online account on the SAGETRACK system powered by ScholarOne (this can take about 30 minutes). From their account, a new submission can be initiated.

TIPS "Look online for book proposal guidelines. No telephone calls. We are committed to music education books that will serve as the very best resources for music educators, students and their parents."

MERIWETHER PUBLISHING, LTD.

P.O. Box 7710, Colorado Springs CO 80903. (719)594-4422. Fax: (719)594-9916. E-mail: ahammelev@meriwether.com. Website: www.meriwetherpublishing.com; www.contemporarydrama.com. **Contact:** Theodore Zape, assoc. editor. Arthur Zapel, assoc. editor Estab. 1969. Publishes paperback originals and reprints. **Pays 10% royalty or negotiates purchase.** Accepts simultaneous submissions. Responds in 6 weeks. Book catalog and ms guidelines for $2 postage.

⊶ We are specialists in theater arts books and plays for middle grades, high schools, and colleges. We publish textbooks for drama courses of all types. We also publish for mainline liturgical churches—drama activities for church holidays, youth activities, and fundraising entertainment. These may be plays, musicals, or drama-related books. Query with synopsis or submit complete script."

NONFICTION "Most of the plays we publish are one-acts, 15-45 min. in length. We also publish full-length two-act musicals or three-act plays, 90 min. in length. We prefer comedies. Musical shows should have large cast for 20-25 performers. Comedy sketches, monologues, and plays are welcome. We prefer simple staging appropriate to middle school, high school, college, college, or church performance. We like playwrights who see the world with a sense of humor. Offbeat themes and treatments are accepted if the playwright can sustain a light touch. In documentary or religious plays we look for good research and authenticity. We are publishing many scenebooks for actors (which can be anthologies of great works excerpts), scenebooks on special themes, and speech and theatrical arts textbooks. We also publish many books of monologs for young performers. We are especially interested in authority-books on a variety of theater-related subjects." "Contemporary Drama Service is now looking for play or musical adaptations of classic stories by famous authors and playwrights. Also looking for parodies of famous movies or historical and/or fictional characters (i.e., Robin Hood, Rip Van Winkle, Buffalo Bill, Huckleberry Finn). Obtains either amateur or all rights."

FICTION Subjects include mainstream, contemporary, plays, and musicals, religious, children's plays and religious Christmas and Easter plays, suspense, all in playscript format, comedy. Plays and musical comedies for middle grades through college only. Query with SASE.

TIPS "Contemporary Drama Service is looking for creative books on comedy, monologs, staging amateur theatricals, and Christian youth activities. Our writers are usually highly experienced in theatre as teachers or performers. We welcome books that reflect their experience and special knowledge. Any good comedy writer of monologs and short scenes will find a home with us."

MESSIANIC JEWISH PUBLISHERS

6120 Day Long Lane, Clarksville MD 21029. (410)531-6644. E-mail: website@messianicjewish.net. Website: www.messianicjewish.net. **Contact:** Janet Chaier, managing editor. Publishes hardcover and trade paperback originals and reprints. **Publishes 6-12 titles/year. Pays 7-15% royalty on wholesale price.** Guidelines available via e-mail.

IMPRINTS Lederer Books

NONFICTION Subjects include religion, Messianic Judaism, Jewish roots of the Christian faith. Text must demonstrate keen awareness of Jewish culture and thought, and Biblical literacy. Jewish themes only. Query with SASE. Unsolicited mss are not returned.

FICTION Subjects include religious. "We publish very little fiction. Jewish or Biblical themes are a must. Text must demonstrate keen awareness of Jewish culture and thought." Query with SASE. Unsolicited mss are not return

TIPS Our audience is Christians, M Be familiar with titles we hav

⊘ MIAMI UNIVERSITY PRESS

356 Bachelor Hall, Miami University, Oxford OH 45056. E-mail: tumakw@muohio.edu. Website: www.muohio.edu/mupress. **Contact:** Keith Tuma, Editor. Estab. 1992.

🔾 *Currently closed to unsolicited mss, except for submissions to novella contest; see website for information on the contest.*

🔑 Publishes 1-2 books of poetry/year and one novella, in paperback editions. Recent poetry titles include *Virgil's Cow,* by Frederick Farryl Goodwin; *Between Cup and Lip*, by Peter Manson; and *Talk Poetry*, by Mairéad Byrne. Recent fiction titles include John Cotter, *Under the Small Lights*, Lee Upton, *The Guide to the Flying Island*, and Cary Holladay, *A Fight in the Doctor's Office.*

MICHIGAN STATE UNIVERSITY PRESS

1405 S. Harrison Rd., Suite 25, East Lansing MI 48823-5202. (517)355-9543. Fax: (517)432-2611. E-mail: msupress@msu.edu. Website: http://msupress.msu.edu/. **Contact:** Martha Bates and Julie Loehr, acquisitions. Estab. 1947. Publishes hardcover and softcover originals. **Pays variable royalty.** Book catalog and ms guidelines for 9×12 SASE or online.

🔾 1405 S. Harrison Road, Suite 25, East Lansing MI 48823-5202. (517) 355-9543. Fax: (517) 432-2611. E-mail: msupress@msu.edu. Acquisitions: Martha Bates and Julie Loehr. Estab. 1947. Michigan State University Press has notably represented both scholarly publishing and the mission of Michigan State University with the publication of numerous award-winning books and scholarly journals. In addition, they publish nonfiction that addresses, in a more contemporary way, social concerns, such as diversity and civil rights. They also publish literary fiction and poetry. MSU Press publishes both hardcover and softcover originals and pays variable royalty. Accepts simultaneous submissions: No. Seasonal catalog and manuscript guidelines are available online.

NONFICTION Subjects include Nonfiction Americana, American Studies, business, economics, creative nonfiction, ethnic, Afro-American studies, government, politics, history, contemporary civil rights, language, literature, literary criticism, regional, Great Lakes regional, Canadian studies, women's studies, environmental studies, and American Indian Studies. Distributes books for: University of Calgary Press, University of Alberta Press, and University of Manitoba Press. Submit proposal/outline and sample chapter. Hard copy is preferred but e-mail proposals are also accepted. Initial submissions to MSU Press should be in the form of a short letter of inquiry and a sample chapter(s), as well as our preliminary Marketing Questionnaire, which can be downloaded from their website. We do not accept: Festschrifts, conference papers, or unrevised dissertations. (Festschrift: A complimentary or memorial publication usually in the form of a collection of essays, addresses, or biographical, bibliographic, scientific, of other contributions). Reviews artwork/photos.

MICROSOFT PRESS

E-mail: 4bkideas@microsoft.com. Website: www.microsoft.com/learning/books. **Contact:** Editor. **Publishes 80 titles/year. 25% of books from first-time authors. 90% from unagented writers.** Book proposal guidelines available online.

NONFICTION Subjects include software. A book proposal should consist of the following information: a table of contents, a resumè with author biography, a writing sample, and a questionnaire. "We place a great deal of emphasis on your proposal. A proposal provides us with a basis for evaluating the idea of the book and how fully your book fulfills its purpose."

MID-LIST PRESS

4324 12th Ave S., Minneapolis MN 55407-3218. (612)822-3733. Fax: (612)823-8387. E-mail: guide@midlist.org. Website: www.midlist.org. Estab. 1989. Publishes hardcover and trade paperback originals. **Publishes 3 titles/year.** Publishes book Publishes titles 12-18 months after acceptance. after acceptance of ms. Accepts simultaneous submissions. Guidelines available online.

> ↾ Mid-List Press publishes books of high literary merit and fresh artistic vision by new and emerging writers."

FICTION No children's, juvenile, romance, young adult. See guidelines.

TIPS "Mid-List Press is an independent press. Mid-List Press."

MILKWEED EDITIONS

1011 Washington Ave. S., Suite 300, Minneapolis MN 55415. (612)332-3192. E-mail: submissions@milkweed.org. Website: www.milkweed.org. Estab. 1979. Publishes hardcover, trade paperback, and electronic originals; trade paperback and electronic reprints. **Publishes 15-20 titles/year. 25% of books from first-time authors. 75% from unagented writers. Pays 7% royalty on retail price. Pays varied advance from $500-10,000.** Publishes book 18 months. after acceptance of ms. Accepts simultaneous submissions. Responds in 6 months to queries, proposals, and mss. Book catalog available online at website. Guidelines available online at website http://www.milkweed.org/content/blogcategory/.

> ● Please consider our previous publications when considering submissions.

NONFICTION Subjects include agriculture, animals, archaeology, art, contemporary culture, creative nonfiction, environment, gardening, gay, government, history, humanities, language, literature, multicultural, nature, politics, literary, regional, translation, women's issues, world affairs. Please consider our previous publications when considering submissions to Milkweed Editions. Submit complete ms with SASE. Milkweed strongly encourages digital submissions through our website. Does not review artwork.

FICTION Subjects include experimental, short story collections, translation, young adult. Novels for adults and for readers 8-13. High literary quality. For adult readers: literary fiction, nonfiction, poetry, essays. For children (ages 8-13): literary novels. Translations welcome for both audiences. No romance, mysteries, science fiction. Query with SASE, submit completed ms.

POETRY Query with SASE; submit completed ms

TIPS "We are looking for excellent writing with the intent of making a humane impact on society. Please read submission guidelines before submitting and acquaint yourself with our books in terms of style and quality before submitting. Many factors influence our selection process, so don't get discouraged. Nonfiction is focused on literary writing about the natural world, including living well in urban environments."

MILKWEEDS FOR YOUNG READERS

Milkweed Editions, 1011 Washington Ave. S., Suite 300, Minneapolis MN 55415. (612)332-3192. Fax: (612)215-2550. E-mail: submissions@milkweed.org. Website: www.milkweed.org. **Contact:** The editors. Estab. 1984. Publishes hardcover and trade paperback originals. **Publishes 3-4 titles/year. 25% of books from first-time authors. 50% from unagented writers. Pays 7% royalty on retail price. Pays variable advance.** Publishes book 1 year after acceptance of ms. Accepts simultaneous submissions. Responds in 6 months to queries. Book catalog for $1.50. Guidelines for #10 SASE or on the website.

> ↾ We are looking first of all for high quality literary writing. We publish books with the intention of making a humane impact on society."

FICTION Subjects include adventure, fantasy, historical, humor, mainstream, contemporary, animal, environmental. Query with SASE.

MITCHELL LANE PUBLISHERS, INC.

Editorial Department, Mitchell Lane Publishers, P.O. Box 196, Hockessin DE 19707. (302)234-9426. Fax: (866)834-4164. E-mail: barbaramitchell@mitchell-lane.com. Website: www.mitchelllane.com. **Contact:** Barbara Mitchell, publisher. Estab. 1993. Publishes hardcover and library bound originals. **Publishes 85 titles/year. 100 queries received/year. 5 mss received/year. 0% of books from first-time authors. 90% from unagented writers. Makes outright purchase on work-for-hire basis.** Publishes book 1 year after acceptance of ms. Responds only if interested to queries. Book catalog available free.

NONFICTION Subjects include ethnic, multicultural. Query with SASE. *All unsolicited mss discarded.*

TIPS "We hire writers on a 'work-for-hire' basis to complete book projects we assign. Send résumé and writing samples that do not need to be returned."

MOMENTUM BOOKS, LLC

117 W. Third St., Royal Oak MI 48067. (248)691-1800. Fax: (248)691-4531. E-mail: info@momentumbooks.com. Website: www.momentumbooks.com. **Contact:** Franklin Foxx, editor. Estab. 1987. **Publishes 6 titles/year. 100 queries received/year; 30 mss received/year. 95% of books from first-time authors. 100% from unagented writers. Pays 10-15% royalty.** Guidelines available online.

☛ Momentum Books publishes Midwest regional nonfiction.

NONFICTION , history, sports, travel, automotive, current events, biography, entertainment. Submit proposal package, outline, 3 sample chapters, marketing outline.

TIPS (Also, custom publishing services are available for authors who are considering self-publishing.)

MONDIAL

203 W. 107th St., Suite 6C, New York NY 10025. (212)851-3252. Fax: (208)361-2863. E-mail: contact@mondialbooks.com. Website: www.mondialbooks.com; www.librejo.com. **Contact:** Andrew Moore, editor. Estab. 1996. Publishes trade paperback originals and reprints. **Publishes 20 titles/year. 2,000 queries received/year. 500 mss received/year. 20% of books from first-time authors. Pays 10% royalty on wholesale price.** Publishes book 4 months after acceptance of ms. Accepts simultaneous submissions. Guidelines available online.

NONFICTION Subjects include alternative, ethnic, gay, lesbian, history, language, literature, literary criticism, memoirs, multicultural, philosophy, psychology, sex, sociology, translation. Submit proposal package, outline, 1 sample chapters. Send only electronically by e-mail.

FICTION Subjects include adventure, erotica, ethnic, gay, lesbian, historical, literary, mainstream, contemporary, multicultural, mystery, poetry, romance, short story collections, translation.

⊕ MOON SHADOW PRESS

Wakestone Press, 200 Brook Hollow Rd., Nashville TN 37205. (615)739-6428. Website: http://www.wakestonepress.com. **Contact:** Frank Daniels III, Editor (Youth Fiction). Estab. 2010. Format publishes in hardcover and paperback originals; e-books. **Publishes 6-8 (1-3/fiction) titles/year. 3% of books from first-time authors. 100% from unagented writers. Pays 7.5-15% royalty. Pays $2,000 advance (negotiable)** Publishes book 18-30 months after acceptance of ms. Accepts simultaneous submissions. Responds to queries in 4 weeks; to mss in 2 months. Catalogs available online at website. Send SASE for writer's guidelines.

IMPRINTS Moon Shadow Press, Frank Daniels III, editor, Youth Fiction

☛ Moon Shadow Press, an imprint of Wakestone Press, was founded on the belief that neither authors nor stories get proper attention. Wakestone looks for authors who, with the right team and support, can break out of the crowded, chaotic catalog of books to get their stories widely read. We love the current confusing pace of the publishing business with its challenges in distirbution, technology, marketing and consumption. We think that these market challenges are an exciting time to bring both new and old stories to readers in a way of forms and formats. Our experience in a wide range of publishing ventures has led us to understand that the media world is an either/and world, where readers want to have both short- and long-form stories, in print and digital formats, in multi-media and one-dimensional media. Our goal is to enable authors to tell and sell their stories and make them a part of our culture. Currently Moon Shadow Press is working on publishing youth titles.

FICTION Subjects include adventure, fantasy, horror, juvenile, Needs work for the series *Galadria: Peter Huddleson and the Rites of Passage*, Miguel Lopez DeLeon. Accepts

TIPS "Be honest, be creative, be interesting."

MOREHOUSE PUBLISHING CO.

Church Publishing Incorporated, 4475 Linglestown Rd., Harrisburg PA 17112. Fax: (717)541-8136. E-mail: dperkins@cpg.org. Website: www.morehousepublishing.org. **Contact:** Davis Perkins. Frank Tedeschi Estab. 1884. Publishes hardcover and paperback originals. **Publishes 35 titles/year. 50% of books from first-time authors. Pays small advance.** Publishes book 18 months after acceptance of ms. Accepts simultaneous submissions. Responds in 2-3 months to queries. Guidelines available online.

8—⚓ Morehouse Publishing publishes mainline Christian books, primarily Episcopal/Anglican works. Currently emphasizing Christian spiritual direction.

NONFICTION Subjects include religion, Christian, women's issues, women's studies, Christian spirituality, liturgies, congregational resources, issues around Christian life. Submit outline, résumé, 1-2 sample chapters, market analysis.

✪ MORGAN JAMES PUBLISHING

Morgan James LLC, 5 Penn Plaza, 23rd Floor, New York NY 10001. (212)655-5470. Fax: (516)908-4496. E-mail: csauer@morganjamespublishing.com. Website: www.morganjamespublishing.com. **Contact:** Rick Frishman, publisher (general nonfiction, business); David Hancock, founder (entrepreneurial business). Estab. 2003. hardcover, trade paperback, & electronic originals. **Publishes 163 titles/year. 4,500 queries/year; 3,700 mss/year. 60% of books from first-time authors. 80% from unagented writers. 20-30% royalty on wholesale price** Publishes book 6 months after acceptance of ms. Accepts simultaneous submissions. Responds in 1 month on queries, proposals & mss. Catalog & guidelines free on request.

NONFICTION Subjects include business, career guidance, child guidance, communications, computers, counseling, economics, education, electronics, finance, government, health, history, law, medicine, money, real estate, religion. "Best if book supports existing platform or business." Submit proposal package, including outline, 3 sample chapters; submit completed ms. Does not review artwork/photos.

TIPS "Study www.morganjamespublishing.com."

MOTORBOOKS

Quayside Publishing Group, Motorbooks, MBI Publishing Company, 400 First Ave. North, Suite 300, Minneapolis MN 55401. (612)344-8100. Fax: (612)344-8691. E-mail: customerservice@quaysidepub.com. Website: www.motorbooks.com; http://www.qbookshop.com/motorbooks.com/. **Contact:** Lee Klancher, senior editor; Darwin Holmstrom (motorcycles); Peter Bodensteiner (racing, how-to); Dennis Pernu (Americana, trains & boats); Steve Gansen (military, aviation, tractors). Estab. 1973. Publishes hardcover and paperback originals. **Publishes 200 titles/year. 300 queries received/year. 50 mss received/year. 95% from unagented writers. Pays $5,000 average advance.** Publishes book 1 year after acceptance of ms. Accepts simultaneous submissions. Responds in 6-8 months to proposals. Book catalog available free. Guidelines for #10 SASE or go to website at http://www.qbookshop.com/uploads/files/Motorbooks%20Submission%20Guidelines.pdf.

IMPRINTS Motorbooks International, Crestline.

8—⚓ Motorbooks is one of the world's leading transportation publishers, covering subjects from classic motorcycles to heavy equipment to today's latest automotive technology. We satisfy our customers' high expectations by hiring top writers and photographers and presenting their work in handsomely designed books that work hard in the shop and look good on the coffee table."

NONFICTION Subjects include Americana, history, hobbies, military, war, photography, translation, nonfiction. State qualifications for doing book. Transportation-related subjects. Query with SASE. Reviews artwork/photos. Send photocopies.

MOTORCYCLING

Imprint of Far Horizons Media Company, P.O. Box 560989, Rockledge FL 32956. (321)690-2224. Fax: (321)690-0853. E-mail: postmaster@farhorizonsmedia.com. Website: www.farhorizonsmedia.com. **Contact:** Acquisitions Editor. Publishes trade paperback originals and limited hardback. **Publishes 15-25 titles/year. 100 queries received/year. 50 mss received/year. 50% of books from first-time authors. 99% from unagented writers.** Publishes book 3 months after acceptance of ms. Responds in 1 month to queries. Guidelines available by e-mail.

Motorcycling publishes books on motorcycling and motorcycling history.

NONFICTION "General interest relating to touring, guide books, how-to subjects, and motorcycling history. We are interested in any title related to these fields. Query with a list of ideas. Include phone number. Our title plans rarely extend past 6 months, although we know the type and quantity of books we will publish over the next 2 years. We prefer good knowledge with simple-to-understand writing style containing a well-rounded vocabulary." Query with SASE. Reviews artwork/photos. Send photocopies and JPEG files on CD.

TIPS "All of our staff and editors are riders. As such, we publish what we would want to read relating to the subject. Our audience in general are active riders at the beginner and intermediate level of repair knowledge and riding skills, and history buffs wanting to learn more about the history of motorcycles in this country. Many are people new to motorcycles, attempting to learn all they can before starting out on that first long ride or even buying their first bike. Keep it easy and simple to follow. Use motorcycle jargon sparingly. Do not use complicated technical jargon, terms, or formulas without a detailed explanation of the same. Use experienced riders and mechanics as a resource for knowledge."

MOUNTAINLAND PUBLISHING, INC.

P.O. Box 150891, Ogden UT 84415. E-mail: editor@mountainlandpublishing.com. Website: www.mountainlandpublishing.com. **Contact:** Michael Combe, managing editor (Fiction, Nonfiction). Estab. 2001. Hardcover, Mass market paperback, and electronic originals. **Publishes 10-12 titles/year. 90% of books from first-time authors. 100% from unagented writers. 15% royalty/minimum** Publishes book 6 months after acceptance of ms. 1 month on queries and proposals; 8 months on mss. Catalog and guidelines available online at website.

We are no longer accepting unsolicited submissions either via mail or e-mail.

NONFICTION Subjects include Americana, creative nonfiction, education, history, humanities, literary criticism, memoirs, military, philosophy, regional, religion, science, spirituality, war, world affairs. "Nonfiction should read like Fiction. It should be captivating to the audience and on an intriguing subject." Query via e-mail. Submit proposal package, including outline, 3 sample chapters. Reviews artwork/photos. Send photocopies.

FICTION Subjects include adventure, contemporary, fantasy, historical, horror, humor, juvenile, literary, mainstream, military, multicultural, mystery, regional, religious, romance, science fiction, short story collections, spiritual, sports, suspense, war, western, young adult. " Fiction should be able to grab readers and hold their attention with dynamic writing, interesting characters, and compelling plot." Submit synopsis, 1 sample chapter via e-mail.

TIPS "Our audience is a new generation of readers who enjoy well told storiers and who want to be entertained. They want characters they can feel close to and/or love to hate. Make sure your ms is ready for print. Publishing companies will not wait for you to finish editing your story. Be confident that the work you are submitting is your best work. Please submit all ms electronically. Submissions received by mail will be returned unopened."

MOUNTAIN PRESS PUBLISHING CO.

P.O. Box 2399, Missoula MT 59806-2399. (406)728-1900 or (800)234-5308. Fax: (406)728-1635. E-mail: info@mtnpress.com. Website: www.mountain-press.com. **Contact:** Jennifer Carey, editor. Estab. 1948. Publishes hardcover and trade paperback originals. **Publishes 15 titles/year. 50% of books from first-time authors. 90% from unagented writers. Pays 7-12% royalty on wholesale price.** Publishes book 2 years after acceptance of ms. Responds in 3 months to queries. Book catalog available online.

We are expanding our Roadside Geology, Geology Underfoot, and Roadside History series (done on a state-by-state basis). We are interested in well-written regional field guides—plants and flowers—and readable history and natural history."

NONFICTION Subjects include animals, history, Western, nature, environment, regional, science, Earth science. No personal histories or journals, poetry or fiction. Query with SASE. Submit outline, sample chapters. Reviews artwork/photos.

TIPS "Find out what kind of books a publisher is interested in and tailor your writing to them; research markets and target your audience. Research other books on the same subjects. Make yours different. Don't present your manuscript to a publisher—sell it. Give the information needed to make a decision on a title. Please learn what we publish before sending your proposal. We are a 'niche' publisher."

⊕ MSI PRESS

38 Monterey St., San Juan Bautista CA 95045. E-mail: editor@msipress.com. Website: www.msipress.com. **Contact:** Betty Leaver, managing ed. (foreign language, humanities, humor, spirituality). Estab. 2003. Trade paperback originals. **Publishes 8-12 titles/year. 10% of books from first-time authors. 100% from unagented writers. 10% royalty on wholesale price.** Publishes book 6 months after acceptance of ms. Accepts simultaneous submissions. 1 month to queries and proposals; 2 months to manuscripts. Catalog available online at website. Guidelines available at e-mail address: info@msipress.com.

NONFICTION Subjects include education, health, medicine, humanities, language, literature, medicine, psychology, spirituality. "We are hoping to expand our spirituality, psychology, and self-help line." Submit proposal package, including: outline, 1 sample chapter, and professional resumè. Reviews artwork/photos; send computer disk.

TIPS "We are interested in helping to develop new writers who have good literacy skills but have limited or no publishing experience. We also have the capacity to work with authors with limited English skills whose first language is Arabic, Russian, Spanish, French, German, or Czech."

Ⓐ MVP BOOKS

MBI Publishing and Quayside Publishing Group, 400 First Ave. N, Suite 300, Minneapolis MN 55401. (612)344-8160. E-mail: jleventhal@mbipublishing.com. Website: www.mvpbooks.com. **Contact:** Josh Leventhal, publisher. Estab. 2009. hardcover and trade paperback originals. **Publishes 15-20 titles/year. Pays royalty or fees. Pays advance.** Publishes book 1 year. after acceptance of ms. 3 months after queries.

> 💬 "We seek authors who are strongly committed to helping us promote and sell their books. Please present as focused an idea as possible in a brief submission. Note your credentials for writing the book. Tell all you know about the market niche, existing competition, and marketing possibilities for proposed book."

> 🔑 We publish books for enthusiasts in a wide variety of sports, recreation, and fitness subjects, including heavily illustrated celebra-

tions, narrative works, and how-to instructional guides."

NONFICTION Subjects include sports (baseball, football, basketball, hockey, surfing, golf, bicycling, martial arts, etc.); outdoor activities (hunting and fishing); health and fitness. No children's books. Query with SASE. "We consider queries from both first-time and experienced authors as well as agented or unagented projects. Submit outline." Reviews artwork/photos. Send sample digital images or transparencies (duplicates and tearsheets only).

MYSTIC RIDGE BOOKS

Subsidiary of Mystic Ridge Productions, Inc., 222 Main St., Suite 142, Farmington CT 06032. Website: www.mysticridgebooks.com. **Contact:** Acquisitions Editor. Estab. "Mystic Ridge Books (and its new children's line, MRB Kidz) is a rapidly growing publishing company - nationally known and respected - whose books are sold at fine booksellers. Our aim is to publish 'can't-put-me-down' books on a variety of interests for adults & children. For adults, we're offering books on personal betterment and happiness, including but not limited to books on: relationships, intimacy, love, and a range of human interests. Look for self-help books, too, in the future. For children, MRB Kidz offers books that delight, entertain, educate, inspire and instill positive values. This line, though new, has drawn rave reviews from the press, teachers, librarians, parents and kids. Its authors have appeared on TV shows throughout the nation.". Publishes hardcover, trade paperback, & mass market paperback originals; trade paperback & mass market paperback reprints. **Publishes 6+ titles/year. 500+ queries received/year. 200+ mss received/year. 50% of books from first-time authors. 90% from unagented writers. Pays 10% royalty on wholesale price.** Publishes book 9 months after acceptance of ms. Accepts simultaneous submissions. Responds in 3 months to queries, proposals, & mss. Book catalog & guidelines available online.

NONFICTION Subjects include audio, Americana, animals, anthropology, archeology, business, economics, child guidance, contemporary culture, cooking, foods, nutrition, creative nonfiction, government, politics, health, medicine, history, hobbies, language, literature, memoirs, money, finance, philosophy, psychology, recreation, science, sex, social sciences, spirituality, translation, womens issues, womens studies. "The writer should have a unique angle on a subject (it would be a plus if they are an expert in their field). The target readership should be fairly large. The writer must also be a good self-promoter, willing to be proactive in getting publicity." Query with SASE. Reviews artwork/photos. Send photocopies.

FICTION Subjects include young adult. "We are only looking for juvenile fiction at this time." Query with SASE.

TIPS "An agent is not necessary. Quality is key. It is helpful if the author has a dynamic, charismatic personality, who is intent on developing a high, public profile. No inquiries by phone, and no queries by certified mail or e-mail."

☺ NAPOLEON & COMPANY

235-1173 Dundas St. East, Toronto ON M4M 3P1, Canada. (416)465-9961. Fax: (416)465-3241. E-mail: napoleon@napoleonandcompany.com. Website: www.napoleonandcompany.com. **Contact:** A. Thompson, editor. Estab. 1990. Publishes hardcover and trade paperback originals and reprints. **Publishes 15 titles/year. 200 queries received/year. 100 mss received/year. 50% of books from first-time authors. 75% from unagented writers.** Publishes book 18 months after acceptance of ms. Accepts simultaneous submissions. Responds in 1 month to queries. Responds in 3 months to proposals. Responds in 6 months to manuscripts. Book catalog and guidelines available online.

○ "Napoleon is not accepting children's picture books at this time. Rendezvous Crime is not accepting mysteries. Check website for updates. We are accepting general adult fiction only for RendezVous Press and Darkstar Fiction."

⚷ Rendezvous publishes adult fiction. Napoleon publishes children's books.

NONFICTION Query with SASE. Submit outline, 1 sample chapter.

TIPS Canadian resident authors only.

NATUREGRAPH PUBLISHERS, INC.

P.O. Box 1047, Happy Camp CA 96039. Fax: (530)493-5240. E-mail: nature@sisqtel.net. Website: www.naturegraph.com. **Contact:** Barbara Brown, owner. Estab. 1946. Publishes trade paperback originals. **Publishes 2 titles/year. 300 queries received/year. 12 mss received/year. 80% of books from first-time authors. 0% from unagented writers.** Publishes book 24 months after acceptance of ms. Accepts simultaneous submissions. Responds in 1 month to queries.

Responds in 2 months to manuscripts. Book catalog for #10 SASE.

NONFICTION Subjects include anthropology, archaeology, multicultural, nature, environment, science, natural history: biology, geology, ecology, astronomy, crafts.

TIPS "Please-always send a stamped reply envelope. Publishers get hundreds of manuscripts yearly."

NBM PUBLISHING

40 Exchange Pl., Ste. 1308, New York NY 10005. E-mail: nbmgn@nbmpub.com. Website: nbmpub.com. **Contact:** Terry Nantier, editor/art director. Estab. 1976.

⚷ Publishes graphic novels for an audience of 18-34 year olds. Types of books include fiction, fantasy, mystery, science fiction, horror and social parodies. Circ. 5,000-10,000.

NEAL-SCHUMAN PUBLISHERS, INC.

100 William St., Suite 2004, New York NY 10038-4512. (212)925-8650. Fax: (212)219-8916. E-mail: charles@neal-schuman.com. E-mail: info@neal-schuman.com. Website: www.neal-schuman.com. **Contact:** Charles Harman, V.P./ director of publishing. Estab. 1976. Publishes trade paperback originals. **Publishes 36 titles/year. 150 queries. 80% of books from first-time authors. 100% from unagented writers. Pays 10-15% royalty on wholesale price. Pays infrequent advance.** Publishes book 5 months after acceptance of ms. Accepts simultaneous submissions. Responds in 1 month to queries, proposals, & mss. Book catalog free. Mss

⚷ Neal-Schuman publishes books about library management, archival science, records management, digital curation, information literary, the Internet and information technology. Especially submitting proposals for undergraduate information studies, archival science, records management, and knowledge management textbooks."

NONFICTION Subjects include computers, electronics, education, software, Internet guides, library and information science, archival studies, records management. Submit proposal package, outline, 1 sample chapter. Reviews artwork. Send photocopies.

TIPS "Our audience are professional librarians, archivists, and records managers."

NEW FORUMS PRESS

New Forums, 1018 S. Lewis St., Stillwater OK 74074. (405)372-6158. Fax: (405)377-2237. E-mail: contact@

newforums.com. E-mail: submissions@newforums.com. Website: www.newforums.com. **Contact:** Doug Dollar, president (interests: higher education, Oklahoma-Regional). Estab. 1981. Hardcover and trade paperback originals. **60% of books from first-time authors. 100% from unagented writers.** Use Author Guidelines online or call (800)606-3766 with any questions.

8—m New Forums Press is an independent publisher offering works devoted to various aspects of professional development in higher education, home and office aides, and various titles of a regional interest. We welcome suggestions for thematic series of books and thematic issues of our academic journals—addressing a single issue, problem, or theory."

NONFICTION Subjects include business, finance, history, literature, money, music, politics, regional, sociology, young adult. "We are actively seeking new authors — send for review copies and author guidelines, and visit our website." Manuscripts should be submitted as a Microsoft Word document, or a similar standard word processor document (saved in RTF rich text), as an attachment to an e-mail sent to submissions@newforums.com. Otherwise, submit your manuscript on 8 ½ x 11 inch white bond paper (one original). The name and complete address, telephone, fax number, and e-mail address of each author should appear on a separate cover page, so it can be removed for the blind review process.

⊕ NEW ISSUES POETRY & PROSE

Western Michigan University, 1903 W. Michigan Ave., Kalamazoo MI 49008-5463. (269)387-8185. Fax: (269)387-2562. E-mail: new-issues@wmich.edu. Website: wmich.edu/newissues. **Contact:** Managing Editor. Estab. 1996. **50% first time authors% of books from first-time authors. 95% unagented writers% from unagented writers.** Publishes book 18 months after acceptance of ms. Accepts simultaneous submissions. Guidelines available online, by e-mail, or by SASE.

POETRY New Issues Poetry & Prose offers two contests annually. The Green Rose Prize is awarded to an author who has previously published at least one full-length book of poems. The New Issues Poetry Prize, an award for a first book of poems, is chosen by a guest judge. Past judges have included Philip Levine, C.K. Williams, C.D. Wright, and Campbell McGrath. New Issues does not read manuscripts outside our contests. Graduate students in the Ph.D. and M.F.A. programs of Western Michigan Univ. often volunteer their time

reading manuscripts. Finalists are chosen by the editors. New Issues often publishes up to two additional manuscripts selected from the finalists.

⊕⊜ NEW LIBRI PRESS

4230 95th Ave. SE, Mercer Island WA 98040. E-mail: stasa@newlibri.com. E-mail: query@newlibri.com. Website: http://www.newlibri.com. **Contact:** Michael Muller, Editor (Nonfiction and foreign writers). Estab. 2011. Format publishes in hardcover, trade paperback, mass market paperback, & electronic originals; hardcover, trade paperback, mass market, & electronic reprints. **Publishes 10 (under no fee model) titles/year. 80% of books from first-time authors. 90% from unagented writers. Pays 50-75% royalty on wholesale price. No advance.** Publishes book 4-6 months after acceptance of ms. Responds in 1 month on queries and mss; 2 months on proposals. Catalog not available yet.

NONFICTION Subjects include agriculture, automotive, business, child guidance, computers, cooking, creative nonfiction, economics, electronics, environment, gardening, hobbies, house and home, nature, parenting, recreation, science, sex, software, translation, travel. "Writers should know we embrace ebooks. This means that some formats and types of books work well and others don't." Prefers e-mail. Submit proposal package, including outline, 2 sample chapters, and summary of market from author's perspective; submit completed ms.

FICTION Subjects include adventure, experimental, fantasy, historical, horror, literary, mainstream, military, mystery, science fiction, translation, war, western, young adult. "Open to most ideas right now; this will change as we mature as a press." As a new press, we are more open than most and time will probably shape the direction. That said, trite as it is, we want good writing that is fun to read. While we currently are not looking for some subgenres, if it is well writeen and a bit off the beaten path, submit to us. We are ebook friendly, which means some fiction may be less likely to currently sell(e.g. picture books would work only on an iPad or Color Nook as of this writing)." Submit proposal package, including snyopsis, 5 sample chapters; submit completed ms.

POETRY "Poetry is not our focus. We will probably only examine poetry in the author-subsidized model." Submit complete ms.

TIPS "Our audience is someone who is comfortable reading an ebook, or someone who is tired of the recycled authors of mainstream publishing, but still wants a good, relatively fast, reading experience. The industry is changing, while we accept for the traditional model, we are searching for writings who are interested in sharing the risk and controlling their own destiny. We embrace writers with no agent."

NEW VICTORIA PUBLISHERS INC.

P.O. Box 13173, Chicago IL 60613-0173. E-mail: queries@newvictoria.com. Website: www.newvictoria. com. **Contact:** Patricia Feuerhaken. Estab. 1977. Trade paperback and hardcover originals. Catalog free on request; for #10 SASE; or online at website. Guidelines free on request; for #10 SASE; or online.

NONFICTION Subjects include alternative, biography, lesbian, history, language, poetry, fiction, literature, memoirs, multicultural, music/dance, mystery, nature, environment, New Age, erotica, translation, women's issues/studies, world affairs, contemporary culture. "We will consider well-researched nonfiction of interest to women, as well as lesbian feminist herstory, or biography of interest to a general as well as academic audience." Query with SASE. Reviews artwork/photos; send photocopies.

FICTION Subjects include adventure, comic books, erotica, fantasy, feminist, gay, ethnic, lesbian, historical, humor, literary, multicultural, mystery, science fiction, spiritual, translation. "We are looking for well-crafted fiction in all genres featuring out lesbian protagonists with a strong sense of self-awareness. Our writers' guidelines are available on our website." Query with SASE.

POETRY Query

TIPS "New writers need to pay attention to structuring your novel and determining the basic conflict."

NEXT DECADE, INC.

39 Old Farmstead Rd., Chester NJ 07930. (908)879-6625. Fax: (908)879-2920. E-mail: barbara@nextdecade.com. Website: www.nextdecade.com. **Contact:** Barbara Kimmel, president (reference); Carol Rose, editor. Publishes trade paperback originals. **Publishes 2-4 titles/year. Pays 8-15% royalty on wholesale price.** Responds in 1 month to queries. Book catalog available online. Guidelines available online.

NONFICTION Subjects include health, medicine, women's, money, finance, multicultural, senior/retirement issues, real estate.

TIPS "We publish books that simplify complex subjects. We are a small, award-winning press that successfully publishes a handful of books each year."

⊘ NINETY-SIX PRESS

Furman University, 3300 Poinsett Hwy., Greenville SC 29613. (864)294-3152. Fax: (864)294-2224. E-mail: gil.allen@furman.edu. **Contact:** Gilbert Allen, editor. Estab. 1991.

○ "The name of the press is derived from the old name for the area around Greenville, South Carolina—the Ninety-Six District. The name suggests our interest in the writers, readers, and culture of the region." Publishes 1-2 paperback books of poetry/year. Books are usually 45-70 pages, digest-sized, professionally printed, perfect-bound, with coated stock covers. The normal first run is 500 paperback copies, and authors are compensated in copies. **"For further information about Ninety-Six Press, click the link at our website to send an e-mail query."**

NORTH LIGHT BOOKS

Imprint of F+W Media, Inc., 4700 E. Galbraith Rd., Cincinnati OH 45236. Website: www.fwmedia.com. Publishes hardcover and trade paperback how-to books. **Publishes 70-75 titles/year. Pays 10% royalty on net receipts and $4,000 advance.** Accepts simultaneous submissions. Responds in 2 months to queries. Book catalog for 9×12 envelope and 6 first-class stamps.

○ This market is for experienced fine artists and crafters who are willing to work with a North Light editor to produce a step-by-step how-to book about the artist's creative process. See also separate listing for F+W Media, Inc., in this section.

⚏ North Light Books publishes art and craft books, including watercolor, drawing, mixed media and decorative painting, knitting, jewelry making, sewing, and needle arts that emphasize illustrated how-to art instruction. Currently emphasizing drawing including traditional, fantasy art, and Japanese-style comics as well as creativity and inspiration."

NONFICTION Subjects include hobbies, watercolor, realistic drawing, creativity, decorative painting, comics drawing, paper arts, knitting, collage and other craft instruction books. Interested in books on acrylic painting, basic drawing, pen and ink, colored pencil, decorative painting, and beading, art, how-to. Do not submit coffee table art books without how-to art instruction. Query with SASE. Submit outline.

⊕ NORTIA PRESS

27525 Puerta Real, Ste. 100-467, Mission Viejo CA 92701. E-mail: acquisitions@nortiapress.com. E-mail: acquisitions@nortiapress.com. Website: www.NortiaPress.com. Estab. 2009. Format publishes in trade paperback and electronic originals. **Publishes 6 titles/year. 0% of books from first-time authors. 80% from unagented writers. Pays negotiable royalties on wholesale price.** Publishes book 7 months after acceptance of ms. Accepts simultaneous submissions. Responds in 1 month on queries and 3 months on proposals. Catalog and guidelines available for SASE with first-class stamps.

○ "Submit a brief, e-mail query for both fiction and nonfiction. Please include a short bio, approximate word count of book, and expected date of completion for nonfiction titles (fiction titles should be completed before sending a query). All unsolicited snail mail will be discarded without review."

NONFICTION Subjects include business, community, economics, ethnic, government, health, humanities, medicine, memoirs, military, psychology, public affairs, religion, science, sex, social sciences, sociology, war, women's issues, women's studies.

FICTION Subjects include comic books, ethnic, feminist, historical, humor, literary, military, multicultural, regional, sports, war. "We focus mainly on literary and historical fiction, but are open to other genres. No vampire stories, science fiction, or erotica, please."

TIPS "We specialize in working with experienced authors who seek a more collaborative and fulfilling relationship with their publisher. As such, we are less likely to accept pitches form first-time authors, no matter how good the idea. As with any pitch, please make your e-mail very brief and to the point, so the reader is not forced to skim it. Always include some biographic information. Your life is interesting."

NOVA PRESS

11659 Mayfield Ave., Suite 1, Los Angeles CA 90049. (310)207-4078. Fax: (310)571-0908. E-mail: novapress@aol.com. Website: www.novapress.net. **Contact:** Jeff Kolby, President. Estab. 1993. Publishes trade paperback originals. **Publishes 4 titles/year.** Publishes book 4-6 months after acceptance of ms. Book catalog available free.

⌗� Nova Press publishes only test prep books for college entrance exams (SAT, GRE, GMAT, LSAT, etc.), and closely related reference books, such as college guides and vocabulary books."

NONFICTION Subjects include: education, software.

NURSESBOOKS.ORG

American Nurses Association, 8515 Georgia Ave., Suite 400, Silver Spring MD 20901-3492. 1-800-274-4ANA. Fax: (301)628-5003. E-mail: anp@ana.org. Website: www.nursesbooks.org. **Contact:** Rosanne Roe, publisher; Eric Wurzbacher, editor/project manager; Camille Walker, business operations coordinator/project manager. Publishes professional paperback originals and reprints. **Publishes 10 titles/year. 50 queries received/year. 8-10 mss received/year. 75% of books from first-time authors. 100% from unagented writers.** Publishes book 4 months after acceptance of ms. Responds in 3 months to proposals and manuscripts. Book catalog available online. Guidelines available free.

⌗➨ Nursebooks.org publishes books designed to help professional nurses in their work and careers. Through the publishing program, Nursebooks.org provides nurses in all practice settings with publications that address cutting-edge issues and form a basis for debate and exploration of this century's most critical health care trends."

NONFICTION Subjects include advanced practice, computers, continuing education, ethics, health care policy, nursing administration, psychiatric and mental health, quality, nursing history, workplace issues, key clinical topics, such as geriatrics, pain management, public health, spirituality and home health. Submit outline, 1 sample chapter, CV, list of 3 reviewers and paragraph on audience and how to reach them. Reviews artwork/photos. Send photocopies.

OAK KNOLL PRESS

310 Delaware St., New Castle DE 19720. (302)328-7232. Fax: (302)328-7274. E-mail: Laura@oakknoll.com. Website: www.oakknoll.com. **Contact:** Laura R. Williams, publishing director. Estab. 1976. Publishes hardcover and trade paperback originals and reprints. **Publishes 40 titles/year. 250 queries received/year. 100 mss received/year. 50% of books from first-time authors. 100% from unagented writers.** Publishes book

12 months after acceptance of ms. Accepts simultaneous submissions. Guidelines available online.

○━➤ Oak Knoll specializes in books about books and manuals on the book arts: preserving the art and lore of the printed word."

NONFICTION Reviews artwork/photos. Send photocopies.

OAK TREE PRESS

140 E. Palmer, Taylorville IL 62568. (217)824-6500. E-mail: oaktreepub@aol.com. E-mail: queryotp@aol.com. Website: www.oaktreebooks.com. **Contact:** Acquisitions Editor (prefers e-mail contact). Billie Johnson, publisher (mysteries, romance, nonfiction); Sarah Wasson, acquisitions editor (all); Barbara Hoffman, senior editor (children's, young adult, educational) Estab. 1998. trade paperback and hardcover books. **Royalties based on sales. No.** Publishes book 6-9 months (contract says 18 months after signing on) after acceptance of ms. Catalog and guidelines available online.

○ "I am always on the lookout for good mysteries, ones that engage quickly. I definitely want to add to our Timeless Love list. I am also looking at a lot of nonfiction, especially in the "how-to" category. We are one of a few publishers who will consider memoirs, especially memoirs of folks who are not famous, and this is because I enjoy reading them myself. In addition, plans are in progress to launch a political/current affairs imprint, and I am actively looking for titles to build this list. Then, of course, there is always that "special something" book that you can't quite describe, but you know it when you see it. "

○━➤ Oak Tree Press is an independent publisher that celebrates writers, and is dedicated to the many great unknowns who are just waiting for the opportunity to break into print. We're looking for mainstream, genre fiction, narrative nonfiction, how-to. Sponsors 3 contests annually: Dark Oak Mystery, Timeless Love Romance and CopTales for crime and other stories of law enforcement professionals."

FICTION "No science fiction or fantasy novels, or stories set far into the future. Next, novels substantially longer than our stated word count are not considered, regardless of genre. We look for manuscripts of 70-90,000 words. If the story really charms us, we will bend some on either end of the range. No right-wing political or racist agenda, gratuitous sex or violence, especially against women, or depict harm of animals."

TIPS "Perhaps my most extreme pet peeve is receiving queries on projects which we've clearly advertised we don't want: science fiction, fantasy, epic tomes, bigoted diatribes and so on. Second to that is a practice I call "over-taping," or the use of yards and yards of tape, or worse yet, the filament tape so that it takes forever to open the package. Finding story pitches on my voice mail is also annoying."

OBERLIN COLLEGE PRESS

50 N. Professor St., Oberlin College, Oberlin OH 44074. (440)775-8408. Fax: (440)775-8124. E-mail: oc.press@oberlin.edu. Website: www.oberlin.edu/ocpress. **Contact:** Linda Slocum, managing editor. Estab. 1969. Publishes hardcover and trade paperback originals. **Publishes 2-3 titles/year. Pays 7½-10% royalty.** Accepts simultaneous submissions. Responds promptly to queries. Responds in 2 months to manuscripts.

POETRY "*FIELD Magazine*—submit 2-6 poems through website "submissions" tab; FIELD Translation Series—query with SASE and sample poems; FIELD Poetry Series—*no unsolicited mss.* Enter mss in FIELD Poetry Prize ($1,000 and a standard royalty contract) held annually in May. Submit electronically through field poetry prize link on website at www.oberlin.edu/ocpress." Submit 2-6 sample poems.

TIPS "Queries for the FIELD Translation Series: send sample poems and letter describing project. Winner of the annual FIELD poetry prize determines publication. Do not send unsolicited manuscripts."

OBRAKE BOOKS

Obrake Canada, Inc., 3401 Dufferin St., P.O. Box 27538, Toronto, ON M6A3B8, Canada. E-mail: editors@obrake.com. Website: www.obrake.com. **Contact:** Echez Godoy, Acquisitions Editor (fiction-suspense, thriller, multicultural, science fiction, literary, romance, short story collection, mystery, ethnic, African based novels, African American characters and interest). Estab. 2006. Publishes hardcover and paperback originals, paperback reprints. **Publishes 10 titles/year.**

○━➤ We're a small independent publisher. We publish mainly thriller, suspense, romance, mystery, multicutural, and ethnic novels and short story collections." Average print order: 1,500.

Debut novel print order: 1,500. **Published 1 new writer(s) last year.** Plans 3 debut novels this year. Averages 10 total titles/year; 7 fiction titles/year. Member Independent Publishers Association PMA (USA), Canadian Booksellers Association (CBA), Book Promoters Association of Canada (BPAC).

TIPS "Visit our website and follow our submission guidelines."

OCEANVIEW PUBLISHING

595 Bay Isles Rd., Suite 120-G, Longboat Key FL 34228. E-mail: submissions@oceanviewpub.com. Website: www.oceanviewpub.com. **Contact:** Robert Gussin, CEO. Estab. 2006. Publishes hardcover and electronic originals. Responds in 3 months on mss. Catalog and guidelines available online.

⚡ Independent publisher of nonfiction and fiction, with primary interest in original mystery, thriller and suspense titles. Accepts new and established writers."

NONFICTION Accepts nonfiction but specializes in original mystery, thriller and suspense titles. Query first.

FICTION Subjects include mystery, suspense, thriller. Accepting adult mss with a primary interest in the mystery, thriller and suspense genres—from new & established writers. No children's or YA literature, poetry, cookbooks, technical manuals or short stories. Within body of e-mail only, include author's name and brief bio (Indicate if this is an agent submission), ms title and word count, author's mailing address, phone number and e-mail address. Attached to the e-mail should be the following: A synopsis of 750 words or fewer. The first 30 pages of the ms. Please note that we accept only Word documents as attachments to the submission e-mail. Do not send query letters or proposals.

● ONEWORLD PUBLICATIONS

185 Banbury Rd., London: 10 Fitzroy Square, London W1T 5HP, Oxford OX2 7AR, United Kingdom. (44)(1865)310597. Fax: (44)(1865)310598. E-mail: submissions@oneworld-publications.com. Website: www.oneworld-publications.com. Estab. 1986. Publishes hardcover and trade paperback originals and trade paperback reprints. **Publishes 50 titles/year. 200 queries received/year. 50 mss received/year. 20% of books from first-time authors. 50% from unagented writers. Pays 10% royalty on wholesale price. For** academic books; varies for trade titles. **Pays $1,000-20,000 advance.** Publishes book 15 months after acceptance of ms. Book catalog available online. Guidelines available online.

⚡ We publish accessible but authoritative books, mainly by academics or experts for a general readership and cross-over student market. Authors must be well qualified. Currently emphasizing current affairs, popular science, history, and psychology; de-emphasizing self-help."

NONFICTION Submit through online proposal form.

FICTION Subjects include politics, history, multicultural, philosophy, psychology, religion, science, sociology, women's issues, women's studies. Focusing on well-written literary and commercial fiction from a variety of cultures and periods, many exploring interesting issues and global problems.

TIPS "We don't require agents—just good proposals with enough hard information."

ONSTAGE PUBLISHING

190 Lime Quarry Rd., Suite 106-J, Madison AL 35758-8962. (256)308-2300, (888)420-8879. E-mail: onstage123@knology.net. Website: www.onstagepublishing.com. **Contact:** Dianne Hamilton, Senior Editor. Estab. 1999.

◗ To everyone who has submitted a ms, we are currently about 18 months behind. We should get back on track eventually. Please feel free to submit your ms to other houses. OnStage Publishing understands that authors work very hard to produce the finished ms and we do not have to have exclusive submission rights. Please let us know if you sell your ms. Meanwhile, keep writing and we'll keep reading for our next acquisitions.

⚡ OnStage Publishing is a small, independent publishing house specializing in children's literature. We currently publish chapter books, middle-grade fiction and YA. At this time, we only produce fiction books for ages 8-18. We will not do anthologies of any kind. Query first for nonfiction projects as nonfiction projects must spark our interest. See our submission guidelines for more information.

TIPS "Study our titles and get a sense of the kind of books we publish, so that you know whether your project is likely to be right for us."

OOLIGAN PRESS

P.O. Box 751, Portland OR 97207-0751. (503)725-9410. E-mail: ooligan@ooliganpress.pdx.edu. Website: www.ooliganpress.pdx.edu. **Contact:** Acquisitions Committee. Estab. 2001. Publishes trade paperback, and electronic originals and reprints. **Publishes 4-6 titles/year. 250-500 queries received/year. 100 mss received/year. 90% of books from first-time authors. 90% from unagented writers. Pays negotiable% royalty on retail price.** Book catalog available online. Guidelines available online.

NONFICTION Subjects include agriculture, alternative, anthropology, archeology, art, architecture, community, contemporary culture, cooking, foods, nutrition, creative nonfiction, education, ethnic, film, cinema, stage, gay, lesbian, government, politics, history, humanities, language, literature, literary criticism, memoirs, multicultural, music, dance, nature, environment, philosophy, regional, religion, social sciences, sociology, spirituality, translation, travel, women's issues, women's studies, world affairs, young adult. Query with SASE. Submit proposal package, outline, 4 sample chapters, projected page count, audience, marketing ideas and a list of similar titles. Reviews artwork/photos.

FICTION Subjects include adventure, ethnic, experimental, fantasy, feminist, gay, lesbian, historical, horror, humor, literary, mainstream, contemporary, multicultural, mystery, plays, poetry, poetry in translation, regional, science fiction, short story collections, spiritual, suspense, translation, young adult, and middle grade. Query with SASE

POETRY Special preference given for translated poetry, prose poetry, and traditional verse. Especially seeks local poets. Can only consider poetry such as rap, spoken word, or slam if it translates well to the written page. Query, submit sample poems, submit complete ms.

TIPS "For children's books, our audience will be middle grades and young adult, with marketing to general trade, libraries, and schools. Good marketing ideas increase the chances of a manuscript succeeding."

OPEN COURT PUBLISHING CO.

70 E. Lake St., Ste. 300, Chicago IL 60601. Website: www.opencourtbooks.com. Estab. 1887. Publishes hardcover and trade paperback originals. **Publishes 20 titles/year. Pays 5-15% royalty on wholesale price.** Publishes book 2 years after acceptance of ms. Book catalog available online. Guidelines available online.

NONFICTION Subjects include philosophy, Asian thought, religious studies and popular culture. Query with SASE. Submit proposal package, outline, 1 sample chapter, TOC, author's cover letter, intended audience.

TIPS "Audience consists of philosophers and intelligent general readers."

⊕ OTTN PUBLISHING

16 Risler St., Stockton NJ 08559. (609)397-4005. Fax: (609)397-4007. E-mail: inquiries@ottnpublishing.com. Website: www.ottnpublishing.com. Estab. 1998. Hardcover and trade paperback originals. **Publishes 5-10 titles/year. 50 queries received/year 50% of books from first-time authors. 100% from unagented writers. Pays outright purchase of $1,200 to $5,000.** Publishes book 9 months after acceptance of ms. Accepts simultaneous submissions. Responds in 6 months on queries. Catalog online at website. Guidelines online at website http://www.ottnpublishing.com/contact.htm.

NONFICTION Subjects include government, history, military, politics, war. Query with SASE.

TIPS Most of our books are published for the school library market, although we do publish some books for an adult audience.

OUR SUNDAY VISITOR, INC.

200 Noll Plaza, Huntington IN 46750. E-mail: jlindsey@osv.com. Website: www.osv.com. Publishes paperback and hardbound originals. **Publishes 40-50 titles/year. Pays variable royalty on net receipts Pays $2,000 average advance** Publishes book 1-2 years from acceptance to publication. after acceptance of ms. Accepts simultaneous submissions. Responds in 3 months to queries. Book catalog for 9×12 envelope and first-class stamps; ms guidelines available online.

- Our Sunday Visitor, Inc. is publishing only those children's books that are specifically Catholic. See website for submission guidelines."

- We are a Catholic publishing company seeking to educate and deepen our readers in their faith. Currently emphasizing devotional, inspirational, catholic identity, apologetics, and catechetics."

NONFICTION Prefers to see well-developed proposals as first submission with annotated outline and definition of intended market; Catholic viewpoints on family, prayer, and devotional books, and Catholic heritage books. Reviews artwork/photos.

TIPS "Stay in accordance with our guidelines."

OUTRIDER PRESS, INC.

2036 North Winds Dr., Dyer IN 46311. (219)322-7270. Fax: (219)322-7085. E-mail: outriderpress@sbcglobal.net. Website: www.outriderpress.com. **Contact:** Whitney Scott, editor. Estab. 1988. Publishes trade paperback originals. **Receives 2,400 queries/year; 200 mss/year. 90% from unagented writers. Pays honorarium** Publishes book 6 months after acceptance of ms. Responds in 6 weeks to queries; 4 months to proposals and to mss. Guidelines available online.

○ Accepts unsolicited mss. Query with SASE. Accepts queries by mail. Include estimated word count, brief bio, list of publishing credits. Agented fiction 10%. Accepts simultaneous submissions, electronic submissions, submissions on disk. Sometimes comments on rejected mss. In affiliation with Tallgrass Writers Guild, publishes an annual anthology with cash prizes. Anthology theme for 2012 is: "'Deep waters: rivers, lakes and seas.' As always, broadly interpreted with a variety of historic/geographic/psychological settings welcomed." Postmark deadline is Feb. 27, 2012. Pays honorarium. Ms guidelines for SASE. Was a *Small Press Review* "Pick" for 2000. Sponsors an anthology competition for short stories, poetry, and creative nonfiction.

NONFICTION Subjects include creative nonfiction, language, literature, general nonfiction.

FICTION Subjects include contemporary, ethnic, experimental, feminist, gay, historical, humor, lesbian, literary, mainstream, short story collections, fantasy (space fantasy, sword and sorcery), family saga, horror (psychological/supernatural), mystery (amateur sleuth, cozy, police procedural, private eye/hardboiled), psychic/supernatural, romance (contemporary, futuristic/time travel), western (frontier saga, traditional). Query with SASE.

TIPS "It's always best to familiarize yourself with our publications. We're especially fond of humor/irony."

RICHARD C. OWEN PUBLISHERS, INC.

P.O. Box 585, Katonah NY 10536. (914)232-3903; (800)262-0787. E-mail: richardowen@rcowen.com. Website: www.rcowen.com. **Contact:** Richard Owen,

publisher. Estab. 1982. Publishes book 2-5 years after acceptance of ms. Accepts simultaneous submissions. Ms guidelines with SASE and 52¢ postage.

✂ Due to high volume and long production time, we are currently limiting to nonfiction submissions only."

NONFICTION Subjects include art, architecture, history, nature, environment, recreation, science, sports, women's issues, women's studies, music, diverse culture, nature. Our books are for kindergarten, first- and second-grade children to read on their own. The stories are very brief—under 1,000 words—yet well structured and crafted with memorable characters, language, and plots.

TIPS "We don't respond to queries or e-mails. Please do not fax or e-mail us. Because our books are so brief, it is better to send an entire manuscript. We publish story books with inherent educational value for young readers—books they can read with enjoyment and success. We believe students become enthusiastic, independent, life-long learners when supported and guided by skillful teachers using good books. The professional development work we do and the books we publish support these beliefs."

P & R PUBLISHING CO.

P.O. Box 817, Phillipsburg NJ 08865. Fax: (908)859-2390. E-mail: editorial@prpbooks.com. Website: www.prpbooks.com. Estab. 1930. Publishes hardcover originals and trade paperback originals and reprints. **Publishes 40 titles/year. 300 queries received/year. 100 mss received/year. 5% of books from first-time authors. 95% from unagented writers. Pays 10-14% royalty on wholesale price.** Accepts simultaneous submissions. Responds in 3 months to proposals. Guidelines available online.

NONFICTION Subjects include history, religion, spirituality, translation. Only accepts electronic submission with completion of online Author Guidelines. Hard copy mss will not be returned.

TIPS "Our audience is evangelical Christians and seekers. All of our publications are consistent with Biblical teaching, as summarized in the Westminster Standards."

PACIFIC PRESS PUBLISHING ASSOCIATION

Trade Book Division, P.O. Box 5353, Nampa ID 83653-5353. (208)465-2500. Fax: (208)465-2531. E-mail: booksubmissions@pacificpress.com. Website: www.

pacificpress.com. **Contact:** Scott Cady, acquisitions editor (children's stories, biography, Christian living, spiritual growth); David Jarnes, book editor (theology, doctrine, inspiration). Estab. 1874. Publishes hardcover and trade paperback originals and reprints. **Publishes 35 titles/year. 35% of books from first-time authors. 100% from unagented writers. Pays 8-16% royalty on wholesale price.** Publishes book up to 24 months after acceptance of ms. Responds in 3 months to queries. Guidelines available online.

⌇➤ We publish books that fit Seventh-day Adventist beliefs only. All titles are Christian and religious. For guidance, see www.adventist. org/beliefs/index.html. Our books fit into the categories of this retail site: www.adventist-bookcenter.com."

NONFICTION Subjects include child guidance, cooking, foods, nutrition, vegetarian only, health, history, nature, environment, philosophy, religion, spirituality, women's issues, family living, Christian lifestyle, Bible study, Christian doctrine, prophecy. Query with SASE or e-mail, or submit 3 sample chapters, cover letter with overview of book. Electronic submissions accepted. Reviews artwork/photos.

FICTION Subjects include religious. "Pacific Press rarely publishes fiction, but we're interested in developing a line of Seventh-day Adventist fiction in the future. Only proposals accepted; no full manuscripts."

TIPS "Our primary audience is members of the Seventh-day Adventist denomination. Almost all are written by Seventh-day Adventists. Books that do well for us relate the Biblical message to practical human concerns and focus more on the experiential rather than theoretical aspects of Christianity. We are assigning more titles, using less unsolicited material—although we still publish manuscripts from freelance submissions and proposals."

PALARI PUBLISHING

P.O. Box 9288, Richmond VA 23227-0288. (866)570-6724. Fax: (866)570-6724. E-mail: dave@palaribooks. com. Website: www.palaribooks.com. **Contact:** David Smitherman, publisher/editor. Estab. 1998. Publishes hardcover and trade paperback originals. **Pays royalty.** Publishes book 1 year after acceptance of ms. Responds in 1 month to queries. Responds in 2-3 months to manuscripts. Guidelines available online.

◯ Member of Publishers Marketing Association.

⌇➤ Palari provides authoritative, well-written nonfiction that addresses topical consumer needs and fiction with an emphasis on intelligence and quality. We accept solicited and unsolicited manuscripts, however we prefer a query letter and SASE, describing the project briefly and concisely. This letter should include a complete address and telephone number. Palari Publishing accepts queries or any other submissions by e-mail, but prefers queries submitted by US mail. All queries must be submitted by mail according to our guidelines. Promotes titles through book signings, direct mail and the Internet.

NONFICTION Subjects include business, economics, memoirs.

FICTION Subjects include adventure, ethnic, gay, lesbian, historical, literary, mainstream, contemporary, multicultural. Tell why your idea is unique or interesting. Make sure we are interested in your genre before submitting. Query with SASE. Submit bio, estimated word count, list of publishing credits. Accepts queries via e-mail (prefer US Mail), fax.

TIPS "Send a good bio. I'm interested in a writer's experience and unique outlook on life."

⊕ PALETTES & QUILLS

330 Knickerbocker Ave., Rochester NY 14615. (585)456-0217. E-mail: palettesnquills@gmail.com. Website: www.palettesnquills.com. **Contact:** Donna M. Marbach, publisher/owner. Estab. 2002.

⌇➤ Palettes & Quills "is at this point, a poetry press only, and produces only a handful of publications each year, specializing in anthologies, individual chapbooks, and broadsides." Wants "work that should appeal to a wide audience." Has published Cornelius Eady (reprints with permission), M.J. Iuppa, Katharyn Howd Machan, Tom Holmes, Liz Rosenberg, Linda Allardt and Michael Meyerhofer. Published 1-2 chapbooks/year, occasional anthologies, and 3-5 broadsides. Query first with 3-5 poems and a cover letter with brief bio and publication credits for individual unsolicited chapbooks. May include previously published poems. Chapbook poets would get 20 copies of a run; broadside poets and artists get 5-10 copies and occasionally paid $10 for reproduction rights. Anthology poets get 1 copy of the anthology. All poets and artists get a discount on purchases that include their work. Palettes & Quills Biennial Chapbook Contest, held biennially. Prize: $200 plus 50 copies of chapbook and discount on purchase of others. Guidelines available for SASE or on website. Entry fee: $20. Next contest is planned for 2012, Past judges: Ellen Bass and Dorianne Laux."From time to time, Palettes & Quills will put out a special call for poems for themed anthologies (e.g. Women Celebrating Women). Specific directions for such calls are posted on the website when they are announced and our available for SASE."

NONFICTION Does not want political and religious diatribes.

FICTION Does not want "poems that are sold blocks of text, long-lined and without stanza breaks. Wildly elaborate free-verse would be difficult and in all likelihood fight with art background, amateurish rhyming poem, overly sentimental poems, poems that use excessive profanity, or which denigrate other people, or political and religious diatribes."

PARADISE CAY PUBLICATIONS

P.O. Box 29, Arcata CA 95518-0029. (800)736-4509. Fax: (707)822-9163. E-mail: info@paracay.com; jim@paracay.com. Website: www.paracay.com. **Contact:** Matt Morehouse, publisher. Publishes hardcover and trade paperback originals and reprints. **Publishes 5 titles/year. 360-480 queries received/year. 240-360 mss received/year. 10% of books from first-time authors. 100% from unagented writers. Pays 10-15% royalty on wholesale price. Makes outright purchase of $1,000-10,000. Does not normally pay advances to first-time or little-known authors.** Publishes book 4 months after acceptance of ms. Responds in 1 month to queries and to proposals. Responds in 2 months to manuscripts. Book catalog and ms guidelines free on request or online.

IMPRINTS Pardey Books.

Paradise Cay Publications, Inc. is a small independent publisher specializing in nautical books, videos, and art prints. Our primary interest is in manuscripts that deal with the instructional and technical aspects of ocean sailing. We also publish and will consider fiction if it has a strong nautical theme."

NONFICTION Subjects include cooking, foods, nutrition, recreation, sports, travel. Must have strong

nautical theme. Include a cover letter containing a story synopsis and a short bio, including any plans to promote their work. The cover letter should describe the book's subject matter, approach, distinguishing characteristics, intended audience, author's qualifications, and why the author thinks this book is appropriate for Paradise Cay. Call first. Reviews artwork/photos. Send photocopies.

FICTION Subjects include adventure, nautical, sailing. All fiction must have a nautical theme. Query with SASE. Submit proposal package, clips, 2-3 sample chapters.

TIPS Audience is recreational sailors. Call Matt Morehouse (publisher).

PARKWAY PUBLISHERS, INC.

421 Fairfield Lane, Blowing Rock NC 28605. (828)295-9829. Fax: (828)295-9829. E-mail: editor@parkway-publishers.com. Website: www.parkwaypublishers.com. **Contact:** Rao Aluri, president. Publishes hardcover and trade paperback originals. **Publishes 5-6 titles/year. 15-20 queries received/year. 20 mss received/year. 75% of books from first-time authors. 100% from unagented writers.** Publishes book 8 months after acceptance of ms.

Parkway Publishers, Inc. is primarily interested in nonfiction manuscripts about western North Carolina in particular and North Carolina and Appalachia in general. We prefer manuscripts of 150 to 250 pages long - double-spaced, 8.5" ×11" pages. We would like to receive a hardcopy rather than an e-mail submission. We are interested in books about the history of region, biographies, and tourist-oriented books. Will consider fiction if it highlights the region."

NONFICTION Subjects include history, biography, tourism, and natural history. Query with SASE. Submit complete ms.

PASSKEY PUBLICATIONS

P.O. Box 580465, Elk Grove CA 95758. (916)712-7446. E-mail: pineappleguides@yahoo.com. Website: www.passkeypublications.com. **Contact:** Christine P. Silva, president. Estab. 2007. Publishes trade paperback originals. **Publishes 15 titles/year. 375 queries/year; 120 mss/year 15% of books from first-time authors. 90% from unagented writers. Pay varies on retail price.** Publishes book 6-12 months after acceptance of ms. Accepts simultaneous submissions. Responds in 1 month on queries, proposals, and mss (for tax & accounting only). All others 1-3 months. Catalog and guidelines online at website www.passkeypublications.com.

IMPRINTS Passkey Publications, PassKey EA Review.

NONFICTION Subjects include business, economics, finance, money, real estate, accounting, taxation, study guides for professional examinations. "Books on taxation and accounting are generally updated every year to reflect tax law changes, and the turnaround on a ms must be less than 3 months for accounting and tax subject matter. Books generally remain in publication only 11 months and are generally published every year for updates." Submit complete ms. Nonfiction mss only. Reviews artwork/photos as part of ms package. Send electronic files on disk, via e-mail, or jump drive.

TIPS "Accepting business, accounting, tax, finance and other related subjects only."

PAUL DRY BOOKS

1616 Walnut St., Suite 808, Philadelphia PA 19103. (215)231-9939. Fax: (215)231-9942. E-mail: pdry@pauldrybooks.com. Website: http://pauldrybooks.com. Hardcover and trade paperback originals, trade paperback reprints. Book catalog available online. Guidelines available online.

○ "Take a few minutes to familiarize yourself with the books we publish. Then if you think your book would be a good fit in our line, we invite you to submit the following: A one- or two-page summary of the work. Be sure to tell us how long- pages or words-in the full book will be; a sample of 20 to 30 pages; your bio. A brief description of how you think the book (and you, the author) could be marketed."

⚷ We publish fiction, both novels and short stories, and nonfiction, biography, memoirs, history, and essays, covering subjects from Homer to Chekhov, bird watching to jazz music, New York City to shogunate Japan."

NONFICTION Subjects include agriculture, contemporary culture, history, literary criticism, memoirs, multicultural, philosophy, religion, translation, Popular Mathematics. Submit proposal package.

FICTION Subjects include literary, short story collections, translation, young adult, novels. Submit sample chapters, clips, bio. sample 2-3 pages, 1 or 2-pages.

TIPS "Our aim is to publish lively books 'to awaken, delight, & educate'—to spark conversation. We publish fiction and nonfiction, & essays covering subjects from Homer to Chekhov, bird watching to jazz music, New York City to shogunate Japan."

PAULINE BOOKS & MEDIA

50 St. Paula's Ave., Boston MA 02130. (617)522-8911. Fax: (617)541-9805. E-mail: design@paulinemedia.com; **editorial@paulinemedia.com**. Website: www.pauline.org. Estab. 1932. Publishes trade paperback originals and reprints. **Publishes 40 titles/year. 15% of books from first-time authors. 5% from unagented writers. 5-15% royalty on wholesale price** Publishes book 11 months after acceptance of ms. Accepts simultaneous submissions. Responds in 3 months to queries, proposals, & mss. Book catalog available online. Guidelines available online & by e-mail.

⚷ Submissions are evaluated on adherence to Gospel values, harmony with the Catholic tradition, relevance of topic, and quality of writing."

NONFICTION Subjects include child guidance, religion, spirituality. No biography/autobiography, poetry, or strictly nonreligious works considered. Submit proposal package, including outline, 1- 2 sample chapters, cover letter, synopsis, intended audience & proposed length. Reviews artwork; send photocopies.

FICTION Subjects include juvenile. Children's fiction only. We are now accepting submissions for easy-to-read and middle-reader chapter fiction. Please see our Writer's Guidelines. "Submit proposal package, including synopsis, 2 sample chapters, & cover letter; complete ms."

TIPS "Manuscripts may or may not be explicitly catechetical, but we seek those that reflect a positive worldview, good moral values, awareness and appreciation of diversity, and respect for all people. All material must be relevant to the lives of young readers and must conform to Catholic teaching and practice."

PAULIST PRESS

997 Macarthur Blvd., Mahwah NJ 07430-9990. (201)825-7300; (800)218-1903. Fax: (800)836-3161. E-mail: info@paulistpress.com; dcrilly@paulistpress.com. Website: www.paulistpress.com. **Contact:** Donna Crilly, editorial. Estab. 1865. Publishes hardcover and electronic originals and electronic reprints. **Publishes 85 titles/year. 250/year 50% of books from first-time authors. 95% from un-**

agented writers. **Pays 6-8%/min, 12%/max royalty on wholesale price; $1,000-2,000 for outright purchase. Pays advance.** Publishes book 12-18 months after acceptance of ms. Accepts simultaneous submissions. Responds in 2 months to queries and proposals; 2-3 months on mss. Book catalog available free on request and online. Guidelines available online and by e-mail.

8—⚓ Paulist Press publishes "ecumenical theology, Roman Catholic studies, and books on scripture, liturgy, spirituality, church history, and philosophy, as well as works on faith and culture. Our publishing is oriented toward adult-level nonfiction. We do not publish poetry."

NONFICTION Subjects include religion. "It should deal with traditional Catholic spirituality, sacraments, church doctrine or practical aids for ministry and prayer, or be intended as a textbook in religion classes in college or high school. Children's books should have strong religious (not just spiritual) or moral content, or deal with learning to be Catholic." Submit proposal package, including: outline, 1 sample chapter; submit completed ms. Reviews artwork/photos. Writers should send photocopies.

FICTION Subjects include picture books (ages 2-5), chapter books (ages 8-12), Christian and Catholic themes. Submit résumé, ms, SASE. Accepts unsolicited mss, but most of our titles have been commissioned.

TIPS "Our typical reader is probably Roman Catholic and wants the content to be educational about Catholic thought and practice, or else the reader is a spiritual seeker who looks for discovery of God and spiritual values which churches offer but without the church connection."

PEACHTREE CHILDREN'S BOOKS

Peachtree Publishers, Ltd., 1700 Chattahoochee Ave., Atlanta GA 30318-2112. (404)876-8761. Fax: (404)875-2578. E-mail: hello@peachtree-online.com. Website: www.peachtree-online.com. **Contact:** Helen Harriss, submissions editor. Publishes hardcover and trade paperback originals. **Publishes 30 titles/year. 25% of books from first-time authors. 25% from unagented writers. Pays royalty on retail price.** Publishes book 1 year or more after acceptance of ms. Accepts simultaneous submissions. Responds in 6 months to queries. Responds in 6 months to manuscripts. Book catalog for 6 first-class stamps. Guidelines available online.

IMPRINTS Freestone; Peachtree Jr.

8—⚓ We publish a broad range of subjects and perspectives, with emphasis on innovative plots and strong writing."

NONFICTION Subjects include animals, child guidance, creative nonfiction, education, ethnic, gardening, health, medicine, history, language, literature, literary criticism, multicultural, music, dance, nature, environment, recreation, regional, science, social sciences, sports, travel. No e-mail or fax queries of mss. Submit complete ms with SASE, or summary and 3 sample chapters with SASE.

FICTION Subjects include juvenile, picture books, young adult. Looking for very well-written middle grade and young adult novels. No collections of poetry or short stories; no romance or science fiction. Submit complete ms with SASE.

PELICAN PUBLISHING COMPANY

1000 Burmaster St., Gretna LA 70053. (504)368-1175. Fax: (504)368-1195. E-mail: editorial@pelicanpub.com. Website: www.pelicanpub.com. **Contact:** Nina Kooij, editor-in-chief. Estab. 1926. Publishes hardcover, trade paperback and mass market paperback originals and reprints. **Publishes 70 titles/year. 15% of books from first-time authors. 95% from unagented writers. Pays royalty on actual receipts. Advance considered.** Publishes book 9-18 months after acceptance of ms. Responds in 1 month to queries. Responds in 3 months to manuscripts. Book catalog and ms guidelines online.

8—⚓ We believe ideas have consequences. One of the consequences is that they lead to a best-selling book. We publish books to improve and uplift the reader. Currently emphasizing business and history titles."

NONFICTION Subjects include Americana, especially Southern regional, Ozarks, Texas, Florida, and Southwest, art, architecture, ethnic, government, politics, special interest in conservative viewpoint, history, popular, multicultural, American artforms, but will consider others: jazz, blues, Cajun, R&B, regional, religion, for popular audience mostly, but will consider others, sports, motivational (with business slant). "We look for authors who can promote successfully. We require that a query be made first. This greatly expedites the review process and can save the writer additional postage expenses." No multiple queries or submissions. Query with SASE. Reviews artwork/photos.

FICTION Subjects include historical, juvenile, regional or historical focus. We publish maybe 1 novel a year, usually by an author we already have. Almost all proposals are returned. No young adult, romance, science fiction, fantasy, gothic, mystery, erotica, confession, horror, sex, or violence. Also no psychological novels. Query with SASE. Submit outline, clips, 2 sample chapters, SASE.

POETRY Pelican Publishing Company is a medium-sized publisher of popular histories, cookbooks, regional books, children's books, and inspirational/motivational books. Considers poetry for "hardcover children's books only (1,100 words maximum), preferably with a regional focus. However, our needs for this are very limited; we publish 20 juvenile titles per year, and most of these are prose, not poetry."

TIPS "We do extremely well with cookbooks, popular histories, and business. We will continue to build in these areas. The writer must have a clear sense of the market and knowledge of the competition. A query letter should describe the project briefly, give the author's writing and professional credentials, and promotional ideas."

☻ PEMMICAN PUBLICATIONS, INC.

150 Henry Ave., Winnipeg MB R3B 0J7, Canada. (204)589-6346. Fax: (204)589-2063. E-mail: pemmican@pemmican.mb.ca. Website: www.pemmican.mb.ca. **Contact:** Randal McIlroy, managing editor (Metis culture & heritage). Estab. 1980. Publishes trade paperback originals and reprints. **Publishes 5-6/year titles/year. 120 queries received/year. 120 mss received/year. 50% of books from first-time authors. 100% from unagented writers. Pays 10% royalty on retail price** Publishes book 1-2 years after acceptance of ms. Accepts simultaneous submissions. Responds in 3 months to queries, proposals & manuscripts. Book catalog available free with SASE. Guidelines available online.

☛ Pemmican Publications is a Metis publishing house, with a mandate to publish books by Metis authors and illustrators and with an emphasis on culturally relevant stories. We encourage writers to learn a little about Pemmican before sending samples. Pemmican publishes titles in the following genres: Adult Fiction, which includes novels, story collections

and anthologies; Nonfiction, with an emphasis on social history and biography reflecting Metis experience; Children's and Young Adult titles; Aboriginal languages, including Michif and Cree."

NONFICTION Subjects include alternative, creative nonfiction, education, ethnic, history, language, literature, military, war, nature, environment. All mss must be Metis culture and heritage related. Submit proposal package including outline and 3 sample chapters. Reviews artwork/photos. Send photocopies.

FICTION Subjects include adventure, ethnic, historical, juvenile, literary, mystery, picture books, short story collections, sports, suspense, young adult. All manuscripts must be Metis culture and heritage related. Submit proposal package including outline and 3 sample chapters.

POETRY Submit 10 sample poems and complete ms.

TIPS "Our mandate is to promote Metis authors, illustrators and stories. No agent is necessary."

PENGUIN GROUP USA

375 Hudson St., New York NY 10014. (212)366-2000. Website: www.penguin.com. **Contact:** Peter Stampfel, Submission Editor, DAW Books. Responds in 3 months generally. Guidelines available online at website.

IMPRINTS *No unsolicited mss.* Submit work through a literary agent. Exceptions are DAW Books and G.P. Putnam's Sons Books for Young Readers, which are accepting submissions. See individual listings for more information. **Penguin Adult Division**: Ace Books, Alpha Books, Avery, Berkley Books, Dutton, Gotham Books, HPBooks, Hudson St. Press, Jove, New American Library, Penguin, The Penguin Press, Perigee, Plume, Portfolio, G.P. Putnam's Sons, Riverhead, Sentinel, Jeremy P. Tarcher, Viking; **Penguin Children's Division:** Dial Books for Young Readers, Dutton Children's Books, Firebird, Grosset & Dunlap, Philomel, Price Stern Sloan, Puffin Books, G.P. Putnam's Sons, Speak, Viking Children's Books, Frederick Warne.

○ "Penguin Young Readers Group: Never send submissions by e-mail or fax. Never send cassettes, CDs, marketing plans, or original artwork. Please mail only one ms at a time and please be sure to retain a copy of your submission. Because confirmation postcards are easily separated from or hidden within the ms, please do not include them with your submission. Please refrain from calling, faxing, or e-mailing to inquire after the status of an unsolicited submission, as we will be unable to assist you. If you have not received a reply from us after 4 months, you can safely assume that we are not interested in publishing your work."

8→ General interest publisher of both fiction and nonfiction.

FICTION "We publish first novels if they are of professional quality. A literary agent is not required for submission. We will not consider mss that are currently on submission to another publisher unless prior arrangements have been made with a literary agent. Please enclose a SASE with your submission for our correspondence. We ask that you only send us disposable copies of your ms, which will be recycled in the event they are not found suitable for publication. We regret that we are no longer able to return submitted ms copies, as the process resulted in too many difficulties with the postal service and unnecessary expense for the prospective authors. It may require up to three months or more for our editors to review a submission and come to a decision. If you want to be sure we have received your manuscript, please enclose a stamped, self-addressed postcard that we will return when your ms. It is not necessary for you to register or copyright your work before publicationit is protected by law as long as it has not been published. When published, we will copyright the book in the author's name and register that copyright with the Library of Congress. DAW Books is currently accepting manuscripts in the science fiction/fantasy genre. We publish science fiction and fantasy novels. The average length of the novels we publish varies but is almost never less than 80,000 words. Do not submit handwritten material." We do not want short stories, short story collections, novellas, or poetry. Send entire ms with a cover letter. No electronic submissions.

TIPS DAW Books is currently accepting manuscripts in the science fiction/fantasy genre. Refer to DAW's Submission Guidelines. For Penguin Young Readers Group submissions, see guidelines at: http://us.penguingroup.com/static/html/aboutus/pyrg-sub-guides.html.

ⒶⓄ PERENNIAL

HarperCollins Publishers, 10 E. 53rd St., New York NY 10022. (212)207-7000. Website: www.harpercol-lins.com. **Contact:** Acquisitions Editor. Estab. 1963. Publishes trade paperback originals and reprints. Book catalog available free.

○ "With the exception of Avon romance, HarperCollins does not accept unsolicited submissions or query letters. Please refer to your local bookstore, the library, or a book entitled *Literary Marketplace* on how to find the appropriate agent for you."

8→ Perennial publishes a broad range of adult literary fiction and nonfiction paperbacks that create a record of our culture.

NONFICTION Subjects include Americana, animals, business, economics, child guidance, cooking, foods, nutrition, education, ethnic, gay, lesbian, history, language, literature, military, war, money, finance, music, dance, nature, environment, and environment, philosophy, psychology, self-help psychotherapy, recreation, regional, religion, spirituality, science, sociology, sports, translation, travel, womens issues, womens studies, mental health, health, classic literature. Our focus is ever-changing, adjusting to the marketplace. Mistakes writers often make are not giving their background and credentials - why they are qualified to write the book. A proposal should explain why the author wants to write this book; why it will sell; and why it is better or different from others of its kind. Agented submissions only.

FICTION Subjects include ethnic, feminist, literary. Agented submissions only.

POETRY Don't send poetry unless you have been published in several established literary magazines already. *Agented submissions only.*

TIPS See our website for a list of titles or write to us for a free catalog.

PETER PAUPER PRESS, INC.

202 Mamaroneck Ave., White Plains NY 10601-5376. E-mail: customerservice@peterpauper.com. Website: www.peterpauper.com. **Contact:** Barbara Paulding, editorial director. Estab. 1928. Publishes hardcover originals. **Publishes 40-50 titles/year. 100 queries received/year. 150 mss received/year. 5% from unagented writers. Makes outright purchase only. Pays advance.** Publishes book 1 year after acceptance of ms. Responds in 2 months to queries. Ms guidelines for #10 SASE or may request via e-mail.

8→ PPP publishes small and medium format, illustrated gift books for occasions and in celebration of specific relationships such as mom, sister, friend, teacher, grandmother, granddaughter. PPP has expanded into the following areas: books for teens and tweens, activity books for children, organizers, books on popular topics of nonfiction for adults and licensed books by best-selling authors."

NONFICTION "We do not publish fiction or poetry. We publish brief, original quotes, aphorisms, and wise sayings. Please do not send us other people's quotes." Query with SASE.

TIPS "Our readers are primarily female, age 10 and over, who are likely to buy a 'gift' book or gift book set in a stationery, gift, book, or boutique store or national book chain. Writers should become familiar with our previously published work. We publish only small- and medium-format, illustrated, hardcover gift books and sets of between 1,000-4,000 words. We have much less interest in work aimed at men."

PFLAUM PUBLISHING GROUP

6162 N. 114th, Milwaukee WI 53225. (414)353-5528. Fax: (414)353-5529. E-mail: kcannizzo@pflaum.com. **Contact:** Karen A. Cannizzo, editorial director. **Publishes 20 titles/year. Payment may be outright purchase, royalty, or down payment plus royalty.** Book catalog and ms guidelines free.

☛ Pflaum Publishing Group, a division of Peter Li, Inc., serves the specialized market of religious education, primarily Roman Catholic. We provide high quality, theologically sound, practical, and affordable resources that assist religious educators of and ministers to children from preschool through senior high school."

NONFICTION Query with SASE.

ⓐⓞ PICADOR USA

Subsidiary of Holtzbrinck Publishers Holdings LLC, 175 Fifth Ave., New York NY 10010. (212)674-5151. Fax: (212)253-9627. E-mail: james.meader@picadorusa.com. Website: www.picadorusa.com. Estab. 1994. Publishes hardcover and trade paperback originals and reprints.

○ *No unsolicited mss or queries. Agented submissions only.*

☛ Picador publishes high-quality literary fiction and nonfiction.

PICCADILLY BOOKS, LTD.

P.O. Box 25203, Colorado Springs CO 80936-5203. (719)550-9887. Fax: (719) 550-8810. Website: www.piccadillybooks.com. **Contact:** Submissions Department.

Estab. 1985. Publishes hardcover originals and trade paperback originals and reprints. **Publishes 5-8 titles/year. 70% of books from first-time authors. 95% from unagented writers. Pays 6-10% royalty on retail price.** Publishes book 1 year after acceptance of ms. Accepts simultaneous submissions. Responds only if interested, unless accompanied by a SASE to queries.

☛ Picadilly publishes nonfiction, diet, nutrition, and health-related books with a focus on alternative and natural medicine."

NONFICTION Subjects include cooking, foods, nutrition, health, medicine, performing arts. "Do your research. Let us know why there is a need for your book, how it differs from other books on the market, and how you will promote the book. No phone calls." "We prefer to see the entire ms, but will accept a minimum of 3 sample chapters on your first inquiry. A cover letter is also required; please provide a brief overview of the book, information about similar books already in print and explain why yours is different or better. Tell us the prime market for your book and what you can do to help market it. Also, provide us with background information on yourself and explain what qualifies you to write this book."

TIPS "We publish nonfiction, general interest, self-help books currently emphasizing alternative health."

PINEAPPLE PRESS, INC.

P.O. Box 3889, Sarasota FL 34230. (941)739-2219. E-mail: info@pineapplepress.com. Website: www.pineapplepress.com. **Contact:** June Cussen, exec. editor. Estab. 1982. Publishes hardcover and trade paperback originals. **Publishes 25 titles/year. 1,000 queries received/year. 500 mss received/year. 10% of books from first-time authors. 95% from unagented writers. Pays rare advance.** Publishes book 12 months after acceptance of ms. Accepts simultaneous submissions. Responds in 1 month to queries and proposals. Responds in 3 months to manuscripts. Book catalog for 9×12 SAE with $1.25 postage. Guidelines available online.

☛ We are seeking quality nonfiction on diverse topics for the library and book trade markets."

NONFICTION Subjects include regional, Florida. We will consider most nonfiction topics when related to Florida. Submit proposal package, outline, 3 sample chapters, and introduction. Reviews artwork/photos. Send photocopies.

FICTION Subjects include regional, Florida. Submit proposal package, 3 sample chapters, clips.

TIPS "Quality first novels will be published, though we usually only do one or two novels per year and they must be set in Florida. We regard the author/editor relationship as a trusting relationship with communication open both ways. Learn all you can about the publishing process and about how to promote your book once it is published. A query on a novel without a brief sample seems useless."

PIÑATA BOOKS

Imprint of Arte Publico Press, University of Houston, 452 Cullen Performance Hall, Houston TX 77204-2004. (713)743-2845. Fax: (713)743-3080. E-mail: submapp@mail.uh.edu. Website: www.artepublicopress. com. **Contact:** Nicolas Kanellos, director. Estab. 1994. Publishes hardcover and trade paperback originals. **Publishes 10-15 titles/year. 40% of books from first-time authors. Pays 10% royalty on wholesale price. Pays $1,000-3,000 advance.** Publishes book 2 years after acceptance of ms. Accepts simultaneous submissions. Responds in 1 month to queries. Responds in 6 months to manuscripts. Book catalog and ms guidelines available via website or with #10 SASE.

☞ Piñata Books is dedicated to the publication of children's and young adult literature focusing on US Hispanic culture by US Hispanic authors."

NONFICTION Subjects include ethnic. Piñata Books specializes in publication of children's and young adult literature that authentically portrays themes, characters and customs unique to U.S. Hispanic culture. Query with SASE. Submit outline, 2 sample chapters, synopsis.

FICTION Subjects include adventure, juvenile, picture books, young adult. Query with SASE. Submit clips, 2 sample chapters, SASE.

POETRY Appropriate to Hispanic theme. Submit 10 sample poems.

TIPS "Include cover letter with submission explaining why your manuscript is unique and important, why we should publish it, who will buy it, etc.

⊘ PLAN B PRESS

P.O. Box 4067, Alexandria VA 22303. (215)732-2663. E-mail: planbpress@gmail.com. Website: www.planbpress.com. **Contact:** Steven Allen May, president. Estab. 1999.

☞ Plan B Press is Ksmall publishing company with an international feel. Our intention is to have Plan B Press be part of the conversation about the direction and depth of literary movements and genres. Plan B Press's new direction is to seek out authors rarely-to-never published, sharing new voices that might not otherwise be heard. Plan B Press is determined to merge text with image, writing with art." Publishes poetry and short fiction. Wants "experimental poetry, concrete/visual work." Has published poetry by Lamont B. Steptoe, Michele Belluomini, Jim Mancinelli, Lyn Lifshin, Robert Miltner, and Steven Allen May. Publishes 1 poetry book/year and 5-10 chapbooks/year. Books/chapbooks are 24-48 pages, with covers with art/graphics.

FICTION Does not want "sonnets, political or religious poems, work in the style of Ogden Nash."

POETRY Does not want "sonnets, political or religious poems, work in the style of Ogden Nash."

PLANNERS PRESS

Imprint of the American Planning Association, 122 S. Michigan Ave., Ste. 1600, Chicago IL 60603. (312)431-9100. Fax: (312)431-9985. E-mail: plannerspress@planning.org. Website: www.planning.org/plannerspress/index.htm. **Contact:** Timothy Mennel, Ph.D. (planning practice, urban issues, land use, transportation). Estab. 1970. Publishes hardcover, electronic, and trade paperback originals; and trade paperback and electronic reprints. **Publishes 12 titles/year. 50 queries received/year. 35 mss received/year. 25% of books from first-time authors. 100% from unagented writers. Pays 10-15% royalty on wholesale price. Pays advance.** Publishes book 15 months after acceptance of ms. Accepts simultaneous submissions. Responds in 1 month to queries. Responds in 2 months to proposals and manuscripts. Book catalog online at website www.planningbooks.com. Guidelines available by e-mail at plannerspress@planning.org.

☞ Our books often have a narrow audience of city planners and frequently focus on the tools of city planning."

NONFICTION Subjects include agriculture, business, economics, community, contemporary culture, economics, environment, finance, government, politics, history, horticulture, law, money, finance, nature, environment, politics, real estate, science, social sciences, sociology, transportation, world affairs. Submit proposal package, including: outline, 1 sample chapter and c.v. Submit completed ms..

TIPS "Our audience is professional planners but also anyone interested in community development, urban affairs, sustainability, and related fields."

⊕ ⊘ PLATYPUS MEDIA, LLC

725 8th St., SE, Washington DC 20003. (202)546-1674. Fax: (202)546-2356. E-mail: submissions@platypus-media.com. Website: www.platypusmedia.com. **Contact:** Tracey Kilby, editorial assistant (children's—early childhood and science, birth, lactation). Estab. 2000. Publishes hardcover and trade paperback originals. **Publishes 3-4 titles/year. 100 queries received/year. 250 mss received/year. 5% of books from first-time authors. 100% from unagented writers. Pays royalty on wholesale price. Makes outright purchase.** Publishes book 9 months after acceptance of ms. Accepts simultaneous submissions. Responds in 2-4 months to queries. Responds in 2-4 months to proposals. Responds in 2-4 months to manuscripts. Book catalog available free. Guidelines available online.

○ "We are eager to review manuscripts for healthcare professionals, parents or children. We are looking for books that help support family life through education, positive images and role models, and entertainment. Platypus Media encourages books dealing with ethnic and cultural diversity in a lighthearted way that reflects the special relationships that can contribute to building close-knit, well-grounded families.","Only authors and illustrators who include a SASE will receive a response. Please be aware that we are a small company and response times may vary from a few weeks to a few months. Authors and Illustrators should send submissions to the Submissions Editor."

⚷ All content should focus on family closeness and child development.

NONFICTION Subjects include child guidance, education, health, medicine, womens issues, womens studies, breastfeeding, childbirth, children's science books. Query with SASE. *All unsolicited mss returned unopened.* Reviews artwork/photos. Send photocopies. No art will be returned. We are particularly interested in artists who can draw realistic images of mothers and babies, both in the human and mammal world.

FICTION Subjects include juvenile. Query with SASE. No electronic submissions.

TIPS Audience includes parents, children, teachers, and parenting professionals. We publish just a handful of books each year and most are generated in-house.

PLEXUS PUBLISHING, INC.

143 Old Marlton Pike, Medford NJ 08055-8750. (609)654-6500. Fax: (609)654-4309. E-mail: jbryans@plexuspublishing.com. Website: www.plexuspublishing.com. **Contact:** John B. Bryans, editor-in-chief/publisher. Estab. 1977. Publishes hardcover and paperback originals. **Pays $500-1,000 advance.** Accepts simultaneous submissions. Responds in 3 months to proposals. Book catalog and book proposal guidelines for 10×13 SASE.

⚷ Plexus publishes regional-interest (southern New Jersey and the greater Philadelphia area) fiction and nonfiction including mysteries, field guides, nature, travel and history. Also a limited number of titles in health/medicine, biology, ecology, botany, astronomy.

NONFICTION Query with SASE.

FICTION Mysteries and literary novels with a strong regional (southern New Jersey) angle. Query with SASE.

⊕ ⊘ POCKET BOOKS

Simon & Schuster, 1230 Ave. of the Americas, New York NY 10020. (212)698-7000. Website: www.simonsays.com. **Contact:** Jennifer Bergstrom, editor-in-chief. Estab. 1939. Publishes paperback originals and reprints, mass market and trade paperbacks. Book catalog available free. Guidelines available online.

○ Pocket Books remains the mass market imprint of Simon & Schusterj in the Gallery family, publishing titles from authors like Stephen King, Mary Higgins Clark, Vince Flynn, Sandra Brown, Greg Iles, Kresley Cole, and Julia London.

⚷ Pocket Books publishes commercial fiction and genre fiction (WWE, Downtown Press, Star Trek).

NONFICTION Subjects include cooking, foods, nutrition. Agented submissions only.

FICTION Subjects include mystery, romance, suspense, psychological suspense, thriller, western, *Star Trek.* Agented submissions only.

POCOL PRESS

Box 411, Clifton VA 20124. (703)830-5862. Website: www.pocolpress.com. **Contact:** J. Thomas Hetrick, editor. Estab. 1999. Publishes trade paperback originals. **Publishes 6 titles/year. 90 queries received/**

year. **20 mss received/year. 90% of books from first-time authors. 100% from unagented writers. Pays 10-12% royalty on wholesale price.** Publishes book less than 12 months after acceptance of ms. Responds in 1 month to queries. Responds in 2 months to manuscripts. Book catalog and guidelines available online.

- ○ "Our authors are comprised of veteran writers and emerging talents."
- ⚷ Pocol Press is dedicated to producing high-quality books from first-time, non-agented authors. However, all submissions are welcome. We're dedicated to good storytellers and to the written word, specializing in short fiction and baseball. Several of our books have been used as literary texts at universities and in book group discussions around the nation. Pocol Press does not publish children's books, romance novels, or graphic novels."

FICTION Subjects include historical, horror, literary, mainstream, contemporary, military, war, mystery, short story collections, thematic, spiritual, sports, western, baseball fiction. "We specialize in thematic short fiction collections by a single author and baseball fiction. Expert storytellers welcome." Query with SASE.

TIPS "Our audience is aged 18 and over. Pocol Press is unique; we publish good writing and great storytelling. Write the best stories you can. Read them to you friends/peers. Note their reaction. Publishes some of the finest fiction by a small press."

POISONED PEN PRESS

6962 E. 1st Ave., #103, Scottsdale AZ 85251. (480)945-3375. Fax: (480)949-1707. E-mail: editor@poisonedpenpress.com; info@poisonedpenpress.com. E-mail: submissions@poisonedpenpress.com. Website: www.poisonedpenpress.com. **Contact:** Jessica Tribble. Estab. 1996. Publishes hardcover originals, and hardcover and trade paperback reprints. **Publishes 36 titles/year. 1,000 queries received/year. 300 mss received/year. 35% of books from first-time authors. 65% from unagented writers. Pays 9-15% royalty on retail price.** Publishes book 10-12 months after acceptance of ms. Responds in 2-3 months to queries and proposals. Responds in 6 months to manuscripts. Book catalog and guidelines available online.

- ⚷ Our publishing goal is to offer well-written mystery novels of crime and/or detection

where the puzzle and its resolution are the main forces that move the story forward."

FICTION Subjects include mystery. Mss should generally be longer than 65,000 words and shorter than 100,000 words. Does not want novels centered on serial killers, spousal or child abuse, drugs, or extremist groups, although we do not entirely rule such works out. "Query with SASE. Submit clips, first 3 pages. We must receive both the synopsis and ms pages electronically as separate attachments to an e-mail message or as a disk or CD which we will not return."

TIPS "Audience is adult readers of mystery fiction."

POPULAR WOODWORKING BOOKS

Imprint of F+W Media, Inc., 4700 Galbraith Rd., Cincinnati OH 45236. (513)531-2690. Website: popularwoodworking.com. **Contact:** David Thiel, executive editor. Publishes trade paperback and hardcover originals and reprints. **Publishes 6-8 titles/year. 30 queries received/year. 10 mss received/year. 20% of books from first-time authors. 95% from unagented writers.** Publishes book 1 year after acceptance of ms. Accepts simultaneous submissions. Responds in 1 month to queries.

- ⚷ Popular Woodworking Books is one of the largest publishers of woodworking books in the world. From perfecting a furniture design to putting on the final coat of finish, our books provide step-by-step instructions and trusted advice from the pros that make them valuable tools for both beginning and advanced woodworkers. Currently emphasizing woodworking jigs and fixtures, furniture and cabinet projects, smaller finely crafted boxes, all styles of furniture. De-emphasizing woodturning, woodcarving, scroll saw projects."

NONFICTION Subjects include hobbies, woodworking/wood crafts. "We publish heavily illustrated how-to woodworking books that show, rather than tell, our readers how to accomplish their woodworking goals." Query with SASE, or electronic query. Proposal package should include an outline and digital photos.

TIPS "Our books are for beginning to advanced woodworking enthusiasts."

POSSIBILITY PRESS

One Oakglade Circle, Hummelstown PA 17036-9525. (717)566-0468. Fax: (717)566-6423. E-mail: info@possibilitypress.com. Website: www.possibilitypress.com. **Contact:** Mike Markowski, publisher. Estab. 1981. Publishes trade paperback originals. **Pub-**

lishes 2-3 titles/year. **90% of books from first-time authors. 100% from unagented writers. Royalties vary.** Responds in 1 month to queries. Catalog available online. Guidelines available online.

IMPRINTS Aeronautical Publishers; Possibility Press; Markowski International Publishers.

8—☞ Our mission is to help the people of the world grow and become the best they can be, through the written and spoken word."

NONFICTION Subjects include psychology, pop psychology, self-help, leadership, relationships, attitude, business, success/motivation, inspiration, entrepreneurship, sales marketing, MLM and home-based business topics, and human interest success stories. Prefers submissions to be mailed. Include SASE. Submit ms in Microsoft Word. Your submission needs to be made both in hard copy and on a CD. Label it clearly with the book title and your name. Be sure to keep a backup CD for yourself. Save your ms as a .doc file name. Save your file a second time with an rtf (Rich Text Format) extension. See guidelines online. Reviews artwork/photos. Do not send originals.

FICTION Parables that teach lessons about life and success.

TIPS "Our focus is on co-authoring and publishing short (15,000-30,000 words) bestsellers. We're looking for kind and compassionate authors who are passionate about making a difference in the world, and will champion their mission to do so, especially by public speaking. Our dream author writes well, knows how to promote, will champion their mission, speaks for a living, has a following and a platform, is cooperative and understanding, humbly handles critique and direction, is grateful, intelligent, and has a good sense of humor."

PPI (PROFESSIONAL PUBLICATIONS, INC.)

1250 Fifth Ave., Belmont CA 94002-3863. (650)593-9119. Fax: (650)592-4519. E-mail: info@ppi2pass.com. Website: www.ppi2pass.com. Estab. 1975. Publishes hardcover, paperback, and electronic products, CD-ROMs and DVDs. **Publishes 10 titles/year. 5% of books from first-time authors. 100% from unagented writers.** Publishes book 4-18 months after acceptance of ms. Accepts simultaneous submissions. Responds in 1 month to queries. Book catalog and ms guidelines free.

8—☞ PPI publishes professional, reference, and licensing preparation materials. PPI wants submissions from both professionals practicing in the field and from experienced instructors. Currently emphasizing engineering, interior design, architecture, landscape architecture and LEED exam review."

NONFICTION Subjects include architecture, science, landscape architecture, engineering mathematics, engineering, surveying, interior design, greenbuilding, sustainable development, and other professional licensure subjects. Especially needs review and reference books for all professional licensing examinations. Please submit ms and proposal outlining market potential, etc. Proposal template available upon request. Reviews artwork/photos.

TIPS "We specialize in books for those people who want to become licensed and/or accredited professionals: engineers, architects, surveyors, interior designers, LEED APs, etc. Exam Prep Lines generally include online and print products such as review manuals, practice problems, sample exams, E-Learning Modules, IPhone Apps, and more. Demonstrating your understanding of the market, competition, appropriate delivery methods, and marketing ideas will help sell us on your proposal."

PRAKKEN PUBLICATIONS, INC.

P.O. Box 8623, Ann Arbor MI 48107-8623. (734)975-2800. Fax: (734)975-2787. E-mail: pam@eddigest.com. E-mail: susanne@eddigest.com. **Contact:** Susanne Peckham, book editor. Sharon K. Miller, art/design/production manager Estab. 1934. Publishes educational hardcover and paperback originals, as well as educational magazines. **Publishes 3 titles/year.** Accepts simultaneous submissions. Responds in 2 months to queries. Book catalog for #10 SASE.

8—☞ We publish books for educators in career/vocational and technology education, as well as books for the machine trades and machinists' education. Currently emphasizing machine trades."

NONFICTION Subjects include education. "We are currently interested in manuscripts with broad appeal in any of the specific subject areas of machine trades, technology education, career-technical education, and reference for the general education field." Submit outline, sample chapters.

TIPS We have a continuing interest in magazine and book manuscripts which reflect emerging issues and trends in education, especially career-technical, industrial, and technology education.

PRESA :S: PRESS

P.O. Box 792, 8590 Belding Rd NE, Rockford MI 49341. E-mail: presapress@aol.com. Website: www. presapress.com. **Contact:** Roseanne Ritzema, editor. Estab. 2003. Presa :S: Press publishes "perfect-bound paperbacks and saddle-stitched chapbooks of poetry.". **Pays 10-25 author\quotes copies.** Publishes book Time between acceptance and publication is 8-12 weeks. after acceptance of ms. Responds to queries in 2-4 weeks; to mss in 8-12 weeks.

- ✎ Wants "imagistic poetry where form is an extension of content, surreal, experimental, and personal poetry." Does not want "overtly political or didactic material." Has published poetry books by Kirby Congdon, John Amen, Hugh Fox, Eric Greinke, Donald Lev, Lyn Lifshin, Glenna Luschei, and Harry Smith. Publishes 2-3 poetry books/year, 1-2 chapbooks/year, and an occasional anthology. Manuscripts are selected through open submission. Books are 64-144 pages, laser-printed on 24 lb. paper, perfect-bound paperback with a laminated, color art cover. Chapbooks are 28-48 pages, laser-printed on 20-24 lb. paper, saddle-stitched with a color art cover. Anthologies are 250-325 pages, laser-printed, perfect-bound paperback with a laminated color art cover. Press runs 500-1,000 copies. Query first, with a few sample poems and a cover letter with brief bio and publication credits. Book/chapbook mss may include previously published poems.

PRICE WORLD PUBLISHING, LLC

1300 W. Belmont Ave., 20g, Chicago IL 60657. Fax: (216)803-0350. E-mail: publishing@priceworldpublishing.com. Website: www.priceworldpublishing.com. **Contact:** Robert Price, President & Executive Editor. Estab. 2002. Trade and mass market paperback and hardcover originals. **Publishes 10-20 titles/year titles/year. 35 queries received/year; 20 mss/year. 50% of books from first-time authors. 50% from unagented writers. Pays 8-15% royalty on wholesale price.**
NONFICTION Subjects include sports, fitness. Submit proposal package, including outline, completed ms; visit www.priceworldpublishing.com for proposal submission information. Reviews artwork/photos; send PDF or MS Word docs.
TIPS "The focus of our editorial scope is sports and fitness, with emphasis on instruction for training and performance. We now welcome all nonfiction proposals—visit our website for more information."

✚ PRINCETON ARCHITECTURAL PRESS

37 E. 7th St., New York NY 10003. (212)995-9620. Fax: (212)995-9454. E-mail: submissions@papress. com. Website: www.papress.com. **Contact:** Editorial Submissions. Publishes hardcover and trade paperback originals. **Publishes 50 titles/year. 300 queries received/year. 150 mss received/year. 65% of books from first-time authors. 95% from unagented writers. Pays royalty on wholesale price.** Publishes book 1 year after acceptance of ms. Accepts simultaneous submissions. Responds in 2 months to queries, proposals and manuscripts. Book catalog available online. Guidelines available online.
NONFICTION Subjects include art, architecture. Submit proposal package, outline, 1 sample chapters, table of contents, sample of art, and survey of competitive titles. Reviews artwork/photos. Do not send originals.
TIPS "Princeton Architecture Press publishes fine books on architecture, design, photography, landscape, and visual culture. Our books are acclaimed for their strong and unique editorial vision, unrivaled design sensibility, and high production values at affordable prices."

PRUETT PUBLISHING

P.O. Box 2140, Boulder CO 80306. (303)449-4919. Fax: (303)443-9019. Website: www.pruettpublishing.com. **Contact:** Jim Pruett, publisher. Estab. 1959. Publishes hardcover and trade paperback originals, trade paperback reprints. **75-80 mss received/year. 90% of books from first-time authors. 90% from unagented writers.** Publishes book 12-18 months after acceptance of ms. Accepts simultaneous submissions. Responds in 1 month to queries; 3 months to proposals and manuscripts.

- ✎ We are focused on the mountain West. Our trade books cover topics that range from fly fishing to hiking and biking, history, nature, and the environment. We also publish textbooks for grade-school students about the history of Colorado."

NONFICTION Subjects include: alternative, Americana, education, history, nature, environment, sports, travel. Query with SASE. Submit outline, 2 sample chapters. Reviews artwork/photos. Send photocopies.
TIPS "We focus on outdoor recreationalists—hikers, fly-fishers, travelers. There has been a movement away from large publisher's mass market books to-

ward small publisher's regional interest books, and in turn distributors and retail outlets are more interested in small publishers. Authors don't need to have a big name to have a good publisher. Look for similar books that you feel are well-produced—consider design, editing, overall quality, and contact those publishers. Get to know several publishers, and find the one that feels right—trust your instincts."

PRUFROCK PRESS, INC.

5926 Balcones Dr., Ste. 220, Austin TX 78731. (512)300-2220. Fax: (512)300-2221. E-mail: info@prufrock.com. Website: www.prufrock.com. **Contact:** Sarah Morrison, Jennifer Robins, Lacy Compton. Publishes trade paperback originals and reprints. Book catalog and ms guidelines free.

    Prufrock Press publishes exciting, innovative and current resources supporting the education of special needs, gifted and advanced learners."

NONFICTION Subjects include child guidance, education. We publish for the education market. Our readers are typically teachers or parents of special needs, gifted and advanced learners. Our product line is built around professional development books for teachers and activity books for children. Our products support innovative ways of making learning more fun and exciting for children. Submit book prospectus (download form on website).

TIPS "We are looking for practical, classroom-ready materials that encourage children to creatively learn and think."

PUCKERBRUSH PRESS

413 Neville Hall, Orono ME 04469. (207)581-3832. Website: http://puckerbrushreview.com. **Contact:** Sanford Phippen, editor. Estab. 1971. Publishes trade paperback originals and reprints of literary fiction and poetry. **Publishes 3-4 titles/year. Pays 10-15% royalty on wholesale price.** Responds in 1 month to queries. Responds in 2 months to proposals. Responds in 3 months to manuscripts. Book catalog for large SASE and 34¢. Guidelines for SASE.

NONFICTION Subjects include language, literature, translation, Belles lettres. No religious subjects, crime per se, tired prose. Query with SASE.

FICTION Subjects include literary, short story collections, novels. Submit complete ms.

POETRY Submit highest literary quality. Submit complete ms. Please submit your poetry, short stories, literary essays and reviews through the link on website. Hard-copy submissions will no longer be accepted.

TIPS "Be to your vision, not to fashion." "For sophisticated readers who retain love of literature. Maine writers continue to be featured."

PUFFIN BOOKS

Imprint of Penguin Group (USA), Inc., 345 Hudson St., New York NY 10014. (212)366-2000. Website: www.penguinputnam.com. **Contact:** Kristin Gilson, editorial director. Sharyn November, senior editor Publishes trade paperback originals and reprints. **Publishes 225 titles/year. Royalty varies. Pays varies advance.** Book catalog for 9×12 SAE with 7 first-class stamps.

    Puffin Books publishes high-end trade paperbacks and paperback reprints for preschool children, beginning and middle readers, and young adults."

NONFICTION Subjects include education, for teaching concepts and colors, not academic, history, women's issues, women's studies. *No unsolicited mss.*

FICTION Subjects include picture books, young adult, middle grade, easy-to-read grades 1-3. We do not publish original picture books. *No unsolicited mss.*

TIPS "Our audience ranges from little children 'first books' to young adult (ages 14-16). An original idea has the best luck."

PURDUE UNIVERSITY PRESS

Stewart Center 370, 504 West State St., West Lafayette IN 47907-2058. (765)494-2038. E-mail: pupress@purdue.edu. Website: www.thepress.purdue.edu. **Contact:** Acquisitions Editor. Estab. 1960. Publishes hardcover and trade paperback originals and trade paperback reprints. **Publishes 20-25 titles/year.** Book catalog and ms guidelines for 9×12 SASE.

IMPRINTS PuP Books

    We look for books that look at the world as a whole and offer new thoughts and insights into the standard debate. Currently emphasizing technology, human-animal issues, business. De-emphasizing literary studies."

NONFICTION Subjects include agriculture, Americana, business, government, politics, health, history, language, literary criticism, philosophy, regional, science, social sciences, sociology. Dedicated to the dissemination of scholarly and professional information, Purdue University Press provides quality resources in several key subject areas including business, technology, health, veterinary medicine, and other selected disciplines in the humanities and sciences. As the scholarly publishing arm of Purdue University and a unit of Purdue Libraries, the Press is also a partner for university faculty and staff, centers and departments, wishing to disseminate the results of their research. Query before submitting.

⊙ PURICH PUBLISHING

Box 23032, Market Mall Post Office, Saskatoon SK S7J 5H3, Canada. (306)373-5311. Fax: (306)373-5315. E-mail: purich@sasktel.net. Website: www.purich-publishing.com. **Contact:** Donald Purich, publisher; Karen Bolstad, publisher. Estab. 1992. Publishes trade paperback originals. **Publishes 3-5 titles/year. 20% of books from first-time authors. 100% from unagented writers. Pays 8-12% royalty on retail price.** Publishes book within 4 months of completion of editorial work, after acceptance of ms. after acceptance of ms. Responds in 1 month to queries. Responds in 3 months to manuscripts. Book catalog available free.

⦿━ Purich publishes books on law, Aboriginal/Native American issues, and Western Canadian history for the academic and professional trade reference market."

NONFICTION , Aboriginal and social justice issues, Western Canadian history. "We are a specialized publisher and only consider work in our subject areas." Query with SASE.

Ⓐ G.P. PUTNAM'S SONS

Penguin Putnam, Inc., 345 Hudson St., New York NY 10014. (212)414-3610. Fax: (212)366-2664. E-mail: susan.kochan@us.penguingroup.com. Website: www.penguinputnam.com; www.us.penguingroup.com. **Contact:** Susan Kochan, associate editorial director. John Rudolph, executive editor;Timothy Travaglini, senior editor; Stacey Barney, editor. **Art Acquisitions:** Cecilia Yung, art director, Putnam and Philomel.

TIPS "Study our catalogs and get a sense of the kind of books we publish, so that you know whether your project is likely to be right for us."

Ⓐ⊘ G.P. PUTNAM'S SONS HARDCOVER

Imprint of Penguin Group (USA), Inc., 375 Hudson, New York NY 10014. (212)366-2000. Fax: (212)366-2664. Website: www.penguinputnam.com. Publishes hardcover originals. **Pays variable royalties on retail price. Pays varies advance.** Accepts simultane-

ous submissions. Request book catalog through mail order department.

NONFICTION Subjects include animals, business, economics, child guidance, contemporary culture, cooking, foods, nutrition, health, medicine, military, war, nature, environment, religion, science, sports, travel, women's issues, women's studies, celebrity-related topics. Agented submissions only. *No unsolicited mss.*

FICTION Subjects include adventure, literary, mainstream, STET, mystery, suspense, women's. Agented submissions only. *No unsolicited mss.*

QUEST BOOKS

Imprint of Theosophical Publishing House, 306 W. Geneva Rd., P.O. Box 270, Wheaton IL 60187. E-mail: submissions@questbooks.net. Website: www.questbooks.net. **Contact:** Richard Smoley, editor. Idarmis Rodriguez, assoc. ed. Estab. 1965. Publishes hardcover and trade paperback originals and reprints. **Publishes 10 titles/year. 150 ms; 350 queries received/year. 20% of books from first-time authors. 80% from unagented writers. Pays royalty on retail price. Pays varying advance.** Publishes book 12 months after acceptance of ms. Accepts simultaneous submissions. Responds in 2 months to queries, proposals, & mss. Book catalog available free. Guidelines available online at: www. questbooks.net/aboutquest. cfm#submission.

⦿━ Quest Books is the imprint of the Theosophical Publishing House, the publishing arm of the Theosophical Society in America. Since 1965, Quest books has sold millions of books by leading cultural thinkers on such increasingly popular subjects as transpersonal psychology, comparative religion, deep ecology, spiritual growth, the development of creativity, and alternative health practices."

NONFICTION Subjects include philosophy, psychology, religion, spirituality, New Age, astrology/psychic. Our speciality is high-quality spiritual nonfiction with a self-help aspect. Great writing is a must. We seldom publish 'personal spiritual awakening' stories. No submissions accepted that do not fit the needs outlined above. No fiction, poetry, children's books, or any literature based on channeling or personal psychic impressions. Submit proposal package, including outline, 1 sample chapter. Prefer online submissions; attachments must be sent as a single file in Microsoft

Word, Rich Text, or PDF formats. Reviews artwork/photos. Hard copies of mss. and artwork will not be returned. Reviews artwork/photos. Writers should send photocopies or transparencies, but note that none will be returned.

TIPS "Our audience includes readers interested in spirituality, particularly the world's mystical traditions. Read a few recent Quest titles and submission guidelines before submitting. Know our books and our company goals. Explain how your book or proposal relates to other Quest titles. Quest gives preference to writers with established reputations/successful publications. Please be advised that proposals or manuscripts WILL NOT BE ACCEPTED if they fall into any of the following categories: Works intended for or about children, teenagers, or adolescents; Fiction or literary works (novels, short stories, essays, or poetry); Autobiographical material (memoirs, personal experiences, or family stories; Works received through mediumship, trance, or channeling; Works related to UFOs or extraterrestrials; Works related to self-aggrandizement (e.g., "how to make a fortune") or "how to" books."

⊘ QUITE SPECIFIC MEDIA GROUP, LTD.

7373 Pyramid Place, Hollywood CA 90046. (323)851-5797. Fax: (323)851-5798. E-mail: info@quitespecific-media.com. Website: www.quitespecificmedia.com. **Contact:** Ralph Pine, editor-in-chief. Estab. 1967. Publishes hardcover originals, trade paperback originals and reprints. **Publishes 12 titles/year. 300 queries received/year. 100 mss received/year. 75% of books from first-time authors. 85% from unagented writers. Pays royalty on wholesale price. Pays varies advance.** Publishes book 18 months after acceptance of ms. Accepts simultaneous submissions. Responds to queries. Book catalog available online. Guidelines available free.

IMPRINTS Costume & Fashion Press; Drama Publishers; By Design Press; Entertainment Pro; Jade Rabbit.

⚷ Quite Specific Media Group is an umbrella company of 5 imprints specializing in costume and fashion, theater and design."

NONFICTION Subjects include fashion, film, cinema, stage, history, literary criticism, translation. Accepts nonfiction and technical works in translations also. For and about performing arts theory and practice: acting, directing; voice, speech, movement; makeup, masks, wits; costumes, sets, lighting, sound; design and ex-

ecution; technical theater, stagecraft, equipment; stage management; producing; arts management, all varieties; business and legal aspects; film, radio, television, cable, video; theory, criticism, reference; theater and performance history; costume and fashion. Query by e-mail please Reviews artwork/photos.

◉ RADCLIFFE PUBLISHING LTD

70 Alston Dr., Bradwell Abbey, Milton Keynes MK13 9HG, United Kingdom. (44)(0)1908-326-941. Fax: (44)(0)-1908-326-960. E-mail: contact.us@radcliffe-publishing.com. Website: www.radcliffe-oxford.com. **Contact:** Andrew Box, managing editor; Gillian Nineham, editorial director. Estab. 1987. **Publishes 90 or fewer titles/year. Pays royalty.** Guidelines available via e-mail.

🖵 "Send proposal to Gillian Nineham. Unsolicited manuscripts, synopses and ideas welcome. We are not interested in non-medical or medical books aimed at lay people. Every proposal we receive is discussed at length in-house, and most are sent out for external review (usually by experts in the field who also fit the intended market profile). The reviewers' comments are passed back to you anonymously for your reference. Often reviewer feedback will elicit further development of the proposal."

NONFICTION Subjects include health, medicine, sociology, nursing, midwifery, health services management and policy. Submit proposal package, outline, resumè, publishing history, bio.

TIPS "Receive book proposal guidelines by e-mail and study them."

RAINBOW PUBLISHERS

P.O. Box 261129, San Diego CA 92196. (858)277-1167. E-mail: editor@rainbowpublishers.com. Website: www.rainbowpublishers.com; www.legacypresskids.com. **Contact:** Editorial Department. Estab. 1979.

TIPS "Our Rainbow imprint publishes reproducible books for teachers of children in Christian ministries, including crafts, activities, games and puzzles. Our Legacy imprint publishes titles for children such as devotionals, fiction and Christian living. Please write for guidelines and study the market before submitting material."

RAIN TOWN PRESS

1111 E. Burnside St. #309, Portland OR 97214. Website: www.raintownpress.com. **Contact:** Misty V'Marie, acquisitions editor. Estab. 2009. **Publishes 1-4 middle readers; 1-4 young adult titles/year. 100% of books from first-time authors. Pays 8-15% royalty on net sales. Does not pay advance.** Publishes book 1 year after acceptance of ms. Accepts simultaneous submissions. Responds to queries and mss in 1-6 months. Catalog available on website. Imprints included in a single catalog. Guidelines available on website for writers, artists, and photographers.

IMPRINTS In The Future: Raintown Kids, Mary Darcy, Misty V'Marie, William Softich, Leah Brown

○ "We are Portland, Oregon's first independent press dedicated to publishing literature for middle grade and young adult readers. We hope to give rise to their voice, speaking directly to the spirit they embody through our books and other endeavors. The gray days we endure in the Pacific Northwest are custom-made for reading a good book—or in our case, making one. The rain inspires, challenges, and motivates us. To that end, we say: "Let it drizzle." "We will soon publish picture books."

NONFICTION Subjects include animals, contemporary culture, environment, health, history, multicultural, nature, sports. "We are a new press and haven't decided yet how we are going to handle/pursue our nonfiction line when the time comes. I think it would almost take a proposal for us to decide." Query. Submit outline/synopsis and 2 sample chapters. See online submission guide for detailed instructions.

FICTION Subjects include fantasy, folktales, graphic novels, hi-lo, problem novels, science fiction, special needs, concept. Query. Submit complete ms. See online submission guide for detailed instructions.

TIPS "The middle grade and YA markets have sometimes very stringent conventions for subject matter, theme, etc. It's most helpful if an author knows his/her genre inside & out. Read, read, read books that have successfully been published for your genre. This will ultimately make your writing more marketable. Also, follow a publisher's submission guidelines to a tee. We try to set writers up for success. Send us what we're looking for."

RANDOM HOUSE AUDIO PUBLISHING GROUP

Subsidiary of Random House, Inc., 1745 Broadway, New York NY 10019. (212)782-9720. Fax: (212)782-9600. Website: www.randomhouse.com.

IMPRINTS Listening Library; Random House Audible; Random House Audio; Random House Audio Assets; Random House Audio Dimensions; Random House Audio Roads; Random House Audio Voices; Random House Price-less.

☛ Audio publishing for adults and children, offering titles in both abridged and unabridged formats on cassettes, compact discs, and by digital delivery."

RANDOM HOUSE INFORMATION GROUP

Division of Random House, Inc., 1745 Broadway, New York NY 10019. (212)782-9000. Website: www.randomhouse.com.

IMPRINTS Fodor's Travel Publications; Living Language; House of Collectibles; Prima Games; The Princeton Review; Random House Español; Random House Puzzles & Games; Random House Reference Publishing.

RANDOM HOUSE LARGE PRINT

Division of Random House, Inc., 1745 Broadway, New York NY 10019. (212)782-9720. Fax: (212)782-9600. Website: www.randomhouse.com. Estab. 1990. **Publishes 60 titles/year.**

☛ Acquires and publishes general interest fiction and nonfiction in large print editions."

RAVEN TREE PRESS

A Division of Delta Publishing Company, 1400 Miller Pkwy., McHenry IL 60050. (800)323-8270. Fax: (800)909-9901. E-mail: raven@deltapublishing.com; raven@raventreepress.com. E-mail: acquisitions@deltapublishing.com. Website: www.raventreepress.com. **Contact:** Check website for most current submission guidelines (children's picture books). Estab. 2000. Publishes hardcover and trade paperback originals. **Publishes 10 titles/year. 1,500 mss received/year. 75% of books from first-time authors. 90% from unagented writers. Pays royalty. Pays variable advance.** Publishes book 2 years after acceptance of ms. Accepts simultaneous submissions. Responds in 2 months to manuscripts. Book catalog available online. Guidelines available online.

NONFICTION "Submission guidelines available online. Do not query or send mss without first checking submission guidelines on our website for most current information."

TIPS "Submit only based on guidelines. No e-mail OR snail mail queries please. Word count is a definite issue, since we are bilingual.", "Submit only based on guidelines. No e-mail OR snail mail queries please. Word count is a definite issue, since we are bilingual." Staff attended or plans to attend the following conferences: BEA, NABE, IRA, ALA and SCBWI.

RECLINER BOOKS

P.O. Box 64128, Calgary AB T2K 1A9, Canada. (403)668-9746. E-mail: info@reclinerbooks.com. E-mail: submission@reclinerbooks.com. Website: www.reclinerbooks.com. **Contact:** Dustin Smith, editor (fiction, literary nonfiction). Estab. 2009. Trade paperback originals. **Publishes 4-8 titles/year. 50% of books from first-time authors. 100% from unagented writers. Pays 10-15% royalty on retail price Pays $250-500 advance.** Publishes book 12 months after acceptance of ms. Accepts simultaneous submissions. Responds in 3 months on queries & proposals; 6 months on mss. Soon available online at www.writtenindust.com/catalogue.html. Guidelines available online at www.writtenindust.com/submission.

NONFICTION Subjects include animals, anthropology, business, creative nonfiction, economics, environment, gay, health, history, language, law, lesbian, literature, medicine, memoirs, money, nature, politics, religion, science, sex, social sciences, sociology, womens issues, womens studies, world affairs, literary nonfiction. "We are currently seeking literary nonfiction titles only, the more literary the better." Submit proposal package, including: outline, 3 sample chapters; submit completed mss. Reviews artwork/photos as part of ms package; send photocopies.

FICTION Subjects include adventure, contemporary, experimental, feminist, gay, historical, humor, lesbian, literary, mainstream, military, multicultural, religious. "We are not currently accepting anything targeted at children, young adults, or science fiction readers." Submit proposal package, including: synopsis, 3 sample chapters, completed mss.

TIPS "Our audience is 24 years and older, 70% female, 30% male, 90% Canadian."

RED DEER PRESS

195 Allstate Pkwy., Markham ON L3R 4TB, Canada. (905)477-9700. Fax: (905)477-9179. E-mail: rdp@reddeerpress.com; dionne@reddeerpress.com; val@reddeerpress.com. Website: www.reddeerpress.com. **Contact:** Richard Dionne, publisher. Estab. 1975.

Red Deer Press has received numerous honors and awards from the Book Publishers Association of Alberta, Canadian Children's Book Centre, the Governor General of Canada and the Writers Guild of Alberta.

TIPS "We're very interested in young adult and children's fiction from Canadian writers with a proven track record (either published books or widely published in established magazines or journals) and for manuscripts with regional themes and/or a distinctive voice. We publish Canadian authors exclusively."

RED HEN PRESS

P.O. Box 3537, Granada Hills CA 91394. (818)831-0649. Fax: (818)831-6659. E-mail: redhenpressbooks.com. Website: www.redhen.org. **Contact:** Mark E. Cull, publisher/editor (fiction). Estab. 1993. Publishes trade paperback originals. **Publishes 10 titles/year. 2,000 queries received/year. 500 mss received/year. 10% of books from first-time authors. 90% from unagented writers.** Publishes book 1 year after acceptance of ms. Accepts simultaneous submissions. Responds in 1 month to queries. Responds in 2 months to proposals. Responds in 3 months to manuscripts. Book catalog available free. Guidelines available online.

The mission of Red Hen Press is to discover, publish, and promote works of literary excellence that have been overlooked by mainstream presses, and to build audiences for literature in two ways: by fostering the literacy of youth and by bringing distinguished and emerging writers to the public stage.

Red Hen Press is not currently accepting unsolicited material. At this time, the best opportunity to be published by Red Hen is by entering one of our contests. Please find more information in our award submission guidelines."

NONFICTION Subjects include ethnic, gay, lesbian, language, literature, memoirs, women's issues, women's studies, political/social interest. Query with SASE. Reviews artwork/photos. Send photocopies.

FICTION Subjects include ethnic, experimental, feminist, gay, lesbian, historical, literary, mainstream, contemporary, poetry, poetry in translation, short story collections. We prefer high-quality literary fiction. Query with SASE.

POETRY Query and submit 5 sample poems.

TIPS "Audience reads poetry, literary fiction, intelligent nonfiction. If you have an agent, we may be too small since we don't pay advances. Write well. Send queries first. Be willing to help promote your own book."

RED SAGE PUBLISHING, INC.

P.O. Box 4844, Seminole FL 33775. (727)391-3847. E-mail: submissions@eredsage.com. Website: www. eredsage.com. **Contact:** Alexandria Kendall, publisher; Theresa Stevens, managing editor. Estab. 1995. **Publishes 4 titles/year. 50% of books from first-time authors. Pays advance.** Guidelines available online.

⚲⇥ Publishes books of romance fiction, written for the adventurous woman.

FICTION Submission guidelines online at http://www.eredsage.com/store/RedSageSubmissionGuidelines_HowToSendSubmission.html

➕◯ RED TUQUE BOOKS, INC.

477 Martin St., Unit #6, Penticton BC V2A 5L2, Canada. (778)476-5750. Fax: (778)476-5651. Website: www.redtuquebooks.ca. **Contact:** David Korinetz, executive editor.

TIPS "Well-plotted, character-Dr.n stories, preferably with happy endings, will have the best chance of being accepted. Keep in mind that authors who like to begin sentences with "and, or, and but" are less likely to be considered. Don't send anything gruesome or overly explicit; tell us a good story, but think PG."

REFERENCE SERVICE PRESS

5000 Windplay Dr., Suite 4, El Dorado Hills CA 95762. (916)939-9620. Fax: (916)939-9626. E-mail: info@rspfunding.com. Website: www.rspfunding.com. **Contact:** Stuart Hauser, acquisitions editor. Estab. 1977. Publishes hardcover originals. **Publishes 10-20 titles/year. 100% from unagented writers. Pays 10% royalty. Pays advance.** Publishes book 6 months after acceptance of ms. Accepts simultaneous submissions. Responds in 2 months to queries. Book catalog for #10 SASE.

⚲⇥ Reference Service Press focuses on the development and publication of financial aid resources in any format (print, electronic, e-book, etc.). We are interested in financial aid publications aimed at specific groups (e.g., minorities, women, veterans, the disabled, undergraduates majoring in specific subject areas, specific types of financial aid, etc.)."

NONFICTION Subjects include agriculture, art, architecture, business, economics, education, ethnic, health, medicine, history, religion, science, sociology, women's issues, women's studies, disabled. Submit outline, sample chapters.

TIPS "Our audience consists of librarians, counselors, researchers, students, re-entry women, scholars, and other fundseekers."

RENAISSANCE HOUSE

465 Westview Ave, Englewood NJ 07631. (800)547-5113. E-mail: raquel@renaissancehouse.net. Website: www.renaissancehouse.net. Publishes book Publishes ms 1 year after acceptance. after acceptance of ms. Accepts simultaneous submissions. Responds to queries/mss in 3 weeks.

⚲⇥ Publishes biographies, folktales, coffee table books, instructional, textbooks, adventure, picture books, juvenile and young adult. Specializes in multicultural and bilingual titles, Spanish-English. Submit outline/synopsis. Will consider e-mail submissions.

REPUBLIC OF TEXAS PRESS

Imprint of Taylor Trade Publishing, and part of Rowman and Littlefield Publishing Group, 5360 Manhattan Circle, #101, Boulder CO 80303. (303)543-7835, ext. 318. E-mail: tradeeditorial@rowman.com. Website: www.rlpgtrade.com. **Contact:** Acquisitions Director. Publishes trade and paperback originals. **Publishes 10-15 titles/year. 95% from unagented writers. Pays industry-standard royalty on net receipts. Pays small advance.** Publishes book 9 months to 1 year after acceptance of ms. Accepts simultaneous submissions. Responds in 2 months to queries.

NONFICTION "Republic of Texas Press specializes in Texas history and general Texana nonfiction, including ethnic, history, nature/environment, regional, sports, travel, women's issues/studies, Old West, Texas military, and ghost accounts." Proposals should be limited to a query letter; an e-mail will generate the quickest response. If querying by e-mail, please note in the memo box "book proposal." Send no attachments unless requested. What we look for at this stage is suitability of the proposed book to our publishing program (see categories) as well as the author's unique qualifications for writing his or her book.

TIPS "Do not submit any original materials, as they will not be returned. Our market is adult."

RIO NUEVO PUBLISHERS

Imprint of Treasure Chest Books, P.O. Box 5250, Tucson AZ 85703. Fax: (520)624-5888. E-mail: info@rionuevo.

com. Website: www.rionuevo.com. **Contact:** Acquisitions Department. Estab. 1975. Publishes hardcover and trade paperback originals and reprints. **Publishes 12-20 titles/year. 20 queries received/year. 10 mss received/ year. 30% of books from first-time authors. 100% from unagented writers. Pays $1,000-4,000 advance.** Publishes book 1 year after acceptance of ms. Accepts simultaneous submissions. Responds in 6 months to queries, proposals and manuscripts. Book catalog available online. Guidelines available via e-mail.

NONFICTION Subjects include animals, cooking, foods, nutrition, gardening, history, nature, environment, regional, religion, spirituality, travel. "We cover the Southwest but prefer titles that are not too narrow in their focus. We want our books to be of broad enough interest that people from other places will also want to read them." Query with SASE. Submit proposal package, outline, 2 sample chapters. Reviews artwork/photos. Send photocopies.

TIPS "We have a general audience of intelligent people interested in the Southwest-nature, history, culture. Many of our books are sold in gift shops throughout the region; we are also distributed nationally by W.W. Norton."

ROCKY MOUNTAIN BOOKS

406-13th Ave. NE, Calgary AB T2E 1C2, Canada. (403)249-9490. Fax: (403)249-2968. E-mail: rmb@heritagehouse.ca. Website: www.rmbooks.com. **Contact:** Fraser Seely, publisher. Publishes trade paperback and hardcover. **Rarely offers advance.** Accepts simultaneous submissions. Responds in 2-6 months to queries. Book catalog and ms guidelines available online at website.

RMB is a dynamic book publisher located in western Canada. We specialize in quality nonfiction on the outdoors, travel, environment, social & cultural issues."

NONFICTION Subjects include nonfiction outdoors, environment, travel & tourism and international mountain culture/history. Our main area of publishing is outdoor recreation guides to Western and Northern Canada.

ROTOVISION

Sheridan House, 112-116A Western Rd., Hove East Sussex BN3 IDD, England. (44)(127)371-6010. Fax: (44)(127)372-7269. E-mail: isheetam@rotovision. com. Website: www.rotovision.com. **Contact:** Isheeta Mustaf. Publishes hardcover and trade paperback originals, and trade paperback reprints. Accepts simultaneous submissions. Book catalog available free. Guidelines available free.

"RotoVision books showcase the works of top writers and designers reflecting excellence and innovation in the visual arts. If you wish to submit a book proposal, in the first instance please familiarise yourself with our publishing portfolio to ensure your proposal fits into our focus area."

NONFICTION Subjects include art, architecture, creative nonfiction, photography, travel, design, graphic design, stage and screen, advertising. Our books are aimed at keen amateurs and professionals who want to improve their skills. Submit an e-mail with "Book Proposal" in the subject line. Reviews artwork/photos. Send transparencies and PDFs.

TIPS "Our audience includes professionals, keen amateurs, and students of visual arts including graphic design, general design, advertising, and photography. Make your approach international in scope. Content not to be less than 35% US."

ROWMAN & LITTLEFIELD PUBLISHING GROUP

4501 Forbes Blvd., Suite 200, Lanham MD 20706. (301)459-3366. Fax: (301)429-5748. E-mail: pbelcher@ rowman.com;jyu@rowman.com. E-mail: See website at: http://www.rowmanlittlefield.com/contact/. Website: www.rowmanlittlefield.com. **Contact:** See website for a detailed list of editors and addresses by subject area at: http://www.rowmanlittlefield.com/ contact/. http://www.rowmanlittlefield.com/Contact/; Janice Braunstein, Assistant Managing Editor, Boulder Estab. 1949. Publishes hardcover and trade paperback originals and reprints. **Pays advance.** Book catalog online. Guidelines available online.

IMPRINTS Lexington Books; Rowman & Littlefield Publishers; Madison Books; Scarecrow Press; Cooper Square.

We are an independent press devoted to publishing scholarly books in the best tradition of university presses; innovative, thought-provoking texts for college courses; and crossover trade books intended to convey scholarly trends to an educated readership. Our approach emphasizes substance and quality of thought over ephemeral trends. We offer a forum for responsible voices representing the diversity of opinion on college campuses, and take special pride in several series designed to provide students with the pros and cons of hotly contested issues."

NONFICTION "Rowman & Littlefield is seeking proposals in the serious nonfiction areas of history, politics, current events, religion, sociology, philosophy, communication and education. All proposal inquiries can be e-mailed or mailed to the respective acquisitions editor listed on the contacts page on our website."

RUKA PRESS

P.O. Box 1409, Washington DC 20013. E-mail: contact@rukapress.com. E-mail: submissions@rukapress.com. Website: www.rukapress.com. **Contact:** Daniel Kohan, owner. Estab. 2010. Publishes in trade paperback originals, electronic. **Publishes 2-4/year titles/year. Pays advance. Royalties are 10-25% on wholesale price.** Publishes book Time between acceptance and publication is 9-12 months after acceptance of ms. Accepts simultaneous submissions. Responds in 1 month to queries, 1 month to proposals. Book catalogue available online. Guidelines available online.

We publish nonfiction books with a strong environmental component for a general audience. We are looking for books that explain things, that make an argument, that demystify. We are interested in economics, science, nature, climate change and sustainability. We like building charts and graphs, tables and timelines. Our politics are progressive, but our books need not be political."

NONFICTION Subjects include environment, nature, science. Submit proposal package, including outline, resume, bio, or CV, and one sample chapter.

TIPS "We appeal to an audience of intelligent, educated readers with broad interests. Be sure to tell us why your proposal is unique, and why you are especially qualified to write this book. We are looking for originality and expertise."

SAFARI PRESS, INC.

15621 Chemical Lane, Bldg. B, Huntington Beach CA 92649-1506. (714)894-9080. Fax: (714)894-4949. E-mail: info@safaripress.com. Website: www.safaripress.com. **Contact:** Jacqueline Neufeld, editor. Estab. 1985. Publishes hardcover originals and reprints, and trade paperback reprints. **Publishes 25-30 titles/year. 70% of books from first-time authors. 80% from unagented writers. Pays 8-15% royalty on wholesale price.** Book catalog for $1. Guidelines available online.

The editor notes that she receives many mss outside the areas of big-game hunting, wing-shooting, and sporting firearms, and these are always rejected.

Safari Press publishes books only on big-game hunting, sporting, firearms, and wingshooting; this includes African, North American, European, Asian, and South American hunting and wingshooting. Does not want books on 'outdoors' topics (hiking, camping, canoeing, etc.).

NONFICTION "We discourage autobiographies, unless the life of the hunter or firearms maker has been exceptional. We routinely reject manuscripts along the lines of 'Me and my buddies went hunting for.. and a good time was had by all!" No outdoors topics (hiking, camping, canoeing, fishing, etc.) Query with SASE. Submit outline.

SAINT MARY'S PRESS

702 Terrace Heights, Winona MN 55987-1318. (800)533-8095. Fax: (800)344-9225. E-mail: submissions@smp.org. Website: www.smp.org. **Contact:** Submissions Editor. Ms guidelines online or by e-mail.

NONFICTION Subjects include religion, prayers, spirituality. Titles for Catholic youth and their parents, teachers, and youth ministers. Query with SASE. Submit proposal package, outline, 1 sample chapter, SASE. Brief author biography.

TIPS "Request product catalog and/or do research online of Saint Mary Press book lists before submitting proposal."

SALMON POETRY

Knockeven, Cliffs of Moher, County Clare , Ireland. 353(0)65 708 1941. Fax: 353(0)65 708 1941. E-mail: info@salmonpoetry.com. E-mail: jessie@salmonpoetry.com. Website: www.salmonpoetry.com. **Contact:** Jessie Lendennie, editor. Estab. 1981. Mass market paperback originals.

"Our list is full until 2011 but I do consider manuscripts on an ongoing basis. E-mail your query, with a short biographical note and 5 -10 poems, to me at jessie@salmonpoetry.com."

POETRY "Salmon Press has become one of the most important publications in the Irish literary world, specialising in the promotion of new poets, particularly women poets. Established as an alternative voice. Walks tightrope between innovation and convention.

Was a flagship for writers in the west of Ireland. Salmon has developed a cross-cultural, internatonal literary dialog, broadening Irish Literature and urging new perspectives on established traditions."

TIPS "If we are broad minded and willing to nurture the individual voice inherent in the work, the artist will emerge."

SALVO PRESS

E-mail: schmidt@salvopress.com. E-mail: query@salvopress.com. Website: www.salvopress.com. **Contact:** Scott Schmidt, publisher. Estab. 1998.

FICTION Adventure, literary, mystery (amateur sleuth, police procedural, private/hard-boiled), science fiction (hard science/technological), suspense, thriller/espionage. "We are a small press specializing in mystery, suspense, espionage and thriller fiction. Our press publishes in trade paperback and most e-book formats." Publishes hardcover, trade paperback originals and e-books in most formats. Books: $5^1/2 \times 8^1/2$; or 6×9 printing; perfect binding. **Published 6 debut authors within the last year.** Averages 6-12 fiction total titles/year, mostly fiction. "Our needs change, check our website." Query by e-mail only at query@salvopress.com. Please place the word "Query" as the subject. Include estimated word count, brief bio, list of publishing credits, "and something to intrigue me so I ask for more." Agented fiction 15%. Responds in 5 minutes to 1 month to queries; 2 months to mss. No simultaneous submissions.

SAMHAIN PUBLISHING, LTD

577 Mulberry St., Ste. 1520, Macon GA 31201. (478)314-5144. Fax: (478)314-5148. E-mail: editor@samhainpublishing.com. Website: samhainpublishing.com. **Contact:** Laurie M. Rauch, executive editor. Estab. 2005. Publishes e-books and paperback originals. POD/offset printing; line illustrations.

○ Preditor and Editors Best Publisher 2006

⌒ Samhain is now accepting submissions for our line of horror novels. We are actively seeking talented writers who can tell an exciting, dramatic and frightening story, and who are eager to promote their work and build their community of readers. We are looking for novels 'either supernatural or non-supernatural, contemporary or historical' that are original and compelling. Authors can be previously unpublished or established, agented or unagented. Content can range from subtle and unsettling to gory and shocking. The writing is what counts."

TIPS "Because we are an e-publisher first, we do not have to be as concerned with industry trends and can publish less popular genres of fiction if we believe the story and voice are good and will appeal to our customers. Please follow submission guidelines located on our website, include all requested information and proof your query/manuscript for errors prior to submission."

SANTA MONICA PRESS LLC

P.O. Box 850, Solana Beach CA 92075. (858)793-1890; (800)784-9553. E-mail: books@santamonicapress.com. Website: www.santamonicapress.com. **Contact:** Acquisitions Editor. Estab. 1994. Publishes hardcover and trade paperback originals. **Publishes 15 titles/year. 25% of books from first-time authors. 75% from unagented writers. Pays 4-10% royalty on wholesale price. Pays $500-2,500+ advance.** Publishes book 6-18 months after acceptance of ms. Accepts simultaneous submissions. Responds in 1-2 months to proposals. Book catalog for 9×12 SASE with $1.31 postage. Guidelines available online.

⌒ At Santa Monica Press, we're not afraid to cast a wide editorial net. Our eclectic list of lively and modern nonfiction titles includes books in such categories as popular culture, film history, photography, humor, biography, travel, and reference."

NONFICTION Subjects include Americana, architecture, art, contemporary culture, creative nonfiction, education, entertainment, film, games, humanities, language, literature, memoirs, regional, social sciences, sports, travel, Biography, coffee table book, general nonfiction, gift book, humor, illustrated book, reference. *All unsolicited mss returned unopened.* Submit proposal package, including outline, 2-3 sample chapters, biography, marketing and publicity plans, analysis of competitive titles, SASE with appropriate postage. Reviews artwork/photos. Send photocopies.

TIPS "Visit our website before submitting to view our author guidelines and to get a clear idea of the types of books we publish. Carefully analyze your book's competition and tell us what makes your book different— and what makes it better. Also let us know what promotional and marketing opportunities you, as the author, bring to the project."

SARABANDE BOOKS, INC.

2234 Dundee Rd., Suite 200, Louisville KY 40205. (502)458-4028. Fax: (502)458-4065. E-mail: info@ sarabandebooks.org. Website: www.sarabandebooks. org. **Contact:** Sarah Gorham, editor-in-chief. Estab. 1994. Publishes trade paperback originals. **Publishes 10 titles/year. 1,500 queries received/year. 3,000 mss received/year. 35% of books from first-time authors. 75% from unagented writers. Pays royalty. 10% on actual income received. Also pays in author's copies. Pays $500-1,000 advance.** Publishes book 18 months after acceptance of ms. Accepts simultaneous submissions. Book catalog available free. contest guidelines for #10 SASE or on website.

○ Charges $10 handling fee with alternative option of purchase of book from website (e-mail confirmation of sale must be included with submission).

⚡ Sarabande Books was founded to publish poetry, short fiction, and creative nonfiction. We look for works of lasting literary value. Please see our titles to get an idea of our taste. Accept submissions through contests and open submissions."

FICTION Subjects include literary, short story collections, novellas, short novels (300 pages maximum, 150 pages minimum).

POETRY Poetry of superior artistic quality; otherwise no restraints or specifications.

TIPS "Sarabande publishes for a general literary audience. Know your market. Read-and buy-books of literature. Sponsors contests for poetry and fiction."

SASQUATCH BOOKS

119 S. Main, Suite 400, Seattle WA 98104. E-mail: ttabor@sasquatchbooks.com. Website: www.sasquatchbooks.com. **Contact:** Gary Luke, editorial director; Terence Maikels, acquisitions editor; Heidi Lenze, acquisitions editor. Estab. 1986. Publishes regional hardcover and trade paperback originals. **Publishes 30 titles/year. 20% of books from first-time authors. 75% from unagented writers. Pays royalty on cover price. Pays wide range advance.** Publishes book 6 months after acceptance of ms. Responds in 3 months to queries. Book catalog for 9×12 envelope and 2 first-class stamps. Guidelines available online.

⚡ Sasquatch Books publishes books for and from the Pacific Northwest, Alaska, and California is the nation's premier regional press. Sasquatch Books' publishing program is a veritable cele-

bration of regionally written words. Undeterred by political or geographical borders, Sasquatch defines its region as the magnificent area that stretches from the Brooks Range to the Gulf of California and from the Rocky Mountains to the Pacific Ocean. Our top-selling Best Places® travel guides serve the most popular destinations and locations of the West. We also publish widely in the areas of food and wine, gardening, nature, photography, children's books, and regional history, all facets of the literature of place. With more than 200 books brimming with insider information on the West, we offer an energetic eye on the lifestyle, landscape, and worldview of our region.

NONFICTION Subjects include animals, art, architecture, business, economics, cooking, foods, nutrition, gardening, history, nature, environment, recreation, regional, sports, travel, women's issues, women's studies, outdoors. "Considers queries and proposals from authors and agents for new projects that fit into our West Coast regional publishing program. We can evaluate query letters, proposals, and complete mss. When you submit to Sasquatch Books, please remember that the editors want to know about you *and* your project, along with a sense of who will want to read your book. We are seeking quality nonfiction works about the Pacific Northwest and West Coast regions (including Alaska to California). The literature of place includes how-to and where-to as well as history and narrative nonfiction." Query first, then submit outline and sample chapters with SASE. Send submissions to The Editors. E-mailed submissions and queries are not recommended. Please include return postage if you want your materials back.

TIPS "We sell books through a range of channels in addition to the book trade. Our primary audience consists of active, literate residents of the West Coast."

⊕ SCHIFFER PUBLISHING, LTD.

4880 Lower Valley Rd., Atglen PA 19310. (610)593-1777. Fax: (610)593-2002. E-mail: info@schifferbooks. com;Schifferbk@aol.com. Website: www.schifferbooks.com. **Contact:** Tina Skinner. Estab. 1975. **Publishes 10-20 titles/year. Pays royalty on wholesale price.** Responds in 2 weeks to queries. Book catalog available free. Guidelines available online.

NONFICTION Art-quality illustrated regional histories. Looking for informed, entertaining writing and lots of subject areas to provide points of entry into the text for non-history buffs who buy a beautiful book because they are from, or love, an area. Full color possible in the case of historic postcards. Fax or e-mail outline, photos, and book proposal.

TIPS "We want to publish books for towns or cities with relevant population or active tourism to support book sales. A list of potential town vendors is a helpful start toward selling us on your book idea."

🅐 ∅ SCHOCKEN BOOKS

Imprint of Knopf Publishing Group, Division of Random House, Inc., 1745 Broadway 21-1, New York NY 10019. (212)572-9000. Fax: (212)572-6030. Website: www.schocken.com. Estab. 1945. Publishes hardcover and trade paperback originals and reprints. **Publishes 9-12 titles/year. Small% of books from first-time authors. Small% from unagented writers. Pays varied advance.** Accepts simultaneous submissions.

○ Does not accept unsolicited mss.

⚷ Schocken publishes quality Judaica in all areas-fiction, history, biography, current affairs, spirituality and religious practices, popular culture, and cultural studies."

🅐 SCHOLASTIC LIBRARY PUBLISHING

A division of Scholastic, Inc., 90 Old Sherman Turnpike, Danbury CT 06816. (203)797-3500. Fax: (203)797-3197. Website: www.scholastic.com/librarypublishing. Estab. 1895. Publishes hardcover and trade paperback originals.

IMPRINTS Grolier; Children's Press; Franklin Watts; Grolier Online.

○ *This publisher accepts agented submissions only.*

⚷ Scholastic Library is a leading publisher of reference, educational, and children's books. We provide parents, teachers, and librarians with the tools they need to enlighten children to the pleasure of learning and prepare them for the road ahead."

🅐 SCHOLASTIC PRESS

Imprint of Scholastic, Inc., 557 Broadway, New York NY 10012. (212)343-6100. Fax: (212)343-4713. Website: www.scholastic.com. Publishes hardcover originals. **Publishes 30 titles/year. 2,500 queries received/ year. 5% of books from first-time authors. Pays royalty on retail price. Pays variable advance.** Publishes book 18-24 months after acceptance of ms. Responds

in 3 months to queries. Responds in 6-8 months to manuscripts.

⚷ Scholastic Press publishes fresh, literary picture book fiction and nonfiction; fresh, literary nonseries or nongenre-oriented middle grade and young adult fiction. Currently emphasizing subtly handled treatments of key relationships in children's lives; unusual approaches to commonly dry subjects, such as biography, math, history, or science. De-emphasizing fairy tales (or retellings), board books, genre, or series fiction (mystery, fantasy, etc.).

NONFICTION *Agented submissions and previously published authors only.*

FICTION Subjects include juvenile, picture books, novels. Wants fresh, exciting picture books and novels-inspiring, new talent. *Agented submissions and previously published authors only.*

TIPS "Be a big reader of juvenile literature before you write and submit!"

SEAL PRESS

1700 4th St., Berkeley CA 94710. (510)595-3664. E-mail: Seal.Press@perseusbooks.com. E-mail: sealacquisitions@avalonpub.com. Website: www.sealpress.com. **Contact:** Acquisitions Editor. Estab. 1976. Publishes trade paperback originals. **Publishes 30 titles/year. 1,000 queries received/year. 750 mss received/year. 25% of books from first-time authors. 50% from unagented writers. Pays 7-10% royalty on retail price. Pays variable royalty on retail price. Pays $3,000-10,000 advance. Pays variable advance.** Publishes book 6-12 months after acceptance of ms. Accepts simultaneous submissions. Responds in 2 months to queries. Book catalog and ms guidelines for SASE or online.

⚷ Seal Press is an imprint of Avalon Publishing Group, feminist book publisher interested in original, lively, radical, empowering and culturally diverse nonfiction by women addressing contemporary issues from a feminist perspective or speaking positively to the experience of being female. Currently emphasizing women outdoor adventurists, young feminists, political issues for women, health issues, and surviving abuse. *Not accepting fiction at this time.*"

NONFICTION Subjects include Americana, child guidance, contemporary culture, creative nonfiction, ethnic, gay, lesbian, memoirs, multicultural, nature, environment, sex, travel, women's issues, women's studies, popular culture, politics, domestic violence, sexual abuse. Query with SASE. Reviews artwork/photos. Send photocopies. No original art or photos accepted.

TIPS "Our audience is generally composed of women interested in reading about women's issues addressed from a feminist perspective."

SEARCH INSTITUTE PRESS

Search Institute, 615 First Ave. NE, Suite 125, Minneapolis MN 55413. (612)399-0200. Fax: (612)692-5553. E-mail: acquisitions@search-institute.org. Website: www.search-institute.org. **Contact:** Editor. Estab. 1958. trade paperback originals. **Publishes 12-15 titles/year. Pays royalty.** Publishes book 12 months after acceptance of ms. Accepts simultaneous submissions. Responds in 6 months on queries, proposals, & mss. Catalog free on request, online at website. Guidelines online at website.

NONFICTION Subjects include career guidance, child guidance, community, counseling, education, entertainment, games, parenting, public affairs, social sciences, youth leadership, prevention, activities. children's picture books, poetry, New Age and religious-themes, memoirs, biographies, and autobiographies. Query with SASE. Does not review artwork/photos.

TIPS "Our audience is educators, youth program leaders, mentors, parents."

SEAWORTHY PUBLICATIONS, INC.

3601 S. Banana River Blvd., A301, Cocoa Beach FL 32931. (262)268-9250. Fax: (262)268-9208. E-mail: orders@seaworthy.com. Website: www.seaworthy.com. **Contact:** Joseph F. Janson, publisher. Publishes trade paperback originals, hardcover originals, and reprints. **Publishes 8 titles/year. 150 queries received/ year. 40 mss received/year. 60% of books from first-time authors. 100% from unagented writers. Pays 15% royalty on wholesale price. Pays $1,000 advance.** Publishes book 6 months after acceptance of ms. Responds in 1 month to queries. Book catalog and guidelines available online.

∑⎯➤ Seaworthy Publications is a nautical book publisher that primarily publishes books of interest to recreational boaters and bluewater cruisers, including cruising guides, how-to books about boating. Currently emphasizing cruising guides."

NONFICTION Subjects include regional, sailing, boating, regional, boating guide books. Regional

guide books, first-person adventure, reference, technical—all dealing with boating. Query with SASE. Submit 3 sample chapters, TOC. Prefers electronic query via e-mail. Reviews artwork/photos. Send photocopies or color prints.

TIPS "Our audience consists of sailors, boaters, and those interested in the sea, sailing, or long-distance cruising."

☺ SECOND STORY PRESS

20 Maud St., Suite 401, Toronto ON M5V 2M5, Canada. Website: www.secondstorypress.ca.

NONFICTION Considers non-sexist, non-racist, and non-violent stories, as well as historical fiction, chapter books. Accepts appropriate material from residents of Canada only. Fiction and nonfiction: Submit complete ms or submit outline and sample chapters by postal mail only. No electronic submissions or queries.

FICTION Considers non-sexist, non-racist, and non-violent stories, as well as historical fiction, chapter books. Accepts appropriate material from residents of Canada only. Fiction and nonfiction: Submit complete ms or submit outline and sample chapters by postal mail only. No electronic submissions or queries.

SENTIENT PUBLICATIONS

1113 Spruce St., Boulder CO 80302. E-mail: contact@sentientpublications.com. Website: www.sentient-publications.com. **Contact:** Connie Shaw, acq. editor. Estab. 2001. Publishes hardcover and trade paperback originals; trade paperback reprints. **Publishes 12 titles/year. 200 queries received/year. 100 mss received/year. 70% of books from first-time authors. 50% from unagented writers. Pays royalty on wholesale price. Pays advance.** Publishes book 6 months after acceptance of ms. Accepts simultaneous submissions. Responds in 1 month to queries; 2 months to proposals and manuscripts. Book catalog available online.

NONFICTION Subjects include audio, alternative, art, architecture, child guidance, contemporary culture, cooking, foods, nutrition, creative nonfiction, education, gardening, health, medicine, history, language, literature, memoirs, nature, environment, New Age, philosophy, photography, psychology, science, sex, social sciences, sociology, spirituality, travel, women's issues, women's studies. "We're especially looking for holistic health books that have something new to say." Submit proposal package, See our website. Submit complete ms. Does not review artwork/photos.

SEVEN FOOTER PRESS / SEVEN FOOTER KIDS

247 West 30th St., 11th Floor, New York NY 10001-2824. E-mail: info@sevenfooterpress.com. Website: www.sevenfooterpress.com. **Contact:** Justin Heimberg, chief creative officer (humor, gift, nonfiction); David Gomberg, president and publisher (children's, illustrated, young adult, sports). Estab. 2004. Publishes hardcover, trade and mass market paperback originals. **Publishes 10-20 titles/year. 200 queries received/year. 50 mss received/year. 50% of books from first-time authors. 50% from unagented writers.** Publishes book 6-12 months after acceptance of ms. Accepts simultaneous submissions. Book catalog available online.

NONFICTION Subjects include creative nonfiction, education, hobbies, regional, sex, sports, travel, college market, games/puzzles, high-concept. We specialize in hip, young audiences. We like books that are socially interactive or offer an experience beyond just reading. Submit proposal package, outline, 2 sample chapters, any visuals or illustrations. Reviews artwork/photos. Send photocopies and scanned artwork or design.

TIPS "The audience for Seven Footer Press titles is Gen X, Gen Y, college, young adults, young professionals, and pop culture fans. The audience for Seven Footer Kids titles is for all children."

⊘ SEVEN STORIES PRESS

140 Watts St., New York NY 10013. (212)226-8760. Fax: (212)226-1411. E-mail: anna@sevenstories.com. Website: www.sevenstories.com. **Contact:** Daniel Simon; Anna Lui. Estab. 1995. Publishes hardcover and trade paperback originals. **Publishes 40-50 titles/year. 15% of books from first-time authors. 50% from unagented writers. Pays 7-15% royalty on retail price. Pays advance.** Publishes book 1-3 years after acceptance of ms. Accepts simultaneous submissions. Responds in 1 month to queries and manuscripts. Book catalog and ms guidelines free.

⌐ Seven Stories Press publishes literary fiction and political nonfiction for social justice. Currently emphasizing politics, social justice, biographies, foreign writings."

NONFICTION Responds only if interested.

FICTION Subjects include literary. Query with SASE. "If no SASE enclosed we'll dispose of them unread."

SHAMBHALA PUBLICATIONS, INC.

300 Massachusetts Ave., P.O. Box 170358, Boston MA 02117. (617)424-0030. Fax: (617)236-1563. E-mail: editors@shambhala.com. Website: www.shambhala.com. **Contact:** Editorial Assistant. Estab. 1969. Publishes hardcover and trade paperback originals and reprints. **Publishes 90-100 titles/year. 2,000 queries received/year. 500-700 mss received/year. 30% of books from first-time authors. 80% from unagented writers. Pays 8% royalty on retail price.** Publishes book 1 year after acceptance of ms. Accepts simultaneous submissions. Responds in 1 month to queries. Responds in 2 months to proposals and manuscripts. Book catalog and ms guidelines free.

◯ To send a book proposal, include a synopsis of the book, a table of contents or outline, a copy of the author's resume or some other brief biographical statement, along with two or three sample chapters (they do not need to be in consecutive order). The chapters should be double-spaced. Include SASE. Publishes very little fiction or poetry.

NONFICTION Subjects include alternative, art, architecture, creative nonfiction, health, medicine, humanities, language, literature, memoirs, philosophy, religion, spirituality, women's issues, women's studies. Query with SASE. Submit proposal package, outline, résumé, 2 sample chapters, synopsis, TOC. Submit complete ms. No e-mail submissions. Reviews artwork/photos.

FICTION Query with SASE. Submit proposal package, outline, résumé, clips, 2 sample chapters, TOC. Submit complete ms.

SHEED & WARD BOOK PUBLISHING

Imprint of Rowman & Littlefield Publishing Group, 4501 Forbes Blvd., Suite 200, Lanham MD 20706. (301)459-3366 ext. 5634. Fax: (301)429-5747. E-mail: sstanton@rowman.com;mboggs@rowman.com. Website: www.sheedandward.com. **Contact:** Sarah Stanton, acquisitions. Publishes hardcover and paperback originals. Book catalog free or on website. Guidelines available online.

⌐ We are looking for books that help our readers, most of whom are college educated, gain access to the riches of the Catholic/Christian tradition. We publish in the areas of history, biography, spirituality, prayer, ethics, ministry, justice, liturgy."

NONFICTION Subjects include religion, spirituality, family life, theology, ethics. Submit proposal package to the appropriate acquisitions editor, including outline, 2 sample chapters, strong cover letter indicating why the project is unique and compelling. Please do not send your entire manuscript. If an acquisitions editor would like to see the complete manuscript, he or she will let you know. Reviews artwork/photos. Send photocopies.

TIPS "We prefer that writers get our author guidelines either from our website or via mail before submitting proposals."

SILVERFISH REVIEW PRESS

P.O. Box 3541, Eugene OR 97403. (541)344-5060. E-mail: sfrpress@earthlink.net. Website: www.silverfishreviewpress.com. Rodger Moody, Series Editor Estab. 1978. Trade paperback originals. **Publishes 2-3 titles/year. 50% of books from first-time authors. 100% from unagented writers.** Guidelines available online.

8—ℸ Sponsors the Gerald Cable Book Award. This prize is awarded annually to a book length manuscript of original poetry by an author who has not yet published a full-length collection. There are no restrictions on the kind of poetry or subject matter; translations are not acceptable. Winners will receive one thousand dollars, publication, and twenty-five copies of the book. The winner will be announced in late March, 2012. Entries must be postmarked by October 15, 2011. Entries may be submitted by e-mail. See website for instructions."

TIPS "Read recent Silverfish titles."

SILVER MOON PRESS

400 East 85th St., New York NY 10028. (800)874-3320. Fax: (212)988-8112. E-mail: mail@silvermoonpress.com. Website: http://silvermoonpress.com/. **Contact:** Hope Killcoyne, managing editor. Publishes hardcover originals. **Publishes 1-2 prep workbooks and 1-2 historical fiction. titles/year. 600 queries received/year. 400 mss received/year. 60% of books from first-time authors. 70% from unagented writers. Pays 7-10% royalty. Pays 500-1,000 advance.** Publishes book 18 months after acceptance of ms. Accepts simultaneous submissions. Responds in 6-12 months to queries. Responds in 6-12 months to proposals. Responds in

6-12 months to manuscripts. Book catalog with 9×12 SASE. Guidelines with #10 SASE.

8—ℸ Publishes educational material for grades 3-8.

NONFICTION Subjects include education, history, language, literature, multicultural. Query with SASE. Submit proposal package, outline, first pages of manuscript.

FICTION Subjects include historical, multicultural, biographical. Query with SASE. Submit proposal package, clips.

TIPS "We do not accept biographies, poetry, or romance. We do not accept fantasy, science fiction, or historical fiction with elements of either. No picture books. Submissions that fit into New York State curriculum topics such as the Revolutionary War, Colonial times, and New York state history in general stand a greater chance of acceptance than those that do not."

Ⓐ⊘ SIMON & SCHUSTER CHILDREN'S PUBLISHING

Division of Simon & Schuster, Inc., 1230 Ave. of the Americas, New York NY 10020. (212)698-7000. Website: www.simonsayskids.com. Publishes hardcover and paperback fiction, nonfiction, trade, library, mass market titles, and novelty books for preschool through young adult readers. **Publishes 650 titles/year.**

IMPRINTS Aladdin Paperbacks; Atheneum Books for Young Readers (Richard Jackson Books, Ginee Seo Books); Libros Para Ninos; Little Simon; Margaret K. McElderry Books; Simon & Schuster Books for Young Readers (Paula Wiseman Books); Simon Pulse; Simon Spotlight.

SKINNER HOUSE BOOKS

The Unitarian Universalist Association, 25 Beacon St., Boston MA 02108. (617)742-2100 ext. 603. Fax: (617)742-7025. E-mail: info@uua.org. Website: www.uua.org/skinner. **Contact:** Mary Benard, senior editor. Estab. 1975. Publishes trade paperback originals and reprints. **Publishes 10-20 titles/year. 50% of books from first-time authors. 100% from unagented writers.** Publishes book 1 year after acceptance of ms. Responds in 3 months to queries. Book catalog for 6×9 SAE with 3 first-class stamps. Guidelines available online.

8—ℸ We publish titles in Unitarian Universalist faith, liberal religion, history, biography, worship, and issues of social justice. We also publish inspirational titles of poetic prose and meditations. Writers should know that Unitarian Universalism is a liberal religious denomination committed to progressive ideals. Currently emphasizing social justice concerns."

NONFICTION Subjects include gay, lesbian, memoirs, religion, women's issues, women's studies, inspirational, church leadership. Query with SASE. Reviews artwork/photos. Send photocopies.

TIPS "From outside our denomination, we are interested in manuscripts that will be of help or interest to liberal churches, Sunday School classes, parents, ministers, and volunteers. Inspirational/spiritual and children's titles must reflect liberal Unitarian Universalist values."

⊕ SLACK, INC.

6900 Grove Rd., Thorofare NJ 08086. (856)848-1000. Fax: (856)853-5991. E-mail: bookspublishing@slack-inc.com. Website: www.slackbooks.com. **Contact:** John Bond, publisher. Estab. 1960. Publishes hardcover and softcover originals. **Publishes 35 titles/year. 80 queries received/year. 23 mss received/year. 75% of books from first-time authors. 100% from unagented writers. Pays 10% royalty. Pays advance.** Publishes book 8 months after acceptance of ms. Accepts simultaneous submissions. Responds in 1 month to queries and proposals. Responds in 3 months to manuscripts. Book catalog and ms guidelines free. Guidelines available online.

⌇ SLACK INC. publishes academic textbooks and professional reference books on various medical topics in an expedient manner.

NONFICTION Subjects include health, medicine, ophthalmology. Submit proposal package, outline, 2 sample chapters, market profile and cv. Reviews artwork/photos. Send photocopies.

⊕ SMALL DOGMA PUBLISHING, INC.

P.O. Box 91023, Lakeland FL 33804. E-mail: submissions@smalldogma.com. Website: www.smalldogma.com. **Contact:** Matt Porricelli, M.B.A., Pres. (fiction, self help, fantasy, sci-fi, religion, lit, poetry). Estab. 2006. Hardcover and electronic originals, trade and mass market paperback originals; trade paperback reprints. **Publishes 20 titles/year. 350 queries; 150 mss 65% of books from first-time authors. 85% from unagented writers. Pays 23-50% royalty on wholesale price** Publishes book 4-6 months after acceptance of ms. Accepts simultaneous submissions. Responds in 2 months on queries & proposals; 3 months on mss. Catalog and guidelines available on website.

NONFICTION Subjects include business, career guidance, contemporary culture, counseling, creative nonfiction, economics, environment, finance, history, hobbies, humanities, literary criticism, military, money, nature, psychology, religion, sociology, travel, war, womens issues, womens studies, world affairs, young adult. "We are dedicated to making a difference and are always looking for new manuscripts that entertain, teach, challenge, inform or inspire." "Please note - We do not accept material with gratuitous violence or sexual content." Submit completed ms along with query letter by e-mail.

FICTION Subjects include adventure, confession, fantasy, historical, humor, juvenile, literary, mainstream, multimedia, mystery, poetry, regional, religious, science fiction, short story collections, suspense, western, young adult. Same as nonfiction. Submit completed ms along with query letter by e-mail.

POETRY Same as fiction Submit complete ms along with query letter by e-mail.

TIPS "Be different. Be passionate about your book. Be willing to do book signings/promotions. How do you plan to reach your target audience? What is your sales/promotion strategy?"

SOFT SKULL PRESS INC.

Counterpoint, 1919 Fifth St., Berkeley CA 94710. (510)704-0230. Fax: (510)704-0268. E-mail: info@softskull.com. Website: www.softskull.com. **Contact:** Fiction or Nonfiction editor (whichever is appropriate).

TIPS "See our website for updated submission guidelines. Submit electronically."

SOHO PRESS, INC.

853 Broadway, New York NY 10003. E-mail: soho@sohopress.com. Website: www.sohopress.com. **Contact:** Bronwen Hruska, Publisher; Katie Herman, editor. Mark Doten, Editor Estab. 1986. Publishes hardcover and trade paperback originals; trade paperback reprints. **Publishes 60-70 titles/year. 15-25% of books from first-time authors. 10% from unagented writers. 7.5-15% royalty on retail price (varies under certain circumstances)** Publishes book 18 months after acceptance of ms. Accepts simultaneous submissions. 3 months on queries and mss. Guidelines available online.

⌇ Soho Press publishes primarily fiction, as well as some narrative literary nonfiction and mysteries set abroad. No electronic submissions, only queries by e-mail.

NONFICTION Subjects include creative nonfiction, ethnic, memoirs. "We do not buy books on proposal. We always need to see a complete ms before we buy a book, though we prefer an initial submission of 3 sample chapters. We do not publish books with color art or photographs or a lot of graphical material." No self-help, how-to, or cookbooks. Submit 3 sample chapters and a cover letter with a synopsis and author bio; SASE. Send photocopies.

FICTION Subjects include ethnic, historical, humor, literary, mystery, In mysteries, we only publish series with foreign or exotic settings, usually procedurals. Submit 3 sample chapters and cover letter with synopsis, author bio, SASE.

TIPS "Soho Press publishes discerning authors for discriminating readers, finding the strongest possible writers and publishing them. Before submitting, look at our website for an idea of the types of books we publish, and read our submission guidelines."

SOLAS HOUSE/TRAVELERS' TALES

853 Alma St., Palo Alto CA 94301. (650)462-2110. Fax: (650)462-2114. E-mail: submit@travelerstales.com. Website: www.travelerstales.com. **Contact:** James O'Reilly and Larry Habegger, series editors; Sean O'Reilly, editor-at-large (sales/publicity). **Publishes 8-10 titles/year. Pays $100 honorarium for anthology pieces.** Accepts simultaneous submissions. Guidelines available online.

IMPRINTS Travelers' Tales Guides; Footsteps; Travelers' Tales Classics.

○ "Due to the volume of submissions, we do not respond unless the material submitted meets our immediate editorial needs. All stories are read and filed for future use contingent upon meeting editorial guidelines."

⚮ Publishes inspirational travel books, mostly anthologies and travel advice books.

NONFICTION Subjects include all aspects of travel.

TIPS "We publish personal nonfiction stories and anecdotes—funny, illuminating, adventurous, frightening, or grim. Stories should reflect that unique alchemy that occurs when you enter unfamiliar territory and begin to see the world differently as a result. Stories that have already been published, including book excerpts, are welcome as long as the authors retain the copyright or can obtain permission from the copyright holder to reprint the material. We do not publish fiction."

SPOUT PRESS

P.O. Box 581067, Minneapolis MN 55458. (612) 782-9629. E-mail: spoutpress@hotmail.com; editors@spoutpress.org. Website: www.spoutpress.org. **Contact:** Carrie Eidem, fiction editor. Estab. 1989. Publishes book 12-15 months after acceptance of ms. Accepts simultaneous submissions. Responds in 1 month to queries; 3-5 months to mss. Ms guidelines for SASE or on website.

○ "Small independent publisher with a permanent staff of five—interested in experimental fiction for our magazine and books." Publishes paperback originals. Books: perfect bound; illustrations. Average print order: 1,000. **Published 1 debut author within the last year.** Distibutes and promotes books through the website, events and large Web-based stores such as Amazon.com. Runs annual. Accepts submissions all year around fall through spring. See website for specific dates and details. Does not accept unsolicited mss. Query with SASE. Accepts queries by mail. Include estimated word count, brief bio, list of publishing credits. Send SASE for return of ms or send a disposable ms and SASE for reply only. Rarely comments on rejected mss. Individual arrangement with author depending on the book.

FICTION Subjects include ethnic, experimental, literary, short story collections.

TIPS "We tend to publish writers after we know their work via publication in our journal, *Spout Magazine*."

SPS STUDIOS, INC.

P.O. Box 1007, Dept. PM, Boulder CO 80306-1007. E-mail: editorial@spsstudios.com. Website: www.sps.com. **Contact:** Editorial Staff. Estab. 1971. **Pays $300/poem, all rights for each of the first 2 submissions chosen for publication (after which payment scale escalates), for the worldwide, exclusive right, $50/poem for one-time use in an anthology.** Responds in up to 6 months. Guidelines available for SASE or by e-mail.

⚮ SPS Studios publishes greeting cards, books, calendars, prints, and other gift items. Looking for poems, prose, and lyrics ("usually non-rhyming") appropriate for publication on greeting cards and in poetry anthologies. Also actively seeking "book-length manuscripts that would be appropriate for book and gift stores. We are also very interested in receiving book and card ideas that would be appropriate for college stores, as well as younger buyers. Poems should reflect a message, feeling, or sentiment that one person would want to share with another. We'd like to receive creative, original submissions about love relationships, family members, friendships, philosophies, and any other aspect of life. Poems and writings for specific holidays (Christmas, Valentine's Day, etc.) and special occasions, such as graduation, anniversary, and get well are also considered. Only a small portion of the material we receive is selected each year and the review process can be lengthy, but be assured every ms is given serious consideration." Submissions must be typewritten, one poem/page or sent by e-mail (no attachments). Include SASE. Simultaneous submissions "discouraged but okay with notification." Accepts fax and e-mail (pasted into body of message) submissions. Submit seasonal material at least 4 months in advance.

STACKPOLE BOOKS

5067 Ritter Rd., Mechanicsburg PA 17055. Fax: (717)796-0412. E-mail: jschnell@stackpolebooks. com. E-mail: cevans@stackpolebooks.com; kweaver@stackpolebooks.com; mallison@stackpolebooks. com; jnichols@stackpolebooks.com. Website: www. stackpolebooks.com. **Contact:** Judith Schnell, editorial director (outdoor sports); Chris Evans, editor (history); Mark Allison, editor (nature); Kyle Weaver, editor (regional/Pennsylvania). Estab. 1935. Publishes hardcover and trade paperback originals, reprints, and ebooks 100/yr. **Pays industry standard advance.** Publishes book 1 year after acceptance of ms. Responds in 1 month to queries. See catalog and guidelines online.

⚬━┓ Stackpole maintains a growing and vital publishing program by featuring authors who are experts in their fields."

NONFICTION Subjects include history, military reference, nature, outdoor sports, crafts and hobbies, regional. "First of all, send your query to an individual editor. The more information you can supply, the better." Reviews artwork/photos.

TIPS "Stackpole seeks well-written, authoritative mss for specialized and general trade markets. Proposals should include chapter outline, sample chapter, illustrations, and author's credentials."

STANDARD PUBLISHING

Standex International Corp., 8805 Governor's Hill Dr., Suite 400, Cincinnati OH 45249. (800)543-1353. E-mail: customerservice@standardpub.com. E-mail: adultministry@standardpub.com; ministrytochildren@standardpub.com; ministrytoyouth@standardpub.com. Website: www.standardpub.com. **Contact:** Acquisitions Editor. Mark Taylor, adult ministry resources; Ruth Frederick, children and youth ministry resources; Diane Stortz, family resources. Estab. 1866. Guidelines and current publishing objectives available online.

⚬━┓ Publishes resources that meet church and family needs in the area of children's ministry.

STANFORD UNIVERSITY PRESS

1450 Page Mill Rd., Palo Alto CA 94304-1124. (650)723-9434. Fax: (650)725-3457. E-mail: info@ www.sup.org. Website: www.sup.org. **Contact:** Stacy Wagner (Asian studies, US foreign policy, Asian-American studies); Kate Wahl (law, political science, public policy); Margo Beth Crouppen (economics, finance, business). Estab. 1925. **Pays variable royalty (sometimes none) Pays occasional advance.** Guidelines available online.

⚬━┓ Stanford University Press publishes scholarly books in the humanities and social sciences, along with professional books in business, economics and management science; also high-level textbooks and some books for a more general audience."

NONFICTION Subjects include anthropology, archeology, business, economics, ethnic, studies, gay, lesbian, government, politics, history, humanities, language, literature, literary criticism, and literary theory, nature, environment, philosophy, psychology, religion, science, social sciences, sociology, political science, law, education, history and culture of China, Japan and Latin America, European history, linguistics, geology, medieval and classical studies. Query with prospectus and an outline. Reviews artwork/photos.

TIPS "The writer's best chance is a work of original scholarship with an argument of some importance."

ST. AUGUSTINE'S PRESS

P.O. Box 2285, South Bend IN 46680-2285. (574)-291-3500. Fax: (574)291-3700. E-mail: bruce@staugustine.net. Website: www.staugustine.net. **Contact:** Bruce Fingerhut, president (philosophy). Publishes hardcover originals and trade paperback originals and reprints. **Publishes 20 titles/year. 350 queries received/year. 300 mss received/year. 2% of books from first-time authors. 95% from unagented writers. Pays 6-15% royalty. Pays $500-5,000 advance.** Publishes book 8 months after acceptance of ms. Accepts simultaneous submissions. Responds in 2-6 months to queries. Responds in 3-8 months to proposals. Responds in 4-8 months to manuscripts. Book catalog available free.

IMPRINTS Carthage Reprints.

8—¬ Our market is scholarly in the humanities. We publish in philosophy, religion, cultural history, and history of ideas only."

NONFICTION Query with SASE. Reviews artwork/photos. Send photocopies.

TIPS "Scholarly and college student audience."

STEEPLE HILL BOOKS

Imprint of Harlequin Enterprises, 233 Broadway, Suite 1001, New York NY 10279. (212)553-4200. Fax: (212)227-8969. Website: www.eharlequin.com. **Contact:** Joan Marlow Golan, executive editor; Melissa Endlich, senior editor (inspirational contemp. romance, historical romance, romantic suspense); Tina Colombo, senior editor (inspirational romantic suspense and historical romance); Emily Rodmell, assistant editor. Estab. 1997. Publishes mass market paperback originals and reprints. **Publishes 144 titles/year. Pays royalty on retail price. Pays advance.** 3 months on proposals & mss. Guidelines available online, free on request, for #10 SASE.

IMPRINTS Love Inspired; Love Inspired Suspense; Love Inspired Historical.

8—¬ This series of contemporary, inspirational love stories portrays Christian characters facing the many challenges of life, faith, and love in today's world."

FICTION " We are looking for authors writing from a Christian worldview and conveying their personal faith and ministry values in entertaining fiction that will touch the hearts of believers and seekers everywhere." Query with SASE, submit completed ms.

TIPS "Drama, humor, and even a touch of mystery all have a place in Steeple Hill. Subplots are welcome and should further the story's main focus or intertwine in a meaningful way. Secondary characters (children,

family, friends, neighbors, fellow church members, etc.) may all contribute to a substantial and satisfying story. These wholesome tales include strong family values and high moral standards. While there is no premarital sex between characters, in the case of romance, a vivid, exciting tone presented with a mature perspective is essential. Although the element of faith must clearly be present, it should be well integrated into the characterizations and plot. The conflict between the main characters should be an emotional one, arising naturally from the well-developed personalities you've created. Suitable stories should also impart an important lesson about the powers of trust and faith."

☺ STELLER PRESS LTD.

13, 4335 W. 10th Ave., Vancouver BC V6R 2H6, Canada. (604)222-2955. Fax: (604)222-2965. E-mail: info@stellerpress.com. Website: www.stellerpress.com. **Contact:** Steve Paton (regional interest, outdoors, gardening, history, travel). **Pays royalty on retail price.**

8—¬ Most titles are specific to the Pacific Northwest, local interest, or by Canadian authors. Currently emphasizing regional interest, gardening, history, outdoors and travel and some fiction. De-emphasizing poetry."

NONFICTION Subjects include gardening, history, nature, environment, regional, travel.

STEMMER HOUSE PUBLISHERS

4 White Brook Rd., P.O. Box 89, Gilsum NH 03448. (800)345-6665. Fax: (603)357-2073. E-mail: info@stemmer.com;editor@stemmer.com. Website: www.stemmer.com. Estab. 1975. **Pays advance.** Publishes book 1-2 years after acceptance of ms. Accepts simultaneous submissions. Book catalog for 5 ½×8 ½ envelope and 2 first-class stamps. Guidelines for #10 SASE.

IMPRINTS The International Design Library®; The NatureEncyclopedia Series.

NONFICTION Subjects include animals, arts, multicultural, nature, environment. Query with SASE.

STERLING PUBLISHING CO.INC.

387 Park Ave. S.10th Floor, New York NY 10016-8810. (212)532-7160. Fax: (212)981-0508. E-mail: ragis@sterlingpub.com; bduquette@sterlingpublishing.com. E-mail: info@sterlingweb.com. Website: www.sterlingpublishing.com/kids. **Contact:** Category Editor; Children's Book Editor; Children's Art Director: Merideth Harte. Brett Duquette Publishes hardcover and

paperback originals and reprints. **Pays royalty. Pays advance.** Accepts simultaneous submissions. Guidelines available online.

IMPRINTS Sterling/Books; Sterling/Ethos; Lark; Sterling/Children's; Sterling/Epicure; Ecosystem; Puzzlewright Press; Union Square Press; Ecosystem; Sandy Creek; Sterling/Innovation; Fall River Press; Metro Books; Flashkids; Quamut; Silver Lining Calendars; Hearst Books.

○ "Our mission is to publish high-quality books that educate, entertain, and enrich the lives of our readers."

⊶ Sterling publishes highly illustrated, accessible, hands-on, practical books for adults and children."

NONFICTION Subjects include alternative, animals, art, architecture, ethnic, gardening, health, medicine, hobbies, New Age, recreation, science, sports, fiber arts, games and puzzles, children's humor, children's science, nature and activities, pets, wine, home decorating, dolls and puppets, ghosts, UFOs, woodworking, crafts, medieval, Celtic subjects, alternative health and healing, new consciousness. Proposals on subjects such as crafting, decorating, outdoor living, and photography should be sent directly to Lark Books at their Asheville, North Carolina offices. Complete guidelines can be found on the Lark site: www.larkbooks.com/submissions. Publishes nonfiction only. Submit outline, publishing history, 1 sample chapter (typed and double-spaced), SASE. Explain your idea. Send sample illustrations where applicable. For Children's books, please submit full mss. We do not accept electronic (e-mail) submissions. Be sure to include information about yourself with particular regard to your skills and qualifications in the subject area of your submission. It is helpful for us to know your publishing history—whether or not you've written other books and, if so, the name of the publisher and whether those books are currently in print. Reviews artwork/photocopies.

TIPS "We are primarily a nonfiction activities-based publisher. We have a picture book list, but we do not publish chapter books or novels. Our list is not trend-Dr.n. We focus on titles that will backlist well. "

STIPES PUBLISHING LLC

P.O. Box 526, Champaign IL 61824-9933. (217)356-8391. Fax: (217)356-5753. E-mail: stipes01@sbcglobal.net. Website: www.stipes.com. **Contact:** Benjamin H. Watts, (engineering, science, business); Robert Watts (agriculture, music, and physical education). Estab. 1925. Publishes hardcover and paperback originals. **Publishes 15-30 titles/year. 50% of books from first-time authors. 95% from unagented writers. Pays 15% maximum royalty on retail price.** Publishes book 4 months after acceptance of ms. Responds in 2 months to queries. Guidelines available online.

⊶ Stipes Publishing is oriented towards the education market and educational books with some emphasis in the trade market."

NONFICTION Subjects include agriculture, business, economics, music, dance, nature, environment, recreation, science. "All of our books in the trade area are books that also have a college text market. No books unrelated to educational fields taught at the college level." Submit outline, 1 sample chapter.

⊕ ST. JOHANN PRESS

P.O. Box 241, Haworth NJ 07641. (201)387-1529. E-mail: d.biesel@verizon.net. Website: www.stjohannpress.com. Estab. 1991. Format publishes in hardcover originals, trade paperback originals and reprints. **Publishes 6-8 titles/year. Receives 15 submissions/year. 50% of books from first-time authors. 95% from unagented writers. Pays 10-15% royalty on wholesale price.** Publishes book 15 months after acceptance of ms. Accepts simultaneous submissions. Responds in 1 month on queries. Catalog online at website. Guidelines free on request.

NONFICTION Subjects include cooking, crafts, foods, history, hobbies, memoirs, military, nutrition, religion, sports (history), war (USMC), Black history in sports. "We are a niche publisher with interests in titles that will sell over a long period of time. For example, the World Football League Encyclopedia, Chicago Showcase of Basketball, will not need to be redone. We do baseball but prefer soccer, hockey, etc." Query with SASE Reviews artwork/photos as part of the ms package. Send photocopies.

TIPS "Our readership is libraries, individuals with special interests, (e.g. sports historians); we also do specialized reference."

STOREY PUBLISHING, LLC

210 MASS MoCA Way, North Adams MA 01247. (800)793-9396. Fax: (413)346-2196. E-mail: webmaster@storey.com. Website: www.storey.com. **Contact:** Deborah Balmuth, editorial director (building, sewing, gift). Estab. 1983. Publishes hardcover and trade paperback originals and reprints. **Publishes 40**

titles/year. **600 queries received/year. 150 mss received/year. 25% of books from first-time authors. 60% from unagented writers. We offer both work-for-hire and standard royalty contracts. Pays advance.** Publishes book within 2 years after acceptance of ms. Accepts simultaneous submissions. Responds in 1 month to queries. Responds in 3 months to proposals andmanuscripts. Book catalog available free. Guidelines available online.

8—➤ We publish practical information that encourages personal independence in harmony with the environment."

NONFICTION Subjects include animals, gardening, nature, environment, home, mind/body/spirit, birds, beer and wine, crafts, building, cooking. Reviews artwork/photos.

ST PAULS/ALBA HOUSE

Society of St. Paul, 2187 Victory Blvd., Staten Island NY 10314-6603. (718)761-0047. Fax: (718)761-0057. E-mail: edmund_lane@juno.com; albabooks@aol.com. Website: www.stpauls.us; www.albahouse.org. **Contact:** Edmund C. Lane, SSP, acquisitions editor. Estab. 1957. Publishes trade paperback and mass market paperback originals and reprints. **Publishes 22 titles/year. 250 queries received/year. 150 mss received/year. 10% of books from first-time authors. 100% from unagented writers. Pays 5-10% royalty.** Publishes book 10 months after acceptance of ms. Responds in 1 month to queries and proposals. Responds in 2 months to manuscripts. Book catalog and ms guidelines free.

NONFICTION Subjects include philosophy, religion, spirituality. Alba House is the North American publishing division of the Society of St. Paul, an International Roman Catholic Missionary Religious Congregation dedicated to spreading the Gospel message via the media of communications. Does not want fiction, children's books, poetry, personal testimonies, or autobiographies. Submit complete ms. Reviews artwork/photos. Send photocopies.

TIPS "Our audience is educated Roman Catholic readers interested in matters related to the Church, spirituality, Biblical and theological topics, moral concerns, lives of the saints, etc."

STRIDER NOLAN PUBLISHING, INC.

702 Cricket Ave., Glenside PA 19038. E-mail: infostridernolan@yahoo.com. Website: www.stridernolanmedia.com. Publishes hardcover, trade paperback.

Publishes 5-10 titles/year. 1,000-2,000 queries received/year. 500-1,000 mss received/year. 50% of books from first-time authors. 50% from unagented writers. Pays royalty on retail price. Accepts simultaneous submissions. Book catalog available online. Guidelines available online.

8—➤ At this time, Strider Nolan is only seeking stories or art for our Visions anthology. Feel free to contact us via e-mail. If you would like to submit a novel to us, we have plenty of material in the pipeline but are always willing to listen. We cannot guarantee anything, so your project would really have to be something special to get us to look at it. We do accept unagented material, although a prior history of published work (even self-published) is preferable. Favored genres include science fiction, horror, and historical fiction (especially westerns or Civil War)."

SUNBURY PRESS, INC.

100 South Front St., Lemoyne PA 17043. E-mail: info@sunburypress.com. E-mail: proposals@sunburypress.com. Website: www.sunburypress.com. Estab. 2004. Format publishes in hardcover and trade paperback originals and reprints; electronic originals and reprints. **Publishes 75 titles/year. 250 queries/year; 150 mss/year 40% of books from first-time authors. 90% from unagented writers. Pays 10% royalty on wholesale price** Publishes book 3 months after acceptance of ms. Accepts simultaneous submissions. Responds in 1 months on queries, proposals, and mss. Catalog available online at website. Guidelines available by e-mail at: proposals@sunburypress.com.

◯ Submit proposal package, including synopsis and 4 sample chapters.

NONFICTION Subjects include Americana, animals, anthropology, archeology, architecture, art, astrology, business, career guidance, child guidance, communications, computers, contemporary culture, counseling, crafts, creative nonfiction, dance, economics, education, electronics, entertainment, ethnic, government, health, history, hobbies, house and home, humanities, language, literature, memoirs, military, money, multicultural, music, nature, New Age, photography, regional, religion, science, sex, spirituality, sports, transportation, travel, war, world affairs, young adult. "We are currently seeking Civil War era memoirs and unpublished or new material regarding the Civil War. We are also seeking biographies / histories of local/regional figures who were noteworthy but unpublished or sparsely published." Reviews artwork.

FICTION Subjects include adventure, confession, contemporary, ethnic, experimental, fantasy, gothic, historical, horror, humor, juvenile, mainstream, military, multicultural, mystery, occult, picture books, poetry, regional, religious, romance, science fiction, short story collections, spiritual, sports, suspense, western, young adult. "We are especially seeking historical fiction regarding the Civil War and books of regional interest."

POETRY Submit complete ms.

TIPS "Our books appeal to very diverse audiences. We are building our list in many categories, focusing on many demographics. We are not like traditional publishers—we are digitally adept and very creative. Don't be surprised if we move quicker than you are accustomed to!"

SUNRISE RIVER PRESS

39966 Grand Ave., North Branch MN 55056. (800)895-4585. Fax: (651)277-1203. E-mail: editorial@sunriseriverpress.com. Website: www.sunriseriverpress.com. **Contact:** Acquisitions Editor. Estab. 1992. **Publishes 30 titles/year. Pays advance.** Accepts simultaneous submissions. Guidelines available online.

○ Sunrise River Press is part of a 3-company publishing house that also includes CarTech Books and Specialty Press. "Sunrise River Press is currently seeking book proposals from health/medical writers or experts who are interested in authoring consumer- geared trade paperbacks on healthcare, fitness, and nutrition topics."

☞ E-mail is preferred method of contact."

NONFICTION Subjects include cooking, foods, nutrition, health, medicine, genetics, immune system maintenance, fitness; also some professional healthcare titles. Check website for submission guidelines. No phone calls, please; no originals.

FICTION "Although we don't solicit article-length manuscripts, short humour contributions or jokes are welcome." Submit online at: http://www2.readersdigest.ca/laugh_submit.html.

SUPERCOLLEGE

3286 Oak Court, Belmont CA 94002. Phone/Fax: (650)618-2221. E-mail: supercollege@supercollege.com. Website: www.supercollege.com. Estab. 1998. Publishes trade paperback originals. **Publishes 8-10 titles/year. 50% of books from first-time au-**thors. **70% from unagented writers. Pays royalty on wholesale price or makes outright purchase.** Publishes book 7-9 months after acceptance of ms. Book catalog and writer's guidelines online.

☞ We only publish books on admission, financial aid, scholarships, test preparation, student life, and career preparation for college and graduate students."

NONFICTION Subjects include education, admissions, financial aid, scholarships, test prep, student life, career prep. Submit complete ms. Reviews artwork/photos. Send photocopies.

TIPS "We want titles that are student and parent friendly, and that are different from other titles in this category. We also seek authors who want to work with a small but dynamic and ambitious publishing company."

⊕ SWAN ISLE PRESS

P.O. Box 408790, Chicago IL 60640-8790. (773)728-3780. E-mail: info@swanislepress.com. Website: www.swanislepress.com. **Contact:** Editor. Estab. 1999. Publishes hardcover and trade paperback originals. **Publishes 3 titles/year. 1,500 queries received/year. 0% of books from first-time authors. Pays 7 ½-10% royalty on wholesale price.** Publishes book 12-18 months after acceptance of ms. Responds in 6 months to queries. Responds in 12 months to manuscripts. Book catalog available online. Guidelines available online.

○ "We do not accept unsolicited mss."

NONFICTION Subjects include art, architecture, creative nonfiction, ethnic, history, humanities, language, literature, literary criticism, memoirs, multicultural, translation. Query with SASE. Submit complete mss only if author receives affirmative response to query. Reviews artwork/photos. Send photocopies.

FICTION Subjects include ethnic, historical, literary, multicultural, poetry, poetry in translation, short story collections, translation. Query with SASE. Submit complete mss. only afte

POETRY Query and submit complete ms.

SWEETGUM PRESS

P.O. Drawer J, 304 Grover, Warrensburg MO 64093. (660)429-5773. Fax: (660)429-3487. E-mail: editors@sweetgumpress.com. Website: www.sweetgumpress.com. **Contact:** R.M. Kinder or Baird Brock, Editors. Estab. 2001. Publishes trade paperback originals. **Publishes 1-2 titles/year. 200 queries received/year. 50 mss received/year. 100% of books from first-time authors. 100% from unagented writers. Pays 10-15%**

royalty on retail price. Publishes book 1 year after acceptance of ms. Accepts simultaneous submissions. Responds in 1 month to queries. Responds in 3-6 months to manuscripts. Book catalog for #10 SASE. Guidelines available online.

○ "Sweetgum has three new titles forthcoming and will not be accepting new submissions for a few months. Please check our website from time to time for updates." Sweetgum accepts work only by midwestern writers. Especially interested in work by Missouri writers.

☞ We will accept only work from midwestern writers."

NONFICTION Subjects include creative nonfiction, history, memoirs, regional, religion. Check website for current calls for manuscript. Then query, following guidelines. Query with SASE and first 3 pages of manuscript. Please do not submit synopses and sample chapters by e-mail unless asked to do so.

FICTION Subjects include experimental, historical, literary, mainstream, contemporary, mystery, regional, short story collections, suspense. Query with SASE and first 3 pages.

TIPS "Right now we are only interested in regional writers. Be straightforward about your goals and experience. Good writing is the most persuasive part of a submission, but make reading easy by sending your work in a professional format."

SWITCHGRASS BOOKS

Northern Illinois University Press, Switchgrass Books, 2280 Bethany Rd., DeKalb IL 60115. Website: www. switchgrass.niu.edu. Estab. 2008. **Publishes 4 titles/year.** Guidelines are free and available online.

☞ E-mail submissions are not accepted.

FICTION "We publish only full-length novels set in or about the Midwest. Switchgrass authors must be from the Midwest, current residents of the region, or have significant ties to it. Briefly tell us in your cover letter why yours is an authentic Midwestern voice." "We will not consider memoirs, short stories, novellas, graphic novels, poetry, or juvenile/YA literature. Agented mss will not be considered." Send your complete ms via U.S. mail. E-mail submissions will not be considered. No queries, calls, or e-mails, please. Please include a resume or C.V.

SYRACUSE UNIVERSITY PRESS

621 Skytop Road, Suite 110, Syracuse NY 13244-5290. (315)443-5534. Fax: (315)443-5545. Website: syracu-

seuniversitypress.syr.edu. **Contact:** Alice R. Pfeiffer, director. Estab. 1943. **Publishes 50 titles/year. 25% of books from first-time authors. 95% from unagented writers.** Publishes book an average of 15 months after acceptance of ms. Book catalog on our website. Guidelines available online.

☞ Currently emphasizing Middle East studies, Jewish studies, Irish studies, peace studies, dissability studies, television and popular culture, Native American studies, gender and ethnic studies, New York State."

NONFICTION Subjects include regional. "Special opportunity in our nonfiction program for freelance writers of books on New York state, sports history, Jewish studies, the Middle East, religious studies, television, and popular culture. Provide precise descriptions of subjects, along with background description of project. The author must make a case for the importance of his or her subject." Submit query with SASE or online, or submit outline and 2 sample chapters. Reviews artwork/photos.

TIPS "We're seeking well-written and well-researched books that will make a significant contribution to the subject areas listed above and will be well-received in the marketplace."

⊜ TAFELBERG PUBLISHERS

Imprint of NB Publishers, P.O. Box 879, Cape Town 8000, South Africa. (27)(21)406-3033. Fax: (27)(21)406-3812. E-mail: nb@nb.co.za. Website: www.tafelberg.com. **Contact:** Danita van Romburgh, editorial secretary.

☞ General publisher best known for Afrikaans fiction, authoritative political works, children's/youth literature, and a variety of illustrated and nonillustrated nonfiction.

NONFICTION Subjects include health, medicine, memoirs, politics. Submit complete ms.

FICTION Subjects include juvenile, romance. Submit complete ms.

TIPS "Writers: Story needs to have a South African or African style. Illustrators: I'd like to look, but the chances of getting commissioned are slim. The market is small and difficult. Do not expect huge advances. Editorial staff attended or plans to attend the following conferences: IBBY, Frankfurt, SCBWI Bologna., "Writers: Story needs to have a South African or African style. Illustrators: I'd like to look, but the chances of getting commissioned are slim. The market is small and difficult. Do not expect huge advances. Editorial staff attended or plans to attend the following conferences: IBBY, Frankfurt, SCBWI Bologna.

☻ TANGLEWOOD BOOKS

P.O. Box 3009, Terre Haute IN 47803. E-mail: ptierney@tanglewoodbooks.com. Website: www.tanglewoodbooks.com. **Contact:** Kairi Hamlin, Acquisitions Editor. Estab. 2003. Publishes book Publishes book 2 years after acceptance. after acceptance of ms. Accepts simultaneous submissions. Responds to mss in up to 18 months.

⚷━ Tanglewood Press strives to publish entertaining, kid-centric books."

NONFICTION Does not generally publish nonfiction.

FICTION Query with 3-5 sample chapters.

TIPS "Please see lengthy 'Submissions' page on our website."

TAYLOR TRADE PUBLISHING

5360 Manhattan Circle, #101, Boulder CO 80303. (303)543-7835. E-mail: rrinehart@rowman.com. E-mail: tradeeditorial@rowman.com. Website: www.rlpgtrade.com. **Contact:** Acquisitions Editor. Rick Rinehart, Editorial Director Publishes hardcover originals, trade paperback originals and reprints. **Publishes 70 titles/year. 15% of books from first-time authors. 65% from unagented writers.** Publishes book 1 year after acceptance of ms. Responds in 2 months to queries. See catalog online at website. Submission guidelines available on website under "Editorial.".

NONFICTION Subjects include child guidance, cooking, foods, nutrition, gardening, health, medicine, history, Texas/Western, nature, environment, sports, contemporary affairs, music, film, theater, art, nature writing, exploration, women's studies, African-American studies, literary studies. All proposals may be sent via e-mail. Proposals should be limited to a query letter; an e-mail will generate the quickest response. If querying by e-mail, please note in the memo box "book proposal." Send no attachments unless requested. If using postal mail, query with SASE. What we look for at this stage is suitability of the proposed book to our publishing program (see categories) as well as the author's unique qualifications for writing his or her book.

✛ TEACHER IDEAS PRESS

Libraries Unlimited, ABC-CLIO, P.O. Box 1911, Santa Barbara CA 93116-1911. Website: www.teacher-ideaspress.com. **Contact:** Sharon Coatney, editor. Contact customer service by phone or e-mail for free updated catalog. Guidelines and catalog available online.

⚷━ Teacher Ideas Press offers books written by teachers for teachers. Our books offer a clear and strong focus on literary and 21st century learning skills. We publish the best in innovative, practical, hands-on lessons and classroom-tested activities, all designed to help you teach 21st century literacy skills and improve student achievement. We are proud to be your partner in promoting excellence in the K-12 classroom. Whether you're a classroom, subject, or special area teacher or a library media specialist, you'll find instructional value in these resources. They include research-based strategies and materials for helping you differentiate for students who are gifted, are at risk, have special needs, or are English language learners. Send us proposals for books to teach reading comprehension, fluency, vocabulary, writing, and information literacy skills in collaboration with the school librarian."

⊘ TEBOT BACH

P.O. Box 7887, Huntington Beach CA 92615-7887. (714)968-0905. E-mail: info@tebotbach.org. Website: www.tebotbach.org. **Contact:** Mifanwy Kaiser, editor/publisher. Publishes book 2 years after acceptance of ms. Responds to queries and mss, if invited, in 3 months.

◯ Tebot Bach (Welsh for "little teapot") publishes books of poetry. Query first via e-mail, with a few sample poems and cover letter with brief bio. Include SASE. Write to order sample books. Sponsors The Patricia Bibby First Book Award (see separate listing in Contests & Awards). An anthology of California poets. Must be current or former resident of California in order to submit, but no focus or theme required for poetry. Query first. Submit up to 6 poems with "California Anthology" written on lower left corner of envelope. Accepts submissions by e-mail (pasted into body of message or as attachment in Word). Deadline for submission is in August of the year call for submissions is announced. Please check the website for calls for submissions. Also publishes *Spillway: A Literary Journal* (see separate listing in Magazines/Journals).

TEMPLE UNIVERSITY PRESS

1852 North 10th St., Philadelphia PA 19122. (215)926-2140. Fax: (215)926-2141. E-mail: tempress@temple.edu. Website: www.temple.edu/tempress/. **Contact:** Alex Holzman, director; Janet Francendese, editor-in-chief; Micah Kleit, executive editor; Mick Gusinde-Duffy, senior acquisitions editor. Estab. 1969. **Publishes 60 titles/year. Pays advance.** Publishes book 10 months after acceptance of ms. Responds in 2 months to queries. Book catalog available free. Guidelines available online.

➤ Temple University Press has been publishing path-breaking books on Asian-Americans, law, gender issues, film, women's studies and other interesting areas for nearly 40 years."

NONFICTION Subjects include ethnic, government, politics, health, medicine, history, photography, regional, Philadelphia, sociology, labor studies, urban studies, Latin American/Latino, Asian American, African American studies, public policy, women's studies. No memoirs, fiction or poetry. Query with SASE. Reviews artwork/photos.

TEN SPEED PRESS

The Crown Publishing Group, Ten Speed Press, Attn: Acquisitions, 2625 Alcatraz Ave. #505, Berkeley CA 94705. (510)559-1600. Fax: (510)524-1052. E-mail: CrownBiz@randomhouse.com. Website: www.randomhouse.com/crown/tenspeed/. Estab. 1971. Publishes trade paperback originals and reprints. **Publishes 120 titles/year. 40% of books from first-time authors. 40% from unagented writers. Pays $2,500 average advance.** Publishes book 1 year after acceptance of ms. Accepts simultaneous submissions. Responds in 3 months to queries; 6-8 weeks to proposals. Book catalog for 9×12 envelope and 6 first-class stamps. Guidelines available online.

IMPRINTS Celestial Arts; Crossing Press; Tricycle Press.

○ "Ten Speed Press has built its reputation on enduring career and business books like Richard Bolles's *What Color Is Your Parachute?* (the bestselling job-hunting book in the world) and acclaimed cookbooks, ranging from the upscale and authoritative *Alinea* by Grant Achatz and *Cooking* by James Peterson to the perennially popular *Moosewood Cook-*

book by Mollie Katzen and *The Bread Baker's Apprentice* by Peter Reinhart. Along the way, the company has also made its mark with an eclectic list of genre-bending titles including the classics *How to Shit in the Woods, Why Cats Paint, The Cannabible Collection*, and *Furry Logic*."

➤ Ten Speed Press publishes authoritative books for an audience interested in innovative ideas. Currently emphasizing cookbooks, career, business, alternative education, and offbeat general nonfiction gift books."

NONFICTION Subjects include business, career guidance, cooking, crafts, relationships, how-to, humor, and pop culture. No fiction. "Please read our submission guidelines online. Before submitting your manuscript, you should first familiarize yourself with our publishing areas and imprints. Note that we do not consider certain genres, including fiction, poetry, memoir, and most photography." Query with SASE. Submit proposal package, sample chapters.

TIPS "We like books from people who really know their subject, rather than people who think they've spotted a trend to capitalize on. We like books that will sell for a long time, rather than nine-day wonders. Our audience consists of a well-educated, slightly weird group of people who like food, the outdoors, and take a light, but serious, approach to business and careers. Study the backlist of each publisher you're submitting to and tailor your proposal to what you perceive as their needs. Nothing gets a publisher's attention like someone who knows what he or she is talking about, and nothing falls flat like someone who obviously has no idea who he or she is submitting to."

TEXAS A&M UNIVERSITY PRESS

College Station TX 77843-4354. (979)845-1436. Fax: (979)847-8752. E-mail: d-vance@tamu.edu. Website: www.tamupress.com. **Contact:** Mary Lenn Dixon, editor-in-chief (presidential studies, anthropology, borderlands, Texas/western history); Shannon Davies, senior editor (natural history, agriculture). Estab. 1974. **Publishes 60 titles/year. Pays royalty.** Publishes book 1 year after acceptance of ms. Responds in 1 month to queries. Book catalog available free. Guidelines available online.

➤ Texas A&M University Press publishes a wide range of nonfiction, scholarly, trade, and crossover books of regional and national interest, reflecting the interests of the university, the broader scholarly community, and the people of our state and region."

NONFICTION Subjects include agriculture, anthropology, archeology, art, architecture, language, literature, military, war, nature, environment, regional, Texas and the Southwest, Mexican-US borderlands studies, nautical archaeology, ethnic studies, presidential studies, history (American, Texas, western, military). Nonreturnable queries; e-mail preferred.

TIPS "Proposal requirements are posted on the website."

TEXAS WESTERN PRESS

The University of Texas at El Paso, 500 W. University Ave., El Paso TX 79968-0633. (915)747-5688. Fax: (915)747-5345. E-mail: twpress@utep.edu; ctavarez@utep.edu. Website: twp.utep.edu. **Contact:** Robert L. Stakes, director. Estab. 1952. Publishes hardcover and paperback originals. **Publishes 1 titles/year. Pays standard 10% royalty. Pays advance.** Responds in 2 months to queries. Book catalog available free. Guidelines available online.

IMPRINTS Southwestern Studies.

Texas Western Press publishes books on the history and cultures of the American Southwest, particularly historical and biographical works about West Texas, New Mexico, northern Mexico, and the U.S. borderlands. The Press also publishes selected books in the areas of regional art, photography, Native American studies, geography, demographics, border issues, politics, and natural history."

NONFICTION Subjects include education, health, medicine, history, language, literature, nature, environment, regional, science, social sciences. "Historic and cultural accounts of the Southwest (West Texas, New Mexico, northern Mexico). Also art, photographic books, Native American and limited regional fiction reprints. Occasional technical titles. Our *Southwestern Studies* use manuscripts of up to 30,000 words. Our hardback books range from 30,000 words and up. The writer should use good exposition in his work. Most of our work requires documentation. We favor a scholarly, but not overly pedantic, style. We specialize in superior book design." Query with SASE, or submit résumé, 2-3 sample chapters, cover letter, description of ms and special features, TOC, list of competing titles.

TIPS "Texas Western Press is interested in books relating to the history of Hispanics in the US. Will experiment with photo-documentary books, and is interested in seeing more contemporary books on border issues. We try to treat our authors professionally, produce handsome, long-lived books and aim for quality, rather than quantity of titles carrying our imprint."

☼ THE ALTHOUSE PRESS

University of Western Ontario, Faculty of Education, 1137 Western Rd., London ON N6G 1G7, Canada. (519)661-2096. Fax: (519)661-3714. E-mail: press@uwo.ca. Website: www.edu.uwo.ca/althousepress. **Contact:** Katherine Butson, editorial assistant. Publishes trade paperback originals and reprints. **Publishes 1-5 titles/year. 50-100 queries received/year. 14 mss received/year. 50% of books from first-time authors. 100% from unagented writers. Pays $300 advance.** Publishes book 8-18 months after acceptance of ms. Accepts simultaneous submissions. Responds in 1-2 months to queries. Responds in 4 months to manuscripts. Book catalog available free. Guidelines available online.

The Althouse Press publishes both scholarly research monographs in education and professional books and materials for educators in elementary schools, secondary schools, and faculties of education. De-emphasizing curricular or instructional materials intended for use by elementary or secondary school students."

NONFICTION Subjects include education, scholarly. "Do not send incomplete manuscripts that are only marginally appropriate to our market and limited mandate." Reviews artwork/photos. Send photocopies.

TIPS "Audience is practising teachers and graduate education students."

THE BOLD STRUMMER, LTD.

P.O. Box 2037, Westport CT 06880-2037. (203)227-8588. Fax: (203)227-8775. E-mail: theboldstrummer@msn.com. Website: www.boldstrummerltd.com. **Contact:** Nicholas Clarke. Estab. 1973. Publishes hardcover and trade paperback originals and reprints. Niche publisher now concentrates solely on books about the guitar, including books about flamenco and all its aspects. Heavy printing. **Publishes 3 titles/year.**

Guitar related reading and instruction books.

NONFICTION Contact through online form.

⊘ THE DENALI PRESS

P.O. Box 021535, Juneau AK 99802-1535. (907)586-6014. Fax: (907)463-6780. E-mail: denalipress@alaska.com. Website: www.denalipress.com. **Contact:** Alan Schorr, editorial director; Sally Silvas-Ottumwa, editorial associate. Estab. 1986. Publishes trade paperback originals. **Publishes 5 titles/year. 50% of books from first-time authors. 80% from unagented writers. Pays 10% royalty on wholesale price. Makes outright purchase. Pays advance.** Publishes book 1 year after acceptance of ms. Accepts simultaneous submissions. Responds in 1 month to queries.

○ "A premier publishing company dedicated to finding, developing, and promoting dynamic Thought Leaders who have a compelling message that must be told. Denali Press has the author in mind first. A designer publishing house that customizes the brand, with the author. We believe that Innovative strategies, purposeful marketing, and collaborative methodology is the new recipe for success. Denali Press - Bringing the Ideas, Innovation, and Execution needed to reach your summit."

⚷➼ The Denali Press looks for reference works suitable for the educational, professional, and library market. Though we publish books on a variety of topics, our focus is most broadly centered on multiculturalism, public policy, Alaskana, and general reference works.

NONFICTION Subjects include Americana, anthropology, archeology, ethnic, government, politics, history, multicultural, recreation, regional. We need reference books—ethnic, refugee, and minority concerns. Query with SASE. Submit outline, sample chapters. *All unsolicited mss returned unopened.*

THE GLENCANNON PRESS

P.O. Box 1428, El Cerrito CA 94530. (510)528-4216. Fax: (510)528-3194. E-mail: merships@yahoo.com. Website: www.glencannon.com. **Contact:** Bill Harris (maritime, maritime children's). Estab. 1993. Publishes hardcover and paperback originals and hardcover reprints. **Publishes 4-5/year, 1 fiction title/year titles/year. Pays 10-20% royalty.** Publishes book 6-24 months after acceptance of ms. Accepts simultaneous submissions. Responds in 1 month to queries; 2 months to mss.

IMPRINTS Smyth: perfect binding; illustrations.

⚷➼ We publish quality books about ships and the sea." Average print order: 1,000. First novel print order: 750. Member PMA, BAIPA. Distributes titles through Baker & Taylor. Promotes titles through direct mail, magazine advertising and word of mouth. Accepts unsolicited mss. Often comments on rejected mss.

FICTION Subjects include adventure, contemporary, ethnic, humor, juvenile, mainstream, military, mystery, war, young adult. Submit complete ms. Include brief bio, list of publishing credits. Send SASE for return of ms or send a disposable ms and SASE for reply only.

TIPS "Write a good story in a compelling style."

THE JOHNS HOPKINS UNIVERSITY PRESS

2715 N. Charles St., Baltimore MD 21218. (410)516-6900. Fax: (410)516-6968. E-mail: jmm@press.jhu.edu. Website: www.press.jhu.edu. **Contact:** Jacqueline C. Wehmueller, executive editor (consumer health, psychology and psychiatry, and history of medicine; jcw@press.jhu.edu); Matthew McAdam, editor (mxm@jhu@press.edu); Robert J. Brugger, senior acquisitions editor (American history; rjb@press.jhu.edu); Vincent J. Burke, exec. editor (biology; vjb@press.jhu.edu); Juliana McCarthy, acquisitions editor (humanities, classics, and ancient studies; jmm@press.jhu.edu); Ashleigh McKown, assistant editor (higher education, history of technology, history of science; aem@press.jhu.edu); Suzanne Flinchbaugh, Associate Editor (Political Science, Health Policy, and Co-Publishing Liaison; skf@press.jhu.edu; Greg Nicholl, Assistant Editor (Regional Books, Poetry and Fiction, and Anabaptist and Pietist Studies; gan@press.jhu.edu). Estab. 1878. Publishes hardcover originals and reprints, and trade paperback reprints. **Publishes 140 titles/year. Pays royalty.** Publishes book 12 months after acceptance of ms.

NONFICTION Subjects include government, politics, health, medicine, history, humanities, literary criticism, regional, religion, science. Submit proposal package, outline, 1 sample chapter, curriculum vita. Reviews artwork/photos. Send photocopies.

THE PERMANENT PRESS

Attn: Judith Shepard, 4170 Noyac Rd., Sag Harbor NY 11963. (631)725-1101. E-mail: judith@thepermanentpress.com; shepard@thepermanentpress.com. Website: www.thepermanentpress.com. **Contact:** Judith and Martin Shepard, acquisitions/publishers. Blog: www.thecockeyedpessimist.com Estab. 1978. Format publishes in hardcover originals. Publishes book Publishes ms within 18 months after acceptance. after acceptance of ms. Responds in weeks or months to queries and submissions.

8—➤ Mid-size, independent publisher of literary fiction. "We keep titles in print and are active in selling subsidiary rights." Average print order: 1,500. Averages 14 total titles. Accepts unsolicited mss. Pays 10-15% royalty on wholesale price. Offers $1,000 advance.

FICTION "Promotes titles through reviews. Literary, mainstream/contemporary, mystery. Especially looking for high-line literary fiction, "artful, original and arresting." Accepts any fiction category as long as it is Kwell-written, original full-length novel.

TIPS "We are looking for good books; be they 10th novels or first ones, it makes little difference. The fiction is more important than the track record. Send us the first 25 pages, it's impossible to judge something that begins on page 302. Also, no outlines—let the writing present itself."

THIRD WORLD PRESS

P.O. Box 19730, Chicago IL 60619. (773)651-0700. Fax: (773)651-7286. E-mail: twpress3@aol.com; GWENMTWP@aol.com. Website: www.thirdworldpressinc. com. **Contact:** Bennett J. Johnson. Estab. 1967. Publishes hardcover and trade paperback originals and reprints. **Publishes 20 titles/year. 200-300 queries received/year. 200 mss received/year. 20% of books from first-time authors. 80% from unagented writers. Compensation based upon royalties. Individual arrangement with author depending on the book, etc.** Publishes book 18 months after acceptance of ms. Accepts simultaneous submissions. Responds in 6 months to queries. Responds in 5 months to manuscripts. Book catalog available free. Guidelines for #10 SASE.

○ Third World Press is open to submissions in July only.

8—➤ We look for the maximum effect of creative expression and cultural enlightenment in all of the written genres, including fiction, nonfiction, poetry, drama, young adult, and children's books which may not have an outlet otherwise. Third World Press welcomes the opportunity to review solicited and unsolicited

manuscripts that explore African-centered life and thought through the genres listed above."

NONFICTION Subjects include anthropology, archeology, education, ethnic, government, politics, health, medicine, history, language, literature, literary criticism, philosophy, psychology, regional, religion, sociology, women's issues, women's studies, Black studies. Query with SASE. Submit outline, 5 sample chapters. Reviews artwork/photos. Send photocopies.

FICTION Subjects include ethnic, feminist, historical, juvenile, animal, easy-to-read, fantasy, historical, contemporary, literary, mainstream, contemporary, picture books, plays, short story collections, young adult, easy-to-read/teen, folktales, historical, African-centered, African-American materials, preschool/picture book. "We primarily publish nonfiction, but will consider fiction by and about Blacks." Query with SASE. Submit outline, clips, 5 sample chapters.

POETRY Ethnic/African-centered and African-American materials. Submit complete ms.

Ⓐ THOMAS DUNNE BOOKS

Imprint of St. Martin's Press, 175 Fifth Ave., New York NY 10010. (212)674-5151. Website: www.thomasdunnebooks.com. Estab. 1986. Publishes hardcover and trade paperback originals, and reprints. Accepts simultaneous submissions. Book catalog and ms guidelines free.

○ "Thomas Dunne Books publishes popular trade fiction and nonfiction. With an output of approximately 175 titles each year, his group covers a range of genres including commercial and literary fiction, thrillers, biography, politics, sports, popular science, and more. The list is intentionally eclectic and includes a wide range of fiction and nonfiction, from first books to international bestsellers."

8—➤ Thomas Dunne publishes a wide range of fiction and nonfiction. Accepts submissions from agents only.

NONFICTION Subjects include government, politics, history, sports, political commentary. Author's attention to detail is important. We get a lot of manuscripts that are poorly proofread and just can't be considered. Agents submit query, or an outline and 1 sample pages. Reviews artwork/photos. Send photocopies.

FICTION Subjects include mainstream, contemporary, mystery, suspense, thrillers, women's. Agents submit query, or submit

⊘ TIGHTROPE BOOKS

602 Markham St., Toronto ON M6G 2L8, Canada. (647)348-4460. E-mail: shirarose@tightropebooks.com. Website: www.tightropebooks.com. **Contact:** Shirarose Wilensky, editor. Estab. 2005. Publishes hardcover and trade paperback originals. **Publishes 12 titles/year. 70% of books from first-time authors. 100% from unagented writers. 5-15% royalty on retail price. $200-300** Publishes book 12 months after acceptance of ms. Accepts simultaneous submissions. Responds if interested. Catalog and guidelines free on request and online.

IMPRINTS Zurita, Latino-Canadian imprint, Halli Villegas, Publisher.

NONFICTION Subjects include alternative lifestyles, architecture, art, contemporary culture, creative nonfiction, ethnic, gay, language, lesbian, literary criticism, literature, multicultural, womens issues. Query with SASE. Submit proposal package, including outline, 1 sample chapter and complete ms. Reviews artwork. Send photocopies.

FICTION Subjects include contemporary, ethnic, experimental, fantasy, feminist, gay, horror, juvenile, lesbian, literary, mainstream, multicultural, poetry, poetry in translation, short story collections, translation, young adult. Query with SASE. Submit proposal package, including: synopsis, 1 sample chapter and completed ms.

POETRY Query. Submit 10 sample poems. Submit complete ms.

TIPS "Audience is young, urban, literary, educated, unconventional."

TILBURY HOUSE, PUBLISHERS

Imprint of Harpswell Press, Inc., 103 Brunswick Ave., Gardiner ME 04345. (800)582-1899. Fax: (207)582-8227. E-mail: tilbury@tilburyhouse.com. Website: www.tilburyhouse.com. **Contact:** Karen Fisk, associate children's book editor. Estab. 1990. **Publishes 10 titles/year. Pays royalty.** Book catalog available free. Guidelines available online.

NONFICTION Regional adult biography/history/maritime/nature, and children's picture books that deal with issues, such as bullying, multiculturalism, etc. Submit complete ms. Reviews artwork/photos. Send photocopies.

⊕ TO BE READ ALOUD PUBLISHING, INC.

P.O. Box 632426, Nacogdoches TX 75963. E-mail: michael@tobereadaloud.org. E-mail: submissions@to-bereadaloud.org. Website: www.tobereadaloud.org. **Contact:** Michael Powell, President (short stories); Stephen Powell, Editor (poetry). Estab. 2006. Publishes trade paperback originals and reprints. **Publishes 4 titles/year. 250 queries received/year. 200 mss received/year. 90% of books from first-time authors. 90% from unagented writers. Makes outright purchase of 100-200.** Publishes book 4 months after acceptance of ms. Accepts simultaneous submissions. Responds in 3 months to queries, proposals, and to manuscripts. Guidelines available via e-mail.

NONFICTION Subjects include community, contemporary culture, creative nonfiction, education, ethnic, military, war, multicultural, philosophy, sociology. "Submissions are for the purpose of supporting high school drama coaches and their oral interpretation competitors. Selections should be written to be read aloud. Selections should be less than 3,000 words." Submit complete ms.

FICTION Subjects include adventure, confession, ethnic, gothic, historical, horror, humor, juvenile, literary, multicultural, mystery, poetry, poetry in translation, science fiction, short story collections, sports, suspense, western. All submissions should be written by authors born in one of the following states: Alabama, Arkansas, Florida, Georgia, Louisiana, Kentucky, Mississippi, North Carolina, South Carolina, Tennessee, Virginia, or West Virginia Submit complete ms. Attach as a Word ".doc"

POETRY Submit complete ms.

TIPS "Our audience is high school drama students. Read your selection aloud before submitting." "We service the UIL of Texas mostly; check their annual categories and write accordingly to match them."

TODD PUBLICATIONS

P.O. Box 1752, Boca Raton FL 33429. (561)910-0440. E-mail: toddpub@aol.com. Website: www.toddpub.info. **Contact:** Barry Klein, president. Estab. 1973. Publishes reference books and trade paperback originals. **Publishes 10 titles/year. 10% of books from first-time authors. 100% from unagented writers.** Publishes book 3 months after acceptance of ms. Accepts simultaneous submissions. Responds in 1 month to proposals. Book listing available via e-mail.

⌐ Todd Publications publishes/distributes reference books and directories of all types."

NONFICTION Subjects include ethnic, health, medicine & fitness. Submit outline and 2 sample chapters.

TOP PUBLICATIONS, LTD.

3100 Independence Pkwy., Suite 311-349, Plano TX 75075. (972)490-9686. Fax: (972)233-0713. E-mail: info@toppub.com. E-mail: submissions@toppub.com. Website: www.toppub.com. **Contact:** Sara Mendoza, Editor. Estab. 1999. Publishes hardcover and paperback originals. **Publishes 2-3 titles/year. 200 queries received/year. 20 mss received/year. 90% of books from first-time authors. 95% from unagented writers. Pays 15-20% royalty on wholesale price. Pays $250-2,500 advance.** Publishes book 8 months after acceptance of ms. Accepts simultaneous submissions. Acknowledges receipt of queries but only responds if interested in seeing manuscript. Responds in 6 months to manuscripts. Tear sheets available on new titles. Guidelines available online.

◯ "Top strives to be an author friendly publisher."

⌘ Primarily a mainstream fiction publisher.

NONFICTION "We are primarily a fiction publisher and do not solicit submissions of nonfiction works."

FICTION Subjects include adventure, historical, horror, juvenile, mainstream, contemporary, military, war, mystery, regional, romance, science fiction, short story collections, suspense, young adult. "It is imperative that our authors realize they will be required to promote their book extensively for it to be a success. Unless they are willing to make this commitment, they shouldn't submit to TOP." Publishes 2-3 ms/year.

TIPS "We recommend that our authors write books that appeal to a large mainstream audience to make marketing easier and increase the chances of success. We only publish a few titles a year so the odds at getting published at TOP are slim. If we reject your work, it probably doesn't have any reflection on your work. We have to pass on a lot of good material each year simply by the limitations of our time and budget."

TORQUERE PRESS

P.O. Box 2545, Round Rock TX 78680. (512)586-3553. Fax: (866)287-2968. E-mail: editor@torquerepress.com. E-mail: submissions@torquerepress.com. Website: www.torquerepress.com. **Contact:** Shawn Clements, submissions editor (homoerotica, suspense, gay/lesbian); Lorna Hinson, senior editor (gay/lesbian romance, historicals). Estab. 2003. Publishes trade paperback originals and electronic originals and reprints. **Publishes 140 titles/year. 500 queries received/year. 200 mss received/year. 25% of books** from first-time authors. 100% from unagented writers. **Pays 8-40% royalty. Pays $35-75 for anthology stories.** Publishes book 6 months after acceptance of ms. Responds in 1 month to queries and proposals. Responds in 2-4 months to manuscripts. Book catalog available online. Guidelines available online.

IMPRINTS Top Shelf (Shawn Clements, editor); Single Shots (Kil Kenny, editor); ScrewDr.rs (M. Rode, editor); High Balls (Vincent Diamond, editor).

FICTION Subjects include adventure, erotica, gay, lesbian, historical, horror, mainstream, contemporary, multicultural, mystery, occult, romance, science fiction, short story collections, suspense, western. "We are a gay and lesbian press focusing on romance and genres of romance. We particularly like paranormal and western romance." Submit proposal package, 3 sample chapters, clips.

TIPS "Our audience is primarily people looking for a familiar romance setting featuring gay or lesbian protagonists. Please read guidelines carefully and familiarize yourself with our lines."

TORREY HOUSE PRESS, LLC

P.O. Box 750196, Torrey UT 84775. (801)810-9THP. E-mail: mark@torreyhouse.com. Website: http://torreyhouse.com. **Contact:** Kirsten Allen, editor: (areas of interest: literary fiction, creative nonfiction). Estab. 2010. hardcover, trade paperback, & electronic originals. **Publishes 10 titles/year. 500 queries/year; 200 mss/year 80% of books from first-time authors. 80% from unagented writers. Pays 5-15% royalty on retail price** Publishes book 6 months after acceptance of ms. Accepts simultaneous submissions. Responds in 2 months to queries, proposals, and mss. Catalog online at website. Guidelines online at website or by e-mail.

◯ Envisions reading audience of the American West literary fiction and creative nonfiction.

⌘ Torrey House Press (THP) publishes literary fiction and creative nonfiction about the issues, people, history, cultures, and landscape of the Colorado Plateau and the American West. Located in the heart of the Plateau in Torrey, Utah, THP sponsors 4 writing contests each year and accepts unsolicited manuscripts. See the website at www.torreyhouse.com for guidelines about submitting your work; peruse the columns and book reviews and read some of THP's favorite fiction and nonfiction excerpts to get a sense of the writing that the company seeks. Follow us at Torrey House Press on Facebook and on our website for contest updates, and please contact us any time with questions."

NONFICTION Subjects include anthropology, creative nonfiction, environment, nature. Query; submit proposal package, including: outline, sample chapter, bio. Does not review artwork.

FICTION Subjects include historical, literary. "THP publishes literary fiction and creative nonfiction about the people, cultures and resource management issues of the Colorado plateau and the American West." Submit proposal package including: synopsis, 3 sample chapters, bio.

POETRY Submit query, 3 sample poems.

TIPS "Include writing experience (none okay) and something about your passion for the land." Sponsors *Torrey House Press writing contest: Fiction and Short Fiction.* **Deadline: check website** - $1000 First Place; $250 Second Place; $100 Third Place.

TRAFALGAR SQUARE BOOKS

P.O. Box 257, 388 Howe Hill Road, N. Pomfret VT 05053-0257. (802)457-1911. Website: www.horseandriderbooks.com. **Contact:** Martha Cook, managing director; Rebecca Didier, senior editor. Estab. 1985. Publishes hardcover and trade paperback originals. **Publishes 12 titles/year. 50% of books from first-time authors. 80% from unagented writers. Pays royalty. Pays advance.** Publishes book 18 months after acceptance of ms. Responds in 1 month to queries, 2 months to proposals, 2-3 months to mss. Catalog free on request and by e-mail.

⊶ We publish high quality instructional books for horsemen and horsewomen, always with the horse's welfare in mind."

NONFICTION Subjects include animals, horses/dogs. We rare consider books for complete novices. Query with SASE. Submit proposal package including outline, 1-3 sample chapters, letter of introduction including qualifications for writing on the subject and why the proposed book is an essential addition to existing publications. Reviews artwork/photos as part of the ms package. We prefer color laser thumbnail sheets or duplicate prints (do not send original photos or art!).

TIPS "Our audience is horse lovers and riders interested in doing what is best in the interest of horses."

TRISTAN PUBLISHING

2355 Louisiana Ave. North, Golden Valley MO 55427. (763)545-1383. Fax: (763)545-1387. E-mail: info@tristanpublishing.com or manuscripts@tristanpublishing.com. Website: www.tristanpublishing.com. **Contact:** Brett Waldman, publisher. Estab. 2002. Hardcover originals. **Publishes 6-10 titles/year. 1,000 queries and manuscripts/year. 15% of books from first-time authors. 100% from unagented writers. Pays royalty on wholesale or retail price; outright purchase.** Publishes book 24 months after acceptance of ms. Accepts simultaneous submissions. Responds in 3 months on queries, proposals, and manuscripts. Catalog and guidelines free on request. Guidelines available online at website.

IMPRINTS Tristan Publishing; Waldman House Press; Tristan Outdoors.

NONFICTION , inspirational. "Our mission is to create books with a message that inspire and uplift in typically 1,000 words or less." Query with SASE; submit completed manuscript. Reviews artwork/photos; send photocopies.

FICTION , inspirational, gift books. Query with SASE; submit completed manuscript.

TIPS "Our audience is adults and children."

TRUMAN STATE UNIVERSITY PRESS

100 E. Normal St., Kirksville MO 63501-4221. (660)785-7336. Fax: (660)785-4480. E-mail: tsup@truman.edu. Website: tsup.truman.edu. **Contact:** Barbara Smith-Mandell (American studies, poetry); Michael Wolfe (early modern studies). **Publishes 13 titles/year.** Guidelines available online.

NONFICTION Early modern, American studies, poetry.

⊕ TUTTLE PUBLISHING

364 Innovation Dr., North Clarendon VT 05759. (802)773-8930. Fax: (802)773-6993. E-mail: info@tuttlepublishing.com. Website: www.tuttlepublishing.com. **Contact:** Editorial Acquisitions. Estab. 1832. Publishes hardcover and trade paperback originals and reprints. **Publishes 125 titles/year. 1,000 queries received/year. 20% of books from first-time authors. 40% from unagented writers. Pays 5-10% royalty on net or retail price, depending on format and kind of book. Pays advance.** Publishes book 18 months after acceptance of ms. Accepts simultaneous submissions. Responds in 8-12 weeks to proposals.

○ "Familiarize yourself with our catalog and/or similar books we publish. Send complete book proposal with cover letter, table of contents, 1-2 sample chapters, target audience description, SASE. No e-mail submissions."

✇➞ Tuttle is America's leading publisher of books on Japan and Asia.

NONFICTION Query with SASE.

23 HOUSE PUBLISHING

405 Moseley St., Jefferson TX 75657. Fax: (214)367-4343. E-mail: editor@23house.com. Website: www.23house.com. **Contact:** Editor. Estab. 1998. Publishes trade paperback originals and electronic book format. Accepts simultaneous submissions. Book catalog and ms guidelines online.

○ "We are looking for regional titles around the U.S., specifically in the folklore and supernatural genre. An idea of the market for the book should be included as part of the proposal."

✇➞ We have produced books in almost every genre."

NONFICTION , Haunted locations, interesting history, etc. "We are looking for regional nonfiction titles that can build an audience in specific locations in the U.S." "Submit proposal via e-mail, and we'll go from there."

FICTION Subjects include horror, mostly, but it is a small part of our catalog.

TIPS "Please check our current needs on the guidelines section of our website. If you're pitching a book to us, we're as interested in the market for it as we are the work itself."

⊕ TYNDALE HOUSE PUBLISHERS

351 Executive Dr., Carol Stream IL 60188. (800)323-9400. Fax: (800)684-0247. Website: www.tyndale.com. Estab. 1962.

✇➞ Tyndale publishes Christian fiction, nonfiction, children's books, and other resources, including Bibles in the New Living Translation (NLT). Tyndale products include many New York Times best sellers, including the popular *Left Behind* fiction series by Tim LaHaye and Jerry B. Jenkins, novels by Karen Kingsbury and Joel C. Rosenberg, plus numerous nonfiction works.

TIPS "We don't have portfolio viewings. Negotiations are different for every project. Have every piece submitted with legible contact information."

ⒶⓄ TYNDALE HOUSE PUBLISHERS, INC.

351 Executive Dr., Carol Stream IL 60188. (800)323-9400. Fax: (800)684-0247. Website: www.tyndale.com. **Contact:** Manuscript Review Committee. Estab. 1962. Publishes hardcover and trade paperback originals and mass paperback reprints. **Pays negotiable royalty. Pays negotiable advance.** Accepts simultaneous submissions. Guidelines for 9×12 SAE and $2.40 for postage or visit website.

✇➞ Tyndale House publishes practical, user-friendly Christian books for the home and family."

NONFICTION Subjects include child guidance, religion, devotional/inspirational. Prefers agented submissions.

FICTION Subjects include romance, Christian (children's, general, inspirational, mystery/suspense, thriller, romance). "Christian truths must be woven into the story organically. No short story collections. Youth books: character building stories with Christian perspective. Especially interested in ages 10-14. We primarily publish Christian historical romances, with occasional contemporary, suspense, or standalones." Agented submissions only. *No unsolicited mss.*

TIPS "All accepted manuscripts will appeal to Evangelical Christian children and parents." "All accepted manuscripts will appeal to Evangelical Christian children and parents."

UNBRIDLED BOOKS

200 North 9th St., Suite A, Columbia MO 65201. Website: http://unbridledbooks.com. Estab. 2004.

✇➞ Unbridled Books is a premier publisher of works of rich literary quality that appeal to a broad audience."

FICTION Please query first by e-mail. Due to the heavy volume of submissions, we regret that at this time we are not able to consider uninvited manuscripts. Please query either Fred Ramey or Greg Michalson, but not both. Send to either of the publishers, but not both, at: Greg Michalson, Co-Publisher, 200 N. 9th St., Ste A, Columbia, MO 65201 or Fred Ramey, Co-Publisher, 2000 Wadsworth Blvd., #195, Lakewood, CO 80214

TIPS "We try to read each ms that arrives, so please be patient."

UNITY HOUSE

Unity, 1901 N.W. Blue Pkwy., Unity Village MO 64065-0001. (816)524-3550. Fax: (816)347-5518. E-mail: unity@unityonline.org. E-mail: sartinson@unityonline.org. Website: www.unityonline.org. **Contact:** Sharon Sartin, exec. asst. Estab. 1889. Publishes hardcover, trade paperback, and electronic originals. **Publishes 5-7 titles/year. 50 queries. 5% of books from first-time authors. 95% from unagented writers. 10-15% royalty on retail price Pays advance.** Publishes book 5 months after acceptance of ms. Responds in 1 month to queries; 2 months to proposals. Catalog free on request & online at website: http://unityonline.org/publications/pdf/productcatalog.pdf. Guidelines free & available online & by e-mail.

⌘— Unity House publishes metaphysical Christian books based on Unity principles, as well as inspirational books on metaphysics and practical spirituality. All manuscripts must reflect a spiritual foundation and express the Unity philosophy, practical Christianity, universal principles, and/or metaphysics.

NONFICTION Subjects include religion, spirituality, metaphysics, new thought. "Writers should be familiar with principles of metaphysical Christianity but not feel bound by them. We are interested in works in the related fields of holistic health, spiritual psychology, and the philosophy of other world religions." Submit proposal package, including: outline, 50 sample chapters. Reviews artwork/photos. Writers should send photocopies.

TIPS "We target an audience of spiritual seekers."

⊕ THE UNIVERSITY OF AKRON PRESS

120 E. Mill St., Suite 415, Akron OH 44325-1703. (330)972-5342. Fax: (330)972-8364. E-mail: uapress@uakron.edu. Website: www.uakron.edu/uapress. **Contact:** Thomas Bacher, Director and Acquisitions. Estab. 1988. Publishes hardcover and paperback originals and reissues. **Publishes 10-12 titles/year. 200-300 queries received/year. 50-75 mss received/year. 40% of books from first-time authors. 80% from unagented writers. Pays 7-15% royalty.** Publishes book 9-12 months after acceptance of ms. Accepts simultaneous submissions. Responds in 2 weeks to queries and proposals. Responds in 3-4 months to solicited manuscripts. Query prior to submitting. Book catalog available free. Guidelines available online.

⌘— The University of Akron Press is the publishing arm of The University of Akron and is dedicated to the dissemination of scholarly, professional, and regional books and other content."

NONFICTION Subjects include Applied politics, early American literature, emerging technologies, history of psychology, history of technology, interdisciplinary studies, Northeast Ohio history and culture, Ohio politics, poetics. Query by e-mail. Mss cannot be returned unless SASE is included.

POETRY Follow the guidelines and submit mss only for contest: www.uakron.edu/uapress/poetry.html

THE UNIVERSITY OF ARKANSAS PRESS

McIlroy House, 105 N. McIlroy Ave., Fayetteville AR 72701. (479)575-3246. Fax: (479)575-6044. E-mail: lmalley@uark.edu; jewatki@uark.edu. Website: uapress.com. **Contact:** Lawrence J. Malley, director and editor-in-chief and Julie Watkins, editor. Estab. 1980. Publishes hardcover and trade paperback originals and reprints. **Publishes 30 titles/year. 30% of books from first-time authors. 95% from unagented writers.** Publishes book 1 year after acceptance of ms. Responds in 3 months to proposals. Book catalog and ms guidelines on website or on request.

⌘— The University of Arkansas Press publishes series on Ozark studies, the Civil War in the West, poetry and poetics, and sport and society."

NONFICTION Subjects include government, politics, history, Southern, humanities, literary criticism, nature, environment, regional, Arkansas. Accepted mss must be submitted on disk. Query with SASE. Submit outline, sample chapters, resume. cv.

UNIVERSITY OF GEORGIA PRESS

330 Research Dr., Athens GA 30602-4901. (706)369-6130. Fax: (706)369-6131. E-mail: books@ugapress.uga.edu. Website: www.ugapress.org. Estab. 1938. Publishes hardcover originals, trade paperback originals, and reprints. **Publishes 85 titles/year. Pays rare, varying advance.** Publishes book 1 year after acceptance of ms. Responds in 2 months to queries. Book catalog and ms guidelines for #10 SASE or online.

NONFICTION Subjects include government, politics, history, American, nature, environment, regional, environmental studies, literary nonfiction. Query with SASE. Submit bio, 1 sample chapter. Reviews artwork/photos. Send if essential to book.

FICTION Short story collections published in Flannery O'Connor Award Competition. Query #1 SASE for guidelines

TIPS "Please visit our website to view our book catalogs and for all manuscript submission guidelines."

UNIVERSITY OF IOWA PRESS

100 Kuhl House, 119 W. Park Road, Iowa City IA 52242-1000. (319)335-2000. Fax: (319)335-2055. E-mail: uipress@uiowa.edu. Website: www.uiowapress.org. **Contact:** Holly Carver, director; Joseph Parsons, acquisitions editor. Estab. 1969. Publishes hardcover and paperback originals. **Publishes 35 titles/year. 30% of books from first-time authors. 95% from unagented writers.** Publishes book 1 year after acceptance of ms. Book catalog available free. Guidelines available online.

🔑 We publish authoritative, original nonfiction that we market mostly by direct mail to groups with special interests in our titles, and by advertising in trade and scholarly publications."

NONFICTION Subjects include anthropology, archeology, creative nonfiction, history, regional, language, literature, nature, environment, American literary studies, medicine and literature. "Looks for evidence of original research, reliable sources, clarity of organization, complete development of theme with documentation, supportive footnotes and/or bibliography, and a substantive contribution to knowledge in the field treated. Use *Chicago Manual of Style*." Query with SASE. Submit outline. Reviews artwork/photos.

FICTION Currently publishes the Iowa Short Fiction Award selections. Competition guidelines available.

POETRY Currently publishes winners of the Iowa Poetry Prize Competition, Kuhl House Poets, poetry anthologies. Competition guidelines available on website.

UNIVERSITY OF NEBRASKA PRESS

1111 Lincoln Mall, Lincoln NE 68588-0630. (800)755-1105. Fax: (402)472-6214. E-mail: pressmail@unl.edu. Website: nebraskapress.unl.edu. **Contact:** Heather Lundine, editor-in-chief. Publishes hardcover and trade paperback originals and trade paperback reprints. Book catalog available free. Guidelines available online.

IMPRINTS Bison Books (paperback reprints of classic books).

🔑 We primarily publish nonfiction books and scholarly journals, along with a few titles per season in contemporary and regional prose and poetry. On occasion, we reprint previously published fiction of established reputation, and we have several programs to publish literary works in translation."

NONFICTION Subjects include agriculture, animals, anthropology, archeology, creative nonfiction, history, memoirs, military, war, multicultural, nature, environment, religion, sports, translation, women's issues, women's studies, Native American studies, American Lives series, experimental fiction by American-Indian writers. Submit book proposal with overview, audience, format, detailed chapter outline, sample chapters, sample bibliography, timetable, CV.

FICTION Series and translation only. Occasionally reprints fiction of established reputation.

POETRY Contemporary, regional.

UNIVERSITY OF NEVADA PRESS

Morrill Hall, Mail Stop 0166, Reno NV 89557. (775)784-6573. Fax: (775)784-6200. Website: www.unpress.nevada.edu. **Contact:** Joanne O'Hare, director. Estab. 1961. Publishes hardcover and paperback originals and reprints. **Publishes 25 titles/year.** Guidelines available online.

NONFICTION Subjects include anthropology, archeology, ethnic, studies, history, regional and natural, nature, environment, regional, history and geography, western literature, current affairs, gambling and gaming, Basque studies. No juvenile books. Submit proposal. No online submissions. Reviews artwork/photos. Send photocopies.

FICTION Submit proposal package, outline, clips, 2-4 sample chapters.

UNIVERSITY OF NEW MEXICO PRESS

1 University of New Mexico, MSC05 3185, Albuquerque NM 87131-0001. (505)277-3324 or (800)249-7737. Fax: (505)277-3343. E-mail: clark@unm.edu; wcwhiteh@unm.edu. Website: www.unmpress.com. **Contact:** W. Clark Whitehorn, Editor-in-Chief. Estab. 1929. Publishes hardcover originals and trade paperback originals and reprints. **Pays variable royalty. Pays advance.** Book catalog available free. Please read and follow the submission query guidelines on the Author Information page online. Do not send entire ms or additional materials until requested. If your book is accepted for publication, you will be notified.

🔑 The Press is well known as a publisher in the fields of anthropology, archeology, Latin American studies, art and photography, architecture and the history and culture of the American West, fiction, some poetry, Chicano/a studies and works by and about American

Indians. We focus on American West, Southwest and Latin American regions."

NONFICTION Subjects include Americana, anthropology, archeology, art, architecture, biography, creative nonfiction, ethnic, gardening, gay, lesbian, government, politics, history, language, literature, memoirs, military, war, multicultural, music, dance, nature, environment, photography, regional, religion, science, translation, travel, women's issues, women's studies, contemporary culture, cinema/stage, crime, general nonfiction. No how-to, humor, juvenile, self-help, software, technical or textbooks. Query with SASE. Reviews artwork/photos. Send photocopies.

POETRY "The Press is well known as a publisher in the fields of anthropology, archeology, Latin American studies, art and photography, architecture and the history and culture of the American West, fiction, some poetry, Chicano/a studies and works by and about American Indians. We focus on American West, Southwest and Latin American regions." Publishes hardcover originals and trade paperback originals and reprints. Pays variable royalty.

UNIVERSITY OF NORTH TEXAS PRESS

1155 Union Circle, #311336, Denton TX 76203-5017. (940)565-2142. Fax: (940) 565-4590. E-mail: ronald. chrisman@unt.edu; Karen.DeVinney@unt.edu. Website: web3.unt.edu/untpress. **Contact:** Ronald Chrisman, director; Karen DeVinney, managing editor. Estab. 1987. Publishes hardcover and trade paperback originals and reprints. **Publishes 14-16 titles/year. 500 queries received/year. 50% of books from first-time authors. 95% from unagented writers.** Publishes book 1-2 years after acceptance of ms. Responds in 1 month to queries. Book catalog for 8 ½×11 SASE. Guidelines available online.

> We are dedicated to producing the highest quality scholarly, academic, and general interest books. We are committed to serving all peoples by publishing stories of their cultures and experiences that have been overlooked. Currently emphasizing military history, Texas history and literature, music, Mexican-American studies."

NONFICTION Subjects include Americana, ethnic, government, politics, history, music, dance, biography, military, war, nature, regional, women's issues/studies. Query with SASE. Reviews artwork/photos. Send photocopies.

FICTION The only fiction we publish is the winner of the Katherine Anne Porter Prize in Short Fiction, an annual, national competition with a $1,000 prize, and publication of the winning manuscript each Fall.

POETRY "The only poetry we publish is the winner of the Vassar Miller Prize in Poetry, an annual, national competition with a $1,000 prize and publication of the winning manuscript each Spring." Query.

TIPS "We publish series called War and the Southwest; Texas Folklore Society Publications; the Western Life Series; Practical Guide Series; Al-Filo: Mexican-American studies; North Texas Crime and Criminal Justice; Katherine Anne Porter Prize in Short Fiction; and the North Texas Lives of Musicians Series.", *Living in the Woods in a Tree: Remember Blaze Foley.*

UNIVERSITY OF OTTAWA PRESS

542 King Edward, Ottawa ON K1N 6N5, Canada. (613)562-5246. Fax: (613)562-5247. E-mail: puo-uop@ uottawa.ca. Website: www.press.uottawa.ca. **Contact:** Eric Nelson, acquisitions editor. Estab. 1936. **Publishes 25-50 titles/year. 20% of books from first-time authors. 95% from unagented writers.** Publishes book 16-18 months after acceptance of ms. Responds in 1 month to queries. Responds in 6 months to manuscripts. Book catalog and ms guidelines free.

> Publishes books for scholarly and serious nonfiction audiences. This is the only bilingual university press in Canada. Currently emphasizing French in North America, translation studies, philosophy, Canadian studies, criminology, international development, governance."

NONFICTION Subjects include education, government, politics, philosophy, sociology, translation, Canadian literature. Send proposals or first chapters to the attention of the acquisitions editor. Replies are not guaranteed. Check website to see if your project fits the scholarly disciplines of the University of Ottawa Press. Submit outline, sample chapters, cv.

TIPS "No unrevised theses! Envision audience of academic specialists and readers of serious nonfiction."

UNIVERSITY OF PENNSYLVANIA PRESS

3905 Spruce St., Philadelphia PA 19104. (215)898-6261. Fax: (215)898-0404. Website: www.pennpress.org. **Contact:** Jerome Singerman, humanities editor; Peter Agree, editor-in-chief and social sciences editor; Jo Joslyn, art and architecture editor; Robert Lockhart, history editor; Bill Finan, politics, international relations. Estab. 1890. Publishes hardcover and paperback originals, and reprints. **Publishes 100+ titles/year. 20-30% of books from first-time authors. 95% from unagented writers. Royalty determined on book-by-book basis. Pays advance.** Publishes book 10 months after delivery of ms after acceptance of ms. Responds in 3 months to queries. Book catalog available online. Guidelines available online.

✊☞ Manuscript submissions are welcome in fields appropriate for Penn Press's editorial program. The Press's acquiring editors, and their fields of responsibility, are listed in the Contact Us section of our Web site. Although we have no formal policies regarding manuscript proposals and submissions, what we need minimally, in order to gauge our degree of interest, is a brief statement describing the manuscript, a copy of the contents page, and a reasonably current vita. Initial inquiries are best sent by letter, in paper form, to the appropriate acquiring editor."

NONFICTION Subjects include Americana, art, architecture, history, American, art, architecture, literary criticism, sociology, anthropology, literary criticism, cultural studies, ancient studies, medieval studies, urban studies, human rights. Follow the *Chicago Manual of Style.* "Serious books that serve the scholar and the professional, student and general reader." *No unsolicited mss.* Query with SASE. Submit outline, resume. Reviews artwork/photos. Send photocopies.

UNIVERSITY OF WISCONSIN PRESS

1930 Monroe St., 3rd Floor, Madison WI 53711. (608)263-1110. Fax: (608)263-1132. E-mail: uwiscpress@uwpress.wisc.edu. E-mail: kadushin@wisc.edu. Website: www.wisc.edu/wisconsinpress. **Contact:** Raphael Kadushin, senior acquisitions editor. Gwen Walker, acquisitions editor Estab. 1937.

○ Test. Ignore editorial comment.

TIPS "Make sure the query letter and sample text are well-written, and read guidelines carefully to make sure we accept the genre you are submitting."

UNIVERSITY PRESS OF KANSAS

2502 Westbrooke Circle, Lawrence KS 66045-4444. (785)864-4154. Fax: (785)864-4586. E-mail: upress@ku.edu. Website: www.kansaspress.ku.edu; facebook: www.facebook.com/kansaspress. **Contact:** Michael J. Briggs, editor-in-chief (military history, political science, law); Ranjit Arab, acquisitions editor (western history, American studies, environmental studies, women's studies); Fred M. Woodward, director, (political science, presidency, regional). Estab. 1946. Publishes hardcover originals, trade paperback originals and reprints. **Publishes 55 titles/year. 600 queries received/year. 20% of books from first-time authors. 98% from unagented writers. Pays selective advance.** Publishes book 10 months after acceptance of ms. Responds in 1 month to proposals. Book catalog and ms guidelines free.

✊☞ The University Press of Kansas publishes scholarly books that advance knowledge and regional books that contribute to the understanding of Kansas, the Great Plains, and the Midwest."

NONFICTION Subjects include Americana, archeology, environment, government, military, nature, politics, regional, sociology, war, womens studies, American History, Native Studies, American Cultural Studies. "We are looking for books on topics of wide interest based on solid scholarship and written for both specialists and informed general readers. Do not send unsolicited, complete manuscripts." Submit outline, sample chapters, cover letter, cv, prospectus. Reviews artwork/photos. Send photocopies.

UNIVERSITY PRESS OF MISSISSIPPI

3825 Ridgewood Rd., Jackson MS 39211-6492. (601)432-6205. Fax: (601)432-6217. E-mail: press@mississippi.edu. Website: www.upress.state.ms.us. **Contact:** Craig Gill, editor-in-chief (regional studies, art, folklore, music). Estab. 1970. Publishes hardcover and paperback originals and reprints. **Publishes 60 titles/year. 20% of books from first-time authors. 90% from unagented writers. Competitive royalties and terms. Pays advance.** Publishes book 1 year after acceptance of ms. Responds in 3 months to queries.

✊☞ University Press of Mississippi publishes scholarly and trade titles, as well as special series, including: American Made Music; Conversations with Comic Artists; Conversations with Filmmakers; Faulkner and Yoknapatawpha; Literary Conversations; Studies in Popular Culture; Hollywood Legends; Caribbean Studies."

NONFICTION Subjects include Americana, art, architecture, ethnic, minority studies, government, politics, history, literature, literary criticism, music, photography, regional, Southern, folklife, literary criticism, popular culture with scholarly emphasis, literary studies. "We prefer a proposal that describes the significance of the work and a chapter outline." Submit outline, sample chapters, cv.

UNLIMITED PUBLISHING LLC

P.O. Box 99, Nashville IN 47448. E-mail: acquisitions@unlimitedpublishing.com. Website: www.unlimitedpublishing.com. **Contact:** Acquisitions Manager (short nonfiction with a clear audience). Publisher (out-of-print books formerly from major publishers) Estab. 2000. **Publishes 25-50 titles/year. Receives 1,000 queries/year; 500 manuscripts/year. 20% of books from first-time authors. 40% from unagented writers. 10-20% Royalty on retail price.** Publishes book 3 months after acceptance of ms. 1 month on queries, proposal, and manuscripts. Catalog online at website http://unlimitedpublishing.com/sitemap.htm.

IMPRINTS Harvardwood Books.

○ "We publish mostly short nonfiction books, often in collaboration with other book publishers, or with nonprofit, charitable and educational institutions worldwide. Our focus on quality and support of worthy causes gives UP books more credibility and public exposure than typical POD book publishing fare."

⚷ We prefer short nonfiction and fiction with a clear audience, and expect authors to be actively involved in publicity. A detailed marketing plan is required with all submissions. Moderate to good computer skills are necessary."

NONFICTION Subjects include agriculture, alternative lifestyles, Americana, animals, anthropology, archaeology, architecture, art, business, career guidance, child guidance, communications, community, computers, contemporary culture, counseling, crafts, creative nonfiction, economics, education, electronics, environment, ethnic, finance, gardening, gay, government, health, history, hobbies, horticulture, humanities, labor, language, law, lesbian, literary criticism, literature, marine subjects, medicine, memoirs, military, money, multicultural, music, nature, parenting, philosophy, politics, psychology, real estate, recreation, regional, religion, science, sex, social sciences, sociology, software, sports, translation, transportation, travel, women's issues, women's studies, world affairs, young adult. "Unlimited Publishing LLC specializes in bringing back out-of-print books originally released by traditional publishers, and in publishing new books by professional writers. Our catalog currently includes books formerly published by many well-known book imprints, including Berkley Books, Houghton Mifflin, Kensington, Macmillan, Penguin, Wiley & Sons, Yale University Press and others. We prefer short nonfiction with a bare minimum of artwork and graphics, but are always interested in quality material, regardless of genre. UP functions like a traditional royalty book publisher, but uses revolutionary new print-on-demand book publishing technologies to slash the cost of getting books in print. UP does not publish books for a fee, nor charge inflated prices for books — from readers OR writers. Our policies are not suitable for vanity publishing or self-publishing. To learn more, please follow the guidelines online at our website." Submit proposal package, including: outline and 10-page excerpt in rich text format, a standard 'save-as option with Microsoft Word', author bio and detailed marketing plan.

FICTION Subjects include adventure, ethnic, experimental, fantasy, feminist, historical, horror, humor, juvenile, literary, mainstream, contemporary, military, war, multicultural, mystery, occult, regional, religious, science fiction fiction, short story collections, spiritual, sports, suspense, translation, war, western, young adult. Submit proposal package by e-mail, including: outline and 10-page excerpt in rich text format, author bio and detailed marketing plan.

TIPS "The growth of online bookselling allows authors and publishers to jointly cultivate a tightly targeted grassroots audience in specialty or niche markets before expanding to mainstream book industry channels based on proven public demand."

⊕ UNTREED READS PUBLISHING

506 Kansas St., San Francisco CA 94107. (415)621-0465. Fax: (415)621-0465. E-mail: general@untreedreads.com. E-mail: submissions@untreedreads.com. Website: www.untreedreads.com. **Contact:** Jay A. Hartman, editor-in-chief (fiction-all genres). K.D. Sullivan, CEO/publisher (nonfiction-all genres, especially business) Estab. 2009. Format publishes in electronic originals and reprints. **Publishes 35 titles/year. Receives 50 submissions/year. 80% of books from first-time authors. 75% from unagented writers. Pays 50-60% royalty on retail price.** Publishes book 3 months after acceptance of ms. Accepts simultaneous submissions. Responds in ½ month on queries, 1

month on proposals, and 1 ½ months on mss. Catalog and guidelines available online at website.

NONFICTION Subjects include agriculture, alternative lifestyles, Americana, animals, anthropology, archeology, architecture, art, astrology, automotive, beauty, business, career guidance, child guidance, cinema, communications, community, computers, contemporary culture, cooking, counseling, crafts, creative nonfiction, dance, economics, education, electronics, entertainment, environment, ethnic, fashion, film, finance, foods, games, gardening, gay, government, health, history, hobbies, horticulture, house and home, humanities, labor, language, law, lesbian, literary criticism, literature, marine subjects, memoirs, military/war, money/finance, multicultural, music/dance, nature/environment/new age, philosophy, photography, psychology, real estate, recreation, regional, religion, science, sex, social sciences, sociology, software, spirituality, sports, translation, transportation, travel, women's issues/studies, world affairs, young adult. "We are very interested in developing our textbook market. Ereaders don't currently support graphs, tables, images, etc. as well as print books; however, we plan to be trendsetters in this as the technology in the ereaders improves. Also we are eager to increase our number of business books. We always look for series or works that could develop into a series." Submit proposal package, including 3 sample chapters. Submit completed mss. Reviews artwork/photos. Send photocopies. Author must provide signed release of permission to use the photographs.

FICTION Subjects include literary. "We look forward to long-terms relationships with our authors. We encourage works that are either already a series or could develop into a series. We are one of the few publishers publishing short stories and are happy to be a resource for these good works. We welcome short story collections. Also, we look forward to publishing children's books, cookbooks, and other works that have been known for illustrations in print as the technology in the multiple ereaders improves. We hope to be a large platform for diverse content and authors. We seek mainstream content, but if you're an author or have content that doesn't seem to always 'fit' into traditional market we'd like to hear from you." No erotica, picture books, poetry, poetry in translation, or romance Submit porposal package with 3 sample chapters. Submit completed ms.

POETRY "We are not accepting individual poems currently, but will accept proposals for poetry collections."

TIPS "For our fiction titles we lean toward a literary audience. For nonfiction titles, we want to be a platform for business people, entrepreneurs, and speakers to become well known in their fields of expertise. However, for both fiction and nonfiction we want to appeal to many audiences."

UPPER ACCESS, INC.

87 Upper Access Rd., Hinesburg VT 05461. (802)482-2988. Fax: (802)304-1005. E-mail: info@upperaccess.com. Website: www.upperaccess.com. **Contact:** Steve Carlson, Publisher. Estab. 1986. Publishes hardcover and trade paperback originals; hardcover and trade paperback reprints. **Publishes 2-3 titles/year. 200 queries received/year. 40 mss received/year. 50% of books from first-time authors. 80% from unagented writers. Pays 10-20% royalty on wholesale price. $200-500 (Advances are tokens of our good faith; author earnings are from royalties a book sells.)** Publishes book 8 months after acceptance of ms. Accepts simultaneous submissions. Responds in 1 month to queries/manuscripts. Catalog online at website. Guidelines available online.

8→ Publishes nonfiction to improve the quality of life.

NONFICTION Subjects include alternative lifestyles, child guidance, community/public affairs, contemporary culture, cooking, foods, nutrition, creative nonfiction, education, ethnic, gardening, government, politics/politics, health, medicine, history, humor, humanities, language, literature, multicultural, nature, environment, philosophy, psychology, science, sex, social sciences, sociology, womens issues, womens studies, world affairs affairs, (gay, lesbian possible). "We are open to considering almost any nonfiction topic that has some potential for national general trade sales." Query with SASE. "We strongly prefer an initial e-mail describing your proposed title. No attachments please. We will look at paper mail if there is no other way, but e-mail will be reviewed much more quickly and thoroughly." Will request artwork, etc. if and when appropriate. "Discuss this with us in your initial e-mail query."

FICTION "Note: Please do not submit fiction, even if it relates to nonfiction subjects. We cannot take novels or poetry of any kind at this time."

TIPS "We target intelligent adults willing to challenge the status quo, who are interested in more self-sufficiency with respect for the environment. Most of our books are either unique subjects or unique or different ways of looking at major issues or basic education on subjects that are not well understood by most of the general public. We make a long-term commitment to each book that we publish, trying to find its market as long as possible."

VANDAMERE PRESS

P.O. Box 149, St. Petersburg FL 33731. Fax: (727) 556-2560. E-mail: webmaster@vandamere.com. Website: www.vandamere.com. **Contact:** Jerry Frank, senior acquisitions editor. Estab. 1984. Publishes hardcover and trade paperback originals and reprints. **Publishes 8-15 titles/year. 1,500 queries received/year and 500 mss received/year. 25% of books from first-time authors. 90% from unagented writers. Pays royalty on revenues generated. Pays advance.** Publishes book 1 year after acceptance of ms. Accepts simultaneous submissions. Responds in 6 months to queries.

○—* *Vandamere* publishes high-quality work with solid, well-documented research and minimum author/political bias."

NONFICTION Subjects include Americana, education, health, medicine, history, military, war, photography, regional, Washington D.C./Mid-Atlantic, disability/healthcare issues. No New Age. Submit outline, 2-3 sample chapters.

FICTION Subjects include adventure, mystery, suspense. Submit clips, 5-1 sample chapters.

TIPS "Authors who can provide endorsements from significant published writers, celebrities, etc., will always be given serious consideration. Clean, easy-to-read, dark copy is essential. Patience in waiting for replies is essential. All unsolicited work is looked at, but at certain times of the year our review schedule will stop. No response without SASE. No electronic submissions or queries!"

VANDERBILT UNIVERSITY PRESS

VU Station B 351813, Nashville TN 37235. (615)322-3585. Fax: (615)343-8823. E-mail: vupress@vanderbilt.edu. Website: www.vanderbiltuniversitypress.com. **Contact:** Michael Ames, director. Publishes hardcover originals and trade paperback originals and reprints. **Publishes 20-25 titles/year. 500 queries received/year. 25% of books from first-time authors. 90% from unagented writers. Pays rare advance.** Publishes book 10 months after acceptance of ms. Accepts simultaneous submissions. Responds in 2 weeks to proposals. Book catalog available free online. Guidelines available online.

○ Also distributes for and co-publishes with Country Music Foundation.

○—* Vanderbilt University Press publishes books on healthcare, social sciences, education, and regional studies, for both academic and general audiences that are intellectually significant, socially relevant, and of practical importance."

NONFICTION Subjects include Americana, anthropology, archeology, education, ethnic, government, politics, health, medicine, history, language, literature, multicultural, music, dance, nature, environment, philosophy, women's issues, women's studies. Submit prospectus, sample chapter, cv. Does not accept electronic submissions. Reviews artwork/photos. Send photocopies.

TIPS "Our audience consists of scholars and educated, general readers."

◆ VANHOOK HOUSE

925 Orchard St., Charleston WV 25302. E-mail: editor@vanhookhouse.com. E-mail: acquisitions@vanhookhouse.com. Website: www.vanhookhouse.com. **Contact:** Jim Whyte, acquisitions, all fiction/ crime/ military/war. Estab. 2009. hardcover and trade paperback originals; trade paperback reprints. **Publishes 6 titles/year. Receives 20 mss/year. 100% of books from first-time authors. 100% from unagented writers. Pays authors 8-10% royalty on wholesale price. Advance negotiable.** Publishes book 6 months. after acceptance of ms. Responds in 1 mo. on queries; 2 months on proposals; 3 months on mss. Book catalog and guidelines free on request and available online at website.

○ "We employ the expertise of individuals qualified to review works falling within their field of study. Be sure of all sources and facts, as VanHook House *will* confirm any and all information. All editing is done in a way to ensure the author's voice remains unchanged."

○—* VanHook House is a small press focused on the talents of new, unpublished authors. We are looking for works of fiction and nonfiction to add to our catalog. No erotica or sci-fi, please.

Query via e-mail. Queries accepted ONLY during submissions periods."

NONFICTION Subjects include agriculture, Americana, animals, anthropology, architecture, art, automotive, business, career guidance, child guidance, communications, community, computers, contemporary culture, cooking, counseling, crafts, creative nonfiction, dance, education, electronics, entertainment, environment, ethnic, foods, games, gardening, government, health, history, house and home, humanities, labor, language, law, literature, marine subjects, medicine, memoirs, military, muticultural, music, nature, New Age, nutrition, philosophy, photography, politics, psychology, public affairs, real estate, recreation, regional, religion, science, sex, social sciences, sociology, software, spirituality, sports, transportation, travel, women's issues/studies, war, world affairs. Reviews artwork.

POETRY "A collection must contain 200 individual poems to be considered." Query; submit 3 poems.

TIPS "Visit our website."

Ⓐ VIKING

Imprint of Penguin Group (USA), Inc., 375 Hudson St., New York NY 10014. (212)366-2000. Website: us.penguingroup.com/static/pages/publishers/adult/viking.html. Estab. 1925. Publishes hardcover and originals. **Publishes 100 titles/year.** Accepts simultaneous submissions.

☛ Viking publishes a mix of academic and popular fiction and nonfiction.

NONFICTION Subjects include business, economics, child guidance, cooking, foods, nutrition, health, medicine, history, language, literature, music, dance, philosophy, womens issues, womens studies. Agented submissions only.

FICTION Subjects include literary, mainstream, contemporary, mystery, suspense. Agented submissions only.

Ⓐ VILLARD BOOKS

Imprint of Random House Publishing Group, 1745 Broadway, New York NY 10019. (212)572-2600. Website: www.atrandom.com. Estab. 1983. Publishes hardcover and trade paperback originals. **Pays negotiable royalty Pays negotiable advance.** Accepts simultaneous submissions.

☛ Villard Books is the publisher of savvy and sometimes quirky, best-selling hardcovers and trade paperbacks."

NONFICTION , Commercial nonfiction. Agented submissions only.

FICTION Commercial fiction. Agented submissions only.

VIVISPHERE PUBLISHING

675 Dutchess Turnpike, Poughkeepsie NY 12603. (845)463-1100, ext. 314. Fax: (845)463-0018. E-mail: cs@vivisphere.com. Website: www.vivisphere.com. **Contact:** Lisa Mays. Estab. 1995. Publishes paperback originals and paperback reprints. **Pays royalty.** Publishes book 3-12 months after acceptance of ms. Accepts simultaneous submissions. Responds in 6-12 months to queries. Book catalog free; ms guidelines free or online.

☛ Cookbooks should have a particular slant or appeal to a certain niche. Also publish out-of-print books."

NONFICTION Subjects include history, military, New Age, Game of Bridge. Vivisphere Publishing is now considering new submissions from any genre. Please see our News & Events board online for more information. Query with SASE. Please submit a *hardcopy* (printed paper copy) or PDF file via e-mail of the first 20 pages, or first chapter of your work, along with your contact information to: Attn: New Submissions, at our address.

FICTION Subjects include feminist, gay, lesbian, historical, horror, literary, contemporary, military, self help, science fiction. Query with SASE.

VOYAGEUR PRESS

Quayside Publishing Group, 400 First Ave. North, Suite 300, Minneapolis MN 55401. (800)458-0454. Fax: (612)344-8691. E-mail: mdregni@voyageurpress.com. Website: http://voyageurpress.com/. **Contact:** Michael Dregni, publisher. Estab. 1972. Publishes hardcover and trade paperback originals. **Publishes 80 titles/year. 1,200 queries received/year. 500 mss received/year. 10% of books from first-time authors. 90% from unagented writers. Pays royalty. Pays advance.** Publishes book 1 year after acceptance of ms. Accepts simultaneous submissions. Responds in 3 months to queries.

IMPRINTS MVP Books.

☛ Voyageur Press (and its sports imprint MVP Books) is internationally known as a leading publisher of quality music, sports, country living, crafts, natural history, and regional books. No children's or poetry books."

NONFICTION Subjects include Americana, cooking, environment, history, hobbies, music, nature, regional, sports, collectibles, country living, knitting and quilting, outdoor recreation. Query with SASE. Submit outline. Send sample digital images or transparencies (duplicates and tearsheets only).

TIPS "We publish books for an audience interested in regional, natural, and cultural history on a wide variety of subjects. We seek authors strongly committed to helping us promote and sell their books. Please present as focused an idea as possible in a brief submission (1-page cover letter; 2-page outline or proposal). Note your credentials for writing the book. Tell all you know about the market niche and marketing possibilities for proposed book. We use more book designers than artists or illustrators, since most of our books are illustrated with photographs."

W&A PUBLISHING

One Peregrine Way, P.O. Box 849, Cedar Falls IA 50613. (319)266-0441; (800)927-8222. Fax: (319)266-1695. E-mail: kgolden@w-apublishing.com. E-mail: editorial@w-apublishing.com. Website: www.w-apublishing.com. **Contact:** Karris Golden, executive editor. Estab. 2006. Hardcover and electronic originals; hardcover reprints. **Publishes 10-12/year titles/year. 90% of books from first-time authors. 100% from unagented writers. Pays 15% royalty.** Publishes book 3-6 months. after acceptance of ms. Accepts simultaneous submissions. 1-2 months on queries and proposals. Catalog available online at website. Guidelines available online at website and by e-mail at editorial@w-apublishing.com.

NONFICTION Subjects include business, economics, finance, money, Investing/trading; investment/trading strategies, systems, and techniques; hot trends; trading/investment psychology; trading guidelines and how-to; new, tested trading/investment methods; anthologies of articles related to the above. "We are always interested in great ideas, fresh voices, and new methods, strategies, and approaches that will educate readers interested in improving their skills as traders and investors." No proposals based on get-rich-quick schemes or 'foolproof, can't lose' strategies. Submit proposal packages, including: outline/synopsis, 1-3 sample chapters(s), table of contents and author's biographical information; prefer e-mailed submissions Writers should send photocopies; scans; computer-generated graphics.

TIPS "Our readers have increased knowledge and awareness of discrete investment products and tools. They are interested in an education and want to learn from practicing financial professionals. Our goal is to offer readers materials highlighting new techniques, in-depth analysis, and solid information that helps them hone their skills and make informed decisions. We are interested in providing accompanying workbook materials in print and electronic form to augment the published book. (We prefer workbook/training materials that are supplemental rather than incorporated into the book.)"

WAKESTONE PRESS

200 Brook Hollow Rd., Nashville TN 37205-3504. (615)739-6428. E-mail: submissions@wakestonepress.com. Website: www.wakestonepress.com. **Contact:** Frank Daniels III, Editor, interested in nonfiction. Estab. 2010. Format publishes hardcover, trade paperback and electronic originals. **Publishes 6+ titles/year. 90% of books from first-time authors. 100% from unagented writers. Pays 7.5%-20% on wholesale price. Outright purchases $10,000-$20,000 maximum. $2,000-$5,000** Publishes book 12-18 months after acceptance of ms. Accepts simultaneous submissions. Responds 1 month to queries and proposals and 2 months to manuscripts. Catalog free by request. Guidelines free by request.

IMPRINTS Wakestone Press LLC; Moonshadow Press (subsidiary): Fiction imprint targeting young adults (10 - up).

NONFICTION Subjects include cooking, creative nonfiction, foods, history, house and home, law, memoirs, New Age, regional, sports, young adult. Submit in Microsoft Word file(s) a proposal package, including: book outline several (2-3) sample chapter(s) and author bio(s). Reviews art work and writers should send digital copies as part of submission file.

FICTION Subjects include erotica, gay, lesbian, occult, young adult. Submit in Microsoft Word file(s) a proposal package, including: book outline several (2-3) sample chapter(s) and author bio(s).

WALKER AND CO.

Walker Publishing Co., 175 Fifth Ave., 7th Floor, New York NY 10010. (212)727-8300. Fax: (212)727-0984. E-mail: rebecca.mancini@bloomsburyusa.com. Website: www.walkeryoungreaders.com. **Contact:** Submissions to Adult Nonfiction Editor limited to agents, published authors, and writers wtih professional credentials in their field of expertise. Children's books to Submissions Editor-Juvenile. Estab. 1959. Publishes hardcover trade originals. Book catalog for 9×12 envelope and 3 first-class stamps.

☛ Walker publishes general nonfiction on a variety of subjects, as well as children's books."

NONFICTION Subjects include business, economics, health, medicine, history, (science and technology), nature, environment, science, sports, mathematics, self-help. *Adult: agented submissions only*; Juvenile: send synopsis.

FICTION Subjects include juvenile, mystery, adult, picture books. Query with SASE. Send complete ms for picture books.

⊕ WAVE BOOKS

1938 Fairview Ave. E., Suite 201, Seattle WA 98102. (206)676-5337. E-mail: info@wavepoetry.com. Website: www.wavepoetry.com. **Contact:** Heidi Broadhead (readings, events, reviews, interviews). Matthew Zapruder, ed.; Heidi Broadhead, man. ed. Estab. 2005. Hardcover and trade paperback originals. Catalog online.

◯ "We are currently not accepting unsolicited manuscripts for consideration."

☛ Wave Books is an independent poetry press based in Seattle, Washington. Dedicated to publishing the best in American poetry by new and established authors, Wave Books was founded in 2005, joining forces with already-established publisher Verse Press. Wave Books seeks to build on and expand the mission of Verse Press by publishing strong innovative work and encouraging our authors to expand and interact with their readership."

POETRY "We are dedicated to publishing the best in American poetry by new & established authors. We seek to build on & expand by publishing strong innovative work & encouraging our authors to expand & interact with their readership through nationwide readings & events, affirming our belief that the audience for poetry is larger & more diverse than commonly thought." No children's, fiction, or nonfiction for Wave library. No magazine contributions right now. Submit with cover letter. Galleys & advance reader's copies are acceptable.

TIPS "Our titles have received critical acclaim in such publications as The Boston Review, Harper's, The New York Times Book Review, The New Yorker, Rolling Stone Publisher's Weekly, The Village Voice, Library Journal, Jacket (Australia)."

♻ WEIGL EDUCATIONAL PUBLISHERS LIMITED

6325 Tenth St. SE, Calgary AB T2H 2Z9, Canada. (403)233-7747. Fax: (403)233-7769. E-mail: linda@weigl.com. Website: www.weigl.com. Estab. 1979. Publishes hardcover originals and reprints, school library softcover. **Publishes 104 titles/year. 100% from unagented writers.** Book catalog available for free.

☛ Textbook publisher catering to juvenile and young adult audience (K-12)." Makes outright purchase. Responds ASAP to queries. Query with SASE.

NONFICTION , animals, education, government, politics, history, nature, environment, science.

WEIGL PUBLISHERS INC.

350 5th Ave. 59th floor, New York NY 10118-0069. E-mail: linda@weigl.com. Website: www.weigl.com. **Contact:** Heather Kissock, acquisitions. Estab. 2000. Publishes book Publishes book 6-9 months after acceptance. after acceptance of ms. Accepts simultaneous submissions. Book catalog available for 9½×11 SASE. Catalog available on website.

☛ Publishes 25 young readers/year; 40 middle readers/year; 20 young adult titles/year. 15% of books by first-time authors. "Our mission is to provide innovative high-quality learning resources for schools and libraries worldwide at a competitive price."

NONFICTION , Young readers: animal, biography, geography, history, multicultural, nature/environment, science. Middle readers: animal, biography, geography, history, multicultural, nature/environment, science, social issues, sports. Young adults: biography, careers, geography, history, multicultural, nature/environment, social issues. Average word length: young readers—100 words/page; middle readers—200 words/page; young adults—300 words/page. Recently published *Amazing Animals* (ages 9 and up, science series); *U.S. Sites and Symbols* (ages 8 and up, social studies series); *Science Q&A* (ages 9 and up, social studies series). Query by e-mail only; will consider e-mail submissions.

WESLEYAN PUBLISHING HOUSE

P.O. Box 50434, Indianapolis IN 46250. E-mail: submissions@wesleyan.org. Website: www.wesleyan.

org/wg. **Contact:** Rachael Stevenson, Associate Production Editor. Estab. 1843. Hardcover and trade paperback originals. **Publishes 25 titles/year. 150-175 submissions received. 50% of books from first-time authors. 90% from unagented writers. Pays royalty on wholesale price** Publishes book 11 months after acceptance of ms. Accepts simultaneous submissions. Responds in 2 months on proposals. Catalog available online at website www.wesleyan.org/wph. Guidelines available online at website www.wesleyan.org/wg.

NONFICTION Subjects include Christianity/religion. No hard copy submissions. Submit proposal package, including outline, 3-5 sample chapters, bio. See writer's guidelines. Does not review artwork.

TIPS "Our books help evangelical Christians learn about the faith or grow in their relationship with God."

⊘ WESLEYAN UNIVERSITY PRESS

215 Long Lane, Middletown CT 06459. (860)685-7711. Fax: (860)685-7712. E-mail: stamminen@wesleyan.edu. Website: www.wesleyan.edu/wespress. Estab. 1959. Publishes hardcover originals and paperbacks. Accepts simultaneous submissions. Book catalog available free. Ms guidelines online or with #10 SASE.

> ⊶ Wesleyan University Press is a scholarly press with a focus on poetry, music, dance and cultural studies."

NONFICTION Subjects include music, dance, film/TV & media studies, science fiction studies, dance and poetry. Submit proposal package, outline, sample chapters, cover letter, CV, TOC, anticipated length of ms and date of completion. Reviews artwork/photos. Send photocopies.

POETRY We do not accept unsolicited manuscripts.

WESTMINSTER JOHN KNOX PRESS

Division of Presbyterian Publishing Corp., 100 Witherspoon St., Louisville KY 40202-1396. Fax: (502)569-5113. E-mail: submissions@wjkbooks.com. Website: www.wjkbooks.com. **Contact:** Jana Riess, acquisitions editor. Publishes hardcover and paperback originals and reprints. **Publishes 70 titles/year. 2,500 queries received/year. 750 mss received/year. 10% of books from first-time authors. Pays royalty on net price.** Responds in 8-10 weeks or longer. Proposal guidelines online.

> ⊶ All WJK books have a religious/spiritual angle, but are written for various markets-scholarly, professional, and the general reader. Westmin-

ster John Knox is affiliated with the Presbyterian Church USA. No phone queries. We do not publish fiction, poetry, memoir, children's books, or dissertations. We will not return or respond to submissions without an accompanying SASE with sufficient postage."

NONFICTION Subjects include religion, spirituality. Submit proposal package according to the WJK book proposal guidelines found online.

⊘ WHITAKER HOUSE

1030 Hunt Valley Circle, New Kensington PA 15068. E-mail: publisher@whitakerhouse.com. Website: www.whitakerhouse.com. **Contact:** Tom Cox, managing editor. Estab. 1970. Publishes hardcover, trade paperback, and mass market originals. **Publishes 50 titles/year. 600 queries received/year. 200 mss received/year. 15% of books from first-time authors. 60% from unagented writers. Pays 5-15% royalty on wholesale price.** Publishes book 7 months after acceptance of ms. Accepts simultaneous submissions. Responds in 3 months to queries, proposals and manuscripts. Book catalog available online. Guidelines available online and by e-mail.

NONFICTION Subjects include religion, Christian. Accepts submissions on topics with a Christian perspective. Subjects include Christian living, prayer, spiritual warfare, healing, gifts of the spirit, etc. Accepts submissions on any topic as long as they have a Christian perspective. Query with SASE. Does not review artwork/photos.

FICTION Subjects include religious, Christian, historial romance, African American romance and Amish fiction. All fiction must have a Christian perspective. Query with SASE.

TIPS "Audience includes those seeking uplifting and inspirational fiction and nonfiction."

⊙ WHITECAP BOOKS, LTD.

351 Lynn Ave., North Vancouver BC V7J 2C4, Canada. (640)980-9852. Fax: (604)980-8197. E-mail: whitecap@whitecap.ca. Website: www.whitecap.ca. **Contact:** Rights & Acquisitions. Publishes hardcover and trade paperback originals. **Publishes 40 titles/year. 500 queries received/year. 1,000 mss received/year. 20% of books from first-time authors. 90% from unagented writers. Pays royalty. Pays negotiated advance.** Publishes book 12 months after acceptance of ms. Accepts simultaneous submissions. Responds

in 2-3 months to proposals. Catalog and guidelines available online at website.

- 🔑 Whitecap Books is a general trade publisher with a focus on food and wine titles. Although we are interested in reviewing unsolicited ms submissions, please note that we only accept submissions that meet the needs of our current publishing program. Please see some of most recent releases to get an idea of the kinds of titles we are interested in."

NONFICTION Subjects include animals, cooking, foods, nutrition, gardening, history, nature, environment, recreation, regional, travel. "Writers should take the time to research our list and read the submission guidelines on our website. This is especially important for children's writers and cookbook authors. We will only consider submissions that fall into these categories: cookbooks, wine and spirits, regional travel, home and garden, Canadian history, North American natural history, juvenile series-based fiction." "At this time, we are not accepting the following categories: self-help or inspirational books, political, social commentary, or issue books, general how-to books, biographies or memoirs, business and finance, art and architecture, religion and spirituality." Submit cover letter, synopsis, SASE via ground mail. See guidelines online at website. Reviews artwork/photos. Send photocopies.

FICTION No children's picture books or adult fiction. See guidelines.

TIPS "We want well-written, well-researched material that presents a fresh approach to a particular topic."

WHITE PINE PRESS

P.O. Box 236, Buffalo NY 14201. (716)627-4665. Fax: (716)627-4665. E-mail: wpine@whitepine.org. Website: www.whitepine.org. **Contact:** Dennis Maloney, editor. Estab. 1973. Trade paperback originals. **Publishes 10-12 titles/year. 500 queries/yearly 1% of books from first-time authors. 100% from unagented writers. Pays in copies** Publishes book 18 months after acceptance of ms. Accepts simultaneous submissions. Reports back in 1 month on queries/proposals; 4 months/mss. Catalog available online at website; for #10 SASE. Guidelines available online at website.

NONFICTION Subjects include language, literature, multicultural, translation, poetry. We are currently not considering nonfiction mss. We do not review artwork/photos

FICTION Subjects include poetry, poetry in translation, translation. "We are currently not reading U.S. fiction. We are currently reading unsolicited poetry only as part of our Annual Poetry Contest. The reading period is July 1 - November 30 for fiction and poetry in translation only." For fiction and poetry in translation ONLY-query with SASE; submit proposal package, including synopsis and 2 sample chapters."

POETRY See above re: poetry contest

WHITTLER'S BENCH PRESS

Dram Tree Books, P.O. Box 7183, Wilmington NC 28406. E-mail: dramtreebooks@ec.rr.com. Website: www.dramtreebooks.com. **Contact:** Fiction Editor. Estab. 2005. Publishes trade paperback originals and reprints. **Publishes 2-6 titles/year. 90% of books from first-time authors. 100% from unagented writers. Pays 10-15% royalty on retail price. Pays $250-500 advance.** Publishes book 1 year after acceptance of ms. Responds in 2 months to queries. Responds in 2 months to proposals. Responds in 4 months to manuscripts. Guidelines available via e-mail.

- 💬 Sign up on facebook to contact.

FICTION Subjects include adventure, historical, humor, military, war, mystery, regional, suspense. Our main focus is on historical fiction, mysteries and humorous novels—and all of it must have some link to North Carolina. When submitting humorous novels you must make us laugh. Think in terms of books by authors like Michael Malone, T.R. Pearson, Clyde Edgerton, Terry Pratchett, etc. Query with SASE. Submit proposal package, 3 sample chapters, clips.

TIPS Our readers are looking for compelling stories that will transport them away from the pressures of the 'real' world for however long they spend with our stories. The North Carolina tie-in is an important part of what will be a Whittler's Bench Press title. Remember they'll be paying good money to be entertained, so give them a story that satisfies. If historical fiction, make sure you get the history right. Finally, always remember: It must have a North Carolina angle of some kind.

WILLIAM ANDREW, INC.

13 Eaton Ave., Norwich NY 13815. (607)337-5000. Fax: (607)337-5090. E-mail: vhaynes@williamandrew.com. Website: www.williamandrew.com. **Contact:** Valerie Haynes, publications editor. Estab. 1989. Publishes hardcover originals. Accepts simultaneous submissions. Book catalog available online.

IMPRINTS Noyes Publications, Plastics Design Library.

☞ We are looking for authors who want to write a book or compile data that can be employed by readers in day-to-day activities."

NONFICTION Subject areas include agricultural/food tech, coatings/paints formulations, cosmetics/toiletries, diffusion/thin films, health/safety, industrial chemicals, MEMS/nanotechnology, materials engineers, packaging, plastics, processing/manufacturing, surface engineering. Submit outline with proposal, SASE Reviews artwork/photos. Send copies.

WILLOW CREEK PRESS

P.O. Box 147, 9931 Highway 70 W., Minocqua WI 54548. (715)358-7010. Fax: (715)358-2807. E-mail: jpetrie@willowcreekpress.com. Website: www.willowcreekpress.com. **Contact:** Jeremy Petrie, vice president of sales. Estab. 1986. Publishes hardcover and trade paperback originals and reprints. **Publishes 25 titles/year. 400 queries received/year. 150 mss received/year. 15% of books from first-time authors. 50% from unagented writers. Pays 6-15% royalty on wholesale price. Pays $2,000-5,000 advance.** Publishes book within 18 months after acceptance of ms. Accepts simultaneous submissions. Responds in 2 months to queries. Guidelines available online.

☞ We specialize in nature, outdoor, and sporting topics, including gardening, wildlife, and animal books. Pets, cookbooks, and a few humor books and essays round out our titles. Currently emphasizing pets (mainly dogs and cats), wildlife, outdoor sports (hunting, fishing). De-emphasizing essays, fiction."

NONFICTION Subjects include animals, cooking, foods, nutrition, gardening, nature, environment, recreation, sports, travel, wildlife, pets. Submit outline, 1 sample chapter, SASE. Reviews artwork/photos.

WILSHIRE BOOK COMPANY

9731 Variel Ave., Chatsworth CA 91311-4315. (818)700-1522. Fax: (818)700-1527. E-mail: mpowers@mpowers.com. Website: www.mpowers.com. **Contact:** Rights Department. Estab. 1947. Publishes trade paperback originals and reprints. **Publishes 25 titles/year. 1,200 queries received/year. 70% of books from first-time authors. 90% from unagented writers. Pays standard royalty. Pays advance.** Publishes book 6-9 months after acceptance of ms. Accepts simultaneous submissions. Responds in 2 months.

NONFICTION Subjects include psychology, personal success. Minimum 30,000 words Submit 3 sample chapters. Submit complete ms. Include outline, author bio, analysis of book's competition and SASE. No e-mail or fax submissions. Reviews artwork/photos. Send photocopies.

FICTION Adult allegories that teach principles of psychological growth or offer guidance in living. Minimum 30,000 words. No standard fiction. Submit 3 sample chapters. Submit complete ms. Include outline, author bio, analysis of book's, competition and SASE.

TIPS "We are vitally interested in all new material we receive. Just as you are hopeful when submitting your manuscript for publication, we are hopeful as we read each one submitted, searching for those we believe could be successful in the marketplace. Writing and publishing must be a team effort. We need you to write what we can sell. We suggest you read the successful books similar to the one you want to write. Analyze them to discover what elements make them winners. Duplicate those elements in your own style, using a creative new approach and fresh material, and you will have written a book we can catapult onto the bestseller list. You are welcome to telephone or e-mail us for immediate feedback on any book concept you may have. To learn more about us and what we publish, and for complete manuscript guidelines, visit our website."

WISCONSIN HISTORICAL SOCIETY PRESS

816 State St., Madison WI 53706. (608)264-6465. Fax: (608)264-6486. E-mail: whspress@wisconsinhistory.org. Website: www.wisconsinhistory.org/whspress/. **Contact:** Kate Thompson, editor. Estab. 1855. Publishes hardcover and trade paperback originals; trade paperback reprints. **Publishes 12-14 titles/year. 60-75 queries received/year. 20% of books from first-time authors. 90% from unagented writers. Pays royalty on wholesale price.** Publishes book 18-24 months after acceptance of ms. Book catalog available free. Guidelines available online.

NONFICTION Subjects include Wisconsin history and culture: archaeology, architecture, cooking, foods, ethnic, history (Wisconsin), memoirs, regional, sports. Submit proposal package, form from website. Reviews artwork/photos. Send photocopies.

TIPS "Our audience reads about Wisconsin. Carefully review the book."

WIZARDS OF THE COAST BOOKS FOR YOUNG READERS

P.O. Box 707, Renton WA 98057. (425)254-2287. E-mail: nina.hess@wizards.com. Website: www.wizards.com. **Contact:** Nina Hess. Estab. 2003. Publishes hardcover and trade paperback originals and trade paperback reprints. **Pays $4,000 advance.**

- Wizards of the Coast publishes only science fiction and fantasy shared-world titles. Currently emphasizing solid fantasy writers. De-emphasizing gothic fiction. Dragonlance; Forgotten Realms; Magic: The Gathering; Eberron. Wizard of the Coast publishes games as well, including Dungeons & Dragons® role-playing game.

TIPS Editorial staff attended or plans to attend ALA conference. Editorial staff attended or plans to attend ALA conference.

WOLF DEN BOOKS

5794 S.W. 40th St., #221, Miami FL 33155. (877)667-9737. E-mail: info@wolfdenbooks.com. Website: www.wolfdenbooks.com. **Contact:** Gail Shivel. Estab. 2000. Publishes hardcover, trade paperback and electronic originals and reprints. **Publishes 2 titles/year. 40 queries received/year. 10 mss received/year. 0% of books from first-time authors. 100% from unagented writers. Pays 7 ½% royalty on retail price.** Publishes book 12 months after acceptance of ms. Accepts simultaneous submissions. Responds in 3 months/queries, 6 months/proposals, 8 months/mss. Book catalog available online. Guidelines available via e-mail.

- "Please do not send postage; mss are not returned."

NONFICTION Subjects include history, humanities, language, literature, literary criticism, philosophy. Query with SASE; submit proposal package, including outline; submit complete ms. Does not review artwork.

WOODBINE HOUSE

6510 Bells Mill Rd., Bethesda MD 20817. (301)897-3570. Fax: (301)897-5838. E-mail: ngpaul@woodbinehouse.com. Website: www.woodbinehouse.com. **Contact:** Nancy Gray Paul, acquisitions editor. Estab. 1985. Publishes trade paperback originals. **Publishes 10 titles/year. 15% of books from first-time authors. 90% from unagented writers. Pays 10-12% royalty.** Publishes book 18 months after acceptance of ms. Accepts simultaneous submissions. Responds in 3 months to queries. Book catalog for 6×9 SAE with 3 first-class stamps. No metered mail or international reply coupons (IRC's) please. Guidelines available online.

- Woodbine House publishes books for or about individuals with disabilities to help those individuals and their families live fulfilling and satisfying lives in their homes, schools, and communities.

NONFICTION Subjects include specific issues related to a given disability (e.g., communication skills, social sciences skills, feeding issues) and practical guides to issues of concern to parents of children with disabilities (e.g., special education, sibling issues). Publishes books for and about children with disabilities. No personal accounts or general parenting guides. Submit outline, and at least 3 sample chapters. Reviews artwork/photos.

FICTION Subjects include picture books, children's. Receptive to stories re: developmental and intellectual disabilities, e.g., autism and cerebral palsy. Submit complete ms with SASE.

TIPS "Do not send us a proposal on the basis of this description. Examine our catalog or website and a couple of our books to make sure you are on the right track. Put some thought into how your book could be marketed (aside from in bookstores). Keep cover letters concise and to the point; if it's a subject that interests us, we'll ask to see more."

WRITER'S DIGEST BOOKS

Imprint of F+W Media, Inc., 4700 E. Galbraith Rd., Cincinnati OH 45236. E-mail: writersdigest@fwmedia.com. Website: www.writersdigest.com. **Contact:** Kelly Messerly, Acquisitions Editor. Estab. 1920. Publishes hardcover originals and trade paperbacks. **Publishes 18-20 titles/year. 300 queries received/year. 50 mss received/year. 30% from unagented writers. Pays average $3,000 advance.** Publishes book 6-12 months after acceptance of ms. Accepts simultaneous submissions. Responds in 3 months to queries. Our catalog of titles is available to view online at www.WritersDigestShop.com.

- Writer's Digest Books accepts query letters and complete proposals via e-mail at writersdigest@fwmedia.com.
- Writer's Digest Books is the premiere source for instructional books on writing and publishing for an audience of aspirational writers. Typical

mss are 80,000 words. E-mail queries strongly preferred; no phone calls please."

NONFICTION "Our instruction books stress results and how specifically to achieve them. Should be well-researched, yet lively and readable. We do not want to see books telling readers how to crack specific non-fiction markets: *Writing for the Computer Market* or *Writing for Trade Publications*, for instance. We are most in need of fiction-technique books written by published authors. Be prepared to explain how the proposed book differs from existing books on the subject." No fiction or poetry Query with SASE. Submit outline, sample chapters, SASE.

TIPS "Most queries we receive are either too broad (how to write fiction) or too niche (how to write erotic horror), and don't reflect a knowledge of our large backlist of 150 titles. We rarely publish new books on journalism, freelancing, magazine article writing or marketing/promotion. We are actively seeking fiction and nonfiction writing technique books with fresh perspectives, interactive and visual writing instruction books, similar to *Pocket Muse*, by Monica Wood; and general reference works that appeal to an audience beyond writers."

YALE UNIVERSITY PRESS

P.O. Box 209040, New Haven CT 06520. (203)432-0960. Fax: (203)432-0948. E-mail: niamh.cunningham@yale.edu. Website: www.yale.edu/yup. **Contact:** Niamh Cunningham, (203)432-0975. Christopher Rogers, editorial director (history and current events); Jean E. Thomson Black, executive editor (science, medicine); Vadim Staklo, Associate Editor (reference books, Annals of Communism, Slavic Studies); William Frucht, Executive Editor (politics, law, and economics); Michelle Komie, Senior Editor (art, architecture); Patricia Fidler, Publisher (art, architecture); Tim Shea, Editor (languages, ESL); Alison Mackeen, Editor (literature, literary studies, media studies); Sarah Miller, Associate Editor, General Interest; Ileene Smith, Exec. Editor-at-large, General Interest; Laura Davulis, Editor (digital development); Jennifer Banks, Senior Editor (Religion, Religious History, Classics). Estab. 1908. Estab. 1908. Publishes hardcover and trade paperback originals. Accepts simultaneous submissions. Book catalog and ms guidelines online.

8→ Yale University Press publishes scholarly and general interest books."

NONFICTION Subjects include Americana, anthropology, archeology, art, architecture, business, economics, education, health, medicine, history, language, literature, military, war, music, dance, philosophy, psychology, religion, science, sociology, women's issues, women's studies. Our nonfiction has to be at a very high level. Most of our books are written by professors or journalists, with a high level of expertise. *Submit proposals only*. We'll ask if we want to see more. *No unsolicited mss*. We won't return them. Submit sample chapters, cover letter, prospectus, cv, table of contents, SASE. Reviews artwork/photos. Send photocopies.

POETRY Publishes 1 book each year. Submit to Yale Series of Younger Poets Competition. Open to poets under 40 who have not had a book previously published. Submit ms of 48-64 pages by November 15. Rules and guidelines available online or with SASE. Submit complete ms.

TIPS "Audience is scholars, students and general readers."

✛ YBK PUBLISHERS, INC.

39 Crosby St., New York NY 10013. E-mail: info@ybkpublishers.com. Website: www.ybkpublishers.com. **Contact:** George Ernsberger, editor-in-chief. Estab. 2000. Publishes hardcover and trade paperback originals. **Publishes 12 titles/year. 90% of books from first-time authors. 100% from unagented writers. Pays -15% royalty on retail price.** Publishes book 3 months after acceptance of ms. Accepts simultaneous submissions. Responds in 1 month only to nonfiction queries, proposals and manuscripts. Book catalog available online. Guidelines available online.

NONFICTION We seek highly directed niche subjects directed at a market that is narrow, identifiable, and economically reachable. Reviews artwork/photos.

TIPS "Our audience wants academic and special interest topics."

◐∅ YEARLING BOOKS

Imprint of Random House Children's Books/Random House, Inc., 1745 Broadway, New York NY 10019. (212)782-9000. Website: www.randomhouse.com/kids.

◔ "Quality reprint paperback imprint for middle grade paperback books." *Does not accept unsolicited mss.*

☻ YOGI IMPRESSIONS BOOKS PVT. LTD.

1711, Centre 1, World Trade Centre, Cuffe Parade Mumbai 400 005, India. E-mail: yogi@yogiimpressions.com. Website: www.yogiimpressions.com. **Contact:** Submissions Editor. Estab. 2000. Guidelines available online.

☞ Yogi Impressions are Self-help, Personal Growth and Spiritual book publishers based in Mumbai, India. Established at the turn of the millennium, at Mumbai, Yogi Impressions publishes books which seek to revive interest in spirituality, enhance the quality of life and, thereby, create the legacy of a better world for future generations."

NONFICTION Subjects include audio, child guidance, multicultural, religion, spirituality, alternative health, enlightened business, self-improvement/personal growth. Submit outline/proposal, bio, 2-3 sample chapters, market assessment, SASE.

⊕ ZENITH PRESS

Quayside Publishing Group, 400 First Ave. N., Suite 300, Minneapolis MN 55401. (612)344-8100; (800)328-0590. Fax: (612)344-8691. E-mail: spearson@quaysidepub.com. E-mail: rkane@quaysidepub.com; spearson@quaysidepub.com. Website: www.qbookshop.com; zenithpress.com. **Contact:** Scott Pearson, Acquisitions Editor. Richard Kane, Senior Acquisitions Editor (American military history, politics/current events) Estab. 2004. hardcover and trade paperback originals, electronic originals and reprints, hardcover and trade paperback reprints. **Publishes 210 titles/year. Receives 250 queries/year; 100 mss/year 25% of books from first-time authors. 50% from unagented writers. Pays authors 8-15% royalty on wholesale price** Publishes book 12 months after acceptance of ms. Accepts simultaneous submissions. Responds in 1 month on queries/proposals/mss. Catalog available online. Guidelines available online at http://www.quaysidepub.com/submissions.php.

☞ Zenith Press publishes an eclectic collection of historical nonfiction and current affairs in both narrative and illustrated formats. Building on a core of military history, particularly from World War II forward, Zenith reaches out to other historical, political, and science topics with compelling narrative hooks or eye-catching photography. From a history of nuclear weapons to contemporary coverage of the wars in Iraq and Afghanistan to an illustrated celebration of the space shuttle program, Zenith Books are engaging stories with historical, military, or science foundations— sometimes all three at once."

NONFICTION Subjects include history, military, politics, science, world affairs. Submit proposal package, including outline, 1-3 sample chapters, and author biography. Reviews artwork. Send digital files.

ZOLAND BOOKS

Steerforth Press, 45 Lyme Rd., Suite 208, Hanover NH 03755. (603)643-4787. Fax: (603)643-4788. Website: www.steerforth.com/zoland/. **Contact:** Editor: Roland Pease (Zoland Poetry annuals). Estab. 1987. Trade paperback originals.

NONFICTION Subjects include translation, travel, (book reviews).

FICTION Subjects include ethnic, experimental, fantasy, historical, horror, humor, literary, military, war, mystery, picture books, plays, poetry, regional, religious, romance, science fiction, short story collections, spiritual, suspense, translation, Folklore.

POETRY Zoland annuals are meant to be read as a continuation of the Zoland Books line. Rather than 3-4 volumes of poetry by individual authors each year, there is instead one Zoland annual that includes a wide swath of individuals previously published by Zoland who were on the radar, and an individual that fits into the larger whole of each annual.

⊕ ZUMAYA PUBLICATIONS, LLC

3209 S. Interstate 35, #1086, Austin TX 78741. E-mail: submissions@zumayapublications.com. E-mail: submissions@zumayapublications.com. Website: www.zumayapublications.com. **Contact:** Elizabeth Burton, executive editor. Estab. 1999. Publishes trade paperback and electronic originals and reprints. **Publishes 20-25 titles/year. 1,000 queries received/year. 100 mss received/year. 75% of books from first-time authors. 98% from unagented writers.** Publishes book 6-24 months after acceptance of ms. Accepts simultaneous submissions. Responds in 6 months to queries and proposals. Responds in 6-9 months to manuscripts. Guidelines available online.

IMPRINTS Zumaya Arcane (New Age, inspirational fiction & nonfiction), Zumaya Boundless (GLBT); Zumaya Embraces (romance/women's fiction); Zumaya Enigma (mystery/suspense/thriller); Zumaya Thresholds (YA/middle grade); Zumaya Otherworlds

(SF/F/H), Zumaya Yesterdays (memoirs, historical fiction, fiction, western fiction).

○ "We are currently closed to submissions until further notice while we endeavor to catch up on our publishing queue. We will begin accepting queries for some imprints in July of 2010. Please review the guidelines page near that time for information on which imprints will be opened when."

NONFICTION Subjects include creative nonfiction, memoirs, New Age, spirituality, ghost stories. "The easiest way to figure out what I'm looking for is to look at what we've already done. Our main nonfiction interests are in collections of ghost stories, ones that have been investigated or thoroughly documented, memoirs that address specific regions and eras and books on the craft of writing. That doesn't mean we won't consider something else." Electronic query only. Reviews artwork/photos. Send digital format.

FICTION Subjects include adventure, fantasy, bisexual, gay, lesbian, historical, horror, humor, juvenile, literary, mainstream, contemporary, multicultural, mystery, occult, romance, science fiction, short story collections, spiritual, suspense, transgender, western, young adult. "We are currently oversupplied with speculative fiction and are reviewing submissions in SF, fantasy and paranormal suspense by invitation only. We are much in need of GLBT and YA/middle grade, historical and western, New Age/inspirational (no overtly Christian materials, please), non-category romance, thrillers. As with nonfiction, we encourage people to review what we've already published so as to avoid sending us more of the same, at least, insofar as the plot is concerned. While we're always looking for good specific mysteries, we want original concepts rather than slightly altered versions of what we've already published." Electronic query only.

TIPS "We're catering to readers who may have loved last year's best seller but not enough to want to read 10 more just like it. Have something different. If it does not fit standard pigeonholes, that's a plus. On the other hand, it has to have an audience. And if you're not prepared to work with us on promotion and marketing, it would be better to look elsewhere."

CONSUMER MAGAZINES

Selling your writing to consumer magazines is as much an exercise of your marketing skills as it is of your writing abilities. Editors of consumer magazines are looking not only for good writing, but for good writing which communicates pertinent information to a specific audience—their readers.

APPROACHING THE CONSUMER MAGAZINE MARKET

Marketing skills will help you successfully discern a magazine's editorial slant, and write queries and articles that prove your knowledge of the magazine's readership. You can gather clues about a magazine's readership—and establish your credibility with the magazine's editor—in a number of ways:

- **READ** the magazine's listing.
- **STUDY** a magazine's writer's guidelines.
- **CHECK** a magazine's website.
- **READ** several current issues of the target magazine.
- **TALK** to an editor by phone.

Writers who can correctly and consistently discern a publication's audience and deliver stories that speak to that target readership will win out every time over writers who submit haphazardly.

WHAT EDITORS WANT

In nonfiction, editors continue to look for short feature articles covering specialized topics. Editors want crisp writing and expertise. If you are not an expert in the area about which you are writing, make yourself one through research. Always query before sending your manuscript. Don't e-mail or fax a query to an editor unless the listing mentions it is acceptable to do so.

Fiction editors prefer to receive complete manuscripts. Writers must keep in mind that marketing fiction is competitive, and editors receive far more material than they can publish. For this reason, they often do not respond to submissions unless they are interested in using the story.

PAYMENT

Most magazines listed here have indicated pay rates; some give very specific payment-per-word rates, while others state a range. Any agreement you come to with a magazine, whether verbal or written, should specify the payment you are to receive and when you are to receive it. Some magazines pay writers only after the piece in question has been published (on publication). Others pay as soon as they have accepted a piece and are sure they are going to use it (on acceptance).

So what is a good pay rate? There are no standards; the principle of supply and demand operates at full throttle in the business of writing and publishing. As long as there are more writers than opportunities for publication, wages for freelancers will never skyrocket. Rates vary widely from one market to the next. Smaller circulation magazines and some departments of the larger magazines will pay a lower rate.

Editors know the listings are read and used by writers with a wide range of experience, from those unpublished writers just starting out, to those with a successful, profitable freelance career. As a result, many magazines publicly report pay rates in the lower end of their actual pay ranges. Experienced writers will be able to successfully negotiate higher pay rates for their material. Newer writers should be encouraged that as their reputation grows (along with their clip file), they will be able to command higher rates. The article "How Much Should I Charge?" gives an idea of pay ranges for different freelance jobs, including those directly associated with magazines.

INFORMATION AT-A-GLANCE

In the Consumer Magazines section, icons identify comparative payment rates (💲-💲💲💲💲). Important information is highlighted in boldface—the "quick facts" you won't find in any other market book, but should know before you submit your work. The word **Contact** identifies the appropriate person to query at each magazine. We also highlight what percentage of the magazine is freelance written; how many manuscripts a magazine buys per year of nonfiction, fiction, poetry, and fillers; and respective pay rates in each category.

ANIMAL

🌑🌑 AKC GAZETTE

American Kennel Club, (212)696-8295. Fax: (212)696-8239. Website: akc.org/pubs/gazette. **Contact:** Tilly Grassa, creative director. **85% freelance written.** Monthly magazine. "Geared to interests of fanciers of purebred dogs as opposed to commercial interests or pet owners. We require solid expertise from our contributors—we are *not* a pet magazine." Estab. 1889. Circ. 60,000. Byline given. Pays on publication. Offers 10% kill fee. Publishes ms an average of 6 months after acceptance. Submit seasonal material 6 months in advance. Accepts queries by mail. Responds in 2 months to queries. Guidelines for #10 SASE.

NONFICTION Needs general interest, how-to, humor, interview, photo feature, travel, dog art, training and canine performance sports. No poetry, tributes to individual dogs, or fiction. **Buys 30-40 mss/year.** Length: 1,000-3,000 words. **Pays $300-500.** Pays expenses of writers on assignment.

PHOTOS Photo contest guidelines for #10 SASE. State availability. Captions, identification of subjects, model releases required. Reviews color transparencies, prints. Pays $50-200/photo.

FICTION Annual short fiction contest only. Guidelines for #10 SASE. Send entries to AKC Publications Fiction Contest, The American Kennel Club, 260 Madison Avenue, New York, NY 10016.

🌑🌑 APPALOOSA JOURNAL

Appaloosa Horse Club, 2720 West Pullman Rd., Moscow ID 83843. (208)882-5578. Fax: (208)882-8150. E-mail: editor@appaloosajournal.com; drice@appaloosajournal.com; artdirector@appaloosajournal.com;. Website: appaloosajournal.com. Laura Vander Hoek, art director, artdirector@appaloosajournal.com. **Contact:** Dana , editor. **40% freelance written.** Monthly magazine covering Appaloosa horses. We seek feature-length (1,500 to 1,800 words) and article-length (600 to 800 words) submissions about breeders, trainers, specific training methods, influential horses, youth and non-pro competitors, breed history, trail riding and artists using Appaloosa subjects. Article-length reports of timely and newsworthy events, such as shows, races and overseas competition, are welcome but must be pre-approved by the editor. Manuscripts exceeding the preferred word length will be evaluated according to relevance and content matter. Lengthy stories, opinion pieces or poorly written pieces will be rejected. Manuscripts may be sent on a CD or via e-mail in Microsoft Word or text-only format. If sent via CD, an accompanying hard copy should be printed, double spaced, following the guidelines. "*Appaloosa Journal* is the authoritative, association-based source for information about the Appaloosa Horse Club, the Appaloosa breed and the Appaloosa industry. Our mission is to cultivate a broader membership base and instill enthusiasm for the breed by recognizing the needs and achievements of the Appaloosa, ApHC members, enthusiasts and our readers. The Appaloosa Horse Club is a not-for-profit organization. Serious inquiries within specified budget only." In photographer's samples, wants to see "high-quality color photos of world-class, characteristic (coat patterned) Appaloosa horses in appealing, picturesque outdoor environments. Send a letter introducing yourself and briefly explaining your work. If you have inflexible preset fees, be upfront and include that information. Be patient. We are located at the headquarters; although an image might not work for the magazine, it might work for other printed materials. Work has a better chance of being used if allowed to keep on file. If work must be returned promptly, please specify. Otherwise, we will keep it for other departments' consideration." Estab. 1946. Circ. 25,000. Byline given. Pays on publication. Publishes ms an average of 3 months after acceptance. Responds in 1 month to queries. Responds in 2 months to mss. Sample copy free. Guidelines available online.

○ *Appaloosa Journal* no longer accepts material for columns.

NONFICTION Needs historical, interview, photo feature. **Buys 15-20 mss/year.** Send complete ms. *Appaloosa Journal* is not responsible for unsolicited materials. All freelance correspondence should be directed to Editor Dana Russell, editor@appaloosajournal.com, subject line "Freelance." Length: 800-1,800 words. **Pays $200-400.**

PHOTOS Contact: Dana Russell, editor. Send photos. Captions, identification of subjects required. Payment varies. Pays $200 for color cover; $25 minimum for color inside. Pays on publication. Credit line given.

➕🌑🌑 AQUARIUM FISH INTERNATIONAL

Bowtie, Inc., P.O. Box 6050, Mission Viejo CA 92690-6050. (949)855-8822. Fax: (949)855-3045. E-mail:

aquariumfish@bowtieinc.com. Website: fishchannel. com. Clay Jackson, editor. **Contact:** Patricia Knight, managing editor. **90% freelance written**. Monthly magazine covering fish and other aquatic pets. Estab. 1988. Byline given. Pays on publication. Accepts queries by mail, e-mail, fax. Responds in 1 month to queries. Responds in 6 months to mss. Guidelines for #10 SASE.

Monthly magazine covering fish and other aquatic pets. 90% freelance written "Our focus is on beginning and intermediate fish keeping; we also run one advanced saltwater article per issue. Most of our articles concentrate on general fish and aquarium care, but we will also consider other types of articles that may be helpful to those in the fishkeeping hobby. Freshwater and saltwater tanks, and ponds are covered."

NONFICTION Needs general interest, species profiles, natural history with home care info, new product, press releases only for Product Showcase section, photo feature, caring for fish in aquariums. Special issues: "We do have 1 annual; freelancers should query.". "No fiction, anthropomorphism, articles on sport fishing, or animals that cannot be kept as pets (i.e., whales, dolphins, manatees, etc.).". **Buys 60 mss/ year.** Send complete ms. Length: 1,500-2,000 words. **Pays 15¢/word.**

PHOTOS Contact: Patricia Knight, managing editor. Purchases 240 freelance photos/year. Send for digital image requirements. State availability. Identification of subjects required. Reviews 35mm transparencies, 4×5 prints. Offers $15-200/photo.

FILLERS Needs facts, gags, newsbreaks. **Buys variable number mss/year.** Length: 50-200 words.

BIRDING WORLD

Sea Lawn, Coast Rd., Cley next the Sea, Holt Norfolk NR25 7RZ United Kingdom. (44)(126)374-0913. E-mail: steve@birdingworld.co.uk. Website: birdingworld.co.uk. **Contact:** Steve Gantlett. "Monthly magazine publishing notes about birds and birdwatching. The emphasis is on rarer British and Western Palearctic birds with topical interest." Estab. 1988. Accepts queries by mail, e-mail. Sample copy for £4.50. Guidelines by e-mail.

NONFICTION Pays £2-4/100 words for unsolicited articles.

PHOTOS Reviews digital images, drawings, maps, graphs, paintings. Pays £10-30/color photos; £5-25/ b&w photos.

CAT FANCY

Fancy Publications, a Divison of BowTie Inc., P.O. Box 6050, Mission Viejo CA 92690. (949)855-8822. Fax: (949)855-3045. E-mail: query@catfancy.com; catsupport@catchannel.com. E-mail: slogan@bowtieinc.com. Website: catfancy.com; catchannel.com. **Contact:** Susan Logan, editor. **90% freelance written.** Monthly magazine covering all aspects of responsible cat ownership. If you have an idea for an article, please send a written query with a self-addressed, stamped envelope. Feature Articles: We are open to working with new contributors and fresh voices in addition to drawing from a talented crop of established contributors. Each month, we provide our readers with a mix of informative articles on various topics, including breed profiles, feline health, nutrition, grooming, behavior, training, as well as lifestyle and special interest articles on cat culture, the human-animal bond and personalities. Length: 100-1,000 words. Query first. "*Cat Fancy* is the undisputed premier feline magazine that is dedicated to better lives for pet cats. Always a presence within the cat world, *Cat Fancy* and its sister website, CatChannel.com are where cat owners, lovers and rescue organizations go for education and entertainment." Estab. 1965. Pays on publication. Editorial lead time 6 months. Responds in 3 months to queries. Guidelines available online.

"With a readership that is highly receptive to its credible advice, news, lifestyle information, *Cat Fancy* and CatChannel.com are the ultimate places to read about cat news, breeds, care and products and services."

NONFICTION Needs how-to, humor, photo feature, travel, behavior, health, lifestyle, cat culture, entertainment. "We no longer publish any fiction or poetry." **Buys 70 mss/year.** Query with published clips. Length: 300-1,000 words. **Pays $50-450.**

PHOTOS "Seeking photos of happy, healthy, well-groomed cats and kittens in indoor settings.". Captions, identification of subjects, model releases required. Pays $200 maximum for color cover; $25-200 for inside. Negotiates payment individually. Credit line given. Buys first North American serial rights.

THE CHRONICLE OF THE HORSE

P.O. Box 46, Middleburg VA 20118-0046. (540)687-6341. Fax: (540)687-3937. E-mail: slieser@chronofhorse.com. Website: chronofhorse.com. **Contact:** Sara Lieser, managing editor. **80% freelance written.**

Weekly magazine covering horses. "We cover English riding sports, including horse showing, grand prix jumping competitions, steeplechase racing, foxhunting, dressage, endurance riding, handicapped riding, and combined training. We are the official publication for the national governing bodies of many of the above sports. We feature news, how-to articles on equitation and horse care and interviews with leaders in the various fields." Estab. 1937. Circ. 18,000. Byline given. Pays for features on acceptance; news and other items on publication. Publishes ms an average of 4 months after acceptance. Submit seasonal material 3 months in advance. Accepts queries by mail, e-mail. Responds in 5-6 weeks to queries. Sample copy for $2 and 9×12 SAE. Guidelines available online.

NONFICTION Needs general interest, historical, history of breeds, use of horses in other countries and times, art, etc., how-to, trailer, train, design a course, save money, etc., humor, centered on living with horses or horse people, interview, of nationally known horsemen or the very unusual, technical, horse care, articles on feeding, injuries, care of foals, shoeing, etc. Special issues: Steeplechase Racing (January); American Horse in Sport and Grand Prix Jumping (February); Horse Show (March); Intercollegiate (April); Kentucky 4-Star Preview (April); Junior and Pony (April); Dressage (June); Horse Care (July); Combined Training (August); Hunt Roster (September); Amateur (November); Stallion (December). No poetry, Q&A interviews, clinic reports, Western riding articles, personal experience or wild horses. **Buys 300 mss/year.** Send complete ms. 6-7 pages **Pays $150-250.**

PHOTOS State availability. Identification of subjects required. Photo captions required with every subject identified. Reviews e-mailed image, prints or color slides; accepts color for color reproduction. Pays $30 base rate. Pays on publication. Buys one-time rights. Credit line given. Prefers first North American rights.

COLUMNS Dressage, Combined Training, Horse Show, Horse Care, Racing over Fences, Young Entry (about young riders, geared for youth), Horses and Humanities, Hunting, Vaulting, Handicapped Riding, Trail Riding, 1,000-1,225 words; News of major competitions (clear assignment with us first), 1,500 words. Query with or without published clips or send complete ms. **Pays $25-200.**

$ COONHOUND BLOODLINES

United Kennel Club, Inc., 100 E. Kilgore Rd., Kalamazoo MI 49002-5584. (269)343-9020. Fax: (269)343-7037. E-mail: vrand@ukcdogs.com. Website: ukcdogs.com. **40% freelance written.** Monthly magazine covering all aspects of the 6 Coonhound dog breeds. Writers must retain the 'slang' particular to dog people and to our readers—many of whom are from the South. Estab. 1925. Circ. 16,000. Byline given. Pays on publication. Publishes ms an average of 6 months after acceptance. Editorial lead time 6 months. Submit seasonal material 6 months in advance. Accepts queries by mail, e-mail, fax, phone. Accepts simultaneous submissions. Responds in 6 weeks to queries. Sample copy for $4.50.

NONFICTION Needs general interest, historical, humor, interview, new product, personal experience, photo feature, breed-specific. Special issues: Six of our 12 issues are each devoted to a specific breed of Coonhound. Treeing Walker (February); English (July); Black & Tan (April); Bluetick (May); Redbone (June); Plott Hound (August), 1,000-3,000 words and photos. **Buys 12-36 mss/year.** Query. Length: 1,000-5,000 words. **Pays variable amount.** Sometimes pays expenses of writers on assignment.

PHOTOS State availability. Captions, identification of subjects required. Reviews contact sheets. Negotiates payment individually.

FICTION Must be about the Coonhound breeds or hunting with hounds. Needs adventure, historical, humorous, mystery. **Buys 3-6 mss/year.** Query. Length: 1,000-3,000 words. **Pay varies.**

$$ DOG FANCY

P.O. Box 6050, Mission Viejo CA 92690-6050. (949)855-8822. Fax: (949)855-3045. E-mail: barkback@dogfancy.com. Website: dogfancy.com. **95% freelance written.** Monthly magazine for men and women of all ages interested in all phases of dog ownership. Estab. 1970. Circ. 268,000. Byline given. Pays on publication. Offers kill fee. Publishes ms an average of 6 months after acceptance. Accepts queries by e-mail. Responds in 2 months to queries. Guidelines available online.

◯ Reading period from January through April.

NONFICTION Needs general interest, how-to, humor, inspirational, interview, photo feature, travel. "No stories written from a dog's point of view." **Buys**

10 or fewer from new writers; 80 mss/year. Query. Length: 800-1,200 words. **Pays 40¢/word.**

PHOTOS State availability of photos. Digital images, only. Offers no additional payment for photos accepted with ms.

COLUMNS News hound, fun dog. **Buys 6 mss/year.** Query by e-mail. **Pays 40¢/word.**

DOGS IN CANADA

Apex Publishing, Ltd., 200 Ronson Dr., Suite 401, Etobicoke ON M9W 5Z9 Canada. (416)798-9778. Fax: (416)798-9671. E-mail: editor@dogsincanada. com. Website: dogsincanada.com. **90% freelance written.** Monthly magazine covering dogs. *"Dogs in Canada* is considered a reliable and authoritative source of information about dogs. The mix of content must satisfy a diverse readership, including knowledgeable dog owners and fanciers as well as those who simply love dogs." Estab. 1889. Circ. 41,769. Byline given. Pays on publication. Offers 50% kill fee. Publishes ms 3-6 months after acceptance. Editorial lead time 4 months. Submit seasonal material 6 months in advance. Accepts queries by mail, e-mail. Responds in 12 weeks to queries. Responds in 3 months to mss. Guidelines for #10 SASE or via e-mail.

NONFICTION Needs Historical, purebred-focused content, health content. Does not want articles written from the dog's point of view. **Buys 10 mss/year.** Send complete ms. Length: 500-1,800 words. **Pays $100 and above.** Sometimes pays expenses of writers on assignment.

PHOTOS Contact: Kelly Caldwell, art director. State availability of or send photos. Identification of subjects, model releases required. Digital photo submissions only. Reviews contact sheets, negatives, transparencies, 5×7 prints, GIF/JPEG files. Negotiates payment individually.

FILLERS Needs anecdotes, short humor. **Buys Accepts less than 10 fillers/year. mss/year.** Length: 150-500 words.

DOGS IN CANADA ANNUAL

Apex Publishing, Ltd., 200 Ronson Drive, Suite 401, Suite 200, Etobicoke ON M9W 5Z9 Canada. (416)798-9778. Fax: (416)798-9671. E-mail: query@dogsincanada.com. Website: dogsincanada.com. **Contact:** Kelly Caldwell, editor-in-chief, art director. **25% freelance written.** Annual magazine covering dogs. Also a small cats section. *Dogs in Canada Annual* is a reliable source of information about dogs. Our mix of content must satisfy a diverse readership, including knowledgeable dog owners, breed enthusiasts, and average pet owners who simply love their dogs. Estab. 1975. Circ. 107,919. Byline given. Pays on acceptance. Offers 50% kill fee. Publishes ms an average of 6 months after acceptance. Editorial lead time 5 months. Submit seasonal material 6 months in advance. Accepts queries by mail, e-mail. Responds in 6 weeks to queries. Responds in 2 months to mss. Guidelines for #10 SASE or by e-mail.

"We encourage writers to query with fresh ideas about dogs and the diverse roles they play in our lives. Basics regarding canine health, nutrition, obedience and behaviour have been extensively explored in the magazine. A fresh perspective on a basic canine issue, or a query regarding an up-and-coming topic will be more likely to catch our attention."

NONFICTION Needs interview, photo feature, travel. Does not want anything written from the dog's perspective. **Buys less than 10 mss/year.** Send complete ms. Length: 500-1,500 words. **Pays $100.** Sometimes pays expenses of writers on assignment.

PHOTOS Contact: Kelly Caldwell, art director. State availability of or send photos. Identification of subjects, model releases required. Reviews contact sheets, negatives, transparencies, 5×7 prints, GIF/JPEG files. Negotiates payment individually.

COLUMNS Query with or without published clips. **Pays $100+.**

FILLERS Needs anecdotes, facts, short humor. **Buys less than 10 mss/year.** Length: 150-500 words. **Pays $100+.**

DOG SPORTS MAGAZINE

4215 S. Lowell Rd., St. Johns MI 48879. (989)224-7225. Fax: (989)224-6033. E-mail: suggestions@dogsports. com. Website: dogsports.com. **Contact:** Cheryl Carlson, editor. **5% freelance written.** Monthly tabloid covering working dogs. "Dog Sports online magazine is for ALL dog trainers. We focus on the "HOW" of dog training. You will find articles on Police K-9 training, Narcotics detection, Herding, Weight Pull, Tracking, Search and Rescue, and how to increase your dog training Business. We bring you the latest in techniques from the field, actual dog trainers that are out there, working, titling and training. French Ring, Mondio,

Schutzhund, N.A.P.D. PPDA, K-9 Pro Sports all are featured, as well as spotlight articles on breeds, trainers, judges, or events.". Estab. 1979. Circ. 2,000. Byline given. Pays on publication. Publishes ms an average of 1 month after acceptance. Editorial lead time 1 month. Submit seasonal material 1 month in advance. Accepts queries by mail, e-mail. Accepts simultaneous submissions. Sample copy free or online.

"If you have ideas about topics, articles, or areas of interest, please drop us an e-mail and let us know how we can make this online magazine the best training tool you've ever had!"

NONFICTION Needs essays, general interest, how-to, working dogs, humor, interview, technical. **Buys 5 mss/year.** Send complete ms. **Pays $50.**

PHOTOS State availability of photos. Captions, identification of subjects required. Reviews prints. Offers no additional payment for photos accepted with ms.

$$ EQUESTRIAN MAGAZINE

United States Equestrian Federation (USEF), 4047 Iron Works Pkwy, Lexington KY 40511. (859)225-6934. Fax: (859)231-6662. E-mail: bsosby@usef.org. Website: usef.org. **Contact:** Brian Sosby, editor. **10-30% freelance written.** Magazine published 10 times/year covering the equestrian sport. Estab. 1937. Circ. 77,000. Byline given. Pays on publication. Offers 50% kill fee. Editorial lead time 1-5 months. Accepts queries by mail, e-mail, fax, phone. Sample copy and writer's guidelines free.

NONFICTION Needs interview, technical, all equestrian-related. **Buys 20-30 mss/year.** Query with published clips. Length: 500-3,500 words. **Pays $200-500.**

PHOTOS State availability of photos. Captions, identification of subjects, model releases required. Reviews contact sheets. Offers $50-200/photo.

COLUMNS Horses of the Past (famous equines); Horse People (famous horsemen/women), both 500-1,000 words. **Buys 20-30 columns. mss/year.** Query with published clips. **Pays $100.**

$ EQUINE JOURNAL

103 Roxbury St., Keene NH 03431. (603)357-4271. Fax: (603)357-7851. E-mail: editorial@equinejournal.com. Website: equinejournal.com. **Contact:** Kelly Ballou, editor. **90% freelance written.** Monthly tabloid covering horses—all breeds, all disciplines. "The Equine Journal is a monthly, all-breed/discipline regional publication for horse enthusiasts. The purpose of our editorial is to educate, entertain and enable amateurs and professionals alike to stay on top of new developments in the field. Every month, the Equine Journal presents feature articles and columns spanning the length and breadth of horse-related activities and interests from all corners of the country." Estab. 1988. Circ. 26,000. Byline given. Pays on publication. Editorial lead time 4 months. Accepts queries by mail, e-mail, fax, phone. Responds in 2 months to queries. Guidelines available online.

NONFICTION Needs general interest, how-to, interview. **Buys 100 mss/year.** Send complete ms. Length: 1,500-2,200 words.

PHOTOS Send photos. Reviews prints. Pays $10.

COLUMNS Horse Health (health-related topics), 1,200-1,500 words. **Buys 12 mss/year.** Query.

$$ FIDO FRIENDLY MAGAZINE

Fido Friendly, Inc., P.O. Box 160, Marsing ID 83639. E-mail: fieldeditor@fidofriendly.com. Website: fidofriendly.com. **95% freelance written.** Bimonthly magazine covering travel with your dog. "We want articles about all things travel related with your dog." Estab. 2,000. Circ. 44,000. Byline given. Pays on publication. Publishes ms an average of 2 months after acceptance. Editorial lead time 1-3 months. Submit seasonal material 3 months in advance. Accepts queries by e-mail. Accepts simultaneous submissions. Responds in 2 weeks to queries. Responds in 1 month to mss Sample copy for $7. Guidelines free.

NONFICTION Contact: Susan Sims, publisher. Needs essays, general interest, how-to, travel with your dog, humor, inspirational, interview, personal experience, travel. No articles about dog's point of view - dog's voice. **Buys 24 mss/yr. mss/year.** Query with published clips. Length: 600-1,200 words. **Pays 10-20¢ for assigned articles. Pays 10-20¢ for unsolicited articles.**

PHOTOS Contact: Susan Sims. Send photos. Captions, identification of subjects, model releases required. Reviews GIF/JPEG files. Offers no additional payment for photos accepted with ms.

COLUMNS Fido Friendly City (City where dogs have lots of options to enjoy restaurants, dog retail stores, dog parks, sports activity.) **Buys 6 mss/yr. mss/year.** Query with published clips. **Pays 10-20¢/word**

FICTION Contact: Susan Sims. Needs adventure, (dog). Nothing from dog's point of view. **Buys 0 mss/year.** Query. Length: 600-1,200 words. **Pays $10¢-20¢.**

$ $ FIELD TRIAL MAGAZINE

Androscoggin Publishing, Inc., P.O. Box 298, Milan NH 03588. (800)615-8392 fax: 1-603-449-2462. Fax: (603)449-2462. E-mail: fieldtrialmag@gmail.com. Website: fieldtrialmagazine.com. **Contact:** Craig Doherty. **75% freelance written.** Quarterly magazine covering field trials for pointing dogs. "Our readers are knowledgeable sportsmen and women who want interesting and informative articles about their sport." Estab. 1997. Circ. 6,000. Byline given. Pays on publication. Publishes ms an average of 6 months after acceptance. Editorial lead time 3 months. Submit seasonal material 6 months in advance. Accepts queries by mail, e-mail, fax. Accepts simultaneous submissions. Responds in 2 weeks to queries. Responds in 2 months to mss. Sample copy free. Guidelines available online.

NONFICTION Needs book excerpts, essays, general interest, historical, how-to, interview, opinion, personal experience. No hunting articles. **Buys 12-16 mss/year.** Query. Length: 1,000-3,000 words. **Pays $100-300.**

PHOTOS Send photos. Captions, identification of subjects required. Offers no additional payment for photos accepted with ms.

FICTION "Fiction that deals with bird dogs and field trials." **Buys 4 mss/year.** Send complete ms. Length: 1,000-2,500 words. **Pays $100-250.**

$ $ FRESHWATER AND MARINE AQUARIUM

Bowtie, Inc., 3 Burroughs, Irvine CA 92618-2804. (949)855-8822. E-mail: emizer@bowtieinc.com. Website: fishchannel.com. Clay Jackson. **Contact:** Ethan Mizer, senior associate editor. **95% freelance written.** The freshwater and marine aquarium hobby. "Our audience tends to be more advanced fish-and coral-keepers as well as planted tank fans. Writers should have aquarium keeping experience themselves. FAMA covers all aspects of fish and coral husbandry." Estab. 1978. Circ. 14,000. Byline given. Pays on publication. Pays $50 kill fee. Publishes ms 6-8 months after acceptance. 3.5 months editorial lead time. Accepts queries by mail, e-mail. Accepts simultaneous submissions. 3 weeks on queries, 2 months on mss. "If we are interested in a query or ms, we'll e-mail an assignment with guidelines included.".

NONFICTION **Contact:** Ethan Mizer, senior associate editor. Needs general interest, how-to, interview, new product, personal experience, technical, aquarium-related articles. Special issues: Three special issues every year. Past issues have included aquarium lighting, invertebrates, planted tanks, food, etc. "No beginner articles, such as keeping guppies and goldfish. If mid-level to advanced aquarists wouldn't get anything new by reading it, don't send it." Writer should query. 1,500-2,000/words. **Pay $300-400; 20¢/word.**

PHOTOS **Contact:** Ethan Mizer. State availability of photos with submission; send photos. Captions are required. GIF/JPEG files, RAW files, transparencies (35 mm). Digitals must be 300 DPI. If article is on keeping unusual fish, photos should be included.

COLUMNS "All of our columns are assigned and written by established columnists." **Pays $250.**

$ THE GREYHOUND REVIEW

P.O. Box 543, Abilene KS 67410. (785)263-4660. E-mail: nga@ngagreyhounds.com. Website: ngagreyhounds.com. **20% freelance written.** Monthly magazine covering greyhound breeding, training, and racing. Estab. 1911. Circ. 3,500. Byline given. Pays on acceptance. Submit seasonal material 2 months in advance. Responds in 2 weeks to queries. Responds in 1 month to mss. Sample copy for $3. Guidelines free.

NONFICTION Needs how-to, interview, personal experience. Do not submit gambling systems. **Buys 24 mss/year.** Query. Length: 1,000-10,000 words. **Pays $85-150.**

REPRINTS Send photocopy. Pays 100% of amount paid for original article.

PHOTOS State availability. Identification of subjects required. Reviews digital images. Pays $10-50 photo.

$ $ $ THE HORSE

P.O. Box 919003, Lexington KY 40591-9003. (859)278-2361. Fax: (859)276-4450. E-mail: schurch@thehorse.com. Website: thehorse.com. **Contact:** Stephanie Church. **85% freelance written.** Monthly magazine covering equine health, care, management and welfare. *The Horse* is an educational/news magazine geared toward the hands-on horse owner. Estab. 1983. Circ. 55,000. Byline given. Pays on acceptance. Publishes ms an average of 6 months after acceptance. Accepts queries by mail, e-mail. Responds in 3 months to queries. Sample copy for $3.95 or online. Guidelines available online.

🔑 *The Horse* is a monthly magazine devoted to equine health care. The publication focuses on educational topics and news and is geared towards the professional, hands-on horse owner. Writers should submit a resume and samples of their writing before submitting a manuscript, and including an e-mail address will expedite our response to you. Query letters or complete mss will be reviewed after this process. The Horse will not accept unsolicited mss. A byline is given and acceptance for publication includes first rights and online rights unless otherwise agreed upon. *The Horse* prefers "how-to topics," technical topics, and topical interviews. It accepts no first-person experiences except from professionals—this is a technical magazine to inform horse owners. Clips (writing samples) should ideally show an ability to organize technical information to maximize the understanding and education of the reader, as well as a smooth, correct writing style. If you have a specific article topic in mind, check to make sure we have not done an article on the topic recently, and do not already have one assigned on it in the near future. You can check recent issues (by issue or via a topical search) and our calendar of upcoming topics. Articles range from short news items at 250 - 4,000 word cover stories; payments vary depending on length of article. If photos are to be submitted with a submission, please do not send originals. Please see the complete Photography Guidelines."

NONFICTION Needs how-to, technical, topical interviews. No first-person experiences not from professionals; this is a technical magazine to inform horse owners. **Buys 90 mss/year.** Query with published clips. Length: 250-4,000 words. **Pays $60-850.**

PHOTOS Send photos. Captions, identification of subjects required. Reviews transparencies. Offers $35-350.

COLUMNS News Front (news on horse health), 100-500 words; Equinomics (economics of horse ownership); Step by Step (feet and leg care); Nutrition; Reproduction; Back to Basics, all 1,500-2,200 words. **Buys Accepts 50 column articles/year. mss/year.** Query with published clips. **Pays $50-450.**

$$$ HORSE&RIDER

2520 55th St., #210, Boulder CO 80301. E-mail: horseandrider@aimmedia.com. Website: horseandrider.com. **Contact:** Julie Preble, assistant editor. **10% freelance written.** Monthly magazine covering Western horse industry, competition, recreation. "*Horse&Rider*'s mission is to enhance the enjoyment and satisfaction readers derive from horse involvement. We strive to do this by providing the insights, knowledge, and horsemanship skills they need to safely and effectively handle, ride, and appreciate their horses, in and out of the competition arena. We also help them find the time, resources, and energy they need to enjoy their horse to the fullest." Estab. 1961. Circ. 164,000. Byline given. Pays on acceptance. "Very little unsolicited freelance accepted." Publishes ms an average of 1 year after acceptance. Editorial lead time 2 months. Submit seasonal material 6 months in advance. Accepts queries by mail (must be on a cd in a digital format), e-mail (preferred). Responds in 3 months to queries and to mss. Sample copy and writer's guidelines online.

💬 "Online magazine carries original content not found in the print edition."

NONFICTION Needs book excerpts, general interest, how-to, horse training, horsemanship, humor, interview, new product, personal experience, photo feature, travel. **Buys 5-10 mss/year.** Send complete ms. Length: 1,000-3,000 words. **Pay depends on length, use, and quality.**

PHOTOS State availability of or send photos. Captions, identification of subjects, model releases required. Negotiates payment individually.

$ HORSE CONNECTION

Horse Connection, LLC, 333 Perry St., Suite 309, Castle Rock CO 80104. (303)663-1300. Fax: (303)663-1331. E-mail: gyoung@horseconnection.com. Website: horseconnection.com. **Contact:** Geoff Young, editor, art director. **90% freelance written.** Magazine published 12 times/year covering horse owners and riders. Our readers are horse owners and riders. They specialize in English riding. We primarily focus on show jumping and hunters, dressage, and three-day events, with additional coverage of driving, polo, and endurance. Estab. 1995. Circ. 25,000. Byline given. Pays on publication. Publishes ms an average of 1 month after acceptance. Editorial lead time 3 months. Submit seasonal material 3 months in advance. Accepts queries by e-mail. Responds in 1 month to queries. Sample copy for $3.50 or online. Guidelines for #10 SASE or online.

NONFICTION Needs humor, interview, personal experience, event reports. No general interest stories about horses. Nothing negative. No western, racing, or breed specific articles. No my first pony stories. **Buys 30-50 mss/year.** Query with published clips. Length: 500-1,000 words. **Pays $25 for assigned articles. Pays $75 for unsolicited articles.** Sometimes pays expenses of writers on assignment.
PHOTOS State availability. Negotiates payment individually.

$$ HORSE ILLUSTRATED

BowTie, Inc., P.O. Box 8237, Lexington KY 40533. (859)260-9800. Fax: (859)260-1154. E-mail: horseillustrated@bowtieinc.com. Website: horseillustrated.com. **Contact:** Elizabeth Moyer, editor. **90% freelance written. Prefers to work with published/established writers but will work with new/unpublished writers.** Monthly magazine covering all aspects of horse ownership. "Our readers are adults, mostly women, between the ages of 18 and 40; stories should be geared to that age group and reflect responsible horse care." Estab. 1976. Circ. 160,660. Byline given. Pays on publication. Publishes ms an average of 8 months after acceptance. Submit seasonal material 6 months in advance. Accepts queries by mail. Responds in 3 months to queries. Guidelines for #10 SASE and are available online at horsechannel.com/horse-magazines/horse-illustrated/submission-guidelines.aspx.
NONFICTION Needs general interest, how-to, horse care, training, veterinary care, inspirational, photo feature. "No little girl horse stories, cowboy and Indian stories or anything not *directly* relating to horses." **Buys 20 mss/year.** Query or send complete ms. Length: 1,000-2,000 words. **Pays $200-400.**
PHOTOS Send high-res digital images on a CD with thumbnails.

$$ JUST LABS

Village Press, 2779 Aero Park Dr., Traverse City MI 49686. (231)946-3712; (800)447-7367. E-mail: jake@villagepress.com; sallystevens@villagepress.com. Website: justlabsmagazine.com. **Contact:** Jason Smith, editor. **50% freelance written**. Bimonthly magazine. "*Just Labs* is targeted toward the family Labrador Retriever, and all of our articles help people learn about, live with, train, take care of, and enjoy their dogs. We do not look for articles that pull at the heart strings (those are usually staff-written), but rather we look for articles that teach, inform, and entertain." Estab. 2001. Circ. 20,000. Byline given. Pays on publication. Offers 40% kill fee. Publishes ms an average of 6 months after acceptance. Editorial lead time 6 months. Submit seasonal material 6-8 months in advance. Accepts queries by mail. Responds in 4-6 weeks to queries. Responds in 2 months to mss. Guidelines for #10 SASE.
NONFICTION Needs essays, how-to, (train, health, lifestyle), humor, inspirational, interview, photo feature, technical, travel. "We don't want tributes to dogs that have passed on. This is a privilege we reserve for our subscribers." **Buys 30 mss/year mss/year.** Query. Length: 1,000-1,800 words. **Pays $250-400 for assigned articles. Pays $250-400 for unsolicited articles.**
PHOTOS Send photos. Captions required. Reviews contact sheets, transparencies, prints, GIF/JPEG files. Offers no additional payment for photos accepted with ms.

$ MINIATURE DONKEY TALK

Miniature Donkey Talk, Inc., PO Box 982, Cripple Creek CO 80813. (719)789-2904. E-mail: mike@donkeytalk.info. Website: miniaturedonkey.net; web-donkeys.com. **Contact:** Mike Gross. **65% freelance written**. Quarterly magazine covering donkeys, with articles on healthcare, promotion, and management of donkeys for owners, breeders, or donkey lovers. Estab. 1987. Circ. 4,925. Byline given. Pays on acceptance. Publishes ms an average of 4 months after acceptance. Editorial lead time 2 months. Submit seasonal material 3 months in advance. Accepts queries by mail, e-mail, fax. Responds in 2 weeks to queries. Responds in 1 month to mss. Sample copy for $5. Guidelines free.
NONFICTION Needs book excerpts, humor, interview, personal experience. **Buys 6 mss/year.** Query with published clips. Length: 700-5,000 words. **Pays $25-150.**
PHOTOS State availability. Identification of subjects required. Reviews 3×5 prints. Offers no additional payment for photos accepted with ms.
COLUMNS Humor, 2,000 words; Healthcare, 2,000-5,000 words; Management, 2,000 words. **Buys 50 mss/year.** Query. **Pays $25-100.**

$$ MUSHING.COM MAGAZINE

PO Box 1195, Willow AK 99688. (907)495-2468. E-mail: editor@mushing.com. Website: mushing.com. **Contact:** Greg Sellentin, Managing Editor. Bimonthly magazine covering "all aspects of the growing sports of dogsledding, skijoring, carting, dog packing, and weight pulling. *Mushing* promotes responsible dog care through feature articles and updates on working animal health care, safety, nutrition, and training." Estab. 1987. Circ. 10,000. Byline given. Pays within 3 months of publication. Publishes ms an average of 4 months after acceptance. Submit seasonal material 4 months in advance. Accepts queries by mail, e-mail, fax, phone. Responds in 8 months to queries. Sample copy for $5 ($6 US to Canada). Guidelines available online.

NONFICTION Needs historical, how-to. Special issues: Iditarod and Long-Distance Racing (January/February); Ski or Sprint Racing (March/April); Health and Nutrition (May/June); Musher and Dog Profiles, Summer Activities (July/August); Equipment, Fall Training (September/October); Races and Places (November/December). Query with or without published clips. "We prefer detailed queries but also consider unsolicited manuscripts. Please make proposals informative yet to the point. Spell out your qualifications for handling the topic. We like to see clips of previously published material but are eager to work with new and unpublished authors, too." Considers complete ms with SASE. Length: 1,000-2,500 words. **Pays $50-250.** Sometimes pays expenses of writers on assignment.

PHOTOS "We look for good quality color for covers and specials." Send photos. Captions, identification of subjects. Reviews digital images only. Pays $20-165/photo.

COLUMNS Query with or without published clips or send complete ms.

FILLERS Needs anecdotes, facts, newsbreaks, short humor, cartoons, puzzles. Length: 100-250 words. **Pays $20-35.**

PAINT HORSE JOURNAL

American Paint Horse Association, P.O. Box 961023, Fort Worth TX 76161-0023. (817)834-2742. E-mail: tonyag@apha.com; avasquez@apha.com. Website: painthorsejournal.com. **10% freelance written. Works with a small number of new/unpublished writers each year.** Monthly magazine for people who raise, breed and show Paint Horses. Estab. 1966. Circ. 12,000. Byline given. Pays on acceptance. Offers negotiable kill fee. Submit seasonal material 3 months in advance. Accepts queries by mail, e-mail, fax. Sample copy for $4.50. Guidelines available online.

NONFICTION Needs general interest, personality pieces on well-known owners of Paints, historical,

Paint Horses in the past—particular horses and the breed in general, how-to, train and show horses, photo feature, Paint Horses. **Buys 4-5 mss/year.** Query. Length: 1,000-2,000 words. **Pays $100-500.**

PHOTOS Photos must illustrate article and must include registered Paint Horses. Send photos. Captions required. Reviews 35mm or larger transparencies, 3×5 or larger color glossy prints, digital images on CD or DVD. Offers no additional payment for photos accepted with accompanying ms.

PET NEW ZEALAND

The Fusion Group, LTD, P.O. Box 37 356, Parnell Auckland 1151 New Zealand. (64)(9)336-1188. Fax: (64)(9)373-5647. E-mail: editorial@petmag.co.nz. Website: petmag.co.nz. Quarterly magazine covering topics for pet owners and animal lovers. "*Pet New Zealand* promotes public awareness of pet issues, educates through practical advice, features heart-warming stories and pet products, and provides expert advice."

Query before submitting.

REPTILES

BowTie, Inc., P.O. Box 6050, Mission Viejo CA 92690. (949)855-8822. E-mail: reptiles@bowtieinc.com. Website: reptilesmagazine.com. **20% freelance written.** Monthly magazine covering reptiles and amphibians. *Reptiles* covers "a wide range of topics relating to reptiles and amphibians, including breeding, captive care, field herping, etc." Estab. 1992. Byline given. Pays on publication. Offers 20% kill fee. Publishes ms an average of 6-8 months after acceptance. Accepts queries by mail, e-mail. Responds in 1 month to queries. Responds in 1-2 months to mss. Sample copy available online. Guidelines available online.

"Submissions from freelance writers are welcome, though we ask that you query first at the e-mail address listed above. When pitching ideas, keep in mind that we do prefer that animal articles, whenever possible, be written by people who have experience keeping and breeding the animals."

NONFICTION Needs general interest, historical, how-to, interview, personal experience, photo feature, travel. **Buys 10 mss/year.** Query. Length: 1,000-2,000 words. **Pays $250-500.**

ROCKY MOUNTAIN RIDER MAGAZINE

P.O. Box 995, Hamilton MT 59840. (406)363-4085. E-mail: editor@rockymountainrider.com; info@rockymountainrider.com. Website: rockymountainrider. com. **Contact:** Natalie Riehl, editor. **90% freelance written**. Monthly regional all-breed magazine for horse owners and enthusiasts. Idaho, Montana, Nevada, Oregon, Utah, Washington, Wyoming. Estab. 1993. Circ. 14,000. Byline given. Pays on publication. Publishes ms an average of 6 months after acceptance. Submit seasonal material 6 months in advance. Accepts queries by mail, e-mail. Accepts simultaneous submissions. Responds in 2 months to queries. Responds in 3 months to mss. Sample copy for $3. Guidelines for #10 SASE.

O—📌 "RMR is looking for positive, human interest stories that appeal to an audience of horse people, ranchers, seniors, and folks who live in the West. Pieces may include profiles of unusual people or animals, history, humor, anecdotes, coverage of regional events and new products. We occasionally excerpt books by regional authors. We aren't looking for many "how to" or training articles, and are not currently looking at any fiction. We sometimes run cowboy poetry, and we always need clean jokes and short humorous pieces with a western theme. Feature articles generally run between 500-2,000 words in length. Fillers should run about 100-500 words. Poetry should be no more than 4-5 stanzas. Please submit articles typed and double-spaced on 8½ × 11 paper. We need photos of Western scenes and people. Photos accompanying articles may be either color or black-and-white. We also need humorous and action shots from various events in the northern Rockies. Send only high-resolution digital photos or physical photos (no slides, contact sheets or negatives)."

NONFICTION Needs articles on horse care, horse health issues, anecdotes, historical, humor, personal experience. **Buys 50 mss/year.** Send complete ms. Length: 500-2,000 words. **Pays $35 per 1,000 words approx.**

PHOTOS Send photos. Captions, identification of subjects required. Reviews 3×5 prints, e-mail digital photos. Pays $5/photo.

POETRY Contact: Natalie Riehl, editor. Needs light verse, traditional. Buys 25 poems/year. Submit maximum 10 poems. Length: 6-36 lines. **Pays $10/poem.**

FILLERS Needs anecdotes, facts, gags, short humor. Length: 200-750 words. **Pays $15-30.**

⊕⊕ TROPICAL FISH HOBBYIST MAGAZINE

TFH Publications, Inc., One TFH Plaza, Neptune City NJ 07753. E-mail: associateeditor@tfh.com. Website: tfhmagazine.com. **Contact:** Associate Editor. **90% freelance written**. Monthly magazine covering tropical fish. Manuscripts should be submitted as e-mail attachments. Estab. 1952. Circ. 35,000. Byline given. Pays on acceptance. Editorial lead time 3 months. Submit seasonal material 6 months in advance. Accepts queries by e-mail. Responds immediately on electronic queries. Guidelines available online.

NONFICTION Buys 100-150 mss/year. Manuscripts should be submitted as e-mail attachments to associateeditor@tfh.com. Most articles are between 10,000 and 20,000 characters-with-spaces long. Please break up the text using subheads to categorize topics. We prefer articles that are submitted with photos. Do not insert photos into the text. Photos must be submitted separately. For more information regarding photos, please visit our Photographer's Guidelines page." Length: 10,000 - 20,000 characters-with-spaces **Pays $100-250.**

PHOTOS State availability. Identification of subjects, model releases required. Reviews prints, slides, high-resolution digital images. Negotiates payment individually.

⊕⊕ USDF CONNECTION

United States Dressage Federation, 4051 Iron Works Parkway, Lexington KY 40511. E-mail: usdressage@usdf.org. Website: usdf.org. **40% freelance written**. Monthly magazine covering dressage (an equestrian sport). All material must relate to the sport of dressage in the US. Estab. 2000. Circ. 35,000. Byline given. Pays on acceptance. Offers 50% kill fee. Publishes ms an average of 3 months after acceptance. Editorial lead time 3 months. Submit seasonal material 6 months in advance. Accepts queries by mail, e-mail. Responds in 1 month to queries. Responds in 1-2 months to mss. Sample copy for $5. Guidelines available online.

NONFICTION Needs book excerpts, essays, how-to, interview, opinion, personal experience. Does not want general interest equine material or stories that lack a US dressage angle. **Buys 40 mss/year.** Query. Length: 650-3,000 words. **Pays $100-500 for assigned articles. Pays $100-300 for unsolicited articles.** Sometimes pays expenses of writers on assignment.

PHOTOS State availability. Captions, identification of subjects required. Reviews prints, GIF/JPEG files. Negotiates payment individually.

COLUMNS Amateur Hour (profiles of adult amateur USDF members), 1,200-1,500 words; Under 21 (profiles of young USDF members), 1,200-1,500 words; Veterinary Connection (dressage-related horse health), 1,500-2,500 words; Mind-Body-Spirit Connection (rider health/fitness, sport psychology), 1,500-2,500 words. **Buys 24 mss/year.** Query with published clips. **Pays $150-400.**

ART AND ARCHITECTURE

⊖⊕ AMERICAN INDIAN ART MAGAZINE

American Indian Art, Inc., 7314 E. Osborn Dr., Scottsdale AZ 85251. (480)994-5445. Fax: (480)945-9533. E-mail: info@aiamagazine.com. E-mail: editorial@aiamagazine.com. Website: aiamagazine.com. **97% freelance written. Works with many new/unpublished writers/year.** Quarterly magazine covering Native American art, historic and contemporary, including new research on any aspect of Native American art north of the US-Mexico border. Estab. 1975. Circ. 22,000. Byline given. Pays on publication. Publishes ms an average of 6 months after acceptance. Accepts queries by e-mail, online submission form. Responds in 6 weeks to queries. Responds in 3 months to mss. Guidelines for #10 SASE or online.

NONFICTION No previously published work or personal interviews with artists. **Buys 12-18 mss/year.** Query. Prefers e-mail submissions as an attachment or on CD (prefers Microsoft Word) Length: 6,000-7,000 words. **Pays $150-300.**

PHOTOS An article usually requires 8-15 photographs. Fee schedules and reimbursable expenses are decided upon by the magazine and the author.

⊖⊕⊕ AMERICANSTYLE MAGAZINE

The Rosen Group, 3000 Chestnut Ave., Suite 304, Baltimore MD 21211. (410)889-3093. Fax: (410)243-7089. E-mail: hoped@rosengrp.com. Website: americanstyle.com. **70% freelance written.** Bimonthly magazine covering arts, crafts, travel, and interior design. "*AmericanStyle* is a full-color lifestyle publication for people who love art. Our mandate is to nurture collectors with information that will increase their passion for contemporary art and craft and the artists who create it. *AmericanStyle*'s primary audience is contemporary craft collectors and enthusiasts. Readers are college-educated, age 35+, high-income earners with the financial means to collect art and craft, and to travel to national art and craft events in pursuit of their passions." Estab. 1994. Circ. 60,000. Pays on publication. Publishes ms an average of 9-12 months after acceptance. Editorial lead time 9-12 months. Submit seasonal material at least 1 year in advance. Accepts queries by mail, e-mail. Sample copy for $3. Guidelines available online.

NONFICTION E-mailed submissions are to be followed by hard copy submissions. Length: 600-800 words. **Pays $400-800.** Sometimes pays expenses of writers on assignment.

PHOTOS Send photos. Captions required. Reviews oversized transparencies, 35mm slides, low resolution e-images. Negotiates payment individually.

COLUMNS Portfolio (profiles of emerging and established artists); Arts Tour; Arts Walk; Origins; One on One, all appx. 600 words. Query with published clips. **Pays $400-600.**

⊖⊕ THE ARTIST'S MAGAZINE

F+W Media, Inc., 4700 E. Galbraith Rd., Cincinnati OH 45236. (513)531-2690, ext. 1489. Fax: (513)891-7153. Website: artistsmagazine.com. **Contact:** Maureen Bloomfield, editor-in-chief. **80% freelance written.** Magazine published 10 times/year covering primarily two-dimensional art for working artists. "Ours is a highly visual approach to teaching serious amateur and professional artists techniques that will help them improve their skills and market their work. The style should be crisp and immediately engaging, written in a voice that speaks directly to artists." Circ. 135,000. Bionote given for feature material. Pays on publication. Offers 8% kill fee. Publishes ms an average of 6 months-1 year after acceptance. Responds in 6 months to queries Sample copy for $5.99. Guidelines available online.

⊙ Sponsors 3 annual contests. Send SASE for more information.

NONFICTION No unillustrated articles. **Buys 60 mss/year.** Length: 500-1,200 words. **Pays $300-500 and up.**

PHOTOS Images of artwork must be in the form of 35mm slides, larger transparencies, or high-quality digital files. Full captions must accompany these.

⊖⊕ ART PAPERS

Atlanta Art Papers, Inc., P.O. Box 5748, Atlanta GA 31107. (404)588-1837. Fax: (404)588-1836. E-mail: editor@artpapers.org. Website: artpapers.org. **Contact:** Sylvie Fortin, editor-in-chief. **95% freelance written.** Bimonthly magazine covering contemporary art and artists. *Art Papers*, about regional and national contemporary art and artists, features a variety of perspectives on current art concerns. Each issue presents topical articles, interviews, reviews from across the US, and an extensive and informative artists' classified listings section. Our writers and the artists they cover represent the scope and diversity of the country's art scene. Estab. 1977. Circ. 12,000. Byline given. Pays on publication. Publishes ms an average of 3 months after acceptance. Editorial lead time 2 months. Submit seasonal material 2 months in advance.

NONFICTION Buys 240 mss/year. Pays $60-325. **unsolicited articles are on spec for unsolicited articles.**

PHOTOS Send photos. Identification of subjects required. Reviews color slides, b&w prints. Offers no additional payment for photos accepted with ms.

COLUMNS Current art concerns and news. **Buys 8-10 mss/year.** Query. **Pays $100-175.**

🌙 AUSTRALIAN ART COLLECTOR

Gadfly Media, Level 1, 579 Harris St., Ultimo, Sydney NSW 2007 Australia. (61)02 8204 1000. Fax: (61)(2)9281-7529. E-mail: josullivan@artcollector. net.au. Website: artcollector.net.au. **Contact:** Jane O'Sullivan. Quarterly magazine covering Australian art collecting. *Australian Art Collector* is the only Australian publication targeted specifically at people who buy art.

NONFICTION Needs expose, general interest, interview. Query.

🌙🌓🌓🌓🌓 AZURE DESIGN, ARCHITECTURE AND ART

460 Richmond St. W, Suite 601, Toronto ON M5V 1Y1 Canada. (416)203-9674. Fax: (416)203-9842. E-mail: editorial@azuremag.com; azure@azureonline.com. Website: azuremagazine.com. **75% freelance written.** Magazine covering design and architecture. Estab. 1985. Circ. 20,000. Pays on publication. Offers variable kill fee. Publishes ms an average of 1 month after acceptance. Editorial lead time up to 45 days. Responds in 6 weeks to queries.

NONFICTION Buys 25-30 mss/year. Length: 350-2,000 words. **Pays $1/word (Canadian).**

COLUMNS Trailer (essay/photo on something from the built environment); and Forms & Functions (coming exhibitions, happenings in world of design),

both 300-350 words. **Buys 30 mss/year.** Query. **Pays $1/word (Canadian).**

🌙🌓🌓 C

C The Visual Arts Foundation, P.O. Box 5, Station B, Toronto ON M5T 2T2 Canada. (416)539-9495. Fax: (416)539-9903. E-mail: amishmorrell@cmagazine.com. Website: cmagazine.com. **Contact:** Amish Morrell, editor. **80% freelance written.** Quarterly magazine covering international contemporary art. *C* provides a vital and vibrant forum for the presentation of contemporary art and the discussion of issues surrounding art in our culture, including feature articles, reviews and reports, as well as original artists' projects. Estab. 1983. Circ. 7,000. Byline given. Pays on publication. Offers kill fee. Offers kill fee Publishes ms an average of 4 months after acceptance. Editorial lead time 3 months. Accepts queries by mail, e-mail, fax. Accepts simultaneous submissions. Responds in 6 weeks to queries. Responds in 4 months to mss. Sample copy for $10 (US). Guidelines for #10 SASE.

NONFICTION Needs essays, general interest, opinion, personal experience. **Buys 50 mss/year.** Length: 1,000-3,000 words. **Pays $150-500 (Canadian), $105-350 (US).**

PHOTOS State availability of or send photos. Captions required. Reviews 35mm transparencies or 8×10 prints. Offers no additional payment for photos accepted with ms.

COLUMNS Reviews (review of art exhibitions), 500 words. **Buys 30 mss/year.** Query. **Pays $125 (Canadian)**

🌓🌓 DIRECT ART MAGAZINE

Slow Art Productions, 123 Warren St., Hudson NY 12534. E-mail: slowart@aol.com; directartmag@aol. com. Website: slowart.com. **75% freelance written.** Semiannual fine art magazine covering alternative, anti-establishment, left-leaning fine art. Estab. 1998. Circ. 10,000. Byline sometimes given. Pays on acceptance. Editorial lead time 2 months. Submit seasonal material 3 months in advance. Accepts queries by mail, e-mail. Accepts simultaneous submissions. Responds in 2 weeks to queries. Responds in 1 month to mss. Sample copy for sae with 9×12 envelope and 10 First-Class stamps. Guidelines for #10 SASE.

NONFICTION Needs essays, exposè, historical, how-to, humor, inspirational, interview, opinion, personal experience, photo feature, technical. **Buys 4-6 mss/**

year. Query with published clips. Length: 1,000-3,000 words. **Pays $100-500.**

PHOTOS State availability of or send photos. Reviews 35mm slide transparencies, digital files on CD (TIF format). Negotiates payment individually.

COLUMNS Query with published clips. **Pays $100-500.**

☼☻☯ ESPACE

Le Centre de Diffusion 3D, 4888 rue Saint-Denis, Montreal QC H2J 2L6 Canada. (514)844-9858. Fax: (514)844-3661. E-mail: espace@espace-sculpture. com. Website: espace-sculpture.com. **Contact:** Serge Fisette, editor. **95% freelance written.** Quarterly magazine covering sculpture events. Estab. 1987. Circ. 1,400. Byline given. Pays on publication. Publishes ms an average of 3 months after acceptance. Editorial lead time 5 months. Submit seasonal material 3 months in advance. Accepts queries by mail. Accepts simultaneous submissions. Sample copy free.

⟒— Canada's only sculpture publication, *Espace* represents a critical tool for the understanding of contemporary sculpture through analysis and reflection. Published 4 times a year, in English and French, *Espace* features interviews, in-depth articles, and special issues related to various aspects of three dimensionality. Foreign contributors guarantee an international perspective and diffusion. Deadlines to submit an article of 1,000 words/max are: March 5th, June 5th, September 5th and December 5th.

NONFICTION Needs essays, exposè. **Buys 60 mss/ year.** Query. Length: 1,000 words. **Pays $65/page and a copy of the magazine.**

PHOTOS Send photos. Reviews transparencies, prints. Offers no additional payment for photos accepted with ms.

☯☯☯☯ METROPOLIS

Bellerophon Publications, 61 W. 23rd St., 4th Floor, New York NY 10010. (212)627-9977. Fax: (212)627-9988. E-mail: edit@metropolismag.com. Website: metropolismag.com. **Contact:** Belinda Lanks, managing editor. **80% freelance written.** Monthly magazine (combined issue July/August) for consumers interested in architecture and design. "*Metropolis* examines contemporary life through design—architecture, interior design, product design, graphic design, crafts, planning, and preservation. Subjects range from the sprawling urban environment to intimate living spaces to small objects of everyday use. In looking for why design happens in a certain way, Metropolis explores the economic, environmental, social, cultural, political, and technological context. With its innovative graphic presentation and its provocative voice, *Metropolis* shows how richly designed our world can be." Estab. 1981. Circ. 45,000. Byline given. Pays 60-90 days after acceptance. Publishes ms an average of 3 months after acceptance. Submit seasonal material 3 months in advance. Accepts queries by mail, e-mail, fax. Responds in 8 months to queries. Sample copy for $7. Guidelines available online.

NONFICTION Contact: Martin Pedersen, executive editor. Needs essays, design, architecture, urban planning issues and ideas, interview, of multi-disciplinary designers/architects. No profiles on individual architectural practices, information from public relations firms, or fine arts. **Buys 30 mss/year.** Send query letters, not complete manuscripts, describing your idea and why it would be good for our magazine. Be concise, specific, and clear. Also, please include clips and a resume. The ideal Metropolis story is based on strong reporting skills and includes an examination of current critical issues. A design firm's newest work isn't a story, but the issues that their work brings to light might be. We do not cover conferences or seminars. Please send these announcements to the general magazine address or e-mail. Send query letters for potential articles for MetropolisMag.com, the online home of *Metropolis* Magazine, to edit@metropolismag.com. The same guidelines. Length: 1,500-4,000 words. **Pays $1,500-4,000.**

PHOTOS Captions required. Reviews contact sheets, 35mm or 4 x 5 transparencies, 8 x 10 b&w prints. Payment offered for certain photos.

COLUMNS The Metropolis Observed (architecture, design, and city planning news features), 100-1,200 words, **pays $100-1,200;** Perspective (opinion or personal observation of architecture and design), 1,200 words, **pays $1,200;** Enterprise (the business/ development of architecture and design), 1,500 words, **pays $1,500;** In Review (architecture and book review essays), 1,500 words, **pays $1,500.** Direct queries to Belinda Lanks, managing editor. **Buys 40 mss/year.** Query with published clips.

☼☯☯ MIX

Parallelogramme Artist-Run Culture and Publishing, Inc., 401 Richmond St. West, Suite 446, Toronto

ON M5V 3A8 Canada. (416)506-1012. E-mail: editor@mixmagazine.com. Website: mixmagazine.com. **95% freelance written**. Quarterly magazine covering Artist-Run gallery activities. *Mix* represents and investigates contemporary artistic practices and issues, especially in the progressive Canadian artist-run scene. Estab. 1975. Circ. 3,500. Byline given. Pays on publication. Offers 40% kill fee. Publishes ms an average of 6 months after acceptance. Editorial lead time 6 months. Submit seasonal material 4 months in advance. Accepts queries by mail, e-mail, fax. Responds in 2 months to queries. Responds in 3 months to mss. Sample copy for $6.95, 8½×10¼ SAE and 6 first-class stamps. Guidelines available online.

NONFICTION Needs essays, interview. **Buys 12-20 mss/year.** Query with published clips. Length: 750-3,500 words. **Pays $100-450.**

REPRINTS Send photocopy of article and information about when and where the article previously appeared.

PHOTOS State availability. Captions, identification of subjects required.

COLUMNS Features, 1,000-3,000 words; Art Reviews, 500 words. Query with published clips. **Pays $100-450.**

💲💲 MODERNISM MAGAZINE

199 George St., Lambertville NJ 08530. (609)397-4104. Fax: (609)397-4409. E-mail: andrea@modernismmagazine.com. Website: modernismmagazine.com. **Contact:** Andrea Truppin, editor-in-chief. **70% freelance written**. Quarterly magazine covering 20th century design, architecture and decorative arts. "We are interested in design, architecture and decorative arts and the people who created them. Our coverage begins in the 1920s with Art Deco and related movements, and ends with 1980s Post-Modernism, leaving contemporary design to other magazines." Estab. 1998. Circ. 35,000. Byline given. Pays on publication. Offers 25% kill fee. Publishes ms an average of 4 months after acceptance. Editorial lead time 6 months. Submit seasonal material 6 months in advance. Accepts queries by mail, e-mail. Accepts simultaneous submissions. Responds in 1 month to queries. Sample copy for $6.95. Guidelines free.

NONFICTION Needs book excerpts, essays, historical, interview, new product, photo feature. No first-person. **Buys 20 mss/year.** "To propose an article, send an e-mail or letter to Andrea Truppin describing your subject matter, angle and illustration

material. Please include a resume and two samples of previously published writing, as well as a sample of unpublished writing. It helps to include images, but for the initial query, these can be low resolution digital files or photocopies. Proposals are submitted on a speculative basis." Length: 1,000-2,500 words. **Pays $300-600.**

REPRINTS Accepts previously published submissions.

PHOTOS State availability of or send photos. Captions, identification of subjects required. Reviews contact sheets, transparencies, prints. Negotiates payment individually.

💲💲 THE MAGAZINE ANTIQUES

Brant Publications, 575 Broadway, New York NY 10012. (212)941-2800. Fax: (212)941-2819. E-mail: tmaedit@brantpub.com (JavaScript required to view). Website: themagazineantiques.com. **Contact:** Editorial. **75% freelance written**. Bimonthly magazine. Articles should present new information in a scholarly format (with footnotes) on the fine and decorative arts, architecture, historic preservation, and landscape architecture. Estab. 1922. Circ. 61,754. Byline given. Pays on publication. Publishes ms an average of 6 months after acceptance. Editorial lead time 6 months. Submit seasonal material 6 months in advance. Responds in 3 weeks to queries. Responds in 6 months to mss. Sample copy for $10.50 for back issue; $5 for current issue. Back Issues / Single Copies - jbrentan@brantpub.com.

NONFICTION Needs historical, scholarly. **Buys 50 mss/year.** "For submission guidelines and questions about our articles, please contact the editorial department at tmaedit@brantpub.com, you need JavaScript enabled to view it. For general inquiries, please call 212.941.2800." Length: 2,850-3,500 words. **Pays $250-500.** Sometimes pays expenses of writers on assignment.

PHOTOS State availability. Captions, identification of subjects required. Reviews contact sheets, negatives, transparencies, prints.

ASSOCIATIONS

💲💲💲💲 AAA LIVING

Pace Communications, 1301 Carolina St., Greensboro NC 27401. Fax: (336)383-8272. E-mail: martha.leonard@paceco.com. Website: aaa.com/aaaliving.

Contact: Martha Leonard. **70% freelance written.** Published 4 times a year/print; 6 times a year/digital. "AAA Living magazine, published for the Auto Club Group of Dearborn, Michigan, is for members of AAA clubs in 8 Midwest states (IL, N. IN, IA, MI, MN, NE, ND, & WI). Our magazine features lifestyle & travel articles about each state and the region, written by knowledgeable resident writers, as well as coverage of affordable, accessible travel getaways nationally & internationally & information about exclusive AAA products & services." Estab. 1917. Circ. 2.5 million. Byline givenmfor feature articles. Pays on acceptance. Offers 10% kill fee. Publishes ms an average of 3 months after acceptance. Editorial lead time 6 months. Submit seasonal material 6 months in advance. Accepts queries by mail, e-mail. Responds in 6 months to mss. Samples available online at aaa.com/aaaliving. Guidelines are not available online.

NONFICTION Needs travel. Query with published clips. Length: 150-1,600 words. **Pays $1/word for assigned articles.** Sometimes pays expenses of writers on assignment.

PHOTOS Send photos. Captions, identification of subjects required. Reviews GIF/JPEG files. Negotiates payment individually.

💲💲 ACTION

United Spinal Association, 75-20 Astoria Blvd., Jackson Heights NY 11370-1177. (718)803-3782, ext. 279. E-mail: action@unitedspinal.org. Website: unitedspinal.org/publications/action. **Contact:** Chris Pierson, managing editor. **75% freelance written.** Bimonthly magazine covering living with spinal cord injury. Estab. 1946. Circ. 12,000. Byline given. Pays on publication. Publishes ms an average of 2-3 months after acceptance. Accepts queries by e-mail. Sample copy for sae. Guidelines for sae.

> 🖍 "The monthly news magazine of the United Spinal Association is a benefit to members of the organization: people with spinal cord injury or dysfunction, as well as caregivers, parents and some spinal cord injury/dysfunction professionals. All articles should reflect this common interest of the audience. Assume that your audience is better educated in the subject of spinal cord medicine than average, but be careful not to be too technical.Within these seemingly narrow confines, however, a wide variety of subjects are possible. Articles that feature members or programs of United Spinal are preferred, but any article that deals with issues of living with SCI will be considered."

NONFICTION Needs essays, general interest, how-to, humor, interview, new product, personal experience, photo feature, travel, medical research. Does not want articles that treat disabilities as an affliction or cause for pity, or that show the writer does not get that people with disabilities are people like anyone else. **Buys 36 mss/year.** Query. "The editor prefers all submissions for Action to be in electronic form. We edit with MSWord and would appreciate writers to submit their articles or columns in Word or similar format, preferably as an attachment to an e-mail (sent to action@unitedspinal.org). Cutting and pasting your document into the e-mail message area is also acceptable. Electronic submissions do not have to be accompanied by hard copy. If you are sending your submission as hard copy, you must let the editor know ahead of time. Hard copy submissions will be accepted only in the event that a writer whose query has been approved has no other means of writing or submitting an article." Length: 1,000-1,800 words. **Pays $400.**

PHOTOS Send photos. Identification of subjects required. Reviews GIF/JPEG files. Offers no additional payment for photos accepted with ms.

COLUMNS The Observatory (personal essays on subjects related to disability), 750 words. **Buys 60 mss/year.** Query with published clips. **Pays $200.**

💲💲💲💲 AMERICAN EDUCATOR

American Federation of Teachers, 555 New Jersey Ave. N.W., Washington DC 20001. E-mail: amered@aft.org. Website: aft.org/newspubs/periodicals/ae/index.cfm. **Contact:** Lisa Hansel. **50% freelance written.** Quarterly magazine covering education, condition of children, and labor issues. *American Educator*, the quaterly magazine of the American Federation of Teachers, reaches over 800,000 public school teachers, higher education faculty, and education researchers and policymakers. The magazine concentrates on significant ideas and practices in education, civics, and the condition of children in America and around the world. Estab. 1977. Circ. 850,000. Byline given. Pays on publication. Offers 50% kill fee. Publishes ms an average of 2-6 months after acceptance. Editorial lead time 1 year. Submit seasonal material 6 months in advance. Accepts queries by mail, e-mail. Accepts simultaneous submissions. Responds in 2 months to queries. Responds in 6 months to mss. Sample copy available online. Guidelines available online.

○ We prefer queries to manuscripts. When sending a manuscript, please keep at least one copy of your article on file, as we cannot be responsible for unsolicited manuscripts. Be sure to include your contact information in the event we need to reach you. Payment varies according to length and topic. The minimum payment for an article is $300.

NONFICTION Needs book excerpts, essays, historical, interview, discussions of educational research. No pieces that are not supportive of the public schools. **Buys 8 mss/year.** Query with published clips. Length: 1,000-7,000 words. **Pays $750-3,000 for assigned articles. Pays $300-1,000 for unsolicited articles.** Pays expenses of writers on assignment.

PHOTOS State availability. Captions, identification of subjects, model releases required. Reviews contact sheets, negatives, transparencies, 8×10 prints, GIF/JPEG files. Negotiates payment individually.

❸❸ DAC NEWS

Detroit Athletic Club, 241 Madison Ave., Detroit MI 48226. (313)442-1034. Fax: (313)442-1047. E-mail: kenv@thedac.com. Website: thedac.com. **20% freelance written.** Magazine published 10 times/year. *DAC News* is the magazine for Detroit Athletic Club members. It covers club news and events, plus general interest features. Estab. 1916. Circ. 5,000. Byline given. Pays on publication. Publishes ms an average of 3 months after acceptance. Editorial lead time 3 months. Submit seasonal material 3 months in advance. Accepts queries by mail, phone. Responds in 1 month to queries. Sample copy free.

NONFICTION Needs general interest, historical, photo feature. No politics or social issues—this is an entertainment magazine. We do not acccept unsolicited manuscripts or queries for travel articles. **Buys 2-3 mss/year.** Length: 1,000-2,000 words. **Pays $100-500.** Sometimes pays expenses of writers on assignment.

PHOTOS Illustrations only. State availability. Captions, identification of subjects, model releases required. Reviews transparencies, 4×6 prints. Negotiates payment individually.

❸❸❸ DCM

AFCOM, 742 E. Chapman Ave., Orange CA 92866. Fax: (714)997-9743. E-mail: afcom@afcom.com; jmoore@afcom.com. Website: afcom.com. **50% freelance written.** Bimonthly magazine covering data center management. *DCM* is the slick, 4-color, bimonthly publication for members of AFCOM, the leading association for data center management. Estab. 1988. Circ. 4,000 worldwide. Byline given. Pays on acceptance for assigned articles and on publication for unsolicited articles. Offers 0-10% kill fee. Publishes ms an average of 3 months after acceptance. Editorial lead time 6-12 months. Submit seasonal material 6 months in advance. Responds in 1-3 weeks to queries. Responds in 1-3 months to mss. Guidelines available online.

○ Prefers queries by e-mail.

NONFICTION Needs how-to, technical, management as it relates to and includes examples of data centers and data center managers. Special issues: The January/February issue is the annual 'Emerging Technologies' issue. Articles for this issue are visionary and product neutral. No product reviews or general tech articles. **Buys 15+ mss/year.** Query with published clips. 2,000 word maximum **Pays 50¢/word and up, based on writer's expertise.**

PHOTOS We rarely consider freelance photos. State availability. Identification of subjects, model releases required. Reviews TIFF/PDF/GIF/JPEG files. Offers no additional payment for photos accepted with ms.

❸❸ THE ELKS MAGAZINE

The Elks Magazine, 425 W. Diversey Pkwy., Chicago IL 60614-6196. (773)755-4740. E-mail: elksmag@elks.org. Website: elks.org/elksmag. **Contact:** Cheryl T. Stachura, editor/publisher. **25% freelance written.** Magazine covers nonfiction only; published 10 times/year with basic mission of being the voice of the elks. All material is written in-house. Estab. 1922. Circ. 1,037,000. Pays on acceptance. Accepts queries by mail, e-mail. Responds in 1 month with a /no on ms purchase Guidelines available online.

○ Each year, the editors buy 20 to 30 articles. These articles consist of previously unpublished, informative, upbeat, entertaining writing on a variety of subjects, including science, technology, nature, Americana, sports, history, health, retirement, personal finance, leisure-time activities, and seasonal topics. Articles should be authoritative (please include sources) and appeal to the lay person.

NONFICTION No fiction, religion, controversial issues, first-person, fillers, or verse. **Buys 20-30 mss/year.** Send complete ms. Length: 1,200-2,000 words. **Pays 25¢/word.**

PHOTOS "If possible, please advise where photographs may be found. Photographs taken and submitted by the writer are paid for separately at $25 each. Send transparencies, slides. Pays $475 for one-time cover rights.". Pays $25/photo.

COLUMNS "The invited columnists are already selected."

$$ HUMANITIES

National Endowment for the Humanities, 1100 Pennsylvania Ave. NW, Washington DC 20506. (202)606-8435. Fax: (202)606-8451. E-mail: dskinner@neh.gov. Website: neh.gov. **50% freelance written.** Bimonthly magazine covering news in the humanities focused on projects that receive financial support from the agency. Estab. 1980. Circ. 6,000. Byline given. Pays on publication. Publishes ms an average of 2 months after acceptance. Editorial lead time 3 months. Submit seasonal material 4 months in advance. Accepts queries by mail, e-mail, fax, phone. Sample copy available online.

NONFICTION Needs book excerpts, historical, interview, photo feature. **Buys 25 mss/year.** Query with published clips. Length: 400-2,500 words. **Pays $300-600.** Sometimes pays expenses of writers on assignment.

PHOTOS Contact: Contact mbiernik@neh.gov. Identification of subjects, model releases required. Offers no additional payment for photos accepted with ms; negotiates payment individually.

COLUMNS In Focus (directors of state humanities councils), 700 words; Breakout (special activities of state humanities councils), 750 words. **Buys 12 mss/year.** Query with published clips. **Pays $300.**

●$$⊘ KIWANIS

3636 Woodview Trace, Indianapolis IN 46268-3196. (317)875-8755; (800)549-2647 [dial 411] (US and Canada only). Fax: (317)879-0204. E-mail: magazine@kiwanis.org. E-mail: shareyourstory@kiwanis.org. Website: kiwanis.org. **Contact:** Jack Brockley, editor. **10% freelance written.** Magazine published 6 times/year for business and professional persons and their families. Estab. 1917. Circ. 240,000. Byline given. Pays on acceptance. Offers 40% kill fee. Publishes ms an average of 6 months after acceptance. Accepts queries by mail, e-mail, fax. Responds in 1 month to queries. Sample copy and writer's guidelines for 9×12 SAE with 5 first class stamps. Guidelines available online.

🗨 No unsolicited mss.

NONFICTION Needs "Most *Kiwanis* content is related to the activities of our Kiwanis clubs.". No fiction, personal essays, profiles, travel pieces, fillers, or verse of any kind. A light or humorous approach is welcomed where the subject is appropriate and all other requirements are observed. **Buys 20 mss/year.** "See guidelines under Share Your Story in the Media Center section on the website. You must be 13 or older to submit your story and/or photographs. If you are age 18 or younger, you must have the permission of your parent or guardian to complete your submission." Length: 500-1,200 words. **Pays $300-600.** Sometimes pays expenses of writers on assignment.

PHOTOS We accept photos submitted with manuscripts. Our rate for a manuscript with good photos is higher than for one without. Identification of subjects, model releases required.

$$ THE LION

300 W. 22nd St., Oak Brook IL 60523-8842. Fax: (630)571-1685. E-mail: rkleinfe@lionsclubs.org. E-mail: magazine@lionsclubs.org. Website: lionsclubs.org. **Contact:** Jay Copp, editor. **35% freelance written. Works with a small number of new/unpublished writers each year.** Monthly magazine covering service club organization for Lions Club members and their families. Estab. 1918. Circ. 490,000. Byline given. Pays on acceptance. Publishes ms an average of 5 months after acceptance. Accepts queries by mail, e-mail, fax, phone. Responds in 1 month to queries. Sample copy and writer's guidelines free.

🗨 "LION Magazine welcomes freelance article submissions with accompanying photos that depict the service goals and projects of Lions clubs on the local, national and international level. Contributors may also submit general interest articles that reflect the humanitarian, community betterment and service activism ideals of the worldwide association. Lions Clubs International is the world's largest service club organization. Lions are recognized globally for their commitment to projects that benefit the blind, visually impaired and people in need."

NONFICTION Needs photo feature, must be of a Lions Club service project, informational (issues of interest to civic-minded individuals). No travel, biography, or personal experiences. **Buys 40 mss/year.** Article length should not exceed 2,000 words, and is subject to editing. No gags, fillers, quizzes or poems are accepted. Photos must be color prints or sent digitally. LION Magazine pays upon acceptance of material. Advance queries save your time and ours. Address all submissions to: Jay Copp, Senior Editor, by mail or e-mail text and .tif or .jpg (300 dpi) photos. Length: 500-1,500 words. **Pays $100-750.** Sometimes pays expenses of writers on assignment.

PHOTOS Purchased with accompanying ms. Photos should be at least 5×7 glossies; color prints or slides are preferred. We also accept digital photos by e-mail. Be sure photos are clear and as candid as possible. Captions required. Total purchase price for ms includes payment for photos accepted with ms.

💲💲 PENN LINES

Pennsylvania Rural Electric Association, 212 Locust St., Harrisburg PA 17108-1266. E-mail: reaenergy@reaenergy.com. Website: reaenergy.com/penn_lines.htm. Monthly magazine covering rural life in Pennsylvania. News magazine of Pennsylvania electric cooperatives. Features should be balanced, and they should have a rural focus. Electric cooperative sources (such as consumers) should be used. Estab. 1966. Circ. 140,000. Byline given. Pays on publication. Publishes ms an average of 3 months after acceptance. Editorial lead time 4 months. Submit seasonal material 4 months in advance. Accepts queries by mail, e-mail. Sample copy available online. Guidelines available online.

NONFICTION Needs general interest, historical, how-to, interview, travel, rural PA only. **Buys 6 mss/year.** Query or send complete ms. Length: 500-2,000 words. **Pays $300-650.**

PHOTOS Captions required. Reviews transparencies, prints, GIF/JPEG files. Negotiates payment individually.

THE ROTARIAN

Rotary International, One Rotary Center, 1560 Sherman Ave., Evanston IL 60201. (847)866-3000. Fax: (847)328-8554. E-mail: rotarian@rotary.org. Website: rotary.org. **40% freelance written.** Monthly magazine for Rotarian business and professional men and women and their families, schools, libraries, hospitals, etc. "Articles should appeal to an international audience and in some way help Rotarians help other people. The organization's rationale is one of hope, encouragement, and belief in the power of individuals talking and working together." Estab. 1911. Circ. 510,000. Byline sometimes given. Pays on acceptance. Offers kill fee. Kill fee negotiable Editorial lead time 4-8 months. Accepts queries by mail, e-mail. Sample copy for $1 (edbrookc@rotaryintl.org). Guidelines available online.

NONFICTION Needs general interest, humor, inspirational, photo feature, technical, science, travel, lifestyle, sports, business/finance, environmental, health/medicine, social issues. No fiction, religious, or political articles. Query with published clips. Length: 1,500-2,500 words. **Pays negotiable rate.** Answer.

REPRINTS "Send tearsheet, photocopy or typed ms with rights for sale noted and information about when and where the material previously appeared." Negotiates payment.

PHOTOS State availability. Reviews contact sheets, transparencies.

COLUMNS Health; Management; Finance; Travel, all 550-900 words. Query.

💲💲💲 SCOUTING

Boy Scouts of America, 1325 W. Walnut Hill Ln., P.O. Box 152079, Irving TX 75015-2079. Website: scoutingmagazine.org. **80% freelance written.** Magazine published 6 times/year covering Scouting activities for adult leaders of the Boy Scouts, Cub Scouts, and Venturing. Estab. 1913. Circ. 1,000,000. Byline given. Pays on acceptance for major features and some shorter features. Publishes ms an average of 18 months after acceptance. Editorial lead time 1 year. Submit seasonal material 1 year in advance. Accepts queries by mail. Accepts simultaneous submissions. Responds in 3 weeks to queries. Responds in 2 months to mss. Sample copy for $2.50 and 9×12 SAE with 4 first-class stamps or online. Guidelines available online.

NONFICTION Needs inspirational, interview. **Buys 20-30 mss/year.** Query with published clips and SASE. A query with a synopsis or outline of a proposed story is essential. Include a SASE. We do not buy fiction or poetry. We pay on acceptance. We purchase first rights unless otherwise specified (purchase does not necessarily guarantee publication). Photos, if of acceptable quality, are usually included in payment for certain assignments. (We normall assign a professional photographers to take photographs for major story assignments.) Payment rates depend on the professional quality the of an article. Payment is from $300 to $500 for a short feature, $650 to $800 for a major article, and more for quality articles by frequent contributors. Writers or photographers should be familiar with the Scouting program and *Scouting* magazine. A sample copy will be sent if you provide a SASE and $2.50. Length: short features of 500 to 700 words; some longer features, up to 1,200 words, usually the result of a definite assignment to a professional writer. **Pays $650-800 for major articles, $300-500 for shorter features.** Pays expenses of writers on assignment.

REPRINTS Send photocopy of article and information about when and where the article previously appeared. First-person accounts of meaningful Scouting experiences (previously published in local newspapers, etc.) are a popular subject.

PHOTOS State availability. Identification of subjects required. Reviews transparencies, prints.

COLUMNS Way It Was (Scouting history), 600-750 words; Family Talk (family—raising kids, etc.), 600-750 words. **Buys 8-12 mss/year.** Query. **Pays $300-500.**

FILLERS Limited to personal accounts of humorous or inspirational Scouting experiences. Needs anecdotes, short humor. **Buys 15-25 mss/year.** Length: 50-150 words. **Pays $25 on publication.**

⬤❸❸ THE TOASTMASTER

Toastmasters International, P.O. Box 9052, Mission Viejo CA 92690-9052. (949)858-8255. E-mail: submissions@toastmasters.org. Website: toastmasters.org. **50% freelance written**. Monthly magazine on public speaking, leadership, and club concerns. "This magazine is sent to members of Toastmasters International, a nonprofit educational association of men and women throughout the world who are interested in developing their communication and leadership skills. Members range from novice to professional speakers and from a wide variety of ethnic and cultural backgrounds, as Toastmasters is an international organization." Estab. 1933. Circ. 235,000 in 11,700 clubs worldwide. Byline given. Pays on acceptance. Publishes ms an average of 1 year after acceptance. Submit seasonal material 3-4 months in advance.

Accepts queries by mail, e-mail. Accepts simultaneous submissions. Responds in 6-8 weeks to queries. Sample copy for 9×12 SASE with 4 first-class stamps. Guidelines available online.

◗ "Our readers are knowledgeable and experienced public speakers; therefore we accept only authentic, well-researched and well-crafted stories. Show, don't tell! Use sources, quotes from experts and other research to back up your views. The best articles have style, depth, emotional impact and take-away value to the reader. A potential feature article needs an unusual hook, compelling story or unique angle. Profiles of colorful, controversial, historically significant, amusing, unusual or unique people are welcome, but keep in mind that our readers live in 92 different countries, so stay away from profiles of American presidents or sports figures. All submissions must be in English, however. Please query first, or send a draft of your proposed article. We recommend you carefully study several issues of the magazine before submitting a query. We are not responsible for unsolicited articles, artwork or photographs, so please don't send anything you can't afford to lose."

NONFICTION Needs how-to, humor, interview, well-known speakers and leaders, communications, leadership, language use. **Buys 50 mss/year.** "Please read our guidelines first, then when you are ready, submit through e-mail. Query with published clips by mail or e-mail (preferred)." Length: 700-2,000 words. **"Compensation for accepted articles depends on whether our submission guidelines are followed, the amount of research involved and the article's general value to us."** Sometimes pays expenses of writers on assignment.

REPRINTS Send typed ms with rights for sale noted and information about when and where the material previously appeared. Pays 50-70% of amount paid for an original article.

❺ TRAIL & TIMBERLINE

The Colorado Mountain Club, 710 10th St., Suite 200, Golden CO 80401. (303)996-2745. Fax: (303)279-3080. E-mail: editor@cmc.org. Website: cmc.org. **Contact:** Editor. **80% freelance written**. Official quarterly publication for the Colorado Mountain Club. "Articles in

Trail & Timberline conform to the mission statement of the Colorado Mountain Club to unite the energy, interest, and knowledge of lovers of the Colorado mountains, to collect and disseminate information "regarding the Colorado mountains in the areas of art, science, literature and recreaetion", to stimulate public interest, and to encourage preservation of the mountains of Colorado and the Rocky Mountain region." Estab. 1918. Circ. 10,500. Byline given. Pays on publication. Publishes ms an average of 2 months after acceptance. Editorial lead time 6 months. Submit seasonal material 6 months in advance. Accepts queries by mail, e-mail. Responds in 1 week to queries. Responds in 1 month to mss. Sample copy for $5. Guidelines available online.

"We encourage submissions from freelance writers who are familiar with our subject matter and our mission statement. Learn more about the club online, or for a sample copy of the magazine, send a SASE and a check for $3 payable to "CMC." Please be sure your article conforms to style and word usage as detailed in *The Associated Press Stylebook*. Finally, payment for articles is on acceptance, which is contingent on a favorable review by our editorial staff, and by outside reviewers, where appropriate.

NONFICTION Needs essays, humor, opinion, Switchbacks, personal experience, photo feature, travel, trip reports. **Buys 10-15 mss/year.** Send complete ms. Length: 500-2,000 words. **Pays $50.**

PHOTOS Send photos. Captions, identification of subjects, model releases required. Send images at 72 dpi, 5 x 7 in. If possible, please post images on a website for us to view. Offers no additional payment for photos accepted with ms.

POETRY **Contact:** Jared Smith, poetry editor. Needs avant-garde, free verse, traditional. Buys 6-12 poems/year. **Pays $50.**

$$$ UPDATE

New York Academy of Sciences, 2 E. 63rd St., New York NY 10021. E-mail: aburke@nyas.org; editorial@nyas.org. Website: nyas.org. **Contact:** Adrienne Burke, Executive Editor. **40% freelance written.** Magazine published 7 times/year covering science, health issues. Scientific newsletter for members of the New York Academy of Sciences. Estab. 2001. Circ. 25,000. Byline sometimes given. Pays on publication. Publishes ms an average of 1 month after acceptance. Editorial lead time 2 months. Submit seasonal material 2 months in advance. Accepts queries by mail. Sample copy available online.

NONFICTION Needs book excerpts, essays, general interest, historical, interview, technical. No science fiction, any pieces exceeding 1,000 words, or subjects that aren't current. **Buys 6-7 mss/year.** Query. Length: 300-1,000 words. **Pays $200-1,200.** Sometimes pays expenses of writers on assignment.

PHOTOS State availability. Captions, identification of subjects, model releases required. Reviews GIF/JPEG files. Negotiates payment individually.

$$$ VFW MAGAZINE

Veterans of Foreign Wars of the United States, 406 W. 34th St., Suite 523, Kansas City MO 64111. (816)756-3390. Fax: (816)968-1169. E-mail: magazine@vfw.org. Website: vfwmagazine.org. Tim Dyhouse, managing editor. **Contact:** Rich Kolb, editor-in-chief. **40% freelance written.** Monthly magazine on veterans' affairs, military history, patriotism, defense, and current events. "*VFW Magazine* goes to its members worldwide, all having served honorably in the armed forces overseas from World War II through the Iraq and Afghanistan Wars." Estab. 1904. Circ. 1.5 million. Byline given. Pays on acceptance. Offers 50% kill fee. Publishes ms 3-6 months after acceptance. Editorial lead time is 6 months. Submit seasonal material 6 months in advance. Accepts queries by mail, e-mail, fax. Responds in 2 months to queries. Sample copy for 9×12 SAE with 5 first-class stamps. Guidelines available by e-mail.

NONFICTION **Contact:** Richard Kolb. Needs general interest, historical, inspirational. **Buys 25-30 mss/year.** Query with 1-page outline, résumé, and published clips. Length: 1,000-1,500 words. **Pays up to $500-$1,000 max. for assigned articles; $500-$750 max. for unsolicited articles.**

PHOTOS Send photos. Reviews contact sheets, negatives, hi-res, GIF/JPEG files, 5×7 or 8×10 prints.

ASTROLOGY, METAPHYSICAL AND NEW AGE

$$ FATE MAGAZINE

Fate Magazine, Inc., P.O. Box 460, Lakeville MN 55044 US. (952)431-2050. Fax: (952)891-6091. E-mail: submissions@fatemag.com. Website: fatemag.com. David Godwin, managing editor. **Contact:** Phyllis

Galde, editor-in-chief. **75% freelance written**. Covering the paranormal, ghosts, ufos, strange science. "Reports a wide variety of strange and unknown phenomena. We are open to receiving any well-written, well-documented article. Our readers especially like reports of current investigations, experiments, theories, and experiences. See topics on website at fatemag.com/fatemagold/WritersGuidelines.pdf.". Estab. 1948. Circ. 15,000. Byline given. Pays after publication. 3-6 months 3-6 months Accepts queries by mail, e-mail, fax. NoAccepts simultaneous submissions. Responds in 1-3 months to queries. Sample copy available for free online, by e-mail. Guidelines available online at fatemag.com/fatemagold/WritersGuidelines.pdf.

💬 "*Fate* prefers first-person accounts and investigations of the topics we cover. We do not publish fiction or opinion pieces or book-length mss."

NONFICTION Contact: Andrew Honigman. Needs general interest, historical, how-to, personal experience, photo feature, technical. We do not publish poetry, fiction, editorial/opinion pieces, or book-length mss. **Buys 100 mss/year mss/year.** Query. 500-4,000 words **Pays 5¢/word.** Pays with merchandise or ad space if requested.

PHOTOS Contact: Andrew Honigman. Buys slides, prints, or digital photos/illustrations with ms. Send photos with submission. GIF/JPEG files; prints (4 x 6). Pays $10.

COLUMNS Contact: Andrew Honigman. True Mystic Experiences: Short reader-submitted stories of strange experiences; My Proof of Survival: Short, reader-submitted stories of proof of life after death, 300-1,000 words Writer should query. **$25**

FILLERS Fillers are especially welcomed and must be be fully authenticated also, and on similar topics. Length: 100-1,000 words. **Pays 5¢/word.**

$ WHOLE LIFE TIMES

Whole Life Media, LLC, 23705 Vanowen St., #306, West Hills CA 91307. (877)807-2599. Fax: (310)933-1693. E-mail: editor@wholelifemagazine.com. Website: wholelifemagazine.com. Bimonthly regional glossy on holistic living. "*Whole Life Times* relies almost entirely on freelance material. We depend on freelancers like you." Open to stories on natural health, alternative healing, green living, sustainable and local food, social responsibility, conscious business, the environment, spirituality and personal growth—anything that deals with a progressive, healthy lifestyle. Estab. 1979. Circ. 58,000. Byline given. Pays within 45 days. 50% kill fee on assigned stories. No kill fee to first-time WLT writers. 2-4 months Accepts queries by mail, e-mail. Sample copy for $3. Guidelines available online and via e-mail.

💬 "We are a regional publication and favor material that somehow links to our area via topics, sources, similar.

NONFICTION Special issues: Healing Arts, Food and Nutrition, Spirituality, New Beginnings, Relationships, Longevity, Arts/Cultures Travel, Vitamins and Supplements, Women's Issues, Sexuality, Science and Metaphysics, eco lifestyle. **Buys 60 mss/year. Payment varies. *WLT* accepts up to 3 longer stories (800-1,100 words) per issue, and pay ranges from $150-200 depending on topic, research required and writer experience. In addition, we have a number of regular departments that pay $75-150 depending on topic, research required and writer experience.**

REPRINTS Rarely publishes reprints.

COLUMNS Local News, Taste of Health, Yoga & Spirit, Healthy Living, Art & Soul. Length: 750-900 words. City of Angels is our FOB section featuring short, newsy blurbs on our coverage topics, generally in the context of Los Angeles. These are generally 200-400 words and pay $25-35 depending on length and topic. This is a great section for writers who are new to us. BackWords is a 750-word personal essay that often highlights a seminal moment or event in the life of the writer and pays $100. One per issue.

$ WITCHES AND PAGANS

BBI Media, Inc., P.O. Box 687, Forest Grove OR 97116. (888)724-3966. E-mail: editor2@bbimedia.com. Website: witchesandpagans.com. Quarterly magazine covering paganism, wicca and earth religions. *Witches and Pagans* is dedicated to witches, wiccans, neo-pagans, and various other earth-based, pre-Christian, shamanic, and magical practitioners. We hope to reach not only those already involved in what we cover, but the curious and completely new as well. Estab. 2002. Circ. 15,000. Byline given. Pays on publication. Offers 100% kill fee. Editorial lead time 3-4 months. Submit seasonal material 6 months in advance. Accepts queries by mail, e-mail, fax, phone. Responds in 1-2 weeks to queries. Responds in 1 month to mss. Sample copy for $6. Guidelines available online.

💬 "Devoted exclusively to promoting and covering contemporary Pagan culture, W&P features exclusive interviews with the teachers, writers and activists who create and lead our traditions, visits to the sacred places and people who inspire us and in-depth discussions of our ever-evolving practices. You'll also find practical daily magic, ideas for solitary ritual and devotion, God/dess-friendly craft-projects, Pagan poetry and short fiction, reviews, and much more in every 96-page issue. *Witches&Pagans* is available in either traditional paper copy sent by postal mail or as a digital PDF-eZine download that is compatible with most computers and readers."

NONFICTION Needs book excerpts, essays, historical, how-to, humor, inspirational, interview, new product, opinion, personal experience, photo feature, religious, travel. Special issues: Features (articles, essays, fiction, interviews, and rituals) should range between 1,000 - 5,000 words. We most often publish items between 1500 - 3000 words; we prefer in-depth coverage to tidbits in most cases, and the upper ranges are usually reserved for lead pieces assigned to specific writers. Send complete ms. Submit all written material in electronic format. Our first choice is Open Office writer file attachments e-mailed directly to editor2@bbimedia.com. This e-mail address is being protected from spambots. You need JavaScript enabled to view it; other acceptable file attachment formats include text files and commonly used word processing programs; you may also paste the text of your ms directly into an e-mail message. Use a plain, legible font or typeface large enough to read easily. Sidebars can be 500-1300 words or so. Reviews have specific lengths and formats, e-mail editor2@bbimedia.com. This e-mail address is being protected from spambots. You need JavaScript enabled to view it . Length: 1,000-4,000 words. **"We offer a standard range of about $.025 per word for all written works except letters to the editor, as well as a contributor's copy of the issue in which your work appears. Occasionally we accept reprints (almost always solicited by us) at a rate of $.01 per word. These rates are *inclusive* of non-exclusive reprint and electronic rights. Short works such as reviews typically get a flat fee of $10. Payment for artwork, photography, and other visual works is negotiated individually; other exchanges, such as subscriptions or advertising space, may be** possible and may be much more generous than cash payments." Sometimes pays expenses of writers on assignment.

PHOTOS State availability. Identification of subjects, model releases required. Reviews GIF/JPEG files. Negotiates payment individually; offers no additional payment for photos accepted with ms.

FICTION Needs adventure, erotica, ethnic, fantasy, historical, horror, humorous, mainstream, mystery, novel concepts, religious, romance, suspense. Does not want faction (fictionalized retellings of real events). Avoid gratuitous sex, violence, sentimentality and pagan moralizing. Don't beat our readers with the Rede or the Threefold Law. **Buys 3-4 mss/year.** Send complete ms. Length: 1,000-5,000 words. **Pays 2¢/word minimum**.

POETRY Needs avant-garde, free verse, haiku, light verse, traditional. Submit maximum 3-5 poems. **Pays $10**.

AUTOMOTIVE AND MOTORCYCLE

💲 AMERICAN MOTORCYCLIST

American Motorcyclist Association, 13515 Yarmouth Dr., Pickerington OH 43147. (614)856-1900. E-mail: grassroots@ama-cycle.org. Website: ama-cycle.org. **Contact:** Bill Wood. **10% freelance written.** Monthly magazine for enthusiastic motorcyclists investing considerable time and money in the sport, emphasizing the motorcyclist, not the vehicle. Monthly magazine of the American Motorcyclist Association. Emphasizes people involved in, and events dealing with, all aspects of motorcycling. Readers are "enthusiastic motorcyclists, investing considerable time in road riding or all aspects of the sport." Estab. 1947. Circ. 260,000. Byline given. Pays on publication. Editorial lead time 3 months. Submit seasonal material 4 months in advance. Accepts queries by mail, e-mail. Responds in 5 weeks to queries. Responds in 6 weeks to mss. Sample copy for $1.50. Guidelines free.

NONFICTION Needs interview, with interesting personalities in the world of motorcycling, personal experience, travel. **Buys 8 mss/year.** Send complete ms. Length: 1,000-2,500 words. **Pays minimum $8/ published column inch.**

PHOTOS Contact: Bill Wood, director of communications; Grant Parsons, managing editor. Buys 10-20 photos/issue. Subjects include: travel, technical, sports, humorous, photo essay/feature and celebrity/personality. Photo captions preferred. Send photos. Captions, identification of subjects required. Reviews transparencies, prints. Pays $50/photo minimum. Pays $50-150/photo; $250 minimum for cover. Also buys photos in photo/text packages according to same rate; pays $8/column inch minimum for story. Pays on publication.

⬦ AUTO RESTORER

Bowtie, Inc., 3 Burroughs, Irvine CA 92618. (949)855-8822, ext. 412. Fax: (949)855-3045. E-mail: tkade@fancypubs.com; editors@mmminc.org. Website: autorestorermagazine.com. **Contact:** Ted Kade, editor. **85.** Covers auto restoration. Monthly magazine covering auto restoration. Our readers own old cars and they work on them. We help our readers by providing as much practical, how-to information as we can about restoration and old cars. Estab. 1989. Circ. 60,000. Pays on publication. 3 months from acceptance to publication Submit seasonal material 4 months in advance. Accepts queries by mail, e-mail, fax. Responds in 2 months to queries. Sample copy for $7. Guidelines free.

> Interview the owner of a restored car. Present advice to others on how to do a similar restoration. Seek advice from experts. Go light on history and nonspecific details. Make it something that the magazine regularly uses. Do automotive how-tos.

NONFICTION Needs how-to, auto restoration, new product, photo feature, technical product evaluation. **Buys 60 mss/year.** Query first. Length: 250-2,000/words **Pays $150/published page, including photos and illustrations.**

PHOTOS Monthly magazine. Emphasizes restoration of collector cars and trucks. Readers are 98% male, professional/technical/managerial, ages 35-65. Buys 47 photos from freelancers/issue; 564 photos/year. Send photos. Model/property release preferred. Photo captions required; include year, make and model of car; identification of people in photo. Reviews photos with accompanying ms only. Reviews contact sheets, transparencies, 5×7 prints. Looks for "technically proficient or dramatic photos of various automotive subjects, auto portraits, detail shots, action photos, good angles, composition and lighting. We're also looking for photos to illustrate how-to articles such as how to repair a damaged fender or how to repair

a carburetor.". Pays $50 for b&w cover; $35 for b&w inside. Pays on publication. Credit line given.

⬦⬦ AUTOMOBILE QUARTERLY

Automobile Heritage Publishing & Communications LLC, 800 E. 8th St., New Albany IN 47150. Fax: (812)948-2816. E-mail: info@autoquarterly.com; tpowell@autoquarterly.com. Website: autoquarterly.com. **Contact:** Tracy Powell, managing editor. **85% freelance written.** Quarterly magazine covering "automotive history, with excellent photography.". Estab. 1962. Circ. 8,000. Byline given. Pays on acceptance. Publishes ms an average of 1 year after acceptance. Editorial lead time 9 months. Responds in 1 month to queries. Responds in 2 months to mss. Sample copy for $19.95.

NONFICTION Needs historical, photo feature, technical, biographies. **Buys 25 mss/year.** Query. Length: 2,500-5,000 words. **Pays approximately 35¢/word or more.** Sometimes pays expenses of writers on assignment.

PHOTOS State availability. Reviews 4 x 5.

⬦⬦⬦⬦ AUTOWEEK

Crain Communications, Inc., 1155 Gratiot Ave., Detroit MI 48207. (313)446-6000. Fax: (313)446-1027. Website: autoweek.com. **Contact:** Roger Hart, Executive Editor. **5% freelance written, most by regular contributors.** Biweekly magazine. *AutoWeek* is a biweekly magazine for auto enthusiasts. Estab. 1958. Circ. 300,000. Byline given. Pays on publication. Publishes ms an average of 1 month after acceptance. Accepts queries by e-mail.

NONFICTION Needs historical, interview. **Buys 5 mss/year.** Query. Length: 100-400 words. **Pays $1/word.**

◑⬦⬦⬦ CANADIAN BIKER MAGAZINE

735 Market St., Victoria BC V8T 2E2 Canada. (250)384-0333. Fax: (250)384-1832. E-mail: edit@canadianbiker.com. Website: canadianbiker.com. **65% freelance written.** Magazine covering motorcycling. Estab. 1980. Circ. 20,000. Byline given. Publishes ms an average of 1 year after acceptance. Editorial lead time 3 months. Accepts queries by mail, e-mail, fax, phone. Responds in 6 weeks to queries. Responds in 6 months to mss. Sample copy for $5 or online. Guidelines free.

> "A family-oriented motorcycle magazine whose purpose is to unite Canadian motorcyclists from coast to coast through the dissemination of information in a non-biased,

open forum. The magazine reports on new product, events, touring, racing, vintage and custom motorcycling as well as new industry information."

NONFICTION Needs general interest, historical, how-to, interview, Canadian personalities preferred, new product, technical, travel. **Buys 12 mss/year.** Send complete ms. Length: 500-1,500 words. **Pays $100-200 for assigned articles. Pays $80-150 for unsolicited articles.**

PHOTOS State availability of or send photos. Captions, identification of subjects, model releases required. Reviews 4×4 transparencies, 3×5 prints. Negotiates payment individually.

⊘ $ $ $ $ CAR AND DRIVER

Hachette Filipacchi Magazines, Inc., 1585 Eisenhower Pl., Ann Arbor MI 48108. (734)971-3600. Fax: (734)971-9188. E-mail: editors@caranddriver.com; tips@caranddriver.com. Website: caranddriver.com. **Contact:** Eddie Alterman, editor-in-chief; Mark Gillies, executive editor. Monthly magazine for auto enthusiasts; college-educated, professional, median 24-35 years of age. Estab. 1956. Circ. 1,300,000. Byline given. Pays on acceptance. Offers 25% kill fee. Accepts queries by mail, e-mail, fax. Responds in 2 months to queries.

NONFICTION Buys 1 mss/year. Pays max $3,000/feature; $750-1,500/short piece. Pays expenses of writers on assignment.

PHOTOS Color slides and b&w photos sometimes purchased with accompanying ms.

$ $ CAR AUDIO AND ELECTRONICS

Source Interlink, 4223 Glencoe Ave ., Suite B121, Marina del Rey CA 90292. E-mail: editor@caraudiomag.com. Website: caraudiomag.com. **30% freelance written**. Monthly magazine covering mobile electronics. Circ. 40,000. Byline given. Pays on publication. Publishes ms an average of 5 months after acceptance. Editorial lead time 4 months. Submit seasonal material 5 months in advance. Accepts queries by mail, e-mail. Accepts simultaneous submissions. Responds in 1 week to queries. Responds in 1 month to mss. Sample copy available online. Guidelines available online.

NONFICTION Needs how-to, photo feature, technical. Does not want personal essays, humor, and so on. **Buys 30 mss/year.** Query. Length: 750-1,200 words. **Pays $150-300.**

PHOTOS State availability of or send photos. Model releases required. Reviews GIF/JPEG files. Negotiates payment individually.

COLUMNS Choices (vehicle feature), 400-500 words. **Buys 5 mss/year.** Query. **Pays $100-150.**

$ $ $ CELEBRITY CAR MAGAZINE

duPont Publishing, Inc., 3051 Tech Dr., St. Petersburg FL 33716. (727)573-9339. Website: dupontregistry.com. **90% freelance written.** Quarterly magazine covering celebrities and cars. *Celebrity Car* is about automotive style and access to a world of exciting cars, offering insight into the celebrities and their automobiles. *Celebrity Car* profiles the automobile collections of musicians, athletes, movie and television stars and industry personalities—all with a passion for cars—in full-color photographs with their vehicles. Estab. 2003. Circ. 120,000. Byline given. Pays on acceptance. Offers $100 kill fee. Publishes ms an average of 2 months after acceptance. Editorial lead time 2 months. Accepts queries by e-mail. Sample copy free. Guidelines free.

NONFICTION Needs interview, automotive luxury. Query. Length: 750-1,000 words. **Pays $750.** Sometimes pays expenses of writers on assignment.

PHOTOS State availability. Captions required. Negotiates payment individually.

$ $ CLASSIC TRUCKS

Primedia/McMullen Argus Publishing, 1733 Alton Parkway, Irvine CA 92606. E-mail: inquiries@automotive.com. Website: classictrucks.com. Monthly magazine covering classic trucks from the 1930s to 1973. Estab. 1994. Circ. 60,000. Byline given. Pays on publication. Editorial lead time 4 months. Submit seasonal material 4 months in advance. Guidelines free.

NONFICTION Needs how-to, interview, new product, technical, travel. Query. Length: 1,500-5,000 words. **Pays $75-200/page. Pays $100/page maximum for unsolicited articles.**

PHOTOS Send photos. Captions, identification of subjects, model releases required. Reviews transparencies, 5 x 7 prints. Negotiates payment individually.

COLUMNS Buys 24 mss/year. Query.

$ $ $ FOUR WHEELER MAGAZINE

831 S. Douglas Street, El Segundo CA 90245. Website: fourwheeler.com. **20% freelance written. Works with a small number of new/unpublished writers each year.** Monthly magazine covering four-wheel-

drive vehicles, back-country driving, competition, and travel adventure. Estab. 1963. Circ. 355,466. Pays on publication. Publishes ms an average of 4 months after acceptance. Submit seasonal material 4 months in advance. Accepts queries by mail.

NONFICTION Query with photos. 1,200-2,000 words; average 4-5 pages when published. **Pays $200-300/feature vehicles; $350-600/travel and adventure; $100-800/technical articles.**

PHOTOS Requires professional quality color slides and b&w prints for every article. Prefers Kodachrome 64 or Fujichrome 50 in 35mm or 2 ¼ formats. Action shots a must for all vehicle features and travel articles. Captions required.

⊘❸❺ FRICTION ZONE

60166 Hop Patch Spring Road,, Mountain Center CA 92561. (951)659-9500. E-mail: amy@friction-zone.com. Website: friction-zone.com. **60% freelance written.** Monthly magazine covering motorcycles. Estab. 1999. Circ. 26,000. Byline given. Pays on publication. Publishes ms an average of 1 month after acceptance. Editorial lead time 6 weeks. Submit seasonal material 2 months in advance. NoResponds in to queries. Sample copy for $4.50 or on website.

NONFICTION Needs general interest, historical, how-to, humor, inspirational, interview, new product, opinion, photo feature, technical, travel, medical (relating to motorcyclists), book reviews (relating to motorcyclists). Does not accept first-person writing. **Buys 1 mss/year.** Query. Length: 1,000-3,000 words. **Pays 20¢/word.** Sometimes pays expenses of writers on assignment.

PHOTOS Send photos. Captions, identification of subjects, model releases required. Reviews negatives, slides. Offers $15/published photo.

COLUMNS Health Zone (health issues relating to motorcyclists); Motorcycle Engines 101 (basic motorcycle mechanics); Road Trip (California destination review including hotel, road, restaurant), all 2,000 words. **Buys 60 mss/year.** Query. **Pays 20¢/word**

FICTION We want stories concerning motorcycling or motorcyclists. No 'first-person' fiction. Query. Length: 1,000-2,000 words. **Pays 20¢/word.**

FILLERS Needs anecdotes, facts, gags, newsbreaks, short humor. Length: 2,000-3,000 words. **Pays 20¢/word.**

❸❺ IN THE WIND

Paisano Publications, LLC, P.O. Box 3000, Agoura Hills CA 91376-3000. (818)889-8740. Fax: (818)889-1252. E-mail: photos@easyriders.net. Website: easyriders.com. **50% freelance written.** Quarterly magazine. "Geared toward the custom (primarily Harley-Davidson) motorcycle rider and enthusiast, *In the Wind* is driven by candid pictorial-action photos of bikes being ridden, and events." Estab. 1978. Circ. 90,000. Byline given. Pays on publication. Publishes ms an average of 9 months after acceptance. Editorial lead time 6 months. Accepts queries by mail, e-mail. Responds in 2 weeks to queries. Responds in 2 months to mss.

NONFICTION Needs photo feature, event coverage. No long-winded tech articles **Buys 6 mss/year.** Length: 750-1,000 words. **Pays $250-600.** Sometimes pays expenses of writers on assignment.

PHOTOS Send SASE for return. Send photos. Identification of subjects, model releases required. Reviews transparencies, digital images, b&w, color prints.

❸❺ RIDER MAGAZINE

Ehlert Publishing Group, 2575 Vista Del Mar Dr., Ventura CA 93001. E-mail: **rider@ridermagazine.com.** Website: ridermagazine.com. **60% freelance written.** Monthly magazine covering motorcycling. *Rider* serves the all-brand motorcycle lifestyle/enthusiast with a slant toward travel and touring. Estab. 1974. Circ. 127,000. Byline given. Pays on publication. Offers 25% kill fee. Publishes ms an average of 6-12 months after acceptance. Editorial lead time 3 months. Submit seasonal material 6 months in advance. Accepts queries by mail. Responds in 2 months to queries. Sample copy for $2.95. Guidelines by e-mail.

NONFICTION Needs general interest, historical, how-to, humor, interview, personal experience, travel. Does not want to see fiction or articles on 'How I Began Motorcycling.' **Buys 40-50 mss/year.** Query. Length: 750-1,800 words. **Pays $150-750.**

PHOTOS Send photos. Captions required. Reviews contact sheets, transparencies, high quality prints, high resolution (4MP+) digital images. Offers no additional payment for photos accepted with ms.

COLUMNS Favorite Rides (short trip), 850-1,100 words. **Buys 12 mss/year.** Query. **Pays $150-750.**

❸❺ ROADBIKE

TAM Communications, 1010 Summer St., Stamford CT 06905. (203)425-8777. Fax: (203)425-8775. E-mail: info@roadbikemag.com. Website: roadbikemag.com. **40% freelance written.** Monthly magazine covering motorcycling tours, project and custom bikes, products, news, and tech. Estab. 1993. Circ. 50,000. Byline given. Pays on publication. Publishes ms an average of 6 months after acceptance. Editorial lead time 4 months. Submit seasonal material 6 months in advance. Accepts queries by mail, e-mail, fax, online submission form. Guidelines free.

💬"Build your tour story around photographs. "All text documents should be formatted as a word doc, typed in New Times Roman, and saved to a CD, DVD, or USB stick. Send it, along with high res images, to: *RoadBike* Re: Tour Submission 1010 Summer St., 3rd Fl. Stamford, CT 06905."

NONFICTION Needs how-to, motorcycle tech, travel, camping, interview, motorcycle related, new product, photo feature, motorcycle events or gathering places with maximum of 1,000 words text, travel. No fiction. **Buys 100 mss/year.** Send complete ms. Length: 1,000-2,500 words. **Pays $15-400.**

PHOTOS Send photos with submission (high resolution digital images only). Captions required. Offers no additional payment for photos accepted with ms.

FILLERS Needs facts.

$$ ROAD KING

Parthenon Publishing, 28 White Bridge Rd., Suite 209, Nashville TN 37205. Website: roadking.com. **25% freelance written**. Bimonthly magazine covering the trucking industry. Byline given. Pays 3 weeks from acceptance. Offers 30% kill fee. Publishes ms an average of 3 months after acceptance. Editorial lead time 3-4 months. Submit seasonal material 4 months in advance. Accepts queries by mail. Accepts simultaneous submissions. Responds in 3-4 weeks to queries. Sample copy for #10 SASE. Guidelines free.

NONFICTION No essays, no humor, no cartoons. **Buys 12 mss/year.** Query with published clips. Length: 100-1,000 words. **Pays $50-500.**

$ TRUCKIN' MAGAZINE

Source Interlink Media, Inc., 1733 Alton Parkway, Irvine CA 92606. E-mail: inquiries@automotive.com. Website: truckinweb.com. Monthly magazine. Written for pickup drivers and enthusiasts. Circ. 186,606. Editorial lead time 3 months.

AVIATION

🌐 AFRICAN PILOT

Published by Wavelengths 10 (Pty) Ltd., P.O. Box 30620, Kyalami 1684 South Africa. +27 11 466-8524. Fax: +27 11 466 8496. E-mail: Editor@Africanpilot.co.za. Website: Africanpilot.co.za. **Contact:** Athol Franz, editor. **50% freelance written**. Circ. 9,000 printed, 7,000 ABC, 6,000 on-line. "*African Pilot* is southern Africa's premier monthly aviation magazine. It publishes a high-quality magazine that is well-known and respected within the aviation community of southern Africa. The magazine offers a number of benefits to readers and advertisers, including a weekly e-mail newsletter, annual service guide, pilot training supplement, executive wall calendar and an extensive website that mirrors the paper edition. The magazine offers clean layouts with outstanding photography and reflects editorial professionalism as well as a responsible approach to journalism. The magazine offers a complete and tailored promotional solution for all aviation businesses operating in the African region." Estab. 2001. Circ. 7,000+ online, 6,000+ print. Byline given. Editorial lead time 2-3 months. Accepts queries by e-mail. Accepts simultaneous submissions. Responds only if interested, send nonreturnable samples. Sample copies available upon request. Writer's guidelines online or via e-mail.

NONFICTION Needs general interest, historical, interview, new product, personal experience, photo feature, technical. No articles on aircraft accidents. **Buys up to 60 mss/year.** Send complete ms. Length: 1,200-2,800 words. Sometimes pays expenses of writers on assignment.

PHOTOS Contact: Athol Franz, editor. Send photos. Captions required. Negotiates payment individually.

$$$$ AIR & SPACE MAGAZINE

Smithsonian Institution, P.O. Box 37012, MRC 951, Washington DC 20013-7012. (202)633-6070. Fax: (202)633-6085. E-mail: editors@si.edu. Website: airspacemag.com. **80% freelance written**. Bimonthly magazine covering aviation and aerospace for a nontechnical audience. 'Emphasizes the human rather than the technological, on the ideas behind the events. Features are slanted to a technically curious, but not necessarily technically knowledgeable, audience. We are looking for unique angles to aviation/aerospace stories, history, events, personalities, current and future technologies, that emphasize the human-interest aspect." Estab. 1985. Circ. 225,000. Byline given. Pays on acceptance. Offers kill fee. Accepts queries by mail, e-mail, fax. Responds in 3 months to queries. Sample copy for $7. Guidelines available online.

NONFICTION Needs book excerpts, essays, general interest, on aviation/aerospace, historical, humor, photo feature, technical. **Buys 50 mss/year.** Query with published clips. Length: 1,500-3,000 words. **Pays $1,500-3,000.** Pays expenses of writers on assignment.
PHOTOS Refuses unsolicited material. State availability. Reviews 35 mm transparencies, digital files.
COLUMNS Above and Beyond (first person), 1,500-2,000 words; Flights and Fancy (whimsy), approximately 800 words. Soundings (brief items, timely but not breaking news), 500-700 words. **Buys 25 mss/year.** Query with published clips. **Pays $150-300.**

$ AUTOPILOT MAGAZINE

The AutoPilot Franchise Systems, 2310 Pendley Rd., Cumming GA 30041. (770)422-1505. Fax: (770)255-1016. E-mail: production@autopilotmagazine.com. Website: autopilotmagazine.com. **70% freelance written**. Bimonthly magazine covering aviation. *AutoPilot Magazine* is a lifestyle magazine for the aviation enthusiast. We currently have four editions circulating, including Alabama, Georgia, Florida and the Mid-Atlantic region. This magazine differs from other aviation publications, because its focus is specifically on the pilot. Estab. 2000. Circ. 90,000 for all four editions. Byline given. Pays on acceptance. Editorial lead time 2-3 weeks. Accepts queries by mail, e-mail, fax, phone. Sample copy free. Guidelines free.
NONFICTION Needs book excerpts, essays, historical, personal experience, photo feature, travel. Query. Length: 500-900 words. **Pays $100.**
COLUMNS Airport Spotlight (general aviation airports), 500-800 words; Pilot Profiles, 500-800 words; Notable Aviation Organizations, 900 words; Aviation Museums, 900 words; Aviation Memorials, 600 words. **Pays $100.**
FILLERS Needs anecdotes.

$$ AVIATION HISTORY

Weider History Group, 19300 Promenade Dr., Leesburg VA 20176. E-mail: aviationhistory@weiderhistorygroup.com. Website: thehistorynet.com. **95% freelance written**. Bimonthly magazine covering military and civilian aviation from first flight to the jet age. "It aims to make aeronautical history not only factually accurate and complete, but also enjoyable to a varied subscriber and newsstand audience." Estab. 1990. Circ. 45,000. Byline given. Pays on publication. Publishes ms an average of 2 years after acceptance. Editorial lead time 6 months. Submit seasonal material 1 year in advance. Accepts queries by mail, e-mail, fax. Accepts simultaneous submissions. Responds in 2 months to queries. Responds in 3 months to mss. Sample copy for $5. Guidelines for #10 SASE or online.
NONFICTION Needs historical, interview, personal experience. **Buys 24 mss/year.** Query. Feature articles should be 3,000-3,500 words, each with a 500-word sidebar where appropriate, author's biography, and book suggestions for further reading **Pays $300.**
PHOTOS State availability of art and photos with submissions, cite sources. We'll order. Identification of subjects required. Reviews contact sheets, negatives, transparencies.
COLUMNS Aviators, Restored, Extremes all 1,500 words or less. Pays $150 and up. Book reviews, 250-500 words, pays minimum $50.

$ BALLOON LIFE

9 Madeline Ave., Westport CT 06880. (203)629-1241. E-mail: bill_armstrong@balloonlife.com. Website: balloonlife.com. **75% freelance written**. Monthly magazine covering sport of hot air ballooning. Readers participate as pilots, crew, and official observers at events and spectators. Estab. 1986. Circ. 7,000. Byline given. Pays on publication. Offers 50-100% kill fee. Publishes ms an average of 3-4 months after acceptance. Submit seasonal material 4 months in advance. Accepts queries by mail, e-mail. Accepts simultaneous submissions. Responds in 2 weeks to queries. Sample copy for 9×12 SAE with $2 postage. Guidelines available online.
NONFICTION Needs book excerpts, general interest, how-to, flying hot air balloons, equipment techniques, interview, new product, technical, events/rallies, safety seminars, balloon clubs/organizations, letters to the editor. **Buys 150 mss/year.** Send complete ms. Length: 1,000-1,500 words. **Pays $50-200.**
PHOTOS Send photos. Captions, identification of subjects required. Reviews transparencies, prints, high-resolution digital images. Offers $15/inside photos, $50/cover.
COLUMNS Crew Quarters (devoted to some aspect of crewing), 900 words; Preflight (a news and information column), 300-500 words; **pays $50.** Logbook (balloon events that have taken place in last 3-4 months), 300-500 words; **pays $20. Buys 60 mss/**

year. Send complete ms.

$$ CESSNA OWNER MAGAZINE

Jones Publishing, Inc., N7450 Aanstad Rd., P.O. Box 5000, Iola WI 54945. (715)445-5000. Fax: (715)445-4053. E-mail: carie@cessnaowner.org. Website: cessnaowner.org. **50% freelance written.** Monthly magazine covering Cessna single and twin-engine aircraft. *Cessna Owner Magazine* is the official publication of the Cessna Owner Organization (C.O.O.). Therefore, our readers are Cessna aircraft owners, renters, pilots, and enthusiasts. Articles should deal with buying/selling, flying, maintaining, or modifying Cessnas. The purpose of our magazine is to promote safe, fun, and affordable flying. Estab. 1975. Circ. 6,000. Byline given. Pays on publication. Publishes ms an average of 3 months after acceptance. Editorial lead time 1 month. Submit seasonal material 3 months in advance. Accepts queries by mail, e-mail, fax, phone. Responds in 2 weeks to queries. Responds in 1 month to mss. Sample copy and writer's guidelines free or on website.

NONFICTION Needs historical, of specific Cessna models, how-to, aircraft repairs and maintenance, new product, personal experience, photo feature, technical, aircraft engines and airframes. Special issues: Engines (maintenance, upgrades); Avionics (purchasing, new products). **Buys 48 mss/year.** Query. Length: 1,500-2,000 words. **Pays 12¢/word.**

PHOTOS Send photos. Captions, identification of subjects required. Reviews 3×5 and larger prints.

$$ FLIGHT JOURNAL

Air Age Publishing, 88 Danbury Road, Rte. 7, Wilton CT 06897. (203)431-9000. Fax: (203)529-3010. E-mail: **flightjournal@airage.com**. Website: flightjournal.com/. Bimonthly magazine covering aviation-oriented material, for the most part with a historical overtone, but also with some modern history in the making reporting. Many articles have an 'I was there' or 'from the cockpit' human-interest emphasis. We are not a general aviation magazine. A typical issue will have 2-3 articles on WWII, one modern jet story; it could be hardware and operations with pilot interviews, or a personal story; one historical piece, e.g., early airlines, barnstormers; one semi-technical piece with historical overtones, e.g., low aspect ratio airplanes. Accepts queries by mail, e-mail, fax. Guidelines available.

NONFICTION Needs expose, historical, humor, interview, new product, personal experience, photo feature, technical. We do not want any general aviation articles like 'My Flight to Baja in my 172,' nor detailed recitations of the technical capabilities of an aircraft. Avoid historically accurate, but bland, chronologies of events. Lengthier pieces should be discussed in advance with the editors. Length: 2,500-3,000 words. **Pays $600.**

PHOTOS See submission guidelines. Reviews 5×7 prints. Negotiates payment individually.

$$ FLYING ADVENTURES MAGAZINE

Aviation Publishing Corporation, P.O. Box 93613, Pasadena CA 91109-3613. (626)618-4000. E-mail: editor@flyingadventures.com;info@flyingadventures.com. Website: flyingadventures.com. **20% freelance written.** Bimonthly magazine covering lifestyle travel for owners and passengers of private aircraft. "Our articles cover upscale travelers." Estab. 1994. Circ. 135,858. features, no departments Pays on acceptance. Editorial lead time 2 weeks to 2 months. Accepts queries by e-mail. Accepts simultaneous submissions. Responds immediately. Sample copy and guidelines free.

NONFICTION Needs travel, Lifestyle. Nothing non-relevant, not our style. See magazine. Query with published clips. Length: 500-1,500 words. **Pays $150-300 for assigned and unsolicited articles.** Sometimes pays expenses of writers on assignment.

COLUMNS Contact: Editor. Numerous Departments, see magazine. **Buys 100+ mss/yr. mss/year.** Query with published clips. **Pays $-$150.**

$$ PIPERS MAGAZINE

Jones Publishing, Inc., N7450 Aanstad Rd., P.O. Box 5000, Iola WI 54945. 866-697-4737. Website: piperowner.org. **50% freelance written.** Monthly magazine covering Piper single and twin engine aircraft. *Pipers Magazine* is the official publication of the Piper Owner Society (P.O.S). Therefore, our readers are Piper aircraft owners, renters, pilots, mechanics, and enthusiasts. Articles should deal with buying/selling, flying, maintaining, or modifying Pipers. The purpose of our magazine is to promote safe, fun and affordable flying. Estab. 1988. Circ. 5,000. Pays on publication. Publishes ms an average of 3 months after acceptance. Editorial lead time 1 month. Submit seasonal material 3 months in advance. Accepts queries by mail, e-mail, fax, phone.

Responds in 2 weeks to queries. Responds in 1 month to mss. Sample copy free. Guidelines free.

NONFICTION Needs historical, of specific models of Pipers, how-to, aircraft repairs and maintenance, new product, personal experience, photo feature, technical, aircraft engines and airframes. **Buys 48 mss/year.** Query. Length: 1,500-2,000 words. **Pays 12¢/word.**

REPRINTS Send mss by e-mail with rights for sale noted and information about when and where the material previously appeared.

PHOTOS Send photos. Captions, identification of subjects required. Reviews transparencies, 3 x 5 and larger prints. Offers no additional payment for photos accepted.

💲💲 PLANE AND PILOT

Werner Publishing Corp., 12121 Wilshire Blvd., 12th Floor, Los Angeles CA 90025-1176. (310)820-1500. Fax: (310)826-5008. E-mail: editor@planeandpilotmag.com. Website: planeandpilotmag.com. **80% freelance written.** Monthly magazine covering general aviation. We think a spirited, conversational writing style is most entertaining for our readers. We are read by private and corporate pilots, instructors, students, mechanics and technicians—everyone involved or interested in general aviation. Estab. 1964. Circ. 150,000. Byline given. Pays on publication. Offers kill fee. Publishes ms an average of 4 months after acceptance. Submit seasonal material 4 months in advance. Responds in 4 months to queries. Sample copy for $5.50. Guidelines available online.

NONFICTION Needs how-to, new product, personal experience, technical, travel, pilot efficiency, pilot reports on aircraft. **Buys 75 mss/year.** Query. Length: 1,200 words. **Pays $200-500.** Pays expenses of writers on assignment.

REPRINTS Send tearsheet, photocopy or typed ms with rights for sale noted and information about when and where the material previously appeared. Pays 50% of amount paid for original article.

PHOTOS Submit suggested heads, decks and captions for all photos with each story. Submit b&w photos, 8 x 10 prints with glossy finish. Submit color photos in the form of 2 ¼×2 ¼, 4×5 or 35mm transparencies in plastic sleeves. Offers $50-300/photo.

COLUMNS Readback (any newsworthy items on aircraft and/or people in aviation), 1,200 words; Jobs & Schools (a feature or an interesting school or program in aviation), 900-1,000 words. **Buys 30 mss/year.** Send complete ms. **Pays $200-500.**

BUSINESS AND FINANCE BUSINESS NATIONAL

💲💲 BUSINESS TRAVELER USA

Varquin, 115 W. 30th St., Suite 202, New York NY 10001. (212)725-3500. Fax: (212)725-2646. E-mail: eva@varquin.com. Website: btusonline.com. **Contact:** Eva Leonard, editor-in-chief. **90% freelance written.** Business travel magazine. Estab. 1988. Circ. 150,000. Byline given. Editorial lead time 2 months. Submit seasonal material 2 months in advance. Accepts queries by mail, e-mail, fax, phone. Accepts simultaneous submissions. Sample copy free.

NONFICTION Needs interview, new product, personal experience, travel. **Buys 100/year mss/year.** Query. Length: 100-1,800 words. **Pays 50¢ a word for assigned articles.**

COLUMNS Query. **Pays $-50¢ a word.**

💲💲💲💲 CORPORATE BOARD MEMBER

Board Member Inc., 5110 Maryland Way, Suite 250, Brentwood TN 37027. Fax: (615)371-0899. E-mail: boardmember@boardmember.com. Website: boardmember.com. **100% freelance written.** Bimonthly magazine covering corporate governance. Our readers are the directors and top executives of publicly-held US corporations. We look for detailed and preferably narrative stories about how individual boards have dealt with the challenges that face them on a daily basis: reforms, shareholder suits, CEO pay, firing and hiring CEOs, setting up new boards, firing useless directors. We're happy to light fires under the feet of boards that are asleep at the switch. We also do service-type pieces, written in the second person, advising directors about new wrinkles in disclosure laws, for example. Estab. 1999. Circ. 60,000. Byline given. Pays on acceptance. Offers 25% kill fee. Publishes ms an average of 3 months after acceptance. Editorial lead time 4-5 months. Submit seasonal material 4-5 months in advance. Accepts queries by e-mail. Responds in 1 week to queries. Responds in 1 week to mss. Sample copy available online. Guidelines by e-mail.

NONFICTION Special issues: Best Law Firms in America (July/August); What Directors Think (November/December). Does not want views from 35,000 feet, pontification, opinion, humor, anything devoid of reporting. **Buys 100 mss/year.** Query. Length: 650-2,500 words. **Pays $1,200-5,000.** Pays expenses of writers on assignment.

$$ DOLLARS AND SENSE: THE MAGAZINE OF ECONOMIC JUSTICE

Economic Affairs Bureau, 29 Winter St., Boston MA 02108. (617)447-2177. Fax: (617)477-2179. E-mail: dollars@dollarsandsense.org. Website: dollarsandsense.org. **10% freelance written.** Bimonthly magazine covering economic, environmental, and social justice. "We explain the workings of the US and international economics, and provide left perspectives on current economic affairs. Our audience is a mix of activists, organizers, academics, unionists, and other socially concerned people." Estab. 1974. Circ. 8,000. Byline given. Pays on publication. Publishes ms an average of 4 months after acceptance. Editorial lead time 3 months. Submit seasonal material 2 months in advance. Accepts queries by mail, e-mail, fax, phone. Sample copy for $5 or on website. Guidelines available online.

NONFICTION Needs exposè, political economics. **Buys 6 mss/year.** Query with published clips. Length: 700-2,500 words. **Pays $0-200.** Sometimes pays expenses of writers on assignment.

PHOTOS State availability. Captions, identification of subjects required. Negotiates payment individually.

$$ ENTREPRENEUR MAGAZINE

Entrepreneur Media, 2445 McCabe Way, Suite 400, Irvine CA 92614. (949)261-2325. Website: entrepreneur.com. **60% freelance written.** *Entrepreneur* readers already run their own businesses. They have been in business for several years and are seeking innovative methods and strategies to improve their business operations. They are also interested in new business ideas and opportunities, as well as current issues that affect their companies. Circ. 600,000. Byline given. Pays on acceptance. Publishes ms an average of 5 months after acceptance. Submit seasonal material 6 months in advance. Accepts queries by mail, e-mail. Responds in 3 months to queries. Sample copy for $7.20. Guidelines available online.

NONFICTION Needs how-to, information on running a business, dealing with the psychological aspects of running a business, profiles of unique entrprenuers, current news/trends (and their effect on small business). **Buys 10-20 mss/year.** Query with published clips. Length: 1,800 words. **Payment varies**

PHOTOS Ask for photos or transparencies when interviewing entrepreneurs; send them with the article.

COLUMNS Snapshots (profiles of interesting entrepreneurs who exemplify innovation in their marketing/sales technique, financing method or management style, or who have developed an innovative product/service or technology); Money Smarts (financial management); Marketing Smarts; Web Smarts (Internet news); Tech Smarts; Management Smarts; Viewpoint (first-person essay on entrepreneurship), all 300 words. **Pays $1/word.**

⊘ FORTUNE

Time, Inc., 1271 Avenue of the Americas, New York NY 10020. (212)522-1212. Fax: (212)522-0810. E-mail: fortune-mail_letters@fortune-mail.com. Website: fortune.com. Bi-weekly magazine. Edited primarily for high-demographic business people. Specializes in big stories about companies, business personalities, technology, managing, Wall Street, media, marketing, personal finance, politics and policy. Circ. 1,066,000. Editorial lead time 6 weeks.

Does not accept freelance submissions.

$$$$ HISPANIC BUSINESS

Hispanic Business, Inc., 425 Pine Ave., Santa Barbara CA 93117-3709. (805)964-4554. Fax: (805)964-5539. Website: hispanicbusiness.com. **40-50% freelance written.** Monthly magazine covering Hispanic business. For more than 2 decades, *Hispanic Business* magazine has documented the growing affluence and power of the Hispanic community. Our magazine reaches the most educated, affluent Hispanic business and community leaders. Stories should have relevance for the Hispanic business community. Estab. 1979. Circ. 220,000 (rate base); 990,000 (readership base). Byline given. Pays on publication. Offers 50% kill fee. Publishes ms an average of 1 month after acceptance. Editorial lead time 1-3 months. Submit seasonal material 2 months in advance. Accepts queries by mail. NoAccepts simultaneous submissions. Responds in 3 weeks to queries. Responds in 1 month to mss. Sample copy free.

NONFICTION Needs interview, travel. **Buys 120 mss/year.** Query résumé and published clips. Length: 650-2,000 words. **Pays $50-1,500.** Sometimes pays expenses of writers on assignment.

PHOTOS State availability. Captions required. Reviews GIF/JPEG files. Negotiates payment individually.

COLUMNS Tech Pulse (technology); Money Matters

(financial), both 800 words. **Buys 40 mss/year.** Query with résumé and published clips. **Pays $50-450.**

✪⑨⑨ HOME BUSINESS REPORT

Impact Communications Ltd, 2625A Alliance St., Abbottsford BC V2S 3J9 Canada. (604)936-5815. Fax: (604)936-5805. E-mail: info@impactcommuni-cationsltd.com. Website: homebusinessreport.com. **95% freelance written**. Quarterly magazine covering home-based business/small business. "Our focus is on practical strategies that small and home-based business owners can use to increase their business success. We prefer articles about real people having real experiences, as opposed to lists of how-tos. We run 2 types of articles: features and Regional Reports, which profile successful Canadian home-based businesses." Estab. 1989. Circ. 125,000. Byline given. Pays on acceptance. Publishes ms an average of 2 months after acceptance. Editorial lead time 1-3 months. Submit seasonal material 3-6 months in advance. Accepts queries by mail, e-mail. Responds in 1-6 weeks to queries. Responds in 1-6 months to mss. Sample copy and writer's guidelines online.

NONFICTION Needs interview, business articles. Special issues: Creating Cash Flow (October). Does not want articles solely on theory or 'puff' pieces that do little more than promote your own business or product. **Buys 35-40 mss/year.** Query. Length: 1,000-3,000 words. **Pays $200-350.**

PHOTOS State availability. Captions required. Offers no additional payment for photos accepted with ms.

✪⑨⑨⑨ MYBUSINESS MAGAZINE

Imagination Publishing, 600 W. Fulton St., Suite 600, Chicago IL 60661. (615)872-5800; (800)634-2669). E-mail: nfib@imaginepub.com. Website: mybusiness-mag.com. **75% freelance written**. Bimonthly magazine for small businesses. "We are a guide to small business success, however that is defined in the new small business economy. We explore the methods and minds behind the trends and celebrate the men and women leading the creation of the new small business economy." Estab. 1999. Circ. 600,000. Byline given. Pays on acceptance. Offers 30% kill fee. Publishes ms an average of 4 months after acceptance. Editorial lead time 4 months. Submit seasonal material 5 months in advance. Accepts queries by mail, e-mail. Accepts simultaneous submissions. Responds in 3 weeks to queries. Sample copy free. Guidelines available online.

NONFICTION Needs book excerpts, how-to, small business topics, new product. **Buys 8 mss/year.** Query with resume and 2 published clips. We accept pitches for feature stories, which fall under one of three categories: Own, Operate and Grow. Story ideas should be small-business focused, with an emphasis on timely problems that small business owners face and real, workable solutions. Trend pieces are also of interest. Copy should be submitted as a Microsoft Word enclosure. Deadlines are 90 days before publication. Length: 200-1,800 words. **Pays $75-1,000.** Pays expenses of writers on assignment.

⑨⑨ THE NETWORK JOURNAL

The Network Journal Communication, 39 Broadway, Suite 2120, New York NY 10006. (212)962-3791. Fax: (212)962-3537. E-mail: editors@tnj.com. Website: tnj.com. **25% freelance written**. Monthly magazine covering business and career articles. *The Network Journal* caters to black professionals and small-business owners, providing quality coverage on business, financial, technology and career news germane to the black community. Estab. 1993. Circ. 25,000. Byline given. Pays on publication. Editorial lead time 2 months. Submit seasonal material 3 months in advance. Accepts queries by mail, e-mail, fax, phone. Accepts simultaneous submissions. Sample copy for $1 or online. Writer's guidelines for SASE or online.

NONFICTION Needs how-to, interview. Send complete ms. Length: 1,200-1,500 words. **Pays $150-200.** Sometimes pays expenses of writers on assignment.

PHOTOS Send photos. Identification of subjects required. Offers $25/photo.

COLUMNS Book reviews, 700-800 words; career management and small business development, 800 words. **Pays $100.**

✪⑨⑨⑨⑨⑨ PROFIT

Rogers Media, 1 Mt. Pleasant Rd., 11th Floor, Toronto ON M4Y 2Y5 Canada. (416)764-1402. Fax: (416)764-1404. Website: profitguide.com. **80% freelance written**. Magazine published 6 times/year covering small and medium businesses. We specialize in specific, useful information that helps our readers manage their businesses better. We want Canadian stories only. Estab. 1982. Circ. 110,000. Byline given. Pays on acceptance. Offers variable kill fee. Publishes ms an average of 2 months after acceptance. Submit seasonal material 6 months in advance. Accepts queries by mail, fax, phone. Responds in 1 month to queries.

Responds in 6 weeks to mss. Sample copy for 9×12 SAE with 84¢ postage. Guidelines free.

NONFICTION Needs how-to, business management tips, strategies and Canadian business profiles. **Buys 50 mss/year.** Query with published clips. Length: 800-2,000 words. **Pays $500-2,000.** Pays expenses of writers on assignment.

COLUMNS Finance (info on raising capital in Canada), 700 words; Marketing (marketing strategies for independent business), 700 words. **Buys 80 mss/ year.** Query with published clips. **Pays $150-600.**

⦿⦿ SFO MAGAZINE

Wasendorf and Associates, One Peregrine Way, Cedar Falls IA 50613. E-mail: editorial@sfomag.com. Website: sfomag.com. **Contact:** Heather Larson-Blakestad. **90% freelance written.** Monthly magazine covering trading of stocks, futures, options, exchange traded funds and currency pairs. We focus on issues and strategies for the retail individual trader. "Our articles are educational and nonpromotional in angle and tone. We try to offer our readers information they can apply immediately to their trading (expository types of articles)." Estab. 2000. Circ. 120,000. Byline given. Pays on publication. Offers 20% kill fee. Publishes ms an average of 2 months after acceptance. Editorial lead time 2.5 months. Accepts queries by e-mail. Accepts simultaneous submissions. Responds in 8 weeks to queries. Sample copy available online. Guidelines by e-mail.

NONFICTION Needs how-to, trading strategies, interview, In-depth on financial regulations, laws, etc. Special issues: See editorial calendar. Each month, we have a 'spotlight' section that takes a look at an issue that may affect the way that an individual retail trader can access or take advantage of the financial markets. These are determined as the year progresses, but general areas of interest would be financial regulation, financial policy, taxes, etc. We do not run book excerpts or material that has been published elsewhere. **Buys 12 mss/year.** Query with published clips. Length: 600-1,800 words. **Pays $250 min. for assigned articles.** Sometimes pays expenses of writers on assignment.

⦿⦿ TECHNICAL ANALYSIS OF STOCKS & COMMODITIES

Technical Analysis, Inc., 4757 California Ave. SW, Seattle WA 98116. (206)938-0570. E-mail: editor@traders.com. Website: traders.com. **95% freelance written.** "Magazine covers methods of investing and trading

stocks, bonds and commodities (futures), options, mutual funds, and precious metals using technical analysis." Estab. 1982. Circ. 65,000. Byline given. Pays on publication. Publishes ms an average of 6 months after acceptance. Responds in 3 months to queries. Sample copy for $8. Guidelines available online.

◯"Eager to work with new/unpublished writers."

NONFICTION Needs how-to, trade, technical, cartoons, trading and software aids to trading, reviews, utilities, real world trading (actual case studies of trades and their results). No newsletter-type, buy-sell recommendations. The article subject must relate to technical analysis, charting or a numerical technique used to trade securities or futures. Almost universally requires graphics with every article. **Buys 150 mss/ year.** Send complete ms. Length: 1,000-4,000 words. **Pays $100-500.**

REPRINTS Send tearsheet with rights for sale noted and information about when and where the material previously appeared.

PHOTOS Contact: Christine M. Morrison, art director. State availability. Captions, identification of subjects, model releases required. Pays $60-350 for b&w or color negatives with prints or positive slides.

COLUMNS Length: 800-1,600 words. **Buys 100 columns. mss/year.** Query. **Pays $50-300**

FILLERS Contact: Karen Wasserman, fillers editor. "Must relate to trading stocks, bonds, options, mutual funds, commodities, or precious metals." **Buys 20 fillers. mss/year.** Length: 500 words. **Pays $20-50.**

BUSINESS REGIONAL

⦿⦿ ALASKA BUSINESS MONTHLY

Alaska Business Publishing, 501 W. Northern Lights Blvd., Suite 100, Anchorage AK 99503-2577. (907)276-4373. Fax: (907)279-2900. E-mail: editor@akbizmag.com. Website: akbizmag.com. **Contact:** Debbie Cutler, managing editor. **90% freelance written.** "Our audience is Alaska businessmen and women who rely on us for timely features and up-to-date information about doing business in Alaska." Estab. 1985. Circ. 12,000-14,000. Byline given. Pays on publication. Offers $50 kill fee. Publishes ms an average of 4 months after acceptance. Editorial lead time 5 months. Submit seasonal material 5 months in advance. Accepts queries by mail, e-mail, fax. Responds in 1 month to queries, 4 months to mss. Sample copy for 9×12 SAE and 4 first-class stamps. Guidelines free.

NONFICTION Needs general interest, how-to, interview, new product, Alaska, opinion, expose, inspire, photo, technical, travel, business. No fiction, poetry, or anything not pertinent to Alaska. **Buys approximately 130 mss/year.** Send complete ms. Length: 500-2,000 words. **Pays $100-350 for assigned articles. Pays $100-300 for unsolicited articles.** Sometimes pays expenses of writers on assignment.

PHOTOS State availability. Captions, identification of subjects required. Reviews negative, GIF/JPEG files. Pays $25-400/photo.

⊘❸❸❸❸ ALBERTA VENTURE

Venture Publishing Inc., 10259 - 105 St., Edmonton AB T5J 1E3 Canada. (780)990-0839. E-mail: admin@albertaventure.com. Website: albertaventure.com. **70% freelance written.** Monthly magazine covering business in Alberta. "Our readers are mostly business owners and managers in Alberta who read the magazine to keep up with trends and run their businesses better." Estab. 1997. Circ. 35,000. Byline given. Pays on publication. Offers 30% kill fee. Publishes ms an average of 2 months after acceptance. Editorial lead time 3 months. Submit seasonal material 3 months in advance. Accepts queries by e-mail. Responds in 2 weeks to queries. Sample copy available online. Guidelines by e-mail.

NONFICTION Needs how-to, business narrative related to Alberta. Does not want company or product profiles. **Buys 75 mss/year.** Query. Length: 1,000-3,000 words. **Pays $300-2,000 (Canadian).** Pays expenses of writers on assignment.

PHOTOS Contact: Contact Kim Larson, art director. State availability. Identification of subjects required. Reviews GIF/JPEG files. Negotiates payment individually.

⊘❸❸ ATLANTIC BUSINESS MAGAZINE

Communications Ten, Ltd., P.O. Box 2356, Station C, St. John's NL A1C 6E7 Canada. (709)726-9300. Fax: (709)726-3013. Website: atlanticbusinessmagazine.com. **80% freelance written.** Bimonthly magazine covering business in Atlantic Canada. We discuss positive business developments, emphasizing that the 4 Atlantic provinces are a great place to do business. Estab. 1989. Circ. 30,000. Byline given. Pays within 30 days of publication. Publishes ms an average of 2 months after acceptance. Editorial lead time 6 months. Accepts queries by mail, e-mail, fax. Sample copy and writer's guidelines free.

NONFICTION Needs expose, general interest, interview, new product. We don't want religious, technical, or scholarly material. We are not an academic magazine. We are interested only in stories concerning business topics specific to the 4 Canadian provinces of Nova Scotia, New Brunswick, Prince Edward Island, and Newfoundland and Labrador. **Buys 36 mss/year.** Query with published clips. Length: 1,200-2,500 words. **Pays $300-750.** Sometimes pays expenses of writers on assignment.

PHOTOS Send photos. Captions, identification of subjects required. Reviews contact sheets, transparencies, prints. Negotiates payment individually.

COLUMNS Query with published clips.

❸ BLUE RIDGE BUSINESS JOURNAL

Landmark, Inc., 302 Second St., 4th Floor, Roanoke VA 24011. (540)777-6460. Fax: (540)777-6471. E-mail: dansmith@bizjournal.com. Website: bizjournal.com. **75% freelance written.** Monthly. We take a regional slant on national business trends, products, methods, etc. Interested in localized features and news stories highlighting business activity. Estab. 1989. Circ. 15,000. Byline given. Pays on acceptance. Publishes ms an average of 1 month after acceptance. Editorial lead time 10 days. Accepts queries by mail, e-mail, fax. Responds immediately. Call the editor for sample copies and/or writer's guidelines. Writers must live in our region.

NONFICTION Special issues: Health Care and Hospitals; Telecommunications; Building and Construction; Investments; Personal Finance and Retirement Planning; Guide to Architectural; Engineering and Construction Services; and Manufacturing and Industry. No columns or stories that are not pre-approved. **Buys 120-150 mss/year.** Query. Length: 500-2,000 words.

PHOTOS State availability. Captions, identification of subjects required. Offers $10/photo.

❸❸ THE BUSINESS JOURNAL

American City Business Journals, Inc., 96 N. Third St., Suite 100, San Jose CA 95112. (408)295-3800. Fax: (408)295-5028. Website: sanjose.bizjournals.com. **Contact:** Moryt Milo, editor. **2-5% freelance written.** Weekly tabloid covering a wide cross-section of industries. Estab. 1983. Circ. 13,200. Byline given. Pays on publication. Offers $75 kill fee. Editorial lead time 1 month. Responds in 2 weeks to queries. Sample copy free. Guidelines free.

💬 "Our stories are written for business people. Our audience is primarily upper-level management."

NONFICTION Buys 300 mss/year. Query. Length: 700-2,500 words. **Pays $175-400.**

PHOTOS State availability. Reviews 5 x 7 prints. Offers $25/photo used.

➕ BUSINESS NH MAGAZINE

55 S. Commercial St., Manchester NH 03101. (603)626-6354. Fax: (603)626-6359. E-mail: hcopeland@BusinessNHmagazine.com. Website: millyardcommunications.com. **Contact:** Heidi Copeland, publisher. **25% freelance written**. Monthly magazine covering business, politics, and people of New Hampshire. "Our audience consists of the owners and top managers of New Hampshire businesses." Estab. 1983. Circ. 15,000. Byline given. Pays on publication. Publishes ms an average of 2 months after acceptance. Accepts queries by e-mail, fax.

NONFICTION Needs how-to, interview. No unsolicited manuscripts; interested in New Hampshire writers only. **Buys 24 mss/year.** Query with published clips and résumé Length: 750-2,500 words. **Payment varies.**

PHOTOS Contact: Graphic Designer. Both b&w and color photos are used. Model/property release preferred. Photo captions required; include names, locations, contact phone number. Payment varies. Pays $450 for color cover; $100 for color or b&w inside. Credit line given. Buys one-time rights. Pays on publication.

💲💲 CINCY MAGAZINE

Great Lakes Publishing Co., Cincinnati Club Building, 30 Garfield Place, Suite 440, Cincinnati OH 45202. (513)421-2533. Fax: (513)421-2542. E-mail: webmaster@cincymagazine.com. Website: cincymagazine.com. **80% freelance written**. Glossy bimonthly color magazine written for business professionals in Greater Cincinnati, published 10 times annually. *Cincy* is written and designed for the interests of business professionals and executives both at work and away from work, with features, trend stories, news and opinions related to business, along with lifestyle articles on home, dining, shopping, travel, health and more. Estab. 2003. Circ. 15,300. Byline given. Pays on publication. Offers 100% kill fee. Publishes ms an average of 3 months after acceptance. Editorial lead time 1-3 months. Submit seasonal material 4 months in advance. Accepts queries by mail, e-mail. No

NONFICTION Needs general interest, interview. Does not want stock advice. Length: 200-2,000 words. **Pays $75-600.**

➕💲💲💲 COLORADOBIZ

WiesnerMedia, 6160 S. Syracuse Way, Suite 300, Greenwood Village CO 80111. (303)662-5283 (cell) (720)771-7332. Fax: (303)694-5385. E-mail: mcote@cobizmag.com. Website: cobizmag.com. Mike Taylor, man. ed. **Contact:** Mike Cote, editor. **70**. Colorado business. "*ColoradoBiz* is a monthly magazine that covers people, issues and trends statewide for a sophisticated audience of business owners and executives." Estab. 1973. Circ. 20,000+. publication 25% 2 months Editorial lead time is 2-3 months. Submit seasonal material 3 months in advance. Accepts queries by e-mail at: mcote@cobizmag.com. Responds in 2 weeks to queries. Sample copy available for $2.95 with SASE. Writer's guidelines free online.

NONFICTION Needs book excerpts, expose, technical, Colorado business. Special issues: Minority business. Does not want humor, first-person, self-promotional **Buys Buys up to 100 mss/year mss/year.** Query with published clips. Length: 300-3,000/words **Pays 40 cents/word; $100 to $1,200.** Sometimes pays expenses of writers on assignment.

PHOTOS Contact: Alese Pickering, art dir. State availability of photos with submission. captions, identification of subjects required. Offers $100-200 per photo.

COLUMNS State of the State, 150 to 300 word briefs on Colorado business issues. **Buys Buys 6 mss/year. mss/year.** Query **Pays 40 cents/word**

💲💲 CORPORATE CONNECTICUT MAGAZINE

Corporate World LLC, P.O. Box 290726, Wethersfield CT 06129. Fax: (860)257-1924. E-mail: editor@corpct.com. Website: corpct.com. **50% freelance written**. Quarterly magazine covering regional reporting, global coverage of corporate/business leaders, entrepreneurs. *Corporate Connecticut* is devoted to people who make business happen in the private sector and who create innovative change across public arenas. Centered in the Northeast between New York and Boston, Connecticut is positioned in a coastal corridor with a dense affluent population who are highly mobile, accomplished and educated. Estab. 2001. Byline given. Pays on publication. Offers 25% kill fee. Publishes ms an average of 2-3 months after acceptance. Editorial lead time 3-6 months. Submit seasonal material 10-12 months in advance. Accepts queries by mail, e-mail. Responds in 2 weeks to queries. Sample copy for #10 SASE.

NONFICTION Query with published clips. **Pays 35¢/word minimum with varying fees for excellence.**

PHOTOS State availability.

$ CRAIN'S DETROIT BUSINESS

Crain Communications, Inc., 1155 Gratiot, Detroit MI 48207. (313)446-0419. Fax: (313)446-1687. E-mail: kcrain@crain.com. Website: crainsdetroit.com. **10% freelance written.** Weekly tabloid covering business in the Detroit metropolitan area—specifically Wayne, Oakland, Macomb, Washtenaw, and Livingston counties. Estab. 1985. Circ. 150,000. Byline given. Pays on publication. Publishes ms an average of 1 month after acceptance. Accepts queries by mail, e-mail. Sample copy for $1.50. Guidelines available online.

Crain's Detroit Business uses only area writers and local topics.

NONFICTION Needs new product, technical, business. **Buys 20 mss/year.** Query with published clips. 30-40 words/column inch **Pays $10-15/column inch.** Pays expenses of writers on assignment.

PHOTOS State availability.

$$ INGRAM'S

Show-Me Publishing, Inc., P.O. Box 411356, Kansas City MO 64141-1356. (816)842-9994. Fax: (816)474-1111. E-mail: editorial@ingramsonline.com. Website: ingramsonline.com. **Contact:** Joe Sweeney, editor in chief. **10% freelance written.** Monthly magazine covering Kansas City business and economic development. "*Ingram's* readers are top-level corporate executives and community leaders, officials and decision makers. Our editorial content must provide such readers with timely, relevant information and insights." Estab. 1975. Circ. 105,000. Byline given. Pays on publication. Publishes ms an average of 1 month after acceptance. Editorial lead time 1 month. Submit seasonal material 5 months in advance. Accepts queries by e-mail. Sample copy free.

Only accepts local writers; guest columnist are not paid articles.

NONFICTION Needs interview, technical. Does not want humor, inspirational, or anything not related to Kansas City business. **Buys 4-6 mss/year.** Query. Length: 500-1,500 words. **Pays $75-200 depending on research/feature length.** Sometimes pays expenses of writers on assignment.

COLUMNS Say So (opinion), 1,500 words. **Buys 12 mss/year. Pays $75-100 max.**

$$ THE LANE REPORT

Lane Communications Group, 201 E. Main St., 14th Floor, Lexington KY 40507. (859)244-3500. Fax: (859)244-3555. E-mail: markgreen@lanereport.com;editorial@lanereport.com. Website: lanereport.com. **70% freelance written.** Monthly magazine covering statewide business. Estab. 1986. Circ. 15,000. Byline given. Pays on publication. Editorial lead time 6 weeks. Submit seasonal material 3 months in advance. Accepts queries by mail, e-mail, fax. Accepts simultaneous submissions. Responds in 1 month to queries. Sample copy and writer's guidelines free.

NONFICTION Needs essays, interview, new product, photo feature. No fiction. **Buys 30-40 mss/year.** Query with published clips. Length: 500-2,000 words. **Pays $150-375.** Sometimes pays expenses of writers on assignment.

PHOTOS State availability. Identification of subjects required. Reviews contact sheets, negatives, transparencies, prints, digital images. Negotiates payment individually.

COLUMNS Technology and Business in Kentucky; Advertising; Exploring Kentucky; Perspective; Spotlight on the Arts, all less than 1,000 words.

$ MERCER BUSINESS MAGAZINE

White Eagle Publishing Company, 1A Quakerbridge Plaza Drive, Suite 2, Mercerville NJ 08619. (609)689-9960. Fax: (609)586-9899. E-mail: info@mercerchamber.org. Website: mercerchamber.org. **100% freelance written.** Monthly magazine covering national and local business-related, theme-based topics. *Mercer Business* is a Chamber of Commerce publication, so the slant is pro-business primarily. Also covers nonprofits, education and other related issues. Estab. 1924. Circ. 8,500. Byline given. Pays on publication. Publishes ms an average of 1 month after acceptance. Editorial lead time 6 weeks. Submit seasonal material 6 weeks in advance. Accepts queries by e-mail. Accepts simultaneous submissions. Responds in 1 week to queries. Sample copy for #10 SASE. Guidelines by e-mail.

NONFICTION Needs humor. Query with published clips. Length: 1,000-1,800 words. **Pays $150 for assigned articles.** Sometimes pays expenses of writers on assignment.

PHOTOS State availability of or send photos. Captions, identification of subjects, model releases required. Offers no additional payment for photos accepted with ms.

FILLERS Needs gags. **Buys 24 mss/year.** Length: 300-500 words.

$$$$$ OREGON BUSINESS

MEDIAmerica, Inc., 715 SW Morrison St,, Suite 800, Portalnd OR 97205. (503)223-0304. Fax: (503)221-6544. E-mail: robind@oregonbusiness.com. Website: oregonbusiness.com. **15-25% freelance written**. Monthly magazine covering business in Oregon. Our subscribers inlcude owners of small and medium-sized businesses, government agencies, professional staffs of banks, insurance companies, ad agencies, attorneys and other service providers. We accept *only* stories about Oregon businesses, issues and trends. Estab. 1981. Circ. 50,000. Byline given. Pays on publication. Editorial lead time 2 months. Accepts queries by mail, e-mail. Sample copy for $4. Guidelines available online.

NONFICTION Query with résumé and 2-3 published clips. Length: 1,200-3,000 words.

COLUMNS First Person (opinion piece on an issue related to business), 750 words; Around the State (recent news and trends, and how they might shape the future), 100-600 words; Business Tools (practical, how-to suggestions for business managers and owners), 400-600 words; In Character (profile of interesting or quirky member of the business community), 850 words. Query with résumé and 2-3 published clips.

$$ PACIFIC COAST BUSINESS TIMES

14 E. Carrillo St., Suite A, Santa Barbara CA 93101. (805)560-6950. E-mail: hdubroff@pacbiztimes.com. Website: pacbiztimes.com. **10% freelance written**. Weekly tabloid covering financial news specific to Santa Barbara, Ventura, San Luis Obispo counties in California. Estab. 2000. Circ. 5,000. Byline given. Editorial lead time 1 month. Accepts queries by e-mail, phone. Sample copy free. Guidelines free.

NONFICTION Needs interview, opinion, personal finance. Does not want first person, promo or fluff pieces. **Buys 20 mss/year.** Query. Length: 500-800 words. **Pays $75-175.** Pays expenses of writers on assignment.

COLUMNS Harvey Mackay (management), 600 words. Query. **Pays $10-50.**

$$ PRAIRIE BUSINESS

Grand Forks (ND), Forum Communications Company, 808 Third Ave., #400, Fargo ND 58103. Fax: (701)280-9092. E-mail: avanormer@prairiebizmag.com. Website: prairiebizmag.com. **Contact:** Ryan Schuster, submissions editor. **30% freelance written.** Monthly magazine covering business on the Northern Plains (North Dakota, South Dakota, Minnesota). "We attempt to be a resource for business owners/managers, policymakers, educators, and nonprofit administrators, acting as a catalyst for growth in the region by reaching out to an audience of decision makers within the region and also venture capitalists, site selectors, and angel visitors from outside the region." Estab. 2000. Circ. 20,000. Byline given. Pays within 2 weeks of mailing date. Publishes ms an average of 1-2 months after acceptance. Editorial lead time 2 months. Submit seasonal material 2 months in advance. Accepts queries by e-mail. Accepts simultaneous submissions. Responds in 2 weeks to queries. Sample copy free. Guidelines free.

NONFICTION Needs interview, technical, basic online research. "Does not want articles that are blatant self-promotion for any interest without providing value for readers." **Buys 36 mss/year.** Query. Length: 800-1,500 words. **Pays 15¢/word.**

PHOTOS E-mail photos. Captions, identification of subjects required. Reviews GIF/JPEG files (hi-res). Offers $30-250/photo.

$ ROCHESTER BUSINESS JOURNAL

Rochester Business Journal, Inc., 45 E. Ave., Suite 500, Rochester NY 14604. (585)546-8303. Fax: (585)546-3398. Website: rbjdaily.com. **10% freelance written.** Weekly tabloid covering local business. The *Rochester Business Journal* is geared toward corporate executives and owners of small businesses, bringing them leading-edge business coverage and analysis first in the market. Estab. 1984. Circ. 10,000. Byline given. Pays on publication. Publishes ms an average of 1 month after acceptance. Editorial lead time 6 weeks. Accepts queries by mail, fax. Responds in 1 week to queries. Sample copy for free or by e-mail. Guidelines available online.

NONFICTION Needs how-to, business topics, news features, trend stories with local examples. Do not query about any topics that do not include several local examples—local companies, organizations, universities, etc. **Buys 110 mss/year.** Query with published clips. Length: 1,000-2,000 words. **Pays $150.**

🅢🅢 SMARTCEO MAGAZINE

SmartCEO, 2700 Lighthouse Point E., Suite 220A, Baltimore MD 21224. (410)342-9510. Fax: (410)675-5280. E-mail: jeanine@smartceo.com. Website: smartceo.com. **Contact:** Jeanine Gajewski. **25% freelance written.** Monthly magazine covering regional business in the Baltimore, MD and Washington, DC areas. "*SmartCEO* is a regional 'growing company' publication. We are not news; we are a resource full of smart ideas to help educate and inspire decision-makers in the Baltimore and DC areas. Each issue contains features, interviews, case studies, columns and other departments designed to help this region's CEOs face the daily challenges of running a business." Estab. 2001. Circ. 34,000. Byline given. Pays on publication. Publishes ms an average of 2 months after acceptance. Editorial lead time 5 months. Submit seasonal material 5 months in advance. Accepts queries by e-mail, phone. Responds in 4 weeks to queries. Responds in 2 months to mss. Sample copy available online. Guidelines by e-mail.

NONFICTION Needs essays, interview, Business features or tips. "We do not want pitches on CEOs or companies outside the Baltimore, MD or Washington, DC areas; no product reviews, lifestyle content or book reviews, please." **Buys 20 mss/year. mss/year.** Query. Length: 2,000-5,000 words. **Pays $300-600.** Sometimes pays expenses of writers on assignment.

PHOTOS Contact: Erica Fromherz, art director. State availability. Identification of subjects required. Reviews GIF/JPEG files.

COLUMNS Project to Watch (overview of a local development project in progress and why it is of interest to the business community), 600 words; Q&A and tip-focused coverage of business issues and challenges (each article includes the opinions of 10-20 CEOs), 500-1,000 words. **Buys 0-5 mss/year mss/year.** Query.

🅢 SOMERSET BUSINESS MAGAZINE

White Eagle Printing Company, P.O. Box 833, 360 Grove Street at Route 22 East, Somerville NJ 08876. (908)218-4300. Fax: (908)722-7823. E-mail: info@somersetbusinesspartnership.com. Website: scbp.org. **100% freelance written.** Monthly magazine covering national and local business-related, theme-based topics. *Somerset Business Magazine* is a Chamber of Commerce publication, so the slant is pro-business primarily. Also covers nonprofits, education and other related issues. Estab. 1924. Circ. 6,500. Pays on publication. Publishes ms an average of 1 month after acceptance. Editorial lead time 6 weeks. Submit seasonal material 6 weeks in advance. Accepts queries by e-mail. Accepts simultaneous submissions. Responds in 1 week to queries. Sample copy for #10 SASE. Guidelines by e-mail.

NONFICTION Needs humor. Query with published clips. Length: 1,000-1,800 words. **Pays $150 for assigned articles.** Sometimes pays expenses of writers on assignment.

PHOTOS State availability of or send photos. Captions, identification of subjects, model releases required. Offers no additional payment for photos accepted with ms.

🅢🅢 VERMONT BUSINESS MAGAZINE

365 Dorset Street, Burlington VT 05403. (802)863-8038. Fax: (802)863-8069. Website: vermontbiz.com. **80% freelance written.** Monthly tabloid covering business in Vermont. Circ. 8,000. Byline given. Pays on publication. Publishes ms an average of 1 month after acceptance. Responds in 2 months to queries. Sample copy for sae with 11×14 envelope and 7 First-Class stamps.

NONFICTION Buys 200 mss/year. Query with published clips. Length: 800-1,800 words. **Pays $100-200.**

REPRINTS Send tearsheet and information about when and where the material previously appeared.

PHOTOS Send photos. Identification of subjects required. Reviews contact sheets. Offers $10-35/photo.

CAREER, COLLEGE AND ALUMNI

🅢🅢 AFRICAN-AMERICAN CAREER WORLD

Equal Opportunity Publications, Inc., 445 Broad Hollow Rd., Suite 425, Melville NY 11747. (631)421-9421. Fax: (631)421-1352. E-mail: info@eop.com. Website: eop.com. **60% freelance written.** Semiannual magazine focused on African-American students and professionals in all disciplines. Estab. 1969. Byline given. Pays on publication. Publishes ms an average of 3 months after acceptance. Editorial lead time 3 months. Accepts queries by mail, e-mail, fax, phone. NoAccepts simultaneous submissions. Sample copy free. Guidelines free.

NONFICTION Needs how-to, get jobs, interview, personal experience. We do not want articles that are too general. Query. Length: 1,500-2,500 words. **Pays $350 for assigned articles.**

⊜⊜ AMERICAN CAREERS

Career Communications, Inc., 6701 W. 64th St., Overland Park KS 66202. (800)669-7795. E-mail: ccinfor@carcom.com. Website: carcom.com; americancareersonline.com. Jerry Kanabel, art director. **Contact:** Mary Pitchford. **10% freelance written.** Student publication covering careers, career statistics, skills needed to get jobs. *American Careers* provides career, salary, and education information to middle school and high school students. Self-tests help them relate their interests and abilities to future careers. Also online publication at americancareersonline.com. Estab. 1989. Circ. 500,000. Byline given. Pays 1 month after acceptance. Accepts queries by mail. Accepts simultaneous submissions. Sample copy for $4. Guidelines for #10 SASE.

NONFICTION No preachy advice to teens or articles that talk down to students. **Buys 5 mss/year.** Query by mail only with published clips Length: 300-1,000 words. **Pays $100-450.**

PHOTOS State availability. Captions, identification of subjects, model releases required. Negotiates payment individually.

⊜⊜ THE BLACK COLLEGIAN

IMDiversity, Inc., 140 Carondelet St., New Orleans LA 70130. (504)523-0154. Website: blackcollegian.com. **25% freelance written.** Semiannual magazine for African-American college students and recent graduates with an interest in career and job information, African-American cultural awareness, personalities, history, trends, and current events. Estab. 1970. Circ. 122,000. Byline given. Pays 1 month after publication. Submit seasonal material 2 months in advance. Accepts queries by mail. Responds in 6 months to queries. Sample copy for $5 (includes postage) and 9×12 SAE. Guidelines for #10 SASE.

NONFICTION Needs book excerpts, expose, general interest, historical, how-to, develop employability, inspirational, interview, opinion, personal experience. Query. Length: 900-1,900 words. **Pays $100-500 for assigned articles.**

PHOTOS State availability of or send photos. Captions, identification of subjects, model releases required. Reviews 8×10 prints.

⊜⊜ EQUAL OPPORTUNITY

Equal Opportunity Publications, Inc., 445 Broad Hollow Rd., Suite 425, Melville NY 11747. (631)421-9421. Fax: (631)421-0359. E-mail: jschneider@eop.com. Website: eop.com. **Contact:** James Schneider, director, editorial & production. **70% freelance written. Prefers to work with published/established writers.** Triannual magazine dedicated to advancing the professional interests of African Americans, Hispanics, Asian Americans, and Native Americans. Our audience is 90% college juniors and seniors; 10% working graduates. An understanding of educational and career problems of minorities is essential. Estab. 1967. Circ. 11,000. Byline given. Pays on publication. Publishes ms an average of 6 months after acceptance. Editorial lead time 6 months. Submit seasonal material 6 months in advance. Accepts queries by mail, e-mail, fax, phone. Responds in 2 weeks to queries. Responds in 1 month to mss. Sample copy and writer's guidelines for 9×12 SAE with 5 first-class stamps.

○ Distributed through college guidance and placement offices.

NONFICTION Needs general interest, specific minority concerns, how-to, job hunting skills, personal finance, better living, coping with discrimination, interview, minority role models, opinion, problems of minorities, personal experience, professional and student study experiences, technical, on career fields offering opportunities for minorites, coverage of minority interests. **Buys 10 mss/year.** Send complete ms. Length: 1,000-2,000 words. **Pays 10¢/word.** Sometimes pays expenses of writers on assignment.

REPRINTS Send information about when and where the material previously appeared. Pays 10¢/word.

PHOTOS Captions, identification of subjects required. Reviews 35mm color slides and b&w.

⊜⊜⊜ HARVARD MAGAZINE

7 Ware St., Cambridge MA 02138-4037. (617)495-5746. Fax: (617)495-0324. E-mail: harvard_magazine@harvard.edu. Website: harvardmagazine.com. **35-50% freelance written.** Bimonthly magazine for Harvard University faculty, alumni, and students. Estab. 1898. Circ. 245,000. Byline given. Pays on publication. Publishes ms an average of 4 months after acceptance. Editorial lead time 1 year. Accepts queries by mail, fax. Responds in 1 month to queries. Responds in 1 month to mss. Sample copy available online.

NONFICTION Needs book excerpts, essays, interview, journalism on Harvard-related intellectual subjects. **Buys 20-30 mss/year.** Query with published clips. Length: 800-10,000 words. **Pays $400-3,000.** Pays expenses of writers on assignment.

⊛⊛ HISPANIC CAREER WORLD

Equal Opportunity Publications, Inc., 445 Broad Hollow Rd., Suite 425, Melville NY 11747. (631)421-9421. Fax: (631)421-1352. E-mail: info@eop.com. Website: eop.com. **60% freelance written**. Semiannual magazine aimed at Hispanic students and professionals in all disciplines. Estab. 1969. Byline given. Pays on publication. Publishes ms an average of 3 months after acceptance. Editorial lead time 3 months. Accepts queries by mail, e-mail, fax, phone. Accepts simultaneous submissions. Responds in 2 weeks to queries. Responds in 2 months to mss. Sample copy free. Guidelines free.

NONFICTION Needs how-to, find jobs, interview, personal experience. Query. Length: 1,500-2,500 words. **Pays $350 for assigned articles.**

⊛ NEXT STEP MAGAZINE

Next Step Publishing, Inc., 2 W. Main St., Suite 200, Victor NY 14564. E-mail: info@NextStepU.com;counselor@NextStepU.com. Website: nextstepmag.com. **75% freelance written**. Bimonthly magazine covering LINK Newsletter, Transfer Guide. "Our magazine is a 5-times-a-school-year objective publication for high school juniors & seniors preparing for college. Articles cover college, careers, life & financial aid." Estab. 1995. Circ. distributed in 20,500+ high schools. Publishes ms an average of 6 months after acceptance. Editorial lead time 6 months. Submit seasonal material 6 months in advance. Accepts queries by e-mail. NoSample copy available online. Guidelines by e-mail.

NONFICTION Needs book excerpts, general interest, how-to, interview, personal experience, travel. Special issues: *Link* is a newsletter published 5 times a year for high school counselors. Articles run 800-1,500 words & should be focused on helping counselors do their jobs better. Past articles have included counseling students with AD/HD, sports scholarships & motivation tactics. **Buys 15 mss/yr. mss/year.** Query. Length: 500-1,000 words. **Pays $75 for assigned articles.**

COLUMNS Contact: Laura Jeanne Hammond. College Planning (college types, making a decision, admissions); Financial Air (scholarships, financial

aid options); SAT/ACT (preparing for the SAT/ACT, study tips), 400-1,000 words; Career Profiles (profile at least 3 professionals in different aspects of a specific industry), 800-1,000 words; Military (careers in the military, different branches, how to join), 400-600 words. **Buys 5-10 mss/yr. mss/year.** Query with or without published clips. **Pay varies, averages $75 per article.**

⊛⊛⊛⊛ NOTRE DAME MAGAZINE

University of Notre Dame, 538 Grace Hall, Notre Dame IN 46556-5612. E-mail: Ndmag@Nd.edu. Website: Magazine.Nd.edu. **Contact:** Art Director. **50% freelance written**. "We are a university magazine with a scope as broad as that found at a university, but we place our discussion in a moral, ethical, and spiritual context reflecting our Catholic heritage." Estab. 1972. Circ. 150,000. Byline given. Pays on acceptance. Publishes ms an average of 1 year after acceptance. Accepts queries by mail, e-mail, fax. Responds in 2 months to queries. Sample copy available online and by request. Guidelines available online.

NONFICTION Needs opinion, personal experience, religious. **Buys 35 mss/year.** Query with published clips. Length: 600-3,000 words. **Pays $250-3,000.** Sometimes pays expenses of writers on assignment.

PHOTOS Contact: Kerry Prugh, art director. State availability. Identification of subjects, model releases required.

COLUMNS CrossCurrents (essays, deal with a wide array of issues—some topical, some personal, some serious, some light). Query with or without published clips or send complete ms.

⊛⊛ OREGON QUARTERLY

5228 University of Oregon, Eugene OR 97403-5228. (541)346-5048. Fax: (541)346-5571. E-mail: quarterly@uoregon.edu. Website: oregonquarterly.com. **85% freelance written**. Quarterly magazine covering people and ideas at the University of Oregon and the Northwest. Estab. 1919. Circ. 100,000. Byline given. Pays on acceptance. Offers 20% kill fee. Publishes ms an average of 3 months after acceptance. Accepts queries by mail (preferred), e-mail ("grumpily"). NoResponds in 2 months to queries Sample copy for 9×12 SAE with 4 first-class stamps. Guidelines available online.

NONFICTION **Buys 30 mss/year.** Query with published clips. Length: 300-3,000 words. **Payment varies—30¢-50C/per word for departments; features**

more. Sometimes pays expenses of writers on assignment.

REPRINTS See Upfront/Excerpts section for examples. Send photocopy and information about when and where the material previously appeared.

PHOTOS State availability of story-related images. Identification of subjects required. Reviews 8×10 prints. Prefers hi-res digital.

FICTION Rarely publishes novel excerpts by UO professors or grads.

[CAN] $$ QUEEN'S ALUMNI REVIEW

Queen's University, 99 University Ave., Kingston ON K7L 3N6 Canada. Fax: (613)533-2060. E-mail: ken.cuthbertson@queensu.ca. Website: alumnireview.queensu.ca. **25% freelance written.** Quarterly magazine. Estab. 1927. Circ. 112,000. Byline given. Pays on publication. Publishes ms an average of 3 months after acceptance. Editorial lead time 3 months. Submit seasonal material 9 months in advance. Accepts queries by mail, e-mail. Responds in 2 weeks to queries. Responds in 2 weeks to mss. Sample copy and writer's guidelines online.

NONFICTION "Does not want religious or political rants, travel articles, how-to, or general interest pieces that do not refer to or make some reference to our core audience." **Buys 10 mss/year.** Send complete ms. Length: 200-2,500 words. **Pays 50¢/word (Canadian) plus 10% e-rights fee for assigned articles.** Sometimes pays expenses of writers on assignment.

PHOTOS Send photos. Identification of subjects required. Reviews transparencies, prints, GIF/JPEG files. Offers $25 minimum or negotiates payment individually.

COLUMNS Potential freelancers should study our magazine before submitting a query for a column. **Buys 10 mss/year.** Query with published clips or send complete ms. **Pays 50¢/word (Canadian).**

$$$ UAB MAGAZINE

UAB Publications and Periodicals (University of Alabama at Birmingham), AB 340, 1530 3rd Ave. S., Birmingham AL 35294-0103. (205)934-9420. Fax: (205)975-4416. E-mail: mwindsor@uab.edu;charlesb@uab.edu; periodicals@uab.edu. Website: uab.edu/uabmagazine. **70% freelance written.** University magazine published 3 times/year covering University of Alabama at Birmingham. *UAB Magazine* informs readers about the innovation and creative energy that drives UAB's renowned research, educational, and health care programs. The magazine reaches active alumni, faculty, friends and donors, patients, corporate and community leaders, media and the public. Estab. 1980. Circ. 33,000. Byline given. Pays on acceptance. Offers 50% kill fee. Publishes ms an average of 3-4 months after acceptance. Editorial lead time 3 months. Accepts queries by mail, e-mail. Sample copy available online. Guidelines free.

NONFICTION Needs general interest, interview. **Buys 40-50 mss/year.** Query with published clips. Length: 500-5,000 words. **Pays $100-1,200.** Sometimes pays expenses of writers on assignment.

$$ WOMAN ENGINEER

Equal Opportunity Publications, Inc., 445 Broad Hollow Rd., Suite 425, Melville NY 11747. (631)421-9421. Fax: (631)421-1352. E-mail: info@eop.com. Website: eop.com. **Contact:** James Schneider, editor. **60% freelance written.** Triannual magazine focusing on advancing careers of women engineering students and professional engineers. Job information for members of minority groups. Estab. 1969. Byline given. Pays on publication. Publishes ms an average of 3 months after acceptance. Editorial lead time 3 months. Accepts queries by mail, e-mail, fax, phone. Accepts simultaneous submissions. Responds in 2 weeks to queries. Responds in 2 months to mss. Sample copy free. Guidelines free.

NONFICTION Needs how-to, find jobs, interview, personal experience. "We do not want anything too general." Query. Length: 1,500-2,500 words. **Pays $350 for assigned articles.**

TIPS "Gear articles to our audience."

$$ WORKFORCE DIVERSITY FOR ENGINEERING & IT PROFESSIONALS

Equal Opportunity Publications, Inc., 445 Broad Hollow Rd., Suite 425, Melville NY 11747. (631)421-9421. Fax: (631)421-1352. E-mail: info@eop.com. Website: eop.com. **60% freelance written.** Quarterly magazine addressing workplace issues affecting technical professional women, members of minority groups, and people with disabilities. Estab. 1969. Byline given. Pays on publication. Publishes ms an average of 3 months after acceptance. Editorial lead time 3 months. Accepts queries by mail, e-mail, fax, phone. Accepts simultaneous submissions. Responds in 2 weeks to queries. Responds in 2 months to mss. Sample copy free. Guidelines free.

NONFICTION Needs how-to, find jobs, interview, personal experience. We do not want articles that are too general. Query. Length: 1,500-2,500 words. **Pays $350 for assigned articles.**

CHILD CARE AND PARENTAL GUIDANCE

$$$ AMERICAN BABY MAGAZINE

Meredith Corp., 375 Lexington Ave., 9th Floor, New York NY 10017. E-mail: abletters@americanbaby.com. Website: americanbaby.com. **70% freelance written.** Monthly magazine covering health, medical and childcare concerns for expectant and new parents, particularly those having their first child or those whose child is between the ages of birth and 2 years old. Mothers are the primary readers, but fathers' issues are equally important. Estab. 1938. Circ. 2,000,000. Byline given. Pays on acceptance. Offers 25% kill fee. Publishes ms an average of 6 months after acceptance. Editorial lead time 5 months. Submit seasonal material 6 months in advance. Accepts queries by mail. Responds in 3 months to queries. Responds in 3 months to mss. Sample copy for 9×12 SAE with 6 first-class stamps. Guidelines for #10 sase.

💬 Prefers to work with published/established writers; works with a small number of new/unpublished writers each year.

NONFICTION Needs book excerpts, essays, general interest, how-to, some aspect of pregnancy or child care, humor, new product, personal experience, fitness, beauty, health. No `hearts and flowers' or fantasy pieces. **Buys 60 mss/year.** Send complete ms. Length: 1,000-2,000 words. **Pays $750-1,200 for assigned articles. Pays $600-800 for unsolicited articles.** Pays expenses of writers on assignment.

REPRINTS Send photocopy and information about when and where the material previously appeared. Pays 50%

PHOTOS State availability. Identification of subjects, model releases required. Reviews transparencies, Prints.

COLUMNS Personal essays (700-1,000 words) and shorter items for Crib Notes (news and features) and Health Briefs (50-150 words) are also accepted. **Pays $200-1,000.**

$ ATLANTA PARENT/ATLANTA BABY

2346 Perimeter Park Dr., Suite 100, Atlanta GA 30341. (770)454-7599. E-mail: atlantaparent@atlantaparent.com. Website: atlantaparent.com. **50% freelance written.** Byline given. Pays on publication. Publishes ms an average of 3 months after acceptance. Submit seasonal material 6 months in advance. Accepts queries by mail, e-mail. Responds in 4 months to queries. Sample copy for $3.

NONFICTION Needs general interest, how-to, humor, interview, travel. Special issues: Private School (January); Camp (February); Birthday Parties (March and September); Maternity and Mothering (May and October); Childcare (July); Back-to-School (August); Teens (September); Holidays (November/December). No religious or philosophical discussions. **Buys 60 mss/year.** Send complete ms. Length: 800-1,500 words. **Pays $5-50.** Sometimes pays expenses of writers on assignment.

REPRINTS Send tearsheet or photocopy with rights for sale noted and information about when and where the material previously appeared. **Pays $30-50**

PHOTOS State availability of or send photos. Reviews 3×5 photos . Offers $10/photo.

$$$$ BABY TALK

Bonnier Corp., 460 No. Orlando Ave., Suite 200, Winter Park FL 32789. (212)522-4327. Fax: (212)522-8699. E-mail: letters@babytalk.com. Website: babytalk.com. Estab. 1935. Circ. 2,000,000. Byline given. Accepts queries by mail, online submission form. Responds in 2 months to queries.

💬 Magazine published 10 times/year. *Baby Talk* is written primarily for women who are considering pregnancy or who are expecting a child, and parents of children from birth through 18 months, with the emphasis on pregnancy through first 6 months of life.

NONFICTION No phone calls. Query with SASE Length: 1,000-2,000 words. **Pays $500-2,000 depending on length, degree of difficulty, and the writer's experience.**

COLUMNS Several departments are written by regular contributors. 100-1,250 words. Query with SASE **Pays $100-1,000.**

$$ BIRMINGHAM PARENT

Evans Publishing LLC, 700-C Southgate Dr.,, Pelham AL 35124. (205)739-0090. Fax: (205)739-0073. E-mail: editor@birminghamparent.com; carol@birminghamparent.com. Website: birminghamparent.com. **Contact:** Carol Muse Evans, publisher/editor. **75% freelance written.** Monthly magazine covering family issues, parenting, education, babies to teens, health care, anything involving parents raising children. "We are a free, local parenting publication in central Alabama. All of our stories carry some type of local slant. Parenting magazines abound: we are the source for the local market." Estab. 2004. Circ. 40,000. Byline given. Pays within 30 days of publication. Offers 20% kill fee. Publishes ms an average of 3-4 months after acceptance. Editorial lead time 3-4 months. Submit seasonal material 4 months in advance. Accepts queries by e-mail. Accepts simultaneous submissions. Responds in 2-3 weeks to queries. Responds in 2-3 months to mss. Sample copy for $3. Guidelines available online.

NONFICTION Needs book excerpts, general interest, how-to, interview, parenting. Does not want first person pieces. Our pieces educate and inform: we don't take stories without sources. **Buys 24 mss/year.** Send complete ms. Length: 350-2,500 words. **Pays $50-350 for assigned articles. Pays $35-200 for unsolicited articles.**

PHOTOS State availability. Captions, identification of subjects, model releases required. Reviews GIF/JPEG files. Negotiates payment individually; offers no additional payment for photos accepted with ms.

COLUMNS Parenting Solo (single parenting), 650 words; Baby & Me (dealing with newborns or pregnancy), 650 words; Teens (raising teenagers), 650-1,500 words. **Buys 36 mss/year.** Query with published clips or send complete ms. **Pays $35-200.**

$ CHESAPEAKE FAMILY

Jefferson Communications, 929 West St., Suite 307, Annapolis MD 21401. (410)263-1641. Fax: (410)280-0255. E-mail: editor@chesapeakefamily.com. Website: chesapeakefamily.com. **Contact:** Mary McCarthy, editor. **80% freelance written.** Monthly magazine covering parenting. *Chesapeake Family* is a free, regional parenting publication serving readers in the Anne Arundel, Calvert, Prince George's, and Queen Anne's counties of Maryland. Our goal is to identify tips, resources, and products that will make our readers' lives easier. We answer the questions they don't have time to ask, doing the research for them so they have the information they need to make better decisions for their families' health, education, and well-being. Articles must have local angle and resources. Estab. 1990. Circ. 40,000. Byline given. Publishes ms an average of 2 months after acceptance. Editorial lead time 3-6 months. Submit seasonal material 4 months in advance. Accepts queries by mail, e-mail, fax. Accepts simultaneous submissions. Guidelines available online.

NONFICTION Needs how-to, parenting topics: sign your kids up for sports, find out if your child needs braces, etc., interview, local personalities, travel, family-fun destinations. No general, personal essays (however, personal anecdotes leading into a story with general applicability is fine). **Buys 25 mss/year.** Send complete ms. Length: 800-1,200 words. **Pays $75-125. Pays $35-50 for unsolicited articles.**

PHOTOS State availability. Model releases required. Reviews prints, GIF/JPEG files. Offers no additional payment for photos accepted with ms, unless original, assigned photo is selected for the cover.

COLUMNS Buys 25 mss/year. Pays $35-50.

$$ CHICAGO PARENT

141 S. Oak Park Ave., Oak Park IL 60302. (708)386-5555. E-mail: ediffin@chicagoparent.com. Website: chicagoparent.com. **60% freelance written.** Monthly tabloid. "*Chicago Parent* has a distinctly local approach. We offer information, inspiration, perspective and empathy to Chicago-area parents. Our lively editorial mix has a 'we're all in this together' spirit, and articles are thoroughly researched and well written." Estab. 1988. Circ. 125,000 in 3 zones covering the 6-county Chicago metropolitan area. Byline given. Pays on publication. Offers 10-50% kill fee. Publishes ms an average of 2 months after acceptance. Editorial lead time 4 months. Submit seasonal material 4 months in advance. Accepts queries by mail. Responds in 6 weeks to queries. Sample copy for $3.95 and 11×17 SAE with $1.65 postage. Guidelines for #10 SASE.

NONFICTION Needs essays, expose, how-to, parent-related, humor, interview, travel, local interest. Special issues: include Chicago Baby and Healthy Child. No pot-boiler parenting pieces, simultaneous submissions, previously published pieces or non-local writers (from outside the 6-county Chicago metropolitan area). **Buys 40-50 mss/year.** Query with published clips. Length: 200-2,500 words. **Pays $25-300 for assigned articles. Pays $25-100 for unsolicited articles.** Pays expenses of writers on assignment.

PHOTOS State availability. Captions, identification of subjects required. Reviews contact sheets, negatives, prints. Offers $0-40/photo; negotiates payment individually.

COLUMNS Healthy Child (kids' health issues), 850 words; Getaway (travel pieces), up to 1,200 words; other columns not open to freelancers. **Buys 30 mss/year.** Query with published clips or send complete ms. **Pays $100.**

💲💲 COLUMBUS PARENT MAGAZINE

Consumer News Service, 34 S. 3rd St., Columbus OH 43215. (614)461-8878. E-mail: jhawes@columbusparent.com. Website: columbusparent.com. **50% freelance written.** Monthly magazine covering parenting. A hip, reliable resource for Central Ohio parents who are raising children from birth to 18. Estab. 1988. Circ. 60,000. Byline given. Pays on publication. Offers 10% kill fee. Publishes ms an average of 2 months after acceptance. Editorial lead time 3 months. Submit seasonal material 5 months in advance. Accepts queries by mail, e-mail, fax. Sample copy available online. Guidelines available online.

NONFICTION Needs general interest, how-to, interview, new product. Does not want personal essays. **Buys 80 mss/year.** Send complete ms. Length: 500-900 words. **Pays 10¢/word.**

PHOTOS State availability. Identification of subjects required. Offers no additional payment for photos accepted with ms.

💲💲💲💲 FAMILYFUN

Disney Publishing, Inc., 47 Pleasant St., Northampton MA 01060. (413)585-0444. Fax: (413)586-5724. E-mail: queries.familyfun@disney.com. Website: familyfun.com. Magazine covering activities for families with kids ages 3-12. "*FamilyFun* is about all the great things families can do together. Our writers are either parents or authorities in a covered field." Estab. 1991. Circ. 2,100,000. Byline sometimes given. Pays on acceptance. Offers 25% kill fee. Editorial lead time 6 months. Submit seasonal material 6 months in advance. Accepts simultaneous submissions. Responds in 3 months to queries. Sample copy for $5. Guidelines available online.

NONFICTION Needs book excerpts, essays, general interest, how-to, crafts, cooking, educational activities, humor, interview, personal experience, photo feature, travel. **Buys dozens of mss/year.** "Query with published clips. Articles are scheduled and assigned at least 5 months in advance of publication. Please send mss and queries by e-mail or standard mail only — not by telephone or fax. We do not accept unsolicited manuscripts for feature stories; we do accept unsolicited manuscripts for the following departments: Let's Go and Success Story. Queries should describe the content, structure, and tone of the proposed article. We receive many queries on the same topics, so please be as specific as possible about what makes your idea unique and why you are qualified to write about it. If appropriate, include photographs or sketches of the finished project, food, or craft. Due to the large volume of submissions, allow 6-8 weeks for a response. Supporting materials, such as photographs and clips, will be returned if accompanied by SASE with correct postage. Please note: Editorial responses to submissions will be sent via e-mail, so please provide an address for our reply." Length: 850-3,000 words. **Pays $1.25/word.** Pays expenses of writers on assignment.

PHOTOS State availability. Identification of subjects, model releases required. Reviews contact sheets, negatives, transparencies. Offers $75-500/photo.

COLUMNS "Everyday Fun, Debbie Way, senior editor (simple, quick, practical, inexpensive ideas and projects—outings, crafts, games, nature activities, learning projects, and cooking with children), 200-400 words; query or send ms; **pays per word or $200 for ideas.** Family Getaways, Becky Karush, associate editor (brief, newsy items about family travel, what's new, what's great, and especially, what's a good deal), 100-125 words; send ms; **pays per word or $50 for ideas.** Creative Solutions, Debra Immergut, senior editor (explains fun and inventive ideas that have worked for writer's own family), 1,000 words; query or send ms; **pays $1,250 on acceptance.** Also publishes best letters from writers and readers following column, send to My Great Idea: From Our Readers Editor, 100-150 words, **pays $100 on publication.**" **Buys 60-80 letters/year; 10-12 mss/year.**

💲 GRAND RAPIDS FAMILY MAGAZINE

Gemini Publications, 549 Ottawa Ave. NW,, Suite 201, Grand Rapids MI 49503-1444. (616)459-4545. Fax: (616)459-4800. E-mail: cvalade@geminipub.com. Website: grfamily.com. Monthly magazine covering local parenting issues. *Grand Rapids Family* seeks to inform, instruct, amuse, and entertain its readers and their families. Circ. 30,000. Byline given. Pays on publication. Offers $25 kill fee. Editorial lead time 3 months. Submit seasonal material 4 months in advance. Accepts simultaneous submissions. Responds in 2 months to queries. Responds in 6 months to mss. Guidelines for #10 SASE.

NONFICTION Query. **Pays $25-50.**

PHOTOS State availability. Captions, identification of subjects, model releases required. Reviews contact sheets. Offers $25/photo.

COLUMNS All local: law, finance, humor, opinion, mental health. **Pays $25**

🟢 HOME EDUCATION MAGAZINE

P.O. Box 1083, Tonasket WA 98855. (800)236-3278 or (509)486-1351. Fax: (509)486-2753. E-mail: articles@homeedmag.com. Website: homeedmag.com. **Contact:** Jeanne Faulconer, articles editor. **80% freelance written.** Bimonthly magazine covering home-based education. "We feature articles which address the concerns of parents who want to take a direct involvement in the education of their children—concerns such as socialization, how to find curriculums and materials, testing and evaluation, how to tell when your child is ready to begin reading, what to do when homeschooling is difficult, teaching advanced subjects, etc." Estab. 1983. Circ. 120,000. Byline given. Pays on publication. Publishes ms an average of 6 months after acceptance. Submit seasonal material 6 months in advance. Accepts queries by mail. Responds in 2 months to queries. Sample copy for $6.50. Writer's guidelines for #10 SASE, via e-mail, or on website.

NONFICTION Needs essays, how-to, related to homeschooling, humor, interview, personal experience, photo feature, technical. **Buys 40-50 mss/year.** Send complete ms. Length: 750-2,500 words. **Pays $50-150.**

PHOTOS Send photos. Identification of subjects required. Reviews enlargements, 35mm prints, CDs. Pays $100/cover; $12/inside photos.

🟢 HOMESCHOOLING TODAY

P.O. Box 244, Abingdon VA 24212. (866)804-4478; (276)628-1686. Fax: (888)333-4478. E-mail: management@homeschooltoday.com. Website: homeschooltoday.com. **Contact:** Kara Murphy, editor. **75% freelance written.** Bimonthly magazine covering homeschooling. "We are a practical magazine for homeschoolers with a broadly Christian perspective." Estab. 1992. Circ. 13,000. Byline given. Pays on publication. Offers 25% kill fee. Publishes ms an average of 1 year after acceptance. Editorial lead time 6 months. Submit seasonal material 1 year in advance. Accepts

simultaneous submissions. Responds in 4 months to mss. Sample copy and writer's guidelines free.

NONFICTION Needs book excerpts, how-to, interview, new product. No fiction. **Buys 30 mss/year.** Send complete ms. Length: 500-2,000 words. **Pays 10¢/word.**

PHOTOS State availability. Captions, identification of subjects required. Offers no additional payment for photos accepted with ms.

🟢 HUDSON VALLEY PARENT

The Professional Image, 174 South St., Newburgh NY 12550. E-mail: editor@excitingread.com. Website: hvparent.com. **95% freelance written.** Monthly magazine covering parents and families. Estab. 1994. Circ. 80,000. Byline given. Pays on publication. Publishes ms an average of 3 months after acceptance. Editorial lead time 4 months. Submit seasonal material 4 months in advance. Accepts queries by e-mail. Responds in 2-4 weeks to mss. Sample copy free. Guidelines available online.

NONFICTION Needs expose, general interest, humor, interview, personal experience. **Buys 20 mss/yr. mss/year.** Query. Length: 700-1,200 words. **Pays $70-120 for assigned articles. Pays $25-35 for unsolicited articles.**

🟢🟢 ISLAND PARENT MAGAZINE

Island Parent Group, 830 Pembroke St., Suite A-10, Victoria BC V8T 1H9 Canada. (250)388-6905. Fax: (250)388-6920. E-mail: mail@islandparent.ca. Website: islandparent.ca. **Contact:** Sue Fast, Editor. **98% freelance written.** Monthly magazine covering parenting. Estab. 1988. Circ. 20,000. Byline given. honorium. Publishes ms an average of 3 months after acceptance. Editorial lead time 3 months. Submit seasonal material 3 months in advance. Accepts queries by e-mail. Responds in 4-6 weeks to queries. Sample copy available online. Guidelines available online.

💬 "Our editorial philosophy is based on the belief that parents need encouragement and useful information. We encourage writers to cover topics of interest to them or that reflect their own experience—we're looking for a variety of perspectives, experiences and beliefs. Our aim is to help readers feel valued, supported and respected. Ideally, we can raise the profile of parenting and help families enjoy each other."

NONFICTION Contact: Sue Fast. Needs book excerpts, essays, general interest, how-to, humor, inspirational, interview, opinion, (does not mean letters to the editor), personal experience, travel. **Buys 80 mss/year. mss/year.** Query. Length: 400-1,800 words. **Pays $35 for assigned articles. Pays $35 for unsolicited articles.**

PHOTOS Send photos. Reviews GIF/JPEG files. Offers no additional payment for photos accepted with ms.

FILLERS Needs anecdotes, facts, gags, newsbreaks, short humor. **Buys 10/year mss/year.** Length: 400-650 words. **Pays $$35.**

💲 KIDS LIFE MAGAZINE

Tuscaloosa's Family Magazine, Kids Life Publishing of Tuscaloosa, LLC, 1426 22nd Ave., Tuscaloosa AL 35401. (205)345-1193. Fax: (205)345-1632. E-mail: kidslife@comcast.net. Website: kidslifemagazine. com. **50% freelance written.** Kids Life Magazine is a FREE publication for families in West Alabama, containing information on child-related events, parenting and family activities offered in the Tuscaloosa area. Kids Life is printed bimonthly and distributed to over 250 locations including malls, local doctor's offices, children's specialty shops, restaurants and child care centers. "*Kids Life Magazine* is a one-stop place for families containing everything the Tuscaloosa area offers our children, from a Calendar of Events to Articles of Interest!" Estab. 1996. Circ. 30,000. Byline given. Editorial lead time 2 months. Submit seasonal material 4 months in advance. Accepts queries by e-mail. Accepts simultaneous submissions. Sample copy free. No guidelines available. "There are no guidelines per se.".

NONFICTION Needs personal experience. **Does not pay.**

PHOTOS Send photos. Reviews GIF/JPEG files. Offers no payment for photos accepted with ms.

COLUMNS Reel Life with Jane (movie reviews), 1,000 words; Single Parenting, 750 words; Spiritual, 725 words. **Buys 3 columns/year mss/year.**

FILLERS Needs facts, gags, short humor. Length: 500 words.

💲 LIVING

Shalom Foundation, 1251 Virginia Ave., Harrisonburg VA 22802. E-mail: mediaforliving@gmail.com. Website: churchoutreach.com. **90% freelance written.** Quarterly tabloid covering family living. Articles focus on giving general encouragement for families of all ages and stages. Estab. 1985. Circ. 250,000. Byline given. Pays on publication. Publishes ms an average of 6-12 months after acceptance. Editorial lead time 4-6 months. Submit seasonal material 6 months in advance. Accepts queries by mail, e-mail. Accepts simultaneous submissions. Responds in 2 months to queries. Responds in 2-4 months to mss. Sample copy for sae with 9×12 envelope and 4 First-Class stamps. Guidelines free.

☛ "We want our stories and articles to be very practical and upbeat. Since we go to every home, we do not assume a Christian audience. Writers need to take this into account. Personal experience stories are welcome, but are not the only approach.Our audience? Children, teenagers, singles, married couples, right on through to retired persons. We cover the wide variety of subjects that people face in the home and workplace. (See theme list in our guidelines online.)"

NONFICTION Needs general interest, how-to, humor, inspirational, personal experience. We do not use devotional materials intended for Christian audiences. We seldom use pet stories and receive way too many grief/death/dealing with serious illness stories to use. We encourage stories from non-white writers (excuse the phrase). We publish in March, June, September, and December so holidays that occur in other months are not usually the subject of articles. **Buys 48-52 mss/year.** Query. Length: 500-1,200 words. **Pays $35-60.**

PHOTOS Contact: Dorothy Hartman. State availability. Captions, identification of subjects, model releases required. Reviews 4×6 prints, GIF/JPEG files. Offers $15-25/photo.

💲 METROFAMILY MAGAZINE

Inprint Publishing, 725 NW 11th St., Suite 204, Oklahoma City OK 73103. (405)3601-2081. E-mail: editor@metrofamilymagazine.com. Website: metrofamilymagazine.com. **Contact:** Mari Farthing, editor. **20% freelance written.** Monthly tabloid covering parenting. Circ. 35,000. Byline given. Pays on publication. No kill fee; assignments given to local writers only. Publishes ms an average of 2-3 months after acceptance. Editorial lead time 2-3 months. Accepts queries by e-mail. Accepts simultaneous submissions. Responds in 3 weeks to queries. Responds in 1 month to mss. Sample copy for sae with 10×13 envelope and 3 First-Class stamps. via e-mail or return with #10 SASE.

💬 "*MetroFamily Magazine* provides local parenting and family fun information for our Central Oklahoma readers."

NONFICTION Needs , Family or mom-specific articles; see website for themes. No poetry, fiction (except for humor column), or anything that doesn't support good, solid family values. Send complete ms. Length: 800-1200 words. **Pays $40-60, plus 1 contributor copy.**

COLUMNS You've Just Gotta Laugh, humor (600 words). **Buys 12 mss/year.** Send complete ms. **Pays $35.**

$ METROKIDS

Kidstuff Publications, Inc., 1412-1414 Pine St., Philadelphia PA 19102. (215)291-5560, ext. 102. Fax: (215)291-5563. E-mail: editor@metrokids.com. Website: metrokids.com. **Contact:** Tom Livingston. **25% freelance written.** Monthly tabloid providing information for parents and kids in Philadelphia and surrounding counties, South Jersey, and Delaware. free monthly magazine, MetroKids, which has served the community since 1990. The Pennsylvania, South Jersey and Delaware editions of MetroKids are available in supermarkets, libraries, day cares and hundreds of other locations. The magazine features the Never a Dull Moment calendar of day-by-day family events; child-focused camp, day care and party directories, and articles that offer parenting advice and insights. Other MetroKids publications include the Family Find-It Book, a guide to area attractions, service providers and community resources; SpecialKids®, a resource guide for families of children with special needs; and Educator's Edition, a directory of field trips, assemblies and school enrichment programs. Estab. 1990. Circ. 115,000. Byline given. Pays on publication. Submit seasonal material 4 months in advance. Accepts queries by e-mail. Guidelines by e-mail.

💬 Responds only if interested.

NONFICTION Needs general interest, how-to, new product, travel, parenting, health. Special issues: Educator's Edition—field trips, school enrichment, teacher, professional development (March & September); Camps (December & June); Special Kids—children with special needs (August); Vacations and Theme Parks (May & June); What's Happening—guide to events and activities (January); Kids 'N Care—guide to childcare (July). **Buys 40 mss/year.** Query with published clips. Length: 800-1,500 words. **Pays $50.**

REPRINTS E-mail summary or complete article and information about when and where the material previously appeared. Pays $35, or $50 if localized after discussion.

COLUMNS Techno Family (CD-ROM and website reviews); Body Wise (health); Style File (fashion and trends); Woman First (motherhood); Practical Parenting (financial parenting advice); Kids 'N Care (toddlers and daycare); Special Kids (disabilities), all 650-850 words. **Buys 25. mss/year.** Query. **Pays $25-50.**

$$ METRO PARENT MAGAZINE

Metro Parent Publishing Group, 22041 Woodward Ave., Ferndale MI 48220-2520. (248)398-3400. Fax: (248)3399-3970. E-mail: jelliott@metroparent.com. Website: metroparent.com. **75% freelance written.** Monthly magazine covering parenting, women's health, education. Circ. 80,000. Byline given. Pays on publication. Publishes ms an average of 3 months after acceptance. Editorial lead time 3 months. Submit seasonal material 3 months in advance. Accepts queries by mail, e-mail. Accepts simultaneous submissions. Responds in 2 weeks to queries. Responds in 3 months to mss. Sample copy for $2.50.

💬 "We are a local magazine on parenting topics and issues of interest to Detroit-area parents. Related issues: *Ann Arbor Parent; African/American Parent; Metro Baby Magazine.*"

NONFICTION Needs essays, humor, inspirational, personal experience. **Buys 100 mss/year.** Send complete ms. Length: 1,500-2,500 words. **Pays $50-300 for assigned articles.**

PHOTOS State availability. Captions required. Offers $100-200/photo or negotiates payment individually.

COLUMNS Women's Health (latest issues of 20-40 year olds), 750-900 words; Solo Parenting (advice for single parents); Family Finance (making sense of money and legal issues); Tweens 'N Teens (handling teen issues), 750-800 words. **Buys 50 mss/year.** Send complete ms. **Pays $75-150.**

$$ PARENT:WISE AUSTIN

Pleticha Publishing Inc., 5501-A Balcones Dr., Suite 102, Austin TX 78731. (512)699-5327. Fax: (512)532-6885. E-mail: editor@parentwiseaustin.com. Website: parentwiseaustin.com. **25% freelance written.**

Monthly magazine covering parenting news, features and issues; mothering issues; maternal feminism; feminism as it pertains to motherhood and work/life balance; serious/thoughtful essays about the parenting experience; humor articles pertaining to the parenting experience. *"Parent:Wise Austin* targets educated, thoughtful readers who want solid information about the parenting experience. We seek to create a warm, nurturing community by providing excellent, well researched articles, thoughtful essays, humor articles, and other articles appealing to parents. Our readers demand indepth, well written articles; we do not accept, nor will we print, 're-worked' articles on boiler plate topics." Estab. 2004. Circ. 32,000. Byline given. Pays on publication. Publishes ms an average of 2 months after acceptance. Editorial lead time 6 months. Submit seasonal material 6 months in advance. Accepts queries by e-mail. NoResponds in 1 week to queries. Responds in 1 month to mss. Sample copy for 41.17 postage. "However, sample copies can be viewed online.". Guidelines available online.

NONFICTION Needs essays, humor, opinion, personal experience, travel, hard news, features on parenting issues. Special issues: Mother's Day issue (May); Father's Day issue (June). "Does not want boiler plate articles or generic articles that have been customized for our market." **Buys 12-20 mss/year.** All articles should be submitted in their entirety—no queries—via e-mail. You should receive a response within 60-days (if not, please e-mail us again to ensure that we received your submission). Please do NOT send us your article via snail mail (snail-mailed submissions will not be read or returned). Length: 500-2,500 words. **Pays $50-200.** Sometimes pays expenses of writers on assignment.

PHOTOS Contact: Contact Nisa Sharma, art director. State availability. Captions, identification of subjects, model releases required. Reviews JPEG files. Offers no additional payment for photos accepted with ms.

COLUMNS My Life as a Parent (humor), 500-700 words; Essay (first-person narrative), 500-1,000 words. **Buys 24-50 mss/year.** Send complete ms. **Pays $50.**

POETRY Needs avant-garde, free verse, haiku, light verse, traditional. "Does not want poetry that does not pertain to parenting or the parenting experience." Buys 3-5 poems/year. Submit maximum 3 poems. Length: 25 lines.

PARENTGUIDE

PG Media, 419 Park Ave. S., Floor 13, New York NY 10016. (212)213-8840. Fax: (212)447-7734. E-mail: jenna@parentguidenews.com. Website: parentguidenews.com. **Contact:** Jenna Hammond, Editor. **80% freelance written**. Monthly magazine covering parenting and family issues. "We are a tabloid-sized publication catering to the needs and interests of parents who have children under the age of 12. Our print publication is distributed in New York City, New Jersey, Long Island, Westchester County, Rockland County, and Queens. Our website (one of the most popular online parenting sites) is read by parents, psychologists, teachers, caretakers, and others concerned about family matters worldwide. Our columns and feature articles cover health, education, child-rearing, current events, parenting issues, recreational activities and social events. We also run a complete calendar of local events. We welcome articles from professional authors as well as never-before-published writers." Estab. 1982. Circ. 285,000. Byline given. Does not offer financial compensation. Publishes ms an average of 5 months after acceptance. Editorial lead time 5 months. Submit seasonal material 6 months in advance. Accepts queries by e-mail. Accepts simultaneous submissions. Sample copy available online. Guidelines free.

NONFICTION Needs how-to, (family-related service pieces), inspirational, interview, personal experience, travel, (education, health, fitness, special needs, parenting).

FICTION Needs confession, humorous, slice-of-life vignettes. Query. Length: 700-1,000 words.

⊖⊖⊖⊖ PARENTING MAGAZINE (EARLY YEARS AND SCHOOL YEARS EDITIONS)

Bonnier Corporation, 2 Park Ave., New York NY 10016. (212)779-5000. Website: parenting.com. Magazine published 10 times/year for mothers of children from birth to 12, and covering both the emotional and practical aspects of parenting. Estab. 1987. Circ. 2,100,000. Byline given. Pays on acceptance. Offers 25% kill fee. Accepts queries by mail. Responds in 2 months. Samples not available. Guidelines for #10 SASE.

○ "For writers new to *Parenting*, the best opportunities are the departments. The pieces there range from 100 to 500 words. Queries for each of these departments should be addressed to the appropriate editor (such as Kids' Health Editor, or Ages & Stages Editor). Put all queries in writing (no phone calls, please), and enclose a SASE for a reply and the return of any materials you submit. Allow about 2 months for a response, due to the large volume of unsolicited queries we receive. We will not consider simultaneous submissions. We do not publish poetry. *Parenting* is available on newsstands; please do not send requests for sample issues."

NONFICTION Contact: Articles Editor. Needs book excerpts, personal experience, child development/behavior/health. **Buys 20-30 mss/year.** Query. Length: 1,000-2,500 words. **Pays $1,000-3,000.** Pays expenses of writers on assignment.

COLUMNS Contact: Query to the specific departmental editor. **Buys 50-60 mss/year.** Query. **Pays $50-400.**

$ PEDIATRICS FOR PARENTS

Pediatrics for Parents, Inc., 35 Starknaught Heights, Gloucester MA 01930. (215)253-4543. Fax: (973)302-4543. E-mail: richsagall@pedsforparents.com. **50% freelance written.** Monthly newsletter covering children's health. "*Pediatrics For Parents* emphasizes an informed, common-sense approach to childhood health care. We stress preventative action, accident prevention, when to call the doctor and when and how to handle a situation at home. We are also looking for articles that describe general, medical and pediatric problems, advances, new treatments, etc. All articles must be medically accurate and useful to parents with children—prenatal to adolescence." Estab. 1981. Circ. 120,000. Byline given. Pays on publication. Publishes ms an average of 4 months after acceptance. Accepts queries by mail, e-mail, fax. Accepts simultaneous submissions. Responds in 1 month to queries. Sample copy available online. Guidelines available online.

NONFICTION No first person or experience. **Buys 25 mss/year.** Send complete ms. Length: 1,000-1,500 words. **Pays $10-25.**

$ PIKES PEAK PARENT

The Gazette/Freedom Communications, 30 S. Prospect St., Colorado Springs CO 80903. Fax: (719)476-1625. E-mail: trudy@pikespeakparent.com. Website: pikespeakparent.com. **10% freelance written.** Monthly tabloid covering parenting, family and grandparenting. We prefer stories with local angle and local stories. We do not accept unsolicited manuscripts. Estab. 1994. Circ. 35,000. Byline given. Pays on publication. Editorial lead time 3 months. Submit seasonal material 4 months in advance. Accepts queries by e-mail. Accepts simultaneous submissions. Responds in 1 month to queries. Sample copy available online.

NONFICTION Needs essays, general interest, how-to, medical related to parenting. **Buys 10 mss/year.** Query with published clips. Length: 800-1,000 words. **Pays $20-120.**

$$$ PLUM MAGAZINE

Groundbreak Publishing, 276 Fifth Ave., Suite 302, New York NY 10001. (212)725-9201. Fax: (212)725-9203. E-mail: editor@plummagazine.com. Website: plummagazine.com. **90% freelance written.** Annual magazine covering health and lifestyle for pregnant women over age 35. *Plum* is a patient education tool meant to be an adjunct to obstetrics care. It presents information on preconception, prenatal medical care, nutrition, fitness, beauty, fashion, decorating, and travel. It also covers newborn health with articles on baby wellness, nursery necessities, postpartum care, and more. Estab. 2004. Circ. 450,000. Byline sometimes given. Pays on publication. Offers 20% kill fee. Publishes ms an average of 3-6 months after acceptance. Editorial lead time 6 months. Submit seasonal material 8 months in advance. Accepts queries by e-mail. Responds in 6 weeks to queries. Sample copy for $7.95. Guidelines by e-mail.

NONFICTION Needs essays, how-to, interview. Query with published clips. Length: 300-3,500 words. **Pays 75¢-$1/word**

$ SACRAMENTO PARENT

Family Publishing Inc., 457 Grass Valley Hwy., Suite 5, Auburn CA 95603. (530)888-0573. Fax: (530)888-1536. E-mail: amy@sacramentoparent.com. Website: sacramentoparent.com. **Contact:** Amy Crelly, editor. **50% freelance written.** Monthly magazine covering parenting in the Sacramento region. We look for articles that promote a developmentally appropriate, healthy and peaceful environment for children. Estab. 1992. Circ. 50,000. Byline given. Pays on publication. Offers 10% kill fee. Publishes ms an average of 2 months after acceptance. Editorial lead time 3 months. Submit seasonal material 4 months in advance. Accepts queries by e-mail. Sample copy free. Guidelines by e-mail.

NONFICTION Needs book excerpts, general interest, how-to, humor, interview, opinion, personal experience. **Buys 36 mss/year.** Query. Length: 300-1,000 words. **Pays $50-200 for original articles.**

COLUMNS Let's Go! (Sacramento regional family-friendly day trips/excursions/activities), 600 words. **Pays $25-45.**

$ SAN DIEGO FAMILY MAGAZINE

1475 Sixth Ave., 5th Floor, San Diego CA 92101-3200. (619)685-6970. Fax: (619)685-6978. E-mail: kirsten@sandiegofamily.com; family@sandiegofamily.com. Website: sandiegofamily.com. **100% freelance written**. Monthly magazine for parenting and family issues. "*SDFM* is a regional family publication. We focus on providing current, informative and interesting editorial about parenting and family life that educates and entertains." Estab. 1982. Circ. 300,000. Byline given. Pays on publication. Publishes ms an average of 1-6 months after acceptance. Editorial lead time 4 months. Submit seasonal material 6 months in advance. Accepts queries by mail, e-mail. Accepts simultaneous submissions. Responds in 1 month to queries. Responds in 2 months to mss. Sample copy for $4.50 to P.O. Box 23960, San Diego CA 92193. Guidelines available online.

NONFICTION Needs essays, general interest, how-to, interview, technical, travel, informational articles. Does not want humorous personal essays, opinion pieces, religious or spiritual. **Buys 350-500 mss/year.** Query. Length: 600-1,250 words. **Pays $22-90.**

REPRINTS Send typed manuscript with rights for sale, ted and information about when and where the material previously appeared. Will respond only if SASE is included.

FICTION "No adult fiction. We only want to see short fiction written for children: 'read aloud' stories, stories for beginning readers (400-500 words)." **Buys 0-12 fillers. mss/year.** Send complete ms.

FILLERS **Buys 0-12 mss/year.** Length: 200-600 words.

$ SCHOLASTIC PARENT & CHILD

Scholastic, Inc., 557 Broadway, New York NY 10012. (212)343-6100. Fax: (212)343-4801. E-mail: parentandchild@scholastic.com. Website: parentandchildonline.com. **Contact:** Nick Friedman, editor-in-chief. Bimonthly magazine published to keep active parents up-to-date on children's learning and development while in pre-school or child-care environment. Circ. 1,224,098. Editorial lead time 10 weeks.

$$ SOUTH FLORIDA PARENTING

1701 Green Rd., Suite B, Deerfield Beach FL 33441. (954)596-5607. Fax: (954)429-1207. E-mail: krlomer@tribune.com. Website: sfparenting.com. **Contact:** Kyara Lomer, ed. **90% freelance written**. Monthly magazine covering parenting, family. "*South Florida Parenting* provides news, information, and a calendar of events for readers in Southeast Florida (Palm Beach, Broward and Miami-Dade counties). The focus is on parenting issues, things to do, information about raising children in South Florida." Estab. 1990. Circ. 110,000. Byline given. Pays on publication. Editorial lead time 4 months. Submit seasonal material 4 months in advance. Accepts queries by e-mail, fax. Responds in 3 months to queries.

💬 Preference given to writers based in South Florida.

NONFICTION Needs how-to (parenting issues), interview/profile, family, parenting and children's issues. Special issues: family fitness, education, spring party guide, fall party guide, kids and the environment, toddler/preschool, preteen. Length: 500-1,000 words. **Pays $40-165.**

REPRINTS **Pays $25-50.**

COLUMNS Dad's Perspective, Family Deals, Products for Families, Health/Safety, Nutrition, Baby Basics, Travel, Toddler/Preschool, Preteen, South Florida News.

$$ SOUTHWEST FLORIDA PARENT & CHILD

The News-Press, 2442 Dr. Martin Luther King, Jr. Blvd., Fort Myers FL 33901. (239)335-4698. Fax: (239)344-4690. E-mail: pamela@swflparentchild.com. Website: gulfcoastmoms.com. **75% freelance written.** Monthly magazine covering parenting. *Southwest Florida Parent & Child* is a regional parenting magazine with an audience of mostly moms but some dads, too. With every article, we strive to give readers information they can use. We aim to be an indispensable resource for our local parents. Estab. 2000. Circ. 25,000. Byline given. Pays on publication. Publishes ms an average of 2-3 months after acceptance. Editorial lead time 2-3 months. Submit seasonal material 3+ months in advance. Accepts queries by mail, e-mail, fax. Accepts simultaneous submissions.

NONFICTION Needs book excerpts, general interest, how-to, humor, interview, new product, personal experience, photo feature, religious, travel. Does not want personal experience or opinion pieces. **Buys 96-120 mss/year.** Send complete ms. Length: 500-700 words. **Pays $25-200.** Sometimes pays expenses of writers on assignment.

PHOTOS State availability of or send photos. Captions, identification of subjects required. Reviews GIF/JPEG files. Negotiates payment individually.

☺⊖⊖⊖⊖⊖ TODAY'S PARENT

Rogers Media, Inc., One Mt. Pleasant Rd., 8th Floor, Toronto ON M4Y 2Y5 Canada. (416) 764-2883. Fax: (416)764-2894. E-mail: editors@todaysparent.com. Website: todaysparent.com. Monthly magazine for parents with children up to the age of 12. Circ. 175,000. Editorial lead time 5 months.

NONFICTION Length: 1,800-2,500 words. **Pays $1,500-2,200.**

COLUMNS Profile (Canadian who has accomplished something remarkable for the benefit of children), 250 words; **pays $250.** Your Turn (parents share their experiences), 800 words; **pays $200.** Beyond Motherhood (deals with topics not directly related to parenting), 700 words; **pays $800.** Education (tackles straightforward topics and controversial or complex topics), 1,200 words; **pays $1,200-1,500.** Health Behavior (child development and discipline), 1,200 words; **pays $1,200-1,500.** Slice of Life (explores lighter side of parenting), 750 words; **pays $650.**

☺⊖⊖⊖⊖ TODAY'S PARENT PREGNANCY & BIRTH

Rogers Media, Inc., One Mt. Pleasant Rd., 8th Floor, Toronto ON M4Y 2Y5 Canada. (416)764-2883. Fax: (416) 764-2894. E-mail: editors@todaysparent.com. Website: todaysparent.com. **Contact:** The Editor. **100% freelance written.** Magazine published 3 times/year. "*P&B* helps, supports and encourages expectant and new parents with news and features related to pregnancy, birth, human sexuality and parenting." Estab. 1973. Circ. 190,000. Pays on acceptance. Publishes ms an average of 8 months after acceptance. Editorial lead time 6 months. Accepts queries by mail. Responds in 6 weeks to queries. Guidelines for SASE.

NONFICTION Buys 12 mss/year. Query with published clips; send detailed proposal. Length: 1,000-2,500 words. **Pays up to $1/word.** Sometimes pays expenses of writers on assignment.

PHOTOS State availability. Pay negotiated individually.

⊖⊖ TOLEDO AREA PARENT NEWS

Adams Street Publishing, Co., 1120 Adams St., Toledo OH 43604. (419)244-9859. E-mail: mattd@toledoparent.com;editor@toledoparent.com. Website: toledoparent.com. Monthly tabloid for Northwest Ohio/Southeast Michigan parents. Estab. 1992. Circ. 40,000. Byline given. Pays on publication. Publishes ms an average of 1 month after acceptance. Editorial lead time 3 months. Accepts queries by mail, e-mail, fax. Responds in 1 month to queries. Sample copy for $1.50.

NONFICTION Needs general interest, interview, opinion. **Buys 10 mss/year.** Length: 1,000-2,500 words. **Pays $75-125.**

PHOTOS State availability. Identification of subjects required. Negotiates payment individually.

⊖⊖ TWINS™ MAGAZINE

30799 Pinetree Road, #256, Cleveland OH 44124. (866) 586-7683. Fax: (866) 586-7683. E-mail: twinseditor@twinsmagazine.com. Website: twinsmagazine.com. **50% freelance written.** "We now publish eight (8) issues per year—4 print/4 digital covering all aspects of parenting twins/multiples. *Twins* is a national/international publication that provides informational and educational articles regarding the parenting of twins, triplets, and more. All articles must be multiple specific and have an upbeat, hopeful, and/or positive ending." Estab. 1984. Circ. 35,000. Byline given. Pays on publication. Editorial lead time 4 months. Submit seasonal material 6 months in advance. Accepts queries by U.S. mail, e-mail only. Response time varies. Sample copy for $5 or on website. Guidelines available online.

NONFICTION Needs personal experience, first-person parenting experience, professional experience as it relates to multiples. Nothing on cloning, pregnancy reduction, or fertility issues. **Buys 12 mss/year.** Send complete ms. Length: 650-1,200 words. **Pays $25-250 for assigned articles. Pays $25-125 for unsolicited articles.**

PHOTOS State availability. Identification of subjects required. Offers no additional payment for photos accepted with ms.

COLUMNS A Word From Dad; Mom-2-Mom; LOL: Laugh Out Loud; Family Health; Resource Round Up; Tales From Twins; & Research. Pays $25-75. **Buys 8-10 mss/year.** Query with or without published clips or send complete ms. **Pays $40-75.**

COMIC BOOKS

$ THE COMICS JOURNAL

Fantagraphics Books, 7563 Lake City Way NE, Seattle WA 98115. (206)524-1967. Fax: (206)524-2104. E-mail: editorial@tcj.com. Website: tcj.com. Magazine covering the comics medium from an arts-first perspective on a six-week schedule. "*The Comics Journal* is one of the nation's most respected single-arts magazines, providing its readers with an eclectic mix of industry news, professional interviews, and reviews of current work. Due to its reputation as the American magazine with an interest in comics as an art form, the *Journal* has subscribers worldwide, and in this country serves as an important window into the world of comics for several general arts and news magazines." Byline given. Accepts queries by mail, e-mail. Guidelines available online.

NONFICTION Needs essays, interview, opinion, reviews. Send complete ms. Length: 2,000-3,000 words. **Pays 4¢/word, and 1 contributor's copy.**

COLUMNS On Theory, Art and Craft (2,000-3,000 words); Firing Line (reviews 1,000-5,000 words); Bullets (reviews 400 words or less). Send inquiries, samples **Pays 4¢/word, and 1 contributor's copy.**

NTH DEGREE

3502 Fernmoss Ct., Charlotte NC 28269. E-mail: submissions@nthzine.com. Website: nthzine.com. **Contact:** Michael Pederson. Estab. 2002.

TIPS "Don't submit anything that you may be ashamed of ten years later."

CONSUMER SERVICE AND BUSINESS OPPORTUNITY

$$ HOME BUSINESS MAGAZINE

United Marketing & Research Co., Inc., P.O. Box 807, 20711 Holt Ave, Lakeville MN 55044. E-mail: editor@homebusinessmag.com; publisher@homebusinessmag.com. Website: homebusinessmag.com. **75% freelance written.** *Home Business Magazine* covers every angle of the home-based business market including: cutting edge editorial by well-known authorities on sales and marketing, business operations, the home office, franchising, business opportunities, network marketing, mail order and other subjects to help readers choose, manage and prosper in a home-based business; display advertising, classified ads and a directory of home-based businesses; technology, the Internet, computers and the future of home-based business; home-office editorial including management advice, office set-up, and product descriptions; business opportunities, franchising and work-from-home success stories. Estab. 1993. Circ. 105,000. Publishes ms an average of 6 months after acceptance. Editorial lead time 6 months. Submit seasonal material 6 months in advance. Accepts queries by e-mail. Accepts simultaneous submissions. Sample copy for sae with 9×12 envelope and 8 First-Class stamps. Guidelines for #10 sase.

NONFICTION Needs book excerpts, general interest, how-to, home business, inspirational, interview, new product, personal experience, photo feature, technical, mail order, franchise, business management, internet, finance network marketing. No non-home business related topics. **Buys 40 mss/year.** Send complete ms. Length: 200-1,000 words. **Pays 20¢/published word for work-for-hire assignments; 50-word byline for unsolicited articles.**

PHOTOS Identification of subjects required. Offers no additional payment for photos accepted with ms.

COLUMNS Marketing & Sales; Money Corner; Home Office; Management; Technology; Working Smarter; Franchising; Network Marketing, all 650 words. Send complete ms.

CONTEMPORARY CULTURE

$$ A&U

Art & Understanding, Inc., 25 Monroe St., Suite 205, Albany NY 12210-2729. (518)426-9010. Fax: (518)**436-5354.** E-mail: mailbox@aumag.org; chaelaumag@me.com. Website: aumag.org. **50% freelance written.** Monthly magazine covering cultural, political, and medical responses to HIV/AIDS. Estab. 1991. Circ. 205,000. Byline given. Pays 3 months after publication. Publishes ms an average of 3 months after acceptance. Editorial lead time 6 months. Accepts queries by mail, e-mail. Accepts simultaneous submissions. Responds in 1 month to queries. Responds in 2 months to mss. Sample copy for $5. Guidelines available online.

NONFICTION Needs AIDS-related book excerpts, essays, general interest, how-to, humor, interview, new product, opinion, personal experience, photo feature, travel, reviews (film, theater, art exhibits, video, music, other media), medical news, artist profiles. **Buys 6 mss/year.** Query with published clips. Length: 800-1,200 words. **Pays $150-300 for assigned articles.**

PHOTOS State availability. Captions, identification of subjects, model releases required.

COLUMNS The Culture of AIDS (reviews of books, music, film), 300 words; Viewpoint (personal opinion), 750 words. **Buys 6 mss/year. mss/year.** Send complete ms. **Pays $50-150.**

FICTION Drama. Send complete ms. Length: less than 1,500 words. **Pays $100.**

POETRY Any length/style (shorter works preferred). **Pays $25.**

☼❸❸❸ ADBUSTERS

Adbusters Media Foundation, 1243 W. 7th Ave., Vancouver BC V6H 1B7 Canada. (604)736-9401. Fax: (604)737-6021. E-mail: editor@adbusters.org. Website: adbusters.org. **50% freelance written.** Bimonthly magazine. We are an activist journal of the mental environment. Estab. 1989. Circ. 90,000. Byline given. Pays 1 month after publication. Accepts queries by mail, e-mail, fax. Accepts simultaneous submissions. Guidelines available online.

NONFICTION Needs essays, expose, interview, opinion. **Buys variable mss/year.** Query. Length: 250-3,000 words. **Pays $100/page for unsolicited articles; 50¢/word for solicited articles.**

FICTION Inquire about themes.

POETRY Inquire about themes.

❸❸ ALBEMARLE

Carden Jennings Publishing Co., Ltd., 375 Greenbrier Dr., Suite 100, Charlottesville VA 22901. (434)817-2000. Fax: (434)817-2020. E-mail: albemarle@cjp.com. Website: cjp.com. **80% freelance written.** Bimonthly magazine covering lifestyle for central Virginia. Lifestyle magazine for central Virginia. Estab. 1987. Circ. 10,000. Byline given. Pays on publication. Offers 30% kill fee. Publishes ms an average of 4 months after acceptance. Editorial lead time 6-8 months. Submit seasonal material 6 months in advance. Accepts queries by mail, e-mail, fax. Accepts simultaneous submissions. Responds in 1 month to queries. Responds in 2 months to mss. Sample copy for sae with 10x12 envelope and 5 first-class stamps. Guidelines for #10 SASE.

NONFICTION Needs essays, historical, interview, photo feature, travel. No fiction, poetry or anything without a direct tie to central Virginia. **Buys 30-35 mss/year.** Query with published clips. Length: 900-3,500 words. **Pays $75-225 for assigned articles and unsolicited articles.** Sometimes pays expenses of writers on assignment.

PHOTOS State availability. Captions, identification of subjects, model releases required. Reviews transparencies. Negotiates payment individually.

COLUMNS Etcetera (personal essay), 900-1,200 words; no food; Leisure (travel, sports), 3,000 words. **Buys 20 mss/year.** Query with published clips. **Pays $75-150.**

❸ BOSTON REVIEW

PO Box 425786, Cambridge MA 02142. (617)324-1360. Fax: (617)452-3356. E-mail: review@bostonreview.net. Website: bostonreview.net. Timothy Donnelly. **Contact:** Dept. Editor. **90% freelance written.** Bimonthly magazine of cultural and political analysis, reviews, fiction, and poetry. "The editors are committed to a society and culture that foster human diversity and a democracy in which we seek common grounds of principle amidst our many differences. In the hope of advancing these ideals, the *Review* acts as a forum that seeks to enrich the language of public debate." Estab. 1975. Circ. 20,000. Byline given. Publishes ms an average of 4 months after acceptance. Accepts simultaneous submissions. Responds in 4 months to queries. Sample copy for $5 or online. Guidelines available online.

○ *Boston Review* is a recipient of the Pushcart Prize in Poetry.

✂ Reads submissions September 15-May 15.

NONFICTION Needs essays (book reviews). "*We do not accept unsolicited book reviews. If you would like to be considered for review assignments, please send your resume along with several published clips.*" **Buys 50 mss/year.** Query with published clips. You may submit query letters and unsolicited nonfiction up to 5,000 words via the online submissions system.

FICTION Contact: Junot Díaz , fiction editor. "I'm looking for stories that are emotionally and intellectually substantive and also interesting on the level of language. Things that are shocking, dark, lewd, comic, or even insane are fine so long as the fiction is *controlled* and purposeful in a masterly way. Subtlety, delicacy, and lyricism are attractive too." Needs ethnic, experimental, contemporary, prose poem. No romance, erotica, genre fiction. **Buys 5 mss/year.** Send complete ms. Length: 1,200-5,000 words. Average length: 2,000 words. **Pays $25-300, and 5 contributor's copies.**

POETRY Contact: Benjamin Paloff and Timothy Donnelly, poetry editors. *Boston Review*, published bimonthly, is a tabloid-format magazine of arts, culture, and politics. "We are open to both traditional and experimental forms. What we value most is originality and a strong sense of voice." Has published poetry by Frank Bidart, Lucie Brock-Broido, Peter Gizzi, Jorie Graham, Allen Grossman, John Koethe, and Karen Volkman. Receives about 5,000 submissions/year, accepts about 30 poems/year. Circulation is 20,000 nationally. Single copy: $5; subscription: $25. Sample: $5. Responds in 2-4 months. Acquires first serial rights. Reviews books of poetry, solicited reviews only. Send materials for review consideration. Reads poetry between September 15 and May 15 each year. Submit maximum 5—6 poems. **Payment varies.**

○ ❸ ❸ BROKEN PENCIL

P.O. Box 203, Station P, Toronto ON M5S 2S7 Canada. E-mail: editor@brokenpencil.com. E-mail: fiction@brokenpencil.com. Website: brokenpencil.com. **80% freelance written**. Quarterly magazine covering arts and culture. *Broken Pencil* is one of the few magazines in the world devoted exclusively to underground culture and the independent arts. We are a great resource and a lively read! *Broken Pencil* reviews the best zines, books, Web sites, videos and artworks from the underground and reprints the best articles from the alternative press. From the hilarious to the perverse, *Broken Pencil* challenges conformity and demands attention. Estab. 1995. Circ. 5,000. Byline given. Pays on publication. Publishes ms an average of 2-3 months after acceptance. Accepts queries by mail, e-mail. Guidelines available online.

NONFICTION Needs essays, general interest, historical, humor, interview, opinion, personal experience, photo feature, travel, reviews. Does not want anything about mainstream art and culture. **Buys 8 mss/year.** Query with published clips. Length: 400-2,500 words. **Pays $100-400.** Sometimes pays expenses of writers on assignment.

PHOTOS Send photos. Identification of subjects required. Reviews prints, GIF/JPEG files. Negotiates payment individually.

COLUMNS Contact: Contact Erin Kobayashi, books editor; James King, ezines editor; Terence Dick, music editor; Lindsay Gibb, film editor. Books (book reviews and feature articles); Ezines (ezine reviews and feature articles); Music (music reviews and feature articles);

Film (film reviews and feature articles), all 200-300 words for reviews and 1,000 words for features. **Buys 8 mss/year.** Query with published clips. **Pays $100-400.**

FICTION Contact: Contact Hal Niedzviecki, fiction editor. We're particularly interested in work from emerging writers. Needs adventure, cond novels, confession, erotica, ethnic, experimental, fantasy, historical, horror, humorous, mystery, novel concepts, romance, science fiction, slice-of-life vignettes. **Buys 8 mss/year.** Send complete ms. Length: 500-3,000 words.

➕ ❸ ❸ BUST MAGAZINE

Bust, Inc., PO Box 1016, Cooper Station, New York NY 10276. E-mail: submissions@bust.com. Website: bust.com. **60% freelance written**. Bimonthly magazine covering pop culture for young women. "*Bust* is the groundbreaking, original women's lifestyle magazine & website that is unique in its ability to connect with bright, cutting-edge, influential young women." Estab. 1993. Circ. 100,000. Byline given. Pays on publication. Publishes ms an average of 4 months after acceptance. Editorial lead time 3-4 months. Submit seasonal material 6 months in advance. Accepts queries by mail, e-mail. Accepts simultaneous submissions. varies. online at bust.com/info/submit.html.

> 💬 "Please include your full name, e-mail address, mailing address, day and night phone number in your submission. If you're e-mailing your submission, please send it as an attachment. If you're mailing your submission and want us to return it to you, please include a SASE. If we're interested in running your piece, we'll get back to you about it. If we aren't, we will try to let you know but it may take a very long time and we can't promise you that we'll be able to. BUST does not accept poetry. If you are submitting a story idea rather than a story, please also send us clips of your previous writing."

NONFICTION Needs book excerpts, exposè, general interest, historical, how-to, humor, inspirational, interview, new product, personal experience, photo feature, travel. Special issues: No dates are currently set, but we usually have a fashion issue, a music issue and a *Men We Love* issue periodically. We do not want poetry; no stories not relating to women. **Buys 60+ mss/yr. mss/year.** Query with published clips. Length: 350-

3,000 words. **Pays 0-$250/max for assigned articles. Pays 0-$250/max for unsolicited articles.** Sometimes pays expenses of writers on assignment.

PHOTOS Contact: Laurie Henzel, Art Director. State availability. Identification of subjects, model releases required. Reviews GIF/JPEG files. Negotiates payment individually.

COLUMNS Contact: Emily Rems, Managing Editor. Books (Reviews of books by women) assigned by us, Music (Reviews of music by/about women), Movies (Reviews of movies by/about women), 300 words; One-Handed-Read (Erotic Fiction for Women), 1,200 words. **Buys 6 mss/yr. mss/year.** Query with published clips. **Pays $-$100.**

FICTION Contact: Lisa Butterworth, Assoc. Editor. Needs erotica. "We only publish erotic fiction. All other content is nonfiction." **Buys 6 mss/yr. mss/year.** Query with published clips. Length: 1,000-1,500 words. **Pays $0-$100.**

⊙ $ CANADIAN DIMENSION

Dimension Publications, Inc., 91 Albert St., Room 2-E, Winnipeg MB R3B 1G5 Canada. (204)957-1519. Fax: (204)943-4617. E-mail: letters@canadiandimension.com. Website: canadiandimension.com. **80% freelance written.** Bimonthly magazine covering socialist perspective. We bring a socialist perspective to bear on events across Canada and around the world. Our contributors provide in-depth coverage on popular movements, peace, labour, women, aboriginal justice, environment, third world and eastern Europe. Estab. 1963. Circ. 3,000. Pays on publication. Publishes ms an average of 6 months after acceptance. Accepts simultaneous submissions. Responds in 6 weeks to queries. Sample copy for $2. Guidelines available online.

NONFICTION Needs interview, opinion, reviews. **Buys 8 mss/year.** Length: 500-2,000 words. **Pays $25-100.**

REPRINTS Send typed manuscript with rights for sale noted and information about when and where the material previously appeared.

⊕ CLOUDBANK: JOURNAL OF CONTEMPORARY WRITING

P.O. Box 610, Corvallis OR 97339-0610. Website: cloudbankbooks.com. **Contact:** Michael Malan, Editor. Biannual journal of contemporary writing open to range of styles; never publishes theme issues. Estab. 2009. up to 6 months Accepts queries by mail. Accepts simultaneous submissions. Responds in 4 months. Guidelines available in magazine, for SASE, by e-mail or on website.

Has published poetry by y madrone, Dennis Schmitz, Christopher Buckley, Paulann Peterson, Vern Rutsala, Penelope Schott.

Prefers submissions from skilled, experienced poets; will consider work from beginning poets. Considers poetry by teens. Previously published includes poetry posted on a public website/blog/forum. Reviews single-books of poetry in 500 words.

FICTION Digest-sized, 84 pages of print, perfect bound; color artwork on cover, includes ads. Receives 1,600 poems/year, accepts about 8%. Press run is 400. Subscribers: 300; shelf sales: 100 distributed free. Single copy $8; subscription: $15. Make checks payable to Cloudbank. Submit 5 poems or less at a time with SASE. Cover letter is preferred. Does not accept fax, e-mail, or disk submissions. Reads year round. Never sends prepublication galleys. 150 lines/max. **Pays $200 prize for one poem or flash fiction piece per issue.**

$$$ COMMENTARY

165 E. 56th St., New York NY 10022. (212)891-1400. Website: commentarymagazine.com. Monthly magazine. Estab. 1945. Byline given. Pays on publication. Publishes ms an average of 2 months after acceptance. Accepts queries by mail.

NONFICTION Needs essays, opinion. **Buys 4 mss/year.** Query. Length: 2,000-8,000 words. **Pays $400-1,200.**

⊙ $ $ COMMON GROUND

Common Ground Publishing, 204-4381 Fraser St., Vancouver BC V5V 4G4 Canada. (604)733-2215. Fax: (604)733-4415. E-mail: admin@commonground.ca. E-mail: editor@commonground.ca. Website: commonground.ca. **90% freelance written.** Monthly tabloid covering health, environment, spirit, creativity, and wellness. "We serve the cultural creative community." Estab. 1982. Circ. 70,000. Byline given. Pays on publication. Publishes ms an average of 1 month after acceptance. Editorial lead time 2 months. Submit seasonal material 3 months in advance. Accepts queries by e-mail. Accepts simultaneous submissions. Responds in 6 weeks to queries. Responds in 3 months to mss. Sample copy for $5. Guidelines available online.

NONFICTION Needs book excerpts, how-to, inspirational, interview, opinion, personal experience, travel,

call to action. Send complete ms. Length: 500-2,500 words. **Pays 10¢/word (Canadian).**
PHOTOS State availability. Captions, True required.

💲💲💲 FIRST THINGS

Institute on Religion & Public Life, 35 East 21st Street,, 6th floor, New York NY 10010. (212)627-1985. E-mail: ft@firstthings.com. Website: firstthings.com. **70% freelance written.** social and intellectual commentary. "Intellectual journal published 10 times/year containing social and ethical commentary in a broad sense, religious and ethical perspectives on society, culture, law, medicine, church and state, morality and mores." Estab. 1990. Circ. 32,000. Byline given. Pays on publication. Publishes ms an average of 4 months after acceptance. Editorial lead time 2 months. Submit seasonal material 5 months in advance. Responds in 3 weeks to mss. Sample copy and writer's guidelines for #10 SASE.
NONFICTION Needs essays, opinion. **Buys 60 mss/year.** Send complete ms. Length: 1,500-6,000 words. **Pays $400-1,000.** Sometimes pays expenses of writers on assignment.
POETRY Contact: Joseph Bettum, poetry editor. Needs traditional. Buys 25-30 poems/year. Length: 4-40 lines. **Pays $50.**

💲💲💲 FLAUNT MAGAZINE

1422 N. Highland Ave., Los Angeles CA 90028. (323)836-1000. E-mail: info@flauntmagazine.com. Website: flaunt.com. **40% freelance written.** Monthly magazine covering culture, arts, entertainment, music, fashion and film. *Flaunt* features the bold work of emerging photographers, writers, artists and musicians. The quality of the content is mirrored in the sophisticated, interactive format of the magazine, using advanced printing techniques, fold-out articles, beautiful papers and inserts to create a visually stimulating, surprisingly readable, and intelligent book that pushes the magazine into the realm of art-object. *Flaunt* has for the last 11 years made it a point to break new ground, earning itself a reputation as an engine of the avant-garde and an outlet for the culture of the cutting edge. *Flaunt* takes pride in reinventing itself each month, while consistently representing a hybrid of all that is interesting in entertainment, fashion, music, design, film, art and literature. Estab. 1998. Circ. 100,000. Byline given. Publishes ms an average of 3 months after acceptance. Editorial lead time 3 months. Submit seasonal material 3 months in advance. Accepts queries by mail, e-mail. Accepts simultaneous submissions. Responds in 2 weeks to queries. Responds in 1 month to mss. Guidelines by e-mail.
NONFICTION Needs book excerpts, essays, expose, general interest, historical, humor, interview, new product, opinion, personal experience, photo feature, travel. Special issues: September and March (fashion issues); February (men's issue); May (music issue). **Buys 20 mss/year.** Query with published clips. Length: 500-5,000 words. **Pays up to $500.** Sometimes pays expenses of writers on assignment.
PHOTOS Contact: Contact: Lee Corbin, art director. State availability. Identification of subjects, model releases required. Reviews contact sheets, transparencies, prints, GIF/JPEG files.
FICTION Contact: Contact Andrew Pogany, senior editor. **Buys 4 mss/year.** Length: 500-5,000 words. **Pays up to $500.**

THE FUTURIST

The World Future, 7910 Woodmont Ave., Suite 450, Bethesda MD 20814. (301)656-8274. Fax: (301)951-0394. E-mail: info@wfs.org. Website: wfs.org. **50% freelance written.** Bimonthly magazine covering technological, social, environmental, economic, and public policy trends related to the future. "Articles should have something new & significant to say about the future. For example, an article noting that increasing air pollution may damage human health is something everyone has already heard. Writers should remember that the publication focuses on the future, especially the period 5 to 50 years ahead. We cover a wide range of subject areas—virtually everything that will affect our future or will be affected by the changes the future will bring. Past articles have focused on technology, planning, resources, economics, religion, the arts, values, and health. For quality of writing, make points clearly and in a way that holds the reader's interest. A reader should not have to struggle to guess an author's meaning. Use concrete examples and anecdotes to illustrate your points; keep sentences short, mostly under 25 words. Avoid the jargon of a particular profession; when technical terms are necessary, explain them." Estab. 1966. Circ. 10,000. Byline given. "We pay only in contributors copies." Publishes ms an average of 4 months after acceptance. Editorial lead time 2 months. Submit seasonal material 3 months in advance. Accepts queries by mail, e-mail. Accepts simultaneous submissions.

Responds in 4 weeks to queries. Guidelines available at: wfs.org/content/writers-guidelines.

NONFICTION Needs book excerpts, essays, expose, general interest, how-to, interview, photo feature, technical. "We don't want articles by authors who aren't experts on what they're writing about, or who can't find expert opinion on the subjects they're covering. Articles we avoid include: (A) overly technical articles that would be of little interest to the general reader; (B) opinion pieces on current government issues; (C) articles by authors with only a casual knowledge of the subject being discussed. *The Futurist* does not publish fiction or poetry. An exception is occasionally made for scenarios presenting fictionalized people in future situations. These scenarios are kept brief." **Buys 5 articles/issue, 30 articles/year. mss/year.** Send complete ms.

●● THE LIST

The List, Ltd., 14 High St., Edinburgh EH1 1TE Scotland. (44)(131)550-3050. Fax: (44)(131)557-8500. Website: list.co.uk. **25% freelance written.** Biweekly general interest magazine covering Glasgow and Edinburgh arts, events, listings, and lifestyle. "*The List* is pitched at educated 18-35 year olds in Scotland. All events listings are published free of charge and are accompanied by informative, independent critical comment offering a guide to readers as to what is worth seeing and why. Articles and features are also included previewing forthcoming events in greater detail." Estab. 1985. Circ. 500,000. Byline given. Pays on publication. Offers 100% kill fee. Publishes ms an average of 2 weeks after acceptance. Editorial lead time 1 month. Submit seasonal material 1 month in advance. Accepts queries by mail, e-mail. NoAccepts simultaneous submissions.

NONFICTION Needs interview, opinion, travel. Query with published clips. 300 words. **Pays £60-80.** Sometimes pays expenses of writers on assignment.

COLUMNS Reviews, 50-650 words, **pays £16-35**; Book Reviews, 150 words; **pays £14**. Comic Reviews, 100 words; **pays £10**. TV/Video Reviews, 100 words; **pays £10**. Record Reviews, 100 words; **pays £10**. Query with published clips.

●●●● MOTHER JONES

Foundation for National Progress, 222 Sutter St., Suite 600, San Francisco CA 94108. (415)321-1700. E-mail: query@motherjones.com. Website: motherjones.com. Mark Murrmann, assoc. photo editor. **80% freelance written.** Bi-monthly magazine covering politics, investigative reporting, social issues, and pop culture. "*Mother Jones* is a 'progressive' magazine—but the core of its editorial well is reporting (i.e., fact-based). No slant required. MotherJones.com is an online sister publication." Estab. 1976. Circ. 240,000. Byline given. Pays on publication. Offers 33% kill fee. Publishes ms an average of 4 months after acceptance. Editorial lead time 4 months. Submit seasonal material 6 months in advance. Responds in 2 months to queries. Sample copy for $6 and 9×12 SAE. Guidelines available online.

○ "*Mother Jones* magazine and *MotherJones.com* will consider solidly reported, hard-hitting, groundbreaking news stories. We're also open to thought-provoking, timely opinion and analysis pieces on important current issues. We're interested in just about anything that will raise our readers' eyebrows, but we focus especially on these areas: national politics, environmental issues, corporate wrongdoing, human rights, and political influence in all spheres.

NONFICTION Needs exposè, interview, photo feature, current issues, policy, investigative reporting. **Buys 70-100 mss/year.** Query with published clips. "Please also include your rèsumè and two or three of your most relevant clips. If the clips are online, please provide the complete URLs. Web pieces are generally less than 1,500 words. Because we have staff reporters it is extremely rare that we will pay for a piece whose timeliness or other qualities work for the Web only. Magazine pieces can range up to 5,000 words. There is at least a two-month lead time. No phone calls please." Length: 2,000-5,000 words. **Pays $1/word.** Sometimes pays expenses of writers on assignment.

COLUMNS Outfront (short, newsy and/or outrageous and/or humorous items), 200-800 words; Profiles of Hellraisers, 500 words. **Pays $1/word.**

TIPS "We're looking for hard-hitting, investigative reports exposing government cover-ups, corporate malfeasance, scientific myopia, institutional fraud or hypocrisy; thoughtful, provocative articles which challenge the conventional wisdom (on the right or the left) concerning issues of national importance; and timely, people-oriented stories on issues such as the environment, labor, the media, healthcare, consumer protection, and cultural trends. Send a great, short query and establish your credibility as a reporter. Explain what you plan to cover and how you will proceed with the reporting. The query should convey your approach, tone and style, and should answer the following: What are your specific qualifications to write on this topic? What 'ins' do you have with your sources? Can you provide full documentation so that your story can be fact-checked?"

$$ NATURALLY

Internaturally, Inc., P.O. Box 317, Newfoundland NJ 07435. (973)697-3552. Fax: (973)697-8313. E-mail: naturally@internaturally.com. Website: internaturally.com. **80% freelance written.** Quarterly magazine covering nudism and naturism. Write about nudists and naturists. More people stories than travel. Estab. 1980. Circ. 30,000. Byline given. Pays on publication. Publishes ms an average of 3 months after acceptance. Editorial lead time 3-6 months. Submit seasonal material 6 months in advance. Accepts queries by mail, phone. Accepts simultaneous submissions. Responds in 2 weeks to queries. Responds in 3 months to mss. Sample copy available online. Guidelines available online.

> 💬 "A full color, glossy magazine with on-line editions, and the foremost naturist/nudist magazine in the U.S.A. with international distribution. Naturally focuses on the clothes-free lifestyle, publishing articles about worldwide destinations, first time nudist experiences, with news information pertaining to the clothes-free lifestyle. Our mission is to demystify the human form, and allow each human to feel comfortable in their own skin, in a non-sexual environment. We offer a range of books, DVD's, magazines, and other products useful to naturists/nudists in their daily lives, and for the education of non-naturists. Travel DVD's featuring resorts to visit, books on Christianity and nudity, nudist plays, memoirs, cartoons, and novellas, as well as towels, sandals, calendars, and more."

NONFICTION Needs book excerpts, essays, expose, general interest, historical, how-to, for first-time visitors to nudist park., humor, inspirational, interview, new product, personal experience, photo feature, travel. Special issues: Free-beach activities, public nude events. We don't want opinion pieces and religious slants. **Buys 50 mss/year mss/year.** Send complete ms. Length: 500-2,000 words. **Pays $80 per page, text or photos min.; $300 max. for assigned articles.**

PHOTOS Send photos. Model releases required. $80 per page min.; $200 front cover max.

COLUMNS Health (nudism/naturism), Travel (nudism/naturism), Celebrities (nudism/naturism). **Buys 8 mss/year mss/year.** Send complete ms.

FICTION Needs humorous. Science fiction. **Buys 6-8 mss/year. mss/year.** Send complete ms. Length: 800-2,000 words. **Pays $-$80 per page.**

POETRY Needs avant-garde, free verse, haiku, light verse, traditional. Buys 3-6/year poems/year. Submit maximum 3 poems.

FILLERS Needs anecdotes, facts, gags, newsbreaks, short humor. **Buys 4 mss/year.**

$ NEW HAVEN ADVOCATE

New Mass Media, Inc., 900 Chapel St., Suite 1100, New Haven CT 06510. (203)789-0010. Fax: (203)787-1418. E-mail: abromage@newhavenadvocate.com. Website: newhavenadvocate.com. **10% freelance written.** Weekly tabloid covering alternative, investigative, cultural reporting. Alternative, investigative, cultural reporting with a strong voice. We like to shake things up. Estab. 1975. Circ. 55,000. Byline given. Pays on publication. Editorial lead time 1 month. Submit seasonal material 2 months in advance. Accepts simultaneous submissions. Responds in 1 month to queries.

NONFICTION Needs book excerpts, essays, expose, general interest, humor, interview. **Buys 15-20 mss/year.** Query with published clips. Length: 750-2,000 words. **Pays $50-150.** Sometimes pays expenses of writers on assignment.

PHOTOS State availability. Captions, identification of subjects, model releases required.

🍁$ POETRY CANADA MAGAZINE

Innersurf Publishing, 375 South Third St., Ste. 323, Burbank CA 91502. Website: poetrycanada.com. **90% freelance written.** "Biannual magazine promoting culture and diversity through art, photography, poetry, and articles. Despite its Canadian root, writers from around the world can submit poetry, book reviews, and articles that will help to advance and inspire the reader to learn more about their craft, society, and environment." Estab. 2003. Circ. 500. Byline given. Pays on publication. Publishes ms an average of 3-12 months after acceptance. Editorial lead time 3-12 months. Submit seasonal material 6 months in advance. Accepts queries by e-mail. NoResponds in 3 days to queries. Sample copy and writer's guidelines online.

NONFICTION Needs general interest, historical, how-to, humor, inspirational, photo feature, art feature. **Buys 60-100 mss/year.** Length: 25-800 words. **Pays $5-100 and a contributor copy**

COLUMNS Book Reviews; Top Ways To; Dead Poets Society; Poets Practice; Interviews. **Buys 12-15 mss/year. Pays $5-100.**

POETRY All types and styles; no line limit.

$$ SHEPHERD EXPRESS

The Brooklyn Company, Inc., 207 E. Buffalo St., Suite 410, Milwaukee WI 53202. (414)276-2222. Fax: (414)276-3312. E-mail: info@expressmilwaukee.com. Website: expressmilwaukee.com. **50% freelance written**. Weekly tabloid covering news and arts with a progressive news edge and a hip entertainment perspective. Home of Sheprd Flickr interactive photo feature—Milwaukee-related photography. Estab. 1982. Circ. 58,000. Pays 1 month after publication. Publishes ms an average of 1 month after acceptance. Submit seasonal material 2 months in advance. Accepts simultaneous submissions. Sample copy for $3.

NONFICTION Needs book excerpts, essays, expose, opinion. **Buys 200 mss/year.** Send complete ms. Length: 900-2,500 words. **Pays $35-300 for assigned articles. Pays $10-200 for unsolicited articles.** Sometimes pays expenses of writers on assignment.

PHOTOS State availability. Captions, identification of subjects, model releases required. Reviews prints. Negotiates payment individually.

COLUMNS Opinions (social trends, politics, from progressive slant), 800-1,200 words; Books Reviewed (new books only: Social trends, environment, politics), 600-1,200 words. **Buys 10 mss/year.** Send complete ms.

$$$ THE SUN

The Sun Publishing Co., 107 N. Roberson St., Chapel Hill NC 27516. (919)942-5282. Fax: (919)932-3101. Website: thesunmagazine.org. **Contact:** Luc Sanders, editorial associate. **90% freelance written**. Monthly magazine. "We are open to all kinds of writing, though we favor work of a personal nature." Estab. 1974. Circ. 69,500. Byline given. Pays on publication. Publishes ms an average of 6-12 months after acceptance. Accepts queries by mail. Responds in 3-6 months to queries. Responds in 3-6 months to mss. Sample copy for $5. Guidelines available online.

NONFICTION Contact: Sy Safransky, editor. Needs essays, personal experience, spiritual, interview. **Buys 50 mss/year.** Send complete ms. 7,000 words maximum **Pays $300-2,000.**

REPRINTS Send photocopy and information about when and where the material previously appeared.

PHOTOS Contact: Sy Safransky, editor. Send photos. Model releases required. Reviews b&w prints. Offers $100-500/photo.

FICTION Contact: Sy Safransky, editor. "We avoid stereotypical genre pieces like science fiction, romance, western, and horror. Read an issue before submitting." **Buys 20/year mss/year.** Send complete ms. 7,000 words maximum **Pays $300-1,500.**

POETRY Contact: Sy Safransky, editor. Needs free verse. Submit up to 6 poems at a time. Considers previously published poems but strongly prefers unpublished work; no simultaneous submissions. "Poems should be typed and accompanied by a cover letter and SASE." Guidelines available with SASE or on website. Responds within 3-6 months. Pays $100-500 on publication plus contributor's copies and subscription. Acquires first serial or one-time rights. Rarely publishes poems that rhyme. **Pays $100-500.**

DISABILITIES

[C]$$ ABILITIES

Canadian Abilities Foundation, 340 College St., Suite 270, Toronto ON M5T 3A9 Canada. (416)923-1885. Fax: (416)923-9829. Website: abilities.ca. **50% freelance written**. Quarterly magazine covering disability issues. *Abilities* provides information, inspiration, and opportunity to its readers with articles and resources covering health, travel, sports, products, technology, profiles, employment, recreation, and more. Estab. 1987. Circ. 20,000. Byline given. Pays on publication. Offers 50% kill fee. Publishes ms an average of 3 months after acceptance. Editorial lead time 3 months. Submit seasonal material 4 months in advance. Accepts queries by mail, e-mail, fax. Responds in 3 months to queries. Sample copy free. Writer's guidelines for #10 SASE, online, or by e-mail.

NONFICTION Needs general interest, how-to, humor, inspirational, interview, new product, personal experience, photo feature, travel. Does not want articles that 'preach to the converted'—this means info that people with disabilities likely already know, such as what it's like to have a disability. **Buys 30-**

40 mss/year. Query or send complete ms. Length: 500-2,500 words. **Pays $50-400 (Canadian) for assigned articles. Pays $50-350 (Canadian) for unsolicited articles.**

REPRINTS Sometimes accepts previously published submissions (if stated as such).

PHOTOS State availability.

COLUMNS The Lighter Side (humor), 700 words; Profile, 1,200 words.

$$$$ ARTHRITIS TODAY

Arthritis Foundation, 1330 W. Peachtree St. NW, Suite 100, Atlanta GA 30309. (404)872-7100. Fax: (404)872-9559. Website: arthritis.org. **50% freelance written.** Bimonthly magazine covering living with arthritis and the latest in research/treatment. *Arthritis Today* is a consumer health magazine and is written for the more than 70 million Americans who have arthritis and for the millions of others whose lives are touched by an arthritis-related disease. The editorial content is designed to help the person with arthritis live a more productive, independent, and pain-free life. The articles are upbeat and provide practical advice, information, and inspiration. Estab. 1987. Circ. 650,000. Byline given. Pays on acceptance. Offers kill fee. Offers kill fee Editorial lead time 6 months. Submit seasonal material 6 months in advance. Accepts queries by mail, online submission form. Accepts simultaneous submissions. Responds in 2 months to queries. Sample copy for 9×11 SAE with 4 first-class stamps. Guidelines available online.

NONFICTION Needs general interest, how-to, tips on any aspect of living with arthritis, inspirational, new product, arthritis related, opinion, personal experience, photo feature, technical, travel, tips, news, service, nutrition, general health, lifestyle. **Buys 12 unsolicited mss/year.** Query with published clips. Length: 150-2,500 words. **Pays $100-2,500.** Pays expenses of writers on assignment.

PHOTOS Send photos. Identification of subjects required. Reviews prints. Negotiates payment individually.

COLUMNS Nutrition, 100-600 words; Fitness, 100-600 words; Balance (emotional coping), 100-600 words; MedWatch, 100-800 words; Solutions, 100-600 words; Life Makeover, 400-600 words.

FILLERS Needs facts, gags, short humor. **Buys 2 mss/year.** Length: 40-100 words. **Pays $80-150.**

$$ CAREERS & THE DISABLED

Equal Opportunity Publications, 445 Broad Hollow Rd., Suite 425, Melville NY 11747. (631)421-9421. Fax: (631)421-0359. E-mail: info@eop.com;jschneider@eop.com. Website: eop.com. **60% freelance written.** Magazine published 6 times/year with Fall, Winter, Spring, Summer, and Expo editions; offering role-model profiles and career guidance articles geared toward disabled college students and professionals, and promotes personal and professional growth. Estab. 1967. Circ. 10,000. Byline given. Pays on publication. Publishes ms an average of 6 months after acceptance. Editorial lead time 6 months. Submit seasonal material 6 months in advance. Accepts queries by mail, e-mail, fax, phone. Accepts simultaneous submissions. Responds in 3 weeks to queries. Sample copy for 9×12 SAE with 5 first-class stamps. Guidelines free.

NONFICTION Needs essays, general interest, how-to, interview, new product, opinion, personal experience. **Buys 30 mss/year.** Query. Length: 1,000-2,500 words. **Pays 10¢/word.** Sometimes pays expenses of writers on assignment.

REPRINTS and information about when and where the material previously appeared.

PHOTOS Captions, identification of subjects, model releases required. Reviews transparencies, prints.

$$ DIABETES HEALTH

365 Bel Marin Keys Blvd, Suite 100, Novato CA 94949. (415)883-1990 ext. 3. Fax: (415)883-1932. Website: diabetesinterview.com. **Contact:** Russell Phillips, managing editor. **40% freelance written.** Monthly tabloid covering diabetes care. *Diabetes Interview* covers the latest in diabetes care, medications, and patient advocacy. Personal accounts are welcome as well as medical-oriented articles by MDs, RNs, and CDEs (certified diabetes educators). Estab. 1991. Circ. 40,000. Byline given. Pays on publication. Publishes ms an average of 2 months after acceptance. Editorial lead time 2 months. Submit seasonal material 2 months in advance. Accepts queries by e-mail, online submission form. Sample copy available online. Guidelines free.

"Accepts solicited submissions from contributing writers for feature-length stories. Our feature stories run at a maximum of 1,500 words. Features should have at least 3-5 outside sources. We also accept shorter opinion pieces, columns (500 words each) and letters to the editor. We are not responsible for returning unsolicited content or photos. All content should be balanced, informative, lively, timely, concise and easy to read for a lay audience. Diabetes Health does not accept manuscripts that promote a product, philosophy or personal view. When discussing products or treatment techniques, you should include experiences of a person with diabetes. Never make sweeping generalizations that cannot be supported by published research or highly credible sources. All manuscripts should be sent as a Word file. Do not fax or mail manuscripts. Do not copy and paste manuscript into the body of an e-mail. All manuscripts will be edited for style, length and substance. Upon receiving a manuscript, we will either query you for additional information or, if the material is unacceptable, return the manuscript with rewrite instructions. Payment varies with experience and is based on the final length as it appears in the magazine. We encourage writers to submit photographs or other art that will help illustrate the story. For more information, contact Russell Phillips."

NONFICTION Needs essays, how-to, humor, inspirational, interview, new product, opinion, personal experience. **Buys 25 mss/year.** Send complete ms. Length: 500-1,500 words. **Pays 20¢/word.**

PHOTOS State availability of or send photos. Negotiates payment individually.

💲💲 DIABETES SELF-MANAGEMENT

R.A. Rapaport Publishing, Inc., 150 W. 22nd St., Suite 800, New York NY 10011-2421. (212)989-0200. Fax: (212)989-4786. E-mail: editor@rapaportpublishing. com. Website: diabetesselfmanagement.com. **Contact:** Editor. **20% freelance written.** Bimonthly magazine. "We publish how-to health care articles for motivated, intelligent readers who have diabetes and who are actively involved in their own health care management. All articles must have immediate application to their daily living." Estab. 1983. Circ. 410,000. Byline given. Pays on publication. Offers 20% kill fee. Submit seasonal material 6 months in advance. Accepts queries by mail, e-mail, fax. Responds in 6 weeks to queries. Sample copy for $4 and 9×12 SAE with 6 first-class stamps or online. Guidelines for #10 SASE.

NONFICTION Needs how-to, exercise, nutrition, diabetes self-care, product surveys, technical, reviews of products available, foods sold by brand name, pharmacology, travel, considerations and prep for people with diabetes. No personal experiences, personality profiles, exposès, or research breakthroughs. **Buys 10-12 mss/year.** Query with published clips. Length: 2,000-2,500 words. **Pays $400-700 for assigned articles. Pays $200-700 for unsolicited articles.**

💲 DIALOGUE

Blindskills, Inc., P.O. Box 5181, Salem OR 97304-0181. E-mail: magazine@blindskills.com. Website: blindskills.com. **60% freelance written.** Bimonthly journal covering visually impaired people. Estab. 1962. Circ. 1,100. Byline given. Pays on publication. Publishes ms an average of 6 months after acceptance. Editorial lead time 3 months. Accepts queries by e-mail. One free sample on request. Available in large print, Braille, 4-track audio cassette, and e-mail. Guidelines available online.

NONFICTION Needs essays, general interest, historical, how-to, life skills methods used by visually impaired people, humor, interview, personal experience, sports, recreation, hobbies. No controversial, explicit sex, religious, or political topics. **Buys 80 mss/year.** Send complete ms. Length: 200-1,000/words. **Pays $15-35 for assigned articles. Pays $15-25 for unsolicited articles.**

COLUMNS All material should be relative to blind and visually impaired readers. Living with Low Vision, 1,000 words; Hear's How (dealing with sight loss), 1,000 words. Technology Answer Book, 800 words. **Buys 80 mss/year.** Send complete ms. **Pays $10-25.**

HEARING HEALTH

Deafness Research Foundation, 363 Seventh Avenue, 10th Floor, New York NY 10001. E-mail: info@drf.org. Website: drf.org/magazine. Magazine covering issues and concerns pertaining to hearing health and hearing loss. Byline given. Pays with contributor copies. Accepts queries by mail, e-mail. Accepts simultaneous submissions. Guidelines available online.

NONFICTION Send complete ms.

REPRINTS Please do not submit a previously published article unless permission has been obtained in writing that allows the article's use in *Hearing Health*.

PHOTOS State availability. Captions required. Reviews high-resolution digital images.

COLUMNS Features (800-1,500 words); First-person stories (500-1,500 words); Humor (500-750 words); Viewpoints/Op-Ed (350-500 words). Send complete ms.

$ KALEIDOSCOPE

Kaleidoscope Press, 701 S. Main St., Akron OH 44311-1019. (330)762-9755. Fax: (330)762-0912. E-mail: mshiplett@udsakron.org. Website: udsakron.org/kaleidoscope.htm. **Contact:** Mildred Shiplett. **75% freelance written. Eager to work with new/unpublished writers**. Semiannual magazine. "Subscribers include individuals, agencies, and organizations that assist people with disabilities and many university and public libraries. Appreciates work by established writers as well. Especially interested in work by writers with a disability, but features writers both with and without disabilities. Writers without a disability must limit themselves to our focus, while those with a disability may explore any topic (although we prefer original perspectives about experiences with disability)." Estab. 1979. Circ. 1,000. Byline given. Pays on publication. Accepts queries by mail, fax. Accepts simultaneous submissions. Responds in 3 weeks to queries. Responds in 6 months to mss. Sample copy for $6 prepaid. Double-space your work, number the pages, & include name. Guidelines available online.

Kaleidoscope has received awards from the American Heart Association, the Great Lakes Awards Competition and Ohio Public Images. *Kaleidoscope* has received awards from the American Heart Association, the Great Lakes Awards Competition and Ohio Public Images.

NONFICTION Needs book excerpts, essays, humor, interview, personal experience, book reviews, articles related to disability. **Buys 8-15 mss/year.** 5,000 words maximum. **Pays $25, plus 2 copies**

REPRINTS Send double-spaced typed manuscript with rights for sale noted and information about when and where the material previously appeared. Reprints permitted with credit given to original publication.

PHOTOS Send photos.

FICTION Contact: Fiction Editor. Short stories, novel excerpts. Traditional and experimental styles. Works should explore experiences with disability. Use people-first language. Needs Well-developed plots, engaging characters, and realistic dialogue. We lean toward fiction that emphasizes character and emotions rather than action-oriented narratives. No fiction that is stereotypical, patronizing, sentimental, erotic, or maudlin. No romance, religious or dogmatic fiction; no children's literature. 5,000 words maximum **Pays $25, and 2 contributor's copies.**

POETRY "Do not get caught up in rhyme scheme. High quality with strong imagery and evocative language. Reviews any style." Buys 12-20 poems/year. Submit maximum 5 poems.

$$ PN

Paralyzed Veterans of America, 2111 E. Highland Ave., Suite 180, Phoenix AZ 85016. (602)224-0500. E-mail: richard@pnnews.com. Website: pn-magazine.com. Monthly magazine covering news and information for wheelchair users. Writing must pertain to people with disabilities—specifically mobility impairments. Estab. 1946. Circ. 40,000. Byline given. Pays on publication. Publishes ms an average of 2-4 months after acceptance. Editorial lead time 3 months. Submit seasonal material 3 months in advance. Accepts queries by mail, e-mail, fax. Sample copy free. Guidelines free.

NONFICTION Needs how-to, interview, new product, opinion. **Buys 10-12 mss/year.** Send complete ms. Length: 1,200-2,500 words. **Pays $25-250.**

$$ SPECIALIVING

P.O. Box 1000, Bloomington IL 61702. (309)962-2003. E-mail: gareeb@aol.com. Website: specialiving.com. **90% freelance written**. Quarterly online magazine covering the physically disabled/mobility impaired. "We are now an online-only magazine. There is no subscription fee. Subject matter is the same. Payment is still the same, (max 800 words). Need photos with ms." Estab. 2001. Circ. 12,000. Byline given. Pays on publication. Editorial lead time 3 months. Submit seasonal material 6 months in advance. Accepts queries by mail, e-mail, fax, phone. Accepts simultaneous submissions. Responds in 3 weeks to queries.

NONFICTION Needs how-to, humor, inspirational, interview, new product, personal experience, technical, travel. **Buys 40 mss/year.** Query. Length: 800 words. **Pays 10¢/word.**

PHOTOS State availability. Captions, identification of subjects required. Reviews GIF/JPEG files. Offers $10/photo; $50/cover photo.

COLUMNS Shopping Guide; Items. **Buys 30 mss/year.** Query.

⊖⊖ SPORTS N SPOKES

The Magazine for Wheelchair Sports and Recreation, The Paralyzed Veterans of America, 2111 E. Highland Ave., Suite 180, Phoenix AZ 85016. (602)224-0500. Fax: (602)224-0507. E-mail: brenda@pnnews.com; richard@pnnews.com. Website: sportsnspokes.com. Richard Hoover, editor. **Contact:** Brenda Martin. Bimonthly magazine covering wheelchair sports and recreation. Writing must pertain to wheelchair sports and recreation. Estab. 1974. Circ. 25,000. Byline given. Pays on publication. Publishes ms an average of 2-3 months after acceptance. Editorial lead time 2-3 months. Submit seasonal material 2-3 months in advance. Accepts queries by mail, e-mail, fax. Sample copy free. Guidelines free.

○ "SPORTS 'N SPOKES is committed to providing a voice for the wheelchair sporting and recreation community."

NONFICTION Needs general interest, interview, new product. **Buys 5-6 mss/year.** Send complete ms. Length: 1,200-2,500 words. **Pays $20-250.**

ENTERTAINMENT

⊖ CINEASTE

Cineaste Publishers, Inc., 243 Fifth Ave., #706, New York NY 10016. (212)366-5720. E-mail: cineaste@cineaste.com. Website: cineaste.com. **30% freelance written.** Quarterly magazine covering motion pictures with an emphasis on social and political perspective on cinema. Estab. 1967. Circ. 11,000. Byline given. Pays on publication. Offers 50% kill fee. Publishes ms an average of 4 months after acceptance. Editorial lead time 3 months. Submit seasonal material 4 months in advance. Accepts queries by mail, e-mail, fax. Responds in 1 month to queries. Sample copy for $5. Writer's guidelines on website.

NONFICTION Needs book excerpts, essays, expose, historical, humor, interview, opinion. **Buys 20-30 mss/year.** Query with published clips. Length: 2,000-5,000 words. **Pays $30-100.**

PHOTOS State availability. Identification of subjects required. Reviews transparencies, 8×10 prints. Offers no additional payment for photos accepted with ms.

COLUMNS Homevideo (topics of general interest or a related group of films); A Second Look (new interpretation of a film classic or a reevaluation of an unjustly neglected release of more recent vintage); Lost and Found (film that may or may not be released or otherwise seen in the US but which is important enough to be brought to the attention of our readers), all 1,000-1,500 words. Query with published clips. **Pays $50 minimum.**

◑⊖ DANCE INTERNATIONAL

Scotiabant Dance Centre, Level 6 677 Davie St., Vancouver BC V6B 2G6 Canada. (604)681-1525. Fax: (604)681-7732. E-mail: Editor@DanceInternational.org. Website: danceinternational.org. **100% freelance written.** Quarterly magazine covering dance arts. Articles and reviews on current activities in world dance, with occasional historical essays; reviews of dance films, video, and books. Estab. 1973. Circ. 4,500. Byline given. Pays on publication. Offers 50% kill fee. Publishes ms an average of 3 months after acceptance. Editorial lead time 3 months. Submit seasonal material 6 weeks in advance. Accepts queries by mail, e-mail, fax, phone. NoResponds in 2 weeks to queries. Responds in 1 month to mss. Sample copy for $7. Guidelines for #10 SASE.

NONFICTION Needs book excerpts, essays, historical, interview, personal experience, photo feature. **Buys 100 mss/year.** Query. Length: 1,200-2,200 words. **Pays $40-150.**

PHOTOS Send photos. Identification of subjects required. Reviews prints. Offers no additional payment for photos accepted with ms.

COLUMNS Dance Bookshelf (recent books reviewed), 700-800 words; Regional Reports (events in each region), 1,200 words. **Buys 100 mss/year.** Query. **Pays $80.**

⊖⊖ DIRECTED BY

Visionary Media, P.O. Box 1722, Glendora CA 91740-1722. Fax: (626)608-0309. E-mail: visionarycinema@yahoo.com. Website: directed-by.com. **10% freelance written.** Quarterly magazine covering the craft of directing a motion picture. "Our articles are for readers particularly knowledgeable about the art and history of movies from the director's point of view. Our purpose is to communicate our enthusiasm and interest in the craft of cinema." Estab. 1998. Circ. 42,000. Byline given. Pays on publication. Offers 25% kill fee. Publishes ms an average of 3 months after acceptance. Editorial lead time 3 months. Submit seasonal material 3 months in advance. Accepts queries by mail, e-mail. Accepts simultaneous submissions. Responds in 6 weeks to queries. Sample copy for $5. Writer's guidelines free or by e-mail.

NONFICTION Needs interview, photo feature, on-set reports. No gossip, celebrity-oriented material, or movie reviews. **Buys 5 mss/year.** Query. Length: 500-7,500 words. **Pays $50-750.** Sometimes pays expenses of writers on assignment.

PHOTOS State availability. Captions, identification of subjects required. Reviews contact sheets. Offers no additional payment for photos accepted with ms.

COLUMNS Trends (overview/analysis of specific moviemaking movements/genres/subjects), 1,500-2,000 words; Focus (innovative take on the vision of a contemporary director), 1,500-2,000 words; Appreciation (overview of deceased/foreign director), 1,000-1,500 words; Final Cut (spotlight interview with contemporary director), 3,000 words; Perspectives (interviews/articles about film craftspeople who work with a featured director), 1,500-2,000 words. **Buys 5 mss/year.** Query. **Pays $50-750.**

$$ FLICK MAGAZINE

Decipher, Inc., 259 Granby St., Norfolk VA 23510. (757)623-3600. Fax: (757)623-8368. E-mail: julie.matthews@decipher.com. Website: flickmagazine.com. **30-40% freelance written.** Mini-magazine distributed in movie theaters that comes out in conjunction with selected movies covering one specific movie per issue. *Flick*'s mission is to match the passion and personality of fans, taking readers inside Hollywood and increasing their connection to the film they are about to view. Estab. 2005. Circ. 2.5 million. Pays on acceptance. Publishes ms an average of 4 months after acceptance. Editorial lead time 4-5 months. Accepts queries by mail, e-mail.

NONFICTION Needs essays, humor, interview, opinion, personal experience. Query. Length: 500-1,000 words. **Pays $200-500.** Sometimes pays expenses of writers on assignment.

PHOTOS Contact: Art Director (jeff.hellerman@decipher.com).

COLUMNS Pays $200-500.

FILLERS Needs gags, short humor. **Buys 5-10 mss/year. Pays $200-500.**

$ IN TOUCH WEEKLY

Bauer Magazine Limited Partnership, 270 Sylvan Ave., Englewood Cliffs NJ 07632. (201)569-6699. E-mail: breakingnews@intouchweekly.com; contactintouch@intouchweekly.com. Website: intouchweekly.com. **10% freelance written.** Weekly magazine covering celebrity news and entertainment. Estab. 2002. Circ. 1,300,000. No byline given. Pays on publication. Editorial lead time 1 week. Accepts queries by e-mail.

NONFICTION Needs interview, gossip. **Buys 1,300 mss/year.** Query. Send a tip about a celebrity by e-mail. Length: 100-1,000 words. **Pays $50.**

$$ MOVIEMAKER MAGAZINE

MovieMaker Media LLC, 27 West 24th Street, Suite 9D, New York NY 10010. (646)405-5170. Fax: (646)405-5172. E-mail: jwood@moviemaker.com;rebecca@moviemaker.com. Website: moviemaker.com. **75% freelance written.** Bimonthly magazine covering film, independent cinema, and Hollywood. "*MovieMaker*'s editorial is a progressive mix of in-depth interviews and criticism, combined with practical techniques and advice on financing, distribution, and production strategies. Behind-the-scenes discussions with Hollywood's top moviemakers, as well as independents from around the globe, are routinely found in *MovieMaker*'s pages. E-mail is preferred submission method, but will accept via mail as well. Please, no telephone pitches. We want to read the idea with clips." Estab. 1993. Circ. 55,000. Byline given. Pays 30 days after newsstand publication. Offers kill fee. Offers variable kill fee. Publishes ms an average of 2 months after acceptance. Editorial lead time 3 months. Submit seasonal material 4 months in advance. Accepts queries by mail, e-mail. NoAccepts simultaneous submissions. Responds in 2-4 weeks to queries. Responds in 4-6 weeks to mss. Sample copy available online. Guidelines by e-mail.

NONFICTION Needs expose, general interest, historical, how-to, interview, new product, technical. **Buys 20 mss/year.** Query with published clips. Length: 800-3,000 words. **Pays $75-500 for assigned articles.**

PHOTOS State availability. Identification of subjects required. Payment varies for photos accepted with ms.

COLUMNS Documentary; Home Cinema (home video/DVD reviews); How They Did It (first-person filmmaking experiences); Festival Beat (film festival reviews); World Cinema (current state of cinema from a particular country). Query with published clips **Pays $75-300.**

$$$ OK! MAGAZINE

Northern & Shell North America Limited, 1155 Avenue of the Americas, New York NY 10036. E-mail: subscription@okmagazine.com. Website: ok-magazine.com. **10% freelance written.** Weekly magazine covering entertainment news. We are a celebrity friendly magazine. We strive not to show celebrities in a negative light. We consider ourselves a cross between *People* and *In Style*. Estab. 2005. Circ. 1,000,000. Byline sometimes given. Pays after publication. Publishes ms an average of 1 month after acceptance. Editorial lead time 2 weeks. Accepts queries by mail, e-mail, fax.

NONFICTION Needs interview, photo feature. **Buys 50 mss/year.** Query with published clips. Length: 500-2,000 words. **Pays $100-1,000.**

PHOTOS Contact: Contact Maria Collazo, photography director.

☼❸❸ RUE MORGUE

Marrs Media, Inc., 2926 Dundas St. West, Toronto ON M6P 1Y8 Canada. E-mail: dave@rue-morgue.com. Website: rue-morgue.com. **Contact:** Dave Alexander, editor-in-chief. **50% freelance written.** Monthly magazine covering horror entertainment. "A knowledge of horror entertainment (films, books, games, toys, etc.)." Estab. 1997. Byline given. Pays on publication. Publishes ms an average of 2-4 months after acceptance. Editorial lead time 2 months. Submit seasonal material 4 months in advance. Accepts queries by e-mail. NoResponds in 6 weeks to queries. Responds in 2 months to mss. Guidelines available by e-mail.

NONFICTION Needs essays, exposè, historical, interview, travel, new product. No reviews. Query with published clips or send complete ms. Length: 500-3,500 words.

COLUMNS Classic Cut (historical essays on classic horror films, books, games, comic books, music), 500-700 words. Query with published clips.

❸❸❸❸ SOUND & VISION

Hachette Filipacchi Media U.S., Inc., 2 Park Avenue,, 10th floor,, New York NY 10016. (212)767-6000. Fax: (212)767-5615. E-mail: soundandvision@bonniercorp.com. Website: soundandvisionmag.com. **Contact:** Mike Mettler, editor-in-chief. **40% freelance written.** Published 8 times/year. "Provides readers with authoritative information on the home entertainment technologies and products that will impact their lives." Estab. 1958. Circ. 400,000. Byline given. Pays on acceptance. Publishes ms an average of 4 months after acceptance. Accepts queries by mail, e-mail, fax. Sample copy for sae with 9×12 envelope and 11 First-Class stamps.

NONFICTION Buys 25 mss/year. Query with published clips. Length: 1,500-3,000 words. **Pays $1,000-1,500.**

❸ TELE REVISTA

Teve Latino Publishing, Inc., P.O. Box 142179, Coral Gables FL 33114-5170. (305)445-1755. Fax: (305)445-3907. E-mail: info@telerevista.com. Website: telerevista.com. **100% freelance written.** Monthly magazine written in Spanish covering Hispanic entertainment (US and Puerto Rico). We feature interviews, gossip, breaking stories, behind-the-scenes happenings, etc. Estab. 1986. Byline sometimes given. Pays on publication. Publishes ms an average of 3 months after acceptance. Editorial lead time 2 months. Submit seasonal material 3 months in advance. Accepts queries by mail, e-mail, fax. Sample copy free.

NONFICTION Needs expose, interview, opinion, photo feature. **Buys 200 mss/year.** Query. **Pays $25-75.**

PHOTOS State availability of or send photos. Captions required. Negotiates payment individually.

COLUMNS Buys 60 mss/year. Query. **Pays $25-75.**

FILLERS Needs anecdotes, facts, gags, newsbreaks, short humor.

∅ TV GUIDE

Gemstar-TV Guide International, Inc., 1211 Avenue of the Americas, 4th Floor, New York NY 10036. (212)852-7500. Fax: (212)852-7470. Website: tvguide.com. Weekly magazine. Focuses on all aspects of network, cable, and pay television programming and how it affects and reflects audiences. Circ. 9,097,762.

○ *Does not buy freelance material or use freelance writers.*

ETHNIC AND MINORITY

❸❸❸❸ AARP SEGUNDA JUVENTUD

AARP, 601 E St. NW, Washington DC 20049. E-mail: segundajuventud@aarp.org. Website: aarpsegundajuventud.org. **75% freelance written.** Bimonthly Spanish language magazine geared toward 50+ Hispanics. With fresh and relevant editorial content and a mission of inclusiveness and empowerment, *AARP Segunda Juventud* serves more than 800,000 Hispanic AARP members and their families in all 50 states, the District of Columbia, Puerto Rico, and the US Virgin Islands. Estab. 2002. Circ. 800,000. Byline given. Pays on acceptance. Offers 33.33% kill fee. Publishes ms an average of 4 months after acceptance. Editorial lead time 2-12 months. Submit seasonal material 4-12 months in advance. Accepts queries by mail, e-mail. Accepts simultaneous submissions. Responds in 4 months to queries. Responds in 4 months to mss. Sample copy available online.

NONFICTION Needs general interest, interview, new product, travel, reviews (book, film, music). **Buys 36 mss/year.** Query with published clips. Length: 200-1,500 words. **Pays $1-2/word.** Sometimes pays expenses of writers on assignment.

PHOTOS Send photos. Captions, identification of subjects, model releases required. Reviews contact sheets, negatives, transparencies, prints, GIF/JPEG files. Negotiates payment individually.

COLUMNS Health; Finance; Travel; Celebrity profile; Encore (Hispanic 50+ individuals re-inventing themselves). **Buys 24 mss/year.** Query with published clips. **Pays $1-2/word.**

FILLERS Needs facts. **Buys 6 mss/year.** Length: 200-250 words. **Pays $1-2/word.**

💲 AIM MAGAZINE

Aim Publication Association, P.O. Box 856, Forest Grove OR 97116. (253)815-9030. E-mail: apiladoone@aol.com; editor@aimmagazine.com;submissions@aimmagazine.org. Website: aimmagazine.org. **75% freelance written. Works with a small number of new/unpublished writers each year.** Quarterly magazine on social betterment that promotes racial harmony and peace for high school, college, and general audience. Publishes material to purge racism from the human bloodstream through the written word. Estab. 1975. Circ. 10,000. Byline given. Pays on publication. Offers 60% kill fee. Publishes ms an average of 3 months after acceptance. Submit seasonal material 6 months in advance. Accepts queries by mail, e-mail. Does not accept previously published submissions.Responds in 2 months to queries. Responds in 1 month to mss. Sample copy and writer's guidelines for $5 and 9×12 SAE with correct postage or online. Guidelines available online: aimmagazine.org/submit.htm.

NONFICTION Needs expose, education, general interest, social significance, historical, Black or Indian, how-to, create a more equitable society, interview, one who is making social contributions to community, book reviews, reviews of plays. No religious material. **Buys 16 mss/year.** Send complete ms. Length: 500-800 words. **Pays $25-35.**

PHOTOS Captions, identification of subjects required. Reviews b&w prints.

FICTION Contact: Ruth Apilado, associate editor. Fiction that teaches the brotherhood of man. Needs

ethnic, historical, mainstream, suspense. Open. No religious mss. **Buys 20 mss/year.** Send complete ms. Length: 1,000-1,500 words. **Pays $25-35.**

POETRY Needs avant-garde, free verse, light verse. No preachy poetry. Buys 20 poems/year. Submit maximum 5 poems. Length: 15-30 lines. **Pays $3-5.**

FILLERS Needs anecdotes, newsbreaks, short humor. **Buys 30 mss/year.** Length: 50-100 words. **Pays $5.**

💲💲 AMBASSADOR MAGAZINE

National Italian American Foundation, 1860 19th St. NW, Washington DC 20009. (202)939-3108. Fax: (202)387-0800. E-mail: don@niaf.org. Website: niaf.org. **Contact:** Don Oldenburg, editor. **50% freelance written.** Quarterly magazine for Italian-Americans covering Italian-American history and culture. We publish nonfiction articles on little-known events in Italian-American history and articles on Italian-American culture, traditions, and personalities living and dead. Estab. 1989. Circ. 25,000. Byline given. Pays on approval of final draft. Offers $50 kill fee. Editorial lead time 3 months. Accepts queries by mail, e-mail, fax. Accepts simultaneous submissions. Responds in 2 months to queries. Sample copy and writer's guidelines free.

NONFICTION Needs historical, interview, photo feature. **Buys 12 mss/year.** Send complete ms. Length: 800-1,500 words. **Pays $250 for photos and article.**

PHOTOS Send photos. Captions, identification of subjects required. Reviews contact sheets, prints. Offers no additional payment for photos accepted with ms.

💲💲💲 B'NAI B'RITH MAGAZINE

2020 K St. NW, 7th Floor, Washington DC 20006. (202)857-6527. E-mail: bbmag@bnaibrith.org. Website: bnaibrith.org. **90% freelance written.** Quarterly magazine specializing in social, political, historical, religious, cultural, `lifestyle,' and service articles relating chiefly to the Jewish communities of North America and Israel. Write for the American Jewish audience, i.e., write about topics from a Jewish perspective, highlighting creativity and innovation in Jewish life. Estab. 1886. Circ. 110,000. Byline given. Pays on publication. Publishes ms an average of 6 months after acceptance. Editorial lead time 3 months. Submit seasonal material 5 months in advance. Accepts queries by mail, e-mail, fax. Accepts simultaneous submissions. Responds in 1 month to queries. Responds in 6 weeks to mss. Sample copy for $2. Writer's guidelines for #10 SASE or by e-mail.

NONFICTION Needs interview, photo feature, religious, travel. No Holocaust memoirs, first-person essays/memoirs, fiction, or poetry. **Buys 14-20 mss/year.** Query with published clips. Length: 1,000-2,500 words. **Pays $300-800 for assigned articles. Pays $300-700 for unsolicited articles.** Sometimes pays expenses of writers on assignment.

PHOTOS Rarely assigned.

⊕⊕ CELTICLIFE MAGAZINE

Clansman Publishing, Ltd., 1454 Dresden Row, Suite 204, Halifax NS B3J 3T5 Canada. (902)425-5716. Fax: (902)835-0080. E-mail: editorial@celticlife.ca. Website: celticlife.ca. **Contact:** Alexa Thompson, editor-in-chief. **95% freelance written.** Quarterly magazine covering culture of North Americans of Celtic descent. "The magazine chronicles the stories of Celtic people who have settled in North America, with a focus on the stories of those who are not mentioned in history books. We also feature Gaelic language articles, history of Celtic people, traditions, music, and folklore. We profile Celtic musicians and include reviews of Celtic books, music, and videos." Estab. 1987. Circ. 5,000 (per issue). Byline given. Pays 2 months after publication. Publishes ms an average of 2 months after acceptance. Editorial lead time 2 months. Submit seasonal material 3 months in advance. Accepts queries by mail, e-mail, fax, phone. Responds in 1 week to queries. Responds in 1 month to mss Sample copy available online. Digital sample and guidelines available online.

⊖80% of content must originate from Canadian citizens or Canadian landed immigrants.

NONFICTION Needs essays, general interest, historical, interview, opinion, personal experience, travel, Gaelic language, Celtic music reviews, profiles of Celtic musicians, Celtic history, traditions, and folklore. No fiction, poetry, historical stories already well publicized. **Buys 100 mss/year.** Query or send complete ms Length: 800-2,500 words. **Pays $50-75 (Canadian). All writers receive a complimentary subscription.**

PHOTOS State availability. Captions, identification of subjects, model releases required. Reviews 35mm transparencies, 5×7 prints, JPEG files (300 dpi). We do not pay for photographs.

COLUMNS Query. **Pays $50-75 (Canadian)**

⊕ FILIPINAS

Filipinas Publishing, Inc., GBM Bldg., 1580 Bryant St., Daly City CA 94015. (650)993-8943. Website: filipinasmag.com. Monthly magazine focused on Filipino-American affairs. *Filipinas* answers the lack of mainstream media coverage of Filipinos in America. It targets both Filipino immigrants and American-born Filipinos, gives in-depth coverage of political, social, and cultural events in the Philippines and in the Filipino-American community. Features role models, history, travel, food and leisure, issues, and controversies. Estab. 1992. Circ. 40,000. Byline given. Pays on publication. Offers $10 kill fee. Publishes ms an average of 5 months after acceptance. Editorial lead time 2 months. Submit seasonal material 4 months in advance. Accepts queries by mail, e-mail, fax. Responds in 3 weeks to queries. Responds in 5 months to mss. Writer's guidelines for 9 ½×4 SASE or on website.

⊖*Unsolicited mss will not be paid.*

NONFICTION Needs expose, general interest, historical, inspirational, interview, opinion, personal experience, travel. No academic papers. **Buys 80-100 mss/year.** Query with published clips. Length: 800-1,500 words. **Pays $50-75.**

PHOTOS State availability. Captions, identification of subjects required. Reviews 2¼×2¼ and 4 x 5 transparencies. Offers $15-25/photo.

COLUMNS Cultural Currents (Filipino traditions and beliefs), 1,000 words; New Voices (first-person essays by Filipino Americans ages 10-25), 800 words; First Person (open to all Filipinos), 800 words. Query with published clips. **Pays $50-75.**

⊕⊕ GERMAN LIFE

Zeitgeist Publishing, Inc., 1068 National Hwy., La-Vale MD 21502. (301)729-6190. Fax: (301)729-1720. E-mail: mslider@germanlife.com. Website: germanlife.com. **50% freelance written.** Bimonthly magazine covering German-speaking Europe. "*German Life* is for all interested in the diversity of German-speaking culture—past and present—and in the various ways that the US (and North America in general) has been shaped by its German immigrants. The magazine is dedicated to solid reporting on cultural, historical, social, and political events." Estab. 1994. Circ. 40,000. Byline given. Pays on publication. Editorial lead time 4 months. Submit seasonal material 6 months in advance. Accepts queries by mail, e-mail. Responds in

2 months to queries. Responds in 3 months to mss. Sample copy for $4.95 and SAE with 4 first-class stamps. Guidelines available online.

NONFICTION Needs general interest, historical, interview, photo feature, travel. Special issues: Oktoberfest-related (October); Seasonal Relative to Germany, Switzerland, or Austria (December); Travel to German-speaking Europe (April). **Buys 50 mss/year.** Query with published clips. Length: 800-1,500 words. **Pays $200-500 for assigned articles. Pays $200-350 for unsolicited articles.**

PHOTOS State availability. Identification of subjects required. Reviews color transparencies, 5×7 color or b&w prints. Offers no additional payment for photos accepted with ms.

COLUMNS German-Americana (regards specific German-American communities, organizations, and/or events past or present), 1,200 words; Profile (portrays prominent Germans, Americans, or German-Americans), 1,000 words; At Home (cuisine, etc. relating to German-speaking Europe), 800 words; Library (reviews of books, videos, CDs, etc.), 300 words. **Buys 30 mss/year.** Query with published clips. **Pays $50-150.**

FILLERS Needs facts, newsbreaks. Length: 100-300 words. **Pays $50-150.**

$$ HADASSAH MAGAZINE

50 W. 58th St., New York NY 10019. (212)688-0227. Fax: (212)446-9521. E-mail: magazine@hadassah.org. Website: hadassah.org. **Contact:** Rachel Fyman Schwartzberg. **90% freelance written**. Monthly magazine. *Hadassah* is a general interest Jewish feature and literary magazine. We speak to our readers on a vast array of subjects ranging from politics to parenting, to midlife crisis to Mideast crisis. Our readers want coverage on social and economic issues, Jewish women's (feminist) issues, the arts, travel and health. Circ. 300,000. Pays on acceptance. NoResponds in 4 months to mss. Sample copy and writer's guidelines with 9×12 SASE.

NONFICTION Buys 10 unsolicited mss/year. Query. Length: 1,500-2,000 words. Sometimes pays expenses of writers on assignment.

PHOTOS "We buy photos only to illustrate articles. Always interested in striking cover photos.". Offers $50 for first photo, $35 for each additional photo.

COLUMNS "We have a family column and a travel column, but a query for topic or destination should be submitted first to make sure the area is of interest and the story follows our format."

FICTION Contact: Zelda Shluker, maaging editor. Short stories with strong plots and positive Jewish values. Needs ethnic, Jewish. No personal memoirs, schmaltzy or shelter magazine fiction. Length: 1,500-2,000 words. **Pays $500 minimum.**

$ INTERNATIONAL EXAMINER

622 S. Washington, Seattle WA 98104-2720. (206)624-3925. Fax: (206)624-3046. E-mail: editor@iexaminer.org. Website: iexaminer.org. **Contact:** Diem Ly, editor-in-chief. **75% freelance written**. Biweekly journal of Asian-American news, politics, and arts. We write about Asian-American issues and things of interest to Asian-Americans. We do not want stuff about Asian things (stories on your trip to China, Japanese Tea Ceremony, etc. will be rejected). , we are in English. Estab. 1974. Circ. 12,000. Pays on publication. Publishes ms an average of 1 month after acceptance. Editorial lead time 1 month. Submit seasonal material 2 months in advance. Accepts simultaneous submissions. Guidelines for #10 SASE.

NONFICTION Needs essays, expose, general interest, historical, humor, interview, opinion, personal experience, photo feature. **Buys 100 mss/year.** Query by mail, fax, or e-mail with published clips 750-5,000 words depending on subject **Pays $25-100.** Sometimes pays expenses of writers on assignment.

REPRINTS Accepts previously published submissions (as long as t published in same area). Send typed ms with rights for sale noted and information about when and where the material previously appeared. Payment negotiable

PHOTOS State availability. Captions, identification of subjects required. Reviews contact sheets. Negotiates payment individually.

FICTION Asian-American authored fiction by or about Asian-Americans. Needs novel concepts. **Buys 1-2 mss/year.** Query.

$$ ITALIAN AMERICA

219 E St. NE, Washington DC 20002. (202)547-2900. Fax: (202)546-8168. E-mail: ddesanctis@osia.org. Website: osia.org. **20% freelance written**. Quarterly magazine. *Italian America* provides timely information about OSIA, while reporting on individuals, institutions, issues, and events of current or historical significance in the Italian-American community. Estab. 1996. Circ. 65,000. Byline given. Pays on publication. Offers 50% kill fee. Publishes ms an average

of 3 months after acceptance. Editorial lead time 3 months. Accepts queries by mail, e-mail, fax. Accepts simultaneous submissions. Sample copy free. Guidelines available online.

NONFICTION Needs historical, little known historical facts that must relate to Italian Americans, interview, opinion, current events. **Buys 8 mss/year.** Query with published clips. Length: 750-1,000 words. **Pays $50-250.**

⊖⊜ JEWISH ACTION

Orthodox Union, 11 Broadway, New York NY 10004. (212)613-8146. Fax: (212)613-0646. E-mail: ja@ou.org; carmeln@ou.org. Website: ou.org/jewish_action. Ed Hamway, art director. **Contact:** Nechama Carmel, editor; Anna Socher, assistant editor. **80% freelance written.** Quarterly magazine covering a vibrant approach to Jewish issues, Orthodox lifestyle, and values. Estab. 1986. Circ. 40,000. Byline given. Pays 2 months after publication. Submit seasonal material 4 months in advance. Accepts queries by mail, e-mail, fax. Responds in 3 months to queries. Sample copy available online. Guidelines for #10 SASE or by e-mail.

○ Prefers queries by e-mail. Mail and fax OK.

NONFICTION "We are not looking for Holocaust accounts. We welcome essays about responses to personal or societal challenges." **Buys 30-40 mss/year.** Query with published clips. Length: 1,000-3,000 words. **Pays $100-400 for assigned articles. Pays $75-150 for unsolicited articles.**

PHOTOS Send photos. Identification of subjects required.

COLUMNS Just Between Us (personal opinion on current Jewish life and issues), 1,000 words. **Buys 4 mss/year.**

FICTION Must have relevance to Orthodox reader. Length: 1,000-2,000 words.

POETRY Buys limited number of poems/year. **Pays $25-75.**

⊜ JULUKA

Mindsgate Media, 220 West 8th St., Palo Verdes Peninsula CA 90731-3708. (866)458-5852. Fax: (310)707-2255. E-mail: info@julukanews.com. Website: facebook.com/. Editorial lead time 1 month. Accepts queries by e-mail.

○ Published in the US for those interested in South Africa. Helps South Africans adapt to life in a new country and provides a forum for networking and exchanging ideas, opinions, and resources.

NONFICTION Needs humor, interview, opinion, personal experience, travel, news, book reviews. **Pays 5¢/word** Sometimes pays expenses of writers on assignment.

PHOTOS Send photos.

COLUMNS Travel, 520 words; Art & Culture (artist profiles/gallery events), 200-400 words; Culture Shock (personal stories about life in North American/stories about emigrating), 500 words; Sports 200-400 words; Human Interest (personal experiences), 300-1,000 words; Guest Editorial, 150-350 words; Reader Profiles, 400-800 words; Money Matters (financial news), 150-300 words; News You Can Use (law/insurance/financial planning), 250-350 words.

⊜ KHABAR

Khabar, Inc., 3790 Holcomb Bridge Rd., Suite 101, Norcross GA 30092. (770)451-7666, ext. 115. E-mail: parthiv@khabar.com;info@khabar.com. Website: khabar.com. **50% freelance written.** "Monthly magazine covering the Asian Indian community in and around Georgia.". Content relating to Indian-American and/or immigrant experience. Estab. 1992. Circ. 27,000. Pays on publication. Offers 25% kill fee. Publishes ms an average of 2 months after acceptance. Editorial lead time 2 months. Submit seasonal material 2 months in advance. Accepts queries by e-mail. Accepts simultaneous submissions. Sample copy free. Guidelines by e-mail.

NONFICTION Needs essays, interview, opinion, personal experience, travel. **Buys 5 mss/year.** Send complete ms. Length: 750-4,000 words. **Pays $100-300 for assigned articles. Pays $75 for unsolicited articles.**

PHOTOS State availability of or send photos. Captions, identification of subjects required. Negotiates payment individually.

COLUMNS Book Review, 1,200 words; Music Review, 800 words; Spotlight (profiles), 1,200-3,000 words. **Buys 5 mss/year.** Query with or without published clips or send complete ms. **Pays $75+.**

FICTION Needs ethnic, Indian American/Asian immigrant. **Buys 5 mss/year.** Query or send complete ms. **Pays $50-100.**

⊖⊖⊖⊜ LATINA MAGAZINE

Latina Media Ventures, LLC, 625 Madison Ave,, 3rd Floor, New York NY 10022. (212)642-0200. E-mail: editor@latina.com. Website: latina.com. **40-50%**

freelance written. Monthly magazine covering Latina lifestyle. *Latina Magazine* is the leading bilingual lifestyle publication for Hispanic women in the US today. Covering the best of Latino fashion, beauty, culture, and food, the magazine also features celebrity profiles and interviews. Estab. 1996. Circ. 250,000. Byline given. Pays on publication. Offers 25% kill fee. Publishes ms an average of 2-3 months after acceptance. Editorial lead time 3 months. Submit seasonal material 4-5 months in advance. Accepts queries by e-mail. Responds in 1 month to queries. Responds in 1-2 months to mss. Sample copy available online.

> Editors are in charge of their individual sections and pitches should be made directly to them. Do not make pitches directly to the editor-in-chief or the editorial director as they will only be routed to the relevant section editor.

NONFICTION Needs essays, how-to, humor, inspirational, interview, new product, personal experience. Special issues: The 10 Latinas Who Changed the World (December). We do not feature an extensive amount of celebrity content or entertainment content, and freelancers should be sensitive to this. The magazine does not contain book or album reviews, and we do not write stories covering an artist's new project. We do not attend press junkets and do not cover press conferences. Please note that we are a lifestyle magazine, not an entertainment magazine. **Buys 15-20 mss/year.** Query with published clips. Length: 300-2,200 words. **Pays $1/word.** Pays expenses of writers on assignment.

PHOTOS State availability. Identification of subjects required. Reviews contact sheets, transparencies, GIF/JPEG files. Negotiates payment individually.

$$$ MOMENT

4115 Wisconsin Ave. NW, Suite 102, Washington DC 20016. (202)363-6422. Fax: (202)362-2514. E-mail: editor@momentmag.com. Website: momentmag.com. **90% freelance written**. Bimonthly magazine. *Moment* is an independent Jewish bimonthly general interest magazine that specializes in cultural, political, historical, religious, and lifestyle articles relating chiefly to the North American Jewish community and Israel. Estab. 1975. Circ. 65,000. Byline given. Pays on publication. Publishes ms an average of 6 months after acceptance. Editorial lead time 3 months. Submit seasonal material 6 months in advance. Accepts queries by mail, e-mail, fax. Accepts simultaneous submissions. Responds in 1 month to queries. Responds in 3 months to mss. Sample copy for $4.50 and SAE. Guidelines available online.

NONFICTION Buys 25-30 mss/year. Query with published clips. Length: 2,500-7,000 words. **Pays $200-1,200 for assigned articles. Pays $40-500 for unsolicited articles.**

PHOTOS State availability. Identification of subjects required. Negotiates payment individually.

COLUMNS 5765 (snappy pieces about quirky events in Jewish communities, news and ideas to improve Jewish living), 250 words maximum; Olam (first-person pieces, humor, and colorful reportage), 600-1,500 words; Book reviews (fiction and nonfiction) are accepted but generally assigned, 400-800 words. **Buys 30 mss/year.** Query with published clips. **Pays $50-250.**

$$ NATIVE PEOPLES MAGAZINE

5333 N. 7th St., Suite C-224, Phoenix AZ 85014. (602)265-4855. Fax: (602)265-3113. E-mail: dgibson@nativepeoples.com; kcoochwytewa@nativepeoples.com. Website: nativepeoples.com. Kevin Coochwytewa, art director. **Contact:** Daniel Gibson, editor; Kevin Coochwytewa, art director. Bimonthly magazine covering Native Americans. High-quality reproduction with full color throughout. The primary purpose of this magazine is to offer a sensitive portrayal of the arts and lifeways of native peoples of the Americas. Estab. 1987. Circ. 40,000. Byline given. Pays on publication. Accepts queries by mail, e-mail, fax. Responds in 2 months to queries. Guidelines available online.

NONFICTION Needs interview, of interesting and leading Natives from all walks of life, with an emphasis on arts, personal experience. **Buys 35 mss/year.** Length: 1,000-2,500 words. **Pays 25¢/word.**

PHOTOS State availability. Identification of subjects required. Reviews transparencies, prefers high res digital images and 35mm slides. Inquire for details. Offers $45-150/page rates, $250/cover photos.

$$$$ PAKN TREGER

National Yiddish Book Center, 1021 West St., Amherst MA 01002. (413)256-4900. E-mail: aatherley@bikher.org; pt@bikher.org; bwolfson@bikher.org. Website: yiddishbookcenter.org. Betsey Wolfson, photography. **Contact:** Anne Atherley, editor's assistant. **50% freelance written**. Magazine published 2 times/year covering modern and contemporary Yiddish and Jewish culture. Estab. 1980. Circ. 20,000.

Byline given. Pays on publication. Publishes ms an average of 3 months after acceptance. Editorial lead time 4 months. Submit seasonal material 3 months in advance. Accepts queries by mail, e-mail, fax. Accepts simultaneous submissions. Responds in 4 weeks to queries. Responds in 3 months to mss. Sample copy available online. Guidelines by e-mail.

NONFICTION Needs Needs pre-publication book excerpts, essays, humor, interview, travel, graphic novels. Does not want personal memoirs or poetry. **Buys 6-10 mss/year.** Query. Length: 1,200-4,000 words. **Pays $800-2,000 for assigned articles. Pays $350-1,000 for unsolicited articles.** Sometimes pays expenses of writers on assignment.

PHOTOS Contact: Betsey Wolfson, designer. State availability. Identification of subjects required. Reviews GIF/JPEG files. Negotiates payment individually.

COLUMNS Let's Learn Yiddish (Yiddish lesson), 1 page Yid/English; Translations (Yiddish-English), 1,200-2,500 words. **Pays $350-1,000.**

FICTION Needs historical, humorous, mystery, novel concepts, serialized, slice-of-life vignettes. **Buys 3 mss/year.** Query. Length: 1,200-6,000 words. **Pays $1,000-2,000.**

💲💲 RUSSIAN LIFE

RIS Publications, P.O. Box 567, Montpelier VT 05601. Website: russianlife.net. **75% freelance written**. Bimonthly magazine covering Russian culture, history, travel, and business. "Our readers are informed Russophiles with an avid interest in all things Russian. But we do not publish personal travel journals or the like." Estab. 1956. Circ. 15,000. Byline given. Pays on publication. Publishes ms an average of 3-6 months after acceptance. Editorial lead time 2 months. Submit seasonal material 3 months in advance. Accepts queries by mail. TrueResponds in 1 month to queries. Sample copy for sae with 9×12 envelope and 6 first-class stamps. Guidelines available online.

NONFICTION Needs general interest, photo feature, travel. No personal stories, i.e., How I came to love Russia. **Buys 15-20 mss/year.** Query. Length: 1,000-6,000 words. **Pays $100-300.**

REPRINTS Accepts previously published submissions rarely.

PHOTOS Send photos. Captions required. Model/property release preferred. Words with local freelancers only. Reviews contact sheets. Negotiates payment individually. Pays $20-50 (color photo with accompanying story), depending on placement in magazine. Pays on publication. Credit line given.

💲💲 SCANDINAVIAN REVIEW

The American-Scandinavian Foundation, 58 Park Ave.@ 38th Street, New York NY 10016. (212)779-3587. E-mail: info@amscan.org. Website: amscan.org. **75% freelance written**. Triannual magazine for contemporary Scandinavia. Audience: Members, embassies, consulates, libraries. Slant: Popular coverage of contemporary affairs in Scandinavia. Estab. 1913. Circ. 4,000. Byline given. Pays on publication. Publishes ms an average of 2 months after acceptance. Editorial lead time 3 months. Submit seasonal material 3 months in advance. Responds in 6 weeks to queries. Sample copy available online. Guidelines free.

NONFICTION Needs general interest, interview, photo feature, travel, must have Scandinavia as topic focus. Special issues: Scandinavian travel. No pornography. **Buys 30 mss/year.** Query with published clips. Length: 1,500-2,000 words. **Pays $300 maximum.**

PHOTOS Captions required. Reviews 3 x 5 transparencies, prints. Pays $25-50/photo; negotiates payment individually.

SKIPPING STONES: A MULTICULTURAL LITERARY MAGAZINE

P.O. Box 3939, Eugene OR 97403-0939. (541)342-4956. Fax: On demand. E-mail: Editor@Skippingstones.org. Website: Skippingstones.org. **Contact:** Arun Toke, editor. **80% freelance written**. Estab. 1988. Circ. 2,200 print, plus web. Byline given. Publishes ms an average of 4-8 months after acceptance. Editorial lead time 3-4 months. Submit seasonal material 4 months in advance. Accepts queries by mail, e-mail. Accepts simultaneous submissions. Responds only if interested, send nonreturnable samples. Sample copy for $6. Writer's guidelines online or for business-sized envelope.

NONFICTION Needs essays, general interest, humor, inspirational, interview, opinion, personal experience, photo feature, travel. No 'preachy' or 'screetchy' articles. **Buys 20-30 mss/year.** Send complete ms..

FICTION Needs adventure, ethnic, historical, humorous, multicultural, international, social issues. **Buys 20 mss/year.** Send complete ms. Length: 300-800 words. **Pays with contributor copies.**

POETRY Only accepts poetry from youth under age 18. Buys 100-150 poems/year. Submit maximum 4 poems. Length: 30 lines maximum.

✿$ WINDSPEAKER

Aboriginal Multi-Media Society of Alberta, 13245-146 St., Edmonton AB T5L 4S8 Canada. (780)455-2700. Fax: (780)455-7639. E-mail: dsteel@ammsa.com. Website: ammsa.com/windspeaker. **Contact:** Debora Steel, editor. **25% freelance written.** Monthly tabloid covering native issues. Focus on events and issues that affect and interest native peoples, national or local. Estab. 1983. Circ. 27,000. Byline given. Pays on publication. Offers kill fee. Publishes ms an average of 1 month after acceptance. Editorial lead time 1 month. Submit seasonal material 2 months in advance. Accepts queries by mail, e-mail, phone. Accepts simultaneous submissions. Sample copy free. Guidelines available online.

NONFICTION Needs opinion, photo feature, travel, news interview/profile, reviews: books, music, movies. Special issues: Powwow (June); Travel supplement (May). **Buys 200 mss/year.** Query with published clips and SASE or by phone. Length: 500-800 words. **Pays $3-3.60/published inch.** Sometimes pays expenses of writers on assignment.

PHOTOS Send photos. Identification of subjects required. Offers $25-100/photo. Will pay for film and processing.

FOOD AND DRINK

$$$ DRAFT

Draft Publishing, **4742 N. 24th St.**, Suite 210, Phoenix AZ 85016. (888)806-4677. E-mail: jessica.daynor@draftmag.com. Website: draftmag.com. **60% freelance written.** Bimonthly magazine covering beer and men's lifestyle (including food, travel, sports and leisure). "*DRAFT* is a national men's magazine devoted to beer, breweries and the lifestyle and culture that surrounds it. Read by nearly 300,000 men aged 21-45, *DRAFT* offers formal beer reviews, plus coverage of food, travel, sports and leisure. Writers need not have formal beer knowledge (though that's a plus!), but they should be experienced journalists who can appreciate beer and beer culture." Estab. 2006. Circ. 275,000. Byline given. Pays on publication. Offers 20% kill fee. Publishes ms an average of 2 months after acceptance. Editorial lead time 4 months. Submit seasonal material 6 months in advance. Accepts queries by e-mail. Accepts simultaneous submissions. Responds in 3 weeks to queries. Sample copy for $3 (magazine can

also be found on most newsstands for $4.99). Guidelines available at draftmag.com/submissions.

NONFICTION Needs features, short front-of-book pieces, how-to's, interviews, travel, food, restaurant and bar pieces, sports and adventure; anything guy-related. Special issues: The editorial calendar is as follows: November/December: Holiday issue; Jan/Feb: Best of issue; May/June: Food issue; Mar/Apr: Travel issue; July/Aug: All-American issue; Sept/Oct Anniversary issue. Do not want unsolicited mss., beer reviews, brewery profiles. **Buys 80/year. mss./year.** Query with published clips. Length: 250-2,500 words. **50-90¢ for assigned articles.** sometimes (limit agreed upon in advance).

PHOTOS Reviews GIF/JPEG files. Offers no additional payment for photos accepted with ms.

COLUMNS Contact: Chris Staten, associate editor, (chris.staten@draftmag.com) for OnTap and OnTap llife, Jessica Daynor, managing editor, for all other departments. 'On Tap' (short FOB pieces on beer-related subjects, 350 words; 'On Tap Life' (short FOB pieces on NON -beer-related subjects (travel, food, sports, home, leisure), 350 words; 'Trek' (travel pieces [need not relate to beer, but it's a plus]), 950 words; 'Taste' (beer-and food-related incident or unique perspective on beer), 750 words. **Buys 50 mss/year. mss./year.** Query with published clips. **Pays 50¢-80¢.**

◔ GOURMET TRAVELLER WINE

ACP Magazines, Ltd., 54-58 Park St., GPO Box 4088, Sydney NSW 2000 Australia. (61)(2)9282-8000. Fax: (61)(2)9267-4361. Website: gourmettravellerwine.com.au. **Contact:** Judy Sarris, editor. Bimonthly magazine for the world of wine, celebrating both local and overseas industries. "*Gourmet Traveller WINE* is for wine lovers: It's for those who love to travel, to eat out and to entertain at home, and for those who want to know more about the wine in their glass." Circ. 22,088.

✂� Target men 25-54, professionals & managers.

NONFICTION Needs general interest, how-to, interview, new product, travel. Query.

➕$$ KASHRUS MAGAZINE

The Kashrus Institute, P.O. Box 204, Brooklyn NY 11204. (718)336-8544. E-mail: **editorial@kashrusmagazine.com**. Website: kashrusmagazine.com. Circ. 10,000. Byline given. Pays on publication. Offers 50% kill fee. Publishes ms an average of 2 months after acceptance. Submit seasonal material 2 months in advance. Accepts queries by mail, phone. Accepts simultaneous submissions. Responds in 2 weeks. Sample copy for $2.

NONFICTION Needs general interest, interview, new product, personal experience, photo feature, religious, technical, travel. Special issues: International Kosher Travel (October); Passover Shopping Guide (March); Domestic Kosher Travel Guide (June). **Buys 8-12 mss/ year.** Query with published clips. Length: 1,000-1,500 words. **Pays $100-250 for assigned articles. Pays up to $100 for unsolicited articles.** Sometimes pays expenses of writers on assignment.

REPRINTS Send tearsheet or photocopy and information about when and where the material previously appeared. Pays 25-50% of amount paid for an original article.

PHOTOS Contact: Rabbi Wikler, editor. No guidelines; send samples or call. State availability. Offers no additional payment for photos accepted with ms.

COLUMNS Book Review (cookbooks, food technology, kosher food), 250-500 words; People In the News (interviews with kosher personalities), 1,000-1,500 words; Regional Kosher Supervision (report on kosher supervision in a city or community), 1,000-1,500 words; Food Technology (new technology or current technology with accompanying pictures), 1,000-1,500 words; Travel (international, national— must include Kosher information and Jewish communities), 1,000-1,500 words; Regional Kosher Cooking, 1,000-1,500 words. **Buys 8-12 mss/year.** Query with published clips. **Pays $50-250.**

TEA A MAGAZINE

Olde English Tea Company, Inc., 3 Devotion Rd., P.O. Box 348, Scotland CT 06264. (860)456-1145. Fax: (860)456-1023. E-mail: teamag@teamag.com. Website: teamag.com. **75% freelance written**. Quarterly magazine covering anything tea related. "*Tea, A Magazine* is an exciting magazine all about tea, both as a drink and for its cultural significance in art, music, literature, history and society." Estab. 1994. Circ. 9,500. Byline given. Pays on publication. Publishes ms an average of 1 year after acceptance. Editorial lead time 9 months. Submit seasonal material 6 months in advance. Responds in 6 months to mss. Guidelines by e-mail.

NONFICTION Needs book excerpts, essays, general interest, historical, how-to, humor, interview, personal experience, photo feature, travel. Send complete ms. **Pays negotiable amount.** Sometimes pays expenses of writers on assignment.

PHOTOS Send photos. Captions, identification of subjects required. Reviews prints, GIF/JPEG files (300 dpi). Negotiates payment individually.

COLUMNS Readers' Stories (personal experience involving tea); Book Reviews (review on tea books). Send complete ms. **Pays negotiable amount**

FICTION Does not want anything that is not tea related. Send complete ms. **Pays negotiable amount.**

POETRY Needs avant-garde, free verse, haiku, light verse, traditional. Does not want anything that is not tea related.

VEGETARIAN JOURNAL

P.O. Box 1463, Baltimore MD 21203-1463. (410)366-8343. E-mail: vrg@vrg.org. Website: vrg.org. *Vegetarian Journal* is 36 pages, magazine-sized, professionally printed, saddle-stapled, with glossy card cover. Press run is 20,000. Sample: $3. "Please, no submissions of poetry from adults; 18 and under only."The Vegetarian Resource Group offers an annual contest for ages 18 and under: $50 savings bond in 3 age categories for the best contribution on any aspect of vegetarianism. "Most entries are essay, but we would accept poetry with enthusiasm." **Deadline:** May 1 (postmark). Details available at website: vrg. org/essay/ Estab. 1982.

❸❸❸❸ WINE ENTHUSIAST MAGAZINE

Wine Enthusiast Companies, 333 North Bedford Rd., Mt. Kisco NY 10549. E-mail: editor@wineenthusiast.net. Website: winemag.com. **40% freelance written**. Monthly magazine covering the lifestyle of wine. "Our readers are upscale and educated, but not necessarily super-sophisticated about wine itself. Our informal, irreverent approach appeals to savvy enophiles and newbies alike." Estab. 1988. Circ. 80,000. Byline given. Pays on acceptance. Offers 25% kill fee. Editorial lead time 4 months. Submit seasonal material 5 months in advance. Accepts queries by e-mail. Responds in 2 weeks to queries. Responds in 2 months to mss.

NONFICTION Needs essays, humor, interview, new product, personal experience. **Buys 5 mss/year. Pays $750-2,500 for assigned articles. Pays $750-2,000 for unsolicited articles. Pays 50¢/word for website.**

PHOTOS Send photos. Reviews GIF/JPEG files. Offers $135-400/photo.

$$ WINE PRESS NORTHWEST

333 W. Canal Dr., Kennewick WA 99336. (509)582-1564. Fax: (509)585-7221. E-mail: edegerman@winepressnw.com. Website: winepressnw.com. **Contact:** Eric Degerman, managing editor. **50% freelance written**. Quarterly magazine covering Pacific Northwest wine (Washington, Oregon, British Columbia, Idaho). "We focus narrowly on Pacific Northwest wine. If we write about travel, it's where to go to drink NW wine. If we write about food, it's what goes with NW wine. No beer, no spirits." Estab. 1998. Circ. 12,000. Byline given. Pays on publication. Offers 20% kill fee. Publishes ms an average of 3 months after acceptance. Editorial lead time 3 months. Submit seasonal material 3 months in advance. Accepts queries by mail, e-mail, fax. Accepts simultaneous submissions. Responds in 1 month to queries. Sample copy free or online. Guidelines free.

NONFICTION Needs general interest, historical, interview, new product, photo feature, travel. No beer, spirits, non-NW (California wine, etc.) **Buys 30 mss/year.** Query with published clips. Length: 1,500-2,500 words. **Pays $300.** Sometimes pays expenses of writers on assignment.

PHOTOS State availability. Identification of subjects required. Reviews contact sheets. Negotiates payment individually.

$$$ WINE SPECTATOR

M. Shanken Communications, Inc., 387 Park Ave. S., New York NY 10016. E-mail: wsonline@mshanken.com. Website: winespectator.com. **20% freelance written. Prefers to work with published/established writers**. Monthly news magazine. Estab. 1976. Circ. 350,000. Byline given. Pays within 30 days of publication. Publishes ms an average of 2 months after acceptance. Submit seasonal material 4 months in advance. Accepts queries by mail, fax. Responds in 3 months to queries. Guidelines for #10 SASE.

NONFICTION Needs general interest, news about wine or wine events, interview, of wine, vintners, wineries, opinion, photo feature, travel, dining and other lifestyle pieces. No winery promotional pieces or articles by writers who lack sufficient knowledge to write below just surface data. Query. Length: 100-2,000 words. **Pays $100-1,000.**

PHOTOS Send photos. Captions, identification of subjects, model releases required. Pays $75 minimum for color transparencies.

GAMES AND PUZZLES

$ THE BRIDGE BULLETIN

American Contract Bridge League, 6575 Windchase Dr., Horn Lake MS 38637-1523. (662)253-3156. Fax: (662)253-3187. E-mail: editor@acbl.org. E-mail: brent.manley@acbl.org. Website: acbl.org. Paul Linxwiler, managing editor. **Contact:** Brent Manley, editor. **20% freelance written**. Monthly magazine covering duplicate (tournament) bridge. Estab. 1938. Circ. 155,000. Byline given. Pays on publication. Publishes ms an average of 3 months after acceptance. Editorial lead time 2 months. Accepts queries by mail, e-mail. Accepts simultaneous submissions.

NONFICTION Needs book excerpts, essays, how-to, play better bridge, humor, interview, new product, personal experience, photo feature, technical, travel. **Buys 6 mss/year.** Query. Length: 500-2,000 words. **Pays $100/page.**

PHOTOS Contact: Brent Manley. State availability. Identification of subjects required. Reviews photos with or without a manuscript. Pays $200 or more for suitable work. Pays on publication. Negotiates payment individually.

$$ CHESS LIFE

United States Chess Federation, P.O. Box 3967, Crossville TN 38557-3967. (931)787-1234. Fax: (931)787-1200. E-mail: dlucas@uschess.org; fbutler@uschess.org. Website: uschess.org. Francesca "Frankie" Butler. **Contact:** Daniel Lucas, editor. **15% freelance written. Works with a small number of new/unpublished writers/year.** Monthly magazine. "*Chess Life* is the official publication of the United States Chess Federation, covering news of most major chess events, both here and abroad, with special emphasis on the triumphs and exploits of American players." Estab. 1939. Circ. 85,000. Byline given. Publishes ms an average of 6 months after acceptance. Submit seasonal material 6 months in advance. Accepts queries by mail, e-mail, fax, phone. TrueAccepts simultaneous submissions. Responds in 3 months to mss. Sample copy and writer's guidelines for 9×11 SAE with 5 first-class stamps.

Also publishes children's magazine, *Chess Life For Kids* every other month. Same submission guidelines apply.

NONFICTION Needs general interest, historical, humor, interview, of a famous chess player or organizer, photo feature, chess centered, technical. No stories about personal experiences with chess. **Buys 30-40 mss/ year.** Query with samples if new to publication 3,000 words maximum. **Pays $100/page (800-1,000 words).** Sometimes pays expenses of writers on assignment.

REPRINTS "Send tearsheet, photocopy or typed ms with rights for sale noted and information about when and where the material previously appeared."

PHOTOS Monthly publication of the U.S. Chess Federation. Emphasizes news of all major national and international tournaments; includes historical articles, personality profiles, columns of instruction, occasional fiction, humor for the devoted fan of chess. Sample copy and photo guidelines free with SASE or on website. Uses about 15 photos/issue; 7-8 supplied by freelancers.. Captions, identification of subjects, model releases required. Reviews b&w contact sheets and prints, and color prints and slides. Pays $25-100 inside; covers negotiable. Pays $25-100 for b&w inside; cover payment negotiable. Pays on publication. Buys one-time rights; "we occasionally purchase all rights for stock mug shots." Credit line given.

FILLERS Submit with samples and clips. Buys first or negotiable rights to cartoons and puzzles. **Pays $25 upon acceptance.**

$$$ GAMES MAGAZINE

Games Publications, a division of Kappa Publishing Group, Inc., 6198 Butler Pike, Blue Bell PA 19422. (215)643-6385. Fax: (215)628-3571. E-mail: games@kappapublishing.com. Website: gamesmagazine-online.com. **50% freelance written.** Online magazine covering puzzles and games. *Games* is a magazine of puzzles, contests, and features pertaining to games and ingenuity. It is aimed primarily at adults and has an emphasis on pop culture. Estab. 1977. Circ. 75,000. Byline given. Pays on publication. Offers 25% kill fee. Publishes ms an average of 4 months after acceptance. Editorial lead time 3 months. Submit seasonal material 6 months in advance. Accepts queries by mail, e-mail. Accepts simultaneous submissions. Responds in 6 weeks to queries. Responds in 3 months to mss. Sample copy for $5. Guidelines for #10 sase.

NONFICTION Needs photo feature, puzzles. **Buys 100 puzzles/year and 3 mss/year.** Query. Length: 1,500-2,500 words. **Pays $300-1,000.** Sometimes pays expenses of writers on assignment.

PHOTOS State availability. Captions, identification of subjects, model releases required. Reviews contact sheets, negatives, transparencies, prints. Negotiates payment individually.

COLUMNS Gamebits (game/puzzle news), 250 words; Games & Books (product reviews), 350 words; Wild Cards (short text puzzles), 100 words. **Buys 50 mss/year.** Query. **Pays $25-250.**

FICTION Needs adventure, interactive, mystery. **Buys 1-2 mss/year.** Query. Length: 1,500-2,500 words. **Pays $500-1,200.**

[+] HIGHLIGHTS HIGH FIVE

807 Church St., Honesdale PA 18431. Fax: (570)251-7847. Website: highlights.com/highfive. **Contact:** Kathleen Ha, Editor. "*Highlights High Five* was created to help you encourage your young child's development—and have fun together at the same time. Based on sound educational principles and widely accepted child-development theories, each monthly issue brings a 40-page, high-quality mix of read-aloud stories and age appropriate activities that will help you set your child firmly on the path to becoming a lifelong learner." "Stories for younger readers should have 170 words or less and should appeal to children ages 2-6." Estab. 2009. At this time accepts very few manuscripts. Most articles are commissioned or written in-house. *Highlights Magazine* does accept freelance writing. See the guidelines on the website. Accepts queries by mail. Guidelines available at website online.

$$ POKER PRO MAGAZINE

Poker Pro Media, 5300 W. Atlantic Ave., Suite 602, Delray Beach FL 33484. E-mail: jwenzel@pokerpromedia.com. Website: pokerpromagazine.com. **75% freelance written.** Monthly magazine covering poker, gambling, nightlife. "We want articles about poker and gambling-related articles only; also nightlife in gaming cities and articles on gaming destinations." Estab. 2005. Circ. 150,000. Byline given. Pays on publication. Publishes ms an average of 1 month after acceptance. Editorial lead time 1 ½ months. Submit seasonal material 2 months in advance. Accepts queries by e-mail. Responds in 1 week to queries. Responds in 1 month to mss. Sample copy by e-mail. Guidelines by e-mail.

NONFICTION Needs book excerpts, essays, expose, general interest, historical, how-to, humor, interview, new product, opinion, personal experience, photo feature, travel. **Buys 125 mss/year mss/year.** Query. Length: 800-2,500 words. **Pays $100-$200**

for assigned articles. Pays $100-$200 for unsolicited articles. Sometimes pays expenses of writers on assignment.

PHOTOS State availability. Captions, identification of subjects, model releases required. Reviews GIF/JPEG files. Negotiates payment individually.

GAY AND LESBIAN INTEREST

$$ THE ADVOCATE

Liberation Publications, Inc., 6380 Wilshire Blvd., Suite 1400, Los Angeles CA 90048. (323)852-7200. Fax: (323)852-7272. E-mail: newsroom@advocate.com. Website: advocate.com. **Contact:** Winston Gieseke, managing editor. Biweekly magazine covering national news events with a gay and lesbian perspective on the issues. Estab. 1967. Circ. 120,000. Byline given. Pays on publication. Responds in 1 month to queries. Sample copy for $3.95. Guidelines by e-mail.

NONFICTION Needs expose, interview, news reporting and investigating. Special issues: gays on campus, coming out interviews with celebrities, HIV and health. Query. Length: 1,200 words. **Pays $550.**

COLUMNS Arts & Media (news and profiles of well-known gay or lesbians in entertainment) is most open to freelancers, 750 words. Query. **Pays $100-500.**

$$ CURVE MAGAZINE

P.O Box 467, New York NY 10034. E-mail: editor@curvemag.com. Website: curvemag.com. **60% freelance written.** Magazine published 10 times/year covering lesbian entertainment, culture, and general interest categories. We want dynamic and provocative articles that deal with issues, ideas, or cultural moments that are of interest or relevance to gay women. Estab. 1990. Circ. 80,000. Byline given. Pays on publication. Offers 25% kill fee. Editorial lead time 6 months. Submit seasonal material 6 months in advance. Accepts queries by mail, e-mail, fax. Sample copy for $4.95 with $2 postage. Guidelines available online.

NONFICTION Needs general interest, photo feature, travel, celebrity interview/profile. Special issues: Sex (February); Travel (March); Fashion + Design (April); Weddings (May); Pride (June); Green/Music (July/August); [Travel/Tech] (September); Sexy & Powerful Women (October); Food/Wine/Holiday (November); Gift Guide (December). No fiction or poetry. **Buys 100 mss/year.** Query. Length: 200-2,000 words. **Pays 15¢/word.**

PHOTOS Send hi-res photos with submission. Captions, identification of subjects, model releases required. Offers $25-100/photo; negotiates payment individually.

$ ECHO MAGAZINE

ACE Publishing, Inc., P.O. Box 16630, Phoenix AZ 85011-6630. (602)266-0550. Fax: (602)266-0773. E-mail: editor@echomag.com. Website: echomag.com. **30-40% freelance written.** Biweekly magazine covering gay and lesbian issues. *Echo Magazine* is a newsmagazine for gay, lesbian, bisexual, and transgendered persons in the Phoenix metro area and throughout the state of Arizona. Editorial content needs to be pro-gay, that is, supportive of GLBT equality in all areas of American life. Estab. 1989. Circ. 15,000-18,000. Byline given. Pays on publication. Publishes ms an average of less than 1 month after acceptance. Editorial lead time 1-2 months. Submit seasonal material 1-2 months in advance. Accepts queries by e-mail. Responds in 2 weeks to queries. Responds in 1 month to mss.

NONFICTION Needs book excerpts, essays, historical, humor, interview, opinion, personal experience, photo feature, travel. Special issues: Pride Festival (April); Arts issue (August); Holiday Gift/Decor (December). No articles on topics unrelated to our GLBT readers, or anything that is not pro-gay. **Buys 10-20 mss/year.** Query. Length: 500-2,000 words. **Pays $30-40.**

PHOTOS State availability. Captions, identification of subjects, model releases required. Reviews contact sheets, GIF/JPEG files. Negotiates payment individually.

COLUMNS Guest Commentary (opinion on GLBT issues), 500-1,000 words; Arts/Entertainment (profiles of GLBT or relevant celebrities, or arts issues), 800-1,500 words. **Buys 5-10 mss/year.** Query. **Pays $30-40.**

$ THE GAY & LESBIAN REVIEW

Gay & Lesbian Review, Inc., P.O. Box 180300, Boston MA 02118. (617)421-0082. E-mail: editor@glreview.com. Website: glreview.com. **100% freelance written.** Bimonthly magazine covers gay and lesbian history, culture, and politics. In-depth essays on GLBT history, biography, the arts, political issues, written in clear, lively prose targeted to the 'literate nonspecialist.' Estab. 1994. Circ. 12,000. Byline given. Pays on publication. Editorial lead time 2 months. Accepts queries by mail, e-mail, phone. Accepts simultaneous submissions. Sample copy free. Guidelines free.

NONFICTION Needs essays, historical, humor, interview, opinion, book reviews. Does not want fiction, memoirs, personal reflections. Query. Length: 1,500-5,000 words. **Pays $100.**

POETRY Needs avant-garde, free verse, traditional. **No payment for poems.**

⑤⑤⑤⑤ THE GUIDE

491 Church Street, Suite 200, Toronto ON M4Y 2C6. (416)925-6665. Fax: (416)925-6674. E-mail: matt.mills@xtra.ca;info@guidemag.com. Website: guidemag.com. **Contact:** Mark Sullivan, man. ed. **75% freelance written.** Monthly magazine on the gay and lesbian news, features, and travel. Estab. 1981. Circ. 45,000. Pays on publication. Offers negotiable kill fee. Publishes ms an average of 2 months after acceptance. Submit seasonal material 4 months in advance. Accepts queries by mail, e-mail. Accepts simultaneous submissions. Responds in 3 months to queries.

NONFICTION Needs book excerpts, if yet unpublished, essays, expose, general interest, historical, humor, interview, opinion, personal experience, photo feature, religious. **Buys 48 mss/year.** Send complete ms. Length: 500-2,500 words. **Pays $100-1,750**

REPRINTS Occasionally buys previously published submissions. Pays 100% of amount paid for an original article.

PHOTOS Send photos. Captions, identification of subjects, model releases required. Reviews contact sheets. Pays $15/image used.

⑤⑤ INSTINCT MAGAZINE

Instinct Publishing, 303 N. Glenoaks Blvd., Suite L-120, Burbank CA 91502. E-mail: editor@instinct-mag.com. Website: instinctmag.com. **Contact:** Mike Wood, editor-in-chief. **40% freelance written.** Gay men's monthly lifestyle and entertainment magazine. "*Instinct* is a blend of *Cosmo* and *Maxim* for gay men. We're smart, sexy, irreverent, and we always have a sense of humor—a unique style that has made us the #1 gay men's magazine in the US." Estab. 1997. Circ. 115,000. Byline given. Pays on publication. Offers 20% kill fee. Editorial lead time 2-3 months. Accepts queries by mail, e-mail. NoAccepts simultaneous submissions. Sample copy available online. Guidelines available online. Register online first.

NONFICTION Needs expose, general interest, humor, interview, celebrity and non-celebrity, travel, ba-

sically anything of interest to gay men will be considered. Does not want first-person accounts or articles. Send complete ms. via online submissions manager Length: 850-2,000 words. **Pays $50-300.** Sometimes pays expenses of writers on assignment.

PHOTOS Captions, identification of subjects, model releases required. Negotiates payment individually.

COLUMNS Health (gay, off-kilter), 800 words; Fitness (irreverent), 500 words; Movies, Books (edgy, sardonic), 800 words; Music, Video Games (indie, underground), 800 words. **Pays $150-250.**

➕⑤⑤ MENSBOOK JOURNAL

47 West Communications, LLC, P.O. Box 148, Sturbridge MA 01566. Fax: (508)347-8150. E-mail: features@mensbook.com. Website: mensbook.com. **Contact:** P.C. Carr, editor/publisher. **75% freelance written.** Quarterly paperback book-serial covering gay men's journal. "We target bright, inquisitive, discerning gay men who share our criticism of the gay culture of pride and want more from gay media. We seek primarily first-person autobiographical pieces—then: biographies, political and social analysis, cartoons, short fiction, commentary, travel, humor." Estab. 2008. Circ. start up. Byline given. Pays on publication. Offers $10 kill fee. Editorial lead time 4 months. Submit seasonal material 6 months in advance. Accepts queries by e-mail. Responds in 4 weeks to queries. Sample copy sent free by pdf. Guidelines online at mensbook.com/writersguidelines.htm.

NONFICTION Contact: P.C. Carr, publisher. Needs first-person pieces; essays; think-pieces; expose; humor; inspirational profiles of courage and triumph over adversity; interview/profile; religion/philosophy vis-a-vis the gay experience; opinion; travel. "We do not want celebrity profiles/commentary, chatty, campy gossip; sexual conjecture about famous people; film reviews." **Buys Buys 25 mss./yr. mss/year.** Query by e-mail. Length: 1,000-2,500 words. **Pays $20-100 for assigned articles and for unsolicited articles.**

FICTION Contact: Payson Fitch, managing editor. Needs adventure, erotica, fantasy, mystery/suspense, slice-of-life vignettes-of-life vignettes. Nothing poorly written. **Buys 10-12 fiction pieces/yr. mss/year.** Send complete ms. Length: 750-3,000 words.

POETRY Contact: J. K. Small, poetry editor. Needs avant-garde, free verse, haiku, light verse, traditional. Buys 8/yr. poems/year.

⊙⊙ METROSOURCE MAGAZINE

MetroSource Publishing, Inc., 137 W. 19th St.,, 2nd Floor, New York NY 10011. (212)691-5127. E-mail: letters@metrosource.com. Website: metrosource.com. **Contact:** Editor. **75% freelance written.** Magazine published 6 times/year. "*MetroSource* is an upscale, glossy, 4-color lifestyle magazine targeted to an urban, professional gay and lesbian readership." Estab. 1990. Circ. 145,000. Byline given. Pays on publication. Publishes ms an average of 2 months after acceptance. Editorial lead time 4 months. Submit seasonal material 4 months in advance. Accepts queries by mail, e-mail, fax, phone. Accepts simultaneous submissions. Sample copy for $5.

NONFICTION Contact: Paul Hagen, editor-in-chief. Needs exposè, interview, opinion, photo feature, travel. **Buys 20 mss/year.** Query with published clips. Length: 1,000-1,800 words. **Pays $100-400.**

PHOTOS Contact: Paul Hagen, editor-in-chief. State availability. Captions, model releases required. Negotiates payment individually.

COLUMNS Book, film, television, and stage reviews; health columns; and personal diary and opinion pieces. Word lengths vary. Query with published clips. **Pays $200.**

⊙⊙ OUTLOOKS

Outlooks Publication Inc., 303 - 1235 17th Ave SW, Calgary Alberta T2C 0C2 Canada. (403)228-1157. Fax: (403)228-7735. E-mail: btaylor@outlooks. ca. Website: outlooks.ca. **100% freelance written.** Monthly national lifestyle publication for Canada's LGBT community. Estab. 1997. Circ. 31,500. Byline given. Pays on publication. Offers 50% kill fee. Publishes ms an average of 2 months after acceptance. Editorial lead time 2 months. Submit seasonal material 3 months in advance. Accepts queries by e-mail. Accepts simultaneous submissions. Responds in 2 weeks to queries. Sample copy available online. Guidelines free.

NONFICTION Needs essays, general interest, humor, interview, photo feature, travel. Query with published clips. Length: 500-1,500 words. **Pays $100-120.** Sometimes pays expenses of writers on assignment.

PHOTOS State availability. Captions required. Reviews contact sheets. Negotiates payment individually.

COLUMNS Book, movie, and music reviews (600-700 words). **Buys 120 mss/year.** Query with published clips.

FICTION Needs adventure, erotica, humorous. **Buys 10 mss/year.** Query with published clips. Length: 1,200-1,600 words. **Pays $120-160.**

⊙ RAINBOW RUMPUS

P.O. Box 6881, Minneapolis MN 55406. E-mail: fictionandpoetry@rainbowrumpus.org; editor@rainbowrumpus.org. Website: rainbowrumpus.org. **Contact:** Beth Wallace, Editor-in-Chief. "Rainbow Rumpus is the world's only online literary magazine for children and youth with lesbian, gay, bisexual, and transgender (LGBT) parents. We are creating a new genre of children's and young adult fiction. Please carefully read and observe the guidelines on our website. Stories should be written from the point of view of children or teens with LGBT parents or other family members, or who are connected to the LGBT community. Stories for 4- to 12-year-old children should be approximately 800 to 2,500 words in length. Stories for 13- to 18-year-olds may be as long as 5,000 words. Stories featuring families of color, bisexual parents, transgender parents, family members with disabilities, and mixed-race families are particularly welcome. Rainbow Rumpus pays $75 per story on publication. We purchase first North American online rights. All fiction and poetry submissions should be sent to our Editor-in-Chief via our Contact page. Be sure to select the "Submissions" category. A staff member will be in touch with you shortly to obtain a copy of your manuscript."

⊙ THE WASHINGTON BLADE

Washington Blade, 529 14thSt., NW, Washington DC 20045. (202)747-2077. Fax: (202)747-2070. E-mail: knaff@washblade.com. Website: washblade. com. **20% freelance written.** Nation's oldest and largest weekly newspaper covering the lesbian, gay, bi-sexual and transgender issues. Articles (subjects) should be written from or directed to a gay perspective. Estab. 1969. Circ. 30,000. Byline given. Submit seasonal material one month in advance. Accepts queries by mail, e-mail, fax. Responds in within one month to queries.

PHOTOS A photo or graphic with feature articles is particularly important. Photos with news stories are appreciated. Send photos by mail or e-mail. . Captions required. Pay varies. Photographers on assignment are paid mutually agreed upon fee.

COLUMNS Send feature submissions to Joey DiGuglielmo, arts editor. Sent opinion submission to Kevin Naff, editor. Pay varies. No sexually explicit material.

○❸❸ XTRA

Pink Triangle Press, 491 Church St., Suite 200, Toronto ON M4Y 2C6 Canada. (416)925-6665; (800)268-9872. Fax: (416)925-6674. E-mail: info.toronto@xtra.ca. E-mail: matt.mills@xtra.ca. Website: xtra.ca. Marcus McCann, managing editor. **Contact:** Matt Mills. **80% freelance written.** Biweekly tabloid covering gay, lesbian, bisexual and transgender issues, news, arts and events of interest in Toronto. *Xtra* is dedicated to lesbian and gay sexual liberation. We publish material that advocates this end, according to the mission statement of the not-for-profit organization Pink Triangle Press, which operates the paper. Estab. 1984. Circ. 45,000. Byline given. Pays on publication. Editorial lead time 1 month. Accepts queries by e-mail. Accepts simultaneous submissions. Responds in 2 weeks to queries. Sample copy available online. Guidelines by e-mail.

NONFICTION Needs book excerpts, essays, interview, opinion, personal experience, travel. US-based stories or profiles of straight people who do not have a direct connection to the LGBT community. Query with published clips. Length: 200-1,600 words. Sometimes pays expenses of writers on assignment. Limit agreed upon in advance

COLUMNS *Xtra* rarely publishes unsolicited columns. **Buys 6 mss/year.** Query with published clips.

GENERAL INTEREST

● AASRA PUNJABI ENGLISH MAGAZINE

P.O. Box 5716, Kent WA 98064. E-mail: aasra@q.com. **Contact:** Sarab Singh, editor. "Aasra Punjabi English Magazine, published bimonthly, features current events mainly Indian, but have featured others, too, of interest. Also features interviews, yoga, and other articles, and poetry." Has published poetry by Joan Robers, Elizabeth Tallmadge, Carmen Arhiveleta. Page count varies. Measures approximately 8.5x11, press printed, staple bound, includes ads. Single copy cost $3 (postage); subscription: $20/year. "The magazine is distributed free in the Seattle area and available through other libraries. We charge postage for a copy to be mailed. Please include $3 to allow us to send you the copy of the magazine. $2 per copy if more than 10 copies are purchased." Reads submissions year round. Sometimes comments on rejected poems. Sometimes published theme issues. Guidelines in magazine. Rights revert to poet upon publication. Best Poem of the Year is awarded one-year free subscription. Estab. 2005. Time between acceptance and publication is 2 months.

❸❸ THE AMERICAN LEGION MAGAZINE

P.O. Box 1055, Indianapolis IN 46206-1055. (317)630-1200. Fax: (317)630-1280. E-mail: magazine@legion.org. E-mail: mgrills@legion.org;hsoria@legion.org. Website: legion.org. **Contact:** Matt Grills. **70% freelance written. Prefers to work with published/established writers, but works with a small number of new/unpublished writers each year.** Monthly magazine. "Working through 15,000 community-level posts, the honorably discharged wartime veterans of The American Legion dedicate themselves to God, country and traditional American values. They believe in a strong defense; adequate and compassionate care for veterans and their families; community service; and the wholesome development of our nation's youth. We publish articles that reflect these values. We inform our readers and their families of significant trends and issues affecting our nation, the world and the way we live. Our major features focus on the American flag, national security, foreign affairs, business trends, social issues, health, education, ethics and the arts. We also publish selected general feature articles, articles of special interest to veterans, and question-and-answer interviews with prominent national and world figures." Estab. 1919. Circ. 2,550,000. Byline given. Pays on acceptance. Publishes ms an average of 6 months after acceptance. Accepts queries by mail, e-mail, fax. Responds in 2 months to queries. Sample copy for $3.50 and 9×12 SAE with 6 first-class stamps. Guidelines for #10 SASE.

NONFICTION Needs general interest, interview. No regional topics or promotion of partisan political agendas. No personal experiences or war stories. **Buys 50-60 mss/year.** Query with SASE should explain the subject or issue, article's angle and organization, writer's qualifications, and experts to be interviewed. Length: 300-2,000 words. **Pays 40¢/word and up.**

❸❸ THE AMERICAN SCHOLAR

Phi Beta Kappa, 1606 New Hampshire Ave. NW, Washington DC 20009. (202)265-3808. Fax: (202)265-0083. E-mail: scholar@pbk.org. Website: theamericanscholar.org. **Contact:** Sandra Costich. **100% free-lance written**. Quarterly magazine dedicated to current events, politics, history, science, culture and the arts. "Our intent is to have articles written by scholars and experts but written in nontechnical language for an intelligent audience. Material covers a wide range in the arts, sciences, current affairs, history, and literature." Estab. 1932. Circ. 30,000. Byline given. Pays on publication. Offers 50% kill fee. Publishes ms an average of 1 year after acceptance. Editorial lead time 6 months. Submit seasonal material 6 months in advance. Accepts queries by mail, e-mail, fax. Responds in 2 weeks to queries. Responds in 2 months to mss. Sample copy for $9. Guidelines for #10 SASE or via e-mail.

NONFICTION Needs essays, historical, humor. **Buys 40 mss/year.** Query. Length: 3,000-5,000 words. **Pays $500 maximum.**

POETRY Contact: Sandra Costich. "We're not considering any unsolicited poetry."

🟢🟢 AVENTURA MAGAZINE

Stern Bloom Media, 425 NW 10th Terrace, Hallandale Beach FL 33009. (305)932-2400. Fax: (305)466-9285. E-mail: editorial@sternbloom.com. Website: aventuramagazine.com. **70% freelance written**. Magazine published 7 times/year covering affluent consumer markets. *AVENTURA Magazine*'s readership identify us as 'the intelligent source to luxury living.' As a horizontally positioned magazine with distribution over 50,000 and readership beyond 125,000, *AVENTURA* is distinguished as the magazine choice for readers pursuing a sophisticated lifestyle and luxury brand. Our typical reader has a household income over $200,000, are well traveled and well-educated. Articles are written for an audience with heightened expectations in all areas of life. Estab. 1998. Circ. 50,000. Byline given. Pays on acceptance. Editorial lead time 3 months. Submit seasonal material 6 months in advance. Accepts queries by e-mail. Responds in 3 weeks to queries. Sample copy free. Guidelines by e-mail.

NONFICTION Needs expose, interview, travel, luxury living. Does not want to see opinions, essays, religious or how-to pieces. **Buys 1-3 mss/year.** Query. Length: words. **Pays $250+.** Sometimes pays expenses of writers on assignment.

PHOTOS State availability. Captions, identification of subjects, model releases required. Reviews GIF/JPEG files. Negotiates payment individually.

🟢 CAPPER'S

Ogden Publications, Inc., 1503 SW 42nd St., Topeka KS 66609-1265. (800)678-4883. E-mail: editor@cappers.com. Website: cappers.com. **Contact:** Hank Will, editor-in-chief. **90%.** Monthly tabloid emphasizing home and family for readers who live mainly in the rural Midwest. "*Capper's* is upbeat, focusing on the homey feelings people like to share, as well as hopes and dreams. Capper's is a bi-monthly rural lifestyle magazine that focuses on small town life, country and rural lifestyles and 'hobby' farms. Buys shared rights. Capper's no longer publishes poetry and fiction. No unsolicited mss accepted; authors must query first. Send queries via e-mail. Articles (except Heart of the Home) are assigned; no editorial calendar is published. A great way to have a first article published is to become a Capper's blogger. For blogger information, send e-mail." Estab. 1879. Circ. 100,000. Byline given. Pays for poetry and fiction on acceptance; articles on publication. Publishes ms an average of 2-12 months after acceptance. Submit seasonal material 6-8 months in advance. Accepts queries by e-mail. Responds in 2-3 to queries. Responds in 6 months to mss. Sample copy available online. Guidelines available online or by e-mail.

NONFICTION Needs , feature-length articles (800-1,500 words with photos) on topics of interest to those living in rural areas, on farms or ranches, or those simply interested in the rural lifestyle; department articles (500-1,500 words with photos) on nostalgia, farm equipment and animals, DIY projects, gardening and cooking. Paid upon publication.

PHOTOS Photos paid upon publication. Pay is negotiable. Photo captions required. Send digital images via e-mail, one at a time, as JPEG files at 300 dpi resolution. Buys shared rights. Send photos. Captions required.

COLUMNS Send complete ms. **Pays approximately $2/printed inch. Payment for recipes is $5. Hints used earn $2 gift certificate.**

➕ CELLAR DOOR POETRY JOURNAL

Dreamland Books, Inc., P.O. Box 1714, Minnetonka MN 55345. E-mail: dreamlandbooks@inbox.com. Website: cellardoorpoetry.com or dreamlandbooksinc.com. Estab. 2011. 12 months Guidelines available on website.

✂ "We publish all forms and subjects of poetry, but will not publish work that promotes pornography or violence. We especially like poetry that can be enjoyed at a very basic level, but may have a much deeper level as well."

POETRY Does not want poetry promoting pornography, violence, racism, sexism, or any form of hate.

THE CHRISTIAN SCIENCE MONITOR

The Home Forum Page, 210 Massachussetts Ave., P02-30, Boston MA 02115. E-mail: homeforum@csmonitor.com. Website: csmonitor.com; csmonitor.com/About/Contributor-guidelines#homeforum. **Contact:** Editors: Susan Leach, Marjorie Kehe. Estab. 1908.

The Christian Science Monitor, an international daily newspaper, regularly features poetry in The Home Forum section. Wants "finely crafted poems that explore and celebrate daily life; that provide a respite from daily news and from the bleakness that appears in so much contemporary verse." Considers free verse and fixed forms. Has published poetry by Diana Der-Hovanessian, Marilyn Krysl, and Michael Glaser. Publishes 1-2 poems/week.

POETRY Submit up to 5 poems at a time. Lines/poem: Prefers short poems under 20 lines. No previously published poems or simultaneous submissions. Accepts e-mail submissions only (by attachment in MS Word, 1 poem/e-mail). Pays $20/haiku; $40/poem. Does not want "work that presents people in helpless or hopeless states; poetry about death, aging, or illness; or dark, violent, sensual poems. No poems that are overtly religious or falsely sweet."

ECLIPSE

Glendale College, 1500 N. Verdugo Rd., Glendale CA 91208. (818)240-1000. Fax: (818)549-9436. E-mail: eclipse@glendale.edu.

"Eclipse is committed to publishing outstanding fiction and poetry. We look for compelling characters and stories executed in ways that provoke our readers and allow them to understand the world in new ways." Annual. Circ. 1,800. Receives 50-100 unsolicited mss/month. Accepts 10 mss/year. Publishes ms 6-12 months after acceptance. **Publishes 8 new writers/year.** Recently published work by Amy Sage Webb, Ira Sukrungruang, Richard Schmitt, George Rabasa. Length: 6,000 words; average length: 4,000 words. Publishes short shorts. Also publishes poetry. Sometimes comments on rejected mss. Send complete ms. Responds in 2 weeks to queries; 4-6

weeks to mss. Accepts simultaneous submissions. Sample copy for $8. Writer's guidelines for #10 SASE or by e-mail. Pays 2 contributor's copies; additional copies $7. Pays on publication for first North American serial rights.

FICTION Contact: Michael Ritterbrown, fiction editor. Needs ethnic, experimental. Does not want horror, religious, science fiction, or thriller mss. Send complete ms Length: 6,000 words.

💲💲 FASHION FORUM

Business Journals, Inc., 1384 Broadway, 11th Floor, New York NY 10018. (212)710-7442. E-mail: jillians@busjour.com. Website: busjour.com. Karen Alberg Grossman, Lisa Montemorra, project manager. **Contact:** Jillian Sprague, managing editor. **80% freelance written.** Semiannual magazine covering luxury fashion (men's 70%, women's 30%), luxury lifestyle. "*Forum* directly targets a very upscale reader interested in profiles and service pieces on upscale designers, new fashion trends and traditional suiting. Lifestyle articles—including wine and spirits, travel, cars, boating, sports, collecting, etc.—are upscale top of the line (i.e., don't write how expensive taxis are)." Circ. 150,000. Byline given. Pays on publication. Offers 50% kill fee. Publishes ms an average of 3-4 months after acceptance. Editorial lead time 6 months. Submit seasonal material 6 months in advance. Accepts queries by mail, e-mail. NoResponds in 2-3 weeks to queries. Guidelines by e-mail.

NONFICTION Needs general interest, interview, travel, luxury lifestyle trends, fashion service pieces. Does not want personal essays. We run a few but commission them. No fiction or single product articles. In other words, an article should be on whats new in Italian wines, not about one superspecial brand. **Buys 20-25 mss/year.** Query. Length: 600-1,500 words. **Pays $300-500.**

PHOTOS State availability. Reviews GIF/JPEG files. Offers no additional payment for photos accepted with ms.

COLUMNS Travel, 1,000-1,500 words; Wine + Spirits, 600-1,200 words; Gourmet, 600-1,200 words; Wheels, 600 words. **Buys 10-15 mss/year.** Query. **Pays $300-500.**

💲💲 GRIT

Ogden Publications, 1503 SW 42nd St., Topeka KS 66609-1265. Website: grit.com. **Contact:** Oscar

"Hank" Will, editor. **90% freelance written. Open to new writers.** Bimonthly magazine. "*Grit* focuses on rural lifestyles, country living and small-scale farming. We are looking for useful, practical information on livestock, gardening, farm equipment, home-and-yard improvement and related topics. We also offer one nostalgia article in each issue—what it was like living on the farm in the Great Depression, how the family kept the peace during holidays, etc. What we expect from anyone who wants to write for us is that they know what the magazine is about." Estab. 1882. Circ. 230,000. Byline given. Pays on publication. Submit seasonal material 6 months in advance. Accepts queries by mail, e-mail. Sample copy and writer's guidelines for $6. Articles from current issue are posted on website. Guidelines online at grit.com/guidelines.aspx.

NONFICTION Query by e-mail to Jean Teller, jteller@grit.com. Assignments are made from queries approximately a year in advance. Send queries for 2012 by May 1, 2012. Main features run 1,000-1,200 words. Department features average 800-1,000 words. **Varies: $75 for a short, newsy article for Grit Gazette to $750 or more for long feature articles. Negotiates individually with writers rather than paying a per-word fee.**

FICTION "We do not accept fiction or poetry submissions."

$$$$ HARPER'S MAGAZINE

666 Broadway, 11th Floor, New York NY 10012. (212)420-5720. Fax: (212)228-5889. E-mail: readings@harpers.org. Website: harpers.org. **90% freelance written.** Monthly magazine for well-educated, socially concerned, widely read men and women who value ideas and good writing. *Harper's Magazine* encourages national discussion on current and significant issues in a format that offers arresting facts and intelligent opinions. By means of its several shorter journalistic forms—Harper's Index, Readings, Forum, and Annotation—as well as with its acclaimed essays, fiction, and reporting, *Harper's* continues the tradition begun with its first issue in 1850: to inform readers across the whole spectrum of political, literary, cultural, and scientific affairs. Estab. 1850. Circ. 230,000. Pays on acceptance. Offers negotiable kill fee. Publishes ms an average of 3 months after acceptance. Responds in 6 weeks to queries. Sample copy for $5.95.

Harper's Magazine will neither consider nor return unsolicited nonfiction manuscripts that have not been preceded by a written query. Harper's will consider unsolicited fiction. Unsolicited poetry will not be considered or returned. No queries or manuscripts will be considered unless they are accompanied by a SASE. All submissions and written queries (with the exception of Readings submissions) must be sent by mail to above address.

NONFICTION Needs humor. No interviews; no profiles. **Buys 2 mss/year.** Query. Length: 4,000-6,000 words.

REPRINTS Accepted for Readings section. Send typed ms with rights for sale ted and information about when and where the article previously appeared.

PHOTOS Contact: Stacey Clarkson, art director. Occasionally purchased with ms; others by assignment. State availability. Pays $50-500.

FICTION Will consider unsolicited fiction. Needs humorous. **Buys 12 mss/year.** Query. Length: 3,000-5,000 words. **Generally pays 50¢-$1/word.**

$$$$ NATIONAL GEOGRAPHIC MAGAZINE

1145 17th St. NW, Washington DC 20036. (202)857-7000. Fax: (202)492-5767. Website: nationalgeographic.com. Chris Johns, editor-in-chief. **60% freelance written. Prefers to work with published/established writers.** Monthly magazine for members of the National Geographic Society. Timely articles written in a compelling, 'eyewitness' style. Arresting photographs that speak to us of the beauty, mystery, and harsh realities of life on earth. Maps of unprecedented detail and accuracy. These are the hallmarks of *National Geographic* magazine. Since 1888, the *Geographic* has been educating readers about the world. Estab. 1888. Circ. 6,800,000.

NONFICTION Query (500 words with clips of published articles by mail to Senior Assitant Editor Oliver Payne. Do not send mss. Length: 2,000-8,000 words. Pays expenses of writers on assignment.

PHOTOS Query in care of the Photographic Division.

$$$ NEWSWEEK

251 W. 57th St., New York NY 10019. E-mail: editors@newsweek.com. Website: newsweek.com. *Newsweek* is edited to report the week's developments on the

newsfront of the world and the nation through news, commentary and analysis. Circ. 3,180,000.

COLUMNS Contact: myturn@newsweek.com. "We are no longer accepting submissions for the print edition. To submit an essay to our website, please e-mail it to: myturn@newsweek.com. The My Turn essay should be: A) an original piece, B) 850-900 words, C) generally personal in tone, and D) about any topic, but not framed as a response to a Newsweek story or another My Turn essay. Submissions must not have been published elsewhere. Please include your full name, phone number and address with your entry. The competition is very stiff-we get 600 entries per month-and we can only print one a week. *Due to the number of submissions we receive, we cannot respond unless we plan to publish your essay;* if your story is tied to current events, it may not be appropriate. We are fully aware of the time and effort involved in preparing an essay, and each manuscript is given careful consideration. For an automated message with further details about My Turn, you may call: (212) 445-4547. **Pays $1,000 on publication.**

❸❸❸ THE NEW YORK TIMES MAGAZINE

620 Eighth Ave., New York NY 10018. (212)556-1234. Fax: (212)556-3830. E-mail: magazine@nytimes.com; thearts@nytimes.com. Website: nytimes.com/pages/magazine. **Contact:** Gerald Marzorati, editor. *The New York Times Magazine* appears in *The New York Times* on Sunday. The *Arts and Leisure* section appears during the week. The *Op Ed* page appears daily. Circ. 1.8 million.

○ "Because of the volume of submissions for the Lives column, the magazine cannot return or respond to unsolicited manuscripts. If you have a query about about the "Lives" page, please write to lives@nytimes.com. For Randy Cohen/The Ethicist, please write to ethicist@nytimes.com."

❸❸❸ THE OLD FARMER'S ALMANAC

Yankee Publishing, Inc., P.O. Box 520, Dublin NH 03444. (603)563-8111. Website: Almanac.com. **95% freelance written**. Annual magazine covering weather, gardening, history, oddities, lore. "*The Old Farmer's Almanac* is the oldest continuously published periodical in North America. Since 1792, it has provided useful information for people in all walks of life: tide tables for those who live near the ocean; sunrise tables and planting charts for those who live on the farm or simply enjoy gardening; recipes for those who like to cook; and forecasts for those who don't like the question of weather left up in the air. The words of the *Almanac*'s founder, Robert B. Thomas, guide us still: 'Our main endeavor is to be useful, but with a pleasant degree of humour.'" Estab. 1792. Circ. 3,750,000. Byline given. Pays on acceptance. Offers 25% kill fee. Publishes ms an average of 9 months after acceptance. Editorial lead time 6 months. Submit seasonal material 1 year in advance. Accepts queries by mail. Responds in 3 weeks to queries. Responds in 2 months to mss. Sample copy for $6 at bookstores or online. Guidelines available online.

NONFICTION Needs general interest, historical, how-to, garden, cook, save money, humor, weather, natural remedies, obscure facts, history, popular culture. No personal recollections/accounts, personal/family histories. Query with published clips. Length: 800-2,500 words. **Pays 65¢/word.** Sometimes pays expenses of writers on assignment.

FILLERS Needs anecdotes, short humor. **Buys 1-2 mss/year.** Length: 100-200 words. **Pays $25.**

TIPS "*The Old Farmer's Almanac* is a reference book. Our readers appreciate obscure facts and stories. Read it. Think differently. Read writer's guidelines online."

❸❸❸ OPEN SPACES

Open Spaces Publications, Inc., PMB 134, 6327-C SW Capitol Hwy., Portland OR 97239-1937. (503)313-4361. Fax: (503)227-3401. E-mail: info@open-spaces.com. Website: open-spaces.com. **95% freelance written**. Quarterly general interest magazine. Estab. 1997. Byline given. Pays on publication. Offers 20% kill fee. Publishes ms an average of 6 months after acceptance. Editorial lead time 9 months. Accepts queries by mail, fax. Accepts simultaneous submissions. Sample copy for $10. Guidelines available online.

○ "*Open Spaces* is a forum for informed writing and intelligent thought. Articles are written by experts in various fields. Audience is varied (CEOs and rock climbers, politicos and university presidents, etc.) but is highly educated and loves to read good writing."

NONFICTION Needs essays, general interest, historical, how-to, if clever, humor, interview, personal experience, travel. **Buys 35 mss/year.** Send complete ms.

1,500-2,500 words; major articles up to 6,000 words. **Pays variable amount.**

PHOTOS State availability. Captions, identification of subjects required.

COLUMNS Contact: David Williams, departments editor. Books (substantial topics such as the Booker Prize, The Newbery, etc.); Travel (must reveal insight); Sports (past subjects include rowing, and swing dancing); Unintended Consequences, 1,500-2,500 words. **Buys 20-25 mss/year.** Send complete ms. **Payment varies**

FICTION Contact: Ellen Teicher, fiction editor. Quality is far more important than type. Read the magazine. Excellence is the issue—not subject matter. **Buys 8 mss/year.** Length: 2,000-6,000 words. **Payment varies.**

POETRY Contact: Susan Juve-Hu Bucharest, poetry editor. Again, quality is far more important than type.

FILLERS Needs anecdotes, short humor, cartoons.

$$$$ OUTSIDE

Mariah Media, Inc., Outside Plaza, 400 Market St., Santa Fe NM 87501. (505)989-7100. Fax: (505)989-4700. Website: outsidemag.com. **60% freelance written.** Monthly magazine covering active lifestyle. Estab. 1977. Circ. 665,000. Byline given. Pays on acceptance. Offers 25% kill fee. Publishes ms an average of 3-6 months after acceptance. Accepts queries by mail. Responds is 6-8 weeks. Guidelines free.

💬 "*Outside* is a monthly national magazine dedicated to covering the people, sports and activities, politics, art, literature, and hardware of the outdoors. Although our features are usually assigned to a regular stable of experienced and proven writers, we're always interested in new authors and their ideas. In particular, we look for articles on outdoor events, regions, and activities; informative seasonal service pieces; sports and adventure travel pieces; profiles of engaging outdoor characters; and investigative stories on environmental issues. Queries should present a clear, original, and provocative thesis, not merely a topic or idea, and should reflect familiarity with the magazine's content and tone. Features are generally 1,500 to 5,000 words in length. Dispatches articles (100 to 800 words) cover timely news, events, issues, and short profiles. Destinations pieces (300 to 1,000 words) include places, news, and advice for adventurous travelers. Review articles (200 to 1,500 words) examine and evaluate outdoor gear and equipment."

NONFICTION Needs book excerpts, new product, travel. **Buys 300 mss./yr. mss/year.** Query with two or three relevant clips along with a sSASE to: Editorial Department, Outside magazine, 400 Market St., Santa Fe, New Mexico, 87501. Length: 100-5,000 words. **Pays $1.50-2/word for assigned articles. Pays $1-1.50/word for unsolicited articles.** Pays expenses of writers on assignment.

COLUMNS Pays $1.50-$2.

$$$$ PARADE

ParadeNet, Inc., 711 Third Ave., New York NY 10017-4014. (212)450-7000. Website: parade.com. **Contact:** Megan Brown, articles editor. **95% freelance written.** Weekly magazine for a general interest audience. Estab. 1941. Circ. 32,000,000. Pays on acceptance. Offers kill fee. Kill fee varies in amount Publishes ms an average of 5 months after acceptance. Editorial lead time 1 month. Accepts queries by mail, online submission form. Accepts simultaneous submissions. Sample copy available online. Guidelines available online.

NONFICTION Spot news events are not accepted, as *Parade* has a 2-month lead time. No fiction, fashion, travel, poetry, cartoons, nostalgia, regular columns, personal essays, quizzes, or fillers. Unsolicited queries concerning celebrities, politicians or sports figures are rarely assigned. **Buys 150 mss/year.** Query with published clips. Length: 1,200-1,500 words. **Pays very competitive amount.** Pays expenses of writers on assignment.

PORTLAND MAGAZINE

165 State, Portland ME 04101. (207)775-4339. E-mail: staff@portlandmonthly.com. Website: portlandmagazine.com. **Contact:** Colin Sargent. Monthly city lifestyle magazine—fiction, style, business, real estate, controversy, fashion, cuisine, interviews and art relating to the Maine area. Estab. 1985. Circ. 100,000. Pays on publication. Accepts queries by mail, e-mail.

NONFICTION Query first. "Clips and a bio note are appreciated, but we take no responsibility for returning unsolicited materials."

FICTION Contact: Colin Sargent, editor. Send complete ms. 700 words or less

PULSAR POETRY MAGAZINE

Ligden Publishers, 34 Lineacre, Grange Park, Swindon, Wiltshire SN5 6DA England. E-mail: pulsar.ed@btopenworld.com. Website: pulsarpoetry.com. **Contact:** David Pike, Editor. Estab. 1992.

Now is a web-zine only. "We will publish poems on the Pulsar web on a quarterly basis, i.e. March, June, September and December. The selection process for poems will not alter and we will continue to publish on a merit basis only, be warned the editor is very picky! See poem submission guidelines online. We encourage the writing of poetry from all walks of life. Wants 'hard-hitting, thought-provoking work; interesting and stimulating poetry.' Does not want 'racist material. Not keen on religious poetry.' Has published poetry by A.C. Evans, Chris Hardy, Kate Edwards, Elizabeth Birchall, and Michael Newman."

POETRY Submit 3 poems at a time. No previously published poems or simultaneous submissions. Accepts e-mail submissions (pasted into body of message). "Send no more than 2 poems via e-mail; file attachments will not be read." Cover letter is preferred. Include SAE with adequate IRCs for a reply only (mss not returned if non-UK). Manuscripts should be typed. Time between acceptance and publication is about 1 month. "Poems can be published in next edition if it is what we are looking for. The editor and assistant read all poems." Seldom comments on rejected poems. Guidelines available for SASE (or SAE and IRC) or on website. Responds within 1 month. Pays 1 contributor's copy. Acquires first rights. "Originators retain copyright of their poems." Staff reviews poetry books and CDs (mainstream); word count varies. Send materials for review consideration.

READER'S DIGEST

The Reader's Digest Association, Inc., Box 100, Pleasantville NY 10572-0100. E-mail: articleproposals@rd.com. Website: rd.com. Monthly magazine.

COLUMNS Life; @Work; Off Base, **pays $300.** Laugh; Quotes, **pays $100.** Address your submission to the appropriate humor category.

READER'S DIGEST (CANADA)

1100 Rene Le vesque Blvd. W., Montreal QC H3B 5H5 Canada. E-mail: originals@rd.com. Website: readersdigest.ca. **30-50% freelance written.** Monthly magazine of general interest articles and subjects. Estab. 1948. Circ. 1,000,000. Byline given. **Pays on acceptance for original works.** Pays on publication for pickups. Offers $500 (Canadian) kill fee. Submit seasonal material 5 months in advance. Accepts queries by mail, online submission form. Guidelines available online.

Only responds to queries if interested. Prefers Canadian subjects.

NONFICTION Needs general interest, how-to, general interest, humor, jokes, inspirational, personal experience, travel, adventure, crime, health. Query with published clips. Proposals can be mailed to the above address. We are looking for dramatic narratives, inspirational stories, articles about crime, adventure, travel and health issues. Download our writer's guidelines. If we are interested in pursuing your idea, an editor will contact you. Length: 2,000-2,500 words. **Pays $1.50-2.50/word (CDN) depending on story type.** Pays expenses of writers on assignment.

REPRINTS Query. Payment is negotiable.

PHOTOS State availability.

REUNIONS MAGAZINE

P.O. Box 11727, Milwaukee WI 53211-0727. (414)263-4567. Fax: (414)263-6331. E-mail: info@reunionsmag.com. Website: reunionsmag.com. **85% freelance written.** Quarterly magazine covering reunions—all aspects and types. "*Reunions Magazine* is primarily for people actively planning family, class, military, and other reunions. We want easy, practical ideas about organizing, planning, researching/searching, attending, or promoting reunions." Estab. 1990. Circ. 20,000. Byline given. publication. Publishes ms an average of 1 year after acceptance. Editorial lead time 6 months. Submit seasonal material 1 year in advance. Accepts queries by mail, e-mail, fax; prefers Word attachments to e-mail. Responds in about 1 year. Sample copy and writer's guidelines for #10 SASE or online.

NONFICTION Needs historical, how-to, humor, interview, new product, personal experience, photo feature, travel, Reunion recipes with reunion anecdote. **Buys 40 mss/year.** Query with published clips. Length: 500-2,500 (prefers work on the short side) **Rarely able to pay any more, but when we can pays $25-50.**

REPRINTS Send tearsheet, photocopy or typed ms with rights for sale noted and information about when and where the material previously appeared. Usually pays $10.

PHOTOS Always looking for vertical cover photos screaming: *Reunion!* Prefers print or e-mail pictures. State availability. Captions, identification of subjects, model releases required. Reviews contact sheets, negatives, 35mm transparencies, prints, TIFF/JPEG files (300 dpi or higher) as e-mail attachments. Offers no additional payment for photos accepted with ms.

FILLERS Must be reunion-related. Needs anecdotes, facts, short humor. **Buys 20-40 fillers/year mss/year.** Length: 50-250 words. **Pays $5.**

$$$$ ROBB REPORT

Curtco Media Labs, 1 Acton Place, Acton MA 01720. (978)264-7500. Fax: (212)264-7501. E-mail: editorial@robbreport.com. Website: robbreport.com. **60% freelance written**. Monthly lifestyle magazine geared toward active, affluent readers. Addresses upscale autos, luxury travel, boating, technology, lifestyles, watches, fashion, sports, investments, collectibles. Estab. 1976. Circ. 111,000. Byline given. Pays on publication. Offers 25% kill fee. Submit seasonal material 5 months in advance. Accepts queries by mail, fax. Responds in 2 months to queries. Responds in 1 month to mss. Sample copy for $10.95, plus shipping and handling. Guidelines for #10 SASE.

NONFICTION Needs new product, autos, boats, aircraft, watches, consumer electronics, travel, international and domestic, dining. Special issues: Home (October); Recreation (March). **Buys 60 mss/year.** Query with published clips. Length: 500-2,000 words. **Pays $1/word.** Sometimes pays expenses of writers on assignment.

PHOTOS State availability. Payment depends on article.

$$ THE SATURDAY EVENING POST

The Saturday Evening Post Society, 1100 Waterway Blvd., Indianapolis IN 46202. (317)634-1100. Website: satevepost.org. **30% freelance written**. Bimonthly general interest, family-oriented magazine focusing on lifestyle, physical fitness, preventive medicine. Ask almost any American if he or she has heard of *The Saturday Evening Post*, and you will find that many have fond recollections of the magazine from their childhood days. Many readers recall sitting with their families on Saturdays awaiting delivery of their *Post* subscription in the mail. *The Saturday Evening Post* has forged a tradition of 'forefront journalism.' The *Satur-*day *Evening Post* continues to stand at the journalistic forefront with its coverage of health, nutrition, and preventive medicine. Estab. 1728. Circ. 350,000. Byline given. Pays on publication. Publishes ms an average of 3 months after acceptance. Submit seasonal material 4 months in advance. Accepts queries by mail, fax. Accepts simultaneous submissions. Responds in 3 weeks to queries. Responds in 6 weeks to mss.

NONFICTION Needs how-to, gardening, home improvement, humor, interview, medical, health, fitness. No political articles or articles containing sexual innuendo or hypersophistication. **Buys 25 mss/year.** Send complete ms. (Buys very few outside mss) Length: 1,000-2,500 words. **Pays $25-400.**

PHOTOS State availability. Identification of subjects, model releases required. Reviews negatives, transparencies. Offers $50 minimum, negotiable maximum per photo.

COLUMNS Travel (destinations); Post Scripts (well-known humorists); Post People (activities of celebrities). Length 750-1,500. **Buys 16 mss/year.** Query with published clips or send complete ms. **Pays $150 minimum, negotiable maximum.**

FICTION Contact: Fiction Editor.

POETRY Needs light verse.

FILLERS Contact: Post Scripts Editor. Needs anecdotes, short humor. **Buys 200 mss/year.** 300 words. **Pays $15.**

$ SENIOR LIVING

Stratis Publishing Ltd, 153, 1581-H Hillside Ave., Victoria BC V8T 2CI Canada. (250)479-4705. Fax: (250)479-4808. E-mail: editor@seniorlivingmag.com. Website: seniorlivingmag.com. **Contact:** Bobbie Jo Reid, managing editor. **100% freelance written**. 12 times per yr. magazine covering active 50+ living. "Inspiring editorial profiling 'seniors' (50+) who are active & lead interesting lives. Include articles on health, housing, accessibility, sports, travel, recipes, etc." Estab. 2004. Circ. 41,000. Byline given. Pays quarterly. Publishes an average of 2-3 months after acceptance. Editorial lead time 3 months. Submit seasonal material 6 months in advance. Accepts queries by e-mail. Accepts simultaneous submissions. Sample copy available online. Guidelines available.

NONFICTION Needs historical, how-to, humor, inspirational, interview, personal experience, travel, active living for 50+. Do not want politics, religion, promotion of business, service or products, humor that demeans 50+ demographic or aging process. **Buys 150 mss/year.** Query. Does not accept previously published material. Length: 500-1,200 words. **Pays $35-150 for assigned articles. Pays $35-150 for unsolicited articles.** Sometimes pays expenses (limit agreed upon in advance).

PHOTOS Send photos. Identification of subjects, model releases required. Reviews GIF/JPEG files. Offers $10-75 per photo.

COLUMNS **Buys 5-6 mss/yr. mss/year.** Query with published clips. **Pays $25-$50.**

$$$$ SMITHSONIAN MAGAZINE

Capital Gallery, Suite 6001, MRC 513, P.O. Box 37012, Washington D.C. 20013-7012. (202)275-2000. Website: smithsonianmag.com. **90% freelance written.** Monthly magazine for associate members of the Smithsonian Institution; 85% with college education. "*Smithsonian Magazine's* mission is to inspire fascination with all the world has to offer by featuring unexpected and entertaining editorial that explores different lifestyles, cultures and peoples, the arts, the wonders of nature and technology, and much more. The highly educated, innovative readers of *Smithsonian* share a unique desire to celebrate life, seeking out the timely as well as timeless, the artistic as well as the academic, and the thought-provoking as well as the humorous." Circ. 2,300,000. Pays on acceptance. Offers 33% kill fee. Publishes ms an average of 6 months after acceptance. Editorial lead time 2 months. Submit seasonal material 3 months in advance. Accepts queries by online submission form only. Responds in 3 weeks to queries from the web form. Sample copy for $5. Guidelines available online.

NONFICTION **Buys 120-130 feature (up to 5,000 words) and 12 short (500-650 words) mss/year.** Use online submission form. **Pays various rates per feature, $1,500 per short piece.** Pays expenses of writers on assignment.

PHOTOS Purchased with or without ms and on assignment. Illustrations are not the responsibility of authors, but if you do have photographs or illustration materials, please include a selection of them with your submission. In general, 35mm color transparencies or black-and-white prints are perfectly acceptable. Photographs published in the magazine are usually obtained through assignment, stock agencies, or specialized sources. No photo library is maintained and photographs should be submitted only to accompany a specific article proposal. Send photos. Captions required. Pays $400/full color page.

COLUMNS Buys 12-15 department articles/year. Length: 1,000-2,000 words. Last Page humor, 550-700 words. Use online submission form. **Pays $1,000-1,500.**

$$$ YES! MAGAZINE

284 Madrona Way NE, Suite 116, Bainbridge Island WA 98110. E-mail: editors@magazine.org. Website: magazine.org. **70% freelance written.** Quarterly magazine covering politics and world affairs; contemporary culture; nature, conservation and ecology. "YES! *Magazine* documents how people are creating a more just, sustainable and compassionate world. Each issue includes articles focused on a theme—about solutions to a significant challenge facing our world—and a number of timely, non-theme articles. Our non-theme section provides ongoing coverage of issues like health, climate change, globalization, media reform, faith, democracy, economy and labor, social and racial justice and peace building. To inquire about upcoming themes, send an e-mail to submissions@magazine.org; please be sure to type 'themes' as the subject line." Estab. 1997. Circ. 55,000. Byline given. Pays on publication. Offers kill fee. varies Publishes ms an average of 1-6 months after acceptance. Editorial lead time 3-6 months. Submit seasonal material 2-6 months in advance. Accepts queries by mail, e-mail. Sample copy and writer's guidelines online.

NONFICTION Needs book excerpts, essays, general interest, how-to, interview, opinion, (does not mean letters to the editor), photo feature. "We don't want stories that are negative or too politically partisan." **Buys 60 mss/year. mss/year.** Query with published clips. Length: 100-2,500 words. **Pays $50-1,250 for assigned articles. Pays $50-600 for unsolicited articles.**

REPRINTS Send photocopy or typed ms with rights for sale noted and information about when and where the material previously appeared.

COLUMNS Signs of Life (positive news briefs), 100-250 words; Commentary (opinion from thinkers and experts), 500 words; Book and film reviews, 500-800 words. **Pays $20-$300.**

HEALTH AND FITNESS

$ $ AMERICAN FITNESS

15250 Ventura Blvd.,, Suite 200, Sherman Oaks CA 91403. (800)446-2322, ext. 200. E-mail: americanfitness@afaa.com. Website: afaa.com. **Contact:** Meg Jordan, editor. **75% freelance written**. Bimonthly magazine covering exercise and fitness, health, and nutrition. "We need timely, in-depth, informative articles on health, fitness, aerobic exercise, sports nutrition, age-specific fitness, and outdoor activity. Absolutely no first-person accounts. Need well-researched articles for professional readers." Estab. 1983. Circ. 42,000. Byline given. Pays 30 days after publication. Publishes ms an average of 6 months after acceptance. Submit seasonal material 4 months in advance. Accepts queries by mail, fax. Accepts simultaneous submissions. Responds in 2 months to queries. Sample copy for $4.50 and SASE with 6 first-class stamps.

NONFICTION Needs historical, history of various athletic events, inspirational, sport's leaders motivational pieces, interview, fitness figures, new product, plus equipment review, personal experience, successful fitness story, photo feature, on exercise, fitness, new sport, travel, activity adventures. No articles on unsound nutritional practices, popular trends, or unsafe exercise gimmicks. **Buys 18-25 mss/year.** Send complete ms. Length: 800-1,200 words. **Pays $200 for features, $80 for news.** Sometimes pays expenses of writers on assignment.

PHOTOS Sports, action, fitness, aquatic aerobics competitions, and exercise class. We are especially interested in photos of high-adrenalin sports like rock climbing and mountain biking. . Captions, identification of subjects, model releases required. Reviews transparencies, prints. Pays $35 for transparencies.

COLUMNS Research (latest exercise and fitness findings); Alternative paths (nonmainstream approaches to health, wellness, and fitness); Strength (latest breakthroughs in weight training); Clubscene (profiles and highlights of fitness club industry); Adventure (treks, trails, and global challenges); Food (low-fat/nonfat, high-flavor dishes); Homescene (home-workout alternatives); Clip 'n' Post (concise exercise research to post in health clubs, offices or on refrigerators). Length: 800-1,000 words. Query with published clips or send complete ms. **Pays $100-200.**

$ $ CLIMBING

Primedia Enthusiast Group, Box 420034, Palm Coast FL 32142-0235. (970)963-9449. Fax: (970)963-9442. E-mail: msamet@climbing.com. Website: climbing.com. Magazine published 9 times/year covering climbing and mountaineering. Provides features on rock climbing and mountaneering worldwide. Estab. 1970. Circ. 51,000. Pays on publication. Editorial lead time 6 weeks. Accepts queries by e-mail. Sample copy for $4.99. Guidelines available online.

"We pride ourselves on running the best, most exciting, and most experimental climbing photography and writing in the world. We're glad that you are interested in helping us convey passion and creativity for the sport. For more information contact Matt Samet: msamet@climbing.com."

NONFICTION Needs interview, interesting climbers, personal experience, climbing adventures, surveys of different areas. Query. Length: 1,500-3,500 words. **Pays 35¢/word.**

PHOTOS State availability. Reviews negatives, 35mm transparencies, prints, digital submissions on CD. Pays $25-800.

COLUMNS Query. **Payment varies**

$ $ $ $ FITNESS MAGAZINE

Meredith Corp., 375 Lexington Ave., New York NY 10017-5514. Website: fitnessmagazine.com. Monthly magazine for women in their 20s and 30s who are interested in fitness and living a healthy life. Circ. 1.5 million. Byline given. Pays on acceptance. Offers 20% kill fee. Responds in 2 months to queries.

Do not call.

NONFICTION Buys 60-80 mss/year. Query. Length: 1,500-2,500 words. **Pays $1,500-2,500.** Pays expenses of writers on assignment.

REPRINTS Send photocopy. Negotiates fee.

COLUMNS Length:600-1,200 words **Buys 30 mss/year.** Query. **Pays $800-1,500.**

$ $ HEALING LIFESTYLES & SPAS

P.O. Box 271207, Louisville CO 80027. (202)441-9557. Fax: (303)926-4099. E-mail: melissa@healinglifestyles.com; editorial@healinglifestyles.com. Website: healinglifestyles.com. **Contact:** Melissa B. Williams, editor-in-chief. **90% freelance written**. Estab. 1996. Circ. 45,000. Pays on publication. Publishes ms an average of 2-10 months after acceptance. Editorial lead time 6 months. Submit seasonal material 6-9 months in advance. Accepts queries by mail, e-mail. Responds in 6 weeks to queries.

○ "*Healing Lifestyles & Spas* is a bimonthly magazine committed to healing, health, and living a well-rounded, more natural life. In each issue we cover retreats, spas, organic living, natural food, herbs, beauty, yoga, alternative medicine, bodywork, spirituality, and features on living a healthy lifestyle."

NONFICTION Needs travel, domestic and international. No fiction or poetry. Query. Length: 1,000-2,000 words. **Pays $150-500, depending on length, research, experience, and availability and quality of images.**

PHOTOS If you will be providing your own photography, you must use slide film or provide a Mac-formatted CD with image resolution of at least 300 dpi. Send photos. Captions required.

COLUMNS All Things New & Natural (short pieces outlining new health trends, alternative medicine updates, and other interesting tidbits of information), 50-200 words; Urban Retreats (focuses on a single city and explores its spas and organic living features), 1,200-1,600 words; Health (features on relevant topics ranging from nutrition to health news and updates), 900-1,200 words; Food (nutrition or spa-focused food articles and recipes), 1,000-1,200 words; Ritual (highlights a specific at-home ritual), 500 words; Seasonal Spa (focuses on a seasonal ingredient on the spa menu), 500-700 words; Spa Origins (focuses on particular modalities and healing beliefs from around the world, 1,000-1,200 words; Yoga, 400-800 words; Retreat (highlights a spa or yoga retreat), 500 words; Spa a la carte (explores a new treatment or modality on the spa menu), 600-1,000 words; Insight (focuses on profiles, theme-related articles, and new therapies, healing practices, and newsworthy items), 1,000-2,000 words. Query.

○❸❺ IMPACT MAGAZINE

IMPACT Productions, 2007 2nd St. SW, Calgary AB T2S 1S4 Canada. (403)228-0605. E-mail: info@impactmagazine.ca. E-mail: claire@impactmagazine.ca. Website: impactmagazine.ca. **Contact:** Claire Young, Editor. **10% freelance written.** Bimonthly magazine covering fitness and sport performance. "A leader in the industry, *IMPACT Magazine* is committed to publishing content provided by the best experts in their fields for those who aspire to higher levels of health, fitness, and sport performance." Estab. 1992. Circ. 90,000. Byline given. Pays 30 days after publication. Offers 25% kill fee. Publishes ms an average of 4-6 months after acceptance. Editorial lead time 6 months. Submit seasonal material 6 months in advance. Accepts queries by e-mail. Accepts simultaneous submissions. Responds in 4 weeks to queries. Sample copy and guidelines available online.

○ "Query first, outlining the parameters of the article, the length, sources, etc. before submitting a completed manuscript. We do not accept as editorial articles that profile and promote a specific business or service. IMPACT Magazine is a bi-monthly publication; submission deadlines are sixteen weeks prior to the publishing date. E-mail the article in a MSWord or text format (Mac or PC format). IMPACT Magazine compensates writers whose qualifications and work meet our specific guidelines (available from the editor). We are happy to accept photos or illustrations and will give photos credit where due. Digital images must be a minimum of 300 dpi."

NONFICTION Needs general interest, how-to, interview, new product, opinion, technical. **Buys 4 mss/year.** Query. Length: 600-1,800 words. **Pays $0.25/max. for assigned articles. Pays $0.25/max. for unsolicited articles.**

PHOTOS State availability. Identification of subjects, model releases required. Reviews contact sheets, GIF/JPEG files (300dpi or greater). Negotiates payment individually.

❸❺ LIVER HEALTH TODAY

Quality Publishing, Inc., P.O. Box 667399, Houston TX 77266. (832)813-3392. Fax: (713)520-1463. E-mail: tlaprade@liverhealthtoday.com. Website: liverhealthtoday.org. **70-80% freelance written.** Quarterly magazine covering hepatitis health news. Estab. 1999. Circ. 25,000. Byline given. Pays on publication. Publishes ms an average of 2 months after acceptance. Editorial lead time 6 months. Submit seasonal material 4 months in advance. Accepts queries by mail, e-mail. Accepts simultaneous submissions. Responds in 6 weeks to queries. Sample copy and writer's guidelines free.

NONFICTION Needs inspirational, interview, new product, personal experience. We do not want any one-source or no-source articles. **Buys 42-48 mss/year.** Query. Tell us about your experience as a liver disease patient or caregiver, and you might see it in the "My Story" section of *Liver Health Today.* "My Story" submissions should be 750-800 words in length and can be sent as a Word attachment to tlaprade@liverhealthtoday.net Length: 1,500-2,500 words. Sometimes pays expenses of writers on assignment.

PHOTOS Send photos. Identification of subjects required. Reviews transparencies, prints, GIF/JPEG files. Offers no additional payment for photos accepted with ms.

COLUMNS General news or advice on Hepatitis written by a doctor or healthcare professional, 1,500-2,000 words. **Buys 12-18 mss/year.** Query. **Pays $375-500.**

⊛⊛⊛⊛ MAMM MAGAZINE

MAMM, LLC, 54 W. 22nd St., 4th Floor, New York NY 10010. (646)365-1355. Fax: (646)365-1369. E-mail: editorial@mamm.com. Website: mamm.com. **80% freelance written**. Magazine published 10 times/year covering cancer prevention, treatment, and survival for women. *MAMM* gives its readers the essential tools and emotional support they need before, during and after diagnosis of breast, ovarian and other gynecologic cancers. We offer a mix of survivor profiles, conventional and alternative treatment information, investigative features, essays, and cutting-edge news. Estab. 1997. Circ. 100,000. Byline given. Pays within 30 days of publication. Offers 50% kill fee. Publishes ms an average of 3 months after acceptance. Submit seasonal material 3-4 months in advance. Accepts simultaneous submissions. Sample copy and writer's guidelines free.

NONFICTION Needs book excerpts, essays, exposè, how-to, humor, inspirational, interview, opinion, personal experience, photo feature, historic/nostalgic. **Buys 90 mss/year.** Query with published clips. Length: 200-3,000 words. **Pays $100-3,000.** Negotiates coverage of expenses of writers on assignment.

PHOTOS Send photos. Identification of subjects required. Reviews contact sheets, negatives. Negotiates payment individually.

COLUMNS Opinion (cultural/political); International Dispatch (experience); Q and A (interview format), all 600 words. **Buys 30 mss/year.** Query with published clips. **Pays $400-800.**

⊘⊛⊛ MAXIMUM FITNESS

CANUSA Publishing, 400 Matheson Blvd. West, Mississauga ON L5R 3MI Canada. E-mail: editorial@maxfitmag.com. Website: maxfitmag.com. Bimonthly magazine. *American Health & Fitness* is designed to help male fitness enthusiasts (18-39) stay fit, strong, virile, and healthy through sensible diet and exercise. Estab. 2006. Circ. 310,000. Byline given. Pays on acceptance. Publishes ms an average of 6 months after acceptance. Editorial lead time 4 months. Submit seasonal material 6 months in advance. Accepts queries by mail, e-mail, fax. Responds in 4 months to queries. Responds in 4 months to mss. Sample copy for $5.

NONFICTION Needs photo feature, bodybuilding and weight training, health & fitness tips, diet, medical advice, workouts, nutrition. **Buys 80-100 mss/year.** Query or send complete ms. Length: 800-1,500 words. **Pays 25-45¢/word for assigned articles.**

COLUMNS Personal Training; Strength & Conditioning; Fitness; Longevity; Natural Health; Sex. **Buys 40 mss/year.** Query or send complete ms.

FILLERS Needs anecdotes, facts, gags, newsbreaks, fitness, nutrition, health, short humor. **Buys 50-100 mss/year.** Length: 100-200 words.

⊛⊛⊛⊛ MEN'S HEALTH

Rodale, 33 E. Minor St., Emmaus PA 18098. (610)967-5171. Fax: (610)967-7725. E-mail: mhletters@rodale.com. Website: menshealth.com. **50% freelance written**. Magazine published 10 times/year covering men's health and fitness. *Men's Health* is a lifestyle magazine showing men the practical and positive actions that make their lives better, with articles covering fitness, nutrition, relationships, travel, careers, grooming, and health issues. Estab. 1986. Circ. 1,600,000. Pays on acceptance. Offers 25% kill fee. Accepts queries by mail, fax. Responds in 3 weeks to queries. Guidelines for #10 SASE.

NONFICTION Buys 30 features/year; 360 short mss/year. Query with published clips. 1,200-4,000 words for features, 100-300 words for short pieces **Pays $1,000-5,000 for features; $100-500 for short pieces.**

COLUMNS Length: 750-1,500 words. **Buys 80 mss/year. Pays $ 750- 2,000.**

⊛⊛⊛ MUSCLE & FITNESS

Weider Health & Fitness, 21100 Erwin St., Woodland Hills CA 91367. (818)884-6800. Fax: (818)595-0463. Website: muscleandfitness.com. **50% freelance written**. Monthly magazine covering bodybuilding and fitness for healthy, active men and women. It contains a wide range of features and monthly departments devoted to all areas of bodybuilding, health, fitness, sport, injury prevention and treatment, and nutrition. Editorial fulfills 2 functions: information and entertainment. Special attention is devoted to how-to advice and accuracy. Estab. 1950. Circ. 500,000. Pays on publication. Publishes ms an average of 2 months after acceptance. Editorial lead time 5 months. Submit seasonal material 6 months in advance. Accepts queries by mail. Responds in 1 month to queries.

NONFICTION Needs book excerpts, how-to, training, humor, interview, photo feature. **Buys 120 mss/year.** Query with published clips. Length: 800-1,800 words. **Pays $400-1,000.** Pays expenses of writers on assignment.

REPRINTS Send photocopy with rights for sale noted and information about when and where the material previously appeared. Payment varies.

☯☯ MUSCLEMAG

RK Publishing, Inc., 400 Matheson Blvd. W., Mississauga ON L5R 3M1. (905)507-3545. Fax: (905)507-2372. E-mail: editorial@emusclemag.com. Website: emusclemag.com. **80% freelance written.** Covers hardcore bodybuilding. "Monthly magazine building health, fitness, and physique." Byline given. Pays on acceptance. Publishes ms an average of 6 months after acceptance. Accepts queries by mail, e-mail. Responds in 4 months to queries. Responds in 4 months to mss. Guidelines available.

NONFICTION Needs how-to, interview, new product, personal experience, photo feature, bodybuilding, strenth training, health, nutrition & fitness. **Pays $80-400 for assigned accepted articles submitted on spec.**

PHOTOS Contact: Rich Baker, photo editor. Send photos. Captions, identification of subjects required. Reviews 35 mm transparencies, 8×10 prints and hi-res digital images 300 DPI or higher.

FILLERS Needs anecdotes, facts, gags, newsbreaks, fitness, nutrition, health, short humor. **Buys 50-100 mss/year.** Length: 100-200 words.

☯$$$ OXYGEN

Canusa Products/St. Ives, Inc., 5775 McLaughlin Rd., Mississauga ON L5R 3P7 Canada. (905)507-3545; (888)254-0767. Fax: (905)507-2372. E-mail: editorial@oxygenmag.com. Website: oxygenmag.com. **70% freelance written.** Monthly magazine covering women's health and fitness. *Oxygen* encourages various exercise, good nutrition to shape and condition the body. Estab. 1997. Circ. 340,000. Byline given. Pays on acceptance. Offers 25% kill fee. Publishes ms an average of 4 months after acceptance. Editorial lead time 3 months. Submit seasonal material 6 months in advance. Accepts queries by mail, fax. Responds in 5 weeks to queries. Responds in 2 months to mss. Sample copy for $5.

NONFICTION Needs expose, how-to, training and nutrition, humor, inspirational, interview, new product, personal experience, photo feature. No poorly researched articles that do not genuinely help the readers towards physical fitness, health and physique. **Buys 100 mss/year.** Send complete ms. with SASE and $5 for return postage. Length: 1,400-1,800 words. **Pays $250-1,000.** Sometimes pays expenses of writers on assignment.

PHOTOS State availability of or send photos. Identification of subjects required. Reviews contact sheets, 35mm transparencies, prints. Offers $35-500.

COLUMNS Nutrition (low-fat recipes), 1,700 words; Weight Training (routines and techniques), 1,800 words; Aerobics (how-tos), 1,700 words. **Buys 50 mss/year.** Send complete ms. **Pays $150-500.**

☯$$$ POZ

CDM Publishing, LLC, 462 Seventh Avenue,, 19th Floor, New York NY 10118. (212)242-2163. Fax: (212)675-8505. Website: poz.com. **25% freelance written.** Monthly national magazine for people impacted by HIV and AIDS. *POZ* is a trusted source of conventional and alternative treatment information, investigative features, survivor profiles, essays and cutting-edge news for people living with AIDS and their caregivers. *POZ* is a lifestyle magazine with both health and cultural content. Estab. 1994. Circ. 125,000. Byline given. Pays 30 days after publication. Offers 25% kill fee. Publishes ms an average of 3 months after acceptance. Editorial lead time 4 months. Submit seasonal material 4 months in advance. Accepts simultaneous submissions. Sample copy and writer's guidelines free.

NONFICTION Needs book excerpts, essays, exposè, historical, how-to, humor, inspirational, interview, opinion, personal experience, photo feature. Query with published clips. We take unsolicited mss on speculation only. Length: 200-3,000 words. **Pays $1/word.** Sometimes pays expenses of writers on assignment.

PHOTOS Send photos. Identification of subjects required. Reviews contact sheets, negatives. Negotiates payment individually.

🜲🜲🜲🜲 SHAPE MAGAZINE

Weider Publications, Inc., 21100 Erwin St., Woodland Hills CA 91367. (818)595-0593. Fax: (818)704-7620. Website: shapemag.com. **70% freelance written. Prefers to work with published/established writers.** Monthly magazine covering health, fitness, nutrition, and beauty for women ages 18-34. *Shape* reaches women who are committed to healthful, active lifestyles. Our readers are participating in a variety of fitness-related activities, in the gym, at home and outdoors, and they are also proactive about their health and are nutrition conscious. Estab. 1981. Circ. 1,600,000. Pays on acceptance. Offers 33% kill fee. Submit seasonal material 8 months in advance. Accepts queries by mail. Responds in 2 months to queries. Sample copy for sae with 9×12 envelope and 4 First-Class stamps. Guidelines available online.

NONFICTION Needs book excerpts, expose, health, fitness, nutrition related, how-to, get fit, health/fitness, recipes. "We rarely publish celebrity question and answer stories, celebrity profiles, or menopausal/hormone replacement therapy stories." **Buys 27 features/year; 36-54 short mss/year.** Query with published clips. 2,500 words/features; 1,000 words/shorter pieces **Pays $1.50/word (on average).**

🜲🜲🜲 SPIRITUALITY & HEALTH MAGAZINE

Spirituality & Health Publishing, Inc., 107 Cass Street, Suite C, Traverse City MI 49684. E-mail: **editors@spiritualityhealth.com** . Website: spiritualityhealth.com. **Contact:** Heather Shaw, man. ed. Bimonthly magazine covering research-based spirituality and health. "We look for formally credentialed writers in their fields. We are nondenominational and non-proselytizing. We are not New Age. We appreciate well-written work that offers spiritual seekers from all different traditions help in their unique journeys." Estab. 1998. Circ. 95,000. Byline given. Pays on acceptance. Offers 50% kill fee. Editorial lead time 4 months. Submit seasonal material 6 months in advance. Accepts queries by e-mail. Accepts simultaneous submissions. Responds in 3-4 months to queries. Responds in 2-4 months to mss. Sample copy and writer's guidelines online.

　　The most open department is Updates & Observations. Read it to see what we use. (All back issues are on the website.) News must be current with a four-month lead time.

NONFICTION Needs book excerpts, how-to, news shorts. Does not want proselytizing, New Age cures with no scientific basis, "how I recovered from a disease personal essays," psychics, advice columns, profiles of individual healers or practitioners, pieces promoting one way or guru, reviews, poetry or columns. Send complete ms. 300 words for news shorts, otherwise 700 -1,500 words. Sometimes pays expenses of writers on assignment. Limit agreed upon in advance

🜲🜲🜲 VIBRANT LIFE

Review and Herald Publishing Association, 55 W. Oak Ridge Dr., Hagerstown MD 21740-7390. (301)393-4019. Website: vibrantlife.com. **80% freelance written. Enjoys working with published/established writers; works with a small number of new/unpublished writers each year.** Bimonthly magazine covering health articles (especially from a prevention angle and with a Christian slant). The average length of time between acceptance of a freelance-written manuscript and publication of the material depends upon the topics: some immediately used; others up to 2 years. Estab. 1885. Circ. 30,000. Byline given. Pays on acceptance. Offers 50% kill fee. Submit seasonal material 9 months in advance. Accepts queries by mail, e-mail, fax. Responds in 1 month to queries. Sample copy for $1. Guidelines available online.

　　Currently closed to submissions.

NONFICTION Needs interview, with personalities on health. **Buys 50-60 feature articles/year and 6-12 short mss/year.** Send complete ms. 500-1,500 words for features, 25-250 words for short pieces. **Pays $75-300 for features, $50-75 for short pieces.**

REPRINTS Send tearsheet and information about when and where the material previously appeared. Pays 50% of amount paid for an original article.

PHOTOS Not interested in b&w photos. Send photos. Reviews 35mm transparencies.

COLUMNS Buys 12-18 department articles/year. Length: 500-650 words. **Pays $75-175.**

🜲🜲🜲🜲 VIM & VIGOR

1010 E. Missouri Ave., Phoenix AZ 85014-2601. (602)395-5850. Fax: (602)395-5853. E-mail: stephaniec@mcmurry.com. **90% freelance written.** Quarterly magazine covering health and healthcare. Estab. 1985. Circ. 800,000. Byline given. Pays on acceptance. Publishes ms an average of 6 months after acceptance.

Sample copy for 9×12 SAE with 8 first-class stamps. Guidelines for #10 SASE.

NONFICTION Send published clips and resume by mail or e-mail. Length: 500-1,200 words. **Pays 90¢-$1/word.** Pays expenses of writers on assignment.

🌑🌑 WHJ/HRHJ

Rian Enterprises, LLC, 4808 Courthouse St., Suite 204, Williamsburg VA 23188. Fax: (757)645-4473. E-mail: info@thehealthjournals.com. Website: williamsburghealth.com; hamptonroadshealth.com. **70% freelance written.** Monthly tabloid covering consumer/family health and wellness in the Hampton Roads area. "Articles accepted of local and national interest. Health-savvy, college educated audience of all gender, ages, and backgrounds. " Estab. 2005. Circ. 81,000. Byline given. Pays on publication. Publishes ms an average of 1-2 months after acceptance. Editorial lead time 4-6 months. Submit seasonal material 4 months in advance. Accepts queries by mail, e-mail, fax. Accepts simultaneous submissions. Only responds to mss of interest. Sample copy available online. Guidelines available online.

NONFICTION Needs book excerpts, essays, expose, general interest, historical, how-to, humor, inspirational, interview, new product, opinion, personal experience, photo feature, technical, travel. Does not want promotion of products, religious material, anything over 2,000 words. **Buys 100 mss/year.** Query with published clips. Length: 400-1,000 words. **Pays 15¢/word, $50/reprint.** Sometimes pays expenses of writers on assignment.

🌑🌑🌑🌑 YOGA JOURNAL

475 Sasome St., Suite 850, San Francisco CA 94111. (415)591-0555. Fax: (415)591-0733. E-mail: queries@yogajournal.com. Website: yogajournal.com. **Contact:** Kaitlin Quistgaard, editor-in-chief. **75% freelance written.** Magazine published 9 times a year covering the practice and philosophy of yoga. "With comprehensive features on the practice, fitness, well-being and everyday balance, we deliver the yoga tradition suited to today's lifestyle. We welcome professional queries for these departments: **Om**: Covers myriad aspects of the yoga lifestyle (150-400 words). This department includes Yoga Diary, a 250-word story about a pivotal moment in your yoga practice. **Eating Wisely.** A popular, 1,400-word department about relationship to food. Most stories focus on vegetarian and whole-foods cooking, nutritional healing, and

contemplative pieces about the relationship between yoga and food. **Well Being.** This 1,500-word department presents reported pieces about holistic health practices." Estab. 1975. Circ. 300,000. Byline given. Pays within 90 days of acceptance. Offers kill fee. Offers kill fee on assigned articles. Publishes ms an average of 10 months after acceptance. Submit seasonal material 7 months in advance. Accepts queries by e-mail. Responds in 6 weeks to queries if interested. Sample copy for $4.99. Guidelines available online.

NONFICTION Needs book excerpts, how-to, yoga, exercise, etc., inspirational, yoga or related, interview, opinion, photo feature, travel, yoga-related. Does not want unsolicited poetry or cartoons. Please avoid New Age jargon and in-house buzz words as much as possible. **Buys 50-60 mss/year.** Query with SASE. Length: 3,000-5,000 words. **Pays $800-2,000.**

REPRINTS Send tearsheet or photocopy with rights for sale noted and information about when and where the material previously appeared.

COLUMNS Health (self-care; well-being); Body-Mind (hatha Yoga, other body-mind modalities, meditation, yoga philosophy, Western mysticism); Community (service, profiles, organizations, events), all 1,500-2,000 words. **Pays $400-800.** Living (books, video, arts, music), 800 words. **Pays $200-250.** World of Yoga, Spectrum (brief yoga and healthy living news/events/fillers), 150-600 words. **Pays $50-150.**

HISTORY

AMERICAN HISTORY

Weider History Group, 19300 Promenade Dr., Leesburg VA 20176-6500. (703)771-9400. Fax: (703)779-8345. Website: historynet.com. **60% freelance written.** Bimonthly magazine of cultural, social, military, and political history published for a general audience. "Presents the history of America to a broad spectrum of general-interest readers in an authoritative, informative, thought-provoking and entertaining style. Lively narratives take readers on an adventure with history, complemented by rare photographs, paintings, illustrations and maps." Estab. 1966. Circ. 95,000. Byline given. Pays on acceptance. Responds in 10 weeks to queries. Sample copy and guidelines for $5 (includes 3rd class postage) or $4 and 9×12 SAE with 4 first-class stamps. Guidelines for #10 SASE.

NONFICTION Key prerequisites for publication are thorough research and accurate presentation, precise English usage, and sound organization, a lively style, and a high level of human interest. *Unsolicited manuscripts not considered.* Inappropriate materials include: book reviews, travelogues, personal/family narratives not of national significance, articles about collectibles/antiques, living artists, local/individual historic buildings/landmarks, and articles of a current editorial nature. **Buys 20 mss/year.** Query by mail only with published clips and SASE. 2,000-4,000 words depending on type of article.

PHOTOS Welcomes suggestions for illustrations.

💲💲 AMERICA'S CIVIL WAR

Weider History Group, 741 Miller Dr., Suite D-2, Leesburg VA 20175-8994. (703)771-9400. Fax: (703)779-8345. E-mail: acwletters@weiderhistorygroup.com. Website: historynet.com. **95% freelance written.** Bimonthly magazine covering popular history and straight historical narrative for both the general reader and the Civil War buff covering strategy, tactics, personalities, arms and equipment. Estab. 1988. Circ. 78,000. Byline given. Pays on publication. Accepts queries by mail, e-mail. Sample copy for $5. Writer's guidelines for #10 SASE.

🖵 "Americascivilwarmag.com is the website of America's Civil War magazine."

NONFICTION Needs historical, book notices, preservation news. **Buys 24 mss/year.** Query. Submit a page outlining the subject and your approach to it, and why you believe this would be an important article for the magazine. Briefly summarize your prior writing experience in a cover note. 3,500-4,000 words and a 500-word sidebar. **Pays $300 and up.**

PHOTOS Send photos with submission or cite sources. Captions, identification of subjects required.

COLUMNS Personality (profiles of Civil War personalities); Men & Material (about weapons used); Commands (about units); Eyewitness to War (historical letters and diary excerpts). Length: 2,000 words. **Buys 24 mss/year.** Query. **Pays $150 and up**

💲 THE ARTILLERYMAN

Historical Publications, Inc., 234 Monarch Hill Rd., Tunbridge VT 05077. (802)889-3500. Fax: (802)889-5627. E-mail: mail@artillerymanmagazine.com. Website: artillerymanmagazine.com. **Contact:** Kathryn Jorgensen, editor. **60% freelance written.** Quarterly magazine covering antique artillery, fortifications, and crew-served weapons 1750-1900 for competition shooters, collectors, and living history reenactors using artillery. Emphasis on Revolutionary War and Civil War but includes everyone interested in pre-1900 artillery and fortifications, preservation, construction of replicas, etc. Estab. 1979. Circ. 1,500. Byline given. Pays on publication. Publishes ms an average of 6 months after acceptance. Accepts queries by mail, e-mail, fax. Accepts simultaneous submissions. Responds in 3 weeks to queries. Sample copy and writer's guidelines for 9×12 SAE with 4 first-class stamps.

NONFICTION Needs historical, how-to, interview, new product, nostalgic, opinion, personal experience, photo feature, technical, travel, reproduce ordinance, equipment/sights/implements/tools/accessories, etc. **Buys 24-30 mss/year.** Send complete ms. 300 words minimum **Pays $20-60.**

REPRINTS Send tearsheet or photocopy and information about when and where the material previously appeared.

PHOTOS Send photos. Captions, identification of subjects required. Pays $5 for 5×7 and larger b&w prints.

🌙 BRITISH HERITAGE

Weider History Group, 19300 Promenade Dr., Leesburg VA 20176. (703)771-9400. Fax: (703)779-8345. E-mail: dana.huntley@weiderhistorygroup.com. Website: thehistorynet.com. Bimonthly magazine covering British travel and culture. "The magazine of travel, culture and adventure, especially written for those who love England, Scotland, Ireland and Wales. A must-read for Anglophiles, British Heritage shows them what they can see and do, how to get there and where to stay, with information that even veteran travelers may overlook." Circ. 77,485. Pays on acceptance. Pays kill fee though never had to. Editorial lead time 6 months. Accepts queries by e-mail. No

NONFICTION Buys 50 mss/year. Query by e-mail. Length: 1,000-2,500 words.

💲💲💲 CIVIL WAR TIMES

Weider History Group, 19300 Promenade Dr., Leesburg VA 20176-6500. (703)779-8371. Fax: (703)779-8345. E-mail: cwt@weiderhistorygroup.com. Website: historynet.com. **90% freelance written. Works with a small number of new/unpublished writers each year.** Magazine published 6 times/year. "*Civil War Times* is the full-spectrum magazine of the Civil War. Specifically, we look for nonpartisan coverage of battles, prominent military and civilian figures, the home front, politics, military technology, common soldier life, prisoners and escapes, period art and photography, the naval war, blockade-running, specific regiments, and much more." Estab. 1962. Circ. 108,000. Pays on acceptance and on publication. Publishes ms an average of 18 months after acceptance. Submit seasonal material 1 year in advance. Responds in 3-6 months to queries. Sample copy for $6. Guidelines for #10 SASE.

NONFICTION Needs interview, photo feature, Civil War historical material. "Don't send us a comprehensive article on a well-known major battle. Instead, focus on some part or aspect of such a battle, or some group of soldiers in the battle. Similar advice applies to major historical figures like Lincoln and Lee. Positively no fiction or poetry." **Buys 20 freelance mss/year.** Query with clips and SASE **Pays $75-800.**

GATEWAY

(formerly *Gateway Heritage*), Missouri History Museum, P.O. Box 11940, St. Louis MO 63112-0040. (314)746-4558. Fax: (314)746-4548. E-mail: vwmonks@mohistory.org. Website: mohistory.org. **75% freelance written.** Annual magazine covering Missouri history and culture. *Gateway* is a popular cultural history magazine that is primarily a member benefit of the Missouri History Museum. Thus, we have a general audience with an interest in the history and culture of Missouri, and St. Louis in particular. Estab. 1980. Circ. 11,000. Byline given. Pays on publication. Offers $100 kill fee. Publishes ms an average of 6 months to 1 year after acceptance. Editorial lead time 6 months. Accepts queries by mail, e-mail, fax. Responds in 1 month to queries. Responds in 2 months to mss. Sample copy for $10. online or send #10 SASE.

NONFICTION Needs book excerpts, interview, photo feature, Interviews; historical, scholarly essays; Missouri biographies; photo essays; viewpoints on events; first-hand historical accounts; book excerpts; regional architectural history; literary history. No genealogies. No genealogies. **Buys 4-6 mss/year.** Query with writing samples. Length: 4,000-5,000 words. **Pays $300-400 (average).**

PHOTOS State availability with submission.

GOOD OLD DAYS

Dynamic Resource Group, 306 E. Parr Rd., Berne IN 46711. Fax: (260)589-8093. E-mail: editor@goodolddaysonline.com. Website: goodolddaysonline.com. **Contact:** Ken Tate, editor. **75% freelance written.** Bi-Monthly magazine of first person nostalgia, 1935-

1965. "We look for strong narratives showing life as it was in the middle decades of the 20th century. Our readership is comprised of nostalgia buffs, history enthusiasts, and the people who actually lived and grew up in this era." Byline given. Pays on contract. Publishes ms an average of 8 months after acceptance. Submit seasonal material 10 months in advance. Accepts queries by fax, online submission form. Responds in 2 months to queries. Sample copy for $2. Guidelines available online.

Queries accepted, but are not necessary.

NONFICTION Needs historical, humor, personal experience, photo feature, favorite food/recipes, year-round seasonal material, biography, memorable events, fads, fashion, sports, music, literature, entertainment. No fiction accepted. **Buys 350 mss/year.** Query or send complete ms. Length: 500-1,500 words. **Pays $20-100, depending on quality and photos.**

PHOTOS Do not send original photos until we ask for them. You may send photocopies or duplicates. Do not submit laser-copied prints. Send photos. Identification of subjects required.

HISTORY MAGAZINE

Moorshead Magazines, 505 Consumers Rd., Suite 312, Toronto ON M2J 4V8 Canada. E-mail: edward@moorshead.com;marc@familychronicle.com. Website: history-magazine.com. **90% freelance written.** Bimonthly magazine covering social history. A general interest history magazine, focusing on social history up to the outbreak of World War II. Estab. 1999. Byline given. Pays on publication. Publishes ms an average of 6 months after acceptance. Editorial lead time 6 months. Submit seasonal material 6 months in advance. Accepts queries by mail, e-mail. Responds in 1 month to queries. Responds in 1 month to mss. Sample copy available online. Guidelines available online.

NONFICTION Needs book excerpts, historical. Does not want first-person narratives or revisionist history. **Buys 50 mss/year.** Query. Length: 400-2,500 words. **Pays $50-250.**

PHOTOS State availability. Captions required. Reviews GIF/JPEG files. Negotiates payment individually.

LEBEN

City Seminary Press, 2150 River Plaza Dr., #150, Sacramento CA 95833. E-mail: editor@leben.us. Website: leben.us. **40% freelance written.** Estab. 2004. Circ. 5,000. Byline given. Pays on acceptance. Offers 25%

kill fee. Publishes ms an average of 6 months after acceptance. Editorial lead time 6 months. Submit seasonal material 6 months in advance. Accepts queries by online submission form. Accepts simultaneous submissions. Responds in 3 weeks to queries. Responds in 2 months to mss. Sample copy for $1.50 (order online or request via e-mail). Guidelines by e-mail.

○ "Quarterly magazine presenting the people and events of Christian history from a Reformation perspective. We are not a theological journal, per se, but rather a popular history magazine."

NONFICTION Needs historical, reformed biography. Does not want articles that argue theological issues. There is a place for that, but not in a popular history/biography magazine aimed at general readership. Query. Length: 500-2,500 words. **Pays up to $100.**

➕ 💲 LIGHTHOUSE DIGEST

Lighthouse Digest, P.O. Box 250, East Machias ME 04630. (207)259-2121. E-mail: Editor@LighthouseDigest.com. Website: lighthousedigest.com. **Contact:** Tim Harrison, editor. **15% freelance written.** Monthly magazine covering historical, fiction and news events about lighthouses and similar maritime stories. Estab. 1989. Circ. 24,000. Byline given. Pays on publication. Publishes ms an average of 4 months after acceptance. Editorial lead time 3 months. Submit seasonal material 3 months in advance. Accepts queries by e-mail. Accepts simultaneous submissions. Responds in 6 weeks to queries. Sample copy free.

NONFICTION Needs expose, general interest, historical, humor, inspirational, personal experience, photo feature, religious, technical, travel. No historical data taken from books. **Buys 30 mss/year.** Send complete ms. 2,500 words maximum **Pays $75.**

PHOTOS Send photos. Captions, identification of subjects required. Reviews prints. Offers no additional payment for photos accepted with ms.

FICTION Needs adventure, historical, humorous, mystery, religious, romance, suspense. **Buys 2 mss/year.** Send complete ms. 2,500 words maximum **Pays $75-150.**

NOSTALGIA MAGAZINE

King's Publishing Group, Inc., P.O. Box 203, Spokane WA 99210. (509)299-4041. E-mail: editor@nostalgiamagazine.net. Website: nostalgiamagazine.net. **90% freelance written.** Bi-monthly magazine covering "stories and photos of personal, historical, nostalgic experiences: I remember when. *Nostalgia Magazine* is a journal that gathers photos, personal remembrance stories, diaries, and researched stories of well-known—and more often little-known—people, places, and events, and puts them into 1 bi-monthly volume. We glean the best of the past to share and enrich life now." Byline given. Publishes ms an average of 1 year after acceptance. Editorial lead time 6 months. Submit seasonal material 6 months in advance. Accepts queries by mail, e-mail. Accepts simultaneous submissions. Responds in 6 months to queries and mss. Sample copy for $5. Writer's guidelines available via e-mail or mail.

NONFICTION Needs book excerpts, expose, general interest, historical, how-to, humor, inspirational, interview, personal experience, photo feature, religious, travel. Does not want genealogies, current events/news, divisive politics (in historical setting sometimes OK), or glorification of immorality. **Buys 120 mss/year.** Send complete ms. Length: 400-2,000 words.

PHOTOS "Photos are as important as the story. We need 1 candid photo per 400 words of fiction.". Send photos. Captions, identification of subjects required. Reviews negatives, transparencies, prints, JPEG files. Offers no payment for photos accepted with ms.

POETRY Needs free verse, light verse, traditional. "Does not want avant-garde, contemporary/modern experiences, simple junk." Buys 3 poems/year. Submit maximum 1 poems. **Pays in copies.**

FILLERS Needs anecdotes, facts, gags, short humor. **Buys 50 fillers/year. mss/year.** Length: 50-200 words. **Pays with copies of the magazine.**

💲 💲 PERSIMMON HILL

National Cowboy & Western Heritage Museum, 1700 NE 63rd St., Oklahoma City OK 73111. (405)478-6404. Fax: (405)478-4714. E-mail: editor@nationalcowboymuseum.org. Website: nationalcowboymuseum.org. **Contact:** Judy Hilovsky. **70% freelance written. Prefers to work with published/established writers; works with a small number of new/unpublished writers each year.** Quarterly magazine for an audience interested in Western art, Western history, ranching, and rodeo, including historians, artists, ranchers, art galleries, schools, and libraries. Estab. 1970. Circ. 7,500. Byline given. Pays on publication. Publishes ms an average of 18 months after acceptance. Responds in 3 months to queries. Sample copy for $10.50, including postage. Writer's guidelines available on website.

NONFICTION Buys 50-75 mss/year. Query by mail with clips. Word length: 1,500 words. **Pays $150-300**

PHOTOS Purchased with ms or on assignment. Captions required. Reviews digital images and b&w prints. Pays according to quality and importance for b&w and color photos.

$$$ TIMELINE

Ohio Historical Society, 1982 Velma Ave., Columbus OH 43211-2497. (614)297-2360. Fax: (614)297-2367. E-mail: timeline@ohiohistory.org. **90% freelance written. Works with a small number of new/unpublished writers each year.** Quarterly magazine covering history, prehistory, and the natural sciences, directed toward readers in the Midwest. Estab. 1984. Circ. 7,000. Byline given. Pays on final edit. Offers $75 minimum kill fee. Publishes ms an average of 1 year after acceptance. Submit seasonal material 6 months in advance. Accepts queries by mail, e-mail, fax. Responds in 3 weeks to queries. Responds in 6 weeks to mss. Sample copy for $12 and 9×12 SAE. Guidelines for #10 SASE.

NONFICTION Needs book excerpts, essays, historical, photo feature. **Buys 22 mss/year.** Query. 1,500-6,000 words. Also vignettes of 500-1,000 words. **Pays $100-800.**

PHOTOS Submissions should include ideas for illustration. Send photos. Captions, identification of subjects, model releases required. Reviews contact sheets, transparencies, 8×10 prints.

$ TOMBIGBEE COUNTRY MAGAZINE

Tombigbee Country Magazine, PO Box 621, Gu-Win AL 35563. (205)412-9750; (205)412-8557. E-mail: tombigbeecountrymagazine@yahoo.com. Website: tombigbeecountry.com. **Contact:** Bo Webster, editor. **50% freelance written.** Monthly magazine covering nostalgia - history. We fancy ourselves as containing up-beat articles that make our readers feel good about themselves. We attempt to build pride in being an American, from the South and from our particular region along the Tombigbee River (now Tennessee-Tombigbee Waterway) in Mississippi, Alabama and Tennessee. We are an old fashioned, country magazine which takes pride in printing articles by everyday, ordinary people, most of which have never been published before. Estab. 2,000. Circ. 10,000. Byline given. Pays on publication. Publishes ms an average of 1 month after acceptance. Editorial lead time 2 months. Submit seasonal material 2 months in advance. Accepts queries by mail, e-mail. Accepts simultaneous submissions. Responds in 1 week to queries. Responds in 1 month to mss. Sample copy $2. Guidelines free.

> "Contributors who submit nonfiction, nostalgia-related articles have the best chance of being published."

NONFICTION Needs book excerpts, essays, general interest, historical, humor, inspirational, personal experience, religious. Special issues: We are eager for stories on personal experience with celebrities—country musicians, famous southerners. We do not want tributes to family members. **Buys 24+ mss/year.** Query. Length: 800-2,000 words. **Pays $24 for assigned articles. Pays $24 for unsolicited articles.**

FILLERS Needs short humor. Length: 25-800 words. **Pays $-0.**

$ THE TOMBSTONE EPITAPH

Tombstone Epitaph, Inc., P.O. BOX, 1880, Tombstone AZ 85638. (520)457-2211. E-mail: info@tombstoneepitaph.com. Website: tombstoneepitaph.com. **60% freelance written.** Monthly tabloid covering American west to 1900 (-1935, if there's an Old West connection). "We seek lively, well-written, sourced articles that examine the history and culture of the Old West." Estab. 1880. Byline given. End of calendar year. Publishes ms an average of 3 months after acceptance. Editorial lead time 3 months. Submit seasonal material 6 months in advance. Accepts queries by e-mail. Responds in 2 weeks to queries. Responds in 1 month to mss. Sample copy for $3. Guidelines by e-mail.

NONFICTION Needs essays, historical, humor, personal experience, (if historically grounded), travel, Past events as interpreted in film, books, magazines, etc. "We do not want poorly sourced stories, contemporary West pieces, fiction, poetry, big 'tell-all' stories." **Buys 25-40 mss/year.** Query. Length: 1,000-5,000 words. **Pays $30-50 for assigned articles. Pays $30 max. for unsolicited articles.**

PHOTOS Send photos/. Captions, identification of subjects required. Reviews GIF/JPEG files. Offers no additional payment for photos accepted with ms.

$$ TRACES OF INDIANA AND MIDWESTERN HISTORY

Indiana Historical Society, 450 W. Ohio St., Indianapolis IN 46202-3269. (317)232-1877. Fax: (317)233-0857.

E-mail: rboomhower@indianahistory.org. Website: indianahistory.org. **Contact:** Ray E. Boomhower, Senior editor. **80% freelance written.** Quarterly magazine on Indiana history. "Conceived as a vehicle to bring to the public good narrative and analytical history about Indiana in its broader contexts of region and nation, *Traces* explores the lives of artists, writers, performers, soldiers, politicians, entrepreneurs, homemakers, reformers, and naturalists. It has traced the impact of Hoosiers on the nation and the world. In this vein, the editors seek nonfiction articles that are solidly researched, attractively written, and amenable to illustration, and they encourage scholars, journalists, and freelance writers to contribute to the magazine." Estab. 1989. Circ. 6,000. Byline given. Publishes ms an average of 6 months after acceptance. Submit seasonal material 1 year in advance. Responds in 3 months to mss. Guidelines available online.

NONFICTION Buys 20 mss/year. Send complete ms. Length: 2,000-4,000 words. **Pays $100-500.**

PHOTOS Send photos. Captions, identification of subjects, True required. Reviews contact sheets, transparencies, photocopies, prints. Pays reasonable photographic expenses.

⊘❶❷❸❹ TRUE WEST

True West Publishing, Inc., P.O. Box 8008, Cave Creek AZ 85327. (888)687-1881. Fax: (480)575-1903. E-mail: editor@twmag.com. Website: twmag.com. Executive Editor: Bob Boze Bell. **Contact:** Megan Saar, Editor-in-Chief. **45% freelance written. Works with a small number of new/unpublished writers each year.** Magazine published 10 times/year covering Western American history from prehistory 1800 to 1930. "We want reliable research on significant historical topics written in lively prose for an informed general audience. More recent topics may be used if they have a historical angle or retain the Old West flavor of trail dust and saddle leather. True West magazine's features and departments tie the history of the American West (between 1800-1930) to the modern western lifestyle through enticing narrative and intelligent analyses." Estab. 1953. Byline given. Pays on publication. Kill fee applicable only to material assigned by the editor, not for stories submitted on spec based on query written to the editor. 50% of original fee should the story have run in the publication. Editorial lead time 6 months. Accepts queries by mail, e-mail. Sample copy for $3. Guidelines available online.

No unsolicited mss. No e-mail submissions, except to ask if we received your proposal and ms. True West seeks to establish long-term relationships with writers who conduct excellent research, provide a fresh look at an old subject, write well, hit deadlines and provide manuscripts at the assigned word length. Such writers tend to get repeat assignments. Send your query and accompanying MSS and photos to: **Meghan Saar**, Editor-in-Chief, Via mail (SASE).

NONFICTION No fiction, poetry, or unsupported, undocumented tales. **Buys 30 mss/year.** Send query to Meghan Saar at editor@twmag.com Length: no more than 1,500 words. **Pays $50-800. "Features pay $150-500 with a $20 payment for each photo the author provides that is published with the article and not already part of True West archives."**

PHOTOS State availability. Captions, identification of subjects, model releases required and verification of permission granted for publication by original owner. Reviews contact sheets, negatives, 4×5 transparencies, 4×5 prints. Offers $20/photo.

FILLERS Needs anecdotes, facts, gags, newsbreaks, short humor. **Buys 30 mss/year.** Length: 50-300 words.

❶❷ WILD WEST

Weider History Group, 19300 Promenade Dr., Leesburg VA 20176-6500. (703)771-9400. Fax: (703)779-8345. E-mail: wildwest@weiderhistorygroup.com. Website: historynet.com. **Contact:** Eric Weider, publisher. **95% freelance written.** Bimonthly magazine covering the history of the American frontier, from its eastern beginnings to its western terminus. "*Wild West* covers the popular (narrative) history of the American West—events, trends, personalities, anything of general interest." Estab. 1988. Circ. 83,500. Byline given. Pays on publication. Publishes ms an average of 2 years after acceptance. Editorial lead time 10 months. Submit seasonal material 1 year in advance. Accepts queries by mail, e-mail. Accepts simultaneous submissions. Responds in 3 months to queries. Responds in 6 months to mss. Sample copy for $6. Writer's guidelines for #10 SASE or online.

NONFICTION Needs historical, Old West. No excerpts, travel, etc. Articles can be adapted from book. No fiction or poetry—nothing current. **Buys 36 mss/year.** Query. 3,500 words with a 500-word sidebar. **Pays $300.**

PHOTOS State availability. Captions, identification of subjects required. Reviews negatives, transparencies. Offers no additional payment for photos accepted with ms.

COLUMNS Gunfighters & Lawmen, 2,000 words; Westerners, 2,000 words; Warriors & Chiefs, 2,000 words; Western Lore, 2,000 words; Guns of the West, 1,500 words; Artists West, 1,500 words; Books Reviews, 250 words. **Buys 36 mss/year.** Query. **Pays $150 for departments; book reviews paid by the word, minimum $40.**

➎➏➏ WORLD WAR II

Weider History Group, 19300 Promenade Dr., Leesburg VA 20176. E-mail: worldwar2@weiderhistorygroup.com. Website: historynet.com. **Contact:** Editor, World War II. **25%. Most of our stories are assigned by our staff to professional writers. However, we do accept written proposals for features and for our Time Travel department.** Bimonthly magazine covering military operations in World War II—events, personalities, strategy, the home front, etc. Estab. 1986. Circ. 146,000. Byline given. Pays on acceptance. Kill fee. Accepts queries by mail, e-mail. Writer's guidelines available on website or for SASE.

NONFICTION No fiction. **Buys 24 mss/year.** Query. Outline the subject and your approach to it, and why you believe this would be an important article. Also summarize briefly your prior writing experience in a cover note. List your sources in standard format at the end of your piece Features: 2,500-4,000 words. **Pay negotiated on a piece by piece basis.**

HOBBY AND CRAFT

➄➄➄➄ AMERICAN CRAFT

American Craft Council, 1224 Marshall Street NE, Suite 200, Minneapolis MN 55413. (612)206-3100. E-mail: letters@craftcouncil.org; mmoses@craftcouncil.org. Website: americancraftmag.org. **75% freelance written.** Bimonthly magazine covering art/craft/design. Estab. 1943. Circ. 40,000. Byline given. Pays 30 days after acceptance. Offers 25% kill fee. Publishes ms an average of 2 months after acceptance. Editorial lead time 3 months. Submit seasonal material 3 months in advance. Accepts queries by mail, e-mail. Accepts simultaneous submissions. Responds in 1 month to queries. Responds in 2 months to mss. Sample copy free. Guidelines by e-mail.

NONFICTION Needs essays, general interest, interview, new product, opinion, photo feature, travel. Query with published clips. Length: 1,200-3,000 words. Pays expenses of writers on assignment.

COLUMNS Critics's Corner (critical essays), 200-2,500 words; Wide World of Craft (travel), 800-1,000 words; Material Culture (material studies), 600-800 words; outskirts (a look at peripheral disciplines), 600-800 words. **Buys 10-12 mss/year.** Query with published clips. **Pays $1-1.50/word.**

➄➄ ANTIQUE TRADER

F+W Media, Inc., 700 E. State St., Iola WI 54990-0001. (715)445-2214. Fax: (715)445-4087. Website: antiquetrader.com. **Contact:** Eric Bradley, editor. **60% freelance written.** Weekly tabloid covering antiques. "We publish quote-heavy stories of timely interest in the antiques field. We cover antiques shows, auctions, and news events." Estab. 1957. Circ. 30,000. Byline given. Pays on publication. Publishes ms an average of 1-3 months after acceptance. Editorial lead time 2 months. Accepts queries by mail, e-mail, fax. Responds in 1 week to queries. Responds in 2 months to mss Sample copy for cover price, plus postage. Guidelines available online.

NONFICTION Needs book excerpts, general interest, interview, personal experience, show and auction coverage. Does not want the same, dry textbook, historical stories on antiques that appear elsewhere. Our readers want personality and timeliness. **Buys 1,000+ mss/year.** Send complete ms. Length: 750-1,200 words. **Pays $50-150, plus contributor copy.**

PHOTOS State availability. Identification of subjects required. Reviews transparencies, prints, GIF/JPEG files. Offers no additional payment for photos accepted with ms.

COLUMNS Dealer Profile (interviews with interesting antiques dealers), 750-1,200 words; Collector Profile (interviews with interesting collectors), 750-1,000 words. **Buys 30-60 mss/year.** Query with or without published clips or send complete ms.

➄ AUTOGRAPH COLLECTOR

Odyssey Publications, 510-A South Corona Mall, Corona CA 92879. (951)734-9636. Fax: (951)371-7139. E-mail: editorev@telus.net. Website: autographmagazine.com. **80% freelance written.** Monthly magazine covering the autograph collecting hobby. The focus of *Autograph Collector* is on documents, photographs, or any collectible item that has been signed by a famous person, whether a current celebrity or historical figure. Articles stress how and where to locate celebrities and autograph material, authenticity of signatures and what they are worth. Byline given. Offers negotiable kill fee. Editorial lead time 2 months. Submit seasonal material 3 months in advance. Accepts queries by mail, e-mail, fax, phone. Responds in 2 weeks to queries. Sample copy and writer's guidelines free.

NONFICTION Needs historical, how-to, interview, personal experience. **Buys 25-35 mss/year.** Query. Length: 1,600-2,000 words. **Pays 5¢/word.** Sometimes pays expenses of writers on assignment.

PHOTOS State availability. Captions, identification of subjects required. Reviews transparencies, prints. Offers $3/photo.

COLUMNS *Autograph Collector* buys 8-10 columns per month written by regular contributors. **Buys 90-100 mss/year.** Query. **Pays $50 or as determined on a per case basis.**

FILLERS Needs anecdotes, facts. **Buys 20-25 mss/year.** Length: 200-300 words. **$15.**

⊙⊙ BEAD & BUTTON

Kalmbach Publishing, P.O. Box 1612, 21027 Crossroads Circle, Waukesha WI 53187. E-mail: editor@beadandbutton.com. Website: beadandbutton.com. **50% freelance written.** "*Bead & Button* is a bimonthly magazine devoted to techniques, projects, designs and materials relating to making beaded jewelry. Our readership includes both professional and amateur bead and button makers, hobbyists, and enthusiasts who find satisfaction in making beautiful things." Estab. 1994. Circ. 100,000. Byline given. Pays on acceptance. Offers $75 kill fee. Publishes ms an average of 4-12 months after acceptance. Accepts queries by mail, e-mail, fax. Guidelines available online.

NONFICTION Needs historical, on beaded jewelry history, how-to, make beaded jewelry and accessories, humor, inspirational, interview. **Buys 20-25 mss/year.** Send complete ms. Length: 750-1,500 words. **Pays $100-400.**

PHOTOS Send photos. Identification of subjects required. Offers no additional payment for photos accepted with ms.

⊙⊙ BLADE MAGAZINE

F+W Media, Inc., 700 E. State St., Iola WI 54990-0001. (715)445-2214. Fax: (715)445-4087. E-mail: joe.kertzman@fwmedia.com. Website: blademag.com. **Contact:** Joe Kertzman, Managing Editor.

5% freelance written. Monthly magazine covering working and using collectible, popular knives. *Blade* prefers in-depth articles focusing on groups of knives, whether military, collectible, high-tech, pocket knives or hunting knives, and how they perform. Estab. 1973. Circ. 39,000. Byline given. Pays on publication. Publishes ms an average of 9 months after acceptance. Editorial lead time 9 months. Submit seasonal material 9 months in advance. Accepts queries by mail, e-mail, fax. Responds in 3 months to queries. Responds in 6 months to mss. Sample copy for $4.99. Guidelines for sae with 8×11 envelope and 3 first-class stamps.

NONFICTION Needs general interest, historical, how-to, interview, new product, photo feature, technical. "We assign profiles, show stories, hammer-in stories, etc. We don't need those. If you've seen the story on the Internet or in another knife or knife/gun magazine, we don't need it. We don't do stories on knives used for self-defense." Send complete ms. Length: 700-1,400 words. **Pays $150-300.**

PHOTOS Send photos. Captions, identification of subjects required. Reviews transparencies, prints, digital images (300 dpi at 1200x1200 pixels). Offers no additional payment for photos accepted with ms.

FILLERS Needs anecdotes, facts, newsbreaks. **Buys 1-2 fillers. mss/year.** Length: 50-200 words. **Pays $25-50.**

⊙ BREW YOUR OWN

Battenkill Communications, 5515 Main St., Manchester Center VT 05255. (802)362-3981. Fax: (802)362-2377. E-mail: edit@byo.com. Website: byo.com; byo.com/about/guidelines. **85% freelance written.** Monthly magazine covering home brewing. "Our mission is to provide practical information in an entertaining format. We try to capture the spirit and challenge of brewing while helping our readers brew the best beer they can." Estab. 1995. Circ. 50,000. Byline given. Pays on acceptance. Offers 25% kill fee. Publishes ms an average of 4 months after acceptance. Editorial lead time 3 months. Submit seasonal material 3 months in advance. Accepts queries by mail, e-mail, fax. Responds in 2 months to queries. Guidelines available online.

NONFICTION Needs historical, how-to, home brewing, humor, related to home brewing, interview, of professional brewers who can offer useful tips to home hobbyists, personal experience, trends. **Buys 75 mss/year.** Query with published clips or description of brewing expertise Length: 800-3,000 words. **Pays $50-350, depending on length, complexity of article, and experience of writer.** Sometimes pays expenses of writers on assignment.

PHOTOS State availability. Captions required. Reviews contact sheets, transparencies, 5×7 prints, slides, and electronic images. Negotiates payment individually.

COLUMNS News (humorous, unusual news about homebrewing), 50-250 words; Last Call (humorous stories about homebrewing), 700 words. **Buys 12 mss/year.** Query with or without published clips. **Pays $75**

CANADIAN WOODWORKING AND HOME IMPROVEMENT

Sawdust Media, Inc., 51 Maple Ave. N., RR #3, Burford ON N0E 1A0 Canada. (519)449-2444. Fax: (519)449-2445. E-mail: pfulcher@canadianwoodworking.com. Website: canadianwoodworking.com. Paul Fulcher, publisher. **20% freelance written.** Bimonthly magazine covering woodworking; only accepts work from Canadian writers. Estab. 1999. Byline given. Pays on publication. Offers 50% kill fee. Accepts queries by e-mail. Sample copy available online. Guidelines by e-mail.

NONFICTION Needs how-to, humor, inspirational, new product, personal experience, photo feature, technical. Does not want profile on a woodworker. Query. Length: 500-4,000 words. **Pays $100-600 for assigned articles. Pays $50-400 for unsolicited articles.**

PHOTOS State availability. Negotiates payment individually.

CARVING MAGAZINE

All American Crafts, P.O. Box 611, Faribault MN 55021. E-mail: editors@carvingmagazine.com. Website: carvingmagazine.com. **95% freelance written.** Quarterly magazine covering woodcarving. *Carving Magazine* specialzing in woodcarving articles including step-by-steps, techniques, profiles and photo galleries. Estab. 2002. Circ. 20,000. Byline given. Pays on publication. Publishes ms an average of 6 months after acceptance. Editorial lead time 6 months. Submit seasonal material 6 months in advance. Accepts queries by mail, e-mail.

NONFICTION Needs general interest, historical, how-to, interview, photo feature. Does not want anything other than woodcarving. **Buys 40 mss/year.** Length: 2,000 words. **Pays $50-100.**

PHOTOS State availability. Captions required. Reviews GIF/JPEG files. Negotiates payment individually.

FILLERS Needs gags.

CERAMICS MONTHLY

600 N. Cleveland Ave., Suite 210, Westerville OH 43082. (614)792-5867. Fax: (614)891-8960. E-mail: editorial@ceramicsmonthly.org. Website: ceramicsmonthly.org. **Contact:** Jessica Knapp, assistant editor. **70% freelance written.** Monthly magazine (except July and August) covering the ceramic art and craft field. "Each issue includes articles on potters and ceramics artists from throughout the world, exhibitions, and production processes, as well as critical commentary, book and video reviews, clay and glaze recipes, kiln designs and firing techniques, advice from experts in the field, and ads for available materials and equipment. While principally covering contemporary work, the magazine also looks back at influential artists and events from the past." Estab. 1953. Circ. 39,000. Byline given. Pays on publication. Editorial lead time 3 months. Submit seasonal material 6 months in advance. Accepts queries by mail, e-mail, fax, phone. Responds in 2 months to mss. Guidelines available online.

NONFICTION Needs essays, how-to, interview, opinion, personal experience, technical. **Buys 100 mss/year.** Send complete ms. Length: 500-3,000 words. **Pays 10¢/word.**

PHOTOS Send photos. Captions required. Reviews digital images, original slides or 2¼ or 4×5 transparencies.

COLUMNS Upfront (workshop/exhibition review), 500-1,000 words. **Buys 20 mss/year.** Send complete ms.

CLASSIC TOY TRAINS

Kalmbach Publishing Co., P.O. Box 1612, 21027 Crossroads Cir., Waukesha WI 53187-1612. (262)796-8776, ext. 524. Fax: (262)796-1142. E-mail: manuscripts@classictoytrains.com. Website: classictoytrains.com. **Contact:** Carl Swanson, editor. **80% freelance written.** Magazine published 9 times/year covering collectible toy trains (O, S, Standard) like Lionel and American Flyer, etc. "For the collector and operator of toy trains, *CTT* offers full-color photos of layouts and collections of toy trains, restoration tips, operating information, new product reviews and information, and insights into the history of toy trains." Estab. 1987. Circ. 50,000. Byline given. Pays on acceptance.

Publishes ms an average of 1 year after acceptance. Editorial lead time 3 months. Submit seasonal material 6 months in advance. Accepts queries by mail, e-mail. Responds in 3 weeks to queries. Responds in 1 month to mss. Sample copy for $5.95, plus postage. Guidelines available online.

NONFICTION Needs general interest, historical, how-to, restore toy trains; design a layout; build accessories; fix broken toy trains, interview, personal experience, photo feature, technical. **Buys 90 mss/year.** Query. Length: 500-5,000 words. **Pays $75-500.** Sometimes pays expenses of writers on assignment.

PHOTOS Send photos. Captions required. Reviews 4×5 transparencies, 5×7 prints or 35mm slides preferred. Also accepts hi-res digital photos. Offers no additional payment for photos accepted with ms or $15-75/photo.

COLLECTORS NEWS

P.O. Box 306, Grundy Center IA 50638. (319)824-6981. Fax: (319)824-3414. E-mail: lkruger@pioneermagazines.com. Website: collectors-news.com. **Contact:** Linda Kruger, Exec. Director. **20% freelance written. Works with a small number of new/unpublished writers each year.** Ten issues/year; magazine-size publication on glossy stock, full cover, covering antiques, collectibles, and nostalgic memorabilia, and modern collectibles. Estab. 1959. Circ. 11,000. Byline given. Pays on publication. Publishes ms an average of 1 year after acceptance. Submit seasonal material 3 months in advance. Accepts queries by e-mail. Responds in 2 weeks to queries. Responds in 6 weeks to mss. Sample copy for $4 and 9×12 SAE. Guidelines free.

NONFICTION Needs general interest, collectibles, antique to modern, historical, relating to collections or collectors, how-to, display your collection, care for, restore, appraise, locate, add to, etc., interview, covering individual collectors and their hobbies, unique or extensive; celebrity collectors, and limited edition artists, technical, in-depth analysis of a particular antique, collectible, or collecting field, travel, hot antiquing places in the US. Special issues: 12-month listing of antique and collectible shows, flea markets, and conventions (January includes events January-December; June includes events June-May); Care & Display of Collectibles (September); holidays (October-December). **Buys 36 mss/year.** Query with sample of writing. Length: 800-1,000 words. **Pays $1.10/column inch.**

PHOTOS Articles must be accompanied by high resolution digital photographs for illustration. A selection of 5-8 images is suggested. Captions required. Reviews hi res color digital images. Payment for photos included in payment for ms.

CQ AMATEUR RADIO

CQ Communications, Inc., 25 Newbridge Rd., Hicksville NY 11801. (516)681-2922. Fax: (516)681-2926. E-mail: cq@cq-amateur-radio.com. E-mail: w2vu@cq-amateur-radio.com. Website: cq-amateur-radio.com. **Contact:** Richard Moseson, editor. **40% freelance written.** Monthly magazine covering amateur (ham) radio. "*CQ* is published for active ham radio operators and is read by radio amateurs in over 100 countries. All articles must deal with amateur radio. Our focus is on operating and on practical projects. A thorough knowledge of amateur radio is required." Estab. 1945. Circ. 60,000. Byline given. Pays on publication. Publishes ms an average of 6 months after acceptance. Editorial lead time 4 months. Submit seasonal material 4 months in advance. Accepts queries by mail, e-mail, fax. Responds in 3 weeks to queries. Responds in 3 months to mss. Sample copy free. Guidelines available online.

NONFICTION Needs historical, how-to, interview, personal experience, technical, all related to amateur radio. **Buys 50-60 mss/year.** Query. Length: 2,000-4,000 words. **Pays $40/published page.**

PHOTOS State availability. Captions, identification of subjects, model releases required. Reviews contact sheets, 4×6 prints, TIFF or JPEG files with 300 dpi resolution. Offers no additional payment for photos accepted with ms.

CREATING KEEPSAKES

Scrapbook Magazine, Primedia Enthusiast Group, 14850 Pony Express Rd., Bluffdale UT 84065. (801)984-2070. E-mail: editorial@CreatingKeepsakes.com. Website: creatingkeepsakes.com. Monthly magazine covering scrapbooks. Written for scrapbook lovers and those with a box of photos high in the closet. Circ. 100,000. Editorial lead time 6 weeks. Accepts queries by mail, e-mail. Guidelines available online.

NONFICTION Query with 2 visuals to illustrate your suggested topic. Length: 800-1,200 words.

DESIGNS IN MACHINE EMBROIDERY

Great Notions News Corp., 2517 Manana Dr., Dallas TX 75220. (888)739-0555. Fax: (413)723-2027. E-mail: eroche@dzgns.com. Website: dzgns.com. **75%**

freelance written. Bimonthly magazine covering machine embroidery. Projects in *Designs in Machine Embroidery* must feature machine embroidery and teach readers new techniques. Estab. 1998. Circ. 50,000. Byline given. Pays on publication. Publishes ms an average of 2 months after acceptance. Editorial lead time 4 months. Submit seasonal material 4 months in advance. Accepts queries by mail, e-mail. NoResponds in 2-3 weeks to queries. Guidelines available online.

NONFICTION Needs how-to, interview, new product, technical. Does not want previously published items. **Buys 60 mss/year.** Query. Length: 250-1,000 words. **Pays $250-500.**

PHOTOS Send photos. Captions, identification of subjects, model releases required. Reviews GIF/JPEG files (300 dpi, 4×6 min.). Offers no additional payment for photos accepted with ms.

💲💲 DOLLHOUSE MINIATURES

68132 250th Ave., Kasson MN 55944. (507)634-3143. E-mail: usoffice@ashdown.co.uk. Website: dhminiatures.com. **80% freelance written**. Monthly magazine covering dollhouse scale miniatures. *Dollhouse Miniatures* is America's best-selling miniatures magazine and the definitive resource for artisans, collectors, and hobbyists. It promotes and supports the large national and international community of miniaturists through club columns, short reports, and by featuring reader projects and ideas. Estab. 1971. Circ. 25,000. Byline given. Pays on acceptance. Editorial lead time 6 months. Submit seasonal material 6 months in advance. Accepts queries by mail. Responds in 1 month to queries. Responds in 2 months to mss. Sample copy for $4.95. Guidelines available online.

NONFICTION Needs how-to, miniature projects of various scales in variety of media, interview, artisans, collectors, photo feature, dollhouses, collections, museums. No articles on miniature shops or essays. **Buys 50-60 mss/year.** Send complete ms. Length: 500-1,500 words. **Pays $50-350 for assigned articles. Pays $0-200 for unsolicited articles.**

PHOTOS Send photos. Captions, identification of subjects required. Reviews 35mm slides and larger, 3×5 prints. Photos are paid for with ms. Seldom buys individual photos.

💲💲 DOLLS

Jones Publishing, Inc., P.O. Box 5000, N7528 Aanstad Rd., Iola WI 54945. (715)445-5000. Fax: (715)445-4053. E-mail: carief@jonespublishing.com;jonespub@jonespublishing.com. Website: dollsmagazine.com. **75% freelance written**. "Magazine published 10 times/year covering dolls, doll artists, and related topics of interest to doll collectors and enthusiasts.". "*Dolls* enhances the joy of collecting by introducing readers to the best new dolls from around the world, along with the artists and designers who create them. It keeps readers up-to-date on shows, sales and special events in the doll world. With beautiful color photography, *Dolls* offers an array of easy-to-read, informative articles that help our collectors select the best buys." Estab. 1982. Circ. 100,000. Byline given. Pays on publication. Accepts queries by mail, e-mail. Responds in 1 month to queries.

NONFICTION Needs historical, how-to, interview, new product, photo feature. **Buys 55 mss/year.** Send complete ms. Length: 750-1,200 words. **Pays $75-300.**

PHOTOS Send photos. Captions, identification of subjects, model releases required. Reviews transparencies. Offers no additional payment for photos accepted with ms.

F+W MEDIA, INC. (MAGAZINE DIVISION)

4700 E. Galbraith Rd., Cincinnati OH 45236. (513)531-2690. E-mail: dave.pulvermacher@fwmedia.com. Website: fwmedia.com. "Each month, millions of enthusiasts turn to the magazines from F+W for inspiration, instruction, and encouragement. Readers are as varied as our categories, but all are assured of getting the best possible coverage of their favorite hobby." Publishes magazines in the following categories: **antiques and collectibles** (*Antique Trader*); **automotive** (*Military Vehicles, Old Cars Report Price Guide, Old Cars Weekly*); **coins and paper money** (*Bank Note Reporter, Coins Magazine, Coin Prices, Numismatic News, World Coin News*); **comics** (*Comics Buyer's Guide*); **construction** (*Frame Building News, Metal Roofing, Rural Builder*); **fine art** (*Collector's Guide, Pastel Journal, Southwest Art, The Artist's Magazine, Watercolor Artist*); **firearms and knives** (*Blade, Gun Digest—The Magazine, Gun-Knife Show Calendar*); **genealogy** (*Family Tree Magazine*); **graphic design** (*HOW Magazine, PRINT*); **horticulture** (*Horticulture*); **militaria** (*Military Trader*); **outdoors and hunting** (*Deer & Deer Hunting, Trapper & Predator Caller, Turkey & Turkey Hunting*); **records and CDs** (*Goldmine*); **sports** (*Sports Collectors Digest*); **woodworking** (*Popular Woodworking Magazine);* **writing** (*Writer's Digest*).

⚪ "Please see individual listings in the Consumer Magazines and Trade Journals sections for specific submission information about each magazine."

💲💲💲 FAMILY TREE MAGAZINE

F+W Media, Inc., 4700 E. Galbraith Rd., Cincinnati OH 45236. (513)531-2690. Fax: (513)891-7153. Website: familytreemagazine.com. **75% freelance written**. Magazine covering family history, heritage, and genealogy research. "*Family Tree Magazine* is a general-interest consumer magazine that helps readers discover, preserve, and celebrate their family's history. We cover genealogy, ethnic heritage, genealogy websites and software, photography and photo preservation, and other ways that families connect with their past." Estab. 1999. Circ. 75,000. Byline given. Pays on acceptance. Offers 25% kill fee. Publishes ms an average of 6 months after acceptance. Editorial lead time 8 months. Submit seasonal material 8 months in advance. Accepts queries by mail, e-mail. Responds in 1 month to queries. Sample copy for $8 from website. Guidelines available online.

NONFICTION Needs book excerpts, historical, how-to, genealogy, new product, photography, computer, technical, genealogy software, photography equipment. **Buys 60 mss/year.** Query with published clips. Length: 250-4,500 words. **Pays $25-800.** Does not pay expenses.

PHOTOS State availability. Captions required. Reviews color transparencies. Negotiates payment individually.

💲💲 FIBERARTS

Interweave Press, 201 E. Fourth St., Loveland CO 80537. (970)613-4654. Fax: (970)669-6117. E-mail: shansen@fiberarts.com. Website: fiberarts.com. **85% freelance written**. "Magazine published 5 times/year covering textiles as art and craft (contemporary trends in fiber sculpture, weaving, quilting, surface design, stitchery, papermaking, basketry, felting, wearable art, knitting, fashion, crochet, mixed textile techniques, ethnic dying, eccentric tidbits, etc.) for textile artists, craftspeople, collectors, teachers, museum and gallery staffs, and enthusiasts." Estab. 1975. Circ. 27,000. Byline given. Pays on publication. Publishes ms an average of 4 months after acceptance. Accepts queries by mail. Sample copy for $7.99. Guidelines available online.

NONFICTION Needs essays, interview, artist, opinion, personal experience, photo feature, technical, education, trends, exhibition reviews, textile news, book reviews, ethnic. Query with brief synopsis, SASE, and visuals. No phone queries. Length: 250-2,000 words. **Pays $70-550.**

PHOTOS Color slides, large-format transparencies, or 300 dpi (5-inch-high) TIFF images must accompany every query. "Please include caption information. The names and addresses of those mentioned in the article or to whom the visuals are to be returned are necessary.".

COLUMNS Commentary (thoughtful opinion on a topic of interest to our readers), 400 words; News and Notes; Profiles; The Creative Process; Travel and Traditions; Collecting; Reviews (exhibits and shows; summarize quality, significance, focus and atmosphere, then evaluate selected pieces for aesthetic quality, content and technique. "Because we have an international readership, brief biographical notes or quotes might be pertinent for locally or regionally known artists). (Do not cite works for which visuals are unavailable; you are not eligible to review a show in which you have participated as an artist, organizer, curator or juror.")

⚪💲 FIBRE FOCUS

17 Robinson Rd., RR4, Waterford ON N0E 1Y0 Canada. (519)443-7104. E-mail: ffpublisher@bell.net. Website: ohs.on.ca. **Contact:** Graham McCracken. **90% freelance written**. Quarterly magazine covering handweaving, spinning, basketry, beading, and other fibre arts. "Our readers are weavers and spinners who also do dyeing, knitting, basketry, feltmaking, papermaking, sheep raising, and craft supply. All articles deal with some aspect of these crafts." Estab. 1957. Circ. 1,000. Byline given. Pays within 30 days after publication. Editorial lead time 6 months. Submit seasonal material 6 months in advance. Responds in 1 month to queries. Sample copy for $8 Canadian. Guidelines available online.

NONFICTION Needs how-to, interview, new product, opinion, personal experience, technical, travel, book reviews. **Buys 40-60 mss/year.** Please contact the *Fibre Focus* Editor before undertaking a project or an article. Manuscripts may be submitted c/o Graham McCracken by phone or e-mail for anything you have to contribute for upcoming issues. **Feature article deadlines: Dec 31, March 31, June 30, Sept 15.** Please read the guidelines for contributing an article to *Fibre Focus.* Word length varies. **Pays $30 Canadian/published page.**

PHOTOS Send photos. Captions, identification of subjects required. Offers additional payment for photos accepted with ms.

$ $ FINE BOOKS & COLLECTIONS

OP Media, LLC, 4905 Pine Cone Drive #2, Durham NC 27707. (800)662-4834. Fax: (919)489-4767. E-mail: rebecca@finebooksmagazine.com. Website: finebooksmagazine.com. **90% freelance written.** Bimonthly magazine covering used and antiquarian bookselling and book collecting. We cover all aspects of selling and collecting out-of-print books. We emphasize good writing, interesting people, and unexpected view points. Estab. 2002. Circ. 5,000. Byline given. Pays on publication. Offers negotiable kill fee. Publishes ms an average of 4 months after acceptance. Editorial lead time 4 months. Submit seasonal material 4 months in advance. Accepts queries by mail, e-mail. Accepts simultaneous submissions. Responds in 1 month to queries. Responds in 2 months to mss. Sample copy for $6.50. Guidelines available online.

NONFICTION Needs book excerpts, essays, expose, general interest, historical, how-to, humor, opinion, personal experience, photo feature, travel. Does not want tales of the gold in my attic vein; stories emphasizing books as an investment. **Buys 40 mss/year.** Query with published clips. Length: 1,000-5,000 words. **Pays $100-400.** Sometimes pays expenses of writers on assignment.

PHOTOS State availability. Captions, identification of subjects required. Reviews GIF/JPEG files. Negotiates payment individually.

COLUMNS Digest (news about collectors, booksellers, and bookselling), 350 words; Book Reviews (reviews of books about books, writers, publishers, collecting), 400-800 words.

$ FINESCALE MODELER

Kalmbach Publishing Co., P.O. Box 1612, Waukesha WI 53187. Website: finescale.com. **80% freelance written. Eager to work with new/unpublished writers.** "Magazine published 10 times/year devoted to how-to-do-it modeling information for scale model builders who build non-operating aircraft, tanks, boats, automobiles, figures, dioramas, and science fiction and fantasy models.". Circ. 60,000. Byline given. Pays on acceptance. Publishes ms an average of 14 months after acceptance. Responds in 6 weeks to queries. Responds in 3 months to mss. Sample copy for SASE with 9×12 envelope and 3 first-class stamps.

🔑 "*Finescale Modeler* is especially looking for how-to articles for armor and aircraft modelers.

NONFICTION Needs how-to, build scale models, technical, research information for building models. Query or send complete ms. Length: 750-3,000 words. **Pays $60/published page minimum.**

PHOTOS "Send original high-res digital images, slides, or prints with submission. You can submit digital images at contribute.kalmbach.com.". Captions, identification of subjects required. Reviews transparencies, color prints. Pays $7.50 minimum for transparencies and $5 minimum for color prints.

COLUMNS *FSM* Showcase (photos plus description of model); *FSM* Tips and Techniques (model building hints and tips). **Buys 25-50 mss/year.** Send complete ms. **Pays $25-50.**

$ $ FINE TOOL JOURNAL

Antique & Collectible Tools, Inc., 27 Fickett Rd., Pownal ME 04069. (207)688-4962. Fax: (207)688-4831. E-mail: ceb@finetoolj.com. Website: finetoolj.com. **90% freelance written.** "Quarterly magazine specializing in older or antique hand tools from all traditional trades. Readers are primarily interested in woodworking tools, but some subscribers have interests in such areas as leatherworking, wrenches, kitchen, and machinist tools. Readers range from beginners just getting into the hobby to advanced collectors and organizations.". Estab. 1970. Circ. 2,500. Byline given. Pays on publication. Offers $50 kill fee. Publishes ms an average of 6 months after acceptance. Editorial lead time 9 months. Submit seasonal material 6 months in advance. Accepts queries by mail, online submission form. Responds in 2 months to queries. Responds in 3 months to mss. Sample copy for $5. Guidelines for #10 SASE.

NONFICTION Needs general interest, historical, how-to, make, use, fix and tune tools, interview, personal experience, photo feature, technical. **Buys 24 mss/year.** Send complete ms. Length: 400-2,000 words. **Pays $50-200.** Pays expenses of writers on assignment.

PHOTOS Send photos. Identification of subjects, model releases required. Reviews 4×5 prints. Negotiates payment individually.

COLUMNS Stanley Tools (new finds and odd types), 300-400 words; Tips of the Trade (how to use tools),

100-200 words. **Buys 12 mss/year.** Send complete ms. **Pays $30-60.**

😊😉 FINE WOODWORKING

The Taunton Press, P.O. Box 5506, Newtown CT 06470-5506. (203)426-8171. Fax: (203)426-3434. E-mail: fw@taunton.com. Website: finewoodworking. com. **Contact:** Tom McKenna. acquisitions. Bimonthly magazine on woodworking in the small shop. "All writers are also skilled woodworkers. It's more important that a contributor be a woodworker than a writer. Our editors (also woodworkers) will provide assistance and travel to shops to shoot all photography needed." Estab. 1975. Circ. 270,000. Byline given. Pays on acceptance. Offers variable kill fee. Submit seasonal material 6 months in advance. Accepts simultaneous submissions. Responds in 1 month to queries. Writer's guidelines free and online.

⚡➤ "We're looking for good articles on almost all aspects of woodworking from the basics of tool use, stock preparation and joinery, to specialized techniques and finishing. We're especially keen on articles about shop-built tools, jigs and fixtures, or any stage of design, construction, finishing and installation of cabinetry and furniture. Whether the subject involves fundamental methods or advanced techniques, we look for high-quality workmanship, thoughtful designs, and safe and proper procedures."

NONFICTION Needs how-to, woodworking. **Buys 120 mss/year.** Send article outline, any helpful drawings or photos, and proposal letter. **Pays $150/magazine page.** Sometimes pays expenses of writers on assignment.

COLUMNS Fundamentals (basic how-to and concepts for beginning woodworkers); Master Class (advanced techniques); Finish Line (finishing techniques); Question & Answer (woodworking Q&A); Methods of Work (shop tips); Tools & Materials (short reviews of new tools). **Buys 400 mss/year. Pays $50-150/published page.**

😊😉 THE HOME SHOP MACHINIST

P.O. Box 629, Traverse City MI 49685. (231)946-3712. Fax: (231)946-6180. E-mail: cfoster@villagepress. com;gbulliss@villagepress.com. Website: home-shopmachinist.net. Craig Foster, managing editor. **Contact:** George Bulliss, editor. **95% freelance written.** Bimonthly magazine covering machining and

metalworking for the hobbyist. Circ. 34,000. Byline given. Pays on publication. Publishes ms an average of 2 years after acceptance. Responds in 2 months to queries. Sample copy free. Guidelines for 9×12 SASE.

NONFICTION Needs how-to, projects designed to upgrade present shop equipment or hobby model projects that require machining, technical, should pertain to metalworking, machining, drafting, layout, welding or foundry work for the hobbyist. No fiction or people features. **Buys 40 mss/year.** Send complete ms. open—whatever it takes to do a thorough job. **Pays $40/published page, plus $9/published photo.**

PHOTOS Send photos. Captions, identification of subjects required. Pays $9-40 for 5×7 b&w prints; $70/page for camera-ready art; $40 for b&w cover photo.

COLUMNS Become familiar with our magazine before submitting. Book Reviews; New Product Reviews; Micro-Machining; Foundry. Length: 600-1,500 words. **Buys 25-30 mss/year.** Query. **Pays $40-70.**

FILLERS Buys 12-15 mss/year. Length: 100-300 words. **Pays $30-48.**

😊😉 KITPLANES

A Primedia Publication, Kitplanes, 302 Argonne Ave., Suite B105, Long Beach CA 90803. E-mail: editorial@kitplanes.com. Website: kitplanes.com. **Contact:** Marc Cook, editor. **50% freelance written. Eager to work with new/unpublished writers.** Monthly magazine covering self-construction of private aircraft for pilots and builders. Estab. 1984. Circ. 72,000. Byline given. Pays on publication. Publishes ms an average of 3 months after acceptance. Submit seasonal material 6 months in advance. Accepts queries by mail, e-mail. Responds in 4 weeks to queries. Responds in 6 weeks to mss Sample copy for $6. Guidelines available online.

NONFICTION Needs general interest, how-to, interview, new product, personal experience, photo feature, technical. No general-interest aviation articles, or My First Solo type of articles. **Buys 80 mss/year.** Query. Length: 500-3,000 words. **Pays $150-500 including story photos.**

PHOTOS State availability of or send photos. Captions, identification of subjects required. Pays $300 for cover photos.

😊😉 KNIVES ILLUSTRATED

2400 East Katella Ave., Suite 300, Anaheim CA 92806. (714)939-9991. Fax: (714)456-0146. E-mail: BVoyles@Beckett.com. Website: knivesillustrated.com. **40-50%**

freelance written. Bimonthly magazine covering high-quality factory and custom knives. We publish articles on different types of factory and custom knives, how-to make knives, technical articles, shop tours, articles on knife makers and artists. Must have knowledge about knives and the people who use and make them. We feature the full range of custom and high tech production knives, from miniatures to swords, leaving nothing untouched. We're also known for our outstanding how-to articles and technical features on equipment, materials and knife making supplies. We do not feature knife maker profiles as such, although we do spotlight some makers by featuring a variety of their knives and insight into their background and philosophy. Estab. 1987. Circ. 35,000. Byline given. Pays on publication. Editorial lead time 3 months. Accepts queries by mail, e-mail, fax. Responds in 2 weeks to queries. Sample copy available. Guidelines for #10 SASE.

NONFICTION Needs general interest, historical, how-to, interview, new product, photo feature, technical. **Buys 35-40 mss/year.** Query. Length: 400-2,000 words. **Pays $100-500.**

PHOTOS Send photos. Captions, identification of subjects, model releases required. Reviews 35mm, 2 ¼ × 2 ¼, 4×5 transparencies, 5×7 prints, electronic images in TIFF, GIF or JPEG Mac format. Negotiates payment individually.

⊕⊕ THE LEATHER CRAFTERS & SADDLERS JOURNAL

222 Blackburn St., Rhinelander WI 54501-3777. (715)362-5393. Fax: (715)362-5391. E-mail: tworjournal@newnorth.net. **100% freelance written.** Bimonthly magazine. "A leather-working publication with how-to, step-by-step instructional articles using patterns for leathercraft, leather art, custom saddle, boot, etc. A complete resource for leather, tools, machinery, and allied materials, plus leather industry news." Estab. 1990. Circ. 8,000. Byline given. Pays on publication. Publishes ms an average of 4 months after acceptance. Submit seasonal material 6 months in advance. Accepts queries by mail, e-mail, fax, phone. Accepts simultaneous submissions. Responds in 1 month to mss. Sample copy for $7. Guidelines for #10 SASE.

NONFICTION Buys 75 mss/year. Send complete ms. Length: 500-2,500 words. **Pays $20-250 for assigned articles. Pays $25-150 for unsolicited articles.**

REPRINTS Send tearsheet or photocopy. Pays 50% of amount paid for an original article.

PHOTOS Send good contrast color print photos and full-size patterns and/or full-size photo-carve patterns with submission. If by e-mail, send instructions in word document format, photos and patterns as attachments. Lack of these reduces payment amount. Captions required.

COLUMNS Beginners; Intermediate; Artists; Western Design; Saddlemakers; International Design; and Letters (the open exchange of information between all peoples). Length: 500-2,500 words on all.

⊕ LINN'S STAMP NEWS

Amos Press, P.O. Box 29, Sidney OH 45365. (937)498-0801. Fax: (937)498-0886. E-mail: linns@linns.com. Website: linns.com. **Contact:** Michael Baadke, Editor. **50% freelance written.** Weekly tabloid on the stamp collecting hobby. "All articles must be about philatelic collectibles. Our goal at *Linn's* is to create a weekly publication that is indispensable to stamp collectors." Estab. 1928. Circ. 33,000. Byline given. Pays within 1 month of publication. Publishes ms an average of 4 months after acceptance. Submit seasonal material 2 months in advance. Responds in 6 weeks to queries. Sample copy online. Guidelines available online.

NONFICTION Needs general interest, historical, how-to, interview, technical, club and show news, current issues, auction realization and recent discoveries. "No articles merely giving information on background of stamp subject. Must have philatelic information included." **Buys 40 mss/year.** Send complete ms. 750 words maximum **Pays $40-75.** Sometimes pays expenses of writers on assignment.

PHOTOS Good illustrations a must. Send scans with submission. Captions required. Reviews digital color at twice actual size (300 dpi). Offers no additional payment for photos accepted with ms.

⊕ LOST TREASURE, INC.

P.O. Box 451589, Grove OK 74345. (866)469-6224. Fax: (918)786-2192. E-mail: managingeditor@losttreasure.com. Website: losttreasure.com. **75% freelance written.** Monthly and annual magazines covering lost treasure. Estab. 1966. Circ. 55,000. Byline given. Pays on publication. Accepts queries by mail, e-mail, fax. Responds in 1 month to queries. Responds in 2 months to mss. Sample copy for #10 SASE. Guidelines for 10×13 SAE with $1.52 postage or online.

NONFICTION **Buys 225 mss/year.** Query on *Treasure Cache* only. Length: 1,000-2,000 words. **Pays 4¢/word.**

PHOTOS Color or b&w prints, hand-drawn or copied maps, art with source credit with mss will help sell your story.We are always looking for cover photos with or without accompanying ms. Pays $100/published cover photo. Must be vertical. Captions required. Pays $5/published photo.

$$ MILITARY VEHICLES

F+W Media, Inc., 700 E. State St., Iola WI 54990-0001. (715)445-4612. Fax: (715)445-4087. Website: militaryvehiclesmagazine.com. **50% freelance written.** Bimonthly magazine covering historic military vehicles. Dedicated to serving people who collect, restore, and drive historic military vehicles. Circ. 18,500. Byline given. Pays on publication. Publishes ms an average of 1 month after acceptance. Accepts queries by mail, e-mail. Accepts simultaneous submissions. Responds in 1 week to queries. Responds in 1 month to mss. Sample copy for $5.

NONFICTION Needs historical, how-to, technical. **Buys 20 mss/year.** Send complete ms. Length: 1,300-2,600 words. **Pays $0-200.**

PHOTOS True required.

COLUMNS **Pays $0-75.**

$ MODEL CARS MAGAZINE

Golden Bell Press, 2403 Champa St., Denver CO 80205. (808)754-1378. E-mail: gregg@modelcarsmag.com. Website: modelcarsmag.com. **25% freelance written.** Magazine published 9 times year covering model cars, trucks, and other automotive models. "*Model Cars Magazine* is the hobby's how-to authority for the automotive modeling hobbiest. We are on the forefront of the hobby, our editorial staff are model car builders, and every single one of our writers have a passion for the hobby that is evident in the articles and stories that we publish. We are the model car magazine written by and for model car builders." Estab. 1999. Circ. 8,500. Byline given. Pays on publication. Publishes ms an average of 2-3 months after acceptance. Editorial lead time 2-3 months. Accepts queries by mail, e-mail. Sample copy for $5.50.

NONFICTION Needs how-to. Length: 600-3,000 words. **Pays $50/page. Pays $25/page for unsolicited articles.** Sometimes pays expenses of writers on assignment.

$ MONITORING TIMES

Grove Enterprises, Inc., 7546 Hwy. 64 W., Brasstown NC 28902-0098. (828)837-9200. E-mail: editor@monitoringtimes.com. Website: monitoringtimes.com. **15% freelance written.** Monthly magazine for radio hobbyists. Estab. 1982. Circ. 15,000. Byline given. Pays on publication. Publishes ms an average of 4 months after acceptance. Submit seasonal material 4 months in advance. Accepts queries by mail, e-mail. Responds in 1 month to queries. Sample copy for 9×12 SAE and 9 first-class stamps. Guidelines available online.

NONFICTION Needs general interest, how-to, humor, interview, personal experience, photo feature, technical. **Buys 50 mss/year.** Query. Length: 1,500-3,000 words. **Pays average of $50/published page.**

REPRINTS Send photocopy and information about when and where the material previously appeared. Pays 50% of amount paid for an original article

PHOTOS Send photos. Captions required.

COLUMNS Query managing editor.

$ NATIONAL COMMUNICATIONS MAGAZINE

Norm Schrein, Inc., P.O. Box 291918, Kettering OH 45429. (937)299-7226. Fax: (937)299-1323. E-mail: norm@bearcat1.com. Website: nat-com.org. **Contact:** Norm Schrein. **100% freelance written.** Bimonthly magazine covering radio as a hobby. Estab. 1990. Circ. 5,000. Byline given. Pays on publication. Publishes ms an average of 2 months after acceptance. Editorial lead time 2 months. Submit seasonal material 2 months in advance. Accepts queries by phone. Accepts simultaneous submissions. Sample copy for $4.

💬 "National Communications is the magazine for every radio user."

NONFICTION Needs how-to, interview, new product, personal experience, photo feature, technical. Does not want articles off topic of the publication's audience (radio hobbyists). **Buys 2-3 mss/year.** Query. Length: 300 words. **Pays $75+.**

PHOTOS Send photos. Captions, identification of subjects required. Reviews GIF/JPEG files. Offers no additional payment for photos accepted with ms.

⊘ OLD CARS REPORT PRICE GUIDE

F+W Media, Inc., 700 E. State St., Iola WI 54990-0001. (715)445-2214. Fax: (715)445-4087. E-mail: ron.kowalke@fwmedia.com; oldcarspg@fwmedia.com. Website:

oldcarspriceguide.net. Bimonthly magazine covering collector vehicle values from 1930-2004. Estab. 1978. Circ. 60,000. Sample copy free.

○ This publication is not accepting freelance submissions at this time.

⊝⊝ PAPER CRAFTS MAGAZINE

Primedia Magazines, 14850 Pony Express Rd., Bluffdale UT 84065. (801)816-8300. Fax: (801)816-8302. E-mail: **ksmith@papercraftsmag.com**. Website: papercraftsmag.com. Magazine published 10 times/year designed to help readers make creative and rewarding handmade crafts. The main focus is fresh, craft-related projects our reader can make and display in her home or give as gifts. Estab. 1978. Circ. 300,000. Byline given. Pays on acceptance. Editorial lead time 6 months. Accepts queries by mail, e-mail. Responds in 1 month to queries. Guidelines for #10 SASE.

NONFICTION Needs how-to. **Buys 300 mss/year.** Query with photo or sketch of how-to project. Do not send the actual project until request. **Pays $100-500.**

⊝ PIECEWORK MAGAZINE

Interweave Press, Inc., 201 E. 4th St., Loveland CO 80537-5655. (800) 272-2193. Fax: (970)669-6117. E-mail: piecework@interweave.com. Website: interweave.com. **90% freelance written**. Bimonthly magazine covering needlework history. *PieceWork* celebrates the rich tradition of needlework and the history of the people behind it. Stories and projects on embroidery, cross-stitch, knitting, crocheting, and quilting, along with other textile arts, are featured in each issue. Estab. 1993. Circ. 30,000. Byline given. Pays on publication. Offers 25% kill fee. Editorial lead time 6 months. Submit seasonal material 6 months in advance. Accepts queries by mail, e-mail, fax, phone. Responds in 6 months to queries. Sample copy and writer's guidelines free.

NONFICTION Needs book excerpts, historical, how-to, interview, new product. No contemporary needlework articles. **Buys 25-30 mss/year.** Send complete ms. Length: 1,000-5,000 words. **Pays $100/printed page.**

PHOTOS State availability of or send photos. Captions, identification of subjects, model releases required. Reviews transparencies, prints.

⊝ POPULAR COMMUNICATIONS

CQ Communications, Inc., 25 Newbridge Rd., Hicksville NY 11801. (516)681-2922. Fax: (516)681-2926. E-mail: editor@popular-communications.com. Web-

site: popular-communications.com. **25% freelance written**. Monthly magazine covering the radio communications hobby. Estab. 1982. Circ. 40,000. Byline given. Pays on publication. Publishes ms an average of 6 months after acceptance. Editorial lead time 3 months. Submit seasonal material 6 months in advance. Accepts queries by mail, e-mail. Responds in 1 month to queries. Responds in 2 months to mss. Sample copy free. Guidelines for #10 SASE.

NONFICTION Needs general interest, how-to, antenna construction, humor, new product, photo feature, technical. **Buys 6-10 mss/year.** Query. Length: 1,800-3,000 words. **Pays $135/printed page.**

PHOTOS State availability. Captions, identification of subjects, model releases required. Negotiates payment individually.

⊝⊝⊝⊝ POPULAR MECHANICS

Hearst Corp., 300 W. 57th St., New York NY 10019. (212)649-2000. E-mail: popularmechanics@hearst.com. Website: popularmechanics.com. **Up to 50% freelance written**. Monthly magazine on technology, science, automotive, home, outdoors. We are a men's service magazine that addresses the diverse interests of today's male, providing him with information to improve the way he lives. We cover stories from do-it-yourself projects to technological advances in aerospace, military, automotive and so on. Estab. 1902. Circ. 1,200,000. Offers 25% kill fee. Publishes ms an average of 6 months after acceptance. Submit seasonal material 6 months in advance.

○ "By submitting your anecdote and/or image, you give Popular Mechanics the right to publish your story and photo in the magazine or on the Website. Popular Mechanics reserves the right to use your real name or a pseudonym, as well as edit text for clarity and conciseness. All submissions become the property of Popular Mechanics. You represent that the information you give us will be truthful in every respect."

NONFICTION Pays $1/word and up.

⊝⊝ POPULAR WOODWORKING MAGAZINE

F+W Media, Inc., 4700 E. Galbraith Rd., Cincinnati OH 45236. (513)531-2690, ext. 11348. E-mail: megan.fitzpatrick@fwmedia.com. Website: popularwoodworking.com. **45% freelance written**. Magazine published 7 times/year. "*Popular Woodworking Magazine* invites woodworkers of all skill levels into a community of professionals who share their hard-won shop experience through in-depth projects and technique articles, which help the readers hone their existing skills and develop new ones for both hand and power tools. Related stories increase the readers' understanding and enjoyment of their craft. Any project submitted must be aesthetically pleasing, of sound construction, and offer a challenge to readers. On the average, we use 2 freelance features per issue. Our primary needs are 'how-to' articles on woodworking. Our secondary need is for articles that will inspire discussion concerning woodworking. Tone of articles should be conversational and informal but knowledgeable, as if the writer is speaking directly to the reader. Our readers are the woodworking hobbyist and small woodshop owner. Writers should have an extensive knowledge of woodworking and excellent woodworking techniques and skills." Estab. 1981. Circ. 180,000. Byline given. Pays on acceptance. Publishes ms an average of 10 months after acceptance. Submit seasonal material 6 months in advance. Accepts queries by mail, e-mail, fax, phone. Responds in 2 months to queries Sample copy for $5.99 and 9×12 SAE with 6 first-class stamps or online. Guidelines available online.

NONFICTION Needs how-to (on woodworking projects, with plans), humor (woodworking anecdotes), technical (woodworking techniques). No tool reviews. **Buys 10 mss/year.** Send complete ms. **Pay starts at $250/published page.**

REPRINTS Send photocopy with rights for sale noted and information about when and where the material previously appeared. Pays 25% of amount paid for an original article.

PHOTOS Photographic quality affects acceptance. Need professional quality, high-resolution digital images of step-by-step construction process. Send photos. Captions, identification of subjects required.

COLUMNS Tricks of the Trade (helpful techniques), End Grain (thoughts on woodworking as a profession or hobby, can be humorous or serious), 500-600 words. **Buys 20 columns/yr. mss/year.** Query.

$ $ THE QUILTER

All American Crafts, Inc., 7 Waterloo Rd., Stanhope NJ 07874. (973)347-6900 ext. 135. E-mail: editors@thequiltermag.com. Website: thequiltermag.com. **Contact:** Laurette Koserowski, editor. **45% freelance written.** Bimonthly magazine on quilting. Estab. 1988. Byline given. Pays on publication. Publishes ms an average of 6 months after acceptance. Submit seasonal material 6 months in advance. Accepts queries by mail, phone. Responds in 6 weeks to queries. Sample copy for sae with 9×12 envelope and 4 First-Class stamps. Guidelines available online.

"Seeking articles about quilters and quilted items to publish in bimonthly magazine, *The Quilter*. This publication is an instructional magazine that features patterns in patchwork and appliquè techniques. The editors accept articles relating to quilting, detailed quilting projects, and profiles of outstanding quilting instructors and their techniques. Holiday items are always welcome. No fiction or poetry is accepted. It is recommended that you submit a query first. Manuscripts must be typewritten, double-spaced on one side of the paper and, if possible, submitted on 3.5" floppy disks or PC-formatted CDs saved in Microsoft Word (.DOC) or text (.TXT) format. Write simple, clear, and thorough directions, including a list of materials, finished sizes, seam allowances, assembly diagrams, appliquè patterns, etc. Be sure patterns are perfectly accurate, and marked clearly with cutting, sewing, and fabric grain directions. Articles about quilts and quilt exhibits must be accompanied by professional quality digital images. If you submit a query, attach a good photograph and description of your project. Include a SASE with sufficient postage for the return of your material. Submissions without a SASE will not be returned. *The Quilter* pays $150 - 250 per article for first North American Rights for original, hitherto unpublished, articles. For quilts, pillows, and other projects, payment is made at a flat rate of $175 - $375 per project. Payment is made upon publication. We respond within approximately six (6) weeks on manuscripts and queries. Send all designs and manuscripts to: *The Quilter* or e-mail editors@thequiltermag.com."

NONFICTION Query with published clips. Length: 350-1,000 words. **Pays $150-250/article for original, unpublished mss. Project payments are a flat rate of $175-$375/project.**

PHOTOS Send photos. Captions, identification of subjects required. Reviews transparencies, prints. Offers $10-15/photo.

COLUMNS Feature Teacher (qualified quilt teachers with teaching involved—with slides); Profile (award-winning and interesting quilters). Length: 1,000 words maximum. **Pays 10¢/word, $15/photo**

⊜⊜ QUILTER'S WORLD

185 Sweet Rd., Lincoln ME 04457. Website: quilters-world.com. **100% freelance written. Works with a small number of new/unpublished writers each year.** Bimonthly magazine covering quilting. "*Quilter's World* is a general quilting publication. We accept articles about special quilters, techniques, coverage of unusual quilts at quilt shows, special interest quilts, human interest articles and patterns. We include 2 articles and 12-15 patterns in every issue. Reader is 30-70 years old, midwestern." Circ. 130,000. Byline given. Pays 45 days after acceptance. Submit seasonal material 10 months in advance. Accepts queries by mail, e-mail. Responds in 3 months to queries. Guidelines available online.

NONFICTION Needs how-to, interview, new product, photo feature feature, technical, quilters, quilt products. Query or send complete ms **Pays $100-$200 for articles; $50-550 for quilt designs**

PHOTOS State availability. Captions required. Reviews Color slides.

⊜ RENAISSANCE MAGAZINE

80 Hathaway Drive, Stratford CT 06615. (800)232-2224. Fax: (800)775-2729. E-mail: editortom@renaissancemagazine.com. Website: renaissancemagazine.com. **90% freelance written.** Bimonthly magazine covering the history of the Middle Ages and the Renaissance. Our readers include historians, reenactors, roleplayers, medievalists, and Renaissance Faire enthusiasts. Estab. 1996. Circ. 33,000. Byline given. Pays on publication. Publishes ms an average of 1 year after acceptance. Editorial lead time 6 months. Submit seasonal material 4 months in advance. Accepts queries by mail, e-mail, fax, phone. Responds in 3 weeks to queries. Responds in 2 months to mss. Sample copy for $9. Guidelines available online.

⊙ The editor reports an interest in seeing costuming how-to articles; and Renaissance Festival insider articles.

NONFICTION Needs essays, expose, historical, how-to, interview, new product, opinion, photo feature, re-

ligious, travel. **Buys 25 mss/year.** Query or send ms Length: 1,000-5,000 words. **Pays 8¢/word.**

PHOTOS State availability. Captions, identification of subjects, model releases required. Reviews contact sheets, negatives, transparencies, prints. Pays $7.50/photo.

⊜⊜ ROCK & GEM

Miller Magazines, Inc., Rock & Gem Submissions, P.O. Box 6925, Ventura CA 93006. (805)644-3824, ext. 29. Fax: (805)644-3875. E-mail: editor@rockngem.com. Website: rockngem.com. **99% freelance written.** Monthly magazine covering rockhounding field trips, how-to lapidary projects, minerals, fossils, gold prospecting, mining, etc. See guidelines. This is not a scientific journal. Its articles appeal to amateurs, beginners, and experts, but its tone is conversational and casual, not stuffy. It's for hobbyists. Estab. 1971. Circ. 55,000. Byline given. Pays on publication. Editorial lead time 4 months. Submit seasonal material 6 months in advance. Accepts queries by mail. Guidelines available online.

⊙Contributor agreement required.

NONFICTION Needs general interest, how-to, personal experience, photo feature, travel. Does not want to see The 25th Anniversary of the Pet Rock, or anything so scientific that it could be a thesis. **Buys 156-200 mss/year.** Send complete ms. Length: 2,000-4,000 words. **Pays $100-250.**

PHOTOS Accepts prints, slides or digital art on disk or CD only (provide thumbnails). Send photos. Captions required. Offers no additional payment for photos accepted with ms.

⊜⊜ SEW NEWS

Creative Crafts Group, 741 Corporate Circle, Suite A, Golden CO 80401. (303)215-5600. Fax: (303)215-5601. E-mail: sewnews@sewnews.com. Website: sewnews.com. **70% freelance written. Works with a small number of new/unpublished writers each year.** Monthly magazine covering fashion, gift, and home-dec sewing. "Our magazine is for the beginning home sewer to the professional dressmaker. It expresses the fun, creativity, and excitement of sewing." Estab. 1980. Circ. 185,000. Byline given. Pays on publication. Publishes ms an average of 6 months after acceptance. Submit seasonal material 6 months in advance. Accepts queries by mail, e-mail, fax. Responds in 2 months to mss. Sample copy for $5.99. Guidelines for #10 SAE with 2 first-class stamps or online.

All stories submitted to *Sew News* must be on disk or CD.

NONFICTION Needs how-to, sewing techniques, interview, interesting personalities in home-sewing field. **Buys 200-240 mss/year.** Query with published clips if available Length: 500-2,000 words. **Pays $25-500.**

PHOTOS Prefers digital images, color photos, or slides. Send photos. Identification of subjects required. Payment included in ms price.

$ SHUTTLE SPINDLE & DYEPOT

Handweavers Guild of America, Inc., 1255 Buford Hwy., Suite 211, Suwanee GA 30024. (678)730-0010. Fax: (678)730-0836. E-mail: hga@weavespindye.org. Website: weavespindye.org. **60% freelance written.** Quarterly magazine. "Quarterly membership publication of the Handweavers Guild of America, Inc., *Shuttle Spindle & Dyepot* magazine seeks to encourage excellence in contemporary fiber arts and to support the preservation of techniques and traditions in fiber arts. It also provides inspiration for fiber artists of all levels and develops public awareness and appreciation of the fiber arts. *Shuttle Spindle & Dyepot* appeals to a highly educated, creative, and very knowledgeable audience of fiber artists and craftsmen, weavers, spinners, dyers, and basket makers." Estab. 1969. Circ. 30,000. Byline given. Pays on publication. Publishes ms an average of 6 months after acceptance. Editorial lead time 8 months. Submit seasonal material 8 months in advance. Accepts queries by mail, e-mail, fax, phone. Sample copy for $8.00 plus shipping. Guidelines available online.

NONFICTION Needs inspirational, interview, new product, personal experience, photo feature, technical, travel. No self-promotional and no articles from those without knowledge of area/art/artists. **Buys 40 mss/year.** Query with published clips. Length: 1,000-2,000 words. **Pays $75-150.**

COLUMNS Books and Videos, News and Information, Calendar and Conference, Travel and Workshop (all fiber/art related).

$ SUNSHINE ARTIST

Palm House Publishing Inc., 4075 L.B. McLeod Rd., Suite E, Orlando FL 32811. (800)597-2573. Fax: (407)228-9862. E-mail: business@sunshineartist.com. Website: sunshineartist.com. Monthly magazine covering art shows in the US. We are the premiere marketing/reference magazine for artists and crafts professionals who earn their living through art shows nationwide. We list more than 2,000 shows monthly, critique many of them, and publish articles on marketing, selling and other issues of concern to professional show circuit artists. Estab. 1972. Circ. 12,000. Byline given. Pays on publication. Publishes ms an average of 3 months after acceptance. Responds in 2 months to queries. Sample copy for $5.

NONFICTION No how-to. **Buys 5-10 freelance mss/year.** Send complete ms. Length: 1,000-2,000 words. **Pays $50-150.**

REPRINTS Send photocopy and information about when and where the material previously appeared.

PHOTOS Send photos. Captions, identification of subjects, model releases required. Offers no additional payment for photos accepted with ms.

$$ TATTOO REVUE

Art & Ink Enterprises, Inc., c/o Outlaw Biker/Art & Ink Publications, 1000 Seaboard Street Suite B4, Charlotte NC 28206-2991. (704)333-3331. Fax: (704)333-3433. E-mail: inked@skinartmag.com. Website: skinart.com. **25% freelance written.** Interview and profile magazine published 4 times/year covering tattoo artists, their art and lifestyle. All writers must have knowledge of tattoos. Features include interviews with tattoo artists and collectors. Estab. 1990. Circ. 100,000. Byline given. Pays on publication. Publishes ms an average of 3 months after acceptance. Editorial lead time 3 months. Submit seasonal material 5 months in advance. Accepts queries by mail, e-mail, fax. Responds in 2 weeks to queries. Sample copy for $5.98. Guidelines for #10 SASE.

NONFICTION Needs book excerpts, historical, humor, interview, photo feature. Special issues: Publishes special convention issues—dates and locations provided upon request. No first-time experiences—our readers already know. **Buys 10-30 mss/year.** Send complete ms. Length: 500-2,500 words. **Pays $25-200.**

PHOTOS Send photos. Captions, identification of subjects, model releases required. Reviews transparencies, prints. Offers $0-10/photo.

COLUMNS **Buys 10-30 mss/year.** Query with or without published clips or send complete ms. **Pays $25-50.**

FILLERS Needs anecdotes, facts, gags, newsbreaks, short humor. **Buys 10-20 mss/year.** Length: 50-2,000 words.

◎ⓢ TEDDY BEAR REVIEW

Jones Publishing, Inc., P.O. Box 5000, Iola WI 54945-5000. (800)331-0038. Fax: (715)445-4053. Website: teddybearreview.com. **65% freelance written. Works with a small number of new/unpublished writers each year.** Bimonthly magazine on teddy bears for collectors, enthusiasts and bearmakers. Estab. 1985. Byline given. Payment upon publication on the last day of the month the issue is mailed. Submit seasonal material 6 months in advance. Sample copy and writer's guidelines for $2 and 9×12 SAE.

NONFICTION Needs historical, how-to, interview. No articles from the bear's point of view. **Buys 30-40 mss/year.** Query with published clips. Length: 900-1,500 words. **Pays $100-350.**

PHOTOS Send photos. Captions required. Reviews transparencies, prints. Offers no additional payment for photos accepted with ms.

◎ⓢ THREADS

Taunton Press, 63 S. Main St., P.O. Box 5506, Newtown CT 06470. (203)426-8171. Fax: (203)426-3434. E-mail: th@taunton.com. Website: threadsmagazine.com. Bimonthly magazine covering garment sewing, garment design, and embellishments (including quilting and embroidery). "We're seeking proposals from hands-on authors who first and foremost have a skill. Being an experienced writer is of secondary consideration." Estab. 1985. Circ. 129,000. Byline given. Offers $150 kill fee. Editorial lead time 4 months. Responds in 1-2 months to queries. Guidelines available online.

NONFICTION $150/page.

COLUMNS Product reviews; Book reviews; Tips; Closures (stories of a humorous nature). Query. **Closures pays $150/page. Each sewing tip printed pays $25.**

◎ⓢ TOY FARMER

Toy Farmer Publications, 7496 106 Ave. SE, LaMoure ND 58458-9404. (701)883-5206. Fax: (701)883-5209. E-mail: info@toyfarmer.com. Website: toyfarmer.com. **70% freelance written.** Monthly magazine covering farm toys. Estab. 1978. Circ. 27,000. Byline given. Pays on publication. Editorial lead time 2 months. Submit seasonal material 3 months in advance. Accepts queries by mail, e-mail, fax, phone. Responds in 1 month to queries. Responds in 2 months to mss. Writer's guidelines available upon request.

○ Youth involvement is strongly encouraged.

NONFICTION Needs general interest, historical, interview, new product, personal experience, technical, book introductions. **Buys 100 mss/year.** Query with published clips. Length: 800-1,500 words. **Pays 10¢/word.** Sometimes pays expenses of writers on assignment.

PHOTOS Must be 35mm originals or very high resolution digital images. State availability.

◎ⓢ TOY TRUCKER & CONTRACTOR

Toy Farmer Publications, 7496 106th Ave. SE, LaMoure ND 58458-9404. (701)883-5206. Fax: (701)883-5209. E-mail: info@toyfarmer.com. Website: toytrucker.com. **40% freelance written.** Monthly magazine covering collectible toys. "We are a magazine on hobby and collectible toy trucks and construction pieces." Estab. 1990. Circ. 6,500. Byline given. Pays on publication. Editorial lead time 2 months. Submit seasonal material 3 months in advance. Accepts queries by mail, e-mail, fax, phone. Responds in 1 month to queries. Responds in 2 months to mss. Writer's guidelines available on request.

NONFICTION Needs historical, interview, new product, personal experience, technical. **Buys 35 mss/ year.** Query. Length: 800-1,400 words. **Pays 10¢/word.** Sometimes pays expenses of writers on assignment.

PHOTOS Must be 35mm originals or very high resolution digital images. Send photos. Captions, identification of subjects, model releases required.

ⓢ WESTERN & EASTERN TREASURES

People's Publishing Co., Inc., P.O. Box 219, San Anselmo CA 94979. Website: treasurenet.com. **100% freelance written.** Monthly magazine covering hobby/sport of metal detecting/treasure hunting. "*Western & Eastern Treasures* provides concise, yet comprehensive coverage of every aspect of the sport/hobby of metal detecting and treasure hunting with a strong emphasis on current, accurate information; innovative, field-proven advice and instruction; and entertaining, effective presentation." Estab. 1966. Circ. 50,000. Byline given. Pays on publication. Publishes ms an average of 4+ months after acceptance. Editorial lead time 4 months. Submit seasonal material 3-4 months in advance. NoResponds in 3 months to mss. Sample copy for sae with 9×12 envelope and 5 First-Class stamps. Guidelines for #10 SASE.

NONFICTION Needs how-to, tips and finds for metal detectorists, interview, only people in metal detecting, personal experience, positive metal detector experiences, technical, only metal detecting hobby-related, helping in local community with metal detecting skills (i.e., helping local police locate evidence at crime scenes—all volunteer basis). Special issues: *Silver & Gold Annual* (editorial deadline February each year)—looking for articles 1,500+ words, plus photos on the subject of locating silver and/or gold using a metal detector. No fiction, poetry, or puzzles. **Buys 150+ mss/year.** Send complete ms. Length: 1,000-1,500 words. **Pays 3¢/word for articles.**

PHOTOS Send photos. Captions, identification of subjects required. Reviews 35mm transparencies, prints, digital scans (minimum 300 dpi). Offers $5 minimum/photo.

§§ WOODSHOP NEWS

Soundings Publications, Inc., 10 Bokum Rd., Essex CT 06426. (860)767-8227. Fax: (860)767-1048. E-mail: editorial@woodshopnews.com. Website: woodshopnews.com. **20% freelance written.** Monthly tabloid covering woodworking for professionals. Solid business news and features about woodworking companies. Feature stories about interesting professional woodworkers. Some how-to articles. Estab. 1986. Circ. 60,000. Byline given. Pays on publication. Publishes ms an average of 3 months after acceptance. Submit seasonal material 4 months in advance. Accepts queries by mail, e-mail, fax. Responds in 1 month to queries. Sample copy available online. Guidelines free.

○ *Woodshop News* needs writers in major cities in all regions except the Northeast. Also looking for more editorial opinion pieces.

NONFICTION Needs how-to, query first, interview, new product, opinion, personal experience, photo feature. Key word is newsworthy. No general interest profiles of folksy woodworkers. **Buys 15-25 mss/year.** Send complete ms. Length: 100-1,200 words. **Pays $50-500 for assigned articles. Pays $40-250 for unsolicited articles.** Pays expenses of writers on assignment.

PHOTOS Captions, identification of subjects required. Reviews contact sheets, prints.

COLUMNS Pro Shop (business advice, marketing, employee relations, taxes, etc., for the professional written by an established professional in the field); Finishing (how-to and techniques, materials, spraybooths, staining; written by experienced finishers), both 1,200-1,500 words. **Buys 18 mss/year.** Query. **Pays $200-300.**

HOME AND GARDEN

§§ THE AMERICAN GARDENER

7931 E. Boulevard Dr., Alexandria VA 22308-1300. (703)768-5700. Fax: (703)768-7533. E-mail: editor@ahs.org; myee@ahs.org. Website: ahs.org. **Contact:** Mary Yee, art director. **60% freelance written.** Bimonthly, 64-page, four-color magazine covering gardening and horticulture. "This is the official publication of the American Horticultural Society (AHS), a national, nonprofit, membership organization for gardeners, founded in 1922. The AHS mission is 'to open the e of all Americans to the vital connection between people and plants, and to inspire all Americans to become responsible caretakers of the earth, to celebrate America's diversity through the art and science of horticulture, and to lead this effort by sharing the society's unique national resources with all Americans.' All articles are also published on members-only website." Estab. 1922. Circ. 20,000. Byline given. Pays on publication. Offers 25% kill fee. Publishes ms an average of 6 months after acceptance. Editorial lead time 6 months. Submit seasonal material at least 1 year in advance. Accepts queries by mail with SASE. NoResponds in 3 months to queries. Sample copy for $5. Writer's guidelines by e-mail and online.

NONFICTION Buys 20 mss/year. Query with published clips. No fax, phone, or e-mail submissions. Length: 1,500-2,500 words. **Pays $300-500, depending on complexity and author's experience.**

REPRINTS Rarely purchases second rights. Send photocopy of article with information about when and where the material previously appeared. Payment varies.

PHOTOS Contact: editor@ahs.org. E-mail or check website for guidelines before submitting. It is very important to include some kind of plant list for your stock so we can determine if you specialize in the types of plants we cover. The list does not have to be comprehensive, but it should give some idea of the breadth of your photo archive. If, for instance, your list contains mostly tulips, pansies, roses, and other popular plants like these, your stock will not be a good match for our articles. Also, if your list does not include the botanical names for all plants, we will not be able to use the photos. We currently still accept slides and transparencies, but prefer digital photos (no photo prints or negatives). In 2012, we will accept only digital photos. Sample slides will be returned if submitted with a self-addressed, stamped envelope or self-addressed and paid FedEx label. . Identification of subjects required. Photo captions required; include complete botanical names of plants including genus, species and botanical variety or cultivar. Pays $350 maximum for color cover; $80-130 for color inside. Pays on publication. Credit line given. Buys one-time North American and nonexclusive rights.

COLUMNS Natural Connections (explains a natural phenomenon—plant and pollinator relationships, plant and fungus relationships, parasites—that may be observed in nature or in the garden), 750-1,200 words. Homegrown Harvest (articles on edible plants delivered in a personal, reassuring voice. Each issue focuses on a single crop, such as carrots, blueberries, or parsley), 800-900 words; Plant in the Spotlight (profiles of a single plant species or cultivar, including a personal perspective on why it's a favored plant), 600 words. **Buys 5 mss/year.** Query with published clips. **Pays $100-250.**

⊖⊛ ATLANTA HOMES AND LIFESTYLES

Network Communications, Inc., 1100 Johnson Ferry Rd., Suite 595, Atlanta GA 30342. (404)252-6670. Fax: (404)252-6673. Website: atlantahomesmag.com. **65% freelance written**. Magazine published 12 times/year. *Atlanta Homes and Lifestyles* is designed for the action-oriented, well-educated reader who enjoys his/her shelter, its design and construction, its environment, and living and entertaining in it. Estab. 1983. Circ. 33,091. Byline given. Pays on publication. Publishes ms an average of 6 months after acceptance. Accepts queries by mail, fax. Responds in 3 months to queries. Sample copy for $3.95. Guidelines available online.

NONFICTION Needs interview, new product, photo feature, well-designed homes, gardens, local art, remodeling, food, preservation, entertaining. We do not want articles outside respective market area, not written for magazine format, or that are excessively controversial, investigative or that cannot be appropriately illustrated with attractive photography. **Buys 35 mss/year.** Query with published clips. Length: 500-1,200 words. **Pays $100-500.** Sometimes pays expenses of writer on assignment

PHOTOS Most photography is assigned. State availability. Captions, identification of subjects, model releases required. Reviews transparencies. Pays $40-50/photo.

COLUMNS Pays $50-200.

⊛ AUSTRALIAN COUNTRY COLLECTIONS

Universal Magazines, Ltd., Unit 5, 6-8 Byfield St., North Ryde NSW 2113 Australia. (61)(2)9887-0399. Fax: (61)(2)9805-0714. E-mail: countrycollections@ universalmagazines.com.au. Website: completecraft. com.au/. Bimonthly magazine featuring a variety of stunning Australian country homes in every issue, creating a sense of country style for our readers' world. "Your country lifestyle magazine, Country Collections caters to those wanting to live the country life wherever they live; be them passionate homemakers, collectors or those aspiring to own a country dream home. Be inspired by the variety of stunning homes and successful tree change stories in every issue." Circ. 30,000.

NONFICTION Needs general interest, inspirational, photo feature. Query.

⊜ BACKHOME

Wordsworth Communications, Inc., P.O. Box 70, Hendersonville NC 28793. (828)696-3838. Fax: (828)696-0700. E-mail: backhome@ioa.com. Website: backhomemagazine.com. **80% freelance written**. Bimonthly magazine. "*BackHome* encourages readers to take more control over their lives by doing more for themselves: productive organic gardening; building and repairing their homes; utilizing renewable energy systems; raising crops and livestock; building furniture; toys and games and other projects; creative cooking. *BackHome* promotes respect for family activities, community programs, and the environment." Estab. 1990. Circ. 42,000. Byline given. Pays on publication. Offers $25 kill fee at publisher's discretion. Publishes ms an average of 1 year after acceptance. Editorial lead time 3 months. Submit seasonal material 6 months in advance. Accepts queries by mail, e-mail, fax, phone. Responds in 6 weeks to queries. Responds in 2 months to mss. Sample copy $5 or online. Guidelines available online.

◯ The editor reports an interest in seeing more renewable energy experiences, *good* small houses, workshop projects (for handy persons, not experts), and community action others can copy.

NONFICTION Needs how-to, gardening, construction, energy, homebusiness, interview, personal experience, technical, self-sufficiency. No essays or old-timey reminiscences. **Buys 80 mss/year.** Query.

Length: 750-5,000 words. **Pays $35 (approximately)/ printed page.**

REPRINTS Send photocopy and information about when and where the material previously appeared. Pays $35/printed page.

PHOTOS Send photos. Identification of subjects required. Reviews color prints, 35mm slides, JPEG photo attachments of 300 dpi. Offers additional payment for photos published.

⊖⊖⊖⊖ BETTER HOMES AND GARDENS

1716 Locust St., Des Moines IA 50309-3023. (515)284-3044. Fax: (515)284-3763. Website: bhg.com. Brenda Lesch, creative director. **Contact:** Doug Crichton, editor-in-chief. **10-15% freelance written.** Magazine "providing home service information for people who have a serious interest in their homes. We read all freelance articles, but much prefer to see a letter of query rather than a finished manuscript." Estab. 1922. Circ. 7,605,000. Pays on acceptance.

NONFICTION Needs travel, education, gardening, health, cars, home, entertainment. "We do not deal with political subjects or with areas not connected with the home, community, and family. No poetry or fiction." **Pay rates vary.**

⊖⊖ BIRDS & BLOOMS

Reiman Publications, 5925 Country Ln., Greendale WI 53129-1404. (414)423-0100. E-mail: editors@birdsandblooms.com. Website: birdsandblooms.com. **15% freelance written.** "Bimonthly magazine focusing on the beauty in your own backyard. *Birds & Blooms* is a sharing magazine that lets backyard enthusiasts chat with each other by exchanging personal experiences. This makes *Birds & Blooms* more like a conversation than a magazine, as readers share tips and tricks on producing beautiful blooms and attracting feathered friends to their backyards.". "See contributor's guidelines at: birdsandblooms.com/contributor-s-guidelines." Estab. 1995. Circ. 1,900,000. Byline given. Pays on publication. Publishes ms an average of 7 months after acceptance. Editorial lead time 2 months. Submit seasonal material 4 months in advance. Accepts queries by mail, online submission form. Accepts simultaneous submissions. Responds in 2 months to queries & mss. Sample copy for $2, 9×12 SAE and $1.95 postage. Guidelines online or for #10 SASE.

NONFICTION Needs essays, how-to, humor, inspirational, personal experience, photo feature, natural

crafting and plan items for building backyard accents. No bird rescue or captive bird pieces. **Buys 12-20 mss/ year.** Send complete ms to us, along with your full name, daytime phone number, e-mail address and mailing address. If you're submitting for a particular column, note that as well. Each reader contributor whose story, photo or short item is published receives a *Birds & Blooms* tote bag. See guidelines online. Length: 250-1,000 words. **Pays $100-400.**

PHOTOS Send photos. Identification of subjects required. Reviews transparencies, prints.

COLUMNS Backyard Banter (odds, ends & unique things); Bird Tales (backyard bird stories); Local Lookouts (community backyard happenings), all 200 words. **Buys 12-20 mss/year.** Send complete ms. **Pays $50-75.**

FILLERS Needs anecdotes, facts, gags. **Buys 25 mss/ year.** Length: 10-250 words. **Pays $10-75.**

⊕⊖ BURKE'S BACKYARD

Burke's Backyard Magazine, Locked Bag 1000, Artarmon NSW 1570 Australia. (61)(2)9414-4800. Fax: (61)(2)9414-4850. E-mail: magazine@burkesbackyard. com.au; photos@burkesbackyard.com.au. Website: burkesbackyard.com.au. Monthly magazine providing trusted, informative ideas and information for Australian homes & gardens. "Our founder is Don Burke. As well as being an expert gardener he's nuts about animals and pets, too. And healthy food, the environment, science, DIY projects and good design anywhere it can be found." Circ. 60,000.

NONFICTION Needs general interest, how-to, new product. Query.

PHOTOS The ideal format is 300dpi (high-resolution) or a JPEG saved to "best quality.".

⊖⊖ CALIFORNIA HOMES

McFadden-Bray Publishing Corp., 417 31st St., Suite B, Newport Beach CA 92663. (949)640-1484. Fax: (949)640-1665. E-mail: edit@calhomesmagazine. com; susan@calhomesmagazine.com; larissa@paper-cakesdesign.com. Website: calhomesmagazine.com. Larissa Linn, art director. **Contact:** Susan McFadden, editor-in-chief. **80% freelance written.** Bimonthly magazine covering California interiors, architecture, some food, travel, history, and current events in the field. Estab. 1997. Circ. 80,000. Byline given. Pays on publication. Offers 50% kill fee. Publishes ms an average of 3 months after acceptance. Editorial lead time 3 months. Submit seasonal material 6 months in advance. Accepts queries by mail, e-mail, fax. Responds in 1 month to queries. Responds in 2 months to mss. Sample copy for $7.50. Guidelines for #10 SASE.

NONFICTION Query. Length: 500-1,000 words. **Pays $250-750.** Sometimes pays expenses of writers on assignment.

PHOTOS State availability. Captions required. Negotiates payment individually.

◐⊘ CANADIAN HOMES & COTTAGES

The In-Home Show, Ltd., 2650 Meadowvale Blvd., Unit 4, Mississauga ON L5N 6M5 Canada. (905)567-1440. Fax: (905)567-1442. E-mail: jnaisby@homesandcottages.com. E-mail: oliver@homesandcottages.com. Website: homesandcottages.com. **Contact:** Oliver Johnson, managing editor. **75% freelance written.** Magazine published 6 times/year covering building and renovating. "Publishes articles that have a technical slant, as well as those with a more general lifestyle feel." Estab. 1987. Circ. 92,340. Byline given. Pays on acceptance. Offers 10% kill fee. Publishes ms an average of 6 months after acceptance. Editorial lead time 3 months. Submit seasonal material 6 months in advance. Accepts queries by mail. Sample copy for SAE. Guidelines for #10 SASE.

NONFICTION Needs humor, building and renovation related, new product, technical. **Buys 32 mss/year.** Query. Length: 800-1,500 words. **Pays $3500-650.** Sometimes pays expenses of writers on assignment.

PHOTOS Bi-monthly. Canada's largest building, renovation and home improvement magazine. Send photos. Captions, identification of subjects required. Reviews transparencies, prints. Negotiates payment individually. Pays on acceptance. Credit line given.

◐⊖⊖ THE CANADIAN ORGANIC GROWER

1205 Rte 915, New Horton NB E4H 1W1 Canada. E-mail: janet@cog.ca; office@cog.ca; publications@cog.ca. Website: cog.ca/magazine.htm. **Contact:** Janet Wallace, managing editor. **100% freelance written.** Quarterly magazine covering organic gardening and farming. "We publish articles that are of interest to organic gardeners, farmers and consumers in Canada. We're always looking for practical how-to articles, as well as farmer profiles. At times, we include news about the organic community, recipes and stories about successful marketing strategies." Estab. 1975. Circ. 4,000. Byline given. Pays on publication. Publishes ms an average of 2-3 months after acceptance.

Editorial lead time 6 months. Submit seasonal material 6 months in advance. Accepts queries by mail, e-mail. Responds in 3 weeks to queries. Responds in 1 month to mss. Sample copy available online. Guidelines available online.

NONFICTION Needs essays, general interest, how-to, garden, farm, market, process organic food, interview, new product, opinion, technical, "If you would like to write an article for *The Canadian Organic Grower*, please e-mail the editor to discuss your idea before you start to write. If you would like to submit a book review, please contact the COG Librarian for detailed guidelines and, if necessary, suggestions about books to review: library@cog.ca.". Does not want "rants." **Buys 25 mss/year.** Query. Length: 500-2,500 words. **Pays $150-350 for assigned articles. Pays $150-350 for unsolicited articles.**

PHOTOS State availability. Captions, identification of subjects required. Reviews prints, GIF/JPEG files. Reviews photos with or without accompanying manuscript. Negotiates payment individually. For each feature article, contributors are paid $100-200 per article (depending on length, scope and quality). Pays on publication. Expenses are not reimbursed unless discussed and approved in advance. We do not pay for opinion pieces or book reviews. Credit line given.

⊖⊖⊖⊖ COASTAL LIVING

Southern Progress Corp., 2100 Lakeshore Dr., Birmingham AL 35209. (205)445-6007. Fax: (205)445-8655. E-mail: mamie_walling@timeinc.com. Website: coastalliving.com. **Contact:** Mamie Walling. "Bimonthly magazine for those who live or vacation along our nation's coasts. The magazine emphasizes home design and travel, but also covers a wide variety of other lifestyle topics and coastal concerns.". Estab. 1997. Circ. 660,000. Pays on acceptance. Offers 25% kill fee. Responds in 2 months to queries. Sample copy available online. Guidelines available online.

NONFICTION Query with clips and SASE. **Pays $1/word.**

PHOTOS State availability.

⊖⊖ COLORADO HOMES & LIFESTYLES

Wiesner Publishing, LLC, 1777 S. Harrison Street, Suite 903, Denver CO 80210. (303)248-2060. Fax: (303)248-2066. E-mail: mabel@coloradohomesmag.com. Website: coloradohomesmag.com. **75% freelance written.** Upscale shelter magazine published 9 times/year containing beautiful homes, landscapes, architecture, calendar, antiques, etc. All of Colorado is included. Geared toward home-related and lifestyle areas, personality profiles, etc. Estab. 1981. Circ. 36,000. Byline given. Pays on acceptance. Offers 15% kill fee. Publishes ms an average of 3 months after acceptance. Editorial lead time 3 months. Submit seasonal material 1 year in advance. Accepts queries by mail, e-mail. Accepts simultaneous submissions. Responds in 2 months to queries. Sample copy for #10 SASE.

NONFICTION No personal essays, religious, humor, technical **Buys 50-75 mss/year.** Query with published clips. Length: 900-1,500 words. **Pays $200-400.** Sometimes pays expenses of writers on assignment. Provide sources with phone numbers

PHOTOS Send photos. Identification of subjects, True required. Reviews transparencies, b&w glossy prints, CDs, digital images, slides.

COUNTRY LIVING

The Hearst Corp., 300 W. 57th St., New York NY 10019. (212)649-3501. E-mail: clmail@hearst.com. Website: countryliving.com. **Contact:** Editorial Dept. Monthly magazine covering home design and interior decorating with an emphasis on country style. Estab. 1978. Circ. 1,600,000.

> "A lifestyle magazine for readers who appreciate the warmth and traditions associated with American home and family life. Each monthly issue embraces American country decorating and includes features on furniture, antiques, gardening, home building, real estate, cooking, entertaining and travel." Verify the market is active and accepting submissions before sending your manuscript via regular mail.

NONFICTION Buys 20-30 mss/year. Send complete ms and SASE. **Payment varies.**

COLUMNS Query first.

💲💲 EARLY AMERICAN LIFE

Firelands Media Group LLC, P.O. Box 221228, Shaker Heights OH 44122-0996. E-mail: queries@firelandsmedia.com. Website: ealonline.com. **60% freelance written**. Bimonthly magazine for people who are interested in capturing the warmth and beauty of the 1600-1840 period and using it in their homes and lives today. They are interested in antiques, traditional crafts, architecture, restoration, and collecting. Estab. 1970. Circ. 90,000. Byline given. Pays on

acceptance. 25% kill fee. Publishes ms an average of 1 year after acceptance. Accepts queries by mail, e-mail. Responds in 3 months to queries. Sample copy and writer's guidelines for 9×12 SAE with $2.50 postage. Guidelines available online at: ealonline.com/editorial/guidelines.php.

NONFICTION Buys 40 mss/year. Query us first before sending ms. Length: 750-3,000 words. **Pays $250-700, additionally for photos.**

PHOTOS We need releases for any photos that include identifiable people or protected sites. We will supply the release forms to you as necessary.

💲💲💲💲 ECOHOME DESIGNS

Hanley Wood, 1 Thomas Cir., #600, Washington DC 20005-5811. E-mail: hgottemoeller@hanleywood.com. Website: hanleywood.com. **Contact:** Hillary Gottemoeller. **75% freelance written**. Semiannual magazine covering sustainable building, green design, predrawn blueprints. "Whether your definition of green building is about the use of sustainable materials or about high performance and energy savings, *Eco-Home Designs* is the perfect place to find the latest editorial about the green building phenomenon as well as predrawn house plans that feature comfortable green designs. Readers will find a wealth of insights about the newest building materials and construction methods, as well as tried-and-true tips on building an energy-efficient custom home." Estab. 2009. Byline given. Pays on acceptance. Offers 50% kill fee. Publishes ms an average of 2 months after acceptance. Editorial lead time 6 months. Submit seasonal material 3 months in advance. Accepts queries by e-mail. Accepts simultaneous submissions. Responds in 1 week to queries. Responds in 1 month to mss. Guidelines available.

NONFICTION Contact: Simon Hyoun, editor. Needs how-to, choose green building materials; practice green building concepts, new product, photo feature, technical. No personal stories of home building experiences. **Buys 12 mss/year.** Query with published clips. Length: 500-1,000 words. **Pays $.80-$1/word for assigned or unsolicited articles.**

💲💲💲 FINE GARDENING

Taunton Press, 63 S. Main St., P.O. Box 5506, Newtown CT 06470-5506. (203)426-8171. Fax: (203)426-3434. E-mail: fg@taunton.com. Website: finegardening.com. Bimonthly magazine. High-value magazine on landscape and ornamental gardening. Articles written by avid gardeners—first person, hands-on gardening experiences. Estab. 1988. Circ. 200,000. Byline given. Pays on acceptance. Publishes an average of 6 months after acceptance. Editorial lead time 1 year. Submit seasonal material 1 year in advance. Accepts queries by mail, e-mail. Guidelines free.

NONFICTION Needs how-to, personal experience, photo feature.

PHOTOS Send photos. Reviews digital images.

💲💲 FINE HOMEBUILDING

The Taunton Press, 63 S. Main St., P.O. Box 5506, Newtown CT 06470-5506. (203)426-8171. Fax: (203)426-3434. E-mail: fh@taunton.com. Website: taunton.com. Bimonthly magazine for builders, architects, contractors, owner/builders and others who are seriously involved in building new houses or reviving old ones. Estab. 1981. Circ. 300,000. Byline given. Pays half on acceptance, half on publication. Offers kill fee. Offers on acceptance payment as kill fee. Publishes ms an average of 1 year after acceptance. Responds in 1 month to queries. Writer's guidelines for SASE and on website.

NONFICTION Query with outline, description, photographs, sketches. **Pays $150/published page.**

PHOTOS Take lots of work-in-progress photos. Color print film, ASA 400, from either Kodak or Fuji works best. If you prefer to use slide film, use ASA 100. Keep track of the negatives; we will need them for publication. If you're not sure what to use or how to go about it, feel free to call for advice.

COLUMNS Tools & Materials, Reviews, Questions & Answers, Tips & Techniques, Cross Section, What's the Difference?, Finishing Touches, Great Moments, Breaktime, Drawing Board (design column). Query with outline, description, photographs, sketches and SASE. **Payment varies**

💲 GARDEN COMPASS

Streamopolis, 1450 Front St., San Diego CA 92101. Website: gardencompass.com. Bert Wahlen, Jr. **Contact:** Jim Fitzpatrick. **70% freelance written.** Bimonthly magazine covering gardening. *Garden Compass* is entertaining and offers sound practical advice for West Coast gardeners. Estab. 1992. Circ. 112,000. Byline given. Pays on publication. Offers $50 kill fee. Publishes ms an average of 10 weeks after acceptance. Editorial lead time 6 months. Submit seasonal material 6 months in advance. Accepts queries by mail, e-mail. NoAccepts simultaneous sub-

missions. Responds in 1 month to queries. Sample copy free.

PHOTOS State availability of or send photos. Identification of subjects required. Reviews contact sheets, transparencies, GIF/JPEG files. Negotiates payment individually.

COLUMNS Pest Patrol (plant posts/diseases), 400-800 words; e-Gardening (garden info on the Web), 400-800 words; Book Review (gardening books), 400-600 words; Fruit Trees, 800-1,200 words. Query with published clips. **Payment varies.**

FILLERS Needs anecdotes, facts, newsbreaks. Length: 30-150 words. **Pays $25.**

💲💲💲💲 HORTICULTURE

F+W Media, Inc., 4700 E. Galbraith Rd., Cincinnati OH 45236. (513)531-2690. Fax: (513)891-7153. E-mail: edit@hortmag.com. Website: hortmag.com. Bimonthly magazine. *Horticulture*, the country's oldest gardening magazine, is designed for active home gardeners. Our goal is to offer a blend of text, photographs and illustrations that will both instruct and inspire readers. Circ. 160,000. Byline given. Offers kill fee. Submit seasonal material 10 months in advance. Accepts queries by mail, e-mail, fax. Responds in 3 months to queries. Guidelines for SASE or by e-mail.

NONFICTION Buys 70 mss/year. Query with published clips, subject background material and SASE. Length: 800-1,000 words. **Pays $500.**

COLUMNS Length: 200-600 words. Query with published clips, subject background material and SASE. Include disk where possible. **Pays $250.**

💲💲💲💲 HOUSE BEAUTIFUL

The Hearst Corp., 300 W. 57th St., 24th Floor, New York NY 10019. (212)903-5000. E-mail: readerservices@housebeautiful.com. Website: housebeautiful.com. Monthly magazine. Targeted toward affluent, educated readers ages 30-40. Covers home design and decoration, gardening and entertaining, interior design, architecture and travel. Circ. 865,352. Editorial lead time 3 months.

○ Query first.

LOG HOME LIVING

Home Buyer Publications, Inc., 4125 Lafayette Center Dr.,, Suite 100, Chantilly VA 20151. (703)222-9411; (800)826-3893. Fax: (703)222-3209. E-mail: editor@loghomeliving.com; ksmith@homebuyerpubs.com.

Website: loghomeliving.com. **90% freelance written.** Monthly magazine for enthusiasts who are dreaming of, planning for, or actively building a log home. Estab. 1989. Circ. 132,000. Byline given. Pays on acceptance. Offers $100 kill fee. Publishes ms an average of 6 months after acceptance. Editorial lead time 6 months. Submit seasonal material 6 months in advance. Accepts queries by mail, e-mail. Responds in 6 weeks to queries. Sample copy for $4. Guidelines available online.

Also publishes *Timber Home Living, Log Home Design Ideas* and *Building Systems.*

NONFICTION Needs how-to, build or maintain log home, interview, log home owners, personal experience, photo feature, log homes, technical, design/decor topics, travel. **Buys 60 mss/year.** Query with SASE. Length: 1,000-2,000 words. **Payment depends on length, nature of the work and writer's expertise.** Pays expenses of writers on assignment.

REPRINTS Send tearsheet, photocopy or typed ms and information about when and where the material previously appeared.

PHOTOS State availability. Reviews contact sheets, 4×5 transparencies, 4×6 prints. Negotiates payment individually.

$$$ MOUNTAIN HOUSE AND HOME

Colorado Resort Publishing, P.O. Box 8, Vail CO 81658. (970)748-2970. E-mail: bharrington@cmnm.org. Website: mountainhouseandhome.com. **80% freelance written**. Quarterly magazine covering building, remodeling Colorado homes. "We cater to an affluent population of homeowners (including primary, second and third homeowners) who are planning to build or remodel their Colorado home in the mountains or on the western slope. While we feature luxury homes, we also have a slant toward green building." Estab. 2005. Circ. 35,000. Byline given. Pays on publication. Publishes ms an average of 2-3 months after acceptance. Editorial lead time 12 months. Submit seasonal material 6 months in advance. Accepts queries by e-mail. Responds in 2-4 weeks to queries. Responds in month to mss. Sample copy available online.

NONFICTION Needs interview, new product, Profiles of Colorado homes and features related to them. We do not want do-it-yourself projects. Query with published clips. **Pays $200-650 for assigned articles. We do not buy articles; we only assign articles.**

PHOTOS Send photos. Captions required. Reviews GIF/JPEG files. We negotiate payment individually.

COLUMNS Your Green Home (tips for environmentally-conscious building, remodeling and living), 300 words. **Buys 4 mss/year. mss/year.** Query.

$$ MOUNTAIN LIVING

Network Communications, Inc., 1777 S. Harrison St., Suite 903, Denver CO 80210. (303)248-2062; (303)248-2063. Fax: (303)248-2064. E-mail: hscott@mountainliving.com; cdeorio@mountainliving.com. Website: mountainliving.com. **Contact:** Holly Scott, publisher; Christine DeOrio, editor-in-chief. **50% freelance written.** Magazine published 10 times/year covering architecture, interior design and lifestyle issues for people who live in, visit, or hope to live in the mountains. Estab. 1994. Circ. 48,000. Byline given. Pays on acceptance. Offers 15% kill fee. Publishes ms an average of 4 months after acceptance. Editorial lead time 6 months. Submit seasonal material 8-12 months in advance. Accepts queries by mail, e-mail. NoResponds in 6 weeks to queries. Responds in 2 months to mss. Sample copy for $7. Guidelines by e-mail.

NONFICTION Needs photo feature, travel, home features. **Buys 30 mss/year.** Query with published clips. Length: 500-1,000 words. **Pays $250-600.** Sometimes pays expenses of writers on assignment.

PHOTOS Provide photos (slides, transparencies, or on disk, saved as TIFF and at least 300 dpi). State availability. All features photography is assigned to photographers who specialize in interior photography. Negotiates payment individually.

COLUMNS ML Recommends; Short Travel Tips; New Product Information; Art; Insider's Guide; Entertaining. Length: 300-800 words. **Buys 35 mss/year.** Query with published clips. **Pays $50-500.**

$$$$ ORGANIC GARDENING

Rodale, 33 E. Minor St., Emmaus PA 18098. E-mail: ogdcustserv@rodale.com. Website: organicgardening.com. **75% freelance written**. Bimonthly magazine. "*Organic Gardening* is for gardeners who enjoy gardening as an integral part of a healthy lifestyle. Editorial shows readers how to grow flowers, edibles, and herbs, as well as information on ecological landscaping. Also covers organic topics including soil building and pest control." Estab. 1942. Circ. 300,000. Byline given. Pays between acceptance and publication. Accepts queries by mail, fax. Responds in 3 months to queries.

NONFICTION Query with published clips and outline **Pays up to $1/word for experienced writers.**

💲💲 ROMANTIC HOMES

Y-Visionary Publishing, 2400 East Katella Avenue,, Suite 300, Orange CA 92868. E-mail: JDeMontravel@Beckett.com. Website: romantichomesmag.com. **70% freelance written**. Monthly magazine covering home decor. *Romantic Homes* is the magazine for women who want to create a warm, intimate, and casually elegant home—a haven that is both a gathering place for family and friends and a private refuge from the pressures of the outside world. The *Romantic Homes* reader is personally involved in the decor of her home. Features offer unique ideas and how-to advice on decorating, home furnishings, and gardening. Departments focus on floor and wall coverings, paint, textiles, refinishing, architectural elements, artwork, travel, and entertaining. Every article responds to the reader's need to create a beautiful, attainable environment, providing her with the style ideas and resources to achieve her own romantic home. Estab. 1994. Circ. 200,000. Byline given. Pays 30-60 days upon receipt of invoice. Publishes ms an average of 4 months after acceptance. Editorial lead time 5 months. Submit seasonal material 6 months in advance. Accepts queries by mail, fax. Accepts simultaneous submissions. Responds in 2 weeks to queries. Responds in 2 months to mss. Guidelines for #10 SASE.

NONFICTION Needs essays, how-to, new product, personal experience, travel. **Buys 150 mss/year.** Query with published clips. Length: 1,000-1,200 words. **Pays $500.**

PHOTOS State availability of or send photos. Captions, identification of subjects, model releases required. Reviews transparencies.

COLUMNS Departments cover antiques, collectibles, artwork, shopping, travel, refinishing, architectural elements, flower arranging, entertaining, and decorating. Length: 400-600 words. **Pays $250.**

💲💲 SAN DIEGO HOME/GARDEN LIFESTYLES

McKinnon Enterprises, Box 719001, San Diego CA 92171-9001. (858)571-1818. Fax: (858)571-1889. E-mail: donoho@sdhg.net. Website: sdhg.net. **30% freelance written**. Monthly magazine covering homes, gardens, food, intriguing people, real estate, art and culture for residents of San Diego city and county. Estab. 1979. Circ. 50,000. Byline given. Pays on publication. Publishes ms an average of 3 months after acceptance. Submit seasonal material 3 months in advance. Accepts queries by mail. Responds in 3 months to queries. Sample copy for $5.

NONFICTION Query with published clips. Length: 500-1,000 words. **Pays $50-375.**

💲💲 SEATTLE HOMES & LIFESTYLES

Network Communications, Inc., 3240 Eastlake Ave. E.,, Suite 200, Seattle WA 98102. (206)322-6699. E-mail: marketing@seattlehomesmag.com; gsmith@seattlehomesmag.com. Website: seattlehomesmag.com. **60% freelance written**. Magazine published 6 times/year covering home design and lifestyles. "*Seattle Homes & Lifestyles* showcases the finest homes and gardens in the Northwest, and the personalities and lifestyles that make this region special. We try to help our readers take full advantage of the resources the region has to offer with in-depth coverage of events, entertaining, shopping, food, and wine. And we write about it with a warm, personal approach that underscores our local perspective." Estab. 1996. Circ. 30,000. Byline given. Pays on acceptance. Offers 25% kill fee. Publishes ms an average of 2 months after acceptance. Editorial lead time 3 months. Submit seasonal material 4 months in advance. Accepts simultaneous submissions. Responds in 4 months to queries.

NONFICTION Needs general interest, how-to, decorating, cooking, interview, photo feature. No essays, travel stories, sports coverage. **Buys 95 mss/year.** Query with published clips via mail. Length: 300-1,500 words. **Pays $150-400.**

PHOTOS State availability. Captions, identification of subjects, model releases required. Reviews contact sheets, transparencies, prints. Negotiates payment individually.

💲💲💲 SU CASA

Hacienda Press, 4100 Wolcott Ave. NE, Suite B, Albuquerque NM 87109. (505)344-1783. Fax: (505)345-3795. E-mail: akellogg@sucasamagazine.com. Website: sucasamagazine.com. **80% freelance written**. Magazine published 5 times/year covering southwestern homes, building, design, architecture for the reader comtemplating building, remodeling, or decorating a Santa Fe style home. Su Casa is tightly focused on Southwestern home building, architecture and design. In particular, we feature New Mexico homes. We also cover alternative construction, far-out homes and contemporary design. Estab. 1995. Circ. 40,000. Byline given. Pays on acceptance. Offers 50% kill fee.

Publishes ms an average of 6 months after acceptance. Editorial lead time 6-9 months. Submit seasonal material 9 months in advance. Accepts queries by mail, e-mail, fax, phone. NoResponds in 1 week to queries. Responds in 1 month to mss. Sample copy free. Guidelines free.

○ All the departments are assigned long term. We encourage writers to pitch feature story ideas. We don't cover trends or concepts, but rather homes that express them.

NONFICTION Needs book excerpts, essays, interview, personal experience, photo feature. Special issues: The summer issue covers kitchen and bath topics. Does not want how-to articles, product reviews or features, no trends in southwest homes. **Buys 30 mss/year.** Query with published clips. Length: 1,000-2,500 words. **Pays $250-1,000.** Sometimes pays expenses of writers on assignment. Limit agreed upon in advance

PHOTOS State availability of or send photos. Captions, identification of subjects, model releases, True required. Reviews GIF/JPEG files. Offers $25-150/photo.

🌑🌑 TEXAS GARDENER

Suntex Communications, Inc., P.O. Box 9005, Waco TX 76714-9005. (254)848-9393. Fax: (254)848-9779. E-mail: info@texasgardener.com. Website: texasgardener.com. **80% freelance written. Works with a small number of new/unpublished writers each year.** Bimonthly magazine covering vegetable and fruit production, ornamentals, and home landscape information for home gardeners in Texas. Estab. 1981. Circ. 20,000. Byline given. Pays on publication. Publishes ms an average of 4 months after acceptance. Submit seasonal material 6 months in advance. Accepts queries by mail, e-mail, fax. Responds in 2 months to queries. Sample copy for $4.25 and SAE with 5 first-class stamps. Writers' guidelines available online at website.

NONFICTION Needs how-to, humor, interview, photo feature. **Buys 50-60 mss/year.** Query with published clips. Length: 800-2,400 words. **Pays $50-200.**

PHOTOS "We prefer superb color and b&w photos; 90% of photos used are color. Send low resolution jpgs files for review to info@texasgardener.com. High resolution jpg files are required for publication if photos are accepted.". Send photos. Identification of subjects, model releases required. Reviews contact sheets, 2 ¼x2 ¼ or 35mm color transparencies, 8×10 b&w prints. Pays negotiable rates.

COLUMNS Between Neighbors. **Pays $25.**

🌑🌑 TEXAS HOME & LIVING

Publications & Communications, Inc., 13581 Pond Springs Rd., Suite 450, Austin TX 78729. (512)381-0576. Fax: (512)331-3950. E-mail: bronas@pcinews.com. Website: texasHomeandLiving.com. **75% freelance written.** Bimonthly magazine. "*Texas Home & Living.*the magazine of design, architecture and Texas lifestyle." Estab. 1994. Circ. 50,000. Byline given. Pays on publication. Offers 100% kill fee. Publishes ms an average of 4 months after acceptance. Editorial lead time 4 months. Submit seasonal material 6 months in advance. Accepts queries by mail, e-mail, fax. Responds in 1 month to queries. Responds in 2 months to mss. Sample copy free. Guidelines available online.

NONFICTION Needs how-to, interview, new product, travel. **Buys 18 mss/year.** Query with published clips. Length: 500-2,000 words. **Pays $200 for assigned articles.** Pays expenses of writers on assignment.

PHOTOS State availability of or send photos. Captions required. Reviews negatives, transparencies, prints. Offers no additional payment for photos accepted with ms.

🌑🌑🌑🌑 THIS OLD HOUSE MAGAZINE

Time Inc., 135 W. 50th St., 10th Floor, New York NY 10020. (212)522-9465. Fax: (212)522-9435. E-mail: toh_letters@thisoldhouse.com. Website: thisoldhouse.com. **40% freelance written.** Magazine published 10 times/year covering home design, renovation, and maintenance. "*This Old House* is the ultimate resource for readers whose homes are their passions. The magazine's mission is threefold: to inform with lively service journalism and reporting on innovative new products and materials, to inspire with beautiful examples of fine craftsmanship and elegant architectural design, and to instruct with clear step-by-step projects that will enhance a home or help a homeowner maintain one. The voice of the magazine is not that of a rarefied design maven or a linear Mr. Fix It, but rather that of an e-wide-open, in-the-trenches homeowner who's eager for advice, tools, and techniques that'll help him realize his dream of a home." Estab. 1995. Circ. 960,000. Byline given. Pays on acceptance. Publishes ms an average of 3-6 months after acceptance. Editorial lead time 3-12 months. Submit seasonal material 1 year in advance. Accepts queries by mail, e-mail.

NONFICTION Needs essays, how-to, new product, technical, must be house-related. **Buys 70 mss/year.** Query with published clips. Length: 250-2,500 words. **Pays $1/word.** Sometimes pays expenses of writers on assignment.

COLUMNS Around the House (news, new products), 250 words. **Pays $1/word.**

$$ VICTORIAN HOMES

Y-Visionary Publishing, LP, 2400 East Katella Avenue,, Suite 300, Anaheim CA 92806. (714)939-9991. Fax: (714)939-9909. E-mail: JMyers@Beckett.com. Website: victorianhomesmag.com. **90% freelance written.** Bimonthly magazine covering Victorian home restoration and decoration. *Victorian Homes* is read by Victorian home owners, restorers, house museum management, and others interested in the Victorian revival. Feature articles cover home architecture, interior design, furnishings, and the home's history. Photography is very important to the feature. Estab. 1981. Circ. 100,000. Byline given. Pays on acceptance. Offers $50 kill fee. Publishes ms an average of 1 year after acceptance. Editorial lead time 4 months. Submit seasonal material 1 year in advance. Accepts queries by mail, e-mail, fax. Accepts simultaneous submissions. Responds in 6 weeks to queries. Responds in 2 months to mss. Sample copy and writer's guidelines for SAE.

NONFICTION Needs how-to, create period style curtains, wall treatments, bathrooms, kitchens, etc., photo feature. **Buys 30-35 mss/year.** Query. Length: 800-1,800 words. **Pays $300-500.** Sometimes pays expenses of writers on assignment.

PHOTOS State availability. Captions required. Reviews 2¼×2¼ transparencies. Negotiates payment individually.

HUMOR

$ FUNNY TIMES

Funny Times, Inc., P.O. Box 18530, Cleveland Heights OH 44118. (216)371-8600. Fax: (216)371-8696. E-mail: info@funnytimes.com. Website: funnytimes.com. **50% freelance written.** Monthly tabloid for humor. *Funny Times* is a monthly review of America's funniest cartoonists and writers. We are the *Reader's Digest* of modern American humor with a progressive/peace-oriented/environmental/politically activist slant. Estab. 1985. Circ. 70,000. Byline given. Pays on publication. Publishes ms an average of 3 months after acceptance. Editorial lead time 2 months. Accepts simultaneous submissions. Responds in 3 months to mss. Sample copy for $3 or 9×12 SAE with 3 first-class stamps ($1.14 postage). Guidelines available online.

NONFICTION Needs essays, funny, humor, interview, opinion, humorous, personal experience, absolutely funny. **Buys 60 mss/year.** Send complete ms. Length: 500-700 words. **Pays $60 minimum.**

COLUMNS Query with published clips.

FICTION Contact: Ray Lesser and Susan Wolpert, editors. Anything funny. **Buys 6 mss/year.** Query with published clips. Length: 500-700 words. **Pays $50-150.**

FILLERS Needs short humor. **Buys 6 mss/year. Pays $20.**

$$ MAD MAGAZINE

1700 Broadway, New York NY 10019. (212)506-4850. Fax: (212)506-4848. E-mail: submissions@madmagazine.com. Website: madmag.com. **100% freelance written.** Monthly magazine always on the lookout for new ways to spoof and to poke fun at hot trends. Estab. 1952. Byline given. Pays on acceptance. Publishes ms an average of 6 months after acceptance. Submit seasonal material 6 months in advance. Responds in 10 weeks to queries. Sample copy available online. Guidelines available online.

NONFICTION "We're not interested in formats we're already doing or have done to death like 'what they say and what they really mean.' Don't send previously published submissions, riddles, advice columns, TV or movie satires, book manuscripts, top 10 lists, articles about Alfred E. Neuman, poetry, essays, short stories or other text pieces." **Buys 400 mss/year. Pays minimum of $500/page.**

INFLIGHT

$$$ GO MAGAZINE

INK Publishing, 68 Jay St., Suite 315, Brooklyn NY 11201. (347)294-1220. Fax: (917)591-6247. E-mail: editorial@airtranmagazine.com. E-mail: trcrosby@mailaaa. Website: airtranmagazine.com. **80% freelance written.** Monthly magazine covering travel. "*Go Magazine* is an inflight magazine covering travel, general interest and light business." Estab. 2003. Circ. 100,000. Byline given. net 45 days upon receipt of invoice. Offers 50% kill fee. Publishes ms an average of 3 months after acceptance. Editorial lead time 4 months. Submit seasonal material 5 months in advance. Accepts queries by e-mail. Sample copy available online. Guidelines by e-mail.

NONFICTION Needs general interest, interview, photo feature, travel, light business. Does not want first-person travelogues. **Buys 200 mss/year.** Query with published clips. Length: 400-2,000 words. **Pay is negotiable.**

PHOTOS Contact: Shane Luitjens, art director. State availability. Reviews GIF/JPEG files. Offers no additional payment for photos accepted with ms.

⊖⊖⊖ HEMISPHERES

Ink Publishing, 68 Jay St., Suite 315, Brooklyn NY 11201. (347)294-1220. Fax: (917)591-6247. E-mail: united.ed@ink-publishing.com. Website: hemispheresmagazine.com. **Contact:** Mike Guy, editor-in-chief. **95% freelance written.** Monthly magazine for the educated, sophisticated business and recreational frequent traveler on an airline that spans the globe. Inflight magazine that interprets 'inflight' to be a mode of delivery rather than an editorial genre. Hemispheres' task is to engage, intrigue and entertain its primary readers—an international, culturally diverse group of affluent, educated professionals and executives who frequently travel for business and pleasure on United Airlines. The magazine offers a global perspective and a focus on topics that cross borders as often as the people reading the magazine. Emphasizes ideas, concepts, and culture rather than products, presented in a fresh, artful and sophisticated graphic environment. Estab. 1992. Circ. 500,000. Byline given. Pays on acceptance. Offers 20% kill fee. Publishes ms an average of 4-6 months after acceptance. Editorial lead time 8 months. Submit seasonal material 8 months in advance. Accepts queries by mail. Responds in 2 months to queries. Responds in 4 months to mss. Sample copy for $7.50. Guidelines for #10 SASE.

NONFICTION Needs general interest, humor, personal experience. No 'in this country' phraseology. 'Too American' is a frequent complaint for queries. Query with published clips. Length: 500-3,000 words. **Pays 50¢/word and up.**

PHOTOS Reviews photos only when we request them. State availability. Captions, identification of subjects, model releases required. Negotiates payment individually.

COLUMNS Making a Difference (Q&A format interview with world leaders, movers, and shakers. A 500-600 word introduction anchors the interview. We want to profile an international mix of men and women representing a variety of topics or issues, but all must truly be making a difference. No puffy celebrity profiles.); 15 Fascinating Facts (a snappy selection of 1- or 2-sentence obscure, intriguing, or travel-service-oriented items that the reader never knew about a city, state, country, or destination.); Executive Secrets (things that top executives know); Case Study (Business strategies of international companies or organizations. No lionizations of CEOs. Strategies should be the emphasis. We want international candidates.); Weekend Breakaway (takes us just outside a major city after a week of business for several activities for an action-packed weekend); Roving Gourmet (insider's guide to interesting eating in major city, resort area, or region. The slant can be anything from ethnic to expensive; not just best. The 4 featured eateries span a spectrum from hole in the wall, to expense account lunch, and on to big deal dining.); Collecting (occasional 800-word story on collections and collecting that can emphasize travel); Eye on Sports (global look at anything of interest in sports); Vintage Traveler (options for mature, experienced travelers); Savvy Shopper (insider's tour of best places in the world to shop. Savvy Shopper (steps beyond all those stories that just mention the great shopping at a particular destination. A shop-by-shop, gallery-by-gallery tour of the best places in the world.); Science and Technology (substantive, insightful stories on how technology is changing our lives and the business world. Not just another column on audio components or software. No gift guides!); Aviation Journal (for those fascinated with aviation; topics range widely.); Terminal Bliss (a great airports guide series); Grape And Grain (wine and spirits with emphasis on education, not one-upmanship); Show Business (films, music, and entertainment); Musings (humor or just curious musings); Quick Quiz (tests to amuse and educate); Travel Trends (brief, practical, invaluable, global, trend-oriented); Book Beat (tackles topics like the Wodehouse Society, the birth of a book, the competition between local bookshops and national chains.

Please, no review proposals.); What the World's Reading (residents explore how current bestsellers tell us what their country is thinking). Length: 1,400 words. Query with published clips. **Pays 50¢/word and up**

FICTION Needs adventure, ethnic, historical, humorous, mainstream, mystery, explorations of those issues common to all people but within the context of a particular culture. **Buys 14 mss/year.** Send complete ms. Length: 1,000-4,000 words. **Pays 50¢/word and up.**

$$$$ SPIRIT MAGAZINE

Pace Communications, Inc., Suite 360, 2811 McKinney Ave., Dallas TX 75204. (214)580-8070. Fax: (214)580-2491. Website: spiritmag.com. Monthly magazine for passengers on Southwest Airlines. Estab. 1992. Circ. 380,000. Byline given. Pays on acceptance. Responds in 1 month to queries. Guidelines available online.

NONFICTION Buys about 40 mss/year. Query by mail only with published clips. 3,000-6,000 words (features). **Pays $1/word.** Pays expenses of writers on assignment.

COLUMNS Length: 800-900 words. **Buys about 21 mss/year.** Query by mail only with published clips.

FILLERS Buys 12 mss/year. 250 words. **variable amount.**

$$$$ US AIRWAYS MAGAZINE

Pace Communications, 1301 Carolina St., Greensboro NC 27401. E-mail: edit@usairwaysmag.com. Website: usairwaysmag.com. Monthly magazine for travelers on US Airways. We focus on travel, lifestyle and pop culture. Estab. 2006. Circ. 441,000. Byline given. Pays on acceptance. Publishes ms an average of 4 months after acceptance. Editorial lead time 3 months. Accepts queries by mail, e-mail. Responds in 6 weeks to queries. Responds in 1 month to mss. Sample copy for $7.50 or online. Guidelines available online.

NONFICTION Needs general interest, personal experience, travel, food, lifestyle, sports. **Buys 200-350 mss/year.** Query with published clips. Length: 100-1,500 words. **Pays $100-1,500.** Sometimes pays expenses of writers on assignment.

PHOTOS State availability. Identification of subjects, model releases required. Reviews contact sheets, negatives, transparencies. Negotiates payment individually.

COLUMNS Several columns are authored by a single writer under long-term contract with US Airways Magazine. Departments open to freelance pitches include: All Over the Map; Alter Ego; Straight Talk; Hands On; Shelf Life; In Gear; Get Personal; and Get Away. All of these departments may be viewed on the magazine's website.

JUVENILE

$ BABYBUG

Carus Publishing, 70 East Lake St., Chicago IL 60601. E-mail: babybug@caruspub.com. Website: cricketmag.com. **Contact:** Marianne Carus, editor-in-chief. **50**. Estab. 1994. Circ. 45,000. Byline given. Accepts simultaneous submissions. Responds in 6 months to mss Guidelines available online.

NONFICTION Buys 10-20 mss/year. Submit complete ms, SASE. Length: 10 words/max **Pays $25**

PHOTOS Pays $500/spread; $250/page.

FICTION Stories must be simple and concrete. Needs rhythmic, rhyming. **Buys 10-20 mss/year.** Length: 2-8 short sentences. **$25 min.**

POETRY Pays $25 minimum on publication. Acquires North American publication rights for previously published poems; rights vary for unpublished poems.

$$$$ BOYS' LIFE

Boy Scouts of America, P.O. Box 152079, 1325 West Walnut Hills Lane, Irving TX 75015-2079. (972)580-2366. Fax: (972)580-2079. Website: boyslife.org. J. D. Owen, editor-in-chief, Michael Goldman, managing editor, Aaron Derr, senior writer. **75% freelance written. Prefers to work with published/established writers; works with small number of new/unpublished writers each year.** *Boys' Life* is a monthly 4-color general interest magazine for boys 7-18, most of whom are Cub Scouts, Boy Scouts or Venturers. Estab. 1911. Circ. 1.1 million. Byline given. Pays on acceptance. Publishes approximately one year after acceptance. Accepts queries by mail. Responds to queries/mss in 2 months. Sample copies for $3.95 plus 9×12 SASE. Guidelines available for SASE and online.

NONFICTION Contact: Send article queries to the attention of the senior editor; column queries to the attention of the associate editor. Needs , Scouting activities and general interests (nature, Earth, health, cars, sports, science, computers, space and aviation, entertainment, history, music, animals, how-to's, etc.). **Buys 60 mss/year.** Query with SASE. No phone queries Averge word length for articles: 500-1,500 words, including sidebars and boxes. Average word length for columns: 300-750. **Pay ranges from $300 and up.** Pays expenses of writers on assignment.

PHOTOS Contact: Photo Director. Photo guidelines free with SASE. Boy Scouts of America Magazine Division also publishes *Scouting* magazine. "Most photographs are from specific assignments that freelance photojournalists shoot for *Boys' Life*. Interested in all photographers, but do not send unsolicited images.". Pays $500 base editorial day rate against placement fees, plus expenses. **Pays on acceptance.** Buys one-time rights.

COLUMNS Contact: Columns query associate editor with SASE for response.

FICTION Needs All fiction is assigned.

$ CADET QUEST MAGAZINE

P.O. Box 7259, Grand Rapids MI 49510-7259. (616)241-5616. Fax: (616)241-5558. E-mail: submissions@calvinistcadets.org. Website: calvinistcadets.org. **Contact:** G. Richard Broene, editor. **40% freelance written. Works with a small number of new/unpublished writers each year.** Magazine published 7 times/year. "*Cadet Quest Magazine* shows boys 9-14 how God is at work in their lives and in the world around them." Estab. 1958. Circ. 7,500. Byline given. Pays on acceptance. Publishes ms an average of 4-11 months after acceptance. Accepts simultaneous submissions. Responds in 2 months to submissions. Sample copy for 9×12 SASE. Guidelines for #10 SASE.

Accepts submissions by mail, or by e-mail (must include ms in text of e-mail). Will not open attachments.

NONFICTION Needs how-to, humor, inspirational, interview, personal experience, informational. Special issues: Write for new themes list in February. Send complete ms. Length: 500-1,500 words. **Pays 4-5¢/word.**

REPRINTS Send typed manuscript with rights for sale noted. Payment varies.

PHOTOS Pays $20-30 for photos purchased with ms.

COLUMNS Project Page (uses simple projects boys 9-14 can do on their own made with easily accessible materials; must provide clear, accurate instructions).

FICTION Considerable fiction is used. Fast-moving stories that appeal to a boy's sense of adventure or sense of humor are welcome. Needs adventure, religious, spiritual, sports, comics. Avoid preachiness. Avoid simplistic answers to complicated problems. Avoid long dialogue and little action. No fantasy, science fiction, fashion, horror or erotica. Send complete ms. Length: 900-1,500 words. **Pays 4-5¢/word, and 1 contributor's copy.**

$$ CALLIOPE

Cobblestone Publishing Co., 30 Grove St., Suite C, Peterborough NH 03458-1454. (603)924-7209. Fax: (603)924-7380. E-mail: cfbakeriii@meganet.net. Website: cobblestonepub.com. Lou Waryncia, editorial director; Ann Dillon, art director. **Contact:** Rosalie Baker & Charles Baker, co-editors. **50% freelance written**. Magazine published 9 times/year covering world history (East and West) through 1800 AD for 8 to 14-year-old kids. Articles must relate to the issue's theme. Lively, original approaches to the subject are the primary concerns of the editors in choosing material. Estab. 1990. Circ. 13,000. Byline given. Pays on publication. Kill fee. Accepts queries by mail. If interested, responds 5 months before publication date. Sample copy for $5.95, $2 shipping and handling, and 10×13 SASE. Guidelines available online.

For themes and queries deadlines, visit the Calliope web site at: cobblestonepub.com/magazine/CAL. 2010 themes included: Isabella of Spain-Queen of a New World; Michelangelo; Dutch East India Company; Exploring Africa with Stanley & Livingstone; Meaning of Numbers; Shades of Indigo; The Nile river, and the Zodiac.

NONFICTION Needs essays, general interest, historical, how-to, crafts/woodworking, humor, interview, personal experience, photo feature, technical, travel, recipes. No religious, pornographic, biased, or sophisticated submissions. **Buys 30-40 mss/year.** Query with writing sample, 1-page outline, bibliography, SASE. 400-1000/feature articles; 300-600 words/supplemental nonfiction. **Pays 20-25¢/word.**

PHOTOS Contact: Ann Dillon, art director. If you have photographs pertaining to any upcoming theme, please contact the editor by mail or fax, or send them with your query. You may also send images on speculation. Model/property release preferred. Reviews b&w prints, color slides. Reviews photos with or without accompanying manuscript. We buy one-time use. Our suggested fee range for professional quality photographs follows: ¼ page to full page b/w $15-100; color $25-100. Please note that fees for non-professional quality photographs are negotiated. Cover fees are set on an individual basis for one-time use, plus promotional use. All cover images are color. Prices set by museums, societies, stock photography houses, etc., are paid or negotiated. Photographs that are promotional in nature (e.g., from tourist agencies, organizations, special events, etc.) are usually submitted at no charge. Pays on publication. Credit line given. Buys one-time rights; negotiable.

FICTION Needs adventure, historical, biographical, retold legends. **Buys 10 mss/year.** Length: 1000 words maximum **Pays 20-25¢/word.**

FILLERS Crossword and other word puzzles (no word finds), mazes, and picture puzzles that use the vocabulary of the issue's theme or otherwise relate to the theme. **Pays on an individual basis.**

CLUBHOUSE MAGAZINE

Focus on the Family, 8605 Explorer Dr., Colorado Springs CO 80920. Website: clubhousemagazine.com. **25% freelance written.** Monthly magazine. *Clubhouse* readers are 8-12 year old boys and girls who desire to know more about God and the Bible. Their parents (who typically pay for the membership) want wholesome, educational material with Scriptural or moral insight. The kids want excitement, adventure, action, humor, or mystery. Your job as a writer is to please both the parent and child with each article. Estab. 1987. Circ. 85,000. Byline given. Pays on acceptance. Publishes ms an average of 12-18 months after acceptance. Editorial lead time 5 months. Submit seasonal material 9 months in advance. Responds in 2 months to mss. Sample copy for $1.50 with 9×12 SASE. Guidelines for #10 SASE.

NONFICTION Contact: Jesse Florea, editor. Needs essays, how-to, humor, inspirational, interview, personal experience, photo feature, religious. Avoid Bible stories. Avoid informational-only, science, or educational articles. Avoid biographies told encyclopedia or textbook style. **Buys 6 mss/year.** Send complete ms. Length: 800-1,200 words. **Pays $25-450 for assigned articles. Pays 15-25¢/word for unsolicited articles.**

FICTION Contact: Jesse Florea, editor. Needs adventure, humorous, mystery, religious, suspense, holiday. Avoid contemporary, middle-class family settings (existing authors meet this need), poems (rarely printed), stories dealing with boy-girl relationships. **Buys 10 mss/year.** Send complete ms. Length: 400-1,500 words. **Pays $200 and up for first time contributor**

and 5 contributor's copies; additional copies available.

FILLERS Needs facts, newsbreaks. **Buys 2 mss/year.** Length: 40-100 words.

COBBLESTONE

Cobblestone Publishing, 30 Grove Street, Suite C, Peterborough NH 03458. (800)821-0115. Fax: (603)924-7380. E-mail: customerservice@caruspub.com. Website: cobblestonepub.com. **50% freelance.** Covers material for ages 9-14. "We are interested in articles of historical accuracy and lively, original approaches to the subject at hand. Our magazine is aimed at youths from ages 9 to 14. Writers are encouraged to study recent COBBLESTONE back issues for content and style. (Sample issues are available for $6.95 plus $2.00 shipping and handling. Sample issues will not be sent without prepayment.) All material must relate to the theme of a specific upcoming issue in order to be considered. To be considered, a query must accompany each individual idea (however, you can mail them all together) and must include the following: a brief cover letter stating the subject and word length of the proposed article, a detailed one-page outline explaining the information to be presented in the article, an extensive bibliography of materials the author intends to use in preparing the article, a SASE. Authors are urged to use primary resources and up-to-date scholarly resources in their bibliography. Writers new to COBBLESTONE should send a writing sample with the query. If you would like to know if your query has been received, please also include a stamped postcard that requests acknowledgment of receipt. In all correspondence, please include your complete address as well as a telephone number where you can be reached. A writer may send as many queries for one issue as he or she wishes, but each query must have a separate cover letter, outline, bibliography, and SASE. All queries must be typed. **Please do not send unsolicited manuscripts - queries only!** Prefers to work with published/established writers. Each issue presents a particular theme, making it exciting as well as informative. Half of all subscriptions are for schools. All material must relate to monthly theme." Circ. 15,000. Byline given. Pays on publication. Offers 50% kill fee. Accepts queries by mail, fax. Accepts simultaneous submissions. Guidelines available on website or for SASE; sample copy for $6.95, $2 shipping/handling, 10×13 SASE.

💬 "Cobblestone stands apart from other children's magazines by offering a solid look at one subject and stressing strong editorial content, color photographs throughout, and original illustrations." *Cobblestone* themes and deadline are available on website or with SASE.

🔑 (Specialized: American History, children/teens ages 9-14)

NONFICTION Needs historical, humor, interview, personal experience, photo feature, travel, crafts, recipes, activities. No material that editorializes rather than reports. **Buys 45-50 mss/year.** Query with writing sample, 1-page outline, bibliography, SASE. 800 words/feature articles; 300-600 words/supplemental nonfiction; up to 700 words maximum/activities. **Pays 20-25¢/word.**

PHOTOS Contact: Editor, by mail or fax, or send photos with your query. Captions, identification of subjects required, model release. Reviews contact sheets, transparencies, prints. $15-100/b&w. Pays on publication. Credit line given. Buys one-time rights. Our suggested fee range for professional quality photographs follows: ¼ page to full page b/w $15 to $100; color $25 to $100. Please note that fees for non-professional quality photographs are negotiated.

FICTION Needs adventure, historical, biographical, retold legends. **Buys 5 mss/year.** 800 words maximum. **Pays 20-25¢/word.**

POETRY Contact: Meg Chorlian. Needs free verse, light verse, traditional. Serious and light verse considered. Must have clear, objective imagery. Buys 3 poems/year. 50 lines maximum **Pays on an individual basis. Acquires all rights.**

FILLERS "Crossword and other word puzzles (no word finds), mazes, and picture puzzles that use the vocabulary of the issue's theme or otherwise relate to the theme." **Pays on an individual basis.**

⊕ $$ CRICKET

Carus Publishing Co., 700 E. Lake St., Suite 300, Chicago IL 60601. (312)701-1720, ext. 10. Website: cricketmag.com. Alice Letvin. **Contact:** Submissions Editor. Monthly magazine for children ages 9-14. "*Cricket* is looking for more fiction and nonfiction for the older end of its 9-14 age range, as well as contemporary stories set in other countries. It also seeks humorous stories and mysteries (not detective spoofs), fantasy and original fairy tales, stand-alone excerpts from unpublished novels, and well-written/researched science articles." Estab. 1973. Circ. 73,000. Byline given. Pays on publication. Accepts queries by mail. Responds in 4-6 months to mss. Guidelines available online.

NONFICTION Submit complete ms, SASE. Length: 200-1,500 words. **Pays 25¢/word maximum.**

REPRINTS with rights for sale noted and information about when and where the material previously appeared.

PHOTOS Commissions all art separately from the text. Tearsheets/photocopies of both color and b&w work are considered. Accepts artwork done in pencil, pen and ink, watercolor, acrylic, oil, pastels, scratchboard, and woodcut. Does not want work that is overly caricatured or cartoony. It is especially helpful to see pieces showing young people, animals, action scenes, and several scenes from a narrative showing a character in different situations and emotional states.

FICTION Needs fantasy, historical, humorous, mystery, science fiction, realistic, contemporary, folk tales, fairy tales, legends, myths. No didactic, sex, religious, or horror stories. **Buys 75-100 mss/year.** Length: 200-2,000 words. **Pays 25¢/word maximum, and 6 contributor's copies; $2.50 charge for extras.**

POETRY Serious, humorous, nonsense rhymes. Buys 20-30 poems/year. 50 lines maximum **Pays $3/line maximum.**

FILLERS Crossword puzzles, logic puzzles, math puzzles, crafts, recipes, science experiments, games and activities from other countries, plays, music, art.

TIPS Writers: "Read copies of back issues and current issues. Adhere to specified word limits. *Please* do not query." Would currently like to see more fantasy and science fiction." Illustrators: "Send only your best work and be able to reproduce that quality in assignments. Put name and address on *all* samples. Know a publication before you submit your style appropriate?" Writers: "Read copies of back issues and current issues. Adhere to specified word limits. *Please* do not query." Would currently like to see more fantasy and science fiction." Illustrators: "Send only your best work and be able to reproduce that quality in assignments. Put name and address on *all* samples. Know a publication before you submit your style appropriate?"

$$ DIG MAGAZINE

Cobblestone Publishing, 30 Grove St., Suite C, Peterborough NH 03458-1454. (603)924-7209. Fax: (603)924-7380. Website: digonsite.com. **Contact:**

CONSUMER MAGAZINES

Rosalie Baker, editor. **75% freelance written**. Magazine published 9 times/year covering archaeology for kids ages 9-14. Estab. 1999. Circ. 20,000. Byline given. Pays on publication. Publishes ms an average of 1 year after acceptance. Editorial lead time 1 year. Accepts queries by mail. Responds in several months. Sample copy for $5.95 with 8×11 SASE or $10 without SASE. Guidelines available online.

NONFICTION Needs personal experience, photo feature, travel, archaeological excavation reports. No fiction. Occasional paleontology stories accepted. **Buys 30-40 mss/year.** Query with published clips. Length: 100-1,000 words. **Pays 20-25¢/word.**

PHOTOS State availability. Identification of subjects required. Negotiates payment individually.

🟡🟢 FACES

Cobblestone Publishing, 30 Grove St., Suite C, Peterborough NH 03458. (603)924-7209; (800)821-0115. Fax: (603)924-7380. E-mail: customerservice@caruspub.com. Website: cobblestonepub.com. **90-100% freelance written**. "Publishes monthly throughout the year, *Faces* covers world culture for ages 9-14. It stands apart from other children's magazines by offering a solid look at one subject and stressing strong editorial content, color photographs throughout, and original illustrations. *Faces* offers an equal balance of feature articles and activities, as well as folktales and legends." Estab. 1984. Circ. 15,000. Byline given. Pays on publication. Offers 50% kill fee. Accepts queries by mail, e-mail. Accepts simultaneous submissions. Sample copy for $6.95, $2 shipping and handling, 10 x 13 SASE. Guidelines with SASE or online.

NONFICTION Needs historical, humor, interview, personal experience, photo feature, travel, recipes, activities, crafts. **Buys 45-50 mss/year.** Query with writing sample, 1-page outline, bibliography, SASE. 800 words/feature articles; 300-600/supplemental nonfiction; up to 700 words/activities. **Pays 20-25¢/word.**

PHOTOS "Contact the editor by mail or fax, or send photos with your query. You may also send images on speculation.". Captions, identification of subjects, model releases required. Reviews contact sheets, transparencies, prints. Pays $15-100/b&w; $25-100/color; cover fees are negotiated.

FICTION Needs ethnic, historical, retold legends/folktales, original plays. 800 words maximum. **Pays 20-25¢/word.**

POETRY Serious and light verse considered. Must have clear, objective imagery. 100 lines maximum. **Pays on an individual basis.**

FILLERS "Crossword and other word puzzles (no word finds), mazes, and picture puzzles that use the vocabulary of the issue's theme or otherwise relate to the theme." **Pays on an individual basis.**

🟡🟢 GIRLS' LIFE

Monarch Publishing, 4529 Harford Rd., Baltimore MD 21214. Website: girlslife.com. **Contact:** Katie Abbondanza, senior editor. Bimonthly magazine covering girls ages 9-15. Estab. 1994. Circ. 2,000,000. Byline given. Pays on publication. Publishes ms an average of 3 months after acceptance. Editorial lead time 4 months. Submit seasonal material 5 months in advance. Accepts queries by mail. Responds in 1 month to queries. Sample copy for $5 or online. Guidelines available online.

NONFICTION Needs book excerpts, essays, general interest, how-to, humor, inspirational, interview, new product, travel, beauty, relationship, sports. Special issues: Back to School (August/September); Fall, Halloween (October/November); Holidays, Winter (December/January); Valentine's Day, Crushes (February/March); Spring, Mother's Day (April/May); and Summer, Father's Day (June/July). **Buys 40 mss/year.** Query by mail with published clips. Submit complete mss on spec only. Length: 700-2,000 words. **Pays $350/regular column; $500/feature.**

PHOTOS State availability. Captions, identification of subjects, model releases required. Reviews contact sheets, negatives, transparencies. Negotiates payment individually.

COLUMNS Buys 20 mss/year. Query with published clips. **Pays $150-450.**

🟢 HIGHLIGHTS FOR CHILDREN

803 Church St., Honesdale PA 18431-1824. (570)253-1080. Fax: (570)251-7847. Website: Highlights.com. Christine French Clark, editor-in-chief. **Contact:** Manuscript Coordinator. **80% freelance written**. Monthly magazine for children up to age 12. "This book of wholesome fun is dedicated to helping children grow in basic skills and knowledge, in creativeness, in ability to think and reason, in sensitivity to others, in high ideals, and worthy ways of living—for children are the world's most important people. We publish stories for beginning and advanced readers. Up to 500 words for beginners (ages 3-7), up to 800

words for advanced (ages 8-12)." Estab. 1946. Circ. approx. 2.5 million. Pays on acceptance. Accepts queries by mail. Responds in 2 months to queries. Sample copy free. Guidelines on website in "About Us" area.

NONFICTION "Generally we prefer to see a manuscript rather than a query. However, we will review queries regarding nonfiction." 800 words maximum **Pays $25 for craft ideas and puzzles; $25 for fingerplays; $150 and up for articles.**

PHOTOS Contact: Cindy Faber Smith, art director. Reviews color 35mm slides, photos, or electronic files.

FICTION "Meaningful stories appealing to both girls and boys, up to age 12. Vivid, full of action. Engaging plot, strong characterization, lively language. Prefers stories in which a child protagonist solves a dilemma through his or her own resources. Seeks stories that the child ages 8-12 will eagerly read, and the child ages 2-7 will like to hear when read aloud (500-800 words). Stories require interesting plots and a number of illustration possiblities. Also need rebuses (picture stories 120 words or under), stories with urban settings, stories for beginning readers (100-500 words), sports and humorous stories, adventures, holiday stories, and mysteries. We also would like to see more material of 1-page length (300 words), both fiction and factual. Needs adventure, fantasy, historical, humorous, animal, contemporary, folktales, multi-cultural, problem-solving, sports. No war, crime or violence. Send complete ms. Length: words. **Pays $150 minimum.**

POETRY Lines/poem: 16 or less ("most poems are shorter"). Considers simultaneous submissions ("please indicate"); no previously published poetry. No e-mail submissions. "Submit typed manuscript with very brief cover letter." Occasionally comments on submissions "if manuscript has merit or author seems to have potential for our market." Guidelines available for SASE. Responds "generally within one month." Always sends prepublication galleys. Pays 2 contributor's copies; "money varies." Acquires all rights.

JACK AND JILL

Children's Better Health Institute, P.O. Box 567, Indianapolis IN 46206-0567. (317)636-8881. E-mail: j.goodman@cbhi.org. Website: jackandjillmag.org. **50% freelance written.** Bimonthly magazine published 6 times/year for children ages 8-12. "Material will not be returned unless accompanied by SASE with sufficient postage. No queries. May hold material being seriously considered for up to 1 year." Es-

tab. 1938. Circ. 200,000. Byline given. Pays on publication. Publishes ms an average of 8 months after acceptance. Submit seasonal material 8 months in advance. Responds in 12 weeks to mss. Guidelines available online.

FICTION Pays 30¢/word minimum.

JUNIOR SCHOLASTIC

Scholastic, Inc., 557 Broadway, New York NY 10012-3902. (212)343-6100. Fax: (212)343-6945. E-mail: junior@scholastic.com. Website: juniorscholastic.com. Magazine published 18 times/year. Edited for students ages 11-14. Circ. 535,000. Editorial lead time 6 weeks.

LADYBUG

Carus Publishing Co., 700 E. Lake St., Suite 300, Chicago IL 60601. (312)701-1720. Website: cricketmag.com. Suzanne Beck, man. art dir. **Contact:** Marianne Carus, editor-in-chief. Monthly magazine for children ages 2-6. "We look for quality literature and nonfiction." Estab. 1990. Circ. 125,000. Byline given. Pays on publication. Responds in 6 months to mss. Guidelines available online.

NONFICTION Buys 35 mss/year. Send complete ms, SASE. Length: 400-700 words. **Pays 25¢/word ($25 minimum).**

PHOTOS Artists should submit tearsheets/photocopies of artwork to be kept in our illustrator files. $500/spread; $250/page.

FICTION Read-aloud stories, picture stories, original retellings of folk and fairy tales, multicultural stories. **Buys 30 mss/year.** 800 words maximum. **Pays 25¢/word ($25 minimum).**

POETRY Needs light verse, traditional. Buys 40 poems/year. Submit maximum 5 poems. 20 lines maximum. **Pays $3/line ($25 minimum).**

FILLERS Learning activities, games, crafts, songs, finger games. See back issues for types, formats, and length.

MAGIC DRAGON

Association for Encouragement of Children's Creativity, P.O. Box 687, Webster NY 14580. E-mail: magicdragon@rochester.rr.com. Website: magicdragonmagazine.com. Quarterly magazine covering children's writing and art (no photography). "All work is created by children up to age 12 (elementary school grades). We consider stories, poems, and artwork. Queries, writing and art accepted by USPS mail and by e-mail.". Estab. 2005. Circ. 3,500. Byline given. Pays 1 contributor copy on publication. Editorial lead time 3-6 months. Submit seasonal material 6 months in advance. Accepts queries by mail, e-mail. Responds in 2 weeks to queries. Sample copy for $4. Guidelines available online.

NONFICTION Needs essays, humor, inspirational, personal experience. Send complete ms. Length: 250 words maximum.

PHOTOS Include a SASE with adequate postage with all original artwork. If it's a copy, make sure the colors and copy are the same and the lines are clear. Include an explanation of how you created the art (crayon, watercolor, paper sculpture, etc).

FICTION Needs adventure, fantasy, historical, humorous.

POETRY Needs free verse, haiku, light verse, traditional. Length: 30 lines maximum.

$$$ ⊘ MUSE

140 S. Dearborn, Suite 1450, Chicago IL 60604. Website: cricketmag.com. Estab. 1996. Circ. 40,000.

$$$$ NATIONAL GEOGRAPHIC KIDS

National Geographic Society, 1145 17th St. NW, Washington DC 20036. Website: kidsnationalgeographic.com. **70% freelance written**. Magazine published 10 times/year. It's our mission to excite kids about their world. We are the children's magazine that makes learning fun. Estab. 1975. Circ. 1.3 million. Byline given. Pays on acceptance. Offers 10% kill fee. $100 Publishes ms an average of 6 months after acceptance. Editorial lead time 6+ months. Submit seasonal material 6+ months in advance. Accepts queries by mail. NoAccepts simultaneous submissions. Sample copy for #10 SAE. Guidelines free.

NONFICTION Needs general interest, humor, interview, technical, travel, animals, human interest, science, technology, entertainment, archaeology, pets. Special issues: "We do not release our editorial calendar. We do not want poetry, sports, fiction, or story ideas that are too young—our audience is between ages 8-14." Query with published clips and resume. Length: 100-1,000 words. **Pays $1/word for assigned articles.** Pays expenses of writers on assignment.

PHOTOS Contact: Jay Sumner, photo director. State availability. Captions, identification of subjects, model releases required. Reviews contact sheets, negatives, transparencies, prints. Negotiates payment individually.

COLUMNS Amazing Animals (animal heroes, stories about animal rescues, interesting/funny animal tales), 100 words; Inside Scoop (fun, kid-friendly news items), 50-70 words. Query with published clips. **Pays $1/word.**

$ NATURE FRIEND MAGAZINE

4253 Woodcock Lane, Dayton VA 22821. (540)867-0764. E-mail: photos@naturefriendmagazine.com. Website: dogwoodridgeoutdoors.com; naturefriendmagazine.com. **Contact:** Kevin Shank, editor. **80% freelance written.** Monthly magazine covering nature. *"Nature Friend* includes stories, puzzles, science experiments, nature experiments—all submissions need to honor God as creator." Estab. 1982. Circ. 13,000. Byline given. Pays on publication. Editorial lead time 4 months. Submit seasonal material 6 months in advance. Accepts simultaneous submissions. Responds in 6 months to mss. Sample copy and writer's guidelines for $10 postage paid.

NONFICTION Needs how-to, nature, science experiments, photo feature, articles about interesting/unusual animals. No poetry, evolution, animals depicted in captivity. **Buys 50 mss/year.** Send complete ms. Length: 250-900 words. **Pays 5¢/word.**

PHOTOS Send photos. Captions, identification of subjects required. Reviews prints. Offers $20-75/photo.

COLUMNS Learning By Doing, 500-900 words. **Buys 12 mss/year.** Send complete ms.

FILLERS Needs facts, puzzles, short essays on something current in nature. **Buys 35 mss/year.** Length: 150-250 words. **5¢/word.**

$$ NEW MOON

New Moon Publishing, Inc., P.O. Box 161287, Duluth MN 55816. (218)728-5507. Fax: (218)728-0314. E-mail: girl@newmoon.org. Website: newmoon.org. **25% freelance written**. Bimonthly magazine covering girls ages 8-14, edited by girls aged 8-14. "In general, all material should be pro-girl and feature girls and women as the primary focus. *New Moon* is for every girl who wants her voice heard and her dreams taken seriously. *New Moon* celebrates girls, explores the passage from girl to woman, and builds healthy resistance to gender inequities. The *New Moon* girl is true to herself and *New Moon* helps her as she pursues her unique path in life, moving confidently into the world." Estab. 1992. Circ. 30,000. Byline given. Pays on publication. Publishes ms an average of 6 months after acceptance. Editorial lead time 6 months. Submit seasonal material 8 months in advance. Accepts queries by mail, e-mail, fax. No-Accepts simultaneous submissions. Responds in 2 months to mss. Sample copy for $7 or online. Guidelines for SASE or online.

NONFICTION Needs essays, general interest, humor, inspirational, interview, opinion, personal experience, written by girls, photo feature, religious, travel, multicultural/girls from other countries. No fashion, beauty, or dating. **Buys 20 mss/year.** Send complete ms. Length: 600 words. **Pays 6-12¢/word.**

PHOTOS State availability. Captions, identification of subjects required. Negotiates payment individually.

COLUMNS Women's Work (profile of a woman and her job relating the the theme), 600 words; Herstory (historical woman relating to theme), 600 words. **Buys 10 mss/year.** Query. **Pays 6-12¢/word**

FICTION Prefers girl-written material. All girl-centered. Needs adventure, fantasy, historical, humorous, slice-of-life vignettes. **Buys 6 mss/year.** Send complete ms. Length: 1,200-1,400 words. **Pays 6-12¢/word.**

POETRY No poetry by adults.

$ SHINE BRIGHTLY

GEMS Girls' Clubs, P.O. Box 7259, Grand Rapids MI 49510. (616)241-5616. Fax: (616)241-5558. E-mail: shinebrightly@gemsgc.org. Website: gemsgc.org. **Contact:** Jan Boone, editor; Kelli Ponstein, managing editor. **80% freelance written. Works with new and published/established writers.** Monthly magazine (with combined June/July, August summer issue). Our purpose is to lead girls into a living relationship with Jesus Christ and to help them see how God is at work in their lives and the world around them. Puzzles, crafts, stories, and articles for girls ages 9-14. Estab. 1970. Circ. 17,000. Byline given. Pays on publication. Publishes ms an average of 1 year after acceptance. Submit seasonal material 1 year in advance. Accepts simultaneous submissions. Responds in 2 months to queries. Sample copy for 9×12 SAE with 3 first class stamps and $1. Guidelines available online.

NONFICTION Needs humor, inspirational, seasonal and holiday, interview, personal experience, avoid the testimony approach, photo feature, query first, religious, travel, adventure, mystery. **Buys 35 unsolicited mss/year.** Send complete ms to shinebrightly@gemsgc.org. Length: 100-900 words. **Pays 3-5¢/word, plus 2 copies.**

REPRINTS Send typed manuscript with rights for sale noted and information about when and where the material previously appeared.

PHOTOS Purchased with or without ms. Appreciate multicultural subjects. Reviews 5×7 or 8×10 clear color glossy prints. Pays $25-50 on publication.

COLUMNS How-to (crafts); puzzles and jokes; quizzes. Length: 200-400 words. Send complete ms. **Pay varies**

FICTION Needs adventure, that girls could experience in their hometowns or places they might realistically visit, ethnic, historical, humorous, mystery, believable only, religious, nothing too preachy, romance, slice-of-life vignettes, suspense, can be serialized. **Buys 20 mss/year.** Send complete ms. Length: 400-900 words. **Pays up to $35.**

POETRY Needs free verse, haiku, light verse, traditional. **Pays $5-15.**

$ SPARKLE

GEMS Girls' Clubs, P.O. Box 7259, Grand Rapids MI 49510. (616)241-5616. Fax: (616)241-5558. E-mail: kelli@gemsgc.org. Website: gemsgc.org. **80% freelance written.** Magazine published 6 times/year that helps girls in first through third grades grow in a stronger relationship with Jesus Christ. *Sparkle*'s mission is to prepare girls for a life of living out their faith. Our mission is to prepare girls to become world changers. We aspire for girls to passionately shadow Jesus, seeking to live, act and talk so that others are drawn toward the savior. Estab. 2002. Circ. 5,000. Byline given. Pays on publication. Offers $20 kill fee. Editorial lead time 3 months. Submit seasonal material 1 year in advance. Accepts queries by mail. Accepts simultaneous submissions. Responds in 3 weeks to queries. Responds in 3 months to mss. Sample copy for 9x13 SAE, 3 first-class stamps, and $1 for coverage/publication cost. Writer's guidelines for #10 SASE or online.

NONFICTION Needs how-to, crafts/recipes, humor, inspirational, personal experience, photo feature, religious, travel. Constant mention of God is not necessary if the moral tone of the story is positive. **Buys 15 mss/year.** Send complete ms. Length: 100-400 words. **Pays $20/article**

PHOTOS Send photos. Identification of subjects required. Reviews at least 5×7 clear color glossy prints, GIF/JPEG files on CD. Offers $25-50/photo.

COLUMNS Crafts; puzzles and jokes; quizzes, all 200-400 words. Send complete ms. **Payment varies.**

FICTION Needs adventure, ethnic, fantasy, humorous, mystery, religious, slice-of-life vignettes. **Buys 10 mss/year.** Send complete ms. Length: 100-400 words. **Pays $20/story.**

POETRY Needs free verse, haiku, light verse, traditional. We do not wish to see anything that is too difficult for a first grader to read. We wish it to remain light. The style can be fun, but also teach a truth. No violence or secular material. Buys 4 poems/year. Submit maximum 4 poems.

FILLERS Needs facts, short humor. **Buys 6 mss/year.** Length: 50-150 words. **Pays $10-15.**

⊕⊕ SPIDER

Cricket Magazine Group, 70 East Lake St., Suite 300, Chicago IL 60601. (312)701-1720. Fax: (312)701-1728. Website: cricketmag.com. **85% freelance written.** Monthly reading and activity magazine for children ages 6 to 9. *Spider* introduces children to the highest quality stories, poems, illustrations, articles, and activities. It was created to foster in beginning readers a love of reading and discovery that will last a lifetime. We're looking for writers who respect children's intelligence. Estab. 1994. Circ. 70,000. Byline given. Pays on publication. Accepts simultaneous submissions. Responds in 6 months to mss. Guidelines available online.

NONFICTION Submit complete ms, bibliography, SASE. Length: 300-800 words. **Pays up to 25¢/word.**

REPRINTS Send photocopy with rights for sale noted and information about when and where the material previously appeared.

PHOTOS For art samples, it is especially helpful to see pieces showing children, animals, action scenes, and several scenes from a narrative showing a character in different situations. Send photocopies/tearsheets. Also considers photo essays (prefers color, but b&w is also accepted). Captions, identification of subjects, model releases required. Reviews contact sheets, transparencies, 8×100 prints.

FICTION Stories should be easy to read. Needs fantasy, humorous, science fiction, folk tales, fairy tales, fables, myths. Length: 300-1,000 words. **Pays up to 25¢/word.**

POETRY Needs free verse, traditional. Submit maximum 5 poems. 20 lines maximum **Pays $3/line maximum.**

FILLERS Recipes, crafts, puzzles, games, brainteasers, math and word activities. 1-4 pages. **Pays for fillers.**

⊕ STONE SOUP

Children's Art Foundation, P.O. Box 83, Santa Cruz CA 95063-0083. (831)426-5557. Fax: (831)426-1161. E-mail: editor@stonesoup.com. Website: stonesoup.com. **Contact:** Ms. Gerry Mandel, editor. **100% freelance written.** Bimonthly magazine of writing and art by children, including fiction, poetry, book reviews, and art by children through age 13. "Audience is children, teachers, parents, writers, artists. We have a preference for writing and art based on real-life experiences; no formula stories or poems." Estab. 1973. Circ. 15,000. Pays on publication. Publishes ms an average of 4 months after acceptance. Submit seasonal material 6 months in advance. Sample copy by phone only. Guidelines available online.

○ "Stories and poems from past issues are available online."

NONFICTION Needs historical, personal experience, book reviews. **Buys 12 mss/year. Pays $40.**

FICTION Contact: Ms. Gerry Mandel, editor. Needs adventure, ethnic, experimental, fantasy, historical, humorous, mystery, science fiction, slice-of-life vignettes, suspense. We do not like assignments or formula stories of any kind. **Buys 60 mss/year.** Send complete ms. Length: 150-2,500 words. **Pays $40 for stories. Authors also receive 2 copies, a certificate, and discounts on additional copies and on subscriptions.**

POETRY Needs avant-garde, free verse. *Stone Soup*, published 6 times/year, showcases writing and art by children ages 13 and under. Wants free verse poetry. Does not want rhyming poetry, haiku, or cinquain. No simultaneous submissions. No e-mail submissions. "Submissions can be any number of pages, any format. Include name, age, home address, and phone number. Don't include SASE; we respond only to those submissions under consideration and cannot return manuscripts." Guidelines available on website. Responds in up to 6 weeks. Acquires all rights. Returns rights upon request. Open to reviews by children. Buys 12 poems/year. **Pays $40/poem, a certificate, and 2 contributor's copies plus discounts.**

⊘⊕⊕ U.S. KIDS

Children's Better Health Institute, 1100 Waterway Blvd, Indianapolis IN 46202-0567. (317)634-1100. Website: uskidsmags.com. **50% freelance written.** Magazine published 8 times/year featuring kids doing extraordinary things, especially activities related to health, sports, the arts, interesting hobbies, the environment, computers, etc. Estab. 1987. Circ. 230,000. Byline given. Pays on publication. Publishes ms an average of 4 months after acceptance. Editorial lead time 6 months. Submit seasonal material 6 months in advance. Responds in 4 months to mss. Sample copy for $2.95 or online. Guidelines for #10 SASE.

○ *U.S. Kids* is being retargeted to a younger audience. Closed to submissions until further notice.

NONFICTION Needs general interest, how-to, interview, science, kids using computers, multicultural. **Buys 16-24 mss/year.** Send complete ms. 400 words maximum **Pays up to 25¢/word.**

PHOTOS State availability. Captions, identification of subjects, model releases required. Reviews contact sheets, negatives, transparencies, color photocopies, or prints. Negotiates payment individually.

COLUMNS Real Kids (kids doing interesting things); Fit Kids (sports, healthy activities); Computer Zone. Length: 300-400 words. Send complete ms. **Pays up to 25¢/word**

FICTION Buys very little fictional material. **Buys 1-2 mss/year.** Send complete ms. 400 words **Pays up to 25¢/word.**

POETRY Needs light verse, traditional. Buys 6-8 poems/year. Submit maximum 6 poems. Length: 8-24 lines. **Pays $25-50.**

FILLERS Needs facts, newsbreaks, short humor, puzzles, games, activities. Length: 200-500 words. **Pays 25¢/word.**

○ MAG

3968 Long Gun Place, Victoria BC V8N 3A9 Canada. E-mail: editor@mag.ca; jude@mag.com. Website: mag.ca. **Contact:** Jude Isabella, Managing Editor; David Garrison, Publisher; Shannon Hunt, Editor. Bimonthly magazine. " Mag is designed to make science accessible, interesting, exciting, and fun. Written for children ages 10 to 15, Mag covers a range of topics including science and technology news, environmental updates, do-at-home projects and articles about Canadian science and scientists." Children's Middle readers: all the sciences-math, engineering, biology, physics, chemistry, etc. Buys 30 mss/year. Generally publishes ms 3 months after acceptance. Emphasis on Canadian writers. Buys 2 illustrations/issue; 10 illustrations/year. Uses color artwork only. Works on assignment only. Reviews ms/illustration packages from artists. Query.

Illustration only: Query with samples. Samples filed. Credit line given. "Looking for science, technology, nature/environment photos based on current editorial needs." Photo captions required. Uses color prints. Provide resume, business card, promotional literature, tearsheets if possible. Will buy if photo is appropriate. Usually uses stock agencies. Original artwork returned at job's completion. Pays $ 70-200 for stories and articles. Estab. 1996. Circ. 22,000. Byline given. Pays on publication. Responds to queries/mss in 6 weeks Sample copies available. Writer's guidelines available on the website under "Contact" information.

NONFICTION Query with published clips. Average Length: 250-800/words

PHOTOS Contact: Sam Logan, Art/Photo Director.

LITERARY AND LITTLE

ACORN

OutOfPocket Press, 122 Calistoga Rd., #135, Santa Rose CA 95409. E-mail: acornhaiku@mac.com. Website: acornhaiku.com. **Contact:** Carolyn Hall, editor. Biannual magazine dedicated to publishing the best of contemporary English language haiku, and in particular to showcasing individual poems that reveal the extraordinary moments found in everyday life. Estab. 1998. Publishes ms an average of 1-3 months after acceptance. Reads submissions in January-February and July-August only. Accepts queries by accepts submissions, mail or e-mail, through e-mail is preferred. NoResponds in 3 weeks to mss. Guidelines and sample poems available online at acornhaiku.com.

POETRY Needs HAIKU. "Decisions made by editor on a rolling basis. Poems judged purely on merit." Sometimes acceptance conditional on minor edits. Often comments on rejected poems. "Does NOT want epigrams, musings, and overt emotion poured into 17 syllables; surreal, science fiction, or political commentary 'ku;' strong puns or raunchy humor. A 5-7-5 syllable count is not necessary or encouraged." Length: 1-5 lines; 17 or fewer syllables.

○ ADVENTURES FOR THE AVERAGE WOMAN

IdeaGems Publications, P.O. Box 4748, Portland ME 04112-4748. (202)746-5160. E-mail: ideagems@aol. com. Website: ideagems.com. **Contact:** Laurie Notch, managing editor. **40-50% freelance written.** Hardcopy periodical AND e-zine containing serial stories (fact and fiction), serial graphic novels, poetry, flash fiction, articles, and artwork on women-centered experiences and adventures. "Monthly feuilleton that includes women-centered adventure, suspense, and mystery stories laced with romance and intrigue. We present a variety of serial stories, flash fiction, articles, and illustrations similar to the days of yore when Dickensian frame stories, dime novels, and penny dreadfuls were all the rage. Most of our tales are made up, but some are based on truth. We also include poetry, photography, and original artwork to add eye-pleasing color to our non-glossy journal. We do not deal with women's issues or offer lifestyle tips. Our stories portray average women in fantastic, nail-biting situations." Estab. 2006. Circ. 2,000. Byline given. Publishes ms an average of 1-3 months after acceptance. Editorial lead time 1-3 months. Submit seasonal material 3 months in advance. Accepts queries by mail, e-mail. Accepts simultaneous submissions. Free sample PDF copy opon request. Guidelines by e-mail and on website.

NONFICTION Needs book excerpts, essays, expose, historical, humor, inspirational, interview, opinion, personal experience, photo feature, photo feature essays of women on the job, technical, travel, exotic journeys—not touristy travelogues, women running their own businesses, encounters with the paranormal. Special issues: New special issue, "TOUGH LIT II" is out now. Dedicated to crime, grit, and suspense writers. Send submissions by January 1. Does not want religious, pornographic, or conservative political material. **Buys 1-4 mss/year.** Query. Length: 500-7,500 words. **"Sorry, we can no longer pay for accepted submissions. We offer free publicity and promotion online and in print plus a complimentary PDF copy."**

PHOTOS Identification of subjects, model releases required. Reviews GIF/JPEG files.

FICTION "We are open to any work of imagination and whimsy where women play central roles. We love stories that tackle issues; however, we do not invite stories with strong religions overtones, racial/gender prejudice, or political bents for the purposes of zealous expostulating. We are not able to review any full-length novels or graphic novels at this time, but you can always send a query and a sample chapter for us to consider." Needs adventure, ethnic, experimental, fantasy, historical, horror, humorous, mystery, novel concepts, romance, science fiction, serialized, slice-of-life vignettes, suspense, "Get us your ghoulish, gory, ghastly, ghostly stories, poems, photos, and artwork for our fearsome fall issue! Send submissions by September 30." New special issue, *TOUGH LIT* is out. Dedicated to crime, grit, and suspense writers. **Buys 1-6 mss/year.** Query. Length: 150-7,500 words. Flash Fiction: 100-500 words. Article: 500 to 2,500 words. Novel excerpt: up to 3 chapters. Short story: 1,500 to 5,000 words.

POETRY Needs avant-garde, free verse, haiku, light verse, traditional. Buys 1-10 poems/year. Submit maximum 2 poems. Length: 3-50 lines.

$ AFRICAN AMERICAN REVIEW

Saint Louis University, 317 Adorjan Hall, 3800 Lindell Blvd., St. Louis MO 63108. (314)977-3688. Fax: (314)977-1514. E-mail: keenanam@slu.edu. Website: aar.slu.edu. Nathan Grant, editor. **65% freelance written**. Quarterly journal covering African-American literature and culture. Essays on African-American literature, theater, film, art and culture generally; interviews; poetry and fiction by African-American authors; book reviews. Estab. 1967. Circ. 2,000. Byline given. Pays on publication. Publishes ms an average of 1 year after acceptance. Editorial lead time 1 year. Responds in 1 week to queries. Responds in 3-6 months to mss. Sample copy for $12. Guidelines available online.

African American Review is the official publication of the Division of Black American Literature and Culture of the Modern Language Association. The magazine received American Literary Magazine Awards in 1994 and 1995. *African American Review* is the official publication of the Division of Black American Literature and Culture of the Modern Language Association. The magazine received American Literary Magazine Awards in 1994 and 1995.

NONFICTION Needs essays, interview. **Buys 30 mss/year.** Query. Length: 6,000-8,500 words.

PHOTOS State availability. Captions required. Pays $100 for covers.

FICTION Contact: Nathan Grant, editor. Needs ethnic, experimental, mainstream. No children's/juvenile/young adult/teen. **Buys 30 mss/year.** Length: No more than 1,500 words. **1 contributor's copy and 5 offprints.**

$ AGNI

Creative Writing Program, Boston University, 236 Bay State Rd., Boston MA 02215. (617)353-7135. Fax: (617)353-7134. E-mail: agni@bu.edu. Website: agnimagazine.org. **Contact:** Sven Birkerts, editor. Biannual magazine. "Eclectic literary magazine publishing first-rate poems, essays, translations, and stories." Estab. 1972. Circ. 3,000 in print, plus more than 60,000 distinct readers online per year. Byline given. Pays on publication. Publishes ms an average of 6 months after acceptance. Editorial lead time 1 year. Accepts queries by mail. Accepts simultaneous submissions. Responds in 2 weeks to queries. Responds in 4 months to mss. Sample copy for $10 or online. Guidelines available online.

○ Reading period September 1-May 31 only. "Online magazine carries original content not found in print edition. All submissions are considered for both." Founding editor Askold Melnyczuk won the 2001 Nora Magid Award for Magazine Editing. Work from *AGNI* has been included and cited regularly in the *Pushcart Prize* and *Best American* anthologies.

FICTION Buys stories, prose poems. "No science fiction or romance." **Buys 20+ mss/year. Pays $10/page up to $150, a one-year subscription, and for print publication: 2 contributor's copies and 4 gift copies.**

POETRY Buys 120+ poems/year. Submit maximum 5 poems. **Pays $20/page up to $150.**

$ $ ALASKA QUARTERLY REVIEW

ESB 208, University of Alaska-Anchorage, 3211 Providence Dr., Anchorage AK 99508. (907)786-6916. E-mail: aqr@uaa.alaska.edu. Website: uaa.alaska.edu/aqr. **95% freelance written**. Semiannual magazine publishing fiction, poetry, literary nonfiction, and short plays in traditional and experimental styles. "*AQR* publishes fiction, poetry, literary nonfiction and short plays in traditional and experimental styles." Estab. 1982. Circ. 2,200. Byline given. Honorariums on publication when funding permits. Publishes ms an average of 6 months after acceptance. Accepts queries by mail. Responds in 1 month to queries. Responds in 6 months to mss. Sample copy for $6. Guidelines available online.

○ *Alaska Quarterly* reports they are always looking for freelance material and new writers.

NONFICTION Buys 0-5 mss/year. Query. Length: 1,000-20,000 words. **Pays $50-200 subject to funding.**

FICTION Contact: Ronald Spatz, fiction editor. "Works in AQR have certain characteristics: freshness, honesty, and a compelling subject. The voice of the piece must be strong—idiosyncratic enough to create a unique persona. We look for craft, putting it in a form where it becomes emotionally and intellectually complex. Many pieces in AQR concern everyday life. We're not asking our writers to go outside themselves and their experiences to the absolute exotic to catch our interest. We look for the experiential and revelatory qualities of the work. We will champion a piece that may be less polished or stylistically sophisticated, if it engages me, surprises me, and resonates for me. The joy in reading such a work is in discovering something true. Moreover, in keeping with our mission to publish new writers, we are looking for voices our readers do not know, voices that may not always be reflected in the dominant culture and that, in all instances, have something important to convey." Needs experimental and traditional literary forms., contemporary, prose poem, novel excerpts, drama: experimental & traditional one-acts. No romance, children's, or inspirational/religious. **Buys 20-26 mss/year; 0-2 mss/year drama. mss./year.** not exceeding 100 pages **Pays $50-200 subject to funding; pays in contributor's copies and subscriptions when funding is limited.**

POETRY Needs avant-garde, free verse, traditional. *Alaska Quarterly Review*, published in 2 double issues/year, is "devoted to contemporary literary art. We publish both traditional and experimental fiction, poetry, literary nonfiction, and short plays." Wants all styles and forms of poetry, "with the most emphasis perhaps on voice and content that displays 'risk,' or intriguing ideas or situations." Has published poetry by Has published poetry by Maxine Kumin, Jane Hirshfield, David Lehman, Pattiann Rogers, Albert Goldbarth, David Wagoner, Robert Pinsky, Linda Pastan, Ted Kooser, Kay Ryan, W. S. Merwin, Sharon Olds and Billy Collins. *Alaska Quarterly Review* is 224-300 pages, digest-sized, professionally printed, perfect-bound, with card cover with color or b&w photo. Receives up to 6,000 submissions/year, accepts 40-90. Subscription: $18. Sample: $6. Pays $10-50 subject to availability of funds; pays in contributor's copies and subscriptions when funding is limited. No light verse. Buys 10-30 poems/year. Submit maximum 10 poems.

Pays $10-50 subject to availability of funds; pays in contributor's copies and subscriptions when funding is limited. Acquires first North American serial rights.

ALIMENTUM, THE LITERATURE OF FOOD

P.O. Box 210028, Nashville TN 37221, Nashville TN 37221. E-mail: submissions@alimentumjournal.com. Website: alimentumjournal.com. **Contact:** Cortney Davis, Poetry Editor. **Byline given.** Biannual magazine covering food in literature. "We're seeking fiction, creative nonfiction, and poetry all around the subject of food or drink. We do not read year-round. Check website for reading periods." Estab. 2005. Accepts queries by mail. Accepts simultaneous submissions. Responds in 1-3 months to mss.

NONFICTION Send complete ms.

FICTION Send complete ms.

POETRY Needs avant-garde, free verse, haiku, light verse, traditional. Submit maximum 5 poem limit/submission. poems.

$ ANDROIDS2 MAGAZINE

Man's Story 2 Publishing Co., 1321 Snapfinger Rd., Decatur GA 30032. E-mail: mansstory2@aol.com. Website: mansstory2.com. **80% freelance written.** Online e-zine. "*Man's Story 2 Magazine* strives to recreate the pulp fiction that was published in the magazines of the 1920s through the 1970s with strong emphasis on 3D graphic art." Estab. 2001. Circ. 500. Pays on publication. Publishes ms an average of 3-6 months after acceptance. Accepts queries by e-mail. Accepts simultaneous submissions. Guidelines available online.

"Story subjects tend to slant toward the damsel in distress."

FICTION Needs adventure, erotica, fantasy, horror, suspense, pulp fiction. **Buys 30-50 mss/year.** Send complete ms. Length: 1,500-3,500 words. **Pays $25.**

$ ARC

Arc Poetry Society, P.O. Box 81060, Ottawa ON K1P 1B1 Canada. E-mail: editor@arcpoetry.ca. Website: arcpoetry.ca. Semiannual magazine featuring poetry, poetry-related articles, and criticism. Our focus is poetry, and Canadian poetry in general, although we do publish writers from elsewhere. We are looking for the best poetry from new and established writers. We often have special issues. Send a SASE for upcoming special issues and contests. Estab. 1978. Circ. 1,500. Byline given. Pays on publication. Publishes ms an average of 6 months after acceptance. Responds in 4 months. Guidelines for #10 SASE.

NONFICTION Needs essays, interview, book reviews. Query first. Length: 500-4,000 words. **Pays $40/printed page (Canadian), and 2 copies.**

PHOTOS Query first. Pays $300 for 10 photos.

POETRY Needs avant-garde, free verse. E-mail submissions not accepted. Buys 60 poems/year. Submit maximum 5 poems. **Pays $40/printed page (Canadian).**

TIPS Please include brief biographical note with submission.

$ ART TIMES

A Literary Journal and Resource for All the Arts, P.O. Box 730, Mount Marion NY 12456-0730. (845)246-6944. Fax: (845)246-6944. E-mail: info@ArtTimesJournal.com. Website: arttimesjournal.com. **Contact:** Raymond J. Steiner. **10% freelance written.** Monthly tabloid covering the arts (visual, theater, dance, music, literary, etc.). "*Art Times* covers the art fields and is distributed in locations most frequented by those enjoying the arts. Our copies are distributed throughout the lower part of the northeast as well as metropolitan New York area; locations include theaters, galleries, museums, schools, art clubs, cultural centers and the like. Our readers are mostly over 40, affluent, art-conscious and sophisticated. Subscribers are located across US and abroad (Italy, France, Germany, Greece, Russia, etc.)." Estab. 1984. Circ. 28,000. Byline given. Pays on publication. Publishes ms an average of 3 years after acceptance. Submit seasonal material 8 months in advance. Accepts simultaneous submissions. Responds in 6 months to queries. Responds in 6 months to mss. Sample copy for sae with 9×12 envelope and 6 first-class stamps. Writer's guidelines for #10 SASE or online.

FICTION Contact: Raymond J. Steiner, fiction editor. Looks for quality short fiction that aspires to be literary. Publishes 1 story each issue. Needs adventure, ethnic, fantasy, historical, humorous, mainstream, science fiction, contemporary. "Nothing violent, sexist, erotic, juvenile, racist, romantic, political, off-beat, or related to sports or juvenile fiction." **Buys 8-10 mss/year.** Send complete ms. 1,500 words maximum **True.**

POETRY Contact: Raymond J. Steiner, poetry editor. Needs avant-garde, free verse, haiku, light verse, traditional. *Art Times*, published monthly (combining

Jan/Feb and July/Aug), is a tabloid newspaper devoted to the fine and performing arts. Focuses on cultural and creative articles and essays, but also publishes some poetry and fiction. Wants "poetry that strives to express genuine observation in unique language. All topics, all forms." *Art Times* is 20-26 pages, newsprint, includes ads. Receives 300-500 poems/month, accepts about 30-35/year. Circulation is 27,000; most distribution is free through galleries, performing arts centers, schools, museums, theatres, etc., in the Northeast Corridor of the U.S. Subscription: $15/year. Sample: $1 with 9×12 SAE and 3 first-class stamps. Submit 4-5 typed poems at a time. Lines/poem: up to 20. No e-mail submissions. Include SASE with all submissions. Has an 18-month backlog. Guidelines available for SASE. Responds in 6 months. Pays 6 contributor's copies plus one-year subscription. "We prefer well-crafted 'literary' poems. No excessively sentimental poetry." Publishes 2-3 poems each issue. Buys 30-35 poems/year. Submit maximum 6 poems. 20 lines maximum. **Offers contributor copies and 1 year's free subscription.**

$ ARTFUL DODGE

Dept. of English, College of Wooster, Wooster OH 44691. (330)263-2577. E-mail: artfuldodge@wooster.edu. Website: wooster.edu/artfuldodge. Annual magazine that takes a strong interest in poets who are continually testing what they can get away with successfully in regard to subject, perspective, language, etc., but who also show mastery of the current American poetic techniques—its varied textures and its achievement in the illumination of the particular. There is no theme in this magazine, except literary power. We also have an ongoing interest in translations from Central/Eastern Europe and elsewhere. Estab. 1979. Circ. 1,000. Accepts queries by mail. NoAccepts simultaneous submissions. Responds in 1-6 months to mss. Sample copy for $7. Guidelines for #10 SASE.

FICTION Contact: Marcy Campbell, fiction editor. Needs experimental, prose poem. We judge by literary quality, not by genre. We are especially interested in fine English translations of significant prose writers. Translations should be submitted with original texts. **Pays 2 contributor's copies and honorarium of $5/page, thanks to funding from the Ohio Arts Council.**

POETRY Contact: Philip Brady, poetry editor. We are interested in poems that utilize stylistic persuasions both old and new to good effect. We are not afraid of poems which try to deal with large social, political, historical, and even philosophical questions—especially if the poem emerges from one's own life experience and is not the result of armchair pontificating. We don't want cute, rococo surrealism, someone's warmed-up, left-over notion of an avant-garde that existed 10-100 years ago, or any last bastions of rhymed verse in the civilized world. Buys 20 poems/year. Submit maximum 6 poems. **Pays $5/page honorarium and 2 contributor's copies.**

BATEAU PRESS

P.O. Box 2335, Amherst MA 01004. E-mail: info@bateaupress.org; ashley@bateaupress.org; submit@bateaupress.org. Website: bateaupress.org. **Contact:** Ashley Schaffer, managing editor. Biannual magazine publishing poetry, flash fiction, short plays, mini reviews, comic strips or graphic narratives, and other illustrations. Byline given. NoAccepts simultaneous submissions. Responds in 1-4 months to mss.

> 💬 "*Bateau* subscribes to no trend but serves to represent as wide a cross-section of contemporary writing as possible. For this reason, readers will most likely love and hate at least something in each issue. We consider this a good thing. To us, it means Bateau is eclectic, open-ended, and not mired in a particular strain."

NONFICTION Send complete ms.

FICTION Send complete ms.

POETRY Needs avant-garde, free verse, haiku, light verse, traditional. Submit maximum 5 poems.

⊕ BELLINGHAM REVIEW

Mail Stop 9053, Western Washington University, Bellingham WA 98225. (360)650-4863. E-mail: bhreview@wwu.edu. Website: wwu.edu/bhreview. Brenda Miller, editor-in-chief. **Contact:** Christopher Carlson, managing editor. **100% freelance written.** Annual small press literary magazine covering poems, stories, and essays. No limitations on form or subject matter. Annual nonprofit magazine published once a year in the Spring. Seeks "Literature of palpable quality: poems stories and essays so beguiling they invite us to touch their essence. The *Bellingham Review* hungers for a kind of writing that nudges the limits of form, or executes traditional forms exquisitely." Estab. 1977. Circ. 1,500. Byline given. Pays on publication when funding allows. Publishes ms an average of 6 months after acceptance. Editorial lead time 6 months. Accepts simultaneous submissions. Responds in 1-6 months. Sample copy for $12. Guidelines available online.

💬 The editors are actively seeking submissions of creative nonfiction, as well as stories that push the boundaries of the form. The Tobias Wolff Award in Fiction Contest runs December 1-March 15; see website for guidelines or send SASE.

NONFICTION Contact: Kate Ver Ploeg, nonfiction editor; K. Toole, nonfiction editor. Needs essays, personal experience. Does not want anything nonliterary. **Buys 4-6 mss/year.** Send complete ms. 9,000 words maximum. **Pays as funds allow, plus contributor copies.**

PHOTOS Contact: Christopher Carlson, managing editor. Pays on publication. $0-75.

FICTION Contact: Josh Browning, fiction editor; Kevin Dickinson, fiction editor; Emily Ehrlich, fiction editor. Literary short fiction. Needs experimental, humorous. Does not want anything nonliterary. **Buys 4-6 mss/year.** Send complete ms. 9,000 words maximum. **Pays as funds allow.**

POETRY Contact: Manda Frederick, poetry editor; Andrew Allison, poetry editor. Needs avant-garde, free verse, traditional. *Bellingham Review*, published twice/year, has no specific preferences as to form. Wants "well-crafted poetry, but are open to all styles." Has published poetry by David Shields, Tess Gallagher, Gary Soto, Jane Hirshfield, Albert Goldbarth, and Rebecca McClanahan. Will not use light verse. Buys 10-30 poems/year. Submit maximum 3-5/poems at a time. poems. Indicate approximate word count on prose pieces. **Pays contributor's copies, a year's subscription, plus monetary payment (if funding allows).**

BIG BRIDGE

Big Bridge Press, P.O. Box 870, Guerniville CA 95446. E-mail: walterblue@bigbridge.org. Website: bigbridge.org. Website covering poetry, fiction, nonfiction, essays, journalism and art. "*Big Bridge* is a webzine of poetry and everything else. If we like it, we'll publish it. We're interested in poetry, fiction, nonfiction essays, journalism and art (photos, line drawings, performance, installations, siteworks, comix, graphics)." Accepts simultaneous submissions. Guidelines available.

💬 "We will begin accepting submissions again in Sept. 2011."

NONFICTION Needs essays, interview, Reviews.

PHOTOS Contact: Terri Carrion, editor. Reviews negatives, prints, GIF/JPEG files. original work.

FICTION Contact: Vernon Frazer, editor. Only accepts electronic submissions.

POETRY Needs avant-garde, free verse, haiku, light verse, traditional.

➕ THE BINNACLE

University of Maine at Machias, 116 O'Brien Ave., Machias ME 04654. E-mail: ummbinnacle@maine.edu. Website: umm.maine.edu/binnacle. **100% freelance written.** Semi-annual alternative paper format covering general arts. "We are interested in fresh voices, not Raymond Carver's, and not the Iowa Workshop's. We want the peculiar, and the idiosyncratic. We want playful and experimental, but understandable. Please see our website for details on our Annual Ultra-Short Competition." (Prize of a minimum of $300.) "We accept submissions for the Fall Edition from March 15 to October 15 and report to writers between October 15 and November 15. We accept submissions for the Spring Edition from September 15 to March 15 and report to writers between March 15 and April 15. We accept submissions for our Ultra-Short Competition between December 1 and February 15 and report to writers between May 15 and June 15." Estab. 1957. Circ. 300. Publishes ms an average of 3 months after acceptance. Editorial lead time 2-3 months. Submit seasonal material 3 months in advance. Accepts queries by e-mail. Does not accept previously published works. Accepts simultaneous submissions. Responds in 1 month to queries. Responds in 3 months to mss. Sample copy for $7. Writer's guidelines online at website or by e-mail.

NONFICTION Needs humor, personal experience. **Buys 1-2 mss/year.** Send complete ms. Length: 100-2,500 words.

PHOTOS Send photos. Reviews prints, GIF/JPEG files. Offers no additional payment for photos accepted with ms.

FICTION Needs ethnic, experimental, humorous, mainstream, slice-of-life vignettes. No extreme erotica, fantasy, horror, or religious, but any genre attuned to a general audience can work. **Buys 10-15 mss/year.** Send complete ms. 2,500 words maximum.

POETRY Needs avant-garde, free verse, haiku, light verse, traditional. No greeting card poetry. Buys 10-15 poems/year. Submit maximum 5 poems. 100 lines maximum.

⊜⊜ BOULEVARD

Opojaz, Inc., 6614 Clayton Rd., Box 325, Richmond Heights MO 63117. (314)862-2643. Fax: (314)862-2982. E-mail: kellyleavitt@boulevardmagazine.org; richardburgin@att.net; richardburgin@netzero.net. E-mail: boulevard.submishmash.com/submit. Website: boulevardmagazine.org. Kelly Leavitt, managing editor. **Contact:** Richard Burgin, editor. **100% freelance written.** Triannual magazine covering fiction, poetry, and essays. "*Boulevard* is a diverse literary magazine presenting original creative work by well-known authors, as well as by writers of exciting promise." Estab. 1985. Circ. 11,000. Byline given. Pays on publication. Offers Publishes ms an average of 9 months after acceptance. Accepts queries by mail. Accepts simultaneous submissions. Responds in 2 weeks to queries. Responds in 3 months to mss. Sample copy for $10. Guidelines available online.

✇➤ "Break in with a touching, intelligent, and original story, poem, or essay."

NONFICTION Needs book excerpts, essays, interview, opinion, photo feature. No pornography, science fiction, children's stories, or westerns. **Buys 10 mss/year.** Send complete ms. Now has online submissions link. 10,000 words maximum. **Pays $20/page, minimum $150.**

FICTION Contact: Richard Burgin, editor. Also sponsors the Short Fiction Contest for Emerging Writers. $1,500 and publication in Boulevard awarded to the winning story by a writer who has not yet published a book of fiction, poetry, or creative nonfiction with a nationally distributed press. All entries must be postmarked by December 31, 2010. Entry fee is $15 for each individual story, with no limit per author. Entry fee includes a one-year subscription to Boulevard (one per author). Make check payable to Boulevard. Needs confession, experimental, mainstream, novel excerpts. "We do not want erotica, science fiction, romance, western, horror, or children's stories." **Buys 20 mss/year.** Send complete ms. Now takes online submissions: pdf, doc, docx, txt, rtf, jpg, gif, mp3, mp4, m4a, zip, tiff, png 8,000 words maximum. **$50-$500 (sometimes higher) for accepted work.**

POETRY Needs avant-garde, free verse, haiku, traditional. *Boulevard*, published 3 times/year, strives "to publish only the finest in fiction, poetry, and nonfiction (essays and interviews). While we frequently publish writers with previous credits, we are very interested in publishing less experienced or unpublished writers with exceptional promise. We've published everything from John Ashbery to Donald Hall to a wide variety of styles from new or lesser known poets. We're eclectic. We are interested in original, moving poetry written from the head as well as the heart. It can be about any topic." Has published poetry by Albert Goldbarth, Molly Peacock, Bob Hicok, Alice Friman, Dick Allen, and Tom Disch. *Boulevard* is 175-250 pages, digest-sized, professionally printed, flat-spined, with glossy card cover. Subscription: $15 for 3 issues, $22 for 6 issues, $25 for 9 issues. "Foreign subscribers, please add $6." Sample: $8 plus 5 first-class stamps and SASE. Make checks payable to Opojaz, Inc. Considers simultaneous submissions with notification; no previously published poems. Guidelines available for SASE, by e-mail, or on website. Responds in less than 2 months. Acquires first-time publication and anthology rights. Does not consider book reviews. "Do not send us light verse. Does not want "poetry that is uninspired, formulaic, self-conscious, unoriginal, insipid." Buys 80 poems/year. Submit maximum 5 poems. Length: 200/max lines. **$25-300 (sometimes higher) depending on length, plus one contributor's copy.**

⊘⊜⊜ BRICK

Brick, P.O. Box 609, Station P, Toronto ON M5S 2Y4 Canada. E-mail: info@brickmag.com. Website: brickmag.com. **90% freelance written.** Semiannual magazine covering literature and the arts. "We publish literary nonfiction of a very high quality on a range of arts and culture subjects." Estab. 1977. Circ. 4,000. Byline given. Pays on publication. 3-5 months Editorial lead time 5 months. Responds in 6 months to mss Sample copy for $15, plus shipping. Guidelines available online.

NONFICTION Needs essays, historical, interview, opinion, travel. No fiction, poetry, personal memoir, or art. **Buys 30-40 mss/year.** Send complete ms. Length: 250-3,000 words. **Pays $75-500 (Canadian).**

PHOTOS : State availability. Reviews transparencies, prints, TIFF/JPEG files. Offers $25-50/photo.

CALYX

Calyx, Inc., P.O. Box B, Corvallis OR 97339. (541)753-9384. Fax: (541)753-0515. E-mail: editor@calyxpress.org. Website: calyxpress.org. **Contact:** The Editor. Biannual journal publishes prose, poetry, art, essays, interviews and critical and book reviews. "*Calyx* exists to publish fine literature and art by women and is committed to publishing the work of all women, including women of color, older women, working class women and other voices that need to be heard. We are committed to discovering and nurturing developing writers." Estab. 1976. Circ. 6,000. Publishes ms an average of 6-12 months after acceptance. Accepts queries by mail, e-mail. Accepts simultaneous submissions. Responds in 4-8 months to mss. Sample copy for $10 plus $4 postage and handling.

> "Annual open submission period is October 1-December 31. Mss received when not open will be returned. Electronic submissions are accepted only from overseas. E-mail for guidelines only."

FICTION All submissions (prose, poetry, art, reviews) should include author's name on each page and be accompanied by a brief (50-word or less) biographical statement, a SASE with forever stamp, phone number, and e-mail address. Even if you indicate that it is unnecessary to return your submission(s), please enclose a SASE for your notification. Prose and poetry should be submitted separately with separate SASEs for each submission category. Length: 5,000 words. **Payment dependent upon grant support. Also receive free issues and 1 volume subscription.**

POETRY *CALYX, A Journal of Art and Literature by Women*, published 3 times every 18 months, contains poetry, prose, art, book reviews, essays, and interviews by and about women. Has published poetry by Maurya Simon, Diane Averill, Carole Boston Weatherford, and Eleanor Wilner. Submit maximum 6 poems at a time poems. **Pays one contributor's copy/poem, plus subscription.**

THE CAPILANO REVIEW

2055 Purcell Way, North Vancouver BC V7J 3H5 Canada. (604)984-1712. E-mail: contact@thecapilanoreview.ca; tcr@capilanou.ca. E-mail: tcr@capilanou.ca. Website: thecapilanoreview.ca. **Contact:** Tamara Lee, managing editor. **100% freelance written.** *The Capilano Review* has a long history of publishing new and established Canadian writers and artists who are experimenting with or expanding the boundaries of conventional forms and contexts. International writers and artists appear in our pages too. Now in its 38th year, the magazine continues to favour the risky, the provocative, the innovative, and the dissident. Tri-annual visual and literary arts magazine that "publishes only what the editors consider to be the very best fiction, poetry, drama, or visual art being produced. *TCR* editors are interested in fresh, original work that stimulates and challenges readers. Over the years, the magazine has developed a reputation for pushing beyond the boundaries of traditional art and writing. We are interested in work that is new in concept and in execution." Estab. 1972. Circ. 800. Byline given. Pays on publication. Publishes ms an average of within 1 year after acceptance. Accepts queries by mail. Only by mail. Does not accept e-mail submissions. Please refer to website for submission guidelines. Responds in 4 months to mss. Sample copy for $10 (outside of Canada, USD). Guidelines for #10 SASE with IRC or Canadian stamps.

PHOTOS Pays $50 for cover and $50/page to maximum of $200 Canadian. Additional payment for electronic rights; negotiable. Pays on publication. Credit line given.

FICTION Send complete ms with SASE and Canadian postage or IRCs. Needs experimental, novel concepts, previously unpublished only, literary. No traditional, conventional fiction. Want to see more innovative, genre-blurring work. **Buys 10-15 mss/year.** Does not accept submissions through e-mail or on disks. 6,000 words **Pays $50-200.**

POETRY Needs avant-garde, free verse, previously unpublished poetry. Buys 40 poems/year. Submit maximum 6-8 poems (with SASE and Canadian postage or IRCs) CAD, subscription, and 2 contributor's copies. Acquires first North American serial rights. poems. Length: No more than 4 pages. **Pays $50-200.**

CHICKEN SOUP FOR THE SOUL PUBLISHING, LLC

Chicken Soup for the Soul Publishing, LLC, Fax: (203)861-7194. E-mail: webmaster@chickensoupforthesoul.com. Website: chickensoup.com. **95% freelance written.** Paperback with 12 publications/year featuring inspirational, heartwarming, uplifting short stories. Estab. 1993. Circ. Over 200 titles; 100 million books in print. Byline given. Pays on publication. Accepts simultaneous submissions.

Responds upon consideration. Guidelines available online.

💬 "Stories must be written in the first person."

NONFICTION No sermon, essay, eulogy, term paper, journal entry, political, or controversial issues. **Buys 1,000 mss/year.** Send complete ms. Length: 300-1,200 words. **Pays $200.**

POETRY Needs traditional. No controversial poetry.

💲💲 CHRYSALIS READER

1745 Gravel Hill Rd., Dillwyn VA 23936. (434)983-3021. E-mail: editor@swedenborg.com; rlawson@sover.net. E-mail: chrysalis@hovac.com. Website: swedenborg. com/chrysalis. **Contact:** Robert F. Lawson, editor. **90% freelance written.** Annual magazine published in the fall. Each issue focuses on a theme: Bridges: Paths Between Worlds (2010), The Marketplace: Exchange (2011) Deadline was Nov. 15, 2010. "*The Chrysalis Reader* is a contemporary journal of spiritual discovery published in honor of Emanuel Swedenborg. Each issue focuses on a meaningful theme that inspires current writings and artwork that address today's questions on spirituality. Essays, fiction, poetry, and artwork give fresh and diverse perspectives from many traditions, personal experiences, and fields of study. As Swedenborg says, 'the essence of a thing cannot come into being unless it unites with a means that can express it." *The Chrysalis Reader* is published annually in the fall. Content of fiction, articles, poetry, etc. should be focused on that issue's theme and directed to the intellectual reader. Estab. 1985. Circ. 2,000. Byline given. Pays on publication. Publishes ms an average of 15 months after acceptance. Accepts queries by mail or e-mail. NoAccepts simultaneous submissions. Responds in 4 weeks to queries. Responds in 6 months to mss. Sample copy for $10. Guidelines and themes by e-mail and online at website.

✂🖙 "*The Chrysalis Reader* audience includes people from numerous faiths and backgrounds. Many of them work in psychology, education, religion, the arts, sciences, or one of the helping professions. The style of writing may be humorous, serious, or some combination of these approaches. Essays, poetry, and fiction that are not evangelical in tone but that are unique in addressing the Chrysalis Reader theme are more likely to be accepted. Our readers are interested in expanding, enriching, or challenging their intellects, hearts, and philosophies, and many also just want to enjoy a good read. For these reasons the editors attempt to publish a mix of writings. Articles and poetry must be related to the theme; however, you may have your own approach to the theme not written in our description."

NONFICTION Needs essays, interviews, personal experiences. Special issues: Upcoming special issues will explore contemporary questions on spirituality. Every anthology has its own theme. 2011 theme: The Marketplace. "We do not want inspirational or religious articles." Manuscripts should be typed, double-spaced, and no longer than 3,000 words. Manuscripts will not be returned to authors without an SASE. Please keep a copy of your submission for your records. It is very important to send for writer's guidelines and sample copies before submitting. Length: 1,500-3,000 words. **Pays $75 for assigned articles.**

PHOTOS Send suggestions for illustrations with submission. Buys original artwork for cover and inside copy; b&w illustrations related to theme. Captions, identification of subjects required. Offers no additional payment for photos accepted with ms.

FICTION Contact: Robert Tucker, fiction editor. Needs adventure, fantasy, historical, science fiction: none of an overtly religious nature. Length: 1,500-3,000 words.

POETRY Contact: Rob Lawson, series editor. "We are interested in all forms of poetry, but none of an overtly religious nature." (Specialized: spirituality; themes) Does not want anything "overly religious or sophomoric." Buys 20 poems/year. Submit maximum of 6 poems. **Pays $75 for prose and $25 for poetry.**

💲💲 CONFRONTATION MAGAZINE

Confrontation Press, English Dept., C. W. Post Campus Long Island University, 720 Northern Blvd., Brookville NY 11548-1300. (516)299-2720. Fax: (516)299-2735. E-mail: confrontation@liu.edu; martin.tucker@liu.edu. Website: liu.edu/confrontation. **Contact:** Jonna Semeiks, editor. **75% freelance written.** Semiannual magazine covering all forms and genres of stories, poems, essays, memoirs, and plays. A special section contains book reviews and cultural commentary. "We are eclectic in our taste. Excellence of style is our dominant concern. We bring new talent to light. We are open to all submissions, each issue contains original work by famous and lesser-known writers and also contains a thematic supplement that 'confront' a topic; the ensuing confrontation is an attempt to see the many sides of an issue rather than a formed conclusion." - Martin Tucker, director Confrontation Publications Estab. 1968. Circ. 2,000. Byline given. Pays on publication. Offers kill fee. Publishes ms an average of 1 year after acceptance. Accepts queries by mail, e-mail, phone. Accepts simultaneous submissions. Responds in 3 weeks to queries. Responds in 2 months to mss. Sample copy for $3.

💬 *Confrontation* has garnered a long list of awards and honors, including the Editor's Award for Distinguished Achievement from CCLP (to Martin Tucker) and NEA grants. Work from the magazine has appeared in numerous anthologies including the *Pushcart Prize, Best Short Stories* and *The O. Henry Prize Stories. Confrontation* does not read mss during June, July, or August and will be returned unread unless commissioned or requested.

NONFICTION Needs essays, personal experience. **Buys 15 mss/year.** Send complete ms. Length: 1,500-5,000 words. **Pays $100-300 for assigned articles. Pays $15-300 for unsolicited articles.**

PHOTOS Semiannual literary magazine. Readers are college-educated lay people interested in literature. Sample copy available for $3. State availability. Photo captions preferred. Reviews photos with or without manuscript. Offers no additional payment for photos accepted with ms. Pays $100-300 for b&w or color cover; $40-100 for b&w inside; $50-100 for color inside. Pays on publication. Credit line given. Buys first North American serial rights; negotiable.

FICTION We judge on quality, so genre is open. Needs experimental, mainstream, novel concepts, if they are self -contained stories, slice-of-life vignettes, contemporary, prose poem. No 'proselytizing' literature or genre fiction. **Buys 60-75 mss/year.** Send complete ms. 6,000 words **Pays $25-250.**

POETRY Contact: Bellinda Kremer, poetry editor. Needs avant-garde, free verse, haiku, light verse, traditional. *Confrontation Magazine*, published semiannually, is interested "in all forms. Our only criterion is high literary merit. We think of our audience as an educated, lay group of intelligent readers. Has published poetry by David Ray, T. Alan Broughton, David Ignatow, Philip Appleman, Jane Mayhall, and Joseph Brodsky. No sentimental verse. No previously published poems. Buys 60-75 poems/year. Submit maximum 6. No more than 10 pages at a time. poems. Lines/poem: Length should generally be kept to 2 pages **Pays $10-100. Pays $5-50 and 1 contributor's copy with discount available on additional copies.**

$ CRAB ORCHARD REVIEW

Southern Illinois University at Carbondale, English Department, Faner Hall, Carbondale IL 62901-4503. (618)453-6833. Fax: (618)453-8224. Website: siu.edu/~crborchd. We are a general interest literary journal published twice/year. We strive to be a journal that writers admire and readers enjoy. We publish fiction, poetry, creative nonfiction, fiction translations, interviews and reviews. Estab. 1995. Circ. 2,200. Publishes ms an average of 9-12 months after acceptance. Accepts simultaneous submissions. Responds in 3 weeks to queries. Responds in 9 months to mss. Sample copy for $8. Guidelines for #10 SASE.

FICTION Contact: Jon Tribble, managing editor. Needs ethnic, excerpted novel. No science fiction, romance, western, horror, gothic or children's. Wants more novel excerpts that also stand alone as pieces. Length: 1,000-6,500 words. **Pays $100 minimum; $20/page maximum, 2 contributor's copies and a year subscription.**

+ $ $ $ DELAWARE BEACH LIFE

Endeavours LLC, Endeavours, LLC, P.O. Box 417, Rehoboth Beach DE 19927. (302)227-9499. E-mail: info@delawarebeachlife.com. Website: delawarebeachlife.com. **Contact:** Terry Plowman, publisher/editor. Covering coastal Delaware. "Delaware Beach Life focuses on coastal Delaware: Fenwick to Lewes. You can go slightly inland as long as there's water and a natural connection to the coast, e.g. Angola or Long Neck." Publishes 8 issues/year. Estab. 2002. Circ. 15,000. Byline given. Pays on acceptance. 50% kill fee. 4 months 6 months editorial lead time. Submit seasonal material 12 months in advance. Accepts queries by e-mail. Accepts previously published mss.Reports in 8 weeks/queries; 6 months/mss Sample copy available online at website. Guidelines free and by e-mail.

💬 "Delaware Beach Life is the only full-color glossy magazine focused on coastal Delaware's culture and lifestyle. Created by a team of the best freelance writers, the magazine takes a deeper look at the wealth of topics that interest coastal residents. Delaware Beach Life features such top-notch writing and photography that it inspires 95% of its readers to save it as a 'coffee-table' magazine."

NONFICTION Needs book excerpts, essays, general interest, humor, interview, opinion, photo feature. Does not want anything not focused on coastal Delaware. Query with published clips. 1,200-3,000/words. **Pays $400-1,000 for assigned articles.** Does not pay expenses of writers on assignment.

PHOTOS Send photos. Photos require captions, identification of subjects. Reviews GIF/JPEG files. Pays $25-100 per photo.

COLUMNS Profiles, History, and Opinion (all coastal DE)—1,200/words each. **Buys Buys 32 mss/year. mss/year.** Query with published clips. **Pays $150-350.**

FICTION Needs adventure, condensed novels, historical, humorous, novel excerpts, Must have coastal theme. Does not want anything not coastal. **Buys 3 mss/year.** Query with published clips. 1,000-2,000/words **True.**

POETRY Needs We use avant-garde, free verse, haiku, light verse, and traditional. Does not want anything not coastal. No erotic poetry. Buys 6 poems/year. Submit maximum 3 poems. 6-15/lines. **Pays $50/max.**

DESCANT

P.O. Box 314, Station P, Toronto ON M5S 2S8 Canada. (416)593-2557. Fax: (416)593-9362. E-mail: info@descant.ca. Website: descant.ca. Quarterly journal. Estab. 1970. Circ. 1,200. Pays on publication. Publishes ms an average of 16 months after acceptance. Editorial lead time 1 year. Accepts queries by mail, e-mail, phone. Sample copy for $8.50 plus postage. Guidelines available online.

> Pays $100 honorarium, plus 1-year's subscription for accepted submissions of any kind.

NONFICTION Needs book excerpts, essays, interview, personal experience, historical.

PHOTOS State availability. Reviews contact sheets, prints. Offers no additional payment for photos accepted with ms.

FICTION Contact: Karen Mulhallen, editor. Short stories or book excerpts. Maximum length 6,000 words; 3,000 words or less preferred. Needs ethnic, experimental, historical, humorous. No gothic, religious, beat. Send complete ms. **Pays $100 (Canadian); additional copies $8.**

POETRY Needs free verse, light verse, traditional. "descant seeks high quality poems and stories in both traditional and innovative form." Annual. Circ. 500-750. Member CLMP. Literary. Submit maximum 6 poems. **Pays $100. Pays on pubication.**

DOWNSTATE STORY

1825 Maple Ridge, Peoria IL 61614. (309)688-1409. E-mail: ehopkins@prairienet.org. Website: wiu.edu/users/mfgeh/dss. Annual magazine covering short fiction with some connection with Illinois or the Midwest. Estab. 1992. Circ. 500. Pays on acceptance. Publishes ms an average of 1 year after acceptance. Accepts simultaneous submissions. Responds ASAP. Sample copy for $8. Guidelines available online.

FICTION Contact: Elaine Hopkins, editor. Needs adventure, ethnic, experimental, historical, horror, humorous, mainstream, mystery, romance, science fiction, suspense, western. No porn. **Buys 10 mss/year.** Length: 300-2,000 words. **Pays $50.**

DUCTS

P.O. Box 3203, Grand Central Station, New York NY 10163. E-mail: fiction@ducts.org; essays@ducts.org. Website: ducts.org. **Contact:** Jonathan Kravetz. DUCTS is a webzine of personal stories, fiction, essays, memoirs, poetry, humor, profiles, reviews and art. "DUCTS was founded in 1999 with the intent of giving emerging writers a venue to regularly publish their compelling, personal stories. The site has been expanded to include art and creative works of all genres. We believe that these genres must and do overlap. DUCTS publishes the best, most compelling stories and we hope to attract readers who are drawn to work that rises above." Semi-annual. Estab. 1999. Circ. 12,000.

ECOTONE

Creative Writing Dept., Univ. of No. Carolina Wilmington, 601 S. College Rd., Wilmington NC 28403. (910)962-2547. Fax: (910)962-7461. E-mail: info@ecotonejournal.com. Website: ecotonejournal.com. Biannual magazine featuring fiction, poetry and nonfiction. "*Ecotone* is a literary journal of place that seeks to publish creative works about the environment and the natural world while avoiding the hushed tones and cliches of much of so-called nature writing. Reading period is Aug. 15 - Apr. 15." Byline given. Accepts simultaneous submissions. Responds in 3-6 months to mss.

NONFICTION Needs personal experience. Send complete ms.

FICTION Needs experimental, mainstream. Send complete ms.

POETRY Needs avant-garde, free verse, haiku, light verse, traditional. Submit maximum 6 poems.

$ EPOCH

Cornell University, 251 Goldwin Smith Hall, Cornell University, Ithaca NY 14853. (607)255-3385. Fax: (607)255-6661. **100% freelance written.** Magazine published 3 times/year. "Well-written literary fiction, poetry, personal essays. Newcomers always welcome. Open to mainstream and avant-garde writing." Estab. 1947. Circ. 1,000. Byline given. Pays on publication. Offers 100% kill fee. Publishes ms an average of 6 months after acceptance. Editorial lead time 6 months. Submit seasonal material 8 months in advance. Accepts queries by mail. Responds in 2 weeks to queries. Responds in 6 weeks to mss. Sample copy for $5. Guidelines for #10 SASE.

NONFICTION Needs essays, interview. No inspirational. **Buys 6-8 mss/year.** Send complete ms. **Pays $5-10/printed page.**

PHOTOS Send photos. Reviews contact sheets, transparencies, any size prints. Negotiates payment individually.

FICTION Contact: Joseph Martin, senior editor. Needs ethnic, experimental, mainstream, novel concepts, literary short stories. No genre fiction. Would like to see more Southern fiction (Southern US). **Buys 25-30 mss/year.** Send complete ms. **Pays $5 and up/printed page.**

POETRY Contact: Nancy Vieira Couto. Needs avant-garde, free verse, haiku, light verse, traditional. Buys 30-75 poems/year. Submit maximum 7 poems. **Pays $5 up/printed page.**

[O] $ $ EVENT

Douglas College, P.O. Box 2503, New Westminster BC V3L 5B2 Canada. (604)527-5293. Fax: (604)527-5095. Website: event.douglas.bc.ca. **100% freelance written.** Magazine published 3 times/year containing fiction, poetry, creative nonfiction, notes on writing, and reviews. We are eclectic and always open to content that invites involvement. Generally, we like strong narrative. Estab. 1971. Circ. 1,250. Byline given. Pays on publication. Publishes ms an average of 8 months after acceptance. Accepts queries by mail, fax. Accepts simultaneous submissions. Responds in 1 month to queries. Responds in 6 months to mss. Sample copy for $5. Guidelines available online.

[O] *Event* does not read mss in July, August, December, and January. No e-mail submissions. All submissions must include SASE (Canadian postage or IRCs only).

FICTION We look for readability, style, and writing that invites involvement. Submit maximum 2 stories. Needs humorous, contemporary. No technically poor or unoriginal pieces. **Buys 12-15 mss/year.** Send complete ms. 5,000 words maximum **Pays $22/page up to $500.**

POETRY Needs free verse. We tend to appreciate the narrative and sometimes the confessional modes. No light verse. Buys 30-40 poems/year. Submit maximum 10 poems. **Pays $25-500.**

$ FICTION

c/o Dept. of English, City College, 138th St. & Covenant Ave., New York NY 10031. Website: fictioninc.com. Semiannual magazine. "As the name implies, we publish only fiction; we are looking for the best new writing available, leaning toward the unconventional. *Fiction* has traditionally attempted to make accessible the inaccessible, to bring the experimental to a broader audience." Estab. 1972. Circ. 4,000. Publishes ms an average of 1 year after acceptance. Accepts simultaneous submissions. Responds in 3 months to mss. Sample copy for $7. Guidelines available online.

[O] Reading period for unsolicited mss is September 15-May 15.

FICTION Needs experimental, humorous, satire, contemporary, literary. translations. No romance, science fiction, etc. **Buys 24-40 mss/year.** Length: 5,000 words. **Pays $114.**

$ FIELD: CONTEMPORARY POETRY & POETICS

Oberlin College Press, 50 N. Professor St., Oberlin OH 44074-1091. (440)775-8408. Fax: (440)775-8124. E-mail: oc.press@oberlin.edu. Website: oberlin.edu/ocpress. **Contact:** Linda Slocum, man. editor. **60% freelance written.** Biannual magazine of poetry, poetry in translation, and essays on contemporary poetry by poets. Estab. 1969. Circ. 1,500. Byline given. Pays on publication. Editorial lead time 4 months. Accepts queries by mail, e-mail, fax, phone, online submission form. Responds in 4-6 weeks to mss. Sample copy for $8. Guidelines available online and for #10 SASE.

[O] "See electronic submission guidelines."

NONFICTION Needs , poetry, poetry in translation.

POETRY Contact: Linda Slocum, man. editor. Buys 120 poems/year. Submit maximum 5 with sase poems. **Pays $15/page.**

FIVE POINTS

Georgia State University, P.O. Box 3999, Atlanta GA 30302-3999. E-mail: info@langate.gsu.edu. Website: webdelsol.com/Five_Points. Triannual. *Five Points* is committed to publishing work that compels the imagination through the use of fresh and convincing language. Estab. 1996. Circ. 2,000. Publishes ms an average of 6 months after acceptance. Sample copy for $7.

FICTION Contact: Megan Sexton, executive editor. **Pays $15/page minimum; $250 maximum, free subscription to magazine and 2 contributor's copies; additional copies $4.**

FREEFALL MAGAZINE

Freefall Literary Society of Calgary, 922 Ninth Ave. SE, Calgary AB T2G 0S4 Canada. E-mail: freefallmagazine@yahoo.com. Website: freefallmagazine.ca. **Contact:** Lynn S. Fraser, managing editor. **100%.** "Magazine published biannually containing fiction, poetry, creative nonfiction, essays on writing, interviews, and reviews. Submit up to 5 poems at once. Pays $25 per poem and one copy of the issue poems appeaer in. Wants prose of all types, up to 3,000 words; pays $10/page to a maximum of $100 per piece and one copy of issue piece appears in. We are looking for exquisite writing with a strong narrative." Estab. 1990. Circ. 1,000. Pays on publication. Accepts queries by mail, e-mail. Writers' guidelines online.

POETRY Magazine published biannually containing fiction, poetry, creative nonfiction, essays on writing, interviews, and reviews. Submit up to 5 poems at once. We are looking for exquisite writing with a strong narrative." Circ.: 1,000. Buys first North American serial rights (ownership reverts to author after one-time publication). Pays on publication. 100% freelance.

FRESHLY BAKED FICTION

Isis International, P.O. Box 510232, Saint Louis MO 63151. (314)315-5200. E-mail: Editor@Freshlybakedfiction.com. Website: Freshlybakedfiction.com. **Contact:** John Ferguson, editor. "*Freshly Baked Fiction* ins a non-genre specific publication. We publish short stories, novellas, poetry, art, and more. Our audience is everyone that loves to read. Our website is free to all and updated daily with new fiction and classic works. *Freshly Baked Fiction* is a place where new and published authors can get opinions and insight from readers and other authors relating to their own work.

Taking advantage of technology, we have set out goals on being the new way people read. We will be offering readers a chance to get daily fiction on eBook readers, via RSS, e-mail, iPhone, and other electronic devices that have yet to hit the market." Estab. 2009. Circ. 8,000+ monthly. Byline given 1 month Accepts queries by e-mail. Accepts simultaneous submissions. Responds in 2 weeks. Sample copy not available. Guidelines available for SASE online.

NONFICTION Needs humor, interview, photo feature, profile, book and movie reviews. **Buys 1000 mss/year.** Send complete ms. 300-25,000 maximum

PHOTOS Send photos with submission. Requires model release and identification of subjects. Reviews GIF/JPEG files, transparencies, prints.

FICTION Needs adventure, condensed novels, confessions, erotica, ethnic, experimental, historical, humorous, mainstream, mystery, romance, slice-of-life vignettes, suspense, western. **Buys 1,000/year mss/year.** Send complete ms. 300-20,000 words maximum

POETRY Needs avant-garde, free verse, haiku, light verse, traditional. Buys 500 poems/year. Submit maximum 5 poems.

GARGOYLE

Paycock Press, 3819 N. 13th St., Arlington VA 22201. (703)525-9296. E-mail: hedgehog2@erols.com. Website: gargoylemagazine.com. **Contact:** Richard Peabody, co-editor, Lucinda Ebersole, co-editor. **75%.** Literary magazine: $5^1{}_2 \times 8^1{}_2$; 200 pages; illustrations; photos. "Gargoyle Magazine has always been a scallywag magazine, a maverick magazine, a bit too academic for the underground and way too underground for the academics. We are a writer's magazine in that we are read by other writers and have never worried about reaching the masses." Annual. Wants "edgy realism or experimental works. We run both." Wants to see more Canadian, British, Australian and Third World fiction. Receives 50-200 unsolicited mss/month. Accepts 10-15 mss/issue. Accepts submissions during June, July, and Aug. Agented fiction 5%. **Publishes 2-3 new writers/year.** Recently published work by Stephanie Allen, Tom Carson, Michael Casey, Kim Chinquee, Susan Cokal, Ramola D., Janice Eidus, Thaisa Frank, James Grady, Colette Inez, Susan Smith Nash, Zena Polin, Wena Poon, Pilar Quintana, Kris Saknussem, Tomaz Salamun, Lynda Sexson, Elisabeth Sheffield, Barry Silesky, Curtis Smith, Patricia Smith, Marilyn Stablein, Ronald Wallace. Length: 30 pages maximum; average length:

5-10 pages. Publishes short shorts. Also publishes literary essays, literary criticism, poetry. Sometimes comments on rejected mss. "We prefer electronic submissions. Please use submission engine online." For snail mail, send SASE for reply, return of ms; or send a disposable copy of ms. Sends galleys to author. Estab. 1976. Circ. 2,000. 12 months Accepts queries by online submission form. Accepts simultaneous submissions. Responds in 1month to queries, proposals, and to mss. Sample copy for $12.95. Catalog available online at FAQ link. "We don't have guidelines; we have never believed in them."

🔑 Receives 150 queries/year; 50 mss/year. Publishes 10% material from first-time author; 75% from unagented writers. Publishes 2 titles/year. Format: trade paperback originals.

NONFICTION Needs memoir, photo feature, creative nonfiction, literary criticism. **Pays 10% of print run and so-so split (after/if) we break even. Sends galleys to author.**

FICTION Needs experimental, poetry, literary, short story collections. No romance, horror, science fiction **Buys 10-15 mss/year.** Query in an e-mail. Reviews artwork. Length: 1,000-4,500 words.

$ THE GEORGIA REVIEW

The University of Georgia, Athens GA 30602-9009. (706)542-3481. Fax: (706)542-0047. E-mail: garev@uga.edu. Website: uga.edu/garev. **Contact:** Stephen Corey, editor. **99% freelance written.** Quarterly journal. Our readers are educated, inquisitive people who read a lot of work in the areas we feature, so they expect only the best in our pages. All work submitted should show evidence that the writer is at least as well-educated and well-read as our readers. Essays should be authoritative but accessible to a range of readers. Estab. 1947. Circ. 3,500. Byline given. Pays on publication. Publishes ms an average of 6 months after acceptance. Accepts queries by mail. Responds in 2 weeks to queries. Responds in 2-3 months to mss. Sample copy for $10. Guidelines available online.

No simultaneous or electronic submissions.

NONFICTION Needs essays. For the most part we are not interested in scholarly articles that are narrow in focus and/or overly burdened with footnotes. The ideal essay for *The Georgia Review* is a provocative, thesis-oriented work that can engage both the intelligent general reader and the specialist. **Buys 12-20 mss/year.** Send complete ms. **Pays $40/published page.**

PHOTOS Send photos. Reviews 5×7 prints or larger. Offers no additional payment for photos accepted with ms.

FICTION We seek original, excellent writing not bound by type. Ordinarily we do not publish novel excerpts or works translated into English, and we strongly discourage authors from submitting these. **Buys 12-20 mss/year.** Send complete ms. Open **Pays $40/published page.**

POETRY We seek original, excellent poetry. Submit 3-5 poems at a time. We do not accept submissions via fax or e-mail. If a submission is known to be included in a book already accepted by a publisher, please notify us of this fact (and of the anticipated date of book publication) in a cover letter. Reads year-round, but submissions postmarked May 15-August 15 will be returned unread. Guidelines available for SASE or on website. Responds in 2-3 months. Always sends prepublication galleys. Pays $4/line, one-year subscription, and 1 contributor's copy. Acquires first North American serial rights. Reviews books of poetry. "Our poetry reviews range from 500-word 'Book Briefs' on single volumes to 5,000-word essay reviews on multiple volumes." Buys 60-75 poems/year. Submit maximum 5 poems. **Pays $3/line.**

$ THE GETTYSBURG REVIEW

Gettysburg College, Gettysburg PA 17325. (717)337-6770. Fax: (717)337-6775. Website: gettysburgreview.com. Quarterly magazine. "Our concern is quality. Manuscripts submitted here should be extremely well written. Reading period September-May." Estab. 1988. Circ. 3,000. Byline given. Pays on publication. Publishes ms an average of 6 months after acceptance. Editorial lead time 1 year. Submit seasonal material 9 months in advance. Accepts queries by mail, fax. Accepts simultaneous submissions. Responds in 1 month to queries. Responds in 3-6 months to mss. Sample copy for $11. Guidelines available online.

NONFICTION Needs essays. **Buys 20 mss/year.** Send complete ms. Length: 3,000-7,000 words. **Pays $30/page.**

FICTION Contact: Mark Drew, assisant editor. High quality, literary. Needs experimental, historical, humorous, mainstream, novel concepts, serialized, contemporary. "We require that fiction be intelligent and

esthetically written." **Buys 20 mss/year.** Send complete ms. Length: 2,000-7,000 words. **Pays $30/page.**
POETRY Buys 50 poems/year. Submit maximum 5 poems. **Pays $2.50/line.**

GLASS: A JOURNAL OF POETRY

No public address available, E-mail: glasspoetry@yahoo.com. Website: glass-poetry.com. **Contact:** Holly Burnside, Editor. Triannual website covering high quality poetry of all styles, forms and schools. "We are not bound by any specific aesthetic; our mission is to present high quality writing. Easy rhyme and 'light' verse are less likely to inspire us. We want to see poetry that enacts the artistic and creative purity of glass." Accepts queries by e-mail. Accepts simultaneous submissions. Responds in 4 months to queries.

⊙ Submissions must follow our guidelines.
POETRY Submit maximum 4 poems.

⊖⊙ GLIMMER TRAIN STORIES

Glimmer Train Press, Inc., 1211 NW Glisan St., Suite 207, Portland OR 97209. Fax: (503)221-0837. E-mail: eds@glimmertrain.org. Website: glimmertrain.org. **90% freelance written.** Quarterly magazine of literary short fiction. "We are interested in literary short stories, particularly by new and lightly published writers." Estab. 1991. Circ. 12,000. Byline given. Pays on acceptance. Publishes ms an average of 18 months after acceptance. Accepts simultaneous submissions. Responds in 2 months to mss. Sample copy for $12 on website. Guidelines available online.
FICTION Buys 40 mss/year. Submit via the website. In a pinch, send paper. up to 12,000 **Pays $700.**

⟳⟲⊖⊙ GRAIN LITERARY MAGAZINE

P.O. Box 67, Saskatoon SK S7K 3K1 Canada. (306)244-2828. Fax: (306)244-0255. E-mail: grainmag@sasktel.net (inquiries only). Website: grainmagazine.ca. **Contact:** Mike Thompson, bus. admin. **100% freelance written**. Quarterly magazine covering poetry, fiction, creative nonfiction. "*Grain* Magazine, published 4 times per year, is an internationally acclaimed literary journal that publishes engaging, surprising, eclectic, and challenging writing and images by Canadian and international writers and artists. *Grain* is digest-sized, professionally printed. Press run is 1,100. Receives about 2,400 submissions/year." Estab. 1973. Circ. 1,600. Byline given. Pays on publication. Editorial lead time 6 months. Accepts queries by mail. Responds in 2 to 4 months. Sample copy for $13. (See

website for U.S. and foreign postage fees.). Guidelines available in magazine, by SASE (or SAE and IRC, fax, e-mail, or website.

⊙ "Queries for submissions of work in other forms, less easy to categorize forms, cross-genre work, are welcome."

NONFICTION No academic papers or reportage. No fax or e-mail submissions. Postal submissions only. Send typed, unpublished material only (we consider work published on-line to be previously published). Please only submit work in one genre at one time. 5,000/words max. **Pays $50-225 CAD (depending on number of pages) and 2 contributor's copies.**
FICTION Contact: fiction editor. Needs 1 or 2 stories. Needs experimental, mainstream, contemporary, prose poem. No romance, confession, science fiction, vignettes, mystery. **Buys 40 mss/year.** Submissions must be typed in readable font (ideally 12 pt., Times Roman or Courier), free of typos, printed on one side only. No staples. You name & address must be on every page. Pieces of more than one page must be numbered. Cover letter with all contact information, title(s) and genre of work is required. 5000/words max. (stories at the longer end of the word count must be of exceptional quality).
POETRY Needs Needs individual poems, sequences, or suites up to a max. of 12 pages. High quality, imaginative, well-crafted poetry. Submit maximum 8 poems and SASE with postage or IRC's. Buys 78 poems/year.

⊖⊙ GUD MAGAZINE

Greatest Uncommon Denominator Publishing, P.O. Box 1537, Laconia NH 03247. E-mail: editor@gudmagazine.com. Website: gudmagazine.com. **99% freelance written**. Semiannual magazine covering literary content and art. "*GUD Magazine* transcends and encompasses the audiences of both genre and literary fiction by featuring fiction, art, poetry, essays and reports, comics, and short drama." Estab. 2006. Byline given. Pays on publication. Publishes ms an average of 6-12 months after acceptance. Editorial lead time 6 months. Submit seasonal material 6 months in advance. Accepts queries by online submission form. Accepts simultaneous submissions. Responds in 6 months to mss. Guidelines available online.
NONFICTION Needs book excerpts, essays, historical, humor, interview, personal experience, photo feature, travel, interesting event. **Buys 2-4 mss/year.** sub-

mit complete ms using online form Length: 1-15,000 words. **Pays $.03/word for first rights.**

PHOTOS Send photos and artwork in electronic format. Model releases required for human images. Reviews GIF/JPEG files. Pays $12.

FICTION Needs adventure, erotica, ethnic, experimental, fantasy, horror, humorous, science fiction, suspense. **Buys 40 mss/year.** Length: 1-15,000 words. **Pays $450.**

POETRY Needs avant-garde, free verse, haiku, light verse, traditional. Does not want anything that rhymes 'love' with 'above.' Buys 12-20 poems/year. **Pays $.03/word for first rights.**

FILLERS Buys comics. Reviews GIF/JPEG files. **Pays $12.**

⊕ GUERNICA

A Magazine of Art and Politics, Attn: Michael Archer, 165 Bennett Ave., 4C, New York NY 10040. E-mail: editors@guernicamag.com; art@guernicamag.com (art/photography); poetry@guernicamag.com; publisher@guernicamag.com. Website: guernicamag.com. **Contact:** Erica Wright, poetry; Dan Eckstein, art/photography. "*Guernica*, published biweekly, is one of the web's most acclaimed new magazines. 2009: Guernica is called a "great online literary magazine" by *Esquire*. *Guernica* contributors come from dozens of countries and write in nearly as many languages." Estab. 2005. Publishes mss 3-4 months from acceptance. Accepts queries by e-mail. NoAccepts simultaneous submissions. Responds in 4 months. Guidelines available online.

> ◯ Received Caine Prize for African Writing, Best of the Net, cited by Esquire as a "great literary magazine."

FICTION Needs Literary, preferably with an international approach. No genre fiction. Submit complete ms with cover letter Attn: Meakin Armstrong to fiction@guernicamag.com. In subject line (please follow this format exactly): "fiction submission." Include bio and list of previous publications. Accepts 26 mss/year. Has published Jesse Ball, Elizabeth Crane, Josh Weil, Justo Arroyo, Sergio Ramírez Mercado, Matthew Derby, E.C. Osondu (Winner of the 2009 Caine Prize for African Writing). Length: 700-2500 words.

POETRY Contact: Erica Wright. Please send 3-5 poems to poetry@guernicamag.com. Attn: Erica Wright. Translations welcome (with rights to publish). Ac-

cepts 15-20 poems/year. Has published James Galvin, Barbara Hamby, Terrance Ha, Richard Howard.

❸ GULF COAST: A JOURNAL OF LITERATURE AND FINE ARTS

University of Houston, Dept. of English, University of Houston, Houston TX 77204-3013. (713)743-3223. E-mail: editors@gulfcoastmag.org. Website: gulfcoastmag.org. Christine Ha, Eric Howerton, Edward Porter, fiction editors. **Contact:** The Editors. Biannual magazine covering innovative fiction, nonfiction, and poetry for the literary-minded. Buys 5-10 ms/year. Receives 300 unsolicited mss/month. Accepts 4-8 mss/issue; 12-16 mss/year. Agented fiction 5%. **Publishes 2-8 new writers/year.** Recently published work by Matt Bell, Megan Mayhew Bergman, Sarah Shun-Lien Bynum, Jenine Capot Crucet, Benjamin Percy, John Weir. Publishes short shorts. Sometimes comments on rejected mss. Estab. 1986. 6 months-1 year Accepts queries by mail, phone. Accepts simultaneous submissions. Responds in 4-6 months to mss. Writer's guidelines for #10 SASE or on website.

NONFICTION Contact: Nonfiction editor. Needs interview, reviews. **Gulf Coast reads general submissions, submitted by post or through the online submissions manager, from September 1 through March 1.** Submissions e-mailed directly to the editors, or postmarked between March 1 and Sept. 1, will not be read or responded to. Please visit our contest page for contest submission guidelines. **Pays $50 per review, and $100 per interview.**

FICTION Contact: Fiction editor. Buys 5-10 ms/year. Receives 300 unsolicited mss/month. Accepts 4-8 mss/issue; 12-16 mss/year. Publishes ms 6 months-1 year after acceptance. Agented fiction 5%. **Publishes 2-8 new writers/year.** Recently published work by Matt Bell, Megan Mayhew Bergman, Sarah Shun-Lien Bynum, Jenine Capot Crucet, Benjamin Percy, John Weir. Publishes short shorts. Sometimes comments on rejected mss. Back issue for $7, 7×10 SASE with 4 first-class stamps. Please do not send multiple submissions; we will read only one submission per author at a given time, except in the case of our annual contests. Needs ethnic, experimental, multicultural, literary, regional, translations, contemporary. No children's, genre, religious/inspirational. **Gulf Coast reads general submissions, submitted by post or through the online submissions manager, from September 1 through March**

1. Submissions e-mailed directly to the editors, or post-marked between March 1 and Sept. 1, will not be read or responded to. Please visit our contest page for contest submission guidelines. Responds in 4-6 months to mss. Accepts simultaneous submissions. **Pays $-$100. POETRY Contact:** Poetry editor. Submit maximum 1-5 poems.

🌑⊘ THE HELIX

Central Connecticut State University English Dept., E-mail: helixmagazine@gmail.com. Website: helixmagazine.org. **The Helix Magazine** is a Central Connecticut State University student run biannual publication. The magazine accepts submission from all over the globe, as it went national in 2007 and global in 2009. The magazine features CCSU student writing, writing from the Hartford County community and an array of submissions from all over the world. The magazine contains multiple genres of literature and art submissions including: poetry, short fiction, playwright, creative nonfiction paintings, photography, watercolor, collage, stencil and computer generated artwork. It is a student run and funded publication. Accepts queries by e-mail.

FICTION "Published once each semester, The Helix is the longest running literary magazine of Central Connecticut State University. We accept submissions of poetry, short fiction pieces, short pieces of drama, creative nonfiction, and art (which includes anything that can be e-mailed in a .jpg format). Our Spring 2011 deadline is March 15. Contributions are invited from all members of the campus community, as well as the literary community at large. Payment for all accepted submissions is a copy of The Helix. Products: Each year we release a spring issue and a fall issue of our literary magazine, The Helix. Needs , There are no requirements placed on those submitting. Art: Scans or Photography Only, 300 DPI Minimum, Size: 10 Inches Minimum, Flat Art Only, TIFF or JPG. Literature: Poetry, Fiction, Nonfiction, Plays, etc. File Formats: (.doc or .docx).

🟢 HOBART

P.O. Box 1658, Ann Arbor MI 48103. E-mail: aaron@hobartpulp.com. Website: hobartpulp.com. Website covering short stories, personal essays, short interviews, comics, roundtable discussions. We tend to like quirky stories like truck driving, mathematics and vagabonding. We like stories with humor (humor-ous but engaging, literary but not stuffy). We want to get excited about your story and hope you'll send your best work. Accepts queries by e-mail. If our response time is longer than 3 mos., feel free to inquire. Responds in 1-3 months to mss.

> 💬 Send submissions to: websubmissions@hobartpulp.com. Query first if you'd like to interview someone for Hobart.

NONFICTION Needs essays, personal., humor, interview, short., Roundtable Discussions. **Pays $50-150.**

🟢 THE HOLLINS CRITIC

P.O. Box 9538, Hollins University, Roanoke VA 24020-1538. E-mail: acockrell@hollins.edu. Website: hollins.edu/academics/critic. **Contact:** Cathryn Hankla. **100% freelance written**. Magazine published 5 times/year. Estab. 1964. Circ. 400. Byline given. Pays on publication. Publishes ms an average of 1 year after acceptance. Accepts queries by online submission form Submit at hollinscriticssubmissions.com. Accepts simultaneous submissions. Responds in 2 months to mss. Sample copy for $3. Guidelines for #10 SASE.

> 💬 No e-mail submissions.

POETRY Needs avant-garde, free verse, traditional. We read poetry only from September 1-December 15. Buys 16-20 poems/year. Submit maximum 5 poems. **Pays $25.**

🟢 THE HUDSON REVIEW

The Hudson Review, Inc., 684 Park Ave., New York NY 10065. Website: hudsonreview.com. **Contact:** Paula Deitz. **100% freelance written**. Quarterly magazine publishing fiction, poetry, essays, book reviews; criticism of literature, art, theatre, dance, film and music; and articles on contemporary cultural developments. Estab. 1948. Circ. 2,000. Byline given. Pays on publication. Publishes ms an average of 6 months after acceptance. Editorial lead time 3 months. Accepts queries by mail. Responds in 6 months. Sample copy for $10. Guidelines for #10 SASE or online.

> 💬 Send with SASE. Mss. sent outside accepted reading period will be returned unread if SASE contains sufficient postage.

NONFICTION Contact: Paula Deitz. Needs essays, general interest, historical, opinion, personal experience, travel. **Buys 4-6 mss/year.** Send complete ms between January 1 and March 31 only 3,500 words maximum **Pays 2½¢/word.**

FICTION Reads between September 1 and November 30 only. **Buys 4 mss/year.** 10,000 words maximum. **Pays 2½¢/word.**

POETRY Reads poems only between April 1 and June 30. Buys 12-20 poems/year. Submit maximum 7 poems. **Pays 50¢/line.**

$ HUNGER MOUNTAIN

Vermont College of Fine Arts, Vermont College of Fine Arts, 36 College St., Montpelier VT 05602. (802)828-8517. E-mail: hungermtn@vermontcollege.edu. Website: hungermtn.org. **30% freelance written.** Semiannual perfect-bound journal covering high quality fiction, poetry, creative nonfiction, interviews, photography, and artwork reproductions. Accepts high quality work from unknown, emerging, or successful writers and artists. No genre fiction, drama, or academic articles, please. Estab. 2002. Byline given. Pays on publication. Publishes ms an average of 1 year after acceptance. Submit seasonal material 6 months in advance. Accepts queries by mail. NoResponds in 1 month to queries. Responds in 3 months to mss. Sample copy for $10. Writer's guidelines for free, online, or by e-mail.

NONFICTION No informative or instructive articles, please. Prose for young adults is acceptable. Query with published clips. **Pays $5/page (minimum $30).** Sometimes pays expenses of writers on assignment.

PHOTOS Send photos. Reviews contact sheets, transparencies, prints, GIF/JPEG files. Slides preferred. Negotiates payment individually.

FICTION Needs adventure, ethnic, experimental, novel concepts, high quality short stories and short shorts. No genre fiction, meaning science fiction, fantasy, horror, erotic, etc. Query with published clips. **Pays $25-100.**

POETRY Needs avant-garde, free verse, haiku, traditional. No light verse, humor/quirky/catchy verse, greeting card verse. Buys 10 poems/year.

$ ILLUMEN

Sam's Dot Publishing, P.O. Box 782, Cedar Rapids IA 52406-0782. E-mail: illumensdp@yahoo.com. Website: samsdotpublishing.com/aoife/cover.htm. **Contact:** Karen L. Newman, ed. **100% freelance written.** Semiannual magazine. "*Illumen* publishes speculative poetry and articles about speculative poetry, and reviews of poetry and collections." Estab. 2004. Circ. 40. Byline given. Offers 100% kill fee. Editorial lead time 2 months. Submit seasonal material 6 months in advance. Accepts queries by e-mail. Responds in 2 weeks to queries. Responds in 3-4 months to mss. Sample copy for $8. Guidelines available online.

NONFICTION Buys 5-8 mss/year. Send complete ms. Length: 2,000 words. **Pays $10 for unsolicited articles.**

POETRY Needs avant-garde, free verse, haiku, light verse, traditional. "Scifaiku is a difficult sell with us because we also publish a specialty magazine—*Scifaikuest*—for scifaiku and related forms." Buys 40-50 poems/year. Submit maximum 5 poems. Length: 200 lines. **Pays 1-2¢/word.**

$ INDIANA REVIEW

Ballantine Hall 465, 1020 E. Kirkwood, Indiana University, Bloomington IN 47405-7103. (812)855-3439. E-mail: inreview@indiana.edu. Website: indiana.edu/~inreview. **100% freelance written.** Biannual magazine. "*Indiana Review*, a nonprofit organization run by IU graduate students, is a journal of previously unpublished poetry and fiction. Literary interviews and essays are also considered. We publish innovative fiction, nonfiction, and poetry. We're interested in energy, originality, and careful attention to craft. While we publish many well-known writers, we also welcome new and emerging poets and fiction writers." Estab. 1976. Circ. 5,000. Byline given. Pays on publication. Publishes ms an average of 3-6 months after acceptance. Accepts queries by mail, e-mail. Accepts simultaneous submissions. Responds in 2 or more weeks to queries. Responds in 4 or more months to mss. Sample copy for $9. Guidelines available online.

🔑 Break in with 500-1,000 word book reviews of fiction, poetry, nonfiction, and literary criticism published within the last 2 years.

NONFICTION Needs essays, interview, creative nonfiction, reviews. No coming of age/slice of life pieces. **Buys 5-7 mss/year.** Send complete ms. 9,000 words maximum. **Pays $5/page ($10 minimum), plus 2 contributor's copies.**

FICTION Contact: Danny Nguyen, fiction editor. "We look for daring stories which integrate theme, language, character, and form. We like polished writing, humor, and fiction which has consequence beyond the world of its narrator." Needs ethnic, experimental, mainstream, novel concepts, literary, short fictions, translations. No genre fiction. **Buys 14-18 mss/year.** Send complete ms.

Length: 250-10,000 words. **Pays $5/page ($10 minimum), plus 2 contributor's copies**.

POETRY Contact: Hannah Faith Notess, poetry editor. "We look for poems that are skillful and bold, exhibiting an inventiveness of language with attention to voice and sonics. Experimental, free verse, prose poem, traditional form, lyrical, narrative." Buys 80 poems/year. Submit maximum 6 poems. 5 lines minimum **Pays $5/page ($10 minimum), plus 2 contributor's copies**.

$ $ INKWELL

Manhattanville College, 2900 Purchase St., Purchase NY 10577. (914)323-7239. Fax: (914)323-3122. E-mail: inkwell@mville.edu. Website: inkwelljournal.org. **100% freelance written**. Semiannual magazine covering poetry, fiction, essays, artwork, and photography. Estab. 1995. Byline given. Pays on publication. Publishes ms an average of 4 months after acceptance. Editorial lead time 4 months. NoAccepts simultaneous submissions. Responds in 1 month to queries. Responds in 4-6 months to mss. Sample copy for $6. Guidelines free.

> *Inkwell* is produced in affiliation with the Master of Arts in Writing program at Manhattanville College, and is staffed by faculty and graduate students of the program.

NONFICTION Needs book excerpts, essays, literary essays, memoirs. Does not want children's literature, erotica, pulp adventure, or science fiction. **Buys 3-4 mss/year.** Send complete ms. 5,000 words maximum **Pays $100-350.**

PHOTOS Send photos/artwork with submission. Reviews 5×7 prints, GIF/JPEG files on diskette/cd. Negotiates payment individually.

FICTION Needs mainstream, novel concepts, literary. Does not want children's literature, erotica, pulp adventure, or science fiction. **Buys 20 mss/year.** Send complete ms. 5,000 words maximum **Pays $75-150.**

POETRY Needs avant-garde, free verse, traditional. Does not want doggerel, funny poetry, etc. Buys 40 poems/year. Submit maximum 5 poems. **Pays $5-10/page.**

INNISFREE POETRY JOURNAL

Cook Communication, E-mail: editor@innisfreepoetry.org. Website: innisfreepoetry.org. **Contact:** Greg McBride. Semiannual online journal publishing contemporary poetry. Estab. 2005. Accepts simultaneous submissions. Guidelines available.

POETRY Needs free verse, traditional.

$ IRREANTUM

The Association for Mormon Letters, P.O. Box 1315, Salt Lake City UT 84110-1315. E-mail: editor@aml-pubs.org. Website: irreantum.org. Literary journal published 2 times/year. "While focused on Mormonism, *Irreantum* is a cultural, humanities-oriented magazine, not a religious magazine. Our guiding principle is that Mormonism is grounded in a sufficiently unusual, cohesive, and extended historical and cultural experience that it has become like a nation, an ethnic culture. We can speak of Mormon literature at least as surely as we can of a Jewish or Southern literature. *Irreantum* publishes stories, one-act dramas, stand-alone novel and drama excerpts, and poetry by, for, or about Mormons (as well as author interviews, essays, and reviews). The journal's audience includes readers of any or no religious faith who are interested in literary exploration of the Mormon culture, mindset, and worldview through Mormon themes and characters either directly or by implication. *Irreantum* is currently the only magazine devoted to Mormon literature." Estab. 1999. Circ. 500. Pays on publication. Publishes ms an average of 3-12 months after acceptance. Accepts queries by e-mail. Accepts simultaneous submissions. Responds in 2 weeks to queries. Responds in 2 months to mss. Sample copy for $6. Guidelines by e-mail.

> Also publishes short shorts, literary essays, literary criticism, and poetry.

FICTION Needs adventure, ethnic, Mormon, experimental, fantasy, historical, horror, humorous, mainstream, mystery, religious, romance, science fiction, suspense. **Buys 12 mss/year.** Length: 1,000-5,000 words. **Pays $0-100.**

$ $ ISLAND

P.O. Box 210, Sandy Bay Tasmania 7006 Australia. (61)(3)6226-2325. E-mail: island.magazine@utas.edu.au. Website: islandmag.com. Quarterly magazine. "*Island* seeks quality fiction, poetry, essays, and articles. A literary magazine with an environmental heart." Circ. 1,500. Accepts queries by E-mail. Sample copy for $15.95 (Australian). Guidelines available online.

NONFICTION Pays $100 (Australian)/1,000 words

FICTION Length: up to 2,500 words. **Pays $100 (Australian).**

POETRY Pays $60.

$ THE JOURNAL

The Ohio State University, 164 W. 17th Ave., Columbus OH 43210. (614)292-4076. Fax: (614)292-7816. E-mail: thejournal@osu.edu; thejournalmag@gmail.com. Website: english.osu.edu/research/journals/thejournal/. **100% freelance written.** Semiannual magazine. "We're open to all forms; we tend to favor work that gives evidence of a mature and sophisticated sense of the language." Estab. 1972. Circ. 1,500. Byline given. Pays on publication. Publishes ms an average of 1 year after acceptance. Accepts queries by mail, online submission form. Accepts simultaneous submissions. Responds in 2 weeks to queries. Responds in 2 months to mss. Sample copy for $7 or online. Guidelines available online.

> "We are interested in quality fiction, poetry, nonfiction, and reviews of new books of poetry. We impose no restrictions on category, type, or length of submission for Fiction, Poetry, and Nonfiction. We are happy to consider long stories and self-contained excerpts of novels. Please double-space all prose submissions. Address correspondence to the Editors. We will only respond to submissions accompanied by a SASE."

NONFICTION Needs essays, interview. **Buys 2 mss/year.** Query. Length: 2,000-4,000 words. **Pays $20 maximum.**

COLUMNS Reviews of contemporary poetry, 1,500 words maximum **Buys 2 mss/year.** Query. **Pays $20.**

FICTION Needs novel concepts, literary short stories. No romance, science fiction or religious/devotional. Open **Pays $20.**

POETRY Needs avant-garde, free verse, traditional. Buys 100 poems/year. Submit maximum 5 poems. **Pays $20.**

$ THE KENYON REVIEW

Finn House, 102 W. Wiggin, Gambier OH 43022. (740)427-5208. Fax: (740)427-5417. E-mail: kenyonreview@kenyon.edu. Website: KenyonReview.org. **Contact:** Marlene Landefeld. **100% freelance written.** Quarterly magazine covering contemporary literature and criticism. "An international journal of literature, culture, and the arts dedicated to an inclusive representation of the best in new writing (fiction, poetry, essays, interviews, criticism) from established and emerging writers." Estab. 1939. Circ. 6,000. Byline given. Pays on publication. Publishes ms an average of 1 year after acceptance. Editorial lead time 1 year. Submit seasonal material 1 year in advance. Responds in 4 months to mss. Sample copy $10, includes postage and handling. Please call or e-mail to order. Guidelines available online.

FICTION Needs condensed novels, ethnic, experimental, historical, humorous, mainstream, contemporary. 3-15 typeset pages preferred **Pays $30-40/page.**

$ THE KIT-CAT REVIEW

244 Halstead Ave., Harrison NY 10528. (914)835-4833. E-mail: kitcatreview@gmail.com. **Contact:** Claudia Fletcher, editor. **100% freelance written.** Quarterly magazine. "*The Kit-Cat Review* is named after the 18th Century Kit-Cat Club, whose members included Addison, Steele, Congreve, Vanbrugh, and Garth. It is part of the collections of the Univ. of Wisconsin, Madison, and the State Univ. of New York, Buffalo. Its purpose is to promote/discover excellence and originality." Estab. 1998. Circ. 500. Byline given. Pays on publication. Publishes ms an average of 6-12 months after acceptance. Accepts queries by mail, phone. Accepts simultaneous submissions. Responds in 1 week to queries. Responds in 2 months to mss. Sample copy for $7 (payable to Claudia Fletcher). Guidelines for SASE.

NONFICTION Needs book excerpts, essays, general interest, historical, humor, interview, personal experience, travel. **Buys 6 mss/year.** Send complete ms with brief bio and SASE 5,000 words maximum **Pays $25-100.**

FICTION Needs ethnic, experimental, novel concepts, slice-of-life vignettes. No stories with O. Henry-type formula endings. Shorter pieces stand a better chance of publication. No science fiction, fantasy, romance, horror, or new age. **Buys 20 mss/year.** Send complete ms. 5,000 words maximum **Pays $25-100 and 2 contributor's copies; additional copies $5.**

POETRY Needs free verse, traditional. No excessively obscure poetry. Buys 100 poems/year. **Pays $20-100.**

+ LULLWATER REVIEW

Emory University, P.O. Box 122036, Emory University, Atlanta GA 30322. Fax: (404)727-7367. E-mail: lullwater@lullwaterreview.com. **Contact:** Arina Korneva, editor-in-chief. **100% freelance written.** Semiannual magazine. "We're a small, student-run literary magazine published out of Emory University in Atlanta, GA with two issues yearly—once in the fall and once in the spring. You can find us in the *Index of American Periodical Verse*, the *American Humanities Index* and as a member of the Council of Literary Magazines and Presses. We welcome work that brings a fresh perspective, whether through language or the visual arts." Estab. 1990. Circ. 2,000. Byline given. Pays on publication. Publishes ms an average of 1-2 months after acceptance. Accepts queries by e-mail. Accepts simultaneous submissions. Responds in 1-3 months to queries. Responds in 3-6 months to mss. Sample copy for $5. Guidelines for #10 SASE.

NONFICTION Needs book excerpts, essays, general interest, historical, humor, inspirational, personal experience, photo feature, travel. **Buys 1-2 mss/year.** Send complete ms. 5,000 words maximum.

PHOTOS **Contact:** Arina Korneva, editor-in-chief. Send photos. Model release and property release are preferred. Must include title of photograph. Reviews photos in JPEG format at 240 dpi. Offers no additional payment for photos accepted with ms.

FICTION Needs adventure, condensed novels, ethnic, experimental, fantasy, historical, humorous, mainstream, mystery, novel concepts, religious, science fiction, slice-of-life vignettes, suspense, western. No romance or science fiction, please. **Buys 5-7 mss/year.** Send complete ms. 5,000 words maximum. **Pays 3 contributor copies.**

POETRY Needs avant-garde, free verse, light verse, traditional. Buys 30-40 poems/year. Submit maximum 6 poems. **Pays 3 contributor copies.**

[+] LYRICAL PASSION POETRY E-ZINE

P.O. Box 17331, Arlington TX 22216. Website: lyricalpassionpoetry.yolasite.com. **Contact:** Raquel D. Bailey, Founding Editor. Founded by award-winning poet Raquel D. Bailey, Lyrical Passion Poetry E-Zine is an attractive monthly online literary magazine specializing in Japanese short form poetry. Publishes quality artwork, well-crafted short fiction and poetry in English by emerging and established writers. Literature of lasting literary value will be considered. Welcomes the traditional to the experimental. Poetry works written in German will be considered if accompanied by translations. Offers annual short fiction and poetry contests. Estab. 2007. Circ. 500 online visitors/month. 1 month from acceptance to publication. 2 months advance on seasonal submissions. Accepts queries by e-mail. Does not want previously published submissions.Accepts simultaneous submissions. Responds in 2 months. Guidelines and upcoming themes available on website.

FICTION Cover letter preferred. Fiction should be typed, double-spaced.

POETRY Needs haiku, senryu, tanka, tan renga, haiga, haibun, cinquain, haiku sequences, micro-poetry, micro-fiction, free verse, (well-crafted) rhyming poetry, prose poetry. **Does not return manuscripts. Multiple submissions are permitted but no more than 3 submissions in a 6 month period.** Does not want: dark, cliché, limerick, erotica, extremely explicit, violent or depressing literature. Submit maximum 10 poems/max at a time **for Japanase short form poetry.** poems. Free verse poetry length: between 1 and 40/lines.

🍁 $ THE MALAHAT REVIEW

The University of Victoria, P.O. Box 1700, STN CSC, Victoria BC V8W 2Y2 Canada. (250)721-8524. E-mail: malahat@uvic.ca (for queries only). Website: malahatreview.ca. **Contact:** John Barton, editor. **100% freelance written. Eager to work with new/unpublished writers.** Quarterly magazine covering poetry, fiction, creative nonfiction, and reviews. "We try to achieve a balance of views and styles in each issue. We strive for a mix of the best writing by both established and new writers." Estab. 1967. Circ. 1,500. Byline given. Pays on acceptance. Publishes ms an average of 6 months after acceptance. Accepts queries by mail. NoResponds in 2 weeks to queries. Responds in 3-10 months to mss. Sample copy for $18.45 (US). Guidelines available online.

NONFICTION Include SASE with Canadian postage or IRCs. **Pays $20/magazine page.**

FICTION Needs general fiction and creative nonfiction. **Buys 12-14 mss/year.** Send complete ms. 8,000 words max. **Pays $20/magazine page.**

POETRY Needs avant-garde, free verse, traditional. Buys 100 poems/year. 5-10 pages **Pays $20/magazine page.**

$ $ MANOA

English Dept., University of Hawaii, Honolulu HI 96822. (808)956-3070. Fax: (808)956-3083. E-mail: mjournal-l@listserv.hawaii.edu. Website: manoajournal.hawaii.edu. **Contact:** Frank Stewart, Poetry Editor. Semiannual magazine. "High quality literary fiction, poetry, essays, personal narrative. In general, each issue is devoted to new work from Pacific and Asian nations. Our audience is international. US writing need not be confined to Pacific settings or subjects. Please note that we seldom publish unsolicited work." Estab. 1989. Circ. 2,000 print, 10,000 digital. Byline given. Pays on publication. Editorial lead time 9 months. Accepts simultaneous submissions. Responds in 3 weeks to queries; 1 month to poetry mss; 6 months to fiction. Sample copy for $15 (US). Guidelines available online.

NONFICTION No Pacific exotica. Query first. Length: 1,000-5,000 words. **Pays $25/printed page.**

FICTION Query first and/or see website. Needs mainstream, contemporary, excerpted novel. No Pacific exotica. **Buys 1-2 in the US (excluding translation) mss/year.** Send complete ms. Length: 1,000-7,500 words. **Pays $100-500 normally ($25/printed page).**

POETRY No light verse. Buys 10-20 poems/year. Submit maximum 5-6 poems. **Pays $25/poem.**

THE MASSACHUSETTS REVIEW

South College, University of Massachusetts, Amherst MA 01003-9934. (413)545-2689. Fax: (413)577-0740. E-mail: massrev@external.umass.edu. Website: massreview.org. Quarterly magazine. Estab. 1959. Circ. 1,200. Pays on publication. Publishes ms an average of 18 months after acceptance. Accepts queries by mail. Accepts simultaneous submissions. Responds in 3 months to mss. Sample copy for $8. Guidelines available online.

Does not respond to mss without SASE.

NONFICTION No reviews of single books. Send complete ms or query with SASE 6,500 words maximum. **Pays $50.**

FICTION Short stories. Wants more prose less than 30 pages. **Buys 10 mss/year.** Send complete ms. 25-30 pages maximum.

POETRY Submit maximum 6 poems. **Pays 50¢/line to $25 maximum.**

MEMOIR (AND)

Memoir Journal, **1316 67th Street, #8,**, Emeryville CA 94608. (415)339-3142. E-mail: submissions@memoirjournal.com. Website: memoirjournal.com. **100% freelance written.** Semiannual magazine covering memoirs. "*Memoir (and)* publishes memoirs in many forms, from the traditional to the experimental. The editors strive with each issue to include a selection of prose, poetry, graphic memoirs, narrative photography, lies and more from both emerging and established authors." Estab. 2006. (Contributors Notes in each issue) Publishes ms an average of 3 months after acceptance. Ac-

cepts queries by mail, e-mail. Accepts simultaneous submissions. Sample copy available online. Guidelines available online.

"We have two reading periods per year, with 4 prizes awarded in each: the *Memoir (and)* Prizes for Prose and Poetry ($100, $250, $500 & publication in publication in print and online, plus 3-6 copies of the journal) and the *Memoir (and)* Prize for Graphic Memoir ($100 & publication in print & online, 6 copies). Deadline: **noon Pacific time, August 16, 2011.**"

NONFICTION Contact: Claudia Sternbach. Needs essays, personal experience, Graphic Memoir. Special issues: Does not publish themed issues. **Buys 40-80 mss/year mss/year.** Send complete ms. Length: 50-10,000 words. **Pays 0 for assigned or unsolicited articles.**

PHOTOS Send photos. Reviews GIF/JPEG files. Offers no additional payment for photos accepted with ms.

POETRY Needs avant garde, free verse, haiku, light verse, traditional. Buys 20-40 poems/year. Submit maximum 5 poems.

MICHIGAN QUARTERLY REVIEW

0576 Rackham Bldg., 915 E. Washington, University of Michigan, Ann Arbor MI 48109-1070. (734)764-9265. E-mail: mqr@umich.edu. Website: umich.edu/~mqr. **75% freelance written.** Quarterly magazine. "An interdisciplinary journal which publishes mainly essays and reviews, with some high-quality fiction and poetry, for an intellectual, widely read audience." Estab. 1962. Circ. 1,000. Byline given. Pays on publication. Publishes ms an average of 1 year after acceptance. Accepts queries by mail. Responds in 2 months to queries. Responds in 2 months to mss. Sample copy for $4. Guidelines available online.

"The Laurence Goldstein Award is a $1,000 annual award to the best poem published in the *Michigan Quarterly Review* during the previous year. The Lawrence Foundation Award is a $1,000 annual award to the best short story published in the *Michigan Quarterly Review* during the previous year."

NONFICTION Buys 35 mss/year. Query. Length: 2,000-5,000 words. **Pays $10/published page.**

FICTION Contact: Fiction Editor. "No restrictions on subject matter or language. We are very selective. We like stories which are unusual in tone and structure, and innovative in language. No genre fiction written for a market. Would like to see more fiction about social, political, cultural matters, not just centered on a love relationship or dysfunctional family." **Buys 10 mss/year.** Send complete ms. Length: 1,500-7,000 words. **Pays $10/published page.**

POETRY Pays $10/published page.

$ MID-AMERICAN REVIEW

Bowling Green State University, Department of English, Box W, Bowling Green OH 43403. (419)372-2725. E-mail: mikeczy@bgsu.edu. Website: bgsu.edu/midamericanreview. **Contact:** Michael Czyzniejewski. **Willing to work with new/unpublished writers.** Bi-annual magazine of the highest quality fiction, poetry, and translations of contemporary poetry and fiction. Also publishes critical articles and book reviews of contemporary literature. "We try to put the best possible work in front of the biggest possible audience. We publish serious fiction and poetry, as well as critical studies in contemporary literature, translations and book reviews." Estab. 1981. Byline given. Pays on publication when funding is available. Publishes ms an average of 6 months after acceptance. Accepts queries by online submission form. Responds in 5 months to mss. Sample copy for $7 (current issue); $5 (back issue); $10 (rare back issues). Guidelines available online.

NONFICTION Needs essays, articles focusing on contemporary authors and topics of current literary interest, short book reviews (500-1,000 words). **Pays $10/page up to $50, pending funding.**

FICTION Contact: Michael Czyzniejewski, fiction editor. Character-oriented, literary, experimental, short short. Needs experimental, Memoir, prose poem, traditional. No genre fiction. Would like to see more short shorts. **Buys 12 mss/year.** 6,000 words **Pays $10/page up to $50, pending funding.**

POETRY Contact: Contacts: Brad Modlin, poetry editor; Angela Gentry and David D. Williams, assistant poetry editors. Buys 60 poems/year. **Pays $10/page up to $50, pending funding.**

$ MILLER'S POND

H&H Press, 980 Locey Creek Rd., Middlebury Center PA 16935. (570)376-3361. E-mail: mail@handhpress.com (C.J. Houghtaling); mpwebeditor@yahoo.com (Julie Damerell). Website: millerspondpoetry.com. **100% freelance written.** Annual magazine featuring poetry with poetry book/chapbook reviews and interviews of poets. E-mail submissions must be on the form from the website. Estab. 1998. Circ. 200. Byline given. Pays on publication. Publishes ms an average of 1 year after acceptance. Editorial lead time 1 year. Accepts queries by mail. Accepts simultaneous submissions. Responds in 10 months to queries. Responds in 10 months to mss. Sample copy for $7, plus $3 postage. Guidelines available online.

NONFICTION Needs interview, 2,000 words, poetry chapbook reviews (500 words). **Buys 1-2 mss/year.** Query or send complete ms. **Pays $5.**

POETRY Needs free verse. No religious, horror, vulgar, rhymed, preachy, lofty, trite, overly sentimental. Buys 30-35 poems/year. Submit maximum 3-5 poems. 40 lines maximum **Pays $2.**

$$$ THE MISSOURI REVIEW

357 McReynolds Hall, University of Missouri, Columbia MO 65211. (573)882-4474. Fax: (573)884-4671. E-mail: tmr@missourireview.com. Website: missourireview.com. **90% freelance written.** Quarterly magazine. Estab. 1978. Circ. 6,500. Byline given. Offers signed contract. Editorial lead time 6 months. Accepts queries by mail. Responds in 2 weeks to queries. Responds in 10 weeks to mss. Sample copy for $8.95 or online. Guidelines available online.

> 💬 "We publish contemporary fiction, poetry, interviews, personal essays, cartoons, special features—such as History as Literature series and Found Text series—for the literary and the general reader interested in a wide range of subjects."

NONFICTION Contact: Evelyn Somers, associate editor. Needs book excerpts, essays. No literary criticism. **Buys 10 mss/year.** Send complete ms. **Pays $1,000.**

FICTION Contact: Speer Morgan, editor. Needs ethnic, humorous, mainstream, novel concepts, literary. No genre or flash fiction. **Buys 25 mss/year.** Send complete ms. no preference. **Pays $30/printed page.**

POETRY Contact: Jason Koo, poetry editor. Publishes 3-5 poetry features of 6-12 pages per issue. Please familiarize yourself with the magazine before submitting poetry. Buys 50 poems/year. **Pays $30/printed page.**

$ MODERN HAIKU

P.O. Box 33077, Santa Fe NM 87594-9998. E-mail: trumbullc@comcast.net. Website: modernhaiku.org. **85% freelance written.** Magazine published 3 times/year. "*Modern Haiku* publishes high quality material only. Haiku and related genres, articles on haiku, haiku book reviews, and translations comprise its contents. It has an international circulation; subscribers include many university, school, and public libraries." Estab. 1969. Circ. 650. Byline given. Pays on acceptance. Publishes ms an average of 6 months after acceptance. Editorial lead time 4 months. Accepts queries by mail, e-mail. Responds in 1 week to queries. Responds in 6-8 weeks to mss. Sample copy for $11 in North America, $13 in Canada, $14 in Mexico, $17 overseas. Guidelines available online.

NONFICTION Needs essays, anything related to haiku. Send complete ms. **Pays $5/page.**

COLUMNS Haiku & Senryu; Haibun; Essays (on haiku and related genres); Reviews (books of haiku or related genres). **Buys 40 essay & review mss/year (most are commissioned). mss/year.** Send complete ms. **Pays $5/page.**

POETRY Needs haiku, senryu, haibun, haiga. Does not want "general poetry, tanka, linked verse forms." Buys 750 poems/year. Submit maximum 24 poems. **Pays $1 per haiku.**

NECROLOGY SHORTS: TALES OF MACABRE AND HORROR

Isis International, P.O. Box 510232, Saint Louis MO 63151. E-mail: editor@necrologyshorts.com; submit@necrologyshorts.com. Website: necrologyshorts.com. **Contact:** John Ferguson, editor. **80%.** Consumer publication published online daily and through Amazon Kindle. Also offers an annual collection. "*Necrology Shorts* is an online publication which publishes fiction, articles, cartoons, artwork, and poetry daily. Embracing the Internet, e-book readers, and new technology, we aim to go beyond the long time standard of a regular publication to bringing our readers a daily flow of entertainment. We will also be publishing an annual collection for each year in print, e-book reader, and Adobe PDF format. Our main genre is suspense horror similar to H.P. Lovecraft and/or Robert E. Howard. We also publish science fiction and fantasy. We would love to see work continuing the Cthulhu Mythos, but we accept all horror. We also hold contests, judged by our readers, to select the top stories and artwork. Winners of contests receive various prizes, including cash." Estab. 2009. Circ. 20,000. Does not currently pay for submissions Acceptance to publication is 1 month. Editorial lead time is 1 month. Submit seasonal material 2 months in advance. Accepts queries by

e-mail. TrueAccepts simultaneous submissions. Responds in 1 month to ms. Sample copy online. Guidelines found on website.

NONFICTION Needs humor, interview, photo feature, profile, reviews. **Buys Buys 1,000 mss/year. mss/year.** Submit complete ms. 300 mininum-25,000 words maximum. Pays expenses of writers on assignment.

PHOTOS Contact: John Ferguson, editor. Send photos with submission. Model releases and identification of subjects required. Reviews GIF/JPEG files, transparences, prints.

COLUMNS Book Review (2,000 words): Movie Review (2,000 words); Biography of Famous Authors (2,000-10,000 words); Interviews of Authors and Artists (2,000-5,000 words). Send complete ms. Buys 500 mss/year.

FICTION Needs fantasy, horror, science fiction. **Buys Buys 1,000 mss/year. mss/year.** Send complete ms. Length: 300-200,000 words.

NEON MAGAZINE

UK. E-mail: neonmagazine@ymail.com. Website: neonmagazine.co.uk. **Contact:** Krishan Coupland. Quarterly website and print magazine covering alternative work of any form of poetry and prose, short stories, flash fiction, photographs, artwork and reviews. "Genre work is welcome. Experimentation is encouraged. We like stark poetry and weird prose. We seek work that is beautiful, shocking, intense and memorable. Darker pieces are generally favored over humorous ones." Accepts queries by e-mail. Reports in 1 month. Query if you have received no reply after 6 weeks. Guidelines available online.

"Note: *Neon* was previously published as *Four-Volts Magazine*."

NONFICTION Needs essays, Reviews. No word limit.

FICTION Needs experimental, horror, humorous, science fiction, suspense. "No nonsensical prose; we are not appreciative of sentimentality." **Buys 8-12 mss/year.** No word limit. **For 1 short story, or 1-2 flash fictions.**

POETRY "No nonsensical poetry; we are not appreciative of sentimentality. Rhyming poetry is discouraged." Buys 24-30 poems/year. No word limit.

NEW ENGLAND REVIEW

Middlebury College, Middlebury VT 05753. (802)443-5075. E-mail: nereview@middlebury.edu. Website:

go.middlebury.edu/nereview; nereview.com. Quarterly magazine. Literary only. Reads September 1-May 31 (postmarked dates). Estab. 1978. Circ. 2,000. Byline given. Pays on publication. Publishes ms an average of 6 months after acceptance. Accepts simultaneous submissions. Responds in 2 weeks to queries. Responds in 3 months to mss. Sample copy for $10 (add $5 for overseas). Guidelines available online.

⬭ No e-mail submissions.

NONFICTION Buys 20-25 mss/year. Send complete ms. 7,500 words maximum, though exceptions may be made. **Pays $10/page ($20 minimum), and 2 copies.**

FICTION Send 1 story at a time, unless it is very short. Serious literary only, novel excerpts. **Buys 25 mss/year.** Send complete ms. Prose length: not strict on word count **Pays $10/page ($20 minimum), and 2 copies.**

POETRY Buys 75-90 poems/year. Submit maximum 6 poems. **Pays $10/page ($20 minimum), and 2 copies.**

❺ NEW LETTERS

University of Missouri-Kansas City, University House, 5101 Rockhill Rd., Kansas City MO 64110-2499. (816)235-1168. Fax: (816)235-2611. E-mail: newletters@umkc.edu. Website: newletters.org. **100% freelance written.** Quarterly magazine. *"New Letters* is intended for the general literary reader. We publish literary fiction, nonfiction, essays, poetry. We also publish art." Estab. 1934. Circ. 5,000. Byline given. Pays on publication. Publishes ms an average of 6 months after acceptance. Editorial lead time 6 months. Submit seasonal material 6 months in advance. Accepts queries by mail. Responds in 1 month to queries. Responds in 3 months to mss. Sample copy for $10 or sample articles on website. Guidelines available online.

⬭ Submissions are not read between May 1 and October 1.

NONFICTION Needs essays. No self-help, how-to, or nonliterary work. **Buys 8-10 mss/year.** Send complete ms. 5,000 words maximum. **Pays $40-100.**

PHOTOS Send photos. Reviews contact sheets, 2x4 transparencies, prints. Pays $10-40/photo.

FICTION Contact: Robert Stewart, editor. Needs ethnic, experimental, humorous, mainstream, contemporary. No genre fiction. **Buys 15-20 mss/year.** Send complete ms. 5,000 words maximum. **Pays $30-75.**

❺ NEW ORLEANS REVIEW

Box 195, Loyola University, New Orleans LA 70118. (504)865-2295. E-mail: noreview@loyno.edu. Website: neworleansreview.org. **Contact:** Christopher Chambers, editor. Biannual magazine publishing poetry, fiction, translations, photographs, and nonfiction on literature, art and film. Readership: those interested in contemporary literature and culture. Estab. 1968. Circ. 1,500. Pays on publication. Accepts queries by online submission form. Accepts simultaneous submissions. Responds in 4 months to mss. Sample copy for $7.

FICTION Contact: Christopher Chambers, editor. Good writing, from conventional to experimental. We are now using an online submission system and require a $3 fee. See website for details. up to 6,500 words. **Pays $25-50 and 2 copies.**

❍❺❺ THE NEW QUARTERLY

St. Jerome's University, 290 Westmount Rd. N., Waterloo ON N2L 3G3 Canada. (519)884-8111, ext. 28290. E-mail: editor@tnq.ca. Website: tnq.ca. **95% freelance written.** Quarterly book covering Canadian fiction and poetry. "Emphasis on emerging writers and genres, but we publish more traditional work as well if the language and narrative structure are fresh." Estab. 1981. Circ. 1,000. Byline given. Pays on publication. Publishes ms an average of 4 months after acceptance. Editorial lead time 6 months. Accepts queries by mail. Accepts simultaneous submissions. Responds in 2 weeks to queries. Responds in 4 months to mss. Sample copy for $16.50 (cover price, plus mailing). Guidelines for #10 SASE or online.

⬭ Open to Canadian writers only.

FICTION *"Canadian work only.* We are not interested in genre fiction. We are looking for innovative, beautifully crafted, deeply felt literary fiction." **Buys 20-25 mss/year.** Send complete ms. 20 pages maximum **Pays $200/story.**

POETRY Needs avant-garde, free verse, traditional. *Canadian work only.* Buys 40 poems/year. Submit maximum 3 poems. **Pays $40/poem.**

❺❺ THE NEW WRITER

P.O. Box 60, Cranbrook Kent TN17 2ZR United Kingdom. (44)(158)021-2626. E-mail: editor@thenewwriter.com. Website: thenewwriter.com. **Contact:** Sarah Jackson, poetry editor. Publishes 6 issues per annum. "Contemporary writing magazine which publishes the best in fact, fiction and poetry." Estab. 1996. Circ. 1,500. Pays on publication. Publishes ms an average of 1 year after acceptance. Accepts queries by e-mail, fax. Accepts simultaneous submissions. Responds in 2 months to queries. Responds in 4 months to mss.

Sample copy for SASE and A4 SAE with IRCs only. Guidelines for SASE.

NONFICTION Query. Length: 1,000-2,000 words. **Pays £20-40.**

FICTION *No unsolicited mss.* Accepts fiction from subscribers only. "We will consider most categories apart from stories written for children. No horror, erotic, or cosy fiction." Query with published clips. Length: 2,000-5,000 words. **Pays £10 per story by credit voucher; additional copies for £1.50.**

POETRY Buys 50 poems/year. Submit maximum 3 poems. 40 lines maximum **Pays £3/poem.**

$ THE NORTH AMERICAN REVIEW

University of Northern Iowa, 1222 W. 27th St., Cedar Falls IA 50614-0516. (319)273-6455. Fax: (319)273-4326. E-mail: nar@uni.edu. Website: webdelsol.com/northamreview/nar/. **90% freelance written.** Bimonthly magazine. "The *NAR* is the oldest literary magazine in America and one of the most respected; though we have no prejudices about the subject matter of material sent to us, our first concern is quality." Estab. 1815. Circ. under 5,000. Byline given. Pays on publication. Publishes ms an average of 1 year after acceptance. Accepts queries by mail. Responds in 4 months to mss. Sample copy for $5. Guidelines available online.

💬 "This is the oldest literary magazine in the country and one of the most prestigious. Also one of the most entertaining—and a tough market for the young writer."

NONFICTION Contact: Ron Sandvik, nonfiction editor. Open **Pays $5/350 words; $20 minimum, $100 maximum.**

FICTION Contact: fiction editor. No restrictions; highest quality only. Needs , Wants more well-crafted literary stories that emphasize family concerns. No flat narrative stories where the inferiority of the character is the paramount concern. Open **Pays $5/350 words; $20 minimum, $100 maximum.**

POETRY No restrictions; highest quality only. Open. **Pays $1/line; $20 minimum, $100 maximum.**

$ NORTH CAROLINA LITERARY REVIEW

East Carolina University, ECU Mailstop 555 English, Greenville NC 27858-4353. (252)328-1537. Fax: (252)328-4889. E-mail: nclrsubmissions@ecu.edu; bauerm@ecu.edu. Website: nclr.ecu.edu. Annual magazine published in summer covering North Carolina writers, literature, culture, history. "Articles should have a North Carolina slant. First consideration is always for quality of work. Although we treat academic and scholarly subjects, we do not wish to see jargon-laden prose; our readers, we hope, are found as often in bookstores and libraries as in academia. We seek to combine the best elements of magazine for serious readers with best of scholarly journal." Estab. 1992. Circ. 750. Byline given. Pays on publication. Publishes ms an average of 1 year after acceptance. Editorial lead time 6 months. Accepts queries by mail, e-mail. Responds in 1 month to queries. Responds in 6 months to mss. Sample copy for $10-25. Guidelines available online.

NONFICTION Needs book excerpts, essays, expose, general interest, historical, humor, interview, opinion, personal experience, photo feature, travel, reviews, short narratives, surveys of archives. No jargon-laden academic articles. **Buys 25-35 mss/year.** Query with published clips. Length: 500-5,000 words. **Pays $50-100 honorarium, extra copies, back issues or subscription (negotiable).**

COLUMNS NC Writers (interviews, biographical/bibliographic essays); Reviews (essay reviews of North Carolina-related fiction, creative nonfiction, or poetry). Query with published clips. **Pays $50-100 honorarium, extra copies, back issues or subscription (negotiable).**

FICTION "Fiction submissions accepted during Doris Betts Prize Competition; see our submission guidelines for detail." **Buys 3-4 mss/year.** Query. 5,000 words maximum. **$50-100 honorarium, extra copies, back issues or subscription (negotiable).**

POETRY *North Carolina poets only.* Buys 5-10 poems/year. Length: 30-150 lines. **$50-100 honorarium, extra copies, back issues or subscription (negotiable).**

FILLERS Buys 2-5 mss/year. Length: 50-500 words. **$50-100 honorarium, extra copies, back issues or subscription (negotiable).**

$ NOTRE DAME REVIEW

University of Notre Dame, 840 Flanner Hall, Notre Dame IN 46556. (574)631-6952. Fax: (574)631-4795. E-mail: english.ndreview.1@nd.edu. Website: nd.edu/~ndr/review.htm. Semiannual magazine. The *Notre Dame Review* is an indepenent, noncommercial magazine of contemporary American and international fiction, poetry, criticism, and art. We are especially interested in work that takes on big issues by making the invisible seen, that gives voice to the voiceless. In addition to showcasing celebrated authors like Seamus Heaney and Czelaw Milosz, the *Notre Dame Review* introduces readers to authors they may have never encountered before, but who are doing innovative and important work. In conjunction with the *Notre Dame Review*, the online companion to the printed magazine, the *Notre Dame Re-view* engages readers as a community centered in literary rather than commercial concerns, a community we reach out to through critique and commentary as well as aesthetic experience. Estab. 1995. Circ. 2,000. Pays on publication. Publishes ms an average of 6 months after acceptance. Accepts simultaneous submissions. Responds in 4 or more months to mss. Sample copy for $6. Guidelines available online.

FICTION Contact: William O'Rourke, fiction editor. "We're eclectic. Upcoming theme issues planned. List of upcoming themes or editorial calendar available for SASE. Does not read mss May-August." No genre fiction. **Buys 100 (90 poems, 10 stories) mss/year.** Length: 3,000 words. **Pays $5-25.**

☉ ONE-STORY

One-Story, LLC, 232 3rd St., #A111, Brooklyn NY 11215. Website: one-story.com. **Contact:** Maribeth Batcha, publisher. **100% freelance written.** Literary magazine covering 1 short story. "*One-Story* is a literary magazine that contains, simply, 1 story. It is a subscription-only magazine. Every 3 weeks subscribers are sent *One-Story* in the mail. *One-Story* is artfully designed, lightweight, easy to carry, and ready to entertain on buses, in bed, in subways, in cars, in the park, in the bath, in the waiting rooms of doctor's offices, on the couch, or in line at the supermarket. Subscribers also have access to a website, where they can learn more about *One-Story* authors, and hear about *One-Story* readings and events. There is always time to read *One-Story*." Estab. 2002. Circ. 3,500. Byline given. Pays on publication. Publishes ms an average of 3-6 months after acceptance. Editorial lead time 3-4 months. Accepts simultaneous submissions. Responds in 2-6 months to mss. Sample copy for $5. Guidelines available online.

> ◔ "Accepts submissions via website only (.rtf files). Receives 100 submissions a week. Submit between June & Sept. Publishes each writer one time only."

FICTION *One-Story* only accepts short stories. Do not send excerpts. Do not send more than 1 story at a time. **Buys 18 mss/year.** Send complete ms. Length: 3,000-8,000 words. **Pays $100.**

OYEZ REVIEW

Roosevelt University, Dept. of Literature & Languages, 430 S. Michigan Ave., Chicago IL 60605-1394. (312)341-3500. E-mail: oyezreview@roosevelt.edu. Website: legacy.roosevelt.edu/roosevelt.edu/oyezreview. **100% freelance written.** Annual magazine of the Creative Writing Program at Roosevelt University, publishing fiction, creative nonfiction, poetry, and art. There are no restrictions on style, theme, or subject matter. Each issue has 100 pages: 92 pages of text and an 8-page black & white spread of one artist's work (usually drawing, painting or photography). In addition to the 8-page spread, the front and back cover feature the artist's work as well, totaling 10 pieces. It has featured work from such writers as Charles Bukowski, James McManus, Carla Panciera, Michael Onofrey, Tim Foley, John N. Miller, Gary Fincke, and Barry Silesky, and visual artists Vivian Nunley, C. Taylor, Jennifer Troyer, and Frank Spidale. Estab. 1965. Circ. 600. Byline given. Pays 2 contributor's copies. Publishes ms an average of 2 months after acceptance. Accepts queries by mail, e-mail. Responds in 3 months Sample copy available by request. Guidelines available online. SASE required. Does not accept e-mail submissions unless from abroad.

> ◔ Reading period is August 1-October 1. Responds by mid-December.

NONFICTION Needs essays, personal experience memoir, literary journalism. **Buys 1-5 mss/year.** Send complete ms. 5,500 words maximum

PHOTOS Accepts b&w artwork. Do not send originals. Porfolio not required. Submit at least 20 black & white images (because we publish 10 images from one artist each year and need several to choose from). Reviews prints, slides, GIF/JPEG files. Offers no additional payment for photos accepted with ms.

FICTION We publish short stories and flash fiction on their merit as contemporary literature rather than the category within the genre. **Buys 1-8 mss/year.** Send complete ms. 5,500 words maximum

POETRY Needs avant-garde, free verse, traditional. Buys 10-20 poems/year. Submit maximum 5 poems. 10 pages maximum

☉ PALABRA

P.O. Box 86146, Los Angeles CA 90086-0146. E-mail: info@palabralitmag.com. Website: palabralitmag.

com. Annual magazine featuring poetry, fiction, short plays, and more. "*PALABRA* is about exploration, risk and ganas—the myriad intersections of thought, language, story and art—*el mas alla of letters*, symbols and spaces into meaning." Byline given. Responds in 3-4 months to mss

NONFICTION Pays $25-35.

FICTION Needs experimental/hybrid, mainstream, novel excerpts, flash fiction, short plays. Does not want genre work (mystery, romance, science fiction, etc.). Send complete ms, unpublished work only. Length: 4,000 words. **Pays $$25-$35.**

POETRY Needs avant garde, free verse, traditional. Submit maximum 5 poems.

⊖⊖⊖ THE PARIS REVIEW

62 White Street, New York NY 10013. (212)343-1333. E-mail: queries@theparisreview.org. Website: theparisreview.org. Nathaniel Rich, fiction editor. **Contact:** Philip Gourevitch, editor. Quarterly magazine. "Fiction and poetry of superlative quality, whatever the genre, style or mode. Our contributors include prominent, as well as less well-known and previously unpublished writers. Writers at Work interview series includes important contemporary writers discussing their own work and the craft of writing." Pays on publication. Accepts queries by mail. Accepts simultaneous submissions. Responds in 4 months to mss. Sample copy for $15 (includes postage). Guidelines available online.

⊙ Address submissions to proper department. Do not make submissions via e-mail.

FICTION Study the publication. Annual Aga Khan Fiction Contest award of $1,000. Send complete ms. no limit **Pays $500-1,000.**

POETRY Contact: Richard Howard, poetry editor. **Pays $35 minimum varies according to length. Awards $1,000 in Bernard F. Conners Poetry Prize contest.**

⊖⊖ PARNASSUS: POETRY IN REVIEW

Poetry in Review Foundation, 205 W. 89th St., #8F, New York NY 10024. (212)362-3492. Fax: (212)875-0148. E-mail: parnew@aol.com. Website: parnassuspoetry.com. **Contact:** Herbert Leibowitz, editor & publisher. Annual magazine covering poetry and criticism. "We now publish one double issue a year." Estab. 1972. Circ. 1,800. Byline given. Pays on publication. Publishes ms an average of 12-14 months after acceptance. Accepts queries by mail. Responds in 2 months to mss. Sample copy for $15.

NONFICTION Needs essays. **Buys 30 mss/year.** Query with published clips. Length: 1,500-7,500 words. **Pays $200-750.**

POETRY Needs avant garde, free verse, traditional. Accepts most types of poetry. Buys Buys 3-4 unsolicited poems/year.

⊖ PLEIADES

Pleiades Press, Department of English, University of Central Missouri, Martin 336, Warrensburg MO 64093. (660)543-4425. Fax: (660)543-8544. E-mail: pleiades@ucmo.edu. Website: ucmo.edu/englphil/pleiades. **Contact:** G.B. Crump, Matthew Eck and Phong Nguyen, prose editors. **100% freelance written.** Semiannual journal (5½×8½ perfect bound). "We publish contemporary fiction, poetry, interviews, literary essays, special-interest personal essays, reviews for a general and literary audience from authors from around the world." Estab. 1991. Circ. 3,000. Byline given. Pays on publication. Publishes ms an average of 9 months after acceptance. Editorial lead time 9 months. Accepts queries by mail. Accepts simultaneous submissions. Responds in 2 months to queries. Responds in 1-4 months to mss. Sample copy for $5 (back issue); $6 (current issue). Guidelines available online.

⊙ "Also sponsors the Lena-Miles Wever Todd Poetry Series competition, a contest for the best book ms by an American poet. The winner receives $1,000, publication by Pleiades Press, and distribution by Louisiana State University Press. Deadline September 30. Send SASE for guidelines."

NONFICTION Contact: Phong Nguyen and Matthew Eck, nonfiction editor. Needs book excerpts, essays, interview, reviews. "Nothing pedantic, slick, or shallow. Do not send submissions after May 31. We resume reading nonfiction Sept. 1." **Buys 4-6 mss/year.** Send complete ms. Length: 2,000-4,000 words. **Pays $10.**

FICTION Contact: Matthew Eck and Phong Nguyen. We read fiction year-round. Needs ethnic, experimental, humorous, mainstream, novel concepts, magic realism. No science fiction, fantasy, confession, erotica. **Buys 16-20 mss/year.** Send complete ms. Length: 2,000-6,000 words. **Pays $10.**

POETRY Contact: Kevin Prufer and Wayne Miller. Needs avant-garde, free verse, haiku, light verse, traditional. "Nothing didactic, pretentious, or overly sentimental. Do not send poetry after May 31. We resume reading poetry on Sept. 1." Buys 40-50 poems/year. Submit maximum 6 poems. **Pays $3/poem, and contributor copies.**

PMS

University of Alabama at Birmingham, HB 217, 1530 3rd Ave. South, Birmingham AL 35294-1260. (205)934-8578. E-mail: kmadden@uab.edu. Website: pms-journal.org/submissions-guidelines. **Contact:** Kerry Madden, Editor-in-Chief. Annual magazine covering poetry, memoirs and short fiction; contains the best work of the best women writers in the world. "This is an all women's literary journal. The subject field is wide open." "Each issue of *PMS* includes a memoir written by a woman who has experienced a historically significant event. *PMS 10* features Masha Hamilton and her authors from the Afghan Women's Writing Project. Writer Donna Thomas's memoir, Kiddie Land, recalls Birmingham's segregated past when Kiddie Land opened to children of all colors. Look for excerpts of *PMS 10* to be online soon." Sample copy for $7.

⭕ Work from PMS has been reprinted in a number of award anthologies: *New Stories from the South 2005, The Best Creative Nonfiction 200 and 2008, Best American Poetry 2003 and 2004, and Best American Essays 2005 and 2007.*

NONFICTION Needs personal experience. Special issues: Each issue includes a memoir written by a woman who is not necessarily a writer but who has experienced something of historic import. Emily Lyons, the nurse who survived the 1998 New Woman All Women Birgmingham clinic bombing by Eric Rudolph; women who experienced the World Trade Center on 9/11; the Civil Rights Movement in Birmingham, the war in Iraq, Hurricane Katrina, and teaching Milton's *Paradise Lost* to inmates at an Alabama state prison have lent us their stories. Length: 4,300 words.

FICTION Length: 4,300 words.

POETRY All submissions should be unpublished original work that we can recycle and be accompanied by a SASE with sufficient postage for either return of your manuscript or notification. Submit maximum 5 poems. **Writers will receive two complimentary copies of the issue of *PMS* in which their work appears and a one-year subscription. Copyright returns to the author after publication in *PMS*.**

💲 POETRY

The Poetry Foundation, 444 N. Michigan Ave., Suite 1850, Chicago IL 60611-4034. (312)787-7070. Fax: (312)787-6650. E-mail: editors@poetrymagazine.org. Website: poetrymagazine.org. Christian Wiman, Editor. **Contact:** Helen Klaviter. **100% freelance written.** Monthly magazine. Estab. 1912. Circ. 31,000. Byline given. Pays on publication. Publishes ms an average of 9 months after acceptance. Accepts queries by mail. Responds in 1 month to queries and to mss. Sample copy for $3.75 or online at website. Guidelines available online.

NONFICTION Buys 14 mss/year. Query. Length: 1,000-2,000 words. **Pays $150/page.**

POETRY Accepts all styles and subject matter. Buys 180-250 poems/year. Submit maximum 4 poems. Open **Pays $10/line ($150 minimum payment).**

💲💲 POETRY NEW ZEALAND

34B Methuen Rd., Avondale Auckland New Zealand. E-mail: alstair@ihug.co.nz. Website: poetrynz.net. "Each issue has 15-20 pages of poetry from a developing or established poet. The rest of the issue is devoted to a selection of poetry from New Zealand and abroad, plus essays, reviews, and general criticism to a total of 112 pages." Estab. 1951. Accepts queries by mail. Responds in 3 months to mss. Guidelines available online.

NONFICTION Submit a copy of the magazine. **Featured poets and essayists receive 1 copy of the magazine and a fee.**

POETRY Accepts any theme/style of poetry. Send complete ms, bio, and SASE.

💲 THE PRAIRIE JOURNAL

Prairie Journal Trust, P.O. Box 68073, 28 Crowfoot Terrace NW, Calgary AB Y3G 3N8 Canada. E-mail: editor@prairiejournal.org (queries only); prairiejournal@yahoo.com. Website: prairiejournal.org. **Contact:** A.E. Burke, literary editor. **100% freelance written.** Semiannual magazine publishing quality poetry, short fiction, drama, literary criticism, reviews, bibliography, interviews, profiles, and artwork. "The audience is literary, university, library, scholarly, and creative readers/writers." Estab. 1983. Circ. 600. Byline given. Pays on publication. Publishes ms an average of 4-6 months after acceptance. Editorial lead time 4-6 months. Accepts queries by mail, e-mail. NoResponds in 2 weeks to queries. Responds in 6 months to mss. Sample copy for $5. Guidelines available online.

💬 "Use our mailing address for submissions and queries with samples sor clippings."

NONFICTION Needs essays, humor, interview, literary. No inspirational, news, religious, or travel. **Buys 25-40 mss/year.** Query with published clips. Length: 100-3,000 words. **Pays $50-100, plus contributor's copy.**

PHOTOS State availability. Offers additional payment for photos accepted with ms.

COLUMNS Reviews (books from small presses publishing poetry, short fiction, essays, and criticism), 200-1,000 words. **Buys 5 mss/year.** Query with published clips. **Pays $10-50.**

FICTION No genre (romance, horror, western—sagebrush or cowboys), erotic, science fiction, or mystery. **Buys 6 mss/year.** Send complete ms. Length: 100-3,000 words. **Pays $10-75.**

POETRY Needs avant-garde, free verse, haiku. No heroic couplets or greeting card verse. Buys 25-35 poems/year. Submit maximum 6-8 poems. Length: 3-50 lines. **Pays $5-50.**

♻️💲 PRISM INTERNATIONAL ·

Department of Creative Writing, Buch E462, 1866 Main Mall, University of British Columbia, Vancouver BC V6T 1Z1 Canada. (604)822-2514. Fax: (604)822-3616. Website: prismmagazine.ca. **100% freelance written. Works with new/unpublished writers.** A quarterly international journal of contemporary writing—fiction, poetry, drama, creative nonfiction and translation. Readership: public and university libraries, individual subscriptions, bookstores—a world-wide audience concerned with the contemporary in literature. Estab. 1959. Circ. 1,200. Pays on publication. Publishes ms an average of 4 months after acceptance. Accepts queries by mail. Responds in 4 months to queries. Responds in 3-6 months to mss. Sample copy for $11, more info online. Guidelines available online.

NONFICTION No reviews, tracts, or scholarly essays. **Pays $20/printed page, and 1-year subscription.**

FICTION For Drama: one-acts/excerpts of no more than 1500 words preferred. Also interested in seeing dramatic monologues. Needs experimental, novel concepts, traditional. "New writing that is contemporary and literary. Short stories and self-contained novel excerpts. Works of translation are eagerly sought

and should be accompanied by a copy of the original. Would like to see more translations. No gothic, confession, religious, romance, pornography, or science fiction." **Buys 12-16 mss/year.** Send complete ms. 25 pages maximum **Pays $20/printed page, and 1-year subscription.**

POETRY Needs avant-garde, traditional. **Buys 10 poems/issue.** Submit maximum 6 poems. **Pays $40/ printed page, and 1-year subscription.**

♻️💲💲 QUEEN'S QUARTERLY

144 Barrie St., Queen's University, Kingston ON K7L 3N6 Canada. (613)533-2667. Fax: (613)533-6822. E-mail: queens.quarterly@queensu.ca. Website: queensu.ca/quarterly. **Contact:** Joan Harcourt, editor. **95% freelance written.** Quarterly magazine covering a wide variety of subjects, including science, humanities, arts and letters, politics, and history for the educated reader. "A general interest intellectual review, featuring articles, book reviews, poetry, and fiction." Estab. 1893. Circ. 3,000. Byline given. Pays on publication. Publishes ms on average 6-12 months after acceptance. Accepts queries by e-mail. Responds in 2-3 months to queries. Free sample copy online. Writer's guidelines online.

💬 Submissions can be sent as e-mail attachment or on hard copy with a S.A.S.E. (if submitting from the US or Int'l, the S.A.S.E. must have Canadian postage or be accompanied by an International Reply Coupon in order to receive a reply and will be responded to by same.) Payment will be determined at time of acceptance.

NONFICTION Contact: Boris Castel, Editor (articles, essays and reviews).

FICTION Contact: Joan Harcourt, Literary Editor (fiction and poetry). Needs , short stories. Submissions over 3,000 words shall not be accepted. Length: 2,500-3,000 words.

POETRY Buys 25 poems/year. Submit maximum 6 poems.

RAIN TAXI

Rain Taxi, Inc., P.O. Box 3840, Minneapolis MN 55403-0840. (612)825-1528. Fax: (612)825-1528. E-mail: info@raintaxi.com. Website: raintaxi.com. **40% freelance written.** Quarterly magazine covering books. "*Rain Taxi* Review of Books, a nonprofit quarterly, is dedicated to covering literature & the arts, including poetry, graphic novels, cultural critique, & quality fiction in all genres. Winner of an

Independent Press Award, *Rain Taxi* is a great vehicle for books & authors that may otherwise get lost in the mainstream media." Estab. 1996. Circ. 18,000. Byline given. Payment in Issues. Publishes ms an average of 2 months after acceptance. Editorial lead time 2 months. Submit seasonal material 3 months in advance. Accepts queries by mail, e-mail. Responds in 2 weeks to queries. Responds in 1 month to mss. Sample copy for $5. Guidelines by e-mail.

NONFICTION Contact: Eric Lorberer, editor. Needs essays, interview, Reviews. **Buys 0 mss/year.** Query. Length: 500-2,000 words. **Pays 0 for assigned or unsolicited articles.**

RATTAPALLAX

Rattapallax Press, 217 Thompson St., Suite 353, New York NY 10012. (212)560-7459. E-mail: info@rattapallax.com. Website: rattapallax.com. **Contact:** Alan Cheuse, fiction editor. **10% freelance written.** Annual magazine covering international fiction and poetry. *Rattapallax* is a literary magazine that focuses on issues dealing with globalization. Estab. 1999. Circ. 3,000. Byline given. Pays on publication. Publishes ms an average of 6 months after acceptance. Editorial lead time 6 months. Submit seasonal material 6 months in advance. Accepts queries by e-mail. Responds in 2 weeks to queries. Responds in 6 months to mss. Sample copy available online. Guidelines available online.

POETRY Needs avant-garde, free verse, traditional. Submit maximum 5 poems. Length: 5-200 lines.

REDACTIONS: POETRY & POETICS

58 So. Main St., 3rd Floor, Brockport NY 14420. E-mail: redactionspoetry@yahoo.com. Website: redactions.com. Every 9 months covering poems, reviews of new books of poems, translations, manifestos, interviews, essays concerning poetry, poetics, poetry movements, or concerning a specific poet or a group of poets; and anything dealing with poetry. Accepts queries by e-mail. Accepts simultaneous submissions.

NONFICTION Needs essays on poetics, reviews of new books of poems, interviews with poets., Art, Translation.

REPRINTS "Please mention first publication in *Redactions.*"

POETRY "Anything dealing with poetry."

RHINO

The Poetry Forum, Inc., P.O. Box 591, Evanston IL 60204. E-mail: editors@rhinopoetry.org. Website: rhinopoetry.org. **Contact:** Ralph Hamilton, Sr., Editor; Helen Degen Cohen, Sr. Editor and Founder. Annual magazine covering high-quality, diverse poetry, short/shorts and translations by new and established writers. "This eclectic annual journal of more than 30 years accepts poetry, flash fiction (1,000 words or less), and poetry-in-translation from around the world that experiments, provokes, compels. More than 80 poets are showcased. The regular call for poetry is from April 1 to October 1st, and the Founder's Contest submission period has been changed to July 1 to October 1st." Accepts simultaneous submissions. Response time may exceed 6 weeks. Guidelines available online.

💬 "Founders' Contest submission period is from July 1 - October 1."

NONFICTION Needs essays, on poetry, humor, translation.

FICTION Needs humorous, flash fiction, (1,000 words or less), poetry, poetry-in-translation. Submit by mail or online. Include SASE for USPS mail only. Short shorts: 1,000 words or less.

POETRY Needs avant-garde, free verse, light verse, traditional. "Please label each poem with your name, address, telephone number, and e-mail address for ease in contacting you." Submit maximum 5 poems.

RIVER STYX MAGAZINE

Big River Association, 3547 Olive St., Suite 107, St. Louis MO 63103. (314)533-4541. E-mail: bigriver@riverstyx.org. Website: riverstyx.org. **Contact:** Richard Newman, Editor. Triannual magazine. "*River Styx* publishes the highest quality fiction, poetry, interviews, essays, and visual art. We are an internationally distributed multicultural literary magazine. Mss read May-November." Estab. 1975. Byline given. Pays on publication. Publishes ms an average of 1 year after acceptance. Accepts queries by mail. Accepts simultaneous submissions. Responds in 4 months to mss. Sample copy for $8. Guidelines available online.

💬 Work published in *River Styx* has been selected for inclusion in past volumes of *New Stories From the South, The Best American Poetry, Beacon's Best, Best New Poets* and *The Pushcart Prize Anthology*

NONFICTION Needs essays, interview. **Buys 2-5 mss/year.** Send complete ms. **Pays 2 contributor copies, plus 1 year subscription; plus cash payment as funds permit.**

PHOTOS Send photos. Reviews 5×7 or 8×10 b&w and color prints and slides. Pays 2 contributor copies, plus 1-year subscription; plus cash as funds permit.

FICTION Contact: Richard Newman, editor. Needs ethnic, experimental, mainstream, novel concepts, short stories, literary. No genre fiction, less thinly veiled autobiography. **Buys 6-9 mss/year.** Send complete ms. no more than 23-30 manuscript pages. **Pays 2 contributor copies, plus 1-year subscription; plus cash payment as funds permit.**

POETRY Needs avant-garde, free verse. *River Styx Magazine*, published 3 times/year in April, August, and December, is "an international, multicultural journal publishing both award-winning and previously undiscovered writers. We feature poetry, short fiction, essays, interviews, fine art, and photography." Wants "excellent poetry—original, energetic, musical, and accessible." Does not want "chopped prose or opaque poetry that isn't about anything." Has published poetry by Jennifer Perrine, Louis Simpson, Molly Peacock, Marilyn Hacker, Yusef Komunyakaa, Andrew Hudgins, and Catie Rosemurgy. *River Styx Magazine* is 100-120 pages, digest-sized, professionally printed on coated stock, perfect-bound, with color cover, includes ads. Receives about 8,000 poems/year, accepts 60-75. Press run is 2,500 (1,000 subscribers, 80 libraries). Subscription: $20/year, $35/2 years. Sample: $9. Sometimes comments on rejected poems. Publishes 1 theme issue/year. Upcoming themes available in magazine or on website. Guidelines available for SASE or on website. Responds in up to 5 months. Pays 2 contributor's copies and one-year subscription, plus a small cash payments as funds permit. Acquires one-time rights. No religious. Buys 40-50 poems/year. Submit maximum 3-5 poems. **Pays 2 contributor copies, plus a 1-year subscription; plus small cash payments as funds permit.**

✪ $ THE SAVAGE KICK LITERARY MAGAZINE

Murder Slim Press, 129 Trafalgar Road West, Gt. Yarmouth Norfolk NR31 8AD United Kingdom. E-mail: moonshine@murderslim.com. Website: murderslim.com/savagekick.html. **100% freelance written.** Semiannual magazine. "*Savage Kick* primarily deals with viewpoints outside the mainstream.honest emotions told in a raw, simplistic way. It is recommended that you are very familiar with the *SK* style before submitting. We have only accepted 8 new writers in 4 years of the magazine. Ensure you have a distinctive voice and story to tell." Estab. 2005. Circ. 500+. Byline given. Pays on acceptance. Publishes ms an average of up to 2 months after acceptance. Accepts queries by mail, e-mail. Accepts simultaneous submissions. Responds in 7-10 days to queries. Guidelines free.

NONFICTION Needs interview, personal experience. **Buys 10-20 mss/year.** Send complete ms. Length: 500-3,000 words. **Pays $25-35.**

COLUMNS Buys up to 4 mss/year. Query. **Pays $25-35.**

FICTION Needs mystery, slice-of-life vignettes, crime. "Real-life stories are preferred, unless the work is distinctively extreme within the crime genre. No Poetry of any kind, no mainstream fiction, Oprah-style fiction, Internet/chat language, teen issues, excessive Shakespearean language, surrealism, overworked irony, or genre fiction (horror, fantasy, science fiction, western, erotica, etc.)." **Buys 10-25 mss/year.** Send complete ms. Length: 500-6,000 words. **Pays $35.**

$ SHENANDOAH

Washington and Lee University, Mattingly House, 2 Lee Ave., Lexington VA 24450-2116. (540)458-8765. Fax: (540)458-8461. E-mail: shenandoah@wlu.edu. Website: shenandoah.wlu.edu/faq.html. **Contact:** R. T. Smith, editor. Triannual magazine. "Unsolicited manuscripts will not be read between January 1 and October 1, 2010. All manuscripts received during this period will be recycled unread." Estab. 1950. Circ. 2,000. Byline given. Pays on publication. Publishes ms an average of 10 months after acceptance. Responds in 3 months to mss. Sample copy for $12. Guidelines available online.

NONFICTION Needs essays, Book reviews. **Buys 6 mss/year.** Send complete ms. **Pays $25/page ($250 max).**

FICTION Needs mainstream, short stories. No sloppy, hasty, slight fiction. **Buys 15 mss/year.** Send complete ms. **Pays $25/page ($250 max).**

POETRY Considers simultaneous submissions "only if we are immediately informed of acceptance elsewhere." No e-mail submissions. All submissions should be typed on 1 side of the paper only, with name and address clearly written on the upper right corner of the ms. Include SASE. Reads submissions September 1-May 15 only. Responds in 3 months. Pays $2.50/line, one-year subscription, and 1 contributor's copy. Acquires first publication rights. Staff reviews books of poetry in 7-10 pages, multi-book format. Send materials for review consideration. (Most reviews are solicited.) "No inspirational, confessional poetry." Buys 70 poems/year. Submit maximum 5 poems. **Pays $2.50/line ($200 max).**

SLIPSTREAM

Dept. W-1, Box 2071, Niagara Falls NY 14301. E-mail: editors@slipstream.org. Website: slipstreampress.org/index.html. **Contact:** Dan Sicoli, co-editor. Annual magazine covering poetry only, black & white photos, drawings and illustrations; A yearly anthology of some of the best poetry and fiction you'll find today in the American small press. "We prefer contemporary urban themes—writing from the grit that is not afraid to bark or bite. We shy away from pastoral, religious, and rhyming verse." Estab. 1980. Chapbook Contest prize is $1,000 plus 50 professionally printed copies of your chapbook. Accepts queries by mail. Accepts simultaneous submissions. Guidelines available online.

 If you're unsure, the editors strongly recommend that you sample a current or back issue of *Slipstream.*

PHOTOS It's better to send scans or photocopies of artwork rather than originals.

POETRY No pastoral, religious, and rhyming verse.

THE SOUTHERN REVIEW

Louisiana State University, Old President's House, Baton Rouge LA 70803-5001. (225)578-5108. Fax: (225)578-5098. E-mail: southernreview@lsu.edu. Website: lsu.edu/tsr. **Contact:** Jeanne Leiby, Editor. **100% freelance written. Works with a moderate number of new/unpublished writers each year; reads unsolicited mss.** Quarterly magazine with emphasis on contemporary literature in the US and abroad. Reading period: September1-June 1. All mss. submitted during summer months will be recycled. Estab. 1935. Circ. 2,900. Byline given. Pays on publication. Publishes ms an average of 6 months after acceptance. Accepts queries by mail. Does not accept previously published work.Responds in 2 months. Sample copy for $8. Guidelines available online.

NONFICTION Buys 25 mss/year. Length: 4,000-10,000 words. **Pays $30/page.**

FICTION Contact: Jessica Faust-Spitzfaden, assistant editor. Short stories of lasting literary merit, with emphasis on style and technique; novel excerpts. "We emphasize style and substantial content. No mystery, fantasy or religious mss." Submit one ms. in any genre at a time. "We rarely publish work that is longer than 8,000 words. We consider novel excerpts if they stand alone." Length: 4,000-8,000 words. **Pays $30/page.**

POETRY Submit maximum 5/time poems. 1-4 pages **Pays $30/page.**

STAND MAGAZINE

School of English, University of Leeds, Leeds LS2 9JT United Kingdom. (44)(113)343-4794. E-mail: stand@leeds.ac.uk. Website: standmagazine.org. "Quarterly literary magazine." Estab. 1952. Pays on publication. Accepts queries by mail. Guidelines available online at website.

 "U.S. submissions can be made through the Virginia office (see separate listing)."

STRUGGLE: A MAGAZINE OF PROLETARIAN REVOLUTIONARY LITERATURE

P.O. Box 28536, Detroit MI 48228. (313)273-9039. E-mail: timhall11@yahoo.com. Website: strugglemagazine.net. **Contact:** Tim Hall, Editor. Quarterly magazine devoted to progressive and revolutionary literature and art expressing the the anti-establishment struggles of the working class and oppressed people in the U.S. and worldwide. Poems, songs, stories, short plays, drawings, cartoons, occasional photos plus editorials by Tim Hall, an anti-revisionist Marxist-Leninist since the 1960's. Publishes material related to "the struggle of the working class and all progressive people against the rule of the rich—including their war policies, repression, racism, exploitation of the workers, oppression of women and immigrants and general culture, etc." Quarterly. Recently published work by Billie Louise Jones, Tyler Plosia, Margaret Dimacou. Accepts multiple submissions. Magazine: 512×812; 36-72 pages; 20 lb. white bond paper; colored cover; illustrations; occasional photos. Estab. 1985. Accepts queries by mail, e-mail. Accepts simultaneous submissions. Responds in 3-4 months to queries generally. Sample copies for $3; $5 for double-size issues; subscriptions $10 for 4 issues; make checks payable to Tim Hall, Special Account, not to *Struggle.*

NONFICTION Needs , Ethnic/multicultural, experimental, feminist, historical, humor/satire, literary, pro-immigrant, regional, science fiction, translations, young adult/teen (10-18), prose poem, senior citizen/retirement. The theme can be approached in many ways, including plenty of categories not listed here. Readers would like fiction about anti-globalization, the fight against racism, prison conditions, neo-conservatism and the Iraq and Afghanistan wars, the struggle of immigrants, and the disillusionment with the Obama Administration as it reveals its craven service to the rich billionaires. No romance, psychic, mystery, western, erotica, religious. Send ms. Receives 10-12 unsolicited mss/month. **Pays 1 contributor's copy. Not copyrighted.**

FICTION "Readers would like fiction about anti-globalization, the fight against racism, prison conditions, neo-conservatism and the Iraq and Afghanistan wars, the struggle of immigrants, and the disillusionment with the Obama Administration as it reveals it craven service to the rich billionaires. Would also like to see more fiction that depicts life, work and struggle of the working class of every background; also the struggles of the 1930s and '60s illustrated and brought to life." Accepts submissions by e-mail, mail. Length: 4,000 words; average length: 1,000-3,000 words.

SUBTROPICS

University of Florida, P.O. Box 112075, 4008 Turlington Hall, Gainesville FL 32611-2075. E-mail: dleavitt@ufl.edu; subtropics@english.ufl.edu. Website: english.ufl.edu/subtropics. **Contact:** David Leavitt. **100% freelance written.** "Magazine published 3 times/year through the University of Florida's English department. *Subtropics* seeks to publish the best literary fiction, essays, and poetry being written today, both by established and emerging authors. We will consider works of fiction of any length, from short shorts to novellas and self-contained novel excerpts. We give the same latitude to essays. We appreciate work in translation and, from time to time, republish important and compelling stories, essays, and poems that have lapsed out of print by writers no longer living." Estab. 2005. Byline given. Pays on acceptance. Publishes ms an average of 6 months after acceptance. Responds in 1 month to queries and mss. Guidelines available online.

NONFICTION Needs essays, literary nonfiction. No book reviews. **Buys 15 mss/year.** Send complete ms. **Pays $1,000.**

FICTION Literary fiction only, including short-shorts. No genre fiction. **Buys 20 mss/year.** Send complete ms. **Pays $500 for short-shorts; $1,000 for full stories.**

POETRY Buys 50 poems/year. Submit maximum 5 poems. **Pays $100.**

THEMA

Box 8747, Metairie LA 70011-8747. E-mail: thema@cox.net. Website: members.cox.net/thema. **100% freelance written.** Triannual magazine covering a different theme for each issue. Upcoming themes for SASE. "*Thema* is designed to stimulate creative thinking by challenging writers with unusual themes, such as 'The Box Under the Bed' and 'Put It In Your Pocket, Lillian'. Appeals to writers, teachers of creative writing, and general reading audience." Estab. 1988. Circ. 350. Byline given. Pays on acceptance. Publishes ms an average of within 6 months after acceptance. Accepts queries by mail. Accepts simultaneous submissions. Responds in 1 week to queries. Responds in 5 months to mss. Sample copy for $10. Guidelines for #10 SASE.

FICTION Contact: Virginia Howard, editor. Needs adventure, ethnic, experimental, fantasy, historical, humorous, mainstream, mystery, novel concepts, religious, science fiction, slice-of-life vignettes, suspense, western, contemporary, sports, prose poem. No erotica. **Buys 30 mss/year.** fewer than 6,000 words preferred **Pays $10-25.**

POETRY Needs avant-garde, free verse, haiku, light verse, traditional. No erotica. Buys 27 poems/year. Submit maximum 3 poems. Length: 4-50 lines. **Pays $10.**

TIME OF SINGING

P.O. Box 149, Conneaut Lake PA 16316. E-mail: timesing@zoominternet.net. Website: timeofsinging.com. **Contact:** Lora Zill, Editor. **100% freelance written.** Quarterly journal (4 issues). "*Time of Singing* publishes 'Christian' poetry in the widest sense, but prefers 'literary' type. Welcome forms, fresh rhyme, well-crafted free verse. Like writers who take chances, who don't feel the need to tie everything up neatly." Estab. 1958. Circ. 250. Byline given. Acceptance to publish time is 1 year. Editorial lead time 6 months. Tell when and where. Submit seasonal material 6 months in advance. Accepts queries by mail, e-mail. Accepts previously published material. Accepts simultaneous submissions. Responds in 3 months to mss. Sample copy for $4/each or 2 for $7. Guidelines for SASE or on website.

POETRY Needs free verse, haiku, light verse, traditional. Does not want sermons that rhyme or greeting card type poetry. Buys 200 poems/year. Submit maximum 5 poems. Length: 3-60 lines. **All contributors receive one copy of the issue in which their work appears and the opportunity to purchase more at the contributor's rate.**

$$$ TIN HOUSE

McCormack Communications, P.O. Box 10500, Portland OR 97210. (503)274-4393. Fax: (503)222-1154. E-mail: info@tinhouse.com; submissions@tinhouse.com. Website: tinhouse.com. **Contact:** Cheston Knapp; Holly Macarthur. **90% freelance written**. "We are a general interest literary quarterly. Our watchword is quality. Our audience includes people interested in literature in all its aspects, from the mundane to the exalted." Estab. 1998. Circ. 11,000. Byline given. Pays on publication. Publishes ms an average of 6 months after acceptance. Editorial lead time 6 months. Submit seasonal material 6 months in advance. Accepts queries by mail, online submission form. Accepts simultaneous submissions. Responds in 6 weeks to queries. Responds in 3 months to mss. Sample copy for $15. Guidelines available online.

NONFICTION Needs book excerpts, essays, interview, personal experience. Send complete ms. 5,000 words maximum **Pays $50-800 for assigned articles. Pays $50-500 for unsolicited articles.** Sometimes pays expenses of writers on assignment.

COLUMNS Lost and Found (mini-reviews of forgotten or underappreciated books), up to 500 words; Readable Feasts (fiction or nonfiction literature with recipes), 2,000-3,000 words; Pilgrimage (journey to a personally significant place, especially literary), 2,000-3,000 words. **Buys 15-20 mss/year.** Send complete ms. **Pays $50-500.**

FICTION Contact: Rob Spillman, fiction editor. Needs experimental, mainstream, novel concepts, literary. **Buys 15-20 mss/year.** Send complete ms. 5,000 words maximum **Pays $200-800.**

POETRY Contact: Brenda Shaunessy, poetry editor. Needs avant-garde, free verse, traditional. "No prose masquerading as poetry." Buys 40 poems/year. Submit maximum 5 poems. **Pays $50-150.**

$$ VERBATIM

Word, Inc., P.O. BOX 1774, Burlingame ILCA 94011. (800)897-3006. E-mail: editor@verbatimmag.com. Website: verbatimmag.com. **75-80% freelance written**. Quarterly magazine covering language and linguistics. "*Verbatim* is the only magazine of language and linguistics for the lay person." Estab. 1974. Circ. 1,600. Byline given. Pays on publication. Publishes ms an average of 6-9 months after acceptance. Editorial lead time 3 months. Submit seasonal material 6 months in advance. Accepts queries by e-mail (only). Responds in 3 weeks to queries. Responds in 2 months to mss. Sample copy for sae with 9×12 envelope and 6 first-class stamps. Guidelines available online.

NONFICTION Needs essays, humor, personal experience. Does not want puns or overly cranky prescriptivism. **Buys 24-28 mss/year.** Query. Submissions only accepted online. **Pays $25-400 for assigned articles. Pays $25-300 for unsolicited articles.**

POETRY "We only publish poems explicitly about language. Poems written in language not enough." Buys 4-6 poems/year. Submit maximum 3 poems. Length: 3-75 lines. **Pays $25-50.**

[+]$ VERSAL

Postbus 3865, Amsterdam 1054 EJ The Netherlands. +31 (0)63 433 8875. E-mail: Info@wordsinhere.com. Website: wordsinhere.com. **Contact:** Megan M. Garr, editor. **Contact: Megan M. Garr, editor. Est. 2002. Circ. 650. "*Versal*, published each May by *wordsinhere*, is the only literary magazine of its kind in the Netherlands and publishes new poetry, prose and art from around the world. *Versal* and the writers behind it are also at the forefront of a growing translocal European literary scene, which includes exciting communities in Amsterdam, Paris and Berlin. *Versal* seeks work that is urgent, involved and unexpected."**. Annual print magazine. "*Versal*, published each May by *worsinhere*, is the only literary magazine of its kind in the Netherlands and publishes new poetry, prose and art from around the world. *Versal* and the writers behind it are also at the forefront of a growing translocal European literary scene, which includes exciting communities in Amsterdam, Paris and Berlin. *Versal* seeks work that is urgent, involved and unexpected." Estab. 2002. Circ. 650. Pays on publication. Publishes ms an average of 3-4 months after acceptance. Accepts queries by e-mail. Accepts simultaneous submissions. Responds in 2 months. Sample copies available for $10. Guidelines available online.

NONFICTION Query.

PHOTOS Contact: Shayna Schapp, assistant art editor.

FICTION Contact: Robert Glick, editor. Needs experimental, mainstream, novel concepts, Flash fiction, prose poetry. **Buys 10 mss/year. pays in copies.**

POETRY Contact: Megan M. Garr, editor. Needs avant-garde, free verse. Buys 35 poems/year. Submit maximum 5 poems. **Pays in copies.**

$ $ VESTAL REVIEW

2609 Dartmouth Dr., Vestal NY 13850. E-mail: submissions@vestalreview.net. Website: vestalreview.net. Semi-annual print magazine specializing in flash fiction. "We accept submissions only through our submission manager." Circ. 1,500. Pays on publication. Publishes ms an average of 3-4 months after acceptance. Accepts queries by e-mail. Accepts simultaneous submissions. Responds in 1 week to queries. Responds in 4 months to mss. Guidelines available online.

> *Vestal Review's* stories have been reprinted in the *Mammoth Book of Miniscule fiction, Flash Writing, E2Ink anthologies*, and in the *WW Norton Anthology Flash Fiction Forward.*

FICTION Needs ethnic, horror, mainstream, speculative fiction. Does not read new submissions in January, June, July, and December. All submissions received during these months will be returned unopened. Length: 50-500 words. **Pays 3-10¢/word and 1 contributor's copy; additional copies $10 (plus postage).**

THE VIEW FROM HERE

E-mail: Editor@Viewfromheremagazine.com. Website: Viewfromheremagazine.com. **Contact:** Mike French, senior editor. Monthly print/weekly online Website covering prose, fiction, and nonfiction essays of personal appeal with a touch of deliberate nonsense combined with editorial comments designed to make you think. "We are a print and online literary magazine with author interview, book reviews, original fiction & poetry and articles. Designed and edited by an international team we bring an entertaining mix of wit, insight and intelligence all packaged in beautifully designed pages that mix the new with the famous. We publish our fiction at *The Front View* and our poetry at *The Rear View,* where we showcase the weird, unusual, thought provoking and occasionally bizarre. We classify ourselves as 'Bohemian Eclectic'—, we coined the term. Our stories and poems will make you wonder, laugh, cry and generally *feel* something." Estab. 2008. Circ. 8,000. Byline given. Authors receive print contributor's copy. Accepts queries by e-mail. Responds

within 2 weeks. Available for $6.89. Guidelines available via e-mail.

NONFICTION Word Length: 5000. Please send an inquiry first if your work is longer than this.

PHOTOS Model and property releases required. Reviews JPEG format.

FICTION Word Limit: 5000. Please send an inquiry first if your work is longer than this.

POETRY Submit maximum 3-5 poems.

$ WEST BRANCH

Stadler Center for Poetry, Bucknell University, Lewisburg PA 17837-2029. (570)577-1853. Fax: (570)577-1885. E-mail: westbranch@bucknell.edu. Website: bucknell.edu/westbranch. Semiannual literary magazine. *West Branch* publishes poetry, fiction, and nonfiction in both traditional and innovative styles. Byline given. Pays on publication. Accepts queries by online submission form. Sample copy for $3. Guidelines available online.

NONFICTION Needs essays, general interest, literary. **Buys 4-5 mss/year.** Send complete ms. **Pays $20-100 ($10/page).**

FICTION Needs novel excerpts, short stories. No genre fiction. **Buys 10-12 mss/year.** Send complete ms. **Pays $20-100 ($10/page).**

POETRY Needs free and formal verse. Buys 30-40 poems/year. Submit maximum 6 poems. **Pays $20-100 ($10/page).**

$ WESTERN HUMANITIES REVIEW

University of Utah, English Department, 255 S. Central Campus Dr., Room 3500, Salt Lake City UT 84112-0494. (801)581-6070. Fax: (801)585-5167. E-mail: whr@mail.hum.utah.edu. Website: hum.utah.edu/whr. **Contact:** Dawn Lonsinger, Managing Editor. A tri-annual magazine for educated readers. Estab. 1947. Circ. 1,000. Pays in contributor copies. Publishes ms an average of 1 year after acceptance. Accepts simultaneous submissions. Sample copy for $10. Guidelines available online.

> Reads mss September 1-April 1. Mss sent outside these dates will be returned unread.

NONFICTION Contact: Barry Weller, editor-in-chief. **Buys 6-8 unsolicited/year mss/year.** Send complete ms. **Pays $5/published page.**

FICTION Contact: Lance Olsen, Fiction Editor. Needs experimental, and innovative voices. Does not want genre (romance, sci-fi, etc.). **Buys 5-8 mss/year**

mss/year. Send complete ms. Length: 5,000 words. **Pays $5/published page (when funds available).**
POETRY Contact: Richard Howard, poetry editor.

WHISKEY ISLAND MAGAZINE

Cleveland State University, English Dept., 2121 Euclid Ave., Cleveland OH 44115-2214. (216)687-2000. E-mail: whiskeyisland@csuohio.edu. Website: csuohio.edu/class/english/whiskeyisland/. Semiannual magazine covering creative writing, original poetry, fiction, nonfiction, and art submissions year round. "This is a nonprofit literary magazine that has been published (in one form or another) by students of Cleveland State University for over 30 years. Also features the Annual Student Creative Writing Contest ($5000-$400-$250)." Accepts queries by mail, e-mail. Accepts simultaneous submissions. Responds in 6 months to mss.

⊙❷❸ WINDSOR REVIEW

Dept. of English, University of Windsor, Windsor ON N9B 3P4 Canada. (519)253-3000. Fax: (519)971-3676. E-mail: uwrevu@uwindsor.ca. Website: uwindsor.ca. Semiannual magazine. "We try to offer a balance of fiction and poetry distinguished by excellence." Estab. 1965. Circ. 250. Pays on publication. Publishes ms an average of 6 months after acceptance. Accepts queries by e-mail. Responds in 1 month to queries; 6 weeks to mss. Sample copy for $7 (US). Guidelines available online.
FICTION Contact: Alistair MacLeod, fiction editor. Needs experimental. No genre fiction (science fiction, romance), but would consider if writing is good enough. Send complete ms. Length: 1,000-5,000 words. **Pays $25, 1 contributor's copy and a free subscription.**
POETRY Submit maximum 6 poems.

❸ THE YALOBUSHA REVIEW

University of Mississippi, P.O. Box 1848, Dept. of English, University MS 38677. (662)915-3175. E-mail: yreditor@yahoo.com. Website: olemiss.edu/yalobusha. Annual literary journal seeking quality submissions from around the globe. Reading period is July 15-November 15. Estab. 1995. Circ. 500. Accepts queries by mail. Does not accept previously published work. Accepts simultaneous submissions. Responds in 2-4 months to mss. Sample copy for $5. Guidelines for #10 SASE.
NONFICTION Contact: Nonfiction Editor. Needs essays, memoir, travel, experimental pieces. Does not want sappy confessional or insights into parenthood. Send complete ms with cover letter and SASE. Length: 10,000 words. **Pays honorarium when funding available.**
FICTION Contact: Fiction Editor. Needs experimental, historical, humorous, mainstream, novel excerpts, short shorts. **Buys 3-6 mss/year.** Send complete ms with cover letter and SASE. Length: 10,000 words. **Pays honorarium when funding available.**
POETRY Contact: Poetry Editor. Needs avant-garde, free verse, traditional. Interested in publishing a variety of voices, both new and established. Submit maximum up to 5 poems. **Send cover letter and SASE. Pays 2 contributor's copies.**

❸ ZAHIR

Zahir Publishing, 315 South Coast Hwy. 101, Suite U8, Encinitas CA 92024. E-mail: zahirtales@gmail.com. Website: zahirtales.com. **Contact:** Sheryl Tempchin, editor. **100% freelance written.** Quarterly online magazine. "We publish literary speculative fiction." Estab. 2003. Byline given. Pays on publication. Publishes ms an average of 2-12 months after acceptance. Accepts queries by mail, e-mail. Responds in 1-2 weeks to queries. Responds in 1-3 months to mss. Writer's guidelines for #10 SASE, by e-mail, or online.
FICTION Needs fantasy, surrealism, magical realism, science fiction, surrealism, magical realism. No children's stories or stories that deal with excessive violence or anything pornographic. **Buys 18-25 mss/year.** Send complete ms. or submit through online submission form. 6,000 words maximum. **Pays $10 and one copy of the annual print anthology.**

❸❸❸ ZOETROPE: ALL-STORY

Zoetrope: All-Story, The Sentinel Bldg., 916 Kearny St., San Francisco CA 94133. (415)788-7500. Website: all-story.com. Quarterly magazine specializing in the best of contemporary short fiction. *Zoetrope: All Story* presents a new generation of classic stories. Estab. 1997. Circ. 20,000. Byline given. Publishes ms an average of 5 months after acceptance. Accepts queries by mail. Accepts simultaneous submissions. Responds in 8 months (if SASE included). Sample copy for $8.00. Guidelines available online.
FICTION Buys 25-35 mss/year. "Writers should submit only one story at a time and no more than two stories a year. Before submitting, non-subscribers should read several issues of the magazine to determine if

their works fit with *All-Story.* Electronic versions of the magazine are available to read, in part, at the website; and print versions are available for purchase by single-issue order and subscription. We consider unsolicited submissions of short stories and one-act plays no longer than 7,000 words. Excerpts from larger works, screenplays, treatments, and poetry will be returned unread. We do not accept artwork or design submissions. We do not accept unsolicited revisions nor respond to writers who don't include an SASE." Send complete ms. by mail to: *Zoetrope:All-Story* Attn: Fiction Editor. **Pays $1,000.**

$ ZYZZYVA

466 Geary Street, Suite 401, San Francisco CA 94102. (415)440-1510. E-mail: editor@zyzzyva.org. Website: zyzzyva.org. **Contact:** Howard Junker. **100% freelance written. Works with a small number of new/unpublished writers each year.** Magazine published in March, August, and November. "We feature work by writers currently living on the West Coast or in Alaska and Hawaii only. We are essentially a literary magazine, but of wide-ranging interests and a strong commitment to nonfiction." Estab. 1985. Circ. 2,500. Byline given. Pays on acceptance. Publishes ms an average of 3 months after acceptance. Accepts queries by mail, e-mail. Responds in 1 week to queries. Responds in 1 month to mss. Sample copy for $7 or online. Guidelines available online.

NONFICTION Needs book excerpts, general interest, historical, humor, personal experience. **Buys 50 mss/year.** Query by mail or e-mail. Open **Pays $50.**

PHOTOS Reviews scans only at 300 dpi, 5½.

FICTION Needs ethnic, experimental, humorous, mainstream. **Buys 60 mss/year.** Send complete ms. Length: 100-7,500 words. **Pays $50.**

POETRY Buys 20 poems/year. Submit maximum 5 poems. Length: 3 200 lines. **Pays $50.**

MEN'S

$$$$ CIGARAFICIONADO

M. Shanken Communications, Inc., 387 Park Ave. S., 8th Floor, New York NY 10016. (212)684-4224. Fax: (212)684-5424. E-mail: gmott@mshanken.com. Website: cigaraficionado.com. **75% freelance written.** Bimonthly magazine for affluent men. Estab. 1992. Circ. 275,000. Byline given. Pays on acceptance. Offers 25% kill fee. Publishes ms an average of 3-6 months after acceptance. Editorial lead time 6 months. Submit seasonal material 6 months in advance. Accepts queries by e-mail. Responds in 1 month to queries. Responds in 2 months to mss. Sample copy free.

NONFICTION Needs general interest. Query. Length: 1,500-4,000 words. **Pays variable amount.** Pays expenses of writers on assignment.

PHOTOS Contact: Contact Sarina Finkelstein, photo editor.

$$$$ KING

Harris Publications, Inc., 1115 Broadway, 8th Floor, New York NY 10010. Fax: (212)807-0216. E-mail: king@harris-pub.com. Website: king-mag.com. **75% freelance written.** Men's lifestyle magazine published 80 times/year. *King* is a general interest men's magazine with a strong editorial voice. Topics include lifestyle, entertainment, news, women, cars, music, fashion, investigative reporting. Estab. 2001. Circ. 270,000. Byline given. Pays on publication. Offers 25% kill fee. Editorial lead time 2-3 months. Submit seasonal material 4 months in advance. Accepts queries by e-mail. Responds in 1 month to queries. Guidelines free.

NONFICTION Needs essays, expose, general interest. Does not want completed articles. Pitches only. Query with published clips. Length: 2,000-5,000 words. **Pays $1-1.50/word.**

MILITARY

$$$ AIRFORCE

Air Force Association of Canada, P.O Box 2460, Stn D, Ottawa ON K1P 5W6 Canada. (613)232-2303. Fax: (613)232-2156. E-mail: vjohnson@airforce.ca. Website: airforce.ca. **5% freelance written.** Quarterly magazine covering Canada's air force heritage. Stories center on Canadian military aviation—past, present and future. Estab. 1977. Circ. 16,000. Byline given. Pays on publication. Publishes ms an average of 6 months after acceptance. Editorial lead time 3 months. Submit seasonal material 3 months in advance. Accepts queries by mail, e-mail, fax, phone. Accepts simultaneous submissions. Responds in 2 weeks to queries. Responds in 1 month to mss. Sample copy free. Guidelines by e-mail.

NONFICTION Needs historical, interview, personal experience, photo feature. **Buys 2 mss/year.** Query with published clips. Length: 1,500-3,500 words.

Sometimes pays expenses of writers on assignment. Limit agreed upon in advance

PHOTOS Send photos. Captions, identification of subjects required. Reviews prints, GIF/JPEG files.

FILLERS Needs anecdotes, facts. About 800 words. **Negotiable.**

⊙⊙ AIR FORCE TIMES

Army Times Publishing Co., 6883 Commercial Dr., Springfield VA 22159. (703)750-8646. Fax: (703)750-8601. E-mail: kmiller@militarytimes.com; airlet@airforcetimes.com. Website: airforcetimes.com. "Weeklies edited separately for Army, Navy, Marine Corps, and Air Force military personnel and their families. They contain career information such as pay raises, promotions, news of legislation affecting the military, housing, base activities and features of interest to military people." Estab. 1940. Byline given. Pays on acceptance. Offers kill fee. Accepts queries by mail, e-mail, phone. Accepts simultaneous submissions. Responds in 1 month to queries. Sample copy for #10 SASE. Guidelines for #10 SASE.

NONFICTION No advice pieces. **Buys 150-175 mss/year.** Query. Length: 750-2,000 words. **Pays $100-500.**

COLUMNS Length: 500-900. **Buys 75 mss/year. Pays $75-125.**

⊙⊙ ARMY MAGAZINE

2425 Wilson Blvd., Arlington VA 22201-3385. (703)841-4300. Fax: (703)841-3505. E-mail: armymag@ausa.org. Website: ausa.org. **70% freelance written. Prefers to work with published/established writers.** Monthly magazine emphasizing military interests. Estab. 1904. Circ. 90,000. Byline given. Pays on publication. Publishes ms an average of 5 months after acceptance. Submit seasonal material 3 months in advance. Accepts queries by mail. Sample copy and Writer's Guidelines for 9×12 SAE with $1 postage or online.

◯*ARMY Magazine* looks for shorter articles.

NONFICTION Needs historical, military and original, humor, military feature-length articles and anecdotes, interview, photo feature. Special issues: "We would like to see more pieces about little-known episodes involving interesting military personalities. We especially want material lending itself to heavy, contributor-supplied photographic treatment. The first thing a contributor should recognize is that our readership is very savvy militarily. 'Gee-whiz' personal reminiscences get short shrift, unless they hold their own in a company in which long military service, heroism and unusual experiences are commonplace. At the same time, *ARMY* readers like a well-written story with a fresh slant, whether it is about an experience in a foxhole or the fortunes of a corps in battle. No rehashed history. No unsolicited book reviews. **Buys 40 mss/year.** Submit complete ms (hard copy and disk). Length: 1,000-1,500 words. **Pays 12-18¢/word.**

PHOTOS Send photos. Captions required. Reviews prints, slides, high resolution digital photos. Pays $50-100 for 8×10 b&w glossy prints; $50-350 for 8×10 color glossy prints and 35mm and high resolution digital photos.

⊙⊙⊙ MILITARY OFFICER

201 N. Washington St., Alexandria VA 22314-2539. (800)234-6622. Fax: (703)838-8179. E-mail: editor@moaa.org. Website: moaa.org. **60% freelance written. Prefers to work with published/established writers.** Monthly magazine for officers of the 7 uniformed services and their families. Estab. 1945. Circ. 389,000. Byline given. Pays on acceptance. Publishes ms an average of 1 year after acceptance. Accepts queries by e-mail. Responds in 3 months to queries. Sample copy available online. Guidelines available online.

NONFICTION "We rarely accept unsolicited manuscripts." **Buys 50 mss/year.** Query with résumé, sample clips Length: 800-2,000 words. **Pays 80¢/word.**

PHOTOS Query with list of stock photo subjects. Images should be 300 dpi or higher. Pays $75-250 for inside color; $300 for cover.

⊙⊙ PROCEEDINGS

U.S. Naval Institute, 291 Wood Rd., Annapolis MD 21402-5034. (410)268-6110. Fax: (410)295-7940. E-mail: articlesubmissions@usni.org. Website: usni.org; navalinstitute.org. **Contact:** Paul Merzlak, editor-in-chief; Amy Voight, photo editor. **80% freelance written**. Monthly magazine covering Navy, Marine Corps, Coast Guard issues. Estab. 1873. Circ. 60,000. Byline given. Pays on publication. Publishes ms an average of 9 months after acceptance. Editorial lead time 3 months. Responds in 2 months to queries. Sample copy for $3.95. Guidelines available online.

NONFICTION Needs essays, historical, interview, photo feature, technical. **Buys 100-125 mss/year.** Send complete ms. 3,000 words **Pays $60-150/printed page for unsolicited articles.**

PHOTOS State availability of or send photos. Reviews transparencies, prints. Offers $25/photo maximum.

COLUMNS Comment & Discussion (letters to editor), 500 words; Commentary (opinion), 700 words; Nobody Asked Me, But. (opinion), less than 700 words. **Buys 150-200 mss/year. mss/year.** Query or send complete ms. **Pays $34-150.**

FILLERS Needs anecdotes. **Buys 20 fillers/year mss/ year.** Length: 100 words. **Pays $25.**

💲💲💲💲 SOLDIER OF FORTUNE

2135 11th Street, Boulder CO 80302-4045. (303)449-3750. E-mail: editorsof@aol.com. Website: sofmag.com. Lt. Col. Robert A. Brown. **Contact:** Lt. Col. Robert A. Brown, editor/publisher. **50% freelance written.** Monthly magazine covering military, para-military, police, combat subjects, and action/adventure. "We are an action-oriented magazine; we cover combat hot spots around the world. We also provide timely features on state-of-the-art weapons and equipment; elite military and police units; and historical military operations. Readership is primarily active-duty military, veterans, and law enforcement." Estab. 1975. Circ. 60,000. Byline given. Offers 25% kill fee. Responds in 3 weeks to queries. Responds in 1 month to mss. Sample copy for $5. Guidelines for #10 SASE.

NONFICTION Needs expose, general interest, historical, how-to, on weapons and their skilled use, humor, interview, new product, personal experience, photo feature, No. 1 on our list, technical, travel, combat reports, military unit reports, and solid Vietnam and Operation Iraqi Freedom articles. No `How I won the war' pieces; no op-ed pieces unless they are fully and factually backgrounded; no knife articles (staff assignments only). All submitted articles should have good art; art will sell us on an article. **Buys 75 mss/ year.** Query with or without published clips or send complete ms. Send mss to articles editor; queries to managing editor Length: 2,000-3,000 words. **Pays $150-250/page.**

REPRINTS Send disk copy, photocopy of article and information about when and where the material previously appeared. Pays 25% of amount paid for an original article

PHOTOS Send photos. Captions, identification of subjects required. Reviews contact sheets, transparencies. Pays $500 for cover photo.

FILLERS Contact: Bulletin Board editor. Needs newsbreaks, military/paramilitary related has to be documented. Length: 100-250 words. **Pays $50.**

MUSIC CONSUMER

➕ ALARM MAGAZINE

Alarm Press, 53 W. Jackson Blvd., Suite 315, Chicago IL 60604. E-mail: info@alarmpress.com. Website: alarmpress.com. **Contact:** Art Director. *ALARM*, published 6 times/year, "does one thing, and it does it very well: it publishes the best new music and art in *ALARM* Magazine and alarmpress.com. From our headquarters in a small Chicago office, along with a cast of contributing writers spread across the country, we listen to thousands of CDs, view hundreds of gallery openings, and attend lectures and live concerts in order to present inspirational artists who are fueled by an honest and contagious obsession with their art." Accepts queries by mail, e-mail. Only responds if interested. Submit by e-mail with the subject line "ALARM Magazine Submissions. Please send your work as part of the body of an e-mail; we cannot accept attachments." Alternatively, submissions may be sent by regular mail to Submissions Dept. "*ALARM* is not responsible for the return, loss of, or damage to unsolicited manuscripts, unsolicited art work, or any other unsolicited materials. Those submitting manuscripts, art work, or any other materials should not send originals.".

💲💲 BLUEGRASS UNLIMITED

Bluegrass Unlimited, Inc., P.O. Box 771, Warrenton VA 20188-0771. (540)349-8181 or (800)BLU-GRAS. Fax: (540)341-0011. E-mail: editor@bluegrassmusic.com. Website: bluegrassmusic.com. **10% freelance written. Prefers to work with published/established writers.** Monthly magazine covering bluegrass, acoustic, and old-time country music. Estab. 1966. Circ. 27,000. Byline given. Pays on publication. Offers negotiated kill fee. Publishes ms an average of 4 months after acceptance. Submit seasonal material 4 months in advance. Accepts queries by mail, e-mail, fax. Responds in 2 weeks to queries. Responds in 2 months to mss. Sample copy free. Guidelines for #10 SASE.

NONFICTION Needs general interest, historical, how-to, interview, personal experience, photo feature, travel. No fan-style articles. **Buys 30-40 mss/ year.** Query. Open **Pays 10-13¢/word.**

REPRINTS Send photocopy with rights for sale noted and information about when and where the material previously appeared. Payment is negotiable.

PHOTOS State availability of or send photos. Identification of subjects required. Reviews 35mm transparencies and 3×5, 5×7 and 8×10 b&w and color prints. Also, reviews/prefers digital 300 dpi or better jpg, tif files, index, contact sheet with digital submissions. Pays $50-175 for color; $25-60 for b&w prints; $50-250 for color prints.

FICTION Needs ethnic, humorous. **Buys 3-5 mss/year.** Query. Negotiable **Pays 10-13¢/word.**

$$ CHAMBER MUSIC

Chamber Music America, 305 Seventh Ave., 5th Floor, New York NY 10001-6008. (212)242-2022. Fax: (212)242-7955. E-mail: egoldensohn@chamber-music.org. Website: chamber-music.org. Bimonthly magazine covering chamber music. Estab. 1977. Circ. 13,000. Byline given. Pays on publication. Offers kill fee. Publishes ms an average of 5 months after acceptance. Editorial lead time 4 months. Accepts queries by mail, phone.

NONFICTION Needs book excerpts, essays, humor, opinion, personal experience, issue-oriented stories of relevance to the chamber music fields written by top music journalists and critics, or music practitioners. No artist profiles, no stories about opera or symphonic work. **Buys 35 mss/year.** Query with published clips. Length: 2,500-3,500 words. **Pays $500 minimum.** Sometimes pays expenses of writers on assignment.

PHOTOS State availability. Offers no payment for photos accepted with ms.

GUITAR WORLD

Future Media US, Inc., The Sounding Board, c/o Guitar World, 149 5th Avenue, 9th Floor, New York NY 10010. (650)872-1642. E-mail: gwedit@aol.com; soundingboard@guitarworld.com. Website: guitarworld.com. Monthly magazine. Written for guitar players categorized as either professionals, semi-professionals or amateur players. Every issue offers broad-ranging interviews that cover technique, instruments, and lifestyles. "To submit a GuitarWorld-Blips story, you must be logged in. If you already have an account on GuitarWorldBlips, please log in. Or join GuitarWorldBlips—it's free and fast. Just fill out the form and enter the URL, title, and description. Your story will appear once we've validated your e-mail address." Circ. 150,000. Editorial lead time 2 months.

⊘ ROLLING STONE

Wenner Media, 1290 Avenue of the Americas, New York NY 10104. (212)484-1616. Fax: (212)484-1664. E-mail: letters@rollingstone.com. Website: rollingstone.com. **Contact:** Jann S. Wenner. Bi-weekly magazine geared towards young adults interested in news of popular music, entertainment and the arts, current news events, politics and American culture. Circ. 1,254,200. Editorial lead time 1 month.

Query before submitting.

$$$ SYMPHONY

American Symphony Orchestra League, 33 W. 60th St., Fifth Floor, New York NY 10023. (212)262-5161. Fax: (212)262-5198. E-mail: clane@americanorchestras.org; jmelick@americanorchestras.org. Website: symphony.org. **Contact:** Chester Lane, senior editor, or Jennifer Melick, managing editor. **50% freelance written.** Bimonthly magazine for the orchestra industry and classical music enthusiasts covering classical music, orchestra industry, musicians. "Writers should be knowledgeable about classical music and have critical or journalistic/repertorial approach." Circ. 18,000. Byline given. Pays on acceptance. Publishes ms an average of 10 weeks after acceptance. Editorial lead time 6 months. Submit seasonal material 8 months in advance. Accepts queries by mail, e-mail. Accepts simultaneous submissions. Guidelines available online.

NONFICTION Needs book excerpts, essays, inspirational, interview, opinion, personal experience, rare, photo feature, rare, issue features, trend pieces (by assignment only; pitches welcome). Does not want to see reviews, interviews. **Buys 30 mss/year.** Query with published clips. Length: 1,500-3,500 words. **Pays $500-900.** Sometimes pays expenses of writers on assignment.

PHOTOS Rarely commissions photos or illustrations. State availability of or send photos. Captions, identification of subjects required. Reviews contact sheets, negatives, prints, electronic photos (preferred). Offers no additional payment for photos accepted with ms.

COLUMNS Repertoire (orchestral music—essays); Comment (personal views and opinions); Currents (electronic media developments); In Print (books); On Record (CD, DVD, video), all 1,000-2,500 words. **Buys 12 mss/year.** Query with published clips.

MYSTERY

$ ELLERY QUEEN'S MYSTERY MAGAZINE

Dell Magazines Fiction Group, 267 Broadway, 4th Floor, New York NY 10017. (212)686-7188. Fax: (212)686-7414. E-mail: elleryqueenmm@dellmagazines.com. Website: themysteryplace.com/eqmm. **100% freelance written**. Featuring mystery fiction. "*Ellery Queen's Mystery Magazine* welcomes submissions from both new and established writers. We publish every kind of mystery short story: the psychological suspense tale, the deductive puzzle, the private eye case—the gamut of crime and detection from the realistic (including the policeman's lot and stories of police procedure) to the more imaginative (including 'locked rooms' and 'impossible crimes'). We look for strong writing, an original and exciting plot, and professional craftsmanship. We encourage writers whose work meets these general criteria to read an issue of *EQMM* before making a submission." Estab. 1941. Circ. 100,000. Byline given. Pays on acceptance. Publishes ms an average of 6-12 months after acceptance. Accepts queries by online submission form. NoAccepts simultaneous submissions. Responds in 3 months to mss. Sample copy for $5.50. Guidelines for SASE or online.

> "EQMM uses an online submission system (eqmm.magazinesubmissions.com) that has been designed to streamline our process and improve communication with authors. We ask that all submissions be made electronically, using this system, rather than on paper. All stories should be in standard manuscript format and submitted in .DOC format. We cannot accept .DOCX.RTF, or .TXT files at this time. For detailed submission instructions, see eqmm.magazinesubmissions.com or our writers guidelines page (themysteryplace.com/eqmm/guidelines)."

FICTION **Contact:** Janet Hutchings, editor. "We always need detective stories. Special consideration given to anything timely and original." Needs mystery. No explicit sex or violence, no gore or horror. Seldom publishes parodies or pastiches. "We do not want true detective or crime stories." **Buys up to 120 mss/year.** EQMM uses an online submission system (eqmm.magazinesubmissions.com) that has been designed to streamline our process and improve communication with authors. We ask that all submissions be made electronically, using this system, rather than on paper. All stories should be in standard manuscript format and submitted in .DOC format. We cannot accept .DOCX.RTF, or .TXT files at this time. For detailed submission instructions, see eqmm.magazinesubmissions.com or our writers guidelines page (themysteryplace.com/eqmm/guidelines). Most stories 2,500-8,000 words. Accepts longer and shorter submissions—including minute mysteries of 250 words, and novellas of up to 20,000 words from established authors **Pays 5-8¢/word; occasionally higher for established authors.**

POETRY Short mystery verses, limericks. Length: 1 page, double spaced maximum.

SUSPENSE MAGAZINE

JRSR Ventures, 26500 W. Agoura Rd., Suite 102-474, Calabasas CA 91302. Fax: (310)626-9670. E-mail: editor@suspensemagazine.com. Website: suspensemagazine.com. **Contact:** John Raab, editor. **100% freelance.** Monthly consumer magazine covering suspense, mystery, thriller, & horror genre. Estab. 2007. Pays on acceptance. Pays 100% kill fee. 6-9 months from acceptance to publishing time. Editorial lead time is 6-9 months Accepts queries by e-mail. Responds in 1-2 weeks on queries, 2-3 months on mss.

NONFICTION Needs true crime. Query. 1,000-3,000/words. **Pays commissions only, by assignment only.** True

COLUMNS Book Reviews (reviews for newly released fiction); Graphic Novel Reviews (reviews for comic books/graphic novels), 250-1,000/words. **Buys 6-12 mss/year mss/year.** Query. **Pays by assignment only**

FICTION Needs horror, mystery, suspense, thrillers. No explicit scenes **Buys 15-30 mss/year.** Query. 500-5,000/words.

NATURE, CONSERVATION AND ECOLOGY

$ ALTERNATIVES JOURNAL

Alternatives, Inc., University of Waterloo, Faculty of Environmental Studies, Waterloo ON N2L 3G1 Canada. (519)888-4442. Fax: (519)746-0292. E-mail: editor@alternativesjournal.ca. Website: alternativesjournal.ca. **Contact:** Nicola Ross, editor-in-chief. **90% freelance written**. Estab. 1971. Circ. 4,800. Byline given. Pays on publication. Offers 50% kill fee. Publishes ms an average of 5 months after acceptance. Editorial lead time 7 months. Submit seasonal material 5 months in advance. Accepts queries by mail, e-mail, fax. Accepts simultaneous submissions. Sample copy free for Canadian writers only. Guidelines available online.

○ Before responding to this call for submissions, please read several back issues of the magazine so that you understand the nature of our publication. We also suggest you go through our detailed submission procedures to understand the types and lengths of articles we accept. Queries should explain, in less than 300 words, the content and scope of your article, and should convey your intended approach, tone and style. Please include a list of people you will interview, potential images or sources for images and the number of words you propose to write. We would also like to receive a very short bio. And if you have not written for Alternatives before, please include other examples of your writing. Articles range from about 500 to 2000 words in length. Keep in mind that our lead time is several months. Articles should not be so time-bound that they will seem dated once published. Alternatives has a limited budget of 10 cents per word for several articles. This stipend is available to professional and amateur writers and students only. Please indicate your interest in this funding in your submission.

NONFICTION Needs book excerpts, essays, expose, humor, interview, opinion. **Buys 50 mss/year.** Query with published clips. Length: 800-3,000 words. **Pays $50-150 (Canadian).** Sometimes pays expenses of writers on assignment.

PHOTOS Contact: Marcia Ruby, production coordinator. State availability. Identification of subjects required. Offers $35-75/photo.

ARIZONA WILDLIFE VIEWS

Arizona Game & Fish Dept., 2221 W. Greenway Rd., Phoenix AZ 85053. (800)777-0015. E-mail: awv@azgfd.gov. Website: azgfd.gov/magazine. **Contact:** Julie Hammonds, assoc. editor. **50% freelance written.** Bi-monthly magazine covering Arizona wildlife, wildlife management and outdoor recreation (specifically hunting, fishing, wildlife watching, boating and off-highway vehicle recreation). *Arizona Wildlife Views* is a general interest magazine about Arizona wildlife, wildlife management and outdoor recreation. We publish material that conforms to the mission and policies of the Arizona Game and Fish Department. In addition to Arizona wildlife and wildlife management, topics include habitat issues, outdoor recreation involving wildlife, boating, fishing, hunting, bird-watching, animal observation, off-highway vehicle use, etc., and historical articles about wildlife and wildlife management. Circ. 22,000. Byline given. Pays on publication. Publishes ms an average of 10 months after acceptance. Editorial lead time 1 year. Submit seasonal material 2 months in advance. Accepts queries by mail, e-mail. Accepts simultaneous submissions. Responds in 1 month to queries. Responds in 2 months to mss. Sample copy free. Guidelines free and available online.

NONFICTION Needs general interest, historical, how-to, interview, photo feature, technical, travel, scientific for a popular audience. Does not want me and Joe articles, anthropomorphism of wildlife or opinionated pieces not based on confirmable facts. **Buys 20 mss/year.** Query. Length: 1,000-2,500 words. **Pays $450-800.**

✪❸❸❸ THE ATLANTIC SALMON JOURNAL

The Atlantic Salmon Federation, P.O. Box 5200, St. Andrews NB E5B 3S8 Canada. (506)529-1033. Fax: (506)529-4438. E-mail: martinsilverstone@videotron.ca. Website: asf.ca. **Contact:** Martin Silverstone. **50-68% freelance written.** Quarterly magazine covering conservation efforts for the Atlantic salmon, catering to the dedicated angler and conservationist. Circ. 11,000. Byline given. Pays on publication. Publishes ms an average of 6 months after acceptance. Submit seasonal material 3 months in advance. Accepts simultaneous submissions. Responds in 2 months to queries. Sample copy for 9×12 SAE with $1 (Canadian), or IRC. Guidelines free.

NONFICTION Needs exposè, historical, how-to, humor, interview, new product, opinion, personal experience, photo feature, technical, travel, conservation. **Buys 15-20 mss/year.** Query with published clips. Length: 2,000 words. **Pays $400-800 for articles with photos.** Sometimes pays expenses of writers on assignment.

PHOTOS State availability. Captions, identification of subjects required. Pays $50 minimum; $350-500 for covers; $300 for 2-page spread; $175 for full page photo; $100 for ½-page photo.

COLUMNS Fit To Be Tied (Conservation issues and salmon research; the design, construction and success of specific flies); interesting characters in the sport and opinion pieces by knowledgeable writers, 900 words; Casting Around (short, informative, entertaining reports, book reviews and quotes from the world of Atlantic salmon angling and conservation). Query. **Pays $50-300.**

⑨⑨ THE BEAR DELUXE MAGAZINE

Orlo, 810 SE Belmont #5, Portland OR 97214. E-mail: bear@orlo.org. Website: orlo.org. **Contact:** Tom Webb, editor-in-chief. **80% freelance written**. Covers fiction/essay/poetry/other. 750-4,500 words. Do not combine submissions, rather submit poetry, fiction and essay in separate packages. News essays, on occasion, are assigned out if they have a strong element of reporting. Artists contribute to *The Bear Deluxe* in various ways, including: editorial illustration, editorial photography, spot illustration, independent art, cover art, graphic design, and cartoons. "*The Bear Deluxe Magazine* is a national independent environmental arts magazine publishing significant works of reporting, creative nonfiction, literature, visual art and design. Based in the Pacific Northwest, it reaches across cultural and political divides to engage readers on vital issues effecting the environment. Published twice per year, *The Bear Deluxe* includes a wider array and a higher-percentage of visual art work and design than many other publications. Artwork is included both as editorial support and as stand alone or independent art. It has included nationally recognized artists as well as emerging artists. As with any publication, artists are encouraged to review a sample copy for a clearer understanding of the magazine's approach. Unsolicited submissions and samples are accepted and encouraged. *The Bear Deluxe* has been recognized for both its editorial and design excellence. Over the years, awards and positive reviews have been handed down from *Print* magazine, *Utne Reader, Literary Arts, Adbusters*, the Bumbershoot Arts Festival, *Orion, Fact Sheet 5*, the Regional Arts and Culture Council, *The Oregonian*, and the *Library Journal*, among others." Estab. 1993. Circ. 19,000. Byline given. Pays on publication. Offers 25% kill fee. Publishes ms an average of 6 months after acceptance. Editorial lead time 6 months. Submit seasonal material 9 months in advance. Accepts queries by mail, e-mail. Accepts simultaneous submissions. Responds in 3-6 months to mail queries. Only responds to e-mail queries if interested. Sample copy for $3. Guidelines for #10 SASE or on website.

> ○ "The magazine is moving away from using the term environmental writing. Quality writing which furthers the magazine's goal of engaging new and divergent readers will garner the most attention." The Orlo Office is open by appointment only.

NONFICTION Needs book excerpts, essays, exposè, general interest, interview, new product, opinion, personal experience, photo feature, travel, artist profiles. Special issues: Publishes 1 theme/2 years. **Buys 40 mss/year.** Query with published clips. Length: 250-4,500 words. Essays: 750-3,000 words. **Pays $25-400, depending on piece.** Sometimes pays expenses.

PHOTOS Contact: Kristin Rogers Brown, art director. State availability. Identification of subjects, model releases required. Reviews contact sheets, transparencies, 8×10 prints. Offers $30/photo.

COLUMNS Reviews (almost anything), 300 words; Front of the Book (mix of short news bits, found writing, quirky tidbits), 300-500 words; Portrait of an Artist (artist profiles), 1,200 words; Back of the Book (creative opinion pieces), 650 words. **Buys 16 mss/year.** Query with published clips. **Pays $25-400, depending on piece.**

FICTION Stories must have some environmental context, but we view that in a broad sense. Needs adventure, condensed novels, historical, horror, humorous, mystery, novel concepts, western. No detective, children's or horror. **Buys 8 mss/year.** Query or send complete ms. Length: 750-4,500 words. **Pays free subscription to the magazine, contributor's copies and $25-400, depending on piece; additional copies for postage**.

POETRY Needs avant-garde, free verse, haiku, light verse, traditional. Buys 16-20 poems/year. Submit maximum 3-5 poems. 50 lines maximum **Pays $20, subscription, and copies.**

FILLERS Needs facts, newsbreaks, short humor. **Buys 10 mss/year.** Length: 100-750 words. **$25, subscription, and copies.**

BIRD WATCHER'S DIGEST

P.O. Box 110, Marietta OH 45750. (740)373-5285; (800)879-2473. Fax: (740)373-8443. E-mail: editor@birdwatchersdigest.com. E-mail: submissions@birdwatchersdigest.com. Website: birdwatchersdigest.com. **Contact:** Bill Thompson III, editor. **60**. Bimonthly magazine covering natural history—birds and bird watching. "*BWD* is a nontechnical magazine interpreting ornithological material for amateur observers, including the knowledgeable birder, the serious novice and the backyard bird watcher; we strive to provide good reading and good ornithology. Works with a small number of new/unpublished writers each year." Estab. 1978. Circ. 125,000. Byline given. Pays on publication. Publishes ms an average of 2 years after acceptance. Submit seasonal material 6 months in advance. TrueResponds in 10-12 weeks to queries. Sample copy for $3.99 or access online. Guidelines available online.

NONFICTION Needs book excerpts, how-to, relating to birds, feeding and attracting, etc., humor, personal experience, travel, limited. No articles on pet or caged birds; none on raising a baby bird. **Buys 45-60 mss/year.** We gladly accept e-mail queries and manuscript submissions but are not able to respond immediately to most inquiries via e-mail. When submitting by e-mail, please make the subject line read "Submission—your topic." Attach your submission to your e-mail in either MS Word (.doc) or RichText Format (.rtf). Please do not copy and paste your submission into the body of the e-mail. Whether submitting by regular mail or e-mail, please include your full contact information on every page. We ask that you allow 10 to 12 weeks for a response. Length: 600-3,500 words. **Pays from $100.**

PHOTOS Reviews transparencies, prints. Pays $75 minimum for transparencies. "Our payment schedule is $75 per image used regardless of size. Images reused on our table of contents page or on our website will be paid an additional $25. There is no payment or contract for photos used in 'My Way', or for photos that have been loaned for courtesy use.".

$$ BIRDWATCHING

Kalmbach Publishing Co., P.O. Box 1612, Waukesha WI 53187-1612. Fax: (262)798-6468. E-mail: mail@birdwatchingdaily.com. Website: birdwatchingdaily.com. Bimonthly magazine for birdwatchers who actively look for wild birds in the field. "*BirdWatching* concentrates on where to find, how to attract, and how to identify wild birds, and on how to understand what they do." Estab. 1987. Circ. 40,000. Byline given. Pays on acceptance. Accepts queries by mail. Guidelines available online.

NONFICTION Needs essays, how-to, attracting birds, interview, personal experience, photo feature, bird photography, travel, birding hotspots in North America and beyond, product reviews/comparisons, bird biology, endangered or threatened birds. No poetry, fiction, or puzzles. **Buys 60 mss/year.** Query with published clips. Length: 500-2,400 words. **Pays $200-450.**

PHOTOS See photo guidelines online. State availability. Identification of subjects required.

$$ EARTH ISLAND JOURNAL

Earth Island Institute, 300 Broadway, Suite 28, San Francisco CA 94133. E-mail: editor@earthisland.org. Website: earthislandjournal.org. **80% freelance written**. Quarterly magazine covering the environment/ecology. We are looking for in-depth, vigorously reported stories that reveal the connections between the environment and other contemporary issues. Our audience, though modest, includes many of the leaders of the environmental movement. Article pitches should be geared toward this sophisticated audience. Estab. 1985. Circ. 10,000. Byline given. Pays on publication. Publishes ms an average of 4 months after acceptance. Editorial lead time 4 months. Submit seasonal material 4 months in advance. Accepts queries by e-mail. Responds in 4 weeks to queries. Responds in 1 month to mss. Sample copy for $5. Guidelines available online.

NONFICTION Needs book excerpts, essays, expose, general interest, interview, opinion, personal experience, photo feature. We do not want product pitches, services, or company news. **Buys 20/year mss/year.** Query with published clips. Length: 750-4,000 words. **Pays 20¢ a word for unsolicited articles.** Sometimes pays expenses of writers on assignment.

PHOTOS Send photos. Reviews contact sheets, GIF/JPEG files. We negotiate payment individually.

COLUMNS Voices (first person reflection about the environment in a person's life.), 750 words. **Buys 4 mss/year mss/year.** Query. **Pays $$50.00.**

💲💲 E THE ENVIRONMENTAL MAGAZINE

Earth Action Network, P.O. Box 5098, Westport CT 06881-5098. (203)854-5559. Fax: (203)866-0602. E-mail: info@emagazine.com. Website: emagazine.com. **60% freelance written.** Bi-monthly magazine. *E Magazine* was formed for the purpose of acting as a clearinghouse of information, news, and commentary on environmental issues. Estab. 1990. Circ. 50,000. Byline given. Pays on publication. Editorial lead time 3 months. Submit seasonal material 6 months in advance. Accepts queries by mail, e-mail, fax. Accepts simultaneous submissions. Sample copy for $5 or online. Guidelines available online.

💬 The editor reports an interest in seeing more investigative reporting.

NONFICTION Needs expose, environmental, how-to, new product, book review, feature (in-depth articles on key natural environmental issues). **Buys 100 mss/year.** Query with published clips. Length: 100-4,000 words. **Pays 30¢/word.**

PHOTOS State availability. Identification of subjects required. Reviews printed samples, e.g., magazine tearsheets, postcards, etc., to be kept on file. Negotiates payment individually.

COLUMNS On spec or free contributions welcome. In Brief/Currents (environmental news stories/trends), 400-1,000 words; Conversations (Q&As with environmental movers and shakers), 2,000 words; Tools for Green Living; Your Health; Eco-Travel; Eco-Home; Eating Right; Green Business; Consumer News (each 700-1,200 words). Query with published clips.

💲💲💲⊘ NATIONAL PARKS MAGAZINE

National Parks Conservation Association, 777 6th St., NW, Suite 700, Washington D.C. 20001-3723. (202)223-6722; (800)628-7275. Fax: (202)454-3333. E-mail: npmag@npca.org. Website: npca.org/magazine/. **Contact:** Scott Kirkwood, editor-in-chief. **60% freelance written. Prefers to work with published/established writers.** Quarterly magazine for a largely unscientific but highly educated audience interested in preservation of National Park System units, natural areas, and protection of wildlife habitat. Estab. 1919. Circ. 340,000. Pays on acceptance. Offers 33% kill fee. Publishes ms an average of 2 months after acceptance. Responds in 3-4 months to queries. Sample copy for $3 and 9×12 SASE or online. Guidelines available online.

NONFICTION Needs expose, on threats, wildlife problems in national parks, descriptive articles about new or proposed national parks and wilderness parks. No poetry, philosophical essays, or first-person narratives. No unsolicited mss. Length: 1,500 words. **Pays $1,300 for 1,500-word features and travel articles.**

💲💲💲💲 NATURAL HISTORY

Natural History, Inc., 105 W. Highway 54,, Suite 265, Durham NC 27713. E-mail: nhmag@naturalhistorymag.com. Website: naturalhistorymag.com. **15% freelance written.** Magazine published 10 times/year for well-educated audience: professional people, scientists, and scholars. Circ. 225,000. Byline given. Pays on acceptance. Publishes ms an average of 3 months after acceptance. Submit seasonal material 6 months in advance.

NONFICTION Buys 60 mss/year. Query by mail or send complete ms Length: 1,500-3,000 words. **Only accepts mss from scientists, reporting on their own research or related research, who want to disseminate their work to a general audience. No honorarium.**

PHOTOS Rarely uses 8×10 b&w glossy prints; pays $125/page maximum. Much color is used; pays $300 for inside, and up to $600 for cover.

COLUMNS Journal (reporting from the field); Findings (summary of new or ongoing research); Naturalist At Large; The Living Museum (relates to the American Museum of Natural History); Discovery (natural or cultural history of a specific place).

🍁💲💲💲 NATURE CANADA

75 Albert St., Suite 300, Ottawa ON K1P 5E7 Canada. (613)562-3447. Fax: (613)562-3371. E-mail: info@naturecanada.ca. Website: naturecanada.ca. Quarterly magazine covering conservation, natural history and environmental/naturalist community. "Editorial content reflects the goals and priorities of Nature Canada as a conservation organization with a focus on our program areas: federally protected areas (national parks, national wildlife areas, etc.), endangered species, and bird conservation through Canada's important bird areas. Nature Canada is written for an audience interested in nature conservation. Nature Canada celebrates, preserves, and protects Canadian nature. We promote the awareness and understanding of the connection between humans and nature and how natural systems support life on Earth.

We strive to instill a sense of ownership and belief that these natural systems should be protected." Estab. 1971. Circ. 27,000. Byline given. Pays on publication. Offers $100 kill fee. Publishes ms an average of 3 months after acceptance. Editorial lead time 4 months. Submit seasonal material 6 months in advance. Responds in 4 months to mss. Sample copy for $5. Guidelines available online.

NONFICTION **Buys 12 mss/year.** Query with published clips. Length: 650-2,000 words. **Pays up to 50¢/word (Canadian).**

PHOTOS State availability. Identification of subjects required. Offers $50-200/photo (Canadian).

$$ NORTHERN WOODLANDS MAGAZINE

Center for Woodlands Education, Inc., 1776 Center Rd., P.O. Box 471, Corinth VT 05039-0471. (802)439-6292. Fax: (802)439-6296. E-mail: dave@northernwoodlands.org. Website: northernwoodlands.org. **40-60% freelance written.** Quarterly magazine covering natural history, conservation, and forest management in the Northeast. "*Northern Woodlands* strives to inspire landowners' sense of stewardship by increasing their awareness of the natural history and the principles of conservation and forestry that are directly related to their land. We also hope to increase the public's awareness of the social, economic, and environmental benefits of a working forest." Estab. 1994. Circ. 15,000. Byline given. Pays 1 month prior to publication Publishes ms an average of 6 months after acceptance. Editorial lead time 6 months. Submit seasonal material 6 months in advance. Accepts queries by mail, e-mail. Accepts simultaneous submissions. Responds in 1 month to queries. Responds in 1-2 months to mss Sample copy available online. Guidelines available online.

NONFICTION No product reviews, first-person travelogues, cute animal stories, opinion, or advocacy pieces. **Buys 15-20 mss/year.** Query with published clips. Length: 500-3,000 words. **Pay varies per piece.** Sometimes pays expenses of writers on assignment.

PHOTOS State availability. Identification of subjects required. Reviews transparencies, prints, high res digital photos. Offers $35-75/photo.

$$ OCEAN MAGAZINE

P.O. Box 84, Rodanthe NC 27968-0084. (252)256-2296. E-mail: Diane@Oceanmagazine.org. Website: Oceanmagazine.org. **Contact:** Diane Buccheri, publisher. **100% freelance written.** "*OCEAN Magazine* serves to celebrate and protect the greatest, most comprehensive resource for life on earth, our world's ocean. *OCEAN* publishes articles, stories, poems, essays, and photography about the ocean—observations, experiences, scientific and environmental discussions—written with fact and feeling, illustrated with images from nature." Estab. 2004. Circ. 40,000. Byline given. Pays on publication. Publishes ms an average of 2-4 months after acceptance. Editorial lead time 3-6 months. Submit seasonal material 3-6 months in advance. Accepts queries by e-mail. .Accepts simultaneous submissions. Responds in 1 day to 2 months. Sample copy available for $3 digital, $8.45 print. Guidelines available online.

NONFICTION Needs book excerpts, essays, general interest, historical, inspirational, interview, opinion, personal experience, photo feature, technical, travel, spiritual. Does not want poor writing. **Buys 24-36 mss/year.** Query. Length: 75-5,000 words. **Pays $75-250.**

PHOTOS **Contact:** Diane Buccheri, publisher. Identification of subjects, model releases required. Reviews 3×5, 4×6, 5×7, 8×100, 10×12 prints, JPEG files. Negotiates payment individually. Buys one-time rights. Reviews 3×5, 4×6, 5×7, 8×100, 10×12 prints, JPEG files. Negotiates payment individually.

FICTION Needs adventure, fantasy, historical, novel concepts, romance, slice-of-life vignettes. **Buys 1-2 mss/year.** Query. Length: 100-2,000 words. **Pays $75-150.**

POETRY Needs avant-garde, free verse, haiku, light verse, traditional. Buys 12 poems/year. Submit maximum 6 poems. **Pays $25-75.**

FILLERS Needs anecdotes, facts. **Buys Reflections facts 4-12 mss/year.** Length: 20-100 words. **Pays $25-75.**

$$$ OUTDOOR AMERICA

Izaak Walton League of America, 707 Conservation Ln., Gaithersburg MD 20878. (301)548-0150. Fax: (301)548-9409. E-mail: oa@iwla.org. Website: iwla.org. **Contact:** Dawn Merritt, communications director. Quarterly magazine covering national conservation efforts/issues related to and involving members of the Izaak Walton League. A 4-color publication, *Outdoor America* is received by League members, as well as representatives of Congress and the media. Our audience, located predominantly in the midwestern and mid-Atlantic states, enjoys traditional recreational pursuits, such as fishing, hiking, hunting, as well as conservation activities and educating youth. All have a keen interest in protecting the future of our natural resources and outdoor recreation heritage. Estab. 1922. Circ. 36,500. Pays on acceptance. Offers 1/3 original rate kill fee. Publishes ms an average of 2 months after acceptance. Accepts queries by mail, e-mail. Responds in 2 months to queries. Sample copy for $2.50. Guidelines available online.

NONFICTION No fiction, poetry, or unsubstantiated opinion pieces. Query or send ms for short columns/news pieces (500 words or less). Features are planned 6-12 months in advance. **Pays $1,000-1,500 for features.**

PHOTOS Send tearsheets or nonreturnable samples. Pays $100-500.

$$$$ SIERRA

85 Second St., 2nd Floor, San Francisco CA 94105. (415)977-5656. Fax: (415)977-5799. E-mail: sierra.magazine@sierraclub.org. Website: sierraclub.org. **Works with a small number of new/unpublished writers each year.** Bimonthly magazine emphasizing conservation and environmental politics for people who are well educated, activist, outdoor-oriented, and politically well informed with a dedication to conservation. Estab. 1893. Circ. 695,000. Byline given. Pays on acceptance. Offers negotiable kill fee. Publishes ms an average of 4 months after acceptance. Accepts queries by mail, fax. Responds in 2 months to queries. Sample copy for $3 and SASE, or online. Guidelines available online.

💬 The editor reports an interest in seeing pieces on environmental heroes, thoughtful features on new developments in solving environmental problems, and outdoor adventure stories with a strong environmental element.

NONFICTION Needs expose, well-documented articles on environmental issues of national importance such as energy, wilderness, forests, etc., general interest, well-researched nontechnical pieces on areas of particular environmental concern, interview, photo feature, photo feature essays on threatened or scenic areas, journalistic treatments of semitechnical topic (energy sources, wildlife management, land use, waste management, etc.). "No 'My trip to .' or 'Why we must save wildlife/nature' articles; no poetry or general superficial essays on environmentalism; no reporting on purely local environmental issues. **Buys 30-36 mss/year.** Query with published clips. Length: 1,000-3,000 words. **Pays $800-3,000.**

REPRINTS Send photocopy with rights for sale noted and information about when and where the material previously appeared. Payment negotiable

PHOTOS Publishes photographs pertaining to the natural world and the environment. "We use high-quality, mostly color photographs and prefer digital files. Photographers interested in submitting work to Sierra are encouraged to send a link to their website, along with a stock listing of regions and subjects of specialty for us to review. Please do not send unsolicited transparencies and prints. We review photographers' stock lists (subject matter and locations in photographs) and samples and keep the names of potential contributors on file. Photographers are contacted only when subjects they have in stock are needed. We typically do not post our photo-needs list online or elsewhere. Sierra does not accept responsibility for lost or damaged transparencies sent on spec or for portfolio review. Please e-mail Photo.Submissions@sierraclub.org.". Send photos. Pays maximum $300 for transparencies; more for cover photos.

COLUMNS Food for Thought (food's connection to environment); Good Going (adventure journey); Hearth & Home (advice for environmentally sound living); Body Politics (health and the environment); Profiles (biographical look at environmentalists); Hidden Life (exposure of hidden environmental problems in everyday objects); Lay of the Land (national/international concerns), 500-700 words; Mixed Media (essays on environment in the media; book reviews), 200-300 words. **Pays $50-500.**

$$$$ WILDLIFE CONSERVATION

2300 Southern Blvd., Bronx NY 10460. (718)220-5100. E-mail: nsimmons@wcs.org; membership@wcs.org. Website: wcs.org. Bimonthly magazine for environmentally aware readers. Offers 25% kill fee. Accepts simultaneous submissions. Responds in 1 month to queries. Sample copy for $4.95 (plus $1 postage). Writer's guidelines available for SASE or via e-mail.

NONFICTION Buys 30 mss/year. Query with published clips. Length: 300-2,000 words. **Pays $1/word for features and department articles, and $150 for short pieces**

PERSONAL COMPUTERS

💲💲💲 SMART COMPUTING

Sandhills Publishing, 131 W. Grand Dr., Lincoln NE 68521. (800)544-1264. Fax: (402)479-2104. E-mail: editor@smartcomputing.com. Website: smartcomputing.com. **45% freelance written**. Monthly magazine. "We focus on plain-English computing articles with an emphasis on tutorials that improve productivity without the purchase of new hardware." Estab. 1990. Circ. 200,000. Byline given. Pays on acceptance. Offers 25% kill fee. Publishes ms an average of 2 months after acceptance. Editorial lead time 4 months. Submit seasonal material 4 months in advance. Accepts queries by mail, e-mail. Accepts simultaneous submissions. Responds in 1 month to queries. Sample copy for $7.99. Guidelines for #10 SASE.

NONFICTION Needs how-to, new product, technical. No humor, opinion, personal experience. **Buys 250 mss/year.** Query with published clips. Length: 800-3,200 words. **Pays $240-960.** Pays expenses of writers on assignment up to $75

PHOTOS Send photos. Captions required. Offers no additional payment for photos accepted with ms.

PHOTOGRAPHY

⊕ APOGEE PHOTO

Apogee Photo, Inc., 11121 Wolf Way, Westminster CO 80031. (904)619-2010 (Florida contact). Website: apogeephoto.com. **Contact:** Marla Meier, editorial director. A free online monthly magazine designed to inform, educate and entertain photographers of all ages and levels. Take online photography courses, read photo articles covering a wide range of photo topics and see listings of photo workshops and tours, camera clubs, and books. Submit your articles for publication.

⌘ Please do a search by subject before submitting your article to see if your article covers a new subject or brings a new perspective on a particular subject or theme.

PHOTOS "Apogee Photo is interested in providing an electronic forum for high quality work from photographic writers and photographers. We will accept articles up to 2000 words on any photographic subject geared towards the beginning to advanced photographer. Articles must have a minimum of 4-6 photographs accompanying them. You must hold the copyright and/or have a copyright release from a 3rd party and you must have signed model releases where applicable for any identifiable person or persons which appear in your photographs.". Accepts reviews of new products, 1,000/words max.

PHOTOGRAPHER'S FORUM MAGAZINE

813 Reddick St., Santa Barbara CA 93103. (805)963-6425. Fax: (805)965-0496. E-mail: julie@serbin.com. Website: pfmagazine.com. **Contact:** Julie Simpson, managing editor. Quarterly magazine for the serious student and emerging professional photographer. Includes feature articles on historic and contemporary photographers, interviews, book reviews, workshop listings, new products.

NONFICTION Needs historical, interview, new product, photo feature, profile, reviews.

POLITICS AND WORLD AFFAIRS

💲💲 CHURCH & STATE

518 C St. NE, Washington DC 20002. (202)466-3234. Fax: (202)466-2587. E-mail: americansunited@au.org. Website: au.org. **10% freelance written**. Monthly magazine emphasizing religious liberty and church/state relations matters. "Strongly advocates separation of church and state. Readership is well-educated." Estab. 1947. Circ. 40,000. Pays on acceptance. Publishes ms an average of 2 months after acceptance. Accepts queries by mail. Accepts simultaneous submissions. Responds in 2 months to queries. Sample copy and writer's guidelines for 9×12 SAE with 3 first-class stamps.

NONFICTION Needs expose, general interest, historical, interview. **Buys 11 mss/year.** Query. Length: 800-1,600 words. **Pays $150-300.** Sometimes pays expenses of writers on assignment.

REPRINTS Send tearsheet, photocopy or typed ms with rights for sale noted and information about when and where the material previously appeared.

PHOTOS Send photos. Captions required. Pays negotiable fee for b&w prints.

💲 COMMONWEAL

Commonweal Foundation, 475 Riverside Dr., Room 405, New York NY 10115. (212)662-4200. Fax: (212)662-4183. E-mail: editors@commonwealmagazine.org. Website: commonwealmagazine.org. **Con-**

tact: Paul Baumann, editor. Biweekly journal of opinion edited by Catholic lay people, dealing with topical issues of the day on public affairs, religion, literature, and the arts. Estab. 1924. Circ. 20,000. Byline given. Pays on publication. Submit seasonal material 2 months in advance. Responds in 2 months to queries. Sample copy free. Guidelines available online.

NONFICTION Needs essays, general interest, interview, personal experience, religious. **Buys 30 mss/year.** Query with published clips. Length: 2,000-2,500 words. **Pays $200-300 for longer manuscripts; $100-200 for shorter pieces.**

COLUMNS Upfronts (brief, newsy reportorials, giving facts, information and some interpretation behind the headlines of the day), 750-1,000 words; Last Word (usually of a personal nature, on some aspect of the human condition: spiritual, individual, political, or social), 800 words.

POETRY Contact: Rosemary Deen, editor. Needs free verse, traditional. *Commonweal*, published every 2 weeks, is a Catholic general interest magazine for college-educated readers. Does not publish inspirational poems. Buys 20 poems/year. Length: 75 lines/poem max **Pays 75¢/line plus 2 contributor's copies. Acquires all rights. Returns rights when requested by the author.**

⊛⊛ THE FREEMAN: IDEAS ON LIBERTY

30 S. Broadway, Irvington-on-Hudson NY 10533. (914)591-7230. Fax: (914)591-8910. E-mail: freeman@fee.org. Website: fee.org. **85% freelance written.** Monthly publication for the layman and fairly advanced students of liberty. Estab. 1946. Byline given. Pays on publication. Publishes ms an average of 5 months after acceptance. Sample copy for 7 ½×10 ½ SASE with 4 first-class stamps.

○ Eager to work with new/unpublished writers.
NONFICTION Buys 100 mss/year. Query with SASE. Length: 3,500 words. **Pays 10¢/word.** Sometimes pays expenses of writers on assignment.

⊛⊛ THE PROGRESSIVE

409 E. Main St., Madison WI 53703. (608)257-4626. Fax: (608)257-3373. E-mail: editorial@progressive.org; mattr@progressive.org. Website: progressive.org. **75% freelance written.** Monthly. Estab. 1909. Byline given. Pays on publication. Publishes ms an average of 6 weeks after acceptance. Accepts queries by mail. Responds in 1 month to queries. Sample copy for 9×12

SASE with 4 first-class stamps or sample articles online. Guidelines available online.
NONFICTION Query. Length: 500-4,000 words. **Pays $500-1,300.**
POETRY Publishes 1 original poem a month. "We prefer poems that connect up—in one fashion or another, however obliquely—with political concerns." **Pays $150.**

⊛ PROGRESSIVE POPULIST

P.O. Box 819, Manchaca TX 78652. (512)828-7245. E-mail: populist@usa.net. Website: populist.com. **90% freelance written.** Biweekly tabloid covering politics and economics. "We cover issues of interest to workers, small businesses, and family farmers and ranchers." Estab. 1995. Circ. 15,000. Byline given. Pays quarterly. Publishes ms an average of 1 month after acceptance. Editorial lead time 3 weeks. Submit seasonal material 1 month in advance. Accepts queries by mail, e-mail, fax, phone. TrueAccepts simultaneous submissions. Sample copy and writer's guidelines free.

NONFICTION Needs essays, exposè, general interest, historical, humor, interview, opinion. "We are not much interested in 'sound-off' articles about state or national politics, although we accept letters to the editor. We prefer to see more 'journalistic' pieces, in which the writer does enough footwork to advance a story beyond the easy realm of opinion." **Buys 400 mss/year.** Query. Length: 600-1,000 words. **Pays $15-50.** Pays writers with contributor copies or other premiums if preferred by writer

REPRINTS Send photocopy with rights for sale noted and information about when and where the material previously appeared.

PHOTOS State availability. Identification of subjects required. Negotiates payment individually.

PSYCHOLOGY AND SELF-IMPROVEMENT

⊛ SPOTLIGHT ON RECOVERY MAGAZINE

R. Graham Publishing Company, 9602 Glenwood Rd., #140, Brooklyn NY 11236. (347)831-9373. E-mail: rgraham_100@msn.com. Website: spotlightonrecovery.com. **85% freelance written.** Quarterly magazine covering self-help, recovery, and empowerment. "This is the premiere outreach and resource magazine in New York. Its goal is to be the catalyst for which the human spirit could heal. Everybody knows somebody who has mental illness, substance abuse issues, parenting problems, educational issues, or someone who is homeless, unemployed, physically ill, or the victim of a crime. Many people suffer in silence. *Spotlight on Recovery* will provide a voice to those who suffer in silence and begin the dialogue of recovery." Estab. 2001. Circ. 1,500-2,500. Byline sometimes given. Pays on publication. Publishes ms an average of 2 months after acceptance. Editorial lead time 1 month. Submit seasonal material 1 month in advance. Accepts queries by mail, e-mail. Accepts simultaneous submissions. Responds in 2 weeks to queries. Responds in 1 month to mss. Sample copy and writer's guidelines free.

NONFICTION Needs book excerpts, interview, opinion, personal experience. **Buys 30-50 mss/year.** Query with published clips. Length: 150-1,500 words. **Pays 5¢/word or $75-80/article.**

PHOTOS State availability. Identification of subjects required. Reviews GIF/JPEG files. Pays $5-10/photo.

COLUMNS Buys 4 mss/year. mss/year. Query with published clips. **Pays 5¢/word or $75-80/column.**

FICTION Needs ethnic, mainstream, slice-of-life vignettes.

FILLERS Needs facts, newsbreaks, short humor. **Buys 2 mss/year. mss/year. Pays 5¢/word.**

REGIONAL

ALABAMA

$ ALABAMA LIVING

Alabama Rural Electric Assn., P.O. Box 244014, Montgomery AL 36124. (334)215-2732. Fax: (334)215-2733. E-mail: dgates@areapower.com. Website: alabamaliving.com. Michael Cornelison, art director. **Contact:** Darryl Gates, editor. **80% freelance written.** Monthly magazine covering topics of interest to rural and suburban Alabamians. "Our magazine is an editorially balanced, informational and educational service to members of rural electric cooperatives. Our mix regularly includes Alabama history, Alabama features, gardening, outdoor, and consumer pieces." Estab. 1948. Circ. 400,000. Byline given. Pays on acceptance. Editorial lead time 4 months. Submit seasonal material 4 months in advance. Accepts queries by mail, e-mail. Accepts simultaneous submissions. Responds in 1 month to queries. Sample copy free.

NONFICTION Needs historical, rural-oriented, Alabama slant, Alabama. Special issues: Gardening (March); Travel (April); Home Improvement (May); Holiday Recipes (December). **Buys 20 mss/year.** Send complete ms. Length: 500-750 words. **Pays $250 minimum for assigned articles. Pays $150 minimum for unsolicited articles.**

REPRINTS Send typed manuscript with rights for sale noted. Pays $100.

PHOTOS Buys 1-3 photos from freelancers/issue; 12-36 photos/year. Pays $100 for color cover; $50 for color inside; $60-75 for photo/text package. **Pays on acceptance.** Credit line given. Buys one-time rights for publication and website; negotiable.

ALASKA

$$ ALASKA MAGAZINE

301 Arctic Slope Ave., Suite 300, Anchorage AK 99518-3035. (907)272-6070. Fax: (907)258-5360. E-mail: tim.woody@alaskamagazine.com; andy.hall@alaskamagazine.com. Website: alaskamagazine.com. Tim Woody, editor; Andy Hall, publisher. **Contact:** Rebecca Luczycki, senior editor, rebecca.luczycki@alaskamagazine.com. **70% freelance written. Eager to work with new/unpublished writers.** Magazine published 10 times/year covering topics uniquely Alaskan. Estab. 1935. Circ. 180,000. Byline given. Pays on publication. Publishes ms an average of 6 months after acceptance. Submit seasonal material 1 year in advance. Accepts queries by mail. Responds in 2 months to queries and to mss. Sample copy for $4 and 9×12 SAE with 7 first-class stamps. Guidelines available online.

NONFICTION Needs historical, humor, interview, personal experience, photo feature, travel, adventure, outdoor recreation (including hunting, fishing), Alaska destination stories. No fiction or poetry. **Buys 40 mss/year.** Length: 100-2,500 words **Pays $100-1,250**

PHOTOS Contact: Tim Woody, editor; Tim Blum, art director. *Alaska Magazine* is dedicated to depicting life in Alaska through high-quality images of its people, places and wildlife. Color photographs from professional free-lance photographers are used extensively and selected according to their creative and technical merits. Send photos. Captions, identification of subjects required. Reviews 35mm or larger transparencies, slides labeled with your name. Pays $50 maximum for b&w photos; $75-500 for color photos; $300 maximum/day; $2,000 maximum/complete job; $300 maximum/full page; $500 maximum/cover. Buys limited rights, first North American serial rights and electronic rights." Each issue of *Alaska* features a 4- to 6-page photo feature. We're looking for themes and photos to show the best of Alaska. We want sharp, artistically composed pictures. Cover photo always relates to stories inside the issue." Photographers on assignment are paid a competitive day-rate and reimbursed for approved expenses. All assignments are negotiated in advance. Buys first North American publication rights and limited electronic rights and pays upon publication.

ARIZONA

💲💲 ARIZONA FOOTHILLS MAGAZINE

Media That Deelivers, Inc., 8132 N. 87th Place, Scottsdale AZ 85258. (480)460-5203. Fax: (480)443-1517. E-mail: editorial@azfoothillsmag.com; editorial@mediathatdeelivers.com. Website: azfoothillsmag.com. **10% freelance written**. Monthly magazine covering Arizona lifesyle. Estab. 1996. Circ. 60,000. Byline given. Pays on publication. Publishes ms an average of 6 months after acceptance. Editorial lead time 6 months. Submit seasonal material at least 4 months in advance. Accepts queries by mail, e-mail. Responds in 1 month to queries. Sample copy for #10 SASE.

NONFICTION Needs general interest, photo feature, travel, fashion, decor, arts, interview. **Buys 10 mss/year.** Query with published clips. Length: 900-2,000 words. **Pays 35-40¢/word for assigned articles.**

PHOTOS Photos may be requested. Captions, identification of subjects, model releases required. Reviews contact sheets, transparencies. Negotiates payment individually.

COLUMNS Travel, dining, fashion, home decor, design, architecture, wine, shopping, golf, performance & visual arts.

💲 PHOENIX MAGAZINE

Cities West Publishing, Inc., 15169 N. Scottsdale Road, Ste. C-310, Scottsdale AZ 85254. (866)481-6970. Fax: (602)604-0169. E-mail: aklawonn@citieswestpub.com. Website: phoenixmag.com. **Contact:** Adam Klawonn, managing editor. **70% freelance written**. Monthly magazine covering regional issues, personalities, events, neighborhoods, customs, and history of metro Phoenix. Estab. 1966. Circ. 60,000.

Byline given. Pays on publication. Publishes ms an average of 3 months after acceptance. Submit seasonal material 1 year in advance. Accepts queries by mail, e-mail. Responds in 2 months to queries. Responds in 2 months to mss. Sample copy for $3.95 and 9×12 SASE with 5 first-class stamps. Guidelines for #10 sase.

NONFICTION Needs general interest, interview, investigative, historical, service pieces (where to go and what to do around town). "We do not publish fiction, poetry, personal essays, book reviews, music reviews, or product reviews, and our travel stories are staff written. With the exception of our travel stories, all of the content in *Phoenix* magazine is geographically specific to the Phoenix-metro region. We do not publish any non-travel news or feature stories that are outside the Phoenix area, and we prefer that our freelancers are located in the Phoenix metro area." **Buys 50 mss/year.** Query with published clips via e-mail. "Include a short summary, a list of sources, and an explanation of why you think your idea is right for the magazine and why you're qualified to write it." Length: 150-2,000 words.

CALIFORNIA

➕💲 CALIFORNIA NORTHERN MAGAZINE

P.O. Box 2268, Sacramento CA 95822. E-mail: submissions@calnorthern.net. Website: calnorthern.net. **Contact:** Casey Mills, editor. **60% freelance written**. Biannual publication exploring the region's cultures, environments, histories, and identities. It provides a rare California-based forum for exceptional essays, long-form journalism, literature, and photography, and distinguishes itself from traditional regional media by balancing its local emphasis with a level of sophistication and depth typically found in larger national publications. Estab. 2010. Circ. 500. Byline given. Pays on publication. Accepts queries by mail, e-mail, fax. Responds in 3 weeks to queries; 2 months to ms. Guidelines by e-mail.

NONFICTION Contact: Richard Mills, executive editor. Needs book excerpts, essays, historical, interview, nostalgic, opinion, personal experience, photo feature, profile. **Buys 6 mss/year.** Query. Length: 1,500-8,500 words. **Pays $.05-.07/word.**

PHOTOS Contact: Paul Barrett, executive editor. Send photos with submission. Reviews GIF/JPEG files.

Negotiates payment individually. "Please submit no more than 10 photos taken in Northern California, along with a brief cover letter telling us about yourself and your work, and why you feel it would be a good fit for the magazine.".

COLUMNS Contact: Richard Mills, executive editor. Notes From The Field: vignettes that provide readers a window into a part of Northern California that is often overlooked, or a well-known place that the writer has a unique connection to. 500-700 words. **Buys 8 mss/year.** Query.

FICTION Contact: Paul Barrett, executive editor. Fiction should be submitted by writers who reside in the region or have some strong connection to it. No genre fiction. **Buys 2 mss/year.** Send complete ms. Accepts 2,000-8,500 words.

POETRY Needs Avant-garde, free verse, haiku, light verse, traditional. Buys 5 poems/year. Submit maximum 3 poems.

⊛⊛ CARLSBAD MAGAZINE

Wheelhouse Media, 2917 State St., Suite 210, Carlsbad CA 92008. (760)729-9099. Fax: (760)729-9011. E-mail: tim@wheelhousemedia.com. Website: clickoncarlsbad.com. **Contact:** Tim Wrisley. **80% freelance written**. Bimonthly magazine covering people, places, events, arts in Carlsbad, California. "We are a regional magazine highlighting all things pertaining specifically to Carlsbad. We focus on history, events, people and places that make Carlsbad interesting and unique. Our audience is both Carlsbad residents and visitors or anyone interested in learning more about Carlsbad. We favor a conversational tone that still adheres to standard rules of writing." Estab. 2004. Circ. 35,000. Byline given. Pays on publication. Publishes ms an average of 6 months after acceptance. Editorial lead time 4 months. Submit seasonal material 6-12 months in advance. Accepts queries by mail, e-mail. Accepts simultaneous submissions. Responds in 2 months to queries and to mss. Sample copy for $2.31. Guidelines by e-mail.

NONFICTION Needs historical, interview, photo feature, home, garden, arts, events. Does not want self-promoting articles for individuals or businesses, real estate how-to's, advertorials. **Buys 3 mss/year.** Query with published clips. Length: 300-2,700 words. **Pays 20-30¢/word for assigned articles. Pays 20¢/word for unsolicited articles.** Sometimes pays expenses of writers on assignment.

PHOTOS State availability. Reviews GIF/JPEG files. Offers $15-400/photo.

COLUMNS Carlsbad Arts (people, places or things related to cultural arts in Carlsbad); Happenings (events that take place in Carlsbad); Carlsbad Character (unique Carlsbad residents who have contributed to Carlsbad's character); Commerce (Carlsbad business profiles); Surf Scene (subjects pertaining to the beach/surf in Carlsbad), all 500-700 words. Garden (Carlsbad garden feature); Home (Carlsbad home feature), both 700-1,200 words. **Buys 60 columns. mss/year.** Query with published clips. **Pays $50 flat fee or 20¢/word.**

⊛ JOURNAL PLUS

654 Osos St., San Luis Obispo CA 93401. (805)544-8711. Fax: (805)546-8827. E-mail: slojournal@fix.net. Website: slojournal.com. **Contact:** Steve Owens, publisher. **60% freelance written**. Monthly magazine that can be read online covering the 25-year old age group and up, but young-at-heart audience. Estab. 1981. Circ. 25,000. Byline given. Pays on publication. Publishes ms an average of 2 months after acceptance. Editorial lead time 2 months. Submit seasonal material 2 months in advance. Accepts queries by mail. Accepts simultaneous submissions. Responds in 2 weeks to queries. Responds in 1 month to mss. Sample copy for 9×12 SAE with $2 postage. Guidelines available online.

NONFICTION Needs historical, humor, interview, personal experience, travel, book reviews, entertainment, health. Special issues: Christmas (December); Travel (October, April). No finance, automotive, heavy humor, poetry, or fiction. **Buys 60-70 mss/year.** Send complete ms. Length: 600-1,400 words. **Pays $50-75.**

PHOTOS Send photos.

⊛ NOB HILL GAZETTE

Nob Hill Gazette, Inc., 5 Third St., Suite 222, San Francisco CA 94103. (415)227-0190. Fax: (415)974-5103. E-mail: cherie@nobhillgazette.com. Website: nobhillgazette.com. **Contact:** Cherie L. Turner. **95% freelance written**. Monthly magazine covering upscale lifestyles in the Bay Area. *Nob Hill Gazette* is for an upscale readership. Estab. 1978. Circ. 82,000. Byline given. Pays on 15th of month following publication. Offers $50 kill fee. Publishes ms an average of 2-3 months after acceptance. Editorial lead time 1-2 months. Submit seasonal material 1-2 months in advance. Accepts queries by e-mail. Responds in 2 weeks to queries. Responds in 2 months to mss. Sample copy available online. Guidelines free.

🖵 "The *Gazette* caters to an audience upscale in taste and lifestyle. Our main purpose is to publicize events that raise millions of dollars for local cultural programs and charities, and to recognize the dedicated volunteers who work behind the scenes. With publisher Lois Lehrman at the helm, each trendsetting issue of our monthly magazine includes about 200 photos and 15 or more local interest stories. Our features, often 'tongue-in-chic', cover art, beauty, books, entertainment, fashion, health, history, interiors, profiles, travels, and much, much more."

NONFICTION Needs general interest, historical, interview, opinion, photo feature, trends, lifestyles, fashion, health, fitness, entertaining, decor, real estate, charity and philanthropy, culture and the arts. Does not want first person articles, anything commercial (from a business or with a product to sell), profiles of people not active in the community, anything technical, anything on people or events not in the Bay Area. **Buys 75 mss/year.** Query with published clips. Length: 1,200-2,000 words. **Pays $100.** Sometimes pays expenses of writers on assignment.

PHOTOS Contact: Contact Shara Hall, photo coordinator. State availability. Captions, identification of subjects required. Reviews GIF/JPEG files. Offers no additional payment for photos accepted with ms.

COLUMNS Contact: Contact Lois Lehrman, publisher. All our columnists are freelancers, but they write for us regularly, so we don't take other submissions.

💲💲 SACRAMENTO NEWS & REVIEW

Chico Community Publishing, 1124 Del Paso Blvd., Sacramento CA 95815-3607. (916)498-1234. Fax: (916)498-7920. E-mail: melindaw@newsreview. com; kelm@newsreview.com. Website: newsreview. com. **Contact:** Melinda Welsh, editor. **25% freelance written.** Alternative news and entertainment weekly magazine. We maintain a high literary standard for submissions; unique or alternative slant. Publication aimed at a young, intellectual audience; submissions should have an edge and strong voice. We have a decided preference for stories with a strong local slant. "Our mission: To publish great newspapers that are successful and enduring. To create a quality work environment that encourages employees to grow

professionally while respecting personal welfare. To have a positive impact on our communities and make them better places to live. " Estab. 1989. Circ. 87,000. Byline given. Pays on publication. Offers 10% kill fee. Publishes ms an average of 2 months after acceptance. Editorial lead time 2 months. Submit seasonal material 2 months in advance. Accepts queries by mail, e-mail. Accepts simultaneous submissions. Responds in 1 month to queries. Responds in 2 months to mss. Sample copy for 50¢. Guidelines available online.

🖵 Prefers to work with Sacramento-area writers.
NONFICTION Needs essays, expose, general interest, humor, interview, personal experience. Does not want to see travel, product stories, business profile. **Buys 20-30 mss/year.** Query with published clips. Length: 750-5,000 words. **Pays $40-500.** Sometimes pays expenses of writers on assignment.

PHOTOS State availability. Identification of subjects required. Reviews 8×10 prints. Negotiates payment individually.

💲💲💲 SAN JOSE

Renaissance Publications, Inc., 25 Metro Dr., Suite 550, San Jose CA 95110. (408)975-9300. Fax: (408)975-9900. E-mail: jodi@sanjosemagazine.com. Website: sanjosemagazine.com. **10% freelance written.** Monthly magazine. "As the lifestyle magazine for those living at center of the technological revolution, we cover the people and places that make Silicon Valley the place to be for the new millennium. All stories must have a local angle, though they should be of national relevance." Estab. 1997. Circ. 60,000. Byline given. Pays on publication. Offers 10% kill fee. Publishes ms an average of 3 months after acceptance. Editorial lead time 18 weeks. Submit seasonal material 6 months in advance. Accepts queries by mail, e-mail, fax. Accepts simultaneous submissions. Responds in 1 month to queries. Sample copy for $5. Guidelines for #10 SASE.

🖵 "Magazine currently being re-launched."
NONFICTION Needs general interest, interview, photo feature, travel. No technical, trade or articles without a tie-in to Silicon Valley. **Buys 12 mss/year.** Query with published clips. Length: 1,000-2,000 words. **Pays 35¢/word.**

PHOTOS State availability. Captions, identification of subjects, model releases required. Offers no additional payment for photos accepted with ms.

COLUMNS Fast Forward (a roundup of trends and personalities and news that has Silicon Valley buzzing; topics include health, history, politics, nonprofits, education, Q&As, business, technology, dining, wine and fashion). **Buys 5 mss/year.** Query. **Pays 35¢/word.**

CANADA/INTERNATIONAL

💲💲 ABACO LIFE

Caribe Communications, P.O. Box 37487, Raleigh NC 27627. (919)859-6782. Fax: (919)859-6769. E-mail: jimkerr@mindspring.com. Website: abacolife.com. **50% freelance written**. Quarterly magazine covering Abaco, an island group in the Northeast Bahamas. *"Abaco Life editorial focuses entirely on activities, history, wildlife, resorts, people and other subjects pertaining to the Abacos. Readers include locals, vacationers, second-home owners, and other visitors whose interests range from real estate and resorts to scuba, sailing, fishing, and beaches. The tone is upbeat, adventurous, humorous. No fluff writing for an audience already familiar with the area."* Estab. 1979. Circ. 10,000. Byline given. Pays on publication. Offers 40% kill fee. Publishes ms an average of 2 months after acceptance. Editorial lead time 2 months. Submit seasonal material 4 months in advance. Accepts queries by mail, e-mail. Accepts simultaneous submissions. Responds in 2 weeks to queries. Responds in 2 months to mss. Sample copy for $2. Guidelines free.

NONFICTION Needs general interest, historical, how-to, interview, personal experience, photo feature, travel. No general first-time impressions. Articles must be specific, show knowledge and research of the subject and area—'Abaco's Sponge Industry'; 'Diving Abaco's Wrecks'; 'The Hurricane of '36.' **Buys 8-10 mss/year.** Query or send complete ms Length: 700-2,000 words. **Pays $400-1,000.**

PHOTOS State availability of or send photos. Captions, identification of subjects, model releases required. Reviews transparencies, prints. Offers $25-100/photo. Negotiates payment individually.

🌐💲💲💲💲 ALBERTAVIEWS

AlbertaViews, Ltd., Suite 208-320 23rd Ave. SW, Calgary AB T2S 0J2 Canada. (403)243-5334 or 1-877-212-5334. Fax: (403)243-8599. E-mail: editor@albertaviews.ab.ca. Website: albertaviews.ab.ca. **50% freelance written**. Bimonthly magazine covering Alberta culture: politics, economy, social issues, and art. We are a regional magazine providing thoughtful commentary and background information on issues of concern to Albertans. Most of our writers are Albertans. Estab. 1997. Circ. 30,000. Byline given. Pays on publication. Offers 50% kill fee. Publishes ms an average of 3 months after acceptance. Editorial lead time 4 months. Submit seasonal material 3 months in advance. Accepts queries by e-mail. Responds in 6 weeks to queries. Responds in 2 months to mss. Sample copy free. Guidelines available online.

🔘No phone queries.

☛ If you are a writer, illustrator or photographer interested in contributing to *Alberta Views*, please see our contributor's guidelines.

NONFICTION Needs essays. **Buys 18 mss/year.** Query with published clips. Length: 3,000-5,000 words. **Pays $1,000-1,500 for assigned articles. Pays $350-750 for unsolicited articles.** Sometimes pays expenses of writers on assignment.

PHOTOS "We are a Mac-based operation, running recent versions of InDesign, Photoshop, Illustrator and Acrobat. All digital images for publication should be 300 dpi, TIFF, JPG or EPS format. We can scan transparencies, prints and illustrations up to 18 x 25 inches. We gratefully accept images from Alberta artists and galleries who wish to showcase their work in the magazine (space permitting). No fee is paid for this usage. All materials will be returned. All photography and illustration for our features is assigned by our art director, and fees are paid based on the artist's experience and qualifications. We buy First North American Serial Rights, and the right to post the article on our website and for internal design re-use. It is the magazine's mandate to feature Alberta artists and photographers, or imagery that is about Alberta. We do our best to avoid the postcard view of our province. If you would like *AlbertaViews* to see your visual work, please send samples to: Art Director, Alberta Views, Suite 208 - 320, 23rd Avenue SW Calgary AB T2S 0J2.". State availability. Negotiates payment individually.

FICTION Only fiction by Alberta writers. **Buys 6 mss/year.** Send complete ms. Length: 2,500-4,000 words. **Pays $1,000 maximum.**

🌐💲💲💲 CANADA'S HISTORY MAGAZINE

Canada's National History Society, Bryce Hall, Main Floor, 515 Portage Ave., Winnipeg MB R3B 2E9 Canada. (204)988-9300, ext. 219; (866)952-3444, ext. 219. Fax: (204)988-9309. E-mail: articlequeries@history-society.ca; aqueries@historysociety.ca. Website: canadasahistory.ca. **50% freelance written**. Bimonthly magazine covering Canadian history. Estab. 1920. Circ. 46,000. Byline given. Pays on acceptance. Offers $200 kill fee. Editorial lead time 4 months. Submit seasonal material 8 months in advance. Accepts queries by e-mail. Accepts simultaneous submissions. Responds in 6 weeks to queries. Responds in 2 months to mss. Sample copy for sae with 9×12 envelope and 2 First-Class stamps. Guidelines available online.

NONFICTION Needs Canadian focus., Subject matter covers the whole range of Canadian history, with emphasis on social history, politics, exploration, discovery and settlement, aboriginal peoples, business & trade, war, culture and sport. Does not want anything unrelated to Canadian history. No memoirs. **Buys 30 mss/year.** Query with the word *query* in the subject line if using e-mail; include published clips, sase is using postal mail. Length: 600-3,500 words. **Pays 50¢/ word for major features.** Sometimes pays expenses of writers on assignment.

PHOTOS State availability. Identification of subjects, model releases required. Offers no additional payment for photos accepted with ms.

COLUMNS Book and other media reviews and Canadian history subjects, 600 words (These are assigned to freelancers with particular areas of expertise, i.e., women's history, labour history, French regime, etc.) **Buys 15 columns. mss/year. Pays $125.**

☺☻☺☻☺ HAMILTON MAGAZINE

Town Media, 1074 Cooke Blvd., Burlington ON L7T 4A8 Canada. (905)522-6117 or (905)634-8003. Fax: (905)634-7661 or (905)634-8804. E-mail: david@ townmedia.ca; info@townmedia.ca. Website: hamiltonmagazine.com. **50% freelance written**. Quarterly magazine devoted to the Greater Hamilton and Golden Horseshoe area. "Mandate: to entertain and inform by spotlighting the best of what our city and region has to offer. We invite readers to take part in a vibrant community by supplying them with authoritative and dynamic coverage of local culture, food, fashion and design. Each story strives to expand your view of the area, every issue an essential resource for exploring, understanding and unlocking the region. Packed with insight, intrigue and suspense, *Hamilton Magazine* delivers the city to your doorstep." Estab. 1978. Byline

given. Pays on publication. Offers 50% kill fee. Editorial lead time 2-3 months. Submit seasonal material 2-3 months in advance. Accepts queries by e-mail. NoResponds in 1 week to queries and to mss. Sample copy for #10 SASE. Guidelines by e-mail.

NONFICTION Needs book excerpts, essays, expose, historical, how-to, humor, inspirational, interview, personal experience, photo feature, religious, travel. Does not want generic articles that could appear in any mass-market publication. Send complete ms. Length: 800-2,000 words. **Pays $200-1,600 for assigned articles. Pays $100-800 for unsolicited articles.** Sometimes pays expenses of writers on assignment.

PHOTOS Contact: Contact Kate Sharrow, art director. State availability of or send photos. Identification of subjects required. Reviews 8×10 prints, JPEG files (8×10 at 300 dpi). Negotiates payment individually.

COLUMNS A&E Art, 1,200-2,000 words; A&E Music, 1,200-2,000 words; A&E Books, 1,200-1,400 words. **Buys 12 columns. mss/year.** Send complete ms. **Pays $200-400.**

☺☻☺ MONDAY MAGAZINE

Black Press Ltd., 818 Broughton St., Victoria BC V8W 1E4 Canada. E-mail: editor@mondaymag.com. Website: mondaymag.com. Grant McKenzie. **10% freelance written**. Weekly tabloid covering local news. "*Monday Magazine* is Victoria's only alternative newsweekly. For more than 35 years, we have published fresh, informative and alternative perspectives on local events. We prefer lively, concise writing with a sense of humor and insight." Estab. 1975. Circ. 40,000. Byline given. Pays 1 month after publication. Publishes ms an average of 1 month after acceptance. Editorial lead time 1-2 months. Submit seasonal material 2 months in advance. Accepts queries by e-mail (preferred). Responds in 6-8 weeks to queries. Responds in up to 3 months to mss See Writer's Guidelines on our website.

NONFICTION Needs exposè, general interest, humor, interview, opinion, personal experience, technical, travel. Special issues: Body, Mind, Spirit (October); Student Survival Guide (August). Does not want fiction, poetry, or conspiracy theories. Send complete ms. Length: 300-2,000 words. **Pays 10¢/word.**

PHOTOS Send photos. Captions, identification of subjects required. Reviews GIF/JPEG files (300 dpi at 4×6). Offers no additional payment for photos accepted with ms.

🍁$$⊘ OUTDOOR CANADA MAGAZINE

25 Sheppard Ave. W., Suite 100, Toronto ON M2N 6S7 Canada. (416)733-7600. Fax: (416)227-8296. E-mail: editorial@outdoorcanada.ca. Website: outdoorcanada.ca. **90% freelance written. Works with a small number of new/unpublished writers each year.** Estab. 1972. Circ. 90,000. Byline given. Pays on publication. Publishes ms an average of 8 months after acceptance. Submit seasonal material 1 year in advance. Accepts queries by mail, e-mail. Responds in 1 month to queries. Guidelines available online.

NONFICTION Needs how-to, fishing, hunting, outdoor issues, outdoor destinations in Canada. **Buys 35-40 mss/year.** Does not accept unsolicited mss. 2,500 words **Pays $500 and up.**

REPRINTS Send information about when and where the article previously appeared. Payment varies

PHOTOS Emphasize people in the Canadian outdoors. Captions, model releases required. Fees negotiable.

FILLERS Buys 30-40 mss/year. Length: 100-500 words. **Pays $50 and up.**

🍁 UP HERE

Up Here Publishing, Ltd., P.O. Box 1350, Yellowknife NT X1A 3T1 Canada. (867)766-6710. Fax: (867)873-9876. E-mail: katharine@uphere.ca; patrick@uphere.ca (for photography). Website: uphere.ca. **Contact:** Katharine Sandiford, editor. **50% freelance written.** Magazine published 8 times/year covering general interest about Canada's Far North. We publish features, columns, and shorts about people, wildlife, native cultures, travel, and adventure in Yukon, Northwest Territories, and Nunavut. Be informative, but entertaining. Estab. 1984. Circ. 22,000. Byline given. Pays on publication. Offers 50% kill fee. Editorial lead time 6 months. Accepts queries by e-mail. Sample copy for $4.95 (Canadian) and 9×12 SASE.

NONFICTION Needs essays, general interest, how-to, humor, interview, personal experience, photo feature, technical, travel, lifestyle/culture, historical. **Buys 25-30 mss/year.** Query. Length: 1,500-3,000 words. **Fees are negotiable.**

PHOTOS *Please* do not send unsolicited original photos, slides. Send photos. Captions, identification of subjects required. Reviews transparencies, prints.

COLUMNS Write for updated guidelines, visit website, or e-mail. **Buys 25-30 mss/year.** Query with published clips.

COLORADO

$ SOUTHWEST COLORADO ARTS PERSPECTIVE MAGAZINE

Shared Vision Publishing, P.O. Box 3042, Durango CO 81302. (970)739-3200. E-mail: director@artsperspective.com. Website: artsperspective.com. **100% freelance written.** Quarterly tabloid covering art. "*Arts Perspective Magazine* offers a venue for all of the arts. Artists, writers, musicians, dancers, performers and galleries are encourage to showcase their work. A resource for supporters of the arts to share a common thread in the continuum of creative expression." Estab. 2004. Circ. 30,000+. Byline given. Pays on publication. Publishes ms an average of 2 months after acceptance. Editorial lead time 2-5 months. Submit seasonal material 2-5 months in advance. Accepts queries by mail, e-mail, phone. Responds in 2 weeks to queries. Responds in 1 month to mss. Sample copy free. artsperspective.com/submissions.php.

PHOTOS Send photos. Identification of subjects, model releases required. Reviews GIF/JPEG files. Offers $15-25 per photo.

POETRY Needs avant-garde, free verse, haiku, light verse, traditional. Buys 4 poems/year. Submit maximum 3 poems. Length: 4-45 lines.

$$ STEAMBOAT MAGAZINE

100 Park Ave., Suite 209, Steamboat Springs CO 80487. (970)871-9413. Fax: (970)871-1922. E-mail: info@steamboatmagazine.com. Website: steamboatmagazine.com. **Contact:** Deborah Olsen. **80% freelance written.** Quarterly magazine showcasing the history, people, lifestyles, and interests of Northwest Colorado. Our readers are generally well-educated, well-traveled, upscale, active people visiting our region to ski in winter and recreate in summer. They come from all 50 states and many foreign countries. Writing should be fresh, entertaining, and informative. Estab. 1978. Circ. 20,000. Byline given. Pays 50% on acceptance, 50% on publication. Submit seasonal material 1 year in advance. Accepts queries by mail, e-mail, fax, phone. Responds in 3 months to queries. Sample copy for $5.95 and SAE with 10 first-class stamps. Guidelines free.

NONFICTION Needs book excerpts, essays, general interest, historical, humor, interview, photo feature, travel. **Buys 10-15 mss/year.** Query with published clips. Length: 150-1,500 words. **Pays $50-300 for as-**

signed articles. Sometimes pays expenses of writers on assignment.

PHOTOS Contact: Corey Copischke. Prefers to review viewing platforms, JPEGs, and dupes. Will request original transparencies when needed. State availability. Captions, identification of subjects required. Pays $50-250/photo.

⊕ TELLURIDE MAGAZINE

Big Earth Publishing, Inc., P.O. Box 964, Telluride CO 81435-0964. (970)728-4245. Fax: (970)728-4302. E-mail: duffy@telluridemagazine.com. Website: telluridemagazine.com. **Contact:** Mary Duffy, editor-in-chief. 75. Telluride: community, events, recreation, ski resort, surrounding region, San Juan Mountains, history, tourism, mountain living. "*Telluride Magazine* speaks specifically to Telluride and the surrounding mountain environment. Telluride is a resort town supported by the ski industry in winter, festivals in summer, outdoor recreation year round and the unique lifestyle all of that affords. As a National Historic Landmark District with a colorful mining history, it weaves a tale that readers seek out. The local/visitor interaction is key to Telluride's success in making profiles an important part of the content. Telluriders are an environmentally minded and progressive bunch who appreciate efforts toward sustainability and protecting the natural landscape and wilderness that are the region's number one draw." Estab. 1982. Circ. 70,000. Byline given. Pays 60 days from publication. $50 Editorial lead time and advance on seasonal subs is 6 months. Accepts queries by e-mail. Responds in 2 weeks on queries; 2 months on mss. Sample copy online at website. Guidelines by e-mail.

NONFICTION Needs historical, humor, nostalgic, personal experience, photo feature, travel, recreation, lifestyle. No articles about places or adventures other than Telluride. **Buys 10 mss/year.** Query with published clips. 1,000-2,000 words. **$200-700 for assigned articles; $100-700 for unsolicited articles.** Does not pay expenses.

PHOTOS Send no more than 20 jpeg comps (low-ers) via e-mail or send CD/DVD with submission. Reviews JPEG/TIFF files. Offers $35-300 per photo; negotiates payment individually.

COLUMNS Telluride Turns (news and current topics); Mountain Health (health issues related to mountain sports, and living at altitude); Nature Notes (explores the flora, fauna, geology and climate of San Juan Mountains); Green Bytes (sustainable & environmentally sound ideas and products for home building), all 500 words. **Buys Buys 40/year mss/year.** Query. **Pays $50-200.**

FICTION "Please contact us; we are very specific about what we will accept." Needs adventure, historical, humorous, slice-of-life vignettes, western, recreation in the mountains. **Buys 2 mss/year.** Query with published clips. 800-1,200 words.

POETRY Needs any poetry; must reflect mountains or mountain living. Buys 1/year poems/year. 3 lines/min. Open/max. **Pays up to to $100.**

FILLERS anecdotes, facts, short humor. **Buys seldom buys fillers. mss/year.** 300-1,000 words. **Pays up to $500.**

CONNECTICUT

⊕ⓈⓈⓈ CONNECTICUT MAGAZINE

Journal Register Co., 35 Nutmeg Dr., Trumbull CT 06611. (203)380-6600. Fax: (203)380-6610. E-mail: cmonagan@connecticutmag.com. Website: connecticutmag.com. **Contact:** Dale Salm. **75% freelance written. "Prefers to work with published/established writers who know the state and live/have lived here.** Monthly magazine for an affluent, sophisticated, suburban audience. We want only articles that pertain to living in Connecticut.". Estab. 1971. Circ. 93,000. Byline given. Pays on publication. Offers 20% kill fee. Publishes ms an average of 4 months after acceptance. Submit seasonal material 4 months in advance. Accepts queries by mail, e-mail, fax. Responds in 6 weeks to queries. Guidelines for #10 SASE.

NONFICTION Needs book excerpts, expose, general interest, interview, topics of service to Connecticut readers. Special issues: Dining/entertainment, northeast/travel, home/garden and Connecticut bride twice/year. Also, business (January) and healthcare 4-6x/year. No personal essays. **Buys 50 mss/year.** Query with published clips. 3,000 words maximum. **Pays $600-1,200.** Sometimes pays expenses of writers on assignment.

PHOTOS Send photos. Identification of subjects, model releases required. Reviews contact sheets, transparencies. Pays $50 minimum/photo.

COLUMNS Business, Health, Politics, Connecticut Calendar, Arts, Dining Out, Gardening, Environment, Education, People, Sports, Media, From the Field (quirky, interesting regional stories with broad

appeal). Length: 1,500-2,500 words. **Buys 50 mss/year.** Query with published clips. **Pays $400-700.**
FILLERS Short pieces about Connecticut trends, curiosities, interesting short subjects, etc. Length: 150-400 words. **Pays $75-150.**

DELAWARE

$$ DELAWARE TODAY

3301 Lancaster Pike, Suite 5C, Wilmington DE 19805. (302)656-1809. Fax: (302)656-5843. E-mail: editors@delawaretoday.com. Website: delawaretoday.com. **50% freelance written.** Monthly magazine geared toward Delaware people, places and issues. All stories must have Delaware slant. No pitches such as Delawareans will be interested in a national topic. Estab. 1962. Circ. 25,000. Byline given. Pays on publication. Offers 50% kill fee. Publishes ms an average of 4 months after acceptance. Editorial lead time 3 months. Submit seasonal material 6 months in advance. Responds in 2 months to queries. Sample copy for $2.95.
NONFICTION Needs historical, interview, photo feature, lifestyles, issues. Special issues: Newcomer's Guide to Delaware. **Buys 40 mss/year.** Query with published clips. Length: 100-3,000 words. **Pays $50-750.** Sometimes pays expenses of writers on assignment.
PHOTOS State availability. Identification of subjects required. Negotiates payment individually.
COLUMNS Business, Health, History, People, all 1,500 words. **Buys 24 mss/year.** Query with published clips. **Pays $150-250.**
FILLERS Needs anecdotes, newsbreaks, short humor. **Buys 10 mss/year.** Length: 100-200 words. **Pays $50-75.**

FLORIDA

$$ EMERALD COAST MAGAZINE

Rowland Publishing, Inc., 1932 Miccosukee Rd., Tallahassee FL 32308. (850)878-0554. Fax: (850)656-1871. E-mail: editorial@rowlandinc.com. Website: emeraldcoastmagazine.com. **25% freelance written.** Bimonthly magazine. Lifestyle publication celebrating life on Florida's Emerald Coast. All content has an Emerald Coast (Northwest Florida) connection. This includes Sandestin, Destin, Fort Walton Beach. Estab. 2000. Circ. 18,000. Byline given. Pays on acceptance. Publishes ms an average of 3 months after acceptance. Editorial lead time 4 months. Submit seasonal material 6 months in advance. Accepts queries by mail, e-mail. Accepts simultaneous submissions. Responds in 3 months to queries. Responds in 3 months to mss. Sample copy for $4. Guidelines by e-mail.
NONFICTION Needs essays, historical, inspirational, interview, new product, personal experience, photo feature. No fiction, poetry, or travel. No general interest—be Northwest Florida specific. **Buys 5 mss/year.** Query with published clips. Length: 1,800-2,000 words. **Pays $100-250.**
PHOTOS Send photos. Captions, identification of subjects, model releases required. Reviews prints, GIF/JPEG files. Negotiates payment individually.

$ FT. MYERS MAGAZINE

And Pat, LLC, 15880 Summerlin Rd., Suite 189, Fort Myers FL 33908. E-mail: ftmyers@optonline.net. Website: ftmyersmagazine.com. **90% freelance written.** Bi-monthly magazine covering regional arts and living for educated, active, successful and creative residents of Lee & Collier counties (FL) and guests at resorts and hotels in Lee County. "Content: Arts, entertainment, media, travel, sports, health, home, garden, environmental issues." Estab. 2001. Circ. 20,000. Byline given. 30 days after publication. Publishes ms an average of 2-6 months after acceptance. Editorial lead time 2-4 months. Submit seasonal material 2-4 months in advance. Accepts queries by e-mail. Accepts simultaneous submissions. Responds in 3 months to queries and to mss. Guidelines available online.
NONFICTION Needs essays, general interest, historical, how-to, humor, interview, personal experience, reviews, previews, news, informational. **Buys 10-25 mss/year.** Send complete ms. Length: 750-1,500 words. **Pays $50-150 or approximately 10¢/word.** Sometimes pays expenses of writers on assignment.
PHOTOS State availability of or send photos. Captions, identification of subjects required. Negotiates payment individually; generally offers $25-100/photo or art.
COLUMNS Media: books, music, video, film, theater, Internet, software (news, previews, reviews, interviews, profiles), 750-1,500 words. Lifestyles: art & design, science & technology, house & garden, health & wellness, sports & recreation, travel & leisure, food & drink (news, interviews, previews, reviews, profiles, advice), 750-1,500 words. **Buys 60 mss/year. mss/year.**

Query with or without published clips or send complete ms. **Pays $50-150.**

💲💲 TALLAHASSEE MAGAZINE

Rowland Publishing, Inc., 1932 Miccosukee Rd., Tallahassee FL 32308. E-mail: editorial@rowlandpublishing.com. Website: rowlandpublishing.com. **20% freelance written.** Bimonthly magazine covering life in Florida's Capital Region. All content has a Tallahassee, Florida connection. Estab. 1978. Circ. 18,000. Byline given. Pays on acceptance. Publishes ms an average of 2 months after acceptance. Editorial lead time 4 months. Submit seasonal material 6 months in advance. Accepts queries by mail, e-mail. Accepts simultaneous submissions. Responds in 3 months to queries & mss. Sample copy for $4. Guidelines by e-mail.

NONFICTION Needs book excerpts, essays, historical, inspirational, interview, new product, personal experience, photo feature, travel, sports, business, Calendar items. No fiction, poetry, or travel. No general interest. **Buys 15 mss/year.** Query with published clips. Length: 500-2,500 words. **Pays $100-350.**

PHOTOS Send photos. Captions, identification of subjects, model releases required. Reviews prints, GIF/JPEG files. Negotiates payment individually.

➕💲💲 WHERE MAGAZINE (WHERE GUESTBOOK, WHERE MAP, WHERE NEWSLETTER)

Morris Visitor Publications, 7300 Corporate Center Dr., Suite 303, Miami FL 33126. Fax: (305)892-1005. E-mail: irene.moore@wheremagazine.com. Website: wheretraveler.com. **40% freelance written.** Monthly magazine covering Miami tourism. We cover Miami only. We are a tourism guide, so features are only about where to go and what to do in Miami. Writers must be very familiar with Miami. Estab. 1936. Circ. 30,000. Byline for features only, but all writers listed on masthead. Pays on publication. Editorial lead time 3 months. Submit seasonal material 3 months in advance. Accepts queries by mail, e-mail. Responds in 1 week to queries Sample copy available online. Guidelines by e-mail.

NONFICTION Needs new product, photo feature, travel, (in Miami). **Buys 0 mss/year.** Query. Length: 500 words.

PHOTOS Send photos. Captions, identification of subjects, model releases required. Reviews GIF/JPEG files. Negotiates payment individually.

COLUMNS Dining; Entertainment; Museums & Attractions; Art Galleries; Shops & Services; Navigating around Miami, 50 words. Queries for writer clips only per page of 1 blurbs per page.

GENERAL REGIONAL

💲💲 BLUE RIDGE COUNTRY

Leisure Publishing, 3424 Brambleton Ave., Roanoke VA 24018. (540)989-6138. Fax: (540)989-7603. E-mail: krheinheimer@leisurepublishing.com. Website: leisurepublishing.com; blueridgecountry.com. **Contact:** Kurt Rheinheimer, editor. **90% freelance written.** Bimonthly, full-color magazine embracing the feel and spirit of the Blue Ridge region, the traditions and recipes, the husbandry and farming, the country stores and bed-and-breakfast inns, the things to visit and learn about—everything that will allow and encourage the reader to take a trip home for the weekend even if he or she has never lived in the region. "The magazine is designed to celebrate the history, heritage and beauty of the Blue Ridge region. It is aimed at adult, upscale readers who enjoy living or traveling in the mountain regions of Virginia, North Carolina, West Virginia, Maryland, Kentucky, Tennessee, South Carolina, Alabama, and Georgia." Estab. 1988. Circ. 425,000. Byline given. Pays on publication. Offers kill fee. Offers $50 kill fee for commissioned pieces only. Publishes ms an average of 8 months after acceptance. Submit seasonal material 6 months in advance. Accepts queries by mail, e-mail, fax; prefer e-mail. Responds in 3-4 months to queries. Responds in 2 months to mss. Sample copy for 9×12 SAE with 6 first-class stamps. Guidelines available online.

NONFICTION Needs essays, general interest, historical, personal experience, photo feature, travel, The photo essay will continue to be part of each issue, but for the foreseeable future will be a combination of book and gallery/museum exhibit previews, and also essays of work by talented individual photographers—though we cannot pay, this is a good option for those who are interested in editorial coverage of their work. Those essays will include short profile, web link and contact information, with the idea of getting them, their work and their business directly in front of 425,000 readers' e. **Buys 25-30 mss/year.** Send complete ms. Length: 200-1,500 words. **Pays $50-250.**

PHOTOS Photos must be shot in region. Outline of region can be found online. Send photos. Identification of subjects required. Reviews transparencies. Pays $40-150 for color inside photo; pays $150 for color cover. Pays on publication. Credit line given.

COLUMNS Inns and Getaways (reviews of inns); Mountain Delicacies (cookbooks and recipes); Country Roads (shorts on regional news, people, destinations, events, history, antiques, books); Inns and Getaways (reviews of inns); On the Mountainside (first-person outdoor recreation pieces excluding hikes). **Buys 30-42 mss/year.** Query. **Pays $25-125.**

$ MIDWEST LIVING

Meredith Corp., 1716 Locust St., Des Moines IA 50309-3038. (515)284-3000. Fax: (515)284-3836. E-mail: midwestliving@meredith.com. Website: midwestliving.com. Bimonthly magazine covering Midwestern families. Regional service magazine that celebrates the interest, values, and lifestyles of Midwestern families. Estab. 1987. Circ. 915,000. Pays on acceptance. Editorial lead time 6 months. Accepts queries by mail, e-mail. Sample copy for $3.95. Guidelines by e-mail.

NONFICTION Needs general interest, good eating, festivals and fairs, historical, interesting slices of Midwestern history, customs, traditions and the people who preserve them, interview, towns, neighborhoods, families,people whose stories exemplify the Midwest spirit an values, travel, Midwestern destinations with emphasis on the fun and affordable. Query.

PHOTOS State availability.

⊘ SOUTHCOMM PUBLISHING COMPANY, INC.

541 Buttermilk Pike, Suite 100, Crescent Springs KY 41017. (678)624-1075. Fax: (678)623-9979. E-mail: cwwalker@southcomm.com. Website: southcomm.com. "Our magazines primarily are used as marketing and economic development pieces, but they are also used as tourism guides and a source of information for newcomers. As such, our editorial supplies entertaining and informative reading for those visiting the communities for the first time, as well as those who have lived in the area for any period of time. We are looking for writers who are interested in writing dynamic copy about Georgia, Tennessee, South Carolina, North Carolina, Alabama, Virginia, Florida, Pennsylvania, Texas, and many other states." Estab. 1985. Byline given. Pays 30 days after acceptance. Publishes ms an average of 1-2 months after acceptance. Accepts queries by mail, e-mail, fax. Sample copy and writer's guidelines free.

NONFICTION "We are not looking for article submissions. We will assign stories to writers in which we're interested. Queries should include samples of published works and biographical information." **Buys 50+ mss/year.** Quer or send complete ms. Length: 100-1,000 words. **Pays $25-200.**

THE OXFORD AMERICAN

201 Donaghey Ave., Main 107, Conway AR 72035. (501)450-5376. Fax: (501)450-3490. E-mail: info@oxfordamerican.org. Website: oxfordamerican.org. Warwick Sabin, Publisher. **Contact:** Carol Ann Fitzgerald, Man. Editor, Wes Enzinna, Assoc. Editor. Quarterly literary magazine from the South with a national audience. Circ. 20,000. Pays on publication. Accepts queries by mail. NoResponds in 2-3 months or sooner to mss. Guidelines available online at oxfordamerican.org/pages/submission-guidelines.

> 💬 "*The Oxford American* will consider only unpublished mss that are from and/or about the South. Especially interested in nonfiction from diverse perspectives. Considers excerpts from forthcoming books."

NONFICTION Needs short and long essays (500 to 3,000 words), general interest, how-to, humor, personal experience, travel, reporting, business. Query with SASE or send complete ms.

PHOTOS Uses photos for the cover and throughout issue. Also uses illustration, original art, and comics. Send photos. Reviews contact sheets, GIF/JPEG files, slides.

COLUMNS Odes, Travel, Politics, Business, Writing on Writing, Southerner Abroad, Reports, Literature.

FICTION Stories should be from or about the South. Send complete ms.

POETRY Poems should be from or about the South. Submit maximum 3-5 poems.

GEORGIA

$$ GEORGIA MAGAZINE

Georgia Electric Membership Corp., P.O. Box 1707, Tucker GA 30085. (770)270-6951. Fax: (770)270-6995. E-mail: aorowski@georgiaemc.com. Website: georgiamagazine.org. **50% freelance written**. We are a monthly magazine for and about Georgians, with a friendly, conversational tone and human interest topics. Estab. 1945. Circ. 509,000. Byline given. Pays on publication. Publishes ms an average of 6 months after acceptance. Editorial lead time 2 months. Submit seasonal material 6 months in advance. Accepts simultaneous submissions. Responds in 1 month to subjects of interest. Sample copy for $2. Guidelines for #10 SASE, or by e-mail.

NONFICTION Needs general interest, Georgia-focused, historical, how-to, in the home and garden, humor, inspirational, interview, photo feature, travel. Query with published clips. 1,000-1,200 words; 800 words for smaller features and departments. **Pays $350-500.**

PHOTOS State availability. Identification of subjects, model releases required. Reviews digital images, websites and prints. Negotiates payment individually.

$$ POINTS NORTH MAGAZINE

All Points Interactive Media Corp., 568 Peachtree Pkwy., Cumming GA 30041-6820. (770)844-0969. Fax: (770)844-0968. E-mail: julie@ptsnorth.com. Website: ptsnorth.com. **15% freelance written.** Monthly magazine covering lifestyle (regional). *Points North* is a first-class lifestyle magazine for affluent residents of suburban communities in north metro Atlanta. Estab. 2000. Circ. 81,000. Byline given. Pays on publication. Offers negotiable (for assigned articles only) kill fee. Publishes ms an average of 3 months after acceptance. Editorial lead time 3 months. Submit seasonal material 6 months in advance. Accepts queries by e-mail only. Responds in 6-8 weeks to queries. Responds in 6-8 months to mss. Sample copy for $3.

NONFICTION Contact: Managing Editor. Needs general interest, only topics pertaining to Atlanta area, historical, interview, travel. **Buys 50-60 mss/year.** Query with published clips. Length: 1,200-2,500 words. **Pays $250-500.**

PHOTOS "We do not accept photos until article acceptance. Do not send photos with query.". State availability. Captions, identification of subjects, model releases required. Reviews slide transparencies, 4×6 prints, GIF/JPEG files. Offers no additional payment for photos accepted with ms.

$$ SAVANNAH MAGAZINE

Morris Publishing Group, P.O. Box 1088, Savannah GA 31402-1088. Fax: (912)525-0611. E-mail: linda.wittish@savannahnow.com. Website: savannahmagazine.com. **95% freelance written.** Bimonthly magazine focusing on homes and entertaining covering coastal lifestyle of Savannah and South Carolina area. "*Savannah Magazine* publishes articles about people, places and events of interest to the residents of the greater Savannah areas, as well as coastal Georgia and the South Carolina low country. We strive to provide our readers with information that is both useful and entertaining—written in a lively, readable style." Estab. 1990. Circ. 16,000. Byline given. Pays on publication. Offers 20% kill fee. Publishes ms an average of 2 months after acceptance. Editorial lead time 2 months. Submit seasonal material 4 months in advance. Accepts queries by mail, e-mail, fax. Accepts simultaneous submissions. Responds in 4 weeks to queries. Responds in 6 weeks to mss. Sample copy free. Guidelines by e-mail.

NONFICTION Needs general interest, historical, humor, interview, travel. Does not want fiction or poetry. Query with published clips. Length: 500-750 words. **Pays $250-450.**

PHOTOS Contact: Contact Michelle Karner, art director. State availability. Reviews GIF/JPEG files. Negotiates payment individually. Offers no additional payment for photos accepted with ms.

HAWAII

$$$ HONOLULU MAGAZINE

PacificBasin Communications, 1000 Bishop St., Suite 405, Honolulu HI 96813. (808)537-9500. Fax: (808)537-6455. E-mail: akamn@honolulumagazine.com; kathrynw@honolulumagazine.com. Website: honolulumagazine.com. **Contact:** A. Kam Napier, editor; Kathryn Drury Wagner, executive editor. **Prefers to work with published/established writers.** Monthly magazine covering general interest topics relating to Hawaii residents. Estab. 1888. Circ. 30,000. Byline given. Pays about 30 days after publication. Where appropriate, kill fee of half of assignment fee. Accepts queries by mail, e-mail. Guidelines available online.

NONFICTION Needs historical, interview, sports, politics, lifestyle trends, all Hawaii-related. "We write for Hawaii residents, so travel articles about Hawaii are not appropriate." Send complete ms. determined when assignments discussed. **Pays $250-1,200.** Sometimes pays expenses of writers on assignment.

PHOTOS Contact: Kristin Lipman, art director. State availability. Captions, identification of subjects, model releases required. Pays $100 for stock, $200 for assigned shot. Package rates also negotiated.

COLUMNS Length determined when assignments discussed. Query with published clips or send complete ms. **Pays $100-300.**

IDAHO

$$ SUN VALLEY MAGAZINE

Valley Publishing, LLC, 111 1st Ave. N. #1M, Meriwether Building, Hailey ID 83333. (208)788-0770. Fax: (208)788-3881. E-mail: edit@sunvalleymag.com. Website: sunvalleymag.com. **95% freelance written.** Quarterly magazine covering the lifestyle of the Sun Valley area. *Sun Valley Magazine* presents the lifestyle of the Sun Valley area and the Wood River Valley, including recreation, culture, profiles, history and the arts. Estab. 1973. Circ. 17,000. Byline given. Pays on publication. Publishes ms an average of 5 months after acceptance. Editorial lead time 1 year. Submit seasonal material 14 months in advance. Accepts queries by mail. Accepts simultaneous submissions. Responds in 5 weeks to queries. Responds in 2 months to mss. Sample copy for $4.95 and $3 postage. Guidelines for #10 SASE.

NONFICTION Needs historical, interview, photo feature, travel. Special issues: Sun Valley home design and architecture, Spring; Sun Valley weddings/wedding planner, summer. Query with published clips. **Pays $40-500.** Sometimes pays expenses of writers on assignment.

REPRINTS Only occasionally purchases reprints.

PHOTOS State availability. Identification of subjects, model releases required. Reviews transparencies. Offers $60-275/photo.

COLUMNS Conservation issues, winter/summer sports, health & wellness, mountain-related activities and subjects, home (interior design), garden. All columns must have a local slant. Query with published clips. **Pays $40-300.**

ILLINOIS

$$$$ CHICAGO MAGAZINE

435 N. Michigan Ave., Suite 1100, Chicago IL 60611. (312)222-8999. E-mail: stritsch@chicagomag.com. Website: chicagomag.com. Richard Babcock, editor. **Contact:** Shane Tritsch, managing editor. **50% freelance written. Prefers to work with published/established writers.** Monthly magazine for an audience which is 95% from Chicago area; 90% college educated; upper income, overriding interests in the arts, politics, dining, good life in the city and suburbs. Most are in 25-50 age bracket, well-read and articulate. "Produced by the city's best magazine editors and writers, Chicago Magazine is the definitive voice on top dining, entertainment, shopping and real estate in the region. It also offers provocative narrative stories and topical features that have won numerous awards. Chicago Magazine reaches 1.5 million readers and is published by Tribune Company." Estab. 1968. Circ. 182,000. Pays on acceptance. Publishes ms an average of 3 months after acceptance. Submit seasonal material 4 months in advance. Accepts queries by mail, e-mail. Responds in 1 month to queries. For sample copy, send $3 to Circulation Department. Guidelines for #10 SASE.

NONFICTION Needs expose, humor, personal experience, think pieces, profiles, spot news, historical articles. Does not want anything about events outside the city or profiles on people who no longer live in the city. **Buys 100 mss/year.** Query; indicate specifics, knowledge of city and market, and demonstrable access to sources. Length: 200-6,000 words. **Pays $100-3,000 and up.** Pays expenses of writers on assignment.

PHOTOS Usually assigned separately, not acquired from writers. Reviews 35mm transparencies, color and b&w glossy prints.

$$$$ CHICAGO READER

Chicago Reader, Inc., 11 E. Illinois St., Chicago IL 60611. (312)828-0350. Fax: (312)828-9926. E-mail: mail@chicagoreader.com. Website: chicagoreader.com. **50% freelance written.** Weekly Alternative tabloid for Chicago. Estab. 1971. Circ. 120,000. Byline given. Pays on publication. Occasional kill fee. Publishes ms an average of 2 weeks after acceptance. Editorial lead time up to 6 months. Accepts queries by mail, e-mail, fax. Accepts simultaneous submissions. Responds if interested. Sample copy free. Writer's guidelines free or online.

NONFICTION Buys 500 mss/year. Send complete ms. Length: 250-2,500 words. **Pays $100-3,000.** Sometimes pays expenses of writers on assignment.

REPRINTS Occasionally accepts previously published submissions.

COLUMNS Local color, 500-2,500 words; arts and entertainment reviews, up to 1,200 words.

$$ CHICAGO SCENE MAGAZINE

233 E. Erie, Suite 603, Chicago IL 60611. Fax: (312)587-7397. E-mail: e-mail@chicago-scene.com. Website: chicago-scene.com. **95% freelance written.** Monthly magazine covering dining, nightlife, travel, beauty, entertainment, fitness, style, drinks. *Chicago Scene Magazine* is the premier news and entertainment publication for Chicago's young professional. Estab. 2001. Byline given. Pays on publication. Publishes ms an average of 2 months after acceptance. Submit seasonal material 3 months in advance. Accepts queries by e-mail. Sample copy available online. Guidelines free.

NONFICTION Needs how-to, interview, new product, travel. Does not want personal experiences, essays, technical. Query with published clips. Length: 600-2,400 words. **Pays $25-250.**

COLUMNS Beauty, 840 words; Dining, 1,260-1,680 words; Drinks, 1,260-1,680 words; Fitness, 420-630 words; Travel, 1,260-1,680 words; Nightlife, 1,050-1,680 words; Personal Style, 420 words. Query with published clips. **Pays $25-250.**

$ ILLINOIS ENTERTAINER

4223 W. Lake Street, Suite 420, Chicago IL 60624. (773)533-9333. Fax: (312)922-9341. E-mail: ieeditors@aol.com. Website: illinoisentertainer.com. **80% freelance written.** Monthly free magazine covering popular and alternative music, as well as other entertainment: film, media. Estab. 1974. Circ. 55,000. Byline given. Pays on publication. Offers 50% kill fee. Publishes ms an average of 2 months after acceptance. Editorial lead time 2 months. Submit seasonal material 2 months in advance. Accepts queries by mail. Accepts simultaneous submissions. Responds in 2 months to queries. Sample copy for $5.

NONFICTION Needs expose, how-to, humor, interview, new product, reviews. No personal, confessional, inspirational articles. **Buys 75 mss/year.** Query with published clips. Length: 600-2,600 words. **Pays $15-160.** Sometimes pays expenses of writers on assignment.

REPRINTS Send typed manuscript with rights for sale noted and information about when and where the material previously appeared. Pays 100% of amount paid for an original article.

PHOTOS Send photos. Captions, identification of subjects, model releases required. Reviews contact sheets, transparencies, 5×7 prints. Offers $20-200/photo.

COLUMNS Spins (LP reviews), 100-400 words. **Buys 200-300 mss/year.** Query with published clips. **Pays $8-25.**

$ MIDWESTERN FAMILY MAGAZINE

P.O. Box 9302, Peoria IL 61612. (309)679-9539; (309)303-7309. E-mail: jrudd@midwesternfamily.com. Website: midwesternfamily.com. **90% freelance written.** Bimonthly magazine covering family living in Central Illinois. *Midwestern Family* is a comprehensive guide to fun, health and happiness for Central Illinois families. Estab. 2003. Circ. 23,000. Byline given. Pays on publication. Publishes ms an average of 2 months after acceptance. Editorial lead time 4-6 weeks. Submit seasonal material 4-6 weeks in advance. Accepts queries by e-mail, online submission form. Responds in 2 weeks to queries. Responds in 4 months to mss. Sample copy for $1.50. Guidelines by e-mail.

NONFICTION Query. Length: 1,000-1,500 words. **Pays $100.** Sometimes pays expenses of writers on assignment.

PHOTOS State availability. Identification of subjects, model releases required. Reviews GIF/JPEG files. Negotiates payment individually.

COLUMNS Home; Fun; Life; Food; Health; Discovery, all 1,000-1,250 words. **Buys 40 mss/year.** Query. **Pays $100.**

$$ NEWCITY

New City Communications, Inc., 770 N. Halsted, Chicago IL 60622. (312)243-8786. Fax: (312)243-8802. Website: newcitychicago.com. **50% freelance written.** Weekly magazine. Estab. 1986. Circ. 50,000. Byline given. Pays 2-12 months after publication. Offers kill fee. Offers 20% kill fee in certain cases. Publishes ms an average of 1 month after acceptance. Editorial lead time 2 months. Submit seasonal material 2 months in advance. Responds in 1 month to mss. Sample copy for $3. For contact and guidelines, see: newcitynetwork.com/editorialart/contributing-to-newcity-guidelines-for-writers-artists-and-photographers/.

NONFICTION Needs essays, exposè, general interest, interview, personal experience, travel, related to traveling from Chicago and other issues particularly affecting travelers from this area, service. **Buys 100 mss/year.** Query by e-mail only Length: 100-4,000 words. **Pays $10-200.** Rarely pays expenses of writers on assignment.

PHOTOS State availability. Captions, identification of subjects, model releases required. Reviews contact sheets.

COLUMNS Lit (literary supplement), 300-2,000 words; Music, Film, Arts (arts criticism), 150-800 words; Chow (food writing), 300-2,000 words. **Buys 50 mss/year.** Query by e-mail **Pays $15-300.**

⊖⊛ NORTHWEST QUARTERLY MAGAZINE

Hughes Media Inc., 728 N. Prospect St., Rockford IL 61101. Fax: (815)316-2301. E-mail: janine@northwestquarterly.com. Website: northwestquarterly.com. **80% freelance written.** Quarterly magazine covering regional lifestyle of Northern Illinois and Southern Wisconsin, and also Kane and McHenry counties (Chicago collar counties), highlighting strengths of living and doing business in the area. Estab. 2004. Circ. 42,000. Byline given. Pays on publication. Publishes ms an average of 4-6 months after acceptance. Editorial lead time 6 months. Submit seasonal material 6 months in advance. Accepts queries by mail, e-mail. Responds in 2 weeks to queries. Responds in 2 months to mss. Sample copy and guidelines by e-mail.

NONFICTION Needs historical, interview, photo feature, regional features. Does not want opinion, fiction, anything unrelated to our geographic region. **Buys 150 mss/year.** Query. Length: 700-2,500 words. **Pays $25-500.** Sometimes pays expenses of writers on assignment.

PHOTOS State availability. Captions required. Reviews GIF/JPEG files. Negotiates payment individually.

COLUMNS Health & Fitness, 1,000-2,000 words; Home & Garden, 1,500 words; Destinations & Recreation, 1,000-2,000 words; Environment & Nature, 2,000-3,000 words. **Buys 120 mss/year.** Query. **Pays $100-500.**

⊖⊛ OUTDOOR ILLINOIS

Illinois Department of Natural Resources, P.O. Box 19225, Dept. NL, Springfield IL 62794-9225. (217)785-4193. E-mail: dnr.editor@illinois.gov. Website: dnr.state.il.us/oi. **25% freelance written.** Monthly magazine covering Illinois cultural and natural resources. *Outdoor Illinois* promotes outdoor activities, Illinois State parks, Illinois natural and cultural resources. Estab. 1973. Circ. 30,000. Byline given. Pays on acceptance. Editorial lead time 4 months. Submit seasonal material 1 year in advance. Accepts queries by mail, e-mail. Responds in 2 weeks to queries. Sample copy free. Guidelines by e-mail.

NONFICTION Needs historical, how-to, humor, interview, photo feature, travel. Does not want first person unless truly has something to say. Query

with published clips. Length: 350-1,500 words. **Pays $100-250.**

PHOTOS Contact: Contact Adele Hodde, photography manager. Captions, identification of subjects, model releases required. Reviews contact sheets, GIF/JPEG files. Negotiates payment individually.

⊖⊛ WEST SUBURBAN LIVING

C2 Publishing, Inc., P.O. Box 111, Elmhurst IL 60126. (630)834-4995. Fax: (630)834-4996. Website: westsuburbanliving.net. **Contact:** Chuck Cozette, Editor. **80% freelance written.** Bimonthly magazine focusing on the western suburbs of Chicago. Estab. 1996. Circ. 25,000. Byline given. Pays on publication. Publishes ms an average of 2-4 months after acceptance. Accepts queries by mail, e-mail, fax. NoSample copy available online.

NONFICTION Needs general interest, how-to, travel. "Does not want anything that does not have an angle or tie-in to the area we cover—Chicago's western suburbs." **Buys 15 mss/year. Pays $100-500.** Sometimes pays expenses of writers on assignment.

PHOTOS State availability. Model releases required. Offers $50-700/photo; negotiates payment individually.

INDIANA

⊖⊛ EVANSVILLE LIVING

Tucker Publishing Group, 223 NW Second St., Suite 200, Evansville IN 47708. (812)426-2115. Fax: (812)426-2134. Website: evansvilleliving.com. **80-100% freelance written.** Bimonthly magazine covering Evansville, Indiana, and the greater area. *Evansville Living* is the only full-color, glossy, 100+ page city magazine for the Evansville, Indiana, area. Regular departments include: Home Style, Garden Style, Day Tripping, Sporting Life, and Local Flavor (menus). Estab. 2000. Circ. 50,000. Byline given. Pays on acceptance. Publishes ms an average of 3 months after acceptance. Editorial lead time 6 months. Submit seasonal material 6 months in advance. Accepts queries by mail, e-mail, fax. Sample copy for $5 or online. Guidelines for free or by e-mail.

NONFICTION Needs essays, general interest, historical, photo feature, travel. **Buys 60-80 mss/year.** Query with published clips. Length: 200-2,000 words. **Pays $100-300.** Sometimes pays expenses of writers on assignment.

PHOTOS State availability. Captions, identification of subjects required. Reviews contact sheets, negatives, transparencies, prints. Negotiates payment individually.

COLUMNS Home Style (home); Garden Style (garden); Sporting Life (sports); Local Flavor (menus), all 1,500 words. Query with published clips. **Pays $100-300.**

💲💲💲 INDIANAPOLIS MONTHLY

Emmis Publishing Corp., 1 Emmis Plaza, 40 Monument Circle,, Suite 100, Indianapolis IN 46204. (317)237-9288. E-mail: dzivan@indymonthly.emmis.com. Website: indianapolismonthly.com. **30% freelance written. Prefers to work with published/established writers.** "*Indianapolis Monthly* attracts and enlightens its upscale, well-educated readership with bright, lively editorial on subjects ranging from personalities to social issues, fashion to food. Its diverse content and attention to service make it the ultimate source by which the Indianapolis area lives.". Estab. 1977. Circ. 45,000. Byline given. Pays on publication. Offers kill fee. Offers negotiable kill fee. Publishes ms an average of 2 months after acceptance. Editorial lead time 3 months. Submit seasonal material 3 months in advance. Accepts queries by mail, e-mail. Responds in 6 weeks to queries. Sample copy for $6.10.

> 💭 "This magazine is using more first-person essays, but they must have a strong Indianapolis or Indiana tie. It will consider nonfiction book excerpts of material relevant to its readers."

NONFICTION Needs book excerpts, by Indiana authors or with strong Indiana ties, essays, expose, general interest, interview, photo feature. No poetry, fiction, or domestic humor; no 'How Indy Has Changed Since I Left Town', 'An Outsider's View of the 500', or generic material with no or little tie to Indianapolis/Indiana. **Buys 35 mss/year.** Query by mail with published clips. Length: 200-3,000 words. **Pays $50-1,000.**

PHOTOS State availability. Captions, identification of subjects, model releases required. Negotiates payment individually.

💲💲 NORTHERN INDIANA LAKES MAGAZINE

1415 W. Coliseum Blvd., Fort Wayne IN 46808. (260)484-0546. Fax: (260)469-0454. E-mail: editor@nilakes.com. Website: nilakes.com. **Contact:** Sue Rawlinson, managing editor. Bimonthly magazine that defines lake living at its best. "*Northern Indiana LAKES Magazine* is the official publication for the good life in northern Indiana. The LAKES country market area is essentially defined as 20 northern Indiana counties: Adams, Allen, DeKalb, Elkhart, Huntington, Jasper, Kosciusko, LaGrange, Lake, LaPorte, Marshall, Newton, Noble, Porter, Pulaski, St. Joseph, Starke, Steuben, Wells and Whitley." Byline given. Pays 2-3 weeks after accepting completed article. Accepts queries by mail. Guidelines by e-mail and online.

NONFICTION Needs general interest, humor, interview, travel. Does not want "personal essays, stories about your vacation, celebrity profiles (with rare exceptions), routine pieces on familiar destinations, completed manuscripts, previously published works." Query with published clips. **Pays 10-50¢/word.**

IOWA

💲💲 THE IOWAN

Pioneer Communications, Inc., 300 Walnut, Suite 6, Des Moines IA 50309. Fax: (515)282-0125. E-mail: editor@iowan.com. Website: iowan.com. **Contact:** Beth Wilson, editor. **75% freelance written.** Bimonthly magazine covering the state of Iowa. "Our mission statement is: To celebrate the people and communities, the history and traditions, and the culture and events of Iowa that make our readers proud of our state." Estab. 1952. Circ. 25,000. Byline given. Pays on acceptance. Offers $100 kill fee. Publishes ms an average of 3 months after acceptance. Editorial lead time 9-10 months. Submit seasonal material 6 months in advance. Accepts queries by mail, e-mail. Responds to queries received twice/year. Sample copy for $4.50 + s&h.

NONFICTION Needs book excerpts, essays, general interest, historical, interview, photo feature, travel. **Buys 30 mss/year.** Query with published clips. Length: 500-1,500 words. **Pays $250-450.** Sometimes pays expenses of writers on assignment.

PHOTOS Send photos. Captions, identification of subjects, model releases required. Reviews contact sheets, GIF/JPEG files (8×10 at 300 dpi min). Negotiates payment individually, according to space rates.

COLUMNS Last Word (essay), 800 words. **Buys 6 mss/year.** Query with published clips. **Pays $100.**

KANSAS

💲💲 KANSAS!

Kansas Department of Commerce, 1000 SW Jackson St., Suite 100, Topeka KS 66612-1354. (785)296-3479. Fax: (785)296-6988. E-mail: ksmagazine@kansas-commerce.com. Website: kansmag.com. **90% freelance written**. Quarterly magazine emphasizing Kansas travel attractions and events. Estab. 1945. Circ. 45,000. Byline and courtesy bylines are given to all content. Pays on acceptance. Purchased content will publish an average of 1 year after acceptance. Submit seasonal material 8 months in advance. Accepts queries by mail. Responds in 2 months to queries. Guidelines available online.

NONFICTION Needs general interest, photo feature, travel. Query by mail. Length: 750-1,250 words. **Pays $200-350.** Mileage reimbursement is available for writers on assignment in the state of Kansas; TBD by assignment editor.

PHOTOS We are a full-color photograph/manuscript publication. Send digital photos (original transparencies only or CD with images available in high resolution) with query. Captions and location of the image (county and city) are required. Pays $25-75 for gallery images, $150 for cover. Assignments also available, welcome queries.

KENTUCKY

💲 BACK HOME IN KENTUCKY

Back Home In Kentucky, Inc., P.O. Box 1555, Shelbyville KY 40066. (502)633-7766. E-mail: bilmatt@aol.com. **Contact:** Bill Mitchell, publisher. **50% freelance written.** "Bimonthly magazine covering Kentucky heritage, people, places, events. We reach Kentuckians and 'displaced' Kentuckians living outside the state.". Estab. 1977. Circ. 8,000. Byline given. Pays on publication. Publishes ms an average of 4-6 months after acceptance. Submit seasonal material 6 months in advance. Responds in 2 months to queries. Sample copy for $3 and 9×12 SAE with $1.23 postage affixed. Guidelines for #10 SASE.

💭 Interested in profiles of Kentucky people and places, especially historic interest.

NONFICTION Needs historical, Kentucky-related eras or profiles, interview, Kentucky residents or natives, photo feature, Kentucky places and events, travel, unusual/little-known Kentucky places, profiles (Kentucky cooks, gardeners, and craftspersons), memories (Kentucky related). No inspirational or religion. No how-to articles. **Buys 20-25 mss/year.** Send complete ms. Length: 500-2,000 words. **Pays $50-200 for assigned articles. Pays $50-100 for unsolicited articles.**

PHOTOS Looking for digital (high resolution) of Kentucky places of interet. Pays $25-$100 per photo. Photo credits given. For inside photos, send photos with submission. Identification of subjects, model releases required. Reviews transparencies, 4×6 prints. Occasionally offers additional payment for photos accepted with ms.

COLUMNS Travel, history, profile, and cookbooks (all Kentucky related), 500-2,000 words. **Buys 10-12 mss/year.** Query with published clips. **Pays $25-50.**

TIPS "We work mostly with unpublished or emerging writers who have a feel for Kentucky's people, places, and events. Areas most open are little known places in Kentucky, unusual history, and profiles of interesting Kentuckians, and Kentuckians with unusual hobbies or crafts."

FORT MITCHELL LIVING

Community Publications, Inc., 179 Fairfield Ave., Bellevue KY 41073. (859)291-1412. Fax: (859)291-1417. E-mail: fortmitchell@livingmagazines.com. Website: livingmagazines.com. **Contact:** Editor. Estab. 1983. Circ. 4,700. Byline given. Pays on publication. Editorial lead time 2 months. Submit seasonal material 3 months in advance. Guidelines by e-mail.

💭 Monthly magazine uses material about the people living in or news about the communities the magazine serves; Fort Mitchell, Fort Wright, Park Hills, Crestview Hills, Villa Hills, Edgewood, Lakeside Park, and Crescent Springs. The magazine does not publish opinion pieces other than those submitted in Letters to the Editor.

NONFICTION Query.

PHOTOS State availability. Captions, identification of subjects, model releases required. Reviews contact sheets, negatives, transparencies, prints, GIF/JPEG files. Negotiates payment individually.

FORT THOMAS LIVING

Community Publications, Inc., 179 Fairfield Ave., Bellevue KY 41073. (859)291-1412. Fax: (859)291-1417. E-mail: fortthomas@livingmagazines.com. Website: livingmagazines.com. **Contact:** Linda Johnson, editor. Monthly magazine covering Fort

Thomas community. "Magazine focuses upon people living and working in Fort Thomas and promoting acitvities of interest to this community." Estab. 1977. Circ. 4,400. Byline given. Pays on publication. Editorial lead time 2 months. Submit seasonal material 3 months in advance. Accepts queries by mail, e-mail. Guidelines by e-mail.

NONFICTION Does not want any material unrelated to Fort Thomas, Kentucky. Query. Prefers e-mail submissions.

💲💲 KENTUCKY LIVING

Kentucky Association of Electric Co-Ops, P.O. Box 32170, Louisville KY 40232. (502)451-2430. Fax: (502)459-1611. E-mail: e-mail@kentuckyliving.com. Website: kentuckyliving.com. **Mostly freelance written. Prefers to work with published/established writers**. Monthly Feature magazine primarily for Kentucky residents. Estab. 1948. Circ. 500,000. Byline given. Pays on acceptance. Publishes ms an average of 12 months after acceptance. Submit seasonal material at least 6 months in advance. Accepts simultaneous submissions. Responds in 1 month to queries. Sample copy for sae with 9×12 envelope and 4 first-class stamps.

NONFICTION Needs , Emphasis on electric industry and ties to Kentucky's electric co-op areas of readership. **Buys 18-24 mss/year.** Send complete ms. **Pays $75-935** Sometimes pays expenses of writers on assignment.

PHOTOS State availability of or send photos. Identification of subjects required. Reviews photo efiles at online link or sent on CD. Payment for photos included in payment for ms.

💲💲 KENTUCKY MONTHLY

P.O. Box 559, Frankfort KY 40602-0559. (502)227-0053; (888)329-0053. Fax: (502)227-5009. E-mail: kymonthly@kentuckymonthly.com; steve@kentuckymonthly.com. Website: kentuckymonthly.com. **Contact:** Stephen Vest, editor. **75% freelance written.** Monthly magazine. "We publish stories about Kentucky and by Kentuckians, including those who live elsewhere." Estab. 1998. Circ. 40,000. Byline given. Pays within 3 months of publication. Publishes ms an average of 3 months after acceptance. Editorial lead time 3 months. Submit seasonal material 4 months in advance. Accepts queries by mail, e-mail, fax. Accepts simultaneous submissions. Responds in 1 month to queries. Responds

in 1 month to mss. Sample copy and writer's guidelines online.

NONFICTION Needs book excerpts, general interest, historical, how-to, humor, interview, photo feature, religious, travel, all with a Kentucky angle. **Buys 60 mss/year.** Query. Length: 300-2,000 words. **Pays $25-350 for assigned articles. Pays $20-100 for unsolicited articles.**

PHOTOS State availability. Captions required. Reviews negatives.

FICTION Needs adventure, historical, mainstream, novel concepts, all Kentucky-related stories. **Buys 10 mss/year.** Query with published clips. Length: 1,000-5,000 words. **Pays $50-100.**

LOUISIANA

➕ 💲💲 PRESERVATION IN PRINT

Preservation Resource Center of New Orleans, 923 Tchoupitoulos St., New Orleans LA 70130. (504)581-7032. Fax: (504)636-3073. E-mail: prc@prcno.org. Website: prcno.org. **30% freelance written.** Monthly magazine covering preservation. We want articles about interest in the historic architecture of New Orleans. Estab. 1974. Circ. 10,000. Byline given. Pays on acceptance. Publishes ms an average of 1 month after acceptance. Editorial lead time 1 month. Submit seasonal material 1-2 months in advance. Accepts queries by mail, e-mail, fax, phone. Accepts simultaneous submissions. Sample copy available online. Guidelines free.

NONFICTION Needs essays, historical, interview, photo feature, technical. **Buys 30 mss/year mss/year.** Query. Length: 700-1,000 words. **Pays $100-200 for assigned articles.** Sometimes pays expenses of writers on assignment.

MAINE

💲 DISCOVER MAINE MAGAZINE

10 Exhcange St., Suite 208, Portland ME 04101. (207)874-7720. Fax: (207)874-7721. E-mail: info@discovermainemagazine.com. Website: discovermainemagazine.com. **100% freelance written.** Monthly magazine covering Maine history and nostalgia. Sports and hunting/fishing topics are also included. Estab. 1992. Circ. 12,000. Byline given. Pays on publication. Publishes ms an average of 2-3 months after acceptance. Editorial lead time 3 months.

Submit seasonal material 3 months in advance. Accepts queries by mail, fax, phone. Accepts simultaneous submissions. Responds in 2 weeks to queries. Responds in 1 month to mss.

NONFICTION Needs historical. Does not want to receive poetry. **Buys 200 mss/year.** Send complete ms. Length: 500-2,000 words. **Pays $20-30**

PHOTOS Send photos. Negotiates payment individually.

MARYLAND

⊖⊖ BALTIMORE MAGAZINE

Inner Harbor E. 1000 Lancaster St., Suite 400, Baltimore MD 21202. (410)752-4200. Fax: (410)625-0280. E-mail: Send correspondence to the appropriate editor. Website: baltimoremagazine.net. Max Weiss—lifestyle, film, sports, general inquiries; Suzanne Loudermilk—Food; Ken Eglehart—business, special editions; John Lewis—arts and culture; Amy Mulvihill—calendar, coming events, party pages. **Contact:** Department Editor. **50-60% freelance written.** Monthly city magazine featuring news, profiles and service articles. "Pieces must address an educated, active, affluent reader and must have a very strong Baltimore angle." Estab. 1907. Circ. 70,000. Byline given. Pays within 1 month of publication. Offers kill fee in some cases Submit seasonal material 4 months in advance. Accepts queries by mail, e-mail (preferred). Sample copy for $4.99. Guidelines available online.

⌐ Unless you already have a great set of feature clips and a powerful idea, the best way to break into *Baltimore* is through the shorter articles that run before and after the features, in the front of the book sections like Up Front, which run from 300-700 words. Another good place to start is our departments beat, such as "Hot Shots" and "Cameo." These stories range from 800 to 2,000 words. To propose one, send a query letter and clips. We generally develop story ideas ourselves and sometimes assign them to freelancers. To be considered for such assignments, send clips and a letter about your specialties.

NONFICTION Needs book excerpts, Baltimore subject or author, essays, expose, general interest, historical, humor, interview, with a Baltimorean, new product, personal experience, photo feature, trav-el, local and regional to Maryland. "Nothing that lacks a strong Baltimore focus or angle. Unsolicited personal essays are almost never accepted. We've printed only two over the past few years; the last was by a 19-year veteran city judge reminiscing on his time on the bench and the odd stories and situations he encountered there. Unsolicited food and restaurant reviews, whether positive or negative, are likewise never accepted." Query by e-mail or mail with published clips or send complete ms. Length: 1,600-2,500 words. **Pays 30-40¢/word.** Sometimes pays expenses.

COLUMNS "The shorter pieces are the best places to break into the magazine." Hot Shot, Health, Education, Sports, Parenting, Politics. Length: 1,000-2,500 words. Query with published clips.

MASSACHUSETTS

⊖⊖ CAPE COD LIFE

Cape Cod Life, Inc., 13 Steeple Street, Ste. 204, P.O. Box 1439, Mashpee MA 02649. (508)419-7381. Fax: (508)477-1225. Website: capecodlife.com. **Contact:** Susan Dewey, managing editor. **80% freelance written.** Magazine published 6 times/year focusing on area lifestyle, history and culture, people and places, business and industry, and issues and answers for year-round and summer residents of Cape Cod, Nantucket, and Martha's Vineyard as well as nonresidents who spend their leisure time here. Cape Cod Life Magazine has become the premier lifestyle magazine for the Cape & Islands, featuring topics ranging from arts and events, history and heritage, beaches and boating as well as a comprehensive resource for planning the perfect vacation. Circ. 45,000. Byline given. Pays 90 days after acceptance. Offers 20% kill fee. Submit seasonal material 6 months in advance. Accepts queries by mail. Responds in 3 months to queries. Responds in 3 months to mss. Sample copy for $5. Guidelines for #10 SASE.

NONFICTION Needs book excerpts, general interest, historical, interview, photo feature, travel, outdoors, gardening, nautical, nature, arts, antiques. **Buys 20 mss/year.** Query. Length: 800-1,500 words. **Pays $200-400.**

PHOTOS Photo guidelines for #10 SASE. Captions, identification of subjects required. Pays $25-225.

$$ CAPE COD MAGAZINE

Rabideau Publishing, P.O. Box 208, Yarmouth Port MA 02765. (508)771-6549. Fax: (508)771-3769. E-mail: editor@capecodmagazine.com. Website: capecodmagazine.com. **80% freelance written.** Magazine published 9 times/year covering Cape Cod lifestyle. Estab. 1996. Circ. 16,000. Byline given. Pays 30 days after publication. Offers 25% kill fee. Publishes ms an average of 3 months after acceptance. Editorial lead time 6 months. Submit seasonal material 1 year in advance. Accepts queries by mail, e-mail. Responds in 3 weeks to queries. Responds in 2 months to mss. Sample copy for $5. Guidelines by e-mail.

NONFICTION Needs book excerpts, essays, general interest, historical, humor, interview, personal experience. Does not want cliched pieces, interviews, and puff features. **Buys 3 mss/year.** Send complete ms. Length: 800-2,500 words. **Pays $300-500 for assigned articles. Pays $100-300 for unsolicited articles.** Sometimes pays expenses of writers on assignment.

PHOTOS State availability of or send photos. Reviews GIF/JPEG files. Negotiates payment individually.

COLUMNS Last Word (personal observations in typical back page format), 700 words. **Buys 4 mss/year.** Query with or without published clips or send complete ms. **Pays $150-300.**

$$ CHATHAM MAGAZINE

Rabideau Publishing, 396 Main St., Suite 8, Hyannis MA 02601. (508)771-6549. Fax: (508)771-3769. E-mail: editor@capecodmagazine.com. Website: chathammag.com. **80% freelance written.** Annual magazine covering Chatham lifestyle. Estab. 2006. Byline given. Pays 30 days after publication. Offers 25% kill fee. Publishes ms an average of 3 months after acceptance. Editorial lead time 6 months. Submit seasonal material 1 year in advance. Accepts queries by mail, e-mail. Responds in 3 weeks to queries. Responds in 2 months to mss. Sample copy for $5. Guidelines by e-mail.

NONFICTION Needs book excerpts, essays, general interest, historical, humor, interview, personal experience. Send complete ms. Length: 800-2,500 words. **Pays $300-500 for assigned articles. Pays $100-300 for unsolicited articles.** Sometimes pays expenses of writers on assignment.

PHOTOS State availability of or send photos. Reviews GIF/JPEG files. Negotiates payment individually.

COLUMNS Hooked (fishing issues), 700 words. **Buys 4 mss/year.** Query with or without published clips or send complete ms. **Pays $150-300.**

$$ PROVINCETOWN ARTS

Provincetown Arts, Inc., 650 Commercial St., P.O. Box 35, Provincetown MA 02657. (508)487-3167. E-mail: cbusa@comcast.net. Website: provincetownarts.org. **90% freelance written.** Annual magazine covering contemporary art and writing. "*Provincetown Arts* focuses broadly on the artists and writers who inhabit or visit the Lower Cape, and seeks to stimulate creative activity and enhance public awareness of the cultural life of the nation's oldest continuous art colony. Drawing upon a 75-year tradition rich in visual art, literature, and theater, *Provincetown Arts* offers a unique blend of interviews, fiction, visual features, reviews, reporting, and poetry." Estab. 1985. Circ. 8,000. Pays on publication. Offers 50% kill fee. Publishes ms an average of 4 months after acceptance. Editorial lead time 6 months. Submit seasonal material 6 months in advance. Accepts simultaneous submissions. Responds in 3 weeks to queries. Responds in 2 months to mss Sample copy for $10. Guidelines for #10 sase.

NONFICTION Needs book excerpts, essays, humor, interview. **Buys 40 mss/year.** Send complete ms. Length: 1,500-4,000 words. **Pays $150 minimum for assigned articles. Pays $125 minimum for unsolicited articles.**

PHOTOS Send photos. Identification of subjects required. Reviews 8×10 prints. Offers $20-$100/photo.

FICTION Contact: Christopher Busa, editor. Needs mainstream, novel concepts. **Buys 7 mss/year.** Send complete ms. Length: 500-5,000 words. **Pays $75-300.**

POETRY Buys 25 poems/yr. poems/year. Submit maximum 3 poems. **Pays $25-100/poem plus 2 contributor's copies. Acquires first rights.**

$$ WORCESTER MAGAZINE

101 Water St., Worcester MA 01604. (508)749-3166. Fax: (508)749-3165. E-mail: editor@worcestermag.com. Website: worcestermag.com. **Contact:** Doreen Manning, editor. **10% freelance written.** Weekly tabloid emphasizing the central Massachusetts region, especially the city of Worcester. Estab. 1976. Circ. 40,000. Byline given. Pays on publication. Publishes ms an average of 3 weeks after acceptance. Submit sea-

sonal material 2 months in advance. Accepts queries by mail, e-mail, fax.

🗨 Does not respond to unsolicited material.

NONFICTION Needs essays, expose, area government, corporate, general interest, historical, humor, opinion, local, personal experience, photo feature, religious, interview (local). **Buys less than 75 mss/year.** Length: 500-1,500 words. **Pays 10¢/word.**

MICHIGAN

$$$ ANN ARBOR OBSERVER

Ann Arbor Observer Co., 201 E. Catherine, Ann Arbor MI 48104. Fax: (734)769-3375. E-mail: hilton@ aaobserver.com. Website: arborweb.com. **50% freelance written.** Monthly magazine. "We depend heavily on freelancers and we're always glad to talk to new ones. We look for the intelligence and judgment to fully explore complex people and situations, and the ability to convey what makes them interesting." Estab. 1976. Circ. 60,000. Byline given in some sections. Pays on publication. Publishes ms an average of 2 months after acceptance. Accepts queries by mail, e-mail, fax, phone. Responds in 3 weeks to queries. Responds in several months to mss. Sample copy for 12½x15 SAE with $3 postage. Guidelines for #10 SASE.

NONFICTION **Buys 75 mss/year.** Length: 100-2,500 words. **Pays up to $1,000.** Sometimes pays expenses of writers on assignment.

COLUMNS Up Front (short, interesting tidbits), 150 words. **Pays $100.** Inside Ann Arbor (concise stories), 300-500 words. **Pays $200.** Around Town (unusual, compelling ancedotes), 750-1,500 words. **Pays $150-200.**

$$ GRAND RAPIDS MAGAZINE

Gemini Publications, Gemini Publications, 549 Ottawa Ave. NW, Suite 201, Grand Rapids MI 49503-1444. (616)459-4545. Fax: (616)459-4800. E-mail: cvalade@ geminipub.com. Website: grmag.com. *Grand Rapids* is a general interest life and style magazine designed for those who live in the Grand Rapids metropolitan area or desire to maintain contact with the community. Estab. 1964. Byline given. Pays on publication. Editorial lead time 2 months. Submit seasonal material 2 months in advance. Sample copy for $2 and an SASE with $1.50 postage. Guidelines for #10 SASE.

NONFICTION Query. **Pays $25-500.**

➕ $$ MICHIGAN HISTORY

The Historical Society of Michigan, 5815 Executive Dr., Lansing MI 48911. (517)332-1828. Fax: (517)324-4370. E-mail: mhmeditor@hsmichigan.org. E-mail: majher@hsmichigan.org. Website: hsmichigan.org. **Contact:** Patricia Majher, editor. Covers exciting stories of Michigan people and their impact on their communities, the nation and the world. *Michigan History* overflows with intriguing feature articles, bold illustrations and departments highlighting history-related books, travel and events 6 time each year. Bimonthly magazine, 64 colorful pages. "A thoroughly entertaining read, Michigan History specializes in stories from Michigan's colorful past. Within its pages, you'll learn about logging, mining, manufacturing, and military history as well as art and architecture, music, sports, shipwrecks, and more. Requires idea queries first." In addition to payment, authors receive 5 free copies of issues in which their work appears. Estab. 1917. Circ. 22,000. Byline given. Pays on publication. 6 months from acceptance to publication. 1 year Accepts queries by mail, e-mail. Guidelines for authors at hsmichigan. org/mhm/pub_guidelines.html.

NONFICTION Needs feature articles, bold illustrations and departments highlighting history-related books, travel and events., Remember the Time features (first-person, factual, personal experiences that happened in Michigan—750 words) pay $100. Other features pay $200-$400, depending on word length and cooperation in gathering photos. "We are not a scholarly journal and do not accept academic papers" **Buys 50-55/mss/year mss/year.** "When you are ready to submit a manuscript, please provide a digital copy of the text, and also list your research sources for fact-checking purposes. Include with your ms a summary of your writing experience and "in the interest of full disclosure" any relationship you have to your subject. You are expected to gather your own graphics (provided digitally and with captions, if possible) or at least suggest possible graphics." Length: 750-2,500 words **$100-400**

PHOTOS Expects writers to provide photos or recommend their source; will pay for photo permissions.

FICTION "We do not want fiction."

$$ TRAVERSE

Prism Publications, Inc., 148 E. Front St., Traverse City MI 49684. (231)941-8174. Fax: (231)941-8391.

Website: mynorth.com. **20% freelance written**. Monthly magazine covering northern Michigan life. "Since 1981, our company, Prism Publications, Inc., has been dedicated to sharing stories and photos that embody life in Northern Michigan. For more than 25 years we have accomplished this through our award-winning flagship publication *Traverse, Northern Michigan's Magazine*." Estab. 1981. Circ. 30,000. Byline given. Pays on acceptance. Offers 10% kill fee. Editorial lead time 1 year. Submit seasonal material 1 year in advance. Accepts queries by mail, fax, phone. Accepts simultaneous submissions. Responds in 2 months to queries. Sample copy for $3. Guidelines for #10 SASE.

NONFICTION Needs book excerpts, essays, general interest, historical, humor, interview, personal experience, photo feature, travel. No fiction or poetry. **Buys 24 mss/year.** Send complete ms. Length: 1,000-3,200 words. **Pays $150-500.** Sometimes pays expenses of writers on assignment.

PHOTOS State availability. Negotiates payment individually.

COLUMNS Up in Michigan Reflection (essays about northern Michigan); Reflection on Home (essays about northern homes), both 700 words. **Buys 18 mss/year.** Query with published clips or send complete ms. **Pays $100-200.**

MINNESOTA

⊗⊗ LAKE COUNTRY JOURNAL MAGAZINE

P.O. Box 978, Brainerd MN 56401. (218)828-6424, ext. 14. Fax: (218)825-7816. E-mail: jodi@lakecountryjournal.com. Website: lakecountryjournal.com. **Contact:** Jodi Schwen, editor or Tenlee Lund, assistant editor. **90% freelance written.** Bimonthly magazine covering central Minnesota's lake country. "We target a specific geographical niche in central Minnesota. The writer must be familiar with our area. We promote positive family values, foster a sense of community, increase appreciation for our natural and cultural environments, and provide ideas for enhancing the quality of our lives." Estab. 1996. Circ. 14,500. Byline given. Pays on publication. Offers 25% kill fee. Publishes ms an average of 6 months after acceptance. Submit seasonal material 1 year in advance. Accepts queries by mail, e-mail. Responds in 2 months to queries. Responds in 3 months to mss. Sample copy for $6. Guidelines available online.

⊶ Break in by "submitting department length first—they are not scheduled as far in advance as features. Always in need of original fillers."

NONFICTION Needs essays, general interest, how-to, humor, interview, personal experience, photo feature. "No articles that come from writers who are not familiar with our target geographical location." **Buys 30 mss/year.** Query with or without published clips Length: 1,000-1,500 words. **Pays $100-200.** Sometimes pays expenses of writers on assignment.

PHOTOS State availability. Identification of subjects, model releases required. Reviews transparencies. Negotiates payment individually.

COLUMNS Profile-People from Lake Country, 800 words; Essay, 800 words; Health (topics pertinent to central Minnesota living), 500 words. **Buys 40 mss/year mss/year.** Query with published clips **Pays $50-75.**

FICTION Needs adventure, humorous, mainstream, slice-of-life vignettes, literary, also family fiction appropriate to Lake Country and seasonal fiction. **Buys 6 mss/year.** Length: 1,500 words. **Pays $100-200.**

POETRY Needs free verse. "Never use rhyming verse, avant-garde, experimental, etc." Buys 6 poems/year. Submit maximum 4 poems. Length: 8-32 lines. **Pays $25.**

FILLERS Needs anecdotes, short humor. **Buys 20 fillers/year mss/year.** Length: 100-300 words. **$25/filler.**

⊗⊗ LAKE SUPERIOR MAGAZINE

Lake Superior Port Cities, Inc., P.O. Box 16417, Duluth MN 55816-0417. (218)722-5002. Fax: (218)722-4096. E-mail: edit@lakesuperior.com. Website: lakesuperior.com. **40% freelance written. Works with a small number of new/unpublished writers each year. Please include phone number and address with e-mail queries.** Bi-monthly magazine covering contemporary and historic people, places and current events around Lake Superior. Estab. 1979. Circ. 20,000. Byline given. Pays on publication. Publishes ms an average of 10 months after acceptance. Submit seasonal material 1 year in advance. Accepts queries by mail, e-mail. Responds in 3 months to queries. Sample copy for $4.95 and 6 first-class stamps. Guidelines available online.

NONFICTION Needs book excerpts, general interest, historical, humor, interview, local, personal experience, photo feature, local, travel, local, city profiles, regional business, some investigative. **Buys 15 mss/year.** Query with published clips. Length: 300-1,800 words. **Pays $60-400.** Sometimes pays expenses of writers on assignment, with assignments.

PHOTOS Quality photography is our hallmark. Send photos. Captions, identification of subjects, model releases required. Reviews contact sheets, 2×2 and larger transparencies, 4×5 prints. Offers $50/image; $150 for covers.

COLUMNS Current events and things to do (for Events Calendar section), less than 300 words; Around The Circle (media reviews; short pieces on Lake Superior; Great Lakes environmental issues; themes, letters and short pieces on events and highlights of the Lake Superior Region); Essay (nostalgic lake-specific pieces), up to 1,100 words; Profile (single personality profile with photography), up to 900 words. Other headings include Destinations, Wild Superior, Lake Superior Living, Heritage, Recipe Box. **Buys 20 mss/year.** Query with published clips. **Pays $60-90.**

FICTION Ethnic, historic, humorous, mainstream, novel excerpts, slice-of-life vignettes, ghost stories. Must be targeted regionally. Wants stories that are Lake Superior related. **Buys 2-3 mss/year.** Query with published clips. Length: 300-2,500 words. **Pays $50-125.**

⑨⑨⑨ MPLS. ST. PAUL MAGAZINE

MSP Communications, 220 S. 6th St., Suite 500, Minneapolis MN 55402. (612)339-7571. Fax: (612)339-5806. E-mail: edit@mspmag.com. E-mail: APlatt@mspmag.com. Website: mspmag.com. Stephanie March (food and dining), StephM@mspmag.com; Stephanie Davila (front-of-the-book Scene + Heard), SDavila@mspcommunications.com; Tad Simons (arts and entertainment subjects), tsimons@mspmag.com; Melissa Colgan (fashion/lifestyle/shopping), MColgan@mspmag.com. **Contact:** Adam Platt, executive editor. Monthly magazine. *Mpls. St. Paul Magazine* is a city magazine serving upscale readers in the Minneapolis-St. Paul metro area. Circ. 80,000. Pays on publication. Editorial lead time 3 months. Accepts queries by mail, e-mail, fax. Sample copy for $10. Guidelines available online.

NONFICTION Needs book excerpts, essays, general interest, historical, interview, personal experience, photo feature, travel. **Buys 150 mss/year.** Query with published clips. Length: 500-4,000 words. **Pays 50-75¢/word for assigned articles.**

MISSISSIPPI

⑨⑨ MISSISSIPPI MAGAZINE

Downhome Publications, 5 Lakeland Circle, Jackson MS 39216. (601)982-8418. Fax: (601)982-8447. E-mail: editor@mismag.com. Website: mississippimagazine.com. **Contact:** Editor. **90% freelance written.** Bimonthly magazine covering Mississippi—the state and its lifestyles. "We are interested in positive stories reflecting Mississippi's rich traditions and heritage and focusing on the contributions the state and its natives have made to the arts, literature, and culture. In each issue we showcase homes and gardens, in-state travel, food, design, art, and more." Estab. 1982. Circ. 40,000. Byline given. Pays on publication. Offers 25% kill fee. Publishes ms an average of 6 months after acceptance. Editorial lead time 6 months. Submit seasonal material 1 year in advance. Accepts queries by mail, fax. Responds in 2 months to queries. Guidelines for #10 SASE or online.

NONFICTION Needs general interest, historical, how-to, home decor, interview, personal experience, travel, in-state. No opinion, political, sports, expose. **Buys 15 mss/year.** Query. Length: 100-1,200 words. **Pays $25-350.**

PHOTOS Send photos with query. Captions, identification of subjects, model releases required. Reviews transparencies, prints, digital images on CD. Negotiates payment individually.

COLUMNS Southern Scrapbook (see recent issues for example), 100-600 words; Gardening (short informative article on a specific plant or gardening technique), 800-1,200 words; Culture Center (story about an event or person relating to Mississippi's art, music, theatre, or literature), 800-1,200 words; On Being Southern (personal essay about life in Mississippi; only ms submissions accepted), 750 words. **Buys 6 mss/year.** Query. **Pays $150-225.**

MISSOURI

⑨⑨ 417 MAGAZINE

Whitaker Publishing, 2111 S. Eastgate Ave., Springfield MO 65809. (417)883-7417. Fax: (417)889-7417. E-mail: editor@417mag.com. Website: 417mag.com.

Contact: Katie Pollock, editor. **50% freelance written.** Monthly magazine. *"417 Magazine* is a regional title serving southwest Missouri. Our editorial mix includes service journalism and lifestyle content on home, fashion and the arts; as well as narrative and issues pieces. The audience is affluent, educated, mostly female." Estab. 1998. Circ. 20,000. Byline given. Pays on acceptance. Publishes ms an average of 2-3 months after acceptance. Editorial lead time 6 months. Accepts queries by e-mail. Responds in 1-2 months to queries. Sample copy by e-mail. Guidelines available online.

NONFICTION Needs essays, expose, general interest, how-to, humor, inspirational, interview, new product, personal experience, photo feature, travel, local book reviews. "We are a local magazine, so anything not reflecting our local focus is something we have to pass on." Buys 175 mss/year. Query with published clips. Length: 300-3,500 words. **Pays $30-500, sometimes more.** Sometimes pays expenses of writers on assignment.

⊙⊙ KANSAS CITY HOMES & GARDENS

Network Communications, Inc., 4121 W. 83rd St., Suite 110, Prairie Village KS 66208. (913)648-5757. Fax: (913)648-5783. E-mail: adarr@nci.com. Website: kchandg.com. Magazine published 8 times annually. *"KCH&G* creates inspirational, credible and compelling content about trends and events in local home and design for affluent homeowners, with beautiful photography, engaging features and expert insight. We help our readers get smarter about where to find and how to buy the best solutions for enhancing their homes." Estab. 1986. Circ. 18,000. Byline given. Pays on publication. Editorial lead time 4 months. Submit seasonal material 4 months in advance. Accepts queries by mail, e-mail, fax. Accepts simultaneous submissions. Responds in 1 month to queries. Responds in 1 month to mss. Sample copy for $5.

NONFICTION Buys 8 mss/year. Query with published clips. Length: 600-1,000 words. **Pays $100-350.** Sometimes pays expenses of writers on assignment.

PHOTOS State availability of or send photos. Identification of subjects required. Reviews transparencies. Offers no additional payment for photos accepted with ms.

⊙⊙ MISSOURI LIFE

Missouri Life, Inc., 515 E. Morgan St., Boonville MO 65233. (660)882-9898. Fax: (660)882-9899. E-mail: query@missourilife.com. Website: missourilife.com. **Contact:** Managing editor. **85% freelance written.** Bimonthly magazine covering the state of Missouri. *"Missouri Life's* readers are mostly college-educated people with a wide range of travel and lifestyle interests. Our magazine discovers the people, places, and events—both past and present—that make Missouri a great place to live and/or visit." Estab. 1973. Circ. 20,000. Byline given. Pays on publication. Editorial lead time 3 months. Submit seasonal material 6 months in advance. Accepts queries by mail, e-mail, fax. Responds in 2 months to queries. Sample copy available for $4.95 and SASE with $2.44 first-class postage. Guidelines available online.

NONFICTION Needs general interest, historical, travel, all Missouri related. Length: 300-2,000 words. **Pays $50-600; 20¢/word.**

PHOTOS State availability in query; buys all rights nonexclusive. Captions, identification of subjects, model releases required. Offers $50-150/photo.

COLUMNS "All Around Missouri (people and places, past and present, written in an almanac style), 300 words; Missouri Artist (features a Missouri artist), 500 words; Made in Missouri (products and businesses native to Missouri), 500 words.

⊙⊙ RELOCATING TO THE LAKE OF THE OZARKS

Cliffside Corporate Center, 2140 Bagnell Dam Blvd., Suite 303E, Lake Ozark MO 65049. (573)365-2323. Fax: (573)365-2351. E-mail: spublishingco@msn.com. Website: relocatingtothelakeoftheozarks.com/. **Contact:** Dave Leathers. Annual relocation guides, free for people moving to the area. Byline given. Pays on publication. Publishes ms an average of 6 months after acceptance. Accepts queries by e-mail. Sample copy for $8.95. Guidelines available online.

NONFICTION Needs historical, travel, local issues. Length: 600-1,000 words.

PHOTOS Purchases images portraying recreational activities, tourism, nature, business development, cultural events, historical sites, and the people of the lake area. Send color positive film in 35mm or larger format, or send high-resoultion digital images. State availability of or send photos. Identification of subjects required. Pays $20-300, depending on size.

⊙ RIVER HILLS TRAVELER

Traveler Publishing Co.,, P.O. Box 220, Valley Park MO 63088-0220. (800)874-8423. Fax: (800)874-8423.

E-mail: stories@rhtrav.com. Website: riverhillstraveler.com. **80% freelance written**. Monthly tabloid covering outdoor sports and nature in the southeast quarter of Missouri, the east and central Ozarks. Topics like those in *Field & Stream* and *National Geographic*. Estab. 1973. Circ. 5,000. Byline given. Pays on publication. Publishes ms an average of 2 months after acceptance. Editorial lead time 2 months. Submit seasonal material 1 year in advance. Accepts queries by e-mail. Accepts simultaneous submissions. Responds in 2 months to queries. Sample copy for SAE or online. Guidelines available online.

NONFICTION Needs historical, how-to, humor, opinion, personal experience, photo feature, technical, travel. No stories about other geographic areas. **Buys 80 mss/year.** Query with writing samples. 1,500 word maximum **Pays $15-50.**

REPRINTS E-mail manuscript with rights for sale noted and information about when and where the material previously appeared.

PHOTOS Send photos. Reviews JPEG/TIFF files. Negotiates payment individually. Pays $35 for covers.

$ RURAL MISSOURI MAGAZINE

Association of Missouri Electric Cooperatives, P.O. Box 1645, Jefferson City MO 65102. E-mail: hberry@ruralmissouri.coop. Website: ruralmissouri.coop. **5% freelance written**. Monthly magazine covering rural interests in Missouri; people, places and sights in Missouri. "Our audience is comprised of rural electric cooperative members in Missouri. We describe our magazine as 'being devoted to the rural way of life.'" Estab. 1948. Circ. 535,000. Byline given. Pays on acceptance. Publishes ms an average of 6 months after acceptance. Editorial lead time 6 months. Submit seasonal material 6 months in advance. Accepts queries by mail, e-mail. NoResponds in 6-8 weeks to queries and to mss. Sample copy available online. Guidelines available online.

NONFICTION Needs general interest, historical. Does not want personal experiences or nostalgia pieces. Send complete ms. Length: 1,000-1,100 words. **Pays variable amount for each piece.**

MONTANA

$$ MONTANA MAGAZINE

Lee Enterprises, P.O. Box 5630, Helena MT 59604-5630. E-mail: editor@montanamagazine.com. E-mail: butch.larcombe@lee.net. Website: montanamagazine.com. **Contact:** Butch Larcombe, editor. **90% freelance written.** Bimonthly magazine. Strictly Montana-oriented magazine that features community profiles, contemporary issues, wildlife and natural history, travel pieces. Estab. 1970. Circ. 40,000. Byline given. Publishes ms an average of 1 year after acceptance. Submit seasonal material 1 year in advance. Accepts simultaneous submissions. Responds in 6 months to queries. Sample copy for $5 or online. Guidelines available online.

Accepts queries by e-mail. No phone calls.

NONFICTION Needs essays, general interest, interview, photo feature, travel. Special issues: Special features on summer and winter destination points. No 'me and Joe' hiking and hunting tales; no blood-and-guts hunting stories; no poetry; no fiction; no sentimental essays. **Buys 30 mss/year.** Query with samples and SASE. Length: 800-1,000 words. **Pays 20¢/word.** Sometimes pays expenses of writers on assignment.

REPRINTS Send photocopy of article with rights for sale and information about when and where the material previously appeared. Pays 50% of amount paid for an original article.

PHOTOS Send photos. Captions, identification of subjects, model releases required. Reviews contact sheets, 35mm or larger format transparencies, 5×7 prints. Offers additional payment for photos accepted with ms.

COLUMNS Memories (reminisces of early-day Montana life), 800-1,000 words; Outdoor Recreation, 1,500-2,000 words; Community Festivals, 500 words, plus b&w or color photo; Montana-Specific Humor, 800-1,000 words. Query with samples and SASE.

NEVADA

$$ NEVADA MAGAZINE

401 N. Carson St., Carson City NV 89701-4291. (775)687-5416. Fax: (775)687-6159. E-mail: editor@nevadamagazine.com. Website: nevadamagazine.com. **Contact:** Editor. **50% freelance written. Works with a small number of new/unpublished writers each year**. Bimonthly magazine published by the state of Nevada to promote tourism. Estab. 1936. Circ. 30,000. Byline given. Pays on publication. Publishes ms an average of 6 months after acceptance. Submit seasonal material 6 months in advance.

Accepts queries by e-mail (preferred). Responds in 1 month to queries.

NONFICTION Length: 700-1,000 words. **Pays $50-500.**

PHOTOS Contact: Query art director Tony deRonnebeck (tony@nevadamagazine.com). Reviews digital images. Pays $35-175; cover, $250.

NEW HAMPSHIRE

$$ NEW HAMPSHIRE MAGAZINE

McLean Communications, Inc., 150 Dow St., Manchester NH 03101. (603)624-1442. E-mail: editor@nhmagazine.com. Website: nhmagazine.com. **50% freelance written**. Monthly magazine devoted to New Hampshire. "We want stories written for, by, and about the people of New Hampshire with emphasis on qualities that set us apart from other states. We feature lifestyle, adventure, and home-related stories with a unique local angle.' Estab. 1986. Circ. 32,000. Byline given. Pays on publication. Offers 25% kill fee. Editorial lead time 3 months. Submit seasonal material 3 months in advance. Accepts queries by mail, e-mail, fax. Accepts simultaneous submissions. Responds in 2 months to queries. Responds in 3 months to mss. Guidelines available online.

NONFICTION Needs essays, general interest, historical, photo feature, business. **Buys 30 mss/year.** Query with published clips. Length: 800-2,000 words. **Pays $50-500.** Sometimes pays expenses of writers on assignment.

PHOTOS State availability. Captions, identification of subjects, model releases required. Possible additional payment for photos accepted with ms.

FILLERS Length: 200-400 words.

NEW JERSEY

$$$$ NEW JERSEY MONTHLY

New Jersey Monthly, LLC, 55 Park Place, P.O. Box 920, Morristown NJ 07963-0920. (973)539-8230. Fax: (973)538-2953. E-mail: research@njmonthly.com. Website: njmonthly.com. **Contact:** Visit the website for appropriate editor contacts. **75-80% freelance written.** Monthly magazine covering just about anything to do with New Jersey, from news, politics, and sports to decorating trends and lifestyle issues. Our readership is well-educated, affluent, and on average our readers have lived in New Jersey 20 years or more. Estab. 1976. Circ. 92,000. Byline given. Pays on completion of fact-checking. Offers 20% kill fee. Publishes ms an average of 3 months after acceptance. Editorial lead time 3 months. Submit seasonal material 6 months in advance. Accepts queries by mail, e-mail, fax, phone. Accepts simultaneous submissions. Responds in 2-3 months to queries.

○ This magazine continues to look for strong investigative reporters with novelistic style and solid knowledge of New Jersey issues.

NONFICTION Needs book excerpts, essays, expose, general interest, historical, humor, interview, personal experience, photo feature, travel, within New Jersey, arts, sports, politics. No experience pieces from people who used to live in New Jersey or general pieces that have no New Jersey angle. **Buys 90-100 mss/year.** Query with published magazine clips and SASE. Length: 250-3,000 words. **Pays $750-2,500.** Pays reasonable expenses of writers on assignment with prior approval.

PHOTOS Contact: Donna Panagakos, art director. State availability. Identification of subjects, model releases required. Reviews transparencies, prints. Payment negotiated.

COLUMNS Exit Ramp (back page essay usually originating from personal experience but written in a way that tells a broader story of statewide interest), 1,200 words. **Buys 12 mss/year.** Query with published clips. **Pays $400.**

FILLERS Needs anecdotes, for front-of-book. **Buys 12-15 mss/year.** Length: 200-250 words. **$100.**

$$ NEW JERSEY SAVVY LIVING

CTB, LLC, P.O. Box 607, Short Hills NJ 07078-0607. (973)966-0997. Fax: (973)966-0210. E-mail: njsavvyliving@ctbintl.com. Website: njsavvyliving.com. **90% freelance written.** Bimonthly magazine covering New Jersey residents with affluent lifestyles. "*Savvy Living* is a regional magazine for an upscale audience, ages 35-65. We focus on lifestyle topics such as home design, fashion, the arts, travel, personal finance, and health and well being." Estab. 1997. Circ. 50,000. Byline given. Pays on publication. Offers $50 kill fee. Publishes ms an average of 3 months after acceptance. Editorial lead time 3 months. Accepts queries by mail. Accepts simultaneous submissions. Response time varies. Sample copy for sae with 9×12 envelope.

NONFICTION Needs interview, people of national and regional importance, photo feature, travel, home/decorating, finance, health, fashion, beauty. No investigative, fiction, personal experience, and non-New Jersey topics (excluding travel). **Buys 50 mss/year.** Query with published clips. Length: 900-2,000 words. **Pays $250-500.**

PHOTOS State availability. Captions, identification of subjects, model releases required. Offers no additional payment for photos accepted with ms.

COLUMNS Savvy Shoppers (inside scoop on buying); Dining Out (restaurant review); Home Gourmet (gourmet cooking and entertaining). **Buys 25 mss/year.** Query with published clips. **Pays $300.**

$$ THE SANDPAPER

The SandPaper, Inc., 1816 Long Beach Blvd., Surf City NJ 08008-5461. (609)494-5900. Fax: (609)494-1437. E-mail: jaymann@thesandpaper.net; curttravers@thesandpaper.net; photo@thesandpaper.net. Website: thesandpaper.net. Ryan Morrill, Photography Editor, Curt Travers, Publisher. **Contact:** Jay Mann, managing editor. Weekly tabloid covering subjects of interest to Long Island Beach area residents and visitors. Each issue includes a mix of news, human interest features, opinion columns, and entertainment/calendar listings. Estab. 1976. Circ. 30,000. Byline given. Pays on publication. Offers 100% kill fee. Publishes ms an average of 1 month after acceptance. Submit seasonal material 3 months in advance. Accepts queries by mail, e-mail, fax, phone. Accepts simultaneous submissions. Responds in 1 month to queries.

COLUMNS Speakeasy (opinion and slice-of-life, often humorous); Commentary (forum for social science perspectives); both 1,000-1,500 words, preferably with local or Jersey Shore angle. **Buys 50 mss/year.** Send complete ms. **Pays $40**

NEW MEXICO

$$ NEW MEXICO MAGAZINE

Lew Wallace Bldg., 495 Old Santa Fe Trail, Santa Fe NM 87501. (505)827-7447. E-mail: queries@nmmagazine.com. Website: nmmagazine.com. **70.** Covers areas throughout the state. "We want to publish a lively editorial mix, covering both the down-home (like a diner in Tucumcari) and the upscale (a new bistro in world-class Santa Fe)." Explore the gamut of the Old West and the New Age. "Our magazine is about the power of place—in particular more than 120,000 sq. miles of mountains, desert, grasslands, and forest inhabited by a culturally rich mix of individuals. It is an enterprise of the New Mexico Tourism Dept., which strives to make potential visitors aware of our state's multicultural heritage, climate, environment, and uniqueness." Estab. 1923. Circ. 100,000. Pays on acceptance. 20% kill fee. Publishes ms an average of 3 months after acceptance. Submit seasonal material 1 year in advance. Accepts queries by mail, e-mail (preferred). Does not accept previously published submissions.Responds to queries if interested. Sample copy for $5. Guidelines for SASE.

○ No unsolicited mss. Does not return unsolicited material.

NONFICTION "Submit your story idea along with a working head and subhead and a paragraph synopsis. Include published clips and a short sum-up about your strengths as a writer. We will consider your proposal as well as your potential to write stories we've conceptualized."

REPRINTS Rarely publishes reprints but sometimes publishes excerpts from novels and nonfiction books.

PHOTOS "Purchased as portfolio or on assignment. Photographers interested in photo assignments should reference submission guidelines on the contributors' page of our website.".

NEW YORK

$$ ADIRONDACK LIFE

P.O. Box 410, Jay NY 12941-0410. (518)946-2191. Fax: (518)946-7461. E-mail: astoltie@adirondacklife.com. Website: adirondacklife.com. **Contact:** Annie Stoltie, editor. **70% freelance written. Prefers to work with published/established writers.** Magazine published 8 issues/year, including special Annual Outdoor Guide, emphasizes the Adirondack region and the North Country of New York State in articles covering outdoor activities, history, and natural history directly related to the Adirondacks. Estab. 1970. Circ. 50,000. Byline given. Pays 30 days after publication. Publishes ms an average of 10 months after acceptance. Submit seasonal material 1 year in advance. Accepts queries by mail, e-mail. Does not accept previously published work.Sample copy for $3 and 9×12 SAE. Guidelines available online.

NONFICTION Special issues: Outdoors (May); Single-topic Collector's issue (September). **Buys 20-25 unsolicited mss/year.** Query with published clips. Accepts queries, but not unsolicited mss, via e-mail. Length: 1,000-4,000 words. **Pays 30¢/word.** Sometimes pays expenses of writers on assignment.

PHOTOS Contact: Kelly Hofschneider, photo editor. "All photos must have been taken in the Adirondacks. Each issue contains a photo feature. Purchased with or without ms on assignment. All photos must be individually identified as to the subject or locale and must bear the photographer's name.". Send photos. Reviews color transparencies, b&w prints. Pays $150 for full page, b&w, or color; $400 for cover (color only,vertical in format). Credit line given.

COLUMNS Special Places (unique spots in the Adirondack Park); Watercraft; Barkeater (personal essays); Wilderness (environmental issues); Working (careers in the Adirondacks); Home; teryears; Kitchen; Profile; Historical Preservation; Sporting Scene. Length: 1,200-2,100 words. Query with published clips. **Pays 30¢/word.**

FICTION Considers first-serial novel excerpts in its subject matter and region.

$ ARTSNEWS

ArtsWestchester, 31 Mamaroneck Ave., White Plains NY 10601. Fax: (914)428-4306. E-mail: jormond@artswestchester.org. Website: artswestchester.org. **Contact:** Jim Ormond, editor. **20% freelance written.** Monthly tabloid covering arts and entertainment in Westchester County, New York. "We profile artists, arts organizations and write teasers about upcoming exhibitions, concerts, events, theatrical performances, etc." Estab. 1975. Circ. 20,000. Byline given. Pays on publication. Editorial lead time 1 month. Submit seasonal material 2 months in advance. Accepts queries by mail, e-mail. Sample copy free.

NONFICTION Query with published clips. Length: 400-500 words. **Pays $75-100.** Pays expenses of writers on assignment.

$$ BUFFALO SPREE MAGAZINE

Buffalo Spree Publishing, Inc., 100 Corporate Pkwy., Suite 200, Buffalo NY 14226. (716)783-9119. Fax: (716)783-9983. E-mail: elicata@buffalospree.com. Website: buffalospree.com. **Contact:** Elizabeth Licata, editor. **90% freelance written.** City regional magazine published 8 times/year. Estab. 1967. Circ. 25,000. Byline given. Pays on publication. Publishes ms an average of 1 month after acceptance. Accepts queries by mail, e-mail, fax. Responds in 6 months to queries. Sample copy for $3.95 and 9×12 SAE with 9 first-class stamps.

NONFICTION Needs interview, travel, issue-oriented features, arts, living, food, regional. Query with rÃˆsumÃˆ and published clips. Length: 1,000-2,000 words. **Pays $125-250.**

CITY LIMITS

Community Service Society of New York, 105 East 22nd St., Suite 901, New York NY 10010. (212)479-3344. Fax: (212)344-6457. E-mail: citylimits@citylimits.org; magazine@citylimits.org. E-mail: editor@citylimits.org. Website: citylimits.org. Jarrett Murphy, editor-in-chief. **Contact:** Mark Anthony Thomas, director. **50% freelance written.** Monthly magazine covering urban politics and policy. *City Limits* is a 29-year-old nonprofit print and online magazine focusing on issues facing New York City and its neighborhoods, particularly low-income communities. The magazine is strongly committed to investigative journalism, in-depth policy analysis and hard-hitting profiles. Estab. 1976. Circ. 5,000. Byline given. Pays on publication. Offers 50% kill fee. Publishes ms an average of 3 months after acceptance. Editorial lead time 2 months. Accepts queries by mail, e-mail, fax. Accepts simultaneous submissions. Responds in 1 month. Sample copy for $2.95. Guidelines free.

🔑 "*City Limits* is devoted to the in-depth investigation of pressing civic issues in New York City. Driven by a mission to inform public discourse, the magazine provides the factual reporting, human faces, data, history and breadth of knowledge necessary to understanding the nuances, complexities and hard truths of the city, its politics and its people."

NONFICTION Needs book excerpts, exposè, humor, interview, opinion, photo feature. No essays, polemics. **Buys 25 mss/year.** Query with published clips. Length: 400-3,500 words. **Pays $150-2,000 for assigned articles. Pays $100-800 for unsolicited articles.** Pays expenses of writers on assignment.

PHOTOS State availability. Model release required for children. Reviews contact sheets, negatives, transparencies. Buys 20 photos from freelancers/issue; 200 photos/year. Pays $100 for color cover; $50-100 for b&w inside. Pays on publication. Credit line given. Buys rights for use in *City Limits* in print and online; higher rate given for online use.

COLUMNS Making Change (nonprofit business); Big Idea (policy news); Book Review, all 800 words; Urban Legend (profile); First Hand (Q&A), both 350 words. **Buys 15 mss/year.** Query with published clips.

$ HUDSON VALLEY LIFE

The Professional Image, 174 South St., Newburgh NY 12550. (845)562-3606. E-mail: editor@excitingread.com. Website: hvlife.com. **Contact:** M.J. Goff, editor. **95% freelance written.** Monthly magazine serving parents and active adults by providing reliable local information of interest. Estab. 1999. Circ. 15,000. Pays on publication. Publishes ms an average of 3 months after acceptance. Guidelines available online.

NONFICTION Needs expose, general interest, humor, interview, personal experience. **Buys 15 mss/yr. mss/year.** Query. Length: 700-1,200 words. **Pays $60-120 for assigned articles. Pays $25-35 for unsolicited articles.**

$$$$ NEW YORK MAGAZINE

New York Media Holdings, LLC, 75 Varick Street, New York NY 10013. Website: newyorkmag.com. **Contact:** Editorial Submissions. **25% freelance written.** Weekly magazine focusing on current events in the New York metropolitan area. Circ. 433,813. Pays on acceptance. Offers 25% kill fee. Submit seasonal material 2 months in advance. Responds in 1 month to queries. Sample copy for $3.50 or on website.

NONFICTION Query by mail. No unsolicited mss. **Pays $1/word.** Pays expenses of writers on assignment.

NORTH CAROLINA

$$ AAA CAROLINAS GO MAGAZINE

6600 AAA Dr., Charlotte NC 28212. Fax: (704)569-7815. Website: aaacarolinas.com. **Contact:** Tom Crosby, VP of communications. **20% freelance written.** Member publication for the Carolina affiliate of American Automobile Association covering travel, auto-related issues. "We prefer stories that focus on travel and auto safety in North and South Carolina and surrounding states." Estab. 1922. Circ. 1.1 million. Byline given. Pays on publication. Editorial lead time 2 months. Accepts queries by mail. Sample copy and writer's guidelines for #10 SASE.

"The online magazine carries original content not found in the print edition. Contact Brendan Byrnes at btbyrnes@mailaaa.com."

NONFICTION Needs travel, auto safety. Length: 750 words. **Pays $150.**

PHOTOS Send photos. Identification of subjects required. Reviews slides. Offers no additional payment for photos accepted with ms.

$$ CARY MAGAZINE

SA Cherokee, Westview at Weston, 301 Cascade Pointe Lane, #101, Cary NC 27513. (919)674-6020. Fax: (919)674-6027. E-mail: editor@carymagazine.com. Website: carymagazine.com. **Contact:** Danielle Stanfield, editor. **40% freelance written.** Bimonthly magazine. "Lifestyle publication for the affluent communities of Cary, Apex, Morrisville, Holly Springs, Fuquay-Varina and RTP. Our editorial objective is to entertain, enlighten and inform our readers with unique and engaging editorial and vivid photography." Estab. 2004. Circ. 23,000. Byline given. Negotiated Editorial lead time 3 months. Submit seasonal material 3 months in advance. Accepts queries by mail, e-mail. Responds in 2-4 weeks to queries. Responds in 1 month to mss. Sample copy for $4.95. Guidelines free.

NONFICTION Needs historical, specific to Western Wake County, North Carolina, inspirational, interview, human interest, personal experience. Don't submit articles with no local connection. **Buys 2 mss/year.** Query with published clips. Sometimes pays expenses of writers on assignment.

PHOTOS Freelancers should state the availability of photos with their submission or send the photos with their submission. Identification of subjects required. Reviews GIF/JPEG files. Negotiates payment individually.

$$ CHARLOTTE MAGAZINE

Morris Visitor Publications, 309 E. Morehead St., Suite 50, Charlotte NC 28202. (704)335-7181. Fax: (704)335-3757. E-mail: richard.thurmond@charlottemagazine.com. Website: charlottemagazine.com. **75% freelance written.** Monthly magazine covering Charlotte life. This magazine tells its readers things they didn't know about Charlotte, in an interesting, entertaining, and sometimes provocative style. Circ. 40,000. Byline given. Pays within 30 days of acceptance. Offers 25% kill fee. Publishes ms an average of 3 months after acceptance. Editorial lead time 3 months. Submit seasonal material 6 months in advance. Accepts queries by mail, e-mail. Accepts simultaneous submissions. Responds in 6 months to mss. Sample copy for 8 ½×11 SAE and $5.

NONFICTION Needs book excerpts, expose, general interest, interview, photo feature, travel. **Buys 35-50 mss/year.** Query with published clips. Length: 200-3,000 words. **Pays 20-40¢/word.** Sometimes pays expenses of writers on assignment.

PHOTOS State availability. Identification of subjects required. Negotiates payment individually.

COLUMNS Buys 35-50 mss/year. Pays 20-40¢/word

$$ FIFTEEN501

Weiss and Hughes Publishing, 189 Wind Chime Ct., Raleigh NC 27615. (919)870-1722. Fax: (919)719-5260. E-mail: djackson@whmags.com. Website: fifteen501.com. **Contact:** Danielle Jackson, editor. **50% freelance written.** Quarterly magazine covering lifestyle issues relevant to residents in the US 15/501 corridor of Durham, Orange and Chatham counties. "We cover issues important to residents of Durham, Orange and Chatham counties. We're committed to improving our readers' overall quality of life and keeping them informed of the lifestyle amenities there." Estab. 2006. Circ. 30,000. Byline given. within 30 days of publication. Offers 25% kill fee. Publishes ms an average of 2 months after acceptance. Editorial lead time 2-3 months. Submit seasonal material 6 months in advance. Accepts queries by mail, e-mail. Accepts simultaneous submissions. Responds in 2-4 weeks to queries. Sample copy available online. Guidelines by e-mail.

NONFICTION Needs general interest, historical, how-to, home interiors, landscaping, gardening, technology, inspirational, interview, personal experience, photo feature, technical, travel. Does not want opinion pieces, political or religious topics. Query. Length: 600-1,200 words. **Pays 35¢/word.** Sometimes pays expenses of writers on assignment.

PHOTOS State availability. Captions, identification of subjects required. Reviews transparencies, GIF/JPEG files. Offers no additional payment for photos accepted with ms.

COLUMNS Around Town (local lifestyle topics), 1,000 words; Hometown Stories, 600 words; Travel (around North Carolina), 1,000 words; Home Interiors/Landscaping (varies), 1,000 words; Restaurants (local, fine dining), 600-1,000 words. **Buys 20-25 mss/year.** Query. **Pays 35¢/word.**

$$ OUR STATE

Mann Media, P.O. Box 4552, Greensboro NC 27404. (336)286-0600. Fax: (336)286-0100. E-mail: editorial@ourstate.com. Website: ourstate.com. **95% freelance written.** Monthly magazine covering North Carolina. *Our State* is dedicated to providing editorial about the history, destinations, out-of-the-way places, and culture of North Carolina. Estab. 1933. Circ. 130,000. Byline given. Pays on publication. Publishes ms an average of 6-24 months after acceptance. Editorial lead time 4-6 months. Submit seasonal material 4 months in advance. Accepts queries by mail, e-mail, fax. Responds in 6 weeks to queries. Responds in 2 months to mss. Sample copy for $6. Guidelines for #10 SASE.

NONFICTION Needs historical, travel, North Carolina culture, folklore. **Buys 250 mss/year.** Send complete ms. Length: 1,400-1,600 words. **Pays $300-500.**

PHOTOS State availability. Reviews 35mm or 4×6 transparencies, digital. Negotiates payment individually.

COLUMNS Tar Heel Memories (remembering something specific about North Carolina), 1,000 words; Tar Heel Profile (profile of interesting North Carolinian), 1,500 words; Tar Heel Literature (review of books by North Carolina writers and about North Carolina), 300 words.

$$ WAKE LIVING

Weiss and Hughes Publishing, 189 Wind Chime Ct., Suite 104, Raleigh NC 27615. (919)870-1722. Fax: (919)719-5260. E-mail: dhughes@wakeliving.com; djackson@whmags.com. Website: wakeliving.com. **Contact:** David Hughes, president/publisher; Danielle Jackson, editor. **50% freelance written.** Quarterly magazine covering lifestyle issues in Wake County, North Carolina. "We cover issues important to residents of Wake County. We are committed to improving our readers' overall quality of life and keeping them informed of the lifestyle amenities here." Estab. 2003. Circ. 40,000. Byline given. Pays within 30 days of publication. Offers 25% kill fee. Publishes ms an average of 2 months after acceptance. Editorial lead time 2-3 months. Submit seasonal material 6 months in advance. Accepts queries by mail, e-mail. NoAccepts simultaneous submissions. Responds in 2-4 weeks to queries. Sample copy available online. Guidelines available online.

NONFICTION Needs general interest, historical, how-to, home interiors, technology, landscaping, gardening, inspirational, interview, personal experience, photo feature, technical, travel. Does not want opinion pieces, political topics, religious articles. Query. Length: 600-1,200 words. **Pays 35¢/word.** Sometimes pays expenses of writers on assignment.

PHOTOS State availability. Captions, identification of subjects required. Reviews transparencies, GIF/JPEG files. Offers no additional payment for photos accepted with ms.

COLUMNS Around Town (local lifestyle topics); Hometown Stories, 600 words; Travel (around North Carolina); Home Interiors/Landscaping, all 1,000 words. Restaurants (local restaurants, fine dining), 600-1,000 words. **Buys 20-25 mss/year.** Query. **Pays 35¢/word.**

NORTH DAKOTA

$$ NORTH DAKOTA LIVING MAGAZINE

North Dakota Association of Rural Electric Cooperatives, 3201 Nygren Dr. NW, P.O. Box 727, Mandan ND 58554-0727. (701)663-6501. Fax: (701)663-3745. E-mail: kbrick@ndarec.com. Website: ndarec.com/dakotaLiving. **20% freelance written.** Monthly magazine covering information of interest to memberships of electric cooperatives and telephone cooperatives. "We publish a general interest magazine for North Dakotans. We treat subjects pertaining to living and working in the northern Great Plains. We provide progress reporting on electric cooperatives and telephone cooperatives." Estab. 1954. Circ. 70,000. Byline given. Pays on acceptance. Publishes ms an average of 6 months after acceptance. Editorial lead time 6 months. Submit seasonal material 6 months in advance. Accepts queries by mail, e-mail. Accepts simultaneous submissions. Sample copy and writer's guidelines not available.

NONFICTION Needs general interest, historical, how-to, humor, interview, new product, travel. **Buys 20 mss/year.** Query with published clips. Length: 1,500-2,000 words. **Pays $100-500 minimum for assigned articles. Pays $300-600 for unsolicited articles.** Sometimes pays expenses of writers on assignment.

PHOTOS State availability. Identification of subjects required. Reviews contact sheets. Negotiates payment individually.

COLUMNS Energy Use and Financial Planning, both 750 words. **Buys 6 mss/year.** Query with published clips. **Pays $100-300.**

FICTION Needs historical, humorous, slice-of-life vignettes, western. **Buys 1 mss/year.** Query with published clips. Length: 1,000-2,500 words. **Pays $100-400.**

OHIO

$$ AKRON LIFE & LEISURE

Baker Media Group, 90 S. Maple St., Akron OH 44302. (330)253-0056. Fax: (330)253-5868. E-mail: kmoorhouse@bakermediagroup.com; editor@bakermediagroup.com. Website: akronlife.com. Georgina Carson, editor. **Contact:** Kathy Moorhouse, art director. **10% freelance written.** Monthly regional magazine covering Summit, Stark, Portage and Medina counties. "*Akron Life & Leisure* is a monthly lifestyles publication committed to providing information that enhances and enriches the experience of living in or visiting Akron and the surrounding region of Summit, Portage, Medina and Stark Counties. Each colorful, thoughtfully designed issue profiles interesting places, personalities and events in the arts, sports, entertainment, business, politics and social scene. We cover issues important to the Greater Akron area and significant trends affecting the lives of those who live here." Estab. 2002. Circ. 15,000. Byline given. Pays on publication. Offers 50% kill fee. Publishes ms an average of 4-6 months after acceptance. Editorial lead time 2+ months. Submit seasonal material 6 months in advance. Accepts queries by mail, e-mail, fax. Sample copy free. Guidelines free.

NONFICTION Needs essays, general interest, historical, how-to, humor, interview, photo feature, travel. Query with published clips. Length: 300-2,000 words. **Pays $0.10 max/word for assigned and unsolicited articles.**

PHOTOS Contact: Kathy Moorhouse, art director. State availability. Captions, identification of subjects, model releases required. Reviews GIF/JPEG files. Negotiates payment individually.

$ BEND OF THE RIVER MAGAZINE

P.O. Box 859, Maumee OH 43537. (419)893-0022. Website: bendoftherivermagazine.com. **98% freelance written. This magazine reports that it is eager to work with all writers. "We buy material that we like whether it is by an experienced writer or not.".** Monthly magazine for readers interested in northwestern Ohio history and nostalgia. Estab. 1972. Circ. 6,500. Byline given. Pays on publication. Publishes ms an average of 1 month after acceptance. Submit seasonal material 2 months in advance. Responds in 1 week to queries. Sample copy for $1.25.

NONFICTION Needs historical. **Buys 75 unsolicited mss/year.** Send complete ms. 1,500 words. **Pays $50 on average.**

$$$ CINCINNATI MAGAZINE

Emmis Publishing Corp., 441 Vine St., Suite 200, Cincinnati OH 45202-2039. (513)421-4300. Fax: (513)562-2746. Website: cincinnatimagazine.com. **Contact:** "See website for appropriate editor.". Monthly magazine emphasizing Cincinnati living. Circ. 38,000. Byline given. Pays on publication. Accepts queries by mail, e-mail. Send SASE for writer's guidelines; view content on magazine website.".

NONFICTION Buys 12 mss/year. Query. Length: 2,500-3,500 words. **Pays $500-1,000.**

COLUMNS Topics are Cincinnati media, arts and entertainment, people, politics, sports, business, regional. Length: 1,000-1,500 words. **Buys 10-15 mss/year.** Query. **Pays $200-400.**

$$$ CLEVELAND MAGAZINE

City Magazines, Inc., 1422 Euclid Ave., Suite 730, Cleveland OH 44115. (216)771-2833. Fax: (216)781-6318. E-mail: gleydura@clevelandmagazine.com; miller@clevelandmagazine.com; kessen@clevelandmagazine.com. Website: clevelandmagazine.com. **Contact:** Kristen Miller, art director. **60% freelance written. Mostly by assignment.** Monthly magazine with a strong Cleveland/Northeast Ohio angle. Estab. 1972. Circ. 50,000. Byline given. Pays on publication. Publishes ms an average of 3 months after acceptance. Editorial lead time 6 months. Submit seasonal material 8 months in advance. Accepts queries by mail, e-mail, fax. Accepts simultaneous submissions. Responds in 2 months to queries.

NONFICTION Needs general interest, historical, humor, interview, travel, home and garden. Query with published clips. Length: 800-4,000 words. **Pays $250-1,200.**

PHOTOS Contact: Kristen Miller, art director. Buys an average of 50 photos from freelancers/issue; 600 photos/year. Model release required for portraits; property release required for individual homes. Photo captions required; include names, date, location, event, phone. Pays on publication. Credit line given. Buys one-time publication, electronic and promotional rights.

COLUMNS Talking Points (opinion or observation-driven essay), approx. 1,000 words Query with published clips. **Pays $300**

$$$ COLUMBUS MONTHLY

P.O. Box 29913, Columbus OH 43229-7513. (614)888-4567. Fax: (614)848-3838. Website: columbusmonthly.com. **40-60% freelance written. Prefers to work with published/established writers.** Monthly magazine emphasizing subjects specifically related to Columbus and Central Ohio. Circ. 35,000. Byline given. Pays on publication. Publishes ms an average of 2 months after acceptance. Responds in 1 month to queries. Sample copy for $6.50.

NONFICTION Buys 2-3 unsolicited mss/year. Query. Length: 250-4,000 words. **Pays $85-900.** Sometimes pays expenses of writers on assignment.

INDIAN HILL LIVING

Community Publications, Inc., 179 Fairfield Ave., Bellevue KY 41074. (859)291-1412. Fax: (859)291-1417. E-mail: indianhill@livingmagazines.com. Website: livingmagazines.com. Monthly magazine covering Indian Hill community. Estab. 1983. Circ. 3,000. Byline given. Pays on publication. Editorial lead time 2 months. Submit seasonal material 3 months in advance. Accepts queries by mail, e-mail, fax. Guidelines by e-mail.

NONFICTION Needs book excerpts, essays, exposè, general interest, historical, humor, inspirational, interview, new product, personal experience, photo feature, travel. Does not want anything unrelated to Indian Hill, Ohio. Query.

PHOTOS State availability. Captions, identification of subjects, model releases required. Reviews contact sheets, negatives, transparencies, prints, GIF/JPEG files. Negotiates payment individually.

COLUMNS Financial; Artistic (reviews, etc.); Historic; Food. Query.

FICTION Needs adventure, historical, humorous, mainstream, slice-of-life vignettes. Query.

POETRY Needs free verse, light verse, traditional. Please query.

FILLERS Please query. Needs anecdotes, short humor.

$$$ OHIO MAGAZINE

Great Lakes Publishing Co., 1422 Euclid Ave., Suite 730, Cleveland OH 44115. (216)771-2833. E-mail: editorial@ohiomagazine.com. Website: ohiomagazine.com. **50% freelance written.** Monthly magazine emphasizing Ohio-based travel, news and feature material that highlights what's special and unique about the state. Estab. 1978. Circ. 80,000. Byline given. Pays on publication. 20% kill fee. Publishes ms an average of 6 months after acceptance. Submit seasonal material 6 months in advance. Accepts queries by mail, e-mail, fax. Responds in 3 months to queries. Responds in 3 months to mss. Sample copy for $3.95 and 9×12 SAE or online. Guidelines available online.

NONFICTION Length: 1,000-3,000 words. **Pays $300-1,200.** Sometimes pays expenses of writers on assignment.

REPRINTS Contact Emily Vanuch, advertising coordinator Pays 50% of amount paid for an original article

PHOTOS Contact: Lesley Blake, art director. Rate negotiable.

COLUMNS Buys minimum 5 unsolicited mss/year. Pays $100-600.

OKLAHOMA

[+]$$ INTERMISSION

Langdon Publishing, 110 E. 2nd St., Tulsa OK 74103-3212. (918)596-2368. Fax: (918)596-7144. E-mail: nhermann@cityoftulsa.org. Website: tulsapac.com. **Contact:** Nancy Hermann, editor-in-chief. **30% freelance written.** Monthly magazine covering entertainment. "We feature profiles of entertainers appearing at our center, Q&As, stories on the events and entertainers slated for the Tulsa PAC." Byline given. Pays on publication. Offers 50% kill fee. Publishes ms an average of 1 month after acceptance. Editorial lead time 2 months. Submit seasonal material 2 months in advance. Accepts queries by mail, e-mail. Accepts simultaneous submissions. Responds in 2 weeks to queries. Sample copy available online. Guidelines by e-mail.

NONFICTION Needs general interest, interview. Does not want personal experience. **Buys 35 mss/year.** Query with published clips. Length: 600-1,400 words. **Pays $100-200.**

COLUMNS Q&A (personalities and artists tied into the events at the Tulsa PAC), 1,100 words. **Buys 12 mss/year.** Query with published clips. **Pays $100-150.**

$$ OKLAHOMA TODAY

P.O. Box 1468, Oklahoma City OK 73101-1468. (405)230-8450; (800)777-1793. Fax: (405)230-8650. E-mail: megan@oklahomatoday.com. Website: oklahomatoday.com. **Contact:** Megan Rossman, associate editor. **80% freelance written. Works with approximately 25 new/unpublished writers each year.** Bimonthly magazine covering people, places, and things Oklahoman. "We are interested in showing off the best Oklahoma has to offer; we're pretty serious about our travel slant but regularly run history, nature, and personality profiles." Estab. 1956. Circ. 45,000. Byline given. Pays on publication. Publishes ms an average of 6 months after acceptance. Submit seasonal material 1 year in advance. Accepts queries by mail, e-mail. Responds in 4 months to queries. Sample copy for $4.95 and 9×12 SASE or online. Guidelines available online.

NONFICTION Needs book excerpts, on Oklahoma topics, historical, Oklahoma only, interview, Oklahomans only, photo feature, in Oklahoma, travel, in Oklahoma. No phone queries. **Buys 20-40 mss/year.** Query with published clips. Length: 250-3,000 words. **Pays $25-750.**

PHOTOS "We are especially interested in developing contacts with photographers who live in Oklahoma or have shot here. Send samples. Photo guidelines for SASE.". . Captions, identification of subjects required. Reviews 4×5, 2&frac14:x2¼, and 35mm color transparencies, high-quality transparencies, slides, and b&w prints. Pays $50-750 for color.

OREGON

🖲🖲 OREGON COAST

4969 Highway 101 N. #2, Florence OR 97439. E-mail: Rosemary@nwmags.com. Website: northwestmagazines.com. **Contact:** Rosemary Camozzi. **65% freelance written.** Bimonthly magazine covering the Oregon Coast. Estab. 1982. Circ. 50,000. Byline given. Pays after publication. Offers 33% (on assigned stories only, not on stories accepted on spec) kill fee. Publishes ms an average of up to 1 year after acceptance. Submit seasonal material 6 months in advance. Accepts queries by mail, e-mail. Responds in 3 months to queries. Sample copy for $4.50. Guidelines available on website.

◯This company also publishes *Northwest Travel*.
NONFICTION Buys 55 mss/year. Query with published clips. Length: 500-1,500 words. **Pays $75-350, plus 2 contributor copies.**
REPRINTS Send tearsheet or photocopy and information about when and where the material previously appeared. Pays an average of 60% of the amount paid for an original article.
PHOTOS Photo submissions with no ms or stand alone or cover photos. Send photos. Captions, identification of subjects, True required. Slides or high-resolution digital.

PENNSYLVANIA

🖲🖲 BERKS COUNTY LIVING

201 Washington St., Suite 525, GoggleWorks Center for the Arts, Reading PA 19601. (610)898-1928. Fax: (610)898-1933. E-mail: fscoboria@berkscountyliving.com. Website: berkscountyliving.com. **Contact:** Francine Scoboria. **90% freelance written.** Bimonthly magazine covering topics of interest to people living in Berks County, Pennsylvania. Estab. 2000. Circ. 36,000. Byline given. Pays on publication. Offers 25% kill fee. Publishes ms an average of 4 months after acceptance. Editorial lead time 3 months. Submit seasonal material 4 months in advance. Accepts queries by mail, e-mail. Accepts simultaneous submissions. Responds in 1 week to queries. Responds in 1 month to mss. Sample copy for sae with 9×12 envelope and 2 First-Class stamps. Guidelines available online.
NONFICTION Needs expose, general interest, historical, how-to, humor, inspirational, interview, new product, photo feature, travel, food, health. **Buys 25 mss/year.** Query. Length: 750-2,000 words. **Pays**

$150-400. Sometimes pays expenses of writers on assignment.
PHOTOS State availability. Captions, identification of subjects, model releases required. Reviews 35mm or greater transparencies, any size prints. Negotiates payment individually.

🖲🖲 MAIN LINE TODAY

Today Media, Inc., 4699 West Chester Pike, Newtown Square PA 19073. (610)848-6037. Fax: (610)325-5215. Website: mainlinetoday.com. **60% freelance written.** Monthly magazine serving Philadelphia's main line and western suburbs. Estab. 1996. Circ. 20,000. Byline given. Pays on publication. Offers 25% kill fee. Publishes ms an average of 3 months after acceptance. Editorial lead time 5 months. Submit seasonal material 5 months in advance. Accepts queries by fax. Accepts simultaneous submissions. Responds in 2 weeks to queries. Responds in 1 month to mss. Sample copy free. Guidelines free.
NONFICTION Needs book excerpts, historical, how-to, humor, interview, opinion, photo feature, travel. Special issues: Health & Wellness Guide (September and March). Query with published clips. Length: 400-3,000 words. **Pays $125-650.** Sometimes pays expenses of writers on assignment.
PHOTOS State availability. Identification of subjects, model releases required. Reviews GIF/JPEG files. Negotiates payment individually.
COLUMNS Profile (local personality); Neighborhood (local people/issues); End of the Line (essay/humor); Living Well (health/wellness), all 1,600 words. **Buys 50 mss/year.** Query with published clips. **Pays $125-350.**

🖲🖲 PENNSYLVANIA

Pennsylvania Magazine Co., P.O. Box 755, Camp Hill PA 17001-0755. (717)697-4660. E-mail: pamag@aol.com. Website: pa-mag.com. **90% freelance written.** Bimonthly magazine covering people, places, events, and history in Pennsylvania. Estab. 1981. Circ. 33,000. Byline given. Pays on acceptance except for articles (by authors unknown to us) sent on speculation. Offers kill fee. 25% kill fee for assigned articles. Publishes ms an average of 9 months after acceptance. Submit seasonal material 9 months in advance. Accepts queries by mail, e-mail. Responds in 4-6 weeks to queries. Sample copy free. Guidelines for #10 SASE or by e-mail.

NONFICTION Nothing on Amish topics, hunting, or skiing. **Buys 75-120 mss/year.** Query. Length: 750-2,500 words. **Pays 15¢/word.**

REPRINTS Send photocopy with rights for sale noted and information about when and where the material previously appeared. Pays 5¢/word.

PHOTOS No original slides or transparencies. Photography Essay (highlights annual photo essay contest entries and showcases individual photographers). Captions, True required. Reviews 35mm 2 ¼×2 ¼ color transparencies, 5×7 to 8×10 color prints, digital photos (send printouts and CD OR DVD or contact eitodro uplo tad to FTP site. Pays $35-45 . Pays $25-35 for inside photos; $150 for covers.

COLUMNS Round Up (short items about people, unusual events, museums, historical topics/events, family and individually owned consumer-related businesses), 250-1,300 words; Town and Country (items about people or events illustrated with commissioned art), 500 words. Include SASE. Query. **Pays 15¢/word.**

$$ PENNSYLVANIA HERITAGE

Pennsylvania Historical and Museum Commission and the Pennsylvania Heritage Society, Commonwealth Keystone Bldg., Plaza Level, 400 North St., Harrisburg PA 17120-0053. (717)787-2407. Fax: (717)346-9099. E-mail: miomalley@state.pa.us. Website: paheritage.org. **75% freelance written. Prefers to work with published/established writers.** Quarterly magazine. *Pennsylvania Heritage* introduces readers to Pennsylvania's rich culture and historic legacy; educates and sensitizes them to the value of preserving that heritage; and entertains and involves them in such a way as to ensure that Pennsylvania's past has a future. The magazine is intended for intelligent lay readers. Estab. 1974. Circ. 10,000. Byline given. Pays on publication. Publishes ms an average of 1 year after acceptance. Accepts queries by mail, e-mail. Responds in 10 weeks to queries. Responds in 8 months to mss. Sample copy for $5 and 9×12 SAE or online. Guidelines for #10 SASE.

> *Pennsylvania Heritage* is now considering freelance submissions that are shorter in length (2,000-3,000 words); pictorial/photographic essays; biographies of famous (and not-so-famous) Pennsylvanians; and interviews with individuals who have helped shape, make, and preserve the Keystone State's history and heritage.

NONFICTION No articles which do not relate to Pennsylvania history or culture. **Buys 20-24 mss/year.** Prefers to see mss with suggested illustrations. Length: 2,000-3,500 words. **Pays $100-500.**

PHOTOS State availability of or send photos. Captions, identification of subjects required. $25-200 for transparencies; $5-75 for b&w photos.

$$ PHILADELPHIA STYLE

Philadelphia Style Magazine, LLC, 141 League St., Philadelphia PA 19147. (215)468-6670. Fax: (215)223-3095. E-mail: info@phillystylemag.com. Website: phillystylemag.com. **Contact:** Sarah Schaffer, editor in chief. **50% freelance written.** "Bimonthly magazine covering upscale living in the Philadelphia region. Topics include: celebrity interviews, fashion (men's and women's), food, home and design, real estate, dining, beauty, travel, arts and entertainment, and more. Our magazine is a positive look at the best ways to live in the Philadelphia region. Submitted articles should speak to an upscale, educated audience of professionals that live in the Delaware Valley." Estab. 1999. Circ. 60,000. Byline given. Pays on publication. Offers 25% kill fee. Publishes ms an average of 3 months after acceptance. Editorial lead time 2-4 months. Submit seasonal material 6 months in advance. Accepts queries by mail, e-mail, fax.

NONFICTION Needs general interest, interview, travel, region-specific articles. "We are not looking for articles that do not have a regional spin." **Buys 100+ mss/year.** Send complete ms. Length: 300-2,500 words. **Pays $50-500.**

COLUMNS Declarations (celebrity interviews and celebrity contributors); Currents (fashion news); Manor (home and design news); Liberties (beauty and travel news); Dish (dining news); Life in the City (fresh, quirky, regional reporting on books, real estate, art, retail, dining, events, and little-known stories/facts about the region), 100-500 words; Vanguard (people on the forefront of Philadelphia's arts, media, fashion, business, and social scene), 500-700 words; In the Neighborhood (reader-friendly reporting on up-and-coming areas of the region including dining, shopping, attractions, and recreation), 2,000-2,500 words. Query with published clips or send complete ms. **Pays $50-500.**

$$$$ PITTSBURGH MAGAZINE

WiesnerMedia, 600 Waterfront Drive, Suite 100, Pittsburgh PA 15222-4795. (412)304-0900. Fax: (412)304-0938. E-mail: editors@pittsburghmagazine.com. Website: pittsburghmag.com. **70% freelance written.** Monthly magazine. "*Pittsburgh* presents issues, analyzes problems, and strives to encourage a better understanding of the community. Our region is Western Pennsylvania, Eastern Ohio, Northern West Virginia, and Western Maryland." Estab. 1970. Circ. 75,000. Byline given. Pays on publication. Offers kill fee. Offers kill fee. Publishes ms an average of 2 months after acceptance. Submit seasonal material 6 months in advance. Accepts queries by mail. Responds in 2 months to queries. Sample copy for $2 (old back issues). Writer's guidelines online or via SASE.

NONFICTION Needs expose, lifestyle, sports, informational, service, business, medical, profile. "We have minimal interest in historical articles and we do not publish fiction, poetry, advocacy, or personal reminiscence pieces." Query in writing with outline and clips. Length: 1,200-4,000 words. **Pays $300-1,500+.**

PHOTOS Query. Model releases required. Pays pre-negotiated expenses of writer on assignment.

$ SUSQUEHANNA LIFE

637 Market St., Lewisburg PA 17837. (800)232-1670. Fax: (570)524-7796. E-mail: susquehannalife@gmail.com. Website: susquehannalife.com. **80% freelance written.** Quarterly magazine covering Central Pennsylvania lifestyle. Estab. 1993. Circ. 45,000. Byline given. Pays on publication. Offers 50% kill fee. Publishes ms an average of 6-9 months after acceptance. Editorial lead time 3-6 months. Submit seasonal material 4-6 months in advance. Accepts queries by e-mail. NoResponds in 4-6 weeks to queries. Responds in 1-3 months to mss. Sample copy for $4.95, plus 5 first-class stamps. Guidelines for #10 SASE.

NONFICTION Needs book excerpts, general interest, historical, how-to, inspirational, related to the region, interview, photo feature, travel. Does not want fiction. **Buys 30-40 mss/year.** Query or send complete ms. Length: 800-1,200 words. **Pays $75-125.** Sometimes pays expenses of writers on assignment.

PHOTOS Send photos. Captions, identification of subjects, model releases required. Reviews contact sheets, prints, GIF/JPEG files. Offers $20-25/photo.

POETRY Must have a Central PA angle.

RHODE ISLAND

$$$ RHODE ISLAND MONTHLY

The Providence Journal Co., 717 Allens Ave.,, Suite 105, Providence RI 02905. (401)649-4800. Website: rimonthly.com. **50% freelance written**. Monthly magazine. *Rhode Island Monthly* is a general interest consumer magazine with a strict Rhode Island focus. Estab. 1988. Circ. 41,000. Byline given. Pays on acceptance. Offers 25% kill fee. Publishes ms an average of 3 months after acceptance. Editorial lead time 3 months. Submit seasonal material 6 months in advance. Accepts queries by mail, e-mail, fax. Responds in 6 weeks to queries. Guidelines free.

NONFICTION Needs expose, general interest, interview, photo feature. **Buys 40 mss/year.** Query with published clips. Length: 1,800-3,000 words. **Pays $600-1,200.** Sometimes pays expenses of writers on assignment.

SOUTH CAROLINA

CHARLESTON MAGAZINE

P.O. Box 1794, Mt. Pleasant SC 29465-1794. (843)971-9811 or (888)242-7624. E-mail: lauren@charlestonmag.com; jed@charlestonmag.com. Website: charlestonmag.com. Jed Drew, publisher. **Contact:** Lauren Brooks Johnson, managing editor. **80% freelance written.** Bimonthly magazine covering current issues, events, arts and culture, leisure pursuits, travel, and personalities, as they pertain to the city of Charleston and surrounding areas. A Lowcountry institution for more than 30 years, *Charleston Magazine* captures the essence of Charleston and her surrounding areas—her people, arts and architecture, culture and events, and natural beauty. Estab. 1972. Circ. 25,000. Byline given. Pays 1 month after publication. Submit seasonal material 4 months in advance. Accepts queries by mail, e-mail, fax. Sample copies may be ordered at cover price from office. Guidelines for #10 sase.

NONFICTION Needs general interest, humor, interview, opinion, photo feature, travel, food, architecture, sports, current events/issues, art. Not interested in 'Southern nostalgia' articles or gratuitous history pieces. **Buys 40 mss/year.** Query with published clips and SASE. Length: 150-1,500 words. **Payment negotiated** Sometimes pays expenses of writers on assignment.

REPRINTS Send photocopy and information about when and where the material previously appeared. Payment negotiable.

PHOTOS Send photos. Identification of subjects required. Reviews contact sheets, transparencies, slides.

COLUMNS Channel Markers (general local interest), 50-400 words; Local Seen (profile of local interest), 500 words; In Good Taste (restaurants and culinary trends in the city), 1,000-1,200 words, plus recipes; Chef at Home (profile of local chefs), 1,200 words, plus recipes; On the Road (travel opportunities near Charleston), 1,000-1,200 words; Southern View (personal experience about Charleston life), 750 words; Doing Business (profiles of exceptional local businesses and entrepreneurs), 1,000-1,200 words; Native Talent (local profiles), 1,000-1,200 words; Top of the Shelf (reviews of books with Southern content or by a Southern author), 750 words.

$$ HILTON HEAD MONTHLY

P.O. Box 5926, Hilton Head Island SC 29938. Fax: (843)842-5743. E-mail: editor@hiltonheadmonthly.com. Website: hiltonheadmonthly.com. **Contact:** Jeff Vrabel, Editor. **75% freelance written.** Monthly magazine covering the people, business, community, environment, and lifestyle of Hilton Head, South Carolina and the surrounding Lowcountry. Our mission is to offer lively, fresh writing about Hilton Head Island, an upscale, environmentally conscious and intensely pro-active resort community on the coast of South Carolina." Circ. 35,000. Byline given. Pays on publication. Offers 50% kill fee. Publishes ms an average of 6 months after acceptance. Editorial lead time 3 months. Submit seasonal material 4 months in advance. Accepts queries by mail, e-mail. NoAccepts simultaneous submissions. Responds in 1 week to queries. Responds in 4 months to mss. Sample copy for $3.

NONFICTION Needs general interest, historical, history only, how-to, home related, humor, interview, Hilton Head residents only, opinion, general humor or Hilton Head Island community affairs, personal experience, travel. Everything is local, local, local, so we're especially interested in profiles of notable residents (or those with Lowcountry ties) and original takes on home design/maintenance, environmental issues, entrepreneurship, health, sports, arts and entertainment, humor, travel and volunteerism. We like to see how national trends/issues play out on a local level." **Buys 225-250 mss/year.** Query with published clips.

PHOTOS State availability. Reviews contact sheets, prints, digital samples. Negotiates payment individually.

COLUMNS News; Business; Lifestyles (hobbies, health, sports, etc.); Home; Around Town (local events, charities and personalities); People (profiles, weddings, etc.). Query with synopsis. **Pays 20¢/word.**

TENNESSEE

$$ AT HOME TENNESSEE

671 N. Ericson Rd., Suite 200, Cordova TN 38018. (901)684-4155. Fax: (901)684-4156. Website: athometn.com. **Contact:** Visit website for editorial e-mail contacts. **50% freelance written.** Monthly magazine. Estab. 2002. Circ. 37,000. Byline given. Pays on publication. Offers 50% kill fee. Editorial lead time 2 months. Submit seasonal material 2-3 months in advance. Accepts queries by e-mail. NoResponds in 1-2 months to queries. Sample copy for $4.99. Guidelines free.

NONFICTION Needs general interest, how-to, interview, travel, landscaping, arts, design. Does not want opinion. Query with published clips. Length: 400-900 words. **Pays $50-200.**

PHOTOS Contact: Nikki Aviotti, creative director. Send photos. Reviews GIF/JPEG files.

$$ MEMPHIS

Contemporary Media, P.O. Box 1738, Memphis TN 38101. (901)521-9000. Fax: (901)521-0129. E-mail: tibbs@memphismagazine.com. Website: memphismagazine.com. **Contact:** Mary Helen Tibbs, editor. **30% freelance written. Works with a small number of new/unpublished writers.** Monthly magazine covering Memphis and the local region. Our mission is to provide Memphis with a colorful and informative look at the people, places, lifestyles and businesses that make the Bluff City unique. Estab. 1976. Circ. 24,000. No byline given. Pays on publication. Submit seasonal material 3 months in advance. Accepts queries by mail, e-mail, fax.

NONFICTION Needs essays, general interest, historical, interview, photo feature, travel, Interiors/exteriors, local issues and events. Special issues: Restaurant Guide and City Guide. **Buys 20 mss/year.** Query with published clips. Length: 500-3,000 words. **Pays 10-30¢/word.** Sometimes pays expenses of writers on assignment.

PHOTOS State availability. Reviews contact sheets, transparencies.

FICTION One story published annually as part of contest. Open only to those within 150 miles of Memphis. See website for details.

$$ MEMPHIS DOWNTOWNER MAGAZINE

Downtown Productions, Inc., 408 S. Front St., Suite 109, Memphis TN 38103. (901)525-7118. Fax:

(901)525-7128. E-mail: editor@memphisdowntowner.com. Website: memphisdowntowner.com. **Contact:** Terre Gorham, editor. **50% freelance written.** Monthly magazine covering features on positive aspects with a Memphis tie-in, especially to downtown. "We feature people, companies, nonprofits, and other issues that the general Memphis public would find interesting, entertaining, and informative. All editorial focuses on the positives Memphis has. No negative commentary or personal judgements. Controversial subjects should be treated fairly and balanced without bias." Estab. 1991. Circ. 30,000. Byline given. Pays on 15th of month in which assignment is published. Offers 25% kill fee. Publishes ms an average of 2-6 months after acceptance. Editorial lead time 3-6 months. Submit seasonal material 3-6 months in advance. Accepts queries by mail, e-mail. Responds in 2 weeks to queries. Sample copy free. Guidelines by e-mail.

NONFICTION Needs general interest, historical, how-to, humor, interview, personal experience, photo feature. **Buys 40-50 mss/year.** Query with published clips. Length: 600-2,000 words. **Pays scales vary depending on scope of assignment, but typically runs 15¢/word.** Sometimes pays expenses of writers on assignment.

PHOTOS State availability. Identification of subjects required. Reviews GIF/JPEG files (300 dpi). Negotiates payment individually.

COLUMNS So It Goes (G-rated humor), 600-800 words; Discovery 901 (Memphis one-of-a-kinds), 1,000-1,200 words. **Buys 6 mss/year.** Query with published clips. **Pays $100-150.**

FILLERS Unusual, interesting, or how-to or what to look for appealing to a large, general audience. Needs facts.

TEXAS

$ HILL COUNTRY SUN

T.D. Austin Lane, Inc., 100 Commons Rd., Suite 7, #319, Dripping Springs TX 78620. (512)484-9715. Fax: (512)847-5162. E-mail: melissa@hillcountrysun.com. Website: hillcountrysun.com. **75% freelance written.** Monthly tabloid covering traveling in the Central Texas Hill Country. "We publish stories of interesting people, places and events in the Central Texas Hill Country." Estab. 1990. Circ. 34,000. Byline given. Pays on acceptance. Publishes ms an average of 2 months after acceptance. Editorial lead time 1 month. Submit seasonal material 2 months in advance. Accepts queries by mail and e-mail. Responds in 1 week to queries. Responds in 1 month to mss. Sample copy free. Guidelines available online.

NONFICTION Needs interview, travel. No first person articles. **Buys 50 mss/year.** Query. Length: 600-800 words. **Pays $50-60.**

PHOTOS State availability of or send photos. Identification of subjects required. No additional payment for photos accepted with ms.

$$$ HOUSTON PRESS

1621 Milam, Suite 100, Houston TX 77002. (713)280-2400. Fax: (713)280-2444. Website: houstonpress.com. **Contact:** Margaret Downing, editor. **40% freelance written.** "Weekly tabloid covering news and arts stories of interest to a Houston audience. If the same story could run in Seattle, then it's not for us.". Estab. 1989. Byline given. Pays on publication. Publishes ms an average of 2 weeks after acceptance. Editorial lead time 2 months. Submit seasonal material 3 months in advance. Sample copy for $3.

NONFICTION Needs expose, general interest, interview, arts reviews. Query with published clips. Length: 300-4,500 words. **Pays $10-1,000.** Sometimes pays expenses of writers on assignment.

PHOTOS State availability. Identification of subjects required. Negotiates payment individually.

$$$ TEXAS HIGHWAYS

Texas Highways Editor, Box 141009, Austin TX 78714-1009. (800)839-4997. Website: texashighways.com. **70% freelance written.** Monthly magazine encourages travel within the state and tells the Texas story to readers around the world. Estab. 1974. Circ. 250,000. Pays on acceptance. Publishes ms an average of 1 year after acceptance. Accepts queries by mail. Responds in 2 months to queries. Guidelines available online.

NONFICTION Query with description, published clips, additional background materials (charts, maps, etc.) and SASE. Length: 1,200-1,500 words. **Pays 40-50¢/word.**

$$$$ TEXAS MONTHLY

Emmis Publishing LP, P.O. Box 1569, Austin TX 78767-1569. (512)320-6900. Fax: (512)476-9007. E-mail: lbaldwin@texasmonthly.com. Website: texasmonthly.com. **Contact:** Jake Silverstein, editor. **10%**

freelance written. Monthly magazine covering Texas. Estab. 1973. Circ. 300,000. Byline given. Pays on acceptance, $1/word and writer's expenses. Publishes ms an average of 1-3 months after acceptance. Editorial lead time 2 months. Submit seasonal material 3 months in advance. Accepts queries by mail, e-mail, fax. NoResponds in 6-8 weeks to queries. Responds in 6-8 weeks to mss. Sample copy for $7. Guidelines available online.

NONFICTION Contact: Contact John Broders, associate editor (jbroders@texasmonthly.com). Needs book excerpts, essays, expose, general interest, interview, personal experience, photo feature, travel. Does not want articles without a Texas connection. **Buys 15 mss/year.** Query. Length: 2,000-5,000 words. Pays expenses of writers on assignment.

PHOTOS Contact: Leslie Baldwin, photo editor.

💲💲 TEXAS PARKS & WILDLIFE

4200 Smith School Rd., Building D, Austin TX 78744. (512)389-8793. Fax: (512)707-1913. E-mail: louie.bond@tpwd.state.tx.us. Website: tpwmagazine.com. For photos: Brandon Jakobeit, assistant art director, brandon.jakobeit@tpwd.state.tx.us. **Contact:** Louie Bond, editor. **80% freelance written.** Monthly magazine featuring articles about "Texas hunting, fishing, birding, outdoor recreation, game and nongame wildlife, state parks, environmental issues.". All articles must be about Texas. Estab. 1942. Circ. 150,000. Byline given. Pays on acceptance. Offers kill fee. Kill fee determined by contract, usually $200-250. Publishes ms an average of 4 months after acceptance. Accepts queries by mail. Responds in 1 month to queries. Responds in 3 months to mss. Sample copy available online. Guidelines available online.

> 🔵 *Texas Parks & Wildlife* needs more short items for front-of-the-book scout section and wildlife articles written from a natural history perspective (not for hunters).

NONFICTION Needs general interest, Texas only, how-to, outdoor activities, photo feature, travel, state parks and small towns. **Buys 60 mss/year.** Query with published clips; follow up by e-mail 1 month after submitting query. Length: 500-2,500 words. **Pays 50¢/word.**

PHOTOS Send photos to photo editor. Captions, identification of subjects required. Reviews transparencies. Offers $65-500/photo.

VERMONT

💲💲 VERMONT LIFE MAGAZINE

One National Life Dr., 6th Fl, Montpelier VT 05620. (802)828-3241. Fax: (802)828-3366. E-mail: editors@vtlife.com. Website: vermontlife.com. **Contact:** Bill Anderson, managing editor. **90% freelance written. Prefers to work with published/established writers.** Quarterly magazine. "*Vermont Life* is interested in any article, query, story idea, photograph or photo essay that have to do with Vermont. As the state magazine, we are most favorably impressed with pieces that present positive aspects of life within the state's borders. We have no rules, however, about avoiding controversy when the presentation of the controversial subject can illustrate some aspect of Vermont's unique character." Estab. 1946. Circ. 52,000. Byline given. Offers kill fee. Publishes ms an average of 9 months after acceptance. Submit seasonal material 1 year in advance. Accepts queries by mail, e-mail. Responds in 1 month to queries. Guidelines available online.

NONFICTION "No Vermont clichés, and please do not send first-person accounts of your vacation trip to Vermont." **Buys 60 mss/year.** 1,500 words average **Pays $100-900 depending on scope of article**

PHOTOS Buys seasonal photographs. Gives assignments but only with experienced photographers. Query in writing. Original digital photos from cameras of at least 6 megapixels. "*Vermont Life* uses only digital photography. Photographs should be current (taken within the last five years).". Metadata for each image must include captions, photographer's name, identification of subjects, date; model releases required. Pays $75-200 inside color; $500 for cover.

VIRGINIA

💲💲 THE ROANOKER

Leisure Publishing Co., Leisure Publishing Co., 3424 Brambleton Ave., Roanoke VA 24018. (540)989-6138. Fax: (540)989-7603. E-mail: jwood@leisurepublishing.com. Website: theroanoker.com. **75% freelance written. Works with a small number of new/unpublished writers each year.** Magazine published 6 times/year. "*The Roanoker* is a general interest city magazine for the people of Roanoke, Virginia and the surrounding area. Our readers are primarily upper-income, well-educated professionals between the ages of 35 and 60. Coverage ranges from hard news and consumer information to restaurant reviews and local history." Estab. 1974. Circ. 12,000. Byline given. Pays on publication. Publishes ms an average of 4 months after acceptance. Submit seasonal material 4 months in advance. Accepts queries by mail, e-mail, fax. Responds in 2 months to queries. Sample copy for $2 and 9×12 SASE with 5 first-class stamps or online.

NONFICTION Needs exposè, historical, how-to, live better in western Virginia, interview, of well-known area personalities, photo feature, travel, Virginia and surrounding states, periodic special sections on fashion, real estate, media, banking, investing. **Buys 30 mss/year.** Send complete ms. 1,400 words maximum **Pays $35-200.**

PHOTOS Send photos. Captions, model releases required. Reviews color transparencies, digital submissions. Pays $25-50/published photograph.

COLUMNS Skinny (shorts on people, Roanoke-related books, local issues, events, arts and culture).

🟢🟢 VIRGINIA LIVING

Cape Fear Publishing, 109 E. Cary St., Richmond VA 23219. (804)343-7539. Fax: (804)649-0306. E-mail: RichardErnsberger@capefear.com. Website: virginialiving.com. **Contact:** Richard Ernsberger, Jr. **80% freelance written**. Bimonthly magazine covering life and lifestyle in Virginia. "We are a large-format (10×13) glossy magazine covering life in Virginia, from food, architecture, and gardening, to issues, profiles, and travel." Estab. 2002. Circ. 70,000. Byline given. Pays on publication. Publishes ms an average of 4-6 months after acceptance. Editorial lead time 2-6 months. Submit seasonal material 1 year in advance. Accepts queries by mail. NoAccepts simultaneous submissions. Responds in 1 month to queries. Responds in 1 month to mss. Sample copy for $5.

NONFICTION Needs book excerpts, essays, expose, general interest, historical, interview, new product, personal experience, photo feature, travel, architecture, design. No fiction, poetry, previously published articles, or stories with a firm grasp of the obvious. **Buys 180 mss/year.** Query with published clips or send complete ms. Length: 300-3,000 words. **Pays 50¢/word.**

PHOTOS Contact: Tyler Darden, art director. Captions, identification of subjects, model releases required. Reviews contact sheets, 6x7 transparencies, 8×10 prints, GIF/JPEG files. Negotiates payment individually.

COLUMNS Beauty; Travel; Books; Events; Sports (all with a unique Virginia slant), all 1,000-1,500 words. **Buys 50 mss/year.** Send complete ms. **Pays $120-200.**

WASHINGTON

➕🟢🟢 PUGET SOUND MAGAZINE

2115 Renee Place, Port Townsend WA 98368. (206)414-1589. Fax: (206)932-2574. E-mail: editorial@puget-soundmagazine.com. Website: pugetsoundmagazine.com. **Contact:** David Petrich. **50% freelance written**. Online magazine covering regional focus on adventure, travel, recreation, art, food, wine, culture, wildlife, plants, and healthy living on the shoreline communities of Puget Sound and the Salish Sea. Olympia WA to Campbell River, BC. Writing from a personal experience, human interest perspective. We do profiles, historic pieces, how to—mostly features on water-centric lifestyles. Estab. 2008. Circ. 30,000 when go to print in 2011 as a quarterly. Byline given. Publishes ms an average of 2 months after acceptance. Editorial lead time 2 months. Accepts queries by mail, e-mail. Accepts simultaneous submissions. Responds in 4 weeks to queries. Sample copy free. Guidelines available online.

NONFICTION Contact: Kathleen McKelvey. Needs book excerpts, essays, general interest, historical, how-to, humor, inspirational, interview, personal experience, photo feature, travel. Special issues: No special issues at this time. Nothing negative, political, pornographic, religious. Send complete ms. Length: 800-2,000 words. **Pays 10¢ for assigned articles and for unsolicited articles.**

PHOTOS Contact: Dave Petrich, graphics/creative. State availability of or send photos. Photos require captions, identification of subjects. Reviews contact sheets. Negotiates payment individually.

FICTION Contact: Katherine McKelvey. Needs adventure, historical, humorous, mainstream, mystery, western. **Buys 6 mss/year.** Query with published clips. Word length: 800-1,000 words. **Pays 10¢.word.**

POETRY Contact: Terry Persun, editor. Needs free verse, traditional. Buys 6/yr. poems/year. Submit maximum 3 poems. Length: 25 lines.

🟢🟢 SEATTLE MAGAZINE

Tiger Oak Publications Inc., 1518 1st Ave. S., Suite 500, Seattle WA 98134. (206)284-1750. Fax: (206)284-

2550. E-mail: rachel.hart@tigeroak.com. Website: seattlemagazine.com. **75% freelance written.** "Monthly magazine serving the Seattle metropolitan area. Articles should be written with our readers in mind. They are interested in social issues, the arts, politics, homes and gardens, travel and maintaining the region's high quality of life.". Estab. 1992. Circ. 45,000. Byline given. Pays on or about 30 days after publication. Offers 25% kill fee. Publishes ms an average of 3 months after acceptance. Editorial lead time 6 months. Submit seasonal material 6 months in advance. Accepts queries by mail, e-mail, fax. Responds in 2 months to queries. Sample copy for #10 SASE. Guidelines available online.

NONFICTION Needs book excerpts, local, essays, expose, general interest, humor, interview, photo feature, travel, local/regional interest. No longer accepting queries by mail. Query with published clips. Length: 200-4,000 words. **Pays $50 minimum.**

PHOTOS State availability. Negotiates payment individually.

COLUMNS Scoop, Urban Safari, Voice, Trips, People, Environment, Hot Button, Fitness, Fashion, Eat and Drink Query with published clips. **Pays $225-400.**

$$$ SEATTLE WEEKLY

Village Voice, 1008 Western Ave., Suite 300, Seattle WA 98104. (206)623-0500. Fax: (206)467-4338. Website: seattleweekly.com. **20% freelance written.** Weekly tabloid covering arts, politics, food, business and books with local and regional emphasis. Estab. 1976. Circ. 105,000. Byline given. Pays on publication. Offers variable kill fee. Publishes ms an average of 1 month after acceptance. Submit seasonal material 2 months in advance. Responds in 1 month to queries. Sample copy for $3. Guidelines available online.

NONFICTION Needs book excerpts, expose, general interest, historical, Northwest, humor, interview, opinion. **Buys 6-8 mss/year.** Query with cover letter, resume, published clips and SASE. Length: 300-4,000 words. **Pays $50-800.** Sometimes pays expenses of writers on assignment.

REPRINTS Send tearsheet. Payment varies.

WISCONSIN

$$ MADISON MAGAZINE

Morgan Murphy Media, 7025 Raymond Rd., Madison WI 53719. (608)270-3600. Fax: (608)270-3636. E-mail: bnardi@madisonmagazine.com. Website: madisonmagazine.com. **Contact:** Brennan Nardi. **75% freelance written.** Monthly magazine. Estab. 1978. Byline given. Pays on publication. Offers 33% kill fee. Publishes ms an average of 2 months after acceptance. Editorial lead time 3 months. Submit seasonal material 3-4 months in advance. Accepts queries by mail, e-mail. Accepts simultaneous submissions. Responds in 3 weeks to queries. Responds in 3 weeks to mss. Sample copy free. Guidelines available online.

NONFICTION Needs book excerpts, essays, expose, general interest, historical, how-to, humor, inspirational, interview, new product, opinion, personal experience, photo feature, religious, technical, travel.

PHOTOS State availability. Reviews contact sheets. Negotiates payment individually.

COLUMNS Your Town (local events) and OverTones (local arts/entertainment), both 300 words; Habitat (local house/garden) and Business (local business), both 800 words. **Buys 120 mss/year.** Query with published clips. **Pays variable amount.**

FILLERS Needs anecdotes, facts, gags, newsbreaks, short humor. Length: 100 words. **Pays 20-30¢/word.**

$$$$ MILWAUKEE MAGAZINE

126 N. Jefferson St., Milwaukee WI 53202. (414)273-1101. Fax: (414)273-0016. E-mail: milmag@milwaukeemagazine.com; bruce.murphy@milwaukeemagazine.com. Website: milwaukeemagazine.com. Ann Christenson, senior editor; Evan Solochek, assistant editor. **Contact:** Bruce Murphy, editor. **40% freelance written.** Monthly magazine. "We publish stories about Milwaukee, of service to Milwaukee-area residents and exploring the area's changing lifestyle, business, arts, politics, and dining." Circ. 40,000. Byline given. Pays on publication. Offers 20% kill fee. Publishes ms an average of 2 months after acceptance. Submit seasonal material 6 months in advance. Accepts queries by mail, e-mail. Responds in 6 weeks to queries. Sample copy for $6. Guidelines available online.

NONFICTION Needs essays, expose, general interest, historical, interview, photo feature, travel, food and dining, and other services. "No articles without a strong Milwaukee or Wisconsin angle. Length: 2,500-5,000 words for full-length features; 800 words for 2-page breaker features (short on copy, long on visuals)." **Buys 30-50 mss/year.** Query with published clips. **Pays $700-2,000 for full-length articles.** Sometimes pays expenses of writers on assignment.

COLUMNS Insider (inside information on Milwaukee, exposé, slice-of-life, unconventional angles on current scene), up to 500 words; Mini Reviews for Insider, 125 words. Query with published clips.

WISCONSIN NATURAL RESOURCES

Wisconsin Department of Natural Resources, P.O. Box 7921, Madison WI 53707-7921. (608)266-1510. Fax: (608)264-6293. E-mail: natasha.kassulke@ wisconsin.gov. E-mail: Natasha Kassulke. Website: wnrmag.com. **30% freelance written.** Bimonthly magazine covering environment, natural resource management, and outdoor skills. "We cover current issues in Wisconsin aimed to educate and advocate for resource conservation, outdoor recreation, and wise land use." Estab. 1931. Circ. 90,000. Byline given. Publishes ms an average of 8 months after acceptance. Editorial lead time 6 months. Submit seasonal material 1 year in advance. Accepts queries by mail, e-mail. Accepts simultaneous submissions. Responds in 3 weeks to queries. Responds in 6 months to mss. Sample copy free. Guidelines available online.

NONFICTION Needs essays, how-to, photo feature, features on current outdoor issues and environmental issues. Does not want animal rights pieces, poetry or fiction. Query. Length: 1,500-2,700 words.

PHOTOS Also seeks photos of pets at state properties like wildlife areas, campsites, and trails. Send photos. Identification of subjects required. Reviews transparencies, JPEG files. Offers no additional payment for photos accepted with ms.

💲💲 WISCONSIN TRAILS

333 W. State St., Milwaukee WI 53201. Fax: (414)647-4723. E-mail: clewis@wistrails.com. Website: wisconsintrails.com. **Contact:** Chelsey Lewis. **40% freelance written**. Bimonthly magazine for readers interested in Wisconsin and its contemporary issues, personalities, recreation, history, natural beauty, and arts. Estab. 1960. Circ. 55,000. Byline given. Pays 1 month from publication. Kill fee 20%, up to $75. Publishes ms an average of 6 months after acceptance. Submit seasonal material 1 year in advance. Accepts queries by mail, e-mail, fax. Responds in 2-3 months to queries. Sample copy for $4.95. Guidelines for #10 SASE or online.

NONFICTION Does not accept unsolicited mss. Query or send outline Length: 250-1,500 words. **Pays 25¢/word.** Sometimes pays expenses of writers on assignment.

PHOTOS Contact: editor@wistrails.com. "Because Wisconsin Trails works primarily with professional photographers, we do not pay writers for accompanying images nor do we reimburse for any related expenses. Photos will be credited and the photographer retains all rights.". Contact editor. $75-250.

WYOMING

💲 WYOMING RURAL ELECTRIC NEWS (WREN)

P.O. Box 549, Gillette WY 82717. (307)682-7527. Fax: (307)634-0728. E-mail: wren@vcn.com. **20% freelance written**. Monthly magazine for audience of small town residents, vacation-home owners, farmers, and ranchers. Estab. 1954. Circ. 41,000. Byline given. Pays on acceptance. Publishes ms an average of 2 months after acceptance. Submit seasonal material 2 months in advance. Accepts queries by mail, e-mail, fax, phone. Responds in 3 months to queries. Sample copy for $2.50 and 9×12 SASE. Guidelines for #10 SASE.

NONFICTION No nostalgia, sarcasm, or tongue-in-cheek. **Buys 4-10 mss/year.** Send complete ms. Length: 500-800 words. **Pays up to $140, plus 4 copies.**

REPRINTS Send tearsheet or photocopy and information about when and where the material previously appeared.

PHOTOS Color only.

RELIGIOUS

ALIVE NOW

1908 Grand Ave., P.O. Box 340004, Nashville TN 37203-0004. E-mail: alivenow@upperroom.org. Website: alivenow.upperroom.org. **Contact:** Gina Manskar. Bimonthly thematic magazine for a general Christian audience interested in reflection and meditation. Circ. 40,000. Guidelines available online.

NONFICTION Length: 250-400 words. **Pays $35 and up.**

FICTION Length: 250-400 words. **Pays $35 and up.**

POETRY Needs "We accept any style.". Length: 10-45 lines.

⊘⊘ AMERICA

106 W. 56th St., New York NY 10019. (212)581-4640. Fax: (212)399-3596. E-mail: america@americamagazine.org. E-mail: articles@americamagazine.org; reviews@americamagazine.org. Website: americamagazine.org. "Published weekly for adult, educated, largely Roman Catholic audience. Founded by the Jesuit order and directed today by Jesuits and lay colleagues, America is a resource for spiritual renewal and social analysis guided by the spirit of charity. The print and web editions of America feature timely and thought-provoking articles written by prestigious writers and theologians, and incisive book, film and art reviews." Estab. 1909. Byline given. Pays on acceptance. Responds in 3 weeks to queries. Guidelines available online.

NONFICTION "We are not interested in purely informational pieces or personal narratives which are self-contained and have no larger moral interest." Length: 1,500-2,000 words. **Pays $50-300.**

POETRY Contact: Rev. James S. Torrens, poetry editor. Only 10-12 poems published a year, thousands turned down. Buys 10-12 poems/year. Length: 15-30 lines.

ANCIENT PATHS

P.O. Box 7505, Fairfax Station VA 22039. E-mail: SSBurris@msn.com. Website: editorskylar.com. **Contact:** Skylar H. Burris, Editor. *Ancient Paths*, published biennially in odd-numbered years, provides "a forum for quality Christian poetry." Wants "traditional rhymed/metrical forms and free verse; subtle Christian themes. Seeks poetry that makes the reader both think and feel." Does not want 'preachy' poetry, inconsistent meter, or forced rhyme; no stream of conscious or avant-garde work; no esoteric academic poetry. Has published poetry by Nicholas Samaras, Paul David Adkins, Ida Fasel, and Donna Farley. *Ancient Paths* is 60+ pages, digest-sized, printed, perfectbound, with glossy cover. Issue 17 will feature the work of multiple poets. Receives about 600 queries/year, accepts 10-20 poets. Press run to be determined. Single copy: $10. Make checks payable to Skylar Burris. Estab. 1998.

⊘ BIBLE ADVOCATE

Bible Advocate, Church of God (Seventh Day), P.O. Box 33677, Denver CO 80233. (303)452-7973. E-mail: bibleadvocate@cog7.org. Website: cog7.org/publications/ba/; cog7.org/ba. **Contact:** Sherri Langton, Associate Editor. **25% freelance written.** Religious magazine published 6 times/year. "Our purpose is to advocate the Bible and represent the Church of God (Seventh Day) to a Christian audience." Estab. 1863. Circ. 13,500. Byline given. Pays on publication. Offers 50% kill fee. Publishes ms an average of 9 months after acceptance. Editorial lead time 3 months. Submit seasonal material 6 months in advance. Accepts queries by mail, e-mail; prefers e-mail; attachments ok. Accepts simultaneous submissions. Responds in 2 months to queries. Sample copy for sae with 9×12 envelope and 3 first-class stamps. Guidelines available online.

NONFICTION Needs inspirational, personal experience, religious, Biblical studies. No articles on Christmas or Easter. **Buys 15-20 mss/year.** Send complete ms and SASE. Length: 1,000-1,200 words. **Pays $25-55.**

REPRINTS E-mail manuscript with rights for sale noted.

PHOTOS Send photos. Identification of subjects required. Reviews prints. We no longer buy photos.

POETRY Contact: Sherri Langton, associate editor. Needs free verse, traditional. *Bible Advocate*, published 6 times/year, features "Christian content—to be a voice for the Bible and for the church." *Bible Advocate* is 32 pages, magazine-sized. Receives about 30-50 poems/year, accepts about 10-20. Press run varies; all distributed free. Submit no more than 5 poems at a time. Lines/poem: 5 minimum, 20 maximum. Considers previously published poems (with notification) and simultaneous submissions. Publishes theme issues. Guidelines available for SASE or on website. Responds in 2 months. Acquires first, reprint, electronic, and one-time rights. No avant-garde. Buys 10-12 poems/year. Submit maximum 5/poems. poems. Length: 5-20 lines. **Pays $20 and 2 contributor's copies.**

FILLERS Needs anecdotes, facts. **Buys 5 mss. mss/year.** Length: 50-400 words. **Pays $10-20.**

♁ THE BREAD OF LIFE MAGAZINE

P.O. Box 127, Burlington ON L7R 3×5 Canada. E-mail: info@thebreadoflife.ca. Website: thebreadoflife.ca. *The Bread of Life*, published semimonthly, is "a Catholic charismatic magazine designed to encourage spiritual growth in areas of renewal in the Catholic Church today." Includes feature articles, poetry, regular columns, quizzes and photography. "It's good if contributors are members of The Bread of Life Renewal Centre, a nonprofit, charitable organization.

All of our contributors do so in humble service to our Lord on a volunteer basis." *The Bread of Life* is 48 pages, digest-sized, professionally printed, saddle-stapled, with glossy paper cover. Receives about 50-60 poems/year, accepts about 25%. Press run is 1,700. Membership: $35/year (includes magazine subscription). Cover letter is preferred. Publishes theme issues. Guidelines available for SAE with IRC. Estab. 1977. TrueAccepts simultaneous submissions.

$$ CATHOLIC DIGEST

P.O. Box 6015, 1 Montauk Ave., Suite 200, New London CT 06320. (800)321-0411. Fax: (860)457-3013. E-mail: queries@catholicdigest.com. Website: catholicdigest.com. **12% freelance written.** Monthly magazine. Publishes features and advice on topics ranging from health, psychology, humor, adventure, and family, to ethics, spirituality, and Catholics, from modern-day heroes to saints through the ages. Helpful and relevant reading culled from secular and religious periodicals. Estab. 1936. Circ. 275,000. Byline given. Pays on publication. Editorial lead time 3 months. Submit seasonal material 4-5 months in advance. Accepts queries by mail, e-mail. Responds in 2 months to mss. Sample copy free. Guidelines available online.

NONFICTION Needs book excerpts, essays, general interest, historical, how-to, humor, inspirational, interview, personal experience, religious, travel. Does not accept unsolicited submissions. Send complete ms. Length: 350-1,500 words. **Pays $200-300.**

REPRINTS Send tearsheet or typed ms with rights for sale noted and information about when and where the material previously appeared. Pays $100.

PHOTOS State availability. "If your query is accepted and you have photos that may be used to accompany your submission, please attach them as JPEG files. Photos must be at least 300 dpi to be used in the magazine. Appropriate credit lines and captions should also accompany the photos.". Reviews contact sheets, transparencies, prints. Negotiates payment individually.

FILLERS Contact: Filler Editor. Open Door (statements of true incidents through which people are brought into the Catholic faith, or recover the Catholic faith they had lost), 350-600 words. Send to opendoor@catholicdigest.com. Good Egg (stories about a Catholic who has demonstrated their faith through commitment to their family, community, and church), 350-600 words. Send to goodegg@catholicdigest.com. **Buys 200 mss/year.** 350-600 words.

$$ CATHOLIC FORESTER

Catholic Order of Foresters, 355 Shuman Blvd., P.O. Box 3012, Naperville IL 60566-7012. Fax: (630)983-3384. E-mail: magazine@catholicforester.org. Website: catholicforester.org. Danielle Marsh, art director. **Contact:** Patricia Baron, assoc. editor. **20% freelance written.** Quarterly magazine for members of the Catholic Order of Foresters, a fraternal insurance benefit society. "*Catholic Forester,*is a quarterly magazine filled with product features, member stories, and articles affirming fraternalism, unity, friendship, and true Christian charity among members. Although a portion of each issue is devoted to the organization and its members, a few freelance pieces are published in most issues. These articles cover varied topics to create a balanced issue for the purpose of informing, educating, and entertaining our readers." Estab. 1883. Circ. 137,000. Pays on acceptance. Editorial lead time 6 months. Submit seasonal material 6 months in advance. TrueResponds in 3 months to mss. Sample copy for sae with 9×12 envelope and 4 First-Class stamps. Guidelines available online.

NONFICTION Needs health and wellness, money management and budgeting, parenting and family life, interesting travels, insurance, nostalgia, humor, inspirational, religious, financial. **Buys 12-16 mss/year.** Send complete ms by mail, fax, or e-mail. Rejected material will not be returned without accompanying SASE Length: 500-1,500 words. **Pays 50¢/word.**

PHOTOS State availability. Negotiates payment individually.

FICTION Needs humorous, religious. **Buys 12-16 mss/year.** Length: 500-1,500 words. **Pays 50¢/word.**

POETRY Needs light verse, traditional. Buys 3 poems/year. 15 lines maximum **Pays 30¢/word.**

$$ CELEBRATE LIFE

American Life League, P.O. Box 1350, Stafford VA 22555. (540)659-4171. Fax: (540)659-2586. E-mail: clmag@all.org. Website: clmagazine.org. **Contact:** Editor. **50% freelance-written.** Bimonthly educational magazine covering "pro-life education and human interest". "We are a religious-based publication specializing in pro-life education through human-interest stories and investigative exposés. Our purpose is to inspire, encourage, motivate, and educate pro-life individuals and activists." Estab. 1979. Circ. 30,000. Byline given. Pays on publication. Submit seasonal material 4 months in advance. Accepts queries by mail, e-mail. No.Accepts simultaneous submissions. Responds in 6 months to mss. For sample copy, send 9×12 SAE envelope and 4 first-class stamps. Guidelines free.

NONFICTION "Nonfiction only; No fiction, poetry, music, allegory, devotionals." Query with published clips or send complete ms. Length: 400-1,500 words.

PHOTOS Identification of subjects required.

💲💲💲 CHARISMA & CHRISTIAN LIFE

Charisma Media, 600 Rinehart Rd., Lake Mary FL 32746. (407)333-0600. Fax: (407)333-7133. E-mail: charisma@charismamedia.com. Website: charismamag.com. **Contact:** Marcus Yoars. **80% freelance written.** Monthly magazine covering items of interest to the Pentecostal or independent charismatic reader. Now also online. "More than half of our readers are Christians who belong to Pentecostal or independent charismatic churches, and numerous others participate in the charismatic renewal in mainline denominations." Estab. 1975. Circ. 250,000. Byline given. Pays on publication. Offers $50 kill fee. Publishes ms an average of 3 months after acceptance. Editorial lead time 4 months. Submit seasonal material 5 months in advance. Accepts queries by mail, e-mail. Sample copy for $4. Guidelines by e-mail and online.

NONFICTION Needs book excerpts, expose, general interest, interview, religious. No fiction, poetry, COLUMNS, or sermons. **Buys 40 mss/year.** Query. Length: 1,800-2,500 words. Pays expenses of writers on assignment.

PHOTOS State availability. Model releases required. Reviews contact sheets, 2 ¼×2 ¼ transparencies, 3×5 or larger prints, TIF/JPEG files. Negotiates payment individually.

💲💲 THE CHRISTIAN CENTURY

104 S. Michigan Ave., Suite 700, Chicago IL 60603-5901. (312)263-7510. Fax: (312)263-7540. E-mail: main@christiancentury.org. E-mail: submissions@christiancentury.org; poetry@christiancentury.org. Website: christiancentury.org. **Contact:** Jill Peláez Baumgaertner, poetry editor. **90% freelance written. Works with new/unpublished writers.** Biweekly magazine for ecumenically-minded, progressive Protestants, both clergy and lay. "We seek manuscripts that articulate the public meaning of faith, bringing the resources of religious tradition to bear on such topics as poverty, human rights, economic justice, international relations, national priorities and popular culture. We are also interested in pieces that examine or critique the theology and ethos of individual religious communities. We welcome articles that find fresh meaning in old traditions and that adapt or apply religious traditions to new circumstances. Authors should assume that readers are familiar with main themes in Christian history and theology, are accustomed to the historical-critical study of the Bible and are already engaged in relating faith to social and political issues. Many of our readers are ministers or teachers of religion at the college level. Book reviews are solicited by our books editor. Please note that submissions via e-mail will not be considered. If you are interested in becoming a reviewer for the *Christian Century*, please send your rèsumè and a list of subjects of interest to Attn: Book reviews. Authors must have a critical and analytical perspective on the church and be familiar with contemporary theological discussion." Estab. 1884. Circ. 37,000. Byline given. Pays on publication. Editorial lead time 1 month. Submit seasonal material 4 months in advance. Accepts queries by mail, e-mail. Responds in 4-6 week to queries. Responds in 2 months to mss. Sample copy for $3.50. Guidelines available online.

NONFICTION Needs essays, humor, interview, opinion, religious. No inspirational. **Buys 150 mss/ year.** Send complete ms; query appreciated, but not essential. Length: 1,000-3,000 words. **Pays variable amount for assigned articles. Pays $100-300 for unsolicited articles.**

PHOTOS State availability. Reviews any size prints.

COLUMNS "We do not accept unsolicited submissions for our regular columns."

POETRY Contact: Jill Pelàez Baumgaertner, poetry editor. Needs avant-garde, free verse, haiku, traditional. (Specialized: Christian; social issues) *The Christian Century*, an "ecumenical biweekly," is a liberal, sophisticated journal of news, articles of opinion, and reviews. Uses approximately 1 poem/issue, not necessarily on religious themes but in keeping with the literate tone of the magazine. Has published poetry by Jeanne Murray Walker, Ida Fasel, Kathleen Norris, Luci Shaw, J. Barrie Shepherd, and Wendell Berry. "Prefer shorter poems." Inquire about reprint permission. No sentimental or didactic poetry. Buys 50 poems/year. Length: 20 lines/max. **Pays usually $20/poem plus 1 contributor's copy and discount on additional copies. Acquires all rights.**

CHRISTIAN HOME & SCHOOL

Christian Schools International, 3350 E. Paris Ave. SE, Grand Rapids MI 49512. (616)957-1070, ext. 239. Fax: (616)957-5022. E-mail: rheyboer@csionline.org. Website: csionline.org/chs. **30% freelance written. Works with a small number of new/unpublished writers each year.** Magazine published 2 times/year during the school year covering family life and Christian education. *Christian Home & School* is designed for parents in the United States and Canada who send their children to Christian schools and are concerned about the challenges facing Christian families today. These readers expect a mature, Biblical perspective in the articles, not just a Bible verse tacked onto the end. Estab. 1922. Circ. 66,000. Byline given. Pays on publication. Publishes ms an average of 4 months after acceptance. Submit seasonal material 4 months in advance. Accepts queries by mail, e-mail. Responds in 1 month to queries. Sample copy and writer's guidelines for 9×12 SAE with 4 first-class stamps. Writer's guidelines only for #10 SASE or online.

○ The editor reports an interest in seeing articles on how to experience and express forgiveness in your home, make summer interesting and fun for your kids, help your child make good choices, and raise kids who are opposites, and promote good educational practices in Christian schools.

NONFICTION Needs book excerpts, interview, opinion, personal experience, articles on parenting and school life. **Buys 30 mss/year.** Send complete ms. Length: 1,000-2,000 words. **Pays $175-250.**

COLUMBIA

1 Columbus Plaza, New Haven CT 06510. (203)752-4398. Fax: (203)752-4109. E-mail: columbia@kofc.org. Website: kofc.org/columbia. **Contact:** Alton Pelowski, managing editor. Monthly magazine for Catholic families. Caters primarily to members of the Knights of Columbus. Estab. 1921. Circ. 1,500,000. Pays on acceptance. Accepts queries by mail, e-mail. Sample copy and writer's guidelines free.

NONFICTION No reprints, poetry, cartoons, puzzles, short stories/fiction. Query with SASE or by e-mail. Length: 750-1,500 words.

CONSCIENCE

Catholics for Choice, 1436 U St. NW, Suite 301, Washington D.C. 20009-3997. (202)986-6093. E-mail: conscience@catholicsforchoice.org. Website: catholicsforchoice.org. **Contact:** Kim Puchir; David Nolan. **80% written by nonstaff writers. Publishes 40 freelance submissions yearly; 10% by unpublished writers, 50% by authors who are new to the magazine, 70% by experts.** "Conscience offers in-depth coverage of a range of topics, including contemporary politics, Catholicism, women's rights in society and in religions, U.S. politics, reproductive rights, sexuality and gender, ethics and bioethics, feminist theology, social justice, church and state issues, and the role of religion in formulating public policy." Estab. 1980. Circ. 12,000. Byline given. Pays on publication. Publishes ms an average of 2 months after acceptance. Accepts queries by mail, e-mail. Responds in 4 months to queries. Sample copy free with 9×12 envelope and $1.85 postage. Guidelines for #10 SASE.

NONFICTION Needs book excerpts, interview, opinion, personal experience, a small amount, issue analysis. **Buys 4-8 mss/year.** Send complete ms. Length: 1,500-3,500 words. **Pays $200 negotiable.**

REPRINTS Send typed manuscript with rights for sale noted and information about when and where the material previously appeared. Pays 20-30% of amount paid for an original article.

PHOTOS Quarterly news journal of Catholic opinion. Sample copies available. Buys up to 25 photos/year. Model/property release preferred. Photo captions preferred; include title, subject, photographer's name. Reviews photos with or without a manuscript. Pays $300 maximum for color cover; $50 maximum for b&w inside. Pays on publication. Credit line given.

COLUMNS Book Reviews, 600-1,200 words. **Buys 4-8 mss/year. Pays $75.**

DECISION

Billy Graham Evangelistic Association, 1 Billy Graham Pkwy., Charlotte NC 28201-0001. (704)401-2432. Fax: (704)401-3009. E-mail: submissions@bgea.org. Website: decisionmag.org. **Contact:** Bob Paulson, editor. **5% freelance written. Works each year with small number of new/unpublished writers.** "Magazine published 11 times/year with a mission to extend the ministry of Billy Graham Evangelistic Association; to communicate the Good News of Jesus Christ in such a way that readers will be drawn to make a commitment to Christ; and to encourage, strengthen and equip Christians in evangelism and discipleship.". Estab. 1960. Circ. 400,000. Byline given. Pays on publication. Publishes ms an average of up to 18 months after acceptance. Editorial lead time 6 months. Submit seasonal material 6 months in advance. Sample copy for sae with 9×12 envelope and 4 first-class stamps. Guidelines available online.

☎ Include telephone number with submission.

NONFICTION Needs personal experience, testimony. **Buys approximately 8 mss/year.** Send complete ms. Length: 400-1,500 words. **Pays $200-400.** Pays expenses of writers on assignment.

PHOTOS State availability. Captions, identification of subjects, model releases required. Reviews prints.

COLUMNS Finding Jesus (people who have become Christians through Billy Graham Ministries), 500-900 words. **Buys 11 mss/year.** Send complete ms. **Pays $200.**

DEVOZINE

1908 Grand Ave., P.O. Box 340004, Nashville TN 37203-0004. E-mail: smiller@upperroom.org. Website: devozine.org. **Contact:** Sandi Miller, Editor. (Specialized: Christian youth ages 12-19; weekly themes)1908 Grand Ave., P.O. Box 340004, Nashville TN 37203-0004. Websites: devozine.org (for youth), devoted2youth.org (for youth workers). E-mail: devozine@upperroom.org. *devozine*, published bimonthly, is a 64-page devotional magazine for youth (ages 12-19) and adults who care about youth. Offers meditations, scripture, prayers, poems, stories, songs, and feature articles to "aid youth in their prayer life, introduce them to spiritual disciplines, help them shape their concept of God, and encourage them in the life of discipleship." Considers poetry by teens. Lines/poem: 10-20. No e-mail submissions; submit by regular mail with SASE or use online submmission form. Include name, age/birth date (if younger than 25), mailing address, e-mail address, phone number, and fax number (if available). Always publishes theme issues (focuses on nine themes/issue, one for each week). Indicate theme you are writing for. Guidelines available for SASE or on website. Pays $25.

$ DOVETAIL

Dovetail Institute for Interfaith Family Resources, 45 Lilac Ave., Hamden CT 06517. E-mail: Debit4RLS@aol.com. Website: dovetailinstitute.org. **75% freelance written.** Quarterly newsletter for interfaith families. "All articles must pertain to life in an interfaith (primarily Jewish/Christian) family. We are broadening our scope to include other sorts of interfaith mixes. We accept all kinds of opinions related to this topic." Estab. 1992. Circ. 1,500. Byline given. Pays on publication. Publishes ms an average of 9 months after acceptance. Editorial lead time 6 months. Submit seasonal material 6 months in advance. Accepts queries by mail, e-mail, fax, phone. Accepts simultaneous submissions. Responds in 3 months to queries. Sample copy available online. Guidelines available online.

NONFICTION Needs book excerpts, interview, opinion, personal experience. No fiction. **Buys 5-8 mss/year.** Send complete ms. Length: 800-1,000 words. **Pays $25, plus online subscription for 800-1,000 words**

PHOTOS Send photos. Identification of subjects, model releases required. Reviews 5×7 prints. Offers no additional payment for photos accepted with ms.

$$ EFCA TODAY

Evangelical Free Church of America, 418 Fourth St., NE, Charlottesville VA 22902. E-mail: dianemc@journeygroup.com. Website: efca.org. **30% freelance written.** Quarterly digital magazine. "*EFCA Today*'s purpose is to unify church leaders around the overall mission of the EFCA by bringing its stories and vision to life, and to sharpen those leaders by generating conversations over topics pertinent to faith and life in this 21st century." Estab. 1931. Byline given. Pays on acceptance. Offers 50% kill fee. Publishes ms an average of 3 months after acceptance. Editorial lead time 5 months. Submit seasonal material 6 months in advance. Accepts queries by mail, e-mail. Rarely accepts previously published material.Responds in 6 weeks. Sample copy for $1 with SAE and 5 first-class stamps. Guidelines by e-mail.

NONFICTION Needs interview, of EFCA-related subjects, feature articles of EFCA interest, highlighting EFCA subjects. No general-interest inspirational articles. Send complete ms. Length: 200-1,100 words and related/approved expenses for assigned articles. **Pays 23¢/word for first rights, including limited subsidiary rights (free use within an EFCA context).**

COLUMNS Engage (out of the church and into the world); Leader to Leader (what leaders are saying, doing, learning); Catalyst (the passion of EFCA's young leaders; Face to Face (our global family), all between 200 and 600/words. Send complete ms. **Pays 23¢/word and related/approved expenses for assigned articles.**

⊜⊜ ENRICHMENT

The General Council of the Assemblies of God, 1445 N. Boonville Ave., Springfield MO 65802. (417)862-2781. Fax: (417)862-0416. E-mail: enrichmentjournal@ag.org. Website: enrichmentjournal.ag.org. **Contact:** Rick Knoth, managing editor. **15% freelance written.** Quarterly journal covering church leadership and ministry. "*Enrichment* offers enriching and encouraging information to equip and empower spirit-filled leaders." Circ. 33,000. Byline given. Pays on publication. 50% kill fee. Publishes ms an average of 1 year after acceptance. Editorial lead time 18 months. Submit seasonal material 18 months in advance. Accepts queries by mail, e-mail. Sample copy for $7. Guidelines free.

NONFICTION Needs religious. Send complete ms. Length: 1,000-3,000 words. **Pays up to 15¢/word.**

⊜ EVANGELICAL MISSIONS QUARTERLY

Billy Graham Center/Wheaton College, P.O. Box 794, Wheaton IL 60187. (630)752-7158. Fax: (630)752-7155. E-mail: emq@wheaton.edu. Website: emqonline.com. **Contact:** Managing Editor. **67% freelance written.** Quarterly magazine covering evangelical missions. This is a professional journal for evangelical missionaries, agency executives, and church members who support global missions ministries. Estab. 1964. Circ. 7,000. Byline given. Pays on publication. Offers negotiable kill fee. Publishes ms an average of 18 months after acceptance. Editorial lead time 1 year. Accepts queries by e-mail. Responds in 2 weeks to queries. Sample copy free. Guidelines available online.

NONFICTION Needs essays, interview, opinion, personal experience, religious, book reviews. No sermons, poetry, straight news. **Buys 24 mss/year.** Query. Length: 800-3,000 words. **Pays $25-100.**

PHOTOS Send photos. Identification of subjects required. Offers no additional payment for photos accepted with ms.

COLUMNS In the Workshop (practical how to's), 800-2,000 words; Perspectives (opinion), 800 words. **Buys 8 mss/year.** Query. **Pays $50-100.**

⊜⊜ FAITH & FRIENDS

The Salvation Army, 2 Overlea Blvd., Toronto ON M4H 1P4 Canada. (416)422-6226. Fax: (416)422-6120. E-mail: faithandfriends@can.salvationarmy.org. Website: faithandfriends.ca. **25% freelance written.** Monthly magazine covering Christian living and religion. "Our mission statement: to show Jesus Christ at work in the lives of real people, and to provide spiritual resources for those who are new to the Christian faith." Estab. 1996. Circ. 50,000. Byline given. Pays on acceptance. Offers $50 kill fee. Publishes ms an average of 3 months after acceptance. Editorial lead time 3 months. Submit seasonal material 6 months in advance. Accepts queries by mail, e-mail. TrueResponds in 1 week to queries and to mss. Sample copy available online. Guidelines by e-mail.

NONFICTION Needs book excerpts, humor, inspirational, interview, personal experience, photo feature, religious, travel. Does not want sermons, devotionals, or Christian-ese. **Buys 12-24 mss/year.** Query. Length: 500-1,250 words. **Pays $50-200.**

PHOTOS Send photos. Captions required. Reviews prints, GIF/JPEG files. Negotiates payment individually.

COLUMNS God in My Life (how life changed by accepting Jesus); Someone Cares (how life changed through someone's intervention), 750 words. **Buys 12-18 mss/year. mss/year.** Query. **Pays $50.**

⊘⊜⊜ FAITH TODAY

Evangelical Fellowship of Canada, MIP Box 3745, Markham ON L3R 0Y4 Canada. (905)479-5885. Fax: (905)479-4742. Website: faithtoday.ca. Bimonthly magazine. "*FT* is the magazine of an association of more than 40 evangelical denominations, but serves evangelicals in all denominations. It focuses on church issues, social issues and personal faith as they are tied to the Canadian context. Writing should explicitly acknowledge that Canadian evangelical context." Estab. 1983. Circ. 18,000. Byline given. Pays on publication. Offers 30-50% kill fee. Publishes ms an average of 4 months after acceptance. Editorial lead time 4 months. Accepts queries by mail, e-mail, fax. Responds in 6 weeks to queries. Sample copy for SASE in Canadian postage. Guidelines available online at faithtoday.ca/writers. "View a sample copy at faithtoday.ca/digitalsample. Or download our app from the iTunes store.".

NONFICTION Needs book excerpts, Canadian authors only, essays, Canadian authors only, interview, Canadian subjects only, opinion, religious, news feature. **Buys 75 mss/year.** Query. Length: 400-2,000 words. **Pays $100-500 Canadian.** Sometimes pays expenses of writers on assignment.

REPRINTS Send photocopy. Rarely used. Pays 50% of amount paid for an original article.

PHOTOS State availability. True required. Reviews contact sheets.

$ FORWARD IN CHRIST

WELS Communication Services, 2929 N. Mayfair Rd., Milwaukee WI 53222-4398. (414)256-3210. Fax: (414)256-3210. E-mail: fic@wels.net. Website: wels. net. John A. Braun, exec. ed. **Contact:** Julie K. Wietzke, managing editor. **5% freelance written.** official monthly magazine covering Wisconsin Evangelical Lutheran Synod (WELS) news, topics, issues. The material usually must be written by or about WELS members. Estab. 1913. Circ. 42,000. Byline given. Pays on publication. Publishes ms an average of 6 months after acceptance. Editorial lead time 3 months. Submit seasonal material 4 months in advance. Accepts queries by mail, e-mail, fax. Responds in 2 months to queries. Sample copy and writer's guidelines free. Guidelines available on website.

NONFICTION Needs personal experience, religious. Query. Length: 550-1,200 words. **Pays $75/page, $125/2 pages.** Sometimes pays expenses of writers on assignment.

PHOTOS State availability. Captions, identification of subjects, model releases required. Reviews contact sheets. Negotiates payment individually.

$ $ GROUP MAGAZINE

Group Publishing, Inc., P.O. Box 481, Loveland CO 80539-0481. (970)669-3836. E-mail: sfirestone@group. com. Website: groupmag.com. **Contact:** Scott Firestone. **50% freelance written.** Bimonthly magazine for Christian youth workers. "*Group* is the interdenominational magazine for leaders of Christian youth groups. *Group's* purpose is to supply ideas, practical help, inspiration, and training for youth leaders." Estab. 1974. Circ. 55,000. Byline sometimes given. Pays on acceptance. Editorial lead time 4 months. Submit seasonal material 5 months in advance. Responds in 8-10 weeks to queries. Responds in 2 months to mss. Sample copy for $2, plus 10x12 SAE and 3 first-class stamps. Guidelines available online.

NONFICTION Needs inspirational, personal experience, religious. No fiction, prose, or poetry. **Buys 30 mss/year.** Query. Length: 200-2,200 words. **Pays $50-250.** Sometimes pays expenses of writers on assignment.

COLUMNS "Try This One" section needs short ideas (100-250 words) for youth group use. These include games, fund-raisers, crowdbreakers, Bible studies, helpful hints, outreach ideas, and discussion starters. "Hands-on Help" section needs mini-articles (100-350 words) that feature practical tips for youth leaders on working with students, adult leaders, and parents. **$50**

$ $ GUIDEPOSTS MAGAZINE

Box 5814, Harlan IA 51593. (800)431-2344. E-mail: submissions@guidepostsmag.com. Website: guideposts.com. **40% freelance written. Works with a small number of new/unpublished writers each year.** Monthly magazine. "*Guideposts* is an inspirational monthly magazine for people of all faiths, in which men and women from all walks of life tell in true, first-person narrative how they overcame obstacles, rose above failures, handled sorrow, gained new spiritual insight, and became more effective people through faith in God." Estab. 1945. Pays on publication. Offers kill fee. Offers 20% kill fee on assigned stories, but not to first-time freelancers. Publishes ms an average of several months after acceptance. Guidelines available online.

> "Many of our stories are ghosted articles, so the writer would not get a byline unless it was his/her own story. Because of the high volume of mail the magazine receives, we regret we *cannot* return manuscripts, and will contact writers only if their material can be used."

NONFICTION Buys 40-60 unsolicited mss/year. Length: 250-1,500 words. **Pays $100-500.** Pays expenses of writers on assignment.

HIGHWAY NEWS

Transport For Christ, P.O. Box 117, 1525 River Rd., Marietta PA 17547. (717)426-9977. Fax: (717)426-9980. E-mail: editor@transportforchrist.org. Website: transportforchrist.org. **Contact:** Inge Koenig. **50% freelance written.** Monthly magazine covering trucking and Christianity. "We publish human interest stories, testimonials, and teachings that have a foundation in Biblical/Christian values. Since truck drivers and their families are our primary readers, we publish works that they will find edifying and helpful." Estab. 1957. Circ. 29,000. Byline given. Publishes ms an average of 1 year after acceptance. Submit seasonal material 1 year in advance. Accepts queries by mail, e-mail, fax. Accepts simultaneous submissions. Responds in 1 month to queries. Responds in

2 months to mss. Sample copy free. Writer's guidelines by e-mail.

💬 Does not pay writers.

NONFICTION Needs essays, general interest, humor, inspirational, interview, personal experience, photo feature, religious, trucking. No sermons full of personal opinions. **Buys Accepts 20-25 mss/year.** Send complete ms. Length: 600-800 words.

PHOTOS Send photos. Captions, identification of subjects, model releases required. Reviews prints, GIF/JPEG files. Does not pay for photos.

COLUMNS From the Road (stories by truckers on the road); Devotionals with Trucking theme, both 600 words. Send complete ms.

FICTION Needs humorous, religious, slice-of-life vignettes. No romance or fantasy. We use very little fiction. **Buys Accepts 1 or fewer mss/year.** Send complete ms. Length: 600-800 words.

POETRY Needs traditional. Accepts very little poetry. Don't send anything unrelated to the trucking industry. Buys Accepts 2 poems/year. Submit maximum 10 poems. Length: 4-20 lines.

FILLERS Needs anecdotes, facts, short humor. Length: 20-200 words.

$ HORIZONS

100 Witherspoon St., Louisville KY 40202-1396. (502)569-5897. Fax: (502)569-8085. E-mail: susan.jackson-dowd@pcusa.org. Website: pcusa.org/horizons/. **Contact:** Susan Jackson Dowd, communications coordinator. Bimonthly. "Magazine owned and operated by Presbyterian women offering information and inspiration for Presbyterian women by addressing current issues facing the church and the world." Estab. 1988. Circ. 25,000. Pays on publication. Publishes ms an average of 4 months after acceptance. Sample copy for $4 and 9×12 SAE. Guidelines for #10 SASE.

FICTION Send complete ms. Length: 800-1,200 words. **Pays $50/600 words and 2 contributor's copies.**

IMAGE: ART, FAITH, MYSTERY

3307 3rd Ave. W., Seattle WA 98119. E-mail: image@imagejournal.org. Website: imagejournal.org. Covers the relationship between faith and art. *Image: Art, Faith, Mystery,* published quarterly, "explores and illustrates the relationship between faith and art through world-class fiction, poetry, essays, visual art, and other arts." Wants "poems that grapple with religious faith, usually Judeo-Christian." Has published work from Philip Levine, Scott Cairns, Annie Dillard, Mary Oliver, Mark Jarman, and Kathleen Norris. *Image* is 136 pages, 10x7, printed on acid-free paper, perfect-bound, with glossy 4-color cover, includes ads. Receives about 800 poems/year, accepts up to 3%. Has 5,000 subscribers (100 are libraries). Subscription: $39.95. Sample: $16 postpaid. Submit up to 4 poems at a time. No previously published poems. No e-mail submissions. Cover letter is preferred. Guidelines available on website. Always sends prepublication galleys. Pays 4 contributor's copies plus $2/line ($150 maximum). Reviews books of poetry in 2,000 words, single- or multi-book format. Send materials for review consideration. Estab. 1989. Circ. 5,000. 1 year Accepts queries by mail. Responds in 3 months

KEYS FOR KIDS

Box 1001, Grand Rapids MI 49501-1001. E-mail: hazel@cbhministries.org. Website: cbhministries.org. **Contact:** Hazel Marett, Fiction Editor. "CBH Ministries is an international Christian ministry based on the Gospel of Jesus Christ, which produces and distributes excellent media resources to evangelize and disciple kids and their families." Estab. 1982.

🔑 For children ages 6-12.

$ LAUSANNE WORLD PULSE

Evangelism and Missions Information Service/Wheaton College, P.O. Box 794, Wheaton IL 60187. (630)752-7158. Fax: (630)752-7155. E-mail: submissions@lausanneworldpulse.com. Website: lausanneworldpulse.com. **60% freelance written.** Online newsletter covering mission news and trends. "We provide current information about evangelical Christian missions and churches around the world. Most articles are news-oriented, although we do publish some features and interviews." Estab. 1965. Circ. 3,000. Byline given. Pays on publication. Publishes ms an average of 2 months after acceptance. Editorial lead time 2 months. Accepts queries by e-mail. Sample copy and writer's guidelines free. Guidelines available online.

NONFICTION Needs interview, photo feature, religious, technical. Does not want anything that does not cover the world of evangelical missions. **Buys 50-60 mss/year.** Query with published clips. Include short bio of 40 words or less and electronic photo, if possible, with article submission. Prefers e-mail. Length: 600-1,000 words.

PHOTOS Send photos. Reviews contact sheets. Pays $25 for use of all photos accompanying an article.

$$ LEADERS IN ACTION

CSB Ministries, P.O. Box 150, Wheaton IL 60189. (630)582-0630. Fax: (630)582-0623. Website: csbministries.org. Magazine published 3 times/year covering leadership issues for CSB Ministries leaders. "*Leaders in Action* is distributed to leaders with CSB Ministries across North America. CSB is a nonprofit, nondenominational agency dedicated to winning and training boys and girls to serve Jesus Christ. Hundreds of churches throughout the U.S. and Canada make use of our wide range of services." Estab. 1960. Circ. 6,000. Byline given. Pays on acceptance. Offers $35 kill fee. Publishes ms an average of 3 months after acceptance. Editorial lead time 3 months. Responds in 1 week to queries. Sample copy for $1.50 and 10×13 SAE with 4 first-class stamps. Guidelines for #10 sase.

NONFICTION **Buys 8 mss/year.** Query. Length: 500-1,500 words. **Pays 5-10¢/word.** Sometimes pays expenses of writers on assignment.

REPRINTS Send typed manuscript with rights for sale noted. Pays 50% of amount paid for an original article.

$$ LIGHT & LIFE MAGAZINE

Free Methodist Church of North America, P.O. Box 535002, Indianapolis IN 46253-5002. (317)244-3660. Fax: (317)244-1247. E-mail: llmauthors@fmcna.org; info@llcom.net. Website: llcomm.org; freemethodistchurch.org. **Contact:** Jason Archer, executive director of communications. **20%.** "Bimonthly magazine for maturing Christians emphasizing a holiness lifestyle, contemporary issues, and a Christ-centered worldview. Includes pull-out discipleship and evangelism tools and encouragement cards, denominational news.". Estab. 1868. Circ. 38,000. Byline given. Pays on acceptance. Accepts queries by mail, e-mail. Responds in 12 weeks. Sample copy for $4. Guidelines available online.

NONFICTION Query. 800-1,500 words (LifeNotes 1,000 words) **Pays 15¢/word, 3 complimentary copies.**

$$ LIGUORIAN

One Liguori Dr., Liguori MO 63057-9999. (636)464-2500. Fax: (636)464-8449; (636)464-2503. E-mail: liguorianeditor@liguori.org. Website: liguorian.org. **Contact:** Cheryl Plass, managing editor. **25% freelance written. Prefers to work with published/established writers.** Magazine published 10 times/year for Catholics. "Our purpose is to lead our readers to a fuller Christian life by helping them better understand the teachings of the gospel and the church and by illustrating how these teachings apply to life and the problems confronting them as members of families, the church, and society." Estab. 1913. Circ. 100,000. Pays on acceptance. Submit seasonal material 8 months in advance. Accepts queries by mail, e-mail, fax, phone. Responds in 3 months to mss. Sample copy for 9×12 SAE with 3 first-class stamps or online. Guidelines for #10 SASE and on website.

NONFICTION "No travelogue approach or unresearched ventures into controversial areas. Also, no material found in secular publications—fad subjects that already get enough press, pop psychology, negative or put-down articles. *Liguorian* does not consider retold Bible stories." **Buys 30-40 unsolicited mss/year.** Length: 400-2,400 words. **Pays 12-15¢/word and 5 contributor's copies.**

PHOTOS Photographs on assignment only unless submitted with and specific to article.

FICTION Needs religious, senior citizen/retirement. Send complete ms. 1,500-2,000 words preferred **Pays 12-15¢/word and 5 contributor's copies.**

$$ LIVE

Gospel Publishing House, 1445 N. Boonville Ave., Springfield MO 65802-1894. (417)862-1447. Fax: (417)862-6059. E-mail: rl-live@gph.org. Website: gospelpublishing.com. **100% freelance written.** Weekly magazine for weekly distribution covering practical Christian living. "LIVE is a take-home paper distributed weekly in young adult and adult Sunday school classes. We seek to encourage Christians in living for God through fiction and true stories which apply Biblical principles to everyday problems." We seek to encourage Christians in living for God through fiction and true stories which apply Biblical principles to everyday problems." Estab. 1928. Circ. 35,000. Byline given. Pays on acceptance. Publishes ms an average of 18 months after acceptance. Editorial lead time 12 months. Submit seasonal material 18 months in advance. Accepts queries by mail, e-mail. Accepts simultaneous submissions. Responds in 2 weeks to queries. Responds in 6 weeks to mss. Sample copy for #10 SASE. Guidelines for #10 SASE or on website: gospelpublishing.com/store/startcat.cfm?cat=tWRITGUID.

NONFICTION Needs inspirational, religious. No preachy articles or stories that refer to religious myths (e.g., Santa Claus, Easter Bunny, etc.) **Buys 50-**

100 mss/year. Send complete ms. Length: 400-1,100 words. **Pays 7-10¢/word.**

REPRINTS Send tearsheet, photocopy or typed ms with rights for sale noted and information about when and where the material previously appeared. Pays 7¢/word.

PHOTOS Send photos. Identification of subjects required. Reviews 35mm transparencies and 3 x 4 prints or larger. Higher resolution digital files also accepted. Offers $35-60/photo.

FICTION Contact: Richard Bennett, editor. Needs religious, inspirational, prose poem. No preachy fiction, fiction about Bible characters, or stories that refer to religious myths (e.g., Santa Claus, Easter Bunny, etc.). No science or Bible fiction. No controversial stories about such subjects as feminism, war or capital punishment. **Buys 20-50 mss/year.** Send complete ms. Length: 800-1,200 words. **Pays 7-10¢/word.**

POETRY Needs free verse, haiku, light verse, traditional. Buys 15-24 poems/year. Submit maximum 3 poems. Length: 12-25 lines. **Pays $35-60.**

[+] $ THE LIVING CHURCH

Living Church Foundation, P.O. Box 514036, Milwaukee WI 53203-3436. (414)276-5420. Fax: (414)276-7483. E-mail: tlc@livingchurch.org. Website: livingchurch.org. John Schuessler, managing editor. **Contact:** Douglas LeBlanc, editor at large. **50% freelance written.** covering news or articles of interest to members of the Episcopal Church. "Weekly magazine that presents news and views of the Episcopal Church and the wider Anglican Communion, along with articles on spirituality, Anglican heritage, and the application of Christianity in daily life. There are commentaries on scripture, book reviews, editorials, letters to the editor, and special thematic issues." Estab. 1878. Circ. 9,500. Byline given. Does not pay unless article is requested. Publishes ms an average of 3 months after acceptance. Editorial lead time 3 weeks. Submit seasonal material 2 months in advance. Accepts queries by mail, e-mail, fax. Responds in 2 weeks to queries. Responds in 1 month to mss. Sample copy free.

NONFICTION Needs opinion, personal experience, photo feature, religious. **Buys 10 mss/year.** Send complete ms. Length: 1,000 words. **Pays $25-100.** Sometimes pays expenses of writers on assignment.

PHOTOS Send photos. Reviews any size prints. Offers $15-50/photo.

COLUMNS Benediction (devotional), 250 words; Viewpoint (opinion), under 1,000 words. Send complete ms. **Pays $50 maximum.**

POETRY Needs light verse, traditional.

$ $ THE LOOKOUT

Standard Publishing, 8805 Governor's Hill Dr., Suite 400, Cincinnati OH 45249. (513)931-4050. Fax: (513)931-0950. E-mail: lookout@standardpub.com. Website: lookoutmag.com. Sheryl Overstreet, assistant editor. **Contact:** Shawn McMullen, editor. **50% freelance written**. Weekly magazine for Christian adults, with emphasis on spiritual growth, family life, and topical issues. "Our purpose is to provide Christian adults with practical, Biblical teaching and current information that will help them mature as believers." Estab. 1894. Circ. 60,000. Byline given. Pays on acceptance. Offers 33% kill fee. Publishes ms an average of 1 year after acceptance. Editorial lead time 9 months. Submit seasonal material 1 year in advance. Accepts queries by mail, e-mail. No previously published materialAccepts simultaneous submissions. Responds in 10 weeks to queries. Responds in 10 weeks to mss. Sample copy for $1. Guidelines by e-mail or online.

💬 Audience is mainly conservative Christians. Manuscripts only accepted by mail.

NONFICTION Needs inspirational, interview, opinion, personal experience, religious. No fiction or poetry. **Buys 100 mss/year.** Send complete ms. Check guidelines. **Pays 11-17¢/word.**

PHOTOS State availability. Identification of subjects required. Offers no additional payment for photos accepted with ms.

$ $ THE LUTHERAN

8765 W. Higgins Rd., 5th Floor, Chicago IL 60631-4183. (770)380-2540. Fax: (773)380-2409. E-mail: lutheran@lutheran.org. Website: thelutheran.org. Michael D. Watson, art director. **Contact:** Daniel J. Lehmann, editor. **15% freelance written.** Monthly magazine for lay people in church. News and activities of the Evangelical Lutheran Church in America, news of the world of religion, ethical reflections on issues in society, personal Christian experience. Estab. 1988. Circ. 300,000. Byline given. Pays on acceptance. Offers 50% kill fee. Publishes ms an average of 6 months after acceptance. Submit seasonal material 4 months in advance. Accepts queries by mail, e-mail. Responds in 6 weeks to queries. Sample copy free. Guidelines available online.

NONFICTION Needs inspirational, interview, personal experience, photo feature, religious. No articles unrelated to the world of religion. **Buys 40 mss/year.** Query with published clips. Length: 250-1,200 words. **Pays $75-600.** Pays expenses of writers on assignment.

PHOTOS Send photos. Captions, identification of subjects required. Reviews contact sheets, transparencies, prints. Offers $50-175/photo.

COLUMNS Contact editor.

$ THE LUTHERAN DIGEST

The Lutheran Digest, Inc., 6160 Carmen Ave. E, Inver Grove Heights MN 55076. (952)933-2820. Fax: (952)933-5708. E-mail: editor@lutherandigest.com. Website: lutherandigest.com. David Tank, editor. **Contact:** Nicholas A. Skapyak, editor. **95% freelance written.** Quarterly magazine covering Christianity from a Lutheran perspective. "Articles frequently reflect a Lutheran Christian perspective, but are not intended to be sermonettes. Popular stories show how God has intervened in a person's life to help solve a problem." Estab. 1953. Circ. 70,000. Byline given. Pays on acceptance. Publishes ms an average of 6 months after acceptance. Editorial lead time 9 months. Submit seasonal material 9 months in advance. Accepts queries by e-mail mss only at Microsoft Word or PDF attachments. Accepts simultaneous submissions. Responds in 1 month to queries. Responds in 4 months to mss. No response to e-mailed manuscripts unless selected for publication. Sample copy for $3.50. Guidelines available online.

NONFICTION Needs general interest, historical, how-to, personal or spiritual growth, humor, inspirational, personal experience, religious, nature, God's unique creatures. Does not want "to see personal tributes to deceased relatives or friends. They are seldom used unless the subject of the article is well known. We also avoid articles about the moment a person finds Christ as his or her personal savior." **Buys 50-60 mss/year.** Send complete ms. Length: 1,500 words. **Pays $35-50.**

REPRINTS Accepts previously published submissions. "We prefer this as we are a digest and 70-80% of our articles are reprints."

PHOTOS "We seldom print photos from outside sources.". State availability.

$ $ MESSAGE MAGAZINE

Review and Herald Publishing Association, 55 West Oak Ridge Dr., Hagerstown MD 21740. (301)393-4099. Fax: (301)393-4103. E-mail: wjohnson@rhpa.org. E-mail: Message@rhpa.org. Website: messagemagazine.org. **Contact:** Washington Johnson. **10-20% freelance written.** Bimonthly magazine. "*Message* is the oldest religious journal addressing ethnic issues in the country. Our audience is predominantly Black and Seventh-day Adventist; however, *Message* is an outreach magazine for the churched and un-churched across cultural lines." Estab. 1898. Circ. 110,000. Byline given. Pays on acceptance. Publishes ms an average of 12 months after acceptance. Editorial lead time 6 months. Submit seasonal material 6 months in advance. Responds in 9 months to queries. Sample copy by e-mail. Guidelines by e-mail and online.

NONFICTION Needs general interest; how-to (overcome depression, overcome defeat, get closer to God, learn from failure, deal with the economic crises, etc.). **Buys variable number of mss/year.** Send complete ms. Length: 800-1,200 words. **Payment varies. Payment upon acceptance.**

PHOTOS State availability. Identification of subjects required.

MESSAGE OF THE OPEN BIBLE

Open Bible Churches, 2020 Bell Ave., Des Moines IA 50315-1096. (515)288-6761. Fax: (515)288-2510. E-mail: andrea@openbible.org. Website: openbible.org. **5% freelance written.** "*The Message of the Open Bible* is the official bimonthly publication of Open Bible Churches. Its readership consists mostly of people affiliated with Open Bible." Estab. 1932. Circ. 2,700. Byline given. Publishes ms an average of 4-6 months after acceptance. Editorial lead time 6 months. Submit seasonal material 6 months in advance. Accepts queries by mail. Responds in 1 month to queries. Responds in 2 months to mss. Sample copy for sae with 9×12 envelope and 3 first-class stamps. Writer's guidelines for #10 SASE or by e-mail (message@openbible.org).

○ Does not pay for articles.

NONFICTION Needs inspirational, teachings or challenges, interview, personal experience, religious, testimonies, news. No sermons. Send complete ms. Maximum 650 words.

PHOTOS State availability. Reviews 5×7 prints, GIF/JPEG files. Doesn't pay for photos.

☼ ⑤ THE MESSENGER OF THE SACRED HEART

Apostleship of Prayer, 661 Greenwood Ave., Toronto ON M4J 4B3 Canada. (416)466-1195. Website: sacredheartcanada.com. **20% freelance written.** "Monthly magazine for Canadian and U.S. Catholics interested in developing a life of prayer and spirituality; stresses the great value of our ordinary actions and lives." Estab. 1891. Circ. 11,000. Byline given. Pays on acceptance. Submit seasonal material 5 months in advance. NoResponds in 1 month to queries. Sample copy for $1 and 7½×10½ SAE. Guidelines for #10 SASE.

FICTION Contact: Rev. F.J. Power, S.J. and Alfred De-Manche, editors. Needs religious, stories about people, adventure, heroism, humor, drama. No poetry. **Buys 12 mss/year.** Send complete ms. Length: 750-1,500 words. **Pays 8¢/word, and 3 contributor's copies.**

⑤ ⑤ MY DAILY VISITOR

Our Sunday Visitor, Inc., 200 Noll Plaza, Huntington IN 46750. (260)356-8400. Fax: (260)356-8472. E-mail: mdvisitor@osv.com. Website: osv.com. **Contact:** Monica and Bill Dodds, editors. **99% freelance written.** Bimonthly magazine of Scripture meditations based on the day's Catholic Mass readings. Circ. 33,000. Byline given. Pays on acceptance. Publishes ms an average of 6 months after acceptance. Accepts queries by mail, e-mail. Responds in 2 months to queries. Sample copy and writer's guidelines for #10 SAE with 3 first-class stamps.

○ Sample meditations and guidelines online. Each writer does 1 full month of meditations on assignment basis only.

NONFICTION Needs inspirational, personal experience, religious. **Buys 12 mss/year.** Query with published clips. 130-140 words times the number of days in month. **Pays $500 for 1 month (28-31) of meditations and 5 free copies.**

⑤ ⑤ ONE

Catholic Near East Welfare Association, 1011 First Ave., New York NY 10022-4195. (212)826-1480. Fax: (212)838-1344. E-mail: cnewa@cnewa.org. Website: cnewa.org. **75% freelance written.** Bimonthly magazine for a Catholic audience with interest in the Near East, particularly its current religious, cultural and political aspects. Estab. 1974. Circ. 100,000. Byline given. Pays on publication. Publishes ms an average of 6 months after acceptance. Accepts queries by mail, fax. Responds in 1 month to queries. Sample copy and writer's guidelines for 7½×10½ SAE with 2 first-class stamps.

NONFICTION Length: 1,200-1,800 words. **Pays 20¢/edited word.**

PHOTOS Photographs to accompany manuscript are welcome; they should illustrate the people, places, ceremonies, etc. which are described in the article. We prefer color transparencies but occasionally use b&w. Pay varies depending on use—scale from $50-300.

⑤ ⑤ ON MISSION

North American Mission Board, SBC, 4200 North Point Pkwy., Alpharetta GA 30022-4176. E-mail: onmission@namb.net. Website: onmission.com. **25% freelance written.** Quarterly lifestyle magazine that popularizes evangelism, church planting and missions. "*On Mission*'s primary purpose is to tell the story of southern baptist missionaries in North America and to help readers and churches become more intentional about personal evangelism, church planting, and missions in North America. *On Mission* equips Christians for leading people to Christ and encourages churches to reach people through new congregations." Estab. 1998. Circ. 200,000. Byline given. Pays on acceptance. Publishes ms an average of 6 months after acceptance. Editorial lead time 9 months. Submit seasonal material 9 months in advance. Accepts queries by mail, e-mail (prefers e-mail). Responds in 6 weeks to queries. Responds in 4 months to mss. Sample copy free or online. Guidelines available online.

NONFICTION Needs how-to, humor, personal experience, stories of sharing your faith in Christ with a non-Christian. **Buys 30 mss/year.** Query with published clips. Length: 350-1,200 words. **Pays 25¢/word, more for cover stories.** Pays expenses of writers on assignment.

PHOTOS Most are shot on assignment. Captions, identification of subjects required.

COLUMNS Buys 8 mss/year. Blog posts Buys 48 per year. Query. **Pays 25¢/word.**

⑤ ⑤ OUR SUNDAY VISITOR

Our Sunday Visitor, Inc., 200 Noll Plaza, Huntington IN 46750. (260)356-8400. Fax: (260)356-8472. E-mail: oursunvis@osv.com; jnorton@osv.com. Website: osv.com. **Contact:** John Norton, editor. **70% freelance written. (Mostly assigned.).** Weekly publication covering world events and culture from a Catholic perspective. "We are a Catholic publishing company seeking to educate and deepen our readers in their faith. Currently emphasizing devotional, inspirational, catholic identity, apologetics, and catechetics." Estab. 1912. Circ. 60,000. Byline given. Pays on acceptance. Publishes ms an average of 2-3 weeks after acceptance. Accepts queries by mail, e-mail. Sample copy for $2. Send a 10×13 SASE with 93 cents in postage affixed.

$$ OUTREACH MAGAZINE

Outreach, Inc., 2230 Oak Ridge Way, Vista CA 92081-2314. (760)940-0600. Fax: (760)597-2314. E-mail: tellus@outreachmagazine.com. Website: outreachmagazine.com. **Contact:** Editor. **80% freelance written.** Bimonthly magazine covering outreach. "*Outreach* is designed to inspire, challenge, and equip churches and church leaders to reach out to their communities with the love of Jesus Christ." Circ. 30,000, plus newsstand. Byline given. Pays on publication. Offers 10% kill fee. Publishes ms an average of 2-4 months after acceptance. Editorial lead time 6 months. Submit seasonal material 6 months in advance. Accepts queries by mail, e-mail, fax. Mail submissions to Editor. Mark Query or Unsolicited manuscript on your envelope. E-mail submissions to editor@outreach.com. No phone calls, please. Accepts simultaneous submissions. Responds in 2 months to queries. Responds in 8 months to mss. Sample copy free. Guidelines free and online.

NONFICTION Needs book excerpts, how-to, humor, inspirational, interview, personal experience, photo feature, religious. Special issues: Vacation Bible School (January); Church Growth—America's Fastest-Growing Churches (Special Issue). Does not want fiction, poetry, non-outreach-related articles. **Buys 30 mss/year.** Query with published clips. Length: 1,500-2,500 words. **Pays $375-600 for assigned articles. Pays $375-500 for unsolicited articles.** Sometimes pays expenses of writers on assignment.

PHOTOS Contact: Tim Downs, art director. Send photos. Identification of subjects required. Reviews GIF/JPEG files. Negotiates payment individually.

COLUMNS Contact: Lindy Lowry, editor. Pulse (short stories about outreach-oriented churches and ministries), 250-350 words; Soulfires (an as-told-to interview with a person about the stories and people that have fueled their passion for outreach), 900 words; Ideas (a profile of a church that is using a transferable idea or concept for outreach), 300 words, plus sidebar; Soulfires (short interviews with known voices about the stories and people that have informed their worldview and faith perspective), 600 words. **Buys 6 mss/year. mss/year.** Query with published clips. **Pays $100-375.**

FILLERS Needs facts, gags. **Buys 6/year. mss/year.** Length: 25-100 words. **negotiated fee.**

$$ PENTECOSTAL EVANGEL

The General Council of the Assemblies of God, 1445 N. Boonville, Springfield MO 65802-1894. (417)862-2781. Fax: (417)862-0416. E-mail: pe@ag.org. Website: pe.ag.org. **5-10% freelance written.** Weekly magazine emphasizing news of the Assemblies of God for members of the Assemblies and other Pentecostal and charismatic Christians. "Articles should be inspirational without being preachy. Any devotional writing should take a literal approach to the Bible. A variety of general topics and personal experience accepted with inspirational tie-in." Estab. 1913. Circ. 180,000. Byline given. Pays on acceptance. Offers 100% kill fee. Publishes ms an average of 6 months or more after acceptance. Editorial lead time 3 months. Submit seasonal material 6 months in advance. Accepts queries by e-mail. Responds in 2 weeks to queries. Responds in 2 months to mss. Sample copy free. Guidelines available online.

NONFICTION Needs book excerpts, general interest, inspirational, personal experience, religious. Does not want poetry, fiction, self-promotional. **Buys 10-15 mss/year.** Send complete ms. Length: 700-1,200 words. **Pays $25-200.**

$ THE PENTECOSTAL MESSENGER

Messenger Publishing House/Pentecostal Church of God, P.O. Box 850, Joplin MO 64802-0850. (417)624-7050. Fax: (417)624-7102. E-mail: charlotteb@pcg.org. Website: pcg.org. **Contact:** Charlotte Beal. Monthly magazine covering Christian, inspirational, religious, leadership news. "Our organization is Pentecostal in nature. Our publication goes out to our ministers and laypeople to educate, inspire and inform them of topics around the world and in our organization that will help them in their daily walk." Estab. 1919. Circ. 5,000. Byline given. Pays on publication. Editorial lead time 6 months. Submit themed material 6 months in advance. Accepts queries by mail. Accepts simultaneous submissions. May contact the *Pentecostal Messenger* for a list of monthly themes.

NONFICTION Needs book excerpts, essays, expose, general interest, inspirational, interview, new product, personal experience, religious. **Buys 12-24 mss/year.** Send complete ms. Length: 750-2,000 words. **Pays $15-40.**

PHOTOS Send photos. Identification of subjects required. Reviews prints. Offers no additional payment for photos accepted with ms.

⊘⊜⊜ THE PLAIN TRUTH

Plain Truth Ministries, 300 W. Green St., Pasadena CA 91129. (800)309-4466. Fax: (626)358-4846. E-mail: managing.editor@ptm.org. Website: ptm.org. **90% freelance written.** Bimonthly magazine. "We seek to reignite the flame of shattered lives by illustrating the joy of a new life in Christ." Estab. 1935. Circ. 70,000. Byline given. Pays on publication. Offers $50 kill fee. Publishes ms an average of 8 months after acceptance. Editorial lead time 6 months. Submit seasonal material 6 months in advance. Accepts queries by mail, e-mail. Accepts simultaneous submissions. Sample copy for sae with 9×12 envelope and 5 First-Class stamps. Guidelines available online.

NONFICTION Needs inspirational, interview, personal experience, religious. **Buys 48-50 mss/year.** Query with published clips and SASE. *No unsolicited mss.* Length: 750-2,500 words. **Pays 25¢/word.**

REPRINTS Send tearsheet or photocopy of article or typed ms with rights for sale ted and information about when and where the article previously appeared with SASE for response. Pays 15¢/word.

PHOTOS State availability. Captions required. Reviews transparencies, prints. Negotiates payment individually.

⊜⊜ POINT

Converge Worldwide (Baptist General Conference), 2002 S. Arlington Heights Rd., Arlington Heights IL 60005. Fax: (847)228-5376. E-mail: bob.putman@convergeww.org. Website: convergeworldwide.org. **5% freelance written.** Nonprofit, religious, evangelical Christian magazine published 4 times/year covering Converge Worldwide. "*Point* is the official magazine of Converge Worldwide (BCG). Almost exclusively uses articles related to Converge, our churches, or by/about Converge people." Circ. 46,000. Byline given. Pays on publication. Offers 50% kill fee. Editorial lead time 6 months. Submit seasonal material 6 months in advance. Accepts queries by e-mail. Responds in 1 month to queries. Responds in 3 months to mss. Sample copy for #10 SASE. Writer's guidelines, theme list free.

NONFICTION Articles about our people, churches, missions. View online at: convergeworldwide.org. before sending anything. **Buys 20-30 mss/year.** Query with published clips. Length: 300-1,500 words. **Pays $60-280.** Sometimes pays expenses of writers on assignment.

PHOTOS State availability. Captions, identification of subjects, model releases required. Reviews prints, some high-resolution digital. Offers $15-60/photo.

COLUMNS Converge Connection (blurbs of news happening in Converge Worldwide), 50-150 words. Send complete ms. **Pays $30.**

⊜⊜ PRAIRIE MESSENGER

Benedictine Monks of St. Peter's Abbey, P.O. Box 190, Muenster SK S0K 2Y0 Canada. 1+ 306 682-1772. Fax: 1+ 306 682-5285. E-mail: Pm.canadian@Stpeterspress.ca. Website: prairiemessenger.ca. **Contact:** Maureen Weber, associate editor. **10% Freelance written.** Weekly Catholic publication published by the Benedictine Monks of St. Peter's Abbey in Muenster, SK. Canada. Has a strong focus on ecumenism, social justice, interfaith relations, aboriginal issues, arts and culture. Estab. 1904. Circ. 5,000. Byline given. Pays on publication. Publishes ms an average of 4 months after acceptance. Submit seasonal material 3 months in advance. Accepts queries by mail, e-mail, fax, phone. TrueAccepts simultaneous submissions. Responds only if interested, send nonreturnable samples. Sample copy for 9×12 SAE with $1 Canadian postage or IRCs. Guidelines available online. "Because of government subsidy regulations, we are no longer able to accept non-Canadian freelance material.".

NONFICTION Needs interview, opinion, religious. "No articles on abortion." **Buys 15 mss/year.** Send complete ms. Length: 500-800 words. **Pays $60** Sometimes pays expenses of writers on assignment.

PHOTOS Send photos. Captions required. Reviews 3×5 prints. Offers $25/photo.

⊜⊜ PRESBYTERIANS TODAY

Presbyterian Church (U.S.A.), 100 Witherspoon St., Louisville KY 40202-1396. (502)569-5637. Fax: (502)569-8632. E-mail: today@pcusa.org. Website: pcusa.org/today. Shellee Marie Layman, art director. **Contact:** Eva Stimson, editor. **25% freelance written. Prefers to work with published/established writers.** Denominational magazine published 10 times/year covering religion, denominational activities, and public issues for members of the Presbyterian Church (U.S.A.). "The magazine's purpose is to increase understanding and appreciation of what the church and its members are doing to live out their Christian faith." Estab. 1867. Circ. 40,000. Byline given. Pays on acceptance. Offers 50% kill fee. Publishes ms an average of 6 months after acceptance. Editorial lead time 3 months. Submit seasonal material 3 months in advance. Accepts queries by mail, e-mail, fax, phone. Responds in 2 weeks to queries. Sample copy free. Guidelines available online.

NONFICTION Needs how-to, everyday Christian living, inspirational, Presbyterian programs, issues, people. **Buys 20 mss/year.** Send complete ms. Length: 1,000-1,800 words. **Pays $300 maximum for assigned articles. Pays $75-300 for unsolicited articles.**

PHOTOS State availability. Identification of subjects required. Reviews contact sheets, transparencies, color prints, digital images. Negotiates payment individually.

🌑🌑 PRISM MAGAZINE

Evangelicals for Social Action, 6 E. Lancaster Ave., Wynnewood PA 19096. (484)384-2990. E-mail: kristyn@esa-online.org. Website: prismmagazine. org. **50% freelance written**. Bimonthly magazine covering Christianity and social justice. "For holistic, Biblical, socially-concerned, progressive Christians." Estab. 1993. Circ. 2,500. Byline given. Pays on publication. Publishes ms an average of 4-6 months after acceptance. Editorial lead time 4 months. Submit seasonal material 4 months in advance. Accepts queries by mail, e-mail. Responds in 1 month to queries. Responds in 3 months to mss. Hardcover sample copy for $3. PDF sample copy free. Request via website. Guidelines on website.

> 💬 "We're a nonprofit, some writers are pro bono. Occasionally accepts previously published material."

NONFICTION Needs essays on culture/faith, interviews, ministry profiles, reviews, etc. **Buys 10-12/ year mss/year.** Send complete ms. Length: 500-3,000 words. **Pays $75 per printed page - about 10¢/word. Pays $25-200 for unsolicited articles.**

PHOTOS Send photos. Reviews prints, JPEG files. Pays $25/photo published; $200 if photo used on cover.

🌑 PURPOSE

616 Walnut Ave., Scottdale PA 15683-1999. (724)887-8500. Fax: (724)887-3111. E-mail: purposeeditor@mpn.net. Website: mpn.net. **Contact:** Carol Duerksen, editor. **75% freelance written.** Monthly magazine for adults, young and old, general audience with varied interests. Magazine focuses on Christian discipleship—how to be a faithful Christian in the midst of everyday life situations. Uses personal story form to present models and examples to encourage Christians in living a life of faithful discipleship. Estab. 1968. Circ. 8,500. Pays on acceptance. Publishes ms an average of 18 months after acceptance. Submit seasonal material 1 year in advance. Accepts queries by e-mail. Accepts simultaneous submissions. Responds in 3 months to queries. Sample copy and writer's guidelines for 6×9 SAE and $2.

NONFICTION Buys 140 mss/year. E-mail submissions preferred.

REPRINTS Send tearsheet, photocopy or typed ms with rights for sale noted and information about when and where the material previously appeared.

PHOTOS Photos purchased with ms must be sharp enough for reproduction; requires prints in all cases. Captions required.

FICTION Contact: Carol Duerksen, editor. Produce the story with specificity so that it appears to take place somewhere and with real people. Needs historical, related to discipleship theme, humorous, religious. No militaristic/narrow patriotism or racism. Send complete ms. Length: 600 words. **Pays up to 7¢ for stories, and 2 contributor's copies.**

POETRY Needs free verse, light verse, traditional. Buys 140 poems/year. Length: 12 lines. **Pays $7.50-20/poem depending on length and quality. Buys one-time rights only.**

QUAKER LIFE

Friends United Meeting, 101 Quaker Hill Dr., Richmond IN 47374. (765)962-7573. Fax: (765)966-1293. E-mail: quakerlife@fum.org. Website: fum.org. **Contact:** Katie Wonsik. **50% freelance written.** A Christian Quaker magazine published 6 times/year that covers news, inspirational, devotional, peace, equality, and justice issues. Estab. 1960. Circ. 3,000. Byline given. Publishes ms an average of 3-6 months after acceptance. Editorial lead time 2-3 months. Submit seasonal material 4-6 months in advance. Accepts queries by mail, e-mail. Accepts simultaneous submissions. Responds in 1 week to queries. Responds in 1-3 months to mss. Sample copy and writer's guidelines free.

NONFICTION Needs book excerpts, general interest, humor, inspirational, interview, personal experience, photo feature, religious, travel, bible study. No poetry or fiction. Query. Length: 400-1,500 words. **Pays 3 contributor's copies.**

PHOTOS Reviews b&w or color prints and JPEG files. Occasionally, line drawings and b&w cartoons are used. Send photos. Does not pay for photos.

COLUMNS News Brief (newsworthy events among Quakers), 75-200 words; Devotional/Inspirational (personal insights or spiritual turning points), 750 words; Ideas That Work (ideas from meetings that could be used by others), 750 words; Book/Media Reviews, 75-300 words.

RAILROAD EVANGELIST

Railroad Evangelist Association, Inc., P.O. Box 5026, Vancouver WA 98668. (360)699-7208. E-mail: rrjoe@ comcast.net. Website: railroadevangelist.com. **80% freelance written.** Magazine published 3 times/year covering the railroad industry. "The *Railroad Evangelist*'s purpose and intent is to reach people everywhere with the life-changing gospel of Jesus Christ. The railroad industry is our primary target, along with model railroad and rail fans." Estab. 1938. Circ. 3,000/issue. Byline sometimes given. Editorial lead time 6 weeks. Submit seasonal material 6 weeks in advance. Accepts queries by mail, e-mail. Sample copy for sae with 10x12 envelope and 3 first-class stamps. Guidelines for #10 SASE.

◯ All content must be railroad related.

NONFICTION Needs inspirational, interview, personal experience, religious. Query. Length: 300-800 words.

PHOTOS State availability. Captions required. Reviews 3×5, 8×10 prints, GIF/JPEG files. Offers no additional payment for photos accepted with ms.

COLUMNS Right Track (personal testimony), 300-800 words; Ladies Line (personal testimony), 300-500 words; Kids Corner (geared toward children), 50-100 words. Query. **Pays in contributor copies.**

FICTION Needs historical, religious. Query. Length: 300-800 words. **Pays in contributor copies.**

POETRY Needs traditional. Length: 10-100 lines. **Pays in contributor copies.**

⊗⊗ REFORM JUDAISM

Union for Reform Judaism, 633 Third Ave., 7th Fl., New York NY 10017-6778. (212)650-4240. Fax: (212)650-4249. E-mail: rjmagazine@urj.org. Website: reformjudaismmag.org. **30% freelance written.** Quarterly magazine of Jewish issues for contemporary Jews. "*Reform Judaism* is the official voice of the Union for Reform Judaism, linking the institutions and affiliates of Reform Judaism with every Reform Jew. *RJ* covers developments within the Movement while interpreting events and Jewish tradition from a Reform perspective." Estab. 1972. Circ. 310,000. Byline given. Pays on publication. Offers kill fee for commissioned articles. Publishes ms an average of 3 months after acceptance. Submit seasonal material 6 months in advance. Accepts simultaneous submissions. Responds in 2 months to queries and to mss Sample copy for $3.50. Guidelines available online.

NONFICTION **Buys 30 mss/year.** Submit complete ms. SASE is preferable and will elicit a faster response. Cover stories: 2,500-3,500 words; major feature: 1,800-2,500 words; secondary feature: 1,200-1,500 words; department (e.g., travel): 1,200 words. **Pays 30¢/published word.** Sometimes pays expenses of writers on assignment.

REPRINTS Send tearsheet, photocopy or typed ms with rights for sale and information about when and where the material previously appeared. Usually doesn't publish reprints.

PHOTOS Send photos. Identification of subjects required. Reviews 8×10/color or slides, b&w prints, and printouts of electronic images. Payment varies.

FICTION Needs humorous, religious, sophisticated, cutting-edge, superb writing. **Buys 4 mss/year.** Send complete ms. Length: 600-2,500 words. **Pays 30¢/published word.**

⊗⊗ RELEVANT

Relevant Media Group, 900 N. Orange Ave., Winter Park FL 32789. (407)660-1411. Fax: (407)660-8555. E-mail: roxanne@relevantmediagroup.com for print queries. ryan@relevantmediagroup.com for online queries. Website: relevantmagazine.com. **80% freelance written.** Bimonthly magazine covering God, life, and progressive culture. *Relevant* is a lifestyle magazine for Christians in their 20s and 30s. Estab. 2002. Circ. 83,000. Byline given. Pays 45 days after publication. Offers 50% kill fee. Publishes ms an average of 6 months after acceptance. Editorial lead time

4 months. Submit seasonal material 5 months in advance. Accepts queries by e-mail. Accepts simultaneous submissions. Responds in 6 weeks to queries. Responds in 3 months to mss. Sample copy available online. Guidelines available online.

NONFICTION Needs general interest, how-to, inspirational, interview, new product, personal experience, religious. Don't submit anything that doesn't target ages 18-34. Query with published clips. Length: 600-1,000 words. **Pays 10-15¢/word for assigned articles. Pays 10¢/word for unsolicited articles.** Sometimes pays expenses of writers on assignment.

$ REVIEW FOR RELIGIOUS

3601 Lindell Blvd., St. Louis MO 63108-3393. (314)633-4610. Fax: (314)633-4611. E-mail: reviewrfr@gmail.com. Website: reviewforreligious.org. **100% freelance written.** Quarterly magazine for Roman Catholic priests, brothers, and sisters. Estab. 1942. Byline given. Pays on publication. Publishes ms an average of 9 months after acceptance. Accepts queries by mail, fax. Responds in 2 months to queries. Guidelines available online.

NONFICTION Not for general audience. Length: 1,500-5,000 words. **Pays $6/page.**

$ RIVER REGION'S JOURNEY

P.O. Box 230367, Montgomery AL 36123. (334)213-7940. Fax: (334)213-7990. E-mail: deanne@readjourneymagazine.com. **Contact:** DeAnne Watson, editor. **50% freelance written.** Monthly magazine covering Christian living. Includes Protestant Christian writing, topical articles on Christian living, and Christian living articles with helpful information for walking with Christ daily. Estab. 1999. Circ. 8,000. Byline given. Pays on publication. Offers 25% kill fee. Publishes ms an average of 6-12 months after acceptance. Editorial lead time 1 year. Submit seasonal material 1 year in advance. Accepts queries by e-mail. Accepts simultaneous submissions. Sample copy for $1.75 and self-addressed magazine-size envelope. Guidelines by e-mail.

NONFICTION Needs inspirational, religious. No fiction, poetry, or autobiography. Submit query or complete ms. Length: 1,300-2,200 words. **Pays $25-50 for assigned articles. Pays $25 for unsolicited articles.**

SACRED JOURNEY

Fellowship in Prayer, Inc., 291 Witherspoon St., Princeton NJ 08542. (609)924-6863. Fax: (609)924-6910. E-mail: submissions@sacredjourney.org. Website: sacredjourney.org. **70% freelance written.** *Sacred Journey*: The Journal of Fellowship in Prayer is a quarterly multi-faith journal published Winter, Spring, Summer and Autumn. Estab. 1950. Circ. 5,000. Editorial lead time 3 months. Submit seasonal material 4 months in advance. Accepts queries by e-mail (preferably). Accepts simultaneous submissions. Responds within 4 months of receipt. Submission is considered permission for publication. We reserve the right to edit. We will make every effort to contact the author with content revisions. Please include or be prepared to provide a bio of 50-words or less and/or a headshot phot to accompany your work, should it be selected for the print journal. Sample copy free. Guidelines available online.

> 💬 "We publish articles, poems, and photographs which convey a spiritual orientation to life, promote prayer, meditation, and service to others and present topics that will foster a deeper spirit of unity among humankind. The spiritual insights, practices, and beliefs of women and men from a broad spectrum of religious traditions are welcomed."

NONFICTION Buys 30 mss/year. Send complete ms. Length: Approx. 750-1,500 words, double-spaced. **"You receive a complimentary one-year subscription to Sacred Journey if you work is selected for publication in the journal or on our website. For publication in the print journal you will also receive 5 copies of the issue in which your work appears."**

PHOTOS "We accept Hi-Res digital photographs and illlustrations for possible publication. Cover photos are typically in color while interior photos are usually in black & white. We favor vertical images, but consider horizontal ones.".

POETRY Does not want poetry highly specific to a certain faith tradition. Nothing laden with specific faith terminology, nor a lot of Bibe quotes or other quotes. Submit maximum 5 per submission poems. Limited to 35 lines (occasionally longer).

[+] $ THE SECRET PLACE

American Baptist Home Mission Societies, ABC/USA, P.O. Box 851, Valley Forge PA 19482-0851. (610)768-2240. E-mail: thesecretplace@abc-usa.org. **100% freelance written.** Quarterly devotional covering Christian daily devotions. Estab. 1937. Circ. 150,000. Byline given. Pays on acceptance. Editorial lead time 1 year. Submit seasonal material 9 months in advance. For free sample and guidelines, send 6×9 SASE.

NONFICTION Needs inspirational. **Buys about 400 mss/year.** Send complete ms. Length: 100-200 words. **Pays $20.**

POETRY Needs avant-garde, free verse, light verse, traditional. Buys 12-15/year poems/year. Submit maximum 6 poems. Length: 4-30 lines. **Pays $20.**

$ SEEK

8805 Governor's Hill Dr., Suite 400, Cincinnati OH 45239. (513)931-4050, ext. 351. E-mail: seek@standardpub.com. Website: standardpub.com. Also contains art and photos in each issue. "Inspirational stories of faith-in-action for Christian adults; a Sunday School take-home paper." Quarterly. Religious/inspirational, religious fiction and religiously slanted historical and humorous fiction. No poetry. List of upcoming themes available online. Accepts 150 mss/year. Send complete ms. Prefers submissions by e-mail. "SEEK corresponds to the topics of Standard Publishing's adult curriculum line and is designed to further apply these topics to everyday life." "Unsolicited mss must be written to a theme list. Submissions for Summer 2012 themes due by July 15, 2011". Estab. 1970. Circ. 27,000. Byline given. Pays on acceptance. Acceptance to publishing time is 1 year. Accepts queries by e-mail. Writer's guidelines online.

NONFICTION Send complete ms. **Pays 7 cents/word for first rights; 5 cents/word for reprint rights.**

REPRINTS Reprints pay 5 cents/word.

$$ SHARING THE VICTORY

Fellowship of Christian Athletes, 8701 Leeds Rd., Kansas City MO 64129. (816)921-0909. Fax: (816)921-8755. E-mail: stv@fca.org. Website: fca.org. **Contact:** Jill Ewert, managing editor. **50% freelance written. Prefers to work with published/established writers, but works with a growing number of new/unpublished writers each year.** Published 9 times/year. "We seek to serve as a ministry tool of the Fellowship of Christian Athletes by informing, inspiring and involving coaches, athletes and all whom they influence, that they may make an impact for Jesus Christ." Estab. 1959. Circ. 80,000. Byline given. Pays on publication. Publishes ms an average of 4 months after acceptance. Submit seasonal material 6 months in advance. Responds in 3 months to queries. Responds in 3 months to mss. Sample copy for $1 and 9×12 SAE with 3 first-class stamps. Guidelines available online.

NONFICTION Needs inspirational, interview, with name athletes and coaches solid in their faith, personal experience, photo feature. **Buys 5-20 mss/year.** Query. Length: 500-1,000 words.

PHOTOS State availability. Reviews contact sheets. Payment based on size of photo.

$ SOCIAL JUSTICE REVIEW

3835 Westminster Place, St. Louis MO 63108-3472. (314)371-1653. Fax: (314)371-0889. E-mail: centbur@juno.com. Website: socialjusticereview.org. **25% freelance written. Works with a small number of new/unpublished writers each year.** Bimonthly magazine. Estab. 1908. Publishes ms an average of 1 year after acceptance. Accepts queries by mail. Sample copy for sae with 9×12 envelope and 3 First-Class stamps.

NONFICTION Query by mail only with SASE. Length: 2,500-3,000 words. **Pays about 2¢/word.**

REPRINTS Send typed manuscript with rights for sale noted and information about when and where the material previously appeared. Pays about 2¢/word.

$ SPIRITUAL LIFE

2131 Lincoln Rd. NE, Washington DC 20002-1199. (888)616-1713; (202)832-5505. Fax: (202)832-5711. E-mail: edodonnell@aol.com. Website: spiritual-life.org. **Contact:** Edward O'Donnell, editor. **80% freelance written. Prefers to work with published/established writers.** Quarterly magazine for largely Christian, well-educated, serious readers. Circ. 12,000. Pays on acceptance. Publishes ms an average of 1 year after acceptance. Responds in 2 months to queries. Sample copy and writer's guidelines for 7x10 or larger SAE with 5 first-class stamps.

NONFICTION Sentimental articles or those dealing with specific devotional practices not accepted. No fiction or poetry. **Buys 20 mss/year.** Length: 3,000-5,000 words. **Pays $50 minimum, and 2 contributor's copies.**

$$ ST. ANTHONY MESSENGER

28 W. Liberty St., Cincinnati OH 45202-6498. (513)241-5615. Fax: (513)241-0399. E-mail: mageditors@americancatholic.org. Website: americancatholic.org. **Contact:** John Feister. **55% freelance written.** Monthly general interest magazine for a national readership of Catholic families, most of which have children or grandchildren in grade school, high school, or college. *St. Anthony Messenger* is a Catholic family magazine which aims to help its readers lead more fully human

and Christian lives. We publish articles which report on a changing church and world, opinion pieces written from the perspective of Christian faith and values, personality profiles, and fiction which entertains and informs. Estab. 1893. Circ. 305,000. Byline given. Pays on acceptance. Publishes ms an average of 1 year after acceptance. Submit seasonal material 6 months in advance. Accepts queries by mail, e-mail, fax. Responds in 3 weeks to queries. Responds in 2 months to mss. Sample copy for 9×12 SAE with 4 first-class stamps. Guidelines available online.

NONFICTION Needs how-to, on psychological and spiritual growth, problems of parenting/better parenting, marriage problems/marriage enrichment, humor, inspirational, interview, opinion, limited use; writer must have special qualifications for topic, personal experience, if pertinent to our purpose, photo feature, informational, social issues. **Buys 35-50 mss/year.** Query with published clips. Length: 2,000-2,500 words. **Pays 20¢/word.** Sometimes pays expenses of writers on assignment.

FICTION Contact: Father Pat McCloskey, O.F.M., editor. Needs mainstream, religious, senior citizen/retirement. "We do not want mawkishly sentimental or preachy fiction. Stories are most often rejected for poor plotting and characterization; bad dialogue—listen to how people talk; inadequate motivation. Many stories say nothing, are 'happenings' rather than stories. No fetal journals, no rewritten Bible stories." **Buys 12 mss/year.** Send complete ms. Length: 2,000-2,500 words. **Pays 16¢/word maximum and 2 contributor's copies; $1 charge for extras.**

POETRY Our poetry needs are very limited. Submit maximum 4-5 poems. Up to 20-25 lines; the shorter, the better. **Pays $2/line; $20 minimum.**

⚫⚫ THE UPPER ROOM

P.O. Box 340004, Nashville TN 37203-0004. (615)340-7252. Fax: (615)340-7267. E-mail: theupperroommagazine@upperroom.org. Website: upperroom.org. **95% freelance written. Eager to work with new/unpublished writers.** Bimonthly magazine offering a daily inspirational message which includes a Bible reading, text, prayer, 'Thought for the Day,' and suggestion for further prayer. Each day's meditation is written by a different person and is usually a personal witness about discovering meaning and power for Christian living through scripture study which illuminates daily life. Circ. 2.2 million (U.S.); 385,000 outside U.S. Byline given. Pays on publication. Publishes ms an average of 1 year after acceptance. Submit seasonal material 14 months in advance. Sample copy and writer's guidelines with a 4×6 SAE and 2 first-class stamps. Guidelines only for #10 SASE or online.

⚫ Manuscripts are not returned. If writers include a stamped, self-addressed postcard, we will notify them that their writing has reached us. This does not imply acceptance or interest in purchase. Does not respond unless material is accepted for publication.

NONFICTION Needs inspirational, personal experience, Bible-study insights. Special issues: Lent and Easter; Advent. No poetry, lengthy spiritual journey stories. **Buys 365 unsolicited mss/year.** Send complete ms by mail or e-mail. Length: 300 words. **Pays $25/meditation.**

⚫⚫ THIS ROCK

Catholic Answers, P.O. Box 199000, San Diego CA 92159. (619)387-7200. Fax: (619)387-0042. Website: catholic.com. **60% freelance written.** Monthly magazine covering Catholic apologetics and evangelization. Our content explains, defends and promotes Catholic teaching. Estab. 1990. Circ. 24,000. Byline given. Pays on acceptance. Offers variable kill fee. Publishes ms an average of 4 months after acceptance. Accepts queries by e-mail. Responds in 2-4 weeks to queries. Responds in 1-2 months to mss. Sample copy available online. Guidelines by e-mail.

NONFICTION Needs book excerpts, essays, religious, conversion stories. **Buys 50 mss/year.** Send complete ms. Length: 1,500-3,000 words. **Pays $200-350.**

COLUMNS Damascus Road (stories of conversion to the Catholic Church), 2,000 words. **Buys 10 mss/year.** Send complete ms. **Pays $200.**

⚫⚫ THRIVE - THE EB ONLINE

Fellowship of Evangelical Baptist Churches in Canada, P.O. Box 457, Guelph ON N1H 6K9 Canada. 519-821-4830, ext. 229. Fax: 519-821-9829. E-mail: eb@fellowship.ca. Website: thrive-magazine.ca; fellowship.ca. **Contact:** Jennifer Bugg, managing editor. **10% freelance written.** Online magazine covering religious, spiritual, Christian living, denominational, and missionary news. "We exist to enhance the life and ministry of the church leaders and members in Fellowship Congregations." Estab. 1953. Byline given. Pays on publication. Publishes ms an average of 6 months after acceptance. Editorial lead time 4 months. Accepts queries by e-mail. Accepts simultaneous submissions. Sample copy available online. Guidelines available online.

NONFICTION Needs religious. No poetry, fiction, puzzles. **Buys 4-6 mss/year.** Send complete ms. Length: 600-2,400 words. **Pays $50.**

$ TOGETHER

Media For Living, 1251 Virginia Ave., Harrisonburg VA 22802. (540)433-5351. E-mail: tgether@aol.com. E-mail: melodiemd@msn.com. Website: churchoutreach.com. **Contact:** Melodie M. Davis, editor. **90% freelance written.** Quarterly tabloid covering religion and inspiration for a nonchurched audience. "*Together* is directed as an outreach publication to those who are not currently involved in a church; therefore, we need general inspirational articles that tell stories of personal change, especially around faith issues. Also, stories that will assist our readers in dealing with the many stresses and trials of everyday life—family, financial, career, community." Estab. 1980. Circ. 20,000. Byline given. Pays on publication. Publishes ms an average of 6-12 months after acceptance. Editorial lead time 6-9 months. Submit seasonal material 6 months in advance. Accepts queries by mail, e-mail. Accepts simultaneous submissions. Responds in 2 months to queries. Responds in 4 months to mss. Sample copy available online. Guidelines available online.

NONFICTION Needs essays, general interest, how-to, humor, inspirational, interview, personal experience, testimony, religious. "No pet stories. We have limited room for stories about illness, dying, or grief, but we do use them occasionally. We publish in March, June, September, and December, so holidays that occur in other months are not usually the subject of articles." **Buys 16 mss/year.** Send complete ms. Length: 500-1,200 words. **Pays $35-60.**

PHOTOS State availability. Captions, identification of subjects, model releases required. Reviews 4×6 prints, TIF/JPEG files. Offers $15-25/photo.

TRICYCLE

92 Vandam St., New York NY 10013. (212)645-1143. Fax: (212)645-1493. E-mail: editorial@tricycle.com. Website: tricycle.com. **80% freelance written**. Quarterly magazine covering the impact of Buddhism on Western culture. *Tricycle* readers tend to be well educated and open minded. Estab. 1991. Circ. 60,000. Byline given. Pays on publication. Offers 25% kill fee. Editorial lead time 3 months. Accepts queries by mail, e-mail, fax. Accepts simultaneous submissions. Responds in 3 months to queries & mss Sample copy for $7.95 or online at website. Guidelines available online.

NONFICTION Needs book excerpts, essays, general interest, historical, humor, inspirational, interview, personal experience, photo feature, religious, travel. **Buys 4-6 mss/year.** Length: 1,000-5,000 words.

PHOTOS State availability. Captions, identification of subjects required. Reviews contact sheets. Negotiates payment individually.

COLUMNS Reviews (film, books, tapes), 600 words; Science and Gen Next, both 700 words. **Buys 6-8 mss/year.** Query.

$$ U.S. CATHOLIC

Claretian Publications, 205 W. Monroe St., Chicago IL 60606. (312)236-7782. Fax: (312)236-8207. E-mail: editors@uscatholic.org. E-mail: submissions@uscatholic.org. Website: uscatholic.org. **100% freelance written**. Monthly magazine covering Roman Catholic spirituality. *U.S. Catholic* is dedicated to the belief that it makes a difference whether you're Catholic. We invite and help our readers explore the wisdom of their faith tradition and apply their faith to the challenges of the 21st century. Estab. 1935. Circ. 40,000. Byline given. Pays on acceptance. Publishes ms an average of 2-3 months after acceptance. Editorial lead time 8 months. Submit seasonal material 6 months in advance. Accepts queries by mail, e-mail, fax, phone. Responds in 1 month to queries. Responds in 2 months to mss. Sample copy for large SASE. Guidelines by e-mail or on website.

🗨 Please include SASE with written ms.

NONFICTION Needs essays, inspirational, opinion, personal experience, religious. **Buys 100 mss/year.** Send complete ms. Length: 2,500-3,500 words. **Pays $250-600.** Sometimes pays expenses of writers on assignment.

PHOTOS State availability.

COLUMNS Pays $250-600.

FICTION Contact: Maureen Abood, literary editor. Accepts short stories. "Topics vary, but unpublished fiction should be no longer than 2,500 words and should include strong characters and cause readers to stop for a moment and consider their relationships with others, the world, and/or God. Specifically religious themes are not required; subject matter is not restricted. E-mail literaryeditor@uscatholic.org. Usually responds in 8-10 weeks. Minimum payment is $300." Needs ethnic, mainstream, religious, slice-of-life vignettes. **Buys 4-6 mss/year.** Send complete ms. Length: 2,500-3,000 words. **Pays $300.**

POETRY Contact: Maureen Abood, literary editor. Needs free verse. Submit 3-5 poems at a time. Lines/poem: 50 maximum. Considers simultaneous submissions; no previously published poems. Accepts e-mail submissions (pasted into body of message; no attachments). Cover letter is preferred. "Always include SASE." Time between acceptance and publication is 3 months. Poems are circulated to an editorial board. Seldom comments on rejected poems. Guidelines available for SASE or on website. Responds in 3 months. Pays $75/poem and 5 contributor's copies. Acquires first North American serial rights. No light verse. Buys 12 poems/year. Submit maximum 5 poems. Length: 50 lines. **Pays $75.**

THE WAR CRY

The Salvation Army, 615 Slaters Lane, Alexandria VA 22314. (703)684-5500. Fax: (703)684-5539. E-mail: war_cry@usn.salvationarmy.org. **5% freelance written.** Biweekly magazine covering evangelism and Christian growth stories. Estab. 1881. Circ. 250,000. Byline given. Pays on acceptance. Publishes ms an average of 2 months - 1 year after acceptance. Editorial lead time 6 weeks. Submit seasonal material 1 year in advance. Responds in 3-4 weeks to mss. Sample copy, theme list, and writer's guidelines free for #10 SASE or online.

NONFICTION Needs inspirational, interview, personal experience, religious. No missionary stories, confessions. **Buys 25 mss/year.** Send complete ms. **Pays 15¢/word for articles.**

PHOTOS Identification of subjects required. Not currently purchasing photos.

FILLERS Needs anecdotes, inspirational. **Buys 10-20 mss/year mss/year.** Length: 200-500 words. **Pays 15¢/word.**

WESLEYAN LIFE

The Wesleyan Publishing House, P.O. Box 50434, Indianapolis IN 46250-0434. (317)774-7909. Fax: (317)774-3924. E-mail: communications@wesleyan.org. Website: wesleyanlifeonline.com. Quarterly magazine of The Wesleyan Church. Estab. 1842. Circ. 50,000. Byline given. Pays on publication. Submit seasonal material 6 months in advance. Accepts simultaneous submissions.

NONFICTION Needs inspirational, religious. No poetry accepted. Send complete ms. Length: 250-400 words. **Pays $25-150.**

WHAT IS ENLIGHTENMENT?

P.O. Box 2360, Lenox MA 01240. (413)637-6015. Website: wie.org. "At EnlightenNext we call ourselves "the magazine for Evolutionaries." We are a niche publication for those "Evolutionaries," for people who are passionate about the evolution of consciousness and culture. We are the place that leading thinkers in science, spirituality, politics, ecology, and business look to for an in-depth perspective on these many areas of life." Accepts queries by mail.

WIE does not accept freelance submissions.

NONFICTION Contact: Reviews Editor. *Unable to accept unsolicited articles at this time.* "We will, however, consider new books for potential review, particularly in the fields of philosophy, science, spirituality, and contemporary culture. Published books and bound galleys are preferred over unbound manuscripts."

WOMAN ALIVE

Christian Publishing and Outreach, Garcia Estate, Canterbury Rd., Worthing West Sussex BN13 1BW United Kingdom. 44)(190)360-4379. E-mail: womanalive@cpo.org.uk. Website: womanalive.co.uk. "Christian magazine geared specifically toward women. It covers all denominations and seeks to inspire, encourage, and provide resources to women in their faith, helping them to grow in their relationship with God and providing practical help and biblical perspective on the issues impacting their lives." Pays on publication. Accepts queries by mail, e-mail. Sample copy for £1.50, plus postage. Guidelines by e-mail.

NONFICTION Needs how-to, personal experience, travel, also, building life skills and discipleship, interviews with Christian women in prominent positions or who are making a difference in their communities/jobs, women facing difficult challenges or taking on new challenges, affordable holiday destinations written from a Christian perspective. Submit clips, bio, article summary, ms, SASE. 750-900/1-page article; 1,200-1,300/2-page article; 1,500-1,600/3-page article. **Pays £75/1-page article; £95/2-page article; £125/3-page article.**

PHOTOS Send photos. Reviews 300 dpi digital images.

RETIREMENT

✪✪✪✪ AARP THE MAGAZINE

AARP, c/o Editorial Submissions, 601 E St. NW, Washington DC 20049. E-mail: aarpmagazine@aarp.org. Website: aarp.org/magazine/. **Contact:** Editorial Submissions. **50% freelance written. Prefers to work with published/established writers.** Bimonthly magazine. *AARP The Magazine* is devoted to the varied needs and active life interests of AARP members, age 50 and over, covering such topics as financial planning, travel, health, careers, retirement, relationships, and social and cultural change. Its editorial content serves the mission of AARP seeking through education, advocacy and service to enhance the quality of life for all by promoting independence, dignity, and purpose. Circ. 21,500,000. Byline given. Pays on acceptance. Offers 25% kill fee. Publishes ms an average of 6 months after acceptance. Submit seasonal material 6 months in advance. Accepts queries by mail, e-mail only. NoResponds in 3 months to queries. Sample copy free. Guidelines available online.

NONFICTION No previously published articles. Query with published clips. *No unsolicited mss.* Length: Up to 2,000 words. **Pays $1/word.** Sometimes pays expenses of writers on assignment.

PHOTOS Photos purchased with or without accompanying mss. Pays $250 and up for color; $150 and up for b&w.

✪ MATURE LIVING

Lifeway Christian Resources, 1 Lifeway Plaza, Nashville TN 37234. (615)251-2000. E-mail: matureliving@lifeway.com. Website: lifeway.com. **Contact:** Rene Holt. **90% freelance written.** "Monthly leisure reading magazine for senior adults 55 and older. *Mature Living* is Christian in content and the material required is what would appeal to 55 and over age group: inspirational, informational, nostalgic, humorous. Our magazine is distributed mainly through churches (especially Southern Baptist churches) that buy the magazine in bulk and distribute it to members in this age group." Estab. 1977. Circ. 320,000. Byline given. Pays on acceptance. Publishes ms an average of 7-8 weeks after acceptance. Submit seasonal material 1 year in advance. Responds in 3 months to mss. Sample copy for 9×12 SAE with 4 first-class stamps. Guidelines for #10 sase.

NONFICTION Needs general interest, historical, how-to, humor, inspirational, interview, personal experience, travel, crafts. No pornography, profanity, occult, liquor, dancing, drugs, gambling. **Buys 100 mss/year.** Length: 600-1,200 words. **Pays $85-115**

PHOTOS State availability. Offers $10-25/photo. Pays on publication.

COLUMNS Cracker Barrel (brief, humorous, original quips and verses), **pays $15**; Grandparents' Brag Board (something humorous or insightful said or done by your grandchild or great-grandchild), **pays $15**; Inspirational (devotional items), **pays $25**; Food (introduction and 4-6 recipes), **pays $50**; Over the Garden Fence (vegetable or flower gardening), **pays $40**; Crafts (step-by-step procedures), **pays $40**; Game Page (crossword or word-search puzzles and quizzes), **pays $40**.

FICTION Contact: David Seay, editor-in-chief. Needs humorous, religious, senior citizen/retirement. No reference to liquor, dancing, drugs, gambling; no pornography, profanity or occult. **Buys 12 mss/year.** Send complete ms. 900-1,200 words preferred **Pays $85-115; 3 contributor's copies.**

POETRY Buys 24 poems/year. Submit maximum 5 poems. Length: 12-16 lines. **Pays $-25.**

✪ MATURE YEARS

The United Methodist Publishing House, 201 Eighth Ave. S., P.O. Box 801, Nashville TN 37202-0801. (615)749-6292. Fax: (615)749-6512. E-mail: matureyears@umpublishing.org. **80% freelance written. Prefers to work with published/established writers.** Quarterly magazine designed to help persons in and nearing the retirement years understand and appropriate the resources of the Christian faith in dealing with specific problems and opportunities related to aging. Estab. 1954. Circ. 55,000. Pays on acceptance. Publishes ms an average of 1 year after acceptance. Submit seasonal material 14 months in advance. Responds in 2 weeks to queries. Responds in 2 months to mss. Sample copy for $6 and 9×12 SAE. Writer's guidelines for #10 SASE or by e-mail.

NONFICTION Needs how-to, hobbies, inspirational, religious, travel, special guidelines, older adult health, finance issues. **Buys 75-80 mss/year.** Send complete ms; e-mail submissions preferred. Length: 900-2,000 words. **Pays $45-125.** Sometimes pays expenses of writers on assignment.

REPRINTS Send tearsheet, photocopy or typed ms with rights for sale noted and information about when and where the material previously appeared. Pays at same rate as for previously unpublished material.

PHOTOS Send photos. Captions, model releases required. Negotiates pay individually.

COLUMNS Health Hints (retirement, health), 900-1,500 words; Going Places (travel, pilgrimage), 1,000-1,500 words; Fragments of Life (personal inspiration), 250-600 words; Modern Revelations (religious/inspirational), 900-1,500 words; Money Matters (personal finance), 1,200-1,800 words; Merry-Go-Round (cartoons, jokes, 4-6 line humorous verse); Puzzle Time (religious puzzles, crosswords). **Buys 4 mss/year.** Send complete ms. **Pays $25-45.**

FICTION Contact: Marvin Cropsey, editor. Needs humorous, religious, slice-of-life vignettes, retirement years nostalgia, intergenerational relationships. "We don't want anything poking fun at old age, saccharine stories, or anything not for older adults. Must show older adults (age 55 plus) in a positive manner." **Buys 4 mss/year.** Send complete ms. Length: 1,000-2,000 words. **Pays $60-125.**

POETRY Needs free verse, haiku, light verse, traditional. Buys 24 poems/year. Submit maximum 6 poems. Length: 3-16 lines. **Pays $5-20.**

RURAL

💲💲 BACKWOODS HOME MAGAZINE

P.O. Box 712, Gold Beach OR 97444. (541)247-8900. Fax: (541)247-8600. E-mail: editor@backwoodshome.com. Website: backwoodshome.com. **90% freelance written.** Bimonthly magazine covering self-reliance. "*Backwoods Home Magazine* is written for people who have a desire to pursue personal independence, self-sufficiency, and their dreams. We offer 'how-to' articles on self-reliance." Estab. 1989. Circ. 38,000. Byline given. Pays on acceptance. Editorial lead time 4-6 months. Submit seasonal material 4-6 months in advance. Accepts queries by mail, e-mail. Sample copy for sae with 9x10 envelope and 6 First-Class stamps. Guidelines free.

NONFICTION Needs general interest, how-to, humor, personal experience, technical. **Buys 120 mss/year.** Send complete ms. Length: 500 words. **Pays $30-200.**

PHOTOS Send photos. Captions, identification of subjects, model releases required. Offers no additional payment for photos accepted with ms.

⊙💲💲 THE COUNTRY CONNECTION

Pinecone Publishing, P.O. Box 100, Boulter ON K0L 1G0 Canada. (866)332-3651; (613)332-3651. Website: pinecone.on.ca. **100% freelance written.** Magazine published 4 times/year covering nature, environment, history, heritage, nostalgia, travel and the arts. *The Country Connection* is a magazine for true nature lovers and the rural adventurer. Building on our commitment to heritage, cultural, artistic, and environmental themes, we continually add new topics to illuminate the country experience of people living within nature. Our goal is to chronicle rural life in its many aspects, giving 'voice' to the countryside. Estab. 1989. Circ. 4,000. Byline given. Pays on publication. Publishes ms an average of 4 months after acceptance. Editorial lead time 4 months. Accepts queries by mail, e-mail, phone. Sample copy for $5.64. Guidelines available online.

NONFICTION Needs general interest, historical, humor, opinion, personal experience, travel, lifestyle, leisure, art and culture, vegan recipes. No hunting, fishing, animal husbandry, or pet articles. **Buys 60 mss/year.** Send complete ms. Length: 500-2,000 words. **Pays 10¢/word.**

PHOTOS Send photos. Captions required. Reviews transparencies, prints, digital photos on CD. Offers $10-50/photo.

FICTION Needs adventure, fantasy, historical, humorous, slice-of-life vignettes, country living. **Buys 10 mss/year.** Send complete ms. Length: 500-1,500 words. **Pays 10¢/word.**

💲💲 FARM & RANCH LIVING

Reiman Media Group, 5925 Country Lane, Greendale WI 53129. (414)423-0100. Fax: (414)423-8463. E-mail: editors@farmandranchliving.com. Website: farmandranchliving.com. **30% freelance written. Eager to work with new/unpublished writers.** Bimonthly magazine aimed at families that farm or ranch full time. *F&RL* is *not* a 'how-to' magazine—it focuses on people rather than products and profits. Estab. 1978. Circ. 400,000. Byline given. Pays on publication. Publishes ms an average of 6 months after acceptance. Submit seasonal material 6 months in advance. Accepts queries by mail, e-mail, fax. Responds in 6 weeks to queries. Sample copy for $2. Guidelines for #10 SASE.

NONFICTION Needs humor, rural only, inspirational, interview, personal experience, farm/ranch related, photo feature, nostalgia, prettiest place in the country (photo/text tour of ranch or farm). No issue-oriented stories (pollution, animal rights, etc.). **Buys 30 mss/year.** Send complete ms. Length: 600-1,200 words. **Pays up to $300 for text/photo package. Payment for Prettiest Place negotiable.**

REPRINTS Send photocopy with rights for sale noted. Payment negotiable.

PHOTOS Scenic. State availability. Pays $75-200 for 35mm color slides.

$$ HOBBY FARMS

Bowtie, Inc., P.O. Box 8237, Lexington KY 40533. Fax: (859)260-9814. E-mail: hobbyfarms@bowtieinc.com. Website: hobbyfarms.com. **75% freelance written.** Bimonthly magazine covering small farms and rural lifestyle. "*Hobby Farms* is the magazine for rural enthusiasts. Whether you have a small garden or 100 acres, there is something in *Hobby Farms* to educate, enlighten or inspire you." Estab. 2001. Circ. 138,000. Byline given. Pays on publication. Publishes ms an average of 6 months after acceptance. Editorial lead time 4 months. Submit seasonal material 6 months in advance. Accepts queries by mail, e-mail. Responds in 2 months to queries. Responds in 2 months to mss. Guidelines free.

"Writing tone should be conversational, but authoritative."

NONFICTION Needs historical, how-to, farm or livestock management, equipment, etc., interview, personal experience, technical, breed or crop profiles. **Buys 10 mss/year.** Send complete ms. Length: 1,500-2,500 words. Sometimes pays expenses of writers on assignment. Limit agreed upon in advance

PHOTOS State availability of or send photos. Identification of subjects, model releases required. Reviews transparencies, GIF/JPEG files. Negotiates payment individually.

$ MOTHER EARTH NEWS

Ogden Publications, 1503 SW 42nd St., Topeka KS 66609-1265. (785)274-4300. E-mail: letters@motherearthnews.com. Website: motherearthnews.com. **Contact:** Cheryl Long, editor-in-chief. **Mostly written by staff and team of established freelancers.** Bimonthly magazine emphasizing country living, country skills, natural health and sustainable technologies for both long-time and would-be ruralists. "*Mother Earth News* promotes self-sufficient, financially independent and environmentally aware lifestyles. Many of our feature articles are written by our Contributing Editors, but we also assign articles to freelance writers, particularly those who have experience with our subject matter (both firsthand adn writing experience." Circ. 350,000. Byline given. Pays on publication. Submit seasonal material 5 months in advance. Responds in 6 months to mss. Sample copy for $5. Guidelines for #10 SASE.

NONFICTION Needs how-to, green building, do-it-yourself, organic gardening, whole foods & cooking, natural health, livestock & sustainable farming, renewable energy, 21st century homesteading, nature-environment-community, green transportation. No fiction, please. **Buys 35-50 mss/year.** "Query. Please send a short synopsis of the idea, a one-page outline and any relevant digital photos, and samples. If available, please send us copies of one or two published articles, or tell us where to find them online." "Country Lore" length: 100-300/words. "Firsthand Reports" length: 1,500-2,000/words **Pays $25-150.**

PHOTOS "We welcome quality photographs for our two departments.".

COLUMNS Country Lore (helpful how-to tips); 100-300/words; Firsthand Reports (first-person stories about sustainable lifestyles of all sorts), 1,500-2,000/words.

OUR LOCAL TABLE MONADNOCK: THE GUIDE TO OUR REGION'S FOOD, FARMS, & COMMUNITY

P.O. Box 1504, Keene NH 03431. E-mail: editor@localtablemonadnock.com. Website: localtablemonadnock.com. **Contact:** Marcia Passos Duffy, managing editor and editorial director. Quarterly Magazine for local food/farms in the Monadnock Region of New Hampshire. Estab. 2010. Circ. 10,000. Pays on publication. Publishes ms an average of 3 months after acceptance. 25% Kill fee. 3 months. Submit seasonal material 3 months in advanced. Accepts queries by e-mail. Reports in 4 weeks on queries; 1 month manuscripts. Sample copy available online. Guidelines are available on website.

"Must be out trends, profiles, etc., of local food and farms in the Monadnock Region of New Hampshire."

NONFICTION Contact: Marcia Passos Duffy, Editorial Director. Needs book excerpts, essays, how-to, interview, opinion, personal experience. 500-1,000.

Pays 10¢ per word. Sometimes pays expenses of writers on assignment. (limit agreed upon in advance)

PHOTOS Contact: Jodi Genest, Creative Director. Freelancers should state of photos with submission. Captions. GIF/JPEG files. Offers no additional payment for photos accepted with ms.

COLUMNS Our Local Farmer (Profile of local farmer in Monadnock Region) up to 800 words; Local Chefs, Local Food (Profile of local chef using local food) up to 800 words; Feature ("How-to" or think piece about local foods) up 1,000; Books/Opinion/Commentary (Review of books, book excerpt, commentary, opinion pieces about local food) up to 500 words. **Buys 10 mss/year.** Query

$ $ RANGE MAGAZINE

Purple Coyote Corp., 106 E. Adams St., Suite 201, Carson City NV 89706. (775)884-2200. Fax: (775)884-2213. E-mail: edit@rangemagazine.com. Website: rangemagazine.com. **70% freelance written.** Quarterly magazine. *RANGE* magazine covers ranching and farming and the issues that affect agriculture. Estab. 1991. Pays on publication. Publishes ms an average of 6 months after acceptance. Accepts queries by e-mail. Responds in 6-8 weeks to queries. Responds in 3-6 months to mss. Sample copy for $2. Guidelines available online.

NONFICTION Needs book excerpts, humor, interview, personal experience, photo feature. No rodeos or anything by a writer not familiar with *RANGE*. Query. Length: 500-2,000 words. **Pays $50-400.**

PHOTOS Contact: C.J. Hadley, editor/publisher. State availability. Captions, identification of subjects required. Reviews 35mm transparencies, 4×6 prints, CDs with contact sheet & captions. Must be high-res digital images. Negotiates payment individually.

$ RURAL HERITAGE

P.O. Box 2067, Cedar Rapids IA 52406. (319)362-3027. E-mail: editor@ruralheritage.com. Website: ruralheritage.com. **98% freelance written. Willing to work with a small number of new/unpublished writers.** Bimonthly magazine devoted to the training and care of draft animals. Estab. 1976. Circ. 9,500. Byline given. Pays on publication. Publishes ms an average of 6 months after acceptance. Submit seasonal material 6 months in advance. Accepts queries by mail, e-mail. Responds in 3 months to queries. Sample copy for $8. Guidelines available online.

NONFICTION Needs how-to, farming with draft animals, interview, people using draft animals, photo feature. No articles on *mechanized* farming. **Buys 200 mss/year.** Query or send complete ms. Length: 1,200-1,500 words. **Pays 5¢/word.**

PHOTOS 6 covers/year, animals in harness $200. Photo guidelines for #10 SASE or online. Captions, identification of subjects required. Pays $10.

POETRY Needs traditional. **Pays $5-25.**

$ $ RURALITE

P.O. Box 558, Forest Grove OR 97116-0558. (503)357-2105. Fax: (503)357-8615. E-mail: curtisc@ruralite.org. Website: ruralite.org. **80% freelance written. Works with new, unpublished writers.** Monthly magazine aimed at members of consumer-owned electric utilities throughout 10 western states, including Alaska. Publishes 48 regional editions. Estab. 1954. Circ. 325,000. Byline given. Pays on acceptance. Accepts queries by mail. Responds in 1 month to queries. Sample copy for 9×12 SAE with $1.28 of postage affixed. Guidelines available online.

NONFICTION Buys 50-60 mss/year. Query. Length: 100-2,000 words. **Pays $50-500.**

REPRINTS Send typed manuscript with rights for sale noted and information about when and where the material previously appeared.

PHOTOS Illustrated stories are the key to a sale. Stories without art rarely make it. Color prints/negatives, color slides, all formats accepted. No black & white. Inside color is $25-100; cover photo is $250-350.

SCIENCE

$ $ AD ASTRA

1155 15th St. NW, Suite 500, Washington DC 20005. (202)429-1600. Fax: (202)463-0659. E-mail: adastra.editor@nss.org. Website: nss.org. **Contact:** Gary Barnhard, Editor-in-Chief. **90% freelance written.** "We publish non-technical, lively articles about all aspects of international space programs, from shuttle missions to planetary probes to plans for the future and commercial space." Needs freelancers for multimedia design. Works with 40 freelancers/year. Uses freelancers for magazine illustration. Buys 10 illustrations/year. "We are looking for original artwork on space themes, either conceptual or representing specific designs, events, etc." Prefers acrylics, then oils and collage." Show a set of slides showing planetary art, spacecraft and people working in space. I do not want to see 'science-fiction' art. Label each slide with name and phone number. Understand the freelance assignments are usually made far in advance of magazine deadline." Estab. 1989. Byline given. Pays on publication. Responds only when interested. Sample copy for 9×12 SASE.

NONFICTION Needs book excerpts, essays, exposè, general interest, interview, opinion, photo feature, technical. No science fiction or UFO stories. Query with published clips. Length: 1,000-2,400 words. **Pays $200-500 for features.**

PHOTOS State availability. Identification of subjects required. Reviews color prints, digital, JPEG-IS, GISS. Negotiates pay.

⊖⊖⊖⊖ AMERICAN ARCHAEOLOGY

The Archaeological Conservancy, 5301 Central Ave. NE, #902, Albuquerque NM 87108-1517. (505)266-9668. Fax: (505)266-0311. E-mail: tacmag@nm.net. Website: americanarchaeology.org. **Contact:** Michael Bawaya, Editor. **60% freelance written**. Quarterly magazine. "We're a popular archaeology magazine. Our readers are very interested in this science. Our features cover important digs, prominent archaeologists, and most any aspect of the science. We only cover North America." Estab. 1997. Circ. 35,000. Byline given. Pays on acceptance. Offers 20% kill fee. Publishes ms an average of 3 months after acceptance. Editorial lead time 3 months. Accepts queries by mail, e-mail, fax. Responds in 3 weeks to queries. Responds in 1 month to mss

NONFICTION No fiction, poetry, humor. **Buys 15 mss/year.** Query with published clips. Length: 1,500-3,000 words. **Pays $1,000-2,000.** Pays expenses of writers on assignment.

PHOTOS Contact: Vicki Singer, art director. State availability. Identification of subjects required. Reviews transparencies, prints. Offers $400-600/photo shoot. Negotiates payment individually.

⊖⊖⊖⊖ ARCHAEOLOGY

Archaeological Institute of America, 36-36 33rd St., Long Island NY 11106. (718)472-3050. Fax: (718)472-3051. E-mail: cvalentino@archaeology.org. E-mail: editorial@archaeology.org. Website: archaeology. org. **Contact:** Editor-in-Chief. **50% freelance written.** *ARCHAEOLOGY* combines worldwide archaeological findings with photography, specially rendered maps, drawings, and charts. Covers current

excavations and recent discoveries, and includes personality profiles, technology updates, adventure, travel and studies of ancient cultures. "*ARCHAEOLOGY* magazine is a publication of the Archaeological Institute of America, a 130-year-old nonprofit organization. The magazine has been published continuously for more than 60 years. We have a total audience of nearly 750,000, mostly in the United States and Canada. Our readership is a combination of the general public, enthusiastic amateurs, and scholars in the field. Publishing bimonthly, we bring our readers all the exciting aspects of archaeology: adventure, discovery, culture, history, technology, and travel. Authors include both professional journalists and professional archaeologists. If you are a scientist interested in writing about your research for *ARCHAEOLOGY*, see tips and suggestions on writing for a general audience online." Estab. 1948. Circ. 750,000. Byline given. Pays on acceptance. Offers 25% kill fee. Submit seasonal material 6 months in advance. Accepts queries by mail, e-mail, fax. Accepts simultaneous submissions. Sample copy and writer's guidelines free. Guidelines online.

> "Our feature-length articles cover the world of archaeology and feature intriguing insights into a period of history or prehistory. Archaeology isn't just about digging, and we're always looking for a new angle on a subject. Recent articles have covered such diverse subjects as Turkey's claim to the world's first temple, a diet for Roman gladiators, Polynesian Mormons in Utah, why flattened foreheads and filed teeth made the Maya beautiful, and how Egypt's Great Pyramid was built."

NONFICTION Needs essays, general interest. "Our reviews department looks for short (250- to 500-word) articles on museums, books, television shows, movies, websites, and games of interest to our readers. While the material reviewed may not be purely archaeological in nature, it should have a strong archaeological element to it. Reviews should not simply summarize the material, but provide a critical evaluation.". **Buys 6 mss/year.** Query preferred. "Preliminary queries should be no more than 1 or 2 pages (500 words max.) in length and may be sent to the Editor-in-Chief by mail or via e-mail to editorial@archaeology.org. We do not accept telephone queries. Check our online index and search to make sure that we have not already published a similar article. Your query should tell us the following: who you are, why you are qualified to cover the subject, how you will cover the subject (with an emphasis on narrative structure, new knowledge, etc.), and why our readers would be interested in the subject." Length: 1,000-3,000 words. **Pays $2,000 maximum.** Sometimes pays expenses of writers on assignment.

PHOTOS Clips and credentials are helpful. While illustrations are not the sole responsibility of the author, it helps to give us a sense of how the article could be illustrated; if possible, e-mail an example of 2 or 3 images that might accompany the article (noting where and from whom such images may be obtained). Please do not e-mail unusually large images or too many images at a time; we will request additional ones if needed. Please do not mail us unsolicited CDs, transparencies, or slides as they will not be returned. If you do not have access to images, referrals to professional photographers with relevant material are appreciated. Send photos. Identification of subjects, True required. Reviews 4×5 color transparencies, 35mm color slides.

COLUMNS Insider is a piece of about 2,500 words dealing with subject matter with which the author has an intimate, personal interest. **Conversation** is a one-page interview in a Q&A format with someone who has made a considerable impact on the field of archaeology or has done something unusual or intriguing. **Letter From.** is an account of a personal experience involving a particular topic or site. "Letters" have included a visit to an alien-archaeology theme park, the account of an archaeologist caught in a civil war, and an overnight stay with the guards at Angkor Wat. "Letters" are usually about 2,500 to 3,000 words in length. **Artifact** is the last editorial page of the magazine. Its purpose is to introduce the reader to a single artifact that reveals something surprising about a site or an historical event. Unusual artifacts recently excavated are preferred and visuals must be of the highest quality. The writer must explain the archaeological context, date, site found, etc., as well as summarize the artifact's importance in about 200 words or less. First person accounts by the actual excavators or specialists are preferred, although exceptions are be made.

TIPS "We reach nonspecialist readers interested in art, science, history, and culture. Our reports, regional commentaries, and feature-length articles introduce readers to recent developments in archaeology worldwide."

✷✷ ASTRONOMY

Kalmbach Publishing, 21027 Crossroads Circle, P.O. Box 1612, Waukesha WI 53187-1612. (800)533-6644. Fax: (262)796-1615. Website: astronomy.com. **50% of articles submitted and written by science writers; includes commissioned and unsolicited.** Monthly magazine covering the science and hobby of astronomy. "Half of our magazine is for hobbyists (who are active observers of the sky); the other half is directed toward armchair astronomers who are intrigued by the science." Estab. 1973. Circ. 122,000. Byline given. Pays on acceptance. Responds in 1 month to queries. Responds in 3 months to mss. Guidelines for #10 SASE or online.

○ "We are governed by what is happening in astronomical research and space exploration. It can be up to a year before we publish a manuscript. Query for electronic submissions."

NONFICTION Needs book excerpts, new product, announcements, photo feature, technical, space, astronomy. **Buys 75 mss/year.** Query. Length: 500-3,000 words. **Pays $100-1,000.**

PHOTOS Send photos. Captions, identification of subjects required; model/property releases preferred. Pays $25/photo.

✷✷✷✷ BIOSCIENCE

American Institute of Biological Sciences, 1900 Campus Commons Drive, Suite 200, Reston VA 20191. (202)628-1500. Fax: (202)628-1509. E-mail: tbeardsley@aibs.org. Website: aibs.org. James Verdier, managing editor, jverdier@aibs.org. **Contact:** Dr. Timothy M. Beardsley, editor-in-chief. **5% freelance written.** Monthly peer-reviewed scientific journal covering organisms from molecules to the environment. "We contract professional science writers to write features on assigned topics, including organismal biology and ecology, but excluding biomedical topics." Estab. 1951. Byline given. Publishes ms an average of 3 months after acceptance. Editorial lead time 2 months. Accepts queries by e-mail. Responds in 2-3 weeks to queries. Sample copy free. Guidelines free.

NONFICTION Does not want biomedical topics. **Buys 10 mss/year.** Query. Length: 1,500-3,000 words. **Pays $1,500-3,000.** Sometimes pays expenses of writers on assignment.

✪✪✪ CHEMICAL HERITAGE

Chemical Heritage Foundation (CHF), 315 Chestnut St., Philadelphia PA 19106-2702. (215)925-2222. E-mail: editor@chemheritage.org. Website: chemheritage.org. **40% freelance written**. The magazine is published three times per year. *Chemical Heritage* reports on the history of the chemical and molecular sciences and industries, on CHF activities, and on other activities of interest to our readers. Estab. 1982. Circ. 20,000. Byline given. Pays on acceptance. Publishes ms an average of 6-12 months after acceptance. Editorial lead time 4 months. Accepts queries by mail, e-mail, phone. Responds in 1 month to queries and to mss. Sample copy free.

NONFICTION Needs book excerpts, essays, historical, interview. No exposes or excessively technical material. Many of our readers are highly educated professionals, but they may not be familiar with, for example, specific chemical processes. **Buys 3-5 mss/ year.** Query. Length: 1,000-3,500 words. **Pays 50¢ to $1/word.**

PHOTOS State availability. Captions required. Offers no additional payment for photos accepted with ms.

COLUMNS Contact: Associate Editor: Jennifer Dionisio, jdionisio@chemheritage.org). Book reviews: 200 or 750 words; CHF collections: 300-500 words; policy: 1,000 words; personal remembrances: 750 words; profiles of CHF awardees and oral history subjects: 600-900 words: buys 3-5 mms/year. **Buys 10 mss/year.** Query.

CHEMMATTERS

1155 16th Street, NW, Washington DC 20036. (202)872-6164. Fax: (202)833-7732. E-mail: chemmatters@acs.org. Website: acs.org/chemmatters. **Contact:** Pat Pages, editor. Covers content covered in a standard high school chemistry textbook. Estab. 1983. Pays on acceptance. 6 months Accepts queries by mail, e-mail. Accepts simultaneous submissions. Responds to queries/mss in 2 weeks. **Sample copies** free for self-addressed stamped envelope 10 inches × 13 inches and 3 first-class stamps. **Writer's guidelines** free for SASE (available as e-mail attachment upon request).

NONFICTION Query with published clips. **Pays $500-$1,000 for article. Additional payment for mss/illustration packages and for photos accompanying articles.**

✪✪✪ COSMOS MAGAZINE

Luna Media Pty Ltd., Level 1, 49 Shepherd St., Chippendale, Sydney NSW 2008 Australia. (61)(2)9310-8500. Fax: (61)(2)9698-4899. E-mail: submissions@cosmosmagazine.com. Website: cosmosmagazine.com. **90% freelance written**. Bimonthly magazine covering science. "An Australian brand with a global outlook, COSMOS internationally respected for its literary writing, excellence in design and engaging breadth of content. Won the 2009 Magazine of the Year and twice Editor of the Year at the annual Bell Awards for Publishing Excellence; the American Institute of Physics Science Writing Award;the Reuters/IUCN Award for Excellence in Environmental Journalism; the City of Sydney Lord Mayor's Sustainability Award and an Earth Journalism Award. COSMOS is the brainchild of Wilson da Silva, a former ABC TV science reporter and past president of the World Federation of Science Journalists. It is backed by an Editorial Advisory Board that includes Apollo 11 astronaut Buzz Aldrin, ABC Radio's Robyn Williams, and is chaired by Dr. Alan Finkel, the neuroscientist and philanthropist who is the Chancellor of Monash University in Melbourne." Estab. 2005. Circ. 25,000. Byline given. Pays on publication. Offers up to 50% kill fee. Publishes ms an average of 1 month after acceptance. Editorial lead time 2 months. Submit seasonal material 3 months in advance. Accepts queries by e-mail, fax. Accepts simultaneous submissions. Responds in 1 month to queries. Responds in 3 months to mss. Guidelines available online.

NONFICTION Needs book excerpts, essays, exposè, historical, humor, interview, opinion, photo feature, travel. **Buys 250 mss/year.** Query with published clips. Length: 700-5,000 words. **Pays 60¢/word for assigned articles. Pays 30¢/word for unsolicited articles.** Sometimes pays expenses of writers on assignment.

PHOTOS State availability. Captions, identification of subjects required. Reviews JPEG files. Pays $10-100/photo; negotiates payment individually.

COLUMNS Travelogue (travel to an intriguing/unusual place that involves science), 1,500-2,000 words. Query. **Pays $1,200-1,700**

FICTION Needs science fiction. No fantasy—science fiction only. **Buys 8 mss/year.** Length: 2,000-4,000 words. **Pays flat $300 per story.**

$$$$ INVENTORS DIGEST

Inventors Digest, LLC, 520 Elliot St., Suite 200, Charlotte NC 28202. (704)369-7312. Fax: (704)333-5115. E-mail: info@inventorsdigest.com. Website: inventorsdigest.com/about-us. **50% freelance written.** Monthly magazine covering inventions, technology, engineering, intellectual property issues. Inventors Digest is committed to educating and inspiring entry- and enterprise-level inventors and professional innovators. As the leading print and online publication for the innovation culture, *Inventors Digest* delivers useful, entertaining and cutting-edge information to help its readers succeed. Estab. 1983. Circ. 40,000. Byline given. Pays on publication. Offers 40% kill fee. Publishes ms an average of 2 months after acceptance. Editorial lead time 2 months. Submit seasonal material 4 months in advance. Accepts queries by mail, e-mail. Responds in 3 weeks to queries. Responds in 1 month to mss. Sample copy available online. Guidelines free.

NONFICTION Needs book excerpts, historical, how-to, secure a patent, find a licensing manufacturer, avoid scams, inspirational, interview, new product, opinion, (does not mean letters to the editor), personal experience, technical. Special issues: Our editorial calendar is available at our website, inventorsdigest.com/images/Inventors%20Digest%20Media%20Kit_R08.pdf. "We don't want poetry. No stories that talk about readers—stay away from 'one should do X' construction. Nothing that duplicates what you can read elsewhere." **Buys 4 mss/year. mss/year.** Query. Length: 2,500 words. **Pays $50-TBD for assigned articles. Pays $50-TBD for unsolicited articles.**

PHOTOS Contact: Mike Drummond. State availability. Identification of subjects required. Reviews GIF/JPEG files. Negotiates payment individually.

COLUMNS Contact: Brandon Phillips. Cover (the most important package-puts a key topic in compelling context), 2,000-3,000 words; Radar (news/product snippets), 1,200; Bookshelf (book reviews), 700; Pro Bono (legal issues), 850; Profile (human interest stories on inventors and innovators), BrainChild (celebration of young inventors and innovators), FirstPerson (inventors show how they've overcome hurdles), 1,000; MeetingRoom (learn secrets to success of best inventor groups in the country), 900; TalkBack (Q&A with manufacturers, retailers, etc. in the innovation industry), Five Questions With.(a conversation with some of the brightest and most controversial minds in Technology, manufacturing, academia and other fields), 800. **Buys 4 mss/year mss/year.** Query. **Pays $$20.**

$$$$ SCIENTIFIC AMERICAN

415 Madison Ave., New York NY 10017. (212)754-0550. Fax: (212)755-1976. E-mail: editors@sciam.com. Website: sciam.com. Monthly magazine covering developments and topics of interest in the world of science. Query before submitting. *Scientific American* brings its readers directly to the wellspring of exploration and technological innovation. The magazine specializes in first-hand accounts by the people who actually do the work. Their personal experience provides an authoritative perspective on future growth. Over 100 of our authors have won Nobel Prizes. Complementing those articles are regular departments written by *Scientific American*'s staff of professional journalists, all specialists in their fields. *Scientific American* is the authoritative source of advance information. Authors are the first to report on important breakthroughs, because they're the people who make them. It all goes back to *Scientific American*'s corporate mission: to link those who use knowledge with those who create it. Estab. 1845. Circ. 710,000.

NONFICTION Pays $1/word average. Pays expenses of writers on assignment.

$$ SKY & TELESCOPE

New Track Media, 90 Sherman St., Cambridge MA 02140. (617)864-7360. Fax: (617)864-6117. E-mail: editors@SkyandTelescope.com. Website: skyandtelescope.com. **15% freelance written.** Monthly magazine covering astronomy. "*Sky & Telescope* is the magazine of record for astronomy. We cover amateur activities, research news, equipment, book, and software reviews. Our audience is the amateur astronomer who wants to learn more about the night sky." Estab. 1941. Circ. 110,000. Byline given. Pays on publication. Publishes ms an average of 6 months after acceptance. Editorial lead time 4 months. Submit seasonal material 1 year in advance. Accepts queries by mail, e-mail, fax. Responds in 3 weeks to queries. Responds in 1 month to mss. Sample copy for $6.99. Guidelines available online.

NONFICTION Needs essays, historical, how-to, opinion, personal experience, photo feature, technical. No poetry, crosswords, New Age, or alternative cosmologies. **Buys 10 mss/year.** Query. Length: 1,500-

2,500 words. **Pays at least 25¢/word.** Sometimes pays expenses of writers on assignment.

PHOTOS Send photos. Identification of subjects required. Reviews contact sheets. Negotiates payment individually.

COLUMNS Focal Point (opinion), 700 words; Books & Beyond (reviews), 800 words; The Astronomy Scene (profiles), 1,500 words. **Buys 20 mss/year.** Query. **Pays 25¢/word.**

⊘$$$$ STARDATE

University of Texas, 1 University Station, A2100, Austin TX 78712. (512)471-5285. Fax: (512)471-5060. Website: stardate.org. **80% freelance written.** Bimonthly magazine covering astronomy. "*StarDate* is written for people with an interest in astronomy and what they see in the night sky, but no special astronomy training or background." Estab. 1975. Circ. 10,000. Byline given. Pays on acceptance. Offers 25% kill fee. Publishes ms an average of 4 months after acceptance. Editorial lead time 6 months. Submit seasonal material 6 months in advance. Accepts queries by mail, e-mail, fax. Responds in 6 weeks to queries. Sample copy and writer's guidelines free.

💬 No unsolicited mss.

NONFICTION Needs general interest, historical, interview, photo feature, technical, travel, research in astronomy. No first-person; first stargazing experiences; paranormal. **Buys 8 mss/year.** Query with published clips. Length: 1,500-3,000 words. **Pays $500-1,500.** Sometimes pays expenses of writers on assignment.

PHOTOS Send photos. Identification of subjects required. Reviews transparencies, prints. Negotiates payment individually.

COLUMNS Astro News (short astronomy news item), 250 words. **Buys 6 mss/year.** Query with published clips. **Pays $100-200.**

$$ WEATHERWISE

Taylor & Francis Group, 325 Chestnut St., Suite 800, Philadelphia PA 19106. (215)625-8900. E-mail: margaret.benner@taylorandfrancis.com. Website: weatherwise.org. **Contact:** Margaret Benner, editor-in-chief. **75% freelance written.** Bimonthly magazine covering weather and meteorology. "*Weatherwise* is America's only magazine about the weather. Our readers range from professional weathercasters and scientists to basement-bound hobbyists, but all share a common interest in craving information about weather as it relates to the atmospheric sciences, technology, history, culture, society, art, etc." Estab. 1948. Circ. 11,000. Byline given. Pays on publication. Publishes ms an average of 6 months after acceptance. Editorial lead time 6-9 months. Submit seasonal material 9 months in advance. Accepts queries by mail, e-mail, fax, phone. Responds in 2 months to queries. Guidelines available online.

NONFICTION Needs book excerpts, essays, general interest, historical, how-to, interview, new product, opinion, personal experience, photo feature, technical, travel. Special issues: Photo Contest (September/October deadline June 2). No blow-by-blow accounts of the biggest storm to ever hit your backyard. **Buys 15-18 mss/year.** Query with published clips. Length: 2,000-3,000 words. **Pays $200-500 for assigned articles. Pays $0-300 for unsolicited articles.**

PHOTOS Captions, identification of subjects required. Reviews contact sheets, negatives, prints, electronic files. Negotiates payment individually.

COLUMNS Weather Front (news, trends), 300-400 words; Weather Talk (folklore and humor), 650-1,000 words. **Buys 12-15 mss/year.** Query with published clips. **Pays $0-200.**

SCIENCE FICTION, FANTASY AND HORROR

AOIFE'S KISS

The Speculative Fiction Foundation, P.O. Box 782, Cedar Rapids IA 52406-0782. E-mail: aoifeskiss@yahoo.com. Website: samsdotpublishing.com. **Contact:** Tyree Campbell, Managing Editor. **100%.** "Aoife's Kiss is a print and online magazine of fantasy, science fiction, horror, sword & sorcery, and slipstream, published quarterly in March, June, September, and December. Aoife's Kiss publishes short stories, poems, illustrations, articles, and movie/book/chapbook reviews, and interviews with noted individuals in those genres." Estab. 2002. Offers 100% kill fee. Editorial lead time is 2 months. Submit seasonal material 2 months in advance. Accepts queries by e-mail. Responds in 2 weeks to queries.

NONFICTION Buys 10-16 mss/year. Send complete ms Length: 4,000 words

FICTION *Aoife's Kiss*, published quarterly, prints "fantasy, science fiction, sword and sorcery, alternate history, dark fantasy short stories, poems, illustrations, and movie and book reviews." Wants "fantasy, science fiction, spooky horror, and speculative poetry with minimal angst." **Buys 16-20 mss/year.** Accepts e-mail submissions (pasted into body of message); no disk submissions. "Submission should include snail mail address and a short (1-2 lines) bio." Reads submissions year round.

APEX MAGAZINE

Apex Publications, LLC, P.O. Box 24323, Lexington KY 40524. (859)312-3974. E-mail: jason@apexbookcompany.com. Website: apexbookcompany. com. **Contact:** Catherynne M. Valente, subm. editor. **100% freelance written.** Monthly e-zine publishing dark speculative fiction. "An elite repository for new and seasoned authors with an other-worldly interest in the unquestioned and slightly bizarre parts of the universe." Estab. 2004. Circ. 10,000 unique visits per month. Byline given. Pays on publication. Offers 30% kill fee. Publishes ms an average of 2 months after acceptance. Editorial lead time 2 months. Submit seasonal material 2 months in advance. Accepts queries by e-mail. Responds in 20-30 days to queries and to mss. Sample copy available online. Guidelines available online.

Apex Publications, LLC, P.O. Box 24323, Lexington KY 40524. (859)312-3974.E-mail: jason@apexbookcompany.com. Website: apexbookcompany.com. Acquisitions: Catherynne M. Valente, subm. editor. Estab. 2004."We want science fiction, fantasy, horror, and mash-ups of all three of "the dark, weird stuff down at the bottom of your little literary heart." Monthly e-zine publishing dark speculative fiction. Circ. 10,000 unique visits per month. Nonfiction Pays writer expenses: No. Buys 24 mss/year. Send complete ms. Length: 100-7,500 words. Pays $0.05/word.Tips "See submissions guidelines at apexbookcompany. com/apex-online/guidelines/."

FICTION Needs , dark speculative fiction. Does not want monster fiction. **Buys 24 mss/year.** Send complete ms. Length: 100-7,500 words. **Pays $20-200.**

ASIMOV'S SCIENCE FICTION

Dell Magazine Fiction Group, 267 Broadway, 4th Floor, New York NY 10007. (212)686-7188. Fax: (212)686-7414. E-mail: asimovssf@dellmagazines. com. Website: asimovs.com. Sheila Williams, editor; Victoria Green, senior art director; June Levine, associate art director. **Contact:** Brian Bieniowski, managing editor. **98% freelance written. Works with a small number of new/unpublished writers each year.** Magazine published 10 times/year, including 2 double issues. "Magazine consists of science fiction and fantasy stories for adults and young adults. Publishes the best short science fiction available." Estab. 1977. Circ. 50,000. Pays on acceptance. Publishes ms an average of 6-12 months after acceptance. Accepts queries by mail. NoResponds in 2 months to queries. Responds in 3 months to mss. Sample copy for $5. Guidelines for #10 SASE or online.

Named for a science fiction "legend," *Asimov's* regularly receives Hugo and Nebula Awards. Editor Gardner Dozois has received several awards for editing including Hugos and those from *Locus* magazine. Named for a science fiction "legend," *Asimov's* regularly receives Hugo and Nebula Awards. Editor Gardner Dozois has received several awards for editing including Hugos and those from *Locus* magazine.

FICTION "Science fiction primarily. Some fantasy and humor but no sword and sorcery. No explicit sex or violence that isn't integral to the story. It is best to read a great deal of material in the genre to avoid the use of some very old ideas. Send complete ms and SASE with *all* submissions." Needs fantasy, science fiction, hard science, soft sociological. No horror or psychic/supernatural. Would like to see more hard science fiction. **Buys Buys 10 mss/issue mss/year.** Length: 750-15,000 words. **Pays 5-8¢/word.**
POETRY 40 lines maximum. **Pays $1/line.**

A COMPANION IN ZEOR

1622 Swallow Crest Dr., Apt. B, Edgewood MD 21040-1751. Website: simegen.com/sgfandom/rimonslibrary/cz/. **Contact:** Karen MacLeod, Editor. Estab. 1978. Accepts queries by mail, e-mail, fax. Guidelines available for SASE, by fax, e-mail, or on website.

"Material used is now limited to creations based solely on works (universes) of Jacqueline Lichtenberg and Jean Lorrah. No other submission types considered. Prefer nothing obscene. Homosexuality not acceptable unless very relevant to the piece. Prefer a 'clean' publication image." Considers poetry written by young writers over 13; "copyright release form (on the web) available for all submissions."

FICTION Accepts fax, e-mail (pasted into body of message), and disk submissions. For regular mail submissions, "note whether to return or dispose of rejected mss." Cover letter is preferred. Sometimes sends prepublication galleys. Always willing to work with authors or poets to help in improving their work." Reviews books of poetry. Poets may send material for review consideration.

$ LEADING EDGE

4087 JKB, Provo UT 84602. E-mail: editor@leadingedgemagazine.com. Website: leadingedgemagazine.com. **90% freelance written.** Semiannual magazine covering science fiction and fantasy. "*Leading Edge* is a magazine dedicated to new and upcoming talent in the field of science fiction and fantasy." Estab. 1980. Circ. 200. Byline given. Pays on publication. Publishes ms an average of 2-4 months after acceptance. Responds in 2-4 months to queries. Sample copy for $5.95. Guidelines available online at website.

Accepts unsolicited submissions.

FICTION Needs fantasy, science fiction. **Buys 14-16 mss/year mss/year.** Send complete ms by mail. Length: 12,500 words maximum **Pays 1¢/word; $10 minimum.**

POETRY Needs avant-garde, haiku, light verse, traditional. "Publishes 2-4 poems per issue. Poetry should reflect both literary value and popular appeal and should deal with science fiction- or fantasy-related themes." Submit maximum 10 poems. Pays $10 for first 4 pages; $1.50/each subsequent page.

THE MAGAZINE OF FANTASY & SCIENCE FICTION

P.O. Box 3447, Hoboken NJ 07030. (201) 876-2551. E-mail: fandsf@aol.com. Website: fandsf.com. **Contact:** Gordon Van Gelder, editor. **100%.** "*The Magazine of Fantasy and Science Fiction* publishes various types of science fiction and fantasy short stories and novellas, making up about 80% of each issue. The balance of each issue is devoted to articles about science fiction, a science column, book and film reviews, cartoons, and competitions." Bimonthly." Estab. 1949. Circ. 40,000. Byline given. Pays on acceptance. Publishes ms an average of 9-12 months after acceptance. Submit seasonal material 8 months in advance. Responds in 2 months to queries. Sample copy for $6. Guidelines for SASE, by e-mail or website.

The *Magazine of Fantasy and Science Fiction* won a Nebula Award for Best Novelet for "The Merchant and the Alchemist's Gate" by Ted Chiang in in 2008. Also won the 2007 World Fantasy Award for Best Short Story for "Journey into the Kingdom" by M. Rickert. Editor Van Gelder won the Hugo Award for Best Editor (short form), 2007 and 2008.

COLUMNS Curiosities (Reviews of odd & obscure books), 270 words max. Accepts 6 mss/year. Query. **Pays $-$50.**

FICTION Contact: Gordon Van Gelder, Editor. "Prefers character-oriented stories. We receive a lot of fantasy fiction, but never enough science fiction." Needs adventure, fantasy, horror, space fantasy, sword & sorcery, dark fantasy, futuristic, psychological, supernatural, science fiction, hard science/technological, soft/sociological. **Buys Accepts 60-90/mss. mss/year.** No electronic submissions. Send complete Ms. Length: up to 25,000 words **Pays 5-9¢/word.**

POETRY *The Magazine of Fantasy & Science Fiction*, published bimonthy, is "one of the longest-running magazines devoted to the literature of the fantastic." Wants only poetry that deals with the fantastic or the science-fictional. Has published poetry by Rebecca Kavaler, Elizabeth Bear, Sophie M. White, and Robert Frazier. "I buy poems very infrequently—just when one hits me right." Seldom comments on rejected poems. Guidelines available for SASE or on website. Responds in up to 1 month. Always sends prepublication galleys. **Pays $50/poem and 2 contributor's copies. Acquires first North American serial rights.**

$ MINDFLIGHTS

Double-Edged Publishing Inc., 9618 Misty Brook Cove, Cordova TN 38016. (901)213-3768. E-mail: editor@mindflights.com; MindFlightsEditors@gmail.com. Website: mindflights.com. **Contact:** Selena Thomason, managing editor. **100% freelance written.** Monthly online magazine and annual print magazine covering science fiction, fantasy, all genres of speculative fiction and poetry, grounded in a Christian or Christian-friendly worldview. "Paving new roads for Christ-reflected short fiction. Not preachy, but still a reflection of the truth and light. Examples of this are in the writings of C.S. Lewis and Tolkien. We strive to provide quality fiction and poetry, all in means that respect traditional values and Christian principles. Be uplifting, encouraging with something interesting to our audience—fans of sci-fi and fantasy who are comfortable with an environment committed to a Christian world view." Estab. 2007. Byline given. Pays on acceptance. Publishes ms an average of 2 months after acceptance. Editorial lead time 3-4 months. Submit seasonal material 4 months in advance. Accepts queries by online submission form. NoResponds in 3-4 weeks to mss. Sample copy available online. Guidelines available online at mindflights.com/guidelines.php.

○ "No postal submissions accepted. See our portal entry and submission process online."

NONFICTION Buys 1 mss/year. Send complete ms. Length: 300-5,000 words. **Pays $5-25.**

REPRINTS "We will consider reprints but strongly prefer previously unpublished works. We rarely accept reprints, and then only if they are exceptional in both quality and fit. Please note that if a work is publicly available on the Internet, it is considered previously published."

FICTION "Illustrations are compensated with $10 gratuity payment." Needs fantasy, science fiction, work with strong speculative element. Does not want to see any work that would be offensive to a Christian audience. **Buys 25 mss/year.** "We only accept submissions via our online form. Send complete ms. after August 1, when we plan to resume taking submissions." Length: 50-5,000 words. **Pays $5-25.**

POETRY Needs avant-garde, free verse, haiku, light verse, traditional. "We accept all forms of poetry, but the work must be speculative in nature." Does not want to see any work that would be offensive to a Christian audience. Buys 25 poems/year. Submit maximum 3 poems. **Pays ½¢ per word, $5/min.-$25/max.**

➕➍ MORPHEUS TALES PUBLISHING

Morpheus Tales, 116 Muriel St., London N1 9QU UK. E-mail: morpheustales@blueyonder.co.uk. Website: morpheustales.com. **Contact:** Adam Bradley, publisher. **100% freelance written.** Quarterly magazine covering horror, science fiction, fantasy. "We publish the best in horror, science fiction and fantasy, both fiction and nonfiction." Estab. 2008. Circ. 1,000. Publishes ms an average of 18 months after acceptance. Editorial lead time 3 months. Submit seasonal material 6 months in advance. Accepts queries by e-mail. Responds in 1 week to queries. Responds in 1 month to mss. Sample copy for $7. Guidelines available online.

NONFICTION Needs book excerpts, essays, general interest, how-to, inspirational, interview, new product, opinion, photo feature, Letters to the editor. All material must be based on horror, science fiction or fantasy genre.

Buys 6 mss/year. Query. Length: 1,000-3,000 words. Sometimes pays expenses of writers on assignment.

PHOTOS Contact: Adam Bradley, publisher. Model and property release are required.

FICTION Needs experimental, fantasy, horror, mystery, novel concepts, science fiction, serialized, suspense. **Buys 20 mss/year.** Send complete ms. Length: 800-3,000 words.

⟳➍💲 ON SPEC

P.O. Box 4727, Station South, Edmonton AB T6E 5G6 Canada. (780)413-0215. Fax: (780)413-1538. E-mail: onspec@onspec.ca. E-mail: onspecmag@gmail.com. Website: onspec.ca. **95% freelance written.** Quarterly magazine covering Canadian science fiction, fantasy and horror. "We publish speculative fiction and poetry by new and established writers, with a strong preference for Canadian authored works." Estab. 1989. Circ. 2,000. Byline given. Pays on acceptance. Publishes ms an average of 6-18 months after acceptance. Editorial lead time 6 months. Accepts queries by mail. Accepts simultaneous submissions. Responds in 2 weeks to queries. 3 months after deadline to mss. Sample copy for $8. Guidelines for #10 SASE or on website.

○ Submission deadlines are February 28, May 31, August 31, and November 30.

FICTION Needs fantasy, horror, science fiction, magic realism, ghost stories, fairy stories. No media tie-in or shaggy-alien stories. No condensed or excerpted novels, religious/inspirational stories, fairy tales. **Buys 50 mss/year.** Send complete ms. Length: 1,000-6,000 words. **Pays $50-180 for fiction. Short stories (under 1,000 words): $50 plus 1 contributor's copy.**

POETRY Needs avant-garde, free verse. No rhyming or religious material. Buys 6 poems/year. Submit maximum 10 poems. Length: 4-100 lines. **Pays $50 and 1 contributor's copy.**

💲 TALES OF THE TALISMAN

Hadrosaur Productions, P.O. Box 2194, Mesilla Park NM 88047-2194. E-mail: hadrosaur@zianet.com. Website: talesofthetalisman.com. **Contact:** David Lee Summers, editor. **95% freelance written.** Quarterly magazine covering science fiction and fantasy. *"Tales of the Talisman* is a literary science fiction and fantasy magazine. We publish short stories, poetry, and articles with themes related to science fiction and fantasy. Above all, we are looking for thought-provoking ideas and good writing. Speculative fiction set in the past, present, and future is welcome. Likewise, contemporary or historical fiction is welcome as long as it has a mythic or science fictional element. Our target audience includes adult fans of the science fiction and fantasy genres along with anyone else who enjoys thought-provoking and entertaining writing." Estab. 1995. Circ. 200. Byline given. Pays on acceptance. Offers 100% kill fee. Publishes ms an average of 9 months after acceptance. Editorial lead time 9-12 months. Submit seasonal material 1 year in advance. Accepts queries by mail, e-mail. Responds in 1 week to queries. Responds in 1 month to mss. Sample copy for $8. Guidelines available online.

○ Fiction and poetry submissions are limited to reading periods of January 1-February 15 and July 1-August 15.

NONFICTION Needs interview, technical, articles on the craft of writing. "We do not want to see unsolicited articles—please query first if you have an idea that you think would be suitable for *Tales of the Talisman*'s audience. We do not want to see negative or derogatory articles." **Buys 1-3 mss/year.** Query. Length: 1,000-3,000 words. **Pays $10 for assigned articles.**

FICTION Contact: David L. Summers, editor. Needs fantasy, space fantasy, sword and sorcery, horror, science fiction, hard science/technological, soft/sociological. "We do not want to see stories with graphic violence. Do not send 'mainstream' fiction with no science fictional or fantastic elements. Do not send stories with copyrighted characters, unless you're the copyright holder." **Buys 25-30 mss/year.** Send complete ms. Length: 1,000-6,000 words. **Pays $6-10.**

POETRY Needs avant-garde, free verse, haiku, light verse, traditional. "Do not send 'mainstream' poetry with no science fictional or fantastic elements. Do not send poems featuring copyrighted characters, unless you're the copyright holder." Buys 24-30 poems/year. Submit maximum 5 poems. Length: 3-50 lines.

✪ VAMPIRES 2 MAGAZINE

Man's Story 2 Publishing Co., 1321 Snapfinger Rd., Decatur GA 30032. E-mail: mansstory2@aol.com. Website: vampires2.us. **Contact:** Glenn Dunn. **80% freelance written.** "Online E-Zine that strives to re-create Vampire Romance in the pulp fiction style of the 1920s through the 1970s with strong emphasis on 3D graphic art." Also features Illustrated Stories, Online Magazine, Online Photo Galleries and more. Estab. 1999. Circ. 500. Pays on publication. Publishes ms an average of 3-6 months after acceptance. Accepts que-

ries by e-mail only. Accepts simultaneous submissions. Guidelines available online.

○ "We Publish Books, Publish Online, and Operate Websites. In 2000 we became one of Writer's Digest top 100 markets for fiction writers and have since become listed with twenty other outstanding writers organizations."

FICTION Needs adventure, erotica, fantasy, horror, suspense, pulp fiction involving vampires. **Buys 30-50 mss/year.** Send complete ms. Length: 1,500-3,500 words. **Pays $25.**

SEX

✪✪ EXOTIC MAGAZINE

X Publishing Inc., 818 SW 3rd Ave., Suite 324, Portland OR 97204. Fax: (503)241-7239. E-mail: webmaster@xmag.com; exoticunderground2004@yahoo.com. Website: xmag.com. Monthly magazine covering adult entertainment, sexuality. "*Exotic* is pro-sex, informative, amusing, mature, intelligent. Our readers rent and/or buy adult videos, visit strip clubs and are interested in topics related to the adult entertainment industry and sexuality/culture. Don't talk down to them or fire too far over their heads. Many readers are computer literate and well-traveled. We're also interested in insightful fetish material. We are not a 'hard core' publication." Estab. 1993. Circ. 120,000. Byline given. Pays 30 days after publication. Accepts queries by fax. Accepts simultaneous submissions. Responds in 2 weeks to queries. Responds in 2 months to mss. Sample copy for SAE with 9×12 envelope and 5 first-class stamps. Guidelines for #10 SASE.

NONFICTION Needs expose, general interest, historical, how-to, humor, interview, travel, News. No men writing as women, articles about being a horny guy, opinion pieces pretending to be fact pieces. **Buys 36 mss/year.** Send complete ms. Length: 1,000-1,800 words. **Pays 10¢/word up to $150.**

REPRINTS Send typed manuscript with rights for sale noted and information about when and where the material previously appeared. Pays 100% of amount paid for an original article.

PHOTOS Rarely buys photos. Most provided by staff. Model releases required. Reviews prints. Negotiates payment individually.

FICTION We are currently overwhelmed with fiction submissions. Please only send fiction if it's really amazing. Needs erotica, slice-of-life vignettes, must present either erotic element or some vice of modern culture, such as gambling, music, dancing. Send complete ms. Length: 1,000-1,800 words. **Pays 10¢/word up to $150.**

$$$$ HUSTLER

HG Inc., 8484 Wilshire Blvd., Suite 900, Beverly Hills CA 90211. Fax: (323)651-2741. Website: hustler.com. **60% freelance written.** Magazine published 13 times/year. *Hustler* is the no-nonsense men's magazine, one that is willing to speak frankly about society's sacred cows and expose its hypocrites. The *Hustler* reader expects honest, unflinching looks at hard topicsÂ³sexual, social, political, personality profile, true crime. Estab. 1974. Circ. 750,000. Byline given. Pays as boards ship to printer. Offers 20% kill fee. Publishes ms an average of 3 months after acceptance. Editorial lead time 4 months. Submit seasonal material 6 months in advance. Accepts queries by mail, e-mail, fax. Responds in 2 weeks to queries. Responds in 1 month to mss. Guidelines for #10 SASE.

> *Hustler* is most interested in well-researched nonfiction reportage focused on sexual practices and subcultures.

NONFICTION Needs book excerpts, expose, general interest, how-to, interview, personal experience, trends. **Buys 30 mss/year.** Query. Length: 3,500-4,000 words. **Pays $1,500.** Sometimes pays expenses of writers on assignment.

COLUMNS Sex play (some aspect of sex that can be encapsulated in a limited space), 2,500 words. **Buys 13 mss/year.** Send complete ms. **Pays $750.**

FILLERS Jokes and Graffilthy, bathroom wall humor. **Pays $50-100.**

$$$$⊘ PENTHOUSE

General Media Communications, 2 Penn Plaza, 11th Floor, New York NY 10121. (212)702-6000. Fax: (212)702-6279. E-mail: pbloch@pmgi.com. Website: penthouse.com. Monthly magazine. *Penthouse* is for the sophisticated male. Its editorial scope ranges from outspoken contemporary comment to photography essays of beautiful women. *Penthouse* features interviews with personalities, sociological studies, humor, travel, food and wine, and fashion and grooming for men. Estab. 1969. Circ. 640,000. Byline given. Pays 2 months after acceptance. Offers 25% kill fee. Editorial lead time 3 months. Accepts simultaneous submissions. Guidelines for #10 SASE.

NONFICTION Needs expose, general interest, to men, interview. **Buys 50 mss/year.** Send complete ms. Length: 4,000-6,000 words. **Pays $3,000.**

COLUMNS Length: 1,000 words. **Buys 25 mss/year.** Query with published clips. **Pays $500.**

⊘ PLAYBOY MAGAZINE

680 North Lake Shore Drive, Chicago IL 60611. (312)373-2700. Fax: (312)587-9046. E-mail: gcole@playboy.com. Website: playboy.com. Gary Cole, contributing editor. Monthly magazine. Estab. 1953.

> *Playboy* no longer accepts unsolicited mss, including fiction, nonfiction or poetry.

SPORTS

ARCHERY AND BOWHUNTING

$$ BOW & ARROW HUNTING

Beckett Media LLC, 2400 E. Katella Ave., Suite 300, Anaheim CA 92806. (714)939-9991, ext. 306. Fax: (714)456-0146. E-mail: JBell@Beckett.com; editorial@bowandarrowhunting.com. Website: bowandarrowhunting.com. **70% freelance written.** Magazine published 9 times/year covering bowhunting. "Dedicated to serve the serious bowhunting enthusiast. Writers must be willing to share their secrets so our readers can become better bowhunters." Estab. 1962. Circ. 90,000. Byline given. Pays on publication. Publishes ms an average of 2 months after acceptance. Submit seasonal material 6 months in advance. Accepts queries by mail, e-mail. Accepts simultaneous submissions. Responds in 1 month to queries. Responds in 6 weeks to mss. Sample copy and writer's guidelines free.

NONFICTION Needs how-to, humor, interview, opinion, personal experience, technical. **Buys 60 mss/year.** Send complete ms. Length: 1,700-3,000 words. **Pays $200-450.**

PHOTOS Send photos. Captions required. Reviews contact sheets, digital images only; no slides or prints accepted. Offers no additional payment for photos accepted with ms.

FILLERS Needs facts, newsbreaks. **Buys 12 mss/year.** Length: 500 words. **Pays $20-100.**

$$ BOWHUNTER

InterMedia Outdoors, 6385 Flank Dr., Suite 800, Harrisburg PA 17112. (717)695-8085. Fax: (717)545-2527.

E-mail: dwight.schuh@imoutdoors.com; curt.wells@imoutdoors.com. Website: bowhunter.com. Mark Olszewski, art director; Dwight Schuh, editor-at-large; Jeff Waring, publisher. **Contact:** Curt Wells, editor. **50% freelance written**. Bi-monthly magazine covering hunting big and small game with bow and arrow. "We are a special-interest publication, produced by bowhunters for bowhunters, covering all aspects of the sport. Material included in each issue is designed to entertain and inform readers, making them better bowhunters." Estab. 1971. Circ. 126,480. Byline given. Pays on acceptance. Submit seasonal material 8 months in advance. Accepts queries by mail, e-mail, fax. Responds in 1 month to queries. Responds in 2 months to mss. Sample copy for $2 and 8 ½×11 SAE with appropriate postage. Guidelines for #10 SASE or on website.

NONFICTION Needs general interest, how-to, interview, opinion, personal experience, photo feature. **Buys 60 plus mss/year.** Query. Length: 250-2,000 words. **Pays $500 maximum for assigned articles. Pays $100-400 for unsolicited articles.** Sometimes pays expenses of writers on assignment.

PHOTOS Contact: Mark Olszewski, art director. Send photos. Captions required. Reviews high-res digital images. Reviews photos with or without a manuscript. Offers $50-300/photo. Pays $50-125 for b&w inside; $75-300 for color inside; $600 for cover, "occasionally more if photo warrants it." **Pays on acceptance**. Credit line given. Buys one-time publication rights.

FICTION Contact: Dwight Schuh, editor. Send complete ms. Length: 500-2,000 words. **Pays $100-350.**

🟢🟢 BOWHUNTING WORLD

Grand View Media Group, 5959 Baker Rd., Suite 300, Minnetonka MN 55345. (888)431-2877. E-mail: molis@grandviewmedia.com; hilary@grandviewmedia.com. Website: bowhuntingworld.com. **Contact:** Mark Olis; Hilary Dyer. **50% freelance written.** Bimonthly magazine with 3 additional issues for bowhunting and archery enthusiasts who participate in the sport year-round. For article or photo submissions, please contact Mark Olis at (888) 431-2877, ext. 4665 or e-mail him at molis@grandviewmedia.com and Hilary Dyer at (888) 431-2877, ext. 4660 or e-mail her at hilary@grandviewmedia.com. Estab. 1952. Circ. 95,000. Byline given. Pays on acceptance. Publishes ms an average of 5 months after acceptance. Responds in

1 week (e-mail queries). Responds in 6 weeks to mss. Sample copy for $3 and 9×12 SAE with 10 first-class stamps. Guidelines for #10 SASE.

💬Accepts queries by mail, but prefers e-mail.

NONFICTION Buys 60 mss/year. Send complete ms. Length: 1,500-2,500 words. **Pays $350-600.**

PHOTOS "We are seeking cover photos that depict specific behavioral traits of the more common big game animals (scraping whitetails, bugling elk, etc.) and well-equipped bowhunters in action. Must include return postage.".

BASEBALL

🟢 JUNIOR BASEBALL

JSAN Publishing LLC, Wilton CT 06897. (203)210-5726. E-mail: jim@juniorbaseball.com. Website: juniorbaseball.com. **Contact:** Jim Beecher, Publisher. **25% freelance written**. Bimonthly magazine covering youth baseball. Focused on youth baseball players ages 7-17 (including high school) and their parents/coaches. Edited to various reading levels, depending upon age/skill level of feature. Estab. 1996. Circ. 20,000. Byline given. Pays on publication. Publishes ms an average of 4 months after acceptance. Editorial lead time 3 months. Submit seasonal material 4 months in advance. Accepts simultaneous submissions. Responds in 2 weeks to queries. Responds in 1 month to mss. Sample copy for $5 and online.

NONFICTION Needs how-to, skills, tips, features, how-to play better baseball, etc., interview, with major league players; only on assignment, personal experience, from coaches' or parents' perspective. No trite first-person articles about your kid. No fiction or poetry. **Buys 8-12 mss/year.** Query. Length: 500-1,000 words. **Pays $50-100.**

PHOTOS Photos can be e-mailed in 300 dpi JPEGs. State availability. Captions, identification of subjects required. Reviews 35mm transparencies, 3 x 5 prints. Offers $10-100/photo; negotiates payment individually.

COLUMNS When I Was a Kid (a current Major League Baseball player profile); Parents Feature (topics of interest to parents of youth ball players); all 1,000-1,500 words. In the Spotlight (news, events, new products), 50-100 words; Hot Prospect (written for the 14 and older competitive player. High school baseball is included, and the focus is on improving the finer points of the game to make the high school team, earn a college scholarship, or attract scouts, written to an adult level), 500-1,000 words. **Buys 8-12 columns mss/year. Pays $50-100.**

TIPS "Must be well-versed in baseball! Having a child who is very involved in the sport, or have extensive hands-on experience in coaching baseball, at the youth, high school or higher level. We can always use accurate, authoritative skills information and good photos to accompany is a big advantage! This magazine is read by experts. No fiction, poems, games, puzzles, etc." Does not want first-person articles about your child.

BICYCLING

💲💲💲 ADVENTURE CYCLIST

Adventure Cycling Assn., Box 8308, Missoula MT 59807. (406)721-1776, ext. 222. Fax: (406)721-8754. E-mail: magazine@adventurecycling.org. Website: adventurecycling.org. **75% freelance written**. Magazine published 9 times/year for Adventure Cycling Association members, emphasizing bicycle tourism and travel. Estab. 1975. Circ. 43,000. Byline given. Pays on publication. Kill fee 25%. Submit seasonal material 12 months in advance. Sample copy and guidelines for 9×12 SAE with 4 first-class stamps. Info available at adventurecycling.org/mag.

NONFICTION Needs first-person bike-travel accounts (U.S. and worldwide), essays, how-to, profiles, photo feature, technical, U.S. or foreign tour accounts. **Buys 20-25 mss/year.** Send complete ms. Length: 1,400-3,500 words. **Inquiries requested prior to complete manuscripts. Pays sliding scale per word.**

PHOTOS State availability.

💲💲 BIKE MAGAZINE

Source Interlink Media, P.O. Box 1028, Dana Point CA 926229. (949)325-6200. Fax: (949)325-6196. E-mail: bikemag@sorc.com. Website: bikemag.com. **Contact:** Joe Parkin, editor. **35% freelance written.** Magazine publishes 8 times/year covering mountain biking. Estab. 1993. Circ. 170,000. Byline given. Pays on publication. Offers 25% kill fee. Publishes ms an average of 2 months after acceptance. Editorial lead time 4 months. Submit seasonal material 6 months in advance. Responds in 2 months to queries. Sample copy for $8. Guidelines for #10 SASE.

NONFICTION Needs humor, interview, personal experience, photo feature, travel. **Buys 20 mss/year.** Length: 1,000-2,500 words. **Pays 50¢/word.** Some-

times pays expenses of writers on assignment. $500 maximum.

PHOTOS Contact: David Reddick, photo editor. Send photos. Captions, identification of subjects required. Reviews color transparencies, b&w prints. Negotiates payment individually.

COLUMNS Splatter (news), 300 words; Urb (details a great ride within 1 hour of a major metropolitan area), 600-700 words. Query year-round for Splatter and Urb. **Buys 20 mss/year. Pays 50¢/word.**

💲💲 CYCLE CALIFORNIA! MAGAZINE

1702-L Meridian Ave., #289, San Jose CA 95125. (408)924-0270. Fax: (408)292-3005. E-mail: tcorral@cyclecalifornia.com. Website: cyclecalifornia.com. **Contact:** Tracy L. Corral. **75% freelance written.** Magazine published 11 times/year covering Northern California bicycling events, races, people. Issues (topics) covered include bicycle commuting, bicycle politics, touring, racing, nostalgia, history, anything at all to do with riding a bike. Estab. 1995. Circ. 26,000 print; 4,700 digital. Byline given. Pays on publication. Publishes ms an average of 3 months after acceptance. Editorial lead time 6 weeks. Submit seasonal material 6 weeks in advance. Accepts queries by mail, e-mail. Accepts simultaneous submissions. Responds in 1 month to queries. Sample copy for 10×13 SAE with 3 first-class stamps. Guidelines for #10 SASE.

NONFICTION Needs historical, how-to, interview, opinion, personal experience, technical, travel. Special issues: Bicycle Tour & Travel (January/February). No articles about any sport that doesn't relate to bicycling, no product reviews. **Buys 36 mss/year.** Query. Length: 500-1,500 words. **Pays 10-15¢/word.**

PHOTOS Contact: Bob Mack, publisher (BMack@cyclecalifornia.com). Send photos. Identification of subjects required. Reviews 3 x 5 prints. Negotiates payment individually.

COLUMNS Buys 2-3 mss/year. Query with published clips. **Pays 10-15¢/word.**

💲💲 VELONEWS

Inside Communications, Inc., 3002 Sterling Circle, Suite 100, Boulder CO 80301. (303)440-0601. Fax: (303)444-6788. E-mail: velonews@pcspublink.com. Website: velonews.com. **40% freelance written.** Monthly tabloid covering bicycle racing. Estab. 1972. Circ. 48,000. Byline given. Pays on publication. Publishes ms an average of 1 month after acceptance. Responds in 3 weeks to queries.

NONFICTION Buys 80 mss/year. Query. Length: 300-1,200 words. **Pays $100-400.**

REPRINTS Send typed manuscript with rights for sale noted and information about when and where the material previously appeared.

PHOTOS State availability. Captions, identification of subjects required.

BOATING

⊘◯ AUSTRALIAN AMATEUR BOATBUILDER

P.O. Box 1254, Burleigh Heights QLD 4220 Australia. (61)(7)5593-8187. Fax: (61)(7)5593-8973. E-mail: info@boatbuilder.com.au. Website: boatbuilder.com.au. Quarterly magazine. "*AABB* is an Australian-based specialist publication devoted exclusively to amateur enthusiasts—monohulls, kayaks, multihulls, offshore, off-the-beach, power, racing and cruising." Estab. 1991. Circ. 9,500.

○ Query before submitting.

◯◯ BOATING WORLD MAGAZINE

Duncan McIntosh Co., 17782 Cowan, Suite C, Irvine CA 92614. (949)660-6150. Fax: (949)660-6172. Website: boatingworld.com. Mike Werling, managing editor, mikew@boatingworld.com. **Contact:** Alan Jones, executive editor. **60% freelance written.** Magazine published 8 times/year covering recreational trailer boats. "Typical reader owns a power boat between 14 and 32 feet long and has 3-9 years experience. Boat reports are mostly written by staff while features and most departments are provided by freelancers. We are looking for freelancers who can write well and who have at least a working knowledge of recreational power boating and the industry behind it." Estab. 1997. Circ. 100,000. Pays on publication. Publishes ms an average of 4 months after acceptance. Accepts simultaneous submissions. Responds in 3 months to queries. Sample copy free. Guidelines for #10 SASE.

NONFICTION Needs general interest, how-to, humor, new product, personal experience, travel. **Buys 20-25 mss/year.** Query. Length: 1,400-1,600 words. **Pays $150-450.** Sometimes pays expenses of writers on assignment.

PHOTOS State availability. Identification of subjects, model releases required. Reviews transparencies, prints, digital images. Offers $50-250/photo.

FILLERS Needs anecdotes, facts, newsbreaks. Length: 250-500 words. **Pays $50-100.**

◯◯◯◯◯ BOAT INTERNATIONAL USA

Boat International Media, 41-47 Hartfield Rd., London SW19 3RQ United Kingdom. (954)522-2628. Fax: (954)522-2240. E-mail: marilyn.mower@boatinternationalmedia.com. Website: boatinternational.com. **Contact:** Marilyn Mower, US editor-in-chief. **80% freelance written.** Magazine published 10 times/year covering luxury superyacht industry. "Luxury yachting publication aimed at the world's discerning yachting audience. We provide the most exclusive access to superyachts over 100 feet worldwide." Estab. 1995. Circ. 55,000. Byline given. Pays on publication. Offers 50% kill fee. Editorial lead time 2 months. Submit seasonal material 4 months in advance. Accepts queries by e-mail. Responds in 2 months to mss. Sample copy for $3.00. Guidelines free.

NONFICTION anything about boats under 50 feet. Travel/destination pieces that are not superyacht related. **Buys 3/year mss/year.** Query. Length: 500-1,500 words. **Pays $300 minimum, $2,000 maximum for assigned articles.** Sometimes pays expenses of writers on assignment.

PHOTOS Contact: Richard Taranto, art director. State availability. Captions required. Reviews contact sheets, GIF/JPEG files. negotiates payment individually.

◯◯◯ CANOE & KAYAK

Source Interlink Media, 236 Avenida Fabricante, Suite 201, San Clemente CA 92672. (425)827-6363. E-mail: jeff@canoekayak.com; joe@canoekayak.com; dave@canoekayak.com. Website: canoekayak.com. Joe Carberry, managing editor; Dave Shively, associate editor. **Contact:** Jeff Moag, editor-in-chief. **75% freelance written.** Bimonthly magazine. *Canoe & Kayak Magazine* is North America's No. 1 paddlesports resource. Our readers include flatwater and whitewater canoeists and kayakers of all skill levels. We provide comprehensive information on destinations, technique and equipment. Beyond that, we cover canoe and kayak camping, safety, the environment, and the history of boats and sport. Estab. 1972. Circ. 70,000. Byline given. Pays on publication. Publishes ms an average of 6 months after acceptance. Editorial lead time 6 months. Submit seasonal material 8 months in advance. Accepts queries by mail, e-mail. Responds in 2 months to queries.

Sample copy and writer's guidelines for 9×12 SAE with 7 first-class stamps.

NONFICTION Needs historical, how-to, canoe, kayak camp, load boats, paddle whitewater, etc., personal experience, photo feature, technical, travel. Special issues: Whitewater Paddling; Beginner's Guide; Kayak Touring; Canoe Journal. No cartoons, poems, stories in which bad judgement is portrayed or 'Me and Molly' articles. **Buys 25 mss/year.** Send complete ms. Length: 400-2,500 words. **Pays $100-800 for assigned articles. Pays $100-500 for unsolicited articles.**

PHOTOS "Some activities we cover are canoeing, kayaking, canoe fishing, camping, canoe sailing or poling, backpacking (when compatible with the main activity) and occasionally inflatable boats. We are not interested in groups of people in rafts, photos showing disregard for the environment or personal safety, gasoline-powered engines unless appropriate to the discussion, or unskilled persons taking extraordinary risks.". State availability. Captions, identification of subjects, model releases required. Reviews 35mm transparencies, 4×6 prints. Offers $75-500/photo.

COLUMNS Put In (environment, conservation, events), 500 words; Destinations (canoe and kayak destinations in US, Canada), 1,500 words; Essays, 750 words. **Buys 40 mss/year.** Send complete ms. **Pays $100-350.**

FILLERS Needs anecdotes, facts, newsbreaks. **Buys 20 mss/year.** Length: 200-500 words. **Pays $25-50.**

$$$ CHESAPEAKE BAY MAGAZINE

Chesapeake Bay Communications, 1819 Bay Ridge Ave., Annapolis MD 21403. (410)263-2662, ext. 32. Fax: (410)267-6924. E-mail: chesapeakeboating@gmail.com. Website: chesapeakeboating.net. Karen Ashley, art director; T. F. Sayles, editor. **Contact:** Ann Levelle, managing editor. **60% freelance written**. Monthly magazine covering boating and the Chesapeake Bay. "Our readers are boaters. Our writers should know boats and boating. Read the magazine before submitting." Estab. 1972. Circ. 46,000. Byline given. Pays within 2 months after acceptance. Publishes ms an average of 1 year after acceptance. Editorial lead time 1 year. Submit seasonal material 1 year in advance. Accepts queries by mail, e-mail, fax, phone. Accepts simultaneous submissions. Responds in 2 months to queries. Responds in 3 months to mss. Sample copy for $5.19 prepaid.

NONFICTION Buys 30 mss/year. Query with published clips. Length: 300-3,000 words. **Pays $100-1,000.** Pays expenses of writers on assignment.

PHOTOS Captions, identification of subjects required. Offers $75-250/photo, $400/day rate for assignment photography. Pays $400 for color cover; $75-250 for color *stock* inside, depending on size; $200-1,200 for *assigned* photo package. Pays on publication. Credit line given. Buys one-time rights.

$$$$ CRUISING WORLD

The Sailing Co., 55 Hammarlund Way, Middletown RI 02842. (401)845-5100. Fax: (401)845-5180. E-mail: elaine.lembo@cruisingworld.com; bill.roche@bonniercorp.com. Website: cruisingworld.com. **Contact:** Manuscripts Editor. **60% freelance written**. Monthly magazine covering sailing, cruising/adventuring, do-it-yourself boat improvements. "*Cruising World* is a publication by and for sailboat owners who spend time in home waters as well as voyaging the world. Its readership is extremely loyal, savvy, and driven by independent thinking." Estab. 1974. Circ. 155,000. Byline given. **Pays on acceptance for articles;** on publication for photography. Publishes ms an average of 18 months after acceptance. Editorial lead time 3 months. Submit seasonal material 1 year in advance. Accepts queries by mail. Responds in 2 months to queries. Responds in 4 months to mss. Sample copy free. Guidelines available online.

NONFICTION Needs book excerpts, essays, expose, general interest, historical, how-to, humor, interview, new product, opinion, personal experience, photo feature, technical, travel. No travel articles that have nothing to do with cruising aboard sailboats from 20-50 feet in length. **Buys dozens mss/year.** Send complete ms. **Pays $50-1,500 for assigned articles. Pays $50-1,000 for unsolicited articles.** Sometimes pays expenses of writers on assignment.

PHOTOS Contact: Bill Roche, art director. Send high-res (minimum 300 DPI) images on CD. Send photos. Captions required. Reviews negatives, transparencies, color slides preferred. Payment upon publication. Also buys stand-alone photos.

COLUMNS Shoreline (sailing news, people, and short features; contact Elaine Lembo), 300 words maximum; Hands-on Sailor (refit, voyaging, seamanship, how-to; contact Mark Pillsbury), 1,000-1,500 words. **Buys dozens of mss/year.** Query with or without published clips or send complete ms.

💲💲 HEARTLAND BOATING

The Waterways Journal, Inc., 319 N. Fourth St., Suite 650, St. Louis MO 63102. (314)241-4310. Fax: (314)241-4207. E-mail: Lbraff@Heartlandboating.com. Website: Heartlandboating.com. **Contact:** John R. Cassady, art director. **90% freelance written**. Magazine published 8 times/year covering recreational boating on the inland waterways of mid-America, from the Great Lakes south to the Gulf of Mexico and over to the east. "Our writers must have experience with, and a great interest in, boating, particularly in the area described above. *Heartland Boating*'s content is both informative and humorous—describing boating life as the heartland boater knows it. The content reflects the challenge, joy, and excitement of our way of life afloat. We are devoted to both power and sailboating enthusiasts throughout middle America; houseboats are included. The focus is on the freshwater inland rivers and lakes of the heartland, primarily the waters of the Arkansas, Tennessee, Cumberland, Ohio, Missouri, Illinois, and Mississippi rivers, the Tennessee-Tombigbee Waterway, The Gulf Intracoastal Waterway, and the lakes along these waterways." Estab. 1989. Circ. 12,000. Byline given. Pays on publication. Editorial lead time 3 months. Accepts queries by mail. Responds only if interested. Sample copy online at website. Choose the Try It For Free! button. Fill out the form, and you will receive 3 free copies. Guidelines for #10 SASE.

Submission window is May 1-July 15.

NONFICTION Needs how-to, articles about navigation maintenance, upkeep, or making time spent aboard easier and more comfortable, humor, personal experience, technical, Great Loop leg trips, along waterways and on-land stops. Special issues: Annual houseboat issue in March looks at what is coming out on the houseboat market for the coming year. **Buys 100 mss/year.** Send complete ms. Length: 850-1,500 words. **Pays $40-285.**

REPRINTS Send tearsheet, photocopy or typed ms and information about when and where the material previously appeared.

PHOTOS Contact: John R. Cassady, art director. Magazine published 8 times/year covering recreational boating on the inland waterways of mid-America, from the Great Lakes south to the Gulf of Mexico and over to the east. Submission period is only between May 1 and July 1. Send photos. Model release is required, property release is preferred, photo captions

are required. Include names and locations. Reviews prints, digital images. Offers no additional payment for photos accepted with ms.

COLUMNS Books Aboard (assigned book reviews), 400 words. Buys 8-10 mss/year. Pays $40. Handy Hints (boat improvement or safety projects), 1,000 words. Buys 8 mss/year. Pays $180. Heartland Haunts (waterside restaurants, bars or B&Bs), 1,000 words. Buys 16 mss/year. Pays $160. Query with published clips or send complete ms.

⊘💲💲 HOUSEBOAT MAGAZINE

Harris Publishing, Inc., 360 B St., Idaho Falls ID 83402. Fax: (208)522-5241. E-mail: blk@houseboatmagazine. com. Website: houseboatmagazine.com. **60% freelance written**. "Monthly magazine for houseboaters, who enjoy reading everything that reflects the unique houseboating lifestyle. If it is not a houseboat-specific article, please do not query.". Estab. 1990. Circ. 25,000. Byline given. Pays on acceptance. Offers 25% kill fee. Publishes ms an average of 3 months after acceptance. Editorial lead time 6 months. Submit seasonal material 6 months in advance. Accepts simultaneous submissions. Responds in 1 month to queries. Sample copy for $5. Guidelines by e-mail.

No unsolicited mss. Accepts queries by mail and fax, but e-mail strongly preferred.

NONFICTION Needs how-to, interview, new product, personal experience, travel. **Buys 36 mss/year.** Query. Length: 1,500-2,200 words. **Pays $200-500.**

PHOTOS Often required as part of submission package. Color prints discouraged. Digital prints are unacceptable. Seldom purchases photos without ms, but occasionally buys cover photos. Captions, model releases required. Reviews transparencies, high-resolution electronic images. Offers no additional payment for photos accepted with ms.

COLUMNS Pays $150-300.

💲💲 LAKELAND BOATING

O'Meara-Brown Publications, Inc., 727 S. Dearborn St., Suite 812, Chicago IL 60605. (312)276-0610. Fax: (312)276-0619. E-mail: ljohnson@lakelandboating. com. Website: lakelandboating.com. **Contact:** Lindsey Johnson, editor. **50% freelance written**. Magazine covering Great Lakes boating. Estab. 1946. Circ. 60,000. Byline given. Pays on publication. Accepts queries by e-mail. Responds in 4 months to queries. Sample copy for $5.50 and 9×12 SAE with 6 first-class stamps. Guidelines free.

NONFICTION Needs book excerpts, historical, how-to, interview, personal experience, photo feature, technical, travel, must relate to boating in Great Lakes. No inspirational, religious, exposÃ' or poetry. **Buys 20-30 mss/year.** Length: 300-1,500 words. **Pays $100-600.**
PHOTOS State availability. Captions required. Reviews prefers 35mm transparencies, high-res digital shots.
COLUMNS Bosun's Locker (technical or how-to pieces on boating), 100-1,000 words. **Buys 40 mss/year.** Query. **Pays $25-200.**

$ LIVING ABOARD

FTW Publishing, P.O. Box 668, Redondo Beach CA 90277. (888)893-7245. Fax: (310)789-3448. E-mail: editor@livingaboard.com. Website: livingaboard.com. **95% freelance written.** Bimonthly magazine covering living on boats/cruising. Estab. 1973. Circ. 10,000. Byline given. Pays on publication. Publishes ms an average of 3-6 months after acceptance. Accepts queries by mail, e-mail, fax. Responds in 1-2 weeks to queries. Responds in 1-2 months to mss. Sample copy available online. Guidelines free.
NONFICTION Needs how-to, buy, furnish, maintain, provision a boat, interview, personal experience, technical, as relates to boats, travel, on the water, Cooking Aboard with Recipes. Send complete ms. **Pays 5¢/word.**
PHOTOS Pays $5/photo; $50/cover photo.
COLUMNS Cooking Aboard (how to prepare healthy and nutritious meals in the confines of a galley; how to entertain aboard a boat), 1,000-1,500 words; Environmental Notebook (articles pertaining to clean water, fish, waterfowl, water environment), 750-1,000 words. **Buys 40 mss/year mss/year.** Send complete ms. **Pays 5¢/word**

$ NORTHERN BREEZES, SAILING MAGAZINE

Northern Breezes, Inc., 3949 Winnetka Ave. N, Minneapolis MN 55427. (763)542-9707. Fax: (763)542-8998. E-mail: info@sailingbreezes.com. Website: sailingbreezes.com. **70% freelance written.** Magazine published 8 times/year for the Great Lakes and Midwest sailing community. Focusing on regional cruising, racing, and day sailing. Estab. 1989. Circ. 22,300. Byline given. Pays on publication. Editorial lead time 1 months. Submit seasonal material 3 months in advance. Accepts queries by mail, e-mail, fax, phone. Responds in 1 month to queries. Responds in 2 months to mss. Sample copy free. Guidelines available online.
NONFICTION Needs book excerpts, how-to, sailing topics, humor, inspirational, interview, new product, personal experience, photo feature, technical, travel. No boating reviews. **Buys 24 mss/year.** Query with published clips. Length: 300-3,500 words.
PHOTOS Send photos. Captions required. Reviews negatives, 35mm slides, 3 x 5 or 4 x 6 prints. "Digital submission preferred.". Offers no additional payment for photos accepted with ms.
COLUMNS This Old Boat (sailboat), 500-1,000 words; Surveyor's Notebook, 500-800 words. **Buys 8 mss/year.** Query with published clips. **Pays $50-150.**
TIPS "Query with a regional connection already in mind."

[C] $ $ PACIFIC YACHTING

OP Publishing, Ltd., 200 West Esplanade, Suite 500, North Vancouver BC V7M 1A4 Canada. (604)998-3310. Fax: (604)998-3320. E-mail: editor@pacificyachting.com. Website: pacificyachting.com. **Contact:** Dale Miller, editor. **90% freelance written.** Monthly magazine covering all aspects of recreational boating in the Pacific Northwest. "The bulk of our writers and photographers not only come from the local boating community, many of them were long-time *PY* readers before coming aboard as a contributor. The *PY* reader buys the magazine to read about new destinations or changes to old haunts on the British Columbia coast and the Pacific Northwest and to learn the latest about boats and gear." Estab. 1968. Circ. 19,000. Byline given. Pays on publication. Publishes ms an average of 6 months after acceptance. Editorial lead time 4 months. Submit seasonal material 6 months in advance. Accepts queries by mail, e-mail, fax. Sample copy for $6.95, plus postage charged to credit card. Guidelines available online.
NONFICTION Needs historical, British Columbia coast only, how-to, humor, interview, personal experience, technical, boating related, travel, cruising, and destination on the British Columbia coast. "No articles from writers who are obviously not boaters!" Query. Length: 800-2,000 words. **Pays $150-500. Pays some expenses of writers on assignment for unsolicited articles.** Pays expenses of writers on assignment.
PHOTOS Send photos. Identification of subjects required. Reviews digital photos transparencies, 4 x 6

prints, and slides. Offers no additional payment for photos accepted with ms. Offers $25-400 for photos accepted alone.

COLUMNS Currents (current events, trade and people news, boat gatherings, and festivities), 50-250 words. Reflections; Cruising, both 800-1,000 words. Query. **Pay varies.**

🐾🐾 PONTOON & DECK BOAT

Harris Publishing, Inc., 360 B. St., Idaho Falls ID 83402. (208)524-7000. Fax: (208)522-5241. E-mail: blk@pdbmagazine.com. Website: pdbmagazine. com. **15% freelance written.** Magazine published 11 times/year. "We are a boating niche publication geared toward the pontoon and deck boating lifestyle and consumer market. Our audience is comprised of people who utilize these boats for varied family activities and fishing. Our magazine is promotional of the PDB industry and its major players. We seek to give the reader a twofold reason to read our publication: to celebrate the lifestyle, and to do it aboard a first-class craft." Estab. 1995. Circ. 84,000. Byline given. Pays on publication. Editorial lead time 2 months. Submit seasonal material 3 months in advance. Accepts simultaneous submissions. Responds in 6 weeks to queries. Responds in 3 months to mss Sample copy and writer's guidelines free.

NONFICTION Needs how-to, personal experience, technical, remodeling, rebuilding. We are saturated with travel pieces; no general boating, humor, fiction, or poetry. **Buys 15 mss/year.** Send complete ms. Length: 600-2,000 words. **Pays $50-300.** Sometimes pays expenses of writers on assignment.

PHOTOS State availability. Captions, model releases required. Reviews transparencies.

COLUMNS No Wake Zone (short, fun quips); Better Boater (how-to). **Buys 6-12 mss/year.** Query with published clips. **Pays $50-150.**

🐾🐾🐾 POWER & MOTORYACHT

Source Interlink Media, 261 Madison Ave., 6th Floor, New York NY 10016. (212)915-4313; (212)915-4000. Fax: (212)915-4328. E-mail: richard.thiel@powerandmotoryacht.com. Website: powerandmotoryacht.com. **Contact:** Richard Thiel, editor-in-chief. **25% freelance written.** Monthly magazine covering powerboats 24 feet and larger with special emphasis on the 35-foot-plus market. "Readers have an average of 33 years experience boating, and we give them accurate advice on how to choose, operate, and maintain

their boats as well as what electronics and gear will help them pursue their favorite pastime. In addition, since powerboating is truly a lifestyle and not just a hobby for them, *Power & Motoryacht* reports on a host of other topics that affect their enjoyment of the water: chartering, sportfishing, and the environment, among others. Articles must therefore be clear, concise, and authoritative; knowledge of the marine industry is mandatory. Include personal experience and information for marine industry experts where appropriate." Estab. 1985. Circ. 157,000. Byline given. Pays on acceptance. Offers 33% kill fee. Publishes ms an average of 4-6 months after acceptance. Editorial lead time 4-6 months. Submit seasonal material 4-6 months in advance. Accepts queries by mail, e-mail. NoResponds in 1 month to queries. Sample copy for 10x12 SASE. Guidelines for #10 SASE or via e-mail.

NONFICTION Needs how-to, interview, personal experience, photo feature, travel. No unsolicited mss or articles about sailboats and/or sailing yachts (including motorsailers or cruise ships). **Buys 20-25 mss/year.** Query with published clips. Length: 800-1,500 words. **Pays $500-1,000 for assigned articles.** Sometimes pays expenses of writers on assignment.

PHOTOS Contact: Aimee Colon, art director. State availability. Captions, identification of subjects required. Reviews 8×10 transparencies, GIF/JPEG files (minimum 300 dpi). Offers no additional payment for photos accepted with ms.

⊘🐾🐾🐾 POWERBOAT

Affinity Group Inc., 2575 Vista Del Mar, Ventura CA 93001. (805)667-4100. Fax: (805)667-4336. E-mail: editdept@powerboatmag.com; jason@powerboatmag.com. Website: powerboatmag.com. Jim Hendricks, editorial director, jhendricks@affinitygroup.com. **Contact:** Jason Johnson, senior editor. **25% freelance written.** Magazine published 11 times/year covering performance boating. Estab. 1973. Circ. 50,000. Byline given. Pays on publication. Offers negotiable kill fee. Publishes ms an average of 3 months after acceptance. Editorial lead time 3 months. Submit seasonal material 4 months in advance. Accepts queries by mail, e-mail, fax. Sample copy available online.

○ No unsolicited mss.

NONFICTION Needs how-to, interview, new product, photo feature. No general interest boating stories. **Buys numerous mss/year.** Query. Length: 300-2,000 words. **Pays $125-1,200.** Sometimes pays expenses of writers on assignment.

PHOTOS State availability. Captions required. Reviews negatives.

☺☉☉ POWER BOATING CANADA

1121 Invicta Drive Unit 2, Oakville ON L6H 2R2 Canada. (800)354-9145. Fax: (905)844-5032. E-mail: editor@powerboating.com. Website: powerboating.com. **70% freelance written.** Bimonthly magazine covering recreational power boating. *Power Boating Canada* offers boating destinations, how-to features, boat tests (usually staff written), lifestyle pieces—with a Canadian slant—and appeal to recreational power boaters across the country. Estab. 1984. Circ. 42,000. Byline given. Pays on publication. Publishes ms an average of 3 months after acceptance. Editorial lead time 2 months. Submit seasonal material 3 months in advance. Responds in 1 month to queries. Responds in 2 months to mss. Sample copy free.

NONFICTION Needs historical, how-to, interview, personal experience, travel, boating destinations. No general boating articles or personal anecdotes. **Buys 40-50 mss/year.** Query. Length: 1,200-2,500 words. **Pays $150-300 (Canadian).** Sometimes pays expenses of writers on assignment.

REPRINTS Send photocopy with rights for sale noted and information about when and where the material previously appeared.

PHOTOS Send photos. Captions, identification of subjects required. Reviews contact sheets, negatives, transparencies, prints. Pay varies; no additional payment for photos accepted with ms.

☉☉☉ SAIL

98 N. Washington St., Suite 107, Boston MA 02114. (617)720-8600. Fax: (617)723-0912. E-mail: sailmag@sailmagazine.com. Website: sailmagazine.com. **Contact:** Peter Nielsen, editor-in-chief. **30% freelance written.** Monthly magazine written and edited for everyone who sails—aboard a coastal or bluewater cruiser, trailerable, one-design or offshore racer, or daysailer. How-to and technical articles concentrate on techniques of sailing and aspects of design and construction, boat systems, and gear; the feature section emphasizes the fun and rewards of sailing in a practical and instructive way. Estab. 1970. Circ. 180,000. Byline given. Pays on acceptance. Publishes ms an average of 1 year after acceptance. Accepts queries by mail, e-mail, fax. Responds in 3 months to queries. Guidelines for SASE or online (download).

NONFICTION Needs how-to, personal experience, technical, distance cruising, destinations. Special issues: Cruising, chartering, commissioning, fitting-out, special race (e.g., America's Cup), Top 10 Boats. **Buys 50 mss/year.** Query. Length: 1,500-3,000 words. **Pays $200-800.** Sometimes pays expenses of writers on assignment.

PHOTOS Prefers transparencies. High-resolution digital photos (300 dpi) are also accepted, as are high-quality color prints (preferably with negatives attached). Captions, identification of subjects, True required. Payment varies, up to $1,000 if photo used on cover.

COLUMNS Sailing Memories (short essay); Sailing News (cruising, racing, legal, political, environmental); Under Sail (human interest). Query. **Pays $50-400.**

☉☉☉ SAILING MAGAZINE

125 E. Main St., Port Washington WI 53074. (262)284-3494. Fax: (262)284-7764. E-mail: editorial@sailingmagazine.net. Website: sailingmagazine.net. Monthly magazine for the experienced sailor. Estab. 1966. Circ. 45,000. Pays after publication. Accepts queries by mail, e-mail. Responds in 2 months to queries.

NONFICTION Needs book excerpts, how-to, tech pieces on boats and gear, interview, personal experience, travel, by sail. **Buys 15-20 mss/year.** Length: 750-2,500 words. **Pays $100-800.**

PHOTOS Captions required. Reviews color transparencies. Pays $50-400.

☉☉ SAILING WORLD

World Publications, 55 Hammarlund Way, Middletown RI 02842. (401)845-5100. Fax: (401)848-5180. E-mail: editorial@sailingworld.com. Website: sailingworld.com. **40% freelance written.** Magazine published 10 times/year covering performance sailing. Estab. 1962. Circ. 60,000. Byline given. Pays on publication. Publishes ms an average of 4 months after acceptance. Responds in 1 month to queries. Sample copy for $5.

NONFICTION Needs how-to, for racing and performance-oriented sailors, interview, photo feature, Regatta sports and charter. No travelogs. **Buys 5-10 unsolicited mss/year.** Query. Length: 400-1,500 words. **Pays $400 for up to 2,000 words.** Does not pay expenses of writers on assignment unless pre-approved.

$$ SEA KAYAKER

Sea Kayaker, Inc., P.O. Box 17029, Seattle WA 98127. (206)789-1326. Fax: (206)781-1141. E-mail: editorial@seakayakermag.com. Website: seakayakermag.com. **Contact:** Editorial department. **95% freelance written.** *Sea Kayaker* is a bimonthly publication with a worldwide readership that covers all aspects of kayak touring. It is well known as an important source of continuing education by the most experienced paddlers. Estab. 1984. Circ. 30,000. Byline given. Pays on publication. Offers 10% kill fee. Publishes ms an average of 6 months after acceptance. Editorial lead time 4 months. Submit seasonal material 4 months in advance. Accepts queries by mail, e-mail, fax, phone. Responds in 2 months to queries. Sample copy for $7.30 (US), samples to other countries extra. Guidelines available online.

NONFICTION Needs essays, historical, how-to, on making equipment, humor, new product, personal experience, technical, travel. Unsolicited gear reviews are not accepted. **Buys 50 mss/year.** Send complete ms. Length: 1,500-5,000 words. **Pays 18-20¢/word for assigned articles. Pays 15-17¢/word for unsolicited articles.**

PHOTOS Send photos. Captions, identification of subjects required. Reviews transparencies, prints. Offers $15-400.

COLUMNS Technique; Equipment; Do-It-Yourself; Food; Safety; Health; Environment; Book Reviews; all 1,000-2,500 words. **Buys 40-45 mss/year.** Query. **Pays 15-20¢/word.**

$$ SOUTHERN BOATING MAGAZINE

Southern Boating & Yachting, Inc., 330 N. Andrews Ave., Ft. Lauderdale FL 33301. (954)522-5515. Fax: (954)522-2260. E-mail: info@southernboating.com. Website: southernboating.com. **Contact:** Louisa Beckett. **50% freelance written.** Monthly boating magazine. Upscale monthly yachting magazine focusing on the Southeast U.S., Bahamas, Caribbean, and Gulf of Mexico. Estab. 1972. Circ. 40,000. Byline given. Pays within 30 days of publication. Publishes ms an average of 2 months after acceptance. Editorial lead time 3 months. Submit seasonal material 3 months in advance. Accepts queries by e-mail. Sample copy for $8.

NONFICTION Needs how-to, boat maintenance, travel, boating related, destination pieces. **Buys 50 mss/year.** Query. Length: 900-1,200 words. **Pays $500-750 with art.**

PHOTOS State availability of or send photos. Captions, identification of subjects, model releases required. Reviews transparencies, prints, digital files. Offers $75/photo minimum.

COLUMNS Weekend Workshop (how-to/maintenance), 900 words; What's New in Electronics (electronics), 900 words; Engine Room (new developments), 1,000 words. **Buys 24 mss/year.** Query first, see media kit for special issue focus. **Pays $600.**

$$$ TRAILER BOATS MAGAZINE

Ehlert Publishing Group, Inc., 20700 Belshaw Ave., Carson CA 90746-3510. Website: trailerboats.com. **Contact:** Jim Hendricks, publisher/editorial director. **50% freelance written.** Monthly magazine covering legally trailerable power boats and related powerboating activities. Estab. 1971. Circ. 100,000. Byline given. Pays on acceptance. Publishes ms an average of 3 months after acceptance. Editorial lead time 3 months. Submit seasonal material 5 months in advance. Responds in 1 month to queries. Sample copy for 9×12 SAE with 7 first-class stamps.

NONFICTION Needs general interest, trailer boating activities, historical, places, events, boats, how-to, repair boats, installation, etc., interview, personal experience, photo feature, technical, travel, boating travel on water or highways, product evaluations. "No 'How I Spent My Summer Vacation' stories, or stories not directly connected to trailerable boats and related activities." **Buys 3-4 unsolicited mss/year.** Query. Length: 1,000-2,500 words. **Pays $150-1,000.** Sometimes pays expenses of writers on assignment.

PHOTOS Send photos. Captions, identification of subjects, model releases required. Reviews transparencies, 2 ¼x2 ¼ and 35mm slides, and high-resolution digital images (300 dpi).

COLUMNS Over the Transom (funny or strange boating photos); Dock Talk (short pieces on boating news, safety, products, profiles of people using boats to do their jobs), all 1,000-1,500 words. **Buys 12-13 mss/year.** Query. **Pays $250-500.**

$ WATERFRONT TIMES

Storyboard Media Inc., 2787 E. Oakland Park Blvd., Suite 205, Ft. Lauderdale FL 33306. (954)524-9450. Fax: (954)524-9464. E-mail: editor@waterfronttimes.com. Website: waterfronttimes.com. **Contact:** Jennifer Heit, editor. **20% freelance written.** Monthly tabloid covering marine and boating topics for the Greater Ft. Lauderdale waterfront community. Estab. 1984. Circ. 20,000. Byline given. Pays on publication. Publishes ms an average of 2 months after acceptance. Submit seasonal material 3 months in advance. Responds in 1 month to queries. Sample copy for SAE with 9×12 envelope and 4 first-class stamps.

NONFICTION Needs interview, of people important in boating, i.e., racers, boat builders, designers, etc. from south Florida, Regional articles on south Florida's waterfront issues; marine communities; travel pieces of interest to boaters, including docking information. Length: 500-1,000 words. **Pays $100-125 for assigned articles.**

PHOTOS Send photos. Reviews JPEG/TIFF files.

WATERWAY GUIDE

P.O. Box 1125, 16273 General Puller Highway, Deltaville VA 23043. (804)776-8999. Fax: (804)776-6111. E-mail: slandry@waterwayguide.com. Website: waterwayguide.com. **Contact:** Susan Landry, editor. **90% freelance written.** Triannual magazine covering intracoastal waterway travel for recreational boats. "Writer must be knowledgeable about navigation and the areas covered by the guide." Estab. 1947. Circ. 30,000. Byline given. Pays on publication. Publishes ms an average of 3 months after acceptance. Editorial lead time 4 months. Submit seasonal material 3 months in advance. Accepts queries by mail, phone. Responds in 6 weeks to queries. Responds in 2 months to mss. Sample copy for $39.95 with $3 postage.

NONFICTION Needs essays, historical, how-to, photo feature, technical, travel. **Buys 6 mss/year.** Send complete ms. Length: 250-5,000 words. **Pays $50-500.**

PHOTOS Send photos. Captions, identification of subjects required. Reviews transparencies, 3 x 5 prints. Offers $25-50/photo.

WATERWAYS WORLD

Waterways World Ltd, 151 Station St., Burton-on-Trent Staffordshire DE14 1BG United Kingdom. 01283 742950. E-mail: richard.fairhurst@wwonline.co.uk. Monthly magazine publishing news, photographs, and illustrated articles on all aspects of inland waterways in Britain, and on limited aspects of waterways abroad. Estab. 1972. Pays on publication. Editorial lead time 2 months. Accepts queries by mail, e-mail. NoGuidelines by e-mail.

NONFICTION Does not want poetry or fiction. Submit query letter or complete ms, SAE.

PHOTOS Captions required. Reviews transparencies, gloss prints, 300 dpi digital images, maps/diagrams.

WAVELENGTH MAGAZINE

Wild Coast Publishing, #6-10 Commercial St., Nanaimo BC V9R 5G2 Canada. (250)244-6437; (866)984-6437. Fax: (250)244-1937; (866)654-1937. E-mail: editor@wavelengthmagazine.com. Website: wavelengthmagazine.com. **Contact:** John Kimantas, editor. **75% freelance written.** Quarterly magazine with a major focus on paddling the Pacific coast. We promote safe paddling, guide paddlers to useful products and services and explore coastal environmental issues. Estab. 1991. Circ. 65,000 print and electronic readers. Byline given. Pays on publication. Publishes ms an average of 4 months after acceptance. Editorial lead time 4 months. Submit seasonal material 4 months in advance. Accepts queries by mail, e-mail. Sample copy available online. Guidelines available online.

NONFICTION Needs how-to, paddle, travel, humor, new product, personal experience, technical, travel, trips. **Buys 25 mss/year.** Query. Length: 1,000-1,500 words. **Pays $50-75.**

PHOTOS State availability. Captions, identification of subjects required. Reviews low-res JPEGs. Offers $25-50/photo.

WOODENBOAT MAGAZINE

WoodenBoat Publications, Inc., P.O. Box 78, 41 WoodenBoat Lane, Brooklin ME 04616-0078. (207)359-4651. Fax: (207)359-8920. E-mail: woodenboat@woodenboat.com. E-mail: matt@woodenboat.com. Website: woodenboat.com. **Contact:** Matt Murphy. **50% freelance written.** Bimonthly magazine for wooden boat owners, builders, and designers. "We are devoted exclusively to the design, building, care, preservation, and use of wooden boats, both commercial and pleasure, old and new, sail and power. We work to convey quality, integrity, and involvement in the creation and care of these craft, to entertain, inform, inspire, and to provide our varied readers with access to individuals who are deeply experienced in the world of wooden boats." Estab. 1974. Circ. 90,000. Byline given. Pays on publication. Offers variable kill fee. Publishes ms an average of 1 year after acceptance. Accepts simultaneous submissions. Responds in 2 months to queries. Responds in 2 months to mss. Sample copy for $5.99. Guidelines available online.

NONFICTION Needs technical, repair, restoration, maintenance, use, design, and building wooden boats. No poetry, fiction. **Buys 50 mss/year.** Query with published clips. Length: 1,500-5,000 words. **Pays $300/1,000 words.** Sometimes pays expenses of writers on assignment.

REPRINTS Send tearsheet or typed ms with rights for sale noted and information about when and where the material previously appeared.

PHOTOS Send photos. Identification of subjects required. Reviews negatives. Pays $15-75 b&w, $25-350 color.

COLUMNS Currents pays for information on wooden boat-related events, projects, boatshop activities, etc. Uses same columnists for each issue. Length: 250-1,000 words. Send complete information. **Pays $5-50.**

$$$ YACHTING

Bonnier Corporation, 2 Park Ave., 9th Floor, New York NY 10016. Fax: (212)779-5479. E-mail: editor@yachtingmagazine.com. Website: yachtingmagazine.com. **Contact:** Editor. **30% freelance written.** Monthly magazine. Monthly magazine written and edited for experienced, knowledgeable yachtsmen. Estab. 1907. Circ. 132,000. Byline given. Pays on acceptance. Editorial lead time 2 months. Submit seasonal material 6 months in advance. Accepts queries by mail, e-mail, fax. Responds in 1 month to queries. Responds in 3 months to mss. Sample copy free. Guidelines available online.

NONFICTION Needs personal experience, technical. **Buys 50 mss/year.** Query with published clips. Length: 750-800 words. **Pays $150-1,500.** Pays expenses of writers on assignment.

PHOTOS Send photos. Captions, identification of subjects, model releases required. Reviews transparencies. Negotiates payment individually.

GENERAL INTEREST

$ OUTDOORS NW

PMB Box 331, 10002 Aurora Ave. N. #36, Seattle WA 98133. (206)418-0747; (800) 935-1083. Fax: (206)418-0746. E-mail: info@outdoorsnw.com. Website: outdoorsnw.com. **80% freelance written.** Monthly magazine covering outdoor recreation in the Pacific Northwest. "Writers must have a solid knowledge of the sport they are writing about. They must be doers." Estab. 1988. Circ. 40,000. Byline given. Pays on publication. Publishes ms an average of 3 months after acceptance. Editorial lead time 2 months. Submit seasonal material 4 months in advance. Accepts queries by mail, e-mail, fax. Accepts simultaneous submissions. Sample copy and writer's guidelines for $3.

Publication changed it's name from Sports Etc.

NONFICTION Needs interview, new product, travel. Query with published clips. Length: 750-1,500 words. **Pays $25-125.** Sometimes pays expenses of writers on assignment.

PHOTOS Send photos. Captions, identification of subjects, model releases required. Reviews electronic images only.

COLUMNS Faces, Places, Puruits (750 words). **Buys 4-6 mss/year.** Query with published clips. **Pays $40-75.**

$ SILENT SPORTS

Journal Community Publishing Group, 600 Industrial Dr., P.O. Box 609, Waupaca WI 54981. (715)258-5546; (800)236-3313. Fax: (715)258-8162. E-mail: info@silentsports.net. Website: silentsports.net. **75% freelance written.** Monthly magazine covering running, cycling, cross-country skiing, canoeing, kayaking, snowshoeing, in-line skating, camping, backpacking, and hiking aimed at people in Wisconsin, Minnesota, northern Illinois, and portions of Michigan and Iowa. "Not a coffee table magazine. Our readers are participants from rank amateur weekend athletes to highly competitive racers." Estab. 1984. Circ. 10,000. Byline given. Pays on publication. Offers 20% kill fee. Publishes ms an average of 3 months after acceptance. Submit seasonal material 4 months in advance. Accepts queries by mail, e-mail, fax. Responds in 3 months to queries. Sample copy and writer's guidelines for 10×13 SAE with 7 first-class stamps.

The editor needs local angles on in-line skating, recreation bicycling, and snowshoeing.

NONFICTION Needs general interest, how-to, interview, opinion, technical, travel. **Buys 25 mss/year.** Query. 2,500 words maximum. **Pays $15-100.** Sometimes pays expenses of writers on assignment.

REPRINTS Send typed manuscript with rights for sale noted and information about when and where the material previously appeared. Pays 50% of amount paid for an original article.

PHOTOS State availability. Reviews transparencies. Pays $5-15 for b&w story photos; $50-100 for color covers.

SPORTS ILLUSTRATED

Time, Inc., Magazine Co., Sports Illustrated Bldg., 135 W. 50th St., New York NY 10020. (212)522-1212. E-mail: story_queries@simail.com. Website: sportsillustrated.cnn.com. Weekly magazine. *Sports Illustrated* reports and interprets the world of sport, recreation, and active leisure. It previews, analyzes, and comments upon major games and events, as well as those noteworthy for character and spirit alone. It features individuals connected to sport and evaluates trends concerning the part sport plays in contemporary life. In addition, the magazine has articles on such subjects as sports gear and swim suits. Special departments deal with sports equipment, books, and statistics. Estab. 1954. Circ. 3,339,000. Accepts queries by mail. Responds in 4-6 weeks to queries.

○ Do not send photos or graphics. Please include a SASE for return of materials.

GOLF

AFRICAN AMERICAN GOLFER'S DIGEST

139 Fulton St., Suite 209, New York NY 10038. (212)571-6559. E-mail: debertcook@aol.com. Website: africanamericangolfersdigest.com. **Contact:** Debert Cook, managing editor. **100% freelance written.** Quarterly magazine covering golf lifestyle, health, travel destinations and reviews, golf equipment, golfer profiles. Editorial should focus on interests of our market demographic of African Americans with historical, artistic, musical, educational (higher learning), automotive, sports, fashion, entertainment, and other categories of high interest to them. Estab. 2003. Circ. 20,000. Byline given. Publishes ms an average of 3 months after acceptance. Editorial lead time 3-6 months. Submit seasonal material 3-6 months in advance. Accepts queries by e-mail. Accepts simultaneous submissions. Responds in 3 weeks to queries. Responds in 3 months to mss. Sample copy for $4.99. Guidelines by e-mail.
NONFICTION Needs how-to, interview, new product, personal experience, photo feature, technical, travel., golf-related. **Buys 3 mss/year.** Query. Length: 250-1,500 words. **Pays 25-50¢/word.**
PHOTOS State availability. Captions, identification of subjects, model releases required. Reviews GIF/JPEG files (300 dpi or higher at 4×6). Negotiates payment individually. Credit line given.

COLUMNS Profiles (celebrities, national leaders, entertainers, corporate leaders, etc., who golf); Travel (destination/golf course reviews); Golf Fashion (jewelry, clothing, accessories). **Buys 3 mss/year.** Query. **Pays 25-50¢/word.**
FILLERS Needs anecdotes, facts, gags, newsbreaks, short humor. **Buys 3 mss/year. mss/year.** Length: 20-125 words. **Pays 25-50¢/word.**

ARIZONA, THE STATE OF GOLF

Arizona Golf Association, 7226 N. 16th St., Suite 200, Phoenix AZ 85020. (602)944-3035. Fax: (602)944-3228. Website: azgolf.org. **Contact:** Brian Foster, director of marketing and communications. **50% freelance written.** Quarterly magazine covering golf in Arizona, the official publication of the Arizona Golf Association. Estab. 1999. Circ. 45,000. Byline given. Pays on acceptance. Editorial lead time 6 months. Submit seasonal material 3 months in advance. Accepts queries by mail. Accepts simultaneous submissions. Sample copy and writer's guidelines free.
NONFICTION Needs book excerpts, essays, historical, how-to, golf, humor, inspirational, interview, new product, opinion, personal experience, photo feature, travel, destinations. **Buys 5-10 mss/year.** Query. Length: 500-2,000 words. **Pays $50-500.** Sometimes pays expenses of writers on assignment.
PHOTOS State availability. Captions, identification of subjects required. Reviews contact sheets. Negotiates payment individually.
COLUMNS Short Strokes (golf news and notes), Improving Your Game (golf tips), Out of Bounds (guest editorial, 800 words). Query.

GOLF CANADA

Chill Media Inc., 77 John St., Suite 4, Oakville ON L6K 3W3 Canada. (905)337-1886. Fax: (905)337-1887. E-mail: scotty@chillmag.ca; stacy@chillonline.ca. Website: golfcanada.ca. Stacy Bradshaw, associate editor. **Contact:** Scott Stevenson, publisher. **80% freelance written**. Magazine published 4 times/year covering Canadian golf. *Golf Canada* is the official magazine of the Royal Canadian Golf Association, published to entertain and enlighten members about RCGA-related activities and to generally support and promote amateur golf in Canada. Estab. 1994. Circ. 159,000. Byline given. Pays on acceptance. Offers 100% kill fee. Editorial lead time 3 months. Submit seasonal material 6 months in advance. Accepts queries by mail, e-mail, fax, phone. Sample copy free.

NONFICTION Needs historical, interview, new product, opinion, photo feature, travel. No professional golf-related articles. **Buys 42 mss/year.** Query with published clips. Length: 750-3,000 words. **Pays 60¢/word, including electronic rights.** Sometimes pays expenses of writers on assignment.

PHOTOS State availability. Captions required. Reviews contact sheets, negatives, transparencies, prints. Negotiates payment individually.

COLUMNS Guest Column (focus on issues surrounding the Canadian golf community), 700 words. Query. **Pays 60¢/word, including electronic rights.**

💲💲 THE GOLFER

59 E. 72nd St., New York NY 10021. (212)867-7070. Fax: (212)867-8550. E-mail: info@thegolferinc.com. Website: thegolfermag.com; thegolferinc.com. **40% freelance written.** Bimonthly magazine covering golf. A sophisticated tone for a lifestyle-oriented magazine. Estab. 1994. Circ. 253,000. Byline given. Pays on publication. Offers negotiable kill fee. Publishes ms an average of 2 months after acceptance. Editorial lead time 2 months. Submit seasonal material 4 months in advance. Accepts queries by mail, e-mail, fax. Accepts simultaneous submissions. Sample copy free.

NONFICTION Needs book excerpts, essays, general interest, historical, how-to, humor, inspirational, interview, new product, opinion, personal experience, photo feature, technical, travel. Send complete ms. Length: 300-2,000 words. **Pays $150-600.**

PHOTOS Send photos. Reviews any size digital files.

💲💲💲 GOLFING MAGAZINE

Golfer Magazine, Inc., 274 Silas Dean Hwy., Wethersfield CT 06109. (860)563-1633. Fax: (646)607-3001. E-mail: tlanders@golfingmagazine.net. Website: golfingmagazineonline.com. **Contact:** Tom Landers, national editor. **30% freelance written.** Bimonthly magazine covering golf, including travel, products, player profiles and company profiles. Estab. 1999. Circ. 175,000. Byline given. Pays on publication. Offers negotiable kill fee. Editorial lead time 2 months. Submit seasonal material 2 months in advance. Accepts queries by mail, e-mail. Sample copy free.

NONFICTION Needs book excerpts, new product, photo feature, travel. **Buys 4-5 mss/year.** Query. Length: 700-2,500 words. **Pays $250-1,000 for assigned articles. Pays $100-500 for unsolicited articles.**

PHOTOS State availability. Captions required. Reviews GIF/JPEG files. Negotiates payment and rights individually.

FILLERS Needs facts, gags. **Buys 2-3 mss/year. Payment individually determined.**

💲💲 GOLF NEWS MAGAZINE

Golf News Magazine, P.O. Box 1040, Rancho Mirage CA 92270. (760)321-8800. Fax: (760)328-3013. E-mail: golfnews@aol.com. Website: golfnewsmag.com. **Contact:** Dan Poppers, editor-in-chief. **40% freelance written.** Monthly magazine covering golf. "Our publication specializes in the creative treatment of the sport of golf, offering a variety of themes and slants as related to golf. If it's good writing and relates to golf, we're interested." Estab. 1984. Circ. 15,000. Byline given. Pays on acceptance. Publishes ms an average of 3 months after acceptance. Editorial lead time 2 months. Submit seasonal material 2 months in advance. Accepts queries by mail, e-mail, fax. Accepts simultaneous submissions. Responds in 3 weeks to queries. Responds in 3 weeks to mss. Sample copy for $2 and 9×12 SAE with 4 first class stamps.

NONFICTION Needs book excerpts, essays, expose, general interest, historical, humor, inspirational, interview, opinion, personal experience, real estate. **Buys 20 mss/year.** Query with published clips. **Pays $75-350.**

PHOTOS State availability. Identification of subjects required. Negotiates payment individually.

COLUMNS Submit ideas. **Buys 10 mss/year.** Query with published clips.

💲💲💲 GOLF TIPS

Werner Publishing Corp., Golf Tips Magazine, Werner Publishing Corporation, 12121 Wilshire Blvd., 12th Floor, Los Angeles CA 90025-1176. (310)820-1500. Fax: (310)826-5008. E-mail: editors@golftipsmag.com. Website: golftipsmag.com. **95% freelance written.** Magazine published 9 times/year covering golf instruction and equipment. We provide mostly concise, very clear golf instruction pieces for the serious golfer. Estab. 1986. Byline given. Pays on publication. Offers 33% kill fee. Publishes ms an average of 2 months after acceptance. Editorial lead time 3 months. Submit seasonal material 4 months in advance. Responds in 1 month to queries. Sample copy free. Guidelines available online.

NONFICTION Needs book excerpts, how-to, interview, new product, photo feature, technical, travel, all golf related. Generally golf essays rarely make it. **Buys 125 mss/year.** Send complete ms. Length: 250-2,000 words. **Pays $300-1,000 for assigned articles. Pays $300-800 for unsolicited articles.** Sometimes pays expenses of writers on assignment.

PHOTOS State availability. Captions, identification of subjects required. Reviews 2 x 2 transparencies. Negotiates payment individually.

COLUMNS Stroke Saver (very clear, concise instruction), 350 words; Lesson Library (book excerpts—usually in a series), 1,000 words; Travel Tips (formatted golf travel), 2,500 words. **Buys 40 mss/year.** Query with or without published clips or send complete ms. **Pays $300-850.**

$$$ MINNESOTA GOLFER

6550 York Ave. S., Suite 211, Edina MN 55435. (952)927-4643; (800)642-4405. Fax: (952)927-9642. E-mail: wp@mngolf.org; editor@mngolf.org. Website: mngolfer.com. **Contact:** W.P. Ryan, editor. **75% freelance written.** Bimonthly magazine covering golf in Minnesota, the official publication of the Minnesota Golf Association. Estab. 1975. Circ. 66,000. Byline given. Pays on acceptance or publication. Editorial lead time 3 months. Accepts queries by mail, e-mail, fax.

NONFICTION Needs historical, interview, new product, travel, book reviews, instruction, golf course previews. Query with published clips. Length: 400-2,000 words. **Pays $50-750.** Sometimes pays expenses of writers on assignment.

PHOTOS State availability. Captions, identification of subjects required. Reviews contact sheets, transparencies, digital images. Negotiates payment individually.

COLUMNS Punch shots (golf news and notes); Q School (news and information targeted to beginners, junior golfers and women); Great Drives (featuring noteworthy golf holes in Minnesota); Instruction.

$$ TEXAS GOLFER MAGAZINE

Texas Golder Media, 15721 Park Row, Suite 100, Houston TX 77084. (888)863-9899. E-mail: george@texasgolfermagazine.com. Website: texasgolfermagazine.com. **Contact:** George Fuller, editor-in-chief. **10% freelance written.** Bi-monthly magazine covering golf in Texas. Estab. 1984. Circ. 50,000. Byline given. Pays 10 days after publication. Publishes ms an average of 2 months after acceptance. Editorial lead time 2 months. Submit seasonal material 3 months in advance. Responds in 2 weeks to queries. Responds in 1 month to mss. Sample copy free. Prefers direct phone discussion for writer's guidelines.

💬 *Texas Golfer Magazine* was created by the merger of two publications: *Gulf Coast Golfer* and *North Texas Golfer*.

NONFICTION Needs book excerpts, humor, personal experience, all golf-related. Travel pieces accepted about golf outside of Texas. **Buys 20 mss/year.** Query. **Pays 25-40¢/word.**

PHOTOS State availability. Captions, identification of subjects required. Reviews contact sheets, prints. No additional payment for photos accepted with ms, but pays $125 for cover photo.

$$ VIRGINIA GOLFER

Touchpoint Publishing, Inc., 600 Founders Bridge Blvd., Midlothian VA 23113. (804)378-2300, ext. 12. Fax: (804)378-2369. E-mail: ablair@vsga.org. Website: vsga.org. **Contact:** Andrew Blair, editor. **65% freelance written.** Bimonthly magazine covering golf in Virginia, the official publication of the Virginia State Golf Association. Estab. 1983. Circ. 45,000. Byline given. Pays on publication. Editorial lead time 6 months. Submit seasonal material 3 months in advance. Accepts queries by mail, e-mail. Accepts simultaneous submissions. Sample copy and writer's guidelines free.

NONFICTION Needs book excerpts, essays, historical, how-to, golf, humor, inspirational, interview, personal experience, photo feature, technical, golf equipment, where to play, golf business. **Buys 30-40 mss/year.** Send complete ms. Length: 500-2,500 words. **Pays $50-200.** Sometimes pays expenses of writers on assignment.

PHOTOS State availability. Captions, identification of subjects required. Reviews contact sheets. Negotiates payment individually.

COLUMNS Chip ins & Three Putts (news notes), Rules Corner (golf rules explanations and discussion), Your Game, Golf Travel (where to play), Great Holes, Q&A, Golf Business (what's happening?), Fashion. Query.

GUNS

[+]$$ GUN DIGEST THE MAGAZINE

F+W Media, 700 E. State St., Iola WI 54990. (715)445-2214. Fax: (715)445-4087. E-mail: kevin.michalowski@fwmedia.com. Website: gundigest.com. **Contact:** Kevin Michalowski, senior editor. **Uses 90% freelancers.** Bimonthly magazine covering firearms. "Gun Digest the Magazine covers all aspects of the firearms community; from collectible guns to tactical gear to reloading and accessories. We also publish gun reviews and tests of new and collectible firearms and news features about firearms legislation. We are 100 percent pro-gun, fully support the NRA and make no bones about our support of Constitutional freedoms." Byline given. Pays on publication. 2 months 3 months 3 months Accepts queries by e-mail. Responds in 3 weeks on queries; 1 month on mss. Free sample copy. Guidelines available via e-mail.

NONFICTION Needs general interest (firearms related), historical, how-to, interview, new product, nostalgic, profile, technical, All submissions must focus on firearms, accessories or the firearms industry and legislation. Stories that include hunting reference must have as their focus the firearms or ammunition used. The hunting should be secondary. Special issues: Gun Digest the Magazine also publishes an annual gear guide and 4 issues each year of Tactical Gear Magazine. Tactical Gear is designed for readers interested in self-defense, police and military gear including guns, knives, accessories and fitness. We do not publish "Me and Joe" hunting stories. **Buys 50-75 mss/year.** Query. 500-3,500 max. **$175-500 for assigned and for unsolicited articles. Does not pay in contributor copies.** Does not pay expenses.

PHOTOS Send photos with submission. Requires captions, identification of subjects. Reviews GIF/JPEG files (and TIF files); 300 DPI submitted on a CD (size). Offers no additional payment for photos accepted with ms.

$$ MUZZLE BLASTS

National Muzzle Loading Rifle Association, P.O. Box 67, Friendship IN 47021. (812)667-5131. Fax: (812)667-5136. E-mail: mblastdop@seidata.com. Website: nmlra.org. **65% freelance written.** Monthly magazine. "Articles must relate to muzzleloading or the muzzleloading era of American history." Estab. 1939. Circ. 18,500. Byline given. Pays on publication. Offers $50 kill fee. Publishes ms an average of 6 months after acceptance. Editorial lead time 4 months. Submit seasonal material 6 months in advance. Responds in 1 month to mss. Sample copy and writer's guidelines free.

NONFICTION Needs book excerpts, general interest, historical, how-to, humor, interview, new product, personal experience, photo feature, technical, travel. No subjects that do not pertain to muzzleloading. **Buys 80 mss/year.** Query. Length: 2,500 words. **Pays $150 minimum for assigned articles. Pays $50 minimum for unsolicited articles.**

PHOTOS Send photos. Captions, model releases required. Reviews 5×7 prints. Negotiates payment individually.

COLUMNS Buys 96 mss/year. Query. **Pays $50-200.**

FICTION Must pertain to muzzleloading. Needs adventure, historical, humorous. **Buys 6 mss/year.** Query. Length: 2,500 words. **Pays $50-300.**

FILLERS Needs facts. **Pays $50.**

$$ SHOTGUN SPORTS MAGAZINE

P.O. Box 6810, Auburn CA 95604. (530)889-2220. Fax: (530)889-9106. E-mail: shotgun@shotgunsportsmagazine.com. Website: shotgunsportsmagazine.com. **Contact:** Linda Martin, Production Coordinator. **50% freelance written. Welcomes new writers.** Monthly magazine covering all the shotgun sports and shotgun hunting—sporting clays, trap, skeet, hunting, gunsmithing, shotshell patterning, shotsell reloading, mental training for the shotgun sports, shotgun tests, anything shotgun. Pays on publication. Publishes ms an average of 1-6 months after acceptance. Sample copy and writer's guidelines available by contacting Linda Martin, production coordinator, or can be downloaded on the website.

NONFICTION Needs Currently needs anything with a 'shotgun' subject. Think pieces, roundups, historical, interviews, etc. No articles promoting a specific club or sponsored hunting trip, etc. Submit complete ms with photos by mail with SASE. Can submit by e-mail. Make Length: 1,500-3,000 words. **Pays $50-150.**

PHOTOS 5×7 or 8×10 b&w or 4-color with appropriate captions. On disk or e-mailed at least 5-inches and 300 dpi (contact Graphics Artist for details). Reviews transparencies (35 mm or larger), b&w, or 4-color. Send photos.

HIKING AND BACKPACKING

$$$$ BACKPACKER MAGAZINE

Cruz Bay Publishing, Inc., an Active Interest Media Co., 2520 55th St., Suite 210, Boulder CO 80301. E-mail: jdorn@backpacker.com. Website: backpacker.com. Dennis Lewon, deputy editor (Features & People), dlewon@backpacker.com; Shannon Davis, senior editor (Destinations), sdavis@backpacker.com; Kristin Bjornsen, associate editor (Skills(, kbjornsen@aimmedia.com; Kristin Hostetter, gear editor (Gear), khostetter1@gmail.com. **Contact:** Jonathan Dorn, editor-in-chief. **50% freelance written.** Magazine published 9 times/year covering wilderness travel for backpackers. Estab. 1973. Circ. 340,000. Byline given. Pays on acceptance. 6 months. Accepts queries by mail (include SASE for returns), e-mail (preferred, with attachments and web links), fax. Responds in 2-4 weeks to queries. Free sample copy. Guidelines available online.

NONFICTION Needs essays, expose, historical, how-to, humor, inspirational, interview, new product, personal experience, technical, travel, BACKPACKER primarily covers hiking. When warranted, we cover canoeing, kayaking, snowshoeing, cross-country skiing, and other human-powered modes of travel. Wilderness or backcountry: The true backpacking experience means getting away from the trailhead and into the wilds. Whether a dayhike or a weeklong trip, out-of-the-way, unusual destinations are what we're looking for. No step-by-step accounts of what you did on your summer vacation—stories that chronicle every rest stop and gulp of water. Query with published clips before sending complete ms. Length: 750-4,000 words. **Pays 60¢-$1/word.**

PHOTOS State availability. Payment varies.

COLUMNS Signpost, News From All Over (adventure, environment, wildlife, trails, techniques, organizations, special interests—well-written, entertaining, short, newsy item), 50-500 words; Getaways (great hiking destinations, primarily North America), includes weekend, 250-500 words, weeklong, 250-1000, multi-destination guides, 500-1500 words, and dayhikes, 50-200 words, plus travel news and other items; Fitness (in-the-field health column), 750-1,200 words; Food (food-related aspects of wilderness: nutrition, cooking techniques, recipes, products and gear), 500-750 words; Know How (ranging from beginner to expert focus, written by people with solid expertise, details ways to improve performance, how-to-do-it instructions, information on equipment manufacturers, and places readers can go), 300-1,000 words; Senses (capturing a moment in backcountry through sight, sound, smell, and other senses, paired with an outstanding photo), 150-200 words. **Buys 50-75 mss/year.**

HOCKEY

💲💲 MINNESOTA HOCKEY JOURNAL

Touchpoint Sports, 505 N. Hwy 169, Ste. 465, Minneapolis MN 55441. (763)595-0808. Fax: (763)595-0016. E-mail: mhj@touchpointsports.com; greg@touchpointsports.com. Website: minnesotahockeyjournal.com. **50% freelance written.** Journal published 4 times/year. Estab. 2000. Circ. 40,000. Byline given. Pays on publication. Editorial lead time 6 months. Submit seasonal material 4 months in advance. Accepts simultaneous submissions. Sample copy and writer's guidelines free.

NONFICTION Needs essays, general interest, historical, how-to, play hockey, humor, inspirational, interview, new product, opinion, personal experience, photo feature, travel, hockey camps, pro hockey, juniors, college, Olympics, youth, etc. **Buys 3-5 mss/year.** Query. Length: 500-1,500 words. **Pays $100-300.**

PHOTOS State availability. Captions, identification of subjects required. Reviews contact sheets. Negotiates payment individually.

💲💲💲 USA HOCKEY MAGAZINE

Touchpoint Sports, 1775 Bob Johnson Dr., Colorado Springs CO 80906. (719)576-8724. Fax: (763)538-1160. E-mail: usah@usahockey.org; info@touchpointsports.com. Website: usahockeymagazine.com; usahockey.com. **Contact:** Harry Thompson, editor-in-chief. **60% freelance written.** Magazine published 10 times/year covering amateur hockey in the US. The world's largest hockey magazine, *USA Hockey Magazine* is the official magazine of USA Hockey, Inc., the national governing body of hockey. Estab. 1980. Circ. 444,000. Byline given. Pays on acceptance or publication. Editorial lead time 6 months. Submit seasonal material 4 months in advance. Accepts simultaneous submissions. Sample copy and writer's guidelines free.

NONFICTION Needs essays, general interest, historical, how-to, play hockey, humor, inspirational, interview, new product, opinion, personal experience, photo feature, travel, hockey camps, pro hockey, juniors, college, NCAA hockey championships, Olympics, youth, etc. **Buys 20-30 mss/year.** Query. Length: 500-5,000 words. **Pays $50-750.** Pays expenses of writers on assignment.

PHOTOS State availability. Captions, identification of subjects required. Reviews contact sheets. Negotiates payment individually.

COLUMNS Short Cuts (news and notes); Coaches' Corner (teaching tips); USA Hockey; Inline Notebook (news and notes). **Pays $150-250.**

FICTION Needs adventure, humorous, slice-of-life vignettes. **Buys 10-20 mss/year. Pays $150-1,000.**

FILLERS Needs anecdotes, facts, gags, newsbreaks, short humor. **Buys 20-30 mss/year.** Length: 10-100 words. **Pays $25-250.**

HORSE RACING

AMERICAN TURF MONTHLY

747 Middle Neck Rd., Great Neck NY 11024. (516)773-4075. Fax: (516)773-2944. E-mail: jcorbett@americanturf.com; editor@americanturf.com. Website: americanturf.com. **Contact:** Joe Girardi, editor; James Corbett, editor-in-chief. **90.** Monthly magazine squarely focused on Thoroughbred racing, handicapping and wagering. *ATM* is a magazine for horseplayers, not owners, breeders, or 12-year-old girls enthralled with ponies. Estab. 1946. Circ. 30,000. Byline given. Pays on publication. Publishes ms an average of 4 months after acceptance. Editorial lead time 2 months. Submit seasonal material 2 months in advance. Accepts queries by mail, e-mail. Responds in 1 month to queries. Sample copy and writer's guidelines free.

> "*American Turf Monthly*, the only handicapping magazine sold on news stands within the U.S. and Canada, has been entertaining horse racing enthusiasts since 1946. Each issue draws the reader into the exhilarating world of horse racing with features written by premier handicapping authors in the sport. The photography and creative design capture the spellbinding highlights of the race tracks to satiate the thrill seeking desire of the wagering player."

NONFICTION No historical essays, bilious 'guest editorials,' saccharine poetry, fiction. Special issues: Triple Crown/Kentucky Derby (May); Saratoga/Del Mar (August); Breeder's Cup (November). **Buys Length: 800-2,000 words. Pays $75-300 for assigned articles. Pays $100-500 for unsolicited articles. mss/year.** Query. Length: 800-2,000 words. **Pays $75-300 for assigned articles. Pays $100-500 for unsolicited articles. No.**

PHOTOS Send photos. Identification of subjects required. Reviews 3 x 5 transparencies, prints, 300 dpi TIFF images on CD. Offers $25 for b&w or color interior; $150 min. for color cover. Pays on publication. Credit line given.

FILLERS newsbreaks, short humor Needs newsbreaks, short humor. **Buys 5 mss/year.** Length: 400 words. **Pays $25.**

🟢🟢 HOOF BEATS

United States Trotting Association, 750 Michigan Ave., Columbus OH 43215. Fax: (614)222-6791. E-mail: hoofbeats@ustrotting.com. Website: hoofbeatsmagazine.com. **60% freelance written.** Monthly magazine covering harness racing and standardbred horses. "Articles and photos must relate to harness racing or standardbreds. We do not accept any topics that do not touch on these 2 subjects." Estab. 1933. Circ. 13,500. Byline given. Pays on publication. Offers 25% kill fee. Publishes ms an average of 2-4 months after acceptance. Editorial lead time 6 months. Submit seasonal material 6 months in advance. Accepts queries by mail, e-mail, fax. Accepts simultaneous submissions. Responds in 2 weeks to queries. Responds in 1 month to mss. Sample copy available online. Guidelines free.

NONFICTION Needs general interest, how-to, interview, personal experience, photo feature, technical. "We do not want any fiction or poetry." **Buys 48-72 mss/year.** Query. Length: 750-3,000 words. **Pays $100-500. Pays $100-500 for unsolicited articles.**

PHOTOS State availability. Identification of subjects required. Reviews contact sheets. We offer $25-100 per photo.

COLUMNS Equine Clinic (standardbreds who overcame major health issues), 900-1,200 words; Profiles (short profiles on people or horses in harness racing), 600-1,000 words; Industry Trends (issues impacting standardbreds & harness racing), 1,000-2,000 words. **Buys 60 mss/year mss/year.** Query. **Pays $100-500.**

HUNTING AND FISHING

🟢🟢 ALABAMA GAME & FISH

Game & Fish, 2250 Newmarket Pkwy., Suite 110, Marietta GA 30067. (770)953-9222. Fax: (770)933-9510. E-mail: Ken.Dunwoody@imoutdoors.com. Website: alabamagameandfish.com. **Contact:** Ken Dunwoody, editorial director. See *Game & Fish*.

🅢🅢 AMERICAN ANGLER

P.O. Box 810, Arlington VA 05250. E-mail: russ.lumpkin@morris.com; steve.walburn@morris.com. Website: flyfishingmagazines.com. **Contact:** Steve Walburn, editor. **95% freelance written.** Bimonthly magazine covering fly fishing. "*American Angler* is devoted exclusively to fly fishing. We focus mainly on coldwater fly fishing for trout, steelhead, and salmon, but we also run articles about warmwater and saltwater fly fishing. (Our sister magazine, Saltwater Fly Fishing, is devoted exclusively to the latter.) Our mission is to supply our readers with well-written, accurate articles on every aspect of the sport—angling techniques and methods, reading water, finding fish, selecting flies, tying flies, fish behavior, places to fish, casting, managing line, rigging, tackle, accessories, entomology, and any other relevant topics. Each submission should present specific, useful information that will increase our readers' enjoyment of the sport and help them catch more fish." Estab. 1976. Circ. 60,000. Byline given. Pays on publication. Publishes ms an average of 6 months after acceptance. Editorial lead time 3 months. Submit seasonal material 5 months in advance. Accepts queries by mail, fax. Accepts simultaneous submissions. Responds in 6 weeks to queries. Responds in 2 months to mss. Sample copy for $6. Guidelines with #10 SASE.

NONFICTION Needs how-to, most important, personal experience, photo feature, seldom, technical. No superficial, broad-brush coverage of subjects. **Buys 45-60 mss/year.** Query with published clips. Length: 800-2,200 words. **Pays $200-400.**

REPRINTS Send information about when and where the material previously appeared. Pay negotiable.

PHOTOS Contact: Wayne Knight, art director: wayne.knight@morris.com. "How-to pieces—those that deal with tactics, rigging, fly tying, and the like—must be accompanied by appropriate photography or rough sketches for our illustrator. Naturally, where-to stories must be illustrated with shots of scenery, people fishing, anglers holding fish, and other pictures that help flesh out the story and paint the local color. Do not bother sending sub-par photographs, as this serves only to irritate the editor. We only accept photos that are well lit, tack sharp, and correctly framed. Photographs are important. A fly-tying submission should always include samples of flies to send to our staff photographer, even if photos of the flies are included.". Send photos. Captions, identification of subjects required. Reviews contact sheets, transparencies. Offers no additional payment for photos accepted with ms. Pays $600 for color cover; $30-350 for color inside. Pays on publication. Credit line given. Buys one-time rights, first rights for covers. "Payment is made just prior to publication. "We don't pay by the word, and length is only one of the variables considered. The quality and completeness of a submission may be more important than its length in determining rates, and articles that include good photography are usually worth more. As a guideline, the following rates generally apply: Feature articles pay $450 (and perhaps a bit more if we're impressed), while short features pay $200 to $400. Generally, these rates assume that useful photos, drawings, or sketches accompany the words.

COLUMNS One-page shorts (problem solvers), 350-750 words. Query with published clips. **Pays $100-300.**

🅢🅢🅢 AMERICAN HUNTER

NRA, 11250 Waples Mill Rd., Fairfax VA 22030-9400. (703)267-1336. Fax: (703)267-3971. E-mail: publications@nrahq.org; americanhunter@nrahq.org, lcromwell@nrahq.org. Website: americanhunter.org. **Contact:** J. Scott Olmsted, editor-in-chief. Monthly magazine for hunters who are members of the National Rifle Association (NRA). "*American Hunter* contains articles dealing with various sport hunting and related activities both at home and abroad. With the encouragement of the sport as a prime game management tool, emphasis is on technique, sportsmanship and safety. In each issue hunting equipment and firearms are evaluated, legislative happenings affecting the sport are reported, lore and legend are retold and the business of the Association is recorded in the Official Journal section." Circ. 1,000,000. Byline given. Pays on publication. Accepts queries by mail, e-mail. Responds in 6 months to queries. Guidelines for #10 SASE.

NONFICTION Special issues: Pheasants, whitetail tactics, black bear feed areas, mule deer, duck hunters' transport by land and sea, tech topics to be decided; rut strategies, muzzleloader moose and elk, fall turkeys, staying warm, goose talk, long-range muzzleloading. Not interested in material on fishing, camping, or firearms knowledge. Query. Length: 1,800-2,000 words. **Pays up to $1,000.**

REPRINTS Copies for author will be provided upon publication. No reprints possible.

PHOTOS Captions preferred. Accepts images in digital format only, no slides. Model release required "for every recognizable human face in a photo.". Pays $125-600/image; $1000 for color cover; $400-1400 for text/photo package. Pays on publication. Credit line given. No additional payment made for photos used with ms.

COLUMNS Hunting Guns, Hunting Loads, destination and adventure, and Public Hunting Grounds. Study back issues for appropriate subject matter and style. Length: 800-1,500 words. **Pays $300-800.**

⊙ ⊛ ARKANSAS SPORTSMAN

Game & Fish, 2250 Newmarket Parkway, Suite 110, Marietta GA 30067. (770)953-9222. Fax: (770)933-9510. E-mail: Ken.Dunwoody@imoutdoors.com. Website: arkansassportsmanmag.com. **Contact:** Ken Dunwoody, editorial director. See *Game & Fish*.

⊙ ⊛ BASSMASTER MAGAZINE

B.A.S.S. Publications, 1170 Celebration Blvd., Suite 200, Celebration FL 32830. (407)566-2277. Fax: (407)566-2072. E-mail: editorial@bassmaster.com. Website: bassmaster.com. **80% freelance written**. Magazine published 11 times/year about largemouth, smallmouth, and spotted bass, offering how-to articles for dedicated beginning and advanced bass fishermen, including destinations and new product reviews. Estab. 1968. Circ. 600,000. Byline given. Pays on acceptance. Publishes ms an average of less than 1 year after acceptance. Editorial lead time 2 months. Submit seasonal material 6 months in advance. Accepts queries by mail, e-mail. Responds in 2 months to queries. Sample copy upon request. Guidelines for #10 SASE.

⊙ Needs destination stories (how to fish a certain area) for the Northwest and Northeast.

NONFICTION Needs historical, how-to, patterns, lures, etc., interview, of knowledgeable people in the sport, new product, reels, rods, and bass boats, travel, where to go fish for bass, conservation related to bass fishing. No first-person, personal experience-type articles. **Buys 100 mss/year.** Query. Length: 500-1,500 words. **Pays $100-300.**

PHOTOS Send photos. Captions, model releases required. Reviews transparencies. Offers no additional payment for photos accepted with ms, but pays $800 for color cover transparencies.

COLUMNS Short Cast/News/Views/Notes/Briefs (upfront regular feature covering news-related events such as new state bass records, unusual bass fishing happenings, conservation, new products, and editorial viewpoints). Length: 250-400 words. **Pays $100-300.**

⊙ ⊛ ⊛ BC OUTDOORS HUNTING AND SHOOTING

OP Publishing Ltd, 200 West Esplanade, Suite 500, Vancouver BC V7M 1A4 Canada. (604)998-3310. Fax: (604)998-3320. E-mail: info@oppublishing.com. E-mail: sswanson@oppublishing.com; mmitchell@outdoorgroupmedia.com; production@outdoorgroupmedia.com. Website: bcoutdoorsmagazine.com. Paul Bielicki, art director/production; Chelsea Whitteker, managing editor. **Contact:** Mike Mitchell, editor. **80% freelance written**. Bi-annual magazine covering hunting, shooting, camping, and backroads. "*BC Outdoors Magazine* publishes 7 sport fishing issues a year with 2 hunting and shooting supplement issues each summer and fall. Our magazine is about the best outdoor experiences in BC. Whether you're camping on an ocean shore, hiking into your favorite lake, or learning how to fly-fish on your favourite river, we want to showcase what our province has to offer to sport fishing and outdoor enthusiasts. *BC Outdoors Hunting and Shooting* provides trusted editorial for trapping, deer hunting, big buck, bowhunting, bag limits, baitling, decoys, calling, camouflage, tracking, trophy hunting, pheasant hunting, goose hunting, hunting regulations, duck hunting, whitetail hunting, hunting regulations, hunting trips and mule deer hunting." Estab. 1945. Circ. 30,000. Byline given. Pays on publication. Offers kill fee. Publishes ms an average of 3 months after acceptance. Accepts queries by e-mail. Writer's guidelines for 8×10 SASE with 7 Canadian first-class stamps. Guidelines available online.

NONFICTION Needs how-to, new or innovative articles on hunting subjects, personal experience, outdoor adventure, outdoor topics specific to British Columbia. **Buys 50 mss/year.** "Please query the publication before submitting. Please do not send unsolicited manuscripts or photos. Your pitch should be no more than 100-words outlining exactly what your story will be. You should be able to encapsulate the essence of your story and show us why our readers would be interested in reading or knowing what you are writing about. Queries need to be clear, succinct and straight to the point. Show us why we should publish your article in 150 words or less." Length: 1,700-2,000 words. **Pays $300-500.**

PHOTOS Bi-annual magazine emphasizing hunting, RV camping, canoeing, wildlife and management issues in British Columbia only. Sample copy available for $4.95 Canadian. Buys 30-35 photos from freelancers/issue; 60-70 photos/year. Family oriented. "By far, most photos accompany manuscripts. We are always on the lookout for good covers—wildlife, recreational activities, people in the outdoors—of British Columbia, vertical and square format. Photos with manuscripts must, of course, illustrate the story. There should, as far as possible, be something happening. Photos generally dominate lead spread of each story. They are used in everything from double-page bleeds to thumbnails.". State availability. Model/property release preferred. Photo captions or at least full identification required.

COLUMNS Column needs basically supplied in-house.

$$ THE BIG GAME FISHING JOURNAL

Informational Publications, Inc., 1800 Bay Ave., Point Pleasant NJ 08742. Fax: (732)223-2449. Website: biggamefishingjournal.com. **90% freelance written.** Bimonthly magazine covering big game fishing. Estab. 1994. Circ. 45,000. Byline given. Pays on publication. Offers 50% kill fee. Editorial lead time 3 months. Submit seasonal material 3 months in advance. Accepts queries by mail, online submission form. Accepts simultaneous submissions. Responds in 2 weeks to queries. Responds in 1 month to mss. Guidelines free.

💬 "We require highly instructional articles prepared by qualified writers/fishermen."

NONFICTION Needs how-to, interview, technical. **Buys 50-70 mss/year.** Send complete ms. Length: 2,000-3,000 words. **Pays $200-400.** Sometimes pays expenses of writers on assignment.

PHOTOS Send photos. Captions required. Reviews transparencies. Offers no additional payment for photos accepted with ms.

$$ CALIFORNIA GAME & FISH

Game & Fish, 2250 Newmarket Parkway, Suite 110, Marietta GA 30067. (770)953-9222. Fax: (770)933-9510. E-mail: Ken.Dunwoody@imoutdoors.com. Website: californiagameandfish.com. See *Game & Fish*

$$ DEER & DEER HUNTING

F+W Media, Inc., 700 E. State St., Iola WI 54990-0001. E-mail: dan.schmidt@fwmedia.com. Website: deeranddeerhunting.com. **Contact:** Dan Schmidt, editor-in-chief. **95% freelance written.** Magazine published 11 times/year covering white-tailed deer. "Readers include a cross section of the deer hunting population—individuals who hunt with bow, gun, or camera. The editorial content of the magazine focuses on white-tailed deer biology and behavior, management principle and practices, habitat requirements, natural history of deer, hunting techniques, and hunting ethics. We also publish a wide range of how-to articles designed to help hunters locate and get close to deer at all times of the year. The majority of our readership consists of 2-season hunters (bow & gun) and approximately one-third camera hunt." Estab. 1977. Circ. 130,000. Byline given. Pays on acceptance. Publishes ms an average of 18 months after acceptance. Editorial lead time 6 months. Submit seasonal material 12 months in advance. Accepts queries by mail, e-mail. Responds in 1 month to queries. Responds in 2 months to mss. Sample copy for 9×12 SASE. Guidelines available online.

NONFICTION Needs general interest, historical, how-to, photo feature, technical. No "Joe and me" articles. **Buys 100 mss/year.** Send complete ms. Length: 1,000-1,700 words. **Pays $150-500 for assigned articles. Pays $150-400 for unsolicited articles.** Sometimes pays expenses of writers on assignment.

PHOTOS Send photos. Captions required. Reviews transparencies. Offers $75-250/photo; $600 for cover photos.

COLUMNS Deer Browse (odd occurrences), 500 words. **Buys 10 mss/year.** Query. **Pays $50-300.**

FICTION Mood deer hunting pieces. **Buys 9 mss/year.** Send complete ms.

FILLERS Needs facts, newsbreaks. **Buys 40-50 mss/year.** Length: 100-500 words. **Pays $15-150.**

$$ THE DRAKE MAGAZINE

1600 Maple St., Fort Collins CO 80521. (949)218-8642. E-mail: info@drakemag.com. Website: drakemag.com. **70% freelance written.** Biannual magazine for people who love fishing. Byline given. Pays 1 month after publication. Publishes ms an average of 1 year after acceptance. Editorial lead time 1 year. Submit seasonal material 1 year in advance. Accepts queries by mail. Responds in 6 months to mss. Guidelines available online.

NONFICTION Needs book excerpts, essays, general interest, historical, humor, interview, opinion, personal experience, photo feature, travel, fishing related. **Buys 8 mss/year.** Query. Length: 250-3,000 words. **Pays 10-20¢/word depending on the amount of work we have to put into the piece.**

PHOTOS State availability. Reviews contact sheets, negatives, transparencies. Offers $25-250/photo.

💲💲💲 FIELD & STREAM

2 Park Ave., New York NY 10016. (212)779-5000. Fax: (212)779-5114. E-mail: fsletters@bonniercorp.com. Website: fieldandstream.com. **50% freelance written.** Monthly magazine. Broad-based service magazine for the hunter and fisherman. Editorial content consists of articles of penetrating depth about national hunting, fishing, and related activities. Also humor, personal essays, profiles on outdoor people, conservation, sportsmen's insider secrets, tactics and techniques, and adventures. Estab. 1895. Circ. 1,500,000. Byline given. Pays on acceptance for most articles. Accepts queries by mail. Responds in 1 month to queries. Guidelines available online.

> 💬 "Writers are encouraged to submit queries on article ideas. These should be no more than a paragraph or 2, and should include a summary of the idea, including the angle you will hang the story on, and a sense of what makes this piece different from all others on the same or a similar subject. Many queries are turned down because we have no idea what the writer is getting at. Be sure that your letter is absolutely clear. We've found that if you can't sum up the point of the article in a sentence or 2, the article doesn't have a point. Pieces that depend on writing style, such as humor, mood, and nostalgia or essays often can't be queried and may be submitted in ms form. The same is true of short tips. All submissions to *Field & Stream* are on an on-spec basis. Before submitting anything, however, we encourage you to *study*, not simply read, the magazine. Many pieces are rejected because they do not fit the tone or style of the magazine, or fail to match the subject of the article with the overall subject matter of *Field & Stream*."

PHOTOS Send photos. Reviews slides (prefers color). When purchased separately, pays $450 minimum for color.

💲💲 FLORIDA GAME & FISH

Game & Fish, 2250 Newmarket Pkwy, Suite 110, Marietta GA 30067. (770)953-9222. Fax: (770)933-9510. E-mail: ken.dunwoody@imoutdoors.com. Website: floridagameandfish.com. **Contact:** Ken Dunwoody, editorial director. See *Game & Fish* website.

> 💬 To query information regarding writing guidelines and submissions for any of our *Game & Fish* magazines, please contact Ken Dunwoody, Editorial Director - *Game & Fish*

💲💲 FLORIDA SPORTSMAN

Wickstrom Communications Division of Intermedia Outdoors, 2700 S. Kanner Hwy., Stuart FL 34994. (772)219-7400. Fax: (772)219-6900. E-mail: editor@floridasportsman.com. Website: floridasportsman.com. **30% freelance written.** Monthly magazine covering fishing, boating, hunting, and related sports—Florida and Caribbean only. *Florida Sportsman* is edited for the boatowner and offshore, coastal, and fresh water fisherman. It provides a how, when, and where approach in its articles, which also includes occasional camping, diving, and hunting stories—plus ecology; in-depth articles and editorials attempting to protect Florida's wilderness, wetlands, and natural beauty. Circ. 115,000. Byline given. Pays on acceptance. Publishes ms an average of 6 months after acceptance. Submit seasonal material 6 months in advance. Accepts queries by mail, e-mail. Responds in 2 months to queries. Responds in 1 month to mss. Sample copy free. Guidelines available at floridasportsman.com/submission_guidelines.

NONFICTION Needs essays, environment or nature, how-to, fishing, hunting, boating, humor, outdoors angle, personal experience, in fishing, etc., technical, boats, tackle, etc., as particularly suitable for Florida specialties. **Buys 40-60 mss/year.** Query. Length: 1,500-2,500 words. **Pays $475.**

PHOTOS Send photos. Hi-res digital images on CD preferred. Reviews 35mm transparencies, 4×5 and larger prints. Offers no additional payment for photos accepted with ms. Pays up to $750 for cover photos.

✪✪ FLW OUTDOORS MAGAZINE

FLW Outdoors, 30 Gamble Lane, Benton KY 42025. E-mail: cmoore@flwoutdoors.com. Website: flwoutdoors.com. **Contact:** Colin Moore, editor. **40% freelance written**. Magazine published 8 times/year in 2 editions (16 magazines/year) covering bass and walleye. "*FLW Outdoors Magazine* caters to all anglers from beginning weekend anglers to hardcore professional anglers. Our magazine seeks to educate as well as entertain anglers with cutting-edge techniques and new product innovations being used by America's top fishermen." Estab. 1979. Circ. 100,000+. Byline given. Pays on acceptance. Publishes ms an average of 4 months after acceptance. Editorial lead time 5 months. Submit seasonal material 1 year in advance. Accepts queries by mail, e-mail. NoSample copy free. Guidelines free.

NONFICTION Needs how-to, new product, photo feature, technical, travel. Does not want me-and-Bubba-went-fishing type stories; stories about author's first trip to catch a certain type of fish; stories in the first person about catching a fish. **Buys 50-75 mss/year.** Query. Length: 2,000-2,500 words. **Pays $400-500.** Sometimes pays expenses of writers on assignment.

PHOTOS State availability. Captions required. Reviews contact sheets, GIF/JPEG files. Offers $50-200/photo.

COLUMNS Destinations; Environment; Boat Tech; Tackle Maintenance. **Buys 20-30 mss/year.** Query. **Pays $100-300.**

✪ FLY FISHERMAN MAGAZINE

6405 Flank Dr., Harrisburg PA 17112. (717)540-6704. Fax: (717)657-9552. Website: flyfisherman.com. Published 6 times/year covering fly fishing. Written for anglers who fish primarily with a fly rod and for other anglers who would like to learn more about fly fishing. Circ. 120,358.

✪✪ FUR-FISH-GAME

2878 E. Main St., Columbus OH 43209-9947. E-mail: ffgcox@ameritech.net. Website: furfishgame.com. **Contact:** Mitch Cox, editor. **65% freelance written**. Monthly magazine for outdoorsmen of all ages who are interested in hunting, fishing, trapping, dogs, camping, conservation, and related topics. Estab. 1900. Circ. 111,000. Byline given. Pays on acceptance. Publishes ms an average of 7 months after acceptance. Responds in 2 months to queries. Sample copy for $1 and 9×12 SAE. Guidelines for #10 SASE.

NONFICTION Query. Length: 500-3,000 words. **Pays $50-250 or more for features depending upon quality, photo support, and importance to magazine.**

PHOTOS Send photos. Captions, True required. Reviews transparencies, color 5×7 or 8×100 prints, digital photos on CD only with thumbnail sheet of small images and a numbered caption sheet. Pays $35 for separate freelance photos.

✪✪ GAME & FISH

2250 Newmarket Pkwy., Suite 110, Marietta GA 30067. (770)953-9222. Fax: (770)933-9510. E-mail: ken.dunwoody@inoutdoors.com. Website: gameandfishmag.com. **90% freelance written**. Publishes 30 different monthly outdoor magazines, each one covering the fishing and hunting opportunities in a particular state or region (see individual titles to contact editors). Estab. 1975. Circ. 570,000. Byline given. Pays 3 months prior to cover date of issue. Offers negotiable kill fee. Publishes ms an average of 7 months after acceptance. Submit seasonal material 8 months in advance. Accepts queries by mail, e-mail, fax. Responds in 3 months to queries. Sample copy for $3.50 and 9×12 SASE. Guidelines for #10 SASE.

> "To query information regarding writing guidelines and submissions for any of our *Game & Fish* magazines, please contact Ken Dunwoody, Editorial Director - Game & Fish."

NONFICTION Length: 1,500-2,400 words. **Pays $150-300; additional payment made for electronic rights.**

PHOTOS Captions, identification of subjects required. Reviews transparencies, prints, digital images. Cover photos $250, inside color $75, and b&w $25.

✪✪ GEORGIA SPORTSMAN

Game & Fish, 2250 Newmarket Parkway, Suite 110, Marietta GA 30067. (770)953-9222. Fax: (770)933-9510. E-mail: Ken.Dunwoody@imoutdoors.com. Website: georgiasportsmanmag.com. **Contact:** Ken Dunwoody, editorial director. See *Game & Fish*

✚✪✪✪ GRAY'S SPORTING JOURNAL

Morris Communications Corp., 735 Broad St., Augusta GA 30901. (706)724-0851. E-mail: russ@lumpkin@morris.com. Website: grayssportingjournal.com. **75% freelance written**. 7 issues per year magazine High-end hunting and fishing—think *Field & Stream* meets *The New Yorker*. "We expect competent, vividly written prose—fact or fiction—that has high entertainment value for a very sophisticated audience of experienced hunters and anglers. We do not consider previously published material. We do, however, occasionally run prepublication book excerpts. To get a feel for what Gray's publishes, review several back issues. Note that we do not, as a rule, publish 'how-to' articles; this is the province of our regular columnists." Estab. 1975. Circ. 32,000. Byline given. Pays on publication. Publishes ms an average of 12 months after acceptance. Editorial lead time 14 months. Submit seasonal material 16 months in advance. Accepts simultaneous submissions. Responds in 3 months to mss. Guidelines available online.

NONFICTION Needs essays, historical, humor, personal experience, photo feature, travel. Special issues: Gray's publishes three themed issues each year: August is always entirely devoted to upland birdhunting; April to fly fishing; December to sporting travel. All other issues—February, May, September, November—focus on seasonally appropriate themes. Each issue always features a travel piece, from exotic destinations to right around the corner. We publish no how-to of any kind. **Buys 20-30 mss/year. mss/year.** Send complete ms. Length: 1,500-12,000 words. **Pays $600-1,000 for unsolicited articles.**

PHOTOS State availability. Reviews contact sheets, GIF/JPEG files. We negotiate payment individually.

FICTION Accepts quality fiction with some aspect of hunting or fishing at the core. Needs adventure, experimental, historical, humorous, slice-of-life vignettes. If some aspect of hunting or fishing isn't at the core of the story, it has zero chance of interesting Gray's. **Buys 20 mss/year mss/year.** Send complete ms. Length: 1,500-12,000 words. **Pays $600-1,000.**

POETRY Needs avant-garde, haiku, light verse, traditional. Buys 7/year poems/year. Submit maximum 3 poems. Length: 10-40 lines.

GREAT PLAINS GAME & FISH

Game & Fish, 2250 Newmarket Parkway, Suite 110, Marietta GA 30067. (770)953-9222. Fax: (770)933-9510. E-mail: Ken.Dunwoody@imoutdoors.com. Website: greatplainsgameandfish.com. **Contact:** Ken Dunwoody, editorial director. See *Game & Fish*

ILLINOIS GAME & FISH

Game & Fish, 2250 Newmarket Pkwy, Suite 110, Marietta GA 30067. (770)953-9222. Fax: (770)933-9510. E-mail: ken.dunwoody@inoutdoors.com. Website: illinoisgameandfish.com. **Contact:** Ken Dunwoody, editorial director. See *Game & Fish*

"To query information regarding writing guidelines and submissions for any of our *Game & Fish* magazines, please contact Ken Dunwoody, Editorial Director - Game & Fish."

INDIANA GAME & FISH

Game & Fish, 2250 Newmarket Pkwy, Suite 110, Marietta GA 30067. (770)953-9222. Fax: (770)933-9510. E-mail: ken.dunwoody@inoutdoors.com. Website: indianagameandfish.com. **Contact:** Ken Dunwoody, editorial director. See *Game & Fish*

"To query information regarding writing guidelines and submissions for any of our *Game & Fish* magazines, please contact Ken Dunwoody, Editorial Director - Game & Fish."

IOWA GAME & FISH

Game & Fish, 2250 Newmarket Pkwy, Suite 110, Marietta GA 30067. (770)953-9222. Fax: (770)933-9510. E-mail: ken.dunwoody@inoutdoors.com. Website: iowagameandfish.com. **Contact:** Ken Dunwoody, editorial director. See *Game & Fish*

"To query information regarding writing guidelines and submissions for any of our *Game & Fish* magazines, please contact Ken Dunwoody, Editorial Director - Game & Fish."

KENTUCKY GAME & FISH

Game & Fish, 2250 Newmarket Pkwy, Suite 110, Marietta GA 30067. (770)953-9222. Fax: (770)933-9510. E-mail: ken.dunwoody@inoutdoors.com. Website: kentuckygameandfish.com. **Contact:** Ken Dunwoody. See *Game & Fish*

"To query information regarding writing guidelines and submissions for any of our *Game & Fish* magazines, please contact Ken Dunwoody, Editorial Director - Game & Fish."

LOUISIANA GAME & FISH

Game & Fish, 2250 Newmarket Pkwy, Suite 110, Marietta GA 30067. (770)953-9222. Fax: (770)933-9510. E-mail: ken.dunwoody@inoutdoors.com. Website: lagameandfish.com. **Contact:** Ken Dunwoody. See *Game & Fish*

"To query information regarding writing guidelines and submissions for any of our *Game & Fish* magazines, please contact Ken Dunwoody, Editorial Director - Game & Fish."

$$ THE MAINE SPORTSMAN

183 State St., Augusta ME 04330. (207)622-4242. Fax: (207)622-4255. E-mail: harry@mainesportsman.com. Website: mainesportsman.com. **80% freelance written.** Monthly tabloid. "Eager to work with new/unpublished writers, but because we run over 30 regular columns, it's hard to get into *The Maine Sportsman* as a beginner." Estab. 1972. Circ. 30,000. Byline given. Pays during month of publication. Publishes ms an average of 3 months after acceptance. Accepts queries by mail, e-mail. Responds in 2 weeks to queries.

NONFICTION **Buys 25-40 mss/year.** Send complete ms via e-mail Length: 200-2,000 words. **Pays $20-300.** Sometimes pays expenses of writers on assignment.

REPRINTS , send typed ms via e-mail or query with rights for sale noted. Pays 100% of amount paid for an original article.

PHOTOS Send color slides, color prints, or JPGs/TIFFs via e-mail. Pays $5-50 for b&w print.

$$ MARLIN

P.O. Box 8500, Winter Park FL 32790. (407)628-4802. Fax: (407)628-7061. E-mail: dave.ferrell@bonniercorp.com. Website: marlinmag.com. **90% freelance written.** Magazine published 8 times/year covering the sport of big game fishing (billfish, tuna, dorado, and wahoo). Our readers are sophisticated, affluent, and serious about their sport—they expect a high-class, well-written magazine that provides information and practical advice. Estab. 1982. Circ. 50,000. Byline given. Pays on acceptance. Publishes ms an average of 3 months after acceptance. Submit seasonal material 3 months in advance. Sample copy free with SASE. Guidelines available online.

NONFICTION Needs general interest, how-to, bait-rigging, tackle maintenance, etc., new product, personal experience, photo feature, technical, travel. No freshwater fishing stories. No 'Me & Joe went fishing' stories. **Buys 30-50 mss/year.** Query with published clips. Length: 800-3,000 words. **Pays $250-500.**

REPRINTS Send photocopy and information about when and where the material previously appeared. Pays 50-75% of amount paid for original article.

PHOTOS State availability. Reviews original slides. Offers $50-300 for inside use, $1,000 for a cover.

COLUMNS Tournament Reports (reports on winners of major big game fishing tournaments), 200-400 words; Blue Water Currents (news features), 100-400 words. **Buys 25 mss/year.** Query. **Pays $75-250.**

$ MICHIGAN OUT-OF-DOORS

P.O. Box 30235, Lansing MI 48909. (517)371-1041. Fax: (517)371-1505. E-mail: magazine@mucc.org. Website: mucc.org. **75% freelance written.** Monthly magazine emphasizing Michigan hunting and fishing with associated conservation issues. Estab. 1947. Circ. 40,000. Byline given. Pays on acceptance. Publishes ms an average of 6 months after acceptance. Submit seasonal material 6 months in advance. Accepts queries by e-mail only. Responds in 1 month to queries. Sample copy for $3.50. Guidelines for free or on website.

NONFICTION Needs expose, historical, how-to, interview, opinion, personal experience, photo feature. All topics must pertain to hunting and fishing topics in Michigan. Special issues: Archery Deer and Small Game Hunting (October); Firearm Deer Hunting (November); Cross-country Skiing and Early-ice Lake Fishing (December or January); Camping/Hiking (May); Family Fishing (June). No humor or poetry. **Buys 96 mss/year.** Send complete ms. Length: 1,000-2,000 words. **Pays $150 minimum for feature stories. Photos must be included with story.**

PHOTOS Captions required. Offers no additional payment for photos accepted with ms; others $20-175.

$$ MICHIGAN SPORTSMAN

Game & Fish, 2250 Newmarket Parkway, Suite 110, Marietta GA 30067. (770)953-9222. Fax: (770)933-9510. E-mail: Ken.Dunwoody@imoutdoors.com. Website: michigansportsmanmag.com. **Contact:** Ken Dunwoody, editorial director. See *Game & Fish*

$$ MID-ATLANTIC GAME & FISH

Game & Fish, 2250 Newmarket Pkwy, Suite 110, Marietta GA 30067. (770)953-9222. Fax: (770)933-9510. Website: midatlanticgameandfish.com. See *Game & Fish*

💬 "To query information regarding writing guidelines and submissions for any of our *Game & Fish* magazines, please contact Ken Dunwoody, Editorial Director - Game & Fish."

$ MIDWEST OUTDOORS

MidWest Outdoors, Ltd., 111 Shore Dr., Burr Ridge IL 60527-5885. (630)887-7722. Fax: (630)887-1958. Website: midwestoutdoors.com. **100% freelance written.** Monthly tabloid emphasizing fishing, hunting, camping, and boating. Estab. 1967. Byline given. Pays on publication. Publishes ms an average of 3 months after acceptance. Submit seasonal material 2 months in advance. Accepts simultaneous submissions. Responds in 3 weeks to queries. Sample copy for $1 or online. Guidelines for #10 SASE or online.

💬"Submissions must be e-mailed to info@midwestoutdoors.com (Microsoft Word format preferred)."

NONFICTION Needs how-to, fishing, hunting, camping in the Midwest, where-to-go (fishing, hunting, camping within 500 miles of Chicago). "We do not want to see any articles on 'my first fishing, hunting, or camping experiences,' 'cleaning my tackle box,' 'tackle tune-up,' 'making fishing fun for kids,' or 'catch and release.'" **Buys 1,800 unsolicited mss/year.** Send complete ms. Length: 1,000-1,500 words. **Pays $15-30.**

PHOTOS Captions required. Reviews slides and b&w prints. Offers no additional payment for photos accompanying ms.

COLUMNS Fishing; Hunting. Send complete ms. **Pays $30.**

$$ MINNESOTA SPORTSMAN

Game & Fish, 2250 Newmarket Parkway, Suite 110, Marietta GA 30067. (770)953-9222. Fax: (770)933-9510. E-mail: Ken.Dunwoody@imoutdoors.com. Website: minnesotasportsmanmag.com. **Contact:** Ken Dunwoody, editorial director. See *Game & Fish*

$$ MISSISSIPPI GAME & FISH

Game & Fish, 2250 Newmarket Pkwy, Suite 110, Marietta GA 30067. (770)953-9222. Fax: (770)933-9510. E-mail: ken.dunwoody@inoutdoors.com. Website: mississippigameandfish.com. **Contact:** Ken Dunwoody. See *Game & Fish*

💬"To query information regarding writing guidelines and submissions for any of our *Game & Fish* magazines, please contact Ken Dunwoody, Editorial Director - Game & Fish."

$$ MISSOURI GAME & FISH

Game & Fish, 2250 Newmarket Parkway, Suite 110, Marietta GA 30067. (770)953-9222. Fax: (678)279-7512. E-mail: Ken.Dunwoody@imoutdoors.com; nick.gilmore@Imoutdoors.com. Website: missourigameandfish.com. **Contact:** Nick Gilmore, editor; Ken Dunwoody, editorial director. See *Game & Fish*

$$ MUSKY HUNTER MAGAZINE

P.O. Box 340, 7978 Hwy. 70 E., St. Germain WI 54558. (715)477-2178. Fax: (715)477-8858. E-mail: editor@muskyhunter.com. Website: muskyhunter.com. **Contact:** Jim Saric, editor. **90% freelance written.** Bimonthly magazine on musky fishing. Serves the vertical market of musky fishing enthusiasts. We're interested in how-to, where-to articles. Estab. 1988. Circ. 37,000. Byline given. Pays on publication. Publishes ms an average of 4 months after acceptance. Submit seasonal material 4 months in advance. Responds in 2 months to queries. Sample copy for 9×12 SAE with $2.79 postage. Guidelines for #10 SASE.

NONFICTION Needs historical, related only to musky fishing, how-to, catch muskies, modify lures, boats, and tackle for musky fishing, personal experience, must be musky fishing experience, technical, fishing equipment, travel, to lakes and areas for musky fishing. **Buys 50 mss/year.** Send complete ms. Length: 1,000-2,500 words. **Pays $100-300 for assigned articles. Pays $50-300 for unsolicited articles.**

PHOTOS Send photos. Identification of subjects required. Reviews 35mm transparencies, 3×5 prints, high resolution digital images preferred. Offers no additional payment for photos accepted with ms.

$$ NEW ENGLAND GAME & FISH

Game & Fish, 2250 Newmarket Pkwy, Suite 110, Marietta GA 30067. (770)953-9222. Fax: (770)933-9510. E-mail: ken.dunwoody@inoutdoors.com. Website: newenglandgameandfish.com. See *Game & Fish*

💬"To query information regarding writing guidelines and submissions for any of our *Game & Fish* magazines, please contact Ken Dunwoody, Editorial Director - Game & Fish."

$$ NEW YORK GAME & FISH

Game & Fish, 2250 Newmarket Pkwy, Suite 110, Marietta GA 30067. (770)953-9222. Fax: (770)933-9510. E-mail: ken.dunwoody@inoutdoors.com. Website: newyorkgameandfish.com. **Contact:** Ken Dunwoody, editorial director. See *Game & Fish*

💬"To query information regarding writing guidelines and submissions for any of our *Game & Fish* magazines, please contact Ken Dunwoody, Editorial Director - Game & Fish."

$$ NORTH AMERICAN WHITETAIL

Game & Fish, 2250 Newmarket Pkwy., Suite 110, Marietta GA 30067. (770)953-9222. Fax: (770)933-9510. Website: northamericanwhitetail.com. **70% freelance written.** Magazine published 8 times/year about hunting trophy-class white-tailed deer in North America, primarily the US. We provide the serious hunter with highly sophisticated information about trophy-class whitetails and how, when, and where to hunt them. We are not a general hunting magazine or a magazine for the very occasional deer hunter. Estab. 1982. Circ. 150,000. Byline given. Pays 65 days prior to cover date of issue. Offers negotiable kill fee. Publishes ms an average of 6 months after acceptance. Submit seasonal material 10 months in advance. Accepts queries by mail, e-mail, phone. Responds in 3 months to mss. Sample copy for $3.50 and 9×12 SAE with 7 first-class stamps. Guidelines for #10 SASE.

NONFICTION Needs how-to, interview. **Buys 50 mss/year.** Query. Length: 1,000-3,000 words. **Pays $150-400.**

PHOTOS Send photos. Captions, identification of subjects required. Reviews 35mm transparencies, color prints, high quality digital images. Offers no additional payment for photos accepted with ms.

COLUMNS Trails and Tails (nostalgic, humorous, or other entertaining styles of deer-hunting material, fictional or nonfictional), 1,200 words. **Buys 8 mss/year.** Send complete ms. **Pays $150.**

NORTH CAROLINA GAME & FISH

Game & Fish, 2250 Newmarket Pkwy, Suite 110, Marietta GA 30067. (770)953-9222. Fax: (770)933-9510. E-mail: ken.dunwoody@inoutdoors.com. Website: ncgameandfish.com. **Contact:** Ken Dunwoody. See *Game & Fish*

"To query information regarding writing guidelines and submissions for any of our *Game & Fish* magazines, please contact Ken Dunwoody, Editorial Director - Game & Fish."

OHIO GAME & FISH

Game & Fish, 2250 Newmarket Pkwy, Suite 110, Marietta GA 30067. (770)953-9222. Fax: (770)933-9510. E-mail: ken.dunwoody@inoutdoors.com. Website: ohiogameandfish.com. **Contact:** Ken Dunwoody. See *Game & Fish*

"To query information regarding writing guidelines and submissions for any of our *Game & Fish* magazines, please contact Ken Dunwoody, Editorial Director - Game & Fish."

OKLAHOMA GAME & FISH

Game & Fish, 2250 Newmarket Pkwy, Suite 110, Marietta GA 30067. (770)953-9222. Fax: (770)933-9510. E-mail: ken.dunwoody@inoutdoors.com. Website: oklahomagameandfish.com. **Contact:** Ken Dunwoody. See *Game & Fish*

"To query information regarding writing guidelines and submissions for any of our *Game & Fish* magazines, please contact Ken Dunwoody, Editorial Director - Game & Fish."

ONTARIO OUT OF DOORS

Ontario Federation of Anglers and Hunters, P.O. Box 8500, Peterborough ON K9J 0B4 Canada. (705)748-0076. Fax: (705)748-9577. Website: ontariooutdoors.com. **Contact:** John Kerr, editor-in-chief. **80% freelance written.** Magazine published 10 times/year covering the outdoors (hunting, fishing). Estab. 1968. Circ. 93,865. Byline given. Pays on acceptance. Publishes ms an average of 6 months after acceptance. Editorial lead time 1 year. Submit seasonal material 2 months in advance. Accepts queries by mail, e-mail, fax. Responds in 3 months to queries. Writer's guidelines free.

NONFICTION Needs interview, opinion, technical, travel, wildlife management. No 'Me and Joe' features. **Buys 100 mss/year.** Length: 500-2,500 words. **Pays $950 maximum for assigned articles.**

FICTION Pays $500 maximum.

THE OUTDOORS MAGAZINE

Elk Publishing, Inc., 531 Main St., Colchester VT 05446. (802)879-2013. Fax: (802)879-2015. E-mail: kyle@elkpublishing.com. Website: outdoorsmagazine.net. **Contact:** Kyle Scanlon, editor. **80% freelance written.** Monthly magazine covering wildlife conservation. Northeast hunting, fishing, and trapping magazine covering news, tips, destinations, and good old-fashioned stories. Estab. 1996. Circ. 20,000. Byline given. Pays on publication. Offers 10% kill fee. Publishes ms an average of 1 year after acceptance. Editorial lead time 1 year. Submit seasonal material 6 months in advance. Accepts queries by mail. Responds in 1 month to queries. Responds in 3 month to mss. Sample copy online or by e-mail. Guidelines free.

NONFICTION Needs book excerpts, essays, expose, general interest, historical, how-to, interview, new product, opinion, personal experience, technical. **Buys 200 mss/year.** Query with published clips. Length: 750-2,500 words. **Pays $20-150 for assigned articles.**

PHOTOS State availability. Identification of subjects required. Reviews contact sheets. Pays $15-75/photo.

COLUMNS **Buys 100 mss/year.** Query with published clips. **Pays $20-60.**

FILLERS Needs anecdotes, facts.

⊘$$ PENNSYLVANIA ANGLER & BOATER

Pennsylvania Fish & Boat Commission, P.O. Box 67000, Harrisburg PA 17106-7000. (717)705-7835. E-mail: ra-pfbcmagazine@state.pa.us. Website: fish.state.pa.us. **40% freelance written.** Bimonthly magazine covering fishing, boating, and related conservation topics in Pennsylvania. Circ. 28,000. Byline given. Pays 2 months after acceptance. Publishes ms an average of 8 months after acceptance. Submit seasonal material 8 months in advance. Responds in 1 month to queries. Responds in 2 months to mss. Sample copy for 9×12 SAE with 9 first-class stamps. Guidelines for #10 SASE.

○ No unsolicited mss.

NONFICTION Needs how-to, and where-to, technical. No saltwater or hunting material. **Buys 75 mss/year.** Query. Length: 500-2,500 words. **Pays $25-300.**

PHOTOS Send photos. Captions, identification of subjects, model releases required. Reviews 35mm and larger transparencies, hi-res digital submissions on CD (preferred). Offers no additional payment for photos accompanying mss.

$$ PENNSYLVANIA GAME & FISH

Game & Fish, 2250 Newmarket Parkway, Suite 110, Marietta GA 30067. (770)953-9222. Fax: (770)933-9510. E-mail: Ken.Dunwoody@imoutdoors.com. Website: pagameandfish.com. **Contact:** Ken Dunwoody. See *Game & Fish*

$$ RACK MAGAZINE

Buckmasters, Ltd., 10350 U.S. Hwy. 80 E., Montgomery AL 36117. (800)240-3337. Fax: (334)215-3535. E-mail: mhandley@buckmasters.com. Website: buckmasters.com. **50% freelance written.** Monthly, July-December magazine covering big game hunting. "All features are either first- or third-person narratives detailing the successful hunts for world-class, big game animals—mostly white-tailed deer and other North American species." Estab. 1998. Circ. 75,000. Byline given. Pays on publication. Publishes ms an average of 9 months after acceptance. Editorial lead time 9-12 months. Submit seasonal material 9 months in advance. Accepts queries by e-mail. Accepts simultaneous submissions. Responds in 1 month to queries. Responds in 2 months to mss. Sample copy free. Guidelines free.

NONFICTION Needs personal experience. "We're interested only in articles chronicling successful hunts." **Buys 40-50 mss/year.** Query. Length: 1,000 words. **Pays $100-325 for assigned and unsolicited articles.**

PHOTOS Send photos. Captions, identification of subjects required. Reviews transparencies, prints, GIF/JPEG files.

$$ ROCKY MOUNTAIN GAME & FISH

Game & Fish, 2250 Newmarket Parkway, Suite 110, Marietta GA 30067. (770)935-9222. Fax: (770)933-9510. E-mail: Ken.Dunwoody@imoutdoors.com. Website: rmgameandfish.com. **Contact:** Ken Dunwoody, editorial director. See *Game & Fish*

$$ SALT WATER SPORTSMAN MAGAZINE

Bonnier Corporation, 460 N. Orlando Ave., Suite 200, Winter Park FL 32789. (407)628-4802. E-mail: john.brownlee@bonniecorp.com. Website: saltwatersportsman.com. **85% freelance written.** Monthly magazine. *Salt Water Sportsman* is edited for serious marine sport fishermen whose lifestyle includes the pursuit of game fish in US waters and around the world. It provides information on fishing trends, techniques, and destinations, both local and international. Each issue reviews offshore and inshore fishing boats, high-tech electronics, innovative tackle, engines, and other new products. Coverage also focuses on sound fisheries management and conservation. Circ. 170,000. Byline given. Pays on acceptance. Offers kill fee. Publishes ms an average of 5 months after acceptance. Submit seasonal material 8 months in advance. Accepts queries by mail, e-mail, fax. Responds in 1 month to queries. Sample copy for #10 SASE. Guidelines available online.

NONFICTION Needs how-to, personal experience, technical, travel, to fishing areas. **Buys 100 mss/year.** Query. Length: 1,200-2,000 words. **Pays $300-750.**

REPRINTS Send tearsheet. Pays up to 50% of amount paid for original article.

PHOTOS Captions required. Reviews color slides. Pays $1,500 minimum for 35mm, 2 ¼×2 ¼ or 8×10 transparencies for cover.

COLUMNS Sportsman's Tips (short, how-to tips and techniques on salt water fishing, emphasis is on building, repairing, or reconditioning specific items or gear). Send complete ms.

$$ SOUTH CAROLINA GAME & FISH

Game & Fish, 2250 Newmarket Pkwy, Suite 110, Marietta GA 30067. (770)953-9222. Fax: (770)933-9510. E-mail: ken.dunwoody@inoutdoors.com. Website: scgameandfish.com. **Contact:** Ken Dunwoody. See *Game & Fish*

💬"To query information regarding writing guidelines and submissions for any of our *Game & Fish* magazines, please contact Ken Dunwoody, Editorial Director - Game & Fish."

$$$$ SPORT FISHING

World Publications, Bonnier Corporation, 460 N. Orlando Ave., Suite 200, Winter Park FL 32789. (407)628-4802. Fax: (407)628-7061. E-mail: missie.prichard@bonniercorp.com. Website: sportfishingmag.com. **50% freelance written**. Magazine published 10 times/year covering saltwater angling, saltwater fish and fisheries. "*Sport Fishing*'s readers are middle-aged, affluent, mostly male, who are generally proficient in and very educated to their sport. We are about fishing from boats, not from surf or jetties." Estab. 1985. Circ. 250,000. Byline given. Pays on acceptance. Offers 25% kill fee. Publishes ms an average of 6-12 months after acceptance. Editorial lead time 2-12 months. Submit seasonal material 1 year in advance. Accepts queries by e-mail. Responds in 1 week to queries. Responds in 1 month to mss. Sample copy for #10 SASE. Guidelines available online.

NONFICTION Needs general interest, how-to. Query. Length: 2,500-3,000 words. **Pays $500-750 for text only; $1,500+ possible for complete package with photos.** Answer.

PHOTOS State availability. Reviews GIF/JPEG files. Offers $75-400/photo.

$$$ SPORTS AFIELD

Field Sports Publishing, 15621 Chemical Lane, Ste. B, Huntington Beach CA 92649. (714)373-4910. E-mail: letters@sportsafield.com. Website: sportsafield.com. **60% freelance written**. Magazine published 6 times/year covering big game hunting. "We cater to the upscale hunting market, especially hunters who travel to exotic destinations like Alaska and Africa. We are not a deer hunting magazine, and we do not cover fishing." Estab. 1887. Circ. 50,000. Byline given. Pays 1 month prior to publication. Publishes ms an average of 6 months after acceptance. Editorial lead time 4 months. Submit seasonal material 5 months in advance. Accepts queries by mail, e-mail. Responds in 2 months to queries and to mss Sample copy for $7.99. Guidelines available online.

NONFICTION Needs personal experience, travel. **Buys 6-8 mss/year.** Query. Length: 1,500-2,500 words. **Pays $500-800.**

PHOTOS Contact: Jerry Gutierrez, art director. State availability. Captions, model releases required. Reviews 35mm slides transparencies, TIFF/JPEG files. Offers no additional payment for photos accepted with ms.

FILLERS Needs newsbreaks. **Buys 30 mss/year.** Length: 200-500 words. **Pays $75-150.**

$$ TENNESSEE SPORTSMAN

Game & Fish, 2250 Newmarket Parkway, Suite 110, Marietta GA 30067. (770)953-9222. Fax: **(678) 279-7512.** E-mail: **E-mail editor: jimmy.jacobs@IMoutdoors.com; Editorial Director: ken.dunwoody@IMoutdoors.com**. Website: tennesseesportsmanmag.com. See *Game & Fish*

$$ TEXAS SPORTSMAN

Game & Fish, 2250 Newmarket Parkway, Suite 110, Marietta GA 30067. (770)953-9222. Fax: (770)933-9510. E-mail: Ken.Dunwoody@imoutdoors.com. Website: texassportsmanmag.com. **Contact:** Ken Dunwoody, editorial director. See *Game & Fish*

$$ TRAPPER & PREDATOR CALLER

F+W Media, Inc., 700 E. State St., Iola WI 54990. (715)445-2214. E-mail: jared.blohm@fwmedia.com. Website: trapperpredatorcaller.com. **75% freelance written**. Tabloid published 10 times/year covering trapping and predator calling, fur trade. "Must have mid-level to advanced knowledge, because *T&PC* is heavily how-to focused." Estab. 1975. Circ. 42,000. Byline given. Pays on publication. Publishes ms an average of 6 months after acceptance. Editorial lead time 1 year. Submit seasonal material 1 year in advance. Accepts queries by e-mail.

NONFICTION Needs how-to, interview, personal experience, travel. **Buys 100 mss/year.** Send complete ms. Length: 1,500-2,500 words. **Pays $250 for assigned articles.**

PHOTOS Send photos. Reviews negatives, prints.

$$ TURKEY & TURKEY HUNTING

a Division of F+W Media, Inc., 700 E. State St., Iola WI 54990-0001. (715)445-4612. E-mail: brian.lovett@

fwmedia.com. Website: turkeyandturkeyhunting. com. **Contact:** Brian Lovett. **50% freelance written**. Bimonthly magazine filled with practical and comprehensive information for wild turkey hunters. Estab. 1982. Circ. 40,000. Byline given. Pays on acceptance. Offers 50% kill fee. Publishes ms an average of 8 months after acceptance. Editorial lead time 1 year. Submit seasonal material 1 year in advance. Accepts queries by mail, e-mail. Responds in 1 month to queries. Responds in 6 months to mss. Sample copy for $4. Ms and photo guidelines online.

NONFICTION Does not want Me and Joe went hunting and here's what happened articles. **Buys 20 mss/ year.** Send complete ms. Length: 1,500-2,500 words. **Pays $275-400.**

PHOTOS Contact: Contact Editor before sending photos. Send photos. Identification of subjects required. Reviews 2 X 2 transparencies, any size prints, digital images with contact sheets. Offers $75-200/ photo. Negotiates payment individually.

💲💲 TURKEY COUNTRY

National Wild Turkey Federation, P.O. Box 530, Edgefield SC 29824-0530. (803)637-3106. Fax: (803)637-0034. E-mail: info@nwtf.net; turkeycountry@nwtf. net. E-mail: klee@nwtf.net. Website: turkeycountrymagazine.com. Gregg Powers, managing editor; P.J. Perea, senior editor; photo editor, Matt Lindler. **Contact:** Karen Lee, editor. **50-60% freelance written.** "Bimonthly educational magazine for members of the National Wild Turkey Federation. Topics covered include hunting, history, restoration, management, biology, and distribution of wild turkey." Estab. 1973. Circ. 180,000. Byline given. Pays on acceptance. Publishes ms an average of 6 months after acceptance. Editorial lead time 1 year. Accepts queries by mail, e-mail. Responds in 2 months to queries Sample copy for $3 and 9×12 SAE. Guidelines available online.

💭 Submit queries by June 1 of each year.

NONFICTION Query (preferred) or send complete ms. Length: 700-2,500 words. **Pays $100 for short fillers; $200-500 for features.**

PHOTOS "We want quality photos submitted with features. Illustrations also acceptable. We are using more and more inside color illustrations. No typical hunter-holding-dead-turkey photos or setups using mounted birds or domestic turkeys. Photos with how-to stories must make the techniques clear (i.e., how to make a turkey call; how to sculpt or carve a bird

in wood).". Identification of subjects, model releases required. Reviews transparencies, high resolution digital images.

FICTION Must contribute to the education, enlightenment, or entertainment of readers in some special way.

💲💲 VIRGINIA GAME & FISH

Game & Fish, 2250 Newmarket Pkwy, Suite 110, Marietta GA 30067. (770)953-9222. Fax: (770)933-9510. E-mail: ken.dunwoody@inoutdoors.com. Website: virginiagameandfish.com. **Contact:** Ken Dunwoody. See *Game & Fish*

💭 "To query information regarding writing guidelines and submissions for any of our *Game & Fish* magazines, please contact Ken Dunwoody, Editorial Director - Game & Fish."

💲💲 WASHINGTON-OREGON GAME & FISH

Game & Fish, 2250 Newmarket Pkwy, Suite 110, Marietta GA 30067. (770)953-9222. Fax: (770)933-9510. E-mail: ken.dunwoody@inoutdoors.com. Website: wogameandfish.com. **Contact:** Ken Dunwoody. See *Game & Fish*

💭 "To query information regarding writing guidelines and submissions for any of our *Game & Fish* magazines, please contact Ken Dunwoody, Editorial Director - Game & Fish."

💲💲 WEST VIRGINIA GAME & FISH

Game & Fish, 2250 Newmarket Parkway, Suite 110, Marietta GA 30067. (770)953-9222. Fax: (770)933-9510. E-mail: ken.dunwoody@imoutdoors.com. Website: wvgameandfish.com. **Contact:** Jimmy Jacobs, Editor. "This is the ultimate resource for West Virginia outdoor enthusiasts that are passionate about hunting, shooting and fishing." Pays kill fee.

💲💲 WISCONSIN SPORTSMAN

Game & Fish, 2250 Newmarket Parkway, Suite 110, Marietta GA 30067. (770)953-9222. Fax: (770)933-9510. E-mail: Ken.Dunwoody@imoutdoors.com. Website: wisconsinsportsmanmag.com. **Contact:** Ken Dunwoody, editorial director. See *Game & Fish*

MARTIAL ARTS

💲💲 BLACK BELT

Black Belt Communications, LLC, 24900 Anza Dr., Unit E, Valencia CA 91355. Fax: (661)257-3028. E-mail: byoung@aimmedia.com. Website: blackbelt-mag.com. **Contact:** Robert Young, executive editor. **80% freelance written. Works with a small number of new/unpublished writers each year.** Monthly magazine emphasizing martial arts for both experienced practitioner and layman. Estab. 1961. Circ. 100,000. Pays on publication. Publishes ms an average of 1 year after acceptance. Accepts queries by mail, e-mail, fax. Accepts simultaneous submissions. Responds in 3 weeks to queries. Guidelines available online.

NONFICTION Needs expose, how-to, interview, new product, personal experience, technical, travel, Informational. We never use personality profiles. **Buys 40-50 mss/year.** Query with outline 1,200 words minimum. **Pays $100-300.**

PHOTOS Very seldom buys photographs without accompanying ms. Captions, model releases required. Total purchase price for ms includes payment for photos.

➕❸❸ JOURNAL OF ASIAN MARTIAL ARTS

Via Media Publishing Co., 941 Calle Mejia, #822, Santa Fe NM 87501. (505)983-1919. E-mail: info@goviamedia.com. Website: goviamedia.com. **90% freelance written.** "Quarterly magazine covering all historical and cultural aspects related to Asian martial arts, offering a mature, well-rounded view of this uniquely fascinating subject. Although the journal treats the subject with academic accuracy (references at end), writing need not lose the reader!". Estab. 1991. Circ. 10,000. Byline given. Pays on publication. Publishes ms an average of 1 year after acceptance. Submit seasonal material 6 months in advance. Responds in 1 month to queries. Responds in 2 months to mss. Sample copy for $10. Guidelines for #10 SASE or online.

NONFICTION Needs essays, expose, historical, how-to, martial art techniques and materials, e.g., weapons, interview, personal experience, photo feature, place or person, religious, technical, travel. No articles overburdened with technical/foreign/scholarly vocabulary, or material slanted as indirect advertising or for personal aggrandizement. **Buys 30 mss/year.** Query with short background and martial arts experience. Length: 1,000-10,000 words. **Pays $150-500.**

PHOTOS State availability. Identification of subjects, model releases required. Reviews contact sheets, negatives, transparencies, prints. Offers no additional payment for photos accepted with ms.

COLUMNS Location (city, area, specific site, Asian or non-Asian, showing value for martial arts, researchers, history); Media Review (film, book, video, museum for aspects of academic and artistic interest). Length: 1,000-2,500 words. **Buys 16 mss/year.** Query. **Pays $50-200.**

FICTION Needs adventure, historical, humorous, slice-of-life vignettes, translation. No material that does not focus on martial arts culture. **Buys 1 mss/year.** Query. Length: 1,000-10,000 words. **Pays $50-500, or copies.**

POETRY Needs avant-garde, free verse, haiku, light verse, traditional. No poetry that does not focus on martial arts culture. Buys 2 poems/year. Submit maximum 10 poems. **Pays $10-100, or copies.**

FILLERS Needs anecdotes, facts, gags, newsbreaks, short humor. **Buys 2 mss/year.** Length: 25-500 words. **Pays $1-50, or copies.**

❸ KUNG FU TAI CHI

Pacific Rim Publishing, 40748 Encyclopedia Circle, Fremont CA 94538. (510)656-5100. Fax: (510)656-8844. E-mail: gene@kungfumagazine.com. Website: kungfumagazine.com. **70% freelance written.** Bimonthly magazine covering Chinese martial arts and culture. "*Kung Fu Tai Chi* covers the full range of Kung Fu culture, including healing, philosophy, meditation, Fengshui, Buddhism, Taoism, history, and the latest events in art and culture, plus insightful features on the martial arts." Circ. 15,000. Byline given. Pays on publication. Editorial lead time 4 months. Submit seasonal material 4 months in advance. Accepts queries by mail, e-mail, fax, phone. Responds in 2 months to queries. Responds in 3 months to mss. Sample copy for $4.99 or online. Guidelines available online.

NONFICTION Needs general interest, historical, interview, personal experience, religious, technical, travel, cultural perspectives. No poetry or fiction. **Buys 70 mss/year.** Query. Length: 500-2,500 words. **Pays $35-125.**

PHOTOS Send photos. Captions, identification of subjects required. Reviews 5×7 prints, GIF/JPEG files. Offers no additional payment for photos accepted with ms.

❸❸ T'AI CHI

Wayfarer Publications, P.O. Box 39938, Los Angeles CA 90039. (323)665-7773. Fax: (323)665-1627. E-mail: taichi@tai-chi.com. Website: tai-chi.com. **Contact:**

Marvin Smalheiser, Editor. **90% freelance written**. Quarterly magazine covering T'ai Chi Ch'uan as a martial art and for health and fitness. "Covers T'ai Chi Ch'uan and other internal martial arts, plus qigong and Chinese health, nutrition, and philosophical disciplines. Readers are practitioners or laymen interested in developing skills and insight for self-defense, health, and self-improvement." Estab. 1977. Circ. 50,000. Byline given. Pays on publication. Publishes ms an average of 3 months after acceptance. Editorial lead time 3 months. Submit seasonal material 6 months in advance. Accepts queries by mail, e-mail, fax. Responds in 3 weeks to queries. Responds in 3 months to mss. Sample copy for $5.99. Guidelines available online.

NONFICTION Needs essays, how-to, on T'ai Chi Ch'uan, qigong, and related Chinese disciplines, interview, personal experience. "Do not want articles promoting an individual, system, or school." Send complete ms. Length: 1,200-4,500 words. **Pays $75-500.**

PHOTOS Send photos. Captions, identification of subjects, model releases required. Reviews color or b&w 4×6 or 5×7 prints, digital files suitable for print production. "Offers no additional payment for photos accepted with ms, but overall payment takes into consideration the number and quality of photos.".

✪ⓈⓈ ULTIMATE MMA

Apprise Media, 2400 E. Katella Ave., Suite 300, Anaheim CA 92806. (714)939-9991. Fax: (714)939-9909. E-mail: djeffrey@beckett.com. Website: ultimatemmamg.com. Monthly magazine covering mixed martial arts, grappling. "We are interested in anything and everything about mixed martial arts.lifestyle to events to training to strategy." Estab. 2,000. Byline given. Pays on publication. Offers 20% kill fee. Publishes ms an average of 1-3 months after acceptance. Editorial lead time 3 months. Submit seasonal material 3 months in advance. Accepts queries by mail, e-mail. Responds in 2 months to mss. Sample copy free. Guidelines free.

NONFICTION Needs book excerpts, expose, general interest, historical, how-to, inspirational, interview, new product, personal experience, photo feature, technical. **Buys 30 mss/year mss/year.** Query. Length: 500-1,500 words. **Pays $150-500 for assigned articles. Pays $150-500 for unsolicited articles.** Sometimes pays expenses of writers on assignment.

COLUMNS Beyond Fighting (lifestyle of fighters); Exercises to bolster MMA game and general fitness.

Buys 30 mss/year mss/year. Query.

MISCELLANEOUS SPORTS

Ⓢ ACTION PURSUIT GAMES

Beckett Media, 2400 E. Katella Ave., Suite 300, Anaheim CA 92806. (714)939-9991. E-mail: editor@actionpursuitgames.com. E-mail: bryansullivanapg@gmail.com; liisa.sullivan@verizon.net. Website: actionpursuitgames.com. Editors Bryan Sullivan and Liisa Sullivan. **Contact:** Daniel Reeves, editor. **60% freelance written**. Monthly magazine covering paintball. Estab. 1987. Circ. 85,000. Byline given. Pays on publication. Publishes ms an average of 2 months after acceptance. Editorial lead time 3 months. Submit seasonal material 6 months in advance. Accepts queries by e-mail. Sample copy for sae with 9×12 envelope and 5 First-Class stamps. Guidelines available online.

NONFICTION Needs essays, expose, general interest, historical, how-to, humor, interview, new product, opinion, personal experience, technical, travel, all paintball-related. No sexually oriented material **Buys 100+ mss/year.** Length: 500-1,000 words. **Pays $100.** Sometimes pays expenses of writers on assignment.

PHOTOS Send photos. Captions, identification of subjects, model releases required. Reviews transparencies, prints. Negotiates payment individually.

COLUMNS Guest Commentary, 400 words; TNT (tournament news), 500-800 words; Young Guns, 300 words; Scenario Game Reporting, 300-500 words. **Buys 24 mss/year. Pays $100.**

FICTION Needs adventure, historical, must be paintball related. **Buys 1-2 mss/year.** Send complete ms. Length: 500 words. **Pays $100.**

POETRY Needs avant-garde, free verse, haiku, light verse, traditional. Buys 1-2 poems/year. Submit maximum 1 poems. Length: 20 lines.

FILLERS Needs anecdotes, gags. **Buys 2-4 mss/year.** Length: 20-50 words. **Pays $25.**

ⓈⓈ AMERICAN CHEERLEADER

Macfadden Performing Arts Media LLC, 110 William St., 23rd Floor, New York NY 10038. (646)459-4800. Fax: (646)459-4900. E-mail: mwalker@americancheerleader.com; acmail@americancheerleader.com. Website: americancheerleader.com. **30% freelance written**. Bimonthly magazine covering high school, college, and competitive cheerleading. We try to keep a young, informative voice for all articles—'for cheerleaders, by cheerleaders.' Estab. 1995. Circ. 200,000. Byline given. Pays on publication. Offers 25% kill fee. Publishes ms an average of 4 months after acceptance. Editorial lead time 3 months. Submit seasonal material 4 months in advance. Accepts queries by mail, e-mail, online submission form. Responds in 4 weeks to queries. Responds in 2 months to mss. Sample copy for $2.95. Guidelines free.

NONFICTION Needs how-to, cheering techniques, routines, pep songs, etc., interview, celebrities and media personalities who cheered. Special issues: Tryouts (April); Camp Basics (June); College (October); Competition (December). No professional cheerleading stories, i.e., no Dallas Cowboy cheerleaders. **Buys 12-16 mss/year.** Query with published clips. Length: 400-1,500 words. **Pays $100-250 for assigned articles. Pays $100 maximum for unsolicited articles.** Sometimes pays expenses of writers on assignment.

PHOTOS State availability. Model releases required. Reviews transparencies, 5×7 prints. Offers $50/photo.

COLUMNS Gameday Beauty (skin care, celeb how-tos), 600 words; Health & Fitness (teen athletes), 1,000 words; Profiles (winning squads), 1,000 words. **Buys 12 mss/year.** Query with published clips. **Pays $100-250.**

$$$ ATV MAGAZINE/ATV SPORT

Ehlert Publishing, 6420 Sycamore Lane, Maple Grove MN 55369. Fax: (763)383-4499. E-mail: jprusak@affinitygroup.com. Website: atvmagonline.com; atvsport.com. **Contact:** John Prusak, editor. **20% freelance written.** Bimonthly magazine covering all-terrain vehicles. Devoted to covering all the things ATV owners enjoy, from hunting to racing, farming to trail riding. Byline given. Pays on magazine shipment to printer. Editorial lead time 6 months. Accepts queries by mail, e-mail, fax. Responds in 3 weeks to queries. Sample copy and writer's guidelines for #10 SASE.

NONFICTION Needs how-to, interview, new product, personal experience, photo feature, technical, travel. **Buys 15-20 mss/year.** Query with published clips. Length: 200-2,000 words. **Pays $100-1,000.** Sometimes pays expenses of writers on assignment.

PHOTOS State availability. Captions, identification of subjects required. Negotiates payment individually.

🍁$ CANADIAN RODEO NEWS

Canadian Rodeo News, Ltd., 272245 RR 2, Airdrie AB T4A 2L5 Canada. (403)945-7393. Fax: (403)945-0936. E-mail: editor@rodeocanada.com. Website: rodeocanada.com. **80% freelance written.** Monthly tabloid covering Canada's professional rodeo (CPRA) personalities and livestock. Read by rodeo participants and fans. Estab. 1964. Circ. 4,000. Byline given. Pays on publication. Publishes ms an average of 1 month after acceptance. Editorial lead time 1 month. Submit seasonal material 1 month in advance. Accepts queries by mail, e-mail, fax. Accepts simultaneous submissions. Responds in 1 month to queries. Responds in 2 months to mss.

NONFICTION Needs general interest, historical, interview. **Buys 70-80 mss/year.** Query. Length: 400-1,200 words. **Pays $30-60.**

REPRINTS Send photocopy of article or typed ms with rights for sale noted and information about when and where the material previously appeared. Pays 100% of amount paid for an original article.

PHOTOS Send photos. Reviews digital only. Offers $15-25/cover photo.

$ FANTASY SPORTS

F+W Media, Inc., 700 E. State St., Iola WI 54990-0001. (715)445-2214. Fax: (715)445-4087. Website: fantasysportsmag.com. **10% freelance written.** Quarterly magazine covering fantasy baseball and football. Fantasy advice—how-to win. Estab. 1989. Circ. 100,000. Byline given. Pays on publication. Offers negotiable kill fee. Publishes ms an average of 3 months after acceptance. Editorial lead time 4 months. Submit seasonal material 4 months in advance. Accepts queries by e-mail. Sample copy free.

$$ FENCERS QUARTERLY MAGAZINE

848 S. Kimbrough, Springfield MO 65806. (417)866-4370. E-mail: editor@fencersquarterly.com. Website: fencersquarterly.com. **60% freelance written.** Quarterly magazine covering fencing, fencers, history of sword/fencing/dueling, modern techniques and systems, controversies, personalities of fencing, personal experience. This is a publication for all fencers and those interested in fencing; we favor the grassroots level rather than the highly-promoted elite. Readers will have a grasp of terminology of the sword and refined fencing skills—writers must be familiar with fencing and current changes and controversies. We are happy to air any point of view on any fencing subject, but the material must be well-researched and logically presented. Estab. 1996. Circ. 5,000. Byline given. Pays prior to or at publication. Offers 25% kill fee.

Publishes ms an average of 6 months after acceptance. Editorial lead time 3 months. Submit seasonal material 6 months in advance. Accepts queries by mail, e-mail. Accepts simultaneous submissions. Sample copy by request. Guidelines available online.

Responds in 1 week or less for e-mail; 1 month for snail mail if SASE; no reply if no SASE and material not usable.

NONFICTION No articles that lack logical progression of thought, articles that rant, `my weapon is better than your weapon' emotionalism, puff pieces, or public relations stuff. **Buys 100 mss/year.** Send complete ms. Length: 100-4,000 words. **Pays $100-200 (rarely) for assigned articles. Pays $10-60 for unsolicited articles.**

PHOTOS Send photos by mail or as e-mail attachment. Prefers prints, all sizes. Captions, identification of subjects, model releases required. Negotiates payment individually.

COLUMNS Cutting-edge news (sword or fencing related), 100 words; Reviews (books/films), 300 words; Fencing Generations (profile), 200-300 words; Tournament Results (veteran events only, please), 200 words. **Buys 40 mss/year.** Send complete ms. **Pays $10-20.**

FICTION Will consider all as long as strong fencing/sword slant is major element. No erotica. Query or send complete ms. 1,500 words maximum. **Pays $25-100.**

POETRY Will consider all which have distinct fencing/sword element as central. No erotica. Submit maximum 10 poems. Up to 100 lines. **Pays $10.**

FILLERS Needs anecdotes, facts, gags, newsbreaks. **Buys 30 mss/year.** 100 words maximum. **Pays $5.**

🟢 LACROSSE MAGAZINE

U.S. Lacrosse, 113 W. University Pkwy., Baltimore MD 21210. (410)235-6882. Fax: (410)366-6735. E-mail: gferraro@uslacrosse.org; blogue@uslacrosse.org. Website: uslacrosse.org. **Contact:** Gabriella O'Brien, art director; Brian Logue, director of communications. **60% freelance written.** *Lacrosse* is the only national feature publication devoted to the sport of lacrosse. It is a benefit of membership in U.S. Lacrosse, a nonprofit organization devoted to promoting the growth of lacrosse and preserving its history. U.S. Lacrosse maintains *Lacrosse Magazine Online* (LMO) at laxmagazine.com. *LMO* features daily lacrosse news and scores directly from lacrosse-play-

ing colleges. *LMO* also includes originally-produced features and news briefs covering all levels of play. Occasional feature articles printed in *Lacrosse* are republished at *LMO*, and vice versa. The online component of *Lacrosse* will do things that a printed publication can't—provide news, scores and information in a timely manner. Estab. 1978. Circ. 235,000. Byline given. Pays on publication. Publishes ms an average of 2 months after acceptance. Editorial lead time 2 months. Submit seasonal material 2 months in advance. Sample copy free. Guidelines free.

NONFICTION Needs book excerpts, general interest, historical, how-to, drills, conditioning, x's and o's, etc., interview, new product, opinion, personal experience, photo feature, technical. **Buys 30-40 mss/year.** Length: 500-1,750 words. **Payment negotiable.** Sometimes pays expenses of writers on assignment.

PHOTOS State availability. Captions, identification of subjects required. Reviews contact sheets, 4×6 prints. Negotiates payment individually.

COLUMNS First Person (personal experience), 1,000 words; Fitness (conditioning/strength/exercise), 500-1,000 words; How-to, 500-1,000 words. **Buys 10-15 mss/year. Payment negotiable.**

🟢🟢 POINTE MAGAZINE

MacFadden Performing Arts Media, LLC, 110 William St., 23rd Floor, New York NY 10038. (646)459-4800. Fax: (646)459-4900. E-mail: pointe@dancemedia.com. Website: pointemagazine.com. Bimonthly magazine covering ballet. *Pointe Magazine* is the only magazine dedicated to ballet. It offers practicalities on ballet careers as well as news and features. Estab. 2000. Circ. 38,000. Byline given. Pays on publication. NoResponds in 1 month to queries. Responds in 1 month to mss. Sample copy for sae with 9×12 envelope and 6 First-Class stamps.

NONFICTION Needs historical, how-to, interview, biography, careers, health, news. **Buys 60 mss/year.** Query with published clips. Length: 400-1,500 words. **Pays $125-400.**

PHOTOS Contact: Colin Fowler, photo editor. State availability. Captions required. Reviews 214x2¼ or 35 mm transparencies, 8×11 prints. Negotiates payment individually.

🟢🟢 POLO PLAYERS' EDITION

9011 Lake Worth Rd., Suite B, Lake Worth FL 33467. (561)968-5208. Fax: (561)968-5208. E-mail: gwen@poloplayersedition.com. Website: poloplayersedition.com. **Contact:** Gwen Rizzo. Monthly magazine on poloÂ³the sport and lifestyle. "Our readers are affluent, well educated, well read, and highly sophisticated." Circ. 6,150. Pays on acceptance. Offers kill fee. Kill fee varies. Publishes ms an average of 2 months after acceptance. Submit seasonal material 3 months in advance. Accepts queries by mail, e-mail, fax. Accepts simultaneous submissions. Responds in 3 months to queries. Guidelines for #10 SAE with 2 stamps.

NONFICTION Needs historical, interview, personal experience, photo feature, technical, travel. Special issues: Annual Art Issue/Gift Buying Guide; Winter Preview/Florida Supplement. **Buys 20 mss/year.** Send complete ms. Length: 800-3,000 words. **Pays $150-400 for assigned articles. Pays $100-300 for unsolicited articles.** Sometimes pays expenses of writers on assignment.

REPRINTS Send tearsheet or typed ms with rights for sale noted and information about when and where the material previously appeared. Pays 50% of amount paid for an original article.

PHOTOS State availability of or send photos. Captions required. Reviews contact sheets, transparencies, prints. Offers $20-150/photo.

COLUMNS teryears (historical pieces), 500 words; Profiles (clubs and players), 800-1,000 words. **Buys 15 mss/year.** Query with published clips. **Pays $100-300.**

PRORODEO SPORTS NEWS

Professional Rodeo Cowboys Association, 101 ProRodeo Dr., Colorado Springs CO 80919. (719)593-8840. Fax: (719)548-4889. Website: prorodeo.com. **Contact:** Neal Reid, managing editor. **10% freelance written.** Biweekly magazine covering professional rodeo. "Our readers are extremely knowledgeable about the sport of rodeo, and anyone who writes for us should have that same in-depth knowledge. Estab. 1952. Circ. 27,000. Byline given. Pays on publication. Publishes ms an average of 1 month after acceptance. Editorial lead time 2 months. Submit seasonal material 2 months in advance. Responds in 2 weeks to queries Sample copy for #10 SASE. Guidelines free.

NONFICTION Needs historical, how-to, interview, photo feature, technical. **Pays $50-100.**

PHOTOS State availability. Identification of subjects required. Reviews digital images and hard copy portfolios. Offers $15-85/photo.

RUGBY MAGAZINE

Rugby Press, Ltd., 459 Columbus Ave., #1200, New York NY 10024. (212)787-1160. Fax: (212)787-1161. E-mail: alex@rugbymag.com. Website: rugbymag.com. **75% freelance written.** Monthly magazine. Estab. 1975. Circ. 10,000. Byline given. Pays on publication. Publishes ms an average of 2 months after acceptance. Editorial lead time 1 month. Submit seasonal material 2 months in advance. Accepts queries by mail, e-mail, fax, phone. Accepts simultaneous submissions. Responds in 2 weeks to queries. Responds in 1 month to mss. Sample copy for $4. Guidelines free.

"*Rugby Magazine* is the journal of record for the sport of rugby in the U.S. Our demographics are among the best in the country."

NONFICTION Needs book excerpts, essays, general interest, historical, how-to, humor, interview, new product, opinion, personal experience, photo feature, technical, travel. **Buys 15 mss/year.** Send complete ms. Length: 600-2,000 words. **Pays $50 minimum.** Pays expenses of writers on assignment.

REPRINTS Send tearsheet or typed ms with rights for sale noted and information about when and where the material previously appeared. Payment varies.

PHOTOS Send photos. Reviews negatives, transparencies, prints. Offers no additional payment for photos accepted with ms.

COLUMNS Nutrition (athletic nutrition), 900 words; Referees' Corner, 1,200 words. **Buys 2-3 mss/year.** Query with published clips. **Pays $50 maximum.**

FICTION Needs cond novels, humorous, novel concepts, slice-of-life vignettes. **Buys 1-3 mss/year.** Query with published clips. Length: 1,000-2,500 words. **Pays $100.**

SKYDIVING

1725 N. Lexington Ave., DeLand FL 32724. (386)736-9779. Fax: (386)736-9786. E-mail: sue@skydiving-magazine.com. Website: skydivingmagazine.com. **Contact:** Sue Clifton, editor. **25% freelance written.** Monthly tabloid featuring skydiving for sport parachutists, worldwide dealers and equipment manufacturers. *Skydiving* is a news magazine. Its purpose is to deliver timely, useful and interesting information about the equipment, techniques, events, people and places of parachuting. Our scope is national. *Skydiving*'s audience spans the entire spectrum of jumpers, from first-jump students to veterans with thousands of skydives. Some readers are riggers with a keen interest in the technical aspects of parachutes, while others are weekend "fun" jumpers who want information to help them make travel plans and equipment purchases. Circ. 14,200. Byline given. Pays on publication. Publishes ms an average of 3 months after acceptance. Accepts simultaneous submissions. Responds in 1 month to queries. Sample copy for $2. Guidelines available online.

NONFICTION No personal experience or human interest articles. Query. Length: 500-1,000 words. **Pays $25-100.** Sometimes pays expenses of writers on assignment.

PHOTOS State availability. Captions required. Reviews 5×7 and larger b&w glossy prints. Offers no additional payment for photos accepted with ms.

FILLERS Needs newsbreaks. Length: 100-200 words. **$25 minimum.**

MOTOR SPORTS

💲 DIRT RIDER

Source Interlink Media, Inc., 1733 Alton Pkwy., Irvine CA 92606. E-mail: drmail@sorc.com. Website: dirtrider.com. Monthly magazine devoted to the sport of off-road motorcycle riding that showcases the many ways enthusiast can enjoy dirt bikes. Circ. 201,342.

💲 THE HOOK MAGAZINE

P.O. Box 51324, Bowling Green KY 42104. (270)202-6742. E-mail: editor@hookmagazine.com; rblively@hotmail.com. Website: hookmagazine.com. **Contact:** Bryan Lively, editor-in-chief. **80% freelance written.** Bimonthly magazine covering tractor pulling. Estab. 1992. Circ. 6,000. Byline given. Pays on publication. Editorial lead time 6 months. Submit seasonal material 6 months in advance. Accepts queries by mail, e-mail, fax. Accepts simultaneous submissions. Responds in 3 weeks to queries. Responds in 2 months to mss. Sample copy for 8 ½×11 SAE with 4 first-class stamps or online. Guidelines for #10 SASE.

⊶ "Our magazine is easy to break into. Puller profiles are your best bet. Features on individuals and their tractors, how they got into the sport, what they want from competing."

NONFICTION Needs how-to, interview, new product, personal experience, photo feature, technical, event coverage. **Buys 25 mss/year.** Send complete ms. Length: 500-1,500 words. **Pays $70 for technical articles; $35 for others.**

PHOTOS Send photos. Captions, identification of subjects, model releases required. Reviews 3×5 prints. Negotiates payment individually.

FILLERS Needs anecdotes, short humor. **Buys 6 mss/ year.** Length: 100 words.

💲💲 ROAD RACER X

Filter Publications, 122 Vista del Rio Dr., Morgantown WV 26508. (304)284-0080. Fax: (304)284-0081. E-mail: letters@roadracerx.com. Website: roadracerx. com. **25% freelance written.** 8 issues per year magazine covering motorcycle road racing. "We cover the sport from a lifestyle/personality perspective. We don't do many technical stories or road tests." Estab. 2003. Circ. 35,000. Byline given. Pays on publication. Publishes ms an average of 2 months after acceptance. Editorial lead time 2 months. Submit seasonal material 1 month in advance. Accepts queries by e-mail. Responds in 1 month to queries. Sample copy for #10 SASE. Guidelines available.

NONFICTION Needs historical, (road racing), interview, (racers). Special issues: "We publish official event programs for several important events, including the Red Bull U.S. Grand Prix & the Miller Motorsports Park World Superbike race. We do not want road tests." **Buys 8 mss/yr. mss/year.** Query. Length: 2,000-3,000 words. **Pays $400-600 for assigned articles. Pays $400-600 for unsolicited articles.** Sometimes pays expenses of writers on assignment. (limit agreed upon in advance)

PHOTOS Contact: Matt Ware. State availability. Reviews GIF/JPEG files. Negotiates payment individually.

COLUMNS Contact: Chris Jonnum. **Buys 8 mss/yr. mss/year.** Query. **Pays $$25-$100.**

💲💲 SAND SPORTS MAGAZINE

Wright Publishing Co., Inc., P.O. Box 2260, Costa Mesa CA 92628. (714)979-2560, ext. 107. Fax: (714)979-3998. E-mail: msommer@hotvws.com. Website: sandsports.net. **Contact:** Michael Sommer, editor. **20% freelance written.** Bimonthly magazine covering vehicles for off-road and sand dunes. Estab. 1995. Circ. 35,000. Byline given. Pays on publication. Editorial lead time 3 months. Submit seasonal material 6 months in advance. Accepts queries by mail. Sample copy and writer's guidelines free.

NONFICTION Needs how-to, technical-mechanical, photo feature, technical. **Buys 20 mss/year.** Query.

1,500 words minimum **Pays $175/page.** Sometimes pays expenses of writers on assignment.

PHOTOS Send photos. Captions, identification of subjects, model releases required. Reviews color slides or high res digital images. Negotiates payment individually.

RUNNING

$ INSIDE TEXAS RUNNING

2470 Gray Falls, Suite 110, Houston TX 77077. (281)759-0555. Fax: (281)759-7766. E-mail: lance@runningmags.com. Website: insidetexasrunning.com. **70% freelance written.** Monthly (except June and August) tabloid covering running and running-related events. Our audience is made up of Texas runners who may also be interested in cross training. Estab. 1977. Circ. 10,000. Byline given. Pays on publication. Publishes ms an average of 2 months after acceptance. Submit seasonal material 2 months in advance. Responds in 1 month to mss. Sample copy for $4.95. Guidelines for #10 SASE.

NONFICTION Special issues: Shoe Review (March); Fall Race Review (September); Marathon Focus (October); Resource Guide (December). **Buys 20 mss/year.** Send complete ms. Length: 500-1,500 words. **Pays $100 maximum for assigned articles. Pays $50 maximum for unsolicited articles.**

REPRINTS Send tearsheet, photocopy or typed ms with rights for sale noted and information about when and where the material previously appeared.

PHOTOS Send photos. Captions required. Offers $25 maximum/photo.

$$ NEW YORK RUNNER

New York Road Runners, 9 E. 89th St., New York NY 10128. (212)860-4455. Fax: (212)423-0879. E-mail: webmaster@nyrr.org. Website: nyrr.org. Quarterly magazine covering running, walking, nutrition, and fitness. Estab. 1958. Circ. 45,000. Byline given. Pays on acceptance. Submit seasonal material 4 months in advance. Accepts queries by mail, e-mail, fax. Responds in 2 months to queries. Sample copy for $3.

💬 Material should be of interest to members of the New York Road Runners.

NONFICTION Needs interview, of runners. **Buys 15 mss/year.** Query. Length: 750-1,000 words. **Pays $50-350.**

COLUMNS Running Briefs (anything noteworthy in the running world), 250-500 words. Query.

$$$$ RUNNER'S WORLD

Rodale, 135 N. 6th St., Emmaus PA 18098. (610)967-8441. Fax: (610)967-8883. E-mail: rwedit@runnersworld.com. Website: runnersworld.com. Christian Evans Gartley, managing editor. **Contact:** David Willey, editor-in-chief. **5% freelance written.** Monthly magazine on running, mainly long-distance running. Estab. 1966. Circ. 500,000. Byline given. Pays on publication. Publishes ms an average of 6 months after acceptance. Submit seasonal material 6 months in advance. Accepts queries by mail. Responds in 2 months to queries. Guidelines available online.

💬 The magazine for and about distance running, training, health and fitness, nutrition, motivation, injury prevention, race coverage, personalities of the sport.

NONFICTION Needs how-to, train, prevent injuries, interview, personal experience. No my first marathon stories. No poetry. **Buys 5-7 mss/year.** Query. **Pays $1,500-2,000.** Pays expenses of writers on assignment.

PHOTOS State availability. Identification of subjects required.

COLUMNS Finish Line (back-of-the-magazine essay, personal experienceÃ³humor). **Buys 24 mss/year.** Send complete ms. **Pays $300**

$$ RUNNING TIMES

Rodale, Inc., c/o Zephyr Media, P.O. Box 20627, Boulder CO 80308. (203)761-1113. Fax: (203)761-9933. E-mail: editor@runningtimes.com. Website: runningtimes.com. **40% freelance written.** Magazine published 10 times/year covering distance running and racing. "*Running Times* is the national magazine for the experienced running participant and fan. Our audience is knowledgeable about the sport and active in running and racing. All editorial relates specifically to running: improving performance, enhancing enjoyment, or exploring events, places, and people in the sport." Estab. 1977. Circ. 102,000. Byline given. Pays on publication. Publishes ms an average of 3 months after acceptance. Editorial lead time 4-6 months. Submit seasonal material 6 months in advance. Accepts queries by mail, e-mail. Responds in 1 month to queries. Responds in 2 months to mss. Sample copy for $8. Guidelines available online.

NONFICTION Needs book excerpts, essays, historical, how-to, training, humor, inspirational, interview, new product, opinion, personal experience, with theme, purpose, evidence of additional research and/or special expertise, photo feature, news, reports. No basic, beginner how-to, generic fitness/nutrition, or generic first-person accounts. **Buys 35 mss/year.** Query. Length: 1,500-3,000 words. **Pays $200-1,000 for assigned articles. Pays $150-300 for unsolicited articles.** Sometimes pays expenses of writers on assignment.

PHOTOS State availability. Identification of subjects required. Negotiates payment individually.

COLUMNS Training (short topics related to enhancing performance), 1,000 words; Sports-Med (application of medical knowledge to running), 1,000 words; Nutrition (application of nutritional principles to running performance), 1,000 words. **Buys 10 mss/year.** Query. **Pays $50-200.**

FICTION Any genre, with running-related theme or characters. Buys 1 ms/year. Send complete ms. Length: 1,500-3,000 words. **Pays $100-500.**

⊕⊕ TRAIL RUNNER

Big Stone Publishing, 417 Main St., Unit N, Carbondale CO 81623. (970)704-1442. Fax: (970)963-4965. E-mail: aarnold@bigstonepub.com. Website: trailrunnermag.com. **Contact:** Michael Benge, editor; Ashley Arnold, associate editor. **50% freelance written.** Bimonthly magazine covering trail running, adventure racing, snowshoeing. Covers all aspects of off-road running. "North America's only magazine dedicated to trail running. In-depth editorial and compelling photography informs, entertains and inspires readers of all ages and abilities to enjoy the outdoors and to improve their health and fitness through the sport of trail running." Estab. 1999. Circ. 29,000. Byline given. Pays on publication. Offers $50 kill fee. Publishes ms an average of 2 months after acceptance. Editorial lead time is 3 months. Submit seasonal material 5 months in advance. Accepts queries by e-mail. Accepts simultaneous submissions. Responds in 4 weeks to queries. Sample copy for $5. Guidelines available online at trailrunnermag.com/contri_guidelines.php.

> ○ "Your well-written query should present a clear, original and provocative story angle, not merely a topic or idea, and should reflect your thorough knowledge of the magazine's content, editorial style and tone."

NONFICTION Needs expose, historical, how-to, humor, inspirational, interview, personal experience, technical, travel, racing. Does not want "My first trail race." **Buys 30-40 mss/year.** Query with one or two writing samples (preferably previously published articles), including your name, phone number and e-mail address. Identify which department your story would be best suited for. **Pays 30¢/word for assigned and unsolicited articles.**

PHOTOS "*Trail Runner* regularly features stunning photography of trail running destinations, races, adventures and faces of the sport.". State availability of photos with submission. Captions, Identification of subjects. Reviews GIF/JPEG files. Offers $50-250/photo.

COLUMNS Contact: Michael Benge, editor, or Ashley Arnold, associate editor. Making Tracks (news, race reports, athlete Q&A, nutrition tips), 300-800 words; Adventure (adventure stories, athlete profiles); Nutrition (sports nutrition, health news), 800-1,000 words; Great Escapes (running destinations/trails), 1,200 words **Buys 30 mss/year. mss/year.** Query with published clips. **Pays 30 cents/word.**

FICTION Pays 25-35 cents/word.

FILLERS Needs anecdotes, facts, newsbreaks, short humor. **Buys 10 mss/year. mss/year.** Length: 75-400 words. **Pays 30 cents/word.**

⊕ WASHINGTON RUNNING REPORT

Capital Running Company, 15739 Crabbs Branch Way, Rockville MD 20855. (301)871-0005. Fax: (301)871-0006. E-mail: kathy@runwashington.com. Website: runwashington.com. **90% freelance written.** Bimonthly tabloid covering running and racing in Washington, DC, metropolitan area, including Baltimore and Richmond metro areas. "*Washington Running Report* is written by runners for runners. Features include runner rankings, training tips and advice, feature articles on races, race results, race calendar, humor, product reviews, and other articles of interest to runners." Estab. 1984. Circ. 35,000. Byline given. Pays on publication. Publishes ms an average of 2-4 months after acceptance. Editorial lead time 1 month. Submit seasonal material 3 months in advance. Accepts queries by mail, e-mail, fax, phone. Accepts simultaneous submissions. Responds in 2-3 weeks to queries. Responds in 1-2 months to mss. Sample copy free.

NONFICTION Needs book excerpts, essays, expose, general interest, historical, how-to, humor, inspirational, interview, new product, opinion, personal experience, photo feature, technical, travel. **Buys 10-**

12 mss/year. Query. Length: 500-2,800 words. **Pays $75 for assigned articles. Pays $50 for unsolicited articles.**

PHOTOS Send photos. Captions, identification of subjects required. Reviews contact sheets, 4×6 prints, GIF/JPEG files. Offers $20-50/photo.

COLUMNS Traveling Runner (races in exotic locales), 1,400 words; Training Tips (how to run faster, racing strategy), 750 words; Sports Medicine (new developments in the field), 750 words. **Buys 3-4 mss/year.** Query with or without published clips or send complete ms. **Pays $50.**

FICTION Needs adventure, cond novels, experimental, fantasy, historical, humorous, mainstream, mystery, slice-of-life vignettes. **Buys 1-2 mss/year.** Send complete ms. Length: 750-1,500 words. **Pays $50.**

FILLERS Needs anecdotes, facts, gags, newsbreaks, short humor. **Buys 6 mss/year.** Length: 50-250 words. **Pays $50.**

SKIING AND SNOW SPORTS

$ AMERICAN SNOWMOBILER

Kalmbach Publishing Co., 21027 Crossroads Circle, P.O. Box 1612, Waukesha WI 53187-1612. E-mail: editor@amsnow.com. Website: amsnow.com. **Contact:** Mark Savage, editor. **30% freelance written.** Magazine published 6 times seasonally covering snowmobiling. Estab. 1985. Circ. 54,000. Byline given. Pays on acceptance. Publishes an average of 4 months after acceptance. Editorial lead time 4 months. Submit seasonal material 6 months in advance. Accepts queries by mail, e-mail, fax. Responds in 1 month to queries. Responds in 2 months to mss. Guidelines available online.

NONFICTION Needs general interest, historical, how-to, interview, personal experience, photo feature, travel. **Buys 10 mss/year.** Query with published clips. Length: 500-1,200 words. **Pay varies for assigned articles. Pays $100 minimum for unsolicited articles.**

PHOTOS State availability. Captions, identification of subjects, model releases required. Offers no additional payment for photos accepted with ms.

$ SKATING

United States Figure Skating Association, 20 First St., Colorado Springs CO 80906-3697. (719)635-5200. Fax: (719)635-9548. E-mail: info@usfigureskating.org. Website: usfsa.org. "Magazine published 10 times/year. *Skating* magazine is the official publication of U.S. Figure Skating, and thus we cover skating at both the championship and grass roots level." Estab. 1923. Circ. 45,000. Byline given. Pays on publication. Publishes ms an average of 3 months after acceptance. Accepts queries by mail, e-mail, fax.

NONFICTION Needs general interest, historical, how-to, interview, background and interests of skaters, volunteers, or other U.S. Figure Skating members, photo feature, technical and competition reports, figure skating issues and trends, sports medicine. **Buys 10 mss/year.** Query. Length: 500-2,500 words. **Payment varies**

PHOTOS Photos purchased with or without accompanying ms. Query. Pays $10 for 8×10 or 5×7 b&w glossy prints, and $25 for color prints or transparencies.

COLUMNS Ice Breaker (news briefs); Foreign Competition Reports; Health and Fitness; In Synch (synchronized skating news); Takeoff (up-and-coming athletes), all 500-2,000 words.

$$$$ SKIING

Bonnier Corporation, 5720 Flatiron Pkwy., Boulder CO 80301. (303)253-6300. E-mail: editor@skiingmag.com. Website: skiingmag.com. **Contact:** Sam Bass, editor. Magazine published 7 times/year for skiers who deeply love winter, who live for travel, adventure, instruction, gear, and news. *Skiing* is the user's guide to winter adventure. It is equal parts jaw-dropping inspiration and practical information, action and utility, attitude and advice. It relates the lifestyles of dedicated skiers and captures their spirit of daring and exploration. Dramatic photography transports readers to spine-tingling mountains with breathtaking immediacy. Reading *Skiing* is almost as much fun as being there. Estab. 1948. Circ. 400,000. Byline given. Offers 40% kill fee. No

NONFICTION Buys 10-15 feature (1,500-2,000 words) and 12-24 short (100-500 words) mss/year. Query. **Pays $1,000-2,500/feature; $100-500/short piece.**

COLUMNS Length: 200-1,000 words. **Buys 2-3 mss/year.** Query. **Pays $150-1,000.**

⊘$$$ SKIING MAGAZINE

Bonnier Corp., 5720 Flatiron Parkway, Boulder CO 80301. (303)448-7600. Fax: (303)448-7638. E-mail: editor@skiingmag.com. Website: skinet.com/skiing. **60% freelance written.** Magazine published 8 times/year. *Skiing Magazine* is a ski-lifestyle publication written and edited for recreational skiers. Its content is intended to help them ski better (technique), buy better (equipment and skiwear), and introduce them to new experiences, people, and adventures. Changing from print to online publication. Estab. 1936. Circ. 430,000. Byline given. Pays on acceptance. Offers 15% kill fee. Publishes ms an average of 3 months after acceptance. Submit seasonal material 8 months in advance. Accepts queries by mail, e-mail. Sample copy with 9×12 SASE and 5 first-class stamps.

○ Does not accept unsolicited mss, and assumes no responsibility for their return.

NONFICTION Needs essays, historical, how-to, humor, interview, personal experience. **Buys 5-10 mss/year.** Send complete ms. Length: 1,000-3,500 words. **Pays $500-1,000 for assigned articles. Pays $300-700 for unsolicited articles.** Pays expenses of writers on assignment.

PHOTOS Sponsors 12-week-long internship based at editorial headquarters in Boulder, Colorado. Intern workload includes: assisting in our photo studio and on assignment, photo retouching, coordinating photography, working with our art department to build cohesive features, invoicing, production workflow, and participating in staff meetings. "We try to keep the grunt work to a minimum. *Skiing Magazine* is a small staff (4 editors and 2 art directors), so interns work closely with staffers. Interns should be dedicated, hard-working, conscientious, and fun-loving, with a career interest in photography. A very strong foundation in the CS3 Creative Suite, as well as previous journalism or photography experience is required. A passion for the sport of skiing helps." All internships are unpaid. E-mail résumé, cover letter, and portfolio to: Niall@skiingmag.com. Send photos. Captions, identification of subjects, model releases required. Offers $75-300/photo.

FILLERS Needs facts, short humor. **Buys 10 mss/year.** Length: 60-75 words. **Pays $50-75.**

⊙⊙ SNOWEST MAGAZINE

Harris Publishing, 360 B St., Idaho Falls ID 83402. (208)524-7000. Fax: (208)522-5241. E-mail: lindstrm@snowest.com. Website: snowest.com. **10-25% freelance written**. Monthly magazine. "*SnoWest* covers the sport of snowmobiling, products, and personalities in the western states. This includes mountain riding, deep powder, and trail riding, as well as destination pieces, tech tips, and new model reviews." Estab. 1972. Circ. 140,000. Byline given. Pays on publication. Publishes ms an average of 2 months after

acceptance. Editorial lead time 6 months. Submit seasonal material 3 months in advance. Sample copy and writer's guidelines free.

NONFICTION Needs how-to, fix a snowmobile, make it high performance, new product, technical, travel. **Buys 3-5 mss/year.** Query with published clips. Length: 500-1,500 words. **Pays $150-300.**

PHOTOS Send photos. Captions, identification of subjects required. Negotiates payment individually.

⊙⊙ SNOW GOER

Affinity Media, 6420 Sycamore Lane, Maple Grove MN 55369. Fax: (763)383-4499. E-mail: JPrusak@affinitygroup.com. Website: snowgoer.com. **Contact:** John Prusak. **5% freelance written**. Magazine published 7 times/year covering snowmobiling. "*Snow Goer* is a hard-hitting, tell-it-like-it-is magazine designed for the ultra-active snowmobile enthusiast. It is fun, exciting, innovative, and on the cutting edge of technology and trends." Estab. 1967. Circ. 66,000. Byline given. Pays on publication. Publishes ms an average of 5 months after acceptance. Editorial lead time 5 months. Submit seasonal material 6 months in advance. Accepts queries by mail, e-mail, fax. Accepts simultaneous submissions. Responds in 3 months to queries. Sample copy for sae with 8×10 envelope and 4 First-Class stamps.

NONFICTION Needs general interest, how-to, interview, new product, personal experience, photo feature, technical, travel. **Buys 6 mss/year.** Query. Length: 500-4,000 words. **Pays $50-500.** Sometimes pays expenses of writers on assignment.

PHOTOS State availability. Captions, identification of subjects required. Reviews contact sheets, prints. Negotiates payment individually.

WATER SPORTS

⊙⊙ DIVER

216 East Esplanade, North Vancouver BC V7L 1A3 Canada. (604)988-0711. Fax: (604)988-0747. E-mail: editor@divermag.com. Website: divermag.com. Magazine published 8 times/year emphasizing sport scuba diving, ocean science, and technology for a well-educated, active readership across North America and around the world. Circ. 30,000. Accepts queries by e-mail.

NONFICTION Query first. Length: 500-3,000 words. **Pays 12.5 cents/word, $25/photo inside, $350 for cover photo.**

PHOTOS Captions, identification of subjects required. Reviews JPEG/TIFF files (300 dpi), slides, maps, drawings.

⊜⊜ ROWING NEWS

The Independent Rowing News, Inc., 85 Mechanic St., Suite 440, Lebanon NH 03766. (603)448-5090. E-mail: editor@rowingnews.com. Website: rowingnews.com. **Contact:** Ed Winchester. **75% freelance written.** Monthly magazine covering rowing (the Olympic sport). We write for a North American readership, serving the rowing community with features, how-to, and dispatches from the rowing world at large. Estab. 1994. Circ. 20,000. Byline given. Pays on publication. Publishes ms an average of 1-2 months after acceptance. Editorial lead time 1-12 months. Submit seasonal material 1-2 months in advance. Responds in 6 weeks to queries. Sample copy available online. Guidelines free.

NONFICTION Needs essays, how-to, rowing only, interview, new product, personal experience, rowing, travel. Everything must be directly related to rowing. **Buys 12 mss/year mss/year.** Query with published clips. Length: 1,500-5,000 words. Sometimes pays expenses of writers on assignment.

PHOTOS True required. Reviews JPEG/TIFF. Negotiates payment individually.

⊘⊜ SURFER MAGAZINE

Source Interlink, P.O. Box 1028, Dana Point CA 92629-5028. (949)325-6212. E-mail: brendon@surfermag.com. Website: surfermag.com. **Contact:** Brendon Thomas. Monthly magazine edited for the avid surfers and those who follow the beach, wave riding scene. Circ. 118,570. Editorial lead time 10 weeks.

◯Query before submitting.

⊜⊜ SWIMMING WORLD MAGAZINE

Sports Publications International, P.O. Box 20337, Sedona AZ 86341. (928)284-4005; *602)522-0778. Fax: (928)284-2477. E-mail: garrettm@swimmingworld.com; editorial@swimmingworldmagazine.com. Website: swimmingworldmagazine.com. **Contact:** Garrett McCaffrey. **30% freelance written.** Bimonthly magazine about competitive swimming. Readers are fitness-oriented adults from varied social and professional backgrounds who share swimming as part of their lifestyle. Submit 250-word synopsis of your article. Estab. 1960. Circ. 50,000. Byline given. Pays on publication. Editorial lead time 2 months. Submit seasonal material 3 months in advance. Accepts queries by mail, e-mail, fax. Accepts simultaneous submissions. Responds in 1 month to queries. Guidelines available online.

◯Included in this publication are *Swimming Technique*, *Swim Magazine*, and *Junior Swimmer*.

NONFICTION Needs book excerpts, essays, expose, general interest, historical, how-to, training plans and techniques, humor, inspirational, interview, people associated with fitness and competitive swimming, new product, articles describing new products for fitness and competitive training, personal experience, photo feature, technical, travel, general health. **Buys 30 mss/year.** Query. Length: 250-2,500 words. **Pays $75-400.**

PHOTOS Send photos. Captions, identification of subjects, model releases required. Reviews high-resolution digital images. Negotiates payment individually.

⊜ THE WATER SKIER

USA Water Ski, 1251 Holy Cow Rd., Polk City FL 33868. (863)324-4341. Fax: (863)325-8259. E-mail: satkinson@usawaterski.org. Website: usawaterski.org. **10-20% freelance written.** Magazine published 7 times/year. *The Water Skier* is the membership magazine of USA Water Ski, the national governing body for organized water skiing in the United States. The magazine has a controlled circulation and is available only to USA Water Ski's membership, which is made up of 20,000 active competitive water skiers and 10,000 members who are supporting the sport. These supporting members may participate in the sport but they don't compete. The editorial content of the magazine features distinctive and informative writing about the sport of water skiing only. Estab. 1951. Circ. 30,000. Byline given. Offers 30% kill fee. Editorial lead time 4 months. Submit seasonal material 6 months in advance. Responds in 2 weeks to queries. Sample copy for $3.50. Guidelines for #10 SASE.

NONFICTION Needs historical, has to pertain to water skiing, interview, call for assignment, new product, boating and water ski equipment, travel, water ski vacation destinations. **Buys 10-15 mss/year.** Query. Length: 1,500-3,000 words. **Pays $100-150.**

REPRINTS Send photocopy. Payment negotiable.

PHOTOS State availability. Captions, identification of subjects required. Reviews contact sheets. Negotiates payment individually.

COLUMNS The Water Skier News (small news

items about people and events in the sport), 400-500 words. Other topics include safety, training (3-event, barefoot, disabled, show ski, ski race, kneeboard, and wakeboard); champions on their way; new products. Query. **Pays $50-100.**

TEEN AND YOUNG ADULT

⊜⊜ CICADA MAGAZINE

Cricket Magazine Group, 70 S. Lake St., Suite 300, Chicago IL 60601. (312)701-1720. Fax: (312)701-1728. E-mail: dvetter@caruspub.com. Website: cicadamag. com. **Contact:** Deborah Vetter, Executive Editor; John Sandford, Art Director. **80% freelance written.** Bimonthly literary magazine for ages 14 and up. Publishes original short stories, poems, and first-person essays written for teens and young adults. Estab. 1998. Circ. 10,000. Byline given. Pays on publication. Accepts simultaneous submissions. Responds in 2 months to mss. Guidelines available online.

NONFICTION Needs essays, personal experience, book reviews. Submit complete ms, SASE. 5,000 words maximum; 300-500 words/book reviews. **Pays up to 25¢/word.**

REPRINTS Send typed manuscript. Payment varies.

PHOTOS Send photocopies/tearsheets of artwork.

FICTION The main protagonist should be at least 14 and preferably older. Stories should have a genuine teen sensibility and be aimed at readers in high school or college. Needs adventure, fantasy, historical, humorous, mainstream, novel concepts, romance, science fiction, contemporary, realistic, novellas (1/issue). 5,000 words maximum (up to 15,000 words/novellas). **Pays up to 25¢/word.**

POETRY Needs free verse, light verse, traditional. 25 lines maximum. **Pays up to $3/line on publication.**

⊘⊜⊜⊜⊜ COSMOGIRL!

The Hearst Corp., 224 W. 57th St., 3rd Floor, New York NY 10019. (212)649-3852. E-mail: inbox@cosmogirl. com. Website: cosmogirl.com. Monthly magazine covering fashion, beauty, photos and profiles of young celebs, advice, health and fitness, dating, relationships and finance. CosmoGIRL! has the voice of a cool older sister. The magazine is conversational, funny, down-to-earth, and honest. We never talk down to our readers, who are 12- to 22-year-old young women. Estab. 1999. Circ. 1,350,000. Byline given. Offers 25% kill fee. Editorial lead time 3-4 months. Accepts queries by mail. Responds in 2 months to queries. Guidelines by e-mail.

NONFICTION Contact: Look at the masthead of a current issue for the appropriate editor. Needs interview, opinion, personal experience. **Pays $1/word.** Pays expenses of writers on assignment.

PHOTOS Put name, phone # and address on back of all photos. Send photos.

⊜ INSIGHT

The Review and Herald Publishing Association, 55 W. Oak Ridge Dr., Hagerstown MD 21740. (301)393-4038. E-mail: insight@rhpa.org. Website: insightmagazine. org. **80% freelance written.** Weekly magazine covering spiritual life of teenagers. *Insight* publishes true dramatic stories, interviews, and community and mission service features that relate directly to the lives of Christian teenagers, particularly those with a Seventh-day Adventist background. Estab. 1970. Circ. 20,000. Byline given. Pays on publication. Publishes ms an average of 4 months after acceptance. Editorial lead time 6 months. Submit seasonal material 6 months in advance. Accepts queries by mail, e-mail, fax. Responds in 1 month to mss. Sample copy for $2 and #10 SASE. Guidelines available online.

> ◯ 'Big Deal' appears in *Insight* often, covering a topic of importance to teens. Each feature contains: An opening story involving real teens (can be written in first-person), Scripture Picture (a sidebar that discusses what the Bible says about the topic) and another sidebar (optional) that adds more perspective and help.

NONFICTION Needs how-to, teen relationships and experiences, humor, interview, personal experience, photo feature, religious. **Buys 120 mss/year.** Send complete ms. Length: 500-2,000 words. **Pays $25-150 for assigned articles. Pays $25-125 for unsolicited articles.**

REPRINTS Send typed manuscript with rights for sale noted and information about when and where the material previously appeared. Pays $50.

PHOTOS State availability. Model releases required. Reviews contact sheets, negatives, transparencies, prints. Negotiates payment individually.

COLUMNS Big Deal (topic of importance to teens) 1,200-1,700 words; Interviews (Christian culture figures, especially musicians), 2,000 words; It Happened to Me (first-person teen experiences containing spiritual insights), 1,000 words; On the Edge (dramatic true stories about Christians), 2,000 words; So I Said.(true short stories in the first person of common, everyday events and experiences that taught the writer something), 300-500 words. Send complete ms. **Pays $25-125.**

$$ LISTEN MAGAZINE

The Health Connection, 55 W. Oak Ridge Dr., Hagerstown MD 21740. (301)393-4010; (301)393-4082. E-mail: editor@listenmagazine.org. Website: listenmagazine.org. **Contact:** Celeste Perrino-Walker, editor. **80% freelance written.** Monthly magazine specializing in tobacco, drug, and alcohol prevention, presenting positive alternatives to various tobacco, drug, and alcohol dependencies. *Listen* is used in many high school classes and by professionals: medical personnel, counselors, law enforcement officers, educators, youth workers, etc. Circ. 12,000. Byline given. Publishes ms an average of 6 months after acceptance. Accepts queries by mail, e-mail. Accepts simultaneous submissions. Responds in 2 months to queries. Sample copy for $2 and 9×12 SASE. Guidelines available online.

NONFICTION **Buys 30-50 unsolicited mss/year.** Query.

REPRINTS Send photocopy of article or typed ms with rights for sale ted and information about when and where the material previously appeared. Pays their regular rates.

PHOTOS Color photos preferred. Captions required. Purchased with accompanying ms.

$$ THE NEW ERA

50 E. North Temple St., Room 2414, Salt Lake City UT 84150-0024. (801)240-2951. Fax: (801)240-2270. E-mail: newera@ldschurch.org. Website: newera.lds.org. **Contact:** Richard M. Romney, managing editor. **20% freelance written.** Monthly magazine for young people (ages 12-18) of the Church of Jesus Christ of Latter-day Saints (Mormon), their church leaders and teachers. Estab. 1971. Circ. 230,000. Byline given. Pays on acceptance. Publishes ms an average of 1 year after acceptance. Submit seasonal material 1 year in advance. Accepts queries by mail, e-mail, fax. Responds in 2 months to queries. Sample copy for $1.50. Guidelines available online.

NONFICTION Needs how-to, humor, inspirational, interview, personal experience, informational. Query. Length: 150-1,200 words. **Pays $25-350/article.**

PHOTOS Uses b&w photos and transparencies with manuscripts. Individual photos used for *Photo of the Month*. Payment depends on use, $10-125 per photo.

COLUMNS What's Up? (news of young Mormons around the world); How I Know; Scripture Lifeline. **Pays $25-125/article.**

POETRY Needs free verse, light verse, traditional, all other forms. Must relate to editorial viewpoint. **Pays $25 and up.**

$$$$ SEVENTEEN

300 W. 57th St., 17th Floor, New York NY 10019. (917)934-6500. Fax: (917)934-6574. Website: seventeen.com. **20% freelance written.** Monthly magazine. *Seventeen* is a young woman's first fashion and beauty magazine. Tailored for young women in their teens and early twenties, *Seventeen* covers fashion, beauty, health, fitness, food, college, entertainment, fiction, plus crucial personal and global issues. Estab. 1944. Circ. 2,400,000. Byline given. Pays on acceptance. Offers 25% kill fee. Publishes ms an average of 6 months after acceptance. Accepts queries by mail. Responds in 3 months to queries.

NONFICTION Length: 1,200-2,500 words. **Pays $1/word, occasionally more.** Pays expenses of writers on assignment.

PHOTOS Photos usually by assignment only.

$$ YOUNG SALVATIONIST

The Salvation Army, P.O. Box 269, Alexandria VA 22313-0269. (703)684-5500. Fax: (703)684-5539. E-mail: ys@usn.salvationarmy.org. Website: use.salvationarmy.org. **Contact:** Captain Amy Reardon. **10% freelance written.** Monthly magazine for high school and early college youth. "Young Salvationist provides young people with biblically based inspiration and resources to develop their spirituality. Only material with Christian perspective with practical real-life application will be considered." Circ. 48,000. Byline given. Pays on acceptance. Publishes ms an average of 6 months after acceptance. Submit seasonal material 6 months in advance. Accepts queries by Accepts complete mss by mail and e-mail. Responds in 2 months to mss. Sample copy for 9×12 SAE with 3 first-class stamps or on website. Writer's guidelines and theme list for #10 SASE or on website.

"Works with a small number of new/unpublished writers each year."

NONFICTION Needs how-to, humor, inspirational, interview, personal experience, photo feature, reli-

CONSUMER MAGAZINES

gious. **Buys 10 mss/year.** Send complete ms. Length: 1,000-1,500 words. **Pays 15¢/word for first rights.**

REPRINTS Send tearsheet, photocopy or typed ms with rights for sale noted and information about when and where the material previously appeared. Pays 10¢/word for reprints.

TRAVEL, CAMPING AND TRAILER

$ AAA GOING PLACES

AAA Auto Club South, 1515 N. Westshore Blvd., Tampa FL 33607. (813)289-5923. Fax: (813)288-7935. **50% freelance written.** Bimonthly magazine on auto tips, cruise travel, tours. Estab. 1982. Circ. 2,500,000. Byline given. Pays on publication. Publishes ms an average of 6 months after acceptance. Submit seasonal material 9 months in advance. Accepts simultaneous submissions. Responds in 2 months to mss. Writer's guidelines for SAE.

NONFICTION Needs historical, how-to, humor, interview, personal experience, photo feature, travel. **Buys 15 mss/year.** Send complete ms. Length: 500-1,200 words. **Pays $50/printed page.**

PHOTOS State availability. Captions required. Reviews 2â—Š2 transparencies, 300 dpi digital images. Offers no additional payment for photos accepted with ms.

COLUMNS What's Happening (local attractions in Florida, Georgia, or Tennessee).

$$ AAA MIDWEST TRAVELER

AAA Auto Club of Missouri, 12901 N. 40 Dr., St. Louis MO 63141. (314)523-7350 ext. 6301. Fax: (314)523-6982. E-mail: dreinhardt@aaamissouri.com. Website: aaa.com/traveler. **Contact:** Deborah Reinhardt, Managing Editor. **80% freelance written.** Bimonthly magazine covering travel and automotive safety. "We provide members with useful information on travel, auto safety and related topics." Estab. 1901. Circ. 500,000. Byline given. Pays on acceptance. Offers $50 kill fee. Editorial lead time 1 year. Submit seasonal material 6 months in advance. Accepts queries by mail, e-mail, fax. Accepts simultaneous submissions. Responds in 1 month to queries. Responds in 1 month to mss. Sample copy with 10×13 SASE and 4 First-Class stamps. Guidelines with #10 SASE.

NONFICTION Needs travel. No humor, fiction, poetry or cartoons. **Buys 20-30 mss/year.** Query; query with published clips the first time. Length: 800-1,200 words. **Pays $400.**

PHOTOS State availability. Captions required. Reviews transparencies, prints. Offers no additional payment for photos accepted with ms.

$ CAMPERWAYS, MIDWEST RV TRAVELER, FLORIDA RV TRAVELER, NORTHEAST OUTDOORS, SOUTHERN RV

Woodall Publications Corp., 2575 Vista Del Mar Dr., Ventura CA 93001. (888)656-6669. E-mail: info@woodallpub.com. Website: woodalls.com. **75% freelance written.** Monthly tabloids covering RV lifestyle. We're looking for articles of interest to RVers. Lifestyle articles, destinations, technical tips, interesting events and the like make up the bulk of our publications. We also look for region-specific travel and special interest articles. Circ. 30,000. Byline given. Pays on acceptance. Offers 50% kill fee. Accepts queries by mail, e-mail. Sample copy free. Guidelines for #10 SASE.

💬 Accepts queries in June, July, and August for upcoming year.

NONFICTION Needs how-to, personal experience, technical, travel. No "Camping From Hell" articles. **Buys approximately 500 mss/year.** Length: 500-2,000 words. **Payment varies.**

PHOTOS Prefers slides and large (5×7, 300 dpi) digital images. State availability. Captions, identification of subjects required. Reviews negatives, 4â—Š5 transparencies, 4â—Š5 prints.

$ CAMPING TODAY

126 Hermitage Rd., Butler PA 16001-8509. (724)283-7401. E-mail: d_johnston01@msn.com. Website: fcrv.org. **Contact:** DeWayne Johnston, editor. **30% freelance written.** Bimonthly official membership publication of the fcrv. "*Camping Today* is the largest nonprofit family camping and RV organization in the U.S. and Canada. Members are heavily oriented toward RV travel. Concentration is on member activities in chapters. Group is also interested in conservation and wildlife. The majority of members are retired." Estab. 1983. Circ. 10,000. Byline given. Pays on publication. Publishes ms an average of 6 months after acceptance. Submit seasonal material 3 months in advance. Accepts simultaneous submissions. Responds in 2 months to queries and to mss. Sample copy and guidelines for 4 first-class stamps. Guidelines for #10 SASE.

NONFICTION Needs humor, camping or travel related, interview, interesting campers, new product, technical, RVs related, travel, interesting places to visit by RV, camping. **Buys 10-15 mss/year.** Query by mail or e-mail or send complete ms with photos. Length: 750-2,000 words. **Pays $50-150.**

REPRINTS Send typed manuscript with rights for sale noted and information about when and where the material previously appeared. Pays 35-50% of amount paid for original article.

PHOTOS Need b&w or sharp color prints. Send photos. Captions required.

●●● CNN TRAVELLER

Highbury House, 47 Brunswick Place, London N1 6EB England. (44)(207)613-6949. E-mail: dha@emphasis.net. Website: cnntraveller.com. **Contact:** Dan Ha, editor. **50% freelance written.** Bimonthly magazine covering travel. *CNN Traveller* takes readers on a fascinating journey to some of the most intriguing and exotic places in the world. It marries the best in travel journalism and photography with the news values of CNN. The magazines takes an issues-led view of travel, getting behind the headlines with articles that are guaranteed to be intriguing and thought-provoking every issue. Estab. 1998. Circ. 106,500. Byline given. Pays 1 month after publication. Offers 50% kill fee. Publishes ms an average of 3 months after acceptance. Editorial lead time 2-6 months. Submit seasonal material 4 months in advance. Accepts queries by e-mail. Sample copy available online. Guidelines free.

NONFICTION Needs book excerpts, travel. **Buys 50 mss/year.** Query with published clips. Length: 600-2,000 words. **Pays £120-400 ($225-750) for assigned articles. Pays £100-400 ($190-750) for unsolicited articles.**

PHOTOS State availability. Captions required. Reviews GIF/JPEG files. Negotiates payment individually.

COLUMNS Buys 10 mss/year. Query with published clips. **Pays £100-200 ($190-375).**

●●● COAST TO COAST MAGAZINE

Affinity Group, Inc., 2575 Vista Del Mar Dr., Ventura CA 93001. (805)667-4100. E-mail: editor@coastresorts.com. Website: coastresorts.com. **80% freelance written.** Quarterly magazine for members of Coast to Coast Resorts. *"Coast to Coast* focuses on North American travel, outdoor recreation, camping and RV parks; circulation is 60,000."* Estab. 1983. Byline given. Pays on acceptance. Offers 33% kill fee. Publishes

ms an average of 4 months after acceptance. Editorial lead time 5 months. Submit seasonal material 5 months in advance. Accepts queries by mail, e-mail, fax. Accepts simultaneous submissions. Responds in 6-8 weeks to queries. Responds in 1-2 months to mss. Sample copy for $4 and 9×12 SASE. Guidelines for #10 SASE.

NONFICTION Needs book excerpts, essays, general interest, how-to, interview, new product, personal experience, photo feature, technical, travel. No poetry, cartoons. **Buys 70 mss/year.** Send complete ms. Length: 800-2,500 words. **Pays $75-1,200.**

REPRINTS Send photocopy and information about when and where the material previously appeared. Pays approximately 50% of amount paid for original article

PHOTOS sharp, color-saturated high-res digital images, particularly of North American destinations and RV travel.

●● FAMILY MOTOR COACHING

8291 Clough Pike, Cincinnati OH 45244. (513)474-3622. Fax: (513)388-5286. E-mail: rgould@fmca.com. Website: fmca.com. **Contact:** Robbin Gould, editor. **80% freelance written. We prefer that writers be experienced RVers.** Monthly magazine emphasizing travel by motorhome, motorhome mechanics, maintenance, and other technical information. *"Family Motor Coaching* magazine is edited for the members and prospective members of the Family Motor Coach Association who own or are about to purchase self-contained, motorized recreational vehicles known as motorhomes. Featured are articles on travel and recreation, association news and activities, plus articles on new products and motorhome maintenance and repair. Approximately 1/3 of editorial content is devoted to travel and entertainment, 1/3 to association news, and 1/3 to new products, industry news, and motorhome maintenance."* Estab. 1963. Circ. 140,000. Byline given. Pays on acceptance. Publishes ms an average of 8 months after acceptance. Submit seasonal material 4 months in advance. Accepts queries by mail, e-mail, fax. Responds in 3 months to queries. Sample copy for $3.99; $5 if paying by credit card. Guidelines with #10 SASE or request PDF by e-mail.

NONFICTION Needs how-to, do-it-yourself motorhome projects and modifications, humor, interview, new product, technical, motorhome travel (various areas of North America accessible by motorhome), bus conversions, nostalgia. **Buys 50-75 mss/year.** Query with published clips. Length: 1,000-2,000 words. **Pays $100-500, depending on article category.**

PHOTOS State availability. Captions, model releases, True required. Offers no additional payment for b&w contact sheets, 35mm 2¼x2¼ color transparencies, or high-res electronic images (300 dpi and at least 4×6 in size).

⊕⊛ HIGHROADS

AAA Arizona, 3144 N. 7th Ave., Phoenix AZ 85013. (602)650-2732. Fax: (602)241-2917. E-mail: highroads@arizona.aaa.com. Website: aaa.com. **50% freelance written**. Bimonthly magazine covering Travel/Automotive. Our magazine goes out to our 470,000+ AAA Arizona members on a bimonthly basis. The mean age of ur audience is around 60 years old. We look for intelligent, engaging writing covering auto and travel-related topics. Byline given. Pays on publication. Offers 30% kill fee. Editorial lead time 6 months. Submit seasonal material 6 months in advance. Accepts queries by mail, e-mail, fax. Accepts simultaneous submissions. Sample copy for #10 SASE. Guidelines by e-mail.

NONFICTION Needs travel, Auto-related. Articles unrelated to travel, automotive or Arizona living. **Buys 21 mss/year.** Query with published clips. Length: 500-2,000 words. **Pays $0.35/word for assigned articles. Pays $0.35/word for unsolicited articles.**

PHOTOS Contact: Sherri Rowland, Art Director. Identification of subjects required. Offers $75-500 per photo.

COLUMNS Contact: Lindsay DeChacco. Weekender (Weekend destinations near Arizona), Road Trip (Day activities in Arizona), Charming Stays (A charming inn or B&B in Arizona); 500 to 700 words. **Buys 10 mss/year. Pays $-$0.35.**

⊕⊛ HIGHWAYS

Affinity Group, Inc., 2575 Vista Del Mar Dr., Ventura CA 93001. (805)667-4100. E-mail: highways@goodsamclub.com. Website: goodsamclub.com/highways. **30% freelance written**. Monthly magazine covering recreational vehicle lifestyle. "All of our readers own some type of RV—a motorhome, trailer, pop-up, tent—so our stories need to include places that you can go with large vehicles, and campgrounds in and around the area where they can spend the night." Estab. 1966. Circ. 975,000. Byline given. Pays on acceptance. Offers 50% kill fee. Publishes ms an average of 6 months after acceptance. Accepts queries by e-mail.

Responds in 2 weeks to queries. Sample copy and writer's guidelines free or online.

NONFICTION Needs how-to, repair/replace something on an RV, humor, technical, travel, all RV related. **Buys 15-20 mss/year.** Query. Length: 800-1,100 words.

PHOTOS Do not send or e-mail unless approved by staff. .

COLUMNS On the Road (issue related); RV Insight (for people new to the RV lifestyle); Action Line (consumer help); Tech Topics (tech Q&A); Camp Cuisine (cooking in an RV); Product Previews (new products). No plans on adding new COLUMNS.

⊛⊕⊛ INTERNATIONAL LIVING

International Living Publishing, Ltd., Elysium House, Ballytruckle, Waterford Ireland (800)643-2479. Fax: 353-51-304-561. E-mail: editor@internationalliving.com. Website: internationalliving.com. **Contact:** Eoin Bassett, managing editor. **50% freelance written**. Monthly magazine covering retirement, travel, investment, and real estate overseas. "We do not want descriptions of how beautiful places are. We want specifics, recommendations, contacts, prices, names, addresses, phone numbers, etc. We want offbeat locations and off-the-beaten-track spots." Estab. 1981. Circ. 500,000. Byline given. Pays on publication. Offers 25-50% kill fee. Publishes ms an average of 3 months after acceptance. Editorial lead time 2 months. Submit seasonal material 3 months in advance. Accepts queries by mail, e-mail, fax. Accepts simultaneous submissions. Responds in 2 months to mss. Sample copy for #10 SASE. Guidelines available online.

NONFICTION Needs how-to, get a job, buy real estate, get cheap airfares overseas, start a business, etc., interview, entrepreneur or retiree abroad, new product, travel, personal experience, travel, shopping, cruises. No descriptive, run-of-the-mill travel articles. **Buys 100 mss/year.** Send complete ms. Length: 500-2,000 words. **Pays $200-500 for assigned articles. Pays $100-400 for unsolicited articles.**

PHOTOS State availability. Identification of subjects required. Reviews contact sheets, negatives, transparencies, prints. Offers $50/photo.

FILLERS Needs facts. **Buys 20 mss/year. mss/year.** Length: 50-250 words. **Pays $25-50.**

⊛ THE INTERNATIONAL RAILWAY TRAVELER

Hardy Publishing Co., Inc., P.O. Box 3747, San Diego CA 92163. (619)260-1332. Fax: (619)296-4220.

E-mail: irteditor@aol.com. Website: irtsociety.com. **100% freelance written**. Monthly newsletter covering rail travel. Estab. 1983. Circ. 3,500. Byline given. Pays within 1 month of the publication date. Offers 25% kill fee. Editorial lead time 4 months. Submit seasonal material 6 months in advance. Responds in 1 month to queries. Responds in 2 months to mss. Sample copy for $6. Guidelines for #10 SASE or via e-mail.

NONFICTION Needs general interest, how-to, interview, new product, opinion, personal experience, travel, book reviews. **Buys 48-60 mss/year.** Send complete ms. Length: 800-1,200 words. **Pays 3¢/word.**

PHOTOS Include SASE for return of photos. Send photos. Captions, identification of subjects required. Reviews contact sheets, negatives, transparencies, 8×10 (preferred) and 5×7 prints, digital photos preferred (minimum 300 dpi). Offers $10 b $20 cover photo. Costs of converting slides and negatives to prints are deducted from payment.

⊘⊘⊘⊘ ISLANDS

Bonnier Corp., 460 N. Orlando Ave., Suite 200, Winter Park FL 32789. (407)628-4802. E-mail: story-ideas@islands.com. Website: islands.com. **80% freelance written**. Magazine published 8 times/year. We cover accessible and once-in-a-lifetime islands from many different perspectives: travel, culture, lifestyle. We ask our authors to give us the essence of the island and do it with literary flair. Estab. 1981. Circ. 250,000. Byline given. Pays on publication. Offers 25% kill fee. Publishes ms an average of 8 months after acceptance. Accepts queries by e-mail. Responds in 2 months to queries. Responds in 6 weeks to mss Sample copy for $6. E-mail us for writer's guidelines.

NONFICTION Needs book excerpts, essays, general interest, interview, photo feature, travel, service shorts, island-related material. **Buys 25 feature mss/year.** Send complete ms. Length: 2,000-4,000 words. **Pays $750-2,500.** Sometimes pays expenses of writers on assignment.

PHOTOS "Fine color photography is a special attraction of *Islands*, and we look for superb composition, technical quality, and editorial applicability. Will not accept or be responsible for unsolicited images or artwork.".

COLUMNS Discovers section (island related news), 100-250 words; Taste (island cuisine), 900-1,000 words; Travel Tales (personal essay), 900-1,100 words; Live the Life (island expat Q&A). Query with

published clips. **Pays $25-1,000.**

JOURNEY MAGAZINE

AAA, 1745 114th Ave. S.E., Bellevue WA 98004. **Contact:** Nicole Meoli, editor. The bimonthly magazine for members of AAA Washington reaches readers in Washington and northern Idaho. Our goal is to present readers with lively and informative stories on lifestyle, travel and automotive topics that encourage them to discover and explore the Northwest and beyond. Articles range from 500 to 1,800 words. We assign stories based on writers' proposals, and rarely accept completed manuscripts. We look for writers who combine sound research and reporting skills with a strong voice and excellent storytelling ability. We adhere to AP style. A solid knowledge of the Pacific Northwest is also required. We create our editorial calendar in the spring for the following calendar year. We encourage you to read several issues of *Journey* to familiarize yourself with our publication before you submit article ideas. *Journey* pays up to $1 per word upon acceptance for first North American rights. Some stories run alternatively in our Western and Puget Sound editions and may also be published on the Website. We run all articles with high-quality photographs and illustrations. If you are a published photographer, let us know but please do not submit any photos unless requested. To be considered for an assignment, mail a query along with three samples of published work. Circ. 550,000. Pays on acceptance Responds within 3 months with SASE.

⊘⊘ MOTORHOME

Affinity Group Inc., 2575 Vista Del Mar Dr., Ventura CA 93001. (805)667-4100. Fax: (805)667-4484. E-mail: info@motorhomemagazine.com. Website: motorhomemagazine.com. **Contact:** Eileen Hubbard, editor. **60% freelance written**. Monthly magazine. "*MotorHome* is a magazine for owners and prospective buyers of motorized recreational vehicles who are active outdoorsmen and wide-ranging travelers. We cover all aspects of the RV lifestyle; editorial material is both technical and nontechnical in nature. Regular features include tests and descriptions of various models of motorhomes, travel adventures, and hobbies pursued in such vehicles, objective analysis of equipment and supplies for such vehicles, and do-it-yourself articles. Guides within the magazine provide listings of manufacturers, rentals, and other sources of equipment and accessories of interest to enthusiasts. Articles must have an RV slant and excellent photography accompanying text." Estab. 1968. Circ. 150,000. Byline given. Pays on acceptance. Offers 30% kill fee. Publishes ms an average of within 1 year after acceptance. Editorial lead time 4 months. Submit seasonal material 6 months in advance. Accepts queries by mail, fax. Responds in 1 month to queries. Responds in 2 months to mss. Sample copy free. Guidelines available online or for #10 SASE.

NONFICTION Needs general interest, historical, how-to, humor, interview, new product, personal experience, photo feature, technical, travel, celebrity profiles, recreation, lifestyle, legislation, all RV related. No diaries of RV trips or negative RV experiences. **Buys 120 mss/year.** Query with published clips. Length: 250-2,500 words. **Pays $300-600.**

PHOTOS Digital photography accepted. Send photos. Captions, identification of subjects, model releases required. Reviews 35mm slides. Offers no additional payment for art accepted with ms. Pays $500 for covers.

COLUMNS Crossroads (offbeat briefs of people, places, and events of interest to travelers), 100-200 words; Keepers (tips, resources). Query with published clips or send complete ms. **Pays $100**

○$$ NORTH AMERICAN INNS MAGAZINE

Harworth Publishing Inc., Box 998, Guelph ON N1H 6N1 Canada. (519)767-6059. Fax: (519)821-0479. E-mail: editor@harworthpublishing.com. Website: innsmagazine.com. *North American Inns* is a national publication for travel, dining and pastimes. It focuses on inns, beds & breakfasts, resorts and travel in North America. The magazine is targeted to travelers looking for exquisite getaways. Accepts queries by e-mail. Guidelines by e-mail.

NONFICTION Needs general interest, interview, new product, opinion, personal experience, travel. Query. Length: 300-600 words. **Pays $175-250 (Canadian).**

FILLERS Short quips or nominations at 75 words are **$25 each**. All stories submitted have to accompany photos. Please e-mail photos to designer@harworthpublishing.com.

$$ NORTHWEST TRAVEL

Northwest Regional Magazines, 4969 Hwy. 101 N., Suite 2, Florence OR 97439. (541)997-8401 or (800)348-8401. Fax: (541)902-0400. E-mail: rosemary@nwmags.com. Website: northwestmagazines.com. **Contact:** Rosemary Camozzi. **60% freelance written**. Bimonthly magazine. "We like energetic writing about popular activities and destinations in the Pacific Northwest. *Northwest Travel* aims to give readers practical ideas on where to go in the region. Magazine covers Oregon, Washington, Idaho, British Columbia, Alaska and western Montana." Estab. 1991. Circ. 50,000. Pays after publication. Publishes ms an average of 8 months after acceptance. Submit seasonal material 6 months in advance. Accepts queries by mail, e-mail. Responds in 3 months to queries. Responds in 3 months to mss. Sample copy for $4.50. Guidelines available online.

NONFICTION Needs historical, interview, rarely, photo feature, travel in Northwest region. No "cliché-ridden pieces on places that everyone covers." **Buys 40 mss/year.** Query with or without published clips. Submit copy on CD or via e-mail. Length: 1,000-1,500 words. **Pays $100-500 for feature articles, and contributor copies.**

REPRINTS Send photocopy and information about when and where the material previously appeared. Pays 25% of amount paid for original article

PHOTOS Provide credit and model release information on cover photos. Digital photos on CD (300 dpi 8 ½x11 ½). State availability. Captions, identification of subjects, True required. Reviews transparencies, prefers dupes. Pays $425 for cover; $100 for stand-alone photos; $100 for Back Page.

COLUMNS Worth a Stop (brief items describing places worth a stop), 350-500 words. **Pays $50-100**. Back Page (photo and large caption package on a specific activity, season, or festival with some technical photo info), 80 words and 1 slide. **Pays $100. Buys 25-30 mss/year.**

$ PATHFINDERS

6325 Germantown Ave., Philadelphia PA 19144. (215)438-2140. Fax: (215)438-2144. E-mail: editors@pathfinderstravel.com. Website: pathfinderstravel.com. **75% freelance written**. Bimonthly magazine covering travel for people of color, primarily African-Americans. We look for lively, original, well-written stories that provide a good sense of place, with useful information and fresh ideas about travel and the travel industry. Our main audience is African-Americans, though we do look for articles relating to other persons of color: Native Americans, Hispanics and Asians. Estab. 1997. Circ. 100,000. Byline given. Pays on publication. Accepts queries by mail, e-mail. Responds in 1 month to queries. Responds in 2 months to mss. Sample copy at bookstores (Barnes & Noble, Borders). Guidelines available online.

NONFICTION Needs essays, historical, how-to, personal experience, photo feature, travel, all vacation travel oriented. No more pitches on Jamaica. We get these all the time. **Buys 16-20 mss/year.** Send complete ms. 1,200-1,400 words for cover stories; 1,000-1,200 words for features. **Pays $200.**

PHOTOS State availability.

COLUMNS Chef's Table, Post Cards from Home; Looking Back; City of the Month, 500-600 words. Send complete ms. **Pays $150.**

$$ PILOT GETAWAYS MAGAZINE

Airventure Publishing LLC, P.O. Box 550, Glendale CA 91209-0550. (818)241-1890. Fax: (818)241-1895. E-mail: info@pilotgetaways.com. Website: pilotgetaways.com. **90% freelance written.** Bimonthly magazine covering aviation travel for private pilots. *Pilot Getaways* is a travel magazine for private pilots. Our articles cover destinations that are easily accessible by private aircraft, including details such as airport transportation, convenient hotels, and attractions. Other regular features include fly-in dining, flying tips, and bush flying. Estab. 1999. Circ. 25,000. Byline given. Pays on publication. Editorial lead time 4 months. Submit seasonal material 9 months in advance. Accepts queries by mail, e-mail, fax, phone. Accepts simultaneous submissions. Responds in 2 weeks to queries. Responds in 2 months to mss. Sample copy and writer's guidelines free.

NONFICTION Needs travel, specifically travel guide articles. "We rarely publish articles about events that have already occurred, such as travel logs about trips the authors have taken or air show reports." **Buys 30 mss/year.** Query. Length: 1,000-3,500 words. **Pays $100-500.**

PHOTOS State availability. Captions, identification of subjects required. Reviews contact sheets, negatives, 35mm transparencies, prints, GIF/JPEG/TIFF files. Negotiates payment individually.

COLUMNS Weekend Getaways (short fly-in getaways), 2,000 words; Fly-in Dining (reviews of airport restaurants), 1,200 words; Flying Tips (tips and pointers on flying technique), 1,000 words; Bush Flying (getaways to unpaved destinations), 1,500 words. **Buys 20 mss/year.** Query. **Pays $100-500.**

$$$ PORTHOLE CRUISE MAGAZINE

Panoff Publishing, 4517 NW 31st Ave., Ft. Lauderdale FL 33309-3403. (954)377-7777. Fax: (954)377-7000. E-mail: editorial@ppigroup.com. E-mail: jlaign@ppigroup.com; jornstein@ppigroup.com. Website: porthole.com. **Contact:** Send queries to both Jeff Laign, editorial director, and Jodi Ornstein, managing editor. **70% freelance written.** Bimonthly magazine covering the cruise industry. *Porthole Cruise Magazine* entices its readers to take a cruise vacation by delivering information that is timely, accurate, colorful, and entertaining. Estab. 1992. Circ. 80,000. Byline given. Pays on publication. Offers 20% kill fee. Publishes ms an average of 6 months after acceptance. Editorial lead time 8 months. Submit seasonal material 5 months in advance. Accepts queries by e-mail. Accepts simultaneous submissions. Guidelines available online.

NONFICTION Needs general interest, cruise related, historical, how-to, pick a cruise, not get seasick, travel tips, humor, interview, crew on board or industry executives, new product, personal experience, photo feature, travel, off-the-beaten-path, adventure, ports, destinations, cruises, onboard fashion, spa articles, duty-free shopping, port shopping, ship reviews. No articles on destinations that can't be reached by ship. **Buys 60 mss/year.** Length: 1,000-1,200 words. **Pays $500-600 for assigned feature articles.**

PHOTOS Contact: Linda Douthat, creative director. State availability. Captions, identification of subjects, model releases required. Reviews digital images and original transparencies. Rates available upon request to ldouthat@ppigroup.com.

$$ RECREATION NEWS

Official Publication of the RecGov.org, 204 Greenwood Rd., Linthicum MD 21090. (410)944-4852. Website: recreationnews.com. **Contact:** Marvin Bond, editor. **75% freelance written.** Monthly guide to leisure-time activities for federal and private industry workers covering Mid-Atlantic travel destinations, outdoor recreation, and cultural activities. Estab. 1982. Circ. 115,000. Byline given. Pays on publication. Publishes ms an average of 6 months after acceptance. Submit seasonal material 10 months in advance. Accepts queries by mail, e-mail, phone. Accepts simultaneous submissions. Responds in 2 months to queries. See sample copy and writer's guidelines online.

NONFICTION Needs Mid-Atlantic travel destinations, outdoor recreation. Special issues: Skiing (December), Golf (April), Theme Parks (July). Query with published clips or links. Length: 600-900 words. **Pays $50-300.**

REPRINTS Send tearsheet or typed ms with rights for sale noted and information about when and where the material previously appeared. Pays $50.

💲💲💲💲 SPA

Bonnier Corp., 415 Jackson St., San Francisco CA 94111. (415)632-1633. Fax: (415)632-1640. Website: spamagazine.com. Bimonthly magazine covering health spas: treatments, travel, cuisine, fitness, beauty. Approachable and accessible, authoritative and full of advice, *Spa* is the place to turn for information and tips on nutrition, spa cuisine/recipes, beauty, health, skin care, spa travel, fitness, well-being and renewal. Byline given. Offers 25% kill fee. Editorial lead time 3 months. Accepts queries by mail. Sample copy for $6.

COLUMNS In Touch (spa news, treatments, destinations); Body (nutrition, health & fitness, spa therapies); Rituals (spa at home, beauty, home, books and music, mind/body).

♻💲💲 SPA LIFE

Harworth Publishing, Inc., P.O. Box 998, Guelph ON N1H 6N1 Canada. (519)767-6059. Fax: (519)821-0479. E-mail: editor@harworthpublishing.com. Website: spalifemagazine.com. "*Spa Life* is about more than just spas. With favorite recipes from featured spa destinations, mouth-watering treats are at your fingertips. *Spa Life* is also dedicated to personal and health issues." Estab. 2000. Accepts queries by e-mail. Guidelines by e-mail.

NONFICTION Needs general interest, interview, new product, personal experience, travel. Length: 300-600 words. **Pays $25-50 (Canadian).**

FILLERS photos e-mailed to: designer@harworthpublishing.com.

🌑💲💲 TIMES OF THE ISLANDS

Times Publications, Ltd., P.O. Box 234, Lucille Lightbourne Bldg., #7, Providenciales Turks & Caicos Islands British West Indies. (649)946-4788. Fax: (649)946-4788. E-mail: timespub@tciway.tc. Website: timespub.tc. **60% freelance written**. Quarterly magazine covering the Turks & Caicos Islands. "*Times of the Islands* is used by the public and private sector to inform visitors and potential investors/developers about the Islands. It goes beyond a superficial

overview of tourist attractions with in-depth articles about natural history, island heritage, local personalities, new development, offshore finance, sporting activities, visitors' experiences, and Caribbean fiction." Estab. 1988. Circ. 10,000. Byline given. Pays on publication. Publishes ms an average of 6 months after acceptance. Editorial lead time 4 months. Submit seasonal material at least 4 months in advance. Accepts queries by e-mail. Accepts simultaneous submissions. Responds in 6 weeks to queries. Responds in 2 months to mss. Sample copy for $6. Guidelines available online.

NONFICTION Needs book excerpts, essays, general interest, Caribbean art, culture, cooking, crafts, historical, humor, interview, locals, personal experience, trips to the Islands, photo feature, technical, island businesses, travel, book reviews, nature, ecology, business (offshore finance), watersports. **Buys 20 mss/year.** Query. Length: 500-3,000 words. **Pays $200-600.**

REPRINTS Send photocopy and information about when and where the material previously appeared. Payment varies

PHOTOS Send photos. Identification of subjects required. Reviews digital photos. Pays $15-100/photo.

COLUMNS On Holiday (unique experiences of visitors to Turks & Caicos), 500-1,500 words. **Buys 4 mss/year. mss/year.** Query. **Pays $200.**

FICTION Needs adventure, sailing, diving, ethnic, Caribbean, historical, Caribbean, humorous, travel-related, mystery, novel concepts. **Buys 2-3 mss/year.** Query. Length: 1,000-3,000 words. **Pays $250-400.**

💲💲 TRAILER LIFE

Affinity Group, Inc., 2575 Vista Del Mar Dr., Ventura CA 93001. Fax: (805)667-4484. E-mail: info@trailerlife.com. Website: trailerlife.com. **40% freelance written**. Monthly magazine. "*Trailer Life* magazine is written specifically for active people whose overall lifestyle is based on travel and recreation in their RV. Every issue includes product tests, travel articles, and other features—ranging from lifestyle to vehicle maintenance." Estab. 1941. Circ. 270,000. Byline given. Pays on acceptance. Offers kill fee. Offers 30% kill fee for assigned articles that are not acceptable. Publishes ms an average of 6 months after acceptance. Editorial lead time 4 months. Submit seasonal material 6 months in advance. Accepts queries by mail. Responds in 2 months to queries. Responds in 2 months to mss. Sample copy free. Guidelines for #10 SASE.

NONFICTION Needs historical, how-to, technical, humor, new product, opinion, personal experience, travel. "No vehicle tests, product evaluations or road tests; tech material is strictly assigned. No diaries or trip logs, no non-RV trips; nothing without an RV-hook." **Buys 75 mss/year.** Query. Length: 250-2,500 words. **Pays $125-700.** Sometimes pays expenses of writers on assignment.

PHOTOS Send photos. Identification of subjects, model releases required. Reviews transparencies, b&w contact sheets . Offers no additional payment for photos accepted with ms, does pay for supplemental photos.

COLUMNS Around the Bend (news, trends of interest to RVers), 100 words. **Buys 70 mss/year.** Query or send complete ms **Pays $75-250.**

⊖⊖⊖⊖⊗ TRAVEL + LEISURE

American Express Publishing Corp., 1120 Avenue of the Americas, New York NY 10036. (212)382-5600. Website: travelandleisure.com. **80% freelance written.** *Travel + Leisure* is a monthly magazine edited for affluent travelers. It explores the latest resorts, hotels, fashions, foods, and drinks, as well as political, cultural, and economic issues affecting travelers. Circ. 925,000. Byline given. Pays on acceptance. Offers 25% kill fee. Accepts queries by mail, e-mail. Responds in 6 weeks to queries. Responds in 6 weeks to mss. Sample copy for $5.50 from (800)888-8728. Guidelines available online.

NONFICTION Needs travel. **Buys 40-50 feature (3,000-5,000 words) and 200 short (125-500 words) mss/year.** Query (e-mail preferred) **Pays $4,000-6,000/feature; $100-500/short piece.** Pays expenses of writers on assignment.

PHOTOS Contact: Photo Dept. Discourages submission of unsolicited transparencies. Captions required. Payment varies.

COLUMNS Length: 2,500-3,500 words. **Buys 125-150 mss/year. Pays $2,000-3,500.**

⊗ TRAVEL NATURALLY

Internaturally, Inc., P.O. Box 317, Newfoundland NJ 07435-0317. (973)697-3552. Fax: (973)697-8313. E-mail: naturally@internaturally.com. Website: internaturally.com. **90% freelance written.** Quarterly magazine covering wholesome family nude recreation and travel locations. *Travel Naturally* looks at

why millions of people believe that removing clothes in public is a good idea, and at places specifically created for that purpose—with good humor, but also in earnest. *Travel Naturally* takes you to places where your personal freedom is the only agenda, and to places where textile-free living is a serious commitment. Estab. 1981. Circ. 35,000. Byline given. Pays on publication. Editorial lead time 4 months. Submit seasonal material 4 months in advance. Accepts queries by mail, e-mail, fax. Accepts simultaneous submissions. Sample copy for $9. Guidelines available online.

NONFICTION Needs general interest, interview, personal experience, photo feature, travel. **Buys 12 mss/year.** Send complete ms. 2 pages. **Pays $80/published page, including photos.**

REPRINTS Pays 50% of original rate.

PHOTOS Send photos. Reviews contact sheets, negatives, transparencies, prints, high resolution digital images.

FILLERS Needs anecdotes, facts, gags, newsbreaks, short humor, poems, artwork. **Payment is pro-rated based on length.**

⊗ TRAVEL SMART

Communications House, Inc., P.O. Box 397, Dobbs Ferry NY 10522. E-mail: travelsmartnow@aol.com. Website: travelsmartnewsletter.com. Monthly newsletter covering information on good-value travel. Estab. 1976. Circ. 20,000. Pays on publication. Accepts queries by mail, e-mail. Responds in 6 weeks to queries. Responds in 6 weeks to mss. Sample copy for sae with 9×12 envelope and 3 First-Class stamps. Guidelines for sae with 9×12 envelope and 3 First-Class stamps.

NONFICTION Query. Length: 100-1,500 words. **Pays $150 maximum.**

⊖⊗⊗ VERGE MAGAZINE

Verge Magazine Inc., P.O. Box 147, Peterborough ON K9J 6Y5 Canada. E-mail: contributing@vergemagazine.org. Website: vergemagazine.org. **Contact:** Zalina Alvi, editor. **60% freelance written.** Quarterly magazine. Each issue takes you around the world, with people who are doing something different & making a difference doing it. This is the magazine resource for those wanting to volunteer, work, study or adventure overseas. "*Verge* is the magazine for people who travel with purpose. It explores ways to get out & see the world by volunteering, working & studying overseas. Our readers are typically young (17-40 yrs.), or young at heart, active, independent travelers. Editorial content is intended to inform & motivate the reader by profiling unique individuals & experiences that are timely & socially relevant. We look for articles that are issue driven & combine an engaging & well-told story with nuts & bolts how-to information. Wherever possible & applicable, efforts should be made to provide sources where readers can find out more about the subject, or ways in which readers can become involved in the issue covered." Estab. 2002. Circ. 10,000. Byline given. Pays on publication. Publishes ms an average of 6 months after acceptance. Submit seasonal material 8-12 months in advance. Accepts queries by mail, e-mail. Responds in 8 weeks to queries. Responds in 2 months to mss. Sample copy for $6 plus shipping. Guidelines available online.

NONFICTION Contact: Julia Steinecke. Needs how-to, humor, interview, travel, News. "We do not want pure travelogues, predictable tourist experiences, luxury travel, stories highighting a specific company or organisation." **Buys 30-40 mss/yr. mss/year.** Send complete ms. Length: 600-1,000 words. **Pays $60-500 for assigned articles. Pays $60-250 for unsolicited articles.**

PHOTOS Send link to online portfolio to editor@vergemagazine.ca or mail portfolio on CD or DVD to *Verge Magazine*. Captions required. Reviews GIF/JPEG files. Negotiates payment individually.

COLUMNS Contact: Julia Steinecke. **Buys 20-30 mss/yr. mss/year.** Query with published clips. **Pays $$60-$250.**

$ $ WOODALL'S REGIONALS

2575 Vista Del Mar Dr., Ventura CA 93001. Website: woodalls.com. Monthly magazine for RV and camping enthusiasts. Woodall's Regionals include *CamperWays, Midwest RV Traveler, Northeast Outdoors, Florida RV Traveler.* Byline given. Accepts queries by mail, e-mail. Responds in 1-2 months to queries. Sample copy free. Guidelines free.

NONFICTION Buys 300 mss/year. Query with published clips. Length: 1,000-1,400 words. **Pays $180-220/feature; $75-100/department article and short piece.**

WOMEN'S

$ $ $ BRIDAL GUIDE

R.F.P., LLC, 330 Seventh Ave., 10th Floor, New York NY 10001. (212)838-7733; (800)472-7744. Fax: (212)308-7165. E-mail: editorial@bridalguide.com. Website: bridalguide.com. **20% freelance written.** Bimonthly magazine covering relationships, sexuality, fitness, wedding planning, psychology, finance, travel. Only works with experienced/published writers. Pays on acceptance. Accepts queries by mail. Responds in 3 months to queries. Responds in 3 months to mss. Sample copy for $5 and SAE with 4 first-class stamps. Writer's guidelines available.

NONFICTION Please do not send queries concerning beauty, fashion, or home design stories since we produce them in-house. We do not accept personal wedding essays, fiction, or poetry. Address travel queries to travel editor. All correspondence accompanied by an SASE will be answered. **Buys 100 mss/year.** Query with published clips from national consumer magazines. Length: 1,000-2,000 words. **Pays 50¢/word.**

PHOTOS Photography and illustration submissions should be sent to the art department.

⊕ ↪ $ $ THE BROADSHEET

Broad Universe, 1600 W Green Tree Rd., Apt 225, Milwaukee WI 53209. E-mail: broadsheet@broaduniverse.org. Website: broaduniverse.org. **Contact:** Lee-Anne Phillips, editor-in-chief. Covers articles about women writers of science fiction, fantasy, and horror genre fiction. "*The Broadsheet* is a small web-based zine published three times a year. *The Broadsheet* accepts art, articles, interviews, book reviews and commentaries about any topic involving women writers and artists in science fiction, fantasy and horror. It also accepts general articles on the writing or marketing of science fiction/fiction/horror. We only print nonfiction. Anyone may submit, whether female or male, new writer or experienced pro. Interviews should be between 3,000 and 5,000 words. Brief articles (2,000 words or less) are preferred for Create, Sell, Read, and Think. However, excellent interviews and articles of shorter or longer lengths will also receive consideration." Pays for articles specifically targeting their marketplace and membership. Estab. 2000. Pays on acceptance. Accepts queries by e-mail. Query first via e-mail, according to topic: For Art: Constance Burris at art@broaduniverse.org. For Read: JJ Pionke at editor1@broaduniverse.org. For Create: Carol Ullmann at editor3@broaduniverse.org. All other topics: Broadsheet Editor Lee-Anne Phillips at broadsheet@broaduniverse.org. Accepts simultaneous submissions.

NONFICTION Contact: JJ Pionke. **Art and Interviews: $50; Create, Sell, Think: $40; Read: $25 for**

the usual brief review; up to $40 for pieces that deliver something more. A brief biography of the contributor, including any link to the artist or author's website, will also run with the piece if so desired. Art and articles appearing in past issues of *The Broadsheet* are made available in our public archives unless the artist or author states otherwise in writing.

✪❸❸❸❸ CHATELAINE

One Mount Pleasant Rd., 8th Floor, Toronto ON M4Y 2Y5 Canada. (416)764-1888. Fax: (416)764-2891. E-mail: storyideas@chatelaine.rogers.com. Website: chatelaine.com. Monthly magazine. "*Chatelaine* is edited for Canadian women ages 25-49, their changing attitudes and lifestyles. Key editorial ingredients include health, finance, social issues and trends, as well as fashion, beauty, food and home decor. Regular departments include Health pages, Entertainment, Money, Home, Humour, How-to." Byline given. Pays on acceptance. Offers 25-50% kill fee. Accepts queries by mail, e-mail (preferred). Responds in 4-6 weeks to 1 month to queries; up to 2 months to proposals. See writers' guidelines online at website.

> ○ "*Does not accept unsolicited manuscripts*. Submit story ideas online."

❸❸ COMPLETE WOMAN

Associated Publications, Inc., 875 N. Michigan Ave., Suite 3434, Chicago IL 60611. (312)266-8680. Fax: (312)573-3020. Website: thecompletewomanmagazine. com. **90% freelance written**. Bimonthly magazine. Estab. 1980. Circ. 300,000. Byline given. Pays 45 days after acceptance. Publishes ms an average of 6 months after acceptance. Editorial lead time 6 months. Submit seasonal material 5 months in advance. Accepts queries by mail. Accepts simultaneous submissions. Responds in 2 months to queries. Responds in 2 months to mss Guidelines with #10 SASE.

> ○ Manuscripts should be written for today's busy women, in a concise, clear format with useful information. Our readers want to know about the important things: sex, love, relationships, career, and self-discovery. Examples of true-life anecdotes incorporated into articles work well for our readers, who are always interested in how other women are dealing with life's ups and downs.

NONFICTION Needs book excerpts, expose, of interest to women, general interest, how-to, beauty/diet-related, humor, inspirational, interview, celebrities, new product, personal experience, photo feature, sex, love, relationship advice. **Buys 60-100 mss/year.** Send complete ms. Length: 800-2,000 words. **Pays $160-500.** Sometimes pays expenses of writers on assignment.

REPRINTS Send tearsheet, photocopy or typed ms with rights for sale noted and information about when and where the material previously appeared.

PHOTOS Photo features with little or no copy should be sent to Kourtney McKay. Send photos. Captions, identification of subjects, model releases required. Reviews 2.25 or 35mm transparencies, 5×7 prints. Pays $35-100/photo.

COUNTRY WOMAN

Reiman Publications, 5400 South 60th St., Greendale WI 53129. (414)423-0100. E-mail: editors@country-womanmagazine.com. Website: countrywomanmagazine.com. **75-85% freelance written**. Bimonthly magazine. *Country Woman* is for contemporary rural women of all ages and backgrounds and from all over the U.S. and Canada. It includes a sampling of the diversity that makes up rural women's lives—love of home, family, farm, ranch, community, hobbies, enduring values, humor, attaining new skills and appreciating present, past and future all within the context of the lifestyle that surrounds country living. Estab. 1970. Byline given. Pays on acceptance. Submit seasonal material 5 months in advance. Accepts queries by mail. Accepts simultaneous submissions. Responds in 2 months to queries. Responds in 3 months to mss. Sample copy for $2 and SASE. Guidelines for #10 SASE.

NONFICTION Needs general interest, historical, how-to, crafts, community projects, decorative, antiquing, etc., humor, inspirational, interview, personal experience, photo feature, packages profiling interesting country women-all pertaining to rural women's interests. Query. 1,000 words maximum.

REPRINTS Send typed manuscript with rights for sale noted and information about when and where the material previously appeared. Payment varies

PHOTOS Uses only excellent quality color photos. No b&w. We pay for photo/feature packages. State availability of or send photos. Captions, identification of subjects, model releases required. Reviews 35mm or 2.25 transparencies, excellent-quality color prints.

COLUMNS Why Farm Wives Age Fast (humor), I Remember When (nostalgia) and Country Decorating. Length: 500-1,000 words. **Buys 10-12 mss/year.**

Query or send ms.

FICTION Contact: Kathleen Anderson, managing editor. Main character *must* be a country woman. All fiction must have a country setting. Fiction must have a positive, upbeat message. Includes fiction in every issue. Would buy more fiction if stories suitable for our audience were sent our way. No contemporary, urban pieces that deal with divorce, drugs, etc. Send complete ms. Length: 750-1,000 words.

POETRY Needs light verse, traditional. Poetry must have rhythm and rhyme! It must be country-related, positive and upbeat. Always looking for seasonal poetry. Buys 6-12 poems/year. Submit maximum 6 poems. Length: 4-24 lines.

$$$$ ELLE

Hachette Filipacchi Media U.S., Inc., 1271 Avenue of the Americas, 41st Floor, New York NY 10020. (212)767-5800. Fax: (212)489-4210. Website: elle.com. Monthly magazine. Edited for the modern, sophisticated, affluent, well-traveled woman in her twenties to early thirties. Circ. 1,100,000. Editorial lead time 3 months.

💬 Query first.

$$$$ FAMILY CIRCLE MAGAZINE

Meredith Corporation, 375 Lexington Ave., 9th Floor, New York NY 10017. Website: familycircle.com. **80% freelance written**. Magazine published every 3 weeks. We are a national women's service magazine which covers many stages of a woman's life, along with her everyday concerns about social, family, and health issues. Submissions should focus on families with children ages 8-16. Estab. 1932. Circ. 4,200,000. Byline given. Offers 20% kill fee. Editorial lead time 4 months. Submit seasonal material 4 months in advance. Responds in 2 months to queries. Responds in 2 months to mss. For back issues, send $6.95 to P.O. Box 3156, Harlan IA 51537. Guidelines available online.

NONFICTION Needs essays, opinion, personal experience, women's interest subjects such as family and personal relationships, children, physical and mental health, nutrition and self-improvement. No fiction or poetry. **Buys 200 mss/year.** Submit detailed outline, 2 clips, cover letter describing your publishing history, SASE or IRCs. Length: 1,000-2,500 words. **Pays $1/word.**

🍁$$$$ FLARE MAGAZINE

One Mt. Pleasant Rd., 8th Floor, Toronto ON M4Y 2Y5 Canada. (416)764-1829. Fax: (416)764-2866. E-mail: editors@flare.com. Website: flare.com. Monthly magazine for women ages 17-35. Byline given. Offers 50% kill fee. Accepts queries by e-mail. Response time varies. Sample copy for #10 SASE. Guidelines available online.

NONFICTION Buys 24 mss/year. Query. Length: 200-1,200 words. **Pays $1/word.** Pays expenses of writers on assignment.

GIRLFRIENDZ

The Word Source, LLC, 6 Brookville Drive, Cherry Hill NJ 08003. E-mail: tobi@girlfriendzmag.com. Website: girlfriendzmag.com; facebook.com/girlfriendz. **80% freelance written**. Bimonthly magazine covering Baby Boomer women. "As a publication by and for Baby Boomer women, we are most interested in entertaining, educating and empowering our readers. Our target is smart women born between 1946 and 1964. We like a little humor in our articles, but only if it's appropriate and subtle. And most importantly, all facts must be checked for accuracy. We insist on well-researched and well-documented information." Estab. 2007. Circ. 30,000. Byline given. Headshot and bio included. "As a startup, we are unable to pay our writers." Editorial lead time 3 months. Submit seasonal material 6 months in advance. Accepts queries by e-mail. Accepts simultaneous submissions. Responds in 2 weeks to queries. Sample copy for $5. Guidelines available online.

NONFICTION Needs book excerpts, exposè, historical, how-to, humor, interview, (celebrities only), new product, articles of interest to women born 1946-1964; especially interested in local and national celebrities. Examples of those we've already profiled: Dr. Ruth, Joan Lunden, Fran Drescher. "We do not want fiction, essays or poetry." **Buys 20 mss/year.** Query. Length: 735-1,200 words. Sometimes pays expenses of writers on assignment.

PHOTOS State availability. Captions, identification of subjects required. Reviews JPEGs and/or PDFs, 300 dpi. Offers no additional payment for photos accepted with mss.

$$$$ GLAMOUR

Conde Nast Publications, Inc., 4 Times Square, 16th Floor, New York NY 10036. (212)286-2860. Fax: (212)286-8336. Website: glamour.com. Cynthia Leive, editor-in-chief. **Contact:** Susan Goodall. Monthly magazine covering subjects ranging from fashion, beauty and health, personal relationships, career, travel, food and entertainment. "*Glamour* is edited for the contemporary woman, and informs her of the trends and recommends how she can adapt them to her needs, and motivates her to take action." Estab. 1939. Circ. 2,320,325. Accepts queries by mail. Not available online.

NONFICTION Needs personal experience, relationships, travel. **Pays 75¢-$1/word**

PHOTOS Only uses professional photographers.

$$$$ GOOD HOUSEKEEPING

Hearst Corp., 300 W. 57th St., 28th Floor, New York NY 10019. (212)649-2200. Website: goodhousekeeping.com. Monthly magazine. "*Good Housekeeping* is edited for the 'new traditionalist.' Articles which focus on food, fitness, beauty, and child care draw upon the resources of the Good Housekeeping Institute. Editorial includes human interest stories, articles that focus on social issues, money management, health news, travel." Circ. 5,000,000. Byline given. Pays on acceptance. Offers 25% kill fee. Submit seasonal material 6 months in advance. Responds in 2-3 months to queries. Responds in 2-3 months to mss. For sample copy, call (212)649-2359. Guidelines for #10 SASE.

NONFICTION Buys 4-6 mss/issue mss/year. Query. Length: 1,500-2,500 words. Pays expenses of writers on assignment.

PHOTOS Contact: Melissa Paterno, art director; Toni Paciello, photo editor. Photos purchased mostly on assignment. State availability. Model releases required. Pays $100-350 for b&w; $200-400 for color photos.

COLUMNS Profiles (inspirational, activist or heroic women), 400-600 words. Query with published clips. **Pays $1/word for items 300-600 words.**

FICTION Contact: Laura Mathews, fiction editor. No longer accepts unagented fiction submissions. Because of heavy volume of fiction submissions, *Good Housekeeping* is not accepting unsolicited submissions at this time. Agented submissions only. 1,500 words (short-shorts); novel according to merit of material; average 5,000 word short stories. **Pays $1,000 minimum.**

$$ GRACE ORMONDE WEDDING STYLE

Elegant Publishing, Inc., P.O. Box 89, Barrington RI 02806. Fax: (401)245-5371. E-mail: jessica@weddingstylemagazine.com. Website: weddingstylemagazine.com. **90% freelance written.** Semiannual magazine covering weddings catering to the affluent bride. Estab. 1997. Circ. 500,000. Pays on publication. Publishes ms an average of 4 months after acceptance. Editorial lead time 1 month. Sample copy available online. Guidelines by e-mail.

💬 Does not accept queries.

PHOTOS State availability. Reviews transparencies. Negotiates payment individually.

$$$$ HARPER'S BAZAAR

The Hearst Corp., 1700 Broadway, 37th Floor, New York NY 10019. (212)903-5000. Website: harpersbazaar.com. Estab. 1867. Circ. 711,000. Byline given. Pays on publication. Offers 25% kill fee. Responds in 2 months to queries.

💬 *Harper's Bazaar* is a monthly specialist magazine for women who enjoy fashion and beauty. It is edited for sophisticated women with exceptional taste. *Bazaar* offers ideas in fashion and beauty, and reports on issues and interests relevant to the lives of modern women.

NONFICTION Buys 36 mss/year. Query with published clips. Length: 2,000-3,000 words. **Payment negotiable**

COLUMNS Length: 500-700 words. **Payment negotiable.**

I DO . . . FOR BRIDES

P.O. Box 2007, Hiram GA 30141. (770)942-0913. E-mail: jgibbs@idoforbrides.com. E-mail: john@idoforbrides.com. Website: idoforbrides.com. **30% freelance written.** Quarterly magazine covering the bridal industry. The magazine includes tips for wedding preparation, bridal attire, honeymoon and wedding destinations. Publishes 4 regional versions: Alabama, Georgia, Tennessee, and Washington DC/Maryland/Virginia. Estab. 1996. Circ. 160,000. Byline given. Publishes ms an average of 8 months after acceptance. Editorial lead time 8 months. Submit seasonal material 8 months in advance. Accepts queries by mail, e-mail. Accepts simultaneous submissions.

NONFICTION Needs book excerpts, essays, general interest, historical, how-to, bridal-related, humor, inspirational, interview, new product, opinion, personal experience, photo feature, religious, travel. **Buys 8 mss/year.** Query. Length: 300-1,000 words. **Pays variable rate.**

⊘ $$$$ LADIES' HOME JOURNAL

Meredith Corp., 125 Park Ave., 20th Floor, New York NY 10017-5516. (212)557-6600. Fax: (212)455-1313. E-mail: lhj@mdp.com. Website: lhj.com. **50% freelance written**. Monthly magazine focusing on issues of concern to women 30-45. They cover a broader range of news and political issues than many women's magazines. *Ladies' Home Journal* is for active, empowered women who are evolving in new directions. It addresses informational needs with highly focused features and articles on a variety of topics: self, style, family, home, world, health, and food. Estab. 1882. Circ. 4.1 million. Pays on acceptance. Offers 25% kill fee. Publishes ms an average of 4-12 months after acceptance. Editorial lead time 4 months. Accepts queries by mail, e-mail. Accepts simultaneous submissions. Responds in 3 months to queries. Guidelines available online.

NONFICTION Send 1-2 page query, SASE, rÂˆsumÂˆ, clips via mail or e-mail (preferred). Length: 2,000-3,000 words. **Pays $2,000-4,000.** Pays expenses of writers on assignment.

PHOTOS *LHJ* arranges for its own photography almost all the time. State availability. Captions, identification of subjects, model releases required. Offers variable payment for photos accepted with ms.

FICTION Only short stories and novels submitted by an agent or publisher will be considered. No poetry of any kind. **Buys 12 mss/year.** Send complete ms. 2,000-2,500

○$$ THE LINK & VISITOR

Baptist Women of Ontario and Quebec, 100-304 The East Mall, Etobicoke ON M9B 6E2 Canada. (416)651-8967. E-mail: rsejames@gmail.com. Website: baptist-women.com. **Contact:** Renee James, editor/director of communications. **50% freelance written**. Magazine published 6 times/year designed to help Baptist women grow their world, faith, relationships, creativity, and mission vision—evangelical, egalitarian, Canadian. Estab. 1878. Circ. 3,500. Byline given. Pays on publication. Publishes ms an average of 6 months after acceptance. Editorial lead time 2 months. Submit seasonal material 4 months in advance. Accepts simultaneous submissions. Sample copy for 9×12 SAE with 2 first-class Canadian stamps. Guidelines available online.

NONFICTION Needs inspirational, interview, religious. **Buys 30-35 mss/year.** Send complete ms. Length: 750-2,000 words. **Pays 5-12¢/word (Canadian).** Sometimes pays expenses of writers on assignment.

PHOTOS State availability. Captions required. Offers no additional payment for photos accepted with ms.

$ LONG ISLAND WOMAN

Maraj, Inc., P.O. Box 176, Malverne NY 11565. E-mail: editor@liwomanonline.com. Website: liwomanonline.com. **40% freelance written**. Monthly magazine covering issues of importance to women—health, family, finance, arts, entertainment, fitness, travel, home. Estab. 2001. Circ. 40,000. Byline given. Pays within 1 month of publication. Offers 33% kill fee. Publishes ms an average of 3 months after acceptance. Editorial lead time 3 months. Submit seasonal material 3 months in advance. Accepts queries by mail, e-mail. Accepts simultaneous submissions. Responds in 8 weeks to queries. Responds in 3 months to mss. Sample copy for $5. Guidelines available online.

○ Responds if interested in using reprints that were submitted.

NONFICTION Needs book excerpts, general interest, how-to, humor, interview, new product, travel, reviews. **Buys 25-30 mss/year.** Send complete ms. Length: 500-1,800 words. **Pays $35-150.**

PHOTOS State availability of or send photos. Captions, identification of subjects, model releases required. Reviews 5×7 prints.

COLUMNS Humor; Health Issues; Family Issues; Financial and Business Issues; Book Reviews and Books; Arts and Entertainment; Travel and Leisure; Home and Garden; Fitness.

$$$$ MARIE CLAIRE

The Hearst Publishing Corp., Feature Submissions, Marie Claire Magazine, 300 W. 57th St., 34th Floor, New York NY 10019-1497. (212)649-5000. Fax: (212)649-5050. E-mail: JoannaColes@hearst.com. Website: marieclaire.com. **Contact:** Joanna Coles, editor-in-chief. Monthly magazine written for today's younger working woman with a smart service-oriented view. Estab. 1937. Circ. 952,223. Editorial lead time 6 months.

○ "Please make sure you are familiar with our content by reading the most previous issues. We prefer to receive story proposals, rather than completed work, so please send a query letter detailing your idea to the address below. If the editors find the subject suitable, they will contact you. Please enclose clips of your previously published materials, which we are unable to return to you. Please allow 4-6 weeks for a response."

$$$$ MS. MAGAZINE

433 S. Beverly Dr., Beverly Hills CA 90212. (310)556-2515. Fax: (310)556-2514. E-mail: mkort@msmagazine.com. Website: msmagazine.com. **70% freelance written.** Quarterly magazine on women's issues and news. Estab. 1972. Circ. 150,000. Byline given. Offers 25% kill fee. Responds in 3 months to queries. Responds in 3 months to mss. Sample copy for $9. Guidelines available online.

NONFICTION Buys 4-5 feature (2,000-3,000 words) and 4-5 short (500 words) mss/year. Query with published clips. Length: 300-3,500 words. **Pays $1/word, 50¢/word for news stories and book review.**

COLUMNS Buys 6-10 mss/year. Pays $1/word.

FICTION "*Ms.* welcomes the highest-quality original fiction and poetry, but is publishing these infrequently as of late."

$$ NA'AMAT WOMAN

350 Fifth Ave., Suite 4700, New York NY 10118. (212)563-5222. Fax: (212)563-5710. E-mail: naamat@naamat.org; judith@naamat.org. Website: naamat.org. **Contact:** Judith Sokoloff, editor. **80% freelance written.** Quarterly magazine covering Jewish issues/subjects. "We cover issues and topics of interest to the Jewish community in the U.S., Israel, and the rest of the world with emphasis on Jewish women's issues." Estab. 1926. Circ. 15,000. Byline given. Pays on publication. Publishes ms an average of 6 months after acceptance. Submit seasonal material 6 months in advance. Accepts queries by mail, e-mail. Accepts simultaneous submissions. Responds in 4 weeks to queries. Responds in 3 months to mss Sample copy for $2. Guidelines by e-mail.

NONFICTION Needs book excerpts, essays, historical, interview, personal experience, photo feature, travel, Jewish topics & issues, political & social issues & women's issues. **Buys 16-20 mss/year.** Send complete ms. **Pays 10-20¢/word for assigned and unsolicited articles.** Some

PHOTOS State availability. Reviews GIF/JPEG files. Negotiates payment individually.

FICTION "We want serious fiction, with insight, reflection and consciousness." Needs novel excerpts, literary with Jewish content. "We do not want fiction that is mostly dialogue. No corny Jewish humor. No Holocaust fiction." **Buys 1-2 mss/year. mss/year.** Query with published clips or send complete ms. Length: 2,000-3,000 words. **Pays 10-20¢/word for assigned articles and for unsolicited articles.**

$$$$ PREGNANCY

Future US, Inc., 4000 Shoreline Ct., Suite 400, S. San Francisco CA 94080-1960. (650)872-1642. E-mail: editors@pregnancymagazine.com. Website: pregnancymagazine.com. **40% freelance written.** Magazine covering products, wellness, technology fashion, and beauty for pregnant women; and products, health, and child care for babies up to 12 months old. "A large part of our audience is first-time moms who seek advice & information about health, relationships, diet, celebrities, fashion, & green living for pregnant women and babies up to 12 mos. old. Our readers are first-time and experienced moms (and dads) who want articles that are relevant to their modern lives. Our goal is to help our readers feel confident and prepared for pregnancy and parenthood by providing the best information for today's parents." Estab. 2000. Circ. 250,000. Offers kill fee. TBD Editorial lead time 5 months. Submit seasonal material 5-6 months in advance. Guidelines available at pregnancy360.com/writers.

NONFICTION Buys 60 mss/yr. mss/year. Length: 350-2,000 words.

P31 WOMAN

Proverbs 31 Ministries, 616-G Matthews-Mint Hill Rd., Charlotte NC 28105. (704)849-2270. E-mail: janet@proverbs31.org. Website: proverbs31.org. Janet Burke. **Contact:** Glynnis Whitwer, editor. **50% freelance written.** Monthly magazine covering Christian issues for women. "The *P31 Woman* provides Christian wives and mothers with articles that encourage them in their faith and support them in the many roles they have as women. We look for articles that have a Biblical foundation and offer inspiration, yet have a practical application to everyday life." Estab. 1992. Circ. 10,000. Byline given. Publishes ms an average of 6 months after acceptance. Editorial lead time 5 months. Submit seasonal material 5-6 months in advance. Accepts queries by mail, e-mail. Accepts simultaneous submissions. Responds in 2-4 weeks to queries. Responds in 1-2 months to mss. Sample copy online or $2 for hard copy. Guidelines available online.

NONFICTION Needs humor, inspirational, personal experience, religious. No biographical stories or articles about men's issues. Send complete ms. Length: 200-1,000 words. **Pays in contributor copies.**

❸❸❸⊘ REDBOOK MAGAZINE

Hearst Corp., Articles Dept., Redbook, 300 W. 57th St., 22nd Floor, New York NY 10019. Website: redbookmag.com/writersguidelines. **Contact:** Submissions Editor. Monthly magazine. "*Redbook* is targeted to women between the ages of 25 and 45 who define themselves as smart, capable, and happy with their lives. Many, but not all, of our readers are going through one of two key life transitions: single to married and married to mom. Each issue is a provocative mix of features geared to entertain and inform them, including: News stories on contemporary issues that are relevant to the reader's life and experience, and explore the emotional ramifications of cultural and social changes; First-person essays about dramatic pivotal moments in a woman's life; Marriage articles with an emphasis on strengthening the relationship; Short parenting features on how to deal with universal health and behavioral issues; Reporting on exciting trends in women's lives." Estab. 1903. Circ. 2,300,000. Pays on acceptance. Publishes ms an average of 6 months after acceptance. Responds in 3 months to queries. Responds in 3 months to mss. Guidelines available online.

NONFICTION Query with published clips and SASE 2,500-3,000 words/articles; 1,000-1,500 words/short articles

⟳ RESOURCES FOR FEMINIST RESEARCH

RFR/DRF (Resources for Feminist Research), OISE, University of Toronto, 252 Bloor St. W., Toronto ON M5S 1V6 Canada. E-mail: rfr@utoronto.ca. Website: oise.utoronto.ca/rfr. Semiannual academic journal covering feminist research in an interdisciplinary, international perspective. Estab. 1972. Circ. 2,500. Byline given. Publishes ms an average of 1 year after acceptance. Editorial lead time 1 year. Accepts queries by e-mail. Responds in 2 weeks to queries. Responds in 6-8 months to mss. Guidelines free.

NONFICTION Needs essays, academic articles and book reviews. Does not want nonacademic articles. Send complete ms. Length: 3,000-5,000 words.

PHOTOS Send photos. Identification of subjects required. Reviews prints, GIF/JPEG files. Offers no additional payment for photos accepted with ms.

❸❸❸❸ SELF

Conde Nast, 4 Times Square, New York NY 10036. (212)286-2860. Fax: (212)286-8110. E-mail: comments@self.com. Website: self.com. Monthly magazine for women ages 20-45. Self-confidence, self-assurance, and a healthy, happy lifestyle are pivotal to *Self* readers. This healthy lifestyle magazine delivers by addressing real-life issues from the inside out, with unparalleled energy and authority. From beauty, fitness, health and nutrition to personal style, finance, and happiness, the path to total well-being begins with *Self*. Circ. 1,300,000. Byline given on features and most short items. Pays on acceptance. Accepts queries by online submission form. Accepts simultaneous submissions. Responds in 1 month to queries. Guidelines for #10 sase.

◯*SELF* magazine does not accept unsolicited mss.

NONFICTION Buys 40 mss/year. Query with published clips. Length: 1,500-5,000 words. **Pays $1-2/word.**

COLUMNS Uses short, news-driven items on health, fitness, nutrition, money, jobs, love/sex, psychology and happiness, travel. Length: 300-1,000 words. **Buys 50 mss/year.** Query with published clips. **Pays $1-2/word.**

❸❸ SKIRT! MAGAZINE

Morris Communications, 7 Radcliffe St., Suite 302, Charleston SC 29403. (843)958-0027. Fax: (843)958-0029. E-mail: submissions@skirt.com. Website: skirt.com. Margaret Pilarski or Melissa Krueger at 843-958-0028. **Contact:** Nikki Hardin, publisher. **50% freelance written.** Monthly magazine covering women's interest. *Skirt!* is all about women—their work, play, families, creativity, style, health, wealth, bodies, and souls. The magazine's attitude is spirited, independent, outspoken, serious, playful, irreverent, sometimes controversial, and always passionate. Estab. 1994. Circ. 285,000. Byline given. Pays on publication. Publishes ms an average of 2 months after acceptance. Editorial lead time 2-3 months. Submit seasonal material 2-3 months in advance. Accepts queries by e-mail (preferred). Accepts simultaneous submissions. Responds in 6-8 weeks to queries. Responds in 1-2 months to mss. Guidelines available online.

NONFICTION Needs essays, humor, personal experience. "Do not send feature articles. We only accept submissions of completed personal essays that will work with our monthly themes available online." **Buys 100+ mss/year.** Send complete ms. We prefer e-mail submissions. Length: 900-1,200 words. **Pays $150-200.**

PHOTOS "We feature a different color photo, painting, or illustration on the cover each month. Each issue also features a b&w photo by a female photographer. Submit artwork via e-mail.". Reviews Slides, high-resolution digital files. Does not pay for photos or artwork, but the artist's bio is published.

🌍$$ THAT'S LIFE!

Bauer Publishing, Academic House, 24-28 Oval Rd., London England NW1 7DT United Kingdom. (44)(207)241-8000. E-mail: stories@thatslife.co.uk. Website: bauer.co.uk. **Contact:** Sophie Hearsey, editor. "Magazine is packed with the most amazing true-life stories, fab puzzles offering big money prizes including family sunshine holidays and even a car! We also have bright, up-to-date fashion, health and beauty pages with top tips and readers' letters. And just to make sure we get you smiling too, there's our rib-tickling rude jokes and 'aren't men' daft tales." Estab. 1995. Circ. 550,000. Submit seasonal material 3 months in advance. Accepts queries by mail. NoResponds in 6 weeks to mss. Guidelines by e-mail.

FICTION Stories should have a strong plot and a good twist. A sexy relationships/scene can feature strongly, but isn't essential—the plot twist is much more important. The writing should be chronological and fast moving. A maximum of 4 characters is advisable. Avoid straightforward romance, historical backgrounds, science fiction, and stories told by animals or small children. Graphic murders and sex crimes—especially those involving children—are not acceptable. Send complete ms. 700 words **£400**.

🍁$$ TODAY'S BRIDE

Family Communications, 65 The East Mall, Toronto ON M8Z SW3 Canada. (416)537-2604. Fax: (416)538-1794. E-mail: info@canadianbride.com. Website: todaysbride.ca; canadianbride.com. **20% freelance written.** Semiannual magazine. Magazine provides information to engaged couples on all aspects of wedding planning, including tips, fashion advice, etc. There are also beauty, home, groom, and honeymoon travel sections. Estab. 1979. Circ. 102,000. Byline given. Pays on acceptance. Editorial lead time 6 months. Accepts queries by mail, e-mail, fax. Accepts simultaneous submissions. Responds in 2 weeks-1 month.

NONFICTION Needs humor, opinion, personal experience. No travel pieces. Send complete ms. Length: 800-1,400 words. **Pays $250-300.**

PHOTOS Send photos. Identification of subjects required. Reviews transparencies, prints. Negotiates payment individually.

$$ WOMAN'S LIFE

A Publication of Woman's Life Insurance Society, 1338 Military St., P.O. Box 5020, Port Huron MI 48061-5020. (800)521-9292, ext. 281. Fax: (810)985-6970. E-mail: wkrabach@womanslife.org. Website: womanslife.org. **Contact:** Wendy Krabach, managing editor. **30% freelance written.** Quarterly magazine published for a primarily female membership to help them care for themselves and their families. Estab. 1892. Circ. 32,000. Byline given. Pays on publication. Publishes ms an average of 1 year after acceptance. Submit seasonal material 6 months in advance. Accepts queries by mail, e-mail, fax. Accepts simultaneous submissions. Responds in 1 year to queries and to mss. Sample copy for sae with 9×12 envelope and 4 first-class stamps. Guidelines for #10 SASE.

💬 "Works only with published/established writers."

NONFICTION **Buys 4-10 mss/year.** Send complete ms. Length: 1,000-2,000 words. **Pays $150-500.**

REPRINTS Send tearsheet, photocopy or typed ms with rights for sale noted and information about when and where the material previously appeared. Pays 15% of amount paid for an original article

PHOTOS Only interested in photos included with ms. Identification of subjects, model releases required.

$$$ WOMAN'S WORLD

Bauer Publishing Co., 270 Sylvan Ave., Englewood Cliffs NJ 07632. (201)569-6699. Fax: (201)569-3584. Website: winit.womansworldmag.com. **Contact:** Stephanie Saible, editor-in-chief. Weekly magazine covering human interest and service pieces of interest to family-oriented women across the nation. *Woman's World* is a women's service magazine. It offers a blend of fashion, food, parenting, beauty, and relationship features coupled with the true-life human interest stories. We publish short romances and mini-mysteries for all women, ages 18-68. Estab. 1980. Circ. 1,625,779. Pays on acceptance. Publishes ms an average of 4 months after acceptance. Submit seasonal material 4 months in advance. Accepts queries by mail. Responds in 2 months to mss. Guidelines for #10 SASE.

○ *Woman's World* is not looking for freelancers to take assigments generated by the staff, but it will assign stories to writers who have made a successful pitch.

NONFICTION Pays $500/1,000 words.

FICTION Contact: Johnene Granger, fiction editor. Short story, romance, and mainstream of 800 words and mini-mysteries of 1,000 words. Each of our stories has a light romantic theme and can be written from either a masculine or feminine point of view. Women characters may be single, married, or divorced. Plots must be fast moving with vivid dialogue and action. The problems and dilemmas inherent in them should be contemporary and realistic, handled with warmth and feeling. The stories must have a positive resolution. Specify Fiction on envelope. Always enclose SASE. Responds in 4 months. No phone or fax queries. Pays $1,000 for romances on acceptance for North American serial rights for 6 months. The 1,000 word mini-mysteries may feature either a 'whodunnit' or 'howdunnit' theme. The mystery may revolve around anything from a theft to murder. However, we are not interested in sordid or grotesque crimes. Emphasis should be on intricacies of plot rather than gratuitous violence. The story must include a resolution that clearly states the villain is getting his or her come-uppance. Submit complete mss. Specify Mini-Mystery on envelope. Enclose SASE. No phone queries. Needs mystery, romance, contemporary. Not interested in science fiction, fantasy, historical romance, or foreign locales. No explicit sex, graphic language, or seamy settings. Send complete ms. Romances—800 words; mysteries—1,000 words. **Pays $1,000/romances; $500/mysteries**.

☺ WOMEN IN BUSINESS

American Business Women's Association (The ABWA Co., Inc.), 9100 Ward Pkwy., P.O. Box 8728, Kansas City MO 64114-0728. (816)361-6621. Fax: (816)361-4991. E-mail: abwa@abwa.org. Website: abwa.org. **Contact:** Rene Street, executive director. **30% freelance written**. Bimonthly magazine covering issues affecting working women. "How-to features for career women on business trends, small-business ownership, self-improvement, and retirement issues. Profiles business women." Estab. 1949. Circ. 45,000. Byline given. Pays on acceptance. Publishes ms an average of 3 months after acceptance. Editorial lead time 3 months. Accepts queries by mail, e-mail, fax. Accepts simultaneous submissions. Responds in 3 weeks to queries. Responds in 2 months to mss. Sample copy for sae with 9×12 envelope and 4 First-Class stamps. Guidelines for #10 SASE.

NONFICTION Needs how-to, interview, computer/Internet. No fiction or poetry. **Buys 3% of submitted mss/year.** Query. Length: 500-1,000 words. **Pays $100/500 words.**

PHOTOS State availability. Identification of subjects required. Reviews prints. Offers no additional payment for photos accepted with ms.

COLUMNS Life After Business (concerns of retired business women); It's Your Business (entrepreneurial advice for business owners); Health Spot (health issues that affect women in the work place). Length: 500-750 words. Query. **Pays $100/500 words**

TRADE JOURNALS

Many writers hope to sell an article to one of the popular, high-profile consumer magazines found on newsstands and in bookstores. Many of those writers are surprised to find an entire world of magazine publishing exists outside the realm of commercial magazines—trade journals. Writers who have discovered trade journals have found a market that offers the chance to publish regularly in subject areas they find interesting, editors who are typically more accessible than their commercial counterparts, and pay rates that rival those of the big-name magazines.

Trade journal is the general term for any publication focusing on a particular occupation or industry. Other terms used to describe the different types of trade publications are business, technical, and professional journals. They are read by truck drivers, bricklayers, farmers, fishermen, heart surgeons, and just about everyone else working in a trade or profession. Trade periodicals are sharply angled to the specifics of the professions on which they report. They offer business-related news, features, and service articles that will foster their readers' professional development.

Editors at trade journals tell us their audience is made up of knowledgeable and highly interested readers. Writers for trade journals have to either possess knowledge about the field in question or be able to report it accurately from interviews with those who do. Writers who have or can develop a good grasp of a specialized body of knowledge will find trade magazine editors who are eager to hear from them.

An ideal way to begin your foray into trade journals is to write for those that report on your present profession. Whether you've been teaching dance, farming, or working as a paralegal, begin by familiarizing yourself with the magazines that serve your current occupation.

ADVERTISING, MARKETING AND PR

⊖⊖⊖ ADVANTAGES MAGAZINE

The Advertising Specialty Institute, 4800 Street Rd., Trevose PA 19053. (215)953-3337. Website: advantagesinfo. com. **40% freelance written**. Monthly magazine covering promotional products (branded T-shirts, mugs, pens, etc.). Estab. 1997. Circ. 40,000. Byline given. Pays on acceptance. Publishes ms an average of 1-2 months after acceptance. Editorial lead time 1 month. Submit seasonal material 1 month in advance. Accepts queries by e-mail, phone. Accepts simultaneous submissions.

> 🖚 "*Advantages* is a 15-issue publication targeted to promotional products salespeople. Its main objective is to be a comprehensive source of sales strategies, information and inspiration through articles, columns, case histories and product showcases. The magazine is presented in a fun and easy-to-read format to keep busy salespeople interested and entertained. The easy-to-use reader response system makes it fast and simple to request product information from suppliers featured in showcases. We want our subscribers to look forward to its arrival and to believe that *Advantages* is the one magazine they can't do without."

NONFICTION **Buys 40 mss/year.** Query. Length: 2,500-3,500 words. **Pays $500-1,000+.**

⊖⊖⊖ BRAND PACKAGING

BNP Media, 155 Pfingsten Rd., Suite 205, Deerfield IL 60015. (847)405-4000. Fax: (847)405-4100. E-mail: acevedoj@bnpmedia.com; hammerbeckp@bnpmedia. com. Website: brandpackaging.com. **Contact:** Pauline Tingas Hammerbeck, editor-in-chief. **15% freelance written**. Magazine published 10 times/year covering how packaging can be a marketing tool. "We publish strategies and tactics to make products stand out on the shelf. Our market is brand managers who are marketers but need to know something about packaging." Estab. 1997. Circ. 33,000. Byline given. Pays on acceptance. Publishes ms an average of 2 months after acceptance. Editorial lead time 3 months. Submit seasonal material 3 months in advance. Accepts queries by mail, fax.

NONFICTION Needs how-to, interview, new product. **Buys 10 mss/year.** Send complete ms. Length: 600-2,400 words. **Pays 40-50¢/word.**

PHOTOS State availability. Identification of subjects required. Reviews contact sheets, 35mm transparencies, 4x5 prints. Negotiates payment individually.

COLUMNS Emerging Technology (new packaging technology), 600 words. **Buys 10 mss/year.** Query. **Pays $150-300.**

⊖ DECA DIMENSIONS

1908 Association Dr., Reston VA 20191. (703)860-5000. Fax: (703)860-4013. E-mail: chuck_beatty@ deca.org. Website: deca.org. **30% freelance written**. Quarterly magazine covering marketing, professional development, business, career training during school year (no issues published May-August). *DECA Dimensions* is the membership magazine for DECA—The Association of Marketing Students—primarily ages 15-19 in all 50 states, the U.S. territories, Germany, and Canada. The magazine is delivered through the classroom. Students are interested in developing professional, leadership, and career skills. Estab. 1947. Circ. 160,000. Byline given. Pays on publication. Editorial lead time 3 months. Submit seasonal material 4 months in advance. Accepts queries by mail, e-mail, fax, phone. Accepts simultaneous submissions.

NONFICTION Needs essays, general interest, how-to, get jobs, start business, plan for college, etc., interview, business leads, personal experience, working, leadership development. **Buys 10 mss/year.** Send complete ms. Length: 800-1,000 words. **Pays $125 for assigned articles. Pays $100 for unsolicited articles.**

COLUMNS Professional Development; Leadership, 350-500 words. **Buys 6 mss/year.** Send complete ms. **Pays $ 75-100.**

⊖ FORMAT MAGAZINE

Decker Publications, 315 5th Ave. NW, St. Paul MN 55112. (651)628-2468. Fax: (651)633-1862. E-mail: news@formatmag.com. Website: formatmag.com. **Contact:** Erik Adler, editor; Daniel Eckler, publisher. **90% freelance written**. Monthly magazine covering the marketing communication industry in Minnesota. Estab. 1954. Circ. 6,000. Byline given. Pays on publication. Editorial lead time 1 months. Accepts queries by e-mail. Accepts simultaneous submissions. Sample copy for #10 sase. Guidelines for #10 SASE or online.

> 🖚 "*Format* Magazine is your source for the most current and compelling information relating to urban aesthetics. *Format* strives to maintain a broad scope, encompassing elements from every corner of the urban art world, in-

cluding, but not limited to: design, electro, graffiti, hip hop, lowbrow, menswear, punk, skate, sneakers, street art, streetwear, tattoo, vinyl toys. *Format Mag* is the primary Internet streetwear magazine featuring urban art, urban fashion, graffiti, designer toys, lowbrow, street art, and sneakers."

NONFICTION Needs general interest, historical, humor, interview, photo feature. **Buys 2 mss/year.** Send complete ms. Length: 300-800 words. **Pays $25-50.**

PHOTOS Send photos. Identification of subjects required. Negotiates payment individually.

COLUMNS Advertising (ad humor), 400 words. **Buys 12 mss/year.** Send complete ms. **Pays $25-50.**

FILLERS Needs anecdotes, facts, gags, newsbreaks, short humor. **Buys 12 mss/year.** Length: 100-300 words. **Pays $10-25.**

$$ FPO MAGAZINE

Auras Custom Publishing, 8435 Georgia Ave., Silver Spring MD 20910. (301)587-4300. Fax: (301)587-6836. E-mail: editor@fpomagazine.com. Website: fpomagazine.com. **Contact:** Rob Sugar, editor. **50% freelance written**. Magazine covering creative and production with occasional issues. "*[FPO] Magazine* is a print and online resource for publication professionals, publishers, editors, designers, and production managers that focuses on the creative side of magazine publishing." Estab. 2007. Circ. 10,000. Byline given. Pays on publication. Offers 25% kill fee. Publishes ms an average of 3-4 months after acceptance. Editorial lead time 3 months. Accepts queries by mail, e-mail, fax, phone. Accepts simultaneous submissions. Sample copy by e-mail. Guidelines available online.

"Until further notice, FPO will suspend its quarterly publication schedule and produce occasional issues."

NONFICTION Needs essays, historical, how-to, humor, interview, new product, technical. Special issues: 100 Top Tips (late Fall 2008). **Buys 10-12 mss/year.** Query. **Pays 50¢/word.**

PHOTOS State availability. Captions, model releases required. Reviews GIF/JPEG files. Negotiates payment individually.

COLUMNS Cover Charge; Re: Write; Re: Design; Creative Briefs, all 500 words. **Buys 20-25 mss/year.** Query. **Pays 50¢/word.**

FILLERS Needs anecdotes, facts, gags, short humor. Length: 100-400 words. **Pays $25-50.**

NETWORKING TIMES

Gabriel Media Group, 11418 Kokopeli Place, Chatsworth CA 91311. (818)727-2000. Website: networkingtimes.com. **Contact:** Josephine Gross, editor-in-chief. **30% freelance written.** "*Networking Times* is an advertisement-free educational journal for professional networkers worldwide, available at major bookstores and by subscription. We don't mention any company names, instead filling the pages with practical information that covers two areas: acquisition of skills and building the right mindset to be successful in the world of marketing today." Estab. 2001. Circ. 12,000. Byline given. Pays on publication. Editorial lead time 3 months. Submit seasonal material 3 months in advance. Accepts queries by e-mail. Sample copy for $7.97 (US), $10.97 (Canada). Guidelines by e-mail.

"*Networking Times* is a bimonthly educational journal focused on personal growth and professional development."

$$ O'DWYER'S PR REPORT

271 Madison Ave., #600, New York NY 10016. Fax: (212)679-2471. E-mail: jack@odwyerpr.com. Website: odwyerpr.com. **Contact:** Jack O'Dwyer. Monthly magazine providing PR articles. "O'Dwyer's has been covering public relations, marketing communications and related fields for over 40 years. The company provides the latest news and information about PR firms and professionals, the media, corporations, legal issues, jobs, technology, and much more through its website, weekly newsletter, monthly magazine, directories, and guides. Many of the contributors are PR people publicizing themselves while analyzing something." Byline given. Accepts queries by mail.

NONFICTION Needs opinion. Query. **Pays $250.**

$$$ PROMO MAGAZINE

Penton Media, 244 W. 17th St., New York NY 10011. (212)358-4183. Fax: (203)358-9900. E-mail: patricia.odell@penton.com. Website: promomagazine.com. **Contact:** Patricia Odell, executive editor. **5% freelance written**. Monthly magazine covering promotion marketing. Estab. 1987. Circ. 25,000. Byline given. Pays on publication. Offers 25% kill fee. Publishes ms an average of 2 months after acceptance. Editorial lead time 3 months. Submit seasonal material 3 months in advance. Responds in 1 month to queries. Sample copy for $5.

💬 *"Promo* serves marketers, and stories must be informative, well written, and familiar with the subject matter."

NONFICTION Needs exposè, general interest, how-to, marketing programs, interview, new product, promotion. No general marketing stories not heavily involved in promotions. Generally does not accept unsolicited mss, query first. **Buys 6-10 mss/year.** Query with published clips. Variable **Pays $1,000 maximum for assigned articles. Pays $500 maximum for unsolicited articles.**

PHOTOS State availability. Captions, identification of subjects, model releases required. Reviews contact sheets, negatives. Negotiates payment individually.

SHOPPER MARKETING

In-Store Marketing Institute, 7400 Skokie Blvd., Skokie IL 60077. (847)675-7400. Fax: (847)675-7494. E-mail: adownes@instoremarketer.org. Website: shoppermarketingmag.com; hoytpub.com/poptimes. **80% freelance written**. Monthly tabloid covering advertising and primarily the in-store marketing industry. "We cover how brands market to the shopper at retail, what insights/research did they gather to reach that shopper and how did they activate the program at retail. We write case studies on large branded fixtures, displays, packaging, retail media, and events. We write major category reports, company profiles, trends features, and more. Our readers are marketers and retailers, and a small selection of P-O-P producers (the guys that build the displays)." Circ. 20,000 Estab. 1988. Byline given. Pays on acceptance. Offers Editorial lead time 2 months. Submit seasonal material 3 months in advance. Accepts queries by e-mail. Accepts simultaneous submissions. Responds in 1 month to queries.

💲💲 SIGN BUILDER ILLUSTRATED

Simmons-Boardman Publishing Corp., 345 Hudson St., 12th Floor, New York NY 10014. (252)355-5806. E-mail: jwooten@sbpub.com; abray@sbpub.com. Website: signshop.com. Associate Editor Ashley Bray. **Contact:** Jeff Wooten, editor. **40% freelance written.** Monthly magazine covering sign and graphic industry. Estab. 1987. Circ. 14,500. Byline given. Pays on acceptance. Offers 10% kill fee. Publishes ms an average of 3 months after acceptance. Editorial lead time 3 months. Submit seasonal material 4 months in advance. Accepts queries by mail, e-mail, fax, phone. Accepts

simultaneous submissions. Responds in 1 month to queries. Sample copy and writer's

💬 *"Sign Builder Illustrated* targets sign professionals where they work: on the shop floor. Our topics cover the broadest spectrum of the sign industry, from design to fabrication, installation, maintenance and repair. Our readers own a similarly wide range of shops, including commercial, vinyl, sign erection and maintenance, electrical and neon, architectural, and awnings."

NONFICTION Needs historical, how-to, humor, interview, photo feature, technical. **Buys 50-60 mss/year.** Query. Length: 1,000-1,500 words. **Pays $250-550 for assigned articles.**

PHOTOS Send photos. Captions, identification of subjects required. Reviews 3x5 prints. Negotiates payment individually.

💲💲 SIGNCRAFT

SignCraft Publishing Co., Inc., P.O. Box 60031, Fort Myers FL 33906. (239)939-4644. Fax: (239)939-0607. E-mail: signcraft@signcraft.com. Website: signcraft.com. **10% freelance written**. Bimonthly magazine covering the sign industry. Estab. 1980. Circ. 14,000. Byline given. Pays on publication. Offers negotiable kill fee. Publishes ms an average of 6 months after acceptance. Accepts queries by mail, e-mail, fax. Responds in 1 month to queries Sample copy and writer's guidelines for $3.

💬 "Like any trade magazine, we need material of direct benefit to our readers. We can't afford space for material of marginal interest."

NONFICTION Needs interview. **Buys 10 mss/year.** Query. Length: 500-2,000 words.

💲💲💲 SOCAL MEETINGS + EVENTS MAGAZINE

Tiger Oak Publications, 251 First Ave. N., Suite 401, Minneapolis MN 55401. Fax: (612)338-0532. E-mail: meghan.mcandrews@tigeroak.com. Website: meetingsmags.com. **80% freelance written**. Quarterly magazine covering meetings and events industry. *SoCal Meetings & Events* magazine is the premier trade publication for meetings planners and hospitality service providers in Southern California. This magazine aims to report on and promote businesses involved in the meetings and events industry. The magazine covers current and emerging trends, people and venues in the meetings and events industry in Southern California. Estab. 1993. Circ. 20,000. Byline given. Pays on acceptance. Offers 20% kill fee. Publishes ms an average of 4 months after acceptance. Editorial lead time 4-6 months. Submit seasonal material 6 months in advance. Accepts queries by mail. Accepts simultaneous submissions. Responds in 1-2 weeks to queries.

NONFICTION Needs general interest, historical, interview, new product, opinion, personal experience, photo feature, technical, travel. **Buys 30 mss/year.** Each query should tell us: -What the story will be about. -How you will tell the story: what sources you will use, how you will conduct research, etc. -Why is the story pertinent to the market audience? Length: 600-1,500 words. **The average department length story (4-700 words) pays about $2-300 and the average feature length story (1,000-1,200 words) pays from $5-600, depending on the story. These rates are not guaranteed and vary.**

PHOTOS State availability. Identification of subjects, model releases required. Negotiates payment individually.

COLUMNS Meet + Eat (restaurant reviews); Facility Focus (venue reviews); Regional Spotlight (city review), 1,000 words. **Buys 30 mss/year.** Query with published clips. **Pays $400-600.**

$$$ TEXAS MEETINGS + EVENTS

Tiger Oak Publications, 900 S. 3rd St., Minneapolis MN 55401. (612)338-4125; (612)548-3180. Fax: (612)548-3181. E-mail: kate.smith@tigeroak.com. Website: meetingsmags.com. **80% freelance written.** Quarterly magazine covering meetings and events industry. Estab. 1993. Circ. 20,000. Byline given. Pays on acceptance. Offers 20% kill fee. Publishes ms an average of 4 months after acceptance. Editorial lead time 4-6 months. Submit seasonal material 6 months in advance. Accepts queries by mail. Accepts simultaneous submissions. Responds in 1-2 weeks to queries.

> "*Texas Meetings & Events* magazine is the premier trade publication for meetings planners and hospitality service providers in the state. This magazine aims to report on and promote businesses involved in the meetings and events industry. The magazine covers current and emerging trends, people and venues in the meetings and events industry in the state."

NONFICTION Needs general interest, historical, interview, new product, opinion, personal experience, photo feature, technical, travel. **Buys 30 mss/year.** Query with published clips. Length: 600-1,500 words. **Pays $400-800.**

PHOTOS State availability. Identification of subjects, model releases required. Negotiates payment individually.

COLUMNS Meet + Eat (restaurant reviews); Facility Focus (venue reviews); Regional Spotlight (city review), 1,000 words. **Buys 30 mss/year.** Query with published clips. **Pays $400-600.**

ART, DESIGN AND COLLECTIBLES

$$ AIRBRUSH ACTION MAGAZINE

Action, Inc., 3209 Atlantic Ave., P.O. Box 438, Allenwood NJ 08720. (732)223-7878; (800)876-2472. Fax: (732)223-2855. E-mail: ceo@airbrushaction.com; editor@airbrushaction.com. Website: airbrushaction.com. **80% freelance written.** Bimonthly magazine covering the spectrum of airbrush applications: automotive and custom paint applications, illustration, T-shirt airbrushing, fine art, automotive and sign painting, hobby/craft applications, wall murals, fingernails, temporary tattoos, artist profiles, reviews, and more. Estab. 1985. Circ. 35,000. Byline given. Pays 1 month after publication. Publishes ms an average of 6 months after acceptance. Editorial lead time 6 months. Submit seasonal material 6 months in advance. Accepts queries by mail, e-mail, fax, phone. Accepts simultaneous submissions.

NONFICTION Needs how-to, humor, inspirational, interview, new product, personal experience, technical. Nothing unrelated to airbrush. Query with published clips. **Pays 15¢/word.**

PHOTOS Digital images preferred. Send photos. Captions, identification of subjects, model releases required. Negotiates payment individually.

COLUMNS Query with published clips.

$$ ANTIQUEWEEK

MidCountry Media, P.O. Box 90, Knightstown IN 46148-0090. (800)876-5133, ext. 189. Fax: (800)695-8153. E-mail: connie@antiqueweek.com; tony@antiqueweek.com. Website: antiqueweek.com. Tony Gregory, publisher. **Contact:** Connie Swaim, managing editor. **80% freelance written.** Weekly tabloid covering antiques and collectibles with 3 editions: Eastern, Central and National, plus monthly *Anti-*

queWest. *AntiqueWeek* has a wide range of readership from dealers and auctioneers to collectors, both advanced and novice. Our readers demand accurate information presented in an entertaining style. Estab. 1968. Circ. 50,000. Byline given. Pays on publication. Offers kill fee. Offers 10% kill fee or $25. Submit seasonal material 1 month in advance. Accepts queries by mail, e-mail. Guidelines by e-mail.

NONFICTION Needs historical, how-to, interview, opinion, personal experience, antique show and auction reports, feature articles on particular types of antiques and collectibles. **Buys 400-500 mss/year.** Query. Length: 1,000-2,000 words. **Pays $50-250.**

PHOTOS All material must be submitted electronically via e-mail or on CD. Send photos. Identification of subjects required.

🕒 THE APPRAISERS STANDARD

New England Appraisers Association, 5 Gill Terrace, Ludlow VT 05149-1003. (802)228-7444. Fax: (802)228-7444. E-mail: llt44@ludl.tds.net. Website: newenglandappraisers.net. **Contact:** Linda L. Tucker, ed. **50% freelance written. Works with a small number of new/unpublished writers each year.** Quarterly publication covering the appraisals of antiques, art, collectibles, jewelry, coins, stamps, and real estate. "The writer should be knowledgeable on the subject, and the article should be written with appraisers in mind, with prices quoted for objects, good pictures, and descriptions of articles being written about." Estab. 1980. Circ. 1,000. Short bio and byline given. Pays on publication. Publishes ms an average of 1 year after acceptance. Submit seasonal material 2 months in advance. Accepts queries by mail, e-mail. Accepts simultaneous submissions. Responds in 1 month to queries. Responds in 2 months to mss. Sample copy for 9×12 SAE with 78¢ postage. Guidelines for #10 SASE.

> "I would like writers to focus on particular types of antiques: i.e. types of furniture, glass, artwork, etc., giving information on the history of this type of antique, good photos, recent sale prices, etc."

NONFICTION Needs interview, personal experience, technical, travel. Send complete ms. Length: 700 words. **Pays $60.**

PHOTOS Send photos. Identification of subjects required. Reviews negatives, prints. Offers no additional payment for photos accepted with ms.

🕒🕒 ART CALENDAR MAGAZINE

Turnstile Publishing, 1500 Park Center Dr., Orlando FL 32835. (407)563-7000. Fax: (407)563-7099. E-mail: khall@artcalendar.com. Website: artcalendar.com. Louise Buyo at lbuyo@professionalartistmag.com. **Contact:** Kim Hall. **75% freelance written.** Monthly magazine. Estab. 1986. Circ. 20,000. Pays on publication. Sample print copy for $5. Guidelines available online.

> "We welcome nuts-and-bolts, practical articles of interest to professional visual artists, emerging or professional. Examples: How-to's, first-person stories on how an artist has built his career or an aspect of it, interviews with artists (business/career-building emphasis), web strategies, and pieces on business practices and other topics of use to artists. The tone of our magazine is practical, and uplifting."

NONFICTION Needs essays, the psychology of creativity, how-to, interview, successful artists with a focus on what made them successful, networking articles, marketing topics, technical articles (new equipment, new media, computer software, Internet marketing.), cartoons, art law, including pending legislation that affects artists (copyright law, Internet regulations, etc.). We like nuts-and-bolts information about making a living as an artist. We do not run reviews or art historical pieces, nor do we like writing characterized by 'critic-speak,' philosophical hyperbole, psychological arrogance, politics, or New Age religion. Also, we do not condone a get-rich-quick attitude. Send complete ms. **Pays $250.**

PHOTOS Reviews b&w glossy or color prints. Pays $25.

COLUMNS If an artist or freelancer sends us good articles regularly, and based on results we feel that he is able to produce a column at least 3 times per year, we will invite him to be a contributing writer. If a gifted artist-writer can commit to producing an article on a monthly basis, we will offer him a regular column and the title contributing editor. Send complete ms.

🕒🕒 ART MATERIALS RETAILER

Fahy-Williams Publishing, P.O. Box 1080, Geneva NY 14456. (315)789-0458. Fax: (315)789-4263. E-mail: tmanzer@fwpi.com. Website: artmaterialsretailer.com. J. Kevin Fahy at kfahy@fwpi.com. **Contact:** J. Kevin Fahy, publisher. **10% freelance written.** Quarterly magazine. Estab. 1998. Byline given. Pays on publication. Editorial lead time 2 months. Submit seasonal material 3 months in advance. Accepts simultaneous submissions. Responds in 3 weeks to queries. Responds in 3 months to mss. Sample copy and writer's

NONFICTION Needs book excerpts, how-to, interview, personal experience. **Buys 2 mss/year.** Send complete ms. Length: 1,500-3,000 words. **Pays $50-250.**

PHOTOS State availability. Identification of subjects required. Reviews transparencies. Offers no additional payment for photos accepted with ms.

FILLERS Needs anecdotes, facts, newsbreaks. **Buys 5 mss/year.** Length: 500-1,500 words. **Pays $50-125.**

☺☺ FAITH + FORM

47 Grandview Terrace, Essex CT 06426. (860)575-4702. E-mail: mcrosbie@faithandform.com. Website: faithandform.com. **Contact:** Michael J. Crosbie, editor-in-chief. **50% freelance written.** Quarterly magazine covering relgious buildings and art. Writers must be knowledgeable about environments for worship, or able to explain them. Estab. 1967. Circ. 4,500. Byline given. Publishes ms an average of 6 months after acceptance. Editorial lead time 6 months. Submit seasonal material 6 months in advance. Accepts queries by online submission form. Accepts simultaneous submissions. Responds in 2 weeks to queries. Responds in 1 month to mss. Sample copy available online. Guidelines available.

○ Magazine devoted to religious art and architecture, is read by artists, designers, architects, clergy, congregations, and all who care about environments for worship.

NONFICTION Needs book excerpts, essays, how-to, inspirational, interview, opinion, personal experience, photo feature, religious, technical. **Buys 6 mss/year.** Query. Length: 500-2,500 words.

PHOTOS State availability. Captions required. Reviews GIF/JPEG files. Offers no additional payment for photos accepted with ms.

COLUMNS News, 250-750 words; Book Reviews, 250-500 words. **Buys 3 mss/year.** Query.

☺☺☺ HOW

F+W Media, Inc., F+W Media, Inc., 4700 E. Galbraith Rd., Cincinnati OH 45236. (513)531-2222. Fax: (513)531-2902. E-mail: bryn.mooth@fwmedia.com; editorial@howdesign.com. Website: howdesign.com. **Contact:** Bryn Mooth. **75% freelance written.** Bi-monthly magazine covering graphic design profession. Estab. 1985.

Circ. 40,000. Byline given. Pays on acceptance. Responds in 6 weeks to queries.

○ *HOW: Design Ideas at Work* strives to serve the business, technological and creative needs of graphic-design professionals. The magazine provides a practical mix of essential business information, up-to-date technological tips, the creative whys and hows behind noteworthy projects, and profiles of professionals who are impacting design. The ultimate goal of *HOW* is to help designers, whether they work for a design firm or for an inhouse design department, run successful, creative, profitable studios.

⊶ "The HOW brand now extends beyond the print magazine to annual events for design professionals, yearly design competitions, digital products and books."

NONFICTION Special issues: Self-Promotion Annual (September/October); Business Annual (November/December); International Annual of Design (March/April); Creativity/Paper/Stock Photography (May/June); Digital Design Annual (July/August). No how-to articles for beginning artists or fine-art-oriented articles. **Buys 40 mss/year.** Query with published clips and samples of subject's work, artwork or design. Length: 1,500-2,000 words. **Pays $700-900.**

PHOTOS State availability. Captions required. Reviews information updated and verified.

COLUMNS Creativity (focuses on creative exercises and inspiration) 1,200-1,500 words. In-House Issues (focuses on business and creativity issues for corporate design groups), 1,200-1,500 words. Business (focuses on business issue for design firm owners), 1,200-1,500 words. **Buys Number of columns: 35. mss/year.** Query with published clips. **Pays $250-400.**

☺☺☺ PRINT

F+W Media, Inc., 38 E. 29th St., 3rd Floor, New York NY 10016. (212)447-1400. Fax: (212)447-5231. E-mail: Aaron.Kenedi@fwmedia.com. Website: printmag.com. **Contact:** Aaron Kenedi. **75% freelance written.** Bimonthly magazine covering graphic design and visual culture. *PRINT*'s articles, written by design specialists and cultural critics, focus on the social, political, and historical context of graphic design, and on the places where consumer culture and popular culture meet. We aim to produce a general interest magazine for professionals with engagingly written text and lavish illustrations. By covering a broad spectrum of topics, both international and local, we try to demonstrate the significance of design in the world at large. Estab. 1940. Circ. 45,000. Byline given. Pays on acceptance. Offers 25% kill fee. Publishes ms an average of 3 months after acceptance. Editorial lead time 3 months. Submit seasonal material 3 months in advance. Accepts queries by e-mail. Responds in 2 weeks to queries. Responds in 1 month to mss.

NONFICTION Needs essays, interview, opinion. **Buys 35-40 mss/year.** Query with published clips. Length: 1,000-2,500 words. **Pays $1,250.**

COLUMNS Query with published clips. **Pays $800.**

⑨ TEXAS ARCHITECT

Texas Society of Architects, 816 Congress Ave., Suite 970, Austin TX 78701. (512)478-7386. Fax: (512)478-0528. Website: texasarchitect.org. **Contact:** Stephen Sharpe, editor. **30% freelance written. Mostly written by unpaid members of the professional society.** Bimonthly journal covering architecture and architects of Texas. "*Texas Architect* is a highly visually-oriented look at Texas architecture, design, and urban planning. Articles cover varied subtopics within architecture. Readers are mostly architects and related building professionals." Estab. 1951. Circ. 12,000. Byline given. Pays on publication. Publishes ms an average of 3 months after acceptance. Submit seasonal material 4 months in advance. Accepts queries by mail, e-mail. Responds in 6 weeks to queries. Guidelines available online.

NONFICTION Needs interview, photo feature, technical, book reviews. Query with published clips. Length: 100-2,000 words. **Pays $50-100 for assigned articles.**

PHOTOS Send photos. Identification of subjects required. Reviews contact sheets, 35mm or 4x5 transparencies, 4x5 prints. Offers no additional payment for photos accepted with ms.

COLUMNS News (timely reports on architectural issues, projects, and people), 100-500 words. **Buys 10 articles/year mss/year.** Query with published clips. **Pays $50-100.**

⑨⑨ THE PASTEL JOURNAL

F+W Media, Inc., 4700 E. Galbraith Rd., Cincinnati OH 45236. (513)531-2690. Fax: (513)891-7153. Website: pasteljournal.com. **Contact:** Anne Hevener. Bimonthly magazine covering pastel art. "*The Pastel Journal* is the only national magazine devoted to the medium of pastel. Addressing the working pro-

fessional as well as passionate amateurs, *The Pastel Journal* offers inspiration, information, and instruction to our readers." Estab. 1999. Circ. 22,000. Byline given. Pays on acceptance. Offers 25% kill fee. Publishes ms an average of 3-6 months after acceptance. Editorial lead time 6 months. Submit seasonal material 6 months in advance. Accepts queries by mail. NoAccepts simultaneous submissions. Responds in 4-6 weeks to queries. Writer's

NONFICTION Needs how-to, interview, new product, profile. Does not want articles that aren't art-related. Review magazine before submitting. Query with or without published clips. Length: 500-2,500 words. **Pays $150-750.**

PHOTOS State availability of or send photos. Captions required. Reviews transparencies, prints, GIF/JPEG files. Offers no additional payment for photos accepted with ms.

⑨⑨ WATERCOLOR ARTIST

F+W Media, Inc., 4700 E. Galbraith Rd., Cincinnati OH 45236. (513)531-2690. Fax: (513)531-2902. Website: watercolorartistmagazine.com. Bimonthly magazine covering water media arts. Estab. 1984. Circ. 53,000. Byline given. Pays on acceptance. Offers 10% kill fee. Publishes ms an average of 3-6 months after acceptance. Editorial lead time 6 months. Submit seasonal material 6 months in advance. Accepts queries by mail. NoAccepts simultaneous submissions. Responds in 4-6 weeks to queries. Sample copy and writer's

"*Watercolor Artist* is the definitive source of how-to instruction and creative inspiration for artists working in water-based media."

NONFICTION Needs book excerpts, essays, how-to, inspirational, interview, new product, personal experience. "Does not want articles that aren't art-related. Review magazine before submitting." **Buys 36 mss/year.** Send query letter with images. Length: 350-2,500 words. **Pays $150-600.**

PHOTOS State availability of or send photos. Captions required. Reviews transparencies, prints, slides, GIF/JPEG files.

AUTO AND TRUCK

⑨ AUTO RESTORER

Bowtie, Inc., 3 Burroughs, Irvine CA 92618. (949)855-8822, ext. 412. Fax: (949)855-3045. E-mail: tkade@fancypubs.com; editors@mmminc.org. Website: autorestorermagazine.com. **Contact:** Ted Kade, editor. 85. Covers auto restoration. Monthly magazine covering auto restoration. Our readers own old cars and they work on them. We help our readers by providing as much practical, how-to information as we can about restoration and old cars. Estab. 1989. Circ. 60,000. Pays on publication. 3 months from acceptance to publication Submit seasonal material 4 months in advance. Accepts queries by mail, e-mail, fax. Responds in 2 months to queries. Sample copy for $7.

✂→ Interview the owner of a restored car. Present advice to others on how to do a similar restoration. Seek advice from experts. Go light on history and nonspecific details. Make it something that the magazine regularly uses. Do automotive how-tos.

NONFICTION Needs how-to, auto restoration, new product, photo feature, technical product evaluation. **Buys 60 mss/year.** Query first. Length: 250-2,000/words **Pays $150/published page, including photos and illustrations.**

PHOTOS Monthly magazine. Emphasizes restoration of collector cars and trucks. Readers are 98% male, professional/technical/managerial, ages 35-65. Buys 47 photos from freelancers/issue; 564 photos/year. Send photos. Model/property release preferred. Photo captions required; include year, make and model of car; identification of people in photo. Reviews photos with accompanying ms only. Reviews contact sheets, transparencies, 5×7 prints. Looks for "technically proficient or dramatic photos of various automotive subjects, auto portraits, detail shots, action photos, good angles, composition and lighting. We're also looking for photos to illustrate how-to articles such as how to repair a damaged fender or how to repair a carburetor.". Pays $50 for b&w cover; $35 for b&w inside. Pays on publication. Credit line given.

⊛⊛ AUTOINC.

Automotive Service Association, P.O. Box 929, Bedford TX 76095. (800)272-7467. Fax: (817)685-0225. E-mail: leonad@asashop.org. Website: autoinc.org. **10% freelance written**. Monthly magazine covering independent automotive repair. The mission of *AutoInc.*, ASA's official publication, is to be the informational authority for ASA and industry members nationwide. Its purpose is to enhance the professionalism of these members through management, technical and legislative articles, researched and written with the high-

est regard for accuracy, quality, and integrity. Estab. 1952. Circ. 14,000. Byline given. Pays on publication. Publishes ms an average of 3 months after acceptance. Editorial lead time 2 months. Accepts queries by mail, e-mail, fax. Accepts simultaneous submissions. Responds in 6 weeks to queries. Responds in 2 months to mss. Sample copy for $5 or online. Guidelines available online.

NONFICTION Needs how-to, automotive repair, technical. No coverage of staff moves or financial reports. **Buys 6 mss/year.** Query with published clips. Length: 1,200 words. **Pays $300.** Sometimes pays phone expenses of writers on assignment.

PHOTOS State availability of or send photos. Captions, identification of subjects, model releases required. Reviews 2â—Š3 transparencies, 3â—Š5 prints, high resolution digital images. Negotiates payment individually.

⊛⊛ BUSINESS FLEET

Bobit Publishing, 3520 Challenger St., Torrance CA 90501-1711. (310)533-2400. E-mail: chris.brown@bobit.com. Website: businessfleet.com. **Contact:** Chris Brown, exec. editor. **10% freelance written**. Bimonthly magazine covering businesses which operate 10-50 company vehicles. Estab. 2000. Circ. 100,000. Byline given. Pays on publication. Offers 25% kill fee. Publishes ms an average of 3 months after acceptance. Editorial lead time 2 months. Submit seasonal material 2 months in advance. Accepts queries by mail, e-mail, fax. Responds in 3 weeks to queries. Responds in 2 months to mss. Sample copy and writer's

◯ "While it's a trade publication aimed at a business audience, *Business Fleet* has a lively, conversational style. The best way to get a feel for our `slant' is to read the magazine."

NONFICTION Needs how-to, interview, new product, personal experience, photo feature, technical. **Buys 16 mss/year.** Query with published clips. Length: 500-2,000 words. **Pays $100-400.**

PHOTOS State availability. Captions required. Reviews 3x5 prints. Negotiates payment individually.

◯⊛⊛ CASP

Rousseau Automotive Communication, 455, Notre-Dame Est, Suite 311, Montreal QC H2Y 1C9 Canada. (514)289-0888 / 1-877-989-0888. Fax: (514)289-5151. E-mail: info@autosphere.ca. Website: autosphere.ca. **30% freelance written**. Magazine published 8 times/year covering the Canadian automotive aftermarket.

"*CASP* presents many aspects of the automotive aftermarket: new products, technology, industry image, HR, management." Estab. 2003. Circ. 18,000. Byline given. Pays on publication. Publishes ms an average of 2 months after acceptance. Editorial lead time 2 months. Submit seasonal material 2 months in advance. Accepts queries by e-mail. Accepts simultaneous submissions. Responds in 2 weeks to queries. Responds in 2 months to mss. Guidelines by e-mail.

NONFICTION Needs general interest, how-to, inspirational, interview, new product, technical. Does not want opinion pieces. **Buys 6 mss/year.** Query with published clips. Length: 550-610 words. **Pays up to $200 (Canadian).**

PHOTOS Send photos. Captions required. Reviews GIF/JPEG files. Offers no additional payment for photos accepted with ms.

FILLERS Needs facts. **Buys 2 mss/year.** Length: 550-610 words. **Pays $0-200.**

💲💲 FENDERBENDER

DeWitt Publishing, 1043 Grand Ave. #372, St. Paul MN 55105. (651)224-6207. Fax: (651)224-6212. E-mail: jniemela fenderbender.com; letters@fenderbender.com. Website: fenderbender.com. **Contact:** Jennifer Niemela, managing editor. **50% freelance written.** Monthly magazine covering automotive collision repair. Estab. 1999. Circ. 58,000. Byline given. Pays on publication. Offers 20% kill fee. Publishes ms an average of 2 months after acceptance. Editorial lead time 3 months. Submit seasonal material 6 months in advance. Accepts queries by e-mail. Accepts simultaneous submissions. Responds in 1-2 months to queries. Responds in 2-3 months to mss. Sample copy for sae with 10x13 envelope and 6 First-Class stamps. Guidelines available online.

NONFICTION Needs exposè, how-to, inspirational, interview, technical. Does not want personal narratives or any other first-person stories. No poems or creative writing manuscripts. Query with published clips. Length: 1,800-2,500 words. **Pays 25-60¢/word.**

PHOTOS Send photos. Captions, identification of subjects, model releases required. Reviews PDF, GIF/JPEG files. Offers no additional payment for photos accepted with ms.

COLUMNS Q&A, 600 words; Shakes, Rattles & Rollovers; Rearview Mirror Query with published clips. **Pays 25-35¢/word.**

💲💲 FLEET EXECUTIVE

NAFA Fleet Management Association, 125 Village Blvd., Suite 200, Princeton NJ 08540. (609)986-1053; (609)720-0882. Fax: (609)720-0881; (609)452-8004. E-mail: publications@nafa.org; info@nafa.org. Website: nafa.org. **10% freelance written.** Magazine published 6 times/year covering automotive fleet management. Estab. 1957. Circ. 4,000. No byline given. Pays on publication. Publishes ms an average of 4 months after acceptance. Editorial lead time 2 months. Accepts queries by mail. Accepts simultaneous submissions. Responds in 1 month to queries. Sample copy available online.

"Generally focuses on car, van, and light-duty truck management in US and Canadian corporations, government agencies, and utilities. Editorial emphasis is on general automotive issues; improving jobs skills, productivity, and professionalism; legislation and regulation; alternative fuels; safety; interviews with prominent industry personalities; technology; association news; public service fleet management; and light-duty truck fleet management."

NONFICTION Needs interview, technical. **Buys 24 mss/year.** Query with published clips. Length: 500-3,000 words. **Pays $500 maximum.**

PHOTOS State availability. Reviews electronic images.

OLD CARS WEEKLY

Division of F+W Media, Inc., 700 E. State St., Iola WI 54990-0001. (715)445-4612. Fax: (715)445-2214. E-mail: angelo.vanbogart@fwmedia.com. Website: oldcarsweekly.com. **Contact:** Angelo Van Bogart. **30% freelance written.** Weekly tabloid for anyone restoring, selling or driving an old car. Estab. 1971. Circ. 55,000. Byline given. Pays within 3 months after publication date. Publishes ms an average of 6 months after acceptance. Call circulation department for sample copy. Guidelines for #10 SASE.

NONFICTION Needs how-to, technical, auction prices realized lists. No Grandpa's Car, My First Car or My Car themes from freelance contributors. **Buys 1,000 mss/year.** Send complete ms. Length: 400-1,600 words. **Payment varies.**

PHOTOS Send photos. Captions, identification of subjects required. Pays $5/photo. Offers no additional payment for photos accepted with ms.

⊖⊖⊖ OVERDRIVE

Randall-Reilly Publishing Co./Overdrive, Inc., 3200 Rice Mine Rd., Tuscaloosa AL 35406. (205)349-2990. Fax: (205)750-8070. E-mail: mheine@randallpub.com. Website: etrucker.com. **Contact:** Max Heine, editorial director. **5% freelance written.** Monthly magazine for independent truckers. Estab. 1961. Circ. 100,000. Byline given. Pays on publication. Offers 10% kill fee. Publishes ms an average of 2 months after acceptance. Responds in 2 months to queries. Sample copy for 9×12 SASE.

NONFICTION Needs essays, exposè, how-to, truck maintenance and operation, interview, successful independent truckers, personal experience, photo feature, technical. Send complete ms. Length: 500-2,500 words. **Pays $300-1,500 for assigned articles.**

PHOTOS Photo fees negotiable.

⊖ PML

PML Consulting, P.O. 365, Ridgecrest CA 98555. E-mail: thom@pmletter.com. Website: pmletter.com/blog. **100% freelance written.** Monthly magazine covering technical tips, personality profiles and race coverage of Porsche automobiles. Estab. 1981. Circ. 1,500. Byline given. Pays on publication. Publishes ms an average of 2 months after acceptance. Editorial lead time 2 months. Submit seasonal material 2 months in advance. Accepts queries by mail, e-mail, fax, phone. Accepts simultaneous submissions. Responds in 2 weeks to queries. Responds in 1 month to mss. Sample copy for $5.

NONFICTION Needs general interest, historical, how-to, humor, interview, new product, personal experience, photo feature, technical, travel, race results. **Buys 30-40 mss/year.** Query with published clips. Length: 500-2,000 words. **Pays $30-50 and up, depending on length and topic.**

PHOTOS Send photos. Captions, identification of subjects, model releases required. Reviews 8×10 b&w prints. Negotiates payment individually.

FILLERS Needs anecdotes, facts, gags, newsbreaks, short humor. **Negotiable amount.**

♻⊖⊖ TIRE NEWS

Rousseau Automotive Communication, 455, Notre-Dame Est, Suite 311, Montreal QC H2Y 1C9 Canada. (514)289-0888; 1-877-989-0888. Fax: (514)289-5151. E-mail: info@autosphere.ca; 104420.662@compuserve.com; daniel.lafrance@autosphere.ca. Website: pub-licationsrousseau.com; autosphere.ca/en/tires.html. Daniel Lafrance, web editor. Bimonthly magazine covering Canadian tire industry. *Tire News* focuses on education/training, industry image, management, new tires, new techniques, marketing, HR, etc. Estab. 2004. Circ. 16,000. Byline given. Pays on publication. Publishes ms an average of 2 months after acceptance. Editorial lead time 2 months. Submit seasonal material 2 months in advance. Accepts simultaneous submissions. Responds in 2 weeks to queries. Responds in 2 months to mss. Guidelines by e-mail.

NONFICTION Needs general interest, how-to, inspirational, interview, new product, technical. Does not want opinion pieces. **Buys 5 mss/year.** Query with published clips. Length: 550-610 words. **Pays up to $200 (Canadian).**

PHOTOS Send photos. Captions required. Reviews GIF/JPEG files. Offers no additional payment for photos accepted with ms.

FILLERS Needs facts. **Buys 2 mss/year.** Length: 550-610 words. **Pays $0-200.**

⊖⊖ TOWING & RECOVERY FOOTNOTES

Dominion Enterprises, 150 Granby St., Norfolk VA 23510. (757)351-8633. Fax: (757)233-7047. E-mail: bcandler@dominionenterprises. Website: trfootnotes.com. **100% freelance written.** Monthly trade newspaper and marketplace for the nation's towing and recovery industry. Estab. 1991. Circ. 25,000. Byline given. Pays within 2-3 weeks of acceptance. Publishes ms an average of 2-3 months after acceptance. Editorial lead time 2 months. Submit seasonal material 2 months in advance. Accepts queries by mail, e-mail, phone. Responds in 2 weeks to queries. Responds in 1 month to mss.

NONFICTION Needs historical, how-to, humor, interview, new product, opinion, personal experience, photo feature, technical. **Buys 500 mss/year.** Query with published clips. Length: 800-2,000 words. **Pays $200-$600 for assigned articles.**

PHOTOS Send photos. Captions, identification of subjects required. Reviews GIF/JPEG files. Negotiates payment individually.

COLUMNS Columns vary from issue to issue; no regular departments available to freelancers; columns are given names appropriate to topic, and often repeat no matter who the author is. **Buys 250 mss/year.** Query with published clips.

◎ ⊜ ⊜ WESTERN CANADA HIGHWAY NEWS

Craig Kelman & Associates, 2020 Portage Ave., 3rd Floor, Winnipeg MB R3J 0K4 Canada. (204)985-9785. Fax: (204)985-9795. E-mail: terry@kelman.ca. Website: highwaynews.ca. **Contact:** Terry Ross, editor. **30% freelance written.** Quarterly magazine covering trucking. "The official magazine of the Alberta, Saskatchewan, and Manitoba trucking associations." Estab. 1995. Circ. 4,500. Byline given. Pays on publication. Publishes ms an average of 2 months after acceptance. Editorial lead time 3 months. Submit seasonal material 3 months in advance. Accepts simultaneous submissions. Responds in 1 month to queries and mss. Sample copy for 10x13 SAE with 1 IRC. Guidelines for #10 SASE.

> "As the official magazine of the trucking associations in Alberta, Saskatchewan and Manitoba, *Western Canada Highway News* is committed to providing leading edge, timely information on business practices, technology, trends, new products/services, legal and legislative issues that affect professionals in Western Canada's trucking industry."

NONFICTION Needs essays, general interest, how-to, run a trucking business, interview, new product, opinion, personal experience, photo feature, technical, profiles in excellence (bios of trucking or associate firms enjoying success). **Buys 8-10 mss/year.** Query. Length: 500-3,000 words. **Pays 18-25¢/word.**

PHOTOS State availability. Identification of subjects required. Reviews 4×6 prints.

COLUMNS Safety (new safety innovation/products), 500 words; Trade Talk (new products), 300 words. Query. **Pays 18-25¢/word.**

AVIATION AND SPACE

⊕ ⊜ ⊜ AEROSAFETY WORLD MAGAZINE

Flight Safety Foundation, 801 N. Fairfax S., Suite 400, Alexandria VA 22314-1774. (703)739-6700. Fax: (703)739-6708. E-mail: donoghue@flightsafety.org. Website: flightsafety.org. **Contact:** J.A. Donoghue, editor-in-chief. Monthly newsletter covering safety aspects of airport operations. Estab. 1974. Accepts queries by mail, e-mail, fax. Sample copy and guidelines online.

> "AeroSafety World continues Flight Safety Foundation's tradition of excellence in aviation safety journalism that stretches back more than 50 years. The new full-color monthly magazine, initially called Aviation Safety World offers in-depth analysis of important safety issues facing the industry, along with several new departments and a greater emphasis on timely news coverage—in a convenient format and eye-catching contemporary design. While AeroSafety World has taken the place of the 7 newsletters the Foundation used to produce, including Airport Operations, the archives remain active and back issues of the newsletters are still available."

NONFICTION Needs technical. Query.

⊜ ⊜ AIRCRAFT MAINTENANCE TECHNOLOGY

Cygnus Business Media, 1233 Janesville Ave., Fort Atkinson WI 53538. (920)563-6388. Fax: (920)569-4603. E-mail: joe.escobar@cygnusb2b.com. Website: amtonline.com. **10% freelance written.** Magazine published 10 times/year covering aircraft maintenance. *Aircraft Maintenance Technology* provides aircraft maintenance professionals worldwide with a curriculum of technical, professional, and managerial development information that enables them to more efficiently and effectively perform their jobs. Estab. 1989. Circ. 41,500 worldwide. Byline given. Pays on publication. Publishes ms an average of 2 months after acceptance. Editorial lead time 3 months. Submit seasonal material 6 months in advance. Accepts queries by online submission form. Accepts simultaneous submissions. Responds in 2 weeks to queries. Responds in 1 month to mss. Guidelines for #10 SASE or by e-mail.

> "Aircraft Maintenance Technology is the source for information for the professional maintenance team. We welcome your questions, comments and suggestions regarding our editorial content - as well as ideas for future stories."

NONFICTION Needs how-to, technical, safety. Special issues: Aviation career issue (August). No travel/pilot-oriented pieces. **Buys 10-12 mss/year.** Query with published clips. Please use the online form to contact us. 600-1,500 words, technical articles 2,000 words **Pays $200.**

PHOTOS State availability. Captions, identification of subjects, model releases required. Offers no additional payment for photos accepted with ms.

COLUMNS Professionalism, 1,000-1,500 words; Safety Matters, 600-1,000 words; Human Factors, 600-1,000 words. **Buys 10-12 mss/year.** Query with published clips. **Pays $200**

AIR LINE PILOT

Air Line Pilots Association, 1625 Massachusetts Ave. NW, Washington D.C. 20036. (703)698-2270. E-mail: magazine@alpa.org. Website: alpa.org. **Contact:** Pete Janhunen, publications manager. **2% freelance written. Prefers to work with published/established writers; works with a small number of new/unpublished writers each year.** Magazine published 10 times/year for airline pilots covering commercial aviation industry information—economics, avionics, equipment, systems, safety—that affects a pilot's life in a professional sense. Also includes information about management/labor relations trends, contract negotiations, etc. **Contact:** Pete Janhunen, publications manager. Circ. 72,000. Estab. 1932. Publication of Air Line Pilots Association. 10 issues/year. Emphasizes news and feature stories for airline pilots. Photo guidelines available online. Estab. 1931. Circ. 90,000. Pays on acceptance. Offers 50% kill fee. Publishes ms an average of 6 months after acceptance. Submit seasonal material 6 months in advance. Responds in 2 months to queries. Sample copy for $2. Guidelines available online.

NONFICTION Needs humor, inspirational, photo feature, technical. **Buys 5 mss/year.** Query with or without published clips or send complete ms and SASE. Length: 700-3,000 words. **Pays $100-600 for assigned articles. Pays $50-600 for unsolicited articles.**

PHOTOS "Our greatest need is for strikingly original cover photographs featuring ALPA flight deck crew members and their airlines in their operating environment. See list of airlines with ALPA Pilots online.". Send photos. Identification of subjects required. Reviews contact sheets, 35mm transparencies, 8×10 prints, digital must be 300 dpi at 8x11. Will review low-res thumbnail images. Offers $10-35/b&w photo, $30-50 for color used inside and $450 for color used as cover. For cover photography, shoot vertical rather than horizontal.

$$ AVIATION INTERNATIONAL NEWS

The Convention News Co., 214 Franklin Ave., Midland Park NJ 07432. (201)444-5075. Fax: (201)444-4647. E-mail: nmoll@ainonline.com; editor@ainonline.com. Website: ainonline.com. Annmarie Yannaco, managing editor at ayannaco@ainonline.com. **Contact:** Nigel Moll, editor. **30-40% freelance written.** Monthly magazine (with daily onsite issues published at 3 conventions and 2 international air shows each year) and twice-weekly AINalerts via e-mail covering business and commercial aviation with news features, special reports, aircraft evaluations, and surveys on business aviation worldwide, written for business pilots and industry professionals. While the heartbeat of *AIN* is driven by the news it carries, the human touch is not neglected. We pride ourselves on our people stories about the industry's `movers and shakers' and others in aviation who make a difference. Estab. 1972. Circ. 40,000. Byline given. **Pays on acceptance and upon receipt of writer's invoice.** Offers variable kill fee. Publishes ms an average of 2 months after acceptance. Editorial lead time 2 months. Submit seasonal material 3 months in advance. Accepts queries by mail, e-mail, fax. Responds in 6 weeks to queries. Responds in 2 months to mss. Sample copy for $10. Writer's guidelines for 9×12 SAE with 3 first-class stamps.

NONFICTION Needs how-to, aviation, interview, new product, opinion, personal experience, photo feature, technical. No puff pieces. Our readers expect serious, real news. We don't pull any punches. *AIN* is not a 'good news' publication: It tells the story, both good and bad. **Buys 150-200 mss/year.** Query with published clips. Do not send mss by e-mail unless requested. Length: 200-3,000 words. **Pays 40¢/word to first timers, higher rates to proven *AIN* freelancers.**

PHOTOS Send photos. Captions required. Reviews contact sheets, transparencies, prints, TIFF files (300 dpi). Negotiates payment individually.

$$ GROUND SUPPORT WORLDWIDE MAGAZINE

Cygnus Business Media, 1233 Janesville Ave., Fort Atkinson WI 53538. (920)563-1622; (800)547-7377 ext. 1389. Fax: (920)563-1699. E-mail: karen.reinhardt@cygnusb2bpub.com; Lisa.Haddican@cygnusb2b.com. Website: groundsupportworldwide.com. **Contact:** Lisa Haddican, managing editor. **20% freelance written.** Magazine published 10 times/year. Estab. 1993. Circ. 15,000. Pays on publication. Publishes ms an average of 2 months after acceptance. Editorial lead time 2 months. Accepts queries by mail, e-mail, fax. Responds in 3 weeks to queries. Responds in 3 months to mss. Sample copy for sae with 9â—Š11 envelope and 5 First-Class stamps.

Our readers are those aviation professionals who are involved in ground support—the

TRADE JOURNALS

equipment manufacturers, the suppliers, the ramp operators, ground handlers, airport and airline managers. We cover issues of interest to this community—deicing, ramp safety, equipment technology, pollution, etc.

NONFICTION Needs how-to, use or maintain certain equipment, interview, new product, opinion, photo feature, technical aspects of ground support and issues, industry events, meetings, new rules and regulations. **Buys 12-20 mss/year.** Send complete ms. Length: 500-2,000 words. **Pays $100-300.**

PHOTOS Send photos. Identification of subjects required. Reviews 35mm prints, electronic preferred, slides. Offers additional payment for photos accepted with ms.

⊝⊝⊝ PROFESSIONAL PILOT

Queensmith Communications, 30 S. Quaker Ln., Suite 300, Alexandria VA 22314. (703)370-0606. Fax: (703)370-7082. E-mail: editor@propilotmag.com; prose@propilotmag.com; publisher@propilotmag.com. Website: propilotmag.com. Murray Smith, publisher. **Contact:** Phil Rose, editor. **75% freelance written.** Monthly magazine covering corporate, non combat government, law enforcement and various other types of professional aviation. The typical reader has a sophisticated grasp of piloting/aviation knowledge and is interested in articles that help him/her do the job better or more efficiently. Estab. 1967. Circ. 40,000. Byline given. Pays on publication. Offers kill fee. Kill fee negotiable. Publishes ms an average of 2-3 months after acceptance. Accepts queries by mail, e-mail, fax.

NONFICTION Buys 40 mss/year. Query. Length: 750-2,500 words. **Pays $200-1,000, depending on length. A fee for the article will be established at the time of assignment.**

PHOTOS Prefers transparencies or high resolution 300 JPEG digital images. Send photos. Captions, identification of subjects required. Additional payment for photos negotiable.

BEAUTY AND SALON

⊝⊝ BEAUTY STORE BUSINESS

Creative Age Communications, 7628 Densmore Ave., Van Nuys CA 91406-2042. (818)782-7328, ext. 353; (800)442-5667. Fax: (818)782-7450. E-mail: mbatist@creativeage.com; mbirenbaum@creativeage.

com; skelly@creativeage.com. Website: beautystorebusiness.com. Shelley Moench-Kelly, managing editor. **Contact:** Manha Batist, editor/online editor. **50% freelance written.** Monthly magazine covering beauty store business management, news and beauty products. Estab. 1994. Circ. 15,000. Byline given. Pays on acceptance. Offers kill fee. Offers negotiable kill fee. Publishes ms an average of 3 months after acceptance. Editorial lead time 3 months. Submit seasonal material 4 months in advance. Accepts queries by mail, e-mail, fax. Responds in 1 week to queries. Responds in 2 weeks, if interested,.

> "The primary readers of the publication are owners, managers, and buyers at open-to-the-public beauty stores, including general-market and multicultural market-oriented ones with or without salon services. Our secondary readers are those at beauty stores only open to salon industry professionals. We also go to beauty distributors."

NONFICTION Needs how-to, business management, merchandising, e-commerce, retailing, interview, industry leaders/beauty store owners. **Buys 20-30 mss/year.** Query. Length: 1,800-2,200 words. **Pays $250-525 for assigned articles.**

PHOTOS Do not send computer art electronically. State availability. Captions, identification of subjects required. Reviews transparencies, computer art (artists work on Macs, request 300 dpi, on CD or Zip disk, saved as JPEG, TIFF, or EPS). Negotiates payment individually.

⊝⊝⊝ COSMETICS

Rogers, 1 Mt. Pleasant Rd., 7th Floor, Toronto ON M4Y 2Y5 Canada. (416)764-1680. Fax: (416)764-1704. E-mail: dave.lackie@cosmetics.rogers.com. Website: cosmeticsmag.com. **Contact:** Dave Lackie, editor. **10% freelance written.** Bimonthly magazine. Estab. 1972. Circ. 13,000. Byline given. Pays on acceptance. Offers 50% kill fee. Publishes ms an average of 3 months after acceptance. Editorial lead time 4 months. Submit seasonal material 4 months in advance. Accepts queries by mail. Responds in 1 month to queries. Sample copy for $6 (Canadian) and 8% GST.

> "Our main reader segment is the retail trade—department stores, drugstores, salons, estheticians—owners and cosmeticians/beauty advisors; plus manufacturers, distributors, agents, and suppliers to the industry."

NONFICTION Needs general interest, interview, photo feature. **Buys 1 mss/year.** Query. Length: 250-1,200 words. **Pays 25¢/word.**

PHOTOS Send photos. Captions, identification of subjects, model releases required. Reviews 2½ up to 8×10 transparencies, 4×6 up to 8×10 prints, 35mm slides, e-mail pictures in 300 dpi JPEG format. Offers no additional payment for photos accepted with ms.

COLUMNS "All articles assigned on a regular basis from correspondents and columnists that we know personally from the industry."

⊗⊗ DAYSPA

Creative Age Publications, 7628 Densmore Ave., Van Nuys CA 91406. (818)782-7328, ext. 301. Fax: (818)782-7450. E-mail: lkossoff@creativeage.com. Website: dayspamagazine.com. **Contact:** Linda Kossoff, exec. editor. **50% freelance written.** Monthly magazine covering the business of day spas, multi-service/skincare salons, and resort/hotel spas. *"Dayspa* includes only well-targeted business and trend articles directed at the owners and managers. It serves to enrich, enlighten, and empower spa/salon professionals." Estab. 1996. Circ. 31,000. Byline given. Pays on acceptance. Publishes ms an average of 4 months after acceptance. Editorial lead time 4 months. Submit seasonal material 4 months in advance. Accepts queries by mail, e-mail, fax, phone, online submission form. Responds in 2 months to queries. Sample copy for $5.

NONFICTION **Buys 40 mss/year.** Query. Length: 1,500-1,800 words. **Pays $150-500.**

PHOTOS Send photos. Identification of subjects, model releases required. Negotiates payment individually.

COLUMNS Legal Pad (legal issues affecting salons/spas); Money Matters (financial issues); Management Workshop (spa management issues); Health Wise (wellness trends), all 1,200-1,500 words. **Buys 20 mss/year.** Query. **Pays $150-400.**

⊗⊗ MASSAGE MAGAZINE

5150 Palm Valley Rd., Suite 103, Ponte Vedra Beach FL 32082. (904)285-6020. Fax: (904)285-9944. E-mail: kmenahan@massagemag.com. Website: massagemag.com. **Contact:** Karen Menahan. **60% freelance written.** Bimonthly magazine covering massage and other touch therapies. Estab. 1985. Circ. 50,000. Byline given. Pays on publication. Publishes ms an average of 2 months-24 months after acceptance. Accepts queries by e-mail. Responds in 2 months to queries. Responds

in 3 months to mss. Sample copy for $6.95. Guidelines available online.

NONFICTION Needs book excerpts, essays, general interest, how-to, interview, personal experience, photo feature, technical, experiential. No multiple submissions Length: 600-2,000 words. **Pays $50-400.**

PHOTOS Send photos with submission via e-mail. Identification of subjects, required. Offers $15-40/photo; $40-100/illustration.

COLUMNS Profiles; News and Current Events; Practice Building (business); Technique; Body/Mind. Length: 800-1,200 words. **$75-300 for assigned articles**

FILLERS Needs facts, newsbreaks. Length: 100-800 words. **Pays $125 maximum.**

⊗⊗ NAILPRO, THE MAGAZINE FOR NAIL PROFESSIONALS

Creative Age Publications, 7628 Densmore Ave., Van Nuys CA 91406. (818)782-7328. Fax: (818)782-7450. E-mail: mjames@creativeage.com. E-mail: nailpro@creativeage.com. Website: nailpro.com. **75% freelance written.** Monthly magazine written for manicurists and nail technicians working in a full-service salon or nails-only salons. Estab. 1989. Circ. 65,000. Byline given. Pays on acceptance. Publishes ms an average of 6 months after acceptance. Editorial lead time 3 months. Submit seasonal material 3 months in advance. Accepts queries by mail, e-mail, fax. Accepts simultaneous submissions. Responds in 6 weeks to queries. Sample copy for $2 and 8 ½x11 SASE.

> "Nailpro covers technical and business aspects of working in a salon and operating nailcare services, as well as the nailcare industry in general.

NONFICTION Needs book excerpts, how-to, humor, inspirational, interview, personal experience, photo feature, technical. No general interest articles or business articles not geared to the nail-care industry. **Buys 50 mss/year.** Query. Length: 1,000-3,000 words. **Pays $150-450.**

PHOTOS Send photos. Identification of subjects, model releases required. Reviews transparencies, prints. Negotiates payment individually. Pays on acceptance.

COLUMNS "All Business (articles on building salon business, marketing & advertising, dealing with employees), 1,500-2,000 words; Attitudes (aspects of operating a nail salon and trends in the nail industry),

1,200-2,000 words." **Buys 50 mss/year.** Query. **Pays $250-350.**

⊘❸❸ NAILS

Bobit Business Media, 3520 Challenger St., Torrance CA 90503. (310)533-2457. Fax: (310)533-2507. E-mail: judy.lessin@bobit.com. Website: nailsmag.com. **Contact:** Judy Lessin, features editor. **10% freelance written.** Monthly magazine. *NAILS* seeks to educate its readers on new techniques and products, nail anatomy and health, customer relations, working safely with chemicals, salon sanitation, and the business aspects of running a salon. Estab. 1983. Circ. 55,000. Byline given. Pays on acceptance. Submit seasonal material 4 months in advance. Accepts queries by mail, e-mail, fax. Responds in 3 months to queries. Sample copy and writer's guidelines for #10 SASE.

NONFICTION Needs historical, how-to, inspirational, interview, personal experience, photo feature, technical. No articles on one particular product, company profiles or articles slanted toward a particular company or manufacturer. **Buys 20 mss/year.** Query with published clips. Length: 1,200-3,000 words. **Pays $200-500.**

PHOTOS State availability. Captions, identification of subjects, model releases required. Reviews contact sheets, transparencies, prints (any standard size acceptable). Offers $50-200/photo.

❸❸ PULSE MAGAZINE

HOST Communications Inc., 2365 Harrodsburg Rd., Suite A325, Lexington KY 40511. (859)226-4429; (859)425-5062. Fax: (859)226-4445. E-mail: mae.manacap-johnson@ispastaff.com. Website: experienceispa.com/ispa/pulse. **Contact:** Mae Manacap-Johnson, editor. **20% freelance written.** Magazine published 10 times/year covering spa industry. Estab. 1991. Circ. 5,300. Byline given. Pays on publication. Publishes ms an average of 1 month after acceptance. Editorial lead time 3 months. Submit seasonal material 4 months in advance. Accepts queries by e-mail. Sample copy for #10 SASE. Guidelines by e-mail.

    "Pulse is the magazine for the spa professional. As the official publication of the International SPA Association, its purpose is to advance the business of the spa professionals by informing them of the latest trends and practices and promoting the wellness aspects of spa. *Pulse* connects people, nurtures their personal and pro-fessional growth, and enhances their ability to network and succeed in the spa industry."

NONFICTION Needs general interest, how-to, interview, new product. Does not want articles focused on spas that are not members of ISPA, consumer-focused articles (market is the spa industry professional), or features on hot tubs (not *that* spa industry). **Buys 8-10 mss/year.** Query with published clips. Length: 800-2,000 words. **Pays $250-500.**

PHOTOS Contact: Contact Rebekah Sellers, assistant editor. Send photos. Captions required. Reviews GIF/JPEG files. Negotiates payment individually.

❸❸ SKIN DEEP

Associated Skin Care Professionals, 25188 Genesee Trail Rd., Suite 200, Golden CO 80401. (800)789-0411. E-mail: cpatrick@ascpskincare.com. Website: ascpskincare.com. **Contact:** Carrie Patrick, ed. **80% freelance written.** Bimonthly magazine covering technical, educational and business information for estheticians with an emphasis on solo practitioners and spa/salon employees or independent contractors. "Our audience is the U.S. individual skin care practitioner who may work on her own and/or in a spa or salon setting. We keep her up to date on skin care trends and techniques and ways to earn more income doing waxing, facials, peels, microdermabrasion, body wraps and other skin treatments. Our product-neutral stories may include novel spa treatments within the esthetician scope of practice. We do not want cover treatments that involve needles or lasers, or invasive treatments like ear candling, colonics or plastic surgery. Successful stories have included how-tos on paraffin facials, aromatherapy body wraps, waxing tips, how to read ingredient labels, how to improve word-of-mouth advertising, and how to choose an online scheduling software package." Estab. 2003. Circ. 8,000+. Byline given. Pays on acceptance. Publishes ms an average of 4-6 months after acceptance. Editorial lead time 4-5 months. Submit seasonal material 7 months in advance. Accepts queries by e-mail. Responds in 2 weeks to queries. Guidelines available.

NONFICTION "We don't run general consumer beauty material and very rarely run a new product that is available through retail outlets. 'New' products means introduced in the last 12 months. We do not run industry personnel announcements or stories on individual spas/salons or getaways. We don't cover hair or nails." **Buys 12 mss/year.** Query. Length: 800-2,300 words. **Pays $75-$300 for assigned articles.**

COLUMNS Ask the Expert (Practical marketing & technical info, how-to (no pay))

😊😊 SKIN INC. MAGAZINE

Allured Business Media, 336 Gundersen Dr., Suite A, Carol Stream IL 60188. (630)653-2155. Fax: (630)653-2192. E-mail: taschetta-millane@allured.com. Website: skininc.com. **Contact:** Melinda Taschetta-Millane, editor. **30% freelance written.** Magazine published 12 times/year. "Manuscripts considered for publication that contain original and new information in the general fields of skin care and make-up, dermatological and esthetician-assisted surgical techniques. The subject may cover the science of skin, the business of skin care and makeup, and plastic surgeons on healthy (i.e., nondiseased) skin." Estab. 1988. Circ. 30,000. Byline given. Pays on publication. Publishes ms an average of 6 months after acceptance. Editorial lead time 6 months. Submit seasonal material 1 year in advance. Accepts queries by mail, e-mail, fax, phone. Responds in 3 weeks to queries. Responds in 1 month to mss. Sample copy and writer's

NONFICTION Needs general interest, how-to, interview, personal experience, technical. **Buys 6 mss/year.** Query with published clips. Length: 2,000 words. **Pays $100-300 for assigned articles. Pays $50-200 for unsolicited articles.**

PHOTOS State availability. Captions, identification of subjects, model releases required. Reviews 3x5 prints. Offers no additional payment for photos accepted with ms.

COLUMNS Finance (tips and solutions for managing money), 2,000-2,500 words; Personnel (managing personnel), 2,000-2,500 words; Marketing (marketing tips for salon owners), 2,000-2,500 words; Retail (retailing products and services in the salon environment), 2,000-2,500 words. Query with published clips. **Pays $50-200.**

FILLERS Needs facts, newsbreaks. **Buys 6 mss/year. mss/year.** Length: 250-500 words. **Pays $50-100.**

BEVERAGES AND BOTTLING

😊😊😊 BAR & BEVERAGE BUSINESS MAGAZINE

Mercury Publications, Ltd., 1740 Wellington Ave., Winnipeg MB R3H 0E8 Canada. (204)954-2085. Fax:

(204)954-2057. E-mail: elaine@mercury.mb.ca; editorial@mercury.mb.ca. Website: barandbeverage.com. **Contact:** Elaine Dufault, assoc. manager. **33% freelance written.** Bimonthly magazine providing information on the latest trends, happenings, buying-selling of beverages and product merchandising. Estab. 1998. Circ. 16,077. Byline given. Pays 30-45 days from receipt of invoice. Offers 33% kill fee. Submit seasonal material 3 months in advance. Accepts simultaneous submissions. Sample copy and writer's guidelines free or by e-mail.

> "Does not accept queries for specific stories. Assigns stories to Canadian writers."

NONFICTION Needs how-to, making a good drink, training staff, etc., interview. Industry reports, profiles on companies. Query with published clips. Length: 500-9,000 words. **Pays 25-35¢/word.**

PHOTOS State availability. Captions required. Reviews negatives, transparencies, 3â—Š5 prints, JPEG, EPS or TIFF files. Negotiates payment individually.

COLUMNS Out There (bar & bev news in various parts of the country), 100-500 words. Query. **Pays $0-100.**

😊😊 THE BEVERAGE JOURNAL

MI Licensed Beverage Association, 920 N. Fairview, Lansing MI 48912. (517)374-9611; (800)292-2896. Fax: (517)374-1165. E-mail: editor@mlba.org. Website: mlba.org. **Contact:** Peter Broderick, editor. **40-50% freelance written.** Monthly magazine covering hospitality industry. Estab. 1983. Circ. 4,200. Pays on publication. Editorial lead time 3 months. Submit seasonal material 3 months in advance. Accepts queries by mail, e-mail. Responds in 2 weeks to queries. Responds in 1 month to mss. Sample copy for $5 or online.

> A monthly trade magazine devoted to the beer, wine, and spirits industry in Michigan. It is dedicated to serving those who make their living serving the public and the state through the orderly and responsible sale of beverages.

NONFICTION Needs essays, general interest, historical, how-to, make a drink, human resources, tips, etc. , humor, interview, new product, opinion, personal experience, photo feature, technical. **Buys 24 mss/year.** Send complete ms. Length: 1,000 words. **Pays $20-200.**

COLUMNS Open to essay content ideas. Interviews (legislators, others), 750-1,000 words; personal experience (waitstaff, customer, bartenders), 500 words. **Buys 12 mss/year.** Send complete ms. **Pays $25-100.**

🌕🌑 PRACTICAL WINERY & VINEYARD

PWV, Inc., 58 Paul Dr., Suite D, San Rafael CA 94903-2054. (415)479-5819. Fax: (415)492-9325. E-mail: office@practicalwinery.com; tina@practicalwiner.com. Website: practicalwinery.com. Carol Caldwell-Ewart, Elinor Pravda, editors. **Contact:** Don Neel, publisher/editor. **50% freelance written.** Bimonthly magazine covering winemaking, grapegrowing, wine marketing. *"Practical Winery & Vineyard* is a technical trade journal for winemakers and grapegrowers. All articles are fact-checked and peer-reviewed prior to publication to ensure 100% accuracy, readability, and practical useful application for readers. NO consumer-focused wine articles, please." Estab. 1979. Circ. 4,000. Byline given. Pays on publication. Publishes ms an average of 6-9 months after acceptance. Editorial lead time 6-9 months. Submit seasonal material 9 months in advance. Accepts queries by mail, e-mail, fax. Responds in 1-2 weeks to queries. Responds in 1 month to mss. Guidelines by e-mail.

NONFICTION Contact: Tina L. Vierra, associate publisher. Needs how-to, technical. Special issues: "Each issue has a specific topic/focus. Please see Editorial Calendar for 2010. We do not want any wine consumer trends, retail info, wine tasting notes; no food, travel, wine lifestyles." **Buys 25 mss/year. mss/year.** Query with published clips. Length: 1,000-3,000 words. **Pays 25-50¢ a word for assigned articles. Pays 25-35¢ a word for unsolicited articles.**

PHOTOS Contact: Tina L. Vierra, associate publisher. State availability. Captions required. Reviews GIF/JPEG files. Offers no additional payment for photos accepted with ms.

🌕🌑🌑 VINEYARD & WINERY MANAGEMENT

P.O. Box 2358, Windsor CA 95492-2358. (707)577-7700. Fax: (707)577-7705. E-mail: tcaputo@vwm-online.com. Website: vwm-online.com. **Contact:** Tina Caputo, editor-in-chief. **70% freelance written.** Bimonthly magazine of professional importance to grape growers, winemakers, and winery sales and business people. "Headquartered in Sonoma County, California, we proudly remain as a leading independent wine trade magazine serving all of North America." Estab. 1975. Circ. 6,500. Byline given. Pays on

publication. Accepts queries by e-mail. Responds in 3 weeks to queries. Responds in 1 month to mss. Guidelines for #10 SASE.

○ "We focus on the management of people and process in the areas of viticulture, enology, winery marketing and finance. Our articles are written with a high degree of technical expertise by a team of wine industry professionals and top-notch journalists. Timely articles and columns keep our subscribers poised for excellence and success."

NONFICTION Needs how-to, interview, new product, technical. **Buys 30 mss/year.** Query. Length: 1,800-5,000 words. **Pays $30-1,000.**

PHOTOS State availability. Captions, identification of subjects required. Reviews contact sheets, negatives, transparencies, digital photos. Black & white often purchased for $20 each to accompany story material; 35mm and/or 4x5 transparencies for $50 and up; 6/year of vineyard and/or winery scene related to story.

🌕🌑 WINES & VINES MAGAZINE

Wine Communications Group, 1800 Lincoln Ave., San Rafael CA 94901. (415)453-9700. Fax: (415)453-2517. E-mail: edit@winesandvines.com; info@winesandvines.com. Website: winesandvines.com. Jerry Gordon, editor. **Contact:** Kerry Kirkham, tech. editor. **50% freelance written.** Monthly magazine covering the North American winegrape and winemaking industry. "Since 1919 *Wines & Vines Magazine* has been the authoritative voice of the wine and grape industry—from prohibition to phylloxera, we have covered it all. Our paid circulation reaches all 50 states and many foreign countries. Because we are intended for the trade—including growers, winemakers, winery owners, wholesalers, restauranteurs, and serious amateurs—we accept more technical, informative articles. We do not accept wine reviews, wine country tours, or anything of a wine consumer nature." Estab. 1919. Circ. 5,000. Byline given. Pays 30 days after acceptance. Publishes ms an average of 3 months after acceptance. Editorial lead time 2 months. Submit seasonal material 4 months in advance. Accepts queries by e-mail. Responds in 2-3 weeks to queries. Sample copy for $5.

NONFICTION Needs interview, new product, technical. "No wine reviews, wine country travelogues, 'lifestyle' pieces, or anything aimed at wine consumers. Our readers are professionals in the field." **Buys 60 mss/year.** Query with published clips. Length: 1,000-2,000 words. **Pays flat fee of $500 for assigned articles.**

PHOTOS Prefers JPEG files (JPEG, 300 dpi minimum). Can use high-quality prints. State availability of or send photos. Captions, identification of subjects required. Does not pay for photos submitted by author, but will give photo credit.

BOOK AND BOOKSTORE

$ THE BLOOMSBURY REVIEW

Dept. WM, Owaissa Communications Co., Inc., P.O. Box 8928, Denver CO 80201. (303)455-3123. Fax: (303)455-7039. E-mail: bloomsb@aol.com. **75% freelance written.** Quarterly tabloid covering books and book-related matters. "We publish book reviews, interviews with writers and poets, literary essays, and original poetry. Our audience consists of educated, literate, nonspecialized readers." Estab. 1980. Circ. 35,000. Byline given. Pays on publication. Publishes ms an average of 4-6 months after acceptance. Accepts queries by mail. Responds in 4 months to queries. Sample copy for $5 and 9×12 SASE. Guidelines for #10 SASE.

NONFICTION Needs essays, interview, book reviews. **Buys 60 mss/year.** Send complete ms. Length: 800-1,500 words. **Pays $10-20. Sometimes pays writers with contributor copies or other premiums if writer agrees.**

PHOTOS State availability of photos. Reviews prints. Offers no additional payment for photos accepted with ms.

COLUMNS Book reviews and essays, 500-1,500 words. **Buys 6 mss/year.** Query with published clips or send complete ms. **Pays $10-20.**

POETRY Contact: Ray Gonzalez, poetry editor. Needs avant-garde, free verse, haiku, traditional. Buys 20 poems/year. Submit maximum 5 poems. **Pays $5-10.**

$$ FOREWORD MAGAZINE

ForeWord Magazine, Inc., 129 ½ E. Front St., Traverse City MI 49684. (231)933-3699. Fax: (231)933-3899. E-mail: victoria@forewordmagazine.com. Website: forewordmagazine.com. Teresa Scollon. **Contact:** Victoria Sutherland, publisher. **95% freelance written.** Bimonthly magazine covering reviews of good books independently published. In each issue of the magazine, there are 3 to 4 feature *ForeSight* articles focusing on trends in popular categories. These are in addition to the 75 or more critical reviews of forthcoming titles from independent presses in our *Review* section. While we try very hard to communicate with publicity departments concerning calls for submissions to the *ForeSight* features, we also hope that publishers will keep these forms handy to track what's happening at *ForeWord*. Look online for our review submission guidelines or view the 2011-2012 editorial calendar. Be sure to read the ForeWord Ten-Point Tip Sheet, which outlines how to make sure you know how to present your book for best results. Estab. 1998. Circ. 20,000 (about 85% librarians, 12% bookstores, 3% publishing professionals). Byline given. Pays 2 months after publication. Publishes ms an average of 2-3 months after acceptance. Editorial lead time 3-4 months. Submit seasonal material 5 months in advance. Accepts queries by mail, e-mail. Responds in 1 month to queries. Responds in 1 month to mss. Sample copy for $10 and 8½×11 SASE with $1.50 postage.

"*ForeWord's* special sections and supplements exist to cover perennial interest areas and emerging trends in the publishing world. Currently, we highlight graphic novels in *Comique*, digital technology in *eWord*, books for a global society in *Polis*, religion titles in *Faith*, and mind/body books in *Spirit*."

NONFICTION Query with published clips. All review submissions should be sent to the Book Review Editor. Submissions should include a fact sheet or press release. Length: 400-1,500 words. **Pays $25-200 for assigned articles.**

THE HORN BOOK MAGAZINE

The Horn Book, Inc., 56 Roland St., Suite 200, Boston MA 02129. (617)628-0225. Fax: (617)628-0882. Website: hbook.com. Cynthia Ritter, editorial assistant. **75% freelance written. Prefers to work with published/established writers.** Bimonthly magazine covering children's literature for librarians, booksellers, professors, teachers and students of children's literature. Estab. 1924. Circ. 9,000. Byline given. Pays on publication. Publishes ms an average of 4 months after acceptance. Submit seasonal material 6 months in advance. Accepts queries by mail, e-mail, fax. Accepts simultaneous submissions. Responds in 3 months to queries. Sample copy and writer's guidelines online.

TRADE JOURNALS

NONFICTION Needs interview, children's book authors and illustrators, topics of interest to the children's bookworld. **Buys 20 mss/year.** Query or send complete ms. Length: 1,000-2,800 words. **Pays honorarium upon publication.**

$ VIDEO LIBRARIAN

8705 Honeycomb Court NW, Seabeck WA 98380. (360)830-9345. Fax: (360)830-9346. E-mail: vidlib@videolibrarian.com. Website: videolibrarian.com. **75% freelance written.** Bimonthly magazine covering DVD reviews for librarians. "*Video Librarian* reviews approximately 225 titles in each issue: children's, documentaries, how-to's, movies, TV, music and anime." Estab. 1986. Circ. 2,000. Byline given. Pays on publication. Publishes ms an average of 2 months after acceptance. Editorial lead time 2 months. Accepts queries by e-mail. Accepts simultaneous submissions. Responds in 1 week to queries. Sample copy for $11.

NONFICTION **Buys 500+ mss/year.** Query with published clips. Length: 200-300 words. **Pays $10-20/review.**

BRICK, GLASS AND CERAMICS

$$ GLASS MAGAZINE

National Glass Association, National Glass Association, 1945 Old Gallows Rd., Suite 750, Vienna VA 22182. (866)342-5642, ext.253. Fax: (703)442-0630. E-mail: editorialinfo@glass.org. Website: glass.org. **10% freelance written. Prefers to work with published/established writers.** Monthly magazine covering the architectural glass industry. Circ. 28,289. Byline given. Pays on acceptance. Offers kill fee. Kill fee varies. Publishes ms an average of 6 months after acceptance. Accepts queries by mail, e-mail, fax. Responds in 2 months to mss. Sample copy for $5 and 9×12 SASE with 10 first-class stamps.

NONFICTION Needs interview, of various glass businesses; profiles of industry people or glass business owners, new product, technical, about glazing processes. **Buys 5 mss/year.** Query with published clips. 1,000 words minimum. **Pays $150-300.**

PHOTOS State availability.

$ STAINED GLASS

Stained Glass Association of America, 9313 East 63rd St., Raytown MO 64133. (800)438-9581. Fax: (816)737-2801. E-mail: quarterly@sgaaonline.com; webmaster@sgaaonline.com. Website: stainedglass.org. **Contact:** Richard Gross, editor & media director. **70% freelance written.** Quarterly magazine. "Since 1906, *Stained Glass* has been the official voice of the Stained Glass Association of America. As the oldest, most respected stained glass publication in North America, *Stained Glass* preserves the techniques of the past as well as illustrates the trends of the future. This vital information, of significant value to the professional stained glass studio, is also of interest to those for whom stained glass is an avocation or hobby." Estab. 1906. Circ. 8,000. Byline given. Pays on publication. Publishes ms an average of 1 year after acceptance. Editorial lead time 6 months. Submit seasonal material 8 months in advance. Accepts queries by mail, e-mail, fax. Responds in 3 months to queries. Sample copy and writer's guideline free.

NONFICTION Needs how-to, humor, interview, new product, opinion, photo feature, technical. **Buys 9 mss/year.** Query or send complete ms but must include photos or slides—very heavy on photos. Length: 2,500-3,500 words **Pays $125/illustrated article; $75/nonillustrated.**

PHOTOS Send photos. Identification of subjects required. Reviews 4x5 transparencies, send slides with submission. Pays $75 for non-illustrated. Pays $125, plus 3 copies for line art or photography.

COLUMNS Columns must be illustrated. Teknixs (technical, how-to, stained and glass art), word length varies by subject. **Buys 4 mss/year.** Query or send complete ms, but must be illustrated.

$$ US GLASS, METAL & GLAZING

Key Communications, Inc., P.O. Box 569, Garrisonville VA 22463. (540)720-5584, ext.114. Fax: (540)720-5687. E-mail: info@glass.com; mheadley@glass.com. Website: usglassmag.com. **Contact:** Megan Headley, editor. **25% freelance written.** Monthly magazine for companies involved in the flat glass trades. Estab. 1966. Circ. 27,000. Byline given. Pays on publication. Publishes ms an average of 3 months after acceptance. Editorial lead time 3 months. Submit seasonal material 2 months in advance. Accepts queries by mail, e-mail, fax. Accepts simultaneous submissions. Responds in 1 month to queries. Responds in 2 months to mss. Sample copy and writer's guidelines online.

NONFICTION **Buys 12 mss/year.** Query with published clips. **Pays $300-600 for assigned articles.**

PHOTOS State availability. Captions, identification of subjects required. Reviews contact sheets. Offers no additional payment for photos accepted with ms.

BUILDING INTERIORS

💲💲 FABRICS + FURNISHINGS INTERNATIONAL

SIPCO Publications + Events, 145 Main St., 3rd Floor, Ossining NY 10591. (914)923-0616. Fax: (914)923-0018; 923-0616. E-mail: marc@sipco.net. Website: sipco.net. Eric Schneider, editor/publisher. **Contact:** March Weinreich. **10% freelance written**. Bimonthly magazine covering commercial, hospitality interior design, manufacturing. *F+FI* covers news from vendors who supply the hospitality interiors industry. Estab. 1990. Circ. 11,000+. Byline given. Pays on publication. Offers $100 kill fee. Editorial lead time 3 months. Submit seasonal material 3 months in advance. Accepts queries by e-mail. Accepts simultaneous submissions. Sample copy available online.

NONFICTION Needs interview, technical. "Does no opinion, consumer pieces. Our readers must learn something from our stories." Query with published clips. Length: 500-1,000 words. **Pays $250-350.**

PHOTOS Send photos. Captions, identification of subjects required. Reviews GIF/JPEG files. Offers no additional payment for photos accepted with ms.

💲💲 KITCHEN & BATH DESIGN NEWS

Cygnus Business Media, 3 Huntington Quadrangle, Suite 301N, Melville NY 11747. Fax: (631)845-7218. E-mail: janice.costa@cygnuspub.com; eliot.sefrin@cygnuspub.com. Website: kitchenbathdesign.com. Eliot Sefrin. **15% freelance written**. Monthly tabloid for kitchen and bath dealers and design professionals, offering design, business and marketing advice to help our readers be more successful. It is not a consumer publication about design, a book for do-it-yourselfers, or a magazine created to showcase pretty pictures of kitchens and baths. Rather, we cover the professional kitchen and bath design industry in depth, looking at the specific challenges facing these professionals, and how they address these challenges. Estab. 1983. Circ. 51,000. Byline given. Pays on publication. Publishes ms an average of 2-3 months after acceptance. Editorial lead time 2 months. Accepts queries by mail, e-mail, fax. Responds in 2-4 weeks to queries. Sample copy available online. Guidelines by e-mail.

NONFICTION Needs how-to, interview. "Does not want consumer stories; generic business stories; I remodeled my kitchen and it's so beautiful stories. This is a magazine for trade professionals, so stories need to be both slanted for these professionals, as well as sophisticated enough so that people who have been working in the field 30 years can still learn something from them." **Buys 16 mss/year.** Query with published clips. Length: 1,100-3,000 words. **Pays $200-650.**

PHOTOS Send photos. Identification of subjects required. Offers no additional payment for photos accepted with ms.

💲💲 QUALIFIED REMODELER

Cygnus Business Media, P.O. Box 803, Fort Atkinson WI 53538. E-mail: Rob.Heselbarth@cygnusb2b.com; christina.koch@cygnusb2b.com. Website: qualifiedremodeler.com. Christina Koch, editor-in-chief. **Contact:** Rob Heselbarth, editorial director. **5% freelance written**. Monthly magazine covering residential remodeling. Estab. 1975. Circ. 83,500. Byline given. Pays on acceptance. Publishes ms an average of 1 month after acceptance. Editorial lead time 3 months. Submit seasonal material 2 months in advance. Accepts queries by mail, e-mail, fax, phone. Sample copy available online.

NONFICTION Needs how-to, business management, new product, photo feature, best practices articles, innovative design. **Buys 12 mss/year.** Query with published clips. Length: 1,200-2,500 words. **Pays $300-600 for assigned articles. Pays $200-400 for unsolicited articles.**

PHOTOS Send photos. Reviews negatives, transparencies. Negotiates payment individually.

COLUMNS Query with published clips. **Pays $400**

💲💲💲💲 REMODELING

HanleyWood, LLC, One Thomas Circle NW, Suite 600, Washington D.C. 20005. (202)452-0800. Fax: (202)785-1974. E-mail: salfano@hanleywood.com; ibush@hanleywood.com. Website: remodelingmagazine.com. **Contact:** Sal Alfano, editorial director. **10% freelance written**. Monthly magazine covering residential and light commercial remodeling. "We cover the best new ideas in remodeling design, business, construction and products." Estab. 1985. Circ. 80,000. Byline given. Pays on publication. Offers 5¢/word kill fee. Publishes ms an average of 3 months after acceptance. Accepts queries by mail, e-mail, fax.

NONFICTION Needs interview, new product, technical, small business trends. **Buys 6 mss/year.** Query with published clips. Length: 250-1,000 words. **Pays $1/word.**

PHOTOS State availability. Captions, identification of subjects, model releases required. Reviews 4x5 transparencies, slides, 8×10 prints. Offers $25-125/photo.

⊖⊖ WALLS & CEILINGS

2401 W. Big Beaver Rd., Suite 700, Troy MI 48084. (313)894-7380. Fax: (248)362-5103. E-mail: wyattj@bnpmedia.com; mark@wwcca.org. Website: wconline.com. Mark Fowler, Editorial Director. **Contact:** John Wyatt, editor. **20% freelance written.** Monthly magazine for contractors involved in lathing and plastering, drywall, acoustics, fireproofing, curtain walls, and movable partitions, together with manufacturers, dealers, and architects. Estab. 1938. Circ. 30,000. Byline given. Pays on publication. Publishes ms an average of 6 months after acceptance. Submit seasonal material 4 months in advance. Accepts queries by mail, e-mail, phone. Accepts simultaneous submissions. Responds in 6 months to queries. Sample copy for 9×12 SAE with $2 postage. Guidelines for #10 SASE.

NONFICTION Needs how-to, drywall and plaster construction and business management, technical. **Buys 20 mss/year.** Query or send complete ms. Length: 1,000-1,500 words. **Pays $50-500.**

PHOTOS Send photos. Captions, identification of subjects required. Reviews contact sheets, negatives, transparencies, prints.

BUSINESS MANAGEMENT

⊖⊖⊖⊖⊖ BEDTIMES

International Sleep Products Association, 501 Wythe St., Alexandria VA 22314-1917. (703)683-8371. E-mail: info@sleepproducts.org; jpalm@sleepproducts.org. Website: sleepproducts.org. **Contact:** Julie Palm, editor. **20-40% freelance written.** Monthly magazine covering the mattress manufacturing industry. "Our news and features are straightforward—we are not a lobbying vehicle for our association. No special slant." Estab. 1917. Circ. 3,800. Byline given. Pays on acceptance. Publishes ms an average of 3 months after acceptance. Editorial lead time 2 months. Accepts queries by e-mail. Accepts simultaneous submissions. Responds in 1 month to queries. Sample copy for $4. Guidelines by e-mail.

NONFICTION No pieces that do not relate to business in general or mattress industry in particular. **Buys 15-25/year mss/year.** Query with published clips. Length: 500-2,500 words. **Pays 50-$1/word for short features; $2,000 for cover story.**

PHOTOS State availability. Identification of subjects required. Negotiates payment individually.

⊖⊖⊖⊖ BLACK MBA MAGAZINE

P&L Publishing Ltd., 9730 S. Western Ave., Suite 320, Evergreen Park IL 60805. (800)856-8092 (toll free); (850)668-7400 (direct). Fax: (708)422-1507. E-mail: elaine@naylor.com. Website: blackmbaonline.com. **Contact:** Elaine Richardson, Naylor LLC, Managing Editor. **80% freelance written.** Online magazine covering business career strategy, economic development, and financial management. Estab. 1997. Circ. 45,000. Byline given. Pays after publication. Offers 10-20% or $500 kill fee. Publishes ms an average of 1 month after acceptance. Editorial lead time 2-3 months. Submit seasonal material 3-4 months in advance. Accepts queries by mail, e-mail, fax.

PHOTOS State availability of or send photos. Identification of subjects required. Reviews ZIP disk. Offers no additional payment for photos accepted with ms.

COLUMNS Management Strategies (leadership development), 1,200-1,700 words; Features (business management, entrepreneurial finance); Finance; Technology. Send complete ms. **Pays $500-1,000.**

⊖⊖⊖ BUSINESS TRAVEL EXECUTIVE

11 Ryerson Ave., Suite 201, Pompton Plains NJ 07444. E-mail: jallison@askbte.com. Website: askbte.com. Editorial Office: 5768 Remington Dr., Winston-Salem, NC 27104, (336)766-1961. **Contact:** Gerald Allison, publisher. **90% freelance written.** Monthly magazine covering corporate procurement of travel services. "We are not a travel magazine. We publish articles designed to help corporate purchasers of travel negotiate contracts, enforce policy, select automated services, track business travelers and account for their safety and expenditures, understand changes in the various industries associated with travel. Do not submit manuscripts without an assignment. Look at the website for an idea of what we publish." Byline given. Pays on publication. Publishes ms an average of 2 months after acceptance. Editorial lead time 0-3 months. Accepts queries by e-mail.

Manuscripts and photographs are welcomed. Please send unsolicited submissions, at your own risk. Please enclose a SASE for return of material.

NONFICTION Needs how-to, technical. **Buys 48 mss/year.** Query. Length: 800-2,000 words. **Pays $200-800.**

COLUMNS Meeting Place (meeting planning and management); Hotel Pulse (hotel negotiations, contracting and compliance); Security Watch (travel safety), all 1,000 words. **Buys 24 mss/year.** Query. **Pays $200-400.**

💲💲 CONTRACTING PROFITS

Trade Press Publishing, 2100 W. Florist Ave., Milwaukee WI 53209. (414)228-7701 / (800)727-7995. Fax: (414)228-1134. E-mail: dan.weltin@tradepress.com. Website: cleanlink.com/cp. **Contact:** Dan Weltin, editor-in-chief. **40% freelance written**. Magazine published 10 times/year covering building service contracting, business management advice. We are the pocket MBA for this industry—focusing not only on cleaning-specific topics, but also discussing how to run businesses better and increase profits through a variety of management articles. Estab. 1995. Circ. 32,000. Byline given. Pays within 30 days of acceptance. Editorial lead time 2 months. Submit seasonal material 3 months in advance. Accepts queries by mail, e-mail. Responds in weeks to queries. Sample copy available online.

NONFICTION Needs expose, how-to, interview, technical. No product-related reviews or testimonials. **Buys 30 mss/year.** Query with published clips. Length: 1,000-1,500 words. **Pays $100-500.**

COLUMNS Query with published clips.

💲💲 CONTRACT MANAGEMENT

National Contract Management Association, 8260 Greensboro Dr., Suite 200, McLean VA 22102. (571)382-0082. Fax: (703)448-0939. E-mail: mckinnona@ncmahq.org. Website: ncmahq.org. **Contact:** Kerry McKinnon, managing editor. **10% freelance written**. Monthly magazine covering contract and business management. Most of the articles published in *Contract Management (CM)* are written by members, although one does not have to be an NCMA member to be published in the magazine. Articles should concern some aspect of the contract management profession, whether at the level of a beginner or that of the advanced practitioner. Estab. 1960. Circ. 23,000. Byline given. Pays on publication. Publishes ms an average of 3 months after acceptance. Editorial lead time

10 weeks. Submit seasonal material 3 months in advance. Accepts queries by mail, e-mail, fax, phone. Accepts simultaneous submissions. Responds in 2 weeks to queries. Responds in 1 month to mss. Sample copy and writer's guidelines free online.

NONFICTION Needs essays, general interest, how-to, humor, inspirational, new product, opinion, technical. No company or CEO profiles—please read a copy of publication before submitting. **Buys 6-10 mss/year.** Query with published clips. Send an inquiry including a brief summary (150 words) of the proposed article to the managing editor before you write the article. Length: 1,500-3,500 words. **Pays $300, association members paid in 3 copies.**

PHOTOS State availability. Captions, identification of subjects required. Offers no additional payment for photos accepted with ms.

COLUMNS Professional Development (self-improvement in business), 1,000-1,500 words; Back to Basics (basic how-tos and discussions), 1,500-2,000 words. **Buys 2 mss/year.** Query with published clips. **Pays $300**

💲💲 EXPANSION MANAGEMENT MAGAZINE

Penton Media, Inc., 1300 E. 9th St., Cleveland OH 44114. (877)530-8801. E-mail: gwood@penton.com. Website: eminfo.org; expansionmanagement.com. **Contact:** Gorton Wood, publisher. **50% freelance written**. Monthly magazine covering economic development. Estab. 1986. Circ. 45,000. Byline given. Pays on acceptance. Publishes ms an average of 1 month after acceptance. Editorial lead time 2 months. Sample copy for $7.

💭 "Part of Industry Week Magazine."

NONFICTION **Buys 120 mss/year.** Query with published clips. Length: 800-1,200 words. **Pays $200-400 for assigned articles.**

PHOTOS Send photos. Captions required. Offers no additional payment for photos accepted with ms.

💲💲💲 EXPO

Red7 Media, 10 Norden Pl., Norwalk CT 06855. (203)899-8438. E-mail: traphael@red7media.com; bmickey@red7media.com. E-mail: tsilber@red7media.com. Website: expoweb.com. **Contact:** Tony Silber, general manager. **80% freelance written**. Magazine covering expositions. Byline given. Pays on publication. Offers 50% kill fee. Editorial lead time 3 months.

Accepts queries by mail, e-mail, fax. Responds in 3 weeks to queries. Guidelines available online.

○"EXPO is published 10 times a year. It includes sales- and marketing-focused features about destinations, case studies and revenue-generating ideas, as well as coverage of new products and services for its audience—show organizers and their managers."

NONFICTION Needs how-to, interview. Query with published clips. Length: 600-2,400 words. **Pays 50¢/word.**

PHOTOS State availability.

COLUMNS Profile (personality profile), 650 words; Exhibitor Matters (exhibitor issues) and EXPOTech (technology), both 600-1,300 words. **Buys 10 mss/year.** Query with published clips.

⊜⊜⊜ FAMILY BUSINESS MAGAZINE

Family Business Publishing Co., Family Business Magazine, 1845 Walnut St., Philadelphia PA 19103. Fax: (215)405-6078. E-mail: bspector@familybusinessmagazine.com. Website: familybusinessmagazine.com. **Contact:** Barbara Spector, editor-in-chief. **50% freelance written.** Quarterly magazine covering family-owned companies. "Written expressly for family company owners and advisors. Focuses on business and human dynamic issues unique to family enterprises. Offers practical guidance and tried-and- solutions for business stakeholders." Estab. 1989. Circ. 6,000. Byline given. Pays on acceptance. Offers 30% kill fee. Publishes ms an average of 9-12 months after acceptance. Editorial lead time 4 months. Submit seasonal material 6 months in advance. Accepts queries by e-mail. Guidelines available online.

NONFICTION Needs how-to, family business related only, interview, personal experience. "No small business articles, articles that aren't specifically related to multi-generational family companies (no general business advice). No success stories—there must be an underlying family or business lesson. **No payment for articles written by family business advisors and other service providers."** **Buys 24 mss/year.** Query with published clips. E-mail queries preferred. Length: 1,500-2,000 words. **Pays $50-1,400 for articles written by freelance reporters.**

PHOTOS State availability. Captions, identification of subjects, model releases required. Offers $50-600 maximum/shoot.

⊜⊜ IN TENTS

Industrial Fabrics Association International, 1801 County Rd. B W, Roseville MN 55113-4061. (651)225-6970; (800)-225-4324. Fax: (651)225-6966; (651)0631-9334. E-mail: srniemi@ifai.com; intents@ifai.com; generalinfo@ifai.com. Website: ifai.com. **Contact:** Susan R. Niemi, Assoc. Publisher. **50% freelance written.** Bimonthly magazine covering tent-rental and special-event industries. Estab. 1994. Circ. 12,000. Byline given. Pays on acceptance. Publishes ms an average of 2 months after acceptance. Editorial lead time 3 months. Accepts queries by mail, e-mail, fax. Sample copy and writer's

NONFICTION Needs how-to, interview, new product, photo feature, technical. **Buys 12-18 mss/year.** Query. Length: 800-2,000 words. **Pays $300-500.**

PHOTOS State availability. Captions, identification of subjects, model releases required. Reviews contact sheets, negatives, prints, digital images. Negotiates payment individually.

⊜⊜ MAINEBIZ

Mainebiz Publications, Inc., 30 Milk St., 3rd Floor, Portland ME 04101. (207)761-8379. Fax: (207)761-0732. E-mail: ccoultas@mainebiz.biz. Website: mainebiz.biz. **Contact:** Carol Coultas, editor. **25% freelance written.** Biweekly tabloid covering business in Maine. *Mainebiz* is read by business decision makers across the state. They look to the publication for business news and analysis. Estab. 1994. Circ. 13,000. Byline given. Pays on publication. Offers 10% kill fee. Publishes ms an average of 1 month after acceptance. Editorial lead time 1 month. Submit seasonal material 2 months in advance. Accepts queries by mail, e-mail. Responds in 3 weeks to queries. Sample copy and guidelines online.

○"If you wish to contribute, please spend some time familiarizing yourself with *Mainebiz*. Tell us a little about yourself, your experience and background as a writer and qualifications for writing a particular story. If you have clips you can send us via e-mail, or Web addresses of pages that contain your work, please send us a representative sampling (no more than 3 or 4, please). Send the text of your query or submission in plain text in the body of your e-mail, rather than as an attached file, as we may not be able to read the format of your file. We do our best to respond to all inquiries, but be aware that we are sometimes inundated."

NONFICTION Needs essays, expose, interview, business trends. Special issues: See website for editorial calendar. **Buys 50+ mss/year.** Query with published clips. Length: 500-2,500 words. **Pays $50-250.**

PHOTOS State availability. Identification of subjects required. Reviews GIF/JPEG files. Negotiates payment individually.

$$ RETAIL INFO SYSTEMS NEWS

Edgell Communications, 4 Middlebury Blvd., Randolph NJ 07869. (973)607-1300. Fax: (973)607-1395. Website: risnews.com. **Contact:** Adam Blair, editor. **65% freelance written.** Monthly magazine covering retail technology. Estab. 1988. Circ. 22,000. Byline sometimes given. Pays on publication. Publishes ms an average of 2 months after acceptance. Editorial lead time 3 months. Submit seasonal material 3 months in advance. Accepts queries by mail. Sample copy available online.

> "Readers are functional managers/executives in all types of retail and consumer goods firms. They are making major improvements in company operations and in alliances with customers/suppliers."

NONFICTION Needs essays, expose, how-to, humor, interview, technical. **Buys 80 mss/year.** Query with published clips. Length: 700-1,900 words. **Pays $600-1,200 for assigned articles.**

PHOTOS State availability of or send photos. Identification of subjects required. Negotiates payment individually.

COLUMNS News/trends (analysis of current events), 150-300 words. **Buys 4 articles/year mss/year.** Query with published clips. **Pays $100-300.**

$$ RETAILERS + RESOURCES

CBA Service Corp., 9240 Explorer Dr., Suite 200, Colorado Springs CO 80920. Fax: (719)272-3510. E-mail: ksamuelson@cbaonline.org. Website: cbaonline.org. **30% freelance written.** Monthly magazine covering the Christian retail industry. "Writers must have knowledge of and direct experience in the Christian retail industry. Subject matter must specifically pertain to the Christian retail audience." Estab. 1968. Byline given. Pays on publication. Publishes ms an average of 3 months after acceptance. Editorial lead time 3 months. Submit seasonal material 6 months in advance. Accepts queries by e-mail. Responds in 2 months to queries. Sample copy for $9.50 or online.

NONFICTION **Buys 24 mss/year.** Query. Length: 750-1,500 words. **Pays 30¢/word.**

$$ RTOHQ: THE MAGAZINE

Association of Progressive Rental Organizations, 1504 Robin Hood Trail, Austin TX 78703. (800)204-2776. Fax: (512)794-0097. E-mail: nferguson@rtohq.org. Website: rtohq.org. **Contact:** Neil Ferguson, editor. **50% freelance written.** Bi-monthly magazine covering the rent-to-own industry. (formerly *Progressive Rental*) *RTOHQ: The Magazine* is the only publication representing the rent-to-own industry and members of APRO. The magazine covers timely news and features affecting the industry, association activities, and member profiles. Awarded best 4-color magazine by the American Society of Association Executives in 1999. Estab. 1980. Circ. 5,500. Byline given. Pays on acceptance. Offers 25% kill fee. Publishes ms an average of 2 months after acceptance. Editorial lead time 2 months. Submit seasonal material 4 months in advance. Accepts queries by mail, e-mail, fax, phone, online submission form. Accepts simultaneous submissions. Responds in 1 month to queries. Responds in 2 months to mss.

NONFICTION Needs expose, general interest, how-to, inspirational, interview, technical, industry features. **Buys 12 mss/year.** Query with published clips. Length: 1,200-2,500 words. **Pays $150-700.**

$$ SECURITY DEALER & INTEGRATOR

Cygnus Publishing, 445 Broad Hollow Rd., Melville NY 11747. (800)547-7377, ext 2730 or 2705. Fax: (631)845-2376. E-mail: deborah.omara@cygnusb2b.com; natalia.kosk@cygnusb2b.com. Website: securityinfowatch.com/magazine. **Contact:** Deborah O'Mara, editor-in-chief; 2730 or Natalia Kosk, assist. editor. **25% freelance written.** Circ. 25,000. Byline sometimes given. Pays 3 weeks after publication. Publishes ms an average of 3 months after acceptance. Accepts queries by e-mail. Accepts simultaneous submissions. Guidelines available online.

> "Security Dealer & Integrator magazine is a leading voice for security resellers and the related security service community, covering business intelligence and technology solutions that effectively mitigate a wide variety of security risks faced by commercial, industrial, government and residential resellers. Content includes vertical market and industry specific needs; new technologies and their impact on

the market; business issues including operations, business development, funding, mergers and acquisitions; and in-depth coverage of the market's vendors."

NONFICTION Needs how-to, interview, technical. No consumer pieces. Query by emai. Length: 1,000-3,000 words. **Pays $300 for assigned articles. Pays $100-200 for unsolicited articles.**

PHOTOS State availability. Captions, identification of subjects required. Reviews contact sheets, transparencies. Offers $25 additional payment for photos accepted with ms.

COLUMNS Closed Circuit TV, Access Control (both on application, installation, new products), 500-1,000 words. **Buys 25 mss/year.** Query by mail only. **Pays $100-150.**

⊖ ⊖ SMART BUSINESS

Smart Business Network, Inc., 835 Sharon Dr., Cleveland OH 44145. (440)250-7000. Fax: (440)250-7001. E-mail: tshryock@sbnonline.com. Website: sbnonline.com. **Contact:** Todd Shryock, managing editor. **5% freelance written.** Monthly business magazine with an audience made up of business owners and top decision makers. "*Smart Business* is one of the fastest growing national chains of regional management journals for corporate executives. Every issue delves into the minds of the most innovative executives in each of our regions to report on how market leaders got to the top and what strategies they use to stay there." Estab. 1989. Byline given. Pays on publication. Offers 50% kill fee. Publishes ms an average of 2 months after acceptance. Editorial lead time 3 months. Submit seasonal material 3 months in advance. Accepts queries by mail, e-mail. Responds in 2 weeks to queries. Responds in 1 month to mss. Sample copy available online. Guidelines by e-mail.

> Publishes local editions in Dallas, Houston, St. Louis, Northern California, San Diego, Orange County, Tampa Bay/St. Petersburg, Miami, Philadephia, Cincinnati, Detroit, Los Angeles, Broward/Palm Beach, Cleveland, Akron/Canton, Columbus, Pittsburgh, Atlanta, Chicago, and Indianapolis.

NONFICTION Needs how-to, interview. No breaking news or news features. **Buys 10-12 mss/year.** Query with published clips. Length: 1,150-2,000 words. **Pays $200-500.**

PHOTOS State availability. Identification of subjects required. Reviews negatives, prints. Offers no additional payment for photos accepted with ms.

⊖ ⊖ STAMATS MEETINGS MEDIA

550 Montgomery St., Suite 750, San Francisco CA 94111. Fax: (415)788-1358. E-mail: tyler.davidson@meetingsfocus.com. Website: meetingsmedia.com. **Contact:** Tyler Davidson, Chief Content Director. **75% freelance written.** Monthly tabloid covering meeting, event, and conference planning. Estab. 1986. Circ. *Meetings East* and *Meetings South* 22,000; *Meetings West* 26,000. Byline given. Pays 1 month after publication. Publishes ms an average of 1 month after acceptance. Editorial lead time 3 months. Submit seasonal material 3 months in advance. Accepts queries by mail, e-mail, fax. Responds in 3 weeks to queries. Sample copy for sae with 9â—Š13 envelope and 5 First-Class stamps.

> "Provides highly targeted audience marketing opportunities through online, live event and print media branded products. Consistent high quality audience qualification requirements and processes combined with award winning staff-written content have kept **Stamats Business Media** at the forefront of each industry market it serves for over 80 years."

> "*Meetings Focus* is the premier one-stop resource for meeting planning professionals who need information on destinations, meeting facilities, meeting room setup ideas, sustainable meetings and other components of successful meetings, conventions, conferences and events in the U.S., Mexico, Canada and the Caribbean."

NONFICTION Needs how-to, travel, as it pertains to meetings and conventions. No first-person fluff—this is a business magazine. **Buys 150 mss/year.** Query with published clips. Length: 1,200-2,000 words. **Pays $500 flat rate/package.**

PHOTOS State availability. Identification of subjects required. Offers no additional payment for photos accepted with ms.

⊖ SUPERVISION MAGAZINE

National Research Bureau, 320 Valley St., Burlington IA 52601. (319)752-5415. E-mail: articles@supervisionmagazine.com. Website: national-research-bureau.com. **Contact:** Todd Darnall. **80% freelance written.** Monthly magazine covering management and supervision. *SuperVision Magazine* explains complex issues in a clear and understandable format. Articles written by both experts and scholars provide practical and concise answers to issues facing today's supervisors and managers. Estab. 1939. Circ. 500. Byline given. Pays on acceptance. Publishes ms an average of 1 month after acceptance. Editorial lead time 1 month. Submit seasonal material 2 months in advance. Accepts queries by e-mail. Guidelines free and online.

NONFICTION Needs personal experience, "We can use articles dealing with motivation, leadership, human relations and communication.". Send complete ms. Length: 1,500-2,000 words. **Pays 4¢/word**

🟢🟢 SUSTAINABLE INDUSTRIES

Sustainable Industries Media, LLC, 230 California St., Suite 410, San Francisco CA 94111. (503)226-7798. Fax: (503)226-7917. E-mail: sarah@sustainableindustries.com. Website: sustainableindustries.com. **Contact:** Sarah Stroud, assoc. editor. **20% freelance written.** Bimonthly magazine covering environmental innovation in business. "We seek high quality, balanced reporting aimed at business readers. More compelling writing than is typical in standard trade journals." Estab. 2003. Circ. 2,500. Byline sometimes given. Pays on publication. Publishes ms an average of 1-3 months after acceptance. Editorial lead time 1-2 months. Accepts queries by mail, e-mail, fax. NoAccepts simultaneous submissions.

NONFICTION Needs general interest, how-to, interview, new product, opinion, news briefs. Special issues: Themes rotate on the following topics: Agriculture & Natural Resources; Green Building; Energy; Government; Manufacturing & Technology; Retail & Service; Transportation & Tourism—though all topics are covered in each issue. No prosaic essays or extra-long pieces. Query with published clips. Length: 500-1,500 words. **Pays $0-500.**

PHOTOS State availability. Reviews prints, GIF/JPEG files. Offers no additional payment for photos accepted with ms.

COLUMNS Guest columns accepted, but not compensated. Business trade columns on specific industries, 500-1,000 words. Query.

🟢 THE STATE JOURNAL

West V Media Management, LLC, 12 Kanawha Blvd. W., Suite 100, Charleston WV 25302. (304)344-1630; (304)720-6512. E-mail: dpage@statejournal.com.

Website: statejournal.com. **Contact:** Dan Page, editor. **30% freelance written.** We are a weekly journal dedicated to providing stories of interest to the business community in West Virginia. Estab. 1984. Circ. 10,000. Byline given. Pays on publication. Publishes ms an average of 3 weeks after acceptance. Submit seasonal material 4 months in advance. Accepts queries by mail, e-mail, fax. Sample copy and writer's guidelines for #10 SASE.

NONFICTION Needs general interest, interview, new product, (all business related). **Buys 400 mss/year.** Query. Length: 250-1,500 words. **Pays $50.**

PHOTOS State availability. Captions required. Reviews contact sheets. Offers $15/photo.

🟢🟢🟢 VENECONOMY/VENECONOMA

VenEconomia, Edificio Gran Sabana, Piso 1, Avendia Abraham Lincoln No. 174, Blvd. de Sabana Grande, Caracas Venezuela. (58)(212)761-8121. Fax: (58)(212)762-8160. E-mail: mercadeo@veneconomia.com. Website: veneconoma.com; veneconomy.com. **70% freelance written.** Monthly business magazine covering business, political and social issues in Venezuela. *VenEconomy*'s subscribers are mostly businesspeople, both Venezuelans and foreigners doing business in Venezuela. Some academics and diplomats also read our magazine. The magazine is published monthly both in English and Spanish—freelancers may query us in either language. Our slant is decidedly pro-business, but not dogmatically conservative. Development, human rights, political and environmental issues are covered from a business-friendly angle. Estab. 1983. Byline given. Pays on publication. Offers 50% kill fee. Publishes ms an average of 1 month after acceptance. Editorial lead time 1-2 months. Submit seasonal material 1 month in advance. Accepts queries by e-mail. NoAccepts simultaneous submissions. Responds in 2 weeks to queries. Responds in 4 months to mss. Sample copy by e-mail.

NONFICTION Contact: Francisco Toro, political editor. Needs essays, expose, interview, new product, opinion. No first-person stories or travel articles. **Buys 50 mss/year.** Query. Length: 1,100-3,200 words. **Pays 10-15¢/word for assigned articles.**

🟢🟢🟢 WORLD TRADE

20900 Farnsleigh Rd., Shaker Heights OH 44122. (424)634-2499; (216)991-4861. E-mail: hardings@worldtradewt100.com; laras@worldtradewt100.com. Website: worldtrademag.com. **Contact:** Lara Sowinski, Managing Editor; Sarah Harding, Publisher. **50% freelance written.** Monthly magazine covering international business. Estab. 1988. Circ. 75,000. Byline given. Pays on publication. Publishes ms an average of 1 month after acceptance. Editorial lead time 3 months. Accepts queries by mail, fax.

NONFICTION Needs interview, technical, market reports, finance, logistics. **Buys 40-50 mss/year.** Query with published clips. Length: 450-1,500 words. **Pays 50¢/word.**

PHOTOS State availability. Identification of subjects required. Reviews transparencies, prints. Negotiates payment individually.

COLUMNS International Business Services, 800 words; Shipping, Supply Chain Management, Logistics, 800 words; Software & Technology, 800 words; Economic Development (US, International), 800 words. **Buys 40-50 mss/year. Pays 50¢/word.**

CHURCH ADMINISTRATION AND MINISTRY

$ CHRISTIAN COMMUNICATOR

9118 W. Elmwood Dr., Ste.1G, Niles IL 60714-5820. (847)296-3964. Fax: (847)296-0754. E-mail: ljohnson@wordprocommunications.com. Website: acwriters.com. **Contact:** Lin Johnson, managing editor. **90% freelance written.** Monthly magazine covering Christian writing and speaking. Circ. 4,000. Byline given. Pays on publication. Publishes ms an average of 6-12 months after acceptance. Editorial lead time 3 months. Submit seasonal material 9 months in advance. Accepts queries by e-mail. Responds in 4-6 weeks to queries. Responds in 6-8 weeks to mss. Sample copy for SAE and 5 first-class stamps. Writer's guidelines for SASE or by e-mail. Also online.

NONFICTION Needs how-to, interview, book reviews. **Buys 90 mss/year.** Query or send complete ms only by e-mail. Length: 650-1,000 words. **Pays $10. $5 for reviews. ACW CD for anecdotes**

COLUMNS Speaking, 650-1,000 words. **Buys 11 mss/year.** Query. **Pays $10.**

POETRY Needs free verse, light verse, traditional. Buys 22 poems/year. Submit maximum 3 poems. Length: 4-20 lines. **Pays $5.**

FILLERS Needs anecdotes, short humor. **Buys 10-30 mss/year.** Length: 75-300 words. **Pays CD.**

THE CHRISTIAN LIBRARIAN

Association of Christian Librarians, P.O. Box 4, Cedarville OH 45314. E-mail: info@acl.org. Website: acl.org. **Contact:** Anne-Elizabeth Powell, editor-in-chief. **80% freelance written.** Magazine published 3 times/year covering Christian librarianship in higher education. *The Christian Librarian* is directed to Christian librarians in institutions of higher learning and publishes articles on Christian interpretation of librarianship, theory and practice of library science, bibliographic essays, reviews, and human-interest articles relating to books and libraries. Estab. 1956. Circ. 800. Byline given. Editorial lead time 3 months. Accepts queries by e-mail to Editor-in-Chief, apowell@pointloma.edu. Responds in 1 month to mss. Sample copy for $5. Guidelines may be found online at acl.org/index.cfm/the-christian-librarian/.

NONFICTION Needs how-to, librarianship, technical, bibliographic essays. No articles on faith outside the realm of librarianship or articles based on specific church denomination. Includes peer reviewed content. Do not send book reviews that haven't been requested by the Review Editor. Send complete ms. Deadlines are: Feb. 15, August 15 Length: 1,000-5,000 words.

$ THE CLERGY JOURNAL

Logos Productions, Inc., 6160 Carmen Ave. E., Inver Grove Heights MN 55076-4422. (800)328-0200. Fax: (888)852-5524. E-mail: editorial@logosstaff.com. Website: logosproductions.com. **Contact:** Rebecca Grothe, editor. **98% freelance written.** Magazine published 10 times/year covering articles for continuing education and practical help for Christian clergy who are currently serving congregations. "The focus of *The Clergy Journal* is personal and professional development for clergy. Each issue focuses on a current topic related to ministers and the church, and also includes preaching illustrations, sermons, and worship aids based on the Revised Common Lectionary. There is an insert in each issue on financial management topics. Most readers are from mainline Protestant traditions, especially Methodist, Presbyterian, Lutheran, and United Church of Christ." Estab. 1924. Circ. 6,000. Byline given. Pays on publication. Publishes ms an average of 9 months after acceptance. Editorial lead time 4 months. Submit seasonal material 9 months in advance. Accepts queries by e-mail. Responds in 2 weeks to queries. Responds in 2 months to mss. Guidelines by e-mail.

NONFICTION Needs religious. **Buys 90 mss/year.** Query or send complete ms. Length: 1,200-1,500 words. **Pays $125 for assigned articles.**

CREATOR MAGAZINE

P.O. Box 3538, Pismo Beach CA 93448. (707)837-9071. E-mail: creator@creatormagazine.com. Website: creatormagazine.com. **Contact:** Bob Burroughs, editor. **35% freelance written.** Bimonthly magazine. Most readers are church music directors and worship leaders. Content focuses on the spectrum of worship styles from praise and worship to traditional to liturgical. All denominations subscribe. Articles on worship, choir rehearsal, handbells, children's/youth choirs, technique, relationships, etc. Estab. 1978. Circ. 6,000. Byline given. Pays on publication. Publishes ms an average of 3 months after acceptance. Editorial lead time 3 months. Submit seasonal material 4 months in advance. Accepts queries by mail. Accepts simultaneous submissions.

Dedicated to "Balanced Music Ministry," Creator does not espouse denominational or other agendas. Issues are full of timely "how-to" articles, reviews of new publications, thought-provoking essays, and our famous Clip Art.

NONFICTION Needs essays, how-to, be a better church musician, choir director, rehearsal technician, etc., humor, short personal perspectives, inspirational, interview, call first, new product, call first, opinion, personal experience, photo feature, religious, technical, choral technique. Special issues: July/August is directed toward adult choir members, rather than directors. **Buys 20 mss/year.** Query or send complete ms. Length: 1,000-10,000 words. **Pays $30-75 for assigned articles. Pays $30-60 for unsolicited articles.**

PHOTOS State availability of or send photos. Captions required. Reviews negatives, 8×10 prints. Offers no additional payment for photos accepted with ms.

COLUMNS Hints & Humor (music ministry short ideas, cute anecdotes, ministry experience), 75-250 words; Inspiration (motivational ministry stories), 200-500 words; Children/Youth (articles about specific choirs), 1,000-5,000 words. **Buys 15 mss/year.** Query or send complete ms. **Pays $20-60.**

GROUP MAGAZINE

Group Publishing, Inc., P.O. Box 481, Loveland CO 80539-0481. (970)669-3836. E-mail: sfirestone@group.com. Website: groupmag.com. **Contact:** Scott Firestone. **50% freelance written.** Bimonthly magazine for Christian youth workers. "*Group* is the interdenominational magazine for leaders of Christian youth groups. *Group*'s purpose is to supply ideas, practical help, inspiration, and training for youth leaders." Estab. 1974. Circ. 55,000. Byline sometimes given. Pays on acceptance. Editorial lead time 4 months. Submit seasonal material 5 months in advance. Accepts queries by mail, e-mail, fax. Responds in 8-10 weeks to queries. Responds in 2 months to mss. Sample copy for $2, plus 10x12 SAE and 3 first-class stamps. Guidelines available online.

NONFICTION Needs inspirational, personal experience, religious. No fiction, prose, or poetry. **Buys 30 mss/year.** Query. Length: 200-2,000 words. **Pays $50-250.**

COLUMNS "Try This One" section needs short ideas (100-250 words) for youth group use. These include games, fund-raisers, crowdbreakers, Bible studies, helpful hints, outreach ideas, and discussion starters. "Hands-on Help" section needs mini-articles (100-350 words) that feature practical tips for youth leaders on working with students, adult leaders, and parents. **Pays $50.**

THE JOURNAL OF ADVENTIST EDUCATION

General Conference of SDA, 12501 Old Columbia Pike, Silver Spring MD 20904-6600. (301)680-5069. Fax: (301)622-9627. E-mail: rumbleb@gc.adventist.org; goffc@gc.adventist.org. Website: jae.education.org/authors. Chandra Goff. **Contact:** Beverly J. Robinson-Rumble, editor. Bimonthly (except skips issue in summer) professional journal covering teachers and administrators in Seventh Day Adventist school systems. Estab. 1939. Circ. 10,500. Byline given. Pays on publication. Publishes ms an average of 1 year after acceptance. Editorial lead time 1 year. Accepts queries by mail, e-mail, fax, phone. Responds in 6 weeks to queries. Responds in 4 months to mss. Sample copy for sae with 10x12 envelope and 5 First-Class stamps. Guidelines available online.

NONFICTION Needs book excerpts, essays, how-to, education-related, personal experience, photo feature, religious, education. "No brief first-person stories about Sunday Schools." Query. Articles submitted on disk or by E-mail as attached files are welcome. Store in MS Word or WordPerfect format. If you submit a CD, be sure to include a printed copy of the article with the CD. Articles should be 6-8 pages long, with a max of 10 pages, including references. Two-part articles will be considered. Length: 1,000-1,500 words. **Pays $25-300.**

PHOTOS No PowerPoint presentations or photos imbedded in Word documents. Include photo of author with submission. State availability of or send photos. Captions required. Model releases. Negotiates payment individually. Payment varies, but may run as high as $250-300 for a photo used as a cover.

$ KIDS' MINISTRY IDEAS

Review and Herald Publishing Association, 55 W. Oak Ridge Dr., Hagerstown MD 21740. (301)393-3178. Fax: (301)393-3209. E-mail: kidsmin@rhpa.org. Website: kidsministryideas.com. **Contact:** Editor. **95% freelance written.** A quarterly resource for children's leaders, those involved in Vacation Bible School and Story Hours, home school teachers, etc. *Kids' Ministry Ideas* provides affirmation, pertinent and informative articles, program ideas, resource suggestions, and answers to questions from a Seventh-day Adventist Christian perspective. Estab. 1991. Circ. 3,000. Byline given. Pays on acceptance. Publishes ms an average of 3 months after acceptance. Editorial lead time 3 months. Submit seasonal material 6 months to one year in advance. Accepts queries by mail, e-mail, fax. Responds in 3 weeks to queries. Responds in 3 months to mss. Sample copy and writer's

🔑 "Kids' Ministry Ideas is a resource that is practical. Material needs to provide specific, helpful how-to's for children's leaders. Articles on a wide range of subjects appear in KMI, but they generally have one thing in common—practical ideas and easy-to-understand instructions that people can implement in their area of ministry. Use of sidebars, boxes, and lists of information is encouraged, as this dilutes copy intensity and makes articles more readable."

NONFICTION Needs inspirational, new product, related to children's ministry, articles fitting the mission of *Kids' Ministry Ideas*. **Buys 40-60 mss/year.** Send complete ms. Length: 300-1,000 words. **Pays $20-100 for assigned articles. Pays $20-70 for unsolicited articles. Writers can expect payment within 5-6 weeks of acceptance. Upon publication, authors are sent one complimentary copy of the issue in which their material appears.**

PHOTOS State availability. Captions required.

COLUMNS Buys 20-30 mss/year. Query. **Pays $20-100.**

$ LAUSANNE WORLD PULSE

Evangelism and Missions Information Service, Institute of Strategic Evangelism/Wheaton College, Lausanne Comittee for World Evangelization, P.O. Box 794, Wheaton IL 60189. (630)752-7158, 7155. Fax: (630)752-7155. E-mail: submissions@lausanneworldpulse.com. Website: worldpulseonline.com. **60% freelance written.** Online newsletter covering mission news and trends. Estab. 1965. Circ. 3,000. Byline given. Pays on publication. Publishes ms an average of 2 months after acceptance. Editorial lead time 2 months. Accepts queries by e-mail. Sample copy and writer's Guidelines online.

💬 "We provide current information about evangelical Christian missions and churches around the world. Most articles are news-oriented, although we do publish some features and interviews."

NONFICTION Needs interview, photo feature, religious, technical. Does not want anything that does not cover the world of evangelical missions. **Buys 50-60 mss/year.** Query with published clips. Include short bio of 40 words or less and electronic photo, if possible, with article submission. Prefers e-mail. Length: 600-1,200 words. **Pays $25-100.**

PHOTOS Send photos. Reviews contact sheets. Pays $25 for use of all photos accompanying an article.

$$ LEADERSHIP JOURNAL

Christianity Today International, 465 Gundersen Dr., Carol Stream IL 60188. (630)260-6200. Fax: (630)260-0114. E-mail: ljeditor@leadershipjournal.net. Website: leadershipjournal.net. Skye Jethani, managing editor. **Contact:** Marshall Shelley, editor-in-chief. **75% freelance written. Works with a small number of new/unpublished writers each year.** Quarterly magazine. "Writers must have a knowledge of and sympathy for the unique expectations placed on pastors and local church leaders. Each article must support points by illustrating from real life experiences in local churches." Estab. 1980. Circ. 48,000. Byline given. Pays on acceptance. Offers 33% kill fee. Publishes ms an average of 6 months after acceptance. Editorial lead time 6 months. Submit seasonal material 6 months in advance. Accepts queries by mail, e-mail, fax. Responds in 2 weeks to queries. Responds in 2 months to mss. Sample copy for free or online.

NONFICTION Needs how-to, humor, interview, personal experience, sermon illustrations. No articles from writers who have never read our journal. No unsolicited ms. **Buys 60 mss/year.** Query with proposal. Send a brief query letter describing your idea and how you plan to develop it. Length: 300-3,000 words. **Pays $35-400.**

COLUMNS Contact: Skye Jethanis, managing editor. Toolkit (book/software reviews), 500 words. **Buys 8 mss/year. mss/year.** Query.

$ MOMENTUM

National Catholic Educational Association, 1005 No. Glebe Rd., Suite 525, Arlington VA 22312. (571)257-0010. Fax: (703)243-0025. E-mail: momentum@ncea.org. Website: ncea.org. **Contact:** Brian E. Gray, editor. **65% freelance written.** Quarterly educational journal covering educational issues in Catholic schools and parishes. "*Momentum* is a membership journal of the National Catholic Educational Association. The audience is educators and administrators in Catholic schools K-12, and parish programs." Estab. 1970. Circ. 20,000. Byline given. Pays on publication. Publishes ms an average of 3 months after acceptance. Accepts queries by e-mail. Sample copy for $5 SASE and 8 first-class stamps. Guidelines available online.

NONFICTION No articles unrelated to educational and catechesis issues. **Buys 40-60 mss/year.** Query and send complete ms. Length: 1,500 words. **Pays $75 maximum.**

PHOTOS State availability of photos. Captions, identification of subjects required. Reviews prints. Offers no additional payment for photos accepted with ms.

COLUMNS : From the Field (practical application in classroom); DRE Directions (parish catechesis), both 700 words. **Buys 10 columns. mss/year.** Query and send complete ms. **Pays $50.**

$$ THE PRIEST

Our Sunday Visitor, Inc., 200 Noll Plaza, Huntington IN 46750-4304. (800)348-2440. Fax: (260)359-9117. E-mail: tpriest@osv.com. Website: osv.com. **Contact:** Editorial Dept. **40% freelance written.** Monthly magazine. Byline given. Pays on acceptance. Editorial lead time 3 months. Submit seasonal material 4 months in advance. Accepts queries by mail, e-mail, fax, phone. Responds in 5 weeks to queries. Responds in 3 months to mss. Sample copy and writer's

💬 "We publish articles that will aid priests in their day-to-day parish ministry. Includes items on spirituality, counseling, administration, theology, personalities, the saints, etc."

NONFICTION Needs essays, historical, humor, inspirational, interview, opinion, personal experience, photo feature, religious. **Buys 96 mss/year.** Send complete ms. Length: 1,500 words. **Pays $200 minimum for assigned articles. Pays $50 minimum for unsolicited articles.**

PHOTOS Send photos. Captions, identification of subjects required. Reviews transparencies, prints. Negotiates payment individually.

COLUMNS Viewpoints (whatever applies to priests and the Church); 1,000 words or less; send complete manuscript

$ RTJ'S CREATIVE CATECHIST

Twenty-Third Publications, P.O. Box 6015, New London CT 06320. (800)321-0411, ext. 188. Fax: (860)437-6246. E-mail: rosanne.coffey@bayard-inc.com. Website: rtjscreativecatechist.com. **Contact:** Rosanne Coffey, editor. Monthly magazine for Catholic catechists and religion teachers. Estab. 1966. Circ. 30,000. Byline given. Pays on acceptance. Publishes ms an average of 3-20 months after acceptance. Editorial lead time 4 months. Submit seasonal material 6 months in advance. Accepts queries by mail, e-mail. Accepts simultaneous submissions. Responds in 1-2 weeks to queries. Responds in 1-2 months to mss. Sample copy for sae with 9×12 envelope and 3 First-Class stamps.

💬 "The mission of *RTJ's Creative Catechist* is to encourage and assist Catholic DREs and catechists in their vocation to proclaim the gospell message and lead others to the joy of following Jesus Christ, *RTJ* provides professional support, theological content, age appropriate methodology and teaching tools."

NONFICTION Needs how-to, inspirational, personal experience, religious, articles on celebrating church seasons, sacraments, on morality, on prayer, on saints. Special issues; Sacraments; Prayer; Advent/Christmas; Lent/Easter. All should be written by people who have experience in religious education, or a good background in Catholic faith. Does not want fiction, poems, plays, articles written for Catholic school teachers (i.e., math, English, etc.), or articles that are academic rather than catechetical in nature. **Buys 35-40 mss/year.** Send complete ms. Length: 600-1,300 words. **Pays $100-125 for assigned articles. Pays $75-125 for unsolicited articles.**

COLUMNS Catechist to Catechist (brief articles on crafts, games, etc., for religion lessons); Faith and Fun (full page religious word games, puzzles, mazes, etc., for children). **Buys 30 mss/year.** Send complete ms. **Pays $20-125.**

$$ TODAY'S CATHOLIC TEACHER

Peter Li Education Group, 2621 Dryden Rd., Suite 300, Dayton OH 45439. (937)293-1415; (800)523-4625 x1139. Fax: (937)293-1310. E-mail: mnoschang@peterli.com. E-mail: bshepard@peterli.com. Website: catholicteacher.com. **Contact:** Betsy Shepard, managing editor. **60% freelance written**. Magazine published 6 times/year during school year covering Catholic education for grades K-12. "We look for topics of interest and practical help to teachers in Catholic elementary schools in all curriculum areas including religion technology, discipline, motivation." Estab. 1972. Circ. 50,000. Byline given. Pays on publication. Publishes ms an average of 2 months after acceptance. Editorial lead time 3 months. Submit seasonal material 6 months in advance. Accepts queries by mail, e-mail, fax. Accepts simultaneous submissions. Responds in 1 month to queries. Responds in 3 months to mss. Sample copy for $3 or on website. Guidelines available online.

NONFICTION Needs essays, how-to, humor, interview, personal experience. No articles pertaining to public education. **Buys 15 mss/year.** Query or send complete ms. Query letters are encouraged. E-mail, write, call, or fax the editor for editorial calendar. Articles may be submitted as hard copy; submission by e-mail with accompanying hard copy is appreciated. Length: 1,500-3,000 words. **Pays $150-300.**

PHOTOS State availability. Captions, identification of subjects, model releases required. Reviews transparencies, prints. Offers $20-50/photo.

$$$ WORSHIP LEADER MAGAZINE

32234 Paseo Adelanto, Suite A, San Juan Capistrano CA 92675. (949)240-9339. Fax: (949)240-0038. E-mail: jeremy@wlmag.com. Website: worshipleader.com. **Contact:** Jeremy Armstrong, managing editor. **80% freelance written**. Bimonthly magazine covering all aspects of Christian worship. *Worship Leader Magazine* exists to challenge, serve, equip, and train those involved in leading the 21st century church in worship. The intended readership is the worship team (all those who plan and lead) of the local church. Estab. 1990. Circ. 40,000. Byline given. Pays on publication. Offers 50% kill fee. Editorial lead time 3 months. Submit seasonal material 6 months in advance. Responds in 6 weeks to queries. Responds in 3 months to mss. Sample copy for $5. Guidelines available online.

🔑 "Worship Leader magazine does not accept unsolicited articles for the print version of the magazine. However we do accept submissions for our Web properties. This is often the first step in creating a relationship with us and our readers, which could lead to more involvement as a writer.Web articles should be between 700 and 900 words and have beneficial qualities to a person who is involved in creating devotional arts or planning a service of worship. Web articles are published on a gratis basis. Please send finished articles to Jeremy Armstrong, jeremy@wlmag.com and potential articles to feedback@wlmag.com.

NONFICTION Needs general interest, how-to, related to purpose/audience, inspirational, interview, opinion. **Buys 15-30 mss/year.** Query with published clips. Length: 1,200-2,000 words. **Pays $200-800 for assigned articles. Pays $200-500 for unsolicited articles.**

PHOTOS State availability. Identification of subjects required. Negotiate payment individually.

$$ YOUR CHURCH

Christianity Today International, 465 Gundersen Dr., Carol Stream IL 60188. (630)260-6200. Fax: (630)260-0451. E-mail: yceditor@yourchurch.net. Website: yourchurch.net. **Contact:** Matt Branaugh, editor. **5-10.** Bimonthly e-mail newsletter covering church administration and products. Articles pertain to the business aspects of ministry pastors are called upon to perform: administration, purchasing, management, technology, building, etc. Estab. 1955. Circ. 75,000 (controlled). Byline given. Pays on acceptance. Publishes ms an average of 3-4 months after acceptance. Editorial lead time 6 weeks. Submit seasonal material 5 months in advance. Accepts queries by mail, e-mail, fax. Responds in 1 month to queries. Responds in 3 months to mss. Sample copy for sae with 9×12 envelope and 4 First-Class stamps.

NONFICTION Needs how-to, new product, technical. **Buys 50-60 mss/year.** Send complete ms. Length: 1,000-4,000 words. **Pays 15-20¢/word.**

YOUTH AND CHRISTIAN EDUCATION LEADERSHIP

Pathway Press, 1080 Montgomery Ave., Cleveland TN 37311. (800)553-8506. Fax: (800)546-7590. E-mail: tammy_hatfield@pathwaypress.org. E-mail: tammy_hatfield@pathwaypress.org. Website: pathwaypress.org. **Contact:** Jonathan Martin, editor. **25% freelance written.** Quarterly magazine covering Christian education. *Youth and Christian Education Leadership* is written for teachers, youth pastors, children's pastors, and other local Christian education workers. Estab. 1976. Circ. 12,000. Pays on publication. Publishes ms an average of 6 months after acceptance. Editorial lead time 3 months. Submit seasonal material 6 months in advance. Accepts queries by mail, e-mail. Accepts simultaneous submissions. Responds in 3 months to mss. Sample copy for $1.25 and 9×12 SASE. Writer's guidelines online or by e-mail.

NONFICTION Needs how-to, humor, in-class experience, inspire, interview, motivational, seasonal short skits. **Buys 16 mss/year.** Send complete ms; include SSN. Send SASE for return of ms. Internet submissions are accepted. They should be sent as attachments to e-mail and not as part of the e-mail message itself. Length: 500-1,000 words. **Pays $25-50.**

PHOTOS State availability. Reviews contact sheets, transparencies. Negotiates payment individually.

COLUMNS Sunday School Leadership; Reaching Out (creative evangelism); The Pastor and Christian Education; Preschool; Elementary; Teen; Adult; Drawing Closer; Kids Church, all 500-1,000 words. Send complete ms with SASE. **Pays $25-50.**

YOUTHWORKER JOURNAL

Salem Publishing, 402 BNA Dr., Suite 400, Nashville TN 37217-2509. E-mail: articles@youthworker.com. Website: youthworker.com. **Contact:** Steve Rabey, editor. **100% freelance written.** Website and bimonthly magazine covering professional youth ministry in the church and parachurch. "We exist to help meet the personal and professional needs of career, Christian youth workers in the church and parachurch. Proposals accepted on the posted theme, according to the writer's guidelines on our website. It's not enough to write well—you must know youth ministry." Estab. 1984. Circ. 20,000. Byline given. Pays on publication. Publishes ms an average of 3 months after acceptance for print; immediately online. Editorial lead time 6 months for print; immediately online. Submit seasonal material 6 months in advance for print. Accepts queries by e-mail, online submission form. Responds within 6 weeks to queries. Sample copy for $5. Guidelines available online.

NONFICTION Needs essays, new product, youth ministry books only, personal experience, photo feature, religious. Query. Length: 250-3,000 words. **Pays $15-200.**

PHOTOS Send photos. Reviews GIF/JPEG files. Negotiates payment individually.

CLOTHING

FOOTWEAR PLUS

9 Threads, 36 Cooper Square, 4th Fl., New York NY 10003. (646)278-1550. Fax: (646)278-1553. E-mail: editorialrequests@9threads.com. Website: footwearplusmagazine.com. **20% freelance written.** Monthly magazine covering footwear fashion and business. "A business-to-business publication targeted at footwear retailers. Covering all categories of footwear and age ranges with a focus on new trends, brands and consumer buying habits, as well as retailer advice on operating the store more effectively." Estab. 1990. Circ. 18,000. Byline given. Pays on publication. Publishes ms an average of 1-2 months after acceptance. Editorial lead time 1-2 months. Accepts queries by e-mail. Sample copy for $5.

NONFICTION Needs interview, new product, technical. Does not want pieces unrelated to footwear/fashion industry. **Buys 10-20 mss/year.** Query. Length: 500-2,500 words. **Pays $1,000 maximum.**

MADE TO MEASURE

The Uniform Magazine, Halper Publishing Co., 633 Skokie Blvd. #490, Northbrook IL 60062. Fax: (847)780-2902. E-mail: mtm@halper.com; frontdesk@theuniformmagazine.com. Website: madetomeasuremag.com. **50% freelance written.** Semiannual magazine covering uniforms and career apparel. A semi-annual magazine/buyers' reference containing leading sources of supply, equipment, and services of every description related to the Uniform, Career Apparel, and allied trades, throughout the entire US. Estab. 1930. Circ. 25,000. Byline given. Pays on acceptance. Publishes ms an average of 2 months after acceptance. Editorial lead time 4 months. Submit seasonal material 4 months in advance. Accepts queries by mail, e-mail. Accepts simultaneous submissions.

Responds in 3 weeks to queries. Sample copy available online.

NONFICTION Needs interview, new product, personal experience, photo feature, technical. **Buys 6-8 mss/year.** Query with published clips. Length: 1,000-3,000 words. **Pays $300-500.**

❾❸❸ TEXTILE WORLD

Billian Publishing Co., 2100 RiverEdge Pkwy., Suite 1200, Atlanta GA 30328. (770)955-5656. Fax: (770)952-0669. E-mail: editor@textileworld.com. Website: textileworld.com. **Contact:** James Borneman, editor-in-chief. **5% freelance written.** Bimonthly magazine covering the business of textile, apparel, and fiber industries with considerable technical focus on products and processes. No puff pieces pushing a particular product. Estab. 1868. Byline given. Pays on publication.

NONFICTION Needs technical, business. **Buys 10 mss/year.** Query. Length: 500 words minimum. **Pays $200/published page.**

CONSTRUCTION AND CONTRACTING

❸❸ AUTOMATED BUILDER

CMN Associates, Inc., 1445 Donlon St., Suite 16, Ventura CA 93003. (805)642-9735; (800)344-2537. Fax: (805)642-8820. E-mail: info@automatedbuilder.com. Website: automatedbuilder.com. **Contact:** Don O. Carlson, editor/publisher. **10% freelance written.** Monthly online magazine specializing in management for industrialized (manufactured) housing and volume home builders. "*Automated Builder* provides management, production and marketing information on all seven segments of home, apartment and commercial construction, including: (1) Production Builders, (2) Panelized Home Manufacturers, (3) HUD-Code (mobile) Home Manufacturers, (4) Modular Home Manufacturers, (5) Component Manufacturers, (6) Special Unit (commercial) Manufacturers, and (7) MH Builders and Builders/Dealers. "The material is technical in content and concerned with new technologies or improved methods for in-plant building and components related to building. Online content is uploaded from the monthly print material." Estab. 1964. Circ. 25,000. Byline given. Pays on acceptance. Publishes ms an average of 3 months after acceptance. Editorial lead time 2 months. Submit seasonal material 2 months in advance. Accepts queries by mail, e-mail, fax. Responds in 2 weeks to queries.

NONFICTION "No architect or plan `dreams.' Housing projects must be built or under construction." **Buys 6-8 mss/year.** Query. Length: 250-500 words. **Pays $350 for stories including photos.**

PHOTOS Monthly. Emphasizes home and apartment construction. Readers are "factory and site builders and dealers of all types of homes, apartments and commercial buildings." Sample copy free with SASE. Buys 4-8 photos from freelancers/issue; 48-96 photos/year. State availability. Captions, identification of subjects required. Offers no additional payment for photos accepted with ms. Pays $350 for text/photo package; $150 for cover. Credit line given "if desired." Buys first time reproduction rights.

❸❸ BUILDERNEWS MAGAZINE

Pacific NW Publishing, BUILDERnews Magazine, 2105 C St., Vancouver WA 98663. (360)906-0793; (800)401-0696. Fax: (360)906-0794. E-mail: editing@bnmag.com. Website: bnmag.com. Estab. 1996. Circ. 35,000. Byline given. Pays on acceptance of revised ms. Publishes ms an average of 1 month after acceptance. Editorial lead time 2 months. Submit seasonal material 3 months in advance. Accepts queries by mail, e-mail, fax. Responds in 1 week to queries. Responds in 1 month to mss. Sample copy for free or online.

NONFICTION Needs how-to, interview, new product, technical. No personal bios unless they teach a valuable lesson to those in the building industry. **Buys 400 mss/year.** Query. Length: 500-2,500 words. **Pays $200-500.**

PHOTOS State availability. Captions, identification of subjects, model releases required. Offers no additional payment for photos accepted with ms.

COLUMNS Engineering; Construction; Architecture & Design; Tools & Materials; Heavy Equipment; Business & Economics; Legal Matters; E-build; Building Green, all 750-2,500 words. Query.

❸❸❸ THE CONCRETE PRODUCER

Hanley-Wood, LLC, 8725 W. Higgins Rd., Suite 600, Chicago IL 60631. (773)824-2400; (773)824-2496. E-mail: ryelton@hanleywood.com; smitchell@hanleywood.com. Website: theconcreteproducer.com. **Contact:** Shelby O. Mitchell, managing editor. **25% freelance written.** Monthly magazine covering concrete production. Our audience consists of producers who have succeeded in making concrete the preferred building material through management, operating, quality control, use of the latest technology, or use of superior materials. Estab. 1982. Circ. 18,000. Byline given. Pays on acceptance. Publishes ms an average of 2 months after acceptance. Editorial lead time 4 months. Accepts queries by mail, e-mail, fax, phone. Responds in 1 week to queries. Responds in 2 months to mss. Sample copy for $4.

NONFICTION Needs how-to, promote concrete, new product, technical. **Buys 10 mss/year.** Send complete ms. Length: 500-2,000 words. **Pays $200-1,000.**

PHOTOS Scan photos at 300 dpi. State availability. Captions, identification of subjects required. Reviews transparencies, prints. Offers no additional payment for photos accepted with ms.

$$ FRAME BUILDING NEWS

A Division of F+W Media, Inc., 700 E. State St., Iola WI 54990-0001. (715)445-4612, ext. 428. Fax: (715)445-4087. E-mail: jim.austin@fw.media.com. Website: framebuildingnews.com. **10% freelance written.** Magazine published 5 times/year covering post-frame building. "*Frame Building News* is the official publication of the National Frame Builders Association, which represents contractors who specialize in post-frame building construction." Estab. 1990. Circ. 20,000. Byline given. Pays on publication. Publishes ms an average of 3 months after acceptance. Editorial lead time 3 months. Submit seasonal material 3 months in advance. Accepts queries by mail. NoAccepts simultaneous submissions.

NONFICTION Needs book excerpts, historical, how-to, interview, new product, opinion, photo feature, technical. No advertorials. **Buys 15 mss/year.** Query with published clips. 750 words minimum. **Pays $100-500 for assigned articles.**

PHOTOS Send photos. Captions, identification of subjects required. Reviews GIF/JPEG files. Negotiates payment individually.

COLUMNS Money Talk (taxes for business); Tech Talk (computers for builders); Tool Talk (tools); Management Insights (business management), all 1,000 words. **Buys 15 mss/year.** Send complete ms. **Pays $0-500.**

$ HARD HAT NEWS

Lee Publications, Inc., 6113 State Highway 5, Palatine Bridge NY 13428. (518)673-3237. Fax: (518)673-2381. E-mail: joncasey88@gmail.com. Website: hardhat.com. **Contact:** Jon Casey, editor. **50% freelance written**. Biweekly tabloid covering heavy construction, equipment, road, and bridge work. "Our readers are contractors and heavy construction workers involved in excavation, highways, bridges, utility construction, and underground construction." Estab. 1980. Circ. 15,000. Byline given. Editorial lead time 2 weeks. Submit seasonal material 2 weeks in advance. Accepts queries by mail, e-mail, fax, phone. Sample copy and writer's

NONFICTION Needs interview, new product, opinion, photo feature, technical. Send complete ms. Length: 800-2,000 words. **Pays $2.50/inch.**

PHOTOS Send photos. Captions, identification of subjects required. Reviews prints, digital preferred. Offers $15/photo.

COLUMNS Association News; Parts and Repairs; Attachments; Trucks and Trailers; People on the Move.

$$ HOME ENERGY MAGAZINE

Home Energy Magazine, 1250 Addison St., 211B, Berkeley CA 94702. (510)524-5405. Fax: (510)981-1406. E-mail: contact@homeenergy.org. Website: homeenergy.org. Alan Meier, publisher. **Contact:** Jim Gunshinan, managing editor. **10% freelance written**. Bimonthly magazine covering green home building and renovation. Estab. 1984. Circ. 5,000. Byline given. Pays on publication. Offers 10% kill fee. Publishes ms an average of 4 months after acceptance. Editorial lead time 4 months. Accepts queries by e-mail. Responds in 2 weeks to queries. Responds in 2 months to mss. Guidelines by e-mail.

○ "Our readers are building contractors, energy auditors, and weatherization professionals. They expect technical detail, accuracy, and brevity."

NONFICTION Needs interview, technical. We do not want articles for consumers/general public. **Buys 6 mss/year. mss/year.** Query with published clips. Length: 900-3,500 words. **Pays 20¢/word; $400 max. for assigned articles. Pays 20¢/word; $400 max. for unsolicited articles.**

$$$ INTERIOR CONSTRUCTION

Ceilings & Interior Systems Construction Association, 405 Illinois Ave., Unit 2B, St. Charles IL 60174. (630)584-1919. Fax: (630)584-2003. E-mail: mgi@comcast.net; cisca@cisca.org. Website: cisca.org. **Contact:** Rick Reuland, publisher. **1-2 features per issue**. Quarterly magazine Acoustics and commercial specialty ceiling construction. Estab. 1950. Circ. 3,000. Byline given. Pays on publication. Publishes ms an average of 1 ½ months after acceptance. Editorial lead time 2-3 months. Accepts queries by e-mail. Sample copy by e-mail. Guidelines available.

NONFICTION Needs new product, technical. Query with published clips. Length: 700-1,700 words. **Pays $400 min., $800 max. for assigned articles.**

$$ KEYSTONE BUILDER MAGAZINE

Pennsylvania Builders Association, 600 N. 12th St., Lemoyne PA 17043. (717)730-4380; 800-692-7339. Fax: (717)730-4396. E-mail: admin@pabuilders.org. Website: pabuilders.org. **10% freelance written.** "Bimonthly trade publication for builders, remodelers, subcontractors, and other affiliates of the home building industry in Pennsylvania." Estab. 1988. Circ. 9,300. Byline given. Pays on publication. Publishes ms an average of 1 year after acceptance. Editorial lead time 3 months. Submit seasonal material 9 months in advance. Accepts queries by mail, e-mail. Accepts simultaneous submissions. Responds in 2 weeks to queries. Responds in 3 months to mss. Guidelines by e-mail.

NONFICTION Needs general interest, how-to, new product, technical. No personnel or company profiles. **Buys 1-2 mss/year.** Send complete ms. Length: 200-500 words. **Pays $200.**

PHOTOS Send photos. Captions, identification of subjects required. Reviews digital images. Negotiates payment individually.

$$ METAL ROOFING MAGAZINE

a Division of F+W Media, Inc., 700 E. Iola St., Iola WI 54990-0001. (715)445-4612, ext. 13281. Fax: (715)445-4087. E-mail: jim.austin@fwmedia.com. Website: metalroofingmag.com. **Contact:** Jim Austin. **10% freelance written.** Bimonthly magazine covering roofing. *Metal Roofing Magazine* offers contractors, designers, suppliers, architects and others in the construction industry a wealth of information on metal roofing—a growing segment of the roofing trade. Estab. 2000. Circ. 26,000. Byline given. Pays on publication. Publishes ms an average of 3 months after acceptance. Editorial lead time 3 months. Submit seasonal material 3 months in advance. Accepts queries by mail. NoAccepts simultaneous submissions.

NONFICTION Needs book excerpts, historical, how-to, interview, new product, opinion, photo feature, technical. No advertorials. **Buys 15 mss/year.** Query with published clips. 750 words minimum. **Pays $100-500 for assigned articles.**

PHOTOS Send photos. Captions, identification of subjects required. Reviews GIF/JPEG files. Negotiates payment individually.

COLUMNS Gutter Opportunities; Stay Cool; Metal Roofing Details; Spec It. **Buys 15 mss/year.** Send complete ms. **Pays $0-500.**

$$ NETCOMPOSITES ENEWS

Composites Worldwide, Inc., 991-C Lomas Santa Fe Dr., MC469, Solana Beach CA 92075-2125. (858)755-1372. E-mail: gordon.bishop@netcomposites.com; info@netcomposites.com. Website: netcomposites.com. **Contact:** Gordon Bishop (UK). **1% freelance written.** Bimonthly newsletter covering advanced materials and fiber-reinforced polymer composites, plus a weekly electronic version called *Composite eNews*, reaching over 15,000 subscribers and many more pass-along readers. *Advanced Materials & Composites News* covers markets, applications, materials, processes, and organizations for all sectors of the global hi-tech materials world. Audience is management, academics, researchers, government, suppliers, and fabricators. Focus on news about growth opportunities. Estab. 1978. Circ. 15,000+. Byline sometimes given. Pays on publication. Publishes ms an average of 1 month after acceptance. Editorial lead time 2 weeks. Submit seasonal material 1 month in advance. Accepts queries by e-mail. Responds in 1 week to queries. Responds in 1 month to mss. Sample copy for #10 SASE.

NONFICTION Needs new product, technical, industry information. **Buys 4-6 mss/year.** Query. 300 words. **Pays $200/final printed page.**

PHOTOS State availability. Captions, identification of subjects, model releases required. Reviews 4x5 transparencies, prints, 35mm slides, JPEGs (much preferred). Offers no additional payment for photos accepted with ms.

$$ POB MAGAZINE

BNP Media, 2401 W. Big Beaver Rd., Suite 700, Troy MI 48084. (248)362-3700. E-mail: pobeditor@bnpmedia.com. Website: pobonline.com. **Contact:** Christine Grahl. **5% freelance written.** Monthly magazine covering surveying, mapping and geomatics. Estab. 1975. Circ. 39,000. Byline given. Pays on publication. Publishes ms an average of 3 months after acceptance. Editorial lead time 3 months. Accepts queries by e-mail, phone. Sample copy and guidelines online.

NONFICTION Query. Please ensure the document is saved in MS-Word or text-only format. Please also include an author byline and biography. Length: 1,700-2,200 words with 2 graphics included. **Pays $400.**

PHOTOS State availability. Captions, identification of subjects required. Reviews GIF/JPEG files. Offers no additional payment for photos accepted with ms.

PRECAST INC./MC MAGAZINE

National Precast Concrete Association, 1320 City Center Dr., Carmel IN 46032. (317)571-9500. Fax: (317)571-0041. E-mail: rhyink@precast.org. Website: precast.org. **Contact:** Ron Hyink, managing editor. **75% freelance written.** Bimonthly magazine covering manufactured concrete products. Estab. 1995. Circ. 8,500. Byline given. Pays on acceptance. Publishes ms an average of 6 months after acceptance. Editorial lead time 3 months. Accepts queries by mail, e-mail, fax. Accepts simultaneous submissions. Responds in 1 month to queries. Responds in 2 months to mss. Sample copy and guidelines online.

NONFICTION Needs how-to, business, interview, technical, concrete manufacturing. No humor, essays, fiction, or fillers. **Buys 8-14 mss/year.** Query or send complete ms. Length: 1,500-2,500 words. **Pays $250-750.**

PHOTOS State availability. Captions required. Offers no additional payment for photos accepted with ms.

RURAL BUILDER

a Division of F+W Media, Inc., 700 E. State St., Iola WI 54990-0001. (715)445-4612, ext. 13644. Fax: (715)445-4087. E-mail: sharon.thatcher@fwmedia.com. Website: ruralbuilder.com. **10% freelance written.** Magazine published 7 times/year covering rural building. "*Builder* serves diversified town and country builders, offering them help managing their businesses through editorial and advertising material about metal, wood, post-frame, and masonry construction." Estab. 1967. Circ. 30,000. Byline given. Pays on publication. Publishes ms an average of 3 months after acceptance. Editorial lead time 3 months. Submit seasonal material 3 months in advance. Accepts queries by mail. NoAccepts simultaneous submissions.

NONFICTION Needs book excerpts, historical, how-to, interview, new product, opinion, photo feature, technical. No advertorials. **Buys 15 mss/year.** Que-

ry with published clips. 750 words minimum. **Pays $100-500.**

PHOTOS Send photos. Captions, identification of subjects required. Reviews GIF/JPEG files. Negotiates payment individually.

COLUMNS Money Talk (taxes for business); Tech Talk (computers for builders); Tool Talk (tools); Management Insights (business management); all 1,000 words. **Buys 15 mss/year.** Send complete ms. **Pays $0-500.**

UNDERGROUND CONSTRUCTION

Oildom Publishing Co. of Texas, Inc., P.O. Box 941669, Houston TX 77094-8669. (281)558-6930, ext. 220. Fax: (281)558-7029. E-mail: rcarpenter@oildom.com; oklinger@oildom.com. Website: oildompublishing.com. Oliver Klinger, publisher. **Contact:** Robert Carpenter, editor. **35% freelance written.** Monthly magazine covering underground oil and gas pipeline, water and sewer pipeline, cable construction for contractors and owning companies. Circ. 38,000. Publishes ms an average of 6 months after acceptance. Accepts queries by mail, e-mail, fax, phone. Responds in 1 month to mss. Sample copy for sae.

NONFICTION Needs how-to, job stories and industry issues. Query with published clips. Length: 1,000-2,000 words. **Pays $3-500.**

PHOTOS Send photos. Captions required. Reviews color prints and slides.

DRUGS, HEALTH CARE AND MEDICAL PRODUCTS

ACP INTERNIST/ACP HOSPITALIST

American College of Physicians, 191 N. Independence Mall W., Philadelphia PA 19106. (215)351-2400. E-mail: acpinternist@acponline.org; acphospitalist@acponline.org. Website: acpinternist.org; acphospitalist.org. Darren Taichman, editor. **Contact:** Janet Colwell, editor; Jessica Berthold, editor of ACP Hospitalist. **40% freelance written.** Monthly magazine covering Internal Medicine/Hospital Medicine. "We write for specialists in internal medicine, not a consumer audience. Topics include clinical medicine, practice management, health information technology, Medicare issues." Estab. 1981. Circ. 85,000 (Internist), 24,000 (Hospitalist). Byline given. Offers kill fee. Negotiable Publishes ms an average of 2 months after acceptance. Editorial lead time 4 months. Submit seasonal material 6 months in advance. Accepts queries by e-mail. Sample copy available online.

NONFICTION Needs interview. Query with published clips. Length: 700-2,000 words. **Pays $500-2,000 for assigned articles.**

PHOTOS Contact: Ryan Dubosar, senior editor. State availability. Reviews TIFF/JPEG files. Negotiates payment individually.

$$ LABTALK

LabTalk, P.O. Box 1945, Big Bear Lake CA 92315. (909)866-5590. Fax: (909)866-5577. E-mail: cwalker@framesdata.com. Website: framesdata.com. **20% freelance written.** Magazine published 6 times/year for the eye wear industry. Estab. 1970. Accepts simultaneous submissions.

$$$ VALIDATION TIMES

Washington Information Source Co., 19-B Wirt St. SW, Leesburg VA 20175. (703)779-8777. Fax: (703)779-2508. E-mail: kreid@fdainfo.com. Website: fdainfo.com. **Contact:** Ken Reid. Monthly newsletters covering regulation of pharmaceutical and medical devices. "We write to executives who have to keep up on changing FDA policies and regulations, and on what their competitors are doing at the agency." Estab. 1999. Byline given. Pays on publication. Publishes ms an average of 1 month after acceptance. Editorial lead time 1 month. Submit seasonal material 1 month in advance. Accepts queries by mail. Responds in 1 month to queries. Sample copy and writer's

NONFICTION Needs how-to, technical, regulatory. No lay interest pieces. **Buys 50-100 mss/year.** Query. Length: 600-1,500 words. **Pays $100/half day; $200 full day to cover meetings, same rate for writing.**

EDUCATION AND COUNSELING

$ ARTS & ACTIVITIES

Publishers' Development Corp., Dept. WM, 12345 World Trade Dr., San Diego CA 92128. (858)605-0242. Fax: (858)605-0247. E-mail: ed@artsandactivities.com. Website: artsandactivities.com. **Contact:** Maryellen Bridge, editor-in-chief. **95% freelance written. Eager to work with new/unpublished writers.** Monthly (except July and August) magazine covering art education at levels from preschool through college for educators and therapists engaged in arts and crafts education and training. Estab. 1932. Circ. 20,000. Byline given. Pays on publication. Publishes ms 6 months to 3 years after acceptance. Submit seasonal material 6 months in advance. Accepts queries by mail, e-mail. Responds in 3 months to queries. Sample copy for sae with 9×12 envelope and 8 First-Class stamps. Guidelines available online.

NONFICTION Needs historical, arts, activities, history, how-to, classroom art experiences, artists' techniques, interview, of artists, opinion, on arts activities curriculum, ideas of how-to do things better, philosophy of art education, personal experience, this ties in with the how-to, articles of exceptional art programs; make it personal, not recipe style. **Buys 80-100 mss/year.** Length:500-1500 words. **Pays $35-150.**

✪$ THE ATA MAGAZINE

11010 142nd St. NW, Edmonton AB T5N 2R1 Canada. (780)447-9400. Fax: (780)455-6481. E-mail: government@teachers.ab.ca. Website: teachers.ab.ca. **Contact:** The Editor. Quarterly magazine covering education. Estab. 1920. Circ. 42,100. Byline given. Pays on publication. Publishes ms an average of 4 months after acceptance. Editorial lead time 2 months. Submit seasonal material 2 months in advance. Accepts queries by mail, e-mail, fax, phone. Accepts simultaneous submissions. Responds in 2 months to queries. Guidelines available online.

NONFICTION Query with published clips. Length: 500-1,500 words. **Pays $75 (Canadian).**

PHOTOS Send photos. Captions required. Reviews 4×6 prints. Negotiates payment individually.

$ THE FORENSIC TEACHER

Wide Open Minds Educational Services, P.O. Box 5263, Wilmington DE 19808. E-mail: admin@theforensicteacher.com. Website: theforensicteacher.com. **Contact:** Mark R. Feil, Ed.D, editor. **70% freelance written.** Quarterly magazine covering forensic education. "Our readers are middle, high and post-secondary teachers who are looking for better, easier and more engaging ways to teach forensics as well as law enforcement and scientific forensic experts. Our writers understand this and are writing from a forensic or educational background, or both. Prefer a first person writing style." Estab. 2006. Circ. 30,000. Byline given. Pays 60 days after publication. Publishes ms an average of 6 months after acceptance. Editorial lead time 6 months. Submit seasonal material 6 months in advance. Accepts queries by mail, e-mail. Accepts simultaneous submissions. Responds in 2 weeks to queries. Responds in 2 months to mss. Sample copy for $5. Guidelines available online.

NONFICTION Needs how-to, personal experience, photo feature, technical, lesson plans. Does not want poetry, fiction or anything unrelated to medicine, law, forensics or teaching. **Buys 18 mss/year.** Send complete ms. Length: 400-2,000 words. **Pays 2¢/word.**

PHOTOS State availability. Captions required. Reviews GIF/JPEG files/pdf. Send photos separately in e-mail, not in the article. Negotiates payment individually.

COLUMNS Needs lesson experiences or ideas, personal or professional experiences with a branch of forensics. "If you've done it in your classroom please share it with us. Also, if you're a professional, please tell our readers how they can duplicate the lesson/demo/experiment in their classrooms. Please share what you know."

FILLERS Needs : facts, newsbreaks. **Buys 15 fillers/year. mss./year.** Length: 50-200 words. **Pays 2¢/word.**

⊖⊖ THE HISPANIC OUTLOOK IN HIGHER EDUCATION

80 Route 4 E., Suite 203, Paramus NJ 07652. (800)549-8280. Fax: (201)587-9105. E-mail: sloutlook@aol.com. Website: hispanicoutlook.com. **50% freelance written.** Biweekly magazine, except in summer. "We're looking for higher education story articles, with a focus on Hispanics and the advancements made by and for Hispanics in higher education." Circ. 28,000. Byline given. Pays on publication. Publishes ms an average of 2 months after acceptance. Editorial lead time 2 months. Submit seasonal material 3 months in advance. Accepts queries by mail, e-mail, fax. Accepts simultaneous submissions.

NONFICTION Needs historical, interview, of academic or scholar, opinion, on higher education, personal experience, all regarding higher education only. **Buys 20-25 mss/year.** Query with published clips. Length: 1,800-2,200 words. **Pays $400 minimum for print articles, and $300 for online articles when accepted.**

PHOTOS Send photos. Reviews color or b&w prints, digital images must be 300 dpi (call for e-mail photo address). Offers no additional payment for photos accepted with ms.

⊖⊖ PTO TODAY

PTO Today, Inc., 100 Stonewall Blvd., Suite 3, Wrentham MA 02093. (800)644-3561. Fax: (508)384-6108.

E-mail: editor@ptotoday.com. Website: ptotoday.com. **Contact:** Craig Bystrynski, editor-in-chief. **50% freelance written.** Magazine published 6 times during the school year covering the work of school parent-teacher groups. "We celebrate the work of school parent volunteers and provide resources to help them do that work more effectively." Estab. 1999. Circ. 80,000. Byline given. Pays on acceptance. Offers 30% kill fee. Publishes ms an average of 4-6 months after acceptance. Editorial lead time 4 months. Submit seasonal material 4 months in advance. Accepts queries by e-mail. Guidelines by e-mail.

NONFICTION Needs general interest, how-to, interview, personal experience. **Buys 20 mss/year.** Query. We review but do not encourage unsolicited submissions. Features run roughly 1,200 to 2,200 words. Average assignment is 1,200 words. Department pieces run 600 to 1,200 words **Payment depends on the difficulty of the topic and the experience of the writer. "We pay by the assignment, not by the word; our pay scale ranges from $200 to $700 for features and $150 to $400 for departments. We occasionally pay more for high-impact stories and highly experienced writers. We buy all rights, and we pay on acceptance (within 30 days of invoice)."**

PHOTOS State availability. Identification of subjects required. Negotiates payment individually.

⊖ SCHOOLARTS MAGAZINE

Davis Art, Production Department, Attn: Article Submissions, 50 Portland St., Worcester MA 01608. E-mail: nwalkup@davisart.com. Website: davisart.com. **Contact:** Nancy Walkup, editor. **85% freelance written.** Monthly magazine (August/September-May/June), serving arts and craft education profession, K-12, higher education, and museum education programs written by and for art teachers. Estab. 1901. Pays on publication (honorarium and 4 copies). Publishes ms an average of 24 months after acceptance. Accepts queries by mail. Responds in 1-2 months to queries. Guidelines available online.

NONFICTION Query or send complete ms and SASE. Mail a CD containing your article's text and photographs, along with signed permission forms (online under Guidelines). No e-mail submissions. Length: 600-1,400 words. **Pays $30-150.**

⊖ TEACHERS OF VISION

A Publication of Christian Educators Association, 227 N. Magnolia Ave., Suite 2, Anaheim CA 92801.

(714)761-1476. E-mail: TOV@ceai.org. Website: ceai. org. **70% freelance written**. Magazine published 4 times/year for Christians in public education. "*Teachers of Vision*'s articles inspire, inform, and equip teachers and administrators in the educational arena. Readers look for teacher tips, integrating faith and work, and general interest education articles. Topics include subject matter, religious expression and activity in public schools, and legal rights of Christian educators. Our audience is primarily public school educators. Other readers include teachers in private schools, university professors, school administrators, parents, and school board members." Estab. 1953. Circ. 10,000. Byline given. Pays on publication. Publishes ms an average of 6 months after acceptance. Editorial lead time 4 months. Submit seasonal material 4 months in advance. Accepts queries by mail, e-mail. Accepts simultaneous submissions. Responds in 1 month to queries. Responds in 3-4 months to mss. Sample copy for sae with 9×12 envelope and 4 first-class stamps. Guidelines available online.

NONFICTION Needs how-to, humor, inspirational, interview, opinion, personal experience, religious. Nothing preachy. **Buys 50-60 mss/year.** Query or send complete ms if 2,000 words or less. Length: 1,500 words. **Pays $40-50.**

PHOTOS State availability of photos. Offers no additional payment for photos accepted with ms.

TEACHING MUSIC

MENC: The National Association for Music Education, 1806 Robert Fulton Dr., Reston VA 20191-4348. E-mail: lindab@menc.org. Website: menc.org. **Contact:** Linda C. Brown, editor. Journal covering music education issued six times a year. *Teaching Music* offers music educators a forum for the exchange of practical ideas that will help them become more effective teachers. Written in an easy-to-read, conversational style, the magazine includes timely information to interest, inform, and inspire music teachers and those who support their work. Byline given. Does not pay writers at this time. Publishes ms an average of 24 months after acceptance. Editorial lead time 12-18 months. Accepts queries by e-mail (preferably in Word). Responds in 2 weeks to queries. Responds in 3 months to mss. Guidelines available online.

NONFICTION Needs how-to, inspirational, personal experience, manuscripts for the Lectern section that describe effective and innovative instructional strategies or thoughtful solutions to problems faced by music educators at all levels, from PreK through college. Major article categories are General Music, Band, Orchestra, Chorus, Early Childhood, Advocacy, and Teacher Education/Professional Development. Send complete ms. Length: 1,000-1,400 words.

PHOTOS Send in color photographs or other graphics that illustrate the main points of their articles. Photographers should obtain permission from the parents/guardians of minors whose photographs are submitted. Release form is online. Send photos after ms accepted.

$$ TEACHING THEATRE

Educational Theatre Association, 2343 Auburn Ave., Cincinnati OH 45219-2819. (513)421-3900. E-mail: jpalmarini@edta.org. Website: edta.org; schooltheatre.org. **Contact:** James Palmarini, editor. **65% freelance written**. Quarterly magazine covering education theater K-12, primary emphasis on middle and secondary level education. Estab. 1989. Circ. 5,000. Byline given. Pays on acceptance. Publishes ms an average of 3 months after acceptance. Editorial lead time 2 months. Accepts queries by mail, e-mail. Accepts simultaneous submissions. Responds in 4-6 weeks to queries. Responds in 3 months to mss. Sample copy for $2. Guidelines available online.

"*Teaching Theatre* emphasizes the teaching, theory, philosophy issues that are of concern to teachers at the elementary, secondary, and—as they relate to teaching K-12 theater—college levels. A typical issue includes an article on acting, directing, playwriting, or technical theatre; a profile of an outstanding educational theatre program; a piece on curriculum design, assessment, or teaching methodology; and a report on current trends or issues in the field, such as funding, standards, or certification."

NONFICTION Needs book excerpts, essays, how-to, interview, opinion, technical theater. **Buys 20 mss/year.** Query. Buys 12-15 articles a year. A typical issue might include an article on theatre curriculum development, a profile of an exemplary theatre education program, a how-to teach piece on acting, directing, or playwriting, and a news story or two about pertinent educational theatre issues and events. Once articles are accepted, authors are asked to supply their work electronically via e-mail (jpalmarini@edta.org) or on

IBM compatible diskettes. Length: 750-4,000 words **Pays $50-350**

PHOTOS State availability. Reviews contact sheets, 5×7 and 8×10 transparencies, prints, digital images (150 dpi minimum). Unless other arrangements are made, payment for articles includes payment for the photos and illustrations.

$$$$ TEACHING TOLERANCE

The Southern Poverty Law Center, 400 Washington Ave., Montgomery AL 36104. (334)956-8200. Fax: (334)956-8488. Website: teachingtolerance.org. **30% freelance written**. Semiannual magazine. Estab. 1991. Circ. 400,000. Byline given. Pays on acceptance. Editorial lead time 6 months. Submit seasonal material 6 months in advance. Accepts queries by mail, fax, online submission form. Sample copy and writer's guidelines free or online.

"*Teaching Tolerance* is dedicated to helping K-12 teachers promote tolerance and understanding between widely diverse groups of students. Includes articles, teaching ideas, and reviews of other resources available to educators."

NONFICTION Needs essays, how-to, classroom techniques, personal experience, classroom, photo feature. No jargon, rhetoric or academic analysis. No theoretical discussions on the pros/cons of multicultural education. **Buys 2-4 mss/year.** Submit outlines or complete mss. Length: 1,000-3,000 words. **Pays $500-3,000.**

PHOTOS State availability. Captions, identification of subjects required. Reviews contact sheets, transparencies.

COLUMNS Essays (personal reflection, how-to, school program), 400-800 words; Idea Exchange (special projects, successful anti-bias activities), 250-500 words; Student Writings (short essays dealing with diversity, tolerance, justice), 300-500 words. **Buys 8-12 mss/year.** Query with published clips. **Pays $50 1,000.**

$ TECH DIRECTIONS

Prakken Publications, Prakken Publications, Inc., P.O. Box 8623, Ann Arbor MI 48107-8623. (734)975-2800. Fax: (734)975-2787. E-mail: susanne@techdirections.com. Website: techdirections.com. **Contact:** Susanne Peckham, managing editor. **100% freelance written. Eager to work with new/unpublished writers.** Monthly (except June and July) magazine covering issues, trends, and activities of interest to science, technical, and technology educators at the elementary through post-secondary school levels. Estab. 1934. Circ. 40,000. Byline given. Pays on publication. Publishes ms an average of 1 year after acceptance. Responds in 1 month to queries. Sample copy for $5. Guidelines available online.

NONFICTION Needs general interest, how-to, personal experience, technical, think pieces. **Buys 50 unsolicited mss/year.** Length: 2,000-3,000 words. **Pays $50-150.**

PHOTOS Send photos. Reviews color prints. Payment for photos included in payment for ms. Will accept electronic art as well.

COLUMNS Direct from Washington (education news from Washington DC); Technology Today (new products under development); Technologies Past (profiles the inventors of last century); Mastering Computers, Technology Concepts (project orientation).

ELECTRONICS AND COMMUNICATION

$$ THE ACUTA JOURNAL

Information Communications Technology in Higher Education, ACUTA, 152 W. Zandale Dr., Suite 200, Lexington KY 40503-2486. (859)278-3338. Fax: (859)278-3268. E-mail: aburton@acuta.org; pscott@acuta.org. Website: acuta.org. **Contact:** Amy Burton; Patricia Scott, communications manager. **20% freelance written.** Quarterly professional association journal covering information communications technology (ICT) in higher education. "Our audience includes, primarily, middle to upper management in the IT/telecommunications department on college/university campuses. They are highly skilled, technology-oriented professionals who provide data, voice, and video communications services for residential and academic purposes." Estab. 1997. Circ. 2,200. Byline given. Pays on publication. Publishes ms an average of 6 months after acceptance. Editorial lead time 6 months. Accepts queries by mail, e-mail, fax, phone. Responds in 1 month to queries. Responds in 2 months to mss. Sample copy for sae with 9×12 envelope and 6 first-class stamps.

NONFICTION Needs how-to, ICT, technical, technology, case study, college/university application of technology. **Buys 6-8 mss/year.** Query. Length: 1,200-4,000 words. **Pays 8-10¢/word.**

PHOTOS State availability. Captions, model releases required. Reviews prints. Offers no additional payment for photos accepted with ms.

⊖⊖ CABLING BUSINESS MAGAZINE

Cabling Publications, Inc., 12035 Shiloh Rd., Suite 350, Dallas TX 75228. (214)328-1717. Fax: (214)319-6077. E-mail: russell@cablingbusiness.com. Website: cablingbusiness.com. Russell Paulov, editor-in-chief. **Contact:** Margaret Patterson, managing editor. **30% freelance written**. Monthly magazine covering telecommunications, cable manufacturing, volP, wireless, broadband, structured cabling. Estab. 1991. Circ. 15,000. Byline given. Pays on publication. Publishes ms an average of 1-2 months after acceptance. Editorial lead time 2 months. Submit seasonal material 2 months in advance. Accepts queries by e-mail. Accepts simultaneous submissions. Responds in 1 week to queries and to mss. Sample copy available online. Guidelines by e-mail.

NONFICTION Needs how-to, interview, new product, opinion, personal experience, technical. No vendor/product specific infomercials. **Buys 6 mss/year.** Query. Length: 1,500-2,500 words. **Pays $400 max. for assigned articles. Pays $400 max. for unsolicited articles.**

PHOTOS State availability. Captions, identification of subjects, model releases required. Reviews GIF/JPEG files. Offers no additional payment for photos accepted with ms.

COLUMNS New Products (latest technology from industry), 350 words; Testing Equipment Q&A (work with specific companies on testing information), Cable Q&A (work with specific companies on cable questions from industry), 800 words; Terminology/Calendar, 200 words. Query. **Pays $400.**

⊖⊖ DIGITAL OUTPUT

Rockport Custom Publishing, LLC, 100 Cummings Center, Suite 321E, Beverly MA 01915. (904)273-2588. E-mail: mdonovan@rdigitaloutput.net; edit@rockportpubs.com. Website: digitaloutput.net. **Contact:** Melissa Donovan, editor. **70% freelance written**. Monthly magazine covering electronic prepress, desktop publishing, and digital imaging, with articles ranging from digital capture and design to electronic prepress and digital printing. *Digital Output* is a national business publication for electronic publishers and digital imagers, providing monthly articles which examine the latest technologies and digital methods and discuss how to profit from them. Our readers include service bureaus, prepress and reprographic houses, designers, commercial printers, wide-format printers, ad agencies, corporate communications, sign shops, and others. Estab. 1994. Circ. 25,000. Byline given. Pays on publication. Offers 10-20% kill fee. Publishes ms an average of 2 months after acceptance. Editorial lead time 3 months. Submit seasonal material 3 months in advance. Accepts queries by mail, e-mail. Responds in 3 weeks to queries. Responds in 1 month to mss. Sample copy for $4.50 or online.

💬 "Each issue of Digital Output in 2011 will focus on these areas to give our readers the most up-to-date information on every aspect of their business. Digital Output magazine will publish 12 issues in 2011, including two Buyers' Guides that mail in January and June." Digital Output magazine provides news and information for the high-growth digita graphics and printing industry. In it's 11th year of publication, the magazine continues to be an authority in the industry, educating subscribers, and reinforcing manufacturer brand awareness. Digital Output helps bridge the information gap between printers, designers, and imagers with its unique, application-driven approach. Free subscription, digital editions, and Buyers'™ Guide available online at digitaloutput.net.

NONFICTION Needs how-to, interview, technical, case studies. **Buys 36 mss/year.** Query with published clips or hyperlinks to posted clips. Length: 1,500-4,000 words. **Pays $250-600.**

PHOTOS Send photos.

⊖⊖⊖ SOUND & VIDEO CONTRACTOR

Penton Media, 6400 Hollis St., Suite 12, Emeryville CA 94608. (818)236-3667. Fax: (913)514-3683. E-mail: cynthia.wisehart@penton.com; Jessaca.Gutierrez@penton.com. Website: svconline.com. Cynthia Wisehart, editor. **Contact:** Jessaca Gutierrez, online editor (913)967-1762. **60% freelance written**. Monthly magazine covering professional audio, video, security, acoustical design, sales, and marketing. Estab. 1983. Circ. 24,000. Byline given. Pays on acceptance. Publishes ms an average of 3 months after acceptance. Editorial lead time 3 months. Accepts queries by mail, e-mail, fax, phone. Accepts simultaneous submissions. Responds ASAP to queries and. Sample copy and writer's

NONFICTION Needs historical, how-to, photo feature, technical, professional audio/video applications, installations, product reviews. No opinion pieces, advertorial, interview/profile, expose/gossip. **Buys 60 mss/year.** Query. Length: 1,000-2,500 words. **Pays $200-1,200 for assigned articles. Pays $200-650 for unsolicited articles.**

COLUMNS Security Technology Review (technical install information); Sales & Marketing (techniques for installation industry); Video Happenings (Pro video/projection/storage technical info), all 1,500 words. **Buys 30 mss/year.** Query. **Pays $200-350.**

⬤⬤ SQL SERVER MAGAZINE

Penton Media, 221 E. 29th St., Loveland CO 80538. (970)663-4700. Fax: (970)667-2321. E-mail: articles@sqlmag.com. Website: sqlmag.com. **Contact:** Amy Eisenberg. **35% freelance written.** Monthly magazine covering Microsoft SQL Server. "*SQL Server Magazine* is the only magazine completely devoted to helping developers and DBAs master new and emerging SQL Server technologies and issues. It provides practical advice and lots of code examples for SQL Server developers and administrators, and includes how-to articles, tips, tricks, and programming techniques offered by SQL Server experts." Estab. 1999. Circ. 20,000. Byline given. "Penton Media pays for articles upon publication. Payment rates are based on the author's writing experience and the quality of the article submitted. We will discuss the payment rate for your article when we notify you of its acceptance." Offers $100 kill fee. Publishes ms an average of 6 months after acceptance. Editorial lead time 4+ months. Accepts queries by mail, e-mail. Responds in 6 weeks to queries. Responds in 2-3 months to mss. Sample copy and guidelines online.

NONFICTION Needs how-to, technical, SQL Server administration and programming. Nothing promoting third-party products or companies. **Buys 25-35 mss/year.** Send complete ms. Length: 1,800-3,000 words. **Pays $200 for feature articles; $500 for Focus articles.**

COLUMNS Contact: R2R Editor. Send all column/department submissions to r2r@sqlmag.com. Reader to Reader (helpful SQL Server hints and tips from readers), 200-400 words. **Buys 6-12 mss/year.** Send complete ms. **Pays $50**

⬤ TECH TRADER MAGAZINE

The Intermedia Group, Ltd., Tech Trader Magazine, 41 Bridge Road,, Glebe NSW 2037 Australia. (61)(2)9660-2113. Fax: (61)(2)9660-0885. E-mail: kymberly@intermedia.com.au. Website: intermedia.com.au. Monthly magazine covering consumer electronics industry. "Tech Trader Magazine delivers the latest news, opinion, features, product reviews, overseas reports, and new products together in one lively publication." Circ. 7,000.

NONFICTION Needs general interest, new product. Query.

ENERGY AND UTILITIES

⬤⬤ ELECTRICAL APPARATUS

Barks Publications, Inc., 400 N. Michigan Ave., Chicago IL 60611-4104. (312)321-9440. Fax: (312)321-1288. **Contact:** Elsie Dickson, associate publisher. Monthly magazine for persons working in electrical and electronic maintenance, in industrial plants and service and sales centers, who install and service electric motors, transformers, generators, controls, and related equipment. Contact staff members by telephone for their preferred e-mail addresses. Estab. 1967. Circ. 16,000. Byline given. Pays on publication. Publishes ms an average of 1 month after acceptance. Accepts queries by mail, fax. Responds in 1 week to queries. Responds in 2 weeks to mss.

NONFICTION Needs technical. Length: 1,500-2,500 words. **Pays $250-500 for assigned articles.**

⬤⬤⬤ ELECTRICAL BUSINESS

CLB Media, Inc., 240 Edward St., Aurora ON L4G 3S9 Canada. (905)727-0077; (905)713-4391. Fax: (905)727-0017. E-mail: acapkun@annexweb.com. Website: ebmag.com. **Contact:** Anthony Capkun, editor. **35% freelance written.** Tabloid published 10 times/year covering the Canadian electrical industry. *Electrical Business* targets electrical contractors and electricians. It provides practical information readers can use right away in their work and for running their business and assets. Estab. 1964. Circ. 18,097. Byline given. Pays on acceptance. Offers 50% kill fee. Publishes ms an average of 1-2 months after acceptance. Editorial lead time 3 months. Submit seasonal material 6 months in advance. Accepts queries by e-mail, phone. NoAccepts simultaneous submissions. Responds in 1 month to queries. Responds in 1 month to mss. Sample copy available online.

NONFICTION Needs how-to, technical. Special issues: Summer Blockbuster issue (June/July); Special Homebuilders' issue (November/December). **Buys 15 mss/year.** Query. Length: 800-1,200 words. **Pays 40¢/word.**

PHOTOS State availability. Captions, identification of subjects, model releases required. Reviews GIF/JPEG files. Negotiates payment individually.

COLUMNS Atlantic Focus (stories from Atlantic Canada); Western Focus (stories from Western Canada, including Manitoba); Trucks for the Trade (articles pertaining to the vehicles used by electrical contractors); Tools for the Trade (articles pertaining to tools used by contractors); all 800 words. **Buys 6 mss/year.** Query. **Pays 40¢/word.**

⊖⊙ PUBLIC POWER

American Public Power Association, 1875 Connecticut Ave. NW, Suite 1200, Washington D.C. 20009-5715. (202)467-2900. Fax: (202)467-2910. E-mail: DBlaylock@publicpower.org. Website: publicpowermedia.org. **Contact:** David L. Blaylock, editor. **60% freelance written. Prefers to work with published/established writers.** Estab. 1942. Byline given. Pays on acceptance. Publishes ms an average of 3 months after acceptance. Accepts queries by mail, e-mail, fax. Responds in 6 months to queries. Sample copy and writer's

NONFICTION Pays $500 and up.

PHOTOS Reviews electronic photos (minimum 300 dpi at reproduction size).

⊖⊙ SOLAR INDUSTRY

Zackin Publications, Inc., P.O. Box 2180, Waterbury CT 06722. (800)325-6745. Fax: (203)262-4680. E-mail: jlillian@solarindustrymag.com. Website: aeronline.com. **Contact:** Jessica Lillian, editor. **5% freelance written. Prefers to work with published/established writers.** Monthly magazine on selling home hearth products—chiefly solid fuel and gas-burning appliances. We seek detailed how-to tips for retailers to improve business. Most freelance material purchased is about retailers and how they succeed. Estab. 1980. Circ. 10,000. Pays on publication. Publishes ms an average of 2 months after acceptance. Submit seasonal material 4 months in advance. Accepts queries by mail, e-mail, fax, phone. Responds in 2 weeks to

queries. Sample copy for sae with 9×12 envelope and 4 First-Class stamps. Guidelines available online.

◗ Industry experts are invited to call with their ideas for bylined articles.

⊶ "Publishes two types of timely articles: Features that examine and analyze solar energy industry trends; and Features that give readers nuts and bolts information about how to improve their operations. These features are written by professional industry staff and contract journalists, and also by industry experts."

NONFICTION Needs how-to, improve retail profits and business know-how, interview, of successful retailers in this field. No general business articles not adapted to this industry. **Buys 10 mss/year.** Query. Length: 1,500 - 2,000 words. **Pays $200.**

PHOTOS State availability. Identification of subjects required. Reviews color transparencies. Pays $25-125 maximum for 5×7 b&w prints.

⊖⊙⊙ TEXAS CO-OP POWER

Texas Electric Cooperatives, Inc., 1122 Colorado St. 24th Floor, Austin TX 78701. (512)486-6242. E-mail: kayen@texas-ec.org. Website: texascooppower.com. **Contact:** Kaye Northcott. **50% freelance written.** Monthly magazine covering rural and suburban Texas life, people, and places. *Texas Co-op Power* provides 1 million households and businesses educational and technical information about electric cooperatives in a high-quality and entertaining format to promote the general welfare of cooperatives, their member-owners, and the areas in which they serve. Estab. 1948. Circ. 1.2 million. Byline given. after any necessary rewrites. Publishes ms an average of 6 months after acceptance. Editorial lead time 4-5 months. Submit seasonal material 6 months in advance. Accepts queries by mail, e-mail, fax, online submission form. Accepts simultaneous submissions. Responds in 1 month to queries. Responds in 3 months to mss. Sample copy available online. Guidelines for #10 sase.

◗ "*Texas Co-op Power* is published by your electric cooperative to enhance the quality of life of its member-customers in an educational and entertaining format."

NONFICTION Needs general interest, historical, interview, photo feature, travel. **Buys 30 mss/year.** Query with published clips. Length: 800-1,200 words. **Pays $400-1,000.**

PHOTOS State availability. Identification of subjects, model releases required. Reviews transparencies, prints. Negotiates payment individually.

ENGINEERING AND TECHNOLOGY

○ ⊖ ⊖ ⊖ CABLING NETWORKING SYSTEMS

12 Concorde Place, Suite 800, North York ON M3C 4J2 Canada. (416)510-6752. Fax: (416)510-5134. E-mail: pbarker@cnsmagazine.com. Website: cabling-systems.com. **Contact:** Paul Barker, editor. **50% freelance written**. Magazine published 6 times/year covering structured cabling/telecommunications industry. Estab. 1998. Circ. 11,000. Byline given. Pays on publication. Publishes ms an average of 1 month after acceptance. Editorial lead time 3 months. Submit seasonal material 1 month in advance. Accepts queries by mail, e-mail, phone. Accepts simultaneous submissions. Sample copy available online.

NONFICTION Needs technical, case studies, features. No reprints or previously written articles. All articles are assigned by editor based on query or need of publication. **Buys 12 mss/year.** Query with published clips. Length: 1,500-2,500 words. **Pays 40-50¢/word.**

PHOTOS State availability. Captions, identification of subjects required. Reviews contact sheets, prints. Negotiates payment individually.

COLUMNS Focus on Engineering/Design; Focus on Installation; Focus on Maintenance/Testing, all 1,500 words. **Buys 7 mss/year.** Query with published clips. **Pays 40-50¢/word.**

○ ⊖ ⊖ ⊖ CANADIAN CONSULTING ENGINEER

Business Information Group, 12 Condorde Pl., Suite 800, Toronto ON M3C 4J2 Canada. (416)510-5119. Fax: (416)510-5134. E-mail: bparsons@ccemag.com. Website: canadianconsultingengineer.com. **Contact:** Bronwen Parsons, editor. **20% freelance written**. Bimonthly magazine covering consulting engineering in private practice. Estab. 1958. Circ. 8,900. Byline given depending on length of story Pays on publication. Offers 50% kill fee. Publishes ms an average of 4 months after acceptance. Editorial lead time 6 months. Responds in 3 months to mss.

NONFICTION Needs historical, new product, technical, engineering/construction projects, environmental/construction issues. **Buys 8-10 mss/year.** Length: 300-1,500 words. **Pays $200-1,000 (Canadian).**

PHOTOS State availability. Negotiates payment individually.

COLUMNS Export (selling consulting engineering services abroad); Management (managing consulting engineering businesses); On-Line (trends in CAD systems); Employment; Business; Construction and Environmental Law (Canada), all 800 words. **Buys 4 mss/year.** Query with published clips. **Pays $250-400.**

⊖ ⊖ COMPOSITES MANUFACTURING MAGAZINE

(formerly *Composites Fabrication Magazine*), American Composites Manufacturers Association, 1010 N. Glebe Rd., Suite 450, Arlington VA 22201. (703)525-0511. Fax: (703)525-0743. E-mail: mskea@acmanet.org; info@acmanet.org. E-mail: mskea@acmanet.org. Website: acmanet.org. **Contact:** Melinda Skea, editor. Monthly magazine covering any industry that uses reinforced composites: marine, aerospace, infrastructure, automotive, transportation, corrosion, architecture, tub and shower, sports, and recreation. Primarily, we publish educational pieces, the how-to of the shop environment. We also publish marketing, business trends, and economic forecasts relevant to the composites industry. Estab. 1979. Circ. 12,000. Byline given. Pays on acceptance. Publishes ms an average of 2-3 months after acceptance. Editorial lead time 2 months. Accepts queries by e-mail. Accepts simultaneous submissions. Responds in 1 week to queries. Responds in 1 month to mss. Guidelines by e-mail.

○ *Composites Manufacturing* invites freelance feature submissions, all of which should be sent via e-mail as a Microsoft Word attachment. Please include photos and any applicable charts/graphs with articles. Digital photos should be 300 dpi and should be provided as a separate file (not embedded in the Word document). A query letter is required and may be directed to Melinda Skea, editor.

NONFICTION Needs how-to, composites manufacturing, new product, technical, marketing, related business trends and forecasts. Special issues: Each January we publish a World Market Report where we cover all niche markets and all geographic areas relevant to the composites industry. Freelance material will be considered strongly for this issue. No need to query company or personal profiles unless there is an extremely unique or novel angle. **Buys 5-10 mss/year.** Query. Length: 1,500-4,000 words. **Pays 20-40¢/word (negotiable).**

COLUMNS We publish columns on HR, relevant government legislation, industry lessons learned, regulatory affairs, and technology. Average word length for columns is 500 words. We would entertain any new column idea that hits hard on industry matters. Query. **Pays $300-350.**

💲💲💲 ENTERPRISE MINNESOTA MAGAZINE

Enterprise Minnesota, Inc., 310 4th Ave. So., Minneapolis MN 55415. (612)373-2900; 800-325-3073. Fax: (612)373-2901. E-mail: editor@mntech.org. Website: enterpriseminnesota.org. **Contact:** Tom Mason, editor. **90% freelance written.** Magazine published 5 times/year. Estab. 1991. Circ. 16,000. Byline given. Pays on publication. Offers 10% kill fee. Publishes ms an average of 3 months after acceptance. Editorial lead time 1 month. Submit seasonal material 1 year in advance. Accepts queries by mail, e-mail, online submission form. Guidelines available online.

NONFICTION Needs general interest, how-to, interview. **Buys 60 mss/year.** Query with published clips. **Pays $150-1,000.**

COLUMNS Feature Well (Q&A format, provocative ideas from Minnesota business and industry leaders), 2,000 words; Up Front (mini profiles, anecdotal news items), 250-500 words. Query with published clips.

💲💲 LD+A

Illuminating Engineering Society of North America, 120 Wall St., 17th Floor, New York NY 10005. (212)248-5000, ext. 108. Fax: (212)248-5017. E-mail: ptarricone@iesna.org. Website: iesna.org. **Contact:** Paul Tarricone, editor. **10% freelance written.** Monthly magazine. Estab. 1971. Circ. 10,000. Byline given. Pays on acceptance. Publishes ms an average of 4 months after acceptance. Editorial lead time 2 months. Submit seasonal material 4 months in advance. Accepts queries by mail, e-mail, fax, phone. Accepts simultaneous submissions. Responds in 2 weeks to queries. Guidelines available online at website.

NONFICTION Needs historical, how-to, opinion, personal experience, photo feature, technical. No articles blatantly promoting a product, company, or individual. **Buys 6-10 mss/year.** Query. Length: 1,500-2,000 words.

PHOTOS Send photos. Captions required. Reviews JPEG/TIFF files. Offers no additional payment for photos accepted with ms.

COLUMNS Essay by Invitation (industry trends), 1,200 words. Query. **Does not pay for columns.**

💲💲 MANUFACTURING & TECHNOLOGY EJOURNAL

Manufacturers Group Inc., P.O. Box 4310, Lexington KY 40544. Fax: (859)223-6709. E-mail: editor@industrysearch.com. Website: mfr.tech.com. **40% freelance written.** Weekly website covering manufacturing & technology. Editorial targets middle and upper management—Presidents, Plant Managers, Engineering, Purchasing. Editorial includes features on operations and management, new plants, acquisitions, expansions, new products. Estab. 1976 (print). Circ. 10,000 plus weekly (e-mail) 5,000 weekly online. Byline given. 30 days followiong publication. Offers 25% kill fee. Publishes ms an average of 2 weeks after acceptance. Editorial lead time 2 weeks. Submit seasonal material 2 weeks in advance. Sample copy available online. Guidelines by e-mail.

NONFICTION Needs new product, opinion, technical, New plants, expansions, acquisitions. Most articles are assignments. Special issues: We have assigned features on timely issues relating to economics, environmental, manufacturing trends, employment. Open to feature suggestions by outline only. Marketing, opinion. General interest, inspirational, personal, travel, book excerpts. You can include up two photo or graphic images and must come as an attachment to your e-mail as JPEGs and no larger than 300 x 300 pixels each Length: 750-1,200 words. **Pays $0.20/word published.**

COLUMNS New Plants (Manufacturing, Technology), Acquisitions (Manufacturing, Technology), New Technology, Expansions (Manufacturing, Technology). Query. **Pays $-$0.20/word.**

💲💲 MINORITY ENGINEER

Equal Opportunity Publications, Inc., 445 Broad Hollow Rd., Suite 425, Melville NY 11747. (631)421-9421. Fax: (516)421-0359. E-mail: jschneider@eop.com; info@eop.com. Website: eop.com. **Contact:** James Schneider, Director, Editorial. **60% freelance written. Prefers to work with published/established writers.** Triannual magazine covering career guidance for minority engineering students and minority professional engineers. Job information. Estab. 1969. Circ.

15,000. Byline given. Pays on publication. Publishes ms an average of 3 months after acceptance. Editorial lead time 3 months. Accepts queries by mail, e-mail, fax, phone. Accepts simultaneous submissions. Responds in 2 weeks to queries. Responds in 2 months to mss. Sample copy and writer's guidelines for 9×12 SAE with 5 first-class stamps.

NONFICTION Needs book excerpts, general interest, on specific minority engineering concerns, how-to, land a job, keep a job, etc., interview, minority engineer role models, opinion, problems of ethnic minorities, personal experience, student and career experiences, technical, on career fields offering opportunities for minority engineers, articles on job search techniques, role models. No general information. Query. Length: 1,500-2,500 words. **Pays $350 for assigned articles.**

💲💲💲💲 **RAILWAY TRACK AND STRUCTURES**

Simmons-Boardman Publishing, 20 S. Clark St., Suite 2450, Chicago IL 60603-1838. (312)683-0130. Fax: (312)683-0131. E-mail: mischa@sbpub-chicago.com. Website: rtands.com. **Contact:** Mischa Wanek-Libman, editor. **1% freelance written.** Monthly magazine covering railroad civil engineering. *"RT&S is a nuts-and-bolts journal to help railroad civil engineers do their jobs better."* Estab. 1904. Circ. 9,500. Byline given. Pays on publication. Offers 90% kill fee. Publishes ms an average of 1 month after acceptance. Editorial lead time 2 months. Submit seasonal material 3 months in advance. Accepts queries by mail, fax, phone. Accepts simultaneous submissions. Responds in 1 month to queries and to mss. Sample copy available online.

NONFICTION Needs how-to, new product, technical. Does not want nostalgia or railroadiana. **Buys 1 mss/year.** Query. Length: 900-2,000 words. **Pays $500-1,000**

PHOTOS State availability. Captions, identification of subjects, model releases required. Reviews GIF/JPEG files. Negotiates payment individually.

💲💲 **WOMAN ENGINEER**

Equal Opportunity Publications, Inc., 445 Broad Hollow Rd., Suite 425, Melville NY 11747. (631)421-9421. Fax: (631)421-0359. E-mail: info@eop.com; jschneider@eop.com. Website: eop.com. **Contact:** James Schneider, editor. **60% freelance written. Works with a small number of new/unpublished writers each**

year. Triannual magazine aimed at advancing the careers of women engineering students and professional women engineers. Job information. Estab. 1968. Circ. 16,000. Byline given. Pays on publication. Publishes ms an average of 3 months after acceptance. Editorial lead time 3 months. Accepts queries by mail, e-mail, fax, phone. Responds in 2 weeks to queries. Responds in 2 months to mss. Sample copy and writer's

NONFICTION Needs how-to, find jobs, interview, personal experience. Query. Length: 1,500-2,500 words. **Pays $350 for assigned articles.**

PHOTOS Captions, identification of subjects required. Reviews color slides but will accept b&w.

ENTERTAINMENT AND THE ARTS

💲💲💲 **AMERICAN CINEMATOGRAPHER**

American Society of Cinematographers, 1782 N. Orange Dr., Hollywood CA 90028. (800)448-0145; (outside U.S. (323)969-4333). Fax: (323)876-4973. E-mail: stephen@ascmag.com. Website: theasc.com. **Contact:** Stephen Pizzello, executive editor. **90% freelance written.** Monthly magazine covering cinematography (motion picture, TV, music video, commercial). *"American Cinematographer is a trade publication devoted to the art and craft of cinematography. Our readers are predominantly film-industry professionals."* Estab. 1919. Circ. 45,000. Byline given. Pays on publication. Offers 50% kill fee. Publishes ms an average of 2-3 months after acceptance. Editorial lead time 2 months. Submit seasonal material 3 months in advance. Accepts queries by mail, e-mail, phone. No-Responds in 2 weeks to queries. Responds in 2 months to mss. Sample copy and writer's

NONFICTION Contact: Stephen Pizzello, editor. Needs interview, new product, technical. No reviews, opinion pieces. **Buys 20-25 mss/year.** Query with published clips. Length: 1,500-4,000 words. **Pays $600-1,200.**

💲💲 **AMERICAN THEATRE**

Theatre Communications Group, 520 8th Ave., 24th Floor, New York NY 10018-4156. (212)609-5900. E-mail: jim@tcg.org. Website: tcg.org. Nicole Estvanik Taylor, managing editor. **Contact:** Jim O'Quinn, editor. **60% freelance written.** Monthly magazine covering theatre. "Our focus is American regional nonprofit theatre. American Theatre typically publishes two or three features and four to six back-of-the-book articles covering trends and events in all types of theatre, as well as economic and legislative developments affecting the arts." Estab. 1982. Circ. 100,000. Byline given. Pays on publication. Editorial lead time 2 months. Submit seasonal material 3 months in advance. Accepts queries by mail, e-mail, online submission form. Accepts simultaneous submissions. Responds in 2 months Sample copy and guidelines online.

⭘ "Writers wishing to submit articles to *American Theatre* should mail or e-mail a query to editor in chief Jim O'Quinn outlining a particular proposal; unsolicited material is rarely accepted. Please include a brief resume and sample clips. Planning of major articles usually occurs at least 3 months in advance of publication. All mss are subject to editing."

⚷ *American Theatre* covers trends and events in all types of theatre, as well as economic and legislative developments affecting the arts. *American Theatre* rarely publishes articles about commercial, amateur or university theatre, nor about works that would widely be classified as dance or opera, except at the editors' discretion. While significant productions may be highlighted in the Critic's Notebook section, *American Theatre* does not review productions (but does review theatre-related books).

NONFICTION Needs book excerpts, essays, exposè, general interest, historical, how-to, humor, inspirational, interview, opinion, personal experience, photo feature, travel. Special issues: Training (January); International (May/June); Season Preview (October). No unsolicited submissions (rarely accepted), no reviews Send query letter to Jim O'Quinn with outlined proposal, published clips. Include brief resumè, SASE. Length: 200-2,000 words. **While fees are negotiated per ms, we pay an average of $350 for full-length (2500-3500 words) features, less for shorter pieces.**

PHOTOS Contact: Kitty Suen, creative dir.; atphoto@tcg.com. Send photos. Captions required. Reviews JPEG files. Negotiates payment individually.

💲💲 BOXOFFICE MAGAZINE

Boxoffice Media, LLC, 230 Park Ave., Suite 1000, New York NY 10169. (212)922-9800. E-mail: help@boxoffice.com; amy@boxoffice.com; peter@boxoffice.com; ken@boxoffice.com. Website: BoxOffice.com; BoxofficeMagazine.com. Amy Nicholson, editor; Peter Cane, publisher; Kenneth James Bacon, creative director. Phil Contrino, boxoffice.com editor: phil@boxoffice. com. **Contact:** Amy Nicholson, editor. **15% freelance written**. Providing news and numbers to the film industry since 1920. Magazine about the motion picture industry for executives and managers working in the film business, including movie theater owners and operators, Hollywood studio personnel and leaders in allied industries. Estab. 1920. Circ. 6,000. Byline given. Pays on publication. Publishes ms an average of 3 months after acceptance. Submit seasonal material 5 months in advance. Accepts queries by mail, e-mail, fax. Sample copy for $5 in US; $10 outside US.

⭘ "BOXOFFICE Magazine has been the premier trade magazine covering The Business of Movies for industry insiders. In November 2010, we began publishing our new fan magazine, available at a theater near you. If you love the movies, you'll love The New BOXOFFICE Magazine. Check out our online edition. In addition to the fastest and most accurate box office on the Internet, we review more than 600 movies a year—every theatrical release in the US and major festival screenings from around the world as well as exclusive features and interviews with top filmmakers and industry executives and the latest news from Hollywood. If you're a film aficionado (for love or money), check out our sister site, boxofficemagazine.com for all the latest on your favorite films and filmmakers."

NONFICTION Needs book excerpts, essays, interview, new product, personal experience, photo feature, technical, investigative all regarding movie theatre business. Query with published clips. Length: 800-2,500 words. **Pays 10¢/word.**

PHOTOS Contact: Kenneth James Bacon, creative director. Monthly trade magazine; the official publication of the National Association of Theater Owners. Sample copy available for $10. State availability. Captions required. Reviews prints, slides and JPEG files. Pays $10/printed photo. Pays on publication. Credit line sometimes given.

💲💲 CAMPUS ACTIVITIES

Cameo Publishing Group, 1520 Newberry Rd., Blair SC 29015. (800)728-2950. Fax: (803)712-6703. E-mail:

info@cameopublishing.com; kirby@cameopublishing.com. Website: campusactivitiesmagazine.com; cameopublishing.com; americanentertainmentmagazine.com. W.C. Kirby, publisher. **Contact:** Ian Kirby, editorial director. **75% freelance written.** Magazine published 8 times/year covering entertainment on college campuses. *Campus Activities* goes to entertainment buyers on every campus in the U.S. Features stories on artists (national and regional), speakers, and the programs at individual schools. Estab. 1991. Circ. 9,872. Byline given. Pays on publication. Offers kill fee. Offers 15% kill fee if accepted and not run. Publishes ms an average of 2 months after acceptance. Editorial lead time 2 months. Submit seasonal material 2 months in advance. Accepts queries by mail, e-mail, fax. Accepts simultaneous submissions. Responds in 1 month to queries. Responds in 2 months to mss. Sample copy for $3.50.

NONFICTION Needs interview, photo feature. Accepts no unsolicited articles. **Buys 40 mss/year.** Query. Length: 1,400-3,000 words. **Pays 13¢/word.**

PHOTOS State availability. Identification of subjects required. Reviews contact sheets, negatives, 3x5 transparencies, 8×10 prints, electronic media at 300 dpi or higher. Negotiates payment individually.

$$ DANCE TEACHER

McFadden Performing Arts Media, 110 William St., 23rd Floor, New York NY 10038. Fax: (646)459-4000. E-mail: khildebrand@dancemedia.com. Website: dance-teacher.com. **Contact:** Karen Hildebrand, editor. **60% freelance written.** Monthly magazine. Estab. 1979. Circ. 25,000. Byline given. Pays on publication. Publishes ms an average of 3 months after acceptance. Submit seasonal material 6 months in advance. Accepts queries by mail, e-mail, fax, phone, online submission form. Responds in 3 months to mss. Sample copy for sae with 9×12 envelope and 6 first-class stamps. Guidelines available online.

"Our readers are professional dance educators, business persons, and related professionals in all forms of dance."

NONFICTION Needs how-to, teach, health, business, legal. Special issues: Summer Programs (January); Music & More (May); Costumes and Production Preview (November); College/Training Schools (December). No PR or puff pieces. All articles must be well researched. **Buys 50 mss/year.** Query. Length: 700-2,000 words. **Pays $100-300.**

PHOTOS Send photos. Reviews contact sheets, negatives, transparencies, prints. Limited photo budget.

$$ DRAMATICS MAGAZINE

Educational Theatre Association, 2343 Auburn Ave., Cincinnati OH 45219-2815. (513)421-3900. Fax: (513)421-7077. E-mail: dcorathers@schooltheatre.org. Website: schooltheatre.org; edta.org. **Contact:** Donald Corathers, editor. **70% freelance written.** Monthly magazine for theater arts students, teachers, and others interested in theater arts education. "*Dramatics* is designed to provide serious, committed young theater students and their teachers with the skills and knowledge they need to make better theater; to be a resource that will help high school juniors and seniors make an informed decision about whether to pursue a career in theater, and about how to do so; and to prepare high school students to be knowledgeable, appreciative audience members for the rest of their lives." Estab. 1929. Circ. 40,000. Byline given. Pays on acceptance. Publishes ms an average of 3 months after acceptance. Submit seasonal material 3 months in advance. Accepts queries by mail, e-mail, fax. Accepts simultaneous submissions. Responds in 3 months to queries. Responds in more than 3 months to mss Sample copy for 9×12 SAE with 5 first-class stamps. Guidelines available online.

NONFICTION Needs how-to, technical theater, directing, acting, etc., humor, inspirational, interview, photo feature, technical. **Buys 30 mss/year.** Send complete ms. Length: 750-3,000 words. **Pays $50-400.**

PHOTOS Query. Purchased with accompanying ms. Reviews high-res JPEG files on CD.

FICTION Drama (one-act and full-length plays). Prefers unpublished scripts that have been produced at least once. No plays for children, Christmas plays, or plays written with no attention paid to the conventions of theater. **Buys 5-9 mss/year.** Send complete ms. **Pays $100-500.**

$$$ EMMY MAGAZINE

Academy of Television Arts & Sciences, 5220 Lankershim Blvd., North Hollywood CA 91601-3109. E-mail: emmymag@emmys.org. Website: emmys.tv. **Contact:** Gail Polevoi, editor. **90% freelance written. Prefers to work with published/established writers.** Bimonthly magazine on television for TV professionals. Circ. 14,000. Byline given. Pays on publication or within 6 months. Offers 25% kill fee. Publishes ms an average of 4 months after acceptance. Accepts queries by mail. Responds in 1 month to queries. Sample copy for sae with 9×12 envelope and 6 first-class stamps. Guidelines available online.

NONFICTION Query with published clips. Length: 1,500-2,000 words. **Pays $1,000-1,200.**

COLUMNS Mostly written by regular contributors, but newcomers can break in with filler items with In the Mix or short profiles in Labors of Love. Length: 250-500 words, depending on department. Query with published clips. **Pays $250-500.**

$$ MAKE-UP ARTIST MAGAZINE

4018 NE 112th Ave., Suite D-8, Vancouver WA 98682. (360)882-3488. E-mail: news@makeupmag.com. Website: makeupmag.com. Michael Key, editor-in-chief. **Contact:** Heather Wisner, managing editor. **90% freelance written.** Bimonthly magazine covering all types of professional make-up artistry. "Our audience is a mixture of high-level make-up artists, make-up students, and movie buffs. Writers should be comfortable with technical writing, and should have substantial knowledge of at least one area of makeup, such as effects or fashion. This is an entertainment-industry magazine so writing should have an element of fun and storytelling. Good interview skills required." Estab. 1996. Circ. 12,000. Byline given. Pays within 30 days of publication. Editorial lead time 6 weeks. Submit seasonal material 2 months in advance. Accepts queries by mail, e-mail, phone. Accepts simultaneous submissions. Sample copy for $7. Guidelines by e-mail.

NONFICTION Needs book excerpts, essays, historical, how-to, humor, inspirational, interview, new product, opinion, personal experience, photo feature, technical, travel. Does not want fluff pieces about consumer beauty products. **Buys 20+ mss/year.** Query with published clips. Length: 500-3,000 words. **Pays 20-50¢/word.**

PHOTOS Send photos. Captions, identification of subjects required. Reviews prints, GIF/JPEG files. Negotiates payment individually.

COLUMNS : Cameo (short yet thorough look at a makeup artist not covered in a feature story), 800 words (15 photos); Lab Tech (how-to advice for effects artists, usually written by a current makeup artist working in a lab), 800 words (3 photos); Backstage (analysis, interview, tips and behind the scenes info on a theatrical production's makeup), 800 words (3 photos). **Buys 30 columns. mss/year.** Query with published clips. **Pays $100.**

$ SCREEN MAGAZINE

Screen Enterprises, Inc., 676 N. LaSalle Blvd., #501, Chicago IL 60654. (312)640-0800. Fax: (312)640-1928. E-mail: editor@screenmag.com. Website: screenmag.com. Kevin Jeong, managing editor, kevin@screenmag.com. **Contact:** Andrew Schneider, editor. **5% freelance written.** Biweekly Chicago-based trade magazine covering advertising and film production in the Midwest and national markets. *Screen* is written for Midwest producers (and other creatives involved) of commercials, AV, features, independent corporate and multimedia. Estab. 1979. Circ. 15,000. Byline given. Pays on publication. Accepts queries by e-mail. Responds in 3 weeks to queries. Sample copy available online.

NONFICTION Needs interview, new product, technical. No general AV; nothing specific to other markets; no no-brainers or opinion. **Buys 26 mss/year.** Query with published clips. Length: 750-1,500 words. **Pays $50.**

PHOTOS Send photos. Captions required. Reviews prints. Offers no additional payment for photos accepted with ms.

$ SOUTHERN THEATRE

Southeastern Theatre Conference, P.O. Box 9868, 3309 Northampton Dr., Greensboro NC 27429-0868. (336)292-6041. E-mail: deanna@setc.org. Website: setc.org. **Contact:** Deanna Thompson, editor. **100% freelance written.** Quarterly magazine covering all aspects of theater in the Southeast, from innovative theater companies, to important trends, to people making a difference in the region. All stories must be written in a popular magazine style but with subject matter appropriate for theater professionals (not the general public). The audience includes members of the Southeastern Theatre Conference, founded in 1949 and the nation's largest regional theater organization. These members include individuals involved in professional, community, college/university, children's, and secondary school theater. The magazine also is purchased by more than 100 libraries. Estab. 1962. Circ. 4,200. Byline given. Pays on publication. Publishes ms an average of 3 months after acceptance. Editorial lead time 3 months. Submit seasonal material 6 months in advance. Accepts queries by mail, e-mail. Responds in 3 months to queries. Responds in 6 months to mss. Sample copy for $10. Guidelines available online.

NONFICTION Needs general interest, innovative theaters and theater programs, trend stories, interview, people making a difference in Southeastern theater. Special issues: Playwriting (Fall issue, all stories submitted by January 1). No scholarly articles. **Buys 15-20 mss/year.** Send complete ms. Length: 1,000-3,000 words. **Pays $50 for feature stories.**

PHOTOS State availability of or send photos. Captions, identification of subjects, model releases required. Reviews transparencies, prints. Offers no additional payment for photos accepted with ms.

COLUMNS *Outside the Box* (innovative solutions to problems faced by designers and technicians), *400 Words* (column where the theater professionals can sound off on issues), 400 words; 800-1,000 words; *Words, Words, Words* (reviews of books on theater), 400 words. Query or send complete ms **No payment for columns.**

FARM

AGRICULTURAL EQUIPMENT

$ AG WEEKLY

Lee Agri-Media, P.O. Box 507, Twin Falls ID 83303. Fax: (208)734-9667. E-mail: mark.conlon@lee.net. Website: agweekly.com. **Contact:** Mark Conlon, editor. **40% freelance written.** Monthly tabloid covering regional farming and ranching with emphasis on Idaho. *Ag Weekly* is an agricultural publication covering production, markets, regulation, politics. Writers need to be familiar with Idaho agricultural commodities. Circ. 12,402. Byline given. Pays on publication. Publishes ms an average of 1 month after acceptance. Editorial lead time 1 month. Submit seasonal material 1 month in advance. Accepts queries by e-mail. Accepts simultaneous submissions. Responds in 2 weeks to queries. Responds in 1 month to mss. Sample copy available online. Guidelines for #10 sase.

NONFICTION Needs interview, new product, opinion, travel, ag-related. Does not want anything other than local/regional ag-related articles. No cowboy poetry. **Buys 100 mss/year.** Query. Length: 250-700 words. **Pays $40-70.**

PHOTOS State availability. Captions required. Reviews GIF/JPEG files. Offers $10/photo.

$$ IMPLEMENT & TRACTOR

Farm Journal, 120 West 4th St., Cedar Falls IA 50613. (319)277-3599. Fax: (319)277-3783. E-mail: mfischer@farmjournal.com or cfinck@farmjournal.com. Website: implementandtractor.com. **Contact:** Margy Fischer or Charlene Finck. **10% freelance written.** Bimonthly magazine covering the agricultural equipment industry. *"Implement & Tractor* offers equipment reviews and business news for agricultural equipment dealers, ag equipment manufacturers, distributors, and aftermarket suppliers." Estab. 1895. Circ. 5,000. Byline given. Pays on publication. Publishes ms an average of 3-4 months after acceptance. Editorial lead time 2 months. Accepts queries by mail, e-mail, fax. Responds in 2 months to queries. Sample copy for $6.

CROPS AND SOIL MANAGEMENT

$$ AMERICAN/WESTERN FRUIT GROWER

Meister Media Worldwide, 37733 Euclid Ave., Willoughby OH 44094. (440)942-2000. E-mail: avazzano@meistermedia.com; deddy@meistermedia.com. Website: fruitgrower.com. **Contact:** Ann-Marie Avazzano, managing editor; David Eddy, editor. **3% freelance written.** Annual magazine covering commercial fruit growing. How-to articles are best. Estab. 1880. Circ. 44,000. Byline given. Pays on publication. Publishes ms an average of 4 months after acceptance. Editorial lead time 2 months. Submit seasonal material 4 months in advance. Accepts queries by mail, e-mail, fax, phone. Responds in 2 weeks to queries. Responds in 2 months to mss. Sample copy and writer's

NONFICTION Needs how-to, better grow fruit crops. **Buys 6-10 mss/year.** Send complete ms. Length: 800-1,200 words. **Pays $200-250.**

PHOTOS Send photos. Reviews prints, slides. Negotiates payment individually.

$$ COTTON GROWER MAGAZINE

Cotton Media Group, 65 Germantown Court, Suite #202, Cordova TN 38018-4246. (901)756-8822. E-mail: mccue@meistermedia.com. **Contact:** Mike McCue, editor. **5% freelance written.** Monthly magazine covering cotton production, cotton markets and related subjects. Readers are mostly cotton producers who seek information on production practices, equipment and products related to cotton. Estab. 1901. Circ. 43,000. Byline given. Pays on acceptance. Publishes ms an average of 2 months after acceptance. Editorial lead time 2 months. Submit seasonal material 2 months in advance. Accepts queries by mail, e-mail, fax, phone. Accepts simultaneous submissions.

NONFICTION Needs interview, new product, photo feature, technical. No fiction or humorous pieces. **Buys 5-10 mss/year.** Query with published clips. Length: 500-800 words. **Pays $200-400.**

PHOTOS State availability. Captions, identification of subjects required. Reviews transparencies. Offers no additional payment for photos accepted with ms.

$ FRUIT GROWERS NEWS

Great American Publishing, P.O. Box 128, Sparta MI 49345. (616)887-9008. Fax: (616)887-2666. E-mail: fgnedit@fruitgrowersnews.com. Website: fruitgrowersnews.com. **Contact:** Matt Milkovich, managing editor. **10% freelance written**. Monthly tabloid covering agriculture. "Our objective is to provide commercial fruit growers of all sizes with information to help them succeed." Estab. 1961. Circ. 16,429. Pays on publication. Publishes ms an average of 2 months after acceptance. Editorial lead time 1-2 months. Submit seasonal material 3 months in advance. Accepts queries by mail, e-mail, fax. Accepts simultaneous submissions. Responds in 2 weeks to queries. Responds in 1 month to mss.

NONFICTION Needs general interest, interview, new product. No advertorials, other puff pieces. **Buys 25 mss/year.** Query with published clips and resume. Length: 600-1,000 words. **Pays $150-250.**

PHOTOS Send photos. Captions required. Reviews prints. Offers $15/photo.

$$ GOOD FRUIT GROWER

Washington State Fruit Commission, 105 S. 18th St., #217, Yakima WA 98901-2177. (509)575-2315. E-mail: jim.black@goodfruit.com. Website: goodfruit.com. **Contact:** Jim Black, managing editor. **20% freelance written**. Semi-monthly magazine covering tree fruit/grape growing. Estab. 1946. Circ. 11,000. Byline given. Pays on acceptance. Publishes ms an average of 3 months after acceptance. Accepts queries by mail, e-mail. Accepts simultaneous submissions. Responds in 1 week to queries. Responds in 1 month to mss.

NONFICTION Buys 50 mss/year. Query. Length: 500-1,500 words. **Pays 40-50¢/word.**

PHOTOS Contact: Jim Black. Reviews GIF/JPEG files. Negotiates payment individually.

$ GRAIN JOURNAL

Country Journal Publishing Co., 3065 Pershing Ct., Decatur IL 62526. (800)728-7511. Fax: (217)877-6647. E-mail: ed@grainnet.com. Website: grainnet.com. **Contact:** Ed Zdrojewski, editor. **5% freelance written**. Bimonthly magazine covering grain handling and merchandising. *Grain Journal* serves the North American grain industry, from the smallest country grain elevators and feed mills to major export terminals. Estab. 1972. Circ. 12,000. Byline sometimes given. Pays on publication. Publishes ms an average of 2 months after acceptance. Editorial lead time 2 months. Submit seasonal material 2 months in advance. Accepts simultaneous submissions.

NONFICTION Needs how-to, interview, new product, technical. Query. 750 words maximum. **Pays $100.**

PHOTOS Send photos. Captions, identification of subjects required. Reviews contact sheets, negatives, transparencies, 3x5 prints, electronic files. Offers $50-100/photo.

$ ONION WORLD

Columbia Publishing & Design, 413-B N. 20th Ave., Yakima WA 98902. (509)248-2452, ext. 105. Fax: (509)248-4056. E-mail: dbrent@columbiapublications.com. Website: onionworld.net. **Contact:** Brent Clement, editor. **25% freelance written**. Monthly magazine covering the world of onion production and marketing for onion growers and shippers. Estab. 1985. Circ. 5,500. Byline given. Pays on publication. Publishes ms an average of 1 month after acceptance. Submit seasonal material 1 month in advance. Accepts queries by e-mail or phone. Accepts simultaneous submissions. Responds in 1 month to queries. Sample copy for sae with 9×12 envelope and 5 First-Class stamps.

NONFICTION Needs general interest, historical, interview. **Buys 30 mss/year.** Query. Length: 1,200-1,250 words. **Pays $100 to $250 per article, depending upon length. Mileage paid, but query first.**

$ SPUDMAN

Great American Publishing, P.O. Box 128, Sparta MI 49345. (208)234-2634. Fax: (616)887-2666. E-mail: bills@spudman.com. Website: spudman.com. **Contact:** Bill Schaefer, Managing Editor. **10% freelance written**. Monthly magazine covering potato industry's growing, packing, processing, chipping. Estab. 1964. Circ. 10,000. Byline given. Pays on publication. Offers $75 kill fee. Publishes ms an average of 2 months after acceptance. Editorial lead time 2 months. Submit seasonal material 4 months in advance. Accepts queries by mail, e-mail. Responds in 2-3 weeks to queries. Sample copy for sae with 8 ½×11 envelope and 3 First-Class stamps. Guidelines for #10 sase.

💲 THE VEGETABLE GROWERS NEWS

Great American Publishing, P.O. Box 128, Sparta MI 49345. (616)887-9008, ext. 102. Fax: (616)887-2666. E-mail: writer@vegetablegrowersnews.com. Website: vegetablegrowersnews.com. **Contact:** Matt Milkovich, managing editor. **10% freelance written.** Monthly tabloid covering agriculture. Estab. 1970. Circ. 16,000. Pays on publication. Publishes ms an average of 2 months after acceptance. Editorial lead time 1-2 months. Submit seasonal material 3 months in advance. Accepts queries by mail, e-mail, fax. Accepts simultaneous submissions. Responds in 2 weeks to queries. Responds in 1 month to mss.

NONFICTION Needs general interest, interview, new product. No advertorials, other puff pieces. **Buys 25 mss/year.** Query with published clips and resume. Length: 800-1,200 words. **Pays $100-125.**

PHOTOS Send photos. Captions required. Reviews prints. Offers $15/photo.

DAIRY FARMING

💲💲 HOARD'S DAIRYMAN

W.D. Hoard and Sons, Co., P.O. Box 801, Fort Atkinson WI 53538. (920)563-5551. Fax: (920)563-7298. E-mail: editors@hoards.com. Website: hoards.com. Tabloid published 20 times/year covering dairy industry. We publish semi-technical information published for dairy-farm families and their advisors. Estab. 1885. Circ. 100,000. Byline given. Pays on acceptance. Publishes ms an average of 4 months after acceptance. Editorial lead time 2 months. Submit seasonal material 3 months in advance. Accepts queries by mail, e-mail, fax. Responds in 2 weeks to queries. Responds in 1 month to mss. Sample copy for 12×15 SAE and $3. Guidelines for #10 sase.

NONFICTION Needs how-to, technical. **Buys 60 mss/year.** Query. Length: 800-1,500 words. **Pays $150-350.**

PHOTOS Send photos. Reviews 2X2 transparencies. Offers no additional payment for photos accepted with ms.

COLUMNS Handy Hints that are published receive $30 and if you include a clear, reproducible photo, that earns you an additional $20. The photo should be at least 240 dpi (dots per inch) and approximately 4" x 6" in size to print well in our magazine. And, when you provide your full mailing address with your hint, payment will be sent promptly. (Hints and photos can also be mailed to the Hoard's Dairyman office).

💲💲 WESTERN DAIRYBUSINESS

Dairy Business Communications, 1200 W. Laurel Avenue, Visalia CA 93277. (800)934-7872; (559)802-3743. Fax: (559)802-3746. E-mail: rgoble@dairybusiness.com. Website: dairybusiness.com. **10% freelance written. Prefers to work with published/established writers.** Monthly magazine dealing with large-herd commercial dairy industry. Rarely publishes information about non-Western producers or dairy groups and events. Estab. 1922. Circ. 11,500. Byline given. Pays on publication. Publishes ms an average of 3 months after acceptance. Submit seasonal material 3 months in advance. Accepts queries by e-mail. Responds in 1 month to queries.

NONFICTION Needs interview, new product, opinion, industry analysis, industry analysis. No religion, nostalgia, politics, or 'mom and pop' dairies. Query, or e-mail complete ms. Length: 300-1,500 words. **Pays $50-400.**

💲💲 WESTERN DAIRY FARMER

Sun Media, 4504 61 Ave., Leduc AB T9E 3Z1 Canada. (780)986-2271. Fax: (780)986-6397. E-mail: john.greig@sunmedia.ca; paul.mahon@sunmedia.ca. Paul Mahon, publisher, editor-in-chief. **Contact:** John Greig, editor. **70% freelance written.** Bimonthly magazine covering the dairy industry. *Western Dairy Farmer* is a trade publication dealing with issues surrounding the dairy industry. The magazine features innovative articles on animal health, industry changes, new methods of dairying, and personal experiences. Sometimes highlights successful farmers. Estab. 1991. Circ. 6,300. Byline given. Pays on publication. Publishes ms an average of 4 months after acceptance. Editorial lead time 2 months. Submit seasonal material 2 months in advance. Accepts queries by mail, e-mail, fax. Responds in 2 weeks to queries; 2 months to mss. Sample copy for 9×12 SAE.

NONFICTION Needs general interest, how-to, interview, new product, personal experience, only exceptional stories, technical. Not interested in anything vague, trite, or not dairy related. **Buys 50 mss/year.** Query or send complete ms Length: 900-1,200 words. **Pays $75-150.**

PHOTOS State availability. Captions, identification of subjects, model releases required. Reviews GIF/JPEG files. Offers no additional payment for photos accepted with ms.

LIVESTOCK

$$ ANGUS BEEF BULLETIN

Angus Productions, Inc., 3201 Frederick Ave., St. Joseph MO 64506-2997. (816)383-5270. Fax: (816)233-6575. E-mail: shermel@angusjournal.com. Website: angusbeefbulletin.com. **Contact:** Shauna Rose Hermel, editor. **45% freelance written.** Tabloid published 5 times/year covering commercial cattle industry. The *Bulletin* is mailed free to commercial cattlemen who have purchased an Angus bull and had the registration transferred to them and to others who sign a request card. Estab. 1985. Circ. 97,000. Byline given. Pays on publication. Publishes ms an average of 3 months after acceptance. Editorial lead time 3 months. Submit seasonal material 3 months in advance. Accepts queries by mail, e-mail. Accepts simultaneous submissions. Responds in 3 weeks to queries. Responds in 3 months to mss. Sample copy for $5. Guidelines for #10 sase.

NONFICTION Needs how-to, cattle production, interview, technical, cattle production. **Buys 10 mss/year.** Query with published clips. Length: 800-2,500 words. **Pays $50-600.**

PHOTOS Send photos. Identification of subjects required. Reviews 5×7 transparencies, 5×7 glossy prints. Offers $25/photo.

$$$ ANGUS JOURNAL

Angus Productions Inc., 3201 Frederick Ave., St. Joseph MO 64506-2997. (816)383-5270. Fax: (816)233-6575. E-mail: shermel@angusjournal.com. Website: angusjournal.com. **40% freelance written.** Monthly magazine covering Angus cattle. The *Angus Journal* is the official magazine of the American Angus Association. Its primary function as such is to report to the membership association activities and information pertinent to raising Angus cattle. Estab. 1919. Circ. 13,500. Byline given. Pays on publication. Publishes ms an average of 3 months after acceptance. Editorial lead time 2 months. Submit seasonal material 3 months in advance. Accepts queries by mail, e-mail, fax. Accepts simultaneous submissions. Responds in 3 weeks to queries. Responds in 2 months to mss. Sample copy for $5. Guidelines for #10 sase.

NONFICTION Needs how-to, cattle production, interview, technical, related to cattle. **Buys 20-30 mss/year.** Query with published clips. Length: 800-3,500 words. **Pays $50-1,000.**

PHOTOS Send photos. Identification of subjects required. Reviews 5×7 glossy prints. Offers $25-400/photo.

$$ THE BRAHMAN JOURNAL

Carl and Victoria Lambert, 915 12th St., Hempstead TX 77445. (979)826-4347. Fax: (979)826-2007. E-mail: info@brahmanjournal.com; vlambert@brahmanjournal.com. Website: brahmanjournal.com. **Contact:** Victoria Lambert, editor. **10% freelance written.** Monthly magazine covering Brahman cattle. This publication provides timely and useful information about one of the largest and most dynamic breeds of beef cattle in the world. In each issue the Brahman Journal reports on Brahman shows, events, and sales as well as technical articles and the latest research as it pertains to the Brahman Breed. Estab. 1971. Circ. 4,000. Byline given. Pays on publication. Publishes ms an average of 2 months after acceptance. Submit seasonal material 3 months in advance. Sample copy for sae with 9×12 envelope and 5 First-Class stamps.

> "We promote, support, and inform the owners and admirers of American Brahman Cattle through honest and forthright journalism."

NONFICTION Needs general interest, historical, interview. Special issues: See 2009 Calendar online. **Buys 3-4 mss/year.** Query with published clips. Length: 1,200-3,000 words. **Pays $100-250.**

$$ THE CATTLEMAN

Texas and Southwestern Cattle Raisers Association, 1301 W. 7th St., Ft. Worth TX 76102-2660. E-mail: lionel@texascattleraisers.org. Website: thecattlemanmagazine.com. **25% freelance written.** Monthly magazine covering the Texas/Oklahoma beef cattle industry. We specialize in in-depth, management-type articles related to range and pasture, beef cattle production, animal health, nutrition, and marketing. We want 'how-to' articles. Estab. 1914. Circ. 15,400. Byline given. Pays on acceptance. Publishes ms an average of 2 months after acceptance. Editorial lead time 2 months. Submit seasonal material 6 months in advance. Accepts queries by mail, e-mail. Guidelines available online.

NONFICTION Needs how-to, interview, new product, personal experience, technical, ag research. Special issues: Editorial calendar themes include: Horses (January); Range and Pasture (February); Livestock Marketing (July); Hereford and Wildlife (August); Feedlots (September); Bull Buyers (October); Ranch Safety (December). Does not want to see anything not specifically related to beef production in the Southwest. **Buys 20 mss/year.** Query with published clips. Length: 1,500-2,000 words. **Pays $200-350 for assigned articles. Pays $100-350 for unsolicited articles.**

PHOTOS Identification of subjects required. Reviews transparencies, prints, digital files. Offers no additional payment for photos accepted with ms.

⊖⊜ FEED LOT MAGAZINE

Feed Lot Magazine, Inc., P.O. Box 850, Dighton KS 67839. (620)397-2838. Fax: (620)397-2839. E-mail: feedlot@st-tel.net. Website: feedlotmagazine.com. **40% freelance written.** Bimonthly magazine that provides readers with the most up-to-date information on the beef industry in concise, easy-to-read articles designed to increase overall awareness among the feedlot community. "The editorial information content fits a dual role: large feedlots and their related cow/calf operations, and large 500pl cow/calf, 100pl stocker operations. The information covers all phases of production from breeding, genetics, animal health, nutrition, equipment design, research through finishing fat cattle. *Feed Lot* publishes a mix of new information and timely articles which directly affect the cattle industry." Estab. 1993. Circ. 12,000. Byline given. Pays on publication. Offers 50% kill fee. Publishes ms an average of 2 months after acceptance. Editorial lead time 2 months. Submit seasonal material 6 months in advance. Accepts queries by mail, e-mail, fax. Responds in 1 month to queries. Sample copy and writer's guidelines for $1.50.

NONFICTION Needs interview, new product, cattle-related, photo feature. Send complete ms. Length: 100-400 words. **Pays 20¢/word.**

⊖ SHEEP! MAGAZINE

Countryside Publications, Ltd., Nathan Griffith, 3831 Trout Rd., Williamsburg WV 24991-7227. (715)785-7979. Fax: (715)785-7414. Website: sheepmagazine. com. **35% freelance written. Prefers to work with published/established writers.** Bimonthly magazine published in north-central Wisconsin. Estab. 1980. Circ. 11,000. Byline given. Pays on publication. Offers $30 kill fee. Submit seasonal material 3 months in advance.

○ "We're looking for clear, concise, useful information for sheep raisers who have a few sheep to a 1,000 ewe flock."

NONFICTION Needs book excerpts, how-to, on innovative lamb and wool marketing and promotion techniques, efficient record-keeping systems, or specific aspects of health and husbandry, interview, on experienced sheep producers who detail the economics and management of their operation, new product, of value to sheep producers; should be written by someone who has used them, technical, on genetics health and nutrition. **Buys 80 mss/year.** Send complete ms. Length: 750-2,500 words. **Pays $45-150.**

PHOTOS Color—vertical compositions of sheep and/or people—for cover. 35mm photos or other visuals improve chances of a sale. Identification of subjects required.

MANAGEMENT

⊖ AG JOURNAL

Arkansas Valley Publishing, P.O. Box 500, La Junta CO 81050. (719)384-1453. Fax: (719)384-8157, 5999. E-mail: publisher@ljtdmail.com. Website: agjournalonline. com. **Contact:** Candi Hill, editor. **20% freelance written.** Weekly journal covering agriculture. Estab. 1949. Circ. 11,000. Byline given. Pays on publication. Publishes ms an average of 2 weeks after acceptance. Editorial lead time 1 month. Submit seasonal material 1 month in advance. Accepts queries by e-mail. Responds in 2 weeks to queries. Sample copy and writer's

○ "The *Ag Journal* covers people, issues and events relevant to ag producers in our 7-state region (Colorado, Kansas, Oklahoma, Texas, Wyoming, Nebraska, New Mexico)."

NONFICTION Needs how-to, interview, new product, opinion, photo feature, technical. Query by e-mail only. **Pays 4¢/word.**

PHOTOS State availability. Captions, identification of subjects required. Offers $8/photo.

⊖⊜ NEW HOLLAND NEWS AND ACRES MAGAZINE

P.O. Box 1895, New Holland PA 17557-0903. (610)621-2253. E-mail: contact@newhollandmediakit.com. Website: newholland.com/na; agriculture.newholland.com.

Contact: Gary Martin, editor. **75% freelance written. Works with a small number of new/unpublished writers each year.** Each magazine published 4 times/year covering agriculture and non-farm country living; designed to entertain and inform farm families and rural homeowners and provide ideas for small acreage outdoor projects. Estab. 1960. Byline given. Pays on acceptance. Offers negotiable kill fee. Publishes ms an average of 8 months after acceptance. Submit seasonal material 8 months in advance. Accepts queries by mail. Responds in 2 months to queries. Sample copy and writer's guidelines for 9×12 SAE with 2 first-class stamps.

○ "Break in with features about people and their unique and attractive country living projects, such as outdoor pets (horses, camels, birds), building projects (cabins, barns, restorations), trees, flowers, landscaping, outdoor activities, part-time farms and businesses, and country-related antique collections."

NONFICTION Buys 40 mss/year. Query. **Pays $700-900.**

PHOTOS Professional photos only. Captions, identification of subjects, model releases required. Reviews color photos in any format. Pays $50-300, $500 for cover shot.

💲⊖ SMALLHOLDER MAGAZINE

Newsquest Media Group, Hook House, Hook Rd., Wimblington, March Cambs PE15 0QL United Kingdom. Phone/Fax: (44)(135)474-1538. E-mail: liz.wright1@btconnect.com. Website: smallholder.co.uk. Accepts queries by e-mail. Sample copy available online. Guidelines by e-mail.

○ "Copy is required at least two months before publication, e.g. 1st April for June. News items may be accepted up until one month before publication, e.g. 1st May for June. The Editor's decision on copy is final and, although every effort will be made to return manuscripts and photos, no responsibility can be accepted."

NONFICTION Length: 700-1,400 words. **Pays 4£/word.**

PHOTOS Send photos. Reviews 300 dpi digital images. Pays £5-50.

MISCELLANEOUS FARM

💲⊖ ACRES U.S.A.

P.O. Box 91299, Austin TX 78709-1299. (512)892-4400. Fax: (512)892-4448. E-mail: editor@acresusa.com.

Website: acresusa.com. "Monthly trade journal written by people who have a sincere interest in the principles of organic and sustainable agriculture." Estab. 1970. Circ. 18,000. Byline given. Pays on publication. Editorial lead time 4 months. Submit seasonal material 6 months in advance. Accepts queries by mail, e-mail, fax. Accepts simultaneous submissions. Sample copy and writer's

NONFICTION Needs expose, how-to, personal experience. Special issues: Seeds (January), Poultry (February), Compost/Compost Tea (April), Cattle & Grazing (May), Dairy (June), Grains (August), Soil Fertility & Testing (October). Does not want poetry, fillers, product profiles, or anything with a promotional tone. **Buys about 50 mss/year.** Send complete ms. Length: 1,000-2,500 words. **Pays 10¢/word**

PHOTOS State availability of or send photos. Captions, identification of subjects required. Reviews GIF/JPEG/TIF files. Negotiates payment individually.

💲💲 BEE CULTURE

P.O. Box 706, Medina OH 44256-0706. Fax: (330)725-5624. E-mail: kim@beeculture.com. Website: beeculture.com. **Contact:** Mr. Kim Flottum, editor. **50% freelance written.** Covers the natural science of honey bees. "Monthly magazine for beekeepers and those interested in the natural science of honey bees, with environmentally-oriented articles relating to honey bees or pollination." Estab. 1873. Pays on publication. Publishes ms an average of 4 months after acceptance. Accepts queries by mail, e-mail, fax, phone. Responds in 1 month to mss. Sample copy for sae with 9×12 envelope and 5 first-class stamps. Guidelines and sample copy available online.

NONFICTION Needs interview, personal experience, photo feature. No how I began beekeeping articles. Highly advanced, technical, and scientific abstracts accepted for review for quarterly Refered section. 2,000 words average. **Pays $200-250.**

REPRINTS Send photocopy and information about when and where the material previously appeared. Pays about the same as for an original article, on negotiation.

PHOTOS Contact: Kim Flottum, Editor. Color prints, 5×7 standard, but 3x5 are OK. Electronic images encouraged. Digital jpg, color only, at 300 dpi best, prints acceptable. Model release required. Photo captions preferred. Pays $50 for cover photos. Photos payment included with article payment.

⊛⊛⊛ PRODUCE BUSINESS

Phoenix Media Network Inc., P.O. Box 810425, Boca Raton FL 33481-0425. (561)994-1118. E-mail: kwhitacre@phoenixmedianet.com; info@producebusiness.com. Website: producebusiness.com. **90% freelance written**. Monthly magazine covering produce and floral marketing. Estab. 1985. Circ. 16,000. Byline given. Pays 30 days after publication. Offers $50 kill fee. Editorial lead time 2 months. Accepts queries by e-mail. No

○ "We address the buying end of the produce/floral industry, concentrating on supermarkets, chain restaurants, etc."

NONFICTION Does not want unsolicited articles. **Buys 150 mss/year.** Query with published clips. Length: 1,200-10,000 words. **Pays $240-1,200.**

REGIONAL FARM

⊛⊛ AMERICAN AGRICULTURIST

5227 Baltimore Pike, Littlestown PA 17340. (717)359-0150. Fax: (717)359-0250. E-mail: jvogel@farmprogress.com. Website: farmprogress.com. **20% freelance written**. Monthly magazine covering "cutting-edge technology and news to help farmers improve their operations.". "We publish cutting-edge technology with ready on-farm application." Estab. 1842. Circ. 32,000. Pays on publication. Publishes ms an average of 3 months after acceptance. Editorial lead time 3 months. Submit seasonal material 3 months in advance. Accepts queries by e-mail, fax. Accepts simultaneous submissions. Responds in 2 weeks to queries. Responds in 1 month to mss. Guidelines for #10 SASE.

NONFICTION Needs how-to, humor, inspirational, interview, new product, personal experience, photo feature feature, technical, "No stories without a strong tie to Mid-Atlantic farming.". **Buys 20 mss/year.** Query. Length: 500-1,000 words. **Pays $300-500.**

PHOTOS Send photos. Captions, identification of subjects, model releases required. Reviews transparencies, JPEG files. Offers $75-200/photo.

COLUMNS Contact: Kathleen O'Connor, editorial assistant. Country Air (humor, nostalgia, inspirational), 300-400 words. **Buys 12 mss/year.** Send complete ms. **Pays $100.**

POETRY Contact: Kathleen O'Connor, editorial assistant. Needs free verse, light verse, traditional. All poetry must have a link to New York farming. Buys 2 poems/year. Length: 12-40 lines. **Pays $50.**

⊛⊛ FLORIDA GROWER

Meister Media Worldwide, 1555 Howell Branch Rd., Suite C-204, Winter Park FL 32789-1170. (407)539-6552. Fax: (407)539-6544. E-mail: fgiles@meistermedia.com; pprusnak@meistermedia.com. Website: growingproduce.com/floridagrower/. Paul Rusnak, managing editor. **Contact:** Frank Giles, editor. **10% freelance written**. "Monthly magazine edited for the Florida farmer with commercial production interest primarily in citrus, vegetables, and other ag endeavors. Our goal is to provide articles which update and inform on such areas as production, ag financing, farm labor relations, technology, safety, education, and regulation". Estab. 1907. Circ. 12,200. Byline given. Pays on publication. Editorial lead time 2 months. Submit seasonal material 3 months in advance. Accepts queries by mail, e-mail, fax, phone. Responds in 1 month to queries. Sample copy for sae with 9×12 envelope and 5 First-Class stamps.

NONFICTION Needs interview, photo feature, technical. Query with published clips. Length: 700-1,000 words. **Pays $150-250.**

PHOTOS Send photos.

⊛ THE LAND

Free Press Co., P.O. Box 3169, Mankato MN 56002-3169. (507)345-4523. E-mail: editor@thelandonline.com. Website: thelandonline.com. **40% freelance written**. Weekly tabloid covering farming in Minnesota and Northern Iowa. Although we're not tightly focused on any one type of farming, our articles must be of interest to farmers. In other words, will your article topic have an impact on people who live and work in rural areas? Prefers to work with Minnesota or Iowa writers. Estab. 1976. Circ. 33,000. Byline given. Pays on acceptance. Publishes ms an average of 2 months after acceptance. Editorial lead time 2 months. Submit seasonal material 2 months in advance. Accepts queries by mail, e-mail. Responds in 3 weeks to queries. Responds in 2 months to mss. Guidelines for #10 SASE.

NONFICTION Needs general interest, ag, how-to, crop, livestock production, marketing. **Buys 80 mss/year.** Query. Length: 500-750 words. **Pays $50-70 for assigned articles.**

PHOTOS Send photos. Reviews contact sheets. Negotiates payment individually.

COLUMNS Query. **Pays $10-50.**

💲💲 MAINE ORGANIC FARMER & GARDENER

Maine Organic Farmers & Gardeners Association, 662 Slab City Rd., Lincolnville ME 04849. (207)763-3043. E-mail: jenglish@tidewater.ne. Website: mofga.org. **40% freelance written. Prefers to work with published/established local writers.** Quarterly newspaper. "The *MOF&G* promotes and encourages sustainable agriculture and environmentally sound living. Our primary focus is organic farming, gardening, and forestry, but we also deal with local, national, and international agriculture, food, and environmental issues." Estab. 1976. Circ. 10,000. Byline and bio offered. Pays on publication. Publishes ms an average of 8 months after acceptance. Submit seasonal material 1 year in advance. Accepts queries by mail, e-mail. Accepts simultaneous submissions. Responds in 2 months to queries. Sample copy for $2 and SAE with 7 first-class stamps; from MOFGA, P.O. Box 170, Unity ME 04988. Guidelines available at mofga.org.

NONFICTION Buys 30 mss/year. Send complete ms. Length: 250-3,000 words. **Pays $25-300.**

FINANCE

♻💲💲💲 ADVISOR'S EDGE

Rogers Media, Inc., 156 Front St. W., 4th Floor, Toronto ON M5J 2L6 Canada. E-mail: donna.kerry@rci.rogers.com. Website: advisorsedge.ca. Philip Porado, exec. editor, philip.porado@advisor.rogers.com. **Contact:** Donna Kerry, publisher. Monthly magazine covering the financial industry (financial advisors and investment advisors). "*Advisor's Edge* focuses on sales and marketing opportunities for the financial advisor (how they can build their business and improve relationships with clients). Estab. 1998. Circ. 36,000. Byline given. Pays on publication. Offers 25% kill fee. Publishes ms an average of 3 months after acceptance. Editorial lead time 3 months. Accepts queries by e-mail. Sample copy available online.

NONFICTION Needs how-to, interview. No articles that aren't relevant to how a financial advisor does his/her job. **Buys 12 mss/year.** Query with published clips. Length: 1,500-2,000 words. **Pays $900 (Canadian).**

♻🗣💲💲💲 AFP EXCHANGE

Association for Financial Professionals, 4520 East-West Hwy., Suite 750, Bethesda MD 20814. (301)907-2862. E-mail: exchange@afponline.org. Website: afponline.org. **20% freelance written.** Monthly magazine covering corporate treasury, corporate finance, B2B payments issues, corporate risk management, accounting and regulatory issues from the perspective of corporations. Welcome interviews with CFOs and senior level practitioners. Best practices and practical information for corporate CFOs and treasurers. Tone is professional, intended to appeal to financial professionals on the job. Most accepted articles are written by professional journalists and editors, many featuring high-level AFP members in profile and case studies. Estab. 1979. Circ. 25,000. Byline given. Pays on publication. Offers kill fee. Pays negotiable kill fee in advance. Editorial lead time 2 months. Submit seasonal material 3 months in advance. Accepts queries by e-mail. Responds in 1 week to queries. Responds in 1 month to mss. Guidelines available online.

NONFICTION Contact: Exchange Magazine Editor. Needs book excerpts, how-to, interview, personal experience, technical. PR-type articles pointing to any type of product or solution **Buys 3-4 year mss/year.** Query. Length: 1,100-1,800 words. **Pays 75¢/word minimum, &1.00 maximum for assigned articles.**

COLUMNS Cash Flow Forecasting (practical tips for treasurers, CFOs); Financial Reporting (insight, practical tips); Risk Management (practical tips for treasurers, CFOs); Corporate Payments (practical tips for treasurers), all 1,000-1,300 words; Professional Development (success stories, career related, about high level financial professionals), 1,100 words. **Buys 10 mss/year.** Query. **Pays $75¢/word-$1.00/word.**

FILLERS Needs anecdotes. **Buys open to consideration mss/year.** Length: 400-700 words. **Pays 75¢.**

💲💲💲 COLLECTIONS & CREDIT RISK

SourceMedia, 550 West Van Buren St., Suite 1110, Chicago IL 60607. E-mail: darren.waggoner@sourcemedia.com; jeffrey.green@sourcemedia.com. Website: creditcollectionsworld.com. **Contact:** Darren Waggoner, chief editor; Jeffrey Green, editorial director. **33% freelance written.** Monthly journal covering debt collections and credit risk management. "*Collections & Credit Risk* is the only magazine that brings news and trends of strategic and competitive importance to collections and credit-policy executives who are driving the collections industry's growth and diversification in both commercial and consumer credit. These executives work for financial institutions, insurance companies, collections agencies, law firms and attorney networks, health-care providers, retailers, telecoms and utility companies, manufacturers, wholesalers, and government agencies." Estab. 1996. Circ. 30,000. Byline given. Pays on acceptance. Offers kill fee. Kill fee determined case by case. Publishes ms an average of 3 months after acceptance. Editorial lead time 3 months. Accepts queries by mail. Sample copy free or online.

NONFICTION Needs interview, technical, business news and analysis. No unsolicited submissions accepted—freelancers work on assignment only. **Buys 30-40 mss/year.** Query with published clips. Length: 1,000-2,500 words. **Pays $800-1,000.**

⑨⑨⑨ CREDIT TODAY

P.O. Box 720, Roanoke VA 24004. (540)343-7500. E-mail: robl@credittoday.net; editor@credittoday. net. Website: credittoday.net. **Contact:** Rob Lawson, publisher. **50% freelance written.** Monthly newsletter covering business or trade credit. Make pieces actionable, personable, and a quick read. Estab. 1997. No byline given. Pays on acceptance. Publishes ms an average of 2 months after acceptance. Editorial lead time 1-2 months. Accepts queries by e-mail. No

NONFICTION Needs how-to, interview, technical. Does not want puff pieces promoting a particular product or vendor. **Buys 20 mss/year.** Send complete ms. Length: 700-1,800 words. **Pays $200-1,400.**

⑨⑨ CREDIT UNION MANAGEMENT

Credit Union Executives Society, 5510 Research Park Dr., Madison WI 53711. (608)271-2664. E-mail: lisa@ cues.org; cues@cues.org. Website: cumanagement.org. **Contact:** Lisa Hochgraf, editor. **44% freelance written.** Monthly magazine covering credit union, banking trends, management, HR, marketing issues. Our philosophy mirrors the credit union industry of cooperative financial services. Estab. 1978. Circ. 7,413. Pays on acceptance. Publishes ms an average of 2 months after acceptance. Editorial lead time 3 months. Submit seasonal material 4 months in advance. Accepts queries by mail. Accepts simultaneous submissions. Responds in 2 weeks to queries. Responds in 1 month to mss. Sample copy and writer's

NONFICTION Needs book excerpts, how-to, be a good mentor/leader, recruit, etc., interview, technical. **Buys 74 mss/year.** Query with published clips. Length: 700-2,400 words. **$250-350 for assigned features.** Phone expenses only

COLUMNS Management Network (book/Web reviews, briefs), 300 words; e-marketing, 700 words; Point of Law, 700 words; Best Practices (new technology/operations trends), 700 words. Query with published clips.

⑨⑨ EQUITIES MAGAZINE, LLC

439 N. Cannon Dr., Suite 220, Beverly Hills CA 90210. (310)271-1700. E-mail: equitymag@aol.com. Website: equitiesmagazine.com; facebook.com/pages/EQUITIES-Magazine/155271407650. **50% freelance written.** "We are a seven-issues-a-year financial magazine covering the fastest-growing public companies in the world. We study the management of companies and act as critics reviewing their performances. We aspire to be `The Shareholder's Friend.' We want to be a bridge between quality public companies and sophisticated investors." Estab. 1951. Circ. 18,000. Byline given. Pays on publication. Publishes ms an average of 2 months after acceptance. Accepts queries by mail. Sample copy for sae with 9×12 envelope and 5 First-Class stamps.

NONFICTION Needs expose, new product, technical. **Buys 30 mss/year.** Query with published clips. Length: 300-1,500 words. **Pays $250-750 for assigned articles, more for very difficult or investigative pieces.**

PHOTOS Send color photos with submission. Identification of subjects required. Reviews contact sheets, negatives, transparencies, prints. Offers no additional payment for photos accepted with ms.

COLUMNS Pays $25-75 for assigned items only.

⑨⑨⑨ THE FEDERAL CREDIT UNION

National Association of Federal Credit Unions, 3138 10th St. N., Arlington VA 22201. (703)522-4770; (800)336-4644. Fax: (703)524-1082. E-mail: sbroaddus@nafcu.org. Website: nafcu.org. **Contact:** Susan Broaddus, managing editor. **30% freelance written.** Estab. 1967. Circ. 8,000. Byline given. Pays on publication. Publishes ms an average of 3 months after acceptance. Submit seasonal material 5 months in advance. Accepts queries by mail, e-mail, fax. Accepts simultaneous submissions. Responds in 2 months to queries. Sample copy for sae with 10x13 envelope and 5 First-Class stamps. Guidelines for #10 sase.

○ "Looking for writers with financial, banking, or credit union experience, but will work with inexperienced (unpublished) writers based on writing skill. Published bimonthly, *The Feder-*

al Credit Union is the official publication of the National Association of Federal Credit Unions. The magazine is dedicated to providing credit union management, staff, and volunteers with in-depth information (HR, technology, security, board management, etc.) they can use to fulfill their duties and better serve their members. The editorial focus includes coverage of management issues, operations, and technology as well as volunteer-related issues."

NONFICTION Needs humor, inspirational, interview. Query with published clips and SASE. Length: 1,200-2,000 words. **Pays $400-1,000.**

PHOTOS Send photos. Identification of subjects, model releases required. Reviews 35mm transparencies, 5×7 prints, high-resolution photos. Offers no additional payment for photos accepted with ms. Pays $50-500.

🟢🟢 SERVICING MANAGEMENT

Zackin Publications, P.O. Box 2180, Waterbury CT 06722. (800)325-6745. Fax: (203)262-4680. E-mail: bates@sm-online.com. Website: sm-online.com. John Clapp, editor. **Contact:** Michael Bates, editor. **15% freelance written**. Monthly magazine covering residential mortgage servicing. Estab. 1989. Circ. 20,000. Byline given. Pays on acceptance. Publishes ms an average of 2 months after acceptance. Accepts queries by mail, e-mail, fax, phone. Responds in 2 weeks to queries. Guidelines available online.

NONFICTION Needs how-to, interview, new product, technical. **Buys 10 mss/year.** Query. Length: 1,500-2,500 words.

PHOTOS State availability. Identification of subjects required. Reviews contact sheets. Offers no additional payment for photos accepted with ms.

COLUMNS Buys 5 mss/year. Query. **Pays $200.**

🟢🟢🟢🟢 USAA MAGAZINE

USAA, 9800 Fredericksburg Rd., San Antonio TX 78288. E-mail: usaamagazine@usaa.com. Website: usaa.com/maglinks. **80% freelance written**. Quarterly magazine covering financial security for USAA members. "Conservative, common-sense approach to personal finance issues. Especially interested in how-to articles and pieces with actionable tips." Estab. 1970. Circ. 4.2 million. Byline given. Pays on acceptance. Offers 25% kill fee. Publishes ms an average of 4 months after acceptance. Editorial lead time 6 months. Submit seasonal material 6 months in ad-

vance. Accepts queries by e-mail. Responds in 6-8 weeks to queries. No mss accepted. Sample copy available online. Guidelines by e-mail.

NONFICTION Needs general interest, (finance), historical, (military), how-to, (personal finance), interview, (military/financial), personal experience, (finance). No poetry, photos, lifestyle unrelated to military or personal finance. **Buys 20 mss/year.** Query with published clips. Length: 750-1,500 words. **Pays $750-1,500 for assigned articles.**

🟢🟢🟢🟢 WEALTH MANAGER

33-41 Newark St., 2nd Floor, Hoboken NJ 07030. (201)526-2344. Fax: (201)526-1260. E-mail: jgreen@sbmedia.com. Website: wealthmanagermag.com. **Contact:** James Green, group editor-in-chief. **90% freelance written**. Magazine published 11 times/year for financial advisors. Estab. 1999. Circ. 50,000. Byline given. Pays on acceptance. Publishes ms an average of 3 months after acceptance. Editorial lead time 4 months. Submit seasonal material 4 months in advance. Accepts queries by e-mail. Responds in 1 month to queries.

💬 "Stories should provide insight and information for the financial adviser. Put yourself on the adviser's side of the table and cover the issues thoroughly from his/her perspective. The piece should delve beneath the surface. We need specific examples, professional caveats, advice from professionals."

NONFICTION Needs book excerpts, interview, technical. Do not submit anything that does not deal with financial planning issues or the financial markets. **Buys 30-40 mss/year.** Query with published clips. Length: 1,500-3,000 words. **Pays $1.50/word for assigned articles.**

FLORIST, NURSERIES AND LANDSCAPERS

🟢🟢 DIGGER

Oregon Association of Nurseries, 29751 SW Town Center Loop W., Wilsonville OR 97070. (503)682-5089; (800) 342-6401. Fax: (503)682-5099. E-mail: ckipp@oan.org; info@oan.org. Website: oan.org. **Contact:** Curt Kipp, publications manager. **50% freelance written**. Monthly magazine covering nursery and greenhouse industry. Our readers are mainly nursery and greenhouse operators and owners who propagate nursery stock/crops, so we write with them in mind. Circ. 8,000. Byline given. Pays on receipt of copy. Offers 100% kill fee. Publishes ms an average of 2 months after acceptance. Editorial lead time 6 weeks. Submit seasonal material 2 months in advance. Accepts queries by mail, e-mail, fax, phone. Sample copy and writer's

◉ "*Digger* is a monthly magazine that focuses on industry trends, regulations, research, marketing and membership activities. In August the magazine becomes "*Digger Farwest Edition*," with all the features of *Digger* plus a complete guide to the annual Farwest Show, one of North America's top-attended nursery industry trade shows."

NONFICTION Needs general interest, how-to, propagation techniques, other crop-growing tips, interview, personal experience, technical. Special issues: Farwest Edition (August)—this is a triple-size issue that runs in tandem with our annual trade show (14,500 circulation for this issue). No articles not related or pertinent to nursery and greenhouse industry. **Buys 20-30 mss/year.** Query. Length: 800-2,000 words. **Pays $125-400 for assigned articles. Pays $100-300 for unsolicited articles.**

PHOTOS State availability. Captions, identification of subjects required. Reviews high-res digital images sent by e-mail or on CD preferred. Offers $25-150/photo.

ⓒ GROWERTALKS

Ball Publishing, 335 N. River St., P.O. Box 9, Batavia IL 60510. (630)588-3401; (630)588—3385. Fax: (630)208-9350. E-mail: jzurko@ballpublishing.com; cbeytes@growertalks.com. Website: growertalks.com. **Contact:** Jen Zurko. **50% freelance written.** Monthly magazine. Estab. 1937. Circ. 9,500. Byline given. Pays on publication. Publishes ms an average of 3 months after acceptance. Editorial lead time 4 months. Submit seasonal material 3 months in advance. Accepts queries by mail, e-mail, fax. Responds in 1 month to queries. Sample copy and writer's

◉ "*GrowerTalks* serves the commercial greenhouse grower. Editorial emphasis is on floricultural crops: bedding plants, potted floral crops, foliage and fresh cut flowers. Our readers are growers, managers, and owners. We're looking for writers who've had experience in the greenhouse industry."

NONFICTION Needs how-to, time- or money-saving projects for professional flower/plant growers, interview, ornamental horticulture growers, personal experience, of a grower, technical, about growing process in greenhouse setting. No articles that promote only one product. **Buys 36 mss/year.** Query. Length: 1,200-1,600 words. **Pays $125 minimum for assigned articles. Pays $75 minimum for unsolicited articles.**

PHOTOS State availability. Captions, identification of subjects, model releases required. Reviews 2½×2½ slides and 3×5 prints. Negotiates payment individually.

ⓒⓒ THE GROWING EDGE

New Moon Publishing, Inc., P.O. Box 1027, Corvallis OR 97339. (541)745-7773. Fax: (541)757-0028. Website: growingedge.com. **Contact:** Jenie Skoy, editor. **85% freelance written.** Bimonthly magazine covering indoor and outdoor high-tech gardening techniques and tips. Estab. 1980. Circ. 20,000. Byline given. Pays on publication. Publishes ms an average of 3 months after acceptance. Submit seasonal material 6 months in advance. Accepts queries by mail, e-mail, online submission form. Responds in 3 months to queries. Sample copy for $3. Guidelines available online.

NONFICTION Needs how-to, interview, personal experience, must be technical, book reviews, general horticulture and agriculture. Query. Ms format: double-spaced typed or word-processed; final, accepted manuscript must be on computer disk (include hard copy); e-mail is acceptable. Length: 500-3,500 words. **Pays 20¢/word (10¢ for first rights, 5¢ for nonexclusive reprint and nonexclusive electronic rights).**

PHOTOS Pays $25-175. Pays on publication. Credit line given.

ⓒⓒ TREE CARE INDUSTRY MAGAZINE

Tree Care Industry Association, 136 Harvey Rd., Suite 101, Londonderry NH 03053. (800)733-2622 or (603)314-5380. Fax: (603)314-5386. E-mail: staruk@tcia.org. Website: treecareindustry.org. **Contact:** Don Staruk, editor. **50% freelance written.** Monthly magazine covering tree care and landscape maintenance. Estab. 1990. Circ. 27,500. Byline given. Pays within 1 month of publication. Publishes manuscripts an average of 3 months after acceptance. Editorial lead time 10 weeks. Submit seasonal material 3 months in advance. Accepts queries by e-mail. Responds within 2 days to queries. Responds in 2 months to manuscripts. View PDFs online.

NONFICTION Needs book excerpts, historical, interview, new product, technical. **Buys 60 manuscripts/ year mss/year.** Query with published clips. Length: 900-3,500 words. **Pays negotiable rate.**

PHOTOS Send photos with submission by e-mail or FTP site. Captions, identification of subjects required. Reviews prints. Negotiate payment individually.

COLUMNS Buys 40 mss/year. Send complete manuscript. **Pays $100 and up.**

GOVERNMENT AND PUBLIC SERVICE

$$ AMERICAN CITY & COUNTY

Penton Media, 6151 Powers Ferry Rd. NW, Suite 200, Atlanta GA 30339. (770)618-0199. Fax: (770)618-0349. E-mail: bill.wolpin@penton.com; lindsay.isaacs@penton.com. Website: americancityandcounty.com. **Contact:** Lindsay Isaacs, managing editor; Bill Wolpin, editorial director. **40% freelance written.** Monthly magazine covering local and state government in the United States. Estab. 1909. Circ. 75,000. Byline given. Pays on publication. Offers 25% kill fee. Publishes ms an average of 2 months after acceptance. Editorial lead time 3 months. Accepts queries by e-mail. Accepts simultaneous submissions. Sample copy available online. Guidelines by e-mail.

NONFICTION Needs new product, local and state government news analysis. **Buys 36 mss/year.** Query. Length: 600-2,000 words. **Pays 30¢/published word.**

PHOTOS State availability. Captions required. Reviews GIF/JPEG files. Negotiates payment individually.

COLUMNS Issues & Trends (local and state government news analysis), 500-700 words. **Buys 24 ms/year. mss/year.** Query. **Pays $150-250.**

$ AMPC TODAY

Associated Mail and Parcel Centers (AMPC), 5411 E. State St., Suite 202, Rockford IL 61108. Fax: (815)316-8256. E-mail: articles@ampc.org. Website: ampc.org. Ellen Peters, editor. **Contact:** Jim Kitzmiller, Exec. Director. **85% freelance articles.** Mail and Parcel Industry/Retail Shipping Stores. "Our readers are the owners and operators of retail shipping and business service stores. These are convenience stores for packing, shipping, and other services including mailbox rental and mail forwarding. The stores are both independent and franchise operated; they are small and generally family or owner operated. The biggest obstacle to success is for the owner to leave the store for training, networking, planning, managing, and sales." Estab. 1984. Circ. 6 months: 2,400. Byline given. Pays on publication. 3 months from acceptance to publication. Editorial lead time: 3 months. Accepts queries by mail, e-mail. Accepts previously published submissions.Accepts simultaneous submissions. Sample copy online at website.

NONFICTION Needs essays, how-to, inspirational, interview, new product, technical, Typical topics can be packing, shipping, mailbox rentals, freight shipping, UPS, FedEx, DHL, USPS, bulk mailing, copy service, binding, laminating, retail fill items, packaging supplies, custom boxes, customer service, store profiles, and diversified profit centers. Send complete ms. 500-2,000/words. **Pays $50-150 for assigned articles and for unsolicited articles.** Pays expenses sometimes (limit agreed upon in advance). Does not pay with contributor copies or other premiums rather than cash.

PHOTOS Send photos with submission. Requires identification of subjects. Review GIF/JPEG files. Offers no additional payment for photos accepted with ms.

COLUMNS Column pays $50-150.

$$ COUNTY

Texas Association of Counties, P.O. Box 2131, Austin TX 78768-2131. (512)478-8753. Fax: (512)481-1240. E-mail: marias@county.org. Website: county.org. **Contact:** Maria Sprow, managing editor. **15% freelance written.** Bimonthly magazine covering county and state government in Texas. "We provide elected and appointed county officials with insights and information that help them do their jobs and enhances communications among the independent office-holders in the courthouse." Estab. 1988. Circ. 5,500. Byline given. Pays on acceptance. Publishes ms an average of 2 months after acceptance. Editorial lead time 2 months. Submit seasonal material 4 months in advance. Accepts queries by mail, e-mail, phone. Responds in 2 weeks to queries. Responds in 1 month to mss. Sample copy and writer's guidelines for 8×10 SAE with 3 first-class stamps.

NONFICTION Needs historical, photo feature, government innovations. **Buys 5 mss/year.** Query with published clips. Length: 1,000-3,000 words. **Pays $500-700.**

PHOTOS State availability. Captions, identification of subjects, model releases required. Negotiates payment individually.

COLUMNS Safety; Human Resources; Risk Management (all directed toward education of Texas county officials), maximum length 1,000 words. **Buys 2 mss/year. mss/year.** Query with published clips. **Pays $500**

$$ FIRE CHIEF

Primedia Business, 330 N. Wabash Ave.,, Suite 2300, Chicago IL 60611. (312)595-1080. Fax: (312)595-0295. E-mail: glenn.bischoff@penton.com. Website: firechief.com. Glenn Bischoff, editor. **60% freelance written.** Monthly magazine. *Fire Chief* is the management magazine of the fire service, addressing the administrative, personnel, training, prevention/education, professional development, and operational issues faced by chiefs and other fire officers, whether in paid, volunteer, or combination departments. We're potentially interested in any article that can help them do their jobs better, whether that's as incident commanders, financial managers, supervisors, leaders, trainers, planners, or ambassadors to municipal officials or the public. Estab. 1956. Circ. 53,000. Byline given. Pays on publication. Offers kill fee. Kill fee negotiable. Publishes ms an average of 6 months after acceptance. Editorial lead time 2 months. Submit seasonal material 4 months in advance. Accepts queries by mail, e-mail, fax. Responds in 1 month to queries. Responds in 2 months to mss. Sample copy and submission guidelines free or online.

NONFICTION Needs how-to, technical. "We do not publish fiction, poetry or historical articles. We also aren't interested in straightforward accounts of fires or other incidents, unless there are one or more specific lessons to be drawn from a particular incident, especially lessons that are applicable to a large number of departments." **Buys 50-60 mss/year.** Query first with published clips. Length: 1,000-10,000 words. **Pays $50-400.**

PHOTOS State availability. Captions, identification of subjects required. Reviews transparencies, prints.

COLUMNS Training Perspectives; EMS Viewpoints; Sound Off; Volunteer Voice; all 1,000-1,800 words.

FIRE ENGINEERING

PennWell Corporation, 21-00 Route 208 S., Fair Lawn NJ 07410. (800)962-6484, ext. 5047. E-mail: dianef@pennwell.com. Website: fireengineering.com. **Contact:** Diane Feldman, executive editor. Monthly magazine covering issues of importance to firefighters. Accepts queries by mail, e-mail. Responds in 2-3 months to mss. Guidelines available online.

NONFICTION Needs how-to, new product,, incident reports, training. Send complete ms.

PHOTOS Reviews electronic format only: JPEG/TIFF/EPS files (300 dpi).

COLUMNS Volunteers Corner; Training Notebook; Rescue Company; The Engine Company; The Truck Company; Fire Prevention Bureau; Apparatus; The Shops; Fire Service EMS; Fire Service Court; Speaking of Safety; Fire Commentary; Technology Today; and Innovations: Homegrown. Send complete ms.

FIRE-RESCUE MAGAZINE

525 B St., Suite 1800, P.O. Box 469012, San Diego CA 92101. (800)266-5367. Fax: (619)699-6396. E-mail: s.pieper@elsevier.com; jfoskett@elsevier.com. Website: firefighternation.com. **Contact:** Shannon Pieper, deputy editor. Covers the fire and rescue markets. Our "Read It Today, Use It Tomorrow" mission weaves through every article and image we publish. Our readers consist of fire chiefs, company officers, training officers, firefighters, and technical rescue personnel. Estab. 1997. Circ. 50,000. Pays on publication. Accepts queries by mail, e-mail. Responds in 1 month to mss. Guidelines available online.

> Read back issues of the magazine to learn our style. Research back issues to ensure we haven't covered your topic within the past three years. Read and follow the instructions on our guidelines page.

NONFICTION Needs general interest, how-to, interview, new product, technical. "All story ideas must be submitted with a cover letter that outlines your qualifications and includes your name, full address, phone, fax, social security or tax ID number, and e-mail address. We accept story submissions in one of the following two formats: query letters and manuscripts." Length: 800-2,200 words. **Features: $100—$200.**

PHOTOS Digital images in jpg, tiff, or eps format at 72 dpi for initial review. We require 300 dpi resolution for publication. If you send images as attachments via e-mail, compress your files with Stuffit, Disk Doubler, etc.

$$ FIREHOUSE MAGAZINE

Patricia Maroder, 3 Huntington Quad., Suite 301N, Melville NY 11747. (631)845-2700. Fax: (631)845-7218. E-mail: editors@firehouse.com. Website: firehouse.com. Harvey Eisner, editor-in-chief. **Contact:** Elizabeth Friszell-Nerouslas, managing editor. **85% freelance written. Works with a small number of new/ unpublished writers each year.** Monthly magazine. *Firehouse* covers major fires nationwide, controversial issues and trends in the fire service, the latest firefighting equipment and methods of firefighting, historical fires, firefighting history and memorabilia. Fire-related books, fire safety education, hazardous-materials incidents, and the emergency medical services are also covered. Estab. 1976. Circ. 75,000. Byline given. Pays on publication. Accepts queries by mail, e-mail, fax, online submission form. Sample copy for sae with 9×12 envelope and 8 first-class stamps. Guidelines available online at firehouse.com/submission-guidelines.

NONFICTION Needs book excerpts, of recent books on fire, EMS, and hazardous materials, historical, great fires in history, fire collectibles, the fire service of teryear, how-to, fight certain kinds of fires, buy and maintain equipment, run a fire department, technical, on almost any phase of firefighting, techniques, equipment, training, administration, trends in the fire service. No profiles of people or departments that are not unusual or innovative, reports of nonmajor fires, articles not slanted toward firefighters' interests. No poetry. **Buys 100 mss/year.** Query. If you have any story ideas, questions, hints, tips, etc., please do not hesitate to call. Length: 500-3,000 words. The average length of each article is between2-3 pages including visuals. **Pays $50-400 for assigned articles.**

PHOTOS *Firehouse* is a visually-oriented publication. Please include photographs (color preferred) with captions (or a description of what is taking place in the photo), illustrations, charts or diagrams that support your ms. The highest priority is given to those submissions that are received as a complete package. Pays $25-200 for transparencies and color prints. Cannot accept negatives.

COLUMNS Training (effective methods); Book Reviews; Fire Safety (how departments teach fire safety to the public); Communicating (PR, dispatching); Arson (efforts to combat it). Length: 750-1,000 words. **Buys 50 mss/year.** Query or send complete ms. **Pays $100-300.**

🟢🟢 LAW ENFORCEMENT TECHNOLOGY MAGAZINE

Cygnus Business Media, P.O. Box 803, 1233 Janesville Ave., Fort Atkinson WI 53538-0803. (920)568-8334. Fax: (920)563-1702. E-mail: officer@corp.officer.com; tabatha.wethal@cygnuspub.com. Website: officer.com. **Contact:** Tabatha Wethal. **40% freelance written**. Monthly magazine covering police management and technology. Estab. 1974. Circ. 30,000. Byline given. Pays on publication. Publishes ms an average of 4 months after acceptance. Editorial lead time 6 months. Responds in 1 month to queries; 2 months to mss Guidelines available online.

NONFICTION Needs how-to, interview, photo feature, police management and training. **Buys 30 mss/ year.** Query. Length: 1,200-2,000 words. **Pays $75-400 for assigned articles.**

🟢🟢 9-1-1MAGAZINE.COM

Official Publications, Inc., 18201 Weston Pl., Tustin CA 92780-2251. (714)544-7776. Fax: (714)838-9233. E-mail: publisher@9-1-1magazine.com. **Contact:** Randall Larson, editor. **85% freelance written**. Trade magazine published 9 times/year for knowledgeable emergency communications professionals and those associated with this respectful profession. "Serving law enforcement, fire, and emergency medical services, with an emphasis on communications, *9-1-1 Magazine* provides valuable information to readers in all aspects of the public safety communications and response community. Each issue contains a blending of product-related, technical, operational, and people-oriented stories, covering the skills, training, and equipment which these professionals have in common." Estab. 1988. Circ. 18,000. Byline given. Pays on publication. Offers 20% kill fee. Publishes ms an average of 4-6 months after acceptance. Accepts queries by mail, e-mail, fax. NoResponds in 1 month to queries and to mss. Sample copy for sae with 9×12 envelope and 5 first-class stamps. Guidelines available online.

NONFICTION Needs new product, photo feature, technical, incident report. **Buys 15-25 mss/year.** Query by e-mail (editor@9-1-1magazine.com). We prefer queries, but will look at manuscripts on speculation. Most positive responses to queries are considered on spec, but occasionally we will make assignments. Each ms should include a 25-word bio of the author. All submissions must include social security number, address, and phone number. Length: 1,000-2,500 words. **Pays 10-20¢/word.**

PHOTOS Send photos. Captions, identification of subjects required. Reviews color transparencies, prints, high-resolution digital (300 dpi). Offers $50-100/interior, $300/cover.

💲💲 PLANNING

American Planning Association, 205 N. Michigan Ave., Suite 1200, Chicago IL 60601. (312)431-9100. Fax: (312)786-6700. E-mail: slewis@planning.org. Website: planning.org. Richard Sessions, art director. **Contact:** Sylvia Lewis, editor. **30% freelance written.** Monthly magazine emphasizing urban planning for adult, college-educated readers who are regional and urban planners in city, state, or federal agencies or in private business, or university faculty or students. Estab. 1972. Circ. 44,000. Byline given. Pays on publication. Publishes ms an average of 2 months after acceptance. Accepts queries by mail, e-mail, fax. Responds in 5 weeks to queries. Sample copy for 9×12 SASE with 6 first-class stamps. Guidelines available online.

NONFICTION Special issues: Transportation Issue; Technology Issue. Also needs news stories up to 500 words. **Buys 44 features and 33 news story mss/year.** Length: 500-3,000 words. **Pays $150-1,500.**

PHOTOS "We prefer authors supply their own photos, but we sometimes take our own or arrange for them in other ways.". State availability. Captions required. Pays $100 minimum for photos used on inside pages and $300 for cover photos.

💲💲 POLICE AND SECURITY NEWS

DAYS Communications, Inc., 1208 Juniper St., Quakertown PA 18951-1520. (215)538-1240. Fax: (215)538-1208. E-mail: jdevery@policeandsecuritynews.com; dyaw@policeandsecuritynews.com. Website: policeandsecuritynews.com. Al Menear, assoc. publisher. **Contact:** James Devery, editor; David Yaw, publisher. **40% freelance written.** Bimonthly periodical on public law enforcement and Homeland Security. Our publication is designed to provide educational and entertaining information directed toward management level. Technical information written for the expert in a manner the nonexpert can understand. Estab. 1984. Circ. 24,000. Byline given. Pays on publication. Publishes ms an average of 2 months after acceptance. Accepts queries by mail, e-mail, fax, phone, online submission form. Accepts simultaneous submissions. Sample copy and writer's guidelines for 10x13 SAE with $2.53 postage.

NONFICTION Contact: Al Menear, articles editor. Needs exposè, historical, how-to, humor, interview, opinion, personal experience, photo feature, tech-nical. **Buys 12 mss/year.** Query. Length: 200-2,500 words. **Pays 10¢/word. Sometimes pays in trade-out of services.**

PHOTOS State availability. Reviews 3x5 prints. Offers $10-50/photo.

FILLERS Needs facts, newsbreaks, short humor. **Buys 6 mss/year.** Length: 200-2,000 words. **10¢/word.**

💲💲💲💲 YOUTH TODAY

American Youth Work Center, 1200 17th St. NW, 4th Floor, Washington DC 20036. (202)785-0764. E-mail: pboyle@youthtoday.org. Website: youthtoday.org. **Contact:** Patrick Boyle. **50% freelance written.** Newspaper published 10 times a year covering businesses that provide services to youth. Audience is people who run youth programs—mostly nonprofits & government agencies. They want help in providing services, getting funding. Estab. 1994. Circ. 9,000. Byline given. Pays on publication. Offers $200 kill fee for features. Editorial lead time 2 months. Accepts queries by mail, e-mail, or disk. Accepts simultaneous submissions. Responds in 2 weeks to queries. Responds in 1 month to mss. Sample copy for $5. Guidelines available online.

💬 "Our freelance writers work for or have worked for daily newspapers, or have extensive experience writing for newspapers and magazines."

NONFICTION Needs exposè, general interest, technical. No feel-good stories about do-gooders. We examine the business of youth work. **Buys 5 mss/yr. mss/year.** Query. Send resumè, short cover letter, a few clips. Length: 600-2,500 words. **Pays $150-2,000 for assigned articles.**

PHOTOS Identification of subjects required. Offers no additional payment for photos accepted with ms.

COLUMNS "Youth Today also publishes 750-word guest columns, called Viewpoints. These pieces can be based on the writer's own experiences or based on research, but they must deal with an issue of interest to our readership and must soundly argue an opinion, or advocate for a change in thinking or action within the youth field." Viewpoints

GROCERIES AND FOOD PRODUCTS

💲💲💲 CONVENIENCE DISTRIBUTION

American Wholesale Marketers Association, 2750 Prosperity Ave., Suite 530, Fairfax VA 22031. Fax:

(703)573-5738. E-mail: info@awmanet.org; tracic@awmanet.org. Website: awmanet.org. **70% freelance written**. Magazine published 10 times/year. "We cover trends in candy, tobacco, groceries, beverages, snacks, and other product categories found in convenience stores, grocery stores, and drugstores, plus distribution topics. Contributors should have prior experience writing about the food, retail, and/or distribution industries. Editorial includes a mix of columns, departments, and features (2-6 pages). We also cover AWMA programs." Estab. 1948. Circ. 11,000. Byline given. Pays on acceptance. Publishes ms an average of 2 months after acceptance. Editorial lead time 3-4 months. Accepts queries by e-mail only. Guidelines available online.

NONFICTION Needs how-to, technical, industry trends, also profiles of distribution firms. No comics, jokes, poems, or other fillers. **Buys 40 mss/year.** Query with published clips. Length: 1,200-3,600 words. **Pays 50¢/word.**

PHOTOS Authors must provide artwork (with captions) with articles.

$$$$ FOOD PRODUCT DESIGN MAGAZINE

P.O. Box 3439, Northbrook IL 60065-3439. (480)990-1101 ext. 1241; (800)581-1811. E-mail: lkuntz@vpico.com. Website: foodproductdesign.com. **Contact:** Lynn Kuntz, editor-in-chief. **50% freelance written**. Monthly magazine covering food processing industry. The magazine written for food technologists by food technologists. No foodservice/restaurant, consumer, or recipe development. Estab. 1991. Circ. 30,000. Byline given. Pays on acceptance. Publishes ms an average of 2 months after acceptance. Editorial lead time 4 months. Sample copy for sae with 9×12 envelope and 5 First-Class stamps.

NONFICTION Needs technical. **Buys 30 mss/year.** Length: 1,500-7,000 words. **Pays $100-1,500.**

PHOTOS State availability. Captions required. Reviews transparencies, prints. Offers no additional payment for photos accepted with ms.

COLUMNS Pays $100-500.

$ FRESH CUT MAGAZINE

Great American Publishing, P.O. Box 128, 75 Applewood Dr. , Suite A, Sparta MI 49345. (616)887-9008. E-mail: news@freshcut.com. Website: freshcut.com. **Contact:** Scott Christie. **20% freelance written**. Monthly magazine covering the value-added and precut fruit and vegetable industry. The editor is interested in articles that focus on what different fresh-cut processors are doing. Estab. 1993. Circ. 16,000. Byline given. Pays on publication. Publishes ms an average of 2 months after acceptance. Editorial lead time 2 months. Accepts queries by mail, e-mail, fax, phone, online submission form. Responds in 1 month to queries. Responds in 2 months to mss. Sample copy for sae with 9×12 envelope. Guidelines for #10 sase.

NONFICTION Needs historical, new product, opinion, technical. **Buys 2-4 mss/year.** Query with published clips.

PHOTOS Send photos. Identification of subjects required. Reviews transparencies. Offers no additional payment for photos accepted with ms.

COLUMNS Packaging; Food Safety; Processing/Engineering. **Buys 20 mss/year.** Query. **Pays $125-200.**

$$$ NATURAL FOOD NETWORK MAGAZINE

760 Market St., Suite 432, San Francisco CA 94102. (847)720-5600. E-mail: news@naturalfoodnet.com. Website: naturalfoodnet.com. **70% freelance written**. Bimonthly magazine covering natural and certified organic food industry (domestic and international). Estab. 2003. Circ. 15,000. Byline given. Pays on publication. Offers 10% up to $50 maximum kill fee. Publishes ms an average of 2 months after acceptance. Editorial lead time 2 months. Submit seasonal material 2 months in advance. Accepts queries by e-mail. Accepts simultaneous submissions. Responds in 1 week to queries. Responds in 1 month to mss.

NONFICTION Does not want work with a consumer angle. **Buys 50 mss/year.** Query. Length: 250-1,500 words. **Pays $250-750.**

PHOTOS State availability. Captions, identification of subjects required. Reviews JPEG files. Offers no additional payment for photos accepted with ms.

COLUMNS Q&A with industry leaders (natural and organic specialists in academia, trade associations and business); Worldview (interviews with internationally recognized leaders in organic food supply), both 750 words. **Buys 6 mss/year.** Query. **Pays $500.**

$$ THE PRODUCE NEWS

800 Kinderkamack Rd., Suite 100, Oradell NJ 07649. (201)986-7990. Fax: (201)986-7996. E-mail: groh@theproducenews.com; jalil@theproducenews.com. Website: theproducenews.com. **Contact:** Daniel Jalil, managing editor. **10% freelance written. Works with**

a small number of new/unpublished writers each year. Weekly magazine for commercial growers and shippers, receivers and distributors of fresh fruits and vegetables, including chain store produce buyers and merchandisers. Estab. 1897. Pays on publication. Publishes ms an average of 2 weeks after acceptance. Accepts queries by mail, e-mail, fax. Responds in 1 month to queries. Sample copy and writer's guidelines for 10X13 SAE and 4 first-class stamps.

NONFICTION Query. **Pays $1/column inch minimum.**

PHOTOS Black & white glossies or color prints. Pays $8-10/photo.

⊖⊖ PRODUCE RETAILER

Vance Publishing Corp., 400 Knightsbridge Pkwy., Lincolnshire IL 60069. (512)906-0733. E-mail: pamelar@produceretailer.com. Website: produceretailer.com. **Contact:** Pamela Riemenschneider, editor. **10% freelance written.** Monthly magazine. *Produce Merchandising* is the only monthly journal on the market that is dedicated solely to produce merchandising information for retailers. Estab. 1988. Circ. 12,000. Byline given. Pays on acceptance. Publishes ms an average of 3 months after acceptance. Editorial lead time 3 months. Accepts queries by mail. Responds in 2 weeks to queries.

○ Our purpose is to provide information about promotions, merchandising, and operations in the form of ideas and examples.

NONFICTION Needs how-to, interview, new product, photo feature, technical, contact the editor for a specific assignment. **Buys 48 mss/year.** Query with published clips. Length: 1,000-1,500 words. **Pays $200-600.** Pays expenses.

PHOTOS Contact: Tony Re, art director. State availability of or send photos. Captions, identification of subjects, model releases required. Reviews color slides and 3x5 or larger prints. Offers no additional payment for photos accepted with ms.

COLUMNS Contact: Contact editor for a specific assignment. **Buys 30 mss/year.** Query with published clips. **Pays $200-450.**

○⊖⊖ WESTERN GROCER MAGAZINE

Mercury Publications Ltd., 1740 Wellington Ave., Winnipeg MB R3H 0E8 Canada. (204)954-2085; (800)337-6372. Fax: (204)954-2057. E-mail: mp@mercury.mb.ca; editorial@mercury.mb.ca. Website: mercury.mb.ca/. **Contact:** Nicole Sherwood, editorial coordinator. **75% freelance written.** Bimonthly magazine covering the grocery industry. Reports for the Western Canadian grocery, allied non-food and institutional industries. Each issue features a selection of relevant trade news and event coverage from the West and around the world. Feature reports offer market analysis, trend views and insightful interviews from a wide variety of industry leaders. The Western Grocer target audience is independent retail food stores, supermarkets, manufacturers and food brokers, distributors and wholesalers of food and allied non-food products, as well as bakers, specialty and health food stores and convenience outlets. Estab. 1916. Circ. 15,500. Byline given. Pays 30-45 days from receipt of invoice. Offers 33% kill fee. Submit seasonal material 3 months in advance. Sample copy and writer's

○ Assigns stories to Canadian writers based on editorial needs of publication.

NONFICTION Needs how-to, interview. Industry reports and profiles on companies. Query with published clips. Length: 500-9,000 words. **Pays 25-35¢/word.**

PHOTOS State availability. Captions required. Reviews negatives, transparencies, 3x5 prints, JPEG, EPS, or TIF files. Negotiates payment individually.

HOME FURNISHINGS AND HOUSEHOLD GOODS

⊖⊖ HOME FURNISHINGS RETAILER

National Home Furnishings Association (NHFA), 3910 Tinsley Dr., Suite 101, High Point NC 27265-3610. (336)801-6156. Fax: (336)801-6102. E-mail: wynnryan@rcn.com. Website: nhfa.org. **Contact:** Mary Wynn Ryan, editor-in-chief. **75% freelance written**. Monthly magazine published by NHFA covering the home furnishings industry. "We hope home furnishings retailers view our magazine as a profitability tool. We want each issue to help them make or save money." Requires writers to have credentials that include specific knowledge of the industry & extensive experience in writing about it. Estab. 1927. Circ. 15,000. Byline given. Pays on acceptance. Publishes ms an average of 6 weeks after acceptance. Editorial lead time 3 months. Accepts queries by mail, e-mail. Responds in 1 month to queries. Sample copy available with proper postage. Guidelines online and for #10 sase.

NONFICTION Query—include resume, writing samples & credentials, published clips. Assigned articles should be submitted by e-mail or on disc. 3,000-5,000 words (features) **Pays $350-500.**

PHOTOS Author is responsible for obtaining photos or other illustrative material. State availability. Identification of subjects required. Reviews transparencies. Negotiates payment individually.

COLUMNS Columns cover business and product trends that shape the home furnishings industry. Advertising and Marketing; Finance; Technology; Training; Creative Leadership; Law; Style and Operations. Length: 1,200-1,500 words. Query with published clips.

HOSPITALS, NURSING AND NURSING HOMES

⊛⊛ CURRENT NURSING IN GERIATRIC CARE

Freiberg Press Inc., P.O. Box 612, Cedar Falls IA 50613. (319)553-0642; (800)354-3371. Fax: (319)553-0644. E-mail: bfreiberg@cfu.net. Website: care4elders.com. **25% freelance written**. Bimonthly trade journal covering medical information and new developments in research for geriatric nurses and other practitioners Estab. 2006. Byline sometimes given. Pays on acceptance. Accepts queries by e-mail.

NONFICTION Query. Length: 500-1,500 words. **Pays 15¢/word for assigned articles.**

PHOTOS State availability.

⊛⊛⊛ HOSPITALS & HEALTH NETWORKS

Health Forum, 1 N. Franklin, 29th Floor, Chicago IL 60606. (312)422-2100. E-mail: rhill@healthforum.com; bsantamour@healthforum.com. Website: hhnmag.com. **Contact:** Richard Hill, editor. **25% freelance written**. Monthly magazine covering hospitals. We are a business publication for hospital and health system executives. We use only writers who are thoroughly familiar with the hospital field. Submit rÂ^sumÂ^ and up to 5 samples of health care-related articles. We assign all articles and do not consider manuscripts. Estab. 1926. Circ. 85,000. Byline given. Pays on acceptance. Offers variable kill fee. Publishes ms an average of 3 months after acceptance. Editorial lead time 2-3 months. Accepts queries by e-mail. Responds in 2-4 months to queries.

NONFICTION Contact: Bill Santamour, managing editor. Needs interview, technical. Query with published clips. Length: 350-2,000 words. **Pays $300-1,500 for assigned articles.**

⊘⊛⊛ LONG TERM CARE

Ontario Long Term Care Association, 345 Renfrew Dr., Third Floor, Markham ON L3R 9S9 Canada. (905)470-8995. Fax: (905)470-9595. E-mail: info@oltca.com. Website: oltca.com. Quarterly magazine covering professional issues and practical articles of interest to staff working in a long-term care setting (nursing home, retirement home). Information must be applicable to a Canadian setting; focus should be on staff and on resident well being. Estab. 1990. Circ. 6,000. Byline given. Pays on publication. Publishes ms an average of 4 months after acceptance. Editorial lead time 3 months. Submit seasonal material 5 months in advance. Responds in 3 months to queries. Guidelines available online.

NONFICTION Needs general interest, how-to, practical, of use to long term care practitioners, inspirational, interview. No product-oriented articles. Query with published clips. Individuals should submit their ideas and/or completed articles to: justwrite@powergate.ca. Electronic versions in either Wordperfect or MS Word are preferred. Length:400-2,500 words. **Pays up to $500 (Canadian).**

PHOTOS Send photos. Captions, model releases required. Reviews contact sheets, 5x5 prints. Offers no additional payment for photos accepted with ms.

COLUMNS Query with published clips. **Pays up to $500 (Canadian).**

⊛⊛⊛ NURSEWEEK

Gannett Healthcare Group, 2353 Hassell Rd., Suite 110, Hoffman Estates IL 60169-2170. (847)490-6666. Fax: (847)490-0419. E-mail: jthew@gannetthg.com. Website: nurse.com. **Contact:** Jennifer Thew, RN. **98% freelance written**. Biweekly magazine covering nursing news. Registered nurses read our magazine, which they receive for free by mail. We cover nursing news about people, practice, and the profession. Estab. 1999. Circ. 155,000. Byline given. Pays on publication. Offers $200 kill fee. Publishes ms an average of 2 months after acceptance. Editorial lead time 2-3 months. Submit seasonal material 4 months in advance. Accepts queries by mail, e-mail, fax, phone. Accepts simultaneous submissions.

○ "Before you begin to write, we recommend that you review several of our magazines for content and style. We also suggest e-mailing your idea to the editorial director in your region (See list online). The editorial director can help you with the story's focus or angle, along with the organization and development of ideas."

NONFICTION Needs interview, personal experience, Articles on innovative approaches to clinical care and evidence-based nursing practice, health-related legislation and regulation, community health programs, healthcare delivery systems, and professional development and management, advances in nursing specialties such as critical care, geriatrics, perioperative care, women's health, home care, long-term care, emergency care, med/surg, pediatrics, advanced practice, education, and staff development. We don't want poetry, fiction, technical pieces. **Buys 20 mss/ year. mss/year.** Query. Length: 600-1,500 words. **Pays $200-800 for assigned or unsolicited articles.**

PHOTOS Send photos. Captions, model releases required. Reviews contact sheets, GIF/JPEG files. Offers no additional payment for photos accepted with ms.

💲💲 NURSING2012

(formerly *Nursing2011*), Lippincott Williams & Wilkins, 323 Norristown Rd., Suite 200, Ambler PA 19002. (215)646-8700. Fax: (215)367-2155. E-mail: patricia.wolf@wolterskluwer.com; nursingeditor@wolterskluwer.com. Website: nursing2011.com; journals. lww.com/nursing/pages/default.aspx. **Contact:** Linda Laskowski-Jones, RN, ACNS-BC, CCRN, CEN, MS, FAWM. **100% freelance written.** Monthly magazine Written by nurses for nurses; we look for practical advice for the direct caregiver that reflects the author's experience. Any form acceptable, but focus must be nursing. Estab. 1971. Circ. over 300,000. Byline given. Pays on publication. Offers 50% kill fee. Publishes ms an average of 18 months after acceptance. Submit seasonal material 8 months in advance. Responds in 2 weeks to queries. Responds in 3 months to mss. Sample copy for $5. Specific instructions and guidelines for submitting articles are readily available on the submission service site. Please read and review them carefully.

○ "Published monthly, *Nursing2012* is widely regarded as offering current, practical contents to its readers, and has won many edito-

rial awards testifying to the quality of its copy and graphics. The editorial and clinical staff, a 18-member Editorial Board of distinguished clinicians and practitioners, and over 100 invited reviewers help ensure the quality of this publication."

NONFICTION Needs book excerpts, exposè, how-to, specifically as applies to nursing field, inspirational, opinion, personal experience, photo feature. No articles from patients' point of view, poetry, etc. **Buys 100 mss/year.** Query. All manuscripts can be submitted online through the journal's submission website at LWWeSubmissions.com. Using this process will expedite review and feedback, and you can see where your ms is in the editorial process at any time after it's accepted. So we strongly encourage you to register there as an author and follow the directions. 3,500 words (continuing ed feature); 2,100 words (features); short features/departments, 700 words. **Pays $50-400 for assigned articles.**

💲 SCHOOL NURSE NEWS

Franklin Communications, Inc., 71 Redner Rd., Morristown NJ 07960. (973)644-4003. Fax: (973)644-4062. E-mail: michael@schoolnursenews.org. Website: schoolnursenews.org. **Contact:** Michael. **10% freelance written.** Magazine published 5 times/year covering school nursing. "Focuses on topics related to the health issues of school-aged children and adolescents (grades K-12), as well as the health and professional issues that concern school nurses. We believe this is an excellent opportunity for both new and experienced writers. School Nurse News publishes feature articles as well as news articles and regular departments, such as Asthma & Allergy Watch, Career & Salary Survey, Oral Health, Nursing Currents, and Sights & Sounds. Manuscripts can include case histories, scenarios of health office situations, updates on diseases, reporting of research, and discussion of procedures and techniques, among others. The author is responsible for the accuracy of content. References should be complete, accurate, and in APA format. Tables, charts and photographs are welcome. Authors are responsible for obtaining permission to reproduce any material that has a pre-existing copyright. The feature article, references, tables and charts should total 8-10 typewritten pages, double-spaced. The author's name should be included only on the top sheet. The top sheet should also include the title of the article, the author's credentials, current position, address and phone." Estab. 1982. Circ. 7,500. Byline given. Pays on publication. Publishes ms an average of 3-6 months after acceptance. Editorial lead time 3-6 months. Submit seasonal material 6 months in advance. Accepts queries by e-mail, fax, phone.

NONFICTION Needs how-to, interview, new product, personal experience. **Buys 1-2 mss/year.** Query. Send via e-mail or forward ms with disk. See guidelines: schoolnursenews.org/SubmitArticle/Guidelines_Dept.pdf. **Pays $100.**

HOTELS, MOTELS, CLUBS, RESORTS AND RESTAURANTS

💲💲 BARTENDER MAGAZINE

Foley Publishing, P.O. Box 158, Liberty Corner NJ 07938. (908)766-6006. Fax: (908)766-6607. Website: bartender.com. **Contact:** Jackie Foley, editor. **100% freelance written. Prefers to work with published/established writers; eager to work with new/unpublished writers.** Quarterly magazine emphasizing liquor and bartending for bartenders, tavern owners, and owners of restaurants with full-service liquor licenses. Estab. 1979. Circ. 150,000. Byline given. Pays on publication. Publishes ms an average of 3 months after acceptance. Submit seasonal material 3 months in advance. Accepts simultaneous submissions. Responds in 2 months to mss. Sample copy for sae with 9×12 envelope and 4 first-class stamps.

NONFICTION Needs general interest, historical, how-to, humor, interview with famous bartenders or ex-bartenders, new product, opinion, personal experience, photo feature, travel, nostalgia, unique bars, new techniques, new drinking trends, bar sports, bar magic tricks. Special issues: Annual Calendar and Daily Cocktail Recipe Guide. Send complete ms and SASE. Length: 100-1,000 words.

PHOTOS Send photos. Captions, model releases required. Pays $7.50-50 for 8×10 b&w glossy prints; $10-75 for 8×10 color glossy prints.

COLUMNS Bar of the Month; Bartender of the Month; Creative Cocktails; Bar Sports; Quiz; Bar Art; Wine Cellar; Tips from the Top (from prominent figures in the liquor industry); One For the Road (travel); Collectors (bar or liquor-related items); Photo Essays. Length: 200-1,000 words. Query by mail only with SASE. **Pays $50-200.**

FILLERS Needs anecdotes, newsbreaks, short humor, clippings, jokes, gags. Length: 25-100 words. **Pays $5-25.**

💲💲 EL RESTAURANTE MEXICANO

P.O. Box 2249, Oak Park IL 60303-2249. (708)488-0100. Fax: (708)488-0101. E-mail: kfurore@restmex.com. Bimonthly magazine covering Mexican and other Latin cuisines. "*El Restaurante Mexicano* offers features and business-related articles that are geared specifically to owners and operators of Mexican, Tex-Mex, Southwestern, and Latin cuisine restaurants and other foodservice establishments that want to add that type of cuisine." Estab. 1997. Circ. 27,000. Byline given. Pays on publication. Publishes ms an average of 3 months after acceptance. Responds in 2 months to queries.

NONFICTION No specific knowledge of food or restaurants is needed; the key qualification is to be a good reporter who knows how to slant a story toward the Mexican restaurant operator. **Buys 4-6 mss/year.** Query with published clips. Length: 800-1,200 words. **Pays $250-300.**

⊘💲💲💲💲 HOSPITALITY TECHNOLOGY

Edgell Communications, 4 Middlebury Blvd., Randolph NJ 07869. (973)252-0100. Fax: (973)252-9020. E-mail: alorden@edgellmail.com. Website: htmagazine.com. **Contact:** Abigail Lorden, editor-in-chief. **70% freelance written.** Magazine published 9 times/year. We cover the technology used in foodservice and lodging. Our readers are the operators, who have significant IT responsibilities. Estab. 1996. Circ. 16,000. Byline given. Pays on acceptance. Publishes ms an average of 1 month after acceptance. Editorial lead time 2 months. Accepts queries by mail, e-mail, fax, phone. Responds in 2 weeks to queries.

○ This publication will not respond to all inquiries—only those that are of particular interest to the editor.

NONFICTION Needs how-to, interview, new product, technical. Special issues: We publish 2 studies each year, the Restaurant Industry Technology Study and the Lodging Industry Technology Study. No unsolicited mss. **Buys 40 mss/year.** Query with published clips. Length: 800-1,200 words. **Pays $1/word.**

TIPS Given the vast amount of inquiries we receive, it's impossible for us to respond to all. We can only respond to those that are of particular interest.

$$$ HOTELIER

Kostuch Publications, Ltd., 23 Lesmill Rd., Suite 101, Toronto ON M3B 3P6 Canada. (416)447-0888. Fax: (416)447-5333. E-mail: rcaira@foodservice.ca. Website: hoteliermagazine.com. **Contact:** Rosanna Caira, editor and publisher. **40% freelance written.** Magazine published 8 times/year covering the Canadian hotel industry. Estab. 1989. Circ. 9,000. Byline given. Pays on publication. Editorial lead time 3 months. Submit seasonal material 2 months in advance. Accepts queries by mail, fax. Sample copy and writer's

NONFICTION Needs how-to, new product. No case studies. **Buys 30-50 mss/year.** Query. Length: 700-1,500 words. **Pays 35¢/word (Canadian) for assigned articles.**

PHOTOS Send photos. Offers $30-75/photo.

$$ INSITE

Christian Camp and Conference Association, P.O. Box 62189, Colorado Springs CO 80962-2189. (719)260-9400. Fax: (719)260-6398. E-mail: editor@ccca.org. Website: ccca.org. **Contact:** Editor. **75% freelance written. Prefers to work with published/established writers.** Bimonthly magazine emphasizing the broad scope of organized camping with emphasis on Christian camps and conference centers. "All who work in youth camps and adult conferences read our magazine for inspiration and to get practical help in ways to serve in their operations." Estab. 1963. Circ. 8,500. Byline given. Pays on publication. Publishes ms an average of 4 months after acceptance. Accepts queries by mail, e-mail. Responds in 1 month to queries. Sample copy for $4.99 plus 9×12 SASE. Guidelines available by request.

NONFICTION Needs general interest, trends in organized camping in general, Christian camping in particular, how-to, anything involved with organized camping, including motivating staff, programming, healthcare, maintenance, and camper follow-up, inspirational, interested in profiles and practical applications of Scriptural principles to everyday situations in camping, interview, with movers and shakers in Christian camping. **Buys 15-20 mss/year.** Query required. Length: 500-1,700 words. **Pays 20¢/word.**

PHOTOS Price negotiable for 35mm color transparencies and high-quality digital photos.

$$ MOUNTAIN RESORT MAGAZINE

Skinner Media, Vail CO 81657. (252)564-9520; Phone/Fax: (252)261-3437. E-mail: editor@mountainresortmag.com. Website: mountainresortmag.com. **50% freelance written.** Bimonthly magazine covering the ski and snowboard resort industry. "We are exclusively an area operations, marketing, and management resource for local, regional, and national mountain destinations. We combine humor with information and images with explanations, and understand the spark it takes to work in black snow pants 175 days a year. We will gladly trade publishing credits for real experience on the front lines. And, we readily understand that although travel writers and old-school journalists are invariably handsome, brilliant, and uber-masters of the sport, they have little cred with those who actually do the job. We do not preach, but utilize the voices in the industry to help share authentic experience." Estab. 2004. Circ. 4,200. Byline given. Pays on acceptance. Offers 20% kill fee. Editorial lead time 2 months. Submit seasonal material 3 months in advance. Accepts queries by e-mail. Accepts simultaneous submissions. Responds in 1 week to queries. Responds in 1 month to mss. Guidelines by e-mail.

NONFICTION Needs historical, how-to, humor, interview, new product, technical. Please do not confuse the retail or travel end of skiing and riding with the operations community (management, marketing, lift operators). **Buys 15 mss/year.** Query. Length: 1,200-2,000 words. **Pays $500**

PHOTOS Please contact the editor if you have taken operations photography. (This does not include pictures of your buddy doing some trick in the park.).

COLUMNS Bullwheel (informative spew about interesting and funny operations developments), 200 words. **Buys 1 ms/year.** Query. **Pays $100 maximum.**

$$$ PIZZA TODAY

Macfadden Protech, LLC, 908 S. 8th St., Suite 200, Louisville KY 40203. (502)736-9500. Fax: (502)736-9502. E-mail: jwhite@pizzatoday.com. Website: pizzatoday.com. Mandy Detwiler, managing editor. **Contact:** Jeremy White, editor-in-chief. **30% freelance written. Works with published/established writers; occasionally works with new writers.** Monthly magazine for the pizza industry, covering trends, features of successful pizza operators, business and management advice, etc. Estab. 1984. Circ. 44,000. Byline given. Pays on acceptance. Publishes ms an average of 2 months after acceptance. Submit seasonal material 3 months in advance. Accepts queries by mail, e-mail, fax. Responds in 2 months to queries. Responds in 3 weeks to mss. Sample copy for sae with 10x13 envelope and 6 first-class stamps. Guidelines for #10 sase and online.

NONFICTION Needs interview, entrepreneurial slants, pizza production and delivery, employee training, hiring, marketing, and business management. No fillers, humor, or poetry. **Buys 85 mss/year.** Length: 1,000 words. **Pays 50¢/word, occasionally more.**

PHOTOS Captions required. Reviews contact sheets, negatives, transparencies, color slides, 5 x 7 prints.

💲💲💲 SANTÉ MAGAZINE

On-Premise Communications, 100 South St., Bennington VT 05201. 802-442-6771. Fax: 802-442-6859. E-mail: mvaughan@santemagazine.com. Website: isantemagazine.com. **Contact:** Mark Vaughan, editor. **75% freelance written.** 9 issues per year magazine covering food, wine, spirits, and management topics for restaurant professionals. "Information and specific advice for restaurant professionals on operating a profitable food and beverage program. Writers should 'speak' to readers on a professional-to-professional basis." Estab. 1996. Circ. 55,000. Byline given. Pays on publication. Offers 50% kill fee. Publishes ms an average of 2 months after acceptance. Editorial lead time 6 months. Submit seasonal material 6 months in advance. Accepts queries by e-mail. Responds in 2 weeks to queries. We do not accept mss. Sample copy available. Guidelines by e-mail.

> "Articles should be concise and to the point and should closely adhere to the assigned word count. Our readers will only read articles that provide useful information in a readily accessible format. Where possible, articles should be broken into stand-alone sections that can be boxed or otherwise highlighted."

NONFICTION Needs interview, Restaurant business news. "We do not want consumer-focused pieces." **Buys 95 mss/year.** Query with published clips. Length: 650-1,800 words.

PHOTOS State availability. Captions required. Reviews 8 x 10 at 300 dpi transparencies, GIF/JPEG files. Offers no additional payment for photos accepted.

COLUMNS "Due to a Redesign, 650 words; Bar Tab (focuses on one bar's unique strategy for success),

1,000 words; Restaurant Profile (a business-related look at what qualities make one restaurant successful), 1,000 words; Maximizing Profits (covers one great profit-maximizing strategy per issue from several sources), Chef's Seminar (highlights one chef's unique style), Appellations (an in-depth look at a high-profile wine-producing region), Distillations (a detailed study of a particular type of spirit), 1,500 words; Provisions (like The Goods only longer; an in-depth look at a special ingredient), 1,500 words. **Buys 95 mss/year. mss/year.** Query with published clips. **Pays $300-$800.**

🔄💲💲 WESTERN HOTELIER MAGAZINE

Mercury Publications, Ltd., 1740 Wellington Ave., Winnipeg MB R3H 0E8 Canada. (204)954-2085. Fax: (204)954-2057. E-mail: mp@mercury.mb.ca; editorial@mercury.mb.ca. Website: mercury.mb.ca/. **Contact:** Nicole Sherwood, editorial coordinator. **33% freelance written.** Quarterly magazine covering the hotel industry. *Western Hotelier* is dedicated to the accommodation industry in Western Canada and U.S. western border states. *WH* offers the West's best mix of news and feature reports geared to hotel management. Feature reports are written on a sector basis and are created to help generate enhanced profitability and better understanding. Circ. 4,342. Byline given. Pays 30-45 days from receipt of invoice. Offers 33% kill fee. Submit seasonal material 3 months in advance. Accepts queries by mail, fax. Accepts simultaneous submissions. Responds in 2 weeks to queries. Sample copy and writer's

NONFICTION Needs how-to, train staff, interview. Industry reports and profiles on companies. Query with published clips. Length: 500-9,000 words. **Pays 25-35¢/word.**

PHOTOS State availability. Captions required. Reviews negatives, transparencies, 3x5 prints, JPEG, EPS or TIF files. Negotiates payment individually.

🔄💲💲 WESTERN RESTAURANT NEWS

Mercury Publications, Ltd., 1740 Wellington Ave., Winnipeg MB R3H 0E8 Canada. (204)954-2085. Fax: (204)954-2057. E-mail: editorial@mercury.mb.ca; mp@mercury.mb.ca. Website: mercury.mb.ca/. **Contact:** Nicole Sherwood, editorial director. **20% freelance written.** Bimonthly magazine covering the restaurant trade. Reports profiles and industry reports on associations, regional business developments, etc. *Western Restaurant News Magazine* is the authoritative voice of the foodservice industry in Western Canada. Offering a total package to readers, *WRN* delivers concise news articles, new product news, and coverage of the leading trade events in the West, across the country, and around the world. Estab. 1994. Circ. 14,532. Byline given. Pays 30-45 days from receipt of invoice. Offers 33% kill fee. Submit seasonal material 3 months in advance. Accepts queries by mail, fax. Accepts simultaneous submissions. Sample copy and writer's

NONFICTION Needs how-to, interview. Industry reports and profiles on companies. Query with published clips. Length: 500-9,000 words. **Pays 25-35¢/ word.**

PHOTOS State availability. Captions required. Reviews negatives, transparencies, 3x5 prints, JPEG, EPS, or TIFF files. Negotiates payment individually. **FILLERS** Length: words.

INDUSTRIAL OPERATIONS

⊘⊜⊜ COMMERCE & INDUSTRY

Mercury Publications, Ltd., 1740 Wellington Ave., Winnipeg MB R3H 0E8 Canada. (204)954-2085. Fax: (204)954-2057. E-mail: editorial@mercury.mb.ca. Website: mercury.mb.ca. **75% freelance written.** Bimonthly magazine covering the business and industrial sectors. Industry reports and company profiles provide readers with an in-depth insight into key areas of interest in their profession. Estab. 1947. Circ. 18,876. Byline given. Pays 30-45 days from receipt of invoice. Offers 33% kill fee. Submit seasonal material 3 months in advance. Accepts queries by mail, e-mail, fax. Accepts simultaneous submissions. Responds in 2 weeks to queries. Sample copy and writer's guidelines free or by e-mail.

○ "Offers new product news, industry event coverage, and breaking trade specific business stories."

NONFICTION Needs how-to, interview. Industry reports and profiles on companies. Query with published clips. Length: 500-9,000 words. **Pays 25-35¢/word.**

PHOTOS State availability. Captions required. Reviews negatives, transparencies, 3x5 prints, JPEG, EPS or TIF files. Negotiates payment individually.

⊜⊜ MODERN MATERIALS HANDLING

Peerless Media, 111 Speen St., Ste 200, Framingham MA 01701. (508)663-1500. E-mail: mlevans@ehpub. com; robert.trebilcock@myfairpoint.net. Website:

mmh.com. **Contact:** Michael Levans, editorial director. **40% freelance written.** Magazine published 13 times/year covering warehousing, distribution centers, inventory. *Warehousing Management* is a national magazine read by managers of warehouses and distribution centers. We focus on lively, well-written articles telling our readers how they can achieve maximum facility productivity and efficiency. Heavy management components. We cover technology, too. Estab. 1945. Circ. 81,000. Byline given. Pays on acceptance (allow 4-6 weeks for invoice processing). Publishes ms an average of 1 month after acceptance. Editorial lead time 3 months. Accepts queries by mail, e-mail, fax.

NONFICTION Needs how-to, new product, technical. Special issues: State-of-the-Industry Report, Peak Performer, Salary and Wage survey, Warehouse of the Year. Doesn't want to see anything that doesn't deal with our topic—warehousing. No general-interest profiles or interviews. **Buys 25 mss/year.** Query with published clips. **Pays $300-650.**

PHOTOS State availability. Captions, identification of subjects required. Reviews negatives, transparencies, prints. Offers no additional payment for photos accepted with ms.

⊘⊕⊜⊜⊜ PEM PLANT ENGINEERING & MAINTENANCE

CLB Media, Inc., 240 Edward St., Aurora ON L4G 3S9 Canada. 905-726-4655. Fax: (905)727-0017. E-mail: avoshart@clbmedia.ca. Website: pem-mag.com. **Contact:** Andre Voshart, editor. **30% freelance written.** Bimonthly magazine looking for informative articles on issues that affect plant floor operations and maintenance. Estab. 1977. Circ. 18,500. Byline given. Pays on publication. Publishes ms an average of 3 months after acceptance. Editorial lead time 4 months. Submit seasonal material 4 months in advance. Accepts simultaneous submissions. Responds in 3 weeks to queries. Responds in 1 month to mss. Guidelines available online.

NONFICTION Needs how-to, keep production downtime to a minimum, better operate an industrial operation, new product, technical. **Buys 6 mss/ year.** Query with published clips. Length: 750-4,000 words. **Pays $500-1,400 (Canadian).**

PHOTOS State availability. Captions required. Reviews transparencies, prints. Negotiates payment individually.

💲💲 **WEIGHING & MEASUREMENT** ✦

WAM Publishing Co., P.O. Box 2247, Hendersonville TN 37077. (615)824-6920. Fax: (615)824-7092. E-mail: wampub@wammag.com. Website: wammag.com. **Contact:** David M. Mathieu, publisher. Bimonthly magazine for users of industrial scales; also now covers material handling & logistics industries. Estab. 1914. Circ. 13,900. Byline given. Pays on acceptance. Offers 20% kill fee. Accepts queries by mail, e-mail, fax, phone, online submission form. Responds in 2 weeks to queries. Sample copy for $2.

NONFICTION Needs interview, with presidents of companies, personal experience, guest editorials on government involvement in business, etc., technical, Profile (about users of weighing and measurement equipment). **Buys 15 mss/year.** Query on technical articles; submit complete ms for general interest material. Length: 1,000-2,500 words. **Pays $175-300.**

INFORMATION SYSTEMS

💲💲💲 **DESKTOP ENGINEERING**

Level 5 Communications, Inc., P.O. Box 1039, Dublin NH 03444. (603)563-1631. Fax: (603)563-8192. E-mail: jgooch@level5com.com. Website: deskeng. com. **Contact:** Features editor. **90% freelance written.** "Monthly magazine covering computer hardware/software for hands-on design and mechanical engineers, analysis engineers, and engineering management. Ten special supplements/year.". Estab. 1995. Circ. 63,000. Byline given. Pays in month of publication. Kill fee for assigned story. Publishes ms an average of 2 months after acceptance. Editorial lead time 3 months. Accepts queries by mail, e-mail, phone. Responds in 2 weeks to queries. Responds in 1 month to mss. Sample copy for free with 8×10 SASE. Writer's guidelines by e-mail.

> 💭 "We welcome ideas for 800 - 1,200 word articles (plus artwork) presenting tutorials, application stories, product reviews or other features. We also welcome ideas for 500 - 700 word guest commentaries for almost any topic related to desktop engineering. For more information on submitting article or commentary ideas, please contact Managing Editor Jamie Gooch via e-mail or at 216-849-6402."

NONFICTION Needs how-to, new product, reviews, technical, design. No fluff. **Buys 50-70 mss/year.** Query. Submit outline before you write an article. Length:

1,000-1,200 words. **Pays per project. Pay negotiable for unsolicited articles.**

PHOTOS "No matter what type of article you write, it must be supported and enhanced visually. Visual information can include screen shots, photos, schematics, tables, charts, checklists, time lines, reading lists, and program code. The exact mix will depend on your particular article, but each of these items must be accompanied by specific, detailed captions.". Send photos. Captions required. Negotiates payment individually.

💲💲💲 **GAME DEVELOPER**

United Business Media LLC, Think Services, 600 Harrison St., 6th Floor, San Francisco CA 94107. (415)947-6000. Fax: (415)947-6090. E-mail: bsheffield@gdmag. com; jen.steele@ubm.com. Website: gdmag.com. **Contact:** Brandon Sheffield, editor-in-chief; Jen Steele. **90% freelance written.** Monthly magazine covering computer game development. Estab. 1994. Circ. 35,000. Byline given. Pays on publication. Publishes ms an average of 3-6 months after acceptance. Editorial lead time 3 months. Submit seasonal material 4 months in advance. Accepts queries by e-mail. Guidelines available online.

NONFICTION Needs how-to, personal experience, technical. **Buys 50 mss/year.** Query. Length: 3,500 words for Feature articles and the Postmortem column; 600-1,200 words for product reviews (game development tools). **Pays $150/page.**

PHOTOS State availability.

💲 **JOURNAL OF INFORMATION ETHICS**

McFarland & Co., Inc., Publishers, P.O. Box 611, Jefferson NC 28640. (336)246-4460. E-mail: hauptman@ stcloudstate.edu. **90% freelance written.** Semiannual scholarly journal covering all of the information sciences. "Addresses ethical issues in all of the information sciences with a deliberately interdisciplinary approach. Topics range from electronic mail monitoring to library acquisition of controversial material to archival ethics. The *Journal*'s aim is to present thoughtful considerations of ethical dilemmas that arise in a rapidly evolving system of information exchange and dissemination." Estab. 1992. Byline given. Pays on publication. Publishes ms an average of 2 years after acceptance. Submit seasonal material 8 months in advance. Accepts queries by mail, e-mail, phone. Sample copy for $30.

NONFICTION Needs essays, opinion, Also book reviews. **Buys 10-12 mss/year.** Send complete ms.

Length: 500-3,500 words. **Pays $25-50, depending on length.**

⊖⊖⊖ SYSTEM INEWS

Penton Technology Media, 748 Whalers Way, Fort Collins CO 80525. (970)203-2914; (800)650-1804. E-mail: editors@systeminetwork.com. Website: iseriesnetwork.com. **40% freelance written.** Magazine published 12 times/year. Programming, networking, IS management, technology for users of IBM AS/400, iSERIES, SYSTEM i, AND IBM i platform. Estab. 1982. Circ. 30,000 (international). Byline given. Pays on publication. Offers 50% kill fee. Publishes ms an average of 3 months after acceptance. Editorial lead time 4 months. Submit seasonal material 4 months in advance. Accepts queries by e-mail. Responds in 3 weeks to queries. Responds in 5 weeks to mss Guidelines available online.

NONFICTION Needs technical. Query. Length: 1,500-2,500 words. **Pays $300/$500 flat fee for assigned articles, depending on article quality and technical depth.**

⊖⊖⊖⊖ TECHNOLOGY REVIEW

MIT, One Main St., 7th Floor, Cambridge MA 02142. (617)475-8000. Fax: (617)475-8042. Website: technologyreview.com. David Rotman, editor. **Contact:** Jason Pontin, editor-in-chief. Magazine published 10 times/year covering information technology, biotech, material science, and nanotechnology. *Technology Review* promotes the understanding of emerging technologies and their impact. Estab. 1899. Circ. 310,000. Byline given. Pays on acceptance. Accepts queries by mail, e-mail.

〇Contact specific editor via e-mail using firstname.lastname@technologyreview.com

NONFICTION Length: 2,000-4,000 words. **Pays $1-3/word.**

INSURANCE

⊖⊖⊖⊖ ADVISOR TODAY

NAIFA, 2901 Telestar Court, Falls Church VA 22042. (703)770-8204. E-mail: amseka@naifa.org. Website: advisortoday.com. **Contact:** Ayo Mseka. **25% freelance written.** Monthly magazine covering life insurance and financial planning. Writers must demonstrate an understanding at what insurance agents and financial advisors do to earn business and serve their clients. Estab. 1906. Circ. 110,000. Pays on acceptance or publication (by mutual agreement with editor). Publishes ms an average of 3 months after acceptance. Editorial lead time 3 months. Submit seasonal material 6 months in advance. Accepts queries by mail, e-mail, fax, phone. Accepts simultaneous submissions. Guidelines available online at advisortoday.com/about/contribute.cfm.

NONFICTION Buys 8 mss/year. We prefer e-mail submissions in Microsoft Word format. For other formats and submission methods, please query first. For all articles and queries, contact Ayo Mseka. Web articles should cover the same subject matter covered in the magazine. The articles can be between 300-800 words and should be submitted to Ayo Mseka. Please indicate where a story has been previously published articles have been accepted. Length: 1,500-6,000 words. **Pays $800-2,000.**

⊖⊖ AGENT'S SALES JOURNAL

Summit Business Media, 5081 Olympic Blvd., Erlanger KY 41018. (720)895-1525. Fax: (727)446-1166. E-mail: astonehouse@sbmedia.com; nmorford@sbmedia.com. Website: agentssalesjournal.com. Nichole Morford, Managing Editor, 720-895-8580, 720-873-8580, nmorford@sbmedia.com. **Contact:** Andy Stonehouse, Editor. **40% freelance written.** Monthly magazine covering life and health insurance industry. We are a how-to publication for life and health-licensed insurance agents. All editorial is nonpromotional and dedicated to helping our readerse do a better job. Circ. 50,000. Byline given. Pays on acceptance. Offers 50% kill fee. Publishes ms an average of 2 months after acceptance. Editorial lead time 2 months. Accepts queries by e-mail. Accepts simultaneous submissions. Sample copy available online.

NONFICTION Contact: Christina Pellett, managing editor. Needs how-to, selling insurance, technical, Industry trend pieces. No articles promoting specific companies, products or services. No consumer-oriented material-please keep in mind audience is insurance agents. **Buys 24 mss/year.** Query with published clips. Length: 1,200-1,700 words. **Pays $350-450 for assigned articles.**

JEWELRY

⊖ THE DIAMOND REGISTRY BULLETIN

580 Fifth Ave., #806, New York NY 10036. (212)575-0444; 888-669-4747. Fax: (212)575-0722. E-mail: diamond58@aol.com; info@diamondregistry.com;.

Website: diamondregistry.com. **50% freelance written**. Monthly newsletter. "Our publication is the first independent insider newsletter of diamond information. Regularly quoted in The New York Times and other financial publications - Fortune, Forbes and Newsweek. The Diamond Registry Bulletin contains analyses and forecasts on diamond supplies prices and trends, worldwide mining updates, exclusive interviews with some of the most important players in the industry and the latest breaking news." Estab. 1969. Pays on publication. Submit seasonal material 1 month in advance. Accepts queries by mail, e-mail. Accepts simultaneous submissions. Responds in about 3 weeks to mss. Sample copy for $5.

NONFICTION Needs how-to, ways to increase sales in diamonds, improve security, etc., interview, of interest to diamond dealers or jewelers, prevention advice (on crimes against jewelers). Send complete ms. Length: 50-500 words. **Pays $75-150.**

$$ THE ENGRAVERS JOURNAL

P.O. Box 318, Brighton MI 48116. (810)229-5725. Fax: (810)229-8320. E-mail: editor@engraversjournal.com. Website: engraversjournal.com. **Contact:** Managing Editor. **70% freelance written**. Monthly magazine covering the recognition and identification industry (engraving, marking devices, awards, jewelry, and signage). "We provide practical information for the education and advancement of our readers, mainly retail business owners." Estab. 1975. Byline given Pays on acceptance. Publishes ms an average of 3-9 months after acceptance. Accepts queries by mail, e-mail, fax. Responds in 2 weeks to mss.

NONFICTION Needs general interest, industry related, how-to, small business subjects, increase sales, develop new markets, use new sales techniques, etc., technical. No general overviews of the industry. Length: 1,000-5,000 words. **Pays $200 and up.**

JOURNALISM AND WRITING

$$$$ AMERICAN JOURNALISM REVIEW

University of Maryland Foundation, 1117 Journalism Bldg., University of Maryland, College Park MD 20742. (301)405-8803. Fax: (301)405-8323. E-mail: rrieder@ajr.umd.edu; editor@ajr.umd.edu. Website: ajr.org. **Contact:** Rem Rieder, editor. **80% freelance written**. Bimonthly magazine covering print, broadcast, and online journalism. Mostly journalists subscribe. We cover ethical issues, trends in the industry, coverage that falls short. Circ. 25,000. Byline given. Pays within 1 month after publication. Offers 25% kill fee. Publishes ms an average of 2 months after acceptance. Editorial lead time 1 month. Accepts queries by mail, e-mail, fax. Responds in 1 month to queries and unsolicited mss. Sample copy for $4.95 pre-paid or online. Guidelines available online.

NONFICTION Needs expose, personal experience, ethical issues. **Buys many mss/year.** Send complete ms. Length: 2,000-4,000 words. **Pays $1,500-2,000.**

$ AUTHORSHIP

National Writers Association, 10940 S. Parker Rd., #508, Parker CO 80134. (303)841-0246. E-mail: natlwritersassn@hotmail.com. Website: webmasternationalwriters.com. Quarterly magazine covering writing articles only. "Association magazine targeted to beginning and professional writers. Covers how-to, humor, marketing issues. Disk and e-mail submissions preferred." Estab. 1950s. Circ. 4,000. Byline given. Pays on acceptance. Editorial lead time 3 months. Submit seasonal material 6 months in advance. Accepts simultaneous submissions. Responds in 2 months to queries. Sample copy for stamped, self-addressed, 8½x11 envelope.

NONFICTION Buys 25 mss/year. Query or send complete ms. Length: 1,200 words. **Pays $10, or discount on memberships and copies.**

PHOTOS State availability. Identification of subjects, model releases required. Reviews 5×7 prints. Offers no additional payment for photos accepted with ms.

$ BOOK DEALERS WORLD

North American Bookdealers Exchange, P.O. Box 606, Cottage Grove OR 97424. (541)942-7455 (ph/fax). E-mail: nabe@bookmarketingprofits.com. Website: bookmarketingprofits.com. **50% freelance written**. Quarterly magazine covering writing, self-publishing, and marketing books by mail. Circ. 20,000. Byline given. Pays on publication. Publishes ms an average of 3 months after acceptance. Accepts simultaneous submissions. Responds in 1 month to queries. Sample copy for $3.

NONFICTION Needs book excerpts, writing, mail order, direct mail, publishing, how-to, home business by mail, advertising, interview, of successful self-publishers, positive articles on self-publishing, new writing angles, marketing. **Buys 10 mss/year.** Send complete ms. Length: 1,000-1,500 words. **Pays $25-50.**

☼❂❂ CANADIAN SCREENWRITER

Writers Guild of Canada, 366 Adelaide St. W., Suite 401, Toronto ON M5V 1R9 Canada. (416)979-7907. Fax: (416)979-9273. E-mail: info@wgc.ca; mparker@wgc.ca. Website: wgc.ca/magazine. **Contact:** Maureen Parker, exec. director. **80% freelance written.** Magazine published 3 times/year covering screenwriting for television, film, radio and digital media. *Canadian Screenwriter* profiles Canadian screenwriters, provides industry news and offers practical writing tips for screenwriters. Estab. 1998. Circ. 4,000. Byline given. Pays on acceptance. Offers 50% kill fee. Publishes ms an average of 1 month after acceptance. Editorial lead time 2 months. Submit seasonal material 2 months in advance. Accepts queries by e-mail. Responds in 1 week to queries. Responds in 1 month to mss. Guidelines by e-mail.

NONFICTION Needs how-to, humor, interview. Does not want writing on foreign screenwriters. The focus is on Canadian-resident screenwriters. **Buys 12 mss/year.** Query with published clips. Length: 750-2,200 words. **Pays 50¢/word.**

PHOTOS State availability. Identification of subjects required. Reviews GIF/JPEG files. Negotiates payment individually.

☼❂ CANADIAN WRITER'S JOURNAL

P.O. Box 1178, New Liskeard ON P0J 1P0 Canada. (705)647-5424. Fax: (705)647-8366. E-mail: editor@cwj.ca. Website: cwj.ca. **Contact:** Deborah Ranchuk, editor. **75% freelance written.** Bimonthly magazine for writers. Digest-size magazine for writers emphasizing short "how-to" articles which convey easily understood information useful to both apprentice and professional writers. General policy and postal subsidies require that the magazine must carry a substantial Canadian content. We try for about 90% Canadian content, but prefer good material over country of origin, or how well you're known. Writers may query, but unsolicited manuscripts are welcome. Estab. 1984. Circ. 350. Byline given. Pays on publication. Publishes ms an average of 2-9 months after acceptance. Accepts queries by mail, e-mail, fax, phone; preference will be given to the article that can be submitted electronically. Responds in 2 months to queries. Sample copy for $8, including postage.

NONFICTION Needs how-to, articles for writers, Humorous and seasonal items. **Buys 200 mss/year.** Query optional. 400-2000/words for articles; 250-500/words for book reviews **Pays $7.50/published magazine page (approx. 450 words), plus one complimentary copy. A $2 premium is paid for electronic submissions.**

FICTION Fiction is published only through semi-annual short fiction contest with April 30 deadline. Send SASE for rules, or see guidelines on website. Does not want gratuitous violence, sex subject matter.

POETRY Poetry must be unpublished elsewhere. Short poems or extracts used as part of articles on the writing of poetry. **$2-5 per poem published, depending on length. SASE required for response.**

❂❂❂ ECONTENT MAGAZINE

Online, Inc., 48 South Main St., Suite 3, Newtown CT 06470-2140. (203)761-1466; (800)248-8466. Fax: (203)761-1444; (203)304-9300. E-mail: michelle.manafy@infotoday.com. Website: econtentmag.com. **Contact:** Michelle Manafy, editor. **90% freelance written.** Monthly magazine covering digital content trends, strategies, etc. *EContent* is a business publication. Readers need to stay on top of industry trends and developments. Estab. 1979. Circ. 12,000. Byline given. Pays within 1 month of publication. Editorial lead time 3-4 months. Accepts queries by e-mail. Responds in 3 weeks to queries. Responds in 1 month to mss. Sample copy and writer's guidelines online.

NONFICTION Needs expose, how-to, interview, new product, opinion, technical, news features, strategic and solution-oriented features. No academic or straight Q&A. **Buys 48 mss/year.** Query with published clips. Submit electronically as e-mail attachment. Length: 500-700 words. **Pays 40-50¢/word.**

PHOTOS State availability. Captions required. Negotiates payment individually.

COLUMNS Profiles (short profile of unique company, person or product), 1,200 words; New Features (breaking news of content-related topics), 500 words maximum. **Buys 40 mss/year.** Query with published clips. **Pays 30-40¢/word**

☼❂ FELLOWSCRIPT

InScribe Christian Writers' Fellowship, *FellowScript*, c/o P.O. Box 6201, Wetaskiwin AB T9A 2E9 Canada. E-mail: fellowscript@gmail.com. Website: inscribe.org. **Contact:** Janet Sketchley, acq. editor. **100% freelance written.** Quarterly writers' newsletter featuring

Christian writing. "Our readers are Christians with a commitment to writing. Among our readership are best-selling authors and unpublished beginning writers. Submissions to us should include practical information, something the reader can immediately put into practice." Estab. 1983. Circ. 200. Byline given. Pays on publication. Publishes ms an average of 6-12 months after acceptance. Editorial lead time 3 months. Submit seasonal material 4 months in advance. Accepts queries by e-mail, prefers full ms by e-mail; postal submissions only accepted from In-Scribe members. Accepts simultaneous submissions. Responds in 1 month to queries or mss Sample copy for $5, 9 x 12 SAE, and 3 first-class stamps (Canadian) or IRCs. Guidelines available online.

NONFICTION Needs essays, exposè, how-to, for writers, interview, new product. Does not want poetry, fiction, personal experience, testimony or think piece, commentary articles. **Buys 30-45 mss/year.** Send complete ms attached in rtf or doc format. Length: 400-1,200 words. **Pays 2 ½¢/word (first rights); 1 ½¢/ word reprints (Canadian funds).**

COLUMNS Book reviews, 150-300 words; Market Updates, 50-300 words. **Buys 1-3. mss/year.** Send complete ms. **Pays 1 copy.**

FILLERS Needs facts, newsbreaks. **Buys 5-10 mss/ year.** Length: 25-300 words. **Pays 1 copy.**

FREELANCE MARKET NEWS

The Writers Bureau Ltd., Sevendale House, 7 Dale St., Manchester M1 1JB England. (44)(161)228-2362. Fax: (44)(161)228-3533. E-mail: fmn@writersbureau. com. Website: freelancemarketnews.com. **15% free-lance written.** Monthly newsletter covering freelance writing. Estab. 1968. Byline given. Pays on acceptance. Publishes ms an average of 3 months after acceptance. Editorial lead time 3 months. Submit seasonal material 3 months in advance. Accepts queries by mail, e-mail, fax. Sample copy, guidelines available online.

"Prefers to receive a complete manuscript rather than a query."

NONFICTION Needs how-to sell your writing/improve your writing. **Buys 12 mss/year.** Length: 700 words **Pays £50/1,000 words.**

COLUMNS New Markets (magazines which have recently been published); Fillers & Letters; Overseas Markets (obviously only English-language publications); Market Notes (established publications accepting articles, fiction, reviews, or poetry). All

should be between 40 and 200 words. **Pays £40/1,000 words.**

FREELANCE WRITER'S REPORT

CNW Publishing, Inc., 45 Main St., P.O. Box A, North Stratford NH 03590-0167. (603)922-8338. E-mail: fwrwm@writers-editors.com. Website: writers-editors.com. **25% freelance written.** Monthly newsletter. "*FWR* covers the marketing and business/office management aspects of running a freelance writing business. Articles must be of value to the established freelancer; nothing basic." Estab. 1982. Byline given. Pays on publication. Publishes ms an average of 6 months after acceptance. Editorial lead time 2 months. Submit seasonal material 2 months in advance. Accepts simultaneous submissions. Responds in 1 week to queries. Responds in 2 weeks to mss. Sample copy for 6x9 SAE with 2 first-class stamps (for back copy); $4 for current copy. Guidelines and sample copy available online.

NONFICTION Needs book excerpts, how-to (market, increase income or profits). "No articles about the basics of freelancing." **Buys 50 mss/year.** Send complete ms by e-mail. Length: Up to 900 words. **Pays 10¢/word.**

MAINE IN PRINT

Glickman Family Library, 314 Forest Ave., Room 318, Portland ME 04102. (207)228-8263. Fax: (207)228-8150. E-mail: maineinprint@mainewriters.org; info@mainewriters.org. Website: mainewriters.org. **Contact:** Joshua Bodwell, exec. director. Quarterly newsletter for writers, editors, teachers, librarians, etc., focusing on Maine literature and the craft of writing. Estab. 1975. Circ. 3,000. Byline given. Pays on publication. Publishes ms an average of 2 months after acceptance. Editorial lead time 2 months. Accepts queries by mail. Accepts simultaneous submissions. Sample copy and writer's

NONFICTION Needs essays, how-to, writing, interview, technical. No creative writing, fiction, or poetry. **Buys 20 mss/year.** Query with published clips. Length: 400-1,500 words. **Pays $25-50 for assigned articles.**

PHOTOS State availability. Offers no additional payment for photos accepted with ms.

COLUMNS Front-page articles (writing related), 500-1,500 words. **Buys 20 articles/year mss/year.** Query. **Pays $25 minimum.**

⊛⊛⊛ MSLEXIA

Mslexia Publications Ltd., P.O. Box 656, Newcastle upon Tyne NE99 1PZ United Kingdom. [(44)(191)233-3860. E-mail: submissions@mslexia.co.uk; postbag@mslexia.co.uk. Website: mslexia.co.uk. **Contact:** Daneet Steffens, editor. **60% freelance written**. Quarterly magazine offering advice and publishing opportunities for women writers, plus poetry and prose submissions on a different theme each issue. "*Mslexia* tells you all you need to know about exploring your creativity and getting into print. No other magazine provides *Mslexia's* unique mix of advice and inspiration; news, reviews, interviews; competitions, events, grants; all served up with a challenging selection of new poetry and prose. *Mslexia* is read by authors and absolute beginners. A quarterly master class in the business and psychology of writing, it's the essential magazine for women who write." Estab. 1998. Circ. 9,000. Byline given. Pays on publication. Offers 50% kill fee. Publishes ms an average of 1 month after acceptance. Editorial lead time 3 months. Submit seasonal material 3 months in advance. Accepts queries by mail, e-mail, phone. NoAccepts simultaneous submissions. Responds in 3 months to mss. Sample copy available online. Writer's guidelines online or by e-mail.

○ This publication does not accept e-mail submissions except from overseas writers.

NONFICTION Needs how-to, interview, opinion, personal experience. No general items about women or academic features. We are only interested in features (for tertiary-educated readership) about women's writing and literature. **Buys 40 mss/year.** Query with published clips. Length: 500-2,200 words. **Pays $70-400 for assigned articles. Pays $70-300 for unsolicited articles.**

COLUMNS We are open to suggestions, but would only commission 1 new column/year, probably from a UK-based writer. **Buys 12 mss/year.** Query with published clips.

FICTION See guidelines on our website. Submissions not on one of our current themes will be returned (if submitted with a SASE) or destroyed. **Buys 30 mss/year.** Send complete ms. Length: 50-2,200 words.

POETRY Needs avant-garde, free verse, haiku, traditional. Buys 40 poems/year. Submit maximum 4 poems.

⊛⊛ NOVEL & SHORT STORY WRITER'S MARKET

F+W Media, Inc., 4700 E. Galbraith Rd., Cincinnati OH 45236. E-mail: adria.haley@fwmedia.com.

Website: writersmarket.com. **Contact:** Adria Haley, managing editor. **85% freelance written**. Annual resource book covering the fiction market. "In addition to thousands of listings for places to get fiction published, we feature articles on the craft and business of fiction writing, as well as interviews with successful fiction writers, editors, and agents. Our articles are unique in that they always offer an actionable takeaway. In other words, readers must learn something immediately useful about the creation or marketing of fiction." Estab. 1981. Byline given. Pays on acceptance plus 45 days. Offers 25% kill fee. Accepts queries by e-mail only. Include "NSSWM query" in the subject line. Responds in 4 weeks to queries.

○ Accepts proposals during the summer.

NONFICTION Needs how-to, write, sell and promote fiction; find an agent; etc., interview, personal experience. **Buys 12-15 mss/year.** Length: 1,500-2,500 words. **Pays $400-650.**

PHOTOS Send photos. Identification of subjects required. Reviews prints, GIF/JPEG files (hi-res). Offers no additional payment for photos accepted with ms.

⊛⊛ POETS & WRITERS MAGAZINE

90 Broad St., Suite 2100, New York NY 10004. (212)226-3586. E-mail: editor@pw.org. Website: pw.org. **Contact:** Suzanne Pettypiece, managing editor. **95% freelance written**. Bimonthly professional trade journal for poets and fiction writers and creative nonfiction writers. Estab. 1987. Circ. 60,000. Byline given. Pays on acceptance of finished draft. Offers 25% kill fee. Publishes ms an average of 4 months after acceptance. Submit seasonal material 4 months in advance. Accepts queries by mail, e-mail. Responds in 2 months to mss. Sample copy for $5.95 to Sample Copy Dept. Guidelines available online.

○ No poetry or fiction submissions.

NONFICTION Needs how-to, craft of poetry, fiction or creative nonfiction writing, interviews, with poets or writers of fiction and creative nonfiction, personal essays about literature, regional reports of literary activity, reports on small presses, service pieces about publishing trends. "We do not accept submissions by fax." **Buys 35 mss/year.** Send complete ms. Length: 500-2,500 (depending on topic) words.

PHOTOS State availability. Reviews b&w prints. Offers no additional payment for photos accepted with ms.

COLUMNS Literary and Publishing News, 500-1,000 words; Profiles of Emerging and Established Poets,

Fiction Writers and Creative Nonfiction Writers, 2,000-3,000 words; Regional Reports (literary activity in US and abroad), 1,000-2,000 words. Query with published clips or send complete ms. **Pays $150-500.**

🟡🟢 QUILL & SCROLL MAGAZINE

Quill and Scroll International Honorary Society for High School Journalists, 100 Adler Journalism Bldg., Room E346, Iowa City IA 52242-2004. (319)335-3457. Fax: (319)335-3989. E-mail: quill-scroll@uiowa.edu. Website: uiowa.edu/~quill-sc. **Contact:** Vanessa Shelton, publisher/editor. **20% freelance written.** Bimonthly magazine covering scholastic journalism-related topics during school year. Our primary audience is high school journalism students working on and studying topics related to newspapers, yearbooks, radio, television, and online media; secondary audience is their teachers and others interested in this topic. Estab. 1926. Circ. 10,000. Byline given. acceptance & publication. Publishes ms an average of 4 months after acceptance. Editorial lead time 2 months. Accepts queries by mail, e-mail. Accepts simultaneous submissions. Responds in 2 weeks to queries. Guidelines available.

> ◑ "We invite journalism students and advisers to submit manuscripts about important lessons learned or obstacles overcome."

NONFICTION Needs essays, how-to, humor, interview, new product, opinion, personal experience, photo feature, technical, travel, types on topic. Articles not pertinent to high school student journalists. Query. Length: 600-1,000 words. **Pays $100-500 for assigned articles. Pays complementary copy - $200 max. for unsolicited articles.**

PHOTOS State availability. Reviews GIF/JPEG files. Offers no additional payment for photos accepted with ms.

🟡🟢🟢 QUILL MAGAZINE

Society of Professional Journalists, 3909 N. Meridian St., Indianapolis IN 46208. Fax: (317)920-4789. E-mail: sleadingham@spj.org. Website: spj.org/quill.asp. **Contact:** Scott Leadingham, editor. **75% freelance written.** Monthly magazine covering journalism and the media industry. *Quill* is a how-to magazine written by journalists. We focus on the industry's biggest issues while providing tips on how to become better journalists. Estab. 1912. Circ. 10,000. Byline given. Pays on acceptance. Offers 25% kill fee. Publishes ms an average of 2 months after acceptance. Editorial

lead time 2-3 months. Submit seasonal material 2-3 months in advance. Accepts queries by e-mail. Accepts simultaneous submissions. Sample copy available online.

NONFICTION Needs general interest, how-to, technical. Does not want personality profiles and straight research pieces. **Buys 12 mss/year.** Query. Length: 800-2,500 words. **Pays $150-800.**

🟡🟢 THE WRITER

Kalmbach Publishing Co., 21027 Crossroads Circle, P.O. Box 1612, Waukesha WI 53187-1612. E-mail: queries@writermag.com. Website: writermag.com. **Contact:** Ronald Kovach, sr. editor. **90% freelance written. Prefers to buy work of published/established writers.** Estab. 1887. Pays on acceptance. Kill fee paid (but rarely used). Accepts queries by mail, e-mail. Sample copy for $5.95. Guidelines available online.

◑ No phone queries.

NONFICTION No phone queries. Responds generally in 1-2 months to submissions. Length: 700-3,400 words. **Pays $50-400.**

🟡🟢 THE WRITER'S CHRONICLE

Association of Writers & Writing Programs (AWP), Carty House MS 1E3, George Mason University, Fairfax VA 22030-4444. (703)993-4301. Fax: (703)993-4302. E-mail: chronicle@awpwriter.org. Website: awpwriter.org. **90% freelance written.** Published 6 times during the academic year; 3 times a semester. Magazine covering the art and craft of writing. *Writer's Chronicle* strives to: present the best essays on the craft and art of writing poetry, fiction and nonfiction; help overcome the over-specialization of the literary arts by presenting a public forum for the appreciation, debate and analysis of contemporary literature; present the diversity of accomplishments and points of view within contemporary literature; provide serious and committed writers and students of writing the best advice on how to manage their professional lives; provide writers who teach with new pedagogical approaches for their classrooms; provide the members and subscribers with a literary community as a compensation for a devotion to a difficult and lonely art; provide information on publishing opportunities, grants and awards; promote the good works of AWP, its programs and its individual members. Estab. 1967. Circ. 35,000. Byline given. Pays on publication. Editorial lead time 3 months. Accepts queries by Electronic queries OK but send submissions by postal mail. Accepts simultaneous submissions. Responds in 2 weeks to queries. Guidelines free and online.

NONFICTION Needs essays, interview, opinion, (does not mean letters to the editor). No personal essays. **Buys 15-20 mss/year.** Send complete ms. Length: 2,500-7,000 words. **Pays $11 per 100 words for assigned articles.**

💲💲💲 WRITER'S DIGEST

F+W Media, Inc., 4700 E. Galbraith Rd., Cincinnati OH 45236. (513)531-2690, ext. 11483. E-mail: wd-submissions@fwmedia.com. Website: writersdigest.com. **75% freelance written.** Magazine for those who want to write better, get published and participate in the vibrant culture of writers. "Our readers look to us for specific ideas and tips that will help them succeed, whether success means getting into print, finding personal fulfillment through writing or building and maintaining a thriving writing career and network." Estab. 1920. Byline given. Pays on acceptance. Offers 25% kill fee. Publishes ms an average of 6-9 months after acceptance. Accepts queries by e-mail only. Responds in 2-4 months to queries. Responds in 2-4 months to mss. Guidelines and editorial calendar available online (writersdigest.com/submissionguidelines).

⭕The magazine does not accept or read e-queries with attachments.

NONFICTION Needs essays, how-to, humor, inspirational, interviews, profiles. Does not accept phone, snail mail, or fax queries. "We don't buy newspaper clippings or reprints of articles previously published in other writing magazines. Book and software reviews are handled in-house, as are most *WD* interviews." **Buys 40 mss/year.** Send complete ms. Length: 800-1,500 words. **Pays 30-50¢/word.**

💲 WRITERS' JOURNAL

Val-Tech Media, P.O. Box 394, Perham MN 56573-0394. (218)346-7921. Fax: (218)346-7924. E-mail: writersjournal@writersjournal.com. Website: writersjournal.com. **Contact:** Leon Ogroske, ed. **60% freelance written.** Bimonthly magazine covering writing. "*Writers' Journal* is read by thousands of aspiring writers whose love of writing has taken them to the next step: writing for money. We are an instructional manual giving writers the tools and information necessary to get their work published. We also print works by authors who have won our writing contests." Estab. 1980. Circ. 15,000. Byline given. Pays on publication.

Publishes ms an average of 4 months after acceptance. Accepts queries by mail, e-mail, fax. Responds in 6 weeks to queries. Responds in 6 months to mss. Sample copy for $6. Guidelines available online.

NONFICTION Needs how-to, write, publish, market. **Buys 25 mss/year.** Send complete ms. Length: 800-2,500 words. **Pays $30.**

PHOTOS Send photos. Model releases required. Reviews transparencies, 8×10 prints, GIF/JPEG files. Offers no addition payment for photos accepted with ms; offers $50/cover photo.

FICTION "We only publish winners of our fiction contests—16 contests/year." Length: 2,000 words.

POETRY Contact: Contact Esther M. Leiper-Esteabrooks, poetry editor. Needs light verse. Does not want anything boring. Buys 30 poems/year. Submit maximum 2 poems. Length: 15 lines. **Pays $5.**

FILLERS Needs facts, gags, short humor. **Buys 20 mss/year.** Length: 10-200 words. **Pays up to $10.**

💲 WRITING THAT WORKS

Communications Concepts, Inc., 7481 Huntsman Blvd., #720, Springfield VA 22153-1648. (703)643-2200. E-mail: concepts@writingthatworks.com. Website: apexawards.com. Monthly newsletter on business writing and communications. Our readers are company writers, editors, communicators, and executives. They need specific, practical advice on how to write well as part of their job. Estab. 1983. Byline sometimes given. Pays within 45 days of acceptance. Publishes ms an average of 3 months after acceptance. Editorial lead time 3 months. Accepts queries by mail, e-mail, online submission form. Responds in 1 month to queries. Sample copy and writer's guidelines online.

NONFICTION Needs how-to. **Buys 90 mss/year.** Accepts electronic final mss. E-mail attached word processing files. Length: 100-600 words. **Pays $35-150.**

COLUMNS Writing Techniques (how-to business writing advice); Style Matters (grammar, usage, and editing); Online Publishing (writing, editing, and publishing for the Web); Managing Publications; PR & Marketing (writing).

FILLERS Short tips on writing or editing. Mini-reviews of communications websites for business writers, editors, and communicators. Length: 100-250 words. **Pays $35.**

💲💲💲💲 WRITTEN BY

7000 W. Third St., Los Angeles CA 90048. (323)782-4522. Fax: (323)782-4800. Website: wga.org. **40%**

freelance written. Magazine published 9 times/year. "*Written By* is the premier magazine written by and for America's screen and TV writers. We focus on the craft of screenwriting and cover all aspects of the entertainment industry from the perspective of the writer. We are read by all screenwriters and most entertainment executives." Estab. 1987. Circ. 12,000. Byline given. Pays on acceptance. Offers 10% kill fee. Publishes ms an average of 2 months after acceptance. Editorial lead time 4 months. Submit seasonal material 4 months in advance. Accepts queries by mail, e-mail, fax, phone, online submission form. Guidelines for #10 SASE.

💬"Guidelines are currently being rewritten."

NONFICTION Needs book excerpts, essays, historical, humor, interview, opinion, personal experience, photo feature, technical, software. No beginner pieces on how to break into Hollywood, or how to write scripts. **Buys 20 mss/year.** Query with published clips. Length: 500-3,500 words. **Pays $500-3,500 for assigned articles.**

PHOTOS State availability. Captions, identification of subjects, model releases required. Reviews transparencies. Offers no additional payment for photos accepted with ms.

COLUMNS Pays $1,000 maximum.

LAW

$$$$ ABA JOURNAL

American Bar Association, 321 N. Clark St., 15th Floor, Chicago IL 60654. (312)988-6018. Fax: (312)988-6014. E-mail: releases@americanbar.org. Website: abajournal.com. **Contact:** Allen Pusey, editor. **10% freelance written.** Monthly magazine covering the trends, people and finances of the legal profession from Wall Street to Main Street to Pennsylvania Avenue. The *ABA Journal* is an independent, thoughtful, and inquiring observer of the law and the legal profession. The magazine is edited for members of the American Bar Association. Circ. 380,000. Byline given. Pays on acceptance. Accepts queries by e-mail, fax. Guidelines available online.

NONFICTION We don't want anything that does not have a legal theme. No poetry or fiction. **Buys 5 mss/year.** We use freelancers with experience reporting for legal or consumer publications; most have law degrees. If you are interested in freelancing for the *Journal*, we urge you to include your resumè and published clips when you contact us with story ideas. Length: 500-3,500 words. **Pays $300-2,000 for assigned articles.**

COLUMNS The National Pulse/Ideas from the Front (reports on legal news and trends), 650 words; eReport (reports on legal news and trends), 500-1,500 words. The *ABA Journal eReport* is our weekly online newsletter sent out to members. **Buys 25 mss/year.** Query with published clips. **Pays $300, regardless of story length**

$$$ BENCH & BAR OF MINNESOTA

Minnesota State Bar Association, 600 Nicollet Mall #380, Minneapolis MN 55402. (612)333-1183; 800-882-6722. Fax: (612)333-4927. E-mail: jhaverkamp@mnbar.org. Website: mnbar.org. **Contact:** Judson Haverkamp, editor. **5% freelance written.** Magazine published 11 times/year. Audience is mostly Minnesota lawyers. *Bench & Bar* seeks reportage, analysis, and commentary on trends and issues in the law and the legal profession, especially in Minnesota. Preference to items of practical/professional human interest to lawyers and judges. Estab. 1931. Circ. 17,000. Byline given. Pays on acceptance. Publishes ms an average of 3 months after acceptance. Responds in 1 month to queries. Guidelines for free online or by mail.

NONFICTION Needs Needs analysis and exposition of current trends, developments and issues in law, legal profession, esp, in Minnesota. Balanced commentary and "how-to" considered. "We do not want one-sided opinion pieces or advertorial." **Buys 2-3 mss/year.** Send query or complete ms. Length: 1,000-3,500 words. **Pays $500-1,500.** Some expenses of writers on assignment.

PHOTOS State availability. Identification of subjects, model releases required. Reviews 5×7 prints. Pays $25-100 upon publication.

$$$$ CALIFORNIA LAWYER

Daily Journal Corp., 44 Montgomery St., Suite 250, San Francisco CA 94104. (213)229-5323. Fax: (415)296-2440. E-mail: sharon_liang@dailyjournal.com. Website: dailyjournal.com. **Contact:** Sharon Liang, legal editor. **30% freelance written.** Monthly magazine of law-related articles and general-interest subjects of appeal to lawyers and judges. "Our primary mission is to cover the news of the world as it affects the law and lawyers, helping our readers better comprehend the issues of the day and to cover changes and trends in the legal profession. Our readers are all California lawyers, plus judges, legislators, and corporate executives. Although we focus on California and the West, we have subscribers in every state. *California Lawyer* is a general interest magazine for people interested in law. Our writers are journalists." Estab. 1981. Circ. 140,000. Byline given. Pays on acceptance. Offers 25% kill fee. Publishes ms an average of 3 months after acceptance. Editorial lead time 3 months. Accepts queries by e-mail. No previously published articles.Sample copy and writer's guidelines for #10 SASE.

NONFICTION Needs essays, general interest, interview, news and feature articles on law-related topics. "We are interested in concise, well-written and well-researched articles on issues of current concern, as well as well-told feature narratives with a legal focus. We would like to see a description or outline of your proposed idea, including a list of possible sources." **Buys 12 mss/year.** Send complete ms. Length: 500-5,000 words. **Pays $50-2,000.**

PHOTOS Contact: Jake Flaherty, art director. State availability. Identification of subjects, model releases required. Reviews prints.

COLUMNS California Esq. (current legal trends), 300 words. **Buys 6 mss/year.** Query with or without published clips. **Pays $50-250.**

$$$$ INSIDECOUNSEL

(formerly *Corporate Legal Times*), 222 S. Riverside Plaza, Suite 620, Chicago IL 60606. (312)654-3500. E-mail: atrent@insidecounsel.com. Website: inside-counsel.com. **Contact:** Ashley Trent, managing editor. **50% freelance written.** Monthly tabloid. Estab. 1991. Circ. 45,000. Byline given. Pays on publication. Publishes ms an average of 3 months after acceptance. Editorial lead time 3 months. Submit seasonal material 3 months in advance. Accepts queries by mail, e-mail. Responds in 3 weeks to queries. Sample copy for $17. Guidelines available online.

NONFICTION Needs interview, news about legal aspects of business issues and events. **Buys 12-25 mss/year.** Query with published clips. Length: 500-3,000 words. **Pays $500-2,000.**

PHOTOS Freelancers should state availability of photos with submission. Identification of subjects required. Reviews color transparencies, b&w prints. Offers $25-150/photo.

$$$ JOURNAL OF COURT REPORTING

National Court Reporters Association, 8224 Old Courthouse Rd., Vienna VA 22180. E-mail: jschmidt@ncrahq.org. Website: ncraonline.org. **Contact:** Jacqueline Schmidt, editor. **10% freelance written.** Monthly (bimonthly July/August and November/December) magazine. "The *Journal of Court Reporting* has two complementary purposes: to communicate the activities, goals and mission of its publisher, the National Court Reporters Association; and, simultaneously, to seek out and publish diverse information and views on matters significantly related to the court reporting and captioning professions." Estab. 1899. Circ. 20,000. Byline sometimes given. Pays on acceptance. Publishes ms an average of 4-5 months after acceptance. Editorial lead time 4 months. Submit seasonal material 4 months in advance. Accepts queries by mail, e-mail. Accepts simultaneous submissions.

NONFICTION Needs book excerpts, how-to, interview, technical, legal issues. **Buys 10 mss/year.** Query. Length: 1,000-2,500 words. **Pays 1,000 max. for assigned articles. Pays $100 max. for unsolicited articles.**

COLUMNS Language (proper punctuation, grammar, dealing with verbatim materials); Technical (new technologies, using mobile technology, using technology for work); Book excerpts (language, crime, legal issues), all 1,000 words; Puzzles (any, but especially word-related games). **Pays $- $100.**

$ LEGAL ASSISTANT TODAY

James Publishing, Inc., Editorial Dept., 118 Steiner Dr., Pittsburgh PA 15236. (412)653-2262. E-mail: skane@conexionmedia.com. Website: legalassistanttoday.com; conexioninternationalltd.com. **Contact:** Sally A. Kane, Esq., editor-in-chief. Bimonthly magazine geared toward all legal assistants/paralegals throughout the United States and Canada, regardless of specialty (litigation, corporate, bankruptcy, environmental law, etc.). How-to articles to help paralegals perform their jobs more effectively are most in demand, as are career and salary information, and timely news and trends pieces. Estab. 1983. Circ. 8,000. Byline given. Pays on publication. Kill fee $25-50. Editorial lead time 10 weeks. Submit seasonal material 3 months in advance. Accepts queries by mail, e-mail, fax, online submission form. Accepts simultaneous submissions. Responds in 2 months to mss. Sample copy and writer's Guidelines available online.

NONFICTION Needs interview, unique and interesting paralegals in unique and particular work-related situations, news (brief, hard news topics regarding paralegals), features (present information to help paralegals advance their careers). Send query letter first; if electronic, send as attachment. **Pays $25-100.**

PHOTOS Send photos.

$$$$$ NATIONAL

The Canadian Bar Association, 500-865 Carling Ave., Ottawa ON K1S 5S8 Canada. (613)237-2925. Fax: (613)237-0185. E-mail: beverleys@cba.org; national@cba.org. Website: cba.org/national. Melanie Raymond, managing editor. **Contact:** Beverley Spencer editor-in-chief. **90% freelance written.** Magazine published 8 times/year covering practice trends and business developments in the law, with a focus on technology, innovation, practice management and client relations. Estab. 1993. Circ. 37,000. Byline given. Pays on acceptance. Offers 50% kill fee. Publishes ms an average of 2 months after acceptance. Editorial lead time 2 months. Accepts queries by e-mail.

NONFICTION Buys 25 mss/year. Query with published clips. Length: 1,000-2,500 words. **Pays $1/word.**

$$ THE NATIONAL JURIST AND PRE LAW

Cypress Magazines, 7670 Opportunity Rd #105, Suite 108, San Diego CA 92111. (858)300-3201; (800)296-9656. Fax: (858)503-7588. E-mail: njpl@cypressmagazines.com; callahan@cypressmagazines.com. Website: nationaljurist.com. **Contact:** Jack Crittenden, editor-in-chief. **25% freelance written.** Bimonthly magazine covering law students and issues of interest to law students. Estab. 1991. Circ. 145,000. Pays on publication. Accepts queries by mail, e-mail, fax, phone.

NONFICTION Needs general interest, how-to, humor, interview. **Buys 4 mss/year.** Query. Length: 750-3,000 words. **Pays $100-500.**

PHOTOS State availability. Reviews contact sheets. Negotiates payment individually.

$$ THE PENNSYLVANIA LAWYER

Pennsylvania Bar Association, P.O. Box 186, 100 South St., Harrisburg PA 17108-0186. E-mail: editor@pabar.org. Website: pabar.org. **25% freelance written. Prefers to work with published/established writers.** Bimonthly magazine published as a service to the legal profession and the members of the Pennsylvania Bar Association. Estab. 1979. Circ. 30,000. Byline given. Pays on acceptance. Publishes ms an average of 6 months after acceptance. Submit seasonal material 6 months in advance. Accepts queries by mail, e-mail, online submission form. Responds in 2 months to queries and to mss. Sample copy for $2. Writer's guidelines for #10 SASE or by e-mail.

NONFICTION Needs how-to, interview, law-practice management, technology. **Buys 8-10 mss/year.** Query. Length: 1,200-2,000 words. **Pays $50 for book reviews; $75-400 for assigned articles. Pays $150 for unsolicited articles.**

PHOTOS State availability. Identification of subjects required. Reviews contact sheets. Negotiates payment individually.

THE PUBLIC LAWYER

American Bar Association Government and Public Sector Lawyers Division, ABA GPS LD, 321 N. Clark St., MS 19.1, Chicago IL 60610. (312)988-5809. Fax: (312)988-5709. E-mail: katherine.mikkelson@americanbar.org. Website: governmentlawyer.org. **60% freelance written.** Semiannual magazine covering government attorneys and the legal issues that pertain to them. "The mission of *The Public Lawyer* is to provide timely, practical information useful to all public lawyers regardless of practice setting. We publish articles covering topics that are of universal interest to a diverse audience of public lawyers, such as public law office management, dealing with the media, politically motivated personnel decisions, etc. Articles must be national in scope." Estab. 1993. Circ. 6,500. Byline given. Publishes ms an average of 4 months after acceptance. Editorial lead time 6 months. Accepts queries by e-mail. Accepts simultaneous submissions. Responds in 1 month to queries. Responds in 2 months to mss. Guidelines available online.

NONFICTION Needs interview, opinion, technical, book reviews. Does not want pieces that do not relate to the status of government lawyers or that are not legal issues exclusive to government lawyers. We accept very few articles written by private practice attorneys. **Buys 6-8 mss/year.** Query. Length: 2,000-5,000 words. **Pays contributor copies.**

PHOTOS State availability. Identification of subjects, model releases required. Reviews GIF/JPEG files. Offers no additional payment for photos accepted with ms.

$$$$ SUPER LAWYERS

Thomson Reuters, 610 Opperman Dr., Eagan MN 55123. (877)787-5290. E-mail: awahlberg@lawandpolitics.com. Website: superlawyers.com. **Contact:** Adam Wahlberg. **100% freelance written.** Monthly magazine covering law and politics. We publish glossy magazines in every region of the country. All serve a legal audience and have a storytelling sensibility. We write profiles of interesting attorneys exclusively. Estab. 1990. Byline given. Pays on acceptance. Offers 25% kill fee. Publishes ms an average of 1 month after acceptance. Editorial lead time 6 months. Submit seasonal material 6 months in advance. Accepts queries by phone, online submission form. Accepts simultaneous submissions.

NONFICTION Needs general interest, historical. Query. Length: 500-2,000 words. **Pays 50¢-$1.50/ word.**

LUMBER

💲💲 PALLET ENTERPRISE

Industrial Reporting Inc., 10244 Timber Ridge Dr., Ashland VA 23005. (804)550-0323. Fax: (804)550-2181. E-mail: chaille@ireporting.com; edb@ireporting.com. Website: palletenterprise.com. **Contact:** Edward C. Brindley, Jr., Ph.D., publisher. **40% freelance written**. Monthly magazine covering lumber and pallet operations. The **Pallet Enterprise** is a monthly trade magazine for the sawmill, pallet, remanufacturing and wood processing industries. Articles should offer technical, solution-oriented information. Anti-forest articles are not accepted. Articles should focus on machinery and unique ways to improve profitability/make money. Estab. 1981. Circ. 14,500. Pays on publication. Editorial lead time 2 months. Submit seasonal material 2 months in advance. Accepts queries by mail, e-mail, fax, phone. Accepts simultaneous submissions. Sample copy available online.

NONFICTION Needs interview, new product, opinion, technical, industry news, environmental, forests operation/plant features. No lifestyle, humor, general news, etc. **Buys 20 mss/year.** Query with published clips. Length: 1,000-3,000 words. **Pays $200-400 for assigned articles. Pays $100-400 for unsolicited articles.**

PHOTOS State availability. Captions, identification of subjects required. Reviews 3x5 prints. Negotiates payment individually.

COLUMNS Green Watch (environmental news/opinion affecting US forests), 1,500 words. **Buys 12 mss/year.** Query with published clips. **Pays $200-400.**

💲💲 SOUTHERN LUMBERMAN

Hatton-Brown Publishers, P.O. Box 2268, Montgomery AL 36102. (334)834-1170. Fax: (334)834-4525. E-mail: rich@hattonbrown.com. Website: southernlumberman.com. **Contact:** Rich Donnell. **20% freelance written. Works with a small number of new/unpublished writers each year**. Monthly journal for the sawmill industry. Estab. 1881. Circ. 15,000. Byline given. Pays on publication. Publishes ms an average of 3 months after acceptance. Submit seasonal material 6 months in advance. Accepts queries by online submission form. Responds in 1 month to queries. Responds in 2 months to mss. Sample copy for $3 and 9×12 SAE with 5 first-class stamps. Guidelines for #10 sase.

NONFICTION Needs how-to, sawmill better, technical, equipment analysis, sawmill features. **Buys 10-15 mss/year.** Send complete ms. Length: 500-2,000 words. **Pays $150-350 for assigned articles. Pays $100-250 for unsolicited articles.**

💲💲 TIMBERLINE

Industrial Reporting, Inc., 10244 Timber Ridge Dr., Ashland VA 23005. (804)550-0323. Fax: (804)550-2181. E-mail: editor@ireporting.com; chaille@ireporting.com. Website: timberlinemag.com. **Contact:** Chaille Brindley, asst. publisher. **50% freelance written**. Monthly tabloid covering the forest products industry. Estab. 1994. Circ. 30,000. Byline given. Pays on publication. Editorial lead time 2 months. Submit seasonal material 2 months in advance. Accepts queries by mail, e-mail, fax, phone. Accepts simultaneous submissions. Sample copy available online.

> "Articles should offer technical, solution-oriented information. Anti-forest products, industry articles are not accepted. Articles should focus on machinery and unique ways to improve profitability and make money."

NONFICTION Contact: Tim Cox, editor. Needs historical, interview, new product, opinion, technical, industry news, environmental operation/plant features. No lifestyles, humor, general news, etc. **Buys 25 mss/year.** Query with published clips. Length: 1,000-3,000 words. **Pays $200-400 for assigned articles. Pays $100-400 for unsolicited articles.**

PHOTOS State availability. Captions, identification of subjects required. Reviews 3x5 prints. Negotiates payment individually.

COLUMNS Contact: Tim Cox, editor. From the Hill (legislative news impacting the forest products industry), 1,800 words; Green Watch (environmental news/opinion affecting US forests), 1,500 words. **Buys 12 mss/year.** Query with published clips. **Pays $200-400.**

⊝⊝ TIMBERWEST

TimberWest Publications, LLC, P.O. Box 610, Edmonds WA 98020-0160. Fax: (425)771-3623. E-mail: diane@forestnet.com. Website: forestnet.com. **Contact:** Diane Mettler, managing editor. **75% freelance written**. Monthly magazine covering logging and lumber segment of the forestry industry in the Northwest. "We publish primarily profiles on loggers and their operations—with an emphasis on the machinery—in Washington, Oregon, Idaho, Montana, Northern California, and Alaska. Some timber issues are highly controversial and although we will report on the issues, this is a pro-logging publication. We don't publish articles with a negative slant on the timber industry." Estab. 1975. Circ. 10,000. Byline given. Pays on acceptance. Editorial lead time 3 months. Accepts queries by mail, fax. Responds in 3 weeks to queries. Sample copy for $2. Guidelines for #10 sase.

NONFICTION Needs historical, interview, new product. No articles that put the timber industry in a bad light—such as environmental articles against logging. **Buys 50 mss/year.** Query with published clips. Length: 1,100-1,500 words. **Pays $350.**

PHOTOS Send photos. Captions, identification of subjects required. Reviews contact sheets, transparencies, prints, GIF/JPEG files. Offers no additional payment for photos accepted with ms.

FILLERS Needs facts, newsbreaks. **Buys 10 mss/year. mss/year.** Length: 400-800 words. **Pays $100-250.**

MACHINERY AND METAL

⊝⊝⊝ AMERICANMACHINIST.COM

Penton Media, 1300 E. 9th St., Cleveland OH 44114-1503. (216)931-9240. Fax: (913)514-6386. E-mail: robert.brooks@penton.com. Website: americanmachinist.com. **Contact:** Robert Brooks, editor-in-chief. **10% freelance written**. Monthly online website covering all forms of metalworking covering all forms of metalworking. Accepts contributed features and articles. "*AmericanMachinist.com* is the oldest magazine dedicated to metalworking in the United States. Our readers are the owners and managers of metalworking shops. We publish articles that provide the managers and owners of job shops, contract shops, and captive shops the information they need to make their operations more efficient, more productive, and more profitable. Our articles are technical in nature and must be focused on technology that will help these shops to become more competitive on a global basis. Our readers are skilled machinists. This is not the place for lightweight items about manufacturing, and we are not interested in articles on management theories." Estab. 1877. Circ. 80,000. Byline sometimes given. Offers 20% kill fee. Publishes ms an average of 1-2 months after acceptance. Editorial lead time 3-6 months. Submit seasonal material 4-6 months in advance. Accepts queries by mail, e-mail, phone. Responds in 1-2 weeks to queries. Responds in 1 month to mss. Sample copy available online.

NONFICTION Needs general interest, how-to, new product, opinion, personal experience, photo feature, technical. Query with published clips. Length: 600-2,400 words. **Pays $300-1,200.**

PHOTOS State availability. Captions, identification of subjects, model releases required. Reviews GIF/JPEG files. Negotiates payment individually.

FILLERS Needs anecdotes, facts, gags, newsbreaks, short humor. **Buys 12-18 mss/year. mss/year.** Length: 50-200 words. **Pays $25-100.**

⊝⊝⊝ CUTTING TOOL ENGINEERING

CTE Publications, Inc., 40 Skokie Blvd., Northbrook IL 60062. (847)714-0175. Fax: (847)559-4444. E-mail: alanr@jwr.com. Website: ctemag.com. **Contact:** Alan Richter, editor. **40% freelance written**. Monthly magazine covering industrial metal cutting tools and metal cutting operations. "*Cutting Tool Engineering* serves owners, managers and engineers who work in manufacturing, specifically manufacturing that involves cutting or grinding metal or other materials. Writing should be geared toward improving manufacturing processes." Circ. 48,000. Byline given. Pays on publication. Offers 50% kill fee. Publishes ms an average of 2 months after acceptance. Editorial lead time 2 months. Accepts queries by mail, fax. Responds in 2 months to mss. Sample copy and writer's

NONFICTION Needs how-to, opinion, personal experience, technical. "No fiction or articles that don't relate to manufacturing." **Buys 10 mss/year.** Length: 1,500-3,000 words. **Pays $750-1,500.**

PHOTOS State availability. Captions required. Reviews transparencies, prints. Negotiates payment individually.

⊙⊝⊝ EQUIPMENT JOURNAL

Pace Publishing, 5160 Explorer Dr., Unit 6, Mississauga ON L4W 4T7 Canada. (416)459-5163. E-mail: Editor@Equipmentjournal.com. Website: Equipmentjournal.

com. **10% freelance written**. 17 times/year. "We are Canada's national heavy equipment newspaper. We focus on the construction, material handling, mining, forestry and on-highway transportation industries." Estab. 1964. Circ. 23,000 subscribers. Byline given. Pays on publication. Publishes ms an average of 1-2 months after acceptance. Editorial lead time 2-3 months. Submit seasonal material 2 months in advance. Accepts queries by mail. Accepts simultaneous submissions. Responds within 7 days. Sample copy and

NONFICTION Needs how-to, interview, new product, photo feature, technical. No material that falls outside of *EJ*'s mandate—the Canadian equipment industry. **Buys 15/year mss/year.** Send complete ms. We prefer electronic submissions. We do not accept unsolicited freelance submissions. Length: 500-1,500 words. **$250-$400 for assigned and unsolicited articles.**

PHOTOS Contact: Nathan Medcalf, editor. State availability. Identification of subjects required. 4 x 6 prints. Negotiates payment individually.

THE FABRICATOR

833 Featherstone Rd., Rockford IL 61107. (815)399-8700. Fax: (815)381-1370. E-mail: kateb@thefabricator.com; timh@thefabricator.com. Website: thefabricator.com. Tim Heston, senior editor. **Contact:** Kate Bachman, editor. **15% freelance written**. Monthly magazine covering metal forming and fabricating. Our purpose is to disseminate information about modern metal forming and fabricating techniques, machinery, tooling, and management concepts for the metal fabricator. Estab. 1971. Circ. 58,000. Byline given. Pays on publication. Editorial lead time 6 months. Accepts queries by mail, e-mail. Responds in 2 weeks to queries. Responds in 1 month to mss. Guidelines available online.

NONFICTION Needs how-to, technical, company profile. Query with published clips. Length: 1,200-2,000 words. **Pays 40-80¢/word.**

PHOTOS Request guidelines for digital images. State availability. Captions, identification of subjects required. Reviews transparencies, prints. Negotiates payment individually.

SPRINGS

Spring Manufacturers Institute, 2001 Midwest Rd., Suite 106, Oak Brook IL 60523-1335. (630)495-8588. Fax: (630)495-8595. E-mail: lynne@smihq.org. Website: smihq.org. **Contact:** Lynne Carr, general man-

ager. **10% freelance written**. Quarterly magazine covering precision mechanical spring manufacture. Articles should be aimed at spring manufacturers. Estab. 1962. Circ. 10,800. Byline given. Pays on publication. Publishes ms an average of 3-6 months after acceptance. Editorial lead time 4 months. Accepts simultaneous submissions. Guidelines available online.

NONFICTION Needs general interest, how-to, interview, opinion, personal experience, technical. **Buys 4-6 mss/year.** Length: 2,000-10,000 words. **Pays $100-600 for assigned articles.**

PHOTOS State availability. Captions required. Reviews prints, digital photos. Offers no additional payment for photos accepted with ms.

STAMPING JOURNAL

Fabricators & Manufacturers Association (FMA), 833 Featherstone Rd., Rockford IL 61107. (815)381-0382. Fax: (815)381-1370. E-mail: kateb@thefabricator.com. Website: thefabricator.com. **15% freelance written**. Bimonthly magazine covering metal stamping. "We look for how-to and educational articles—nonpromotional." Estab. 1989. Circ. 35,000. Byline given. Pays on publication. Editorial lead time 6 months. Accepts queries by mail, e-mail, fax, phone. Responds in 2 weeks to queries. Responds in 2 months to mss. Sample copy and writer's

NONFICTION Needs how-to, technical, company profile. Special issues: Forecast issue (January). No unsolicited case studies. **Buys 5 mss/year.** Query with published clips. 1,000 words **Pays 40-80¢/word.**

PHOTOS State availability. Captions, identification of subjects required. Reviews contact sheets. Negotiates payment individually.

TODAY'S MACHINING WORLD

Screw Machine World, Inc., 4235 W. 166th St., Oak Forest IL 60452. (708)535-2200. Fax: (708)535-0103. E-mail: emily@todaysmachiningworld.com; lloydgraff-tmw@yahoo.com. Website: todaysmachiningworld.com. **Contact:** Emily or Lloyd. **40% freelance written**. Monthly magazine covering metal turned parts manufacturing U.S./global. "We hire writers to tell a success story or challenge regarding our industry. There are **no** advertorials coming from advertisers." Estab. 2001. Circ. 18,500. Byline given. Pays on publication. Offers $500 kill fee. Publishes ms an average of 2 months after acceptance. Editorial lead time 2-4 months. Submit seasonal material 2 months in advance. Responds in 1 month to mss.

NONFICTION Needs general interest, how-to. We do not want unsolicited articles. **Buys 12-15 mss/year. mss/year.** Query. Length: 1,500-2,500 words. **Pays $1,500-2,000 for assigned articles.**

PHOTOS State availability. Captions required. Reviews GIF/JPEG files. Negotiates payment individually.

COLUMNS Shop Doc (manufacturing problem/solution), 500 words. Query. **Pays $-$250.**

THE WORLD OF WELDING

Hobart Institute of Welding Technology, 400 Trade Square East, Troy OH 45373. (937)332-5603. Fax: (937)332-5220. E-mail: hiwt@welding.org. Website: welding.org. **10% freelance written.** Quarterly magazine covering welding training and education. "The content must be educational and must contain welding topic information." Estab. 1930. Circ. 6,500. Byline given. Publishes ms an average of 3 months after acceptance. Editorial lead time 3 months. Submit seasonal material 3 months in advance. Accepts queries by mail, e-mail, fax. Accepts simultaneous submissions. Responds in 1 week to queries. Responds in 3 months to mss.

NONFICTION Needs general interest, historical, how-to, interview, personal experience, photo feature, technical, welding topics. Query with published clips.

PHOTOS Send photos. Captions, identification of subjects, model releases required. Reviews GIF/JPEG files. Offers no additional payment for photos accepted with ms.

FICTION Needs adventure, historical, mainstream, welding. Query with published clips.

FILLERS Needs facts, newsbreaks.

MAINTENANCE AND SAFETY

🌍🌍 AMERICAN WINDOW CLEANER MAGAZINE

12 Publishing Corp., 750-B NW Broad St., Southern Pines NC 28387. (910)693-2644. Fax: (910)246-1681. Website: awcmag.com. Bob Lawrence, Karen Grinter, creative director. **Contact:** Gary Mauer. **20% freelance written.** Bimonthly magazine window cleaning. Articles to help window cleaners become more profitable, safe, professional, and feel good about what they do. Estab. 1986. Circ. 8,000. Byline given. Pays on acceptance. Offers 33% kill fee. Publishes ms an average of 4-8 months after acceptance. Editorial lead time 2 months. Submit seasonal material 3 months in advance. Responds in 2 weeks to queries. Responds in 1 month to mss. Guidelines available online.

NONFICTION Needs how-to, humor, inspirational, interview, personal experience, photo feature, technical, add on business. We do not want PR-driven pieces. We want to educate—not push a particular product. **Buys 20 mss/year.** Query. Length: 500-5,000 words. **Pays $50-250.**

PHOTOS State availability. Captions required. Reviews contact sheets, transparencies, 4×6 prints. Offers $10 per photo.

COLUMNS Window Cleaning Tips (tricks of the trade); 1,000-2,000 words; Humor-anecdotes-feel good-abouts (window cleaning industry); Computer High-Tech (tips on new technology), all 1,000 words **Buys 12 mss/year.** Query. **Pays $50-100.**

🌍🌍 EXECUTIVE HOUSEKEEPING TODAY

The International Executive Housekeepers Association, 1001 Eastwind Dr., Suite 301, Westerville OH 43081-3361. (614)895-7166. Fax: (614)895-1248. E-mail: ldigiulio@ieha.org. Website: ieha.org. **Contact:** Laura DiGiulio, editor. **50% freelance written.** Monthly magazine for nearly 5,000 decision makers responsible for housekeeping management (cleaning, grounds maintenance, laundry, linen, pest control, waste management, regulatory compliance, training) for a variety of institutions: hospitality, healthcare, education, retail, government. Estab. 1930. Circ. 5,500. Byline given. Publishes ms an average of 6 months after acceptance. Editorial lead time 2 months. Submit seasonal material 3 months in advance. Accepts queries by mail, e-mail, fax, phone.

NONFICTION Needs general interest, interview, new product, related to magazine's scope, personal experience, in housekeeping profession, technical. **Buys 30 mss/year.** Query with published clips. Length: 500-1,500 words.

COLUMNS Federal Report (OSHA/EPA requirements), 1,000 words; Industry News; Management Perspectives (industry specific), 500-1,500 words. Query with published clips.

MANAGEMENT AND SUPERVISION

🌍🌍🌍 HUMAN RESOURCE EXECUTIVE

LRP Publications Magazine Group, P.O. Box 980, Horsham PA 19044-0980. (215)784-0910. Fax: (215)784-0275. E-mail: kfrasch@lrp.com. E-mail: afreedman@lrp.com. Website: hronline.com. **Contact:** Kristen B.

Frasch, managing editor. **30% freelance written**. Estab. 1987. Circ. 75,000. Byline given. Pays on acceptance. Offers kill fee. Pays 50% kill fee on assigned stories. Publishes ms an average of 2 months after acceptance. Accepts queries by mail, e-mail, fax. Responds in 1 month to mss. Guidelines available online.

NONFICTION Needs book excerpts, interview. **Buys 16 mss/year.** Query with published clips. News, editorial and byline submissions: Anne Freedman, Web Editor, afreedman@lrp.com Length: 1,800 words. **Pays $200-1,000.**

PHOTOS State availability. Identification of subjects required. Reviews contact sheets. Offers no additional payment for photos accepted with ms.

$$ INCENTIVE

Northstar Travel Media LLC, 100 Lighting Way, Secaucus NJ 07094-3626. (201)902-2000; (201)902-1975. E-mail: lcioffi@ntmllc.com. Website: incentivemag. com. **Contact:** Lori Cioffi, Editorial Director. Monthly magazine covering sales promotion and employee motivation: managing and marketing through motivation. Estab. 1905. Circ. 41,000. Byline given. Pays on acceptance. Publishes ms an average of 3 months after acceptance. Accepts queries by mail, e-mail, fax. Responds in 1 month to queries. Responds in 2 months to mss. Sample copy for sae with 9×12 envelope.

NONFICTION Needs general interest, motivation, demographics, how-to, types of sales promotion, buying product categories, using destinations, interview, sales promotion executives, travel, incentive-oriented, corporate case studies. **Buys 48 mss/year.** Query with published clips. Length: 1,000-2,000 words. **Pays $250-700 for assigned articles. does not pay for unsolicited articles. for unsolicited articles.**

$$ PLAYGROUND MAGAZINE

Harris Publishing, 360 B St., Idaho Falls ID 83402. (208)542-2271. Fax: (208)522-5241. E-mail: lindstrm@playgroundmag.com. Website: playgroundmag. com. **Contact:** Lane Lindstrom, editor. **25% freelance written**. Magazine published quarterly covering playgrounds, play-related issues, equipment and industry trends. *"Playground Magazine* targets park and recreation management, elementary school teachers and administrators, child care facilities and parent-group leader readership. Articles should focus on play and the playground market as a whole, including aquatic play and surfacing."* Estab. 2000. Circ. 35,000. Byline given. Pays on publication. Publishes ms an average

of 6 months after acceptance. Editorial lead time 2 months. Submit seasonal material 1 year in advance. Accepts queries by mail, e-mail. Accepts simultaneous submissions. Responds in 1 month to queries. Responds in 2 months to mss. Sample copy for $5. Guidelines for #10 sase.

NONFICTION Needs how-to, interview, new product, opinion, personal experience, photo feature, technical, travel. *Playground Magazine* does not publish any articles that do not directly relate to play and the playground industry. **Buys 4-6 mss/year.** Query. Length: 800-1,500 words. **Pays $50-300 for assigned articles.**

PHOTOS State availability of or send photos. Captions, identification of subjects, model releases required. Reviews 35mm transparencies, GIF/JPEG files (350 dpi or better). Offers no additional payment for photos accepted with ms.

COLUMNS Dream Spaces (an article that profiles a unique play area and focuses on community involvement, unique design, or human interest), 800-1,200 words. **Buys 2 mss/year.** Query. **Pays $100-300.**

MARINE AND MARITIME INDUSTRIES

$$ CURRENTS

Marine Technology Society, 5565 Sterrett Pl., Suite 108, Columbia MD 21044-2665. (410)884-5330. Fax: (410)884-9060. E-mail: publications@mtsociety.org. Website: mtsociety.org. **Contact:** Susan Branting, managing editor. **0% freelance written**. Bimonthly newsletter covering commercial, academic, scientific marine technology. Estab. 1963. Circ. 3,200. Byline given. Pays on acceptance. Editorial lead time 1-2 months. Accepts queries by e-mail. Accepts simultaneous submissions. Responds in 4 weeks to queries Sample copy free editorial comments.

NONFICTION Needs interview, technical. **Buys 1-6 mss/year.** Query. Length: 250-500 words. **Pays $100-500 for assigned articles.**

$$ MARINE BUSINESS JOURNAL

330 N. Andrews Ave., Ft. Lauderdale FL 33301. (954)522-5515. Fax: (954)522-2260. E-mail: louisa@ marinebusiness.com. Website: marinebusinessjournal.com. **Contact:** Louisa Beckett, editor. **25% freelance written**. Bimonthly magazine that covers the recreational boating industry. *The Marine Business Journal* is aimed at boating dealers, distributors and

manufacturers, naval architects, yacht brokers, marina owners and builders, marine electronics dealers, distributors and manufacturers, and anyone involved in the U.S. marine industry. Articles cover news, new product technology, and public affairs affecting the industry. Estab. 1986. Circ. 26,000. Byline given. Pays on publication. Publishes ms an average of 1 month after acceptance. Accepts queries by mail, e-mail. Responds in 2 weeks to queries. Sample copy for $2.50, 9×12 SAE with 7 first-class stamps.

NONFICTION Buys 20 mss/year. Query with published clips. Length: 500-1,000 words. **Pays $200-500.**

PHOTOS State availability. Captions, identification of subjects, model releases required. Reviews 35mm or larger transparencies, 5×7 prints. Offers $50/photo.

PROFESSIONAL MARINER

Navigator Publishing, PO Box 461510, Escondido CA 92046. (207)772-2466, ext. 204. Fax: (207)772-2879. E-mail: editors@professionalmariner.com; jgormley@professionalmariner.com. Website: professionalmariner.com. **Contact:** John Gormley, editor. **75% freelance written.** Bimonthly magazine covering professional seamanship and maritime industry news. Estab. 1993. Circ. 29,000. Byline given. Pays on publication. Editorial lead time 3 months. Accepts queries by mail, e-mail, fax, phone. Accepts simultaneous submissions.

NONFICTION Buys 15 mss/year. Query. varies; short clips to long profiles/features. **Pays 25¢/word.**

PHOTOS Send photos. Captions, identification of subjects required. Reviews prints, slides. Negotiates payment individually.

WORK BOAT WORLD

Baird Publications, 135 Sturt St., Southbank VIC 3006 Australia. (61)(3)9645-0411. Fax: (61)(3)9645-0475. E-mail: marinfo@baird.com.au. Website: bairdmaritime.com. Monthly magazine covering all types of commercial, military and government vessels to around 130 meters in length. Maintaining close contact with ship builders, designers, owners and operators, suppliers of vessel equipment and suppliers of services on a worldwide basis, the editors and journalists of *Work Boat World* seek always to be informative. They constantly put themselves in the shoes of readers so as to produce editorial matter that interests, educates, informs and entertains. Estab. 1982.

NONFICTION Needs general interest, how-to, interview, new product. Query.

MEDICAL

ADVANCE FOR RESPIRATORY CARE & SLEEP MEDICINE

Merion Publications, Inc., 2900 Horizon Dr., King of Prussia PA 19406-0956. (800)355-5627, ext. 1324. Fax: (610)278-1425. E-mail: sgeorge@advanceweb.com; advance@merion.com. Website: advanceweb.com. **Contact:** Sharlene George, editor. **50% freelance written.** Biweekly magazine covering clinical, technical and business management trends for professionals in pulmonary, respiratory care, and sleep. "ADVANCE for Respiratory Care & Sleep Medicine welcomes original articles, on speculation, from members of the respiratory care and sleep professions. Once accepted, manuscripts become the property of *ADVANCE for Respiratory Care & Sleep Medicine* and cannot be reproduced elsewhere without permission from the editor. An honorarium is paid for published articles. **For information on preparing your manuscript, please** download our Writer's Guidelines (PDF format)." Estab. 1988. Circ. 45,500. Byline given. Pays on publication. Offers 75% kill fee. Publishes ms an average of 6 months after acceptance. Editorial lead time 1 month. Submit seasonal material 3 months in advance. Accepts queries by mail, e-mail. Accepts simultaneous submissions. Responds in 2 weeks to queries. Responds in up to 6 months to mss. Sample copy and guidelines online.

NONFICTION Needs technical. "We do not want to get general information articles about specific respiratory care related diseases. For example, our audience is all too familiar with cystic fibrosis, asthma, COPD, bronchitis, Alpha 1 Antitrypsin Defiency, pulmonary hypertension and the like." Buys 2-3 mss/year. Query. E-mail article & send printout by mail. 1,500-2,000/words. Double-spaced, 4-7 pages. **Pays honorarium.**

PHOTOS State availability. Captions, identification of subjects, model releases required. Reviews GIF/JPEG files. Negotiates payment individually.

ADVANCE NEWSMAGAZINES

Merion Publications Inc., 2900 Horizon Dr., King of Prussia PA 19406. Fax: (610)278-1425. Website: advanceweb.com. More than 30 magazines covering allied health fields, nursing, age management, long-term care and more. Byline given. Pays on publication. Editorial lead time 3 months. Accepts queries by e-mail only. Guidelines available online.

NONFICTION Needs interview, new product, personal experience, technical. Query with published clips. Include name, phone & fax no. for verification. Length: 2,000 words.

COLUMNS Phlebotomy Focus, Safety Solutions, Technology Trends, POL Perspectives, Performance in POCT & Eye on Education

$$$ AHIP COVERAGE

America's Health Insurance Plans, 601 Pennsylvania Ave. NW, South Bldg., Suite 500, Washington DC 20004. (202)778-8493. Fax: (202)331-7487. E-mail: ahip@ahip.org. Website: ahip.org. **75% freelance written**. Bimonthly magazine geared toward administrators in America's health insurance companies. Articles should inform and generate interest and discussion about topics on anything from patient care to regulatory issues. Estab. 1990. Circ. 12,000. Byline given. Pays within 30 days of acceptance of article in final form. Offers 30% kill fee. Publishes ms an average of 2 months after acceptance. Editorial lead time 2 months. Submit seasonal material 4 months in advance. Accepts queries by mail, e-mail, fax. Accepts simultaneous submissions.

NONFICTION Needs book excerpts, how-to, how industry professionals can better operate their health plans, opinion. We do not accept stories that promote products. Send complete ms. Length: 1,800-2,500 words. **Pays 65¢/word minimum.** Pays phone expenses of writers on assignment.

$ AT THE CENTER

At the Center Webzine, P.O. Box 309, Fleetwood PA 19522. (800)588-7744 ext. 2. Fax: (800)588-7744. E-mail: publications@rightideas.us. Website: atcmag. com. **20% freelance written**. Webzine published 4 times/year that provides encouragement and education to the staff, volunteers, and board members working in crisis pregnancy centers. Estab. 2000. Circ. 30,000. Byline given. Pays on publication. Publishes ms an average of 1 year after acceptance. Editorial lead time 6 months. Submit seasonal material 1 year in advance. Accepts queries by mail, e-mail, fax. Accepts simultaneous submissions. Responds in 1 month to queries. Responds in 3-4 months to mss. Online at atcmag.com. Writer's guidelines for #10 SASE or by e-mail.

NONFICTION Buys about 12 mss/year. Query. Length: 800-1,200 words. **Pays $150 for assigned articles. Pays $50-150 for unsolicited articles.**

$$$ BIOTECHNOLOGY HEALTHCARE

BioCommunications LLC, 780 Township Line Rd., Yardley PA 19067. (267)685-2783. Fax: (267)685-2966. E-mail: editors@biotechnologyhealthcare.com. Website: biotechnologyhealthcare.com. **75% freelance written**. Bimonthly magazine. "We are a business magazine (not an academic journal) that covers the economic, regulatory, and health policy aspects of biotech therapies and diagnostics. Our audience includes third-party payers, employer purchasers of healthcare, public healthcare agencies, and healthcare professionals who prescribe biotech therapies. Articles should be written in business magazine-style prose and should be focused on the concerns of these audiences." Estab. 2004. Circ. 36,000 (digital); 12,431 (print). Byline given. Pays on acceptance. Offers $300 kill fee. Publishes ms an average of 3 months after acceptance. Editorial lead time 4 months. Accepts queries by mail, e-mail, fax. NoResponds in 2 weeks to queries. Responds in 1 month to mss. Sample copy available online. Guidelines by e-mail.

NONFICTION Needs book excerpts, essays, how-to, manage the cost of biologics, case studies, interview, opinion, technical, about biotech therapies, diagnostics, or devices, regulatory developments, cost analyses studies, coverage of hot-button issues in the field. **Buys 24 mss/year.** Query with published clips. Length: 1,650-3,300 words. **Pays 75-85¢/word. Pays $300-1,870 for unsolicited articles.**

PHOTOS Contact: Philip Denlinger, design director. State availability. Captions, identification of subjects required. Reviews contact sheets, 4×6 or larger, color only prints, PowerPoint slides, TIF files that are 200 dpi or higher. Negotiates pay individually.

COLUMNS Our columns are 'spoken for,' but I am always interested in pitches for new columns from qualified writers. **Buys 18 mss/year.** Query with published clips. **Pays $300 minimum for a full piece; 75¢/word maximum for ms 600-1,200 words**

FILLERS Needs gags. **Buys 3 cartoons mss/year. Pays $300 for cartoons upon publication.**

$$ BIOWORLD PERSPECTIVES

3525 Piedmont Rd., Bldg. 6, Suite 400, Atlanta GA 30305. (404)784-9093. Fax: (404)585-3072. E-mail: amanda.lanier@ahcmedia.com. Website: bioworld.

com. **Contact:** Amanda Lanier, Managing Editor. **70% freelance written.** Weekly e-zine covering Biotechnology. "We're open to a variety of articles, so long as there's a tie-in to biotech. So far, topics have included Michael Moore's film, *Sicko*, Michael Crichton's book, *Next* and its presentation of biotech patents, a comparison of real biotech innovations to those mentioned in sci-fi, personal accounts of people's experiences with diseases, critiques of science education in the West, and how immigration impacts the biotech industry. Usually there is some connection to current events, an ethical debate, or a top-of-mind issue." Estab. 2007. Circ. 4,500. Byline given. Pays on publication. Publishes ms an average of 1 month after acceptance. Editorial lead time 2 months. Submit seasonal material 2 months in advance. Accepts queries by e-mail. Responds in 2 weeks to queries.

NONFICTION Needs essays, humor, inspirational, interview, opinion, personal experience. **Buys 25 mss/year.** Query with published clips. Length: 1,000-1,200 words.

💲💲 JEMS

Elsevier Public Safety, 525 B St., Suite 1900, San Diego CA 92101. Fax: (619)699-6396. E-mail: jems.editor@elsevier.com; a.j.heightman@elsevier.com; je.berry@elsevier.com. Website: jems.com. **Contact:** A.J. Heightman, MPA, EMT-P, editor-in-chief. **95% freelance written.** Monthly magazine directed to personnel who serve the pre-hospital emergency medicine industry: paramedics, EMTs, emergency physicians and nurses, administrators, EMS consultants, etc. Estab. 1980. Circ. 45,000. Byline given. Pays on publication. Publishes ms an average of 6 months after acceptance. Submit seasonal material 6 months in advance. Accepts queries by mail, e-mail, fax, online submission form. Responds in 2-3 months to queries. Sample copy and writer's Guidelines available online.

NONFICTION Needs essays, expose, general interest, how-to, humor, interview, new product, opinion, personal experience, photo feature, technical, continuing education. **Buys 50 mss/year.** Query. All story ideas must be submitted via our online system at ees.elsevier.com/jems. **Pays $200-400.**

PHOTOS State availability. Identification of subjects, model releases required. Reviews 4×6 prints, digital images. Offers $25 minimum per photo.

COLUMNS Length: 850 words maximum. Query with or without published clips. **Pays $50-250.**

💲💲💲 MANAGED CARE

780 Township Line Rd., Yardley PA 19067-4200. (267)685-2784. Fax: (267)685-2966. E-mail: editors_mail@managedcaremag.com. Website: managedcaremag.com. **Contact:** John Marcille, editor. **75% freelance written.** Monthly magazine. "We emphasize practical, usable information that helps HMO medical directors and pharmacy directors cope with the options, challenges, and hazards in the rapidly changing health care industry." Estab. 1992. Circ. 44,000. Byline given. Pays on acceptance. Offers 20% kill fee. Publishes ms an average of 6 weeks after acceptance. Editorial lead time 3 months. Submit seasonal material 4 months in advance. Accepts queries by mail, e-mail, fax. Responds in 3 weeks to queries. Responds in 2 months to mss. Writer's guidelines on request.

NONFICTION Needs book excerpts, general interest, trends in health-care delivery and financing, quality of care, and employee concerns, how-to, deal with requisites of managed care, such as contracts with health plans, affiliation arrangements, accreditation, computer needs, etc., original research and review articles that examine the relationship between health care delivery and financing. Also considered occasionally are personal experience, opinion, interview/profile, and humor pieces, but these must have a strong managed care angle and draw upon the insights of (if they are not written by) a knowledgeable managed care professional. **Buys 40 mss/year.** Query with published clips. Length: 1,000-3,000 words. **Pays 75¢/word.**

PHOTOS State availability. Reviews contact sheets, negatives, transparencies, prints. Negotiates payment individually.

💲💲💲💲 MEDICAL ECONOMICS

24950 Country Club Blvd., Suite 200, North Ormsted OH 44070. (440)243-8100. Fax: (440)891-2683. E-mail: tschultz@advanstar.com. Website: medicaleconomics.modernmedicine.com. **Contact:** Robert A. Feigenbaum, articles editor. Semimonthly magazine (24 times/year). Circ. 210,000. Pays on acceptance. Offers 25% kill fee. Accepts queries by mail, e-mail, fax. Sample copy available online. Guidelines available online at medicaleconomics.modernmedicine.com/writersguide.

NONFICTION We do not want overviews or pieces that only skim the surface of a general topic. We address physician readers in a conversational, yet no-

nonsense tone, quoting recognized experts on office management, personal finance, patient relations, and medical-legal issues. Mss should be double-spaced, with a heading that includes your name, address, daytime phone, and if you have them, fax number and e-mail address. Be sure to include your CV. Send the manuscript and other information to manuscripts@ advanstar.com as either message text or a Word attachment. If the ms was mailed to us between January 1 and October 31, it will be entered automatically in that year's writing contest. Length: 1,000-1,800 words. **Pays $1,200-2,000 for assigned articles.** Expenses over $100 must be approved in advance—receipts required. Will negotiate an additional fee for photos, if accepted for publication.

PHOTOS Will negotiate an additional fee for photos accepted for publication.

MIDWIFERY TODAY

P.O Box 2672, Eugene OR 97402. (541)344-7438. Fax: (541)344-1422. E-mail: mgeditor@midwiferytoday. com. Website: midwiferytoday.com. **Contact:** Sarah Harwell, managing editor. **95% freelance written.** Quarterly magazine. Estab. 1986. Circ. 3,000. Byline given. Publishes ms an average of 5 months after acceptance. Editorial lead time 3-9 months. Submit seasonal material 6 months in advance. Accepts queries by e-mail. Accepts simultaneous submissions. Responds in 2 weeks to queries. Responds in 1 month to mss. Sample copy and guidelines online.

NONFICTION Needs book excerpts, essays, how-to, humor, inspirational, interview, opinion, personal experience, photo feature, clinical research, herbal articles, birth stories, business advice. **Buys 60 mss/year.** Send complete ms. Length: 300-3,000 words.

PHOTOS Contact: Cathy Guy, layout designer. State availability. Model releases required. Reviews prints, GIF/JPEG files. $15-$50 per photo.

COLUMNS News: "In My Opinion" (150-750 words). **Buys 8 columns. mss/year.** Send complete ms.

POETRY Needs avant-garde, haiku, light verse, traditional. Does not want poetry unrelated to pregnancy or birth. Does not want poetry that is "off subject or puts down the subject." Buys 4/year poems/year. Maximum line length of 25 **Pays 2 contributor's copies. Acquires first rights.**

FILLERS Contact: Jan Tritten. Needs anecdotes, facts, newsbreaks. Length: 100-600 words.

(S)(S)(S)(S) **MODERN PHYSICIAN**

Crain Communications, 360 N. Michigan Ave., 5th Floor, Chicago IL 60601. (312)649-5439. Fax: (312)280-3183. E-mail: dburda@modernhealthcare.com. Website: modernphysician.com. **Contact:** David Burda, editor. **10% freelance written.** Monthly magazine covering business and management news for doctors. *Modern Physician* offers timely topical news features with lots of business information—revenues, earnings, financial data. Estab. 1997. Circ. 24,000. Byline given. Pays on acceptance. Publishes ms an average of 2 months after acceptance. Editorial lead time 2 months. Accepts queries by mail, e-mail. Responds in 6 weeks to queries. Writer's guidelines sent after query.

NONFICTION Length: 750-1,000 words. **Pays 75¢-$1/word. (Does not pay for Guest Commentaries.)**

TIPS "Read the publication, know our audience, and come up with a good story idea that we haven't thought of yet."

(S) **THE NEW ZEALAND JOURNAL OF PHYSIOTHERAPY**

New Zealand Society of Physiotherapists, P.O. Box 27386, Wellington New Zealand. (64)(4)801-6500. Fax: (64)(4)801-5571. E-mail: nzsp@physiotherapy. org.nz. Website: physiotheraphy.org.nz. "Acadmic journal publishing papers relevant to the theory and practice of physiotheraphy." No

NONFICTION Send complete ms.

(S) **THE NEW ZEALAND MEDICAL JOURNAL**

Dept. of Surgery, Christchurch Hospital, P.O. Box 4345, Christchurch New Zealand. (64)(3)364-1277. Fax: (64)(3)364-1683. E-mail: nzmj@cdhb.govt.nz. Website: nzma.org.nz/journal. **Contact:** Brennan Edwardes, production editor. Accepts queries by e-mail. NoGuidelines available online.

All submissions to the journal are via e-mail.
NONFICTION Send complete ms.

(S)(S)(S) **OPTICAL PRISM**

250 The East Mall, Suite 1113, Toronto ON M9B 6L3 Canada. (416)233-2487. Fax: (416)233-1746. E-mail: info@opticalprism.ca. Website: opticalprism. ca. **30% freelance written.** Magazine published 10 times/year covering Canada's optical industry. We cover the health, fashion and business aspects of the optical industry in Canada. Estab. 1982. Circ. 10,000.

Byline given. Pays on publication. Publishes ms an average of 2 months after acceptance. Editorial lead time 3 months. Submit seasonal material 3 months in advance. Accepts queries by mail, e-mail. Accepts simultaneous submissions.

NONFICTION Needs interview, related to optical industry. Query. Length: 1,000-1,600 words. **Pays 40¢/word (Canadian).**

COLUMNS Insight (profiles on people in the eyewear industry—also sometimes schools and businesses), 700-1,000 words. **Buys 5 mss/year.** Query. **Pays 40¢/word.**

⊛⊛ PLASTIC SURGERY NEWS

American Society of Plastic Surgeons, 444 E. Algonquin Rd., Arlington Heights IL 60005. Fax: (847)981-5458. E-mail: mss@plasticsurgery.org. Website: plasticsurgery.org. **Contact:** Mike Stokes, managing editor. **15% freelance written.** Monthly tabloid covering plastic surgery. *Plastic Surgery News* readership is comprised primarily of plastic surgeons and those involved with the specialty (nurses, techs, industry). The magazine is distributed via subscription and to all members of the American Society of Plastic Surgeons. The magazine covers a variety of specialty-specific news and features, including trends, legislation and clinical information. Estab. 1960. Circ. 6,000. Byline given. Pays on acceptance. Offers 25% kill fee. Publishes ms an average of 1-2 months after acceptance. Editorial lead time 1-3 months. Accepts queries by e-mail. Accepts simultaneous submissions. Responds in 2 weeks to queries. Responds in 3 months to mss. Sample copy for 10 First-Class stamps. Guidelines by e-mail.

NONFICTION Needs expose, how-to, new product, technical. Does not want celebrity or entertainment based pieces. **Buys 20 mss/year.** Query with published clips. Length: 1,000-3,500 words. **Pays 20-40¢/word.**

COLUMNS Digital Plastic Surgeon (technology), 1,500-1,700 words.

⊛⊛ PODIATRY MANAGEMENT

Kane Communications, Inc., P.O. Box 750129, Forest Hills NY 11375. (718)897-9700. Fax: (718)896-5747. E-mail: bblock@podiatrym.com. Website: podiatrym.com. Magazine published 9 times/year for practicing podiatrists. "Aims to help the doctor of podiatric medicine to build a bigger, more successful practice, to conserve and invest his money, to keep him posted on the economic, legal, and sociological changes that affect him." Estab. 1982. Circ. 16,500. Byline given. Pays on publication. $75 kill fee. Submit seasonal material 4 months in advance. Accepts queries by e-mail. Accepts simultaneous submissions. Responds in 2 weeks to queries. Sample copy for $5 and 9×12 SAE. Guidelines for #10 SASE.

NONFICTION Buys 35 mss/year. Length: 1,500-3,000 words. **Pays $350-600.**

⊛⊛ PRIMARY CARE OPTOMETRY NEWS

SLACK Inc., 6900 Grove Rd., Thorofare NJ 08086. (856)848-1000; (800)257-8290. Fax: (856)848-6091. E-mail: editor@pconsupersite.com. Website: pconsupersite.com. **Contact:** Nancy Hemphill, editor-in-chief. **5% freelance written.** Monthly tabloid covering optometry. *Primary Care Optometry News* strives to be the optometric professional's definitive information source by delivering timely, accurate, authoritative and balanced reports on clinical issues, socioeconomic and legislative affairs, ophthalmic industry and research developments, as well as updates on diagnostic and thereapeutic regimens and techniques to enhance the quality of patient care. Estab. 1996. Circ. 39,000. Byline given. Pays on publication. Offers 50% kill fee. Publishes ms an average of 2 months after acceptance. Editorial lead time 2 months. Accepts queries by mail, e-mail, fax, phone. Responds in 2 weeks to queries. Sample copy available online. Guidelines by e-mail.

NONFICTION Needs how-to, interview, new product, opinion, technical. **Buys 20 mss/year.** Query. Length: 800-1,000 words. **Pays $350-500.**

PHOTOS State availability. Captions, model releases required. Reviews GIF/JPEG files. Offers no additional payment for photos accepted with ms.

COLUMNS What's Your Diagnosis (case presentation), 800 words. **Buys 40 mss/year.** Query. **Pays $100-500.**

⊛⊛ SOUTHERN CALIFORNIA PHYSICIAN

LACMA Services, Inc., 707 Wilshire Blvd., Suite 3800, Los Angeles CA 90017. (213)226-0335. Fax: (213)226-0350. E-mail: cheryle@lacmanet.org. Website: socalphysician.net. **Contact:** Cheryl England, publisher/editor. **25% freelance written.** Monthly magazine covering non-technical articles of relevance to physicians. "We want professional, well-researched articles covering policy, issues, and other concerns of physicians. No personal anecdotes or patient viewpoints." Estab. 1908. Circ. 18,000. Byline given. Pays on acceptance. Offers 10% kill fee. Publishes ms an average of 2-3 months after acceptance. Editorial lead time 2-3 months. Accepts queries by e-mail. Accepts simultaneous submissions. Responds in 4 weeks to queries. Responds in 2 months to mss. Sample copy available online.

NONFICTION Needs general interest. **Buys 12-24 mss/year. mss/year.** Query with published clips. Length: 600-3,000 words. **Pays $200-600 for assigned articles.**

PHOTOS State availability.

COLUMNS Medical World (tips/how-to's), 800-900 words. Query with published clips. **Pays $$200-$600.**

⊘ $$ STRATEGIC HEALTH CARE MARKETING

Health Care Communications, 11 Heritage Lane, P.O. Box 594, Rye NY 10580. (914)967-6741. Fax: (914)967-3054. E-mail: healthcomm@aol.com. Website: strategichealthcare.com. **Contact:** Michele von Dambrowski, Publisher. **90% freelance written.** Monthly newsletter covering health care marketing and management in a wide range of settings, including hospitals, medical group practices, home health services, and managed care organizations. Emphasis is on strategies and techniques employed within the health care field and relevant applications from other service industries. Works with published/established writers only. Estab. 1984. Byline given. Pays on publication. Offers 25% kill fee. Publishes ms an average of 2 months after acceptance. Accepts queries by mail, e-mail. Responds in 1 month to queries. Sample copy for sae with 9×12 envelope and 3 first-class stamps. Guidelines sent with sample copy only.

NONFICTION Needs how-to, interview, new product, technical. **Buys 50 mss/year.** Query. Length: 700-3,000 words. **Pays $100-500.** Sometimes pays expenses of writers on assignment with prior authorization.

MUSIC TRADE

$ CLASSICAL SINGER MAGAZINE

Classical Publications, Inc., P.O. Box 1710, Draper UT 84020. (801)254-1025, ext. 14. Fax: (801)254-3139. E-mail: editorial@classicalsinger.com. Website: classicalsinger.com. **Contact:** Sara Thomas. Monthly magazine covering classical singers. Estab. 1988. Circ. 7,000. Byline given, plus bio and contact info Pays on publication. Publishes ms an average of 3 months after acceptance. Editorial lead time 3 months. Submit seasonal material 3 months in advance. Accepts queries by e-mail. Responds in 1 month to queries. Potential writers will be given password to website version of magazine and writer's guidelines online.

NONFICTION Needs book excerpts, expose, carefully done, how-to, humor, interview, new product, personal experience, photo feature, religious, technical, travel, crossword puzzles on opera theme. Does not want reviews unless they are assigned. Query with published clips. Length: 500-3,000 words. **Pays 5Â¢/word ($50 minimum). Writers also receive 10 copies of the magazine.** Pays telephone expenses of writers with assignments when Xerox copy of bill submitted.

PHOTOS Send photos. Captions required.

⊘ $ INTERNATIONAL BLUEGRASS

International Bluegrass Music Association, 2 Music Circle S., Suite 100, Nashville TN 37203. (615)256-3222. Fax: (615)256-0450. E-mail: info@ibma.org. Website: ibma.org; discoverbluegrass.com. **10% freelance written.** Bimonthly newsletter. "We are the business publication for the bluegrass music industry. IBMA believes that our music has growth potential. We are interested in hard news and features concerning how to reach that potential and how to conduct business more effectively." Estab. 1985. Circ. 4,500. Byline given. Pays on publication. Publishes ms an average of 2 months after acceptance. Submit seasonal material 4 months in advance. Accepts queries by mail, e-mail, phone. Accepts simultaneous submissions. Responds in 1 month to queries. Sample copy for sae with 6x9 envelope and 2 First-Class stamps.

NONFICTION Needs book excerpts, essays, how-to, conduct business effectively within bluegrass music, new product, opinion. No interview/profiles/feature stories of performers (rare exceptions) or fans. **Buys 6 mss/year.** Query. Length: 1,000-1,200 words. **Pays up to $150/article for assigned articles.**

PHOTOS Send photos. Captions, identification of subjects, required. Offers no additional payment for photos accepted with ms.

$$$ MIX MAGAZINE

Penton Media, 249 W. 17th St., New York NY 10011. Fax: (510)653-5142; (212)204-4200. E-mail: tkenny@

mixonline.com; gpetersen@mixonline.com. Website: mixonline.com. **Contact:** Tom Kenny, Group Editorial Director. **50% freelance written.** Monthly magazine covering pro audio. *Mix* is a trade publication geared toward professionals in the music/sound production recording and post-production industries. We include stories about music production, sound for picture, live sound, etc. We prefer in-depth technical pieces that are applications-oriented. Estab. 1977. Circ. 50,000. Byline given. Pays on publication. Offers 50% kill fee. Publishes ms an average of 3 months after acceptance. Editorial lead time 10 weeks. Submit seasonal material 3 months in advance. Responds in 2 weeks to queries. Responds in 1 month to mss. Sample copy for $6.

NONFICTION Needs how-to, interview, new product, technical, project/studio spotlights. Special issues: Sound for picture supplement (April, September), Design issue. **Buys 60 mss/year.** Query. Length: 500-2,000 words. **Pays $300-800 for assigned articles. Pays $300-400 for unsolicited articles.**

PHOTOS State availability. Captions, identification of subjects required. Reviews 4x5 transparencies, prints. Negotiates payment individually.

[$] [$] THE MUSIC & SOUND RETAILER

Testa Communications, 25 Willowdale Ave., Port Washington NY 11050. (516)767-2500. E-mail: bberk@testa.com. Website: msretailer.com. **10% freelance written.** Monthly magazine covering business to business publication for music instrument products. *The Music & Sound Retailer* covers the music instrument industry and is sent to all dealers of these products, including Guitar Center, Sam Ash, and all small independent stores. Estab. 1983. Circ. 11,700. Byline given. Pays on publication. Offers $100 kill fee. Editorial lead time 1 month. Submit seasonal material 2 months in advance. Accepts queries by e-mail. Accepts simultaneous submissions. Responds in 2 weeks to queries. Responds in 1 month to mss. Sample copy for #10 sase.

NONFICTION Needs how-to, new product, opinion, (does not mean letters to the editor), personal experience. Concert and CD reviews are never published; interviews with musicians. **Buys 25 mss/year.** Query with published clips. Length: 1,000-2,000 words. **Pays $300-400 for assigned articles. Pays $300-400 for unsolicited articles.**

PHOTOS Send photos. Captions required. Reviews GIF/JPEG files. Offers no additional payment for photos accepted with ms.

MUSIC CONNECTION

Music Connection, Inc., 14654 Victory Blvd., Encino CA 91436. (818)995-0101. Fax: (818)995-9235. E-mail: markn@musicconnection.com. Website: musicconnection.com. **40% freelance written.** Monthly magazine geared toward working musicians and/or other industry professionals, including producers/engineers/studio staff, managers, agents, publicists, music publishers, record company staff, concert promoters/bookers, etc. Found in select major booksellers and all Guitar Centers in America. Check out our Digital Edition (including video and audio content) at musicconnection.com/digital. Estab. 1977. Circ. 75,000. Byline given. Pays after publication. Offers kill fee. Kill fee varies. Publishes ms an average of 2 months after acceptance. Editorial lead time 2 months. Submit seasonal material 2 months in advance. Sample copy for $5.

NONFICTION Needs how-to, music industry related, interview, new product, technical. Query with published clips. Length: 1,000-5,000 words. **Payment varies.**

MUSIC EDUCATORS JOURNAL

MENC: The National Association for Music Education, Sage Publications, Inc., 2455 Teller Rd., Thousand Oaks CA 91320. (805)499-0721. Fax: (805)499-8096. E-mail: ellaw@menc.org. Website: sagepub.com. **Contact:** Ella Wilcox, Acqusitions. Quarterly music education journal published in March, June, September, and December. "Offers scholarly and practical articles on music teaching approaches and philosophies, instructional techniques, current trends and issues in music education in schools and communities and the latest in products and services. Especially welcome are topics of value, assistance, or inspiration to practicing music teachers." Accepts queries by e-mail. Articles should not have been previously published elsewhere.Sample copy available. Guidelines available online.

NONFICTION Needs , "Music Educators Journal (MEJ) encourages music education professionals to submit manuscripts about all phases of music education in schools and communities, practical instructional techniques, teaching philosophy, and current issues in music teaching and learning. The main goal of MEJ is to advance music education.". Authors should avoid personal asides that are not relevant to the primary topic, as well as content that promotes a person, performing group, institution, or product. Submissions should be grounded in the professional literature. Articles with no citations or reference to previous work in the area will not be considered for publication. Manuscripts should be submitted electronically to mc.manuscriptcentral.com/mej. Length: 1,800-3,500/words **Each author receives two copies of the issue in which his or her article appears; authors may also order additional copies.**

PHOTOS "Up to three photographs are a welcome part of accepted articles. Each photograph must be accompanied by a short caption and photo credit information. credit information. All minors must have parental or guardian's permission for their images to be used. Please contact Ella Wilcox at ellaw@menc.org if you feel it is necessary to have more than three photographs included with your article. Acceptable file formats for photographs include TIFF, EPS, and JPEG, and PDF Microsoft Application Files are acceptable. 2011-02-01."

❸❸❸ OPERA NEWS

Metropolitan Opera Guild, Inc., 70 Lincoln Center Plaza, New York NY 10023-6593. (212)769-7080. Fax: (212)769-8500. E-mail: info@operanews.com. Website: operanews.com. **Contact:** Kitty March. **75% freelance written**. Monthly magazine for people interested in opera; the opera professional as well as the opera audience. Estab. 1936. Circ. 105,000. Byline given. Pays on publication. Publishes ms an average of 4 months after acceptance. Editorial lead time 4 months. Accepts queries by e-mail. Sample copy for $5.

NONFICTION Needs historical, interview, informational, think pieces, opera, CD, and DVD reviews, book reviews. We do not accept works of fiction or personal remembrances. No phone calls, please. Query. Length: 1,500-2,800 words. **Pays $450-1,200.**

❸ OVERTONES

American Guild of English Handbell Ringers, P.O. Box 1765, Findlay OH 45839. E-mail: editor@agehr.org. Website: agehr.org. **Contact:** J.R. Smith, publications director. **80% freelance written**. Bimonthly magazine covering English handbell ringing and conducting. "AGEHR is dedicated to advancing the musical art of handbell/handchime ringing through education, community and communication. The purpose of 'Overtones' is to provide a printed resource to

support that mission. We offer how-to articles, inspirational stories and interviews with well-known people and unique ensembles." Estab. 1954. Circ. 8,000. Byline given. Pays on publication. Publishes ms an average of 4 months after acceptance. Editorial lead time 4 months. Submit seasonal material 4 months in advance. Accepts queries by mail, e-mail. Responds in 1 month to queries and to mss. Sample copy by e-mail. Guidelines by e-mail.

NONFICTION Needs essays, general interest, historical, how-to, inspirational, interview, religious, technical. Does not want product news, promotional material. **Buys 8-12 mss/year.** Send complete ms. Length: 1,200-2,400 words. **Pays $120.**

PHOTOS State availability of or send photos. Captions required. Reviews 8×10 prints, JPEG/TIFF files. Offers no additional payment for photos accepted with ms.

COLUMNS Handbells in Education (topics covering the use of handbells in school setting, teaching techniques, etc.); Handbells in Worship (topics and ideas for using handbells in a church setting); Tips & Tools (variety of topics from ringing and conducting techniques to score study to maintenance); Community Connections (topics covering issues relating to the operation/administration/techniques for community groups); Music Reviews (recommendations and descriptions of music following particular themes, i.e., youth music, difficult music, seasonal, etc.), all 800-1,200 words. Query. **Pays $80.**

❸❸ VENUES TODAY

18350 Mount Langley, #201, Fountain Valley CA 92708. Fax: (714)378-0040. E-mail: linda@venuestoday.com. Website: venuestoday.com. **Contact:** Linda Deckard, editor-in-chief. **70% freelance written**. Weekly magazine covering the live entertainment industry and the buildings that host shows and sports. "We need writers who can cover an exciting industry from the business side, not the consumer side. The readers are venue managers, concert promoters, those in the concert and sports business, not the audience for concerts and sports. So we need business journalists who can cover the latest news and trends in the market." Estab. 2002. Byline given. Pays on publication. Publishes ms an average of 1 month after acceptance. Editorial lead time 1-2 months. Submit seasonal material 1-2 months in advance. Accepts queries by mail, e-mail, fax. NoAccepts simultaneous submissions. Responds in 1 week to queries. Sample copy available online.

NONFICTION Needs interview, photo feature, technical, travel. Does not want customer slant, marketing pieces. Query with published clips. Length: 500-1,500 words. **Pays $100-250.**

PHOTOS State availability. Captions, identification of subjects required. Reviews GIF/JPEG files. Negotiates payment individually.

COLUMNS Venue News (new buildings, trend features, etc.); Bookings (show tours, business side); Marketing (of shows, sports, convention centers); Concessions (food, drink, merchandise). Length: 500-1,200 words. **Buys 250 mss/year. mss/year.** Query with published clips. **Pays $100-250.**

FILLERS Needs gags. **Buys 6 mss/year. Pays $100-300.**

PAPER

💲💲 THE PAPER STOCK REPORT

McEntee Media Corp., 9815 Hazelwood Ave., Cleveland OH 44149. (440)238-6603. Fax: (440)238-6712. E-mail: ken@recycle.cc. Website: recycle.cc. **Contact:** Ken McEntee. Biweekly newsletter covering market trends, news in the paper recycling industry. Audience is interested in new innovative markets, applications for recovered scrap paper, as well as new laws and regulations impacting recycling. Estab. 1990. Circ. 2,000. Byline given. Pays on publication. Publishes ms an average of 1 month after acceptance. Editorial lead time 2 months. Submit seasonal material 2 months in advance. Accepts queries by mail, e-mail, fax, phone. Accepts simultaneous submissions. Responds in 1 month to queries. Sample copy for #10 SAE with 55¢ postage.

NONFICTION Needs book excerpts, essays, expose, general interest, historical, interview, new product, opinion, photo feature, technical, all related to paper recycling. **Buys 0-13 mss/year.** Send complete ms. Length: 250-1,000 words. **Pays $50-250 for assigned articles. Pays $25-250 for unsolicited articles.**

PHOTOS State availability. Identification of subjects required. Reviews contact sheets. Negotiates payment individually.

💲💲 RECYCLED PAPER NEWS

McEntee Media Corp., 9815 Hazelwood Ave., Cleveland OH 44149. (440)238-6603. Fax: (440)238-6712.

E-mail: rpn@recycle.cc; ken@recycle.cc. Website: recycle.cc. **Contact:** Ken McEntee. **10% freelance written.** Monthly newsletter. "We are interested in any news impacting the paper recycling industry, as well as other environmental issues in the paper industry, i.e., water/air pollution, chlorine-free paper, forest conservation, etc., with special emphasis on new laws and regulations." Estab. 1990. Pays on publication. Publishes ms an average of 2 months after acceptance. Editorial lead time 1 month. Submit seasonal material 1 month in advance. Accepts queries by mail, e-mail, fax, phone. Accepts simultaneous submissions. Responds in 2 months to queries. Sample copy for 9×12 SAE and 55¢ postage. Guidelines for #10 sase.

NONFICTION Needs book excerpts, essays, how-to, interview, new product, opinion, personal experience, photo feature, technical, new business, legislation, regulation, business expansion. **Buys 0-5 mss/year.** Query with published clips. **Pays $10-500.**

COLUMNS Query with published clips. **Pays $10-500.**

PETS

ANIMAL SHELTERING

2100 L St., Washington D.C. 20037. (301)258-3008. Fax: (301)721-6468. E-mail: asm@hsus.org. Website: animalsheltering.org. Carrie Allan, editor. **Contact:** Shevaun Brannigan, production/marketing manager. **20%.** A magazine for animal care professionals and volunteers, dealing with animal welfare issues faced by animal shelters, animal control agencies, and rescue groups. Emphasis on news for the field and professional, hands-on work. Readers are shelter and animal control directors, kennel staff, field officers, humane investigators, animal control officers, animal rescuers, foster care volunteers, general volunteers, shelter veterinarians, and anyone concerned with local animal welfare issues. Estab. 1978. Circ. 6,000. Sample copies are free. Please contact Shevaun Brannigan at sbrannigan@hsus.org to obtain one. Contact asm@hsus.org for guidelines.

NONFICTION Approximately 6-10 submissions published each year from non-staff writers; of those submissions, 50% are from writers new to the publication. "**Payment varies depending on length and complexity of piece. Longer features generally $400-600; short news pieces generally $200. We rarely take**

unsolicited work, so it's best to contact the editor with story ideas."

🔕 DOG SPORTS MAGAZINE

4215 S. Lowell Rd., St. Johns MI 48879. (989)224-7225. Fax: (989)224-6033. E-mail: suggestions@dogsports. com. Website: dogsports.com. **Contact:** Cheryl Carlson, editor. **5% freelance written**. Monthly tabloid covering working dogs. "Dog Sports online magazine is for ALL dog trainers. We focus on the "HOW" of dog training. You will find articles on Police K-9 training, Narcotics detection, Herding, Weight Pull, Tracking, Search and Rescue, and how to increase your dog training Business. We bring you the latest in techniques from the field, actual dog trainers that are out there, working, titling and training. French Ring, Mondio, Schutzhund, N.A.P.D. PPDA, K-9 Pro Sports all are featured, as well as spotlight articles on breeds, trainers, judges, or events.". Estab. 1979. Circ. 2,000. Byline given. Pays on publication. Publishes ms an average of 1 month after acceptance. Editorial lead time 1 month. Submit seasonal material 1 month in advance. Accepts queries by mail, e-mail. Accepts simultaneous submissions. Sample copy free or online.

NONFICTION Needs essays, general interest, how-to, working dogs, humor, interview, technical. **Buys 5 mss/year.** Send complete ms. **Pays $50.**

PHOTOS State availability of photos. Captions, identification of subjects required. Reviews prints. Offers no additional payment for photos accepted with ms.

🔕🔕 PET AGE

H.H. Backer Associates, Inc., 18 S. Michigan Ave., Suite 1100, Chicago IL 60603. (312)578-1818. Fax: (312)578-1819. E-mail: cfoster@hhbacker.com. Website: petage.com. **Contact:** Cathy Foster, managing editor. **90% freelance written**. Monthly magazine for pet/pet supplies retailers, covering the complete pet industry. Prefers to work with published/established writers. Will consider new writers. Estab. 1971. Circ. 23,022. Byline given. Pays on acceptance. Publishes ms an average of 3 months after acceptance. Sample copy and writer's guidelines available.

NONFICTION No profiles of industry members and/or retail establishments or consumer-oriented pet articles. **Buys 80 mss/year.** Query with published clips. Length: 1,500-2,200 words. **Pays 15¢/word for assigned articles.** Pays documented telephone expenses.

🔕🔕 PET PRODUCT NEWS INTERNATIONAL

BowTie News, P.O. Box 6050, Mission Viejo CA 92690. (949)855-8822. Fax: (949)855-3045. E-mail: scollins@ bowtieinc.com; lmacdonald@bowtieinc.com. Website: bowtieinc.com. Lisa MacDonald, marketing director. **Contact:** Sherri Collins, editor. **70% freelance written**. Monthly magazine covers business/legal and economic issues of importance to pet product retailers, suppliers, and distributors, as well as product information and animal care issues. "*Pet Product News* covers business/legal and economic issues of importance to pet product retailers, suppliers, and distributors, as well as product information and animal care issues. We're looking for straightforward articles on the proper care of dogs, cats, birds, fish, and exotics (reptiles, hamsters, etc.) as information the retailers can pass on to new pet owners." Estab. 1947. Circ. 26,000. Byline given. Pays on publication. Offers $50 kill fee. Editorial lead time 3 months. Submit seasonal material 4 months in advance. Accepts queries by mail, fax. Responds in 2 weeks to queries. Sample copy for $5.50. Guidelines for #10 sase.

NONFICTION Needs general interest, interview, new product, photo feature, technical. No cute animal stories or those directed at the pet owner. **Buys 150 mss/year.** Query. Length: 500-1,500 words. **Pays $175-350.**

COLUMNS The Pet Dealer News™ (timely news stories about business issues affecting pet retailers), 800-1,000 words; Industry News (news articles representing coverage of pet product suppliers, manufacturers, distributors, and associations), 800-1,000 words; Pet Health News™ (pet health and articles relevant to pet retailers); Dog & Cat (products and care of), 1,000-1,500 words; Fish & Bird (products and care of), 1,000-1,500 words; Small Mammals (products and care of), 1,000-1,500 words; Pond/Water Garden (products and care of), 1,000-1,500 words. **Buys 120 mss/year.** Query. **Pays $150-300.**

PLUMBING, HEATING, AIR CONDITIONING AND REFRIGERATION

🔕🔕🔕 HEATING PLUMBING AIR CONDITIONING

One Mount Pleasant Rd., Toronto ON M4Y 2Y5 Canada. (416)764-1549. E-mail: kerry.turner@hpacmag.

rogers.com. Website: hpacmag.com. **Contact:** Kerry Turner, editor. **20% freelance written.** Monthly magazine. For a prompt reply, enclose a sheet on which is typed a statement either approving or rejecting the suggested article which can either be checked off, or a quick answer written in and signed and returned. Estab. 1923. Circ. 16,500. Pays on publication. Publishes ms an average of 3 months after acceptance. Accepts queries by mail, e-mail, phone. Responds in 2 months to queries.

NONFICTION Needs how-to, technical. Length: 1,000-1,500 words. **Pays 25¢/word.**

$$ SNIPS MAGAZINE

BNP Media, 2401 W. Big Beaver Rd., Suite 700, Troy MI 48084. (248)244-6416. Fax: (248)362-0317. E-mail: mcconnellm@bnpmedia.com. Website: snipsmag.com. **2% freelance written.** Monthly magazine for sheet metal, heating, ventilation, air conditioning, and metal roofing contractors. Estab. 1932. Publishes ms an average of 3 months after acceptance. Accepts queries by mail, e-mail, fax, phone. Call for writer's guidelines.

NONFICTION Under 1,000 words unless on special assignment. **Pays $200-300.**

PHOTOS Negotiable.

PRINTING

$$ THE BIG PICTURE

ST Media Group International, 11262 Cornell Park Dr., Cincinnati OH 45242. (513)263-9377. E-mail: gregory.sharpless@stmediagroup.com; lauren.mosko@stmediagroup.com. Website: bigpicture.net. **Contact:** Gregory Sharpless. **20% freelance written.** Monthly magazine covering wide-format digital printing. "*The Big Picture* covers wide-format printing as well as digital workflow, finishing, display, capture, and other related topics. Our 21,500 readers include digital print providers, sign shops, commercial printers, in-house print operations, and other print providers across the country. We are primarily interested in the technology and work processes behind wide-format printing, but also run trend features on segments of the industry (innovations in point-of-purchase displays, floor graphics, fine-art printing, vehicle wrapping, textile printing, etc.)." Estab. 1996. Circ. 21,500 controlled. Byline given. Pays on publication. Offers 20% kill fee. Publishes ms an average of 2 months after acceptance. Editorial lead time 2 months. Accepts queries by e-mail. Accepts simultaneous submissions. Responds in 2 weeks to queries. Responds in 1 month to mss. Sample copy available online. Guidelines available.

NONFICTION Needs how-to, interview, new product, technical. Does not want broad consumer-oriented pieces that don't speak to the business and technical aspects of producing print for pay. **Buys 15-30 mss/year. mss/year.** Query with published clips. Length: 1500-2500 words. **Pays $500-700 for assigned articles.** Sometimes (limit agreed upon in advance)

PHOTOS Send photos. Reviews GIF/JPEG files hi-res. Offers no additonal payment for photos accepted with ms.

$$ IMPRESSIONS

Nielsen Business Media, 1145 Sanctuary Pkwy., Suite 355, Alpharetta GA 30004. (770)291-5574. Fax: (770)777-8733. E-mail: mderryberry@impressionsmag.com'; jlaster@impressionsmag.com. Website: impressionsmag.com. Jamar Laster, Managing Editor. **Contact:** Marcia Derryberry, editor-in-chief. **30% freelance written.** Monthly magazine covering computerized embroidery and digitizing design. Readable, practical business and/or technical articles that show our readers how to succeed in their profession; published 13 times a year. Estab. 1994. Circ. 20,000. Byline given. Pays on publication. Publishes ms an average of 3 months after acceptance. Editorial lead time 3 months. Submit seasonal material 6 months in advance. Accepts queries by mail, e-mail. Accepts simultaneous submissions. Sample copy for $10.

NONFICTION Needs how-to, embroidery, sales, marketing, design, general business info, interview, new product, photo feature, technical, computerized embroidery. **Buys 40 mss/year.** Query. Length: 800-2,000 words. **Pays $200 and up for assigned articles.**

PHOTOS Send photos. Reviews transparencies, prints. Negotiates payment individually.

$$ IN-PLANT GRAPHICS

North American Publishing Co., 1500 Spring Garden St., Suite 1200, Philadelphia PA 19130. (215)238-5321. Fax: (215)238-5457. E-mail: bobneubauer@napco.com. Website: ipgonline.com. **Contact:** Bob Neubauer, editor. **40% freelance written.** Estab. 1951. Circ. 23,100. Byline given. Pays on publication. Publishes ms an average of 3 months after acceptance. Editorial lead time 2 months. Submit seasonal material 3 months in advance. Accepts queries by mail, e-mail, fax. Guidelines available online.

NONFICTION Needs new product, graphic arts, technical, graphic arts/printing/prepress. No articles on desktop publishing software or design software. No Internet publishing articles. **Buys 5 mss/ year.** Query with published clips. Length: 800-1,500 words. **Pays $350-500.**

PHOTOS State availability. Captions, identification of subjects required. Reviews transparencies, prints. Negotiates payment individually.

💲💲 SCREEN PRINTING

ST Media Group International, 11262 Cornell Park Dr., Cincinnati OH 45242. (513)421-2050, ext. 331. Fax: (513)421-5144. E-mail: ben.rosenfield@stmediagroup.com. Website: screenweb.com. **Contact:** Ben Rosenfield. **30% freelance written**. Monthly magazine for the screen printing industry, including screen printers (commercial, industrial, and captive shops), suppliers and manufacturers, ad agencies, and allied professions. Works with a small number of new/unpublished writers each year. Estab. 1953. Circ. 17,500. Byline given. Pays on publication. Publishes ms an average of 3 months after acceptance. Accepts queries by mail, e-mail, fax. Sample copy available. Guidelines for #10 sase.

NONFICTION Unsolicited mss not returned. **Buys 10-15 mss/year.** Query. **Pays $400 minimum for major features.**

PHOTOS Cover photos negotiable; b&w or color. Published material becomes the property of the magazine.

PROFESSIONAL PHOTOGRAPHY

💲💲 NEWS PHOTOGRAPHER

National Press Photographers Association, Inc., 6677 Whitemarsh Valley Walk, Austin TX 78746. E-mail: magazine@nppa.org. Website: nppa.org. Published 12 times/year. *"News Photographer magazine is dedicated to the advancement of still and television news photography. The magazine presents articles, interviews, profiles, history, new products, electronic imaging, and news related to the practice of photojournalism."*. Estab. 1946. Circ. 11,000. Byline given. Pays on acceptance. Offers 100% kill fee. Publishes ms an

average of 4 months after acceptance. Editorial lead time 2 months. Submit seasonal material 2 months in advance. Accepts queries by mail, e-mail, fax, phone. Accepts simultaneous submissions. Responds in 1 month to queries. Sample copy for sae with 9×12 envelope and 3 First-Class stamps.

NONFICTION Needs historical, how-to, interview, new product, opinion, personal experience, photo feature, technical. **Buys 10 mss/year.** Query. 1,500 words **Pays $300.**

PHOTOS State availability. Captions, identification of subjects required. Reviews high resolution, digital images only. Negotiates payment individually.

💲💲 THE PHOTO REVIEW

140 E. Richardson Ave., Suite 301, Langhorne PA 19047. (215)891-0214. Fax: (215)891-9358. E-mail: info@photoreview.org. Website: photoreview.org. **50% freelance written**. Quarterly magazine covering art photography and criticism. *"The Photo Review publishes critical reviews of photography exhibitions and books, critical essays, and interviews. We do not publish how-to or technical articles."* Estab. 1976. Circ. 2,000. Byline given. Pays on publication. Publishes ms an average of 9-12 months after acceptance. Editorial lead time 3 months. Submit seasonal material 6 months in advance. Accepts queries by mail. Accepts simultaneous submissions. Responds in 2 months to queries. Responds in 3 months to mss. Sample copy for $7. Guidelines for #10 SASE.

NONFICTION Needs interview, photography essay, critical review. No how-to articles. **Buys 20 mss/year.** Send complete ms. 2-20 typed pages **Pays $10-250.**

REAL ESTATE

💲💲 AREA DEVELOPMENT ONLINE

Halcyon Business Publications, Inc., 400 Post Ave., Westbury NY 11590. (516)338-0900, ext. 211. Fax: (516)338-0100. E-mail: gerri@areadevelopment.com. Website: areadevelopment.com. **Contact:** Geraldine Gambale, editor. **80% freelance written. Prefers to work with published/established writers.** Bimonthly magazine covering corporate facility planning and site selection for industrial chief executives worldwide. Estab. 1965. Circ. 45,000. Byline given. Pays on publication. Publishes ms an average of 2 months after acceptance. Accepts queries by mail, e-mail, fax.

Responds in 3 months to queries. Guidelines for #10 sase.

NONFICTION Needs historical, if it deals with corporate facility planning, how-to, experiences in site selection and all other aspects of corporate facility planning, interview, corporate executives and industrial developers. **Buys 75 mss/year.** Query. Length: 1,500-2,000 words. **Pays 40¢/word.**

PHOTOS State availability. Captions, identification of subjects required. Reviews JPEGS of at least 300 dpi. Negotiates payment individually.

○⊜♥⊕⊕ CANADIAN PROPERTY MANAGEMENT

Mediaedge Communications Inc., 5255 Yonge St., Suite 1000, Toronto ON M2N 6P4 Canada. (416)512-8186. Fax: (416)512-8344. E-mail: paulm@mediaedge.ca. Website: mediaedge.ca. **10% freelance written.** Magazine published 8 times/year covering Canadian commercial, industrial, institutional (medical and educational), residential properties. *Canadian Property Management* magazine is a trade journal supplying building owners and property managers with Canadian industry news, case law reviews, technical updates for building operations and events listings. Building and professional profile articles are regular features. Estab. 1985. Circ. 12,500. Byline given. Pays on publication. Publishes ms an average of 3 months after acceptance. Editorial lead time 2 months. Submit seasonal material 2 months in advance. Accepts queries by mail, e-mail, fax, phone. Accepts simultaneous submissions. Responds in 3 weeks to queries. Responds in 2 months to mss. Sample copy for $5, subject to availability.

NONFICTION Needs interview, technical. No promotional articles (i.e., marketing a product or service geared to this industry) Query with published clips. Length: 700-1,200 words. **Pays 35¢/word.**

PHOTOS State availability. Captions, identification of subjects, model releases required. Reviews transparencies, 3x5 prints, digital (at least 300 dpi). Offers no additional payment for photos accepted with ms.

⊕⊕ THE COOPERATOR

Yale Robbins, Inc., 102 Madison Ave., 5th Floor, New York NY 10016. (212)683-5700. Fax: (646)405-9768. E-mail: editorial@cooperator.com. Website: cooperator.com. **70% freelance written.** Monthly tabloid covering real estate in the New York City metro area. *The Cooperator* covers condominium and cooperative issues in New York and beyond. It is read by condo unit owners and co-op shareholders, real estate professionals, board members and managing agents, and other service professionals. Estab. 1980. Circ. 40,000. Byline given. Pays on publication. Publishes ms an average of 3 months after acceptance. Submit seasonal material 3 months in advance. Accepts queries by mail, e-mail, fax. Responds in 1 month to queries. Sample copy and writer's

NONFICTION Needs interview, new product, personal experience. No submissions without queries. Query with published clips. Length: 1,500-2,000 words. **Pays $325-425.**

PHOTOS State availability.

COLUMNS Profiles of co-op/condo-related businesses with something unique; Building Finance (investment and financing issues); Buying and Selling (market issues, etc.); Design (architectural and interior/exterior design, lobby renovation, etc.); Building Maintenance (issues related to maintaining interior/exterior, facades, lobbies, elevators, etc.); Legal Issues Related to Co-Ops/Condos; Real Estate Trends, all 1,500 words. **Buys 100 mss/year.** Query with published clips.

⊕⊕ FLORIDA REALTOR MAGAZINE

Florida Association of Realtors, 7025 Augusta National Dr., Orlando FL 32822-5017. (407)438-1400. Fax: (407)438-1411. E-mail: flrealtor@floridarealtors.org. Website: floridarealtormagazine.com. **Contact:** Doug Damerst, editor-in-chief. **70% freelance written.** Journal published 10 times/year covering the Florida real estate profession. "As the official publication of the Florida Association of Realtors, we provide helpful articles for our 115,000 members. We report new practices that lead to successful real estate careers and stay up on the trends and issues that affect business in Florida's real estate market." Estab. 1925. Circ. 112,205. Byline given. Pays on publication. Publishes ms an average of 2 months after acceptance. Editorial lead time 3 months. Accepts queries by mail, e-mail, fax. Sample copy available online.

NONFICTION No fiction or poetry. **Buys varying number of mss/year.** Query with published clips. Length: 800-1,500 words. **Pays $500-700.**

PHOTOS State availability of photos. Captions, identification of subjects, model releases required. Negotiates payment individually.

COLUMNS Some written in-house: Law & Ethics, 900

words; Market It, 600 words; Technology & You, 800 words; ManageIt, 600 words. **Buys varying number of columns mss/year. Payment varies.**

$$ OFFICE BUILDINGS MAGAZINE

Yale Robbins, Inc., 102 Madison Ave., New York NY 10016. (212)683-5700. Fax: (646)405-9751. E-mail: info@yrinc.com. Website: officebuildingsmagazine.com. **15% freelance written.** Covers market statistics, trends. Annual magazine published in 12 separate editions covering market statistics, trends, and thinking of area professionals on the current and future state of the real estate market. Estab. 1987. Circ. 10,500. Byline sometimes given. Pays 1 month after publication. Offers kill fee. Editorial lead time 2 months. Accepts queries by mail, e-mail, fax. Sample copy and writer's

NONFICTION **Buys 15-20 mss/year.** Query with published clips. Length: 1,500-2,000 words. **Pays $600-700.**

$$ PROPERTIES MAGAZINE

Properties Magazine, Inc., P.O. Box 112127, 3826 W. 158th St., Cleveland OH 44111. (216)251-0035. Fax: (216)251-0064. E-mail: kkrych@propertiesmag.com. Website: propertiesmag.com. **Contact:** Kenneth C. Krych, editor. **25% freelance written.** Monthly magazine covering real estate, residential, commerical construction. *Properties Magazine* is published for executives in the real estate, building, banking, design, architectural, property management, tax, and law community—busy people who need the facts presented in an interesting and informative format. Estab. 1946. Circ. over 10,000. Byline given. Pays on publication. Publishes ms an average of 2 months after acceptance. Editorial lead time 2 months. Submit seasonal material 2 months in advance. Accepts queries by mail, fax. Responds in 3 weeks to queries. Sample copy for $3.95.

NONFICTION Needs general interest, how-to, humor, new product. Special issues: Environmental issues (September); Security/Fire Protection (October); Tax Issues (November); Computers In Real Estate (December). **Buys 30 mss/year.** Send complete ms. Length: 500-2,000 words. **Pays 50¢/column line.**

PHOTOS Send photos. Captions required. Reviews prints. Offers no additional payment for photos accepted with ms. Negotiates payment individually.

COLUMNS **Buys 25 mss/year.** Query or send complete ms. **Pays 50¢/column line.**

○$$ REM

2255 B #1178 Queen St. East, Toronto ON M4E 1G3 Canada. (416)425-3504. E-mail: jim@remonline.com. Website: remonline.com. **Contact:** Jim Adair, managing editor. **35% freelance written.** Monthly Canadian trade journal covering real estate. "*REM* provides Canadian real estate agents and brokers with news and opinions they can't get anywhere else. It is an independent publication and not affiliated with any real estate board, association, or company." Estab. 1989. Circ. 45,000. Pays on acceptance. Offers 25% kill fee. Publishes ms an average of 2 months after acceptance. Editorial lead time 3 months. Submit seasonal material 3 months in advance. Accepts queries by mail, e-mail, fax. Accepts simultaneous submissions.

NONFICTION Needs book excerpts, expose, inspirational, interview, new product, personal experience. "No articles geared to consumers about market conditions or how to choose a realtor. Must have Canadian content." **Buys 60 mss/year.** Query. Length: 500-1,500 words. **Pays $200-400.**

PHOTOS Send photos. Captions, identification of subjects required. Reviews transparencies, prints, GIF/JPEG files. Offers $25/photo.

$$ ZONING PRACTICE

American Planning Association, 205 N. Michigan Ave., Suite 1200, Chicago IL 60601-5927. (312)431-9100. Fax: (312)786-6700. E-mail: zoningpractice@planning.org. Website: planning.org/zoningpractice/index.htm. **90% freelance written.** Monthly newsletter covering land-use regulations including zoning. "Our publication is aimed at practicing urban planners and those involved in land-use decisions, such as zoning administrators and officials, planning commissioners, zoning boards of adjustment, land-use attorneys, developers, and others interested in this field. The material we publish must come from writers knowledgeable about zoning and subdivision regulations, preferably with practical experience in the field. Anything we publish needs to be of practical value to our audience in their everyday work." Estab. 1984. Circ. 2,900. Byline given. Pays on publication. Offers 50% kill fee. Publishes ms an average of 3 months after acceptance. Editorial lead time 6 months. Accepts queries by mail, e-mail, fax, phone. Responds in 2 weeks to queries. Responds in 1 month to mss. planning.org/zoningpractice/contribguidelines.htm.

NONFICTION Needs technical. "See our description. We do not need general or consumer-interest articles about zoning because this publication is aimed at practitioners." **Buys 12 mss/year.** Query. Length: 3,000-5,000 words. **Pays $300 min. for assigned articles.**

PHOTOS State availability. Captions required. Reviews GIF/JPEG files. Negotiates payment individually.

RESOURCES AND WASTE REDUCTION

$$ COMPOSTING NEWS

McEntee Media Corp., 9815 Hazelwood Ave., Cleveland OH 44149. (440)238-6603. Fax: (440)238-6712. E-mail: ken@recycle.cc. Website: compostingnews.com. **Contact:** Ken McEntee, editor. **5% freelance written.** Monthly newsletter about the composting industry. "We are interested in any news impacting the composting industry including new laws, regulations, new facilities/programs, end-uses, research, etc." Estab. 1992. Circ. 1,000. Pays on publication. Publishes ms an average of 1 month after acceptance. Editorial lead time 1 month. Submit seasonal material 1 month in advance. Accepts queries by mail, e-mail, fax, phone. Accepts simultaneous submissions. Responds in 2 months to queries. Sample copy for 9×12 SAE and 55¢ postage. Guidelines for #10 sase.

💬 "*Composting News* features the latest news and vital issues of concern to the producers, marketers and end-users of compost, mulch and other organic waste-based products."

NONFICTION Needs book excerpts, essays, general interest, how-to, interview, new product, opinion, personal experience, photo feature, technical, new business, legislation, regulation, business expansion. **Buys 0-5 mss/year.** Query with published clips. Length: 100-5,000 words. **Pays $10-500.**

COLUMNS Query with published clips. **Pays $10-500.**

$$$ EROSION CONTROL

Forester Communications, Inc., 2946 De La Vina St., Santa Barbara CA 93105. (805)682-1300. Fax: (805)682-0200. E-mail: eceditor@forester.net. Website: erosioncontrol.com. **60% freelance written.** Magazine published 7 times/year covering all aspects of erosion prevention and sediment control. "*Erosion Control* is a practical, hands-on, 'how-to' professional journal. Our readers are civil engineers, landscape architects, builders, developers, public works officials, road and highway construction officials and engineers, soils specialists, farmers, landscape contractors, and others involved with any activity that disturbs significant areas of surface vegetation." Estab. 1994. Circ. 20,000. Byline given. Pays 1 month after acceptance. Publishes ms an average of 3 months after acceptance. Editorial lead time 4 months. Submit seasonal material 4 months in advance. Accepts queries by mail, e-mail, fax, phone. Responds in 3 weeks to queries. Sample copy and writer's

NONFICTION Needs photo feature, technical. **Buys 15 mss/year.** Query with published clips. Length: 3,000-4,000 words. **Pays $700-850.**

PHOTOS Send photos. Captions, identification of subjects, model releases required. Reviews transparencies, prints. Offers no additional payment for photos accepted with ms.

$$ MSW MANAGEMENT

P.O. Box 3100, Santa Barbara CA 93130. (805)682-1300. Fax: (805)682-0200. E-mail: editor@forester.net. Website: mswmanagement.com. **Contact:** John Trotti, group editor. **70% freelance written.** Bimonthly magazine. "*MSW Management* is written for public sector solid waste professionals—the people working for the local counties, cities, towns, boroughs, and provinces. They run the landfills, recycling programs, composting, incineration. They are responsible for all aspects of garbage collection and disposal; buying and maintaining the associated equipment; and designing, engineering, and building the waste processing facilities, transfer stations, and landfills." Estab. 1991. Circ. 25,000. Byline given. Pays 30 days after acceptance Editorial lead time 4 months. Submit seasonal material 4 months in advance. Accepts queries by mail, e-mail, fax, phone. Accepts simultaneous submissions. Responds in 6 weeks to queries. Responds in 2 months to mss. Sample copy and writer's Guidelines available online.

NONFICTION Needs photo feature, technical. "No rudimentary, basic articles written for the average person on the street. Our readers are experienced professionals with years of practical, in-the-field experience. Any material submitted that we judge as too fundamental will be rejected." **Buys 15 mss/year.** Query. Length: 3,000-4,000 words. **Pays $350-750.**

PHOTOS Send photos. Captions, identification of subjects, model releases required. Reviews transparencies, prints. Offers no additional payment for photos accepted with ms.

⑨⑨⑨ STORMWATER

Forester Media Inc., 2946 De La Vina St., Santa Barbara CA 93105. (805)682-1300. Fax: (805)682-0200. E-mail: sweditor@forester.net. Website: stormh2o.com. **10% freelance written**. Magazine published 8 times/year. "*Stormwater* is a practical business journal for professionals involved with surface water quality issues, protection, projects, and programs. Our readers are municipal employees, regulators, engineers, and consultants concerned with stormwater management." Estab. 2000. Circ. 20,000. Byline given. Pays 1 month after acceptance. Publishes ms an average of 3 months after acceptance. Editorial lead time 4 months. Submit seasonal material 4 months in advance. Accepts queries by mail, e-mail. Responds in 3 weeks to queries.

NONFICTION Needs technical. **Buys 8-10 mss/year.** Query with published clips. Length: 3,000-4,000 words. **Pays $500-900.**

PHOTOS Send photos. Captions, identification of subjects, model releases required. Offers no additional payment for photos accepted with ms.

⑨⑨ WATER WELL JOURNAL

National Ground Water Association, 601 Dempsey Rd., Westerville OH 43081. Fax: (614)898-7786. Website: ngwa.org. Each month the *Water Well Journal* covers the topics of drilling, rigs and heavy equipment, pumping systems, water quality, business management, water supply, on-site waste water treatment, and diversification opportunities, including geothermal installations, environmental remediation, irrigation, dewatering, and foundation installation. It also offers updates on regulatory issues that impact the ground water industry. Byline given. Pays on publication. Publishes ms an average of 3 months after acceptance. Editorial lead time 6 weeks. Submit seasonal material 3 months in advance. Accepts queries by mail. Responds in 2 weeks to queries. Responds in 1 month to mss.

NONFICTION Needs essays, sometimes, historical, sometimes, how-to, recent examples include how-to chlorinate a well; how-to buy a used rig; how-to do bill collections, interview, new product, personal experience, photo feature, technical, business management.

No company profiles or extended product releases. **Buys up to 30 mss/year.** Query with published clips. Length: 1,000-3,000 words. **Pays $150-400.**

PHOTOS State availability. Captions, identification of subjects required. Offers $50-250/photo.

SELLING AND MERCHANDISING

⑨ THE AMERICAN SALESMAN

National Research Bureau, 320 Valley St., Burlington IA 52601. (319)752-5415. E-mail: articles@salestrainingandtechniques.com. Website: national-research-bureau.com; salestrainingandtechniques.com. **80%**. Monthly magazine covering sales and marketing. *The American Salesman Magazine* is designed for sales professionals. Its primary objective is to provide informative articles which develop the attitudes, skills, personal and professional qualities of sales representatives, allowing them to use more of their potential to increase productivity and achieve goals. Byline given. Publishes ms an average of 1 month after acceptance. Editorial lead time 1 month. Submit seasonal material 2 months in advance. Accepts queries by e-mail. Guidelines by e-mail.

NONFICTION Needs personal experience. **Buys 24 mss mss/year.** Send complete ms. Length: 500-1,000 words. **Pays 4¢/word.**

⑨⑨ BALLOONS & PARTIES MAGAZINE

PartiLife Publications, 65 Sussex St., Hackensack NJ 07601. (201)441-4224. Fax: (201)342-8118. E-mail: mark@balloonsandparties.com. Website: balloonsandparties.com. **Contact:** Mark Zettler, publisher. **10% freelance written**. International trade journal published bi-monthly for professional party decorators and gift delivery businesses. "BALLOONS & Parties Magazine is published six times a year by PartiLife Publications, L.L.C. for the balloon, party and event fields. New product data, letters, manuscripts and photographs should be sent attention: Editor and should include sender's full name, address and telephone number. SASE required on all editorial submissions. All submissions considered for publication unless otherwise noted. Unsolicited materials are submitted at sender's risk and BALLOONS & Parties/PartiLife Publications, L.L.C. assumes no responsibility for unsolicited materials." Estab. 1986. Circ. 7,000. Byline given. Pays on publication. Publishes ms an average of 3 months after acceptance. Submit seasonal material 6 months in advance. Accepts queries by mail, e-mail, fax, phone. Responds in 6 weeks to queries. Sample copy for sae with 9×12 envelope.

NONFICTION Needs essays, how-to, interview, new product, personal experience, photo feature, technical, craft. **Buys 12 mss/year.** Send complete ms. Length: 500-1,500 words. **Pays $100-300 for assigned articles. Pays $50-200 for unsolicited articles.**

● C&I RETAILING

Convenience & Impulse Retailing; Berg Bennett, Pty Ltd., Suite 6, The Atrium, 340 Darling St., Balmain NSW 2041 Australia. (61)(2)9555-1355. Fax: (61)(2)9555-1434. E-mail: magazine@c-store.com.au. Website: c-store.com.au. Bimonthly magazine covering retail store layout, consumer packaged goods, forecourt, impulse retailing as well as convenience food. Circ. 21,323.

NONFICTION Needs general interest, how-to, new product, industry news. Query.

●● CASUAL LIVING MAGAZINE

Reed Business Information, 7025 Albert Pick Rd., Suite 200, Greensboro NC 27409-9519. (336)605-1115. Fax: (336)605-1158. E-mail: cingram@casualliving.com; jburkhart@casualliving.com. Website: casualliving.com. **Contact:** Cinde Ingram, editor-in-chief. **10% freelance written.** Monthly magazine covering outdoor furniture and accessories, barbecue grills, spas and more. We write about new products, trends and casual furniture retailers plus industry news. Estab. 1958. Circ. 10,000. Pays on publication. Publishes ms an average of 1-2 months after acceptance. Editorial lead time 1-2 months. Submit seasonal material 2 months in advance. Accepts queries by mail, e-mail. Responds in 2 weeks to queries. Sample copy available online.

NONFICTION Needs how-to, interview. **Buys 20 mss/year.** Query with published clips. Length: 300-1,000 words. **Pays $300-700.**

PHOTOS Contact: Jesse Burkhart, editorial assistant. Identification of subjects required. Reviews GIF/JPEG files. Negotiates payment individually.

●●●● CONSUMER GOODS TECHNOLOGY

Edgell Communications, 4 Middlebury Blvd., Randolph NJ 07869. (330)864-0848. Fax: (973)252-9020; (973)607-1395. E-mail: aackerman@edgellmail.com.

Website: consumergoods.com. **Contact:** Alliston Ackerman, editor. **40% freelance written.** Monthly tabloid benchmarking business technology performance. Estab. 1987. Circ. 25,000. Byline given. Pays on publication. Publishes ms an average of 2 months after acceptance. Editorial lead time 3 months. Accepts queries by e-mail. Sample copy available online. Guidelines by e-mail.

NONFICTION Needs essays, expose, interview. **Buys 60 mss/year.** Query with published clips. Length: 700-1,900 words. **Pays $600-1,200.**

PHOTOS Identification of subjects, model releases required. Negotiates payment individually.

COLUMNS Columns 400-750 words—featured columnists. **Buys 4 mss/year.** Query with published clips. **Pays 75¢-$1/word**

●● CONVENIENCE STORE DECISIONS

Harbor Communications, 420 Queen Anne Rd., Suite 4, Teaneck NJ 07666. (201)837-2177. E-mail: jlofstock@csdecisions.com. Website: c-storedecisions.com; csdecisions.com. **Contact:** John Lofstock, editor-in-chief, group editorial director. **15-20% freelance written.** Monthly magazine covering convenience retail/petroleum marketing. "*CSD* is received by top-level executives in the convenience retail and petroleum marketing industry. Writers should have knowledge of the industry and the subjects it encompasses." Estab. 1990. Circ. 42,000. Byline given. Pays on publication. Editorial lead time 2-4 months. Submit seasonal material 3 months in advance. Accepts queries by mail, e-mail, fax. NoAccepts simultaneous submissions. Responds in 3 weeks to queries. Sample copy and writer's

NONFICTION Needs interview, retailers, photo feature, technical. No self-serving, vendor-based stories. **Buys 12-15 mss/year.** Query with published clips. Length: 400-2,000 words. **Pays $200-600 for assigned articles.**

●● COUNTRY SAMPLER'S COUNTRY BUSINESS

Emmis Publishing LP, 707 Kautz Rd., St. Charles IL 60174. (630)377-8000; (888)228-7624. Fax: (630)377-8194. E-mail: cbiz@sampler.emmis.com. E-mail: swagner@sampler.emmis.com. Website: country-business.com. **Contact:** Susan Wagner, editor. **50% freelance written.** Magazine published 7 times/year covering independent retail, gift and home decor. *Country Business* is a trade publication for independent retailers of gifts and home accents. Estab. 1993. Circ. 32,000. Byline given. Pays 1 month after acceptance of final ms. Offers $50 kill fee. Publishes ms an average of 4-6 months after acceptance. Editorial lead time 4-6 months. Submit seasonal material 8-10 months in advance. Accepts queries by mail, e-mail, fax. Accepts simultaneous submissions. Usually responds in 4-6 weeks (only if accepted). Sample articles are available on website. Guidelines by e-mail.

NONFICTION Needs how-to, pertaining to retail, interview, new product, finance, legal, marketing, small business. No fiction, poetry, fillers, photos, artwork, or profiles of businesses, unless queried and first assigned. **Buys 20 mss/year.** Send resume and published clips to: Writers Query, Country Business. Send complete ms. Length: 1,000-2,500 words. **Pays $275-500 for assigned articles. Pays $200-350 for unsolicited articles.** Limit agreed upon in advance

COLUMNS Display & Design (store design and product display), 1,500 words; Retailer Profile (profile of retailer—assigned only), 1,800 words; Vendor Profile (profile of manufacturer—assigned only), 1,200 words; Technology (Internet, computer-related articles as applies to small retailers), 1,500 words; Marketing (marketing ideas and advice as applies to small retailers), 1,500 words; Finance (financial tips and advice as applies to small retailers), 1,500 words; Legal (legal tips and advice as applies to small retailers), 1,500 words; Employees (tips and advice on hiring, firing, and working with employees as applies to small retailers), 1,500 words. **Buys 15 mss/year.** Query with published clips or send complete ms. **Pays $250-350.**

$$ NICHE

The Rosen Group, 3000 Chestnut Ave., Suite 304, Baltimore MD 21211. (410)889-3093, ext. 231. Fax: (410)243-7089. E-mail: info@rosengrp.com; hoped@rosengrp.com. Website: nichemag.com. **Contact:** Hope Daniels, editor-in-chief. **80% freelance written.** Quarterly trade magazine for the progressive craft gallery retailer. Each issue includes retail gallery profiles, store design trends, management techniques, financial information, and merchandising strategies for small business owners, as well as articles about craft artists and craft mediums. Estab. 1988. Circ. 25,000. Byline given. Pays on publication. Publishes ms an average of 9 months after acceptance. Editorial lead time 9 months. Submit seasonal material 1 year in advance. Accepts queries by mail, e-mail, fax. Responds in 6-8 weeks to queries. Responds in 3 months to mss. Sample copy for $3.

NONFICTION Needs interview, photo feature, articles targeted to independent retailers and small business owners. **Buys 20-28 mss/year.** Query with published clips. **Pays $300-700.**

PHOTOS Send photos. Captions required. Reviews transparencies, slides, e-images. Negotiates payment individually.

COLUMNS Retail Details (short items at the front of the book, general retail information); Artist Profiles (biographies of American Craft Artists); Retail Resources (including book/video/seminar reviews and educational opportunities pertaining to retailers). Query with published clips. **Pays $25-100.**

$$ TRAVEL GOODS SHOWCASE

Travel Goods Association, 301 North Harrison St., Suite 412, Princeton NJ 08540-3512. (877)842-1938. Fax: (877)842-1938. E-mail: info@travel-goods.org; cathy@travel-goods.org. Website: travel-goods.org. **Contact:** Cathy Hays. **5-10% freelance written.** Magazine published quarterly covering travel goods, accessories, trends, and new products. "*Travel Goods Showcase* contains articles for retailers, dealers, manufacturers, and suppliers about luggage, business cases, personal leather goods, handbags, and accessories. Special articles report on trends in fashion, promotions, selling and marketing techniques, industry statistics, and other educational and promotional improvements and advancements." Estab. 1975. Circ. 21,000. Byline given. Pays on acceptance. Offers $50 kill fee. Publishes ms an average of 2 months after acceptance. Editorial lead time 3 months. Submit seasonal material 2 months in advance. Accepts queries by mail, e-mail. Responds in 2 weeks to queries. Responds in 1 month to mss. Sample copy and writer's

NONFICTION Needs interview, new product, technical, travel, retailer profiles with photos. No manufacturer profiles. **Buys 3 mss/year.** Query with published clips. Length: 1,200-1,600 words. **Pays $200-400.**

$$$ VERTICAL SYSTEMS RESELLER

Edgell Communications, Inc., 4 Middlebury Blvd., Suite 1, Randolph NJ 07869. (973)252-0100. Fax: (973)252-9020. E-mail: alorden@edgellmail.com. Website: verticalsystemsreseller.com. **Contact:** Abigail Lorden, editor-in-chief. **60% freelance written.** Monthly journal covering channel strategies that build business. Estab. 1992. Circ. 30,000. Byline given. Pays on acceptance. Publishes ms an average of 2 months after acceptance. Editorial lead time 3 months. Accepts queries by mail, e-mail, fax. Accepts simultaneous submissions. Responds in 2 weeks to queries. Responds in 2 months to mss. Sample copy available online.

NONFICTION Needs interview, opinion, technical, technology/channel issues. **Buys 36 mss/year.** Query with published clips. Length: 1,000-1,700 words. **Pays $200-800 for assigned articles.**

PHOTOS Send photos. Identification of subjects, model releases required. Offers no additional payment for photos accepted with ms.

$$$ VM+SD

ST Media Group International, 11262 Cornell Park Dr., Cincinnati OH 45242. (513)421-2050. Fax: (513)421-5144. E-mail: steve.kaufman@stmediagroup.com. Website: vmsd.com. **Contact:** Anne DiNardo, editor. **10% freelance written.** Monthly magazine covering retailing store design, store planning, visual merchandising, brand marketing. "Our articles need to get behind the story, tell not only what retailers did when building a new store, renovating an existing store, mounting a new in-store merchandise campaign, but also why they did what they did: specific goals, objectives, strategic initiatives, problems to solve, target markets to reach, etc." Estab. 1872. Circ. 20,000. Byline given. Pays on acceptance. Offers $100 kill fee. Publishes ms an average of 1-2 months after acceptance. Editorial lead time 2-3 months. Submit seasonal material 3-4 months in advance. Accepts queries by e-mail.

NONFICTION **Buys 2-3 mss/year.** Query. Length: 500-1,000 words. **Pays $400-1,000.**

SPORT TRADE

$$ AQUATICS INTERNATIONAL

Hanley Wood, LLC, 6222 Wilshire Blvd., Suite 600, Los Angeles CA 90048. Fax: (503)288-4402. E-mail: gthill@hanleywood.com. Website: aquaticsintl.com. **Contact:** Gary Thill, editor. Magazine published 10 times/year covering public swimming pools and waterparks. Devoted to the commercial and public swimming pool industries. The magazine provides detailed information on designing, building, maintaining, promoting, managing, programming and outfitting aquatics facilities. Estab. 1989. Circ. 30,000. Byline given. Pays on publication. Publishes ms an average of 3 months after acceptance. Editorial lead time 3 months. Responds in 1 month to queries. Sample copy for $10.50.

NONFICTION Needs how-to, interview, technical. **Buys 6 mss/year.** Send query letter with published clips/samples. Length: 1,500-2,500 words. **Pays $525 for assigned articles.**

$$ ARROWTRADE MAGAZINE

Arrow Trade Publishing Corp., 3479 409th Ave. NW, Braham MN 55006. (320)396-3473. Fax: (320)396-3206. E-mail: arrowtrade@northlc.com. Website: arrowtrademag.com. **60% freelance written.** Bimonthly magazine covering the archery industry. "Our readers are interested in articles that help them operate their business better. They are primarily owners or managers of sporting goods stores and archery pro shops." Estab. 1996. Circ. 10,500. Byline given. **Pays on publication.** Publishes ms an average of 2 months after acceptance. Editorial lead time 2 months. Accepts queries by mail, e-mail, fax. Responds in 2 weeks to queries. Responds in 2 weeks to mss. Sample copy for sae with 9×12 envelope and 10 First-Class stamps.

NONFICTION Needs interview, new product. Generic business articles won't work for our highly specialized audience. **Buys 24 mss/year. mss/year.** Query with published clips. Length: 1,800-3,800 words. **Pays $350-550.** Somestimes.

PHOTOS Send photos. Captions required. Must provide digital photos on CD or DVD. Offers no additional payment for photos accepted with ms.

COLUMNS Product Focus (digging into the design and function of an innovative single product); Behind the Brand (profiling a firm that's important to the bowhunting industry). **Buys 18 mss/year. mss/year.** Query with published clips. **Pays $250-375.**

$$ BOATING INDUSTRY

Ehlert Publishing Group, 6420 Sycamore Lane, Suite 100, Maple Grove MN 55369. ((763)383-4448. Fax: (763)383-4499. E-mail: lwalz@affinitygroup.com; mgruhn@affinitygroup.com. Website: boating-industry.com. Matt Gruhn, Group Publisher/Editorial Director of the Trade Group; Liz Walz - Editor-in-Chief, Phone: 315/692-4533. **Contact:** Liz Walz, editor-in-chief. **10-20% freelance written.** Bimonthly magazine covering recreational marine industry management. "We write for those in the industry—not the consumer. Our subject is the business of boating. All of our articles must be analytical and predictive, telling our readers where the industry is going, rather than where it's been." Estab. 1929. Circ. 23,000. Byline given. Pays on acceptance. Offers 50% kill fee. Publishes ms an average of 2 months after acceptance. Editorial lead time 2 months. Submit seasonal material 2 months in advance. Accepts queries by mail, e-mail, fax. Responds in 1 month to queries. Sample copy available online.

NONFICTION Needs technical, business. **Buys 30 mss/year.** Query with published clips. Length: 250-2,500 words. **Pays $25-250.**

$$ BOWLING CENTER MANAGEMENT

Luby Publishing, 122 S. Michigan Ave., Suite 1506, Chicago IL 60603. (312)341-1110. Fax: (312)341-1469. E-mail: mikem@lubypublishing.com. Website: bcmmag.com. **50% freelance written**. Monthly magazine covering bowling centers, family entertainment. "Our readers are looking for novel ways to draw more customers. Accordingly, we look for articles that effectively present such ideas." Estab. 1995. Circ. 12,000. Byline given. Pays on acceptance. Publishes ms an average of 3 months after acceptance. Editorial lead time 3 months. Submit seasonal material 6 months in advance. Accepts queries by e-mail. Accepts simultaneous submissions. Responds in 2-3 weeks to queries. Sample copy for $10.

NONFICTION Needs how-to, interview. **Buys 10-20 mss/year.** Query. Length: 750-1,500 words. **Pays $150-350.**

$$ GOLF COURSE MANAGEMENT

Golf Course Superintendents Association of America, 1421 Research Park Dr., Lawrence KS 66049-3859. (800)472-7878. Fax: (785)832-3665. E-mail: bsmith@gcsaa.org. E-mail: shollister@gcsaa.org. Website: gcsaa.org. Teresa Carson, science editor. **Contact:** Scott Hollister, editor-in-chief. **50% freelance written**. Monthly magazine covering the golf course superintendent. *GCM* helps the golf course superintendent become more efficient in all aspects of their job. Estab. 1924. Circ. 40,000. Byline given. Pays on acceptance. Publishes ms an average of 6 months after acceptance. Editorial lead time 6 months. Submit seasonal material 6 months in advance. Accepts simultaneous submissions. Responds in 3 weeks to queries. Responds in 1 month to mss. Sample copy and writer's Guidelines available online.

NONFICTION Needs how-to, interview. No articles about playing golf. **Buys 40 mss/year.** Query for either feature, research, or superintendent article. Submit electronically, preferably as e-mail attachment. Send one-page synopsis or query for feature article to Scott Hollister, shollister@gcsaa.org. For research article, submit to Teresa Carson, tcarson@gcsaa.org. If you are a superintendent, contact Seth Jones, sjones@gcsaa.org. Length: 1,500-2,000 words. **Pays $400-600.**

$$ INTERNATIONAL BOWLING INDUSTRY

B2B Media, Inc., 13245 Riverside Dr., Suite 501, Sherman Oaks CA 91423. Fax: (818)789-2812. E-mail: info@bowlingindustry.com. Website: bowlingindustry.com. **40% freelance written**. Monthly magazine covering ownership and management of bowling centers (alleys) and pro shops. "*IBI* publishes articles in all phases of bowling center and bowling pro shop ownership and management, among them finance, promotion, customer service, relevant technology, architecture and capital improvement. The magazine also covers the operational areas of bowling centers and pro shops such as human resources, food and beverage, corporate and birthday parties, ancillary attractions (go-karts, gaming and the like), and retailing. Articles must have strong how-to emphasis. They must be written specifically in terms of the bowling industry, although content may be applicable more widely." Estab. 1993. Circ. 10,200. Byline given. Pays on acceptance. Offers $50 kill fee. Publishes ms an average of 3 months after acceptance. Submit seasonal material 3 months in advance. Accepts queries by mail, e-mail, fax. Accepts simultaneous submissions. Responds in 2 weeks to queries. Responds in 1 month to mss. Sample copy for #10 SASE.

💬 "An online bowling industry magazine for bowling center owners, operators and professionals in the business of bowling. "

NONFICTION Needs how-to, interview, new product, technical. **Buys 40 mss/year.** Send complete ms. Length: 1,100-1,400 words. **Pays $250.**

PHOTOS State availability. Identification of subjects required. Reviews JPEG photos. Offers no additional payment for photos accepted with ms.

$$ NSGA RETAIL FOCUS

National Sporting Goods Association, 1601 Feehanville Dr., Suite 300, Mt. Prospect IL 60056-6035. (847)296-6742. Fax: (847)391-9827. E-mail: info@

nsga.org. Website: nsga.org. **Contact:** Bruce Hammond. **20% freelance written. Works with a small number of new/unpublished writers each year.** Bimonthly magazine. *NSGA Retail Focus* serves as a bimonthly trade journal for sporting goods retailers who are members of the association. Estab. 1948. Circ. 2,000. Byline given. Pays on publication. Offers kill fee. Publishes ms an average of 1 month after acceptance. Submit seasonal material 6 months in advance. Accepts queries by e-mail. Sample copy for sae with 9×12 envelope and 5 first-class stamps.

NONFICTION Needs interview, photo feature. No articles written without sporting goods retail business people in mind as the audience. In other words, no generic articles sent to several industries. **Buys 12 mss/year.** Query with published clips. **Pays $150-300.**

PHOTOS State availability. Reviews high-resolution, digital images. Payment negotiable.

COLUMNS Personnel Management (succinct tips on hiring, motivating, firing, etc.); Sales Management (in-depth tips to improve sales force performance); Retail Management (detailed explanation of merchandising/inventory control); Store Design; Visual Merchandising, all 1,500 words. **Buys 12 columns/year. mss/year.** Query. **Pays $150-300.**

$$ POOL & SPA NEWS

Hanley Wood, LLC, 6222 Wilshire Blvd., Suite 600, Los Angeles CA 90048. (323)801-4972. Fax: (323)801-4986. E-mail: etaylor@hanleywood.com. Website: poolspanews.com. **Contact:** Erika Taylor, editor. **15% freelance written.** Semimonthly magazine covering the swimming pool and spa industry for builders, retail stores, and service firms. Estab. 1960. Circ. 16,300. Pays on publication. Publishes ms an average of 2 months after acceptance. Accepts queries by mail, e-mail. Responds in 1 month to queries. Sample copy for $5 and 9×12 SAE and 11 first-class stamps.

NONFICTION Needs interview, technical. Send resume with published clips. Length: 500-2,000 words. **Pays $150-550.**

$$ REFEREE

Referee Enterprises, Inc., P.O. Box 161, Franksville WI 53126. Fax: (262)632-5460. E-mail: submissions@referee.com. Website: referee.com. **Contact:** Julie Sternberg, managing editor. **75% freelance written.** Monthly magazine covering sports officiating. *Referee* is a magazine for and read by sports officials of all kinds with a focus on baseball, basketball, football, softball, and soccer officiating. Estab. 1976. Circ. 40,000. Byline given. Pays on acceptance. Offers kill fee. Kill fee negotiable. Publishes ms an average of 6 months after acceptance. Editorial lead time 6 months. Accepts queries by mail, e-mail. Responds in 2 weeks to queries. Responds in 1 month to mss. Sample copy for #10 sase. Guidelines available online.

NONFICTION Needs book excerpts, essays, historical, how-to, sports officiating related, humor, interview, opinion, photo feature, technical, as it relates to sports officiating. "We don't want to see articles with themes not relating to sport officiating. General sports articles, although of interest to us, will not be published." **Buys 40 mss/year.** Query with published clips. Length: 500-3,500 words. **Pays $50-400.**

PHOTOS State availability. Identification of subjects required. Reviews contact sheets, negatives, transparencies, prints. Offers $35-40 per photo.

$$ THE RINKSIDER

Target Publishing Co., Inc., 2470 E. Main St., Columbus OH 43209. (614)235-1022. Fax: (614)235-3584. E-mail: story@rinksider.com; editor@rinksider.com. Website: rinksider.com. **Contact:** Suzy Weinland, editor. **90% freelance written.** Bimonthly magazine of interest to owners/operators of roller skating facilities, promotions, games, snack bars, roller hockey competitive programs, music, decor, features on new or successful skating centers, competitive amusements, etc. Estab. 1953. Circ. 1,600. Byline given. Pays on publication. Offers 100% (unless poorly done) kill fee. Publishes ms an average of 2 months after acceptance. Editorial lead time 1 month. Accepts queries by e-mail. Accepts simultaneous submissions. Responds in 2 weeks to queries. Responds in 1 month to mss. Sample copy for $5.

NONFICTION Needs essays, historical, how-to, humor, inspirational, interview, new product, personal experience, photo feature, travel. Does not want opinion pieces. Query with published clips. Length: 250-1,000 words. **Pays $75-200.**

PHOTOS Send photos. Reviews prints. Offers no additional payment for photos accepted with ms.

COLUMNS Finance; Roller Skating News; Marketing; Technology. **Buys 20 mss/year.** Query with published clips. **Pays $75-200.**

💲💲 SKI AREA MANAGEMENT

Beardsley Publications, P.O. Box 644, 45 Main St. N, Woodbury CT 06798. (303)652-0285. Fax: (303)652-0461. E-mail: samedit@saminfo.com. E-mail: rick@saminfo.com. Website: saminfo.com. **Contact:** Rick Kahl, editor. **85% freelance written.** Bimonthly magazine covering everything involving the management and development of ski resorts. We are the publication of record for the North American ski industry. We report on new ideas, developments, marketing, and regulations with regard to ski and snowboard resorts. Everyone from the CEO to the lift operator of winter resorts reads our magazine to stay informed about the people and procedures that make ski areas successful. Estab. 1962. Circ. 4,500. Byline given. Pays on publication. Offers kill fee. Offers kill fee. Editorial lead time 2 months. Submit seasonal material 3 months in advance. Accepts queries by mail, e-mail. Responds in 2 weeks to queries. Sample copy for 9×12 SAE with $3 postage or online. Guidelines for #10 sase.

NONFICTION Needs historical, how-to, interview, new product, opinion, personal experience, technical. We don't want anything that does not specifically pertain to resort operations, management, or financing. **Buys 25-40 mss/year.** Query. Length: 500-2,500 words. **Pays $50-400.**

PHOTOS Send photos. Identification of subjects required. Reviews transparencies, prints. Offers no additional payment for photos accepted with ms.

➕💲💲 SKI PATROL MAGAZINE

National Ski Patrol, 133 So. Van Gordon St., Suite 100, Lakewood CO 80228 United States. (303)988-1111, ext. 2625. Fax: (303)988-3005. E-mail: editor@nsp.org; chorgan@nsp.org. Website: nsp.org. **Contact:** Candace Horgan, Editor. **80.** Covers the National Ski Patrol, skiing, snowboarding, and snowsports safety. "Ski Patrol Magazine is a tri-annual publication for the members and affiliates of the National Ski Patrol. Topics are related to patrolling, mountain rescue, and the ski industry." Estab. 1962. Circ. 26,000. Byline given. Pays on publication. Editorial lead time is 3 months. Submit seasonal material 3 months in advance. Accepts queries by mail, e-mail, fax. If you choose to fax, be sure to include a cover page that indicates your intent to submit to *Ski Patrol Magazine.* "We cannot consider your manuscript if it is being reviewed by other publishers or if it has already been published. You must guarantee the originality of your work. If you write about other people's ideas, be sure to credit them where appropriate." Accepts simultaneous submissions. Reponds in 1-2 weeks on queries; 2 months on decisions Sample copy available for SASE with $1.90 postage. Guidelines available for SASE with 1 first-class stamp.

NONFICTION Needs essays, expose, general interest, historical, how-to, humor, interview, nostalgic, opinion, personal experience, photo feature, profile, technical. **Buys 10-15 mss/year.** Query with published clips. Length: 700/min - 3,000/max Does not pay expenses of writers on assignment.

COLUMNS OEC, Medical; MTR, Transport/Rescue; Sweep, Personal Experience, 1,000/words each **Buys 8-12 mss/year. mss/year.** Query with published clips. **Pays $100/min - $200/max**

💲💲 THOROUGHBRED TIMES

Thoroughbred Times Co., Inc., 2008 Mercer Rd., P.O. Box 8237, Lexington KY 40533. (859)260-9800. E-mail: tlaw@thoroughbredtimes.com. **10% freelance written.** Weekly tabloid written for professionals who breed and/or race thoroughbreds at tracks in the U.S. and around the world. Articles must help owners and breeders understand racing to help them realize a profit. Estab. 1985. Circ. 20,000. Byline given. Pays on publication. Offers 50% kill fee. Publishes ms an average of 1 month after acceptance. Submit seasonal material 2 months in advance. Responds in 2 weeks to mss.

NONFICTION Needs historical, interview, technical. **Buys 52 mss/year.** Query. Length: 500-2,500 words. **Pays 10-20¢/word.**

PHOTOS State availability. Identification of subjects required. Reviews prints. Offers $50/photo.

COLUMNS Vet Topics; Business of Horses; Pedigree Profiles; Bloodstock Topics; Tax Matters; Viewpoints; Guest Commentary.

STONE, QUARRY AND MINING

⟳💲💲 CANADIAN MINING JOURNAL

Business Information Group, 12 Concorde Place, Suite 800, Toronto ON M3C 4J2 Canada. (416)510-6742. Fax: (416)510-5138. E-mail: rnoble@canadianminingjournal.com. Website: canadianminingjournal.com. **Contact:** Russell Noble, editor. **5% freelance written.** Magazine covering mining and mineral exploration by Canadian companies. *Canadian Mining*

Journal provides articles and information of practical use to those who work in the technical, administrative, and supervisory aspects of exploration, mining, and processing in the Canadian mineral exploration and mining industry. Estab. 1882. Circ. 11,000. Byline given. Pays on publication. Publishes ms an average of 3 months after acceptance. Submit seasonal material 3 months in advance. Accepts queries by mail, e-mail, fax, phone. Responds in 1 week to queries. Responds in 1 month to mss.

NONFICTION Needs opinion, technical, operation descriptions. **Buys 6 mss/year.** Query with published clips. Length: 500-1,400 words. **Pays $100-600.**

PHOTOS State availability. Captions, identification of subjects, required. Reviews 4×6 prints or high-resolution files. Negotiates payment individually.

COLUMNS Guest editorial (opinion on controversial subject related to mining industry), 600 words. **Buys 3 mss/year.** Query with published clips. **Pays $150.**

TIPS I need articles about mine sites it would be expensive/difficult for me to reach. I also need to know the writer is competent to understand and describe the technology in an interesting way.

⊖⊖ COAL PEOPLE MAGAZINE

Al Skinner, Inc., 629 Virginia St. W, P.O. Box 6247, Charleston WV 25362. (304)342-4129. Fax: (304)343-3124. E-mail: alskinner@ntelos.net; cpm@ntelos.net. Website: coalpeople.com. **Contact:** Christina Karawan, managing editor; Al Skinner, editor. **50% freelance written**. Monthly magazine. Most stories are about people or historical—either narrative or biographical on all levels of coal people, past and present—from coal execs down to grass roots miners. Most stories are upbeat—showing warmth of family or success from underground up! Estab. 1976. Circ. 14,300. Byline given. Pays on publication. Publishes ms an average of 3 months after acceptance. Submit seasonal material 2 months in advance. Accepts queries by e-mail. Responds in 3 months to mss. Sample copy for sae with 9×12 envelope and 10 first-class stamps.

NONFICTION Needs book excerpts, and film if related to coal, historical, coal towns, people, lifestyles, humor, including anecdotes and cartoons, interview, for coal personalities, personal experience, as relates to coal mining, photo feature, on old coal towns, people, past and present. Special issues: Calendar issue for more than 300 annual coal shows, association meetings, etc. (January); Surface Mining/Reclamation Award (July); Christmas in Coal Country (December). No poetry, fiction, or environmental attacks on the coal industry. **Buys 32 mss/year.** Query with published clips. Length: 750-2,500 words. **Pays $150-250.**

⊖ CONTEMPORARY STONE & TILE DESIGN

Business News Publishing Co., 210 Route 4 East, Suite 311, Paramus NJ 07652. (201)291-9001, ext. 8611. Fax: (201)291-9002. E-mail: jennifer@stoneworld.com. Website: stoneworld.com. **Contact:** Jennifer Adams, managing editor. Quarterly magazine covering the full range of stone and tile design and architecture—from classic and historic spaces to current projects. Estab. 1995. Circ. 21,000. Byline given. Pays on publication. Publishes ms an average of 3 months after acceptance. Submit seasonal material 6 months in advance. Responds in 3 weeks to queries. Sample copy for $10.

NONFICTION Needs interview, prominent architect/designer or firm, photo feature, technical, architectural design. **Buys 8 mss/year.** Query with published clips. Length: 1,500-3,000 words. **Pays $6/column inch.**

PHOTOS State availability. Captions, identification of subjects required. Reviews transparencies, prints. Pays $10/photo accepted with ms.

COLUMNS Upcoming Events (for the architecture and design community); Stone Classics (featuring historic architecture); question and answer session with a prominent architect or designer. Length: 1,500-2,000 words. **Pays $6/inch**

⊖⊖ PIT & QUARRY

Questex Media Group, 600 Superior Ave. East, Suite 1100, Cleveland OH 44114. (216)706-3725; (216)706-3747. Fax: (216)706-3710. E-mail: info@pitandquarry.com; dconstantino@questex.com. Website: pitandquarry.com. **Contact:** Darren Constantino, editor-in-chief. **10-20% freelance written**. Monthly magazine covering nonmetallic minerals, mining, and crushed stone. Audience has knowledge of construction-related markets, mining, minerals processing, etc. Estab. 1916. Circ. 23,000. Byline given. Pays on acceptance. Publishes ms an average of 2 months after acceptance. Editorial lead time 2 months. Accepts queries by e-mail. Accepts simultaneous submissions. Responds in 1 month to queries. Responds in 4 months to mss.

NONFICTION Needs how-to, interview, new product, technical. No humor or inspirational articles. **Buys 3-4 mss/year.** Query. Length: 2,000-2,500 words. **Pays $250-500 for assigned articles. Pays nothing for unsolicited articles.**

PHOTOS State availability. Identification of subjects, model releases required. Offers no additional payment for photos accepted with ms.

COLUMNS Brand New; Techwatch; E-business; Software Corner; Equipment Showcase. Length: 250-750 words. **Buys 5-6 mss/year.** Query. **Pays $250-300.**

💲 STONE WORLD

BNP Media, 210 Route 4 E., Suite 203, Paramus NJ 07652. (201)291-9001. Fax: (201)291-9002. E-mail: michael@stoneworld.com. Website: stoneworld. com. **Contact:** Michael Reis, editor-in-chief. Monthly magazine on natural building stone for producers and users of granite, marble, limestone, slate, sandstone, onyx and other natural stone products. Estab. 1984. Circ. 21,000. Byline given. Pays on publication. Publishes ms an average of 4 months after acceptance. Submit seasonal material 6 months in advance. Responds in 2 months to queries. Sample copy for $10.

NONFICTION Needs how-to, fabricate and/or install natural building stone, interview, photo feature, technical, architectural design, artistic stone uses, statistics, factory profile, equipment profile, trade show review. **Buys 10 mss/year.** Send complete ms. Length: 600-3,000 words. **Pays $6/column inch.**

TOY, NOVELTY AND HOBBY

💲💲 MODEL RETAILER

Kalmach Publishing, 21027 Crossroads Circle, P.O. Box 1612, Waukesha WI 53187. (262)796-8776. Fax: (262)796-1142. E-mail: hmiller@modelretailer.com. E-mail: editor@modelretailer.com. Website: modelretailer.com. **Contact:** Hal Miller, editor. **5% freelance written.** Monthly magazine covering the business of hobbies, from financial and shop management issues to industry trends and the latest product releases. *Model Retailer* covers the business of hobbies, from financial and shop management issues to industry trends and the latest product releases. Our goal is to provide hobby shop entrepreneurs with the tools and information they need to be successful retailers. Estab. 1987. Circ. 6,000. Byline given. Pays on acceptance.

Publishes ms an average of 3 months after acceptance. Editorial lead time 3 months. Submit seasonal material 6 months in advance. Accepts queries by mail, e-mail, fax. Sample copy and writer's Guidelines available online.

NONFICTION Needs how-to, business, new product. No articles that do not have a strong hobby or small retail component. **Buys 2-3 mss/year.** Query with published clips. The magazine pays for one-time print and electronic publication rights to freelance manuscripts and images. Freelance stories generally are assigned in advance, but we welcome proposals for feature articles and columns, or the submission of articles sent on speculation. Payment is made upon acceptance of the material for publication. Feature material generally should be limited to 1,500 or fewer words. You may send the ms as an e-mail attachment or via mail. Length: 750-1,500 words. **Pays $250-500 for assigned articles. Pays $100-250 for unsolicited articles.**

PHOTOS State availability. Captions, identification of subjects required. Reviews 4×6 prints. Negotiates payment individually.

COLUMNS Shop Management; Sales Marketing; Technology Advice; Industry Trends, all 500-750 words. **Buys 2-3 mss/year.** Query with published clips. **Pays $100-200.**

PEN WORLD

Masterpiece Litho, Inc., Houston TX (713)869-9997. Fax: (713)869-9993. E-mail: editor@penworld.com. Website: penworld.com. **Contact:** Laura Chandler, editor. Magazine published 6 times/year. Published for writing instrument enthusiasts. Circ. 30,000.

TRANSPORTATION

💲💲 METRO MAGAZINE

Bobit Publishing Co., 3520 Challenger St., Torrance CA 90503. (310)533-2400. Fax: (310)533-2502. E-mail: info@metro-magazine.com. E-mail: alex.roman@bobit.com. Website: metro-magazine.com. **Contact:** Alex Roman, managing editor. **10% freelance written.** Magazine published 10 times/year covering transit bus, passenger rail, and motorcoach operations. METRO's coverage includes both public transit systems and private bus operators, addressing topics such as funding mechanisms, procurement, rolling stock maintenance, privatization, risk management and sustainability. *Metro Magazine* delivers business, government policy, and technology developments that are *industry specific* to public transportation. Estab. 1904. Circ. 20,500. Byline given. Pays on acceptance. Offers 10% kill fee. Publishes ms an average of 2 months after acceptance. Editorial lead time 3 months. Submit seasonal material 3 months in advance. Accepts queries by e-mail. Responds in 2 weeks to queries. Responds in 1 month to mss. Sample copy for $8. Guidelines by e-mail.

NONFICTION Needs how-to, interview, of industry figures, new product, related to transit—bus and rail—private bus, technical. **Buys 6-10 mss/year.** Query. Length: 400-1,500 words. **Pays $80-400.**

PHOTOS State availability. Captions, identification of subjects, model releases required. Negotiates payment individually.

COLUMNS Query. **Pays 20¢/word**

$$ SCHOOL BUS FLEET

Bobit Business Media, 3520 Challenger St., Torrance CA 90503. (310)533-2400. Fax: (310)533-2502. E-mail: sbf@bobit.com. Website: schoolbusfleet.com. Magazine covering school transportation of K-12 population. "Most of our readers are school bus operators, public and private." Estab. 1956. Circ. 24,000. Byline given. Pays on acceptance. Offers kill fee. Offers 25% kill fee or $50. Publishes ms an average of 3 months after acceptance. Editorial lead time 3 months. Submit seasonal material 3 months in advance. Accepts queries by mail, e-mail, fax. Responds in 1 month to queries. *Not currently accepting submissions.*.

NONFICTION *Not currently accepting submissions.*

TRAVEL TRADE

$$ CRUISE INDUSTRY NEWS

Cruise Industry News, 441 Lexington Ave., Suite 809, New York NY 10017. (212)986-1025. Fax: (212)986-1033. E-mail: oivind@cruiseindustrynews.com. Website: cruiseindustrynews.com. **Contact:** Oivind Mathisen, editor. **20% freelance written.** Quarterly magazine covering cruise shipping. "We write about the business of cruise shipping for the industry. That is, cruise lines, shipyards, financial analysts, etc." Estab. 1991. Circ. 10,000. Byline given. Pays on acceptance or on publication Offers 25% kill fee. Publishes ms an average of 4 months after acceptance. Editorial lead time 3 months. Accepts queries by mail. Response time varies. Sample copy for $15. Guidelines for #10 sase.

NONFICTION Needs interview, new product, photo feature, business. No travel stories. **Buys more than 20 mss/year.** Query with published clips. Length: 500-1,500 words. **Pays $.50/word published.**

PHOTOS State availability. Pays $25-50/photo.

$$ LEISURE GROUP TRAVEL

Premier Tourism Marketing, 621 Plainfield Rd., Suite 406, Willowbrook IL 60527. (630)794-0696. Fax: (630)794-0652. E-mail: editorial@ptmgroups.com. Website: premiertourismmarketing.com. **Contact:** Randy Mink, managing editor. **35% freelance written.** Bimonthly magazine covering group travel. We cover destinations and editorial relevant to the group travel market. Estab. 1994. Circ. 15,012. Byline given. Pays on publication. Editorial lead time 6 months. Submit seasonal material 6 months in advance. Accepts queries by mail, e-mail. Sample copy available online.

NONFICTION Needs travel. **Buys 75 mss/year.** Query with published clips. Length: 1,200-3,000 words. **Pays $0-1,000.**

⭘ LL&A MAGAZINE

Media Diversified, Inc., 96 Karma Rd., Markham ON L3R 4Y3 Canada. (905)944-0265. Fax: (416)296-0994. E-mail: info@mediadiversified.com. Website: llanda.com. **5% freelance written.** Quarterly magazine for the luggage, leathergoods and accessories market. Serving the travel, business & fashion accessory products industry. Estab. 1966. Circ. 12,000. Byline given. Pays on publication. Editorial lead time 6 weeks. Accepts queries by e-mail.

NONFICTION Needs general interest, how-to, new product, technical.

$$ MIDWEST MEETINGS®

Hennen Publishing, 302 6th St. W, Brookings SD 57006. (605)692-9559. Fax: (605)692-9031. E-mail: info@midwestmeetings.com; editor@midwestmeetings.com. Website: midwestmeetings.com. **Contact:** Serenity J. Knutson, editor. **20% freelance written.** Quarterly magazine covering meetings/conventions industry. We provide information and resources to meeting/convention planners with a Midwest focus. Estab. 1996. Circ. 28,500. Byline given. Pays on acceptance. Publishes ms an average of 5 months after acceptance. Editorial lead time 3 months. Submit seasonal material 3 months in advance. Accepts queries by mail, e-mail, fax. Guidelines by e-mail.

NONFICTION Needs essays, general interest, historical, how-to, humor, interview, personal experience, travel. Does not want marketing pieces related to specific hotels/meeting facilities. **Buys 15-20 mss/ year.** Send complete ms. Length: 500-1,000 words. **Pays 5-50¢/word.**

PHOTOS Send photos. Captions, identification of subjects required. Reviews GIF/JPEG files (300 dpi). Offers no additional payment for photos accepted with ms.

⑨⑨⑨ RV BUSINESS

G&G Media Group, 2901 E. Bristol St., Suite B, Elkhart IN 46514. (800)831-1076; (574)266-7980, ext. 13. Fax: (574)266-7984. E-mail: bhampson@rvbusiness.com; bhampson@g-gmediagroup.com. Website: rvbusiness.com. **Contact:** Bruce Hampson, editor. **50% freelance written.** Monthly magazine covers a specific audience of people who manufacture, sell, market, insure, finance, service and supply, components for recreational vehicles. *RV Business* caters to a specific audience of people who manufacture, sell, market, insure, finance, service and supply, components for recreational vehicles. Estab. 1972. Circ. 21,000. Byline given. Pays on acceptance. Offers kill fee. Offers kill fee. Publishes ms an average of 2 months after acceptance. Editorial lead time 3 months. Accepts queries by mail, e-mail.

NONFICTION Needs new product, photo feature, industry news and features. No general articles without specific application to our market. **Buys 300 mss/year.** Query with published clips. Length: 125-2,200 words. **Pays $50-1,500.**

COLUMNS Top of the News (RV industry news), 75-400 words; Business Profiles, 400-500 words; Features (indepth industry features), 800-2,000 words. **Buys 300 mss/year.** Query. **Pays $50-1,500.**

⑨⑨ SCHOOL TRANSPORTATION NEWS

STN Media Co., 5334 Torrance Blvd., 3rd Fl., Torrance CA 90503. (310)792-2226. Fax: (310)792-2231. E-mail: ryan@stnonline.com. Website: stnonline.com. **Contact:** Ryan Gray, editor-in-chief. **20% freelance written.** Monthly magazine covering school bus and pupil transportation industries in North America. "Contributors to *School Transportation News* must have a basic understanding of K-12 education and automotive fleets and specifically of school buses. Ar-

ticles cover such topics as manufacturing, operations, maintenance and routing software, GPS, security and legislative affairs. A familiarity with these principles is preferred. Additional industry information is available on our website. New writers must perform some research of the industry or exhibit core competencies in the subject matter." Estab. 1991. Circ. 23,633. Byline given. Pays on publication. Editorial lead time 1-2 months. Submit seasonal material 3 months in advance. Accepts queries by e-mail. Accepts simultaneous submissions.

NONFICTION Needs book excerpts, general interest, historical, humor, inspirational, interview, new product, personal experience, photo feature, technical. "Does not want strictly localized editorial. We want articles that put into perspective the issues of the day." Query with published clips. Length: 600-1,200 words. **Pays $150-300.**

PHOTOS Contact: Contact Vince Rios, director. No Answer. Captions, model releases required. Reviews GIF/JPEG files. Offers $150-200/photo.

COLUMNS Creative Special Report, Cover Story, Top Story; Book/Video Reviews (new programs/publications/training for pupil transporters), both 600 words. **Buys 40 mss/year.** Query with published clips. **Pays $150.**

⑨⑨ SPECIALTY TRAVEL INDEX

Alpine Hansen, P.O. Box 458, San Anselmo CA 94979. (415)455-1643. E-mail: info@specialtytravel.com. Website: specialtytravel.com. **90% freelance written.** Semi-annual magazine covering adventure and special interest travel. Estab. 1980. Circ. 35,000. Byline given. Pays on receipt and acceptance of all materials. Editorial lead time 3 month. Submit seasonal material 3 months in advance. Accepts queries by mail, e-mail. Writer's guidelines on request.

NONFICTION Needs how-to, personal experience, photo feature, travel. **Buys 15 mss/year.** Query. Length: 1,250 words. **Pays $300 minimum.**

PHOTOS State availability. Captions, identification of subjects required. Reviews EPS/TIFF files. Negotiates payment individually.

⑨ STAR SERVICE TRAVEL 42

NORTHSTAR Travel Media, 200 Brookstown Ave., Suite 301, Winston-Salem NC 27101. (336)714-3328. Fax: (336)714-3168. E-mail: csheaffer@ntmllc.com. Website: starserviceonline.com;TRAVEL-42.COM. "Eager to work with experienced writers as well as those working from a home base abroad, planning trips that would allow time for hotel reporting, or living in major ports for cruise ships. Worldwide guide to destinations, accommodations and cruise ships, sold to travel professionals on subscription basis. Estab. 2011. No byline given. Pays 1 month after acceptance. Accepts queries by e-mail preferred.

VETERINARY

💲💲 VETERINARY ECONOMICS

Advanstar Veterinary Healthcare Communications, Advanstar Communications, Veterinary Group, 8033 Flint, Lenexa KS 66214. (800)255-6864. Fax: (913)871-3808. E-mail: ve@advanstar.com. Website: vetecon. com. **20% freelance written.** Monthly magazine covering veterinary practice management. We ad-dress the business concerns and management needs of practicing veterinarians. Estab. 1960. Circ. 54,000. Byline given. Pays on publication. Publishes ms an average of 6 months after acceptance. Editorial lead time 3 months. Submit seasonal material 3 months in advance. Accepts queries by mail, e-mail, fax. Accepts simultaneous submissions. Responds in 3 months to queries. Guidelines available online.

NONFICTION Needs how-to, interview, personal experience. **Buys 24 mss/year.** Send complete ms. Length: 1,000-2,000 words. **Pays $50-400.**

PHOTOS Send photos. Captions, identification of subjects required. Reviews transparencies, prints. Offers no additional payment for photos accepted with ms.

COLUMNS Practice Tips (easy, unique business tips), 200-300 words. Send complete ms. **Pays $40.**

NEWSPAPERS

Over the past several years, newspapers have been struggling, but it would be foolish to think they're dead or dying. There are still thousands of dailies and weeklies covering city and regional beats across the country. And while most newspapers have been forced to consolidate efforts and cut staff to remain competitive, they still need to provide newsworthy content to fill pages, which opens the door of opportunity for freelancers.

Staff writers will continue to handle the obvious stories of national, regional and local importance, but a freelancer can make sales by searching out those stories of real interest that are not as obvious, as well as the stories that demand special connections or a certain sensitivity to write. Your uniqueness as a freelancer is something you should communicate in your query letter. (For more information on query letters, read "Query Letter Clinic.")

LISTINGS

In addition to smaller circulation newspapers, *Writer's Market* lists many of the highest circulation newspapers in the country. As a result of these being the highest circulation newspapers, the information they freely share with freelancers is scarce. While it is always advised that you query before submitting to a newspaper, that rule holds especially for the higher circulation papers.

Most newspapers have several departments with a specific editor handling all the material within each. It is important that you take the extra step to find out who the current contact is for the department you wish to submit your query. While it can seem like a lot of legwork, that is exactly the kind of professionalism that will be required if you expect to successfully freelance for newspapers.

$ ABLE NEWSPAPER

Melmont Printing, P.O. Box 395, Old Bethpage NY 11804. Fax: (516)939-0540. E-mail: ablenews@aol.com. Website: www.ablenews.com. Estab. 1991. Circ. 30,000. Accepts 20% of material on one-time basis. 30 features purchased/year. All news including, but not limited to, legislation, advocacy, health, transportation, and housing issues "*Able* focuses on news for people with disabilities." Accepts queries by e-mail, fax. Buys first rights. Pays on publication. Byline given. Sample copy and guidelines free.

NEEDS Query with published clips. Length: 400-600 words. **Pays $50 minimum.**

🌐 THE AGE

Fairfax Media Limited, P.O. Box 257C, Melbourne VIC 8001 Australia. (61)(3)9601-2250. E-mail: newsdesk@theage.com.au. Website: www.theage.com.au. Estab. 1854. Circ. 200,000. Daily. Pays on Pays on publication. "Nominal kill fee on commissioned pieces which do not run."

💬 Query before submitting.

🍁 $ THE ANGLICAN JOURNAL

The Anglican Journal Board of Directors, 80 Hayden St., Toronto ON M4Y 3G2 Canada. (416)924-9192. Fax: (416)921-4452. E-mail: editor@anglicanjournal.com. Website: www.anglicanjournal.com. Estab. 1875. Circ. 175,000. Accepts 10-15% of material on one-time basis. Monthly, except for July and August *The Anglican Journal* covers news of interest to Anglicans in Canada and abroad. Accepts queries by mail, e-mail, fax. Buys all rights. Pays on publication. Editorial lead time 2 months. Offers 50% kill fee. Byline given. Accepts simultaneous submissions. Sample copy free. Guidelines available by e-mail.

NEEDS No poetry or fiction. Query. Length: 600-1,000 words. **Pays 25¢ (Canadian)/word.** Sometimes pays expenses of writers on assignment.

$ ANTIQUE SHOPPE NEWSPAPER

Specialty General Service Publications, Inc., P.O. Box 2175, Keystone Heights FL 32656. (352)475-1679. Fax: (352)475-5326. E-mail: antshoppe@aol.com. Website: www.antiqueshoppefl.com. Estab. 1986. Circ. 20,000. Accepts 25% of material under contract. Accepts 25% of material on one-time basis. 100 features purchased/year. Works with 10-12 writers/year. Accepts queries by mail, e-mail, phone. Responds in 1 week to queries. Buys one-time rights. Pays on publication. Editorial lead time 3-4 weeks. Byline given. Accepts simultaneous submissions. Returns submission with SASE. Sample copy and guidelines free.

NEEDS Query with published clips. Length: 1,000-1,750 words. **Pays $50.**

AQUARIUS

1035 Green St., Roswell GA 30075. (770)641-9055. Fax: (770)641-8502. E-mail: felica@aquarius-atlanta.com; gloria@aquarius-atlanta.com. Website: www.aquarius-atlanta.com/. **Contact:** Felica Hicks, creative director; Gloria Parker, publisher/editor. Estab. 1991. Circ. 50,000; readership online: 110,000. "Our mission is to publish a newspaper for the purpose of expanding awareness and supporting all those seeking spiritual growth. We are committed to excellence and integrity in an atmosphere of harmony and love. Published monthly before the first of each month. articles by the 1st. We accept articles, artwork and photography which are in accordance with our mission. We reserve the right to accept, reject or edit any material we receive but do our best to honor the integrity of the author/artist. We do not endorse any particular program or advertiser. We simply offer our readers information on various subject matters for potentially educating those who already make a difference by doing business in a growing consciousness field. It is expected that all material is submitted 'in good faith' with no intent to mislead or harm others. It is the readers responsibility to make intuitive decisions that are right for them."

⊘ ARIZONA DAILY STAR

Pulitzer Newspapers, P.O. Box 26807, Tucson AZ 85726-6807. (520)573-4220. Fax: (520)573-4141. E-mail: letters@azstarnet.com. Website: www.azstarnet.com. Other Address: 4850 S. Park Ave., Tucson AZ 85714-3395. Circ. 100,000. Daily.

💬 Query before submitting. Mostly staff written.

⊘ THE ARIZONA REPUBLIC

Gannett Newspapers, 200 E. Van Buren St., Phoenix AZ 85004. (602)444-6397. E-mail: newstips@arizonarepublic.com. Website: www.arizonarepublic.com. Letters to the Editor: P.O. Box 2244, Phoenix AZ 85002. Fax: (602)444-8933. Estab. 1890. Circ. 486,000. Daily.

🖐 Generally, stories written and submitted by the public are not accepted for publication.

💲 ASIAN PAGES

Kita Associates, Inc., P.O. Box 11932, St. Paul MN 55111-1932. (952)884-3265. Fax: (952)888-9373. E-mail: asianpages@att.net. Website: www.asianpages. com. Estab. 1990. Circ. 75,000. Accepts 40% of material on one-time basis. 50-60 features purchased/year. Biweekly *Asian Pages* celebrates the achievements of the Asian community in the Midwest and promotes a cultural bridge among the many different Asian groups that the newspaper serves." Accepts queries by mail. Responds in 1 month to queries. Responds in 2 months to mss. Buys first North American serial rights. Pays on publication. Editorial lead time 4 months. Offers 50% kill fee. Byline given. Accepts simultaneous submissions. Sample copy for SASE with 9x12 envelope and 3 first-class stamps. Guidelines for #10 SASE.

NEEDS "All articles must have an Asian slant. We're interested in articles on the Asian New Years, banking, business, finance, sports/leisure, home and garden, education, and career planning." No culturally insensitive material. Send complete ms. Length: 500-700 words. **Pays $40.**

COLUMNS Query with exceptional ideas for our market and provide 1-2 sample columns. Buys 100 mss/year.

⊘ ATLANTA JOURNAL-CONSTITUTION

Cox Newspapers, Inc., 72 Marietta St., NW, Atlanta GA 30303. (404)526-5151. Fax: (404)526-5610. Website: www.ajc.com. Circ. 405,000. Daily.
🖐 Mostly staff written.

⊘ THE BALTIMORE SUN

Tribune Co., 501 N. Calvert St., P.O. Box 1377, Baltimore MD 21278. (410)332-6000. Fax: (410)323-2898. E-mail: feedback@baltimoresun.com. Website: www.baltimoresun.com. Circ. 304,000. Daily.
🖐 Mostly staff written.

BOOKPAGE

Promotion, Inc., 2143 Belcourt Ave., Nashville TN 37212. (615)292-8926. Fax: (615)292-8249. Website: www.bookpage.com. Circ. 500,000. Monthly. "*Book-Page* reviews almost every category of new books including popular and literary fiction, biography, memoir, history, science, and travel." Accepts queries by e-mail only. Editorial lead time 3 months. Byline given. Guidelines free.
🖐 "*BookPage* editors assign all books to be reviewed, choosing from the hundreds of advance review copies we receive each month. We do not publish unsolicited reviews. We also publish additional reviews and interviews on our Website, BookPage.com."

BOSTON GLOBE

The New York Times Co., P.O. Box 55819, Boston MA 02205. (617)929-2000. Fax: (617)929-2098. Website: www.boston.com/globe/. Estab. 1872. Circ. 448,000. Daily. Accepts queries by e-mail, fax. Guidelines available online.
🖐 Mostly staff written. Break in with Op-Ed piece.

NEEDS Send complete ms. around 700 words.

⊘ BOSTON HERALD

Herald Media, Inc., One Herald Square, Boston MA 02118. (617)426-3000. Fax: (617)542-1315. Website: www.bostonherald.com. Circ. 247,000. Daily.
🖐 Mostly staff written.

THE BUFFALO NEWS

Berkshire Hathaway, Inc., P.O. Box 100, Buffalo NY 14240. (716)849-4444. Fax: (716)847-0207. E-mail: citydesk@buffnews.com. Website: www.buffalonews.com. Circ. 190,000. Daily. Accepts queries by mail.
NEEDS Send complete ms.

⊘ THE CHARLOTTE OBSERVER

Knight Ridder, P.O. Box 30308, Charlotte NC 28230. (704)358-5000. Fax: (704)358-5022. E-mail: localnews@charlotteobserver.com. Website: www.charlotteobserver.com. Estab. 1886. Circ. 242,000. Daily.
🖐 Mostly staff written.

⊘ CHICAGO SUN-TIMES

Sun-Times Media Group, Inc., 350 N. Orleans, Chicago IL 60654. (312)321-3000. Fax: (312)321-3084. Website: www.suntimes.com. Circ. 450,000. Daily.
🖐 Mostly staff written, but accepts freelance queries by mail.

⊘ CHICAGO TRIBUNE

Tribune Co., 435 N. Michigan Ave., Chicago IL 60611. (312)222-3232. Fax: (312)222-2550. Website: www.chicagotribune.com. Estab. 1847. Circ. 689,000. Daily.
🖐 Mostly staff written.

CHRISTIAN JOURNAL

1032 W. Main, Medford OR 97501. (541)773-4004. Fax: (541)773-9917. E-mail: info@thechristianjournal.org. Website: www.thechristianjournal.org. Estab. 1998. Circ. 15,000. Accepts 80% of material on one-time basis. "It is the purpose of the *Christian Journal* to encourage the reader with Christian support articles—personal experiences, stories about ministry, hope in God, poetry, uplifting short pieces, etc. The best chance of getting printed is to submit articles on the issue's theme." Accepts queries by e-mail. Responds in 2 weeks to queries. Responds in 1-2 months to mss. Editorial lead time 1-2 months. Byline and e-mail given. Accepts simultaneous submissions. Sample copy for SASE with 9x12 envelope and 3 First-class stamps. Guidelines available online.

NEEDS Query or send complete ms. Length: up to 500 words.

COLUMNS Health; Senior Views; both 500 words.

⊘ THE CINCINNATI ENQUIRER

Gannett Newspapers, 312 Elm St., Cincinnati OH 45202. (513)768-8000. Fax: (513)768-8340. Website: www.enquirer.com. Circ. 191,000. Daily.

💬 Mostly staff written.

⊘ THE COLUMBUS DISPATCH

The Dispatch Printing Co., 34 S. 3rd St., Columbus OH 43215. (614)461-5000. Fax: (614)461-7580. Website: www.dispatch.com. Circ. 261,000. Daily.

💬 Mostly staff written.

⊘ THE COMMERCIAL APPEAL

E.W. Scripps Co., 495 Union Ave., Memphis TN 38103. (901)529-2345. Fax: (901)529-2522. Website: www.commercialappeal.com. Estab. 1841. Circ. 161,000. Daily.

💬 Mostly staff written.

$ CONSTRUCTION EQUIPMENT GUIDE

470 Maryland St., Ft. Washington PA 19034. (800)523-2200 or (215)885-2900. Fax: (215)885-2910. E-mail: editorial@cegltd.com. Website: www.cegltd.com; constructionequipmentguide.com. **Contact:** Craig Mongeau, editor-in-chief. Estab. 1957. Circ. 120,000. Accepts 30% of material on one-time basis. 200-600 features purchased/year. Four regional biweekly newspapers Biweekly trade newspaper, now online. Emphasizes construction equipment industry, including projects ongoing throughout the country. Readers are males and females of all ages; many are construction executives, contractors, dealers and manufacturers. Free sample copy. "Construction Equipment Guide covers the nation with it's four regional newspapers, offering construction and industry news and information along with new and used construction equipment for sale from dealers in your area. Now we extend those services and information to the internet. Making it as easy as possible to find the news and equipment that you need and want." Accepts queries by mail, e-mail, fax, phone. Buys all rights. Pays on publication. Byline given. Sample copy and guidelines free.

NEEDS Query with published clips. Length: 150-1,800 words. **Word rate negotiable.**

⊘ THE COURIER-JOURNAL

Gannett Newspapers, P.O. Box 740031, Louisville KY 40201. (502)582-4011. Fax: (502)582-4200. Website: www.courier-journal.com. Estab. 1868. Circ. 223,000. Daily.

💬 Mostly staff written.

$ CREATIVE LOAFING

Creative Loafing, Inc., 384 Northyrds Blvd., Suite 600, Atlanta GA 30313. Fax: (404)420-1402. Website: www.atlanta.creativeloafing.com. Estab. 1972. Circ. 150,000. Accepts 20% of material under contract. Accepts 5% of material on one-time basis. Weekly. Accepts queries by e-mail. Pays on publication. Editorial lead time 1 week. Byline given. Sample copy available online.

NEEDS Buys one-shot features. Query with or without published clips, include résumé

⊘ DAILY NEWS (CA)

MediaNews Group, P.O. Box 4200, Woodland Hills CA 91365. (818)713-3000. Fax: (818)713-0058. E-mail: dnforum@dailynews.com. Website: www.dailynews.com. Estab. 1911. Circ. 177,000. Daily.

💬 Mostly staff written.

⊘ DAILY NEWS (NY)

Daily News LP, 450 W. 33rd St., New York NY 10001. (212)210-2100. Fax: (212)643-7832. E-mail: news@edit.nydailynews.com. Website: www.nydailynews.com. Circ. 737,000. Daily.

💬 Mostly staff written.

⊘ THE DALLAS MORNING NEWS

A.H. Belo Corp., P.O. Box 655237, Dallas TX 75265. (214)977-8429. Fax: (214)977-8319. E-mail: metro@

dallasnews.com. Website: www.dallasnews.com. Estab. 1885. Circ. 515,000. Daily.

💬 Mostly staff written.

⊘ DAYTON DAILY NEWS

Cox Newspapers, Inc., P.O. Box 1287, Dayton OH 45401. (937)222-5700. Fax: (937)225-2088. Website: www.daytondailynews.com. Estab. 1898. Circ. 134,000. Daily.

💬 Mostly staff written.

⊘ DENVER POST

MediaNews Group, 101 W. Colfax Ave., Denver CO 80202. (303)820-1010. Fax: (303)820-1201. E-mail: newsroom@denverpost.com. Website: www.denverpost.com. Circ. 300,000. Daily.

💬 Mostly staff written. Contact specific editor.

⊘ DES MOINES REGISTER

Gannett Newspapers, P.O. Box 957, Des Moines IA 50304. (515)284-8000. Fax: (515)286-2504. E-mail: metroiowa@dmreg.com. Website: www.desmoinesregister.com. Estab. 1849. Circ. 155,000. Daily.

💬 Mostly staff written.

⊘ THE DETROIT NEWS

Gannett Newspapers, 615 W. Lafayette Blvd., Detroit MI 48226. (313)222-6400. Fax: (313)222-2335. E-mail: metro@detnews.com. Website: www.detnews.com. Circ. 233,000. Daily.

💬 Mostly staff written.

$ ENTERTAINMENT TODAY

Best Publishing, Inc., 2325 W. Victory Blvd., Burbank CA 91506. Fax: (818)566-4295. E-mail: enttoday@artnet.net. Estab. 1967. Circ. 210,000. Accepts 40% of material on one-time basis. 6-12 features purchased/year. Weekly. Accepts queries by mail, e-mail, fax. Responds in 2-5 months to queries. Buys one-time rights. Editorial lead time 3 months. Byline given. Accepts simultaneous submissions. Sample copy available online. Guidelines available by e-mail.

NEEDS Query with published clips. Length: 675-1,850 words.

COLUMNS Book Report (book review, often entertainment-related), 415-500 words; Disc Domain (CD reviews), 250-400 words. Buys 6-12 mss/year.

⊘ EXPRESS

Washington Post Co., 1515 N. Court House Rd., Arlington VA 22201-2909. (703)469-2800. Fax: (703)469-2831. E-mail: inbox@readexpress.com. Website: www.readexpress.com. Circ. 175,000. Daily.

💬 Query before submitting. Mostly staff written.

$ FARM WORLD

MidCountry Media, P.O. Box 90, Knightstown IN 46148-1242. (800)876-5133. Fax: (800)318-1055. E-mail: davidb@farmworldonline.com. Website: www.farmworldonline.com. Estab. 1955. Circ. 36,000. Accepts 60-70% of material on one-time basis. 1,000 features purchased/year. Accepts queries by mail, e-mail, fax. Buys first, electronic rights. Makes work-for-hire assignments. Editorial lead time 1 month. Byline given. Sample copy and guidelines available online.

NEEDS "We've seen a lot, but we are always looking for ways farmers are able to succeed in the current crisis. New issues include biofuels - ethanol and biodiesel, GMOs and other biotech; trade; marketing; and farmland preservation. The environment and new regulations are also of concern to farmers." We don't want first-person accounts. No unsolicited columns, no opinion, no humor, no nostalgia. Query. Length: 1,000 words maximum. **Pays $55 (less than 400 words); $85 (more than 400 words). All stories go online.** Pays expenses of writers on assignment.

⊘ THE FLORIDA TIMES-UNION

Morris Multimedia, Inc., P.O. Box 1949, Jacksonville FL 32231. (904)359-4111. Fax: (904)359-4478. E-mail: jaxstaff@jacksonville.com. Website: www.jacksonville.com. Estab. 1883. Circ. 171,000. Daily.

💬 Mostly staff written.

⊘ FORT WORTH STAR-TELEGRAM

Knight Ridder, 400 W. 7th, Fort Worth TX 76102. (817)390-7400. Fax: (817)390-7789. E-mail: newsroom@star-telegram.com. Website: www.star-telegram.com. Estab. 1906. Circ. 228,000. Daily.

💬 Mostly staff written.

⊘ THE FRESNO BEE

McClatchy Newspapers, 1626 E St., Fresno CA 93786. (559)441-6111. Fax: (559)441-6436. E-mail: metro@fresnobee.com. Website: www.fresnobee.com. Circ. 165,000. Daily.

💬 Mostly staff written.

THE HAPPY HERALD NEWSPAPER

Star Publications, Inc., P.O. Box 810548, Boca Raton FL 33481. E-mail: editorial@happyherald.com. Website: www.happyherald.com. Estab. 1995. Circ. 75,000. Accepts 50% of material under contract. Accepts 70% of material on one-time basis. 12 features purchased/ year. Monthly. Accepts queries by e-mail. Responds in 2 months to queries. Responds in 2 months to mss. Pays on publication. Editorial lead time 2-3 months. Byline given. Accepts simultaneous submissions. Sample copy available online. Guidelines available online.

💬 Include Attention: Editorial Department in the subject line of e-mail queries.

NEEDS Buys one-shot features. Length: 200-500 words.

⊘ THE HARTFORD COURANT

Tribune Co., 285 Broad St., Hartford CT 06115. (860)241-6200. Fax: (860)241-3865. Website: www.ctnow.com. Circ. 190,000. Daily.

💬 Mostly staff written. Submit story ideas to the appropriate section editor (e-mail addresses provided on website).

$ HOME TIMES FAMILY NEWSPAPER

Neighbor News, Inc., P.O. Box 22547, West Palm Beach FL 33416. (561)439-3509. E-mail: hometimes2@aol.com. Website: hometimesnewspaper.org. **Contact:** Dennis Lombard, editor & publisher. Estab. 1990. Circ. 4,000. Accepts 100% of material on one-time basis. 12 features purchased/year. Works with Works with several local stringers. writers/year. Monthly tabloid mailed to subscribers throughout Palm Beach and Treasure Coast in Southeast Florida. "*Home Times* is a conservative newspaper written for the general public but with a Biblical worldview and family-values slant. It is not religious or preachy." Responds in 2-4 weeks to full articles only. Buys one-time and reprint rights. Makes work-for-hire assignments. Pays on publication. Editorial lead time Editorial lead time is 8 weeks. Byline given. Accepts simultaneous submissions. Accepts SASE returns. Sample copy for $3. Guidelines for #10 SASE.

NEEDS One shot features. Does not want devotionals. Send complete ms. Length: 500-1,000 words. **Pays up to $50 for assigned articles.** Sometimes pays expenses of writers on assignment.

COLUMNS Home & Family; Arts & Entertainment, Science, Sports, Advice, Lifestyles; Personal Finances, all shorts and features. Buys 12 mss/year.

⊘ HOUSTON CHRONICLE

Hearst Newspapers, P.O. Box 4260, Houston TX 77210. (713)362-7171. Fax: (713)362-6677. E-mail: online@chron.com. Website: www.houstonchronicle.com. Circ. 548,000. Daily.

💬 Mostly staff written.

⊘ THE INDIANAPOLIS STAR

Gannett Newspapers, P.O. Box 145, Indianapolis IN 46206. (317)444-4000. Fax: (317)444-6600. E-mail: info@indystar.com. Website: www.indystar.com. Estab. 1903. Circ. 255,000. Daily.

💬 Mostly staff written.

$ ITALIAN TRIBUNE

Italian Tribune Publishing Co., Inc., 427 Bloomfield Ave., Newark NJ 07107. (973)485-6000. E-mail: mail@italiantribune.com. Website: www.italiantribune.com. Estab. 1931. Circ. 67,000. Accepts 15% of material under contract. Accepts 10% of material on one-time basis. 100+ features purchased/year. Works with 20+ writers/year. Weekly. Accepts queries by mail, e-mail. Responds in 2 weeks to queries. Responds in 1 month to mss. Buys one-time rights. Pays on publication. Editorial lead time 3 weeks. Byline given. Accepts simultaneous submissions. Returns submission with SASE. Sample copy free. Guidelines available online.

NEEDS Buys one-shot features. Buys article series. No book reviews or nostalgia (of the my grandparents made sauce every Sunday). Query. Length: 100-1,200 words.

COLUMNS Travel (profile Italian spots/attractions of interest), 700-1,000 words. Buys 50+ mss/year.

$$ JOURNAL NEWSPAPER GROUP

Metropolitan Graphics, 4610 200th St. SW, Suite F, Lynnwood WA 98036. Fax: (425)670-0511. E-mail: editor@journal-newspapers.com. Website: www.journal-newspapers.com. Estab. 1973. Circ. 100,000. Accepts 50%% of material under contract. Accepts 10%% of material on one-time basis. 60 features purchased/year. Works with 10-15 writers/year. Monthly. Accepts queries by e-mail. Responds in 2 weeks to queries. Pays on publication. Editorial lead time 3 wks. Byline given. Sample copy available online.

NEEDS Buys one-shot features. "We do not want feature stories not local to our area (North King, South Snohomish counties); hard news; politics, religion or anything of a controversial nature; personal essays."

Query with published clips. Length: 600-1,000 words. **Pays $100 for assigned articles.**

COLUMNS Arts & Entertainment (local), Senior Lifestyles (local), Health & Fitness (current), 700 words; General Features, 800 words.

THE KANSAS CITY STAR

Knight Ridder, 1729 Grand Blvd., Kansas City MO 64108. (816)234-4636. Fax: (816)234-4926. E-mail: thestar@kcstar.com. Website: www.kcstar.com. Estab. 1880. Circ. 273,000. Daily.

Mostly staff written.

LAS VEGAS REVIEW-JOURNAL

Stephens Media Group, P.O. Box 70, Las Vegas NV 89125. (702)383-0211. Fax: (702)383-4676. Website: www.lvrj.com. Estab. 1905. Circ. 170,000. Daily.

Mostly staff written.

$ $ L.A. WEEKLY

6715 Sunset Blvd., Los Angeles CA 90028. (323)465-9909. Fax: (323)465-3220. Website: www.laweekly.com. **Contact:** Drex Heikes, editor. Estab. 1978. Circ. 225,000. Accepts 30% of material on one-time basis. *L.A. Weekly* provides a fresh, alternative look at Los Angeles. We have arts coverage, news analysis, investigative reporting, and a comprehensive calendar section. "LA Weekly has been decoding Los Angeles for its readers, infiltrating its subcultures, observing and analyzing its shifting rhythms, digging up its unreported stories and confronting the city's political leaders. From the beginning, the paper has found success by drawing in readers with comprehensive calendar listings and cultural coverage, and then keeping those readers loyal with bold news and political coverage and in-depth feature stories by some of the country's finest writers. LA Weekly has won more awards from the Association of Alternative Newsweeklies than any other paper in the country, and in 2007 was awarded the Pulitzer Prize for criticism by food writer Jonathan Gold." Accepts queries by mail, online e-mail, fax. Responds in 1 month to queries. Responds in 4 months to mss. Buys first North American serial, electronic rights. Pays on publication. Offers 33% kill fee. Byline given. Sample copy available online.

NEEDS We assign many articles to freelancers, but accept very few unsolicited manuscripts. Query with published clips. **Pays 37¢/word.**

LEXINGTON HERALD-LEADER

McClatchy, 100 Midland Ave., Lexington KY 40508. (859)231-3100. Fax: (859)231-1659. Website: www.kentucky.com. Circ. 113,000. Daily.

Mostly staff written.

$ LIVING

Media For Living, 1251 Virginia Ave., Harrisonburg VA 22802-2434. E-mail: mediaforliving@gmail.com. Website: www.livingforthewholefamily.com. **Contact:** Dorothy Hartman. Estab. 1992. Circ. 250,000. Accepts 90% of material on one-time basis. 40-50 features purchased/year. Quarterly. "*Living* is a quarterly 'good news' paper published to encourage and strengthen family life at all stages, directed to the general newspaper-reading public." Responds in 2 months to queries. Responds in 6 months to mss. Pays on publication. Editorial lead time 6 months. Byline given. Accepts simultaneous submissions. Sample copy for SASE with 9x12 envelope and 4 First-class stamps. Guidelines available by e-mail.

NEEDS Send complete ms. Length: 500-1,000 words. **Pays $35-60.**

$ LIVING LIGHT NEWS

Living Light Ministries, 5306 89th St., #200, Edmonton AB T6E 5P9 Canada. (780)468-6397. Fax: (780)468-6872. E-mail: shine@livinglightnews.com. Website: www.livinglightnews.org. **Contact:** Jeff Caporale, Editor. Estab. 1995. Circ. 75,000. Accepts 100% on One Time Basis.% of material on one-time basis. Buys 50 features. features purchased/year. Bimonthly. "Our publication is a seeker-sensitive, evangelical, outreach-oriented newspaper focusing on glorifying God and promoting a personal relationship with Him." Accepts queries by e-mail, phone. Responds in 2 weeks to queries and to mss. Buys first North American serial, first, one-time, second serial (reprint), simultaneous, all rights. Makes work-for-hire assignments. Editorial lead time Editorial lead time: 2 months. Offers 100% kill fee. Byline sometimes given. Accepts simultaneous submissions. Sample copy for 10x13 SAE with $3.50 in IRCs. Guidelines available online.

NEEDS Profiles on 'celebrity Christians' in sports, business and entertainment, plus amazing stories of hope, redemption and transformation through Jesus Christ. No issue-oriented, controversial stories. Query with published clips. Length: 300-1,000 words. **Pays $30-100 for assigned articles.** Sometimes pays expenses of writers on assignment. pays expenses of writers on assignment.

COLUMNS Buys 40 columns/year. mss/year.

⊘ LONG BEACH PRESS-TELEGRAM

MediaNews Group, 300 Oceangate, Long Beach CA 90844. (562)435-1161. Fax: (562)437-7892. Website: www.presstelegram.com. Circ. 100,000. Daily.

Query before submitting. Mostly staff written.

LOS ANGELES JEWISH JOURNAL

3580 Wilshire Blvd., Suite 1510, Los Angeles CA 90010. (213)368-1661. Fax: (213)368-1684. E-mail: editor@jewishjournal.com. Website: www.jewishjournal.com. Estab. 1985. Circ. 65,000 (weekly). Accepts 33% of material on one-time basis. 120 features purchased/year. Works with 20 writers/year. Weekly. Our mission is to serve the Jewish community through the practice of quality journalism. Accepts queries by e-mail. Responds in 1-4 weeks to queries. Buys first North American serial, electroic rights. Pays on publication. Editorial lead time 2 weeks. Offers 33% kill fee. Byline given. Returns submission with SASE. Sample copy available online. Guidelines available online.

NEEDS Query. Length: 750-1,500 words. **Pays $100 for assigned articles.**

⊘ LOS ANGELES TIMES

Tribune Co., 202 W. 1st St., Los Angeles CA 90012. (213)237-5000. Fax: (213)237-4712. E-mail: op-ed@latimes.com. Website: www.latimes.com. Circ. 945,000. Daily.

Mostly staff written. Break in on the Op-Ed page.

⊘ METRO NEW YORK

Metro International, 44 Wall St., New York NY 10005-2401. (212)952-1500. Fax: (212)952-1242. E-mail: letters@metro.us. Website: www.metro.us. Circ. 300,000. Daily.

Query before submitting. Mostly staff written.

⊘ MIAMI HERALD

Knight Ridder, 1 Herald Plaza, Miami FL 33132. (305)350-2111. Fax: (305)376-5287. E-mail: nationalnews@herald.com. Website: www.herald.com. Estab. 1903. Circ. 328,000. Daily.

Mostly staff written.

⊘ MILWAUKEE JOURNAL SENTINEL

Journal Communications, P.O. Box 661, Milwaukee WI 53201. (414)224-2413. Fax: (414)224-2047. Website: www.jsonline.com. Estab. 1837. Circ. 257,000. Daily.

Mostly staff written.

$ NAVY TIMES

Army Times Publishing Co., 6883 Commercial Dr., Springfield VA 22159. (703)750-8636. Fax: (703)750-8767. E-mail: aneill@atpco.com. Website: www.navytimes.com. Estab. 1950. Circ. 90,000. 100 features purchased/year. Weekly. Pays on publication. Accepts simultaneous submissions. Guidelines free.

NEEDS Query. Length: 500-1,000 words. **Payment negotiable.**

$ NEW LIVING

New Living, Inc., 1212 Route 25A, Suite 1B, Stony Brook NY 11790. (631)751-8819. E-mail: newliving@aol.com. Website: www.newliving.com. Estab. 1991. Circ. 100,000. Accepts 10% of material on one-time basis. Monthly. Accepts queries by e-mail. Responds in 6 weeks to queries. Makes work-for-hire assignments. Pays on publication. Editorial lead time 2 months. Byline given. Sample copy for 9x12 SAE with $1.21 postage. Guidelines for #10 SASE.

NEEDS Needs only feature articles on holistic/natural health topics. Query. Length: 800-1,700 words. **Pays $25-100.**

⊘ THE NEWS & OBSERVER

McClatchy Newspapers, P.O. Box 191, Raleigh NC 27602. (919)829-4500. Fax: (919)829-4529. Website: www.newsobserver.com. Estab. 1865. Circ. 169,000. Daily.

Mostly staff written.

NEWS & RECORD

Landmark Communications, P.O. Box 20848, Greensboro NC 27401. (336)373-7000. Fax: (336)373-7382. Website: www.news-record.com. Other Address: 200 E. Market St., Greensboro NC 27401-2950. Circ. 92,000. Accepts 5% of material under contract. Accepts 2% of material on one-time basis. 20 features purchased/year. Works with 10 writers/year. Daily. Responds in 2 weeks to queries. Buys first, electroic rights. Editorial lead time 6 weeks. Byline given. Accepts simultaneous submissions. Returns submission with SASE. Sample copy available online.

Query before submitting. Mostly staff written.

NEEDS Buys one-shot features. Buys article series. No advertorial. Query. Word length varies. **Payment negotiable.**

⊘ NEWSDAY

Tribune Co., 235 Pinelawn Rd., Melville NY 11747. (631)843-2020. Fax: (631)843-2953. E-mail: news@ newsday.com. Website: www.newsday.com. Estab. 1940. Circ. 579,000. Daily.

🖰 Mostly staff written.

⊘ THE NEWS JOURNAL

Gannett Newspapers, P.O. Box 15505, Wilmington DE 19850. (302)324-2500. Fax: (302)324-2595. Website: www.delawareonline.com. Circ. 119,000. Daily.

🖰 Mostly staff written.

⊘ THE NEWS TRIBUNE

McClatchy Newspapers, P.O. Box 11000, Tacoma WA 98411. (253)597-8742. Fax: (253)597-8274. Website: www.tribnet.com. Estab. 1880. Circ. 130,000. Daily.

🖰 Mostly staff written.

⊘ NEW YORK POST

News America Publishing, Inc., 1211 Avenue of the Americas, New York NY 10036. (212)930-8000. Fax: (212)930-8540. Website: www.nypost.com. Circ. 620,000. Daily.

🖰 Mostly staff written.

⊘ THE NEW YORK TIMES

The New York Times Co., 229 W. 43rd St., New York NY 10036. (212)556-1234. Fax: (212)556-3815. E-mail: news-tips@nytimes.com. Website: www.nytimes.com. Estab. 1851. Circ. 1,130,000. Daily.

🖰 Mostly staff written.

⊘ THE OKLAHOMAN

Oklahoma Publishing Co., P.O. Box 25125, Oklahoma City OK 73125. (405)478-7171. Fax: (405)475-3970. Website: www.newsok.com. Circ. 222,000. Daily.

🖰 Mostly staff written; submit story ideas through the website.

⊘ OMAHA WORLD-HERALD

MediaNews Group, 1314 Douglas St., Omaha NE 68102. (402)444-1000. Fax: (402)345-0183. Website: www.omaha.com. Estab. 1885. Circ. 200,000. Daily.

🖰 Mostly staff written.

⊘ THE OREGONIAN

Advance Publications, 1320 SW Broadway, Portland OR 97201. (503)221-8327. Fax: (503)227-5306. E-mail: newsroom@news.oregonian.com. Website: www.oregonian.com. Circ. 250,000. Daily news

🖰 Mostly staff written.

⊘ ORLANDO SENTINEL

Tribune Co., 633 N. Orange Ave., Orlando FL 32801. (407)420-5000. Fax: (407)420-5350. Website: www.orlandosentinel.com. Circ. 266,000. Daily.

🖰 Mostly staff written.

⊘ THE PALM BEACH POST

Cox Newspapers, Inc., P.O. Box 24700, West Palm Beach FL 33416. (561)820-4100. Fax: (561)820-4407. E-mail: pbonline@pbpost.com. Website: www.pbpost.com. Estab. 1894. Circ. 181,000. Daily.

🖰 Mostly staff written.

⊘⊘ PARENTS' PRESS

1454 Sixth St., Berkeley CA 94710-1431. (510)524-1602. Fax: (510)524-0912. E-mail: parentsprs@aol.com. Website: www.parentspress.com. Estab. 1980. Circ. 75,000. Accepts 25% of material on one-time basis. 10-12 features purchased/year. Monthly. Accepts queries by mail, e-mail. all rights, including electronic, second serial (reprint), and almost always Northern California exclusive rights. Accepts simultaneous submissions. Sample copy for $3. Guidelines available online.

🖰 Does not download attachments to e-mail.

NEEDS We require a strong Bay Area focus in almost all articles. Use quotes from experts and Bay Area parents. Please, no child-rearing tips or advice based on personal experience. Special issues: Pregnancy; Birth & Baby; Family Travel; Back to School. Send complete ms. Length: 300-1,500 words. **Pays $50-500 for assigned articles.**

⊘ PHILADELPHIA INQUIRER

Knight Ridder, P.O. Box 8263, Philadelphia PA 19101. (215)854-2000. Fax: (215)854-5099. E-mail: inquirer.letters@phillynews.com. Website: www.philly.com. Estab. 1829. Circ. 386,000. Daily.

🖰 Mostly staff written.

⊘ PITTSBURGH TRIBUNE-REVIEW

Richard M. Scaife Publisher, Inc., 503 Martindale St., Pittsburgh PA 15212. Website: www.pittsburghLIVE.

com. Estab. 1992. Circ. 100,000 daily; 200,000 Sunday. Accepts 5-10% of material under contract. Accepts 5-10% of material on one-time basis. Daily. Accepts queries by mail, e-mail. Buys first, electroic rights. Makes work-for-hire assignments. Pays on publication. Editorial lead time 2 weeks. Byline given. Returns submission with SASE. Sample copy available online. Guidelines available by e-mail.

NEEDS Buys one-shot features. Query with published clips. **Payment varies. for no answer.**

COLUMNS Editorial Page; Features; Suburban; Sports; Business.

THE PLAIN DEALER

Newhouse Newspapers, 1801 Superior Ave. E., Cleveland OH 44114. (216)999-5000. Fax: (216)999-6366. E-mail: editor@cleveland.com. Website: www.cleveland.com. Circ. 373,000. Daily.

Mostly staff written.

THE POST AND COURIER

Evening Post Publishing Co., 134 Columbus St., Charleston SC 29403. (843)577-7111. Fax: (843)937-5579. Website: www.charleston.net. Estab. 1803. Circ. 118,000. Daily.

Mostly staff written.

THE PRESS-ENTERPRISE

Belo Corp., 3450 14th St., Riverside CA 92501. (909)684-1200. Fax: (909)368-9024. Website: www.pe.com. Circ. 188,000. Daily.

Mostly staff written.

THE PROVIDENCE JOURNAL

75 Fountain St., Providence RI 02902. (401)277-7000. Fax: (401)277-7346. E-mail: pjnews@projo.com. Website: www.projo.com. Estab. 1829. Circ. 165,000. Daily.

Mostly staff written.

QUEENS LEDGER WEEKLY COMMUNITY NEWSPAPER GROUP

Queens Ledger/Greenpoint Star Inc., 69-60 Grand Ave., Maspeth NY 11378. (718)639-7000. E-mail: news@queensledger.com. Website: www.queensledger.com. Estab. 1873. Circ. 150,000. Weekly. Accepts queries by e-mail. Responds in 1 week to queries. Responds in 1 month to mss. Pays on publication. Editorial lead time 2 days. Byline given. Accepts simultaneous submissions.

NEEDS Buys one-shot features. Buys article series. Query with published clips or send complete ms. **Pays**

$20-50 for assigned articles. Sometimes pays expenses of writers on assignment.

COLUMNS Local sports column, 300 words; local political column, 500 words, community business column. Write about as many local people and events as possible. Buys 100s mss/year.

QUICK

508 Young St., Dallas TX 75202-4893. (214)977-7888. Fax: (214)977-8319. Website: www.quickdfw.com. Circ. 150,000. Daily.

Query before submitting. Mostly staff written.

RICHMOND TIMES-DISPATCH

Media General, Inc., P.O. Box 85333, Richmond VA 23293. (804)649-6000. Fax: (804)775-8059. E-mail: news@timesdispatch.com. Website: www.timesdispatch.com. Circ. 217,000. Daily.

Mostly staff written.

ROCKY MOUNTAIN NEWS

E.W. Scripps Co., P.O. Box 719, Denver CO 80201. (303)892-5000. Fax: (303)892-2841. E-mail: metro@rockymountainnews.com. Website: www.rockymountainnews.com. Circ. 300,000. Daily.

Mostly staff written. Contact specific editor.

SACRAMENTO BEE

McClatchy Newspapers, P.O. Box 15779, Sacramento CA 95816. (916)321-1000. Fax: (916)321-1109. Website: www.sacbee.com. Estab. 1857. Circ. 300,000. Daily.

Mostly staff written.

ST. LOUIS POST-DISPATCH

Pulitzer Newspapers, Inc., 900 N. Tucker Blvd., Saint Louis MO 63101. (314)340-8000. Fax: (314)340-3050. E-mail: pdeditor@post-dispatch.com. Website: www.post-dispatch.com. Estab. 1878. Circ. 286,000. Daily.

Mostly staff written.

ST. PETERSBURG TIMES

490 First Ave. S., Saint Petersburg FL 33701. (727)893-8111. Fax: (727)893-8675. E-mail: local@sptimes.com. Website: www.sptimes.com. Estab. 1884. Circ. 354,000. Daily.

Mostly staff written.

THE SAN DIEGO UNION-TRIBUNE

P.O. Box 120191, San Diego CA 92112. (619)299-3131. Fax: (619)293-1896. E-mail: letters@uniontrib.com.

Website: www.uniontrib.com. Estab. 1868. Circ. 346,000. Daily.

💬 Mostly staff written.

$ SAN FRANCISCO BAY GUARDIAN

135 Mississippi St., San Francisco CA 94107-2536. (415)255-3100. Fax: (415)255-8762. E-mail: corbett@sfbg.com. Website: www.sfbg.com. Estab. 1966. Circ. 140,000. Accepts 40% of material on one-time basis. Responds in 2 months to queries. Buys first rights. Byline given. Guidelines available online.

NEEDS City Editor (news); J.H. Tompkins (arts & entertainment); Lynn Rapoport (culture). Publishes incisive local news stories, investigative reports, features, analysis and interpretation, how-to, consumer and entertainment reviews. Most stories have a Bay Area angle. Freelance material should have a public interest advocacy journalism approach. Query with 3 clips. Sometimes pays expenses of writers on assignment.

$$ SAN FRANCISCO CHRONICLE

Hearst Newspapers, 901 Mission St., San Francisco CA 94103. (415)777-1111. Fax: (415)543-7708. E-mail: metro@sfchronicle.com. Website: www.sfgate.com. Circ. 500,000. Daily. Guidelines available online.

💬 Very competitive market.

NEEDS Query. Length: 250-2,000 words. **Pays up to $500.**

⊘ SAN JOSE MERCURY NEWS

Knight Ridder, 750 Ridder Park Dr., San Jose CA 95190. (408)920-5000. Fax: (408)288-8060. E-mail: letters@sjmercury.com. Website: www.mercurynews.com. Estab. 1851. Circ. 275,000. Daily. Guidelines available online.

💬 Mostly staff written. Contact specific editor.

⊘ SARASOTA HERALD-TRIBUNE

The New York Times Co., P.O. Box 1719, Sarasota FL 34230. (941)953-7755. Fax: (941)957-5276. E-mail: editor.letters@herald-tribune.com. Website: www.heraldtribune.com. Circ. 116,000. Daily.

💬 Query before submitting. Mostly staff written.

⊘ SEATTLE POST-INTELLIGENCER

Hearst Newspapers, P.O. Box 1909, Seattle WA 98111. (206)448-8000. Fax: (206)448-8166. E-mail: citydesk@seattlepi.com. Website: www.seattlepi.com. Estab. 1863. Circ. 155,000. Daily.

💬 Mostly staff written.

$ SENIOR LIVING NEWSPAPERS

Metropolitan Radio Group, 2010 S. Stewart St., Springfield MO 65804. 1-877-479-4705. Fax: (417)862-9079. E-mail: elefantwalk@msn.com. Estab. 1995. Circ. 45,000. Accepts 25-50% of material on one-time basis. 65 features purchased/year. Monthly. For people 55+. Positive and upbeat attitude on aging, prime-of-life times. Slant is directed to mid-life and retirement lifestyles. Readers are primarily well-educated and affluent retirees, homemakers, and career professionals. Accepts queries by mail, e-mail. Responds in 2 weeks to queries. Responds in 1 month to mss. Buys first, second serial (reprint), electroic rights. Editorial lead time 3 months. Byline given. Sample copy for SASE with 9x12 envelope and 5 First-class stamps.

NEEDS No youth-oriented, preachy, sugar-coated, technical articles. Send complete ms. 600 words maximum. **Pays $5-35.**

$ SENIOR TIMES

Senior Publishing, P.O. Box 30965, Columbus OH 43230. (614)337-2055. Fax: (614)337-2059. E-mail: seniortimes@insight.rr.com. Estab. 1983. Circ. 25,000. Accepts 50% of material under contract. Accepts 25% of material on one-time basis. 200 features purchased/year. Works with 25 writers/year. Accepts queries by e-mail. Editorial lead time 1 month. Byline given. Accepts simultaneous submissions. Sample copy for #10 SASE.

NEEDS Query or send complete ms. Length: 500-1000 words. **Pays $15-30.**

⊘ THE STAR-LEDGER

Newhouse Newspapers, 1 Star Ledger Plaza, Newark NJ 07102. (973)392-4141. Fax: (973)392-5845. E-mail: eletters@starledger.com. Website: www.nj.com/starledger. Circ. 407,000. Daily.

💬 Mostly staff written.

⊘ STAR TRIBUNE

McClatchy Newspapers, 425 Portland Ave., Minneapolis MN 55488. (612)673-4000. Fax: (612)673-4359. E-mail: metrostate@gw.startribune.com. Website: www.startribune.com. Circ. 375,000. Daily.

💬 Mostly staff written.

$$ SYRACUSE NEW TIMES

Alltimes Publishing, LLC, 1415 W. Genesee St., Syracuse NY 13204. E-mail: menglish@syracusenewtimes.com. E-mail: editorial@syracusenewtimes.com. Website: newtimes.rway.com. **Contact:** Molly English. Estab. 1969. Circ. 40,000. 250-300 features purchased/year. Works with 10-20 writers/year. Weekly tabloid covering news, sports, arts, and entertainment *"Syracuse New Times is an alternative weekly that is topical, provocative, irreverent, and intensely local."* 50% freelance written. Publishes ms an average of 1 month after acceptance. Submit seasonal material 3 months in advance. Accepts queries by mail. Responds in 2 weeks to queries; 1 month to mss. Buys one-time, electronic rights. Pays on publication. Editorial lead time 2-4 weeks. Byline given. Accepts simultaneous submissions. SASE returns. Sample copy available online. Guidelines for #10 SASE.

NEEDS Essays, general interest Buys one-shot features. Wellness; Continuing Education; seasonal supplements (Autumn Times, Winter Times). No humor or anything not local to Syracuse. Query with published clips. Length: 500-3,000 words. **Pays $75-200 for assigned articles.** Sometimes pays expenses of writers on assignment.

⊘ THE TAMPA TRIBUNE

Media General, Inc., P.O. Box 191, Tampa FL 33601. (813)259-7600. Fax: (813)225-7676. E-mail: news@tampatrib.com. Website: www.tampatrib.com. Circ. 238,000. Daily.

　◯ Mostly staff written.

⊘ THE TENNESSEAN

Gannett Newspapers, 1100 Broadway, Nashville TN 37203. (615)259-8000. Fax: (615)259-8093. E-mail: newstips@tennessean.com. Website: www.tennessean.com. Estab. 1812. Circ. 181,000. Daily.

　◯ Mostly staff written.

❸❸❸ TIMES PUBLICATIONS

Strickbine Publishing, 3200 N. Hayden, Suite 210, Scottsdale AZ 85251. (480)348-0343. Fax: (480)348-2109. E-mail: shanna@timespublications.com. Website: www.timespublications.com. **Contact:** Shanna Hogan, features editor. Estab. 1997. Circ. 111,000. Accepts queries by e-mail. Buys first North American serial, electronic rights. Pays on publication. Byline given. Accepts simultaneous submissions.

NEEDS Exposé (investigations into Arizona businesses, consumer issues, crimes), 1,200-2,500 words; Inspirational, 1,000-2,000 words; Interview/Profile (notable Arizona personalities), 1,000-1,500 words; General Interest (local trends and national trends localized), 1,000-1,500 words; Humor (satirical news stories), 400-500 words; Photo Feature (full-page photo stories); Food Reviews; Travel Articles and Columns. "No travel or opinion articles. If you are not brutally interested in composing the piece, then we will not be mildly interested in publishing it." Query with published clips. Length: 1,000-2,500 words. **Pays 30¢-$1/word for assigned articles.** Sometimes pays expenses of writers on assignment.

⊘ TOWN CRIER

P.O. Box 1020, 75 E. North St., Geneva NY 14456. (315)789-4168. Fax: (315)789-0144. E-mail: info@thetowncrier.com. Website: www.thetowncrier.com. Circ. 70,000. Daily.

　◯ Mostly staff written.

⊘ TRIBUNE-REVIEW (GREENSBURG)

Tribune-Review Publishing Co., 622 Cabin Hill Dr., Greensburg PA 15601-1692. (724)834-1151. Fax: (724)838-5171. Website: www.triblive.com. Circ. 65,000. Daily.

　◯ Mostly staff written.

❸❸ THE TRUCKER

Trucker Publications, Inc., P.O. Box 3413, Little Rock AR 72203-3413. (800)666-2770. E-mail: editor@thetrucker.com. Website: www.thetrucker.com. Estab. 1987. Circ. 100,000. 10-15 features purchased/year. Biweekly. Content must be written to appeal to and inform audience that includes over-the-road drivers as well as CEOs. Accepts queries by mail, e-mail, phone. Responds in 2 weeks to queries. Makes work-for-hire assignments. Pays on publication. Editorial lead time 3 weeks. Offers kill fee. Offers negotiable kill fee. Byline given. Sample copy for 10x13 SAE and $2.53 postage. Guidelines for #10 SASE.

NEEDS Send for editorial calendar. Timely industry news only. No unsolicited manuscripts, please. Query by phone Length: 300-1,200 words. **Pays $25-250.** Sometimes pays expenses of writers on assignment.

⊘ TUCSON CITIZEN

Gannett Newspapers, P.O. Box 26767, Tucson AZ 85726-6767. (520)573-4561. Fax: (520)573-4569. Website: www.tucsoncitizen.com. Other Address: 4850 S. Park Ave., Tucson AZ 85714-3395. Circ. 100,000. Daily.

　◯ Query before submitting. Mostly staff written.

USA TODAY

Gannett Newspapers, 7950 Jones Branch Dr., McLean, VA 22108 (703)854-3400. Fax: (703)854-2078. E-mail: editor@usatoday.com. Website: www.usatoday.com. Circ. 2,250,000. Daily.

○ Mostly staff written.

VENTURA COUNTY REPORTER

700 E. Main St., Ventura CA 93001. (805)648-2244. Fax: (805)648-2245. E-mail: editor@vcreporter.com. Website: www.vcreporter.com. **Contact:** Michael Sullivan, editor. Circ. 35,000. Accepts 50% of material on one-time basis. Weekly tabloid covering local news (entertainment and environment). Accepts queries by mail, e-mail, fax. Responds in 1 month to queries. Buys first North American serial rights. Pays on publication. Byline given.

○ Works with a small number of new/unpublished writers each year.

NEEDS Length: 2,000-3,000 words. **Pay varies.**

COLUMNS Entertainment, Dining News, Features, Environmental News.

THE VIRGINIAN-PILOT

Landmark Communications, Inc., P.O. Box 449, Norfolk VA 23501. (757)446-2000. Fax: (757)446-2414. Website: www.pilotonline.com. Circ. 201,000. Daily.

○ Mostly staff written.

THE WALL STREET JOURNAL

Dow Jones & Co., Inc., 200 Liberty St., New York NY 10281. (212)416-2000. Fax: (212)416-2255. E-mail: edit.features@wsj.com. Website: www.wsj.com. Circ. 1,890,000. Daily. Accepts queries by e-mail. Guidelines available online.

○ Op-Ed pieces must be exclusive to *Journal*.

NEEDS Submit by e-mail complete ms, cover letter, and contact info. Length: 600-1,200 words.

WISCONSIN STATE JOURNAL

Capital Newspapers, P.O. Box 8056, Madison WI 53708-8056. (608)252-6100. Fax: (608)252-6119. Website: www.wisconsinstatejournal.com. Circ. 89,000.

○ Query before submitting. Mostly staff written.

NEWSPAPERS

SCREENWRITING

Writers do not get into screenwriting for the fame. Most of the glory shines on the directors, actors and actresses. That said, every great movie and TV show relies on a great script crafted by a screenwriter. Plus, successful screenwriters can bring in a healthy income.

To break into TV you must have spec scripts—work written for free that serves as a calling card and gets you in the door. A spec script showcases your writing abilities and gets your name in front of influential people. Whether a network has invited you in to pitch some ideas, or a movie producer has contacted you to write a first draft for a feature film, the quality of writing in your spec script got their attention and that may get you the job.

It's a good idea to have several spec scripts, whether it's sitcom (half-hour comedies), episodic (one-hour series), or movie of the week (two-hour dramatic movies). For TV and cable movies, you should have completed original scripts and a few for episodic TV shows.

In choosing spec script shows, remember one thing: Don't write a script for a show you want to work on. If you want to write for *CSI*, for example, you'll send a *Cold Case* script and vice versa. It may seem contradictory, but it's standard practice. It reduces the chances of lawsuits, and writers and producers can feel very proprietary about their shows and stories.

An original movie script contains characters you create, with story lines you design, allowing you more freedom than in TV. However, your writing must still convey believable dialogue and realistic characters, with a plausible plot and high-quality writing carried through roughly 120 pages.

Many novice screenwriters tend to write too many visual cues and camera directions into their scripts. Your goal should be to write something readable, like a "compressed novella." Write succinct resonant scenes and leave the camera technique to the director and producer.

3N1 ENTERTAINMENT

P.O. Box 491085, Los Angeles CA 90049. (310)773-1147. Fax: (310)268-9168. E-mail: info@3n1ent.com. Website: www.3n1ent.com. Feature films, Production, TV Series.

3 RING CIRCUS FILMS

1040 N. Sycamore Ave., Hollywood CA 90038 United States. (323)466-5300. Fax: (323)466-5310. E-mail: info@3ringcircus.tv. Website: www.3ringcircus.tv. Production credits include *One*, *Cherish*, *Dream With the Fishes*.

44 BLUE PRODUCTIONS

4040 Vineland Ave., Suite 105, Studio City CA 91604. (818)760-4442. Fax: (818)760-1509. E-mail: reception@44blue.com. Website: www.44blue.com.

ALLIED ARTISTS, INC.

2251 N. Rampart Blvd., 1479, Las Vegas NV 89128. (702)991-9011. E-mail: query@alliedartistsonline.com. Website: www.alliedartistsonline.com. Produces material for broadcast and cable television, home video, and film. Buys 3-5 scripts/year. Works with 10-20 writers/year. Buys first or all rights. Accepts previously produced material. Submit synopsis, outline. Responds in 2 months to queries. Responds in 3 months to mss. Pays in accordance with writer's guild standards.

NEEDS Films, videotapes social issue TV specials (30-60 minutes), special-interest home video topics, positive values feature screenplays.

BIZAZZ MEDIA

3760 Grand View Blvd., Los Angeles CA 90066. (310)390-9360. E-mail: rupert@bizazzmedia.com. Website: www.bizazzmedia.com. **Contact:** Rupert Hitzig. "Bizazz Media is a full service video production company, built around Emmy and Peabody Award winning Producer Rupert Hitzig and a diverse cast of creative professionals with experienced vision. We specialize in the production of documentaries, electronic press kits, marketing videos, corporate videos, industrial videos, and training films. Whether it's for broadcast, non-broadcast presentation, or the Internet, our productions are engaging, informative, and never dull!"

BRITISH LION FILMS

Los Angeles CA (818)990-7750. Fax: (818)789-2901. E-mail: petersnell@britishlionfilms.com. Website:

www.britishlionfilms.com. **Contact:** Peter Snell. British Lion is continually evaluating literary material for future production as well as remakes of their past films.

HUGHES CAPITAL ENTERTAINMENT

22817 Ventura Blvd., #471, Woodland Hills CA 91364. (818)484-3205. Fax: (818)484-3205. E-mail: info@trihughes.com. Website: www.trihughes.com. **Contact:** Patrick Hughes, producer; Karen Rabesa, VP production/development. "Hughes Capital Entertainment (founded by Patrick Hughes) started as a creative film finance company and has grown to become a major management and production company that produces and develops major motion pictures, TV shows, books, and other creative content and manages a broad and talented group of individuals and companies including screenwriters, best-selling authors, directors, show creators, producers, singers/songwriters/, music producers, game creators, visual effects and animation companies, documentary filmmakers, and more. Produces 2 movies/year." Note for Script/Story Submissions: HCE does not accept unsolicited submissions. Please do not email scripts, novels, or show ideas. You will not receive a response and your material will not be reviewed. Send query and synopsis, or submit complete ms. Mostly accepts agented submissions. Responds in 3 weeks to queries.

✂━📌"We are looking to produce and develop feature-length screenplays, produced stage plays, well-developed pitches, and detailed treatments. Focus is on broad comedies, urban comedies, socially smart comedies, family films (family adventure), ground-breaking abstract projects, and new writers/directors with an extremely unique and unparalleled point of view. Don't focus on budget, cast, or locations. The story is key to getting things done here."

THE MARSHAK/ZACHARY CO.

8840 Wilshire Blvd., 1st Floor, Beverly Hills CA 90211. Fax: (310)358-3192. E-mail: marshakzachary@aol.com; alan@themzco.com. **Contact:** Alan W. Mills, associate. "Audience is film goers of all ages and television viewers.". Buys 3-5 scripts/year. Works with 10 writers/year. Rights purchased vary. Query with synopsis. Responds in 2 weeks to queries. Responds in 3 months to mss. Payment varies

MONAREX HOLLYWOOD CORP.

11605 W. Pico Blvd., Suite 200, Los Angeles CA 90064. (310)478-6666. Fax: (310)478-6866. E-mail: monarexcorp@aol.com. **Contact:** Chris D. Nebe, President. All audiences. Buys 3-4 scripts/year. Works with 5-10 writers/year. Buys all rights. Query with synopsis. Responds in 1 month to queries. Pays in accordance with writer's guild standards.

NHO ENTERTAINMENT

8931 Beverly Blvd., #249, Los Angeles CA 90048. E-mail: info@nho.la. Website: www.nhoentertainment.com. **Contact:** Mark Costa, partner. All audiences. Buys 5 scripts/year. Works with 10 writers/year. Buys all rights. Accepts previously produced material. Query with synopsis, resume, writing samples, production history via e-mail. Responds in 1 month to queries. Pays in accordance with writer's guild standards.
NEEDS films, videotapes, multi kits, tapes, cassettes.

SPENCER PRODUCTIONS, INC.

P.O. Box 2247, Westport CT 06880. E-mail: spencerprods@yahoo.com. **Contact:** Bruce Spencer, general manager; Alan Abel, creative director. Produces material for high school students, college students and adults. Occasionally uses freelance writers with considerable talent. Query. Responds in 1 month to queries. Payment negotiable.

TOO NUTS PRODUCTIONS, L.P.

925 Lakeville St., Petaluma CA 94952. (310)967-4532. E-mail: info@toonutsproductions.com. **Contact:** Ralph Scott and Daniel Leo Simpson, co-executive producers. "Produces illustrated kids books, art books, audio CDs, DVDs, internet animation shorts for internet, music-based kidlit properties, and half-hour tv/video with a twist. Among our projects in development: 'Catscans,' Our Teacher is a Creature, Toad Pizza, The Salivating Salamander, The Suburban Cowboys, The Contest-Ants, The De-Stinktive Skunk, and Sneeks Peaks. Audience for all projects except art books is children, 5-12. Always looking for talented, new kidlit illustrators as well.". Buys 4-10 scripts/year. Works with 4-6 writers/year. Buys both first rights and all rights Query with synopsis. Submit resume. Submit writing samples. Submit production history. creative but brief cover letter/e-mail; Works with 20% first time writers. Illustrators query with creative but brief cover letter, samples of work by e-mail or hyperlink to your online portfolio. Responds in less than 3 months to queries. Responds in 6 months to mss. pays royalty and makes outright purchase
☞ Really good original—clean—content.
NEEDS Videotapes, multi kits, tapes, one-page synopses, audio CDs, CD-ROMs. "Please do not submit anything with violence, chainsaws, axes, ice picks, and general blood and guts. We're producing for children, not monsters, or those who aspire to become them."

VALEO FILMS

P.O. Box 250, Orange Lake FL 32681. (352)591-4714. E-mail: screenplays@valeofilms.com. Website: www.valeofilms.com. Query by e-mail or mail.
☞ Currently considering projects that contain one or more of the following: character or story driven, identifies moral values, romance/love story, educational/documentary, presents the human condition, strong visual imagery, coming of age/learning, or intellectual drama/mystery.

PLAYWRITING

Where TV and movies have a diminished role for writers in the collaboration that produces the final product, whether a show or a film, theater places a very high value on the playwright. This may have something to do with the role of the scripts in the different settings.

Screenplays are often in a constant state of "in progress," where directors make changes; producers make changes; and even actors and actresses make changes throughout the filming of the TV show or movie. Plays, on the other hand, must be as solid as a rock, because the script must be performed live night after night.

As a result, playwrights tend to have more involvement in the productions of their scripts, a power screenwriters can only envy. Counterbalancing the greater freedom of expression are the physical limitations inherent in live performance: a single stage, smaller cast, limited sets and lighting, and, most importantly, a strict, smaller budget. These conditions not only affect what but also how you write.

FOR MORE INFORMATION

To find out more about writing and submitting plays, contact the Dramatists Guild (dramaguild.com) and the Writers Guild of America (wga.org). Both organizations are great for networking and for learning the basics needed to build a successful career crafting plays.

ABINGDON THEATRE CO.

312 W. 36th St., 6th Floor, New York NY 10018. (212)868-2055. Fax: (212)868-2056. E-mail: literary@ abingdontheatre.org. Website: abingdontheatre.org. **Contact:** Literary Manager: Kim T. Sharp. Produces 2-3 Mainstage and 2-3 Studio productions/year. Professional productions for a general audience. Submit full-length script in hard copy, cast breakdown, synopsis and development history, if any. No one-acts or musicals. Include SASE for return of manuscript.

NEEDS All scripts should be suitable for small stages.

ACT II PLAYHOUSE

P.O. Box 555, Ambler PA 19002-0555. (215)654-0200. Fax: (215)654-9050. Website: act2.org. **Contact:** Stephen Blumenthal, literary manager. Produces 4 plays/ year. Submit query and synopsis. Include SASE for return of submission.

NEEDS Contemporary comedy, drama, musicals. Full length. 6 character limitation; 1 set or unit set. Does not want period pieces. Limited number of scenes per act.

ACTORS THEATRE OF LOUISVILLE

316 W. Main St., Louisville KY 40202-4218. (502)584-1265. Fax: (502)561-3300. E-mail: awegener@actorstheatre.org. Website: actorstheatre.org. **Contact:** Amy Wegener, literary manager. Produces approximately 25 new plays of varying lengths/year. "Professional productions are performed for subscription audience from diverse backgrounds. Agented submissions only for full-length plays, will read 10-page samples of unagented full-length works. Open submissions to National Ten-Minute Play Contest (plays 10 pages or less) are due November 1."

NEEDS Full-length and 10-minute plays and plays of ideas, language, humor, experiment and passion.

ⓐ ACT THEATRE

A Contemporary Theatre, Kreielsheimer Place, 700 Union St., Seattle WA 98101. (206)292-7660. Fax: (206)292-7670. E-mail: artistic@acttheatre.org. Website: acttheatre.org. Produces 5-6 mainstage plays/ year. "ACT performs a subscription-based season on 3 stages: 2 main stages (a thrust and an arena) and a smaller, flexible 99-seat space. Although our focus is towards our local Seattle audience, some of our notable productions have gone on to other venues in other cities." *Agented submissions only* or through theatre professional's recommendation. No unsolicited sub-

missions. Query and synopsis only for Northwest playwrights.

NEEDS ACT produces full-length contemporary scripts ranging from solo pieces to large ensemble works, with an emphasis on plays that embrace the contradictions and mysteries of our contemporary world and that resonate with audiences of all backgrounds through strong storytelling and compelling characters.

ALLEYWAY THEATRE

One Curtain Up Alley, Buffalo NY 14202. (716)852-2600. Fax: (716)852-2266. E-mail: newplays@alleyway.com. Website: alleyway.com. **Contact:** Literary Manager. Produces 4-5 full-length, 6-12 one-act plays/year. Submit complete script; include CD for musicals. Alleyway Theatre also sponsors the Maxim Mazumdar New Play Competition. See the Contest & Awards section for more information.

NEEDS "Works written uniquely for the theatre. Theatricality, breaking the fourth wall, and unusual settings are of particular interest. We are less interested in plays which are likely to become TV or film scripts."

ALLIANCE THEATRE

1280 Peachtree St. NE, Atlanta GA 30309. (404)733-4650. Fax: (404)733-4625. Website: alliancetheatre. org. **Contact:** Literary Intern. Produces 11 plays/year. Professional production for local audience. Only accepts agent submissions and unsolicited samples from Georgia residents only. Electronic correspondence preferred. Query with synopsis and sample or submit through agent. Enclose SASE.

NEEDS Full-length scripts and scripts for young audiences no longer than 60 minutes.

⊘ AMERICAN CONSERVATORY THEATER

30 Grant Ave., 6th Floor, San Francisco CA 94108-5800. (415)834-3200. Website: act-sf.org. **Contact:** Pink Pasdar, associate artistic director. Produces 8 plays/year. Plays are performed in Geary Theater, a 1,000-seat classic proscenium. No unsolicited scripts.

⊛ ANCHORAGE PRESS PLAYS, INC.

Dramatic Publishing, 311 Washington St., Woodstock IL 60098. (800)448-7469 (US & CA); (815)338-7170 (all other countries). Fax: (800)334-5302. E-mail: applays@bellsouth.net. Website: applays.com. **Contact:**

Linda Habjan, submissions coordinator. Publishes 4-6 plays/year. "We are an international agency for plays for young people. First in the field since 1935. We are primarily a publisher of theatrical plays with limited textbooks. "Publishes solicited hardcover and trade paperback originals. "Anchorage Press PLAYS, Inc serves a specialty field of TYA - Theatre for Young Audiences. We publish play scripts and license the performance rights for plays to be presented, by skilled performers, before audiences of children, youth, teens, and young adults or a family audience. Anchorage also has a limited number of plays of faith that are more suitable for a family audience or teen/adult audience in subject complexity. Representing the playwrights of these works, Anchorage serves as the licensing agency for the performance rights. We also publish and distribute a select number of books for the field." "A play manuscript must be computer-printed with dark ink. It should be submitted by mail to (Submissions, Anchorage Press Plays, Linda Habjan, Submissions Editor, 311 Washington St., Woodstock, IL 60098) and accompanied by a SASE. Manuscripts will not be accepted via fax or e-mail. Please send a play script only after it has had staged productions, workshop readings, peer reviews, and rewrites. We cannot accept plays for publication that have not been produced. (Please send information about productions: programs, reviews, etc.) **Send your final version**. We will consider plays with 2 or more characters. See more guidelines online at website.".

NEEDS Drama, stage plays, for children and young people.

❶ ARENA STAGE

1101 6th St. SW, Washington DC 20024. (202)554-9066. Fax: (202)488-4056. Website: arenastage.org. **Contact:** Mark Bly, senior dramaturg. Produces 8 plays/year. Only accepts scripts from writers with agent or theatrical representation.

NEEDS "Plays that illuminate the broad canvas of American work, with a commitment to aesthetic, cultural, and geographic diversity. Arena is committed to showcasing the past, present, and future of American theatre." Seeks only full-length plays and musicals in all genres.

ARIZONA THEATRE CO.

P.O. Box 1631, Tucson AZ 85702. (520)884-8210. Fax: (520)628-9129. Website: arizonatheatre.org. **Contact:** Literary Department. Produces 6-8 plays/year. "Arizona Theatre Company is the State Theatre of Arizona and plans the season with the population of the state in mind." Only Arizona writers may submit unsolicited scripts, along with production history (if any), brief bio, and self-addressed envelope. Out-of-state writers can send a synopsis, 10-page sample dialogue, production history (if any), brief bio, and self-addressed envelope.

NEEDS Full length plays of a variety of genres and topics and full length musicals. No one-acts.

ARTISTS REPERTORY THEATRE

1515 SW Morrison, Portland OR 97205. (503)241-1278. Fax: (503)241-8268. Website: artistsrep.org. Produces Plays performed in professional theater with a subscriber-based audience. Send synopsis, résumé, and sample (max 10 pages). No unsolicited mss accepted.

NEEDS Full-length, hard-hitting, emotional, intimate, actor-oriented shows with small casts (rarely exceeds 10-13, usually 2-7). Language and subject matter are not a problem. No one-acts or children's scripts.

ART STATION THEATRE

5384 Manor Dr., Stone Mountain GA 30083. (770)469-1105. E-mail: info@artstation.org. Website: artstation. org. **Contact:** Jon Goldstein, program manager. Produces 3 plays/year. ART Station Theatre is a professional theater located in a contemporary arts center in Stone Mountain, GA, which is part of Metro Atlanta. Audience consists of middle-aged to senior, suburban patrons. Query with synopsis and writing samples.

NEEDS Full length comedy, drama and musicals, preferably relating to the human condition in the contemporary South. Cast size no greater than 6.

ASIAN AMERICAN THEATER CO.

55 Teresita Blvd., San Francisco CA 94127. E-mail: darryl@asianamericantheater.org. Website: asianamericantheater.org. Produces 4 plays/year. Produces professional productions for San Francisco Bay Area audiences. Submit complete script.

NEEDS The new voice of Asian American theater. No limitations in cast, props or staging.

⊘ ASOLO THEATRE CO.

5555 N. Tamiami Trail, Sarasota FL 34234. (941)351-9010. Fax: (941)351-5796. Website: asolo.org. **Contact:** Michael Donald Edwards, Production Artistic Dir. Produces 7-8 plays/year. A LORT theater with 2 intimate performing spaces.

NEEDS Play must be full length. We operate with a resident company in rotating repertory.

ATTIC THEATRE & FILM CENTRE

5429 W. Washington Blvd., Los Angeles CA 90016-1112. (323)525-0600. Website: attictheatre.org. **Contact:** Literary Manager. Produces 4 plays a year. "We are based in Los Angeles and play to industry and regular Joes. We use professional actors; however, our house is very small, and the salaries we pay, including the royalties are very small because of that."

BAILIWICK REPERTORY

Bailiwick Arts Center, 1229 W. Belmont Ave., Chicago IL 60657-3205. (773)883-1090. Fax: (773)883-2017. E-mail: newworks@bailiwickchicago.com. Website: bailiwick.org. **Contact:** David Zak, artistic director. Produces 5 mainstage plays (classic and newly commissioned) each year; 12 one-acts in annual Directors Festival. Pride Performance Series (gay and lesbian), includes one-acts, poetry, workshops, and staged adaptations of prose. Submit year-round. One-act play fest runs July-August. "When submitting your work, please include the following: For non-musicals: Cover letter with contact information and a brief synopsis PDF version of the script. For musicals: Cover letter with contact information and brief synopsis, PDF version of the script, 2-3 mp3's of what you consider to be the best songs from the score.".

NEEDS We need daring scripts that break the mold. Large casts or musicals are OK. Creative staging solutions are a must.

BAKER'S PLAYS PUBLISHING CO.

45 W. 25th St., New York NY 10010. E-mail: publications@bakersplays.com. Website: bakersplays.com. **Contact:** Managing Editor. **Publishes 20-30 straight plays and musicals. Works with 2-3 unpublished/unproduced writers annually. 80% freelance written. 75% of scripts unagented submissions.** Plays performed by amateur groups, high schools, children's theater, churches and community theater groups. Submit complete script with news clippings, resume, production history. Submit complete cd of music with musical submissions. See our website for more information about e-submissions.

NEEDS We are finding strong support in our new division—plays from young authors featuring contemporary pieces for high school production.

MARY BALDWIN COLLEGE THEATRE

Mary Baldwin College, Staunton VA 24401. Fax: (540)887-7139. Website: mbc.edu/theatre/. **Contact:** Terry K. Southerington, professor of theater. Produces 5 plays/year. 10% of scripts are unagented submissions. "An undergraduate women's college theater with an audience of students, faculty, staff and local community (adult, somewhat conservative)." Query with synopsis.

NEEDS "Full-length and short comedies, tragedies, and music plays geared particularly toward young women actresses, dealing with women's issues both contemporary and historical. Experimental/studio theater not suitable for heavy sets. Cast should emphasize women. No heavy sex; minimal explicit language."

BARTER THEATRE

P.O. Box 867, Abingdon VA 24212-0867. (276)628-2281. Fax: (276)619-3335. E-mail: ddramaturge@bartertheatre.com. Website: bartertheatre.com. **Contact:** Dramaturge. Produces 17 plays/year. The Barter Players produces professional children's productions with 100% of roles written for adults. Recently produced plays include: The Legend of Sleepy Hollow and James and the Giant Peach. Query with synopsis, character breakdown and set description. Will consider simultaneous submissions and previously performed work. Responds only if interested.

◯ *Does not accept unsolicited mss.*

NEEDS "Creative, interesting material for children K-12. We are seeking shows for students that go hand in hand with school standards of learning that can be performed by 6 actors. We are also seeking summer shows for young children for casts of 12-15. Works that talk down to the audience will not be considered."

BLOOMSBURG THEATRE ENSEMBLE

226 Center St., Bloomsburg PA 17815. E-mail: jsatherton@bte.org. Website: bte.org. **Contact:** J. Scott Atherton, manager of admin. and development. Produces 9 plays/year. Professional productions for a non-urban audience. Submit query and synopsis.

NEEDS Because of our non-urban location, we strive to expose our audience to a broad range of theatre—both classical and contemporary. We are drawn to language and ideas and to plays that resonate in our community. We are most in need of articulate comedies and cast sizes under 6.

TIPS Because of our non-urban setting we are less interested in plays that focus on dilemmas of city life in particular. Most of the comedies we read are cynical. Many plays we read would make better film scripts; static/relationship-heavy scripts that do not use the 'theatricality' of the theatre to an advantage.

BOARSHEAD THEATER

425 S. Grand Ave., Lansing MI 48933-2122. (517)484-7800, 7805. Fax: (517)484-2564. Website: boarshead. org. **Contact:** George Orban. Produces 8 plays/year (6 mainstage, 2 Young People's Theater productions in-house), 4 or 5 staged readings. Mainstage Actors' Equity Association company; also Youth Theater—touring to schools by our intern company. Submit synopsis, character breakdown, 20 pages of sample dialogue, bio, production history (if any) via mail only.

NEEDS Thrust stage. Cast usually 8 or less; occasionally up to 20; no one-acts and no musicals considered. Prefers staging which depends on theatricality rather than multiple sets. Send materials for full-length plays (only) to Kristine Thatcher, artistic director. For Young People's Theater, send one-act plays (only); 4-5 characters.

CALIFORNIA THEATRE CENTER

P.O. Box 2007, Sunnyvale CA 94087. (408)245-2979. Fax: (408)245-0235. E-mail: resdir@ctcinc.org. Website: ctcinc.org. **Contact:** Will Huddleston. Produces 15 children's plays for professional productions. 75% of plays/musicals written for adult roles; 20% for juvenile roles. Query with synopsis, character breakdown and set description. Send to: Will Huddleston. Will consider previously performed work. Submissions returned with SASE.

NEEDS Prefers material suitable for professional tours and repertory performance; one-hour time limit, limited technical facilities. Recently produced *Brave Irene*, adapted by Joan Cushing (children's lit, for grades K and up); *Dear Mr. Henshaw*, adapted by Gayle Cornelison from Beverley Cleary (children's classic, for grades 2 and up).

CELEBRATION THEATRE

7985 Santa Monica Blvd., #109-1, Los Angeles CA 90046. Fax: (323)957-1826. E-mail: celebrationthtr@earthlink.net. Website: celebrationtheatre.com. **Contact:** Literary Management Team. Produces 4 plays/year. Performed in a small theatre in Los angeles. For all audiences, but with gay and lesbian characters at the center of the plays. Submit query and synopsis.

NEEDS Produce works with gay and lesbian characters at the center of the narrative. There aren't any limitations, but simple productions work best. Don't send coming-out plays/stories.

CHILDSPLAY, INC.

900 S. Mitchell Dr., Tempe AZ 85281. (480)921-5700. Fax: (480)921-5777. E-mail: info@childsplayaz.org. Website: childsplayaz.org. Produces 5-6 plays/year. Professional touring and in-house productions for youth and family audiences. Submit synopsis, character descriptions and 7- to 10-page dialogue sample.

NEEDS Seeking theatrical plays on a wide range of contemporary topics. Our biggest market is K-6. We need intelligent theatrical pieces for this age group that meet touring requirements and have the flexibility for in-house staging. The company has a reputation, built up over 30 years, of maintaining a strong aesthetic. We need scripts that respect the audience's intelligence and support their rights to dream and to have their concerns explored. Innovative, theatrical and small is a constant need. Touring shows limited to 5 actors; in-house shows limited to 6-10 actors.

ⓐ CLEVELAND PLAY HOUSE

8500 Euclid Ave., Cleveland OH 44106. E-mail: sgordon@clevelandplayhouse.com. Website: clevelandplayhouse.com. **Contact:** Seth Gordon, associate artistic director. Produces 10 plays/year. We have five theatres, 100-550 seats. Submit 10-page sample with synopsis. Will return submissions if accompanied by SASE.

NEEDS All styles and topics of new plays.

COLONY THEATRE CO.

555 N. Third St., Burbank CA 91502. (818)558-7000. Fax: (818)558-7110. E-mail: colonytheatre@colonytheatre.org. Website: colonytheatre.org. **Contact:** Michael David Wadler, literary manager. Produces 6 plays/year. Professional 276-seat theater with thrust stage. Casts from resident company of professional actors. Submit query and synopsis.

NEEDS Full length (90-120 minutes) with a cast of 4-12. Especially interested in small casts of 4 or fewer. No musicals or experimental works.

CREEDE REPERTORY THEATRE

P.O. Box 269, Creede CO 81130-0269. (719)658-2541. E-mail: litmgr@creederep.com. Website: creederep.org. **Contact:** Frank Kuhn, Literary Manager. Produces 6 plays/year. Plays performed for a smaller audience.

Submit synopsis, 10-page dialogue sample, letter of inquiry, resume; electronic submissions only.

NEEDS "Special consideration given to plays focusing on the cultures and history of the American West and Southwest."

DALLAS CHILDREN'S THEATER

Rosewood Center for Family Arts, 5938 Skillman, Dallas TX 75231. E-mail: artie.olaisen@dct.org. Website: dct.org. **Contact:** Artie Olaisen, assoc. artistic director. Produces 10 plays/year. "Professional theater for family and student audiences." Query with synopsis, number of actors required, any material regarding previous productions of the work, and a demo tape or lead sheets (for musicals). No materials will be returned without a SASE included.

NEEDS "Seeking substantive material appropriate for youth and family audiences. Most consideration given to full-length, non-musical works, especially classic and contemporary adaptations of literature. Also interested in social, topical, issue-oriented material. Very interested in scripts which enlighten diverse cultural experiences, particularly Hispanic and African-American experiences. Prefers scripts with no more than 15 cast members; 6-12 is ideal."

DETROIT REPERTORY THEATRE

13103 Woodrow Wilson, Detroit MI 48238-3686. (313)868-1347. Fax: (313)868-1705. **Contact:** Barbara Busby, literary manager. Produces 4 plays/year. Professional theater, 194 seats operating on A.E.A. SPT contract Detroit metropolitan area. Submit complete ms in bound folder, cast list, and description with SASE.

NEEDS Wants issue-oriented works. Cast limited to no more than 7 characters. No musicals or one-act plays.

DIVERSIONARY THEATRE

4545 Park Blvd., Suite 101, San Diego CA 92116. (619)220-6830. E-mail: dkirsch@diversionary.org. Website: diversionary.org. **Contact:** Dan Kirsch, executive and artistic director. Produces 5-6 plays/year. "Professional non-union full-length productions of gay, lesbian, bisexual and transgender content. Ideal cast size is 2-6." Submit application and 10-15 pages of script.

DIXON PLACE

161 Chrystie St., Ground Floor, New York NY 10002. (212)219-0736. Fax: (212)219-0761. Website: dixonplace.org. **Contact:** Leslie Strongwater, artistic director. Produces 12 plays/year. Does not accept submissions from writers outside the NYC area. Looking for new work, not already read or workshopped in full in New York. To help us be more efficient in the reviewing of submissions, please read about our ongoing series on the website and submit proposals directly to the series you think is the "best fit". Keep in mind that you are sending an idea or proposal for a performance. Your proposal does not need to be a polished piece when you submit the work, and if selected, it should still be in a 'work-in-progress' stage when you perform it. If you would like your submission materials returned, please include a self-addressed, stamped envelope. We will not return submission materials without a SASE. Works chosen are provided an honorarium, rehearsal time, inclusion in our season brochures, website presence, and technical assistance. If you have any questions, please e-mail us.

NEEDS Particularly interested in non-traditional, either in character, content, structure and/or themes. We almost never produce kitchen sink, soap opera-style plays about AIDS, coming out, unhappy love affairs, getting sober or lesbian parenting. We regularly present new works, plays with innovative structure, multi-ethnic content, non-naturalistic dialogue, irreverent musicals and the elegantly bizarre. We are an established performance venue with a very diverse audience. We have a reputation for bringing our audience the unexpected. Submissions accepted year-round.

Ⓐ DORSET THEATRE FESTIVAL

Box 510, Dorset VT 05251-0510. (802)867-2223. Website: dorsettheatrefestival.org. Produces 5 plays/year (1 a new work). Our plays will be performed in our Equity theater and are intended for a sophisticated community. Agented submissions only.

NEEDS Looking for full-length contemporary American comedy or drama. Limited to a cast of 6.

DRAMATICS MAGAZINE

2343 Auburn Ave., Cincinnati OH 45219. (513)421-3900. Fax: (513)421-7077. E-mail: info@edta.org; dcorathers@schooltheatre.org. Website: schooltheatre.org; edta.org. **Contact:** Don Corathers, editor. For high school theater students and teachers. Submit complete script.

NEEDS 'We are seeking one-acts to full-lengths that can be produced in an educational theater setting."

EAST WEST PLAYERS

120 N. Judge John Aiso St., Los Angeles CA 90012. (213)625-7000. Fax: (213)625-7111. E-mail: jliu@east-westplayers.org. Website: eastwestplayers.org. **Contact:** Jeff Liu, literary manager. Produces 4 plays/year. Professional 240-seat theater performing under LOA-BAT contract, presenting plays which explore the Asian Pacific American experience." Submit ms with title page, résumé, cover letter, and SASE.

NEEDS Whether dramas, comedies, or musicals, all plays must either address the Asian American experience or have a special resonance when cast with Asian American actors.

ELDRIDGE PUBLISHING CO. INC.

P.O. Box 14367, Tallahassee FL 32317. (850)385-2463. E-mail: editorial@histage.com. Website: histage.com or 95church.com. **Contact:** Nancy Vorhis, Editor. Publishes approximately 25 plays/year. Publishes new plays for junior high, senior high, church, and community audience. Query with synopsis (acceptable). Please send CD with any musicals.

THE ENSEMBLE STUDIO THEATRE

549 W. 52nd St., New York NY 10019. (212)247-4982. Fax: (212)664-0041. E-mail: firman@ensemblestudiotheatre.org. Website: ensemblestudiotheatre.org. **Contact:** Linsay Firman, Literary Manager. Produces 250 projects, readings, workshops and productions/year for off-off Broadway developmental theater in a 100-seat house, 60-seat workshop space. Do not fax mss or resumes. Please check website for current submission guidelines and deadlines.

NEEDS "Full-length plays with strong dramatic actions and situations and solid one-acts, humorous and dramatic, which can stand on their own. Special programs include Going to the River Series, which workshops new plays by African-American women, and the Sloan Project, which commissions new works on the topics of science and technology. Seeks original plays with strong dramatic action, believable characters and dynamic ideas. We are interested in writers who respect the power of language. No verse-dramas or elaborate costume dramas or musicals. Accepts new/unproduced work only."

ENSEMBLE THEATRE OF CINCINNATI

1127 Vine St., Cincinnati OH 45248. (513)421-3555. Fax: (513)562-4104. E-mail: lynn.meyers@cincyetc.com. Website: cincyetc.com. **Contact:** D. Lynn Mey-ers, producing artistic director. Produces 12 plays/year, including a staged reading series. Professional year-round theater. Query with synopsis, submit complete ms or submit through agent.

NEEDS Dedicated to good writing of any style for a small, contemporary cast. Small technical needs, big ideas.

FOUNTAIN THEATRE

5060 Fountain Ave., Los Angeles CA 90029. (323)663-2235. Fax: (323)663-1629. E-mail: ftheatre@aol.com. Website: fountaintheatre.com. **Contact:** Simon Levy, dramaturg. Produces both a theater and dance season. Produced at Fountain Theatre (99-seat equity plan). *Professional recommendation only.* Query with synopsis to Simon Levy, producing director/dramaturg.

NEEDS Original plays, adaptations of American literature, material that incorporates dance or language into text with unique use and vision.

THE FREELANCE PRESS

670 Centre St., Suite 8, Dover MA 02130. (617)524-7045. E-mail: info@freelancepress.org. Website: freelanceplayers.com. **Contact:** Narcissa Campion, managing director. "The musicals published by The Freelance Press are designed for music and theater educators who are seeking age-appropriate material for their students. Our plays and scores are developed by a national network of arts programs and children's theaters. Playwrights and composers, working directly with young actors and singers, have created shows to match the voices, interests and sensibilities of young people, ages 8-18." Submit complete ms with SASE.

NEEDS "We publish original musical theater to be performed by young people, dealing with issues of importance to them. Also adapt 'classics' into musicals for 8- to 16-year-old age groups to perform. Large cast, flexible."

SAMUEL FRENCH, INC.

45 W. 25th St., New York NY 10010. (212)206-8990. Fax: (212)206-1429. E-mail: publications@samuelfrench.com. Website: samuelfrench.com. **Contact:** Editorial Department. Publishes 50-60 titles/year. Publishes paperback acting editions of plays. Receives 1,500 submissions/year, mostly from unagented playwrights. 10% of publications are from first-time authors; 20% from unagented writers.

NEEDS Comedies, mysteries, children's plays, high school plays.

WILL GEER THEATRICUM BOTANICUM

P.O. Box 1222, Topanga CA 90290. (310)455-2322. Fax: (310)455-3724. Website: theatricum.com. **Contact:** Ellen Geer, artistic director. Produces 4 classical and 1 new play if selected/year. Professional productions for summer theater. Botanicum Seedlings new plays selected for readings and one play each year developed. Contact: Jennie Webb. Send synopsis, sample dialogue and tape if musical.

NEEDS Socially relevant plays, musicals; all full-length. Cast size of 4-10 people. "We are a large outdoor theatre—small intimate works could be difficult."

⊘ GEORGE STREET PLAYHOUSE

9 Livingston Ave., New Brunswick NJ 08901. (732)246-7717. Website: georgestplayhouse.org. **Contact:** Literary Associate. Produces 6 plays/year. Professional regional theater (LORT C). Proscenium/thurst stage with 367 seats. *No unsolicited scripts. Agent or professional recommendation only.*

GEVA THEATRE CENTER

75 Woodbury Blvd., Rochester NY 14607. (585)232-1366. **Contact:** Marge Betley, literary manager. Produces 7-11 plays/year. Professional and regional theater, modified thrust, 552 seats; second stage has 180 seats. Subscription and single-ticket sales. Query with sample pages, synopsis, and resume.

NEEDS Full-length plays, translations, adaptations.

Ⓐ THE GOODMAN THEATRE

170 N. Dearborn St., Chicago IL 60601-3205. (312)443-3811. Fax: (312)443-3821. E-mail: artistic@goodmantheatre.org. Website: goodman-theatre.org. **Contact:** Tanya Palmer, literary manager. Produces 9 plays/year. The Goodman is a professional, not-for-profit theater producing a series in both the Albert Theatre and the Owen Theatre, which includes an annual New Play Series. The Goodman does not accept unsolicited scripts, nor will it respond to synopsis of plays submitted by playwrights unless accompanied by a stamped, self-addressed postcard. The Goodman may request plays to be submitted for production consideration after receiving a letter of inquiry or telephone call from recognized literary agents or producing organizations.

NEEDS Full-length plays, translations, musicals; special interest in social or political themes.

Ⓐ GRETNA THEATRE

P.O. Box 578, Mt. Gretna PA 17064. Fax: (717)964-2189. E-mail: larryfrenock@gretnatheatre.com. Website: gretnatheatre.com. **Contact:** Larry Frenock, producing artistic director. Musicals and plays are produced at a professional equity theater during summer. Rarely produce new work for mainstage; will consider small cast musicals for children of one hour or less duration. Will accept submissions from writers or agents.

NEEDS Subject, language and content are important factors in this open-air theatre.

Ⓐ HARTFORD STAGE CO.

50 Church St., Hartford CT 06103. (860)525-5601. Fax: (860)525-4420. Website: hartfordstage.org. **Contact:** Scripts Manager. Produces 6 plays/year. Regional theater productions with a wide range in audience. Hartford Stage accepts scripts by agent submission or professional recommendation. As a dedicated supporter of our community, we also accept scripts from Connecticut residents. (Please note, we do not accept one-act plays, or unsolicited material. For questions, contact our scripts manager.

NEEDS Classics, new plays, musicals.

HORIZON THEATRE CO.

P.O. Box 5376, Atlanta GA 31107. (404)523-1477. Fax: (404)584-8815. Website: horizontheatre.com. **Contact:** Literary Manager. 5+ plays/year, and workshops 6 plays as part of New South Playworks Festival Professional productions. Accepts unsolicited résumés, samples, treatments, and summaries with SASE.

NEEDS "We produce contemporary plays that seek to bridge cultures and communities, utilizing a realistic base but with heightened visual or language elements. Particularly interested in comedy, satire, plays that are entertaining and topical, but thought provoking. Also particular interest in plays by women, African-Americans, or that concern the contemporary South. No more than 8 in cast."

ILLINOIS THEATRE CENTRE

371 Artists' Walk, P.O. Box 397, Park Forest IL 60466. (708)481-3510. Fax: (708)481-3693. E-mail: ilthctr@sbcglobal.net. Website: ilthctr.org. Produces 8 plays/year. Professional Resident Theatre Company in our own space for a subscription-based audience. Query with synopsis or agented submission.

NEEDS All types of 2-act plays, musicals, dramas. Prefers cast size of 6-10.

INDIANA REPERTORY THEATRE

140 W. Washington St., Indianapolis IN 46204-3465. (317)635-5277. E-mail: rroberts@irtlive.com. Website: irtlive.com. "Modified proscenium stage with 600 seats; thrust stage with 300 seats." Send synopsis with résumé via e-mail to the dramaturg. No unsolicited scripts. Submit year-round (season chosen by January).

NEEDS Full-length plays, translations, adaptations, solo pieces. Also interested in adaptations of classic literature and plays that explore cultural/ethnic issues with a midwestern voice. Special program: Discovery Series (plays for family audiences with a focus on youth). Cast size should be 6-8.

INTERACT THEATRE CO.

The Adrienne, 2030 Sansom St., Philadelphia PA 19103. (215)568-8077. Fax: (215)568-8095. E-mail: pbonilla@interacttheatre.org. Website: interacttheatre.org. **Contact:** Peter Bonilla, literary associate. Produces 4 plays/year. Produces professional productions for adult audience. Query with synopsis and bio. No unsolicited scripts.

NEEDS Contemporary dramas and comedies that explore issues of political, social, cultural or historical significance. Virtually all of our productions have political content in the foregound of the drama. Prefer plays that raise interesting questions without giving easy, predictable answers. We are interested in new plays. Limit cast to 8. No romantic comedies, family dramas, agit-prop.

ⓐ INTIMAN THEATRE

201 Mercer St., Seattle WA 98109. (206)269-1901. Fax: (206)269-1928. E-mail: literary@intiman.org. Website: intiman.org. **Contact:** Sheila Daniels. Produces 6 plays/year. LORT C Regional Theater in Seattle. Best submission time is October through March. *Agented submissions only* or by professional recommendation.

NEEDS Well-crafted dramas and comedies by playwrights who fully utilize the power of language and character relationships to explore enduring themes. Prefers nonnaturalistic plays and plays of dynamic theatricality.

JACKIE WHITE MEMORIAL NATIONAL CHILDREN'S PLAYWRITING CONTEST

Columbia Entertainment Company, 309 Parkade, Columbia MO 65202-1447. (573)874-5628. E-mail: bybetsy@yahoo.com. Website: cectheatre.org. **Contact:** Betsy Phillips, Contest Director.

JEWEL BOX THEATRE

3700 N. Walker, Oklahoma City OK 73118-7099. (405)521-7031. Fax: (405)525-6562. **Contact:** Charles Tweed, production director. Produces 6 plays/year. Amateur productions. 3,000 season subscribers and general public.

NEEDS Annual Playwriting Competition: Send SASE in September-October. Deadline: mid-January.

JEWISH ENSEMBLE THEATRE

6600 W. Maple Rd., West Bloomfield MI 48322. (248)788-2900. E-mail: e.orbach@jettheatre.org. Website: jettheatre.org. **Contact:** Evelyn Orbach, artistic director. Produces 4-6 plays/year. Professional productions at the Aaron DeRoy Theatre (season), The Detroit Institue of Arts Theatre, and Scottish Rite Cathedral Theatre (schools), as well as tours to schools. Submit complete script.

NEEDS We do few children's plays except original commissions; we rarely do musicals. Cast limited to a maximum of 8 actors

⊕ KITCHEN DOG THEATER

3120 McKinney Ave., Dallas TX 75204. (214)953-2258. Fax: (214)953-1873. E-mail: admin@kitchendogtheater.org. Website: kitchedogtheater.org. **Contact:** Chris Carlos, co-artistic director. Produces 5 plays/year. "Kitchen Dog Theater is a place where questions of justice, morality, and human freedom can be explored. We choose plays that challenge our moral and social consciences, invite our audiences to be provoked, challenged, and amazed. We have 2 performance spaces: a 100-seat black box and a 150-seat thrust." Submit complete manuscript with SASE.

NEEDS "We are interested in experimental plays, literary adaptations, historical plays, political theater, gay and lesbian work, culturally diverse work, and small musicals. Ideally, cast size would be 1-5, or more if doubling roles is a possibility. No romantic/light comedies or material that is more suited for television than the theater."

KUMU KAHUA

46 Merchant St., Honolulu HI 96813. (808)536-4222. Fax: (808)536-4226. E-mail: kumukahuatheatre@hawaiiantel.net. Website: kumukahua.org. Produces 5 productions, 3-4 public readings/year. Plays performed at new Kumu Kahua Theatre, flexible 120-seat theater, for community audiences. Submit complete script.

NEEDS Plays must have some interest for local Hawai'i audiences.

LILLENAS PUBLISHING CO.

P.O. Box 419527, Kansas City MO 64141-6527. (816)931-1900. Fax: (816)412-8390. E-mail: drama@lillenas.com. Website: lillenasdrama.com. **Contact:** Drama Editor. "We publish on 2 levels: 1) Program Builders—seasonal and topical collections of recitations, sketches, dialogues, and short plays; 2) Drama Resources which assume more than 1 format: a) full-length scripts; b) one-acts, shorter plays, and sketches all by 1 author; c) collection of short plays and sketches by various authors. All program and play resources are produced with local churches and Christian schools in mind. Therefore there are taboos." Queries are encouraged, but synopses and complete scripts are read. This publisher is interested in collections of and individual sketches. There is also a need for short pieces that are seasonal and on current events.

NEEDS 98% of Program Builders materials are freelance written. Scripts selected for these publications are outright purchases; verse is minimum of 25¢/line, prose (play scripts) are minimum of $5/double-spaced page. "Lillenas Drama Resources is a line of play scripts that are, for the most part, written by professionals with experience in productions as well as writing. While we do read unsolicited scripts, more than half of what we publish is written by experienced authors whom we have already published."

⊘⊘ LONG WHARF THEATRE

222 Sargent Dr., New Haven CT 06511. (203)787-4284. Fax: (203)776-2287. E-mail: gordon.edelstein@longwharf.org. Website: longwharf.org. **Contact:** Gordon Edelstein, artistic dir. Produces 6 plays/year on its 2 stages. "Professional regional theatre has been and continues to be an incubator of new works, including last season's *A Civil War Christmas* by Paula Vogel and *Coming Home* by Athol Fugard. Long Wharf Theatre has received New York Drama Critics Awards, Obie Awards, the Margo Jefferson Award for Production of New Works and more." *Agented submissions or professional recommendations only.*

NEEDS Full-length plays, translations, adaptations. Special interest: Dramatic plays and comedies about human relationships, social concerns, ethical and moral dilemmas.

LOS ANGELES DESIGNERS' THEATRE

P.O. Box 1883, Studio City CA 91614-0883. **Contact:** Richard Niederberg, artistic dir. Produces 8-20 plays/

year. "Professional shows/industry audience." Submit proposal only (i.e., 1 page in #10 SASE) We want highly commercial work without liens, 'understandings,' or promises to anyone. Does not return submissions accompanied by a SASE.

NEEDS All types. "No limitations—We seek design challenges. No boring material. Shorter plays with musical underscores are desirable; nudity, street language, and political themes are OK."

MAGIC THEATRE

Fort Mason Center, Bldg. D, 3rd Floor, San Francisco CA 94123. (415)441-8001. Fax: (415)771-5505. E-mail: info@magictheatre.org. Website: magictheatre.org. **Contact:** Mark Routhier, director of artistic development. Produces 6 mainstage plays/year, plus monthly reading series and several festivals each year which contain both staged readings and workshop productions. Regional theater. Bay area residents can send complete ms or query with cover letter, résumé, 1-page synopsis, SASE, dialogue sample (10-20 pages). Those outside the Bay area can query or submit through an agent.

NEEDS Plays that are innovative in theme and/or craft, cutting-edge sociopolitical concerns, intelligent comedy. Full-length only, strong commitment to multicultural work.

🌢 MALTHOUSE THEATRE

113 Sturt St., Southbank VIC 3006 Australia. (61)(3)9685-5100. Fax: (61)(3)9685-5111. E-mail: admin@malthousetheatre.com.au. Website: malthousetheatre.com.au. **Contact:** Michael Kantor, artistic director. We are dedicated to contemporary Australian theatre. Writers should have had at least 1 professional production of their work. Proposals are called for on March 1, July 1, and October 1. Mail 1-page synopsis, brief author bio, and 10-page sample. Responds in 3 months if interested.

⊘⊘ MANHATTAN THEATRE CLUB

311 W. 43rd St., 8th Floor, New York NY 10036. (212)399-3000. Fax: (212)399-4329. E-mail: questions@mtc-nyc.org. Website: mtc-nyc.org. **Contact:** Raphael Martin, literary manager. Produces 7 plays/year. 1 Broadway and 2 Off-Broadway theatres, using professional actors. *Solicited and agented submissions only.* No queries.

NEEDS We present a wide range of new work, from this country and abroad, to a subscription audience.

We want plays about contemporary concerns and people. All genres are welcome. MTC also maintains an extensive play development program.

Ⓐ MCCARTER THEATRE

91 University Place, Princeton NJ 08540. E-mail: literary@mccarter.org. Website: mccarter.org. **Contact:** Literary Manager. Produces 5 plays/year; 1 second stage play/year. Produces professional productions for a 1,077-seat and 360-seat theaters. Agented submissions only.

NEEDS Full length plays, musicals, translations.

◑ MELBOURNE THEATRE COMPANY

129 Ferrars St., Southbank VIC 3006 Australia. (61)(3)9684-4500. Fax: (61)(3)9696-2627. E-mail: info@mtc.com.au. Website: mtc.com.au. **Contact:** Aiden Fennessey, associate director. "MTC produces classic plays, modern revivals and the best new plays from Australia and overseas. Victorian work is given emphasis. MTC does not accept unsolicited manuscripts and it is our strict policy to return them unread. MTC does not produce work from previously unproduced Australian playwrights. New Australian plays generally come from three sources: by the commissioning of established writers; by the invitation to submit work to emerging writers with a track record and the potential to write for a mainstream subscription audience; and through a recommendation from an industry body, such as the Australian Script Centre or any of the major playwriting competitions."

MERIWETHER PUBLISHING, LTD.

885 Elkton Dr., Colorado Springs CO 80907-3557. Fax: (719)594-9916. E-mail: editor@meriwether.com. Website: meriwether.com. **Contact:** Ted Zapel, associate editor. "We publish how-to theatre books and DVD's. We are interested in materials for middle school, high school, and college-level students only." Query with synopsis/outline, résumé of credits, sample of style, and SASE. Catalog available for $2 postage.

NEEDS "Musicals for a large cast of performers, one-act or two-act comedy plays with large casts, and book mss on theatrical arts subjects. We are now looking for scenebooks with special themes: scenes for young women, comedy scenes for 2 actors, etc. These need not be original, provided the compiler can get letters of permission from the original copyright owner. We are interested in textbook for theater arts subjects. We

will consider elementary-level church plays, but no elementary-level children's plays."

Ⓐ⊘ METROSTAGE

1201 N. Royal St., Alexandria VA 22314. (703)548-9044. Fax: (703)548-9089. E-mail: info@metrostage.org. Website: metrostage.org. **Contact:** Carolyn Griffin, producing artistic director. Produces 5-6 plays/year. Professional productions for 130-seat theatre, general audience. Agented submissions only.

NEEDS Contemporary themes, small cast (up to 6 actors), unit set.

MILWAUKEE CHAMBER THEATRE

158 N. Broadway, Milwaukee Chamber Theatre, Milwaukee WI 53202. (414)276-8842. Fax: (414)277-4477. E-mail: mail@chamber-theatre.com. Website: chamber-theatre.com. **Contact:** Jaque Troy, Education Director/Literary Manager. Produces 5 plays/year. Plays produced for adult and student audience. Submit query and synopsis. Submissions accompanied by a SASE will be returned.

NEEDS Produces literary, thought-provoking, biographical plays. Plays require small-unit settings. No plays for a large cast.

NEBRASKA THEATRE CARAVAN

6915 Cass St., Omaha NE 68132. Fax: (402)553-6288. E-mail: info@omahaplayhouse.com. Website: omahaplayhouse.com. **Contact:** Alena Furlong, development director. Produces 4-5 plays/year. Nebraska Theatre Caravan is a touring company which produces professional productions in schools, arts centers, and small and large theaters for elementary, middle, high school and family audiences. Submit query and synopsis.

NEEDS All genres are acceptable bearing in mind the student audiences. We are truly an ensemble and like to see that in our choice of shows; curriculum ties are very important for elementary and hich school shows; 75 minutes for middle/high school shows. No sexually explicit material.

THE NEW GROUP

410 W. 42nd St., New York NY 10036. (212)244-3380. Fax: (212)244-3438. E-mail: info@thenewgroup.org. Website: thenewgroup.org. **Contact:** Ian Morgan, associate artistic director. Produces 4 plays/year. Off-Broadway theater. Submit 10-page sample, cover letter, résumé, synopsis, and SASE. No submissions that

have already been produced in NYC. Include SASE for return of script.

NEEDS We produce challenging, character-based scripts with a contemporary sensibility. Does not want to receive musicals, historical scripts or science fiction.

NEW JERSEY REPERTORY COMPANY

179 Broadway, Long Branch NJ 07740. (732)229-3166. Fax: (732)229-3167. E-mail: njrep@njrep.org. Website: njrep.org. **Contact:** Literary Manager. Produces 6-7 plays/year and 20-25 script-in-hand readings. Professional productions year-round. Previously unproduced plays and musicals only. Submit via e-mail with synopsis, cast breakdown, playwright bio. For musicals, e-mail mp3 of songs or send CD.

NEEDS Full-length plays with a cast size no more than 4. Simple set.

NEW REPERTORY THEATRE

200 Dexter Ave., Waterton MA 02472. (617)923-7060. Fax: (617)923-7625. E-mail: artistic@newrep.org. Website: newrep.org. **Contact:** Rick Lombardo, producing artistic director. Produces 5 plays/year. Professional theater, general audience. Query with synopsis and dialogue sample.

NEEDS Idea laden, all styles, full-length only. New musicals.

NEW STAGE THEATRE

1100 Carlisle, Jackson MS 39202. (601)948-3533. Fax: (601)948-3538. E-mail: mail@newstagetheatre.com. Website: newstagetheatre.com. Produces 8 plays/year. Professional productions, 8 mainstage, 3 in our 'second space.' We play to an audience comprised of Jackson, the state of Mississippi and the Southeast. Submit query and synopsis.

NEEDS Southern themes, contemporary issues, small casts (5-8), single set plays.

NEW THEATRE

4120 Laguna St., Coral Gables FL 33146. (305)443-5373. Fax: (305)443-1642. E-mail: tvodihn@new-theatre.org. Website: new-theatre.org. **Contact:** Tara Vodihn, literary manager. Produces 7 plays/year. Professional productions. Submit query and synopsis.

NEEDS Interested in full-length, non-realistic, moving, intelligent, language-driven plays with a healthy dose of humor. No musicals or large casts.

NEW YORK STATE THEATRE INSTITUTE

37 First St., Troy NY 12180. (518)274-3200. Fax: (518)274-3815. E-mail: nysti@capital.net. Website: nysti.org. **Contact:** Patricia DiBenedetto Snyder, producing artistic director. Produces 6 plays/year. Professional regional productions for adult and family audiences. Submit query and synopsis.

NEEDS "We are not interested in material for 'mature' audiences. Submissions must be scripts of substance and intelligence geared to family audiences."

NEW YORK THEATRE WORKSHOP

83 E. 4th St., New York NY 10003. Fax: (212)460-8996. E-mail: litern@nytw.org. Website: nytw.org. **Contact:** Literary Department. Produces four to five full productions and approximately 50 readings/year. "NYTW is renowned for producing intelligent and complex plays that expand the boundaries of theatrical form and in some new and compelling way address issues that are critical to our times. Plays are performed off-Broadway. Audience is New York theater-going audience and theater professionals." Prefer e-mail submissions. Type "synopsis submission." If mailing: Query with cover letter, synopsis, 10-page dialogue sample, 2 letters of recommendation; SASE if requesting return of materials. Include tape/CD/video where appropriate.

NEEDS Full-length plays, translations/adaptations, music theater pieces; proposals for performance projects. Socially relevant issues, innovative form, and language.

NORTHLIGHT THEATRE

9501 Skokie Blvd., Skokie IL 60077. (847)679-9501. Fax: (847)679-1879. E-mail: kleahey@northlight.org. Website: northlight.org. **Contact:** Kristin Leahey, Dramaturg. Produces 5 plays/year. "We are a professional, equity theater, LORT C. We have a subscription base of over 8,000 and have a significant number of single ticket buyers." Query with 10-page dialogue sample, synopsis, resume/bio, and SASE/SASPC for response.

NEEDS Full-length plays, translations, adaptations, musicals. Interested in plays of 'ideas'; plays that are passionate and/or hilarious; accessible plays that challenge, incite, and reflect the beliefs of our society/community. Generally looking for cast size of 6 or fewer, but there are exceptions made for the right play.

ODYSSEY THEATRE ENSEMBLE

2055 S. Sepulveda Blvd., Los Angeles CA 90025-5621. (310)477-2055. Fax: (310)444-0455. Website: odyssey-theatre.com. **Contact:** Sally Essex-Lopresti, director of literary programs. Produces 9 plays/year. Plays performed in a 3-theater facility. All 3 theaters are Equity 99-seat theater plan. We have a subscription audience of 4,000 for a 9-play main season. No unsolicited material. Query with resume, synopsis, 10 pages of sample dialogue, and cassette if musical. Does not return scripts without SASE.

NEEDS Full-length plays only with either an innovative form and/or provocative subject matter. We desire highly theatrical pieces that explore possibilities of the live theater experience. We are not reading one-act plays or light situation comedies.

OMAHA THEATER CO./ROSE THEATER

2001 Farnam St., Omaha NE 68102. (402)345-9718. E-mail: jlarsonotc@msn.com. Website: rosetheater.org. **Contact:** James Larson, artistic director. Produces 6-10 plays/year. "Our target audience is children, preschool through high school, and their parents." Submit query and synopsis. Send SASE.

NEEDS Plays must be geared to children and parents (PG rating). Titles recognized by the general public have a stronger chance of being produced. Cast limit: 25 (8-10 adults). No adult scripts.

ONE ACT PLAY DEPOT

Box 335, Spiritwood Saskatchewan S0J 2M0 Canada. E-mail: submissions@oneactplays.net. Website: oneactplays.net. "Accepts unsolicited submissions only in February of each year." Submit complete script by mail or via e-mail as a plain .txt file.

NEEDS : one-act plays. Does not want musicals or farces. Do not mail originals. Plays should run between ten and sixty minutes.

O'NEILL MUSIC THEATER CONFERENCE

Eugene O'Neill Theater Center, 305 Great Neck Rd., Waterford CT 06385. (860)443-5378. Fax: (860)443-9653. E-mail: theaterlives@theoneill.org. Website: theoneill.org. **Contact:** Jill A. Anderson, general manager. "At The Music Theater Conference, creative artists are in residence with artistic staff and an equity company of actors/singers. Public and private readings, script in hand, piano only." An open submission process begins in the fall of each year and concludes in May. The conference takes place in July

and August at the O'Neill Theater Center. Works are accepted based on their readiness to be performed, but when there is still enough significant work to be accomplished that a fully staged production would be premature. For guidelines and application deadlines, send SASE or see guidelines online.

THE O'NEILL PLAYWRIGHTS CONFERENCE

305 Great Neck Rd., Waterford CT 06385. (860)443-5378. Fax: (860)443-9653. E-mail: info@theoneill.org; litoffice@theoneill.org. Website: theoneill.org. **Contact:** Martin Kettling, literary manager. Produces 7-8 plays/year. The O'Neill Theater Center operates under an Equity LORT contract. Please send #10 SASE for guidelines in the fall, or check online. Decision by late April. We accept submissions September 1-October 1 of each year. Conference takes place during June/July each summer. Playwrights selected are in residence for one month and receive a four-day workshop and two script-in-hand readings with professional actors and directors.

OREGON SHAKESPEARE FESTIVAL

15 S. Pioneer St., Ashland OR 97520. Fax: (541)482-0446. Website: osfashland.org. **Contact:** Director of Literary Development and Dramaturgy. Produces 11 plays/year. OSF directly solicits playwright or agent, and does not accept unsolicited submissions.

PHILADELPHIA THEATRE CO.

230 S. Broad St., Suite 1105, Philadelphia PA 19102. (215)985-1400. Fax: (215)985-5800. Website: philadelphiatheatrecompany.org. **Contact:** Literary Office. Produces 4 plays/year. "Under the direction of Sara Garonzik since 1982, Philadelphia Theatre Company has introduced more than 140 new plays and musicals to audiences in Philadelphia, New York and around the country, establishing the Company's national reputation for artistic quality, risk-taking and diverse programming." Agented submissions only.

NEEDS Philadelphia Theatre Company produces contemporary American plays and musicals.

TIPS Our work is challenging and risky—look to our history for guidance.

PIONEER DRAMA SERVICE, INC.

P.O. Box 4267, Englewood CO 80155-4267. (303)779-4035. Fax: (303)779-4315. E-mail: editors@pioneerdrama.com. Website: pioneerdrama.com. **Contact:**

Lori Conary, submissions editor. Plays are performed for audiences of all ages. All submissions automatically entered in Shubert Fendrich Memorial Playwriting Contest. Guidelines for SASE.

PITTSBURGH PUBLIC THEATER

621 Penn Ave., Pittsburgh PA 15222. (412)316-8200. Fax: (412)316-8216. Website: ppt.org. **Contact:** Dramaturg. Produces 7 plays/year. O'Reilly Theater, 650 seats, thrust seating. Submit full script through agent, or query with synopsis, cover letter, 10-page dialogue sample, and SASE.

NEEDS Full-length plays, adaptations and musicals.

PLAYSCRIPTS, INC.

450 7th Ave., Suite 809, New York NY 10023. Phone/Fax: (866)639-7529. E-mail: submissions@playscripts.com. Website: playscripts.com. Audience is professional, community, college, high school and children's theaters worldwide. See website for complete submission guidelines. Materials accompanied by SASE will be returned; however, e-mail submissions are strongly preferred.

NEEDS We are open to a wide diversity of writing styles and content. Unsolicited musicals are not accepted.

THE PLAYWRIGHTS' CENTER'S PLAYLABS

2301 Franklin Ave. E., Minneapolis MN 55406. (612)332-7481. Fax: (612)332-6037. E-mail: info@pwcenter.org. Website: pwcenter.org. PlayLabs is a 2-week developmental workshop for new plays. The program is held in Minneapolis and is open by script competition. Up to 5 new plays are given reading performances and after the festival, a script sample and contact link are posted on the Center's website. Announcements of playwrights by May 1. Playwrights receive honoraria, travel expenses, room and board.

NEEDS We are interested in playwrights with ambitions for a sustained career in theater, and scripts that could benefit from development involving professional dramaturgs, directors, and actors. US citizens or permanent residents only. Participants must attend entire festival. Submission deadline in October; see website for application and exact deadline. No previously produced materials.

PLAYWRIGHTS HORIZONS

416 W. 42nd St., New York NY 10036. (212)564-1235. Fax: (212)594-0296. Website: playwrightshorizons.

org. **Contact:** Adam Greenfield, literary manager (plays); send musicals Attn: Kent Nicholson, Director of Musical Theater. Produces 6 plays/year. Plays performed off-Broadway for a literate, urban, subscription audience. Submit complete ms with author bio; include CD for musicals.

NEEDS "We are looking for new, full-length plays and musicals by American authors."

PLAYWRIGHTS' PLATFORM

398 Columbus Ave., #604, Boston MA 02116. Website: playwrightsplatform.org. **Contact:** Regina Eliot-Ramsey, president. Produces approximately 50 readings/year "Our website contains all information regarding The Platform. The Platform provides dues paying members with the opportunity to read their plays before an audience. Meetings are held at Rosen Auditorium, Brennan Library, Lasell College, Auburndale, MA 02466. Scripts should not be mailed. Readings must be requested through the calendar coordinator. Only dues paying members can submit scripts and are allowed to participate in Platform productions. The Platform produces a short play festival each year in June, held at the Boston Playwrights Theatre, Boston, MA. Only dues paying members can participate. Short one acts, and scenes from full-length plays can be read throughout the calendar year. The festival only produces plays with running times of 20 minutes or less. Members come from the northeast region and are not limited to Massachusetts. There are no restrictions on content." Submit script and SASE (or e-mail or hand deliver).

NEEDS "Any types of plays. We will not accept scripts we think are sexist or racist. Massachusetts residents only. There are no restrictions on length or number of characters, but it's more difficult to schedule full-length pieces."

Ⓐ PLAYWRIGHTS THEATRE OF NEW JERSEY

P.O. Box 1295, Madison NJ 07940-1295. (973)514-1787. Fax: (973)514-2060. Website: ptnj.org. **Contact:** Alysia Souder, director of program development. Produces 3 plays/year. We operate under a Small Professional Theatre Contract (SPT), a development theatre contract with Actors Equity Association. Readings are held under a staged reading code.

NEEDS Any style or length; full length, one acts, musicals.

PORTLAND STAGE CO.

P.O. Box 1458, Portland ME 04104. (207)774-1043. Fax: (207)774-0576. E-mail: info@portlandstage.org. Website: portlandstage.org. **Contact:** Daniel Burson, literary manager. Produces 7 plays/year. Professional productions at Portland Stage Company. Send first 10 pages with synopsis.

NEEDS Developmental Staged Readings: Little Festival of the Unexpected.

Ⓐ PRIMARY STAGES CO., INC.

307 W. 38th St., Suite 1510, New York NY 10018. (212)840-9705. Fax: (212)840-9725. E-mail: tessa@primarystages.org. **Contact:** Tessa LaNeve, literary manager. Produces 4 plays/year. All plays are produced professionally off-Broadway at 59E59 Theatres' 199 seat theatre. Agented submissions only Guidelines online.

NEEDS Full-length plays, small cast (6 or fewer) musicals. New York City premieres only. Small cast (1-6), unit set or simple changes, no fly or wing space.

PRINCE MUSIC THEATER

100 S. Broad St., Suite 650, Philadelphia PA 19110. (215)972-1000. Fax: (215)972-1020. Website: princemusictheater.org. **Contact:** Marjorie Samoff, producing artistic director. Produces 4 musicals/year. "Professional musical productions. Drawing upon operatic and popular traditions as well as European, African, Asian and South American forms, new work and new voices take center stage." Send synopsis and sample audio tape with no more than 4 songs.

NEEDS Song-driven music theater, varied musical styles. Nine-member orchestra, 10-14 cast, 36x60 stage.

PRINCETON REP COMPANY

44 Nassau St., Suite 350, Princeton NJ 08542. E-mail: prcreprap@aol.com. Website: princetonrep.org. **Contact:** New Play Submissions. Plays are performed in site-specific venues, outdoor amphitheatres, and indoor theatres with approximately 199 seats. Princeton Rep Company works under Actors' Equity contracts, and its directors are members of the SSDC. Query with synopsis, SASE, résumé, and 10 pages of sample dialogue. Submissions accompanied by a SASE will be returned.

NEEDS Stories that investigate the lives of middle and working class people. Love stories of the rich, famous, and fatuous. If the play demands a cast of thousands, please don't waste your time and postage. No drama or comedy set in a prep school or ivy league college.

THE PUBLIC THEATER

425 Lafayette St., New York NY 10003. (212)539-8500. Website: publictheater.org. **Contact:** Literary Department. Produces 6 plays/year. Professional productions. Query with synopsis, 10-page sample, letter of inquiry, cassette with 3-5 songs for musicals/operas.

NEEDS Full-length plays, translations, adapatations, musicals, operas, and solo pieces. All genres, no one-acts.

Ⓞ PULSE ENSEMBLE THEATRE

248 W. 35th St., 15th Floor, New York NY 10001. (212)695-1596. Fax: (212)695-1596. E-mail: theatre@pulseensembletheatre.org. Website: pulseensembletheatre.org. **Contact:** Brian Richardson. Produces 3 plays/year. No unsolicited submissions. Only accepts new material through the Playwright's Lab. Include SASE for return of submission.

NEEDS Meaningful theater. No production limitations.

THE PURPLE ROSE THEATRE CO.

137 Park St., Chelsea MI 48118. (734)433-7782. Fax: (734)475-0802. Website: purplerosetheatre.org. **Contact:** Guy Sanville, artistic director. Produces 4 plays/year. "PRTC is a regional theater with an S.P.T. equity contract which produces plays intended for Midwest/Middle American audience. It is dedicated to creating opportunities for Midwest theatre professionals." Query with synopsis, character breakdown, and 10-page dialogue sample.

NEEDS Modern, topical full length, 75-120 minutes. Prefers scripts that use comedy to deal with serious subjects. 8 cast maximum. No fly space, unit set preferable. Intimate 168 seat 3/4 thrust house.

Ⓢ QUEENSLAND THEATRE COMPANY

P.O. Box 3310, South Brisbane QLD 4101 Australia. (61)(7)3010-7600. Fax: (61)(7)3010-7699. E-mail: mail@qldtheatreco.com.au. Website: qldtheatreco.com.au. **Contact:** Michael Gow, artistic director. "Seeks timeless classics, modern classics, and new plays from Australia and overseas. Only considers unsolicited scripts if the playwright has had at least 1 play professionally produced if the script has been submitted by an agent, or recommended by a professional theatre company or script development agency."

NEEDS "Works specifically aimed at child/youth audiences are less likely to be considered."

🌑 RED LADDER THEATRE CO.

3 St. Peter's Buildings, York St., Leeds LS9 1AJ United Kingdom. (44)(113)245-5311. E-mail: rod@redladder. co.uk. Website: redladder.co.uk. **Contact:** Rod Dixon, artistic director. Produces 2 plays/year. Our work tours nationally to young people, aged 13-25, in youth clubs, community venues and small scale theatres. Submit query and synopsis.

NEEDS One hour in length for cast size no bigger than 5. Work that connects with a youth audience that both challenges them and offers them new insights. We consider a range of styles and are seeking originality. Small scale touring. Does not want to commission single issue drama. The uses of new technologies in production (DVD, video projection). Young audiences are sophisticated.

RESOURCE PUBLICATIONS

160 E. Virginia St., Suite 290, San Jose CA 95112-5876. (408)286-8505. Fax: (408)287-8748. E-mail: editor@ rpinet.com. Website: resourcepublications.com. Audience includes laity and ordained seeking resources (books/periodicals/software) in Christian ministry, worship, faith formation, education, and counseling (primarily Roman Catholic, but not all). Submit query and synopsis via e-mail.

NEEDS Needs materials for those in pastoral ministry, faith formation, youth ministry, and parish administration. No fiction, children's books, or music.

ROUND HOUSE THEATRE

P.O. Box 30688, Bethesda MD 20824. (240)644-1099. Fax: (240)644-1090. E-mail: roundhouse@roundhousetheatre.org. Website: roundhousetheatre.org. **Contact:** Danisha Crosby, associate producer. Produces 5-7 plays/year. "Professional AEA Theatre that is recognized nationally as a center for the development of literary works for the stage. Our critically-acclaimed Literary Works Project features new adaptations of contemporary and classical novels, re-interpreted through a theatrical prism for today's audiences. We give these stories a fresh voice, a bold visual presence, and a new relevance in our ever-changing society. The project has garnered 10 Helen Hayes Award nominations and strong notices in the regional

and national press." Query with synopsis; no unsolicited scripts accepted.

SALTWORKS THEATRE CO.

569 N. Neville St., Pittsburgh PA 15213. (412)621-6150. Fax: (412)621-6010. E-mail: nalrutz@saltworks.org. Website: saltworks.org. **Contact:** Norma Alrutz, executive director. Produces 8-10 plays/year. Submit query and synopsis.

NEEDS Wants plays for children, youth, and families that address social issues like violence prevention, sexual responsibility, peer pressures, tobacco use, bullying, racial issues/diversity, drug and alcohol abuse (grades 1-12). Limited to 5 member cast, 2 men/2 women/1 either.

SEATTLE REPERTORY THEATRE

P.O. Box 900923, Seattle WA 98109. E-mail: bradena@seattlerep.org. Website: seattlerep.org. **Contact:** Braden Abraham, associate artistic director. Produces 8 plays/year. Send query, resume, synopsis and 10 sample pages.

NEEDS "The Seattle Repertory Theatre produces eclectic programming. We welcome a wide variety of writing."

SECOND STAGE THEATRE

307 W. 43rd St., New York NY 10036-6406. (212)787-8302. Fax: (212)397-7066. Website: 2st.com. **Contact:** Sarah Bagley, literary manager. Produces 6 plays/year. "Second Stage Theatre gives new life to contemporary American plays through 'second stagings'; provides emerging authors with their Off-Broadway debuts; and produces world premieres by America's most respected playwrights. Adult and teen audiences." Query with synopsis and 10-page writing sample or agented submission.

NEEDS We need socio-political plays, comedies, musicals, dramas—full lengths for full production.

◐ SHAW FESTIVAL THEATRE

P.O. Box 774, Niagara-on-the-Lake ON L0S 1J0 Canada. (905)468-2153. Fax: (905)468-7140. Website: shawfest.com. **Contact:** Jackie Maxwell, artistic director. Produces 12 plays/year. Professional theater company operating 3 theaters (Festival: 869 seats; Court House: 327 seats; Royal George: 328 seats). Shaw Festival presents the work of George Bernard Shaw and his contemporaries written during his lifetime (1856-1950) and in 2000 expanded the mandate to include contemporary works written about the period of his lifetime. Query with SASE or SAE and IRC's, depending on country of origin.

NEEDS We operate an acting ensemble of up to 75 actors; and we have sophisticated production facilities. During the summer season (April-November) the Academy of the Shaw Festival organizes workshops of new plays commissioned for the company.

SOUTH COAST REPERTORY

P.O. Box 2197, Costa Mesa CA 92628-2197. (714)708-5500. Fax: (714)545-0391. Website: scr.org. **Contact:** Kelly Miller, Literary Manager. Produces 14 plays/year. Professional nonprofit theater; a member of LORT and TCG. "We operate in our own facility which houses the 507-seat Segerstrom stage and 336-seat Julianne Argyros stage. We have a combined subscription audience of 18,000. We commit ourselves to exploring the most urgent human and social issues of our time, and to merging literature, design and performance in ways that test the bounds of theatre's artistic possibilities." Query with synopsis and 10 sample pages of dialogue, and full list of characters.

NEEDS "We produce full-length contemporary plays, as well as theatre for young audiences, scripts geared toward a 4th grade target audience with a running time of approximately 65 minutes. We prefer plays that address contemporary concerns and are dramaturgically innovative. A play whose cast is larger than 15-20 will need to be extremely compelling, and its cast size must be justifiable."

STAGE LEFT THEATRE

3408 N. Sheffield, Chicago IL 60657. (773)883-8830. E-mail: scripts@stagelefttheatre.com. Website: stagelefttheatre.com. **Contact:** Kevin Heckman, literary manager. Produces 3-4 plays/year. "Professional productions (usually in Chicago), for all audiences (usually adult)." Submit script through an agent or query with cover letter, 10-page excerpt, 1-page synopsis, SASE, supporting material, and résumé.

NEEDS any length, any genre, any style that fits the Stage Left mission—to produce plays that raise debate on political and social issues. We do have an emphasis on new work.

Ⓐ STAMFORD THEATRE WORKS

307 Atlantic St., Stamford CT 06901. (203)359-4414. Fax: (203)356-1846. E-mail: stwct@aol.com. Website: stamfordtheatreworks.org. **Contact:** Steve Karp, pro-

ducing director. Produces 4-6 plays/year. Professional productions for an adult audience. *Agented submissions* or queries with a professional recommendation. Include SASE for return of submission.

NEEDS Plays of social relevance; contemporary work. Limited to unit sets; maximum cast of about 8.

Ⓐ STEPPENWOLF THEATRE CO.

758 W. North Ave., 4th Floor, Chicago IL 60610. (312)335-1888. Fax: (312)335-0808. Website: steppenwolf.org. **Contact:** Joy Meads, literary manager. Produces 9 plays/year. "Steppenwolf Theatre Company's mission is to advance the vitality and diversity of American theater by nurturing artists, encouraging repeatable creative relationships and contributing new works to the national canon. 500-, 250- and 100-seat performance venues. Many plays produced at Steppenwolf have gone to Broadway. We currently have 20,000 savvy subscribers." Agented submissions only with full scripts. Others please check our website for submission guidelines. Unrepresented writers may send a 10-page sample along with cover letter, bio, and synopsis.

NEEDS Actor-driven works are crucial to us, plays that explore the human condition in our time. We max at around 10 characters.

Ⓐ STUDIO ARENA THEATRE

710 Main St., Buffalo NY 14202. (716)856-8025. E-mail: jblaha@studioarena.com. Website: studioarena.org. **Contact:** Jana Blaha, executive assistant. Produces 6-8 plays/year. Professional productions. Agented submissions only.

NEEDS Full-length plays. No fly space.

TEATRO VISIÓN

1700 Alum Rock Ave., Suite 265, San José CA 95116. (408)272-9926. Fax: (408)928-5589. E-mail: elisamarina@teatrovision.org. Website: teatrovision.org. **Contact:** Elisa Marina Alvarado, artistic director. Produces 3 plays/year. Professional productions for a Latino population. Query with synopsis or submit complete ms.

NEEDS We produce plays by Latino playwrights—plays that highlight the Chicano/Latino experience.

THE TEN-MINUTE MUSICALS PROJECT

P.O. Box 461194, West Hollywood CA 90046. E-mail: info@tenminutemusicals.org. Website: tenminutemusicals.org. **Contact:** Michael Koppy, producer.

Produces 1-10 plays/year. "Plays performed in Equity regional theaters in the US and Canada. Deadline August 31; notification by November 30." Complete guidelines and information at website.
NEEDS Looking for complete short stage musicals 7-14 minutes long. Limit cast to 10 (5 women, 5 men).

THEATER AT LIME KILN

P.O. Box 1244, Lexington VA 24450. Website: theateratlimekiln.com. Produces 3 (1 new) plays/year. Outdoor summer theater (May through October) and indoor space (October through May, 144 seats). Submit query and synopsis. Include SASE for return of submitted materials.
NEEDS Plays that explore the history and heritage of the Appalachian region. Minimum set required.

THEATER BY THE BLIND

306 W. 18th St., New York NY 10011. (212)243-4337. Fax: (212)243-4337. E-mail: gar@nyc.rr.com. Website: tbtb.org. **Contact:** Ike Schambelan, artistic director. Produces 2 plays/year. Off Broadway, Theater Row, general audiences, seniors, students, disabled. If play transfers, we'd like a piece. Submit complete script.
NEEDS Genres about blindness.

THEATRE BUILDING CHICAGO

1225 W. Belmont Ave., Chicago IL 60657. (773)929-7367 ext. 229. Fax: (773)327-1404. E-mail: allan@theatrebuildingchicago.org. Website: theatrebuildingchicago.org. **Contact:** Allan Chambers, artistic director. "Develops and produces readings of new musicals and Stages festival of new music, some works developed in our writers' workshop. Some scripts produced are unagented submissions. Developmental readings and workshops performed in 3 small off-Loop theaters are seating 148 for a general theater audience, urban/suburban mix." Submit synopsis, sample scene, CD or cassette tape and piano/vocal score of three songs, and author bios along with Stages Festival application, available on our website.
NEEDS "Musicals *only*. We're interested in all forms of musical theater including more innovative styles. Our production capabilities are limited by the lack of space, but we're very creative and authors should submit anyway. The smaller the cast, the better. We are especially interested in scripts using a younger (35 and under) ensemble of actors. We mostly look for authors who are interested in developing their scripts through workshops, readings and production. We rarely work on one-man shows or 'single author' pieces."

THEATRE IV

114 W. Broad St., Richmond VA 23220. (804)783-1688. Fax: (804)775-2325. E-mail: j.serresseque@theatreivrichmond.org. Website: theatreiv.org. **Contact:** Janine Serresseque. Produces approximately 20 plays/year. National tour of plays for young audiences—maximum cast of 5, maximum length of an hour. Mainstage plays for young audiences in 600 or 350 seat venues. Submit query and synopsis. Include SASE for return of submission.
NEEDS Touring and mainstage plays for young audiences. Touring—maximum cast of 5, length of 60 minutes.

$ THEATRE THREE

P.O. Box 512, 412 Main St., Port Jefferson NY 11777-0512. (631)928-9202. Fax: (631)928-9120. Website: theatrethree.com. **Contact:** Jeffrey Sanzel, artistic director. "We produce an Annual Festival of One-Act Plays on our Second Stage. Deadline for submission is September 30. Send SASE for festival guidelines or visit website." Include SASE. No e-mail submissions. Guidelines online.
NEEDS One-act plays. Maximum length: 40 minutes. Any style, topic, etc. We require simple, suggested sets and a maximum cast of 6. No adaptations, musicals or children's works.

Ⓐ THEATRE THREE

2800 Routh St., #168, Dallas TX 75201. (214)871-3300. Fax: (214)871-3139. E-mail: admin@theatre3dallas.com. Website: theater3dallas.com. **Contact:** Jac Alder, executive producer-director. Produces 7 plays/year. Professional regional theatre, in-the-round. Audience is college age to senior citizens. Query with synopsis; agented submissions only.
NEEDS Musicals, dramas, comedies, bills of related one-acts. Modest production requirement; prefer casts no larger than 10. Theatre Three also produces in a studio theatre (its former rehearsal hall) called Theatre Too. The space is variously configured according to demands of the show. Shows in that space include cabaret type revues, experimental work, dramas with small casts and staged readings or concert versions of musicals.

THEATRE WEST

3333 Cahuenga Blvd. W., Hollywood CA 90068-1365. (323)851-4839. Fax: (323)851-5286. E-mail: theatrewest@theatrewest.org. Website: theatrewest.org. **Contact:** Chris DiGiovanni and Doug Haverty, moderators of Workshop. "We operate a 168 seat theater under a letter of agreement with Actors Equity, including a TYA contract for young audiences." Submit script, résumé and letter requesting membership. **NEEDS** Full-length plays only, no one-acts. Uses minimalistic scenery, no fly space.

THEATREWORKS

P.O. Box 50458, Palo Alto CA 94303. (650)463-1950. Fax: (650)463-1963. E-mail: kent@theatreworks.org. Website: theatreworks.org. **Contact:** Kent Nicholson, new works director. Produces 8 plays/year. Specializes in development of new musicals. Plays are professional productions intended for an adult audience. Submit synopsis, 10 pages of sample dialogue, and SASE. Include SASE for return of submission. **NEEDS** TheatreWorks has a high standard for excellence. We prefer well-written, well-constructed plays that celebrate the human spirit through innovative productions and programs inspired by our exceptionally diverse community. There is no limit on the number of characters, and we favor plays with multi-ethnic casting possibilities. We are a LORT C company. Plays are negotiated per playwright. Does not want one-acts, plays with togas. We are particularly interested in plays with musical elements.

⊘ THEATREWORKS/USA

151 W. 26th St., 7th Floor, New York NY 10001. (212)647-1100. Fax: (212)924-5377. Website: twusa. org. Produces 3-4 plays/year. "The theatre is an arena for previously unproduced plays, and works towards their future development. Professional equity productions for young audiences. Weekend series at Equitable Towers, NYC. Also, national and regional tours of each show." Submit query and synopsis only. *No unsolicited submissions.*

UNICORN THEATRE

3828 Main St., Kansas City MO 64111. (816)531-7529 ext. 23. Fax: (816)531-0421. Website: unicorntheatre. org. **Contact:** Herman Wilson, literary assistant. Produces 6-8 plays/year. "We are a professional Equity Theatre. Typically, we produce plays dealing with contemporary issues." Send complete script (to Herman Wilson) with brief synopsis, cover letter, bio, character breakdown. Send #10 SASE for results. Does not return scripts. **NEEDS** Prefers contemporary (post-1950) scripts. Does not accept musicals, one-acts, or historical plays.

URBAN STAGES

555 8th Avenue #1800, New York NY 10018. (212)421-1380. Fax: (212)421-1387. E-mail: lschmiedel@urbanstages.org. Website: urbanstages.org. **Contact:** Lauren Schmiedel, managing director. Produces 2-4 plays/year. Professional productions off Broadway—throughout the year. General audience. Submit complete script. Enter Emerging Playwright Award competition. There is a reading fee of $10 per script. Prize is $1,000, plus NYC production. **NEEDS** Full-length; generally 1 set or styled playing dual. Good imaginative, creative writing. Cast limited to 3-6.

UTAH SHAKESPEAREAN FESTIVAL

New American Playwright's Project, 351 W. Center St., Cedar City UT 84720-2498. (435)586-7884. Fax: (435)865-8003. **Contact:** Charles Metten, director. Produces 9 plays/year. Travelling audiences ranging in ages from 6-80. Programming includes classic plays, musicals, new works. Submit complete script; no synopsis. No musicals. Returns submissions accompanied by a SASE. **NEEDS** "The USF is only interested in material that explores characters and ideas that focus on the West and our western experience, spirit, and heritage. Preference is given to writers whose primary residence is in the western United States. New plays are for staged readings only. These are not fully mountable productions. Cast size is a consideration due to the limited time of rehearsal and the actors available during the USF production period. Does not want plays that do not match criteria or plays longer than 90 pages."

WALNUT STREET THEATRE

Ninth and Walnut Streets, Philadelphia PA 19107. (215)574-3550. Fax: (215)574-3598. **Contact:** Literary Office. Produces 10 plays/year. Our plays are performed in our own space. WST has 3 theaters—a proscenium (mainstage), 1,052 seats; and 2 studios, 79-99 seats. We have a subscription audience—the largest in the nation. If you have written a play or musical that you feel is appropriate for the Walnut Street Theatre's Mainstage or Independence Studio on 3, please send the following:

1-2 page synopsis, 5-10 page excerpt from the scrip, a character breakdown, bios for the playwright, composer, lyricist, and any other artistic collaborators, Demo CD with tracks clearly labeled (musicals only). Include SASE for return of materials.

NEEDS Full-length dramas and comedies, musicals, translations, adaptations, and revues. The studio plays must have a cast of no more than 4 and use simple sets.

WILLOWS THEATRE CO.

636 Ward St., Martinez CA 94553-1651. Website: willowstheatre.org. Produces 6 plays/year. Professional productions for a suburban audience. Accepting only commercially viable, small-medium size comedies right now. Guidelines are online at website. Send synopsis, character breakdown, resume, SASE. Do not send full script unless invited to do so. Do not e-mail submission or e-mail the office for information on your submission.

NEEDS Commercially viable, small-medium size musicals or comedies that are popular, rarely produced, or new. Certain stylized plays or musicals with a contemporary edge to them (e.g., *Les Liasons Dangereuses, La Bete, Candide*). No more than 15 actors. Unit or simple sets with no fly space, no more than 7 pieces. We are not interested in 1-character pieces.

Ⓐ THE WILMA THEATER

265 S. Broad St., Philadelphia PA 19107. (215)893-9456. Fax: (215)893-0895. E-mail: wcb@wilmatheater.org. Website: wilmatheater.org. **Contact:** Walter Bilderback, dramaturg and literary manager. Produces 4 plays/year. LORT-D 300-seat theater, 5,000 subscribers. *Agented submissions only* for full mss. Accepts queries with cover letter, résumé, synopsis, and sample if recommended by a literary manager, dramaturg, or other theater professional. Electronic inquiries and submissions preferred. Will not respond to mailed queries unless self-addressed stamp envelope or postcard is included.

NEEDS Full-length plays, translations, adaptations, and musicals from an international repertoire with emphasis on innovative, bold staging; world premieres; works with poetic dimension; plays with music; multimedia works; social issues, particularly the role of science in our lives. Prefers maximum cast size of 12. Stage 44'x46'.

WOMEN'S PROJECT AND PRODUCTIONS

55 West End Ave., New York NY 10023. (212)765-1706. Fax: (212)765-2024. Website: womensproject.org. **Contact:** Megan E. Carter, Associate Artistic Director. Produces 3 plays/year. Professional Off-Broadway productions. Agented submissions only. Please see website for submission guidelines and details.

NEEDS "We are looking for full-length plays written by women."

Ⓐ WOOLLY MAMMOTH THEATRE CO.

641 D St. NW, Washington DC 20004. (202)289-2443. E-mail: elissa@woollymammoth.net. Website: woollymammoth.net. **Contact:** Elissa Goetschius, literary manager. Produces 5 plays/year. Produces professional productions for the general public. Solicited submissions only.

NEEDS We look for plays with a distinctive authorial voice. Our work is word and actor driven. One-acts and issue-driven plays are not used. Cast limit of 5

GREETING CARDS

Greeting cards are an intricate part of American culture. There are, of course, cards tied to holidays, birthdays, graduations, and weddings. There are "thinking of you" cards, condolences cards, thank you cards, get well cards, and humor cards. And many of these cards are specialized to mom, dad, mother-in-law, father-in-law, son, daughter, cousin, and even ex-girlfriend's roommate from college (OK, that may be stretching it—but only slightly). Point is, they are here; they've all got a special message to deliver; and someone has to write them.

FREELANCE REALITIES

Writers who make a decent income writing greeting cards are almost always staff writers or those who are on contract. Freelance writers do not typically earn enough to use greeting card sales as any more than a supplemental source of income. In the most recent "How Much Should I Charge?" survey, freelancers made $50 on the low end to $300 on the high end per card. And that is from a more experienced set of freelancers. It is known that some freelancers settle for payment as low as $5 to $10 per card idea, which makes it harder for newer writers to negotiate higher payments.

FOR MORE INFORMATION

To learn even more about the greeting card industry, check out the Greeting Card Association (GCA) website at www.greetingcard.org. It provides industry statistics, tips, and information on specific greeting card companies.

⊘ AMERICAN GREETINGS

One American Rd., Cleveland OH 44144-2398. (216)252-7300. Fax: (216)252-6778. Website: www.americangreetings.com.

NEEDS Humorous.

BLUE MOUNTAIN ARTS, INC.

P.O. Box 1007, Boulder CO 80306. (303)449-0536. Fax: (303)447-0939. E-mail: editorial@sps.com. Website: www.sps.com. Bought over 200 freelance ideas last year. Submit seasonal/holiday material 4 months in advance. Buys worldwide, exclusive rights, or anthology rights. Pays on publication. Request writer's guidelines through website.

NEEDS "Submissions should reflect a message, feeling, or sentiment that one person would want to share with another. Full book manuscripts or proposals are also accepted for possible publication by our book division, Blue Mountain Press."

$ ASHLEIGH BRILLIANT ENTERPRISES

117 W. Valerio St., Santa Barbara CA 93101. (805)682-0531. E-mail: ashleigh@west.net; ashleigh@ashleighbrilliant.com. Website: www.ashleighbrilliant.com. **Contact:** Ashleigh Brilliant, president. Catalog and sample set for $2.

NEEDS "Messages should be of a highly original nature, emphasizing subtlety, simplicity, insight, wit, profundity, beauty and felicity of expression. Accompanying art should be in the nature of oblique commentary or decoration rather than direct illustration. Messages should be of universal appeal, capable of being appreciated by all types of people and of being easily translated into other languages. Because our line of cards is highly unconventional, it is essential that freelancers study it before submitting."

➲ DESIGNER GREETINGS

11 Executive Ave., Edison NJ 08817. (732)662-6700. Fax: (732)662-6701. E-mail: Submissions@Designergreetings.com. Website: www.Designergreetings.com. **Contact:** Andy Epstein, creative director. **Purchases 200-300 verses/year.** Submit seasonal/holiday material 6 months in advance. Buys greeting card rights. Pays on acceptance. Guidelines online.

NEEDS Conventional, humorous, informal, inspirational, juvenile, sensitivity, soft line, studio. Accepts rhymed and unrhymed verse ideas.

EPHEMERA, INC.

P.O. Box 490, Phoenix OR 97535. (541)535-4195. Fax: (541)535-5016. Website: www.ephemera-inc.com. **Contact:** Editor. **Receives 2,000 submissions/year.** Buys nearly 200 slogans for novelty buttons, stickers, and magnets each year. Buys all rights. Pays on acceptance. Writer's guidelines for SASE or online Complete full-color catalog online or for $4

NEEDS "We produce irreverent, provocative, and outrageously funny buttons, magnets, and stickers. You'll find them in cutting-edge shops that sell cards, gifts, books, music, coffee, pipes, porn, etc. We're looking for snappy slogans about politics, women and bitchiness, work, parenting, coffee, booze, pot, drugs, religion, food, aging, teens, gays and lesbians, sexual come-ons and put-downs, etc. Pretty please, don't limit yourself to these topics. Surprise us!"

⊘ HALLMARK CARDS

P.O. Box 419034, Kansas City MO 64141. Website: www.hallmark.com.

KATE HARPER DESIGNS

Website: http://kateharperdesigns.com/guidelines.html. **Contact:** Kate Harper. Pays on acceptance. Writer's guidelines online or via e-mail.

KALAN LP

97 S. Union Ave., Lansdowne PA 19050. (610)623-1900. E-mail: editorial@kalanlp.com. Website: www.submitfunnystuff.com. **Contact:** David Umlauf. **Receives 500-800 submissions/year.** Bought 80-100 freelance ideas last year. Submit seasonal/holiday material 8-10 months in advance. Buys all rights. Pays on acceptance. Guidelines available for free.

NEEDS Humorous. Accepts rhymed and unrhymed verse ideas.

KOEHLER COMPANIES, INC.

8758 Woodcliff Rd., Bloomington MN 55438. (952)942-5666. Fax: (952)942-5208. E-mail: bob@koehlercompanies.com. Website: www.koehlercompanies.com. **Receives 100 submissions/year.** Bought 25 freelance ideas last year. Pays on acceptance.

NEEDS Humorous, inspirational.

MARIAN HEATH GREETING CARDS

9 Kendrick Rd., Wareham MA 02571. Website: www.rencards.com. **Receives 75-100 submissions/year.** Bought 200-250 freelance ideas last year. Submit seasonal/holiday material 4 months in advance. Buys

greeting card rights. Pays on publication. Guidelines with #10 SASE.

NEEDS Accepts wide range of writing styles—casual or coversational, meaningful, inspirational, humorous. Prefers unrhymed verse ideas.

MOONLIGHTING CARDS

P.O. Box 4670, Vallejo CA 94590. Fax: (707)554-9366. E-mail: robin@moonlightingcards.com. Website: www.moonlightingcards.com. Submit seasonal/holiday material 12 months in advance. Pays on publication. Guidelines online.

NEEDS Announcements, conventional, humorous, informal, inspirational, invitations, juvenile, sensitivity, soft line, studio. Prefers unrhymed verse ideas. Send as many ideas at one time as you like. But if we see you have not paid attention to our guidelines, we will not sort through 100 queries to find 1 gem.

NOVO CARD PUBLISHERS, INC.

100 Shepard Ave., Wheeling IL 60090. (847)947-8090. Fax: (847)947-8775. E-mail: art@novocard.net. Website: www.novocard.net. **Receives 500 submissions/year.** Bought 200 freelance ideas last year. Submit seasonal/holiday material 8 months in advance. Buys worldwide greeting card rights. Pays on acceptance. Guidelines and market list available.

NEEDS Announcements, conventional, humor, informal, inspirational, invitations, juvenile, soft line.

OATMEAL STUDIOS

P.O. Box 138WP, Rochester VT 05767. (802)767-3171. E-mail: dawn@oatmealstudios.com. Website: www.oatmealstudios.com. Bought 200-300 ideas last year. Pays on acceptance. Market list for #10 SASE.

NEEDS Humorous. Will review concepts. Prefers unrhymed verse ideas.

THE PAPER MAGIC GROUP, INC.

401 Adams Ave., Scranton PA 18501. (800)278-4085. Website: www.papermagic.com. **Receives 500 submissions/year.** Submit seasonal/holiday material 6 months in advance. Pays on acceptance. No market list.

NEEDS Christmas boxed cards only. Submit Christmas sentiments only.

PAPYRUS DESIGN

500 Chadbourne Rd., Fairfield CA 94533. Fax: (707) 428-0641. Website: www.papyrusonline.com. **Contact:** Nikki Burton. Bought 35 ideas last year.

NEEDS Submit 10 ideas per batch. Inspirational, humor, sentimental, contemporary, romance, friendship, seasonal, and everyday categories. "Prefers unrhymed verse, but on juvenile cards rhyme is OK."

P.S. GREETINGS

5730 N. Tripp Ave., Chicago IL 60646. (773)267-6150. Fax: (773)267-6055. E-mail: artdirector@psgreetings.com. Website: www.psgreetings.com. Bought 200-300 freelance ideas last year. Submit seasonal/holiday material 6 months in advance. Pays on acceptance. Writer's guidelines/market list for #10 SASE or online.

NEEDS Conventional, humorous, inspirational, invitations, juvenile, sensitivity, soft line, studio. Accepts rhymed and unrhymed verse ideas.

RECYCLED PAPER GREETINGS

111 N. Canal St., Chicago IL 60606. (800)777-9494. Website: www.recycledpapergreetings.com. Bought 3,000 freelance ideas last year.

NEEDS "Please send ideas for specific occasions, such as birthday, friendship, thank you, miss you, and thinking of you."

ROCKSHOTS, INC.

20 Vandam St., New York NY 10013. (212)243-9661. Fax: (212)604-9060. Website: www.rockshots.com. Bought 75 greeting card verse (or gag) freelance ideas last year. Buys greeting card rights. Guidelines for #10 SASE.

NEEDS Humorous. "Looking for a combination of sexy and humorous come-on type greeting (sentimental is not our style); and insult cards (looking for cute insults). Card gag can adopt a sentimental style, then take an ironic twist and end on an offbeat note."

SNAFU DESIGNS, INC.

2500 University Ave. W., Suite C-10, St. Paul MN 55114. E-mail: info@snafudesigns.com. Website: www.snafudesigns.com. Buys all rights. Pays on acceptance. Guidelines for #10 SASE.

NEEDS Humorous, informal. "Specifically seeking birthday, friendship, thank you, anniversary, congratulations, get well, new baby, Christmas, wedding, pregnancy, retirement, Valentines Day and Mother's Day ideas."

CONTESTS & AWARDS

The contests and awards listed in this section are arranged by subject. Nonfiction writers can turn immediately to nonfiction awards listed alphabetically by the name of the contest or award. The same is true for fiction writers, poets, playwrights and screenwriters, journalists, children's writers, and translators. You'll also find general book awards, fellowships offered by arts councils and foundations, and multiple category contests.

New contests and awards are announced in various writer's publications nearly every day. However, many lose their funding or fold—and sponsoring magazines go out of business just as often. We have contacted the organizations whose contests and awards are listed here with the understanding that they are valid through 2011-2012.

To make sure you have all the information you need about a particular contest, always send a SASE to the contact person in the listing before entering a contest. The listings in this section are brief, and many contests have lengthy, specific rules and requirements that we could not include in our limited space. Often a specific entry form must accompany your submission.

When you receive a set of guidelines, you will see that some contests are not applicable to all writers. The writer's age, previous publication, geographic location, and length of the work are common matters of eligibility. Read the requirements carefully to ensure you don't enter a contest for which you are not qualified. You should also be aware that every year, more and more contests, especially those sponsored by "little" literary magazines, are charging entry fees.

Winning a contest or award can launch a successful writing career. Take a professional approach by doing a little extra research. Find out who the previous winner of the award was by investing in a sample copy of the magazine in which the prize-winning article, poem, or short story appeared. Attend the staged reading of an award-winning play. Your extra effort will be to your advantage in competing with writers who simply submit blindly.

PLAYWRITING & SCRIPTWRITING

ACCOLADE COMPETITION

P.O. Box 9117, La Jolla CA 92038. (858)454-9868. E-mail: info@accoladecompetition.org. Website: accoladecompetition.org. Film, TV, New Media, and Videography awards. Next call for entry deadline: February 25. Submissions in other than English must be subtitled or include transcript. Multiple entries are allowed and each entry may be entered in multiple categories. Submit on DVD in NTSC or PAL format. Entries will not be returned. Deadline: August. Prize: Awards: Best of Show, Awards of Excellence, & Honorable Mention. Winners are eligible to receive an Accolade statuette. The Accolade statuette is a constellation of 24K gold-plated stars mounted on a piano finished base of rosewood. It has been called the most beautiful award in the industry. Judging conducted in-house.conducted in-house. Staff is selective. Entries judged to be potential Best of Show winners may be sent to outside judges for additional review.

ACTORS CHOICE AWARDS

The Screenwriting Conference in Santa Fe, LLC, 7 Avenida Vista Grand, B7-121, Santa Fe NM 87508. (866)424-1501. Fax: (505)424-8207. E-mail: write-on@scsfe.com. Website: scsfe.com. Deadline: April 25. Prize: All 5 winners receive certificates and free submission to the PAGEawards screenwriting competition. In addition, scripts are forwarded to all producers/agents/managers/executives attending The Hollywood Connection component of SCSFe.

ANNUAL AUSTIN FILM FESTIVAL SCREENPLAY & TELEPLAY COMPETITION

Austin Film Festival, 1801 Salina St., Austin TX 78702. (512)478-4795. Fax: (512)478-6205. E-mail: screenplaydirector@austinfilmfestival.com. Website: austinfilmfestival.com. **Contact:** Matt Dy, Screenplay. Teleplay Competition Director. 18th Annual Austin Film Festival Screenplay & Teleplay Competition. The Austin Film Festival is looking for quality screenplays which will be read by industry professionals. AFF provides 'Readers' notes' to all Second Rounders (top 10%) and higher for no charge. Two main categories: Drama Category and Comedy Category. Two optional Award Categories (additional entry of $20 per category); Latitude Productions Award and Dark Hero

Studios Sci-Fi Award. Teleplay Competition: The teleplay competition is now open to pilots as well as spec scripts. Two main categories: Half-hour Sitcom and One-Hour Drama/Comedy. Deadline: May 15 (early); June 1 (late). Prize: $5,000 in Comedy and Drama; $2,500 for Sponsored Award and Sci-Fi Award.

THE ANNUAL BLANK THEATRE COMPANY YOUNG PLAYWRIGHTS FESTIVAL

The Blank Theatre Co., 1301 Lucile Ave., Los Angeles CA 90026-1519. (323)662-7734. Fax: (323)661-3903. E-mail: info@theblank.com. Website: youngplaywrights.com. Offered annually for unpublished work to encourage young writers to write for the theater by presenting their work as well as through our mentoring programs. Open to all writers 19 or younger on the submission date. Deadline: March 15. Prize: Workshop of the winning plays by professional theater artists

ANNUAL DENISE RAGAN WIESENMEYER ONE ACT FESTIVAL

Attic Theatre Ensemble, 5429 W. Washington Blvd., Los Angeles CA 90016-1112. (323)525-0600. E-mail: info@attictheatre.org. Website: attictheatre.org. **Contact:** Literary Manager. "Offered annually for unpublished and unproduced work. Scripts should be intended for mature audiences. Length should not exceed 30 minutes. Guidelines online. Electronic submissions only." Deadline: December 31. Prize: 1st Place: $300; 2nd Place: $150.

ANNUAL NATIONAL PLAYWRITING COMPETITION

Wichita State University, School of Performing Arts, 1845 Fairmount, Box 153, Wichita KS 67260-0153. (316)978-3646. Fax: (316)978-3202. E-mail: bret.jones@wichita.edu. **Contact:** Bret Jones, Director of Theatre. The contest will be open to all undergraduate and graduate students enrolled at any college or university in the United States. Please indicate school affiliation. All submissions must be original, unpublished and unproduced. Both full-length and one act plays may be submitted. Full length plays in one or more acts should be a minimum of 90 minutes playing time. Two or three short plays on related themes by the same author will be judged as one entry. The total playing time should be a minimum of 90 minutes. One act plays should be a minimum of 30 minutes playing time to a maximum of 60 minutes playing time. Musicals should be a minimum of 90 minutes playing time and must include a CD of the accompanying music. Scripts should contain no more than 4-6 characters and setting must be suitable for an 85-seat Black box theatre. Eligible playwrights may submit up to two entries per contest year. One typewritten, bound copy should be submitted. Scripts must be typed and arranged in professional play script format. See information provided in *The Dramatist's Sourcebook* or the following website: pubinfo.vcu.edu/artweb/playwriting/format.html for instruction on use of professional format. Two title pages must be included: one bound and the other unbound. The unbound title page should display the author's name, address, telephone number and e-mail address if applicable. The bound title page should only display the name of the script; do not include any personal identifying information on the bound title page. Scripts may be submitted electronically to the following web address bret.jones@wichita.edu. Submit in PDF format. Please include ALL information requested for mail in scripts with your electronic submission. Deadline: January 16. Prize: Production by the Wichita State University Theatre. Winner will be announced after March 15. No entry may be withdrawn after March 1st. Judging will be conducted by a panel of three or more selected from the school faculty and may also include up to three experienced, faculty approved WSU School of Performing Arts students.

APPALACHIAN FESTIVAL OF PLAYS & PLAYWRIGHTS

Barter Theatre, Box 867, Abingdon VA 24212-0867. (276)619-3316. Fax: (276)619-3335. E-mail: apfestival@bartertheatre.com. Website: bartertheatre.com/festival. **Contact:** Nick Piper, associate director/director. "With the annual Appalachian Festival of New Plays & Playwrights, Barter Theatre wishes to celebrate new, previously unpublished/unproduced plays by playwrights from the Appalachian region. If the playwrights are not from Appalachia, the plays themselves must be about the region." Deadline: March 31. Prize: $250, a staged reading performed at Barter's Stage II theater, and some transportation compensation and housing during the time of the festival. There may be an additional award for the best staged readings.

BEVERLY HILLS FILM FESTIVAL SCREENPLAY COMPETITION

Beverly Hills Film Festival, 9663 Santa Monica Blvd, Suite 777, Beverly Hills CA 90210. (310)779-1206. E-mail: info@beverlyhillsfilmfestival.com. Website: beverlyhillsfilmfestival.com/. Please indicate if the submission is complete, or work in progress. Also include 1) Synopsis of the Script (in English); 2) A statement from the writer on the script; 3) Biography of the writer; 4) Stills if any; 5) Poster and/or press booklet. Deadline: Jan. 25.

BUNTVILLE CREW'S AWARD BLUE

Buntville Crew, 118 N. Railroad Ave., Buckley IL 60918-0445. E-mail: buntville@yahoo.fr. **Contact:** Steven Packard, artistic director. "Presented annually for the best unpublished/unproduced play script under 15 pages, written by a student enrolled in any Illinois high school. Submit 1 copy of the script in standard play format, a brief biography, and a SASE (scripts will not be returned). Include name, address, telephone number, age, and name of school." Deadline: May 31. Prize: Cash prize and possible productions in Buckley and/or New York City. Judged by panel selected by the theater.

BUNTVILLE CREW'S PRIX HORS PAIR

Buntville Crew, 118 N. Railroad Ave., Buckley IL 60918-0445. E-mail: buntville@yahoo.fr. Website: buntville@yahoo.com. **Contact:** Steven Packard, artistic director. "Annual award for unpublished/unproduced play script under 15 pages. Plays may be in English, French, German, or Spanish (no translations, no adaptations). Submit 1 copy of the script in standard play format, a résumé, and a SASE (scripts will not be returned). Include name, address, and telephone number." Deadline: May 31. Prize: $200 and possible production in Buckley and/or New York City. Judged by panel selected by the theater.

CALIFORNIA YOUNG PLAYWRIGHTS CONTEST

Playwrights Project, 2590 Truxton Rd., Ste. 202, San Diego CA 92106-6145. (619)239-8222. Fax: (619)239-8225. E-mail: write@playwrightsproject.org. Website: playwrightsproject.org. Playwrights Project, 2590 Truxton Rd.,Ste. 202, San DiegoCA, 92106-6145. (619)239-8222. Fax: (619)239-8225. E-mail: write@playwrightsproject.org. Website: playwrightsproject.org. **Open to Californians under age 19.** Annual contest. Estab. 1985. "Our organization and the contest is designed to nurture promising young writers. We hope to develop playwrights and audiences for live theater. We also teach playwriting." Submissions required to be unpublished and not produced professionally. Submissions made by the author. Deadline for entries: June 1. SASE for contest rules and entry form. No entry fee. Award is professional productions of 2-4 short plays each year at a professional theatre in San Diego, plus royalty. Judging by professionals in the theater community, a committee of 5-7; changes somewhat each year. Works performed in San Diego at a professional theatre. Writers submitting scripts of 10 or more pages receive a detailed script evaluation letter upon request. **Contact:** Cecelia Kouma, Executive Director. "Offered annually for previously unpublished plays by young writers to stimulate young people to create dramatic works, and to nurture promising writers. Scripts must be a minimum of 10 standard typewritten pages; send 2 copies. Scripts will *not* be returned. If requested, entrants receive detailed evaluation letter. Writers must be California residents under age 19 as of the deadline date. Guidelines available online." Deadline: June 1. Prize: Professional production of 2-4 winning plays at a professional theatre in San Diego, plus royalty.

CHRISTIAN SCREENWRITER

P.O. Box 447, Bloomfield NJ 07003. (201)306-5093. E-mail: info@christianscreenwrite.com. Website: christianscreenwrite.com. Contemporary Christian screenplays only. The contest is "looking for films that spread the messages and principles and Christianity." Deadline: July, 2011-September 2011. Prize: Cash prizes offered for top three winners.

COE COLLEGE PLAYWRITING FESTIVAL

Coe College, 1220 First Ave. NE, Cedar Rapids IA 52402-5092. (319)399-8624. Fax: (319)399-8557. E-mail: swolvert@coe.edu. Website: theatre.coe.edu. **Contact:** Susan Wolverton. "Offered biennially for unpublished work to provide a venue for new works for the stage. We are interested in full-length productions, not one-acts or musicals. There are no specific criteria although a current resumè and synopsis is requested. Open to any writer." Deadline: November 1 (even years). Notification: January 15 (odd years). Prize: $500, plus 1-week residency as guest artist with airfare, room and board provided.

THE CONTEST OF CONTEST WINNERS

ScriptDoctor, 555 E. Limberlost Dr., Suite 1067, Tucson AZ 85705. E-mail: thedoc@scriptdoctor.com. Website: scriptdoctor.com. **Contact:** Howard Allen. Must be at least 18 years of age. Screenplays have won or placed in other competitions. No entry may have earned money or other consideration for mor than $5,000. Deadline: December. Prize: Cash $1,000 and notes from a ScriptDoctor partner.

⚌ CREATIVE WORLD AWARDS (CWA) INTERNATIONAL SCREENWRITING COMPETITION

4712 Admiralty Way #268, Marina del Rey CA 90292. E-mail: info@creativeworldawards.com. Website: creativeworldawards.com. **Contact:** Marlene Neubauer/Heather Waters. "CWA's professionalism, industry innovation, and exclusive company list make this competition a leader in the industry. Several past entrants have gotten optioned and several more are in negotiation. Newly added categories for short film scripts and television. Check out the website for more details." All screenplays must be in English and in standard spec screenplay format. See website's FAQ page for more detailed information. Deadline: See website. Prize: Over $25,000 in cash and prizes awarded in 10 categories.

DRURY UNIVERSITY ONE-ACT PLAY CONTEST

Drury University, 900 N. Benton Ave., Springfield MO 65802-3344. E-mail: msokol@drury.edu. **Contact:** Mick Sokol. Offered in even-numbered years for unpublished and professionally unproduced plays. One play per playwright. Guidelines for SASE or by e-mail. Deadline: December 1.

DUBUQUE FINE ARTS PLAYERS ANNUAL ONE-ACT PLAY CONTEST

Dubuque Fine Arts Players, PO Box 1160, Dubuque IA 52004-1160. E-mail: contact@dbqoneacts.org. Website: dbqoneacts.org. "Annually, we select 3 one-act plays each year, award cash prizes and produce the winning plays in October; plays for submission must be unpublished and unproduced. Applications may be submitted online or by US mail, as listed on our website." Application Deadline: January 31 annually. Prize: Prizes: 1st Place: $600; 2nd Place: $300; 3rd Place: $200. All plays are read at least twice and as many as 6 times by community readers; final judging is done by a group of 3 directors and 2 other qualified judges.

EERIE HORROR FILM FESTIVAL SCREENPLAY COMPETITION

P.O, Box 98, Edinboro PA 16412. E-mail: info@eeriehorrorfest.com. Website: eeriehorrorfilmfestival.com/. There is also a student contest for ages 10-17. Entries must be in the horror film genre. There are contests for features as well as short scripts. Only Horror, Sci-fi, supernatural, and suspense genres will be considered.

ESSENTIAL THEATRE PLAYWRITING AWARD

The Essential Theatre, 1414 Foxhall Lane, #10, Atlanta GA 30316. (404) 212-0815. E-mail: pmhardy@aol.com. Website: essentialtheatre.com. **Contact:** Peter Hardy. "Offered annually for unproduced, full-length plays by Georgia resident writers. No limitations as to style or subject matter." Deadline: April 23. Prize: $600 and full production.

FESTIVAL OF NEW AMERICAN PLAYS

Firehouse Theatre Project, 1609 W. Broad St., Richmond VA 23220. (804)355-2001. E-mail: info@firehousetheatre.org. Website: firehousetheatre.org. **Contact:** Carol Piersol, artistic director. "Annual contest designed to support new and emerging American playwrights. Scripts must be full-length and previously unpublished/unproduced. (Readings are acceptable if no admission was charged.) Submissions should be mailed in standard manuscript form with no fancy binding. This means no disks, no e-mails. Scripts should be secured simply with a binder clip only. All author information must be on a title page separate from the body of the manuscript and no reference to the author is permitted in the body of the script. Scripts must be accompanied by a letter of recommendation from a theater company or individual familiar with your work. Letters of recommendation do not need to be specific to the play submitted; they may be general recommendations of the playwright's work. All letters must be received with the script, not under separate cover. Scripts received without a letter will not be considered. Due to the volume of mail, manuscripts cannot be returned. All American playwrights welcome to submit their work." Deadline: June 30 postmark. Prize: 1st Place: $1,000 and a staged reading; 2nd Place: $500 and a staged reading. All plays are initially read by a panel of individuals with experience in playwriting and literature. Previous judges have included Lloyd Rose (former *Washington Post* theatre critic), Bill Patton (frequent Firehouse director), Richard Toscan (dean of the Virginia Commonwealth University School for the Arts), and Israel Horovitz (playwright). All finalists are asked to sign a contract with the Firehouse Theatre Project that guarantees performance rights for the staged reading in January and printed credit for Firehouse Theatre Project if the play is produced/published in the future.

FLICKERS: RHODE ISLAND INTERNATIONAL FILM FESTIVAL FEATURE SCREENPLAY COMPETITION

P.O. Box 162, Newport RI 02840. (401)861-4445. Fax: (401)490-6735. E-mail: georget@film-festival.org. Website: film-festival.org/enterascreenplay.php. FLICKERS: The Rhode Island International Film Festival is calling for Screenplay Entries for its15th annual festival, which takes place August 9-14, 2011 in historic Providence, Rhode Island. The Festival is accepting screenplays in all genres. Screenplays must have been written after 2008. Scripts not to exceed 130 pages. The purpose of the contest is to promote, embolden and cultivate screenwriters in their quest for opportunities in the industry. Deadline: July 15.

GIMME CREDIT SCREENPLAY COMPETITION

4470 W. Sunset Blvd., #278, Los Angeles CA 90027. (310)499-1475. E-mail: submissions@gimmecreditcompetition.com. Website: gimmecreditcompetition.com/. Short (30 pages) scripts only. Only short screenplays of up to thirty (30) pages for submissions to the short category and five (5) pages for the super short category, not including the cover page, will be accepted. All live action genres, including short plays and original teleplays, are acceptable. Variety is encouraged. Screenplays must not have been previously sold, optioned or produced in any form. In the event an entry is sold, optioned or produced after being received, the author(s) must notify us IMMEDIATELY. Deadline: June 16-October 6. Screenplays are evaluated based on the following criteria: story and structure, dialogue, character, feasibility and their ending. During the second round of judging, a script's feasibility is examined further, along with an emphasis on originality and marketability.

GOTHAM SCREEN FILM FESTIVAL AND SCREENPLAY CONTEST

291 Broadway, Suite 701, New York NY 10007. E-mail: info@gothamscreen.com. Website: gothamscreen. com. "Submit via Withoutabox account or download form at Website." "The contest is open to anyone. Feature length screenplays should be properly formatted and have an approximate length of 80-120 pages. On the cover page, please put the title, the writer's name(s) and the contact details." Deadline: September. Prize: $2,500. In addition, excerpts from selected contest entries will be performed live by professional actors at a staged reading during the festival.

☺ GOVERNOR GENERAL'S LITERARY AWARD FOR DRAMA

Canada Council for the Arts, 350 Albert St., P.O. Box 1047, Ottawa ON K1P 5V8 Canada. (613)566-4414, ext. 5573. Fax: (613)566-4410. Website: canadacouncil.ca/prizes/ggla. Offered for the best English-language and the best French-language work of drama by a Canadian. Publishers submit titles for consideration. Deadline depends on the book's publication date: Books in English: March 15, June 1 or August 7. Books in French: March 15 or July 15. Prize: Each laureate receives $25,000; nonwinning finalists receive $1,000.

HOLIDAY SCREENPLAY CONTEST

P.O. Box 450, Boulder CO 80306. (303)629-3072. E-mail: Cherubfilm@aol.com. Website: HolidayScreenplayContest.com. "Scripts must be centered on a holiday. The screenplay must be centered around one Holiday (New Year's Day, President's Day, Valentine's Day, St. Patrick's Day, April Fool's Day, Easter, 4th of July, Halloween, Thanksgiving, Hanukkah, Christmas, Kwanzaa, or any other world holiday you would like to feature). This contest is limited to the first 400 entries." Screenplays must be in English. Screenplays must not have been previously optioned, produced, or purchased prior to submission. Multiple submissions are accepted but each submission requires a separate online entry and separate fee. Screenplays must be between 90 - 125 pages. Deadline: November 30th. Prize: Up to $500.

HORROR SCREENPLAY CONTEST

Cherub Productions, P.O. Box 540, Boulder Co 80306. (303)629-3072. E-mail: Cherubfilm@aol.com. Website: horrorscreenplaycontest.com. "This contest is looking for horror scripts." This contest is limited to the first 600 entries. Screenplays must be between 90-125 pages. More than $5000 in cash and prizes.

L.A. DESIGNERS' THEATRE-COMMISSIONS

L.A. Designers' Theatre, P.O. Box 1883, Studio City CA 91614-0883. (323)650-9600 or (323)654-2700 T.D.D. Fax: (323)654-3210. E-mail: ladesigners@gmail. com. **Contact:** Richard Niederberg, artistic director. "Quarterly contest to promote new work and push it onto the conveyor belt to filmed or videotaped entertainment. All submissions must be registered with copyright office and be unpublished. Material will not be returned. Do not submit anything that will not fit in a #10 envelope. No rules, guidelines, fees, or entry forms. Just present an idea that can be commissioned into a full work. Proposals for uncompleted works are encouraged. Unpopular political, religious, social, or other themes are encouraged; 'street' language and nudity are acceptable. Open to any writer." Deadline: March 15, June 15, September 15, December 15. Prize: Production or publication of the work in the Los Angeles market. We only want 'first refusal.'

MCKNIGHT ADVANCEMENT GRANT

The Playwrights' Center, 2301 Franklin Ave. E., Minneapolis MN 55406-1099. (612)332-7481, ext. 10. Fax: (612)332-6037. Website: pwcenter.org. Offered annually for either published or unpublished playwrights to recognize those whose work demonstrates exceptional artistic merit and potential and whose primary residence is in the state of Minnesota. The grants are intended to significantly advance recipients' art and careers, and can be used to support a wide variety of expenses. Applications available mid-October. Guidelines for SASE. Additional funds of up to $2,000 are available for workshops and readings. The Playwrights' Center evaluates each application and forwards finalists to a panel of 3 judges from the national theater community. Applicant must have been a citizen or permanent resident of the US and a legal resident of the state of Minnesota since July 1, 2009. (Residency must be maintained during fellowship year.) Applicant must have had a minimum of 1 work fully produced by a professional theater at the time of application. Deadline: January 21. Prize: $25,000 which can be used to support a wide variety of expenses, including writing time, artistic costs of residency at a theater or arts organization, travel and study, production, or presentation

MOONDANCE INTERNATIONAL FILM FESTIVAL

970 9th St., Boulder CO 80302. (303)545-0202. E-mail: director@moondancefilmfestival.com. Website: moondancefilmfestival.com. WRITTEN WORKS SUBMISSIONS: feature screenplays, short screenplays, feature & short musical screenplays, feature & short screenplays for children, 1, 2 or 3-act stageplays, mini-series for TV, television movies of the week, television pilots, libretti, musical film scripts, short stories, radio plays & short stories for children. Submission service: withoutabox.com/login/1240. Postmark Deadline: May 31.

MOVING ARTS PREMIERE ONE-ACT COMPETITION

Moving Arts, P.O. Box 481145, Los Angeles CA 90048. (323)666-3259. E-mail: info@movingarts.org. Website: movingarts.org. **Contact:** Steve Lozier. Offered annually for unproduced one-act plays in the Los Angeles area (single set; maximum cast of 8 people recommended). All playwrights are eligible except Moving Arts resident artists. No more than 40 pages. "We have a blind submission policy. The playwright's name should appear only on the cover letter and no where on the script. Scripts are not returned. Please see website for additional guidelines before submitting. Deadline: see website. Prize: 1st Place: $200, plus a full production during festival; finalists get program mention and possible production.

NANTUCKET FILM FESTIVAL SCREENPLAY COMPETITION

Nantucket Film Festival, 68 Jay St., Suite 425, Brooklyn NY 11201. (646)480-1900. Fax: (646)365-3367. E-mail: info@nantucketfilmfestival.org. Website: nantucketfilmfestival.org/. Screenplays must be standard feature film length (90-130 pages) and standard U.S. format only.

NATIONAL CHILDREN'S THEATRE FESTIVAL

Actors' Playhouse at the Miracle Theatre, 280 Miracle Mile, Coral Gables FL 33134. (305)444-9293, ext. 615. Fax: (305)444-4181. E-mail: maulding@actorsplayhouse.org. Website: actorsplayhouse.org. Purpose of contest: to bring together the excitement of the theater

arts and the magic of young audiences through the creation of new musical works and to create a venue for playwrights/composers to showcase their artistic products. Submissions must be unpublished. Submissions are made by author or author's agent. Deadline for entries: April 1 annually. Visit website or send SASE for contest rules and entry forms. Entry fee is $10. Awards: first prize of $500, full production, and transportation to Festival weekend based on availability. Past judges include Joseph Robinette, Moses Goldberg and Luis Santeiro. E-mail: maulding@actorsplayhouse.org. actorsplayhouse.org. **Contact:** Earl Maulding. "Offered annually for unpublished musicals for young audiences. Target age is 4-12. Script length should be 45-60 minutes. Maximum of 8 actors to play any number of roles. Prefer settings which lend themselves to simplified scenery. Bilingual (English/Spanish) scripts are welcomed. Call or visit website for guidelines. Open to any writer." Deadline: April 1. Prize: $500 and full production.

NATIONAL LATINO PLAYWRIGHTS AWARD

Arizona Theatre Co., 343 S. Scott Ave, Tucson AZ 85701. (520)884-8210. Fax: (520)628-9129. E-mail: jbazzell@arizonatheatre.org. Website: arizonatheatre.org. **Contact:** Jennifer Bazzell, Literary Manager. Offered annually for unproduced, unpublished plays over 50 pages in length. Plays may be in English, bilingual, or in Spanish (with English translation). The award recognizes exceptional full-length plays by Latino playwrights on any subject. Open to Latino playwrights currently residing in the US, its territories, and/or Mexico. Guidelines online or via e-mail. Deadline: Dec31. Prize: $1,000

DON AND GEE NICHOLL FELLOWSHIPS IN SCREENWRITING

Academy of Motion Picture Arts & Sciences, 1313 N. Vine St., Hollywood CA 90028-8107. (310)247-3010. E-mail: nicholl@oscars.org. Website: oscars.org/nicholl. "Offered annually for unproduced feature film to identify talented new screenwriters. Open to writers who have not earned more than $5,000 writing for films or TV." Deadline: May 1. Prize: Up to five $30,000 fellowships awarded each year.

NICKELODEON WRITING FELLOWSHIP

Nickelodeon, 231 W. Olive Ave., Burbank CA 91502. (818)736-3663. E-mail: info.writing@nick.com. Website: nickwriting.com, facebook.com/nickwriting, twitter@nickwriting. **Contact:** Karen Kirkland, Executive Director. Offered annually for unpublished scripts. You must be 18 years or older to participate. You must posses and present evidence of idenitity and United States employment eligibility (valid for the duration of the fellowship program). Deadline: February 28, 2012. Prize: The Fellowship provides a salaried position for up to one year and offers hands-on experience writing spec scripts and pitching story ideas in both live action and animation television. As part of their script writing, each fellow will be assigned to an Executive in Charge of Production and have an opportunity to write a spec script for an on-air Nickelodeon show. In addition, all fellows are integrated into the activities of both the development and production departments. This allows the fellows an opportunity to attend storyboard pitches, notes meetings, records, table reads, show pitches and show tapings, all while being exposed to top creators and key production crews. Experienced readers and Nickelodeon Development and Production employees and executives read all submissions.

ONE-ACT PLAY CONTEST

Tennessee Williams/New Orleans Literary Festival, 938 Lafayette St., Suite 328, New Orleans LA 70113. (504)581-1144. E-mail: info@tennesseewilliams.net. Website: tennesseewilliams.net/contests. **Contact:** Paul J. Willis. "Annual contest for an unpublished play." "The One-Act Play Competition is an opportunity for playwrights to see their work fully produced before a large audience during one of the largest literary festivals in the nation, and for the festival to showcase undiscovered talent." Deadline: November 1 yearly. Prize: $1,500, a VIP All Access Pass ($500 value), publication, and a staged reading at the festival. The play will also be fully produced at the following year's festival. The Tennessee Williams/New Orleans Literary Festival reserves the right to publish. Judged by an anonymous expert panel.

ONE IN TEN SCREENPLAY CONTEST

Cherub Productions, P.O. Box 540, Boulder CO 80306. E-mail: Cherubfilm@aol.com. Website: OneInTen-ScreenplayContest.com. Scripts that provide a positive potrayal of gays and lesbians. "A requirement of the competition is that at least one of the primary characters in the screenplay be gay or lesbian (bisexual, transgender, questioning, and the like) and that gay and lesbian characters must be portrayed positively. All writers are encouraged to enter!" Deadline: September 1. Prize: $1,000 top prize.

THE PAGE INTERNATIONAL SCREENWRITING AWARDS

The PAGE Awards Committee, 7510 Sunset Blvd., #610, Hollywood CA 90046-3408. E-mail: info@PAGEawards.com. Website: PAGEawards.com. **Contact:** Zoe Simmons, contest coordinator. Annual competition to discover the most talented new screenwriters from across the country and around the world. "Each year, awards are presented to 31 screenwriters in 10 different genre: action/adventure, comedy, drama, family film, historical film, science fiction, thriller/horror, short film script, TV drama pilot, and TV sitcom pilot. Guidelines and entry forms are online. The contest is open to all writers 18 years of age and older who have not previously earned more than $25,000 writing for film and/or television. Please visit contest website for a complete list of rules and regulations." Deadline: January 15 (early); March 1 (regular); April 1 (late). Prize: Over $50,000 in cash and prizes, including a $25,000 grand prize, plus gold, silver, and bronze prizes in all 10 categories. Most importantly, the award-winning writers receive extensive publicity and industry exposure. Judging is done entirely by Hollywood professionals, including industry script readers, consultants, agents, managers, producers, and development executives. Entrants retain all rights to their work.

SCREENPLAY FESTIVAL

11693 San Vicente Blvd., Ste. 806, Los Angeles CA 90046. (424)248-9221. Fax: (866)770-2994. E-mail: info@screenplayfestival.com. Website: screenplayfestival.com. Entries in the feature-length competition must be more than 60 pages; entries in the short screenplay contest must be fewer than 60 pages. The Screenplay Festival was established to solve two major problems: Problem Number One: It is simply too difficult for talented writers who have no 'connections' to gain recognition and get their material read by legitimate agents, producers, directors and investors. Problem Number Two: Agents, producers, directors, and investors complain that they cannot find any great material, but they will generally not accept 'unsolicited material.' This means that unless the script comes from a source that is known to them, they will not read it. Screenplay Festival was established to help eliminate this 'chicken and egg' problem. By accepting all submitted screenplays and judging them based upon their quality — not their source or their standardized formatting or the quality of the brads holding them together — Screenplay Festival looks to give undiscovered screenwriters an opportunity to rise above the crowd. Deadline: Sept. 1; early deadline: July 1.

SCRIPTAPALOOZA SCREENPLAY COMPETITION

Supported by Writers Guild of America west Registry, the Writers Guild of Canada and Write Brothers, 7775 Sunset Blvd., #200, Hollywood CA 90046. (323)654-5809. E-mail: info@scriptapalooza.com. Website: scriptapalooza.com. **Contact:** Mark Andrushko, pres. "Annual competition for unpublished scripts from any genre. Open to any writer, 18 or older. Submit one copy of a 90- to 130-page screenplay. Body pages must be numbered, and scripts must be in industry-standard format. All entered scripts will be read and judged by more than 90 production companies." Early Deadline: January 7; Deadline: March 5; Late Deadline: April 15.5. Prize: 1st Place: $10,000 and software package from Write Brothers, Inc.; 2nd Place, 3rd Place, and 10 Runners-Up: Software package from Write Brothers, Inc. The top 100 scripts will be considered by over 90 production companies.

SCRIPTAPALOOZA TELEVISION WRITING COMPETITION

7775 Sunset Blvd., PMB #200, Hollywood CA 90046. (323)654-5809. E-mail: info@scriptapalooza.com. Website: scriptapaloozatv.com. "Seeking talented writers who have an interest in American television writing." Prize: $500, $200, and $100 in each category (total $3,200), production company consideration. Categories: sitcoms, pilots, one-hour dramas and reality shows. Entry fee: $40; accepts Paypal credit card or make checks payable to Scriptapalooza. **Deadline: April 15 and October 1 of each year.** Length: standard television format whether one hour, one-half hour or pilot. Open to any writer 18 or older. Guidelines available now for SASE or on website. Accepts inquiries by e-mail, phone. "Pilots should be fresh and new and easy to visualize. Spec scripts should stay current with the shows, up-to-date story lines, characters, etc." Winners announced February 15 and August 30. For contest results, visit website. "Biannual competition accepting entries in 4 categories: reality shows, sitcoms, original pilots, and 1-hour dramas. There are more than 25 producers, agents, and managers reading the winning scripts. Two past winners won Emmys because of Scriptapalooza and 1 past entrant now writes for Comedy Central." Deadline: October 1 and April 15. Prize: 1st Place: $500; 2nd Place: $200; 3rd Place: $100 (in each category).

"SHOOT IN PHILADELPHIA" SCREENWRITING COMPETITION

Greater Philadelphia Film Office, 1515 Arch St., 11th Floor, Philadelphia PA 19102. (215)686-2668. Fax: (215)686-3659. E-mail: sip@film.org. Website: film. org. Screenplays must be "shootable" primarily in the Greater Philadelphia area (includes the surrounding counties). All genres and storytelling approaches are acceptable. Feature length screenplays must be between 85-130 pages in length. TV pilot scripts must be 35-50 pages. There are different awards, such as an award for the best script for writers under 25, as well as the best script for a regional writer. See the website for full details. Prize: $10,000 grand prize, with other prizes offered.

● SHRIEKFEST HORROR/SCI-FI FILM FESTIVAL & SCREENPLAY COMPETITION

12214 Via Santa Marta, Sylmar CA 91342. E-mail: shriekfest@aol.com. Website: shriekfest.com. **Contact:** Denise Gossett/Todd Beeson. "No, we don't use loglines anywhere, we keep your script private." "We accept award winning screenplays, no restrictions as long as it's in the horror/thriller or scifi/fantasy genres. We accept shorts and features. No specific lengths." "Our awards are to help screenwriters move their script up the ladder and hopefully have it made into a film. Our winners take that win and parlay it into agents, film deals, and options." Deadline: March 20, May 22 and July 10. Prize: Trophies, product awards, usually cash. Our awards are updated all year long as sponsors step onboard. The winners go home with lots of stuff. "We have at least 20-30 judges and they are all in different aspects of the entertainment industry, such as producers, directors, writers, actors, agents."

SHUBERT FENDRICH MEMORIAL PLAYWRITING CONTEST

Pioneer Drama Service, Inc., P.O. Box 4267, Englewood CO 80155. (303)779-4035. Fax: (303)779-4315. E-mail: editors@pioneerdrama.com. E-mail: submissions@pioneerdrama.com. Website: pioneerdrama.

com. Pioneer Drama Service, Inc., P.O. Box 4267, Englewood CO 80155-4267. Fax: (303)779-4315. E-mail: submissions@pioneerdrama.com. Website: pioneerdrama.com. **Director:** Lori Conary, Submissions Editor. Annual contest. Estab. 1990. Purpose of the contest: "To encourage the development of quality theatrical material for educational and family theater." Previously unpublished submissions only. Open to all writers not currently published by Pioneer Drama Service. Deadline for entries: December 31. SASE for contest rules and guidelines or view online. No entry fee. Cover letter, SASE for return of ms, and proof of production or staged reading must accompany all submissions. Awards $1,000 royalty advance and publication. Upon receipt of signed contracts, plays will be published and made available in our next catalog. Judging by editors. All rights acquired with acceptance of contract for publication. Restrictions for entrants: Any writers currently published by Pioneer Drama Service are not eligible. **Contact:** Lori Conary, Submissions Editor. Offered annually for unpublished, but previously produced, submissions to encourage the development of quality theatrical material for educational and community theater. Rights acquired only if published. Authors already published by Pioneer Drama are not eligible. Contest submissions must also meet standard submission guidelines. Deadline: December 31 (postmarked). Prize: $1,000 royalty advance and publication.

SOUTHEASTERN THEATRE CONFERENCE NEW PLAY PROJECT

Dept. of Theatre & Dance, Austin Peay State Univ., 681 Summer St., Clarksville TN 37044. E-mail: hardinb@apsu.edu. Website: setc.org. **Contact:** Chris Hardin, chair. "Annual award for full-length plays or related one acts. No musicals or children's plays. Submissions must be unproduced/unpublished. Readings and workshops are acceptable. Submit application, and 1 copy of script as an e-mail attachment. Visit website for application. Entries will be accepted between March 1st and June 1st. One submission per playwright only." Eligibility: Playwrights who reside in the SETC region (or who are enrolled in a regionally accredited educational institution in the SETC region) or who reside outside the region but are SETC members are eligible for consideration. SETC Region states include Alabama, Florida, Georgia, Kentucky, Mississippi, North Carolina, South Carolina, Tennes-

see, Virginia, West Virginia. Mission: The SETC New Play Project is dedicated to the discovery, development and publicizing of worthy new plays and playwrights. Deadline: June 1. Prize: $1,000 and a staged reading.

SOUTHERN PLAYWRIGHTS COMPETITION

Jacksonville State University, 700 Pelham Rd. N., Jacksonville AL 36265-1602. (256)782-5469. Fax: (256)782-5441. E-mail: jmaloney@jsu.edu; swhitton@jsu.edu. Website: jsu.edu/depart/english/southpla.htm. **Contact:** Joy Maloney, Steven J. Whitton. "Offered annually to identify and encourage the best of Southern playwriting. Playwrights must be a native or resident of Alabama, Arkansas, District of Columbia, Florida, Georgia, Kentucky, Louisiana, Missouri, North Carolina, South Carolina, Tennessee, Texas, Virginia, or West Virginia." Deadline: January 15. Prize: $1,000 and production of the play.

SOUTHWEST WRITERS

3721 Morris N.E., Albuquerque NM 87111. (505)265-9485. Fax: (505)265-9483. E-mail: swwriters@juno.com. Website: southwestwriters.com. 3721 Morris NE, Suite A, Albuquerque NM 87111. (505)265-9485. Fax: (505)265-9483. E-mail: swwriters@juno.com. Website: southwestwriters.org. Non-profit organization dedicated to helping members of all levels in their writing. Members enjoy perks such as networking with professional and aspiring writers; substantial discounts on mini-conferences, workshops, writing classes, and annual and quarterly SWW writing contest; monthly newsletter; two writing programs per month; critique groups, critique service (also for non-members); discounts at bookstores and other businesses; and website linking. Cost of membership: Individual, $60/year, $100/2 years; Two People, $50 each/year; Student, $40/year; Student under 18, $25/year; Outside U.S.$65/year; Lifetime, $750. See website for information. The SouthWest Writers Writing Contest encourages and honors excellence in writing. In addition to competing for cash prizes and the coveted Storyteller Award, contest entrants may receive an optional written critique of their entry from a qualified contest critiquer. Submit first 20 pages and 1 page synopsis (using industry-standard formatting, Courier font, brad-bound). Deadline: May 1-May 16. Prize: Up to $1,000 grand prize. All mss will be screened by a panel and the top 10 in each category will be sent to appropriate editors or literary agents to determine the final top 3 places. The top 3 winners will also receive a critique from the judging editor or literary agent. Contacting any judge about an entry is an automatic disqualification. 12. Entrants retain all rights to their entries. By entering this contest, you agree to abide by the rules, agree that decisions by the judges are final, and agree that no refunds will be awarded.

☿ THEATRE IN THE RAW ONE-ACT PLAY WRITING CONTEST

Theatre In the Raw, 3521 Marshall St., Vancouver BC V5N 4S2 Canada. (604)708-5448. E-mail: theatreintheraw@telus.net. Website: theatreintheraw. ca. Biennial contest for an original one-act play, presented in proper stage-play format, that is unpublished and unproduced. The play (with no more than 6 characters) cannot be longer than 25 double-spaced, typed pages equal to 30 minutes. Scripts must have page numbers. Scripts are to be mailed only & will not be accepted by e-mail. 1st PLACE: $200, at least 1 dramatic reading or staging of the play at a Theatre In the Raw Cafe/Venue, or as part of a mini-tour program for the One-Act Play Series Nights; 3RD PLACE: $75. Winners announced JUNE 30, 2012.][COSTS: ENTRY FEE OF $25 FOR EACH ONE-ACT SUBMITTED (FOR TWO PLAYS: $45 - FOR THREE PLAYS: $70 - FOR FOUR PLAYS: $90) (payable to Theatre In the Raw)] Deadline: December 31. Prize: 1st Place: $200, at least 1 dramatic reading or staging of the play at a Theatre In the Raw Cafe/Venue, or as part of a mini-tour program for the One-Act Play Series Nights; 2nd Place: $100; 3rd Place: $75. Winners announced June 30, 2012.

TRUSTUS PLAYWRIGHTS' FESTIVAL

Trustus Theatre, Box 11721, Columbia SC 29211-1721. (803)254-9732. Fax: (803)771-9153. E-mail: shammond@trustus.org. Website: trustus.org. **Contact:** Sarah Hammond, literary manager. Offered annually for professionally unproduced full-length plays; cast limit of 8. Prefers challenging, innovative dramas and comedies. No musicals, plays for young audiences, or "hillbilly" southern shows. Send SASE or consult Trustus website for guidelines and application. Deadline: for 2013 festival: December 1, 2011-February 28, 2012. Prize: $500 and a 1-year development period with full production and travel/accommodations to attend the public opening.

VERMONT PLAYWRIGHT'S AWARD

The Valley Players, P.O. Box 441, Waitsfield VT 05673. (802)583-6767. E-mail: valleyplayer@madriver.com. Website: valleyplayers.com. **Contact:** Sharon Kellerman. Offered annually for unpublished, nonmusical, full-length plays suitable for production by a community theater group to encourage development of playwrights in Vermont, New Hampshire, and Maine. Deadline: February 1. Prize: $1,000.

☿ THE HERMAN VOADEN NATIONAL PLAYWRITING COMPETITION

Drama Department, Queen's University, Kingston ON K7L 3N6 Canada. (613)533-2104. E-mail: carolanne. hanna@queensu.ca; drama@queensu.ca. Website: queensu.ca/drama. **Contact:** Carol Anne Hanna. Offered every 2 years for unpublished plays to discover and develop new Canadian plays. See website for deadlines and guidelines. Open to Canadian citizens or landed immigrants. Prize: $3,000, $2,000, and 8 honorable mentions. 1st- and 2nd-prize winners are offered a 1-week workshop and public reading by professional director and cast. The 2 authors will be playwrights-in-residence for the rehearsal and reading period.

WATERFRONT FILM FESTIVAL AND INDIE SCREENPLAY COMPETITION

P.O. Box 387, Saugatuck MI 49453. (269)857-8351. E-mail: screenplay@waterfrontfilm.org. Website: waterfrontfilm.org. The contest is now accepting entries from writers in any state. Previously, the contest was only for local writers. Scripts must be 80-130 pages in length. Entries are accepted through Withabox. Deadline: April 1. Prize: Prize includes cash, an industry reception in the winner's honor, lodging, and VIP pass to the festival.

WORLDFEST-HOUSTON INDEPENDENT INTERNATIONAL FILM FESTIVAL

9898 Bissonnet St., Suite 650, Houston TX 77036. (713)965-9955. Fax: (713)965-9960. E-mail: entry@worldfest.org. Website: worldfest.org. **Contact:** Entry Coordinator. Competition for all genres of screenplays, plus 10 other competition categories of films, and videos. Deadline: December 15. Prize: Cash prizes, options, production deals, workshops, master classes, and seminars.

YEAR END SERIES (YES) FESTIVAL OF NEW PLAYS

Dept. of Theatre, Nunn Dr., Northern Kentucky University, Highland Heights KY 41099-1007. (859)572-

6362. Fax: (859)572-6057. E-mail: forman@nku.edu. **Contact:** Sandra Forman, project director. "Receives submissions from May 1 until September 30 in even-numbered years for the festivals which occur in April of odd-numbered years. Open to all writers." Deadline: October 1. Prize: $500 and an expense-paid visit to Northern Kentucky University to see the play produced

YOUNG PLAYWRIGHTS FESTIVAL NATIONAL PLAYWRITING COMPETITION

Young Playwrights, Inc., PO Box 5134, New York NY 10185. (212)594-5440. Fax: (212)594-5441. E-mail: literary@youngplaywrights.org. Website: young-playwrights.org. **Contact:** Literary Department, P.O. BOX 5134, New York, NY 10185. The Young Playwrights Inc. Festival National Playwriting Competition is offered annually to identify talented American playwrights aged 18 or younger. Please include your address, phone number, e-mail address, and date of birth on the title page. Open to US residents only. Deadline: January 2 (postmarked). Prize: Winners receive an invitation to New York City for the annual Young Playwrights, Inc. Writers Conference and a professionally staged reading of their play. Entrants retain all rights to their work.

YOUNG PLAYWRIGHTS INC. WRITE A PLAY! NYC COMPETITION

Young Playwrights, Inc., P.O. Box 5134, New York NY 10185. (212)594-5440. Fax: (212)684-4902. E-mail: literary@youngplaywrights.org. Website: youngplaywrights.org. **Contact:** Literary Department. "Offered annually for stage plays of any length (no musicals, screenplays, or adaptations) by NYC elementary, middle, and high school students only." Deadline: March 1. Prize: varies.

ANNA ZORNIO MEMORIAL CHILDREN'S THEATRE PLAYWRITING COMPETITION

University of New Hampshire, Dept. of Theatre and Dance, PCAC, 30 Academic Way, Durham NH 03824-3538. (603)862-3044. E-mail: mike.wood@unh.edu. Website: unh.edu/theatre-dance/zornio. University of New Hampshire, Department of Theatre and Dance, Paul Creative Arts Center, 30 Academic Way. Durham NH 03824-3538. (603)862-3038. Fax: (603)862-0298. E-mail: mike.wood@unh.edu. Website: unh.edu/theatre-dance/zornio. **Contact:** Michael Wood. Contest every 4 years; next contest is November 2012 for 2013-2014 season. Estab. 1979. Purpose of the award: "to honor the late Anna Zornio, an alumna of The University of New Hampshire, for dedication to and inspiration of playwriting for young people, K-12th grade. Open to playwrights who are residents of the U.S. and Canada. Plays or musicals should run about 45 minutes." Unpublished submissions only. Submissions made by the author. Deadline for entries: March 2, 2012. No entry fee. Awards $500 plus guaranteed production. Judging by faculty committee. Acquires rights to campus production. For entry form and more information visit unh.edu/theatre-dance/zornio. **Contact:** Michael Wood. "Offered every 4 years for unpublished well-written plays or musicals appropriate for young audiences with a maximum length of 60 minutes. May submit more than 1 play, but not more than 3. All plays will be performed by adult actors and must be appropriate for a children's audience within the K-12 grades. Guidelines and entry forms available as downloads on the website. Open to all playwrights in US and Canada. All ages are invited to participate." Deadline: March 2, 2012. Prize: Up to $500. The play is also produced and underwritten as part of the 2013-2014 season by the UNH Department of Theatre and Dance. Winner will be notified on or after Dec. 15, 2012.

ARTS COUNCILS & FELLOWSHIPS

☉ ADVANCED ARTIST AWARD

Government of Yukon, Box 2703, (L-3), Whitehorse YT Y1A 2C6 Canada. (867)667-8789. Fax: (867)393-6456. E-mail: artsfund@gov.yk.ca. Website: tc.gov.yk.ca/arts.html. Grants to senior artists toward projects that contribute to their artistic development. Open to all disciplines. Open only to Yukon artists. Deadline: April 1 and October 1. Prize: Level A artists: up to $5,000; Level B artists: up to $2,500. peer assessment (made up of senior Yukon artists representing the various disciplines seen in applicants for that round).

AKC GAZETTE ANNUAL FICTION CONTEST

260 Madison Ave., New York NY 10016. (212)696-8333. The *Gazette* sponsors an annual fiction contest for short short stories on some subject relating to purebred or mixed breed dogs. Fiction for our maga-

zine needs a slant toward the serious fancier with real insight into the human/dog bond. Deadline: Begins April 15. until January 31 (postmark).$500, $250 and $100 for top 3 entries. Top entry published in AKC magazines. Guidelines online or for SASE. Annual contest for short stories under 2,000 words. Contest requirements available for SASE or online. Send entries to AKC Publications Fiction Contest, The American Kennel Club, 260 Madison Avenue, New York, NY 10016. The *Gazette* sponsors an annual fiction contest for short short stories on some subject relating to purebred or mixed breed dogs. Fiction for our magazine needs a slant toward the serious fancier with real insight into the human/dog bond and breed-specific purebred behavior. Deadline: Begins April 15. until January 31 (postmark). Prize: $500, $250 and $100 for top 3 entries. Top entry published in AKC magazines. Panel.

ALABAMA STATE COUNCIL ON THE ARTS FELLOWSHIP-LITERATURE

Alabama State Council on the Arts, 201 Monroe St., Montgomery AL 36130-1800. (334)242-4076, ext. 224. Fax: (334)240-3269. E-mail: randy.shoults@arts.alabama.gov. Website: arts.alabama.gov. **Contact:** Randy Shoults. "Literature fellowship offered every year (for previously published or unpublished work) to set aside time to create and improve skills. Two-year Alabama residency required. Guidelines available." Deadline: March 1. Prize: $10,000 or $5,000

ARROWHEAD REGIONAL ARTS COUNCIL INDIVIDUAL ARTIST SUPPORT GRANT

Arrowhead Regional Arts Council, 1301 Rice Lake Rd., Suite 120, Duluth MN 55811. (218)722-0952 or (800)569-8134. E-mail: info@aracouncil.org. Website: aracouncil.org. Applicants must live in the 7-county region of Northeastern Minnesota. Award to provide financial support to regional artists wishing to take advantage of impending, concrete opportunities that will advance their work or careers. Deadline: August, November, March. Prize: Up to $3,000. ARAC Board.

DELAWARE DIVISION OF THE ARTS

820 N. French St., Wilmington DE 19801. (302)577-8278. Fax: (302)577-6561. E-mail: kristin.pleasanton@state.de.us. Website: artsdel.org. Award "to help further careers of emerging and established professional artists." For Delaware residents only. Prize:

$10,000 for masters; $6,000 for established professionals; $3,000 for emerging professionals. Judged by out-of-state, nationally recognized professionals in each artistic discipline. No entry fee. Guidelines available after May 1 on website. Accepts inquiries by e-mail, phone. Expects to receive 25 fiction entries. Deadline: August 1. Open to any Delaware writer. Results announced in December. Winners notified by mail. Results available on website. "Follow all instructions and choose your best work sample." Award "to help further careers of emerging and established professional artists." For Delaware residents only. Prize: $10,000 for masters; $6,000 for established professionals; $3,000 for emerging professionals. Judged by out-of-state, nationally recognized professionals in each artistic discipline. No entry fee. Guidelines available after May 1 on website. Accepts inquiries by e-mail, phone. Expects to receive 25 fiction entries. Deadline: August 1. Open to any Delaware writer. Results announced in December. Winners notified by mail. Results available on website. "Follow all instructions and choose your best work sample." **Contact:** Kristin Pleasanton, coordinator. "Award to help further careers of emerging and established professional artists. For Delaware residents only." Deadline: August 1. Prize: $10,000 for masters; $6,000 for established professionals; $3,000 for emerging professionals. out-of-state, nationally recognized professionals in each artistic discipline.

DOBIE PAISANO PROJECT

The Graduate School, The Univ. of Texas at Austin, 1 University Ave., Mail Stop G0400, Austin TX 78712. Fax: (512)471-7620. E-mail: adameve@mail.utexas.edu. Website: utexas.edu/ogs/Paisano. **Contact:** Dr. Michael Adams. "The annual Dobie-Paisano Fellowships provide solitude, isolation, and an extended period of time to live and work at J. Frank Dobie's 258 acre ranch outside of Austin, Texas. At the time of the application, the applicant must: be a native Texan; have lived in Texas at some time for at least 3 years; or have published writing that has a Texas subject. Criteria for making the awards include quality of work, character of proposed project, and suitability of the applicant for ranch life at Paisano, the late J. Frank Dobie's ranch near Austin, TX. Applicants must submit examples of their work in triplicate. Guidelines for SASE or online." Deadline is January 15, 2012 for fellowships in 2012-2013. Winners are announced in early May. Prize: The Ralph A. Johnston memorial Fellowship is for a period of 4 months with a stipend of $5,000 per month. It is aimed at writers who have already demonstrated some publishing and critical success. The Jesse H. Jones Writing Fellowship is for a period of approximately 6 months with a stipend of $3,000 per month. It is aimed at, but not limited to, writers who are early in their careers.

DOCTORAL DISSERTATION FELLOWSHIPS IN JEWISH STUDIES

Foundation for Jewish Culture, 330 7th Ave., 21st Floor, New York NY 10001. (212)629-0500, ext. 215. Fax: (212)629-0508. E-mail: grants@jewishculture. org. Website: jewishculture.org. **Contact:** Paul Zakrzewski. Open annually to students who have completed their course work and need funding for research in order to finish their dissertation thesis or a PhD in a Jewish field of study. Deadline: TBA. Prize: $8,000-10,000 grant

GAP (GRANTS FOR ARTIST PROJECTS) PROGRAM

Artist Trust, 1835 12th Ave., Seattle WA 98122. (206)467-8734 ext. 11. Fax: (206)467-9633. E-mail: miguel@artisttrust.org. Website: artisttrust.org. **Contact:** Director of Programs. The GAP grant is awarded annually to 60 artists of all disciplines including writers. The award is meant to help finance a specific project, which can be in very early stages or near completion. Full-time students are not eligible. Open to Washington state residents only. Deadline: May 10. Prize: Up to $1,500 for artist-generated projects.

JENNY MCKEAN MOORE VISITING WRITER

English Dept. George Washington Univ., Rome Hall, 801 22nd St. NW, Suite 760, Washington DC 20052. (202)994-6180. Fax: (202)994-7915. E-mail: tvmallon@gwu.edu. Website: columbian.gwu.edu/ departmentsprograms/english/creativewriting/activitiesevents. Offers fellowship for a visiting lecturer in creative writing, currently about $55,000 for 2 semesters. Stipend varies slightly from year to year, depending on endowment payout. Teaching duties involve 2 workshops per semester—one for undergraduate students, the other free to the community. Apply with résumé and writing sample of 25 pages or less. Books may be submitted but will not be returned without SASE. Awarded to writers in different genres each year, typically alternating between poets and fiction writers. For the 2012-13 academic year we will be looking for a poet. (Check website for specific genre each year.) Deadline: November 11. **Contact:** Thomas Mallon, Director of Creative Writing. "The position is filled annually, bringing a visiting writer to The George Washington University. During each semester the Writer teaches one creative-writing course at the university as well as a community workshop. Each year we seek someone specializing in a different genre—fiction, poetry, creative nonfiction. For the 2012-13 academic year we will be looking for a poet. Guidelines for application will be announced in *The Writer's Chronicle*. Annual stipend between $50,000 and $60,000, plus reduced-rent townhouse on campus (not guaranteed)." Application Deadline: November 1. Prize: Annual stipend varies, depending on endowment performance; most recently, stipend was $58,000, plus reduced-rent townhouse (not guaranteed).

LITERARY GIFT OF FREEDOM

A Room of Her Own Foundation, P.O. Box 778, Placitas NM 87043. E-mail: info@aroomofherownfoundation.org. Website: aroomofherownfoundation.org. **Contact:** Tracey Cravens-Gras, associate director. Award offered every other year to provide very practical help—both materially and in professional guidance and moral support with mentors and advisory council—to women who need assistance in making their creative contribution to the world. Guidelines, deadlines and application available at aroomofherownfoundation.org. Open to any female resident of the US. Prize: Award is $50,000 over 2 years in support of the production of a particular creative project.

MASSACHUSETTS CULTURAL COUNCIL ARTIST FELLOWSHIP PROGRAM

Massachusetts Cultural Council, 10 St. James Ave., 3rd Floor, Boston MA 02116-3803. (617)727-3668. Fax: (617)727-0044. E-mail: mcc@art.state.ma.us. Website: massculturalcouncil.org; artsake.massculturalcouncil.org. **Contact:** Dan Blask, prog. coordinator. Awards in poetry, fiction/creative nonfiction, and dramatic writing (among other discipline categories) are given in recognition of exceptional original work (check website for award amount). Criteria: Artistic excellence and creative ability, based on work submitted for review. Must be 18 years or older and a legal residents of Massachusetts for the last 2 years and at time of award. This excludes students in directly-related degree programs and grant recipients within the last 3 years. Judged by independent peer panels composed of artists and arts professionals.

NEBRASKA ARTS COUNCIL INDIVIDUAL ARTISTS FELLOWSHIPS

Nebraska Arts Council, 1004 Farnam St., Plaza Level, Omaha NE 68102. (402)595-2122. Fax: (402)595-2334. E-mail: jayne.hutton@nebraska.gov. Website: nebraskaartscouncil.org. **Contact:** J.D. Hutton. Offered every 3 years (literature alternates with other disciplines) to recognize exemplary achievements by originating artists in their fields of endeavor and support the contributions made by Nebraska artists to the quality of life in this state. Generally, distinguished achievement awards are $5,000 and merit awards are $1,000-2,000. Funds available are announced in September prior to the deadline. Must be a resident of Nebraska for at least 2 years prior to submission date; 18 years of age; and not enrolled in an undergraduate, graduate, or certificate-granting program in English, creative writing, literature, or related field. Deadline: November 15.

NORTH CAROLINA ARTS COUNCIL REGIONAL ARTIST PROJECT GRANTS

North Carolina Arts Council, Dept. of Cultural Resources, MSC #4632, Raleigh NC 27699-4634. (919)807-6500. Fax: (919)807-6532. E-mail: david. potorti@ncdcr.gov. Website: ncarts.org. Open to any writer living in North Carolina. See website for contact information for the local arts councils that distribute these grants. $500-3,000 awarded to writers to pursue projects that further their artistic development. **Contact:** David Potorti, Literature Director. Deadline: Generally late summer/early fall. Prize: $500-3,000 awarded to writers to pursue projects that further their artistic development. Open to any writer living in North Carolina. See website for contact information for the local arts councils that distribute these grants.

NORTH CAROLINA WRITERS' FELLOWSHIPS

North Carolina Arts Council, Dept. of Cultural Resources, Raleigh NC 27699-4632. (919)807-6500. Fax: (919)807-6532. E-mail: davidpotorti@ncdcr.gov. Website: ncarts.org. North Carolina Arts Council, Dept. of

Cultural Resources, Raleigh NC 27699-4632. (919)807-6500. Fax: (919)807-6532. E-mail: david.potorti@ncdcr.gov. Website: ncarts.org. Acquisitions: David Potorti, literature director and arts editor. Offered every even year to support writers of fiction, poetry, literary nonfiction, literary translation, and spoken word. See website for guidelines and other eligibility requirements. Writers must be current residents of North Carolina for at least 1 year, must remain in residence in North Carolina during the grant year, and may not pursue academic or professional degrees while receiving grant. Fellowships offered to support writers in the development and creation of their work. Deadline: Next offered in fall, 2012, see website for details. $10,000 grant. Reviewed by a panel of literature professionals (writers and editors). North Carolina Arts Council, Dept. of Cultural Resources, Raleigh NC 27699-4632. (919)807-6500. Fax: (919)807-6532. E-mail: david.potorti@ncdcr.gov. Website: ncarts. org. Acquisitions: David Potorti, literature director and arts editor. Offered every even year to support writers of fiction, poetry, literary nonfiction, literary translation, and spoken word. See website for guidelines and other eligibility requirements. Writers must be current residents of North Carolina for at least 1 year, must remain in residence in North Carolina during the grant year, and may not pursue academic or professional degrees while receiving grant. Fellowships offered to support writers in the development and creation of their work. Deadline: Next offered in fall, 2012, see website for details. $10,000 grant. Reviewed by a panel of literature professionals (writers and editors). **Contact:** David Potorti, literature director. North Carolina Arts Council, Dept. of Cultural Resources, Raleigh NC 27699-4632. (919)807-6500. Fax: (919)807-6532. E-mail: david.potorti@ncdcr.gov. Website: ncarts.org. Acquisitions: David Potorti, literature director and arts editor. Offered every even year to support writers of fiction, poetry, literary nonfiction, literary translation, and spoken word. See website for guidelines and other eligibility requirements. Writers must be current residents of North Carolina for at least 1 year, must remain in residence in North Carolina during the grant year, and may not pursue academic or professional degrees while receiving grant. Fellowships offered to support writers in the development and creation of their work. Deadline: Next offered in fall, 2012, see website for details. $10,000 grant. Reviewed by a panel of literature professionals (writers and editors). Contest offered to support writers in the development and creation of their work. Prize: $10,000 grant. Reviewed by a panel of literature professionals (writers and editors).

RHODE ISLAND ARTIST FELLOWSHIPS AND INDIVIDUAL PROJECT GRANTS

Rhode Island State Council on the Arts, One Capitol Hill, 3rd Floor, Providence RI 02908. (401)222-3880. Fax: (401)222-3018. E-mail: Cristina.DiChiera@arts.ri.gov. Website: arts.ri.gov. **Contact:** Cristina DiChiera, director of individual artist programs. Annual fellowship competition is based upon panel review of mss for poetry, fiction, and playwriting/screenwriting. Project grants provide funds for community-based arts projects. Rhode Island artists may apply without a nonprofit sponsor. Applicants for all RSCA grant and award programs must be at least 18 years and not currently enrolled in an arts-related degree program. Online application and guidelines can be found at arts.ri.gov/grants/guidelines/. Deadline: April 1 and October 1. Prize: Fellowship awards: $5,000 and $1,000. Grants range from $500-10,000 with an average of around $3,000.

SCREENPLAY FESTIVAL

11693 San Vicente Blvd., Ste. 806, Los Angeles CA 90049. (424)248-9221. Fax: (866)770-2994. E-mail: info@screenplayfestival.com. Website: screenplayfestival.com. This festival is an opportunity to give all scriptwriters a chance to be noticed and have their work read by the power players. Deadline: Sept. 1; early deadline is July 1. Prize: In all categories, there is a $1,000 prize.

WALLACE STEGNER FELLOWSHIPS

Creative Writing Program, Stanford University, Dept. of English, Stanford CA 94305-2087. (650)723-0011 or (650)725-1208. Fax: (650)723-3679. E-mail: cablaza@stanford.edu. Website: creativewriting.stanford.edu. **Contact:** Christina Ablaza, program assistant. "A 2-year, non-degree granting program at Stanford offered annually for emerging writers to attend the Stegner workshop to practice and perfect their craft under the guidance of the creative writing faculty. Guidelines available online." Deadline: December 1 (postmarked). Prize: Living stipend (currently $26,000/year) and required workshop tuition of $7,479/year and health insurance

VERMONT ARTS COUNCIL

136 State St., Montpelier VT 05633-6001. (802)828-5425. Fax: (802)828-3363. E-mail: info@vermontartscouncil.org. Website: vermontartscouncil.org. **Contact:** Sonia Rae. Annual grants awarded once per year for specific projects. Creation Grants (awards of $3,000) for "artists working in any medium including writers, visual artists and performing artists. Contact Sonia Rae at (802)828-5425 or by e-mail at srae@vermontartscouncil.org. For Community Arts Grants and Arts Learning Grants of up to $5,000, for not-for-profit organizations (including writing programs and not-for-profit presses), contact Stacy Raphael (802)828-3778 or by e-mail at sraphael@vermontartscouncil.org. Rolling grants are available in the following categories: Artist Development Grants of up to $1,000 providing professional development funds for individual artists and Technical Assistance Grants of up to $1,000 providing grants for organizational development to non-profit arts organizations. Contact Sonia Rae at (802)828-5425 or by e-mail at srae@vermontartscouncil.org. Open to Vermont residents only. Prize: $250-5,000

WISCONSIN INSTITUTE FOR CREATIVE WRITING FELLOWSHIP

6195B H.C. White Hall, 600 N. Park St., Madison WI 53706. E-mail: rfkuka@wisc.edu. Website: wisc.edu/english/cw. **Contact:** Ron Kuka, program coordinator. Fellowship provides time, space and an intellectual community for writers working on first books. Receives approximately 300 applicants a year for each genre. Prize: $27,000 for a 9-month appointment. Judged by English Department faculty and current fellows. **Entry fee:** $45, payable to the Department of English. **Deadline: February.** "Candidates must not yet have published, or had accepted for publication, a book by application deadline." Open to any writer with either an M.F.A. or Ph.D. in creative writing. Please enclose a SASE for notification of results. Results announced by May 1. "Send your best work. Stories seem to have a small advantage over novel excerpts." Fellowship provides time, space and an intellectual community for writers working on first books. Receives approximately 300 applicants a year for each genre. Prize: $27,000 for a 9-month appointment. Judged by English Department faculty and current fellows. **Entry fee:** $45, payable to the Department of English. Applicants should submit up to 10 pages of poetry and a résumé or vita directly to the program during February. An applicant's name must not appear on the writing sample (which must be in ms form) but rather on a separate sheet along with address, social security number, phone number, e-mail address and title(s) of submission(s). Candidates should also supply the names and phone numbers of two references. Accepts inquiries by e-mail and phone. **Deadline: February**. "Candidates must not yet have published, or had accepted for publication, a book by application deadline." Open to any writer with either an M.F.A. or Ph.D. in creative writing. Please enclose a SASE for notification of results. Results announced by May 1. "Send your best work." Fellowship provides time, space and an intellectual community for writers working on first books. Receives approximately 300 applicants a year for each genre. Judged by English Department faculty and current fellows. "Candidates must not yet have published, or had accepted for publication, a book by application deadline." Open to any writer with either an M.F.A. or Ph.D. in creative writing. Please enclose a SASE for notification of results. Results announced by May 1. "Send your best work. Stories seem to have a small advantage over novel excerpts." Applicants should submit up to 10 pages of poetry or one story of up to 30 pages and a résumé or vita directly to the program during the month of February. An applicant's name must not appear on the writing sample (which must be in ms form) but rather on a separate sheet along with address, social security number, phone number, e-mail address and title(s) of submission(s). Candidates should also supply the names and phone numbers of two references. Accepts inquiries by e-mail and phone. Deadline: Feb. Prize: $27,000 for a 9-month appointment

FICTION

AMERICAN SCANDINAVIAN FOUNDATION TRANSLATION PRIZE

58 Park Ave., New York NY 10016. E-mail: info@amscan.org. Website: amscan.org. American Scandinavian Foundation, 58 Park Ave., New York NY 10016. (212) 879-9779. Fax: (212) 686-2115. E-mail: info@amscan.org. Website: amscan.org. **Contact:** Valerie Hymas. Award to recognize excellence in fiction, poetry and drama translations of Scandinavian writers born after 1800. Prize: $2,000 grand prize; $1,000 prize. No entry fee. Cover letter should include name,

address, phone, e-mail and title. Deadline: June 1. Entries must be unpublished. Length: no more than 50 pages for drama, fiction; no more than 35 pages for poetry. Open to any writer. Guidelines available in January for SASE, by fax, phone, e-mail or on website. American Scandinavian Foundation, 58 Park Ave., New York NY 10016. (212) 879-9779. Fax: (212) 686-2115. E-mail: info@amscan.org. Website: amscan.org. Award to recognize excellence in fiction, poetry and drama translations of Scandinavian writers born after 1800. Prize: $2,000 grand prize; $1,000 prize. No entry fee. Cover letter should include name, address, phone, e-mail and title. Deadline: June 1. Entries must be unpublished. Length: no more than 50 pages for drama, fiction; no more than 35 pages for poetry. Open to any writer. Guidelines available in January for SASE, by fax, phone, e-mail or on website. Accepts inquiries by fax, e-mail, phone. Results announced in November. Winners notified by mail. Results available for SASE or by fax, e-mail, website. **Contact:** Valerie Hymas. American Scandinavian Foundation, 58 Park Ave., New York NY 10016. (212) 879-9779. Fax: (212) 686-2115. E-mail: info@amscan.org. Website: amscan.org. Cover letter should include name, address, phone, e-mail and title. Entries must be unpublished. Length: no more than 50 pages for drama, fiction; no more than 35 pages for poetry. Open to any writer. Accepts inquiries by fax, e-mail, phone. Results announced in November. Winners notified by mail. Results available for SASE or by fax, e-mail, website. Guidelines available in January for SASE, by fax, phone, e-mail or on website. Award to recognize excellence in fiction, poetry and drama translations of Scandinavian writers born after 1800. Deadline: June 1. Prize: $2,000 grand prize; $1,000 prize.

AMERICAN SHORT STORY CONTEST

American Short Fiction, P.O. Box 301209, Austin TX 78703. (512)538-1305. Fax: (512)538-1306. Website: americanshortfiction.org. P.O. Box 301209, Austin TX 78703. (512)538-1305. Fax: (512)538-1306. Website: americanshortfiction.org. Acquisitions: Jill Meyers, editor. "Contest offered annually to reward and recognize short stories under 1,000 words." Submissions accepted only via the online submission manager on website. Please see website for full guidelines. Feb. 15-May 1. 1st Place: $500 and publication; 2nd Place: $250 and publication. Costs $15 for up to three 1,000 word entries. **Contact:** Jill Meyers, editor. "Contest offered annually to reward and recognize short stories under 1,000 words." Submissions accepted only via the online submission manager on website. Please see website for full guidelines. Feb. 15-May 1. Prize: 1st Place: $500 & publication; 2nd Place: $250 & publication.

ANNUAL GIVAL PRESS NOVEL AWARD

Gival Press, LLC, P.O. Box 3812, Arlington VA 22203. (703)351-0079. E-mail: givalpress@yahoo.com. Website: givalpress.com. **Contact:** Robert L. Giron. "Offered annually for a previously unpublished original novel (not a translation). It must be in English with at least 30,000-100,000 words of literary quality. Guidelines online, via e-mail, or by mail with SASE." Deadline: May 30. Prize: $3,000, plus publication of book with a standard contract.

ANNUAL GIVAL PRESS SHORT STORY AWARD

Gival Press, LLC, P.O. Box 3812, Arlington VA 22203. (703)351-0079. E-mail: givalpress@yahoo.com. Website: givalpress.com. **Contact:** Robert L. Giron. "Offered annually for a previously unpublished original short story (not a translation). It must be in English with at least 5,000-15,000 words of literary quality. Guidelines by mail with SASE, by e-mail, or online." To award the best literary short story submitted. Deadline: August 8. Prize: $1,000, plus publication on website. The editor narrows entries to the top ten; previous winner chooses the top 5 and selects winner—all done anonymously.

BEST LESBIAN EROTICA

BLE 2010, 31-64 21st St., #319, Long Island City NY 11106. E-mail: kwarnockble@gmail.com. Categories: Novel excerpts, short stories, other prose; poetry will be considered but is not encouraged. No entry fee. Include cover page with author's name, title of submission(s), address, phone, fax, e-mail. All submissions must be typed and double-spaced. You may submit double-sided copies. Length: 5,000 words. You may submit 2 different pieces of work. Submit 2 hard copies of each submission. Will only accept e-mail copies if the following conditions apply: You live outside of North America or Europe, the cost of postage would be prohibitive from your home country, the post office system in your country is dreadful (U.S. does not count); the content of your submission may be illegal to send via postal mail in your home

country. Accepts both previously published and unpublished material, but does not accept simultaneous submissions to another annual erotica anthology. Open to any writer. All submissions must include SASE or an e-mail address for response. If no e-mail address, then please include SASP. No mss will be returned. **Contact:** Kathleen Warnock, series editor. Categories: Novel excerpts, short stories, other prose. No entry fee. Include cover page with author's name/pen name if using one, title of submission(s), address, phone, e-mail. All submissions must be typed and double-spaced. You may submit double-sided copies. Length: 5,000 words. You may submit 2 different pieces of work. Submit 2 hard copies of each submission. Will only accept e-mail copies if the following conditions apply: You live outside of North America or Europe, the cost of postage would be prohibitive from your home country, the post office system in your country is dreadful (U.S. does not count); the content of your submission may be illegal to send via postal mail in your home country. Accepts both previously published and unpublished material, but does not accept simultaneous submissions to another annual erotica anthology. Open to any writer. All submissions must include SASE or an e-mail address for response. If no e-mail address, then please include SASP. No mss will be returned. Acquisitions: Kathleen Warnock, series editor. Payment $100 for each published story.

THE CAINE PRIZE FOR AFRICAN WRITING

The Menier Gallery, Menier Chocolate Factory, 51 Southwark St., London SE1 1RU United Kingdom. (44)(207)378-6234. Fax: (44)(207)378-6235. E-mail: info@caineprize.com. Website: caineprize.com. **Contact:** Nick Elam. "Annual award for a short story (3,000-10,000 words) in English by an African writer. An 'African writer' is normally taken to mean someone who was born in Africa; who is a national of an African country; or whose parents are African, and whose work has reflected African sensibilities. Entries must have appeared for the first time in the 5 years prior to the closing date for submissions, which is January 31 each year. Publishers should submit 6 copies of the published original with a brief cover note (no pro forma application). Guidelines for SASE or online." Deadline: January 31. Prize: $15,000 (£10,000). a panel of judges appointed each year.

☺ CANADIAN AUTHORS ASSOCIATION MOSAID TECHNOLOGIES INC. AWARD FOR FICTION

P.O. Box 581, Stn. Main, Orillia ON L3V 1V5 Canada. (705)653-0323 or (866)216-6222. E-mail: admin@canauthors.org. Website: canauthors.org. **Contact:** Anita Purcell. Offered annually for a full-length novel by a Canadian citizen or permanent immigrant. Entry form required. Obtain entry form from contact name or download from website. Deadline: December 15. Prize: $2,000 and a silver medal

THE ALEXANDER PATTERSON CAPPON FICTION AWARD

New Letters, University of Missouri-Kansas City, 5101 Rockhill Rd., Kansas City MO 64110. (816)235-1168. Fax: (816)235-2611. E-mail: newletters@umkc.edu. Website: newletters.org. **Contact:** Ashley Kaine. Offered annually for unpublished work to discover and reward new and upcoming writers. Buys first North American serial rights. Open to any writer. Deadline: May 18. Prize: 1st Place: $1,500 and publication in a volume of *New Letters*; runner-up will receive a complimentary copy of a recent book of poetry or fiction courtesy of BkMk Press. All entries will be given consideration for publication in future issues of *New Letters*.

KAY CATTARULLA AWARD FOR BEST SHORT STORY

Texas Institute of Letters, P.O. Box 609, Round Rock TX 78680. (512) 238-1871. E-mail: tilsecretary@yahoo.com. Website: texasinstituteofletters.org/. Offered annually for work published January 1-December 31 of previous year to recognize the best short story. The story submitted must have appeared in print for the first time to be eligible. Writers must have been born in Texas, must have lived in Texas for at least 2 consecutive years, or the subject matter of the work must be associated with Texas. See website for guidelines. Deadline: Jan. 1. Prize: $1,000. **Contact:** W.K. (Kip) Stratton, acquisitions. Offered annually for work published January 1-December 31 of previous year to recognize the best short story. The story submitted must have appeared in print for the first time to be eligible. Writers must have been born in Texas, must have lived in Texas for at least 2 consecutive years, or the subject matter of the work must be associated with Texas. See website for guidelines. Deadline: January 1. Prize: $750.

CHIZINE SHORT STORY CONTEST

Dorchester Publications, 200 Madison Ave, Suite 2000, New York NY 10016. Website: chizine.com. Website: chizine.com. **Contact:** Brett Alexander Savory, editor-in-chief. Held annually "to find the top three dark fiction stories." Competition/award for short stories. Prize: 7¢/word, up to 4,000 words. Judged by a revolving panel of writers and editors of dark fiction selected by the Editor-in-Chief of Chizine. No entry fee. Guidelines available in May. Accepts inquiries by e-mail. **Submissions accepted June 1st through 30th.** Entries should be unpublished. Contest open to anyone. Cover letter and ms should include name, address, e-mail, word count, short story title. Writers may submit own work. Results announced end of July. Winners and honorable mentions notified by e-mail. Results made available to entrants on website. **Contact:** Brett Alexander Savory, Editor-in-Chief. Held annually "to find the top three dark fiction stories." Competition/award for short stories. Prize: 7¢/word, up to 4,000 words. Judged by a revolving panel of writers and editors of dark fiction selected by the Editor-in-Chief of Chizine. No entry fee. Guidelines available in May. Accepts inquiries by e-mail. **Submissions accepted June 1st through 30th.** Entries should be unpublished. Contest open to anyone. Cover letter and ms should include name, address, e-mail, word count, short story title. Writers may submit own work. Results announced end of July. Winners and honorable mentions notified by e-mail. Results made available to entrants on website.

✚ COPTALES CONTEST

Sponsored by Oak Tree Press, 140 E. Palmer St., Taylorville IL 62568. E-mail: oaktreepub@aol.com. Website: oaktreebooks.com. "The goal of the CopTales Contest is to discover and publish new authors, or authors shifting to a new genre. This annual contest is open to writers who have not published in the crime fiction, nonfiction, and true crime genre in the past three years, as well as completely unpublished authors. Deadline: July 31. The prize consists of a Publishing Agreement, and launch of the title. Winners or runners up who are offered publishing agreements are asked to transfer rights. Publishing industry professionals prescreen the entries; publisher makes final selection." $25 entry fee. **Contact:** Billie Johnson, award director. Guidelines and entry forms are available for SASE. The goal of the CopTales Contest is to discover and publish new authors, or authors shifting to a new genre. This annual contest is open to writers who have not published in the mystery genre in the past three years, as well as completely unpublished authors. Deadline: July 31. Prize: The prize consists of a Publishing Agreement, and launch of the title. Winners or runners up who are offered publishing agreements are asked to transfer rights. Publishing industry professionals prescreen the entries; publisher makes final selection.

CRAZYHORSE FICTION PRIZE

College of Charleston, Dept. of English, 66 George St., Charleston SC 29424. (843)953-7740. Fax: (843)953-7740. E-mail: crazyhorse@cofc.edu. Website: crazyhorsejournal.org. Contact: Editors. Phone/Fax: (843)953-7740. E-mail: crazyhorse@cofc.edu. Website: crazyhorsejournal.org. The journal's mission is to publish the entire spectrum of today's fiction, essays, and poetry—from the mainstream to the avant-garde, from the established to the undiscovered writer. The editors are especially interested in original writing that engages in the work of honest communication. *Crazyhorse* publishes writing of fine quality regardless of style, predilection, subject. Contest open to any writer. Entry fee: $16 (covers 1-yr subscription to *Crazyhorse*; make checks payable to Crazyhorse). To enter, please send up to 25 pages of prose. **Deadline: January 15th of each year**; see website. Prize: $2,000 and publication in *Crazyhorse*. Judged by anonymous writer whose identity is disclosed when the winners are announced in April. **Contact:** Editors. The journal's mission is to publish the entire spectrum of today's fiction, essays, and poetry—from the mainstream to the avant-garde, from the established to the undiscovered writer. The editors are especially interested in original writing that engages in the work of honest communication. *Crazyhorse* publishes writing of fine quality regardless of style, predilection, subject. Contest open to any writer. To enter, please send up to 25 pages of prose. Send SASE or see website. **Deadline: January 15th of each year**; see website. Prize: $2,000 and publication in *Crazyhorse*. Judged by anonymous writer whose identity is disclosed when the winners are announced in April.

DARK OAK MYSTERY CONTEST

Oak Tree Press, 140 E. Palmer St., Taylorville IL 62568. (217)824-6500. E-mail: oaktreepub@aol.com. Website: oaktreebooks.com. Offered annually for an un-published mystery manuscript (up to 85,000 words) of any sort from police procedurals to amateur sleuth novels. Acquires first North American, audio and film rights to winning entry. Open to authors not published in the past 3 years. Entry fee: $35/mss. E-mail: oaktreepub@aol.com. **Contact:** Editor (prefers e-mail contact). Offered annually for an unpublished mystery manuscript (up to 85,000 words) of any sort from police procedurals to amateur sleuth novels. Acquires first North American, audio and film rights to winning entry. Open to authors not published in the past 3 years. Deadline: July 31. Prize: Publishing Agreement, and launch of the title.

⊕ THE FAR HORIZONS AWARD FOR SHORT FICTION

The Malahat Review, University of Victoria, P.O. Box 1700, Stn CSC, Victoria BC V8W 2Y2 Canada. (250)721-8524. Fax: (250)472-5051. E-mail: malahat@uvic.ca. Website: malahatreview.ca. **Contact:** John Barton, Editor. Open to "emerging short fiction writers from Canada, the United States, and elsewhere" who have not yet published their fiction in a full-length book (48 pages or more). Submissions must be unpublished. No simultaneous submissions. Submit one piece of short fiction, 3,500 words maximum; no restrictions on subject matter or aesthetic approach. Include separate page with author's name, address, e-mail, and title; no identifying information on mss. pages. No e-mail submissions. Do not include SASE for results; mss will not be returned. Guidelines available on website. Deadline: May 1 of odd-numbered years. Prize: Offers $1,000 CAD, publication in Fall issue of *The Malahat Review* (see separate listing in Magazines/Journals). Announced in Fall on website, Facebook page, and in quarterly e-newsletter, *Malahat Lite*.

FIRSTWRITER.COM INTERNATIONAL SHORT STORY CONTEST

firstwriter.com, United Kingdom. Website: firstwriter.com. **Contact:** J. Paul Dyson, managing editor. "Accepts short stories up to 3,000 words on any subject and in any style." Deadline: April 1. Prize: total about $300. Ten special commendations will also be awarded and all the winners will be published in *firstwriter* magazine and receive a $36 subscription voucher, allowing an annual subscription to be taken out for free All submissions are automatically considered for publication in *firstwriter* magazine and may be published there online. *firstwriter* magazine editors.

🌀 FISH UNPUBLISHED NOVEL AWARD

Fish Publishing, Durrus, Bantry, Co. Cork Ireland. E-mail: info@fishpublishing.com. Website: fishpublishing.com. **Contact:** Clem Cairns. A competition for the best unpublished novel entered. Deadline: September 30. Prize: 1st Prize: Publication of winning novel and cash. "This is not an annual award, but is run every so often."

GLIMMER TRAIN'S FAMILY MATTERS CONTEST

Glimmer Train Press, Inc., 1211 NW Glisan St., Suite 207, Portland OR 97209. Fax: (503)221-0837. E-mail: eds@glimmertrain.org. Website: glimmertrain.org. **Contact:** Linda Swanson-Davies. Offered for unpublished stories about family. Word count should not exceed 12,000. All shorter lengths welcome. See complete writing guidelines and submit online at website. Open in the months of April and October. Winners will be called two months after the close of each competition, and results announced in their respective bulletins, on their website, and in a number of additional print and online publications. Represented in recent editions of the Pushcart Prize, O. Henry, New Stories from the Midwest, and Best American Short Stories Anthologies. Prize: 1st Place: $1,200, publication in *Glimmer Train Stories*, and 20 copies of that issue; 2nd Place: $500; 3rd Place: $300.

GLIMMER TRAIN'S FICTION OPEN

Glimmer Train, Inc., Glimmer Train Press, Inc., 1211 NW Glisan St., Suite 207, Portland OR 97209. (503)221-0836. Fax: (503)221-0837. E-mail: eds@glimmertrain.org. Website: glimmertrain.org. Offered quarterly for unpublished stories on any theme. Word count should not exceed 20,000. Prize: 1st place: $2,000, publication in Glimmer Train Stories, and 20 copies of that issue; 1st/2nd runners-up: $1,000/$600 respectively, and possible publication in Glimmer Train Stories. Entry fee: $18/story. **Contest open during the months of March, June, September and December.** Represented in recent editions of the Pushcart Prize, O. Henry, New Stories From The South, New Stories From The Midwest, and Best American Short Stories Anthologies. **Contact:** Linda Swanson-Davies. "Open to all writers. No theme restrictions. Word count range: 2000-20,000. See complete writ-

ing guidelines and submit online at website. Open all during the months of March, June, September and December. Winners will be called 2 months after the close of each competition and results will be announced in their respective bulletin month, on their website, and in a number of additional print and online publications." Prize: 1st Place $2,000, publication in *Glimmer Train Stories*, and 20 copies of that issue; 2nd Place $1,000 and consideration for publication; 3rd Place $600.

GLIMMER TRAIN'S SHORT-STORY AWARD FOR NEW WRITERS

Glimmer Train Press, Inc., 1211 NW Glisan St., Suite 207, Portland OR 97209. (503)221-0836. Fax: (503)221-0837. E-mail: eds@glimmertrain.org. Website: glimmertrain.org. Offered quarterly for any writer whose fiction hasn't appeared in a nationally-distributed publication with a circulation over 5,000. Word count should not exceed 12,000 words. Stories must be previously unpublished. **Entry fee**: $15/story. **Contest open in the months of February, May, August, and November**. Make your submissions online at glimmertrain.org. Prize: First place: receives $1,200, publication in Glimmer Train Stories, and 20 copies of that issue. First/second runners-up receive $500/$300, respectively, and possible publication in Glimmer Train Stories. Winners will be called and results announced two months after the close of each contest. "We are very open to the work of new writers. Of the 100 distinguished short stories listed in a recent edition of the Best American Short Stories, 10 first appeared in Glimmer Train Stories, more than in any other publication, including the New Yorker. 3 of those 10 were the author's first publication." **Contact:** Linda Swanson-Davies. "Offered for any writer whose fiction hasn't appeared in a nationally distributed print publication with a circulation over 5,000. Word count: should not exceed 12,000 words. All shorter lengths welcome. Open quarterly during the months of February, May, August, and November. See complete writing guidelines and submit online at website. Winners will be called 2 months after the close of each competition, and results will be announced in their respective bulletin month, on their website, and in a number of additional print and online publications." Prize: Winner receives $1,200, publication in *Glimmer Train Stories*, and 20 copies of that issue; 2nd Place: $500; 3rd Place: $300.

GLIMMER TRAIN'S VERY SHORT FICTION AWARD (JANUARY)

Glimmer Train Press, Inc., 1211 NW Glisan St., #207, Portland OR 97209. (503)221-0836. Fax: (503)221-0837. E-mail: eds@glimmertrain.org. Website: glimmertrain.org. eds@glimmertrain.org; glimmertrain.org; Contact: Linda Swanson-Davies. Award to encourage the art of the very short story. "We want to read your original, unpublished, very short story—word count not to exceed 3,000 words." Prize: $1,200 and publication in Glimmer Train Stories and 20 author's copies (1st place); First/Second runners-up: $500/$300 respectively and possible publication. Entry fee: $15/story. **Contest open in the months of January and July.** Open to all writers. Make your submissions online at glimmertrain.org. Winners will be called and results announced two months after the close of each contest. **Contact:** Linda Swanson-Davies. "Offered to encourage the art of the very short story. Word count: 3,000 maximum. Open January 1-31. See complete writing guidelines and submit online at website. Winners will be called and results will be announced in their April bulletin and in a number of additional print and online publications." Prize: Winner receives $1,200, publication in *Glimmer Train Stories* and 20 copies of that issue; 2nd Place: $500; 3rd Place: $300.

GLIMMER TRAIN'S VERY SHORT FICTION CONTEST (JULY)

Glimmer Train Press, Inc., 1211 NW Glisan St., 207, Portland OR 97209. (503)221-0836. Fax: (503)221-0837. E-mail: eds@glimmertrain.org. Website: glimmertrain.org. **Contact:** Linda Swanson-Davies. "Offered to encourage the art of the very short story. Word count: 3,000 maximum. Open July 1-31. See complete writing guidelines and submit online at website. Winners will be called and results will be announced in their October bulletin, on their website, and in a number of additional print and online publications." Prize: First Place: $1,200, publication in Glimmer Train Stories, and 20 copies of that issue; 2nd Place: $500; 3rd Place: $300.

☺ GOVERNOR GENERAL'S LITERARY AWARD FOR FICTION

Canada Council for the Arts, 350 Albert St., P.O. Box 1047, Ottawa ON K1P 5V8 Canada. (613)566-4414, ext. 5573. Fax: (613)566-4410. Website: canadacouncil.ca/prizes/ggla. Offered annually for the best English-language and the best French-language work of fiction by a Canadian. Publishers submit titles for consideration. Deadline depends on the book's publication date. Books in English: March 15, June 1 or August 7. Books in French: March 15 or July 15. Prize: Each laureate receives $25,000; non-winning finalists receive $1,000.

G. S. SHARAT CHANDRA PRIZE FOR SHORT FICTION

BkMk Press, University of Missouri-Kansas City, 5100 Rockhill Rd., Kansas City MO 64110-2499. (816)235-2558. Fax: (816)235-2611. E-mail: bkmk@umkc.edu. Website: umkc.edu/bkmk. "Offered annually for the best book-length ms collection (unpublished) of short fiction in English by a living author. Translations are not eligible. Initial judging is done by a network of published writers. Final judging is done by a writer of national reputation. Guidelines for SASE, by e-mail, or on website." $25 fee. Deadline: January 15 (postmarked). Prize: $1,000, plus book publication by BkMk Press. BkMk Press, Univ. of Missouri-Kansas City, 5100 Rockhill Rd., Kansas City MO 64110-2499. Phone: (816)235-2558. Fax: (816)235-2611. E-mail: bkmk@umkc.edu. Website: umkc.edu/bkmk. "Offered annually for the best book-length ms collection (unpublished) of short fiction in English by a living author. Translations are not eligible. Initial judging is done by a network of published writers. Final judging is done by a writer of national reputation. Guidelines for SASE, by e-mail, or on website." Deadline: January 15 (postmarked). Prize: $1,000, plus book publication by BkMk Press.

☺ LYNDALL HADOW/DONALD STUART SHORT STORY COMPETITION

Fellowship of Australian Writers (WA), P.O. Box 6180, Swanbourne WA 6910. (61)(8)9384-4771. Fax: (61)(8)9384-4854. E-mail: admin@fawwa.org.au. Website: fawwa.org.au. Annual contest for unpublished short stories (maximum 3,000 words). "We reserve the right to publish entries in a FAWWA publication or on its website." Guidelines online or for SASE. Deadline: June 1. Prize: 1st Place: $400; 2nd Place; $100; Highly Commended: $50.

L. RON HUBBARD'S WRITERS OF THE FUTURE CONTEST

P.O. Box 1630, Los Angeles CA 90078. (323)466-3310. E-mail: contests@authorservicesinc.com. Website:

writersofthefuture.com. **Contact:** Contest Administrator. "Offered for unpublished work to find, reward, and publicize new speculative fiction writers so they may more easily attain professional writing careers." Open to new and amateur writers who have not professionally published a novel or short novel, more than 1 novelette, or more than 3 short stories. Eligible entries are short stories or novelettes (under 17,000 words) of science fiction or fantasy. Guidelines for SASE, online, or via e-mail. No entry fee. Entrants retain all rights to their stories. Deadline: December 31, March 31, June 30, September 30. Prize: Awards quarterly 1st Place: $1,000; 2nd Place: $750; and 3rd Place: $500. Annual Grand Prize: $5,000. Judged by professional writers only.

INDIANA REVIEW FICTION CONTEST

BH 465/Indiana University, 1020 E. Kirkwood Ave., Bloomington IN 47405-7103. (812)855-3439. Fax: (812)855-4253. E-mail: inreview@indiana.edu. Website: indianareview.org. Contest for fiction in any style and on any subject. Prize: $1,000, publication in the Indiana Review and contributor's copies. Judged by guest judges. 2010 prize judged by Dan Chaon. Entry fee: $15 fee (includes a year's subscription). Deadline: Mid-October. Entries must be unpublished. Mss will not be returned. No previously published work, or works forthcoming elsewhere, are eligible. Simultaneous submissions accepted, but in the event of entrant withdrawal, contest fee will not be refunded. Length: 35 pages maximum, double spaced. Open to any writer. Cover letter must include name, address, phone number and title of story. Entrant's name should appear only in the cover letter, as all entries will be considered anonymously. Results announced January. Winners notified by mail. For contest results, send SASE. "We look for a command of language and structure, as well as a facility with compelling and unusual subject matter. It's a good idea to obtain copies of issues featuring past winners to get a more concrete idea of what we are looking for." See website for updates to guidelines. **Contact:** Alessandra Simmons, Editor. Contest for fiction in any style and on any subject. Mss will not be returned. No works forthcoming elsewhere, are eligible. Simultaneous submissions accepted, but in the event of entrant withdrawal, contest fee will not be refunded. Length: 35 pages maximum, double spaced. Open to any writer. Cover letter must include name, address, phone number and title

of story. Entrant's name should appear only in the cover letter, as all entries will be considered anonymously. Results announced January. Winners notified by mail. For contest results, send SASE. "We look for a command of language and structure, as well as a facility with compelling and unusual subject matter. It's a good idea to obtain copies of issues featuring past winners to get a more concrete idea of what we are looking for." See website for updates to guidelines. Entries must be unpublished. Deadline: Mid-October. Prize: $1,000, publication in the Indiana Review and contributor's copies. Judged by guest judges. 2010 prize judged by Dan Chaon.

◑◐ INTERNATIONAL 3-DAY NOVEL CONTEST

Box 2106 Station Terminal, Vancouver BC V6B 3T5 Canada. E-mail: info@3daynovel.com. Website: 3daynovel.com. **Contact:** Melissa Edwards. "Offered annually for the best novel written in 3 days (Labor Day weekend). To register, send SASE (IRC if from outside Canada) for details, or entry form available online. Open to all writers. Writing may take place in any location." Deadline: Friday before Labor Day weekend. Prize: 1st place receives publication; 2nd place receives $500; 3rd place receives $100.

JACK DYER FICTION PRIZE

Crab Orchard Review, Dept. of English, Southern Illinois Univ. Carbondale, Carbondale IL 62901-4503. E-mail: jtribble@siu.edu. Website: craborchardreview. siuc.edu. Crab Orchard Review, Dept. of English, Faner Hall, Southern Illinois University Carbondale, Carbondale IL 62901-4503. Website: siu.edu/~crborchd. **Contact:** Jon Tribble, managing editor. Offered annually for unpublished short fiction. Crab Orchard Review acquires first North American serial rights to all submitted work. Open to any writer. Prize: $1,500 and publication. Judged by editorial staff (pre-screening); winner chosen by genre editor. Entry fee: $15/entry (can enter up to 3 stories, each story submitted requires a separate fee and can be up to 6,000 words), which includes a 1-year subscription to Crab Orchard Review. Guidelines available after January for SASE or on website. Deadline: Reading period for entries is February 1 through April 1. Entries must be unpublished. Length: 6,000 words maximum. U.S. citizens only. "Please note that no stories will be returned." Results announced by end of October. Winners notified by mail. Contest results on website or send SASE.

"Carefully read directions for entering and follow them exactly. Send us your best work. Note that simultaneous submissions are accepted for this prize, but the winning entry must NOT be accepted elsewhere. No electronic submissions." **Contact:** Jon C. Tribble, man. editor. "Offered annually for unpublished short fiction. *Crab Orchard Review* acquires first North American serial rights to all submitted work. Open to any writer. Open to US citizens only." March 1 - April 30. Prize: $2,000 and publication and one-year subscription to *Crab Orchard Review*.

JAMES JONES FIRST NOVEL FELLOWSHIP

Wilkes University, Creative Writing Department, 245 S. River St., Wilkes-Barre PA 18766. (570)408-4534. Fax: (570)408-3333. E-mail: Jamesjonesfirstnovel@wilkes.edu. Website: wilkes.edu/pages/1159.asp. Offered annually for unpublished novels, novellas, and closely-linked short stories (all works in progress). "The award is intended to honor the spirit of unblinking honesty, determination, and insight into modern culture exemplified by the late James Jones." The competition is open to all American writers who have not previously published novels. Deadline: March 1. Prize: $10,000; 2 runners-up get $750 honorarium

JERRY JAZZ MUSICIAN NEW SHORT FICTION AWARD

Jerry Jazz Musician, 2207 NE Broadway, Portland OR 97232. E-mail: jm@jerryjazzmusician.com. Website: jerryjazz.com. Three times a year, *Jerry Jazz Musician* awards a writer who submits, in our opinion, the best original, previously unpublished work of approximately 3,000-5,000 words. The winner will be announced via a mailing of our *Jerry Jazz* newsletter. Publishers, artists, musicians, and interested readers are among those who subscribe to the newsletter. Additionally, the work will be published on the home page of *Jerry Jazz Musician* and featured there for at least 4 weeks. The *Jerry Jazz Musician* reader tends to have interests in music, history, literature, art, film, and theater—particularly that of the counter-culture of mid-20th century America. Guidelines available online. Deadline: September, January, and May. Prize: $100 Judged by the editors of *Jerry Jazz Musician*.

JOANNA CATHERINE SCOTT NOVEL EXCERPT PRIZE

National League of American Pen Women, Nob Hill, San Francisco Bay Area Branch, The Webhallow House, 1544 Sweetwood Dr., Broadmoor Village CA 94015-2029. E-mail: pennobhill@aol.com. Website: soulmakingcontest.us. Joanna Catherine Scott Novel Excerpt Prize. National League of American Pen Women, Nob Hill, San Francisco Bay Area Branch. The Webhallow House, 1544 Sweetwood Dr., Broadmoor Village, CA 94015-1717. Phone: (650)756-5279. Fax: (650)756-5279. E-mail: pennobhill@aol.com. Website: soulmakingcontest.us. Contact: Eileen Malone. Open annually to any writer. $5/entry (make checks payable to NLAPW, Nob Hill Branch). Deadline: November 30. Prizes: 1st Place: $100; 2nd Place: $50; 3rd Place: $25. **Contact:** Eileen Malone. "Send first chapter or the first 20 pages, whichever comes first. Include a 1-page synopsis indicating category at top of page. Identify with 3X5 card only. Open annually to any writer." Deadline: November 30. Prize: 1st Place: $100; 2nd Place: $50; 3rd Place: $25.

⊕ JESSE JONES AWARD FOR FICTION

P.O. Box 609, Round Rock TX 78680. (214)363-7253. E-mail: dpayne@smu.edu. Website: texasinstituteofletters.org. Offered annually by Texas Institute of Letters for work published January 1-December 31 of year before award is given to recognize the writer of the best book of fiction entered in the competition. Writers must have been born in Texas, have lived in the state for at least 2 consecutive years at some time, or the subject matter of the work should be associated with the state. President changes every two years. See website for guidelines. Deadline: Jan. 1. Prize: $6,000. **Contact:** W.K. (Kip) Stratton, acquisitions. Offered annually by Texas Institute of Letters for work published January 1-December 31 of year before award is given to recognize the writer of the best book of fiction entered in the competition. Writers must have been born in Texas, have lived in the state for at least 2 consecutive years at some time, or the subject matter of the work should be associated with the state. President changes every two years. See website for guidelines. Deadline: January 1. Prize: $6,000.

JUST DESSERTS SHORT-SHORT FICTION CONTEST

Passages North, Dept. of English, Northern Michigan University, 1401 Presque Isle Ave., Marquette MI 49855. (906)227-1203. Fax: (906)227-1096. E-mail: passages@nmu.edu. Website: myweb.nmu.edu/~passages. **Contact:** Kate Myers Hanson. Offered every 2 years to publish new voices in literary fiction (maximum

1,000 words). Guidelines available for SASE or online. Deadline: Submit October 31-January 31. Prize: $1,000, and publication for the winner; 2 honorable mentions also published; all entrants receive a copy of *Passages North*.

THE LAWRENCE FOUNDATION AWARD

Prairie Schooner, 123 Andrews Hall, P.O. Box 880334, Lincoln NE 68588-0334. (402)472-0911. Fax: (402)472-9771. E-mail: jengelhardt2@unlnotes.unl.edu. Website: unl.edu/. **Contact:** Hilda Raz. Offered annually for the best short story published in *Prairie Schooner* in the previous year. Prize: $1,000

THE LEDGE ANNUAL FICTION AWARDS COMPETITION

The Ledge Magazine, 40 Maple Avenue, Bellport NY 11713. E-mail: info@theledgemagazine.com. Website: theledgemagazine.com. **Contact:** Timothy Monaghan, editor-in-chief. Stories must be unpublished and 7,500 words or less. There are no restrictions on form or content. Guidelines online or for SASE. Deadline: Feb. 28. Prize: 1st Place: $1,000 and publication; 2nd Place: $250 and publication; 3rd Place: $100 and publication.

LITERAL LATTÉ FICTION AWARD

Literal Latté, 200 E. 10th St., Suite 240, New York NY 10003. (212)260-5532. E-mail: litlatte@aol.com. Website: literal-latte.com. **Contact:** Edward Estlin, contributing editor. "Award to provide talented writers with 3 essential tools for continued success: money, publication, and recognition. Offered annually for unpublished fiction (maximum 10,000 words). Guidelines online. Open to any writer." Deadline: January 15. Prize: 1st Place: $1,000 and publication in *Literal Latté*; 2nd Place: $300; 3rd Place: $200; also up to 7 honorable mentions.

THE MARY MACKEY SHORT STORY PRIZE

Soul-Making Literary Competition, National League of American Pen Women, Nob Hill, San Francisco Bay Area, The Webhallow House, 1544 Sweetwood Dr., Broadmoor Village CA 94015-2029. E-mail: pennobhill@aol.com. Website: soulmakingcontest. us. The Mary Mackey Short Story Prize. "One story/ entry, up to 5,000 words. All prose works must be typed, page numbered, and double-spaced. Identify only with 3X5 card. Open annually to any writer." $5/entry (make checks payable to NLAPW, Nob Hill

Branch). Needs fiction, short stories. Deadline: November 30. Prizes: 1st Place: $100; 2nd Place: $50; 3rd Place: $25. **Contact:** Eileen Malone. "One story/entry, up to 5,000 words. All prose works must be typed, page numbered, and double-spaced. Identify only with 3X5 card. Open annually to any writer." Deadline: November 30. Prize: 1st Place: $100; 2nd Place: $50; 3rd Place: $25.

❶❷❸ THE MALAHAT REVIEW NOVELLA PRIZE

The Malahat Review, University of Victoria, P.O. Box 1700 STN CSC, Victoria BC V8W 2Y2 Canada. (250)721-8524. E-mail: malahat@uvic.ca. Website: malahatreview.ca. **Contact:** John Barton, Editor. "Held in alternate years with the Long Poem Prize. Offered to promote unpublished novellas. Obtains first world rights. After publication rights revert to the author. Open to any writer." Submit novellas between 10,000 and 20,000 words in length. Include separate page with author's name, address, e-mail, and novella title; no identifying information on mss. pages. No e-mail submissions. Do NOT include SASE for results; mss will not be returned. Guidelines available on website. Deadline: February 1 (even years). Prize: $1,500 CAD and one year's subscription. 2010 winner was Tony Tulathimutte. Winner and finalists contacted by e-mail. Winner published in summer issue of *The Malahat Review* and announced on website, Facebook page, and in quarterly e-newsletter, *Malahat Lite*.

MARY KENNEDY EASTHAM FLASH FICTION PRIZE

National League of American Pen Women, Nob Hill, San Francisco Branch, The Webhallow House, 1544 Sweetwood Dr., Broadmoor Village CA 94015-2029. E-mail: pennobhill@aol.com. Website: soulmaking-contest.us. **Contact:** Eileen Malone. "Three flash fiction (short-short) stories per entry, under 500 words. Previously published material is accepted. Indicate category on each story. Identify only with 3X5 card. Open annually to any writer." Deadline: November 30. Prize: 1st Place: $100; 2nd Place: $50; 3rd Place: $25.

MARY MCCARTHY PRIZE IN SHORT FICTION

Sarabande Books, P.O. Box 4456, Louisville KY 40204. (502)458-4028. Fax: (502)458-4065. E-mail: info@ sarabandebooks.org. Website: sarabandebooks.org. **Contact:** Kirby Gann, managing editor. Offered annually to publish an outstanding collection of stories, novellas, or short novel (less than 250 pages). All finalists considered for publication. Deadline: January 1-February 15. Prize: $2,000 and publication (standard royalty contract).

⊕ MICRO AWARD

c/o Alan Presley, PSC 817 Box 23, FPO AE 09622-0023. E-mail: admin@microaward.org. Website: microaward.org. The Micro Award (4th annual) was established to recognize outstanding flash fiction from both print and electronic media. It is open to all genres. Senior editors may submit two stories; authors may submit one. Guidelines and entry forms are available for a SASE or see website. No entry fee. Submissions required to be previously published that have appeared in print between Jan. 1 and Dec. 31. It is open to anyone who has a story not exceeding 1,000 words in length available for public display. No rights are acquired or purchased when writers enter work for this award. It judged by a panel of 3 judges. The author of the winning story will received $500 (US). **Contact:** Alan Presley. Annual contest. The Micro Award was established to recognize outstanding flash fiction from both print and electronic media. It is open to all genres. Self-published stories are eligible. An author may submit one story of his or her own; the senior editor of a magazine or anthology, or any staff member designated by him or her, may submit two stories if both are from his or her own publication and neither is self-written. Submissions must be previously published and must have appeared in print between Jan. 1, 2011 and Dec. 31. The Micro Award was established to recognize outstanding flash fiction (in English) from both print and electronic media. Mailed submissions must be postmarked from Oct. 1 to Dec. 31, 2011 and received by Jan. 15, 2012. E-mailed submissions should be sent to admin@microaward.org from Oct. 1 to Dec. 31. The text of the story must be inserted in the body of the e-mail or attached as a Rich Text file. It is also permissible to include the URL information for a story or stories accessible online. Prize: The author of the winning story will receive $500 (US). A panel of 3 judges.

C. WRIGHT MILLS AWARD

The Society for the Study of Social Problems, 901 McClung Tower, University of Tennessee, Knoxville TN 37996-0490. (865)689-1531. Fax: (865)689-1534. E-mail: mkoontz3@utk.edu. Website: sssp1.org. **Con-**tact: Michele Smith Koontz, administrative officer & meeting manager. "Offered annually for a book published the previous year that most effectively critically addresses an issue of contemporary public importance; brings to the topic a fresh, imaginative perspective; advances social scientific understanding of the topic; displays a theoretically informed view and empirical orientation; evinces quality in style of writing; and explicitly or implicitly contains implications for courses of action." Deadline: January 15. Prize: $500 stipend

NATIONAL WRITERS ASSOCIATION NOVEL WRITING CONTEST

The National Writers Association, 10940 S. Parker Rd. #508, Parker CO 80134. (303)841-0246. Fax: (303)841-2607. E-mail: natlwritersassn@hotmail.com. Website: nationalwriters.com. Annual contest "to help develop creative skills, to recognize and reward outstanding ability, and to increase the opportunity for the marketing and subsequent publication of novel manuscripts." Prize: 1st place: $500; 2nd place: $300; 3rd place: $200. Judges' evaluation sheets sent to each entry with SASE. Categories: Open to any genre or category. Judged by editors and agents. Entry fee: $35. Opens December 1. **Deadline: April 1.** Entries must be unpublished. Length: 20,000-100,000 words. Open to any writer. Contest forms are available on the NWA website or an attachment will be sent if you request one through e-mail or with an SASE. Address: 10940 S. Parker Rd. #508, Parker CO 80134. **Contact:** Sandy Whelchel, director. Annual contest to help develop creative skills, to recognize and reward outstanding ability, and to increase the opportunity for the marketing and subsequent publication of novel mss. Deadline: April 1. Prize: 1st Place: $500; 2nd Place: $250; 3rd Place: $150.

THE NELLIGAN PRIZE FOR SHORT FICTION

Colorado Review/Center for Literary Publishing, 9105 Campus Delivery, Dept. of English, Colorado State University, Ft. Collins CO 80523-9105. (970)491-5449. E-mail: creview@colostate.edu. Website: nelliganprize.colostate.edu. "The Nelligan Prize for Short Fiction was established in memory of Liza Nelligan, a writer, editor, and friend of many in Colorado State University's English Department, where she received her master's degree in literature in 1992. By giving an award to the author of an outstanding short story each year, we hope to honor Liza Nelligan's life, her passion for writing, and her love of fiction." Annual. Competition/award for short stories. Prize: $1,500 plus publication in Colorado Review. Receives approximately 900 stories. All entries are read blind by Colorado Review's editorial staff. 15 entries are selected to be sent on to a final judge. Entry fee: $15. Send credit card information or make checks payable to Colorado Review. Payment also accepted via our online submission manager link from website. Guidelines available in August 2011. Accepts inquiries by e-mail, phone. **Entry deadline March 12, 2012.** Entries must be unpublished and under 50 pages. Anyone may enter contest. With the exception of Colorado State University students or friends or students of the judge of the contest. Cover letter should include name, address, phone, e-mail, and novel/story title. "Authors should provide two cover sheets: one with name, address, phone, e-mail, and title of story, and a second with only the title of the story. Manuscripts are read 'blind,' so authors'names should not appear anywhere else in the manuscript." Writers may submit own work. "Successful short story writers are those who are reading contemporary short fiction (short story collections, literary magazines, annual prize anthologies), reading about the craft, and actively engaging in the practice of writing." Results announced in July of each year. Winners notified by phone. Results made available to entrants with SASE. **Contact:** Stephanie G'Schwind, editor. Offered annually to an unpublished short story. Guidelines for SASE or online. Deadline: March 12. Prize: $1,500 and publication of story in *Colorado Review*.

FRANK O'CONNOR AWARD FOR SHORT FICTION

descant, Texas Christian University's literary journal, TCU Box 297270, Fort Worth TX 76129. (817)257-6537. Fax: (817)257-6239. E-mail: descant@tcu.edu. Website: descant.tcu.edu. **Contact:** Dan Williams and Alex Lemon, editors. Offered annually for unpublished short stories. Publication retains copyright but will transfer it to the author upon request. Deadline: September-March. Prize: $500.

ON THE PREMISES CONTEST

On The Premises, LLC, 4323 Gingham Court, Alexandria VA 22310. (202) 262-2168. E-mail: questions@onthepremises.com. Website: onthepremises.com. "*On the Premises* aims to promote newer and/or relatively

unknown writers who can write what we feel are creative, compelling stories told in effective, uncluttered and evocative prose. Each contest challenges writers to produce a great story based on a broad premise that our editors supply as part of the contest." Competition/award for short stories. Prize: First prize is $180, Second prize $140, Third prize $100, and Honorable Mentions recieve $40. All prize winners are published in *On the Premises* magazine in HTML and PDF format. Entries are judged blindly by a panel of judges with professional editing and writing experience. No entry fee. Submissions are accepted by e-mail only. Contests held every four months. Check website for exact dates. Entries should be unpublished. Open to everyone. Length: min 1,000 words, max 5,000. E-mail should include name, address, e-mail, novel/story title, with ms attached. No name or contact info should be in ms. Writers may submit own work. "Write something compelling, creative and well-crafted. Above all, clearly use the contest premise. Results announced within 2 weeks of contest deadline. Winners notified via newsletter and with publication of *On the Premises*. Results made available to entrants on website, in publication. **Contact:** Tarl Roger Kudrick or Bethany Granger, co-publishers. Prize: First prize is $180, Second prize $140, Third prize $100, and Honorable Mentions recieve $40. All prize winners are published in *On the Premises* magazine in HTML and PDF format.

PATERSON FICTION PRIZE

PCCC, Poetry Center, One College Blvd., Paterson NJ 07505-1179. (973)684-6555. Fax: (973)523-6085. E-mail: mgillan@pccc.edu. Website: pccc.edu/poetry. The Poetry Center at Passaic County Community College, One College Blvd., Paterson NJ 07505-1179. (973) 684-6555. Fax: (973 523-6085. E-mail: mgillan@pccc.edu. Website: pccc.edu/poetry. **Contact:** Maria Mazziotti Gillan, executive director. Award "to encourage recognition of high-quality writing." Offered annually for a novel or collection of short fiction published the previous calendar year. Prize: $1,000. Judges rotate each year. No entry fee. Deadline: April 1. Open to any writer. Guidelines available for SASE or online. **Contact:** Maria Mazziotti Gillan, executive director. Offered annually for a novel or collection of short fiction published the previous calendar year. Guidelines for SASE or online. Deadline: April 1. Prize: $1,000.

PEN/FAULKNER AWARDS FOR FICTION

PEN/Faulkner Foundation, 201 E. Capitol St., Washington DC 20003. (202)675-0345. Fax: (202)675-0360. E-mail: jneely@penfaulkner.org. Website: penfaulkner.org. PEN/Faulkner Foundation, 201 E. Capitol St., Washington DC 20003. (202) 898-9063. Fax: (202) 675-0363. E-mail: jneely@penfaulkner.org. Website: penfaulkner.org. **Contact:** Jessica Neely, PEN/Faulkner Foundation Executive Director. Offered annually for best book-length work of fiction by an American citizen published in a calendar year (short story collections are eligible). Prize: $15,000 (one winner); $5,000 (4 finalists). Judged by three writers chosen by the directors of the Pen/Faulkner Foundation. No entry fee. **Deadline: October 31.** Open to US citizens only, but they need not be US residents. Writers and publishers submit four copies of eligible titles published during the current year. No juvenile or self-published books. Deadline: October 31. Prize: $15,000 (one Winner); $5,000 (4 Finalists). **Contact:** Jessica Neely, Executive Director. Offered annually for best book-length work of fiction by an American citizen published in a calendar year. Deadline: October 31. Prize: $15,000 (one Winner); $5,000 (4 Finalists)

EDGAR ALLAN POE AWARD

1140 Broadway, Suite 1507, New York NY 10001. E-mail: mwa@mysterywriters.org. Website: mysterywriters.org. Mystery Writers of America, Inc.1140 Broadway, Suite 1507, New York NY Edgar Allan Poe Award. Mystery Writers of American. 1140 Broadway, Suite 1507, New York NY 10001. (212)888-8171. Fax: (212)888-8107. E-mail: mwa@mysterywriters.org. Website: mysterywriters.org. Annual award. Estab. 1945. Purpose of the award: to honor authors of distinguished works in the mystery field. Previously published submissions only. Submissions made by the author, author's agent; "normally by the publisher." Work must be published/produced the year of the contest. Deadline for entries: Must be received by November 30. Submission information can be found at: mysterywriters.org. No entry fee. Awards ceramic bust of "Edgar" for winner; scrolls for all nominees. Judging by professional members of Mystery Writers of America (writers). Nominee press release sent in mid January. Winner announced at the Edgar® Awards Banquet, held in late April/early May. Mystery Writers of America is the leading association for professional crime writers in the United States.

Members of MWA include most major writers of crime fiction and non-fiction, as well as screenwriters, dramatists, editors, publishers, and other professionals in the field. We welcome everyone who is interested in mysteries and crime writing to join MWA. Work must be published/produced the year of the contest. Purpose of the award: to honor authors of distinguished works in the mystery field. Previously published submissions only. Submissions made by the author, author's agent; "normally by the publisher." Submission information can be found at: mysterywriters.org. No entry fee. Judging by professional members of Mystery Writers of America (writers). Nominee press release sent in mid-January. Winner announced at the Edgar® Awards Banquet, held in late April/early May. Deadline: Must be received by Nov. 30. Prize: Awards ceramic bust of "Edgar" for winner; scrolls for all nominees.

THE KATHERINE ANNE PORTER PRIZE FOR FICTION

Nimrod International Journal, The University of Tulsa, 800 S. Tucker Dr., Tulsa OK 74104. (918)631-3080. Fax: (918)631-3033. E-mail: nimrod@utulsa.edu. Website: utulsa.edu/nimrod. **Contact:** Francine Ringold. "This annual award was established to discover new, unpublished writers of vigor and talent. Open to US residents only." Deadline: April 30. Prize: Prizes: 1st Place: $2,000 and publication; 2nd Place: $1,000 and publication. *Nimrod* retains the right to publish any submission. The *Nimrod* editors select the finalists and a recognized author selects the winners.

☺ THE ROGERS WRITERS' TRUST FICTION PRIZE

The Writers' Trust of Canada, 90 Richmond St. E., Suite 200, Toronto ON M5C 1P1 Canada. (416)504-8222. Fax: (416)504-9090. E-mail: info@writerstrust.com. Website: writerstrust.com. **Contact:** Amanda Hopkins. "Awarded annually for a distinguished work of fiction—either a novel or short story collection—published within the previous year. Presented at the Writers' Trust Awards event held in Toronto each Fall. Open to Canadian citizens and permanent residents only." Deadline: August 2011 . Prize: $25,000 and $2,500 to four finalists.

RROFIHE TROPHY

Open City, Open City Magazine & Books, 270 Lafayette St., #1412, New York NY 10012. E-mail: rrofihe@yahoo.com. Website: opencity.org/the-rrofihe-trophy.

Contact: Rick Rofihe, editor. "Eighth annual contest for an unpublished short story (up to 5,000 words). Stories should be typed, double-spaced, with the author's name and contact information on the first page, and name and story title on the upper right corner of remaining pages. Limit 1 submission/author. Author must not have been previously published in *Open City*. Enclose SASE to receive names of winner and honorable mentions. All mss are nonreturnable and will be recycled. Acquires First North American serial rights (from winner only)." Deadline: October 15 (postmarked). Prize: $500, a trophy, and publication in *Open City*. Judge: Rick Rofihe.

SASKATCHEWAN FICTION AWARD

Saskatchewan Book Awards, Inc., 205B-2314 11th Ave., Regina SK S4P 0K1 Canada. (306)569-1585. Fax: (306)569-4187. E-mail: director@bookawards. sk.ca. Website: bookawards.sk.ca. **Contact:** Jackie Lay, executive director, book submissions. Offered annually for work published September 15, 2010- October 31. This award is presented to a Saskatchewan author for the best book of fiction (novel or short fiction), judged on the quality of writing. Deadline: November 1. Prize: $2,000.

MARY WOLLSTONECRAFT SHELLEY PRIZE FOR IMAGINATIVE FICTION

Rosebud, C/O Rosebud Magazine, N3310 Asje Rd., Cambridge WI 53523. (608)423-4750. E-mail: jrodclark@smallbytes.net. Website: rsbd.net. **Contact:** J. Roderick Clark, editor. Biennial (odd years) contest for any kind of unpublished imaginative fiction/short stories, 4,000 words or less. Entries are welcome any time. Acquires first rights. Open to any writer. Deadline: September 1 in odd years. Prize: Grand prize: $1,000. 4 runner-ups receive $100. All winners published in *Rosebud*.

STEVEN TURNER AWARD FOR BEST FIRST WORK OF FICTION

6335 W. Northwest Hwy., #618, Dallas TX 75225. (214)363-7253. E-mail: dpayne@mail.smu.edu. Website: texasinstituteofletters.org. Offered annually for work published January 1-December 31 for the best first book of fiction. Writers must have been born in Texas, have lived in the state for at least 2 consecutive years at some time, or the subject matter of the work should be associated with the state. Needs fiction, novels, and short stories. Guidelines online.

Deadline: January 3. Prize: $1,000. **Contact:** Darwin Payne. Offered annually for work published January 1-December 31 for the best first book of fiction. Writers must have been born in Texas, have lived in the state for at least 2 consecutive years at some time, or the subject matter of the work should be associated with the state. Needs fiction, novels, and short stories. Guidelines online. Deadline: January 3. Prize: $1,000. Contact: Darwin Payne (dpayne@mail.smu. edu). Website: texasinstituteofletters.org. Deadline: January 3. Prize: $1,000.

THOMAS H. RADDALL ATLANTIC FICTION PRIZE

Writers' Federation of Nova Scotia, 1113 Marginal Rd., Halifax NS B3H 4P7 Canada. (902)423-8116. Fax: (902)422-0881. E-mail: director@writers.ns.ca. Website: writers.ns.ca. Writers' Federation of Nova Scotia. 1113 Marginal Rd., Halifax NSB 3H 4P7 Canada. Phone: (902)423-8116. Fax: (902)422-0881. E-mail: director@writers.ns.ca. Website: writers.ns.ca. Contact: Nate Crawford, executive director. Established in 1990. "Full-length books of fiction written by Atlantic Canadians, and published as a whole for the first time in the previous calendar year, are eligible. Entrants must be native or resident Atlantic Canadians who have either been born in Newfoundland, Prince Edward Island, Nova Scotia, or New Brunswick, and spent a substantial portion of their lives living there, or who have lived in 1 or a combination of these provinces for at least 24 consecutive months prior to entry deadline date." No fee or form required. Accepts fiction, novels, short stories." The purpose is "To recognize the best Atlantic Canadian adult fiction." Deadline: First Friday in December$15,000. **Contact:** Nate Crawford, executive director. "Full-length books of fiction written by Atlantic Canadians, and published as a whole for the first time in the previous calendar year, are eligible. Entrants must be native or resident Atlantic Canadians who have either been born in Newfoundland, Prince Edward Island, Nova Scotia, or New Brunswick, and spent a substantial portion of their lives living there, or who have lived in 1 or a combination of these provinces for at least 24 consecutive months prior to entry deadline date." "Publishers: Send 4 copies and a letter attesting to the author's status as an Atlantic Canadian, and the author's current mailing address and telephone number."

"To recognize the best Atlantic Canadian adult fiction." Deadline: First Friday in December. Prize: $15,000.

THOROUGHBRED TIMES FICTION CONTEST

P.O. Box 8237, Lexington KY 40533. (859)260-9800. Fax: (859)260-9812. E-mail: fiction@thoroughbredtimes.com. Website: thoroughbredtimes.com. **Contact:** Tom Law. Offered every 2 years for unpublished work to recognize outstanding fiction written about the Thoroughbred racing industry. Maximum length: 5,000 words. *Thoroughbred Times* receives first North American serial rights and reserves the right to publish any and all entries in the magazine. Deadline: December 31. Prize: 1st Place: $600 and publication in *Thoroughbred Times*; 2nd Place: $300 and publication; 3rd Place: $200 and publication

[+] $ TIMELESS LOVE CONTEST

Sponsored by Oak Tree Press, 140 E. Palmer St., Taylorville IL 62568. E-mail: oaktreeepub@aol.com. Website: oaktreebooks.com. **Contact:** Billie Johnson. Annual contest for unpublished authors or authors shifting to a new genre. Guidelines and entry forms are available for SASE. The goal of the contest is to discover and publish new authors, or authors shifting to a new genre. Deadline: July 31 (same every year). Prize: Publishing Agreement, and launch of the title. Winners or runners up who are offered publishing agreements are asked to transfer rights. Judged by publishing industry professionals who prescreen entries; publisher makes final selection.

TOM HOWARD/JOHN H. REID SHORT STORY CONTEST

c/o Winning Writers, 351 Pleasant St., PMB 222, Northampton MA 01060-3961. (866)946-9748. E-mail: johnreid@mail.qango.com. Website: winningwriters.com. Now in its 19th year. Prizes of $3,000, $1,000, $400 and $250 will be awarded, plus six Most Highly Commended Awards of $150 each. Submit any type of short story, essay or other work of prose. You may submit work that has been published or won prizes elsewhere, as long as you own the online publication rights. $15 entry fee. Submit online or by mail. Early submission encouraged. This contest is sponsored by Tom Howard Books and assisted by Winning Writers. Judges: John H. Reid and Dee C. Konrad. See the complete guidelines and past winners. Make checks payable to Winning Writers (U.S. funds only, please). Guidelines available in July on website. Prefers inquiries by e-mail. **Deadline: March 31.** "Both published and unpublished works are accepted. In the case of published work, the contestant must own the online publication rights." Open to all writers. Length: 5,000 words max per entry. Cover letter should include name, address, phone, e-mail, story title, place(s) where story was previously published (if any). Only the title should be on the actual ms. Writers may submit own work. "Read past winning entries at winningwriters.com/contests/tomstory/ts_pastwinners.php." Winners notified by e-mail. Results made available to entrants on website. **Contact:** John Reid. "Both unpublished and published work accepted (maximum 5,000 words). Guidelines for SASE or online." Now in its 19th year. Submit any type of short story, essay or other work of prose. You may submit work that has been published or won prizes elsewhere, as long as you own the online publication rights. $15 entry fee. Submit online or by mail. Early submission encouraged. This contest is sponsored by Tom Howard Books and assisted by Winning Writers. Judges: John H. Reid and Dee C. Konrad. See the complete guidelines and past winners. Make checks payable to Winning Writers (U.S. funds only, please). Guidelines available in July on website. Prefers inquiries by e-mail. **Deadline: March 31.** "Both published and unpublished works are accepted. In the case of published work, the contestant must own the online publication rights." Open to all writers. Length: 5,000 words max per entry. Cover letter should include name, address, phone, e-mail, story title, place(s) where story was previously published (if any). Only the title should be on the actual ms. Writers may submit own work. "Read past winning entries at winningwriters.com/contests/tomstory/ts_pastwinners.php." Winners notified by e-mail. Results made available to entrants on website. Deadline: March 31. Prize: 1st Place: $3,000; 2nd Place: $1,000; 3rd Place: $400; 4th Place: $250; and 6 most highly commended awards of $150 each. The winners will be published on the Winning Writers website. Judged by John H. Reid; assisted by Dee C. Konrad.

24-HOUR SHORT STORY CONTEST

WritersWeekly.com, P.O. Box 2399, Bangor ME 04402. E-mail: writersweekly@writersweekly.com. Website: writersweekly.com/misc/contest.php. **Contact:** Angela Hoy. "Quarterly contest in which registered entrants receive a topic at start time (usually noon Central Time) and have 24 hours to write a story on that topic. All submissions must be returned via e-mail. Each contest is limited to 500 people. Guidelines via e-mail or online." Deadline: Quarterly—see website for dates. Prize: 1st Place: $300; 2nd Place: $250; 3rd Place: $200. There are also 20 honorable mentions and 60 door prizes. The top 3 winners' entries are posted on WritersWeekly.com (non-exclusive electronic rights only). Writers retain all rights to their work. Angela Hoy (publisher of WritersWeekly.com and Booklocker.com).

WAASMODE FICTION CONTEST

Passages North, Dept. of English, Northern Michigan University, 1401 Presque Isle Ave, Marquette MI 49855. (906)227-1203. Fax: (906)227-1096. E-mail: passages@nmu.edu. Website: myweb.nmu.edu/~passages. **Contact:** Kate Myers Hanson. Offered every 2 years to publish new voices in literary fiction (maximum 5,000 words). Guidelines for SASE or online. In association with the Just Desserts Contest, we have our Waasmode Short Fiction Prize which is also $1,000 first price and publication. It is a 7,500 word maximum word count. It is also given every other year. When we are not having our fiction contest, we are having our poetry and non fiction contests. Elinor Benedict Poetry Prize -$1,000 first prize and publication. $10 for up to three poems entry fee ($3 for each additional poem after that). Thomas J. Hruska Memorial Prize in Nonfiction-$1,000 first prize and publication. $10 per essay entry fee. Deadline: Submit October 15-February 15. Prize: $1,000 and publication for winner; 2 honorable mentions are also published; all entrants receive a copy of *Passages North*.

GARY WILSON SHORT FICTION AWARD

descant, Texas Christian University's literary journal, TCU, Box 297270, Fort Worth TX 76129. (817)257-6537. Fax: (817)257-6239. E-mail: descant@tcu.edu. Website: descant.tcu.edu. Box 297270, Fort Worth TX 76129. Phone: (817)257-6537; Fax: (817)257-6239. E-mail: descant@tcu.edu. Website: descant.tcu.edu. David Kuhne, editor. Offered annually for an outstanding story in an issue. **Contact:** David Kuhne, editor. Offered annually for an outstanding story in an issue. Prize: $250.

WORLD FANTASY AWARDS

P.O. Box 43, Mukilteo WA 98275-0043. E-mail: sfexecsec@gmail.com. Website: worldfantasy.org. Awards

"to recognize excellence in fantasy literature worldwide." Offered annually for previously published work in several categories, including life achievement, novel, novella, short story, anthology, collection, artist, special award-pro and special award-nonpro. Works are recommended by attendees of current and previous 2 years' conventions and a panel of judges. Prize: Bust of HP Lovecraft. Judged by panel. No entry fee. Guidelines available in December for SASE or on website. **Deadline: June 1.** Entries must be previously published. Published submissions from previous calendar year. Word length: 10,000-40,000 for novella, 10,000 for short story. "All fantasy is eligible, from supernatural horror to Tolkien-esque to sword and sorcery to the occult, and beyond." Cover letter should include name, address, phone, e-mail, word count, title and publications where submission was previously published, submitted to the address above and the panel of judges when they appear on the website. Results announced November 1 at annual convention. For contest results, visit website. **Contact:** Peter Dennis Pautz, president. Awards "to recognize excellence in fantasy literature worldwide." Offered annually for previously published work in several categories, including life achievement, novel, novella, short story, anthology, collection, artist, special award-pro and special award-nonpro. Works are recommended by attendees of current and previous 2 years' conventions and a panel of judges. Judged by panel. No entry fee. Guidelines available in December for SASE or on website. Entries must be previously published. Published submissions from previous calendar year. Word length: 10,000-40,000 for novella, 10,000 for short story. Deadline: June 1. Prize: Bust of HP Lovecraft

WOW! WOMEN ON WRITING QUARTERLY FLASH FICTION CONTEST

Wow! Women on Writing, 740 S. Van Buren St., Suite D, Placentia CA 92870. E-mail: contestinfo@wow-womenonwriting.com. Website: wow-womenonwriting.com/contest.php. **Contact:** Angela Mackintosh, CEO. Contest offered quarterly. "We are open to all themes and genres, although we do encourage writers to take a close look at our literary agent guest judge for the season if you are serious about winning." Entries must be 250-750 words. Deadline: August 31, November 30, February 28, May 31. Prize: 1st Place: $300 cash prize, $25 Amazon Gift Certificat, book from our sponsor, story published on WOW! Women On Writing, interview on blog; 2nd Place: $200 cash prize, $25 Amazon Gift Certificat, book from our sponsor, story published on WOW! Women On Writing, interview on blog; 3rd Place: $100 cash prize, $25 Amazon gift certificate, book from our sponsor, story published on WOW! Women On Writing, interview on blog; 7 Runners Up: $25 Amazon gift certificate, book our sponsor, story published on WOW! Women on Writing interview on blog;10 honorable mentions: $20 gift certificate from Amazon, book from our sponsor, story title and name published on WOW!Women On Writing.

WRITERS' JOURNAL ANNUAL ROMANCE CONTEST

Val-Tech Media, P.O. Box 394, Perham MN 56573. (218)346-7921. Fax: (218)346-7924. E-mail: writersjournal@writersjournal.com. Website: writersjournal.com. Offered annually for previously unpublished works. Cover letter should include name, address, phone, e-mail, word count and title; just title on ms. Results announced in January/February issue. Winners notified by mail and on website. Enclose SASE for winner's list. Receives fewer than 150 entries.

WRITERS' JOURNAL ANNUAL SHORT STORY CONTEST

Val-Tech Media, P.O. Box 394, Perham MN 56573. (218)346-7921. Fax: (218)346-7924. Val-Tech Media, P.O. Box 394, Perham MN 56573. (218) 346-7921. Fax: (218) 346-7924. Contact: Leon Ogroske. "Offered annually for previously unpublished short stories. Open to any writer. Guidelines for SASE or online." Receives fewer than 250 entries. Needs fiction, short stories. Deadline: May 30. 1st Place: $350; 2nd Place: $125; 3rd Place: $75; plus honorable mentions. Prize-winning stories and selected honorable mentions are published in *Writers' Journal* November/December issue. Winners list published in WRITERS' Journal and on website. Entry fee: $10 reading fee. **Contact:** Leon Ogroske. "Offered annually for previously unpublished short stories. Open to any writer. Guidelines for SASE or online." Deadline: May 30. Prize: 1st Place: $350; 2nd Place: $125; 3rd Place: $75; plus honorable mentions. Prize-winning stories and selected honorable mentions are published in *Writers' Journal* November/December issue. Winners list published in WRITERS' Journal and on website. Entry fee: $10 reading fee.

NONFICTION

ANTHEM ESSAY CONTEST

The Ayn Rand Institute, P.O. Box 57044, Irvine CA 92619-7044. (949)222-6550. Fax: (949)222-6558. E-mail: essay@aynrand.org. Website: aynrand.org/contests. "Offered annually to encourage analytical thinking and excellence in writing (600-1,200 word essay), and to expose students to the philosophic ideas of Ayn Rand. For information contact your English teacher or guidance counselor or visit our website. Open to 8th, 9th and 10th graders." Deadline: March 20. Prize: 1st Place: $2,000; 2nd Place (5): $500; 3rd Place (10): $200; Finalist (45): $50; Semifinalist (175): $30.

ATLAS SHRUGGED ESSAY CONTEST

The Ayn Rand Institute, P.O. Box 57044, Irvine CA 92619-7044. (949)222-6550. Fax: (949)222-6558. E-mail: essay@aynrand.org. Website: aynrand.org/contests. "Offered annually to encourage analytical thinking and excellence in writing, and to expose students to the philosophic ideas of Ayn Rand. Essays are judged both on style and content. Essay length: 800-1,600/ words. Guidelines on website. Open to 12th graders and college undergraduate and graduate students." Deadline: September 17. Prize: 1st Place: $10,000; 2nd Place (3 awards): $2,000; 3rd Place (5 awards): $1,000; Finalists (20 awards): $100; Semifinalists (20 awards): $50.

BRITISH CZECH AND SLOVAK ASSOCIATION WRITING COMPETITION

24 Ferndale, Tunbridge Wells Kent TN2 3NS England. E-mail: prize@bcsa.co.uk. Website: bcsa.co.uk. **Contact:** Prize Administrator. "Annual contest for original writing (1,500-2,000 words) in English on the links between Britain and the Czech/Slovak Republics, or describing society in transition in the Republics since 1989. Entries can be fact or fiction. Topics can include history, politics, the sciences, economics, the arts, or literature." Deadline: June 30. Prize: 1st Place: £300; 2nd Place: £100.

CANADIAN AUTHORS ASSOCIATION LELA COMMON AWARD FOR CANADIAN HISTORY

74 Mississaga St. E., Orillia ON L3V 1A5 Canada. (705)719-3926. Fax: 1(866)393-1401. E-mail: admin@canauthors.org. Website: canauthors.org. **Contact:** Anita Purcell. Offered annually for a work of historical

nonfiction on a Canadian topic by a Canadian author. Entry form required. Obtain entry form from contact name or download from website. Deadline: December 15. Prize: $2,000 and a silver medal. The CAA Awards Chair appoints a trustee for this award. That trustee selects two judges. The identities of the trustee and judges are confidential throughout the judging process. Decisions of the trustee and judges are final, and they may choose not to award a prize. A shortlist of the best three entries in each category is announced in May. The winners are announced at the gala awards banquet during the annual CanWrite! conference in June.

CANADIAN LIBRARY ASSOCIATION STUDENT ARTICLE CONTEST

Canadian Library Association, 1150 Morrison Dr., Ottawa ON K2H 8S9 Canada. (613)232-9625, ext. 322. Fax: (613)563-9895. Website: cla.ca. **Contact:** Judy Green. Offered annually to unpublished articles discussing, analyzing, or evaluating timely issues in librarianship or information science. Open to all students registered in or recently graduated from a Canadian library school, a library techniques program, or faculty of education library program. Submissions may be in English or French. Deadline: March 31. Prize: 1st Place: $150 and trip to CLA's annual conference; 1st runner-up: $150 and $75 in CLA/ALA publications; 2nd runner-up: $100 and $75 in CLA/ALA publications.

THE DOROTHY CHURCHILL CAPPON CREATIVE NONFICTION AWARD

New Letters, University of Missouri-Kansas City, 5101 Rockhill Rd., Kansas City MO 64110. (816)235-1168. Fax: (816)235-2611. E-mail: newletters@umkc.edu. Website: newsletters.org. **Contact:** Ashley Kaine. Contest is offered annually for unpublished work to discover and reward emerging writers and to give experienced writers a place to try new genres. Acquires first North American serial rights. Open to any writer. Guidelines for SASE or online. Deadline: Third week of May. Prize: 1st Place: $1,500 and publication in a volume of *New Letters*; runner-up will receive a copy of a recent book of poetry or fiction courtesy of BkMk Press. All entries will receive consideration for publication in future editions of *New Letters*.

MORTON N. COHEN AWARD

Modern Language Association of America, 26 Broadway, 3rd Floor, New York NY 10004-1789. (646)576-5141. Fax: (646)458-0030. E-mail: awards@mla.org. Website: mla.org. **Contact:** Coordinator of Book Prizes. Awarded in odd-numbered years for a distinguished edition of letters. At least 1 volume of the edition must have been published during the previous 2 years. Editors need not be members of the MLA. Deadline: May 1. Prize: A cash award and a certificate to be presented at the Modern Language Association's annual convention in January.

THE SHAUGHNESSY COHEN PRIZE FOR POLITICAL WRITING

The Writers' Trust of Canada, 90 Richmond St. E., Suite 200, Toronto ON M5C 1P1 Canada. (416)504-8222. Fax: (416)504-9090. E-mail: info@writerstrust.com. Website: writerstrust.com. **Contact:** Amanda Hopkins, program coordinator. "Awarded annually for a nonfiction book of outstanding literary merit that enlarges our understanding of contemporary Canadian political and social issues. Presented at the Politics & the Pen event each spring in Ottawa. Open to Canadian citizens and permanent residents only." Prize: $25,000 and $2,500 to four finalists.

CARR P. COLLINS AWARD FOR NONFICTION

The Texas Institute of Letters, P.O. Box 609, Round Rock TX 78680. (512) 238-1871. E-mail: tilsecretary@yahoo.com. Website: texasinstituteofletters.org/. **Contact:** W.K. (Kip) Stratton, acquisitions. Offered annually for work published January 1-December 31 of the previous year to recognize the best nonfiction book by a writer who was born in Texas, who has lived in the state for at least 2 consecutive years at one point, or a writer whose work has some notable connection with Texas. See website for guidelines. Deadline: January 1. Prize: $5,000.

THE DONNER PRIZE

The Award for Best Book on Canadian Public Policy, The Donner Canadian Foundation, 349 Carlaw Ave., Toronto ON M4M 2T1 Canada. (416)368-8253 or (416)368-3763. E-mail: sherry@mdgassociates.com. Website: donnerbookprize.com. **Contact:** Sherry Naylor. "Offered annually for nonfiction published January 1-December 31 that highlights the importance of public policy and to reward excellent work in this field. Entries must be published in either English or French. Open to Canadian citizens." Deadline:

November 30. Prize: $30,000; Five shortlist authors get $5,000 each.

EDUCATOR'S AWARD

The Delta Kappa Gamma Society International, P.O. Box 1589, Austin TX 78767-1589. (888)762-4685. Fax: (512)478-3961. Website: dkg.org. **Contact:** Educator's Award Committee. "Offered annually for quality research and nonfiction published January-December of previous year. This award recognizes educational research and writings of female authors whose work may influence the direction of thought and action necessary to meet the needs of today's complex society. The book must be written by 1 or 2 women who are citizens of any country in which The Delta Kappa Gamma Society International is organized: Canada, Costa Rica, Denmark, Estonia, Finland, Germany, Great Britain, Guatemala, Iceland, Mexico, The Netherlands, Norway, Puerto Rico, Sweden, US, Panama. Guidelines (required) for SASE. Deadline: February 1. Prize: $2,500

EVANS BIOGRAPHY & HANDCART AWARDS

Mountain West Center for Regional Studies, Utah State University, 0735 Old Main Hill, Logan UT 84322-0700. (435)797-0299. Fax: (435)797-1092. E-mail: elaine.thatcher@usu.edu. Website: mountainwest.usu.edu/evans.aspx. **Contact:** Elaine Thatcher, program coordinator. "Offered to encourage the writing of biography about people who have played a role in the interior West. Publishers or authors may nominate books. Criteria for consideration: Work must be a biography or autobiography on someone who lived in or significantly contributed to the history of the Interior West; Biennial must be submitted for consideration for publication year's award; new editions or reprints are not eligible; mss are not accepted. Submit 6 copies." Deadline: January 1 in odd-numbered years for books published in the two previous calendar years. Prize: $10,000 and $1,000.

DINA FEITELSON RESEARCH AWARD

International Reading Association, Division of Research & Policy, 800 Barksdale Rd., Newark DE 19714-8139. (302)731-1600, ext. 423. Fax: (302)731-1057. E-mail: research@reading.org. Website: reading.org. **Contact:** Marcella Moore. "This is an award for an exemplary work published in English in a refereed journal that reports on an empirical study investigating aspects of literacy acquisition, such as phonemic awareness, the alphabetic principle, bilingualism, or cross-cultural studies of beginning reading. Articles may be submitted for consideration by researchers, authors, et al. Copies of the applications and guidelines can be downloaded in pdf format from the website." Deadline: September 1. Prize: Monetary award and recognition at the International Reading Association's annual convention.

GEORGE FREEDLEY MEMORIAL AWARD

Theatre Library Association, Benjamin Rosenthal Library, Queens College, CUNY, 65-30 Kissena Blvd., Flushing NY 11367. (718)997-3672. Fax: (718)997-3753. E-mail: Brooke.Stowe@liu.edu. Website: tla.library.unt.edu. **Contact:** Brooke Stowe, chair of the Theatre Library Association Awards. Offered for a book published in the US within the previous calendar year on a subject related to live theatrical performance (including cabaret, circus, pantomime, puppetry, vaudeville, etc.). Eligible books may include biography, history, theory, criticism, reference, or related fields. Deadline: March 15 of year following eligibility. Prize: $500 and a certificate to the winner; $200 and certificate for honorable mention

GORDON W. DILLON/RICHARD C. PETERSON MEMORIAL ESSAY PRIZE

American Orchid Society, Inc., American Orchid Society, 16700 AOS Ln., Delray Beach FL 33446-4351. (561)404-2040. Fax: (561)404-2045. E-mail: jwatson@aos.org. Website: aos.org. **Contact:** Jim Watson, Editor, *Orchids*. The Gordon W. Dillon \ Richard C. Peterson Memorial Essay Prize is an annual writing competition. The winner receives a cash prize and a certificate suitable for framing. Open to amateur and professional writers, it was established to honor the memory of two former editors of the *AOS Bulletin* (now *Orchids*). The theme is announced each May in *Orchids* magazine. All themes deal with an aspect of orchids. Acquires one-time rights." "Published since 1932, *Orchids* magazine (formerly known as the AOS Bulletin) is just one of the many benefits of membership to the AOS. See website for more about membership in the AOS. We are always interested in hearing from our readers! If you have an article idea that you wish to submit, please read our Submission Guidelines." Deadline: November 30. Prize: Cash award and a certificate. Winning entry usually published in the June issue of *Orchids* magazine.

✿ GOVERNOR GENERAL'S LITERARY AWARD FOR LITERARY NON-FICTION

Canada Council for the Arts, 350 Albert St., P.O. Box 1047, Ottawa ON K1P 5V8 Canada. (613)566-4414, ext. 5573. Fax: (613)566-4410. Website: canadacouncil.ca/prizes/ggla. **Contact:** Lori Knoll. Offered annually for the best English-language and the best French-language work of literary nonfiction by a Canadian. Deadline depends on the book's publication date: Books in English: March 15, June 1 or August 7. Books in French: March 15 or July 15. Prize: Each laureate receives $25,000; non-winning finalists receive $1,000.

ALBERT J. HARRIS AWARD

International Reading Association, Division of Research and Policy, 800 Barksdale Rd., Newark DE 19714-8139. (302)731-1600, ext. 423; (800)336-7323. Fax: (302)731-1057. E-mail: research@reading.org. Website: reading.org. **Contact:** Marcella Moore. "Offered annually to recognize outstanding published works focused on the identification, prevention, assessment, or instruction of learners experiencing difficulty learning to read. Articles may be nominated by researchers, authors, and others. Copies of the applications and guidelines can be downloaded in PDF format from the website." Deadline: September 1. Prize: Monetary award and recognition at the International Reading Association's annual convention.

HENDRICKS MANUSCRIPT AWARD

The New Netherland Institute, Cultural Education Center, Room 10C45, 310 Madison Ave., Albany NY 12230. Fax: (518)473-0472. E-mail: fnn@mail.nysed.gov. Website: nnp.org. **Contact:** Charles Gehring. Offered annually for the best published or unpublished ms focusing on any aspect of the Dutch colonial experience in North America. Deadline: March 15. Prize: $5,000 a 5-member panel of scholars.

HOWARD R. MARRARO PRIZE

Modern Language Association of America, 26 Broadway, 3rd Floor, New York NY 10004-1789. (646)576-5141. Fax: (646)458-0030. E-mail: awards@mla.org. Website: mla.org. **Contact:** Coordinator of Book Prizes. Offered in even-numbered years for a scholarly book or essay on any phase of Italian literature or comparative literature involving Italian, published in previous year. Authors must be members of the MLA. Deadline: May 1. Prize: A cash award and a certificate to be presented at the Modern Language Association's annual convention in January.

JAMES RUSSELL LOWELL PRIZE

Modern Language Association of America, 26 Broadway, 3rd Floor, New York NY 10004-1789. (646)576-5141. Fax: (646)458-0030. E-mail: awards@mla.org. Website: mla.org. **Contact:** Coordinator of Book Prizes. Offered annually for literary or linguistic study, or critical edition or biography published in previous year. *Open to MLA members only.* Deadline: March 1. Prize: A cash award and a certificate to be presented at the Modern Language Association's annual convention in January.

JOHN GUYON LITERARY NONFICTION PRIZE

Crab Orchard Review, English Department, Southern Illinois Univ. Carbondale, Carbondale IL 62901-4503. E-mail: jtribble@siu.edu. Website: craborchardreview.siuc.edu. **Contact:** Jon C. Tribble, managing editor. "Offered annually for unpublished work. This competition seeks to reward excellence in the writing of creative nonfiction. This is not a prize for academic essays. *Crab Orchard Review* acquires first North American serial rights to submitted works. Open to US citizens only." March 1 - April 30. Prize: $2,000 and publication.

KATHERYN KROTZER LABORDE LITERARY NONFICTION PRIZE

National League of American Pen Women, Nob Hill, San Francisco Branch, The Webhallow House, 1544 Sweetwood Dr., Broadmoor Village CA 94015-1717. E-mail: pennobhill@aol.com. Website: soulmakingcontest.us. **Contact:** Eileen Malone. All prose works must be typed, page numbered, and double-spaced. Each entry up to 3,000 words. Identify only with 3×5 card. Open annually to any writer. Deadline: November 30. Prize: 1st Place: $100; 2nd Place: $50; 3rd Place: $25.

KENNETH W. MILDENBERGER PRIZE

Modern Language Association of America, 26 Broadway, 3rd Floor, New York NY 10004-1789. (646)576-5141. Fax: (646)458-0030. E-mail: awards@mla.org. Website: mla.org. **Contact:** Coordinator of Book Prizes. Offered annually for a publication from the previous year in the field of language culture, literacy, or literature with a strong application to the teaching of languages other than English. Author need not be a member. Deadline: May 1. Prize: A cash award, and a certificate, to be presented at the Modern Language Association's annual convention in January and a year's membership in the MLA.

KATHERINE SINGER KOVACS PRIZE

Modern Language Association of America, 26 Broadway, 3rd Floor, New York NY 10004-1789. (646)576-5141. Fax: (646)458-0030. E-mail: awards@mla.org. Website: mla.org. **Contact:** Coordinator of Book Prizes. Offered annually for a book published during the previous year in English or Spanish in the field of Latin American and Spanish literatures and cultures. Books should be broadly interpretive works that enhance understanding of the interrelations among literature, the other arts, and society. Author must be a current member of the MLA. Deadline: May 1. Prize: A cash award and a certificate to be presented at the Modern Language Association's annual convention in January.

LAMAR YORK PRIZE FOR NONFICTION CONTEST

The Chattahoochee Review, Georgia Perimeter College, 2101 Womack Rd., Dunwoody GA 30338-4497. (770)274-5479. E-mail: lhetrick@gpc.edu. Website: chattahoochee-review.org. **Contact:** Anna Schachner, Editor. Offered annually for unpublished creative nonfiction and nonscholarly essays up to 5,000 words. *The Chattahoochee Review* buys first rights only for winning essay/ms for the purpose of publication in the summer issue. Deadline: October 1-January 31. Prize: $1,000, plus publication for 1 or more winners. Judged by the editorial staff of *The Chattahoochee Review*.

⊘ TONY LOTHIAN PRIZE

under the auspices of the Biographers' Club, 119a Fordwych Rd., London NW2 3NJ United Kingdom. (44)(20)8452 4993. E-mail: anna@annaswan.co.uk. Website: biographersclub.co.uk. **Contact:** Anna Swan, Prize Administrator. "Entries should consist of a 10-page synopsis and 10 pages of a sample chapter for a proposed biography, plus cv, sources and a note on the market for the book. Open to any writer who has not previously been published or commissioned or written a book." Deadline: August 1. Prize: £2,000. Judges have included Michael Holroyd, Victoria Glendinning, Selina Hastings, Frances Spalding, Lyndall

Gordon, Anne de Courcy, Nigel Hamilton, Anthony Sampson, and Mary Lovell.

RICHARD J. MARGOLIS AWARD

c/o Margolis & Bloom, LLP, 535 Boylston St., 8th floor, Boston MA 02116. (617)267-9700, ext. 517. E-mail: harry@margolis.com. Website: margolis.com/award. **Contact:** Harry S. Margolis. Sponsored by the Blue Mountain Center, this annual award is given to a promising new journalist or essayist whose work combines warmth, humor, wisdom, and concern with social justice. Submit 3 copies of at least 2 examples of your published or unpublished work (maximum 30 pages) and a short biographical note. Deadline: July 1. Prize: $5,000 and a 1-month residency at the Blue Mountain Center—a writers and artists colony in the Adirondacks in Blue Mountain Lake, New York.

MINA P. SHAUGHNESSY PRIZE

Modern Language Association of America, 26 Broadway, 3rd Floor, New York NY 10004-1789. (646)576-5141. Fax: (646)458-0030. E-mail: awards@mla.org. Website: mla.org. **Contact:** Coordinator of Book Prizes. Offered annually for a scholarly book in the fields of language, culture, literacy or literature with strong application to the teaching of English published during preceding year. Authors need not be members of the MLA. Deadline: May 1. Prize: A cash prize, a certificate, to be presented at the Modern Language Association's annual convention in January, and a one-year membership in the MLA.

MLA PRIZE FOR A DISTINGUISHED BIBLIOGRAPHY

Modern Language Association of America, 26 Broadway, 3rd Floor, New York NY 10004-1789. (646)576-5141. Fax: (646)458-0030. E-mail: awards@mla.org. Website: mla.org. **Contact:** Annie Reiser, Coordinator of Book Prizes. Offered in even-numbered years for enumerative and descriptive bibliographies published in monographic, book, or electronic format in the 2 years prior to the competition. Open to any writer or publisher. Deadline: May 1. Prize: A cash prize and a certificate to be presented at the Modern Language Association's annual convention in January.

MLA PRIZE FOR A DISTINGUISHED SCHOLARLY EDITION

Modern Language Association of America, 26 Broadway, 3rd Floor, New York NY 10004-1789. (646)576-

5141. Fax: (646)458-0030. E-mail: awards@mla.org. Website: mla.org. **Contact:** Coordinator of Book Prizes. Offered in odd-numbered years. To qualify for the award, an edition should be based on an examination of all available relevant textual sources; the source texts and the edited text's deviations from them should be fully described; the edition should employ editorial principles appropriate to the materials edited, and those principles should be clearly articulated in the volume; the text should be accompanied by appropriate textual and other historical contextual information; the edition should exhibit the highest standards of accuracy in the presentation of its text and apparatus; and the text and apparatus should be presented as accessibly and elegantly as possible. Editor need not be a member of the MLA. Deadline: May 1. Prize: A cash award and a certificate to be presented at the Modern Language Association's annual convention in January.

MLA PRIZE FOR A FIRST BOOK

Modern Language Association of America, 26 Broadway, 3rd Floor, New York NY 10004-1789. (646)576-5141. Fax: (646)458-0030. E-mail: awards@mla.org. Website: mla.org. **Contact:** Coordinator of Book Prizes. Offered annually for the first book-length scholarly publication by a current member of the association. To qualify, a book must be a literary or linguistic study, a critical edition of an important work, or a critical biography. Studies dealing with literary theory, media, cultural history, and interdisciplinary topics are eligible; books that are primarily translations will not be considered. Deadline: April 1. Prize: A cash award and a certificate to be presented at the Modern Language Association's annual convention in January.

MLA PRIZE FOR INDEPENDENT SCHOLARS

Modern Language Association of America, 26 Broadway, 3rd Floor, New York NY 10004-1789. (646)576-5141. Fax: (646)458-0030. E-mail: awards@mla.org. Website: mla.org. **Contact:** Coordinator of Book Prizes. Offered annually for a book in the field of English, or another modern language, or literature published in the previous year. Authors who are enrolled in a program leading to an academic degree or who hold tenured or tenure-track positions in higher education are not eligible. Authors need not be members of MLA. Guidelines and application form for SASE. Deadline: May 1. Prize: A cash award, a certificate, and a year's membership in the MLA.

LINDA JOY MYERS VIGNETTE MEMOIR PRIZE

National League of American Pen Women, Nob Hill, San Francisco Branch, Webhallow House, 1544 Sweetwood Dr., Broadmoor Village CA 94015-2029. E-mail: pennobhill@aol.com. Website: soulmaking-contest.us. **Contact:** Eileen Malone. "One memoir/entry, up to 1,500 words, double spaced. Previously published material is acceptable. Indicate category on first page. Identify only with 3X5 card. Open annually to any writer." Deadline: November 30. Prize: 1st Place: $100; 2nd Place $50; 3rd Place $25.

NATIONAL WRITERS ASSOCIATION NONFICTION CONTEST

The National Writers Association, 10940 S. Parker Rd., #508, Parker CO 80134. (303)841-0246. Fax: (303)841-2607. E-mail: natlwritersassn@hotmail.com. Website: nationalwriters.com. 10940 S. Parker Rd.#508, Parker CO 80134. (303)841-0246. **Executive Director:** Sandy Whelchel. Annual contest. Estab. 1971. Purpose of contest: "to encourage and recognize those who excel in nonfiction writing." Submissions made by author. Deadline for entries: December 31. SASE for contest rules and entry forms. Entry fee is $18. Awards 3 cash prizes; choice of books; Honorable Mention Certificate. "Two people read each entry; third party picks three top winners from top five." Judging sheets sent if entry accompanied by SASE. Condensed version of 1st place may be published in Authorship. **Contact:** Sandy Whelchel, director. "Annual contest to encourage writers in this creative form and to recognize those who excel in nonfiction writing." Deadline: December 31. Prize: 1st Place: $200; 2nd Place: $100; 3rd Place: $50.

THE FREDERIC W. NESS BOOK AWARD

Association of American Colleges and Universities, 1818 R St. NW, Washington DC 20009. (202)387-3760. Fax: (202)265-9532. E-mail: info@aacu.org. Website: aacu.org. **Contact:** Bethany Sutton. Offered annually for work published in the previous year. Each year the Frederic W. Ness Book Award Committee of the Association of American Colleges and Universities recognizes books which contribute to the understanding and improvement of liberal education. Guidelines for SASE or online. "Writers may nominate their own work; however, we send letters of invitation to publishers to nominate qualified books." Deadline: May 1. Prize: $2,000 and a presentation at the association's annual meeting—transportation and 1 night hotel for meeting are also provided.

OUTSTANDING DISSERTATION OF THE YEAR AWARD

International Reading Association, 800 Barksdale Rd., P.O. Box 8139, Newark DE 19714-8139. (302)731-1600, ext. 423; (800)336-7323. Fax: (302)731-1057. E-mail: research@reading.org. Website: reading.org. **Contact:** Marcella Moore. "This award is offered annually to recognize dissertations in the field of reading and literacy. *Applicants must be members of the International Reading Association.* Copies of the applications and guidelines can be downloaded in PDF format from the website." Deadline: October 1.

FRANK LAWRENCE AND HARRIET CHAPPELL OWSLEY AWARD

Southern Historical Association, Dept. of History, University of Georgia, Athens GA 30602-1602. (706)542-8848. Fax: (706)542-2455. Website: uga.edu/sha. **Contact:** Southern Historical Association. Offered in odd-numbered years for recognition of a distinguished book in Southern history published in even-numbered years. Publishers usually submit the books. Deadline: March 1.

PRESERVATION FOUNDATION CONTESTS

The Preservation Foundation, Inc., 2213 Pennington Bend, Nashville TN 37214. E-mail: preserve@storyhouse.org. Website: storyhouse.org. **Contact:** Richard Loller, Publisher. "Two contests offered annually for unpublished nonfiction. General nonfiction category (1,500-5,000 words)—any appropriate nonfiction topic. Travel nonfiction category (1,500-5,000 words)—must be true story of trip by author or someone known personally by author. E-mail entries only (no mss). **First entry in each category is free; $10 fee for each additional entry (limit 3 entries/category).** Open to any previously unpublished writer. Defined as having earned no more than $750 by creative writing in any previous year." Deadline: August 31. Prize: 1st Place: $100 in each category; certificates for finalists.

PHILLIP D. REED MEMORIAL AWARD FOR OUTSTANDING WRITING ON THE SOUTHERN ENVIRONMENT

Southern Environmental Law Center, 201 W. Main St., Suite 14, Charlottesville VA 22902-5065. (434)977-4090. Fax: (434)977-1483. E-mail: cmccue@selcva.org. Website: SouthernEnvironment.org/phil_reed. **Contact:** Cathryn McCue, writing award coordinator. Offered annually for nonfiction pieces that most effectively tell stories about the South's environment. Categories include Journalism and Book. Entries must have been published during the previous calendar year and have a minimum of 3,000 words. Guidelines online or for SASE. Deadline: early January. Prize: $1,000 for winner in each category. See southernenvironment.org/about/phil_reed.

☼ EVELYN RICHARDSON NONFICTION AWARD

Writers' Federation of Nova Scotia, 1113 Marginal Rd., Halifax NS B3H 4P7 Canada. (902)423-8116. Fax: (902)422-0881. E-mail: talk@writers.ns.ca. Website: writers.ns.ca. **Contact:** Nate Crawford, executive director. "This annual award is named for Nova Scotia writer Evelyn Richardson, whose book *We Keep a Light* won the Governor General's Literary Award for nonfiction in 1945. There is **no entry fee** or form. Full-length books of nonfiction written by Nova Scotians, and published as a whole for the first time in the previous calendar year, are eligible. Publishers: Send 4 copies and a letter attesting to the author's status as a Nova Scotian, and the author's current mailing address and telephone number." Deadline: First Friday in December. Prize: $2,000.

☼ SASKATCHEWAN NONFICTION AWARD

Saskatchewan Book Awards, Inc., 205B-2314 11th Ave., Regina SK S4P 0K1 Canada. (306)569-1585. Fax: (306)569-4187. E-mail: director@bookawards.sk.ca. Website: bookawards.sk.ca. **Contact:** Jackie Lay, executive director. Offered annually for work published September 15-October 31. This award is presented to a Saskatchewan author for the best book of nonfiction, judged on the quality of writing. Deadline: November 1. Prize: $2,000 CAD.

☼ SASKATCHEWAN SCHOLARLY WRITING AWARD

Saskatchewan Book Awards, Inc., 205B-2314 11th Ave., Regina SK S4P 0K1 Canada. (306)569-1585. Fax: (306)569-4187. E-mail: director@bookawards.sk.ca. Website: bookawards.sk.ca. **Contact:** Jackie Lay, exec. dir., book submissions. Offered annually for work published September 15-October 31 annually. This award is presented to a Saskatchewan author for the best contribution to scholarship. The work must recognize or draw on specific theoretical work within a community of scholars, and participate in the creation and transmission of scholarly knowledge. Deadline: November 1. Prize: $2,000.

ALDO AND JEANNE SCAGLIONE PRIZE FOR ITALIAN STUDIES

Modern Language Association of America, 26 Broadway, 3rd Floor, New York NY 10004-1789. (646)576-5141. Fax: (646)458-0030. E-mail: awards@mla.org. Website: mla.org. **Contact:** Coordinator of Book Prizes. Offered in odd-numbered years for a scholarly book on any phase of Italian literature or culture, or comparative literature involving Italian, including works on literary or cultural theory, science, history, art, music, society, politics, cinema, and linguistics, preferably but not necessarily relating other disciplines to literature. Books must have been published in year prior to competition. *Authors must be members of the MLA.* Deadline: May 1. Prize: A cash award and a certificate to be presented at the Modern Language Association's annual convention in January.

ALDO AND JEANNE SCAGLIONE PRIZE FOR STUDIES IN GERMANIC LANGUAGES & LITERATURE

Modern Language Association of America, 26 Broadway, 3rd Floor, New York NY 10004-1789. (646)576-5141. Fax: (646)458-0030. E-mail: awards@mla.org. Website: mla.org. **Contact:** Coordinator of Book Prizes. Offered in even-numbered years for outstanding scholarly work appearing in print in the previous 2 years and written by a member of the MLA on the linguistics or literatures of the Germanic languages. Works of literary history, literary criticism, and literary theory are eligible; books that are primarily translations are not eligible. Deadline: May 1. Prize: A cash award, and a certificate to be presented at the Modern Language Association's annual convention in January.

ALDO AND JEANNE SCAGLIONE PRIZE FOR STUDIES IN SLAVIC LANGUAGES AND LITERATURES

Modern Language Association of America, 26 Broadway, 3rd Floor, New York NY 10004-1789. (646)576-5141. Fax: (646)458-0030. E-mail: awards@mla.org. Website: mla.org. **Contact:** Coordinator of Book Prizes. Offered in odd-numbered years for books

published in the previous 2 years. Membership in the MLA is not required. Works of literary history, literary criticism, philology, and literary theory are eligible; books that are primarily translations are not eligible. Deadline: May 1. Prize: A cash award and a certificate to be presented at the Modern Language Association's annual convention in January.

CHARLES S. SYDNOR AWARD

Southern Historical Association, Dept. of History, University of Georgia, Athens GA 30602. (706)542-8848. Fax: (706)542-2455. Website: uga.edu/sha. **Contact:** Southern Historical Association. Offered in even-numbered years for recognition of a distinguished book in Southern history published in odd-numbered years. Publishers usually submit books. Deadline: March 1.

THE LINCOLN PRIZE

Gettysburg College and Gilder Lehrman Institute of American History, 300 N. Washington St., Campus Box 435, Gettysburg PA 17325. (717)337-8255. Fax: (717)337-6596. E-mail: lincolnprize@gettysburg.edu. Website: gettysburg.edu/civilwar/prize_andscholarships/lincoln_prize/. Offered annually for the "finest scholarly work in English on the era of the American Civil War. The award will usually go to a book published in the previous year; however articles, essays, and works of fiction may be submitted." For more information visit the website.

THOMAS J. HRUSKA MEMORIAL PRIZE IN NONFICTION

Passages North, Dept. of English, Northern Michigan University, 1401 Presque Isle Ave., Marquette MI 49855. Website: myweb.nmu.edu/~passages. **Contact:** Kate Myers Hanson, Acquisitions. Thomas J. Hruska Memorial Prize in Nonfiction. Send SASE for announcement of winners. Author's name may appear anywhere on ms or cover letter. Manuscripts will not be returned. All entrants receive a contest issue. Honorable mentions will also be chosen for each contest and may or may not be published according to the needs of the editors. Deadline: Feb. 15. Prize: $1,000 first prize and publication.

✚ TILIA KLEBENOV JACOBS RELIGIOUS ESSAY COMPETITION

Category in the Soul-Making Literary Competition, National League of American Pen Women, The Webhallow House, 1544 Sweetwood Dr., Broadmoor Village CA 94015-2029. E-mail: pennobhill@aol.com. Website: soulmakingcontest.us. "Call for thoughtful writings of up to 3,000 words. No preaching, no proselytizing. Previously published material is accepted. Indicate category on cover of page and on identifying 3x5 card. Open annually to any writer." **Contact:** Eileen Malone. "Call for thoughtful writings of up to 3,000 words. No preaching, no proselytizing. Previously published material is accepted. Indicate category on cover of page and on identifying 3x5 card. Open annually to any writer." Deadline: November 30. Prize: 1st Place: $100; 2nd Place $50; 3rd Place $25.

⊕ TORREY HOUSE CREATIVE LITERARY NONFICTION CONTEST

Creative Literary Nonfiction Contest, Torrey House, Website: torreyhouse.com. "Submit great stories of the West that promote appreciation of our beautiful land. Length: 2,000 - 10,000 words. Show us the power of the Colorado Plateau. Contest submissions must be original and not previously published. Please, no stories written for children for contest entries. Include two title pages: one with your name and contact information and one with the title of your piece only. Double space your submissions and use a 12-point font, with numbered pages that include the title of the piece as a header. Please e-mail us your material as a document attachment with *Contest: your entry's title* in the subject line and *yourentrystitle* as the filename. Send your entry to mail@torreyhouse.com. The entry fee is $25 per submission and is non-refundable. You are welcome to enter more than one piece; each will be considered a separate submission and must be accompanied by the $25 fee. Please use the PayPal button "Buy Now" online to make your payment and be sure to include the same e-mail address you use on your submission so we know you paid. Deadline: May 31. First prize: $1,000; Second prize: $250; Third prize: $100. All winners published in Torrey House Press annual journal."

☯ THE WRITERS' TRUST NONFICTION PRIZE

The Writers' Trust of Canada, 90 Richmond St. E., Suite 200, Toronto ON M5C 1P1 Canada. (416)504-8222. Fax: (416)504-9090. E-mail: info@writerstrust. com. Website: writerstrust.com. **Contact:** Amanda Hopkins. "Offered annually for a work of nonfiction published in the previous year. Award presented at The Writers' Trust Awards event held in Toronto each Fall. Open to Canadian citizens and permanent residents only." Deadline: August 2011. Prize: $25,000 (Canadian), and $2,500 to four finalists.

WRITING FOR CHILDREN & YOUNG ADULTS

AMERICAN ASSOCIATION OF UNIVERSITY WOMEN AWARD IN JUVENILE LITERATURE

4610 Mail Service Center, Raleigh NC 27699-4610. (919)733-9375. E-mail: michael.hill@ncdcr.gov. Annual award. Purpose of award: to recognize the year's best work of juvenile literature by a North Carolina resident. Book must be published during the year ending June 30. Submissions made by author, author's agent or publisher. Deadline for entries: July 15. SASE for contest rules. Awards a cup to the winner and winner's name inscribed on a plaque displayed within the North Carolina Office of Archives and History. Judging by Board of Award selected by sponsoring organization. Requirements for entrants: Author must have maintained either legal residence or actual physical residence, or a combination of both, in the state of North Carolina for three years immediately preceding the close of the contest period. Only published work (books) eligible. North Carolina Literary and Historical Association, 4610 Mail Service Center, Raleigh NC 27699-4610. (919) 807-7290. Fax: (919) 733-8807. E-mail: michael.hill@ncdcr.gov. **Contact:** Michael Hill, awards coordinator. Award's purpose is to "select the year's best work of literature for young people by a North Carolina writer." Annual award for published books. Award: cup. Competition receives 10-15 submissions per category. Judged by three-judge panel. No entry fee. **Deadline: July 15.** Entries must be previously published. Contest open to "residents of North Carolina (three-year minimum)." Guidelines available July 15. For guidelines, send SASE, fax, e-mail or call. Accepts inquiries by fax, e-mail, phone. Winners announced October 15. Winners notified by mail. List of winners available for SASE, fax, e-mail.

⊕ CHILDREN'S AFRICANA BOOK AWARD

African Studies Association, c/o Rutgers University, 132 George St., New Brunswick NJ 08901. E-mail: harrietmcguire@earthlink.net. Website: africanstudies. org. Outreach Council of the African Studies Association, c/o Rutgers University, 132 George St. New Brunswick NJ 08901. (732)932-8173. Fax: (732)932-3394. Website: africanstudies.org. Administered by Africa Access, P.O. Box 8028, Silver Spring MD 20910. (301)585-9136. E-mail: africaaccess@aol.com. Website: africaaccessreview.org. **Chairperson**: Brenda Randolph. Annually. Estab. 1991. Purpose of contest: "The Children's Africana Book Awards are presented annually to the authors and illustrators of the best books on Africa for children and young people published or republished in the U.S. The awards were created by the Outreach Council of the African Studies Association (ASA) to dispel stereotypes and encourage the publication and use of accurate, balanced children's materials about Africa. The awards are presented in 2 categories: Young Children and Older Readers. Since 1991, 63 books have been recognized." Entries must have been published in the calendar year previous to the award. No entry fee. Awards plaque, ceremony in Washington D.C., announcement each spring, reviews published at Africa Access Review website and in *Sankofa: Journal of African Children's & Young Adult Literature*. Judging by Outreach Council of ASA and children's literature scholars. "Work submitted for awards must be suitable for children ages 4-18; a significant portion of books' content must be about Africa; must by copyrighted in the calendar year prior to award year; must be published or republished in the US. New in 2010, the jury has added designation of 'Noteworthy Books,' flagged for special attention by teachers and librarians. Award winners, Honor Books and Noteworthy books will all be featured in our publicity materials." **Contact:** Harriet McGuire.

PATERSON PRIZE FOR BOOKS FOR YOUNG PEOPLE

The Poetry Center at Passaic County Community College, One College Blvd., Paterson NJ 07505-1179. (973)523-6085. Fax: (973)523-6085. E-mail: mgillan@pccc.edu. Website: pccc.edu/poetry. Part of the Poetry Center's mission is "to recognize excellence in books for young people." Published submissions only. Submissions made by author, author's agent or publisher. Must be published between January 1-December 31 of year previous to award year. Deadline for entries: March 15. SASE for contest rules and entry forms or visit website. Awards $500 for the author in either of 3 categories: PreK-Grade 3; Grades 4-6, Grades 7-12.

Judging by a professional writer selected by the Poetry Center. Contest is open to any writer/illustrator. **Contact:** Maria Mazziotti Gillan, exec. director. At above address or visit pccc.edu/poetry and go to prizes."Offered annually for books published the previous calendar year. Three categories: pre-kindergarten-grade 3; grades 4-6; grades 7-12. Open to any writer." Fiction; nonfiction; poetry; juvenile; novels; short stories. Deadline: March 15. $500 in each category. Deadline: March 15. Prize: $500 in each category.

PEN/PHYLLIS NAYLOR WORKING WRITER FELLOWSHIP

PEN American Center, 588 Broadway, Suite 303, New York NY 10012. (212)334-1660, ext. 108. Fax: (212)334-2181. E-mail: awards@pen.org. Website: pen.org/awards. **Contact:** awards coordinator. Open to a writer of children's or young adult fiction in financial need, who has published at least two books for children or young adults to be eligible. Annual contest. Submissions by nomination from a PEN member. Unpublished submissions of high literary caliber only. The nominator should write a letter of support, describing in some detail how the candidate meets the criteria for the Fellowship. The nominator should also provide: 1) A list of the candidate's published work, accompanied by copies of reviews, where possible. 2) Three copies of the outline of the current novel in progress, together with 50-75 pages of the text. Picture books are not eligible. 3) On a separate piece of paper, a brief description of the candidate's recent earnings and a statement about why monetary support will make a particular difference in the applicant's writing life at this time. If the candidate is married or living with a domestic partner, please include a brief description of total family income and expenses. Deadline: Feb. 3. Prize: Awards $5,000 "Upon nomination by an editor or fellow writer, a panel of judges will select the winning book."

POCKETS FICTION-WRITING CONTEST

P.O. Box 340004, Nashville TN 37203-0004. E-mail: pockets@upperroom.org;theupperroommagazine@upperroom.org. Website: pockets.upperroom.org. **Contact:** Lynn W. Gilliam, senior editor. *Pockets* is a devotional magazine for children between the ages of 6 and 11. Contest offered annually for unpublished work to discover new children's writers. Prize: $1,000 and publication in *Pockets*. Categories: short stories. Judged by *Pockets* staff and staff of other Upper Room

Publications. No entry fee. Guidelines available on website or send #10 SASE. **Deadline: Must be postmarked between March 1-August 15.** Entries must be unpublished. Because the purpose of the contest is to discover new writers, previous winners are not eligible. No violence, science fiction, romance, fantasy or talking animal stories. Word length 1,000-1,600 words. Open to any writer. Winner announced November 1 and notified by U.S. mail. Contest submissions accompanied by SASE will be returned Nov. 1. "Send SASE with 4 first-class stamps to request guidelines and a past issue, or go to: pockets.upperroom. org." **We do not accept manuscripts sent by fax or e-mail.**

QUILL AND SCROLL INTERNATIONAL WRITING/PHOTO CONTEST

School of Journalism, Univ. of Iowa, 100 Adler Journalism Bldg., Iowa City IA 52242-2004. E-mail: quill-scroll@uiowa.edu; vanessa-shelton@uiowa.edu. Website: uiowa.edu/~quill-sc. Quill and Scroll, School of Journalism and Mass Communication, University of Iowa, Iowa City IA 52242-2004. (319)335-3457. Fax: (319)335-3989. E-mail: quill-scroll@uiowa.edu. Website: uiowa.edu/~quill-sc. **Open to students.** Annual contest. Previously published submissions only. Submissions made by the author or school newspaper adviser. Must be published within the last year. Deadline for entries: February 5. Visit website for more information and entry forms. Entry fee is $2/entry. Engraved plaque awarded to sweepstakes winners. Judging by various judges. Quill and Scroll acquires the right to publish submitted material in its magazine or website if it is chosen as a winning entry. Requirements for entrants: must be students in grades 9-12 for high school division. Entry form available on website. **Contact:** Vanessa Shelton. Annual contest. Currently enrolled high school students, including Quill and Scroll members and non-members, are invited to enter the International Writing and Photo Contest. Awards are made in each of the 12 divisions. Winners will receive Quill and Scroll's National Award Gold Key and, if seniors, are eligible to apply for one of the scholarships offered by Quill and Scroll. Work appearing online or in print is acceptable.

RITA WILLIAMS YOUNG ADULT PROSE PRIZE

National League of American Pen Women, Nob Hill, San Francisco Branch, The Webhallow House, 1544

Sweetwood Dr., Broadmoor Vlg. CA 94015-2029. E-mail: pennobhill@aol.com. Website: soulmaking-contest.us. Up to 3,000 words in story, essay, journal entry, creative nonfiction, or memoir by writer in grades 9-12. Indicate age and category on each first page. Identify with 3x5 card only. Open annually to young adult writers. No e-mail entries or those mailed special delivery, certified or registered will be accepted. Do enclose SASE in your entry package if you wish to receive contest results. Deadline: November 30. Prize: 1st Place: $100; 2nd Place: $50; 3rd Place: $25.

⊘ SASKATCHEWAN CHILDREN'S LITERATURE AWARD

Saskatchewan Book Awards, Inc., 205B-2314 11th Ave., Regina SK S4P 0K1 Canada. (306)569-1585. Fax: (306)569-4187. E-mail: director@bookawards.sk.ca. Website: bookawards.sk.ca. Estab. 1995. Purpose of contest: to celebrate Saskatchewan books and authors and to promote their work. Previously published submissions only. Submissions made by author, author's agent or publisher by September 15, 2010-October 31. SASE for contest rules and entry forms. Entry fee is $25 (Canadian). Awards $2,000 (Canadian). Judging by three children's literature authors outside of Saskatchewan. Requirements for entrants: Must be Saskatchewan resident; book must have ISBN number; book must have been published within the last year. Award-winning book will appear on TV talk shows and be pictured on bookmarks distributed to libraries, schools and bookstores in Saskatchewan. **Contact:** Jackie Lay, executive director, book submissions. Offered annually for work published September 15, 2010-October 31. This award is presented to a Saskatchewan author for the best book of children's or young adult's literature, judged on the quality of writing. Deadline: November 1.

⊕ SYDNEY TAYLOR BOOK AWARD

Association of Jewish Libraries, P.O. Box 1118, Teaneck NJ 07666. E-mail: chair@sydneytaylorbookaward. org; heidi@cbiboca.org. Website: sydneytaylorbookaward.org. **Contact:** Barbara Bietz, chair. Offered annually for work published during the current year. "Given to distinguished contributions to Jewish literature for children. One award for younder readers, one for older readers, and one for teens." Publishers submit books. Deadline: December 31, but we cannot guarantee that books received after December 1 will be considered. Guidelines on website. Awards certificate, cash award, and gold or silver seals for cover of winning book.

TOMÁS RIVERA MEXICAN AMERICAN CHILDREN'S BOOK AWARD

601 University Dr., San Marcos TX 78666-4613. (512)245-2357. Website: education.txstate.edu/about/Map-Directions.html. Contact Dr. Jesse Gainer for information and send copy of book. No entry fee. Awards $2,000 per book. Judging of nominations by a regional committee, national committee judges finalists. Annual ceremony honoring the book and author/illustrator is held during the fall at Texas State University-San Marcos in collaboration with the Texas Book Festival. **Contact:** Dr. Jesse Gainer, Director. Competition open to adults. Annual contest. Competition open to adults. Annual contest. Estab. 1995. Purpose of award: "To encourage authors, illustrators and publishers to produce books that authentically reflect the lives of Mexican Americans appropriate for children and young adults in the United States." Unpublished mss not accepted. Submissions made by "any interested individual or publishing company." Must be published during the two years prior to the year of consideration for the appropriate category "Works for Younger Children" or " Works for Older Children". Contact Dr. Jesse Gainer for information and send copy of book. Annual ceremony honoring the book and author/illustrator is held during the fall at Texas State University-San Marcos in collaboration with the Texas Book Festival. Deadline: Nov. 1 of publication year. Prize: Awards $2,000 per book. Judging of nominations by a regional committee, national committee judges finalists.

WORK-IN-PROGRESS GRANT

Society of Children's Book Writers and Illustrators (SCBWI), 8271 Beverly Blvd., Los Angeles CA 90048. (323)782-1010. E-mail: scbwi@scbwi.org. Website: scbwi.org. Four grants—one designated specifically for a contemporary novel for young people, one for nonfiction, one for an unpublished writer, one general fiction—to assist SCBWI members in the completion of a specific project. Open to SCBWI members only. Applications received only between February 15 and March 15.

WRITE A STORY FOR CHILDREN COMPETITION

Academy of Children's Writers, P.O. Box 95, Huntingdon Cambridgeshire PE28 5RL England. Phone/Fax: (44)(148)783-2752. E-mail: enquiries@childrens-writers.co.uk. Website: childrens-writers.co.uk. **Contact:** Contest Director. Annual contest for the best unpublished short story writer for children. Guidelines and entry forms online or send SAE/IRC. Open to any unpublished writer over the age of 18. Deadline: March 31. Prize: 1st Place: £2,000; 2nd Place: £300; 3rd Place: £200. Judgesd by a panel appointed by the Academy of Children's Writers.

WRITE IT NOW!

SmartWriters.com, 10823 Worthing Ave., San Diego CA 92126-2220. E-mail: editor@SmartWriters.com. Website: SmartWriters.com. SmartWriters.com, 10823 Worthing Ave.San Diego CA 92126-2665. (858)689-2665. E-mail: editor@smartwriters.com. Website: SmartWriters.com. Estab. 1994. Annual contest. "Our purpose is to encourage new writers and help get their manuscripts into the hands of people who can help further their careers." Unpublished submissions only. Submissions made by author. Deadline for entries: May 1. SASE for contest rules and entry forms; also see website. Entry fee is $15 for initial entry, $10 for additional entries. Awards a cash prize, books about writing, and an editorial review of the winning manuscripts. Judging by published writers and editors. Requirement for entrants: "This contest is open to all writers age 18 and older. There are 5 categories: Young Adult, Mid-grade, Picture Book, Nonfiction, and Illustration." See website for more details, FAQ, and rules updates. **Contact:** Roxyanne Young, Editorial Director. Annual contest. "Our purpose is to encourage new writers and help get their manuscripts into the hands of people who can help further their careers." Unpublished submissions only. Submissions made by author. SASE for contest rules and entry forms; also see website. Requirement for entrants: "This contest is open to all writers age 18 and older. There are 5 categories: Young Adult, Mid-grade, Picture Book, Nonfiction, and Illustration." See website for more details, FAQ, and rules updates. Deadline for entries: May 1. Prize: Awards a cash prize, books about writing, and an editorial review of the winning manuscripts Judged by published writers and editors.

GENERAL

⊘ AUSTRALIAN CHRISTIAN BOOK OF THE YEAR AWARD

Australian Christian Literature Society, c/o SPCK-Australia, P.O. Box 198, Forest Hill Victoria 3131 Australia. E-mail: acls@spcka.org.au. Website: spcka.org.au. **Contact:** Book of the Year Coordinator. "Annual contest for an Australian Christian book published between April 1 and March 31." Deadline: March 31.

JAMIE CAT CALLAN HUMOR PRIZE

National League of American Pen Women, The Webhallow House, 1544 Sweetwood Dr., Broadmoor Village CA 94015-2029. E-mail: pennobhill@aol.com. Website: soulmakingcontest.us. **Contact:** Eileen Malone. "Any form, 2,500 words or less, one piece per entry. Previously published material is accepted. Indicate category on cover page. Identify only with 3X5 card. Open annually to any writer." Deadline: November 30. Prize: 1st Place: $100; 2nd Place: $50; 3rd Place: $25.

♻ DAFOE BOOK PRIZE

J.W. Dafoe Foundation, 351 University College, University of Manitoba, Winnipeg MB R3T 2M8 Canada. E-mail: ferguss@cc.umanitoba.ca. **Contact:** Dr. James Fergusson. The Dafoe Book Prize was established to honor John Dafoe, editor of the *Winnipeg Free Press* from 1900 to 1944, and is awarded each year to the book that best contributes to our understanding of Canada and/or its relations abroad by a Canadian or author in residence. Books must be published January-December of previous publishing year — i.e., 2011 Award is for books published in 2010. Co-authored books are eligible, but not edited books consisting of chapters from many different authors. Submit 4 copies of book. Authors must be Canadian citizens or landed immigrants. Deadline: December 6. Prize: $10,000. Judged by board members and academics.

THE FOUNTAINHEAD ESSAY CONTEST

The Ayn Rand Institute, P.O. Box 57044, Irvine CA 92619-7044. E-mail: essay@aynrand.org. Website: aynrand.org/contests. "Offered annually to encourage analytical thinking and excellence in writing, and to expose students to the philosophic ideas of Ayn Rand. For information contact your English teacher or guidance counselor, or visit our website. Length: 800-1,600 words. Open to 11th and 12th graders."

Deadline: April 26. Prize: 1st Place: $10,000; 2nd Place (5): $2,000; 3rd Place (10): $1,000; Finalist (45): $100; Semifinalist (175): $50.

THE JANE GESKE AWARD

Prairie Schooner, 123 Andrews Hall, P.O. Box 880334, Lincoln NE 68588-0334. (402)472-0911. Fax: (402)472-9771. E-mail: jengelhardt2@unl.edu. Website: prairieschooner.unl.edu/. **Contact:** Kwame Dawes. Offered annually for work published in *Prairie Schooner* in the previous year. Prize: $250.

INDEPENDENT PUBLISHER BOOK AWARDS

Jenkins Group/Independent Publisher Online, 1129 Woodmere Ave., Ste. B, Traverse City MI 49686. (231)933-4954, ext. 1011. Fax: (231)933-0448. E-mail: jimb@bookpublishing.com. Website: independentpublisher.com. "The Independent Publisher Book Awards were conceived as a broad-based, unaffiliated awards program open to all members of the independent publishing industry. The staff at *Independent Publisher* magazine saw the need to bring increased recognition to the thousands of exemplary independent, university, and self-published titles produced each year. The IPPY Awards reward those who exhibit the courage, innovation, and creativity to bring about change in the world of publishing. Independent spirit and expertise comes from publishers of all areas and budgets, and we judge books with that in mind. Entries will be accepted in 67 categories. Open to any published writer." Costs: $75-95. Needs: fiction, nonfiction, poetry, novels, translations. Offered annually for books published between January 1 and December 31. Deadline: March 20. Prizes: Gold, silver and bronze medals for each category; foil seals available to all. Judged by a panel of experts representing the fields of design, writing, bookselling, library, and reviewing. **Contact:** Jim Barnes. "The Independent Publisher Book Awards were conceived as a broad-based, unaffiliated awards program open to all members of the independent publishing industry. The staff at *Independent Publisher* magazine saw the need to bring increased recognition to the thousands of exemplary independent, university, and self-published titles produced each year. The IPPY Awards reward those who exhibit the courage, innovation, and creativity to bring about change in the world of publishing. Independent spirit and expertise comes from publishers of all areas and budgets, and we judge books with that in mind. Entries will be accepted in 67 categories. Open to any published writer." Offered annually for books published between January 1 and December 31. Deadline: March 20. Prize: Gold, silver and bronze medals for each category; foil seals available to all. Judged by a panel of experts representing the fields of design, writing, bookselling, library, and reviewing.

MLA PRIZE IN UNITED STATES LATINA & LATINO AND CHICANA & CHICANO LITERARY AND CULTURAL STUDIES

Modern Language Association of America, 26 Broadway, 3rd Floor, New York NY 10004-1789. (646)576-5141. Fax: (646)458-0030. E-mail: awards@mla.org. Website: mla.org. **Contact:** Coordinator of Book Prizes. Award for an outstanding scholarly study in any language of United States Latina & Latino and Chicana & Chicano literature or culture. Open to current MLA members only. Authors or publishers may submit titles. Deadline: May 1. Prize: A cash award, and a certificate to be presented at the Modern Language Association's annual convention in January.

OHIOANA WALTER RUMSEY MARVIN GRANT

Ohioana Library Association, 274 E. First Ave., Suite 300, Columbus OH 43201. (614)466-3831. Fax: (614)728-6974. E-mail: ohioana@ohioana.org. Website: ohioana.org. Award "to encourage young, unpublished writers 30 years of age or younger." Competition for short stories. Prize: $1,000. **No entry fee.** Up to 6 pieces of prose may be submitted; maximum 60 pages, minimum 10 pages double-spaced, 12-point type. Deadline: January 31. Entries must be unpublished. Open to unpublished authors born in Ohio or who have lived in Ohio for a minimum of five years. Must be 30 years of age or younger. Guidelines for SASE or on website. Winner notified in May or June. Award given in October. **Contact:** Linda Hengst. "Offered annually to encourage young writers; open to writers age 30 or under who have not published a book. Entrants must have been born in Ohio or have lived in Ohio for at least 5 years. Enter 1-6 pieces of prose totaling 10-60 pages (double space, 12 pt. font)." Deadline: January 31. Prize: $1,000.

DAVID RAFFELOCK AWARD FOR PUBLISHING EXCELLENCE

National Writers Association, 10940 S. Parker Rd., #508, Parker CO 80134. (303)841-0246. Fax: (303)841-2607. E-mail: natlwritersassn@hotmail.com. Website: nationalwriters.com. **Contact:** Sandy Whelchel, executive director. Award to "assist published authors in marketing their work and promoting them." Prize: publicity tour, including airfare, and services of a publicist (valued at $5,000). Categories: novels and short story collections. Judged by publishers and agents. Entry fee: $100. Deadline: May 1. Published works only. Open to any writer. Guidelines for SASE, by e-mail or on website. Winners announced in June at the NWAF conference and notified by mail or phone. List of winners available for SASE or visit website.

BYRON CALDWELL SMITH AWARD

The University of Kansas, Hall Center for the Humanities, 900 Sunnyside Ave., Lawrence KS 66045. (785)864-4798. E-mail: vbailey@ku.edu. Website: hallcenter.ku.edu. **Contact:** Victor Baily, director. Offered in odd years. To qualify, applicants must live or be employed in Kansas and have written an outstanding book published within the previous 2 calendar years. Translations are eligible. Guidelines for SASE or online. Deadline: March 1. Prize: $1,500.

TEXAS INSTITUTE OF LETTERS AWARD FOR MOST SIGNIFICANT SCHOLARLY BOOK

The Texas Institute of Letters, P.O. Box 609, Round Rock TX 78680. (512) 238-1871. E-mail: tilsecretary@yahoo.com. Website: texasinstituteofletters.org. **Contact:** W.K. (Kip) Stratton, acquisitions. "Offered annually for submissions published January 1-December 31 of previous year to recognize the writer of the book making the most important contribution to knowledge. Writer must have been born in Texas, have lived in the state at least 2 consecutive years at some time, or the subject matter of the book should be associated with the state. See website for guidelines." Deadline: Jan. 1. Prize: $2.500.

☉ THE WRITERS' TRUST ENGEL/FINDLEY AWARD

The Writers' Trust of Canada, 90 Richmond St. E., Suite 200, Toronto ON M5C 1P1 Canada. (416)504-8222. Fax: (416)504-9090. E-mail: info@writerstrust.com. Website: writerstrust.com. **Contact:** Amanda Hopkins. "The Writers' Trust Engel/Findley Award is presented annually at The Writers' Trust Awards Event, held in Toronto each Fall, to a Canadian writer for a body of work in hope of continued contribution to the richness of Canadian literature. Open to Canadian citizens and permanent residents only." Prize: $25,000

JOURNALISM

THE AMERICAN LEGION FOURTH ESTATE AWARD

The American Legion, 700 N. Pennsylvania, Indianapolis IN 46204. (317)630-1253. E-mail: pr@legion.org. Website: legion.org/whatsnew/fourthestate. Offered annually for journalistic works published the previous calendar year. Subject matter must deal with a topic or issue of national interest or concern. Entry must include cover letter explaining entry, and any documentation or evidence of the entry's impact on the community, state, or nation. No printed entry form. Guidelines for SASE or on website. Deadline: January 31. Prize: $2,000 stipend to defray expenses of recipient accepting the award at The American Legion National Convention in August.

AMY WRITING AWARDS

The Amy Foundation, P.O. Box 16091, Lansing MI 48901. (517)323-6233. Fax: (517)321-2572. E-mail: amyfoundtn@aol.com. Website: amyfound.org. "Offered annually to recognize creative, skillful writing that applies biblical principles. Submitted articles must be published in a secular, non-religious publication (either printed or online) and must be reinforced with at least one passage of scripture. The article must have been published between January 1 and December 31 of the current calendar year." Deadline: January 31. Prize: 1st Prize: $10,000; 2nd Prize: $5,000; 3rd Prize: $4,000; 4th Prize: $3,000; 5th Prize: $2,000; and 10 prizes of $1,000.

FRANK LUTHER MOTT-KAPPA TAU ALPHA RESEARCH AWARD IN JOURNALISM

University of Missouri School of Journalism, 76 Gannett Hall, Columbia MO 65211-1200. (573)882-7685. E-mail: umcjourkta@missouri.edu. Website: kappaterualpha.org. **Contact:** Dr. Keith Sanders, exec. dir., Kappa Tau Alpha. "Offered annually for best researched book in mass communication. Submit 6 copies; no forms required." Deadline: December 9. Prize: $1,000

O. HENRY AWARD FOR MAGAZINE JOURNALISM

The Texas Institute of Letters, P.O. Box 609, Round Rock TX 78680. Website: texasinstituteofletters.org/.

Contact: W.K. (Kip) Stratton. "Offered annually for work published January 1-December 31 of previous year to recognize the best-written work of journalism appearing in a magazine or weekly newspaper. Judged by a panel chosen by the TIL Council. Writer must have been born in Texas, have lived in Texas for at least 2 consecutive years at some time, or the subject matter of the work should be associated with Texas. See website for guidelines." Deadline: January 1. Prize: $1,000.

SCIENCE IN SOCIETY AWARDS

National Association of Science Writers, Inc., P.O. Box 7905, Berkeley CA 94707. (510)647-9500. E-mail: director@nasw.org. Website: nasw.org. **Contact:** Tinsley Davis. Offered annually for investigative or interpretive reporting about the sciences and their impact on society. Categories: books, commentary and opinions, science reporting, and science reporting with a local or regional focus. Material may be a single article or broadcast, or a series. Works must have been first published or broadcast in North America between June 1 and May 31 of the previous year. Deadline: February 1. Prize: $2,500, and a certificate of recognition in each category.

☉ SOVEREIGN AWARD

The Jockey Club of Canada, P.O. Box 66, Station B, Toronto ON M9W 5K9 Canada. (416)675-7756. Fax: (416)675-6378. E-mail: jockeyclub@bellnet.ca. Website: jockeyclubcanada.com. **Contact:** Stacie Roberts, exec. dir. "Offered annually to recognize outstanding achievement in the area of Canadian thoroughbred racing journalism published January 1-December 31 of the previous year." "Submissions for these media awards must be of Canadian Thoroughbred racing or breeding content. They must have appeared in a media outlet recognized by The Jockey Club of Canada. The writer may submit no more than 1 entry/category. A printed, hard copy of the print category submission must be provided along with an e-mailed copy of the submission. Submissions to the photograph category should be e-mailed in jpeg hi-res format and must be followed by a mailed hard copy of the submission as well as proof of publishing with a tearsheet or on-line printout. Submission to the Outstanding Film/Video/Broadcast category should be made by sending a letter detailing what the video is about, the names of the editor, producer, etc., and a VHS or Beta tape of the program, including the date the show aired and where." Deadline: December 31.

THE MADELINE DANE ROSS AWARD

Overseas Press Club of America, 40 West 45th Street, New York NY 10036. (212)626-9220. Fax: (212)626-9210. E-mail: sonya@opcofamerica.org. Website: opcofamerica.org. **Contact:** Sonya Fry, Executive Director. "Offered annually for best international reporting in the print medium showing a concern for the human condition. Work must be published by US-based publications or broadcast. Printable application available online." Deadline: Late January; date changes each year. Prize: $1,000 and certificate

STANLEY WALKER AWARD FOR NEWSPAPER JOURNALISM

The Texas Institute of Letters, P.O. Box 609, Round Rock TX 78680. (512) 238-1871. E-mail: tilsecretary@yahoo.com. Website: texasinstituteofletters.org/. **Contact:** W.K (Kip) Stratton, acquisitions. Offered annually for work published January 1-December 31 of previous year to recognize the best writing appearing in a daily newspaper. Writer must have been born in Texas, have lived in the state for 2 consecutive years at some time, or the subject matter of the article must be associated with the state. See website for guidelines. Deadline: Jan. 1. Prize: $1,000.

TRANSLATION

ALDO AND JEANNE SCAGLIONE PRIZE FOR A TRANSLATION OF A LITERARY WORK

Modern Language Association, 26 Broadway, 3rd Floor, New York NY 10004-1789. (646)576-5141. Fax: (646)458-0030. E-mail: awards@mla.org. Website: mla.org. **Contact:** Coordinator of Book Prizes. Offered in even-numbered years for the translation of a book-length literary work appearing in print during the previous year. Translators need not be members of the MLA. Deadline: April 1. Prize: A cash award and a certificate to be presented at the Modern Language Association's annual convention in January.

ALDO AND JEANNE SCAGLIONE PRIZE FOR A TRANSLATION OF A SCHOLARLY STUDY OF LITERATURE

Modern Language Association of America, 26 Broadway, 3rd Floor, New York NY 10004-1789. (646)576-

5141. Fax: (646)458-0030. E-mail: awards@mla.org. Website: mla.org. **Contact:** Coordinator of Book Prizes. Offered in odd-numbered years for an outstanding translation into English of a book-length work of literary history, literary criticism, philology, or literary theory published during the previous biennium. Translators need not be members of the MLA. Deadline: May 1. Prize: A cash award and a certificate to be presented at the Modern Language Association's annual convention in January.

DIANA DER-HOVANESSIAN TRANSLATION PRIZE

New England Poetry Club, 2 Farrar St., Cambridge MA 02138. (617)744-6034. E-mail: contests@nepoetryclub.org. Website: nepoetryclub.org/contests.htm. $250 for a translation from any language into English. Send a copy of the original. Funded by John Mahtesian. **Contact:** NEPC Contest Coordinator. Annual contest for a translation from any language into English. Send a copy of the original. Funded by John Mahtesian. Entries should be original unpublished poems in English. No poem should be entered in more than one contest nor have won a previous contest. Poems should be typed and submitted in duplicate with author's name address and e-mail on one copy only. Label poems with contest name. No entries will be returned. NEPC will not engage in correspondence regarding poems or contest decisions. Entries should be sent by regular mail only. Special Delivery or signature required mail will be returned by the Post Office. Deadline: May 31. Prize: $250. Judges are well-known poets and sometimes winners of previous NEPC contests.

FENIA AND YAAKOV LEVIANT MEMORIAL PRIZE IN YIDDISH STUDIES

Modern Language Association of America, 26 Broadway, 3rd Floor, New York NY 10004-1789. (646)576-5141. Fax: (646)458-0030. E-mail: awards@mla.org. Website: mla.org. **Contact:** Coordinator of book prizes. This prize is to honor, in alternating years, an outstanding English translation of a Yiddish literary work or an outstanding scholarly work in any language in the field of Yiddish. Offered in even-numbered years. Open to MLA members and nonmembers. Authors or publishers may submit titles. Guidelines for SASE or by e-mail. Deadline: May 1. Prize: A cash prize, and a certificate, to be presented at the Modern Language Association's annual convention in January.

SOEURETTE DIEHL FRASER AWARD FOR BEST TRANSLATION OF A BOOK

P.O. Box 609, Round Rock TX 78680. E-mail: tilsecretary@yahoo.com. Website: texasinstituteofletters.org. **Contact:** W.K. (Kip) Stratton, acquisitions. Offered every 2 years to recognize the best translation of a literary book into English. Translator must have been born in Texas or have lived in the state for at least 2 consecutive years at some time. Deadline: January 1. Prize: $1,000.

☉ GOVERNOR GENERAL'S LITERARY AWARD FOR TRANSLATION

Canada Council for the Arts, 350 Albert St., P.O. Box 1047, Ottawa ON K1P 5V8 Canada. (613)566-4414, ext. 5573. Fax: (613)566-4410. Website: canadacouncil.ca/prizes/ggla. Offered for the best English-language and the best French-language work of translation by a Canadian. Publishers submit titles for consideration Deadline: March 15, June 1, or August 7, depending on the book's publication date. Prize: Each laureate receives $25,000; non-winning finalists receive $1,000.

LOIS ROTH AWARD FOR A TRANSLATION OF A LITERARY WORK

Modern Language Association, 26 Broadway, 3rd Floor, New York NY 10004-1789. (646)576-5141. Fax: (646)458-0030. E-mail: awards@mla.org. Website: mla.org. **Contact:** Coordinator of Book Prizes. Offered every 2 years (odd years) for an outstanding translation into English of a book-length literary work published the previous year. Translators need not be members of the MLA. Deadline: April 1. Prize: A cash award and a certificate to be presented at the Modern Language Association's annual convention in January.

PEN AWARD FOR POETRY IN TRANSLATION

PEN American Center, 588 Broadway, Suite 303, New York NY 10012. (212)334-1660, ext. 108. E-mail: awards@pen.org. Website: pen.org. **Contact:** Literary awards manager. This award recognizes book-length translations of poetry from any language into English, published during the current calendar year. All books must have been published in the US. Translators may be of any nationality. US residency/citizenship not required. Nominations must be received between September 1, 2010 and February 3. Early submissions are strongly recommended. Three copies of book-length translations published between January 1, 2010, and December 31, 2010, may be submitted by publishers, agents, or the translators themselves. Self-published books are not eligible. Books with more than two translators are not eligible. How to submit: 1) Pay the $50 entry fee online and proceed to checkout. If paying by check, skip to step 2. 2) Fill out the online submission form and click Submit Form. 3) Mail three copies of the candidate's book, your printed submission form, and proof of online payment or a check to above address. Deadline: February 3. Prize: $3,000. a single translator of poetry appointed by the PEN Translation Committee.

PEN TRANSLATION PRIZE

PEN American Center, 588 Broadway, Suite 303, New York NY 10012. (212)334-1660, ext. 108. Fax: (212)334-2181. E-mail: awards@pen.org. **Contact:** Literary Awards Manager. Offered for a literary book-length translation into English published in the calendar year. No technical, scientific, or reference books. Publishers, agents, or translators may submit 3 copies of each eligible title. All eligible titles must have been published in the US. Self-published books are not eligible. 1) Pay the $50 entry fee online and proceed to checkout. If paying by check, skip to step 2. 2) Fill out the online submission form and click Submit Form. 3) Mail three copies of the candidate's book, your printed submission form, and proof of online payment or a check Nominations must be received between September 1, 2010 and February 3. Early submissions are strongly recommended. Prize: $3,000

POETRY

☉ ACORN-PLANTOS AWARD FOR PEOPLES POETRY

Acorn-Plantos Award Committee, 36 Sunset Ave., Hamilton ON L8R 1V6 Canada. E-mail: jeffseff@allstream.net. **Contact:** Jeff Seffinga. "Annual contest for work that appeared in print in the previous calender year. This award is given to the Canadian poet who best (through the publication of a book of poems) exemplifies populist or peoples poetry in the tradition of Milton Acorn, Ted Plantos, et al. Work may be entered by the poet or the publisher; the award goes to the poet. Entrants must submit 5 copies of each title. Poet must be a citizen of Canada or a landed immigrant. Publisher need not be Canadian." Deadline:

June 30. Prize: $500 (CDN) and a medal. Judged by a panel of poets in the tradition who are not entered in the current year.

ALLEN GINSBERG POETRY AWARDS

The Poetry Center at Passaic County Community College, One College Blvd., Paterson NJ 07505-1179. (973)684-6555. Fax: (973)523-6085. E-mail: mgillan@pccc.edu. Website: pccc.edu/poetry. The Allen Ginsberg Poetry Awards offer annual prizes of 1st Prize: $1,000, 2nd Prize: $200, and 3rd Prize: $100. All winning poems, honorable mentions, and editor's choice poems will be published in Paterson Literary Review (see separate listing in Magazines/Journals). Winners will be asked to participate in a reading that will be held in the Paterson Historic District. Submissions must be unpublished. Submit up to 5 poems (no poem more than 2 pages long). Send 4 copies of each poem entered. Include cover sheet with poet's name, address, phone number, e-mail address and poem titles. Poet's name should not appear on poems. Include SASE for results only; poems will not be returned. Guidelines available for SASE or on website. **Entry fee:** $18 (includes subscription to Paterson Literary Review). Write "poetry contest" in memo section of check and make payable to PCCC. **Deadline:** April 1 (postmark). Winners will be announced the following summer by mail and in newspaper announcements. 2010 winners Rafaella Del Bourgo and Kathleen Spivack (1st), Joyce Madelon Winslow and Francine Witte (2nd), and Kim Farrar (3rd). **Contact:** Maria Mazziotti Gillan, exec. director. "Offered annually for unpublished poetry to honor Allen Ginsberg's contribution to American literature. The college retains first publication rights. Open to any writer." Deadline: April 1. Prize: First Prize: $1,000; Second Prize: $200; Third Prize: $100.

⊕ ANGELS & DEVILS POETRY COMPETITION

Holland Park Press Ltd, 116 Gloucester Terrace, London England W2 6HP UK. **Contact:** Bernadette Jansen op de Haar PhD. "Write a poem of no more than 30 lines about family relationships. You can write in English or Dutch. We are looking for poems that look at one's relatives in an original way; we are especially interested in poems that use a personal experience to create general empathy, provided it touches on relationships, everything goes—happy or sad, touching or funny—as long as it expresses your original voice in content as well as form." Stating date: 2 April 2011;

Closing Date: 31 December 2011. Prize: £100 ($160) plus publication in our online magazine organised by Holland Park Press.

ANNUAL GIVAL PRESS OSCAR WILDE AWARD

Gival Press, LLC, P.O. Box 3812, Arlington VA 22203. (703)351-0079. E-mail: givalpress@yahoo.com. Website: givalpress.com. **Contact:** Robert L. Giron. "Award given to the best previously unpublished original poem—written in English of any length, in any style, typed, double-spaced on 1 side only—which best relates gay/lesbian/bisexual/transgendered life, by a poet who is 18 or older. Entrants are asked to submit their poems without any kind of identification (with the exception of titles) and with a separate cover page with the following information: name, address (street, city, and state with zip code), telephone number, e-mail address (if available) and a list of poems by title. Checks drawn on American banks should be made out to Gival Press, LLC." Deadline: June 27 (postmarked). Prize: $100 (USD), and the poem, along with information about the poet, will be published on the Gival Press website.

ART AFFAIR POETRY CONTEST

P.O. Box 54302, Oklahoma City OK 73154. E-mail: okpoets@aol.com. Website: shadetreecreations.com. The annual Art Affair Poetry Contest offers 1st Prize: $40 and certificate; 2nd Prize: $25 and certificate; and 3rd Prize: $15 and certificate. Honorable Mention certificates will be awarded at the discretion of the judges. Open to any poet. Poems must be unpublished. Multiple entries accepted with entry fee for each and may be mailed in the same packet. Submit original poems on any subject, in any style, no more than 60 lines (put line count in the upper right-hand corner of first page). Include cover page with poet's name, address, phone number, and title of poem. Do not include SASE; poems will not be returned. Guidelines available on website. **Deadline:** October 1, 2011 (postmark). **Entry Fee:** $3/poem. Make check payable to Art Affair. Winners' list will be published on the Art Affair website in December. 2010 winners were Sally Clark, Moriah Erickson, and Colleen Cleary. **Contact:** Barbara Shepherd, Acquisitions. The annual Art Affair Poetry Contest. Open to any poet. Multiple entries accepted with entry fee for each and may be mailed in the same packet. Guidelines available on website. Winners' list will be published on the Art

Affair website in December. 2010 winners were Sally Clark, Moriah Erickson, and Colleen Cleary. Poems must be unpublished. Submit original poems on any subject, in any style, no more than 60 lines (put line count in the upper right-hand corner of first page). Include cover page with poet's name, address, phone number, and title of poem. Do not include SASE; poems will not be returned. Deadline: October 1, 2011 (postmark). Prize: Prizes: 1st Prize: $40 and certificate; 2nd Prize: $25 and certificate; and 3rd Prize: $15 and certificate. Honorable Mention certificates will be awarded at the discretion of the judges.

BARBARA BRADLEY PRIZE

New England Poetry Club, P.O. Box 190076, Boston MA 02119. E-mail: contests@nepoetryclub.org. Website: nepoetryclub.org/contests.htm. Lyric poem under 21 lines written by a woman. Contest is free to all full time students and paid up members of New England Poetry Club. Only one poem per contest. Annual. Entries should be original unpublished poems in English. Poem should not be entered in any other contest nor have won a previous contest. Poem should be typed and submitted in duplicate with author's name, address and e-mail on one copy only. Label poem with contest name. No entries will be returned. NEPC will not engage in correspondence regarding poems or contest decisions. Entries should be sent by regular mail only. Special Delivery or signature required mail will be returned by the Post Office. Judges are well-known poets and sometimes winners of previous NEPC contests. Deadline is May 31 Submit only in April or May. Prize: $200. **Contact:** NEPC Contest Coordinator. Offered annually for a lyric poem under 21 lines, written by a woman. It must be submitted only in April and May contests. Entries should be sent by regular mail only. Special Delivery or signature required mail will be returned by the Post Office. Entries should be original unpublished poems in English. No poem should be entered in more than one contest nor have won a previous contest. Poems should be typed and submitted in duplicate with author's name, address, and e-mail on one copy only. Label poems with contest name. No entries will be returned. NEPC will not engage in correspondence regarding poems or contest decisions. Deadline: May 31. Prize: $200. Judges are well-known poets and sometimes winners of previous NEPC contests.

BLUE MOUNTAIN ARTS/SPS STUDIOS POETRY CARD CONTEST

P.O. Box 1007, Boulder CO 80306. (303)449-0536. Fax: (303)447-0939. E-mail: poetrycontest@sps.com. Website: sps.com. "We're looking for original poetry that is rhyming or non-rhyming, although we find no-rhyming poetry reads better. Poems may also be considered for possible publication on greeting cards or in book anthologies. Contest is offered biannually. Guidelines available online." Deadline: December 31 and June 30. Prize: 1st Place: $300; 2nd Place: $150; 3rd Place: $50. Blue Mountain Arts editorial staff.

THE FREDERICK BOCK PRIZE

Poetry, 444 North Michigan Ave., Suite 1850, Chicago IL 60610. (312)787-7070. E-mail: poetry@poetrymagazine.org. Website: poetrymagazine.org. Offered annually for poems published in *Poetry* during the preceding year (October through September). *Poetry* buys all rights to the poems published in the magazine. Copyrights are returned to the authors on request. Any writer may submit poems to *Poetry*. Prize: $500

BOULEVARD EMERGING POETS CONTEST

PMB 325, 6614 Clayton Rd., Richmond Heights MO 63117. E-mail: kellyleavitt@boulevardmagazine.org. Website: boulevardmagazine.org. Annual Emerging Poets Contest offers $1,000 and publication in *Boulevard* (see separate listing in Magazines/Journals) for the best group of 3 poems by a poet who has not yet published a book of poetry with a nationally distributed press. "All entries will be considered for publication and payment at our regular rates." Submissions must be unpublished. Considers simultaneous submissions. Submit 3 poems, typed; may be a sequence or unrelated. On page one of first poem type poet's name, address, phone number, and titles of the 3 poems. Include ASP for notification of receipt of ms; mss will not be returned. Guidelines available on website. **Entry fee:** $15/group of 3 poems, $15 for each additional group of 3 poems; includes one-year subscription to *Boulevard*. Make checks payable to Boulevard. **Deadline:** June 1 (postmark). Judge: editors of *Boulevard* magazine. "No one editorially or financially affiliated with *Boulevard* may enter the contest." **Contact:** Kelly Leavitt, managing editor.

BRITTINGHAM PRIZE IN POETRY; FELIX POLLAK PRIZE IN POETRY

University of Wisconsin Press, Dept. of English, 600 N. Park St., University of Wisconsin, Madison WI

53706. E-mail: rwallace@wisc.edu. Website: wisc.edu/
wisconsinpress/poetryguide.html. **Contact:** Ronald
Wallace, contest director. "Offered for unpublished
book-length mss of original poetry. Submissions must
be received by the press during the month of September, accompanied by a required SASE for contest results. Does not return mss. One entry fee covers both
prizes. Guidelines for SASE or online." Prize: $2,500
($1,000 cash prize and $1,500 honorarium for campus
reading) and publication of the 2 winning mss.

GERALD CABLE BOOK AWARD

Silverfish Review Press, P.O. Box 3541, Eugene OR
97403. (541)344-5060. E-mail: sfrpress@earthlink.
net. Website: silverfishreviewpress.com. Offers annual award of $1,000, publication by Silverfish Review
Press, and 25 author copies to a book-length ms of
original poetry by an author who has not yet published a full-length collection. No restrictions on the
kind of poetry or subject matter; no translations. Individual poems may have been previously published
elsewhere, but must be acknowledged. Considers simultaneous submissions (notify immediately of acceptance elsewhere). Submit at least 48 pages of poetry,
no names or identification on ms pages. Include separate title sheet with poet's name, address, and phone
number. Include SASP for notification of receipt and
SASE for results; no mss will be returned. Accepts
e-mail submissions in Word, plain text, or rich text;
send entry fee and SASE by regular mail. Guidelines
available for SASE, by e-mail, or on website. **Entry
fee:** $20. Make checks payable to Silverfish Review
Press. **Deadline:** October 15 (postmark). Winner announced in March. Copies of winning books available
through website. "All entrants who enclose a booksize
envelope and $2.23 in postage will receive a free copy
of a recent winner of the book award." **Contact:** Rodger Moody, Editor. "Purpose is to publish a poetry
book by a deserving author who has yet to publish a
full-length book collection. For guidelines send SASE,
or request by e-mail." Deadline: October 15. Prize:
$1,000, 25 copies, and publication by the press for a
book-length ms of original poetry.

CIDER PRESS REVIEW BOOK AWARD

777 Braddock Lane, Halifax PA 17032. E-mail: edi-
tor@ciderpressreview.com. Website: ciderpressre-
view.com/bookaward/. The annual Cider Press Review Book Award offers $1,500, publication, and 25
author's copies. CPR acquires first publication rights.

Initial print run is not less than 1,000 copies. Submissions must be unpublished as a collection, but individual poems may have been previously published
elsewhere. Submit book-length ms of 48-80 pages.
"Submissions can be made online using the submission form on the website or by mail. If sending by mail,
include 2 cover sheets—1 with title, author's name,
and complete contact information; and 1 with title
only, all bound with a spring clip. Check website for
change of address coming in the future. Include SASE
for results only if no e-mail address included; notification via e-mail and on the website; manuscripts
cannot be returned. Online submissions must be in
Word for PC or PDF format, and should not include
title page with author's name. The editors strongly
urge contestants to use online delivery if possible."
Entry fee: $25. All entrants will receive a copy of the
winning book and a one-issue subscription to *Cider
Press Review*. 2010 winner was Liz Robbins. Deadline:
submit September 1-November 30 (postmark). 2011
judge: Jeane Marie Beaumont. Acquisitions: Contest
Director. Estab. 1999. **Contact:** Contest Director. Online submissions must be in Word for PC or PDF format, and should not include title page with author's
name. The editors strongly urge contestants to use
online delivery if possible."

CLEVELAND STATE UNIVERSITY POETRY CENTER PRIZES

Cleveland State University Poetry Center, 2121 Euclid Ave., Cleveland OH 44115-2214. (216)687-3986.
Fax: (216)687-6943. E-mail: poetrycenter@csuohio.
edu. Website: csuohio.edu/poetrycenter. **Contact:**
Rita Grabowski, poetry center manager. Offered annually to identify, reward, and publish the best unpublished book-length poetry ms (minimum 48 pages) in
2 categories: First Book Award and Open Competition (for poets who have published at least one collection with a press run of 500). Submission implies
willingness to sign standard contract for publication
if manuscript wins. Does not return mss. Guidelines
for SASE or online. Deadline: Submissions accepted
November 1-February 15. Prize: First Book and Open
Book Competitions award publication and a $1000
advance against royalties for an original manuscript
of poetry in each category

✚ CLOCKWISE CHAPBOOK AWARD

Tebot Bach, 20592 Minerva Ln., Huntington Beach
CA 92646. (714)968-4677. Fax: (714)968-4677. E-mail:

mifanwy@tebotbach.org. Website: tebotbach.org. Clockwise Chapbook Award. Annual contest to honor winning entry. Must be previously unpublished poetry for the full collection; individual poems may have been published. Open to any writer. Address: 20592 Minerva Ln., Huntington Beach, CA 92646. Phone/Fax: (714) 968-4677. E-mail: mifanwy@tebotbach.org. Go to Website: tebotbach.org for guidelines. Deadline: April 15. Entry fee: $15. Guidelines online at website. Prize: $500 award, chapbook publication. Judged by Gail Wrongsky. Acquires First North American Rights for entire collection. **Contact:** Gail Wrongsky. Must be previously unpublished poetry for the full collection; individual poems may have been published. Purpose of award is to honor the winning entry. Deadline: April 15. Prize: $500 award, chapbook publication. Judged by Gail Wronsky.

CLOUDBANK CONTEST

P.O. Box 610, Corvallis OR 97339-0610. Website: cloudbankbooks.com. E-mail: michael@cloudbankbooks.com. Website: cloudbankbooks.com. Contact: Michael Malan. A nominating process must be met before a writer's entry will be considered. Biannual poetry contest open to all. $200 1st place prize and publication. Also, author receives an extra copy of the issue in which their poem appears. Judged by Michael Malan (final) and Reading Board (initial). For contest submissions, the writer's name, address, e-mail address, and the titles of the poems being submitted should be typed on a cover sheet only, not on the pages of poems or short fiction. No electronic submissions. Please do not send more than five poems or short prose pieces (500 words or less) for the contest or regular submissions. The $15 entry fee covers up to 5 poems. The check should be made out to *Cloudbank*. All writers who enter the contest will receive a one-year (two-issue) subscription to *Cloudbank* magazine.

THE COLORADO PRIZE FOR POETRY

Colorado Review/Center for Literary Publishing, Dept. of English, Colorado State University, 9105 Campus Delivery, Ft. Collins CO 80523-9105. (970)491-5449. E-mail: creview@colostate.edu. Website: coloradoprize.colostate.edu. The annual Colorado Prize for Poetry awards an honorarium of $1,500 and publication of a book-length ms. Submission must be unpublished as a collection, but individual poems may have been published elsewhere. Submit mss of 48-100 pages of poetry (no set minimum or maximum) on any subject, in any form, double- or single-spaced. Include 2 titles pages: one with ms title only, the other with ms title and poet's name, address, and phone number. Enclosed SASP for notification of receipt and SASE for results; mss will not be returned. Guidelines available for SASE or by e-mail. **Entry fee:** $25; includes one-year subscription to *Colorado Review* (see separate listing in Magazines/Journals). **Deadline:** submission period was October 1-January 14 for 2011. Winner was Eric Baus. 2011 judge was Cole Swensen. **Contact:** Stephanie G'Schwind, editor.

CRAB ORCHARD SERIES IN POETRY FIRST BOOK AWARD

Dept. of English, Mail Code 4503, Faner Hall 2380, Southern Illinois Univ. Carbondale, Carbondale IL 62901. E-mail: jtribble@siu.edu. Website: craborchardreview.siuc.edu. Dept. of English, Mail Code 4503, Faner Hall 2380, Southern Illinois University Carbondale, 1000 Faner Dr., Carbondale IL 62901. Website: siu.edu/~crborchd. Established 1995. **Contact:** John Tribble, series editor. The Crab Orchard Series in Poetry First Book Award offers $2,500 ($1,000 prize plus $1,500 honorarium for a reading at Southern Illinois University Carbondale) and publication. "Manuscripts should be 50-75 pages of original poetry, in English, by a U.S. citizen or permanent resident who has neither published, nor committed to publish, a volume of poetry 40 pages or more in length (individual poems may have been previously published). Current students and employees of Southern Illinois University and authors published by Southern Illinois University Press are not eligible." See guidelines for complete formatting instructions. Guidelines available for SASE or on website. **Entry fee:** $25/submission; includes a copy of the summer/fall Crab Orchard Review (see separate listing in Magazines/Journals). Make checks payable to Crab Orchard Series in Poetry. **Deadline:** see guidelines or check website.

CRAB ORCHARD SERIES IN POETRY OPEN COMPETITION AWARDS

Dept. of English, Mail Code 4503, Faner Hall 2380, Southern Illinois Univ. Carbondale, Carbondale IL 62901. E-mail: jtribble@siu.edu. Website: craborchardreview.siuc.edu. The Crab Orchard Series in Poetry Open Competition Awards offer two winners $3,500 and publication of a book-length ms. "Cash prize totals reflect a $1,500 honorarium for each winner for a reading at Southern Illinois University Carbondale. Publication contract is with Southern Illinois University Press. Entrants must be U.S. citizens or permanent residents." Submissions must be unpublished as a collection, but individual poems may have been previously published elsewhere. Considers simultaneous submissions, but series editor must be informed immediately upon acceptance. Manuscripts should be typewritten or computer-generated (letter quality only, no dot matrix), single-spaced; clean photocopy is recommended as mss are not returned. See guidelines for complete formatting instructions. Guidelines available for SASE or on website. **Entry fee:** $25/submission; includes a copy of the winning Crab Orchard Review (see separate listing in Magazines/Journals). Make checks payable to Crab Orchard Series in Poetry. **Deadline:** see guidelines or check website. 2010 winners were Brian Barker (*The Black Ocean)* and Camille Dungy (*Smith Blue).* **Contact:** Jon Tribble, series editor. The Crab Orchard Series in Poetry Open Competition Awards. Entrants must be U.S. citizens or permanent residents. Submissions must be unpublished as a collection, but individual poems may have been previously published elsewhere. Considers simultaneous submissions, but series editor must be informed immediately upon acceptance. Manuscripts should be typewritten or computer-generated (letter quality only, no dot matrix), single-spaced; clean photocopy is recommended as mss are not returned. See guidelines for complete formatting instructions. Guidelines available for SASE or on website. 2010 winners were Brian Barker (*The Black Ocean)* and Camille Dungy (*Smith Blue).* Deadline: see guidelines or check website. Prize: Offers two winners $3,500 and publication of a book-length ms. Cash prize totals reflect a $1,500 honorarium for each winner for a reading at Southern Illinois University Carbondale. Publication contract is with Southern Illinois University Press.

THE ROBERT DANA PRIZE FOR POETRY

Anhinga Press, Drawer W, P.O. Box 10595, Tallahassee FL 32302. (850)442-1408. Fax: (850)442-6323. E-mail: info@anhinga.org. Website: anhinga.org. The annual Anhinga Prize awards $2,000, a reading tour of Florida, and publication of a book-length poetry ms. Guidelines available for SASE or on website. **Entry fee:** $25. **Deadline:** submit February 15-May 1. Past judges include Donald Hall, Joy Harjo, Robert Dana, Mark Jarman, and Tony Hoagland. Past winners include Frank X. Gaspar, Julia Levine, Keith Ratzlaff, and Lynn Aarti Chandhok, and Rhett Iseman Trull. **Contact:** Rick Campbell, poetry editor. Offered annually for a book-length collection of poetry by an author who has not published more than 1 book of poetry. Guidelines for SASE or on website. Open to any writer writing in English. Deadline: February 15-May 1. Prize: $2,000, and publication

DANCING POETRY CONTEST

704 Brigham Ave., Santa Rosa CA 95404-5245. (707)528-0912. E-mail: jhcheung@comcast.net. Website: dancingpoetry.com. 704 Brigham Ave., Santa Rosa CA 95404-5245. (707)528-0912. E-mail: jhcheung@comcast.net. Website: dancingpoetry.com. Annual contest offers three Grand Prizes of $100 each, six 1st Prizes of $50, twelve 2nd Prizes of $25, and thirty 3rd Prizes of $10. The 3 Grand Prize-winning poems will be choreographed, costumed, danced, and videotaped at the annual Dancing Poetry Festival at Palace of the Legion of Honor, San Francisco; Natica Angilly's Poetic Dance Theater Company will perform the 3 Grand Prize-winning poems. In addition, all prizes include an invitation to read your prize poem at the festival, and a certificate suitable for framing. Submissions must be unpublished or poet must own rights. Submit 2 copies of any number of poems, 40 lines maximum (each), with name, address, phone number on 1 copy only. Foreign language poems must include English translations. No entries by fax or e-mail. Entry form available for SASE. Entry fee: $5/poem or $10 for 3 poems. Deadline: May 15 annually. Competition receives about 500-800 entries. Winners will be announced by August 1; Ticket to festival will be given to all prize winners. Artist Embassy International has been a nonprofit educational arts organization since 1951, "Furthering intercultural understanding and peace through the universal language of the arts." **Contact:** Judy Cheung, contest chair. Annual contest offers three Grand Prizes of $100 each, six 1st Prizes of $50, twelve 2nd Prizes of $25, and thirty 3rd Prizes of $10. The 3 Grand Prize-winning poems will be choreographed, costumed, danced, and videotaped at the annual Dancing Poetry Festival at Palace of the Legion of Honor, San Francisco; Natica Angilly's Poetic Dance Theater Company will perform the 3 Grand Prize-winning poems. In addition, all prizes include an invitation to read your

prize poem at the festival, and a certificate suitable for framing. Submissions must be unpublished or poet must own rights. Submit 2 copies of any number of poems, 40 lines maximum (each), with name, address, phone number on 1 copy only. Foreign language poems must include English translations. No entries by fax or e-mail. Entry form available for SASE. Competition receives about 500-800 entries. Winners will be announced by August 1; ticket to festival will be given to all prize winners. Artist Embassy International has been a nonprofit educational arts organization since 1951, "furthering intercultural understanding and peace through the universal language of the arts." Deadline: May 15 annually.

DANIEL VAROUJAN AWARD

New England Poetry Club, P.O. Box 190076, Boston MA 02119. E-mail: contests@nepoetryclub.org. Website: nepoetryclub.org/contests.htm. For an unpublished poem (not a translation) to honor a poet killed by the Turks in the 1915 genocide destroying 3/4ths of the Armenian population. Funded by royalties from translations by Diana Der-Hovanessian. Send entries to contest coordinator, P.O. Box 190076 Boston, MA 02119. $10/up to 3 entries; made payable to New England Poetry Club. Members free. Deadline: May 31. Prize: $1,000. Entries should be sent by regular mail only. Special Delivery or signature required mail will be returned by the Post Office. Entries should be original unpublished poems in English. No poem should be entered in more than one contest nor have won a previous contest. Poems should be typed and submitted in duplicate with author's name, address, and e-mail on one copy only. Label poems with contest name. No entries will be returned. NEPC will not engage in correspondence regarding poems or contest decisions. **Contact:** Contest Coordinator. For an unpublished poem (not a translation) to honor a poet killed by the Turks in the 1915 genocide destroying 3/4ths of the Armenian population. Funded by royalties from translations by Diana Der-Hovanessian. Send entries to contest coordinator. Entries should be sent by regular mail only. Special Delivery or signature required mail will be returned by the Post Office. Entries should be original unpublished poems in English. No poem should be entered in more than one contest nor have won a previous contest. Poems should be typed and submitted in duplicate with author's name, address, and e-mail on one copy only.

Label poems with contest name. No entries will be returned. NEPC will not engage in correspondence regarding poems or contest decisions. Deadline: May 31. Prize: $1,000. Judges are well-known poets and sometimes winners of previous NEPC contests.

DREAM HORSE PRESS NATIONAL POETRY CHAPBOOK PRIZE

P.O. Box 2080, Felton CA 95001-2080. E-mail: dreamhorsepress@yahoo.com. Website: dreamhorsepress.com. "The Dream Horse Press National Poetry Chapbook Prize offers an $500, publication, and 25 copies of a handsomely printed chapbook." All entries will be considered for publication. Submissions may be previously published in magazines/journals but not in books or chapbooks. Considers simultaneous submissions with notification. "Submit 20-28 pages of poetry in a readable font with table of contents, acknowledgments, bio, e-mail address for results, and entry fee. Poet's name should not appear anywhere on the manuscript." Accepts multiple submissions (with separate fee for each entry). Manuscripts will be recycled after judging. Guidelines available on website. **Entry fee:** $15. Make checks/money orders made payable to Dream Horse Press. **Deadline:** June 30. Recent previous winners include Amy Holman, Cyntha Arrieu-King, Charles Sweetman and Jason Bredle. 2010 judge: C.J. Sage. **Contact:** J.P. Dancing Bear, Editor/Publisher. "The Dream Horse Press National Poetry Chapbook Prize offers an $500, publication, and 25 copies of a handsomely printed chapbook." All entries will be considered for publication. Submissions may be previously published in magazines/journals but not in books or chapbooks. Considers simultaneous submissions with notification. "Submit 20-28 pages of poetry in a readable font with table of contents, acknowledgments, bio, e-mail address for results, and entry fee. Poet's name should not appear anywhere on the manuscript." Accepts multiple submissions (with separate fee for each entry). Manuscripts will be recycled after judging. Guidelines available on website. **Entry fee:** $15. Make checks/money orders made payable to Dream Horse Press. **Deadline:** June 30.

ERIKA MUMFORD PRIZE

New England Poetry Club, MA E-mail: contests@nepoetryclub.org. Website: nepoetryclub.org/contests.htm. $250 for a poem in any form about foreign culture or travel. Funded by Erika Mumford's family and friends. **Contact:** Contest Coordinator. Offered annually for a poem in any form about foreign culture or travel. Entries should be sent by regular mail only. Special Delivery or signature required mail will be returned by the Post Office. Entries should be original unpublished poems in English. No poem should be entered in more than one contest nor have won a previous contest. Poems should be typed and submitted in duplicate with author's name, address, and e-mail on one copy only. Label poems with contest name. No entries will be returned. NEPC will not engage in correspondence regarding poems or contest decisions. Deadline: May 31. Prize: $250. Judges are well-known poets and sometimes winners of previous NEPC contests.

FIRMAN HOUGHTON PRIZE

New England Poetry Club, P.O. Box 19007, Boston MA 02119. E-mail: contests@nepoetryclug.org. Website: nepoetryclub.org/contests.htm. Prize: $250 For a lyric poem in honor of the former president of NEPC. **Contact:** NEPC Contest Coordinator. Offered annually for a lyric poem in honor of the former president of NEPC. Entries should be sent by regular mail only. Special Delivery or signature required mail will be returned by the Post Office. Entries should be original unpublished poems in English. No poem should be entered in more than one contest nor have won a previous contest. Poems should be typed and submitted in duplicate with author's name, address, and e-mail on one copy only. Label poems with contest name. No entries will be returned. NEPC will not engage in correspondence regarding poems or contest decisions. Deadline: May 31. Prize: $250. Judges are well-known poets and sometimes winners of previous NEPC contests.

FISH POETRY PRIZE

Durrus, Bantry Co. Cork Ireland. Website: fishpublishing.com. Fish Poetry Prize. Durrus, Bantry, Co. Cork, Ireland. E-mail: info@fishpublishing.com. Website: fishpublishing.com. "For poems up to 200 words. First Prize €1,000. Deadline 30 March 2011. Results 30 April 2011. Entry €14. Age Range: Adult. The best 10 will be published in the 2011 Fish Anthology, launched in July at the West Cork Literary Festival by Brian Turnr, the judge. Entries must not have been published before. Enter on-line or by post. Geographical area covered: Worldwide. See our website for full details of competitions, and information on the Fish Editorial and Critique Services, and the Fish

Online Writing Courses." The 2011 Fish Short Story Prize will open on 1 June and close 30 Sept 2011. **Fish Poetry Prize.** "For poems up to 200 words. Deadline 30 March 2011. Results 30 April 2011. Age Range: Adult. The best 10 will be published in the 2011 Fish Anthology, launched in July at the West Cork Literary Festival by Brian Turner. Entries must not have been published before. Entry on-line or by post. Geographical area covered: Worldwide. See our website for full details of competitions, and information on the Fish Editorial and Critique Services, and the Fish Online Writing Courses." Do not put your name or address or any other details on the poem, use a separate sheet. Receipt of entry will be acknowleged by e-mail. Poems will not be returned. Maximum words for each poem is 200, and you may enter as many as you wish, provided there is an entry fee for each one. Full details and rules are online. Entry is deemed to be acceptance of these rules. Publishing rights of the10 winning poems are held by Fish Publishing for one year after the publication of the Anthology. Last year the prize was won by Catherine Phil MacCarthy with *Limbo*. The aim of the competitions is to discover and publish new writers. March 30. Prize: First Prize €1,000 Judged by Brian Turner.

FOUR WAY BOOKS POETRY PRIZES

Four Way Books, P.O. Box 535, Village Station, New York NY 10014. E-mail: editors@fourwaybooks.com. Website: fourwaybooks.com. The Four Way Books Levis Poetry Prize. Open to all poets, regardless of publication history. Publication of a book-length collection of poetry (approximately 48 pages of text to 80, recommended). $1000.00 honorarium. Submissions guidelines will be posted on this site at the end of December. For guidelines send a SASE or download from website. Four Way Books runs different prizes annually. The Intro Prize in Poetry, The Four Way Books Levis Poetry Prize. Open to all poets, regardless of publication history. $1000.00 honorarium. Submissions guidelines will be posted on this site at the end of December. For guidelines send a SASE or download from website. Deadline: March 31. Prize: $1,000 and book publication 2011 contest Judged by Claudia Rankine.

GIVAL PRESS POETRY AWARD

Gival Press, LLC, P.O. Box 3812, Arlington VA 22203. (703)351-0079. E-mail: givalpress@yahoo.com. Website: givalpress.com. **Contact:** Robert L. Giron, editor.

"Offered annually for a previously unpublished poetry collection as a complete ms, which may include previously published poems; and previously published poems must be acknowledged & poet must hold rights. The competition seeks to award well-written, original poetry in English on any topic, in any style. Guidelines for SASE, by e-mail, or online. Entrants are asked to submit their poems without any kind of identification (with the exception of the titles) and with a separate cover page with the following information: name, address (street, city, state, and zip code), telephone number, e-mail address (if available), short bio, and a list of the poems by title. Checks drawn on American banks should be made out to Gival Press, LLC." Deadline: December 15 (postmarked). Prize: $1,000, publication, and 20 author's copies. The editor narrows entries to the top 10; previous winner selects top 5 and chooses the winner—all done anonymously.

GOLDEN ROSE AWARD

New England Poetry Club, P.O. Box 190076, Boston MA 02119. Website: nepoetryclub.org. "Given annually to the poet who has done the most for the art in the previous year or in a lifetime. Chosen by board." Contest open to members and nonmembers. **Contact:** N. Smith. "Given annually to the poet who has done the most for the art in the previous year or in a lifetime. Chosen by board." Contest open to members and nonmembers.

☮ GOVERNOR GENERAL'S LITERARY AWARD FOR POETRY

Canada Council for the Arts, 350 Albert St., P.O. Box 1047, Ottawa ON K1P 5V8 Canada. (613)566-4414, ext. 5573. Fax: (613)566-4410. Website: canadacouncil.ca/prizes/ggla. Offered for the best English-language and the best French-language work of poetry by a Canadian. Publishers submit titles for consideration. Deadline depends on the book's publication date in English: March 15, June 1, or August 7. Books in French: March 15 or July 15. Prize: Each laureate receives $25,000; non-winning finalists receive $1,000.

☮ THE GRIFFIN POETRY PRIZE

The Griffin Trust for Excellence in Poetry, 363 Parkridge Crescent, Oakville ON L6M 1A8 Canada. (905)618-0420. E-mail: info@griffinpoetryprize.com. Website: griffinpoetryprize.com. **Contact:** Ruth Smith. Offered annually for work published between January 1 and December 31. Deadline: December 31. Prize: Two $65,000 (Canadian) prizes. One prize will go to a living Canadian poet or translator, the other to a living poet or translator from any country, which may include Canada. a panel of qualified English-speaking judges of stature. Judges are chosen by the Trustees of The Griffin Trust For Excellence in Poetry.

INDIANA REVIEW POETRY PRIZE

Indiana Review, Ballantine Hall 465, Indiana University, Bloomington IN 47405-7103. (812)855-3439. Fax: (812)855-9535. E-mail: inreview@indiana.edu. Website: indianareview.com. Offered annually for unpublished work. Judged by guest judges; 2011 prize will be judged by Marie Howe. Open to any writer. Send no more than 3 poems per entry. Guidelines on website and with SASE request. This year's deadline: March 25. Prize: $1,000. Costs: $15 fee (includes a 1-year subscription) Open to any writer. **Contact:** Alessandra Simmons, Editor. Offered annually for unpublished work. Open to any writer. Send no more than 3 poems per entry. Guidelines on website and with SASE request. Open to any writer. This year's deadline: March 25. Prize: $1,000. Judged by guest judges; 2011 prize will be judged by Marie Howe.

IOWA POETRY PRIZES

University of Iowa Press, 119 West Park Rd., 100 Kuhl House, Iowa City IA 52242. (319)335-2000. Fax: (319)335-2055. E-mail: uipress@uiowa.edu. Website: uiowapress.org. The University of Iowa Press, 119 West Park Rd., 100 Kuhl House, Iowa City IA 52242-1000. (319)335-2000. E-mail: uipress@uiowa.edu. Website: uiowapress.org. The University of Iowa Press offers the annual Iowa Poetry Prizes for book-length mss (50-150 pages) originally in English by new or established poets. Winners will be published by the Press under a standard royalty contract. Poems from previously published books may be included only in mss of selected or collected poems, submissions of which are encouraged. Considers simultaneous submissions if Press is immediately notified if the book is accepted by another publisher. Guidelines available on website. **Entry fee:** $20. **Deadline:** postmarked during April only. Offered annually to encourage poets and their work. Submissions must be postmarked during the month of April; put name on title page only. This page will be removed before your manuscript is judged. Open to writers of English (US citizens or not). Manuscripts will not be returned. Previous winners are not eligible. Charges $20 reading fee. Deadline: April 30.

JANICE FARRELL POETRY PRIZE

The Soul-Making Literary Competition, National League of American Pen Women, Nob Hill, San Francisco Branch, The Webhallow House, 1544 Sweetwood Dr., Broadmoor Village CA 94015-2029. E-mail: pennobhill@aol.com. Website: soulmaking-contest.us. Annual contest. "Poetry may be double- or single-spaced. One-page poems only, and only 1 poem/page. All poems must be titled. 3 poems/entry. Indicate category on each poem. Identify with 3X5 card only. Open to all writers." $5/entry (make checks payable to NLAPW, Nob Hill Branch). Deadline: November 30. Prizes: 1st Place: $100; 2nd Place: $50; 3rd Place: $25. Judged by a local San Francisco successfully published poet. **Contact:** Eileen Malone. "Poetry may be double- or single-spaced. One-page poems only, and only 1 poem/page. All poems must be titled. 3 poems/entry. Indicate category on each poem. Identify with 3X5 card only. Open annually to all writers." Deadline: November 30. Prize: 1st Place: $100; 2nd Place: $50; 3rd Place: $25. Judged by a local San Francisco successfully published poet.

RANDALL JARRELL POETRY COMPETITION

North Carolina Writers' Network, Appalachian State University, Department of English, Box 32052, Boone NC 28608. E-mail: mailtlkenned@uncg.edu. Website: ncwriters.org. **Contact:** Terry L. Kennedy. Offered annually for unpublished work "to honor Randall Jarrell and his life at UNC-Greensboro by recognizing the best poetry submitted." Competition is open any writer who is a legal resident of North Carolina or a member of the NC Writers Network. Deadline: March 1. Prize: The contest awards the winner publication in *The Crucible* literary journal and $200.

JEAN PEDRICK PRIZE

New England Poetry Club, 2 Farrar St., Cambridge MA 02138. Prize for a chapbook published in the last two years. Funded by club dues. Send to 2 Farrar St., Cambridge MA 02138. $5 handling fee for non-members. Deadline: May 31. Prize: $100. Contests are free to all full time students and paid up members of New England Poetry Club. Non-members pay $10 for three contests and $3 additional per additional entry. Only one poem per contest. "New England Poetry board

members can enter only the Gretchen Warren competition." **Contact:** N. Smith. "Prize for a chapbook published in the last 2 years. Funded by club dues. Send to address above. Contests are free to all full time students and paid up members of New England Poetry Club. Non-members pay $10 for 3 contests and $3 additional per additional entry. Only one poem per contest. New England Poetry board members can enter only the Gretchen Warren competition." Deadline: May 31 (annually). Prize: $100.

JOHN CIARDI PRIZE FOR POETRY

BkMk Press, University of Missouri-Kansas City, 5100 Rockhill Rd., Kansas City MO 02903-1803. (816)235-2558. E-mail: bkmk@umkc.edu. Website: umkc.edu/bkmk. 5100 Rockhill Rd., Kansas City MO 02903-1803. Phone: (816)235-2558. Fax: (816)235-2611. E-mail: bkmk@umkc.edu. Website: umkc.edu/bkmk. Contact: Ben Furnish. "Offered annually for the best book-length collection (unpublished) of poetry in English by a living author. Translations are not eligible. Initial judging is done by a network of published writers. Final judging is done by a writer of national reputation. Guidelines for SASE, by e-mail, or on website." $25 fee. Deadline: January 15 (postmarked). Prize: $1,000, plus book publication by BkMk Press. "Offered annually for the best book-length collection (unpublished) of poetry in English by a living author. Translations are not eligible. Guidelines for SASE, by e-mail, or on website." Deadline: January 15 (postmarked). Prize: $1,000, plus book publication by BkMk Press. Judged by a network of published writers. Final judging is done by a writer of national reputation.

KATE TUFTS DISCOVERY AWARD

Claremont Graduate University, 160 E. 10th St., Harper East B7, Claremont CA 91711-6165. (909)621-8974. Fax: (909)607-8438. E-mail: tufts@cqu.edu. Website: cgu.edu/tufts. The Kate Tufts Discovery Award ($10,000) is for a first book. 2011 winner is Atsuro Riley (Romey's Order). To be considered for the 2012 awards, books must have been published between September 1, 2010 and August 31. Entry form and guidelines available for SASE or on website. Check website for updated deadlines and award information. **Contact:** Wendy Martin, program director. "The Kate Tufts Discovery Award ($10,000) is for a first book. 2011 winner is Atsuro Riley (Romey's Order). To be considered for the 2012 awards, books must have been published between September 1, 2010 and August 31. Entry form and guidelines available for SASE or on website. Check website for updated deadlines and award information." Prize: $10,000.

KATHLEEN MCCLUNG SONNETT COMPETITION

Category in the Soul-Making Literary Competition., National League of American Pen Women, The Webhallow House, 1544 Sweetwood Dr., Broadmoor Village CA 94015-2029. E-mail: pennobhill@aol.com. Website: soulmakingcontest.us. Contact: Eileen Malone, pennobhill@aol.com. Website: soulmakingcontest.us. "Call for Shakespearean and Petrarchan sonnets on the theme of the 'beloved.' Previously published material is accepted. Indicate category on cover page and on identifying 3x5 card. Open annually to any writer." Deadline: November 30. Prize: 1st Place: $100; 2nd Place: $50; 3rd Place: $25. **Contact:** Eileen Malone. "Call for Shakespearean and Petrarchan sonnets on the theme of the 'beloved.' Previously published material is accepted. Indicate category on cover page and on identifying 3x5 card. Open annually to any writer." Deadline: November 30. Prize: 1st Place: $100; 2nd Place: $50; 3rd Place: $25.

KATHRYN HANDLEY PROSE POEM PRIZE

National League of American Pen Women, Nob Hill, San Francisco Branch, The Webhallow House, 1544 Sweetwood Dr., Colma CA 94015-2029. E-mail: pennobhill@aol.com. Website: soulmakingcontest.us. Kathryn Handley Prose Poem Prize open annually to all writers. $5/entry fee (make checks payable to NLAPW, Nob Hill Branch). Poetry may be double- or single-spaced. 1-page poems only, and only 1 prose poem/page. 3 poems/entry. Indicate category on each poem. Identify only with 3X5 card. Open annually to all writers. $5/entry fee (make checks payable to NLAPW, Nob Hill Branch). Deadline: November 30. Prizes: 1st Place: $100; 2nd Place: $50; 3rd Place: $25. **Contact:** Eileen Malone. Kathryn Handley Prose Poem contest open annually to all writers. Poetry may be double- or single-spaced. 1-page poems only, and only 1 prose poem/page. 3 poems/entry. Indicate category on each poem. Identify only with 3X5 card. Deadline: November 30. Prize: 1st Place: $100; 2nd Place: $50; 3rd Place: $25.

BARBARA MANDIGO KELLY PEACE POETRY AWARDS

Nuclear Age Peace Foundation, PMB 121, 1187 Coast Village Rd., Suite 1, Santa Barbara CA 93108-2794. (805)965-3443. Fax: (805)568-0466. E-mail: wagingpeace@napf.org. Website: wagingpeace.org. Offers an annual series of awards "to encourage poets to explore and illuminate positive visions of peace and the human spirit." Awards $1,000 to adult contestants, $200 to youth in each 2 categories (13-18 and 12 and under), plus Honorable Mentions in each category. Submissions must be unpublished. Submit up to 3 poems in any form, unpublished and in English; maximum 30 lines/poem. Send 2 copies; put name, address, e-mail, phone number, and age (for youth) in upper right-hand corner of 1 copy of each poem. Title each poem; do not staple individual poems together. "Any entry that does not adhere to ALL of the contest rules will not be considered for a prize. Poets should keep copies of all entries as we will be unable to return them." Guidelines available for SASE or on website. **Entry fee:** Adult: $15 for up to 3 poems; 13-18: $5 for up to 3 poems; no fee for 12 and under. **Deadline:** July 1 (postmark). Judges: a committee of poets selected by the Nuclear Age Peace Foundation. Winners will be announced by October 1 by mail and on website. Winning poems from current and past contests are posted on the Foundation's website. "The Nuclear Age Peace Foundation reserves the right to publish and distribute the award-winning poems, including Honorable Mentions." "he Barbara Mandigo Kelly Peace Poetry Contest was created to encourage poets to explore and illuminate positive visions of peace and the human spirit. The annual contest honors the late Barbara Kelly, a Santa Barbara poet and longtime supporter of peace issues. Awards are given in 3 categories: adult (over 18 years), youth between 12 and 18 years, and youth under 12. All submitted poems should be unpublished." Deadline: July 1 (postmarked). Prize: Adult: $1,000; Youth (13-18): $200; Youth (12 and under): $200. Honorable Mentions may also be awarded. A committee of poets selected by the Nuclear Age Peace Foundation. The foundation reserves the right to publish and distribute the award-winning poems, including honorable mentions.

TIPS "Poets should keep copies of all entries as we will be unable to return them. Copies of the winning poems from the 2003 Awards will be posted on the

Nuclear Age Peace Foundation website after October 1, 2009."

THE LAUREATE PRIZE FOR POETRY

The National Poetry Review, P.O. Box 2080, Aptos CA 95001-2080. E-mail: editor@nationalpoetryreview.com. Website: nationalpoetryreview.com. The National Poetry Review. Submit via e-mail and paypal (see website for instructions: nationalpoetryreview.com) or via mail to P.O. Box 2080, Aptos CA 95001-2080. E-mail: editor@nationalpoetryreview.com. Acquisitions: C. J. Sage, editor. Poems must be uncommitted (not accepted for first publication elsewhere). Honors one new poem that The National Poetry Review believes has the greatest chance, of those entered, of standing the test of time and becoming part of the literary canon. Deadline: September 30. Prize $500, plus publication in *The National Poetry Review*. Costs $15 (personal checks only; no money orders) Tips Simultaneous submission acceptable, but if the work is selected byTNPR for the prize or for publication, it must be withdrawn from elsewhere unless you have withdrawn it from us 2 weeks before our acceptance. Multiple submissions are acceptable with a reading fee for each group of 3 poems. 10-page limit per group. [See separate listing in Magazines Journals.] **Contact:** C.J. Sage, Editor. *The National Poetry Review* is 72 pages, perfect-bound, with full-color cover. Accepts less than 1% of submissions received. Single copy: $15; subscription: $15/year. Make checks payable to TNPR only. Submit via e-mail and paypal (see website for instructions: nationalpoetryreview.com) or via mail. Poems must be uncommitted (not accepted for first publication elsewhere). Honors one new poem that The National Poetry Review believes has the greatest chance, of those entered, of standing the test of time and becoming part of the literary canon. Deadline: September 30. Prize $500, plus publication in *The National Poetry Review*.

TIPS Simultaneous submission acceptable, but if the work is selected by TNPR for the prize or for publication, it must be withdrawn from elsewhere unless you have withdrawn it from us 2 weeks before our acceptance. Multiple submissions are acceptable with a reading fee for each group of 3 poems. 10-page limit per group. [See separate listing in Magazines Journals.]

THE LEDGE ANNUAL POETRY CHAPBOOK CONTEST

The Ledge Magazine, 40 Maple Ave., Bellport NY 11713. E-mail: info@theledgemagazine.com. Website: theledgemagazine.com. The Ledge Press, 40 Maple Ave., Bellport NY 11713. Website: theledgemagazine.com. The Ledge Poetry Chapbook Contest offers an annual prize of $1,000, publication by The Ledge Press, and 25 chapbook copies. Considers simultaneous submissions. Accepts multiple submissions with separate entry fee for each. " No restrictions on form or content. Excellence is the only criterion." Submit 16-28 pages of poetry with bio and acknowledgements, if any. Include title page with poet's name, address, phone number, and e-mail address (if applicable). Include SASE for results or return of ms. Guidelines available on website. **Entry fee:** $18; all entrants will receive a copy of the winning chapbook upon publication. **Deadline:** October 31. Sample chapbooks available for $8 postpaid. Winner announced in March. **Contact:** Timothy Monaghan, Editor-in-Chief. Offered annually to publish an outstanding collection of poems. No restrictions on form or content. Send 16-28 pages, titles page, bio, acknowledgments, SASE. Guidelines online or for SASE. Open to any writer. Deadline: October 31. Prize: $1,000 and publication and 25 copies of the chapbook.

THE LEVINSON PRIZE

Poetry, 444 North Michigan Ave., Suite 1850, Chicago IL 60611. (312)787-7070. Fax: (312)787-6650. E-mail: poetry@poetrymagazine.org. Website: poetrymagazine.org. Offered annually for poems published in *Poetry* during the preceding year (October-September). *Poetry* buys all rights to the poems published in the magazine. Copyrights are returned to the authors on request. Prize: $500.

LEVIS READING PRIZE

Virginia Commonwealth Univ., Dept. of English, P.O. Box 842005, Richmond VA 23284-2005. (804)828-1329. Fax: (804)828-8684. E-mail: tndidato@vcu.edu. Website: has.vcu.edu/eng/resources/levis_prize.htm. **Contact:** Thom Didato. "Offered annually for books of poetry published in the previous year to encourage poets early in their careers. The entry must be the writer's first or second published book of poetry. Previously published books in other genres, or previously published chapbooks or self-published material, do not count as books for this purpose." Deadline: January 15. Prize: $1,500 honorarium and an expense-paid trip to Richmond to present a public reading.

THE RUTH LILLY POETRY PRIZE

The Modern Poetry Association, 444 North Michigan Ave., Suite 1850, Chicago IL 60610. E-mail: poetry@poetrymagazine.org. Website: poetrymagazine.org. Offered annually to a poet whose accomplishments in the field of poetry warrant extraordinary recognition. No applicants or nominations are accepted. Deadline: Varies. Prize: $100,000.

LITERAL LATTÉ POETRY AWARD

Literal Latté, 200 E. 10th St., Suite 240, New York NY 10003. (212)260-5532. E-mail: LitLatte@aol.com. Website: literal-latte.com. **Contact:** Jenine Gordon Bockman, editor. "Offered annually to any writer for unpublished poetry (maximum 2,000 words per poem). All styles welcome. Winners published in *Literal Latt*è." Acquires first rights. Deadline: Postmark by July 15. Prize: 1st Place: $1,000; 2nd Place: $300; 3rd Place: $200. The Editors.

MAY SARTON AWARD

New England Poetry Club, P.O. Box 190076, Boston MA 02119. Given intermittently to a poet who inspires other poets. Chosen by the board. $250 prize. Given intermittently to a poet who inspires other poets. Chosen by the board. Prize: $250.

NAOMI LONG MADGETT POETRY AWARD

Lotus Press, Inc., P.O. Box 21607, Detroit MI 48221. E-mail: lotuspress@comcast.net. Website: lotuspress.org. "Naomi Long Madgett Poetry Award. Offered annually to recognize an unpublished poetry ms by an African American. E-mail: lotuspress@comcast.net. Wwebsite: lotuspress.org. Contact: Constance Withers. Guidelines for SASE, by e-mail, or online." Deadline: January 2 - March 31. $500 and publication by Lotus Press. **Contact:** Constance Withers. "Offered annually to recognize an unpublished poetry ms by an African American. Guidelines for SASE, by e-mail, or online." Deadline: January 2 - March 31. Prize: $500 and publication by Lotus Press.

NATIONAL WRITERS ASSOCIATION POETRY CONTEST

The National Writers Association, 10940 S. Parker Rd. #508, Parker CO 80134. (303)841-0246. Fax: (303)841-2607. E-mail: natlwritersassn@hotmail.com. Website: nationalwriters.com. **Contact:** Sandy Whelchel, director. Annual contest to encourage the writing of poetry, an important form of individual expression but with a limited commercial market. E-mail Sandy for a form until new website is formed. Deadline: Oct. 1. Prize: 1st Place: $100; 2nd Place: $50; 3rd Place: $25.

HOWARD NEMEROV SONNET AWARD

320 Hunter Dr., Evansville IN 47711. E-mail: mona.3773@yahoo.com. Website: theformalist.evansville.edu/contest.html. Although The Formalist has ceased publication, it continues to sponsor the annual Howard Nemerov Sonnet Award. Offers $1,000 prize; winner and 11 finalists will be published in Measure: A Review of Formal Poetry (see separate listing in Magazines/Journals). Submit original, unpublished sonnets, no translations; sonnet sequences acceptable, but each sonnet will be considered individually. Poets may enter as many sonnets as they wish. Poet's name, address, phone number, and e-mail address should be listed on the **back** of each entry. Enclose SASE for contest results; mss will not be returned. Guidelines available for SASE or on website. **Entry fee**: $3/sonnet. Make all checks payable to The Formalist. Entry fees from outside U.S. must be paid in U.S dollars via check drawn on a U.S. bank or by cash. **Deadline:** November 15 (postmark). 2010 winner was Catherine Chandler. 2010 judge was A. E. Stallings. **Contact:** Mona Baer, contest coordinator. Offered annually for an unpublished sonnet to encourage poetic craftsmanship and to honor the memory of the late Howard Nemerov, third US Poet Laureate. Acquires first North American serial rights for those sonnets chosen for publication. Upon publication all rights revert to the author. Open to the international community of writers. Guidelines available online or for SASE. Poets may enter as many sonnets as they wish. Poet's name, address, phone number, and e-mail address should be listed on the **back** of each entry. Enclose SASE for contest results; mss will not be returned. Guidelines available for SASE or on website. **Entry fee**: $3/sonnet. Make all checks payable to The Formalist. Entry fees from outside U.S. must be paid in U.S dollars via check drawn on a U.S. bank or by cash. 2010 winner was Catherine Chandler. 2010 judge was A. E. Stallings. Deadline: November 15. Prize: $1,000 and publication in *Measure: A Review of Formal Poetry*.

THE JOHN FREDERICK NIMS MEMORIAL PRIZE

Poetry, 444 North Michigan Ave., Suite 1850, Chicago IL 60611. (312)787-7070. E-mail: poetry@poetrymagazine.org. Website: poetrymagazine.org. Offered annually for poems published in *Poetry* during the preceding year (October-September). Judged by the editors of *Poetry*. *Poetry* buys all rights to the poems published in the magazine. Copyrights are returned to the authors on request. Prize: $500.

GUY OWEN AWARD

Southern Poetry Review, Dept. of Languages, Literature, and Philosophy, Armstrong Atlantic State University, 11935 Abercorn St., Savannah GA 31419-1997. (912)344-3196. E-mail: james.smith@armstrong.edu. Website: southernpoetryreview.org. **Contact:** James M. Smith, Jr. Send 3-5 unpublished poems (maximum 10 pages) and SASE for response only. Include contact information on cover sheet only. All entries considered for publication. Please indicate simultaneous submissions. Deadline: March 1-June 15 (postmarked). Prize: $1,000 and publication of winning poem in *Southern Poetry Review*. Final judge will be a distinguished poet.

PAUMANOK POETRY AWARD

English Department, Knapp Hall, Farmingdale State College of New York, 2350 Broadhollow Rd., Route 110, Farmingdale NY 11735. E-mail: brownml@farmingdale.edu. Website: farmingdale.edu. Offers 1st Prize of $1,500 plus an all-expense-paid feature reading in their 2012-2013 visiting writers series. **(Please note: travel expenses within the continental U.S. only.)** Also awards two 2nd Prizes of $750 plus expenses for a reading in the series. Submit cover letter, 1 paragraph literary bio, and 3-5 poems (no more than 10 pages total), published or unpublished. Include cover page with name, address, and phone number. Guidelines available for SASE or on website. **Entry fee:** $25. Make checks payable to Farmingdale State University of New York, VWP. **Deadline:** by September 15 (postmark). Include SASE for results (to be mailed by late December); results also posted on website. Competition receives over 600 entries. 2010 winners were Mary Jo Bang (1st Prize) and Ellen Bass and Kathleen Spivack (runners-up). **Contact:** Margery L. Brown, director, Visiting Writers Program. "Offered annually for published or unpublished poems. Send cover letter, 1-paragraph bio, 3-5 poems (name and address on each poem). Include SASE for notification of winners. (Send photocopies only; mss will *not* be returned.)" Deadline: September 15. Prize: 1st Place: $1,500, plus expenses for a reading in series; Runners-up (2): $750, plus expenses for a reading in series.

PEARL POETRY PRIZE

Pearl Editions, 3030 E. Second St., Long Beach CA 90803. (562)434-4523. Fax: (562)434-4523. E-mail: pearlmag@aol.com. Website: pearlmag.com. The annual Pearl Poetry Prize awards $1,000, publication, and 25 author's copies for a book-length ms. Guidelines available for SASE or on website. **Entry fee:** $20. **Deadline:** submit May 1-June 30 only. 2009 winner was Kim roberts (*Animal Magnetism*). 2012 judge: Andrea Carter Brown. **Contact:** Marilyn Johnson, editor/publisher. "Offered annually to provide poets with further opportunity to publish their poetry in book-form and find a larger audience for their work. Mss must be original works written in English. Guidelines for SASE or online. Open to all writers." Deadline: June 30. Prize: $1,000 and publication by Pearl Editions

PEN/JOYCE OSTERWEIL AWARD FOR POETRY

PEN American Center, 588 Broadway, Suite 303, New York NY 10012. (212)334-1660, ext. 108. E-mail: awards@pen.org. Website: pen.org. **Contact:** Nick Burd, literary awards program manager. *Candidates may only be nominated by members of PEN*. This award recognizes the high literary character of the published work to date of a new and emerging American poet of any age, and the promise of further literary achievement. Nominated writer may not have published more than 1 book of poetry. Offered in odd-numbered years and alternates with the PEN/Voelcker Award for Poetry. Deadline: Feb. 3. Prize: $5,000. a panel of 3 judges selected by the PEN Awards Committee.

PEN/VOELCKER AWARD FOR POETRY

PEN American Center, 588 Broadway, Suite 303, New York NY 10012. (212)334-1600, ext. 108. E-mail: awards@pen.org. Website: pen.org. *Candidates may only be nominated by members of PEN*. Award given to an American poet whose distinguished and growing body of work to date represents a notable and accomplished presence in American literature. Offered in even-numbered years. Last year was in 2010; will be offered in 2012. **Contact:** Nick Burd, Literary awards program manager. Deadline: Feb. 3 (nominations). Prize: $5,000 stipend. a panel of 3-5 poets or other writers.

PERUGIA PRESS PRIZE

Perugia Press, P.O. Box 60364, Florence MA 01062. E-mail: info@perugiapress.com. Website: perugiapress.

com. The Perugia Press Prize for a first or second poetry book by a woman offers $1,000 and publication. Poet must be a living U.S. resident with no more than 1 previously published book of poems (chapbooks don't count). Submissions must be unpublished as a collection, but individual poems may have been previously published in journals, chapbooks, and anthologies. Considers simultaneous submissions if notified of acceptance elsewhere. Submit 48-72 pages (white paper) "with legible typeface, pagination, and fastened with a removable clip. No more than 1 poem per page." Two cover pages required: 1 with ms title, poet's name, address, telephone number, and e-mail address; and 1 with ms title only. Include table of contents and acknowledgments page. Electronic submissions available through our website. No translations or self-published books. Multiple submissions accepted if accompanied by separate entry fee for each. Include SASE for winner notification only; mss will be recycled. Guidelines available on website. **Entry fee:** $25. Make checks payable to Perugia Press. **Deadline:** submit August 1-November 15 (postmark). "Use USPS or electronic submission, not FedEx or UPS." Winner announced by April 1 by e-mail or SASE (if included with entry). Judges: panel of Perugia authors, booksellers, scholars, etc. **Contact:** Susan Kan. "The contest is for first or second poetry books by women. Some poems in the submission may be previously published, but the ms as a whole must be unpublished. Send SASE or visit our website for guidelines. The contest is open to women poets who are US residents and who have not published more than 1 book." Deadline: Nov. 15. Prize: $1,000 and publication

POETS OUT LOUD PRIZE

Poets Out Loud, Fordham University at Lincoln Center, 113 W. 60th St., Room 924-I, New York NY 10023. (212)636-6792. Fax: (212)636-7153. E-mail: pol@fordham.edu. Website: fordham.edu/pol. Annual competition for an unpublished, full-length poetry ms (50-80 pages). Deadline: October 15. Prize: $1,000 book publication, and book launch in POL reading series

MARGARET REID POETRY CONTEST FOR TRADITIONAL VERSE

c/o Winning Writers, 351 Pleasant St., PMB 222, Northampton MA 01060-3961. E-mail: johnreid@mail.qango.com. Website: winningwriters.com. Offers annual award of 1st Prize: $3,000; 2nd Prize: $1,000; 3rd Prize: $400; 4th Prize: $250; 5 High Dis-

tinction Awards of $200 each; and 6 Most Highly Commended Awards of $150 each. The top 10 entries will be published on the Winning Writers website. Submissions may be published or unpublished, may have won prizes elsewhere, and may be entered in other contests. Submit poems in traditional verse forms, such as sonnets, ballads, odes, blank verse, and haiku. No limit on number of lines or number of poems submitted. No name on ms pages; type or computer-print on letter-size white paper, single-sided. Guidelines available for SASE or on website. Submit online or by mail. **Entry fee:** $8 USD for every 25 lines (exclude poem title and any blank lines from count). **Deadline:** November 15-June 30. 2010 winner was Philip Brown ("South Sea Odyssey"). 2010 judges: John H. Reid and Dee C. Konrad. Winners announced in December at WinningWriters.com; entrants who provide valid e-mail addresses also receive notification. **Contact:** John Reid. "Seeks poems in traditional verse forms, such as sonnets." Both unpublished and published work accepted. Guidelines for SASE or on website. Deadline: June 30. Prize: 1st Place: $3,000; 2nd Place: $1,000; 3rd Place: $400; 4th Place: $250; 6 Most Highly Commended awards of $150 each. The top 10 entries will be published on the Winning Writers website. Judged by John H. Reid and Dee C. Konrad.

ROANOKE-CHOWAN POETRY AWARD

The North Carolina Literary & Historical Assoc., 4610 Mail Service Center, Raleigh NC 27699-4610. (919)807-7290. Fax: (919)733-8807. E-mail: michael.hill@ncdcr.gov. Website: history.ncdcr.gov/affiliates/lit-hist/awards/awards.htm. (Specialized: NC resident authors) Offers annual award for "an original volume of poetry published during the 12 months ending June 30 of the year for which the award is given." Open to "authors who have maintained legal or physical residence, or a combination of both, in North Carolina for the 3 years preceding the close of the contest period." Submit 3 copies of each entry. Guidelines available for SASE or by fax or e-mail. **Deadline:** July 15. Competition receives about 15 entries. 2010 winner was Joseph R. Bathanti , professor in Appalachian State University's Department of English and co-director of the creative writing program there for Bathantiâ's poetry collection *Restoring Sacred Art*, in which Bathanti shares rich ethnic associations, religious themes and vivid memories. The collectionwas published by Star

CONTESTS & AWARDS

Cloud Press. **Contact:** Michael Hill, awards coordinator. (Specialized: NC resident authors) Offers annual award for "an original volume of poetry published during the 12 months ending June 30 of the year for which the award is given." Open to "authors who have maintained legal or physical residence, or a combination of both, in North Carolina for the 3 years preceding the close of the contest period." Submit 3 copies of each entry. Guidelines available for SASE or by fax or e-mail. **Deadline:** July 15. Competition receives about 15 entries. Winner announced October 15.

☉ SASKATCHEWAN POETRY AWARD

Saskatchewan Book Awards, Inc., 205B-2314 11th Ave., Regina SK S4P 0K1 Canada. (306)569-1585. Fax: (306)569-4187. E-mail: director@bookawards. sk.ca. Website: bookawards.sk.ca. **Contact:** Jackie Lay, book submissions. Offered annually for work published September 15, 2010- October 31. This award is presented to a Saskatchewan author for the best book of poetry, judged on the quality of writing. Deadline: First deadline: November 1. Prize: $2,000

SLIPSTREAM ANNUAL POETRY CHAPBOOK COMPETITION

Slipstream, Box 2071, Niagara Falls NY 14301. E-mail: editors@slipstreampress.org. Website: slipstream-press.org. The annual Slipstream Poetry Chapbook Contest awards $1,000, publication of a chapbook ms, and 50 author's copies. All entrants receive copy of winning chapbook and an issue of Slipstream (see separate listing in Magazines/Journals). Considers simultaneous submissions if informed of status. Accepts previously published work with acknowledgments. Submit up to 40 pages of poetry, any style, format, or theme. Manuscripts will not be returned. Guidelines available for SASE or on website. **Entry fee:** $20. **Deadline:** December 1. Latest winner is David Chorlton (*From the Age of Miracles*). Winner announced late spring/early summer. **Contact:** Dan Sicoli, co-editor. "Offered annually to help promote a poet whose work is often overlooked or ignored. Open to any writer." Winner is featured prominently on the Slipstream website for one year, as well as in all Slipstream catalogs, press releases, and promotional material. Winning chapbooks are submitted by Slipstream for review by various national and international poetry/writing pubications and may also be featured in the Grants & Awards section of Poets & Writers magazine. Deadline: December 1. Prize: $1,000 and 50 copies of

published chapbook. (Everyone who enters receives a copy of the winning chapbook plus one complimentary issue of *Slipstream* magazine.

HELEN C. SMITH MEMORIAL AWARD FOR POETRY

The Texas Institute of Letters, P.O. Box 609, Round Rock TX 78680. (512) 238-1871. E-mail: tilsecretary@ yahoo.com. Website: texasinstituteofletters.org/. Offered annually for the best book of poems published January 1-December 31 of previous year. Poet must have been born in Texas, have lived in the state at some time for at least 2 consecutive years, or the subject matter must be associated with the state. See website for guidelines. Deadline: Jan. 1. Prize: $1,200. **Contact:** W.K. (Kip) Stratton, acquisitions. Offered annually for the best book of poems published January 1-December 31 of previous year. Poet must have been born in Texas, have lived in the state at some time for at least 2 consecutive years, or the subject matter must be associated with the state. See website for guidelines. Deadline: January 1. Prize: $1,200.

THE SOW'S EAR POETRY COMPETITION

P.O. Box 127, Millwood VA 22646. E-mail: rglesman@ gmail.com. Website: sows-ear.kitenet.net. The Sow's Ear Poetry Review (see separate listing in Magazines/Journals) sponsors an annual contest for unpublished poems. Offers $1,000 and publication in The Sow's Ear Poetry Review. Submit up to 5 unpublished poems. Include separate sheet with poem titles, poet's name, address, phone number, and e-mail address (if available). "We will check with finalists regarding publication status of poems before sending to final judge." Poet's name should not appear on poems. Include SASE for results only; entries will not be returned. Guidelines available for SASE, by e-mail, or on website. **Entry fee:** $27 for up to 5 poems. Contestants receive a year's subscription. Make checks payable to The Sow's Ear Poetry Review. Submit in September or October. **Deadline:** November 1 (postmark). Past judges include Gregory Orr and Marge Piercy. "Four criteria help us judge the quality of submissions: 1) Does the poem make the strange familiar or the familiar strange, or both? 2) Is the form of the poem vital to its meaning? 3) Do the sounds of the poem make sense in relation to the theme? 4) Does the little story of the poem open a window on the Big Story of the human situation?" **Contact:** Robert G. Lesman, Managing Editor. The Sow's Ear Poetry Review (see separate listing in Magazines/Journals) sponsors an annual contest for unpublished poems. Offers $1,000 and publication in The Sow's Ear Poetry Review. Submit up to 5 unpublished poems. Include separate sheet with poem titles, poet's name, address, phone number, and e-mail address (if available). "We will check with finalists regarding publication status of poems before sending to final judge." Poet's name should not appear on poems. Include SASE for results only; entries will not be returned. Guidelines available for SASE, by e-mail, or on website. **Entry fee:** $27 for up to 5 poems. Contestants receive a year's subscription. Make checks payable to The Sow's Ear Poetry Review. Submit in September or October. **Deadline:** November 1 (postmark). Past judges include Gregory Orr and Marge Piercy. "Four criteria help us judge the quality of submissions: 1) Does the poem make the strange familiar or the familiar strange, or both? 2) Is the form of the poem vital to its meaning? 3) Do the sounds of the poem make sense in relation to the theme? 4) Does the little story of the poem open a window on the Big Story of the human situation?"

SPIRE PRESS POETRY CHAPBOOK CONTEST

217 Thompson St., Suite 298, New York NY 10012. E-mail: editor@spirepress.org. Website: spirepress.org. Offers annual award of publication with royalty contract and promotion; author payment (see guidelines for each year). Submissions must be unpublished. Considers simultaneous submissions as long as Spire Press is informed. Submit a chapbook ms of 21-40 pages of poetry in any form (shorter poems preferred). Include SASE. Competition receives 400 entries/year. Past winners include Elizabeth Rees (*Now That We're Here*), Christina Olson (*Before I Came Home Naked*), Lori Romero (*The Emptiness That Makes Other Things Possible*), and Anthony Russell White (*Faith of Leaping*). Winners will be announced on website after contest deadline. Copies of winning chapbooks available through website, Amazon, selected bookstores, and Spire Press. Offers annual award of publication with royalty contract and promotion; author payment (see guidelines for each year). Submissions must be unpublished. Considers simultaneous submissions as long as Spire Press is informed. Submit a chapbook ms of 21-40 pages of poetry in any form (shorter poems preferred). Include SASE. Competition receives 400 entries/year. Past winners include

Elizabeth Rees (*Now That We're Here*), Christina Olson (*Before I Came Home Naked*), Lori Romero (*The Emptiness That Makes Other Things Possible*), and Anthony Russell White (*Faith of Leaping*). Winners will be announced on website after contest deadline. Copies of winning chapbooks available through website, Amazon, selected bookstores, and Spire Press. Deadline: May 31. Prize: Award: $500 + 20 copies and publishing contract.

THE EDWARD STANLEY AWARD

Prairie Schooner, 123 Andrews Hall, P.O. Box 880334, Lincoln NE 68588-0334. (402)472-0911. Fax: (402)472-9771. E-mail: jengelhardt2@unlnotes.unl.edu. Website: prairieschooner.unl.edu. **Contact:** Editor in Chief. Offered annually for poetry published in *Prairie Schooner* in the previous year. Prize: $1,000.

WALLACE E. STEGNER FELLOWSHIPS

Creative Writing Program, Stanford University, Stanford CA 94305-2087. (650)723-0011. Fax: (650)723-3679. E-mail: cablaza@stanford.edu. Website: creativewriting.standford.edu. Offers 5 fellowships in poetry of $26,000 plus tuition of over $7,000/year for promising writers who can benefit from 2 years of instruction and criticism in the program. "We do not require a degree for admission. No school of writing is favored over any other. Chronological age is not a consideration." Accept applications between September 1 and December 1 (postmark). Applicants may apply online. Competition receives about 1,700 entries/year. **Contact:** Christina Ablaza, Program Assistant. Offers 5 fellowships in poetry and fiction of $26,000 plus tuition of over $7,000/year for promising writers who can benefit from 2 years of instruction and criticism in the program. "We do not require a degree for admission. No school of writing is favored over any other. Chronological age is not a consideration." Accept applications between September 1 and December 1 (postmark). Applicants may apply online. Competition receives about 1,700 entries/year.

THE ELIZABETH MATCHETT STOVER MEMORIAL AWARD

Southwest Review, Southern Methodist University, P.O. Box 750374, Dallas TX 75275-0374. (214)768-1037. Fax: (214)768-1408. E-mail: swr@mail.smu.edu. Website: smu.edu/southwestreview. **Contact:** Jennifer Cranfill, Senior Editor and Willard Spiegelman, Editor-In-Chief. "Offered annually to the best works of poetry that have appeared in the magazine in the previous year. Please note that mss are submitted for publication, not for the prizes themselves. Guidelines for SASE and online." Prize: $300 Jennifer Cranfill and Willard Spiegelman.

STROKESTOWN INTERNATIONAL POETRY COMPETITION

Strokestown International Poetry Festival, Strokestown Poetry Festival Office, Strokestown, County Roscommon Ireland. (+353) 71 9633759. E-mail: office@strokestownpoetry.org. Website: strokestownpoetry.org. **Contact:** Director. This annual competition was established to promote excellence in poetry, and participation in the reading and writing of it. Acquires first publication rights. Deadline: January 24. Prize: 1st Prize: 4,000 euros (approximately $3,900) for a poem in English of up to 70 lines, plus others totalling about $3,000 dollars. Up to 10 shortlisted poets will be invited to read at the Strokestown International Poetry Festival and paid a reading fee. Peter Fallon, James Harpur, Mary O' Donoghue.

TEXAS INSTITUTE OF LETTERS BOB BUSH MEMORIAL AWARD FOR FIRST BOOK OF POETRY

Texas Institute of Letters, P.O. Box 609, Round Rock TX 78680. Website: texasinstituteofletters.org. Offered annually for best first book of poetry published in previous year. Writer must have been born in Texas, have lived in the state at least 2 consecutive years at some time, or the subject matter should be associated with the state. Deadline: Jan. 1. Prize: $1,000. **Contact:** W.K. (Kip) Stratton, acquisitions. Offered annually for best first book of poetry published in previous year. Writer must have been born in Texas, have lived in the state at least 2 consecutive years at some time, or the subject matter should be associated with the state. Deadline: Jan. 1. Prize: $1,000.

TOM HOWARD/JOHN H. REID POETRY CONTEST

Tom Howard Books, c/o Winning Writers, 351 Pleasant St., PMB 222, Northampton MA 01060-3961. (866)946-9748. Fax: (413)280-0539. E-mail: johnreid@mail.qango.com. Website: winningwriters.com/poetry. E-mail: johnreid@mail.qango.com. Website: winningwriters.com/poetry. Contact: John Reid, award director Offers annual award of 1st Prize: $3,000; 2nd

Prize: $1,000; 3rd Prize: $400; 4th Prize: $250; 5 High Distinction Awards of $200 each; and 6 Most Highly Commended Awards of $150 each. The top 10 entries will be published on the Winning Writers website. Submissions may be published or unpublished and may have won prizes elsewhere. Considers simultaneous submissions. Submit poems in any form, style, or genre. "There is no limit on the number of lines or poems you may submit." No name on ms pages; type or computer-print on letter-size white paper, single-sided. Submit online or by regular mail. Guidelines available for SASE or on website. **Entry fee:** $7 USD for every 25 lines (exclude poem titles and any blank lines from line count). **Deadline:** December 15-September 30. Competition receives about 1,000 entries/year. 2010 winner was Carmine Dandrea ("On the Silk Road"). 2011 judges: John H. Reid and Dee C. Konrad. Winners announced in February at WinningWriters.com. Entrants who provide valid e-mail addresses will also receive notification. **Contact:** John Reid, award director. Offers annual awards. The top 10 entries will be published on the Winning Writers website. Submissions may be published or unpublished and may have won prizes elsewhere. Poetry may be in any style or theme. Your entry should be your own original work. You may submit the same poem simultaneously to this contest and to others, and you may submit poems that have been published or won prizes elsewhere, as long as you own the online publication rights. "There is no limit on the number of lines or poems you may submit." Guidelines available for SASE or on website. Competition receives about 1,000 entries/year. 2010 winner was Carmine Dandrea ("On the Silk Road"). Winners announced in February at WinningWriters.com. Entrants who provide valid e-mail addresses will also receive notification. No name on ms pages; type or computer-print on letter-size white paper, single-sided. Submit online or by regular mail. **Entry fee:** $7 USD for every 25 lines (exclude poem titles and any blank lines from line count). Deadline: December 15-September 30. Prize: 1st Prize: $3,000; 2nd Prize: $1,000; 3rd Prize: $400; 4th Prize: $250; 5 High Distinction Awards of $200 each; and 6 Most Highly Commended Awards of $150 each 2011 judges: John H. Reid and Dee C. Konrad.

TRANSCONTINENTAL POETRY AWARD

Pavement Saw Press, 321 Empire St., Montpelier OH 43543. (419)485-0524. E-mail: info@pavementsaw.org.

Website: pavementsaw.org. The Transcontinental Poetry Award offers $1,000, publication, and a percentage of the print run for a first or second book. "Each year, Pavement Saw Press will seek to publish at least 1 book of poetry and/or prose poems from manuscripts received during this competition, which is open to anyone who has not previously published a volume of poetry or prose. Poets who have not published a book, who have published 1collection, or who have published a second collection of fewer than 40 pages, or who have published a second full-length collection with a print run of no more than 500 copies are eligible. More than 1prize may be awarded." Submit 48-70 pages of poetry (1 poem/page), paginated and bound with a single clip. Include 2 cover sheets: 1 with ms title, poet's name, address, phone number, and e-mail, if available, the second with ms title only (this sheet should be clipped to ms). Also include one-page cover letter (a brief biography, ms title, poet's name, address, and telephone number, e-mail, and poet's signature) and acknowledgments page (journal, anthology, chapbook, etc., and poem published). Include SASP for acknowledgment of receipt; SASE unnecessary as result will be sent with free book and no mss will be returned. Guidelines available for SASE or on website. **Entry fee:** $20; electronic submissions $27. "All U.S entrants will receive books, chapbooks, and journals equal to, or more than, the entry fee. Add $3 (USD) for other countries to cover the extra postal charge if sending by mail." Make checks payable to Pavement Saw Press. **Deadline:** reads submissions in June, July, and until August 15 (must have August 15 or earlier postmark). **Contact:** David Baratier, editor. "Offered annually for a first or second book of poetry. Judged by the editor and a guest judge. Guidelines available online." Deadline: August 15. Prize: $1,000, 50 copies for judge's choice, and standard royalty contract for editor's choice. All writers receive 2 free books for entering.

TUFTS POETRY AWARDS

Center for Arts & Humanities at Claremont Graduate, University, 160 E. 10th St., Harper East B7, Claremont CA 91711-6165. (909)621-8974. E-mail: tufts@cgu.edu. Website: cgu.edu/tufts. The annual Kingsley Tufts Poetry Award offers $100,000 for a work by an emerging poet, "one who is past the very beginning but has not yet reached the acknowledged pinnacle of his/her career." 2011 winner is Chase Twichell (*Horses Where*

the Answers Should Have Been). The Kate Tufts Discovery Award ($10,000) is for a first book. 2011 winner is Atsuro Riley (*Romey's Order*). To be considered for the 2012 awards, books must have been published between September 1, 2010 and August 31. Entry form and guidelines available for SASE or on website. Check website for updated deadlines and award information. **Contact:** Wendy Martin, Program Director. The annual Kingsley Tufts Poetry Award offers $100,000 for a work by an emerging poet, "one who is past the very beginning but has not yet reached the acknowledged pinnacle of his/her career." 2011 winner is Chase Twichell (*Horses Where the Answers Should Have Been*). The Kate Tufts Discovery Award ($10,000) is for a first book. 2011 winner is Atsuro Riley (*Romey's Order*). To be considered for the 2012 awards, books must have been published between September 1, 2010 and August 31. Entry form and guidelines available for SASE or on website. Check website for updated deadlines and award information.

♻ UTMOST CHRISTIAN POETRY CONTEST

Utmost Christian Writers Foundation, 121 Morin Maze, Edmonton AB T6K 1V1 Canada. E-mail: nnharms@telusplanet.net. Website: utmostchristianwriters.com. The Novice Christian Poetry Contest opened for entries on April 1, 2011—For Christian poets only! $2,000 in cash prizes. Deadline: August 31. See rules and entry form online at website. **Contact:** Nathan Harms, Exec. Director. The purpose of this annual contest is "to promote excellence in poetry by poets of Christian faith. All entries are eligible for most of the cash awards, but there is a special category for rhyming poetry with prizes of $300 and $100. All entries must be unpublished." Deadline: February 28. Prize: 1st Place: $1,000; 2nd Place: $600; ten prizes of $100 are offered for honorable mention. Rights are acquired to post winning entries on the organization's website. Judged by a committee of the Directors of Utmost Christian Writers Foundation (who work under the direction of Barbara Mitchell, chief judge).

CHAD WALSH POETRY PRIZE

Beloit Poetry Journal, P.O. Box 151, Farmington ME 04938. (207)778-0020. E-mail: bpj@bpj.org. Website: bpj.org. **Contact:** Lee Sharkey and John Rosenwald, editors. "Offered annually to honor the memory of poet Chad Walsh, a founder of the *Beloit Poetry Journal*." The editors select an outstanding poem or group of poems from the poems published in the journal that year. Prize: $3,000 in 2010

WAR POETRY CONTEST

Winning Writers, 351 Pleasant St., PMB 222, Northampton MA 01060-3961. (866)946-9748. Fax: (413)280-0539. E-mail: adam@winningwriters.com. Website: winningwriters.com. Offers annual award of 1st Prize: $2,000; 2nd Prize: $1,200; 3rd Prize: $600; 12 Honorable Mentions of $100 each. All prizewinners receive online publication at WinningWriters.com; selected finalists may also receive online publication. Submissions must be unpublished. Considers simultaneous submissions. Submit 1-3 poems of up to 500 lines total on the theme of war, any form, style, or genre. No name on ms pages, typed or computer-printed on letter-size white paper, single-sided. Submit online or by regular mail. Guidelines available for SASE or on website. **Entry fee:** $15 for group of 1-3 poems. **Deadline:** November 15-May 31. Competition receives about 650 entries/year. 2010 winner was Gerardo Mena for *So I Was a Coffin*. 2010 final judge: Jendi Reiter. Winners announced on November 15 at WinningWriters.com and in free e-mail newsletter. Entrants who provided valid e-mail addresses will also receive notification. (See separate listing for the Wergle Flomp Humor Poetry Contest in this section and for Winning Writers in the Additional Resources section.) **Contact:** Adam Cohen. "This annual contest seeks outstanding, unpublished poetry on the theme of war. Up to 3 poems can be submitted, with a maximum total of 500 lines. English language only; translations accepted if you wrote the original poem." Submit online or by mail. Guidelines for SASE or see website. Nonexclusive right to publish submissions on WinningWriters.com, in e-mail newsletter, and in press releases. Deadline: November 15-May 31. Prize: 1st Place: $2,000 and publication on WinningWriters.com; 2nd Place: $1,200 and publication; 3rd Place: $600 and publication; Honorable Mentions (12): $100 and publication. 2010 winner was Gerardo Mena for *So I Was a Coffin*. Final Judge: award-winning poet Jendi Reiter.

WERGLE FLOMP HUMOR POETRY CONTEST

Winning Writers, 351 Pleasant St., PMB 222, Northampton MA 01060-3961. (866)946-9748. Fax: (413)280-0539. E-mail: adam@winningwriters.com. Website: winningwriters.com. Offers annual award

of 1st Prize: $1,500; 2nd Prize: $800; 3rd Prize: $400; plus 12 Honorable Mentions of $75 each. Both published and unpublished poems are welcome. Final judge: Jendi Reiter. See the complete guidelines and past winners. All prizewinners receive online publication at WinningWriters.com. Submissions may be previously published. Considers simultaneous submissions. Submit 1 humorous poem of any length, in any form. See website for examples." Entries accepted only through website; no entries by regular mail. Guidelines available on website. **Entry fee:** none. **Deadline:** April 1, 2012. Competition receives about 750 entries/year. Winners announced at WinningWriters.com and in free e-mail newsletter. "Please read the past winning entries and the judge's comments published at WinningWriters.com." Guidelines are a little unusual—please follow them closely. See separate listing for the War Poetry Contest in this section and for Winning Writers in the Additional Resources section. **Contact:** Adam Cohen. "This annual contest seeks today's best humor poems. One poem of any length should be submitted. The poem should be in English. Inspired gibberish is also accepted. See website for guidelines, examples, and to submit your poem. nonexclusive right to publish submissions on WinningWriters.com, in e-mail newsletter, and in press releases." Deadline: August 15-April 1. Prize: 1st Place: $1,500; 2nd Place: $800; 3rd Place: $400. Twelve Honorable Mentions get $75 each. All prize winners receive publication at WinningWriters.com. Non-US winners will be paid in US currency (or PayPal) if a check is inconvenient. Final judge is Jendi Reiter.

WHITE PINE PRESS POETRY PRIZE

White Pine Press, P.O. Box 236, Buffalo NY 14201. E-mail: wpine@whitepine.org. Website: whitepine.org. **Contact:** Dennis Maloney, editor. Offered annually for previously published or unpublished poets. Manuscript: Up to 80 pages of original work; translations are not eligible. Poems may have appeared in magazines or limited-edition chapbooks. Open to any US citizen Deadline: November 30 (postmarked). Prize: $1,000 and publication. Final Judge is a poet of national reputation. All entries are screened by the editorial staff of White Pine Press.

THE J. HOWARD AND BARBARA M.J. WOOD PRIZE

Poetry, 444 North Michigan Ave., Suite 1850, Chicago IL 60611. (312)787-7070. E-mail: poetry@poetrymagazine.org. Website: poetrymagazine.org. Offered annually for poems published in *Poetry* during the preceding year (October-September). *Poetry* buys all rights to the poems published in the magazine. Copyrights are returned to the authors on request. Prize: $5,000.

WRITERS' JOURNAL POETRY CONTEST

Val-Tech Media, P.O. Box 394, Perham MN 56573. (218)346-7921. Fax: (218)346-7924. E-mail: writers-journal@writersjournal.com. Website: writersjournal.com. "Contest offered for previously unpublished poetry. Receives fewer than 300 entries. Guidelines for SASE or online."$3/poem. Deadline: April 30, August 30, December 30. 1st Place: $50; 2nd Place: $25; 3rd Place: $15. First place, second place, third place, and selected honorable mention winners will be published in *WRITERS' Journal* magazine. **Contact:** Esther M. Leiper-Estabrooks. "Offered for previously unpublished poetry. Receives fewer than 300 entries. Guidelines for SASE or online." Deadline: April 30, August 30, December 30. Prize: 1st Place: $50; 2nd Place: $25; 3rd Place: $15. First place, second place, third place, and selected honorable mention winners will be published in *WRITERS' Journal* magazine.

ZONE 3 POETRY AWARD

ZONE 3, Austin Peay State University, P.O. Box 4565, Clarksville TN 37044. (931)221-7031. Fax: (931)221-7149. E-mail: wallacess@apsu.edu. Website: apsu.edu/zone3/. **Contact:** Susan Wallace, managing editor. "Offered annually for unpublished poetry. Previous judges include Carolyn Forché, Margie Piercy, Maxine Kumin, Stephen Dunn, Mark Jarman, and Michael Collier. Open to any poet." Deadline: December 31. Prize: $500.

MULTIPLE WRITING AREAS

AMERICAN MARKETS NEWSLETTER COMPETITION

American Markets Newsletter, 1974 46th Ave., San Francisco CA 94116. E-mail: sheila.oconnor@juno.com. **Contact:** Sheila O'Connor. "Accepts fiction and nonfiction up to 2,000 words. Entries are eligible for cash prizes and all entries are eligible for worldwide syndication whether they win or not. Here's how it works: Send us your double-spaced manuscripts with your story/article title, byline, word count, and address on the first page above your article/story's first paragraph (no need for separate cover page). There

is no limit to the number of entries you may send." Deadline: December 31 and July 31. Prize: 1st Place: $500; 2nd Place: $200; 3rd Place: $100. a panel of independent judges.

ARIZONA AUTHORS' ASSOCIATION ANNUAL NATIONAL LITERARY CONTEST AND BOOK AWARDS

Arizona Authors' Association, 6145 W. Echo Ln., Glendale AZ 85302. (623)847-9343. E-mail: info@azauthors.com. Website: azauthors.com. Offered annually for previously unpublished poetry, short stories, essays, novels, and articles. Awards for published books in fiction, anthology, nonfiction, and children's. Winners announced at an award banquet in Glendale in November, and short pieces and excerpts published in *Arizona Literary Magazine*. Deadline: July 1. Prize: $100 and publication, and/or feature in the *Arizona Literary Magazine*. Additional prizes awarded by Five Star Publications.

◎ ATLANTIC WRITING COMPETITION FOR UNPUBLISHED MANUSCRIPTS

Writers' Federation of Nova Scotia, 1113 Marginal Rd., Halifax NS B3H 4P7. (902)423-8116. Fax: (902)422-0881. E-mail: director@writers.ns.ca; talk@writers.ns.ca. Website: writers.ns.ca. Writer's Federation of Nova Scotia, 1113 Marginal Rd. Halifax NS B3H 4P7 Canada. (902)423-8116. Fax: (902)422-0881. E-mail: talk@writers.ns.ca. Website: writers.ns.ca/awc.html. Annual contest. Purpose is to encourage emerging writers in Atlantic Canada to explore their talents by sending unpublished work to any of five categories: novel, short story, poetry, writing for younger children, writing for juvenile/young adult. Unpublished submissions only. Only open to residents of Atlantic Canada who are unpublished in category they enter. Visit website for more information. "Annual contest for beginners to try their hand in a number of categories: novel, short story, poetry, writing for younger children, writing for juvenile/young adult. Only 1 entry/category is allowed. Established writers are also eligible, but must work in an area that's new to them. Because our aim is to help Atlantic Canadian writers grow, judges return written comments when the competition is concluded. Anyone residing in the Atlantic Provinces for at least 6 months prior to the contest deadline is eligible to enter."$35 fee for novel ($30 for WFNS members); $25 fee for all other categories ($20 for WFNS members). Needs poetry, essays, juvenile, novels, articles, short stories. Full-length books of adult poetry written by Atlantic Canadians, and published as a whole for the first time in the previous calendar year, are eligible. Entrants must be native or resident Atlantic Canadians who have either been born in Newfoundland, Prince Edward Island, Nova Scotia, or New Brunswick, and spent a susbstantial portion of their lives living there, or who have lived in one or a combination of these provinces for at least 24 consecutive months prior to entry deadline date. Publishers: Send 4 copies and a letter attesting to the author's status as an Atlantic Canadian and the author's current mailing address and telephone number.poetryDeadline: First Friday in December. Prize: $2,000. **Contact:** Nate Crawford, program coordinator. "Annual contest for beginners to try their hand in a number of categories: novel, short story, poetry, writing for younger children, writing for juvenile/young adult. Only 1 entry/category is allowed. Established writers are also eligible, but must work in an area that's new to them. Because our aim is to help Atlantic Canadian writers grow, judges return written comments when the competition is concluded. Anyone residing in the Atlantic Provinces for at least 6 months prior to the contest deadline is eligible to enter." Deadline: First Friday in December. Prize: **Novel**—1st Place: $200; 2nd Place: $150; 3rd Place: $75. **Writing for Younger Children and Juvenile/Young Adult**—1st Place: $150; 2nd Place: $75; 3rd Place: $50. **Poetry and Short Story**—1st Place: $150; 2nd Place: $75; 3rd Place: $50. a team of 2-3 professional writers, editors, booksellers, librarians, or teachers.

AWP AWARD SERIES

Mail Stop 1E3, George Mason Univ., Fairfax VA 22030. E-mail: awp@awpwriter.org. Website: awpwriter.org. The AWP Award Series was established in cooperation with several university presses in order to publish and make fine fiction and nonfiction available to a wide audience. Offered annually to foster new literary talent. Guidelines for SASE and on website. Categories: novel ($2,000), Donald Hall Prize in Poetry ($5,000), Grace Paley Prize in Short Fiction ($5,000), and creative nonfiction ($2,000). Entry fee: $30 for nonmembers, $15 for members. Entries must be unpublished. "This information should appear in cover letter only." Open to any writer. Guidelines available on website in November. No phone calls, please. Manuscripts published previously in their entirety, including self-publishing, are not eligible. No mss returned. Results announced in August. Winners notified by mail or phone. For contest results send SASE, or visit website. No phone calls, please. **Contact:** Supriya Bhatnagar, Dir. of Publications. The AWP Award Series was established in cooperation with several university presses in order to publish and make fine fiction and nonfiction available to a wide audience. Offered annually to foster new literary talent. Guidelines for SASE and on website. Entries must be unpublished. "This information should appear in cover letter only." Open to any writer. Guidelines available on website in November. No phone calls, please. Mss published previously in their entirety, including self-publishing, are not eligible. No mss returned. Results announced in August. Winners notified by mail or phone. For contest results send SASE, or visit website. No phone calls, please. Cover letter should include name, address, phone number, e-mail and title. "This information should appear in cover letter only." Mss must be postmarked between Jan. 1 - Feb. 28. Prize: novel ($2,000), Donald Hall Prize in Poetry ($5,000), Grace Paley Prize in Short Fiction ($5,000), and creative nonfiction ($2,000).

THE BASKERVILLE PUBLISHERS POETRY AWARD & THE BETSY COLQUITT POETRY AWARD

descant, Texas Christian University's literary journal, TCU, Box 297270, Fort Worth TX 76129. (817)257-6537. Fax: (817)257-6239. E-mail: descant@tcu.edu. Website: descant.tcu.edu. "Annual award for an outstanding poem published in an issue of *descant*." Deadline: September - April. $250 for Baskerville Award; $500 for Betsy Colquitt Award. Publication retains copyright, but will transfer it to the author upon request. **Contact:** Dan Williams and Alex Lemon. "Annual award for an outstanding poem published in an issue of *descant*." Deadline: September - April. Prize: $250 for Baskerville Award; $500 for Betsy Colquitt Award. Publication retains copyright, but will transfer it to the author upon request.

THE BOSTON AUTHORS CLUB BOOK AWARDS

The Boston Authors Club, 79 Moore Road, Wayland MA 01778. E-mail: lawson@bc.edu. Website: bostonauthorsclub.org. **Contact:** Alan Lawson. Julia Ward Howe Prize offered annually in the spring for books published the previous year. Two awards are given:

one for trade books of fiction, nonfiction, or poetry, and the second for children's books. Authors must live or have lived within 100 miles of Boston within the past five years. No picture books or subsidized publishers. There must be two copies of each book submitted, accompanied by a $25 submission fee for each pair of books." Deadline: January 15. Prize: $1,000 in each category.

THE BRIAR CLIFF REVIEW FICTION, POETRY, AND CREATIVE NONFICTION COMPETITION

The Briar Cliff Review, Briar Cliff University, 3303 Rebecca St., Sioux City IA 51104-0100. E-mail: curranst@briarcliff.edu; jeanne.emmons@briarcliff.edu. Website: briarcliff.edu/bcreview. The Briar Cliff Review, Briar Cliff University, 3303 Rebecca St., Sioux City IA 51104-0100. (712) 279-5321. Fax: (712) 279-5410. E-mail: curranst@briarcliff.edu. Website: briarcliff.edu/bcreview. **Contact:** Tricia Currans-Sheehan, editor. Purpose of Award: "to reward good writers and showcase quality writing." Offered annually for unpublished poem, story and essay. Prize: $ 1,000, and publication in Spring issue. All entrants receive a copy of the magazine with winning entries. Judged by editors. "We guarantee a considerate reading." Entry fee: $20. Guidelines available in August for SASE. Inquiries accepted by e-mail. **Deadline: Submissions between August 1 and November 1.** No mss returned. Entries must be unpublished. Length: 6,000 words maximum. Open to any writer. Results announced in December or January. Winners notified by phone or letter around December 20. "Send us your best. We want stories with a plot." The Briar Cliff Review (see separate listing in Magazines/Journals) sponsors an annual contest offering $1,000 and publication to each First Prize winner in fiction, poetry, and creative nonfiction. Previous year's winner and former students of editors ineligible. Winning pieces accepted for publication on the basis of First-Time Rights. Considers simultaneous submissions, "but notify us immediately upon acceptance elsewhere." Submit 3 poems, single-spaced on 8½x11 paper, no more than 1 poem/page. Include separate cover sheet with author's name, address, e-mail, and poem title(s); no name on ms. Include SASE for results only; mss will not be returned. Guidelines available on website. **Entry fee:** $20 for 3 poems. "All entrants receive a copy of the magazine (a $15 value) containing the winning en-

tries." **Deadline:** November 1. Judge: the editors of The Briar Cliff Review. **Contact:** Tricia Currans-Sheehan, editor. Offered annually for unpublished poetry, fiction and essay. No mss returned. Award to reward good writers and showcase quality writing. Deadline: August 1-November 1. Prize: $1,000 and publication in Spring issue. Entrants receive copy of the magazine (a $15 value) with winning entries. Judged by editors of *The Briar Cliff Review*. "We guarantee a considerate reading."

☉ BURNABY WRITERS' SOCIETY CONTEST

E-mail: info@bws.bc.ca. Website: bws.bc.ca; http:burnabywritersnews.blogspot.com. Offered annually for unpublished work. Open to all residents of British Columbia. Categories vary from year to year. Send SASE for current rules. Purpose is to encourage talented writers in all genres. Prize: 1st Place: $200; 2nd Place: $100; 3rd Place: $50; and public reading. Entry fee: $5. For complete guidelines, see website or burnabywritersnews.blogspot.com. **Contact:** Eileen Kernaghan. "Offered annually for unpublished work. Open to all residents of British Columbia. Categories vary from year to year. Send SASE for current rules. For complete guidelines see website or burnabywritersnews.blogspot.com." Purpose is to encourage talented writers in all genres. Deadline: May 31. Prize: 1st Place: $200; 2nd Place: $100; 3rd Place: $50; and public reading.

☉ CANADIAN AUTHORS ASSOCIATION AWARDS PROGRAM

P.O. Box 581, Orillia ON L3V 1V5 Canada. (705)653-0323 or (866)216-6222. Fax: (705)653-0593. E-mail: admin@canauthors.org. Website: canauthors.org. **Contact:** Anita Purcell. Offered annually for fiction, poetry, history, and drama. Entrants must be Canadians by birth, naturalized Canadians, or landed immigrants. Entry form required for all awards. Obtain entry form from contact name or download from website. Deadline: December 15. Prize: Cash and a silver medal.

CBC LITERARY AWARDS/PRIX LITTÉRAIRES RADIO-CANADA

CBC Radio/Radio Canada, Canada Council for the Arts, *enRoute* magazine, P.O. Box 6000, Montreal QC H3C 3A8 Canada. (877)888-6788. E-mail: literary_awards@cbc.ca. Website: cbc.ca/literaryawards. **Con-

tact: Carolyn Warren, executive producer. The CBC Literary Awards Competition is the only literary competition that celebrates original, unpublished works in Canada's 2 official languages. There are 3 categories: short story, poetry, and creative nonfiction. Submissions to the short story and creative nonfiction must be 1,000-2,500 words; poetry submissions must be 2,000-2,500 words. Poetry submissions can take the form of a long narrative poem, a sequence of connected poems, or a group of unconnected poems. Canadian citizens, living in Canada or abroad, and permanent residents of Canada are eligible to enter. Deadline: November. Prize: There is a first prize of $6,000 and second prize of $4,000 for each category, in both English and French, courtesy of the Canada Council for the Arts. In addition, winning entries are published in Air Canada's *enRoute* magazine and broadcast on CBC radio. First publication rights are granted by winners to *enRoute* magazine and broadcast rights are given to CBC radio. Submissions are judged blind by a jury of qualified writers and editors from around the country. Each category has 3 jurors.

THE CITY OF VANCOUVER BOOK AWARD

Cultural Services Dept., 111 W. Hasting St., Suite 501, Vancouver BC V6B 1H4 Canada. (604) 829-2007. Fax: (604)871-6005. E-mail: marnie.rice@vancouver.ca. Website: vancouver.ca/bookaward. "Offered annually for books published in the previous year which exhibit excellence in the categories of content, illustration, design, and format. The book must contribute significantly to the appreciation and understanding of the city of Vancouver and heighten awareness of 1 or more of the following: Vancouver's history, the city's unique character, or achievements of the city's residents. The book may be fiction, nonfiction, poetry, or drama written for adults or children, and may deal with any aspects of the city—history, geography, current affairs, or the arts. Guidelines online." Prize: $2,000.

COLORADO BOOK AWARDS

Colorado Center for the Book, 1490 Lafayette St., Suite 101, Denver CO 80218. (303)894-7951, ext. 21. Fax: (303)864-9361. E-mail: long@coloradohumanities.org. Website: coloradocenterforthebook.org. Offered annually for work published by December of previous year. "The purpose is to champion all Colorado authors, editors, illustrators, and photographers, and in particular, to honor the award winners raising the pro-

files of both their work and Colorado as a state whose people promote and support reading, writing, and literacy through books. The categories are generally: children's literature, young adult and juvenile literature, fiction, genre fiction (romance, mystery/thriller, science fiction/fantasy, historical), biography, history, anthology, poetry, pictorial, graphic novel/comic, creative nonfiction, and general nonfiction, as well as other categories as determined each year. Open to authors who reside or have resided in Colorado." Cost: $53 fee. Needs fiction, nonfiction, poetry, juvenile, novels. Deadline: January 16, 2012. Offered annually for work published by December of previous year. "The purpose is to champion all Colorado authors, editors, illustrators, and photographers, and in particular, to honor the award winners raising the profiles of both their work and Colorado as a state whose people promote and support reading, writing, and literacy through books. The categories are generally: children's literature, young adult and juvenile literature, fiction, genre fiction (romance, mystery/thriller, science fiction/fantasy, historical), biography, history, anthology, poetry, pictorial, graphic novel/comic, creative nonfiction, and general nonfiction, as well as other categories as determined each year. Open to authors who reside or have resided in Colorado." Cost: $53 fee. Needs fiction, nonfiction, poetry, juvenile, novels. Deadline: January 16, 2012. **Contact:** Margaret Coval, Exec. Director, or Jennifer Long, Prog. Adjudicator. Offered annually for work published by December of previous year. "The purpose is to champion all Colorado authors, editors, illustrators, and photographers, and in particular, to honor the award winners raising the profiles of both their work and Colorado as a state whose people promote and support reading, writing, and literacy through books. The categories are generally: children's literature, young adult and juvenile literature, fiction, genre fiction (romance, mystery/thriller, science fiction/fantasy, historical), biography, history, anthology, poetry, pictorial, graphic novel/comic, creative nonfiction, and general nonfiction, as well as other categories as determined each year. Open to authors who reside or have resided in Colorado." Deadline: January 16, 2012.

COMMONWEALTH CLUB OF CALIFORNIA BOOK AWARDS

595 Market St., San Francisco CA 94105. (415)597-6724. Fax: (415)597-6729. E-mail: gdobbins@commonwealthclub.org. Website: commonwealthclub.

org/bookawards. Annual contest. Estab. 1932. Purpose of contest: the encouragement and production of literature in California. Juvenile and Young Adult categories included. Previously published submissions; must be published from January 1 to December 31, no self published or on-demand entries. SASE for contest rules and entry forms. No entry fee. Awards gold and silver medals. Judging by the Book Awards Jury. The contest is only open to California writers/illustrators (must have been resident of California when ms was accepted for publication). Winning entries are displayed at awards program and advertised in newsletter. Award to honor excellence in literature written by California residents. Prize: $2,000, gold medal; $300, silver medal. Categories: fiction, first work of fiction, nonfiction, juvenile, young adult, poetry, Californiana, contribution to publishing. Judged by jury. No entry fee. Entries must be previously published. California residents only. Writer or publisher may nominate work. Guidelines available in January on website. Results announced in Spring. Winners notified by phone. For contest results, send e-mail. Annual awards "consisting of not more than two gold and eight silver medals" plus $2,000 cash prize to gold medal winners and $300 to silver medal winners. For books of "exceptional literary merit" in poetry, fiction, and nonfiction (including work related to California and work for children), plus 2 "outstanding" categories. Submissions must be previously published. Submit at least 3 copies of each book entered with an official entry form. (Books may be submitted by author or publisher.) Open to books, published during the year prior to the contest, whose author "must have been a legal resident of California at the time the manuscript was submitted for publication." Entry form and guidelines available for SASE or on website. **Deadline:** December 31. Competition receives approximately 50 poetry entries/year. Most recent award winners were Czeslaw Milosz and Carolyn Kizer. **Contact:** Wendy Wanderman, Associate Program Director. "Offered annually for published submissions appearing in print January 1-December 31 of the previous year. Purpose of award is the encouragement and production of literature in California. Can be nominated by publisher as well. Open to California residents (or residents at time of publication)." Deadline: December 31. Prize: Medals and cash prizes to be awarded at publicized event. Judged by jury.

TIPS "Guidelines available on website."

CORDON D 'OR - GOLD RIBBON ANNUAL INTERNATIONAL CULINARY ACADEMY AWARDS

The 'Accolade of the 21st Century', Cordon d 'Or - Gold Ribbon Inc., P.O. Box 40868, St. Petersburg FL 33743. (727)347-2437. E-mail: cordondor@aol.com. Website: goldribboncookery.com. **Contact:** Noreen Kinney. "Contest promotes recognition of food authors, writers, and culinary magazines and websites, food stylists and food photographers and other professionals in the culinary field. See website: cordondorcuisine.com for full details. Open to any writer. All categories can be found on the website. The only criteria is that all entries must be in the English language." Deadline: Nov. 30. Prize: Cordon d 'Or - Gold Ribbon Crystal Globe Trophies (with stands and engraved marble bases) will be presented to winners. An outstanding winner chosen by the judges from among all entries will also win a cash award of $1,000. Judged by professionals in the fields covered in the awards program.

CWW ANNUAL AWARDS COMPETITION

Council for Wisconsin Writers, Website: wisconsinwriters.org. **Contact:** Geoff Gilpin; Marilyn Taylor; Karla Huston, awards co-chairs; and Carolyn Washburne, Christopher Latham Sholes Award and Major Achievement Award Co-Chair. Offered annually for work published by Wisconsin writers the previous calendar year. Nine awards: major/life achievement alternate years; short fiction; short nonfiction; nonfiction book; poetry book; fiction book; children's literature; Lorine Niedecker Poetry Award; Sholes Award for Outstanding Service to Wisconsin Writers Alternate Years; Essay Award for Young Writers. Open to Wisconsin residents. Guidelines on website. Rules and entry form on website. Deadline: January 31 (postmark). Prize: Prizes: $500 and a certificate. Essay Contest: $150. This year only the Essay Award for Young Writers prize will be $250.

DANA AWARDS IN THE NOVEL, SHORT FICTION, ESSAY AND POETRY

danaawards.com, 200 Fosseway Dr., Greensboro NC 27445. (336)644-8028. E-mail: danaawards@pipeline.com; danaawards@gmail.com. Website: danaawards.com. **Contact:** Mary Elizabeth Parker, chair. Four awards offered annually for unpublished work written in English. Purpose is monetary award for work that has not been previously published or received monetary award, but will accept work published simply for friends and family. Works previously published online are not eligible. No work accepted by or for persons under 16 for any of the 4 awards. Awards: **Novel**—For the first 40 pages of a novel completed or in progress. **Fiction**—Short fiction (no memoirs) up to 10,000 words. **Essay**—personal essay, memoir, or creative non-fiction up to 10,000 words. **Poetry**—For best group of 5 poems based on excellence of all 5 (no light verse, no single poem over 100 lines). Deadline: October 31 (postmarked). Prize: Awards: $1,000 for each of the 4 awards.

EATON LITERARY AGENCY'S ANNUAL AWARDS PROGRAM

Eaton Literary Agency, P.O. Box 49795, Sarasota FL 34230. (941)366-6589. Fax: (941)365-4679. E-mail: eatonlit@aol.com. Website: eatonliterary.com. Offered biannually for unpublished mss. Prize: $2,500 (over 10,000 words); $500 (under 10,000 words). Judged by an independent agency in conjunction with some members of Eaton's staff. No entry fee. Guidelines available for SASE, by fax, e-mail, or on website. Accepts inquiries by fax, phone and e-mail. Deadline: **March 31** (mss under 10,000 words); **August 31** (mss over 10,000 words). Entries must be unpublished. Open to any writer. Results announced in April and September. Winners notified by mail. For contest results, send SASE, fax, e-mail or visit website. **Contact:** Richard Lawrence, V.P. "Offered annually for unpublished mss." Deadline: March 31 (mss under 10,000 words); August 31 (mss over 10,000 words). Prize: $2,500 (over 10,000 words); $500 (under 10,000 words). Judged by an independent agency in conjunction with some members of Eaton's staff.

THE ERIC HOFFER AWARD

Best New Writing, P.O. Box 11, Titusville NJ 08560-0011. Fax: (609)818-1913. E-mail: info@hopepubs.com. Website: hofferaward.com. **Contact:** Christopher Klim, chair. Annual contest recognizing excellence in publishing. "This contest recognizes excellence in independent publishing in 15 distinct categories. Honors by press type (academic, independent, small press, and self-published) and category (art, poetry, general fiction, commercial fiction, children, young adult, culture, memoir, business, reference, home, health, self-help/spiritual, legacy fiction, and legacy nonfiction. Also awards the Montaigne

Medal for most thought provoking book and the Da Vinci Eye for best cover. Results published in the US Review of Books." Deadline: January 21. Prize: $2,000 Judged by authors, editors, agents, publishers, book producers, artists, experienced category readers, and health and business professionals.

THE VIRGINIA FAULKNER AWARD FOR EXCELLENCE IN WRITING

Prairie Schooner, 123 Andrews Hall, P.O. Box 880334, Lincoln NE 68588-0334. (402)472-0911. Fax: (402)472-9771. E-mail: jengelhardt2@unl.edu. Website: prairieschooner.unl.edu. Offered annually for work published in Prairie Schooner in the previous year. Prize: $1,000. Categories: short stories, essays, novel excerpts and translations. Judged by Editorial Board. No entry fee. Guidelines for SASE or on website. Accepts inquiries by fax and e-mail. "We only read mss from September 1 through May 1." Winning entry must have been published in Prairie Schooner in the year preceeding the award. Results announced in the Spring issue. Winners notified by mail in February or March. **Contact:** Kwame Dawes. "Offered annually for work published in *Prairie Schooner* in the previous year." Prize: $1,000.

○ FREEFALL SHORT PROSE AND POETRY CONTEST

Freefall Literary Society of Calgary, 922 9th Ave. SE, Calgary AB T2G 0S4 Canada. E-mail: freefallmagazine@yahoo.ca. Website: freefallmagazine.ca. **Contact:** Lynn C. Fraser, Managing Editor. Offered annually for unpublished work in the categories of poetry (5 poems/entry) and prose (3,000 words or less). The purpose of the award in both categories is to recognize writers and offer publication credits in a literary magazine format. Contest rules and entry form online. First Canadian serial rights (ownership reverts to author after one-time publication). Deadline: December 31. Prize: 1st Place: $300 (Canadian); 2nd Place: $150 (Canadian); 3rd Place: $75 Honourable Mention: $25. All prizes include publication in the spring edition of *FreeFall Magazine*. Winners will also be invited to read at the launch of that issue if such a launch takes place. Honorable mentions in each category will be published and may be asked to read. Travel expenses not included. Judged by current guest editor for issue (who are also published authors in Canada).

GEORGETOWN REVIEW

Georgetown Review, 400 East College St., Box 227, Georgetown KY 40324. (502) 863-8308. Fax: (502) 863-8888. E-mail: gtownreview@georgetowncollege.edu. Website: georgetownreview.georgetowncollege.edu. Annual. Publishes short stories, poetry, and creative nonfiction. Reading period: September 1-December 31. Also sponsors yearly writing contest for short stories, poetry, and creative nonfiction." Prize: $1,000 and publication; runners-up receive publication. Receives about 300 entries for each category. Entries are judged by the editors. Entry fee: $10 for first entry, $5 for each one thereafter. Make checks payable to Georgetown College. Guidelines available in July. Accepts inquiries by e-mail. **Entry deadline is Oct. 15th.** Entries should be unpublished. Contest open to anyone except family, friends of the editors. "We're just looking to publish quality work. Sometimes our contests are themed, so check the website for details." Results announced Feb. or March. Winners notified by e-mail. Results made available to entrants with SASE. Annual. Contact: Steve Carter. E-mail: gtownreview@georgetowncollege.edu. Publishes short stories, poetry, and creative nonfiction. Reading period: September 1-December 31. Also sponsors yearly writing contest for short stories, poetry, and creative nonfiction." Prize: $1,000 and publication; runners-up receive publication. Receives about 300 entries for each category. Entries are judged by the editors. Entry fee: $10 for first entry, $5 for each one thereafter. Make checks payable to Georgetown College. Guidelines available in July. Accepts inquiries by e-mail. **Entry deadline is Oct. 15th.** Entries should be unpublished. Contest open to anyone except family, friends of the editors. "We're just looking to publish quality work. Sometimes our contests are themed, so check the website for details." Results announced Feb. or March. Winners notified by e-mail. Results made available to entrants with SASE. Cover letter, ms should include name, address, phone, e-mail, novel/story title. Writers may submit own work. **Contact:** Steve Carter, editor. "Annual. Publishes short stories, poetry, and creative nonfiction. Reading period Sept. 1 - Dec. 31. Also sponsors yearly writing contest for short stories, poetry, and creative nonfiction." Receives about 300 entries for each category. Entries are judged by the editors. Guidelines available in July. Accepts inquiries by e-mail. Contest open to anyone except family, friends of the editors. "Sometimes our contests are themed, so check the website for details." Results announced Feb. or March. Winners notified by e-mail. Results made available to entrants with SASE. Cover letter, ms should include name, address, phone, e-mail, novel/story title. Writers may submit own work. Entries should be unpublished. Purpose is to publish quality work. Deadline: Oct. 15. Prize: $1,000 and publication; runners-up receive publication.

GRANTS FOR ARTIST'S PROJECTS

Artist Trust, 1835 12th Ave, Seattle WA 98122. (206) 467-8734, ext. 11. Fax: (206) 467-9633. E-mail: miguel@artisttrust.org. Website: artisttrust.org. "The GAP Program provides support for artist-generated projects, which can include (but are not limited to) the development, completion or presentation of new work." Annual. Prize: maximum of $1,500 for projects. Accepted are poetry, fiction, graphic novels, experimental works, creative non-fiction, screen plays, film scripts and teleplays. Entries are judged by work sample as specified in the guidelines. Winners are selected by a discipline-specific panel of artists and artist professionals. No entry fee. Guidelines available in March. Accepts inquiries by mail, phone. Submission period is March-May. **Deadline is May 10.** Website should be consulted for exact date. Entries can be unpublished or previously published. Washington state residents only. Length: 8 pages max for poetry, fiction, graphic novels, experimental work and creative nonfiction; up to 12 pages for screen plays, film scripts and teleplays. All mss must be typed with a 12-point font size or larger and cannot be single-spaced (except for poetry). Include application with project proposal and budget, as well as resume with name, address, phone, e-mail, and novel/story title. "GAP awards are highly competitive. Please follow guidelines with care." Results announced in the fall. Winners notified by e-mail. Results made available to entrants by e-mail and on website. "The GAP Program provides support for artist-generated projects, which can include (but are not limited to) the development, completion or presentation of new work." Annual. Prize: maximum of $1,500 for projects. Accepted are poetry, fiction, graphic novels, experimental works, creative non-fiction, screen plays, film scripts and teleplays. Entries are judged by work sample as specified in the guidelines. Winners are selected by a discipline-specific panel of artists and artist professionals. No entry fee. Guidelines available in March.

Accepts inquiries by mail, phone. Submission period is March-May. **Deadline is May 10.** Website should be consulted for exact date. Entries can be unpublished or previously published. Washington state residents only. Length: 8 pages max for poetry, fiction, graphic novels, experimental work and creative nonfiction; up to 12 pages for screen plays, film scripts and teleplays. All mss must be typed with a 12-point font size or larger and cannot be single-spaced (except for poetry). Include application with project proposal and budget, as well as resume with name, address, phone, e-mail, and novel/story title. "GAP awards are highly competitive. Please follow guidelines with care." Results announced in the fall. Winners notified by e-mail. Results made available to entrants by e-mail and on website. **Contact:** Monica Miller, Director of Programs. "The GAP grant is awarded annually to 60 artists of all disciplines including writers. The award is meant to help finance a specific project, which can be in very early stages or near completion. Full-time students are not eligible. Open to Washington state residents only. Up to $1,500 for artist-generated projects." Deadline: May 10.

HACKNEY LITERARY AWARDS

1305 2nd Avenue North, #103, Birmingham AL 35203. (205)226-4921. E-mail: info@hackneyliteraryawards. org. Website: hackneyliteraryawards.org. **Contact:** Myra Crawford, PhD, chair. Offered annually for unpublished novels, short stories (maximum 5,000 words) and poetry (50 line limit). Guidelines on website. Deadline: September 30 (novels), November 30 (short stories and poetry). Prize: $5,000 in annual prizes for poetry and short fiction ($2,500 national and $2,500 state level; 1st Place: $600; 2nd Place: $400; 3rd Place: $250), plus $5,000 for an unpublished novel. Competition winners will be announced on the website each March.

THE JULIA WARD HOWE/BOSTON AUTHORS AWARD

The Boston Authors Club, 33 Brayton Rd., Brighton MA 02135. (617)783-1357. E-mail: bostonauthors@ aol.com; lawson@bc.edu. Website: bostonauthorsclub. org. This annual award honors Julia Ward Howe and her literary friends who founded the Boston Authors Club in 1900. It also honors the membership over 110 years, consisting of novelists, biographers, historians, governors, senators, philosophers, poets, playwrights, and other luminaries. There are 2 categories: trade books and books for young readers (beginning with chapter books through young adult books). Works of fiction, nonfiction, memoir, poetry, and biography published in 2010 are eligible. Authors must live or have lived (college counts) within a 100-mile radius of Boston within the last 5 years. Subsidized books, cook books and picture books are not eligible. Fee is $25 per title. Deadline: January 15. Prize: $1,000 in each category. **Contact:** Alan Lawson. "This annual award honors Julia Ward Howe and her literary friends who founded the Boston Authors Club in 1900. It also honors the membership over 110 years, consisting of novelists, biographers, historians, governors, senators, philosophers, poets, playwrights, and other luminaries. There are 2 categories: adult books and books for young readers (beginning with chapter books through young adult books). Fee is $25 per title. Works of fiction, nonfiction, memoir, poetry, and biography published in 2010 are eligible. Authors must live or have lived (college counts) within a 100-mile radius of Boston during the last 5 years. Subsidized books and picture books are not eligible." Deadline: January 15, 2012. Prize: $1,000 in each category.

INDIANA REVIEW K (SHORT-SHORT/PROSE-POEM) CONTEST

BH 465/Indiana University, 1020 E. Kirkwood Ave., Bloomington IN 47405-7103. (812)855-3439. Fax: (812)855-4253. E-mail: inreview@indiana.edu. Website: indianareview.edu. Competition for fiction and prose poems no longer than 500 words. Prize: $1,000 plus publication, contributor's copies and a year's subscription. All entries considered for publication. Judged by guest judges; 2010 prize judged by Alberto Rios. Entry fee: $15 fee for no more than 3 pieces (includes a year's subscription, two issues). Make checks payable to Indiana Review. **Deadline: June.** Entries must be unpublished. Guidelines available in March for SASE, by phone, e-mail, on website, or in publication. Length: 500 words, 3 mss per entry. Open to any writer. Cover letter should include name, address, phone, e-mail, word count and title. No identifying information on ms. "We look for command of language and form." Results announced in August. Winners notified by mail. For contest results, send SASE or visit website. See website for detailed guidelines. Competition for fiction and prose poems no longer than 500 words. Prize: $1,000 plus publication, contributor's copies and a year's subscription. All entries considered for publication. Judged by guest judges; 2010 prize judged by Alberto Rios. Entry fee: $15 fee for no more than 3 pieces (includes a year's subscription, two issues). Make checks payable to Indiana Review. **Deadline: June.** Entries must be unpublished. Guidelines available in March for SASE, by phone, e-mail, on website, or in publication. Length: 500 words, 3 mss per entry. Open to any writer. Cover letter should include name, address, phone, e-mail, word count and title. No identifying information on ms. "We look for command of language and form." Results announced in August. Winners notified by mail. For contest results, send SASE or visit website. See website for detailed guidelines. **Contact:** Alessandra Simmons, editor. Maximum story/poem length is 500 words. Offered annually for unpublished work. Check website for guidelines. Deadline: Early June. Prize: $1,000 Judged by Alberto Rios, guest judge for 2010.

IOWA AWARD IN POETRY, FICTION, & ESSAY

The Iowa Review, 308 EPB, Iowa City IA 52242. (319)335-0462. Fax: (319)335-2535. Website: iowareview.org. Deadline: January 1-31 (postmarked). Prize: $1,000 and publication.

JUDITH SIEGEL PEARSON AWARD

Wayne State Univ./Family of Judith Siegel Pearson, 5057 Woodward Ave., Suite 9408, Detroit MI 48202. (313)577-2450. Fax: (313)577-8618. E-mail: rhonda@wayne.edu. Offers an annual award of up to $500 for the best creative or scholarly work on a subject concerning women. The type of work accepted rotates each year: fiction in 2011, drama in 2012, poetry in 2013 (poetry, 20 pages maximum), essays in 2014. Open to all interested writers and scholars. Submissions must be unpublished. Guidelines available for SASE or by fax or e-mail. Offers an annual award of up to $500 for the best creative or scholarly work on a subject concerning women. The type of work accepted rotates each year: fiction in 2011, drama in 2012, poetry in 2013 (poetry, 20 pages maximum), essays in 2014. Open to all interested writers and scholars. Submissions must be unpublished. Submit 4-10 poems (20 pages maximum). Guidelines available for SASE or by fax or e-mail. **Contact:** Rhonda Agnew, Contest Coordinator. Annual award for the best creative or scholarly work on a subject concerning women. The type of work accepted rotates each year: fiction in 2011, drama in 2012, poetry in 2013

(poetry, 20 pages maximum), essays in 2014. Open to all interested writers and scholars. Submissions must be unpublished. Submit 4-10 poems (20 pages maximum). Guidelines available for SASE or by fax or e-mail. Winner announced April 2011. No late or electronic submissions accepted. Deadline: Feb. 25. Prize: Offers an annual award of up to $500

LET'S WRITE LITERARY CONTEST

The Gulf Coast Writers Association, P.O. Box 10294, Gulfport MS 39505. E-mail: writerpllevin@gmail.com. Website: gcwriters.org. **Contact:** Philip Levin. "The Gulf Coast Writers Association sponsors this nationally recognized contest which accepts unpublished poems and short stories from authors all around the United States. This is an annual event which has been held for over 20 years." Deadline: April 15. Prize: 1st Prize: $80; 2nd Prize: $50; 3rd Prize: $20.
TIPS "See guidelines online."

✪ BRENDA MACDONALD RICHES FIRST BOOK AWARD

Saskatchewan Book Awards, Inc., 205B-2314 11th Ave., Regina SK S4P 0K1 Canada. (306)569-1585. Fax: (306)569-4187. E-mail: director@bookawards.sk.ca. Website: bookawards.sk.ca. **Contact:** Jackie Lay, executive director, book submissions. Offered annually for work published September 15, 2010-October 31. This award is presented to a Saskatchewan author for the best first book, judged on the quality of writing. Books from the following categories will be considered: children's; drama; fiction (short fiction by a single author, novellas, novels); nonfiction (all categories of nonfiction writing except cookbooks, directories, how-to books, or bibliographies of minimal critical content); poetry. Deadline: November 1. Prize: $2,000 CAD.

✪ MANITOBA BOOK AWARDS

c/o Manitoba Writers' Guild, 206-100 Arthur St., Winnipeg MB R3B 1H3 Canada. (204)942-6134 or (888)637-5802. Fax: (204)942-5754. E-mail: info@mbwriter.mb.ca. Website: bookpublishers.mb.ca/mba/. Offered annually: The McNally Robinson Book of Year Award (adult); The McNally Robinson Book for Young People Awards (8 and under and 9 and older); The John Hirsch Award for Most Promising Manitoba Writer; The Mary Scorer Award for Best Book by a Manitoba Publisher; The Carol Shields Winnipeg Book Award; The Eileen McTavish Sykes Award for Best First Book; The Margaret Laurence Award for Fiction; The Alexander Kennedy Isbister Award for Non-Fiction; The Manuela Dias Book Design of the Year Award; The Best Illustrated Book of the Year Award; and the biennial Le Prix Littéraire Rue-Deschambault. Guidelines and submission forms available online (accepted until mid-January). Open to Manitoba writers only. Prize: Prizes: Several prizes up to $5,000 (Canadian).

THE MCGINNIS-RITCHIE MEMORIAL AWARD

Southwest Review, P.O. Box 750374, Dallas TX 75275-0374. (214)768-1037. Fax: (214)768-1408. E-mail: swr@mail.smu.edu. Website: smu.edu/southwestreview. **Contact:** Jennifer Cranfill, senior editor and Willard Spiegelman, editor-in-chief. "The McGinnis-Ritchie Memorial Award is given annually to the best works of fiction and nonfiction that appeared in the magazine in the previous year. Manuscripts are submitted for publication, not for the prizes themselves. Guidelines for SASE or online." Prize: Two cash prizes of $500 each. Jennifer Cranfill and Willard Spiegelman.

MIDLAND AUTHORS AWARD

Society of Midland Authors, P.O. Box 10419, Chicago IL 60610-0419. E-mail: writercc@aol.com. Website: midlandauthors.com. "Established in 1915, the Society of Midland Authors Award (SMA) is presented to one title in each of six categories 'to stimulate creative effort,' one of SMA's goals, to be honored at the group's annual awards banquet in May." Annual. Competition/award for novels, story collections (by single author). Prize: cash prize of at least $300 and a plaque that is awarded at the SMA banquet. Categories: children's nonfiction and fiction, adult nonfiction and fiction, adult biography, and poetry. Judging is done by a panel of three judges for each category that includes a mix of experienced authors, reviewers, book sellers, university faculty and librarians. No entry fee. Guidelines available in September-November with SASE, on website, in publication. Accepts inquiries by e-mail, phone. **Deadline: Feb. 1.** Entries must be published in the prior calendar year, e.g. 2007 for 2008 award. "The contest is open to any title with a recognized publisher that has been published within the year prior to the contest year." Open to authors or poets who reside in, were born in, or have strong ties to a Midland state, which includes Illinois, Indiana, Iowa, Kansas, Michigan, Minnesota, Missouri,

Nebraska, North Dakota, South Dakota, Ohio and Wisconsin. SMA only accepts published work accompanied by a completed award form. Writers may submit own work. Entries can also be submitted by the publisher's rep. "Write a great story and be sure to follow contest rules by sending a copy of the book to each of the three judges for the given category who are listed on SMA's website." Results announced at the SMA Awards Banquet each May. Other announcements follow in the media. Winners notified by mail, by phone. Results made available to entrants on website, in our monthly membership newsletter. Results will also go to local media in the form of press releases. **Contact:** Carol Jean Carlson. Offered annually for published fiction, nonfiction, poetry, biography, children's fiction, and children's nonfiction published in the previous calendar year. Authors must reside in, have been born in, or have strong connections to the states of Illinois, Indiana, Iowa, Kansas, Michigan, Minnesota, Missouri, Nebraska, North Dakota, South Dakota, Wisconsin, or Ohio. Guidelines online. Deadline: February 15. Prize: Monetary award given to winner in each category.

NATIONAL OUTDOOR BOOK AWARDS

921 S. 8th Ave., Stop 8128, Pocatello ID 83209. (208)282-3912. E-mail: wattron@isu.edu. Website: noba-web.org. **Contact:** Ron Watters. "Nine categories: History/biography, outdoor literature, instructional texts, outdoor adventure guides, nature guides, children's books, design/artistic merit, natural history literature, and nature and the environment. Additionally, a special award, the Outdoor Classic Award, is given annually to books which, over a period of time, have proven to be exceptionally valuable works in the outdoor field. Application forms and eligibilty requirements are available online." Deadline: September 1. Prize: Winning books are promoted nationally and are entitled to display the National Outdoor Book Award (NOBA) medallion.

☙ THE NOMA AWARD FOR PUBLISHING IN AFRICA

Kodansha Ltd., Japan, P.O. Box 128, Witney, Oxon OX8 ORN UK. (44)(1993)775-235. Fax: (44)(1993)709-265. E-mail: maryljay@aol.com. Website: nomaaward.org. P.O. Box 128, Witney, Oxon 0X8 5XU. United Kingdom. E-mail: maryljay@aol.com. Website: nomaaward.org. **Contact:** Mary Jay. Sponsored by Kodansha Ltd. Award "to encourage publication of works by African writers and scholars in Africa, instead of abroad as is still too often the case at present." Categories: scholarly or academic; books for children; literature and creative writing, including fiction, drama and poetry. Judged by a committee of African scholars and book experts and representatives of the international book community. Chairman: Walter Bgoya. No entry fee. Entries must be previously published. Guidelines and entry forms available in December by fax, e-mail or on website. Submissions are through publishers only. "Publisher must complete entry form and supply six copies of the published work." Maximum number of entries per publisher is three. Results announced in October. Winners notified through publisher. List of winners available from Secretariat or on website. "The award is for an outstanding book. Content is the overriding criterion, but standards of publication are also taken into account." Deadline: Feb. 28. **Contact:** Mary Jay, Noma Award Managing Comm. secretary. "The Noma Award, sponsored by Kodansha LTD., Japan, is open to African writers and scholars whose work is published in Africa. The spirit within which the annual award is given is to encourage and reward genuinely autonomous African publishers, and African writers. The award is given for an outstanding new book in any of these 3 categories: scholarly or academic; books for children; and literature and creative writing (including fiction, drama, poetry, and essays on African literature). Entries must be submitted by publishers in Africa, who are limited to 3 entries (in any combination of the eligible categories). The award is open to any author who is indigenous to Africa (a national, irrespective of place of domicile). Guidelines at website or from Secretariat." No entries or award to be held in 2010. Prize: $10,000 (US). "The managing committee is an impartial committee chaired by Mr. Walter Bgoya, comprising African scholars, book experts, and representatives of the international book community. This Managing Committee is the jury. The jury is assisted by independent opinion and assessment from a large and distinguished pool of subject specialists from throughout the world, including many in Africa."

NORTHERN CALIFORNIA BOOK AWARDS

Northern California Book Reviewers Association, c/o Poetry Flash, 1450 Fourth St. #4, Berkeley CA 94710. (510)525-5476. E-mail: editor@poetryflash.org. Website: poetryflash.org. , c/o Poetry Flash, Berkeley CA 94710. (510)525-5476. Fax: (510)525-6752. E-mail: editor@poetryflash.org. Website: poetryflash.org. **Contact:** Joyce Jenkins. Annual Northern California Book Award for outstanding book in literature, open to books published in the current calendar year by Northern California authors. Annual award. NCBR presents annual awards to Bay Area (northern California) authors annually in fiction, nonfiction, poetry and children's literature. Purpose is to encourage writers and stimulate interest in books and reading." Previously published books only. Must be published the calendar year prior to spring awards ceremony. Submissions nominated by publishers; author or agent could also nominate published work. Deadline for entries: December. No entry forms. Send 3 copies of the book to attention: NCBR. No entry fee. Awards $100 honorarium and award certificate. Judging by voting members of the Northern California Book Reviewers. Books that reach the "finals" (usually 3-5 per category) displayed at annual award ceremonies (spring). Nominated books are displayed and sold at the Northern California Book Awards in the spring of each year; the winner is asked to read at the San Francisco Public Library's Main Branch. Northern California Book Awards, c/o Poetry Flash, 1450 Fourth St. #4, Berkeley CA 94710. (510) 525-5476. Fax: (510) 525-6752. E-mail: editor@poetryflash.org. Website: poetryflash.org. "Offers annual awards to recognize "the best of Northern California (from Fresno north) fiction, poetry, nonfiction, and children's literature, as chosen by the Northern California Book Reviewers Association." NCBA translation award is selected by Center for the Art of Translation and the NCBR submissions must be published in the calendar year. Submit 3 copies of each book entered. The authors of the submitted books must live in Northern California. Guidelines on website. Deadline: December 1. NCBR also presents the Fred Cody Award for Lifetime Achievement for a body of work and service to the literary community. The Fred Cody Award does not accept applications. Estab. 1981. Northern California Book Awards, c/o Poetry Flash, 1450 Fourth St. #4, Berkeley CA 94710. (510) 525-5476. Fax: (510) 525-6752. E-mail: editor@poetryflash.org. Website: poetryflash.org. "Offers annual awards to recognize "the best of Northern California (from Fresno north) fiction, poetry, nonfiction, and children's literature, as chosen by the Northern California Book Reviewers Association." NCBA translation award is selected by Center for the Art of Translation and the NCBR submissions must be published in the calendar year. Submit 3 copies of each book entered. The authors of the submitted books must live in Northern California. Guidelines on website. Deadline: December 1. NCBR also presents the Fred Cody Award for Lifetime Achievement for a body of work and service to the literary community. The Fred Cody Award does not accept applications. Estab. 1981. **Contact:** Joyce Jenkins, exec. director. (Specialized: Northern California). Purpose is "to recognize "the best of Northern California (from Fresno north) fiction, poetry, nonfiction, and children's literature, as chosen by the Northern California Book Reviewers Association." Deadline: Dec. 1.

OHIOANA BOOK AWARDS

Ohioana Library Association, 274 E. 1st Ave., Suite 300, Columbus OH 43201-3673. (614)466-3831. Fax: (614)728-6974. E-mail: ohioana@ohioana.org. Website: ohioana.org. Ohioana Library Association, 274 E. 1st Ave., Suite 300, Columbus OH 43201-3673. (614)466-3831. Fax: (614)728-6974. E-mail: ohioana@ohioana.org. Website: ohioana.org. Offered annually to bring national attention to Ohio authors and their books, published in the last 2 years. (Books can only be considered once.) Categories: Fiction, nonfiction, juvenile, poetry, and books about Ohio or an Ohioan. Writers must have been born in Ohio or lived in Ohio for at least 5 years, but books about Ohio or an Ohioan need not be written by an Ohioan. Prize: certificate and glass sculpture. Judged by a jury selected by librarians, book reviewers, writers and other knowledgeable people. Each winter the jury considers all books received since the previous jury. No entry fee. **Deadline: December 31**. A copy of the book must be received by the Ohioana Library by December 31 prior to the year the award is given; literary quality of the book must be outstanding. No entry forms are needed, but they are available July 1 of each year. Specific questions should be sent to Ohioana. Results announced in August or September. Winners notified by mail in May. Ohioana Library Association, 274 E. 1st Ave., Suite 300, Columbus OH 43201-3673. (614)466-3831. Fax: (614)728-6974. E-mail: ohioana@ohioana.org. Website: ohioana.org. **Contact**: Linda Hengst, executive director. Offered annually to bring national attention to Ohio authors and their books, published

in the last 2 years. (Books can only be considered once.) Categories: Fiction, nonfiction, juvenile, poetry, and books about Ohio or an Ohioan. Writers must have been born in Ohio or lived in Ohio for at least 5 years, but books about Ohio or an Ohioan need not be written by an Ohioan. Prize: certificate and glass sculpture. Judged by a jury selected by librarians, book reviewers, writers and other knowledgeable people. Each winter the jury considers all books received since the previous jury. No entry fee. **Deadline: December 31**. **Contact:** Linda Hengst, executive director. "Offered annually to bring national attention to Ohio authors and their books (published in the last 2 years). Categories: Fiction, nonfiction, juvenile, poetry, and books about Ohio or an Ohioan. Books about Ohio or an Ohioan need not be written by an Ohioan. For other book categories, writers must have been born in Ohio or lived in Ohio for at least 5 years." Deadline: December 31.

OREGON BOOK AWARDS

224 NW 13th Ave., Ste. 306, #219, Portland OR 97209. E-mail: susan@literary-arts.org. Website: literary-arts.org. Literary Arts, 224 NW 13th Ave., Ste. 306, Portland OR 97209. (503)227-2583. E-mail: susan@literary-arts.org. Website: literary-arts.org. The annual Oregon Book Awards celebrate Oregon authors in the areas of poetry, fiction, nonfiction, drama and young readers' literature published between August 1, 2010 and July 31. Prize: Finalists are invited on a statewide reading tour and are promoted in bookstores and libraries across the state. Judged by writers who are selected from outside Oregon for their expertise in a genre. Past judges include Mark Doty, Colson Whitehead and Kim Barnes. Entry fee determined by initial print run; see website for details. Deadline: last Friday in August. Entries must be previously published. Oregon residents only. Accepts inquiries by phone and e-mail. Finalists announced in January. Winners announced at an awards ceremony in November. List of winners available in April. Literary Arts, 224 NW 13th Ave., Ste. 306, Portland OR 97209. (503)227-2583. E-mail: susan@literary-arts.org. Website: literary-arts.org. **Contact:** Susan Denning. The annual Oregon Book Awards celebrate Oregon authors in the areas of poetry, fiction, nonfiction, drama and young readers' literature published between August 1, 2010 and July 31. Prize: Finalists are invited on a statewide reading tour and are promoted

in bookstores and libraries across the state. Judged by writers who are selected from outside Oregon for their expertise in a genre. Past judges include Mark Doty, Colson Whitehead and Kim Barnes. Entry fee determined by initial print run; see website for details. Deadline: last Friday in August. Entries must be previously published. Oregon residents only. Finalists announced in January. Winners announced at an awards ceremony in November. List of winners available in April. **Contact:** Susan Denning. Literary Arts, 224 NW 13th Ave., Ste. 306, Portland OR 97209. (503)227-2583. E-mail: susan@literary-arts.org. Website: literary-arts.org. The annual Oregon Book Awards celebrate Oregon authors in the areas of poetry, fiction, nonfiction, drama and young readers' literature published between August 1, 2010 and July 31. Prize: Finalists are invited on a statewide reading tour and are promoted in bookstores and libraries across the state. Judged by writers who are selected from outside Oregon for their expertise in a genre. Past judges include Mark Doty, Colson Whitehead and Kim Barnes. Entry fee determined by initial print run; see website for details. Deadline: last Friday in August. Entries must be previously published. Oregon residents only. Accepts inquiries by phone and e-mail. Finalists announced in January. Winners announced at an awards ceremony in November. List of winners available in April.

PEN CENTER USA LITERARY AWARDS

PEN Center USA, P.O. Box 6037, Beverly Hills CA 90212. (424)258-1180. E-mail: awards@penusa.org. Website: penusa.org. PEN Center USA Literary Awards. PEN Center USA. Offered for work published or produced in the previous calendar year. Open to writers living west of the Mississippi River. Award categories: fiction, poetry, research nonfiction, creative nonfiction, translation, children's/young adult, drama, screenplay, teleplay, journalism. Guidelines and submission form available on website. for SASE or download from website. $35 Entry Fee. Deadline for book categories: 4 copies must be received by December 31. Deadline for non-book categories: 4 copies must be received by January 31. PEN Center USA Literary Awards. PEN Center USA. Offered for work published or produced in the previous calendar year. Open to writers living west of the Mississippi River. Award categories: fiction, poetry, research nonfiction, creative nonfiction, translation, children's/

young adult, drama, screenplay, teleplay, journalism. Guidelines and submission form available on website. for SASE or download from website.Entry fee: $35 Entry fee. Deadline for book categories: 4 copies must be received by December 31. Deadline for non-book categories: 4 copies must be received by January 31. **Contact:** Literary Awards Coordinator. Offered for work published or produced in the previous calendar year. Open to writers living west of the Mississippi River. Award categories: fiction, poetry, research nonfiction, creative nonfiction, translation, children's/young adult, drama, screenplay, teleplay, journalism. Guidelines and submission form available on website. for SASE or download from website. Deadline for book categories: 4 copies must be received by December 31. Deadline for non-book categories: 4 copies must be received by January 31.

THE PINCH LITERARY AWARD IN FICTION AND POETRY

The Univ. of Memphis/Hohenberg Foundation, Dept. of English, 435 Patterson Hall, Memphis TN 38152. (901)678-4591. E-mail: editor@thepinchjournal.com. Website: thepinchjournal.com. Offered annually for unpublished short stories of 5,000 words maximum or up to three poems. Guidelines on website. Cost: $20/ which is put toward one issue of *The Pinch*. Deadline: March 15. Prize: 1st Place Fiction: $1,500 and publication; 1st Place Poetry: $1,000 and publication. Offered annually for unpublished short stories of 5,000 words maximum or up to three poems. Guidelines on website. Deadline: March 15. Prize: 1st Place Fiction: $1,500 and publication; 1st Place Poetry: $1,000 and publication.

PNWA LITERARY CONTEST

Pacific Northwest Writers Association, PMB 2717-1420 NW Gilman Blvd, Ste 2, Issaquah WA 98027. (425)673-2665. Fax: (206)824-4559. E-mail: staff@pnwa.org. Website: pnwa.org. **Open to students.** Annual contest. Purpose of contest: "Valuable tool for writers as contest submissions are critiqued (2 critiques)." Unpublished submissions only. Submissions made by author. Deadline for entries: February 18. Entry fee is $35/entry for members, $50/entry for nonmembers. Awards $700-1st; $300-2nd. Awards in all 12 categories. **Contact:** Kelli Liddane. "Annual contest for unpublished writers. Over $12,000 in prize monies. Categories include: Mainstream; Historical; Romance; Mystery/Thriller; Science Fiction/Fantasy; Young Adult Novel; Nonfiction Book/Memoir; Screenwriting; Poetry; Adult Short Story; Children's Picture Book/Chapter Book; Adult Short Topics. Each entry receives 2 critiques. Guidelines online." Deadline: February 18. Prize: 1st Place: $700; 2nd Place: $300. Each prize is awarded in all 12 categories.

PRAIRIE SCHOONER BOOK PRIZE

Prairie Schooner and the University of Nebraska Press, 123 Andrews Hall, University of Nebraska, Lincoln NE 68588-0334. (402)472-0911. E-mail: jengelhardt2@unlnotes.unl.edu; jengelhardt2@unl.edu. Website: prairieschooner.unl.edu. Annual. Competition/award for story collections. Prize: $3,000 and publication through the University of Nebraska Press for one book of short fiction and one book of poetry. Entry fee: $25. Make checks payable to Prairie Schooner. Deadline: Submissions are accepted between January 15 and March 15; check website for updates. Entries should be unpublished. Send full manuscript (the author's name should not appear anywhere on the ms). Send two cover pages: one listing only the title of the ms, and the other listing the title, author's name, address, telephone number, and e-mail address. Send SASE for notification of results. All mss will be recycled. You may also send an optional SAS postcard for confirmation of receipt of ms. Winners notified by phone, by e-mail. Results made available to entrants on website, in publication. The annual Prairie Schooner Book Prize Series offers $3,000 and publication of a book-length collection of poetry by the University of Nebraska Press. Individual poems may have been previously published elsehwere. Considers simultaneous submissions if notified immediately of acceptance elsewhere. Submit at least 50 pages of poetry with acknowledgments page (if applicable). Poet's name should not appear on ms pages. Xeroxed copies are acceptable. Bind with rubber band or binder clip only. Include 2 cover pages: one with poet's name, address, phone number, and e-mail address; the other with ms title only. Include SASP for acknowledgment of receipt of ms and #10 SASE for results only; mss will not be returned. Guidelines available for SASE, by e-mail, or on website. **Entry fee:** $25. Make checks payable to Prairie Schooner . **Deadline:** January 15-March 15 annually. 2008 winner was Kara Candito (*Taste of Cherry*). Winners announced on website in early July, with results mailed shortly thereafter. (See separate listing for Prairie Schooner in Magazines/Journals.)

Contact: Kwame Dawes, editor. "Annual book series competition publishing 1 book-length collection of short fiction and 1 book-length collection of poetry. **Submission Period: January 15-March 15.**" Prize: $3,000 and publication through the University of Nebraska Press (1 award in fiction and 1 award in poetry). Kwame Dawes, editor of *Prairie Schooner*, and members of the Book Series Literary Board.

PUDDING HOUSE CHAPBOOK COMPETITION

Pudding House Publications, 81 Shadymere Ln., Columbus OH 43213. (614) 986-1881. E-mail: jen@puddinghouse.com. Website: puddinghouse.com. **Contact:** Jennifer Bosveld. "Ms must be 10-36 pages (prefers around 24-28 pages). Up to four poems may be previously published but not the entire collection as a whole. Guidelines on website." Deadline: September 30. Prize: Winner receives $500, publication, and 20 copies of the chapbook.

RANDOM HOUSE, INC. CREATIVE WRITING COMPETITION

One Scholarship Way, P.O. Box 297, St. Peter MN 56082. (212)782-0316. Fax: (212)940-7590. E-mail: creativewriting@randomhouse.com. Website: randomhouse.com/creativewriting. Offered annually for unpublished work to NYC public high school seniors. Three categories: poetry and graphic novel, fiction & drama and personal memoir. Prize: 72 awards given in literary (3) and nonliterary (2) categories. Awards range from $500-10,000. Categories: short stories and poems. Judged by various city officials, executives, authors, editors. No entry fee. Guidelines available in October on website and in publication. **Deadline: Literature Entries -February 11 for 2011 and Graphic Novel- April 1.** Entries must be unpublished. Word length: 2,500 words or less. Applicants must be seniors (under age 21) at a New York high school. No college essays or class assignments will be accepted. Results announced mid-May. Winners notified by mail and phone. For contest results, send SASE, fax, e-mail or visit website. **Contact:** Melanie Fallon Hauska, director. Offered annually for unpublished work to NYC public high school seniors. Four categories: poetry, fiction/drama, personal essay and graphic novel. Applicants must be seniors (under age 21) at a New York high school. No college essays or class assignments will be accepted. Deadline: February 11 for all categories except graphic novel, which is April 1. Prize: Awards range from $500-10,000.

THE RBC BRONWEN WALLACE AWARD FOR EMERGING WRITERS

The Writers' Trust of Canada, 90 Richmond St. East, Suite 200, Toronto, Ontario M5C 1P1 Canada. (416)504-8222. Fax: (416)504-9090. E-mail: info@writerstrust.com. Website: writerstrust.com. **Contact:** Amanda Hopkins. Presented annually to "a Canadian writer under the age of 35 who is not yet published in book form. The award, which alternates each year between poetry and short fiction, was established in memory of poet Bronwen Wallace." Prize: $5,000 and $1,000 to two finalists.

REGINA BOOK AWARD

Saskatchewan Book Awards, Inc., 205B-2314 11th Ave., Regina SK S4P 0K1 Canada. (306)569-1585. Fax: (306)569-4187. E-mail: director@bookawards. sk.ca. Website: bookawards.sk.ca. **Contact:** Jackie Lay, executive director, book submissions. Offered annually for work published September 15, 2010-October 31. In recognition of the vitality of the literary community in Regina, this award is presented to a Regina author for the best book, judged on the quality of writing. Books from the following categories will be considered: children's; drama; fiction (short fiction by a single author, novellas, novels); nonfiction (all categories of nonfiction writing except cookbooks, directories, how-to books, or bibliographies of minimal critical content); poetry. Deadline: November 1. Prize: $2,000 CAD.

SASKATCHEWAN BOOK OF THE YEAR AWARD

Saskatchewan Book Awards, Inc., 205B, 2314 11th Ave., Regina SK S4P OK1 Canada. (306)569-1585. Fax: (306)569-4187. E-mail: director@bookawards. sk.ca. Website: bookawards.sk.ca. **Contact:** Jackie Lay, exec. dir., book submissions. Offered annually for work published September 15-October 31 annually. This award is presented to a Saskatchewan author for the best book, judged on the quality of writing. Books from the following categories will be considered: children's; drama; fiction (short fiction by a single author, novellas, novels); nonfiction (all categories of nonfiction writing except cookbooks, directories, how-to books, or bibliographies of minimal critical

content); poetry. Visit website for more details. Deadline: November 1. Prize: $3,000.

SASKATOON BOOK AWARD

Saskatchewan Book Awards, Inc., 205B-2314 11th Ave., Regina SK S4P 0K1 Canada. (306)569-1585. Fax: (306)569-4187. E-mail: director@bookawards.sk.ca. Website: bookawards.sk.ca. **Contact:** Jackie Lay, executive director, book submissions. Offered annually for work published September 15, 2010-October 31. In recognition of the vitality of the literary community in Saskatoon, this award is presented to a Saskatoon author for the best book, judged on the quality of writing. Books from the following categories will be considered: children's; drama; fiction (short fiction by a single author, novellas, novels); nonfiction (all categories of nonfiction writing except cookbooks, directories, how-to books, or bibliographies of minimal critical content); poetry. Deadline: November 1. Prize: $2,000 CAD.

MARGARET & JOHN SAVAGE FIRST BOOK AWARD

Halifax Public Libraries, 60 Alderney Dr., Dartmouth NS B2Y 4P8 Canada. (902)490-5991. Fax: (902)490-5889. E-mail: mackenh@halifaxpubliclibraries.ca. Website: halifax.ca/bookawards. **Contact:** Heather MacKenzie. "Recognizes the best first book of fiction or nonfiction written by a first-time published author residing in Atlantic Canada. Books may be of any genre, but must contain a minimum of 40% text, be at least 49 pages long, and be available for sale. No anthologies. Publishers: Send 4 copies of each title and submission form for each entry." Children's Books not accepted. Deadline: December 2.

THE MONA SCHREIBER PRIZE FOR HUMOROUS FICTION & NONFICTION

15442 Vista Haven Place, Sherman Oaks CA 91403. E-mail: brad.schreiber@att.net. Website: brashcyber. com. **Contact:** Brad Schreiber. "The purpose of the contest is to award the most creative humor writing, in any form less than 750 words, in either fiction or nonfiction, including but not limited to stories, articles, essays, speeches, shopping lists, diary entries, and anything else writers dream up." Deadline: December 1. Prize: 1st Place: $500; 2nd Place: $250; 3rd Place: $100. Brad Schreiber, author, journalist, consultant, and instructor at MediaBistro.com. Complete rules and previous winning entries on website.

KAY SNOW WRITERS' CONTEST

9045 SW Barbur Blvd. #5A, Portland OR 97219-4027. (503)452-1592. Fax: (503)452-0372. E-mail: wilwrite@teleport.com. Website: willamettewriters.com. Annual contest. **Open to students.** Purpose of contest: "to encourage beginning and established writers to continue the craft." Unpublished, original submissions only. Submissions made by the author. Deadline for entries: April 23rd. SASE for contest rules and entry forms. Entry fee is $10, Williamette Writers' members; $15, nonmembers; free for student writers grades 1-12. Awards cash prize of $300 per category (fiction, nonfiction, juvenile, poetry, script writing), $50 for students in three divisions: 1-5, 6-8, 9-12. Judges are anonymous. Contest offered annually to "offer encouragement and recognition to writers with unpublished submissions." Acquires right to publish excerpts from winning pieces 1 time in their newsletter. Entry fee is $10 for Williamette Writers' members; $15, nonmembers; free for student writers grades 1-12. **Deadline: April 23.** Prize winners will be honored at the two-day August Willamette Writers' Conference. Press releases will be sent to local and national media announcing the winners, and excerpts from winning entries may appear in our newsletter. Entry fee is $10 for Williamette Writers' members; $15, nonmembers; free for student writers grades 1-12. Submissions must be unpublished. Submit up to 2 poems (1 entry fee), maximum 5 pages total, on any subject, in any style or form, single-spaced, 1 side of paper only. Entry form and guidelines available for SASE or on website. **Deadline:** January 15-April 23 (postmarked) for 2011. Competition receives 150 entries. "Write and send in your very best poem. Read it aloud. If it still sounds like the best poem you've ever heard, send it in." **Contact:** Lizzy Shannon, contest director. "Contest offered annually to offer encouragement and recognition to writers with unpublished submissions. Acquires right to publish excerpts from winning pieces one time in their newsletter." Annual contest. Open to students. Unpublished, original submissions only. Submissions made by the author. SASE for contest rules and entry forms. Purpose of contest is "to encourage beginning and established writers to continue the craft." Deadline for entries: April 23. Prize: Awards cash prize of $300 per category (fiction, nonfiction, juvenile, poetry, script writing), $50 for students in three divisions: 1-5, 6-8, 9-12. Judges are anonymous.

SOUL-MAKING LITERARY COMPETITION

Nob Hill, San Francisco Bay Area Branch, 1544 Sweetwood Dr., Broadmoor Vlg CA 94015-1717. (650)756-5279. Fax: (650)756-5279. E-mail: PenNobHill@aol.com. Website: soulmakingcontest.us. Annual open contest offers cash prizes in each of 11 literary categories, including poetry and prose poem. 1st Prize: $100; 2nd Prize: $50; 3rd Prize: $25. Submissions in some categories may be previously published. Submit 3 one-page poems on soul-making theme; any form for open poetry category. No names or other identifying information on mss; include 3x5 card with poet's name, address, phone, fax, e-mail, title(s) of work, and category entered. Include SASE for results only; mss will not be returned. Guidelines available on website. **Entry fee:** $5/entry. **Deadline:** November 30. Competition receives 300 entries/year. Names of winners and judges are posted on website. Winners announced in January by SASE and on website. Winners are invited to read at the Koret Auditorium, San Francisco. Event is televised. **Contact:** Eileen Malone, Award Director.

☺ SUBTERRAIN ANNUAL LITERARY AWARDS COMPETITION: THE LUSH TRIUMPHANT

P.O. Box 3008 MPO, Vancouver BC V6B 3X5 Canada. E-mail: subter@portal.ca. Website: subterrain.ca. subTERRAIN Magazine, P.O. Box 3008 MPO, Vancouver BC V6B 3X5 Canada. (604) 876-8710. Fax: (604) 879-2667. E-mail: subter@portal.ca. Website: subterrain.ca. Offered annually to foster new and upcoming writers. Prize: $750 (Canadian) cash prizes in each category, publication, and 1-year subscription to subTERRAIN. Categories: short stories, poetry, nonfiction. Judged by an editorial collective. Entry fee: $25. Entrants may submit as many entries in as many categories as they like. All entrants receive a year's subscription. Guidelines on Website. **Deadline: May 15.** Entries must be unpublished. Length: Fiction: 3,000 words maximum; Poetry: a suite of 5 related poems (max 15 pages); creative nonfiction: max 4,000 words. Results announced on Website. "All entries must be previously unpublished material. Submissions will not be returned, so do not send originals." Entrants may submit as many entries in as many categories as they like. Fiction: max. 3,000 words. Poetry: a suite of 5 related poems (max. 15 pages). Creative Nonfiction: (based on fact, adorned with fiction): max. 4,000 words. Deadline: May 15. $3,000 in cash prizes. See website for prize information. All entries MUST be previously unpublished material and not currently under consideration in any other contest or competition. Deadline: May 15. Prize: Winners in each category will receive $750 cash (plus payment for publication) and publication in the Winter issue. First runner-up in each category will received a $250 cash prize and be published in the Spring issue of *subTerrain*. All entrants receive a complimentary 1-year subscription to *subTerrain*.

⊕ TOMMY AWARD FOR EXCELLENCE IN WRITING

International Book Management Corporation, 3468 Babcock Blvd., Pittsburgh PA 15237-2402. (412)837-2423. E-mail: info@internationalbookmanagement.com; editor@writersnewsweekly.com. Website: writersnewsweekly.com. The Tommy Award For Writing Excellent recognizes and rewards excellence in full length literary works in adult fiction and nonfiction. Books must be published in the U.S. between June 1 and May 31 of the following year. Textbooks, e-books, children's books, young adult books, poetry and audio-books will not be considered, nor will manuscripts. Judges will selected one winner and may designate up to two Honorable Mention books in each of the following categories: fiction, nonfiction, shosrt story collection. Books can be submitted by the publisher or the author. A copy of each book submitted should be mailed directly to: International Book Management Corporation, 3468 Babcock Blvd., Pittsburgh, PA 15237. Please send submissions as soon as possible after publication. No books will be accepted after May 21. There will be no extensions to this deadline. Winners and honorable mentions will be announced on August 15th. The awards are presented in October. Winners receive a certificate and trophy. An author interview and book review of the winning submission will appear on WritersNewsWeekly. Entries will not be returned. International Book Management Corp. reserves the right to donate or dispose of entries. No entry fee. More more information contact International Management at: info@internationalbookmanagement.com. **Contact:** Christopher Stokum and Sarah Schiavoni. The Tommy Award For Writing Excellent recognizes and rewards excellence in full length literary works in adult fiction and nonfiction. Books must be published in the U.S. between June 1 and May 31 of the following year. Textbooks, e-books, children's books, young adult books, poetry and audio-books will not be considered, nor will manuscripts. Judges will selected one winner and may designate up to two Honorable Mention books in each of the following categories: fiction, nonfiction, shosrt story collection. Books can be submitted by the publisher or the author.

◑ TORONTO BOOK AWARDS

City of Toronto c/o Toronto Protocol, 100 Queen St. W., City Clerk's Office, 2nd floor, West, City Hall, Toronto ON M5H 2N2 Canada. (416)392-7805. Fax: (416)392-1247. E-mail: bkurmey@toronto.ca. Website: toronto.ca/book_awards. The Toronto Book Awards honor authors of books of literary or artistic merit that are evocative of Toronto. Annual award for short stories, novels, poetry or short story collections. Prize: $15,000. Each short-listed author (usually 4-6) receives $1,000 and the winner receives the remainder. Categories: No separate categories—novels, short story collections, books of poetry, biographies, history, books about sports, children's books—all are judged together. Judged by jury of five who have demonstrated interest and/or experience in literature, literacy, books and book publishing. No entry fee. Cover letter should include name, address, phone, e-mail and title of entry. Six copies of the entry book are also required. **Deadline: last week of March.** Entries must be previously published. Guidelines available in September on website. Accepts inquires by fax, e-mail, phone. Finalists announced in June; winners notified in September at a gala reception. Guidelines and results available on website. **Contact:** Bev Kurmey, protocol officer. "Offered annually for previously published fiction or nonfiction books for adults or children that are evocative of Toronto." Deadline: March 31. Prize: Awards total $15,000; $1,000 goes to shortlist finalists (usually 4-6) and the remainder goes to the winner. Judged by independent judging committee of 5 people chosen through an application and selection process.

WESTMORELAND POETRY & SHORT STORY CONTEST

Westmoreland Arts & Heritage Festival, 252 Twin Lakes Rd., Latrobe PA 15650-9415. (724)834-7474. Fax: (724)850-7474. E-mail: info@artsandheritage.com. Website: artsandheritage.com. **Contact:** Diana Morreo. Offered annually for unpublished work. Two categories: Poem & Short Story. Short story entries no longer than 4,000 words. Family-oriented festival and contest. Deadline: March 15. Prize: Up to $1,000 in prizes.

WILLA LITERARY AWARD

Women Writing the West, 8547 East Arapaho Road, Box J-541, Greenwood Village CO 80112-1436. (801)573-5309. E-mail: alicetrego@mac.com. Website: womenwritingthewest.org. **Contact:** Alice D. Trego, contest director. The Willa Literary Award honors the best in literature featuring women's stories set in the West published each year. Women Writing the West (WWW), a nonprofit association of writers and other professionals writing and promoting the Women's West, underwrites and presents the nationally recognized award annually (for work published between January 1 and December 31). The award is named in honor of Pulitzer Prize winner Willa Cather, one of the country's foremost novelists. The award is given in 7 categories: historical fiction, contemporary fiction, original softcover, nonfiction, memoir/essay nonfiction, poetry, and children's/young adult fiction/nonfiction. Deadline: February 1. Prize: Each winner receives $100 and a trophy. Each finalist receives a plaque. Award announcement is in early August, and awards are presented to the winners and finalists at the annual WWW Fall Conference. professional librarians not affiliated with

WORLD'S BEST SHORT SHORT STORY FICTION CONTEST, NARRATIVE NONFICTION CONTEST & SOUTHEAST REVIEW POETRY CONTEST

English Department, Florida State University, Tallahassee FL 32306. E-mail: southeastreview@gmail.com. Website: southeastreview.org. English Department, Florida State University, Tallahassee FL 32306. E-mail: southeastreview@gmail.com. Website: southeastreview.org. Contact: Katie Cortese, acquisitions editor. "Annual award for unpublished short-short stories (500 words or less), poetry, and narrative nonfiction (6,000 words or less)." $15 reading fee for up to 3 stories or poems, $15 reading fee per nonfiction entry, fiction, nonfiction, poetry, short stories. Deadline: March 15. Prize: $500 per category. Winners and finalists will be published in *The Southeast Review*. English Department, Florida State University, Tallahassee FL 32306. E-mail: southeastreview@gmail.com. Website: southeastreview.org. Contact:

Katie Cortese, acquisitions editor. "Annual award for unpublished short-short stories (500 words or less), poetry, and narrative nonfiction (6,000 words or less)." $15 reading fee for up to 3 stories or poems, $15 reading fee per nonfiction entry, fiction, nonfiction, poetry, short stories. Deadline: March 15. Prize: $500 per category. Winners and finalists will be published in *The Southeast Review*. **Contact:** Katie Cortese, acquisitions editor. "Annual award for unpublished short-short stories (500 words or less), poetry, and narrative nonfiction (6,000 words or less)." Deadline: March 15. Prize: $500 per category. Winners and finalists will be published in *The Southeast Review*.

WRITER'S DIGEST WRITING COMPETITION

Writer's Digest, a publication of F+W Media, Inc., 700 E. State Street, Iola WI 54990. (513)531-2690, ext. 1328. E-mail: writing-competition@fwmedia.com; nicole.florence@fwmedia.com. Website: writersdigest.com. 80th Annual. Writing contest with 10 categories: Inspirational Writing (spiritual/religious, maximum 2,500 words); Memoir/Personal Essay (maximum 2,000 words); Magazine Feature Article (maximum 2,000 words); Short Story (genre, maximum 4,000 words); Short Story (mainstream/literary, maximum 4,000 words); Rhyming Poetry (maximum 32 lines); Nonrhyming Poetry (maximum 32 lines); Stage Play (first 15 pages and 1-page synopsis); TV/Movie Script (first 15 pages and 1-page synopsis). Entries must be original, in English, unpublished*/unproduced (except for Magazine Feature Articles), and not accepted by another publisher/producer at the time of submission. *Writer's Digest* retains one-time publication rights to the winning entries in each category. $15/first poetry entry; $10/additional poem. All other entries are $20/first ms; $15/additional msfiction, poetry, juvenile, scripts, articles, short stories. Deadline: May 2/late entry May 20, additional fee for late entries. Add $5 per manuscript or poem to Entry Fee(s) on all entries submitted between May 3 and May 20. Grand Prize: $3,000 and a trip to New York City to meet with editors and agents; 1st Place: $1,000, ms critique and marketing advice from a *Writer's Digest* editor, commentary from an agent, and $100 of Writer's Digest Books; 2nd Place: $500 and $100 of Writer's Digest Books; 3rd Place: $250 and $100 of Writer's Digest Books;

4th Place: $100 and $50 of *Writer's Digest* Books; 5th Place: $50 and $50 of *Writer's Digest* Books; 6th-10th place $25. **Contact:** Nicki Florence.

WRITERS-EDITORS NETWORK ANNUAL INTERNATIONAL WRITING COMPETITION

Florida Freelance Writers Association, P.O. Box A, North Stratford NH 03590-0167. E-mail: contest@writers-editors.com. Website: writers-editors.com. Estab. 1984. Categories include children's literature (length appropriate to age category). Entry form online at website. Entry fee is $5 (members), $10 (non-members) or $10-20 for entries longer than 3,000 words. Awards $100 first prize, $75 second prize, $50 third prize, certificates for honorable mentions. Judging by librarians, editors and published authors. Judging criteria: interest and readability within age group, writing style and mechanics, originality, salability. Deadline: March 15. For copy of official entry form, send #10 SASE or visit website. List of winners on website.

GENERAL INDEX

B

M

P